WEBSTER'S

DICTIONARY

&

THESAURUS

WITH

COMPUTER

REFERENCE SECTION

Table Of Contents

Rules of Spelling

1. The most common way to form the plural of a
   noun is to add an s.
   (Example: girl, girls; town, towns; hall,halls.)

2. The plural of nouns which end in *y* following a
   consonant are formed by dropping the *y* and
   adding *ies.*
   *(Example: country, countries; baby, babies;
   family, families.)*

3. The plural of nouns which end in *y* following a
   vowel are formed by adding an *s.*
   (Example: toy, toys; boy, boys; family, families)

Each entry and phonetics are in **bold type** followed
by the part of speech in *italics.*

Subentries are in **bold type** after the main
definition.

Edited and proof read by
Carol Suplicki
Gina Molino

Cover design by:
MJ Studios

ISBN 1-57122-145-X

ABBREVIATIONS USED IN THIS DICTIONARY

abbr.	abbreviation	meteor.	meteorol
adv.	adverb	milit.	military
aeron	aeronautics	mus.	music
anal.	analogy	mythol.	mythology
anat.	anatomy	n.	noun
araha.	arahaic	naut.	nautical
arch.	architecture	orig.	original
astron.	astronomy	ornith.	ornithology
Bib.	Biblical	pathol.	pathology
biochem.	biochemistry	photog.	photography
biol.	biology	phys.	physics
bot.	botany	physiol.	physiology
Brit.	British	prep.	preposition
chem.	chemistry	pron.	pronoun
conj.	conjunction	psychol.	psychology
elect.	electricity	psychi.	psychiatry
fig.	figuratively	suf.	suffix
geol.	geology	syn.	synonym
gram.	grammar	theatr.	theatrical
interj.	interjection	usu.	usually
math.	mathematics	v.	verb
mech.	mechanics	var.	variant
med.	medical	zool.	zoology

PRONUNCIATION SYMBOLS
USED IN THIS DICTIONARY

ā	space
â	ware
ä	father
a	abridge
e	hem
ė	herd
ē	spree
I	hip
ī	smile
ŋ	angry
o	cob
o	collect
ö	movie
ō	rose
u	cut
ū	amuse
ü	turn

A, a (ā) *n.* The first letter of the English alphabet; the highest grade, meaning excellent or best.

aah (ä) *v.* To exclaim in joy.

AAR *abbr.* Against all risks.

aard-vark (ärd´värk˝) *n.* A burrowing African animal, which resembles the anteater and feeds on ants and termites.

aard-wolf (ärd´wülf) *n.* A hyena-like mammal, feeding chiefly on carrion and insects.

Aar-on's-beard (âr´ onz bērd´) *n.* A dwarf evergreen shrub, having conspicuous hairlike stamens and yellow flowers.

AB *abbr.* One of the major blood types. One who possesses it may donate blood to type AB and receive blood from types A, B, AB, and O.

A.B. *abbr.* Bachelor of Arts; academic degree.

a-ba (*a* bä´) *n.* A striped fabric, woven of goat's or camel's hair; an outer garment made from this fabric or silk, worn by Arabs.

a-ba-ca (ä˝bä kä´) *n.* A plant from the Philippines whose leafstalks are the source of Manila hemp.

a-back (*a* bak´) *adv.* Unexpectedly; by surprise; startled; confused.

a-bac-te-ri-al (ā bak tir´ ē al) *adj.* Not caused by bacteria.

ab-a-cus (ab´ *a* k*a*s) *n.* A frame holding parallel rods with beads, used for manual computation, especially by the Chinese.

a-baft (*a* baft´) *adv.* On or toward the stern, aft, or hind part of a ship.

ab-a-lo-ne (ab˝*a* lō´nē) *n.* A member of the genus of gastropod mollusks that will cling to rocks and have a shell which is flat and lined with mother of pearl.

a-ban-don (*a* ban´d*o*n) *v.* To yield utterly; to desert; to forsake; to withdraw protection, support, or help, to give up all rights or interest. **abandonment** *n.*

a-ban-doned (*a* ban´d*o*nd) *adj.* To be deserted; to be forsaken.

a-ban-don-ee (*a* ban˝don ē´) *n.* The person to whom a thing is abandoned.

a-ban-don-ment (*a* ban´d*o*n m*e*nt) *n.* The state of being abandoned; or the act of abandoning; to surrender, relinquishment; free from constraint.

a-base (*a* bās´) *v.* To lower in rank, prestige, position, or estimation; to cast down, to humble.

a-base-ment (*a* bās´m*e*nt) *n.* A state of depression, degradation, or humiliation.

a-bash (*a* bash´) *v.* To embarrass; to disconcert; to make ashamed or uneasy.

a-bash-ment (*a* bash´m*e*nt) *n.* The state of something being abashed.

a-bate (*a* bāt´) *v.* To deduct; to make less; to reduce in quantity, value, force, or intensity. **abater** *n.* **abatable** *adj.*

a-bate-ment (*a* bāt´m*e*nt) *n.* The process of abating something; the amount which is abated.

ab-a-tis (ab´*a* tē´) *n.* The collection of felled trees of which the smaller branches have already been cut off.

A battery *n.* A type of battery used for the purpose of heating the filaments of electron tubes.

ab-at-toir (ab˝*a* twär´) *n.* The public slaughterhouse.

ab-ax-i-al (ab ak´sē*a*l) *adj.* To be positioned or situated out of the axis of something.

abb (ab) *n.* A type of low grade wool that is from the inferior parts of a fleece.

Ab-ba (ab´*a*) *n.* The ecclestical title that is used in some Eastern churches.

ab-ba-cy (ab´*a* sē) *n.* A jurisdiction or an office of an abbot.

ab-ba-tial (*a* bā´sh*a*l) *adj.* To be pertaining or related to an abbey or abbot.

ab-be (a bā´) *n.* A French title given to a priest; one who devoted himself to divinity, or who had pursued a course of study in a theological seminary.

ab-bess (ab´is) *n.* The female superior of an abbey of nuns and possessing the same authority as an abbot.

ab-bey (ab´ē) *n.* An abbey church, a monastery, or convent.

ab-bot (ab´ot) *n.* The male head of a monastery.

ab-bre-vi-ate (a brē´vē āt˝) *v.* To make briefer; to abridge; to shorten; to reduce to a briefer form, as a word or phrase.

ab-bre-vi-a-tion (a brē˝vē ā´shan) *n.* A shortened form of a word or phrase, used to represent the full form. **abbreviator** *n.* **abbreviatory** *adj.*

ABC (ā´bē˝sē´) *n.* The rudiments of writing, reading, and spelling.

ab-di-ca-ble (ab´di ka bl) *adj.* To be pertaining to the one that may renounce.

ab-di-cate (ab´di kāt˝) *v.* To relinquish power or responsibility formally; to renounce. **abdication** *n.*

ab-di-ca-tor (ab´di kā˝tėr) *n.* Person who abdicates.

ab-do-men (ab´do men) *n.* That part of the human body that lies between the thorax and the pelvis; it contains the stomach, spleen, liver, kidneys, bladder, pancreas, and the intestines. **abdominally** *adv.*

ab-dom-i-nal (ab dom´i nal) *adj.* Having to do with the abdomen; in, on, or for the abdomen.

ab-dom-i-nous (ab dom´i nus) *adj.* Abdominal; having a large belly.

ab-du-cens nerve *n.* The 6th cranial motor nerves that supply the eye muscles.

ab-du-cent (ab dū´sent) *adj.* Pulling back, or drawing away.

abducent muscles *n.* Muscles that pull back certain parts of the body from the mesial line.

ab-duct (ab dukt´) *v.* To carry away wrongfully, as by force or fraud; to kidnap; to draw aside or away.

ab-duc-tion (ab duk´shan) *n.* An action of abducting. *Med.* Descriptive of the movement of a limb or part of a limb away from the midline of the body.

ab-duc-tor (ab duk´tėr) *n.* A person who or that which abducts; *Med.* muscle that moves certain body parts from the axis of the body.

a-beam (a bēm´) *adv.* At right angles to the keel of a ship.

a-be-ce-dar-i-an (ā˝bē sē dâr´ē an) *n.* A person who teaches the letters of the alphabet, or a person learning the letters. A beginner in any area of learning.

a-be-ce-da-ry (ā´bē sē´da rē) *adj.* Formed by or pertaining to the letters of the alphabet.

a-bed (a bed´) *adv.* In bed; on a bed; to bed; restricted to bed.

a-bel-mosk (ā´bel mosk˝) *n.* A type of herb which is found in Asia and the East Indies and the musky seeds are used to flavor coffee and for perfumes.

Aberdeen Angus (ab´er dēn ang´gus) *n.* A type of black hornless cattle and whose origin is in Scotland.

ab-er-rant (ab er´ent) *adj.* Straying from the right way or usual course; not being proper or truthful; abnormal or exceptional. **aberrantly** *adv.*

ab-er-ra-tion (ab˝er ā´shan) *n.* The disorder of the mind; deviation from a type or standard. **aberrational** *adj.*

a-bet (a bet´) *v.* To incite, encourage, or assist by countenance, aid, or approval. **abetment** *n.* **abetter** *n.*

a-bey-ance (a bā´ans) *n.* State of expectation, for an occupant or holder; a feeling or state of temporary suspension.

a-bey-ant (a bā´ant) *adj.* Temporarily inactive.

ab-hor (ab hor´) *v.* To dislike intensely; to loathe. **abhorrer** *n.* **abhorrence** *n.*

ab-hor-rence (ab hor´rens) *n.* The state of abhorring.

ab-hor-rent (ab hor´ent) *adj.* To be feeling abhorrence; hating; detesting.

a-bid-ance (a bīd´ans) *n.* The state of abiding; compliance.

a-bide (a bīd´) *v.* To tolerate; to bear; to remain; to last; to conform to; to comply with. **abider** *n.*

a-bid-ing (a bī´ding) *adj.* To be enduring.

ab-i-gail (ab e gāl) n. A personal maid of a lady.

-a-bil-i-ty (*e* bil *et* ē) *n. suffix* Tendency to act in a specified manner or way.

a-bil-i-ty (*a* bil´i tē) *n.* State of being able; possession of qualities necessary; competence; skill; a particular talent.

ab-i-o-gen-i-sis (ab˝ē ō jen´i sis) *n.* An origination of something living from something that is not living. **abiogenetically** *adv.*

abi-o-log-i-cal (ā bī *e* lăj i k*e*l) *adj.* Not being made or produced by organisms.

a-bi-otic (ā bīī ˝ăt ik) *adj.* Not being biotic.

ab-ir-ri-tant (ab ir´i t*a*nt) *n.* A lotion used to reduce irritation.

ab-ject (ab´jekt) *adj.* Sunk to a low condition; groveling; mean; despicable; worthless. **abject** *n.* A person who is an outcast.

abjection (ab jek´sh*a*n) *n.* A state which is downcast. **abjectness** *n.*

ab-ju-ra-tion (ab˝ jü rā´sh*a*n) *n.* The process of abjuring.

ab-jure (ab jür´) *v.* To renounce solemnly or on oath; to repudiate; to forswear, to abstain or reject. **abjurer** *n.*

abl *abbr.* Ablative.

ab-lac-tate (ab lak´tāt) *v.* The act of weaning small infants from the breast.

ab-lac-ta-tion (ab˝laktā´sh*a*n)*n.* The weaning from the breast.

ab-late (a blāt´) *v.* To remove something by cutting or erosion.

ab-la-tion (ab lā´sh*a*n) *n.* A removal of a part; a process of ablating. *Med.* Removal of a part of the body by surgery

a-blaze (*a* blāz´) *adv.* On fire; brilliantly lighted up; very excited; angry.

a-ble (ā´bl) *adj.* Having sufficient ability; capable or talented. **able** *adj. suffix* To be worthy of. **ableness** *n.* **ably** *adv.*

a-ble–bod-ied (ā´bl bod´ēd) *adj.* Having a sound, strong body; competent for physical service.

ab-le-gate (ab´l*e* gāt´) *n.* Papal envoy to a newly appointed dignitary.

able seaman *n.* A seaman who is experienced to perform routine tasks at sea.

a-bloom (*a* blŏm´) *adj.* To be abounding with blooms such as a plant.

ab-lu-ent (ab´lŏ *e*nt) *adj.* Cleansing by water

or liquids. *n.* Something that washes off impurities; a detergent or soap.

ab-lut-ed (ab´lŏt ed) *adj.* To be washed and clean.

ab-lu-tion (ab lŏ´sh*a*n) *n.* The act of washing, cleansing, or purification by a liquid, usually water; specifically, a washing of the body as a part of religious rites. **ablutionary** *adj.*

a-bly (ā´blē) *adv.* To do something in an able manner.

abn *abbr.* Airborne.

Ab-na-ki *n.* A person who is a member of the Amerindian people of southern Quebec and Maine.

ab-ne-gate (ab´n*a* gāt´) *v.* To deny; to refuse or renounce; to relinquish or surrender.

ab-ne-ga-tion (ab˝n*e* gā´sh*a*n) *n.* The act of relinquishing rights; denial.

ab-ne-ga-tor (ab´n*a* gāt´*e*r) *n.* A person who denies or renounces.

ab-nor-mal (ab nor´m*e*l) *adj.* Descriptive of that which is unusual, not normal; irregular; unnatural. **abnormally** *adv.* **abnormality** *n.*

abnormal psychology *n.* A type of psychology that deals with the behaviors of people.

ab-nor-mal-i-ty (ab˝nor mal´i tē) *n. pl.* **abnormalities** The quality or state of being abnormal; deviation from rule or type; peculiarity; that which is abnormal.

a-board (*a* bōrd´) *adv.* On board a ship or other vehicle.

a-bode (*a* bōd´) *n.* A dwelling place; home; place of residence; habitation.

a-boil (*a* boil´) *adj.* To be at the point of which something, such as a fluid, will boil.

a-bol-ish (*a* bol´ish) *v.* To put an end to; to annul, to do away with; nullify; destroy; to put out of existence. **abolishment** *n.*

a-bol-ish-a-ble (*a* bol´ish *a* bl) *adj.* Capable of being abolished.

a-bol-ish-er (*a* bol´ish *e*r) *n.* A person who abolishes.

ab-o-li-tion (ab˝*o* lish´*a*n) *n.* The state of being abolished. **abolitionary** *adj.*

ab-o-li-tion-ism (ab˝o lish´a niz˝um) *n.* The measures that will foster abolition.

ab-o-ma-sum (ab˝o mā´sum) *n.* The fourth digestive stomach of the ruminant, lying next to the third stomach or omasum.

A-bomb (ā bom) *n.* An atomic bomb; a very destructive bomb where energy is released in an explosion with enormous force and heat.

a-bom-i-na-ble (a bom´i na bal) *adj.* Detestable; repugnant; loathsome. **abominably** *adv.* **abominableness** *n.*

abominable snowman *n.* A type of animal that has been reported to exist in the Himalayas; having features similar to those of man.

a-bom-i-nate (a bom´i nāt) *v.* To loathe intensely; to detest; to hate extremely; to abhor.

a-bom-in-a-tion (a bom˝i nā´shan) *n.* An extreme hatred, the act of abominating; detestation; hateful vice.

ab-o-ral (ab ōr´al) *adj.* To be situated away from the mouth.

ab-o-rig-i-nal (ab˝o rij´i nal) *adj.* To be the first in a region and may be primitive when compared with a more advanced type.

ab-o-rig-i-ne (ab˝o rij´i nē) *n.* The first inhabitants of a country; *pl.* original animals and flowers of an area or region.

a-bor-ning (a bor´ning) *adv.* While being produced or made, before completion or fulfillment.

a-bort (a bort´) *v.* To terminate or cause to terminate an operation or procedure before completion; to miscarry in giving birth.

a-bor-ti-fa-cient (a bor˝ti fā´shant) *n.* Something used to produce an abortion, usually refers to a drug induced abortion.

a-bor-tion (a bor´shan) *n.* Induced termination of pregnancy before the fetus can survive; something malformed.

a-bor-tion-ist (a bor´sha nist) *n.* Something which will produce or cause an abortion; a person who induces abortions, especially illegal ones.

a-bor-tive (a bor´tiv) *adj.* Delivered in an immature state; to be developed incom-

pletely. **abortiveness** *n.*

a-bound (a bound´) *v.* To have plenty; to exist in large numbers.

a-bout (a bout´) *adv.* Approximately; on every side, here and there.

a-bout–face (a bout˝fās´) *n.* A complete reversal of opinion or direction. **aboutface** *v.* To alter one's position so as to face the opposite direction; to reverse one's opinion completely.

a-bout–ship (a bout˝ship´) *v.* To change the course of a ship.

a-bove (a buv´) *adv.* Higher or greater than; in or at a higher place.

a-bove–all *adv.* To be before all other considerations.

a-bove-board (a buv´bōrd˝) *adv.* To do something in a straightforward manner.

a-bove-ground (a buv´ground˝) *adj.* To be located or positioned above the level or surface of the ground.

abp *abbr.* Archbishop.

abr *abbr.* Abridgment.

ab-ra-ca-dab-ra (ab˝ra ka dab´ra) *n.* A word believed by some to have magical powers, used in casting spells; nonsense, foolish talk.

a-bra-dant (a brād´ant) *n.* A material used for polishing and grinding, as sand, or glass. **abradant** *adj.* Having an abrasive surface and quality.

a-brade (a brād´) *v.* To wear or rub off; to grate off; abrasive, scouring.

a-bra-sion (a brā´zhan) *n.* The injury to the skin by scraping the outer layer; any scraped surface; the grinding of a surface using friction.

a-bra-sive (a brā´siv) *n.* A substance employed in grinding or abrading. *adj.* to tend to abrade.

ab-re-act (ab˝rē akt´) *v.* To release an emotion that is forgotten in psychoanalysis.

ab-re-ac-tion (ab˝rē ak´shan) *n.* To eliminate a bad experience by reliving it.

a-breast (a brest´) *adv.* Side by side.

a-bri (a brē´) *n.* A place of refuge; shelter.

a-bridge (a brij´) *v.* To make smaller,

fewer, or shorter while maintaining essential contents. **abridger** *n.* **abridgable** *or* **abridgeable** *adj.*

a-bridg-ment (ā brij´ment) *n.* The state of being abridged.

a-broach (*a* brōch´) *adv.* In agitation or action.

a-broad (*a* brod´) *adv.* Widely; in many places; outside one's country; at large.

ab-ro-gate (ab´ro gāt´) *v.* To cancel; to put an end to; to repeal. **abrogation** *n.* **abro-gable** *adj.* **abrogative** *adj.*

ab-rupt (*a* brupt´) *adj.* Happening or coming suddenly with no warning; very gruff; steep, craggy of rocks, precipices, etc.; sudden; brusque, without notice to prepare the mind for the event.

ab-rup-tion (*a* brup´shan) *n.* The sudden breaking away of something.

ab-rupt-ly (*a* brupt´lē) *adv.* In an abrupt manner, sudden and without any notice.

ab-rupt-ness (*a* brupt´nis) *n.* The state or quality of being abrupt; precipitousness; suddenness; unceremonious haste or vehemence.

abs *abbr.* Abstract.

ab-scess (ab´ses) *n.* An infected place in the body which becomes sore and swollen, often tender or painful and contains pus, the body's natural response to bacterial infection or an infection **abscessed** *adj.*

ab-scind (ab sind´) *v.* To cut off; to sever; to pare away; to separate.

ab-scise (ab sīz´) *v.* To part or separate with abscission.

abscisic acid *n.* A type of plant hormone that will promote leaf abscission and dormancy.

ab-scis-sa (ab sis´a) *n.* Any part of the diameter or transverse axis of a conic section, as an ellipse.

ab-scis-sion (ab sizh´an) *n.* A natural separation of fruit, flowers, or the leaves of a plant.

ab-scond (ab skond´) *v.* To remove oneself, as to flee from justice. **absconder** *n.*

ab-seil (ăp´zīl) *n.* A means of descending from a steep cliff by securing a line at the peak.

ab-sence (ab´sens) *n.* Being absent, not present; inattention.

ab-sent (ab´sent) *adj.* Not present; away; lacking; nonexistent. **absently** *adv.*

ab-sen-tee (ab sen tē´) *n.* A person who is absent.

absentee ballot *n.* A type of ballot which is submitted to an election by a voter who is not able to be at the polls.

ab-sen-tee-ism (ab sen tē´iz˝um) *n.* The chronic absence from something, such as school.

absentee voter *n.* A person who is allowed to vote in an election with an absentee ballot.

ab-sent–mind-ed (ab´sent mīn´did) *adj.* Always forgetting things; dreaming or thinking of something else; not paying attention.

absent without leave *adj.* To be absent without permission from the place of duty in the armed forces.

ab-sinthe (ab´sinth) *n.* A type of green liqueur which has been flavored by wormwood.

ab-so-lute (ab´so löt˝) *adj.* Unconditional; without restraint; perfect; complete. **abso-luteness** *n.* **absolutely** *adv.*

absolute ceiling *n.* The height above the sea level which is the highest point a plane is able to fly in a horizontal position.

absolute humidity *n.* An amount of water vapor that is present in a unit of volume of air.

absolute pitch *n., Mus.* In a standard scale, the exact position of a tone in terms of the number of vibrations per second.

absolute scale *n., Phys.* Temperature scale, based on absolute zero.

absolute temperature *n.* Temperature that is measured from absolute zero.

absolute unit *n.* Units in an absolute system of units.

absolute value *n., Math.* Regardless of the sign, the numerical value of a real number quantity.

ab-so-lu-tion (ab˝sa lö´shan) *n.* The state or act of being absolved; forgiven, discharged.

ab-so-lut-ism (ab´*so* **lŏ˝tiz˝***u***m)** *n.* The exercise or principle of absolute power in government.

ab-so-lut-ize (ab *so*löt iz**)** *v.* To make something absolute.

ab-sol-u-to-ry (ab sol´ū tōr˝ē) *adj.* In an absolving manner; having the capacity to absolve.

ab-solve (ab zolv´) *v.* To set free or release from duties, guilt, debt, or penalty. **absolvable** *adj.*

ab-so-nant (ab´*so* **nant)** *adj.* Contrary, discordant; dissonant; incongruous, abhorrent.

ab-sorb (ab sorb´) *v.* To take in; to take up the full attention; to engage one's whole attention. **absorbable** *adj.*

ab-sorb-en-cy (ab sorb´*en* **sē)** *n.* The state of being absorbent.

ab-sor-bent (ab sor´bent) *adj.* To be able to absorb something. **absorbent** *n.* Capable of absorbing light rays, fluids; performing the function of absorption.

ab-sorb-ing(absor´bing)*adj.*Exceptionally interesting.

ab-sorp-tion (ab sorp´sh*a***n)** *n.* The act of giving full attention or having great interest. *Med.*The process of assimilating food or other substances into the body, which may take place by a number of means, through the gastrointestinal tract, the skin, or through the mucous membranes of the eyes, nose, etc.

ab-stain (ab stān´) *v.* To refrain from doing something. **abstainer** *n.*

ab-ste-mi-ous (ab stē´mē us) *adj.* Showing moderation in the use of drink and food. **abstemiousness** *n.* **abstemiously** *adv.*

ab-sten-tion (ab sten´sh*a***n)** *n.* The act of holding off from using or doing something.

ab-sterge (ab stürj´) *v.* To make clean by wiping; to wash away.

ab-ster-gent (ab stür´jent) *adj.* Having purgative or cleaning properties. *n.* a detergent or anything that aids in cleaning.

ab-stract (ab strakt´) *v.* To remove from, reduce, or summarize. **abstractedness** *n.*

ab-stract-ed (ab strak´tid) *adj.* Absorbed in thought; Absent in mind; inattentive.

ab-strac-tion (ab strak´sh*a***n)** *n.* The act of separating, withdrawing; something abstract.

ab-strac-tion-ism (ab strak sh*e* **niz***e***m)** *n.* Practice of making abstract art.

ab-strac-tive (ab strak´tiv) *adj.* Having the power or quality of abstracting.

ab-strict (ab strikt) *v.* To cause an abstraction.

ab-stric-tion (ab strik´sh*a***n)** *adj.* A forming of spores with the cutting off of parts of the sporophore.

ab-struse (ab strŏs´) *adj.* Difficult or hard to understand, comprehend. **abstruseness** *n.* **abstrusely** *adv.*

ab-surd (ab sürd´) *adj.* Contrary to reason; clearly untrue or unreasonable. **absurdity** *n.* **absurdness** *n.*

ab-surd-ism (ab sürd iz em) *n.* The philosophy which is based on the idea and belief that man lives in a meaningless universe and the search for order will bring him and the universe into conflict. **absurdist** *n.*

a-bub-ble (*a*´**beb** *e***l)** *adj.* To be in the process of bubbling.

a-build-ing (*a*´**bil din)** *adj.* To be in the process of constructing or building.

a-bu-li-a (*a* **bū´lē** *a***)** *n., Psychol.* Form of mental derangement where volition is lost or impaired.

a-bun-dance (*a* **bun´d***a***ns)** *n.* Ample supply; plenty; amount more than enough.

a-bun-dant (*a* **bun´d***a***nt)** *adj.* Plentiful; sufficient; overflowing, abounding.

a-bun-dant-ly (*a* **bun´d***a***nt lē)** *adv.* In sufficient degree; amply; plentifully; enough.

a-buse (*a* **būz´)** *v.* To use in an improper or wrong way. **abuse** *n.* Improper treatment or employment; improper use or application; misuse. **abuser** *n.*

a-bu-sive (*a* **bū´siv)** *adj.* Practicing abuse; bad treatment toward another. **abusiveness** *n.*

a-but (*a* **but´)** *v.* To border; to touch at one end; to be contiguous to; to join at a border or boundary; to form a point or line of contact, used with *on, upon, against*.

a-bu-ti-lon (*a* būt´*i* lon˝) *n*. A member of the genus of mallow family that has lobed leaves and bell-shaped flowers.

a-but-ment (*a* but´m*e*nt) *n*. Support at the end of an arch or bridge.

a-but-tal (*a* but´*a*l) *n*. The bordering part of a piece of land.

a-but-ting (*a* but´ing) *adj*. To abut or to serve as an abutment of something.

a-buzz (*a* buz) *adj*. To be filled with a buzzing.

a-bys-mal (*a* biz´m*a*l) *adj*. Immeasurably deep or low; profound.

a-byss (*a* bis´) *n*. A deep crack or gap in the earth. **abyssal** *adj*.

Abyssinian cat *n*. A type of breed of cat of African origin that has short brownish hair.

ac *abbr*. Account.

AC *abbr*. Alternating current.

a-ca-cia (*a* kā´sh*a*) *n*. Thorny tree or shrub of warm climates.

acad *abbr*. Academy.

ac-a-deme (ak˝*a* dēm´) *n*. The place where instruction is given to pupils.

ac-a-dem-ic (ak˝*a* dem´ik) *adj*. Higher education; relating to classical or liberal studies, rather than vocational.

ac-a-dem-i-cal (ak˝*a* dem´i k*a*l) *n*. Member of an academy; students and officers of a college or school.

academic freedom *n*. The freedom for one to teach or learn without an interference from the government.

ac-a-de-mi-cian (*a* kad*e* mish´*a*n) *n*. A person who follows a philosophical tradition.

ac-a-dem-i-cism (ak˝*a* dem´i siz ˝*u*m) *n*. The system of teaching at an academy.

academic year *n*. A period of sessions of school which will usually start in September and end in June.

a-cad-e-my (*a* kad´*e* mē) *n. pl.* **academies** A private school for special training, as in music, art, or military. A school holding a rank between a college and an elementary school.

Aca-di-an (*a* kā´dē *a*n) *n*. A person who is a native of Acadia.

AC and U *abbr*. Association of Colleges and Universities.

a-can-tha (*a* kan´th*a*) *n*. The prickle of a plant; an animal's spine; one of the acute processes of the vertebrae of animals.

ac-an-tha-ceous (ak *a*n thā´shus) *adj*. Armed with prickles.

a-can-thine (*a* kan´thin) *adj*. Pertaining to or resembling the plant acanthus.

a-can-tho-ceph-a-la (*a* kan˝th*a* sef´ *a* l*a*) *n*. A member of the group of intestinal worms that have a hooked proboscis and will absorb food out of the digestive tract.

a-can-tho-ceph-a-lan (*a* kan˝th*a* sef´ *a* l*a*n) *adj*. Having spines or hooks on the head, as certain intestinal worms (the Acanthocephala), which are attached within the bodies of animals.

a-can-thoid (*a* kan˝thoid) *adj*. Having the shape of a spine.

ac-an-thop-ter-yg-i-an (ak˝*a*n thop˝ter ij ´ē *a*n) *n*. A fish, as the bluegill, with spine-like fins.

a-can-thous (*a* kan´thus) *adj*. Spiny.

a-can-thus (*a* kan´thus) *n*. A prickly plant, native to the Mediterranean region.

a cap-pel-la (ä˝k*a* pel´*a*) *adj*. Singing without instrumental accompaniment.

ac-a-ri-a-sis (ak˝*a* rī´*a* sis) *n*. An infestation that is caused by mites.

ac-a-rid (ak´*a* rid) *n*. A member of the order of arachnids that includes ticks and mites.

ac-a-roid (ak´*a* roid˝) *adj*. Having the resemblance of a mite.

acaroid resin *n*. A type of resin that is alcohol soluble and is obtained from the Australian grass trees.

a-car-pel-ous (ā kär´p*e* lus) *adj*. To be without carpels.

a-car-pous (ā kär´pus) *adj*. Barren; not producing fruit.

a-cat-a-lec-tic (ā kat˝*a* lek´tik) *adj*. Not stopping short; having the complete number of syllables in a line of verse.

a-cau-date (ā kä´dāt) *adj*. Having no tail.

ac-au-les-cent (ak˝a les′ent) *adj., Bot.* Stemless.

ACC *abbr.* Air Coordinating Committee.

ac-cede (ak sēd′) *v.* To consent; to agree; to arrive at a certain condition or state.

ac-cel-er-ate (ak sel′a rāt˝) *v.* To make work or run faster; to increase the speed; to hasten; to quicken; to cause to advance faster, to increase study courses. **acceleration** *n.*

ac-cel-er-a-tion (ak sel˝a rā′shan) *n.* The process of accelerating something.

ac-cel-er-a-tive (ak sel′e rā˝tiv) *adj.* To be pertaining to acceleration.

ac-cel-er-a-tor (ak sel′e rā˝tor) *n.* Something that accelerates something else.

ac-cel-er-om-e-ter (ak sel˝e rom′i tėr) *n.* An instrument used to measure and record the acceleration of aircraft speed.

ac-cent (ak′sent) *n.* An effort to make one syllable more prominent than the others. **accentless** *adj.*

ac-cen-tu-al (ak sen′chö al) *adj.* To be pertaining to or having an accent.

accentual verse *n.* A verse where the accentuation is the basis of the rhythm.

ac-cen-tu-ate (ak sen′chö āt˝) *v.* To emphasize; to make a portion more or pronounced.

ac-cept (ak sept′) *v.* To take what is given; to believe to be true; to agree, to receive. **accepter** *n.* **acceptor** *n.*

ac-cept-able (ak sep′ta bl) *adj.* Satisfactory; proper; good enough. **acceptableness** *n.* **acceptability** *n.* **acceptably** *adv.*

ac-cep-tance (ak sep′tans) *n.* Approval or belief; an accepting or being accepted.

ac-cep-tant (ak sep′tant) *adj.* To be willing to accept something.

ac-cep-ta-tion (ak˝sep tā′shan) *n.* The act of receiving or accepting; favorable reception.

ac-cept-ed (ak sep′tid) *adj.* Commonly approved; generally thought of as right or normal; conventional.

ac-cep-tive (ak sep′tiv) *adj.* Willing to accept or receive.

ac-cess (ak′ses) *n.* Entrance, admission; near approach; admittance; the state of being approachable; passage that allows communication.

ac-ces-si-bil-i-ty (ak ses˝i bil′i tē) *n.* The quality of being accessible.

ac-ces-si-ble (ak ses′i bl) *adj.* Able to be attained or approached; easy of access.

ac-ces-sion (ak sesh′an) *n.* In Computer Science, the act of obtaining data from storage; the ability to store data.

ac-ces-so-ri-al (ak˝si sōr′ē al) *adj.* To be pertaining to an accessory.

ac-ces-so-ri-ly (ak ses′sa ri lē) *adv.* An accessory; supplementary; not as principal but as a subordinate.

ac-ces-so-ri-ness (ak ses′sa rē nes) *n.* The state of being accessory, or of being or acting in a secondary character.

ac-ces-so-rize (ak ses′sō riz) *v.* To wear with accessories.

ac-ces-so-ry (ak ses′o rē) *adj.* Contributing; aiding in producing some effect, or acting in subordination to the principal agent; contributing to a general effect.

accessory nerve *n.* The pair of 11th cranial nerves which supply to the muscles of the upper chest, shoulders, back, and pharynx.

access road *n.* A type of road which will provide access to an area.

ac-ciac-ca-tu-ra (ä chä˝ka tür′a) *n., Mus.* A short note, one half-step below, and struck at the same time as, the main note.

ac-ci-dence (ak′si dens) *n.* A book that contains the rudiments of grammar; the elementary parts of a subject.

ac-ci-dent (ak′si dent) *n.* A happening that is not planned or expected.

ac-ci-den-tal (ak˝si den′tal) *adj.* Happening by chance or accident; unexpected.

ac-ci-den-tal-ly (ak˝si den′tal lē) *adv.* In an accidental manner; not intentionally; by chance.

accident insurance *n.* A type of insurance protecting the person against loss due to the injury which may be caused by an accident.

accident–prone *adj.* To have a greater than average amount of accidents.

ac-cip-i-ter (ak sip′i tėr) *n.* A type of

short-winged hawk that has a flight pattern that is darting and low. **accipitrine** *adj.*

ac-claim *(a klām´)* *v.* To greet with strong approval or loud applause; to hail or cheer.

ac-cla-ma-tion (ak˝la mā´shan) *n.* An expression of approval that can be quite loud

ac-cli-mate (a kli´mit) *v.* To get used to a different climate or new surroundings.

ac-cli-ma-ti-za-tion (a klī´ma tī zā˝shan) *n.* The result of acclimatizing.

ac-cli-ma-tize (a klī´ma tīz˝) *v.* To change to or to adapt to a change in altitude, climate, or temperature.

ac-cliv-i-ty *(a kliv´i tē)* *n.* An ascending slope.

ac-co-lade (ak´a lād´) *n.* Award; ceremony used in conferring knighthood. *Arch.* A curved molding above an arched opening.

ac-com-mo-date (a kom´a dāt˝) *v.* To give room or lodging; to make fit; to adjust.

ac-com-mo-dat-ing (a kom´a dā˝ting) *adj.* Ready to help; willing to please; obliging.

ac-com-mo-da-tion (a kom´a dā´shan) *n.* Adjustment; change to fit new conditions; help or convenience.

accommodation ladder *n.* A type of ladder which will hang over the ship for the purpose of getting into smaller boats easier.

ac-com-mo-da-tive (a kom´a dā ˝tiv) *adj.* Giving accommodation; adaptive.

ac-com-mo-da-tor (a kom´a dā˝ tôr) *n.* Someone or something that will accommodate.

ac-com-pa-ni-ment *(a kum´pa ni ment)* *n.* Something that goes well with another.

ac-com-pa-nist (a kum´pa nist) *n.* A person who plays a musical accompaniment.

ac-com-pa-ny (a kum´pa nē) *v.* To be together with; to go along with; to go with or attend as a companion or associate; to go together; to be associated or connected with.

ac-com-plice (a kom´plis) *n.* Companion who helps another break the law; a partner or partaker in guilt, usually a subordinate.

ac-com-plish (a kom´plish) *v.* To perform; to carry out; to complete; to do.

accomplisher *n.*

ac-com-plish-a-ble (a kom´plish a bl) *adj.* Being capable of accomplishment.

ac-com-plished (a kom´plisht) *adj.* Trained, perfected, proficient, finished; consummated; skilled.

ac-com-plish-ment (a kom´plish ment) *n.* The act of accomplishing or carrying into effect; fulfillment; attainment; a-chievement.

ac-cord (a kord´) *n.* Harmony; agreement. **accord** *v.* To grant or award.

ac-cord-ance (a kor´dans) *n.* The state of being in accord; agreement with a person.

ac-cord-ant (a kor´dant) *adj.* Agreeable; of the same mind; conformable.

ac-cord-ant-ly (a kor´dant lē) *adv.* In accordance or agreement.

ac-cord-ing-ly (a kor´ding lē) *adv.* In a way that is proper and fitting.

according to *prep.* Attested by.

ac-cor-di-on (a kor´dē an) *n.* A musical instrument fitted with bellows and button keyboard, played by pulling out and pressing together the bellows to force air through the reeds.

ac-cor-di-on-ist (akär´dē an ist) *n.* A player of the accordion.

ac-cost (a kost´) *v.* To come close to and to speak first in an unfriendly manner.

ac-couche-ment (a kösh´mänt) *n.* Childbirth; confinement.

ac-cou-cheur (ä kö shoer´) *n.* A surgeon who attends women in childbirth.

ac-cou-cheuse (ä kö shoez´) *n.* Midwife.

ac-count (a kount´) *n.* A description; a statement of debts and credits in money transactions; a record; a report.

ac-count-a-bil-i-ty (a koun˝ta bil´i tē) *n.* Being accountable, answerable.

ac-count-a-ble (a kount´ta bl) *adj.* Liable to be held responsible; able to be explained. **accountably** *adv.*

ac-coun-tan-cy (a kount´tan sē) *n.* The profession of an accountant.

ac-count-ant (*a* koun´tant) *n*. A person who keeps or examines accounts; a profession.

account executive *n*. Administrator of a client's account; a business service.

ac-count-ing (*a* koun´ting) *n*. A report on how accounts have been balanced; the system of keeping business records or accounts.

accounting machine *n*. A type of device that will subtract, add, and totals data that is placed into it.

ac-cou-tre (*a* kō´tėr) *v*. To give or to provide with furnishings.

ac-cred-it (*a* kred´it) *v*. To authorize someone; to give official power.

ac-cres-cent (*a* kres´ent) *adj*. Increasing; growing.

ac-crete (*a* krēt´) *v*. To grow together or join.

ac-cre-tion (*a* krē´shan) *n*. The process of enlarging something. **accretionary** *adj*.

ac-cru-al (*a* krō´al) *n*. Process or act of accruing; something accrued.

ac-crue(*a* krō´) *v*. To result naturally; to increase at certain times.

acct *abbr*. Account.

ac-cul-tur-a-tion (*a* kul˝cha rā´ shan) *n*. The modification of one's culture with a prolonged interaction involving another culture.

ac-cum-ben-cy (*a* kum´ben sē) *n*. State of being accumbent.

ac-cum-bent (*a* kum´bent) *adj*. Leaning or reclining; lying against anything.

ac-cu-mu-late (*a* kū´mya lāt˝) *v*. To collect or gather over a period of time; to pile up.

ac-cum-u-la-tion (*a*kū˝mya lā´shan) *n*. A mass that has been collected; growth by continuous increases.

ac-cu-mu-la-tive (*a* kū´mya lā˝tiv) *adj*. Causing an accumulation; cumulative; heaping up.

ac-cum-u-la-tor (*a* kū´mya lā˝tor) *n*. One who or that which accumulates.

ac-cu-ra-cy (ak´yur *a* sē) *n. pl.* **accuracies** Exactness; precision; the fact of being accurate or without mistakes.

ac-cu-rate (ak´yur it) *adj*. Without mistakes or errors; careful and exact; correct. **accurately** *adv*.

ac-curse (*a* kürs´) *v*. To curse.

ac-curs-ed (a kür´sid) *adj*. Sure to end badly; under a curse; unpleasant or annoying; very bad. **accursedness** *n*.

ac-cu-sa-tion (ak˝ū zā´shan) *n*. A charge that a person is guilty of breaking the law.

ac-cu-sa-tive (a kū´za tiv) *adj*. Relating to the direct object of a preposition or of a verb.

ac-cuse (*a* kūz´) *v*. To find fault with; to blame; to charge someone with doing wrong or breaking the law. **accuser** *n*.

ac-cused (*a* kūzd´) *n*. A person charged with a crime; a defendant in a court of law.

ac-cus-tom (*a* kus´tom) *v*. To familiarize by habit.

ac-cus-tomed (*a* kus´tomd) *adj*. Often practiced; familiar; usual.

ace (ās) *n*. The face of a die or a playing card marked with one spot; in tennis and some other sports, a score made by a serve that is not returned.

ACE *abbr*. American Council on Education.

a-ce-di-a (*a* sē´dē *a*) *n*. Loss of interest for living.

a-cel-lu-lar (ā sel´ū lar) *adj*. Having no cells.

a-cen-tric (ā sen´trik) *adj*. To be missing a centromere.

a-ceph-a-lous (ā sef´*a* lus) *adj*. To be without a head.

a-ce-quia (*a* sā´kya) *n*. A type of ditch which can be used for irrigation.

ac-er-ate (as´e rāt˝) *adj*. Pointed and sharp.

a-cerb (*a* sürb´) *adj*. To be acid in one's mood; critical; bitter, sour, harsh to the taste.

a-cer-bi-ty (*a* sür´bi tē) *n*. Sourness, with roughness of taste.

ac-er-o-la (*a* e ´rō le) *n*. A type of West Indian shrub that yields cherrylike fruits.

a-ce-rous (ā sēr´us) *adj*. Without horns.

a-cer-vate (*a* sür´vit) *adj*. To be living or growing in heaps. **acervately** *adv*.

a-ces-cent (*a* ses´ent) *adj*. Slightly sour, turning sour.

ac-e-tab-u-lar-ia (as˝i tab´yu lar´ē a) *n.* A type of single-celled alga found in the warm seas which look like mushrooms in shape.

ac-e-tab-u-lum (as˝i tab´yu lum) *n.* The socket of the hipbone. **acetabular** *adj.*

ac-e-tal (as´i tal˝) *n., Chem.* The liquid formed by imperfect oxidation of alcohol.

ac-et-a-min-o-phen (as et e min e fen) *n.* A compound which is used for the purpose of relieving pain and fever.

ac-e-tate (as´i tāt˝) *n.* Salt formed by union of acetic acid with a base, used in making rayon and plastics.

a-cet-ic (a sē´tik) *adj.* To be pertaining to or related to vinegar or acetic acid.

acetic acid (a sē´tik as´id) *n.* The main ingredient of vinegar; a sour, colorless liquid that has a sharp smell.

a-cet-i-fi-ca-tion (a set´i fi kā´shan) *n.* The act of acetifying or making sour; the process of making vinegar.

a-ce-ti-fi-er (a set´i fī˝ēr) *n.* Equipent used in making vinegar.

a-ce-ti-fy (a set´i fī˝) *v.* To change or to turn into acetic acid. **acetification** *n.*

ac-e-tom-e-ter (as˝i tom´i tēr) *n.* Instrument for determining the purity or strength or of acetic acid in a solution.

ac-e-to-phe-net-i-din (as˝i tō fe net´i din) *n.* A type of compound which is used for relief of pain and fever.

a-ce-tous (a sē´tus) *adj.* To be pertaining to vinegar.

a-cet-y-lene (a set´e lēn˝) *n.* A highly inflammable, poisonous, colorless gas that burns brightly with a hot flame, used in blowtorches for cutting metal and welding.

ache (āk) *v.* To give or have a dull, steady pain; to want very much; to long for.

a-chene (ā kēn´) *n.* A type of indehiscent one-seeded fruit that has developed from an ovary. **achenial** *adj.*

a-chiev-a-ble (a chēv´a bl) *adj.* Being capable to be achieved or performed; attainable.

a-chieve (a chēv´) *v.* To set or reach by trying hard; to do; to succeed in doing; to accomplish. **achiever** *n.* **achievable** *adj.*

a-chieve-ment (a chēv´ment) *n.* Something achieved by work, courage, skill.

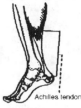
Achilles tendon

Achilles tendon (a kil´ēz ten´don) *n.* The tendon that connects the heelbone and calf muscles.

a-chlor-hy-dri-a (ā˝klōr hī´drē a) *n.* Absence of hydrochloric acid from gastric juices.

a-chon-drite (ā kon drīt) *n.* A type of stony meteorite that does not have rounded grains.

a-chon-dro-pla-sia (ā kon˝dro plā´zha) *n.* The failure of the development in a normal manner of the cartilage which results in dwarfism. **achondroplastic** *adj.*

ach-ro-mat-ic (ak˝ro mat´ik) *adj.* The transmitting of light without decomposing it into primary colors.

a-chro-ma-tin (ā krō´ma tin) *n., Biol.* The portion in the nucleus of a cell that is unstainable.

a-chro-ma-tism (ā krō´m a tiz´um) *n.* A quality of giving of images practically free from extraneous colors.

a-chro-ma-tous (ā krō´ma tus) *adj.* Having no color; of a lighter color than is usual or normal.

achy (āk´ē) *adj.* To have aches.

a-cic-u-la (a sik´yu la) *n.* Spine of an animal or plant.

ac-id (as´id) *n.* A chemical compound containing hydrogen that forms a salt when combined with a base, dissolves in water, has a very sour taste, makes litmus paper turn red.

ac-id-fast (as´id fast˝) *adj.* Not easily decolorized by acid.

acid head *n.* A user of the drug LSD.

a-cid-ic (a sid´ik) *adj, Chem.* Pertaining to acid; to contain a large amount of an acid constituent.

a-cid-i-fi-er (a sid´i fī˝ēr) *n.* Any chemical that produces an acid effect.

a-cid-i-fy (a sid´ifī˝) *v.* To make some

substance acid.

ac-i-dim-e-ter (as˝i dim´itèr) *n., Chem.* Instrument used for measuring the amount of acid in a particular volume or weight of a solution.

a-cid-i-ty (*a* sid´i tē) *n.* Condition or quality of being acid.

ac-i-do-phile (as´i dō fil˝) *n., Biol.* Tissue, cell, organism, or substance that shows an affinity towards an acidic environment.

ac-i-do-phil-ic (as˝i dō fil´ik) *adj.* Having the quality to be easily stained with acid; thriving in acid.

ac-i-do-sis (as˝i dō´sis) *n.* The abnormally high concentration of acid in body tissues and blood.

acid rain *n.* Acid precipitation that falls as rain.

acid rock *n.* Lyrics from Rock music that suggest drug-related experiences.

a-cid-u-late (*a* sij´*u* lāt´) *v.* To become or make somewhat acid.

a-cid-u-lous (*a* sij´*u* lus) *adj.* To be slightly acid in taste.

ac-i-na-ceous (as˝i nā´shus) *adj.* Full of seeds or kernels.

ac-i-nac-i-form (as˝i nas´i form˝) *adj.* Formed like or resembling a scimitar sword.

ac-i-nar (as *e* n*e*r) *adj.* To be pertaining to an acinus.

ac-i-nus (as´i nus) *n.* A sac of a racemose gland which is lined with secreting cells.

ack *abbr.* Acknowledge; acknowledgment.

ack-ack (ak´ak˝) *n.* Anti-aircraft fire.

ac-know-ledge (ak nol´ij) *v.* To admit the truth, existence or reality. **acknowledge-able** *adj*

ac-knowl-edg-ment (ak nol´ij m*e*nt) *n.* To acknowledge or own up to something; recognition; confession; something that is given or done in return for a favor.

a-clin-ic (ā klin´ik) *adj.* Applied to an imaginary line that is near the earth's equator.

ACLS *abbr.* American Council of Learned Societies.

ac-me (ak´mē) *n.* The highest point of attainment; peak.

ac-ne (ak´nē) *n.* An inflammation of the sebaceous glands, or oil-secreting organs, of the skin, manifested by eruptions of hard, inflamed pimples. Increased production of androgens, hormones, in both male and female during puberty causes the sebaceous glands to become active and secrete large amounts of sebum, which block the glands and hair follicles.

a-cock (*a* kok´) *adj.* To be in a cocked position.

ac-o-lyte (ak´*o* lit´) *n.* An altar boy or someone who assists a priest at Mass.

ac-o-nite (ak´*a* nit˝) *n.* A poisonous plant with flowers resembling hoods; sometimes called monkshood.

a-corn (ā´kon) *n.* A fern or moss-type plant that has no seed leaves.

acorn squash *n.* An acorn-shaped squash with yellow flesh and a ridged rind.

acorn tube *n.* A small vacuum tube which is like an acorn in shape.

acorn worm *n.* A member of the group of burrowing wormlike marine animals having an acorn-shaped proboscis.

a-cot-y-le-don (ā˝kot˝*e* lēd´*o*n) *n.* A plant as a fern or moss, which does not have seed leaves.

a-cous-tic (*a* kŏ´stik) *adj.* Having to do with sound or the sense of hearing; the sense of sound; absorbing sound. **acoustical** *n.* **acoustically** *adv.*

acoustic nerve *n.* The nerve that serves the ear.

a-cous-tics (*a* kŏ´stiks) *n.* The scientific study of sound; total effect of sound, especially in an enclosed space. **acoustician** *n.*

ACP *abbr.* American College of Physicians.

acpt *abbr.* Acceptance.

ac-quaint (*a* kwānt´) *v.* To make familiar; to let know, to make aware; to inform.

ac-quaint-ance (*a* kwān´t*a*ns) *n.* A person whom one knows but not as a close friend. **acquaintanceship** *n.*

ac-quaint-ed (*a* kwān´tid) *adj.* Being with, but not close or intimate.

ac-qui-esce (ak˝wē es´) *v.* To agree without arguing; to comply without protest, to comply. **acquiescent** *adj.*

ac-qui-es-cence (ak˝wē es´ens) *n.* The act of giving or acquiescing a quiet; a yielding.

ac-quir-a-ble (a kwī er´ a bl) *adj.* Capable of being acquired.

ac-quire (a kwier´) *v.* To secure control or possession; to become the owner.

acquired immunity *n.* Immunity against disease one develops during a lifetime.

ac-quire-ment (a kwī er´ ment) *n.* The act of acquiring something, as a skill gained by learning.

ac-qui-si-tion (ak˝wi zish´an) *n.* Something that is acquired; the act of acquiring.

ac-quis-i-tive (a kwiz´i tiv) *adj.* Eager to gain and possess things; greedy.

ac-quis-i-tive-ly (a kwiz´i tiv lē) *adv.* An acquisitive manner.

ac-quis-i-tive-ness (a kwiz´i tiv nis) *n.* The quality of being acquisitive.

ac-quit (a kwit´) *v.* To rule that a person accused of something is not guilty; to conduct oneself; to behave.

ac-quit-tal (a kwit´al) *n.* The act of acquitting. To settle a debt or obligation.

ac-quit-tance (a kwit´ans) *n.* A discharge from a debt or any other liability.

a-cre (ā´kėr) *n.* A measurement of land that equals 43,560 square feet.

a-cre-age (ā´kėr ij) *n.* The total number of acres in a section of land.

ac-rid (ak´rid) *adj.* Having a sharp, bitter, or irritating taste or smell. **acridity** *n.* **acridness** *n.* **acridly** *adv.*

ac-ri-mo-ni-ous (ak˝ri mō´nē us) *adj.* Sharp or bitter in speech or manner. **acrimoniousness** *n.* **acrimoniously** *adv.*

ac-ri-mo-ny (ak´ri mō˝nē) *n.* Sharpness or severity of temper; bitterness of expression.

a-crit-i-cal (ā krit´i kal) *adj., Med.* Not critical.

ac-ro-bat (ak´ro bat˝) *n.* One who is skilled in gymnastic feats. **acrobatic** *adj.*

ac-ro-bat-ics (ak˝ro bat´iks) *n.* The performance of an acrobat.

ac-ro-car-pous (ak˝ro kär´pus) *adj., Bot.* Applied to mosses whose fruit terminates the growth of a primary root.

ac-ro-cen-tric (ak rō sen trik) *adj.* To have a centromere that is located so one chromosomal arm is longer than the other arm.

ac-ro-dont (ak´ro dont) *adj.* Having rootless teeth that are joined to the ridges of the upper and lower jaws. *n.* Animals possessing such teeth.

a-crop-e-tal (a krop´i tal) *adj., Bot.* Starting at the base and going toward the highest or narrowest point.

ac-ro-pho-bi-a (ak˝ro fō´bē a) *n.* Unusual fear of heights.

ac-ro-spire (ak´ro spīėr˝) *n.* The first leaf that rises above the ground as grain starts to germinate.

a-cross (a kros´) From side to side; to one side from the other.

across the board (a kros´the bōrd´) *adj.* Designates win, place, and show in one bet on the same contestant.

a-cros-tic (a kro´stik) *n.* A series of lines or a poem in which certain letters in each line form a name or motto.

ac-ro-tism (ak´ro tiz˝um) *n.* The weakness or absence of the pulse.

a-cryl-ic (a kril´ik) *n.* Relating to or of acrylic acid or its derivatives.

acrylic fiber *n.* A fiber which is made of chemicals, used in making fabrics.

ac-ry-lo-ni-trile (ak˝re lō nī´tril) *n.* A liquid organic compound used to make acrylic fibers and rubber.

ACT *abbr.* American College Test.

act (akt) *n.* Doing something; a thing done; deed; an action; a showing of emotion which is not real or true; a law; decree; one of the main parts of a play, opera, etc.

act (akt) *v.* To exert power; to produce effects; to be in action or motion; to behave, demean, or conduct oneself; to perform, as an actor; to substitute for; as, to *act* as captain; to transact; to do or perform; to represent as real; to feign or counterfeit. **act as** To serve as; perform the function or duties of. **act on** To act or obey in accordance with; to affect. **act out** To demonstrate or perform. **act out**

Psychol. To express openly subconscious emotions. **act up** To behave in a manner that is unruly or capricious.

act-a-ble (akt´abl) *adj.* Capable of being acted or performed. **actability** *n.*

actg *abbr.* Acting.

ac-tin (ak´tin) *n.* A type of protein that is in the muscle and becomes active in muscle contractions.

act-ing (ak´ting) *adj.* Temporarily performing the duties, services, or functions of another person.

ac-tin-i-a (ak tin´ ē a) *n.* A sea anemone; having a mouth surrounded by tentacles in circle.

ac-tin-ic (ak tin´ik) *adj.* Pertaining to rays, the chemical rays of the sun.

ac-tin-i-form (ak tin´iform˝) *adj.* Bearing a resemblance to an actinia.

ac-tin-ism (ak´ti niz˝um) *n.* The radiation of heat or light.

ac-tin-o-gen (ak tin´o jen˝) *n.* An element which is radioactive.

ac-tin-o-graph(aktin´o graf˝)*n.* Instrument used to measure and register variations of actinic or chemical influence in the solar rays.

ac-ti-nom-e-ter (ak˝ti nom´itèr) *n.* Instrument for measuring the intensity of the sun's actinic rays.

ac-ti-no-my-cin (ak˝ti nōmīs´in) *n.* One of the yellow-red or red polypeptide antibiotics that is separated from soil bacteria.

ac-ti-non (ak´ti non˝) *n.* A radioactive, gaseous, existing for only a few seconds, and is isotopic with radon.

ac-tion (ak´shan) *n.* The process of doing or acting; an effect produced by something; a lawsuit.

ac-tion-able (ak´sha na bl) *adj.* To be affording ground for a suit at law.

ac-tion-less (ak shen les) *adj.* To be characterized by inaction and lack of movement.

action painting *n.* A style of painting where paint is often smeared or dribbled to give a thickly textured surface.

ac-ti-vate (ak´ti vāt˝) *v.* To put into action. **activation** *n.*

ac-tive (ak´tiv) *adj.* Working; full of action; busy; lively; quick, constant. **activeness** *n.* **actively** *adv.*

active immunity *n.* A type of immunity where the effects are long lasting and acquired through a response to antigens.

active transport *n.* A type of movement across a membrane of a cell with the use of energy.

ac-tiv-ism (ak´ti viz˝um) *n.* A practice based on direct action to affect changes in government and social conditions.

ac-tiv-i-ty (ak tiv´i tē) *n.* Being active, in motion; normal power of body or mind.

act of God *n.* An unforeseeable, uncontrollable happening caused by nature.

ac-tor (ak´tor) *n.* A person who acts in movies, plays, television shows, etc.

ac-tress (ak´tris) *n.* A female actor.

ac-tu-al (ak´chö al) *adj.* Acting or existing in fact or reality; as it really is; true. **actualness** *n.*

ac-tu-al-i-ty (ak˝chö al´i tē) *n.* The state of being actual; something that is actual or real.

ac-tu-al-ize (ak´chö a līz˝) *v.* To realize; to make actual.

ac-tu-al-ly (ak´chö a lē) *adv.* In truth.

ac-tu-ar-y (ak´chö er˝ē) *n.* A person who will figure or calculate insurance.

ac-tu-ate (ak´chö āt˝) *v.* To put into motion or action. **actuation** *n.*

ac-tu-a-tor (ak´chö ā˝tèr) *n.* Something that will control something else indirectly.

a-cu-i-ty (a kū´i tē) *n.* A sharp perception of something.

a-cu-le-ate (a kū´lē it) *adj.* To have a sting.

a-cu-men (a kū´men) *n.* The quickness of perception; mental acuteness, the keenness of insight.

a-cu-mi-nate (a kū´mi nat˝) *adj.* To taper to a point which is slender in shape.

ac-u-punc-ture (ak´ū pungk´chur) *n.* A traditional Chinese means of treating some illnesses or of lessening pain by putting thin needles into certain parts of the body.

a-cute (a kūt´) *adj.* Extremely sensitive; sharp and quick, as pain; shrewd. **acute-**

ness *n.* **acutely** *adv.*

acute accent *n.* A mark to indicate heavy stress on a syllable.

a-cute-ly (*a* kūt´lē) *adv.* In an acute manner; keenly, discrimination.

a-cute-ness (*a* kūt´nis) *n.* The quality of being acute; sharpness; keenness.

ACV *abbr.* Actual cash value.

ad (ad) *n.* An advertisement.

AD *abbr. Anno Domini* Latin for "in the year of the Lord."

ad-age (ad´ij) *n.* A proverb; a wise or true saying.

a-da-gi-o (*a* dä´jō) *adj.* Term used in music to tell how fast a piece should be played.

Ad-am (ad´am) *n.* The first man named in the Bible, the husband of Eve.

ad-a-mant (ad´*a* mant) *adj.* Standing firm; not giving in easily; unyielding.

Adam's apple *n.* A projection in the throat, especially noticeable in men, formed by the trachea or a cartilage at the upper end of the windpipe.

a-dapt (*a* dapt´) *v.* To fit or suit; to change oneself as to adjust to new conditions. **a-daptedness** *n.*

a-dapt-a-ble (*a*dap´tabl) *adj.* Being capable of adapted. Able to adjust oneself without difficulty to new, unfamiliar, or unexpected conditions. **adaptability** *n.*

ad-ap-ta-tion (ad˝*a*p tā´shan) *n.* An act of changing so as to fit or become suitable.

a-dapt-er (*a* dap´tėr) *n.* One who or that which adapts; a connecting device where parts fit together.

ad-ax-i-al (ad ak´sē *a*l) *adj.* To be positioned on one side of the axis.

ADC *abbr.* Aid to Dependent Children. *abbr.* Air Defense Command.

add (ad) *v.* To join or put something with another so that there will be more; to cause an increase. **add up** To make sense; to be reasonable; to arrive or to come to the expected total of a group of numbers. **addable, addible** *adj.*

ad-dax (ad´aks) *n.* An African antelope with spiral twisted horns.

ad-dend (ad´end) *n.* The number that is add-

ed to another number.

ad-den-dum (*a* den´d*u*m) *n. pl.* **addenda** An addition; an appendix to a book or literacy work; something which is added.

ad-der (ad´ėr) *n.* A common poisonous snake found in America and Europe.

ad-der's–tongue (ad´ėrz tung˝) *n.* A type of fern which has a fruiting spike that is just like the tongue of a serpent.

ad-dict (ad´ikt) *n.* A person with a habit so strong that he cannot easily give it up. **addiction** *n.* **addicted** *v.*

Addison's disease *n.* A condition that occurs when the adrenal glands cease to function properly and fail to produce adequate quantities of the hormones called steroids.

ad-di-tion (*a*dish´an) *n.* An adding of numbers to find their total; the act of joining one thing to another. **additionally** *adv.*

ad-di-tion-al (*a* dish´*a* nal) *adj.* Supplementary; additional; added.

ad-di-tive (ad´i tiv) *n.* A substance added to another in small amounts to alter it.

ad-dle (ad´el) *v.* To become or make confused; to spoil, as eggs.

addn *abbr.* Addition.

ad-dress (ad dres´) *v.* To direct or aim; to speak to; to give attention to. **address** *n.* The location to which mail or goods can be sent to a person, business, or organization. *Computer Science* The location, in the memory of a computer, where data is kept, to which data is sent, or from where data is drawn.

ad-dress-ee (ad dres´ē) *n.* The person to whom a letter or package is addressed.

ad-duce (ad dōs´) *v.* To offer as proof or give as a reason. **adducer** *n.*

ad-du-cent (ad dō´sent) *adj.* Bringing together or forward.

ad-duct (ad dukt´) *v.* To move or draw, such as a limb, toward the median axis of the body.

ad-duc-tion (ad duk´shan) *n.* The state

of being adducted.

ad-duc-tor *n.* The type of muscle which will draw a part of the body toward the median line of the body.

a-demp-tion (*a* demp´shn) *n., Law* Act of revoking a legacy.

ad-e-nine (ad´*e* nin) *n., Chem.* White, crystalline alkaloid, that is obtained from tea, glandular organs, or from uric acid; used chiefly in medicine.

ad-e-ni-tis (ad´*e* nī t*es*) *n.* The swelling or inflammation of lymph nodes.

ad-e-no-car-ci-no-ma (ad´*e* nō kăr˝s*i* nō´ m*a*) *n.* A type of malignant tumor which originates in the glandular epithelium, mainly in the stomach, large intestine, gallbladder, pancreas, uterus or prostate gland. **adenocarcinomatous** *adj.*

ad-e-noi-dal (ad *e* noid l) *adj.* To be pertaining to or related to the adenoids.

ad-e-noids (ad´*e* noid˝) *n.* Lymphoid tissue growths in the upper part of the throat behind the nose, that may need to be removed surgically.

ad-e-no-ma (ad˝*e*nō´m*a*)*n.,Pathol.* Benign tumor that originates in a gland.

a-den-o-sine tri-phos-phate (*a* den´*o* sēn˝ trī fos´fāt) *n.* A nucleotide occurring in all cells, representing the reserve energy of muscle that is important to many biochemical processes that produce or require energy.

adenosis *n.* A disease of a gland, particularly the abnormal development of glandular tissue.

a-dept (ad´ept) *adj.* Highly skilled; expert. **adeptly** *adv.* **adeptness** *n.*

ad-e-qua-cy (ad´*e* kwa sē) *n.* The state of being good enough to fill a requirement.

ad-e-quate (ad´*e* kwit) *adj.* Sufficient; good enough for what is needed. **adequateness** *n.* **adequately** *adv.*

ad eun-dem (ad˝ē an´d*em*) *adj.* To, in, or of the same rank.

ad-here (ad hēr´) *v.* To stay attached; to stick and not come loose; to stay firm in support.

ad-her-ence (ad hēr´*ens*) *n.* The quality of adhering.

ad-her-end (ad hēr´end) *n.* A surface to which an adhesive is able to adhere.

ad-her-ent (ad hēr´*ent*) *n.* A person who follows a leader, party, or belief; a believer or supporter.

ad-he-sion (ad hē´zh*an*) *n.* The act or state of sticking to something or of being stuck together.

ad-he-sive (ad hē´siv) *adj.* Tending to stick and not come loose; cling; having a sticky surface. **adhesiveness** *n.* **adhesively** *adv.*

adhesive tape *n.* A type of tape that has an adhesive on one side.

ad hoc (ad hok´) *adv.* For this particular purpose, without larger applications.

ad hoc committee *n.* Committee established for one specific reason.

ad ho-mi-nem (ad hō´mi nem˝) *adj.* Appealing to one's prejudices and personal feelings rather than his intellect and reason.

ad-i-a-bat-ic (ad˝ē*a* bat´ik) *adj.* Of physical changes without gain or loss of heat.

ad-i-aph-o-ra (ad ē af´o r*a*) *n.* Things morally indifferent; matters that have no moral merit or demerit.

ad-i-aph-o-rous (ad˝ē af´or us) *adj.* Indifferent or nonessential, morally; neutral.

a-dieu (*a* dö´) *interj.* French word for goodby.

ad interim *adj.* In the meantime.

a-di-os (ä˝dē ōs˝) *interj.* Spanish for goodby.

ad-i-pose (ad´*i* pōs˝) *n.* Fat; animal fat stored in the cells of adipose tissue.

adipose tissue *n.* A type of connective tissue where fat is stored in the body, mainly directly under the skin acting as an insulation and a source of energy.

ad-i-po-si-ty (ad˝*i* po´si tē) *n.* Obesity.

adj. *abbr.* Adjective; adjacent; adjourned.

ad-ja-cen-cy (*a* jā´s*en* sē) *n.* The state of being adjacent.

ad-ja-cent (*a* jā´sent) *adj.* Nearby; bordering upon; adjoining; neighboring.

adjacent angles *n.* Two angles with a side in common, having the same vertex.

ad-jec-ti-val (aj˝ik tī´val) *adj.* Belonging to or similar to an adjective.

ad-jec-tive (aj´ik tiv) *n.* A word used to describe a noun or pronoun, indicating which, what kind of, how many, or whose.

ad-join (a join´) *v.* To be next to; to be in or nearly in contact with.

ad-join-ing (a joi´ning) *adj.* Being adjacent; contiguous; neighboring; or in the closest relative position to.

ad-join-ing (a joi´ning) *adj.* To be touching at a point.

ad-journ (a jern) *v.* To close a meeting or session for a time; to move from one location to another.

ad-journ-ment (a jern´ment) *n.* The act of adjourning; the period when a legislature or other public body adjourns its meetings.

ad-judge (a juj´) *v.* To decide by judicial procedure. To pronounce or declare formally by law; to sentence or condemn; to adjudicate upon; to rule upon; to settle.

ad-ju-di-cate (a jō´di kāt˝) *v.* To settle a dispute judicially. **adjudicator** *n.* **adjudicative** *adj.*

ad-ju-di-ca-tion (a jō˝di kā´shan) *n.* Judicial decision. **adjudicatory** *adj.*

ad-junct (aj´ungkt) *n.* Something less important added to something with more importance. **adjunctly** *adv.* **adjunctive** *adj.*

ad-junc-tion (a jungk˝shan) *n.* Act of adjoining.

ad-jure (ajer´) *v.* To ask urgently; to command solemnly. **adjuration** *n.*

ad-just (ajust´) *v.* To arrange or change; to make work correctly; to regulate. **adjustability** *n.*

ad-just-a-ble (a just´a bl) *adj.* Anything that can be adjusted.

ad-just-ed (a just´ed) *adj.* To have attained or achieved a relationship with the environment that is harmonious.

ad-just-er (a just´ėr) *n.* A person who investigates property or personal damage and makes estimates for settlements.

ad-just-ment (a just´ment) *n.* The act or process of changing; a settlement of a suit or claim.

ad-ju-tan-cy (aj´u tan sē) *n.* The rank of an adjutant.

ad-ju-tant (aj´u tant) *n.* An administrative staff officer who serves as a secretary to the commanding officer.

adjutant general *n., Mil.* The chief administrative officer of a major military unit responsible for adminstration.

ad-ju-vant (aj´u vant) *n.* Assistant. *Med.* The substance added to a prescription to aid in the operation of the principal ingredient.

ad lib (ad lib´) *v.* To improvise; to compose or make up spontaneously.

ad-man (ad´man˝) *n.* A person who works in the business of advertising.

ad-meas-ure (ad mezh´ėr) *v.* To judge the dimensions, size, or capacity of something; to measure.

ad-meas-ure-ment (ad mezh´ur ment) *n.* The measure of something, or dimensions ascertained.

ad-min-is-ter (ad min´i stėr) *v.* To direct or manage; to give or carry out instructions. **administrable** *adj.*

ad-min-is-tra-tion (ad min˝i strā´shan) *n.* The people who manage a school, company, or organization; the act of administering.

ad-min-is-tra-tive (ad min´i strā˝tiv) *adj.* The pertaining to or resulting from management or administration.

ad-min-is-tra-tor (ad min´i strā˝tor) *n.* A person who administers or directs, an executive; a manager.

ad-mi-ra-ble (ad´mer a bl) *adj.* Worthy of being admired or praised; excellent.

ad-mi-ral (ad´mir al) *n.* The highest rank for a naval officer; the commanding officer of a navy or a fleet of ships.

ad-mi-ral-ty (ad´mir al tē) *n.* The department of the British navy; the court and law dealing with ships and shipping.

ad-mire (ad mīer´) *v.* To hold a high opinion; to regard with wonder, delight, and pleased approval; to regard with admiration. **admiringly** *adv.* **admirer** *n.*

ad-mis-si-bil-i-ty (ad mis´i bil˝i tē) *n.*

Quality of being admissible.

ad-mis-si-ble (ad mis´i bl) *adj.* Capable of being admitted, accepted or allowed.

ad-mis-sion (ad mish´an) *n.* The right or act of being admitted; an admitting of the truth of something; a confession.

ad-mit (ad mit´) *v.* To take or accept as being the truth; to permit or give the right to enter. **admittedly** *adv.*

ad-mit-tance (ad mit´ans) *n.* Permission to enter.

ad-mit-ted-ly (ad mit´id lē) *adv.* One's own admission or confession.

ad-mix-ture (ad miks´cher) *n.* Blend; mingling.

ad-mon-ish (ad mon´ish) *v.* To warn a person to correct a fault; to criticize in a gentle way. **admonisher** *n.*

ad-mo-ni-tion (ad˝mo nish´an) *n.* A mild criticism or warning.

a-do (a dō´) *n.* Fuss or trouble.

a-do-be (a dō´bē) *n.* A brick or building material made from clay and straw and then dried in the sun.

ad-o-les-cence (ad˝o les´ans) *n.* The period of physical and psychological development between childhood and adulthood; also known as youth.

ad-o-les-cent (ad˝oles´ent) *n.* A person in the transitional period between childhood and adulthood.

a-dopt (adopt´) *v.* To legally take into one's family and raise as their own. **adoption** *n.*

a-dop-tion (a dop´shan) *n.* Act of adopting, or the state of being adopted.

a-dor-a-bil-i-ty (a dōr˝´a bil´i tē) *n.* The quality of being adorable.

a-dor-a-ble (a dōr´a bl) *adj.* Very likable; charming. **adorably** *adv.*

a-dore (a dōr´) *v.* To love greatly; to worship or honor highly; to like very much, regard with admiration. **adorer** *n.*

a-dorn (a dorn´) *v.* To add splendor or beauty.

a-dorn-ment (a dorn´ment) *n.* Something that adorns; decoration; ornament; the act of adorning.

ad rem *adj.* Relevant to a point at issue.

ad-re-nal (a drē´nal) *adj.* Pertaining to the product of the adrenal gland, that is located on or near the kidney.

adrenal gland *n.* A small endocrine gland that consists of a medulla and cortex, located near the kidney.

ad-ren-er-gic (ad˝re nėr´jik) *adj., Med.* Liberated or activated by adrenaline or a similar substance.

a-drift (adrift´) *adv.* Drifting; floating freely without being steered; having no clear purpose or aim.

a-droit (a droit´) *adj.* Skillful and clever in difficult circumstances. **adroitly** *adv.*

ad-sci-ti-tious (ad˝si tish´us) *adj.* Derived from without; adventitious.

ad-script (ad´skript) *adj.* Written to the right of and in line with another letter or symbol.

ad-sorb (ad sorb´) *v.* To collect and hold as molecules of gases, liquids; to become adsorbed. **adsorbable** *adj.*

ad-sorb-ate (ad sor´bāt) *n.* The adsorbed substance in the process of adsorption.

ad-sor-bent (ad sorb´ent) *adj.* Having the ability or tendency to adsorb; adsorbing.

ad-u-late (aj´u lāt´) *v.* To give greater praise or flattery than is proper or deserved.

ad-u-la-tion (aj˝u lā´shan) *n.* Praise in excess, or beyond what is merited; high compliment.

a-dult (a dult´) *n.* A man or woman who is fully grown; a mature person. **adult** *adj.* Having reached full size and strength. **adulthood** *n.*

a-dul-ter-ate (a dul´te rāt´) *v.* To make impure or of less quality by adding improper ingredients.

a-dul-ter-a-tion (adul˝terā´shan) *n.* The act of adulterating, or the state of being adulterated; an adulterated substance.

a-dul-ter-er (a dul´tėr ėr) *n.* A person guilty of adultery.

a-dul-ter-ess (adul´ter is) *n.* A woman guilty of adultery.

a-dul-ter-ine (adul´tėr in) *adj.* Born of or involving adultery; impure.

a-dul-ter-ous (*a* **dult´***er* **us)** *adj.* Guilty of adultery; pertaining to adultery.

a-dul-ter-y (*a* **dul´***te* **rē)** *n.* The act of sexual intercourse between a married person and someone other than the husband or wife.

ad-um-brate (ad um´brāt) *v.* To give a faint shadow or brief outline of; to over-shadow.

a-dust (a dust´) *adj.* Scorched; parched; looking as if burned or scorched.

ad va-lo-rem (ad *va* **lōr´um)** *adj.* According to value.

adv *abbr.* Adverb; advertisement.

ad-vance (ad vans´) *v.* To move ahead; to make or become higher; to increase in value or price. *adj.* Something made or given ahead of time.

ad-vanced (ad vanst´) *adj.* Ahead in time; beyond beginning status.

ad-vance-ment (ad vans´ment) *n.* A promotion in position; progression; money ahead of time.

ad-van-tage (ad van´taj) *n.* A better chance or more forcible position; a condition, thing or event that can help or benefit; the first point, after deuce scored in the game of tennis.

ad-van-ta-geous (ad˝vantā´jus)*adj.* Giving advantage; favorable.

ad-vene (ad vēn´) *v.* To accede or become added to.

ad-vent (ad´vent) *n.* A coming or arrival; the four Sundays before Christmas.

ad-ven-ti-ti-a (ad˝ven tish´ē a) *n.* An external connective tissue which covers an organ.

ad-ven-ture (ad ven´ch*u***r)** *n.* An exciting and dangerous experience that is remembered; an unusual experience; uncertain outcome. **adventure** *v.*

ad-ven-tur-er (ad ven´ch*u***r r)** *n.* A person who looks for adventure; one who seeks wealth and social position; bold. **adventurous** *adj.*

ad-ven-ture-some (ad ven´ch*u***r sum)** *adj.* Inclined toward taking risks; daring; bold.

ad-ven-tur-ess (ad ven´ch*u***r es)***n.* A female adventurer.

ad-ven-tur-ous (ad ven´sh*u***r us)***adj.* Liking or seeking adventure; courageous; enterprising; full of hazard; attended with risk. **adventurously** *adv.*

ad-verb (ad´verb) *n.* A word used with a verb, adjective, or another adverb to tell when, where, how, what kind, or how much.

ad-ver-bi-al (ad ver´bē*a***l)** *adj.* Pertaining to or having the structure or character of an adverb.

ad-ver-bi-al-ly (ad ver´bē al ē) *adv.* In the manner of an adverb.

ad ver-bum (ad ver´b*u***m)** *adv.* Exactly word for word.

ad-ver-sar-y (ad´ver ser˝ē) *n.* An enemy, or a person having hostility toward another person or group of people.

ad-ver-sa-tive (ad ver´s*a* **tiv)** *adj.* Expressing difference, or opposition.

ad-verse (ad´vers)*adj.* Opposed; not helpful; against someone or something. **adverseness** *n.* **adversely** *adj.*

ad-ver-si-ty (ad ver´si tē) *n.* Bad luck or misfortune; calamity; state of unhappiness.

ad-vert (ad vert´) *v.* To turn the attention or mind; to regard, notice or observe.

ad-vert-ence (ad ver´t*e***ns)** *n.* Regard; notice; attention.

ad-ver-tise (ad´ver tīz˝) *v.* To draw public attention to a product you wish to sell, by printed broadcast media. **advertiser** *n.*

ad-ver-tise-ment (ad˝ver tīz´ment) *n.* A public notice designed to advertise something.

ad-ver-tis-ing (ad´ver tī˝zing) *n.* The job of preparing advertisements for publication or broadcast.

ad-vice (ad vīs´) *n.* Suggestion or recommendation regarding a decision or course of action.

ad-vis-a-bil-i-ty (ad vī˝*za* **bil´***i* **tē)** *n.* Quality of being advisable.

ad-vis-a-ble (ad vī˝*za* **bl)** *adj.* Fit to be done; advised. **advisability** *n.* **advisableness** *n.*

ad-vise (ad vīz´) *v.* To counsel; to inform; to give information to; to give notice.

ad-vised (ad vīzd′) *adj.* Prudent; cautious; informed; thoughtfully considered.

ad-vis-ed-ness (ad vīz′id nis) *n.* The state of being advised; caution.

ad-vise-ment (ad vīz′ment) *n.* Careful thought and consideration.

ad-vis-er (ad vī′zėr) *n.* A person who gives an opinion or advises.

ad-vi-so-ry (ad vī′z o rē) *adj.* Exercising or having the power to advise; giving or containing advice.

ad-vo-ca-cy (ad′vo ka sē) *n.* Act of advocating.

ad-vo-cate (ad′vo kit) *v.* To write or speak in favor of or support. **advocate** *n.*

ad-y-na-mi-a (ad″e nā′mē a) *n.* Deficiency of vital power; weakness.

ad-y-tum (ad′i tum) *n.* The innermost shrine or sanctuary; in ancient temples, the sanctuary where only priests were permitted to enter.

adz (adz) *n.* An instrument, similar to the ax type used for chipping timber.

ad-zu-ki bean (ad zŏ′kē bēn) *n.* An annual, bushy bean, cultivated in Japan.

AEC *abbr.* Atomic Energy Commission.

a-e-des (ā ē′ dēz) *n.* A mosquito that transmits yellow fever.

ae-gis (ē′jis) *n.* Protection; support or sponsorship.

Ae-o-li-an (ēō′lē an) *adj.* Pertaining to the wind; sounded by the wind.

aeolian harp *n.* Box with an opening over which are stretched strings of equal length that produce sound when wind blows over them.

ae-on (ē′on) *n.* A period of time of indefinite length.

aer-ate (âr′āt) *v.* To purify by exposing to the open air.

aer-a-tor (âr′ā tor) *n.* An apparatus for making carbonated beverages.

aer-i-al (âr′ē al) *adj.* Of or in the air; pertaining to aircraft. *n.* An antenna for television or radio. **aerially** *adv.*

aerial bomb *n., Mil.* A bomb that is dropped from an aircraft.

aerial combat *n., Mil.* Air combat between planes of battling forces.

aer-i-al-ist (âr′ē a list) *n.* An acrobat who does stunts high above the ground on a wire or trapeze.

aerial ladder *n.* A ladder that may be extended to different heights.

aerial mine *n., Mil.* Mine made to be dropped from an aircraft.

aer-ie (âr′ē) *n.* The nest of a predatory bird, built on a cliff or other high places.

aer-i-form (âr′i form″) *adj.* Having the form or nature of air.

aer-i-fy (âr′i fī″) *v.* To blow air into; to fill with air; to combine with air.

aer-o (âr′ō) *adj.* Having to do with air, aircraft, or the flying of aircraft.

aer-o-bal-lis-tics (âr″ō ba lis′iks) *n.* The ballistics of projectiles dropped, fired, or launched from aircraft.

aer-o-bics (â rō′ biks) *n.* Strenuous exercise that increases oxygen to the heart and lungs, therefore strengthening them.

aer-o-bi-o-sis (âr″ō bī ō′sis) *n.* Life in an atmosphere of oxygen or air.

aer-o-dyne (âr′o dīn″) *n.* Heavier-than-air aircraft, as the conventional airplane.

aer-o-em-bo-lism (âr″ō em′bo lizm) *n.* Occlusion of blood vessels by nitrogen gas bubbles that form when the body undergoes rapid decrease in air pressure.

aer-og-ra-phy (â rog′rafē) *n.* Description of the air or atmosphere; meteorology.

aer-ol-o-gist (âr ol′o jist) *n.* One who is versed in aerology.

aer-o-me-chan-ic (âr″ō me kan′ik) *n.* Mechanic in aviation.

aer-o-me-chan-ics (âr″ō me kan′iks) *n.* A study of air and other gases in motion.

aer-o-med-i-cine (âr′o med′isin) *n.* Branch of medicine that is concerned with the disorders that may occur during flying.

aer-o-naut (âr′o not″) *n.* Balloonist.

aer-o-nau-tics (âr″o no′tiks) *n.* The science of designing, constructing and operating aircraft. **aeronautic** *adj.*

ae-ron-o-my (â ron′o mē) *n.* Study of chemical and physical phenomena located in the upper regions of the atmosphere.

acr-o-pause (âr´ o poz˝) *n*. The region in the upper atmosphere where aircraft cannot fly.

aer-o-phore (âr´o fōr˝) *n*. Portable equipment for purifying air.

aer-o-plane (âr´o plān˝) *n*. British word for airplane.

aer-o-sol (âr´o sōl) *n*. A liquid substance under pressure within a metal container.

aer-o-sphere (âr´o sfēr˝) *n*. Body of air above the earth's atmosphere.

aer-o-train (är´a trān) *n*. A train which runs at high speed.

Ae-sop (ē´sǎp) *n*. Greek writer of fables from the sixth century B.C.

aes-thet-ic (es thet´ik) *adj*. Having a love for beauty; pertaining to the sense or study of beauty or taste.

aes-thet-ics (es thet´iks) *n*. The study of the nature of beauty. **aesthetically** *adv*.

a-far (a fär´) *adv*. Far off; far away.

af-fa-ble (af´a bl) *adj*. Good natured, easy to talk to; friendly. **affably** *adv*.

af-fa-bil-i-ty (af´a bil´i tē) *n*. Quality of being sociable.

af-fair (a fâr´) *n*. An event or happening; matters of business or public concern.

af-fect (a fekt´) *v*. To move emotionally; to feel sympathetic or sad; to bring about a change in. **affected** *adj*.

af-fec-ta-tion (af´ek tā´shan) *n*. Artificial behavior that is meant to impress others. False pretense, artificial show or appearance.

af-fect-ing (a fek´ting) *adj*. Power to excite emotion; suited to affect.

af-fect-ing-ly (afek´ting lē) *adv*. In an affecting or impressive manner.

af-fec-tion (a fek´shan) *n*. A tender or fond feeling towards another.

af-fec-tion-al (a fek´sha nal) *adj*. Pertaining to or implying the affections.

af-fec-tion-ate (a fek´sha nit) *adj*. Loving and gentle. Warmly attached; kind; fond; loving. **affectionately** *adv*. In an affectionate manner; fondly; tenderly; kindly.

af-fen-pin-scher (af˝en pin´sher) *n*. A small dog breed with stiff red, black, or gray coat, pointed ears, and shaggy hairs about the eyes, nose.

af-fi-ance (a fī´ans) *v*. To bind by promise of marriage; to betroth.

af-fi-da-vit (af´i dā´vit) *n*. A written statement by a person swearing that something is the truth.

af-fil-i-ate (a fil´ē āt´) *v*. To join in, connect, or associate with. **affiliation** *n*.

af-fine (a fin´) *n*. Relative by marriage.

af-fin-i-ty (a fin´i tē) *n*. A special attraction with kinship; a natural attraction or liking.

af-firm (a ferm´) *v*. To declare positively and be willing to stand by the truth.

af-fir-ma-tion (af˝ir mā´shan) *n*. Act of asserting or affirming something as being true; that which is asserted; confirmation; ratification.

af-firm-a-tive (a fer´ma tiv) *adj*. Asserting the fact is true. **affirmative** *n*.

af-fix (af´iks) *n*. To attach; to fasten; to add at the end. **affix** *n*. A prefix or suffix added to a word.

af-fla-tus (a flā´tus) *n*. Creative inspiration.

af-flict (aflikt´) *v*. To cause suffering or pain; to cause mental suffering.

af-flic-tion (aflik´shan) *n*. A state of distress or acute pain of the body or mind.

af-flu-ence (af´löens) *n*. Riches, wealth; abundance; plentiful supply of worldly goods.

af-flu-ent (af´lö ent) *adj*. Prosperous; rich; having all the wealth or money needed. **affluently** *adv*.

af-ford (a fōrd´) *v*. To be able to provide; to have enough money to spare.

af-for-est (a for´ist) *v*. To turn open land into forest. **afforestation** *n*.

af-fran-chise (afran´chīz) *v*. To make free; to grant full citizenship.

af-fray (a frā´) *n*. Brawl or noisy fight.

af-freight (a frāt´) *v*. To hire, for the transportation of freight or goods.

af-fright (a frīt´) *v*. To impress with sudden terror or fear of; to frighten unexpectedly or suddenly.

af-front (afrunt´) *v*. To insult one to his face; to confront.

af-fuse (*a* fūz´) *adj.* Pour upon; to sprinkle with a liquid.

af-fu-sion (*a* fū´zh*a*n) *n.* The act of sprinkling or pouring liquid on, as to baptize.

af-ghan (af´g*a*n) *n.* A crocheted or knitted cover in colorful designs.

Afghanistan *n.* A country in southwestern Asia, between Pakistan and Iran.

a-field (*a*fēld´) *adv.* Away from home or the usual path.

a-fire (*a*fīr´) *adv.* Burning.

a-flame (*a* flām´) *adj.* Burning; in flames; glowing.

AFL–CIO *abbr.* American Federation of Labor and Congress of Industrial Organizations.

a-float (*a* flōt´) *adv.* Floating on the surface of water; circulating.

a-flut-ter (*e* ´flet er) *adj.* Nervously excited.

a-foot (*a* fet´) *adj.* In the progress of happening; walking; on foot.

a-fore (*a*fōr´) *adv.* Before as in place or time.

a-fore-men-tioned (*a* fōr´men˝sh*a*nd) *adj.* Mentioned before.

a-fore-said (*a* fōr´sed˝) *adj.* Having spoken of something before; mentioned previously in the same discourse.

a-fore-thought (*a* fōr´thot) *adj.* Premeditated; planned beforehand; thought of previously.

a-foul (*a* foul´) *adv.* Tangled; entangled in a collision.

a-fraid (*a* frād´) *adj.* Hesitant; filled with fear; reluctant.

A–frame (ā frām) *n.* A structure for a house; a style or model.

a-fresh (*a* fresh´) *adj.* Once more; again. **afresh** *adv.* After a pause.

Africa *n.* A continent located in the Eastern Hemisphere, south of Europe and between the Atlantic and Indian Oceans.

Af-ri-kaans (af´r*i* käns´) *n.* The spoken language of the Republic of South Africa.

Af-ro (af´rō) *n.* A bushy hair style; African in style.

aft (aft) *adv.* At, close to, near, or toward the rear of an aircraft or stern of a ship.

af-ter (af´ter) *adv.* In the rear. **after** *prep.* Following.

af-ter-birth (af´ter berth˝) *n.* The placenta and fetal matter released by the uterus after childbirth.

af-ter-bod-y (af´ter bod˝ē) *n.* Companion body that follows a satellite; a section of a spacecraft that enters the atmosphere unprotected behind the nose cone or other protected body for entry.

af-ter-burn-er (af´ter be˝ner) *n.* Auxiliary combustion chamber attached to, or within, the tail pipe of some jet engines, where hot unused oxygen of exhaust gases from fuel already burned is used to burn a second fuel to give an increase in thrust.

af-ter-care (af´ter kâr˝) *n., Med.* The care and treatment required by a patient who is convalescing.

af-ter-clap (af´ter klap˝) *n.* Startling repercussion, followed by an affair assumed to be finished.

af-ter-deck (af´ter dek˝) *n.* Section of a deck that is abaft the middle of a ship.

af-ter-ef-fect (af´ter i fekt˝) *n.* An effect coming after; a delayed effect.

af-ter-life (af´ter līf˝) *n.* Life following death; future or succeeding period in a person's life.

af-ter-math (af´ter math˝) *n.* Consequence; result.

af-ter-noon (af´ter nön˝) *n.* The part of the daytime that follows noon, between noon and evening.

af-ter-piece (af´ter pēs˝) *n.* Short dramatic entertainment that is performed after the main performance.

af-ter-taste (af´ter tāst˝) *n.* A taste which comes after eating or drinking.

af-ter-thought (af´ter thot˝) *n.* An idea occurring later.

af-ter-time (af´ter tīm˝) *n.* Coming after time; the future.

af-ter-ward *or* **af-ter-wards** (af´ter ward) *adv.* In later time.

af-ter-world (af´ter werld˝) *n.* The world

that is assumed to be the place of existence after death.

a-gain (*a* gen´) *adv.* Moreover; another time; once more.

a-gainst (*a*genst´) *prep.* In exchange for; in preparation for.

a-gape (*a* gāp´) *adv.* With expectation; in wonder; open-mouthed.

ag-ate (ag´it) *n.* The type of quartz that has bands of colors.

agate line *n.* Unit of measurement used in advertising.

a-ga-ve (*a* gā´vē) *n.* Fleshy-leaved tropical American plant.

age (āj) *n.* The length of time from beginning to a certain date; the time of life when a person has full legal rights; the age of 21. **age** *v.* To grow or become old; to mature.

aged (ā´jid) *adj.* Grown or become old. **agedness** *n.* **agedly** *adv.*

age-ism (ā jiz em) *n.* Discrimination based on a person's age.

age-less (āj´lis) *adj.* Existing forever; never seems to grow old.

a-gen-cy (ā´jen sē) *n.* A business or service that acts for others; action; active influence; power.

a-gen-da (*a* jen´da) *n.* Program or list of things to be done.

a-gen-e-sis (ā jen´i sis) *n., Med.* The lack of, or an imperfect development.

a-gent (ā´jent) *n.* One who acts as the representative of another; one who acts or exerts power.

a-gen-tial (ā jen´shal) *adj.* Pertaining to an agency or agent.

ag-er-a-tum (aj˝e rā´tum) *n.* A tropical American plant from the aster family.

ag-gior-na-men-to(e jór ne ´men tō) *n.* Bringing up to date.

ag-glom-er-ate (*a* glom´e rāt´) *v.* To collect; to form into a mass. **agglomerate** *n.*

ag-glu-ti-nate (*a* glŏt´i nāt˝) *v.* To join by adhesion; to cause red blood cells to clump together.

ag-glu-ti-nin (e ´glü n en) *n.* A substance that causes agglutination; a group or mass formed by the union of separate elements.

ag-grade (*a*grād´) *v.* To raise the level or grade of a river valley.

ag-gran-dize (ag´ran dīz˝) *n.* To enlarge, to extend; to increase.

ag-gra-vate (ag´ravāt˝) *v.* To annoy; to make worse.

ag-gra-va-tion (ag˝ra vā´shan) *n.* Act of making worse or aggravating; irritation; annoyance.

ag-gre-gate (ag´re git) *adj.* To gather together into a mass or whole.

ag-gress (*a* gres´) *v.* To commit the first act of offense or hostility.

ag-gres-sion (*a* gresh´an) *n.* Hostile action or behavior; an unprovoked assault.

ag-gres-sive (*a* gres´iv) *adj.* Offensive; distressing; pushy; afflicting.

ag-gres-sor (*a*gres´er) *n.* An invader.

ag-grieved (*a*grēvd´) *adj.* Wronged or injured.

a-ghast (*a*gast´) *adj.* Appalled; struck with amazement.

ag-ile (aj´il) *adj.* Marked by the ability to move quickly and easily; nimble.

ag-i-o (aj´ēō˝) *n.* The difference in value between one kind of money or another.

ag-i-o-tage (aj´ē *a* tij) *n.* Business of a person who deals in foreign exchange.

ag-i-tate (aj´i tāt˝) *v.* To disturb; to upset; to stir or move with violence; to try to arouse the public interest. **agitation** *n.*

ag-i-ta-tor (aj´i tā˝tor) *n.* One who or that which stirs up public discontent, agitates, or arouses.

a-gleam (*a* glēm´) *adj.* Gleaming.

ag-let (ag´lit) *n.* A metal tag at the end of a shoelace.

a-gley (*a*glā´) *adv.* Wrong; awry.

a-glim-mer (*a* glim´er) *adv.* Glimmering.

a-glit-ter (*a* glit´er) *adj.* Glittering.

a-glow (*a* glō´) *adj.* Glowing.

ag-nail (ag´nāl) *n.* Inflammation of a fingernail or toenail; hangnail.

ag-nate (ag´nāt) *n.* Any male relation on the father's side.

ag-no-men (ag nō´men) *n.* An additional word, phrase or nickname, often used to designate a person in place of their real name.

ag-nos-tic (ag nos´tik) *n.* One who doubts that there is a God or life hereafter. **agnosticism** *n.*

a-go (a gō´) *adj.* In the past; gone by.

a-gog (a gog´) *adj.* Excited; eagerly expectant.

ag-o-nal (ag´o nal) *adj.* Relating to or having the characteristic of agony.

agonic line (ā gä˝ik līn) *n.* The imaginary line on the earth's surface, that joins places having no magnetic declination and where the magnetic needle points to the true north as well as magnetic north.

ag-o-nize (ag´onīz˝) *v.* To afflict with great anguish or to suffer, agony. **agonized** *adj.* **agonizing** *adj.*

ag-o-ny (ag´o nē) *n., pl.* **agonies** Intense mental distress or physical pain; anguish.

ag-o-ra-pho-bi-a (ag˝or afō´bē a) *n.* Fear of open spaces.

agr *or* **agric** *abbr.* Agricultural; agriculture.

a-graffe (a graf´) *n.* The ornamental clasp used for hooking parts of clothing together.

a-gran-u-lo-cy-to-sis (a gran˝yu lo sī tō´ sis) *n.* Destructive blood disease that is distinguished by a decrease of the leukocytes.

a-graph-i-a (a graf´ē a) *n.* The cerebral disorder, in which a patient expresses ideas by written signs.

a-grar-i-an (agrâr´ē an) *adj.* Pertaining to or of land and its ownership; pertaining to farming; agricultural.

a-grar-i-an-ism (a grâr´ē a nizm) *n.* The movement and doctrine advocating equal divisions of lands and property.

a-gree (a grē´) *v.* To give assent; to consent; to share an understanding or opinion; to be beneficial or suitable; to correspond.

a-gree-a-ble (a grē´a bl) *adj.* Pleasant; pleasing; willing; ready to consent. **agreeableness** *n.* **agreeably** *adv.*

a-gree-ment (a grē´ment) *n.* Harmony; concord; state or act of agreeing.

ag-ri-busi-ness (ag re biz nesnez) *n.* Big business farming, embracing the production, distribution, and processing of farm

products and the manufacture of farm equipment.

ag-ri-cul-ture (ag´ri kul˝chur) *n.* Raising of livestock; farming and cultivating the crops. **agriculturalist** *n.*

ag-ri-ol-o-gy (ag˝rē ol´o jē) *n.* The study of human customs, especially those customs of man in a civilization of lesser development.

ag-ro-bi-ol-o-gy (ag˝rō bīāl´o jē) *n.* The science of plant nutrition and life in relation to the production of crops.

a-grol-o-gy (a grol´o jē) *n.* Study of soils.

ag-ro-tech-ny (ag´ro tek nē) *n.* The branch of agricultural science dealing with the conversion of raw farm products into manufactured commodities.

a-ground (a ground´) *adv.* Stranded; on the ground; to run ashore; beached. **aground** *adj.* Stranded; on the ground; to run ashore; beached.

a-gue (ā´gū) *n.* Fever accompanied by chills or shivering and sweating. **aguish** *adj.*

a-head (a hed´) *adv.* Before; in advance; to or at the front of something.

a-hoy (a hoi´) *interj.* A nautical call or greeting.

aid (ād) *v.* To give help or assistance.

aide (ād) *n.* A person who acts as an official assistant; aide-de-camp.

AIDS *n.* Disease that destroys the body's immunological system; Acquired Immune Deficiency Syndrome.

aid station *n.* Medical installation in an isolated area where all treatments of sick and wounded casualties are performed.

ai-guille (ā gwēl´) *n.* The needlelike tops of rocks and mountain masses.

ail (āl) *v.* To feel sick; to make ill or uneasy.

ai-lan-thus (ā lan´thus) *n.* A tree with numerous pointed leaves.

ai-ler-on (ā´le ron˝) *v.* Movable control flap on the trailing edge of an airplane wing.

ail-ment (āl´ment) *n.* A mild illness.

aim (ām) *v.* To direct a weapon; to direct purpose. **aim** *n.* Intention.

aim-less (ām´lis) *adj.* Lacking of purpose.

ain't (ānt) *contr.* Am not, are not, is not, has not, or have not.

ai-o-li *n.* Rich garlic-flavored mayonnaise.

air (âr) *n.* An odorless, tasteless, colorless, gaseous mixture; primarily composed of nitrogen (78%) and oxygen (21%); the sky; a breeze. **on the air** Broadcasting.

air-borne (âr´bōrn´) *adj.* Carried through or by the air.

air brake (âr brāk) *n.* Brake operated by the power of compressed air.

air-brush (âr´bersh) *n.* Machine using compressed air to spray paint and other liquids on a surface.

air conditioner *n.* Equipment used to lower the temperature and humidity of an enclosure.

air-craft (âr´kraft´) *n.* A machine that flies, such as a helicopter, airplane, or glider.

air-craft car-ri-er (âr´kraft˝ kar´ē er) *n.* A large ship which carries airplanes on which they can be landed and launched.

air-crew (âr´krö) *n.* A crew that mans an airplane and are responsible for flying and navigating the aircraft.

air-drop (âr´drop´) *n.* Delivery of supplies made by parachute from an airplane while in flight.

air–dry (âr´drī˝) *v.* To dry by exposing to the air.

air-field (âr´fēld˝) *n.* Paved runways at an airport; landing strip.

air-flow (âr´flō˝) *n.* The motion of the air around a body as relative to the surface of a body immersed in it.

air-foil (âr´foil´) *n.* Part of an airplane which controls stability, lift, thrust, etc.

Air Force (âr fōrs) *n.* Aviation branch of armed forces.

air-frame (âr´frām˝) *n.* The structure of a rocket or airplane without an engine.

air freight *n.* Freight that is transported from one location to another by air.

air gun (âr gun) *n.* Gun which is operated by compressed air.

air hole *n.* A hole that is used to discharge or admit air into an area.

air-ing (âr´ing) *n.* Exposing something in the open air.

air lane *n.* The regular route of travel for airplanes.

air letter (âr let´é) *n.* A letter that is transported by means of an aircraft

air-lift (âr´lift´) *n.* System of transporting supplies or troops by air when ground routes are blocked.

air-line (âr´līn˝) *n.* An air transportation company or system.

air-lin-er (âr´lī´nėr) *n.* A large passenger airline.

air lock *n.* Airtight compartment between regions of unequal pressure.

air-mail *or* **air–mail (âr´māl´)** *n.* Mail sent by means of air.

air-man (âr´man) *n.* A person enlisted in the air force.

air-man-ship (âr´man ship˝) *n.* The skill in navigating or piloting an airplane.

air-plane (âr´plān´) *n.* A vehicle capable of flight, heavier than air, and propelled by jet engines or propellers.

air pocket *n.* A condition in the atmosphere that can cause an airplane to lose altitude quickly.

air-port (âr´pōrt´) *n.* A terminal station for passengers where aircraft take off and land.

air raid *n.* Bombing attack by enemy military aircraft.

air-ship (âr´ship´) *n.* Dirigible; a self-propelled lighter-than-air aircraft.

air-sick-ness (âr´sik´nis) *n.* Nausea resulting from flight in an aircraft. **airsick** *adj.*

air-speed (âr´spēd˝) *n.* Speed of an aircraft while airborne.

air-strip (âr´strip˝) *n.* Concrete runway on an airfield; a minimally equipped airfield.

air-tight (âr´tīt˝) *adj.* Impermeable by air or gas. **airtightness** *n.*

air-wave (âr´wāv˝) *n.* The medium of television and radio transmission and communication

air-way (âr´wā˝) *n.* An air lane; the designated route along which an airplane must travel.

air-wor-thy (âr´wer˝thē) *adj.* Fit to fly. **airworthiness** *n.*

air-y (âr´ē) *adj.* Open to the air; breezy; light as air; graceful or delicate. **airiness** *n.* **airily** *adv.*

aisle (īl) *n.* Passageway between rows of seats, as in a church, auditorium, or airplane, or meeting place. **aisled** *adj.*

a-jar (a jär´) *adv. adj.* Partially opened.

AK *abbr.* Alaska.

AKA *abbr.* Also known as.

a-kim-bo (akim´bō) *adj.* Bent; with a crook. **akimbo** *adv.* Bent; with a crook.

a-kin (akin´) *adj.* Related, as in family; similar in quality or character.

AL *abbr.* American Legion; Alabama.

Alabama *n.* A state located in the southeastern part of the United States, statehood December 14, 1819, state capital Montgomery

al-a-bas-ter (al´a bas˝tėr) *n.* A dense, translucent, tinted or white, fine-grained gypsum. **alabastrine** *adj.*

a la carte (ä˝la kärt´) *n.* Separate price for each item on the menu.

a-lack (a lak´) *interj.* An exclamation expressive of sorrow.

a-lac-ri-ty (a lak´ri tē) *n.* Readiness; cheerfulness; eagerness; briskness.

a la mode (al´a mōd˝) *n.* Served with ice cream, as pie; fashionable.

a-larm (a lärm´) *n.* A warning of danger; sudden feeling of fear; the bell or buzzer of a clock. **alarm** *v.* To frighten or warn by an alarm. **alarming** *adv.*

alarm clock *n.* A clock that is equipped with either a buzzer or bell, that can be set to sound at a specified time.

a-larm-ist (a lär´mist) *n.* Someone who needlessly alarms others. **alarmism** *n.*

a-las (a las´) *interj.* Expressive of anxiety or regret.

Alaska *n.* A state located in the northwestern part of the United States, statehood January 3, 1959, capital Juneau.

a-late *or* **a-lat-ed (ā´lāt, ā´lā ted)** *adj.* Winged; having wings. **alation** *n.*

alb (alb) *n.* White linen robe worn by clergy during Mass.

al-ba-core (al´ba kōr˝) *n.* Large marine fish; major source of canned tuna.

Albania *n.* A country located in SE Europe.

Al-ba-ni-an (al bā´nē an) *n.* An inhabitant or native of Albania.

al-ba-ta (al bā´ta) *n.* Alloy that consists of a combination of tin, nickel, zinc, and copper.

al-ba-tross(al´batros˝) *n.* Large, web-footed, long-winged sea bird.

al-be-do (al bē´dō) *n., Astron.* Measurement of light rays upon a satellite or planet.

al-be-it (ol bē´it) *conj.* Although; even though.

al-bi-no (al bī´nō) *n.* An animal or person with an abnormal whiteness of the skin and hair and pink colored eyes.

al-bum (al´bum) *n.* A book for photographs, autographs, stamps; a book of collections.

al-bu-men (al bū´men) *n.* White of an egg.

al-bu-min (al bū´men) *n.* Several proteins found in the white of eggs, blood serum, milk, and plant and animal tissue.

al-bu-min-oid (al bū´mi noid˝) *n.* A substance resembling albumen.

al-bu-min-ous (al bū´mi nus) *adj.* Relating to, having the properties of or containing albumen.

al-bu-mi-nu-ri-a (al bū˝mi ne´rē a) *adj., Pathol.* The condition where the urine contains albumen, that often indicates diseased kidneys.

al-bur-num (al ber´num) *n.* The white and softer section of the wood from exogenous plants that lays between the inner bark and the heartwood.

al-caz-ar (al´ka zär˝) *n.* A Spanish fortress or palace.

al-che-my (al´ke mē) *n.* Traditional chemical philosophy concerned primarily with changing base metals into gold.

al-co-hol (al′k*o* **hol″)** *n.* Intoxicating liquor containing alcohol; ethanol; a series of related organic compounds.

al-co-hol-ic (al″k*o* **ho′lik)** *adj.* Resulting from alcohol; containing or preserved in alcohol; suffering from alcoholism. **alcoholic** *n.* A habitual drunkard.

al-co-hol-ism (al′k*o* **ho liz″***u***m)** *n.* Excessive alcohol consumption; a habit or addiction.

al-co-hol-om-e-ter (al″k*o* **ho lom′i tėr)** *n.* Instrument for determining the quantity of pure alcohol in liquid.

al-co-hol-ize (al′k*o* **ho līz″)** *v.* Saturate or treat something with alcohol.

al-cove (al′kōv) *n.* Recess or partly enclosed extension of a room.

al-de-hyde (al′*de* **hīd″)** *n.* Any of a class of highly reactive compounds obtained by oxidation of alcohols.

al-der (ol′dėr) *n.* Tree of the birch family, grows in marshy soil.

al-der-man (ol′dėr m*a***n)** *n.* Member of a municipal legislative body.

ale (āl) *n.* Beverage similar to, but more bitter than beer, made from malt by fermentation.

ale-house (āl′hous″) *n.* Place where ale and beer are sold for drinking on the premises.

a-lem-bic (*a* **lem′bik)** *n.* A glass or metal vessel formerly used in distillation.

a-leph-null (ä′lef′nul″) *n., Math.* Smallest infinite nonordinal number.

a-lert (*a* **lert′)** *adj.* Vigilant; brisk; watchful; active. **alert** *n.* A signal by siren of air attack. **alertly** *adv.* **alertness** *n.*

al-ex-an-drine (al″ig zan′drin) *n.* Line of English verse in iambic hexameter; probably from poems dealing with Alexander the Great.

a-lex-in (*a* **lek′sin)** *n.* Any of certain substances found in normal blood-serum, capable of destroying bacteria.

a-lex-i-phar-mic (*a***lek″s***i* **fär′mik)** *adj.* Acting as a means of warding off disease or the effects of poison.

al-fa (al′f*a***)** *n.* A code word in communications to represent the letter A.

al-fal-fa (al fal′f*a***)** *n.* Plant with purple flowers, resembling the clover, widely grown for forage.

al-for-ja (al for′j*a***)** *n.* Leather pouch or saddlebag.

al-fres-co (al fres′kō) *adv.* In the fresh air; outside. *adj.* In the fresh air; outside.

al-gae (al′jē) *n.* Various primitive, chiefly aquatic, one-celled or multi-cellular plants, as the seaweed.

al-ge-bra (al′j*e* **bra)** *n.* Generalization of math in which symbols represent members of a specified set of numbers and are related by operations that hold for all numbers in the set. **algebraic** *adj.* **algebraical, algebraically** *adv.*

al-go-pho-bi-a (al″g*o* **fō′bē** *a***)** *n.* The extreme fear of pain.

a-li-as (ā′lē *a***s)** *n. pl.* **aliases** Assumed name. **alias** *adv.* Otherwise known as.

al-i-bi (al′*i* **bī″)** *n.* A form of defense, an attempt by a defendant to prove he was elsewhere when a crime was committed; an excuse.

a-li-en (āl′yen) *adj.* Owing allegiance to a government or country, not one's own; unfamiliar; repugnant; from another region or country. **alien** *n.* A stranger; a foreigner.

al-ien-a-ble (āl′ye na bl) *adj.* Able to be transferred to the ownership of another. **alienability** *n.*

al-ien-age (āl′ye nij) *n.* Alien's legal status.

al-ien-ate (āl′ye nāt″) *v.* To cause to become indifferent or unfriendly.

al-ien-ist (āl′ye nist) *n.* A psychiatrist accepted by a court as an expert on mental stability.

a-light (*a* **līt′)** *v.* To settle; to come down; to dismount. **alight** *adj. & adv.* Burning, lighted.

a-lign *or* **a-line (***a* **līn′)** *v.* To arrange in a line; to take one side of an argument or cause. **aligner** *n.*

a-lign-ment *or* **a-line-ment (***a* **līn′m** *e***nt)** *n.* Arrange or position in a straight line.

a-like (*a* **līk′)** *adj.* Similar, having close resemblance. **alike** *adv.* In the same manner, way, or degree.

al-i-ment (al´i ment) *n.* Nourishment; food. **alimentation** *n.* **alimental** *adj.*

al-i-men-ta-ry (al˝i men´ta rē) *adj.* Pertaining to nutrition or food.

alimentary canal *n.* The tube of the digestive system from the mouth to the anus, including the pharynx, esophagus, stomach, and intestines.

al-i-men-ta-tion (al˝i men tā´shan) *n.* The process or act of affording nutriment. **alimentative** *adj.*

al-i-mo-ny (al´i mō˝nē) *n.* Court ordered allowance for support, usually given by a man to his former wife following a divorce or legal separation.

A–line *adj.* Having a close-fitting top and a flared bottom.

al-i-phat-ic (al˝i fat´ik) *adj.* Having to do with organic chemical compounds where the carbon atoms are linked in open chains.

al-i-quant (al´i kwant) *adj.* Applied to a number which will not divide into another number equally.

a-li-un-de (ā˝lē un´dē) *adv.* From another source or means .

a-live (a līv´) *adj.* Living; having life; in existence or effect; full of life.

a-li-yah (ā´lē yä) *n.* Immigration of Jews to Israel.

a-liz-a-rin (a liz´ėr in) *n.* A red-orange compound used in dyes.

al-ka-li (al´ka lī˝) *n. pl.* **alkalies** *or* **alkalis** A hydroxide or carbonate of an alkali metal, whose aqueous solution is slippery, bitter, caustic, and basic in reactions.

alkali flat *n.* A plain containing an excess of alkali in its soil.

alkali metal *n.* Any of the mostly basic metals comprising lithium, sodium, potassium, francium, etc.

al-ka-line (al´ka līn˝) *adj.* Of, relating to, or containing an alkali. **alkalinity** *n.*

al-ka-lin-ize (al´ka li nīz) *adj.* To make alkaline.

al-ka-loid (al´ka loid) *n.* Any of various nitrogen containing organic bases obtained from plants. **alkaloidal** *adj.*

al-ka-lo-sis (al˝ka lō´sis) *n.* Unusually high alkali content in the blood and tissues.

al-ka-net (al´ka net˝) *n.* A plant whose root yields a red dye.

al-kyd res-in (al´kid rez´en) *n.* Group of sticky resins coming from phthalic acid and glycerol, that are used primarily in paints and adhesives.

all (awl) *adj.* Total extent or total entity; being a whole number, amount, or quantity; every.

Al-lah (al´a) *n.* The Moslem supreme being.

al-lan-to-is (a lan´tō is) *n.* A sac that is developed from the posterior end of the abdominal cavity in reptiles, birds, and some mammals.

all–a-round (ol´a round˝) *n.* Variance of all–round.

al-lay (alā´) *v.* To relieve; to lessen; to calm; to pacify. **allayer** *n.*

al-le-ga-tion (al˝e gā´shan) *n.* The act or result of alleging.

al-lege (a lej´) *v.* To affirm; to assert to be true; to declare without proof.

Allegheny Mountains *n.* Section of the Appalachians extending from Pennsylvania to Virginia.

al-le-giance (a lē´jans) *n.* Loyalty to one's nation, cause, or sovereign; obligations of a vassal to an overlord.

al-le-giant (a lē´ja˝nt) *n.* A person who owes allegiance.

al-le-go-ry (al´e gōr˝ē) *n. pl.* **allegories** A dramatic, literary, or pictorial device in which each object, character, and event symbolically illustrates a religious or moral principle. **allegoric, allegorical** *adj.* **allegorically** *adv.* **allegorist** *n.*

al-le-gret-to (al˝e gret´ō) *adv., Mus.* Slower than allegro but faster than andante. **allegretto** *adj.*

al-le-gro (a lā´grō) *adv., Mus.* Faster than allegretto but slower than presto. **allegro** *adj.* **allegro** *n.*

al-lele (a lēl´) *n.* Any of a group of possible mutational forms of a gene. **allelism** *n.* **allelic** *adj.*

al-le-lu-ia (al˝e lö´ya) *interj.* Expressing praise to God or of thanksgiving.

al-ler-gen (al´ėr jen˝) *n.* Substance which causes an allergy. **allergenic** *adj.*

al-ler-gic (a ler´jik) *adj.* Pertaining to allergy; extremely sensitive.

al-ler-gist (al´ėr jist) *n.* A doctor specializing in allergies.

al-ler-gy (al´ėr jē) *n. pl.* **allergies** Pathological or abnormal reaction to environmental substances, as foods, dust, pollens, or microorganisms.

al-le-vi-ate (a lē´vē āt˝) *v.* To make more bearable. **alleviation** *n.* **alleviator** *n.*

al-ley (al´ē) *n. pl.* **alleys** Narrow passageway between or behind buildings.

al-li-a-ceous (al˝ē ā´shus) *adj.* Having the properties of an onion or garlic.

al-li-ance (a lī´ans) *n.* A union, relationship, or connection by kinship, marriage, or common interest; a confederation of nations by a formal treaty; an affinity.

al-lied (a līd´) *adj.* United by agreement, or other means.

al-li-ga-tor (al´i gā˝tor) *n.* Large amphibious reptile with very sharp teeth, powerful jaws, and a shorter snout than the related crocodile.

alligator pear *n.* An avocado.

alligator snapper *n.* A turtle.

al-lit-er-ate (a lit´e rāt˝) *v.* To arrange or form words beginning with the same sound, compose or arrange.

al-lit-er-a-tion (a lit˝e rā´shan) *n.* Occurrence of two or more words having the same initial sound. **alliterative** *adj.*

al-li-um (al´ē um) *n.* Any bulb plant, such as garlic or onion.

al-lo-cate (al´o kāt˝) *v.* To assign; to allot. **allocation** *n.*

al-lo-cu-tion (al˝o kū´shan) *n.* Speaking to.

al-log-a-mous (a log´amus) *adj.* Having the property of reproduction by cross-fertilization.

al-lo-graph (al´o graf˝) *n.* Something written by one person on behalf of another.

al-lo-nym (al´o nim) *n.* The name of another person assumed by an author.

al-lot (a lot´) *v.* To distribute or set aside as a share of something, to divide, assign, or parcel out in parts or portions.

al-lot-ment (a lot´ment) *n.* A shared part, or portion granted or distributed.

al-lo-tropy (al´o trōpē) *n.* One of two or more existing forms of a chemical element. **allotropic, allotropical,** *adj*

al-lot-tee (a lot ē) *n.* One to whom an allotment is made.

all out (ol´out´) *adv.* With every possible effort or resource.

all-o-ver (ol´ō˝vėr) *n.* A design or pattern that covers the entire surface.

al-low (a lou´) *v.* To make a provision for, to permit; to permit to have; to admit; to concede. **allowable** *adj.* **allowably** *adv.*

al-low-ance (a lou´ans) *n.* The act of allowing something, such as a regular amount of money or food; a price discount.

al-loy (aloi´) *v.* Something that has been added to; item reduced purity or value.

all right *adj.* Acceptable; meets satisfaction; correct; safe; *Slang* Good; of sound character; dependable. **all right** *adv.* Satisfactorily; correctly; unhurt

all–round (ol´round´) *adj.* Versatile, including all aspects.

all-spice (ol´spīs˝) *n.* Tropical American tree bearing aromatic berries, used as a spice.

all–star (ol stär) *adj.* Composed entirely of star performers.

all-time (ol tim) *adj.* Of all time.

all told *adv.* Everything taken into account.

al-lude (a lōd´) *n.* To refer to something indirectly, to hint at. **allusion** *n.* **allusive** *adj.* **allusively** *adv.*

al-lure (a lür´) *v.* To entice; to tempt. **allure** *n.* Attraction; charm; enticement; prospect of attracting. **allurement** *n.* **allurer** *n.* **alluringly** *adv.*

al-lu-sion (a lö´zhan) *n.* The act of referring to something indirectly; a hint.

al-lu-sive (a lö´siv) *adj.* Reference to something that is not fully expressed.

al-lu-vi-um (a lö´vē um) *n.* Sediment deposited by flowing water as in a river bed. **alluvial** *adj.*

al-ly (*a* lī') *v.* To connect or unite in a formal or close relationship or bond. **ally** *n.* One united with another in a formal or personal relationship.

alma mater *n.* College, school, or university one has attended; the anthem of that college, school, or university.

al-ma-nac (ol'm*a* nak") *n.* Annual publication having calendars with weather forecasts, astronomical information, and other useful facts.

al-man-dine (al'm*a*n dēn") *n.* A name given to the violet variety of the ruby sinel or sapphire; purple Indian garnet.

al-might-y (ol mī'tē) *adj.* Having absolute power. *n.* The Almighty God.

al-mond (ä'm*o*nd) *n.* An oval, edible nut with a soft, light-brown shell; tree bearing such nuts.

al-most (ol'mōst) *adv.* Not quite; slightly short of.

alms (ämz) *n.* Goods or money given to the poor in charity.

alms-house (ämz'hous") *n.* A poorhouse.

al-ni-co (al'ni kō") *n.* A powerful permanent magnet alloy of aluminum, iron, nickel, and other elements.

al-oe (al'ō) *n.* Any of various mostly African plants having fleshy, spiny-toothed leaves; a cathartic drug made from the juice of the leaves of this plant.

a-loft (*a* loft') *adv.* Toward the upper rigging of a ship; in or into a high place; in the air.

a-lo-ha (*a* lō'*a*) *interj.* Hawaiian expression of greeting or farewell.

a-lone (*a* lōn') *adj.* Away from other people; single; solitary; excluding anyone or anything else; with nothing further; sole; only; unaccompanied by others. **alone** *adv.* **aloneness** *n.*

a-long (*a* long') *adv.* In a line with; following the length or path; in association; together; as a companion.

a-long-shore (*a*long'shōr) *adv.* The area near, along, or by the shore, either on land or in the water.

a-long-side (*a* long'sīd") *adv.* Along, at, near, or to the side of; side by side with.

a-loof (*a*lōf') *adj.* Indifferent; distant. **aloofness** *n.* **aloofly** *adv.*

a-loud (*a* loud') *adv.* Orally; audibly.

a-low (*a* lō') *adv.* In a low place, as in the ship's hold.

alp (alp) *n.* High mountain.

al-pac-a (al pak'*a*) *n.* South American mammal related to the llama; the wool of the alpaca.

al-pen-glow (al'p*e*n glō") *n.* A reddish glow seen on the summits of mountains near sunrise or sunset.

al-pen-horn (al'p*e*n horn) *n.* Long curved horn used to call cows to pasture.

al-pen-stock (al'p*e*n stok") *n.* Long staff with an iron point used by mountain climbers.

al-pes-trine (al pes'trin) *adj.* Pertaining to mountain regions; growing at very high elevations but not above the timberline.

al-pha (al'f*a*) *n.* First letter of the Greek alphabet.

alpha and omega *n.* The beginning and the end; the first and last letters of the Greek alphabet.

al-pha-bet (al'f*a* bet") *n.* The letters of a language, arranged in an order fixed by custom.

al-pha-bet-i-cal (al f*a* bet i kel) *adj.* Arranged in the traditional order of the letters of a language. **alphabetically** *adv.*

al-pha-bet-ize (al'f*a* bi tīz") *v.* To arrange in alphabetical order.

alpha decay *n.* Decay of an atomic nucleus as it emits an alpha particle.

Alpha ray *n.* A stream of alpha particles.

Alps *n.* The major mountain system of south central Europe, forming an arc from Southern France to Albania.

al-read-y (ol red'ē) *adv.* By this or a specified time.

al-sike (al'sik) *n.* A European perennial clover with white or light pink flowers.

al-so (ol′sō) *adv.* Likewise; besides; in addition.

al-so–ran (ol′sō ran″) *n.* One defeated in a competition.

alt *abbr.* Alteration; alternate; altitude.

al-tar (ol′tėr) *n.* An elevated structure before which religious ceremonies may be held or sacrifices offered.

altar boy *n.* A boy who assists the celebrant in a religious cermony.

al-tar-piece (ol′tėr pēs″) *n.* A carving or painting placed above and behind an altar.

altar rail *n.* A railing in front of a church's altar separating the body of the church from the sanctuary.

al-ter (ol′tėr) *v.* To make change or become different; to modify; to castrate or spay, as an animal. **alteration** *n.*

al-ter-a-tive (ol′te rā″tiv) *adj.* Tending to alter or produce alterations.

al-ter-ca-tion (ol″tėr kā′shan) *n.* Noisy and heated quarrel.

alter ego *v.* An intimate friend; another aspect of oneself.

al-ter-nate (ol′tėr nāt″) *v.* To happen or follow in turn; to occur in successive turns. **alternate** *n.* Substitute. **alternately** *adv.*

alternating current *n.* Electric current that reverses direction at regular intervals.

al-ter-na-tive (ol′ter′n ativ) *n.* A choice between two or more possibilities; one of the possibilities to be chosen. **alternative** *adj.* Allowing a choice. **alternatively** *adv.*

al-ter-na-tor (ol′tėr nā″tėr) *n.* Electric generator producing alternating current.

alt-horn (alt′horn″) *n.* An alto saxhorn, often substituted for the French horn in bands.

al-though (ol thō′) *conj.* Even though.

al-tim-e-ter (al tim′i tėr) *n.* Instrument for measuring and indicating altitude.

al-ti-tude (al′ti tūd″) *n.* The height of a thing above a reference level; above the earth's surface; above sea level.

al-to (al′tō) *n.* Low female singing voice; the range between soprano and tenor.

al-to-geth-er (ol′to geth′ėr) *adv.* Entirely; with all included or counted.

al-tru-ism (al′trŏ iz″um) *n.* Selfless concern for the welfare of others. **altruist** *n.* **altruistic** *adj.* **altruistically** *adv.*

al-um (al′um) *n.* Any one of several similar double sulfates.

a-lu-mi-na (a lŏ′mi na) *n.* Any of several forms of aluminum oxide.

a-lu-mi-num (a lŏ′mi num) *n.* A silvery-white, ductile metallic element used to form many hard, light, corrosion-resistant alloys.

a-lum-na (a lum′na) *n. pl.* **alumnae** Female graduate or former student of a school, college, or university.

a-lum-nus (a lum′nus) *n. pl.* **alumni** A male graduate or former student of a school, college, or university.

al-ve-o-lar (al vē′o lėr) *adj.* Containing or pertaining to sockets, specifically the part of the jaws where the teeth arise.

al-ways (ol′wāz) *adv.* Continuously; forever; on every occasion; at all times.

a-lys-sum (a lis′um) *n.* Herbs of the mustard family bearing small yellow or white racemose flowers with hairy leaves.

am (am) *v.* First person, singular, present tense of be.

AM *abbr.* Ante meridian, Latin for "before noon."

AMA *abbr.* American Medical Association.

a-mal-gam (a mal′gam) *n.* An alloy of mercury with other metals, as with tin or silver; a blend of diverse elements.

a-mal-ga-mate (a mal′ga māt″) *v.* To mix so as to make a unified whole; to blend. **amalgamation** *n.* **amalgamator** *n.*

a-man-dine (a man dēn′) *adj.* Made with or garnished with almonds.

am-a-ranth (am′aranth″) *n.* Various weedy plants that have greenish or purplish flowers; an imaginary flower that never fades.

am-a-ran-thine (am″a ran′thin) *adj.* Relating to an amaranth; never fading.

am-a-ryl-lis (am″a ril′is) *n.* A bulbous plant with large, lily-like, reddish or white flowers.

a-mass (*a* mas´) *v*. To gather a great mass or number of; to accumulate.

am-a-teur (am´*a* cher˝) *n*. One who engages in an activity as a pastime rather than as a profession; one who lacks expertise. **amateurish** *adj*.

am-a-tive (am´*a* tiv) *adj*. Disposed or disposing of love; full of love; inclined to love.

am-a-tol (am´*a* tol˝) *n*. An explosive consisting of ammonium nitrate and trinitrotoluene (TNT).

am-a-to-ry (am´*a* tōr˝ē) *adj*. Of or expressive of sexual love.

am-au-ro-sis (am˝o rō´sis) *n*. A partial or complete loss of sight due to the loss of power in the optic nerve or retina.

a-maze (*a*māz´) *v*. To astound; to affect with surprise or wonder. **amazingly** *adv*. **amazedness** *n*. **amazing** *adj*.

a-maze-ment (*a* māz´ment) *n*. The quality or state of being amazed or astounded.

Am-a-zon (am´*a* zon˝) *n*. A river of South America, beginning in the Andes and flowing through North Brazil to the Atlantic.

am-a-zon-ite (am´*a* zo nīt˝) *n*. A semi-precious green variety of microcline found near the Amazon River.

amb *abbr*. Ambassador.

am-bass-a-dor (am bas´*a* dor) *n*. Official representative of the highest rank, accredited by one government to another. **ambassadorial** *adj*. **ambassadorship** *n*.

am-ber (am´bėr) *n*. A hard, translucent, yellow, brownish-yellow, or orange fossil resin, used for jewelry and ornaments; medium to dark orange yellow.

am-ber-gris (am´bėr grēs˝) *n*. A waxy, grayish substance produced by sperm whales, and used in making perfumes.

am-bi-dex-trous (am˝bi dek´str*u*s) *adj*. Capable of using both the right and left hands with equal facility.

am-bi-ence (am´bē*e*ns) *n*. Environment; surrounding atmosphere.

am-bi-ent (am´bē *e*nt) *adj*. Surrounding; all sides.

am-bi-gu-i-ty (am˝b*i* gū´i tē) *n*. The quality

of being obscure or ambiguous.

am-big-u-ous (am big´ū us) *adj*. Doubtful; uncertain, open to interpretation. **ambiguousness** *n*. **ambiguously** *adv*.

am-bi-tion (am bish´*a*n) *n*. Strong desire to achieve; will to succeed; the goal or object desired.

am-bi-tious (am bish´us) *adj*. Challenging. **ambitiousness** *n*. **ambitiously** *adv*.

am-biv-a-lence (am biv´*a* l*e*ns) *n*. Existence of mutually different feelings about a person or thing.

am-bi-vert (am´bivürt˝) *n*. A person having the characteristics of both introvert and extrovert.

am-ble (am´bl) *v*. To move at a leisurely pace. **ambler** *n*.

am-bly-o-pi-a (am˝blē ō´pē *a*) *n*. Dullness or dimness of eyesight without apparent change or defect in the organs.

am-boi-na wood (am boi´n*a* wod) *n*. A curled and mottled wood used in cabinet making.

am-bro-sia (am´brō´zh*a*) *n*. Food of the Greek Gods and immortals; food having exquisite flavor or fragrance.

am-bu-lance (am˝būl*a*ns) *n*. Vehicle equipped to transport the injured or sick.

am-bu-lant (am´bū l*a*nt) *adj*. To move from one place to another.

am-bu-la-to-ry (am´bū l*a* tōr˝ē) *n*. Any sheltered part of a building intended as a passageway for walking. *adj*. Moving about; movable; able to walk.

am-bus-cade (am˝b*u* skād´) *n*. A trap; to place in ambush.

am-bush (am´bush) *n*. Surprise attack made from a hidden position. **ambush** *v*. **ambusher** *n*. **ambushment** *n*.

ameba *or* **amoeba** (*a* mē´b*a*) *n*. A minute single-celled, semi-fluid organism of indefinite, changeable form.

a-mel-io-rate (*a* mēl´y*u* rāt˝) *v.* To make better or more tolerable; to improve. **ameliorator** *n.* **ameliorative** *adj.*

a-men (ā´men´) *interj.* Used at the end of a prayer to express solemn approval.

a-me-na-bil-i-ty (*a* mē˝n*a* bil´*i* tē) *n.* State of being amenable.

a-me-na-ble (*a* mē´n*a* bl) *adj.* Responsive; tractable; accountable. **amenableness** *n.*

a-mend (*a* mend´) *v.* To correct; to improve; to rectify. **amendable** *adj.* **amender** *n.*

a-mend-ment (*a* mend´m*e*nt) *n.* Correction, reformation or improvement; a legislative bill change or the parliamentary procedure where such alteration is made.

a-mends (*a* mendz´) *n.* Compensation for insult or injury.

a-men-i-ty (*a* men´i tē) *n. pl.* **amenities** Agreeableness; means of comfort or convenience.

Amer *abbr.* America; American.

a-merce (*a* m*u*rs´) *v.* To punish by a fine decided by the court. **amercement** *n.*

a-merce-ment (*a* m*u*rs´m*e*nt) *n.* Fine imposed on an offender at the discretion of the court.

A-mer-i-ca (*a* mer´ik *a*) *n.* United States of America; North America; South America.

A-mer-i-can (*a* mer´i k*a*n) *n.* A native of one of the Americas or a U.S. citizen.

American eagle *n.* The bald eagle, an endangered species.

A-mer-i-can-ism (*a* mer´i k*a* niz˝um) *n.* Language usage, trait, or tradition of the U.S.

American plan *n.* A hotel plan where a guest is charged a fixed daily rate for service, room, and meals.

Am-er-ind (am´*e* rind) *n.* American Indian or an Eskimo.

am-e-thyst (am´i thist) *n.* Violet or purple form of transparent corundum or quartz, used as a gemstone. **amethystine** *adj.*

am-e-tro-pi-a (am˝i trō´pē *a*) *n.* An abnormal condition of the eye where images fail to focus upon the retina.

a-mi-a-ble (ā´mē *a*bl) *adj.* Friendly and pleasant. **amiableness** *n.* **amiability** *n.* **amiably** *adv.*

am-i-ca-ble (am´i k*a* bl) *adj.* Harmonious; friendly; peaceable. **amicability** *n.* **amicableness** *n.* **amicably** *adv.*

a-mi-cus cu-ri-ae (*a* mī˝k*u*s kūr´ē ē˝) *n.* A professional who is asked for or volunteers information on some matter of law that directly affects a particular case.

a-mid (*a* mid´) *prep.* In the middle of; surrounded by, among.

a-mid-ships (*a* mid´ships) *adv.* Halfway between the bow and the stern.

a-midst (*a* midst´) *prep.* In the middle of; surrounded by; during.

a-mi-go (*a* mē´gō) *n.* A friend.

A-mish (ä´mish) *n. pl.* Mennonites that settled mostly in southeastern Pennsylvania in the late 1600's. **Amish** *adj.*

a-miss (*a* mis´) *adj.* Out of order or place; in an improper or wrong way.

am-i-ty (am´i tē) *n.* Relationships that are friendly, as between two states.

am-me-ter (am´mē˝tèr) *n.* A tool measuring electric current.

am-mo (am´ō) *n.* Ammunition.

am-mo-nia (*a* mōn´ya) *n.* Colorless, pungent gas.

ammonium hydroxide *n.* A colorless, basic aqueous solution of ammonia.

am-mu-ni-tion (am ye ´nish en) *n.* Projectiles that can be propelled or discharged from guns; any means of defense.

am-ne-sia (am nē´zha) *n.* The partial or complete loss of memory. **amnesiac** *n.*

am-nes-ty (am´ni stē) *n. pl.* **amnesties** Pardon for political offenders.

am-ni-on (am´nē on) *n.* The innermost membrane that surrounds the fetus of birds, mammals, and reptiles.

a-moe-ba Variant of ameba.

a-mong (*a* mung´) *prep.* In or through the midst of; between one another.

a-mon-til-la-do (*a* mon˝ti lä´dō) *n. pl.* **amontillados** A pale, dry sherry.

a-mor-al (ā mor´*a*l) *adj.* Neither moral nor immoral. **amorality** *n.* **amorally** *adv.*

am-o-rous (am´ėr us) *adj.* Inclined to or indicative of sexual love. **amorousness** *n.*

a-mor-phous (a mor´fus) *adj.* Lacking definite form; shapeless; general; vague.

am-or-tize (am´ėr tīz˝) *v.* To liquidate a loan by installment payments; a loan. **amortization** *n.*

a-mount (a mount´) *n.* Aggregate, sum or total quantity. **amount** *v.* To be equivalent.

a-mour (a mur´) *n.* A forbidden love affair. **amour–propre** *n.* Self-respect.

am-pe-lop-sis (am˝pe lop´sis) *n.* Any plant having climbing woody vines or shrubs.

am-per-age (am´pėr ij) *n.* Strength of an electric current, expressed in amperes.

am-pere (am´pēr) *n.* Unit of electric current equal to a flow of one amp per second.

am-pere-turn (am´pēr türn˝) *n.* One complete turn of convolution of a conducting coil, through which one ampere of electric current passes.

am-per-sand (am´pėr sand˝) *n.* The character or sign that represents and (&).

am-phet-a-mine (am fet´a mēn˝) *n.* Colorless volatile liquid; a drug.

amphi *prefix* Around, on both sides, all around on all sides.

am-phib-i-an (am fib´ē an) *n.* An organism, as a frog or toad, developing from an aquatic state into an air-breathing state; aircraft that can take off and land on land or water; a vehicle that can move on land or water.

am-phi-bole (am´fi bōl˝) *n.* A silicate mineral of varying composition, that usually consists of a magnesium, silicate of calcium, and one or more other metals.

am-phi-pod (am´fi pod˝) *n.* One of an order of small crustaceous animals having a laterally compressed body and commonly found in fresh and salt water.

am-phi-the-a-ter (am´fi thē˝a tėr) *n.* A round or oval building having tiers of seats rising around an arena.

am-pho-ra (am´for a) *n. pl.* **amphorae** *or* **amphoras** Ancient Greek jar with two handles and a narrow neck, used to carry oil or wine.

am-pho-ter-ic (am˝fo ter´ik) *adj.* Able to react chemically either as an acid or base.

am-ple (am´pel) *adj.* Sufficient; abundant; large. **ampleness** *n.*

am-pli-dyne (am´pli dīn˝) *n.* Direct-current generator.

am-pli-fi-ca-tion (am˝pli fi kā´shan) *n.* An enlargement; an example or product of amplifying.

am-pli-fi-er (am´pli fī˝ėr) *n.* That which amplifies or enlarges.

am-pli-fy (am´pli fī˝) *v.* To make larger, more extended; to explain in greater detail.

am-pli-tude (am´pli tŏd) *n.* Maximum value of a periodically varying quantity; greatness of size; fullness.

amplitude modulation *n.* The encoding of a carrier wave by variation of its amplitude in accordance with a signal.

am-ply (am´plē) *adv.* In sufficient manner.

am-pul *or* **am-pule (am´pūl)** *n.* A small, sealed vial containing a hypodermic injection solution.

am-pu-tate (am´pū tāt´) *v.* To cut off; to remove, as a limb from one's body. **amputation** *n.*

am-pu-tee (am˝pū tē´) *n.* A person who has had one or more limbs amputated.

amt *abbr.* Amount.

amu *n., Phys.* Atomic mass unit.

a-muck (a muk´) *adv.* In an uncontrolled manner; a murderous frenzy; out of control.

am-u-let (am´ū lit) *n.* A charm worn as protection against evil or injury.

Amur *n.* A river of East Asia.

a-muse (a mūz´) *v.* To entertain in an agreeable, pleasing way. **amusement** *n.*

amusement park *n.* A commercially operated park with recreational facilities for entertainment.

am-yl-ase (am´elās˝) *n.* Any of the enzymes that change starch into sugar.

am-y-lol-y-sis (am˝e lol´i sis) *n.* The conversion of starch into soluble products.

a-my-o-to-ni-a (ā˝mī o tō´nē) *adj.* Deficiency of muscle tone.

an (an) *adj.* One; one sort of; each; form

of "a" used before words beginning with a vowel or with an unpronounced "h" as in elephant or honor.

a-na (ā′na) *n.* A collection of memorable sayings, information, or anecdotes about a person or place.

a-nach-ro-nism (a nak′ro niz″um) *n.* An error in chronology; connecting of a thing, person or happening with another that came later in history; anything that is out of place in history; any error which implies the misplacing, usually earlier, of person or events in time.

an-a-co-lu-thic (an″a ko lŏ′ thik) *adj.* Lacking grammatical sequence; inconsistency within a sentence.

an-a-con-da (an″a kon′ da) *n.* A large tropical South American snake which kills its prey by crushing it to death in its coils.

an-a-dem (an′a dem″) *n.* A wreath for the head.

a-nad-ro-mous (a nad′ro mus) *adj.* Migrating up river from the sea to breed in fresh water, as a salmon.

anaemia *n.* Variant of anemia.

an-aes-the-sia (an″is thē′zha) *n.* Variant of anesthesia.

an-a-gram (an′agram″) *n.* Word formed by transposing the letters of another word. **anagrammatical** *adj.*

a-nal (ān′al) *adj.* Of or relating to the anus.

anal *abbr.* Analogous; analogy; analysis; analytic.

a-nal-cime (a nal′sim) *n.* A white or slightly colored mineral with frequent occurrence in igneous rock masses.

an-a-lects (an′a lekts″) *n.* Selected miscellaneous extracts or small pieces selected from different authors and combined.

an-al-ge-sia (an″al jē′zē a) *n.* Inability to feel pain while awake. **analgesic** *adj.*

an-al-get-ic (an″al jed′ik) *n.* A remedy or treatment that removes pain.

analog computer *n.* A computer which calculates by using physical analogs, where numerical data is represented by measurable quantities as lengths, electrical signals, or voltage.

a-nal-o-gous (a nal′o gus) *adj.* Similar; corresponding in certain ways. **analogously** *adv.*

an-a-logue (an′a log″) *n.* Something that bears resemblance to something else.

a-nal-o-gy (a nal′o jē) *n. pl.* **analogies** Connection between things that are otherwise dissimilar; a conclusion or opinion that if two things are alike in some respects they must be alike in others.

an-al-pha-bet (an al′fa bet) *n.* A person who is totally illiterate; one who cannot read.

a-nal-y-sis (a nal′i sis) *n.* Breaking up or separation of something into its parts so as to examine them and see how they fit together; result.

an-a-lyst (an′a list) *n.* A person who analyzes or who is skilled in analysis.

analytic geometry *n.* The study of geometry properties where procedures of algebraic reasoning are applied.

an-a-lyze (an′a līz″) *v.* To make an analysis of.

an-am-ne-sis (an″am nē′sis) *n.* The recalling to mind of things past; recollection; reminiscence.

an-a-pest (an′a pest″) *n.* Metrical foot make up of two short syllables followed by one long one. **anapestic** *adj.*

a-naph-o-ra (a naf′or a) *n.* The repetition of the same word or words at the beginning of two or more successive clauses or verses.

an-a-plas-ty (an′a plas″tē) *n.* Plastic surgery.

an-arch (an′ärk) *n.* A leader who excites disorder or revolt.

an-ar-chic (an är′kik) *adj.* Of, like, or promoting confusion or disorder.

an-ar-chism (an′ar kiz″um) *n.* Belief that all forms of government act in an unnecessary and unfair way against the liberty of a person and should be done away with.

an-ar-chist (an′ar kist) *n.* One who rebels

with violent revolution against the established order.

an-ar-chy (an´ar kē) *n.* Lack of political authority, disorder and confusion; the absence of any purpose or standard.

an-as-tig-mat(a nas´tig mat˝) *n.* System of lenses where astigmatic defects are overcome.

a-nas-to-mo-sis (a nas˝to mō´sis) *n.* Connection or union of branches, as of rivers, leaf veins, or blood vessels. **anastomotic** *adj.* Pertaining to anastomosis

a-nas-tro-phe (a nas´tro fē) *n.* Changing the normal syntactic order of words.

a-nath-e-ma (a nath´a ma) *n.* Curse; ban; or excommunication. **anathematize** *v.*

a-nat-o-mist (a nat´o mist) *n.* A person who is skilled in dissection; one who analyzes critically.

a-nat-o-mize (a nat´o miz˝) *v.* To examine in great detail; to analyze; in biology, to cut in pieces for the purpose of displaying or examining the structure.

a-nat-o-my (a nat´o mē) *n. pl.* **anatomies** The branch of morphology dealing with the structure of an organ or organism; a detailed analysis; the art of dissecting or artificially separating the different parts of an organized body, to discover their situation, structure, and function. **anatomical** *adj.* **anatomic** *adj.*

an-ces-tor (an´ses tėr) *n.* A person who comes before one in a family line; someone earlier than a grandparent; forefather. **ancestral** *adj.*

an-ces-try (an´ses trē) *n. pl.* **ancestries** Line of descent; lineage ancestors collectively

an-chor (ang´kėr) *n.* Heavy metal device that is lowered into the water by a chain to keep a ship from drifting. **anchor** *v.* To attach or fix firmly.

an-chor-age (ang´kėr ij) *n.* A place for anchoring a ship; a strong support that keeps something steady.

an-cho-ret (ang´kėr it) *n.* A hermit; a re-

cluse.

an-cho-rite (ang´kė rīt˝) *n.* One who lives in seclusion for religious reasons; a religious hermit.

anchor man *n.* The main member of a team of newscasters.

an-cho-vy (an´chō vē) *n.* A very small fish of the herring family; usually salted, canned in oil, and used for making sauces and relishes.

an-cien ré-gime (on sē´an rā jēm´) *n.* Ancient or old system of government; system no longer prevailing.

an-cient (ān´shent) *adj.* Anything belonging to the early history of people; very old. **ancientness** *n.* **anciently** *adv.*

an-con (ang´kon) *n.* The upper end of the ulna or elbow used as architectural support.

and (and) *conj.* Together with; along with; as well as; added to; as a result; plus; also.

an-dan-te (an dan´tē) *adv. Mus.* Rather slow in tempo. **andante** *adj.*

an-dan-ti-no (an˝dan tē´nō) *adj. Mus.* Slightly faster in tempo than andante.

An-des *n.* A mountain system stretching the length of west South America, from Venezuela to Tierra del Fuego.

an-des-ite (an´di zīt˝) *n.* A dark grayish rock consisting mostly of feldspar.

and-i-ron (and´ī ėrn) *n.* Heavy metal support for logs or wood in a fireplace.

andr *n.* The male sex; masculine.

an-dro-gen (an´dro jen) *n.* Hormone that develops and maintains masculine characteristics. **androgenic** *adj.*

an-drog-y-nous (an droj´i nus) *adj.* Having the characteristics or nature of both male and female; having both staminate and pistillate flowers in the same cluster with the male flowers uppermost. **androgynal** *n.* **androgyny** *n.*

an-droid (an´droyd) *n.* In science fiction, a synthetic man made to look like a human.

an-ec-dote (an´ik dōt˝) *n.* Short account of a story of some happening or about some person. **anecdotal** *adj.* **anecdotic** *adj.* **anecdotist** *n.*

an-e-cho-ic (an˝e kō´ik) *adj.* Neither having nor producing echoes.

a-ne-mi-a (a nē´mē a) *n.* The condition in which a person's blood does not have enough red corpuscles or hemoglobin and, therefore, does not carry a normal amount of oxygen.

a-ne-mic (a nē´mik) *adj.* Of or having anemia.

an-e-mom-e-ter (an˝e mom´i tėr) *n.* Instrument for measuring wind force and speed.

a-nem-o-ne (a nem˝o nē´) *n.* A plant with purple, white, or red cup-shaped flowers.

an-e-moph-i-lous(an˝emof´ilus) *adj.* Wind-pollinated.

a-nem-o-scope (a nem´o skōp˝) *n.* A device that indicates the direction of the wind.

a-nent (a nent´) *prep.* Regarding; concerning.

an-er-oid (an´e roid˝) *adj.* Capability to function without fluid.

an-es-the-sia (an˝is thē´zha) *n.* Condition in which one has no feeling of heat, touch, or pain in all or part of the body.

an-es-the-si-ol-o-gy (an˝is thē˝zē ol´o jē) *n.* The medical study and use of anesthetics. **anesthesiologist** *n.*

an-es-thet-ic (an˝is thet´ik) *adj.* Taking away the feeling of pain. **anesthetic** *n.* Drug, gas, or substance used to bring on anesthesia before surgery.

an-es-the-tize (a nes´thi tīz˝) *v.* To bring on unconsciousness by giving anesthetics; to remove the capacity to feel pain in a localized area.

an-eu-rysm (an´yu riz˝um) *n.* A dilation of a blood vessel or artery, that is due to the pressure of blood acting on a part weakened by disease or injury.

a-new (a nŏ´) *adv.* Again; once more; in a new way.

an-gel (ān´jel) *n.* An immortal being attendant upon God; a very kind and lovable person; a helping or guiding spirit.

an-gel-fish (ān´jel fish˝) *n.* Several tropical fishes with a flattened body.

an-gel-i-ca (an jel´i ka) *n.* A plant with aromatic seed, used as flavoring.

an-ger (ang´gėr) *n.* Feeling of extreme hostility; rage; wanting to fight back.

an-gi-na (an jī´na) *n.* A disease marked by painful choking spasms and attacks of suffocation pain. **anginous** *adj.* **anginose** *adj.* **anginal** *adj.*

an-gi-na pec-to-ris (an jī´na pek´to ris) *n.* Severe pain in the chest, associated with feelings of apprehension and suffocation.

an-gi-ol-o-gy (an˝jē ol´o jē) *n.* The study of blood vessels and lymphatics.

an-gi-o-sperm (an´jē o spürm˝) *n.* A plant with its seeds in a closed ovary.

an-gle (ang´gl) *v.* A shape made by two straight lines meeting in a point or two surfaces meeting along a line.

angle iron *n.* A bar of iron, in the form of an L-shape.

an-gler (ang´glėr) *n.* A fisherman; a fish having a fleshy mouth appendages used to attract small fish as prey.

an-gle-worm (ang´gl würm˝) *n.* Earthworm, used as fishing bait.

An-gli-can (ang´gli kan) *n.* Member of the church of England or any of its related churches.

an-gli-cize (ang´gli sīz˝) *v.* To make English in form, idiom, or character.

an-gling (ang´gling) *n.* The act of fishing with a hook and line.

An-glo *n.* A root word meaning "English."

Anglo–Saxon *n.* A member of one of the Germanic peoples who settled in Britain in the 5th and 6th centuries A.D.

An-go-la *n.* A country located on the southwestern coast of Africa.

an-go-ra (an gōr´a) *n.* The long silky hair of the Angora rabbit or Angora goat; yarn or fabric made from the hair of an Angora goat or rabbit.

an-gri-ly (aŋ´gri lē) *adv.* To threaten in an angry manner.

an-gry (aŋ´grē) *adj.* Feeling or showing

anger; having a menacing aspect; inflamed.

angst (ăngkst) *n.* Anguish; feeling of anxiety.

an-guish (aŋ´gwish) *n.* Great suffering, from worry, grief, or pain; agony.

an-gu-lar (aŋ´gū lêr) *adj.* Having angles or sharp corners; measured by an angle or degrees of an arc; forming an angle. gaunt, bony, lean. **angularity** *n.* **angularly** *adv.*

an-hy-dride (an hī´drīd) *n.* Chemical compound formed from another by removing the water.

an-hy-drous (an hī´drus) *adj.* Does not contain any water.

an-i-line (an´i lin) *n.* Colorless, oily, poisonous liquid, used to make rubber, dyes, resins, pharmaceuticals, and varnishes.

an-i-mad-vert (an˝i mad vŭrt´) *v.* To make an ill-natured or unfair criticism, a critical remark. **animadversion** *n.*

an-i-mal (an´i mal) *n.* Any being other than a human being; any four-footed creature; beast. **animalize** *v.*

an-i-mal-cule (an˝i mal´kūl) *n.* Microscopic or minute animal.

animal husbandry *n.* That branch of agriculture pertaining to the care and breeding of domestic animals.

an-i-mal-ism (an´i ma liz˝um) *n.* The qualities or characteristic of being an animal.

an-i-mate (an´i māt´) *v.* To give liveliness, life or spirit to; to cause to act; to inspire. **animatedly** *adv.* **animation** *n.*

a-ni-ma-to (ä˝ni mä´tō) *adv. Mus.* In a lively or animated manner; used as a direction.

an-i-ma-tor (an e māter) *n.* One who animates, such as an artist or technician who produces an animation, as a cartoon or movie film.

an-i-mé (an´i mā˝) *n.* Resin that is exuded from a large tropical tree from which varnish, lacquers, and flavorings are produced.

an-i-mism (an´i miz˝um) *n.* A belief in primitive tribes that natural objects and forces have souls. **animist** *n.*

an-i-mos-i-ty (an˝i mos´i tē) *n. pl.* **animosities** Hostility; bitterness; hatred.

an-i-mus (an´o mus) *n.* Feeling of animosity.

an-i-on (an´ī˝on) *n.* An ion with a negative charge that is attracted to an anode; electrolysis.

an-ise (an´is) *n.* A plant with yellowish-white flower clusters and licorice-flavored seeds.

an-i-seed (an´i sēd´) *n.* Seed used for flavoring and in medicine.

an-i-sette (an˝i set´) *n.* Anise-flavored liqueur.

ankh (angk) *n.* A cross having a loop at the top, serving especially in ancient Egypt as a symbol of enduring life.

an-kle (ang´kl) *n.* Joint that connects the foot with the leg; slender section of the leg immediately above this joint.

an-klet (ang´klit) *n.* A short sock, an ornament worn around the ankle.

an-ky-lo-sis (ang˝ki lo´sis) *n.* Stiffness, fixation or immovability of a joint, due to a disease or as a result of surgery.

an-la-ge (än´lä ge) *n.* The first recognizable accumulation of cells in a developing organ or part.

ann *abbr.* Annals; annual; annuity.

an-nals (an´alz) *n. pl.* Descriptive record; history. **annalist** *n.*

an-nat-to (a nat´ō) *n.* The red dye made from the pulp from around the seeds of a small tropical American tree.

an-neal (a nēl´) *v.* To heat and then cool glass slowly to make it less brittle.

an-nex (a neks´) *v.* To add or join a smaller thing to a larger one. **annexation** *n.*

an-ni-hi-late (a nī´i lāt˝) *v.* To destroy completely; totally. **annihilator** *n.* **annihilation** *n.*

an-ni-ver-sa-ry (an i vŭr´sa rē) *n. pl.* **anniversaries** The date on which something happened at an earlier time; this event celebrated on this date each year.

an-no-tate (an´ō tāt˝) *v.* To use notes to give one's opinions. **annotator** *n.*

an-no-ta-tion (an˝ō tā´shan) *n.* Critical note from some passage of a book.

an-nounce (a nouns´) *v.* To proclaim; to

give notice.

an-nounce-ment (*a* nouns'ment) *n.* The act of announcing or being announced; giving notice; public notification.

an-nounc-er (*a* noun'sėr) *n.* A performer on radio or television who provides program continuity and gives commercial and other points of interest.

an-noy (*a* noi') *v.* To bother; to irritate; to make slightly angry. **annoying** *adj.* **annoyingly** *adv.*

an-noy-ance (*a* noi'ans) *n.* A nuisance; irritation; act of annoying.

an-noy-ing (*a* noi'ing) *adj.* Causing irritation; troublesome.

an-nu-al (an'ū al) *adj.* Recurring or done at the same time each year; a yearly publication, as a yearbook. **annually** *adv.*

an-nu-i-tant (*a* nŏ'i tant) *n.* Person who receives an annuity.

an-nu-i-ty (*a* nŏ'i tē) *n. pl.* **annuities** Annual payment of an income or allowance.

an-nul (*a* nul') *v.* To cancel a marriage or a law; to do away with; to put an end to. **annullable** *adj.* **annulment** *n.*

an-nu-lar (an'yu lėr) *adj.* Shaped like or forming a ring. **annularly** *adv.*

an-nun-ci-ate (*a* nun'sē āt') *v.* To proclaim; to announce.

an-nun-ci-a-tion (*a* nun'sē ā'shan) *n.* The act of announcing or being announced; an announcement.

a-no-ci-as-so-ci-a-tion (*a* nō'sē *a* sō'' sē ā'shan) *n.* Method of treatment before, during, and after a surgical operation, in order to prevent shock and other harmful effects.

an-ode (an'ōd) *n.* Positively charged electrode. **anodic** *adj.* **anodically** *adv.*

an-o-dize (an'o dīz'') *v.* To coat a metallic surface by electrolysis with a protective oxide.

a-noint (*a* noint') *v.* To apply oil in a religious ceremony. **anointment** *n.*

a-nom-a-ly (*a* nom'a lē) *n. pl.* **anomalies** Anything irregular or abnormal. **anomalistic** *adj.* **anomalous** *adj.*

a-non (*a* non') *adv.* Soon; in a short period of time.

a-non-y-mous (*a* non'i mus) *adj.* An unknown or withheld name, agency, lacking a name. **anonymity** *n.* **anonymousness** *n.* **anonymously** *adv.*

a-no-rak (ä'no räk) *n.* Parka; a hooded jacket.

an-o-rex-i-a (an''o rek'sē *a*) *n.* The loss of appetite that is accompanied by psychotic symptoms.

an-os-mi-a (an oz'mē *a*) *adj.* The loss or deficiency of the sense of smell.

an-oth-er (*a* nuth'ėr) *adj.* Additional; one more different, but of the same character.

an-ox-i-a (an ok'sē ā) *n.* Lack of oxygen supply in the body tissue and the complications that result from this lack of oxygen.

ans *abbr.* Answer.

an-ser-ine (an'se rīn'') *adj.* Related to or resembling a goose.

an-swer (an'sėr) *n.* A written or spoken reply, as to a question; a result or solution, as to a problem. **answer** *v.* To respond correctly; to be responsible for.

an-swer-a-ble (an'sėr *a* bl) *adj.* Responsible; obliged to give an account.

ant (ant) *n.* A small insect, usually without wings; which lives in or on the ground, or in wood in large colonies. **ant** *abbr.* Antenna; antonym.

an-ta (an'ta) *n.* A rectangular or square pillar.

ant-ac-id (ant as'id) *n.* A substance which neutralizes or weakens acids.

an-tag-o-nism (an tag'o niz''um) *n.* Hostility; condition of being against; the feeling of unfriendliness toward.

an-tag-o-nize (an tag'o nīz'') *v.* To arouse hostility; to make an enemy of someone.

ant-al-ka-line (ant al'ka līn'') *adj.* Having the property of preventing or neutralizing alkalies.

Ant-arc-tic (ant ärk'tik) *n.* Large area of land completely covered with ice; the South Pole.

ant-eat-er (ant´ē˝tėr) *n.* Animal with a long snout and a long, sticky tongue, feeding mainly on ants.

an-te-cede (an˝ti sēd´) *v.* To go before; to precede in time.

an-te-ce-dent (an˝ti sēd´ent) *adj.* One event that precedes another; previous.

an-te-date (an´ti dāt˝) *v.* To precede in time; to give an earlier date than the actual date.

an-te-lope (an´te lōp˝) *n.* A slender, long-horned, swift-running, hoofed mammal.

ante meridiem *n.* Time before noon, abbreviated as "A.M."

an-te-mor-tem (an´tē mor´tem) *adj.* Preceding death.

an-te-mun-dane (an˝tē mun´dān) *adj.* Before the creation of the world.

an-ten-na (an ten´a) *n. pl.* **antennae** Slender feelers on the head of an insect, lobster, crab, etc.; wire or set of wires used in radio and television to send and receive signals.

an-te-pe-nult (an˝tē pē´nult) *n.* The third syllable from the end of a word. **antepenultimate** *adj.* **antepenultimate** *n.*

an-te-ri-or (an tēr´ē or) *adj.* Toward or at the front; coming before; earlier.

an-te-room (an´tē rōm˝) *n.* Waiting room; a room leading to a larger, more important room.

an-te-vert (an˝tē vert´) *v.* To turn forward.

an-them (an´them) *n.* Hymn of praise or loyalty; an official song of a country, school, etc.

an-ther (an´thėr) *n.* The part of the flower where the pollen is located at the end of a stamen.

an-ther-id-i-um (an˝the rid´ē um) *n.* The male reproductive organ in plants such as ferns and mosses.

an-tho-cy-a-nin (an˝tho sī´a nin) *n.* Any of the pigments producing blue to red coloring in flowers and plants.

an-thol-o-gist (an thol´o jist) *n.* A person who compiles an anthology.

an-thol-o-gy (an thol´o jē) *n.* A collection of stories, poems, or other writings.

an-thra-cite (an´thra sīt˝) *n.* Coal with a high carbon content and low volatile matter; hard coal. **anthracitic** *adj.*

an-thrax (an´thraks) *n.* The infectious, usually fatal disease found in animals such as cattle and sheep; disease that can be transmitted to man.

an-throp-ic (an throp´ik) *adj.* Relating to man, or to the period of mankind's existence on earth.

an-thro-po-cen-tric (an˝thro pō sen´trik) *adj.* To interpret reality in terms of human experience and values.

an-thro-po-gen-e-sis (an˝thro pō jen´i sis) *n.* The study of the origin and development of the human race.

an-thro-poid (an´thro poid˝) *n.* Gorillas or chimpanzees resembling man.

an-thro-pol-o-gist (an˝thro pol´o jist) *n.* A person who specializes in anthropology.

an-thro-pol-o-gy (an˝thro pol´o jē) *n.* The science that studies the origin, culture, and mental development of man, in the past and present. **anthropologic** *adj.* **anthropological** *adj.* **anthropologically** *adv.*

an-thro-po-mor-phism (an˝thro po mor´fiz˝um) *n.* The ascribing of human motivation and human characteristics to something that is not human. **anthropomorphic** *adj.*

an-ti (an´tī) *n.* One who opposes a group, policy, practice, or proposal.

an-ti-anx-i-ety (an´tī aŋ´zī et ē) *adj.* Preventing or relieving anxiety.

anti-ballistic missile *n.* A missile designed to destroy a ballistic missile.

an-ti-bi-ot-ic (an˝ti bī ot´ik) *n.* A substance, as streptomycin or penicillin, that is produced by organisms, as fungi and bacteria, effective in the destruction of microorganisms and used widely to prevent or treat diseases.

an-ti-bod-y (an´ti bod˝ē) *n.* Proteins generated in the blood that react to foreign proteins or carbohydrates of certain types, neutralizing them and producing immunity against certain microorganisms or their toxins.

an-tic (an´tik) *n.* Mischievous caper or act.

An-ti-christ (an´ti krīst˝) *n.* A great enemy

of Christ. **Antichristian** *adj.*

an-tic-i-pate (an tis´i pāt) *v.* To look forward; to act in advance of; to foresee. **anticipator** *n.* **anticipatory** *adj.*

an-tic-i-pa-tion (an tis´i pā´sh*a***n)** *n.* The act of looking forward; expectation of a future event.

an-ti-cli-max (an˝ti kl*i***´maks)** *n.* A letdown or decline; a commonplace conclusion; a series of significant events or happenings. **anticlimactic** *adj.* **anticlimactically** *adv.*

an-ti-co-ag-u-lant (an˝tē kō ag´ū l*a***nt)** *n.* Any agent which hinders the coagulation of the blood.

an-ti-dote (an´ti dōt˝) *n.* A substance that counteracts an injury or poison.

an-ti-en-zyme (an˝tē en´zīm) *n.* A substance or inhibitor which retards, or prevents enzymatic action.

an-ti-freeze (an´ti frēz˝) *n.* Substance, as ethylene glycol, that is mixed with water or liquid to lower the freezing point.

an-ti-gen (an´ti j*e***n)** *n.* Substance, when introduced into the body, stimulates the production of antibodies. **antigenic** *adj.* **antigenically** *adv.* **antigenicity** *n.*

an-ti-his-ta-mine (an˝ti his´t*a* **mēn˝)** *n.* A drug used to relieve the symptoms of allergies and colds by interfering with the production of histamines.

an-ti-knock (an´ti nok˝) *n.* Substance added to gasoline to reduce engine knock, making the vehicle run smoother.

Antilles *n.* The main group of islands in the West Indies, forming a chain that separates the Caribbean from the Atlantic.

antilog (an´ti läg˝) *abbr.* Antilogarithm

an-ti-log-a-rithm (an˝ti lo´g*a* **rith˝***u***m)** *n.* The number corresponding to a given logarithm.

an-ti-ma-cas-sar (an˝ti m*a* **kas´***a***r)** *n.* A protective covering for the backs or arms of chairs and sofas, used to prevent soiling.

an-ti-mat-ter (an˝tē mat˝*e***r)** *n.* A form of matter that is composed of antiparticles.

an-ti-mo-ni-al (an˝ti mō ´nē *a***l)** *adj.* Containing or of antimony.

an-ti-mo-ny (an´ti mō˝nē) *n.* Silver-white

metallic element used in chemistry, medicine, and alloys, etc.

an-tin-o-my (an tin´o mē) *n.* An opposition or contradiction.

an-ti-ox-i-dant (an˝tē ok´si d*a***nt)** *n.* A substance that inhibits or opposes oxidation.

an-ti-par-ti-cle (an˝tē pär´ti k*a***l)** *n.* Identically matched atomic particles, but with exactly opposite electrically charged magnetic properties and spin.

an-ti-pasto (an˝ti pä´stō) *n.* Appetizer including cheese, fish, vegetables, and smoked meat served with oil and vinegar.

an-tip-a-thy (an tip´*a* **thē)** *n. pl.* **antipathies** Feeling of repugnance or opposition. **antipathetic,antipathetical** *adj.* **antipathetically** *adv.*

an-ti-per-spi-rant (an tip*e***r rp***e* **r***e***nt)** *n.* Substance applied to the underarm to reduce excessive perspiration.

an-ti-phlo-gis-tic (an˝tē flō jis´tik) *n.* A medicine which counteracts inflammation.

an-tiph-o-ny (an tif´o nē) *n.* One that echoes or answers another; responsive chanting or singing.

an-ti-pode (an´ti pōd˝) *n.* A direct opposite. **antipodal** *adj.*

an-ti-pro-ton (an˝tē prō˝ton) *n.* The antiparticle of a proton.

an-ti-py-rine (an˝tē pī´rin) *n.* A white, crystalline powder used to reduce fever, pain or rheumatism.

an-ti-quar-y (an´t*i* **kwer˝ē)** *n.* A person devoted to the study of old or rare relics.

an-ti-quate (an´t*i* **kwāt˝)** *v.* To make old, obsolete or outdated by substituting something new or more practical.

an-ti-quat-ed (an´t*i* **kwā˝tid)** *adj.* Obsolete; out of use, style or fashion; behind the times.

an-tique (an tēk´) *adj.* Belonging to or of ancient times. *n.* An object that is over 100 years old. **antique** *v.*

an-tiq-ui-ty (an tik´wi tē) *n. pl.* **antiquities** Quality of being ancient or old; well used.

an-ti–Sem-ite (ant i–´sem *e* **īt)** *n.* A person

hostile toward Jews, either religious or racial. **anti-Semitic** *adj.* **anti-Semitism** *n.*

an-ti-sep-sis (an˝ti sep´sis) *n.* Condition of being free from pathogenic bacteria and the method of obtaining this condition.

an-ti-sep-tic (an˝ti sep´tik) *adj.* Pertaining or capable of producing antisepsis; thoroughly clean. **antiseptically** *adj.*

an-ti-so-cial(an˝tē sō´shal)*adj.*Unsociable; opposed to society.

an-tith-e-sis (an tith´i sis) *n. pl.* **antitheses** Direct opposition or contrast. **antithetical** *adj.* **antithetic** *adj.*

an-ti-tox-ic (an˝ti tok´sik) *adj.* Counteracting poisons or toxic influences.

an-ti-tox-in (an˝ti tok´sin) *n.* An antibody formed in the body, capable of neutralizing a specific toxin or infective agency used in treating or producing immunity against certain infectious diseases.

an-ti-trust (an´tē trust˝) *adj.* Having to do with the regulation of trusts, monopolies, and cartels.

an-ti-tus-sive (an˝ti tus´iv) *adj.* Capable of controlling or preventing a cough.

an-ti-ven-in (an˝tē ven´in) *n.* An antitoxin to a venom, produced in the blood by repeated injections of such venom.

an-ti-viv-i-sec-tion-ist(an˝tē viv i sek´shan ist) *n.* A person opposed to scientific experiments on living animals.

ant-ler (ant´lėr) *n.* One of a pair of bony growths on the head of a member of the deer family. **antlered** *adj.*

an-to-nym (an´to nim) *n.* A word opposite in meaning to another word.

an-trorse (an trors´) *adj.* Forward or upward direction.

an-u-re-sis (an˝ū rē´sis) *n.* Unable to bring about the act of urination.

an-u-ri-a (a nūr´ē a) *n.* The inability to urinate.

a-nus (ā´nus) *n.* The lower opening of the alimentary canal.

an-vil (an´vil) *n.* A heavy block of steel or iron on which metal is formed.

anx-i-e-ty (ang zī´i tē) *n.* A state of uncertainty; disturbance of the mind regarding uncertain events.

anx-ious (angk´shus) *adj.* Troubled in mind or worried about some uncertain matter or event. **anxiousness** *n.*

an-y (en´ē) *adj.* One; no matter which; some; every; and quantity or part.

an-y-bo-dy (en´ē bod´ē) *pron.* Anyone; any person.

an-y-how (en´ē hou˝) *adv.* By any means; in any way; whatever.

an-y-more (en´ē mōr´) *adv.* At present and from now on.

an-y-one (en´ē wun˝) *pron.* Any person; anybody.

an-y-place (en´ē plās˝) *adv.* Anywhere.

an-y-thing (en´ē thing˝) *pron.* Any occurrence, object or matter.

an-y-time (en ĕ tim) *adv.* At any time whatever.

an-y-way (en´ē wā˝) *adv.* Nevertheless; anyhow; in any manner; carelessly.

an-y-where (en´ē hwâr˝) *adv.* In, at, or to any place; to any degree or extent.

a-or-ta (ā or´ta) *n. pl.* **aortas** *or* **aortae** The main artery that carries blood away from the heart; distributes blood to all of the body except the lungs. **aortal** *adj.* **aortic** *adj.*

a-ou-dad (ā yu dad´) *n.* Wild sheep of North Africa having long curved horns and a growth of hair on the neck and chest similar to a beard.

a-pace (a pās´) *adv.* At a rapid or quick pace.

A-pache (a pashê´) *n. pl.* **Apaches** A member of the Athapaskan-speaking tribe of Indians in North America, settled in the Southwest U.S. and North Mexico.

a-part (a pärt´) *adv.* Separate or at a distance; in pieces; to pieces; to set aside. **apartness** *n.*

a-part-heid (a pärt´hāt) *n.* In the Republic of South Africa, an official policy of political, social, and economic discrimination and segregation against non-whites.

a-part-ment (a pärt´ment) *n.* A suite or

room in a building equipped for individual living.

apartment building *n.* A building containing separate residential apartments.

ap-a-thy (ap´a thē) *n.* The lack of emotions or feelings. **apathetic** *adj.*

ap-a-tite (ap´a tīt˝) *n.* Mineral used as a source of phosphorus compounds.

ape (āp) *n.* A large mammal such as a gorilla, chimpanzee, or monkey; a very clumsy, coarse person. **aped** *v.*

Apennines *n.* A mountain range in Italy extending the length of the peninsula.

a-pe-ri-tif (ä per˝i tēf´) *n.* A drink of alcoholic liquor consumed before a meal.

ap-er-ture (ap´ér chér) *n.* An opening or open space; a mouth, hole, a passage.

a-pex (ā´peks) *n. pl.* **apexes** *or* **apices** The highest point; tip; top.

aph-a-nite (af´a nīt˝) *n.* Fine-grained igneous rock whose separate grains are invisible to the naked eye.

a-pha-sia (a fā´zha) *n.* Any partial or total loss of the ability to express ideas, resulting from brain damage. **aphasiac** *n.* **aphasic** *adj.* **aphasic** *n.*

a-phe-li-on (a fē´lē on) *n.* The point in an orbit farthest from the sun.

a-phid (ā´fid) *n.* Small insects that suck sap from plants.

a-phis-li-on (ā´fis lī˝an) *n.* Any of various insect larvae that feed on aphids or plant lice.

a-pho-ni-a (ā fō´nē a) *n.* A loss of voice to a whisper.

aph-o-rism (af´o riz˝um) *n.* Brief statement of truth or principal. **aphorist** *n.* **aphoristic** *adj.* **aphoristically** *adv.*

a-pho-tic (ā fō´tik) *adj.* Without light.

aph-ro-dis-i-ac (af˝ro diz´ē ak˝) *adj.* Increasing or arousing the sexual desire or potency.

Aph-ro-di-te (af˝ro dī´tē) *n.* Greek goddess of love and beauty.

a-pi-ar-y (ā´pē er˝ē) *n.* Place where bees are kept and raised for their honey.

ap-i-cal (ap´i kal) *adj.* Relating to or formed with the tip of a tongue; belonging to the

pointed end of a cone-shaped body.

a-pi-cul-ture (ā´pi kul˝chér) *n.* The keeping of bees; beekeeping.

a-piece (a pēs´) *adv.* For or to each one.

a-pla-cen-tal (ā˝pla sen´tal) *adj.* Applied to those mammals having or developing no placenta.

a-pla-sia (a plā˝zha) *n.* Incomplete or defective development of a tissue or organ.

ap-lite (ap´līt) *n.* A fine-grained granite, consisting mainly of quartz and feldspar.

a-plomb (a plom´) *n.* Assurance; poise; self-confidence.

apmt *abbr.* Appointment.

APO *abbr.* Army Post Office.

apo- *pref.* Lack of; separation of; being away from.

Apoc *abbr.* Apocalypse; Apocrypha; Apocryphal.

A-poc-a-lypse (a pok´a lips) *n.* The last book of the New Testament; Revelation. **apocalyptical** *adj.* **apocalyptic** *adj.*

a-poc-o-pe (a pok´o pē) *n.* The loss of the last of one or more sounds, letters or syllables at the end of a word.

a-poc-ry-pha (a pok´ra fa) *n.* Fourteen books not included in the Old Testament by Protestants, considered uncanonical because they are not part of the Hebrew scriptures; eleven of the books are accepted in the Roman Catholic Church.

a-poc-ry-phal (a pok´ri fal) *adj.* False; of questionable authenticity.

a-pog-a-my (a pog´a mē) *n.* Development or reproduction by processes other than fertilization.

ap-o-gee (ap´o jē˝) *n.* The point most distant from earth in the moon's orbit.

ap-o-graph (ap´o graf˝) *n.* A transcript or copy, as a manuscript.

a-pol-it-i-cal (ā po lit´i kal) *adj.* Having no interest for or involvement in political affairs.

A-pol-lo (a pol´ō) *n.* Greek sun god; very handsome young man.

a-pol-o-get-ic (a pol´o jet´ik) *adj.* Making an expression of apology. **apologetical** *adv.* **apologetically** *adv.*

a-pol-o-gist (*a* pol´*o* jist) *n.* A person who speaks in defense of a cause, faith or an institution.

a-pol-o-gize (*a* pol´*o* jīz´) *v.* To make an apology.

a-pol-o-gy (*a* pol´*o* jē) *n. pl.* **apologies** A statement expressing regret for an action or fault; a formal justification or defense.

a-poph-y-sis (*a* pof´i sis) *n.* An expanded or projecting part of a bone.

ap-o-plex-y (ap´*o* plek˝sē) *n.* Sudden loss of muscular control, consciousness, and sensation resulting from a rupture or blockage of the blood vessel in the brain.

a-port (*a* pōrt´) *adv., Naut.* To the left side of a ship.

ap-o-si-o-pe-sis (ap˝*o* sī˝*o* pē´sis) *n.* Sudden stopping short and leaving a thought or statement unfinished for the sake of effect.

a-pos-ta-sy (*a* pos´ta sē) *n. pl.* **apostasies** Desertion of one's political party, religious faith, or cause.

a-pos-tate (*a* pos´tāt) *n.* One who forsakes his faith or principles.

a-pos-ta-tize (*a* pos´ta tīz´) *v.* To abandon religious faith, principles, or party.

a-pos-te-ri-o-ri (ā˝po stēr˝ē ōr´ī) *adj.* Inductive; reasoning from facts to principles or from effect to cause.

a-pos-tle (*a* pos´el) *n.* A person sent on a mission; the first Christian missionary to go into a new area or group; the person who first initiates a moral reform or introduces an important system or belief; a member of a Mormon council of twelve men. **apostleship** *n.*

Apostle's Creed *n.* A Christian statement of belief in God, used in public worship.

a-pos-to-late (*a* pos´to lāt´) *n.* A group of people dedicated to spreading a religion or a doctrine.

ap-os-tol-ic (ap˝*o* stol´ik) *adj.* Relating to an apostle; living by the teachings of the New Testament and the apostles. **apostolicity** *n.*

Apostolic Father *n.* The church father of the first or second century A.D.

a-pos-tro-phe (*a* pos´tro fē) *n.* The mark (') used to indicate the removal of letters or figures, the plural of letters or figures, and the possessive case; the act of turning away; addressing the usually absent person or a usually personified thing rhetorically.

a-pos-tro-phize (*e*´päs tre fiz) *v.* To make use of apostrophe.

apothecaries' measure *n.* A measurement used mainly by pharmacists; a measurement of capacity.

a-poth-e-car-y (*a* poth´*e* ker˝ē) *n. pl.* **apothecaries** A person who prepares and sells drugs for medical uses; a drug-gist; pharmacist.

apo-the-ci-um (*e* thē shē *e*m) *n.* A single-celled structure in many lichens and fungi that consists of a cupped body bearing asci on the exposed flat or concave surface.

ap-o-thegm (ap´*o* them˝) *n.* A short, essential, and instructive formulation or saying. **apothegmatical** *adj.* **apotheg-matic** *adj.*

apo-the-o-sis (*a* poth˝ē ō´sis) *n.* The perfect way to explain or define something or someone. **apotheosize** *v.*

app *abbr.* Apparatus; appendix.

ap-pall (*a* pol´) *v.* To overcome by shock or dismay; to weaken; to fail; to become pale.

ap-pall-ing (*a* pol´ing) *adj.* Dismay or disgust caused by an event or a circumstance, disgusting. **appallingly** *adv.*

Ap-pa-loo-sa (ap e´lü se) *n.* A horse from the north-western American region; which has a mottled skin, vertically striped hooves, and a dotted or blotched patch of white hair over the rump.

ap-pa-nage (ap´*a* nij) *n.* A rightful adjunct; provision for a younger offspring or child; a section of property or privilege appropriated by or to a person as his share.

ap-pa-rat-chik (äp e´räch ik) *n.* A member of the Communist party.

ap-pa-ra-tus (ap˝*a* rat´us) *n. pl.* **apparatuses** Appliance or an instrument designed and used for a specific operation.

ap-par-el (*a par´el*) *v*. To dress or put on clothing; to adorn or embellish. **apparel** *n*. Clothing. *Naut*. The sails and rigging of a ship.

ap-par-ent (*a par´ent*) *adj*. Clear and opened to the eye and mind; open to view, visible. **apparently** *adv*. **apparentness** *n*.

apparent time *n*. Time of day so indicated by a sundial or the sun.

ap-pa-ri-tion (*ap˝a rish´an*) *n*. An unusual or unexpected appearance; the act of being visible; a ghostly figure. **apparitional** *adj*.

ap-par-i-tor (*a par´i tor*) *n*. An official person sent to carry out the order of a judge, court, or magistrate.

ap-peal (*a pēl´*) *n*. Power to arouse a sympathetic response; an earnest plea; a legal preceding where a case is brought from a lower court to a higher court for a re-hearing. **appeal** *v*. To make a request; to ask another person for corroboration, vindication, or decision on a matter of importance. **appealable** *adj*.

ap-pear (*a pēr´*) *v*. To come into existence; to come into public view; to come formally before an authorized person.

ap-pear-ance (*a pēr´ans*) *n*. The action or process of appearing; an outward indication or showing.

ap-pease (*apēz´*) *v*. To give peace; to cause to stop or subside; to calm; to pacify. **appeasable** *adj*. **appeasement** *n*.

ap-pel-late (*a pel´it*) *adj*. Having the power to hear and review the decisions of the lower courts.

ap-pel-la-tion (*ap˝e lā´shan*) *n*. Identifying by a name or title.

ap-pel-la-tive (*a pel´a tiv*) *adj*. Having to do with the giving of names; relating to or of a common noun. **appellatively** *adv*.

ap-pend (*a pend´*) *v*. To add an appendix or supplement, as to a book; to attach.

ap-pend-age (*a pen´dij*) *n*. Something added to something more important or larger; a subordinate or a dependent person.

ap-pen-dec-to-my (*ap˝en dek´to mē*) *n*. The surgical removal of the appendix.

ap-pen-di-ci-tis (*a pen˝di sī´tis*) *n*. Inflam-

mation of the vermiform appendix.

ap-pen-dix (*a pen´diks*) *n. pl*. **appendixes** *Med*. A medical term that refers to a small hollow blind process or the vermiform appendix. Also, supplementary material usually found at the end of something that has been written.

ap-per-ceive (*ap˝ėr sēv*) *v*. To be conscious of perceiving; to have apperception of something.

ap-per-cep-tion (*ap˝ėr sep´shan*) *n*. The mental understanding of something perceived in terms of previous experience. **apperceptively** *adv*. **apperceptive** *adj*.

ap-per-tain (*ap˝ėr tān´*) *v*. To belong to or connect with, as a rightful part.

ap-pe-tence (*ap´i tens*) *n*. Appetite; a strong natural craving.

ap-pe-tite (*ap´i tīt˝*) *n*. The craving or desire for food. **appetitive** *adj*.

ap-pe-tiz-er (*ap´i tī˝zėr*) *n*. Food or drink served before a meal to stimulate the appetite.

ap-pe-tiz-ing (*ap´i tī˝zing*) *adj*. Appealing to the appetite; tempting.

appl *abbr*. Applied.

ap-plaud (*a plod´*) *v*. To express or show approval by clapping the hands. **applaudable** *adj*.

ap-plause (*a ploz´*) *n*. The expression of public approval. **applausive** *adj*.

ap-ple (*ap´l*) *n*. The round, red, yellow, or green edible fruit of a tree.

ap-ple-jack (*ap´pl jak˝*) *n*. Brandy distilled from hard cider.

apple maggot *n*. A two-winged fly whose larva burrows into and feeds on apples.

ap-ple–pie (*ap´l pī˝*) *adj*. Perfect; excellent; relating to American values as being honest or simple.

ap-pli-ance (*a plī ans*) *n*. A piece of equipment or device designed for a particular use.

ap-pli-ca-ble (*ap´li ka bl*) *adj*. Appropriate; suitable; capable of being applied. **applicability** *n*. **applicableness** *n*.

ap-pli-cant (*ap´li kant*) *n*. A person who applies for a job or position.

ap-pli-ca-tion (ap *li* kā´sh*a*n) *n.* The act of putting something to use; the act of super imposing or administering; request or petition; a form used to make a request.

ap-pli-ca-tive (ap´*li* kā˝tiv) *adj.* Practical; applied; having an application.

ap-pli-ca-tor (ap´*li* kā˝t*o*r) *n.* A device used to apply a substance; one who applies.

ap-plies *adj.* Putting something to practical use to solve definite problems.

ap-ply (*a* pli´) *v.* To make a request in the form of a written application; to put into use for a practical purpose or reason; to put into operation or to bring into action; to employ with close attention.

ap-pog-gia-tu-ra (*e* päj *e* tur *e*) *n.* A music note or tone that precedes an essential melodic note or tone and usually is written as a note of smaller size.

ap-point (*a* point´) *v.* To arrange something; to fix or set officially, designate. **appointable** *adj.* **appointer** *n.*

ap-poin-tee (*a* poin tē´) *n.* Someone that is appointed.

ap-point-ive (*a* poin´tiv) *adj.* Something related to or filled by appointment.

ap-point-ment (*a* point´m*e*nt) *n.* The act of appointing or designating; arrangement for a meeting; a non-elective position or office; engagement or meeting.

ap-por-tion (*a* pōr´h*a*n) *v.* To divide and share according to a plan or agreement. **apportionment** *n.*

ap-pose (*a* pōz´) *v.* To apply one thing to another; to put before. **apposable** *adj.*

ap-po-site (ap´*o* zit) *adj.* Highly appropriate or pertinent; applicable. **appositeness** *n.* **appositely** *adv.*

ap-po-si-tion (ap´*o* zish´*a*n) *n.* A grammatical construction where a noun or noun phrase is followed by another; the explanatory equivalent. **appositional** *adj.*

ap-pos-i-tive (*a* poz´i tiv) *adj.* Relating to or standing in apposition.

ap-prais-al (*a* prā´z *a*l) *n.* The evaluation of property by an authorized person.

ap-praise (*a* prāz´) *v.* To estimate the value, worth, or status of a particular item.

appraisement *n.* **appraising** *adj.*

ap-prais-er (*a* prāz´ėr) *n.* One who gives an expert judgment of the value of something.

ap-pre-cia-ble (*a* prē´shē *a* bl) *adj.* Capable of being measured or perceived, noticed, or estimated. **appreciably** *adv.*

ap-pre-ci-ate (*a* prē´shē āt˝) *v.* To recognize the worth, quality, or significance; to value very highly; to be aware of; to realize; to increase in price or value. **appreciatory** *adj.*

ap-pre-ci-a-tion (*a* prē˝shē ā´sh*a*n) *n.* The expression of admiration, gratitude, or approval; increase in value.

ap-pre-cia-tive (*a* prē´sha tiv) *adj.* Having or showing appreciation.

ap-pre-hend (ap˝ri hend´) *v.* To anticipate with anxiety, dread or fear; to recognize the meaning of; to grasp; to understand.

ap-pre-hen-si-ble (ap˝ri hen´si bl) *adj.* Capable of being apprehended.

ap-pre-hen-sion (ap˝ri hen´sh*a*n) *n.* The act of or comprehending power to comprehend; suspicion or fear of future events.

ap-pre-hen-sive (ap˝ri hen´siv) *adj.* Viewing the future with anxiety or fear. **apprehensively** *adv.*

ap-pren-tice (*a* pren´tis) *n.* A person who is learning a trade, art, or occupation under a skilled worker for a prescribed period of time. **apprentice** *v.* To work as an apprentice under the supervision of a skilled worker. **apprenticeship** *n.*

ap-pressed (*a* prest´) *adj.* Pressed close to or lying flat against.

ap-prise (*a* prīz´) *v.* To give notice, to inform; to learn; verbal or written.

ap-proach (*a* prōch´) *v.* To come near to or draw closer; to be close in appearance. **approach** *n.* Access to or reaching something.

ap-proach-a-ble (*a* prō´cha bl) *adj.* Capable of being approached; accessible.

ap-pro-bate (ap´robāt˝) *v.* To express approval, or satisfaction of; to approve.

ap-pro-ba-tion (ap˝ro bā´sh*a*n) *n.* A formal approval.

ap-pro-pri-ate (*a* prō′prē āt″) *v.* To take possession of; to take without permission. **appropriate** *adj.* Suitable for a use or occasion; fitting. **appropriately** *adv.* **appropriator** *n.* **appropriateness** *n.*

ap-pro-pri-a-tion (*a* prō″prē ā′shan) *n.* Money set apart for a particular use; the act or instance of appropriating.

ap-prov-able (*a* prŏv′*a* bl) *adj.* Something or someone that is capable of being approved. **approvably** *adv.*

ap-prov-al (*a* prŏ′val) *n.* The act of approving; subject to acceptance or refusal.

ap-prove (*a* prŏv′) *v.* To regard or express a favorable opinion; to give formal or official approval. **approvingly** *adv.*

approx *abbr.* Approximate; approximately.

ap-prox-i-mate (*a* prok′s*i* māt″) *adj.* Located close together; almost accurate or exact. *v.* To bring close or near to; to approach; to estimate; to be near the same. **approximately** *adv.*

ap-prox-i-ma-tion (*a* prok″s*i* mā′sh *a*n) *n.* An approximate amount or estimate.

appt *abbr.* Appoint; appointment; appointed.

ap-pur-te-nance (*a* pür′te n*a*ns) *n.* Something that belongs with another more important thing; an accessory that is passed along with.

ap-pur-te-nant (*a* per′te n*a*nt) *adj.* Constitutes a legal attachment.

Apr *abbr.* April.

a-prax-ia (*a* prak′sē *a*) *n.* Inability to execute complex coordinate movement. **apractic** *adj.* **apraxic** *adj.*

a-pri-cot (ap′r*i* kot″) *n.* An oval, orange-colored fruit resembling the peach and plum in flavor, varying in color, normally a medium orange.

A-pril (ā′pr*i*l) *n.* The fourth month of the calendar year.

April fool *n.* A trick or joke played on another person on April Fools' Day.

April Fools' Day *n.* The first day of April, marked by practical joke playing.

a-pri-o-ri (ā″prī ōr′ī) *adj.* Based on theory rather than personal experience; deductive.

a-pron (ā′pr*o*n) *n.* A garment used to protect clothing; paved area around an airport terminal building or airport hangar; waterfront edge of a wharf or pier.

apron string *n.* Dominance or complete control over someone.

ap-ro-pos (ap″r*o* pō′) *adv.* At a good time; by the way.

apse (aps) *n.* A semicircular or polygonal projection of a building or church.

ap-si-dal (ap′sed l) *adj.* Relating to an apse.

apt (apt) *adj.* Unusually qualified or fitting; appropriate; having a tendency; suitable; quick to understand. **aptly** *adv.*

ap-ter-al (ap′tèr *a*l) *adj.* Having no columns along each side.

ap-ter-yx (ap′te riks) *n.* A New Zealand bird, having no tail and very short rudimentary wings.

ap-ti-tude (ap′ti töd″) *n.* A natural talent or ability; quickness in learning or understanding.

aq *abbr.* Aqua; aqueous.

aq-ua (ak′wa) *n. pl.* **aquae** *or* **aquas** Water; aquamarine.

aq-ua-board (ak′wa bord) *n.* Surfboard used to teach water skiing.

aq-ua-cade (ak′wa kād″) *n.* Water entertainment, consisting of swimming and diving exhibitions, with musical accompaniment.

aq-ua-lunger *n.* A scuba diver.

aq-ua-ma-rine (ak″wa m*a* rēn′) *n.* A color of pale blue to light green; a mineral that is blue, blue-green, or green in color.

aq-ua-naut (ak′wa not″) *n.* A scuba diver who lives inside and outside of an underwater shelter for an extended period of time.

aq-ua-plane (ak′wa plān″) *n.* A board towed by a speeding boat, ridden by a person while standing.

aq-ua pu-ra (ak′wa pū′ro) *n.* Very pure water.

aqua regia (ak′wa rē′jē *a*) *n.* Mixture of hydrochloric and nitric acids that dissolves platinum or gold.

aq-ua-relle (ak˝wa rel´) *n.* A transparent water-color drawing.

a-quar-ist (a kwâr´ist) *n.* A person who takes care of an aquarium.

a-quar-i-um (a kwâr´ē um) *n.* An artificial pond where living plants and aquatic animals are maintained and exhibited.

A-quar-i-us (a kwâr´ē us) *n.* The eleventh sign of the zodiac; a person born under this sign; (Jan. 20 - Feb. 18).

a-quat-ic (a kwat´ik) *adj.* Anything occurring on or in the water.

aq-ua-vit (ä´kwa vēt˝) *n.* Clear, dry Scandinavian liquor flavored with caraway seeds.

aq-ua vi-tae (ak´wa vī´tē) *n.* A very strong liquor; alcohol.

aq-ue-duct (ak´wi dukt˝) *n.* A conduit for carrying a large quantity of flowing water; a bridge-like structure supporting a canal over a river.

aq-ue-ous (ā´kwē us) *adj.* Like or resembling water; dissolved in water; watery.

aqueous humor *n.* The clear fluid in the chamber of the eye between the cornea and lens.

aq-ui-cul-ture *or* **aq-ua-cul-ture (ak´wi kul´chèr)** *n.* The cultivation of produce in natural water; hydroponics; fish breeding. **aquicultural** *adj.*

aq-ui-fer (ak´wi fèr) *n.* The layer of underground gravel, sand, or rocks where water collects.

aq-ui-line (ak´wi līn˝) *adj.* Resembling or related to an eagle; hooked or curved like the beak on an eagle.

a-quiv-er (a kwiv er) *adj. Slang* Trembling.

ar *abbr.* Arrival; arrive.

AR *abbr.* Arkansas; acknowledgment of receipt; army regulation; accounts receivable.

Ar-ab (ar´ab) *n.* A resident or native of Arabia; a member of the Semitic people of North Africa and the Middle East.

ar-a-besque (ar˝a besk´) *n.* An intricate style or design of interwoven leaves, flowers, and geometric forms.

Arabia (a rā´be a) *n.* Peninsula of south-

west Asia between the Persian Gulf and the Red Sea. **Arabian** *adj. & n.*

Ar-a-bic (ar´a bik) *adj.* Relating to Arabs, their culture, or their language.

Arabic numeral *n.* One of the number symbols: 0,1,2,3,4,5,6,7,8,9.

Ar-ab-ist (ar´a bist) *n.* Specialist in the Arabic culture or in the Arabic language.

ar-a-ble (ar´a bl) *adj.* Land that is suitable for cultivation by plowing.

a-rach-nid (a rak´nid) *n.* Arthropods that are mostly air-breathing, having four pairs of legs but no antennae; an insect as a spider or scorpions. **arachnid** *adj.*

a-rach-noid (arak´noid) *adj.* Having hair that gives an appearance of being covered with cobweb.

Ar-a-ma-ic (ar a mā´ik) *n.* A Semitic language used in Southwestern Asia, known since the ninth century B.C. This commercial language was adopted by non-Aramaean people.

Aramaic alphabet *n.* The commercial alphabet for many countries of southwest Asia, dating from the ninth century B.C.

a-ra-ne-id (a rā´nē id) *n.* A breed of spider.

Araucanian *n.* A member from a group of Indian people of south central Chile.

ar-ba-lest (är´ba list) *n.* Military weapon from medieval times with a steel bow, used to throw balls and stones.

ar-bi-ter (är´bi tèr) *n.* A person chosen to decide a dispute, having absolute power of determining and judging.

ar-bi-tra-ble (är´bi tra bl) *adj.* Subject to arbitration.

ar-bit-ra-ment (är bi´tra ment) *adj.* The settling of a dispute; the power or right of deciding.

ar-bi-trar-y (är´bi trer˝ē) *adj.* Something based on whim or impulse. **arbitrarily** *adv.* **arbitrariness** *n.*

ar-bi-tra-tion (är˝bi trā´shan) *n.* The hearing and determination of a case in controversy, by a person or persons chosen by the parties.

ar-bi-tra-tor (är´bi trā˝tor) *n.* A person chosen to settle a dispute or controversy between parties.

ar-bor (är´bor) *n.* A garden shelter that is shady and covered with or made of climbing plants. **arborous** *adj.*

Arbor Day *n.* A day assigned as a day for planting trees.

ar-bo-re-al (är bōr´ē al) *adj.* Resembling or related to a tree; living in trees or among trees. **arboreally** *adv.*

ar-bo-re-ous (är bōr´ē us) *adj.* Living in a wooded area; an area surrounded by trees.

ar-bo-re-tum (är˝bo rē´tum) *n.* A place for studying and exhibiting trees, shrubs, and plants cultivated for educational and for scientific purposes.

ar-bo-ri-cul-ture (är´bor i kul˝chèr) *n.* The ornamental cultivation of shrubs and trees. **arboriculturist** *n.*

ar-bor-ist (är bo rest) *n.* A specialist in the maintenance and care of trees.

ar-bo-ri-za-tion (är˝bor i zā´shan) *n.* The formation of an arrangement or figure of a bush or shrub.

ar-bo-rize (är bo rīz) *v.* To branch repeatedly and freely.

ar-bor-vi-tae (är´bor vī´tē) *n.* An evergreen tree of the pine family that has closely overlapping or compressed scale leaves, often grown for hedges and for ornamental decorations; a common name for certain coniferous trees.

ar-bo-vi-rus (är bo ´vi res) *n.* Various viruses transmitted by arthropods, including the causative agents for yellow fever and encephalitis.

ar-bu-tus (är bū´tus) *n.* A fragrant pinkish flower that blossoms early in the spring.

arc (ärk) *n.* Something that is curved or arched; the luminous discharge of electric current across a gap of two electrodes.

ARC *abbr.* American Red Cross.

ar-cade (är kād´) *n.* An arched covered passage-way supported by columns; a long arched gallery or building.

ar-cad-ed *adj.* Furnished with arcades or arches.

ar-ca-dia (är kā´dē a) *n.* The ancient Greek area usually chosen as background for poetry; region of simple quiet and pleasure; a mountainous district in ancient Greece.

ar-cane (är kān´) *adj.* Secret; hidden; obscure.

arch (ärch) *n.* A structure that spans over an open area and gives support. **archly** *adv.* **archness** *n.*

ar-chae-ol-o-gy (är˝kē ol´o jē) *n.* Scientific study of ancient times and ancient peoples. **archaeological** *adj.* **archaeologist** *n.*

ar-chae-or-nis (är˝kē or´nis) *n.* Extinct bird that dates back to the upper Jurassic period.

ar-cha-ic (är kā´ik) *adj.* Something that belongs to an earlier time; characteristic of an earlier language, now used only in special cases.

archaic smile *n.* An expression that resembles a smile, characteristic of early Greek sculptures.

ar-cha-ism (är´kē iz˝um) *n.* Something that is outdated or old fashioned, as an expression or word. **archaistic** *adj.* **archaist** *n.*

arch-an-gel (ärk´ān˝jel) *n.* The highest in order of angels. **archangelic** *adj.*

arch-bish-op (ärch´bish´op) *n.* A bishop of the highest rank who has the supervision over the other bishops.

arch-dea-con (ärch´dē´kon) *n.* A clergyman who has the duty of assisting a bishop. **archdeaconate** *n.*

arch-di-o-cese (ärch˝dī´o sēs) *n.* The territory or district of an archbishop, in which he oversees. **archdiocesan** *adj.*

arch-du-cal (ärch´dō´kal) *adj.* Pertains to an archduke.

arch-duch-ess (ärch´duch´is) *n.* A woman who has a rank and right equal to that of an archduke; the wife or widow of an archduke.

arch-duch-y (ärch´duch´ē) *n.* The territory of an archduchess or of an archduke.

arch-duke (ärch'dūk') *n.* A royal prince of the imperial family of Austria. **archdukedom** *n.*

arch-en-e-my (ärch'en'emē) *n.* One who is a chief enemy.

arch-er (är'chėr) *n.* A person who is trained in the uses or skill of the bow and arrow.

ar-cher-y (är'che rē) *n.* The practice or art of shooting with a bow and arrow; the equipment used by an archer.

ar-che-spore (är'ki spōer) *n.* A single cell or group of cells from which a mother spore is formed.

ar-che-type (är'ki tīp') *n.* An original from which other things are patterned.

arch-fiend (ärch'fēnd') *n.* A chief or principal fiend; a person of great wickedness, especially Satan.

ar-chi-pel-a-go (är"ki pel'a gō") *n.* Any water space scattered with many islands; a group of islands.

ar-chi-tect (är'ki tekt') *n.* A person who may design and or supervise the construction of large structures.

ar-chi-tec-ton-ic (är"ki tek ton'ik) *adj.* To resemble architecture in organization or structure. **architectonically** *adv.*

ar-chi-tec-ture (är'ki tek"chėr) *n.* The art or science of designing and building structures; a method or style of construction or building. **architectural** *adj.*

ar-chi-trave (är'ki trāv) *n.* In classical architecture, a horizontal piece supported by the columns of a building.

ar-chives (är'kīv) *n.* Public documents or records; the place where archives are kept. **archival** *adj.* **archivist** *n.*

ar-chi-volt (är'ki vōlt") *n.* An ornamental molding around an arched opening.

arch-way (ärch'wā") *n.* A passage or way under an arch; an arch over a passage.

arc lamp *n.* Electric lamp which produces light as when a current passes between two incandescent electrodes.

arc-tic (ärk'tik) *adj.* Extremely cold or frigid; relating to the territory north of the Arctic Circle. **arctic** *n.* A waterproof boot that covers or comes just above the ankle.

Arctic Circle *n.* Parallel of the latitude that is approximately 66.5 degrees north of the equator.

ar-cu-ate (är'kū it) *adj.* Curved or bent in the form of a bow.

-ard *or* **-art** *suff.* A person who is characterized by performing something excessively.

ar-dor (är'dėr) *n.* Extreme warmth or passion; emotion; intense heat.

ar-du-ous (är'jū us) *adj.* Taking much effort to bring forth; difficult.

are (är) *v.* First, second, and third person plural and second person singular of the verb "to be."

ar-e-a (âr'ē a) *n.* A flat or level piece of ground. **areal** *adj.*

ar-e-a code (â'ē a) *n.* The three-digit number assigned to each telephone area in the United States, used to call another area in the U.S.

ar-e-a-way (âr'ē a wā") *n.* A sunken space that offers access, light and air to a basement; a sunken area forming a passageway to a basement.

a-re-ca (e'rē ke) *n.* Tall palm of southeast Asia that has white flowers and red or orange egg-shaped nuts.

a-re-na (a rē'na) *n.* Enclosed area for public entertainment, such as football games, concerts, etc.

ar-e-na-ceous (är"e na'shus) *adj.* Having the properties of sand.

arena theater *n.* A theater with the stage located in the center and the audience seated around the stage.

aren't (ärnt) *contr.* Are not.

ar-gen-tif-er-ous (är"jen tif'ėr us) *adj.* Producing or containing silver.

Ar-gen-ti-na (ar jen tē'na) *n.* Country of southeastern South America.

ar-gen-tine (är'jen tin) *n.* A white metal having the appearance of silver; or various metals that resembles it.

ar-gen-tite (är"jen tīt') *n.* A lustrous ore.

ar-gil (är'jil) *n.* Clay or potter's earth; potter's clay.

ar-gil-la-ceous (är je'lā shes) *adj.* Resembling or containing clay.

ar-gon (är´gon) *n.* A colorless, odorless, gaseous element found in the air and in volcanic gases and is used in electric bulbs and electron tubes.

ar-go-sy (är´go sē) *n. pl.* **argosies** A fleet of ships; a large merchant ship.

ar-got (är´gō) *n.* An often secret, specialized vocabulary.

ar-gu-a-ble (är´gū a bl) *adj.* Open to argument; questionable. **arguably** *adv.*

ar-gue (är´gū) *v.* To debate, to offer reason for or against a subject; to dispute, argue, or quarrel; to persuade or influence, to debate over an opinion. **argument** *n.* **arguer** *n.*

ar-gu-men-ta-tion (är´gya men tā´shan) *n.* The process or art of arguing; debating.

ar-gu-men-ta-tive (är´gya men´ta tiv) *adj.* Given to argument; debating or disputing.

Ar-gus-eyed (är´gus īd´) *adj.* Watchful; extremely observant; vigilantly observant.

argus pheasant *n.* A large South Asian bird with long tail feathers brilliantly colored with eye-like spots.

ar-gyle *or* **ar-gyll (är´gīl)** *n.* A pattern knitted with varicolored, diamond-shaped designs.

ar-hat (är´hat) *n.* A Buddhist monk who is greatly respected; has reached the stage of enlightenment.

a-ri-a (är´ē a) *n.* A vocal piece with accompaniment sung in solo; part of an opera.

a-ri-bo-fla-vin-o-sis (ā˝rī bo flā˝vi nō´sis) *n., Med.* A vitamin deficiency, in which the mucous membrane of the mouth becomes irritated and some discoloration of the tongue may occur.

ar-id (ar´id) *adj.* Insufficient rain; dry; lacking in interest or feeling; dull.

Ar-ies (âr´ēz) *n.* The first sign of the zod-iac; a person born under this sign: (March 21 - April 19).

a-right (a rīt) *adv.* Correctly; rightly; in a right way or form.

ar-il (ar´il) *n.* The extra covering of the seed of some plants, such as the nutmeg.

a-rise (a rīz´) *v.* To come from a source; to come to attention; to come into view; to mount; to move to a higher place; to get out of bed.

a-ris-ta (a ris´ta) *n, pl.* **aristae** *or* **aristas** Bristle-like appendage or structure.

ar-is-toc-ra-cy (ar˝i stok´ra sē) *n.* A government by the best individuals or by a small privileged class; class or group viewed as superior; the hereditary privileged ruling nobility or class.

a-rith-me-tic (a rith´me tik) *adj.* Branch of math that deals with addition, subtraction, multiplication, division. **arithmetical** *adj.* **arithmetically** *adv.*

arithmetic mean *n.* The number received by dividing the sum of a set of quantities by the number of quantities in the set.

arithmetic progression *n.* A progression in which the difference between any term and the one before or after is constant, as 2,4,6,8, etc.

-ar-i-um *suff.* The place or thing connected to or relating with.

Arizona *n.* A state located in the southwestern part of the United States, statehood February 14, 1912, capital Phoenix.

ark (ärk) *n.* The ship Noah built for survival during the Great Flood; the chest which contained the Ten Commandments on stone tablets, carried by the Jews; something that gives protection; a safe place.

Arkansas *n.* A state located in the south-central part of the United States, statehood June 15, 1836, capital Little Rock.

arm (ärm) *n.* The part between the shoulder and the wrist; upper limb of the human body. **arm** *v.* To furnish with protection against danger.

Arm *abbr.* Armenian.

ar-ma-da (är mä´da) *n.* A fleet of warships; a large force of moving things.

ar-ma-dil-lo (är˝ma dil´ō) *n.* A burrowing nocturnal animal with an armor-like covering of jointed, bony plates.

Ar-ma-ged-don (är˝ma ged´on) *n.* A final battle between the forces of good and evil.

ar-ma-ment (är´ma ment) *n.* Military supplies and weapons; the process of preparing for battle.

ar-ma-ture (är´ma chėr) *n.* The main moving part of an electric device or machine; a piece of soft iron that connects the poles of a magnet.

arm-chair (ärm´châr˝) *n.* A chair with armrests or supports. **armchair** *adj.* Remote from the direct dealing with problems.

armed forc-es (ärmd foŕ ces) *n.* The combined air, military, and naval forces of a nation.

arm-ful (ärm´fel˝) *n. pl.* **armfuls** *or* **armsful** As much as the arm can hold.

arm-hole (ärm´hōl˝) *n.* The opening in a garment for the arm.

ar-mi-ger (är´mi jėr) *n.* One entitled to bear arms; a squire.

ar-mi-stice (är´mi stis) *n.* The temporary suspension of combat by mutual agreement; truce.

Armistice Day *n.* The armistice ending of World War I; title used before the official adoption of Veterans Day in 1954.

arm-let (ärm´lit) *n.* A band worn on the upper arm.

ar-moire (ärm wär) *n.* A large wardrobe or cupboard.

ar-mor (är´mor) *n.* Covering used in combat to protect the body, made from a heavy metal. **armor** *v.* **armored** *adj.*

ar-mor-clad (är´mor klad˝) *adj.* Encased in, covered, or protected with armor.

ar-mor-er (är´mor ėr) *n.* A person who makes armor; one who assembles, repairs, and tests firearms.

ar-mor-y (är´mo rē) *n, pl.* **armories** The supply of arms for attack or defense; the place where military equipment is stored.

ar-oid (ar´oid) *n.* Any araceous plant.

ar-o-mat-ic (ar˝o mat´ik) *adj.* Fragrant; giving out an aroma; sweet-scented; pleasant scent.

arm-pit (ärm´pit˝) *n.* The hollow area under the arm where it joins the shoulder.

arm-rest (ärm rest) *n.* The support for the arm, as on a chair.

arm-twist-ing (ärm twis tin) *n.* The use of direct personal pressure to achieve a desired effect.

arm wrestling *n.* A game in which two opponents sit face to face gripping right hands, with elbows securely on a table, making an attempt to bring the opponent's arm down flat onto the table.

ar-my (är´mē) *n. pl.* **armies** A group of persons organized for a country's protection; the land forces of a country.

ar-my-worm (är mē werm) *n.* Moth whose larvae travels in multitudes from one area to another destroying grain and grass.

ar-ni-ca (är´ni ka) *n.* Plant of the genus Arnica with yellow flowers from which a form of a tincture, as a liniment, is made.

a-ro-ma (a rō´ma) *n.* A distinctive fragrance or pleasant odor, fragrance. **aromatical** *adj.* **aromatic** *adj.*

a-round (a round´) *adv.* To or on all sides; in succession or rotation; from one place to another; in a circle or circular movement.

a-round–the–clock *adj.* Lasting continuously for a period of 24 hours.

a-rouse (a rouz´) *v.* To wake up from a sleep; to stir; to excite. **arousal** *n.*

ar-peg-gi-o (är pej´ē ō˝) *n.* Tones of a chord produced in succession and not simultaneously.

arr *abbr.* Arranged; arrival; arrive.

ar-rack (ar´ak) *n.* An alcoholic beverage distilled from the juices of the coconut palm, from the Far or Near East.

ar-raign (a rān´) *v.* To be called before a court to answer a charge or indictment; to accuse of imperfection, inadequacy, or of wrong doing. **arraignment** *n.*

ar-range (a rānj´) *v.* To put in correct order or proper sequence; to prepare for something; to take steps to organize something; to bring about an understanding or an agreement; to prepare or change a musical composition for instruments or voices other than those that it was written for.

ar-range-ment (*a* rānj´m*e*nt) *n.* The state or being arranged; something made by arranging things or parts together.

ar-rant (ar´*a*nt) *adj.* Extreme; being notoriously without moderation. **arrantly** *adv.*

ar-ras (ar´*a*s) *n.* A screen or wall hanging of tapestry.

ar-ray (*a* rā´) *v.* To place or set in order; to draw up; to decorate or dress in an impressive attire. **arrayer** *n.*

ar-rear-age (*a* rēr´ij) *n.* The condition of having something unpaid or overdue

ar-rears (*a* rēr´) *n.* The state of being behind something, as an obligation, payment, etc.; an unfinished duty.

ar-rest (*a* rest´) *n.* To stop or to bring an end to; to capture; to seize; to hold in custody by the authority of law. **arrester** *n.* **arrestor** *n.* **arrestment** *n.*

ar-rest-ee (*a* res ´tē) *n.* A person under arrest.

ar-rest-ing (*a* res´ting) *adj.* Very impressive or striking; catching the attention. **arrestingly** *adv.*

ar-rhyth-mi-a (*a* rith´mē *a*) *n.* The alteration in rhythm of the heartbeat, either in force or time.

ar-rhyth-mic (*a* rith´mik) *adj.* Lacking regularity or rhythm.

ar-ris (ar´is) *n.* The line where two meeting surfaces of a body form an angle, as in moldings.

ar-riv-al (*a* rī´v*a*l) *n.* The act of arriving.

ar-rive (*a* rīv´) *v.* To reach or get to a destination.

ar-ri-vé (ar˝ē vā´) *n.* One who has climbed quickly to a position of status or wealth.

ar-ri-viste (ar˝ē vēst´) *n.* A person who has achieved success through dubious means.

ar-ro-gance (ar´*o* g*a*ns) *n.* An overbearing manner, intolerable presumption; an insolent pride.

ar-ro-gant (ar´*o* g*a*nt) *adj.* Overbearing manner; proud and assuming, self-important. **arrogantly** *adv.*

ar-ro-gate (ar´*o* gāt˝) *v.* To demand unduly or presumptuously.

ar-row (ar´ō) *n.* A weapon shot from a bow; a sign or mark to show direction.

ar-row-head (ar´ō hed˝) *n.* The striking end of an arrow, usually shaped like a wedge. **arrowheaded** *adj.*

ar-row-root (ar´ō rŏt˝) *n.* A starch-yielding plant of tropical America.

ar-row-wood (ar´ō wed˝) *n.* Shrubs with tough pliant shoots that were formerly used in making arrowheads.

ar-rowy (´ar *e* wē) *adj.* To move swiftly; something that resembles an arrow.

ar-roy-o (*a* roi´ō) *n.* The dry bed of a stream or creek; a gully or channel.

ARS *abbr.* Agricultural Research Service.

ar-se-nal (är´s*e* n*a*l) *n.* A collection of weapons; a place where arms and military equipment are manufactured or stored.

ar-se-nic (är´s*e* nik) *n.* A solid, poisonous element, steel-gray in color, used to make insecticide or weed killer. **arsenic** *adj.* **arsenical** *adj.*

ar-sine (är sēn´) *n.* A colorless, inflammable, extremely poisonous gas having an odor like garlic.

ar-son (är´s*o*n) *n.* The fraudulent burning of property. **arsonist** *n.* **arsonous** *adj.*

art (ärt) *n.* A human skill of expression of other objects by painting, drawing, sculpture, etc.; a branch of learning.

ar-te-ri-al (är tēr´ē *a*l) *adj.* Having to do with an artery or the oxygenated blood contained in the arteries.

ar-te-ri-og-ra-phy (är tēr˝ē äg´r*a* fē) *n.* The visualization of an artery or arterial system after the injection of a radiopaque substance.

ar-te-ri-ole (är tēr´ē ōl˝) *n.* One of the small terminal twigs of an artery that ends in capillaries.

ar-te-ri-o-scle-ro-sis (är tēr˝ē ō skle rō´sis) *n.* A disease that causes the thickening of arteries walls and impedes circulation of the blood.

ar-ter-y (är´te rē) *n. pl.* **arteries** A blood vessel that carries blood from the heart to the other parts of the body; a major means for transportation. **arterial** *adj.*

ar-te-sian (är tē′zhun) *adj.* The perpendicular boring into the ground, at often great depths, which allows water to rise to the surface of the soil, by subterranean pressure.

ar-te-sian well (är tē′zhun wel) *n.* A well that produces water without a pump.

art form *n.* The recognized form of an artistic expression.

art-ful (ärt′fel) *adj.* Showing or performed with skill or art; devious; cunning. **artfully** *adv.* **artfulness** *n.*

art glass *n.* Glass designed for decorative purposes; novelty glassware.

ar-thral-gia (är thral′je) *n.* Pain that occurs in one or more joints. **arthralgic** *adj.*

ar-thrit-ic (är thrit′ik) *n.* A person who has arthritis. *adj.* Affected with arthritis; showing effects associated with aging.

ar-thri-tis (är thrī′tis) *n.* Inflammation of joints due to infectious or metabolic causes.

ar-thro-mere (ärthro mēr″) *n.* Segmented part of an articulate or jointed animal.

ar-thro-pod (är′thro pod″) *n.* An animal with jointed limbs and segmented body, as a spider. **arthropodal** *adj.* **arthropodan** *adj.* **arthropodous** *adj.*

ar-thro-spore (är′thro spōr″) *n.* A thick-walled vegetative cell which has passed into a resting state.

ar-ti-ad (är′tē ad″) *n.* An element with an even atomic number.

ar-ti-choke (är′ti chōk) *n.* A plant with a thistle-like head, which can be cooked and eaten as a vegetable.

ar-ti-cle (är′ti kal) *n.* A term or clause in a contract; a paragraph or section; a condition or rule; an object, item or commodity.

ar-tic-u-lar (är tik′yu lėr) *adj.* Related to or of a joint.

ar-tic-u-late (är tik′yu lit) *adj.* Able to express oneself clearly, effectively, or readily; speaking in distinct words, or syllables. **articulateness** *n.* **articulator** *n.* **articulately** *adv.*

ar-ti-fact (är′ti fakt′) *n.* Something made by man showing human modification or workmanship.

ar-ti-fice (är′ti fis) *n.* An artful or clever skill; ingenuity.

ar-ti-fi-cial (är″ti fish′al) *adj.* Not genuine; made by man; not found in nature. **artificially** *adv.*

artificial horizon *n.* The aeronautical indicator of an airplane designed to give a surface that is constantly perpendicular to the vertical and therefore is parallel to the horizon.

artificial respiration *n.* A method by which air is rhythmically forced into and out of the lungs of a person whose breathing has ceased.

ar-til-ler-ist (är til′e rist) *n.* A person skilled in guns.

ar-til-ler-y (är til′e rē) *n.* Weapons, such as cannons; troops that are trained in the use of guns and other means of defense.

ar-ti-o-dac-tyl (är″tē ō dak′til) *n.* A hoofed mammal with even-numbered toes.

ar-ti-san (är′ti zan) *n.* A person skilled in any art or trade.

art-ist (är′tist) *n.* A person who practices the fine arts of painting, sculpture, etc.

ar-tiste (är tēst′) *n.* One who is an expert in the theatrical profession.

ar-tis-tic (är tis′ik) *adj.* Relating to the characteristic of an artist or art.

art-ist-ry (är′ti strē) *n.* The artistic ability, or quality of workmanship or effect.

art-less (ärt′lis) *adj.* Lacking knowledge, art, or skill; crude; natural; simple. **artlessly** *adv.* **artlessness** *n.*

art-mo-bile (ärt mō bēl) *n.* A trailer that carries an art collection for exhibition on road tours.

art-work (ärt werk) *n.* The artistic work of an artist.

ARV *abbr.* American Revised Version.

Ar-y-an (âr′ē an) *adj.* Relating to or of the Indo-European family of languages.

ar-y-te-noid (ar″i tē′noid) *adj.* Pertaining to the two cartilages of the larynx, where the vocal cords are attached.

as (az) *adv.* In the manner like; of the same

degree or amount; similar to.

AS *abbr.* After sight, airspeed, Anglo-Saxon.

ASA *abbr.* American Society of Appraisers; American Statistical Association.

as-a-fet-i-da (as˝*a* fet´i d*a*) *n.* A gum resin having a strong garlic-like odor, formally used in medicine as an antispasmodic.

asb *abbr.* Asbestos.

as-bes-tos (as bes´tus) *n.* A noncombustible, fibrous, mineral form of magnesium silicate that is used especially in fireproofing. **asbestine** *adj.*

ASCAP *abbr.* American Society of Composers, Authors, and Publishers.

ASCE *abbr.* American Society of Civil Engineers.

as-cend (*a* send´) *v.* To rise up from a lower level; to climb; to mount; to walk up. **ascendible** *adj.* **ascendable** *adj.*

as-cen-dant *or* **as-cen-dent** (*a* sen´d*a*nt) *adj.* Rising; moving up.

as-cent (*a* sent´) *n.* A way up; a slope; the act of rising.

as-cer-tain (as˝ér tān´) *v.* To find out for certain; to make sure, confirm. **ascertainment** *n.* **ascertainable** *adj.*

as-cet-ic (*a* set´ik) *n.* One who retires from the world and practices strict self-denial as spiritual discipline; hermit.

as-cet-i-cism (*a* set´i siz˝*u*m) *n.* The practice of strict self-denial through personal and spiritual discipline.

ascorbic acid *n.* The anti-scorbutic vitamin abundant in citrus fruits, tomatoes, and green vegetables.

as-cot (as´k*o*t) *n.* A scarf or broad tie that is placed under the chin.

as-cribe (*a* skrīb´) *v.* To assign or attribute to something. **ascribable** *v.*

ASCU *abbr.* Association of State Colleges and Universities.

ASE *abbr.* American Stock Exchange.

a-sep-tic (*a* sep´tik) *adj.* Free or freed from septic material.

a-sex-u-al (ā sek´shö *a*l) *adj.* Lacking sexual reproductive organs; without sex. **asexuality** *n.*

asg *abbr.* Assigned, assignment.

ash (ash) *n.* A type of tree with a hard, tough elastic wood; the grayish dust remaining after something has burned.

a-shamed (*a* shāmd´) *adj.* Feeling guilt, disgrace, or shame; feeling unworthy or inferior. **ashamedly** *adv.*

ash-can (ash´kan˝) *n.* A metal receptacle container for refuse.

a-shore (*a* shōr´) *adv.* On or to the shore.

ash-tray (ash´trā) *n.* A container or receptacle for discarding tobacco ashes and cigarette and cigar butts.

Ash Wednesday *n.* The first day of Lent.

ASI *abbr.* Airspeed indicator.

a-side (*a* sīd´) *adv.* Out of the way; to a side; to one side; something that is said in an undertone and not meant to be heard by someone.

ask (ask) *v.* To request; to require or seek information. **asker** *n.*

a-skance (*a* skans´) *adv.* With a side glance; with suspicion or distrust.

a-skew (*a* skū´) *adv. or adj.* Out of line, not straight.

a-slant (*a* slänt´) *adv.* In a slanting direction.

a-sleep (*a* slēp´) *adv.* In a state of sleep; lacking sensation; numb; not alert.

a-slope (*a* slōp´) *adv.* In a slanting or sloping position or direction.

ASME *abbr.* American Society of Mechanical Engineers.

a-so-cial (ā sō´sh*a*l) *adj.* Selfish, not social; withdrawn.

as-par-a-gus (*a* spar´*a* gus) *n.* A vegetable with tender shoots, very succulent when cooked.

as-pect (as´pekt) *n.* The situation, position, view, or appearance of something.

aspect ratio *n.* The ratio of one dimension to another.

as-pen (as´pen) *n.* A tree known as the trembling poplar, having leaves that flutter even in a very light breeze.

as-per-i-ty (*a* sper´i tē) *n. pl.* **asperities** Roughness in manner.

as-per-sion (*a* sper´zh*a*n) *v.* False charges or slander; defamation; maligning.

as-phalt (as folt) *n.* A sticky, thick, blackish-brown mixture of petroleum tar used in paving roads and roofing buildings.

as-phyx-ia (as fik´sē a) *n.* Lack of oxygen or an excess of carbon dioxide in the system resulting in suspended animation or loss of consciousness.

as-phyx-i-ate (as fik´sē at˝) *v.* To suffocate, to prevent from breathing; choking. **asphyxiation** *n.*

as-pic (as´pik) *n.* A savory jelly made from fish, meat, or vegetable juices.

as-pi-rate (as´pi rāt˝) *v.* To give pronunciation with a full breathing sound; to draw out using suction. **aspiration** *n.*

as-pi-ra-tor (as´pi rā˝tor) *n.* A machine that moves air, liquids, or granular substances by the means of suction.

as-pire (a spīr´) *v.* To desire with ambition; to strive towards something that is higher. **aspiringly** *adv.* **aspirer** *n*

as-pi-rin (as´pi rin) *n.* Medication used for the relief of pain and fever.

ass (as) *n.* A hoofed animal; a donkey; a stupid or foolish person.

as-sail (a sāl´) *v.* To attack violently with words or blows. **assailant** *n.*

as-sas-sin (a sas´in) *n.* Murderer, especially one that murders a politically important person either for fanatical motives or for hire.

as-sas-si-nate (a sas´i nāt˝) *v.* To murder a prominent person by secret or sudden attack. **assassination** *n.* **assassinator** *n.*

as-sault (a solt´) *n.* A very violent physical or verbal attack on a person. **assaulter** *n.*

as-say (a sā´) *n.* To evaluate or to assess; to try; to attempt. **assayer** *n.*

as-sem-blage (a sem´blij) *n.* A collection of things or people; artistic composition made from junk, scraps; and miscellaneous materials.

as-sem-ble (a sem´bl) *v.* To put together the parts of something; to come together as a group. **assembly** *n.*

assembly line *n.* The arrangement of workers, machines, and equipment which allows work to pass from operation to operation

in the correct order until the product is assembled.

as-sem-bly-man (a sem´blē man) *n.* A member of an assembly line.

as-sent (a sent´) *v.* To agree on something. **assenter** *n.*

as-sert (a sert´) *v.* To declare or state positively, to maintain; to defend. **asserter** *n.* **assertor** *n.*

as-ser-tion (a ser´shan) *n.* Maintaining claim; the act of affirming.

as-sess (a ses´) *v.* To fix or assign a value to something. **assessor** *n.*

as-sess-ment (a ses´ment) *n.* The official determination of value for tax purposes.

as-set (as´et) *n.* A valuable quality or possession; all of the property of a business or a person that can be used to cover liabilities.

as-sev-er-ate (a sev´e rāt˝) *v.* To state positively, firmly, and seriously.

as-sid-u-ous (a sij´ŏ us) *adj.* Devoted; constant in application; attentive; industrious.

as-sign (a sīn´) *v.* To designate as to duty; to give or allot; to attribute; to transfer. **assignable** *adj.*

assigned risk *n.* A poor risk for insuring; one that insurance companies would normally refuse but are forced to insure by state law.

as-sign-ee (a sī nē´) *n.* The person appointed to act for another; the person to whom property or the right to something is legally transferred.

as-sign-ment (a sīn´ment) *n.* A given amount of work or task to undertake; a post, position, or office to which one is assigned.

as-sim-i-late (a sim´i lāt˝) *v.* To take in, to understand; to make similar; to digest or to absorb into the system. **assimilator** *n.* **assimilation** *n.*

as-sist (a sist´) *v.* To give support, to aid, to give help. **assistance** *n.*

as-sis-tant (a sis´tant) *n.* One who assists; helper.

as-size (a sīz´) *n.* A fixed or customary

standard.

assn *abbr.* Association.

assoc *abbr.* Associate.

as-so-ci-a-ble (*a* sō´shē *a* bl) *adj.* Capable of being associated, joined; linked, or connected in thought.

as-so-ci-ate (*a* sō´shē it) *v.* To connect or join together. *n.* A partner, colleague, or companion.

as-so-ci-a-tion (*a* sō˝sē ā´sh*a*n) *n.* An organized body of people having a common interest; a society. **associational** *adj.*

as-so-nance (*as´o* n*a*ns) *n.* The repetition of sound in words or syllables.

as-sort (*a* sort´) *v.* To distribute into groups of a classification or kind. **assorter** *n.* **assortative** *adj.*

as-sort-ed (*a* sort´id) *adj.* Made up of different or various kinds.

as-sort-ment (*a* sort´m*e*nt) *n.* The act or state of being assorted; a collection of different things.

ASSR *abbr.* Autonomous Soviet Socialist Republic.

asst *abbr.* Assistant.

as-suage (*a* swāj´) *v.* To quiet, pacify; to put an end to by satisfying.

as-sua-sive (*a* swā´siv) *adj.* Having a smooth, pleasant effect or quality.

as-sume (*a* sōm´) *v.* To take upon oneself to complete a job or duty; to take responsibility for; to take for granted. **assumable** *adj.* **assumably** *adv.*

as-sum-ing (*a* sōm´ing) *adj.* Putting on airs of superiority; overbearing.

as-sump-tion (*a* sump´sh*a*n) *n.* An idea or statement believed to be true without proof.

as-sur-ance (*a* sher´*a*ns) *n.* A statement made to inspire confidence of mind or manner; freedom from uncertainty or self-doubt; self-reliance.

as-sure (*a* sher´) *v.* To give the feeling of confidence; to make sure or certain.

as-sured (*a* sherd´) *adj.* Satisfied as to the truth or certainty. **assuredly** *adv.*

as-sur-er (*a* sher´ėr) *n.* A person who gives assurance.

as-sur-gent (*a* ser´j*e*nt) *adj.* Moving or directed upward.

assy *abbr.* Assembly.

as-ter (*as´*tėr) *n.* A plant having white, bluish, purple, or pink daisy-like flowers.

a-ste-ri-a (*a* stēr´ē *a*) *n.* A gem stone, as a sapphire cut to show asterism.

as-ter-isk (*as´te* risk) *n.* The character (*) used to indicate letters omitted or as a reference to a footnote.

a-stern (*a* stern´) *adv. & adj.* Toward the rear or back of an aircraft or ship.

as-ter-oid (*as´te* roid˝) *n.* One of thousands of small planets between Jupiter and Mars.

asth-ma (*az´*m*a*) *n.* A respiratory disease marked by labored breathing, accompanied by wheezing, and often coughing and gasping for breath. **asthmatic** *adj.* **asthmatically** *adv.*

as though *conj.* As if.

a-stig-ma-tism (*a* stig´m*a* tiz˝*u*m) *n.* A defect of the lens of an eye resulting in blurred or imperfect images.

a-stir (*a* ster´) *adj.* To be out of bed, awake; in motion.

ASTM *abbr.* American Society for Testing and Materials.

as to *prep.* With reference to or regard to; concerning; according to.

as-ton-ish (*a* ston´ish) *v.* To strike with sudden fear, wonder, or surprise.

as-ton-ish-ing (*a* ston´i shing) *adj.* Causing surprise or astonishment.

as-ton-ish-ment (*a* ston´ish m*e*nt) *n.* The state of being amazed or astonished.

as-tound (*a* stound´) *v.* To fill with wonder and bewilderment, amazement. **astounding** *adj.* **astoundingly** *adv.*

ASTP *abbr.* Army Specialized Training Program.

as-tra-gal (*as´*tr*a* gal) *n.* A narrow, half-round molding.

as-tra-khan (*as´*tr*a* k*a*n) *n.* The curly fur from a young lamb of the southeast U.S.S.R.

as-tral (as´tr*a***l)** *adj.* Resembling, or related to the stars.

a-stray (*a* **strā´)** *adv.* Away from a desirable or proper path or development.

a-stride (*a* **strīd´)** *prep.* One leg on either side of something; placed or lying on both sides of; extending across or over.

as-trin-gent (*a* **strin´j***e***nt)** *adj.* Able to draw together or to constricting tissue. **astringency** *n.*

as-tro-dome (as´tr*o* **dōm˝)** *n.* A large stadium covered by a dome.

as-tro-labe (as´tr*o* **lāb˝)** *n.* Instrument formerly used to determine the altitude of a celestial body.

as-trol-o-gy (*a* **strol´***o* **jē)** *n.* The study of the supposed influences of the planets and stars and their movements and positions on human affairs. **astrological** *adj.* **astrologer** *n.*

astron *abbr.* Astronomer; Astronomy.

as-tro-naut (as´tr*o* **not˝)** *n.* A person who travels in a spacecraft beyond the earth's atmosphere.

as-tro-nau-tics (as´tr*o* **no´tiks)** *n.* The technology and science of the construction and operation of a spacecraft. **astronautical** *adj.* **astronautically** *adv.*

as-tro-nom-i-cal (as˝tr*o* **nom´i k***a***l)** *adj.* Relating to astronomy; something inconceivable or enormously large. **astronomically** *adv.*

as-tron-o-my (*a* **stron´***o* **mē)** *n.* The science of the celestial bodies and their motion, magnitudes, and constitution.

as-tro-phys-ics (as˝trō fiz´iks) *n.* Branch of astronomy dealing with the chemical and physical constitution of the celestial bodies. **astrophysical** *adj.*

as-tute (*a* **stōt´)** *adj.* Sharp in discernment; very shrewd; cunning; keen. **astutely** *adv.* **astuteness** *n.*

a-sun-der (*a* **sun´d***e***r)** *adv.* Separate into parts or positions apart from each other.

ASV *abbr.* American Standard Version.

a-sy-lum (*a* **sī´lum)** *n.* A refuge or institution for the care of the needy or sick; a place of security and retreat; an institution providing help and care for the destitute or insane; home for the mentally ill.

a-sym-met-ric (ā˝s*i* **me´trik)** *adj.* Something that is not symmetrical.

a-syn-de-ton (*a* **sin´di ton˝)** *n.* A figure of speech in which conjunctions are omitted.

at (at) *prep.* To indicate presence, occurrence, or condition; used as a function word to indicate a certain time.

AT *abbr.* Ampereturn; air temperature.

at-a-rac-tic (at˝*a* **rak´tik)** *n.* A tranquilizer; a drug that decreases anxiety or tension.

a-tav-ic (*a* **tav´ik)** *adj.* Pertaining to, remote ancestor.

at-a-vism (at´*a* **viz˝***u***m)** *n.* The reappearance of a hereditary characteristic that skipped several generations. **atavistic** *adj.*

a-tax-ia (*a* **tak´sē** *a***)** *n.* Any nervous disorder with an inability to coordinate voluntary muscular movements.

at-el-ier (at´el yā˝) *n.* An artist's workshop.

a tem-po (ä tem´pō) *adv.* A direction to return to the original speed; in time.

a-the-ism (ā´thē iz˝*u***m)** *n.* The disbelief that God exists.

a-the-ist (ā´thē ist) *n.* A person who does not believe in God. **atheistic** *adj.* **atheistical** *adj.*

Ath-ens *n.* The capital city of Greece.

ath-er-o-ma (ath˝erō´m*a***)** *n.* Condition where there is a deposit of fats within the inner walls of an artery.

ath-e-to-sis (ath˝i tō´sis) *n.* Condition where the hands and feet continually perform involuntary, irregular, slow movements.

a-thirst (*a* **therst´)** *adj.* Having a strong, eager desire for something.

ath-lete (ath´lēt) *n.* A person who participates in sports, as football, basketball, soccer, etc.

athlete's foot *n.* A contagious skin infection of the feet.

ath-let-ic (ath let´ik) *adj.* Relating to athletes; physically strong and active.

ath-ro-cyte (ath´ro sīt˝) n. A cell capable of ingesting foreign matter and storing it.

a-thwart (a thwort´) adv. Opposition to the expected or right; from one side to another.

a-tilt (a tilt´) adj. & adv. Inclined upward or tilted in some way.

At-lan-ta n. The capital city of Georgia.

Atlantic Ocean n. The second largest ocean.

at-las (at´las) n. A collection or book of maps.

ATM abbr. Automatic Teller Machine; a banking terminal that allows a customer to deposit or withdraw money by inserting a card and entering a private number code.

at-mom-e-ter (at mom´i tėr) n. Instrument for measuring the evaporating capacity of air.

at-mos-phere (at´mos fēr˝) n. A gaseous mass that surrounds a celestial body, as the earth; a predominant mood or feeling.

atmospheric pressure n. The pressure in the atmosphere due solely to the weight of the atmospheric gases above the point concerned.

at-oll (at´ol) n. An island of coral that encircles a lagoon either partially or completely.

at-om (at´om) n. A tiny particle, the smallest unit of an element.

atom bomb or **atom-ic bomb** n. A bomb that explodes violently due to the sudden release of atomic energy, occurring from the splitting of nuclei of a heavy chemical element.

atomic energy n. Energy that is released by changes in the nucleus of an atom.

a-ton-al (ā tōn´al) adj. Marked by the deliberate avoidance of a traditional key or tonal center. **atonality** n. **atonally** adv.

a-tone (a tōn´) v. To give satisfaction; to make amends.

a-tone-ment (a tōn´ment) n. Amends for an injury or a wrong doing; the reconciliation between God and man.

a-top (a top´) adj. On the top of something.

a-tri-um (ā´trē um) n. One of the heart chambers; the main hall of a Roman house. **atrial** adj.

a-tro-cious (a trō´shus) adj. Extremely cruel or evil, horrible. **atrociously** adv. **atrociousness** n.

a-troc-i-ty (a tros´i tē) n. pl. **atrocities** The condition of being atrocious; horrible; an inhuman, atrocious act.

a-tro-phy (a´trō fē) v. To decrease in size; to waste away.

att abbr. Attached; attention; attorney.

at-tac-ca (a tä´ka) v., Mus. Direction at the end of a movement to proceed, immediately, with the following movement.

at-tach (a tach´) v. To bring together; to fasten or become fastened; to bind by personal attachments; to tie together. **attachable** adj.

at-ta-che (at´a shā´) n. An expert on the diplomatic staff of an embassy.

attache case n. A briefcase or a small suitcase.

at-tached (a tacht´) adj. Permanently fixed; joined; cemented; bound.

at-tach-ment (a tach´ment) n. The state of being attached; a tie of affection or loyalty; the supplementary part of something.

at-tack (a tak´) v. To threaten with force, to assault; to start to work on with vigor.

at-tain (a tān´) v. To arrive at or reach a goal, accomplished. **attainability** n. **attainable** adj. **attainableness** n.

at-tain-der (a tān´dėr) n. The loss of civil rights that occurs following a criminal conviction, forfeiture of rights.

at-tain-ment (a tān´ment) n. Accomplishment; an achievement, to find guilty of a crime such as a felony.

at-taint (a tānt´) v. To disgrace or stain; to achieve or obtain by effort.

at-tar (at´ar) n. The fragrant oil from flowers.

at-tempt (a tempt´) v. To make an effort to do something. **attempt** n.

at-tend (a tend´) v. To be present; to take

charge of or to look after.

at-ten-dance (*a* ten´d*a*ns) *n.* The fact or act of attending; the number of times a person attends.

at-ten-dant (*a* ten´d*a*nt) *n.* One who provides a service for another.

at-ten-tion (*a* ten´sh*a*n) *n.* Observation, notice, or mental concentration.

at-ten-tive (*a* ten´tiv) *adj.* Observant; paying or giving attention. **attentively** *adv.* **attentiveness** *n.*

at-ten-u-ate (*a* ten´ū āt´´) *v.* To lessen the force, amount or value; to become thin; to weaken. **attenuation** *n.*

at-test (*a* test´) *v.* To give testimony or to sign one's name as a witness; to declare as truth. **attestation** *n.*

at-tic (at´ik) *n.* The space directly below the roof of a building.

at-tire (*a* tīr´) *n.* A person's dress or clothing. *v.* To clothe; to dress.

at-ti-tude (at´*i* töd´´) *n.* A mental position; the feeling one has for oneself.

at-ti-tu-di-nize (at´i töd´i nīz´´) *v.* To assume affected attitudes or postures.

attn *abbr.* Attention.

at-torn (*a* tern´) *v.* To transfer to another; to turn over.

at-tor-ney (*a* ter´nē) *n.* A person with legal training who is appointed by another to transact business for him.

attorney general *n.* The chief law officer of a state or nation.

at-tract (*a* trakt´) *v.* To draw by appeal; to cause to draw near by appealing qualities.

at-trac-tion (*a* trak´sh*a*n) *n.* The capability of attracting; something that attracts or is meant to attract.

at-trac-tive (*a* trak´tiv) *adj.* Having the power of charming, or quality of attracting. **attractively** *adv.* **attractiveness** *n.*

at-trib-ute (*a* trib´yŏt) *v.* To explain by showing a cause.

attribute *n.* A characteristic of a thing or person. **attributable** *adj.*

at-tri-tion (*a* trish´*a*n) *n.* Wearing down by friction; a rubbing against.

at-tune (*a* tūn´) *v.* To bring something into harmony; to put in tune; to adjust.

atty *abbr.* Attorney.

atty gen *abbr.* Attorney general.

a-twit-ter (*a* twit´ėr) *adj.* Very excited; or nervously concerned about something.

at wt *abbr.* Atomic weight.

a-typ-i-cal (ā tip´*i* k*a*l) *adj.* Not conforming to the typical type; differant than the usual. **atypically** *adv.*

au-bade (ō ´bäd) *n.* A poem or song for lovers who part at dawn; a love song in the morning.

au-ber-gine (ō´bėr zhēn´) *n.* Eggplant, or the fruit from the plant.

au-burn (o´burn) *adj.* A reddish-brown color; moderately brown; used in describing the color of a person's hair.

au cou-rant (ō kŏ rän´) *adj.* Fully familiar or informed.

auc-tion (ok´sh*a*n) *n.* A public sale of merchandise to the highest bidder.

auction bridge *n.* A variation in the game of bridge in which tricks made in excess of the contract are scored toward game.

auc-tion-eer (ok˝sh*a* nēr´) *n.* A person whose profession is the act of selling by auction.

auc-to-ri-al (ok tōr´ē *a*l) *adj.* Having to do with an author.

au-da-cious (o dā´shus) *adj.* Bold, daring, or fearless; insolent. **audaciously** *adv.* **au-dacity** *n.*

au-di-ble (o´d*i* bl) *adj.* Capable of being heard.

au-di-ence (o´dē *e*ns) *n.* A group of spectators or listeners; the opportunity to express views; a formal hearing or conference.

au-di-o (o´dē ō˝) *adj.* Of or relating to sound or its high-fidelity reproduction.

au-di-om-e-ter (o˝dē om´i tēr) *n.* Instrument for testing hearing.

au-dit (o´dit) *n.* Verification or examination of financial accounts or records.

au-di-tion (o dish´*a*n) *n.* A trial performance given by an entertainer as to demonstrate ability.

au-di-tor (o´di t*o*r) *n.* A person who listens

or hears; one who audits accounts.

au-di-to-ri-um (o″di tōr′ē um) *n.* A large room in a public building or a school that holds many people.

au-di-to-ry (o′di tōr″ē) *adj.* Related to the organs or sense of hearing.

au fait (ō fe′) *adj.* Well-versed; experienced.

au-ger (o′gėr) *n.* The tool which is used for the purpose of putting holes in the ground or wood.

aught (ot) *n.* Zero (0).

aug-ment (og ment′) *v.* To add to or increase; to enlarge. **augmentation** *n.* **augmenter** *n.* **augmentable** *adj.*

aug-ment-a-tive (ogmen′ta tiv) *adj.* Having the power of augmenting.

au jus (ō zhŏs′) *adj.* Served in the juices obtained from roasting.

auk (ok) *n.* Sea bird with a stocky body and short wings, living in the arctic regions.

au na-tu-rel (ō nă tŏ rel′) *adj.* Of a natural state.

aunt (ănt) *n.* A sister of a person's father or mother; the wife of one's uncle.

au-ra (or′a) *n. pl.* **auras** *or* **aurae** An emanation said to come from a person's or an animal's body.

au-ral (or′al) *adj.* Relating to the ear or the sense of hearing. **aurally** *adv.*

au-re-ate (or′ē it) *adj.* Of a brilliant golden color.

au-re-ole (or′ē ōl″) *n.* A halo.

au re-voir (ō″ re vwär′) *interj.* Used in expressing farewell; goodbye until we meet again.

au-ri-cle (or′i kal) *n.* The two upper chambers of the heart.

au-ric-u-lar (o rik′yu lėr) *adj.* Relating to the sense of hearing or of being in the shape of the ear.

au-ric-ul-ate (o rik′yu lit) *adj.* Shaped like the ear; having ears or some kind of expansions resembling ears.

au-ri-fer-ous (o rif′ėr us) *adj.* Producing or yielding gold; containing gold.

au-ro-ra (o rōr′a) *n.* The brilliant display of moving and flashing lights in the night sky, believed to be caused by electrically

charged particles. **auroral** *adj.*

aus-cul-ta-tion (o″skul tā′shan) *n.* The act of listening to sounds of the internal parts of the body, particularly of the chest.

aus-tere (o stēr′) *adj.* Stern in manner and appearance. **austerity** *n.*

aus-tral (o′stral) *adj.* Southern.

Aus-tri-a *n.* Country of central Europe.

au-then-tic (o then′tik) *adj.* Real; genuine; worthy of acceptance.

au-then-ti-cate (o then′ti kāt″) *v.* To prove something is true or genuine; real; not an imitation. **authentication** *n.* **authenticity** *n.* **authenticator** *n.*

au-thor (a′thor) *n.* A person who writes an original literary work. **author** *v.*

au-thor-i-tar-i-an (a thor″i târ′ē an) *adj.* Demanding blind submission and absolute, unquestioned obedience to authority. **authoritarianism** *n.* **authoritorian** *n.* **authoritative** *adj.*

au-thor-i-ty (a thor′i tē) *n. pl.* **authorities** A group or person with power; a government; an expert.

au-thor-i-za-tion (o″thor i zā′shan) *n.* The act of authorizing something.

au-thor-ize (o′ tho rīz″) *v.* To give authority, to approve, to justify.

au-thor-ship (a′thor ship) *n.* The character of being an author.

au-tism (o′tiz″um) *n.* Absorption in a self-centered mental state, such as fantasies, daydreams or hallucinations in order to escape from reality. **autistic** *adj.*

au-to (o′tō) *abbr.* Automatic; automobile.

au-to-bahn (ou′tō bän″) *n.* Highway in Germany.

au-to-bi-og-ra-pher (o″to bī og′ra fėr) *n.* A person who writes an autobiography.

au-to-bi-og-ra-phy (o″to bī og′ra fē) *n. pl.* **autobiographies** The life story of a person, written by that person.

au-toch-tho-nous (o″tok′tho nus) *adj.* Native to an area.

au-toc-ra-cy (o tok′ra sē) *n.* Government by one person who has unlimited power. **autocrat** *n.* **autocratic** *adj.*

au-to-di-dact (o′tō di dakt″) *n.* A person

who has taught himself. **autodidactic** *adj.*

au-to-graph (o′to graf˝) *n.* A handwritten signature.

au-to-in-tox-i-ca-tion (a˝tō in tok˝si kā′shan) *n.* Self-poisoning caused by metabolic wastes of other toxins in the body.

au-to-ki-net-ic (a˝tō ki net′ik) *adj.* Self-moving, automatic.

au-tol-o-gous (o tăl′o gus) *adj.* Transplanted, grafted, or relocated within the same body, as using one part to repair another.

au-tol-y-sis (o tol′i sis) *n.* Digestion of tissue by ferments generated in its cells.

au-to-mate (o′to māt˝) *v.* To operate by automation; to convert something to automation, to automatize.

au-to-mat-ic (o˝to mat′ik) *adj.* Operating with very little control; self-regulating. **automatically** *adv.*

au-to-ma-tion (o˝to mā′shan) *n.* The equipment and techniques used to acquire automation.

au-to-mo-bile (o˝to mo bēl′) *n.* A four-wheeled passenger vehicle commonly propelled by an internal-combustion engine.

au-to-mo-tive (o to mō′tiv) *adj.* Relating to self-propelled vehicles.

au-to-nom-ic (o˝to nom′ik) *adj.* Pertaining to the autonomic system of the nervous system.

autonomic nervous system *n.* The part of the body's nervous system which is regulated involuntarily.

au-ton-o-mous (o ton′o mus) *adj.* Self-governing; subject to its own laws.

au-ton-o-my (o ton′o mē) *n.* Independence; self-government.

au-to-phyte (o′to fit˝) *n.* A plant capable of synthesizing its own food from basic inorganic substance.

au-to-pi-lot (o′tō pī′lot) *n.* The device for automatically steering aircraft and ships.

au-top-sy (o′top sē) *n. pl.* **autopsies** Postmortem examination; the examination of a body after death to find the cause of death. **autopsic** *adj.* **autopsical** *adj.*

au-to-stra-da (o˝tō′sträd e) *n.* An expressway in Italy.

au-to-tox-in (o˝to tok′sin) *n.* Toxic or poisonous principle formed within the body and acts against it.

au-to-type (o′to tīp˝) *n.* Photographic process that uses a carbon pigment.

au-tumn (o′tum) *n.* The season between summer and winter. **autumnal** *adj.*

aux-il-ia-ry (og zil′ya rē) *adj.* Providing help or assistance to someone; giving support.

auxiliary verb *n.* Verbs that accompany a main verb and express the mood, voice, or tense.

aux-in (ok′sin) *n.* The hormone in a plant that stimulates growth.

av *abbr.* Average.

av *or* **ave** *abbr.* Avenue.

a-vail (a vāl′) *v.* To be of advantage or use; to use. **avail** *n.* The advantage toward attaining a purpose or goal.

a-vail-a-bil-i-ty (a vā˝la bil′i tē) *n.* The state of being available.

a-vail-a-ble (a vā′la bl) *adj.* Ready or present for immediate use; accessible. **availably** *adv.* **availableness** *adj.*

av-a-lanche (av′a lanch˝) *n.* A large amount of rock or snow that slides down a mountainside.

a-vant–garde (a vänt′ gärd′) *n.* The people who apply and invent new ideas and styles in a certain field.

av-a-rice (av′ar is) *n.* One's desire to have wealth and riches.

av-a-ri-cious (av˝a rish′us) *adj.* Miserly.

a-vast (a vast′) *interj., Naut.* A command to stop or cease.

a-ve (ä′vā) *interj.* Farewell.

a-vel-lan (avel′an) *adj.* Having the shape of a cross.

a-venge (a venj′) *v.* To take revenge for something; to vindicate by inflicting pain. **avenger** *n.*

av-ens (av′inz) *n.* The popular name of perennial herbs of the rose family having purple, white or yellow flowers.

av-e-nue (av′e nū˝) *n.* A street lined with

trees; a way of achieving something; sometimes called an "avenue of attack."

a-ver (*a* ver´) *v.* To be firm and to state positively. **averment** *n.*

av-er-age (av´ėr ij) *n.* Something that is typical or usual, not being exceptional; common.

a-ver-ment (*a* vŭr´ment) *n.* A positive declaration.

a-verse (*a* vers´) *adj.* Having a feeling of distaste or repugnance. **averseness** *n.* **aversely** *adv.*

a-ver-sion (*a* ver´zhan) *n.* A feeling of strong dislike, or distaste for something.

a-vert (*a* vert´) *v.* To prevent or keep from happening; to turn aside or away from; to direct away.

a-vi-an (ā´vē *an*) *adj.* Relating to birds.

a-vi-a-rist (ā´vē *a* rist) *n.* One who maintains a cage, or enclosure for birds.

a-vi-ar-y (ā´vē er˝ē) *n.* A place where birds are kept; enclosure for the breeding, and housing of birds.

a-vi-ate (ā´vē āt) *v.* To navigate a plane.

a-vi-a-tion (ā˝vē ā´shan) *n.* The operation of planes and other aircraft; design and manufacture of planes.

a-vi-a-tor (ā´vē ā˝tor) *n.* Pilot of an aircraft.

a-vi-cul-ture (ā´vi kul˝chur) *n.* Raising and breeding of birds.

av-id (av´id) *adj.* Greedy; eager; enthusiastic. **avidly** *adv.*

a-vi-fau-na (ā´vi fo na) *n.* A name for the birds of a certain period or region.

a-vi-on-ics (ā˝vē on´iks) *n.* The development and application of electronic and electrical devices for use in airplanes, missiles, and spacecraft. **avionic** *adj.* Pertaining to the field of avionics

a-vir-u-lent (ā vir´yu lent) *adj.* Nonpathogenic; not virulent.

a-vi-ta-min-o-sis (ā vī˝ta mi nō´sis) *n.* A disease resulting from or caused by a vitamin deficiency.

av-o-ca-do (av˝okä´dō) *n.* The pear-shaped edible fruit from the

avocado tree, having a large seed and yellowish-green pulp.

av-o-ca-tion (av˝o kā´ shan) *n.* A pleasurable activity that is in addition to the regular work a person must do; a hobby.

a-void (*a* void´) *v.* To stay away from; to shun; to prevent or keep from happening; to elude. **avoidably** *adv.*

a-void-a-ble (*a* void´*a* bl) *adj.* That which can be avoided; able to get away from.

a-void-ance (*a* void´ans) *n.* The act of making something void.

a-vo-set (av´o set˝) *n.* A wading bird with very long legs, black and white variegated feathers and a long slender bill bent upward at the tip.

a-vouch (*a* vouch´) *v.* To assert; to guarantee; to maintain; to vouch for; to admit. **avouchment** *n.*

a-vow (*a* vou´) *v.* To state openly on a subject; to confess; to own up to. **avower** *n.* **avowedly** *adv.*

a-vow-al (*a* vou´al) *n.* Open declaration; acknowledge frankly.

a-vowed (*a* voud´) *adj.* Acknowledged.

a-vulse (*a* vuls´) *v.* To detach with force.

a-vun-cu-lar (*a* vung´kyu lėr) *adj.* Pertaining to an uncle.

a-wait (*a* wāt´) *v.* To wait for something; to expect; to be ready.

a-wake (*a* wāk´) *v.* To wake up; to be alert or watchful.

a-wak-en (*a* wā´ken) *v.* To awake or rouse from sleep.

a-ward (*a* word´) *v.* To give or confer as being deserved, needed, or merited. *n.* A judgment or decision; a prize. **awardable** *adj.* **awarder** *n.*

a-ware (*a* wâr´) *adj.* Being conscious or mindful of something; informed.

a-wash (*a* wosh´) *adj.* Flooded; afloat; to be washed by water; washed about; washed over by the tide.

a-way (*a* wā´) *adv.* At a distance; to another place; apart from.

awe (o) *n.* A feeling of wonder mixed with reverence. **awe** *v.*

a-wea-ry (*a* wē˝rē) *adj.* Tired; weary.

a-weath-er (a weth´ér) *adj.* On the weather side of a ship, as opposed to the alee.

a-weigh (a wā´) *adj.* To hang just clear of a ship's anchor.

awe-some (o´sum) *adj.* Expressive of awe. **awesomeness** *n.* **awesomely** *adv.*

awe-strick-en (o´strik˝en) *adj.* Impressed with awe.

aw-ful (o´ful) *adj.* Very unpleasant or dreadful. **awfully** *adv.*

aw-ful-ness (o´ful nis) *n.* The state or quality of being awful.

a-while (a hwīl´) *adv.* For a short time.

a-whirl (a hwerl´) *adj.* To spin around.

awk-ward (ok´ward) *adj.* Not graceful; clumsy; to cause embarrassment. **awkwardly** *adv.* **awkwardness** *n.*

awl (ol) *n.* Tool used to make holes in leather.

awn (on) *n.* The part of a piece a grass which resembles a bristle. **awned** *adj.*

awn-ing (o´ning) *n.* Structure that serves as a shelter over a window; roof-like.

a-wry (a rī´) *adv.* In a twisted or turned position.

ax *or* **axe (aks)** *n.* A tool with a steel head attached to a wooden handle used to chop wood.

ax-i-al (aks´ē al) *adj.* Pertaining to an axis.

axial skeleton *n.* The part of the human skeleton that includes the head and trunk.

ax-il-la (ak sil´a) *n.* The armpit; the area under a bird's wing.

ax-il-lar (ak´si lar) *n.* The underwing, weaker feathers of a bird.

ax-il-lar-y (ak´si ler˝ē) *adj.* Growing from the axil of something as a plant.

ax-i-ol-o-gy (ak´sē ol´o jē) *n.* The study of values and their nature especially in religion and ethics.

ax-i-om (ak´sē um) *n.* Statement recognized as being true; something assumed to be true without proof.

ax-i-o-mat-ic *adj.* Obvious; self-evident.

ax-is (ak´sis) *n. pl.* **axes** The line around an object or body that rotates or may be thought to rotate.

ax-le (ak´sel) *n.* A spindle or shaft around which a wheel or pair of wheels revolve.

ax-le-tree (ak´sel trē˝) *n.* A bar which a wheel turns upon.

ax-om-e-ter (ak som´e tèr) *n.* An optician's measuring tool used in adjusting frames of eyeglasses to the center of the eyes.

ax-on (ak´son) *n.* A single, long, nerve cell that carries transmitted nerve impulses away from the body of a cell.

a-yah (ä´ya) *n.* A native nursemaid or maid in India.

aye (ā) *interj.* Yes, a sound of affirmation; indeed.

a-yah (ä´ya) *n.* A native maid of India.

aye (i) *n.* An affirmative vote.

a-zal-ea (a zāl´ya) *n.* A shrub of the genus Rhododendron group, grown for its many colored flowers.

az-i-muth (az´i muth) *n.* Usually recognized as an angle, in air navigation is measured clockwise from the magnetic or true north.

a-zo-ic (a zō´ik) *adj.* Time period which occurred before life first appeared on the earth.

a-zon-ic (ā zon´ik) *adj.* Not confined to a particular zone.

az-o-te-mi-a (az˝o tē´mē a) *n.* Nitogenous waste in the blood, in large amounts that results from the kidney malfunctioning.

az-oth (az´oth) *n.* Mercury, the first principle of all known metals.

a-zot-ic (a zot´ik) *adj.* Pertaining to a zote.

az-o-tu-re-a (az˝o tyür´ē a) *n.* The over abundance of urea in the urine.

AZT *abbr.* Azidothymidine; a drug that relieves the symptoms of AIDS (Acquired Immune Deficiency Syndrome), allowing a longer and better life. Approved in early 1987 by the Federal Government for prescription use.

az-ure (azh´ur) *n.* The blue color of the sky.

az-ur-ite (azh´u rīt˝) *n.* A mineral that consists of a blue basic carbonate of copper.

az-ym (az´īm) *n.* Unleavened bread.

B, b (bē) *n.* The second letter of the English alphabet; a student's grade rating of good, but not excellent.

ba-ba (bä bä) *n.* A rich cake soaked in rum.

ba-bas-su (bäb *e* sü) *n.* The tall palm cultivated for the oil its nuts yield.

bab-ble (bab´bl) *v.* To reveal secrets; to chatter senselessly; to talk foolishly.

babe (bāb) *n.* A very young child or infant.

ba-bel (bā´bel) *n.* Babbling noise of many people talking at the same time.

ba-biche (b*a* bēsh´) *n.* A thong or lacing made from animal skin; rawhide.

ba-boon (ba bŏn´) *n.* A species of the monkey family with a large body and big canine teeth.

ba-bu (bä´bŏ) *n.* A Hindu gentleman.

ba-bul (b*e*´bül) *n.* An acacia tree in northern Africa and Asia which yields gum arabic as well as fodder and timber.

ba-bush-ka (b*a* besh´k*a*) *n.* A kerchief folded into a triangle and worn as a covering on the head.

ba-by (bā´bē) *n. pl.* **babies** A young child; infant. **babyish** *adj.*

baby's breath *n.* A tall herb bearing numerous small, fragant, white or pink flowers.

baby–sit (bā bē sit) *v.* To assume the responsibility and care for a child or children during the absence of the parents.

bac-ca-lau-re-ate (bak´*a* lor´ē it) *n.* A degree given by universities and colleges; an address given to a graduating class.

bac-ca-rat (bäk *e* ´rä bak) n. A game of cards played by any number of players betting against a banker.

bac-cha-nal (bak *e* nal) *adj.* Revelling in or characterized by intemperate drinking; riotous; noisy.

bac-cha-na-lia (bak´ *a* nä´lē *a*) *n.* A Roman festival celebrated with dancing and song.

bach (bach) *v. Slang* to live by oneself as does a bachelor.

bach-e-lor (bach´e lor) *n.* An unmarried male; the first degree one can receive from a four year university.

ba-cil-lus (ba sil´us) *n. pl.* **bacilli** A rod-like microscopic organism which can cause

certain diseases.

bac-i-tra-cin (bas˝i trā´sin) *n.* An antibiotic used topically against cocci.

back (bak) *n.* The rear part of the human body from the neck to the end of the spine, also the rear part of an animal; a position in the game of football, in which the player lines up behind the front line of players; the final nine holes of an 18-hole golf course.

back-ache (bak´ā˝) *n.* A pain in the back.

back-bite (bak´bīt˝) *v.* To gossip or speak in a nasty way about a person who is not present.

back-board (bak´bōrd˝) *n.* A board that gives support when placed under or behind something.

back-bone (bak´bōn˝) *n.* The spinal column or spine of the vertebrates; the strongest support, or strength; the back of a book with the title and the author's names.

back-drop (bak´drop˝) *n.* A curtain or scene behind the back of a stage set.

back-er (bak´ér) *n.* Someone who gives support or aid to a cause; one who supports or aids another.

back-field (bak´ field) *n.* Football players who are positioned behind the line of scrimmage; the area where the backfield lines up for play.

back-fill (bak´fil) *n.* Earth, stone, or rubbish used to fill excavations around completed foundations.

back-fire (bak´fiér˝) *n.* Premature explosion of unburned exhaust gases or ignited fuel of an internal-combustion engine; a result which is the opposite of that which had been planned; a fire deliberately set to check an advancing forest or prairie fire. **backfire** *v.*

back-gam-mon (bak´gam˝on) *n.* A game played by two people where each player tries to move his counters on the board, at the same time trying to block his opponent.

back-ground (bak´ground˝) *n.* The area or surface behind which objects are represented; conditions leading up to a happening; the collection of a person's complete experience, education, or knowledge; out of view; low profile.

background music *n.* Music played to accompany the action of a motion picture, or television drama.

back-hand (bak´hand˝) *n.* A stroke in the game of tennis, made with the back of the hand facing outward. **backhand** *v.*

back-handed (bak´han˝did) *adj.* Using the back of the hand, a backward slope as in handwriting.

back-haul (bak´hol) *n.* The return trip of an airplane or other vehicle, when carrying cargo.

back-hoe (bak´ hō) *n.* An excavating machine used to dig foundations for homes, etc.

back-ing (bak´ing) *n.* Support or aid; a supply in reserve.

back judge *n.* A football official who keeps the official time and identifies eligible pass receivers.

back-lash (bak´lash˝) *n.* A violent backward movement or reaction; a snarl in a fishing line. **backlasher** *n.*

back-log (bak´log˝) *n.* The accumulation of unfinished work; a reserve supply.

back-pack (bak´pak) *n.* A piece of equipment used to carry items on the back, mounted on a lightweight frame, and constructed of nylon or canvas.

back-ped-al (bak´ped˝al) *v.* To move backward or retreat.

back-rest (bak´rest˝) *n.* A support given to the back.

back room *n.* A room in the rear of a building for inconspicuous group meetings.

back-saw (bak´so˝) *n.* Saw with metal ribs on its back side.

back-seat (bak´set) *n.* The seat in the back of an automobile, etc.; an inferior position.

back-side (bak´sīd[˝) *n.* The buttocks.

back-slide (bak´slīd) *v.* To lapse back into a less desirable condition, as in a religious practice. **backslider** *n.* **backsliding** *v.*

back-spin (bak´spin˝) *n.* A spin which ro-

tates in the reverse direction.

back-stage (bak˝stāj´) *n.* The area behind the performing area in a theatre. **backstage** *adj.*

back-stitch (bak´stich˝) *n.* A hand stitch made by inserting the needle a stitch to the right and bringing it up an equal stitch to the left.

back-stop (bak´stop˝) *n.* Something that prevents a ball from being hit out of play; baseball.

back-stretch (bak´strech˝) *n.* The opposite of the homestretch on a racecourse.

back-stroke (bak´strōk˝) *n.* A swimming stroke performed while on the back.

back-swept (bak´swept˝) *adj.* Slanting or swept backward.

back-sword (bak´sōrd) *n.* A sword with only one sharp edge.

back talk *n.* A smart or insolent reply; disrespectful.

back-track (bak´trak˝) *v.* To reverse a policy; to retrace previous steps. **backtracking** *v.*

back-up (bak´up˝) *n.* One that serves as an alternative or substitute.

back-ward (bak´ward) *adv.* Toward the back; to or at the back; in a reverse order. **backwardness** *n.* **backwards** *adv.*

back-wash (bak´wosh˝) *n.* A backward flow of water.

back-wa-ter (bak´wotėr) *n.* A body of water turned back by an obstruction.

back-woods (bak´wedz˝) *n. pl.* A sparsely populated, heavily wooded area. **backwoodsman** *n.*

back-yard (bak´yärd) *n.* An area to the rear of a house.

ba-con (bā´kon) *n.* Side and back of a pig, salted and smoked.

bac-ter-e-mia (bak tēr´ē mēa) *n.* The presence of bacteria or microorganisms in the blood.

bac-ter-ia (bak tēr´ē a) *n. pl.* The plural of bacterium.

bac-te-ri-cide (bak tēr´i sīd[˝) *n.* A substance that kills bacteria.

bac-te-ri-ol-o-gy (bak tēr˝ē ol´ o jē) *n.*

Scientific study of bacteria and its relationship to medicine, etc.

bac-te-ri-o-phage (bak tēr˝ē o fāj´) *n.* Any of a group of viruses commonly found in sewage or body products.

bac-te-ri-ol-y-sis (bak tēr˝ē *o* stā´sis) *n.* The process of dissolution or destruction of bacteria.

bac-te-ri-um (bak tēr´ē um) *n. pl.* **-ria** Any of various forms of numerous unicellular microorganisms that cause disease, some are used in industrial work. **bacterial** *adj.*

bad (bad) *adj.* Naughty or disobedient; unfavorable; inferior; poor; spoiled; invalid. **badly** *adv.* **badness** *n.*

bad-der-locks (bad´ėr loks˝) *n.* A blackish seaweed sometimes eaten as a vegetable in Europe.

badge (baj) *n.* An emblem worn for identification.

badg-er (baj´ėr) *n.* A sturdy burrowing mammal. **badger** *v.* To trouble persistently.

bad-lands (bad´landz˝) *n. pl.* Area with sparse life, peaks, and eroded ridges.

bad-min-ton (bad´min t*o*n) *n.* A court game played with long-handled rackets and a shuttlecock.

baf-fle (baf´fl) *v.* To puzzle; to perplex. **baffle** *n.* A device that checks or regulates the flow of gas, sound, or liquids.

bag (bag) *n.* A flexible container used for holding, storing, or carrying something; a square white canvas container used to mark bases in baseball. **bagful** *n.* **baggy** *adj.*

ba-gasse (b*a* gas´) *n.* Plant residue.

bag-a-telle (bag˝*a* tel´) *n.* A game played with a cue and balls on an oblong table.

ba-gel (bā´g*e*l) *n.* A hard, glazed, round roll with a chewy texture and a hole in the middle.

bag-gage (bag´ij) *n.* The personal belongings of a traveler.

bag-gy (bag´ē) *adj.* Loose. **baggily** *adv.*

bag-man (bag´m*a*n) *n.* A person who collects illicit payments for another.

bag-pipe (bag´pīp˝) *n. pl.* **bagpipes** A wind instrument with a leather bag and melody pipes. **bagpiper** *n.*

ba-guette (ba get´) *n.* A gem in the shape of a long, narrow rectangle.

bag-wig (bag wig) *n.* An 18th century wig with the hair in the back contained in a small silk bag.

bag-worm (bag´werm˝) *n.* A type of moth larva that lives in a silk case covered with plant debris, very destructive to evergreens.

bail (bāl) *n.* The security or money given to guarantee the appearance of a person for trial, handle of a pail. *v.* To remove water from a boat by dipping and emptying the water overboard; to free from water. **bailor** *n.* **bailer** *n.*

bail-iff (bā´lif) *n.* The officer who guards prisoners and keeps order in a courtroom.

bail-i-wick (bā´li wik) *n.* The office or district of a bailiff.

bails-man (bālz´m*a*n) *n.* The person who puts up the bail for another.

bait (bāt) *v.* To lure; to entice. **bait** *n.* Food that is used to catch or trap an animal.

baize (bāz) *n.* A coarse woolen or cotton cloth.

bake (bāk) *v.* To cook in an oven; to harden or dry. **baker** *n.* **baking, baked** *v.*

baker's dozen *n.* Thirteen.

bak-er-y (bā´k*a* rē) *n.* A store where baked goods are made and sold.

baking powder *n.* A leavening agent used in baking consisting of carbonate, an acid substance, and flour or starch.

baking soda *n.* Sodium bicarbonate.

bak-sheesh (bak´shēsh) *n.* A tip or gratuity.

bal-a-lai-ka (bal˝*a* lī k*a*) *n.* A three-stringed musical instrument.

bal-ance (bal´*a*ns) *n.* Device for determining the weight of something; the agreement of totals in the debit and credit of an account.

balance beam *n.* A narrow wooden beam, approximately 4 feet off the ground used for balancing feats in gymnastics.

balance of trade *n.* The difference in a-mount of value between the exports and the imports of a country.

balance sheet *n.* An itemized statement showing the financial condition of a corporation as of a specific date.

bal-co-ny (bal´ko̅ ne̅) *n. pl.* **balconies** Gallery or platform projecting from the wall of a building.

bald (bold) *adj.* Lacking hair on the head. **bald-ish** *adj.* **baldness** *n.*

bal-da-chin (bal´da̅ kin) *n.* An embroidered fabric of silk and gold used to carry over an important person or sacred object.

bald eagle *n.* The eagle of North America that is dark when young, but has a white head and neck feathers when mature.

bal-der-dash (bol´de̅r dash˝) *n.* Nonsense.

bal-dric (bol drik) *n.* A broad belt, stretch-ing from the right or left shoulder di-agonally across the body, either as an orna-ment or to suspend a sword or horn.

bale (ba̅l) *n.* A large, bound package or bundle.

ba-leen (ba̅ le̅n´) *n.* A whalebone.

bale-fire (ba̅el fi̅er)*n.* A signal fire; an alarm fire.

bale-ful (ba̅el fel) *adj.* Destructive; deadly; foreboding.

balk (bok) *v.* To refuse to go on; to stop short of something. *n.* A rafter or crossbeam extending from wall to wall. **balky** *adj.* **balking** *v.*

bal-kan-ize (bol ke nī̅z) *v.* To partition, as an area, into various small, politically in-effective divisions.

ball (bol) *n.* A round body or mass; a pitched baseball that is delivered outside of the strike zone.

bal-lad (bal´ad) *n.* A narrative story or poem of folk origin; a romantic song.

bal-lade (bol la̅d´) *n.* A verse form con-sisting of three stanzas with recurrent rhymes and a refrain for each part.

bal-lad-eer (bal e di er) *n.* A person who sings ballads.

bal-last (bal´ast) *n.* Heavy material placed in a vehicle to give stability and weight.

ball bearing *n.* A bearing that reduces friction by separating the stationary parts from the moving ones.

bal-le-ri-na (bal˝e re̅´na) *n.* A female ballet dancer in a company.

bal-let (ba la̅´) *n.* An artistic expression of dance by choreographic design.

ballistic missile *n.* A projectile that is self-powered, is guided during ascent, and has a free-fall trajectory at descent.

bal-lis-tics (ba lis´tiks) *n.* The science of motion in flight; the firing characteristics of a firearm.

bal-lo-net (bal˝o net´) *n.* A compartment within the interior of a balloon or airship to control ascent and descent.

bal-loon (ba lo̅n´) *n.* A bag inflated with gas lighter than air which allows it to float in the atmosphere, often having a basket or compartment for carrying passengers; a bag made of rubber that is used as a child's toy.

balloon tire *n.* An automobile tire con-taining air at low pressure to absorb the shock of bumpy areas in the road.

bal-lot (bal´ot) *n.* A slip of paper used in secret voting. *v.* To vote by ballot.

bal-lotte-ment (be lät ment) *n.* A method of diagnosing pregnancy, in which a sudden shock is imparted to the fetus, as through the uterine wall, causing it to move suddenly.

ball-park (bol pärk) *n.* A stadium where ball games are played.

ball-point (bol´point˝) *n.* A pen that has a small self-inking writing point.

bal-ly-hoo (bal´e̅ ho̅˝) *n.* Exaggerated ad-vertising.

balm (bäm) *n.* A fragrant ointment that soothes, comforts, and heals.

bal-ma-caan (bal me kan´) *n.* A loose overcoat made of woolens and having raglan sleeves, short collar and a closing which may be buttoned up to the thoat.

bal-ne-ol-o-gy (bal ne̅ äl e je̅) *n.* The study of the effects of baths employed in therapy.

ba-lo-ney (*ba* lō´nē**)** *n., Slang* Nonsense.

bal-sa (bol´*sa***)** *n.* American tree that is very light in weight.

bal-sam (bol´*sam***)** *n.* A fragrant ointment from different trees; a plant cultivated for its colorful flowers.

bal-us-ter (bal´*u* stėr**)** *n.* The upright post that supports a handrail.

bal-us-trade (bal *e* **strãd)** *n.* A row of small columns or balusters, joined by a rail, serving as an enclosure for altars, balconies, staircases, and terraces.

bam-boo (bam bŏ´) *n.* Tropical, tall grass with hollow, pointed stems.

bam-boo-zle (bam bŏ´zl) *v.* To trick or deceive. **bamboozled, bamboozling** *v.*

ban (ban) *v.* To prohibit; to forbid. **banning, banned** *v.*

ba-nal (bãn´*al***)** *adj.* Trite; lacking freshness.

ba-nan-a (*ba* nan´*a***)** *n.* The crescent-shaped usually yellow, edible fruit of a tropical plant.

band (band) *n.* A strip used to trim, finish, encircle, or bind; the range of a radio wave length; a group of musicians who join together to play their instruments.

band-age (ban´dij) *n.* A strip of cloth used to protect an injury. **bandage** *v.*

ban-dan-na (ban dan´*a***)** *n.* A brightly colored cotton or silk handkerchief.

ban-deau (ban dō´) *n.* A narrow band worn in the hair; a narrow brassiere.

ban-de-ri-lla (ban *de*´rē ya**)** *n.* A decorated dart that the banderillero thrusts into the neck of the bull in a bullfight.

ban-di-coot (ban´di kŏt˝) *n.* A very large rat of India which is destructive to the rice fields and gardens.

ban-dit (ban´dit) *n. pl.* **bandits, banditti** A gangster or robber. **banditry** *n.*

band-mas-ter (band master) *n.* The conductor and trainer of a band or musicians.

ban-do-leer (ban˝*do* lēr´**)** *n.* A belt worn over the shoulder with pockets for cartridges.

ban-dore (ban dōr´) *n.* A three-stringed instrument resembling a guitar.

band-stand (band´stand˝) *n.* A raised platform on which an orchestra or band perform.

ban-dy (ban´dē) *adv.* Bent; crooked; curved outward. **bandying** *v.*

bane (bãn) *n.* A cause of destruction or ruin. **baneful** *adj.* **banefully** *adv.*

bang (bang) *n.* A sudden loud noise; short hair cut across the forehead. *v.* To move or hit with a loud noise.

bangalore torpedo *n.* A metal tube containing explosive material and a firing mechanism for severing barbed wire and detonate mines.

ban-gle (bang´gel) *n.* A bracelet worn around the wrist or ankle.

ban-ish (ban´ish) *v.* To leave; to drive away; to remove from the mind; to condemn to exile. **banisher, banishment** *n.* **banished, banishing** *v.*

ban-is-ter (ban´i stėr) *n.* The upright supports of a handrail on a staircase.

ban-jo (ban´jō) *n.* A stringed instrument similar to a guitar. **banjoist** *n.*

bank (bangk) *n.* A slope of land adjoining water; an establishment that performs financial transactions. **bankable** *adj.*

bank acceptance *n.* A draft which is accepted or acknowledged by the bank on which it is drawn.

bank draft *n.* A bill of exchange drawn by a bank on another bank.

bank note *n.* A promissory note issued by a bank and payable on demand.

bank roll *n.* The money that one possesses.

bank-rupt (bangk´rupt) *n.* A person who is legally insolvent and whose remaining property is divided among creditors. **bankrupt** *v.* **bankruptcy** *n.*

ban-ner (ban´ėr) *n.* A piece of cloth, such as a flag, that is used as a standard by a commander or monarch. *adj.* Outstanding.

ban-nock (ban´*a***k)** *n.* Unleavened or flat cake made from barley or oatmeal.

banns (banz) *n. pl.* The announcement of a forthcoming marriage.

ban-quet (bang´kwit) *n.* An elaborate dinner or feast.

ban-shee (ban´shē) *n.* A spirit in folklore whose appearance warns a family of approaching death of a member.

ban-tam (bant *e***m)** *n.* A tiny domestic fowl of any or varied breeds, characterized by its small size and feathered shanks.

ban-ter (bant *er***)** *v.* To attack with jokes or jests; to make fun of.

ban-yan (ban´y*a***n)** *n.* A tree from the tropics whose aerial roots grow downward to form additional roots.

bap-tism (bap tiz*e***m)** *n.* A Christian sacrament of spiritual rebirth through the application of water.

bap-tize (bap tīz´) *v.* To immerse or sprinkle with water during baptism. **baptizer** *n.*

bar (bär) *n.* A rigid piece of material used as a support; a barrier or obstacle; a counter where a person can receive drinks. *v.* To prohibit or exclude.

barb (bärb) *n.* A sharp projection that extends backward making it difficult to remove; a breed of horses from Africa noted for their speed and endurance. **barbed** *adj.*

bar-bar-i-an (bär bâr´ē *a***n)** *n.* A person or culture thought to be primitive and therefore inferior. **barbarous** *adj.* **barbaric** *adj.*

bar-be-cue (bär´b*e* **kū´)** *n.* An outdoor fireplace or pit for roasting meat; such as chicken, ribs, and steaks. **barbecue** *v.*

barbed (bärbd) *adj.* Made with sharp points at intervals.

barbed wire *n.* Wire that is twisted with sharp points.

bar-bel (bär b*e***l)** *n.* A fresh-water fish having four beardlike appendages on its upper jaw.

bar-bell (bär´bel´) *n.* A bar with weights at both ends, used for exercise.

bar-ber (bär´bėr) *n.* A person whose business is cutting and dressing hair and also shaving and trimming beards.

bar-ber-ry (bär´be rē) *n.* A shrub having yellow flowers and oblong red berries.

bar-ber-shop (bär b*e***r shäp)** *n.* The place of business where hair is cut; impromptu unaccompanied vocal harmonizing of popular songs, usually consisting of four

or more men.

bar-bet (bär b*e***t)** *adj.* One of a group of tropical birds having a large conical beak.

bar-bette (bär bet´) *n.* A cylinder protecting a gun turret on a warship.

bar-bi-tal (bär´bi tal´) *n.* A white addictive administered in the form of sodium salt.

bar-bi-tu-rate (bär ´bich *e* **ret)** *n.* A derivative of barbituric acid.

bar-ca-role (bär´lk*a* **rōl´)** *n.* A Venetian boat song with a strong and weak beat which suggests a rowing rhythm.

bard (bärd) *n.* A poet; a piece of armor for a horse's neck. **bardic** *adj.*

bare (bär) *adj.* Exposed to view; without coloring. **bare** *v.* **bareness** *n.*

bare-back (bär´bak´) *adv. & adj.* Riding a horse without a saddle.

bare-foot (bär fût) *adj.* With the feet bare; without shoes or stockings.

ba-rege (b*e***´rezh)** *n.* A sheer fabric for women's clothing.

bare-ly (bär´lē) *adv.* Sparsely; by a very little amount.

barf (bärf) *v., Slang* To vomit.

bar-fly (bär flī) *n., Slang* One who spends time drinking alcoholic beverages at bars.

bar-gain (bär´gin) *n.* A contract or agreement on the purchase or sale of an item; a purchase made at a favorable or good price, to negotiate over a price of something that is being sold or bought. **bargainer** *n.*

bargain basement *n.* A section in a store where goods are sold at lower prices.

bargaining agent *n.* In collective bargaining, the union chosen by a group of employees to represent them in labor contract negotiations.

barge (bärj) *n.* A flat-bottomed boat. *v.* To intrude abruptly.

barge-board (bärj´bōrd´) *n.* A board which conceals roof timbers that project over gables.

barg-ee (bär ´jē) *n.* One of the crew of a barge or canal boat.

barge-man (bärj´m*a***n)** *n.* A deckhand of a barge.

bar graph *n.* A graphic representation of statistics by means of bars of various, proportionate lengths.

bar-i-tone (bar´i tōn˝) *n.* A male voice in the range between tenor and bass.

bark (bärk) *n.* The outer protective covering of a tree; the abrupt, harsh sound made by a dog. **bark** *v.*

bark beetle *n.* A beetle that bores under the bark of trees; any of the small beetles of which make burrows between the bark and the wood of woody plants.

bar-keep-er (bär kē per) *n.* One who owns or tends a bar where liquor is served.

bar-ken-tine (bär´ken tēn˝) *n.* A three-masted ship with fore-and-aft rigging.

bar-ker (bär´kėr) *n.* A person in the circus who stands at the entrance and advertises the show.

bar-ley (bär´lē) *n.* A type of grain used for food and for making whiskey and beer.

bar-low (bär lō) *n.* A sturdy jackknife.

barm (bärm) *n.* A yeast which forms on fermenting malt liquors.

bar mitzvah *n.* A Jewish boy who, having reached the age of 13, assumes the moral and religious duties of an adult; the ceremony that recognizes a boy as a bar mitzvah.

barn (bärn) *n.* A farm building used to shelter animals and to store farm equipment and products.

bar-na-cle (bär´na kl) *n.* A fish with a hard shell that remains attached to an underwater surface.

barn dance *n.* A social gathering in a barn featuring square dancing.

barn-storm (bärn´storm) *n.* A tour through rural areas to obtain votes during a political campaign.

barn-yard (bärn yärd) *n.* The area adjacent to and immediately surrounding a barn.

bar-o-gram (bar e gram) *n.* A tracing of atmospheric pressure changes that have been recorded by a barograph.

bar-o-graph (bar e graf) *n.* A self-registering barometric instrument for recording variations in the pressure of the atmosphere.

ba-rom-et-er (ba rom´i tėr) *n.* An instrument that records the weight and pressure of the atmosphere.

bar-on (bar´on) *n.* The lowest rank of nobility in Great Britain. **baroness** *n.* **baronial** *adj.*

ba-rong (ba rong) *n.* A thin-edged knife or sword.

ba-roque (ba rōk´) *adj.* An artistic style characterized by elaborate and ornate forms.

bar-o-tal-gi-a *n.* An ailment of the middle ear resulting from high altitude flying without a pressurized cabin.

ba-rouche (ba rōsh´) *n.* A four-wheeled carriage.

barque (bärk) *n.* A sailing vessel of any kind. *Naut.* A three-masted vessel with only fore-and-aft sails on the mizzen mast, the other two masts being square-rigged.

bar-rack (bar´ak) *n.* A building for housing soldiers.

bar-ra-cu-da (bar˝a kö´da) *n. pl.* **-da, -das** A fish with a large, narrow body, found in the Atlantic Ocean.

bar-rage (bär´ij) *n.* A concentrated outpouring or discharge of missiles from small arms; an artificial dam to increase the depth of water for use in irrigation or navigation.

barrage balloon *n.* A balloon used in coordination with other balloons in strategic military areas as a station for suspension of wires or nets to protect the areas from low-flying enemy aircraft.

bar-ra-tor (bar et er) *n.* One who frequently incites suits at law; an encourager of litigation.

bar-ra-try (bar´a trē) *n.* The unlawful breach of duty by a ship's crew that results in injury to the ship's owner.

barre (bär) *n.* A waist-high bar attached to the walls of a ballet school, used for body support while practicing.

bar-rel (bar´el) *n.* Wooden container with round, flat ends of equal size and sides that bulge.

barrel chair *n.* A high-backed, heavily upholstered easy chair.

bar-ren (bar´en) *adj.* Lacking vegetation; sterile.

bar-rette (b*a* **ret´)** *n.* A clasp or small bar used to hold hair in place.

bar-ri-cade (bar´*i* kād˝) *n.* Barrier; to stop up, or block off, by a barricade.

bar-ri-er (bar´ē ėr) *n.* A structure that restricts or bars entrance.

barrier reef *n.* A coral reef parallel to shore separated by a lagoon.

bar-room (bär´röm˝) *n.* A building or room where a person can purchase alcoholic beverages sold at a counter.

bar-row (bar´ō) *n.* A rectangular, flat frame with handles; a wheelbarrow.

bar-tend-er (bär´ten˝dėr) *n.* A person who serves alcoholic drinks and other refreshments at a bar.

bar-ter (bär´tėr) *v.* To trade something for something else without the exchange of money; one commodity for another. **bartering, bartered** *v.* **barterer** *n.*

bar-ti-zan (bär´ti z*a***n)** *n.* A small structure serving as a lookout.

bar-y-on (bar ē ăn) *n.* Any of the heavier subatomic particles having masses greater than a neutron.

basal metabolism *n.* The amount of energy required by a person to maintain minimum vital functions.

ba-salt (bo solt´) *n.* A greenish-black volcanic rock.

base (bās) *n.* The fundamental part; the point from which something begins; headquarters; the lowest part; the bottom. **base** *v.*

baseless *adj.* Without a base; without grounds or foundation. **basely** *adv.* **baseness** *n.*

base-ball (bās´bol˝) *n.* A game played with a ball and bat; the ball used in a baseball game.

base-board (bäs´bōrd˝) *n.* A molding that covers the area where the wall meets the floor.

base hit *n.* In baseball, a batted ball which enables the batter to reach base safely.

base line *n.* Any line or specified quantity used as a point of reference.

base-ment (bās´ment) *n.* The foundation of a building or home.

base metal *n.* A metal or alloy of relatively inferior value as compared with gold and silver.

base pay *n.* Wages as determined by the amount earned during a given work period exclusive of bonuses, overtime, etc.

base rate *n.* The rate of pay for a stated output or period of labor.

bash (bash) *v.* To smash with a heavy blow; *Slang* A party. **bash** *v.*

bash-ful (bash´f*u***l)** *adj.* Socially shy. self-conscious. **bashfully** *adv.*

ba-sic (bā´sik) *adj.* Forming the basis; fundamental. **basically** *adv.*

BASIC *n.*, *Computer* A common computer programming language. (Beginner's All-purpose Symbolic Instruction Code.)

ba-sic-i-ty (bā ´sis *e***t ē)** *n.* The power of an acid to unite with one or more atoms of a base.

basic skills *n.* A term used in education to denote those skills in any given field which must be acquired as fundamental to further learning.

ba-si-fy (bā s*e* **fī)** *v.* To cause to become alkaline.

bas-il (baz´*i***l)** *n.* An herb used as seasoning in cooking.

ba-sil-i-ca (b*a* **sil´i k***a***)** *n.* An early Christian church building; an ancient Roman building, rectangular in shape, with a middle and two side aisles divided by columns, and an apse.

bas-i-lisk (bas´*i* **lisk)** *n.* A tropical American lizard.

ba-sin (bā´s*i***n)** *n.* A sink; a washbowl; a round open container used for washing; an area that has been drained by a river system.

ba-sis (bā´sis) *n.* *pl.* **bases** The main part; foundation.

bask (bask) *v.* To relax in the warmth of the sun.

bas-ket (bas´kit) *n.* An object made of woven material, as straw, cane, or other flexible items. **basketry** *n*.

bas-ket-ball (bas'kit bol) *n*. A game played on a court with two teams; each team trying to throw the ball through the basketball hoop at the opponents' end of the court.

basket hilt *n*. A basketlike hilt of a sword, serving to cover and protect the hand.

bas-ket-ry (bas ke trē) *n*. Basketwork; the procedure, skill, or craft of basket making.

basket stitch *n*. A stitch in embroidery in which the threads are interlaced as basketry.

basket weave *n*. A textile woven to resemble the surface of a basket.

bas mitzvah *n*. A Jewish girl who having reached the age of thirteen, assumes the moral and religious duties of an adult.

ba-so-phil (bā se fil) *n*. A tissue or cell having a natural inclination for basic stains.

bas-re-lief (bā ri lēf) *n*. A mode of sculpturing figures on a flat surface, the figures being raised above the surface.

bass (bas) *n. pl.* **basses** A fresh water fish, one of the perch family.

bass drum *n*. A large drum with a low booming sound.

basset hound (bas'sit) *n*. A breed of short-legged hunting dogs with very long ears.

bass fiddle *n*. The largest, lowest-pitched of the violin-type musical instruments.

bass horn *n*. A tuba.

bas-si-net (bas˝a net') *n*. A basket on legs used as an infant's crib; a basket made of wicker with a covering or hood over one end, used as an infant's bed.

bas-soon (ba sŏn') *n*. A woodwind instrument with a low-pitched sound.

bast (bast) *n*. The inner bark of exogenous trees, consisting of several layers of fibers.

bastard wing *n*. A group of stiff feathers attached to the bone of a bird's wing that represents the thumb.

baste (bāst) *v*. To run a loose stitch to hold a piece of material in place for a short time; to moisten meat while cooking it by pouring on liquids.

bas-tille (ba stēl') *n*. A tower in France used as a jail.

bas-ti-na-do (bas te nā ō) *n*. A beating with a stick or cudgel; a mode of punishment in oriental countries.

bast-ing (bā sting) *n*. The long stitches by which pieces of garments are temporarily sewn to each other.

bat (bat) *n*. A wooden stick made from strong wood; a nocturnal flying mammal. **batter** *n*.

bat boy *n*. A boy who takes care of the equipment of a baseball team.

batch (bach) *n*. A group of work entered on a computer at one time; a quantity (as of cookies, etc.) baked at one time.

bate (bāt) *v*. To abate, lessen, or reduce; to diminish.

ba-teau (ba tō) *n*. A light, broad, and flat-bottomed boat.

batement light *n*. A section of a window having vertical sides and a curved or inclined bottom.

bat-fowl-ing (bat faul-ing) *n*. A mode of catching birds at night by means of a light and nets.

bath (bath) *n. pl.* **baths** The act of washing the body.

bathe (bāth) *v*. To take a bath.

bath-house (bath haus) *n*. A house or building fitted up for bathing; a structure, as at the seaside, serving as a dressing room for bathers; a building for bathing equipped with medical facilities.

ba-thom-e-ter (ba thom'i tėr) *n*. An instrument which is used to measure the depth of water.

bath-robe (bath rōb) *n*. A long, loose garment worn before and after a bath or shower, and as leisure wear in the home.

bath-tub (bath teb) *n*. A tub to bathe in.

bath-y-scaphe (bath'i skāf˝) *n*. A submersible ship for deep sea exploration.

bath-y-sphere (bath'i sfier) *n*. A diving sphere used for observation of deep-sea life.

ba-tik (ba tēk') *n*. A method of dying

fabric, in which parts not to be dyed are coated with wax.

ba-tiste (b*a* tēst´) *n.* A sheer, soft fabric.

bat-on (b*e* ´tăn) *n.* The wand used by a conductor for beating time; the stick used by a band's drum major.

bat-tal-ion (b*e*´tal˝yon) *n.* A body of troops; a large group of any kind.

bat-tery (bat´*e* rē) *n.* A group of heavy guns.

bat-ting (bat´ing) *n.* Cotton wool in rolls or sheets, used as stuffing or lining.

bat-tle (bat´l) *n.* A struggle; combat between opposing forces. **battle** *v.* To engage in a war or battle.

bat-tle–ax (bat l aks) *n.* An ax formerly used as a weapon of war. *Slang* A woman with a bad temper or domineering nature.

battle cruiser *n.* A large armed warship.

battle cry *n.* A shout of troops rushing into or engaged in battle; any campaign slogan.

battle fatigue *n.* A neurosis suffered by soldiers after prolonged combat duty and exposure to danger.

bat-tle-field (bat l fēld) *n.* The field or scene of a land battle.

bat-tue (ba tü) *n.* A sport in which game is driven by a body of beaters from under cover into a limited area where the animals may be easily shot.

baux-ite (bok sīt) *n.* A mineral consisting essentially of a hydrated aluminum oxide, used as a source of alum and aluminum.

baw-bee (bo bē) *n.* An old Scottish coin of little value, anything of insignificant value.

bawd (bod) *n.* A prostitute. **bawdy** *adj.*

bawl (bol) *v.* To cry very loudly.

bay (bā) *n.* The inlet of a body of water; a main division or compartment; an animal that is reddish brown in color.

ba-ya-dere (bī *e* dif *er*) *adj.* Stripes on fabrics, running crosswise.

bay antler *n.* The second branch from the base of a stag's horn.

bay-ber-ry (bā´ber˝ē) *n.* Evergreen shrub used for decorations and making candles.

bay leaf *n.* The leaf of the bay tree, dried for use as a flavoring in cooking.

bay-o-net (bā´*o* nit) *n.* A spear-like weapon.

bay-ou (bī ō) *n.* An arm or outlet of a lake, river.

bay rum *n.* A fragrant liquid from the leaves of the bayberry used in cosmetics and medicine.

bay salt *n.* Coarse-grained salt, especially that obtained by evaporation of seawater.

ba-zaar (b*a* zär´) *n.* A fair where a variety of items are sold as a money-making project for charity, clubs, churches, or other such organizations.

ba-zoo-ka (b*a* zō´k*a*) *n.* Weapon for firing rockets.

BBA *abbr.* Bachelor of Business Administration.

BC *abbr.* Before Christ.

BD *abbr.* Bank draft.

be (bē) *v.* To occupy a position; to exist; used with the present participle of a verb to show action; used as a prefix to construct compound words, as behind, before, because, etc.

beach (bēch) *n.* Pebbly or sandy shore of a lake, ocean, sea, or river.

beach-comb-er (bēch kōm*er*) *n.* One who earns a living by collecting redeemable wreckage along ocean beaches; a beach-front vagrant.

beach-head (bēch hed) *n.* A seashore area taken and held by the attacking force in an amphibious invasion.

bea-con (bē´k*a*n) *n.* A coastal guiding or signaling device.

bead (bēd) *n.* A small round piece of material with a hole for threading. **bead** *v.* To adorn with beads. **beading** *n.*

bead-roll (bēd rōl) *n.* A list of persons for whom prayers are to be said.

bead-work (bēd werk) *n.* Ornamental work made with beads.

bea-gle (bē´gl) *n.* A small breed of hunting dog with short legs.

beak (bēk) *n.* The bill of a bird; resembling a beak. **beaked** *adj.*

beak-er (bē´k*er*) *n.* Large, wide-mouthed cup for drinking; a cylindrical, glass laboratory vessel with a lip for pouring.

beak-i-ron (bēk īern) *n.* The horn or tapering end of an anvil.

beam (bēm) *n.* Large, oblong piece of wood or metal used in construction. *v.* To shine.

bean (bēn) *n.* An edible seed or seed pod.

bean caper *n.* A small tree growing in warm climates, the flower buds of which are used as capers.

bean curd *n.* A soft vegetable cheese usually found in the Orient.

bear (bâr) *n.* A shaggy, carniverous mammal. *Slang* A rough or gruff person. **bear** *v.* To endure; to carry; to support. **bearable** *adj.* **bearability, bearer** *n.*

bearberry *n.* A creeping or trailing evergreen shrub of the heath family, growing in cooler areas in parts of the northern hemisphere, having red berry-like drupes, the bright green leaves used as an astringent and tonic.

bear-cat (bâr´kat) *n.* A panda.

beard (bērd) *n.* Hair growing on the chin and cheeks. **bearded** *adj.* **beardless** *adj.*

bear-grass (bâr´gras) *n.* Any of several American plants having grass-like foliage.

bearing rein *n.* The rein by which the head of a horse is held up in driving.

bear-skin (bâr´skin˝) *n.* The skin of a bear.

beast (bēst) *n.* A four-legged animal. *Slang* A brutal person. **beastly** *adj.*

beast of burden *n.* An animal used to perform heavy work and transport heavy materials.

beat (bēt) *v.* To strike repeatedly; to defeat. *adj.* Exhausted, very tired; fatigue. **beat, beater** n.

beat-en (bēt´n) *adj.* Made smooth by beating or treading; worn by use; conquered; vanquished.

beat-er (bē´tėr) *n.* One who or that which beats; an instrument for pounding, stirring, or pulverizing substances.

be-a-tif-ic (bē˝a tif´ik) *adj.* Giving or showing extreme bliss or joy.

be-at-i-tude (bē at´i tŏd˝) *n.* The highest form of happiness; heavenly bliss.

beat-nik (bēt´nik) *n.* A person who lives a nonconformist life; a member of the beat generation.

beau (bō) *n.* Sweetheart; dandy.

beau monde *n.* People of distinguished family, wealth, fame and fashion.

beau-ti-cian (bū tish´an) *n.* One whose business is to improve the appearance of a person's hair, nails, and complexion.

beau-ti-fi-ca-tion (bū˝ti fi kā´shon) *n.* The act of beautifying or rendering beautiful; decoration; adornment; embellishment.

beau-ti-ful (būti ful) *adj.* Having the qualities that constitute beauty; highly pleasing to the eye, the ear, or the mind.

beau-ty (bū´tē) *n.* Quality that is pleasing to the eye. **beautifully** *adv.*

beauty shop *n.* An establishment where a person may receive hair care, a nail manicure, and other beauty treatments.

beaux arts *n.* The fine arts, as painting and sculpture.

bea-ver (bē´vėr) *n.* A large semiaquatic rodent with webbed feet and flat tail which yields valuable fur for coats, hats, etc.

be-bop (bē´bop˝) *n., Slang* Jazz music.

be-calm (bē käm´) *v.* To make quiet or calm. **becalming** *v.*

be-cause (bē koz´) *conj.* For a reason; since.

because of *prep* On account of; as a result of.

bech-a-mel (bā´sha mel˝) *n.* A white sauce, seasoned occasionally with onion and nutmet.

beck (bek) *n.* A summons; a call.

beck-et (bek´it) *n.* A loop for holding something in place.

beck-on (bek´n) *v.* To summon someone with a nod or wave.

be-cloud (bē koud´) *v.* To darken; to obscure; to cause confusion about.

be-come (bē kum´) *v.* To come, to be, or to grow. **becoming** *adj.*

be-com-ing (bē kuming) *adj.* Suitable; proper; appropriate; befitting.

bed (bed) *n.* Furniture for sleeping; a piece of planted or cultivated ground. **bedding**

n. **bed** *v.*

be-daub (bē daub´) *v.* To daub over; to soil with anything thick, slimy, and dirty.

be-dazzle (bē daz´l) *v.* To confuse with bright lights. **bedazzling** *adj.* **bedazzle** *v.*

bed bolt *n.* A bolt for fastening something, as a machine, to its bed or foundation.

bed-ding (bed´ing) *n.* Bedclothes; material used as a bed for animals; a foundation.

bed-bug (bed´bug˝) *n.* A wingless insect that sucks blood and infests human homes, especially beds.

bed-fast (bed´fast˝) *adj.* Confined to a bed; bed-ridden.

bed-fel-low (bed´fel˝ō) *n.* One who occupies the same bed with another; a collaborator.

be-diz-en (bē diz´n) *v.* To deck out with clothes or finery; dress or adorn gaudily.

bed-lam (bed´lam) *n.* A state or situation of confusion.

bed-pan (bed´pan˝) *n.* A necessary utensil for urination or defecation by bedridden persons.

bed-plate (bed´plāt˝) *n.* The soleplate or foundation plate of an engine or machine.

be-drag-gled (bē drag´l) *adj.* Limp and wet; soiled as though pulled through mud.

bed-room (bed´rŏm) *n.* A sleeping room.

bed-sore (bed´sōr˝) *n.* A sore which may occur on a bedridden person's body that is subjected to most pressure.

bed-spread (bed´spred˝) *n.* A decorative outer bedcover.

bed-spring (bed´spring˝) *n.* A spring used to support the mattress on a bed.

bed-stead (bed´sted˝) *n.* Framework used to support a bed.

bed-straw (bed´stro) *n.* A perennial plant formerly used to stuff a mattress.

bee (bē) *n.* A hairy-bodied insect characterized by structures for gathering pollen and nectar from flowers.

beech (bēch) *n.* A tree of light-colored bark, with edible nuts.

beef (bēf) *n. pl.* **beefs** *or* **beeves** A cow, steer, or bull that has been fattened for consumption of its meat. **beefy** *adj.*

beef cattle *n.* Cattle raised for food.

beef-eat-er (bēf´ē˝tė) *n.* A consumer of beef.

bee fly *n.* A fly that resembles a bee.

bee-hive (bē´hīv˝) *n.* A dome-shaped hive, that serves as a natural home for bees.

bee-keep-er (bē´kē˝pėr) *n.* A person who raises bees for their honey; a person who raises bees as a means of livelihood.

bee-line (bē´līn˝) *n.* Shortest distance between two locations.

beep (bēp) *n.* A warning sound coming from a horn.

beer (bēr) *n.* An alcoholic beverage.

bees-wax (bēz´waks) *n.* The wax from bees that is used for their honeycombs.

beet (bēt) *n.* The root from a cultivated plant that can be used as a vegetable or a source of sugar.

bee-tle (bēt´l) *n.* An insect with modified, horny front wings, which cover the membranous back wings when it is at rest.

be-fall (bi fol´) *v.* To happen or occur to.

be-fit (bi fit´) *v.* To be suitable; appropriate. **befitting** *adj.*

be-fool (bi fŏl´) *v.* To make a fool of; to deceive.

be-fore (bi fōr´) *adv.* Earlier; previously. *prep.* In front of.

be-fore-hand (bi fōr´hand˝) *adv.* At a time prior to; in advance.

be-foul (bi foul´) *v.* To soil.

be-friend (bi frend´) *v.* To be a friend to someone.

beg (beg) *v.* To make a living by asking for charity. **beggar** *n.* **beggarly** *adj.*

be-gan (bi gan) *v.* The past tense of begin.

be-get (bi get´) *v.* To cause or produce; to cause to exist.

be-gin (bi gin´) *v.* To start; to come into being; to commence. **beginner** *n.* **beginning** *n.*

be-gone (bi gon´) *v. interj.* Go away; depart.

be-go-nia (bi gōn´ya) *n.* A tropical plant with waxy flowers and showy leaves.

be-grime (bi grīm´) *v.* To make dirty; to soil with grime.

be-grudge (bi gruj´) *v.* To envy someone's

possessions or enjoyment.

be-guile (bi gīl´) *v.* To deceive; to delight; to charm.

be-guine (bi gēn´) *n.* A popular dance of the islands which resembles the rumba.

be-gum (bē´gum) *n.* A Muslim woman.

be-gun (bi gun) *v.* The past participle of begin.

be-half (bi haf´) *n.* The support or interest of another person.

be-have (bi hāv´) *v.* To function in a certain manner; to conduct oneself in a proper manner. **behavior, behaviorism** *n.* **behaving** *n.*

be-hav-ior (bi hāv´yė) *n.* Manner of behaving or acting; conduct.

be-head (bi hed´) *v.* To remove the head from the body; to decapitate.

be-held *v.* Past participle of behold.

be-hind (bi hīnd´) *adv.* To or at the back; late or slow in arriving.

be-hold (bi hōld´) *v.* To look at; to see.

be-hoove (bi hŏv´) *v.* To benefit or give advantage.

beige (bāzh) *n. & adj.* A light brownish, grey color.

being (bē´ing) *n.* One's existence.

be-jew-el (bi jō´el) *v.* To adorn with jewels.

be-la-bor (bi lā´bėr) *v.* To work on or to discuss beyond the point where it is necessary; to carry to absurd lengths.

be-lat-ed (bi lā´ted) *adj.* Tardy; late, delayed. **belatedly** *adv.* **belatedness** *n.*

bel canto (bel´ kan´tō) *n.* Operatic singing with rich lyricism and brilliant vocal means.

belch (belch) *v.* To expel stomach gas through the mouth.

be-lea-guer (bi lē´gėr) *v.* To surround with an army as to preclude escape; to blockade; to harass.

bel-fry (bel´frē) *n. pl.* **belfries** The tower that contains the bell of a church.

be-lief (bi lēf´) *n.* Something that is trusted or believed.

be-lieve (bi lēv´) *v.* To accept as true or real; to hold onto religious beliefs. **believable** *adj.* **believer** *n.*

be-lit-tle (bi lit´l) *v.* To think or speak in a

slighting manner of someone or something.

bell (bel) *n.* A metal instrument that gives a ringing sound when struck.

bell-boy (bel boi˝) *n.* A hotel employee who serves guests by carrying luggage or running errands.

bel-la-don-na (bel˝a don´a) *n.* A poisonous plant with black berries; a medicine extracted from the belladonna plant.

bell–bot-toms (bel bät emz) *n. pl.* Pants with legs that flare at the bottom.

belles–let-tres (bel le´tra) *n. pl.* Literature that is regarded not for its value, but for its artistic quality.

bel-lig-er-ent (be lij´ėr ent) *adj.* Hostile and inclined to be aggressive. **belligerence, belligerent** *n.* **belligerently** *adv.*

bel-low (bel´ō) *v.* To make a deep, powerful roar like a bull. **bellow** *n.* **bellowing** *adj.*

bel-lows (bel´ōz) *n.* An instrument that produces air in a chamber and expels it through a short tube.

bell pepper *n.* A bell-shaped sweet pepper.

bell-wort (bel´wert) *n.* An herb of the lilly family with yellow bell-shaped flowers.

bel-ly (bel´ē) *n. pl.* **bellies** The abdomen or the stomach.

bel-ly-ache (bel´ē āk˝) *n.* Pain in the stomach or abdomen.

bel-ly-but-ton (bel´ē but˝on) *n.* Navel.

be-long (bi long´) *v. pl.* **belongings** *n.* To be a part of. **belonging** *n.*

be-loved (bi luv´id) *adj.* To be dearly loved.

be-low (bi lō´) *adv.* At a lower level or place. *prep.* To be inferior to.

belt (belt) *n.* A band worn around the waist; a zone or region that is distinctive in a special way.

belt-way (belt´wā) *n.* A highway that encircles an urban area.

be-lu-ga (be lö´ga) *n.* A large white whale whose roe is used to make caviar.

be-moan (bi mōn´) *v.* To moan or mourn for.

be-muse (bi mūz´) v. To bewilder or confuse; to be lost in thought. **bemused** adj. **bemusing** v.

bench (bench) n. A long seat for more than two people; the seat of the judge in a court of law.

bench-er (ben´chėr) n. A person who sits on a bench as a judge or a member of Parliament.

bench mark n. A mark cut into some durable material, as stone, to serve as a guide in a line of levels for the determination of altitudes over any region.

bench penalty n. In the game of hockey, a penalty against a team due to a minor infraction of the rules, requiring a player to be removed from the ice for a period of two minutes.

bench show n. A dog show or exhibition where awards are given for physical merit.

bench warrant n. A warrant issued by a judge against a person guilty of contempt.

bend (bend) v. To arch; to change the direct course; to deflect. **bender** n. **bending** v.

bend-er (ben´dėr) n. A person who or something that bends. *Slang* A drinking binge.

bends (bendz) n. pl. Stomach and chest pains caused by the reduction of air pressure in the lungs, the result of rising too quickly from deep ocean levels.

beneath (bi nēth´) adv. To be in a lower position; below; underneath.

ben-e-dict (ben´i dikt) n. A previously confirmed bachelor who was recently married.

ben-e-dic-tion (ben˝i dik´shan) n. A blessing given at the end of a religious service.

ben-e-fac-tion (ben´e fak˝shan) n. A charitable donation; a gift. **benefactor** n.

ben-e-fice (ben´e fis) n. Fixed capital assets of a church that provide a living.

be-nef-i-cence (be nef´i sens) n. The quality of being kind or charitable.

be-nef-i-cent (be nef´sent) adj. Performing acts of charity and kindness; doing good.

ben-e-fi-cial (ben˝e fish´al) adj. Advantageous; helpful; contributing to a valuable end. **beneficially** adv.

ben-e-fi-ci-ar-y (ben´e fish´ē er˝ē) n. The person named to the estate of another in case of death.

ben-e-fit (ben´e fit) n. Aid; help; an act of kindness; a social event or entertainment to raise money for a person or cause. **benefit** v.

be-nev-o-lence (be nev´o lens) n. The inclination to be charitable.

be-nev-o-lent (be nev´o lent) adj. Doing good; organized for good works.

ben-ga-line (beng´ga lēn˝) n. A fabric with narrow transverse cords, usually made of rayon, cotton, or silk and similar to poplin.

be-night-ed (bi nī´tid) adj. Overtaken by night.

be-nign (bi nīn´) adj. Having a gentle and kind disposition; gracious; not malignant. **benignly** adv.

be-nig-nan-cy (bi nig´nan sē) n. The condition of being benevolent, gentle, mild.

be-nig-nant (bi nig´nant) adj. Kind; gracious; favorable; beneficial.

ben-i-son (ben´i zen) n. A blessing; benediction.

ben-ne (ben´ē) n. An East Indian plant known as Sesame, from which edible oil is extracted.

bent (bent) adj. Curved, not straight. **bent** n. A fixed determination; purpose.

ben-thos (ben´thos) n. The whole amount of total of all organisms that live under water either near the shore or at great depths.

be-numb (bi num´) v. To dull; to make numb.

ben-zal-de-hyde (ben zal´de hīd˝) n. An aromatic liquid used in flavoring and perfumery.

ben-zene (ben´zēn) n. A flammable toxic liquid used as a motor fuel.

be-queath (bi kwēth´) v. To give or leave to someone by will; to hand down, legacy. **bequeathal** n.

be-quest (bi kwest´) n. Something that is bequeathed.

be-rate (bi rāt´) v. To scold severely.

ber-ceuse (ber suz´) n. A lullaby.

bere (bēr) *n.* A barley species.

be-reave (bi rēv′) *v.* To deprive; to suffer the loss of a loved one. **bereft** *adj.* **bereavement** *n.*

be-ret (be rā′) *n.* A round, brimless woolen cap.

berg (berg) *n.* A large mass of ice; iceberg.

ber-ga-mot (bür′ga mot″) *n.* A pear-shaped orange, the rind of which has a fragrant oil used in perfumery.

ber-i-ber-i (ber′ē ber′ē) *n.* Nervous disorder from the deficiency of vitamin B producing partial paralysis of the extremities.

ber-ry (ber′ē) *n. pl.* **berries** An edible fruit, such as a strawberry or blackberry.

ber-serk (bėr serk′) *adj.* Destructively violent.

berth (berth) *n.* Space at a wharf for a ship or boat to dock; a built-in bunk or bed on a train or ship.

ber-yl (ber′il) *n.* A mineral composed of silicon, oxygen, and beryllium that is the major source of beryllium; a precious stone which is exceptionally hard.

be-ryl-li-um (bi ril′ē um) *n.* A corrosion-resistant, rigid, lightweight metallic element.

be-seech (bi sēch′) *v.* To ask or request earnestly.

be-set (bi set′) *v.* To set, stud, or surround with something.

be-set-ting (bi set′ing) *adj.* Habitually attacking.

be-show (bi shō′) *n.* An edible fish of the western coast of North America.

be-side (bi sīd′) *prep.* At the side of; next to.

be-sides (bi sīdz′) *adv.* Along the side of; over and above.

be-siege (bi sēj′) *v.* To surround with troops; to harass with requests.

be-smear (bi smir′) *v.* To soil; to smear.

be-smirch (bi smürch′) *v.* To tarnish.

be-som (bē′zum) *n.* A broom made of twigs that are attached to a handle, used to sweep floors.

be-sot (bi sot′) *v.* To make mentally dull, as with drink.

be-spat-ter (bi spat′ėr) *v.* To splash; to soil.

be-speak (bi spēk′) *v.* To indicate; to speak; to foretell. **bespoken** *adj.*

be-sprin-kle (bi spring′kl) *v.* To sprinkle over; to cover by scattering.

best (best) *adj.* Exceeding all others in quality or excellence; most suitable, desirable, or useful. **best** *v.*

bes-tial (bēs′chal) *adj. pl.* **-ities** Of or relating to an animal; brutish, having the qualities of a beast. **bestially** *adv.* **bestiality** *n.*

bes-tial-i-ty (bes″chē al′i tē) *n.* The quality of a beast; beastliness.

bes-ti-ar-y (bes′chē er″ē) *n.* A medieval collection of fables about imaginary and real animals, each with a moral.

be-stir (bi stėr′) *v.* To rouse into action; to stir; to put into brisk or vigorous action.

best man *n.* The attendant of a bridegroom at a wedding.

be-stow (bi stō′) *v.* To present or to give honor.

be-strew (bi strö) *v.* To scatter over.

be-stride (bi strīd′) *v.* To step over or to straddle.

best seller *n.* A book or an article which has a high volume of sale.

bet (bet) *n.* An amount risked on a stake or wager. *abbr.* Between.

be-ta (bā′ta) *n.* The first letter of the Greek alphabet.

be-take (bi tāk′) *v.* To cause oneself to make one's way; move or to go.

beta particle *n.* High-speed positron or electron coming from an atomic nucleus that is undergoing radioactive decay.

be-ta-tron (bā′ta tron″) *n.* Accelerator in which electrons are propelled by the inductive action of a rapidly varying magnetic field.

Bethlehem *n.* The birthplace of Jesus.

be-tide (bi tīd′) *v.* To happen to; to take place.

be-to-ken (bi tō′ken) *v.* To show by a visible sign.

be-tray (bi trā′) *v.* To be disloyal or unfaithful; to indicate; to deceive; treachery. **betrayal** *n.*

be-troth (bi trōth´) v. To promise to take or give in marriage. **betrothal** n.

be-trothed (bi trōthd´) n. A person to whom one is engaged to marry.

bet-ta (bā´t a**)** n. A brightly colored freshwater fish of southeastern Asia.

bet-ter (bet´ẻr) adj. More suitable, useful, desirable, or higher in quality. v. To improve oneself. **betterment** n.

bet-tor, bet-ter (bet´ẻr) n. A person who makes bets or wagers.

be-tween (bi twēn´) prep. The position or time that separates; in the middle or shared by two.

be-twixt (bi twikst´) prep. Not knowing which way one should go; between.

bev-el (bev´el) n. The angle at which one surface meets another when they are not at right angles.

bev-er-age (bev´ẻr ij) n. A refreshing liquid for drinking other than water.

bev-y (bev´ē) n. pl. **-bevies** A collection or group; a flock of birds.

be-wail (bi wāl´) v. To express regret or sorrow.

be-ware (bi wâr´) v. To be cautious; to be on guard.

be-wilder (bi wil´dẻr) v. To confuse; to perplex or puzzle. **bewilderment** n.

be-witch (bi wich´) v. To fascinate or captivate completely, to cast a spell over. **bewitchery** n. **bewitchment** v.

bey (bā) n. The Turkish title of respect and honor.

be-yond (bē ond´) prep. Outside the reach or scope of; something past or to the far side.

bez-el (bez´el) n. A flange or groove that holds the beveled edge of an object such as a gem in a ring mounting.

be-zique (be **zēk´)** n. A card game that uses a deck of 64 cards, similar to pinochle.

bhang (bang) n. An intoxicant or narcotic obtained from the leaves and flowering tops of hemp used in India for swallowing or smoking.

bi- pref. Two; occurring two times; used when constructing nouns.

bi-a-ly (bē ´al ē) n. A baked roll with onions on the top.

bi-an-nu-al (bī an´ū al**)** adj. Taking place twice a year; semiannual. **biannually** adv.

bi-as (bī´as**)** n. A line cut diagonally across the grain of fabric; prejudice. v. To be or to show prejudice. **biasness** n. **biased** v. **biased** adj.

bi-au-ral (bī or´al**)** adj. Hearing with both ears.

bib (bib) n. A cloth that is tied under the chin of small children to protect their clothing.

bibb (bib) n. A piece of timber bolted to the ship's mast for support.

Bi-ble (bī´bl) n. The holy book of Christianity, containing the Old and New Testaments. **Biblically** adv.

Bible Belt n. The section of the United States where the Protestant Fundamentalists prevail.

Bib-li-cal (bib´li k**al)** adj. Pertaining to, or contained in the Bible.

Bib-li-cist (bib´li sist) n. A person who accepts the Bible literally.

bib-li-og-ra-phy (bib lē og´ra fē) n. pl. **bibliographies** A list of work by a publisher or writer; a list of sources of information. **bibliographer** n.

bib-lio-phile (bib´lē o **fīl´)** n. A person who collects books.

bib-li-ot-ics (bib˝lē ot´iks) n. The study of handwriting to determine authorship, often used to determine authorship.

bib-u-lous (bib´ya les**)** adj. Inclined to drink; of or related to drinking.

bi-cen-ten-ni-al (bī˝sen ten´ē al**)** adj. Happening once every 200 years. **bicentennial** n. Anniversary or celebration of 200 years.

bi-ceps (bī´seps) n. Large muscle in the front of the upper arm and at the back of the thigh. **bicipital** adj.

bick-er (bik´er) v. To quarrel or argue. **bicker** n.

bi-con-cave (bī kon´kāv) adj. Bowing in on two sides.

bi-cul-tur-al (bī kul'chur al) *adj.* Having or containing two distinct cultures.

bi-cus-pid (bī kus'pid) *n.* A tooth with two roots.

bi-cy-cle (bī'si kl) *n.* A two-wheeled vehicle propelled by pedals. **bicyclist** *n.*

bid (bid) *v.* To request something; to offer to pay a certain price. *n.* One's intention in a card game. **bidder** *n.*

bid-dy (bid'ē) *n.* A young chicken; hen. *Slang* A fussy woman.

bide (bīd) *v.* To remain; to wait.

bi-det (bi'dā) *n.* A basin for bathing the genital and anal areas.

bi-en-ni-al (bī en'ē el) *adj.* Occurring every two years; lasting or living for only two years. **biennially** *adv.* **biennial** *n.*

bi-en-ni-um (bī en'ē um) *n.* Period of two years.

bier (bēr) *n.* A stand on which a coffin is placed before burial.

bi-fo-cal (bī fō'kal) *adj.* Having two different focal lengths.

bi-fo-cals (bī *fō*'kal) *n. pl.* Lenses used to correct both close and distant vision.

bi-fur-cate (bī'fer kāt) *v.* To divide into two parts. **bifurcation** *n.* **bifurcately** *adj.*

big (big) *adj.* Very large in dimensions, intensity, and extent; grown-up; bountiful; powerful. **bigness** n.

big-a-my (big'a mē) *n. pl.* **bigamies** The act of marrying one person while still married to another. **bigamist** *n.*

big brother *n.* A person who befriends and acts as a counselor for a young boy, who usually doesn't have a father.

Big Dipper *n.* Cluster of seven stars that form a bowl and handle.

big-head (big'hed') *adj.* A conceited person. **bigheadedness** *n.*

big-heart-ed (big'här'tid) *adj.* Being generous and kind.

big-horn (big'horn') *n.* A sheep from the mountainous western part of N. America.

bight (bīt) *n.* The slack in a rope; a bend in the shoreline.

big league *n.* Major league.

big-ot (big'ot) *n. pl.* **-ries** A person who is fanatically devoted to one group, religion, politics, or race. **big-otry** *n.*

big shot *n., Slang* An important or influential person.

big top *n.* The largest tent of a circus; a circus.

big wheel *n., Slang* An influential person.

big-wig (big wig) *n.* A person of authority or importance.

bike (bīk) *n.* A bicycle. **biker** *n.* **bike** *v.*

bi-ki-ni (bi kē'nē) *n.* A scanty, two-piece bathing suit. **bikinied** *adj.*

bi-lan-der (bil'an dėr) *n.* A small merchant vessel having two masts.

bi-lat-er-al (bī lat'er al) *adj.* Having or relating to two sides. **bilaterally** *adv.*

bilbo (bil'bō') *n.* An iron bar with sliding shackles to confine prisoners on shipboard.

bile (bīl) *n.* A brownish-yellow alkaline liquid that is secreted by the liver to help digest fats. **biliary** *adj.*

bi–lev-el (bī lev el) *adj.* Divided into 2 floor levels.

bilge (bilj) *n.* Lowest inside part of the hull of a ship.

bilge keel *n.* A projection like a fin along a ship on either side to check rolling.

bi-lin-gual (bī ling'gwal) *adj.* Able to speak two languages with equal ability.

bil-ious (bil'yus) *adj.* Suffering gastric distress from a sluggish gallbladder or liver.

bilk (bilk) *v.* To cheat or swindle.

bill (bil) *n.* Itemized list of fees for services rendered; a document presented containing a formal statement of a case complaint or petition; the beak of a bird. **biller** *n.*

bil-la-bong (bil'a bong') *n.* A blind channel coming from a river; a dry stream bed which fills up after seasonal rains.

bill-board (bil'bōrd') *n.* A place for displaying advertisements.

billed (bild) *adj.* Having a bill or beak.

bil-let (bil'it) *n.* An official document which provides a member of the military with board and lodging.

bill-fold (bil'fōld) *n.* Pocket-sized wallet

for holding money, identification, and personal information.

bil-liards (bil'yardz) *n.* Game played on a table with cushioned edges.

bil-lion (bil'yon) *n.* A thousand million.

bil-lion-aire) *n.* A person whose wealth equals at least one billion dollars.

bill of lading *n.* A form issued by the carrier for promise of delivery of merchandise listed.

Bill of Rights *n.* The first ten amendments to the United States Constitution.

bill of sale *n.* A formal instrument for the transfer of personal property.

bil-low (bil'ō) *n.* Large swell of water or smoke; wave. **billowy** *adj.*

billy club *n.* A short wooden club used for protection or defense.

billy goat *n.* A male goat.

bi-man-u-al (bī man'ūal) *adj.* Involving the use of both hands.

bi-met-al-lism (bī met'al iz"um) *n.* The use of two metals, gold and silver, as legal tenders.

bi-month-ly (bī munth'lē) *adj. pl.* **-lies** Occurring every two months.

bin (bin) *n.* An enclosed place for storage.

bi-na-ry (bī'na rē) *adj.* Made of two different components or parts.

bind (bīnd) *v.* To hold with a belt or rope; to bandage; to fasten and enclose pages of a book between covers. **binding** *n.*

bind-er (bīnd'ēr) *n.* A notebook for holding paper; payment or written statement legally binding an agreement.

bind-er-y (bīn'da rē) *n. pl.* **-eries** The place where books are taken to be bound.

binge (binj) *n.* Uncontrollable self-indulgence; a spree.

bin-go (bing'gō) *n.* A game of chance in which a person places markers on numbered cards in accordance with numbers drawn by a caller.

bin-na-cle (bin'a kal) *n.* A place where a ship's compass is contained.

bi-noc-u-lar (bi nok'ū lēr) *n.* A device design-

ed for both eyes to bring objects that are far away into focus. **binocularity** *n.* **binocularly** *adv.*

bi-o-chem-is-try (bī"ō kem'i strē) *n.* Chemistry of substances and biological processes.

bi-o-de-grad-a-ble (bī di grā e bel) *adj.* Decomposable by natural processes. **biodegradability, biodegradation** *n.*

bi-o-feed-back (bīo fēd bak) *n.* The technique of controlling involuntary bodily functions, such as blood pressure and heartbeat.

bi-o-geo-chem-is-try (bī'o jē ō'kem e strē) *n.* Science dealing with the relation of earth chemicals to plant and animal life.

bi-og-ra-pher (bī og'ra fer) *n.* The person who writes a biography.

bi-o-haz-ard (bī ō haz erd) *n.* Biological material that threatens humans and or their environment, if infective.

biological warfare *n.* Warfare that uses organic biocides or disease-producing microorganisms to destroy crops, livestock, or human life.

bi-ol-o-gist (bī ol'o jist) *n.* A person skilled in or who studies biology.

bi-ol-o-gy (bī ol'o jē) *n.* Science of living organisms and the study of their structure, reproduction, and growth. **biological** *adj.*

bi-o-med-i-cine (bī"ō med'i sin) *n.* Medicine that has to do with human response to environmental stress.

bi-on-ics (bī 'ān iks) *n.* Application of biological principles to the study and design of engineering systems, as electronic systems.

bi-o-phys-ics (bī"ō fiz'iks) *n.* The physics of living organisms. **biophysical** *adj.*

bi-op-sy (bī'op sē) *n. pl.* **biopsies** The examination for the detection of a disease in tissues, cells, or fluids removed from a living organism.

bi-ot-ic (bī ot'ik) *adj.* Related to specific life conditions or to life itself.

bi-o-tin (bī'o tin) *n.* Part of the vitamin B complex found in liver, milk, yeast, and egg yolk.

bi-par-ti-san (bī pär´ti zan) *adj.* Supported by two political parties; working together. **bipartisanship** *n.*

bi-par-tite (bī pär´tīt´) *adj.* Having two parts.

bi-ped (bī´ped) *n.* An animal having two feet.

bi-plane (bī´plān´) *n.* A glider or airplane with wings on two levels.

bi-pod (bī´pod) *n.* Stand supported by two legs.

bi-po-lar (bī pō´lar) *adj.* Having or related to two poles; concerning the earth's North and South Poles.

bi-ra-cial (bī rā´shal) *adj.* Composed of or for members of two races.

bi-ra-mose (bī rā´mōs) *adj.* Having, or consisting of, two branches.

birch (berch) *n.* A tree providing hard, close-grained wood.

birch-bark (berch´bärk´) *n.* A light-weight canoe made from birch tree bark.

bird (berd) *n.* A warm-blooded, egg-laying animal whose body is covered by feathers.

bird bath *n.* A shallow basin for birds to bathe in.

bird-brain (berd´brān´) *n., Slang* A person who acts in a silly fashion.

bird-house (berd´hous´) *n.* A box used outdoors to shelter birds.

bird-ie (ber´dē) *n.* A stroke under par in the game of golf; a shuttlecock.

bi-ret-ta (bi ret´a) *n.* Cap worn by Roman Catholic clergy, square in shape.

birth (berth) *n.* The beginning of existence. *v.* To bring forth a baby from the womb.

birth certificate *n.* An official record of a person's birth date and place of birth.

birth control *n.* A technique used to control or prevent the number of children born by lessening the chances of conception.

birth-day (berth´dā) *n.* The day a person is born and the anniversary of that day.

birth-mark (berth´märk´) *n.* A blemish or mark on the skin present at birth.

birth-place (berth´plās´) *n.* The place of birth.

birth-rate (berth´rāt) *n.* The ratio of the number of births to a given population over a specified period of time.

birth-right (berth´rīt´) *n.* Privilege granted by virtue of birth especially to the first born.

birth-stone (berth´stōn´) *n.* A gemstone that represents the month a person was born in.

birth-wort (berth´wert) *n.* An herb with aromatic roots used in medicine to aid in childbirth.

bis (bis) *adv.* Again; encore.

bis-cuit (bis´kit) *n.* Small piece of bread made with baking soda or baking powder; a cookie, or cracker.

bi-sect (bī sekt´) *v.* To divide or cut into two equal parts. **bisection** *n.*

bi-sex-u-al (bī sek´shö al) *adj.* Sexually relating to both sexes. **bisexuality** *n.* **bisexually** *adv.*

bish-op (bish´op) *n.* A Christian clergyman with high rank. **bishopric** *n.*

bis-muth (biz´muth) *n.* A white, crystalline metallic element.

bi-son (bī´son) *n.* A large buffalo of northwestern America, with a dark-brown coat and short, curved horns.

bisque (bisk) *n.* A creamy soup made from fish or vegetables; unglazed clay.

bis-sex-tile (bī seks´til) *adj.* Related to the extra day occurring in a leap year.

bis-tort (bis´tort) *n.* An American herb with twisted roots used as astringents.

bis-tou-ry (bis´to rē) *n.* A small, narrow surgical knife.

bis-tro (bis´trō) *n. pl.* **bistros** A bar or small nightclub. **bistroic** *adj.*

bit (bit) *n.* A tiny piece or amount of something; a tool designed for boring or drilling, such as drilling for oil; metal mouthpiece of a horse bridle; in computer science, either of two characters, as the binary digits zero and one, of a language that has only two characters; and a unit of information; storage capacity, as a computer memory.

bite (bīt) v. To cut, tear, or crush with the teeth. **bite** n. **bitingly** adv.

bit-stock (bit´stok˝) n. A brace that secures a drilling bit.

bit-ter (bit´ẽr) adj. Having a sharp, unpleasant taste. **bitterly** adv. **bitterness** n.

bit-tern (bit´ern) n. A small to medium-sized heron with a booming cry.

bit-ter-root (bit´ẽr röt) n. A Rocky Mountain herb with fleshy roots and pink flowers.

bit-ter-sweet (bit´ẽr swēt˝) n. A woody vine whose root, when chewed, has first a bitter, then a sweet taste.

bituminous coal n. Coal that contains a high ratio of bituminous material and burns with a smoky flame.

bi-valve (bī´valv˝) n. A mollusk that has a hinged two-part shell, a clam or oyster.

biv-ou-ac (biv´ŏ ak˝) n. A temporary military camp in the open air. v. To camp overnight in the open air.

bi-week-ly (bī wēk´lē) n. Occurring every two weeks.

bi-year-ly (bī yēr´lē) n. Occurring every two years.

bi-zarre (bi zär´) adj. Extremely strange or odd. **bizarrely** adv. **bizarreness** n.

bi-zon-al (bī´zōn´al) adj. Pertaining to two combined zones.

blab (blab) v. To reveal a secret by indiscreetly talking; to gossip.

blab-ber (blab´ẽr) v. To chatter; to blab. **blabber** n. **blabbering** v.

blab-ber-mouth (blab´ẽr mouth˝) n., *Slang* A person who gossips.

black (blak) adj. Very dark in color; depressing; cheerless; darkness, the absence of light. n **blackly** adv.

black–and–blue (blak´and blö´) adj. Discolored skin caused by bruising.

black–and–white (blak´and hwīt´) adj. Having been put down in writing or print.

black-ball (blak´bol) n. A vote that prevents a person's admission to an organization or club.

black bass n. An American freshwater game fish.

black belt n. The rank of expert in karate.

black-ber-ry (blak´ber˝ē) n. *pl.* **-berries** A thorny plant with black edible berries that have small seeds.

black-bird (blak´berd˝) n. A small bird, the males of the species having mostly all black feathers.

black-board (blak´bōrd) n. Hard, slate-like board written on with chalk.

black box n. The container that protects the tape recordings of airline pilots from water and fire, normally recoverable in the event of an accident.

black-en v. To make black.

black eye n. A bruise or discoloration around the eye.

black-eyed pea n. Cowpea.

black–eyed Susan n. A North American plant with orange-yellow petals and dark brown centers; the official state flower of Maryland.

black-fin (blak´fin˝) n. A whitefish of certain northern lakes of the U.S.

black flag v. To signal a race car driver to return to the pits; a pirate's flag with skull and crossbones.

black-heart-ed (blak´här˝tid) adj. Having a wicked and heartless disposition.

black-jack (blak´jak˝) n. A card game in which each player tries to accumulate cards with points higher than that of the dealer, but not more than 21 points.

black light n. Ultraviolet or invisible infrared light.

black-list (blak´list˝) n. A list which contains the names of people who are to be boycotted.

black lung n. A disease of the lungs usually contracted by coal miners from prolonged working in coal mines.

black magic n. Witchcraft.

black-mail (blak´māl´) n. The threat of exposing a past discreditable act or crime; money paid to avoid exposure, extortion and intimidation. **blackmailer** n.

black market (blak´mär´kit) n. The illegal buying or selling of merchandise or items.

black-ness (blak´nis) n. The quality or state of being black.

black-out (blak´out˝) n. The temporary loss of electrical power. black out v. To conceal lights that might be seen by enemy aircraft; to temporarily lose consciousness.

black pepper n. A pungent condiment used for seasoning when cooking.

black sheep n. A person who is considered a loser by a respectable family.

black-smith (blak´ smith˝) n. A person who shapes iron with heat and a hammer; the person who makes or repairs horse shoes.

black-snake (blak´snāk˝) n. A harmless snake very black in color of the United States.

black–tie adj. The wearing of semiformal evening wear by men.

black-top (blak´top˝) n. Asphalt, used to pave or surface roads.

black walnut n. A walnut of eastern North America.

black widow n. A spider that is extremely poisonous.

blad-der (blad´ėr) n. The expandable sac in the pelvis that holds urine.

blade (blād) n. The cutting part of a knife; the leaf of a plant or a piece of grass.

blah (blä) n. A feeling of general dissatisfaction.

blame (blām) v. To hold someone guilty for something; to find fault. blameless n. blamelessly adv. blamelessness n.

blame-wor-thy (blām´wur´thē) adj. Deserving blame.

blanch (blanch) v. To remove the color from something, as to bleach; to pour scalding hot water over fresh vegetables.

bland (bland) adj. Lacking taste or style. blandly adv. blandness n.

blan-dish (blan´dish) v. To coax by flattery.

blank (blangk) adj. Having no markings or writing; empty; confused, no interest or emotion as showed on a persons face or look. blankly adv. blankness n.

blank check n. Carte blanche; freedom of action.

blan-ket (blang´kit) n. A woven covering used on a bed.

blank verse n. A poem of lines that have rhythm but do not rhyme.

blan-quette (blän ket´) n. A stew with a white sauce, usually served with onions or mushrooms.

blare (blâr) v. To make or cause a loud sound.

blar-ney (blär´nē) n. Talk that is deceptive or nonsense. blarney v.

blas-pheme (blas fēm´) v. To speak with irreverence. blasphemously adv. blasphemousness n.

blas-phem-ous (blas´ fa mus) adj. Containing or exhibiting blasphemy.

blast (blast) n. A strong gust of air; the sound produced when a horn is blown. blasted adj.

blast–off (blast´of˝) n. The launching of a space ship.

blat (blat) v. To cry, as a calf; to bleat, as a sheep.

bla-tan-cy (blā´tan sē) n. The quality or state of being offensively loud or clamorous.

bla-tant (blāt´ant) adj. Unpleasant; offensively loud; shameless.

blath-er (blath´ėr) v. To talk, but not making sense. blatherer n.

blath-er-skite (blath´ėr skīt˝) n. One given to voluble, empty talk.

blaze (blāz) n. A bright burst of fire; a sudden outburst of anger; a trail marker; a white mark on an animal's face. blaze v.

bla-zer (blā´zėr) n. A jacket with notched collar and patch pockets.

bla-zon (blāz n) v. To make known; to announce. blazoner n.

bldg abbr. Building.

bleach (blēch) v. To remove the color from a fabric; to become white.

bleach-ers (blē´chėrz) n. pl. Seating for spectators in a stadium.

bleak (blēk) adj. Discouraging and depressing; barren; cold; harsh. bleakness n. bleakly adv.

blear-y (blēr´ē) adj. Unclearly defined; blurred vision from fatigue or lack of sleep.

bleat (blēt) n. The cry of a sheep or goat.

bleed (blēd) *v.* To lose blood, as from an injury; to extort money; to mix or allow dyes to run together.

bleeding heart *n.* A plant with pink flowers; a person who feels very sympathetic toward the underprivileged.

bleep (blēp) *n.* A signal with a quick, loud sound.

blem-ish (blem´ish) *n.* A flaw or defect.

blench (blench) *v.* To turn aside from lack of courage.

blend (blend) *v.* To mix together smoothly, to obtain a new substance, combine together. **blend** *n.* **blender** *n.*

bless (bles) *v.* To honor or praise; to confer prosperity or well-being.

bless-ed (bles´id) *adj.* Holy; enjoying happiness. **blessedly** *adv.*

bless-ing (bles´ing) *n.* A short prayer before a meal.

blight (blīt) *n.* A disease of plants that can cause complete destruction.

blimp (blimp) *n.* A large aircraft with a non-rigid gas-filled hull.

blind (blīnd) *adj.* Not having eyesight; something that is not based on facts. *n.* A shelter that conceals hunters.

blind alley *n.* A mistaken direction.

blind as a bat *adj.* Having poor vision.

blind date *n.* A date between two strangers that has been arranged by a third party.

blind-ers (blīn´dėr) *n. pl.* Flaps that are attached to the bridle of a horse, restricting side vision.

blind-fold (blīnd´fōld˝) *v.* To cover the eyes with a cloth; to block the vision, to interfere with sight. **blindfolded** *adj.*

blind-ing (blī´ ding) *adj.* Making blind; preventing from seeing clearly.

blindman's buff *n.* A game in which a person is blindfolded and then tries to catch another player.

blind spot *n.* The point in the retina that is insensitive to light.

blink (blingk) *v.* To squint; to open and close the eyes quickly; to take a quick glance.

blink-er (bling´kėr) *n.* A signaling light that displays a message; a light on a car used to indicate turns.

blintz (blints) *n.* A very thin pancake rolled and stuffed with cottage cheese or other fillings.

blip (blip) *v.* To remove; erase sounds from a recording. *n.* The brief interruption as the result of blipping.

bliss (blis) *n.* To have great happiness or joy. **blissful** *adj.* **blissfully** *adv.*

blis-ter (blis´tėr) *n.* The swelling of a thin layer of skin that contains a watery liquid. **blister** *v.* **blisteringly** *adj.*

blithe (blīth) *adj.* Carefree or casual. **blithery** *adv.* **blitheness** *n.*

blitz (blits) *n.* A sudden attack; an intensive and forceful campaign.

bliz-zard (bliz´ard) *n.* A severe winter storm characterized by wind and snow.

blk *abbr.* Black, block.

bloat (blōt) *v.* To swell or puff out. **bloat** *n.* **bloated** *adj.*

blob (blob) *n.* A small shapeless mass.

bloc (blok) *n.* A united group formed for a common action or purpose.

block (blok) *n.* A solid piece of matter; the act of obstructing or hindering something. **blockage** *n.* **blocker** *n.*

block-ade (blo kād´) *n.* The closure of an area. **blockader** *n.* **blockade** *v.*

block and tackle *n.* An apparatus with ropes and pulleys used for hoisting and lifting heavy objects.

block-bust-er (blok´bus˝tėr) *n.* A large-scale demolition bomb.

block-er (blok´ėr) *n.* One who or that which blocks.

block-head (blok´hed˝) *n.* A strong-willed person; a stupid fellow; a person slow in understanding.

block letter *n.* A letter or type face in sans serif.

block-y (blok´ē) *adj.* Similar to a block in form; stocky; chunky.

blond (blond) *adj.* A golden or flaxen color. **blondish** *adj.*

blonde (blond) *adj.* A woman or girl with blond hair.

blood (blud) *n.* The red fluid circulated by

the heart throughout the body that carries oxygen and nutrients to all parts of the body.

blood bank *n*. A place where blood is processed, typed, and stored for future needs.

blood bath *n*. A massacre.

blood cell *n*. A basic, structural unit of the blood.

blood count *n*. The determination of the number of white and red corpuscles in a specific amount of blood.

blood-curd-ling(blud´kerd˝ling) *adj*. Terrifying; horrifying.

blood group *n*. One of several classifications into which human blood can be divided, definded as A, B, and O.

blood-hound (blud´hound˝) *n*. A breed of dogs with a very keen sense of smell, used to tract animals and humans.

blood-let-ting (blud´let˝ing) *n*. The act of bleeding a vein as part of medical therapy.

blood-line (blud līn) *n*. The pedigree of animals.

blood poisoning *n*. The invasion of the blood by a toxin produced by bacteria,also known as septicemia.

blood pressure *n*. A pressure exerted by the blood against the walls of the blood vessels; a measure of heart efficiency.

blood-red (blud´red) *adj*. Of the deep red color of blood.

blood-shed (blud´shed˝) *n*. The shedding or spilling of blood; taking of life.

blood-shot (blud´shot˝) *adj*. Redness; irritation especially of the eyes.

blood-stained (blud´stānd˝) *adj*. Stained with blood.

blood-stream (blud´strēm˝) *n*. The circulation of blood in the vascular system.

blood sugar *n*. The presence of glucose in the blood.

blood type *n*. Blood group.

blood vessel *n*. Any canal in which blood circulates, such as a vein, artery, or capillary.

blood-y (blud´ē) *adj*. Stained with blood; having the characteristics of containing blood. **bloodiness** *n*. **bloodied** *adj*.

bloom (blŏm) *v*. To bear flowers; to flourish; to have a healthy look; radiance. **blooming** *adj*.

bloom-ers (blŏ´mėrz) *n. pl*. Loose trousers that are gathered at the knee or just below.

bloop-er (blŏ´pėr) *n*. An embarrassing blunder made in public; in baseball, a high pitch lobbed to the batter.

blos-som (blos´om) *n*. A flower or a group of flowers of a plant that bears fruit. *v*. To flourish; to grow; to develop. **blossomy** *adj*.

blot (blot) *n*. A spot or stain. *v*. To dry with an absorbent material.

blotch (bloch) *n*. An area of a person's skin that is discolored; inflamed. **blotch** *adj*. **blotchily** *adj*.

blot out *v*. To obliterate or obscure; to make unimportant.

blot-ter (blot´ėr) *n*. A piece of paper used to blot ink; a book for temporary entries.

blotting paper *n*. A porous paper used to absorb excess ink.

blouse (blous) *n*. A loosely fitting shirt or top.

blow (blō) *v*. To move or be in motion because of a current of air. *n*. A sudden hit with a hand or fist. **blower** *n*.

blow–by–blow *adj*. Minutely detailed in description.

blow dry *v*. To dry one's hair with a hand-held hair dryer.

blow-hole (blō´hōl˝) *n*. A hole in the ice that enables aquatic mammals to come up and breathe; the nostril of a whale and other cetaceans.

blow-out(blō´out˝) *n*. The sudden deflation of a tire that occurs while driving.

blow-pipe (blō´pīp˝) *n*. A long metal tube used by a glass blower in order to form shapes made from glass.

blow-torch (blō´torch˝) *n*. A hand-held tool that generates a flame hot enough to melt soft metals.

blow-up (blō´up˝) *n*. An explosion of a violent temper, a disagreement; an enlarged picture or photograph.

blow up *v*. Inflate the truth.

BLT *abbr.* Bacon, lettuce and tomato sandwich often served with mayonnaise.

blub-ber (blub′ėr) *n.* The fat removed from whales and other marine mammals from which oil comes from. **blubbery** *adj.*

blub-ber-y (blub′a rē) *adj.* Abounding in or resembling blubber.

bludg-eon (bluj′an) *n.* A stick with a loaded end used as a weapon.

blue (blō) *n.* A color the same as the color of a clear sky; the hue that is between violet and green; the color worn by the Union Army during the Civil War.

blue baby *n.* An infant with a bluish colored skin, caused by inadequate oxygen in the blood.

blue-bird (blō′berd″) *n.* A small North American songbird related to the robin.

blue blood *n.* A member of a socially prominent family.

blue law *n.* A law regulating work, commerce, etc. on Sundays.

blue—pen-cil (blō′pen′sal) *v.* To correct or edit something before it is printed.

blue cat *n.* A large bluish catfish of the Mississippi valley.

blue cheese *n.* A cheese ripened by veins of greenish blue mold.

blue crab *n.* A large edible blue crab found in the Atlantic and Gulf coasts.

blue-fish (blō′fish″) *n.* A game fish of the tropical waters of the Atlantic and Indian Oceans.

blue-gill (blō′gil″) *n.* A sunfish found in the eastern and central sections of the United States, sought for both eating and sport fishing.

blue-grass (blō′gras″) *n.* Folk music of the southern United States, played on guitars and banjos.

blue jay *n.* A bird having mostly blue colored feathers.

blue-nose (blō′nōz″) *n.* A person who advocates a rigorous moral code.

blue-print (blō′print″) *n.* A reproduction of technical drawings or plans, using white lines on a blue background.

blue ribbon *n.* The award given for placing first in a contest.

blues (blōz) *n. pl.* A style of jazz from African-American songs; a state of depression.

blue spruce *n.* An evergreen tree from the Rocky Mountains.

bluff (bluf) *v.* To deceive or mislead; to intimidate by showing more confidence than the facts can support. *n.* A steep and ridged cliff. **bluffly** *adv.* **bluffness** *n.*

blun-der (blun′dėr) *n.* An error or mistake caused by ignorance. *v.* To move clumsily. **blunderer** *n.* **blundering** *v.*

blunt (blunt) *adj.* Frank and abrupt; a dull end or edge. **bluntly** *adv.*

blur (bler) *v.* To smudge or smear; to become hazy. **blurringly** *adv.*

blurt (blert) *v.* To speak impulsively.

blush (blush) *v.* To be embarrassed from modesty or humiliation and to turn red in the face; to feel ashamed. *n.* Make-up used to give color to the cheekbones. **blushful** *adj.* **blushingly** *adv.*

blus-ter (blus′tėr) *n.* A violent and noisy wind in a storm. **bluster** *v.* **blusterer** *n.*

blvd *abbr.* Boulevard

bo-a (bō′a) *n.* A large nonvenomous snake of the Boidea family which coils around prey and crushes it.

boar (bōr) *n.* A male pig; wild pig.

board (bōrd) *n.* A flat piece of sawed lumber; a flat area on which games are played. *v.* To receive lodging, meals or both, usually for pay; to enter a ship, train, or plane. **boarder** *n.* **board-like** *adj.*

board-er (bōrd er) *n.* A person who lives in someone's house and is provided food as well as lodging.

board game *n.* A game played by moving pieces or objects on a board.

board-ing-house (bōrding haus) *n.* A house in which meals and lodging are provided.

board-walk (bōrd′wok″) *n.* A wooden walkway along a beach.

boast (bōst) v. To brag about one's own accomplishments. **boaster, boastfulness** n. **boastful** adj. **boastfully** adv.

boat (bōt) n. A small open craft or ship.

bo-tel (bō tel´) n. A hotel having docks to accommodate people traveling by boat.

boat-er (bō´tėr) n. A straw hat.

boat-house (bōt´hous˝) n .A house or shed for storing or sheltering boats.

boat-man (bōt´man) n. A man who works on boats.

boat-swain (bō´san) n. Warrant or petty officer in charge of the rigging, cables, anchors, and crew of a ship.

bob (bob) v. To cause to move up and down in a quick, jerky movement.

bob-bin (bob´in) n. A spool that holds thread in a sewing machine.

bob-by (bob´ē) n. An English police officer.

bobby socks n. pl. An ankle sock, usually worn by teenaged girls.

bob-cat (bob´kat˝) n. A wildcat of North America, with reddish-brown fur, small ears, and a short tail.

bo-beche (bō besh´) n. A glass collar on a candlestick to catch the wax drippings from the candle.

bob-o-link (bob´a lingk˝) n. An American song bird, the male has black, yellowish, and white feathers.

bob-sled (bob´sled˝) n. Racing sled which has steering controls on the front runners. **bobsled** v. **bobsledder** n.

bob-white (bob´hwīt˝) n. A game bird of the eastern United States; the common North American quail.

bo-cac-cio (bō kä´chō) n. A large rockfish found primarily off the Pacific coast.

bock (bäk) n. A dark rich beer of Germany.

bode (bōd) v. To foretell by omen or sign.

bo-de-ga (bō dā´ ga) n. A wineshop and grocery store.

bod-ice (bod´is) n. The piece of a dress that extends from the shoulder to the waist. A woman's laced outer garment covering the waist and bust.

bod-ied (bod´ēd) adj. Having a body.

bod-i-less (bod´ē lis) adj. Having no body or material form.

bod-kin (bod´kin) n. A small instrument with a sharp point for making holes in fabric or leather goods.

bod-y (bod´ē) n. The main part of something; the physical part of a person; a human being. **bodily** adv.

body building n. The development and toning of the body through diet and exercise.

bod-y-guard (bod´ē gärd˝) n. A person hired to protect another person.

body stocking n. A sheer one-piece garment for the torso.

body-surf (bod´ē serf) v. To ride on a wave without a surfboard. **bodysurfer** n.

bog (bog) n. A poorly drained, spongy area.

bo-gey (bō´gē) n. In golf, one stroke over par for a hole. **bogeyed** v.

bo-gey-man (bō´gē man) n. An imaginary figure used in threatening children.

bog-gle (bog´l) v. To pull away from with astonishment. **boggle** n.

bo-gus (bō´gas) adj. Something that is counterfeit; worthless in value.

bo-hea (bō hē´) n. A black tea from China.

boil (boil) v. To raise the temperature of water or other liquid until it bubbles; to evaporate; reduce in size by boiling. n. A very painful, pus-filled swollen area of the skin caused by bacteria in the skin.

boil-er (boil´ėr) n. A vessel that contains water and is heated for power.

bois-ter-ous (boi´stėr us) adj. Violent, rough and stormy; undisciplined. **boisterously** adv. **boisterousness** n.

bo-la (bō´la) n. A weapon with two or more stones or balls at the end of a cord, which is hurled in the air to entangle an animal.

bold (bōld) adj. Courageous; showing courage; distinct and clear; conspicuous; confident. **boldly** adv. **boldness** n.

bold-face (bōld´fās˝) n. A style of printing type with heavy thick lines.

bole (bōl) n. A tree trunk.

bo-le-ro (ba lâr´o) n. A short jacket without sleeves, worn open in the front.

boll (bōl) n. A rounded capsule that contains seeds, as from the cotton plant.

bol-lard (bōl erd) *n.* A post of wood on a wharf to fasten mooring lines.

boll weevil *n.* A small beetle whose larvae damage cotton bolls.

bo-lo-gna (ba lō'nē) *n.* A seasoned, smoked sausage.

bolo tie *n.* A tie made of cord and fastened with an ornamental clasp.

bol-ster (bōl'stèr) *n.* A long, round pillow.

bolt (bōlt) *n.* A threaded metal pin designed with a head at one end and a removable nut at the other; a thunderbolt; a quick flash of lightning; a large roll of material. *v.* To run or move suddenly.

bolt-er *n.* One who bolts.

bomb (bom) *n.* A weapon that is detonated upon impact releasing destructive material as gas or smoke. *Slang* A complete and total failure.

bom-bard (bom bärd') *v.* To attack repeatedly with missiles or bombs. **bombarder** *n.* **bombardment** *n.*

bom-bar-dier (bom˝bèr dēr') *n.* A crew member who releases the bombs from a military aircraft.

bom-bast (bom'bast) *n.* Very ornate speech. **bombastic** *adj.* **bombastically** *adv.*

bom-ba-zine (bom˝ba zēn') *n.* Silk or cotton fabric woven with diagonal ribbing.

bombe (bom) *n.* A frozen dessert with one mixture molded and filled with another.

bombed *adj., Slang* Drunk.

bomb-er (bom'èr) *n.* A military aircraft that carries and drops bombs.

bona fide *adj.* Performed in good faith; genuine; authentic.

bo-nan-za (ba nan'za) *n.* A profitable pocket or vein of ore; great prosperity.

bon-bon (bon'bon˝) *n.* Chocolate or fondant candy with a creamy, fruity, or nutty center.

bond (bond) *n.* Something that fastens or binds together; a duty or binding agreement; an insurance agreement in which the agency guarantees to pay the employer in the event an employee is accused of causing financial loss. **bonded** *adj.*

bond-age (bon'dij) *n.* Slavery; servitude,

restraint of a person's freedom.

bond-ed *adj.* Secured by a bond to insure safe guard money or goods.

bond-er-ize (bän'de rīz˝) *v.* To coat with a solution for protection against corrosion.

bond paper *n.* A superior grade of paper used for stationery goods.

bond servant *n.* One who agrees to work without pay.

bonds-man (bondz'man) *n.* One who agrees to provide bond for someone else.

bone (bōn) *n.* The calcified connecting tissue of the skeleton. **bone** *v.*

bone–dry (bōn dīr) *adj.* Completely without water.

bone-head (bön'hed˝) *n., Slang* A stupid person. **boneheaded** *adj.*

bon-er (bō'nèr) *n., Slang* A mistake or blunder.

bon-fire (bon'fī˝er) *n.* An open outdoor fire.

bon-go (bong'gō) *n.* A pair of small drums played with the hands.

bon-i-face (bon'a fās˝) *n.* The proprietor of an hotel, inn, etc.

bo-ni-to (ba nē'tō) *n.* A game fish related to the tuna.

bon-kers (bän kerz) *adj., Slang* Acting in a crazy fashion.

bon-net (bon'it) *n.* A woman's hat that ties under the chin.

bon-ny (bon'ē) *adj.* Attractive or pleasing; pretty.

bon-sai (bōn'si) *n.* A small ornamental shrub grown in a shallow pot.

bon ton *n.* High style or fashion.

bo-nus (bō'nas) *n. pl.* **bonuses** Something that is given over and above what is expected.

bon vivant *n.* One who lives well or luxuriously.

bon voyage *n.* A farewell wish for a traveler to have a pleasant and safe journey.

bon-y (bō'nē) *adj.* Pertaining to, consisting

of, or resembling bone.

boo (bŏ) *n.* Verbal expression showing disapproval or contempt.

boo–boo (bŏ bŏ) *n., Slang* A mistake, blunder, or minor injury.

boo-by (bŏ´bē) *n.* A small fish-eating seabird found in the tropical seas.

booby prize *n.* A prize given for the worst performance.

booby hatch *n., Slang* An insane asylum.

boog-ie (bŭg´ē) *v., Slang* To dance, especially to rock and roll music.

boo-hoo *interj & n.* A word imitating the sound of noisy weeping.

book (bŭk) *n.* A group of pages fastened along the left side and bound between a protective cover; literary work that is written or printed. **Book** The Bible.

book-store (bŭk´stōr) *n.* A place of business that sells reading material, especially books.

book-bind-ing (bŭk´bīn˝ding) *n.* The act or trade of binding books.

book-case (bŭk´kās˝) *n.* A piece of furniture with shelving for storing books.

book-ing (bŭk´ing) *n.* A scheduled engagement.

book-keep-er (bŭk´kē˝pėr) *n.* A person who keeps accounts and records business.

book-keep-ing (bŭk´kē˝ping) *n.* The business of recording the accounts and transactions of a business. **bookkeeper** *n.*

book-let (bŭk´lit) *n.* A small book.

book-man (bŭk´man) *n.* A person interested or versed in books.

book-mark (bŭk´mark˝) *n.* Something inserted in a book to mark where to begin.

book-re-port (bŭk´rē pōrt´) *n.* A written or oral review of a book, given after reading the book.

book-match (bŭk´mach˝) *v.* To match a design.

book of account *n.* A book or records used for recording business transactions.

book review *n.* A critical review of a book that is usually written.

book seller *n.* A person who specializes in selling books.

book shelf *n.* An open shelf area used to display and store books.

book-stall (bŭk´sal˝) *n.* A counter or stand where second-hand books are sold.

book value *n.* The value of something as shown in books of the same business.

boom (bŏm) *n.* A deep, resonant sound; a long pole extending to the top of a derrick giving support to guide lifted objects. *v.* To cause to flourish or grow swiftly.

boo-me-rang (bŏ´ma rang˝) *n.* A curved, flat missile that can be thrown so that it returns to the thrower. **boomerang** *v.*

boom town *n., Slang* A town with sudden prosperity or growth.

boon (bŏn) *n.* Something that is pleasant or beneficial; a blessing; favor.

boon-docks *n. pl., Slang* Back country; an out-of-the-way place.

boon-dog-gle (bŏn´dog˝al) *n.* A useless activity; a waste of time; a useless article produced with little skill.

boor (ber) *n.* A person with clumsy manners and little refinement; rude person. **boorishly** *adv.* **boorishness** *n.*

boost (bŏst) *v.* To increase; to raise or lift by pushing up from below. **boost** *n.* An increase in something.

booster cable *n.* Electric cables used to jump start a battery from another battery or power source.

boot (bŏt) *n.* A protective covering for the foot; any protective sheath or covering. *Computer Science* To load a computer with an operating system or other software.

boot-ed (bŏ´tid) *adj.* Equipped with boots, as for riding.

boot camp *n.* A military training camp for new recruits.

boo-tee (bŏ tē´) *n.* A soft, knitted sock for a baby.

booth (bŏth) *n.* A small enclosed compartment or area; display area at trade shows for displaying merchandise for sale; an area in a restaurant with a table and benches.

boot-jack (bŏt′jak″) *n.* A device shaped like a V, used to pull boots off.

boot-leg (bŏt′leg″) *v., Slang* To sell, make, or transport liquor illegally.

boot-less (bŏt′lĕs) *adj.* Without profit or advantage; useless.

booze (bōz) *n., Slang* An alcoholic drink.

bor *abbr.* Borough.

bo-ra (bōr′a) *n.* A cold wind of the Adriatic.

bo-rac-ic (bō ras′ik) *adj.* Pertaining to, or produced from borax.

bo-rax (bōr′aks) *n.* A crystalline compound used in manufacturing detergents and pharmaceuticals.

bor-der (bor′dėr) *n.* A surrounding margin or edge; a political or geographic boundary. *v.* To have the edge or boundary adjoining.

bor-der-ing (bor′dėr ing) *n.* A border or edging.

bor-der-land (bor′dėr land″) *n.* Land near or on a border; an indeterminate situation.

bor-der-line (bor′dėr līn″) *n.* A line or mark indicating a border.

bore (bōr) *v.* To make a hole through or in something using a drill; to become tired, repetitious, or dull. **boredom** *n.*

bo-re-al (bōr′ē al) *adj.* Located in or of the north.

bore-dom (bōr′dam) *n.* State of being bored.

bor-er (bōr′ėr) *n.* A tool used to bore holes.

boric acid *n.* A colorless or white mixture that is used as a preservative and as a weak antiseptic.

bor-ing (bōr′ ing) *adj.* That which is tiresome, causes boredom.

born (born) *adj.* Brought into life or being.

born–again *adj.* Having accepted Jesus Christ as one's personal savior.

bo-ron (bōr′on) *n.* A soft, brown nonmetallic element used in nuclear reactor control elements, abrasives, and flares.

bor-ough (ber′ō) *n.* A self-governing incorporated town, found in some United States cities; an incorporated British town that sends one or more representatives to Parliament.

bor-row (bor′ō) *v.* To receive money with

the intentions of returning it; to use another's idea as one's own.

borscht (borsh) *n.* Hot or cold beet soup.

bor-stal (bor′stal) *n.* An institution for delinquent boys and girls.

bort (bort) *n.* Imperfect diamond fragments used as an abrasive.

bor-zoi (bor′zoi) *n.* A breed of longhaired dogs of the greyhound family.

BOS *abbr.* Basic Operating System; the program that handles the routine functions of computer operations, such as accessing the diskdrive, displaying information on the screen, handling input and output, etc.

bosh (bosh) *n.* Foolish talk.

bos-ky (bosk′ē) *adj.* Thickly covered with trees or shrubs; related to a wooded area.

bos-om (bez′am) *n.* The female's breasts; the human chest; the heart or center of something. **bosomy** *adj.*

boss (bos) *n.* An employer or supervisor for whom one works. **boss** *v.* To command or supervise. **bossy** *adj.*

bossa nova *n.* A Brazilian dance resembling the samba.

boss-i-ness (bo′sē nes) *n.* The quality of being domineering.

boss-y (bo′sē) *adj.* Tending to be domineering.

Boston cream pie *n.* A layer cake having a filling of cream between layers.

Boston terrier *n.* A breed of small smooth-coated terriers.

bo-tan-i-cal (ba tan′i kal) *adj.* Relating to plants.

bot-a-nist (bot′a nist) *n.* A person skilled in botany.

bot-a-nize (bot′a nīz) *v.* To collect and study plants while on a field trip.

bot-a-ny (bot′a nē) *n.* The science of plants.

botch (boch) *v.* To ruin something by clumsiness; to repair clumsily. **botch** *n.* A sore; patchwork. **botcher** *n.*

both (bōth) *adj.* Two in conjunction with one another.

both-er (both′ėr) *v.* To pester, harass, or irritate; to be concerned about something.

bothersome *adj.* bothering *v.*

bot-o-pho-bi-a *n.* Fear of underground places.

bot-tle (bot´al) *n.* A receptacle, usually made of glass, with a narrow neck and a top that can be capped or corked; formula or milk that is fed to a baby.

bot-tle–nosed dolphin *n.* A stout-bodied whale having a prominent beak and dorsal fin.

bottle gourd *n.* A type of gourd.

bot-tle-fed (bot´al fed˝) *adj.* Fed from a bottle.

bot-tle-neck (bot´al nek˝) *n.* A narrow, obstructed passage, highway, road, etc.; a hindrance to progress or production.

bot-tom (bot´am) *n.* The lowest or deepest part of anything; the base; underside; the last; the land below a body of water. *Informal* The buttocks. **bottomless** *adj.* **bottomed** *adj.* **bottomer** *n.*

bot-tom-less (bot´am lis) *adj.* Extremely deep; seemingly without a bottom. **bottomlessness** *n.* **bottomlessly** *adv.*

bottom line *n.* The end result; lowest line of a financial statement, showing net loss or gain.

bot-tom-most (bot´om mīst˝) *adj.* Being at the very bottom.

bottom round *n.* A cut of beef taken above the upper leg and below the rump.

bot-u-lism (boch´a liz˝am) *n.* Food poisoning, often fatal, caused by bacteria that grows in improperly prepared food.

bou-clé (bō klā) *n.* An uneven yarn which forms loops at different intervals.

bouf-fant (bō fänt´) *adj.* Full; puffed out.

bou-gain-vil-lae-a (bō˝gan vil´ē a) *n.* A flower of the 4 o'clock family with purple or red floral flowers.

bough (bou) *n.* The large branch of a tree.

bou-gie (bō´jē) *n.* A candle.

bouil-la-baisse (bōl˝ya bās´) *n.* A fish stew using at least 2 kinds of fish which is highly seasoned.

bouil-lon (bel´yon) *n.* A clear broth made from meat.

bouillon cube *n.* A compressed cube of seasoned meat extract.

boul-der (bōl´der) *n.* A large round rock. **bouldered, bouldery** *adj.*

boul-e-vard (bül´a värd) *n.* A broad city street lined with trees.

bou-le-ver-se-ment (bü laver semänt) *n.* Violent disorder.

bounce (bouns) *v.* To rebound or cause to rebound; to leap or spring suddenly; to be returned by a bank as being worthless or having no value. **bounced** *v.*

bounce-a-ble (bouns´abl) *adj.* That which may bounce.

bounce back *v.* To recover rapidly from shock, illness or defeat.

bounc-er (boun´ser) *n.* A person who removes disorderly people from a public place.

bounc-ing (boun´sing) *adj.* Healthy; vigorous; robust; lively and spirited.

bound (bound) *n.* A leap or bounce. *v.* To limit; to be tied.

bound-a-ry (boun´da rē) *n. pl.* **boundaries** A limit or border.

bound-en (boun´dan) *adj.* Under an obligation or agreement.

bound-er (boun´der) *n.* A vulgar person.

bound-less (bound´lis) *adj.* Without limits. **boundlessly** *adv.* **boundlessness** *n.*

boun-te-ous (boun´tē as) *adj.* Plentiful or generous; giving freely. **bounteously** *adv.* **bounteousness** *n.*

boun-ti-ful (boun´ti fal) *adj.* Abundant; plentiful. **bountifully** *adv.*

bounty (boun´tē) *n.* Generosity; an inducement or reward given for the return of something; a good harvest.

bounty hunter *n.* A person who hunts and captures outlaws when a reward is offered.

bou-quet (bō kā´) *n.* A group of cut flowers; the aroma of wine.

bour-bon (ber´bon) *n.* Whiskey distilled from fermented corn mash.

bour-geois (ber´zhwä) *n. pl.* A member of the middle class. **bourgeois** *adj.*

bout (bout) *n.* A contest or match; the length of time spent in a certain way.

bou-tique (bō tēk´) *n.* A small retail shop

that sells specialized gifts, accessories, and fashionable clothes.

bou-ton-niere (böt˝o nēr´) *n.* A flower worn in the buttonhole of a man's jacket.

bou-zou-ki (bö zü kē) *n.* A long-necked stringed instrument resembling a mandolin.

bo-vine (bō´vīn) *adj.* Of or relating to an ox or cow. **bovinely** *adv.*

bow (bou) *n.* The front section of a boat or ship; bending of the head or waist to express a greeting or courtesy; a weapon made from a curved stave and strung taut to launch arrows; a rod strung with horsehair, used for playing stringed instruments.

bowd-ler-ize (bōd´la rīz˝) *v.* To expurgate. **bowdlerization** *n.*

bow-el (bou´al) *n.* The digestive tract located below the stomach; the intestines.

bow-er (bou´ėr) *n.* A shelter constructed from tree boughs; an anchor.

bow-er-bird (bou´ėr bėrd) *n.* A bird from the Australian region of which the male builds a passage with twigs and branches to attract the female.

bow-er-y (bou´a rē) *n.* A district in New York City.

bowie knife *n.* A single-edged thick-bladed hunting knife.

bowl (bōl) *n.* A hemispherical container for food or liquids; a bowl-shaped part, as of a spoon or ladle; a bowl-shaped stadium. *v.* To participate in the game of bowling. **bowled** *adj.* **bowlful** *n.*

bow-leg (bō´leg˝) *n.* An outward curvature of the leg at the knee.

bowl-er (bō´ler) *n.* A person that bowls.

bow-line (bō´lin) *n.* A rope to keep the edge of a square sail taut.

bowl-ing (bō´ling) *n.* A game in which a person rolls a ball down a wooden alley in order to knock down a triangular group of ten wooden bowling pins.

bowling alley *n.* A building containing alleys or lanes for the game of bowling.

bowl over *v.* To astound; to be astounded.

bow-man (bou´man) *n.* An oarsman in the front of a boat.

bow saw (bō´so˝) *n.* A saw with a narrow blade in a bow-shaped frame.

bow-sprit (bou´sprit) *n.* A spar that projects forward from the stem of a ship.

bow tie *n.* A short necktie tied with a bow at the collar.

bow window *n.* A rounded bay window.

box (boks) *n.* A small container or chest, usually with a lid; a special area in a theater that holds a small group of people; a shrub or evergreen with leaves and hard wood that is yellow in color. *v.* To fight with the fists.

box-car (boks´kär˝) *n.* An enclosed railway car used for the transportation of freight.

box elder *n.* A North American maple.

box-er (bok´sėr) *n.* A person who boxes professionally; a German breed of dog with short hair, brownish coat, and a square nose or muzzle.

box-ing (bok´sing) *n.* A sport in which two opponents hit each other using padded gloves on their hands, forming fists.

boxing glove *n.* A pair of leather gloves heavily padded on the back used in the sport of boxing.

box kite *n.* A tailless kite with open-ended boxes at each end.

box office *n.* An office where theatre tickets are purchased.

box social *n.* An affair at which box lunches are auctioned off to raise money.

box spring *n.* A cloth-covered frame which supports the mattress.

box turtle *n.* A North American land tortoise.

box-wood (boks´wed) *n.* A plant with very heavy tough hard wood.

boy (boi) *n.* A male youth or child. **boyhood** *n.* **boyish** *adj.* **boyishly** *adv.*

boy-cott (boi´kot) *v.* To abstain from dealing with, buying, or using as a means of protest.

boy friend *n.* A male companion.

Boy Scout *n.* A boy who belongs to a worldwide organization that emphasizes citizenship training and character development.

boy-sen-ber-ry (boi´zan ber˝ē) *n.* A trailing hybrid which bears fruit developed by crossing blackberries and raspberries.

bra (brä) *n.* Brassiere.

brace (brās) *n.* A device that supports or steadies something. **brace** *v.*

brace-let (brās´lit) *n.* An ornamental band for the wrist.

brac-er (brā´sér) *n.* A person who or that which braces; a tonic or stimulating drink.

bra-ce-ro (brä´serō) *n.* A Mexican laborer.

brack-en (brak´an) *n.* A large species of fern with tough stems and finely divided fronds.

brack-et (brak´it) *n.* A support attached to a vertical surface that projects in order to hold a shelf or other weight. *v.* To enclose a word in brackets ( ).

brack-ish (brak´ish) *adj.* Containing salt; distasteful. **brackishness** *n.*

bract (brakt) *n.* A leaf-like plant below a flower cluster or flower. **bracteate, bracteal, bracted, bracteolate** *adj.*

brad (brad) *n.* A nail that tapers to a small head. **bradding** *v.*

brad-awl (brad´ol) *n.* A tool used to make holes for brads or screws.

brag (brag) *v.* To assert or talk boastfully. **bragger** *n.* **braggy** *adj.*

brag-ga-do-ci-o (brag˝ a dō´shēō˝) *n. pl.* A cockiness or arrogant manner; empty bragging.

brag-gart (brag´art) *n.* A person who brags.

braid (brād) *v.* To interweave three or more strands of something; to plait. **braider, braiding** *n.* **braided** *adj.*

braille (brāl) *n.* A system of printing for the blind, consisting of six dots, two across and four directly under the first two. Numbers and letters are represented by raising certain dots in each group of six.

brain (brān) *n.* The large mass of nerve tissue enclosed in the cranium, responsible for the interpretation of sensory impulses, control of the body, and coordination; the center of thought and emotion in the body. **braininess** *n* **brainlessness** *n.* **brainy** *adj.*

brain case *n.* The bony cranium or skull that surrounds the brain.

brain child *n.* A product of one's imagination.

brain-less (brān´les) *adj.* Without good judgement; silly; stupid.

brain-pan (brān´pan˝) *n.* The cranium.

brain-sick (brān´sik˝) *adj.* Mental disordered; Crazy; deranged.

brain-wash (brān´wosh˝) *v.* To subject someone to the techniques of brainwashing.

brain-y (brā´nē) *adj.* Provided with brains.

braise (brāz) *v.* To cook by first browning in a small amount of fat, adding a liquid such as water, and then simmering in a covered container. **braising** *v.*

brake (brāk) *n.* A device designed to stop or slow the motion of a vehicle or machine. **brake** *v.* **brakeless** *n.*

brake fluid *n.* The liquid contained in hydraulic brake cylinders.

brake-man (brāk´man) *n.* A train crew member who assists the conductor; the man who operates the brake on a bobsled.

bram-ble (bram´bl) *n.* A prickly shrub or plant such as the raspberry or blackberry bush.

bran (bran) *n.* The husk of cereal grains that is separated from the flour.

branch (branch) *n.* An extension from the main trunk of a tree. **branch** *v.* To divide into different subdivisions.

branch office *n.* Another office of the same business or industry.

brand (brand) *n.* A trademark or label that names a product; a mark of disgrace or shame; a piece of charred or burning wood; a mark made by a hot iron to show ownership. **brander** *n.*

brand–new (brand´nō´) *adj.* Unused and new.

bran-dish (bran´dish) *v.* To wave or flourish a weapon.

brand-ling (brand´ling) *n.* A small earthworm.

brand name *n.* A company's trademark.

bran-dy (bran´dē) *n. pl.* **brandies** An alcoholic drink made from fermented fruit juices or wine. **brandied** *adj.* **brandy** *v.*

brant (brant) *n.* A wild goose which breeds in the Arctic but migrates southward.

brash (brash) *adj.* Hasty, rash, and unthinking; insolent; impudent.

brass (bras) *n.* An alloy of zinc, copper and other metals in lesser amounts. *Slang.* A high-ranking officer in the military.

bras-sard (bras´ärd) *n.* A piece of armor to protect the arm.

brass band *n.* A band with brass and percussion instruments only.

brass-bound (bras´bound˝) *adj.* Having a border made of brass or a similar metal.

bras-siere (bra zēr´) *n.* A woman's undergarment with cups to support the breasts.

brass tacks *n. pl.* The details of immediate, practical importance.

brass-y (bras´ē) *adj.* Of or like brass; brazen or impudent.

brat (brat) *n.* An ill-mannered child.

brat-wurst (brat werst) *n.* A fresh pork sausage.

bra-va-do (bra vä´dō) *n.* A false showing of bravery.

brave (brāv) *adj.* Having or displaying courage. *n.* An American Indian warrior **brave** *v.*

brav-er-y (brā´va rē) *n.* The quality of or state of being brave.

bra-vo (brā´vō) *Interj.* Expressing approval.

bra-vu-ra (brä vō´ra) *n.* A musical passage which takes technical skill.

brawl (brol) *n.* A noisy argument or fight. **brawl** *v.* **brawler** *n.*

brawn (brän) *n.* Well-developed and solid muscles. **brawniness** *n.*

brawn-y (brän ē) *adj.* Having large strong muscles; strong.

bray (brā) *v.* To make a loud cry like a donkey.

braze (brāz) *v.* To solder using a nonferrous alloy that melts at a lower temperature than that of the metals being joined together.

bra-zen (brā´zan) *adj.* Made of brass; shameless or impudent.

bra-zier (brā´zhėr) *n.* A person who works

with brass; a metal pan that holds burning charcoal or coals.

breach (brēch) *n.* Ruptured, broken, or torn condition or area; a break in friendly relations. *v.* To break the law or obligation.

breach of promise *n.* The violation of a promise.

bread (bred) *n.* A leavened food made from a flour or meal mixture and baked. *Slang* Money. **bread** *v.* To cover with bread crumbs before cooking.

bread and butter *adj.* Being the basis of one's livelihood.

bread-fruit (bred´frōt˝) *n.* A tropical tree with lobed leaves and edible fruit.

bread-stuff (bred´stuf˝) *n.* Bread; a cereal product; meal, grain, or flour.

breadth (bredth) *n.* The distance or measurement from side to side; width.

bread-win-ner (bred´win˝ėr) *n.* The one whose pay supports a household.

break (brāk) *v.* To separate into parts with violence or suddenness; to collapse or give way; to change suddenly. *Informal* A stroke of good luck.

break-age (brā´kij) *n.* Things that are broken.

break-a-way (brāk´ a wā˝) *n.* A breaking away; a start, as of competitors in a contest.

break-down (brāk´doun˝) *n.* Failure to function; a mental or nervous collapse.

breaker (brā´kėr) *n.* A wave that breaks into foam.

break-fast (brek´fost) *n.* The first meal of the day.

break in *v.* To enter using force; to intrude upon a conversation.

breaking point *n.* The point of stress at which a material or a person gives away.

break-out (brāk´out˝) *n.* A forceful breaking from restraint, sometimes an escape.

break-up *n.* A disruption; a dissolution of connection.

breast (brest) *n.* The milk-producing glandular organs on a woman's chest; the area of the body from the neck to the abdomen.

breast-bone (brest´bōn˝) *n.* The sternum.

breast-plate (brest′plāt″) *n.* A metal plate worn on the chest for protection; the underside of a turtle.

breast wall *n.* A retaining wall.

breath (breth) *n.* The air inhaled and exhaled in breathing; a very slight whisper, fragrance or breeze.

breathe (brēth) *v.* To draw air into and expel from the lungs; to take a short rest.

breath-er (brē′thėr) *n.* A small opening in an otherwise airtight enclosure; one that breathes.

breath-ing (brē′thing) *n.* The act of one that breathes; respiration.

breath-less (breth′lis) *adj.* Gasping for breath; out of breath. **breathlessly** *adv.* **breathlessness** *n.*

breath-tak-ing (breth′tā″king) *adj.* Astonishing; awesome. **breathtakingly** *adv.*

breech (brēch) *n. pl.* **-es** The buttocks; the hind end of the body; the part of a gun or firearm located at the rear of the bore. *pl.* Trousers that fit tightly around the knees.

breech delivery *n.* Delivery of a fetus when the buttocks, or the feet appear first in the birth canal.

breeches buoy *n.* A canvas seat used to haul persons from one ship to another or in rescue operatons from ship to shore.

breech-load-er (brēch′lō″dėr) *n.* A cannon or smaller firearm loaded from the back instead of the muzzle.

breed (brēd) *v.* The genetic strain of domestic animals, developed and maintained by mankind. **breeding** *n.*

breeze (brēz) *n.* A slight gentle wind; something that is accomplished with very little effort.

breezy *adj.* Brisk, cool.

breez-i-ness (brē′zē nes) *n.* The state of abounding with a breeze.

Bre-ton (bret′on) *n.* A native of Brittany.

breve (brēv) *n.* The curved mark over a vowel to indicate a short or unstressed syllable

bre-vet (bra vet′) *n.* A commission given a military officer with a higher rank than which he is being paid for.

bre-vi-ar-y (brē′vē er″ē) *n.* A book that contains prayers and psalms for the canonical hours.

brev-i-pen-nate (brev″e pen′āt) *adj.* Having short wings.

brev-i-ros-trate (bre″e ros′trāt) *adj.* Having a short bill or beak.

brev-i-ty (brev′i tē) *n. pl.* **brevities** Of brief duration; conciseness.

brew (brō) *v.* To make beer from malt and hops by boiling, infusion, and fermentation.

brewer *n.* A person whose occupation is to brew malt liquors.

brew-age (brō′ij) *n.* Fermented beverage.

brew-er-y (brō′a rē) *n.* A building or plant where beer or ale is brewed.

brew-ing (brō′ing) *n.* The process of making ale, or other fermented liquor.

bri-ard (brē är′) *n.* A breed of large strong black dogs of France.

brib-a-ble (brīb′a bl) *adj.* Capable of being bribed.

bribe (brīb) *v.* To influence or induce by giving a token or anything of value for a service. **bribe** *n.* **bribable** *adj.*

brib-er-y (brī′ba rē) *n.* The practice of giving or receiving a bribe.

bric-a–brac (brik′a brak″) *n.* A collection of small objects.

brick (brik) *n.* A molded block of baked clay, usually rectangular in shape.

brick-bat (brik′bat″) *n.* A piece of a brick used as a weapon when thrown as a missile.

brick-kiln (brik′kil″) *n.* A furnance in which bricks are baked at a high temperature.

brick-lay-er (brik′lā″ėr) *n.* A person who lays bricks as a profession.

brick red *n.* A yellowish or brownish red.

bri-dal (brīd′al) *adj.* Relating to a bride or a nuptial ceremony.

bridal wreath *n.* A flower grown for its small white flowers used in bouquets.

bride (brīd) *n.* A women just married or about to be married.

bride-groom (brīd′grōm″) *n.* A man just

married or about to be married.

brides-maid (brīdz'mād") *n.* A woman who attends a bride at her wedding.

bridge (brij) *n.* A structure that provides passage over a depression or obstacle; a card game for four players.

bridge-head (brij'hed") *n.* A military position secured by advance troops in enemy territory, giving protection for the main attack force.

bridge-work (brij'werk") *n.* The construction of dental work.

bri-dle (brīd'al) *n.* A harness used to restrain or guide a horse. *v.* To restrain or control. **bridler** *n.* **bridling** *v.*

bridle path *n.* A path or road used only for riding horseback.

Brie cheese *n.* A soft, salted, white cream cheese using bacteria or mold for ripening.

brief (brēf) *n.* A concise, formal statement of a client's case. *adj.* Short in duration. *v.* To summarize or inform in a short statement. **briefly** *adv.* **briefness** *n.*

brief case *n.* A small, flat, flexible case for holding and carrying papers or books.

brief-ing (brē'fing) *n.* The act of giving essential information.

brief-less (brēf'lis) *adj.* Having no legal clients.

brief-ly (brēf'lē) *adv.* In a brief way or short span of time.

bri-er (brī'ér) *n.* A woody, thorny, or prickly plant. **briery** *adj.*

bri-er-root (brī'ér rüt) *n.* A root which is used to make tobacco pipes.

brig (brig) *n.* A prison on a ship; a twin-masted, square-rigged sailing ship.

bri-gade (bri gād') *n.* A military unit organized for a specific purpose.

brig-a-dier (brig"a dēr') *n.* An officer in the British army.

brigadier general *n.* A commissioned officer in the armed forces who ranks above a colonel.

brig-and (brig'and) *n.* A person who lives as a robber; bandit.

brig-an-dine (brig'an dēn") *n.* A medieval body armor.

brig-an-tine (brig'an tēn") *n.* A square-rigged two-masted ship.

bright (brīt) *adj.* Brilliant in color; vivid; shining and emitting or reflecting light; happy; cheerful; lovely. **brightness** *n.*

bright-en (brīt'n) *v.* To make things brighter. **brightener** *n.* **brightened** *v.*

bril-liant (bril'yant) *adj.* Very bright and shiny; sparkling; radiant; extraordinarily intelligent; showing cleverness. **brilliantly** *adv.* **brilliantness** *adv.*

bril-lian-tine (bril'yan tēn") *n.* A light woven fabric similar to alpaca.

brim (brim) *n.* The edge or rim of a cup. **brimmed** *v.* **brimless** *adj.*

brim-ful (brim'fel) *adj.* Completely full.

brim-mer (brim'ėr) *n.* A cup or other container that is full to the top.

brim-stone (brim'stōn") *n.* Sulfur.

brin-dle (brin'dl) *adj.* Having dark streaks or flecks on a gray or tawny background.

brine (brīn) *n.* Water saturated with salt; the water contained in the oceans and seas.

bring (bring) *v.* To carry with oneself to a certain place; to cause, act, or move in a special direction.

bring about *v.* To effect; to accomplish; to cause to happen.

bring down *v.* To cause to come down; to lower; to humiliate.

bring forth *v.* To produce, as young or fruit; to beget; to cause.

bring forward *v.* To present for consideration.

bring in *v.* To introduce; to supply.

bring out *v.* To emphasize; to reveal; to publish.

bring to light *v.* To reveal.

bring to mind *v.* To recall what has been forgotten or out of thought.

bring to pass *v.* To effect; to cause to happen.

brink (bringk) *n.* The upper edge or margin of a very steep slope.

bri-oche (brē'ōsh) *n.* A roll made from flour, eggs, butter, and yeast.

bri-o-lette (brē"a let') *n.* A pear-shaped diamond cut into facets.

bri-quette (bri ket´) *n.* A small brick-shaped piece of charcoal.

brisk (brisk) *adj.* Moving or acting quickly; being sharp in tone or manner; energetic, invigorating or fresh, pertaining to weather. **briskly** *adv.* **briskness** *n.*

bris-ket (bris´kit) *n.* The meat from the lower chest or breast of an animal.

bris-ling (bris´ling) *n.* A small fish that is processed like a sardine.

bris-tle (bris´al) *n.* Short, stiff, coarse hair. *v.* To react in angry defiance and manner. **bristly** *adj.*

britch-es (brich´iz) *n. pl.* Trousers.

brit-tle (brit´l) *adj.* Very easy to break; fragile. **brittleness** *n.*

bro *abbr.* Brother.

broach (brōch) *n.* A tapered and serrated tool used for enlarging and shaping a hole. **broach** *v.*

broad (brod) *adj.* Covering a wide area; from side to side; clear; bright. **broadly** *adv.* **broadness** *n.*

broad arrow *n.* A barbed arrow head.

broad-brim (brod´brim˝) *n.* A hat having a broad brim.

broad-cast (brod´kast˝) *v.* To transmit a program by television; to make widely known. **broadcaster** *n.*

broad-cloth (brod´kloth˝) *n.* A textured woolen cloth with a lustrous finish.

broad-en (brod´n) *v.* To become or make broad or broader.

broad gauge *n.* A railroad gauge that is wider than the standard gauge of 56 1/2 inches.

broad jump *n.* A jump for distance either from a stationary position or with a running start.

broad-loom (brod´lōm˝) *adj.* Woven on a wide loom. *n.* Carpet woven in this manner.

broad-mind-ed (brod´mīn´did) *adj.* Tolerant of varied views; liberal. **broadmindedness** *n.*

broad-side (brod´sīd˝) *n.* The side of a ship that is above the water line; a sheet of paper printed on both sides and then folded.

broad-sword (brod ´sōrd˝) *n.* A sword having a broad, flat cutting blade.

Broad-way (brod´wā˝) *n.* The New York theatre district; a famous street in New York.

bro-cade (brō kād´) *n.* A silk fabric with raised patterns in silver and gold.

broc-co-li (brok´a lē) *n.* A green vegetable from the cauliflower family, eaten before the small buds open.

bro-chette (brō shet´) *n.* A skewer used in cooking.

bro-chure (brō sher´) *n.* A booklet or pamphlet.

brock-et (brok´it) *n.* A small deer of South America.

bro-gan (brō´gan) *n.* A sturdy oxford shoe.

brogue (brōg) *n.* A strong regional accent; a heavy shoe with a hobnail sole.

broil (broil) *v.* To cook by exposure to direct radiant heat.

broil-er (broi´lèr) *n.* A device, usually a part of a stove, that is used for broiling meat; a young chicken.

broke (brōk) *adj.* Penniless; completely without money.

bro-ken (brō´ken) *adj.* Separated violently into parts. **brokenly** *adj.* **brokenness** *n.*

broken–down *adj.* Shattered or collapsed; ruined.

bro-ken-heart-ed (brō´ken här´tid) *adj.* Overcome by despair or grief.

broken home *n.* A family situation in which the parents are not living together.

bro-ker (brō´kèr) *n.* A person who acts as a negotiating agent for contracts, sales, or purchases in return for payment.

bro-ker-age (brō´kèr ij) *n.* The establishment of a broker.

brome-grass (brōm´gras˝) *n.* A type of tall grasses having sagging spikelets.

bro-me-li-ad (brō´mē lē ad) *n.* The family of tropical American plants including the pineapple.

bro-mide (brō´mīd) *n.* A compound of bromine with other elements; a sedative; a common place, idea or notion; one who is tiresome. **bromidic** *adj.*

bro-mine (brō´mēn) *n.* A nonmetallic element of a deep red, toxic liquid that gives off a disagreeable odor.

bro-mo (brō mō) *n.* An effervescent mixture used as a sedative or a headache remedy.

bron-chi-al (brong´kē al) *adj.* Pertaining to the bronchi or their extensions, in which air flows through to reach the lungs, the trachea. **bronchially** *adv.*

bron-chi-tis (brong kī´tis) *n.* An acute inflammation of the bronchial tubes.

bron-cho-scope (brong´ka skōp´) *n.* A tubular instrument which is illuminated for inspecting the bronchi.

bron-chus (brong´kus) *n.* Either of two main branches of the trachea that lead directly to the lungs.

bron-co (brong´kō) *n.* A wild horse of western North America.

bron-co-bust-er (brong´kō bus˝tėr) *n.* The man who breaks wild horses.

bron-to-saur (bron´ta sor˝) *n.* A very large dinosaur which grew to a height of 12 feet and a length of over 70 feet.

bronze (bronz) *n.* An alloy of tin, copper, and zinc; moderate olive brown to yellow in color. **bronze** *v.* **bronze** *adj.*

Bronze Age *n.* Human culture between the Iron Age and the Stone Age.

brooch (brōch) *n.* A large decorative pin.

brood (brŏd) *n.* The young of an animal; a family of young. *v.* To produce by incubation; to hatch; to think about at length.

brood-er (brŏd er) *n.* An enclosed heated area for raising young chickens.

brook (brek) *n.* A small freshwater stream that contains many rocks.

brook trout *n.* A cold-water fish of eastern North America.

broom (brŏm) *n.* A long-handled implement used for sweeping; a shrub with small leaves and yellow flowers.

broom-stick (brŏm´stik˝) *n.* The handle of a broom.

bros *abbr.* Brothers.

broth (broth) *n.* The liquid in which fish, meat, or vegetables have been cooked; also called stock.

broth-el (broth´l) *n.* A house of prostitution; whorehouse.

broth-er (bruth´ėr) *n.* A male who shares the same parents as another person. **brotherly** *adj.* **brotherliness** *n.*

broth-er–in–law (bruth´ėr in lo˝) *n.* The brother of one's spouse; the husband of one's sister; the husband of one's spouse's sister.

broth-er-hood (bruth´ėr hed˝) *n.* The state of being brothers; one that is related to another for a particular purpose.

broth-er-li-ness (bruth´ėr lē nes) *n.* State of being brotherly.

broth-er-ly *adj.* Characteristic of, or befitting brothers.

brough-am (brō´am) *n.* A vehicle without a cover over the driver's seat.

brought *v.* The past tense of bring.

brow (brou) *n.* The ridge above the eye where the eyebrow grows.

brow-beat (brou´bēt˝) *v.* To bully; dominate; intimidate. **browbeating** *v.*

brown (broun) *n.* A color between yellow and red; a dark or tanned complexion.

Brown Betty *n.* A pudding baked with apples, spices, and bread crumbs.

brown bread *n.* Bread made from whole wheat flour.

brown-ie (brou´nē) *n.* A good-natured elf believed to perform helpful services; a square, chewy piece of chocolate cake.

brown-out (broun´out˝) *n.* An interruption of electrical power.

brown sugar *n.* Sugar with crystals covered by a film or refined dark syrup.

Brown Swiss *n.* A breed of brown dairy cattle, originally from Switzerland.

browse (brouz) *v.* To look over something in a leisurely and casual way.

bruise (brōz) *n.* An injury that ruptures small blood vessels and discolors the skin without breaking it.

brum-by (brem bē) *n.* An unbroken horse.

brum-ma-gem (brum´a jam) *n.* Something inferior.

brunch (brunch) *n.* A combination of a

late breakfast and an early lunch.

bru-net *or* **bru-nette (brŏ net´)** *n.* A person with dark brown hair.

bru-ni-zem (brŏ˝ na zem´) *n.* A dark-colored soil found in some of the areas in the Mississippi Valley.

Brunswick stew *n.* A stew with vegetables and meats.

brunt (brunt) *n.* The principal shock, or force.

brush up *v.* To refresh one's memory or skills.

brush discharge *n.* A discharge of low-intensity electric current with dimly luminous circuit ends.

brush-wood (brush´wod˝) *n.* A thicket of densely growing bushes, shrubs, or brushes.

brush-work (brush´werk) *n.* Something that requires the use of a brush.

brush-y (brush´ē) *adj.* Overgrown with brush.

brusque (brusk) *adj.* Being blunt or short in manner or speech; harsh. **brusquely** *adv.* **brusqueness** *n.*

Brus-sels lace (brus´elz lās´) *n.* A fine bobbin or needlepoint lace with a floral dsign.

brussels sprout *n.* The small head of a green vegetable, resembling the cabbage.

bru-tal (brŏt´al) *adj.* Very harsh or cruel treatment. **brutally** *adv.*

bru-tal-i-ty (brŏ tal´i tē) *n.* A brutal course of action; ruthless or inhuman behavior.

bru-tal-ize (brŏ tal īz) *v.* To make inhuman, insensitive.

brute (brŏt) *n.* A person characterized by physical power rather than intelligence; a person who behaves like an animal, crude. **brutish** *adj.*

brux-ism (brek siz em) *n.* The unconscious grinding of the teeth during sleep.

bry-o-ny (brī´a nē) *n.* A vine of the gourd family having large leaves and fruit.

bry-o-phyte (brī´a fit˝) *n.* A species of non-flowering plant which includes the liverworts.

bub-ble (bub´l) *n.* A small round object, usually hollow; a small body of gas contained in a liquid. *v.* To produce bubbles.

bubble gum *n.* A chewing gum that can be blown into bubbles.

bub-bler (bub´lėr) *n.* A drinking fountain where water bubbles upward.

bubble top *n.* A protective, clear plastic top used on official automobiles.

bub-bly (bub blē) *adj.* Something containing or full of bubbles. *Slang* Champagne.

bu-bo (bū´bō) *n.* Inflammatory swelling of the lymphatic glands, especially in the area of the groin or armpits.

bubonic plague *n.* The contagious and normally fatal disease that is transmitted by fleas from infected rats, characterized by fever, diarrhea, chills, and vomiting.

buc-ca-neer (buk˝a nēr´) *n.* A pirate preying on Spanish ships in the West Indies in the 17th century; an unscrupulous adventurer.

buck (buk) *n.* The adult male deer; a male animal; the lowest grade in the military category. **buck** *v.* To arch the back and move so as to throw a rider; to oppose the system. *Slang* A dollar.

buck-board (buk´bōrd˝) *n.* An open carriage with four wheels and a seat attached to a flexible board.

buck-et (buk´it) *n.* A vessel used to carry liquids or solids; a pail.

bucket brigade *n.* A line of people who pass buckets of water from hand to hand in order to extinguish a fire.

bucket seat *n.* A separate seat with a rounded or molded back.

buck-eye (buk´ī) *n.* A tree with flower clusters and glossy brown nuts.

buck-hound (buk´hound˝) *n.* A dog in hunting deer and other wild animals; smaller than a staghound.

buckle (buk´l) *v.* To warp, crumple, or bend under pressure. **buckle** *n.* Metal clasp for fastening one end to another. **buckler** *n.*

buckle down *v.* To apply oneself.

buck-o (buk´ō) *n*. A person who is domineering.

buck passer *n*. One who passes blame or responsibility to someone else.

buck-ram (buk´ram) *n*. A coarse, stiff fabric that is sized with glue and used for interlinings in garments and in book bindings.

buck-shee (buk´shē) *n*. An extra portion of rations.

buck-shot (buk´shot˝) *n*. A coarse lead shot for shotgun shells.

buck-skin (buk´skin˝) *n*. A soft leather; a light colored horse; riding breeches made from buckskin. **buckskin** *adj*.

buck-tail (buk´tāl˝) *n*. A lure used by fishermen.

buck-tooth (buk´tōth˝) *n*. A large, prominently projecting front tooth.

buck-wheat (buk´hwēt˝) *n*. A plant with small edible seeds that are often ground into flour and used as a cereal grain.

bu-col-ic (bū kol´ik) *n*. A pastoral poem; someone that is rural or countrified.

bud (bud) *n*. Something that has not developed completely; a small structure that contains flowers or leaves that have not developed.

bud-dy (bud´ē) *n*. A good companion, partner, or friend.

buddy system *n*. A mutual agreement in which two people are paired for safety in hazardous situations.

budge (buj) *v*. To give way to; to cause to move slightly.

bud-ger-i-gar (buj´a rē gär˝) *n*. A small Australian parrot.

bud-get (buj´it) *n*. The total amount of money allocated for a certain purpose. **budget** *v*.

budg-et-eer (buj˝i tēr´) *n*. A person who prepares a budget for someone.

buff (buf) *n*. A leather made mostly from skins of buffalo, elk, or oxen, having the color of light to moderate yellow.

buf-fa-lo (buf´a lō) *n*. A wild ox with heavy forequarters, short horns, and a large muscular hump. *v*. To bewilder, to intimidate.

buff-er (buf´er) *n*. A tool used to polish or shine; in computer science, a part of the memory used to hold information temporarily while data transfers from one place to another. *v*. To lessen, absorb, or protect against the shock of an impact.

buffer zone *n*. A neutral separation between conflicting forces.

buffer state *n*. A smaller neutral state lying between possibly rival larger states.

buf-fet (ba fā´) *n*. A meal placed on a side table so that people may serve themselves; a side table for serving food. *v*. To strike sharply with the hand.

buffing wheel *n*. The round surface of a wheel covered with cloth used to polish or shine something.

buffle head *n*. A North American diving duck.

buf-foon (ba fŏn´) *n*. A clown; a stupid person; an uneducated person.

buff stick *n*. A small stick covered with leather or the like, used in polishing fingernails.

bug (bug) *n*. Any small insect; a concealed listening device. *v*. To bother or annoy. **bugged, bugging** *v*.

bug-a-boo (bug´a bŏ) *n*. A source of concern or fear.

bug-bane (bug´bān) *n*. An herb of the buttercup family but with white flowers.

bug-eye (beg ī) *n*. A small boat with a flat bottom.

bug-gy (bug´ē) *n*. A small carriage pulled behind a horse.

bu-gle (bū´gal) *n*. A brass instrument without keys or valves. **bugle** *v*. **bugler** *n*.

bu-gle-weed (bū´gal wēd) *n*. A genus of the mint family which is a mild narcotic.

bug-seed (bug´sēd˝) *n*. An annual herb of the goosefoot family.

buhr-stone (ber´stōn˝) *n*. A rock used to make a grinding stone.

build (bild) *v*. To erect by uniting materials into a composite whole; to fashion or create; to develop or add to. **build** *n*. The form or structure of a person.

build-er (bil′dėr) *n.* A person who supervises the construction of a building project.

build-ing (bil′ding) *n.* A roofed and walled structure for permanent use.

build-up (bild′up″) *n.* A collection of materials for a future need.

built–in (bilt′in′) *adj.* Containing something within a structure.

bulb (bulb) *n.* A rounded underground plant such as a tulip that lies dormant in the winter and blooms in the spring; an incandescent light for electric lamps. **bulbed, bulbaceous** *adj.*

bul-bous (bul′bus) *adj.* Resembling a bulb in shape.

bul-bul (bel′bel) *n.* A songbird often mentioned in poetry.

bulge (bulj) *n.* A swelling of the surface caused by pressure from within. **bulge** *v.*

bulgy *adj.* *n.* Wheat prepared for human consumption.

bu-lim-i-a (bū lim′ēa) *n.* An eating disorder in which a person overeats and then throws up in order to remain thin.

bulk (bulk) *n.* A large mass; anything that has great size, volume, or units. **bulky** *adj.*

bulk-age (bulk āg) *n.* A substance that increases the bulk of material in the intestine, therefore stimulating peristalsis.

bulk-head (bulk′hed″) *n.* The partition that divides a ship into compartments; a retaining wall along a waterfront.

bulk-y (bül′kē) *adj.* Having great bulk; out of proportion. **bulkiness** *n.*

bul-la (bül′a) *n.* A blister or vesicle.

bull-dog (bül′dog″) *n.* A short-haired dog with a stocky build and an undershot lower jaw.

bull-doze (bül′dōz″) *v.* To move or dig up with a bulldozer. *Slang* To bully.

bull-doz-er (bül′dō″zėr) *n.* A tractor-like machine with a large metal blade in front for moving earth and rocks.

bul-let (bül′it) *n.* A cylindrical projectile that is fired from a gun.

bul-le-tin (bül′i tan) *n.* A broadcasted statement of public interest; a public notice.

bulletin board *n.* A board on which messages and notices are posted.

bullet proof *adj.* Capable of resisting the force of a bullet.

bull-fight (bül′fit″) *n.* A Spanish or Mexican spectacle in which men known as matadors engage in fighting bulls.

bull-frog (bül′frog″) *n.* A deep-voiced frog.

bull-head-ed (bül′hed′id) *adj.* Headstrong and stubborn.

bull horn *n.* A hand-held loudspeaker.

bul-lion (bül′yan) *n.* Refined gold or silver in the uncoined state.

bull-ish (bül′ish) *adj.* Tending to cause or hopeful of rising prices, as in the stock market.

bull–neck (bül′nek) *n.* A thick powerful neck like that of a bull.

bull-ock (bül′ok) *n.* A castrated bull.

bull pen *n.* The area where pitchers warm up during a baseball game.

bull session *n.* An informal group discussion.

bull's eye (bülz′ī) *n.* The center of a target.

bull-snake (bül′snāk″) *n.* A harmless snake native to North America.

bull-ter-ri-er (bül″ter′ē ėr) *n.* A breed of dog crossed between a terrier and a bulldog.

bull tongue *n.* A plow with a vertically placed blade, used in the cultivation of cotton.

bul-ly (bül′ē) *n.* *pl.* **bullies** A person who is mean or cruel to weaker people.

bul-rush (bül′rush″) *n.* Tall grass as found in a marsh.

bul-wark (bül′wėrk) *n.* A strong protection or support.

bum (bum) *n.* One who begs from others; one who spends time unemployed. One who devotes all his time to fun and recreation. **bum** *v.* To loaf.

bum-ble-bee (bum′bl bē″) *n.* A large hairy bee.

bum-boat (bum′bōt″) *n.* A boat that has commodities for sale to ships in port or off shore.

bum-mer (bum´ẽr) *n., Slang* Depressing. One who lives by begging; a looter, esp a Civil War soldier who plundered; in a quarry or mine, the man in charge of the conveyors.

bump (bump) *v.* To collide with, knock, or strike something. *n.* A swelling or lump on a person's body.

bump-er (bum´pẽr) *n.* A device on the front of vehicles that absorbs shock and prevents damage.

bump-kin (bump´kin) *n.* An awkward, stupid, or unsophisticated country person. **bumpkinish** *adj.*

bump-tious (bump´shus) *adj.* Crudely self-assertive and forward; pushy. **bumptiously** *adv.* **bumptiousness** *n.*

bump-y (bum´pē) *adj.* Being uneven; having ups and downs.

bun (bun) *n.* Any of a variety of plain or sweet small breads; tightly rolled hair that resembles a bun.

bunch (bunch) *n.* A cluster or group of items that are the same.

bunch-flow-er (bench flu er) *n.* A summer-blooming herb of the lily family usually found in the eastern and southern part of the United States.

bun-co (bung´kō) *n.* A game of confidence; a swindling scheme.

bun-dle (bun´dl) *n.* Anything wrapped or held together. *Slang* A large amount of money. **bundle** *v.* **bundler** *n.*

bundle up *v.* To dress warmly, usually using many layers of clothing.

bung (bung) *n.* The cork used to plug the bunghole in a large cask.

bun-ga-low (bung´ga lō˝) *n.* A small one-story cottage.

bung-hole (bung´hōl) *n.* A filling hole in a barrel or through which it is filled, then closed by a plug.

bun-gle (bung´gl) *v.* To work or act awkwardly or clumsily. **bungler** *n.*

bun-ion (bun´yan) *n.* An inflamed, painful swelling of the first joint of the big toe.

bunk (bungk) *n.* A narrow bed that is built in; one of a tier of berths on a ship.

bunk bed *n.* A bed having two sections, one on top of the other.

bun-ker (bung´kẽr) *n.* A tank for storing fuel on a ship; an embankment or a sand trap creating a hazard on a golf course.

bunk-house (bungk´hous˝) *n.* A building used as sleeping quarters usually on a ranch.

bun-kum (bung´kam) *n.* Meaningless talk.

bun-ny (bun´ē) *n. pl.* **bunnies** A small rabbit.

bunt (bunt) *v.* To tap a pitched ball with a half swing. *n.* The center of a square sail.

bunt-ing (bun´ting) *n.* A hooded blanket for a baby; a variety of stout-billed birds.

buoy (bŏ´ē) *n.* A floating object to mark a channel or danger. *v.* To stay afloat.

buoy-an-cy (boi´an sē) *n.* The tendency of an object or body to remain afloat in liquid or to rise in gas or air.

buoy-ant (boi ent) *adj.* Having the quality of floating or rising in a fluid.

bur. *abbr* Bureau

bur-ble (bür´bl) *n.* A gentle, bubbling flow; a bubbling speech pattern.

bur-bot (ber´bat) *n.* A freshwater fish of the cod family.

bur-den (ber´dan) *n.* Something that is hard to bear; a duty or responsibility; a ship's capacity for carrying cargo. **burden** *v.* **burdensome** *adj.*

bur-dock (ber´dok) *n.* A coarse plant with purplish flowers.

bu-reau (būr´ō) *n. pl.* **bureaus** *or* **bureaux** A low chest for storing clothes; a branch of the government or a subdivision of a department.

bu-reauc-ra-cy (bū rok´ra sē) *n. pl.* **bureaucracies** A body of nonelected officials in a government; the administration of a government through bureaus.

bu-reau-crat (bū´ra krat˝) *n.* A government official who has great authority in his own department.

bu-reau-crat-ic (bū´ra krat ic) *adj.* Having the characteristics of a bureaucrat.

bu-rette (bū ret´) *n.* A glass tube for measuring quantities of liquid or gas that are discharged or taken in.

burg (berg) *n.* A town or city.

burg-age (ber´gij) *n.* A tenure held under the king for a yearly rent.

bur-gee (ber´jē) *n.* A flag used by ships for signals or identification.

bur-geon (ber´j*a*n) *v.* To put forth new life as in leaves, buds, etc.

burg-er (ber´gėr) *n., Slang* A hamburger.

bur-gess (ber´jis) *n.* A representative of the legislature of colonial Maryland and Virginia.

burgh (bürg) *n.* A borough or chartered towns in Scotland.

burgh-er (bür´gėr) *n.* The inhabitant of a borough; a citizen.

bur-glar (ber´glėr) *n.* A person who steals personal items from another person's home.

bur-glar-i-ous (bėr glâr´ē us) *adj.* Relating or pertaining to a burglary.

bur-glar-ize (ber´gl*a* rīz˝) *v.* To commit burglary.

bur-glar-proof (ber´gl*a*r prüf) *adj.* Protected against burglary.

bur-gla-ry (ber´gl*a* rē) *n.* The breaking into and entering of a private home with the intent to steal.

bur-go-mas-ter (ber´g*a* mas˝tėr) *n.* The chief magistrate in certain countries of Europe.

bur-i-al (ber´ē *a*l) *n.* The process or act of burying, especially the act of burying a deceased person.

bu-rin (būr´in) *n.* An engraver's cutting tool; a flint tool with a beveled point.

burl (berl) *n.* A woody, often flat and hard, hemispherical growth on a tree.

bur-la-der-o (ber l*e* der´ō) *n.* A wooden barrier to protect the bullfighter from the charge of the bull.

bur-lap (ber´lap) *n.* A coarse cloth woven from hemp or jute.

bur-lesque (bėr lesk´) *n.* Theatrical entertainment with comedy and mocking imitations. **burlesque** *adj.* **burlesquely** *adv.*

bur-ley (ber´lē) *n.* A tobacco grown in Kentucky.

bur-ly (ber´lē) *adj.* Very heavy and strong. **burlily** *adv.* **burliness** *n.*

burn (bern) *v.* To be destroyed by fire; to consume fuel and give off heat, char or scorch. *n.* An injury produced by fire, heat, or steam; the firing of a rocket engine in space. **burnable** *adj.* **burningly** *adv.* **burn** *v.*

burn-er (bern´ėr) *n.* The part of a fuel-burning device where the fire is contained.

bur-net (bėr net´) *n.* An herb of the rose family with pinnate leaves and spikes of flowers.

burn in *v.* To increase the density of a photograph while enlarging, by extending the exposure.

bur-nish (ber´nish) *v.* To make shiny by rubbing; to polish. **burnishing** *adj.*

bur-noose (bėr nös´) *n.* A one-piece hooded cloak.

burn-out (bürn´out˝) *n.* Worn out with excessive use; complete rocket fuel depletion.

burnt (bernt) *adj.* Affected by burning.

burp (berp) *n.* A belch. **burp** *v.* To expel gas from the stomach.

burp gun *n.* Small submachine gun.

bur-ro (ber´ō) *n.* A small donkey.

bur-row (ber´ō) *n.* A tunnel dug in the ground by an animal. **burrow** *v.* To construct by tunneling through the earth.

bur-sa (ber´s*a*) *n.* A sac between the bone and the tendon.

bur-sar (ber´sėr) *n.* The person or official in charge of monies at a college.

bur-sa-ry (ber´s*a* rē) *n.* The treasury of a college; a grant to a needy student.

burse (bers) *n.* A square cloth used in a Communion service.

bus-i-ly (biz´*e* lē) *adv.* In a busy manner.

busi-ness-like (biz´nis līk˝) *adj.* Conforming with the methods of business.

bur-si-tis (ber sī´tis) *n.* An inflammation of the small sac between a tendon of the knee, elbow, or shoulder joints.

burst (berst) *adj.* To explode or experience a sudden outbreak; to suddenly become visible or audible. **burst** *n.* A sudden explosion or outburst.

bur-ton (ber´ton) *n.* A single or double blocking tackle used for hoisting.

bur-y (ber´ē) *v.* To hide by covering with earth; to inter a body at a funeral service.

bus (bus) *n. pl.* **busses** A large passenger vehicle; a small hand truck; a conductor for collecting electric currents. *abbr.* Business.

bus-boy (bus´boi˝) *n.* A waiter's assistant; one who removes dirty dishes from a table and then resets it.

bus-by (buz´bē) *n.* A fur hat that is worn in certain regiments of the British Army.

bush (bush) *n.* A low plant with branches near the ground; a dense tuft or growth; land that is covered intensely with undergrowth.

bush-buck (bush´buk˝) *n.* A small African antelope with spirally twisted horns.

bush-fire *n.* A fire burning out of control in the bush.

bush lima *n.* A lima bean grown on small bushes instead of poles.

bush basil *n.* A small annual herb.

bush bean *n.* A variety of green beans grown on bushes.

bushed (busht) *adj., Slang* Extremely exhausted; tired.

bush-el (bush´l) *n.* A unit of dry measurement which equals four pecks or 2,150.42 cubic inches; a container that holds a bushel.

bush-ing (bush´ing) *n.* A metal lining that reduces friction.

bush basil *n.* A cultivated herb.

bush jacket *n.* A cotton jacket, with four patch pockets and resembles a shirt.

bush league *n.* An inferior class or team.

bush-mas-ter (besh´mas˝tėr) *n.* The largest New World venomous snake.

bush pilot *n.* A pilot who flies a plane into remote areas.

bush-whack (besh´hwak˝) *v.* To travel through thick woods by cutting bushes and small trees; to ambush. **bushwacker** *n.*

bush-y (besh´ē) *adj.* Overgrown with a dense growth of bushes.

busi-ness (biz´nes) *n.* A person's profes-

sional dealings or occupation; an industrial or commercial establishment.

business administration *n.* A class of study in universities and colleges that teach the general information of business principles and practices.

business card *n.* A card which informs business associates which company you represent.

business cycle *n.* The cycle of economic activity consisting of growth, decline, recession and recovery.

business man *n.* A male representative of a company; a business executive.

business woman *n.* A female representative of a company or business executive.

bus-ing (bus´ing) *n.* The practice of busing children to a school outside their area to establish racial balance.

busk-er (bes ker) *n.* A person who entertains on the street corner.

bus-kin (bus´kin) *n.* A boot that reaches halfway to the knee; tragedy as that of an ancient Greek drama.

busman's holiday *n.* Vacation or holiday where a person follows the same practice of his usual occupation.

buss (bus) *n.* A kiss.

bust (bust) *n.* A sculpture that resembles the upper part of a human body; the breasts of a woman. **bust** *v.* To break or burst; to become short of money. *Slang* To place a person under arrest.

bus-ter (bus´tėr) *n.* A sturdy child; a person who breaks horses; sudden violent wind coming from the south.

bus-tle (bus´al) *n.* A padding that gives extra bulk to the back of a woman's skirt. **bustle** *v.* To move energetically; to make a show of being busy.

bus-y (biz´ē) *adj.* Full of activity; engaged in some form of work. **busyness** *n.*

bus-y-bod-y (biz´ē bod˝ē) *n.* An inquisitive person who interferes with someone else's business.

busy-work (biz´ē werk) *n.* Work that looks productive but really is not and only keeps a person looking busy or occupied.

but (but) *conj.* On the contrary to; other than; if not; except for the fact.

bu-tane (bū´tān) *n.* A gas produced from petroleum, used as a fuel refrigerant and aerosol propellant.

butch-er (bech´ėr) *n.* One who slaughters animals and dresses them for food.

butcher block *n.* A block of heavily laminated hardwood used as a cutting or work surface for the kitchen or butcher store.

butch-er's–broom (bech´ėrz brŏm˝) *n.* A leafless plant of the lily family with twigs used in brooms.

butcher knife *n.* A heavy kitchen knife with a broad blade.

butch-er-y (büch´a rē) *n.* A butcher's shop; the trade or business of a butcher.

bu-te-o (bū´tē o˝) *n.* Hawks with broad wings and soaring flight.

but-ler (but´lėr) *n.* A male servant of a household.

butt (but) *n.* The object of ridicule; the thick large or blunt end of something. **butt** *v.* To hit with horns or the head; to be joined at the end.

butte (būt) *n.* A small mountain with steep precipitous sides with a smaller summit area than a mesa.

but-ter (but´ėr) *n.* A yellow substance churned from milk.

but-ter–and–eggs (but´ėr an egz´) *n.* A perennial herb of the snap dragon family with yellow and orange flowers.

butter bean *n.* A dried lima bean.

butter clam *n.* A delicately flavored clam of the Pacific coast.

but-ter-fat (but´ėr fat˝) *n.* The natural fat from milk that floats to the top of unpasteurized milk.

but-ter-fin-gers (but´ėr fing˝gerz) *n.* An awkward or clumsy person.

but-ter-fly (but´ėr flī) *n. pl.* **butterflies** A narrow-bodied insect with four broad, colorful wings; a person  occupied with the pursuit of pleasure; a swimming stroke.

butterfly bush *n.* A variety of shrub having showy flowers that attract butterflies.

butterfly chair *n.* A chair constructed from cloth supportd by a frame of metal tubing.

butterfly fish *n.* A fish with variegated colors and or broad expanded spiny-fins.

butterfly weed *n.* An orange flowered milkweed of eastern North America.

but-ter-milk (but´ėr milk˝) *n.* The liquid that remains after butter has been churned from milk. Cultured milk made by adding suitable bacteria to sweet milk.

but-ter-nut (but´ėr nut˝) *n.* The edible nut of the walnut family.

but-ter-scotch (but´ėr skäch) *n.* Candy made from butter, brown sugar, corn syrup, and water.

butter up *v.* To charm with flattery.

but-ter-wort (but´ėr wert˝) *n.* An herb of the bladderwort family whose leaves produce a secretion which captures insects.

but-ter-y (but´a rē) *n.* A liquor storeroom.

butt in *v.* To meddle in someone's affairs.

but-tocks (but´akz) *n. pl.* The two round fleshy parts of the rump.

but-ton (but´on) *n.* A small disk that interlocks with a buttonhole to close a piece of garment; a badge bearing a stamped design or slogan; a small or immature mushroom. **buttoned** *v.* **buttonless** *n.*

but-ton-hole (but´on hōl˝) *n.* The slit through which a button is inserted to close a piece of garment.

buttonhole stitch *n.* A tightly worked loop stitch used to make a firm edge on a button hole.

but-ton-hook (but´ n huk˝) *n.* An offensive play in football; a hook used to draw buttons through buttonholes.

button snakeroot *n.* A plant having a rose-purple flower head; coarse herb.

but-ton-wood (but´an woud˝) *n.* A massive tree that provides useful timber.

but-ton-y (but´a nē) *adj.* Having a number

of buttons.

but-tress (bu´tris) *n.* A support made of either brick or stone and built against or projecting from a building or wall used for the purpose of giving stability; a support or prop.

butt shaft *n.* A barbless arrow.

butt-stock (but´stok˝) *n.* The stock of a firearm that is situated behind the breech mechanism.

butt weld *n.* A weld that is formed by joining the flat ends of two pieces of metal at a white heat.

butyl alcohol *n.* Chemically related form of alcohol that contains the butyl radical, used in manufacturing perfumes, lacquers and other organic compounds.

bu-tyr-a-ceous (bū˝ta rā´shus) *adj.* Having the qualities of butter.

bu-ty-rin (bū´tėr in) *n.* A yellowish liquid fat that is present in butter, and is formed from butyric acid.

bux-om (buk´som) *adj.* Lively; full of life; happy; pleasantly plump, cheerful. **buxomness** *n.*

bux-om-ly (buk´som lē) *adv.* Vigorously; briskly.

buy (bī) *v.* To purchase in exchange for money; to acquire possession of something.. *n.* Anything that is bought.

buy-er (bī´ėr) *v.* A person who buys from a store or an individual; a person employed to make purchases for a company.

buyer's market *n.* A market of plentiful goods giving buyers a wide range of choice and price.

buy off *v.* To obtain release from, as a responsibility, by a payment.

buy out *v.* To obtain release from a responsibility, by making a payment; to purchase shares in a business concern or investment.

buy up *v.* To buy extensively or freely.

buzz (buz) *v.* To make a low vibrating sound, as a bee; the continuous humming sound of a bee.

buz-zard (buz´ėrd) *n.* A broad-winged vulture from the same family as the hawk. *Slang.* A mean, old cantankerous man.

buzz-er (buz´ėr) *n.* An electrical signaling device that makes a buzzing sound; one that buzzes.

buzz saw *n.* A circular power saw named for the sound it makes when cutting wood.

buzz-word (buz´werd) *n.* An important sounding technical word or phrase, which might have little meaning .

by (bī) *prep.* Up to and beyond; to go past; not later than; next to; according to; beside or near; according to; in relation to.

by and large *adv.* In general.

by–blow (bī´blō˝) *n.* A side or accidental blow.

bye (bī) *n.* A position in which a contestant has no opponent after pairs are drawn for a tournament, and, therefore, advances to the next round; something that is aside from the main consideration or course.

bye–bye (bī bī) *Slang* Farewell.

by-gone (bī´gon˝) *adj.* Gone by; past; former; departed; out of date..

by-law (bī´lo) *n.* A rule or law governing internal affairs of a group or organization.

by-line (bī līn) *n.* A side or secondary line.

by–name (bī´nām˝) *n.* A nickname or secondary name.

by–past (bī˝past˝) *adj.* Past; bygone.

by–path (bī´path) *n.* A road or path secondary to the main road or path; an obscure path.

by–play (bī´plā˝) *n.* Something separate from the main part or purpose.

by–product *n.* Something that is industrially produced as a secondary product.

by–road (bī rōd) *n.* A side road; a road other than the main or usual road.

by-street *n.* A side or secondary street.

byte (bīt) *n.* In computer science, a sequence of adjacent binary digits operated on as a unit.

by the way *adv.* Incidentally; used as in passing.

by-way (bī wā) *n.* A secondary or little traveled road; a little known aspect.

by-word (bī werd) *n.* A frequent or commonly used phrase or word; a proverbial saying.

C, c (sē) The third letter of the English alphabet; the Roman numeral for 100.

CA *abbr.* California.

cab (kab) *n.* A taxicab; the compartment where a person sits to drive a large truck or machinery.

ca-bal (ka bal´) *n.* A group that conspires against a government or other public institution.

ca-bal-le-ro (kab˝al yâr´ō) *n.* A Spanish gentleman; in southwestern United States.

ca-ban-a (ka ban´a) *n.* A small building or shelter on the beach or at the side of a pool.

ca-bane (ka ban´) *n.* The framework of struts attached to the top of the fuselage that supported the wings of early model airplanes.

cab-a-ret (kab´a rā´) *n.* A restaurant that provides dancing and live entertainment.

cab-bage (kab´ij) *n.* A plant with large, edible green leaves, eaten as a vegetable.

cabbage butterfly *n.* A whitish butterfly which feeds on cabbage leaves.

cabbage palm *n.* Any palm having an edible leaf bud.

cabbage rose *n.* A rose with a large, round, compact pink flower.

cabbage tree *n.* Any of several palm trees with large terminal leaf buds which are eaten like cabbage.

cabbage worm *n.* A caterpillar that feeds on cabbage leaves.

cab-by (kab´ē) *n.* Cab driver.

cab-in (kab´ in) *n.* A small, roughly-built house, especially one made from logs; the living quarters on a ship; the area of an airplane for the passengers and crew members.

cabin boy *n.* A person employed to serve officers and passengers of a ship.

cabin class *n.* A class of accommodations for passengers on a ship.

cab-i-net (kab´i nit) *n.* A unit for displaying and storing dishes and other objects; a selected group of people appointed by the head of state to officially advise and to take charge of the different government departments.

cab-i-net-maker (kab´i nit mā´kėr) *n.* A person who specializes in the construction of furniture.

cab-i-net-work (kab´i nit würk˝) *n.* High quality woodwork, such as in furniture or shelving.

cabin pressure *n.* The air pressure in an airplane cabin.

ca-ble (kā´bl) *n.* A heavy rope made from fiber or steel; a bound group of insulated conductors; a cablegram.

cable car *n.* A vehicle used to carry passengers on a cable.

ca-ble-gram (kā´bl gram˝) *n.* A telegram carried or transmitted overseas by underwater cable.

ca-ble-laid (kā´bl lād˝) *adj.* Relating to a three rope pattern formed by three strands of rope, laid together with a left-handed twist.

cable length *n.* A nautical unit of length, figured as either 100 or 120 fathoms or 720 feet.

cable railroad *n.* Railroads used to climb steep inclines, by pulling with a motor powered cable buried under the road.

cable–stitch *n.* A knitting stitch resembling the look of a cable having a raised and twisted cablelike pattern.

cable television *n.* A private television system which picks up signals from television stations and transmits them by cable.

ca-ble-way (kā´bl wā˝) *n.* A conveying means in which one or two wire cables are suspended between two structures.

cab-o-chon (kab´ a shon˝) *n.* A precious stone that has been polished but not cut into facets.

ca-boo-dle (ka bōd´l) *n., Slang* The entire unit, amount, or collection.

ca-boose (ka bōs´) *n.* The last car of a train, that contains the eating and sleeping quarters for the crew.

cab-o-tage (kab´ a tij) *n.* Coastal navigation; the carrying of cargo or passengers within the borders of a nation.

ca-bret-ta (k*a* bret´*a*) *n*. Sheepskin used in the making of shoes and gloves.

ca-bril-la (k*a* bril´*a*) *n*. Any of several sea basses.

cab-ri-ole (kab´rē ōl) *n*. A gracefully curved furniture leg, often ending in an animal's paw or other ornamental finish, used for chairs and other types of furniture.

cab-ri-o-let (kab´rē *o* lā) *n*. A light-weight one-horse carriage with a single seat and two wheels; a type of automobile similar to a convertible.

cab-stand (kab´stand˝) *n*. An area where taxicabs wait for hire.

ca-ca-o (k*a* kā´ō) *n*. Any tree of the chocolate family; the dried seed of the cacao tree from which chocolate and cocoa are made.

cach-a-lot (kash´*a* lot´) *n*. A sperm whale.

cache (kash) *n*. A safe place to hide and conceal goods. **cache** *v*.

cache-pot (kash´pot˝) *n*. An ornamental flower pot holder.

ca-chet (k*a* shā´) *n*. A mark of distinction or authenticity; a seal on a letter or an important document showing that it is official.

ca-chou (k*a* shō) *n*. A small lozenge used to sweeten the breath.

ca-chu-cha (k*a* chō´ch*a*) *n*. A Spanish solo dance in three-quarter time, similar to the bolero.

cack-le (kak´l) *v*. To laugh with the characteristic shrill noise a hen makes after laying an egg; to talk or laugh with a similar sound. **cackler** *n*.

cac-o-e-thes (kak˝ō ē´thēz) *n*. A strong compulsion; a bad habit.

ca-coph-o-ny (k*a* kof´*a* nē) *n*. A harsh and disagreeable sound. **cacophonous** *adj*. **cacophonously** *adv*.

cac-ta-ceous (kak tā´shus) *adj*. A cactus family of plants.

cac-toid (kak´toid) *adj*. Resembling the cactus.

cac-tus (kak´t*u*s) *n*. *pl*. **-es, -ti** A leafless plant with a thick, prickly surface, which grows primarily in hot and dry regions.

ca-cu-mi-nal (k*a* kū´m*i* nl) *adj*. Pertaining to the sound produced by curling the top of the tongue back to a point of contact with the hard palate.

cad (kad) *n*. An ungentlemanly man. **caddish** *adj*.

ca-das-tre or **ca-das-ter** (k*a* das´tèr) *n*. An official survey of the value, or worth, and ownership of an area's real estate. This survey is used in assessing taxes.

ca-dav-er (k*a* dav´èr) *n*. The body of a person who has died; pale and gaunt.

ca-dav-er-ous (k*a* dav´èr us) *adj*. Pale and gaunt. **cadaveric** *adj*.

cad-die (kad´ē) *n*. *pl*. **caddies** A person employed by a golfer to assist him by carrying his clubs during the game of golf.

cad-dis (kad´is) *n*. A woolen fabric; worsted ribbon, yarn or binding.

cad-dish (kad´is) *adj*. Unprincipled; like a cad; ungentlemanly.

cad-dis-worm (kad´is wûrm˝) *n*. The caddisfly's aquatic larvae that is used in fishing bait.

cad-dy (kad´ē) *n*. A small box or chest for keeping small items or trinkets.

cade (kād) *adj*. Of an animal's offspring, abandoned by the mother and brought up by human beings.

ca-delle (k*a* del´) *n*. A black beetle, that eats stored grain.

ca-dence (kād´ens) *n*. A rhythmic movement or flow.

ca-den-za (k*a* den´z*a*) *n*. An elaborate ornamental section for a soloist near the end of a concerto.

ca-det (k*a* det´) *n*. A student in training at a naval or military academy. **cadet** *n*.

cadge (kaj) *v*. To beg or to receive by begging; to mooch. **cadger** *n*.

cad-mi-um (kad´mē *u*m) *n*. A metallic element, bluish-white in color, that is used in storage batteries and solders; A white, ductile metallic element resembling tin in appearance; used in the manufacture of certain alloys, in plating of metals and metal wires for rust-proofing, in the nickel-cadmium storage battery, as a barrier in the control of atomic fission, and in miscellaneous manufactured products. **cadmic** *adj.*

cad-re (ka´dra) *n.* The group of trained personnel that forms the heart of an organization.

ca-du-ce-us (ka dŏ´sē us) *n.* The symbol of the medical profession, a winged staff entwined with two serpents entwined around it.

ca-du-ci-ty (ka dŏ´si tē) *n.* The tendency to fall; senility; the infirmity of old age.

Cae-sar (sē´zėr) *n.* The title given to Roman emperors who followed Caesar Augustus.

Caesar, Gauis Julis *n.* Roman general and statesman.

caesarean operation *n.* The operation by which a fetus is removed from the uterus by cutting through the walls of the abdomen and uterus.

cae-su-ra (si zher´a) *n.* A pause or break in a line of verse or poetry; a pause or division in a verse; a separation, by the ending of a word or by a pause in the sense, of syllables rhythmically connected.

caf-e-te-ri-a (kaf´i tēr´ē a) *n.* A restaurant where a person chooses his own food and then carries it on a tray to his table.

caf-feine (ka fēn´) *n.* A stimulant found in coffee, tea, and dark colas; a slightly bitter alkaloid used as a stimulant and diuretic, and found in coffee and tea.

caf-tan (kaf´tan) *n.* A loose-fitting, full-length garment worn in the Near East.

cage (kāj) *n.* A box-like structure enclosed with bars or grating for the confinement of animals. **cage** *v.*

cag-er (kā´jer) *n.* A machine used to move cars on or off a cage.

ca-gey (kā´jē) *adj.* Shrewd, wary, or cautious.

ca-hier (kä yā´) *n.* A number of sheets of paper or leaves of a book placed together, as for binding; a report of the proceedings of any body, as a legislature.

ca-hoot (ka hŏt´) *n.* A questionable relationship with an associate.

cai-man (kā´man) *n.* Crocodilians, similar to alligators, found in South and Central America.

cairn terrier *n.* A small, short-legged Scottish terrier with a shaggy, rough coat.

cais-son (kā´san) *n.* A waterproof structure that is used for construction work underwater.

caisson disease *n.* A painfully paralyzing, and sometimes fatal sickness that results from lowering of air pressure too radidly, as in the change from the compressed air of a diving unit to the surface air pressure, causing dissolved nitrogren to be released as bubbles in the blood and tissues; more commonly known as the bends.

cai-tiff (kā´tif) *n.* A miserable person; a vile person.

caj-e-put (kaj´ i put) *n.* A tree of East India that yields an aromatic oil used in medicine as a stimulant, antispasmodic and in certain skin disorders treatments.

ca-jole (ka jōl´) *v.* To wheedle or coax someone into doing something.

Ca-jun (kā´jan) *n.* A native of Louisiana descended from French-speaking immigrants.

cake (kāk) *n.* A sweet food made from flour, eggs, and shortening. **cake** *v.*

cal-a-bash (kal´a bash´) *n.* A large hard-shelled gourd that can be used as a utensil.

cal-a-ba-zil-la (kal´a ba zē´a) *n.* A wild squash of Mexico and the southwestern United States, from which it's unrippen fruit is used as a substitute for soap.

cal-a-boose (kal´a bŏs´) *n., Slang* A jail.

ca-la-di-um (ka lā´dē um) *n.* Tropical plants having large, beautiful leaves of variegated colors, cultivated as a pot plant for its foliage.

cal-a-man-der (kal´a man˝dėr) *n.* A variety of extremely hard wood from an East India tree.

cal-a-mine (kal´a mīn´) *n.* A pink powder of zinc oxide and ferric oxide mixed with mineral oils to form a lotion for skin irritations such as poison ivy.

cal-a-mint (kal´a mint) *n.* Any of the plants in the mint family.

ca-lam-i-ty (ka lam´i tē) *n. pl.* -ies Misfortune or great distress, adversity or mishap great misery. **calamitous** *adj.* **calamitously** *adj.*

cal-a-mon-din (kal´a mun˝din) *n.* Citrus tree, native to the Philippines; with fruit that resembles the mandarin orange.

cal-a-mus (kal´amus) *n.* A cane or its aromatic root; any palm that yields rattan or canes. The quill of a feather.

ca-lan-do (kä län´dō) *adv.* Music that becomes gradually slower and softer in sound; diminishing.

cal-ca-ne-us (kāl kä´nē us) *n.* The largest bone of the tarsus; the heel bone in man.

cal-car (kal´kä) *n.* A spurlike node on the leg of a bird.

cal-car (kal´kär) *n.* An oven or reverberating furnace, used in glassworks.

cal-car-e-ous (kal kâr´ē us) *adj.* Having the characteristics of or made up of calcium, calcium carbonate, or lime stone.

cal-ce-i-form (kal´sē a form˝) *adj.* Having the form of a shoe, as the petals of some orchids.

cal-cic (kal´ sik) *adj.* Pertaining to lime; containing calcium.

cal-cif-ic (kal sif´ik) *adj.* Forming salts of calcium.

cal-ci-fi-ca-tion (kal´si fi kā˝shan) *n.* Process of changing a substance through the deposition of lime.

cal-ci-fuge (kal´si fūj˝) *n.* A plant that cannot thrive in limestone or in soil saturated with lime.

cal-ci-fy (kal´si fī´) *v.* To become or make chalky or stony. **calcification** *n.*

cal-ci-mine (kal´si mīn´) *n.* A tinted or white liquid that contains water, glue, coloring matter, and zinc oxide; a white or light-colored wash composed of whiting, glue, and water, used to paint walls or ceilings, but which cannot withstand washing.

cal-cine (kal´sīn) *v.* To heat to a high temperature without melting, but causing loss of moisture and reduction. **calcination** *n.*

cal-cite (kal´sīt) *n.* Calcium carbonate mineral, that is found in crystal forms including limestone, chalk and marble.

cal-ci-um (kal´sē um) *n.* The alkaline element that is found in teeth and bones; the element symbolized by Ca.

calcium chloride *n.* A deliquescent salt, white in color, used in its dry state as a dehumidifying agent and in its moist state for controlling ice and dust on roads; a white, absorbant, lumpy, or crystalline salt, derived from calcium carbonate.

calcium hydroxide *n.* A strong alkali, in powder form used in mortar, plaster and cement.

calcium light *n.* A bright, white light produced by heating lime to incandescence in a hot flame.

calcium phosphate *n.* Any of several forms of combined phosphorous and calcium.

calc-tu-fa (kalk´tō˝fa) *n.* An alluvial formation of calcium carbonate.

cal-cu-late (kal´kū lāt) *v.* To figure by a mathematical process, to evaluate; to estimate. **calculable** *adj.* **calculably** *adv.* **calculative** *adj.*

cal-cu-lat-ed (kal´kū lā´tid) *adj.* Worked out beforehand with careful estimation, mathematical calculating.

cal-cu-lat-ing (kal´kū lā´ting) *adj.* Shrewd consideration of self-interest.

cal-cu-la-tion (kal˝kū lā´shan) *n.* The act or the result of mathematical calculating.

cal-cu-la-tor (kal´kū lā´tėr) *n.* A machine with a keyboard for automatic mathematical operation.

cal-cu-lus (kal´kū lus) *n. pl.* -es A stone in the gallbladder or kidneys; the mathematics of integral and differential calculus.

cal-de-ra (kal der´a) *n.* A large crater formed by the collapse of the main part of a volcano, caused by violent volcanic action.

cal-dron (kol´drøn) *n.* A large boiler or kettle.

cal-e-fac-to-ry (kal e´fak terē) *n.* A room in a monastery that is heated and used as a sitting room.

cal-en-dar (kal´an dėr) *n.* A system for showing time divisions by years, months, weeks, and days; the twelve months in a year.

cal-en-der (kal´an dėr) *n.* A machine that makes paper and cloth smooth and glossy.

ca-len-dri-cal *adj.* Having to do with a calendar of calendar units.

cal-ends (kal´endz) *n.* The first day of the new moon.

ca-len-du-la (ka len´ja la) *n.* A marigold; the dried flowers of this plant, used to promote healing.

cal-en-ture (kal´an chėr) *n.* A delirium caused in the tropics due to the exposure to excessive heat.

ca-les-cence (ka les´ans) *n.* Growing warmth; growing heat.

calf (kaf) *n. pl.* **calves** The young offspring of the domestic cow; the young of large animals as the whale and elephant.

calf-skin (kaf´skin´) *n.* The hide or skin of a calf, or leather made from it.

cal-i-ber (kal´i bėr) *n.* The inner diameter of a tube or gun; the quality or worth of something.

cal-i-co (kal´i kō) *n.* Cotton fabric with figured patterns.

ca-lic-u-lus (ka lik´ya lus) *n.* A small cuplike object.

California *n.* A state located on the western coast of the United States, statehood September 9, 1850, state capital Sacramento.

cal-i-for-nite (kal a for´nīt) *n.* Mineral that resembles jade.

cal-i-pash (kal´i pash´) *n.* The greenish substance which lies under the upper shell of a turtle that is edible and regarded as a delicacy in the form of turtle soup.

cal-i-per (kal´i pėr) *n.* An instrument with two curved, hinged legs, used to measure inner and outer dimensions.

ca-liph (kā´lif) *n.* A religious and secular head in Islam. **caliphate** *n.*

cal-is-then-ics (kal´is then´iks) *n.* Exercises that develop muscular tone and promote good physical condition.

calk (kok) *n.* A projection tilted downward on the shoe of a horse to prevent slipping; a similar device on the sole of a shoe or boot.

call (kol) *v.* To call out to someone; to name or designate; to telephone; to pay a short visit; to demand payment; in card games, to demand the opponent show his cards; to stop officially. **call** *n.*

cal-la *or* **cal-la lily (kal´a)** *n.* A family of white and yellow flowers enclosing a club-like flower stalk.

call-a-ble (ko le bel) *adj.* Capable of being called or summonsed; subject to call or summons.

call-board (kol´bōrd) *n.* Bulletin board; bulletin board hung in a theater for notifications of rehearsals or changes in casting

call-boy (kal´boi) *n.* The person who notifies actors when it is time to go on stage.

call down *v.* To reprehend.

call for *v.* To fetch; demand; send for.

call girl *n.* A prostitute with whom a date can be arranged by telephone.

cal-lig-ra-pher (ka lig´ra fėr) *n.* A person who writes beautiful handwriting.

cal-lig-ra-phy (ka lig´ra fē) *n.* The art of writing with a pen using different slants and positions.

call-ing (ko´ling) *n.* The occupation or profession of a person.

cal-liope (ka lī´ø pē´) *n.* A keyboard musical instrument that is fitted with steam whistles.

Cal-lis-to (ka lis´tō) *n.* The largest of Jupiter's moons.

call loan *n.* A stock market loan, used to finance purchases of securities.

call money *n.* Money loaned on call or available for call loans.

call number *n.* A classification number usually combining letters and numerals to designate subject and author, indicating the shelf location of a book in a library.

call off *v.* To cancel, as that which has been planned; to speak or read out loud.

cal-lose (kal´us) *n.* An occasional carbohydrate or periodic component of plant cell walls, as on sieve plantes, where it forms the callus.

cal-los-i-ty (ka los'i tē) *n.* The condition of being callous or hardened; abnormal thickness and hardness of the skin and other tissues.

cal-lous (kal'us) *adj.* Having calluses; to be without emotional feelings; unfeeling **callously** *adv.* **callousness** *n.*

call rate *n.* The interest which is charged on a loan repayable on demand.

call sign *n.* A sign used as a radio signal by aircraft to identify themselves to friendly forces.

call-up *n.* The total number of men ordered to report for military duty during a specified time.

call up *v.* To telephone; to put up for discussion; to select for service in the armed forces.

cal-lus (kal'us) *n. pl.* **-luses** A thickening of the horny layer of the skin.

calm (kom) *adj.* Absence of motion; having little or no wind, storms, or rough water.

cal-ma-tive (kal'ma tiv) *n.* A tranquilizer.

cal-o-mel (kal'ø mel') *n.* A white, tasteless compound used as a purgative.

cal-o-rie (kal'a rē) *n. pl.* **-ries** A measurement of the amount of heat or energy produced by food. **caloric** *adj.* **calorific** *adj.*

cal-o-rif-ic (kal a rif'ik) *adj.* Capable of producing heat or causing heat.

cal-o-rim-e-ter (kal ø rim'i tèr) *n.* An instrument for measuring heat; any of several apparatuses for measuring quantities of heat absorbed or produced by a body.

ca-lotte (ka lot') *n.* A small domed cap for the skull.

cal-trop (kal'trop) *n.* Plants having spiny heads or fruit.

cal-u-met (kal'ya met') *n.* A pipe used by the North American Indians during ceremonies; also known as a peace pipe.

ca-lum-ni-ate (ka lum'nē āt") *v. pl.* **-nies** To slander; to malign.

cal-um-ny (kal'am nē) *n. pl.* **-ies** A statement that is malicious, false, and damaging to someone's reputation.

cal-va-dos (kal"va dōs') *n.* An applejack; brandy, distilled from hard apple cider.

Cal-va-ry (kal'va rē) *n.* The location where Jesus Christ was crucified.

calve (kav) *v.* To give birth to a calf.

Cal-vin-ism (kal'vi niz'am) *n.* The doctrine of John Calvin, marked by a strong emphasis on the sovereignty of God.

calx (kalks) *n.* The oxide or ashy residue that remains after metals or minerals have been subjected to combustion.

ca-lyp-so (ka lip'sō) *n. pl.* **calypsos** Improvised ballad of the West Indies with lyrics on topical or humorous subjects.

ca-lyp-tra (ka lip'tra) *n.* A hoodlike part connected with the organs of fructification in flowering plants.

ca-lyx (kā' liks) *n. pl.* **calyxes, calyces** The outer cover of a flower.

cam (kam) *n.* A curved wheel used to produce a reciprocating motion.

ca-ma-ra-de-rie (kä'ma rä'de rē) *n.* Good–will among friends.

cam-a-ril-la (kam"a ril'a) *n.* A group of private unofficial secret counselors or advisers.

cam-ber (kam'bèr) *n.* A slight curve upward in the middle.

cam-bist (kam'bist) *n.* A person who is well versed in the science of monetary exchange; a dealer in bills of exchange.

cam-bi-um (kam'bē um) *n.* The layer of soft cellular tissue between the bark and wood in trees and shrubs responsible for secondary growth.

Cam-bo-di-a (kam bō' de an) *n.* A country located in Southeastern Asia.

cam-bric (kām'brik) *n.* A cotton fabric or white linen.

cambric tea *n.* A mixture of hot water and milk, with sugar and, often a little tea.

came (kām) *n.* A grooved lead bar that is used to hold together the panes of glass in lattice work or stained-glass windows. *v.* Past tense of to come.

cam-el (kam'el) *n.* An animal used in desert regions, having either one or two humps on its back.

ca-mel-lia (ka mēl′ya) *n.* A greenhouse shrub with shiny green leaves and various colored flowers, used in corsages.

ca-mel-o-pard (ka mel′ø pärd) *n.* A giraffe.

camel's hair *n.* The cloth made of camel's hair.

Camembert cheese *n.* A rich, soft, unpressed cheese characterized by a distinct flavor and odor produced by the presence of a mold.

cam-e-o (kam′ē ō′) *n.* A gem usually cut with one layer contrasting another, serving as a background; a brief appearance by a famous performer in a single scene on a television show or in a movie.

cam-er-a (kam′er a) *n.* An apparatus for taking photographs in a lightproof enclosure with an aperture and shuttered lens through which the image is focused and recorded on photosensitive film.

cam-er-al (kam′ėr al) *adj.* Pertaining to public revenues or finances.

camino real *n.* Highway; main road.

cam-i-on (kam′ē an) *n.* A sturdy cart for transporting heavy loads.

ca-mise (ka mēz′) *n.* A loose smock or shirt.

cam-i-sole (kam′i sōl′) *n.* A woman's short, sleeveless undergarment.

cam-let (kam′lit) *n.* A rich fabric made from goat's hair, a durable waterproof cloth.

cam-o-mile (kam′a mīl) *n.* A herb with strongly scented flowers and flowers that are used medicinally.

cam-ou-flage (kam′a fläzh′) *v.* To disguise by creating the effect of being part of the natural surroundings. **camouflage** *n.*

camp (kamp) *n.* A temporary lodging or makeshift shelter.

cam-paign (kam pān′) *n.* An organized operation designed to bring about a particular political, commercial, or social goal. **campaign , campaigner** *n.*

cam-pa-ni-le (kam′pa nē′lē) *n. pl.* **-iles** A free-standing bell tower that is associated with a church.

cam-pan-u-late (kam pan′ya lit) *adj.* Shaped like a bell, usually as a description for flower petals.

camp-er (kam′pėr) *n.* A person who camps in makeshift shelters for recreation; a vehicle specially equipped for casual travel and camping.

cam-pes-tral (kam pes′tral) *adj.* Relating to the fields or country setting.

camp-fire (kamp′fir′) *n.* An outdoor fire used for cooking and for heat while camping.

camp-ground (kamp graund) *n.* A specially prepared area for camping.

cam-phor (kam′fėr) *n.* A crystalline compound used as an insect repellent. **camphoric** *adj.*

cam-pim-e-ter (kam pim′i tėr) *n.* An apparatus used to measure color range of sensitivity of the retina.

campo santo *n.* A burial ground; a cemetary.

camp-site (kamp sīt) *n.* The area used for camping.

cam-pus (kam′pus) *n.* The buildings and grounds of a college, school, or university.

cam-shaft (kam′shaft′) *n.* The shaft of an engine that is fitted with cams.

can (kan) *v.* To know how to do something; to be physically or mentally able; to have the ability to do something; to preserve fruit or vegetables by sealing in an airtight container. *n.* An airtight container.

Ca-naan (kā′nan) *n.* In biblical times, known as the Promised Land.

Can-a-da (kan yä′da) *n.* The Commonwealth nation located in the northern half of North America. **Canadian** *n.*

ca-nal (ka nal′) *n.* A man-made water channel for irrigating land.

canal boat *n.* A long, narrow boat or barge, either self-propelled or towed, used on canals.

can-a-lic-u-lus *n.* A tubular or canal-like passage or channel, as in a bone.

ca-nal-ize (ka nal′īz) *v.* To convert into canals; to make new canals.

ca-nard (ka närd′) *n.* An untrue story circulated as true; a hoax.

ca-nar-y (ka när′ē) *n. pl.* **-ies** A green

or yellow songbird which is popular as a caged bird.

Canary Islands *n.* A group of islands off the coast of Spain and the northwest coast of Africa.

ca-nas-ta (k*a* **nas´t***a***)** *n.* A card game using two decks of cards which each player or partnership tries to meld in groups of three or more cards of the same rank; a meld of seven cards that are of the same rank in canasta.

can-can (kan´kan) *n.* A dance performed by women, characterized by high kicking while holding up the front of a full skirt.

can-cel (kan´s*el***)** *v.* To invalidate or annul; to cross out; to neutralize; in mathematics, to cross out; to neutralize; in mathematics, to remove a common factor from the numerator and the denominator of a fraction; in computer science, to abort or stop a procedure or program. **cancellation** *n.*

can-cel-la-tion (kan˝s*a* **lā´sh***a***n)** *n.* The act of making void, or invalid; a mark used to cancel something.

can-cer (kan´ser) *n.* A malignant tumor that invades healthy tissue and spreads to other areas; the disease marked by such tumors. **cancerous** *adj.*

Cancer (kan´ser) *n.* The fourth sign of the zodiac; a person born between June 21 - July 22.

can-cri-zans *adj.* Going or moving backward.

can-de-la-bra (kan´d*e* **lä´br***a***)** *n. pl.* **candelabrum** A decorative candlestick with several branching arms for candles.

can-did (kan´did) *adj.* Free from bias, malice, or prejudice; honest and sincere.

can-di-date (kan´di dāt´) *n. pl.* A person who aspires to or is nominated or qualified for a membership, award, or office. **candidacy** *n.* **candidature** *n.*

can-died (kan´dēd) *adj.* Preserved; encrusted with sugar.

can-dle (kan´dl) *n.* A slender, cylindrical mass of wax or tallow containing a linen or cotton wick which is burned to produce light. *v.* To hold something between the eye and a light, as to test eggs for blood clots,

growths, or fertility. **candler** *n.*

can-dle-ber-ry (kan´dl ber˝ē) *n.* Wax myrtle, used in making candles.

can-dle-light (kan´dl līt´) *n.* The light emitted from a candle.

can-dle-pin (kan´dl pin˝) *n.* A gently tapered bowling pin that resembles a slender candle.

can-dle-pow-er (kan´dl pou´*e***r)** *n.* The illuminating power of a standard candle, used as a unit of measurement of light.

can-dle-stick (kan´dl stik˝) *n.* Holder with an opening or spike for a candle.

can-dle-wick (kan´dl wik˝) *n.* The wick of a candle.

can-dle-wood (kan´dl wüd˝) *n.* Resinous wood used for torch lights, or as a substitute for candles.

can-dor (kan´d*e***r)** *n.* Straightforwardness; frankness of expression.

can-dy (kan´dē) *n. pl.* **-ies** A confection made from sugar and flavored in a variety of ways. *v.* To preserve, cook, coat, or saturate with syrup or sugar.

candy striper *n.* A teenage volunteer worker a hospital.

can-dy-tuft (kan´dē tuft´) *n.* A variety of plants with white, purple, or reddish flower clusters.

cane (kān) *n.* A pithy or hollow, flexible, jointed stem of bamboo or rattan that is split for basketry or wicker work; a walking stick. **cane** *v.*

cane-brake (kān´brāk) *n.* A thick growth of cane.

ca-nel-la (k*a* **nel´***a* **)** *n.* The cinnamonlike bark from a tree of a West Indian, used as medicine and a condiment.

can-er (kā´n*e***r)** *n.* A person who weaves cane, especially for chair seats and backs.

cane sugar *n.* Sugar obtained from the sugar cane, sucrose.

ca-nine (kā´nīn) *adj.* Relating to or resembling a dog; of the dog family.

Canis Major (kā´nis mā´j*e***r)** *n.* A constellation in the Southern Hemisphere that contains the Dog Star.

can-is-ter (kan´i st*e***r)** *n.* A container made

of thin metal, used to store dry foods, such as flour, sugar, coffee, and tea; the cylinder that explodes and scatters shot when fired from a gun.

can-ker (kang´kėr) *n.* An ulcerated sore in the mouth.

can-na (kan´a) *n.* Tropical plant with large leaves and showy flowers.

can-na-bin (kan´a bin) *n.* A poisonous resin that comes from Indian hemp.

canned (kand) *adj.* Preserved and sealed under pressure.

cannel coal *n.* A glistening grayish-black, hard, bituminous coal, that burns with a bright flame.

can-ner (kan´ėr) *n.* A person responsible for canning meat, fish, and fruit for preservation.

can-ner-y (kan´e rē) *n. pl.* **-ies** A company that processes canned meat, vegetables, and other foods.

can-ni-bal (kan´i bal) *n.* Any animal who survives by eating one of its own kind; a person who survives by eating the flesh of human beings. **cannibalism, cannibalization** *n.* **cannibalistic** *adj.*

can-ni-bal-ize (kan´i ba līz´) *v.* To remove parts from a plane for use as replacements in another plane.

can-ni-kin (kan´i kin) *n.* A small can; a cup.

can-non (kan´øn) *n. pl.* **cannons** A heavy war weapon made of metal and mounted on wheels or a base for discharging projectiles.

can-non-ade (kan˝a nād´) *n.* A continued heavy discharge of a cannon.

can-non-ball (kan´an bol´) *n.* An iron projectile fired from a cannon.

cannon bone *n.* The bone that extends from the knee or hock joint to the fetlock joint.

can-non-eer (kan˝a nēr´) *n.* Artillery gunner.

can-nu-la (kan´ya la) *n.* A small tube of metal or the like which draws off fluid or injects medicine into the body.

can-ny (kan´ē) *adj.* Thrifty; careful; cautious; shrewd. **cannily** *adv.,* **canniness** *n.*

can-not (kan´ot) *v.* Can not.

ca-noe (ka nŏ´) *n.* A

light-weight, slender boat with pointed ends which moves by paddling. **canoe** *v.* **canoeist** *n.*

can-on (kan´øn) *n.* The laws established by a church council; a priest serving in a collegiate church or cathedral; clergyman. **canonical** *adj.*

can-on-i-cal (ka non´i kal) *n.* The most convenient and simplest form of an equation.

can-on-ize (kan´a nīz´) *v.* To officially declare a deceased person a saint; to place in the catalogue of the saints; to glorify. **canoniza** *n.*

can-on-i-za-tion (kan´a ni zā˝shan) *n.* Process of being named to sainthood.

can-o-py (kan´o pē) *n. pl.* **-ies** A cloth covering used as an ornamental structure over a bed; the supporting surface of a parachute; the transparent cover over the cockpit of an airplane.

cant (kant) *n.* The external angle of a building. *v.* To throw off by tilting.

can't (kant) *cont.* Can not.

can-ta-bi-le (kän tä´bi lā´) *n.* A lyrical, flowing style of music.

can-ta-loupe (kan´ta lōp´) *n.* A sweet-tasting, orange–colored muskmelon.

can-tan-ker-ous (kan tang´kėr us) *adj.* Bad-tempered and argumentative. **cantankerously** *adv.*

can-ta-ta (kan tä´ta) *n.* A drama that is sung but not acted.

can-ta-trice (kän˝tä trē´che) *n.* A professional female singer.

can-teen (kan tēn´) *n.* A small metal container for carrying water or other liquids to drink; a place where a person can buy refreshments.

can-ter (kan´tėr) *n.* An easy lope just a little slower than a gallop, but faster than a trot.

can-ti-cle (kan´ti kl) *n.* A hymn or chant sung in church.

can-ti-lev-er (kan´ti lev´ėr) *n.* A long structure, such as a beam, supported only at one end.

can-ton (kan´ton) *n.* A small area of a

country divided into parts. **cantonal** *adj.*

can-ton-ment (kan ton´ment) *n.* One or more temporary billets for troops.

can-tor (kan´tėr) *n.* The chief singer in a synagogue.

can-thar-is (kan thar´is) *n.* A preparation obtained from dried, crushed blister beetles, used in medicine.

cant hook *n.* A wooden lever with a movable iron hook near the lower end, used for grasping and canting or turning over logs.

can-thus (kan´thus) *n.* The angle formed by the junction of the upper and lower eyelids.

can-ti-lev-er (kan´ti lev˝ėr) *n.* A projecting beam or member that is supported at only one end.

can-to (kan´tō) *n.* A major part or division of a long poem.

can-tus (kan´tus) *n.* A church song or melody.

can-vas (kan´vas) *n.* A heavy fabric used in making tents and sails for boats; a piece of canvas used for oil paintings.

can-vass (kan´vas) *v.* To travel through a region to solicit opinions or votes; to take a poll or survey. **canvasser** *n.*

can-yon (kan´yun) *n.* A deep and narrow gorge with steep sides.

cap (kap) *n.* A covering for the head, usually brimless and made of a soft material; the final or finishing touch to something; a small explosive charge that is used in cap guns.

ca-pa-ble (kā´pa bl) *adj.* Having the ability to perform in an efficient way; qualified. **capability** *n.* **capably** *adv.*

ca-pa-cious (ka pā´shus) *adj.* Having a lot of room or space.

ca-pac-i-tance (ka pas´i tans) *n.* The property of a body or circuit which allows it to store an electrical charge. **capacitive** *adj.*

ca-pac-i-tate (ka pas´i tāt˝) *v.* To make capable; to qualify.

ca-pa-ci-tive (ka pas´i tiv) *adj.* Coupling or connector that joins circuits by means of a condenser.

ca-pac-i-tor (ka pas´i tėr) *n.* The circuit element composed of metallic plates that are separated by a dielectric and are used to store a charge temporarily.

ca-pac-i-ty (ka pas´i tē) *n. pl.* **-ies** The ability to contain, receive, or absorb; having the aptitude or ability to do something; the maximum production or output; in computer science, the total amount of data or information that can be processed, stored, or generated.

cap–a–pie *adv.* From head to foot; all over.

ca-par-i-son (ka par´i san) *n.* An ornamental covering for a horse, saddle, or harness.

cape (kāp) *n.* A sleeveless covering for the shoulders that fastens at the neck; a piece or point of land that extends into a lake or sea.

cap-e-lin (kap´a lin) *n.* A small edible fish, allied to the smelt; codfish.

Ca-pel-la (ka pel´a) *n.* A brilliant star of the first magnitude.

ca-per (kā´pėr) *n.* A prank; antic.

cap-er-cail-lie (kap˝ėr kāl´yē) *n.* The largest wood grouse of the Old World.

cape-skin (kāp skin) *n.* A light flexible leather made from the skins of goats from which gloves are frequently made.

ca-pi-as (kā pē as) *n.* An arrest warrant authorizing the act of taking a person or possessions into custody.

cap-il-lar-i-ty (kap˝i lar´i tē) *n.* The action of molecules on the surface of a liquid in contact with a solid.

cap-il-lary (kap´i ler´ē) *n. pl.* **-ies** Any of the small vessels that connect the veins and arteries. *adj.* Having a hair-like bore; very fine or small in size.

cap-il-lar-y at-trac-tion *n.* The apparent attraction between a liquid and a solid in capillarity.

cap-i-tal (kap´i tal) *n.* The town or city that is designated as the seat of government for a nation or state; material wealth in the form of money or property that is used to produce more wealth; funds that are contributed to a business by the stockholders or owners; net worth of a company or business.

capital account *n*. An account that shows an individual person or shareholder's financial interest in a business.

capital assets *n*. Business assets that are of a fixed, or permanent nature and not commonly bought and sold.

capital gain *n*. The gains from the sale of capital assets.

cap-i-tal-ism (kap´i ta liz´um) *n*. The economic system in which the means of distribution and production are privately owned and operated for private profit.

cap-i-tal-ist (kap´i ta list) *n*. A person who invests in a business; a person who has extensive wealth employed in business enterprises, to invest and manage freely. **capitalistic** *adj*.

capital levy *n*. Levy put on capital assets apart from the income tax.

capital punishment *n*. The death penalty.

cap-i-ta-tion (kap´i tā´shan) *n*. A census or tax of equal amount for each person.

cap-i-tol (kap´i tol) *n*. The building used for meetings of the state legislative body; the building in Washington DC where the United States congress meets.

ca-pit-u-late (ka pich´u lāt´) *v*. To surrender under terms of an agreement. **capitulator** *n*. **capitulatory** *adj*.

ca-pit-u-lum (ka pich´u lum) *n*. The rounded part of a bone; a rounded or flattened cluster of flowers.

ca-pon (kā´pon) *n*. A young rooster that has been castrated to improve the meat for eating.

ca-pote (ka pōt´) *n*. A long hooded cloak with a close-fitting caplike bonnet worn by women and children.

ca-price (ka prēs´) *n*. A sudden change of action or mind without adequate reason; a whim; an impulse **capricious** *adj*. **capriciousness** *n*.

ca-pri-cious (ka prish´us) *adj*. Apt to change opinions unpredictably; subject to change.

Capricorn (kap´ri korn´) *n*. The tenth sign of the zodiac; a person born between December 22 - January 19.

cap-ri-fi-ca-tion (kap´ri fi kā´shan) *n*. The artificial pollination of figs, by hanging flowering branches of the wild fig in the trees, attracting the fig wasps that transfer the pollen to the edible figs.

cap-ri-fig (kap´ri fig´) *n*. Uncultivated form of the common fig.

cap-ri-ole (kap´rē ōl´) *n*. A spring or standing still leap given by a horse in exhibitions; a playfull leap.

capric acid *n*. A fatty acid, found in coconut oil, used for synthetic dyes, perfumes and flavorings.

cap-si-cum (kap´sa kum) *n*. The name for many species plants cultivated for their seed pods, when dried and prepared, are used as a gastric and intestinal stimulant.

cap-size (kap´sīz) *v*. To overturn in a boat.

cap-stan (kap´stan) *n*., *Naut*. A drum-like apparatus rotated to hoist weights by winding in a cable on a ship or boat.

cap-stone (kap´stōn´) *n*. A finishing stone of a structure; a crowning achievement.

cap-su-late (kap´sa lāt´) *adj*. Formed into a capsule.

cap-su-lated (kap´sa lā´tid) *adj*. Formed or in a capsule-like state. **capsulation** *n*.

cap-sule (kap´sul) *n*. A small gelatinous case for a dose of oral medicine; a fatty sac that surrounds an organ of the body, as the kidney, and protects it; a summary in a brief form. **sular** *adj*.

cap-tain (kap´tan) *n*. The chief leader of a group; the commander or master of a ship. *Naval* The commissioned naval officer who ranks below a commodore or rear admiral; the designated spokesperson of a team; to lead. **captaincy** *n*. **captainship** *n*.

cap-tion (kap´shan) *n*. A subtitle; a description of an illustration or picture.

cap-tious (kap´shus) *adj*. Deceptive; critical.

cap-ti-vate (kap´ti vāt´) *v*. To hold the attention, fascinate, or charm a person or group of people. **captivation** *n*. **captivator** *n*.

cap-tive (kap´tiv) *n.* A person being held as a prisoner.

cap-tiv-i-ty (kap tiv´i tē) *n.* The period of being captive.

cap-ture (kap´cher) *v.* To take something or someone by force. **capturer** *n.*

ca-puche (ka pōsh) *n.* A hood or cowl.

cap-y-ba-ra (kap˝i bär´a) *n.* A rodent that lives in rivers of South America, and feeds on vegetables and fish.

car (kär) *n.* An automobile; an enclosed vehicle, as a railroad car.

ca-ra-ca-ra (kär´a kär´a) *n.* Various vulture-like birds of the falcon family.

car-ack (kar´ak) *n.* A large, merchant vessel, of the 15th and 16th centuries.

car-a-cole (kar´a kōl˝) *n.* A half turn to the right or left executed by a trained saddle horse.

ca-rafe (ka raf´) *n.* A glass bottle for serving wine or water.

car-a-mel (kar´a mel) *n.* A chewy substance primarily composed of sugar, butter, and milk.

car-a-mel-ize (kar´a ma līz) *v.* To make into caramel.

ca-ran-gid (ka ran´jid) *n.* Fishes belonging to or resembling the *Carnidae* family, which includes spiny-finned fishes and other imported species.

car-a-pace (kar´a pās˝) *n.* The hard, bony shield covering an animal's back, as a turtle's shell.

car-at (kar´at) *n.* The unit of weight for gems that equals 200 milligrams.

car-a-van (kar´a van´) *n.* A group of people traveling together.

car-a-vel (kar´a vel˝) *n.* A small 15th and 16th century ship having broad bows, formerly used by the Spanish and Portuguese; a small fishing boat.

car-a-way (kar´a wā´) *n.* An aromatic seed used in cooking.

car-ba-mate (kär´ba māt˝) *n.* A salt of carbamic acid.

car-ba-zole (kär´ba zōl˝) *n.* A white, basic cyclic compound, found in coal tar, used in making dyes, explosives, insecticides and

lubricants.

car-bide (kär´bīd) *n.* A carbon compound with a more electropositive element.

car-bine (kär´bīn) *n.* A short-barreled rifle, light in weight.

car-bi-nol *n.* Methyl alcohol, or similar alchol, such as isopropyl alcohol.

carbocyclic compound *n.* Organic compounds having a ring formation made up of carbon atoms, as benzene.

car-bo-hy-drate (kär´bō hī´drāt) *n.* A group of compounds, including starches, celluloses, and sugars that contain carbon, hydrogen, and oxygen.

car-bo-late (kär´bo lāt) *n.* A carbolic acid salt.

car-bo-lat-ed (kär´bo lā˝ tid) *adj.* Containing carbolic acid.

car-bon (kär´bøn) *n.* A nonmetallic element that occurs as a powdery noncrystalline solid; the element symbolized by C. **carbonization** *n.* **carbonize** *v.* **carbonous** *n.*

car-bo-na-do (kär˝ bo nä´dō) *n.* A piece of meat that has been scored before cooking or grilling.

car-bon-ate (kär´bo nāt´) *v.* To add or charge with carbon dioxide gas, as in a beverage. **bonation** *n.*

carbon black *n.* Any of various finely sectioned or divided forms of carbon obtained or derived from incomplete combustion of natural gas.

carbon copy *n.* A copy made with carbon paper. *Slang* An exact copy of anything, person or thing.

carbon dating *n.* Process that determines the age of old materials such as archeological and geological specimens.

carbon dioxide *n.* A colorless, odorless, nonflammable gas, absorbed from the atmosphere by the photosynthesis of plants and returned by the respiration of people and animals.

carbon disulfide *n.* A colorless or yellowish, flammable and poisonous liquid; used as a solvent for rubber.

carbon fin *n.* A jet vane made of carbon

and placed in the jet stream of a rocket.

carbonic acid *n.* A weak dibasic acid, that reacts with bases to form carbonates, and decomposes into water plus carbon dioxide.

carbonium ion *n.* An organic ion having a positive charge at a carbon position.

car-bon-ize (kär´bo nīz˝) *v.* To change into carbon or a carbonic residue, as by partial combustion.

carbon monoxide *n.* An odorless, colorless very toxic gas, formed by the incomplete combustion of carbon, burns with a blue flame; highly poisonous when inhaled.

carbon paper *n.* A thin gelatin-coated sheet of paper with dark pigmented coating on one side, when placed between two sheets of paper transfers whatever is written or typed on the top sheet of paper to the one placed on bottom of it.

carbon process *n.* A photographic printing on paper coated with sensitized gelatin mixed with carbon or other pigment.

carbon tetrachloride *n.* A colorless, non-flammable, poisonous liquid used in cleaning fluid and fire extinguishers.

car-boy (kär´boi) *n.* A large, strong, glass bottle, often cushioned in a protective container, used for corrosive liquids.

car-bun-cle (kär´bung kl) *n.* An infection of the skin and deeper tissue which is red, inflamed, full of pus, and painful.

car-bu-ret (kär´bu rāt˝) *n.* To combine with carbon, or mix with carbon compounds.

car-bu-re-tor (kär´ba rā´tėr) *n.* The device in gasoline engines that mixes vapor, fuel, and air for efficient combustion.

car-ca-jou (kär´ka jö˝) *n.* The American name for the wolverine.

car-cass (kär´kas) *n.* The dead body of an animal; something that no longer has life.

car-cin-o-gen (kär sin´ o jen) *n.* A substance or agent that produces cancer.

car-ci-no-ma (kär´si nō´ma) *n.* A malignant tumor; cancer. **cinomatous** *adj.*

car-ci-no-ma-to-sis *n.* A state in which multiple carcinomas develop at the exact same time.

card (kärd) *n.* A small piece of pasteboard or very stiff paper, used in a wide variety of ways, as a greeting card, a business card, a postcard, etc.

car-da-mom (kär´da mum) *n.* The aromatic capsular fruit of various East India herb plants of the ginger family.

card catalog *n.* An alphabetical arrangement of books, arranged systematically on individual cards, found in libraries.

car-di-ac (kär´dē ak´) *adj.* Relating to the heart.

cardi-ac massage *n.* A procedure performed to restore proper circulation for a heart in distress.

car-di-gan (kär´digan) *n.* A sweater with an opening down the front.

car-di-nal (kär´di nal) *adj.* Of prime importance; principal. *n.* An official of the Catholic Church who ranks just below the Pope and who is appointed by him.

cardinal virtues *n. pl.* Four natural virtues; justice, prudence, temperance, and fortitude.

car-di-o-gram (kär´dē o gram´) *n.* The curve or tracing made by a cardiograph and used in the diagnosis of heart defects; the record of a heart's action made by a cardiograph.

car-di-oid *n.* A somewhat heart-shaped mathematical curve, being the path of a point on the circumference of a circle which rolls on another circle of equal size.

car-di-ol-o-gy (kär´dē ol´o jē) *n.* The study of the heart, its diseases, and treatments. **cardiologist** *n.*

car-di-o-pul-mo-nar-y (kärd ē ō´pul me ner ē) *adj.* Relating to the heart and lungs.

cardiopulmonary resuscitation *n.* A procedure used to restore normal breathing after cardiac arrest by using mouth-to-mouth resuscitation, clearing the air passages to the lungs, heart massage by chest compressions and if necessary the use of drugs.

car-di-o-vas-cu-lar (kär´dē ō vas´kū lėr) *adj.* Involving and relating to the heart and the blood vessels.

car-di-tis (kär dī´tis) *n.* Inflammation of

the heart muscles.

car-doon (kär dŏn´) *n*. A perennial plant of the Mediterranean regions, and related to the artichoke, eaten as a vegetable.

card-shark (kärd´shärp˝) *n*. A person who cheats when playing cards.

care (kâr) *n*. A feeling of concern, anxiety, or worry; guardianship or custody. *v*. To show interest or regard.

ca-reen (ka rēn´) *v*. To lurch or twist from one side to another while moving rapidly.

ca-reer (ka rēr´) *n*. The profession or oc-cupation a person takes in life. **career** *adj*.

ca-reer-ism (ka rēr´iz um) *n*. The practice of giving one's all to a career, often at the sacrifice of one's integrity and family re-sponsibility.

care-free (kâr´frē´) *adj*. Free from all cares, worries, and concerns.

care-less (kâr´lis) *adj*. Not showing or receiving care; being heartless; lacking in consideration.

care-ful (kâr´ful) *adj*. Exercising care; cau-tious; watchful.

ca-ress (ka res´) *v*. To gently show affection by touching or stroking. **caress** *n*.

care-tak-er (kâr´tā˝kėr) *n*. One who takes care of land or maintains a building in the owner's absence.

care-worn (kâr´wōrn˝) *adj*. Showing the effects of anxiety; drained due to prolonged overwork.

car-fare (kär´fâr˝) *n*. Passenger fare on a public vehicle, such as a bus.

car-go (kär´gō) *n*. Freight; the goods and merchandise carried on a ship, plane, or other vehicle.

car-hop (kär´hop´) *n*. A person who waits on customers at a drive-in restaurant.

Caribbean Sea *n*. An arm of the Atlantic Ocean bounded by the coasts of South and Central America and the West Indies.

car-i-bou (kar´i bŏ˝) *n*. A large antlered deer of northern North America.

car-i-ca-ture (kar´a ka chėr) *n*. An exaggerated representation, picture or description, in which peculiarities or defects of person or thing are ridiculously exaggerated.

car-i-ca-ture (kar´a ka chėr) *v*. To make caricature of; to represent in a ridiculous and exaggerated fashion.

car-ies (kâr´ēz) *n*. The decay of a bone or tooth.

car-il-lon (kar´i lon) *n*. A set of tuned bells in a tower, that are usually played by a keyboard.

car-i-o-ca (kar˝ē ō´ka) *n*. A South Amer-ican dance and its accompanying music, variation of the samba.

car-min-a-tive (kär min´a tiv) *adj*. Ex-pelling gas from the body.

car-mine (kär min) *n*. A vivid red color; crimson; deep purplish red.

car-nage (kär´nij) *n*. A bloody slaughter; war; massacre.

car-nal (kär´nal) *adj*. Relating to sensual desires. **carnality** *n*. **carnally** *adv*.

car-nall-ite (kär´na līt˝) *n*. A mineral con-sisting of a hydrous potassium-mag-nesium chloride which provides a valuable source of potassium.

car-nas-si-al (kär nas´ē al) *adj*. Of or pertaining to teeth of a carnivore adapted for cutting rather than tearing flesh.

car-na-tion (kär nā´shan) *n*. A fragrant perennial flower in a variety of colors.

carnauba wax *n*. Wax obtained from the Brazilian wax palm, and used as a base in polishes.

car-nel-ian (kär nēl´yan) *n*. A clear red chalcedony that is used as a gem.

car-ni-val (kär´ni val) *n*. A traveling amusement show with side shows, a Ferris wheel, and merry-go-rounds; any kind of a happy celebration; the period of festivity preceding Lent.

car-ni-vore (kär´ni vōr´) *n*. A flesh-eating animal. **carnivorous** *adj*. **carnivorously** *adv*. **carnivorousness** *n*.

car-ob (kar´ob) *n*. A Mediterranean tree, the pods of which, are known as locust beans, contains a sweet pulp.

car-ol (kar´ol) *n* A song to celebrate joy

or praise. **caroler** *n.* **carol** *v.*

car-o-tene (kar′o tēn″) *n.* Pigment of orange or red found in some vegteables and animal fats, can be turned into vitamin A.

ca-rot-i-noid (ka rot′e noid″) *n.* Red and yellow pigments found in plants, and animals.

ca-rouse (ka rouz′) *v.* To be rowdy and to be in a drunken state. **carouser** *n.*

carp (kärp) *v.* To find unreasonable fault with something or someone; to complain unduly. *n.* A freshwater fish that contains many small bones but can be eaten with caution.

car-pal (kär′pal) *adj.* Pertaining to the wrist and the bones in the wrist.

car-pel (kär′pel) *n.*, *Bot.* A seed vessel or pistil.

car-pen-ter (kär′pen tèr) *n.* A person who builds and repairs wooden structures. **carpentry** *n.*

car-pet (kär′pit) *n.* A thick, woven or felt floor covering that helps to insulate the floors. **carpet** *n.*

car-pet bag (kär′pit bag′) *n.* An old-fashioned traveling bag made from carpet.

car-pet bag-ger (kär′pit bag′er) *n.* A person from the North who traveled to the South after the Civil War to seek political or financial gain.

carpet beetle *n.* Small dermestid beetles which attack and damage woolens.

car-pet-ing (kär′pit ing) *n.* Material for carpets; carpets in general.

carpet weed *n.* A plant of North American that forms a dense mat on the ground as it grows.

car-pol-o-gy *n.* The division of botany relating to the structure of seeds and seed vessels.

car-port (kär′port) *n.* A roof attached to the side of a building to give shelter for a vehicle.

carp-suck-er (kärp′suk″er) *n.* North American freshwater fish, similar to the carp.

car-pus (kär′pus) *n.* The bones of the wrist or the wrist itself.

car-riage (kar′ij) *n.* A horse-drawn cart for

passengers.

car-ri-er (kar′ē er) *n.* A person who carries; an association acting as an insurer; an organization engaged in transporting passengers or goods for hire.

carrier aircraft *n.* Aircraft based on, and operating from, an aircraft carrier.

carrier pigeon *n.* A pigeon trained to carry messages; a homing pigeon.

carron oil *n.* Ointment composed of equal parts of limewater and olive oil, used as a treatment for burns and scalds.

car-rot (kar′ot) *n.* An orange vegetable that is an edible root.

car-rou-sel (kar′a sel′) *n.* A merry-go-round.

car-ry (kar′ē) *v.* To transport from one place to another; to bear the burden, weight, or responsibility of; to keep or have available for sale; to maintain on business books for future settlement.

car-ry-all (kar′ē ol″) *n.* A capacious bag or suitcase for carrying items.

carrying charge *n.* The amount charged over the regular price a merchandise sold on installments.

carry on *n.* Luggage carried on an airplane by passengers.

car sickness *n.* Nausea caused by motion.

cart (kärt) *n.* A two-wheeled vehicle for moving heavy goods; a small lightweight vehicle that can be moved around by hand. **carter** *n.*

carte blanche *n.* Unrestricted authority to make decisions.

car-tel (kär tel′) *n.* A group of independent companies that have organized to control prices, production, etc.

Carter, James Earl Jr. (Jimmy) *n.* The 39th president of the United States 1977-1981.

car-ti-lage (kär′ti lij) *n.* A tough, elastic substance of connective tissue attached to the surface of bones near the joints. **cartilaginous** *adj.*

car-ti-lag-i-nous (kär″ti laj′i nus) *adj.* Having or resembling cartilage.

car-to-gram (kär′to gram″) *n.* A map

giving simplified statistical information by using shading.

car-tog-ra-pher (kär tog′ra fẽr) *n*. One who makes and or publishes maps.

car-tog-ra-phy (kär tog′ra fẽ) *n*. The art of developing charts and maps. **cartographer** *n*. **cartographic** *adj*.

car-ton (kär′ ton) *n*. A container made from cardboard.

car-toon (kär tön′) *n*. A caricature depicting a humorous situation; animated cartoons produced by photographing a series of action drawings. **cartoonist** *n*.

car-tridge (kär′trij) *n*. A case made of metal, pasteboard, etc., that contains a charge of powder; the primer and shot or projectile for a firearm.

cartridge paper *n*. A durable, strong paper used for making cartridges.

car-tu-lar-y *n*. A record or register of title deeds and other documents; the keeper of such a records or archives.

cart-wheel (kärt′hwẽl′) *n*. A sideways hand spring with the arms over the head and the legs spread like the spokes of a wheel.

car-va-crol *n*. A thick, colorless oil.

carve (kärv) *v*. To slice meat or poultry; to cut into something; to create, as sculpture. **carver** *n*.

car-vel–built (kär′vel bilt″) *adj*. Pertaining to a ship or boat built with the planks meeting flush and not overlapping.

cary-at-id (kar′ẽ at′id) *n*. A supporting column sculptured in the form of a female figure.

car-y-op-sis (kar″ẽ op′ss) *n*. A small, one-seeded, dry, indehiscent fruit in which the seed and fruit fuse in a single grain.

ca-sa-ba (ka sä′ba) *n*. A sweet, edible winter melon having a yellow skin.

cas-cade (kas kād′) *n*. A waterfall that flows over steep rocks.

cas-ca-ril-la (kas″ka ril′a) *n*. The bitter aromatic bark of a West Indian shrub used for making incense and as a tonic.

case (kās) *n*. A particular occurrence or instance; an injury or disease; an argument, supporting facts, or reasons that justify a situation; a box or housing to carry things in, as a briefcase; in the law, a suit of action brought against a person.

ca-se-a-tion (kā″sē ā′shan) *n*. The separation of casein from coagulating milk, to form a soft cheesy substance or curd.

case-book (kās′buk″) *n*. A book containing detailed records of cases, that is used for reference and instruction in law, psychology, sociology, and medicine.

case history *n*. A factual information about an individual's personal history.

ca-sein (kā′sēn) *n*. A dairy protein that is used in foods and in manufacturing adhesives and plastics.

case law *n*. Law made by decided cases that serve as precedents.

case-ment *n*. A window sash opening by swinging on hinges, which are generally attached to the upright side of its frame.

case system *n*. A method of teaching law based primarily on reported cases instead of textbooks.

case-work *n*. Social work with direct contact and consideration of a patient, his family, and their problems.

case-worm *n*. A caddisworm, so called from the case which it constructs to protect its body.

cash *n*. Money, or an equivalent, as a check, paid at the time of making a purchase.

cash-ew (kash′ö) *n*. A tropical American tree that produces an edible nut that can be eaten raw or roasted.

cash flow *n*. Reported net income after taxes; the liquidity of a corporation plus amounts charged off plus noncash charges.

cash-ier (ka shēr′) *n*. An employee who handles cash as part of his job description; an officer in a bank in charge of receiving or distributing money.

cashier's check *n*. A check drawn by a bank upon its own funds and signed by its cashier.

cash items *n*. Items such as, government bonds, bank deposits, securities, and the like that are considered equivalent to cash in a corporate statement.

cash-mere (kazh´mēr) *n.* The wool from the Kashmir goat; the yarn made from this wool.

cas-ing (kās ing) *n.* A protective covering; a supporting frame as used around a door or window.

ca-si-no (k*a* **sē´nō)** *n. pl.* **-nos** A public establishment open especially for gambling.

cask (kask) *n.* A large wooden vessel or barrel; the quantity that a cask will hold.

cas-ket (kas´kit) *n.* A coffin; a small chest or box.

Caspian Sea *n.* Salt lake between western Asia and southeastern Europe.

cas-que (kask) *n.* A helmet. **casqued** *adj.*

cas-sa-va (k*a* **sä´va)** *n.* A slender erect shrub grown in the tropics.

cas-se-role (kas´*e* **rōl´)** *n.* A dish in which the food is baked and also served; food cooked and served in this manner.

cas-sette (k*a* **set´)** *n.* A cartridge of magnetic tape used in tape recorders to play and record.

cas-sit-er-ite (k*a* **sit´***a* **rīt˝)** *n.* A brown or black mineral that consists of tin dioxide, the chief source of metallic tin.

cas-sock (kas´*o***k)** *n.* A close-fitting garment worn by members of the clergy.

cas-so-war-y (kas´*o* **wer˝ē)** *n.* A large, three-toed, flightless ratite bird; closely related to emu.

cast (kast) *v.* To hurl or throw with force; to direct or turn; to shed; to give a certain part or role; to deposit or give a vote on something; to make or throw, as with a fishing line. *Naut.* To fall off, to veer; to be shipwrecked or marooned at sea. *n.* A dresing made from plaster of paris used on a broken bone.

cas-ta-net (kas´*ta* **net´)** *n. pl.* **-nets** An instrument made from a pair of ivory or hardwood shells, held in the palm of the hand and clapped together with the fingers.

cast-a-way (kast´*a* **wā´)** *adj.* Throw away. *n.* One who is shipwrecked or discarded.

caste (kast) *n.* A social separation based on a profession, hereditary, or financial hierarchy.

cas-tel-lat-ed (kas´t*e* **lā´tid)** *adj.* Adorned by battlements and turrets.

cast-er (kas´tèr) *n.* A small set of swiveling rollers that are fastened under pieces of furniture and the like.

cas-ti-gate (kas´t*i* **gāt´)** *v.* To punish or criticize severely. **castigation** *n.* **castigator** *n.*

cast-ing (kas´ting) *n.* The act of one that casts.

casting vote *n.* A deciding vote cast by a president or chairman to break a tie.

cast iron *n.* A hard, brittle, commercial alloy of iron, carbon, and silicon that is cast into a mold.

cas-tle (kas´*e***l)** *n.* A fort or fortified dwelling for nobility; any large house or place of refuge; a stronghold.

cast-off (kas tof) *adj.* Discarded; thrown away; thrown to the side.

cas-tor (kas t*e***r)** *n.* A beaver; a beaver hat, or a hat that resembles one.

castor bean *n.* The poisonous seed of the castor-oil plant.

castor oil *n.* A pale fatty oil from castor beans, used as a cathartic and lubricant.

cas-trate (kas´trāt) *v.* To remove the testicles; to remove the ovaries; to spay, to remove something from. **castration** *n.*

ca-su-al (kazh´ö*a***l)** *adj.* Informal; occurring by chance; uncertain. **casually** *adv.* **casualness** *n.*

cas-u-al-ism (kazh´ö*a* **liz˝***u***m)** *n.* The state of things where chance prevails; the belief that all things exist or are governed by chance or accident.

ca-su-al-ty (kazh´ö*a***l tē)** *n. pl* **-ies** One who is injured or killed in an accident. *Milit.* A soldier who is killed, wounded, taken prisoner by the enemy, or missing in action.

casualty insurance *n.* Insurance against damage or loss as in an accident, burglary or libility.

cas-u-ist (kazh´ö ist) *n.* A person who studies and resolves cases of conscience or conduct.

cat (kat) *n.* A small domesticated animal,

a pet; any of the animals in the cat family, such as the lion, lynx, tiger, etc.

ca-tab-o-lism (ka tab´o liz˝um) *n.* In living organisms, a breaking down of more complex molecules into simpler ones, involving the release of energy.

cat-a-chre-sis (kat˝a krē´sis) *n.* Misuse of a word context.

cat-a-clysm (kat´a kliz um) *n.* A sudden and violent event; an extensive flood; a deluge. **cataclysmic** *adj.* **cataclysmal** *adj.*

cat-a-comb (kat´a kŏm˝) *n.* An underground passage with small rooms for coffins.

ca-tad-ro-mous (ka tad´ro mus) *adj.* Of fish living in freshwater and going down to the sea to spawn.

cat-a-falque (kat´a falk´) *n.* The structure that supports a coffin during a state funeral.

cat-a-lep-sy (kat´a lep´sē) *n.* A condition in which there is a rigidity of the muscles, causing the patient to remain in a fixed position or posture. **cataleptic** *adj.*

cat-a-log (kat´a log) *n.* A publication containing a list of names, objects, etc.

ca-tal-pa (katal´pa) *n.* A hardy, small ornamental tree found in Asia and America and noted for its heart-shaped leaves and pale showy flowers.

cat-a-lyst (kat´a list) *n., Chem.* Any substance that alters and decreases the time it takes a chemical reaction to occur.

cat-a-ma-ran (kat´a ma ran´) *n.* A boat with twin hulls.

cat-am-ne-sis (kat˝am nē´sis) *n.* The medical hisory of a patient taken during, or after recovering from, an illness.

cat-a-mount (kat´amount˝) *n.* A wild cat; as the cougar or lynx.

cat-a-pla-sia (kat˝a plā´zha) *n.* The reverting of cells or tissues to an earlier or more primitive stage.

cat-a-plex-y (kat´a plek˝sē) *n.* A sudden loss of muscle power caused by a strong emotional shock.

cat-a-pult (kat´a pult´) *n.* An ancient military device for throwing arrows or stones; a device for launching aircraft from the deck of a ship. **catapult** *v.*

cat-a-ract (kat´a rakt˝) *n.* A large waterfall or downpour. *Pathol.* A disease of the lens of the eye, causing total or partial blindness.

ca-tarrh (ka tär´) *n., Pathol.* Inflammation of the nose and throat. **catarrhal** *adj.*

ca-tas-ta-sis (ka tas´ta sis) *n.* The climax of a play.

ca-tas-tro-phe (ka tas´tro fē) *n.* A terrible and sudden disaster; a calamity. **catastophic** *adj.* **catastrophically** *adv.*

cat-a-to-ni-a (kat˝a tō´nē a) *n.* The state of suspended animation and the loss of voluntary motion.

ca-taw-ba (ka to´ba) *n.* A pale red native American grape that is cultivated into a wine of the same name. **Catawba,** tribe of American Indians.

cat-bird (kat´berd´) *n.* A song bird of North America with slate-gray feathers.

cat block *n.* A heavy pulley block with hook, used in hoisting an anchor.

cat-boat (kat´bōt´) *n.* A broad beamed, light draft sailboat, usually having a cat rig and centerboard, with a single mast set extended by a long boom and gaff.

cat-call (kat´kol´) *n.* A shrill whistle to express derision or disapproval.

catch (kach) *v.* To take; to seize or capture; to reach in time; to intercept; to become entangled or fastened. **catch** *n.*

catch-all (kach´ol´) *n.* A container or bag for odds and ends.

catch basin *n.* A filter placed at the entrance of a drain or sewer in order to catch and retain matter that might clog the system.

catch crop *n.* A fast-growing crop raised between main crops, or as a substitute for a main crop failure.

catch-er (kach´er) *n.* A person who catches; in baseball. *Slang* The position behind the batter.

catch-fly (kach´flī˝) *n.* Any of various plants, with viscid stems in which small insects are sometimes caught.

catch-ment (kach´ment) *n.* The act of catching water; a drainage system that catches water, as a reservoir.

catch on *v.* To understand, learn; to become popular.

catch-word *n.* A word or phrase often repeated; an expression repeated until it represents an idea, party, school, or product.

Catch-22 *n.* The situation where alternatives can cancel each other, leaving no means of settling a dilemma or problem.

cat-e-chize (kat´a kiz˝) *v.* To teach or instruct orally by means of questions and answers.

cat-e-chu *n.* Any of several dry, earthy, or resinous astringent substances obtained from the wood of tropical plants of Asia and used for medicine, dyeing, or tanning.

cat-e-gor-i-cal (kat´a gor´i kal) *adj.* Absolute; certain; related to or included in a category without qualification. **categorically** *adv.*

cat-e-go-rize (kat´a go rīz´) *v.* To place in categories.

cat-e-go-ry (kat´a gōr´ē) *n. pl.* **-ries** A general group to which something belongs.

cat-e-nate (kat´e nāt˝) *v.* To connect in a series; links; to concatenate.

ca-ter (kā´tèr) *v.* To provide a food service; to bring directly to a location. **caterer** *n.*

cat-er-pil-lar (kat´a pil´er) *n.* The very fuzzy, worm-like, brightly-colored spiny larva of a moth or butterfly.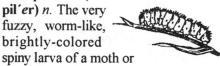

cat-er-waul (kat´er wol´) *n.* The harsh cry made by cats at mating time; cat-like cry. **caterwaul** *v.*

cat-fish (kat´fish´) *n.* A scaleless, freshwater fish that has long barbels or whiskers around the mouth.

cat-gut (kat´gut´) *n.* A thin, tough cord made from the fried intestines of sheep.

cat-head (kat´hed) *n.* A strong projecting piece of timber or iron near a ship's bow to which the anchor is raised and secured.

ca-the-dral (ka thē´dral) *n.* A large and important church, containing the seat of a bishop.

cath-e-ter (kath´i tèr) *n., Med.* A thin, flexible tube that is inserted into the body cavity for drainage and to draw urine from the bladder. **catheterize** *v.*

ca-thex-is *n.* The channeling of psychic energy in an object.

cath-ode (kath´ōd) *n.* The negatively charged electrode which receives positively charged ions during electrolysis.

cathode ray *n.* A stream of electrons projected from the heated cathode of a vacuum tube under the propulsion of a very strong electric field.

cathode–ray tube *n.* The vacuum tube on which images are found, used in a computer screen.

Catholic (kath´o lik) *n.* A member of the Roman Catholic Church.

Ca-thol-i-cism (ka thol´i sizm) *n.* The doctrine, practice, and faith of the Roman Catholic Church.

ca-thol-i-con (ka thol´ kon) *n.* A remedy for all diseases; cure–all.

cat-i-on (kat´ī on) *n.* A positively charged ion that is attracted in electrolytes to a negative electrode. **cationic** *adj.*

cat-kin (kat´kin) *n.* The spikelike blossom of the willow, birch trees that resemble a cat's tail.

cat-nap (kat´nap´) *n.* A short nap.

cat–o'–nine–tails (kat´o nīn´tālz´) *n.* A hand–made whip with nine knotted cords fastened to a handle.

ca-top-tric (ka top´trik) *adj.* Pertaining or relating to a reflected light or a mirror.

ca-top-trics (ka top´trik) *n.* The branch of optics that relates to a mirror or reflected light.

cat rig *n.* A rig consisting of a single mast set well forward and carrying one large sail extended by a long boom and gaff.

CAT scan *n.* A cross-sectional picture produced by a scanner, used to x-ray the body by using computerized axial tomography.

CAT scanner *n.* The machine used to produce a cross-sectional picture of the body.

cat's–eye (kats´ī) *n.* A hard, semi-transparent gem having an opalescent reflections from within; marble having eyelike concentric circles.

cat's foot *n.* The herb called ground ivy.

cat-sup (kat´sup) *n. Variation of* ketchup. A condiment made from tomatoes, water, sugar, and other spices.

cat-tail (kat´tāl´) *n.* A long marsh plant that has minute brown flowers and long leaves, used in making chair seats and in dried flower arrangements.

cat-ta-lo (kat´a lō) *n.* An animal developed by breeding domesticated cattle and the American buffalo.

cat-tle (kat´al) *n. pl.* Farm animals raised for meat and dairy products.

cat-tle-man (kat´al man) *n.* A person in the business of raising or tending cattle.

cat-tleya (kat´lē a) *n.* A tropical American orchid characterized by a showy hooded flower.

cat-ty (kat´ē) *adj.* Malicious or spiteful. **cattily** *adv.* **cattiness** *n.*

cat-ty--cor-nered (kat´ē kor´nėrd) *adj.* Not straight; sitting at an angle.

cat-walk (kat´wok˝) *n.* Any very narrow path, as along-side a bridge.

Cau-ca-sian (ko kā´ zhan) *n.* An inhabitant of Caucasus. *adj.* Relating to a major ethnic division of the human race; of or relating to the white race.

cau-cus (ko´kus) *n.* A meeting of a political party to make policy decisions and to select candidates. **caucus** *v.*

cau-dad (kod´al) *adj.* Toward the tail or posterior end of the body.

caudal anesthesia *n.* Insensibility to pain in the lower portion of the body, due to the injection of an anesthetic drug into the caudal part of the spinal canal.

cau-dex (ko´deks) *n.* The woody base of a perennial plant, including roots and stem.

cau-dle (kod´al) *n.* A warm drink usually made of spices, ale, and mixed with bread, eggs, and sugar.

caught *v.* Past tense of catch.

caul-dron (kol´dron) *n.* A large metal kettle or boiler.

cau-li-flow-er (ko´li flou´er) *n.* A vegetable related to broccoli and cabbage.

cauliflower ear *n.* An external ear which has become misshapen through injury and has excessive scar tissues.

caulk (kok) *v.* To seal seams and edges against leakage of water and air with some substance. **caulker** *n.*

caus-al (ko´zal) *adj.* Relating to or constituting a cause or causes; implying, involving, or expressing a cause or causes.

cau-sa-tion (ko zā´shan) *n.* The act or process of causing or producing an effect.

cause (koz) *v.* To produce a result, consequence, or effect. *n.* A goal, principle; a reason; motive. **causer** *n.*

cau-se-rie (kō´za rē´) *n.* A short informal conversation or chat.

cause-way (koz´wā´) *n.* A paved highway through a marsh tract; raised road over water.

caus-tic (ko´stik) *n.* A curve to which all light rays originating from a point and reflected by a curved surface are tangent.

cau-ter-ize (ko´ta rīz´) *v.* To sear or burn with a hot blade or instrument or fire, as in deseased tissue, a hot iron. **cauterization** *n.*

cau-ter-y (ko´ta rē) *n.* A very hot instrument used to destroy tissue that does not seem normal.

cau-tion (ko´shan) *n.* A warning; careful planning. **cautionary** *adj.*

cau-tious (ko´shus) *adj.* Very careful.

cav-al-cade (kav´al kād´) *n.* A group of horse-drawn carriages or riders, forming a procession.

cav-a-lier (kav´a lėr´) *n.* A very gallant gentleman; a knight.

cav-al-ry (kav´al rē) *n. pl.* **-ies** Army troops trained to fight on horseback or in armored vehicles. **cavalryman** *n.*

ca-vate (kā´vāt) *adj.* Hollowed or dug out; giving the appearance of a cave.

cav-a-ti-na (kav˝a tē´na) *n.* A simple operatic song or solo.

cave (kāv) *n.* An underground tomb or chamber with an opening at the ground surface.

ca-ve-at (kā´vē at´) *n.* A formal legal notice to stop the proceedings until both sides have a hearing; a warning or caution.

cave dweller *n.* A person, as a prehistoric man, who lives in caves.

cave–in *n.* The action of collapsing or caving in; a place where the ground has fallen in.

cave-man (kāv man) *n.* A person who lives in caves; especially of the Stone Age; a person who acts in a very rough primitive manner.

ca-vern (kav´ern) *n.* A very large underground cave. **cavernous** *adj.*

cav-i-ar *or* **cav-i-are (kav´ē är´)** *n.* The eggs of large fish, eaten as an appetizer.

cav-il (kav´il) *v.* To raise captious and trivial objections; to find fault without good reason.

cav-i-ty (kav´i tē) *n.* *pl* **cavities** A decayed place in a tooth; a hollow or hole.

cay (kā) *n.* A range or reef of sand or coral alying near the surface of the water.

cay-man (kā´mam) *n.* A tropical American crocodile which is fundamentally similar to the alligator.

cay-use (kī ūs´) *n.* A small native range horse of the western United States.

CD *abbr.* Compact disk; civil defense; certificate of deposit.

Ceasar salad *n.* A green salad made with an olive oil and lemon juice dressing and topped with anchovies.

cease (sēs) *v.* To come to an end or put an end to; to stop.

cease-fire (sēs´fī´er) *v.* To stop fighting, usually as a result of a truce.

cease-less (sēs´lis) *adj.* Endless; without a stop or pause; continual; without intermission. **ceaselessly** *adv.*

cecropia moth *n.* A large silkworm moth of the eastern United States whose larva feeds on the leaves of many trees.

ce-cum (se´kum) *n.* The pouch where the large intestine begins.

ce-dar (sē´dėr) *n.* An evergreen tree with fragrant, red dishwood.

cedar waxwing *n.* A bird of North American with light brown feathers which often feeds on juniper berries.

cede (sēd) *v.* To formally resign and surrender to another, usually by treaty.

ce-dil-la (si dil´a) *n.* A diacritical mark placed under the letter c (ç) in the French vocabulary to indicate a modification or alteration of the usual phonetic sound.

cei-ba *n.* A large silk-cotton tree, having large pods filled with seeds imbedded with silky floss that yields the fiber kapok.

ceil-ing (sē´ling) *n.* The overhead covering of a room; the maximum limit to something; the maximum height for visibility under specified condi tions for aircraft.

ceiling unlimited *n.* A cloudless or almost cloudless sky.

ceiling zero *n.* A cloud ceiling at a height of 50 feet or lower.

ceil-om-e-ter (sē lom´i tėr) *n.*, *Meteor.* A photo-electric instrument for measuring and recording the height of a cloud ceiling.

cel-a-don (sel´a don˝) *n.* A pale-green ceramic glaze, used in Chinese porcelains and stonewares.

cel-an-dine (sel´an dīn˝) *n.* A biennial herb of the poppy family which emits a bright orange-colored juice when its leaves or stems are crushed. The juice from this plant is used in medicine as a diuretic, purgative and fungicide.

cel-e-brate (sel´e brāt´) *v.* To observe with ceremonies, rejoicing, or festivity. **celebration** *n.*

cel-e-brat-ed (sel´e brā´tid) *adj.* Famous, well-known.

cel-e-bra-tion (sel e´brā shen) *n.* The act of celebrating; to demonstrate satisfaction in a festive way.

cel-leb-ri-ty (se leb´ri tē) *n. pl.* **-ies** A famous person.

ce-ler-i-ac (se ler´ē ak˝) *n.* A variety of celery, grown for its knobby edible turnip-like root.

ce-ler-i-ty (se ler´i tē) *n.* Swiftness; speed; rapid motion.

cel-er-y (sel´e rē) *n.* A green vegetable with

an edible stalk.

ce-les-ta (se les'ta) *n.* A musical instrument which produces bell-like tones when the keyboard and metal plates are struck by hammers.

ce-les-tial (se les'chel) *adj.* Heavenly; spiritual.

celestial body *n.* Any body of matter in the universe, such as a planet, star, or comet.

celestial equator *n.* The great circle of the celestial sphere, midway between the celestial poles, assumed to be the extension of the plane of the earth's equator.

celestial globe *n.* A globe that depicts the celestial bodies.

celestial mechanics *n.* Study of the influence of gravitational fields on the motions of celestial bodies.

celestial navigation *n.* Navigation by which a geographical location is determined by the position of celestial bodies.

celestial pole *n.* The two points on the celestial sphere around which the stars appear to revolve.

ce-li-ac (sē'lē ak˝)*adj.* Relating or pertaining to the cavity of the abdomen.

celiac disease *n.* A chronic nutritional disease of young children, common in the tropics, characterized by anemia, sore tongue, and diarrhea.

cel-i-bate (sel'a bit) *n.* A person who remains unmarried because of religious vows; one who is sexually abstinent. **celibacy** *n.* **celibate** *adj.*

cell (sel) *n.* A prison; a small room; the smallest unit of any organism that is capable of independent function, is composed of a small mass of cytoplasm, usually encloses a central nucleus, and is surrounded by a membrane or a rigid cell wall; a cavity of an ovary or pericarp that is seed-bearing. *Electr.* The part of a battery that generates the electricity; in computer science, the loca tion in memory that holds a single unit of information; a byte.

cel-lar (sel'er) *n.* An underground area, beneath a building, used for storage.

cel-lar-ette (sel˝a ret') *n.* A cabinet or case for holding bottles of liquors or wines.

cell-block (sel'blok˝) *n.* A group or section of cells in a prison.

cell division *n.* The process of dividing both the cytoplasm and nucleus of a cell into two, in the process of reproduction.

cel-list (chel'ist) *n.* A person who plays the cello.

cell membrane *n.* The thin membrane enclosing the protoplasmic material of the cell; the cell wall.

cel-lo (chel'ō) *n.* A base instrument of the violin family. **list** *n.*

cel-lo-phane (sel'ø fān´) *n.* A transparent paper–like material made from treated cellulose that has been processed in thin, clear strips.

cel-lu-lar (sel'ya lėr) *adj.* Consisting of cells.

cel-lu-lase (sel'ya lās˝) *n.* An enzyme that hydrolyzes cellulosic; obtained from a fungus, and used in medicine, septic systems, and brewing.

cel-lu-lite (sel ye līt) *n.* A fatty deposit or area under the skin found in the hips, thighs, and buttocks.

cel-lu-lose (sel'ya lōs´) *n.* A carbohydrate that is insoluble in ordinary solvents and forms the fundamental material for the structure of plants.

cell wall *n.* The definite boundary, formed by the protoplasm, that surrounds a biological cell.

ce-ment (si ment´) *n.* A construction material made up of powdered, calcined rock and clay materials which when added with water, set up as a hard, solid mass.

ce-men-ta-tion (sē˝men tā'shan) *n.* The process of heating a solid, immersed in a powdered substance, so that the solid is changed by chemical combination with the powder.

ce-men-tum (si men'tum) *n.* The external layer of bony tissue that forms the outer surface of a tooth within the gum.

cem-e-ter-y (sem´i ter´ē) *n. pl.* **-ies** The place for burying the dead.

ce-no-bite (sē´no bīt˝) *n.* One of the religious groups that live in a convent or community.

ce-nog-a-my (sē nog´amē) *n.* The practice of having spouces in common, as primitive tribes.

cen-ser (sen´sėr) *n.* A vessel or container for burning incense.

cen-sor (sen´sėr) *n.* A person who examines films and printed materials to determine what might be objectionable and offensive. **censorship** *n.*

cen-sor-ship (sen´sėr ship˝) *n.* The practice of censoring; the authority of a censor.

cen-sure (sen´shur) *n.* An expression of criticism and disapproval.

cen-sus (sen´sus) *n.* An official count of the population.

cent (sent) *n.* One; one hundredth of a dollar.

cen-tare (sen´târ) *n.* A square meter.

cen-taur (sen´tor) *n.* In Greek mythology, a monster that has a man's arms, head, and trunk, but a horse's body and legs.

cen-te-nar-i-an (sen´te nâr´ē an) *n.* A person who has reached the age of 100 or more.

cen-te-na-ry (sen´te ner´ē) *n.* A period or age of 100 years; a century.

cen-ter (sen´tėr) *n.* The place of equal distance from all sides; the heart; in sports, a person who holds the middle position, as in the forward line.

cen-ter-piece (sen´tėr pēs˝) *n.* A decoration placed center of a table; something that is of the central importance.

center punch *n.* A hand punch having a short steel bar with a hard conical point used to center drill bits.

cen-tile (sen´tīl) *n.* A scale of comparison from lowest to highest, derived at by dividing into 100 ranks with the lowest as the first.

centile rank *n.* A score that shows percent of a total distribution is below a certain score.

cen-ti-me-ter (sen´ti mē˝tėr) *n.* A metric system of measurement; hundredth part of a meter; slightly more than 0.39 of an inch.

cen-ti-pede (sen´ti pēd´) *n.* A flat arthropod with numerous body segments and legs.

cen-to (sen´tō) *n.* A literary or musical composition made up of parts from other sources.

cen-tral (sen´tral) *adj.* In, near, or at the center; of primary importance. **centrally** *adv.* **centralize** *v.*

cen-tral-i-za-tion (sen˝tra li zā´shan) *n.* The concentration of authority within any groups or organizations.

central nervous system *n.* The nervous system that consists of the spinal cord and the brain.

cen-trif-u-gal (sen trif´ū gal) *adj.* Moving or directing away from a center location.

cen-tri-fuge (sen´tri fūj˝) *n.* A machine for inducing artificial gravity, used to test the ability of flying personnel, animal subjects, and equipment to withstand the above normal gravitational forces.

cen-tro-bar-ic (sen˝tro bar´ik) *adj.* Having to do with the center of gravity; possessing a center of gravity.

cen-tro-sphere (sen´tro sfēr˝) *n.* The thick material in the central part of the earth.

cen-tu-ry (sen´cha rē) *n. pl.* **-ies** A period consisting of 100 years.

ceph-a-lal-gia (sef˝a lal´ja) *n.* Headache.

ce-phal-ic (se fal´ik) *adj.* Relating or pertaining to the head.

ceph-a-li-za-tion (sef˝a li zā´shan) *n.* An evolutionary tendency in the development of animals to localization of sensory and neural organs or parts in or near the head.

ceph-a-lo-pod (sef˝a lo pod˝) *n.* Any class of mollusks, including the octopus, cuttlefish, and squids, having a tubular siphon under the head.

ceph-a-lo-tho-rax (sef˝a lō thōr´aks) *n.* The outer division of the body in crustaceans, spiders, etc. which consists of the united head and thorax.

ce-ram-ic (se ram´ik) *adj.* Of or relating

to a brittle material made by firing a nonmetallic-mineral, such as clay.

ceramics (se ram´iks) *n.* The art of making a ceramic piece.

cer-a-mist (ser´*a* mist) *n.* A person who works with ceramics.

ce-rar-gy-rite (se rär´jē rīt˝) *n.* Native chloride of silver, having the appearance of horn, and forms an important ore of silver.

ce-rate (sēr´āt) *n.* A thick ointment made by mixing oils with wax, resin, and medicinal ingredients.

cer-car-i-a (ser kâr´ē *a*) *n.* A larval stage of worms, characterized by an oval or tadpoleshape.

cere (sēr) *n.* A protuberance or wax-like skin growth that contains the nostrils, located at the base of the bill of a bird.

ce-re-al (sēr´ē *a*l) *n.* An edible grain eaten as a breakfast food.

cer-e-bel-lum (ser´*e* bel´*u*m) *n. pl.-bellums* The part of the brain responsible for the coordination of voluntary muscular movements.

cerebral (ser´*e* br*a*l) *adj.* Pertaining to the cerebrum or brain; relating to intellect.

cerebral hemisphere *n.* The two convoluted lateral halves into which the cerebrum is divided.

cerebral hemorrhage *n.* The rupture of a blood vessel or artery in the brain, therefore allowing blood to escape.

cerebral palsy *n.* A disability that usually occurres at birth and impairs motor function and speech; paralysis, due to brain damage prior to birth or during delivery.

cer-e-brate (ser´*e* brāt˝) *v.* To have or exhibit brain action; to think; to use the mind.

cer-e-brum (ser´*e* br*u*m) *n. pl.* -**brums** *or* -**bra** The brain structure that is divided into two cerebral hemispheres and occupies most of the cranial cavity.

cere-cloth (sēr´kloth˝) *n.* Cloth waterproofed with wax; formally used to wrap dead bodies as a means of preserving.

cere-ment (sēr´m*e*nt) *n.* A shroud for wrapping a corpse; any burial cloth.

cer-e-mo-ni-al (ser´*e* mō´nē *a*l) *adj.* Mark by or relating to a ceremony for a perticular occasion. **ceremonially** *adv.*

cer-e-mo-ny (ser´*e* mō´nē) *n. pl.* -**ies** A ritual or formal act performed in a certain manner. **ceremonious** *adj.*

ce-rise (se rēs´) *n.* The color of deep purplish red.

ce-rite (sēr´īt) *n.* A rare mineral, of a pale rose-red color.

cer-met (sür´met) *n.* A strong heat-resistant compound, made by bonding a metal and a ceramic substance.

ce-ro (sēr´ō) *n.* Either of two large sport and food fishes of the mackerel family, found in the warmer parts of the western Atlantic ocean.

ce-ro-plas-tic (sēr˝*o* plas´tik) *adj.* Pertaining to art modeling in wax.

cer-tain (ser´t*a*n) *adj. pl.* -**ties** Being very sure of something; without any doubt; inevitable; not mentioned but assumed. **tainly** *adv.* **certainty** *n.*

cer-tain-ty (ser´t*a*n tē) *n.* The state or quality of being certain; a fact or truth certainly established; something that is certain.

cer-tif-i-cate (ser tif´*i* kāt´) *n.* A document stating the truth or accuracy of something; a document that certifies fulfillment of duties or requirements, as of a course of study.

cer-tif-i-ca-tion (ser´t*i* fi kā´sh*a*n) *n.* A certified statement.

certified check *n.* A check certified as good for payment by the bank upon which it is drawn.

certified mail *n.* First-class mail accompanied by a receipt to be signed by the addressee and returned to the sender.

certified public accountant *n.* A public accountant who has met the requirements of state government and has been granted a certificate from the state in which he/she works or practices.

cer-ti-fy (ser´t*i* fī´) *v.* To testify in writing that something is true or a fact.

cer-ti-o-ra-ri (sėr˝shē o rår´ē) *n.* A writ from a superior court to call up the records of an inferior court for trial or review.

cer-ti-tude (sėr´ti tŏd˝) *n.* Certainty; state of being or feeling certain.

ce-ruse (sēr´ŏs) *n.* White lead as a pigment, used in painting and cosmetics.

cer-ve-lat (sėr´ve lat˝)*n.* A kind of highly seasoned, dry sausage, usually of young pork salted.

cer-vi-cal (sėr´vi kal) *adj.* Relating to the neck of the cervix.

cer-vi-ci-tis (sėr˝vi sī´tis) *n.* Inflammation of the uterine cervix.

cer-vix *n.* The neck, esp. the back of the neck; the narrow outer end of the uterus.

Ce-sar-ean (si zâr´ē an) *n.* A surgical operation which involves cutting through the abdomen and the uterus to remove or deliver a baby when normal delivery cannot or should not be accomplished.

ce-si-um (sē´zē um) *n.* An electro-metal, white in color, from the alkali group, used in photoelectric cells.

ces-sa-tion (se sā´shan) *n.* The act of stopping or ceasing.

ces-sion (sesh´on) *n.* The act of giving up territory or rights to another.

cess-pipe (ses´pŏl˝) *n.* An underground pipe for carrying off drainage from a cesspool.

cess-pool (ses´pŏl´) *n.* A pit or hole for the collection of drainage from toilets, and sinks and other waste water.

ces-tode (ses´tŏd) *adj.* Belonging to the class or group of internally parasitic flatworms, including the tapeworm.

ces-tus (ses´tus) *n.* A hand-covering of leather, often loaded with lead or iron, worn by gladiators.

ce-ta-cean (si tā´shan) *n.* Marine mammals that include whales, dolphins, and porpoises.

ce-tane (sē´tān) *n.* A colorless, oily hydrocarbon liquid, used an an additive to improve diesel fuel.

cetane number *n.* The measure of diesel fuel ignition; rating similar to the octane number rating for gasoline.

chafe (chāf) *v.* To become sore by rubbing; to irritate.

chaff (chaf) *n.* The husks of corn and other debris separated from the corn by thrashing, sifting; straw or hay cut up as for food for cattle.

chaf-fer (chā´fėr) *v.* To bargain; to haggle.

chaf-finch (chaf´inch) *n.* A European bird of the finch family of which the male has a reddish breast plumage.

chafing dish (chā´fing dish) *n.* A dish for cooking food and keeping it warm at the table.

cha-grin (sha grin´) *n.* A feeling of distress caused by disappointment, failure, or humiliation. **chagrin** *v.*

chain (chān) *n.* A connection of several links; anything that confines or restrains. **gang** Prisoners that are chained together. **reaction** Series of events that directly affect one another.

chain letter *n.* A letter sent to a number of people with a request to send copies to a specified number of other people for a supposed gain or advantage.

chain reaction *n.* Series of events each of which is initiated by the preceding one.

chain saw *n.* A power saw having teeth on a continuous band or chain.

chain-smoke (chān´smŏk´) *v.* To smoke cigarettes one right after another.

chain store *n.* One of a group of stores owned and operated by one owner or company.

chair (châr) *n.* A seat with four legs and a back, intended for one person; a seat of office; the chairman. *Slang* Electric chair. **lift** A chair suspended from cables that is used to carry people and snow equipment up or down the ski slopes.

chair-man (châr´man) *n. pl.* **-men** The person presiding over a committee, board, or other meeting, chairman of the board. **chairmanship** *n.* **chairperson** *n.*

chair–warm-er(châr´wor˝mėr)*n., Slang,* An idle person; one who puts forth little energy.

chaise (shāz) *n.* A one-horse vehicle for two

people.

chaise lounge (shāz´long´) *n.* A chair that reclines and gives support for a person's legs and feet; a kind of reclining-chair with an elongated seat.

chal-ced-o-ny (kal sed´o nē) *n.* A translucent quartz, often pale blue or grayish with a waxlike shine.

chal-co-cite (kal´ko sīt´) *n.* Native sulfide of copper, a mineral having a dark-gray to black color and a metallic shine, occurring in crystals, and forms an important ore of copper.

cha-let (sha lā´) *n.* A cottage that has a gently sloping and overhanging roof.

chal-ice (chal´is) *n.* A drinking goblet or cup.

chalk (chok) *n.* A soft mineral made from fossil seashells, used for marking on a surface, such as a slate board. **chalky** *adj.*

chalk-board (chok bōerd) *n.* A blackboard made from slate.

chalk-stone (chok ´stōn˝) *n.* A chalk-like mass in the small joints of person affected with gout.

chalk up *v.* To credit or attribute to.

chal-lah *or* **cha-lah (käl e)** *n.* A loaf of leavened white bread that is usually braided and eaten by Jews on holidays and the Sabbath.

chal-lenge (chal´inj) *n.* A demand for a contest; a protest. *v.* To call into question. **challenger** *n.*

chal-lis (shal´ē) *n.* A lightweight printed cloth in rayon, cotton, or wool.

chal-one (kā lōn) *n.* A secretion of endocrine origin which inhibits bodily activity.

cha-lu-meau (shal˝ū mō) *n.* Woodwind instrument having the lowest register of the clarinet.

cha-lyb-e-ate (ka lib´ē it) *n.* Water or medicine that contains iron.

cham-ber (chām´bėr) *n.* A bedroom in a large private home; a judge's office; a meeting place or hall for a legislative body; the com-partment of a gun that holds the charge.

chamber-lain (chām´bėr lin) *n.* The high-ranking person or official of a royal court; an officer charged with the direction and management of the private apartments of a monarch or nobleman..

chamber-maid (chām´bėr mād´) *n.* A maid who takes care of bedrooms at a hotel.

chamber music *n.* Instrumental ensemble music suited for performance in a private or small room.

chamber of commerce *n.* Organization of business people and merchants who meet in an effort to promote, and regulate commercial and industrial interests in their area.

cham-bray (sham´brā) *n.* A variety of gingham, that is commonly woven with a colored warp and white filling threads, giving the plain color a frosted appearance.

cham-fer (cham´fėr) *n.* A small gutter cut in wood or other hard materials; a beveled edge.

cham-ois (sham´ē) *n.* A small goatlike antelope living in the mountains of Europe and Western Asia; a soft pliant leather made from the skins of the chamois, dressed with fish oil; fabric made as an imitation for chamois leather, also known as a chamois.

champ (chămp) *v.* To crush with the teeth; to chew vigorously or noisily; to show impatience in waiting.

cham-pagne (sham pān´) *n.* A white sparkling wine.

cham-per-ty (cham pert ē) *n.* An illegal proceeding whereby a person not a party or otherwise concerned in a suit bargains to aid a plaintiff or defendant in consideration of a share of any proceeds gained from the suit.

cham-pi-gnon (sham´pin yen) *n.* The common edible meadow mushroom.

cham-pi-on (cham´pē an) *n.* The holder of first place in a contest; one who defends another person.

champion-ship (cham´pē an ship´) *n.* The competition that determines a winner.

champ-le-ve (shän le vā´) *adj.* Of enameled work or decoration, in which the metal is ground or cut out or depressed in other means to receive enamel.

chance (chans) *n.* The random existence of something happening; a gamble or a risk, unexpected. **chance** *v.*

chance-ful (chans´ful) *adj.* Eventful; full of chances or accidents; hazardous.

chan-cel (chan´sel) *n.* The area of a church that contains the altar and choir.

chan-cel-lor (chan´se lėr) *n.* The chief director or minister of state in certain countries in Europe. **chancellorship** *n.*

chance–med-ley (chans´med˝lē) *n.* A sudden, accidental homicide; a violent altercation; haphazard action.

chan-cer-y (chan´se rē) *n.* The office for the safekeeping of official records.

chan-cre (shang´kėr) *n.* A lesion that is the first indication of syphilis.

chan-croid (shang´kroid) *n.* A sore or lesion in the genital area that is similar to a chancre, but does not involve syphilis.

chanc-y (chan´sē) *adj.* Risky; dangerous.

chan-de-lier (shan´de lėr´) *n.* A light fixture with many branches for lights that is suspended from the ceiling.

chan-delle (shan del´) *n.* An abrupt, climbing turn of an airplane in which the momentum of the plane provides additional acceleration for a higher rate of climb and to simultaneously change direction.

chan-dler (chand´lėr) *n.* A person who makes and sells candles. **chandlery** *n.*

change (chānj) *v.* To become or make different; to alter; to put with another; to use to take the place of another; to freshen a bed by putting clean coverings on. *n.* Coins; money given back when the payment exceeds the bill. **changeable** *adj.* **changeably** *adv.* **changeability** *n.* **changer** *n.*

change-a-ble (chān je bel) *adj.* Liable or capable to change; subject to alteration; unstable.

change-less (chānj les) *adj.* Constant; absence of change; without variation; steadfast.

change of heart *n.* A revised opinion; an entirely new decision.

change of life *n.* The process of menopause for women; the period in a woman's life when she stops having regular monthly periods.

chan-nel (chan´el) *n.* The deepest part of a stream, river, or harbor; the course that anything moves through or past; a groove. **channel** *v.*

chant (chant) *n.* A melody in which all words are sung on the same note. *v.* To celebrate with a song. **chanter** *n.*

chan-te-relle (shant e rel) *n.* An edible English mushroom of a rich yellow color and pleasant aroma.

chan-teuse (shan tōs´) *n.* A professional female singer and entertainer, one who performs in cabarets or nightclubs.

chan-ti-cleer (chan´ti klēr´) *n.* A rooster.

Cha-nu-kah (chä´ne kä´) *n. Variation of* Hanukkah

cha-os (kā´os) *n.* Total disorder. **chaotic** *adj.* **chaotically** *adv.*

chap (chap) *n., Slang* A fellow; a man. *v.* To dry and split open from the cold and wind.

chap-ar-ral (chap˝a ral´) *n.* A thicket of low–growing evergreen oaks.

chaparral cock *n.* A terrestrial bird of the southwestern United States; also known as the roadrunner.

chaparral pea *n.* A thorny bush which is found in dense thickets in western United States.

chap-book (chap´būk˝) *n.* A small book which contains poems, popular stories, fairy tales, ballads, or songs.

chap-el (chap´el) *n.* A place to worship, usually contained in a church.

chap-er-on *or* **chap-er-one (shap´e rōn´)** *n.* An older woman who supervises younger people. **chaperone** *v.*

chap-fall-en (chap´fo˝len) *adj.* Having the lower jaw depressed and hanging loosely from exhaustion or humiliation.

chap-i-ter (chap´i tėr) *n.* The upper part or capital of a column.

chap-lain (chap´lin) *n.* A clergyman who conducts religious services for a group.

chap-let (chap´lit) *n*. A garland for the head; a string of beads.

chaps (chaps) *n*. Leather overpants, without a seat, worn over trousers by cowboys to provide protection for their legs.

chap-ter (chap´tėr) *n*. One division of a book; a branch of a fraternity, religious order, or society.

chapter house *n*. The building in which a chapter of a fraternity or other organization meets.

cha-que-ta (chä ke´tä) *n*. A leather jacket worn by cowboys of western United States.

char (chär) *n*. Name given to a species of scaled trouts.

char-a-cin (kar´a sin) *n*. A member of the family of freshwater fishes, brightly colored for use in aquariums.

char-ac-ter (kar´ik tėr) *n*. A quality or trait that distinguishes an individual or group; a person that is portrayed in a play; a distinctive quality or trait. *adj*. Distinctive; peculiar.

char-ac-ter-i-za-tion (kar˝ik tė i zā´shan) *n*. The act of characterizing; portrayal; description; artistic representation.

char-ac-ter-ize (kar´ik te rīz´) *v*. To describe the character or quality of; to be characteristic of.

cha-rade (sha rād´) *n*. A game in which words are represented or acted out by pantomime, and the other players must guess the word or phrase.

char-coal (chär´kōl´) *n*. A carbonaceous material resulting from the imperfect combustion of organic matter, such as wood; material used to draw pictures.

chard (chärd) *n*. On edible white beet with large, succulent leaves.

charge (chärj) *v*. To give responsibility; to ask a price; to accuse; to impute something to; to commnd; to record a debt owed. *n*. Management; custody; supervision; an expense or price. *Slang* A thrill; excited. chargeable *adj*.

charge account *n*. A credit arrangement account where a customer may make immediate purchases and delay payment.

charge d'affaires *n*. A subordinate official who is in charge of diplomatic business during the temporary absence of an ambassador or minister.

charg-er (chär´jėr) *n*. An apparatus for recharging a battery.

char-i-ot (char´ē ot) *n*. An ancient horse-drawn vehicle used to fight battles. charioteer *n*.

char-i-ot-eer (char˝ē o tēr) *n*. One who drives a chariot.

char-i-ta-ble (char´i ta bl) *adj*. Pertaining to or characterized by good will or tenderness toward others; benevolent and kind to the poor.

char-i-ty (char´i tē) *n*. Money or help given to aid the needy; an organization, fund, or institution whose purpose is to aid those in need.

cha-ri-va-ri (sha riv´a rē´) *n*. A mock serenade to newlyweds, performed with horns, tin pans, etc.

char-kha (chär´ka) *n*. A spinning wheel used in India for spinning cotton.

char-la-tan (shär´la tan) *n*. One who falsely claims to possess knowledge or a skill he does not have; impostor. charlatanism *n*.

charley horse *n*. A severe muscle cramp especially of the quadriceps, characterized by pain and stiffness.

char-lock (chär lok) *n*. The wild mustard, often troublesome in grainfields.

char-lotte (shär´lot) *n*. A dessert consisting of fruit, custard, or whipped cream and cake or ladyfingers,

charm (chärm) *n*. The ability to delight or please; a small ornament that has a special meaning, usually worn on a bracelet.

char-meuse (shär mōz´) *n*. A soft, variety of satin.

char-nel (chär´nel) *n*. A special room or building that contains the bones or bodies of the dead.

char-qui (chär´kē) *n*. Jerked beef; beef dried by exposure to the sun.

charr (chär) *n*. A kind of fish, the char.

chart (chärt) *n.* A map, graph, or table that gives information in a form that is easy to read. **chart** *v.*

char-ta-ceous *adj.* Resembling paper: applied to the paper-like texture of leaves or bark.

char-ter (chär´tėr) *n.* An official document that grants certain privileges and rights. *v.* To lease or hire a vehicle or aircraft.

char-tist (chär´tist) *n.* An analyst of stock market prices, whose predictions are based on charts and graphics of past performance and information.

char-treuse (shär tröz´) *n.* A light yellowish green.

char-wom-an (chär´wŭm˝an) *n.* A cleaning woman employed by the day for odd jobs in a large office building, also hired for around the house jobs.

char-y (châr´ē) *adj.* Wary; cautious; not wasting time, resources, or money. **charily** *adv.* **chariness** *n.*

chase (chās) *v.* To follow quickly; to pursue; to run after. **chase** *n.* **chaser** *n.*

chasm (kaz´um) *n.* A very deep crack in the earth's surface.

chas-sis (shas´ē) *n.* The rectangular framework that supports the body and engine of a motor vehicle.

chaste (chāst) *adj.* Morally pure; modest; not guilty of participating in sexual intercourse.

chas-ten *v.* To inflict suffering upon for purposes of moral improvement; discipline or subdue, as by adversity.

chas-tise (chas tīz´) *v.* To severely reprimand; to punish by beating; as flogging. **chastisement** *n.*

chas-u-ble (chaz´ū bl) *n.* The vestment without sleeves worn over the alb by a priest when celebrating mass.

chat (chat) *v.* To converse in a friendly manner.

cha-toy-ant (sha toi´ant) *adj.* Having a changeable undulating luster or color. *n.* Any gem, as a cat's-eye, which is cut in a cabochon and reflects a single band of light.

chat-tel (chatel) *n.* An item of tangible movable personal property.

chat-ter-box (chat´ėr boks˝) *n.* One who talks incessantly; a very talkative person..

chatter mark *n.* A mark left by a chattering tool; one of a series of irregular cracks made on surfaces over which a glacier passes.

chauf-feur (shō´fėr) *n.* A person who is hired to drive an automobile for another person.

chaus-sure (shō syr´) *n.* A boot, shoe, slipper; a foot covering.

chau-vin (shō´vin) *n.* Anyone possessed by an absurdly enthusiasm for a cause.

chau-vin-ism (shō ve nizem) *n.* Unreasonable belief in the superiority of one's own group or organization. **chauvinist** *n.* **chauvinistic** *adj.*

chaw (cho) *v.* To chew; to chew tobacco.

cheap (chēp) *adj.* Inexpensive; low in cost; of poor quality. **cheap** *adv.* **cheaply** *adv.* **cheapness** *n.*

cheapen (chē´pen) *v.* To lessen the value; to make cheap.

cheap-skate (chēp´skāt´) *n.* A person who is very cheap and refuses to spend money.

cheat (chēt) *v.* To deprive of by deceit; to break the rules. **cheater** *n.*

check (chek) *v.* To control or restrain; to examine for correctness or condition. *n.* The act of verifying, comparing, or testing; a bill one receives at a restaurant; a written order on one's bank to pay money from funds on deposit; the act of comparing item to item; a move in chess which threatens a king and which forces the opponent to move the king to safety.

check-book (chek´bek´) *n.* A book containing blank checks for a checking account.

check-ers (chek´ėrz) *n.* A game played by two people each moving twelve men on a red and black checkered board.

check-er-bloom (chek´ėr blöm˝) *n.* A mallow herb with pink to purple flowers which grows in the western United States.

check-er-board (chek´ėr bōrd˝) *n.* A game board used to play various games; a pattern that is arranged like a checkerboard.

checking account *n.* A bank account by which the depositor can draw checks.

check list *n.* An alphabetical or systematic list of names of persons or things, intended for purposes of reference.

check-mate (chek'māt') *n.* The move in chess which places the opponent's king in a check from which escape is impossible, *Slang* To give a person no room to move, to defeat. **checkmate** *v.*

check-point (chek'point) *n.* A point where inspections are made.

check-rein (chek'rān') *n.* A short rein looped over a hook on a saddle, to prevent a horse from lowering its head.

check-room (chek'rŏm') *n.* A room where luggage, packages, or clothing are checked for safekeeping for a limited time.

check-up (chek'up') *n.* A complete physical examination.

ched-dar (ched'ėr) *n.* A firm, smooth cheese which ranges in flavor from mild to sharp.

cheek (chēk) *n.* The fleshy part of the face just below the eye and above and to the side of the mouth.

cheek-bone (chēk'bōn') *n.* The facial bone below the eyes.

cheeky (chē'kē) *adj.* Insolent; impudent.

cheep (chēp) *n.* To utter high-pitched sounds.

cheer (chēr) *v.* To give courage to; to instill with courage or hope; to make glad or happy; to shout with encouragement or applause. *n.* Good spirits; happiness.

cheerful (chēr'ful) *adj.* Having good spirits.

cheer-leader (chēr'lē'der) *n.* Someone who leads cheers at a sporting event.

cheer-less (chēr'lis) *adj.* Without joy, gladness, or comfort; lacking the qualities that cheer.

cheese (chēz) *n.* A food made from the curd of milk that is seasoned and aged.

cheese-burg-er (chēz'bür'gėr) *n.* A hamburger topped with a slice of cheese.

cheese-cake (chēz'kāk') *n.* A dessert cake made from cream cheese, cottage cheese, eggs, and sugar, and which may be topped with a variety of fruit.

cheese-cloth (chēz'kloth') *n.* A loosely-woven cotton gauze.

cheese-par-ing (chēz'pâr'ing) *n.* Something worthless and insignificant.

chee-tah (chē'ta) *n.* A swift-running, long-legged African wildcat.

chef (shef) *n.* A male cook who manages a kitchen; the head cook.

che-la (kē'la) *n.* The pincer-like claw of an arachnid.

che-lo-ni-an (ki lō'nē an) *n.* Tortoise; the tortoise family.

chem-i-cal (kem'i kal) *adj.* Of or related to chemistry. **chemically** *adv.*

chemical engineering *n.* A branch of chemistry that deals with the industrial application of chemistry.

chemical warfare *n.* Tactical warfare using asphyxiating, poisonous, and corrosive gases.

chem-i-lum-i-nes-cence (kem"i lō"mi nes'ans) *n.* Light produced due to chemical reactions at low temperatures.

chemin de fer *n.* A card game similar to baccarat.

che-mise (she mēz') *n.* A woman's loose undergarment which resembles a slip; a loose-fitting dress that hangs straight down from the shoulders.

chem-i-sorp-tion (kem"ē sorp'shan) *n.* Adsorption during a reaction between two or more chemicals.

chem-ist (kem'ist) *n.* A person who is versed in chemistry.

chem-is-try (kem'i strē) *n.* The scientific study of the composition, structure, and properties of substances and their reactions.

che-mo-au-to-tro-phic (kem"ō a"to trof' ik) *adj.* Being an autotrophic organism which oxidizes energy from an inorganic compound.

chem-o-pro-phy-lax-is (kem"ō prō"fa lak'sis) *n.* The prevention of infectious disease by the use of chemical drugs or agents.

chem-os-mo-sis (kem"oz mō'sis) *n.* The chemical action between substances that occurs through an intervening membrane.

chem-o-syn-the-sis (kem″o sin′thi sis) *n.* The process by which organic compounds are formed from organic components by energy derived from chemical reactions.

chem-o-tax-is (kem″o tak′sis) *n.* The orientation or movement of a cell or organism toward or away from a chemical stimulus.

che-mo-ther-a-py (kem′o ther′a pē) *n.* The treatment of a disease, such as cancer, with chemicals. **chemotherapeuti** *adj.*

che-mot-ro-pism (ki mo′tro piz″um) *n.* The turning or bending of a plant or other organism in relation to chemical stimuli.

chem-ur-gy (kem′ü jē) *n.* A branch of applied chemistry dealing with industrial utilization of organic raw materials, especially from farm products.

che-nille (she nēl′) *n.* A fuzzy, soft cord used to make rugs, bedspreads, and other fabrics.

cher-ish (cher′ish) *v.* To treat with love; to hold dear.

Cher-o-kee (cher′o kē′) *n.* A tribe of Iroquoian Indians who formerly lived in northern Georgia and North Carolina, now living in the state of Oklahoma.

Cherokee rose *n.* A smooth-stemmed climbing, white Chinese rose.

che-root (she rōt′) *n.* A cigar that is cut off square at both ends.

cher-ry (cher′ē) *n. pl.* **-ies** A fruit tree bearing a small, round, deep, or purplish red fruit with a small, hard stone.

cherry laurel *n.* Evergreen shrub with clusters of white blossoms and black shiny fruit.

cher-ry-stone (cher′ē stōn) *n.* A small quahog; the pit or seed of the cherry fruit.

cher-so-nese (kür′so nēz″) *n.* A peninsula.

chert (chürt) *n.* A compact siliceous rock resembling flint and composed essentially of chalcedonic or opaline silica, either alone or in combination.

cher-ub (cher′ub) *n. pl.* **-cherubs** A beautiful young child; a representation of an angel resembling a child with a rosy face and wings.

cher-vil (chür′vil) *n.* An aromatic herb of the carrot family, leaves of which are used in soups and salads.

chess (ches) *n.* A game played on a chessboard by two people, each of whom has sixteen pieces and tries to checkmate his opponent's king in order to win the game.

chess-board (ches bōerd) *n.* A game board with sixty-four squares, which can be used to play chess or checkers.

chess-man (ches man) *n.* Any of the pieces necessary to play chess.

chest (chest) *n.* The part of the upper body that is enclosed by the thorax; the ribs; a box usually having a hinged lid, used for storage.

ches-ter-field (ches′tėr fēld′) *n.* An overcoat with concealed buttons and a velvet collar.

chest-nut (ches′nut′) *n.* A tree bearing edible reddish-brown nuts; a nut from a chestnut tree.

chestnut blight *n.* A fungus-caused disease characterized by bark lesions, that attacks chestnut trees.

cheval glass *n.* A full-length mirror that may be tilted.

chev-ron (shev′orn) *n.* An insignia or emblem consisting of stripes that meet at an angle, indicating rank, length of service, or merit.

chew (chö) *v.* To crush or grind with the teeth; to masticate. *n.* The act of chewing. **chewer** *n.* **chewy** *adj.*

chewing gum *n.* A sweet blend of various flavors made from chicle for chewing.

che-wink (chi wingk′) *n.* A bird of the finch family, most common in eastern North America.

chew the fat *v., Slang* To chat about trivial matters.

Chi-an-ti (kē än′tē) *n.* A dry red or white wine from Italy.

chi-a-ro-scu-ro (kē är′o sker′ō) *n.* The distribution of shade and light in a picture.

chi-ca-lo-te (chē″kä la′te) *n.* A white-flowered, poppy plant of Mexico and the southwestern United States.

Chi-ca-na (chi′käne) *n.* An American woman with Mexican ancestry.

chi-cane (shi kān´) v. To quibble over.

chick (chik) n. A young chicken or bird. *Slang* A young woman.

chick-a-dee (chik´a dē´) n. A North American bird with dark feathers on the throat and the top of the head.

chick-a-ree (chik´a rē˝) n. A red squirrel of North America.

chick-en (chik´en) n. A domestic fowl; the edible meat of a chicken. *Slang* Cowardly; afraid; losing one's nerve.

chicken feed n. Food for chickens. *Slang* Very little money; small change.

chicken–hearted (chik´en här´tid) adj. Timid or cowardly.

chicken out v., *Slang* To back out, because of the loss of nerve; to surrrender.

chicken pox n. A contagious childhood disease, characterized by skin eruptions and fever.

chicken switch n., *Slang* A mechanical device used by an astronaut, to eject himself from the spacecraft if there is a malfunction.

chick-pea (chik´pē´) n. A bushy plant from Mediterranean regions and central Asia bearing edible pea-like seeds.

chick-weed (chik´wēd´) n. A small, weedy plant with small white flowers.

chic-le (chik´el) n. The milky juice of a tropical tree; the principal ingredient of chewing gum.

chic-o-ry (chik´o rē) n. pl. -ies An herb with blue flowers used in salads, the dried, roasted roots of which are used as a coffee substitute.

chide (chīd) v. To scold or find fault, rebuke. chider n.

chief (chēf) n. The person of highest rank, Slang Boss. chiefly adj.

chief-ly (chēf´lē) adv. For the most part; mostly; most importantly.

Chief of Staff n. A ranking officer of the Armed Forces who advises the Secretary of Defense and the President of the United States.

chief-tain (chēf´tan) n. The head of a group, clan, or tribe.

chif-fon (shi fon´) n. A sheer fabric made from rayon or silk. adj. In cooking, having a fluffy texture.

chif-fo-nier (shif´ø nēr´) n. A tall chest of drawers with a mirror at the top.

chig-ger (chig´er) n. A mite that attaches itself to the skin and causes intense itching.

chi-gnon (shēn´yon) n. A roll of hair worn at the back of the neck; a large roll, knot, or twist of hair worn at the back of the head.

chig-oe (chig´ō) n. A tropical flee that closely resembles the common flea.

chil-blain (chil´blān´) n. An inflammation of the hands and feet caused by exposure to cold.

child (chīld) n. pl. children A young person of either sex; adolescent; a person between infancy and youth. childish adj.

child abuse n. Sexual or physical mistreatment of a child by a parent, guardian, or other adult.

child-birth (chīld´berth´) n. The act of giving birth.

child-hood (chīld´hed) n. The time or period of being a child.

child-like (chīld´līk´) adj. Characteristic of a child.

chil-i (chilē) n. A hot pepper; a thick sauce made of meat and chili powder.

chil-i-ad (kil´ē ad˝) n. A group of one thousand; a period of 1000 years.

chili con carne n. A spicy dish made of chili powder, beans, ground meat, and tomato sauce.

chill (chil) v. To be cold, often with shivering; to reduce to a lower temperature. n. A feeling of cold.

chill-y (chil´ē) adj. Very cold; without warmth of temperature or feeling.

chime (chīm) n. A group or set of bells tuned to a scale. v. To announce on the hour, by sounding a chime.

chime in v. To break into a conversation,

usually in an unwelcome manner.

chi-me-ra (ki mēr´a) *n.* An absurd fantasy; an imaginary monster with a goat's body, a lion's head, and a serpent's tail.

chi-mer-ic (ki mer´ik) *adj.* Pertaining to or being chimera; unreal; imaginary.

chim-ney (chim´nē) *n.* A flue for smoke to escape, as from a fireplace. **sweep** A person who cleans chimneys as an occupation.

chimney pot *n.* A pipe of earthenware of sheet metal placed at the top of chimneys.

chimney sweep *n.* A person whose occupation is cleaning chimney flues of soot.

chim-pan-zee (chim´pan zē´) *n.* An anthropoid ape with large ears and dark brown hair, smaller and more intelligent than the gorilla.

chin (chin) *n.* The lower part of the face. *v.* To lift oneself up while grasping an overhead bar until the chin is level with the bar.

chi-na (chī´na) *n.* An earthenware or porcelain made in China.

chi-na-ber-ry (chī´na ber˝ē) *n.* Small Asian tree widely planted in the southern United States for shade and ornamental uses.

China rose *n.* The name given to a number of varieties of garden rose derived from a shrubby Chinese rose.

chi-na-ware (chī´na wâr˝) *n.* Tableware made of china or porcelain.

chin-chil-la (chin chil´a) *n.* A rodent from South America raised for its soft fur.

chine (chīn) *n.* The spine or backbone of animals.

Chi-nese (chī nēz´) *n.* A native of China.

Chinese cabbage *n.* A lettuce-like plant, a long head of light green leaves.

Chinese lantern *n.* A decorative illuminated lantern made of colored paper.

Chinese puzzle *n.* A complicated, intricate puzzle; something intricate.

chink (chingk) *n.* A narrow crack.

chi-no (chē´nō) *n.* A heavy cotton twill used for military uniforms.

chi-noi-se-rie (shēn woz˝e rē) *n.* A style of Chinese art and ornamentation that reflects Chinese qualities, characterized by intricate patterns and motifs.

chin-qua-pin (ching´ka pin) *n.* The dwarf chestnut of the United States; the edible nut.

chintz (chints) *n.* A printed cotton fabric which is glazed.

chintz-y (chint´sē) *adj.* Cheap.

chip (chip) *n.* A small piece that has been broken or cut from another source; a disk used in the game of poker; in Computer Science, an integrated circuit engraved on a silicone substrate. **chip** *v.*

chip-munk (chip´mungk) *n.* A striped rodent of the squirrel family.

chipped beef *n.* A smoked dried beef, sliced very thin and often served in a cream sauce.

chip-per (chip´ėr) *adj.* Cheerful; happy.

chi-rog-ra-phy (kī rog´ra fē) *n.* Penmanship; handwriting.

chi-ro-man-cy (kī´ro man˝sē) *n.* The ability of foretelling one's fortune by reading the lines of his hand.

chi-rop-o-dist (kī rop´o dist) *n.* One who treats ailments and irregularities of both the hands and feet.

chi-ro-prac-tic (kī´ro prak´tik) *n.* A method of therapy in which the body is manipulated to adjust the spine. **chiropract** *n.*

chirp (cherp) *n.* The high-pitched sound made by a cricket or certain small birds. **chirp** *v.*

chirr (chür) *v.* To make a short vibrant or trilling sound, as a grasshopper.

chis-el (chiz´el) *n.* A tool with a sharp edge which is used to shape and cut metal, wood, or stone.

chis-eled (chiz´eld) *adj.* Formed or shaped with a chisel.

chit (chit) *n.* A voucher indicating the amount owed for food or drink; a lively girl.

chit-chat (chit´chat´) *n.* Casual conversation or small talk.

chi-tin (kī´tin) *n.* The substance that forms the hard outer cover of insects.

chi-ton (kīt´n) *n.* An ancient garment for both sexes, usually worn at knee-length for men and full-length for women.

chit-ter-lings (chit´ėr ling) *n. pl.* The small intestines of a pig, used as food.

chiv-al-ry (shiv´al rē) *n. pl.* **-ies** The brave and courteous qualities of an ideal knight.

chive (chīv) *n.* An herb used as flavoring in cooking.

chlo-ral (klōral) *n.* A pungent colorless oily liquid first prepared from chlorine and alcohol; used in making DDT.

chlo-ral-ose (klōr´a lōs˝) *n.* A crystalline compound of combining chloral dextrose, used in medicine as a hypnotic.

chlo-rate (klōr´āt) *n.* A chloric acid salt.

chlo-ride (klōr´īd) *n.* A compound of chlorine with a double positive element.

chlo-rin-ate (klō´i nāt˝) *v.* To combine or treat with chlorine or a chlorine compound; to disinfect.

chlo-rine (klōr´ēn) *n.* A greenish-yellow compound used to purify water, bleach, and disinfectant.

chlo-rite (klōr´īt) *n.* A name for a group of usually green minerals, hydrous silicates of aluminum, ferrous iron, and magnesium.

chlo-ro-ben-zene (klōr˝o ben´zēn) *n.* A clear, colorless, and very flammable liquid, obtained from chlorination of benzene; used to manufacture DDT.

chlo-ro-form (klōr´i form˝) *n.* A colorless, volatile liquid of an agreeable smell and taste; used as a veterinary anesthetic.

chlo-ro-phyll (klōr´a fil) *n.* The green pigment that is found in photosynthetic organisms.

chlo-ro-pic-rin (klō˝o pik´rin) *n.* A slightly oily, colorless, poisonous liquid that causes vomiting and tears used as a soil fumigant.

chlo-ro-sis (kla rō´sis) *n.* Iron-deficiency in a plant, from lack of iron in the soil or other causes.

chlor-prop-amide(klōr prōp´ amīd) *n.* An oral drug used to lower blood sugar, used to treat mild diabetes.

chock (chok) *n.* A wedge or block placed under a wheel to prevent motion. **chock** *v.*

choc-o-late (cho´ko lit) *n.* A preparation of ground and roasted cacao nuts that is usually sweetened; a candy or beverage made from chocolate. **chocolaty** *adj.*

Choc-taw (chok´to) *n.* A member of the tribe of North American Indians from the Muskhogean group, now residing in Oklahoma.

choice (chois) *n.* To select or choose; the opportunity, right, or power to choose.

choir (kwīr) *n.* An organized group of singers that usually perform in a church.

choir-boy (kwīr´boi˝) *n.* A boy who sings in a choir.

choir-mas-ter (kwī´mas˝tėr) *n.* The director of a choir, a conductor.

choke (chōk) *v.* To stop normal breathing by an obstruction in the windpipe; to strangle.

chok-er (chō´kėr) *n.* A necklace that fits tightly around the neck.

chol-e-cys-tec-to-my (kol˝i si stek´to mē) *n.* The surgical removal of the gall bladder.

chol-er (kol´ėr) *n.* Anger, wrath; the state of easily provoked anger.

chol-er-a (kol´ėr a) *n.* Any of several infectious diseases of man and domestic animals usually showing signs of severe gastrointestinal symptoms.

chol-er-ic (kol´ėr ik) *adj.* Easily irritated; hot-tempered; inclined to excessive anger.

cho-les-ter-ol (ka les´te rōl´) *n.* A fatty crystalline substance that is derived from bile and is present in most gallstones, the brain, and blood cells.

cho-line (kō´lēn) *n.* A basic substance that occurs in many animal and plant products and is a member of the vitamin-B complex essential to the function of the liver.

chol-la (chōl´yä) *n.* A very spiny, treelike cacti of southwestern United States and Mexico.

choose (chōz) *v.* To select or pick out; to prefer; to make a choice. **choosy** *or* **chosen** *adj.* **choosey** *adj.*

choos-y (chō´zē) *adj.* Hard to please; particular, selective.

chop (chop) v. To cut by making a sharp downward stroke; to cut into bits or small pieces.

chopper (chop´ėr) n., *Slang* A helicopter.

choppy (chop´ē) adj. Rough; irregular; jerky.

chop-sticks (chop´stik) n. pl Slender sticks of ivory or wood, held between thumb and fingers and used chiefly in oriental countries as an eating tool, used to bring food to the mouth.

cho-ral (kōr´al) adj. Pertaining to, written for, or sung by a choir or chorus, adapted. **chorally** adv.

cho-rale (ko ral´) n. A Protestant hymn with a simple melody, sung in unison.

chord (kord) n. The sounding of three or more musical notes simultaneously.

chord-al (kor´dial) adj. Relating to music characterized by harmony rather than by counterpoint.

chord organ n. An electronic organ with push buttons that produce programed simple chords.

chore (chōr) n. A daily task; a task that becomes unpleasant or burdensome.

cho-re-a (ko rē´a) n. An acute nervous disease especially of children, marked by irregular and uncontrollable movement of muscles.

cho-re-og-ra-phy (kōr´ē og´ra fē) n. The creation of a dance routine for entertainment. **choreographic** adj. **choreograph** v. **chore-ographically** adv.

cho-ri-o-al-lan-to-is (kōr˝ē ō a lan´tō is) n. Vascular fetal membrane formed in the fetal tissue of birds, reptiles, and some mammals.

chor-is-ter (kor´i stėr) n. A choirboy or a member of a choir; a singer in a choir.

cho-rog-ra-phy (ko rog´ra fē) n. The art of mapping, or of describing particular regions, countries, or districts.

chor-tle (chor´tl) v. To chuckle with glee, especially in triumph or joy. **chortle** n. **chortler** n.

cho-rus (kōr´us) n. pl. -ses A group of people who sing together; the repeated verses of a song.

chose (shōz) v. The past tense of choose.

cho-sen (chō´zen) adj. Selected or preferred above all.

chow-der (chou´dėr) n. A soup dish made with fish or clams, often having a milk base.

chow hall n., *Slang* A large dining room, a military mess hall.

Christ (krīst) n. Jesus; The Messiah; God's son who died to save Christians from sin.

chris-ten (kris´n) v. To baptize; to give a Christian name at baptism; to use for the first time. **christening** n.

Chris-tian (kris´chan) n. A believer and follower of the teachings of Jesus. **Christianly** adv. **Christianity** n.

Christ-mas (kris´mas) n. December 25th, the anniversary of the birth of Jesus Christ, observed as a holiday or holy day.

chro-ma (krō´ma) n. The purity or quality of a color, that combines hue and saturation.

chro-mat-ic (krō mat´ik) adj. Relating to color.

chrome alum n. A dark-violet salt in dyeing, tanning, and photography.

chro-mo-lith-o-graph (krō˝mō li thog´ra fē) n. A picture printed in colors by means of the lithographic process.

chro-mo-plast (krō´mo plast˝) n. A plastid, or mass of protoplasm, containing red or yellow pigment.

chro-mo-pro-tein (kro˝mo prō´tēn) n. A protein compound, as hemoglobin, with a metal-containing pigment or a carotenoid.

chro-mo-some (kro´mo sōm´) n. One of several small bodies in the nucleus of a cell, containing genes responsible for the determination and transmission of hereditary characteristics.

chro-mo-sphere (krō´mo sfēr˝) n. A gaseous layer surrounding the sun above the photosphere, consisting primarily of hydrogen.

chron-ic (kron´ik) adj. Long duration; frequently recurring; continuing for long periods of time; suffering from a disease for a long time. **chronically** *adv.*

chron-i-cle (kron´i kal) *n.* A record of events written in the order in which they occurred. **chronicle** *v.* **chronicler** *n.*

chron-o-graph (kron´o graf˜) *n.* An astronomical instrument for recording the exact instant of occurrences.

chro-nol-o-gy (kro nol´o jē) *n.* The science of measuring times, periods or years when past events or transactions took place, and arranging them in order of occurrence.

chro-nom-e-ter (kro nom´i tėr) *n.* An instrument for measuring time, as a clock, watch, or sundial.

chron-o-scope (kron´o skōp˜) *n.* An instrument for precise measuring of extremely short-lived phenomena.

chrys-a-lis (kris´a lis) *n.* *pl.- ses* The enclosed pupa from which a moth or butterfly develops.

chry-san-the-mum (kri san´the mum) *n.* A cultivated plant having large, showy flowers.

chrys-o-ber-yl (kris´o ber˜il) *n.* A mineral, usually of a yellow or greenish color, sometimes used as a gem.

chrys-o-lite (kris´o līt˜) *n.* A native silicate that varies from yellow to green in color, and in some forms used as a gem.

chtho-ni-an (thō´nē an) *adj.* Dwelling beneath the surface of the earth.

chub (chub) *n.* A freshwater fish related to the carp.

chub-by (chub´ē) *adj.* Plumb; rounded. **chubbiness** *n.*

chuck (chuk) *v.* To tap or pat affectionately under the chin. *Slang* To throw out or to throw away; to quit; to give up. *n.* A cut of beef extending from the neck to the ribs.

chuck-hole (chuk´hōl´) *n.* A hole in the street or the pavement.

chuck-le (chuk´ul) *v.* To laugh quietly with satisfaction. **chuckler** *n.*

chug (chug) *n.* A short, dull, explosive noise, as from a malfunctioning engine.

chuk-ka (chuk´a) *n.* An ankle-length of boot often made of leather, and laced through pairs of eyelets or a buckle.

chum (chum) *n.* A close friend or pal.

chunk (chungk) *n.* A thick piece of anything; a large quantity of something; a lump.

church (cherch) *n.* A building for Christian worship; a congregation of public Christian worship.

churl (cherl) *n.* A rude or rustic person. **churlish** *adj.* **churlishness** *n.*

churn (chėrn) *n.* The container in which cream or milk is beaten vigorously to make butter. *v.* To agitate in a churn in order to make butter; to agitate violently.

churr (chür) *n.* The vibrant or whirring noise made by insects and some birds, such as a partridge.

chute (shōt) *n.* An incline passage through which water, coal, etc., may travel to a destination. *Slang* A parachute.

chut-ney (chut´nē) *n.* An agreeable condiment of fruit, spices, and herbs.

chyme (kīm) *n.* The semi-liquid mass into which food is expelled and converted by gastric secretion during digestion.

ci-ca-da (si kā da) *n.* The popular and generic name of insects with a stout body, large transparent wings and a wide blunt head.

ci-der (sī´dėr) *n.* The juice from apples.

ci-gar (si gär´) *n.* Rolled tobacco leaves used for smoking.

cig-a-rette (sig´a ret´) *n.* A small amount of tobacco rolled in thin paper for smoking.

cil-i-a (sil´ē a) *n.* The hairs that grow from the edge of the eyelids; eyelashes.

cil-i-ar-y (sil´ē er˜ē) *adj.* Pertaining to the eyelids or eyelashes.

cil-ice (sil´is) *n.* A stiff undergarment made of horse or camel hair, formally worn by monks.

cinch (sinch) *n.* The strap for holding a saddle. *v.* To assure. *Slang* Something easy to do.

cin-cho-na (sin kō´na) *n.* A tree in South America whose bark yields quinine.

cin-cho-nine *n.* An alkaloid obtained from the bark of several species of cinchona, along with quinine, and one of the medicinal active principles of this bark, being valuable to reduce fever.

cin-chon-ism (sin´ko niz˝um) *n.* A disorder of the body characterized by dizziness, ear ringing, temporary deafness, and headache, the result of overdoses of cinchona or its alkaloids.

cinc-ture (singk´chėr) *n.* A belt or cord to put around the waist. *v.* To encircle or surround with a cincture.

cin-der (sin´dėr) *n.* A piece of something that is partially burned. **cindery** *adj.*

cin-e-ma (sin´a ma) *n. pl.* **-mas** A motion picture; a motion picture theater; the business of making a motion picture.

cin-e-mat-o-graph (sin´e mat´o graf´) *n.* A movie projector or camera.

cin-e-ma-tog-ra-p hy (sin´e ma tog´ra fē) *n.* The art of photographing a motion picture. **cinematographer** *n.*

cin-e-rar-i-um (sin˝a râ´ē um) *n.* A place for receiving the ashes of the dead after cremation.

ci-ne-re-ous (si nēr´ē us) *adj.* Resembling the color of wood ashes.

cin-na-bar (sin´a bär´) *n.* A mineral which is the principal source of mercury.

cin-na-mon (sin´a møn) *n.* The aromatic inner bark of a tropical Asian tree, used as a spice, reddish brown in color.

ci-pher (sī´fėr) *n.* The symbol for the absence of quantity; 0; secret writing that has a prearranged key or scheme.

cir-cle (ser´kl) *n.* A process that ends at its starting point; a group of people having a common interest or activity.

cir-cuit (ser´kit) *n.* The closed path through which an electric current flows.

circuit breaker *n.* A switch that automatically interrupts the flow of an electric current in an overloaded circuit.

circuit court *n.* The lowest court of record, located in two or more locations within one jurisdiction.

cir-cuit-ry (sür´ki trē) *n.* The arrangement or detailed plan of an electric circuit.

cir-cu-lar (ser´kū lėr) *adj.* Moving in a circle or round-like fashion; relating to something in a circle; having free motion, as the air. **circularity** *n.*

cir-cu-late (ser´kū lāt´) *v.* To pass from place to place or person to person; to distribute in a wide area. **circulation** *n.* **culator** *n.* **circulatory** *adj.*

cir-cu-la-tion (sür˝kū lā´shan) *n.* The movement, or flow of blood through the vessels by the pumping action of the heart; the passing or transmission from one person to another.

cir-cum-cise (ser´kum sīz´) *v.* To remove the foreskin on the male penis, sometimes as a religious rite. **circumcision** *n.*

cir-cum-fer-ence (ser kum´fėr ens) *n.* The perimeter or boundary of a circle. **circumferential** *adj.*

cir-cum-flex (ser´kum fleks´) *n.* A mark indicating the quality or sound of vowels as they appear in words.

cir-cum-gy-ra-tion (sėr˝kym jī rā´shan) *n.* A movement in a circular course.

cir-cum-ja-cent (sėr˝kum jā´sent) *adj.* Bordering on all sides; surrounding.

cir-cum-lo-cu-tion (sėr˝kum lō kū´shan) *n.* The use of more or unnecessarily large words to express an idea.

cir-cum-lu-nar (sür˝cum lö´nėr) *adj.* Revolving about or surrounding the moon.

cir-cum-scribe (ser´kum skrīb´) *v.* To confine something within drawn boundaries; to surround.

cir-cum-spect (sür´kum spekt˝) *adj.* Examining carefully all circumstances and possible consequences.

cir-cum-stance (ser´kum stans´) *n.* A fact or condition that must be considered when making a decision.

cir-cum-stan-tial (ser´kum stan´shal) *adj.* Incidental; not essential; dependent on circumstances.

cir-cum-stan-ti-ate (ser´kum stan´shē āt) *adj.* Providing support or circumstantial evidence.

cir-cum-vent (ser´kum vent´) *v.* To outwit or gain advantage; to avoid or go around. **circumvention** *n.* **circumventive** *adj.*

cir-cum-vo-lu-tion (sŭr˝kum vo lŏ´shan) *n.* The act or rolling or turning around an axis; a single complete turn.

cir-cum-volve (sŭr˝kum volv´) *v.* To revolve about.

cir-cus (ser´kus) *n. pl.* -cuses Entertainment featuring clowns, acrobats, and trained animals.

cirque (sŭrk) *n.* A deep steep-walled circular space, a natural amphitheater.

cir-rho-sis (si rō´sis) *n.* A liver disease that is ultimately fatal. **cirrhotic** *adj.*

cir-ri-ped (sir´i ped˝) *n.* A marine crustacean, with thin, bristly, modified feet used to gather food and which becomes parasitic as an adult.

cir-ro-cu-mu-lus (sir˝ō kū´mū lus) *n.* A cloud of high altitude, consisting of small white rounded masses.

cir-ro-stra-tus (sir˝ō strā´tus) *n.* A whitish fairly uniformed layer of cloud or haze.

cir-rus (sir´us) *n. pl.* **cirri** A high altitude, white, wispy cloud.

cis-co (sis´kō) *n.* Any of various species of whitefish found in the Great Lakes area.

cis-tern (sis´tern) *n.* A man-made tank or artificial reservoir for holding rain water.

cis-tron (sis´tron) *n.* The segment of DNA; the smallest single functional unit of genetic substance, considered equivalent to a gene in molecular biology.

cit-a-del (sit´a del) *n.* A fortress commanding a city; a stronghold.

ci-ta-tion (sī tā´shan) *n.* An official summons from a court; a quotation used in literary or legal material; an honor.

cite (sīt) *v.* To bring forward as proof; to summon to action; to rouse; to summon to appear in court. **citeable** *adj.*

cith-a-ra (sith´er a) *n.* An ancient Greek stringed instrument that resembles the modern guitar.

cit-i-zen (sit´i zen) *n.* A resident of a town or city; a native or naturalized person entitled to protection from a government; a native or naturalized, as opposed to alien, member of a state or nation. **citizenry, citizenship** *n.*

citizen's band *n.* A two-way radio frequency band for private use.

cit-ral (si´tral) *n.* A liquid aldehyde with a strong lemon odor, obtained from oils of lemons or oranges, or synthetically manufactured, and used in perfumery and flavoring.

cit-ric a-cid (si´trik) *n.* A colorless acid found in lime, lemon, and other juices; the acid derived from lemons and similar fruits or obtained by the fermentation of carbohydrates, and used to flavor foods, beverages, and pharmaceuticals.

cit-ri-cul-ture (si´tri kul˝cher) *n.* The cultivation of citrus fruits.

cit-ron (si´tran) *n.* A fruit resembling a lemon, but less acidic and larger in size; a pale yellow thick-skinned fruit resembling the lemon in shape and texture, but larger and less acid, borne by a semi-tropical tree.

cit-ron-el-la (si˝tra nel´a) *n.* A fragrant grass of southern Asia, found in many oils and used in making insect repellant, liniment, perfume, and soap.

cit-rus (sit´rus) *n. pl.* **citrus, citruses** Any of a variety of trees bearing fruit with thick skins, as limes, oranges, lemons, and grapefruits.

cit-tern (sit´ern) *n.* An ancient stringed instrument, somewhat resembling a guitar but with a more flat pear-shaped body.

cit-y (sit´ē) *n.* A place larger than a town.

city council *n.* The legislative body of a municipality or city with administrative and legislative power.

city editor *n.* An editor for a local newspaper responsible for local news coverage and staff assignments and duties.

civ-et (siv´it) *n.* A cat-like mammal that secretes a musky fluid from the genital glands, which is used in perfumery.

civ-ic (siv´ik) *adj.* Relating to or of a citizen, city, or citizenship.

civ-ics (siv´iks) *n.* The social or political science of the rights and duties of citizens.

civ-il (siv´il) *adj.* Relating to citizens; relating to the legal proceedings concerned with the rights of private individuals.

civil aviation *n.* Aviation by commercial or private concerns as separated from military aviation.

civil defense *n.* A civilian program of volunteers ready to provide protection in case of a natural disaster, invasion, or enemy attack.

civil disobedience *n.* Refusal to obey government laws or demands for the purpose of bringing about modifications.

ci-vil-ian (si vil´yen) *n.* A person not serving in the military, as a firefighter, or as a policeman.

civ-i-li-za-tion (siv´i li zā´shan) *n.* A high level of social, cultural, and political development.

civ-i-lize (siv´i līz´) *v.* To bring out of a state of savagery into one of education and refinement.

civil rights *n. pl.* The nonpolitical rights guaranteed to citizens; the rights provided by the 13th and 14th amendments of the United States Constitution.

civil service *n.* The administrative or executive service of a government or international agency separate from the armed forces.

civil war *n.* A war between two opposing regions or citizens of the same country.

clack (klak) *n.* A sharp, abrupt sound, continuous talk; chatter.

clack valve *n.* A hinged valve in pumps with a single flap, that permits the flow of fluid in one direction only.

claim (klām) *v.* To ask for one's due; to hold something to be true; to make a statement that something is true; to demand. **claim** *n.* **claimant** *n.*

clair-voy-ance (klâr voi´ans) *n.* The ability to visualize in the mind distant objects or objects hidden from the senses; a mesmeric state. **clairvoyant** *n.*

clam (klam) *n.* Any of various marine and freshwater bivalve mollusks. *Slang* To become silent; to clam up.

clam-bake (klam´bāk´) *n.* An outside gathering in which clams are cooked over hot coals.

clam-ber (klam´bėr) *v.* To climb by using both the hands and feet. **clamberer** *n.*

clam-my (klam´ē) *adj.* Damp, cold, and sticky. **clammily** *adv.* **clamminess** *n.*

clam-or (klam´ėr) *n.* A loud noise or outcry; a vehement protest or demand. **clamourous** *adj.* **clamorously** *adv.*

clamp (klamp) *n.* A device designed for holding or fastening things together.

clamp down *v.* The action of making or increasing restrictions or regulations.

clam-shell (klam´shel´) *n.* The shell of a clam; a dredging bucket having two hinged jaws.

clamshell door *n.* Either of a pair of cargo-loading doors on the tail or underside of an airplane, that swing apart and open out and away from each other.

clan (klan) *n.* A large group of people who are related to one another by a common ancestor. **clannish** *adj.* **clannishly** *adv.* **clansman** *n.* **clanswoman** *n.*

clan-des-tine (klan des´tin) *adj.* Kept or done in secrecy for a purpose.

clang (klang) *v.* To cause or make a loud, ringing, metallic sound.

clan-gor (klang´ėr) *n.* A loud series of clangs.

clank (klangk) *n.* A sharp, quick, metallic sound.

clap (klap) *v.* To applaud; to strike the hands together with an explosive sound.

clap-board (klab´ord) *n.* A narrow board with one end thicker than the other, used to cover the outside of buildings so as to weatherproof the inside.

clap-per (klap´ėr) *n.* The mechanical part of a bell that hits against the inside of the bell.

claque (klak) *n.* A group hired to attend and applaud at a performance.

clar-en-don (klar´en don) *n.* A condensed style of printing type, similar to roman but with thicker lines.

clar-et (klar´it) *n.* A red Bordeaux table wine; similar red wines produced elsewhere.

clar-i-fy (klar´i fī´) v. To become or make clearer. **clarification** n.

clar-i-net (klar´i net´) n. A woodwind instrument with a single reed. **clarinetist** n.

clar-i-ty (klar´i tē) n. The state or quality of being clear.

clark-i-a (klär´kē a) n. A flowering annual herb of the evening-primrose family.

cla-ro (klä´ō) n. A light-colored and typically mild cigar.

clar-y (klâr´ē) n. An aromatic mint herb used as a potherb and for medicinally.

clash (klash) v. To bring or strike together; to collide; to conflict.

clasp (klasp) n. A hook to hold parts of objects together; a grasp or grip of the hands. **clasp** v.

clasp knife n. A large one-bladed folding knife with a catch to hold the blade out.

class (klas) n. A group or set that has certain social or other interests in common; a group of students who graduate at the same time.

clas-sic (klas´ik) adj. Belonging in a certain category of excellence; having a lasting artistic worth.

clas-si-cal (klas´i kal) adj. Relating to the style of the ancient Roman or Greek classics; standard and authoritative, not experimental or new.

clas-si-cism (klas´i siz´um) n. A belief in the esthetic principles of ancient Rome and Greece.

clas-si-cist (klas´i sist) n. A classical scholar; a follower of classicism.

clas-si-fi-ca-tion (klas´i fi kā´shan) n. The act of classifying; to systematically bring together those things which most resemble each other; arrange in categories.

clas-si-fied (klas´i fīd) adj. Arranged or divided into classes; withheld from the general public; confidential; secret.

classified ad n. An advertisement published in a newspaper

clas-si-fy (klas´i fī´) v. To arrange or assign items, people, etc., into the same class or category. **classification** n.

class-mate (klas´māt˝) n. A member of the same class in a school or college.

class-room (klas´rŏm˝) n. A room where students meet for classes and to study.

clas-tic (klas´tik) adj. Breaking up or made of fragments or parts.

clat-ter (klat´er) v. To make or to cause a rattling sound. **clatter** n.

clause (klos) n. A group of words which are part of a simple compound, or complex sentence, containing a subject and predicate.

claus-tro-pho-bia (klo´stro fō´bē a) n. A fear of small or enclosed places.

cla-ve (klä´vā) n. One of a pair of cylindrical hardwood sticks or blocks of wood, held in the hands and clicked together to the rhythm of music.

clav-i-chord (klav´i kord´) n. A keyboard instrument which is one step down from the piano.

clav-i-cle (klav´i kl) n. The bone that connects the breastbone and the shoulder blade.

cla-vier (kla vēr´) n. An instrument with a keyboard, such as the harpsichord.

claw (klo) n. A sharp, curved nail on the foot of an animal; the pincer of certain crustaceans, such as the crab, lobster, etc.

claw hammer n. A hammer with two curv-ed claws at one end of the head, for pulling out nails.

clay (klā) n. A fine-grained, pliable earth that hardens when fired, used to make pottery, bricks, and tiles.

clay pigeon n. A saucer-shaped clay disk that is thrown into the air in skeet and trapshooting.

clean (klēn) adj. Free from impurities, dirt, or contamination; neat in habits.

clean—cut n. Distinctly outlined or defined; cut so the surface or edge is smooth and clean; a wholesome and neat appearance.

clean out v., *Slang* To empty, as a store; to deprive of resources.

cleanse (klenz) *v.* To make pure or clean. **cleanser** *n.*

clean-up (klēn´up˝) *n.* An act or instance of cleaning; *Slang* A large profit on a bet or investment.

clear (klēr) *adj.* Free from precipitation and clouds; able to hear, see, or think easily; distinctly, free from doubt or confusion; free from a burden, obligation, or guilt. **clearly** *adv.* **clearness** *n.*

clearance (klēr´ans) *n.* The distance that one object clears another by; a permission to proceed.

clear-head-ed (klēr´hed´id) *adj.* Having a clear understanding of something.

clearing house *n.* Stock Exchange and the Board of Trade, similar clearing houses exist for the facilitation of trading in stocks, grain, or other commodities.

clear sailing *n.* The accomplishment of attaining a certain goal without interference.

clear-wing (klēr´wing˝) *n.* A moth with large transparent wings for the most part without scales.

cleat (klēt) *n.* A metal projection that provides support, grips, or prevents slipping.

cleav-a-ble (klē´va bl) *adj.* Capable of being separated or divided.

cleav-age (klē´vij) *n.* The process, act, or result of splitting; the cleft a woman displays in low-cut clothes.

cleave (klēv) *v.* To divide or split by a cutting blow, along a natual division line, as the grain of wood; split; to penetrate or pass through.

cleav-er (klē´vėr) *n.* A knife used by butchers.

cleek (klēk) *n.* A large iron hook, used to suspend a pot over a fire.

clef (klef) *n.* A symbol indicating which pitch each line and space represents on a musical staff.

cleft (kleft) *n.* A space or opening made by partially splitting; a crevice.

clem-a-tis (klem´a tis) *n.* The generic name of woody climbing plant having three leaflets on each individual leaf, usually having white, red, purple or pink blossoms.

clem-ent (klem´ent) *adj.* Merciful; mild.

clench (klench) *v.* To clinch; to hold firmly, as with the hands or teeth, close tightly.

clep-sy-dra (klep´si dra) *n.* A name for common devices used for measuring time by the regulated discharge of water; a water clock.

clep-to-ma-ni-a *n.* Compulsive stealing.

clere-sto-ry (klēr´stōr˝ē) *n.* An outside wall of a building or room that rises above an adjoining roof and contains a series of windows allowing daylight to the interior.

cler-gy (klėr´jē) *n.* The group of men and women who are ordained as religious leaders and servants of God.

cler-gy-man (klėr´jē man) *n.* A member of the clergy.

cler-ic (kler´ik) *adj.* Pertaining to the clergy; clerical.

cler-i-cal (kler´i kal) *adj.* Trained to handle office duties.

clerical collar *n.* A narrow stiff, slender white collar worn buttoned at the back of the neck by certain members of the clergy.

clerk (klork) *n.* A worker in an office who keeps accounts, records, and correspondence up to date; a person who works in the sales department of a store.

Cleveland, Stephen Grover *n.* The 22nd and 24th president of the United States from, 1885-1889 and 1893-1897.

clev-er (klev´ėr) *adj.* Mentally quick; showing dexterity and skill. **cleverly** *adv.* **cleverness** *n.*

clev-is (klev´is) *n.* A piece of metal, usually U-shaped, having a pin or bolt that connects the two sides; shackle.

clew (klō) *n.* A ball of thread, cord, or yarn; a lower corner or loop of a sail.

click (klik) *v.* To make a small sharp sound; to move, strike or produce with a click.

cli-ent (klī´ent) *n.* A person who secures the professional services of another.

cli-en-tele (klī´en tel´) *n.* A collection of patients, customers, or clients.

cliff (klif) *n.* A high, steep edge or face of

a rock.

cliff dweller *n.* A member of the prehistoric aboriginal tribes in the southwestern U.S. who built their homes in natural recesses or rock ledges of canyon walls and cliffs.

cliff-hanger (klif´hang´ėr) *n.* Anything which causes suspense and anticipation until the final outcome is known.

cli-mate (klī´mit) *n.* The weather conditions of a certain region generalized or averaged over a period of years; the prevailing atmosphere. **climatic** *adj.* **climatically** *adv.*

cli-ma-tol-o-gy (klī˝ma tol´o jē) *n.* The science that deals with climates, an investigation of their phenomena.

cli-max (klī´maks) *n.* The point of greatest intensity and fullest suspense; the culmination.

climb (klīm) *v.* To move to a higher or lower location; to advance in rank or status. **climbable** *adj.* **climber** *n.*

climbing iron *n.* An iron frame with spikes attached that can be strapped to boots as a help in climbing poles, trees, or ice-covered areas.

clinch (klinch) *v.* To secure; to fasten; to settle definitively. **clinch** *n.*

cling (kling) *v.* To hold fast to; to grasp or stick; to hold on and resist emotional separation. **clinger** *n.*

clin-ic (klin´ik) *n.* A medical establishment connected with a hospital; a center that offers instruction or counseling.

clinical thermometer *n.* An instrument used in medical practice to measure the body temperature.

cli-ni-cian (kli nish´an) *n.* A physician or one qualified in clinical method skills.

clink (klingk) *v.* To cause a light ringing sound.

clink-er (kling´ker) *n.* An overbaked, hard yellowish Dutch brick used for paving. *n.,* *Slang* A blunder; a flop.

clink-er–built *adj.* Having external plates overlapping one another; as the clapboards of a house.

clin-quant (kling´kant) *adj.* Glittering with tinsel or gold.

clip (klip) *v.* To cut off; to curtail; to cut short. *n.* Something that grips, holds, or clasps articles together.

clip artist *n., Slang* A person who makes a profession of robbing or swindling.

clip-board (klip´bōrd´) *n.* A small writing board, having a spring clip, usually at the top, to hold sheets of paper.

clip joint *n. ,Slang* a place of entertainment notorious for overcharging or defrauding its customers.

clip-per (klip´ėr) *n.* A sailing vessel that travels at a high rate of speed.

clip-per (klip´ėr) *n.* A tool used for cutting.

clique (klēk) *n.* A small and exclusive group of people.

cloak (klōk) *n.* A loose outer garment that conceals or covers.

clob-ber (klob´ėr) *v., Slang* To hit repeatedly and violently.

cloche (klōsh) *n.* A bell-shaped, close-fitting hat.

clock (klok) *n.* An instrument that measures time. *v.* To time with a watch, clock, stop-watch, etc.

c l o c k - w i s e (klok´wīz˝) *adv.* In the direction the hands of a clock rotate.

clod (klod) *n.* A large piece or lump of earth; a stupid, ignorant person.

clod-hop-per (klod´hop˝ė) *n.* A country bumpkin; a clumsy and uncouth person.

clog (klog) *v.* To choke up. *n.* A shoe with a wooden sole.

clois-ter (kloi´stėr) *v.* To confine or seclude in a cloister or convent.

clone (klōn) *n.* An identical reproduction grown from a single cell of the original. **clone** *v.*

clop (kläp) *v.* To produce a hollow sound, as if done by a horse's hoof or wooden shoe.

close (klōs) *adj.* Near, as in time, space, or relationship; nearly even, as in competition; fitting tightly. *v.* To shut. **close-**

ness *n.*

closed (klōzd) *adj.* Forming a self-contained barrier; limited as to season for hunting or fishing.

closed circuit *n.* An unbroken circuit permitting a signal to be transmitted by wire to a limited number of receivers.

closed–end *adj.* Issued to the fully authorized fixed capitalization of shares.

closed shop *n.* A place of business in which, by contract between the employer and the labor union, only union members can work.

close–grained (klōs′grānd′) *adj.* Having a closely compact, fine-grained texture.

close–out (klōz′out″) *n.* A clearance sale of merchandise usually at a reduced price.

close shave *n., Slang.* A narrow escape.

clos-et (kloz′it) *n.* A small cabinet, compartment, or room for storage. **closet** *v.*

close-up (klōs′up′) *n.* A picture taken at close range; a close view or examination of something.

clo-sure (klō′zhėr) *n.* The act or condition of being closed; an end or conclusion.

clot (klot) *n.* A thick or solid mass, as of blood. **clot** *v.*

cloth (kloth) *n.* *pl.* **cloths** A knitted, woven, or matted piece of fabric, used to cover a table; the professional clothing of the clergy.

clothe (klōth) *v.* To provide clothes; to cover with clothes; to wrap.

clothes (klōz) *n.* Cloth items of a person that can be worn and are washable; dress.

clothes-line (klōz′līn) *n.* A strong rope, or cord on which clothes may be hung to dry.

clothes-pin (klōz′pin″) *n.* A forked piece of wood or plastic, or a spring-loaded clamp used to fasten articles on a line to dry.

cloth-ing (klō thing) *n.* Garments in general; clothes.

clo-ture (klō′shėr) *n.* A parliamentary action that calls for an immediate vote.

cloud (kloud) *n.* A visible body of water or ice particles floating in the atmosphere; something that obscures; a cloud of dust or smoke. **cloudy** *adj.* **cloudiness** *n.*

cloud-burst (kloud′bürst″) *n.* A sudden and violent rainfall or downpour of rain.

cloud cover *n.* Complete or partial cover of the sky by clouds.

cloud-i-ly (kloud′i lē) *adv.* In an obscure or cloudy manner.

clout (klout) *n.* A heavy blow with the hand. *Slang* The amount of influence or pull a person may have. **clout** *v.*

clove (klōv) *n.* A spice from an evergreen tree; a small bud that is part of a larger group, as a clove of garlic.

clo-ver (klō′vėr) *n.* A plant that has a dense flower and trifoliolate leaves.

clover-leaf (klō′vėr lēf′) *n.* A junction of highways that cross each other at different levels and are connected by curving ramps.

clown (kloun) *n.* A professional comedian who entertains by jokes, tricks, and funny actions; a circus comedian who dresses in outlandish costumes and wears heavy makeup on his face. **clownish** *adj.*

cloy (kloi) *v.* To make one sick or disgusted with too much sweetness. **cloyingly** *adv.*

club (klub) *n.* A heavy wooden stick, used as a weapon; a group of people who have organized themselves with or for a common purpose.

club car *n.* A railroad passenger car with comfortable chairs, tables, beverage bar, or buffet; a lounge car.

club-foot (klub′füt″) *n.* A short misshapen foot that was twisted out of position from birth.

club-house (klub′hous″) *n.* A house or building occupied by a club or used for club activities.

clue (klö) *n.* Reliable information that leads to the solution of a problem, crime or mystery.

clump (klump) *n.* A group of things in a cluster or group; a shapeless mass. *v.* To plant or place in a clump.

clum-sy (klum′zē) *adj.* Lacking coordination, grace, or dexterity; not tactful or skillful. **clumsily** *adv.* **clumsiness** *n.*

clus-ter (klus′tėr) *n.* A bunch; a group.

clutch (kluch) *v.* To seize or attempt to

seize and hold tightly. *n.* A tight grasp; a device for connecting and disconnecting the engine and the drive shaft in an automobile or other mechanism.

clut-ter (klut´ėr) *n.* A confused mass of disorder.

coach (kōch) *n.* An automobile that is closed and usually has four doors and four wheels; a trainer or director of athletics, drama, etc.

coach-man (kōch´mam) *n.* A man employed to drive a carriage or coach.

co-ad-ju-tor (kō aj u tėr) *n.* An assistant.

co-ag-u-la-bil-i-ty (kō ag´ū la bil´i tē) *n.* The capacity of being coagulated.

co-ag-u-lant (kō ag´ū lant) *n.* A substance that causes coagulation.

co-ag-u-late (kō ag´ū lāt´) *v.* To clot or congeal. **coagulation** *n.*

coal (kōl) *n.* A mineral widely used as a natural fuel; an ember.

coal-er (kō´lėr) *n.* A person who sells or provides coal; something used to haul or transport coal.

co-a-lesce (kō´a les´) *v.* To come together or to grow as one.

co-ali-tion (kō´a lish´an) *n.* A temporary alliance.

co-apt (kō apt´) *v.* To fit together and make fast, as in the setting of broken bones.

co-arc-tate (kō ärk´tāt) *adj.* Pressed together; compressed; enclosed in a rigid case.

coarse (kōrs) *adj.* Lacks refinement; of inferior or low quality; having large particles; harsh. **coarseness** *v.*

coast (kōst) *v.* To move without propelling oneself; to use the force of gravity alone; to slide or glide along. *n.* The land bordering the sea. **coaster** *n.*

coastal current *n.* A current, running parallel to the shoreline, having a comparatively steady flow.

coaster brake *n.* A brake operated by reverse pressure on the pedal as with a bicycle.

coast-line (kōst´līn˝) *n.* The shoreline; the land forming the boundary between land and water.

coast-ward (kōst´wėrd) *adv.* Toward the coast.

coat (kōt) *n.* An outer garment with sleeves, worn over other clothing; a layer that covers a surface. **coating** *n.*

co-au-thor (kō o´thėr) *n.* A person who writes with the assistance of one or more other authors.

coax (kōks) *v.* To persuade by tact, gentleness, or flattery. **coaxingly** *adv.*

co-ax-i-al (kō ak´sē al) *adj.* Having common coincident axes.

coaxial cable *n.* A transmission cable consisting of two or more insulated conductors capable of transmitting television, telegraph, signals of high frequency.

cob (kob) *n.* A male swan; a corncob; a thick-set horse that has short legs.

co-balt (kō´bolt) *n.* A hard, lustrous metallic element that resembles iron and nickel.

cob-ble (kob´l) *v.* To make or repair shoes; to make or put together roughly. **cobbler, cobble** *n.*

CO-BOL (kō´bōl) *n.* In Computer Science, computer programming that is simple and based on English.

co-bra (ko´bra) *n.* A venomous snake from Asia or Africa. When excited, the neck dilates into a broad hood.

cob-web (kob´web´) *n.* The fine thread from a spider which is spun into a web and used to catch prey.

co-caine (kō kān´) *n.* An alkaloid used as an anesthetic and narcotic.

co-cain-ism (kō kā´niz um) *n., Pathol.* The addiction to the use of cocaine.

coc-cyx (kok´siks) *n.* The small bone at the bottom of the spinal column.

coch-i-neal (koch´i nēl´) *n.* A brilliant scarlet dye prepared from the dried, pulverized bodies of certain female insects of tropical America.

coch-le-a (kok´lē a) *n.* The spiral tube of the inner ear, forming an essential part for hearing.

cock (kok) *n.* The adult male in the domestic fowl family; the rooster; the hammer of a firearm and the readiness for firing. *v.* To raise in preparation for hitting; to ready a firearm for firing.

cock-ade (ko kād′) *n.* A knot of ribbon or something similar worn on a hat as a badge.

cock-a-too (kok′a tō′) *n.* A crested parrot of the East Indies.

cock-a-trice (kok′a tris) *n.* A mythical serpent said to be hatched from a cock's egg, deadly to those who meet its glance or feel its breath.

cock-boat(kok′bōt″) *n.* A small boat, used as a tender.

cock-crow (kok′krō″) *n.* The time at which cocks crow; early morning; dawn.

cock-eye (kok′) *n.* An eye that squints; or anything setting off center.

cock-eyed (kok′īd) *adj., Slang* Absurdly wrong; slightly crazy; foolishly twisted to one side.

cock-i-ly (kok′i lē) *adv.* In a cocky manner.

cock-le (kok′el) *n.* European bivalve mollusk of the edible species, having ridged, somewhat heart-shaped shells.

cock-le-shell (kok′el shel″) *n.* The shell of a cockle; a flimsy boat.

cock-loft (kok′loft) *n.* A small loft in the top of a house; a small garret.

cock-pit (kok′pit′) *n.* The compartment of an airplane where the pilot and the crew sit.

cock-roach (kok′rōch′) *n.* A flat-bodied, fast running, chiefly nocturnal insect, many of which are household pests.

cock-shy (kok′shi″) *n.* The act of throwing something at a mark or target.

cock-sure (kok′shür′) *adj.* Perfectly sure or certain; sometimes on inadequate grounds.

cock-tail (kok′tāl″) *n.* Any of various iced drinks, containing alcoholic beverages as gin, whiskey, or brandy and mixed with other flavoring ingredients.

co-co (kō′kō) *n.* The fruit obtained from the coconut palm.

co-coa (kō′kō) *n.* The powder from the roasted husked seed kernels of the cacao.

cocoa butter *n.* A pale fatty substance obtained from cacao beans, used in cosmetics and lotions.

co-co-nut (kō′ko nut) *n.* The nut of the coconut palm, having a hard-shell, with a white edible meat, and contains a milky liquid.

coconut palm *n.* A tall, slender tropical palm tree.

co-coon (ko kŏn′) *n.* The protective fiber or silk pupal case that is spun by insect larvae.

cod (kod) *n.* A large fish of the North Atlantic that is important as food.

C.O.D. *abbr.* Collect On Delivery.

cod-dle (kod′el) *v.* To cook just below the boiling point; to simmer.

code (kōd) *n.* A system of set rules; a set of secret words, numbers, or letters used as a means of communication; in *Computer Science*, the method of representing information or data by using a set sequence of characters, symbols, or words. **code** *v.*

code conversion *n., Computer* The conversion of information from one code to another.

co-de-fend-ant (kō″di fen′dant)) *n.* One or more defendants in a legal action; a joint defendant.

co-dex (kō′deks) *n.* An ancient manuscript of the classics or Scriptures.

codg-er (koj′ér) *n.* An odd or eccentric old man.

cod-i-fy (kod′i fī) *v.* To reduce to a code.

codling moth *n.* A small moth, the larva of which lives and feeds on fruit trees.

co-ed (kō′ed′) *adj.* For, open to or including both men and women; to include both sexes.

co--ed-u-ca-tion (kō′ej e kā′shan) *n.* An educational system for both men and women at the same institution. **coeducational** *adj.*

co-erce (kō ers′) *v.* To restrain or dominate with force; to compel by law, authority, fear, or force.

co-e-qual (kō ē′kwal) *adj.* Equal with one another, person or thing.

co-e-ta-ne-ous (kō″i tā′nē us) *adj.* Beginning to grow or exist at the same time.

co-e-ter-nal (kō″i tür′nal) *adj.* Equally or jointly eternal with another.

co-e-val (kō ē′val) *adj.* Of the same time period. **coeval** *n.*

co-ex-ec-u-tor (kō˝ig zek′ū tėr) *n.* A joint executor of a will.

co-ex-ist (kō´ig zist´) *v.* To exist at the same time or together; the ability to live peaceably with others in spite of differences. **coexistence** *n.*

co-ex-ten-sive (kō˝ik sten′siv) *adj.* Having the same boundaries.

cof-fee (ko′fē) *n.* A beverage prepared from ground beans of the coffee tree.

coffee cake *n.* A sweet rich bread containing raisins or nuts and often shaped into a ring or braid and topped with icing.

coffee house *n.* A restaurant which specializes in different brands of coffee and other light refreshment.

cof-fee-pot (ko′fē pot´) *n.* An appliance used for brewing and or serving coffee.

coffee shop *n.* A small restaurant that serves snacks and light meals.

cof-fer (ko′fėr) *n.* A strongbox or chest made for valuables.

cof-fin (ko′fin) *n.* A box in which a corpse is buried.

cog (kog) *n.* A tooth or one of a series of teeth on the rim of a wheel in a machine or a mechanical device.

co-gent (kō´jent) *adj.* Compelling; forceful; convincing.

cog-i-tate (koj´i tāt´) *v.* To think carefully about or to ponder; give thought to. **cogitation** *n.* **cogitative** *adj.*

co-gnac (kōn′yak) *n.* A fine brandy made in France.

cog-nate (kog′nāt) *adj.* From a common ancestor; identical or similar in nature; related.

cog-na-tion (kog nā′shan) *n.* Relationship by blood.

cog-ni-za-ble (kog′ni za bl) *adj.* Capable of being noticed or observed.

cog-ni-zance (kog′ni zans) *n.* Perception of fact; awareness; recognition; observation.

cog-ni-zant (kog′ni zant) *adj.* Obtained knowledge through personal experiences.

cog-nize (kog nīz´) *v.* To recognize as an object of thought; to perceive; understand.

cog-no-men (kog nō′men) *n. pl.* **cognomens** A person's surname; nickname.

cog-nos-ci-ble (kog nos′ibl) *adj.* Capable of being known; knowable.

cog-wheel (kog′hwēl˝) *n.* A wheel with cogs or teeth; a gear wheel.

co-hab-it (kō hab′it) *v.* To live together as husband and wife.

co-heir (kō âr´) *n.* A joint heir; a person who shares an inheritance with another.

co-here (kō hēr´) *v.* To stick or hold together.

co-her-ent (kō hēr′ent) *adj.* Sticking together; consistent; to remain united.

co-he-sion (kō hē′zhan) *n.* The act or state of sticking together.

co-he-sive (kō hē′siv) *adj.* Sticking together.

co-hort (kō´hort) *n.* A group of people who are united in one effort; an accomplice.

coif (koif) *n.* A close-fitting hat that is worn under a nun's veil.

coif-feur (kwä fyür´) *n.* A male hairdresser.

coil (koil) *n.* A series of connecting rings. *v.* To wind in spirals.

coin (koin) *n.* A flat, rounded piece of metal used as money. *v.* To invent or make a new phrase or word.

co-in-cide (kō´in sīd´) *v.* To happen at the same time; to agree exactly.

co-in-ci-dence (kō in´si dens) *n.* Two events happening at the same time by accident but appearing to have some connection.

co-in-ci-den-tal (kō in˝si den′tal) *adj.* Involving or resulting from a coincidence; happening or existing at the same time.

co-in-ci-dent (kō in´si dent) *adj.* Occupying the same place, position or time simultaneously.

co-in-her-it-ance (kō˝in her′i tans) *n.* Joint inheritance.

co-in-stan-ta-ne-ous (kō˝in stan tā′nē us) *adj.* Happening at the same time or instant.

co-in-sur-ance (kō˝in shür′ans) *n.* Insurance jointly assumed by another or others.

co-in-sure (kō″in shür′) *v.* To insure jointly with another.

co-i-tus (kō′i t*u*s) *n.* Physical union of male and female sexual organs; sexual intercourse.

coke (kōk) *n.* A solid, carbonaceous fuel made by heating soft coal until some of its gases have been removed. *Slang* Cocaine.

co-l-an-der (kul′*a*n dėr) *n.* A utensil with a perforated bottom, used for washing or draining food and straining liquids.

cold (kōld) *adj.* Having a low temperature; feeling uncomfortable; without sufficient warmth; lacking in affection or sexual desire; frigid. *n.* An infection of the upper respiratory tract resulting in coughing, sneezing, etc. **coldness** *n.*

cold--blooded (kōld′blud′id) *adj.* Done without feeling; having a body temperature that varies according to the temperature of the surroundings. **coldbloodedly** *adv.*

cold boot *n., Computer Science* The boot performed when power is turned on for the first time each day.

cold cream *n.* A heavy, oily, cosmetic cream used for cleansing and lubricating the skin.

cold cuts *n. pl.* A selection of freshly sliced cold meats.

cold feet *n., Colloq.* Loss of courage or confidence for carrying out some undertaking proposed or begun.

cold front *n.* The zone between two masses of air in which the cooler mass is in process of replacing the warmer.

cold shoulder *n.* An open show of coldness, or unsympathetic treatment of another person.

cold sweat *n.* A chill characterized by perspiration, often induced by a state of nervousness.

cold wave *n.* A considerable fall in termperature which occurs rapidly and affects a wide area.

cole (kōl) *n.* A plant such as the cabbage or a vegetable of the same family.

co-lec-to-my (k*o* lek′t*o* mē) *n., Surg.* Complete or partial removal of the colon or large intestine.

cole-slaw (kōl′slä) *n.* A salad made of raw, chopped or shredded cabbage leaves.

col-ic (kol′ik) *n.* A sharp pain in the abdomen caused by muscular cramps or spasms, occurring most often in very young babies.

col-i-se-um (kol′i sē′*u*m) *n.* A large amphitheater used for sporting games.

co-lit-is (k*o* lī′tis) *n., Pathol.* Inflammation of the colon.

col-lab-o-rate (k*o* lab′*o* rāt′) *v.* To cooperate or work with another person. **collaboration** *n.* **collaborator** *n.*

col-lapse (k*o* laps′) *v.* To fall; to give way; to fold and assume a smaller size; to lose all or part of the air in a lung.

col-lar (kol′ėr) *n.* The upper part of a garment that encircles the neck and is often folded over.

col-lar-bone (kol′ėr bōn′) *n., Anat.* The clavicle, located near the neck.

col-lard (kol′*a*rd) *n.* A smooth-leaved vegetable of the kale family.

col-late (k*o* lāt′) *v.* To compare in a critical fashion; to assemble in correct sequence or order.

col-lat-er-al (k*o* lat′ėr *a*l) *adj.* Serving to support; guaranteed by stocks, property, bonds, etc.

col-league (kol′ēg) *n.* Someone who works in the same profession or official body.

col-lect (k*o* lekt′) *v.* To gather or assemble; to gather donations or payments. **collectible** *n.* **collection** *n.*

col-lec-tion (k*o* lek′sh*a*n) *n.* The act or process of collecting or gathering.

col-lec-tive (k*o* lek′tiv) *adj.* Formed by a number of things or persons.

col-lec-tiv-i-ty (kol″ek tiv′i tē) *n.* Collective character; the state of being collective.

col-lege (kol′ij) *n.* An institution of higher education which grants a bachelor's degree; a school of special instruction or special fields.

col-le-gian (k*o* lē′j*a*n) *n.* A student or graduate of a college.

col-lide (ko līd´) v. To come together with a direct impact; to clash; to come into conflict.

col-li-mate (kol´i māt) v. To adjust or to bring into line; make parallel.

col-lin-e-ar (ko lin´ė ar) adj. Lying in or passing through the same straight line.

col-li-sion (ko lizh´on) n. The act of striking or colliding together.

col-lo-cate (kol´o kāt´) v. To compare facts and arrange in correct order; to set or place with, or in relation to.

col-lo-di-on (ko lō´dē on) n. A highly flammable spray solution used to protect wounds and used for photographic plates.

col-loid (kol´oid) n. A glue-like substance, such as gelatin, that cannot pass through animal membranes.

col-lo-quy (kol´o kwē) n. pl. -quies A formal conversation or conference.

col-lude (ko lōd´) v. To act together through a secret understanding.

col-lusion (ko lō´zhan) n. A secret agreement between two or more people for an illegal purpose.

co-logne (ko lōn´) n. A perfumed substance of fragrant oils and alchol.

co-lon (kō´lon) n. A punctuation mark (:) used to introduce an example or series; used to separate words and numbers; the section of the large intestine that extends from the cecum to the rectum. **colonic** adj.

colo-nel (ker´nel) n. An officer in the armed forces that ranks above a lieutenant colonel and below a brigadier general.

co-lo-ni-al (ko lō´nē al) adj. Pertaining to a colony or colonies.

co-lo-ni-al-ism (ko lō´nē a liz˝um) n. The colonial system; the control over an area of people; a policy based on such control.

col-o-ny (kol´o nē) n. pl -ies A group of emigrants living in a new land away from, but under the control of, the parent country; a group of insects, as ants.

col-o-phon (kol´o fon´) n. The inscription at the end of a book that gives the publication facts.

col-or (kul´ėr) n. The aspect of things apart from the shape, size, and solidity; a hue or tint that is caused by the different degrees of light that are reflected or emitted by them. **colored** adj. **colorful** adj. **coloring** n.

Col-o-ra-do n. A state located in the western central part of the United States, statehood August 1, 1876, state capital Denver.

col-or-a-tion (kul´o rā´shan) n. The arrangement of different colors or shades.

col-or-bear-er (kul´ė bâr˝ėr) n. The person in charge of carrying the colors, as of a military formation.

col-or–blind (kul´ėr blīnd´) adj. Unable to distinguish colors, either totally or partially.

col-or-cast (kul´ėr käst˝) n. A television broadcast or program presented in color.

col-or-fast (kul´ėr fast´) adj. Color that will not run or fade with washing or wearing. **colorfastness** n.

color guard n. A person in charge of the colors, the flag, as of a military unit.

col-or-ist (kul´ėr ist) n. A person who colors or works with colors.

col-or-less (kul´ėr lis) adj. Destitute or lacking color; washed-out.

co-los-sal (ko los´al) adj. Very large or gigantic in degree or size.

co-los-sus (ko los´us) n. Something that is very large, as a huge state, thing, or person.

col-por-teur (kol´pōr˝tėr) n. A person who travels from place to place distributing or peddling religious materials and Bibles.

colt (kōlt) n. A very young male horse. **coltish** adj.

Columbus, Christopher n. The person credited with finding the New World.

col-umn (kol´um) n. A decorative and or supporting pillar used in construction; a vertical division of typed or printed lines on paper.

co-lum-nar (ko lum´nėr) adj. Of, pertaining to, or relating to columns.

col-lum-ni-a-tion (ko lum˝nē ā´shan) n. The arrangement of columns in a structure.

col-um-nist (kol´um nist) *n.* A person who writes a newspaper or magazine column.

co-ma (kō´ma) *n.* A deep sleep or unconsciousness caused by an illness or injury.

co-ma-tose (kom´a tōs´) *adj.* Unconscious.

comb (kōm) *n.* A toothed instrument made from a material such as plastic used for smoothing and arranging the hair; the fleshy crest on the head of a fowl.

com-bat (kom bat´) *v.* To fight against; to oppose; to contend. *n.* A struggle; a fight or contest especially with armed conflict, as a battle, war with others. **combatant** *n.*

com-ba-tive (kom bat´iv) *adj.* Marked by eagerness to fight.

comb-er (kō´mér) *n.* A machine or person that combs wool or cotton.

com-bin-a-ble (kom bī´na bl) *adj.* That which may be combined.

com-bi-na-tion (kom´bi nā´shan) *n.* The process of combining or the state of being combined; a series of numbers or letters needed to open certain locks.

com-bine (kom bīn´) *v.* To unite; to merge. *n.* A farm machine that harvests by cutting, threshing, and cleaning the grain.

com-bo (kom´bō) *n.* A small jazz group of three or four musicians who dances.

com-bust (kom bust´) *adj.* To burn up.

com-bus-ti-bil-i-ty (kom bus´ti bil´i tē) *n.* The state of being combustible.

com-bus-ti-ble (kom bus´ti bl) *adj.* Having the capability of burning. *n.* A combustible material as paper or wood.

com-bus-tion (kom bus´chan) *n.* The chemical change that occurs rapidly and produces heat and light; a burning; fire **combustive** *adj.*

come (kum) *v.* To arrive; to approach; to reach a certain position, state, or result; to appear; to come into view.

come about *v.* To come to pass.

come across *v.* To find by chance; to produce an impression

come along *v.* To improve.

come back *v.* To return to health or to a former position or success.

co-me-di-an (ko mē´dē an) *n.* An actor of comedy.

come down *v.* To be humbled; to lose rank or position.

com-e-dy (kom´i dē) *n. pl.* **-ies** A humorous, entertaining performance with a happy ending; a real-life comical situation. **comedic** *adj.*

come in *v.* To enter; to become fashionable; to be brought into use.

co-mes-ti-ble (ko mes´ti bl) *n.* Something that is fit to eat. *adj.* Fit to eat.

com-et (kom´it) *n.* A celestial body that moves in an orbit around the sun, consisting of a solid head that is surrounded by a bright cloud with a long, vaporous tail.

com-fort (kum´fèrt) *v.* To console in time of grief or fear; to make someone feel better; to help; to assist, to have relief or satisfaction; solace. **comfort** *n.* **comfortingly** *adv.*

com-fort-a-ble (kumf´ta bl) *adj.* In a state of comfort; financially secure, content and happy. **comfortably** *adv.*

com-fort-er (kum´fèr tèr) *n.* A heavy blanket or quilt; someone who comforts.

com-ic (kom´ik) *adj.* Characteristic of comedy. *n.* A comedian; comic book. **Comics** Comic strips.

com-i-cal (kom´i kal) *adj.* Amusing; humorous.

comic strip *n.* Narrative cartoons appearing in sequence, usually found in newspapers.

com-ing (kum ing) *n.* Approach; instance of arriving.

com-ma (kom´a) *n.* The punctuation mark (,) used to indicate separation of ideas or a series in a sentence.

com-mand (ko mand´) *v.* To rule; to give orders; to dominate. *n., Computer Science* The instruction given that specifies an operation to be performed.

com-man-deer (kom˝an dèr´) *v.* To force into active military service; to seize.

com-mand-er (kom˝an dèr´) *n.* The person authorized to command; a leader or chief officer.

com-mand-ment (ko mand´ment) *n.* The

act, or power of commanding; a command or mandate.

com-mem-o-rate (ko mem´o rāt´) v. To honor the memory of; to create a memorial to. **commemorative** n. **commemoration** n. **commemorator** n.

com-mence (ko mens´) v. To begin; to start.

com-mence-ment (ko mens´ment) n. A graduation ceremony.

com-mend (ko mend´) v. To give praise; to applaud. **mendable** adj. **commendably** adv. **commendation** n.

com-men-da-tion (kom´en dā´shan) n. The act of commending; praise; a favorable representation in words that commends.

com-men-su-rate (ko men´sèr it) adj. Equal in duration, extent, or size. **commensuration** n.

com-ment (kom´ent) n. A statement of criticism, analysis, or observation.

com-men-tar-y (kom´en ter˝ē) n. A series of comments.

com-mer-cial (ko mer´shal) adj. Of or relating to a product; supported by advertising. n. An advertisement on radio or television.

com-mer-cial-ize (ko mür´sha līz˝) v. To render commercial in character, methods, or spirit; to exploit for profit.

com-min-gle (ko ming´gel) v. To mix together; to mingle in one mass; to blend throughly.

com-mi-nute (kom´i nŏt˝) v. To make small or fine; to reduce to minute particles; to pulverize.

com-mis-er-ate (ko miz´e rat´) v. To display or feel sympathy for someone. **commiserative** adj. **commiseration** n.

com-mis-sar (kom´i sär´) n. An official of the Communist Party whose duties include the enforcement of party loyalty and political indoctrination.

com-mis-sar-i-at (kom˝i sâr´ē at) n. The department of an army which supplies food for the troops.

com-mis-sar-y (kom´i ser´ē) n. pl. -ies A store that sells food and supplies on a military base.

com-mis-sion (ko mish´on) n. The percentage of the money received from a total, that is paid to a person for his service in the area of sales.

com-mis-sure n. A joint, or line of union; the junction between two anatomical parts.

com-mit (ko mit) v. To put in trust or charge; consign for safe-keeping or preservation.

com-mit-ment (ko mit´ment) n. The act of committing; the agreement to do something in the future.

com-mit-tal (ko mit´al) n. Commitment.

com-mit-tee (k o mit´ē) n. A group of persons appointed or elected to perform a particular task or function. **committeeman** n. **committeewoman** n.

com-mode (ko mōd´) n. A movable washstand with storage underneath; a toilet; a low chest of drawers or bureau.

com-mo-di-ous (ko mō´dē us) adj. Roomy; spacious. **modiously** adv.

com-mod-i-ty (ko mod´i tē) n. Something valuable or useful.

com-mo-dore (kom´o dōr´) n. A naval officer ranking above a captain and below a rear admiral; the senior captain of a naval squadron or of a merchant fleet.

com-mon (kom´on) adj. Having to do with, belonging to, or used by an entire community or public; vulgar; unrefined.

com-mon-age (kom´o nij) n. Community property; anything in common.

com-mon-al-ty (kom´o nal tē) n. The common people; general group.

common denominator n. The number that can be divided evenly by all denominators of a number of fractions.

com-mon-er (kom´o nè) n. Common people.

common fraction n. A fraction where both the denominator and numerator are whole numbers.

common law n. Unwritten law based on judicial decisions, customs, and usages.

common–law marriage n. A marriage of mutual agreement and cohabitation, but not considered a legal marriage by most laws and jurisdictions.

common multiple *n., Math.* A multiple of each of two or more numbers, quantities, or expressions.

com-mon-place (kom´on plās´) *n.* A trite or obvious observation; something easily taken for granted.

common room *n.* A room usually in schools, colleges, or universities that serves a variety of purposes.

common sense *n.* Sound practical judgment; but often unsophisticated.

common time *n.* Musical time or tempo with four beats to a measure.

common touch *n.* The personal quality of appealing to common people.

com-mon-weal-th (kom´on welth´) *n.* The common good of the whole group of people.

com-mo-tion (ko mō´shan) *n.* Disturbance; mental excitement; total confusion.

com-move (ko mōv´) *v.* To move violently; to excite.

com-mu-nal (ko mūn´al) *adj.* Relating to a community; characterized by common sharing or collective ownership by members of a community.

com-mu-nal-i-ty (kom´ū nal´it ē) *n.* Group solidarity; communal character; similar opinions of a group.

com-mune (ko mūn´) *v.* To converse; to talk together; discuss; to exchange ideas. *n.* A small rural community.

com-mu-ni-ca-ble (ko mū´ni ka bl) *adj.* Capable of being transmitted, as with a disease. **communicability** *n.* **communicab-ly** *adv.*

com-mu-ni-cate (ko mū´ni kāt´) *v.* To make known; to cause others to partake or share something.

com-mu-ni-ca-tion (ko mū´ni kā´shan) *n.* The act of transmitting ideas through writing or speech; the means to transmit messages between person or places.

com-mu-ni-ca-tive (ko mū´ ni kā˝tiv) *adj.* Inclined to communicate; talkative.

com-mun-ion (ko mūn´yan) *n.* The mutual sharing of feelings and thoughts; a religious fellowship between members of a church.

com-mun-ion (ko mūn´yan) *n.* A sacrament in which bread and wine are consumed to commemorate the death of Christ.

com-mu-nism (kom´ū niz´um) *n.* A system of government in which goods and production are commonly owned; the theory of social change and struggle toward communism through revolution.

com-mu-ni-ty (ko mū´ni tē) *n. pl.* **-ies** A group of people living in the same area and under the same government; a class or group having common interests and likes; the state of being held in common; common possession, enjoyment, liability, etc.; common character; agreement; identity.

community center *n.* A place provided by a residential community for members recreational, social, or educational activities.

community chest *n.* A general fund collected from voluntary contributions by members of a community for the support of local charity.

community property *n.* Jointly held property by both husband and wife.

com-mu-nize (kom´ū nīz´) *v.* To transfer individual ownership to community or state owned.

com-mut-a-ble (ko mū´ta bl) *adj.* Exchangeable.

com-mu-ta-tive (ko mū´ ta tiv) *adj.* Of or pertaining to commutation.

com-mute (ko mūt´) *v.* To travel a long distance to one's job each day; to exchange or to substitute.

com-muter (ko mū´tėr) *n.* One who travels a long distance on a regular basis.

com-pact (kom pakt´) *adj.* Packed together or solidly united; firmly and closely united.

com-pact-i-ble (kom pakt´i bl) *adj.* Having the qualities for being compacted.

com-pac-tor (kom pak tōr) *n.* A device for compressing trash into a small mass for disposal.

com-pan-ion (kom pan´yon) *n.* An associate; a person employed to accompany or assist another; one hired to travel or live with another. **companionship** *n.*

com-pan-ion-a-ble (kom pan´yo na bl) *adj.* Friendly; sociable. **companionably** *adv.*

com-pan-ion-ate (kom pan´yo nit) *adj.* Of or relating to companions.

com-pan-ion-way (kom pan´yon wā´) *n.*, Naut. A stairway leading from a ship's deck to the cabin below.

com-pa-ny (kum´pa nē) *n.* *pl.* **-ies** The gathering of persons for a social purpose; a number of persons who are associated for a common purpose, as in business; a business.

company union *n.* A union affiliated with only the employees of a single company, and not affiliated with a national union.

com-pa-ra-ble (kom´par a bl) *adj.* Capable of comparison; worthy of comparison; similar. **comparability** *n.* **comparably** *adv.* **comparative** *adj.*

com-pare (kom pâr´) *v.* To speak of or represent as similar or equal to; to note the similarities or likenesses of.

com-par-i-son (kom par´i son) *n.* Likeness; similarity. *Gram.* Modification of a verb or adjective that indicates the positive, comparative, or superlative degree.

comparison–shop *v.* To shop in different stores; to compare prices in order to get the best buy.

com-part (kom pärt´) *v.* To divide into parts according to a plan.

com-part-ment (kom pärt´ment) *n.* One of the sections into which an enclosed area is divided.

com-pass (kum´pas) *n.* An instrument used to determine geographic direction; an enclosed area or space; the extent of reach of something; range or area; scope. **compasses** A device shaped like a V that is used for drawing circles.

com-pas-sion (kom pash´on) *n.* Sympathy for a person who is suffering or distressed

in someway. **compassionate** *adj.*

com-pa-thy (kom´pa thē) *n.* Feelings of grief or joy shared with another.

com-pat-i-ble (kom pat´i bl) *adj.* Able to function, exist, or live together harmoniously. **compatibility** *n.* **compatibly** *adv.*

com-pa-tri-ot (kom pā´trēot) *n.* A person of the same country.

com-peer (kom pēr´) *n.* A person that is a peer or equal.

com-pel (kom pel´) *v.* To urge or force action.

com-pel-la-tion (kom˝pe lā´shan) *n.* The act of addressing someone.

com-pen-di-ous (kom pen´dē us) *adj.* Containing the substance of a comprehensive subject in a brief form.

com-pen-dium (kom pen´dēum) *n.* *pl.* **-diums** A short summary.

com-pen-sa-ble (kom pen´sa bl) *adj.* That is or is entitled to compensation.

com-pen-sate (kom´pen sāt´) *v.* To make up for; to make amends; to pay; to neutralize or counter balance. **compensation** *n.* **compensatory** *adj.*

com-pete (kom pēt´) *v.* To contend with others; to engage in a contest or competition.

com-pe-tent (kom´pi tent) *adj.* Having sufficient ability; being capable. **competence** *n.* **competency** *n.*

com-pe-ti-tion (kom´pi tish´an) *n.* The act of rivalry or competing; a trial of skill or ability; a contest between teams or individuals. **competitive** *adj.*

com-pi-la-tion (kom˝pi lā´shan) *n.* The act or process of collecting or compiling.

com-pet-i-tor (kom pet´i tėr) *n.* One who competes against another.

com-pile (kom pīl´) *v.* To put together material gathered from a number of sources; in Computer Science, to convert our language into machine language. **compilation** *n.* **compiler** *n.*

com-pla-cence (kom plā´sens) *n.* A feeling of secure self-satisfaction.

com-pla-cent (kom plā´sent) *adj.* Pleased with one's merits or advantages; self-satisfied.

com-plain (kom plān´) v. To express grief, pain, uneasiness, or discontent.

com-plain-ant (kom plā´nant) n. A person filing a formal charge.

com-plaint (kom plānt´) n. An expression of pain, dissatisfaction, or resentment; a cause or reason for complaining; a grievances.

com-plai-sance (kom plā´sans) n. The willingness to please, to oblige, to help. **complaisant** adj.

com-plai-sant (kom plā´ sant) adj. Marked by a need to please; obliging; gracious.

com-ple-ment (kom´plement) n. Something that perfects, completes, or adds to. **complementary** adj.

com-ple-men-tal (kom˝ple men´tal) adj. Relating to or forming a complement.

complementary colors n. pl. Primary or secondary colors in the spectrum, when combined produce a neutral color.

com-plete (kom plēt´) adj. Having all the necessary parts; whole; concluded. **completion** n.

com-ple-tion (kom plē´shan) n. The process or act of completing.

com-plex (kom pleks´) adj. Consisting of various intricate parts. **complexity** n. **complexly** adv.

com-plex-ion (kom plek´shan) n. The natural color and texture of the skin, also the disposition of the mind and body. **complexioned** adj.

com-plex-i-ty n. The state or quality of being complex; intricacy; something complex.

com-pli-ance (kom plī´ans) n. The act of agreeing passively to a request, rule, or demand; the tendency to yield to others. **compliant** adj. **compliancy** n.

com-pli-ant (kom plī´ant) adj. Ready to comply; yielding; obliging.

com-pli-cate (kom´pli kāt´) v. To make or become involved or complex.

com-pli-ca-tion (kom˝pli kā´sham) n. The situation of complicating or the state of being complicated; entanglement; complexity; something complicated.

com-plic-i-ty (kom plis´i tē) n. An involvement or association with a crime.

com-pli-er (kom plī´ėr) n. One who complies.

com-pli-ment (kom´pli ment) n. An expression of praise or admiration.

com-pli-men-ta-ry (kom´pli men´ta rē) adj. Conveying a compliment.

com-ply (kom plī´) v. To agree, to consent to, or obey a command or wish; requirements. **complier** n.

com-po-nent (kom pō´nent) n. A constituent part.

com-port (kom pōrt´) v. To behave or conduct oneself in a certain way.

com-port-ment (kom pōrt´ment) n. Behavior; demeanor; deportment.

com-pose (kom pōz´) v. To make up from elements or parts; to produce or create a song; to arrange, as to typeset; artistic composition. **composer** n.

com-posed (kom pōzd´) adj. Calm.

com-pos-er (kom pō´zėr) n. One who composes; a person who writes an original work.

com-pos-ite (kom poz´it) adj. Made up from separate elements or parts; combined or compounded. Characteristic of a plant with densely clustered flowers.

com-po-si-tion (kom´po zish´on) n. The act of putting together artistic or literary work; a short essay written for an assignment in school. **compositional** adj.

com-post (kom´pōst) n. A fertilizing mixture that consists of decomposed vegetable matter.

com-po-sure (kom pō´zhėr) n. Tranquility; calm self-possession.

com-pote (kom´pōt) n. Fruit that is preserved or stewed in syrup; a dish used for holding fruit, candy, etc.

com-pound (kom´pound) n. The combination of two or more parts, elements, or ingredients; In grammar, a new word that is composed of two or more words joined with a hyphen or written as a solid word. *Chem.* A definite substance that results from combining specific radica n. Elements in certain or fixed proportions. *v.* To combine; to increase. **compoundable** *adj.*

compound fracture *n.* A broken bone that breaks and protrudes through the skin.

compound interest *n.* Interest computed on the original principal plus accrued interest.

compound sentence *n.* A sentence compiled of two or more independent clauses.

compound word *n.* A word made up of two or more words that retain their separate form and signification.

com-pre-hend (kom'pri hend') *v.* To perceive, to grasp mentally, or to understand fully; to comprise; to include. **comprehension** *n.*

com-pre-hen-si-ble (kom'pri hen'si bl) *adj.* Capable of being understood. **comprehensibility** *n.* **comprehensibly** *adv.*

com-pre-hen-sion (kom"pri hen'shan) *n.* The act of understanding or comprehending; the knowledge gained.

com-pre-hen-sive (kom'pri hen'siv) *adj.* Large in content or scope.

com-press (kom'pres) *v.* To press together into a smaller space; to condense. *n.* A soft pad sometimes medicated, for applying cold, heat, moisture, or pressure to a part of the body. **compression, compressibility** *adj.* **compressible** *adj.*

compressed air *n.* Air that is under greater pressure than the atmosphere.

com-pres-sive (kom pres'iv) *adj.* Having the power to compress; tending to compress.

com-pres-sor (kom pres'ėr) *n.* Something that compresses; a machine that is used for compressing air to utilize its expansion.

com-prise (kom prīz') *v.* To consist of; to be made up of. **comprisable** *adj.*

com-pro-mise (kom'pro mīz') *n.* The process of settling or the settlement of differences between opposing sides, with each side making concessions. **compromiser** *n.* **compromise** *v.*

comp-trol-ler (kon trō'lėr) *n.* A person appointed to examine and verify accounts.

com-pul-sion (kom pul'shan) *n.* The act or state of being compelled; an irresistible urge or impulse to act irrationally.

compulsive (kom pul'siv) *adj.* An act or state of being compelled.

com-pul-so-ry (kom pul'so rē) *adj.* Enforced, mandatory.

com-punc-tion (kom pungk'shan) *n.* Anxiety arising from guilt or awareness.

com-pur-ga-tion (kom"pėr gā'shan) *n.* The clearing of an accused person by the oaths of persons who swear his innocence.

com-put-a-ble (kom pūt'a bl) *adj.* Capable of being computed.

com-pu-ta-tion (kom"pū tā'shan) *n.* The action or act of computing. The operation of a computer.

com-pute (kom pūt') *v.* To ascertain or determine by the use of mathematics; to determine something by the use of a computer. **computability** *n.* **computation** *n.* **computable** *adj.*

com-put-er (kom pū'tėr) *n.* A person who computes; a high speed, electronic machine which performs logical calculations, processes, stores, and retrieves programmed information.

com-put-er-ese (kom pū'trēz) *n.* The jargon used by computer technologists.

com-put-er-i-za-tion (kom pū"te rī zā'shan) *n.* The operation or procedure of computerizing.

com-puter-ize (kom pū'te rīz') *v.* To process or store information on a computer; to switch from manual operations to computers.

computer language *n.* The various codes and information that are used to give data and instructions to computers.

computer program *n.* A system used to find and correct a problem on a computer.

com-rade (kom'rad) *n.* An associate, friend, or companion who shares one's interest or occupation. **comradeship** *n.*

con (kon) *v.* To study carefully. *Slang* To swindle or trick.

co-na-tus (kō nā'tus) *n.* A natural impulse, tendency or striving.

con brio (kon brē'ō) *adv.* In a brisk or vigorous manner.

conc *abbr.* Concentrated; concentration or concentrate.

con-cat-e-nate (kon kat´e nāt´) *v.* To join, connect, or link together. **concatenate** *adj.* **concatenation** *n.*

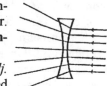

con-cave(kon´kāv) *adj.* Hollowed and curved inward. **concavely** *adv.* **concave** *n.*

con-cav-i-ty (kon kav´i tē) *n.* A concave surface; quality of being concave.

con-ceal (kon sēl´) *v.* To keep from disclosure, sight, or knowledge; to hide or withhold. **concealable** *adj.* **concealer** *n.* **concealment** *n.*

con-cede (kon sēd´) *v.* To grant or yield to a right or privilege; to acknowledge as true. **conceder** *n.* **conceded** *adj.*

con-ceit (kon sēt´) *n.* An exaggerated personal opinion of one's own importance.

con-ceit-ed (kon sē´tid) *adj.* Having an exaggerated or excessively high opinion of oneself.

con-ceive (kon sēv´) *v.* To become pregnant; to create a mental image. **conceivability** *n.* **conceivable** *adj.* **conceivably** *adv.*

con-cen-ter (kon sen´tėr) *v.* To converge or draw to a common center.

con-cen-trate (kon´sen trāt´) *v.* To give intense thought to; to draw to a common point; to intensify by removing certain elements; to become compact. **concentrative** *adj.* **concentrator** *n.*

con-cen-tra-tion (kon´sen trā´shan) *n.* The state of being concentrated or the act of concentrating; the process or act of giving complete attention to a certain problem or task.

concentration camp *n.* An enclosed camp or prison where political prisoners, aliens, or prisoners of war are confined.

con-cen-tric (kon sen´trik) *adj.* Having a common center, as circles or spheres.

con-cept (kon´sept) *n.* A generalized idea formed from particular occurrences or instances; an opinion. **conceptual** *adj.*

con-cep-tion (kon sep´shon) *n.* The union of sperm and egg; a mental thought or plan.

con-cern (kon sėrn´) *n.* Something to consider; sincere interest; something that affects one's business or affairs. *v.* To be interested in; to be involved with. **concerned** *adj.*

con-cern-ing(konsür´ning)*prep.* Relating to; regarding.

con-cern-ment (kon sürn´ment) *n.* Relation or bearing; something in which one is interested or concerned.

con-cert (kon´sėrt) *n.* A musical performance for a group of people; agreement in purpose, action, or feeling. *v.* To act or plan together. **concerted** *adj.*

con-cer-ti-no (kon´cher tē´nō) *n.* A short concerto.

con-cer-to (kon cher´tō) *n.* *pl.* **-tos, -ti** A composition that features one or more solo instruments.

con-ces-sion (kon sesh´an) *n.* The act of conceding; something that has been conceded; a tract of land that is granted by a government for a particular use.

con-ces-sion-aire (kon sesh´o nâr´) *n.* The operator or holder of a concession.

con-ces-sive (kon ses´iv) *adj.* Tending or serving to concede; making for a concession.

conch (kongk) *n.* A tropical marine mollusk having a large spiral shell and flesh that is edible.

con-chol-o-gy (kong kol´o jē) *n.* The study of mollusks and shells. **conchological** *adj.* **conchologist** *n.*

con-cil-i-ar (kon sil´ē ėr) *adj.* Pertaining to, or issued by a council.

con-cil-i-ate (k on sil´ē āt´) *v.* To win over or to gain a friendship. **conciliation** *n.* **conciliator** *n.* **conciliatory** *adj.*

con-cin-ni-ty (kon sin´i tē) *n.* Harmonious adaptation of parts to a whole.

con-cise (kon sīs´) *adj.* Short and to the point.

con-ci-sion (kon sizh´on) *n.* Concise quality or state.

con-clave (kon´klāv) *n.* A private or secret meeting; the private meeting of the Roman Catholic cardinals to elect a new pope.

con-clude (kon klōd´) *v.* To close or bring to an end; to bring about an agreement; to arrive at a decision; to resolve.

con-clu-sion (kon klō´zham) *n.* The close or end; the final decision, the last main division of a discourse.

con-clu-sive (kon klō´siv) *adj.* Putting an end to any questions or doubt.

con-coct (kon kokt´) *v.* To make by combining ingredients; to devise or to plan. **con-coction** *n.*

con-com-i-tant (kon kom´i tant) *adj.* Accompanying. **concomitance** *n.* **concomitantly** *adv.*

con-cord (kon´kord) *n.* Accord; harmony; friendly and peaceful relationships.

con-cor-dance (kon kor´dans) *n.* A condition of concord or agreement; the alphabetical index of major words used by an author, listed in the order of use in a book.

con-cor-dant (kon kor´dant) *adj.* Exist in agreement; harmonious. **concordantly** *adv.*

con-cor-dat (kon kor´dat) *n.* An agreement between a pope and a grovernment; a compact.

con-course (kon´kōrs) *n.* A large, open space for the assembling or passage of crowds.

con-cres-cence (kon kres´ens) *n.* Increase by the addition of particles; growing together.

con-crete (kon´krēt) *adj.* Pertaining to a specific instance or thing; naming a specific class of things. *n.* A construction material made from sand, gravel, and cement. *v.* To bring together in one body or mass. **concretely** *adv.* **concreteness** *n.*

con-cre-tion (kon krē´shan) *n.* The act or process of concreting; the state of being concreted; something concreted.

con-cu-bine (kong´kū bīn´) *n.* A woman living with a man and not being legally married to him. **concubinage** *n.*

con-cu-pis-cence (kon kū´pi sens) *n.* A strong sexual desire; lust.

con-cur (kon kėr´) *v.* To agree or express approval; to cooperate; to happen at the same time; to coincide. **concurrence** *n.*

con-cur-rence (kon kėr´ans) *n.* The act of concurring; a agreement in opinion simultaneous happening in time and place.

con-cur-rent (kon kėr´ant) *adj.* Referring to an event that happens at the same time as another; acting together.

con-cuss (kon kus´) *v.* To affect with a concussion.

con-cus-sion (kon kush´on) *n.* A sudden and violent jolt; a violent injury to an organ, especially the brain. **concussive** *adj.*

con-demn (kon dem´) *v.* To find to be wrong; to show the guilt; to announce judgment upon; to officially declare unfit for use. **condemnable** *adj.* **condemnatory** *adj.* **condemnation** *n.*

con-den-sate (kon den´sāt) *n.* A product of condensation, water from steam.

con-den-sa-tion (kon´den sā´shan) *n.* The act of condensing.

con-dense (kon dens´) *v.* To make more dense, concentrated or compact. **condensability** *n.* **condensation** *n.* **condenser** *n.* **condensable** *adj.* **condensible** *adj.*

con-de-scen-sion (kon´di sen´shan) *n.* The act of condescending; a patronizing behavior.

con-dign (kon dīn´) *adj.* Well deserved; appropriate.

con-di-ment (kon´di ment) *n.* A relish, spice, or sauce used to season food.

con-dis-ci-ple (kon´di sī´pl) *n.* A fellow student.

con-di-tion (kon dish´on) *n.* The mode or state of existence of a thing or person; a circumstance that is found to be necessary to the occurrence of another; a provision in a contract or will that leaves room for modification or changes at a future date. *Slang* A sickness or ailment.

con-di-tion-al (kon dish´a nal) *adj.* Tentative; depending on a condition; implying or expressing a condition. *Gram.* A mood, clause, tense, or condition. **conditionality** *n.* **conditionally** *adv.*

con-di-tion-ed (kon dish´ond) *adj.* Prepared for a certain process or action by past experience.

con-do (kon dō) *n. Slang* Condominium.

con-dole (kon dōl´) *v.* To express sympathetic sorrow at the loss or misfortunes of an-other.

con-dom (kon´dom) *n.* A thin rubber sheath used to cover the penis, serving as an anti-venereal or contraceptive purpose during sexual intercourse.

con-do-min-i-um (kon´do min´ē um) *n.* A joint ownership; an apartment in which all units are owned separately; a building in which the units are owned by each tenant.

con-do-na-tion (kon˝dō nā´shan) *n.* The pardoning of a wrong act.

con-done (kon dōn´) *n.* To overlook; to forgive; to disregard. **condoner** *n.*

con-dor (kon´dor) *v.* One of the largest flying birds, with a bare head and a white downy neck. A very large American vulture with a bare neck and head with dull black plumage and white patches on the wings and neck.

con-du-cive (kon dō´siv) *adj.* Contributing towards or promotion; helpful.

con-duct (kon dukt´) *v.* To lead and direct a performance of a band or orchestra; to guide or show the way; to lead; to direct or control the course of; to transmit heat, electricity, or sound. *n.* Behavior. **conductibility** *n.* **conduction** *n.*

con-duc-tiv-i-ty (kon˝duk tiv´i tē) *n.* The quality of conducting heat, sound or electricity.

con-duc-tor (kon duk´tėr) *n.* A person who conducts a musical ensemble; one who is in charge of a railroad or streetcar. *Phys.* Any substance that conducts light, electricity, heat, or sound.

con-duit (kon´dwit) *n.* A pipe used to pass electric wires or cable through; a channel or pipe that water passes through.

con-du-pli-cate (kon dō´pli kit) *adj.* Doubled or folded lengthwise.

cone (kōn) *n.* A solid body that is tapered evenly to a point from a base that is circular; a wafer that is cone-shaped and used for holding ice cream.

cone-nose (kōn´nōz˝) *n.* A large blood-sucking insect, a species of assassin bug infesting houses in the southern and western United States.

con-fab (kon´fab) *n.* Discussion.

con-fab-u-late (kon fab´ū lāt´) *v.* To chat or speak informally. **confabulation** *n.* **confabulator** *n.* **confabulatory** *adj.*

con-fec-tion-er-y (kon fek´sha ner´ē) *n.* Candy and sweets as a whole; a store that sells candy and sweets. **confection** *n.*

con-fec-tion-a-ry (kon fek´sha ner˝ē) *adj.* Of or pertaining to confections or their making; sweets.

con-fec-tion-er (kon fek´sha nėr) *n.* A person who manufactyres or sells candies and other sweets.

con-fed-er-a-cy (kon fed´ėr a sē) *n. pl.* **-ies** The union of eleven southern states that seceded from the United States during the Civil War of 1861- 1865 and established the Confederate State of America.

con-fed-er-ate (kon fed´ėr it) *n.* An ally or friend; a person who supports the Confederacy. **confederate** *v.*

con-fed-er-a-tion (kon fed˝e rā´shan) *n.* An act of confederating; the state of being confederated.

con-fer (kon fer´) *v.* To consult with another; to hold a conference; to give or grant. **conferment** *n.* **conferral** *n.* **conferrer** *n.* **conferrable** *adj.*

con-fer-ence (kon´fėr ens) *n.* A formal meeting for discussion; a league of churches, schools, or athletic teams.

con-fess (kon fes´) *v.* To disclose or admit to a crime, fault, sin, or guilt; to tell a priest or God of one's sins.

con-fes-sion (kon fesh´on) *n.* The act of confessing.

con-fes-sion-al (kon fesh´o nal) *n.* The small enclosure where a priest hears confessions.

con-fes-sor (kon fes´ẽr) *n*. A person who confesses; one who acknowledges a fault.

con-fet-ti (kon fet´ē) *n*. Small pieces of paper thrown during a celebration.

con-fide (kon fīd´) *v*. To entrust a secret to another. **confider** *n*. **confiding** *adj*. **confidingly** *adv*.

con-fi-dence (kon´fi dens) *n*. A feeling of self-assurance; a feeling of trust in a person; reliance; good faith. **confident** *adj*.

con-fi-den-tial (kon´fi den´shal) *adj*. Hold as a secret; having another's entrusted confidence on spoken or witten matters. **confidentiality** *n*. **confidentially** *adv*.

con-fid-ing (kon´fid ing) *adj*. Trusting; reposing confidence; trustful.

con-fig-u-ra-tion (kon fig´ū rā´shan) *n*. An arrangement of parts or things; the arrangement of elements. **configurationally** *adv*.

con-fig-ure (kon fig´ūr) *v*. To make or arrange for operation in a certain form or particular way.

con-fine (kon fīn´) *v*. To keep within a certain boundary or limits. **confines** *n*. **confinement** *n*. **confiner** *n*.

con-firm (kon fẽrm´) *v*. To establish or support the truth of something; to make stronger; to ratify and bind by a formal approal. **confirmable** *adj*. **confirmatory** *adj*.

con-fir-ma-tion (kon´fẽr mā´shan) *n*. The act of confirming to show proof; a religious rite that admits a person to full membership in a church.

con-fir-ma-to-ry (kon fẽr´ma tōr˝ē) *adj*. Giving additional strength; serving to confirm.

con-firm-ed (kon fẽrmd´) *adj*. Fixed.

con-fis-cate (kon´fi skāt´) *v*. To seize for public use; to officially seize. **confiscation** *n*. **confiscator** *n*.

con-fla-gra-tion (kon˝fla grā´shan) *n*. A large fire, or the burning of a large mass of combustibles.

con-flate (kon´flāt) *v*. To combine two different ideas into a whole. **conflation** *n*.

con-fla-tion (kon flā´shan) *n*. The result of merging various elements; blend.

con-flict (kon flikt´) *n*. A battle; clash; a disagreement of ideas, or interests, opposition. **conflict** *v*. **conflictive** *adj*.

conflict of interest *n*. The conflict when the private financial interests of a public officer stand to benefit by the influence from this position.

con-flu-ence (kon´flŏ ens) *n*. The flowing together of two streams or rivers; the point where the two join. **confluent** *n*. **confluently** *adv*.

con-flu-ent (kon´flŏ eny) *adj*. Flowing or coming together; run together.

con-flux (kon´fluks) *n*. A flowing together; a meeting or joining; a crowd.

con-fo-cal (kon fō´kal) *adj*. Of the same focus.

con-form (kon form´) *v*. To be similar in form or character; to adhere to prevailing customs or modes. **conformable** *adj*. **conformably** *adv*.

con-form-a-ble (kor´ma bl) *adj*. Corresponding in form, manners, or opinions.

con-for-ma-tion (kon´for mā´shan) *n*. The manner in which something is shaped, structured, or arranged.

con-form-i-ty (kon for´mi tē) *n*. Likeness; harmony; accordance.

con-found (kon found´) *v*. To amaze, confuse, or perplex; to confuse one thing for another.

con-found-ed (kon foun´ded) *adj*. Annoying bothersome.

con-fra-ter-ni-ty (kon˝fra tẽr´ni tē) *n*. A brotherhood society devoted to a purpose.

con-frere (kon´frâr) *n*. A fellow colleague; a fraternity or profession.

con-front (kon frunt´) *v*. To put or stand face to face with defiance; to face; to stand or be in front of, providing resistance, as an obstacle; to meet in hostility; to oppose. **confrontation** *n*. **confrontational** *adj*.

con-fuse (kon fūz´) *v*. To mislead or bewilder; to jumble or mix up. **confusedness** *n*. **confusingly** *adv*.

con-fu-sion (kon fū´zhan) *n*. The state of being confused.

con-fu-ta-tion (kon˝fū tā´shan) *n*. The disproving, or proving to be false or invalid.

con-fute (kon fūt´) v. To prove to be invalid or false. confutable adj. confutation n. confutative adj.

con-geal (kon jēl´) v. To jell; to solidify; to change from a liquid to a solid form.

con-ge-la-tion (kon″je lā´shan) n. That which is congealed or solidified or the state of being congealed.

con-ge-ner (kon ´je nèr) n. A member of the same genus as another plant or animal.

con-gen-ial (kon jēn´yal) adj. Having similar character habits, or tastes; sociable; friendly. congeniality n. congenially adv.

con-gen-i-tal (kon jen´i tal) adj. Existing from the time of birth, but not from heredity.

conger eel n. A large scaleless eel used for food along the coasts of Europe.

con-gest (kon jest´) v. To enlarge with an excessive accumulation of blood; to clog. congestion n. congestive adj.

con-glo-bate (kon glō´bāt) v. To form or gather into a ball or small spherical body.

con-glo-ba-tion (kon″glō bā´shan) n. The act of or gathering into a ball; a round body.

con-glom-er-ate (kon glom´ér it) n. A business consisting of many different companies; gravel that is embedded in cement material.

congo snake n. A snakelike amphibian, having small forelimbs, each with several toes, and attaining a length of three feet.

con-gou (kong´gō) n. A black tea from China.

con-grat-u-late (kon grach´u lāt´) v. To acknowledge an achievement with praise. congratulator n. congratulatory adj.

con-grat-u-la-tions (kon grach″ lā´shans) n. pl. The expression of or the act of congratulating.

con-grat-u-la-to-ry (kon grach´u la tōr″ē) adj. Expressing congratulations.

con-gre-gate (kong´gre gāt´) v. To assemble together in a crowd. congregator n.

con-gre-ga-tion (kong´gre gā´shan) n. A group of people meeting together for worship.

con-gre-ga-tion-al (kong″gre gā´shal) adj.

Of or pertaining to a congregation; recognizing the importance and governing power of the congregation.

Con-gress (kong´gris) n. The United States legislative body, consisting of the Senate and the House of Representatives. Congressional adj. Congressionally adv.

con-gress-man (kong´gris man) n. An elected member of the United States House of Representatives.

con-gress-wom-an (kong´gris wem´an) n. A woman elected as a member of the United States House of Representatives.

con-gru-ent (kong´grō ent) adj. Agreeing to conform; in mathematics, having exactly the same size and shape.

con-gru-ous (kong´grō us) adj. Being in agreement; appropriate or fitting.

con-ic or con-i-cal (kon´ik) adj. Related to and shaped like a cone.

co-nid-i-um (kō nid´ē um) n. A propagative body or cell, asexual in its origin and functions.

co-ni-fer (kōni fèr) n. Evergreen trees and shrubs, that include the pine, fir, spruce, and other conebearing trees.

co-ni-ine (kō´nē ēn″) n. A highly poisonous alkaloid found in hemlock.

conj abbr. Conjunction.

con-jec-ture (kon jek´chèr) n. A guess or conclusion based on incomplete evidence. conjecturable, conjectural adj. conjecture v.

con-join (kon join´) v. To unite; join together.

con-ju-gal (kon´ju gal) adj. Pertaining to the relationship or marriage of husband and wife.

con-ju-gate (kon´ju git) adj. To change the form of a verb; to join in pairs. conjugately adv. conjugative adj. conjugator n.

con-junct (kon jungkt´) adj. Combined; joined together.

con-junc-tion (kon jungk´shan) n. The act of joining; the state of being joined. Gram. A word used to join or connect other words, phrases, sentences, or clauses.

con-junc-ti-va (kon´jungk tī´va) *n. pl.* **-vas, -vae** The membrane lining of the eyelids.

con-junc-tive (kon jungk´tiv) *adj.* Connective; joining. *Gram.* Serving as a conjunction.

con-junc-ti-vi-tis (kon jungk´ti vī´tis) *n.,* Pathol. Inflammation of the membrane that lines the eyelids.

con-jur-a-tion (kon˝ju rā´shan) *n.* The act of binding by an oath; a solemn appeal.

con-jure (kon´jėr) *v.* To bring into the mind; to appeal or call on solemnly; to practice magic.

con man *n., Slang.* A confidence man; a swin-dler.

con-nate (kon´āt) *adj.* Existing from birth; born or originating together.

con-nect (ko nekt´) *v.* To join; to unite; to associate, as to relate. **connectedly** *adv.* **connector** *n.* **connecter** *n.*

con-nect-ed (ko nek´tid) *adj.* Linked, bound or fastened together; joined in order or sequence.

Con-nect-i-cut *n.* A state located in the north eastern part of the United States; statehood January 9, 1788; state capital Hartford.

connecting rod *n.* A rod or bar connecting movable parts.

con-nec-tion (ko nek´shan) *n.* An association of one person or thing to another; a union, link, or bond; an influential group of friends or associates.

con-nec-tive (ko nek´tiv) *adj.* Capable of connecting; tending to connect. *n.* something that connects as a word.

connective tissue *n.* Tissue which connects, supports, or surrounds other tissues or organs.

con-nip-tion (ko nip´shan) *n.* A fit of alarm or hysterical excitement.

con-nive (kon nīv´) *v.* To ignore a known wrong, therefore implying sanction; to conspire; to cooperate in secret. **connivance** *n.*

con-nois-seur (kon´o ser´) *n.* A person whose expertise in an area of art or taste

allows him to be a judge; an expert. **connoisseurship** *n.*

con-no-ta-tion (kon´o tā´shan) *n.* The associative meaning of a word in addition to the literal meaning. **connotative** *adj.*

con-note (ko nōt´) *v.* To imply along with the literal meaning.

con-nu-bi-al (ko nō´bē al) *adj.* Having to do with marriage or the state of marriage. **connubiality** *n.* **connubially** *adv.*

con-quer (kong´kėr) *v.* To subdue; to win; to overcome by physical force.

con-quest (kon´kwest) *n.* The process or act of conquering; acquisition by force.

con-qui-an *n.* A card game for two players with 40 cards; the game from which all rummy games originate.

con-quis-ta-dor (kon kwis´ta dor´) *n. pl.* **-dors** A Spanish conqueror of the sixteenth century.

con-san-guin-e-ous (kon´sang gwin´ē us) *adj.* Having the same blood; descended from the same ancestor. **consanguineously** *adv.*

con-science (kon´shens) *n.* The ability to recognize right and wrong regarding one's own behavior.

conscience clause *n.* A clause inserted in a law, that relieves persons whose religious beliefs forbid their compliance.

conscience money *n.* Money paid to relieve the conscience, usually paid anonymously, to cover obligations previously evaded.

con-sci-en-tious (kon´shē en´shus) *adj.* Honest; scrupulous; careful.

con-scious (kon´shus) *adj.* Aware of one's own existence and environment; aware of facts or objects.

con-script (kon´skript) *n.* One who is drafted or forced to enroll for a service or a job.

con-se-crate (kon´se krāt´) *v.* To declare something to be holy; to dedicate to sacred uses.

con-se-cra-tion (kon˝se krā´shan) *n.* The act or state of consecrating.

con-se-cu-tion (kon˝se kū´shan) *n.* Sequence; succession; logical sequence.

con-sec-u-tive (kon sek´ū tiv) *adj.* Following in uninterrupted succession. **consecutively** *adv.* **consecutiveness** *n.*

con-sen-sus (kon sen´sus) *n.* A general agreement; a collective opinion.

con-sent (kon sent´) *v.* To agree; an acceptance. **consenter** *n.*

con-se-quence (kon´se kwens´) *n.* The natural result from a preceding condition or action; the effect.

con-se-quent (kon´se kwent´) *adj.* Following as a natural result or effect logical conclusion. **consequently** *adv.*

con-se-quen-tial (kon´se kwen´shal) *adj.* Having or showing self-importance. **consequentially** *adv.*

con-serv-a-tive (kon sėr´va tiv) *adj.* Opposed to change; desiring the preservation of the existing order of things; moderate; cautious; wanting to conserve. **conservatively** *adv.* **conservativeness** *n.*

con-ser-va-tor (kon´sėr vā tor) *n.* A person who preserves; a person or institution responsible for protecting another's interests.

con-ser-va-to-ry (kon sėr´va tōr´ē) *n.* *pl.* **-ries** A school of dramatic art or music; a greenhouse.

con-serve (kon sėrv´) *v.* To save something from decay, loss, or depletion; to maintain; to preserve fruits with sugar. *n.* A mixture of several fruits cooked together with sugar and sometimes raisins or nuts. **conservable** *adj.* **conserver** *n.*

con-sider (kon sid´ėr) *v.* To seriously think about; to examine mentally; to believe or hold as an opinion; to deliberate.

con-sid-er-a-ble (kon sid´ėr a bl) *adj.* Large in amount or extent; important; worthy of consideration. **considerably** *adv.*

con-sid-er-a-tion (kon sid´e rā´shan) *n.* The taking into account of circumstance before forming an opinion; care and thought; a kind or thoughtful treatment or feeling. **considering** *prep.*

con-sign (kon sīn´) *v.* To commit to the care of another; to deliver or forward, as merchandise; to put aside, as for specific use. **consignee** *n.* **consignable** *adj.* **consignor** *n.* **consignment** *n.*

con-sign-ee (kon´sī nē´) *n.* The person to whom goods are consigned.

con-sign-ment *n.* The act of consigning; goods sent or delivered to an agent for sale.

con-sist (kon sist´) *v.* To be made up of.

con-sis-ten-cy (kon sis´ten sē) *n.* *pl.* **-cies** Agreement or compatibility among ideas, events, or successive acts; the degree of texture, viscosity, or density; coherence. **consistent** *adj.*

con-sis-to-ry (kon sis´to rē) *n.* *pl.* **-ries** In the Roman Catholic Church, the assembly of all cardinals with the pope presiding over them.

con-so-ci-ate (kon sō´shē āt´) *v.* To bring together or into association.

con-so-ci-a-tion (kon sō´sē ā´shan) *n.* Association in; fellowship; an association or union of churches.

con-so-la-tion (kon´so lā´shan) *n.* Comfort; the act of consoling; a person who offers consolation.

con-sole (kon sōl´) *v.* To give comfort to someone. **consolable** *adj.* **consolation** *n.* **consolingly** *adv.*

console table *n.* A table fixed to a wall by consoles or brackets wall.

con-sol-i-date (kon sol´i dāt´) *v.* To combine in one or to form a union of; to form a compact mass. **consolidation** *n.* **consolidator** *n.*

consolidated school *n.* A public school, formed by combining schools from several districts.

con-som-mé (kon´so mā´) *n.* A strong, clear soup made from the stock of meat.

con-so-nant (kon´so nant) *n.* A sound produced by complete or partial blockage of the air from the mouth, as the sound of b, f, k, s, t; the letter of the alphabet that represents such a sound. *adj.* In agreement. **consonantal** *adj.* **consonantly** *adv.*

con-sort (kon´sort) *n.* A spouse; companion or partner. *v.* To unite or keep in company.

con-sor-ti-um (kon sor´shē *u*m) *n. pl.* -tia An association with banks or corporations that require vast resources.

con-spe-cif-ic (kon˝spi sif´ik) *adj.* Of the same species.

con-spec-tus (kon spek´tus) *n.* A general summary; a digest; a resume.

con-spic-u-ous (kon spik´ū us) *adj.* Noticeable. conspicuously *adv.*

con-spir-a-cy (kon spir´*a* sē) *n. pl.* -ies A plan or act of two or more persons to do an evil act.

con-spir-a-tor-ial (kon spir˝*a* tōr´ē *a*l) *adj.* Relating to a conspiracy or conspirators.

con-spire (kon spīr´) *v.* To plan a wrongful act in secret; to work or act together, to plot against others. conspirator *n.*

con-sta-ble (kon´st*a* bl) *n.* A peace officer.

con-stab-u-lar-y (kon stab´ū ler˝ē) *adj.* Relating to the jurisdiction of a constable.

con-stant (kon´st*a*nt) *adj.* Faithful; unchanging; steady in action, purpose, and affection. *Math.* A quantity that remains the same throughout a given problem. constancy, constantly *adv.*

con-ster-na-tion (kon´stėr nā´sh*a*n) *n.* Sudden confusion or amazement.

con-sti-pa-tion (kon´st*i* pā´sh*a*n) *n.* A condition of the bowels characterized by difficult or infrequent evacuation.

con-stit-u-en-cy (kon stich´ŏ *e*n sē) *n. pl.* -cies A group of voters that is represented by an elected legislator.

con-stit-u-ent (kon stich´ŏ *e*nt) *adj.* Having the power to elect a representative. *n.* A necessary element or part.

con-sti-tu-tion (kon´sti tŏ´sh*a*n) *n.* The fundamental laws that govern a nation; structure or composition. constitutional *adj.* constitutionality *n.* constitutionally *adv.*

con-sti-tu-tion-al (kon˝sti tŏ´sh*a* n*a*l) *adj.* Pertaining or relating to the composition of a thing; essential. *n.* Exerise taken to benefit one's health.

con-sti-tu-tion-al-ism (kon˝sti tŏ´sh*a* na liz˝*u*m) *n.* The adherence, theory or principle of constitutional rule or authority.

con-sti-tu-tive (kon´sti tŏ˝tiv) *adj.* Having the power to form, compose, enact, or establish.

con-strain (kon strān´) *v.* To restrain by physical or moral means. constrained *adj.*

con-straint (kon strānt´) *n.* The threat or use of force; confinement; restriction.

con-strict (kon strikt´) *v.* To squeeze, compress, or contract. constriction *n.* constrictive *adj.* constrictively *adv.*

con-stric-tor (kon strik´tėr) *n.* One that constricts; a snake that crushes its prey in its coils.

con-struct (kon strukt´) *v.* To create, make, or build. constructor *n.* constructer *n.*

con-struc-tion (kon struk´sh*a*n) *n.* The act of constructing or building something. *Gram.* The arrangement of words in a meaningful clause or sentence. constructional *adj.*

con-struc-tive (kon struk´tiv) *adj.* Useful; helpful; building, advancing, or improving; resulting in a positive conclusion. constructively *adv.* constructiveness *n.*

con-strue (kon strö´) *v.* To interpret; to translate; to analyze grammatical structure.

con-sul (kon´s*u*l) *n.* An official that resides in a foreign country and represents his or her government's commercial interests and citizens. consular *adj.*

con-sul-ate (kon´s*u* lit) *n.* The official premises occupied by a consul.

con-sult (kon sult´) *v.* To seek advice or information from; to compare views. consultant *n.* consultation *n.*

con-sult-ant (kon sul´t*a*nt) *n.* A person who consults; one who offers professional advice or services for a fee.

con-sume (kon söm´) *v.* To ingest; to eat or drink; to destroy completely; to absorb; to engross. consumable *n.*

con-sum-er (kon sö´mėr) *n.* A person who buys services or goods.

con-sum-mate (kon´s*u* māt´) *v.* To conclude; to make a marriage complete by the initial act of sexual intercourse.

con-sump-tion (kon sump´sh*a*n) *n.* Fulfillment; the act of consuming; the quantity consumed; tuberculosis.

con-sump-tive (ko**n sump´tiv)** *adj.* Tending to destroy or waste away; affected with or pertaining to pulmonary tuberculosis. **consumptively** *adv.* **consumptiveness** *n.*

con-tact (kon´takt) *n.* The place, spot, or junction where two or more surfaces or objects touch; the connection between two electric conductors. **contacts** Contact lens; thin lens of plastic or glass with an optical prescription, worn directly on the cornea of the eye.

contact lens *n.* A prescription lens for correcting vision, which is applied directly to the cornea of the eye.

con-ta-gion (k on tā´jo**n)** *n.* The transmitting of a disease by contact. **contagious** *adj.* **contagiously** *adv.* **contagiousness** *n.*

con-ta-gi-um *n.* A virus by which a contagious disease is communicated.

con-tain (kon tān´) *v.* To include or enclose; to restrain or hold back. **containable** *adj.* **containment** *n.*

con-tain-er (kon tā´nė**r)** *v.* Something that holds or carries, as a box or can.

con-tain-er-i-za-tion (kon tā´nė**r i zā´sh**o**n)** *n.*The procedure of shipping a large amount of goods in one container.

container ship *n.* A ship that is designed to carry containerized cargo.

con-tam-i-nate (kon tam´*i* **nāt´)** *v.* To pollute or make inferior by adding undesireable elements; to taint; to infect; to make dirty or to soil. **contaminant** *n.* **contamination** *n.*

con-tam-i-na-tion (kon tam˝*i* **nā´sh**o**n)** *n.* The act or state of contaminating, or of being contaminated.

con-temn (kon tem´) *v.* To scorn or despise.

con-tem-plate (kon´tem plāt´) *v.* To look over; to ponder; to consider thoughtfully. **contemplative, contemplation** *n.*

con-tem-pla-tion(kon˝templā´sho**n)** *n.* The act of serious contemplating; thoughtful; attentive consideration.

con-tem-po-ra-ne-ous (kon tem´po **rā´nē us)** *adj.* Occurring or living at the same time; contemporary. **contemporaneously** *adv.* **contemporaneousness** *n.*

con-tempt (kon tempt´) *n.* The act of viewing something as mean, vile, or worthless scorn; legally, the willful disrespect or disregard of authority. **contemptible** *adj.* **contemptibleness** *n.* **contemptibly** *adv.*

con-tempt-i-ble (kon temp´ti bl) *adj.* Worthy of contempt; deserving scorn.

con-temp-tu-ous (kon temp´chö us) *adj.* Feeling or showing contempt. **contemptuously** *adv.*

con-tend (kon tend´) *v.* To dispute; to fight; to debate; to argue. **contender** *n.*

con-tent(kon´tent) *n.* Something contained within; the subject matter of a book or document; the proportion of a specified part. *adj.* Satisfied. **contentment** *n.* **contentedly** *adv.* **contented** *adj.*

con-tent-ed (kon ten´tid) *adj.* Satisfied with one's circumstances, possessions, or status.

con-ten-tion (kon ten´sha**n)** *n.* Competition; rivalry; controversy; argument. **contentious** *adj.* **contentiously** *adv.*

con-tent-ment (kon tent´ment) *n.* Feeling of or being contented; a satisfaction of mind.

con-ter-mi-nous (kon tėr´m*i* **nus)** *adj.* Having the same or common boundaries or limits.

con-test (kon´test) *n.* A competition; strife; conflict. *v.* To challenge. **contestable** *adj.* **contestant** *n.* **contester** *n.*

con-text (kon´tekst) *n.* A sentence, phrase, or passage so closely connected to a word or words that it affects their meaning; the environment in which an event occurs.

con-tex-ture (kon teks´chėr) *n.* The act of interweaving several parts into a whole.

con-tig-u-ous (k on tig´ū us) *adj.* Situated next to or near in time; meeting or joining at the surface or border.

con-ti-nent (kon´t*i* **nent)** *n.* One of the seven large masses of the earth; Asia, Africa, Australia, Europe, North America, South America and Antarctica.

con-ti-nen-tal (kon´t*i* **nen´tal)** *adj.* Of or

characteristic of a continent.

continental divide *n.* A divide separating rivers or streams that flow to opposite sides of a continent.

con-tin-gent (k*o***n tin´jent)** *adj.* Likely to happen; happening by chance.

con-tin-u-al (k*o***n tin´u** *a***l)** *adj.* Continuing indefinitely; proceeding without interruption; not intermittent.

con-tin-u-a-tion (k*o***n tin˝ū ā´sh***a***n)** *n.* The act of continuing or prolonging; extension or carrying on after an interruption.

con-tin-ue (k*o***n tin´ū)** *v.* To maintain without interruption a course or condition; to resume; to postpone or adjourn a judicial proceeding. **continuance** *n.* **continuer** *n.*

continued fraction *n.* A fraction with a denominator which contains a fraction and a numerator which contains a fraction.

con-tin-u-ing (k*o***n tin´ū ing)** *adj.* Enduring or lasting; continuous.

con-ti-nu-i-ty (k*o***n´ti n***o***˝´i tē)** *n. pl.* **-ties** The quality of being continuous.

con-tin-u-ous (k*o***n tin´ū us)** *adj.* Uninterrupted. **continuously** *adv.*

con-tort (k*o***n tort´)** *v.* To severely twist out of shape.

con-tor-ted (k*o***n tor´tid)** *adj.* Twisted to an extreme degree or violent manner.

con-tor-tion-ist (k*o***n tor´sh***a*** nist)** *n.* An acrobat who exhibits unnatural body positions.

con-tour (k*o***n´tur)** *n.* The outline of a body, figure, or mass.

contour feather *n.* One of the medium size feathers which form the surface plumage of a bird and determines the external contour of the body.

contour line *n.* A line on a map carried along the surface connecting points that have the same elevation.

contour map *n.* A topographic map where with contour lines are shown by the relative spacing of lines known as contour intervals.

con-tra-band (k*o***n´tr***a*** band´)** *n.* Illegal or prohibited traffic; smuggled goods.

con-tra-bass (k*o***n´tr***a*** bās´)** *n.* A double bass, also called a contrabassoon.

con-tra-cep-tion (k*o***n´tr***a*** sep´sh***a***n)** *n.* The voluntary prevention of impregnation. **contraceptive** *n.*

con-tract (k*o***n´trakt)** *n.* A formal agreement between two or more parties to perform the duties as stated; an oral, written, or implied agreement between two or more persons.

con-trac-tion (k*o***n trak´sh***a***n)** *n.* The act of contracting; a shortening of a word by omitting a letter or letters and replacing them with an apostrophe (’).

con-trac-tile (k*o***n trak´tīl)** *adj.* Having the power to contract.

con-trac-tor (k*o***n´trak tėr)** *n.* A person who contracts to perform work at a certain price or rate.

con-trac-ture (k*o***n trak´chėr)** *n.* A permanent shortening of a muscle or tendon producing deformity.

con-tra-dict (k*o***n´tr***a*** dikt´)** *v.* To express the opposite side or idea; to be inconsistent. **contradictable** *adj.* **contradictory** *adj.* **contradicter** *n.*

con-tra-dic-tion (k*o***n˝tr***a*** dik´sh***a***n)** *n.* A statement that implies by the truth and falseness about something; direct opposition.

con-tra-dic-to-ry (k*o***n˝tr***a*** dik´t***o*** rē)** *adj.* Opposite; being inconsistent with one another; opposite.

con-trail (k*o***n´trāl)** *n.* The visible water vapor left in the sky by a plane.

con-tral-to (k*o***n tral´tō)** *n. pl.* **-tos** The lowest female singing voice.

con-trap-tion (k*o***n trap´sh***a***n)** *n.* A gadget.

con-tra-puntal (k*o***n´tr***a*** pun´tal)** *adj.* Relating to counterpoint.

con-tra-ri-wise (k*o***n´trer ē wīz˝)** *adv.* In a contrary manner; vice versa; on the contrary.

con-trar-y (k*o***n´trer ē)** *adj.* Unfavorable; incompatible with another. **contrarily** *adv.* **contrariness** *n.*

con-trast (k*o***n trast´)** *v.* To note the differences between two or more people, things, etc. **contrastable** *adj.*

con-tra-vene (k*o***n´tr***a*** vēn´)** *v.* To be contrary; to violate; to oppose; to go against.

con-tre-danse (kon´tri dans˝) *n.* A graceful folk dance, in which the partners stand opposite one another in two lines.

con-trib-ute (kon trib´ūt) *v.* To give something to someone; to submit for publication. **contribution** *n.* **contributor** *n.* **contributive** *adj.* **contributory** *adj.* **contributively** *adv.*

con-tri-bu-tion (kon˝tri bū´shan) *n.* The act of contributing or something contributed.

con-trib-u-to-ry (kon trib´ū tōr˝ē) *adj.* Contributing to a common fund; furnishing something toward a result.

con-trite (kon trīt´) *adj.* Grieving for sin or shortcoming. **contritely** *adv.*

con-triv-ance (kon trī´vans) *n.* The act of or thing contriving, devising, or planning.

con-trol (kon trōl´) *v.* To have the authority or ability to regulate, direct, or dominate a situation. **controllable** *adj.*

con-trol-ler (kon trō lėr) *n.* The chief accounting officer of a business, also called the comptroller.

controlling interest *n.* The majority stock ownership in a corporation, which exerts control over policy.

control tower *n.* A lookout tower at an airfield or airport having the necessary equipment and personnel to direct air and ground traffic in takeoffs and landings.

con-tro-ver-sy (kon´tro vėr´sē) *n.* A dispute; a debate; a quarrel **controversial** *adj.*

con-tro-vert (kon´tro vert´) *v.* To contradict.

con-tu-ma-cy (kon´tu ma sē) *n.* Stubborn rebelliousness to authority.

con-tu-me-li-ous (kon˝tu mē´lē us) *adj.* Indicating or expressing humiliation.

con-tu-me-ly (kon´tu me lē) *n.* *pl* -lies Rude treatment. **contumelious** *adj.*

con-tuse (kon tōz´) *v.* To injure the body without breaking the flesh.

con-tu-sion (kon tō´zhen) *n.* A severe bruise or injury to the body; without breaking of the skin.

co-nun-drum (ko nun´drum) *n.* A riddle with an answer that involves a pun; a question or problem with only a surmise for an answer.

con-va-lesce (kon´va les´) *v.* To grow strong after a long illness, recovery time. **convalescence** *n.* **convalescent** *adj.*

con-va-les-cence (kon˝va les´ens) *n.* Gradual recovery of health and strength after a sickness.

con-vect (kon vekt´) *v.* To move or transfer heat by convection.

con-vec-tion (kon vek´shan) *n.* The transfer of heat by the movement of air, gas, or heated liquid between areas of unequal density, upward flow of warm air. **convectional** *adj.*

con-vec-tor (kon vek´tėr) *n.* A heating unit for circulating heat by convection.

con-vene (kon vēn´) *v.* To meet or assemble formally; meeting. **convenable** *adj.*

con-ven-ience (kon vēn´yans) *n.* The quality of being convenient or suitable.

con-ve-nient (kon vē´nyant) *adj.* Suitable and agreeable to the needs or purpose.

con-vent (con´vent) *n.* A local house or community of a religious order, a home for nuns.

con-ven-ti-cle (kon ven´ti kl) *n.* A secret meeting for religious study or worship.

con-ven-tion (kon ven´shan) *n.* A formal meeting; a regulatory meeting between people, states, or nations on matters that affect all of them.

con-ven-tion-al (kon ven´sha nal) *adj.* Commonplace, ordinary.

con-ven-tu-al (kon ven´chö al) *n.* A member of a conventual community or monastery.

con-verge (kon vėrj´) *v.* To come to a common point. **covergence** *n.* **covergent** *adj.*

con-vers-a-ble (kon vėr´sa bl) *adj.* Pleasant and easy to talk to.

con-ver-sa-tion (kon´vėr sā´shan) *n.* An informal talk, verbal discussion with someone or a group of people, oral communication. **conversational** *adj.* **conversationally** *adv.*

converse (kon vėrs´) *v.* To involve oneself

in conversation with another.

con-ver-sion (kon vėr´zhan) *n*. The act or state of changing to adopt new opinions or beliefs; a formal acceptance of a different religion. **conversional** *adj*.

con-vert-er (kon vėr´tėr) *n*. One who converts; a machine or device that accepts information in one form and converts to another.

con-vert-i-ble (kon vėr´ti bl) *adj*. A car with a top that folds back or can be removed completely.

convertible life insurance *n*. A limited type of life insurance, such as group or term that allows the policy holder to change the policy into an expanded or more permanent form.

convertible stock *n*. Preferred stock which may upon exercise of the owner's option, be exchanged for common stock

con-vex (kon´veks) *adj*. Curved outward like the outer surface of a ball.

con-vexo–con-cave (kon vekso kon kāv´) *adj*. Convex on one side greater than on the other side, as an eyeglass lens.

con-vey (kon vā´) *v*. To transport; to pass information on to someone else; to conduct. **conveyable** *adj*.

con-vey-ance (kon vā´ans) *n*. The action of conveying; the legal transfer of property or the document effecting it.

con-vict (kon vikt´) *v*. To prove someone guilty. *n*. A prisoner.

con-vic-tion (kon vik´shan) *n*. The act of being convicted.

con-vince (kon vins´) *v*. To cause to believe without doubt. **convincingly** *adv*.

con-viv-i-al (kon viv´ē al) *adj*. Relating to entertainment and good company.

con-vo-ca-tion (kon´vo kā´shan) *n*. A formal or ceremonial assembly or meeting.

con-voke (kon vōk´) *v*. To call together for a formal meeting.

con-vo-lute (kon´vo lŏt˝) *adj*. Twisted; rolled up together.

con-vo-lu-tion (kon˝vo lŏ´shan) *n*. A rolling, folding or coiling together; a rolled up or coiled condition.

con-voy (kon´voi) *n*. A group of cars, trucks,

etc., traveling together. *v*. To escort or guide.

con-vulse (kon vuls´) *v*. To move or shake violently. **convulsive** *adj*.

con-vul-sion (kon vul´shan) *n*. A violent involuntary muscular contraction.

cook (kuk) *v*. To apply heat to food before eating; to prepare food for a meal. *n*. A person who prepares food.

cook-book (kuk´buk´) *n*. A book containing directions for preparing and cooking food.

cook-ie (kuk´ē) *n*. *pl*. *-ies* A sweet, flat cake.

cool (kŏl) *adj*. Without warmth; indifferent or unenthusiastic. *Slang* First-rate; composure.

cool-ant (kŏ´lant) *n*. The cooling agent that circulates through a machine.

cool-head-ed (kŏl´hed´id) *adj*. Calm; not easily excited.

Coolidge, John Calvin *n*. The 30th president of the United States, from 1923-1929.

coon (kŏn) *n*., *Informal* A raccoon.

coop (kŏp) *n*. A cage or enclosed area to contain animals, as chickens.

co–op (kō´op) *n*. A cooperative.

co-op-er-ate (kō op´e rāt´) *v*. To work together toward a common cause. **cooperation** *n*. **cooperator** *n*.

co-op-er-ation *n*. The action of cooperating; the combination of persons for purposes of production, or distribution for their joint benefit and success; a common effort.

co-op-er-a-tive (kō op´e rā´tiv) *adj*. Willing to cooperate with others. **cooperatively** *adv*. **cooperativeness** *n*.

co–opt (kō opt´) *v*. To elect or choose as a new member.

co-or-di-nate (kō or´di nāt´) *v*. To be equal in rank, importance, or degree; to plan a wardrobe or outfit so that it goes well together. *n*. Any of a set of numbers which establishes position on a graph, map, chart, etc. **coordinately** *adv*. **coordinator** *n*.

co-or-di-na-tion (kō or'di nā´shan) *n.* The state of being coordinated.

coot (kŏt) *n.* A short-winged bird. *Slang* A silly old man.

coot-ie (kŏ´tē) *n.*, *Slang* A body louse.

cop (kop) *n.*, *Informal* A police officer.

co-pal (kō´pal) *n.* A hard, fossil resin from various tropical trees, used in making varnishes.

co-par-ce-nar-y (kō pär´se nėr˝ē) *n.* Joint ownership; joint heirship.

co-part-ner (kō pärt´nėr) *n.* A partner with others; a sharer.

cope (kōp) *v.* To strive; to struggle or contend with something. *n.* The long cape worn by a priest on special ceremonial occasions.

cop-ier (kop´ē ėr) *n.* A machine that makes copies of original material.

co-pi-lot (kō´pī´ot) *n.* The assistant pilot on an aircraft.

coping saw *n.* A saw having a very narrow blade stretched in a U-shape frame, and used to cut curves and fancy patterns.

co-pi-ous *adj.* Yielding something in large quantity; abundant. **copiously** *adv.*

cop—out *n.*, *Slang* A way to avoid responsibility; a person who cops out.

cop-per (kop´ėr) *n.* A metallic element that is a good conductor of electricity and heat, reddish-brown in color.

cop-per-head (kop´ėr hed´) *n.* A venomous snake found in the eastern United States, having brownish-red markings.

cop-per-plate (kop´ėr plāt) *n.* A copper plate on which something is engraved.

cop-per-smith (kop´ėr smith˝) *n.* A person who works in copper.

cop-ra (kop´ra) *n.* Dried coconut meat that yields coconut oil.

copse (kops) *n.* A thicket made up of trees or small bushes.

cop-ter (kop´tėr) *n.*, *Slang* A helicopter.

cop-u-la (kop´ū la) *n.*, *Gram.* A word or words which connect a subject and predicate.

cop-u-late (kop´ū lāt´) *v.* To have sexual intercourse. **copulation** *n.*

copy (kop´ē) *v. pl. -ies* To reproduce an original. *n.* A single printed text.

cop-y-boy (kop´ē boi˝) *n.* A person, usually employed in a newspaper office, who carries copy and runs errands.

copy edit *v.* To edit and correct a written copy for publication. **copy editor** *n.*

copy-right (kop´ē rīt) *n.* The statutory right to sell, publish, or distribute a literary or artistic work.

copy writer *n.* A person who writes copy for advertisements.

co-quette (kō ket´) *n.* A woman who flirts. **coquettish** *adj.*

coquilla nut *n.* The nut or fruit of a South American palm.

co-qui-na (kō kē´na) *n.* A small clam used for making broth or chowder.

cor-a-cle (kor´a kl) *n.* A small boat made by covering a wicker frame with hide or leather.

cor-a-coid (kor´a koid˝) *adj.* Relating or referring to a bony process or cartilage in various vertebrates, as birds and reptiles.

cor-al (kor´al) *n.* The stony skeleton of a small sea creature, often used for jewelry.

coral bells *n.* The alumroot plant cultivated in many varieties for its tiny coral flowers.

Coral Sea *n.* An arm of the southwest Pacific, located southeast of New Guinea and northeast of Australia.

coral reef *n.* A marine mound formed chiefly of broken pieces and grains of coral that have become a hard mass.

coral snake *n.* A venomous snake of tropical America and the southern United States, brightly colored with red, black, and yellow rings.

cor-beil (kor´bel) *n.* A sculptured basket of flowers and fruits.

cor-bi-na *n.* A spotted whiting fish of the California coast.

cord (cord) *n.* A string or twine; an insulated wire used to supply electricity to another source; a measurement for firewood that equals 128 cubic feet; a raised rib of fabric, as corduroy. **corder** *n.*

cord-age (kor´dij) *n.* Cords or ropes used

on the rigging of ship.

cor-dial (kor´jəl) *adj.* Warm-hearted and sincere. *n.* A liqueur. **cordiality** *n.* **cordially** *adv.*

cor-di-er-ite (kor´dē e rīt´) *n.* A silicate of aluminum, iron, and magnesium in shades of blue, having a vitreous luster.

cor-di-form (kor´di form´) *adj.* Heart-shaped.

cord-ing (kor´ding) *n.* A heavy cord used for ornamental purposes.

cord-ite (kor´dīt) *n.* A smokeless gunpowder.

cor-don (kor´don) *n.* A circle of men or ships positioned to guard or enclose an area; an ornamental ribbon or braid worn as an insignia of honor.

cor-du-roy (kor´du roi´) *n.* A durable cotton fabric which has a ribbed pile.

core (kōr) *n.* The innermost or central part of something; the inedible center of a fruit that contains the seeds. *v.* To remove the core from a piece of fruit.

co-re-op-sis (kōr´ē op´sis) *n.* A familiar garden herb grown for its showy flowers.

co-re-spon-dent (kō´ri spon´dent) *n.* A person charged with having committed adultery with the defendant in a divorce case.

co-ri-a-ceous (kōr´ē ā´shus) *adj.* Consisting of or resembling leather.

co-ri-an-der (kōr´ē an´dėr) *n.* A herb plant of the carrot family.

co-ri-um (kōr´ē um) *n.* The vascular layer of the skin beneath the epidermis.

cork (kork) *n.* The elastic bark of the oak tree used for bottle stoppers and craft projects.

cork-age (kor´kij) *n.* The fee that must be paid when one consumes a bottle of liquor not purchased on the premises.

cork-screw (kork´skrö´) *n.* A pointed metal spiral attached to a handle used for removing corks from bottles.

cork-wood (kork´wüd) *n.* The light and porous wood of certain trees and shrubs of the southeastern United States.

cor-mo-rant (kor´mėr ant) *n.* Any bird of the voracious waterbirds having a long neck, webbed feet, and a pouch under the mouth for holding and catching fish.

corn (korn) *n.* An American-cultivated cereal plant bearing seeds on a large ear or cob; the seed of this plant; a horny thickening of the skin, usually on the toe.

cor-na-ceous (kor nā´shus) *adj.* A family of plants, mostly trees and shrubs that include the dogwood and the tupelo.

Corn Belt *n.* The major corn growing states of the United States; Illinois, Indiana, Iowa, Kansas, Missouri, Nebraska, and Ohio.

corn borer *n.* Moths of European origin, that bore in corn.

corn bread *n.* A bread made from crushed cornmeal, eggs, flour, and milk.

corn cob (korn´kob´) *n.* The woody core around which the corn kernels grow.

corn cockle *n.* A common weed that grows among crops and along the side of the road.

corn-crib (korn´krib´) *n.* The building used for storing and drying corn.

cor-ne-a (kor´nē a) *n.* The transparent membrane of the eyeball. **corneal** *adj.*

cor-ner (kor´nėr) *n.* The point formed when two surfaces or lines meet and form an angle; the location where two streets meet.

corner back *n.* In football, the defensive halfback who defends the flank and covers the pass receiver.

corner-stone (kor´nėr stōn´) *n.* A stone that forms part of the corner of a building, usually laid in place with a special ceremony.

cor-net (kor net´) *n.* A three valved, brass musical instrument. **cornetist** *n.*

cor-nice (kor´nis) *n.* The horizontal projecting molding which finishes a wall or building.

cor-niche (kor´nish) *n.* A road built along the edge of a cliff.

corn meal *n.* Meal made from corn.

corn-row (korn rō) *v.* To braid the hair in rows very close to the head.

corn-starch (korn´stärch´) *n.* A starch

made from corn and used to thicken food while cooking.

corn syrup *n.* A sweet syrup made from cornstarch, containing maltose, dextrins, and dextrose.

cor-nu (kor′nū) *n.* A horn-shaped structure.

cor-nu-co-pi-a (kor′nu kō′pē a) *n.* A curved goat's horn overflowing with flowers, fruit, and corn to signify prosperity.

cor-nute (kor nŏt′) *adj.* Having horns; horn-shaped.

corn whiskey *n.* A whiskey distilled, often illegally, from a mash of corn grain.

corn-y (kor′nē) *adj., Slang* Trite or mawkishly old-fashioned.

cor-ol-lary (kor′oler″ē) *n. pl.* **-ies** Something that naturally or incidentally follows or accompanies.

cor-o-nar-y (kor′o ner′ē) *adj.* Of or relating to the two arteries that supply blood to the heart muscles. **coronary** *n.*

coronary thrombosis *n.* A blocking of the coronary artery of the heart.

cor-o-ner *n.* A public officer, of a county or municipality, whose chief function is to investigate, any death not clearly due to natural causes.

cor-o-net (kor′ o nit) *n.* A small, lessor, or inferior crown.

co-ro-no-graph (ko rō′no graf′) *n.* A telescope used for observing and photographing the corona of the sun.

cor-po-ral (kor′pēr al) *n.* The lowest noncommissioned officer. *adj.* Relating to or affecting the body.

cor-po-rate (kor′pēr it) *adj.* Combined into one joint body; relating to a corporation.

cor-po-ra-tion (kor′po rā′shan) *n.* A group of merchants united in a trade guild; any group or persons that act as one.

cor-po-re-al (kor pōr′ē al) *adj.* Of a physical nature.

corps (kōrps) *n. pl.* **corps** A branch of the armed forces; the body of persons under common direction.

corpse (korps) *n.* A dead body.

cor-pu-lent (kor′pū lent) *adj.* Having a large or bulky body.

corpus callosum *n.* The large band of nervous tissue uniting the two cerebral hemispheres in the brain of man and other mammals.

cor-pus-cle (kor′pu sel) *n.* A minute particle or living cell, especially as one in the blood. **corpuscular** *adj.*

corpus delicti (kor′pus di lik′tī) *n.* The essential evidence pertaining to a crime.

cor-rade (ko rād′) *v.* To rub together; to wear away by abrasion.

cor-ral (ko ral′) *n.* An enclosure for containing animals. *v., Slang* To take possession of.

cor-rect (ko rekt′) *v.* To make free from fault or mistakes. **corrective** *n.* **correctable** *adj.* **correctible** *adj.* **correctional** *n.* **correction** *n.* **correctness** *n.* **correctly** *adv.*

cor-rel-a-tive (ko rel′a tiv) *adj.* Having a mutual relation.

cor-re-spond (kor′i spond′) *v.* To communicate by letter or written words; to be harmonious, equal or similar. **correspondingly** *adv.*

cor-re-spond-ent (kor″i spond′) *n.* Something that corresponds to something else; a person who has regular business dealings with another.

cor-ri-dor (kor′i dėr) *n.* A long hall with rooms on either side; a piece of land that forms a passage through a foreign land.

cor-ri-gen-dum (kor′i jen′dum) *n. pl.* **-da** An error in print that is accompanied by its correction.

cor-ri-gi-ble (kor′i ji bl) *adj.* Able to correct; capable of being corrected.

cor-ri-val (ko rī′val) *n.* A competitor.

cor-rob-o-rate (k o rob′o rāt′) *v.* To support a position or statement with evidence. **corroboration** *n.* **corroborative** *adj.*

cor-rode (ko rōd′) *v.* To eat away through chemical action. **corrosive** n. **corrodible** *adj.* **corrosion** *n.*

cor-ro-sion (ko rō zhan) *n.* The process of corroding, eating, or wearing away; the chemical effect of acids on metals.

cor-ro-sive (ko rō′siv) *n.* That which has

the power or quality of wearing away gradually.

cor-ru-gate (kor´u gāt´) v. To form, draw or bend into folds or alternate grooves and ridges.

corrugated iron n. Galvanized sheet iron or sheet steel, shaped and strengthened by bending into equal parallel grooves and ridges.

cor-rupt (ko rupt´) adj. Dishonest; evil. v. To become or make corrupt. **corrupter** n.

cor-rup-tion (ko rup´shan) n. Impaired of integrity.

cor-sage (kor säzh´) n. A small bouquet of flowers worn on a woman's shoulder or wrist.

cor-sair (kor´sâr) n. A pirate; a fast moving vessel.

cor-set (kor´sit) n. An undergarment that is tightened with laces and reinforced with stays, worn to give shape and support to a woman's body. **corsetiere** n.

cor-tege (kor tezh´) n. A ceremonial procession; a funeral procession.

cor-tex (kor´teks) n. pl. **-tices** The external layer of an organ, especially the gray matter that covers the brain; the bark of trees and the rinds of fruits.

cor-ti-sone (kor´ti sōn´) n. A hormone produced by the adrenal cortex, used in the treatment of rheumatoid arthritis.

co-run-dum (ko run´dum) n. An aluminum oxide used as an abrasive.

cor-us-cate (kor´u skāt´) v. To sparkle. **coruscation** n.

cor-vette (kor vet´) n. An armed warship smaller than a destroyer, used as an escort vessel.

cor-vine (kor´vīn) adj. Birds including and resembling the crow, and ravens.

co-ry-za (ko rī´za) n. An acute inflammation of the upper respiratory system.

co-sign (kō sig´n) v. To sign a document jointly.

co-sig-na-to-ry (kō sig´na tōr´ē) n. pl. **-ies** One who jointly cosigns a document.

cos lettuce n. A kind of lettuce; romaine.

cos-met-ic (koz met´ik) n. A preparation designed to beautify the face.

cos-mic (koz´mik) adj. Of or relating to cosmos; forming a part of the material universe.

cosmic dust n. Very fine particles existing in or of the universe.

cosmic ray n. An extremely high frequency and energy content that comes from outer space and bombards the atoms of the earth's atmosphere.

cos-mog-o-ny (koz mog´o nē) n. The creation of the universe.

cos-mog-ra-phy n. The general science description of the heavens and the earth, dealing with the whole makeup of nature.

cos-mo-naut (koz mo not) n. A Soviet astronaut.

cos-mop-o-lis (koz mop´o lis) n. A city inhabited by people from many lands.

cos-mo-pol-i-tan (koz´mo pol´i tan) adj. Being at home anywhere in the world.

cos-mop-o-lite (koz mop´o līt´) n. A cosmopolitan person.

cos-mos (koz´mos) n. An orderly and harmoniously systematic universe.

Cos-sack (kos´ak) n. A member of a group of people of southern Russia, famous as horsemen.

cos-set (kos´it) v. To pamper; pet.

cost (kost) n. The amount paid or charged for a purchase. **cost** v. **costly** adj.

cos-ta (kos´ta) n. A part of a leaf or the interior wing of an insect that most resembles a rib.

cos-tard (kos´tard) n. A large English cooking apple.

cos-tive (kos´tiv) adj. Affected with or causing constipation.

cost-mar-y (kost´mâr¨ē) n. A perennial plant, with fragrant leaves, used as a potherb, in salads.

cos-tume (kos´tŏm) n. A suit, dress, or set of clothes characteristic of a particular season or occasion; clothes worn by a person playing a part or dressing up in a disguise.

cot (kot) n. A small, often collapsible bed.

cote (kōt) n. A shelter for small animals

as a coop or shed.

co-til-lion (kō til′yαn) *n.* A dance that consists of beautiful and intricate patterns.

cot-tage (kot′ij) *n.* A small house, usually for vacation use.

cotter pin *n.* A metal pin, with flared ends that can be spread apart after inserting through a hole.

cot-ton (kot′on) *n.* A plant or shrub cultivated for the fiber surrounding its seeds; a fabric created by the weaving of cotton fibers; yarn spun from cotton fibers.

cotton candy *n.* Spun sugar candy.

cotton gin *n.* A machine for separating the seeds, hulls, and other foreign matter from cotton.

cot-ton-mouth (kot′on mouth′) *n.* The water moccasin. *Slang* Having a dry mouth.

cot-ton-seed (kot′on sēd″) *n.* The seed of the cotton plant, the oil of which can be used as a substitute for olive oil and in cooking.

cotton stainer *n.* A red, dark brown, or black insect that damages the developing seeds of cotton.

cot-ton-weed (kot′on wēd″) *n.* A weedy plant with stems and leaves covered with a soft, fine hair.

couch (kouch) *n.* A piece of furniture, such as a sofa or bed on which one may sit or recline for rest or sleep. *v.* To phrase in a certain manner; to lie in ambush.

cou-gar (kō′gėr) *n.* A large brown cat, also called a mountain lion, panther, and puma.

cough (kof) *v.* To suddenly expel air from the lungs with an explosive noise.

could (küd) *v.* Past tense of can.

could-n't (küd′ent) Could not.

cou-lisse (kō lēs′) *n.* A piece of wood, with a groove in which something slides.

cou-loir (kōl wär′) *n.* A gully or mountainside gorge.

cou-lomb (kō′lom) *n.* The unit of quantity used to measure electricity; the amount conveyed by one amphere in one second.

cou-ma-rone *n.* A colorless liquid compound, found in coal tar and used to form thermoplastic resins used in printing inks,

and adhesives.

coun-cil (koun′sil) *n.* A group of people assembled for consultation or discussion; an official legislative or advisory body. **councilman,** *n.*

coun-sel (koun′sel) *n.* Professional advice given through consultation; a lawyer engaged in a trial or management of a court case.

coun-sel-ing (koun′se ling) *n.* The act or process of giving professional advice.

coun-sel-or (koun′se lėr) *n.* One who gives advice; a lawyer.

count (kount) *v.* To name or number so as to find the total number of units involved; to name numbers in order; to take account of in a tally or reckoning; to rely or depend on something or someone; to have significance. *n.* A nobleman found in various countries throughout Europe, having rank corresponding to that of a British earl; a tally.

count-down (kount′doun′) *n.* An audible counting in descending order to mark the time remaining before an event.

coun-te-nance (kount′te nαns) *n.* The face as an indication of mood or character; bearing or expression that would suggest approval or sanction.

coun-ter (koun′tėr) *n.* A level surface over which transactions are conducted, on which food is served, or on which articles are displayed; a person or device that counts to determine a number or amount. *v.* To move or act in a contrary, or opposing direction or wrong way.

coun-ter-act (koun′tėr akt′) *v.* To oppose and, by contrary action, make ineffective.

coun-ter-attack (koun′tėr a tak′) *n.* An attack made in response to an enemy attack. **counterattack** *v.*

coun-ter-balance (koun′tėr bal′αns) *n.* A force or influence that balances another; a weight that balances another. **counterbalance** *v.*

coun-ter-bore (koun′tėr bōr″) *v.* To bore out a hole for creating a flat-bottomed enlargement for the head of a screw.

coun-ter-claim (koun´tėr klām´) n. A contrary claim made to offset another.

coun-ter-clock-wise (koun´tėr klok´wīz´) adj. & adv. In a direction contrary to that in which the hands of a clock move.

coun-ter-cul-ture (koun´tēr kul´chėr) n. A culture with values opposite those of traditional society.

coun-ter-es-pi-o-nage (koun´tėr es´pē o näzh´) n. Espionage aimed at discovering and thwarting enemy espionage.

coun-ter-feit (koun´tėr fit) v. To closely imitate or copy with the intent to deceive; to forge. adj. Marked by false pretense. n. Something counterfeit.

coun-ter-foil (koun´tėr foil´) n. A stub, as on a check or ticket, usually serving as a record of the transaction.

coun-ter-in-tel-ligence (koun´tėr in tel´i jens) n. An intelligence agency function designed to block information, deceive the enemy, prevent sabotage, and gather military and political material and information.

coun-ter-ir-ri-tant (koun´tėr ir´i tant) n. An irritation that diverts attention from another. counterirritant adj.

coun-ter-man (koun´tėr man) n. One who works at a counter.

coun-ter-mand (koun´tėr mand´) v. To reverse or revoke a command by issuing a contrary order. n. An order which reverses or contradicts a previous order.

coun-ter-of-fensive (koun´tėr o fen´siv) n. A military offensive designed to thwart an enemy attack.

coun-terpane (koun´tėr pān´) n. A covering.

coun-terpart (koun´tėr pärt´) n. One that matches or complements another.

coun-ter-plea (koun´tėr plē) n. A plea made in answer to a previous plea.

coun-ter-plot (koun´tėr plot´) n. A plot that prevents another from occuring.

coun-ter-point (koun´tėr point´) n., Mus. The combining of melodies into a harmonic relationship while retaining the linear character.

coun-ter-poise (koun´tėr poiz´) n. An equal and opposing force or power.

coun-ter-pose (koun´tėr pōz´) v. To place in opposition.

coun-ter-pro-duc-tive (koun´tėr pro duk´tiv) adj. Tending to hinder rather than aid in the attainment of a goal.

coun-ter-pro-pos-al (koun´tėr pro pō´zal) n. A return proposal for one that has been rejected.

coun-ter-punch (koun´tėr punch) n. A punch given in quick retaliation, as a boxing punch.

coun-ter-re-vo-lu-tion (koun´tėr rev´o lō´shan) n. A revolution designed to overthrow a government previously seated by a revolution.

coun-ter-shaft (koun´tėr shaft´) n. A shaft driven by a belt or gearing from a main shaft and transmits motion to a working part.

coun-ter-sign (koun´tėr sīn´) n. A signature confirming the authenticity of a document already signed by another; a sign or signal given in response to another. countersign v.

coun-ter-sink (koun´tėr singk´) n. A funnel-shaped enlargement on the outer end of a drilled hole designed to allow the head of a nail or screw to lie flush with or below the surface; a tool for making a countersink. v. To set the head, as of a nail or screw at or below the surface.

coun-ter-spy (koun´tėr spī´) n. A spy against the espionage actions of a country.

coun-ter-ten-or (koun´tėr tēn´ėr) n. An adult tenor with a very high range, and able to sing in an alto range.

counter-vail (koun´tėr vāl´) v. To counteract.

coun-ter-weight (koun´tėr wāt´) n. An equivalent weight, used as a counterbalance, compensate for. counterweight v.

count-ess (koun´tis) n. The wife or widow of an earl or count; a woman who, in her own right, holds the rank of earl or count.

counting house n. A building or room used for keeping books and transacting or conducting business.

count-less (kount´lis) *adj.* Too many or too numerous to be counted.

coun-tri-fy (kun´tri fī˝) *v.* To emply country life; rustic; unsophisticated.

coun-try (kun´trē) *n. pl.* *-ies* A given area or region; the land of one's birth, residence, or citizenship; a state, nation, or its territory.

country club *n.* A suburban club for recreational and social activities.

coun-try-man (kun´trē man) *n.* A compatriot; one living in the country or having country ways.

country music *n.* Music derived from the folk style of the southern United States and from the cowboy.

coun-try-side (kun´trē sīd´) *n.* A rural area or its inhabitants.

coun-ty (koun´tē) *n. pl.* *-ies* A territorial division for local government within a state.

coup (kö) *n.* A brilliant, sudden move that is usually highly successful.

cou-ple (kup´l) *n.* A pair; something that joins two things together; a few. *v.* To join in marriage or sexual union.

cou-pler (kup´lẻr) *n.* One who or that which couples; a device that transfers electrical energy from one circuit to another.

cou-plet (kup´lit) *n.* Two rhyming lines of poetry in succession.

cou-pling (kup´ling) *n.* A mechanical devices for uniting or connecting parts or things.

cou-pon (kö´pon) *n.* A statement of interest due, to be removed from a bearer bond and presented for payment when it is payable; a form surrendered to obtain a product, service, or discount on same; a form to be clipped from a magazine or paper and mailed for discounts or gifts.

cour-age (kür´ij) *n.* Mental or moral strength to face danger without fear. **courageous** *adj.* **courageously** *adv.*

cou-ri-er (kür´ē ẻr) *n.* A messenger; a person who carries contraband for another.

course (kōrs) *n.* The act of moving in a path from one point to another; the path over which something moves; a period of time; a series or sequence; a series of studies.

court (kört) *n.* The residence of a sovereign or similar dignitary; a sovereign's family and advisors; an assembly for the transaction of judicial business; a place where trials are conducted; an area marked off for game playing. *v.* To try to win favor or dispel hostility.

cour-te-ous (kẻr´tē us) *adj.* Marked by respect for and consideration of others.

cour-te-san (kör´ti zan) *n.* A prostitute; one who associates with or caters to high-ranking or wealthy men.

cour-te-sy (kẻr´ti sē) *n. pl.* *-ies* Courteous behavior; general allowance despite facts.

court-house (kört´hous´) *n.* A building for holding courts of law.

court-i-er (kör´tē ẻr) *n.* One in attendance at a royal court.

court-ly (kört´lē) *adj.* Dignified; elegant; polite.

court of appeals *n.* A court that hears appeals from a lower court.

court-room (kört´röm˝) *n.* A room for holding a court of law.

court-ship (kört´ship) *n.* The act or period of courting.

court-yard (kört´yärd´) *n.* An open space enclosed by walls.

cous-in (kuz´in) *n.* A child of one's uncle or aunt; a member of a culturally similar race or nationality.

couth (köth) *adj.* Having breeding, polish, or refinement.

cou-ture (kö tür´) *n.* The business of designing and selling women's clothing; dressmaker.

covalent bond *n.* The nonionic chemical bond produced by the sharing of an electron pair by two atoms in a chemical process.

cove (kōv) *n.* A small inlet or bay, generally sheltered; a deep recess or small valley in the side of a mountain.

cov-e-nant (kuv´e nant) *n.* A formal, binding agreement; a promise or pledge.

cov-er (kuv´ẻr) *v.* To place something on or over; to lie over; to spread over; concealment, to guard from attack; to hide or conceal, book binding. *Slang* To be all-encompassing; to act as a stand-in during another's absence; to have within one's gun sights. **cover** *n.*

cov-er-age (kuv´ėr ij) *n.* A provision for something by contract; that which is covered.

cov-er-all (kuv´ėr al´) *n.* A loose one-piece outer garment used to cover other clothing.

cover charge *n.* A charge, at night clubs or restaurants, in addition to the bill for food and drink, used to pay for the entertainment.

cover crop *n.* A crop planted to prevent soil erosion.

covered wagon *n.* A canvas covered wagon with high curved hoops supported by bowed strips of metal or wood.

cov-er-let (kuv´ėr lit) *n.* A bedspread.

cov-et (kuv´it) *v.* To wish for enviously; to crave possession of that which belongs to someone else.

cov-ey (kuv´ē) *n.* A small group of birds, especially quail or partridges.

cow (kou) *n. pl.* **cows** The mature female of cattle or of any species when the adult male is referred to as a bull.

cow-ard (kou´ard) *n.* One who shows great fear or timidity. **cowardice** *n.*

cow-bane (kou´bān˝) *n.* Any of several poisonous parsleylike plants, as the water hemlock.

cow-ber-ry (kou´ber˝) *n.* The berry or fruit of various shrubs that grow in pastures and fields.

cow-boy (kou´boi) *n.* A man who tends cows and horses on a large ranch or farm and does this work while on horseback.

cow-hide (kou´hīd˝) *n.* The hide of a cow from which leather is made.

cowl (koul) *n.* A hood or long hooded cloak such as that of a monk; a covering for a chimney that is designed to improve the air draft; the top portion at the front of an automobile where the windshield and dashboard are attached.

cow-lick (kou´lik˝) *n.* A lock of hair grow-ing in a different direction than the other hair.

cowl-ing (kou´ling) *n.* A removable metal covering for an engine.

cow-pox (kou´poks˝) *n.* A disease of cattle which appears on the teats of the animal in the form of blisters or vesicles.

cow-slip (kou´slip) *n.* A common British primrose with yellow or purple flowers.

cox-a (kok´sa) *n.* The joint of the hip.

cox-comb (koks´kōm) *n.* A conceited foolish person.

cox-swain (kok´san) *n.* One who steers a boat or racing shell.

coy (koi) *adj.* Quieting or shy, or to pretending to be so. **coyness** *n.*

coy-o-te (kī ō´tē) *n.* A small wolf-life animal that is native to North America.

co-yo-til-lo (kō˝ yō tēl´ yō) *n.* A small shrub of the southwestern United States and Mexico, bearing poisonous fruit.

coy-pu (koi´pŏ) *n.* A beaverlike, semiaquatic mammal, valued for its soft brown fur.

coz-en (kuz´en) *v.* To swindle, cheat, deceive, win over, or induce to do something by coaxing or trickery. **cozener** *n.*

co-zy (kō´zē) *adj.* Comfortable and warm; snug. *n.* A cover placed over a teapot to retain the warmth. **cozily** *adv.*

crab (krab) *n. pl.* **crabs** Any one of numerous chiefly marine crustaceans with a short, broad shell, four pairs of legs, and one pair of pincers; sideways motion of an airplane headed into a crosswind. **crabs** Infestation with crab lice.

crab apple *n.* A small, brightly colored, sour wild apple, its fruit used in making jelly.

crab-bed (krab´id) *adj.* Morose or peevish; difficult to read or understand. **crabbedly** *adv.* **crabbedness** *n.*

crab-by (krab bē) *adj.* Cross and ill-tempered.

crab-grass (krab gras) *n.* A grass with stems that root freely and is often a weedy pest in lawns.

crab louse *n.* A small, wingless, blood-sucking, insect parasitic that infests the pubic hair of the human body.

crack (krak) *v.* To make a loud explosive sound; to break, snap, or split apart; to break without completely separating; to go at a good speed; to break with a sudden, sharp sound; to solve; to reduce petroleum compounds to simpler forms by heating. *n.* A sharp, witty remark; a weakness caused by decay or age; an attempt or try. *Slang* A highly dangerous and addictive form of cocaine.

crack down *n.* The sudden act of disciplinary actions.

crack-ing (krak´ing) *adj., Slang* To begin quickly.

crack-le (krak´el) *v.* To make sharp, sudden, repeated noises; to develop a network of fine cracks.

crack-pot (krak´pot˝) *n., Slang* An eccentric person.

crack–up (krak´up˝) *n.* A breakdown of a person's health, especially mental and emotional.

cra-dle (krād´el) *n.* A small bed for infants, usually on rockers or rollers; a framework of support, such as that for a telephone receiver; a small platform on casters used by mechanics when working under a vehicle; a device used for rocking in panning for gold.

craft (kraft) *n.* A special skill or ability; a trade that requires dexterity or artistic skill; the ability to use cunning and skill in deceiving; an aircraft, boat, or ship.

craft union *n.* A labor union limited to and composed of people of the same craft or occupation.

crag (krag) *n.* A steep, jagged rock or cliff. **cragged** *adj.* **craggy** *adj.*

cram (kram) *v.* To pack tightly or stuff; to thrust in a forceful manner; to eat in a greedy fashion; to prepare hastily for an exam.

cram-bo (kram´bō) *n.* A game in which one person gives a word or a line of verse to which another finds a rhyme.

cramp (kramp) *n.* A painful involuntary contraction of a muscle; sharp abdominal pain.

cram-pon (kram´pon) *n.* A hooked apparatus used to raise objects.

cran-age (krā´nij) *n.* To load or unload goods from a ship by using a crane.

cran-ber-ry (kran´ber˝ē) *n. pl.* **-berries** A North American shrub which grows in damp soil and bears edible, tart red berries.

cran-dall (kran´dal) *n.* A hammerlike tool for working with soft stone.

crane (krān) *n.* A large bird with long legs and a long neck; a machine used for lifting or moving heavy objects. *v.* To strain or stretch the neck.

cranial index *n.* The ratio multiplied by 100 of the full breadth of the skull to its maxi-mum or full length.

cranial nerve *n.* Any of the nerves that originate in the lower part of the brain and come through openings in the skull.

cra-ni-ol-o-gy (krā˝nē ol´o jē) *n.* The science that deals with the size, shape, and other characteristics of human skulls.

cra-ni-um (krā´nē um) *n. pl.* **crania** The skull, especially the part in which the brain is enclosed. **cranial** *adj.*

crank (krangk) *n.* An arm bent at right angles to a shaft and turned to transmit motion; an eccentric person; a bad-tempered person; a grouch. *v.* To operate or start by crank.

crank-case (krangk´kās´) *n.* The housing of a crankshaft.

crank-pin (krangk´pin˝) *n.* A cylinder at the outer end of a crank, to which the connecting rod is attached.

crank-shaft (krangk´shaft´) *n.* A shaft propelled by a crank.

crank-y (krang´kē) *adj.* Grouchy, irritable.

cran-ny (kran´ē) *n. pl.* **-ies** A small break or crevice; an obscure nook or corner.

crap-pie (krap´ē) *n.* A small sunfish of the central parts of the United States.

craps (kraps) *v.* A gambling game played

with two dice.

crap-shoot-er (krap´shŏ´tėr) *n.* A person who plays craps.

crap-u-lous *adj.* Associated with drunkenness, sick from excessive consumption of liquor.

crash (krash) *v.* To break violently or noisily; to damage in landing, usually an airplane; to collapse suddenly, usually a business; to cause to make a loud noise; to enter into without an invitation. *Slang* To spend the night in a particular place; to return to normalcy from a drug-induced state. *n.* In computer science, the unplanned termination of a computer operation or program.

crass (kras) *adj.* Insensitive and unrefined.

crate (krāt) *n.* A container, usually made of wooden slats, for protection during shipping or storage. **crate** *v.*

cra-ter (krā´tėr) *n.* A bowl-shaped depression at the mouth of a volcano; a depression formed by a meteorite; a hole made by an explosion. **cratered** *adj.*

cra-vat (kra vat´) *n.* A necktie.

crave (krāv) *v.* To desire intensely.

cra-ven (krā´ven) *adj.* Completely lacking courage.

crav-ing (krāv ing) *n.* A great desire; an intense longing.

craw (kro) *n.* The crop of a bird; the stomach of a lower animal.

craw-fish (kro´fish´) *n.* A crayfish.

crawl (krol) *v.* To move slowly by dragging the body along the ground in a prone position; to move on hands and knees; to progress slowly.

crawl space *n.* An unfinished area beneath the first floor of a building which provides access to wiring and plumbing.

cray-on (krā´on) *n.* A stick of white or colored chalk or wax used for writing or drawing.

craze (krāz) *v.* To make insane or as if insane; to become insane; to develop a fine mesh of narrow cracks. *n.* Something that lasts for a short period of time; a fad.

cra-zy (krā´zē) *adj.* Insane; impractical; unusually fond. **craziness** *n.*

crazy bone *n.* The elbow; the funny bone.

crazy quilt *n.* A patch quilt without a particular pattern.

creak (krēk) *v.* A squeaking or grating noise. **creaky** *adj.* **creakily** *adv.*

cream (krēm) *n.* The yellowish, fatty part of milk, containing a great amount of butterfat; something having the consistency of cream; the best part; a pale yellow-white color. **creaminess** *n.* **creamy** *adj.*

cream cheese *n.* Any of various soft, mild, unripened cheeses made from whole sweet milk and enriched with cream.

cream-er (krē´mėr) *n.* A device in which milk is placed to facilitate the formation of cream.

cream-er-y (krē´me rē) *n.* An establishment that engages in the production of butter, milk and cheese products.

crease (krēs) *n.* A line or mark made by folding and pressing a pliable substance. **crease** *v.*

creas-er (krēs´ėr) *n.* A sewing machine attachment for creasing leather or cloth.

cre-ate (krē āt´) *v.* To bring something into existence; to give rise to.

cre-a-tion (krē ā´shan) *n.* The act of creating; something that is created; the universe.

cre-a-tive (krē ā´tiv) *adj.* Marked by the ability to create; inventive; imaginative. **creatively** *adv.* **creativeness** *n.*

crea-tor (krē ā´tėr) *n.* One that creates. **Creator.** God.

crea-ture (krē´chėr) *n.* Something created; a living being.

cre-dence (krēd´ens) *n.* Belief.

cre-den-dum (kri den´dum) *n.* Something to be believed; an article of faith.

cre-den-za (kri den´za) *n.* A buffet or sideboard, usually without legs.

cred-i-ble (kred´i bl) *adj.* Offering reasonable grounds for belief, confidence in truth and reliance. **credibility** *n.* **credibly** *adv.*

cred-it (kred´it) *n.* An amount at a person's disposal in a bank; recognition by name for a contribution; acknowledgment; recognition by a learning institution that a student has completed a requirement leading to a degree.

credit card *n.* A card establishing the right of its holder to buy merchandise on credit.

cred-i-tor (kred′i tėr) *n.* One who gives goods or money on credit; the person or establishment to whom a debt is owed.

cred-u-lous (krej′u lus) *adj.* Gullible; ready to believe on slight or uncertain evidence; easily deceived.. **credulously** *adv.* **credulousness** *n.*

creed (krēd) *n.* A brief authoritative statement of religious belief.

creek (krēk) *n.* A narrow stream. **up the creek** In a difficult or perplexing situation.

creel (krēl) *n.* A wicker basket for holding fish.

creep (krēp) *v.* To advance at a slow pace; to go timidly or cautiously; to grow along a surface, clinging by means of tendrils or aerial roots.

creep-er (krē′pėr) *n.* A breed of birds with short legs; who creep around on bushes or trees.

cre-mate (krē′māt) *v.* To reduce to ashes by burning.

cre-ma-tor (krē′mā tėr) *n.* A person who cremates; the furnace where bodies are cremated.

Cre-ole (krē′ōl) *n.* A person of European descent born in Spanish America or the West Indies; a person of mixed African and European ancestry.

cre-o-sol (krē′o līzd″) *n.* A colorless oily liquid from wood tar and guaiacum resin.

cre-o-sote (krē′o sōt′) *n.* An oily liquid mixture obtained by distilling coal tar, used especially as a wood preservative.

crepe paper *n.* A decorative paper, with a puckered or wrinkled texture.

crepe rubber *n.* A synthetic rubber in the form of crinkled sheets used for shoe soles.

crept *v.* The past tense of creep.

cre-pus-cu-lar (kri pus′kū lėr) *adj.* Of, resembling, or relating to twilight.

cre-pus-cule (kri pus′kūl) *n.* Pertaining to twilight; glimmering; dusk.

cre-scen-do (kri shen′dō) *adv.* In music,

gradually increasing in loudness.

cres-cent (kres′ent) *n.* The shape of the moon in its first and fourth quarters, defined with a convex and a concave edge.

cres-cive (kres′iv) *adj.* Increasing or growing.

cress (kres) *n.* Any of numerous plants with sharp-tasting edible leaves.

cres-set (kres′it) *n.* A lamp or firepan mounted as a torch or carried on a pole as a lantern.

crest (krest) *n.* A tuft or comb on the head of a bird or animal; the top line of a mountain or hill.

crest-fall-en (krest′fo″len) *adj.* Dejected; discouraged; having a hanging head.

cre-ta-ceous (kri tā′shus) *adj.* Composed of, or having the qualities of chalk.

cre-tin (krē′tin) *n.* One afflicted with cretinism; a person with marked mental deficiency.

cre-tin-ism (krēt′e niz′um) *n.* A condition marked by physical stunting and mental deficiency.

cre-tonne (kri ton′) *n.* A strong cotton or linen cloth, used especially for curtains and upholstery; a cotton cloth with various textures of surface printed with pictorial and other patterns.

cre-vasse (kre vas′) *n.* A deep crack or crevice.

crev-ice (krev′is) *n.* A narrow crack.

crew (krö) *n.* A group of people that work together; the whole company belonging to an aircraft or ship.

crew-el (krö′el) *n.* Slackly twisted worsted yarn, used in embroidery.

crib (krib) *n.* A small bed with high sides for an infant; a feeding bin for animals.

crib-bage (krib′ij) *n.* A game of cards, for two, three or four players.

crib-ri-form (krib′ri form″) *adj.* Having the form of a sieve; pierced with many small openings.

crick (krik) *n.* A painful muscle spasm

condition of the neck or back.

crick-et (krik´it) *n.* A leaping orthopteran insect, the male of the species producing a high pitched chirping sound by rubbing the front wings together; a game played with a bat and ball by two teams of eleven players each.

cri-er (krī´ėr) *n.* One who calls out public notices.

crime (krīm) *n.* An act or the commission of an act that is forbidden by law.

crim-i-nal (krim´i nal) *adj.* Relating to a crime. *n.* A person who commits a crime.

criminal law *n.* The law of crimes and punishment.

crim-i-nate (krim´ināt˝) *v.* To involve in a crime.

crim-i-nol-o-gy (krim˝i nol´o jē) *n.* Scientific study of crime.

crimp (krimp) *v.* To cause to become bent or crinkled; to pinch in or together.

crim-son (krim´zon) *n.* A deep purplish color. *v.* To make or become crimson.

cringe (krinj) *v.* To shrink or recoil in fear.

crin-kle (kring´kl) *v.* To wrinkle. **crinkle** *n.* **crinkly** *adj.*

crin-o-line (krin´o lin) *n.* An open-weave fabric used for lining and stiffening garments.

cri-o-sphinx (krī´o sfingks˝) *n.* A sphinx with the head of a ram.

crip-ple (krip´l) *n.* One who is lame or partially disabled; something flawed or imperfect. *adj.* Being a cripple. *v.* To deprive one of the use of a limb or limbs.

cri-sis (krī´sis) *n. pl.* **crises** An unstable or uncertain time or state of affairs, the outcome of which will have a major impact; the turning point for better or worse in a disease or fever, hectic situation.

crisp (krisp) *adj.* Easily broken; brittle; brisk or cold; sharp; clear. *v.* To make or become crisp. **crisply** *adv.* **crispness** *n.* **crispy** *adj.*

crisp-er (kris´pėr) *n.* A compartment within a refrigerator used to keep fruits and vegetables fresh, an instrument used for crisping cloth.

criss-cross (kris´kros´) *v.* To mark with crossed lines; to mark with intersecting lines, crossing. **crisscross** *adj.*

cri-te-ri-on (krī tēr´ē on) *n. pl.* **criteria** A standard by which something can be judged.

crit-ic (krit´ik) *n.* A person who is critical; a person who examines a subject and expresses an opinion as to its value; a person who judges or evaluates art or artistic creations, as a theatre critic.

crit-i-cal (krit´i kal) *adj.* Very important, as a critical decision; tending to criticize harshly. **critically** *adv.*

crit-i-cism (krit´i siz´um) *n.* The act of criticizing, usually in a severe or negative fashion.

crit-i-cize (krit´i sīz´) *v.* To be a critic; to find fault with; to judge critically; to blame.

cri-tique (kri tēk´) *n.* A written estimate of the merits of a performance.

croak (krōk) *n.* A hoarse, raspy cry such as that made by a frog. *v.* To utter a croak. *Slang* To die.

cro-chet (krō shā´) *n.* The needlework achieved by looping thread with a hooked needle.

crock (krok) *n.* An earthenware pot or jar most often used for cooking or storing food.

crock-et (krok´it) *n.* An ornament in the form of curved and bent foilage.

croc-o-dile(krok´o dīl´) *n.* Any of various large, thick-skinned, long-bodied reptiles of tropical and subtropical regions.

crocodile tears *n. pl.* Insincere or false grief.

cro-cus (krō´kus) *n. pl.* **crocuses** A plant having solitary, long-tubed flowers and slender, linear leaves.

croft (kroft) *n.* A small piece of ground or farm worked by the tenant who lives on the property.

crois-sant (krwä sän´) *n.* A crescent-shaped roll of flaky bread dough.

crone (krōn) *n.* A witch-like, withered old woman.

cro-ny (krō′nē) *n. pl.* **-ies** A close friend.

crook (krük) *n.* A bent or hooked implement; a bend or curve; a person given to dishonest acts. *v.* To bend or curve.

crook-ed (krük′id) *adj.* Dishonest; bent; not straight; deformed.

croon (krōn) *v.* To sing in a gentle, low voice; to make a continued moaning sound.

crop (krop) *n.* A plant which is grown and then harvested for use or for sale; a riding whip. *v.* To cut off short; to appear unexpectedly.

cro-quet (krō kā′) *n.* An outdoor game played by driving wooden balls through hoops with long-handled mallets.

cro-quette (krō ket′) *n.* A small patty or roll of minced food that is breaded and deep fried.

cro-qui-gnole (krō′ki nōl) *n.* A method of styling the hair by winding the hair toward the head on curlers, in a circular style.

cross (kros) *n.* A structure consisting of an upright post and a crossbar, used especially by the Romans for execution, such as the cross on which Jesus was crucified; something that tries one's virtue or patience; a medal with the shape of the cross *n.* Used as a Christian emblem; a mark formed by the intersection of two lines. *v.* In biology, to interbreed a plant or an animal with one of a different kind; to go over; to intersect; to turn against; to go against. *adj.* Ill-tempered.

cross-bar (kros′bär′) *n.* A horizontal bar or line.

cross-bill (kros′bil″) *n.* A bird belonging to the finch family.

cross-bones (kros′bōnz′) *n.* Two leg or arm bones placed crosswise, as in a skull and crossbones.

cross-bow (kros′bō′) *n.* A weapon consisting chiefly of a bow mounted crosswise near the end of a wooden stock.

cross-breed (kros′brēd′) *v.* To produce a hybrid plant or animal by interbreeding different breeds and varieties.

cross–check *v.* To check again.

cross-current (kros′kér′ent) *n.* A current flowing against another; a conflicting tendency.

cross-road (kros′rōd″) *n.* A road that crosses another.

cross street *n.* A street crossing another street.

cross-walk (kros′wok″) *n.* A specially marked lane for pedestrians to cross a street or highway.

crotch (kroch) *n.* The angle formed by the junction of two parts, such as branches, part of the human body where the legs join, a pair of pants where the legs meet. **crotched** *adj.*

crotch-et (kroch′it) *n.* A peculiar opinion or preference.

crouch (krouch) *v.* To bend at the knees and lower the body close to the ground. **crouch** *n.*

croup (krōp) *n.* A spasmodic laryngitis, especially of children, marked by a loud, harsh cough and difficulty in breathing. **croupy** *adj.*

crou-pi-er (krō′pē ér) *n.* One who collects and pays bets at a gambling table.

crous-tade (krō städ′) *n.* A crisp shell, either fried or baked, in which to serve foods.

crou-ton (krō′ton) *n.* A small piece of toasted or fried bread.

crow (krō) *n.* A large, black bird.

crow-bar (krō′bär) *n.* A steel or iron bar with a forked end, used as a lever.

crowd (kroud) *n.* A large group of people gathered together. *v.* To assemble in large numbers; to press close.

crown (kroun) *n.* A circular ornament or head covering made of precious metal and jewels, worn as the headdress of a sovereign; the highest point; the topmost part of the skull; the tile representing the championship of a sport; a reward or honor for achievement; the part of a tooth that rises above the gum line. *v.* To place a checker on another checker to make a king; to adorn something with a crown; to hit on the head.

crown antler *n.* A topmost branch of a stag's horn.

crown glass *n.* A glass containing silicon, potassium or sodium, which is blown and whirled into a form.

CRT *abbr.* Cathode Ray Tube.

cru-cial (krö´shal) *adj.* Extremely important; critical.

cru-ci-ble (krö´si bl) *n.* A vessel used for melting and calcining materials at high temperatures; a severe or hard test of someone.

cru-ci-fy (krö´si fï´) *v.* To put to death by nailing to a cross; to treat cruelly; to torment.

crude (kröd) *adj.* Unrefined; lacking refinement or tact; haphazardly made. *n.* Unrefined petroleum. **crudely** *adv.*

cruel (krö´el) *adj.* Inflicting suffering; causing pain. **cruelly** *adv.* **cruelty** *n.*

cru-et (krö´it) *n.* A small glass bottle normally used as a container for oil or vinegar.

cruise (kröz) *v.* To drive or sail about for pleasure; to move about the streets at leisure; to travel at a speed that provides maximum efficiency. **cruise** *n.*

crul-ler (krul´ër) *n.* A light, sweet cake cut in a twisted circular form and fried in deep fat.

crumb (krum) *n.* A small fragment of material, particularly bread.

crum-ble (krum´bl) *v.* To break into small pieces. **crumbly** *adj.*

crump (krump) *v.* To crunch with the teeth. *n.* A crunching sound

crum-ple (krum´pel) *v.* To bend or crush out of shape; to cause to collapse; to be crumpled.

crunch (krunch) *v.* To chew with a crackling noise; to run, walk, etc., with a crushing noise. **crunch** *n.*

cru-ral (krür´al) *adj.* Pertaining to the thigh or leg.

crus (krus) *n.* The part of the leg or hind limb between the femur or thigh and the ankle.

cru-sade (krö säd´) *n.* Any of the military expeditions undertaken by Christian leaders during the 11th, 12th, and 13th centuries to recover the Holy Land from the Moslems. **crusade** *v.*

crush (krush) *v.* To squeeze or force by pressure so as to damage or injure; to reduce to particles by pounding or grinding; to put down or suppress, overwhelm. **crushable** *adj.* **crusher** *n.*

crust (krust) *n.* The hardened exterior or surface of bread; a hard or brittle surface layer; the outer layer of the earth; the shell of a pie, normally made of pastry. *v.* To cover or become covered with crust.

crus-ta-cean (kru stä´shan) *n.* Any one of a large class of aquatic arthropods, including lobsters and crabs, with a segmented body and paired, jointed limbs.

crutch (kruch) *n.* A support usually designed to fit in the armpit and to be used as an aid in walking; any support or prop.

crux (kruks) *n.* An essential or vital moment; a main or central feature.

cry (krï) *v.* To shed tears; to call out loudly; to utter a characteristic call or sound; to proclaim publicly.

cry-o-gen (krï´ö jen) *n.* A substance for producing or obtaining low temperatures.

cry-o-lite *n.* A fluoride of sodium-aluminum and used to make aluminum and soda.

cry-om-e-ter (krï om´i tër) *n.* A thermometer for measuring low temperatures.

cry-o-phyte (krï´ö fït) *n., Bot.* A plant that grows on snow and ice, usually an alga, but sometimes a moss, or fungus.

crypt (kript) *n.* An underground chamber or vault primarily used to bury the dead.

crypt-a-nal-y-sis (krip˝ta nal´i sis) *n.* The study of solving written codes or cyphers.

cryp-tic (krip´tik) *adj.* Intended to be obscure; serving to conceal.

cryp-tog-ra-phy (krip tog´ra fë) *n.* The writing and deciphering of messages in secret code. **cryptographer** *n.*

crys-tal (kris´tal) *n.* Quartz that is transparent or nearly transparent; a body that is formed by the solidification of a chemical element; a clear, high-quality glass. **crystalline** *adj.*

crystal ball *n.* A glass globe foretell the future.

crys-tal-lize (kris´ta līz´) *v.* To cause to form crystals or assume crystalline form; to cause to take a definite form; to coat with crystals, especially sugar crystals.

CT *abbr.* Connecticut.

cten-o-phore (ten´o fōr´) *n.* Any of the free-swimming aquatic animals.

cub (kub) *n.* The young of the lion, wolf, or bear; an awkward child or youth.

cu-ba-ture (kū´ba chèr) *n.* The determination of the cubic contents.

cub-by-hole (kub´ē hōl´) *n.* A small enclosed area.

cube (kūb) *n.* A regular solid with six equal squares, having all its angles right angles.

cu-beb (kū´beb) *n.* The spicy fruit or dried unripe berry of an East Indian climbing shrub of the pepper family.

cube root *n.* A number whose cube is a given number.

cubic (kū´bik) *adj.* Having the shape of a cube; having three dimensions; having the volume of a cube with the edges of a specified unit.

cubic (kū´bik) *adj.* Having the shape of a cube; having three dimensions; having the volume of a cube with the edges of a specified unit.

cu-bi-cle (kū´bi kl) *n.* A small partitioned area.

cub-ism (kū´biz um) *n.* An art style that portrays the subject matter with geometric forms. **cubist** *n.*

cu-bit (kū´bit) *n.* An ancient unit of measurement that equals approximately eighteen to twenty inches.

Cub Scout *n.* A member of the Boy Scout organization from the ages of eight to ten.

cuck-oo (kŏ´kŏ) *n. pl.* **cuckoos** A European bird, gray in color, which lays its eggs in the nests of other birds; Silly.

cu-cu-li-form (kū kū´li form) *adj.* Pertaining to birds, which includes road runners and cuckoos.

cu-cum-ber (kū´kum bèr) *n.* A fruit with a green rind and white, seedy flesh.

cu-cur-bit (kū kèr´bit) *n.* A plant from the gourd family.

cud (kud) *n.* Food forced up into the mouth of a ruminating animal from the first stomach and chewed again.

cud-dle (kud´l) *v.* To caress fondly and hold close; to snuggle. **cuddle** *n.* **cuddly** *adj.*

cudg-el (kuj´el) *n.* A short, thick stick; a heavy club.

cue (kū) *n.* A signal given to an actor or someone making a speech, letting him know it is his turn; a long rod for playing pool and billiards.

cue ball *n.* The white ball that is struck with the cue in billiards and pool.

cues-ta (kwes´ta) *n.* A hill with a gradual incline on one face and a steep incline on the other.

cuff (kuf) *n.* The lower part of a sleeve; the part of the pant legs which is turned up. *v.* To strike someone.

cuffs (kufs) *n.* Handcuffs.

cui-rass (kwi ras´) *n.* A piece of armor for the breast and back, used for protection.

cui-sine (kwi zēn´) *n.* A style of cooking and preparing food; the food prepared.

cu-let (kū´lit) *n.* The small flat facet forming the bottom of a gem.

cu-lex (kū´leks) *n.* A large group of mosquitoes found in North America and Europe.

cu-li-nar-y (kū´li ner´ē) *adj.* Relating to cooking.

cull (kul) *v.* To select the best from a group, to gather only the best. **culler** *n.*

culm (kulm) *n.* Coal dust or refuse coal; slack.

cul-mi-nate (kul´mi nāt´) *v.* To reach or rise to the highest point. **culmination** *n.*

cu-lotte (kŏ lot´) *n.* A woman's full pants made to look like a skirt.

cul-pa-ble (kul´pa bl) *adj.* Meriting blame. **culpability** *n.*

cul-prit (kul´prit) *n.* A person guilty of a crime.

cult (kult) *n.* A group or system of religious worship. **cultic** *adj.* **cultist** *n.*

cul-ti-vate (kul´ti vāt´) *v.* To improve land for planting by fertilizing and plowing; to improve by study; to encourage. **cultivatable** *adj.* **cultivation** *n.* **cultivator** *n.*

cul-ture (kul´chėr) *n.* The act of developing intellectual ability with education; a form of civilization, particularly the beliefs, arts, and customs. *Biol.* The growth of living material in a prepared nutrient media. **culture** *v.*

cul-vert (kul´vėrt) *n.* A drain that runs under a road or railroad.

cum-ber (kum´bėr) *v.* To burden someone.

cum-ber-some (kum´bėr sum) *adj.* Clumsy; arkward. **cumbersomely** *adj.*

cum-in (kum´im) *n.* A small plant of the parsley family cultivated for its aromatic.

cum-mer-bund (kum´ėr bund´) *n.* A wide sash worn by men in formal attire.

cu-mu-late (kū´mū lāt´) *v.* To heap or build up; amass; accumulate.

cu-mu-la-tive (kū´mū lā˝tiv) *adj.* Increasing by successive additions.

cu-mu-lus (kū´mū lus) *n.* *pl.* **cumuli** A white, fluffy cloud with a rounded top and a flat base.

cu-ne-ate (kū´nē it) *adj.* Narrowly triangular and tapering to a point at the base.

cu-ne-i-form (kū nē´i form´) *n.* Wedge-shaped characters used in ancient Babylonian, Assyrian, and Sumerian writing.

cun-ning (kun´ing) *adj.* Crafty; sly. **cunningly** *adv.*

cup (kup) *n.* A small, open container with a handle, used for drinking; a measure of capacity that equals 1/2 pint, 8 ounces, or 16 tablespoons.

cu-pel (kū´pel) *n.* A small, cuplike porous vessel, usually made of bone ash, used in assaying, to separate gold and silver from lead.

Cu-pid (kū´pid) *n.* The god of love in Roman mythology.

cu-pid-ity (kū pid´i tē) *n.* An excessive desire for material gain.

cu-po-la (kū´po la) *n.* A rounded roof; a small vaulted structure that usually rises above a roof.

cu-pre-ous (kū´prē us) *adj.* Consisting of copper.

cur (kür) *n.* A mongrel; a dog of mixed breeds.

cu-rate (kūr´it) *n.* A member of the clergy that assists the priest.

cu-ra-tor (kū rā´tėr) *n.* A person in charge of a museum.

curb (kürb) *n.* Something that restrains or controls; the raised border along the edge of a street. **curb** *v.*

curd (kürd) *n.* The coagulated portion of milk used for making cheese.

cure (kūr) *n.* Recovery from a sickness; a medical treatment; the process of preserving food with the use of salt, smoke, or aging.

cur-few (kür´fū) *n.* An order for people to clear the streets at a certain hour; the hour at which an adolescent has been told to be home by his or her parents.

cu-ri-o (kür´ē ō´) *n.* An unusual or rare object.

cu-ri-o-sa (kür˝ē ō´sa) *n.* Books written on unusual or erotic subjects.

cu-ri-os-i-ty (kūrē os´i tē) *n.* The strong desire to know something; something that arouses interest.

cu-ri-ous (kür´ē us) *adj.* Questioning; inquisitive; eager for information. **curiousity** *n.* **curiously** *adv.*

cu-ri-um (kür´ē um) *n.* An artifically produced radioactive trivalent element.

curl (kürl) *v.* To twist into curves; shape like a coil. *n.* A ringlet of hair. **curler** *n.* **curliness** *n.* **curly** *adj.*

cur-lew (kür´lö) *n.* A migratory bird with long legs and a long slender curved bill.

curling iron *n.* A rod-shaped metal instrument, that curls or waves the hair when the locks are twined around the heated rod.

cur-mudg-eon (kėr muj´on) *n.* An ill-tempered person.

curn (kŭrn) *n*. A grain; a small quantity or number.

cur-rant (kŭr´ant) *n*. A small seedless raisin.

cur-ren-cy (kŭr´en sē) *n*. *pl*. -cies Money in circulation.

cur-rent (kŭr´ent) *adj*. Belonging or occurring in the present time. *n*. Water or air that has a steady flow in a definite direction. **currently** *adv*.

current assets *n*. The assets of a company that can be readily converted to cash.

current liabilities *n*. Debts of a business or corporation.

cur-ri-cle (kėr´i kl) *n*. A two-wheeled carriage, drawn by two horses.

cur-ric-u-lum (ku rik´ū lum) *n*. *pl*. -la, -lums The courses offered in a school.

cur-ri-er (kŭr´ē er) *n*. One who works with leather after it is tanned.

cur-ry (kŭr´ē) *v*. To groom a horse with a brush. *n*. A pungent spice used in cooking.

curse (kŭrs) *n*. A prayer or wish for harm to come to someone or something. **cursed** *adj*. **curse** *v*.

cursor (kŭr´sor) *n*. In computer science, the flashing square, underline, or other indicator on the CRT screen of a computer that shows where the next character will be deleted or inserted.

cur-sive (kėr´siv) *n*. A flowing writing in which the letters are joined together. **cursively** *adv*.

cur-so-ry (kŭr´so rē) *adj*. Rapidly done, often without care and not paying attention to details.

curt (kėrt) *adj*. Abrupt; rude, as in manner or speech. **curtly** *adv*. **curtness** *n*.

cur-tail (kėr´tāl´) *v*. To shorten. **curtailment** *n*.

cur-tain (kŭr´tan) *n*. A piece of material that covers a window and can be either drawn to the sides or raised.

curtain call *n*. The reappearance of a cast member in response to the applause of the audience at the end of a performance.

cur-tate (kŭr´tāt) *adj*. Shortened or reduced; abbreviated.

cur-ti-lage (kŭr´ti lij) *n*. The piece of land occupied by a house and its yard.

curt-sy (kŭrt´sē) *n*. *pl* -sies A respectful gesture made by bending the knees and lowering the body. **curtsy** *v*.

curve (kŭrv) *n*. A continuously curved line without angles.

cur-vet (kŭr´vit) *n*. A prancing leap of a horse in which the hind legs are raised just before the forelegs touch the ground in quick succession so that all four legs are in midair for an instant.

cu-shaw (ka shaw) *n*. A crooknecked squash.

cush-ion (kŭsh´on) *n*. A pillow with a soft filling. *v*. To absorb the shock or effect.

cusk *n*. A large edible marine fish related to a cod, mostly located in the north Atlantic.

cus-pid (kus´pid) *n*. A pointed canine tooth, cuspidate tooth.

cus-pi-dor (kus´pi dor´) *n*. A spittoon.

cuss (kus) *v*. To use profanity.

cus-tard (kus´tėrd) *n*. A mixture of milk, eggs, sugar, and flavoring that is baked.

cus-to-di-an (ku stō´dē an) *n*. One who has the custody or care of something or someone.

cus-to-dy (kus´to dē) *n*. *pl*. -dies The act of guarding; the care and protection of a minor.

cus-tom (kus´tom) *n*. An accepted practice of a community or people; the usual manner of doing something. **customs** The tax one must pay on imported goods. **customary** *adj*. **customarily** *adv*.

cus-tom-ar-y (kus´tomer¯ē) *adj*. According to or based on a custom or established usage.

custom–built (kus´tom bilt´) *adj*. Built to one's special orders.

cus-tomer (kus´to mėr) *n*. A person with whom a merchant or business person must deal, usually on a regular basis.

custom house *n*. An office or building where customs are paid and ships are cleared for entering or leaving a country.

cut (kut) *v.* To penetrate with a sharp edge, as with a knife; to omit or leave something out; to reap or harvest crops in the fields. *Slang* To cut class; to share in the profits.

cut back *v.* To reduce; to prune.

cute (kūt) *adj.* Attractive in a delightful way.

cut glass *n.* Glass shaped and ornamented with patterns by using a cutting instrument.

cut-lass *or* **cut-las (kut´las)** *n.* A thick, short, curved sword.

cut-lery (kut´le rē) *n.* Cutting instruments used at the dinner table and used to prepare food for cooking.

cut-let (kut´lit) *n.* A thin piece of meat for broiling or frying, usually lamb or veal.

cut-off (kut´of´) *n.* A short cut; the act of cutting something off.

cut-offs (kut´ofs) *n., Slang* Blue jeans that have been cut above the knee and made into shorts.

cut-out (kut´out´) *n.* Something intended to be cut or already cut out. *v.* To shape by cutting; to eliminate.

cut–rate (kut´rāt´) *adj.* Offering merchandise at a lower than normal price.

cut-ter (kut´ėr) *n., Naut.* A fast-sailing vessel with a single mast.

cut-throat (kut´thrōt´) *n.* A murderer; a thug.

cut up (kut´up´)´ *v.* To act foolishly; to behave like a clown; to cut into pieces.

cut-work (kut´würk´) *n.* A type of ornamental embroidery in which a design is stitched and the material inside the design is cut away.

cu-vette (kŏ vet´) *n.* A small vessel or tube used in a laboratory.

cyc-la-men (sik´la men) *n.* A plant with red, white, or pink flowers.

cy-cle (sī´kl) *n.* A recurring time in which an event occurs repeatedly; a bicycle or motorcycle. **cyclical** *adj.* **cyclically** *adv.*

cy-clist (sī´klist) *n.* A person who rides a cycle.

cy-clone (sī´klōn) *n.* A storm with wind rotating about a low pressure center, accompanied by destructive weather. **cyclonic** *adj.*

cy-clo-tron (sī´klo tron´) *n.* Machine that obtains high-energy electrified particles by whirling at a high speed in a strong magnetic field.

cyg-net (sig´nit) *n.* A young swan.

cyl-in-der (sil´in dėr) *n.* A long, round body that is either hollow or solid. **cylindrical** *adj.*

cym-bal (sim´bal) *n.* A pair of brass plates which produce a clashing tone when struck together.

cyn-ic (sin´ik) *n.* One who believes that all people have selfish motives. **cynical** *adj.* **cynicism** *n.*

cy-no-sure (sī´no shŏr´) *n.* A person or object that attracts admiration and interest.

cy-press (sī´pres) *n.* An evergreen tree that grows in a warm climate and bears small, scale-like needles.

cyst (sist) *n.* An abnormal sac or vesicle which may collect and retain fluid.

cystic fibrosis *n.* A congenital disease, that usually developes in childhood and results in disorders of the lungs and pancreas.

cys-ti-tis (si stī´tis) *n.* An inflammation of the bladder.

cy-tol-ogy (sī tol´o jē) *n.* The scientific study of cell formation, function, and structure, life cycle of a cell. **cytological** *adj.* **cytologic** *adj.* **cytologist** *n.*

cy-to-gen-e-sis (sī´to jen´i sis) *n.* The origin, development, and changes of cells in animal and vegetable structures.

cy-tol-y-sis (sī tol´i sis) *n.* The degeneration of cells.

cy-to-plasm (sī´to plaz˝um) *n.* The living substance or protoplasm of a cell external to the nuclear membrane.

czar (zär) *n.* An emperor or king or one of the former emperors or kings of Russia. *Slang* One who has authority.

czar-das (chär´däsh) *n.* Hungarian dance to music that starts out slow and ends with a fast whirl.

czar-ism (zär´iz um) *n.* The former Russian system of government; a dictatorship.

D, d (dē) The fourth letter of the English alphabet; the Roman numeral for 500.

DA *abbr.* District Attorney.

dab (dab) *v.* To touch quickly with light, short strokes.

dab-ble (dab´l) *v.* To play in a liquid, as water, with the hands; to work in or play with in a minor way. **dabbler** *n.*

dab-chick (dab´chik˝) *n.* A small diving and swimming bird.

dace (dās) *n.* A small freshwater fish.

dachshund (daks´hend˝) *n.* A small dog with very short legs, drooping ears, and a long body.

dac-ty-lol-o-gy (dak˝ti lol´o jē) *n.* The art of communicating thoughts or ideas by using the hands and fingers; the language of the deaf.

dad (dad) *n., Informal* Father.

dad-dy (dad´ē) *n. pl.* **-dies** *Informal* Father.

dad-dy–long-legs (dad´ē long´legz´) *n.* An insect with very long legs and a rounded body that resembles a spider.

da-do (dā´dō) *n.* The part of an interior wall, often finished with wallpaper, paint or fabric.

dae-dal (dēd´al) *adj.* Having and showing artistic skill.

daf-fo-dil (daf´o dil) *n.* A bulbous plant with solitary yellow flowers.

daft (daft) *adj.* Insane; crazy; foolish. **daftly** *adv.* **daftness** *n.*

dag-ger (dag´ėr) *n.* A pointed, short-edged weapon which is used for stabbing.

dah (dä) *n.* The dash used in the code of telegraphy or radio, represented by a tone interval approximately three times as long as the dot.

da-ha-be-ah (dä˝ha bē´a) *n.* A passenger boat used on the Nile river.

dahl-ia (dal´ya) *n.* A perennial plant having tuberous roots and showy purple, red, yellow, or white flowers.

da-hoon (da hön´) *n.* An evergreen shrub native to the southern United States.

dai-ly (dā´lē) *adj. pl.* **-lies** To occur, appear, or happen every day of the week. *n.* A newspaper which is published daily.

daily double *n.* A bet that is won by picking the winners of two specified races occurring on the same day.

dain-ty (dān´tē) *adj. pl.* **-ties** Having or showing refined taste; delicately beautiful. **daintily** *adv.* **daintiness** *n.*

dai-qui-ri (dī´ki rē) *n.* A cocktail made with rum and lime juice.

dair-y (dâr´ē) *n. pl.* **-ies** A commercial establishment which processes milk for resale. **dairymaid** *n.* **dairyman** *n.*

dairy cattle *n.* Cows raised for their milk.

dai-sy (dā´zē) *n. pl.-ies* A plant having flowers with yellow disks and white rays.

dale (dāl) *n.* A small valley.

dal-ly (dal´ē) *v.* To waste time; to dawdle; to flirt. **dallier** *n.* **dalliance** *n.*

Dal-ma-tian (dal mā´shan) *n.* A breed of dog with short, smooth white hair with black spots. *adj.* Pertaining to Dalmatia or its people.

dal-ton-ism (dal´to niz˝um) *n.* Color blindness; unable to differentiate between red and green.

dam (dam) *n.* A barrier constructed for controlling or raising the level of water; female animal who has had offspring.

dam-age (dam´ij) *n.* An injury to person or property; in law, the compensation given for loss or injury. **damage** *v.* **damageable** *adj.* **damagingly** *adv.*

dam-an (dam´an) *n.* A small, rabbit-like animal.

dam-a-scene (dam´a sēn˝) *v.* To form designs in metal, by inlaying with gold or other precious metals, or by etching.

dam-ask (dam´ask) *n.* An elaborately patterned, reversible fabric, originally made of silk.

damask rose *n.* A color of deep pink or rose.

dame (dām) *n.* A mature woman or matron. *Slang.* A woman. **Dame** *Brit.* A title given to a woman, the female equivalent of a British Lord.

dame's violet *n.* A perennial plant with fragrant spikes of white or purple flowers.

dam-mar (dam'ẽr) *n.* A resin from various coniferous trees which is for making colorless varnish.

damn (dam) *v.* To swear or curse at; to pronounce as bad, worthless, or a failure.

damp (damp) *adj.* Between dry and wet; of or relating to poisonous gas or foul air found in a mine. **dampish** *adj.* **damply** *adv.*

dam-sel (dam'zel) *n.* A maiden; a young unmarried woman.

dam-son (dam'zon) *n.* The tree that produces an oval purple plum of the same name.

dance (dans) *v.* To move rhythmically to music using improvised or planned steps and gestures. **dance** *n.* **dancer** *n.*

dan-de-lion (dan'de lī˝on) *n.* A plant considered a weed in North America, having yellow flowers and green notched leaves, sometimes used in salads and in making wines.

dan-dle (dan'dl) *v.* To move a child or infant up and down on the knees or in the arms with a gentle movement. **dandler** *n.*

dan-druff (dan'druf) *n.* A scaly material which forms on the scalp and is shed from time to time.

dan-dy (dan'dē) *n. pl.* **dandies** A man who is very interested in an elegant appearance and fine clothes. *Informal adj.* Excellent very fine. **dandily** *v.* **dandy, dandyish,** *adj.,* **dandyism** *n.*

dan-ger (dān'jẽr) *n.* An exposure to injury, evil, or loss.

dan-ger-ous (dān'jẽr us) *adj.* Unsafe. **dangerously** *adv.* **dangerousness** *n.*

dan-gle (dang'gl) *v.* To hang loosely and swing to and fro; to have an unclear grammatical relation in a sentence.

dank (dangk) *adj.* Uncomfortably damp; wet and cold. **dankly** *adv.* **dankness** *n.*

dan-seuse (dän soez') *n. pl.* **-seuses** A female ballet dancer.

dap-per (dap'ẽr) *adj.* Stylishly dressed.

dap-ple (dap'l) *v.* To make variegated or spotted in color.

da-querre-o-type (da ger'o tīp') *n.* A very early photographic process which used silver-coated metallic plates that were sensitive to light.

dar-by (där'bē) *n.* A tool for leveling a plaster.

dare (dâr) *v.* To have the boldness or courage to under take an adventure; to challenge a person as to show proof of courage. **dare** *n.* **daring** *adj.* **daringly** *adv.*

dare-devil (dâr'dev'il) *n.* A person who is bold or reckless. **daredevilry** *n.* **daredeviltry** *n.*

dark (därk) *adj.* Dim; to have little or no light; to be difficult to comprehend; of a deep shade of color, as black or almost black. **dark** To do in secret; to be in a state of ignorance.

dark adaptation *n.* The manner in which the eye adjusts to reduced amount of light.

Dark Ages *n.* The early part of the Middle Ages.

dark-en *v.* To become or make dark or darker. **darkish** *adj.* **darkly** *adv.*

dark horse *n.* A competitor about whom nothing certain is known.

dark lantern *n.* A handheld lantern whose light can be blocked by a cover at the opening.

dar-kle (där'kl) *v.* To darken or grow dark.

darkling beetle *n.* A brown or black hard-bodied beetle which feeds on decayed plants, stored grain, and fungi.

dark-room (därk'rōm) *n.* A room protected from actinic rays of light, for handling photographic materials sensitive to light.

dar-ling (där'ling) *n.* A favorite person; someone who is very dear; a person tenderly loved. **darlingly** *adv.*

darn (därn) *v.* To mend a hole by filling the gap with interlacing stitches.

dart (därt) *n.* A pointed missile either shot or thrown. **darts** *pl.* The game of throwing darts at a usually round target.

dash (dash) *v.* To break or shatter with a striking violent blow; to move quickly; to rush; to finish or perform a duty in haste. **dash** *n.* **dasher** *n.*

das-tard (das'tėrd) *n.* A coward; a sneak. **dastardliness** *n.* **dastardly** *adj.*

das-y-ure (das'ē ur) *n.* A small carnivorous marsupials native from Australia and Tasmania.

da-ta (dā'ta) *n. pl.* The figures or facts from which conclusions may be drawn.

data bank *n.* In computer science, the location in a computer where information is stored.

data processing *n.* In computer science, the business of handling and storing information using computers and other available machines.

date (dāt) *n.* A particular point in time; a day, month, or year; the exact time at which something happens; a social engagement; a person's partner on such an occasion.

date-line (dāt'līn') *n.* The line or phrase at the beginning of a periodical giving the date and place of publication; the 180th meridian on a map or globe which is where a day begins.

date palm *n.* A palm that bears dates.

da-tum (dā'tum) *n. pl.* **-ta** A single piece of information.

daub (dob) *v.* To coat or smear with grease, plaster, or an adhesive substance, to defile, to put on without taste. **dauber** *n.*

daugh-ter (do'tėr) *n.* The female offspring of a man or woman; a female descendant of any age. **daughterly** *adj.*

daughter–in–law *n.* A son's wife.

daunt (dont) *v.* To intimidate or discourage.

dav-en-port (dav'en pört') *n.* A large sofa or couch.

Davis, Jefferson *n.* President of the Confederate States of America from 1861-1865.

dav-it (dav'it) *n.* A small crane on the side of a ship, for lifting its boats.

da-vy (dā'vē) *n.* A miner's lamp.

daw-dle (dod'l) *v.* To waste; to take more time than is needed. **dawdler** *n.*

dawn (don) *n.* The beginning of a new day, to begin to understand, expand, or develop, to grow lighter. **dawning** *n.*

day (dā) *n.* The period of time that falls between dawn and nightfall; the time that is represented by one rotation of the earth upon its axis, twenty-four hours; the large portion of a day spent in a particular way.

day-care (dā' kâr) *n.* A service provided for working mothers and fathers, offering daytime supervision, training, and safekeeping for their children while they work.

day-dream (dā'drēm″) *n.* A visionary fancy that appears when awake.

day laborer *n.* A person who works during the day, an unskilled laborer.

daylight saving time *n.* The time of the year, beginning in the spring, when clocks are moved ahead by one hour.

Day of Atonement *n.* Yom Kippur.

daze (dāz) *v.* To bewilder or stun with a heavy blow or shock. **dazedly** *adv.*

DBA *abbr.* Doing business as.

DC *abbr.* District of Columbia.

D–day *n., Milit.* June 6, 1944, the day on which the Allies invaded France in World War II.

dea-con (dē'kon) *n.* The clergyman who ranks immediately below a priest. **deaconess** *n.* **deaconry** *n.* **deaconship** *n.*

de-ac-ti-vate (dē ak'ti vāt″) *v.* To cause to become inactive.

dead (ded) *adj.* Without life; no longer in existence or use; dormant; quiet; in law, no longer in force.

dead-beat (ded'bēt') *n., Slang* A person who avoids paying his debts.

dead-en (ded'en) *v.* To weaken in sensitivity.

dead-end (ded'end') *n.* A point from which one cannot progress; a street having no outlet.

dead heat *n.* A contest where entrants finish at the same time.

dead-line (ded'līn') *n.* A time limit when something must be finished.

dead-ly (ded'lē) *adj.* Very dangerous; likely to cause death.

dead pan *adj., Slang* Having no expression on one's face.

dead reckoning *n., Naut.* A method of

computing a vessel's position by compass and log without the use of astronomical observation.

Dead Sea *n.* The salt lake between Jordan and Israel.

deaf (def) *adj.* Totally or partially unable to hear; refusing or unwilling to listen.

deal (dēl) *v.* To distribute or pass out playing cards; to be occupied or concerned with a certain matter; to discuss, consider, or take affirmative action. *n.* An indefinite amount; a business transaction. **dealer** *n.*

deal-ing (dē´ling) *n., Slang* Involved in the buying and selling of illegal drugs.

dean (dēn) *n.* The head administrator of a college, high school, or university supervising students. **deanship** *n.*

dear (dēr) *adj.* Greatly cherished; loved. **dearly** *adv.* **dearness** *n.*

death (deth) *n.* Termination; the permanent cessation of all vital functions.

death-bed (deth´bed´) *n.* The bed on which a person dies; the last hours.

death-blow (deth´blō˝) *n.* An event or blow that is fatal.

death mask *n.* A cast of a person's face that is taken just after death.

death rate *n.* Ratio of deaths to the population of a certain area.

death-trap (deth´trap´) *n.* An unsafe structure.

death-watch (deth´woch´) *n.* A vigil kept on a person who is dying.

deb (deb) *n.* A debutante.

de-ba-cle (dā bä´kl) *n.* A sudden downfall, failure, or collapse.

de-bar (di bär´) *v.* To bar from a place; to preclude; to prohibit.

de-bark (di bärk´) *v.* To disembark.

de-base (di bās´) *v.* To lower in character or value; demean. **debasement** *n.*

de-bate (di bāt´) *v.* To discuss or argue opposing points; to consider; to deliberate. **debate** *n.* **debatable** *adj.* **debatably** *adv.* **debater** *n.*

de-bauch (di boch´) *v.* To lead away from morals; to corrupt. **debauchery** *n.* **debauchment** *n.*

de-bauch-er-y *n.* The excessive indulgence in sensual pleasures.

de-ben-ture (di ben´chėr) *n.* A voucher given as an acknowledgment of debt.

de-bil-i-tate (di bil´i tāt´) *v.* To make feeble or weak. **debilitation** *n.* **debilitative** *adj.*

deb-it (deb´it) *n.* A debt or item recorded in an account *v.* To enter a debt in a ledger; to charge someone with a debt.

deb-o-nair (deb˝o nâr´) *adj.* Characterized by courtesy and charm.

dé-bride-ment (di brēd´ment) *n.* Removal of contaminated tissue from a wound in order to prevent the spread of infection.

de-brief (dē brēf´) *v.* To interrogate or question in order to obtain information.

de-bris (de brē´) *n.* Scattered or discarded remains or waste.

debt (det) *n.* That which someone owes, as money, services, or goods; an obligation to pay or render something to another.

debt-or (det´ėr) *n.* A person owing a debt to another.

de-bug (dē bug) *v.* To find and remove a concealed electronic listening device; in computer science, to remove errors in a computer program.

de-bunk (di bungk´) *v., Informal* To expose false pretensions, to show the error in false opinions, statements or claims.

de-but (dā bū´) *n.* A first public appearance; the formal introduction to society; the beginning of a new career. **debut** *v.*

deb-u-tante (deb´ū tänt´) *n.* A young woman making her debut in society.

dec-ade (dek´ād) *n.* A period of ten years; a set or group of ten.

de-ca-dence (dek´a dens) *n.* A process of decay or deterioration; a period or condition of decline, as in morals. **decadent** *adj.* **decadently** *adv.*

dec-a-dent (dek´a dent) *adj.* Deteriorating; being in a state of decline. *n.* One who is decadent.

dec-a-gon (dek´a gon´) *n., Geom.* A polygon with ten

sides and ten angles. **decagonal** *adj.* **dec-agonally** *adv.*

dec-a-gram *or* **del-a- gram (dek´a gram´)** *n.* In the metric system, a measure of weight equal to 10 grams.

de-cal (dē´kal) *n.* A design or picture transferred by decalcomania.

de-cal-co-ma-nia (di kal˝ko mā´nē a) *n.* The process of transferring pictures or designs printed on special paper to glass, wood, and other materials.

dec-a-li-ter *or* **dek-a-li-ter (dek´a lē´tėr)** *n.* In the metric system, a measure of capacity equal to 10 liters.

dec-a-logue *or* **dec-a-log (dek´a log´)** *n.* The Ten Commandments.

dec-a-me-ter *or* **dek-a-me-ter (dek´a mē´tėr)** *n.* In the metric system, a measure of length equal to 10 meters.

de-cam-e-ter (de kam´et ėr) *n.* A line of verse or consisting of ten metrical feet.

de-camp (di kamp´) *v.* To break camp; to leave or depart suddenly.

de-cant (di cant´) *v.* To pour off liquid without disturbing the sediments; to pour from one container to another. **decantation** *n.*

de-cant-er (di kan´tėr) *n.* A decorative stoppered bottle for serving wine or other liquids.

de-cap-i-tate (di kap´i tāt´) *v.* To cut off the head; to behead **decapitation** *n.* **decapitator** *n.*

de-car-bon-ize (dē kär´bo nīz) *v.* To remove carbon from a substance or motor.

de-cath-lon (di kath´lon) *n.* An athletic event with ten different track and field events in all of which each contestant participates, an olympic event.

de-cay (di kā´) *v.* To decline in quantity or quality; to rot. *Phys.* To diminish or disintegrate by radioactive decomposition.

de-cease (di sēs´) *v.* To die, one's life ends **decedent** *n.* A deceased person.

de-ceit (di sēt´) *n.* Deception; the quality of being deceptive; falseness, concealment. **deceitful** *adj.* **deceitfully** *adv.*

de-ceive (di sēv´) *v.* To mislead by falsehood; to lead into error; to delude. **de-ceivable** *adj.* **deceiver** *n.*

de-cel-er-ate (dē sel´e rāt) *n.* To decrease in velocity. **deceleration** *n.*

De-cem-ber (di sem´bėr) *n.* The 12th month of the year, having 31 days.

de-cen-ni-al (di sen´ē al) *adj.* Happening once every 10 years; continuing for ten years. **decennially** *adv.*

de-cent (dē´sent) *adj.* Adequate; satisfactory; kind; generous; characterized by propriety of conduct, speech, or dress; respectable. *Informal* Properly or adequately clothed; respectable. **decently** *adv.* **decentness** *n.*

de-cen-tral-ize (dē sen´tra līz˝) *v.* To divide the administrative functions of a central authority among several local authorities; to reorganize into smaller and more dispersed parts. **decentralization** *n.*

de-cep-tion (di sep´shan) *n.* The act of deceiving; the factor state of being deceived; anything which deceives or deludes.

de-cep-tive (di sep´tiv) *adj.* Having the tendency or power to deceive. **deceptively** *adv.* **deceptiveness** *n.*

dec-i-are (des´ē âr´) *n.* In the metric system, one tenth of an are.

de-ci-bel (des´i bl´) *n.* A measurement of sound; one tenth of a bel.

de-cide (di sīd´) *v.* To settle; to determine, as a controversy or contest; to determine the conclusion or issue of; to make up one's mind. **decider** *n.*

de-cid-ed *adj.* Definite or unquestionable; exhibiting, determination, resolute. **decidedly** *adv.* **decidedness** *n.*

de-cid-u-ous (di sij´ŏ us) *adj., Biol.* Shedding or falling off at maturity or at a certain season, such as fruit, leaves, petals, antlers, or snake skins.

dec-i-gram (des´i gram´) *n.* In the metric system, the tenth part of a gram.

dec-i-li-ter (des´i lē´tėr) *n.* In the metric system, the tenth part of a liter.

de-cil-lion (di sil´yon) *n.* The cardinal number written as one followed by thirty-three zeros; a thousand nonillions.

dec-i-mal (des´i mal) *n.* A proper fraction based on the number 10 and indicated by the use of a decimal point; every decimal place indicating a multiple of a power of 10; a number with a decimal point; a decimal fraction or one of its digits.

decimal point *n.* A period placed to the left of a decimal fraction.

dec-i-mate (des´i māt´) *v.* To destroy or kill a large proportion of something; to select by lot and kill one out of every ten. **decimation** *n.*

dec-i-meter (des´i mē´tėr) *n.* In the metric system, the tenth part of a meter.

de-ci-pher (di sī´fėr) *v.* To determine the meaning of something obscure, as a poor handwriting; to translate from code or cipher into plain text; to decode.

de-ci-sion (di sizh´an) *n.* The act of deciding; a judgment or conclusion reached by deciding; in boxing, a victory decided when there has not been a knockout.

de-ci-sive (di sī´siv) *adj.* Ending uncertainty or dispute; conclusive; characterized by firmness; unquestionable; unmistakable. **decisively** *adv.*

dec-i-stere (des´i stēr´) *n.* In the metric system, a cubic decimeter, or the tenth part of a stere.

deck (dek) *n.* A set of playing cards. *Naut.* A horizontal platform that covers or extends across a vessel, and serves as both a floor and a roof. **hit the deck** To rise from bed; to get up early; to be ready for action. **on deck** Present and ready for action. **all decked out** To decorate or dress elegantly. *v.* To knock someone or something down with a punch.

deck chair *n.* A reclining chair that folds, and is often used on patios, beaches, lawns, and ship decks.

de-claim (di klām´) *v.* To speak or deliver loudly and rhetorically; to give a formal speech; to attack verbally. **declamation** *n.* **declamatory** *adj.*

de-clar-ant (di klâr´ant) *n.* One who makes a declaration.

de-clare (di klâr´) *v.* To make known or clear; to state formally or officially; to say emphatically; to avow; to assert; to make full claim to, as goods liable to duty; to proclaim an opinion or choice for or against something. **declarer, declaration** *n.* **declarative** *adj.*

de-class (dē klas´) *v.* To remove from one's class; to lose standing.

de-clas-si-fy (dē klas´i fī´) *v.* To remove the security classification of a document, information considered important to national security of a nation. **declassification** *n.*

de-clen-sion (di klen´shan) *n.* A descent; a sloping downward; a decline; a deviation, as from a belief. *Gram.* The inflection of nouns, pronouns, and adjectives according to case, number, and gender **declensional** *adj.*

dec-li-nate (dek´li nāt´) *adj.* Bending downward.

dec-li-na-tion (dek´li nā´shan) *n.* The act of bending downward or inclining; deviation, as in conduct or direction; the angle formed between the direction of a compass needle and the true north; a polite refusal.

de-cline (di klīn´) *v.* To reject or refuse something; to grow frail gradually, as in health; to bend or incline to the side or downward; to refuse politely. *Gram.* To give the inflected form of a noun, pronoun, or adjective. *n.* The act or result of deterioration, to decline in heath. **declinable** *adj.* **declinational** *adj.* **declination** *n.* **decliner** *n.* **decline** *n.*

de-cliv-i-ty (di klīv´i tē) *n. pl.* **-ties** A steep downward slope or surface. **declivitous** *adj.* **declivous** *adj.*

de-coct (di kokt´) *v.* To extract by boiling; to condense. **decoction** *n.*

de-code (dē kōd´) *v.* To convert from a coded message into plain language. **decoder** *n.*

de-col-or-a-tion (dē kul˝ėr ā´shan) *n.* The removal or loss of color.

de-com-pen-sa-tion (dē˝kom pen sā´shan) *n.* The inability of the heart to sustain a constant heart beat.

de-com-pose (dē′kom pōz′) v. To decay; to separate into constituent parts. **decomposable** adj. **decomposer** n. **decomposition** n.

de-com-pound (dē″kom pound′) adj. Having compound divisions.

de-com-press (dē′kom pres′) v. To relieve of pressure; to bring a person back to normal air pressure, reduce pressure on an organ, as divers or caisson workers. **decompression** n.

de-com-pres-sion (dē″kom presh′an) n. The process of decreasing air pressure from a chamber; adjustment to normal atmospheric pressure.

de-con-ges-tant (dē′kon jes tant′) n. An agent that relieves congestion.

de-con-tam-i-nate (dē″kon tam′i nāt) v. To make free of contamination by destroying or neutralizing poisonous chemicals, radio activity, or other harmful elements. **decontamination** n. **decontaminator** n.

de-con-trol (dē′kon trōl′) v. To free from the control of, especially from governmental control.

de-cor (dā kor′) n. The style of decorating a room, office, or home.

dec-o-rate (dek′o rāt′) v. To adorn or furnish with fashionable or beautiful things; to confer a decoration or medal upon. **decorator** n.

dec-o-ra-tion (dek′o rā′shan) n. The process, art, or act of decorating; a thing or group of things which decorate; an emblem, badge, medal, or award.

Decoration Day n. Memorial Day, the day set aside to honor all fallen soldiers with special services and flowers placed on their graves.

dec-o-ra-tive (dek′ėr a tiv) adj. Suitable for decoration; ornamental. **decoratively** adv. **decorativeness** n.

dec-o-ra-tor (dek′o rā″tėr) n. A person who decorates, a profession who decorates the interior of houses or buildings.

dec-o-rous (dek′ėr us) adj. Marked by decorum; seemly; proper, as dress or speech. **decorously** adv. **decorousness** n.

de-cor-ti-cate (dē kor′ti kāt″) v. To strip or remove the bark; to peel.

de-co-rum (di kōr′um) n. Proper behavior; good or fitting conduct.

de-coy (di koi′) n. An artificial animal used to lure game, especially ducks; a means to mislead, trap, or lure into danger.

de-crease (di krēs′) v. To grow or cause to grow gradually less or smaller; to diminish. n. The process or act of decreasing or the resulting state; a decline.

de-cree (di krē) n. An authoritative and formal order or decision; a judicial judgment. **decree** v.

dec-re-ment (dek′re ment) n. The process or act of decreasing; the amount lost by gradual waste or diminution.

de-crep-it (di krep′it) adj. Broken down or worn out by old age or excessive use. **decrepitly** adv. **decrepitude** n.

de-cre-scen-do (dē′kri shen′dō) n. pl. -dos Music A gradual decrease in force or loudness. **decrescendo** adv.

de-crim-i-nal-ize (dē′krim inal īz) v. To remove the criminal classification of; to no longer prohibit.

de-cry (di krī′) v. To disparage or condemn openly; to denounce. **decrier** n.

de-cum-bent (di kum′bent) adj. To lie down; reclining.

dec-u-ple (dek′ü pel) adj. Tenfold; containing groups of ten.

de-curved (dē kürvd′) adj. Bent or curved downward.

de-cus-sate (di kus′āt) v. To arrange in pairs at acute right angles.

de-dans (de däns) n. The open gallery for spectator's viewing, as a tennis court.

ded-i-cate (ded′i kāt′) v. To set apart, as for sacred uses; to set apart for special use, duty, or purpose; to address or inscribe a work of literature, art or music to someone; to commit oneself to a certain cause, course of action, or thought; to unveil or open to the public, a book inscribed to a person or cause. **dedication** n. **dedicatory** adj.

ded-i-ca-tion (ded″i kā′shan) n. The act

of dedicating or devotion to a sacred use or meaning.

de-dif-fer-en-ti-a-tion (dē dif´e ren˝ shē ā´shan) *n.* A reversion of specialized cells to a more generalized state, often prior to a major or more important change.

de-duce (di dōs´) *v.* To derive a conclusion by reasoning. **deducible** *adj.*

de-duct (di dukt´) *v.* To subtract or take away from; to subtract or separate, in numbering, estimating, or calculating;

de-duc-tion (di duk´shan) *n.* The act of deducing or subtracting; an amount that is or may be deducted; the process or act of deducting. **deductive** *adj.* **deductively** *adv.*

deed (dēd) *n.* Anything performed or done; a notable achievement or feat; in law, a legal document, especially one relating to the transference of property. **deedless** *adj.*

deem (dēm) *v.* To judge or consider.

deep (dēp) *adj.* Extending far below a surface; extending far backward from front to rear or far inward from an outer surface; penetrating to or coming from a depth; hard to understand; extreme; intense; vivid and rich in shade; low in pitch; resonant. *n., Naut.* The interval between two fathoms marked in succession. **to go off the deep end** To become excited or hysterical. **the deep** *Poet.* The ocean or sea. **deeply** *adv.* **deepness** *n.*

deep-en (dē´pen) *v.* To become or make deep or deeper.

deep-freeze *v.* To quick-freeze. *Slang* An appliance for storing frozen foods.

deep-root-ed (dēp´rō´tid) *adj.* Firmly implanted, said of beliefs; of or relating to a plant with very long roots.

deep-seat-ed (dēp´sē´tid) *adj.* Deeply rooted or lodged far below the surface.

deep-six (dēp´siks) *v., Slang* To throw overboard; to get rid of; to toss out.

deer (dēr) *n. pl.* **deer** A hoofed ruminant mammal having deciduous antlers, usually in the male only, as the elk, moose, and reindeer.

deer fly *n.* Any of the various bloodsucking flies.

deer-skin (dēr´skin´) *n.* A deer's hide or the leather made from it.

de-es-ca-late (dē es´ka lāt) *v.* To decrease or be decreased gradually, as in intensity, scope, or effect.

de-face (di fās´) *v.* To spoil or mar the appearance or surface of something.

de fac-to (dē fak´tō) *adj.* Really or actually exercising authority.

de-fal-cate (di fal´kāt) *v.* To embezzle; to misuse funds. **defalcation** *n.*

def-a-ma-tion (def´a mā´sham) *n.* The publishing of slanderous words for the purpose of injuring someone's reputation.

de-fame (di fām´) *v.* To slander or libel, lies. **defamation** *n.* **defamatory** *n.* **defamer** *n.*

de-fault (di folt´) *v.* To neglect to fulfill an obligation or requirement, as to pay money due or to appear in court; to forfeit by default. *n.* The failure to participate or compete in a competition.

de-fea-sance (di fē´zans) *n.* A condition of rendering null or void.

de-feat (di fēt´) *v.* To win a victory; to beat; to prevent the successful outcome of; to frustrate; to baffle; in law, to make void; to annul.

de-feat-ism (di fē´tiz um) *n.* The practice of those accepting defeat as inevitable; failure.

def-e-cate (def´e kāt˝) *v.* To discharge feces from the bowels. **defecation, defecator** *n.*

de-fect (dē´fekt) *n.* The lack of something desirable or necessary for completeness or perfection; a fault or imperfection. **defection, defector** *n.*

de-fec-tion (di fek´shan) *n.* The conscious abandonment of a person or cause to which one is bound by allegiance or duty.

de-fec-tive (di fek´tiv) *adj.* Having a defect; imperfect. *Grammar* Lacking one or more of the infected forms normal for its class. *Psychol.* Having less than normal intelligence. **defectively** *adv.*, **defective-**

ness *n.*

de-fend (di fend´) *v.* Protect.

de-fend-ant (di fen´d*a*nt) *n.* The person charged in a criminal or civil lawsuit.

de-fense (di fens´) *n.* The action of defending.

defense mechanism *n.* The unconscious mental process of self-protection against an invading microorganism.

de-fen-si-ble (d*i* fen´s*i* bl) *adj.* Capable of being defended against injury or assault.

de-fen-sive (di fen´siv) *adj.* Serving to defend against aggression.

de-fer (di fer´) *v.* To delay or postpone, to put off doing. **deferment** *n.*

de-fer-ves-cence (dē˝fêr ves´*e*ns) *n.* A reducing of fever.

de-fi-ance (di fī´*a*ns) *n.* The instance or act of defying; a challenge. **defiant** *adj.* **defiantly** *adv.*

deficiency disease *n.* A disease due to the lack of dietary elements, such as vitamins or minerals.

de-fi-cient (di fish´ent) *adj.* Lacking in a necessary element.

def-i-cit (def´i sit) *n.* Deficiency in amount.

deficit spending *n.* The practice of spending public funds beyond income.

de-file (di fīl´) *v.* To soil or make unclean; violate one's reputation.

de-fine (di fīn´) *v.* To identify the essential qualities; to make clear.

de-fin-i-en-dum (di fin˝ē en´d*u*m) *n.* The term or expression to be defined, defining as in a dictionary entry.

de-fin-i-ens (di fin´ē *e*nz) *n.* A description, expression or statement that defines something.

def-i-nite (def´i nit) *adj.* Clearly defined; having distinct limits; not vague or general.

de-fin-i-tive (di fin´i tiv) *adj.* Serving to provide a final solution.

def-i-nit-ize (def´i ni tīz˝) *v.* To make final or definite.

def-la-grate (def´l*e* grāt˝) *v.* To set fire to; to cause to burn rapidly with intense heat.

de-flate (di flāt´) *v.* To cause to collapse by removing gas or air; to remove self-esteem

or conceit. To reduce or restrict money or spending so that prices decline. **deflation** *n.*, **deflationary** *adj.*

de-flect (di flekt´) *v.* To turn aside; to swerve from a course. **deflectable, deflective** *adj.*, **deflection, deflector** *n.*

de-flower (di flou´êr) *v.* To rob one's virginity; to violate; to rob of charm or beauty.

de-fog (dē fog) *v.* To remove fog from, as from the inside of an automobile. **defogger** *n.*

de-fo-li-ant (dē fō´lē ant) *n.* A chemical sprayed or dusted on plants or trees to cause the leaves to drop off. **defoliate** *v.*

de-force (di fōrs´) *v.* To withhold or keep by force or violence, from the rightful owner.

de-for-est (dē for´ist) *v.* To clear of forests or trees. **deforestation** *n.*

de-form (di form´) *v.* To distort the form of; to be distorted; to mar the beauty or excellence of; to spoil the natural form of. **deformable** *adj.*, **deformation** *n.*

de-fraud (de frod´) *v.* To cheat; to swindle. **defrauder** *n.*

de-fray (di frā´) *v.* To provide for or to make payment on something. **defrayable** *adj.* **defrayal** *n.*

de-frock (dē frok´) *v.* To deprive a priest or minister, the right to practice the functions of his office.

de-frost (di frost´) *v.* To cause to thaw out; to remove the ice or frost from, free of ice. **defroster** *n.*

deft (deft) *adj.* Skillful and neat in one's actions. **deftly** *adv.* **deftness** *n.*

de-funct (di fungkt´) *adj.* Dead; deceased. **defunctive** *adj.* **defunctness** *n.*

de-fuse (dē fūz´) *v.* To remove the fuse from; to make less dangerous or hostile.

de-fy (di fī´) *v. pl.* **-fies** To confront or resist boldly and openly; to challenge someone to do something or not do something; to dare, to provoke. **defier** *n.*

deg *abbr.* Degree.

De Gaulle, Charles *n.* (1890-1970) French general and statesmen.

de-gauss (dē gous´) v. To neutralize the magnetic field of something.

de-gen-er-ate (di jen´e rāt´) v. To decline in quality, value, or desirability; to deteriorate; to become worse. *adj.* Morally depraved or sexually deviant. **degenerate, degeneracy** *n.*, **degeneratively, degenerative** *adv.*

de-glu-ti-tion (dē˝glü tish´an) n. The act or process of swallowing.

de-grade (dē grād´) v. To reduce in rank, status, or grade; to demote; to reduce in quality or intensity. **degraded** *adj.* **degradedly** *adv.* **degradedness** *n.*

de-gree (di grē´) n. One of a succession of stages or steps; relative manner, condition or respect; the academic title given by an institution of learning upon completion of a course of study or as an honorary distinction; a unit on a temperature or thermometer scale; in law, a measure of severity, as murder in the first degree. *Gram.* A form used in the comparison of adjectives and adverbs. **by degrees** Little by little. **to a degree** Somewhat.

de-gres-sion (di gresh´an) n. Descent; the decrease in rate below a certain amount.

de-hisce (di his´) v. To open, along a natural line, as the capsules or seedpods of a plant.

de-horn (dē horn) v. To remove the horns from an animal.

de-hu-man-ize (dē hū´ma nīz´) v. To deprive of human qualities, especially to make mechanical and routine.

de-hu-mid-i-fy (dē´hū mid´i fī´) v. To remove the moisture from. **dehumidifier** *n.*

de-hy-drate (dē hī´drāt) v. To cause to lose moisture or water. **dehydration** *n.*

de-hyp-no-tize v. To bring out of the hypnotic state.

de-ice (dē īs´) v. To rid of or keep free of ice. **deicer** *n.*

deic-tic (dīk´tik) adj. Demonstrating or pointing out directly.

de-i-fy (dē´i fī´) v. To glorify or idealize; to raise in high regard; to worship as a god, divine Being. **deification** *n.*

deign (dān) v. To think it barely worthy of one's dignity; to condescend.

Dei gratia adv. By the grace of God.

de-ism (dē´iz um) n. A belief in the existence of God but a denial of the validity of revelation.

de-ist (dē´ist) n.One who believes in the existence of God.

de-i-ty (dē´i tē) n. The essential nature or rank of a god; divine character.

dé-jà vu (dā zhä vy´) n. The feeling of having experienced something at a prior time when actually experiencing something for the first time.

de-ject (di jekt´) v. To lower the spirits; to dishearten, downcast. **dejection** *n.* **dejectedness** *n.* **dejectedly** *adv.*

de-jec-tion (di jek´shan) n. The state or condition of being dejected; depression; melancholy.

de ju-re (dē jer´ē) adv. By right; legally or rightfully.

dek-a-stere n. In the metric system, a measure of volume equal to 10 steres.

del abbr. Delete.

de-lam-i-nate (dē lam´i nāt´) v. To split into thin layers.

Del-a-ware (del´a wâr´) n. A state located on the eastern coast of the United States, statehood December 7, 1787, state captial Dover.

de-lay (di lā´) v. To put off until a later time; to defer; to cause to be late or detained; to linger; to waste time; to procrastinate. *n.* The time period that someone is delayed, putting off. **delayer** *n.*

de-le (dē´lē) n., *Printing.* A mark in typesetting which indicates something is to be deleted or taken out of the manuscript.

de-lec-ta-ble (di lek´ta bl) adj. Giving great pleasure; delightful; savory; delicious. **delectability.** *n.*

de-lec-ta-tion (dē˝ lek tā´shan) n. Enjoyment or pleasure.

del-e-gate (del´e git) n. A person with the power to act as a representative for another; a deputy or agent; a person appointed or elected to represent a territory in the House of Representatives, where he may speak but not vote; a member of the lower legislature in Maryland, Virginia, and West Virginia. *v.* To entrust and commit to another.

del-e-ga-tion (del′e gā′shan) *n.* The act of delegating or the state of being delegated; a person or group of people appointed to represent others.

de-lete (di lēt′) *v.* To cancel; to take out, eliminate, to mark out. **deletion** *n.*

del-e-te-ri-ous (del′i tēr′ē us) *adj.* Causing moral or physical injury; harmful. **deleteriously** *adv.* **deleteriousness** n.

delft (delft) *n.* A glazed earthenware, usually blue and white in color, originating in Delft, Holland, in 1310.

Delhi *n.* A city in north central India.

del-i (del ē) *n., Slang* A delicatessen.

de-lib-er-ate (di lib′e rāt′) *v.* To say or do something intentionally; to plan in advance. *adj.* Premeditated; to be leisurely or slow in manner or motion. **deliberateness** *n.* **deliberation** *n.* **deliberately** *adv.* **deliberative** *adj.*

de-lib-er-a-tion (di lib″e rā′shan) *n.* The act of careful consideration beforemaking a decision.

del-i-ca-cy (del′i ka sē) *n. pl.* -cies A select or choice food; the quality or state of being delicate.

del-i-cate (del′i kit) *adj.* Pleasing to the senses; exquisite and fine in workmanship, texture, or construction; pleasing, as in color, taste, or aroma; sensitive and subtle in perception, feeling, or expression; frail in constitution; easily broken or damaged; considerate of the feelings of others. **delicately** *adv.,* **delicateness** *n.*

del-i-ca-tes-sen (del′i ka tes′en) *n.* A store which sells cooked meats, preserved cheeses, pickles, and other delicacies.

de-li-cious (di lish′us) *adj.* Extremely enjoyable and pleasant to the taste. **deliciously** *adv.* **deliciousness** *n.*

de-li-cious (di lish′us) *n.* A variety of red, sweet apples.

de-lict (di likt′) *n.* An offense; a misdemeanor.

de-light (di līt′) *n.* A great joy or pleasure. *v.* To give or take great pleasure; to rejoice; to gratify or please highly. **delighted** *adj.* **delightedly** *adv.*

de-light-ful (di līt′ful) *adj.* Extremely pleasing. **delightfully** *adv.*

Delilah (di lī le) *n.* The Philistine woman who betrayed Samson by cutting off his hair, thus depriving him of his strength; a pleasant but treacherous woman.

de-lim-it (di lim′it) *v.* To give or prescribe the limits of.

de-lin-e-ate (di lin′ē āt) *v.* To represent by a drawing; to draw or trace the outline of something; to sketch; to represent in gestures or words. **delineation** *n.*

de-lin-quent (di ling′kwent) *adj.* Neglecting to do what is required by obligation or law; falling behind in a payment. *n.* A juvenile who is out of control, as violating the law. **delinquency** *n.* **delinquent** *n.* **delinquently** *adv.*

del-i-quesce (del′i kwes′) *v., Chemical* To become liquid by absorbing atmospheric moisture; to melt; to turn to water **deliquescent** *adj.*

de-lir-i-ous (di lēr′ē us) *adj.* Having the characteristic of or pertaining to delirium.

de-lir-i-um (di lēr′ē um) *n.* A temporary or sporadic mental disturbance associated with fever, shock, or intoxication and marked by excitement, incoherence, and hallucination; uncontrolled excitement and emotion. **delirious** *adj.* **deliriously** *adv.* **deliriousness** *n.*

de-liver (di liv′er) *v.* To surrender; to hand over; to set free; to liberate; to give or send forth; to assist in the birth of an offspring; to do what is expected or desired; to take to the intended recipient. **to be delivered of** To give **deliverance, deliverer** *n.*

de-liv-er-ance (di liv′ėr ans) *n.* The condition or act of delivering from captivity, danger, or oppression.

de-liv-er-y (di liv′e rē) *n. pl.* **deliveries** The act of conveying or delivering; a transferring or handing over; the process or act of giving birth, as parturition; the act or manner of throwing.

dell (del) *n*. A small, secluded, usually wooded valley.

de-louse (dē lous´) *v*. To free or remove lice from.

del-phin-ium (del fin´ē *u*m) *n*. Any of a genus of perennial plants of the crowfoot with spurred flowers which are usually blue.

del-ta (del´ta) *n*. The fourth letter in the Greek alphabet; a typically triangular shaped silt deposit at or in the mouth of a river; anything triangular in shape.

delta ray *n*. An electron ejected from matter ionizing radiation.

delta wing *n*. An aircraft with wings that sweep back.

de-lude (di lōd´) *v*. To mislead the mind or judgment; to deceive; to cause to be deceived.

del-uge (del´ūj) *v*. To flood with water; to overwhelm; to destroy. *n*. A great flood.

de-lu-sion (di lō´zhan) *n*. A false, fixed belief held in spite of contrary evidence, false impression. **delusional** *adj*.

de luxe *or* **de-luxe (de leks´)** *adj*. High elegance or luxury.

delve (delv) *v*. To search for information with careful investigation.

Dem *abbr*. Democratic; Democrat.

de-mag-net-ize (dē mag´ni tīz´) *v*. To remove the magnetic properties of. **demagnetization, demagnetizer** *n*.

dem-a-gogue (dem´*a* gog´) *n*. A person who leads the populace by appealing to emotions and prejudices. **demagoguery** *n*. **demagogy** *n*.

de-mand (di mand´) *v*. To ask for in a firm tone; to claim as due; to have the need or requirement for; in law, to summon to court; to make a formal claim to property. *Econ.* The ability and desire to purchase something; the quantity of merchandise wanted at a certain price. **in demand** Sought after; desired. **on demand** On request or presentation; a note payable whenever the lender demands it. **demandable** *adj*. **demander** *n*.

demand deposit *n*. A deposit which may be withdrawn by the depositor at any time.

de-mand-ing (di man´ding) *adj*. Requiring much effort, time or a high degree of attention or precision.

demand note *n*. A written promise to pay a note or sum of money upon demand.

de-mar-cate (di mär´kāt) *v*. To set boundaries or limits; to separate or limit. **demarcation** *n*.

de-mar-ca-tion (dē´mär kā´shan) *n*. The act of defining the limits or boundaries of something.

de-mean (di mēn´) *v*. To behave or conduct oneself in a particular manner; to degrade; to humble oneself or another.

de-mean-or (di mē ner) *n*. A person's conduct toward others; a person's general behavior.

de-ment-ed (di men´tid) *adj*. Insane.

de-men-tia (di men´sha) *n*. An irreversible deterioration of intellectual faculties.

de-mer-it (dē mer´it) *n*. A fault; a defect; a mark against one's record, especially for bad conduct in school.

de-mesne (di mān´) *n*. A manor house with the adjoining lands; a domain; a region; in law, lands held in one's own power.

dem-i-god (dem´ē god´´) *n*. A mythological, semidivine being, especially the offspring of a mortal and a god.

dem-i-john (dem´i jon´) *n*. A large, narrow-necked bottle usually enclosed in wicker.

de-mil-i-ta-rize (dē mil´i ta rīz´) *v*. To remove the military characteristics from, free from the military control. **demilitarization** *n*.

dem-i-mon-daine (dem´ē mon dān´) *n*. A woman who belongs to the demimonde.

dem-i-monde (dem´ē mond´) *n*. A class of women who are supported by wealthy protectors or lovers.

demi-rep (dem´ē rep´´) *n*. A woman of doubtful reputation.

de-mise (di mīz´) *n*. Death; in law, a transfer of an estate by lease or will.

de-mis-sion (di mish´an) *n*. Resignation

or relinquishment.

dem-i-tasse (dem´i tas´) *n.* A small cup of very strong coffee; the name of the cup used to hold this beverage.

dem-i-volt (dem´ē vōlt´) *n.* A half turn made by a horse with the forelegs raised.

dem-o (dem ō) *n. pl.* **-os** *Slang* A demonstration to show product use and purpose of an item.

de-mo-bi-lize (dē mō´bi līz´) *v.* To disband; to release from the military service.

de-moc-ra-cy (di mok´ra sē) *n. pl.* **-cies** A form of government exercised either directly by the people or through their elected representatives; rule by the majority; the practice of legal, political, or social equality.

·dem-o-crat (dem´o krat´) *n.* One who prefers a democracy; one who believes in social and political equality. *adj.* Marked by or advocating democracy. **democratically** *adv.*, **democratize** *v.*

dem-o-crat-ic (dem´´o krat´ik) adj. Pertaining to the nature of democracy; upholding democracy.

Democratic Party *n.* One of the two major political parties in the United States, the other being the Republican Party.

de-mod-ed (dē mō´did) *adj.* Out of fashion.

de-mod-u-late (dē moj´u lāt´) *v.* To detect or intercept a modulated signal.

de-mog-ra-phy (di mog´ra fē) *n.* Study of the characteristics of human population, such as growth, size, and vital statistics. **demographic** *adj.* **demographically** *adv.*

de-mol-ish (di mol´ish) *v.* To tear down; to raze; to completely do away with; to end. **demolisher** *n.* **demolishment** *n.*

dem-o-li-tion (dem´o lish´an) *n.* The process of demolishing, especially destruction with explosives.

de-mon (dē´mon) *n.* An evil spirit; a devil. *Informal* A person of great skill or zeal.

de-mon-e-tize (dē mon´i tīz´) *v.* To deprive the currency of its standard value; to withdraw currency from use.

de-mo-ni-ac (di mō´nē ak´) *adj.* Like or befitting a demon; to be influenced or possessed by or as by demons; of, resembling,

or suggestive of a demon.

de-mon-ol-o-gy (dē´mo nol´o jē) *n.* The belief or study in demons.

de-mon-stra-ble (di mon´stra bl) *adj.* Obvious or apparent, proven. **demonstrability** *n.* **demonstrably** *adv.*

dem-on-strate (dem´on strāt´) *v.* To show or prove by reasoning or evidence; to make a public protest, to march or picket to seek public attention, to prove beyond doubt. **demonstration** *n.*

de-mon-stra-tive (d emon´strativ) *adj.* Serving to point out or demonstrate; able to prove beyond any doubt; conclusive and convincing. *Grammar.* Indicating the object or person referred to; a demonstrative pronoun. **demonstratively** *adv.*, **demonstrativeness** *n.*

dem-on-stra-tor (dem´on strā´´tėr) *n.* One who exhibits the operation of something, one who participates.

de-mor-al-ize (di mor´a līz´) *v.* To undermine the morale or confidence of someone; to degrade; to corrupt. **demoralization** *n.* **demoralizer** *n.*

de-mote (di mōt´) *v.* To reduce in rank, grade, or position. **demotion** *n.*

de-mount *v.* To remove from its mounting, setting, or place of support.

de-mul-cent (di mul´sent) *n.* A soothing substance; any medicine which lessens the effects of irritation, as mucilaginous substances,. **demulcent** *adj.*

de-mur (di mėr´) *v.* To take issue; to object. **demurral** *n.*

de-mure (di mūr´) *adj.* Reserved and modest; coy. **demurely** *adv.*

de-murrer (di mėr´ėr) *n.* In law, a plea to dismiss a lawsuit on the grounds that the plaintiff's statements are insufficient to prove claim.

den (den) *n.* The shelter for a wild animal; a small room in a home used for private study or relaxation.

den-a-ry (den´arē) *adj.* Pertaining to the number ten.

de-na-tion-al-ize (dē nash´a na līz´´) *v.* To deprive a person of national status, attachments or characteristics.

de-na-ture (dē nā´chẻr) v. To change the nature or natural qualities of, especially to make unfit for consumption, without impairing its usefulness. **denaturant** n. **denaturation** n.

den-dri-form adj. Having the form or appearance of a tree.

den-drite (den´drīt) n., Physiol. The branching process of a nerve cell which conducts impulses toward the cell body. **dendritic** adj. **dendritically** adv.

den-drol-ogy (den drol´o jē) n. The botanical study of trees.

de-ne-go-ti-ate (dē˝ni gō´shē āt˝) v. Of agreements of an economical or political nature.

den-gue (deng´gā) n., Pathol. An infectious tropical disease transmitted by mosquitoes, characterized by severe joint pains and fever.

de-ni-al (di nī´al) n. A refusal to comply with a request; refusal to acknowledge the truth of a statement; abstinence; self-denial.

den-i-grate (den´i grāt´) v. To slander; to defame, to degrade.

den-im (den´im) n. A strong, twilled cotton used for jeans, overalls, and work clothes.

den-i-zen (den´i zen) n. An inhabitant or a person who frequents a place.

Den-mark (den märk) n. A country of northern Europe consisting of a group of islands and a peninsula between the Baltic and North Seas.

de-nom-i-nate (di nom´i nāt´) v. To give a name to; to designate.

de-nom-i-na-tion (di nom´i nā´shan) n. The name of a group or classification; the act of calling by name or naming; an organization of similar religious congregations. **denominational** adj.

de-nom-i-na-tor (di nom´i nā´tẻr) n. In mathematics, the term for the bottom half of a fraction, which indicates the number of equal parts into which the unit is divided; a common characteristic or trait.

de-no-ta-tion (dē´nō tā´shan) n. The meaning of, or the object or objects des-

ignated by a word; an indication, as a sign. **denotative** adj.

de-note (di nōt´) v. To make known; to point out; to indicate; to signify; to designate; to mean, said of symbols or words. **denotable** adj. **denotative** adj.

de-noue-ment (dā´nŏ mon´) n. The final solution of a novel, play, or plot.

de-nounce (di nouns´) v. To attack or condemn openly and vehemently; to accuse formally; to announce the ending of something in a formal way. **denouncer** n.

dense (dens) adj. Compact; thick; as in a forest or jungle; close; slow to understand; stupid, hardheaded **densely** adv. **denseness** n.

den-si-tom-e-ter (den˝si tom´ite) n. An instrument for determining optical or photographic density.

den-si-ty (den´si tē) n. pl. -ties The state or quality of being dense or close in parts; the quantity or amount of something per unit measure, area, volume, or length; compactness.

dent (dent) n. A small surface depression made by striking or pressing. v. To put a dent in something; to make meaningful progress or headway.

den-tal (den´tal) adj. Pertaining to the teeth; of or pertaining to dentistry.

dental floss n. A strong, waxed or unwaxed thread used to clean the particles of food between teeth.

dental hygienist n. A licensed dental professional who provides preventive dental care, as cleaning and instruction on how to care for teeth at home.

den-tate (den´tāt) adj. Having teeth, or toothlike projections.

den-ti-cle (den´ti kl) adj. Having a small pointed projection.

den-ti-frice (den´ti fris) n. A preparation in powder or paste form for cleaning the teeth.

den-ti-lin-gual (den˝ti ling´gwal) adj. Of speech sounds that are uttered with the cooperation of the tongue and teeth.

den-tine or **den-tin (den´tin)** n. The hard,

calcified part of the tooth beneath the enamel, containing the pulp chamber and root canals.

den-tist (den'tist) *n.* A licensed person whose profession is the diagnosis, treatment, and prevention of diseases of the gums and teeth. **dentistry** *n.*

den-tist-ry (den'ti strē) *n.* The profession of a dentist, one that deals with the diagnosis, prevention, and treatment of the teeth and malformations of the mouth and gums.

den-ti-tion (den tish'an) *n.* The kind, number, and arrangement of teeth, as in humans and other animals; the process of cutting teeth.

den-ture (den'chėr) *n.* A set of artificial teeth either partial or full; also called a dental plate.

de-nude (di nŏd') *v.* To remove all covering; to be or cause to be naked. To come into view by erosion. **denudation** *n.*

Denver *n.* The capital of the state of Colorado.

de-ny (di nī') *v.* To declare untrue; to refuse to acknowledge or recognize; to withhold; to refuse to grant. **deny oneself** To refuse oneself something desired; selfdenial.

de-o-dar (dē'o dä) *n.* A species of an East Indian cedar tree valued for its wood.

de-o-dor-ant (dē ō'dėr ant) *n.* A product designed to prevent, mask, or destroy unpleasant odors.

de-o-dor-ize (dē ō'do rīz') *v.* To destroy, modify, or disguise the odor of. **deodorization** *n.* **deodorizer** *n.*

de-on-tol-o-gy (dē˝on tol'o jē) *n.* The study of moral obligation.

de-ox-i-dize (dē ok'si dīz') *v.* To remove the oxygen from; to reduce from the state of an oxide. **deoxidization , deoxidate** *n.* **deoxidizer** *n.*

de-ox-y-ri-bo-nu-cle-ic acid (dē ok'sirī'bō nŏ klē'ik as'id) *n.* An ucleic acid which forms a principal constituent of the genes and is known to play a role of importance in the genetic action of the chromosomes, also known as DNA.

dep *abbr.* Depart; deposit; deputy.

de-part (di pärt') *v.* To leave; to go away; to deviate. **life** To die.

de-part-ment (di pärt'ment) *n.* The distinct division or part of something, as in a business, college, or store. *Informal* An area of special activity or knowledge. **departmental** *adj.*

de-part-men-tal-ize (di pärt men'ta līz') *v.* To divide into organized departments **departmentalization** *n.*

department store *n.* A store selling various types of merchandise in several different departments.

de-par-ture (di pär'chėr) *n.* The act of taking leave or going away; a divergence; a deviation; the act of starting out on a new course of action or going on a trip.

de-paup-er-ate (di po'pėr it) *adj.* Poorly developed in physical form or size.

de-pend (di pend') *v.* To rely on; to trust with responsibilities; to be determined or conditioned.

de-pend-a-ble (di pen'da bl) *adj.* Capable of being depended upon; trustworthy. **dependability** *n.* **dependableness** *n.* **dependably** *adv.*

de-pend-ence *or* **de-pend-ance (di pen'dens)** *n.* The quality or state of being dependent; trust or reliance; the state of being contingent on or determined by something else.

de-pend-en-cy *or* **de-pend-an-cy (di pen'den sē)** *n. pl.* **dependencies** The state of being dependent; a territory separate from but still subject to another state, territory, or country.

de-pend-ent (di pen'dent) *adj.* Depending or needing the help of another for support; determined by or contingent on something or someone else. *n. also* **dependant** A person who depends on another person for financial support. **dependently** *adv.*

de-per-son-al-ize (dē pėr'so na liz') *v.* To deprive of personal quality or identity.

de-pict (di pikt') *v.* To represent in a sculpture or a picture; to describe or represent in words. **depiction** *n.*

dep-i-late (dep'i lāt') *v.* To remove the hair

from. **depilation** *n.* **depilator** *n.*

de-pil-a-to-ry (di pil′*a* **tōr′ē)** *n. pl.*-**ries**
A chemical which removes hair, usually
in cream or liquid form.

de-plane (dē plān′) *v.* To disembark or leave
an aircraft.

de-plete (di plēt′) *v.* To exhaust, empty, or
use up a supply of something.

de-plor-a-ble (di plōr′*a* **bl)** *adj.* Grievous;
lamentable; very bad; wretched, **deplor-
ability** *n.* **deplorably** *adv.*

de-plore (di plōr′) *v.* To have, show, or feel
great disapproval of something.

de-ploy (di ploi′) *v.* To spread out; to place
or position according to plans.

de-plume (dē plŏm′) *v.* To deprive of feathers or plumage; to pluck.

de-pone (di pōn′) *v.* To testify; depose.

de-po-nent (di pō′n*e***nt)** *n.* A person who
testifies under oath giving sworn testimony, especially in writing.

de-pop-u-late (dē pop′ū lāt′) *v.* To quickly
remove or lower the population greatly, as
by massacre or disease. **depopulation** *n.*

de-port (di pōrt′) *v.* To banish or expel
someone from a country; to behave in a
specified manner. **deportation** *n.*

de-por-tee (dē″pōr tē′)*n.* One who has been
deported, or one under order for deportation.

de-port-ment (di pōrt′m*e***nt)** *n.* One's conduct; behavior.

de-pose (di pōz) *v.* To remove from a powerful position or office; in law, to declare
or give testimony under oath. **deposable**
adj. **deposal** *n.*

de-pos-it (di poz′it) *v.* To put, place, or set
something down; to entrust money to a
bank; to put down in the form of a layer,
as silt; to give as security or partial
payment, mineral deposits, such as oil, coal
or other minerals. **deposit** *n.* **depositor** *n.*

dep-o-si-tion (dep′*o* **zish′***a***n)** *n.* The act of
deposing, as from an office; that which is
deposited; in law, written testimony given
under oath.

de-pos-i-to-ry (di poz′i tor′ē) *n. pl.* -**ries**
A place where anything is deposited for

safekeeping.

de-pot (dē′pō) *n.* A railroad station. *Milit.*
The place where military materials are
manufactured, stored, and repaired; an
installation for processing personnel; a
warehouse or storehouse.

dep-ra-va-tion (dep″ra vā′sh*a***n)** *n.* The
act of corrupting; the state of being depraved.

de-prave (di prāv′) *v.* To render bad or
worse; in morals, to corrupt or pervert.
depraved *adj.* **depravity** *n.*

dep-re-cate (dep′re kāt′) *v.* To express
regret for or disapproval of; to belittle.
deprecatingly *adv.* **deprecation** *n.* **dep-
recator** *n.*

de-pre-ci-ate (di prē′shē āt′) *v.* To lessen
in value or price. **depreciation** A loss
in efficiency or value resulting from age
or usage; the decline in the purchasing
value of money. **depreciator** *n.* **depre-
ciative** *adj.* **depreciatory** *adj.*

de-pre-ci-a-tion (di prē′shē āt″) *n.* A loss
in efficiency or value resulting from age
or usage; the decline in the purchasing
value of money.

de-press (di pres′) *v.* To make gloomy;
to lower the spirits of; to lessen in energy
or vigor; to press down; to lower; to diminish in value or price. **depressor** *n.*

de-pres-sant (di pres′*a***nt)** *adj.* Acting to
lower the nervous or functional activities.
n. A sedative; a depressant agent.

de-pressed (di prest′) *adj.* Dejected; sad;
low in spirits; lower than, even with, or
below the surface; reduced in amount,
value, or power.

depressed area *n.* An area or region characterized by severe unemployment.

de-pres-sion (di presh′*a***n)** *n.* The state of
being or the act of depressing; a severe
decline in business, accompanied by increasing unemployment and falling prices.
Psych. A condition of deep dejection characterized by lack of response to stimulation and withdrawal.

dep-ri-va-tion (dep″ri vā′sh*a***n)** *n.* The act
or state of being deprived.

de-prive (di prīv´) v. To take something away from; to keep from using, acquiring, or enjoying. **deprivable** adj.

depth (depth) n. The degree or state of being deep; the distance or extent backward, downward, or inward; the most intense part of something; intensity of richness of sound or color; the range of one's comprehension. **depths** pl. A deep part or place; an intense state of feeling or being.

depth charge n. A drum-shaped bomb which is designed to detonate under water at a desired depth.

depth perception n. The visual ability to judge the relationship of space between objects at varying distances and angles.

dep-u-ta-tion (dep´ū tā´shan) n. A person or persons who are acting for another or others; the act of deputing or the state of being deputed.

de-pute (de pūt´) v. To appoint as a deputy, an agent, or other figure of authority; to delegate; to transfer.

dep-u-tize (dep´ū tīz´) v. To act as a deputy; to appoint as a deputy.

dep-u-ty (dep´ū tē) n. pl. **-ties** The person designated or authorized to act for in the absence of, or to assist another, generally a sheriff; a member of a legislative body in certain countries.

de-rac-in-ate (di ras´i nāt´) v. To uproot. **deracination.** n.

de-rail (dē rāl´) v. To run off the rails; to cause a train to run off the rails. *Slang* To change a plan or program.

de-range (di rānj´) v. To disturb the arrangement or normal order of; to unbalance the reason; to make insane. **derangement** n.

der-by (dèr´bē) n. pl. **-bies** An annual horse race especially for three year olds; a race open to all contestants; a stiff hat made from felt with a round crown and a narrow, curved brim.

de-reg-u-late (dē´reg ye lāt) v. To decontrol or remove from regulation or control.

der-e-lict (der´e likt) adj. Neglectful of obligations; remiss. n. Abandoned or deserted, as a ship at sea; a vagrant; a social outcast.

der-e-lic-tion (der´e lik´shan) n. Voluntary neglect, as of responsibility; the fact or state of being abandoned.

de-ride (di rīd´) v. To ridicule; to treat with scornful mirth. **derider** n. **derision** n. **deridingly** adv. **derisive** adj.

de ri-gueur (de ri ger´) adj. Prescribed or required by manners, custom, or fashion.

der-i-va-tion (der´i vā´shan) n. The act of or process of deriving; the process used to form new words by the addition of affixes to roots, stems, or words.

de-riv-a-tive (di riv´a tiv) adj. Of or relating to something derived.

de-rive (di rīv´) v. To receive or obtain from a source. *Chemical* To produce a compound from other substances by chemical reaction.

der-mal (der´mel) adj. Relating to or of the skin.

der-ma-ti-tis (der´ma tī´tis) n., Pathol. An inflammation of the skin.

der-mat-o-gen (der mat´o jen) n. The cellular layer at the tip of a plant root where the epidermis is produced.

der-ma-tol-o-gy (der´ma tol´o jē) n. The medical study of the skin and the diseases related it. **dermatologist** n.

der-ma-to-sis (dür˝ma tō´sis) n. A disease of the skin or skin tisssue.

der-o-gate (der´o gāt´) v. To take or cause to take away from; to distract; to cause to become inferior. **derogation** n.

de-rog-a-tory (di rog´a tōr´ē) adj. Having the effect of belittling; lessening. **derogatorily** adv.

der-rick (der´ik) n. A machine which uses a tackle to lift heavy loads; the framework over the open hole of an oil well, used to support the heavy objects necessary to drill the well.

der-ri-ere (der´ē âr) n. The buttocks.

der-ring–do (der´ing dö´) n. A courageous or daring action or spirit.

der-rin-ger (der´in jèr) n. A short-barreled, large-bored, pocket-sized pistol.

der-ris (der´is) n. An East Indian leguminous plant, a source of an insecticide.

der-vish (dĕrvish) *n.* A member of a Moslem religious order, some of whom express their devotion in whirling dances.

de-salt (dēsôt´) *v.* To remove the salt from sea or saline water.

des-cant (des´kant) *v.* To play or sing a varied melody.

de-scend (di send´) *v.* To move from a higher to a lower level; to pass through inheritance; to come from a particular family. *Astron.* Moving toward the horizon.

de-scen-dant *or* **de-scen-dent (di sen´dent)** *adj.* Proceeding downward; descending from an ancestor.

de-scen-dent (di sen´dant) *n.* One who descends from another individual; an offspring.

de-scent (di sent´) *n.* A slope; lowering or decline, as in level or status.

de-scribe (di skrīb´) *v.* To explain in written or spoken words; to draw or trace the figure of. **describable** *adj.* **describer** *n.*

de-scrip-tion (di skrip´shan) *n.* The technique or act of describing; an account or statement that describes. **descriptive** *adj.*

de-scry (di skrī´) *v.* To catch sight of; to discover by observation. **descrier** *n.*

des-e-crate (des´e krāt´) *v.* To violate something sacred, turning it into something common or profane. **desecration** *n.*

de-seg-re-gate (dē seg´re gāt´) *v.* To remove or eliminate racial segregation in, work, school, military. **desegregation** *n.*

de-sen-si-tize (dē sen´si tīz´) *v.* To make less sensitive; to eliminate the sensitivity of an individual, tissue, or organ, as to an allergen. **desensitizer** *n.* **desensitization** *n.*

des-ert (di sĕrt´) *v.* To abandon or forsake. *Milit.* To be absent without leave with the plan of not returning, AWOL. *n.* A dry, barren region incapable of supporting any considerable population or vegetation without an artificial water supply.

de-ser-tion (di zĕr´shan) *n.* The act of deserting or leaving; in law, the willful abandonment of one's spouse, children, or both.

de-serve (di zĕrv´) *v.* To be worthy of or entitled to.

de-served *adj.* Merited; earned. **deserving** *adj.* **deservingly** *adv.*

des-ic-cant (des´i kant) *n.* A silica gel used to absorb moisture; any material used to absorb moisture.

des-ic-cate (des´i kāt´) *v.* To preserve by drying, such as food; dehydrate. **desiccation** *n.* **desiccative** *adj.*

de-sid-er-a-tum (di sid´e rā´tum) *n.* *pl.* -ta A desired and necessary thing.

de-sign (di zīn´) *v.* To draw and sketch preliminary outlines; to invent or create in the mind; to have as an intention or goal. *n.* An artistic or decorative piece of work; a project; a plan; a well thought-out intention. **designer** *n.*

des-ig-nate (dez´ig nāt´) *v.* To assign a name or title to; to point out; to specify; to appoint or select, as to an office, to set apart. **designate** *adj.* **designation** *n.*

de-sign-ing (di zī´ning) *adj.* Of or relating to the art or act of making designs; scheming or plotting; crafty. **designingly** *adv.*

des-i-nence *n.* Termination or ending, as of a line of verse.

de-sir-a-ble (di zīĕr´a bl) *adj.* Pleasing, attractive, or valuable; worthy of desire. **desirability** *n.* **desirableness** *n.*

de-sire (di zīĕr´) *v.* To long for; to wish; to crave; to request or ask for; to have sexual appetite.

de-sir-ous (di zīĕr´us) *adj.* Having a craving or strong desire.

de-sist (di zist´) *v.* To stop doing something; to cease from an action.

desk (desk) *n.* A table or piece of furniture usually with drawers or compartments and a top for writing; a stand or table to hold reading materials; a department in a newspaper office, as the copy desk.

des-mid (des´mid) *n.* Microscopic, unicellular freshwater green algae.

Des Moines *n.* The capital of the state of Iowa.

des-o-late (des´o lit) *adj.* Made unfit for habitation; useless; forlorn; forsaken. **desolately** *adv.*

des-o-la-tion (des´o la´shan) *n.* A wasteland; the condition of being ruined or deserted; loneliness.

de-spair (di spâr´) *v.* To lose or give up hope; to abandon all purpose. **despair** *n.* **despairing** *adj.* **despairingly** *adv.*

des-per-a-do (des´pe rä´dō) *n. pl.* **-does** *or* **-dos** A dangerous, desperate, or violent criminal.

des-per-ate (des´pèr it) *adj.* Rash, violent, reckless, and without care, as from despair; intense; overpowering.

des-per-a-tion (des´pe rä´shan) *n.* The state of being desperate.

des-pi-ca-ble (des´pi ka bl) *adj.* Deserving scorn or contempt. **despicably** *adv.*

de-spite-ful *adj.* Full of despite or spite; malicious.

de-spise (di spīz´) *v.* To regard with contempt; to regard as worthless. **despiser** *n.*

de-spite (di spīt´) *prep.* Not withstanding; in spite of.

de-spoil (di spoil´) *v.* To rob; to strip of property or possessions by force. **despoiler** *n.* **despoilment** *n.* **despoliation** *n.*

de-spond (di spond´) *v.* To lose hope, courage, or spirit. **despondently** *adv.*

de-spon-den-cy (di spon´den sē) *n.* A dejection of spirits from loss of courage or hope. **despondent** *adj.*

de-spond-ent (di spon´dent) *adj.* Having the feeling of extreme discouragement.

des-pot (des´pot) *n.* An absolute ruler; a tyrant. **despotic** *adj.* **despotically** *adv.* **despotism** *n.*

des-pot-ism (des´po tiz˝um) *n.* A system where a ruler has unlimited power or authority.

des-qua-mate (des´kwa māt˝) *v.* To remove in scales, as the epidermis in certain diseases; to peel off.

des-sert (di zèrt´) *n.* A serving of sweet food, as pastry, ice cream, or fruit, as the last course of a meal.

dessert wine *n.* A sweet wine served with or after dessert.

des-ti-na-tion (des´ti nä´shan) *n.* The point or place to which something or someone is directed; the purpose or end for which something is created or intended.

des-tine (des´tin) *v.* To be determined in advance; to design or appoint a distinct purpose.

des-ti-ny (des´ti nē) *n. pl.* **-nies** The inevitable loss or fate to which a person or thing is destined; fate; a predetermined course of events.

des-ti-tute (des´ti tōt´) *adj.* Utterly impoverished; not having; extremely poor, without the necessities of life.

de-stroy (di stroi´) *v.* To ruin; to tear down; to demolish; to kill; to make useless or ineffective.

de-stroy-er (di stroi´er) *n.* One that destroys. A small maneuverable warship.

de-struct (di strukt´) *n., Aeros.* The deliberate destruction of a defective or dangerous missile or rocket after launch.

de-struc-ti-ble (di struk´ti bl) *adj.* Capable of being destroyed. **destructibility** *n.*

de-struc-tion (di struk´shan) *n.* The state of or the act of being destroyed. **destructive** *adj.* **destructively** *adv.* **destructiveness** *n.*

de-struc-tive (di struk´tiv) *adj.* Causing destruction; designed or having the tendency to destroy.

des-ue-tude (des´wi töd´) *n.* A condition or state of disuse.

de-sul-fur-ize (dē sul´fū rīz´) *v.* To remove sulfur from. **desulfurizer** *n.* **desulfurizationer** *n.*

des-ul-to-ry (des´ul tōr´ē) *adj.* Something that occurs by chance; lacking continuity; aimless.

de-tach (di tach´) *v.* To unfasten, disconnect, or separate; to extricate oneself; to withdraw.

de-tached (di tacht´) *adj.* Separate; apart.

de-tach-ment (di tach´ment) *n.* The process of separating. *Milit.* A shipment of military equipment or personnel from a larger unit for special duty.

de-tail (di tāl) *n.* A part or item considered separately. *Milit.* Military personnel selected for a particular duty.

de-tain (di tān´) *v.* To stop; to keep from proceeding; to delay.

de-tect (di tekt´) *v.* To find out or perceive; to expose or uncover, as a crime. **detectible** *adj.* **detection** *n.* **detector** *n.*

de-tec-tive (di tek´tiv) *n.* A person whose work is to investigate crimes, discover evidence, and capture criminals.

de-tec-tor (di tek´tėr) *n.* One who or that which detects; various devices or instruments for indicating the state or presence of something.

de-tent (di tent´) *n.* A pawl.

de-ten-tion (di ten´shan) *n.* The act of or state of being detained; in law, a time or period of temporary custody which precedes disposition by a court.

de-ter (di ter´) *v.* To prevent or discourage someone from acting by arousing fear, uncertainty, intimidation, or other stronge motion. **determent** *n.*

de-terge *v.* To cleanse; to wash or clear away unclean or offending matter from.

de-ter-gent (di ter´jent) *n.* A cleansing agent which is chemically different from soap. **detergency** *n.* **detergence** *n.*

de-te-ri-o-rate (di tēr´ē o rāt´) *v.* To worsen; to depreciate, to reduce in quality and value, degenerate or decompose. **deterioration** *n.* **deteriorative** *adj.*

de-ter-mi-na-ble (di tür´mi na bl) *adj.* Capable of being determinded, definitely decided.

de-ter-mi-nate (di ter´mi nit) *adj.* Definitely fixed or limited; conclusive. *Bot.* The terminating in a bud or flower, as each axis of an inflorescence. **determinately** *adv.* **determinateness** *n.*

de-ter-mi-na-tion (di tür´mi nā´shan) *n.* The act of deciding definitely; a firm resolution; adherence to purposes or aims.

de-ter-mine (di ter´min) *v.* To settle or decide conclusively or authoritatively; to limit to extent or scope; to fix or ascertain; to give direction or purpose to; in law, to

come to an end. **determinable** *adj.* **determinably** *adv.* **determination** *n.*

de-ter-mined (di ter´mind) *adj.* Showing or having a fixed purpose; resolute; firm. **determinedly** *adv.*

de-ter-min-ism (di tür´mi niz˝um) *n.* A doctrine that happenings are the inevitable outcome of preceding conditions, and that man's actions are determined by inherited or environmental influences and are not based on a free will.

de-ter-rent (di ter´ent) *n.* Something which deters. *adj.* Serving to deter; restrain from doing. **deterrently** *adv.*

de-test (di test´) *v.* To dislike strongly. **detestable** *adj.* **detestably** *adv.*

de-tes-ta-tion (dē˝te stā´shan) *n.* Extreme dislike or hatred; adhorrence.

de-throne (dē thrōn´) *v.* To remove from the throne, to depose, as a king.

det-i-nue (det´i nö) *n.* The unlawful detention of a person's property, or a common-law action to recover the personal property so detained.

det-o-nate (det´o nāt´) *v.* To explode suddenly and violently. **detonation** *n.*

det-o-na-tor (det´o nā´tėr) *n.* The device, such as a fuse or percussion cap, used to detonate an explosive.

de-tour (dē´ter) *n.* A road used temporarily instead of a main road; a deviation from a direct route or course of action.

de-tox-i-fy (dē tok´si fī´) *v.* To free oneself from dependence on drugs or alcohol, to remove from one's system the effects of. **detoxification** *n.*

de-tract (di trakt´) *v.* To take away from; to diminish; to divert. **detraction** *n.* **detractor** *n.* **detractive** *adj.*

de-train (dē trān´) *v.* To leave or cause to leave a railroad train. **detrainment** *n.*

det-ri-ment (de´tri ment) *n.* Damage; injury; loss; something which causes damage, injury, or loss. **detrimental** *adj.* **detrimentally** *adv.*

de-tri-tus (di trī´tus) *n.* Loose fragments or particles formed by erosion, glacial action, and other forces; debris.

de-trun-cate (di trung´kāt) *v.* To cut off; to shorten.

deuce (dŏs) *n.* Two; a playing card or the side of a die with two spots or figures; in tennis, a tie in which each side has 40 points. *Informal* The devil, bad luck, or a mild oath.

De-us *n.* God.

deu-te-ri-um (dŏ tēr´ē um) *n.* The isotope of hydrogen which contains one more neutron in its nucleus than hydrogen does.

Deu-ter-on-o-my *n.* The fifth book of the Old Testament.

deut-sche mark (doi´che märk) *n.* The standard monetary unit of East and West Germany, equivalent to 100 pfennigs.

de-val-u-ate (dē val´ū āt´) *v.* To reduce or lessen the value of. **devaluation** *n.*

dev-as-tate (dev´a stāt´) *v.* To destroy; to ruin; to overwhelm; to overpower. **devastation** *n.*

de-vel-op (di vel´up) *v.* To bring out or expand the potentialities; to make more elaborate; to enlarge; to advance from a lower to a higher stage or from an earlier to a later stage of maturation. *Photog.* To process an image upon a sensitized plate that has been exposed to *v.* The action of light. **developer** *n.* **development** *n.* **developmental** *adj.*

de-vel-op-ment (di vel´up ment) *n.* The act or process of developing; the gradual growth or advancement; a developed section of land where homes are built.

de-vest (di vest´) *v.* To deprive of a right; to take away; divest.

de-vi-ate (dē´vē āt´) *v.* To turn away from a specified prescribed behavior or course, different from the normal patterns of a person or thing. **deviation** *n.*

de-vi-a-tion (dē´vē ā´shan) *n.* The act of turning aside from the right way or course.

de-vice (di vīs´) *n.* Something constructed and used for a specific purpose, as a machine; a crafty or evil scheme or plan; an ornamental design; a motto or an emblem.

dev-il *or* **Devil (dev´il)** *n.* The spirit of evil, the ruler of Hell; Satan; a wicked or male-volent person; a daring, clever, and energetic person; a printer's apprentice, also called a printer's devil. **the devil to pay** Trouble to be expected as a consequence of something.

dev-il-fish (dev´il fish´) *n. pl.* -**fishes** Any of the large cephalopods, as the octopus.

dev-il-ment (dev´il ment) *n.* Mischief.

devil's advocate *n.* One who argues about something with which he or she may not disagree, as for the sake of argument.

devil's food cake *n.* A chocolate cake made from dark chocolate, flour, and eggs.

de-vi-ous (dē´vē us) *adj.* Leading away from the straight, regular, or direct course; rambling; straying from the proper way. *Slang* Underhanded. **deviously** *adv.* **deviousness** *n.*

de-vise (di vīz´) *v.* To form in the mind; to contrive; to plan; to invent; in law, to transmit or give by will. *n.* The act of bequeathing lands; a clause in a will conveying real estate.

de-vi-see (di vī zē´) *n.* In law, the person to whom a devise is made.

de-vi-sor (di vī´zėr) *n.* In law, the person who devises property.

de-vi-tal-ize (dē vīt´a līz´) *v.* To make weak; to destroy the vitality.

de-void (di void´) *adj.* Empty; utterly lacking; without.

de-voir (de vwär´) *n.* The act or expression of courtesy or respect; duty or responsibility.

dev-o-lu-tion (dev´o lö´shan) n. The act of devolving; passage onward from stage to stage; the passing of property by succession or inheritance.

de-volve (di volv´) *v.* To pass duty or authority on to a successor.

de-vote (di vōt´) *v.* To apply time or oneself completely to some activity, purpose, or cause. **devotement** *n.*

de-vot-ed (di vō´tid) *adj.* Feeling or showing devotion; set apart, as by a vow. **devotedly** *adv.* **devotedness** *n.*

dev-o-tee (dev´o tē´) *n.* An enthusiastic supporter; one who is deeply devoted to anything; one marked by religious ardor.

de-vo-tion (di vō´sh*a***n)** *n.* A strong attachment or affection, as to a person or cause; zeal or ardor in the performance of religious duties or acts; the state or act of being devoted. **devotional** *adj.* **devotionally** *adv.*

de-vour (di vour´) *v.* To destroy or waste; to eat up greedily; to engulf. **devourer** *n.*

de-vout (di vout´) *adj.* Extremely and earnestly religious; showing sincerity; displaying piety or reverence, a devotion to religion and religious activities. **devoutly** *adv.* **devoutness** *n.*

dew (dö) *n.* Moisture condensed from the atmosphere in minute drops onto cool surfaces; something which is refreshing or pure.

dew-ber-ry (dö´ber´ē) *n.* The fruit of many species of trailing blackberries; the plant which bears such fruit.

dew-claw (dö´klo´) *n.* A rudimentary toe in some dogs and other mammals.

dew-lap (dö´lap´) *n.* The loose skin under the throat and neck of cattle and certain dogs.

dew point *n.* The temperature at which condensation of vapor occurs.

dew-y–eyed (dö´ē īd´) *adj.* Showing youthful innocence.

dex-ter (dek´ster) *adj.* Pertaining to or situated on the right side.

dex-ter-i-ty (dek ster´i tē) *n.* Proficiency or skill in using the hands or body; cleverness.

dex-ter-ous *or* **dex-trous (dek´strus)** *adj.* Skillful or adroit in the use of the hands, body, or mind. **dexterously** *adv.* **dexterousness** *n.*

dex-tran (dek´str*a***n)** *n.* A white gum-like substance, produced by bacterial action and used as a plasma substitute.

dex-trin (dek´strin) *n.* A group of water soluble gummy substances obtained from starch by the action of heat or weak acids and used as an adhesive.

dex-trose (dek´strōs) *n.* Sugar found in animal and plant tissue and derived synthetically from starches.

dia *abbr.* Diameter.

di-a-base (dī´*a*** bās˝)** *n.* A minor intrusive rock.

di-a-be-tes (dī´*a*** bē´tis)** *n., Pathol.* A metabolic disorder characterized by deficient insulin secretion, leading to excess sugar in the urine and blood, extreme hunger, and thirst.

di-a-bet-ic (dī´*a*** bet´ik)** *adj., Med.* Pertaining to, or affected with diabetes.

di-a-bol-ic *or* **di-a-bol-i-cal (dī´***a*** bol´ik)** Wicked; proceeding from the devil; satanic or infernal. **diabolically** *adv.* **diabolicalness** *n.*

di-a-chron-ic (dī´*a*** kron´ik)** *adj.* Dealing with the phenomena or study of language changes over a period of time.

di-a-crit-ic (dī´*a*** krit´ik)** *n.* A mark near or through a phonetic character or combination of characters, to indicate a special phonetic value or to distinguish words otherwise graphically identical. **diacritical** *adj.* **diacritic** *adj.*

di-a-dem (dī´*a*** dem´)** *n.* A crown or headband worn to symbolize or indicate royalty or honor.

di-ag-no-sis (dī´*a***g nō´sis)** *n. pl.* **diagnoses** An analysis and examination to identify a disease; the result of diagnosis. **diagnose** *v.* **diagnostician** *n.*

di-ag-nos-tics *adj.* Branch of medicine dealing with diagnosis.

di-ag-nos-tic (dī´*a***g nos´tik)** *adj.* A symptom by which a disease is known.

di-ag-o-nal (dī ag´o n*a***l)** *adj.* In mathematics, joining two opposite corners of a polygon which are not adjacent. *n.* A diagonal or slanting plane or line; in a diagonal pattern.

di-a-gram (dī´*a*** gram˝)** *n.* A sketch, plan, drawing, or outline designed to demonstrate or clarify the similarity among parts of a whole or to illustrate how something works. **diagram** *v.*, **diagrammatic, diagrammatical** *adj.*

di-al (dī´*a***l)** *n.* Any graduated circular plate or face upon which a measurement, as pressure or temperature, is indicated by means of a needle or pointer; the face of a clock, watch, or sundial; a control for selecting a radio or television station. *v.* To make a call by means of a dial telephone.

di-a-lect (dī´a lekt˝) *n.* Manner of speaking; a form of a language prevailing in a particular region or area.

di-a-lec-tic (dī´a lek´tik) *n.* The act or practice of argument or exposition in which the conflict between contradictory facts or ideas is resolved. **dialect** *adj.* **dialectic** *adj.*

di-a-lec-tol-o-gy (dī´a lek tol´o jē) *n.* The systematic study of dialects.

di-a-logue *or* **dialog (dī´a log´)** *n.* A conversation involving two or more persons; a conversational passage in a literary work.

di-al-y-sis (dī al´i sis) *n. pl.* **-ses** The separation of substances in solution, which is accomplished by passing them through membranes or filters. **dialysis** A form of *dialysis* used to cleanse the blood of impurities and wastes when the kidneys are unable to perform this function.

di-a-mag-net-ic (dī´a mag net´ik) *adj.* Pertaining to a class of substances which, are slightly repelled by a magnet.

di-am-e-ter (dī am´i tėr) *n.* In mathematics, a straight line which passes through the center of a circle or sphere and stops at the circumference or surface; a measurement of that distance.

di-a-met-ri-cal *or* **diametric (dī´a me´trik)** Along or relating to a diameter; exactly opposite; contrary. **diametrically** *adv.*

dia-mond (dī´mond) *n. pl.* **-s** A very hard, highly reflective, colorless, or whitecrystallineofcarbon used as a gem;a playing card with a red, lozenge-shaped figure; a precious gem; in baseball, the shape of a baseball field.

diamond anniversary *n.* The 60th or 75th anniversary.

diamondback rattlesnake *n.* A large, venomous rattlesnake of the south and western United States and Mexico.

Diamond State *n.* The nickname of the state of Delaware.

di-a-pa-son (dī´a pā´zon) *n.* The full range of a voice or an instrument; in a pipe organ, either of two principal stops which form the tonal basis for the entire scale.

dia-pause (dī´a poz˝) *n.* A period of inactivity or forced dormancy in insects during which growth stops.

di-a-pe-de-sis (dī˜a pi dē´sis) *n.* The passage of blood cells through the capillary walls into the tissues.

di-a-per (dī´pėr) *n.* A folded piece of soft, absorbent material placed between a baby's legs and fastened at the waist. *v.* To put a diaper on.

di-aph-a-nous (dī af´a nus) *adj.* Of such fine texture as to be transparent or translucent; delicate; almost totally transparent. **diaphanously** *adv.*

di-a-phone (dī´a fōn˝) *n.* A low-pitched fog horn, that produces a blast of two tones, the sound of which can be heard from a distance.

di-a-phragm (dī´a fram´) *n., Anat.* The muscular wall which separates the abdominal and thoracic cavities. *Photog.* The disk with an adjustable aperture that can control the amount of light which passes through the lens of a telescope, camera, etc.; a contraceptive device *n.* usually made of a rubber or rubber-like material and shaped like a cap to cover the uterine cervix.

di-a-pos-i-tive (dī˜a poz´i tiv) *n.* A transparent photograph.

di-a-rist (dī´a rist) *n.* A person who keeps a diary.

di-ar-rhe-a *or* **di-ar-rhoe-a (dī´arē´a)** *n.* A disorder of the intestines causing frequent, loose bowel movements.

di-ar-thro-sis (dī˜ār thrō´sis) *n.* A freely movable joint in which the bones revolve in every direction, as in the shoulder or leg joint.

di-a-ry (dī´a rē) *n. pl.* **-ries** A daily record, especially a personal record of one's activities, experiences, or observations; a journal; a book for keeping such records.

di-as-ta-sis (dī as′ta sis) *n.* Dislocation of bones without a fracture.

di-as-to-le (dī as′to lē′) *n., Physiol.* The normal rhythmic dilatation and relaxation of the heart cavities during which they fill with blood. **diastolic** *adj.*

di-as-tro-phism (dī as′tro fiz′um) *n., Geol.* Any of the processes through which the earth's crust, as mountains and continents, are formed.

di-a-ther-my (dī′a thėr′mē) *n. pl.*-mies *Med.* The generation of heat in the body tissues by high-frequency electromagnetic waves; the application of electric current to produce heat in tissues below the skin for therapeutic purposes. **diathermic** *adj.*

di-ath-e-sis (dī ath′i sis) *n.* Predisposition toward a condition or certain diseases rather than to others.

di-a-tom (dī′a tom) *n.* Any of various tiny planktonic algae whose walls contain silica.

di-a-tom-ic (dī′a tom′ik) *adj.* Having two atoms in a molecule.

di-a-ton-ic (dī′a ton′ik) *adj., Music* Relating to a standard major or minor scale of eight tones without the chromatic intervals.

di-a-tribe (dī′a trīb′) *n.* A bitter, often malicious criticism or denunciation.

diazo dye *n.* A dye produced by the chemical reaction of materials after being absorbed by the fibers of a fabric.

dib-ble (dib′l) *n.* A gardener's pointed tool used to make holes in soil, especially for planting bulbs or seedlings. **dibble** *v.*

dice (dīs) *n. pl.* Two or more small cubes of wood, bone, or ivory having the sides marked with dots from one to six; a game of chance. *v.* To gamble with dice; to cut food into small cubes.

di-chot-o-mous (di kot′o mus) *adj.* Dividing into two parts.

di-chot-o-my (dī kot′o mē) *n. pl.* -mies A division into two mutually exclusive subclasses. *Bot.* The branching of something in which each successive axis forks into two equally developed branches. **dichotomous** *adj.*

di-chro-mate (dī krō′māt) *n., Chem.* A chemical compound with two chromium atoms per anion.

di-chro-mat-ic (dī′krō mat′ik) *adj., Zool.* Having two color phases within the species apart from the changes due to age or sex. *Pathol.* Having the ability to see only two of the three primary colors.

di-chro-scope (dī′kro skōp″) *n.* Instrument used for testing the dichroism of crystals.

Dickens, Charles John Huffam *n.* (1812-1870). English novelist.

dick-er (dik′ėr) *v.* To haggle or work towards a deal or bargain.

dick-ey *or* **dickie** *or* **dicky** *n. pl.* **dickeys** *or* **dickies** A woman's blouse front worn under a jacket or low-necked dress; the detachable shirt front for a man; a small bird.

di-cot-y-le-don (dī kot′a lēd′on) *n.* A plant which has two seed leaves. **dicotyledonous** *adj.*

di-crot-ic (dī krot′ik) *adj.* Having a double arterial heartbeat for one.

dic-tate (dik′tāt) *v.* To read or speak aloud for another to record or transcribe; to give commands, terms, rules, or other orders with authority. *n.* A directive or guiding principle. **dictation** *n.*

dictating machine *n.* A machine that records and reproduces speech.

dic-ta-tion (dik tā′shan) *n.* The act of recording words for reproduction in writing.

dic-ta-tor (dik′tā tėr) *n.* A person having absolute authority and supreme governmental powers; one who dictates. **dictatorship** *n.*

dic-ta-to-ri-al (dik′ta tōr′ē al) *adj.* Tending to dictate; relating to or characteristic of a dictator; one who has total control. **dictatorially** *adv.*

dic-tion (dik′shan) *n.* The selection and arrangement of words in speaking and writing; the manner of uttering speech sounds.

dic-tion-ar-y (dik′sha ner′ē) *n. pl.* -ies A reference book containing alphabetically arranged words together with their definitions and usages.

dic-tum (dik´tum) *n. pl.* **-ta** *or* **-tums** An authoritative or positive utterance; a pronouncement; a saying that is popular.

did (did) *v.* Past tense of do.

di-dac-tic *or* **didactical (dīdak´ti kal)** *adj.* Being inclined to teach or moralize excessively. **didactically** *adv.* **didacticism** *n.*

did-dle (did l) *v.* To cheat; to swindle; to waste valuable time.

did-n't (did´ant) Did not.

di-do (dī´dō) *n. pl.* **-dos** *or* **-does** *Informal* A mischievous caper; an antic.

did-y-mous (did´i mus) *adj.* Produced in pairs; twins.

die (dī) *v.* To expire; to stop living; to cease to exist; to fade away; to cease operation or functioning, as an engine. **diehard** To resist defeat or death to the end; to be determined not to give up. **off** To be removed one after another by dieing as flowers.

die-back (dī´bak´) *n.* A condition in woody plants in which branches are killed by parasites, viruses, fungi, or conditions of environment.

die casting *n.* The process of giving an alloy or metal a desired shape; the act of cutting, stamping, or shaping with or as with a die.

die–hard (dī´härd´) *n.* A person who resists change.

diel-drin (dēl´drin) *n.* A highly toxic and persistent chemical which is used as an insecticide.

di-e-lec-tric (dī´i lek´trik) *n., Elect.* A nonconductor of electricity.

di-er-e-sis (dī er´i sis) *n. pl.* **-ses** The mark over a vowel indicating that it is to be pronounced in a separate syllable.

die-sel (dē´zel) *n.* A diesel engine or a vehicle driven by a diesel engine.

diesel engine *n.* An internal-combustion engine in which an airfuel mixture is ignited by the heat generated from the high compression in the cylinder.

die-sink-er (dī´sing´ker) *n.* A person who engraves metal dies.

die-stock (dī´stok´) *n.* A stock used to hold the dies used in cutting threads.

di-et (dī´it) *n.* A regulated selection of food and drink, especially one followed for medical or hygienic reasons; something that is taken or provided regularly; an assembly or legislature.

di-e-tar-y (dī´i ter´ē) *adj.* Relating to a diet or the rules of dieting. *n.* The kinds and amount of food available for an individual or a group of people.

di-e-tet-ics (dī´i tet´iks) *n. pl.* The study of diet and or the regulations of a diet. **dietetical** *adj.* **dietetic** *adj.* **dietetically** *adv.* **dietitian** *n.* **dietician** *n.*

diet kitchen *n.* A kitchen that prepares and dispenses special diets, as one located in a hospital or nursing home.

dif-fer (dif´er) *v.* To have different opinions; to disagree.

dif-fer-ence (dif´er ens) *n.* The quality, state, or degree of being different or unlike; a controversy or cause for a disagreement; in mathematics, the amount by which a number or quantity is less or greater than another.

dif-fer-ent (dif´er ent) *adj.* Not the same; separate; other; marked by a difference; unlike; differing from the ordinary. **differently** *adv.* **differentness** *n.*

dif-fer-en-tia (dif´e ren´shē a) *n. pl.* **-tiae** A specific difference; something that distinguishes a species from others of the same genus.

dif-fer-en-tial (dif´e ren´shal) *adj.* Relating to or showing a difference or differences. *n.* The amount or degree to which similar things differ.

differential calculus *n.* In mathematics, the difference or variation of a function with respect to changes in independent variables.

differential gear *n., Mech.* A coupling consisting of a train of gears used to connect two or more shafts to allow different rates of wheel rotation, as on curves.

dif-fer-en-ti-ate (dif´e ren´shē āt´) *v.* To show, state, or distinguish the difference; to become or make different. **differenti-**

ation *n*.

dif-fi-cult (dif'i kult') *adj*. Hard to do, deal with, or accomplish; hard to please.

dif-fi-cul-ty (dif'i kul'tē) *n. pl.* **-ties** The quality or state of being difficult; something that requires great effort; conflicts or problems.

dif-fi-dence (dif'i dens) *n*. Lack of self-confidence.

dif-fi-dent (dif'i dent)*adj*. Lacking confidence in oneself; unsure. **diffidence** *n*. **diffidently** *adv*.

dif-flu-ent (dif'lŏ ent) *adj*. Have the tendency to flow away.

dif-fuse (di fūz') *v*. To pour out and spread freely in all directions; to scatter.

dif-fu-sive (di fū'siv)*adj*. Tending to diffuse.

dig (dig) *v*. To turn up, break up, or remove the earth with a shovel; to discover or learn by investigation or research. *Slang* To understand, like, appreciate or enjoy. *Informal* To work intensively.

dig-a-my (dig'a mē) *n*. Second marriage; the act of marrying after the first marriage has been legally ended.

di-gas-tric (dī gas'trik) *n*. A double muscle separated by a median tendon, that pulls the lower jaw downward and backward.

di-gest (di jest') *v*. To change ingested food into usable form; to mentally assimilate; to endure; to tolerate patiently; to decompose or soften with moisture or heat. **digestibility** *n*. **digestible** *adj*. **digestive** *adj*.

di-gest-ion (di jes'chan) *n*. The chemical and muscular action of transforming food into an absorbable state.

dig-ger (dig'ėr) *n*. A person who or equipment that digs.

dig-it (dij'it) *n*. A toe or finger; the Arabic numerals 0 through 9.

dig-i-tal (dij'i tal) *adj*. Pertaining to or like the fingers or digits; expressed in digits, especially for computer use; reading in digits, as a clock.

digital computer *n*. In computer science, a computer using data that is represented as digits to perform operations.

dig-i-tal-is (dij'i tal' is) *n*. The foxglove plant; a drug prepared from dried leaves of foxglove, used as a heart stimulant.

di-glot (dī'glot) *adj*. Using two languages; bilingual.

dig-ni-fied (dig'ni fid') *adj*. Showing or possessing dignity; poised.

dig-ni-fy (dig'ni fī') *v*. To give dignity or distinction to something.

dig-ni-tary (dig'ni ter'ē) *n. pl.* **-ies** A person of high rank, notability, and influence.

dig-ni-ty (dig'ni tē) *n. pl.* **-ties** The quality or state of being excellent; the quality of being poised or formally reserved in appearance and demeanor; a high rank, office, or title.

di-graph (dī'graf) *n*. A pair of letters, as the ea in seat or oa in boat, that represents a single sound. **digraphic** *adj*.

di-gress (di gres') *v*. To turn away or aside from the main subject in a discourse; to wander. **digression** *n*. **digressive** *adj*. **digressively** *adv*.

dik-dik (dik'dik') *n*. A very small African antelope.

dike (dīk) *n*. An embankment made of earth, built to hold and control flood waters, also known as a levee; also used in irrigation of crops.

di-lap-i-date (di lap'i dāt') *v*. To cause to decay or fall into partial ruin through neglect.

di-lap-i-dat-ed (di lap'i dā'tid) *adj*. Being in a state of decay or disrepair. **dilapidation** *n*.

dil-a-ta-tion *n*. The state of being expanded or distended; something which is dilated. *Med*. Enlargement of a passageway for medical examination.

di-late (dī lāt') *v*. To become or make enlarged; to expand, extend in all directions. **dilatable** *adj*. **dilation** *n*. **dilator** *n*.

di-lat-ed (dī lā'tid) *adj*. Expanded in all directions.

dil-a-tom-e-ter (dil'a tom'i tėr) *n*. An instrument for measuring thermal expansion of substances.

dil-a-to-ry (dil'a tōr'ē) *adj*. Tending to cause decay; characterized by delay; slow;

tardy. **dilatorily** *adv.*

di-lem-ma (di lem´*a***)** *n.* A predicament requiring a choice between equally undesirable alternatives.

dil-et-tante (dil´i tan´tē) *n. pl.* **-tantes** One who has an amateurish and superficial interest in something.

dil-i-gence (dil´i j*ens***)** *n.* The constant effort to accomplish what is undertaken.

dil-i-gent (dil´i j*ent***)** *adj.* Showing painstaking effort and application in whatever is undertaken; industrious; constant in effort to accomplish what is undertaken. **diligence** *n.* **diligently** *adv.*

dill (dil) *n.* An aromatic herb with aromatic leaves and seeds used as seasoning.

dil-ly (dil ē) *n. pl.* **-lies** *Slang* Someone or something that is remarkable or extraordinary.

dil-ly–dal-ly (dil´ē dal´ē) *v.* To waste time with indecision or hesitation.

di-lute (di lōt´) *v.* To weaken, thin, or reduce the concentration of by adding a liquid, reduce strength. **dilution** *n.*

dim (dim) *adj.* Dull; lacking sharp perception or clarity of understanding; obscured or darkened from faintness of light; pessimistic or negative. **dim** *v.,* **dimly** *adv.,* **dimness** *n.*

dim *n. abbr.* Dimension.

dime (dīm) *n.* A United States coin worth ten cents or one tenth of a dollar.

dime novel *n.* A melodramatic paperback novel.

di-men-sion (di men´sh*an***)** *n.* A measurable extent, as length, thickness, or breadth. **dimensions** *pl.* The magnitude or scope of something. **dimensional** *adj.* **dimensionality** *n.*

dim-er-ous (dim´*ė***r us)** *adj.* Consisting of two parts.

di-min-ish (di min´ish) *v.* To become or make smaller or less; to reduce in power, rank, or authority; to decrease; to taper. **diminishable** *adj.* **diminishment** *n.* **diminution** *n.*

dim-in-ished (di min´isht) *adj.* Reduced; lessened.

di-min-u-en-do (di min´ū en´do) *adv.* Gradually lessening in volume. **diminuendo** *n.*

di-min-u-tive (di min´ū tiv) *adj.* Very small; tiny.

dim-is-so-ry (dim´i sōr¨ē) *adj.* Granting leave to depart.

dim-i-ty (dim´i tē) *n. pl.* **-ties** A sheer cotton fabric woven with cords, stripes, or checks.

dim-mer (dim´ėr) *n.* A rheostat used to reduce the intensity of an electric light.

dim-ple (dim´pl) *n.* A slight depression in the surface of the skin, especially one made visible in the cheek by smiling; a slight surface depression. **dimple** *v.*

dim-wit (dim´wit) *n., Slang* A simple-minded or stupid person. **dimwitted** *adj.* **dimwittedly** *adv.* **dimwittedness** *n.*

din (din) *n.* A loud, confused, harsh noise.

dine (dīn) *v.* To eat dinner.

din-er (dī´nėr) *n.* A dining car on a train; a restaurant usually shaped like a railroad car.

di-nette (dī net´) *n.* A small room or alcove which is used as a dining room.

ding (ding) *v.* To sound as a bell when struck; to making a ringing sound.

ding–a–ling *n., Slang* A silly person.

din-ghy (ding´gē) *n. pl.* **-ghies** A small row boat; an inflatable rubber raft.

din-gle (ding´gl) *n.* A valley between hills.

din-gus (ding´us) *n.* Something whose name is unknown.

din-ky (ding´kē) *adj., Informal* Insignificant or small.

din-ner (din´ėr) *n.* The last meal of the day, taken usually between the hours of 5:00 and 7:00 P.M.; a banquet or formal meal.

din-ner-ware (din´ėr w*er***)** *n.* The tableware used in serving a meal.

di-no-saur (dī´no sor´) *n. , Paleon.* A group of extinct reptiles from the Mesozoic period, some of which were the largest land animals known to exist.

di-no-there (dī´no thēr˝) *n.* A huge, extinct, two-tusked mammal closely associated to the elephant.

dint (dint) *n.* Means; force; effort. *v.* To drive with force.

di-oc-ese (dī´o sēs´) *n.* The territory under the jurisdiction of a bishop. **diocesan** *adj.*

di-ode (dī´ōd) *n.* An electron tube which permits electrons to pass in only one direction, used as a rectifier.

di-o-ra-ma (dī´o ram´a) *n.* A miniature scene in three dimensions.

dip (dip) *v.* To let or put down into a liquid momentarily; to lift up and out by scooping or bailing; to be baptized by immersion; to make candles by repeatedly immersing wicks in wax or tallow; to sink or go down suddenly. *n.* A sauce made of liquid, into which something is to be dipped; a depression or hollow. *Slang* A silly person.

diph-the-ri-a (dif thēr´ē a) *n., Pathol.* An acute contagious disease caused by bacillus and characterized by formation of a false membrane in the throat and other air passages by weakness and by fever.

diph-thong (dif´thong) *n.* A blend of a single speech sound which begins with one vowel sound and moves to another in the same syllable, as oi in oil, oi in coil or oy in toy.

diph-y-o-dont (dif´ē o dont˝) *adj.* The successive development of two sets of teeth; as most people do.

di-plex (dī´pleks) *adj.* Pertaining to sending two simultaneous signals over the same communications path.

di-plo-ma (di plō´ma) *n.* A document issued by a college, school, or university testifying that a student has earned a degree or completed a course of study.

di-plo-ma-cy (di plō´ma sē) *n. pl.* **-cies** The art or practice of conducting international negotiations; skill and tact in dealing with people.

dip-lo-mat (dip´lo mat´) *n.* A person employed in diplomacy. **diplomatic** *adj.*

dip-per (dip´ėr) *n.* One that dips; a container for dipping; a long-handled cup for dipping water. *Astron.* The Big Dipper and the Little Dipper, two northern constellations.

dip-so-ma-ni-a (dip´so mā´nē a) *n.* An insatiable craving for alcohol. **dipsomaniac** *adj.*

dip-ter-ous (dip´tėr us) *adj.* Pertaining to or of animal shaving a single pair of wings such as the fly, gnat, and mosquito.

dip-tych (dip´tik) *n.* A pair of painted or carved panels which are hinged together.

dir *abbr.* Director.

dire (dīr) *adj.* Dreadful or terrible in consequence. **direly** *adv.* **direfully** *adv.* **direness** *n.*

di-rect (dī rekt´) *v.* To control or regulate the affairs of; to command or order; to direct or tell someone the way; to cause something to move in a given or direct course; to indicate the destination of a letter; to supervise or instruct the performance of a job; to move or lie in a straight line; to do something immediate. *adj.* Without compromise; absolute; in the exact words of a person, as a direct quote.

direct current *n.* An electrical current which flows in only one direction.

di-rect-ed (di rek´tid) *adj.* Guided, controlled; supervised.

di-rec-tion (di rek´shan) *n.* The act of directing; an order or command; the path or line along which something points, travels or lies. **directional** *adj.*

di-rec-tive (di rek´tiv) *n.* A regulation or order from someone with authority.

di-rect-ly (di rekt´lē) *adv.* Immediately; at once; in a direct manner or line; doing without an agent, medium, or go-between.

di-rec-tor (di rek´tėr) *n.* A person who manages or directs; one of a group of persons who supervises the affairs of an institute, corporation or business. **directorship** *n.*

di-rec-to-ry (di rek´to rē) *n. pl.* **-ries** A book-listing data, alphabetically or classified, containing the names and addresses of a specific group, persons, organizations, inhabitants, or businesses.

di-rec-tress (di rek´tris) *n.* A female manager of a business or production.

direct tax *n.* A tax which is charged directly to the taxpayer.

dirge (dėrj) *n.* A slow mournful song; a funeral hymn.

dir-i-gi-ble (dir´i ji bl) *n.* A lighter-than-air plane which may be steered by means of its own motive power.

dirk (dėrk) *n.* A dagger.

dirn-dl (dėrn´dl) *n.* A lady's full-skirted dress with a gathered waistband.

dirt (dėrt) *n.* Soil or earth; obscene or profane language; scandalous or hateful gossip. *Minera.* Broken ore or rock; washed-down earth, containing precious metal. **dirt-bike** A light-weight motorbike used on rough roads, surfaces, or trails. **dirt-cheap** Extremely cheap.

dirty (dėr´tē) *adj.* Not clean; grimy; indecent; obscene; mean; despicable; lacking in brightness or clarity; relating to excessive radioactive fallout. *v.* To become or make soiled. **dirtiness** *n.*

dirty tricks *n. pl., Informal* Unethical behavior, especially in politics.

dis-a-bil-i-ty (dis´a bil´i tē) *n.* The condition or state of being mentally or physically disabled or unable.

dis-a-ble (dis ā bl) *v.* To make powerless or to incapacitate;to disqualify legally.

dis-a-buse (dis´a būz´) *v.* To free from delusion, misunderstanding, or misconception.

dis-ac-cord. Lack harmony; disagreement.

dis-ad-van-tage (dis´ad van´tij) *n.* A circumstance thatis unfavorable; loss or damage; detriment. **disadvantage** *v.*

dis-af-fect (dis´a fekt´) *v.* To weaken or destroy the affection or loyalty of. **disaffection, disaffectedly** *adv.* **disaffected** *adj.*

dis-af-firm (dis´a fėrm´) *v.* To deny; to refuse to confirm.

dis-af-for-est (dis´a fot´ist) *v.* To strip trees from the forest.

dis-a-gree (dis´a grē´) *v.* To vary in opinion; to differ; to argue; to quarrel; to be unfavorable or unacceptable.

dis-a-gree-able (dis´a grē´a bl) *adj.* Offensive or unpleasant. **disagreeably** *adv.*

dis-al-low (dis´a lou´) *v.* To refuse to allow; to reject as invalid or untrue. **disallowance** *n.*

dis-ap-pear (dis´a pēr´) *v.* To vanish; to drop from sight. **disappearance** *n.*

dis-ap-point (dis´a point´) *v.* To fail to satisfy the desires, hopes, or expectations of. **disappointment** *n.*

dis-ap-point-ment (dis˝a point´ment) *n.* The emotion of being disappointed.

dis-ap-pro-ba-tion (dis´ap ro bā´shan) *n.* Disapproval; condemnation.

dis-ap-prove (dis´a prōv´) *v.* To refuse to approve; to reject; to condemn. **disapproval** *n.*

dis-arm (dis ärm´) *v.* To make harmless; to deprive or take away the weapons or any means of attack or defense.

dis-ar-range (dis´a rānj´) *v.* To disturb the order of something.

dis-ar-ray (dis´a rā´) *n.* A state of confusion or disorder; an upset or turmoil.

dis-as-sem-ble (dis´a sem´bl) *v.* To take apart.

dis-as-so-ci-ate (dis´a sō´shēāt´) *v.* To break away from or to detach oneself from an association. **disassociation** *n.*

dis-as-ter (di zas´tėr) *n.* An event that causes great ruin or distress; a sudden and crushing misfortune. **disastrous** *adj.* **disastrously** *adv.*

dis-a-vow (dis´a vou´) *v.* To disclaim or deny any responsibility for or knowledge of. **disavowal** *n.*

dis-band (dis band´) *v.* To disperse; to break up. **disbandment** *n.*

dis-bar (dis bär´) *v.* In law, to be expelled officially from the legal profession. **disbarment** *n.*

dis-be-lieve (dis´bi lēv´) *v.* To refuse to believe in something. **disbelief** *n.* **disbeliever** *n.*

dis-burse (dis bėrs´) *v.* To pay out; to give out. **disbursement** *n.* **disbursal** *n.* **disburser** *n.*

disc *or* **disk (disk)** *n., Informal* A phonograph record.

disc *abbr.* Discount.

dis-card (di skärd´) *v.* To remove a playing card from one's hand; to throw out. *n.* The act of discarding; something which is cast aside or rejected. **discarder** *n.*

dis-cern (di sèrn´) *v.* To detect visually; to detect with senses other than that of vision; to comprehend mentally; to perceive as separate and distinct. **discerner** *n.* **discernment** *n.* **discernible** *adj.*

dis-cerp-ti-ble *adj.* Capable of being torn apart; divisible.

dis-charge (dis chärj´) *v.* To relieve of a charge, duty, load, or burden; to release as from confinement, custody, care, or duty; to dismiss from employment; to send forth; to shoot or fire a weapon; to get rid of; to release from service or duty; to fulfill an obligation, duty, or debt. *n.* The act of discharging or the condition of being discharged.

dis-ci-ple (di sī´pl) *n.* One who accepts and assists in spreading the doctrines of another. **Disciple** One of Christ's followers.

dis-ci-plin-ary (dis´i pli ner˝ē) *adj.* Intended to enforce discipline.

dis-ci-pline (dis´i plin) *n.* Training which corrects, molds, or perfects the mental faculties or moral character; behavior which results from such training; obedience to authority or rules; punishment meant to correct poor behavior. *v.* To train or develop by teaching and by control; to bring order to; to penalize. **disciplinary** *adj.*

dis-claim (dis klām´) *v.* To disavow any claim to or association with; to deny the authority of; to renounce or give up a claim on. **disclaimer** *n.*

dis-close (di sklōz´) *v.* To make known; to bring into view. **disclosure** *n.*

dis-co (dis kō) *n. pl.* **-cos** A discotheque; a nightclub for dancing.

dis-cog-ra-phy (di skog´ra fē) *n.* A systematic and descriptive list of phonograph records; as to the performer and date released.

dis-coid (dis´koid) *adj.* Having the form or related to a disk; flat and circular.

dis-color (dis kul´èr) *v.* To alter or change the color of. **discoloration** *n.*

dis-com-fit (dis kum´fit) *v.* To defeat in battle; to make upset or uneasy. **discomfiture** *n.*

dis-com-fort (dis kum´fèrt) *n.* Physical or mental uneasiness; pain; an inconvenience. *v.* To make uncomfortable.

dis-com-mend (dis˝ko mend) *v.* To blame; to be viewed unfavorably.

dis-com-mode (dis´ko mōd´) *v.* To inconvenience.

dis-com-pose (dis´kom pōz´) *v.* To disrupt the composure or serenity of; to unsettle; to destroy the order of. **discomposure** *n.*

dis-con-cert (dis´kon sèrt´) *v.* To upset; to discompose; to perturb. **disconcertingly** *adv.*

dis-con-nect (dis´ko nekt´) *v.* To sever or break the connection of or between, to detach. **disconnection** *n.*

dis-con-nect-ed (dis´kon nek´tid) *adj.* Not connected; separate.

dis-con-so-late (dis kon´so lit) *adj.* Without consolation; dejected; cheerless; sorrowful. **disconsolately** *adv.*

dis-con-tent (dis´kon tent´) *n.* Lack of contentment; dissatisfaction. *v.* To make unhappy; malcontent. **discontent** *v.* **discontentedly** *adv.* **discontented** *adj.*

dis-con-tent-ed (dis˝kon ten´tid) *adj.* Not pleased with one's circumstances.

dis-con-tin-ue (dis´kon tin´ū) *v.* To come or bring to an end; to break the continuity of; to interrupt; to stop trying, taking, or using. **discontinuation** *n.*

dis-cord (dis´kord) *n.* Lacking accord or harmony; a harsh combination of musical sounds. **discordant** *adj.*

dis-cord-ance *n.* Disagreement; opposition.

dis-co-theque (dis˝kō tek´) *n.* A nightclub where music is provided for dancing.

dis-count (dis´kount) *v.* To sell or offer for sale at a price lower than usual; to leave out of account; to disregard; to give discounts; to underestimate the importance of something. *n.* A reduction from the full amount of a debt or from the standard price; the act or practice of discounting; a deduction taken or an allowance made. **discountable** *adj.*

dis-coun-te-nance (dis koun´te nans) *v.* To look upon with disfavor; to make uneasy.

dis-cour-age (di skėr´ij) *v.* To deprive or be deprived of enthusiasm or courage; to hinder by disfavoring; deterring or dissuading. **discouragement** *n.*

dis-course (dis´kōrs) *n.* A conversation; a formal and lengthy discussion of a subject. *v.* To write or converse extensively. **discourser** *n.*

dis-cour-te-ous (dis kėr´tē us) *adj.* Lacking consideration or courteous manners. **discourteously** *adv.* **discourtesy** *n.*

dis-cov-er (di skuv´ėr) *v.* To make known or visible; to observe or learn of for the first time; to explore. **discoverable** *adj.* **discoverer** *n.* **discovery** *n.*

dis-cred-it (dis kred´it) *v.* To mar the reputation of or disgrace someone or something; to injure the reputation of. *n.* Loss of credit or reputation; doubt; disbelief. **discred-itable** *adj.* **discreditably** *adv.*

dis-creet (di skrēt´) *adj.* Tactful; careful of appearances; modest. **discreetly** *adv.* **discreetness** *n.*

dis-crep-an-cy (di skrep´an sē) *n. pl.* **-cies** A difference in facts; an instance of being discrepant. **discrepant** *adj.*

dis-crete (di skrēt´) *adj.* Separate; made up of distinct parts.

dis-cre-tion (di skresh´shan) *n.* The quality or act of being discreet; the ability to make responsible choices; power to decide; the result of separating or distinguishing.

dis-crim-i-nate (di skrim´i nāt˝) *v.* To distinguish or differentiate between someone or something on the basis of race, sex, class, or religion; to act prejudicially.

dis-cur-sive (di skėr´siv) *adj.* Covering a wide field of subjects in a quick manner; rambling from subject to subject. **discursively** *adv.* **discursiveness** *n.*

dis-cus (dis´kus) *n.* A heavy disk made of wood, rubber, or metal, which is hurled for distance in athletic competitions; a brightly-colored, disk-shaped freshwater fish of South America.

dis-cuss (di skus´) *v.* To investigate by argument or debate; to consider or examine something through discourse.

dis-cus-sant (di skus´ant) *n.* A participant in a discussion.

dis-cus-sion (di skush´an) *n.* The act of discussing between two or more people about a subject that they may or may not agree on.

dis-dain (dis dān´) *v.* To treat contemptuously; to look on with scorn.

dis-ease (di zēz´) *n.* A condition of the living animal, plant body, or one of its parts which impairs normal functioning; a condition of ill health. **diseased** *adj.*

dis-em-bark (dis´em bärk´) *v.* To go or put ashore from a ship; unload.

dis-em-body (dis´em bod´ē) *v.* To release or free the soul or physical existence.

dis-em-bow-el (dis´em bou´el) *v.* To remove the bowels or entrails; to eviscerate. **disembowelment** *n.*

dis-en-chant (dis´en chant´) *v.* To free from false beliefs or enchantment. **disenchantingly** *adv.* **disenchanting** *adj.*

dis-en-cum-ber (dis´en kum´bėr) *v.* To relieve of hardships; to free from encumbrance; unburden.

dis-en-fran-chise (dis´en fran´chīz) *v.* To disfranchise. **disenfranchisement** *n.*

dis-en-gage (dis´en gāj´) *v.* To free from something that holds or otherwise engages; to set free. **disengagement** *n.*

dis-en-tan-gle (dis´en tang´gl) *v.* To relieve of entanglement, confusion, etc; unravel. **disentanglement** *n.*

dis-e-qui-lib-ri-um (dis ē˝kwi lib´rē um) *n.* The lack of balance.

dis-es-tab-lish (dis´e stab´lish) *v.* To deprive of the privileges of an establishment; bring about the end.

dis-es-teem (dis´e stēm´) *v.* To regard with little esteem. *n.* Lack of esteem.

dis-fa-vor (dis fā´vėr) *n.* Disapproval; the

state of being disliked. **disfavor** v.

dis-fig-ure (dis fig´ūr) v. To mar, deface, or deform the appearance of something or someone. **disfigurement** n.

dis-fran-chise (dis fran´chīz) v. To deprive of a legal right or privilege, especially the right to vote. **disfranchisement** n.

dis-gorge (dis gorj´) v. To discharge by the throat or mouth; to regurgitate; to give up on request or under pressure; to discharge violently or as a result of force; to discharge the contents of; to spew forth violently.

dis-grace (dis grās´) n. The state of having lost grace, favor, respect, or honor; something that disgraces. v. To bring reproach or shame to; to humiliate by a superior showing; to cause to lose favor or standing. **disgracer, disgracefulness** n. **disgraceful** adj. **disgracefully** adv.

dis-grun-tle (dis grun´tl) v. To make dissatisfied or discontented.

dis-guise (dis gīz´) v. To alter the customary appearance or character of in order to prevent recognition; to conceal the actual existence or character of. n. Clothes and or make-up assumed to disguise one's identity or to copy that of another; an artificial manner; the act of disguising someone or thing. **disguisedly** adv. **disguiser** n. **disguisable** adj.

dis-gust (dis gust´) v. To affect with nausea, repugnance, or aversion; to cause one to become impatient or lose attention. n. A marked aversion to something distasteful; repugnance. **disgustedly** adv. **disgustfully** adv. **disgustingly** adv.. **disgusting** adj. **disgustful** adj.

dish (dish) n. A concave vessel on which food is served; the amount a dish holds; the food served in a dish; a particularly prepared food; fashion; a directional microwave antenna having a concave reflector. Slang Something that is favored; an attractive woman. v. To make sarcastic cutting remarks; to put food into a dish.

dis-ha-bille (dis´a bēl´) n. The state of being carelessly dressed; undress.

dis-har-mo-ny (dis här´mo nē) n. Lack of harmony or agreement; discord.

dish-cloth (dish´kloth´) n. A cloth used for washing dishes; also called a dishrag.

dis-heart-en (dis här´ton) v. To cause to lose spirit or courage; to discourage, demoralize, or dispirit.

di-shev-el (di shev´el) v. To mess up or disarrange; to throw into disorder or disarray.

dis-hon-est (dis on´ist) adj. Lack of honesty; arising from or showing fraud or falseness. **dishonesty** n. **dishonestly** adv.

dis-hon-or (dis on´ér) n. The deprivation of honor; disgrace; the state of one who has lost honor; a cause of disgrace; failure to pay a financial obligation. v. To bring disgrace on something or someone; to fail to pay.

dish-rag (dish´rag´) n. A dishcloth.

dish-wash-er (dish´wosh´ér) n. A person or a machine which washes dishes.

dis-il-lu-sion (dis´i lö´zhan) v. To deprive of illusion; to disenchant.

dis-in-cline (dis´in klīn´) v. To make or to be unwilling; to be or cause to be not interested.

dis-in-fect (dis´in fekt´) v. To cleanse and make free from infection, especially by destroying harmful microorganisms; to sterilize. **disinfection** n.

dis-in-gen-u-ous (dis´in jen´ū us) adj. Lacking frankness, sincerity, or simplicity; crafty; not straightforward.

dis-in-her-it (dis´in her´it) v. To deliberately deprive of inheritance; to depose of previously held privileges.

dis-in-te-grate (dis in´te grāt´) v. To break or reduce into separate elements, parts, or small particles; to destroy the unity or integrity of; to explode; to undergo a change in structure, as an atomic nucleus. **disintegration** n. **disintegrator** n.

dis-inter (dis´in tèr) v. To exhume or dig up something buried; to bring to light, disclose, uncover, or expose.

dis-in-ter-est-ed (dis in´tèr ist ed) adj. The state of being unbiased, impartial, unselfish, or not interested; free from selfish motive or interest. **disinterest** *n.* **disinterestedly** *adv.*

dis-join (dis join′) *v.* To end the joining of; to become detached; to disconnect.

dis-junct (dis jungkt′) *adj.* Disjoined; separated; discontinuous.

disk *or* **disc (disk)** *n.* A thin, flat, circular object; in computerscience, a round, flat plate coated with a magnetic substance on which data for a computer is stored; a fairly flat, circular, metal object used to break up soil; the implement employing such tools.

disk jockey *n.* One who conducts a radio program of music, news and other entertainment.

disk operating system *n.* In computer science, the software which controls the disk drives and disk accessing; abbreviated as DOS.

disk pack *n.* In computer science, a computer storage device which has several magnetic disks to use and store as a unit.

dis-like (dis līk′) *v.* To regard with aversion or disapproval. *n.* Distaste.

dis-lo-cate (dis′lō kāt′) *v.* To put out of place or proper position. *Medical* To displace a bone from a socket or joint.

dis-lodge (dis loj′) *v.* To remove or drive out from a dwelling or position; to force out of a settled position.

dis-loy-al (dis loi′al) *adj.* Not loyal; untrue to personal obligations or duty. **disloyally** *adv.* **disloyalty** *n.*

dis-mal (diz′mal) *adj.* Causing gloom or depression; depressing; lacking in interest or merit. **dismally** *adv.* **dismalness** *n.*

dis-man-tle (dis man′tl) *v.* To strip of dress or covering or to strip of furniture and equipment; to take or tear apart; **dismantlement** *n.*

dis-may (dis mā′) *v.* To deprive or be deprived of courage or resolution through the pressure of sudden fear or anxiety. **dismay** *n.* **dismayingly** *adv.*

dis-mem-ber (dis mem′ber) *v.* To cut, pull off or disjoin the limbs, members, or parts of. **dismemberment** *n.*

dis-miss (dis mis′) *v.* To discharge or allow to leave; to remove from position or service as an employee; to bar from attention or serious consideration; in law, to disallow or reject any further judicial consideration on a claim or action. **dismissal** *n.* **dismissible** *adj.*

dis-mount (dis mount′) *v.* To get down from; to remove from a seat, setting, or support; to take apart; to disassemble.

dis-o-be-di-ence (dis′o bē′dē ens) *n.* Refusal to obey.

dis-o-bey (dis′o bā′) *v.* To refuse or fail to obey; to be disobedient. **disobedient** *adj.* **disobediently** *adv.*

dis-o-blige (dis′o blīj′) *v.* To act contrary to the wishes of; to neglect or refuse to act in accordance with the wishes of; to of-fend; to inconvenience. **disobligingly** *adv.*

dis-or-der (dis or′der) *n.* Breach of peace or public order; lack of good order; an abnormal physical or mental condition; an ailment. *v.* To disturb the order of; to disturb the normal or regular functions of. **disorderly** *adj.* **disorderliness** *n.*

dis-or-dered (dis or′derd) *adj.* Lacking order; confused.

dis-or-gan-ize (dis or′ga nīz′) *v.* To destroy or break up the organization, unity, or structure of. **disorganization** *n.*

dis-o-ri-ent (dis ōr′ē ent) *v.* To cause to lose one's bearings.

dis-own (dis ōn′) *v.* To refuse to acknowledge or claim as one's own.

dis-par-age *v.* To bring reproach or discredit upon; lower the estimation of.

dis-pa-rate (dis′pėr it) *adj.* Altogether dissimilar; unequal. **disparately** *adv.* **disparateness** *n.*

dis-par-i-ty (di spar′i tē) *n.* Inequality; difference in condition excellence.

dis-pas-sion-ate (dis pash′o nit) *adj.* Free from bias or passion; impartial.

dis-patch *or* **des-patch (di spach′)** *v.* To send off to a particular destination or on specific business; to dispose of quickly; to kill summarily. *n.* The act of dispatching; a message sent with speed; a message;

news story sent to a newspaper. **dis-patcher** *n.*

dis-pel (di spel´) *v.* To drive off or away.

dis-pen-sa-ble (di spen´sa bl) *adj.* Capable of being dispensed or administered.

dis-pen-sa-ry (di spen´sa rē) *n.* A place where medicine is dispensed.

dis-pense (di spens´) *v.* To give out; to distribute; to administer; to let go or exempt. **with** To get rid of; to forgo. **dispense** *n.* **dispenser** *n.*

dis-perse (di spėrs´) *v.* To break up or scatter in various directions; to spread or distribute from a common source; to distribute. **dispersible** *adj.* **dispersion** *n.* **dispersal** *n.*

di-spir-it (di spir´it) *v.* To deprive of or be deprived of spirit; to discourage or be discouraged. **dispiritedly** *adv.*

dis-place (dis plās) *v.* To change the position of; to take the place of; to discharge from an office; to cause a physical displacement of. **displacement** *n.*

dis-play (di splā´) *v.* To put forth or spread; to put in view; to show off. *n.* The act of displaying; in computer science, a device which gives information in a visual form such as on a cathode-ray tube (computer screen or CRT.)

dis-please (dis plēz´) *v.* To cause the disapproval or annoyance of; to cause displeasure. **displeasingly** *adv.* **displeasure** *n.*

dis-pose (di spōz´) *v.* To put in place; to finally settle or come to terms. **of** To get rid of; to attend to or settle; to transfer or part with, as by selling. **dispose** *adj.* **disposable** *adj.*

dis-po-si-tion (dis˝po zish´an) *n.* Prevailing mood, temper or emotion; final arrangements.

dis-pos-sess (dis´po zes´) *v.* To deprive of possession or ownership of land, possessions, or property. **dispossession** *n.*

dis-pro-por-tion(dis´propōr´shan)*n.* Lack of proportion, symmetry or proper relation. **disproportionate, disproportion** *v.* **disproportional***adj.* **disproportionately***adj.*

dis-prove (dis prōv´) *v.* Prove to be false

or erroneous **disproof** *n.* **disprovable** *adj.*

dis-put-a-ble (di spū´ta bl) *adj.* Capable of being disputed.

dis-pu-ta-tion (dis´pū tā´shan) *n.* The act of disputing; a debate.

dis-pute (di spūt´) *v.* To debate or argue; to question the validity of; to strive against or to resist. *n.* A verbal controversy; a quarrel. **disputable** *adj.* **disputably** *adv.* **disputant** *n.* **disputer** *n.*

dis-qual-i-fy (dis kwol´i fī´) *v.* To deprive of the required properties or conditions; to deprive of a power or privilege; to make ineligible for a prize or further competition. **disqualification** *n.*

dis-quiet (dis kwī´it) *v.* To take away the tranquillity of; to trouble. **disquieting** *adj.* **disquietingly** *adv.*

dis-qui-si-tion (dis´kwi zish´on) *n.* A formal inquiry into or discussion of a subject.

dis-re-gard (dis´ri gärd´) *v.* To ignore; to neglect; to pay no attention to; to treat without proper attention. **disregard** *n.* **disregardful** *adj.*

dis-re-la-tion (dis˝ri lā´shan) *n.* The lack of a fitting or suitable connection.

dis-re-pair (dis´ri pâr´) *n.* The state of being in need of repair, usually due to neglect.

dis-re-pute (dis´ri pūt´) *n.* A state of being held in low esteem; loss of a good reputation; disgrace. **disreputable** *adj.*

dis-re-spect (dis´ri spekt´) *n.* Lack of respect or reverence. **disrespect** *v.* **disrespectful** *adj.* **disrespectfully** *adv.*

dis-re-spect-ful *adj.* Displaying a lack of respect.

dis-robe (dis rōb´) *v.* To undress.

dis-rupt (dis rupt´) *v.* To throw into disorder or confusion; upset; to cause to break down. **disrupter, disruption** *n.* **disruptive** *adj.*

dis-sat-is-fac-tion (dis˝sat is fak´shan) *n.* The feeling of discontent; a lack of satisfaction.

dis-sat-is-fy (dis sat´is fī) *v.* To fail to satisfy; to disappoint; **dissatisfied** *adj.*

dis-sect (di sekt´) *v.* To cut into pieces; to

expose the parts of something, such as an animal, for examination; to analyze in detail. **dissector** *n*.

dis-sem-ble (di sem´bl) *v*. To conceal or hide the actual nature of; to put on a false appearance; to conceal facts, intentions or motives. **dissembler** *n*.

dis-sem-i-nate (di sem´i nāt´) *v*. To scatter or spread, as if by sowing, over a wide area. **dissemination** *n*. **disseminator** *n*.

dis-sem-i-nule (di sem´i nūl´) *n*. The regenerative part of a plant.

dis-sen-sion (di sen´shan) *n*. Difference of opinion; discord; strife.

dis-sent (di sent´) *v*. To differ in opinion or thought. *n*. Difference of opinion; refusal to go along with an established church.

dis-sep-i-ment (di sep´i ment) *n*. A partition between cells of animals and plants.

dis-ser-ta-tion (dis´ėr tā´shan) *n*. A formal written discourse or treatise, especially one submitted for a doctorate.

dis-serv-ice (dis sėr´vis) *n*. An ill turn; an ill service, injury, or harm.

dis-sev-er (di sev´ėr) *v*. To sever; to divide; to separate. **disseverance** *n*.

dis-si-dent (dis´i dent) *adj*. Strong and open difference with an opinion or group. **dissident** *n*. **dissidence** *n*.

dis-sil-i-ent (di sil´ēent) *adj*. Bursting open with force.

dis-sim-i-lar (di sim´i lėr) *adj*. Different; not the same; unlike. **dissimilarity** *n*.

dis-si-mil-i-tude (dis´si mil´i tōd´) *n*. Lack of resemblance; unlikeness.

dis-sim-u-late (di sim´ū lāt´) *v*. To conceal under a false appearance; to dissemble.

dis-si-pate (dis´i pāt´) *v*. To disperse or drive away; to squander or waste; to separate into parts and scatter or vanish; to become dispersed; to lose irreversibly. **dissipation** *n*.

dis-so-cial (di sō´shal) *adj*. Unsuitable; unsocial.

dis-so-ci-ate (di sō´shē āt´) *v*. To break from the association with another person or organization. **dissociation** *n*.

dis-sol-u-ble (dis sol´ū bl) *adj*. Capable of being dissolved.

dis-so-lute (dis´o lŏt´) *adj*. Loose in morals; lacking moral restraint. **dissolutely** *adv*. **dissoluteness** *n*.

dis-so-lu-tion (dis´o lŏ´shan) *n*. The act or process of changing from a solid to a fluid form; the separation of body and soul; death.

dis-solve (di zolv´) *v*. To pass into solution, such as dissolving sugar in water; to overcome, as by emotion; to fade away; to become decomposed; to terminate. **dissolvable** *adj*.

dis-sol-vent (di zol´vent) *n*. A substance that converts a solid substance into a liquid.

dis-so-nance (dis´o nans) *n*. Lack of agreement; a conflict. *Music* A harsh or disagreeable combination of sounds; discord. **dissonant** *adj*. **dissonantly** *adv*.

dis-suade (di swād´) *v*. To alter the course of action; to turn from something by persuasion or advice. **dissuader** *n*. **dissuasion** *n*. **dissuasive** *adj*.

dis-taff (dis´taf) *n*. A staff rotation for holding the flax, tow, or wool in spinning; the female side of a family; women in general.

dis-tal (dis´tal) *n*. Relatively remote from the point of attachment or origin; farthest from the center. **distally** *adv*.

dis-tance (dis´tans) *n*. Separation in time or space; the degree of separation between two points; the space that separates any two specified points in time; the quality or state of being distant; aloofness. **distance** *v*. To put space between; to keep at a distance.

dis-tant (dis´tant) *adj*. Apart or separate by a specified amount of time or space; situated at a great distance; coming from, going to, or located at a distance; remotely related. **distantly, distantness** *n*.

dis-taste (dis tāst´) *n*. Feeling an aversion to; to have an offensive taste; dislike. **distasteful** *adj*. **distastefully** *adv*. **distastefulness** *n*.

dis-tem-per (dis tem´pėr) *n*. Bad humor or temper; a highly contagious viral disease of dogs, marked by fever and by respiratory and sometimes nervous symptoms; a method of painting. **distemper** v. To throw out of order.

dis-tend (di stend´) v. To expand from internal pressure. **distensible** adj. **distention** n. **distension** n.

dis-tich (dis´tik) n. A couple of poetic verses that make sense.

dis-till (di stil´) v. To extract by distillation; to give off in drops. **distilled** adj. **distiller** n. **distillery** n.

dis-til-late (dis´ti lit) n. The condensed substance separated by distillation.

dis-til-la-tion (dis˝ti lā´shan) n. The act or process of heating a liquid or other substance until it sends off a gas or vapor and then cooling the gas of vapor until it returns to a liquid or solid form, thus separating impurities.

dis-tinct (di stingkt´) adj. Distinguished from all others; separated or distinguished by some feature; not the same in number or kind; different; clearly seen; unquestionable; one of a kind. **distinctly** adv. **distinctness** n.

dis-tinc-tion (di stingk´shan) n. The act of distinguishing; a difference; a special honor or recognition.

dis-tinc-tive (di stingk´tiv) adj. Serving to give style or distinction to something. **distinctiveness** n.

dis-tin-guish (di sting´gwish) v. To recognize as being different; to discriminate; to make something different or noticeable. **distinguishable** adj. **distinguished** adj. **distinguishably** adv.

dis-tort (di stort´) v. To twist or bend out of shape; to twist the true meaning of; to give a misleading account of. *Slang* Blow out of shape. **distortion** n.

dis-tract (di strakt´) v. To draw or divert one's attention away from something; to cause one to feel conflicting emotions. **distraction** n.

dis-trac-tion (di strak´shan) n. The act of distracting; that which distracts.

dis-trait (di strā´) adj. Absent-minded.

dis-traught (di strot´) adj. Deeply agitated with doubt or anxiety; crazed.

dis-tress (di stres´) v. To cause suffering of mind or body. **distress** n. Pain or suffering; severe physical or mental strain; a very painful situation. **distressingly** adv.

dis-trib-ute (di strib´ūt) v. To divide among many; to deliver or give out; to classify. **distribution** n. **distributive** adj.

dis-trib-u-tor (di strib´ūt er) n. One who distributes, as a wholesaler; a device that directs electrical current to spark plugs of an engine.

dis-trict (dis´trikt) n. An administrative or political section of a territory; a distinctive area. **district** v.

district attorney n. The public prosecuting officer of a judicial district.

District of Columbia n. The capital of the United States of America; the only part of the continental United States which is not a state, is not part of a state, and does not have a voting congress person in the House of Representatives or an elected senator.

dis-trust (dis trust´) n. Suspicion; doubt. **distrust** v. To doubt; to suspect; to question someone or thing. **distrustful** adj. **distrustfully** adv.

dis-turb (di sterb´) v. To destroy the tranquillity or composure of; to unsettle mentally or emotionally; to interrupt or interfere with; to bother. **disturber** n.

dis-turb-ance (di ster´bans) n. The act or state of disturbing.

dis-un-ion (dis ūn´yon) n. The termination of a union; separation.

dis-u-nite (dis´ū nīt´) v. To divide or separate.

dis-u-ni-ty (dis´ū nit´ē) n. Discord; lack of unity.

dis-use (dis ūs´) n. The state of not using; out of use.

dis-u-til-i-ty (dis˝ū til´i tē) n. The state of causing inconvenience or fatigue; harm; counterproductive.

di-syl-la-ble (dī´sil a bl) n. A word having two syllables.

ditch (dich) *n.* A trench in the earth; a trench made by digging in the earth, particularly for draining wet land. **ditch** *v.* To dig a ditch in; to surround with a ditch. *Slang* To discard; to get rid of something; to land a disabled aircraft on water.

ditch digger *n.* A person or machine that digs ditches.

ditch reed *n.* A tall reed with broad flat leaves found in damp areas of North America.

dith-er (dith´ėr) *n.* A state of nervousness or indecision; commotion.

dit-to (dit´ō) *n. pl.* **dittos** An exact copy; the same as stated before. **ditto mark** The pair of marks (") used to substitute for the word *ditto*. **ditto** *adv.*

dit-ty (dit´ē) *n. pl.* **ditties** A short, simple song.

ditty bag *n.* A small bag used by sailors to hold small articles, such as thread, buttons, and other small personal effects.

di-u-ret-ic (dī´ū ret´ik) *adj.* Tending to cause an increase in the flow of urine. **diuretic** *n.* A drug given to increase the amount of urine produced.

di-ur-nal (dī er´nal) *adj.* Having a daily cycle or recurring every day; of, relating to, or occurring in the daytime; opening in the daytime and closing at night.

di-va (dē´vä) *n. pl.* **divas** *or* **dive** A prima donna; a female opera star.

di-van (di van´) *n.* A long, backless and armless sofa or couch.

di-var-i-cate (dī var´i kāt) *v.* To spread apart; branch off.

dive (dīv) *v.* To plunge into water head first; to plunge downward at a sharp angle; to submerge; to rush headlong. **dive** *n.* The act or an instance of diving; a submerging of a submarine; a sharp decline. *Slang* A disreputable bar; in boxing, a faked knockout; in football, an offensive play in which the ball carrier plunges into the line for short yardage.

dive–bomb *v.* To bomb something from an airplane by making a steep dive toward the target and releasing the bomb. **dive–bomb-**

er *n.*

div-er (dī´vėr) *n.* A person who dives; a person who stays underwater for prolonged periods by having air supplied either from the surface or from compressed air tanks.

di-verge (di vėrj´) *v.* To move or extend in different directions from a common point; to differ in opinion or manner. **divergence** *n.* **divergent** *adj.*

di-vers (dī´vėrz) *adj.* Various; several.

di-verse (di vers´) *adj.* Different; unlike in characteristics; having various forms or qualities. **diversely** *adv.*

di-ver-si-fy (di ver´si fī´) *v.* To give variety to something; to engage in varied operations; to distribute over a wide range of types or classes. **diversification** *n.*

di-ver-sion (di ver´zhan) *n.* The act of diverting from a course, activity or use; something that diverts or amuses. **diversionary** *adj.*

di-ver-sion-ist *n.* A person characterized by political deviation; one engaged in diversionary activites.

di-ver-si-ty (di ver´si tē) *n. pl.* **diversities** A difference; variety; unlikeness.

di-vert (di vert´) *v.* To turn from a set course; to give pleasure by distracting the attention from something that is burdensome or oppressive. **diversionary** *adj.* **diversion** *n.*

di-vest (di vest´) *v.* To undress or strip, especially of clothing or equipment; to deprive or dispossess of property, authority, or title; to take away from a person. **divestment** *n.*

di-vide (di vīd´) *v.* To separate into parts, areas, or groups; to separate into pieces or portions and give out in shares;to cause to be apart; in mathematics, to perform mathematical division on a number. **divide** *n.* An act of dividing; a dividing ridge between drainage areas. **dividable** *adj.*

div-i-dend (div´i dend´) *n.* An individual share of something distributed; a bonus;

a number to be divided; a sum or fund to be divided and distributed.

divider *n.* One who divides something; a partition between separate sections in a large area.

div-i-na-tion (div˝*i* nā´sh*a*n) *n.* The act or practice of foretelling future events, or discovering obscure things.

di-vine (di vīn´) *adj.* Of, relating to, preceding from, or pertaining to God. *Informal* Extremely pleasing. **divine** *n.* A clergyman or theologian. **divine** *v.* To foretell. **divineness** *n.* **divinely** *adv.*

divining rod *n.* A forked branch or stick that supposedly indicates the location of underground water or minerals by bending downward when held over a source.

di-vi-sion (di vizh´*o*n) *n.* Separation; something which divides, separates, or marks off; the act, process, or instance of separating or keeping apart; the condition or an instance of being divided in opinion; in mathematics, the process of discovering how many times one quantity is contained in another. *Military* A self-sufficient tactical unit capable of independent action.

di-vi-sive (di vī´siv) *adj.* Tending to create dissension or disunity. **divisiveness** *n.*

di-vi-sor (di vī´zẻr) *n.* In mathematics, the number by which a dividend is to be divided.

di-vorce (di vōrs´) *n.* The legal dissolution of a marriage; the complete separation of things. **divorce** *v.* **divorcee** *n.*

div-ot (div´ot) *n.* A square of turf or sod; a piece of turf torn up by a golf club while making a shot.

di-vulge (di vulj´) *v.* To reveal or make known; to disclose; to reveal a secret.

di-vul-sion (di vul´sh*a*n) *n.* The act of pulling apart; violent separation.

Dix-ie (dik˝sē) *n.* The southern states of the continental United States.

Dix-ie-crat (dik´sē krat´) *n.* A Democrat who supported a 1948 presidential ticket opposing the civil rights stand of the Democrats. **Dixiecratic** *adj.*

dix-ie-land (dik´sē land´) *n.* Distinctly

American jazz music, usually played by a small band and characterized by ensemble and solo improvisation.

di-zy-got-ic (dī˝zī got´ik) *adj.* Describing fraternal, as in twins.

diz-zy (diz´ē) *adj.* Having a whirling sensation in the head with loss of proper balance; mentally confused; caused by or marked by giddiness; extremely rapid. **dizzily** *adv.* **dizzy** *v.*

DMZ *abbr.* Demilitarized zone.

DNA *abbr.* Deoxyribonucleic acid.

do (dö) *v.* To bring to pass; to bring about; to perform or execute; to put forth; to exert; to bring to an end. **do** *n.* A festive get-together; a command to do something. *Mus.* The first tone of a scale. **do away with** To destroy; to kill. **do in** To tire completely; to kill. **do up** To adorn or dress lavishly; to wrap and tie.

DOA *abbr.* Dead on arrival.

Do-ber-man pin-scher (dō´bẻr m*a*n pin´ shẻr) *n.* A medium-sized, slender, smooth-coated dog.

do-cent (dō´s*e*nt) *n.* A teacher at a college or university; a guide or lecturer in a museum.

doc-ile (dos´il) *adj.* Easily led, taught, or managed. **docility** *n.*

dock (dok) *n.* A landing slip or pier for ships or boats; a loading area for trucks or trains; an enclosure where the defendant sits or stands in a criminal trail. *Bot.* A weedy plant with small flower clusters. **dock** *v.* To haul or guide into a dock; to become docked. *Aeros.* To connect, as in two or more spacecrafts.

dock-age (dok´ij) *n.* A charge for the use of a dock; docking facilities.

dock-et (dok´it) *n.* A brief written summary of a document; an agenda; an identifying statement about a document placed on its cover.

dock-yard (dok´yärd) *n.* A shipyard; a place where ships are repaired or built.

doc-tor (dok´tẻr) *n.* A person trained and licensed to practice medicine, such as a physician, surgeon, veterinarian, or den-tist; a person holding the highest degree offered by a university. **doctor** *v.* To restore to good condition; to practice medicine; to administer medical treatment; to tamper with; to alter for a desired end and self gain. **doctoral** *adj.*

doc-tor-ate (dok´tėr it) *n.* The degree, status, or title of a doctor.

doc-tri-naire (dok˝tri nâr´) *n.* One who tries to put something into effect with little regard to practical difficulties.

doc-trine (dok´trin) *n.* Something taught as a body of principles; a statement of fundamental government policy especially in international relations. **doctrinal** *adj.*

doctrine of descent *n.* The theory or belief that all existing plants and animals are direct descendants from previous plants and animals.

doc-u-ment (dok´ū mẹnt) *n.* An official paper utilized as the basis, proof, or support of something. **document** *v.* To furnish documentary evidence of; to prove with, support by, or provide by documents.

doc-u-men-ta-ry (dok´ū men´ta rē) *adj.* Relating to or based on documents; an artistic way of presenting facts. **documentary** *n.*

doc-u-men-ta-tion (dok˝ū men tā´shạn) *n.*The act or use of documentary evidence.

dod-der (dod´ėr) *v.* To tremble, shake, or totter from weakness or age. **dodder** *n.* *Bot.* A parasitic, twining vine.

do-dec-a-gon (dō dek´agon) *n.* A polygon with twelve sides and twelve angles.

dodge (doj) *v.* To avoid by moving suddenly; to evade a responsibility by trickery or deceit; to shift position suddenly; to move quickly **dodge** *n.*

do-do (dō´dō) *n. pl.* **dodoes** *or* **dodos** An extinct flightless bird, formerly present on the island of Mauritius. *Informal* One hopelessly behind the times. *Slang* A stupid person; an unimaginative person.

doe (dō) *n. pl.* **does** *or* **doe** A mature female deer; any of various mammals, as the hare or kangaroo.

does-n't (duz´ent) *contr.* Does not.

dog (dog) *n.* A usually domesticated, carnivorous mammal, raised in a variety of breeds, probably descended from the common wolf; any of various animals, such as the dingo. *Slang* A mean, worthless person; a despicable fellow; an undesirable piece of merchandise; an unattractive woman or girl; a theatrical flop.

dog days *n. pl.* The hot, sultry part of summer between mid-July and September.

dog-fight (dog´fīt˝) *n.* An aerial combat between planes.

dog-ged (do´gid) *adj.* Stubbornly determined; obstinate. **doggedly** *adv.* **doggedness** *n.*

doggie bag *n.* A container used to carry home leftover food from a meal eaten at a restaurant.

dog-ma (dog´ma) *n.* A rigidly held doctrine proclaimed to be true by a religious group; a principle or idea considered to be the absolute truth.

dog-mat-ic (dog mat´ik) *adj.* Marked by an authoritative assertion of unproved or unprovable principles. **dogmatically** *adv.*

do—good-er (dō´ged´ėr) *n., Informal* An earnest but usually impractical and often naive and ineffectual humanitarian or reformer.

dog paddle *n.* A beginner's swimming stroke in which the arms and legs move up and down. **dog—paddle** *v.*

dog-tooth *n.* Eyetooth; a pointed human tooth between the incisors and the bicuspids.

dog-wood *n.* Any of several trees or shrubs with heads of small flowers having showy, white-to-pinkish, petallike blooms.

do-jo (dō´jō´) *n.* A school of instruction in the Japanese martial arts.

dol-drums (dōl´drumz) *n* A period of listlessness or despondency. *Naut.* The ocean region near the equator where there is very little wind.

dole (dōl) *n.* The distribution of food,

money, or clothing to the needy; a grant of government funds to the unemployed; something portioned out and distributed bit by bit. **dole** *adj.*

dole-ful (dōl'fŭl) *adj.* Filled with grief or sadness. **dolefully** *adv.* **dolefulness** *n.*

dol-er-ite (dol'e rīt") *n.* An igneous rock, similar to basalt, whose composition can not be determined without a microscope.

dol-i-cho-ce-phal-ic (dol"i kō se fal'ik) *adj.* Having a long head; with the width of the skull small in proportion to the length from back to front.

doll (dol) *n.* A child's toy having a human form. *Slang* A woman; an attractive person. **dolled up** To dress up elegantly, as for a special occasion.

dol-lar (dol'ĕr) *n.* A coin, note, or token representing one dollar; the standard monetary unit of the United States.

dol-lop (dol'op) *n.* A lump or blob of a semi-liquid substance; an indefinite amount or form.

dol-ly (dol'ē) *n. pl.* **dollies** A doll; a low, flat frame on wheels or rollers used to move heavy loads; a wheeled apparatus for moving a motion picture or television camera toward or away from the action.

dol-men (dōl'man) *n.* A prehistoric monument made up of a huge stone set on upright stones.

do-lor-ous (dol'ĕr us) *adj.* Marked by grief or pain; sad; mournful. **dolorously** *adv.* **dolorousness** *n.*

dol-phin (dol'fin) *n.* Any of various small cetaceans with the snout in the shape of a beak and the neck vertebrae partially fused.

dolt (dōlt) *n.* A stupid person.

do-main (dō mān') *n.* A territory under one government; a field of activity or interest.

dome (dōm) *n.* A roof resembling a hemisphere; something suggesting a dome.

do-mes-tic (do mes'tik) *adj.* Of or relating to the home, household or family life; interested in household affairs and home life; tame or domesticated; of or relating to

policies of one's country; originated in a particular country. **domestic** *n.* A household servant. **domestically** *adv.* **domesticity** *n.*

domestic animal *n.* An animal, reclaimed from a wild state, adapted to live and breed in a tame condition with man.

do-mes-ti-cate (do mes'ti kāt") *v.* To tame, as an animal.

dom-i-cile (dom'i sīl') *n.* A dwelling place, house, or home; residence. **domicile** *v.* **domiciliary** *adj.*

dom-i-nant (dom'i nant) *adj.* Having the most control or influence; most overwhelming; in genetics, producing a typical effect even when paired with an unlike gene for the same characteristic. **dominance** *n.* **dominantly** *adv.*

dom-i-nate (dom'i nāt") *v.* To rule or control; to exert the supreme determining or guiding influence on; to occupy the most prominent position in or over something. **dominator** *n.*

dom-i-na-tion (dom"i nā'shan) *n.* The exercise of supreme power; dominion.

dom-i-neer (dom'i nēr') *v.* To govern with overbearing control.

Dominica Island *n.* Republic in the East Caribbean.

Dominican Republic *n.* Country occupying the east part of Hispaniola.

do-min-ion (do min'yan) *n.* The power of supreme authority; controlling.

Dominion Day (do min'yan dā') *n.* Canada Day.

dom-i-no (dom'i nō") *n. pl.* **dominoes** *or* **dominos** A long, loose, hooded cloak usually worn with a half mask as a masquerade costume; a person wearing a domino; the mask itself; a small rectangular block of wood or plastic with the face marked with dots. **dominos** *n. pl.* A game containing 28 of such pieces.

domino theory *n.* The theory that if a certain event occurs, a series of similar events will follow.

Don (don) *n.* Sir; used as a courtesy title with a man's name in Spanish-speaking countries; a Spanish gentleman; a head, fellow, or tutor at an English university; a Mafia leader.

don (don) *v.* To put something on; to dress.

do-na-tion (dō nā′shən) *n.* The act of giving or bestowing a gift especially to needy or to charity.

done (dun) *adj.* Completely finished or through; doomed to failure, defeat, or death; cooked adequately.

do-nee (dō nē′) *n.* A recipient of a gift.

done for *adj.* Mortally stricken; doomed; left with no opportunity for recovery; ruined.

don-key (dong′kē) *n. pl.* **donkeys** The domesticated ass. *Informal* A stubborn person.

do-nor (dō′nėr) *n.* One who gives, donates, or contributes.

Don Quixote (don″kē hō′tē) *n.* The idealistic hero of Cervantes' *Don Quixote;* an impractical idealist.

don't (dōnt) *contr.* Do not.

dood-le (dōdel) *v.* To scribble, design, or sketch aimlessly, especially when preoccupied. **doodle** *n.*

doom (dōm) *n.* To pronounce judgment, particularly an official condemnation to a severe penalty or death; an unhappy destiny. **doom** *v.* To condemn; to make certain the destruction of.

dooms-day (dōmz′dā″) *n.* Judgment day; a dreaded day of judgment or reckoning; the end of the world.

door (dōr) *n.* A barrier, normally swinging or sliding, by which an entry is closed and opened; a means of entrance or exit.

door-knob *n.* The handle that is turned to release the door latch.

door-mat *n.* A small rug or mat placed near an entrance for wiping dirt from the shoes.

door-sill *n.* The threshold of a doorway.

door-step *n.* A step raised above the level of the ground outside an outer door.

dope (dōp) *n.* A preparation for giving a desired quality to a substance or surface, such as an antiknock added to gasoline. *Slang* A narcotic, especially one that is addictive; a stupid person; facts and details;

all the details.

dope-ster (dōp′stėr) *n.* One who forecasts the outcome of future sports events, an election, or other contests.

dor-king (dor′king) *n.* A domestic fowl, having five claws on each foot.

dor-mant (dor′mant) *adj.* A sleep; a state of inactivity or rest. **dormancy** *n.*

dor-mi-to-ry (dor′mi tōr″ē) *n.* A large room that contains a number of beds; as at a college.

dor-nick (dor′nik) *n.* A small stone, or a chunk of rock.

dor-sal (dor′sal) *adj.* Of, relating to, or situated on or near the back.

dor-si-ven-tral (dor′si ven″tral) *adj.* Having distinct differences in the dorsal and ventral surfaces.

dor-sum (dor′sum) *n.* The back; the whole surface of an animal's back.

do-ry (dōr′ē) *n. pl.* **dories** A small flat bottomed boat with high, flaring sides and a sharp bow.

DOS *abbr.* Disk operating system.

dos-age (dō′sij) *n.* The administration of medicine in a measured dose; the amount administered.

dose (dōs) *n.* The measured quantity of a therapeutic agent to be taken at one time or at stated intervals. *Med.* The prescribed amount of radiation to which a certain part of the body is exposed.

dos-si-er (dos′ē ā′) *n.* A complete file of documents or papers giving detailed information about a person or affair.

dot (dot) *n.* A small round spot; a mark made by or as if by a writing implement; a small round mark used in punctuation; a precise moment in time; a short click or buzz forming a letter or part of a letter in the Morse code.

dot-age (dō′tij) *n.* Feebleness or imbecility, epecially in old age.

dote (dōt) *v.* To show excessive affection or fondness; to exhibit mental decline, especially as a result of senility. **doter** *n.*

dou-ble (dub′l) *adj.* Twice as much; composed of two like parts; designed for two.

Bot. Having more than the usual number of petals. **double** *n.* An actor who takes the place of another for scenes calling for special skill; in baseball, a two-base hit. **double** *v.* In baseball, to make a double; to make or become twice as great; to fold in two; to turn and go back; to serve an additional purpose. **doubly** *adv.*

double–breasted *adj.* Pertained to a coat or vest, one half of the front overlaps over the other.

double–cross *v., Slang* To betray. **double cross** *n.* The betrayal of a peron, a colleague or associate.

double–deck-er (dub´l dek´ėr) *n.* A vehicle, as a ship or other means of transportation, with two decks for passengers; a sandwich with three slices of bread and two layers of filling.

double dip *n.* A person holding a salaried position while receiving a pension from a previous job.

double entendre (dub´l än tän´dre) *n.* A double meaning; a word or expression capable of two interpretations or meanings.

double–faced *adj.* Deceitful; taking two sides; hypocritical.

dou-ble-head-er (dub´l hed´ėr) *n.* Two games played consecutively on the same day or night.

double indemnity *n.* A clause in a life insurance or an accident policy where the company agrees to double the policy's face value in case of accidental death.

double jointed *adj.* Having unusually flexible joints which allow connected parts to bend at abnormal angles.

double take *n.* A delayed second look or reaction to what first appeared normal.

doubt (dout) *v.* To be uncertain or mistrustful about something; to distrust. **doubt** *n.* **doubter** *n.*

dough (dō) *n.* A soft mixture of flour, liquids, and other ingredients which is baked to make bread, pastry, and other foods. *Slang* Money. **doughy** *adj.*

dough-nut *or* **donut (dō´nut˝)** *n.* A small cake made of rich, light dough which is

deep-fat fried.

dough-ty (dou´tē) *adj.* Marked by valor; brave.

dour (der) *adj.* Stern and forbidding; morose and ill-tempered.

douse (dous) *v.* To plunge into liquid; to throw water on; to drench; to extinguish. **douser** *n.*

dove (duv) *n.* Any of numerous pigeons; a gentle, innocent person. **dovish** *adj.*

dow-a-ger (dou´a jėr) *n.* A widow holding a title or property from her dead husband; a dignified, elderly woman.

dow-dy (dou´dē) *adj.* Not neat or tidy; not stylish. **dowdyish** *adj.* **dowdiness** *n.*

dow-el (dou´el) *n.* A round wooden pin which fits tightly into an adjacent hole to fasten together the two pieces.

dow-er (dou´ėr) *n.* The part of a deceased man's estate that is given to his widow by law. **dower** *v.* To provide with a dower.

down (doun) *adv.* Toward or in a lower physical condition; from a higher to a lower position; the direction that is opposite of up; a lower or worse condition or status; from a past time or past generations of people; partial payment at the time of purchase. **down** *v.* To put something in writing; to bring, strike, put, or throw down; in football, any of a series of plays during which a team must advance at least ten yards in order to retain possession of the ball. **down** *n.* A grassy highland used for grazing; soft, fluffy feathers of a young bird; a soft hairy growth, such as that on a peach.

down-er *n., Slang* A depressant or sedative drug; a barbiturate; something that is depressing.

downpour *n.* A heavy rain, an unusually sudden rain.

Down's syndrome *n.* Extreme mental deficiency; a condition in which a child is born with a broad, short skull, slanting eyes, and broad hands with short fingers;

Mongolism.

down-ward (doun´wėrd) *adv.* From a higher to a lower place. **downwardly** *adj.*

down-wind (doun´wind´) *adv. & adj.* In the direction toward which the wind blows.

dow-ry (dou´rē) *n.* The money, goods, or estate which a woman brings to her husband in marriage; a gift.

dowse (douz) *v.* To search for with a divining rod to find underground water or minerals. **dowser** *n.*

dox-ol-o-gy (dok sol´o jē) *n. pl.* **doxologies** A hymn or verse in praise of God.

doz-en (duz´en) *n.* Twelve of a kind; a set of twelve things. **dozen** *adj.* **dozenth** *adj.*

drab (drab) *adj.* Of a light, dull brown or olive brown color; commonplace or dull. **drabness** *n.*

drach-ma (drak´ma) *n. pl.* **drachmas** *or* **drachmae** A silver coin of ancient Greece.

draft (draft) *n.* A current of air; a sketch or plan of something to be made; a note for the transfer of money; the depth of water a ship draws with a certain load. *Milit.* A mandatory selection of men for service. **draft** *v.* To draw a tentative plan or sketch. **draft** *adj.* The drawing of a liquid from a keg or tap.

draftee *n.* A person who is drafted for military service.

drag (drag) *v.* To pull along or haul by force; to move with painful or undue slowness; to bring by force; to proceed slowly; to lag behind. *Slang* To puff on a pipe, cigarette, or cigar. **drag** *n.* Something which retards motion or action; a tool used under water to detect or collect objects; something which is boring or dull. *Slang* Someone or something that is bothersome; a street; a race. **dragger** *n.*

drag-on (drag´on) *n.* A mythical, giant, serpent-like, winged, fire-breathing monster.

drag-on-et (drag´o net´) *n.* A little dragon; any small, brightly colored marine fish found in shallow tropical waters.

drag-on-fly (drag´on flī´) *n.* A large, harmless insect which holds its wings in a horizontal position when at rest; during its naiad stage it has rectal gills.

drag queen *n., Slang* A male homosexual who dresses in female clothing, especially one who performs as a female publicly.

drain (drān) *n.* To draw off liquid gradually; to use up; to exhaust physically or emotionally; to flow off gradually. **drain** *n.* A means, such as a trench or channel, by which liquid matter is drained; something which causes depletion. **drainer** *n.*

drainage *n.* A system, process or act of draining.

drainpipe *n.* A pipe for draining.

drake (drāk) *n.* A male duck.

dram (dram) *n.* A small drink; a small portion; a measurement equaling approximately .06 ounces.

dra-ma (drä´ma) *n.* A composition in prose or verse, especially one to be presented on the stage, recounting a serious story; a play. **dramatic** *adj.*

dra-mat-ics (dra mat´iks) *n.* Amateur theatrical productions; the study of theatrical arts; excessive emotional behavior.

dram-a-tist (dram´a tist) *n.* A playwright.

drank *v.* Past tense of drink.

drape (drāp) *v.* To cover or adorn with something; to arrange or hang in loose folds. **drape** *n.* The manner in which a cloth hangs or falls.

dras-tic (dras´tik) *adj.* Acting extremely harsh or severe. **drastically** *adv.*

draught (draft) *n. & v.* A variation of draft.

draughts (drafts) *n. pl.* The game of checkers, as referred to by the British.

draw (dro) *v.* To move or cause to move toward a direction or to a position as if by leading; to take out for use; to withdraw funds as from a bank or savings account; to take in air; to sketch on paper or pad; to elicit a response; to attract; to formulate from evidence at hand; to displace water in floating; to provoke; to end something undecided or tied; to write in a set form.

draw-back (dro´bak´) *n.* An undesirable feature.

draw-bridge (drå´brij´) *n.* A bridge that can be raised or lowered to allow ships and boats to pass.

draw-er (dror) *n.* One that draws pictures; a sliding box or receptacle in furniture. **drawers** *n. pl.* An article of clothing for the lower body.

draw-ing (drau´ing) *n.* An act of drawing; the process of deciding something by choosing lots; the art of representing something or someone by means of lines; the amount drawn from an account.

drawl (draul) *v.* To speak slowly with prolonged vowels.

drawn *adj.* Haggard.

dray (drā) *n.* A low, heavy cart without sides, used for hauling.

dread (dred) *v.* To fear greatly; to anticipate with alarm, anxiety, or reluctance. **dread** *n.* A great fear.

dread-ful (dred´ful) *adj.* Inspiring dread; very distasteful or shocking; awful. **dreadfully, dreadfulness** *n.*

dream (drēm) *n.* A series of thought images, or emotions which occur during the rapid eye movement or REM state of sleep; an experience in waking life that has the characteristics of a dream; a daydream; something notable for its beauty or enjoyable quality; something that is strongly desired; something that fully satisfies a desire. **dreamful, dreamlike** *adj.* **dreamfully** *adv.* **dreamfulness** *n.*

dreamer *n.* A person who indulges in daydreams; a person living in a world of imagination.

drea-ry (drēr´ē) *adj.* Bleak and gloomy; dull. **drearily** *adv.* **dreariness** *n.*

dredge (drej) *n.* An apparatus used to remove sand or mud from the bottom of a body of water; a boat or barge equipped with a dredge. **dredge** *v.* To dig, gather, or deepen with a dredging machine; to use a dredge; in cooking, to coat with a powdered substance, expecially flour or corn meal. **dredger** *n.*

dregs (dregz) *n.* The sediment of a liquid; the least desirable part.

drench (drench) *v.* To wet thoroughly; to throw water on. **drencher** *n.*

dress (dres) *n.* An outer garment for women and girls; covering or appearance appropriate to a particular time. **dress** *v.* To set straight; to put clothes on; to arrange in a straight line at proper intervals; to provide with clothing; to kill and prepare for market; to put on or wear formal or fancy clothes.

dressmaker *n.* A person who makes or alters women's clothing.

dress rehearsal *n.* A rehearsal, complete with costumes and stage props.

drew *v.* Past tense of draw.

drib-ble (drib´l) *v.* To drip; to slobber or drool; to bounce a ball repeatedly; to move in short bounces. **dribbler** *n.*

dried-up (drīd´up´) *adj.* Lacking moisture; wrinkled and shriveled.

drift (drift) *v.* To be driven or carried along by or as if by currents of air or water; to move along the line of least resistance; to move about aimlessly; to be carried along with no guidance or control; to accumulate in piles, as sand; to deviate from a set course; in the western United States, to drive livestock slowly to allow grazing. **drifter** *n.*

driftwood *n.* Wood floating on, or washed ashore by, water.

drill (dril) *n.* A tool used in boring holes; the act of training soldiers in marching and the manual of arms; a physical or mental exercise to perfect a skill by regular practice; a marine snail which is destructive to oysters by boring through their shells and feeding on them. **drill** *v.* To make a hole with a drill; to train by repeated exercise.

drill-mas-ter (dril´mas˝tėr) *n., Milit.* A noncommissioned officer who instructs in military drill.

drill press *n.* A drilling machine where the drill is pressed upon the work by power or lever.

drink (dringk) *v.* To take liquid into the mouth and swallow; to take in or suck up; to receive into one's consciousness; to partake of alcoholic beverages. **drink** *n.* A liquid suitable for swallowing; alcoholic beverages; a sizable body of water. **drinkable** *adj.* **drinker** n.

drip (drip) *v.* To fall in drops. **drip** *n.* Liquid or moisture that falls in drops; the sound made by falling drops. *Slang* A dull or unattractive person.

drip coffee *n.* Coffee made by allowing boiling water to drip slowly through ground coffee.

drip-dry (drip´drī´) *adj.* Made of a washable fabric which dries without wrinkling and needs no ironing. **drip-dry** *v.*

drive (drīv) *v.* To propel, push, or press onward; to repulse by authority; to force into a particular act or state; to operate or be conveyed in a vehicle; to supply a moving force; to impress convincingly with force; in sports, to hit a ball hard in a game; to rush or advance violently. **drive** *n.* The act of driving; a trip taken in a vehicle; the means or apparatus by which motion is transmitted to a machine; an organized movement or campaign to accomplish something; initiative; the act of urging animals together. *Milit.* A full-scale military offensive.

drive-in *n.* A place of business which allows consumers to be accommodated while remaining in their vehicles.

driv-el (driv´el) *v.* To slobber; to talk nonsensically. **drivel** *n.*

driver's license *n.* A legal permit that allows the holder to drive a motor vehicle.

drive shaft *n.* A shaft that transmits mechanical power.

driz-zle (driz´el) *n.* A fine, quiet, gentle rain. **drizzle** *v.*

droit (droit) *n.* A legal right or claim.

droll (drōl) *adj.* Whimsically comical. **drollery** *n.*

drom-e-dar-y (drom´e der´ē) *n. pl.* **dromedaries** A one-humped camel, found in northern Africa and western Asia.

drone (drōn) *n.* A male bee, especially a honey bee, which has no sting, performs no work, and produces no honey; a person who depends on others for his survival; an unmanned boat or aircraft controlled by a remote control device. **drone** *v.* To make a low, continuous humming sound; to speak monotonously.

drool (drōl) *v.* To let saliva dribble from the mouth. *Slang* To make an exaggerated expression of desire. **drool** *n.*

droop (drōp) *v.* To hang or bend downward; to become depressed. **droop** *n.* **droopiness** *n.* **droopy** *adj.*

drop (drop) *n.* A tiny, pear-shaped or rounded mass of liquid; a small quantity of a substance; the smallest unit of liquid measure; the act of falling; a swift decline; the vertical distance from a higher to a lower level; a delivery of something by parachute. **drop** *v.* To fall in drops; to descend from one area or level to another; to fall into a state of collapse or death; to pass into a given state or condition; to end or terminate an association or relationship with; to deposit at a specified place. **drop behind** To fall behind. **drop by** To pay a brief visit. **drop out** To quit school without graduating; to withdraw from society.

drop shipment *n.* A shipment of merchandise delivered directly to a retailer by the manufacturer but billed by the wholesaler or distributor.

drop-sy (drop´sē) *n., Med.* A diseased condition in which large amounts of fluid collect in the body tissues and cavities.

dross (dros) *n.* An impurity which forms on the surface of molten metal; inferior, trivial, or worthless matter.

drought (drout) *n.* A prolonged period of dryness, that effects crops; a chronic shortage of something.

drove (drōv) *n.* A herd being driven in a body; a crowd in motion. **drove** *v.* Past tense of drive.

drown (droun) *v.* To kill or die by suffocating in a liquid; to overflow; to cause not to be heard by making a loud noise;

to drive out.

drowse (drouz) *v.* To doze. **drowse** *n.*

drows-y (drou´zē) *adj.* Sleepy; tending to induce sleep. **drowsiness** *n.*

drub (drub) *v.* To hit with a stick; to abuse with words; to defeat decisively.

drudge (druj) *n.* A person who does tiresome or menial tasks. **drudge** *v.* **drudgeries, drudgery** *n.*

drug (drug) *n.* A substance used in the treatment of disease or illness; a narcotic. **drug** *v.* To take drugs for narcotic effect; to mix or dose with drugs.

drug-get (drug´it) *n.* A durable cloth of wool and other fibers used chiefly as a floor covering.

drug-gist (drug´ist) *n.* A pharmacist; the owner or operator of a drugstore.

drug-store (drug´stōr´) *n.* A retail business place where prescriptions for medicines are filled and miscellaneous merchandise is sold.

drum (drum) *n.* A musical percussion instrument consisting of a hollow frame with a cover stretched across one or both ends, played by beating with sticks or the hands; something with the shape of a drum; a cylindrical container; a metal container holding a capacity between 12 and 110 gallons; any of various percoid fishes that make a drumming noise. **drum** *v.* To beat a drum; to tap rhythmically or incessantly; to instill by repetition; to dismiss in disgrace. **drum up** To invent or devise; to go out and actively pursue new accounts or business.

drunk (drungk) *adj.* Intoxicated with alcohol which impairs the physical and mental faculties of a person; overwhelmed by strong feeling or emotion. **drunk** *n.* A drunkard.

drunk-ard (drungk´kèrd) *adj.* A person who is intoxicated by liquor.

drunk-om-e-ter (drung kom´i tèr) *n.* An instrument for measuring the alcoholic content in the bloodstream by testing the breath.

drupe (drŏp) *n.* A fruit, as the peach, usually having one large pit or seed.

dry (drī) *adj.* Free from moisture or liquid; having little or no rain; devoid of running water; not liquid; thirsty; eaten without a garnish, such as jelly; humorous in a shrewd, impersonal way; not sweet, as in dry wines. *Informal* Opposed to the sale or consumption of alcoholic beverages. **dry** *v.* To remove the water from. **dryly** *adv.* **dryness** *n.*

dry-ad (drī´ad) *n.* A wood nymph.

dry–clean (drī´klēn) *v.* To clean cloth or fabrics with chemical solvents, as benzenes, rather than water.

dry fly *n.* An artificial fly, designed to float, used in fishing.

dry goods *n.* Textile fabrics and related products as distinguished from foodstuffs and hardware.

drying oil *n.* An oily, organic liquid such as linseed which, when spread thinly and exposed to the air, hardens to a tough, elastic film.

du-al (dŏ´al) *adj.* Made up or composed of two parts; having a double purpose.

dub (dub) *v.* To confer knighthood upon; to nickname; to give a new sound track to; to add to a film, radio, or television production; to transpose sound already recorded. **dub** *n.* **dubber** *n.*

du-bi-ous (dŏ´bē us) *adj.* Causing doubt; unsettled in judgment; reluctant to agree; questionable as to quality or validity; verging on impropriety. **dubiousness** *n.* **dubiously** *adv.*

du-cal (dŏ´kal) *adj.* Pertaining to a duke or dukedom.

duch-ess (duch´is) *n.* The wife or widow of a duke; a female holding a ducal title in her own right.

duck (duk) *n.* Any of various swimming birds with short necks and legs; the flesh of any of these birds used as food. *Slang* A person. **duck**

v. To lower the head and body quickly; to evade; to plunge quickly under water.

duck-pins (duk´pinz˝) *n.* A type of bowling game that uses a smaller ball and shorter and thicker pins than regulation tenpins.

duck-weed (duk´wēd˝) *n.* A small aquatic plant which floats free on still water.

duct (dukt) *n.* A bodily tube or canal, especially one carrying a secretion; a tubular passage through which something flows.

duc-tile (duk´til) *adj.* Capable of being drawn into a fine strand or wire; easily influenced or persuaded.

dud (dud) *n., Informal* A bomb, shell, or explosive round which fails to detonate; something which turns out to be a failure. **dud**spl., *Slang* Clothing; personal belongings.

dude (dōd) *n. Informal* A city person vacationing on a ranch; a man who is a fancy dresser. *Slang* A fellow.

dudg-eon (duj´on) *n.* A sullen, displeased, or indignant mood.

due (dō) *adj.* Owed; payable; owed or owing as a natural or moral right; scheduled or expected to occur. **due** *n.* Something that is deserved or owed. **dues** *n. pl.* A fee or charge for membership.

du-el (dō´el) *n.* A premeditated combat between two people, usually fought to resolve a point of honor; a struggle which resembles a duel. **duel** *v.* **duelist** *n.*

due process of law *n.* A course of formal proceedings that are carried out in accordance with established rules and principles for protecting and enforcing individual rights.

du-et (dō et´) *n.* A musical composition for two performers or musical instruments.

duff (duf) *v.* To manipulate so as to make anything pass for something new or different; misrepresent.

duf-fel (duf´el) *n.* A coarse woolen material with a thick nap.

duffel bag *n.* A large cloth bag for carrying personal belongings.

duffer *n.* An incompetent or clumsy person; something counterfeit or worthless.

dug (dug) *n.* The nipple of a female mammal.

dug-out (dug´out˝) *n.* A boat made by hollowing out a large log; a shelter that protects the players at a baseball game.

duke (dōk) *n.* A noble ranking below a prince and above a marquis. **dukes** *n. pl. Slang* The fists. **dukedom** *n.*

dul-cet (dul´sit) *adj.* Melodious; pleasing to the ear; having an agreeable, soothing quality.

dul-ci-mer (dul´si mèr) *n.* A musical stringed instrument played with two small picks or by plucking.

dull (dul) *adj.* Stupid; lacking in intelligence or understanding; insensitive; having a blunt edge or point; not intensely felt; arousing no interest or curiosity; not bright; overcast or gloomy; unclear. **dull** *v.* To make or become dull; to blunt or to make blunt. **dullness** *n.* **dully** *adv.*

du-ly (dō´lē) *adv.* In a proper or due manner.

dumb (dum) *adj.* Unable to speak; temporarily speechless. *Informal* Stupid; not bright. **dumbly** *adv.* **dumbness** *n.*

dumb-bell (dum´bel˝) *n.* A short bar with two adjustable weighted disks attached to each end, used in pairs for calisthenic exercise.

dumb-waiter (dum´wā˝tèr) *n.* A small elevator, usually found in the kitchen of a home, which is used to convey goods, as food or dishes, from one floor to another.

dum-dum (dum´dum˝) *n.* A soft-nosed, small arms bullet designed to expand on contact.

dum-found *or* **dumb-found (dum found´)** *v.* To confound with amazement. **dumfounded** *adj.*

dum-my (dum´ē) *n. pl.* **dummies** One who is habitually silent; one who is stupid; the exposed hand in bridge; a bridge player whose hand is a dummy; an imitation or copy of something, used as a substitute; a person or agency secretly in the service of another.

dump (dump) *v.* To throw down or discard in a mass; to empty material out of a container or vehicle; in computer science, to reproduce data stored in the working memory onto an external storage medium. **dump** *n.* A place where garbage or trash is dumped. *Milit.* A military storage facility. *Slang.* A dilapidated, messy or disreputable place.

dump-ling (dump´ling) *n.* A small mass of dough cooked in soup or stew; sweetened dough wrapped around fruit, baked, and served as dessert.

dumps *n.* A dull or gloomy state of mind; as down in the dumps.

dump truck *n.* A transport truck with a body that can be tilted to unload the contents through a rear opening.

dun (dun) *v.* To press a debtor for payment. **dun** *n.* A brownish gray to dull grayish brown color. **dun** *adj.*

dunce (duns) *n.* A slow-witted person.

dune (dūn) *n.* A ridge or hill of sand that has been blown or drifted by the wind.

dung (dung) *n.* The excrement of animals; manure.

dun-ga-ree (dun˝ga rē´) *n.* A sturdy, coarse, cotton fabric, especially blue denim; pants or overalls made from this material.

dun-geon (dun´jon) *n.* A dark, confining, underground prison chamber.

dunk (dungk) *v.* To dip a piece of food into liquid before eating; to submerge someone in a playful fashion.

du-o (dō´ō) *n. pl.* **duos** An instrument duet; two people in close association.

du-o-de-num (dū´o dē´num) *n. pl.* **duodena** *or* **duodenums** The first portion of the small intestine, extending from the lower end of the stomach to the jejunum. **duodenal** *adj*

du-o-logue (dō´o log˝) *n.* A dialogue between two persons.

dupe (dōp) *n.* A person who is easily manipulated or deceived. **dupe** *v.* To deceive or trick.

du-ple (dō´pl) *adj.* Having two members, parts, or elements; double.

du-plex (dō´pleks) *adj.* Double; having two parts. **duplex** *n.* Anything that has two parts; an apartment with rooms on two adjoining floors.

du-pli-cate (dō´pli kit) *adj.* Identical with another; existing in or consisting of two corresponding parts. **duplicate** *n.* Either of two things which are identical; an exact copy of an original. **duplicate** *v.* To make an exact copy of. **duplication** *n.*

du-plic-i-ty (dō plis´i tē) *n.* The practice of contradictory speech or thoughts with the intent to deceive; double-dealing.

du-ra-ble (der´a bl) *adj.* Able to continue for a prolonged period of time without deterioration. **durability** *n.*

du-ra ma-ter (dor´a mā´tèr) *n.* The tough fibrous membrane that covers the brain and spinal cord.

du-ra-tion (de rā´shan) *n.* The period of time during which something exists or lasts; continuance in time.

du-ress (de res´) *n.* Constraint by fear or force; in law, coercion illegally applied; forced restraint.

dur-ing (dur´ing) *prep.* Throughout the time of; within the time of.

durum wheat (dèr´um hwēt) *n.* A variety of wheat that yields a flour used for the production of spaghetti, macaroni, and related foods.

dusk (dusk) *n.* The earliest part of the evening, just before darkness; semidarkness, before night.

dust (dust) *n.* Fine, dry particles of matter; the earth, as a place of burial; the surface of the ground; a scorned condition. **dust** *v.* To remove the dust from; to sprinkle or cover with a powdery material.

dust jacket *n.* A removable paper cover for a hardback book, used to protect the binding.

Dutch (duch) *n.* The people of the Netherlands; the language of the Netherlands. **Dutch** *adj.* **Dutchman** *n.*

Dutch elm disease *n.* A fungus which affects elm trees, eventually killing them.

Dutch treat *n.* An outing during which each

person pays his or her own way.

duty (dŏ'tē) *n. pl.* **duties** Something which a person must or ought to do; a moral obligation; a service, action, or task assigned to one, especially in the military; a government tax on imports.

DVM *abbr.* Doctor of Veterinary Medicine.

dwarf (dworf) *n. pl.* **dwarfs** *or* **dwarves** A human being, plant, or animal of a much smaller than normal size. **dwarf** *v.* To stunt the natural growth of; to cause to seem small by comparison. **dwarfish** *adj.*

dwarf-ism (dwor'fiz"m) *n.* The condition of stunted growth.

dwell (dwel) *v.* To live, as an inhabitant; to continue in a given place or condition; to focus one's attention. **dweller** *n.*

dwell-ing (dwel'ing) *n.* A house or building in which one lives.

DWI *abbr.* Driving while intoxicated.

dwin-dle (dwin'dl) *v.* To waste away; to become steadily less.

dy-ar-chy (dī'är kē) *n.* A type of government where the power is vested in two rulers.

dye (dī) *n.* To fix a color in or to stain materials; to color with or become colored by a dye. **dye** *n.* A color imparted by a dye; a coloring matter or material.

dye-wood (dī'wed") *n.* A type of wood from which coloring material is taken for the purpose of dyeing things.

dy-ing (dī'ing) *adj.* Coming to the end of life; about to die.

dy-nam-ic (dī nam'ik) *adj.* Marked by energy and productive activity or change; of or relating to energy, motion, or force. **dynamically** *adv.*

dy-nam-ics (dī nam'iks) *n.* The part of physics which deals with force, energy, and motion and the relationship between them.

dy-na-mism (dī'na miz"um) *n.* A kind of theory that explains the universe in terms of forces. **dynamist** *n.* **dynamistic** *adj.*

dy-na-mite (dī'na mīt") *n.* An explosive composed of nitroglycerin or ammonium nitrate and an absorbent material, usually packaged in stick form. **dynamite** *v.* To

blow up with or as if with dynamite.

dy-na-mo (dī'na mō") *n.* A person who is very energetic.

dy-na-mom-e-ter (dī'no mom'i ter) *n.* A type of device that is used for the purpose of measuring mechanical force. **dynamometric** *adj.*

dy-na-mo-tor (dī'na mō"ter) *n.* A combined electrical motor and generator.

dy-nap-o-lis (dī nap' ō lis) *n.* A type of city that has been planned for orderly growth along a traffic artery.

dy-nas-ty (dī'na stē) *n. pl.* **dynasties** A succession of rulers from the same family; a family or group which maintains great power, wealth, or position for many years. **dynastic** *adj.*

dys-cra-sia (dis krā'zha) *n.* A condition of the body that is abnormal.

dys-en-ter-y (dis'en ter"ē) *n.* An infection of the lower intestinal tract which produces pain, fever, and severe diarrhea. **dysenteric** *adj.*

dys-func-tion (dis fungk'shan) *n.* An abnormal functioning; not working proper. **dysfunctional** *adj.*

dys-gen-e-sis (dis'jen e sis") *n.* The defective development of the gonads of one's body such as in Turner's syndrome.

dys-gen-ic (dis'jen ik) *adj.* To be biologically defective.

dys-lex-i-a (dis lex'ēa) *n.* An impairment in one's ability to read; unable to read. **dyslexic** *adj.*

dys-men-or-rhea (dis'men or ē"a) *n.* A menstruation of the woman that is a painful, abnormal condition. **dysmenorrheic, dysmenorrheal** *adj.*

dys-pep-sia (dis pep'sha) *n.* Indigestion. **dyspeptic** *adj.*

dys-pro-si-um (dis prō'sē um) *n.* A metallic element used in nuclear research, symbolized by Dy.

dys-tro-phy (is'tro fē) *n.* Atrophy of muscle tissue; any of various neuromuscular disorders, especially muscular dystrophy. **dystrophia** *adj.*

dz *abbr.* Dozen.

E, e (ē) The fifth letter of the English alphabet. *Mus.* The third tone in the natural scale of C.

each (ēch) *adj.* Everyone of two or more considered separately. *adv.* To or for each; apiece.

each other *pron.* Each in reciprocal action or relation; one another.

ea-ger (ē´gėr) *adj.* Marked by enthusiastic interest or desire; having a great desire or wanting something. **eagerly** *adv.*

eager beaver *n.* A person who is overly or extremely zealous.

ea-gle (ē´gl) *n.* A large, powerful bird of prey having a powerful bill, broad strong wings, and soaring flight; a United States gold coin worth ten dollars; a score of two under par on a hole in golf.

eagle-eyed *adj.* Having exceptional vision.

eagle ray *n.* A type of stingray which has broad pectoral fins.

eag-let (ē´glit) *n.* The young of an eagle.

ear (ēr) *n., Anat.* The hearing organ in vertebrates, located on either side of the head; any of various organs capable of detecting vibratory motion; the ability to hear keenly; attention or heed; something that resembles the external ear. **ears** Listen closely. **ear** Without reference to written music.

ear-ache (ēr´āk˝) *n.* The pain which is associated with the ear.

ear-drop (ēr´drop˝) *n.* A type of earring which has a pendant attached to it.

ear-drum (ēr´drum˝) *n.* The tympanic membrane which is located inside the ear.

eared (ērd) *adj.* Having ears.

eared seal *n.* Type of seal which has small well-developed external ears such as the fur seal and the sea lions.

ear-flap *n.* A covering for the ears which may be an extension of a cap.

ear-ful (ēr´ful) *n.* Gossip or news about someone.

ear-ing (ēr´ing) *n.* A line which is attached to a sail and is used for the purpose of

attaching the sail to the gaff or yard.

earl (erl) *n.* A British title for a nobleman ranking above a viscount and below a marquis. **earldom** *n.*

ear-lap *n.* The lobe of the ear; the whole external ear.

earless seal *n.* A type of seal which does not have external ears such as the hair seal.

earl marshal *n.* In England, an officer who is the royal attendant on ceremonial occasions.

ear-lobe (ēr´lōb) *n.* The part of the ear which hangs below the pinna and is the location for earrings.

ear-lock (ēr´läk) *n.* A section of the hair which hangs in front of the ear.

ear-ly (er´lē) *adj.* Occurring near the beginning of a period of time; a development or a series; distant in past time; before the usual or expected time; occurring in the near future. *adv.* Near the beginning of time; far back in time. **earlier** *adj.*

Early American *n.* The style of architecture, furniture and fabric which has the characteristic of colonial America.

early bird *n.* An early riser; a person who arrives early.

early on *adv.* During on early stage.

ear-mark (ēr´märk˝) *n.* A mark which has been placed on the ear of an animal for identification.

earmuff (ēr´muf˝) *n.* A pair of ear coverings which are attached with a band and worn over the head to cover the ears.

earn (ern) *v.* To receive payment in return for work done or services rendered; to gain as a result of one's efforts. **earner** *n.*

ear-nest (er´nist) *n.* A serious mental state; payment in advance to bind an agreement; a pledge. *adj.* Characterized by an intense and serious state of mind; having serious intent. **earnestly** *adv.* **earnestness** *n.*

earn-ings (er´ningz) *n. pl.* Something earned, such as a salary.

ear-phone (ēr´fon˝) *n.* A device that takes electrical energy and converts it into sound.

ear pick *n.* A tool or device which is used to remove the wax from the ear.

ear-plug (ēr plug) *n.* A device which is inserted into the ear to prevent water or sound from entering.

ear-ring (ēr´ring˝) *n.* A piece of jewelry which is worn on the earlobe for decoration.

ear-shot *n.* The distance a sound can be heard.

earth (erth) *n.* The third planet from the sun and the planet on which there is life; the outer layer of the world; ground; soil; dirt.

earth-born (erth´born˝) *adj.* Being born on this earth.

earth-en *adj.* Made of earth.

earth-en-ware *n.* The ceramic ware which is fired at a low heat.

earth-ling (erth´ling) *n.* One who inhabits the earth.

earth-ly (erth´lē) *adj.* Belonging to this earth.

earth-quake (erth´kwāk˝) *n.* A trembling or violent shaking of the crust of the earth.

earth science *n.* A type of science which studies the earth or its parts.

earth-star (erth´stär˝) *n.* A type of fungus whose outer layer splits into the shape of a star.

earth-ward (erth´werd) *adv.* To be moving towards the earth.

earth-worm (erth´werm˝) *n.* A type of annelid worm which lives in the soil.

ear-wig (ēr´wig˝) *n.* A type of insect that has a pair of cerci at the end of its body and antennae which are jointed; any of numerous beetlelike insects.

ease (ēz) *n.* A state of being comfortable; freedom from pain, discomfort, or care; freedom from labor or difficulty; an act of easing or a state of being eased. *v.* To free from pain or discomfort; to lessen the pressure or tension; to make less difficult; to move or pass with freedom. **ease** Free from discomfort. Standing silently with the feet apart, as in a military formation. **easeful** *adj.* **easefully** *adv.*

ea-sel (ē´zel) *n.* A frame used by artists to support a canvas or picture.

eas-i-ly *adv.* Without difficulty.

east (ēst) *n.* The direction opposite of west; the direction in which the sun rises. **easterly, eastward, eastwards** *adv.*

East Berlin *n.* The capital of East Germany.

Easter (ē´stėr) *n.* A Christian festival which celebrates the resurrection of Christ.

Easter egg *n.* An egg that is dyed bright colors and associated with the celebration of Easter.

Easter lily *n.* A type of lily that blooms in the early spring.

east-er-ly *adj.* Coming from or toward the east, as the wind.

easy (ē´zē) *adj.* Capable of being accomplished with little difficulty; free from worry or pain; not hurried or strenuous; something readily obtainable. **easily** *adv.* **easiness** *n.*

easy going (ē´zē gō´ing) *adj.* Taking life easy; without worry, concern, or haste.

easy mark *n.* A person who is easily overcome. *Slang* One who can easily be victimized or tricked.

eat (ēt) *v.* To chew and swallow food; to erode; to consume with distress or agitation; to take a meal. **crow** To accept what one has been fighting against. **out** To grieve bitterly. **words** To retract what has been said. **hand** To accept the domination of another. **one's heart** *n.* **one's** *n.* **eater** *n.*

eat-ery *n.* A type of restaurant.

eat out *v.* To eat in a restaurant or not at home.

eaves (ēvz) *n. pl.* The overhanging edge of a roof.

eaves-drop (ēvz´drop˝) *v.* To listen to what is said without the speakers knowing one is listening.

ebb (eb) *n.* The return of the tide towards the sea; a time of decline. *v.* To recede, as the tide does; to fall or flow back; to weaken.

eb-bet *n.* A type of green newt.

ebb tide *n.* The tide while at ebb; a period of decline.

eb-o-nite (eb′o nī′t′) *n.* A type of hard rubber.

eb-o-ny (eb′o nē) *n. pl.* **-nies** The dark, hard, colored wood from the center of the ebony tree of Asia and Africa. *adj.* Re-sembling ebony; black.

e-bul-lient (i bul′yent) *adj.* Filled with enthusiasm. **ebullience** *n.* **ebulliently** *adv.*

eb-ul-li-tion (eb′u lish′an) *n.* The process of boiling or bubbling; a sudden release of emotion.

ec-cen-tric (ik sen′trik) *adj.* Differing from an established pattern or accepted norm; deviating from a perfect circle; not located at the geometrical center. *n.* An odd or erratic person; a disk or wheel with its axis not situated in the center. **eccentrically** *adv.* **eccentricity** *n.*

ec-chy-mo-sis *n.* The escaping of blood into the surrounding tissues.

ec-cle-si-as-ti-cal (i klē′zē as′tik) *n.* A clergyman; a person officially serving a church. *adj.* Of or relating to a church.

ec-cle-si-ol-ogy (i klē′zē ol″a jē) *n.* A study of the architecture of a church.

ec-crine *adj.* To be producing a fluid secretion which does not remove cytoplasm for the secreting cell.

eccrine gland *n.* A sweat gland that produces an eccrine secretion.

ec-dy-sis (ek′di sis) *n.* The act of shedding the outer cuticular layer such as the insects.

ece-sis (i sē′sis) *n.* An establishment of animals in a new habitat.

ech-e-lon (esh′e lon′) *n.* A formation, as of military aircraft or naval vessels, resembling a series of steps where each rank is positioned slightly to the right or left of the preceding one; a level of command or authority; a hierarchy.

echid-na (i kid′na) *n.* A type of toothless spiny-coated nocturnal mammal found in Australia and feeds on ants.

echi-no-derm (i kī′no dėrm″) *n.* A member of the phylum Echinodermata having a radially symmetrical shape such as the starfish.

ech-o (ek′ō) *n. pl.* **-oes** Repetition of a sound by reflecting sound waves from a surface; the sound produced by such a reflection; a repetition; the reflection of transmitted radar signals by an object. *v.* To repeat or be repeated by; to imitate.

echo chamber *n.* A room that has sound-reflecting walls and it is used for the production of hollow sounds.

ech-o-lo-ca-tion (ek″ō lō kā′shan) *n.* A method for locating objects with the use of sound waves.

echo sounder *n.* A tool or device which is used to determine the depth of a body of water.

é-clair *n.* An oblong chocolate pastry puff, usually filled with custard or whipped cream.

ec-lamp-si-a *n.* A form of toxemia, marked by convulsions of a recurrent nature, and happening during pregnancy or childbirth.

ec-lec-tic (i klek′tik) *adj.* Having components from diverse sources or styles. **eclectic** *n.*

e-clipse (i klips′) *n.* A total or partial blocking of one celestial body by another. *v.* To fall into obscurity or decline; to cause an eclipse of; to overshadow.

e-clip-tic (i klip′tik) *n., Astron.* The circle formed by the intersection of the plane of the earth's orbit and the celestial sphere.

ec-logue *n.* A short pastoral poem in the form of a dialogue.

e-clo-sion *n.* The act of hatching from an egg of a larva.

ec-o-cide *n.* The deliberate destruction of the natural environment, caused by pollutants.

e-col-o-gy (i kol′o jē) *n.* The branch of science concerned with the interrelationship of organisms and their environments; the relationship between living organisms and their environments. **ecologic** *adj.* **ecologically** *adv.* **ecologist** *n.*

ec-o-nom-ic (ē′ko nom′ik) *adj.* The science relating to the development, production, and management of material wealth; relating to the necessities of life.

ec-o-nom-i-cal (ē′ko nom′i kal) *adj.* Not

wasteful; frugal; operating with little waste. **economically** *adv.*

ec-o-nom-ics (ē′ko nom′iks) *n. pl.* The science which treats production, distribution, and consumption of commodities. **economist** *n.*

e-con-o-mize (i kon′o mīz′) *v.* To manage thriftily; to use sparingly. **economizer** *n.*

e-con-o-my (i kon′o mē) *n. pl.* -**mies** Careful management of money, materials, and resources; a reduction in expenses; a system or structure for the management of resources and production of goods and services.

eco-phys-i-ol-ogy *n.* A study of the relationships of the environment and the physiology of organisms.

eco-spe-cies (ek′ō spē″shēz) *n.* The subdivision of cenospecies.

eco-sphere (ek′ō sfēr″) *n.* The section of the universe which is inhabitable by living organisms.

ec-o-tone *n.* A transition area between two adjacent plant communities, where both organisms compete for dominance.

ec-ru (ek′rŏ) *n.* A light yellowish brown, as the color of unbleached linen.

ec-sta-sy (ek′sta sē) *n. pl.* -**sies** The state of intense joy or delight. **ecstatic** *adj.* **ecstatically** *adv.*

ec-to-derm (ek′to dėrm″) *n.* An outer cellular membrane of a diploblastic animal.

ec-to-morph (ek′to morf″) *n.* A body structure, characterized by linearity and leanness.

ec-to-par-a-site *n.* An external parasite.

ec-top-ic *adj.* To be occurring in an abnormal place or position.

ectopic pregnancy *n.* A pregnancy that takes place elsewhere in the body such as the fallopian tubes.

ec-to-therm *n.* An animal which is classified as cold-blooded.

Ec-ua-dor *n.* A country located in northwestern South America.

ec-u-men-i-cal (ek′ū men′i kal) *adj.* Worldwide or general in extent, application, or influence; promoting unity among Christian churches or religions. **ecumenically** *adv.*

ecumenism *n.*

ec-ze-ma (ek′se ma) *n.* A noncontagious inflammatory skin condition, marked by itching and scaly patches. **eczematous** *adj.*

edaph-ic (i daf′ik) *adj.* Pertaining to or relating to the soil. **edaphically** *adv.*

ed-dy (ed′ē) *n. pl.* -**dies** A current, as of water, running against the direction of the main current, especially in a circular motion. **eddy** *v.*

eddy current *n.* A current of electricity which is induced by an alternating magnetic field.

Eddy, Mary Baker *n.* (1821-1910). American founder of Christian Science.

e-del-weiss (ād′el vīs′) *n.* An Alpine plant having woolly leaves and small flowers.

ede-ma (i dē′ma) *n.* An accumulation of serous fluid in the connective tissue that is abnormal. **edematous** *adj.*

E-den (ēd′en) *n.* The garden which was the first home of Adam and Eve; a delightful area; a paradise. **Edenic** *adj.*

eden-tate (ē den′tāt) *adj.* To be without teeth.

eden-tu-lous (ē den′che lus) *adj.* To be without teeth.

edge (ej) *n.* The thin, sharp, cutting side of a blade; keenness; sharpness; the border where an object or area begins or ends; an advantage. *v.* To furnish with an edge or border; to sharpen; to move gradually. **on edge** Tense.

edged *adj.* To have a specified edge.

edge-less *adj.* To be without an edge.

edge tool *n.* A tool with a sharp cutting edge.

edge-wise *adv.* With the edge directed toward the front.

edg-ing (ej′ing) *n.* Something which can make or form an edge.

ed-i-ble (ed′i bl) *adj.* Safe or fit for consumption. **edibility** *n.* **edible** *n.*

e-dict (ē′dikt) *n.* A public decree; an order or command officially proclaimed.

edif-i-ca-to-ry *adj.* To be suitable for edification.

ed-i-fice (ed´i fĭs) *n.* A massive building or structure.

ed-i-fy (ed´i fī´) *v.* To benefit and enlighten, morally or spiritually. **edification** *n.*

Edison, Thomas Alva *n.* (1847-1931). An American inventor.

ed-it (ed´it) *v.* To prepare and correct for publication; to compile for an edition; to delete or change. **editor** *n.*

e-di-tion (i dish´an) *n.* The form in which a book ispublished; the total number of copies printed at one time; one similar to an original version.

ed-i-tor *n.* A person who edits or prepares literary matter as a profession.

ed-i-to-ri-al (ed´i tōr´ē al) *n.* An article in a newspaper or magazine which expresses the opinion of a publisher or editor. *adj.* Of or relating to an editor or an editor's work; being or resembling an editorial. **editorially** *adv.*

ed-i-to-ri-al-ist *n.* A person who writes editorials for a paper or other publication.

editor in chief *n.* The editor who is in charge of an editorial staff.

ed-i-tress *n.* A woman who is an editor.

EDP *abbr.* Electronic data processing.

EDT *abbr.* Eastern Daylight Time.

ed-u-ca-ble *adj.* To be capable of being educated.

ed-u-cate (ej´e kāt´) *v.* To supply with training or schooling; to supervise the mental or moral growth of. **educator** *n.*

ed-u-cat-ed *adj.* To have an education.

ed-u-ca-tion (ej´e kā´shan) *n.* The process of being educated. **educationally** *adv.*, **educational** *adj.*

ed-u-ca-tor (ej´e kā˝tėr) *n.* Someone who educates.

e-duce (i dōs´) *v.* To call forth or bring out; to develop from given facts.

edul-co-rate (i dul´ko rāt´) *v.* To make something pleasant.

eel (ēl) *n. pl.* **eel** *or* **eels** A snake-like marine or freshwater fish without scales or pelvic fins.

eel-grass (ēl´gras˝) *n.* A type of a marine plant that is under the water having narrow leaves.

eel-pout (ēl´pout˝) *n.* A type of marine fish which resembles blennies.

eel-worm (ēl´wėrm˝) *n.* A type of nematode worm.

ee-rie *or* **ee-ry (ēr´ē)** *adj.* Suggesting or inspiring the supernatural or strange; spooky. **eerily** *adv.* **eeriness** *n.*

ef-face (i fās´) *v.* To remove or rub out. **effacer** *n.* **effacement** *n.*

ef-fect (i fekt´) *n.* Something produced by a cause; the power to produce a desired result; the reaction something has on an object; a technique which produces an intended impression. **take effect** To become operative. **effecter** *n.*

ef-fec-tive (i fek´tiv) *adj.* Producing an expected effect or proper result. **effectiveness** *n.*

ef-fec-tiv-i-ty *n.* The state of being effective.

ef-fec-tor (i fek´tėr) *n.* An organ of the body that is active when it has been stimulated.

ef-fec-tu-al (i fek´chŏ al) *adj.* To be able to produce an effect that is desired.

ef-fec-tu-al-ly *adv.* With a great effect.

ef-fec-tu-ate *v.* To achieve; to accomplish.

ef-fem-i-nate (i fem´i nit) *adj.* Having a more woman-like quality or trait than a man. **effeminacy** *n.* **effeminately** *adv.*

ef-fen-di (i fend´ē) *n.* A man who has an education or property.

ef-fer-ent (ef´ėr ent) *adj.*, *Physiol.* Carrying away or outward from a central organ or part. **efferent** *n.* **efferently** *adv.*

ef-fer-vesce (ef´ėr ves´) *v.* To foam with the escaping of a gas for something. **effervescently** *adv.*, **effervescence** *n.*, **effervescent** *adj.*

ef-fete (i fēt´) *adj.* Exhausted of effectiveness or force; worn-out; decadent.

ef-fi-ca-cious (ef´i kā´shus) *adj.* Producing an intended effect. **efficaciously** *adv.*

ef-fi-cien-cy (i fish´en sē) *n.* The degree of being efficient.

efficiency engineer *n.* A person who analyzes methods, or procedures, to determine the desired results with minimum cost, time and effort.

ef-fi-cient (i fish´ent) *adj.* Adequate in performance with a minimum of waste or effort; giving a high ratio of output.

ef-fi-gy (ef´i jē) *n. pl.* **-gies** A life-size sculpture or painting representing a crude image or dummy of a hated person.

ef-flo-resce (ef´lo res´) *v.* To become covered by a powdery crust.

ef-flo-res-cence (ef´lo res´ens) *n.* A time of flowering; a slow process of development; the highest point. **efflorescent** *adj.*

ef-flu-ence (ef´lŏ ens) *n.* An act of flowing out; something that flows out or forth. **effluent** *n.*

ef-flu-vi-um (i flŏ´vē um) *n. pl.* **-via** *or* **-viums** An unpleasant vapor from something. **effluvial** *adj.*

ef-flux (ef´luks) *n.* The passing away of someone or something. **effluxion** *n.*

ef-fort (ef´ėrt) *n.* Voluntary exertion of physical or mental energy; a difficult exertion; a normally earnest attempt or achievement; something done through exertion. *Phys.* A force applied against inertia. **effortless** *adj.*

ef-fort-ful *adj.* To be requiring effort.

ef-fron-ter-y (i frun´te rē) *n. pl.* **-ies** Shameless boldness; impudence.

ef-ful-gent *adj.* Shining brilliantly; radiant. **effulgence** *n.*

ef-fuse (i fūz´) *v.* To give off; to pour out.

ef-fu-sion (i fū´zhan) *n.* An instance of pouring forth; an unrestrained outpouring of feeling. **effuse** *v.* **effusive** *adj.* **effusively** *adv.*

eg *abbr.* For example.

e-gad *Interj.* An exclamation expressing surprise.

egal-i-tar-i-an (i gal´i târ´ē an) *adj.* Being marked by egalitarianism. **egalitarian** *n.*

egest (ē jest´) *v.* To defecate or rid the body of waste. **egestive** *adj.,* **egestion** *n.*

egg (eg) *n.* The hard-shelled reproductive cell of female animals, especially one produced by a chicken, used as food. *v.* To incite to action.

egg-beat-er (eg´bē´tėr) *n.* A kitchen tool with rotating blades used to mix, blend, or beat food.

egg case *n.* A case which encloses an egg for the purpose of protecting it.

egg–cup *n.* A type of cup which is used to hold an egg so that it may be eaten in the shell.

egg-head (eg´hed´) *n., Informal* An intellectual; highbrow.

egg-head-ed *adj.* To have the characteristics of one who is an egghead.

egg-nog (eg´nog´) *n.* A drink of beaten eggs, sugar, and milk or cream, often mixed with alcohol.

egg-plant (eg´plant´) *n.* A widely cultivated perennial plant which yields an egg-shaped edible fruit.

egg-roll *n.* A thin egg-dough casing filled with minced vegetables and sometimes meat or seafood which is fried.

egg-shell *n.* The shell or calcareous covering of an egg.

egg timer *n.* A sandglass which is used for the purpose of timing the cooking of an egg.

egg tooth *n.* The sharp prominence which is located on the tip of a bird's beak for the purpose of breaking through the egg at the time of its birth.

eg-lan-tine (eg´lan tin´) *n.* The sweetbrier, a type of rose.

e-go (ē´gō) *n.* The self thinking, feeling, and acting distinct from the external world. *Physiol.* The conscious aspect that most directly controls behavior and is most in touch with reality.

ego–de-fense *n.* A mechanism that is psychological and protects the self-image.

e-go-cen-tric (ē´gō sen´trik) *adj.* Thinking, observing, and regarding oneself as the object of all experiences. **egocentric** *n.* **egocentricity** *n.*

e-go-ism *n.* The habit of valuing everything with the end result for the benefit of oneself only.

e-go-ist *n.* A self-centered or selfish person.

e-go-ma-ni-a (ē´gō mā´nē a) *n.* Self obsession. **egomaniac** *n.* **egomaniacal** *adj.*

e-go-tism *n.* The practice of too frequently using the word I; hence, a practice of speaking or writing too much about oneself.

ego trip *n., Slang* Something which satisfies the ego.

e-gre-gious (i grē´jus) *adj.* Outstandingly or remarkably bad; flagrant. **egregiously** *adv.* **egregiousness** *n.*

e-gress (ē´gres) *n.* The act of coming out; emergence; a means of departing; exit.

e-gret (ē´grit) *n.* Any of several species of white wading birds having long, drooping plumes.

E-gypt *n.* A county located in northeast Africa and southwest Asia.

eh *interj.* An utterance used to ask for confirmation of something just spoken.

ei-der (ī´dėr) *n.* A large sea duck found in northern regions, having soft down which is used for comforters, pillows,etc.

ei-der-down (ī´dėr doun˝) *n.* The down of the eider duck.

ei-det-ic (ī det´ik) *adj.* Involving vivid recall.

ei-do-lon (ī dō´lon) *n.* An image that is unsubstantial.

eight (āt) *n.* The cardinal number which follows seven. **ball** In a bad spot. **eighth** *adj.*

eight ball (āt´bol˝) *n.* The black ball marked with the number eight, in the game of pool. **behind the eight ball** *Slang* In an extremely bad spot.

eigh-teen (ā´tēn´) *n.* The number that follows seventeen. **eighteenth** *adj.& n.*

eight-fold (āt´fōld˝) *n.* To be eight times as much or greater.

eighth *adj.* Next in order after the seventh; being of eight equal units or parts.

eighth note *n.* A musical note having the time value of 1/8 a whole note.

eightpenny nail *n.* A nail which is under three inches and over two inches.

ein-korn *n.* The type of wheat that can be found in Europe and it has one grain.

Einstein, Albert *n.* (1879-1955). A German born American physicist.

ein-stein-i-um (īn stī´nē um) *n.* A synthetic,

radioactive, metallic element.

Eisenhower, Dwight David *n.* (1890-1969). The 34th president of the United States, from 1953-1961.

ei-stedd-fod (ā steth´vod) *n.* A periodical festival of the Welsh people. **eisteddfodic** *adj.*

ei-ther (ē´thėr) *pron.* One or the other. *conj.* Used before the first of two or more alternatives linked by or. *adj.* One or the other of two. *adv.* Likewise; also.

e-jac-u-late (i jak´ū lāt´) *v.* To eject abruptly, as in semen; to utter suddenly and briefly; to exclaim. **ejaculation** *n.* **ejaculatory** *adj.*

e-ject (i jekt´) *v.* To throw out; to expel. **ejection** *n.* **ejector** *n.*

ejection seat *n.* An emergency escape seat designed to propel an occupant from an airplane.

ejec-tor *n.* Someone that ejects.

e-ject-ment (i jekt´ment) *n.* An act for a recovery of possession of real property.

eke out *v.* To obtain with great effort; to make do.

EKG *abbr.* Electrocardiogram.

ekis-tics *n.* The science which deals with the settlements of humans.

e-lab-o-rate (i lab´o rāt´) *adj.* Planned or carried out with great detail; very complex; intricate. *v.* To work out or complete with great detail; to give more detail. **elaborateness** *n.* **elaboration** *n.*

e-land (ē´land) *n.* A large African antelope with a tan coat and spirally horns.

el-a-pid (el´a pid) *n.* A member of the family of poisonous snakes that have grooved fangs.

e-lapse (i laps´) *v.* To slip or glide away; to pass away silently.

elapsed time *n.* The amount of time that has been taken to go through a course such as with a race.

elas-mo-branch (i las´mo brangh˝) *n.* A member of the class of fishes that have lamellate gills, such members include the sharks, chimaeras, and rays.

elas-tase *n.* The enzyme found in the pancreatic juice which will digest elastin.

e-las-tic (i las´tik) *adj.* Complying with changing circumstances; capable of easy adjustment. **elastically** *adv.* **elasticity** *n.*

e-las-tic-i-ty *n.* The quality or state of being elastic; flexibility.

elas-ti-cized *adj.* Being made with elastic.

elastic scattering *n.* The scattering of particles due to an elastic collision.

elas-tin (i las´tin) *n.* A type of protein which is similar to collagen.

elas-to-mer (i las´tamèr) *n.* The elastic substances which resemble rubber.

e-late (i lāt´) *v.* To make proud of.

el-a-ter (el´*a* tèr) *n.* The structure of a plant which aids in the distribution of spores.

elat-er-ite (i lat´erīt´´) *n.* A mineral resin which is dark brown and occurs in flexible masses.

e-la-tion *n.* The quality or state of exaltation or joy; a feeling of great happiness.

E layer *n.* The layer in the ionosphere above the earth that is able to reflect radio waves.

el-bow (el´bō) *n.* A sharp turn, as in a river or road, which resembles an elbow. *Anat.* The outer joint of the arm between the upper arm and forearm. *v.* To push or shove aside with the elbow.

elbow grease *n.* An energy that is exerted with physical labor.

el-bow-room (el´bō rōm´) *n.* Ample room to move about; enough space for comfort.

eld-er (el´dèr) *adj.* Older. *n.* One who is older than others; a person of great influence; an official of the church. *Bot.* A shrub bearing reddish fruit.

el-der-ber-ry (el´dèr ber´´ē) *n.* An edible red or black berry which can be found in the honeysuckle family.

el-der-ly (el´dèr lē) *adj.* Pertaining to later life; older. **elderliness** *n.*

elder statesman *n.* A highly respected senior member of an organization or group.

el-dest (el´dist) *adj.* The oldest in age or seniority.

eldest hand *n.* The one in a game of cards who receives the cards first in the deal.

elec *abbr.* Electricity; electric.

ele-cam-pane (el´´*e* kam pān´) *n.* A type of European herb which has yellow flowers.

e-lect (i lekt´) *v.* To choose or select by vote, as for an office; to make a choice. *adj.* Singled out on purpose; elected but not yet inaugurated. *n.* One chosen or set apart, especially for spiritual salvation.

e-lect-able *adj.* To be capable of being elected. **electability** *n.*

e-lec-tion (i lek´shan) *n.* The process of electing someone.

e-lec-tion-eer (i lek´´shanēr) *v.* To help with the candidate's election.

e-lec-tive (i lek´tiv) *adj.* Pertaining to an election. **electiveness** *n.* **electively** *adv.*

e-lec-tor (i lek´tèr) *n.* A person who is able to vote.

e-lec-tor-al *adj.* Pertaining to an elector.

e-lec-tor-ate (i lek´tèr it) *n.* A group of people who are able to vote in an election.

e-lec-tress (i lek´tris) *n.* A wife of the German elector.

e-lec-tric *or* **e-lec-tri-cal (i lek´trik)** *adj.* Relating to electricity; emotionally exciting. **electrically** *adv.*

electric eye *n.* A photoelectric cell; an electric device where the electric current is controlled by variations of light.

electrical storm *n.* A storm which contains lightening.

electric chair *n.* The chair which is used to electrocute someone.

electric eel *n.* A large fish which is shaped like an eel that is able to give off an electric shock.

e-lec-tri-cian (i lek trish´an) *n.* A person whose job it is to install or maintain electric equipment.

e-lec-tric-i-ty (i lek tris´i tē) *n. phys., Chem.* A force that causes bodies to attract or repel each other, responsible for a natural phenomena as lightning; electric current as a power source; emotional excitement.

electric organ *n.* A section of tissue which is capable of producing electricity such as with the electric eel.

electric ray *n.* A type of ray which has a pair of electric organs and is found in warm waters.

e-lec-tri-fi-ca-tion *n.* The state of being electrified.

e-lec-tri-fy (i lek′tri fi˝) *v.* To charge something or someone with electricity.

e-lec-tro-a-nal-y-sis *n.* The chemical ana l-ysis by electrolysis.

e-lec-tro-car-di-o-gram (i lek′trō kăr′dēo gram′) *n.* The record produced by an electro-cardiograph machine.

e-lec-tro-car-di-o-graph (i lek′trō kăr′dēo graf′) *n.* An electric instrument which detects and records the heartbeat.

e-lec-tro-cute (i lek′tro kūt′) *v.* To kill or execute by the use of electric current. **electrocution** *n.*

e-lec-trode (i lek′trōd) *n.* A conductor by which an electric current enters or leaves.

e-lec-tro-de-pos-it *n.* The deposit which is formed at an electrode.

e-lec-tro-di-al-y-sis *n.* A dialysis which is accelerated with an electromotive force.

e-lec-tro-dy-nam-ics (i lek′trō dī nam′iks) *n. Phys.* The study of the interactions of an electric current with magnets. **electrodynamic** *adj.*

e-lec-tro-dy-na-mom-e-ter *n.* An instrument used to measure electric currents by the electrodynamic action.

e-lec-trol-y-sis (i lek trol′i sis) *n. , Chem., Phys.* A chemical decomposition by an electric current; destruction of tumors or hairroots by an electric current.

e-lec-tro-lyte *n.* A substance whose solutions are capable of conducting electric current.

e-lec-tro-mag-net (i lek′trō mag′nit) *n.* A magnet consisting of a soft iron core magnetized by an electric current passing through a wire which is coiled around the core.

e-lec-tro-mag-net-ism *n.* The study of the relation between electric currents and magnetism.

e-lec-trom-e-ter (i lek trom′i tèr) *n.* An instrument for detecting or measuring electric potential or differences between two con-

ductors.

e-lec-tro-mo-tive (i lek′tro mō′tiv) *adj.* Of, pertaining to, or tending to produce electric current.

e-lec-tron (i lek′tron) *n., Elect.* A subatomic particle with a negative electric charge found outside of an atoms nucleus.

e-lec-tro-neg-a-tive *adj.* Having a charge of negative electricity.

e-lec-tron-ics *n.* The branch of physics that studies the behavior and applies the effects of the flow of electrons in vacuum tubes, gases, and semiconductors.

electron microscope *n.* An instrument which utilizes the short wave length of an electron beam, to produce magnification and the resolution of minute structures for which a light microscope is insufficient.

e-lec-tro-stat-ic (i lek′tro stat′ik) *adj.* Pertaining to static electric charges.

e-lec-tro-stat-ics (i lek′tro stat′iks) *n. pl., Phys.* The physics of static electric charges.

e-lec-tro-sur-ger-y (i lek˝trō sèr′je rē) *n.* The treatment of a disease by means of electricity.

e-lec-tro-ther-a-py (i lek˝trō ther′a pē) *n.* The treatment of a disease by brief electric shocks.

e-lec-tro-type (i lek′tro tīp′) *n.* A duplicate metal plate made by electroplating a mold of the original plate which is used in printing. **electrotype** *v.*

e-lec-tro-va-lence (i lek˝trō vā′lens) *n.* The valence which is characterized by a transfer of electrons from one atom to another.

electrovalent bond *n.* The bond which forms between ions of opposite charges.

e-lec-trum (i lek′trum) *n.* A type of pale yellow alloy of silver and gold.

el-e-doi-sin *n.* A protein that comes from the salivary glands of the octopus.

el-ee-mos-y-nar-y (el˝e mos′i ner˝˝ē) *adj.* Of, pertaining to, or contributed as charity.

el-e-gance (el′e gans) *n.* Refinement in appearance, movement, or manners; elegant quality. **elegant** *adj.*

el-e-gant *adj.* Marked by elegance; tasteful or luxurious in dress, or manners; gracefully refined, in habits, tastes, or a literary style; excellent inkind or quality; having a graceful distinction in appearance; pleasingly superior in style.

e-le-git *n.* The writ of execution by which any or all of a defendant's goods or property are held by his creditor until the debt is paid.

el-e-gy (el´i jē) *n. pl.* **-gies** A poem expressing sorrow and lamentation for one who is dead.

el-e-ment (el´e ment) *n.* A constituent part. *Chem. & Phys.* A substance not separable into less complex substances by chemical means. **elements** *pl.* The conditions of the weather.

el-e-men-tal (el˝emen´tal) *adj.* Relating to an element, as an uncombined chemical element; relating to the basic constituent of something; fundamental; dealing with the rudiments of something; resembling the great force of nature. **elementally** *adv.*

el-e-men-ta-ry (el´e men´ta rē) *adj.* Fundamental, essential; referring to elementary school; introducing fundamental principles.

elementary school *n.* A school including the grades of first to sixth.

el-e-mi (el´emē) *n.* A fragrant oleoresins which is obtained from topical trees and is used in inks and varnishes.

e-len-chus *n.* An argument which contradicts another argument by proving the contrary to its conclusion.

el-e-phant (el´e fant) *n.* A large mammal having along, flexible trunk and curved tusks.

elephant grass *n.* A cattail which is used for the purpose of making baskets.

elephant seal *n.* A kind of seal that is almost extinct and has a long inflatable proboscis.

el-e-phan-ti-a-sis (el˝e fan tī´a sis) *n., Pathol.* The enormous enlargement of affected parts along with hardening, caused by obstruction of lymphatics from parasitic worms.

el-e-phan-tine (el´e fan´tin) *adj.* To have a lot of strength or to be great in size.

elephant shrew *n.* A small, mouselike insectivorous animal of Africa, with a long snout similar to the snout of an elephant.

el-e-vate (el´e vāt´) *v.* To lift up or raise; to promote to a higher rank.

el-e-vat-ed (el´e vā˝tid) *adj.* To be above something such as the ground.

elevated railroad *n.* A railroad which operated on an elevated track.

el-e-va-tion (el˝e vā´shan) *n.* The height of something which is elevated or above the ground.

el-e-va-tor (el´evā˝tėr) *n.* A platform or cage which raises cargo or person inside it to another level such as in a skyscraper or other building.

e-lev-en (i lev´en) *n.* A cardinal number with a sum equal to ten plus one. **eleventh** *adj. & adv.*

el-e-von (el´e von˝) *n.* A surface which is controlled by an airplane and operated as an elevator.

elf (elf) *n. pl.* **elves** An imaginary being with magical powers, often mischievous; a small, mischievous child. **elfish** *adj.*

e-lic-it (i lis´it) *v.* To bring or draw out; to evoke.

e-lide (i līd´) *v.* To omit, especially to slur over in pronunciation, as a vowel, consonant, or syllable. **elision** *n.*

el-i-gi-ble (el´i ji bl) *adj.* Worthy of being chosen. **eligibly** *adv.*, **eligibility** *n.*

e-lim-i-nate (i lim´i nāt´) *v.* To get rid of, remove; to leave out, to omit; to excrete, as waste. **elim-ination** *n.* **eliminator** *n.* **eliminative** *adj.* **eliminatory** *adj.*

e-li-sion *n.* The act of omitting something as an unstressed vowel or syllable in pronunciation or verse.

e-lite (i lēt´) *n.* The most skilled members of a group; a small, powerful group; a type size yielding twelve characters to the inch. **elite** *adj.*

elit-ism (i lē´tiz um) *n.* A rule by the elite

of a country or of a society.

e-lix-ir (i lik´sẽr) *n., Phar.* A sweetened aromatic liquid of alcohol and water, used as a vehicle for medicine; a medicine regarded as a cure-all; a sovereign remedy.

Elizabeth I *n.* (1533-1603). Queen of England and Ireland from 1558 until 1603. **Elizabethan** *adj. & n.*

elk (elk) *n. pl.* **elks** *or* **elk** The largest deer of Europe and Asia. **Elk** A member of a major benevolent and fraternal order.

elk-hound *n.* A type of dog with a short, compact body, originally raised in Norway and used for hunting game.

ell (el) *n.* An extension of a building at right angles to the main structure.

ellagic acid *n.* A crystalline compound that is obtained from oak galls.

el-lipse (i lips´) *n.* A closed curve, somewhat oval in shape.

el-lip-sis (i lip´sis) *n.* An ommision of a few words which are understood in a sentence.

el-lip-tic *or* **el-lip-ti-cal (i lip´ti kal)** *adj.* Of, pertaining to, or shaped like an ellipse.

elm (elm) *n.* Any of various valuable timber and shade trees with arching branches.

elm bark beetle *n.* Type of beetle leading to the Dutch elm disease.

elm leaf beetle *n.* An orange-yellow beetle of the Old World.

el-o-cu-tion (el´o kū´shan) *n.* The art of effective public speaking. **elocutionary** *adj.* **elocutionist** *n.*

elo-dea *n.* A submerged aquatic seed herb.

e-loign (i loin´) *v.* To take someone or something to a place which is a great distance away.

elon-gate (i long´gāt) *v.* To stretch out in length.

elon-ga-tion *n.* The state of being elongated or stretched out in length.

e-lope (i lōp´) *v.* To run away, especially in order to get married, usually without parental permission. **elopement** *n.* **eloper** *n.*

el-o-quence *n.* The practice of using language with fluency.

el-o-quent (el´o kwent) *adj.* Having the power to speak fluently and persuasively;

vividly expressive. **eloquence** *n.* **eloquently** *adv.*

else (els) *adj.* Different; other; more; additional. *adv.* In addition; besides.

else-where (els´hwâr´) *adv.* To or in another place.

e-lu-ci-date (i lū´si dāt´) *v.* To make clear, clarify; to explain. **elucidator** *n.* **elucidation** *n.*

elu-cu-brate *v.* To work something out with an effort that is studious.

e-lude (i lūd´) *v.* To evade or avoid; to escape understanding.

e-lu-sion (i lū´zhan) *n.* An evasion of an order or of a problem that one may have.

e-lu-sive (i lū´siv) *adj.* Tending to evade something or someone. **elusively** *adv.*

e-lute (ē lūt´) *v.* To remove material from what has absorbed it with the use of a solvent. **elution** *n.*

e-lu-tri-ate (i lū´trē āt´) *v.* To remove something by washing. **elutriator** *n.*

e-lu-vi-al *adj.* Related to eluviation.

e-lu-vi-a-tion (i lū´vē ā´shan) *n.* Transportation of material that is in the soil by water.

e-lu-vi-um *n.* Fine soil, dust, or sand produced by the decomposition and weathering of rock.

E-ly-si-um (i lizh´ē um) *n., Mythol.* A place of exquisite happiness; a paradise. **Elysian** *adj.*

el-y-tron (el´i tron˝) *n.* An anterior wing of a beetle which protects the functional wings.

em *n., Print* A unit of measure for printed matter that is equal to the width of the letter M.

e-ma-ci-ate (i mā´shē āt´) *v.* To become or cause to become extremely thin from the loss of appetite. **emaciation** *n.*

em-a-nate (em´a nāt´) *v.* To come or give forth, as from a source. **emanation** *n.*

em-a-na-tion *n.* Something that emanates, flows, or comes from any source, substance, or body.

e-man-ci-pate (i man´si pāt´) *v.* To liberate; to set free from bondage. **emanci-**

pation *n.* emancipator *n.*

e-mar-gin-ate (i mär´ji nāt) *adj.* To have a margin notched; having a shallow notch at the apex. **emargination** *n.*

e-mas-cu-late (i mas´kū lāt´) *v.* To castrate; to deprive of masculine vigor. **emasculation** *n.* **emasculator** *n.*

em-balm (em bäm´) *v.* To treat a corpse with preservatives in order to protect from decay. **embalmer** *n.*

em-bank (em bangk´) *v.* To support, protect, or defend with a bank of earth or stone. **embankment** *n.*

em-bar-go (em bär´gō) *n. pl.* **-goes** A prohibition or restraint on trade, as a government order forbidding the entry or departure of merchant vessels, for example the oil embargo of 1973. **embargo** *v.*

em-bark (em bärk´) *v.* To board a ship; to set out on a venture. **embarkation** *n.*

em-bar-rass (em bar´as) *v.* To cause to feel self-conscious; to confuse; to burden with financial difficulties. **embarrassment** *n.*

em-bar-rass-ment *n.* The state of being embarrassed; confusion of mind.

em-bas-sage *n.* The commission which has been entrusted to an ambassador.

em-bas-sy (em´ba sē) *n. pl.* **-sies** The headquarters of an ambassador.

em-bat-tle (em bat´l) *v.* To prepare or arrange for battle.

em-bay (em bā´) *v.* To shelter.

em-bay-ment *n.* The formation of a bay.

em-bed (em bed´) *v.* To fix or enclose tightly in a surrounding mass.

em-bel-lish (em bel´ish) *v.* To adorn or make beautiful with ornamentation; to decorate; to heighten the attractiveness by adding ornamental details. **embellishment** *n.*

em-ber (em´bėr) *n.* A small piece of glowing coal or wood, as in a dying fire. **embers** *pl.* The smoldering ashes or remains of afire.

em-bez-zle (em bez´l) *v.* To take money or other items fraudulently.

em-bit-ter (em bit´ėr) *v.* To make bitter; to create feelings of hostility. **embitterment** *n.*

em-blaze (em blāz´) *v.* To set something ablaze.

em-bla-zon (em blā´zon) *v.* To decorate in bright colors.

em-blem (em´blem) *n.* A symbol of something; a distinctive design. **emblematic** *adj.* **emblematical** *adj.*

em-ble-ments *n.* The crops from annual cultivation of the land that lawfully belong to the tenant.

em-bod-y (em bod´ē) *v.* To give a bodily form to; to personify. **embodiment** *n.*

em-bold-en (em bōl´den) *v.* To encourage; to make bold.

em-bo-lism (em´bo liz´um) *n.* The blockage of a blood vessel, as by an air bubble or a detached clot.

em-bo-lus *n.* An abnormal particle such as an air bubble that circulates in the bloodstream.

em-bon-point *n.* Plumpness; stoutness.

em-bos-om *v.* To enclose; to shelter closely; to cherish.

em-boss (em bos´) *v.* To shape or decorate in relief; to represent in relief.

em-bou-chure (äm´be sher´) *n.* The part of a wind instrument, as the mouthpiece, that is applied to the lips to produce a musical tone.

em-bowed *adj.* Bent or curved outward.

em-bow-er (em bou´ėr) *v.* To enclose, cover, or shelter.

em-brace (em brās´) *v.* To clasp or hold in the arms; to hug; to surround; to take in mentally or visually. *n.* The act of embracing; a hug.

em-brac-er-y *n.* An attempt to influence or corrupt a jury, by bribes or promises.

em-bran-gle *v.* To entangle; to confuse.

em-bra-sure (em brā´zhėr) *n., Arch.* A flared opening in a wall, as for a door or window.

em-bro-cate (em´brō kāt´) *v.* To moisten and rub an injured part of the body with a liquid medicine. **embrocation** *n.*

em-broi-der (em broi´dėr) *v.* To decorate with ornamental needlework; to add fictitious details. **embroidery** *n.*

em-broil (em broil´) v. To involve in contention or violent actions; to throw into confusion. **embroilment** n.

em-bry-o (em´brē ō´) n. pl. **-os** An organism in its early developmental stage, before it has a distinctive form; in the human species, the first eight weeks of development, especially before birth or germination; a rudimentary stage. **embryonic** adj.

em-bry-og-e-ny n. The development and formation of embryos; the study of this formation and development.

em-bry-ol-o-gy (em´brē ol´o jē) n. The science concerned with the origin, structure, and growth of embryos. **embryological** adj. **embryologist** n.

em-bry-o-phyte n. A plant that produces an embryo and has vascular tissue.

em-bry-o-tic adj. In the beginning stage.

em-cee (em´sē´) n., Informal A master of ceremonies. **emcee** v.

e-mend (i mend´) v. To correct or remove faults. **emendation** n. **emender** n.

em-er-ald (em´ėr ald) n. A bright-green, transparent variety of beryl, used as a gemstone.

e-merge (i mėrj´) v. To rise into view; to come into existence. **emergence** n. **emergent** adj.

e-mer-gence n. The outgrowth on the surface of a plant.

e-mer-gen-cy (i mėr´jen sē) n. pl. **-cies** A sudden and unexpected situation requiring prompt action.

e-mer-gent adj. Emerging; unexpected; calling for immediate action.

e-mer-i-tus (i mer´i tus) adj. Retired from active duty but retaining the honorary title held immediately before retirement. **emeritus** n.

e-mersed adj. Standing out of or rising above the surrounding water surface.

Emerson, Ralph Waldo n. (1803-1882). An American poet and writer of essays.

em-er-y (em´e rē) n. A grainy, mineral substance having impure corundum, used for polishing and grinding.

e-met-ic (e met´ik) adj. A medicine used to induce vomiting. **emetic** n.

em-e-tine n. An alkaloid that is extracted from the ipecac root used as an expectorant.

em-i-grate (em´i grāt´) v. To move from one country or region to settle elsewhere. **emigrant** n. **emigration** n.

e-mi-gre (em´i grā´) n. A refugee.

em-i-nent (em´i nent) adj. High in esteem, rank, or office; conspicuous; outstanding. **eminently** adv.

eminent domain n. The right of a government to take or control property for public use.

e-mir (e mēr´) n. A Moslem prince.

em-is-sar-y (em´i ser´ē) n. pl. **-ies** A person sent out on a mission.

e-mis-sion n. The act of emitting; something emitted.

e-mit (i mit´) v. To send forth; to throw or give out. **emission** n.

e-mol-lient (i mol´yent) n. A substance for the soothing and softening of the skin. **emollient** adj.

e-mol-u-ment (i mol´ū ment) n. Profit; returns arising from employment; compensation, as a salary or perquisite.

e-mote (i mōt´) v. To show emotion, as in acting.

e-mo-tion (i mō´shan) n. A strong surge of feeling; any of the feelings of fear, sorrow, joy, hate, or love; a particular feeling, as love or hate.

e-mo-tion-al-ize v. To give an emotional quality to.

e-mo-tive adj. Having to do with or relating to emotions.

em-pa-thize v. To regard with empathy.

em-pa-thy (em´pa thē) n., Physiol. Identification with and understanding the feelings of another person. **empathetic** adj. **empathic** adj.

em-pen-nage (äm´pe näzh´) n. The rear section or tail of an aircraft.

em-per-or (em´pėr ėr) n. The ruler of an empire.

em-pha-sis (em´fa sis) n. pl. **-ses** Significance or importance attached to anything.

em-phat-ic (em fat´ik) *adj.* Expressed or spoken with emphasis. **emphatically** *adv.*

em-phy-se-ma *n.* A condition caused by the presence of air in body tissues or organs.

em-pire (em´pīėr) *n.* The territories or nations governed by a single supreme authority.

em-pir-ic *n.* One who relies only on practical experience.

em-pir-i-cal *or* **em-pir-ic (em pir´i kal)** *adj.* Depending on or gained from observation or experiment rather than from theory and science. **empirically** *adv.*

em-place *v.* To put into place or position.

em-place-ment *n.* A platform for guns or military equipment.

em-ploy (em ploi´) *v.* To engage the service or use of; to devote time to an activity. **employer** *n.* **employment** *n.*

em-ploy-ee *or* **em-ploy-e (em ploi´ē)** *n.* A person who works for another in return for salary or wages.

em-ploy-er *n.* One that employs; one for whom someone works for and usually under their direction.

em-ploy-ment *n.* The act of employing.

em-poi-son *v.* To embitter.

em-po-ri-um (em pōr´ē um) *n.* *pl.* **-riums** *or-* **ria** A large store which carries general merchandise.

em-pow-er (em pou´ėr) *v.* To authorize; to delegate; to license.

em-press (em´pris) *n.* A woman who rules an empire; an emperor's wife or widow.

emp-ty (emp´tē) *adj.* Containing nothing; vacant; lacking substance. *v.* To empty. **emptily** *adv.* **emptiness** *n.*

emp-ty–hand-ed *adj.* Having nothing in the hands; without gain.

em-py-e-ma *n.* The collection of pus in a body cavity.

em-py-re-an (em´pi rē´an) *n.* Pertaining to the highest part of heaven; the sky.

e-mu (ē´mū) *n.* A swift-running Australian bird which is related to the ostrich.

em-u-late (em´ū lāt´) *v.* To strive to equal, especially by imitating. **emulation** *n.* **em-**

ulous *adj.*

em-u-la-tion *n.* The act of emulating; desire to equal or excel others.

em-u-lous *adj.* Eager to imitate, equal, or excel another.

e-mul-sion (i mul´shan) *n.,* *Chem.* A suspended mixture of small droplets, one within the other. *Photog.* A light-sensitive coating on photographic paper, film, or plates. **emulsive** *adj.*

en-a-ble (en ā´bl) *v.* To supply with adequate power, knowledge, or opportunity; to give legal power to another.

en-act (en akt´) *v.* To make into law; to decree. **enactment** *n.*

e-nam-el (i nam´el) *n.* A decorative or protective coating fused on a surface, as of pottery; a paint that dries to a hard, glossy surface; the hard outermost covering of a tooth. *v.* To apply, inlay, or decorate with enamel.

e-nam-el-ware *n.* A type of metalware which has been covered with a coating of enamel.

en-amine *n.* A type of amine that has a double bond linkage.

en-am-or (en am´ėr) *v.* To inflame with love; to charm.

en-an-tio-morph (i nan´tē o morf˝) *n.* A pair of chemical compounds which have molecular structures that are alike.

ena-tion *n.* The outgrowth from a surface of an organ.

en bloc *adv.* As a unit.

enc *or* **encl** *abbr.* Enclosed; enclosure.

en-cage *v.* To confine; trap.

en-camp (en kamp´) *v.* To form or stay in a camp. **encampment** *n.*

en-cap-su-late (en kap´su lāt´) *v.* To enclose or encase in a capsule. **encapsulation** *n.*

en-cap-su-lat-ed *adj.* To be surrounded with a membranous envelope.

en-case (en kās´) *v.* To close within a case.

en-case-ment (en kās´ment) *n.* The state of being encased.

en-caus-tic (en ko´stik) *n.* A type of paint which is made with melted beeswax.

en-ceinte *n.* A wall or enclosure around a town.

en-ce-phal-ic (en˝se fal´ik) *adj.* Pertaining to the brain.

en-ceph-a-li-tis (en sef´a lī´tis) *n., Pathol.* Inflammation of the brain.

en-ceph-a-lo-gram *n.* An X-ray picture of the brain.

en-ceph-a-log-ra-phy *n.* The technique or act of taking X-ray photographs of the brain.

en-ceph-a-lo-my-eli-tis (en sef´a lō mī e lī´tis) *n.* The inflammation of the spinal cord and the brain.

en-ceph-a-lon *n.* The brain.

en-ceph-a-lop-a-thy *n.* The disease of the brain that alters structure.

en-chain (en chān´) *v.* To put in chains.

en-chant (en chant´) *v.* To put under a spell; to bewitch; to charm; to delight greatly. **enchantment** *n.*

en-chant-ing *adj.* Delightful; bewitching; charming.

en-chant-ment (en chant´ment) *n.* The state in which something or someone is enchanted.

en-chant-ress *n.* A female who does magic such as a sorceress.

en-chase (en chās´) *v.* To carve a relief into something.

en-chi-la-da (en˝chi lä´da) *n.* A kind of rolled tortilla and is covered with chili-seasoned tomato sauce.

en-chi-rid-i-on *n.* A handbook; a manual.

en-ci-pher (en sī´fėr) *v.* To convert something such as a message into a cipher.

en-cir-cle (en sėr´kl) *v.* To form a circle around; to move around. **encirclement** *n.*

en-clasp (en klasp´) *v.* To hold onto someone or something.

en-clave (en´klāv) *n.* A country surrounded by a foreign country; a cultural group living within a larger group.

en-clit-ic *adj.* Pertaining to a word connected to a preceding word, closely related without an independent accent.

en-close (en klōz´) *v.* To surround on all sides; to put in the same envelope or package with something else. **enclosure** *n.*

en-clo-sure *n.* The action of enclosing something; state of being enclosed.

en-code (en kōd´) *v.* To conver or change a message into a code. **encoder** *n.*

en-co-mi-ast (en kō´mē ast´) *n.* A person who praises. **encomiastic** *adj.*

en-co-mi-um (en kō´mē um) *n. pl.* **-miums** or **-mia** High praise.

en-com-pass (en kum´pas) *v.* To surround; to form a circle; to enclose.

en-core (äng´kōr) *n.* An audience's demand for a repeat performance; a performance in response to an encore. *v.* To call for an encore.

en-cor-ing *v.* To call for an encore.

en-coun-ter (en koun´tėr) *n.* An unplanned or unexpected meeting or conflict. *v.* To come upon unexpectedly; to confront in a hostile situation.

en-coun-ter group *n.* A therapy group formed to increase people's sensitivity and to reveal their feelings so that they openly relate to others.

en-cour-age (en kėr´ij) *v.* To inspire with courage or hope; to support. **encouragement** *n.* **encouragingly** *adv.*

en-crim-son (en krim´zon) *v.* To color or to make something the shade of crimson.

en-croach (en krōch´) *v.* To intrude upon the rights or possessions of another. **encroacher** *n.* **encroachment** *n.*

en-crust (en krust´) *v.* To cover with a crust; to crust. **encrustation** *n.*

en-cum-ber (en kum´bėr) *v.* To hinder or burden with difficulties or obligations. **encumbrance** *n.*

en-cum-brance *n.* An item which encumbers. **encumbrancer** *n.*

en-cyc-li-cal (en sik´li kal) *n., Rom. Cath. Ch.* A papal letter to the bishops of the world.

en-cy-clo-pe-di-a (en sī´klo pē´dēa) *n.* A comprehensive work with articles covering a broad range of subjects.

en-cy-clo-pedic (en sī˝klo pē´dik) *adj.* Pertaining to an encyclopedia.

en-cy-clo-pe-dist (en sī˝klo pē´dist) *n.* A

person who writes an encyclopedia.

en-cyst (en sist´) *v.* To become enclosed in a sac. **encystment** *n.*

en-cys-ta-tion *n.* A process of making or forming a cyst.

end (end) *n.* A part lying at a boundary; the terminal point at which something concludes; the point in time at which something ceases; a goal; a fragment; a remainder; in football, either of the players in the outermost position on the line of scrimmage. *v.* To come or bring to a termination; to ruin or destroy; to die.

en-dam-age (en dam´ij) *v.* To cause damage to something or to someone.

end-amoe-ba (en˝da mē´ba) *n.* A member of the genus that contains amoebas. **end-amoebic** *adj.*

en-dan-ger (en dān´jėr) *v.* To expose or put into danger or imperil. **endangerment** *n.*

en-dan-gered *adj.* Threatened with extinction; to put in danger.

en-darch (en´därk) *adj.* To be formed from the center outward. **endarchy** *n.*

end-ar-ter-ec-to-my *n.* The removal of the inner layer of an artery with surgery.

end-brain (end´brān˝) *n.* The anterior part of the forebrain; the telencephalon, a subdivision of the forebrain.

end bulb *n.* The bulbous termination on a sensory nerve fiber.

en-dear (en dēr´) *v.* To make beloved or dear. **endearingly** *adv.*

en-dear-ment (en dēr´ment) *n.* The state of being endeared.

en-deav-or (en dev´ėr) *n.* An attempt to attain or do something. **endeavor** *v.*

en-dem-ic (en dem´ik) *adj.* Peculiar to a particular area or people.

en-der-mic (en dėr´mik) *adj.* To act through the skin. **endermically** *adv.*

end-ex-ine *n.* A membranous inner layer of the exine.

end-ing (en´ding) *n.* Something which indicates an end.

en-dive (en´dīv) *n.* A herb with crisp succulent leaves, used in salads; a plant related to the endive.

end-less (end´lis) *adj.* To be without an end.

end line *n.* The line which marks the boundary of a playing field.

end-most (end´mōst˝) *adj.* To be at the very end.

en-do-bi-ot-ic (en˝dō bī´t´ik) *adj.* To be living within the host's tissues.

en-do-car-di-tis (en˝dō kär dī´tis) *n.* An inflammation of the lining of the heart.

en-do-car-di-um (en˝dō kär´dē um) *n.* The membrane lining of the cavities of the heart.

en-do-carp *n.* The inner layer of a fruit wall.

en-do-chon-dral *adj.* To be occurring in cartilage of the body.

en-do-crine (en´do krin) *adj.* To be making secretions which are distributed in the body by the blood.

endocrine gland *n.* The gland which makes an endocrine secretion.

en-do-cri-nol-o-gy (en´dō kri nol´ojē) *n.* The area of science or study of the endocrine glands and various secretions. **endocrinologist** *n.*

en-do-cy-to-sis *n.* The act of taking substances into a cell with phagocytosis.

en-do-derm (en´do dėrm˝) *n.* The inner germ layer in an embryo and becomes the epithelium of the digestive tract.

en-do-der-mis (en´do dėr´mis) *n.* The most inner layer in the cortex of a plant.

en-do-don-tia *n.* Dentistry that specializes in the diseases of the tooth's pulp.

en-do-en-zyme (en˝dō en´zīm) *n.* A kind of enzyme which functions inside the cell.

en-do-er-gic *adj.* To be absorbing energy.

en-do-eryth-ro-cyt-ic *adj.* To be occurring without the red cells of the blood.

en-dog-a-my (en dog´a mē) *n.* The marriage that can only take place within a specific group due to customs. **endogamous** *adj.*

en-dog-e-nous (en doj´e nus) *adj., Biol.* Originating or growing from within.

en-do-lymph *n.* A clear watery fluid in the labyrinth of the ear.

en-do-me-tri-um *n.* The membrane that lines the woman's uterus.

en-do-morph (en´do morf˝ *n.* A type of body structure characterized by a heavy rounded body build, often having the tendency to become fat.

en-do-mor-phic *adj.* To be pertaining to endomorphism.

en-do-nu-cle-ase *n.* An enzyme that will break down a chain of nucloetides.

en-do-par-a-site (en˝dō par´a sīt˝) *n.* A kind of parasite that is able to live in the host's internal organs.

en-do-phyte (en´do fīt˝) *n.* A kind of plant which is able to live with another plant.

en-do-plasm (en´do plaz˝um) *n.* The fluid part of the cytoplasm. **endoplasmic** *adj.*

en-dor-phin *n.* Hormones with tranquilizing and pain-killing capabilities, secreted by the brain.

en-dorse (en dors´) *v.* To write one's signature on the back of a check, so as to obtain the cash indicated on the front, or on the back of a car title, so as to show transfer of ownership. **endorsement** *n.*

en-do-scope (en´do skōp´) *n., Med.* An instrument used to examine a bodily canal or hollow organ. **endoscopic** *adj.* **endoscopy** *n.*

en-do-skel-e-ton (en˝dō skel´i ton) *n.* A skeleton which is on the inside of one's body.

en-do-sperm (en´do spėrm˝) *n.* The tissue in seed plants which is nutritious.

en-do-ste-al *adj.* To be pertaining to the endosteum. **endosteally** *adv.*

end-os-te-um (en dos´tē um) *n.* A vascular connective tissue which lines the medullary cavities found in the bone.

en-do-sul-fan *n.* A kind of insecticide used for the control of crop insects.

en-do-the-ci-um (en˝dō thē shē um) *n.* The lining which is in a mature anther.

en-do-therm (en˝dō thėrm) *n.* An animal that is warm-blooded.

en-do-tox-in (en˝dō tok´sin) *n.* A kind of poisonous substance which can be found in bacteria.

en-do-tra-che-al *adj.* To be placed within the trachea of the body.

en-dow (en dou´) *v.* To supply with a permanent income or income-producing property; to bestow upon. **endowment** *n.*

en-do-zo-ic *adj.* To be living in an animal.

end-pa-per *n.* A piece of paper placed on the front or the back cover of a book.

end point *n.* The point which marks the completion process.

end product *n.* A final product of a group of processes.

en-drin *n.* A type of insecticide.

end table *n.* A table that is about the height of the couch.

en-due (en dŏ´) *v.* To put on.

en-dur-able *adj.* Being able to endure. **endurably** *adv.*

en-dur-ance *n.* An ability to withstand stress or hardship.

en-dure (en der´) *v.* To undergo; to sustain; to put up with; to tolerate; to bear. **endurable** *adj.*

en-dur-ing *adj.* Lasting.

en-duro *n.* A kind of long race that will stress endurance.

end-ways *adv.* In, on or toward the end.

end-wise *or* **end-ways** On end; lengthwise.

en-e-ma (en´e ma) *n.* The injection of a liquid into the rectum for cleansing; the liquid injected.

en-e-my (en´e mē) *n. pl.* **enemies** One who seeks to inflict injury on another; a foe; a hostile force or power.

en-er-get-ic (en˝ėr jet´ik) *adj.* Relating to energy. **energetically** *adv.*

en-er-get-ics (en˝ėr jet´iks) *n.* An area of mechanics dealing with energy.

en-er-gize (en´ėr jīz˝) *v.* To bring or put forth energy.

en-er-gy (en´ėr jē) *n. pl.* **energies** Capacity or tendency for working or acting; vigor; strength; vitality of expression. *Phys.* The capacity for doing work; usable heat or electric power.

energy level *n.* On a stable state of constant energy.

en-er-vate (en´ėr vāt´) *v.* To deprive of

vitality or strength; to weaken.

enfant terrible *n.* A person who has unconventional actions and causes embarrassment.

en-fee-ble (en fē′bl) *v.* To weaken; to make feeble. **enfeeblement** *n.*

en-fet-ter (en fet′ėr) *v.* To tie up in fetters.

en-fi-lade (en′fi lād″) *n.* An arrangement of things where they are parallel and opposite such as with rooms.

en-fleu-rage (ăn floe răzh′) *n.* The process to extract perfumes for flowers.

en-fold (en fōld′) *v.* To enclose; to wrap in layers; to embrace.

en-force (en fōrs′) *v.* To compel obedience; to impose by force or firmness. **enforceable** *adj.* **enforcement** *n.* **enforcer** *n.*

en-fran-chise (en fran′chīz) *v.* To grant with civil rights, as the right to vote; to give a franchise to. **enfranchisement** *n.*

eng *abbr.* Engineer.

Eng *abbr.* English.

en-gage (en gāj′) *v.* To employ or hire; to secure or bind,as by a contract; to pledge oneself, especially to marry; to undertake conflict; to participate. *Mech.* To interlock.

en-gaged (en gājd′) *adj.* To be involved in activity.

en-gage-ment (en gāj′ment) *n.* The state of being engaged.

en-gag-ing *adj.* To draw the attention of others.

en-gen-der (en jen′dėr) *v.* To give rise to; to exist; to cause.

en-gine (en′jin) *n.* A machine which converts energy into mechanical motion; a mechanical instrument; a locomotive.

en-gined *adj.* To have an engine.

en-gi-neer (en″jĭ nēr′) *n.* person who works in the field of engineering.

en-gi-neer-ing *n.* The art of executing a practical application of scientific and mathematical knowledge; the activities of an engineer.

en-gird *v.* To encompass.

en-gla-cial *adj.* To be frozen or embedded within a glacier

Eng-land *n.* Great Britian, also a part of the United Kingdom.

Eng-lish (ing′glish) *adj.* Of, relating to, or characteristic of England, its people, language; the language of the United States and other countries that are or were formerly under English control. **Englishman, Englishwoman** *n.*

English Channel *n.* A section of the Atlantic Ocean which separates England from France.

en-glid *v.* To make something bright with light.

en-glut *v.* To gulp or swallow down.

en-gorge (en gorj′) *v.* To swallow greedily. *Pathol.* To fill an artery with blood. **engorgement** *n.*

en-graft (en graft′) *v., Bot.* To join or fasten, as if by grafting.

en-grail *v.* To decorate or indent the edge of with concave curves or notches.

en-grave (en grāv′) *v.* To carve or etch into a surface; to carve, cut, or etch into a stone, metal, or wood for printing; to print from plates made by such a process. **engraver** *n.*

en-grav-ing (en grā′ving) *n.* The act or technique of one that engraves; the impression printed from an engraved plate.

en-gross (en grōs′) *v.* To occupy the complete attention of; to copy or write in a large, clear hand. **engrossingly** *adv.*

en-gulf (en gulf′) *v.* To enclose completely; to submerge; to swallow.

en-hance (en hans′) *v.* To make greater; to raise to a higher degree.

en-har-mon-ic *adj.* Pertaining to a style of music; relating to music notes that are written differently but sound the same.

en-heart-en *v.* To give renewed hope.

e-nig-ma (e nig′ma) *n.* One that baffles; anything puzzling; a riddle.

en-isle *v.* To make an island of; to isolate.

en-jamb-ment *or* **en-jambe-ment (en jam′ment)** *n.* Construction of a sentence from one line of a poem to the next, allowing related words to fall on different lines.

en-join (en join′) *v.* To command to do something; to prohibit, especially by legal action. **enjoiner** *n.*

en-joy (en joi´) *v.* To feel joy or find pleasure in; to have the use or possession of. **enjoyable** *adj.* **enjoyably** *adv.* **enjoyment** *n.*

en-kin-dle *v.* To kindle; to set on fire; to make bright.

en-lace *v.* To encircle.

en-large (en lärj´) *v.* To make larger; to speak or write in greater detail. **enlargement** *n.* **enlarger** *n.*

en-large-ment *n.* The act of enlarging or state of being enlarged.

en-light-en (en līt´en) *v.* To give a broadening or revealing knowledge; to give spiritual guidance or light to. **enlightenment** *n.*

en-list (en list´) *v.* To secure the help or active aid of. *Milit.* To signup for service with the armed forces. **enlistment** *n.*

en-liv-en (en lī´ven) *v.* To make livelier, cheerful or vigorous. **enlivener** *n.*

en masse (än mas´) *adv.* All together; grouped.

en-mesh (en mesh´) *v.* To catch in a net; to entangle.

en-mi-ty (en´mi tē) *n. pl.* **enemities** Deep hatred; hostility.

en-ne-ad *n.* A collection or group of nine.

en-ne-a-gon (en´ē a gon˝) *n.* A closed plane figure having nine angles and nine sides.

en-ne-a-he-dron (en˝ē a hē´dron) *n.* A solid figure with nine faces.

en-no-ble (en nō´bl) *v.* To make noble or honor-able inquality or nature; to confer the rank of nobility. **ennoblement** *n.*

en-nui (än wē´) *n.* Boredom; weariness.

e-nol-o-gy *n.* The science that deals with wine and the wine making.

e-nor-mi-ty (i nor´mi tē) *n. pl.* **-ties** Excessive wickedness; an outrageous offense or crime.

e-nor-mous (i nor´mus) *adj.* Very great in size or degree. **enormously** *adv.* **enormousness** *n.*

e-nough (i nuf´) *adj.* Adequate to satisfy demands or needs. *adv.* To a satisfactory degree.

en-phy-tot-ic *adj.* Denoting a regional plant disease which occurs regularly but not severely.

en prise *adj.* Of a chess piece, liable or exposed to capture.

en-quire (en kwīêr´) *v.* Variation of inquire.

en-rage (en rāj´) *v.* To put or throw into a rage.

en-rap-ture (en rap´chêr) *v.* To enter into a state of rapture; to delight.

en-rich (en rich´) *v.* To make rich or richer; to make more productive.

en-robe *v.* To clothe or cover with; to attire.

en-roll *or* **en-rol (en rōl´)** *v.* To enter or write a name on a roll, register, or record; to place one's name on a roll, register, or record. **enrollment** *n.* **enrollment** *n.*

en route *adv.* On or along the way.

en-san-guine *v.* To stain or make bloody; to crimson.

en-sconce (en skons´) *v.* To settle securely; to shelter.

en-scroll *v.* To write or record on a scroll.

en-sem-ble (än säm´bl) *n.* A group of complementary parts that are in harmony; a coordinated outfit of clothing; a group of people performing together; music for two or more performers.

en-shrine (en shrīn´) *v.* To place in a shrine; to hold sacred. **enshrinement** *n.*

en-shroud (en shroud´) *v.* To cover with a shroud.

en-sign (en´sīn) *n.* An identifying flag or banner, as one displayed on a ship or aircraft. *Milit.* A commissioned officer of the lowest rank in the U.S. Navy or Coast Guard.

en-si-lage (en´si lij) *n.* The process of storing and preserving green fodder in a silo; fodder that has been stored. **ensile** *v.*

en-slave (en slāv´) *v.* To make a slave of; to put in bondage. **enslavement** *n.*

en-snare (en snâr´) *v.* To catch; to trap.

en-snarl *v.* To tangle or involve in a snarl.

en-sphere (en sfēr´) *v.* To enclose in or as if made into a sphere.

en-sue (en sö´) *v.* To follow as a consequence.

en-sure (en sher´) *v.* To make certain of.

en-ta-ble-ment *n.* A platform that supports a statue, as on a pedestal.

en-tail (en tāl´) *v.* To have as a necessary accompaniment or result; to restrict the inheritance of property to a certain line of heirs. **entailment** *n.*

en-tan-gle (en tang´gl) *v.* To tangle; to complicate; to confuse. **entanglement** *n.*

en-tente (än tänt´) *n., Fr.* A mutual agreement between governments for cooperative action; the parties to an entente.

en-ter (en´tėr) *v.* To go or come into; to penetrate; to begin; to become a member of or participant in; in law, to make a record of.

en-ter-ec-to-my (en˝te rek´tomē) *n.* Removal of a section of the intestine.

en-ter-ic (en ter´ik) *adj.* Relating to or part of the intestines.

en-ter-i-tis *n.* Inflammation of the intestines.

en-ter-o-hep-a-ti-tis *n.* An infectious disease that is often fatal, a disease that affects the intestines and liver of some wild birds, chickens or turkeys.

en-ter-os-to-my *n.* A surgical incision into the intestine through the abdominal wall, allowing for drainage or feeding.

en-ter-prise (en´tėr priz´) *n.* A large or risky undertaking; a business organization; boldness and energy in practical affairs.

en-ter-tain (en´tėr tān´) *v.* To harbor or give heed to; to accommodate; receive as a guest; to amuse. **entertainer** *n.*

en-er-tain-ment *n.* The act of entertaining; the accommodating of guests.

en-thrall (en throl´) *v.* To fascinate; to captivate. **enthrallment** *n.*

en-throne (en thrōn´) *v.* To place on a throne. **enthronement** *n.*

en-thu-si-asm (en thö´zē az´um) *n.* Intense feeling for a cause; eagerness. **enthusiast** *n.* **enthusiastic** *adj.* **enthusiastically** *adv.*

en-thu-si-ast *n.* A person full of enthusiasm for something.

en-thu-si-as-tic *adj.* Filled with enthusiasm.

en-thuse *v.* To arouse enthusiasm; to exhibit enthusiasm.

en-tice (en tīs´) *v.* To attract by arousing desire. **enticer** *n.* **enticement** *n.*

en-tire (en tīer´) *adj.* Having no part left out; whole; complete. **entirely** *adv.*

en-ti-tle (en tī´tl) *v.* To give a name to; to furnish with a right. **entitlement** *n.*

en-ti-ty (en´ti tē) *n. pl.* **entities** The fact of real existence; something that exists alone.

en-tomb (en tömb´) *v.* To place in a tomb. **entombment** *n.*

en-to-mol-o-gy (en´to mol´o jē) *n.* The study of insects. **entomologist** *n.* **entomologic** *adj.* **entomological** *adj.*

en-to-moph-a-gous *adj.* Feeding on insects.

en-to-moph-i-lous *adj.* Relating to a plant that is pollinated by insects.

en-to-mos-tra-can *adj.* A subclass of crustaceans which have a moderately simple organization.

en-tou-rage *n.* One's associate.

en-to-zo-on *n.* An internal parasite; an intestinal worm.

en-trails (en´trālz) *n. pl.* Internal organs of man or animals.

en-train-ment *n.* The process where droplets of gas molecules next to a moving stream are carried along by the stream.

en-trance (en´trans) *n.* To fascinate; enchant.

en-trance (en trans´) *n.* The act of entering; the means or place of entry; the first appearance of an actor in a play; the act of entering into a place; the power or liberty of entering; admission. *v.* To fascinate; enchant. **entrancement** *n.* **entrancingly** *adv.*

en-trant *n.* One beginning a new course of life; becoming a member for the first time of an association.

en-trap (en trap´) *v.* To catch in a trap. **entrapment** *n.*

en-treat (en trēt´) *v.* To make an earnest request of or for.

en-tre-chat *n.* A ballet leap where the feet are struck together a number of times.

en-tree *n.* A dish served as the main course.

en-tre-mets *n.* A side dish served at the table.

en-trench (en trench´) *v.* To dig a trench, as for defense; to fix or sit firmly. **entrenchment** *n.*

en-tre-pre-neur (än´tre pre nėr´) *n.* A person who launches or manages a business venture. **entrepreneurial** *adj.*

en-tre-sol *n.* One lower story positioned between two others of greater height.

en-trust (en trust´) *v.* To transfer to another for care or performance; to give as a trust or responsibility.

en-try (en trē´) *n. pl.* **entries** An opening or place for entering; an item entered in a book, list, or register.

en-twine (en twīn´) *v.* To twine about or together.

e-nu-mer-ate (i nŏ´me rāt´) *v.* To count off one by one. **enumeration** *n.*

e-nun-ci-ate (i nun´sē āt´) *v.* To pronounce with clarity; to announce; proclaim. **enunciation** *n.*

en-u-re-sis *n.* The incontinence or involuntary discharge of urine.

en-vel-op *v.* To cover, as by wrapping or folding; to enwrap or wrap up; to surround entirely.

en-ve-lope (en´ve lōp´) *n.* Something that covers or encloses; a paper case, especially for a letter, having a flap for sealing. *v.* To completely enclose.

en-ven-om (en ven´om) *v.* To make poisonous; to embitter.

en-vi-a-ble (en´vē a bl) *adj.* Highly desirable. **enviably** *adv.*

en-vi-ron *n.* To surround; to encircle.

en-vi-ron-ment (en vī´ron ment) *n.* Surroundings; the combination of external conditions which affect the development and existence of an individual, group, or organism. **environmental** *adj.* **environmentally** *adv.*

en-vi-ron-men-tal-ist *n.* A person who seeks to preserve the natural environment.

en-vi-rons (en vī´ronz) *n. pl.* A surrounding region; a place; outskirts, especially of a city.

en-vis-age (en viz´ij) *v.* To have or form a mental image of; to visualize.

en-vi-sion (en vizh´an) *v.* To picture in one's mind, or to one's self.

en-voy (en´voi) *n.* A messenger or agent; a diplomatic representative who is dispatched on a special mission.

en-vy (en´vē) *n. pl.* **envies** A feeling of discontent or resentment for someone else's possessions or advantages; any object of envy. *v.* To feel envy because of or toward. **envious** *adj.*

en-wind (en wīnd´) *v.* To coil about.

en-wreathe (en rēth´) *v.* To encircle.

en-zo-ot-ic *n.* A disease affecting the animals of an area.

en-zyme (en´zīm) *n., Biochem.* Proteins produced by living organisms that function as biochemical catalysts in animals and plants. **enzymatic** *adj.*

en-zy-mol-o-gy *n.* The branch of science dealing with the nature and activity of enzymes.

Eo-cene (ē´o sēn˝) *adj.* Pertaining to the epoch of Tertiary which is between the Oligocene and the Paleocene time periods.

eo-hip-pus (ē˝ō hip´us) *n.* A type of small primitive horse which had four toes and from the Lower Eocene time period.

e-o-li-an (ē ō´lē an) *adj.* Caused by or transmitted by the wind.

eo-lith (ē´o lith) *n.* A kind of flint which is very crudely chipped.

Eo-lith-ic *adj.* To be pertaining to the early time period of the Stone Age.

e-on (ē´on) *n.* An indefinite period of time.

eo-sin (ē´o sin) *n.* A type of red dye that is obtained with the action of bromine on flourescein.

eo-sin-o-phil (ē´o sin´o fil) *n.* A type of leukocyte which has cytoplasmic inclusions.

eo-sin-o-phil-ia *n.* The abnormal increase of the number of eosinophils of the blood and may be caused by an allergic state or infection.

eo-sin-o-phil-ic *adj.* To be pertaining to eosinophilia.

EP *abbr.* Estimated position.

e-pact (ē´pakt) *n.* A period of time which

has been added to harmonize the lunar with the solar calendar.

ep-archy (ep´är kē) *n.* The diocese of the Eastern church.

ep-au-let *or* **ep-au-lette (ep´e let´)** *n.* A shoulder ornament, as on a military uniform.

ep-ei-rog-e-ny (ep˝i roj´e nē) *n.* A deformation in the crust of the earth which causes the broader features of relief to form.

e-pen-the-sis (e pen´thi sis) *n.* An insertion of a sound into the body of a word.

e-pergne (i pėrn´) *n.* An ornamental centerpiece for holding flowers or fruit, used on a dinner table.

ep-ex-e-ge-sis (ep ek˝si jē´sis) *n.* The additional explanatory matter.

e-phah *n.* The ancient Hebrew unit of dry measure which is equal to a little over a bushel.

e-phebe (i-fēb´) *n.* A youth man especiallt one entering manhood.

e-phe-bus *n.* A young person of Greece in the ancient times.

e-phe-dra *n.* A type of desert shrubs with leaves that are reduced to scales and its nodes.

e-phed-rine (i fed´rin) *n., Chem.* A white, odorless alkaloid used to relieve nasal congestion.

e-phem-er-al (i fem´ėr al) *adj.* To last a very short time. **ephemerally** *adv.*

e-phem-er-al *n.* Anything or living for a short time.

e-phem-er-ality *n.* The state of being ephemeral.

e-phem-er-id *n.* A short-lived insect.

e-phem-er-is (i fem´ėr is) *n.* A statement of the positions of a celestial body at regular intervals.

eph-od *n.* A type of apron which was worn in the rites of the ancient Hebrew times.

eph-or *n.* A Spartan magistrates who had power over the king.

epi- *prefix* Attached to; upon.

ep-i-blast (ep´i blast˝) *n.* The layer which is the outside of the blastoderm.

e-pib-o-ly (i pib´o lē) *n.* The act of one part

growing about another part. **epibolic** *adj.*

ep-ic (ep´ik) *n.* A long narrative poem celebrating the adventures and achievements of a hero. **epic** *adj.*

ep-i-cal *n.* A narrative poem in elevated style, centered upon a hero, and describing extraordinary achievements.

ep-i-ca-lyx (ep´i kā´liks) *n.* An involucre which resembles the calyx.

ep-i-can-thic fold *n.* A fold of the upper eyelid skin over the inner angie of the eye.

ep-i-car-di-um (ep´i kär´dē um) *n.* The visceral part of the heart's pericardium.

ep-ic dra-ma *n.* A drama of the twentieth century that provokes critical thought.

ep-i-cene (ep´i sēn) *adj.* To have the characteristics that are typical of the other sex.

ep-i-cen-ter (ep´i sen´tėr) *n.* The part of the earth's surface directly above the focus of an earthquake.

ep-i-chlo-ro-hy-drin *n.* A toxic liquid that has a chloroform color.

ep-i-con-ti-nen-tal *adj.* To be located on a continent.

ep-i-cot-yl *n.* The part of a seedlings, stem that lies immediately above the cotyledons.

epic theater *n.* The theater where an epic drama may be seen.

ep-i-cure (ep´i kūr´) *n.* One having refined tastes, especially in food and wine.

ep-i-cur-ism *n.* The taste of an epicure.

ep-i-cy-cle (ep´i sī˝kal) *n.* The path or circle in which a plant will move; a small circle, the center of which moves around in the circumference of a larger circle.

ep-i-cy-clic train (ep´i si´klik) *n.* A type of train with gear wheels.

ep-i-dem-ic (ep´i dem´ik) *adj.* Breaking out suddenly and affecting many individuals at the same time in a particular area, especially true of a contagious disease; anything that is temporarily widespread, as a fad. **epidemic** *n.*

ep-i-de-mi-ol-o-gy (ep´i dē˝mē ol´o jē) *n.* The science concerned with the control and study of epidemic diseases.

ep-i-den-drum *n.* A member of the genus that contains the tropical American orchids.

ep-i-der-mis (ep´*i* dėr´mis) *n., Anat.* The outer, non-vascular layer of the skin. **epidermal** *adj.*

e-pi-der-moid *adj.* To resemble the epidermal cells.

e-pi-dia-scope (ep˝i dī*a* skōp˝) *n.* Projector which is used for things which are opaque.

ep-i-did-y-mis (ep˝i did´*i* mis) *n.* The convoluted efferent tubes in the back of the testis.

ep-i-dote (ep´dōt˝) *n.* A mineral which occurs in grains and is sometimes used as a gem.

ep-i-du-ral *adj.* To be outside the dura mater.

ep-i-fau-na *n.* The benthic fauna which lives on the sea floor.

ep-i-fo-cal *adj.* Directly above the true center of the disturbance, of an earthquake.

ep-i-gas-tric (ep˝*i* gas´trik) *adj.* Being over the stomach.

ep-i-ge-al *adj.* To be growing above the surface of the ground.

ep-i-gene *adj.* Formed on the surface of the earth.

ep-i-ge-net-ic (ep˝i j*e* net´ik) *adj.* To be formed after the laying of rock.

ep-i-glot-tis (ep´*i* glot´is) *n., Anat.* The leaf-shaped, elastic cartilage at the base of the tongue that covers the windpipe during the act of swallowing. **epiglottal** *adj.*

ep-i-gone (ep´*i* gōn˝) *n.* A follower. **epigonism** *n.*

ep-i-gram (ep´*i* gram´) *n.* A clever, brief, pointed remark or observation; a terse, witty poem or saying. **epigrammatic** *adj.*

ep-i-gram-ma-tize (ep˝i gram´*a* tīz˝) *v.* To make or create an epigram.

ep-i-graph (ep´*i* graf´) *n.* An inscription on a tomb, monument, etc.; a motto or quotation placed at the beginning of a literary work.

e-pig-ra-phy (i pig´r*a* fē) *n.* The study and interpretation of inscriptions.

e-pig-y-nous *adj.* Being adnate to the ovary

surface and appearing to grow from the top.

ep-i-la-tion *n.* A removal of hair.

ep-i-lep-sy (ep´*i* lep´sē) *n., Pathol.* A nervous disorder marked by attacks of unconsciousness with or without convulsions. **epileptic** *adj.*

ep-i-lep-ti-form (ep˝*i* lep´t*i* form˝) *adj.* To be resembling epilepsy.

ep-i-lep-to-gen-ic *adj.* Tending to be able to induce epilepsy.

ep-i-lep-toid (ep˝*i*lep´toid) *adj.* To be showing symptoms of epilepsy.

ep-i-logue *or* **ep-i-log (ep´*i* log´)** *n.* A short speech given by an actor to the audience at the end of a play; an appended chapter placed at the end of a novel or book, etc.

ep-i-mor-pho-sis *n.* A type of regeneration, in invertebrate animals, which involves cell proliferation and subsequent differiation.

e-pi-my-si-um (ep˝*i* miz´ē *u*m) *n.* The connective tissue sheath of a muscle.

e-pi-nas-ty (ep´*i* nas˝tē) *n.* A movement where the leaf of a plant is bent down and outward.

ep-i-neph-rine *or* **ep-i-neph-rin (ep´*i* nef´ rin)** *n.* A hormone secreted by the adrenal medulla of the adrenal glands that raises the blood pressure and quickens the pulse, used in synthesized form as a cardiovascular stimulant.

e-pi-nue-ri-um (ep˝*i* ner´ē *u*m) *n.* The connective sheath of a nerve trunk.

ep-i-phan-ic *adj.* To have the character of an epiphany.

e-piph-a-ny (i pif´*a* nē) *n.* The Christian festival held on January 6th, celebrating the manifestation of Christ to the Gentiles as represented by the Magi; also known as the Twelfth Day.

ep-i-phe-nom-e-nal (ep˝ē f*e* nom´ i n*a*l) *adj.* To be pertaining to an epiphenumenon.

e-piph-o-ra *n.* The excessive flow of tears due to a disorder of the lacrimal glands.

e-piph-y-se-al (ep˝*i* fiz´ē *a*l) *adj.* To be pertaining to an epiphysis.

e-piph-y-sis *n.* A part or section of a bone which is separated from the main body of the bone by a layer of cartilage, and which later becomes united with the bone through further ossification.

ep-i-phyte (ep´i fīt´) *n.* A plant that receives its nourishment from the air and rain while growing on another plant, as an orchid, moss, or lichen. **epiphytic** *adj.*

ep-i-phy-tot-ic *adj.* A plant disease that recurs and attacks many plants in a widespread area. *n.* An epidemic of such a disease.

ep-i-scia *n.* A member of the genus of tropical American herbs having hairy foliage.

e-pis-co-pa-cy (i pis´ko pa sē) *n. pl.* **-cies** The government of a church by bishops; an episcopate.

e-pis-co-pal (i pis´ko pal) *adj.* Pertaining to or governed by bishops.

E-pis-co-pa-lian (i pis˝ko pāl´yan) *n.* A member of the Protestant Episcopal Church.

e-pis-co-pate (i pis´ko pit) *n.* The term, rank, or position of a bishop; bishops as a group.

ep-i-scope *n.* The projector which is used for items that are opaque.

ep-i-sode (ep´i sōd´) *n.* A section of a poem, novel, etc., that is complete in itself; an occurrence; an incident. **episodic** *adj.*

e-pi-some *n.* The gene that can replicate autonomously in the bacterial cytoplasm.

e-pis-te-mol-o-gy *n.* The study of the origin, grounds, methods, of knowledge, with reference to its limits.

e-pi-ster-num (ep˝i stèr´num) *n.* An anterior part of the sternum.

e-pis-tle (i pis´l) *n.* A formal letter. **Epistle** One of the letters in the New Testament. **epistolary** *adj.*

epistle side *n.* The right side of an altar as one faces it.

ep-i-taph (ep´i taf´) *n.* An inscription, as on a tomb or gravestone, in memory of a deceased person.

e-pit-a-sis (i pit´ asis) *n.* The portion of a play that develops the main action and leads it to a catastrophe.

ep-i-tha-la-mi-um *n.* A song in the honor of the groom and the bride.

ep-i-the-li-oma (ep˝i thē˝lē ō´ma) *n.* A tumor either malignant or benign that is derived from epithelial tissue.

ep-i-the-li-um (ep´i thē´lē um) *n. pl.* **-liums** *or* **- lia** *Biol.* The thin, membranous tissue consisting of one or more layers of cells, forming the covering of the outer bodily surface and most of the internal surfaces and organs. **epithelial** *adj.* **epithelioid** *adj.*

ep-i-the-lize *v.* To convert to epithelium.

ep-i-thet (ep´i thet´) *n.* A term, word, or phrase used to characterize a person or thing; an abusive phrase or word.

e-pit-o-me (i pit´o mē) *n.* A concise summary, as of a book; an extreme or typical example.

e-pit-o-mize (i pit´o mīz´) *v.* To be a perfect example.

e-pi-zo-ic (ep´i zō´ik) *adj.* To be living upon the body of an animal.

e-pi-zo-ot-ic *adj.* Pertaining to a disease which will effect a group of animals of the same kind. **epizootically** *adv.*

ep-och (ep´ok) *n.* A point in time marking the beginning of a new era. **epochal** *adj.*

ep-ode (ep´ōd) *n.* Type of lyric poem.

ep-onym (ep´o nim) *n.* The one that something is named for. **eponymic** *adj.*

ep-o-pee (ep´o pē˝) *n.* A type of epic poem.

ep-ox-ide *n.* A kind of epoxy compound.

ep-ox-i-dize *v.* To change something into an epoxide.

ep-ox-y (e pok´sē) *n. pl.* **epoxies** *Chem.* A durable, corrosion-resistant resin used especially in surface glues and coatings. **epoxy** *v.*

ep-si-lon (ep´si lon´) *n.* The fifth letter of the Greek alphabet.

Ep-som salts (ep´som sält) *n. pl.* A hydrated magnesium sulfate, used as a purge or to reduce inflammation.

eq *abbr.* Equation.

eq-ua-ble (ek´wa bl) *adj.* Not changing or varying; free from extremes; evenly proportioned; uniform; not easily upset. **equability** *n.*

e-qual (ē′kwal) *adj*. Of the same measurement, quantity, or value as another; having the same privileges or rights.

e-qualed *v*. To be equal to another.

e-qual-i-tar-i-an *n*. A person who adheres to the doctrine of equality for all men.

e-qual-i-ty (i kwol′i tē) *n*. The state of being equal.

e-qual-ize (ē′kwa līz′) *v*. To become or make equal or uniform. **equalizer** *n*.

e-qual-ly *adv*. Doing something in an equal manner or method.

equal opportunity employer *n*. An employer who does not discriminate on the basis of age, race, sex, religion, etc.

e-qual sign *n*. The sign in math, (=), which denotes equality in an equation or etc.

e-qua-nim-i-ty (ē′kwa nim′i tē) *n*. Composure.

e-quate (i kwāt′) *v*. To consider or make equal.

e-qua-tion (i kwā′zhan) *n*. The act or process of being equal; a mathematical statement expressing the equality of two quantities, usually shown as (=).

e-qua-tion-al *adj*. To be involving an equation. **equationally** *adj*.

e-qua-tor (i kwā′tėr) *n*. The great imaginary circle around the earth; a line lying in a plane perpendicular to the earth's polar axis. **equatorial** *adj*.

e-qua-to-ri-al *adj*. Pertaining to, or near an equator.

equatorial plane *n*. The plane in a cell which is perpendicular to a spindle of a cell and between the pole when it is dividing.

eq-ua-tor-ward *adj*. To be moving toward the equator of the earth.

eq-uer-ry (ek′we rē) *n. pl*. **equerries** The officer in charge of the horses of royalty; the personal attendant to a member of the British royal family.

e-ques-tri-an (i kwes′trē an) *adj*. Pertaining or relating to horsemanship. *n*. The person who rides or performs on a horse. **equiangular** *Geom*. Having all angles equal. **equestrienne** *n*.

e-ques-tri-enne *n*. A woman who rides a horse.

e-qui-an-gu-lar (ē″kwē ang′gū lėr) *adj.*, *Geom*. Having all angles equal.

e-qui-ca-lor-ic (ē″kwi ka lor′ik) *adj*. Being capable to yield equal amounts of energy that is required in the body.

e-qui-dis-tant (ē″kwi dis′tant) *adj*. Having equal distances. **equidistance** *n*., **equidistancally** *adj*.

e-qui-lat-er-al (ē′kwi lat′ėr al) *adj*. Having all sides equal. **equilibrium** *pl*. -ums *Phys*. The state of balance between two opposing forces or influences; any state of compromise, adjustment, or balance. **equilateral** *n*.

e-qui-lat-er-al hy-per-bo-la *n*. A type of hyperbola that has the asymptotes and right angles.

e-quil-i-brant *n*. A system of forces, that counterbalances to produce equilibrium.

e-quil-i-brate (i kwil′i brāt″) *v*. To keep something in equilibrium.

e-qui-li-brist (i kwil′i brist) *n*. A person who can balance himself in positions which are unnatural. **equilibristic** *adj*.

e-qui-lib-ri-um (ē″kwi lib′rē um) *n. pl*. **equilibriums** *Phys*. The state of balance between two opposing forces or influences; any state of compromise, adjustment, or balance.

e-qui-mol-al (ē″kwi mō′lal) *adj*. To have an equal concentration of moles.

e-qui-mo-lar *adj*. Pertaining to an equal amount or number of moles.

e-quine (ē′kwīn) *adj*. Pertaining to or like a horse. **equine** *n*.

e-qui-nox (ē′kwi noks′) *n*. Either of the two times a year when the sun crosses the celestial equator and the days and nights are equal in time. **equinoctial** *adj*.

e-quip (i kwip′) *v*. To furnish or fit with whatever is needed for any undertaking or purpose; to dress for a certain purpose or reason.

eq-ui-page (ek′wi pij) *n*. A carriage that is equipped with horses and attendants.

e-quip-ment (i kwip′ment) *n*. The state or act of being equipped; the material one is provided with for a special purpose.

e-qui-poise (ē´kwi poiz´) *n.* A state of balance.

e-qui-pol-lence (ē˝kwi pol´ens) *n.* The state of being equipollent.

e-qui-pol-lent (ē˝kwi pol´ent) *adj.* To have the same effect. **equipollently** *adv.*, **equipollent** *n.*

e-qui-pon-der-ant *adj.* To be balanced equally.

e-qui-pon-der-ate (ē˝kwi pon´de rāt˝) *v.* To make things equal in their weights.

e-qui-po-tent (ē˝wi pōt´ent) *adj.* To have equal effects for development of something.

e-qui-prob-able *adj.* To have the same degree of mathematical probability.

e-qui-se-tum (ēk˝wi sē tum) *n.* A type of perennial plant which can spread by creeping rhizomes such as the scouring rush.

eq-ui-ta-ble (ek´wi ta bl) *adj. pl.* -ties Being impartial in treatment or judgment. **equitableness** *n.* **equitably** *adv.*

eq-ui-tant (ek´wi tant) *adj.* To be overlapping one another at the base such as the iris.

eq-ui-ta-tion (ek´wi tā´shan) *n.* The art or act of horse riding.

eq-ui-ty (ek´wi tē) *n. pl.* **equities** Fairness or impartiality; the value of property beyond a mortgage or liability;in law, justice based on the concepts of fairness and ethics.

e-quiv-a-lent (i kwiv´a lent) *adj.* Being equal or virtually equal, as in effect or meaning. **equivalence** *n.* **equivalency** *n.* **equivalent** *n.* **equivalently** *adv.*

e-quiv-o-cal (i kwiv´o kal) *adj.* Ambiguous; questionable. **equivocally** *adv.*

e-quiv-o-cate (i kwiv´o kāt´) *v.* To intentionally use evasive or vague language. **equivocation** *n.* **equivocator** *n.*

e-qui-voque (ek´wi vōk˝) *n.* A double meaning.

-er *n. suff.* A thing or person that performs the action of the root verb; a person concerned with a trade or profession, as a banker, teacher, etc.; one who lives in or comes from a certain area, as a northerner, midwesterner, etc.; used to form the comparative usage degree of adverbs and adjectives.

e-ra (ēr´a) *n.* An extended period of time that is reckoned from a specific date or point in the past and used as the basis of a chronology.

e-rad-i-cate (i rad´i kāt´) *v.* To destroy utterly; to remove by the roots. **eradicator** *n.* **eradication** *n.* **eradicable** *adj.*

e-rase (i rās´) *v.* To remove something written. *Slang* To kill. **erasable** *adj.* **eraser** *n.* **erasure** *n.*

e-ras-er *n.* An implement, such as a piece of cloth or rubber, used to erase or remove writing or other marks.

e-ras-ure *n.* The act of erasing; obliteration.

er-bi-um (er bē um) *n.*, *Chem.* A soft, metallic, silvery, rare-earth element, symbolized by Er.

ere (âr) Prior to; before.

e-rect (i rekt´) *adj.* In a vertical position; standing up straight. *v.* To construct; build. *Physiol.* The state of erectile tissue, as through an influx of blood. **erectly** *adv.* **erectness** *n.* **erector** *n.* **erection** *n.*

e-rec-tile *adj.* Capable of being set upright.

ere-long (âr long´) *adv.*, *Archaic* Before long.

er-e-mite (er´em mīt´) *n.* A hermit.

e-rep-sin *n.* A proteolytic mixture that contains peptidases and is found in intestinal secretions.

er-e-thism *n.* The abnormal irritability in any organ or tissue.

erg (erg) *n.*, *Phys.* A unit of work or energy.

er-go (er´gō) *conj. & adv.* Consequently; therefore.

er-go-graph *n.* An implement used to measure and record muscular work completed.

er-gom-e-ter *n.* A device used to measure the work done by a set of muscles.

er-go-no-vine *n.* A crystalline alkaloid made from ergot and used to prevent hemorrhaging after child-birth or an abortion.

er-gos-ter-ol (er gos´te rōl´) *n.*, *Biochem.* A steroid alcohol synthesized by yeast from sugars, converted under ultraviolet radiation to vitamin D.

er-got (er´got) *n*. The disease of rye and other cereal plants; a drug used to contract involuntary muscles and to control hemorrhage.

er-got-a-mine *n*. An alkaloid extracted from ergot, used in treating migraines and stimulating labor contractions.

er-got-ism (er´go tiz˝um) *n*. The toxic condition that is produced by eating grain products or grasses that have been infected with ergot fungus.

E-rie *n*. One of America's five Great Lakes.

er-is-tic *adj*. Pertaining to controversy; controversial.

er-mine (er´min) *n*.
A weasel whose fur changes from brown to white depending on the season.

e-rode (i rōd) *v*. To wear away gradually by constant friction;to corrode; to eat away.

e-rog-e-nous (i roj´e nus) *adj*. Responsive to sexual stimulation.

e-ro-sion (i rō´zhan) *n*. The state or process of being eroded. **erosional** *adj*.

e-ro-sive (i rō´siv) *adj*. Eroding or tending to erode. **erosiveness** *n*.

e-rot-ic (i rot´ik) *adj*. Pertaining to or promoting sexual desire. **erotically** *adv*. **eroticism** *n*.

e-rot-ica (i rot´i ka) *n*. *pl*. Art or literature with an erotic quality.

e-rot-i-cism *n*. Use of sexually stimulating themes.

err (er) *v*. To make a mistake; to sin.

er-rand (er´and) *n*. A short trip to carry a message or to perform a specified task, usually for someone else.

er-rant (er´ant) *adj*. Wandering or traveling about in search of adventure; straying from what is proper or customary. **errantry** *n*.

er-rat-ic (i rat´ik) *adj*. Lacking a fixed course. *Med*. Irregular; inconsistent. **erratically** *adv*.

er-ra-tum (i rā´tum) *n*. *pl*. **-ta** An error in printing or writing.

er-ro-ne-ous (e rō´nē us) *adj*. To have or contain an error. **erroneously** *adv*. **erroneousness** *n*.

er-ror (er´or) *n*. Something said, believed, or done incorrectly; a mistake; the state of being wrong or mistaken; in baseball, a misplay by a team member who is not batting.

er-satz (er´zäts) *adj*. A substitute that is usually inferior; artificial.

erst-while (ėrst´hwīl´) *adj*., *Archaic* Former.

er-u-bes-cence *n*. The instance of turning red; blushing.

e-ruct (i rukt´) *v*. To belch.

e-ruc-tate *n*. The act of belching wind from the stomach.

er-u-dite (er´ū dīt´) *adj*. Scholarly.

er-u-di-tion (er´ū dish´an) *n*. Great learning.

e-rum-pent *adj*. Bursting forth.

e-rupt (i rupt´) *v*. To burst forth violently and suddenly; to explode with steam, lava, etc., as a volcano or geyser; to break out in a skin rash or pimples.

e-rup-tion *n*. A bursting forth; an outburst.

-ery *n*. *suff*. A place of business; a business, or a place where something is performed or done, bakery; the collection of things; practice or act of something; the qualities or characteristics of something; slavery.

e-ryn-go *n*. Plant consisting of coarse herbs having toothed or spiny leaves.

er-y-sip-e-las (er´i sip´e las) *n*. An acute, inflammatory, and very uncomfortable skin disease resulting from streptococcus.

e-ryth-ro-blast *n*. One of the nucleated cells found in bone marrow from which the red blood cells are formed.

e-ryth-ro-cyte (i rith´ro sīt´) *n*. A disk-shaped blood cell that contains hemoglobin and is responsible for the red color of blood.

e-ryth-ro-cy-tom-e-ter *n*. An instrument used to count red blood cells.

e-ryth-ro-my-cin *n*. An antibiotic used to treat amoebic and other diseases.

es-ca-lade *n*. A scaling or mounting by

means of ladders.

es-ca-late (es′k*a* **lāt′)** *v.* To intensify, increase, or enlarge. **escalation** *n.*

es-ca-la-tor (es′k*a* **lā′tėr)** *n.* A moving stairway with steps attached to an endless belt.

es-cal-lop (e skol′*o***p)** *n. & v.* Variation of scallop.

es-ca-pade (es′k*a* **pād′)** *n.* Reckless or playful behavior; a prankish trick.

es-cape (e skāp′) *v.* To break free from capture, confinement, restraint, etc; to fade from the memory; to enjoy temporary freedom from unpleasant realities. **escape** *n.* **escapee** *n.* **escaper** *n.*

es-ca-pee *n.* A person who has escaped, from prison.

escape hatch *n.* Emergency exit.

es-cape-ment (e skāp′m*e***nt)** *n., Mech.* A device used in time pieces to control the movement of the wheel and supply energy impulses to a pendulum or balance; a typewriter mechanism that controls the horizontal movement of the carriage.

escape velocity *n., Phys.* The minimum veloc-ity that a rocket or anybody must attain to escape or overcome the gravitational field.

escape wheel *n., Mech.* The rotating notched wheel in an escapement.

es-cap-ism *n.* An escape from unpleasant realities through daydreams or other mental diversions. **escapist** *adj.*

es-ca-role (es′k*a* **rōl′)** *n.* Endive leaves used for salads.

es-carp *n.* The inner wall of a ditch surrounding a rampart.

es-carp-ment *n.* A steep slope or drop; a long cliff formed by erosion.

-escense *n. suff.* To give off light in a certain way, as florescence.

-escent *adj. suff.* To give off light in a special way, as phosphorescent; beginning to be.

es-chew (es chō′) *v.* To shun or avoid.

es-cort (es′kort) *n.* A group or individual person accompanying another so as to give protection or guidance; a male who accompanies a female in public.

es-cri-toire (es′kri twär′) *n.* A writing desk.

es-crow (es′krō) *n.* In law, a written deed, contract, or money placed in the custody of a third party until specified conditions are met.

es-cu-do *n. pl.* **escudos** The monetary unit of Portugal.

es-cu-lent *adj.* Fit for eating.

es-cutch-eon (e skuch′*o***n)** *n.* A shield-shaped surface with an emblem bearing a coat of arms; a protective plate, as for a keyhole.

-ese *n. & adj. suff.* An inhabitant or native of; in the language or style of.

Es-ki-mo (es′ki mō″) *n. pl.* **eskimo** *or* **eskimos** One of a Mongoloid people living in the Arctic.

Eskimo dog *n.* A large dog of a sturdy, broad-chested breed used to draw sleds.

e-soph-a-gus (i sof′*a* **g***u***s)** *n. pl.* **esophagi** *Anat.* The muscular, membranous tube through which food passes on the way from the mouth to the stomach. **esophageal** *adj.*

es-o-ter-ic (es′*o* **ter′ik)** *adj.* Confidential; kept secret; understood or meant for only a particular and often very small group

ESP *abbr.* Extrasensory perception.

esp *abbr.* Especially..

es-pa-drille (es′p*a* **dril′)** *n.* A shoe with a canvas upper and a flexible sole.

es-pal-ier (e spal′yėr) *n.* A flat framework used to train shrubs to grow a particular way. **espalier** *v.*

es-par-to *n.* Any of two or three types of grass.

es-pe-cial (e spesh′*a***l)** *adj.* Having a very special place; apart or above others; exceptional. **especially** *adv.*

Es-pe-ran-to (es″perän′tō) *n.* An artificial language with a vocabulary based on words in many European languages.

es-pi-al *n.* Observation; discovery.

es-pi-o-nage (es′pē *o* **näzh′)** *n.* The act or practice of spying to obtain secret intelligence.

es-pla-nade (es′pl*a* **nād′)** *n.* A flat, open stretch of land along a shoreline.

es-pou-sal (e spou′z*a***l)** *n.* Support or

adoption, as of a cause; a wedding.

es-pouse (e spouz′) v. To make something one's own; to take as a spouse; to marry; to give in marriage.

es-pres-so (e spres′ō) n. pl. **espressos** A strong coffee brewed by steam pressure from darkly-roasted beans.

es-prit (e sprē′) n. Spirit; wit; mental liveliness.

es-prit de corps (e sprē′ de kor′) n. A group's spirit of enthusiasm and devotion to the common goals of the group.

es-py (e spi) v. To catch a quick view or sight of.

Esq abbr. Esquire.

-esque adj. suff. Resembling.

es-quire (e skwīer′) n. The title of courtesy or respect; sometimes written as Esq. behind a man's last name.

-ess n. suff. Female.

es-say (es′ā) n. A short composition that deals with a single topic and expresses the author's viewpoint on a subject; an effort or attempt. **essayer** n. **essayist** n.

es-sence (es′ ens) n. The real nature in which something consists; the most important element; an immaterial spirit; being.

Es-sene (es′ēn) n. A member of an ascetic Jewish sect of ancient Palestine.

es-sen-tial (e sen′shal) adj. Necessary; indispensable; containing, of, or being an essence. **essential** n. **essentiality** n. **essentialness** n. **essentially** adv.

es-sen-tial-ism n. The theory that there are definite traditional concepts, standards, and procedures that are indispensable to a society.

essential oil n. Oils from plants, possessing the characteristic odor of the plant, and volatilizing completely when heated: used in making perfumes and flavors.

es-so-nite n. A yellow to brown gem.

est abbr. Established; estimate.

EST abbr. Eastern Standard Time.

-est adj. & adv. suff. Used to form the superlative degree of adverbs and adjectives.

es-tab-lish (e stab′lish) v. To make permanent, stable, or secure; to install; to

create or find; to cause to be accepted or recognized; to prove.

es-tab-lish-ment (e stab′lish ment) n. The state of being established; a place of business or residence; those collectively who occupy positions of influence and status in a society.

es-tate (e stāt′) n. A usually large or extensive piece of land containing a large house; in law, the nature, degree, and extent of ownership or use of property.

es-teem (e stēm′) v. To regard with respect.

es-ter (es′tėr) n., Chem. Any of a class of organic compounds formed by the reaction of an acid with an alcohol.

Esther n. In the Old Testament, the Jewish queen and wife of King Ahasuerus of Persia, who saved her people from massacre.

es-the-sia n. Sensibility; feeling.

es-thet-ic (es thet′ik) adj. Variation of aesthetic.

es-ti-ma-ble (es′ti ma bl) adj. Worthy of respect or admiration. **estimableness** n. **estimably** adv.

es-ti-mate (es′ti māt′) v. To form or give an approximate opinion or calculation. n. A preliminary opinion or statement of the approximate cost for certain work. **estimation** n.

es-ti-ma-tion n. Judgment; the act of estimating or appraising something.

es-ti-val (es′ti val′) adj. Pertaining to or of summer.

es-ti-vate (es′ti vāt′) v. To pass the summer in a state of dormancy.

Es-to-ni-a (e stō′nē a) n. A former country located in western Europe, now a part of the U.S.S.R.

es-trange (e stranj′) v. To arouse hatred or indifference where there had been love and caring; to disassociate or remove oneself. **estrangement** n.

es-tray n. A domestic animal, as a dog or cat found wandering without an owner.

es-tro-gen (es′tro jen) n., Biochem. Any of various steroid hormones that regulate female reproductive functions and secondary sex characteristics. **estrogenic** *adj.*

es-trone *n.* A female sex hormone, used to treat estrogen deficiency.

es-tu-ar-y (es′chŏ er′ē) *n. pl.* **estuaries** The wide mouth of a river where the current meets the sea and is influenced by tides.

ET *abbr.* Eastern Time; extra terrestrial.

et al *abbr.* And others.

et-a-mine *n.* A lightweight fabric of cotton, silk, or wool.

etc *abbr.* And so forth.

etch (ech) *v.* To engrave or cut into the surface by the action of acid; to sketch or outline by scratching lines with a pointed instrument. **etcher** *n.*

etch-ing (ech′ing) *n.* The process of engraving in which lines are scratched with a sharp instrument on a plate covered with wax or other coating after which the exposed parts are subjected to the corrosive action of an acid; a picture or impression made from an etched plate.

e-ter-nal (i tèr′nal) *adj.* Existing without beginning or end; unending; meant to last indefinitely. **eternal** *n.* **eternality** *n.* **eternalness** *n.* **eternally** *adv.*

e-ter-ni-ty (i tèr′ni tē) *n. pl.* **-ties** Existence without beginning or end; forever; the immeasurable extent of time; the endless time after a person dies.

eth-ane (eth′ān) *n., Chem.* An odorless, colorless, gaseous hydrocarbon from the methane series that is contained in crude petroleum and in illuminating gas.

eth-a-nol (eth′a nōl′) *n., Chem.* The alcohol obtained after the distillation of certain fermented sugars or starches; the intoxicant in liquors, wines, and beers; alcohol.

e-ther (ē′thèr) *n., Chem.* A highly flammable liquid compound with a characteristic odor, used as a solvent and an anesthetic; the clear upper regions of space.

e-the-re-al (i thēr′ē al) *adj.* Very airy and light; highly refined; delicate; heavenly. **ethereally** *adv.*

eth-ic (eth′ik) *n. pl.* **-ics** The system of moral values; the principle of right or good conduct.

eth-i-cal (eth′i kal) *adj.* Relating to or of ethics; conforming to right principles of conduct as accepted by a specific profession, as medicine. **ethically** *adv.*

eth-moid *adj.* Pertaining to a bone of the skull located at the root of the nose, and contains a number of perforations for the filaments of the olfactory nerve.

eth-nic (eth′nik) *adj.* Relating to or of a national, cultural, or racial group. **ethnicity** *n.*

eth-no-cen-tric *adj.* Pertaining to the belief that a person's own culture is better than other ethnic groups.

eth-nog-ra-phy (eth nog′ra fē) *n. pl.* **-phies** The branch of anthropology dealing with the classification and description of primitive human cultures.

eth-nol-o-gy (eth nol′o jē) *n. pl.* **-gies** The branch of anthropology that is concerned with the study of ethnic and racial groups, their cultures, origins, and distribution.

e-thos *n.* The characteristic spirt of people; character or disposition.

eth-yl (eth′il) *n., Chem.* An organic radical occurring in ether and alcohol; a univalent hydrocarbon radical; any gasoline that is treated with tetraethyl lead to reduce engine knock. **ethylic** *adj.*

ethyl acetate *n.* A colorless, flammable, fragrant liquid, used as paint or lacque solvent, and in perfumes.

ethyl alcohol *n.* Grain alcohol; used as a solvent, and as an intermediate in beverages.

eth-yl-ene (eth′i lēn′) *n., Chem.* A colorless, flammable gas refined from natural gas and petroleum and used as a fuel.

eth-yl-ene gly-col *n., Chem.* A colorless, syrupy alcohol used as an antifreeze, solvent, and lubricant.

eth-yl e-ther *n., Chem.* Ether.

e-ti-ol-o-gy (ē′tē ol′o jē) *n.* The science and study of causes or origins. *Med.* The theory of the cause of a particular disease. **etiologic** *adj.* **etiological** *adj.* **etiologically** *adv.* **etiologist** *n.*

et-i-quette (et′i kit) *n.* The prescribed rules,

forms and practices, established for behavior in polite society or in official or professional life.

-ette *n. suff.* Small; female.

e-tui *n.* A small case holding small articles.

et-y-mol-o-gy (et´*i* mol´*o* jē) *n. pl.* -gies The history of a word as shown by breaking it down into basic parts, tracing it back to the earliest known form, and indicating its changes in form and meaning; the branch of linguistics that deals with etymologies. **etymological** *adj.* **etymologist** *n.*

et-y-mon (et´*i* mon´) *n. pl.* -mons *or* -ma The earlier form of a word in the same language or in the ancestral language.

eu-caine *n.* A white,crystalline powder, used as a local anesthetic.

eu-ca-lyp-tus (ū´k*a* lip´t*u*s) *n. pl.* -tuses *or* -ti A large, native Australian tree with very aromatic leaves that yield an oil used medicinally.

Eu-cha-rist (ū´k*a*rist) *n.* The Christian sacrament of Communion in which bread and wine are consecrated and received in the remembrance of the passion and death of Christ. **Eucharistic** *adj.*

eu-chre (ū´kėr) *n.* A card game for two to four players played with 32 cards in which the winning side must take three of five tricks. *Informal* To trick or cheat.

eu-di-om-e-ter *n.* An instrument used in the analysis and volume measurement of gases.

eu-di-om-e-try *n.* The measurement and analysis of gases using a eudiometer.

eu-gen-ics (ū jen´iks) *n.* The science of improving the physical and mental qualities of human beings through genetics. **eugenic** *adj.* **eugenicist** *n.*

eu-gle-na *n.* Microscopic green protozoa having a single flagellum and a red eyespot, having both animal and plant traits and used in biological research.

eu-la-chon *n.* The candlefish, found on the north Pacific coast, from the smelt family

eu-la-mel-li-branch *n.* Bivalve mollusk, as the clam, oyster, and fresh-water mus-sel.

eu-lo-gize (ū´l*o* jīz´) *v.* To deliver a eulogy for; to speak in commendation of another.

eulogist *n.* **eulogizer** *n.*

eu-lo-gy (ū´l*o* jē) *n. pl.* -gies A speech that honors a person or thing, usually delivered at a funeral; high praise. **eulogistic** *adj.*

eu-nuch (ū´n*u*k) *n.* A castrated man.

eu-on-y-mus *n.* Shrubs, vines, or small trees found in northern areas of the United States.

eu-pep-sia *n.* Good digestion.

eu-phe-mism (ū´f*e* miz´*u*m) *n.* A substitution for a word or expression that is thought to be too strong, blunt, or painful for another person. **euphemistic** *adj.* **euphemistically** *adv.*

eu-pho-ni-um *n.* A musical instrument that resembes the baritone tuba, but has a higher range and mellower tone.

eu-pho-ny (ū´f*o* nē) *n. pl.* -nies The agreeable sound of spoken words. **euphonious** *adj.* **euphoniously** *adv.*

eu-pho-ri-a (ū fōr´ē *a*) *n.* A very strong feeling of elation or well-being.

eu-phu-ism *n.* An ornate style of writing with frequent use of alliteration, antitheses, and mythological similes.

eu-re-ka (ū rē´k*a*) An expression of triumph or achievement.

eu-rhyth-mics *n.* The art of gracefully dance motions of the body that are inspired through physical sensibility to music.

eu-ri-pus *n.* An area where the tide flows with dangerous and violent force.

Eu-ro-pe-an (ūr˝*o* pē´*a*n) *adj.* Derived from or related to Europe or its inhabitants; relating to a person of European descent.

eu-ro-pi-um (ū rō´pē *u*m) *n., Chem.* A soft, silvery-white, rare-earth element used in nuclear research, symbolized by Eu.

eu-ry-therm *n.* An organism with the ability to adjust physically to wide varying degrees of heat and cold.

eu-sta-chian tube (ū stā´shan tŏb) *n., Anat.* The passage between the middle ear and the pharynx that equalizes the air pressure between the tympanic cavity and the atmosphere.

eu-tha-na-sia (u´th*a* nā´zh*a*) *n.* The act

or practice of putting to death painlessly a person suffering from an incurable disease; also called mercy killing.

eu-then-ics (ū then´iks) *n*. The study of improving the physical and mental qualities of human beings by controlling the environmental factors. **euthenist** *n*.

eu-the-ri-an *adj*. Referring to a large group.

eu-tro-phy *n*. Healthful, normal nutrition.

e-vac-u-ate (i vak´ū āt´) *v*. To leave a threatened area, town, building, etc.; to empty; to remove the contents. *Physiol*. To discharge or eject, as from the bowels. **e-vacuation** *n*. **evacuator** *n*.

e-vac-u-a-tion *n*. The process of evacuating.

e-vac-u-ee (i vak´ū ē´) *n*. A person who is evacuated from a hazardous place.

e-vade (i vād´) *v*. To baffle; to elude; to get away from by using cleverness or tricks.

e-val-u-ate (i val´ū āt´) *v*. To examine carefully; to determine the value of; to appraise. **evaluation** *n*. **evaluator** *n*.

ev-a-nesce (ev´a nes´) *v*. To disappear; to fade away.

ev-a-nes-cent (ev´a nes´ent) *adj*. Vanishing or passing quickly; fleeting. **evanescence** *n*. **evanescently** *adv*.

e-van-gel-i-cal (ē´van jel´i kal) *adj*. Relating to the Christian gospel, especially the four Gospels of the New Testament; maintaining the doctrine that the Bible is the only rule of faith.

e-van-gel-ism (i van´je liz´ūm) *n*. The zealous preaching and spreading of the gospel.

e-van-gel-ist *or* **Evangelist (i van´je list)** *n*. One of the four writers of the New Testament Gospels Matthew, Mark, Luke, or John; a zealous Protestant preacher or missionary. **evangelistic** *adj*.

e-van-gel-ize (i van´je līz) *v*. To preach the gospel; to convert to Christianity. **evangelization** *n*.

e-van-ish *v*. To vanish.

e-vap-o-rate (i vap´o rāt´) *v*. To convert into vapor; to remove the liquid or moisture from fruit, milk, etc., so as to concentrate or dry it. **evaporative** *adj*. **evaporator** *n*.

evaporated milk *n*. A type of milk that is concentrated by evaporation.

e-vap-o-rim-e-ter *n*. An instrument for ascertaining the quantity of a fluid that evaporates in a given time.

evap-o-rite *n*. A type of sedimentary rock which originates by evaporation of sea water. **evaporitic** *adj*.

e-vap-o-tran-spi-ra-tion *n*. The process by which the earth's surface loses moisture by evaporation.

e-va-sion (i vā´zhan) *n*. The act or means of evading.

e-va-sive (i vā´siv) *adj*. Being intentionally vague; equivocal. **evasively** *adv*. **evasiveness** *n*.

eve (ēv) *n*. The evening before a special day or holiday; the period immediately preceding some event; evening.

Eve *n*. The first woman created by God; the wife of Adam.

e-vec-tion (i vek´shan) *n*. The perturbation of the orbital motion of the moon that is caused due to the attraction of the sun.

e-ven (ē´ven) *adj*. Having a flat, smooth, and level surface; having no irregularities; smooth; on the same line or plane; equally matched; not owing or having anything owed to one; exactly divisible by 2; opposed to odd. **even** *Informal* To end with neither profit or loss, as in business. **even One's full measure of revenge. break** *adv*. **evenly** *adv*. **evenness** *n*.

e-ven-fall (ē´ven fal´) *n*. The fall or the beginning of the evening.

e-ven-hand-ed (ē´ven han´did) *adj*. Fair; impartial. **evenhandedly** *adv*. **evenhandedness** *n*.

eve-ning (ēv´ning) *n*. The time between sunset and bedtime.

evening dress *n*. Formal attire for evening.

evening primrose *n*. A biennial herb with conspicuous yellow flowers that open in the evening.

eve-nings (ēv´ningz) *adv*. To be done or to occur in the evening repeatedly.

eve-ning star *n*. The brightest planet visible in the west just after sunset, especially Ve-nus.

e-ven–mind-ed *adj.* Not easily disturbed, or prejudiced.

e-ven-song (ē´ven song´) *n.* An evening prayer.

e-vent (i vent´) *n.* A significant occurrence; something that takes place; the actual or possible set of circumstances; a real or contingent situation; the final outcome; one of the parts of a sports program. **eventful** *adj.* **eventfully** *adv.* **eventfulness** *n.*

e-vent-ful (i vent´ful) *adj.* To be rich in e-vents.

e-ven-tide (ē´ven tīd´) *n.* Evening.

e-ven-tu-al (i ven´chŏ al) *adj.* Happening or expected to happen in due course of time. **eventually** *adv.*

e-ven-tu-al-i-ty (i ven´chŏ al´i tē) *n. pl.*-ties A likely or possible occurrence; the conceivable outcome.

e-ven-tu-ate (i ven´chŏ āt´) *v.* To result ultimately; to come out eventually.

ev-er (ev´ėr) *adv.* At any time; on any occasion; by any possible chance or conceivable way; at all times; throughout the entire course of time.

ev-er-bloom-ing *adj.* To be blooming more throughout the growing season.

Everest, Mount *n.* A mountain in the Himalayas, measuring 29,028 feet high.

ev-er-glade (ev´ėr glād´) *n.* A tract of low, swampy land.

ev-er-green (ev´ėr grēn´) *adj.* A tree that has green foliage throughout the year.

ev-er-last-ing (ev´ėr las´ting) *adj.* Lasting or existing forever; eternal. *n.* One of several plants, chiefly of the aster family, whose flowers keep their form and color when dried. **everlastingly** *adv.*

ev-er-more (ev´ėr mōr´) *adv., Poet.* For and a tall time to come; always.

e-vert (i vėrt´) *v.* To turn inside out or outward.

e-ver-tor *n.* A muscle that causes an outward rotation of a part.

eve-ry*adj.* From time to time; occasionally. **every other** Each alternate. **way** *Informal* In every way or direction and with very little

order.

eve-ry-body (ev´rē bod´ē) *pron.*Every person.

eve-ry-day (ev´rē dā´) *adj.* Happening every day; daily; suitable for ordinary days.

eve-ry-one (ev´rē wun´)*pron.* Everybody; every person.

eve-ry-place *adv.* Everywhere.

eve-ry-thing (ev´rē thing´) *pron.*All things; whatever exists; whatever is needed, relevant, or important; the essential thing; the only thing that really matters.

eve-ry-where (ev´rē hwâr´) *adv.* In, at, or to everyplace.

e-vict (i vikt´) *v.* To put out or expel a tenant by legal process. **evictor** *n.* **eviction** *n.*

e-vict-ee *n.* The person who is being evicted from a place of residence or business.

ev-i-dence (ev´i dens) *n.* Signs or facts on which a conclusion can be based. That which makes evident an indication of something; *v.* To indicate clearly.

ev-i-dent (ev´i dent) *adj.* Easily understood or seen; obvious. **evidently** *adv.*

e-vil (ē´vil) *adj.* Morally bad or wrong; causing injury or any other undesirable result; marked by misfortune or distress; low in public esteem. **One** Satan.

e-vil–mind-ed (ē´vil mīn´did) *adj.* Obsessed with vicious or evil thoughts or intentions. **evil–mindedly** *adv.* **evil–mindedness** *n.*

e-vil-do-er *n.* A person who does evil to another. **evildoing** *n.*

e-vince (i vins´) *v.* To demonstrate or indicate clearly; to give an outward sign of having a quality or feeling.

e-vis-cer-ate (i vis´e rāt´) *v.* To remove the vital part of something; to remove the entrails. **evisceration** *n.*

e-voke (i vōk´) *v.* To call or summon forth; to draw forth or produce a reaction; to summon up the spirits by or as by incantations. **evocation** *n.* **evocative** *adj.* **evocatively** *adv.*

ev-o-lu-tion (ev´o lō´shan) *n.* The gradual process of development or change. *Biol.* The theory that all forms of life originated by descent from earlier forms. **evolutionary** *adj.* **evolutionism** *n.* **evolutionist** *n.*

e-volve (i volv´) *v.* To develop or change gradually. *Biol.* To be developed by evolutionary processes; to develop or work out. **evolvement** *n.*

e-vul-sion *n.* The act of pulling out.

ewe (ū) *n.* A female sheep.

ewe-neck *n.* A neck like that of a ewe, with a concave arch.

ew-er (ū´ėr) *n.* A large, wide-mouthed pitcher or jug.

ex *n.* The letter x. *Slang* A former spouse. *abbr.* Example; exchange.

ex- (eks) *pref.* Out of; former.

ex-ac-er-bate (ig zas´ėr bāt´) *v.* To make more severe or worse; to aggravate. **exacerbation** *n.*

ex-act (ig zakt´) *adj.* Perfectly complete and clear in every detail; accurate in every detail with something taken as a model; similar. *v.* To be extremely careful about accuracy and detail; to force unjustly for the payment of something; to insist upon as a strict right or obligation; to call for or require. **exaction** *n.* **exactness** *n.* **exactly** *adv.*

ex-acting (eg zak´ting) *adj.* Making severe demands; rigorous; involving constant attention, hard work, etc. **exactingly** *adv.* **exactingness** *n.*

ex-ac-tion *n.* Extortion; fees, or contributions levied with injustice.

ex-act-i-tude (ig zak´ti tōd´) *n.* The quality of being exact.

ex-ag-ger-ate (ig zaj´e rāt´) *v.* To look upon or to represent something as being greater than it really is; to make greater in intensity or size than would be normal or expected. **exaggerated** *adj.* **exaggerative** *adj.* **exaggeration** *n.* **exaggerator** *n.*

ex-ag-ger-a-tion *n.* An overstatement; an overstatement of something

ex-alt (ig zolt´) *v.* To raise in character, honor, rank, etc.; to praise or glorify; to increase the intensity of. **exalted** *adj.* **exaltedly** *adv.* **exalter** *n.* **exaltation** *n.*

ex-am (ig zam´) *n., Slang* An examination.

ex-am-i-na-tion (ig zam´i nā´shan) *n.* A test of skill or knowledge; the act of examining or the state of being examined; medical testing and scrutiny. **examinational** *adj.*

ex-am-ine (ig zam´in) *v.* To observe or inspect; to test by questions or exercises, as to fitness or qualification. **examinee** *n.* **examiner** *n.*

ex-ample (ig zam´pl) *n.* One that is representative as a sample; one worthy of imitation; an object or instance of punishment, reprimand, etc.; a previous instance or case that is identical with or similar to something that is under consideration; a problem or exercise in algebra, arithmetic, etc. **set an example** To act in such a way as to arouse others to imitation.

ex-an-the-ma *n.* An eruption or rash on the skin; one with fever.

ex-as-per-ate (ig zas´pė rāt´) *v.* To make frustrated or angry; to irritate. **exasperatingly** *adv.* **exasperation** *n.*

ex-ca-vate (eks´ka vāt´) *v.* To dig a hole or cavity; to form or make a tunnel, hole, etc., by digging, scooping, or hollowing out; to remove or uncover by digging; to unearth. **excavation** *n.* **excavator** *n.*

ex-ceed (ik sēd´) *v.* To surpass in quality or quantity; to go beyond the limit; to be superior. **exceeding** *adj.*

ex-ceed-ing *adj.* Great in extent, quantity.

ex-ceed-ing-ly *adv.* Greater than; to an extraordinary degree or extreme.

ex-cel (ik sel´) *v.* To surpass or to do better than others.

ex-cel-lence (ek´se lens) *n.* The state or quality of being superior or excellent; a superior trait or quality.

ex-cel-lent (ek´se lent) *adj.* The best quality; exceptionally good. **excellently** *adv.*

ex-cel-si-or (ik sel´sē ėr) *n.* Long, firm

wood-shavings used in packing to protect delicate materials. *adj.* Upward; higher.

ex-cept (ik sept´) *prep.* With the omission or exclusion of; aside from; not including; leaving out.

ex-cept-ing (ik sep´ting) *prep.* With the exception that.

ex-cep-tion (ik sep´shan) *n.* The act of or state of being excepted; something that is excluded from or does not conform to a general class, rule, or principle; criticism or objection.

ex-cep-tion-a-ble (ik sep´sha nal) *adj.* Open to objection or exception. **exceptionability** *n.* **exceptionably** *adv.*

ex-cep-tion-al (ik sep´sha nal) *adj.* Being an exception to the rule; unusual; well a-bove average. **exceptionally** *adv.*

ex-cerpt (ik sėrpt´) *n.* A passage from a book, speech, etc. *v.* To select and cite.

ex-cess (ik ses´) *n.* The amount or condition of going beyond what is necessary, usual, or proper; overindulgence, as in drink or food.

ex-ces-sive (ik ses´iv) *adj.* Exceeding what is usual, necessary, or proper; extreme. **excessively** *adv.* **excessiveness** *n.*

exch *abbr.* Exchange.

ex-change (iks chānj) *v.* To give in return for something else; to trade; to return as unsatisfactory and get a replacement. *n.* The substitution of one thing for another; a place where brokers meet to buy, sell, or trade; the mutual receiving and giving of equal sums or money. **exchangeable** *adj.*

ex-change-ee (iks chān jē) *n.* A person participating in an exchange program.

exchange rate *n.* The value of the currency from one country to another.

ex-cheq-uer (eks´chek ėr) *n.* The treasury of a nation or organization; financial resources; funds. *Slang* One's total financial resources.

ex-cide (ik sīd´) *v.* To cut out.

ex-cip-i-ent *n.* Inert substance, as sugar or jelly, used a vehicle for an active medicine.

ex-cise (ek sīz´) *n.* The indirect or internal tax on the production, consumption, or sale

of a commodity, such as liquor or tobacco, that is produced, sold, and used or trans-ported within a country.

ex-cise (ik sīz´) *v.* To remove surgically. **excision** *n.*

ex-cit-a-ble (ik sī´ta bl) *adj.* To be easily excited. **excitably** *adv.* **excitability** *n.* **excitableness** *n.*

ex-cit-ant *n.* A stimulant.

ex-ci-ta-tion *n.* The act of exciting.

ex-cit-a-tive *adj.* Having power to excite; tending to excite.

ex-cite (ik sīt´) *v.* To stir up strong feeling, action, or emotion; to stimulate the emo-tions of; to bring about; to induce. **excit-ation** *n.* **excitement** *n.* **excitedly** *adv.* **excitingly** *adv.*

ex-cit-ed *adj.* Emotionally stimulated.

ex-cit-ing *adj.* Producing excitement; thrill-ing.

ex-claim (ik sklām´) *v.* To cry out abruptly; to utter suddenly, as from emotion.

ex-cla-ma-tion (ek´skla mā´shan) *n.* An abrupt or sudden forceful utterance. **excla-matory** *adj.*

exclamation point *n.* A punctuation mark (!) used after an interjection or excla-mation.

ex-clo-sure *n.* An area closed off.

ex-clude (ik sklōd´) *v.* To keep out; to omit from consideration; to put out.

ex-clu-sion *n.* Excluding or the state of being excluded; that which is excluded or expelled.

ex-clu-sive (ik sklō´siv) *adj.* Intended for the sole use and purpose of a single in-dividual or group; intended for or possessed by a single source; having no duplicate; the only one; complete; undi-vided. **exclusively** *adv.* **exclusiveness** *n.* **exclusivity** *n.*

ex-cog-i-tate *v.* To contrive; devise.

ex-com-mu-ni-cate (eks´ko mū´nikāt´) *v.* To deprive the right of church mem-bership. **excommunication** *n.*

ex-co-ri-ate (ik skōr´ē āt´) *v.* To tear the skin or wear off; to censure harshly. **exco-riation** *n.*

ex-cre-ment (ek´skre ment) *n.* Bodily waste, especially feces. **excremental** *adj.*

ex-cres-cent (ik skres´ent) *adj.* Growing abnormally out of something else.

ex-cre-ta (ik skrē´ta) *n. pl.* Excretions from the body such as sweat, urine, etc.

ex-crete (ik skrēt´) *v.* To throw off or eliminate waste matter by normal discharge from the body. **excretion** *n.* **excretory** *adj.*

ex-cru-ci-ate *v.* To cause extreme pain to.

ex-cru-ci-at-ing (ik skrŏ´shē ā´ting) *adj.* Intensely painful; agonizing.

ex-cul-pate (ek´skul pāt´) *v.* To free from wrong doing; to prove innocent of guilt. **exculpation** *n.* **exculpatory** *adj.*

ex-cur-sion (ik sker´zhan) *n.* A short trip, usually made for pleasure; a trip available at a special reduced fare. *Phys.* The oscillating movement between two points; also, half of this total distance. **excursionist** *n.*

ex-cur-sive (ik sker´siv) *adj.* To go in one direction and then another; rambling; digressive.

ex-cus-a-to-ry *adj.* Making an excuse.

ex-cuse (ik skūz´) *v.* To ask forgiveness or pardon for oneself; to grant pardon or forgiveness; to overlook or accept; to apologize for; to justify; to allow one to leave; to release. *n.* A reason, justification, or explanation. **excuse** *Informal* An inferior example for something. **poor** *adj.* **excusable** *adj.* **excusably** *adv.*

ex-ec (ig zek´) *abbr.* Executive; executor.

ex-e-cra-ble (ek´si kra bl) *adj.* Extremely bad; detestable; revolting. **execrableness** *n.* **execrably** *adv.*

ex-e-crate (ek´si krāt´) *v.* To detest; to feel or express detestation for; to abhor. **execration** *n.* **execrator** *n.*

ex-e-cute (ek´se kūt´) *v.* To carry out; to put into effect; to validate, as by signing; to carry out what has been called for in a will; to put to death by the legal authority.

ex-e-cu-tion (ek´se kū´shan) *n.* The act of executing a job or task; a putting to death as a result of a legal decision, as the death penalty.

ex-e-cu-tion-er *n.* A person who puts others to death; a person who carries out a legal execution.

ex-ec-u-tive (ig zek´ū tiv) *n.* A manager or administrator in an organization; the branch of the government responsible for activating or putting the laws of a country into effect and for carrying out plans or policies. **executively** *adv.*

executive council *n.* The cabinet of a provincial government in Canada.

ex-ec-u-tor (ig zek´yu tėr) *n.* The person appointed to carry out the reading and execution of a will. **executorial** *adj.*

ex-ec-u-to-ry *adj.* Executive; pertaining to what is yet to be performed.

ex-e-ge-sis (ek´si jē´sis) *n. pl.* **-ses** An interpretation or explanation of a text. **exegetic** *adj.* **exegetically** *adv.*

ex-e-get-ics *n.* The science that lays down the principles and art of scriptural interpretation.

ex-em-plar (ig zem´plėr) *n.* Something that serves as a worthy model or imitation; a typical example.

ex-em-pla-ry (ig zem´pla rē) *adj.* Serving as a model; worthy of imitation; commendable.

ex-em-pli-fy (ig zem´pli fī´) *v.* To show by giving examples; to be an example of. **exemplification** *n.*

ex-em-plum *n.* An anecdote or story narrated to illustrate a moral.

ex-empt (ig zempt´) *v.* To free or excuse from an obligation or duty to which others are subject. **exempt** *adj.* **exemption** *n.*

ex-en-ter-ate (ek sen´te rāt´) *v.* To surgically remove the contents of a body cavity.

ex-e-quy *n.* A funeral ceremony.

ex-er-cise (ek´sėr sīz´) *n.* The act of performing drills; the act of training or developing oneself; something that is done to maintain or increase a skill, such as practice on the piano. **exercises** *pl.* A ceremony, etc., such as a graduation. **exercise** *v.* **exerciser** *n.*

ex-ergue *n.* The small area located below the main surface on a coin or medal; anything written in this space.

ex-ert (ig zèrt´) v. To put into action, as influence or force; to put oneself through a strenuous effort. **exertion** n.

ex-ha-la-tion n. The process of exhaling; that which is exhaled or emitted.

ex-hale (eks hāl´) v. To breathe out; the opposite of inhale; to breathe forth or give off, as air, vapor, or aroma.

ex-haust (ig zost´) v. To make extremely tired; to drain oneself of resources, strength, etc. n. The escape or discharge of waste gases, working fluid, etc.; the waste gases, etc. that escape; the device through which waste gases are released or expelled. **exhaustible** adj. **exhaustion** n.

ex-haust-ed adj. Completely consumed; tired.

ex-haus-tion n. Extreme fatigue.

ex-haus-tive (ig zos´tiv) adj. Tending to exhaust or that which exhausts. **exhaustively** adv.

ex-hib-it (ig zib´it) v. To display, as to put up for public view; to bring documents or evidence into a court of law. **exhibitionism** n. The practice of deliberately drawing undue attention to one-self. **exhibition** n. **exhibitor, exhibitionist** n.

ex-hi-bi-tion-ism (ek˝si bish´a niz˝um) n. The practice of deliberately drawing undue attention to oneself. **exhibitionist** n.

ex-hil-a-rate (ig zil´a rāt´) v. To elate, make cheerful, or refresh. **exhilaration** n. **exhilarative** adj.

ex-hort (ig zort´) v. To urge by earnest appeal or argument; to advise or recommend strongly. **exhortation** n.

ex-hor-ta-tion n. The practice of exhorting; language intended to encourage.

ex-hume (ig zōm´) v. To dig up and remove from a grave; to disinter. **exhumation** n.

ex-i-gen-cy (ek´si jen sē) n. pl. -cies The quality or state of being exigent. usually pl. A pressing need or necessity. **exigence** n. **exigent** adj.

ex-i-gent adj. Urgent; demanding prompt attention or action.

ex-ig-u-ous (ig zig´ū us) adj. Extremely

small; scanty. **exiguity** n.

ex-ile (eg´zīl) n. The separation by necessity or choice from one's native country or home; banishment; one who has left or been driven from his or her country. v. To banish or expel from one's native country or home.

ex-ist (ig zist´) v. To have actual being or reality; to live.

ex-is-tence (ig zis´tens) n. The fact or state of existing, living, or occurring; the manner of existing. **existent** adj.

ex-is-ten-tial (eg´zi sten´shal) adj. Based on experience; of or relating to existentialism. **existentially** adv.

ex-is-ten-tial-ism (eg´zi sten´sha liz´um) n. A philosophy that stresses the active role of the will rather than of reason in facing problems posed by a hostile universe. **existentialist** n.

ex-it (eg´zit) n. A way or passage out; the act of going away or out; the departure from a stage, as in a play. **exit** v.

ex-o-bi-ol-o-gy (ek´sō bī ol´o jē) n. The search for and study of extraterrestrial life. **exobiologist** n.

ex-o-crine adj. Secreting externally through a duct.

ex-o-don-tia n. The branch of dentistry that deals with tooth extraction.

ex-o-dus (ek´so dus) n. A going forth; a departure of large numbers of people, as that of Moses and the Israelites as described in Exodus, the second book of the Old Testament.

ex-o-en-zyme (ek´sō en´zīm) n. The exzyme that performs its function outside the cell which produced it.

ex officio (eks o fish´ē ō´) adj. & adv. By virtue of or because of office or position.

ex-og-e-nous (ek soj´e nus) n., Biol. That which is derived from external causes.

ex-on-er-ate (ig zon´e rāt´) v. To free or clear one from accusation or blame; to relieve or free from responsibility. **exoneration** n.

ex-oph-thal-mos n. The protrusion of an

eyeball from the eye socket, caused by the excessive activity of the thyroid gland.

ex-or-bi-tant (ig zor´bi tant) *adj.* Beyond usual and proper limits, as in price or demand. **exorbitance** *n.* **exorbitantly** *adv.*

ex-or-cise (ek´sor sīz´) *v.* To cast out or expel an evil spirit by prayers or incantations; to free from an evil spirit. **exorciser** *n.* **exorcism** *n.* **exorcist** *n.*

ex-or-di-um *n.* The beginning of anything.

ex-o-skel-e-ton *n.* An external protective covering , as the shell of crustaceans, the carapace of turtles, and the scales and fins of fish.

ex-o-sphere (ek´sō sfēr´) *n., Meteor.* The region of the earth's atmosphere starting about 400 miles up.

ex-o-ter-ic *adj.* Pertaining only to the external; not belonging to the inner or select circle.

ex-o-ther-mic (ek´sō ther´mik) *adj.* Releasing rather than absorbing heat.

ex-ot-ic (ig zot´ik) *adj.* Belonging by nature or origin to another part of the world; foreign; strangely different and fascinating. **exotically** *adv.*

ex-ot-i-cism *n.* The tendency to adopt what is exotic.

exp *abbr.* Expenses; export; express.

ex-pand (ik spand´) *v.* To increase the scope, range, volume, or size; to open up or spread out; to develop more fully in form or details. **expandable** *adj.* **expander** *n.*

ex-panse (ik spans´) *n.* A wide, open stretch.

ex-pan-sion (ik span´shan) *n.* The act of or state of being expanded; the amount of increase in range, size, or volume.

ex-pan-sive (ik span´siv) *adj.* Capable of expanding or inclined to expand; characterized by expansion; broad and extensive; open and generous; outgoing. **expansively** *adv.* **expansiveness** *n.*

ex par-te (eks pär´tē) *adj. & adv.* In law, giving only one side or point of view.

ex-pa-ti-ate (ik spā´shē āt´) *v.* To elaborate; to talk or write at length. **expatiation** *n.*

ex-pa-tri-ate (eks pa´trē āt´) *v.* To leave one's country and reside in another; to send into exile; to banish. **expatriate** *n.* **expatriation** *n.*

ex-pect (ik spekt´) *v.* To look forward to something as probable or certain; to look for as proper, right, or necessary. *Slang* To presume or suppose.

ex-pec-tan-cy (ik spek´tan sē) *n. pl.* **-cies** The action or state of expecting; expectation; an object or amount of expectation.

ex-pec-tant (ik spek´tant) *adj.* Expecting; pregnant. **expectantly** *adv.*

ex-pec-ta-tion (ek´spek tā´shan) *n.* The state or act of expecting; something that is expected and looked forward to. **expectations** *pl.* Something expected in the future.

ex-pec-to-rant (ik spek´to rant) *adj.* Promoting the discharge by spitting of the mucus from the respiratory tract. *n.* Any medicine that is used to promote expectoration.

ex-pec-to-rate (ik spek´to rāt) *v.* To spit. **expectoration** *n.*

ex-pe-di-en-cy (ik spē´dē en sē) *n. pl.***-cies** The state or quality of being expedient.

ex-pe-di-ent (ik spē´dē ent) *adj.* Promoting narrow or selfish interests; pertaining to or prompted by interest rather than by what is right. **expediently** *adv.*

ex-pe-dite (ek´spi dīt´) *v.* To speed up the progress or process of something; to do with quick efficiency. **expediter** *n.* **expeditor** *n.*

ex-pe-di-tion (ek´spi dish´an) *n.* A journey of some length for a definite purpose; the person or group and equipment that engage in such a journey; promptness.

ex-pe-di-tion-ar-y *adj.* Relating to or being an expedition; sent on military service abroad.

ex-pe-di-tious (ek´spi dish´us) *adj.* Quick; speedy. **expeditiously** *adv.* **expeditiousness** *n.*

ex-pel (ik spel´) *v.* To drive or force out, as to dismiss from a school. **expellable** *adj.* **expeller** *n.* **expulsion** *n.*

ex-pend (ik spend´) *v.* To consume; to pay out or use up.

ex-pend-a-ble (ik spen´da bl) *adj*. Available for spending. *Milit.* Equipment or supplies that can be sacrificed. **expendability** *n*.

ex-pen-di-ture (ik spen´di chêr) *n*. An amount spent; the act or process of expending.

ex-pense (ik spens´) *n*. The outlay or consumption of money; the amount of money required to buy or do something. **expenses** *pl*. The funds that have been allotted or spent to cover incidental costs; the charges incurred by an employee while at or pertaining to work. *Informal* The reimbursement for such charges incurred.

ex-pen-sive (ik spen´siv) *adj*. Costing a lot of money; high-priced.

ex-pe-ri-ence (ik spēr´ē ens) *n*. The actual participation in something or the direct contact with; the knowledge or skill acquired from actual participation or training in an activity or event; one's total judgments or reactions based on one's past. **experience** *v*.

ex-pe-ri-enced *adj*. To be knowledgeable through actual practices,etc.

ex-per-i-ment (ik sper´i ment) *n*. The act or test performed to demonstrate or illustrate a truth; the conducting of such operations. **experimental** *adj*. **experimentally** *adv*. **experimentation** *n*.

ex-pert (ik spert´) *n*. A person having great knowledge, experience, or skill in a certain field. *adj*. Skilled as the result of training or experience. **expertly** *adv*.

ex-per-tise (ek´spêr tēz´) *n*. A specialized knowledge, ability, or skill in a particular area.

ex-pi-ate (ek´spē āt´) *v*. To atone for; to make amends for. **expiation** *n*. **expiator** *n*. **expiatory** *adj*.

ex-pi-ra-tion *n*. The act of breathing out; emission of breath; exhalation.

ex-pire (ik spīêr´) *v*. To come to an end; to breathe out, as from the mouth; to exhale. **expiration** *n*.

ex-plain (ik splān´) *v*. To make understandable; to clarify; to give reasons for; to account for; to give an explanation for.

explainable *adj*. **explanatory** *adj*. **explainer** *n*. **explanation** *n*.

ex-pla-na-tion *n*. The act of explaining; the clearing up of a misunderstanding.

ex-plant *v*. To transfer, as live fragments of plant or animal tissue, to a nutrient material.

ex-ple-tive (ek´sple tiv) *n*. An exclamation, often profane. *adj*. A word added merely to fill out a sentence.

ex-pli-ca-ble (ek´spli ka bl) *adj*. Capable of explanation.

ex-pli-cate (ek´spli kāt´) *v*. To clear up the meaning of. **explication** *n*. **explicator** *n*. **explicative** *adj*.

ex-plic-it (ik splis´it) *adj*. Plainly expressed; specific; unreserved in expression; straight forward. **explicitly** *adv*. **explicitness** *n*.

ex-plode (ik splōd´) *v*. To cause to burst or blow up violently with a loud noise; to increase rapidly without control; to show to be false.

ex-ploit (ek´sploit) *n*. A deed or act that is notable. *v*. To use to the best advantage of; to make use of in a selfish or uneth-ical way. **exploitable** *adj*. **exploitative** *adj*. **exploitation** *n*. **exploiter** *n*.

ex-plo-ra-tion *n*. Travel for purposes of discovery.

ex-plore (ik splōr´) *v*. To examine and investigate in a systematic way; to travel through unfamiliar territory. **exploration** *n*. **explorer** *n*. **exploratory** *adj*.

ex-plor-er *n*. One who explores unknown areas.

ex-plo-sion (ik splō´zhan) *n*. A sudden, violent release of energy; the sudden, violent outbreak of personal feelings.

ex-plo-sive (ik splō´siv) *adj*. Marked by or pertaining to an explosion. *n*. A chemical preparation that explodes. **explosively** *adv*. **explosiveness** *n*.

ex-po-nent (ik spō´nent) *n*. A person who represents or speaks for a cause or group; in mathematics, a number or symbol that indicates the number of times an expression is used as a factor. **exponential** *adj*.

ex-port (ik spōrt´) v. To carry or send merchandise or raw materials to other countries for resale or trade. n. A commodity exported. **exportable** adj. **exportation** n.

ex-por-ta-tion n. The conveying of commodities abroad.

ex-pose (ik spōz´) v. To lay open, as to criticism or ridicule; to lay bare and uncovered; to reveal the identity of someone; to deprive of the necessities of heat, shelter, and protection. Photog. To admit light to a sensitized film or plate. **exposer** n.

ex-po-si-tion (ek´spo zish´an) n. A statement of intent or meaning; a detailed presentation of subject matter; a commentary or interpretation; a large public exhibition. **expositor** n. **expository** adj.

ex-pos-i-tor n. A person who explains.

ex post facto (eks´ pōst´fak´tō) adj. After the fact and retroactive.

ex-pos-tu-late (ik spos´cha lāt´) v. To reason earnestly with someone about the inadvisability of his or her actions in an effort to correct or dissuade that person. **expostulatory** adj. **expostulation** n.

ex-po-sure (ik spō´zhėr) n. The act or state of being exposed; an indication of which way something faces. Photog. The act of exposing a sensitive plate or film; the time required for the film or plate to be exposed.

ex-pound (ik spound´) v. To give a detailed statement of something; to explain the meaning at length. **expounder** n.

ex-press (ik spres´) v. To formulate in words; to verbalize; to state; to communicate through some medium other than words or signs; to squeeze or press out, as juice from fruit; to send goods, etc., by a fast or rapid means of delivery. adj. Explicit; precise. **expressly** adv.

ex-press-age n. The shipping of parcels by express.

ex-pres-sion (ik spresh´an) n. Communication of opinion, thought, or feeling; the outward indication or manifestation of a condition, feeling, or quality; a particular phrase or word from a certain region of the country; a facial aspect or look that conveys a feeling; in mathematics, a symbol, sign, or set of that indicates something.

ex-pres-sion-ism (ik spresh´a niz´um) n. An early 20th Century movement in the fine arts that emphasizes subjective expression of the artist's inner experiences rather than realistic representation. **expressionistic** adj. **expressionist** n.

ex-pres-sive (ik spres´iv) adj. Of or characterized by expression; serving to indicate or express; full of expression. **expressively** adv. **expressiveness** n.

ex-press-ly adv. In direct terms.

ex-press-way (ik spres´wā´) n. A multilane highway designed for rapid travel.

ex-pro-pri-ate (eks prō´prē āt´) v. To transfer or take property from the owner for public use; to deprive a person of property or ownership. **expropriation** n.

ex-pul-sion (ik spul´shan) n. The act of expelling or the state of being expelled.

ex-punge (ik spunj´) v. To delete or remove; to erase. **expunger** n.

ex-pur-gate (ek´spėr gāt´) v. To remove obscene or objectionable material from a play, book, etc., before it is available to the public. **expurgation** n.

ex-qui-site (ek´skwi zit) adj. Delicately or intricately beautiful in design or craftsmanship; highly sensitive; keen or acute, as in pain or pleasure. **exquisitely** adv. **exquisiteness** n.

ex-san-gui-nate (eks sang´gwa nāt´´) v. To remove the blood from.

ex-scind v. To cut off.

ex-sert-ed adj. Standing out; projected, beyond an encompassing part.

ex-tant (ek´stant) adj. Still in existence; not lost or destroyed; surviving.

ex-tem-po-ra-ne-ous (ik stem´´po rā´nē us) adj. Acting or performing with little or no advance preparation; spoken with regard to content, but not memorized or read word for word.

ex-tem-po-re (ik stem´po rē) adj. Extemporaneously.

ex-tem-po-rize (ik stem´po rīz´) v. To make, do, or perform with little or no advance preparation; to improvise to meet circumstances. **extemporization** *n.*

ex-tend (ik stend´) *v.* To stretch or open to full length; to make longer, broader, or wider; to continue; to prolong; to put forth or hold out, as the hand; to exert to full capacity; to offer something.

ex-tend-ed *adj.* Stretched out; straightened.

ex-tend-er (ik sten´dėr) *n.* A substance added to another to dilute, modify, or adulterate.

ex-ten-sion (ik sten´sh*a***n)** *n.* The act or state of being extended; an agreement with a creditor that allows a debt or further time to pay a debt. *Phys.* The property of matter by virtue of which it occupies space.

ex-ten-sive (ik sten´siv) *adj.* Widespread; far-reaching; having a wide range; broad in scope. **extensively** *adv.*

ex-ten-sor *n.* A muscle which serves to straighten any part of the body, as an arm or a leg.

ex-tent (ik stent´) *n.* The degree, dimension, or limit to which anything is extended; the area over which something extends; the size.

ex-ten-u-ate (ik sten´ū āt´) *v.* To minimize the seriousness of something as a crime or fault. **extenuation** *n.* **extenuating** *adj.*

ex-te-ri-or (ik stēr´ē ėr) *adj.* Pertaining to or of the outside; the external layer.

ex-te-ri-or-ize *v.* To expose, as an internal organ from the body for surgery.

ex-ter-mi-nate (ik stėr´mi nāt´) *v.* To annihilate; to destroy completely. **extermination** *n.* **exterminator** *n.*

ex-ter-nal (ik stėr´n*a***l)** *adj.* For, of, or on the outside; acting from the outside; pertaining to foreign countries; outside; exterior. **externals** *pl.* Outward or superficial circumstances. **externally** *adv.*

ex-tern *or* **externe (ek´stėrn)** *n.* A person that is associated with but not officially residing in a hospital or an institution.

ex-tinct (ik stingk´) *adj.* Inactive; no longer existing; extinguished. **extinction** *n.*

ex-tinc-tion *n.* The act of extinguishing; a coming to an end.

ex-tine *n.* The outer coat of a pollen grain.

ex-tin-guish (ik sting´gwish) *v.* To put an end to; to put out; to make extinct. **extinguishable** *adj.* **extinguisher** *n.*

ex-tir-pate (ek´stėr pāt´) *v.* To pull up by the roots; to destroy wholly, completely. **extirpation** *n.* **extirpator** *n.*

ex-tol *also* **ex-toll (ik stō´)** To praise highly. **extoller** *n.* **extolment** *n.*

ex-tort (ik stort´) *v.* To obtain money from a person by threat, oppression, or abuse of authority. **extortion** *n.* **extortionist** *n.*

ex-tor-tion *n.* The practice of extorting money; illegal compulsion to pay money.

ex-tra (ek´str*a***)** *adj.* Over and above what is normal, required, or expected. *n.* An extra edition of a newspaper that covers news of special importance; a performer hired for a small part in a movie.

ex-tract (ik strakt´) *v.* To pull or draw out by force; to obtain in spite of resistance; to obtain from a substance as by pressure or distillation; in mathematics, to determine the root of a number. *n.* A passage taken from a larger work; a concentrated substance used in cooking. **extractable** *adj.* **extractible** *adj.* **extractor** *n.*

ex-trac-tion (ik strak´sh*a***n)** *n.* The process or act of extracting; that which is extracted; one's origin or ancestry.

ex-trac-tive *n.* That which may be extracted.

ex-tra-cur-ric-u-lar (ek´str*a*** k***a*** rik´ūlėr)** *adj.* Pertaining to or of activities not directly a part of the curriculum of a school or college; outside the usual duties.

ex-tra-dite (ek´str*a*** dīt´)** *v.* To obtain or surrender by extradition. **extraditable** *adj.*

ex-tra-di-tion (ek´str*a*** dish´***a***n)** *n.* The legal surrender of an alleged criminal to the jurisdiction of another country, government, or state for trial.

ex-tra-dos (ek´str*a*** dos´)** *n. pl.* **-dos** *or* **-doses** The exterior or upper curve of an arch.

ex-tra-ga-lac-tic (ek´str*a*** g***a*** lak´tik)** *adj.* Coming from beyond the galaxy; situated beyond the galaxy.

ex-tra-ju-di-cial *adj.* Out of the ordinary course of a legal procedure.

ex-tra-mar-i-tal (ek′stra mar′i tal) *adj.* Adulterous.

ex-tra-mu-ral (ek′stra mūr′al) *adj.* Taking place outside of an educational building or institution; involving teams from different schools.

ex-tra-ne-ous (ik strā′ne us) *adj.* Coming from without; foreign; not vital or essential. **extraneously** *adv.*

ex-tra-or-di-nar-y (ik stror′di ner″ē) *adj.* Beyond what is usual or common; remarkable.

ex-traor-di-nar—ily (ik stror′i nâr′īlē) *adv.*

ex-trap-o-late (ik strap′o lāt″) *v.* To infer the possibility beyond the strict evidence of a series of events, facts, or observations; in mathematics, to infer the unknown information by projecting or extending known information. **extrapolation, extrapolator** *n.,* **extrapolative** *adj.*

ex-tra-sen-so-ry (ek′stra sen′so rē) *adj.* Beyond the range of normal sensory perception.

extrasensory perception *n.* The ability to foresee something before it actually happens; the ability to know something without any factual knowledge.

ex-tra-ter-res-tri-al (ek′stra te res′trē al) *adj.* Occurring or originating outside the earth or its atmosphere.

ex-tra-ter-ri-to-ri-al (ek′stra ter′itōr′ē al) *adj.* Pertaining to or of extraterritoriality; situated outside of the territorial limits.

ex-tra-ter-ri-to-ri-al-i-ty *n.* An exemption from local legal jurisdiction, as that extended to foreign diplomats.

ex-trav-a-gant (ik strav′a gant) *adj.* Overly lavish in expenditure; wasteful; exceeding reasonable limits; immoderate; unrestrained. **extravagance** *n.* **extravagantly** *adv.*

ex-trav-a-gan-za (ik strav′a gan′za) *n.* A lavish, spectacular, showy entertainment.

ex-tra-vas-cu-lar *adj.* Being outside of the blood vessels or the vascular system.

ex-tra-ve-hic-u-lar (ek′stra vē hik′ūlar) *adj.* Occurring or done outside a vehicle,

especially a spacecraft in flight.

ex-treme (ik strēm′) *adj.* Greatly exceeding; going far beyond the bounds of moderation; exceeding what is considered moderate, usual, or reasonable; final; last; of the highest or utmost degree; one of the two ends of farthest limits of anything; in mathematics, the first or last term of a proportion or series; a drastic measure. **extremely** *adv.* **extremeness** *n.*

ex-trem-ist *n.* A person who advocates or resorts to extreme measures or holds extreme views. **extremism** *n.*

ex-trem-i-ty (ik strem′i tē) *n. pl.* **-ties** The utmost or farthest point; the greatest degree of distress or peril; an extreme measure; an appendage or limb of the body; a hand or foot.

ex-tri-cate (ek′stri kāt′) *v.* To free from hin-drance, entanglement, or difficulties; to dis-engage. **extrication** *n.*

ex-trin-sic (ik strin′sik) *adj.* Not inherent; outside the nature of something; from the outside; external. **extrinsically** *adv.*

ex-trorse *adj.* Directed outward, or away from the axis.

ex-tro-vert *or* **extravert (ek′strō vėrt′)** *Psychol.* A person who is more interested in people and things outside himself than in his own private feelings and thoughts. **extroversion** *n.*

ex-trude (ik strōd′) *v.* To push or thrust out; to shape by forcing through dies under pressure; to project or protrude. **extrusion** *n.* **extrusive** *adj.*

ex-u-ber-ance *n.* An expression in speech of being exuberant.

ex-u-ber-ant (ig zō′bėr ant) *adj.* Full of high-spirits, vitality, vigor, and joy; plentiful; abundant. **exuberance** *n.*

ex-ude (ig zōd′) *v.* To give off; to ooze or trickle forth, as sweat. **exudation** *n.*

ex-ult (ig zult′) *v.* To be jubilant; to rejoice greatly. **exultant** *adj.* **exultation** *n.*

ex-ur-bi-a (eks ėr′bē a) *n.* The often well-to-do residential area outside the suburbs of a large city. **exurbanite** *n.*

ey-as (ī′as) *n.* A type of bird which is unfledged.

eye (ī) *n.* An organ of sight consisting of the cornea, iris, pupil, retina, and lens; a look; gaze; the ability to judge, perceive, or discriminate. **storm** *Meteor.* The central area of a hurricane or cyclone. **wind** *Naut.* The direction from which the wind blows. **eye**To get someone's attention. **eye** To be in complete agreement.

eye-ball (ī′bol″) *n.* The ball of the eye, enclosed by the socket and eyelids and connected at the rear to the optic nerve.

eye-bank *n.* A place where corneas removed from a recently-deceased person are stored for future use in restoring the sight of someone having a corneal defect.

eye–catch-er *n.* Something that is capable to attract the eye easily.

eye-bolt (ī′bōlt″) *n.* A type of bolt which on its head is a loop.

eye-bright *n.* A type of herb that has opposite cut leaves.

eye-brow (ī′brou″) *n.* The short hairs covering the bony ridge over the eye.

eyebrow pencil *n.* A type of cosmetic pencil which is used to color the eyebrows.

eye-cup (ī′kup″) *n.* A kind of cup which is oval and small and is used to cover the eye for the application of liquid into the eye.

eyed *adj.* To have an eye or many eyes.

eyed-ness *n.* A preference one has for the use of one eye over the other.

eye-ful (ī′fel′) *n. pl.* **-fuls** A satisfying or complete view. *Slang* A beautiful person.

eye-glass (ī′glas″) *n.* A corrective lens used to assist vision. **eyeglasses** *pl.* A pair of corrective lenses set in a frame.

eye-hole (ī′hōl″) *n.* An opening to pass a hook, pin, rope, etc., through; a peephole.

eye-lash (ī′lash′) *n.* The stiff, curved hairs growing from the edge of the eyelids.

eye lens *n.* In an eyepiece, the lens which is located near the eye.

eye-let (ī′lit) *n.* A small perforation or hole for a hook or cord to fit through in closing a fastening; the metal ring reinforcing an eyelet.

eye-lid (ī′lid″) *n.* Either of two folds of skin and muscle that open and close over an eye.

eye-lin-er *n.* Makeup used to highlight the outline of the eyes.

eye–open-er (ī′ō″pe nėr) *n.* That which opens the eyes or enlightens, as a startling revelation. *Slang.* A drink of liquor taken early in the morning.

eye-piece (ī′pēs″) *n.* The lens or combination of lenses of an optical instrument closest to the eye.

eye-point *n.* The position where the eye is placed in the using of an optical instrument.

eye-pop-per *n.* A thing which will astonish.

eye-shade *n.* A type of visor which is used to shield the eyes from light which is strong.

eye-shot (ī′shot″) *n.* The range or area that one is able to see objects.

eye-sight (ī′sīt′) *n.* The faculty or power of sight; the range of vision.

eye-sore (ī′sōr″) *n.* Something ugly that offends the sight.

eye-spot (ī′spot″) *n.* The pigmented cells which cover a sensory termination; a spot of color.

eye-stalk (ī′stolk″) *n.* A movable peduncle of the decapod crustacean that bears an eye at the tip.

eye-strain (ī′strān′) *n.* Fatigue or discomfort of the eyes, caused by excessive or improper use and marked by symptoms such as pain and headache.

eye-tooth (ī′tōth′) *n. pl.* **teeth** One of the canine teeth of the upper jaw.

eye-wash (ī′wosh″) *n.* A medicinal wash for the eye. *Slang.* Nonsense; bunk; meaningless or deceptive language.

eye-wink (ī′wingk″) *n.* A glance or wink; an event or occurrence that happens in an instant.

eye-wit-ness (ī′wit″nis″) *n.* A person who has seen something and can testify to it firsthand.

F, f (ef) The sixth letter of the English alphabet; in music, the fourth tone in the scale of C major; a failing grade.

F *abbr.* Fahrenheit, female.

fa-ba-ceous *adj.* Related to or belonging to the bean family of plants.

fa-ble (fā´bl) *n.* A brief, fictitious story embodying a moral and using persons, animals, or inanimate objects as characters; a false-hood; a lie. **fabulist** *n.* **fabler** *n.*

fab-ric (fab´rik) *n.* A cloth produced by knitting, weaving, or spinning fibers; a structure or framework, as the social fabric.

fab-ri-cate (fab´ri kāt´) *v.* To make or manufacture; to build; to construct by combining or assembling parts; to make up in order to deceive; to invent, as a lie or story. **fabrication** *n.* **fabricator** *n.*

fab-u-list *n.* A creater of fables.

fab-u-lous (fab´ya lus) *adj.* Past the limits of belief; incredible. *Slang* Very successful or pleasing. **fabulously** *adv.*

fa-cade (fa säd´) *n., Arch.* The face or front of a building; an artificial or false appearance.

face (fās) *n.* The front surface of the head from ear to ear and from forehead to chin; external appearance, look, or aspect; the value written on the printed surface of a note or bond; the principal, front, finished, or working surface of anything; the most prominent or significant surface of an object. *v.* To confront with awareness. **face up** To recognize the existence of something and confront it bravely. **faced, facing** *v.*

face–hard-en (fās´här˝den) *v.* To harden the surface of metal or steel by chilling.

face–lift-ing *or* **face–lift** *n.* The plastic surgery for tightening facial tissues and improving the facial appearance. *v.* To modernize.

face–off *n.* The action of facing off in hockey, lacrosse, etc.

face–saver *n.* Something that preserves one's self-esteem or dignity. **face–saving** *adj.*

face brick *n.* A brick used for facing the exterior of a house or building.

face card *n.* In playing cards, a king, queen, or jack of a suit.

fac-et (fas´it) *n.* One of the flat, polished surfaces cut upon a gemstone; the small, smooth surface on a bone or tooth; a phase, aspect, or side of a person or subject. **faceted** *or* **facetted** *adj.*

fa-ce-ti-ae (fa sē´shē ē´) *n.* Humorous or witty writings or remarks.

fa-ce-tious (fa sē´shus) *adj..* Given to or marked by playful jocularity; humorous. **facetiously** *adv.* **facetiousness** *n.*

face value *n.* The apparent value of something; the value printed on the face of a bill or bond.

fa-cial (fā´shal) *adj.* Near, of, or for the face; a massage or other cosmetic treatment for the face. **facially** *adv.*

fac-ile (fas´il) *adj.* Requiring little effort; easily achieved or performed; arrived at without due care, effort, or examination; superficial. **facilely** *adv.* **facileness** *n.*

fa-cil-i-tate (fa sil´i tāt´) *v.* To make easier. **facilitation** *n.* **facilitator** *n.*

fa-cil-i-ty (fa sil´i tē) *n. pl.* **-ies** Ease in performance, moving, or doing something; something that makes an operation or action easier.

fac-ing (fā´sing) *n.* The lining or covering sewn to a garment; any outer protective or decorative layer applied to a surface.

fac-sim-i-le (fak sim´i lē) *n.* An exact copy, as of a document; the method of transmitting drawings, messages, or such by an electronic method.

fact (fakt) *n.* Something that actually occurred or exists; something that has real and demonstrable existence; actuality.

fac-tion (fak´shan) *n.* A group or party within a government that is often self-seeking and usually in opposition to a larger group; conflict within a party; discord. **factional** *adv.* **factionalism** *n.*

fac-tious (fak´shus) *adj.* Given to dissension; creating friction; divisive. **factiously** *adv.*

fac-ti-tious (fak tish´us) *adj.* Produced artificially; lacking authenticity or genuineness. **factitiously** *adv.*

fac-tor (fak′tėr) *n.* One who transacts business for another person on a commission basis; one of the elements or causes that contribute to produce the result; in mathematics, one of two or more quantities that when multiplied together give or yield a given product; in biology, a gene. **factorship** *n.* **factorable** *adj.* **factorage** *n.*

fac-to-ry (fak′to rē) *n. pl.* -ies An establishment where goods are manufactured; a plant.

fac-to-tum (fak tō′tum) *n.* An employee who performs all types of work.

fac-tu-al (fak′chŏ al) *adj.* Containing or consisting of facts, literal and exact. **factually** *adv.*

fac-tu-al-ism *n.* An adherence to factual evidence; a theory that places great emphasis on fact.

fac-u-la *n.* Any bright patch on the sun's surface.

fac-ture (fak′chėr) *n.* The process, manner or act of construction; making.

fac-ul-ty (fak′ul tē) *n. pl.* -ies A natural ability or power; the inherent powers or capabilities of the body or mind; the complete teaching staff of a school or any other educational institution.

fad (fad) *n.* A temporary fashion adopted with wide enthusiasm. **faddish** *adj.* **faddishness** *n.* **faddist** *n.*

fade (fād) *v.* To lose brightness, brilliance, or loudness gradually; to vanish slowly; to lose freshness, vigor, or youth; to disappear gradually.

fa-er-ie (fā′e rē) *n., variation of* **fairy.**

fag (fag) *v.* To exhaust by hard work. *n.* An English public school student required to perform menial tasks for an upperclassman. *Slang* A homosexual; a cigarette.

fa-ga-ceous *adj.* Having to do with shrubs and trees of the beech family.

fag end *n.* The frayed end of a rope or cloth; a remnant; the last part.

fag-ot *or* **fag-got (fag′ot)** *n.* A bundle of twigs, sticks, or branches that are used for fuel.

fag-ot-ing (fag′o ting) *n.* A method of orna-menting cloth by pulling out horizontal threads and tying the remaining vertical threads into hourglass-shaped bunches.

Fahr-en-heit (far′en hīt′) *adj.* Of or relating to the temperature scale in which the freezing point of water is 32 degrees and the boiling point of water is 212 degrees under normal atmospheric pressure.

fa-ience (fī äns′) *n.* Earthenware that is decorated with a colorful opaque glaze.

fail (fāl) *v.* To be totally ineffective, unsuccessful; to go bankrupt; to receive an academic grade below the acceptable standards; to issue such a grade; to omit or neglect. **failing, failed** *v.*

fail-ing (fā′ling) *n.* A minor fault; a defect.

faille (fīl) *n.* A ribbed material of cotton, silk, or rayon.

fail–safe (fāl′sāf′) *adj.* Of or relating to a system designed to prevent equipment failure or to compensate automatically for a mechanical failure; guaranteed not to fail.

fail-ure (fāl′yėr) *n.* The fact or state of failing;a breaking down in health, action, strength, or efficiency; a situation in which a business becomes insolvent or bankrupt; in school, a failing grade.

faint (fānt) *adj.* Having little strength or vigor; feeble; lacking brightness or clarity; dim. *n.* A sudden, temporary loss of consciousness; a swoon. **faintly** *adv.* **faintness** *n.*

faint-hearted (fānt′här′tid) *adj.* Lacking courage or conviction; cowardly; timid. **faintheartedness** *n.*, **faintheartedly** *adv.*

fair (fâr) *adj.* Visually light in coloring; pleasing to the eye; beautiful; impartial; free from blemish or imperfection; moderately large or good; not stormy; without precipitation. *n.* A periodic gathering for the buying and selling of goods and merchandise; a competitive exhibit of agricultural products, livestock, machinery, and other goods; a fund-raising event for a charity.

fair ball *n.* A ball that is situated, falls or

remains in the area bounded by the foul lines.

fair–haired *adj.* Having blonde or light colored hair; favored, favorite.

fair-ish *adj.* Reasonably or fairly good.

fair–mind-ed (fâr´mīn´did) *adj.* Just and impartial.

fair–trade agree-ment (fâr´trād´ *a* grē˝ment) *n.* A commercial agreement between a manufacturer and a seller under which a product cannot be sold at less than a minimum price set by the manufacturer.

fair-way (fâr´wā´) *n.* The part of a golf course between the tees and putting greens; the usual course through a harbor or channel.

fair-weather (fâr´weth˝ėr) *adj.* Friendly only during good times.

fair-y (fâr´ē) *n. pl.* -ies A tiny imaginary being, capable of working good or ill.

fair-y-land *n.* Any delightful, enchanting place; the land of the fairies.

fairy tale *n.* An incredible or fictitious tale of fanciful creatures; a tale about fairies.

fait accompli *n.* An accomplished fact or deed that is ireversible.

faith (fāth) *n.* A belief in the value, truth, or trust worthiness of someone or something; belief and trust in God, the Scriptures, or other religious writings; a system of religious beliefs.

faith-ful (fāth´ful) *adj.* True and trustworthy in the performance of duty, the fulfillment of promises or obligations, etc. **faithfully** *adv.* **faithfulness** *n.*

faith-less (fāth´lis) *adj.* Not being true to one's obligations or duties; lacking a religious faith; unworthy of belief or trust. **faithlessly** *adv.* **faithlessness** *n.*

fake (fāk) *adj.* Having a false or misleading appearance; not genuine. *v.* To make a brief, deceptive movement in order to mislead one's opponent in certain sports. **fake** *n.* **faker** *n.* **fakery** *n.*

fa-kir (fa kėr) *n.* A Moslem or Hindu religious mendicant, performing feats of endurance or magic.

fal-cate *adj.* Hooked like a sickle; curved.

fal-chion *n.* A broad, short and slightly curv-ed sword used in medieval times.

fal-con (fol´kon) *n.* A bird of prey noted for its powerful wings, keen vision, and swiftness of attack upon is prey. **falconer, falconry** *n.*

fal-con-er *n.* A person who breeds and trains hawks for hunting.

fal-con-ry *n.* The sport or arat of training falcons.

fall (fol) *v.* To drop down from a higher place or position due to the removal of support or loss of hold or attachment; to collapse; to become less in rank or importance; to drop when wounded or slain; to be overthrown by another government; to come as though descending as night falls; to pass into a specified condition, as to fall asleep; to cut down or fell, as a tree; to surrender, as a city or fort. **on** To recede; to retreat. **on** To fail in. **for** To be deceived by. **in** In the military, to meet and go along with. **out** In the military, to leave ranks. **of** To fail to meet a standard or to reach a particular place. **under** To be classified, as to be included. **man** The disobedience of Adam and Eve that began or resulted in original sin. A moral lapse or loss of innocence; autumn. **fall back** *n.* **fall down** *n.* **short** *n.*

fal-la-cious (fa lā´shus) *adj.* Containing or based on fundamental errors in reasoning; deceptive; misleading. **fallaciousness** *n.* **fallaciously** *adv.*

fal-la-cy (fal´*a* sē) *n. pl.* **fallacies** A deception; an error.

fall–off *n.* A decrease in something.

fall-out (fol´out´) *n.* The descent of minute particles of radioactive material or debris after a nuclear explosion; an incidental result or side effect.

fall-back *n.* A place or position to which one can retreat.

fall guy *n., Slang* A person left to receive the blame or penalties; scapegoat.

fal-li-ble (fal´i bl) *adj.* Capable of making an error; liable to be deceived or misled; apt to be erroneous. **fallibility** *n.*

fall-ing—out (fo´ling out´) *n. pl.* **fallings—out** A fight, disagreement, or quarrel. **star** A meteor, often visible as a result of being ignited by the atmospheric friction.

falling star *n.* A meteor, often visible as a result of being ignited by the atmospheric friction.

fal-lo-pi-an tube (*fa* lō´pē *a*n) *n.* One of a pair of long, slender ducts serving as a passage for the ovum from the ovary to the uterus.

fal-low (fal´ō) *n.* Ground that has been plowed but left unseeded during the growing season. *adj.* Light yellowish-brown in color. **fallowness** *n.*

fallow deer *n.* A European deer, about three feet high at the shoulders and spotted white in the summer.

false (fols) *adj.* Contrary to truth or fact; incorrect; deliberately untrue or deceptive; treacherous; unfaithful; not natural or real; artificial; in music, an incorrect pitch. *adv.* Faithless in manner. **falsely** *adv.* **falseness** *n.* **falsity** *n.*

false face *n.* A mask used for a disguise at Halloween.

false-hood (fols´hed) *n.* The act of lying; an intentional untruth.

false ribs *n. pl.* Ribs that are not united directly with the sternum. In man there are five on each side.

fal-set-to (fol set´ō) *n.* A high singing voice, usually male, that is artificially high. **falsetto** *adv.*

fal-si-fy (fol´si fī´) *v.* To give an untruthful account of; to misrepresent; to alter or tamper with in order to deceive; to forge. **falsifying, falsified** *v.* **falsifier** *n.*

fal-ter (fol´tėr) *v.* To be uncertain or hesitant in action or voice; to waver; to move with unsteadiness. **falteringly** *adv.*

fame (fām) *n.* Public esteem; a good reputation. **famed** *adj.*

fa-mil-iar (*fa* mil´yėr) *adj.* Being well-acquainted with; common; having good and complete knowledge of something; unconstrained or informal. *n.* A close friend or associate. **familiarly** *adv.*

fa-mil-i-ar-i-ty (*fa* mil´ē ar´i tē) *n. pl.* **-ties** An acquaintance with or the knowledge of something; an established friendship; an undue liberty or informality.

fa-mil-iar-ize (*fa* mil´ya rīz´) *v.* To make oneself or someone familiar with something. **familiarizing, familiarized** *v.* **familiarization** *n.*

fam-i-ly (fam´i lē) *n. pl.* **-ies** Parents and their children; a group of people connected by blood or marriage and sharing common ancestry; the members of a household; a group or class of like things; in science, a taxonomic category higher than a genus and below an order. **family** *adj.*

family name *n.* A surname or last name.

family tree *n.* A genealogical diagram showing family descent; the ancestors and descendants of a family.

fam-ine (fam´in) *n.* A widespread scarcity of food; a drastic shortage of or scarcity of anything; severe hunger; starvation.

fam-ish (fam´ish) *v.* To starve or cause to starve. **famished** *adj.*

fa-mous (fā´mus) *adj.* Well-known; renowned. *Slang* Excellent; admirable. **famously** *adv.* **famousness** *n.*

fan (fan) *n.* A device for putting air into motion, especially a flat, lightweight, collapsible, wedge-like shape; a machine that rotates thin, rigid vanes. *Slang* An enthusiastic devotee or admirer of a sport, celebrity, diversion, etc. *v.* To move or stir up air with a fan; to direct air upon; to cool or refresh with or as with a fan; to spread like a fan; in baseball, to strike out. **fanned, fanning** *v.*

fa-nat-ic (*fa* nat´ik) *n.* One who is moved by a frenzy of enthusiasm or zeal. **fanatical** *adj.* **fanatically** *adv.* **fanaticism** *n.*

fa-nat-i-cism *n.* Excessive vigor, behavior marked by such zeal or enthusiasm.

fan-ci-er (fan´sē ėr) *n.* A person having a special enthusiasm for or interest in something.

fan-ci-ful (fan´si *fu*l) *adj.* Existing or produced only in the fancy; indulging in fancies; exhibiting invention or whimsy in design. **fancifully** *adv.* **fancifulness** *n.*

fan-cy (fan´sē) *n. pl.* **fancies** Imagination of a fantastic or whimsical nature; a notion or idea not based on evidence or fact; a whim or caprice; judgment or taste in art, style, etc. *adj.* Adapted to please the fancy; highly decorated. *v.* To imagine; to visualize; to believe without proof or conviction; to suppose; to breed, as animals, for conventional points of beauty. **fanciness** *n.*

fan-cy–free (fan´sē frē´) *adj.* Unattached; not in love; carefree.

fan-cy-work (fan´sē werk´) *n.* Decorative or ornamental needle work.

fan-dan-go (fan dang´gō) *n.* A Spanish or Spanish-American dance in triple time; the music for this dance.

fan-fare (fan´fâr) *n.* A short, loud trumpet flourish; a spectacular public display.

fang (fang) *n.* A long, pointed tooth or tusk an animal uses to seize or tear at its prey; one of the hollow, grooved teeth with which a poisonous snake injects its venom. **fanged** *adj.*

fan-jet (fan´jet´) *n.* An aircraft with turbojet engines.

fan-light *n.* A semicircular window, above a door or larger window.

fan-ny *n. pl.* **fannies** *Slang* The buttocks.

fan mail *n.* Mail received by a public figure from admirers.

fan-palm *n.* A palm with usually large fan-shaped leaves.

fan-tail (fan´tāl´) *n.* Any fan-shaped tail or end; a variety of domestic pigeons having fan-like tail feathers. **fantailed** *adj.*

fan-ta-sia (fan´tā´zha) *n.* A composition structured according to the composer's fancy and not observing any strict musical form.

fan-ta-sied *adj.* Present only in one's imagination.

fan-ta-size *v.* To create mental fantasies; to imagine or indulge in fantasies. **fantasizing, fantasized** *v.*

fan-tas-tic (fan tas´tik) *adj.* Existing only in the fancy; unreal; wildly fanciful or exaggerated; impulsive or capricious; coming from the imagination or fancy. *Slang* Superb; wonderful.

fan-ta-sy (fan´ta sē) *n. pl.* **-ies** A creative imagination; a creation of the fancy; an unreal or odd mental image;a whimsical or odd notion; a highly or ingeniously imaginative creation; in psychology, the sequence of pleasant mental images fulfilling a wish.

fan-toc-ci-ni *n.* A puppet show where the puppets are operated by concealed wires or strings.

fan-wort *n.* A type of water-lily.

far (fär) *adv.* From, to, or at a considerable distance; to or at a certain distance, degree, or point; very remote in time, quality or degree, *adj.& adv.* Remote in space or time; extending widely or at great lengths; extensive or lengthy. **far and away** Decidedly. **far and wide** Everywhere. **far be it from me** Having no audacity or desire. **in so far as** To the extent that. **to go far** To accomplish a lot; to have success; to last a long time or to cover a great extent. **farther, further, farthest, furthest** *adj.*

far-ad (far´ad) *n.* A unit of capacitance equal to that of a capacitor having a charge of one coulomb on each plate and a potential difference of one voit between the plates.

far-a-way (fär´a wā´) *adj.* Very distant; remote; absent-minded; dreamy.

farce (färs) *n.* A theatre comedy employing exaggerated or ludicrous situations; a ridiculous situation or action; a seasoned stuffing. **farcical** *adj.*

far-cy *n.* A disease of the lymphatic glands and skin, affecting horses and cattle.

fare (fâr) *v.* To be in a specific state; to turn out. *n.* A fee paid for hired transportation; food or a variety of foods.

Far East *n.* The countries of eastern Asia, including China, Japan, Korea, Manchuria, and the adjacent islands.

fare–thee–well (fâr´thē wel´) *n.* The most extreme degree; perfection.

fare-well (fâr˝wel´) *n.* Good-by; a departure. *adj.* Closing; parting.

far--fetched (fär´fecht´) *adj.* Neither natural nor obvious; highly improbable.

far–flung (fär´flung´) *adj.* Widely distributed over a great distance.

fa-ri-na (*fa* rē ´n*a*) *n.* A fine meal obtained chiefly from nuts, cereals, potatoes, or Indian corn, used as a breakfast food or in puddings.

far-i-na-ceous (far˝*i* nā´shus) *adj.* Made from, rich in, or composed of starch; mealy.

farm (färm) *n.* Land that is cultivated for agricultural production; land used to breed and raise domestic animals; the area of water used for the breeding and raising of a particular type of aquatic animal, such as fish; the raising of livestock or crops as a business; in baseball, a minor league club for training its recruits. **farm out** To send work out to be done elsewhere. **farmer** *n.*

farm-er *n.* A person who raises crops or animals.

farm-house (färm´hous˝) *n.* The homestead on a farm.

farm-land (färm´land´) *n.* Land that is suitable for agricultural production.

farm-stead (färm´sted˝) *n.* A farm, including its land and all of the buildings.

farm team *n.* A minor league baseball team.

farm-yard (färm´yärd˝) *n.* The area surrounded by farm buildings and enclosed for confining stock.

far–off (fär´of´) *adj.* Distant; remote.

far–out *adj., Slang* Very unconventional.

far-a-go (*fa* rä´gō) *n. pl.* **faragoes** A confused mixture.

far–reaching (fär´rē´ching) *adj.* Having a wide-range, effect, or influence.

far-row (far´ō) *n.* A litter of pigs.

far–seeing (fär´sē´ing) *adj.* Having foresight; prudent; wise; having the ability to see distant objects clearly.

far-sight-ed (fär´sī´tid) *adj.* Able to see things at a distance more clearly than things nearby; having foresight; wise. **farsight-**

edly *adv.* **farsightedness** *n.*

far-ther (fär´thĕr) *adv.* To or at a more distant point. *adj.* More remote or distant.

far-ther-most *adj.* Most distant; farthest.

far-thest (fär´thist) *adj.* To or at the greatest distance.

far-thing (fär´thing) *n.* Something of little worth; a former British coin worth 1/4 of a penny.

far-thin-gale (fär´thing gāl˝) *n.* A support hoop worn under the skirts of the women in the 16th and 17th centuries.

fas-ci-cle *n.* A small bundle; a single part of a book published in installments.

fas-ci-nate (fas´*i* nāt´) *v.* To attract irresistibly, as by beauty or other qualities; to captivate; to hold motionless; to spellbind. **fascinating** *adj.* **fascinatingly** *adv.* **fascination** *n.* **fascinator** *n.*

fas-cism (fash´iz *u*m) *n.* A one-party system of government marked by a centralized dictatorship, stringent social and economic controls, and often belligerent nationalism. **fascist** *n.,* **fascistic** *adj.*

fash-ion (fash´*a*n) *n.* The mode or manner of dress, living, and style that prevails in society, especially in high society; good form or style; current style or custom; a piece of clothing made up in the current style. *v.* To make into a given shape or form; to make fitting. **fashionable, fashionableness** *adj.,* **fashionably** *adj.*

fast (fäst) *adj.* Swift; rapid; performed quickly; constant; steadfast; firmly secured; sound or deep, as sleep; permitting or suitable for quick movement; requiring rapidity of motion or action; acting or moving quickly. *v.* To give up food, especially for a religious reason. *n.* A period prescribed for fasting.

fast-back *n.* A car with a downward slope from the roof to the rear.

fast-en (fas´*e*n) *v.* To join something else; to connect; to securely fix something; to shut or close; to focus steadily.

fast–food *adj.* Of or relating to a restaurant that specializes in foods prepared and served quickly.

fas-tid-i-ous (fa stid´ē us) *adj.* Exceedingly delicate or refined; hard to please in matters of taste. **fastidiously** *adv.*

fas-tig-i-ate *adj.* Pointed at the top; tapering upward to a point.

fast–talk *v.*, *Slang* To affect or influence someone with deceptive talk. **fast–talking** *v.*, **fast–talker** *n.*

fast–track *adj.* High-powered and aggressive.

fat (fat) *adj.* Having superfluous flesh or fat; obese; plump; containing much fat or oil; rich or fertile; as land; abundant; plentiful; profitable; thick; broad. **a fat chance** *Slang.* Very little or no chance at all. *n.* Any of a large class of yellowish to white, greasy liquid or solid substances that are widely distributed in animal and plant tissues; consisting of various fatty acids and glycerol, generally odorless, tasteless, and colorless, the richest or most desirable part. **fatness, fattiness** *n.* **fatty** *adj.*

fat-al (fāt´al) *adj.* Causing death; deadly; bringing ruin or disaster; destructive; decisively important; fateful; brought about by fate; destined; inevitable. **fatally** *adv.*

fa-tal-ism (fāt´a liz´um) *n.* The belief that events or things are predetermined by fate and cannot be altered. **fatalist** *n.* **fatalistic** *adj.* **fatalistically** *adv.*

fa-tal-i-ty (fā tal´i tē) *n. pl.* -ies A death caused by a disaster or accident; the capability of causing death or disaster; the quality or state of being subject to or determined by fate.

fat-back (fat´bak˝) *n.* The strip of unsmoked salt pork taken from the upper part of a pork side.

fat cat *n.*, *Slang* A powerful and wealthy person; a rich person who contributes greatly to a political campaign.

fate (fāt) *n.* The force or power held to predetermine events; fortune; inevitability; the final result or outcome; unfortunate destiny; doom. **fated** *adj.* **fateful** *adj.* Determining destiny; governed by fate; bringing death or disaster. **fatefully** *adv.* **fatefulness** *n.*

fa-ther (fā´thėr) *n.* The male parent; any male forefather; ancestor; a male who establishes or founds something. **Father** A priest; one of the early Christian writers who formulated doctrines and codified observances. To beget; to act as a father toward. **fatherhood** *v.* **fatherliness** *n.* **fatherly** *adj.*

fa-ther–in–law *n.* The father of one's spouse.

fa-ther-land (fā thėr land) *n.* The land where one was born; the native country of one's ancestors.

Father's Day *n.* A day set aside to honor all fathers, occurring on the third Sunday of June.

fath-om (fath´om) *n.* A unit of length that is equal to six feet or approximately 1. 83 m, used mostly in measuring marine depths. *v.* To understand fully.

fath-om-less *adj.* Too deep to measure; too difficult to understand.

fa-tigue (fa tēg´) *n.* The state or condition of extreme tiredness or weariness from prolonged physical or mental exertion. **fatigues** Military clothes for heavy work and field duty. To become or make tired; to exhaust. **fatiguing, fatigued** *v.*

fats-hed-era *n.* An ornamental foliage plant with glossty leaves.

fat–sol-u-ble *adj.* Pertaining to something soluble in fat or oil.

fat-ten (fat´en) *v.* To make or become fat; to increase the amount of something. **fattening, fattened** *v.*

fat-ty (fat´ē) *adj.* Greasy; oily; having an excess of fat.

fatty acid *n.* Any of a class of organic acids derived from hydrocarbons, occurring in plant and animal fats.

fa-tu-i-ty (fa tö´i tē) *n.* Stupidity; foolishness.

fat-u-ous (fach´ŏ us) *adj.* Silly and foolish in a self-satisfied way. **fatuously** *adv.* **fatuousness** *n.*

fau-ces *n. pl.* The passage at the back of the mouth to the pharynx, formed by the membranous, muscular arches extending downward from each side of the soft palate. **faucial** *adj.*

fau-cet (fo´sit) *n.* A fixture with an adjustable valve used to draw liquids from a pipe or cask.

faugh (fo) *interj.* An exclamation of contempt or disgust.

fault (folt) *n.* An impairment or defect; a weakness; a minor offense or mistake; a break in the earth's crust allowing adjoining surfaces to shift in a direction parallel to the crack; a bad serve, as in tennis. *v.* To criticize. **at fault** Open to blame; in the wrong. **faultily** *adv.* **faultlessly** *adv.* **faultless** *adj.* **faulty** *adj.*

fault-finder (folt´fin˝dėr) *n.* One who finds fault; a petty critic. **faultfinding** *n. & adj.*

fault-less *adj.* Without fault or flaw.

fault-y *adj.* Containing defects; having imperfections.

faun (fon) *n.* A woodland deity represented in Roman mythology as part goat and part man.

fau-na (fo´na) *n. pl.* **faunas** *or* **faunae** Animals living within a given area or environment. **faunal** *adj.*

Faust *n.* A German doctor of legend who sold his soul to the devil for youth, power, and worldly experience.

fau-vism (fo´viz um) *n.* An art movement noted for the use of very flamboyant colors and bold, often distorted forms.

faux pas (fo pä´) *n.* A false step; a social blunder.

fa-vo-ni-an *adj.* Pertaining or relating to the west wind.

fa-vor (fā´vėr) *n.* A helpful or considerate act; the attitude of friendliness or approbation; the condition of being held in the regard; approval or support. **favors** Consent to sexual intimacy, especially as granted by a woman; a token of love or remembrance; a small gift given to each guest at a party. To benefit; to give advantage; to prefer or like one more than another; to support or approve; to look like or resemble; to treat with special care. **favorer** *v.* **favoringly** *n.*

fa-vor-a-ble (fā´vėr a bl) *adj.* Beneficial;

advantageous; building up hope or confidence; approving; promising. **favorableness** *n.* **favorably** *adv.*

fa-vored *adj.* Regarded and treated with preferential favor; enjoying special advantages.

fa-vor-ite (fā´vėr it) *n.* Anything regarded with special favor or preferred above all others; in sports, the contestant considered to be the most likely winner. **favorite** *adj.*

favorite son *n.* A person favored by his own state delegates for nomination at a national political convention.

fa-vor-it-ism (fā´vėr i tiz´um) *n.* Preferential treatment; a display of often unjust partiality.

fa-vour (fā´vėr) *n. & v.* British variety of favor.

fa-vus *n.* A fungus that attacks the scalp of humans and the skin of fowls and mammals.

fawn (fon) *n.* A young deer less than a year old; a light yellowish-brown color. *v.* To show cringing fondness; to display slavish affection. **fawningly** *adv.*

fawn lily *n.* A herb having single nodding flowers and leaves with light brown or white spots.

fay (fā) *n.* A fairy or elf.

faze (fāz) *v.* To worry; to disconcert. **fazed, fazing** *v.*

FB *abbr.* Freight bill.

FBI *abbr.* Federal Bureau of Investigation.

fe-al-ty (fē´al tē) *n. pl.* **fealties** The obligation of allegiance owed to a feudal lord by his vassal or tenant; faithfulness; loyalty.

fear (fēr) *n.* The agitated feeling caused by the anticipation or the realization of danger; an uneasy feeling that something may happen contrary to one's hopes; a feeling of deep, reverential awe and dread. *v.* To be apprehensive; to suspect. **fearfulness** *n.* **fearful** *adj.* **fearfully** *adv.*

fear-ful *adj.* Afraid; apprehensive; causing fear or alarm.

fear-less (fēr´lis) *adj.* Without fear; brave; courageous. **fearlessly** *adv.*

fear-some (fēr´sum) *adj.* Causing fear; timid. **fearsomely** *adv.* **fearsomeness** *n.*

fea-si-ble (fē´zi bl) *adj.* Capable of being put into effect or accomplished; practical. **feasibility** *n.* **feasibly** *adv.*

feast (fēst) *n.* A delicious meal; a banquet; a day or days of celebration set aside for a religious purpose or in honor of some person, event, or thing. *v.* To provide with pleasure. **feasting** *v.* **feaster** *n.*

feat (fēt) *n.* A notable act or achievement.

feath-er (feth´ẽr) *n.* One of the light, hollow-shafted structures that form the covering of birds. **a feather in one's cap** An achieve-ment one should be proud of; in rowing, to turn the oar blade following each stroke so that the blade is more or less horizontal as it is carried back to the position for reentering the water.

feather bed (feth´ẽr bed) *n.* A mattress stuffed with feathers; a bed with a feather mattress.

feather-bedding (feth´ẽr bed″ing) *n.* The practice that requires an employer to hold back on production or to employ more workers than needed because of union rules of safety regulations.

feather-edge (feth´ẽr ej´) *n.* A very thin, fragile edge.

feather-stitch (feth´ẽr stich´) *n.* An embroidery stitch that resembles a feather, accomplished by taking one or more short stitches alternately on either side of a straight line.

feather-weight (feth´ẽr wāt´) *n.* A boxer weighing between 118 and 127 pounds; any person or thing that is light in weight.

fea-ture (fē´chẽr) *n.* The appearance or shape of the face; the main presentation at a movie theater; a special article in a magazine or newspaper that is given special prominence. **feature** *v.*

Feb *abbr.* February.

feb-ri-fuge (feb´ri fūj´) *n.* A medicine used to reduce fever.

feb-rile (fē´bril) *adj.* Feverish.

Feb-ru-ary (feb´rŏ er″ē) *n.* The second month of the year, having 28 days or, in a leap year, 29 days.

fe-ces (fē´sēz) *pl. n.* Waste that is excreted from the bowels; excrement. **fecal** *adj.*

feck-less (fek´lis) *adj.* Ineffective; weak; careless and irresponsible. **fecklessly** *adv.*

fe-cund (fē´kund) *adj.* Fruitful; productive. **fecundity** *n.*

fe-cun-date (fē´kun dāt´) *v.* To make fertile. **fecundation** *n.*

fed *v.* Past tense of feed.

fed *v. abbr.* Federal, federated.

fed-er-al (fed´ẽr al) *adj.* Of, relating to, or formed by an agreement between two or more states or groups in which each retains certain controlling powers while being united under a central authority; of or pertaining to the United States central government. **Federal** Pertaining to or of the central government of Canada; of or supporting the Union in the American Civil War. **federally** *adv.*

fed-er-al-ism *n.* The organization or system of a federal government; the advocacy or support of this system. **federalist** *n.*

Federalist Party *n.* The political party of 1787-1830 which advocated the adoption of the U.S. Constitution and the formation of a strong national government.

fed-er-a-l-ize (fed´ẽr a līz´) *v.* To join or unite in a federal union; to bring under the control of the federal government. **federalizing, federalized** *v.*, **federalization** *n.*

fed-er-ate (fed´e rāt´) *v.* To unite in a federal union or alliance.

fed-er-a-tion (fed″e rā´shan) *n.* The joining together of two or more states or groups into a union or confederacy.

fe-do-ra (fi dōr´a) *n.* A soft hat with a low crown creased lengthwise and a brim that can be turned up or down.

fed up *adj., Slang.* Extremely annoyed or disgusted.

fee (fē) *n.* A fixed charge, compensation, or payment for something; a charge for professional services; an inherited estate in land.

fee-ble (fē´bl) *adj.* Very weak; lacking in

strength; lacking force; ineffective. **feeble-ness** *n*. **feebly** *adv*.

feeble minded (fē´bl mīn´did) *adj*. Mentally deficient; intellectually subnormal. **feeble mindedness** *n*.

feed (fēd) *v*. To supply with food; to provide as food; to consume food; to keep supplied, as with fuel for a fire; to enter data into a computing machine; to draw support or encouragement. *n*. The mechanical part, as of a sewing machine, that keeps supplying material to be worked on. *Slang* A meal.

feed-back (fēd´bak˝) *n*. The return to the input of a portion of the output of a machine; the return of data for corrections or control.

feed lot *n*. A place where livestock are fattended for market.

feed-stock *n*. Raw materials required for an industrial process.

feel (fēl) *v*. To examine, explore, or perceive through the sense of touch; to perceive as a physical sensation; to believe; to consider; to be aware of; to be emotionally affected by; to think; to suppose; to judge; to experience the full force or impact of; to produce a sensory impression of being soft, hard, hot or cold; to produce an indicated overall condition, impression, or reaction. **feeling** *v*.

feel-er (fē´lėr) *n*. Any action, hint, or proposal intended to draw out views and the intentions of another; one who or that which feels; an organ of touch.

feel-ing (fē´ling) *n*. The sensation that is perceived by touch; a physical or emotional sensation; compassion; a generous, sympathetic attitude; the impression produced upon a person by an object, place, etc.

feet *n*. The plural of foot.

feign (fān) *v*. To make a false show of; to dream up a false story and tell it as the truth; to fabricate; to imitate so as to deceive. **feigned** *adj*.

feint (fānt) *n*. A deceptive or misleading movement intended to draw defensive action away from the real target.

feist *n*. A small dog.

feist-y *adj*. Excited; agitated; frisky and exhuberant; quarrelsome.

feld-spar (feld´spär˝) *n*. Any of a large group of crystalline materials largely made up of silicates of aluminum.

fe-lic-i-tate (fi lis´i tāt´) *v*. To congratulate; to wish happiness. **felicitation** *n*.

fe-lic-i-tous (fi lis´i tus) *adj*. Most appropriate; well chosen; pertinent or effective in manner or style. **felicitouly** *adv*.

fe-lic-i-ty (fi lis´ i tē) *n. pl*. **felicities** Happiness; bliss; an instance or source of happiness; an agreeably pertinent or effective style.

fe-line (fē´līn) *adj*. Of or relating to cats, including wild and domestic cats; resembling a cat, as in stealth or agility. **felinity** *n*. **feline** *n*. **felinely** *adv*.

fell (fel) *v*. Past tense of fall; to strike or cause to fall down; to finish a seam with a flat, smooth strip made by joining edges, then folding under and stitching flat. *n*. Timber cut down during one season; an animal's hide; pelt. *adj*. Cruel and fierce; lethal.

fel-lah (fel´a) *n. pl*. **fellahin** *or* **fellaheen** An Arab peasant or laborer.

fel-low (fel´ō) *n*. A boy or man; an associate, comrade; the counterpart; one of a pair. *Informal* A boyfriend.

fel-low-man *n*. Another person or human being.

fel-low-ship (fel´ō ship´) *n*. A friendly relationship; the condition or fact of having common interests, ideals, or experiences; the status of being a fellow at a college or university, also the financial grant made to a fellow.

fel-ly (fel´ē) *n. pl*. **fellies** The rim of a wooden wheel, into which spokes are inserted.

fel-on (fel´on) *n*. A person who has committed a felony; an inflammation in the terminal joint or at the cuticle of a finger or toe.

fel-o-ny (fel´o nē) *n. pl. felonies* A serious crime, such as rape, murder, or burglary, punishable by a severe sentence. **felonious** *adj.* **feloniously** *adv.* **feloniousness** *n.*

fel-site *n.* A dense igneous rock consisting of minute crystals of feldspar and quartz.

felt (felt) *v.* Past tense of feel. *n.* An unwoven fabric made from pressed animal fibers, as wool or fur; a piece of fabric or material made of felt.

fem *abbr.* Feminine.

fe-male (fē´māl) *n.* The sex that produces ova or bears young; a plant with a pistil but no stamen, which is capable of being fertilized and producing fruit. *adj.* Of or relating to the sex that produces ova or bears young; suitable to this sex having a bore, slot, or hollow part designed to receive a projecting part, as a plug or prong.

fem-i-nine (fem´i nin) *adj.* Pertaining to or of the female sex; female; characterized by qualities generally attributed to women; lacking in manly qualities. *Gram.* Applicable to females only or to persons or things classified as female. **femininely** *adv.* **feminineness** *n.* **femininity** *n.*

fem-i-nism (fem´i niz´um) *n.* The movement advocating the granting of the same social, political, and economic rights to women as the ones granted to men. **feminist** *n.* **feministic** *adj.*

fem-i-nize *v.* To make feminine or to give a feminine quality to..

femme fa-tale (fem´fa tal´) *n. pl.* **fatales** A seductive or charming woman.

fe-mur (fē´mėr) *n. pl.* **femurs** *or* **femora** The bone extending from the pelvis to the knee. **femoral** *adj.*

fen (fen) *n.* A low, marshy land; a bog.

fence (fens) *n.* A structure made from rails, stakes, or strung wire that functions as a boundary or barrier. *Slang* A seller and recipient of stolen goods; the location where such goods are sold. *v.* To close in, surround, or separate as if by a fence. **on the fence** Neutral or undecided. **fencer** *n.*

fenc-ing (fen´sing) *n.* The sport of using

a foil or saber; the practice of making quick, effective remarks or retorts, as in a debate; the material used to make fences; fences collectively.

fend (fend) *v.* To ward off or to keep off; to offer resistance. **fending, fended** *v.*

fend-er (fen´dėr) *n.* The protective device over the wheel of a car or other vehicle; a metal guard set in front of an open fireplace; the projection on the front of a locomotive or streetcar, designed to push obstructions from the tracks, also known as cow-catcher.

fe-nes-tra *n.* A natural hole in the bone between the tympanum and the inner ear; a small transparent area often found in wings of butterflies.

fen-es-tra-tion (fen´i strā´shan) *n.* The design and position of doors and windows in a building.

fen-nel (fen´el) *n.* A tall herb from the parsley family which produces an edible stalk and aromatic seeds used as a flavoring.

fen-nel-flow-er *n.* A herb whose seeds are used in the East as medicine.

fen-u-greek *n.* An herb indigenous to western Asia but extensively cultivated elsewhere for its mucilaginous seeds, which are used for food, seasoning, and in veterinary medicine.

fe-ral (fēral) *adj.* Not tame nor domesticated; returned to a wild state; existing in an untamed state.

fer–de–lance (fer˝de lans´) *n.* A large, venomous snake of tropical America, with gray and brown markings.

fe-ri-a *n.* Any week day of a church calendar on which no feast falls.

fer-ment (fer ment´) *n.* Any substance or agent producing fermentation, as yeast, mold, or enzyme; excitement; unrest; agitation. **fermentability** *n.* **fermenter** *n.* **fermentable** *adj.*

fer-men-ta-tion (fe˝men tā´shan) *n.* The decomposition of complex organic compounds into simpler substances; the conversion of glucose into ethyl alcohol through the action of zymase; great agitation; commotion.

fer-mi-on *n*. An artifically produced radio-active metallic element.

fer-mi-um (fer´mē *u***m)** *n*. A metallic radio-active element, symbolized by Fm.

fern (fern) *n*. Any of a number of flowerless, seedless plants, having fronds with divided leaflets and reproducing by spores.

fe-ro-cious (fe rō´shus) *adj*. Extremely savage, fierce, cruel, or blood thirsty. *Slang* Very intense. **ferociously** *adv*. **ferociousness** *n*. **ferocity** *n*.

fer-ret (fer´it) *n*. A small, red-eyed polecat of Europe, often domesticated and trained to hunt rodents or rabbits. *v*. To search out by careful investigation; to drive out of hiding. **ferreter** *n*. **ferrety** *adj*.

fer-ric (fer´ik) *adj*. Pertaining to or containing iron.

ferric oxide *n*. A dark compound that occurs as hematite ore and rust.

fer-rif-er-ous *adj*. Producing or containing iron.

Ferris wheel *n*. A large, power-driven wheel with suspended compartments in which passengers ride for amusement.

fer-ro-con-crete *n*. A building material made of concrete and embedded steel rods.

fer-ro-mag-net-ic (fer˝ō mag net´ik) *adj*. Relating to or being typical of substances, as iron and nickel, that are readily magnetized. **ferromagnetism** *n*.

fer-rous (fer´us) *adj* . Pertaining to or containing iron.

fer-rule (fer´ul) *n*. A cap or ring used near or at the end of a stick, as a walking cane, to reinforce it or prevent splitting.

fer-ry (fer´ē) *n. pl.* **ferries** A boat or other craft used to transport people, vehicles, and other things across a body of water. **ferry** *v*.

ferry-boat *n*. A boat used to transport passengers or goods.

fer-tile (fer´til) *adj., Biol.* Having the ability to reproduce; rich in material required to maintain plant growth. **fertility** *n*. **fertileness** *n*.

fer-ti-li-za-tion *n*. The process of making

productive; the application of a fertilizer.

fer-til-ize (fer´ti līz´) *v*. To make fertile; to cause to be fruitful; to begin the biological reproduction by supplying with sperm or pollen. **fertilized, fertilizing** *v*. **fertilizable** *adj*. **fertilization** *n*.

fer-til-iz-er (fer´ti lī´zėr) *n*. A material that fertilizes, such as nitrates or manure which enriches soil.

fer-ule (fer´ul) *n*. A flat stick sometimes used to punish children. **ferule** *v*.

fer-vent (fer´vent) *adj*. Passionate; ardent; very hot. **fervency** *n*. **ferventness** *n*. **fervently** *adv*.

fer-vid (fer´vid) *adj*. Fervent to an extreme degree; impassioned; very hot; burning. **fervidly** *adv*. **fervidness** *n*.

fer-vor (fer´vėr) *n*. Great emotional warmth or intensity.

fes-cue (fes´kū) *n*. A type of tough grass, often used as pasturage.

fes-tal (fes´tal) *adj*. Pertaining to or typical of a festival, holiday, or feast.

fes-ter (fes´tėr) *v*. To develop or generate pus; to be a constant source of irritation or resentment.

fes-ti-val (fes´ti val) *n*. A particular holiday or celebration; a regularly occurring occasion.

fes-tive (fes´tiv) *adj*. Relating to or suitable for a feast or other celebration. **festively** *adv*. **festiveness** *n*.

fes-tiv-i-ty (fe stiv´i tē) *n. pl.* -ies A festival; gladness and rejoicing.

fes-toon (fe stön´) *n*. A garland of flowers, leaves, colored paper, or ribbon hanging in loops between two points. *v*. To decorate, fashion into, or link together by festoons. **festoonery** *n*.

fet-a *n*. A white Greek cheese made of goat's or ewe's milk and preserved in brine.

fe-tal (fēt´al) *adj*. Relating to or like a fetus.

fetal position *n*. The bodily position of a fetus with the spine curved, the head bowed forward, and the arms and legs drawn in toward the chest.

fetch (fech) *v*. To go after and return with;

to draw forth; to elicit; to bring as a price; to sell for; to strike a blow. **fetching, fetched** *v.* **fetcher** *n.*

fetch-ing *adj.* Very attractive or pleasing to the eye.

fete (fāt) *n.* A festival or feast; a very elaborate outdoor celebration. **fete** *v.*

fet-e-ri-ta *n.* A grain sorghum with compact heads of large white seeds, cultivated in the United States for grain and forage.

fet-id (fet´id) *adj.* Having a foul odor; stinking. **fetidly** *adv.* **fetidness** *n.*

fet-ish (fet´ish) *n.* An object that is regarded as having magical powers; something that one is devoted to excessively or irrationally. *Psychiatry* A nonsexual object that arouses or gratifies sexual desires. **fetishistic** *adj.* **fetishist** *n.*

fet-lock (fet´lok´) *n.* A tuft of hair that grows just above the hoof at the back of the leg of a horse.

fe-tol-o-gy *n.* The medical study of a fetus. **fetologist** *n.*

fet-ter (fet´ėr) *n.* A chain or other bond put around the ankles to restrain movement, preventing escape; anything that prevents free movement.

fet-tle (fet´l) *n.* State; the condition of something.

fe-tus (fē´tus) *n.* The individual unborn organism carried within the womb from the time major features appear; especially in humans, the unborn young after the eighth week of development.

feud (fūd) *n.* A bitter quarrel between two families, usually lasting over a long period of time. **feud** *v.*

feu-dal (fūd´al) *adj.* Relating to or characteristic of feudalism. **feudalize** *v.* **feudally** *adv.*

feu-dal-ism (fūd´a liz˝um) *n.* The political, social, and economic organization produced by the feudal system. **feudalist** *n.* **feudalistic** *adj.*

feu-da-to-ry (fū´da tōr´ē) *n. pl.* **feudatories** One holding a feudal fee. *adj.* Owing feudal homage or allegiance.

fe-ver (fē´vėr) *n.* Abnormally high body temperature and rapid pulse; a craze; a heightened emotion or activity. **feverish** *adj.* **feverishly** *adv.* **feverishness** *n.*

fever blister *n.* A cold sore.

fe-ver-few *n.* A perennial European herb plant that bears small white flowers and primitively used as a medicine to reduce fever.

fe-ver-wort *n.* An herb in the honeysuckle family with emetic and purgative uses.

few (fū) *adj.* Small in number; not many. *n.* A select or limited group.

few-er *adj.* Pertaining to a smaller number.

few-ness *n.* Being few in quantity.

fey (fā) *adj.* Seemingly spellbound; having clairvoyance; acting as if under a spell.

fez (fez) *n.* A red felt, black-tasseled hat worn by Egyptian men.

fi-bril *n.* A very fine filament.

fi-bril-lar *adj.* Pertaining to fibers.

fi-bro-vas-cu-lar *adj.* Composed of a fibrous conductive tissue which conveys fluid from one part to another.

fi-ne (fē´na) *n., Mus.* The end.

fi-an-ce (fē´än sā´) *n.* A man to whom a woman is engaged to be married.

fi-an-cee (fē´än sā´) *n.* A woman to whom a man is engaged to be married.

fi-as-co (fē as´kō) *n. pl.* **fiascoes** A complete or total failure.

fi-at (fī´at) *n.* A positive and authoritative order or decree.

fib (fib) *n.* A trivial lie. **fibber** *n.*

fi-ber (fī´bėr) *n.* A fine, long, continuous piece of natural or synthetic material made from a filament of asbestos, spun glass, textile, or fabric; internal strength; character. **fibrous** *adj.*

fi-ber-board (fībėr bōrd˝) *n.* A tough, pliable building material made of plant fibers, as wood, compressed into rigid sheets.

fi-ber-glass (fī´bėr glas´) *n.* A flexible, nonflammable material of spun glass used for textiles, insulation, and other purposes.

fiber optics *n. pl.* Light optics transmitted through very fine, flexible glass rods by internal reflection. **fiber optic** *adj.*

fiber-scope *n.* The flexible fiber optic instrument used to view otherwise inaccessible objects.

fib-ril-la-tion (fi′bri lā′shɑn) *n., Pathol.* The rapid and uncoordinated contraction of the muscle fibers of the heart.

fi-brin (fi′brin) *n., Biochem.* An insoluble protein that promotes the clotting of blood. **fibrinous** *adj.*

fi-brin-o-gen (fi brin′o jɛn) *n., Biochem.* A complex blood plasma protein that is converted to fibrin during the process of blood clotting.

fi-broid (fi′broid) *adj.* Made up or resembling fibrous tissue.

fib-u-la (fib′ū lɑ) *n.,* *Anat.* The outer and smaller bone of the lower limb or hind leg, in humans located between the knee and ankle.

-fic *adj., suffix* Making; causing; rendering.

-fication *n., suffix* Making; production.

fi-chu (fish′ŏ) *n.* A lightweight triangular scarf, worn about the neck and fastened loosely in front.

fick-le (fik′l) *adj.* Inconstant in purpose or feeling; changeable. **fickleness** *n.*

fic-tile *adj.* Capable of being molded; relating to soft clay or earthenware.

fic-tion (fik′shɑn) *n.* Something that is created or imaginary; a literary work that is produced by the imagination and not based on fact. **fictional** *adj.*

fic-tion-al-i-za-tion *n.* The procedure of narrating an actual event in a fictional form.

fic-tion-eer *n.* An author who writes inferior fiction in large quantities.

fic-ti-tious (fik tish′us) *adj.* Nonexistent; imaginary; not genuine; false; not real. **fictitiously** *adv.* **fictitiousness** *n.*

fid-dle (fid′l) *n.* A violin. *v.* To play the violin; to fidget or make nervous or restless movements; to spend time in a careless way. *Naut.* A rack used at the table to prevent things from sliding off. **fit as a fiddle** To enjoy good or perfect health. **second fiddle** To be put into a position subordinate to that of another. **fiddling, fiddled** *v.* **fiddler** *n.*

fiddler catfish *n.* A freshwater, scaleless fish with long whisker-like feelers used for navigation; ranging in size from 8 to 14 inches in length and having a light taste and tender texture.

fiddler crab *n.* A small burrowing crab found mostly off the Atlantic coast of the United States, the male being much larger than the female.

fid-dle-sticks (fid′l stiks″) *interj.* Used to express mild disgust, annoyance; nonsense.

fid-dling *adj.* Trifling; trivial; insignificant.

fi-de-ism *n.* A tenet that certain premises, as of religion and philosophy, need no rational explanation but should be accepted on faith.

fi-del-i-ty (fi del′i tē) *n. pl.* **fidelities** Faithfulness or loyalty to obligations, vows, or duties. *Elect.* The degree to which a phonograph, tape recorder, or other electronic equipment receives and transmits input signals without distortion.

fidg-et (fij′it) *v.* To move nervously or restlessly. **fidgets** *n. pl.* The condition of being nervous or restless. **fidgeter** *n.* **fidgetiness** *n.* **fidgety** *adj.*

fi-du-ci-ary (fi dū′shē er″ē) *adj.* Relating to or pertaining to the holding of something in trust. *n.* An agent; a trustee.

fie (fi) *interj.* An expression of disgust or impatience in response to an unpleasant surprise.

fief (fēf) *n.* A feudal estate in land.

field (fēld) *n.* A piece of land with few or no trees; a cultivated piece of land devoted to the growing of crops; an area in which a natural resource such as oil is found; an airport; the complete extent of knowledge, research, or study in a given area; in sports, the bounded area in which an event is played; the members of a team actually engaged in active play; in business, the area away from the home office. *Milit.* A region of active operations or maneuvers. *Physics* A region of space that is marked by a physical property, as electromagnetic force, with a determinable value at each point in the region. **fielder** *n.*

field artillery *n.* Artillery that has been mounted for use in the fields.

field corn *n.* Corn grown in large fields and used as livestock food.

field day *n.* A day full of pleasurable activities, usually out of doors. *Slang.* The opportunity to express oneself with the greatest pleasure or success.

field event *n.* An event at an athletic meet other than races, such as jumping and throwing.

field glass *n., often* **field glasses** A compact, portable binocular instrument for viewing distant objects.

field house *n.* An enclosed building used for various indoor sports and for storing equipment and providing a dressing area.

field magnet *n.* A magnet providing the magnetic field in a generator or electric motor.

field marshal *n.* An army official in Europe who ranks just below the commander in chief.

field mouse *n.* A small mouse inhabiting fields and meadows.

field of force *n.* A region where the force of a single agent, as an electric current, is operative.

fiend (fēnd) *n.* An evil spirit or demon; a person who is totally engrossed in something. *Slang* An addict. **fiendish** *adj.* **fiendishly** *adv.* **fiendishness** *n.*

fierce (fērs) *adj.* Savage and violent in nature. *Slang* Very difficult or disagreeable. **fiercely** *adv.* **fierceness** *n.*

fier-y (fiėr´ē) *adj.* Containing or composed of fire; brightly glowing; blazing; hot and inflamed; full of spirit or intense with emotion. **fieriness** *n.*

fi-es-ta (fē es´ta) *n.* A religious holiday or festival.

fife (fīf) *n.* A small, shrill-toned instrument similar to a flute.

fif-teen (fif´tēn) *n.* The cardinal number equal to 14 + 1. **fifteenth** *n., adj. & adv.* **fifteen** *adj.*

fifth (fifth) *n.* The ordinal of five; one of five equal parts. *Mus.* The space between a tone and another tone five steps from it. **fifth** *adj. & adv.*

Fifth Amendment *n.* An amendment to the United States Constitution, ratified in 1791, guaranteeing due process of law and that no person "shall be forced to testify against himself."

fifth column *n.* During wartime, the private civilians within defense lines who secretly assist the enemy. **fifth columnist** *n.*

fifth wheel *n.* A superfluous thing or person.

fif-ty (fif´tē) *n.* The cardinal number equal to 5 X 10; 50th **fiftieth** *n., adj. & adv.* **fifty** *adj.*

fifty-fifty *adj., Slang* Divided into two equal portions or parts.

fig (fig) *n.* A tree or shrub bearing a sweet, pear-shaped, edible fruit; the fruit of the fig tree.

fight (fīt) *v.* To struggle against; to quarrel; to argue; to make one's way by struggling; to participate in wrestling or boxing until a final decision is reached. *n.* A physical battle; struggle; strife; conflict; combat. **fighting** *v.*

fight-er (fī´tėr) *n.* A person who fights. *Milit.* A fast, highly maneuverable airplane used in combat.

fig-ment (fig´mėnt) *n.* An invention or fabrication.

fig-ur-a-tion *n.* The process of shaping into a particular figure; the resulting figure or shape.

fig-u-ra-tive (fig´ūr *a* tiv) *adj.* Based on, like, or containing a figure of speech; metaphorical; representing by means of a figure or symbol. **figuratively** *adv.*

fig-ure (fig´ūr) *n.* A symbol or character that represents a number; anything other than a letter; the visible form, silhouette, shape, or line of something; the human form or body; an individual, especially a prominent one; the impression or appearance that a person makes; *n.* a design or pattern, as in a fabric; a figure of speech; a series of movements, as in a dance.

figures *pl.* In mathematics, calculations; an amount shown in numbers. *v.* To represent; to depict; to compute.

figure eight *n.* A skating maneuver shaped like an 8; anything shaped like the number 8.

fig-ure-head (fig´ūr hed´) *n.* A person with nominal leadership but no real power; a carved figure on a ship's bow.

figure of speech *n.* An expression, as a metaphor or hyperbole, where words are used in a more forceful, dramatic, or illuminating way.

figure skating *n.* A type of skating where a skater traces or outlines prescribed figures or patterns.

fig-u-rine (fig´yu rēn´) *n.* A small sculptured or molded figure; a statuette.

fi-ji *n.* A native of the Figi Islands.

fil-a-ment (fil´a ment) *n.* A very thin, finely spun fiber, wire, or thread; the fine wire enclosed in an electric lamp bulb which is heated electrically to incandescence. **filamentary, filamentous** *adj.*

fi-lar *adj.* Of or pertaining to a thread; *opt.* having threads across the field of vision.

fil-a-ture *n.* The act of forming into threads; the reeling of silk cocoons; a reel for drawing off silk from cocoons; an establishment for reeling silk.

fil-bert (fil´bert) *n.* The edible nut of the hazel tree or the tree it grows on.

filch (filch) *v.* To steal. **filcher** *n.*

file (fil) *n.* A device for storing papers in proper order; a collection of papers so arranged; a line of persons, animals, or things placed one behind another; a hard, steel instrument with ridged cutting surfaces, used to smooth or polish. *v.* To march as soldiers; to make an application, as for a job. **filling, filed** *v.*

file-fish *n.* Any of various saltwater fishes of the family Monacanthidae, with spiny or granular skin, as the triggerfish.

fi-let (fi lā´) *n.* A filet of meat or fish; lace or net with a pattern of squares.

filet mignon *n.* A small, tender cut of beef from the inside of the loin.

fil-i-al (fil´ē al) *adj.* Of or relating to a son or daughter; pertaining to the generation following the parents. **filially** *adv.*

fil-i-buster (fil´i bus´ter) *n.* An attempt to prolong, prevent, or hinder legislative action by using delaying tactics such as long speeches; using time. **filibuster** *v.* **filibusterer** *n.*

fil-i-gree (fil´i grē´) *n.* Delicate, lace-like ornamental work made of silver or gold intertwisted wire. **filigree** *v. & adj.*

fil-ing (fi´ling) *n. often* **filings** Particles removed by a file.

Fil-i-pi-no (fil´i pē´nō) *n.* A native or inhabitant of the Philippines. **Filipino** *adj.*

fill (fil) *v.* To put into or hold as much of something as can be contained; to supply fully, as with food; to put together or make up what is indicated in an order or prescription; to meet or satisfy a requirement or need; to occupy an office or position; to insert something, as to fill in a name or address. *Naut.* To trim the yards so the sails will catch the wind. *n.* A built-up piece of land or the material, as earth or gravel, used for it. **to fill in on** To give someone additional information of facts about something. **to fill out** To become or make fuller or more rounded.

fill-er (fil´er) *n.* Something that is added to increase weight or bulk or to take up space; a material used to fill cracks, pores, or holes in a surface before it is completed.

fil-let *or* **fi-let (fil´it)** *n.* A narrow ribbon or band for holding the hair; a strip of boneless fish or meat. *v.* To slice, bone, or make into fillets.

fill–in *n.* A person or thing that fills the place of another; a review usually, orally of important information.

fil-ling (fil´ing) *n.* That which is used to fill something, especially the substance put into a prepared cavity in a tooth; the horizontal threads crossing the wrap in weaving.

filling station *n.* A retail business, also know as a service station where vehicles are serviced with gasoline, oil, water, and air for tires.

fil-lip (fil´ip) *n.* A snap of the finger that has been pressed down by the thumb and then suddenly released; something that arouses or excites. **fillip** *v.*

fil-lis-ter *n.* A plane for grooves; a groove, on a window sash that holds the glass and putty.

Fillmore, Millard *n.* The 13th president of the United States, from 1850-1853.

fill out *v.* To become fuller, to put on weight.

fill up *v.* To fill completely to the top; to occupy fully.

fil-ly (fil´ē) *n.* A young female horse less than four years of age; a young girl.

film (film) *n.* A thin covering, layer, or membrane. *Photog.* A photosensitive strip or sheet of flexible cellulose material that is used to make photographic negatives or transparencies; the film containing the pictures projected on a large screen; the motion picture itself. *v.* To cover with or as if with a film; to make a movie.

film-dom (film´dom) *n.* The movie industry or business.

film-strip (film´strip´) *n.* A strip of film containing graphic matter for still projection on a screen.

fil-ose *adj.* Threadlike.

fil-ter (fil´tėr) *n.* A device, as cloth, paper, charcoal, or any other porous substance, through which a liquid or gas can be passed to separate out suspended matter. *Photog.* A colored screen that controls the kind and intensity of light waves in an exposure. *v.* To pass liquids through a filter; to strain. **filterer** *n.* **filterability** *n.* **filterable** *adj.* **filtrable** *adj.*

filter bed *n.* A sand or gravel bed, used to filter water or sewage.

filter tip *n.* A cigarette or cigar tip that filters the smoke before it's inhaled.

filth (filth) *n.* Anything that is dirty or foul; something that is considered offensive.

filth-y (fil´thē) *adj.* Highly unpleasant; morally foul; obscene. **filthily** *adv.* **filthiness** *n.*

fil-trate (fil´trāt) *v.* To pass or cause to pass through something. *n.* Anything which has passed through the filter. **filtrating, filtrated** *v.* **filtration** *n.*

fin (fin) *n.* A thin membranous extension of the body of a fish or other aquatic animal, used for swimming and balancing. *Slang* A five dollar bill.

fi-na-gle (fi nā´gl) *v., Slang* To get something by trickery or deceit. **finagling** *adj.* **finagler** *n.*

fi-nal (fin´al) *adj.* Pertaining to or coming to the end; last or terminal. **finality** *n.* **finally** *adv.*

finals *n. pl.* Something decisively final, as the last of a series of athletic contests; the final academic examination.

fi-na-le (fi nal´ē) *n.* The last part, as the final scene in a play or the last part of a musical composition.

fi-nal-ist (fin´a list) *n.* A contestant taking part in the final round of a contest.

fi-nal-i-ty *n.* The state of being final, or irrevocable.

fi-nal-ize (fin´a līz´) *v.* To put into final and complete form. **finalized, finalizing** *v.* **finalization, finalizer** *n.*

fi-nal-ly *adv.* Conclusively or decisively.

fi-nance (fi nans´) *n.* The science of monetary affairs. **finances** Monetary resources; funds. *v.* To supply the capital or funds for something; to sell or provide on a credit basis. **financial** *adj.* **financially** *adv.*

fin-an-cier (fin´an sēr´) *n.* An expert who deals with large-scale financial affairs; makes loans.

fin-back *n.* A common whalebone whale that grows to a length of 60 feet or more, found off the Atlantic and Pacific coasts of the United States.

finch (finch) *n.* A small bird, as a grosbeak, canary, or goldfinch, having a short stout bill.

find (find) *v.* To come upon unexpectedly; to achieve; to attain; to ascertain; to determine; to consider; to regard; to recover or regain something; to detect the true identity or nature of something or someone.

find-er (fin´dėr) *n.* A person who finds; the device on a camera that indicates what will be in the picture.

find-er's fee *n.* A sum of money paid to a person who introduces a company to a new customer.

find-ing (fin´ding) *n.* Something that is found or discovered. **findings** *pl.* Conclusions or statistics that are the result of a study, examination, or investigation.

fine (fin) *adj.* Superior in skill or quality; very enjoyable and pleasant; light and delicate in workmanship, texture, or structure; made up or composed of very small parts. *Slang* To be in good health; very well. *n.* The sum of money required as the penalty for an offense. **fineness** *n.* **fine** *v.* **finely** *adj.*

fine arts *n. pl.* The arts of drawing, painting, sculpture, architecture, literature, music, and drama.

fine-ness *n.* The state of being fine.

fin-er-y (fi´ne rē) *n. pl.* **fineries** Elaborate jewels and clothes.

fines *n. pl.* A ground or powdered material; a collection of very small particles in a mixture of different sizes.

fine-spun *adj.* Developed with extreme delicacy; overrefined.

fi-nesse (fi nes´) *n.* A highly refined skill; the skillful handling of a situation.

fin-ger (fing´gėr) *n.* One of the digits of the hand, usually excluding the thumb; that part of a glove made to fit the finger; anything resembling the finger. *Mus.* The use of the fingers in playing an instrument.

fin-ger-board *n.* The strip of wood on the neck of a stringed instrument against which the strings are pressed by the fingers in order to play.

finger bowl *n.* A small bowl which contains water for cleansing the fingers at the table after eating.

fin-ger-ing (fing´gėr ing) *n., Mus.* The technique of playing a musical instrument with the fingers; the marking that indicates which fingers are to be used.

fin-ger-ling *n.* A small young fish, especially a salmon or trout.

fin-ger-nail (fing´gėr nāl´) *n.* The transparent covering on the dorsal surface of the tip of each finger.

finger painting *n., Art.* The technique of using the fingers to apply or spread paint on wet paper.

fin-ger-print (fing´gėr print´) *n.* An inked impression of the pattern formed by the ridges of the skin on the tips of each finger and thumb. **fingerprint** *v.*

fin-i-al (fin´ē al) *n.* The ornamental projection or terminating part, as on a lamp shade.

fin-i-cal *adj.* Finicky.

fin-ick-y (fin´i kē) *adj.* Hard to please; choosy. **finickiness** *n.*

fi-nis (fin´is) *n.* The end.

fin-ish (fin´ish) *v.* To bring to an end; to conclude; to reach the end; to consume all. *Slang* To kill, defeat, or destroy. *n.* The last stage or conclusion of anything; the perfection or polish in manners, speech, or education; the surface quality or appearance of paint, textiles, or other materials. *adj.* Having a glossy polish. **finishing** *v.* **finisher** *n.* **finished** *adj.*

finishing school *n.* A private school for young girls that emphasizes cultural studies and prepares one for social activities.

fi-nite (fi´nīt) *adj.* Having bounds or limits; of or relating to a number which can be determined, counted, or measured. **finitely** *adv.* **finiteness** *n.*

fink (fingk) *n., Slang* A person that breaks a strike; an unsavory person.

Finn (fin) *n.* A native or inhabitant of Finland.

fin-nan had-die (fin´an had´ē) *n.* Smoked haddock.

fin-ny (fin´ē) *adj.* Having or suggesting fins or fin-like extensions.

fipple flute *n.* A straight, flutelike instrument, with finger holes and a whistle type mouthpiece.

fir (fėr) *n.* An evergreen tree with flat needles and erect cones.

fire (fiėr) *n.* The chemical reaction of burning, which releases heat and light. *v.* To have great enthusiasm; to ignite or cause to become ignited; to bake in a kiln; to discharge a firearm or explosive; to let a person go from a job; to dismiss. **firing** *v.*

fire alarm *n.* A safety device to signal the outbreak of a fire.

fire-arm (fiėr´ärm´) *n.* A small weapon used for firing a missile; a pistol or rifle using an explosive charge.

fire-ball (fiėr´bol´) *n.* A very bright meteor; a hot, incandescent sphere of air and vaporized debris. *Slang* A remarkably energetic person or thing.

fire blight *n.* A highly destructive disease, caused by a bacterium, that affects apple and pear trees with their leaves appearing to be burnt.

fire-boat *n.* A boat equipped with fire fighting equipment.

fire-box *n.* A box that contains a fire alarm; the compartment in which the fuel of a locomotive or furnace is burned.

fire-brand (fiėr´brand´) *n.* A piece of glowing or burning wood; one who stirs up or agitates conflict or trouble.

fire-break (fiėr´brāk´) *n.* A strip of land that is cleared to prevent a fire from spreading.

fire-brick (fiėr´brik´) *n.* A highly heat-resistant brick, used to line furnaces and fireplaces.

fire-bug (fiėr´bug´) *n.* One who enjoys setting fire to buildings or homes; a pyromaniac.

fire clay *n.* A type of clay capable of withstanding high tempatures and used in making firebricks, crucibles, etc.

fire control *n., Milit.* The planned and controlled delivery of gunfire on a target; the control or extinction of fires.

fire-crack-er (fiėr´krak˝ėr) *n.* A small paper cylinder charged with an explosive that is set off to make noise.

fire-damp (fiėr´damp´) *n.* Gas, mainly methane, occurring naturally in coal mines and forming explosive mixtures with air.

fire department *n.* The department or organization for prevention and extinguishing of fires.

fire drill *n.* A practice drill, for a fire company and firemen, in the correct manner for extinguishing fires; a drill for schools, or other individuals, for training in the proper manner to exit the building in case of fire.

fire-eat-er *n.* A magician or performer who pretends to eat fire.

fire engine *n.* A large motor vehicle equipped to carry fire fighters and their equipment to a fire.

fire escape *n.* A structure, often metal, used as an emergency exit from a building.

fire extinguisher *n.* A portable apparatus that contains fire-extinguishing chemicals, which are ejected through a short nozzle and hose.

fire fighter *n.* A person who fights fires as an occupation.

fire-fly (fiėr´flī´) *n.* A beetle that flies at night, having an abdominal organ that gives off a flashing light.

fire-guard *n.* A person in charge of watching for and extinguishing fires. A metal frame inserted in front of a fireplace as protection.

fire-house (fiėr´hous´) *n.* The building used to house fire fighting equipment and personnel.

fire irons *n. pl.* Equipment that includes tongs, shovel, and a poker used to tend a fire, usually in a fireplace.

fire-light *n.* The light produced from an open fire, as a campfire or fireplace.

fire-lock *n.* A gunlock with a slow match to ignite the priming.

fire-man (fiėr′man) *n. pl.* **firemen** A person employed to prevent or extinguish fires; one who tends fires.

fire-place (fiėr′plās′) *n.* An open recess in which a fire is built, especially the base of a chimney that opens into a room.

fire-plug (fiėr′plug′) *n.* A hydrant for supplying water in the event of a fire.

fire-power *n., Milit.* The capacity to deliver fire or missiles, as from a weapon, military unit, or ship.

fire-proof (fiėr′prŏf′) *adj.* Resistant to fires. **fireproof** *v.*

fire sale *n.* A sale in which goods, damaged by fire, smoke or water are offered at reduced prices.

fire screen *n.* A protective screen, of metal, placed before a fireplace to prevent flying sparks.

fire-side *n.* The area near the side of the fireplace.

fire station *n.* A building used to house firefighting equipment and firemen.

fire tower *n.* A forest fire lookout station.

fire-trap (fiėr′trap′) *n.* A building made from such construction or built in such a way that it would be hard to escape from if there were a fire.

fire wall *n.* A fireproof wall in a building used as a barrier to forestall or prevent a fire from spreading.

fire-ward-en *n.* An officer in a community, responsible for preventing and or extinguishing fires.

fire-wa-ter *n., Slang.* A strong alcoholic liquor.

fire-works (fiėr′werks′) *n.* Explosives used to generate colored lights, smoke, and noise for entertainment or celebrations.

fir-ing *n.* The act of one who fires; process of maturing ceramic items by heating to a very high degree of heat.

firing line *n.* In combat, the front line from which gunfire is delivered; the vulnerable front position of a pursuit or activity.

firing pin *n.* A pin that strikes the cartridge primer or detonator of a firearm.

firing range *n.* An area equipped with targets for shooting practice; the distance from a target at which a weapon can be fired effectively.

firing squad *n.* A military detachment assigned to carry out an execution by shooting; a squad assigned to fire guns at the burial of a person buried with military honors.

firm (ferm) *adj.* Relatively solid, compact, or unyielding to pressure or touch; steadfast and constant; strong and sure. *n.* A partnership of two or more persons for conducting a business. *v.* To become or make firm or firmer.

firm-ly *adv.* Unwaveringly; resolutely. **firmness** *n.*

fir-ma-ment (fer′ma ment) *n.* The expanse of the heavens; the sky.

firn (firn) *n.* Snow that is partially consolidated by thawing and freezing but has not converted to glacial ice.

first (ferst) *adj.* Preceding all others in the order of numbering; taking place or acting prior to all others; earliest; ranking above all in importance or quality; foremost. *adv.* Above or before all others in time, order, rank, or importance; for the very first time. *n.* The ordinal number that matches the number 1 in a series, 1st; the transmission gear producing the lowest driving speed in an automotive vehicle. **firstly** *adv.*

first aid *n.* The emergency care given to a person before full treatment and medical care can be obtained.

First Amendment *n.* The amendment to the Constitution of the United States which forbids Congress to interfere with religion, free speech, free press, the right to assemble peaceably, or the right to petition the government, ratified in 1791.

first base *n., Baseball.* The base that must be touched first by a base runner; the position of the player for defending the area around first base; the first step toward a goal.

first-born (ferst′born′) *adj.* First in order.

n. The child who is born first.

first class *n.* The best quality or highest rank; a class of sealed mail that consists partly or wholly of written matter; the best or most luxurious accommodations on a plane, ship, etc.

first–degree burn *n.* A mild burn characterized by heat, pain, and redness of the skin surface but not exhibiting blistering or charring of tissues.

first-hand (ferst´hand´) *adj.* Coming directly from the original source. **firsthand** *adv.*

first lady *or* **First Lady** *n.* The wife of the President of the United States or the wife or hostess of the chief executive of a state, city, or other country.

first lieutenant *n., Milit.* A commissioned officer ranking above a 2nd lieutenant and below a captain.

first-ling *n.* The first of its class; the first product or result

first-ly *adv.* In the first place.

first mortgage *n.* A priority lien on real or personal property that ranks above all other liens, except those imposed by law.

first–night-er *n.* A person at the first night performances of an opera or at the theater.

first offender *n.* One legally convicted for the first time of an offense against the law.

first papers *n. pl.* The first papers filed by an applicant for citizenship

first person *n.* A category for verbs or pronouns indicating the speaker or writer of a sentence in which they are used.

first-rate (ferst´rāt´) *adj.* Of the finest rank, quality, or importance. **first-rate** *adv.*

first reading *n.* The first submitting of a bill before a quorum.

first sergeant *n.* A noncommissioned officer, the chief assistant to the commander, in charge of the personnel management.

first–string *adj.* Being a regular and not a substitute; first-rate.

first water *n.* The highest quality, applied to diamonds and other precious stones.

firth (ferth) *n.* A narrow inlet of the sea.

fis-cal (fis´kal) *adj.* Relating to or of the finances or treasury of a nation or a branch

of government; financial. **fiscally** *adv.*

fish (fish) *n. pl.*
fish *or* **fishes** An aquatic animal having fins, gills for breathing, and usually scales; the flesh of fish used as food. **like a fish**

out of water Not at ease or comfortable.
v. To try to catch fish; to seek or find one's way; to grope; to try and obtain something in an artful or indirect way. **fishing** *v.*

fish–and–chips *n.* Deep fried fish and French fried potatoes.

fish bowl *n.* A bowl usually made of glass, serving as a small aquarium for fish; a lack of privacy.

fish cake *n.* A mixture of shredded fish as codfish, mixed with mashed potato, seasoned, and rolled into a ball and fried. Also **fish ball**.

fish-er-man (fish´ẽr man) *n. pl.* **fishermen** A person who fishes commercially or for sport and relaxation; a commercial fishing boat.

fish-er-y (fish´e rē) *n. pl.* **fisheries** The business of catching, processing, or selling fish; a fish nursery or hatchery.

fish-hook *n.* A barbed hook, used for catching fish.

fish story *n.* An extravagant, boastful story that is probably not true.

fish-tail (fish´tāl´) *v.* To swing from side to side while moving forward, as the motion of the rear end of a vehicle.

fish-wife (fish´wīf´) *n. pl.* **fishwives** A very coarse, abusive woman.

fish-y (fish´ē) *adj.* Resembling fish, as in taste or odor; improbable; highly suspicious. **fishily** *adv.* **fishiness** *n.*

fis-sile (fis´il) *adv.* Capable of being separated or split into. *Physics* Fissionable. **fissility** *n.*

fis-sion (fish´an) *n.* The process or act of splitting into parts. *Physics* The exploding of the nucleus of an atom that leads to the formation of more stable atoms and the release of large quantities of energy. **fis-sionable** *adj.*

fis-si-ped (fis´i ped˝) *adj.* Having toes that are separated.

fis-sure (fish´ėr) *n.* A narrow opening, crack, or cleft in a rock. **fissure** *v.*

fist (fist) *n.* The hand closed tightly with the fingers bent into the palm. *Slang* The hand.

fist-fight *n.* A fight between two or more people without protection for the hands.

fist-ful *n. pl.* **fistfuls** A hand full.

fis-tu-la (fis´che la) *n. pl.* **fistulas** *or* **fistulae** *Pathol.* A duct or other passage formed by the imperfect closing of a wound or abscess and leading either to the body surface or to another hollow organ. **fistulous** *adj.*

fit (fit) *v.* To be the proper size and shape; to be in good physical condition; to possess the proper qualifications; to be competent; to provide a time or place for something; to belong. *adj.* Adapted or adequate for a particular circumstance or purpose. *Med.* A convulsion; an impulsive and irregular exertion or action. **fitter, fitness** *n.*

fitch (fich) *n.* The polecat of the Old World or its fur.

fit-ful (fit´ful) *adj.* Characterized by irregular actions; capricious; restless. **fitfully** *adv.* **fitfulness** *n.*

fit-ter *n.* One who or that which fits; one who fits or alters garments; one who puts together the parts of machinery; a person who installs fittings or fixtures; one who outfits or supplies.

fit-ting (fit´ing) *adj.* Suitable or proper. *n.* The act of trying on clothes for alteration; a piece of equipment or an appliance used in an adjustment. **fittingly** *adv.*

five (fiv) *n.* The cardinal number equal to 4 + 1; any symbol of this number, as 5; anything with five units, parts, or members. **five** *adj.& pron.*

five–and–ten *n.* A store that sells inexpensive items; formally selling items either at 5¢ or 10¢. Also **five and dime.**

five–star *adj.* Of first or top class; of the best quality.

fix (fiks) *v.* To make stationary, firm, or stable; to direct or hold steadily; to place or set definitely; to make rigid; to arrange or adjust; to prepare, as a meal. *n.* A position of embarrassment or difficulty. *Naut.* The position of a ship determined by observations, radio, or bearings. *Slang* The injection of a narcotic, such as heroin. **fixing, fixed** *v.*

fix-a-tion (fik sā´shan) *n.* The act or state of being fixed; a strong, often unhealthy preoccupation. **fixate** *v.*

fix-a-tive (fik´sa tiv) *adj.* Serving to fix; making permmanent. *n.* Something that sets or fixes; a substance added to perfume to prevent rapid evaporation.

fixed (fikst) *adj.* Make permanent or firm; securely placed or fastened; firmly implanted. **fixedly** *adv.* **fixedness** *n.*

fixed asset *n.* An item of value having a relatively permanent nature, used in operating a business, but not intended to be converted to cash

fix-er (fik´sėr) *n.* A person who uses his influence to gain special privileges, or immunity from the law; one that adjusts matters by negotiations.

fix-ing (fik´sing) *n.* The act or process of one who or that which fixes; *pl. colloq.* appropriate accompaniments.

fix-i-ty (fik´si tē) *n.* The quality or state of being fixed or stable.

fix-ture (fiks´chėr) *n.* Anything that is fixed or installed, as a part or appendage of a house; any article of personal property affixed to reality to become a part of and governed by the law of real property.

fizz (fiz) *n.* A hissing or bubbling sound; effervescence; tiny gas bubbles. **fizz** *v.*

fiz-zle (fiz´l) *v.* To fail after making a promising start. *n.* A hissing or sputtering sound.

fizz-y (fiz´ē) *adj.* Bubbly.

Fl *or* **FL** *abbr.* Florida.

flab (flab) *n.* Excessive, loose, and flaccid body tissue. **flabby** *adj.* **flabbiness** *n.*

flab-ber-gast (flab´ėr gast) *v.* To astound; to amaze.

flab-by (flab´ē) *adj.* Hanging loosely; lacking firmness; week or feeble.

flac-cid (flak´sid) *adj.* Lacking resilience or firmness. **flaccidity** *n.* **flaccidly** *adv.*

flac-on (flak´on) *n.* A small, stoppered decorative bottle.

flag (flag) *n.* A piece of cloth, usually oblong, bearing distinctive colors and designs to designate a nation, state, city, or organization. *Bot.* Any of various iris or cattail plants with long-blade-shaped leaves. *v.* To mark with or adorn with flags for identification or ornamentation; to grow weak or tired.

Flag Day *n.* June 14, 1777, the day on which Congress proclaimed the Stars and Stripes the national standard of the United States.

flag-el-lant (flaj´e lant) *n.* One who whips himself or has himself whipped by another for religious motives or for sexual excitement. **flagellation** *n.*

flag-el-late (flaj´e lāt´) *v.* To punish by whipping; to scourge.

flag-eo-let (flaj˝o let´) *n.* A small flutelike wind instrument, with a tubular mouthpiece, and six or more holes.

flag-ging (flag´ing) *adj.* Weakening; declining; becoming progressively weaker.

flag-man (flag´man) *n.* A person who signals with or as with a flag.

flag of truce *n.* *Milit.* A white flag carried to indicate a desire for a conference or parley with the enemy.

flag-on (flag´on) *n.* A vessel or container with a handle, spout, and hinged lid, used for holding wines or liquors.

flag-pole (flag´pōl´) *n.* The pole on which a flag is displayed.

flag rank *n.* A naval rank above captain.

fla-grant (flā´grant) *adj.* Obvious; glaring; disgraceful; notorious; outrageous. **flagrance** *n.* **flagrancy** *n.* **flagrantly** *adv.*

flag-ship (flag´ship˝) *n.* The ship which carries commander and displays his flag.

flag-stone (flag´stōn˝) *n.* A flat stone used for paving.

flag–wav-ing (flag´wā˝ving) *n.* An overly passionate appeal or sentimental show of one's devotion to a country or a cause.

flair (flâr) *n.* An aptitude or talent for something; a dashing style.

flak (flak) *n.* Antiaircraft fire; abusive or excessive criticism.

flake (flāk) *n.* A small, flat, thin piece which has split or peeled off from a surface. *Slang* Odd-ball; eccentric. **flake** *v.* **flakily** *adv.* **flakiness** *n.* **flaky** *adj.*

flak-y (flā´kē) *adj.* Consisting of flakes; flakelike. **flakily,** *adv.* **flakiness,** *n.*

flam-bé (flām bā) *adj., Cooking.* Served with flaming liquor.

flam-boy-ant (flam boi´ant) *adj.* Extravagantly ornate; showy; florid; brilliant and rich in color. **flamboyance** *n.* **flamboyancy** *n.* **flamboyantly** *adv.*

flame (flām) *n.* A mass of burning vapor or gas rising from a fire, often having a bright color and forming a tongue-shaped area of light; something that resembles a flame in motion, intensity, or appearance; a bright, red-yellow color; violent and intense emotion or passion. *Slang* A sweetheart. **flaming, flamed, flame** *v.*

fla-men-co (flā meng´kō) *n.* A fiery percussive dance of the Andalusian gypsies with strong and often improvised rhythms.

flame-out (flām´out´) *n.* The combustion failure of a jet aircraft engine while in flight.

flame-proof (flām´prōf´) *adj.* Resistent to flames or burning.

flame-throw-er (flām´thrō˝ėr) *n.* A weapon or device that shoots a stream of flaming fuel.

fla-min-go (fla ming´gō) *n.* A large, long-necked, tropical wading bird, having very long legs, and pink or red plumage.

flam-ma-ble (flam´a bl) *adj.* Capable of catching fire and burning rapidly. **flammability** *n.* **flammable** *n.*

flange (flanj) *n.* A projecting rim or collar used to strengthen or guide a wheel or other object, keeping it on a fixed track.

flank (flangk) *n.* The fleshy part between the ribs and the hip on either side of the body of an animal or human being; the lateral part of something. *Milit.* The right or left side of a military bastion or formation. *v.* To be stationed at the side of something. **flanker** *n.*

flan-nel (flan´el) *n.* A woven fabric made of wool or a wool, cotton, or synthetic blend.

flan-nels *n. pl.* Trousers made of flannel. **flannelly** *adj.*

flan-nelet-te *n.* Cotton flannel.

flap (flap) *v.* To move up and down; to cause to swing or sway loosely; to strike with something flexible. To sway or swing loosely, as in the wind; to flutter; to beat or strike a blow with something broad and flexible.

flap-doo-dle (flap´dödel) *n., Slang.* Nonsense.

flap-jack *n.* A griddlecake.

flap-per (flap´er) *n.* A young woman of the 1920's whose dress and behavior were considered unconventional; a young bird not yet able to fly.

flare (flâr) *v.* To blaze up or burn with a bright light; to break out suddenly or violently, as with emotion or action; to open or spread outward. **flaring, flared** *v.,*

flare-back *n.* A blast of flame, back or out in an opposite direction from the normal operation.

flare-up (flâr´up˝) *n.* A sudden bursting or an abrupt outburst of anger; a sudden outbreak of disease.

flash (flash) *v.* To burst forth repeatedly or suddenly into a brilliant fire or light; to occur or appear briefly or suddenly. *n.* A short and important news break or transmission. **flashed, flashing** *v.*

flash-back (flash´bak´) *n.* The interruption in the continuity of a story, motion picture, drama, or novel to give a scene that happened earlier.

flash bulb *n.* An electric flash lamp used to illuminate briefly a subject that is being photographed.

flash card *n.* A card printed with numbers or words and displayed briefly as a learning drill.

flash flood *n.* A violent and sudden flood occurring after a heavy rain.

flash-ing *n.* Sheet metal used to cover and waterproof the angle between a chimney and roof. **flashingly** adv.

flash-light (flash´līt˝) *n.* A sudden bright light used in taking photographic pictures; a small, portable electric light.

flash-o-ver (flash´ō˝vėr) *n.* A disruptive abnormal electrical discharge through the air or around the surface of a liquid.

flash point *n.* The lowest temperature at which the vapor of a combustible liquid will ignite or burn.

flash-y (flash´ē) *adj.* Showing brilliance for a moment; tastelessly showy; gaudy. **flashily** adv. **flashiness** *n.*

flask (flask) *n.* A small container made of glass and used in laboratories.

flat (flat) *adj.* Extending horizontally with no curvature or tilt; stretched out level, prostrate or prone; lacking flavor or zest; deflated. *Mus.* Below the correct pitch. *n.* An apartment that is entirely on one floor of a building. **flat broke** Having little or no money. **to fall flat** Failing to achieve. **flatly** adv. **flatness** *n.*

flat-bed *n.* A truck that has a shallow rear platform without sides.

flat-boat (flat´bōt˝) *n.* A large flat-bottomed boat with square ends, used to transport freight in shallow water.

flat-car (flat´kär˝) *n.* A railroad car having no roof or sides.

flat-foot (flat´fet˝) *n. pl.* -feet A condition in which the arch of the foot is flat. *Slang* A police officer. **flatfooted** *adj.*

flat–hat *v., Slang.* To fly a plane recklessly; to fly dangerously low. **flat–hatter** *n.*

flat–out *adv.* In a direct way; at top speed. *adj.* Out-and-out.

flat-ten (flat´en) *v.* To make flat; to knock down. **flattener** *n.*

flat-ter (flat´ėr) *v.* To praise extravagantly, especially without sincerity; to gratify the vanity of; to portray favorably; to show as more attractive. **flatterer** *n.* **flattering**

adj. **flatteringly** *adv.*

flat-ter-y (flat´e rē) *n.* Excessive, often insincere compliments.

flat-top (flat´top˝) *n.* A United States aircraft carrier; a short haircut having a flat crown.

flat-u-lent (flach´u lent) *adj.* Marked by or affected with gases generated in the intestine or stomach; pretentious without real worth or substance. **flatulence** *n.* **flatulently** *adv.*

flat-ware (flat´wâr˝) *n.* Tableware that is fairly flat and designed usually of a single piece, as plates; table utensils, as knives, forks, and spoons.

flat-wise *adv.* With the flat side or surface presented, instead of the edge, in an expressed position.

flaunt (flont) *v.* To display showily. **flaunting** *v.*, **flaunter** *n.* **flauntingly** *adv.*

flau-tist (flo´tist) *n.* A flutist.

fla-vor (flā´vėr) *n.* A distinctive element in the taste of something; a distinctive, characteristic quality; a flavoring. *v.* To impart flavor to. **flavorful, flavorsome** *adj.*

fla-vor-ing (flā´vėr ing) *n.* A substance, as an extract or something else that is used to increase the flavor.

flaw (flo) *n.* A defect or blemish that is often hidden and that may cause failure under stress; a weakness in character; a fault in a legal paper that may nullify it. **flaw** *v.*

flaw-less *adj.* Without flaws or defects; perfect. **flawlessly** *adv.* **flawlessness** *n.*

flax (flaks) *n.* A plant with blue flowers, seeds that yield linseed oil, and slender stems from which a fine textile fiber is derived.

flax-en *adj.* Made of or pertaining to flax; pale yellow or golden as flax fiber.

flay (flā) *v.* To remove the skin of; to scold harshly.

flea (flē) *n.* A small, wingless, bloodsucking, parasitic jumping insect; a parasite of warm-blooded animals.

flea-bane *n.* A popular name for composite plants once believed to drive away fleas.

flea–bitten (flē´bit´en) *adj.* Bitten or covered by fleas. *Slang* Shabby.

fleam (flēm) *n., Surg.* A sharp instrument used in surgery for opening veins.

flea market *n.* A place where antiques and used items and goods are sold.

fleck (flek) *n.* A tiny spot or streak; a small flake or bit. *v.* To mark with flecks.

fledg-ling *or* **fledge-ling (flej´ling)** *n.* A young bird with newly acquired feathers; a person who is inexperienced; a beginner.

flee (flē) *v.* To run away; to move swiftly away. **fleeing** *v.* **fleer** *n.*

fleece (flēs) *n.* A coat of wool covering a sheep; the soft wool covering a sheep. *v.* To shear the fleece from; to swindle; to cover with fleece. **fleecer, fleeciness** *n.* **fleecily** *adv.* **fleecy** *adj.*

fleer (flēr) *v.* To laugh or grimace in a coarsely or mockingly manner; jeer. **fleeringly** *adv.*

fleet (flēt) *n.* A number of warships operating together under the same command; a number of vehicles, as taxicabs or fishing boats, operated under one command. *adj.* Moving rapidly or nimbly. **fleetly** *adv.* **fleetness** *n.*

fleet admiral *n.* The highest rank in the U.S. Navy with an insignia of five stars.

fleet-ing (flē´ting) *adj.* Passing swiftly or rapidly. **fleetingly** *adv.* **fleetingness** *n.*

flesh (flesh) *n.* Soft tissue of the body of a human or animal, especially skeletal muscle; the meat of animals as distinguished from fish or fowl; the pulpy substance of a fruit or vegetable; the body as opposed to the mind or soul; mankind in general; one's family. *v.* To arouse the hunting instinct of dogs by feeding fresh meat.

flesh and blood *n.* Human nature together with its weaknesses; one biologically connected to another.

flesh color *n.* A creamy-pinkish color, used to resemble a Caucasian person's skin. **flesh–colored** *adv.*

flesh-er (flesh´ėr) *n.* A person who or a tool that removes flesh from hides.

flesh-ly (flesh´lē) *adj.* Of or pertaining to the body; sensual; worldly. **fleshliness** *n.*

flesh-pot (flesh´pot˝) *n.* A place were physical gratification is received.

flesh-y (flesh´ē) *adj.* Of, resembling, or suggestive of flesh; firm and pulpy; juicy as fruit. **fleshiness** *n.*

fletch *v.* To equip with a feather, as an arrow.

fleur-de-lis (fler˝de lē´) *n.* *pl.* **fleurs-de-lis** A heraldic emblem consisting of a three- petaled iris, at one time used as the armorial emblem of French sovereigns; the emblem of Quebec Province.

flew *v.* Past tense of fly.

flex (fleks) *v.* To bend the arm repeatedly; to contract a muscle. **flexing, flexed** *v.*

flex-i-ble (flek´si bl) *adj.* Capable of being bent or flexed; pliable; responsive to change; easily yielding. **flexibility** *n.* **flexibly** *adv.*

flex-or (flek´sėr) *n.* A muscle that serves to bend a body joint.

flex time *n.* A system which allows employees to set their own work schedules within a wide range of hours.

flex-ure (flek´shėr) *n.* The state of being flexed or bent; a bent part. **flexural** *adj.*

flick (flik) *n.* A light, quick snapping movement or the sound accompanying it. *v.* To strike or hit with a quick, light stroke; to cause to move with a quick movement. *Slang* A movie.

flick-er (flik´ėr) *v.* To burn or shine unsteadily, as a candle. *n.* A wavering or unsteady light; a North American woodpecker having a brownish back and a spotted breast. **flickering** *v.*

fli-er *or* **fly-er (flī´ėr)** *n.* One who or that which flies, especially an aviator; a daring or risky venture; a printed advertisement or handbill for mass distribution.

flight (flīt) *n.* The act or manner of flying; a scheduled airline trip; a group that flies together; a swift or rapid passage or movement, as of time; a group of stairs leading from one floor to another; an instance of fleeing.

flight attendant *n.* A person employed to assist passengers on an aircraft.

flight bag *n.* A lightweight piece of luggage having flexible sides and outside pockets.

flight deck *n.* The uppermost deck of an aircraft carrier, serving as a runway for airplanes. *Aeron.* The forward compartment of some aircraft.

flight engineer *n.* An airplane crew member responsible for the mechanical performance of the aircraft while in flight.

flight path *n.* *Aeron.* The path made or followed by an airborne airplane, guided missile, or a spacecraft in flight.

flight-y (flī´tē) *adj.* Inclined to act in a fickle fashion; marked by irresponsible behavior, impulse, or whim; easily excited, skittish; moved by sudden and irrational whims; given to flights of fancy; fickle; capricious; slightly delirious or light-headed; mildly crazy. **flightiness** *n.*

flim-flam (flim´flam´) *n., Slang* A swindle; trick; hoax. **flimflam** *v.*

flim-sy (flim´zē) *adj.* Lacking in physical strength or substance; unconvincing. **flimsiness** *n.* **flimsily** *adv.*

flinch (flinch) *v.* To wince or pull back, as from pain; to draw away. **flincher** *n.*

flin-ders *n. pl.* Fragments; splinters.

fling (fling) *v.* To throw or toss violently; to throw oneself completely into an activity. *n.* An act of casting away; a casual attempt; a period devoted to self-indulgence; unrestraint.

flint (flint) *n.* A hard quartz that produces a spark when struck by steel; an implement used by primitive man; an alloy used in lighters to ignite the fuel. **flinty** *adj.*

flint corn *n.* Indian corn, with a thick, hard, horny wall kernels.

flint glass *n.* A heavy brilliant, lustrous glass that contains lead oxide and used chiefly for optical lenses.

flint-y (flin´tē) *adj.* Consisting or composed of flint; very hard; resembling flint.

flip (flip) *v.* To turn or throw suddenly with a jerk; to strike or snap quickly and lightly.

Slang To go crazy; to become upset or angry; to react enthusiastically. **flip** *n.* **flipper** *adj.*

flip–flop (flip´flop˝) *n.* The sound or motion of something flapping loosely; a backward somersault; a sudden reversal of direction or point of view; an electronic device or a circuit capable of assuming either of two stable states.

flip-pant (flip´ant) *adj.* Marked by or showing disrespect, impudence, or the lack of seriousness. **flippancy** *n.* **flippantly** *adv.*

flip-per (flip´er) *n.* A broad flat limb, as of a seal, adapted for swimming; a paddle-like rubber shoe used by skin divers and other swimmers.

flip side *n.* The reverse or opposite side.

flirt (flert) *v.* To make teasing romantic or sexual overtures; to act so as to attract attention; to move abruptly; to dart. *n.* A person who flirts; a snappy, quick, jerky movement. **flirtation, flirtatiousness** *n.* **flirtatious** *adj.*

flit (flit) *v.* To move rapidly or abruptly.

flit-ter (flit´er) *v.* To flutter. **flitter** *n.*

float (flōt) *n.* An act or instance of floating; something that floats on the surface of or in a liquid; a device used to buoy the baited end of a fishing line; a floating platform anchored near a shoreline, used by swimmers or boats; a vehicle with a platform used to carry an exhibit in a parade; a drink consisting of ice cream floating in a beverage. *v.* To be or cause to be suspended within or on the surface of a liquid; to be or cause to be suspended in or move through the air as if supported by water; to drift randomly from place to place; to move lightly and easily; to place a security on the market; to obtain money for the establishment or development of an enterprise by issuing and selling securities. **floating** *v.* **floatable** *adj.* **floater** *n.*

float-a-tion (flō tā´shan) *n.* Flotation.

float-er (flō´ter) *n.* One that which floats; one without a permanent residence or employment. An insurance that insures household or personal property, while in transit.

floating dock *n.* A floating dock for a ship, that can be lowered to allow a ship to enter and then raised to keep the ship above water.

floating island *n.* A mass of earth and vegetation that floats on the surface of water and resembles an island; a custard dessert topped with meringue.

floating rib *n.* One of the four lower ribs in the human being that are not attached to the other ribs.

float-plane (flōt´plān˝) *n., Aeron.* A sea airplane equipped with buoyant landing gear.

flock (flok) *n.* A group of animals of all the same kind, especially birds, sheep, geese, etc., living, feeding or kept together; a group under the direction of a single person, especially the members of a church; a large number. *v.* To travel as if in a flock.

floe (flō) *n.* A large, flat mass of floating ice or a detached part of such a mass.

flog (flog) *v.* To beat hard with a whip or stick. **flogger** *n.*

flood (flud) *n.* The great deluge depicted in the Old Testament; an overflow of water onto land that is normally dry; an overwhelming quantity. *v.* To overwhelm with or as if with a flood; to fill abundantly or overwhelm; to supply the carburetor of an engine with an excessive amount of fuel; in football, to send more than one pass receiver into the same defensive area.

flood-gate (flud´gāt´) *n.* A valve for controlling the flow or depth of a large body of water.

flood-light (flud´līt´) *n.* An electric lamp that gives off a broad and intensely bright beam of light. **floodlight** *v.*

flood plain *n.* Level land along the course of a stream or river that was formed by soil deposited by floods, may be submerged by floodwaters.

flood tide *n.* The rising tide; an enormous amount.

flood–water *n.* The water from a flood.

floor (flōr) *n.* The level base of a room; the lower inside surface of a structure; a ground surface; the right, as granted under parliamentary rules, to speak to a meeting or assembly; an area dividing a building into stories. *v.* To cover or furnish with a floor; to knock down; to overwhelm; to puzzle; to press the accelerator of a vehicle to the floorboard.

floor-age (flōr´ij) *n.* The total floor space in a building **flooring**

floor-board (flōr´bōrd´) *n.* A board in a floor; the floor of an automobile.

floor exercise *n.* A competitive gymnastics event with tumbling maneuvers performed on a mat.

floor lamp *n.* A lamp with a base that rests on the floor.

floor show *n.* Entertainment consisting of singing, dancing; nightclub acts.

floor-walk-er(flōr´wo´kėr)*n.* A department store employee who supervises the sales force and gives assistance to customers.

floo-zy (flō´zē) *n. pl.* **floozies** *Slang* A sleazy, loose woman; a prostitute.

flop (flop) *v.* To fall down clumsily; to move about in a clumsy way. *Slang* To completely fail; to go to bed. **flop** *n.*

flop house (flop´hous´) *n.* A cheap, rundown hotel.

flop-o-ver (flop´ō´vėr) *n.* Defective television reception in which the picture continually crosses the screen in a vertically direction.

flop-py (flop´ē) *adj.* Flexible and loose. **floppily** *adv.,* **floppiness** *n.*

floppy disk *n.* In computer science, a flexible plastic disk coated with magnetic material, used to record and store computer data.

flo-ra (flōr´a) *n. pl.* **floras** *or* **florae** Plants growing in a specific region or season.

flo-ral (flōr´al) *adj.* Of or pertaining to flowers.

flo-res-cence (flō res´ens) *n.* A state or process of blossoming. **florescent** *adj.*

flor-id (flōr´id) *adj.* Flushed with a rosy color or redness; ornate. **floridness** *n.*

floridly *adv.*

Flor-ida *n.* A state located on the southeastern coast of the United States, statehood March 3, 1845, state capital Tallahassee.

Florida moss *n.* A type of Spanish moss that usually hangs from tree branches.

flo-rif-er-ous *adj.* Producing flowers; blooming.

flo-rist (flōr´ist) *n.* One who grows or sells flowers and also artificial ones made of silk or silk-like fibers.

flo-ris-tics *n.* A branch of the science dealing with the distribution and study of plants upon the earth.

floss (flos) *n.* A loosely-twisted embroidery thread; a soft,silky fiber, such as the tassel on corn; dental floss. *v.* To clean between the teeth with dental floss. **flossed, flossing** *v.*

flo-ta-tion (flō tā´shan) *n.* The act or state of floating.

flo-til-la (flō til´a) *n.* A fleet of small vessels; a group resembling a small fleet.

flot-sam (flot´sam)*n.* Any goods remaining afloat after a ship has sunk.

flounce (flouns) *n.* A gathered piece of material attached to the upper edge of another surface, as on a curtain. *v.* To move with exaggerated tosses of the body. **flouncy** *adj.*

floun-der (floun´dėr) *v.* To struggle clumsily, as to gain footing; to act or speak in a confused way. *n.* Any of various edible marine flatfish. **floundering** *v.*

flour (flour) *n.* A soft, fine, powder-like substance obtained by grinding the meal of grain, especially wheat. *v.* To coat or sprinkle with flour. **flourly** *adj.*

flour-ish (flėr´ish) *v.* To thrive; to fare well; to prosper and succeed. *n.* A decorative touch or stroke, especially in handwriting; a dramatic act or gesture; a musical fanfare, as of trumpets. **flourished, flourishing** *v.*

flout (flout) *v.* To have or show open contempt for. **floutingly** *adv.*

flow (flō) *v.* To move freely, as a fluid; to

circulate, as blood; to proceed or move steadily and easily; to rise; to derive; to be abundant in something; to hang in a loose, free way. **flow** *n.*

flow-age (flō´ij) *n.* An overflowing; a flooded condition; floodwater.

flow chart *n.* A diagram that shows the progress of a series of operations on a particular project.

flow-er (flou´ėr) *n.* A cluster of petals, bright in color, near or at the tip of a seed-bearing plant; blossoms; the condition of highest development; the peak; the best example or representative of something. *v.* To produce flowers; to bloom; to develop fully.

flow-er-age (flou´ėr ij) *n.* The process, or state of flowering; flowers collectively; floral or decoration.

flow-er-et (flou´ėr it) *n.* A small flower; a floret.

flower girl *n.* A young girl who carries and sometimes scatters flowers at a wedding.

flow-er-pot (flou´ėr pot˝) *n.* A container in which to grow plants.

flow-er-y (flou´e rē) *adj.* Relating to flowers, as a fragrance. **flowerily,** *adv.*

flow-ing (flō´ing) *adj.* Moving at a smooth steady pace; moving with ease; smoothly and gracefully, having a bountiful supply. **flowingly** *adv.* **flowingness** *n.*

fl oz *abbr.* Fluid ounce.

flu (flō) *n., Informal* Influenza.

flub (flub) *v.* To bungle or botch; to make a mess of. **flub** *n.*

fluc-tu-ant *adj.* Unstable; in a state of constant change; fluctuating. *Med.* Of a boil or abscess, having a compressible semiliquid of which the center requires lancing.

fluc-tu-ate (fluk´chŏ āt´) *v.* To shift irregularly; to change; to undulate.

flue (flō) *n.* A conduit or passage through which air, gas, steam, or smoke can pass.

flu-ent (flō´ent) *adj.* Having an understanding of a language use; flowing smoothly and naturally; flowing or capable of flowing. **fluency** *n.* **fluently** *adv.*

flue pipe *n.* An organ pipe in which the tone is produced by air current that strikes the lip and causing the air inside to vibrate.

fluff (fluf) *n.* A ball, tuft, or light cluster of loosely gathered fibers of cotton or wool. *Slang* A mistake made by an actor or announcer in reading or announcing something. *v.* To make or become fluffy by patting with the hands. *Informal* To make an error in speaking or reading.

flu-id (flō´id) *n.* A substance, as water or gas, capable of flowing. *adj.* Changing readily, as a liquid. **fluidity, fluidness** *n.* **fluidly** *adv.*

fluid ounce *n.* A United States unit of liquid capacity that is equal to one-sixteenth pint.

fluke (flōk) *n.* A flatfish, especially a flounder; a flattened, parasitic trematode worm; the triangular head of an anchor at the end of either of its arms; a barb or point on an arrow; an unexpected piece of good luck. **fluky** *adj.*

flung *v.* Past tense of fling.

flunk (flungk) *v., Slang* To fail in, as an examination or course; to give a failing grade to. **flunking, flunked** *v.*

flun-ky *or* **flun-key (flung´kē)** *n.* A liveried servant; a person who does menial work.

flu-o-res-cence (flō˝o res´ens) *n., Chem. Phys.* Emission of electromagnetic radiation, especially of visible light, resulting from and occurring during the absorption of radiation from another source; the radiation emitted. **fluorescence** *v.* **fluorescent** *adj.*

fluorescent lamp *n.* A tubular electric lamp in which ultraviolet light is reradiated as visible light.

fluor-i-date *v.* To add a sodium compound to water in order to prevent tooth decay. **fluoridating** *v.* **fluoridation** *n.*

fluor-i-da-tion (flür˝i dā´shan) *n.* The addition of fluoride to drinking water to help prevent tooth decay.

flu-o-ride (flō´o rīd˝) *n.* A compound of fluorine with another element or a radical.

flu-o-rine (flō´o rēn˝) *n.* A pale yellow, corrosive, and extremely reactive gaseous element, symbolized by F.

fluor-o-scope (fler´o skōp˝) *n.* A device for observing shadows projected upon a flourescent screen of an optically opaque object, as the human body, which may be viewed by transmission of x-rays through the object. **fluoroscope** *v.* **fluoroscopic** *adj.* **fluoroscopy** *n.*

flur-ry (flur´ē) *n. pl.* **flurries** A sudden gust of wind; a brief, light fall of snow or rain, accompanied by small gusts; a sudden burst of activity or commotion. **flurried** *adj.* **flurry** *v.*

flush (flush) *v.* To flow or rush out suddenly and abundantly; to become red in the face; to blush; to glow with a reddish color; to purify or wash out with a brief, rapid gush of water; to cause to flee from cover, as a game animal or bird. *n.* Glowing freshness or vigor; a hand in certain card games, as poker, in which all the cards are the same suit. *adj.* Having a heightened reddish color; abundant; affluent, prosperous; having surfaces that are even; arranged with adjacent sides close together; having margins aligned with no indentations; direct as a blow. *adv.* In an even position with another surface. **flushed, flushing** *v.*

flus-ter (flus´tėr) *v.* To make or become nervous or confused.

flute (flōt) *n.* A high-pitched, tubular woodwind instrument equipped with finger holes and keys; a decorative groove in the shaft of a column; a small grooved pleat, as in cloth. **fluting** *n.* **fluted** *adj.*

flut-ist *n.* A flute player.

flut-ter (flut´ėr) *v.* To flap or wave rapidly and irregularly; to fly as with a light, rapid beating of the wings; to beat erratically, as one's heart; to move about in a restless way. **flutter** *n.* **fluttery** *adj.*

flutter kick *n.* An alternate kicking motion in swimming.

flux (fluks) *n.* A flowing or discharge; a constant flow or movement; a state of constant fluctuation or change; a substance that promotes the fusing of metals and prevents oxide formation. *v.* To make fluid; to melt; to apply a flux to.

fly (flī) *v.* To move through the air on wings or wing-like parts; to travel by air; to float or cause to float in the air; to escape; to flee; to pass by swiftly or quickly; to hit a fly ball. *n.* A folded piece of cloth that covers the fastening of a garment, especially trousers; a fly ball one has batted over the field; any of numerous winged insects, including the housefly and the tsetse; a fishing lure that resembles an insect. **fly off the handle** To react explosively. **flyable** *adj.*

fly agaric *n.* A poisonous mushroom,

fly-away (flī´a wā˝) *adj.* Fluttering; flighty.

fly-boy *n., Slang.* A pilot of the United States Air Force.

fly–by–night (flī´bī nīt˝) *adj.* Unstable or temporary; financially unsound.

fly-catch-er *n. Ornith.* A singing, perching birds, that feeds on insects caught in flight.

fly-er *n. Var.* of flier.

fly-ing *adj.* Moving through the air; moving rapidly; capable for flight.

flying colors *n. pl.* Complete excellence.

flying machine *n.* A powered aircraft apparatus for navigating, an early type of plane.

flying saucer *n.* An unidentified, flying disk-shaped or saucer-shaped, airborne object reported as seen in the air.

flying squirrel *n.* A nocturnal squirrel of North America, with folds of skin connecting the fore and hind legs which enables it to make gliding leaps.

fly-leaf (flī´lēf˝) *n.* A blank page or end paper of a book.

fly-o-ver (flī´ō˝vėr) *n.* A low-altitude flyover of aircraft; the act of flying over the earth by one or more aircraft. *Brit.* A highway overpass.

fly-pa-per *n.* A paper coated with a sticky often poisonous substance which kills flies.

fly-speck (flī´spek˝) *n.* A speck from the

excrement of a fly; a minute spot; *fig.* Something small and insignificant.

fly-trap *n.* A trap to catch flies.

fly-weight (fli´wāt´) *n.* A boxer who belongs to the lightest weight class, weighing 112 pounds or less.

fly-wheel (fli´hwēl´) *n.* A rotating wheel heavy enough to regulate the speed of a machine shaft.

FM *abbr.* Frequency modulation.

foal (fōl) *n.* The young animal, as a horse, especially one under a year old. *v.* To give birth to a foal.

foam (fōm) *n.* A mass of bubbles produced on the surface of a liquid by agitation; froth; a firm, spongy material used especially for insulation and upholstery. *v.* To cause to form foam. **foam at the mouth** To be very angry. **foaminess, foamy** *adj.*

foam rubber *n.* A spongy rubber, of fine texture which is whipped prior to vulcanization, used in pillows and mattresses.

fob (fob) *n.* A chain or ribbon attached to a pocket watch and worn dangling from a pocket; an ornament or seal worn on a fob. *v.* To dispose of by fraud, deceit, or trickery; to put off by excuse.

f.o.b. *n.* Freight On Board, an agreement that shipping charges on goods purchased and placed aboard a common freight carrier will be paid by the seller after the merchandise is delivered. Also **F.O.B.**

focal infection *n. Pathol.* A persistent bacterial infection, localized in an area or organ which may enter the bloodstream and cause symptoms in other parts of the body.

focal length *n.* The distance to the focus from a lens surface or concave mirror.

fo-cus (fō´kus) *n. pl.* **focuses** *or* **foci** A point in an optical system at which rays converge or from which they appear to diverge; the clarity with which an optical system delivers an image; adjustment for clarity; a center of activity or interest *v.* To produce a sharp, clear image of; to adjust a lens in order to produce a clean image; to direct; to come together at a point of focus. **focal** *adj.* **focally** *adv.*.

fod-der (fod´ėr) *n.* A coarse feed for livestock, made from chopped stalks of corn and hay.

foe (fō) *n.* An enemy in war; an opponent or adversary.

foe-tal (fēt´al) *adj. Var.* of fetal.

foe-tus (fē´tus) *n. Var.* of fetus.

fog (fog) *n.* A vapor mass of condensed water which lies close to the ground; a state of mental confusion or bewilderment. *v.* To obscure or cover with, as if with fog. **foggily** *adv.* **fogginess** *n.* **foggy** *adj.*

fog bank *n.* A distant mass of fog.

fog-horn (fog´horn´) *n.* A horn sounded in fog to give warning.

fo-gy *or* **fo-gey (fō´gē)** *n.* A person with old-fashioned attitudes and ideas.

foi-ble (foi´bl) *n.* A minor flaw, weakness, or failing.

foil (foil) *v.* To prevent from being successful; to thwart. *n.* A very thin, flexible sheet of metal; one that serves as a contrast; a fencing sword having a light, thin, flexible blade and a blunt point. **foiled, foiling** *v.*

foist (foist) *v.* To pass off something as valuable or genuine.

fold (fōld) *v.* To double or lay one part over another; to bring from an opened to a closed position; to put together and intertwine; to envelop or wrap; to blend in by gently turning one part over another. *Slang* To give in; to stop production; to fail in business. *n.* A line, layer, pleat or crease formed by folding; a folded edge; an enclosed area for domestic animals; a flock of sheep; a people united by common aims and beliefs; a church and its members. **folding, folded** *v.*

fold-a-way (fōld´a wā´) *adj.* Designed to be folded and put out of the way.

fold-er (fōl´dėr) *n.* One that folds; a folded page as a circular; a protective covering, for loose papers.

fol-de-rol (fol´de ro˝´) *n.* Nonsense; a pretty but useless ornament.

folding door *n.* A door made of hinged sections that can be folded together.

fo-li-age (fō´lē ij) *n.* The leaves of growing plants and trees; a cluster of flowers and branches.

fo-li-o (fō´lē ō´) *n.* A large sheet of paper folded once in the middle; a folder for loose papers; a book that consists of folios; a page number.

folk (fōk) *n.* *pl.* **folk** *or* **folks** An ethnic group of people forming a nation or tribe; people of a specified group. A person's parents, family, or relatives.

folk dance *n.* A dance originated among the common people of a country.

folk-lore *n.* The traditional customs, beliefs, and songs of a group of people that are handed down from generation to generation in the form of stories. **folklorist,** *n.* **folkloric, folkloristic,** *adj.*

folk song *n.* A traditional song of a nation, sung by local people, usually in a number of different versions, melodies and repetitive verses.

folk tale *n.* A traditional anonymous and placeless legend originating and passed down orally from one generation to another.

fol-li-cle (fol´i kl) *n.* A small anatomical cavity or sac.

fol-low (fol´ō) *v.* To proceed or come after; to pursue; to follow the course of; to obey; to come after in time or position; to ensue; to result; to attend to closely; to understand the meaning of. **following, followed** *v.*

follow out *v.* To carry to a conclusion; to follow to the end.

follow through *v.* To extend or carry through, as the part of the stroke after the ball has been hit; to pursue an activity, esp. to completion.

follow up *n.* The act of following up; a letter sent to enhance a previous communication or notice. *v.* To pursue closely to a conclusion.

fol-ly (fol´ē) *n.* *pl.* **follies** Lack of good judgment; an instance of foolishness; an excessively costly and often unprofitable undertaking.

fo-ment (fō ment´) *v.* To rouse; to incite; to treat therapeutically with moist heat.

foment, fomentation *n.*

fond (fond) *adj.* Affectionate liking; cherished with great affection; deeply felt. **fondly** *adv.* **fondness** *n.*

fon-dant (fon´dant) *n.* A sweet, soft preparation of sugar used in candies and icings; a candy made chiefly of fondant.

fon-dle (fon´dl) *v.* To stroke, handle, or caress affectionately and tenderly. **fondled, fondling** *v.*

fond-ly (fond´lē) *adv.* In an affectionately manner.

fon-due (fon dō) *n.* A preparation of melted cheese, with white wine; a dish consisting of small pieces of food dipped into hot liquid.

font (font) *n.* A receptacle in a church that holds baptismal or holy water; an assortment of printing type of the same size and face.

food (fōd) *n.* A substance consisting essentially of carbohydrates and protein used to sustain life and growth in the body of an organism; nourishment, as in solid form; something that sustains or nourishes. **food for thought** Something to think about, something to ponder.

food chain *n.* A sequence of plants and animals in which each uses the next usu. smaller or lower member as a food source.

food poisoning *n.* An acute gastrointestinal ailment caused by bacteria or toxic products produced by the bacteria that contaminate food.

food-stuff (fōd´stuff´) *n.* A substance having food value.

fool (fōl) *n.* One lacking good sense or judgment; one who can easily be tricked or made to look foolish. *v.* To dupe; to act in jest; to joke. *Slang* To amuse oneself. **fooling** *v.*

fool-er-y (fō´le rē) *n.* Foolish conduct; a foolish action.

fool-ish (fō´lish) *adj.* Marked by lacking good sense; unwise. **foolishly** *adv.* **foolhardiness** *n.*

fool-proof *adj.* Infallible.

foot (fūt) *n.* *pl.* **feet** The lower extremity

of the vertebrate leg upon which one stands; a unit of measurement equal to 12 inches; a basic unit of verse meter that consists of a group of syllables; the end lower or opposite the head; the lowest part. *v.* To go on foot; to walk or run. To pay the bill. **on foot** Walking rather than riding.

foot-age *n.* Length expressed in feet; as the footage of a film; the total number of running feet; as newsreel footage.

foot-and-mouth disease *n.* A highly contagious febrile virus disease of cattle and other hooved animals marked by ulcerating blisters in the mouth, around the hooves, on the teats, and udder.

foot-ball (fŭt´bol) *n.* A game played by two teams on a long rectangular field having goals at either end whose object is to get the ball over a goal line or between goal posts by running, passing or kicking; the oval ball used in the game of football.

foot-board (fŭt´bōrd´) *n.* A small platform to support the feet; a board forming the upright piece across the foot of a bed.

foot-bridge (fŭt´brij´) *n.* A bridge for pedestrians.

foot-ed (fŭt´id) *adj.* Having a foot or feet; having a certain number of feet: esp. used in combination; as, a four-footed animal.

foot-fall (fŭt´fol´) *n.* A footstep; the sound of a footstep.

foot-gear (fŭt´gēr´) *n.* Articles used to cover and protect the feet, as shoes or boots.

foot-hill (fŭt´hil´) *n.* A low hill at or near the foot of a mountain or a higher hill.

foot-hold (fŭt´hōld´) *n.* A place providing support for the foot, as in climbing; a position usable as a base for advancement.

foot-ing (fŭt´ing) *n.* Secure and stable position for placement of the feet; a foundation.

foot-less *adj.* Without feet.

foot-lights *n. pl. Theatr.* A row of lights positioned acrossed the front of a stage. The theater as a profession.

foot-locker (fŭt´lok´ẽr) *n.* A small trunk for personal belongings, designed to be placed at the foot of a bed.

foot-loose (fŭt´lōs´) *adj.* Free to move as one pleases; having no ties.

foot-note (fŭt´nōt´) *n.* A note of reference, explanation, or comment usually below the text on a printed page; a commentary. **footnote** *v.*

foot-pace (fŭt´pās´) *n.* A walking pace; a stairway landing.

foot-pad (fŭt´pad´) *n.* A person who goes on foot and robs other pedestrians.

foot-path (fŭt´path´) *n.* A narrow path for people on foot.

foot-print (fŭt´print´) *n.* The outline or impression of the foot on a surface.

foot-rest (fŭt´rest´) *n.* A support for the feet used for resting the feet.

foot soldier *n.* An infantryman.

foot-sore (fŭt´sōr´) *adj.* Having sore or tender feet.

foot-stalk (fŭt´stok´) *n., Zool.* A supportive structure that resembles a stalk; *Bot.* A stem.

foot-step (fŭt´step´) *n.* A footprint; the distance covered by a step.

foot-stool (fŭt´stōl´) *n.* A low stool for resting the feet.

foot-wear (fŭt´wâr´) *n.* Articles, as shoes or boots, worn on the feet.

foot-work (fŭt´werk´) *n.* The use of the feet, as in boxing.

fop (fop) *n.* A man unduly concerned with his clothes or appearance; a dandy. **foppery, foppishness** *n.* **foppish** *adj.*

for (for) *prep.* Used to indicate the extent of something; used to indicate the number or amount of; considering the usual characteristics of; on behalf of someone; to be in favor of. *conj.* Because; in as much as; with the purpose of.

for-age (for´ij) *n.* Food for cattle or other domestic animals; a search for supplies or food. *v.* To make a raid so as to find supplies; to plunder or rummage through, especially in search of provisions.

for-as-much as *conj.* In view of the fact that; since.

for-ay (for´ā) *n.* A raid to plunder; act of war. **foray** *v.*

for-bade *or* **for-bad** *v.* Past tense of forbid.

for-bear (for´bâr´) *v.* To refrain from; to cease from. **forbearance** *n.*

for-bear-ance (for bâr´ans) *n.* The act of forbearing; a refraining from something; as a debt or obligation.

for-bid (fèr bid´) *v.* To command someone not to do something; to prohibit by law; to prevent.

for-bid-den *adj.* Prohibited; not permitted.

forbidden fruit *n., Bib.* Forbidden fruit of the tree of the knowledge of good and evil, in the Garden of Eden from which Adam and Eve partook; an illegal pleasure or immoral indulgence.

forbidding (fèr bid´ing) *adj.* Very difficult; disagreeable.

force (fōrs) *n.* Energy or power; strength; the use of such power; intellectual influence; a group organized for a certain purpose. *Phys.* Something that changes the state of rest or the body motion or influence. *v.* To compel to do something or to act; to obtain by coercion; to bring forth, as with effort; to move or drive against resistance; to break down by force; to press or impose, as one's will. **in force** In large numbers; in effect. **forceable, forceful** *adj.* **forcer** *n.,* **forcefully** *adv.*

force–feed *v.* To force food by employing force; to force to take.

force-meat (fōrs´mēt´) *n.* Finely ground meat, fish, or poultry, used in stuffing or served separately.

for-ceps (for´seps) *n.* *pl.* An instrument resembling a pair of tongs used for manipulating, grasping or extracting, especially in surgery.

force pump *n.* A pump which draws and forces a liquid by means of pressure or force directly applied, in contrast to a lift pump.

forc-i-ble (fōr´si bl) *adj.* Accomplished or achieved by force; marked by force. **forcibly** *adv.*

ford (fōrd) *n.* A shallow place in a body of water that can be crossed without a boat. *v.* To wade across a body of water.

Ford, Gerald Rudolph *n.* The 38th president of the United States, from 1974-1977.

Ford, Henry *n.* (1863-1947). American automobile maker.

for-do, fore-do (for dö) *v.* To overpower, or overcome.

fore (fōr) *adj. & adv.* Situated in, at, or toward the front; forward. *n.* The front of something. *interj.* A cry used by a golfer to warn others that a ball is about to land in their direction.

fore–and–aft (fōr´and aft´) *adj.* Lying or going lengthwise on a ship; from stem to stern.

fore-arm (fōr ärm´) *v.* To prepare in advance, as for a battle. *n.* The part of the arm between the elbow and the wrist.

fore-bear *or* **for-bear (fōr´bâr´)** *n.* An ancestor.

fore-bode (fōr bōd´) *v.* To give an indication or warning in advance; to have a premonition of something evil. **foreboding** *n.* **forbodingly** *adv.*

fore-brain (fōr´brān´) *n., Anat.* The anterior of the three primary divisions of the developing vertebrate brain, or the corresponding segments of the adult vertebrate brain.

fore-cast (fōr´kast´) *v.* To estimate or calculate in advance, especially to predict the weather. **forecast, forecaster** *n.*

fore-cas-tle (fōk´sal) *n.* The part of a ship's upper deck located forward of the foremast; living quarters for the crew at the bow of a merchant ship.

fore-close (fōr klōz´) *v.* To recall a mortgage in default and take legal possession of the mortgaged property; to exclude; to shut out. **foreclosure** *n.*

fore-clo-sure *n.* The act of foreclosing, esp. of foreclosing a mortgage.

fore-doom (fōr döm´) *n.* A predestination of doom or misfortune.

fore-fa-ther (fōr´fo´thèr) *n.* An ancestor.

fore-fin-ger (fōr´fing´gèr) *n.* The finger

next to the thumb.

fore-foot (fōr´fet´) *n.* A front foot of an animal, insect, etc.

fore-front (fōr´frunt) *n.* The foremost or very front of something; the vanguard.

fore-go (fōr gō´) *v.* To go before; to precede in time, place, etc. **foregoing** *v.*

fore-go-ing *adj.* Before; previous.

fore-gone (fōr gon´) *adj.* Already finished or gone.

foregone conclusion *n.* An inevitable result; a conclusion determined before argument or consideration of the evidence.

fore-ground (fōr´ground´) *n.* The part of a picture or landscape represented as nearest to the viewer.

fore-hand (fōr´hand´) *n.* A stroke in tennis in which the palm of the hand holding the racket faces toward the direction of the stroke. **forehand** *adj & adv.*

fore-head (for´id) *n.* The part of the face that is above the eyebrows and extends to the hair.

for-eign (for´in) *adj.* Situated outside one's native country; belonging to; located in or concerned with a country or region other than one's own; involved with other nations; occurring in a place or body in which it is not normally located.

foreign affairs *n.* Diplomatic, commercial, or any other matters having to do with international relations.

for-eign-er *n.* A person from a different place or country; an alien.

fore-know *v.* To have previous knowledge of; to know beforehand.

fore-knowl-edge (fōr´nol´ij) *n.* Prior knowledge of something; knowledge beforehand.

fore-leg *n.* A front or anterior legs, of an animal or chair.

fore-lock (fōr´lok´) *n.* A lock of hair growing from the front of the scalp and hanging over the forehead.

fore-man (fōr´man) *n.* The person who oversees a group of people; the spokesperson for a jury. **forewoman** *n.*

fore-mast (fōr´mast´) *n., Naut.* The forward mast of a sailing vessel; the mast nearest the bow of a ship.

fore-most (fōr´mōst´) *adj. & adv.* First in rank, position, time, or order.

fore-name *n.* The name that precedes the family surname; one's first name.

fore-noon (fōr´ nŏn´) *n.* The period between sunrise and noon.

fo-ren-sic (fo ren´sik) *adj.* Of, relating to, or used in courts of justice or formal debate. **forensically** *adv.*

forensic medicine *n.* A science dealing with the application of medicine in legal problems.

fore-or-dain (fōr´or dān´) *v.* Appoint or dispose of in advance; predestine.

fore-part (fōr´port´) *n.* The first or earliest part of a period of time.

fore-quar-ter *n.* The front portion of the body of an animal, as of lamb or beef.

fore-run-ner *n.* One sent or going before to give notice of the approach of others; a harbinger.

fore-said (fōr´sed´) *adj.* Spoken before; aforesaid.

fore-sail (fōr´sāl) *n., Naut.* The sail carried on the foremast of a square-rigged vessel.

fore-see (fōr sē´) *v.* To know or see beforehand. **foreseeable** *adj.* **foreseer** *n.*

fore-shad-ow (fōr shad´ō) *v.* To represent or warn of beforehand.

fore-shore (fōr´shōr´) *n.* The part of a shore uncovered at low tide.

fore-short-en (fōr´shor´ten) *v.* To shorten parts of an object in order to give the illusion of depth.

fore-sight (fōr´sīt´) *n.* The act or capacity of foreseeing; the act of looking forward; concern for the future; prudence. **foresighted** *adj.* **foresightedness** *n.*

fore-skin (fōr´skin´) *n.* A fold of skin that covers the glans of the penis.

for-est (for´ist) *n.* A large tract of land covered with trees; something resembling a forest, as in quantity or density. *v.* To cover with trees. **forested** *adj.* **forestland** *n.*

fore-stall (fōr stol´) *v.* To exclude, hinder, or prevent by prior measures.

forest ranger *n.* An officer in charge of

patrolling or protecting a public forest.

fore-taste (for tāst´) v. To sample or indicate beforehand. **foretasting, fortasted** v. **fore-taste** n.

fore-tell (fōr tel´) v. To tell about in advance; to predict. **fortelling** v. **foreteller** n.

fore-thought (fōr´thot´) n. Prior thought or planning; a plan for the future.

fore-to-ken (fōr tō´ken) v. To warn beforehand. **foretoken** n.

fore-top n., Naut. A platform at the head of a ship's foremast.

for-ev-er (for ev´ër) adv. For eternity; without end.

fore-warn (fōr worn´) v. To warn in advance. **forwarned** v.

fore-word (fōr´werd´) n. An introductory statement preceding the text of a book.

fore-yard n., Naut. The lower yard on the foremast.

for-feit (for´fit) n. Something taken away as punishment;a penalty; something that is placed in escrow and redeemed on payment of a fine; a forfeiture. v. To lose or give up the right to by some offense or error. **forfeiter** n. **forfeitable** adj.

for-fei-ture n. The act of forfeiting; something forfeited; a penalty.

for-gath-er (for gath´ër) v. To come together; to convene; to assemble. **forgathering, forgathered** v.

forge (fōrj) n. A furnace where metals are heated and wrought; a smithy; a workshop that produces wrought iron. v. To form by heating and hammering; to give shape to; to imitate falsely; to advance slowly but steadily; to defraud; to counterfeit. **forging, forged** v. **forger, forgery** n.

for-get (fër get´) v. To lose the memory of; to fail to become mindful or aware of at the right time. **forgetful** adj. **forgetable** adj. **forgetfully** adv. **forgetfulness** n.

for-give (fër giv´) v. To pardon; to give up resentment of; to cease to feel resentment against. **forgiveness** n. **forgivable** adj.

for-giv-ing adj. Disposed to forgive; inclined to overlook offenses; compassionate.

for-go or **fore-go (for gō´)** To give up or refrain from. **forgoer** n.

fork (fork) n. A tool consisting of a handle at one end of which are two or more prongs; the division of something into two or more parts that continue, as in a river or road.

forked (forkt) adj. Shaped like or having a fork.

fork-lift (fork´lift˝) n. A self-propelled industrial vehicle with a prolonged platform for hoisting and transporting heavy objects.

for-lorn (for lorn´) adj. Abandoned or left in distress; hopeless; being in a poor condition. **forlornly** adv. **forlornness** n.

form (form) n. The shape or contour of something; a body of a living being; the basic nature of or particular state of something; the way in which something exists; variety; manner, as established by custom or regulation; the style or manner determined by etiquette or custom; performance according to established criteria; fitness with regard to training or health; procedure of words, as in a ceremony; a document having blanks for insertion of information; style in musical or literary composition; the design or style of a work of art. v. To construct or conceive in the mind. suf. Having the form or shape of; cuneiform.

for-mal (for´mal) adj. Of or pertaining to the outward aspect of something; relating or concerned with the outward form of something; adhering to convention, rule, or etiquette; based on accepted conventions. **formally** adv.

for-mal-de-hyde (for mal´de hīd) n. A colorless, gaseous chemical used chiefly as a preservative and disinfectant in synthesizing other compounds.

for-mal-i-ty n. The condition or state of being formal; an established form that is required.

for-mat (for´mat) n. A general style of a publication; the general form or layout of a publication. v. In computer science, to produce data in a specified form.

for-ma-tion (for mā´shan) *n.* The act or proccess of forming or the state of being formed; the manner in which something is formed; a given arrangement, as of troops, as a square or in a column.

for-ma-tive (for´ma tiv) *adj.* Forming or having the power to form; of or pertaining to formation, growth, or development.

for-mer (for´mèr) *adj.* Previous; preceding in place; being the first of two persons or things mentioned or referred to.

for-mer-ly *adv.* Previously.

form-fit-ting (form´fit˝ing) *adj.* Following closely to the contours of the body.

for-mi-da-ble (for´mi da bl) *adj.* Extremely diffcult; exciting fear by reason of size or strength. **formidably** *adv.*

form letter *n.* A standardized format of an impersonal letter sent to different people or to a large number of people.

for-mu-la (for´mū la) *n. pl.* **formulas** *or* **formulae** A prescribed method of words or rules for use in a certain ceremony or procedure; a nutritious food for an infant in liquid form. *Math.* A combination or rule used to express an algebraic or symbolic form. *Chem.* A symbolic representation of the composition of a chemical compound. **formulaic** *adj.*

for-mu-late (for´mū lāt´) *v.* To state or express as a formula. **formulation, formulator** *n.* **formulating, formulated** *v.*

for-ni-ca-tion (for˝ni kā´shan) *n.* Voluntary sexual intercourse between two unmarried people. **fornicate** *v.* **fornicator** *n.*

for-sake (for sāk´) *v.* To abandon or renounce; to give up. **forsaking** *v.*

for-sooth (for sōth´) *adv.* In truth; certainly.

for-swear (for swâr´) *v.* To renounce emphatically or upon oath; to forsake; to swear falsely; to perjure oneself.

for-syth-i-a (for sith´ē a) *n.* An Asian shrub cultivated for its early-blooming, bright, yellow flowers.

fort (fōrt) *n.* A fortified structure or enclosure capable of defense against an enemy; a permanent army post.

forte (fōrt) *n.* An activity one does with excellence; a person's strong point; the part of a sword blade between the middle and the hilt.

forth (fōrth) *adv.* Out into plain sight, as from seclusion; forward in order, place, or time.

forth-com-ing (fōrth´kum´ing) *adj.* Ready or about to appear or occur; readily available.

forth-right (fōrth´rīt˝) *adj.* Straightforward; direct; frank. **forthrightly** *adv.* **forthrightness** *n.*

forth-with (fōrth˝with´) *adv.* At once; promptly; immediately.

for-ti-fi-ca-tion *n.* The act of fortifying; something that fortifies, strengthens, or defends. A fortified place as a fort.

for-ti-fy (for´ti fī˝) *v.* To strengthen and secure with military fortifications; to provide physical strength or courage to; to strengthen; to enrich food, as by adding vitamins, minerals, etc. **fortification, fortifier** *n.* **fortifying, fortified** *n.*

for-tis-si-mo (for tis´i mō´) *adv., Mus.* Very loudly, as a direction.

for-ti-tude (for´ti tŏd˝) *n.* Strength of mind in adversity, pain, or peril, allowing a person to withstand pain.

fort-night (fort´nīt˝) *n.* A period of two weeks. **fortnightly** *adj. & adv.*

FOR-TRAN (for´tran) *n.* In computer science, a programming language for problems that are expressed in several different algebraic terms.

for-tress (for´tris) *n.* A fort.

for-tu-i-tous (for tŏ´i tus) *adj.* Occurring by chance; lucky; fortunate.

for-tu-i-ty *n.* The state of being fortuitous.

for-tu-nate (for´chu nit) *adj.* Brought about by good fortune; having good fortune.

for-tune (for´chan) *n.* A hypothetical force that unpredictably determines events and issues favorably and unfavorably; success that results from luck; possession of material goods; a very large amount of money.

fortune hunter *n.* A person who seeks

wealth through marriage.

for-tune-tell-er (for´chan tel˝ėr) *n.* A person who claims to predict the future. **fortunetelling** *n. & adj.*

for-ty (for´tē) *n. pl.* **forties** The cardinal number equal to four times ten. **fortieth** *n., adj. & adv.*

for-ty-nin-er (for˝tē nī´nėr) *n.* A United States pioneer in the 1849 California gold rush.

forty winks *n., Slang* A short nap.

for-um (fōr´um) *n. pl.* **forums** *or* **fora** A public marketplace in an ancient Roman city, where most legal and political business was transacted; a judicial assembly.

for-ward (for´wėrd) *adj.* At, near, or toward a place or time in advance; overstepping the usual bounds in an insolent or presumptuous way; extremely unconventional, as in political opinions; socially advanced. *n.* A player in football at the frontline of offense or defense. *v.* To send forward or ahead; to help advance onward. **forwardly** *adv.* **forwardness** *n.*

forward pass *n. Football,* An offensive pass thrown in the direction of the opponent's goal.

fos-sil (fos´il) *n.* The remains of an animal or plant of a past geologic age preserved in the rocks of the earth's surface; one that is outdated. **fossilization** *n.* **fossilize** *v.*

fos-ter (fo´stėr) *v.* To give parental care to; to nurture; to encourage. *adj.* Giving or receiving parental care.

foster child *n.* A child supported financially or cared for by a someone who is not their natural parents; the child so cared for.

foster parent *n.* A person who financially supports, or cares for, a child who is not his own.

foul (foul) *adj.* Revolting to the senses; spoiled or rotten; covered with offensive matter; morally offensive; vulgar or obscene; unfavorable; dishonorable; indicating the limiting lines of a playing area. *adj.* **in a foul way** *v.* To physically contact or entangle; to become foul or dirty; to dishonor; to obstruct; to entangle; to make

or hit a foul. **foul up** *Slang* To make a mistake. **foully** *adv.,* **foulness** *n.*

fou-lard *n.* A soft, lightweight silk usu. decorated with a printed pattern.

foul ball *n.* A batted baseball that lands in foul territory.

foul-mouthed *adj.* Using profane, vile, or obscene language.

foul play *n.* A violent act, often murder; an infringement of sporting rules.

found (found) *v.* To establish; to set up, often with funds to permit continuation and maintenance; to establish the basis or lay the foundation of; to melt metal and pour into a mold; to make by casting molten metal. **founder** *n.*

foun-da-tion (foun dā´shan) *n.* The act of founding or establishing; the basis on which anything is founded; an institution supported by an endowment; a cosmetic base for make up.

foun-dry (foun´drē) *n. pl.* **foundries** An establishment where metal is cast.

fount (fount) *n.* A fountain; an abundant source.

foun-tain (foun´tan) *n.* A natural spring or jet of water coming from the earth; an artificially created spray of water; a basin-like structure from which such a stream comes; a point of origin or source.

fountain pen *n.* A pen having a reservoir of ink that automatically feeds the writing point.

four (fōr) *n.* The cardinal number that equals 3 + 1; anything consisting of four units. **four** *adj. & pron.*

four-fold *adj.* Consisting of four units; quadruple.

four-hand-ed *adj.* Involving four players, as a game of cards; engaged in by four people.

four–poster *n.* A bed having four tall posts at each corner, originally for the support of a canopy.

four-score (fōr´skōr´) *adj.* Being four times twenty; eighty.

four-teen (fōr´tēn´) *n.* The cardinal number that equals 13 + 1; anything consisting of fourteen units. **fourteen** *adj. & pron.* **fourteenth** *n., adj. & adv.*

fourth (fōrth) *n.* The ordinal number matching the number four in a series; the fourth forward gear of a transmission in a motor vehicle. **fourth** *adj. & adv.*

Fourth of July *n.* American Independence Day celebrated as a national holiday.

four–wheel *adj.* An automotive transmission in which all four wheels are linked to the source of driving power.

fowl (foul) *n. pl.* **fowl** *or* **fowls** A bird used as food or hunted as game, as the duck, goose, etc.; the edible flesh of a fowl. To hunt or catch wild fowl. **fowler** *n.*.

fox (foks) *n.* A wild mammal having a pointed snout, upright ears, and a long bushy tail; the fur of a fox; a sly or crafty person. *v.* To outwit; to trick.

fox-hole (foks´hōl˝) *n.* A shallow pit dug by a soldier as cover against enemy fire.

fox-hound (foks´hound˝) *n.* A large dog breed developed for fox hunting.

fox-ing *n.* The pieces or piece of leather used to cover the upper front portion of a shoe.

fox terrier *n.* A small dog having a wiry or smooth white coat with dark markings.

fox trot *n.* A ballroom dance in 4/4 or 2/4 time consisting of a variety of rhythmic steps.

fox-y (fok´sē) *adj.* Like a fox; sly or crafty; sharp *Slang* Very pretty. **foxily** *adv.*

foy-er (foi´ėr) *n.* The public lobby of a hotel, theater, etc.; an entrance hall.

fpm *abbr.* Feet per minute.

fps *abbr.* Feet per second.

Fr *abbr.* Father (clergyman).

fra-cas (frā´kas) *n.* A noisy quarrel or disturbance; fight or dispute.

frac-tion (frak´shan) *n.* A small part; a disconnected part or fragment of anything; in mathematics, an indicated quantity less than a whole number that is expressed as a decimal. *Chem.* A component of a compound separated from a substance by distilling. **fractional** *adj.*

frac-tion-al *adj.* Relating or pertaining to a fraction or fractions.

frac-ture (frak´chėr) *n.* The act of breaking; the state of being broken. *Med.* The breaking or cracking, as in a bone.

frag-ile (fraj´il) *adj.* Easily damaged or broken; frail; tenuous; flimsy. **fragilely** *adv.* **fragility** *n.*

frag-ment (frag´ment) *n.* A part detached or broken; part unfinished or incomplete. *v.* To break into fragments. **fragmentation** *n.*

frag-men-tal *adj.* Fragmentary; Geol. Pertaining to rocks made up of fragments of older rocks.

frag-men-tary *adj.* Composed of fragments.

frag-men-tate *v.* To fragment.

frag-ment-ed *adj.* To reduce to fragments; lacking unity.

fra-grance *n.* The quality of being fragrant.

fra-grant (frā´grant) *adj.* Having an agreeable, especially sweet odor. **fragrance** *n.* **fragrantly** *adv.*

frail (frāl) *adj.* Delicate; weak; easily damaged. **frailly** *adv.* **frailness** *n.*

frame (frām) *v.* To put into a frame, as a picture; to build; to design; to adjust or adapt for a given purpose; to provide with a frame. *Slang* To incriminate so as to make a person appear guilty. *n.* Something made up of parts and joined together, such as a skeletal structure of a body; the pieces of wood or metal which surround a picture, photograph, or work of art; general structure; one exposure on a roll of film. **frame-up** *Slang* An act or actions which serve to frame someone or to make someone appear guilty when he is not. **framer** *n.* **framing, framed** *v.*

frame-work *n.* A structure composed of parts fitted together.

fram-ing *n.* The act, process, or manner of constructing or contriving anything.

fran-chise (fran´chīz) *n.* A privilege or right granted to a person or group by a government; the constitutional right to vote; authorization to sell a manufacturer's products; the territory within which a privilege or immunity is authorized. **franchise** *v.* **franchisee, franchiser** *n.*

Franco, Francisco *n.* (1892-1975). Spanish dictator.

Franco–American *n.* An American of French descent. **Franco-American** *adj.*

fran-gi-ble (fran′ji bl) *adj.* Breakable. **frangibility** *n.*

frank (frangk) *adj.* Sincere and straightforward. *v.* To mark mail officially so that no charge is made for delivery. *n.* The right to send mail without charge; a signature or mark on mail indicating that mail can be sent without charge; mail sent without charge; to mail free. **frankly** *adv.* **frankness** *n.*

Frank-fort *n.* The capital of Kentucky.

frank-furt-er (frangk′fer ter) *n.* A smoked sausage made of beef or beef and pork.

frank-in-cense (frang′kin sens′) *n.* An aromatic gum resin obtained from African and Asian trees used as incense and in medicine.

Franklin, Benjamin *n.* (1706-1790). American statesman, scientist and inventor.

Franklin stove *n.* A stove made of cast iron and shaped like a fireplace, which utilizes metal baffles to increase its energy efficiency.

fran-tic (fran′tik) *adj.* Emotionally out of control with worry or fear. **frantically** *adv.* **franticly** *adv.*

frat *n., Slang.* A college fraternity.

fra-ter *n.* A fraternity brother; a comrade.

fra-ter-nal (fra ter′nal) *adj.* Pertaining to or relating to brothers; of, pertaining to, or befitting a fraternity. *Biol.* Of or relating to a twin or twins that developed from separately fertilized ova. **fraternalism** *n.* **fraternally** *adv.*

fra-ter-ni-ty *n.* The relationship of a brother; a class of men associated for a common interest.

frat-er-nize (frat′er nīz′) *v.* To associate with others in a friendly way; to mingle intimately with the enemy, often in violation of military law. **fraternizing, frat-**ernized *v.*

frat-ri-cide (fra′tri sīd′) *n.* The killing of one's brother or sister; one who has killed his brother or sister. **fratricidal** *adj.*

fraud (frod) *n.* A deliberate and willful deception perpetrated for unlawful gain; a trick or swindle; an impostor; a cheat.

fraud-u-lent (fro′ju lent) *adj.* Marked by or practicing fraud. **fraudulence** *n.* **fraudulently** *adv.*

fraught (frot) *adj.* Full of or accompanied by something specified.

fray (frā) *n.* A brawl, or fight; a heated argument or dispute. *v.* To wear out by rubbing; to irritate one's nerves.

fraz-zle (fraz′el) *v., Slang* To wear out; to completely fatigue. **frazzle** *n.*

freak (frēk) *n.* A seemingly capricious event; a whimsical quality or disposition. *Slang* A drug addict; a highly individualistic rebel; a person with an extreme physical abnormality; a fan or enthusiast. **freak out** To experience hallucinations or paranoia induced by a drug; to make or become highly excited. **freakish, freaky** *adj.* **freakily** *adv.*

freck-le (frek′l) *n.* One of the small, brownish, often sun induced spots on the skin usually due to precipitation of pigment increasing in number and intensity on exposure to the sun.

free (frē) *adj.* Not imprisoned; not under obligation; politically independent; possessing political liberties; not affected by a specified circumstance or condition; exempt; costing nothing; not being occupied or used; too familiar; forward; liberal, as with money. *adv.* In a free way; without charge. *v.* To set at liberty; to release or rid; to untangle. **freely** *adv.* **freeness** *n.*

free agent *n.* A person who is released from a contract.

free-boot-er *n.* A pirate; a plunderer.

free-born *adj.* Born free; not in vassalage or servitude.

free-dom (frē′dom) *n.* The condition or state of being free; political independence; possession of political rights; boldness of expression; liberty; unrestricted access or use.

free enterprise *n.* A doctrine or type of economy under which private business is allowed to operate with minimum governmental control; capitalist economy.

free fall *n.* The unguided descent of a body through the air; that portion of a parachute jump occurring before the parachute opens; the hypothetical state of unrestrained movement in a gravitational field.

free-for-all *n.* A competition, fight, or debate open to all, without any rules or regulations; a brawl or fight that is out of control.

free-form *adj.* Having an irregular shape; unrestrained by any set pattern or rules; unconventional.

free-hand *adv.* Drawn by hand without the assistance by any measuring or guiding instruments.

free-handed *adj.* Openhanded; generous.

free lance (frēlans) *n.* One whose services are without long-term commitments to any one employer.

free on board *adv.* Without charge for delivery to the buyer for the placing of merchandise on board a carrier at a specified point. F.O.B.

free-spoken *adj.* Speaking freely without reserve; outspoken.

free-standing (frē'stan'ding) *adj.* Standing alone without any support; free of any apparent support or attachments.

free-stone *n.* Any stone, as limestone, that which can be easily cut and worked without splitting; a fruit having an easily removeable stone as certain varieties of peaches.

free throw *n., Basketball* An unhindered shot at the basket, worth one point if successful, awarded because of a foul by an opponent.

free trade *n.* International exchange between nations or states which is unrestricted.

free-way (frē'wā') *n.* A highway with more than two lanes.

free will *n.* The ability to choose freely; the belief that a human being's choices can be made freely, without external constraint.

adj. Done willingly.

free world *n.* All countries outside the Communist rule.

freeze (frēz) *v.* To become ice or a similar solid through loss of heat; to preserve by cooling at an extremely low temperature; to become nonfunctional through the formation of ice or frost; to feel uncomfortably cold; to make or become rigid; to become suddenly motionless, rigid or inactive, as though through fear; to set prices at a certain level; to forbid further use of. *n.* An act of freezing or the state of being frozen; a cold snap. **freezing** *v.*

freeze-dry (frēz'drī) *v.* To preserve by drying in a frozen state under a high vacuum. **freeze-dried.**

freezer (frēz'ėr) *n.* One that freezes or keeps cold; an insulated cabinet for freezing and storing perishable foods.

freight (frāt) *n.* A service of transporting commodities by air, land or water; the price paid such transportation; a train that transports goods only. *v.* To carry as cargo.

freight-age *n.* Freight; the transportation of goods.

freight-er (frā'tėr) *n.* A ship used for transporting cargo.

French (french) *n.* The language of France; of or pertaining to the people of France. **Frenchman, Frenchwoman** *n.*

French Canadian *n.* A person from Canada whose first language is French.

French fries *n. pl.* The thin strips of potatoes which have been fried crisp in deep fat.

French fry *v.* To fry in deep fat.

fren-zy (fren'zē) *n. pl.* **frenzies** A state of extreme excitement or violent agitation; temporary insanity or delirium.

fre-quen-cy *n.* The state of being frequent.

fre-quent (frē'kwent) *adj.* Happening or appearing often or time after time. *v.* To go to a place repeatedly. **frequenter** *n.* **frequentness** *n.* **frequently** *adv.*

fres-co (fres'kō) *n. pl.* **-coes** *or* **-cos** The art of painting on moist plaster with water-based paint; a picture so painted.

fresh (fresh) *adj*. Newly-made, gathered, or obtained; not spoiled, musty, or stale; new; different; not soiled; pure and clean; having just arrived; refreshed; revived. *Slang* Impudent; disrespectful. **freshly** *adv*.

fresh-en *v*. To make fresh; to revive; renew.

fresh-man (fresh´man) *n*. A student in the first year of studies in a high school, university, or college; a beginner.

fresh-wa-ter *adj*. Pertaining to water without salt.

fret (fret) *v*. To be anxious or irritated; to wear away; to make by erosion; to ripple water. *n*. An ornamental design, composed of repeated symmetric figures; a ridge of metal fixed across the fingerboard of a stringed instrument, as a guitar.

fret-ful *adj*. Irritable.

fret saw *n*. A small saw used to cut curved lines.

fret-work *n*. Ornamental work.

Freud, Sigmund *n*. (1856-1939). Austrian psychoanalyst. **Freudian** *adj. & n*.

Fri *abbr*. Friday.

fri-a-ble (frī´a bl) *adj*. Easily crumbled or pulverized brittle. **friableness** *n*.

fri-ar (frī´ér) *n*. A member of a mendicant Roman Catholic order.

fric-as-see (frik´a sē´) *n*. A dish of meat or poultry stewed in gravy. **fricassee** *v*.

fric-tion (frik´shan) *n*. The rubbing of one surface or object against another; a conflict or clash. *Phys*. A force that retards the relative motion of two touching objects. **frictional** *adj*.

Fri-day (frī´dā) *n*. The sixth day of the week.

friend (frend) *n*. Someone who is personally well known by oneself and for whom one holds warm regards; a supporter of a cause or group. **Friend** A member of the Society of Friends; a Quaker. **friendless** *adj*. **friendship** *n*.

friend-ly *adj*. Characteristic of a friend; like a friend; showing kindness and goodwill.

frieze (frēz) *n*. A decorative horizontal band along the upper part of a wall in a room.

frig-ate (frig´it) *n*. A square-rigged warship

of the 17th to mid19th centuries; U.S. warship smaller than a cruiser but larger than a destroyer.

fright (frīt) *n*. Sudden violent alarm or fear; a feeling of alarm. *Slang* Something very unsightly or ugly.

fright-ful *adj*. Causing intense fright or alarm.

fright-en (frīt´en) *v*. To fill with fear; to force by arousing fear. **frightening** *adj*. **frighteningly** *adv*.

frig-id (frij´id) *adj*. Very cold; lacking warmth of feeling or emotional warmth; sexually unresponsive. **frigidity** *n*. **frigidness** *n*. **frigidly** *adv*.

frill (fril) *n*. A decorative ruffled or gathered border. *Slang* A superfluous item.

fringe (frinj) *n*. An edging that consists of hanging threads, cords, or loops.

fringe benefit *n*. Any employment benefit, such as paid holidays, pensions, or insurance, given in addition to salary.

frip-per-y (frip´e rē) *n. pl*. **fripperies** Showy and often cheap ornamentation; a pretentious display.

frisk (frisk) *v*. To skip or leap about playfully; to search someone for a concealed weapon by running the hands over the clothing quickly.

frit-ter (frit´ér) *v*. To squander or waste little by little. *n*. A small fried cake made of plain batter, often containing fruits, vegetables, or fish. **frittering** *v*.

fri-vol-i-ty *n*. The quality of being frivolous.

friv-o-lous (friv´o lus) *adj*. Trivial; insignificant; lacking importance; not serious; silly. **frivolousness** *n*. **frivolously** *adv*.

frizz (friz) *v*. To form into small, tight curls. **frizziness** *n*. **frizzily** *adv*. **frizzy** *adj*.

friz-zly *adj*. Frizzed, as hair; very curly.

fro (frō) *adv*. Away from; back, as running to and fro.

frock (frok) *n*. A smock or loose-fitting robe; a robe worn by monks.

frog (frog) *n*. Any of various small, smooth-skinned, web-footed, largely aquatic, tailless, leaping amphibians; an ornamental braid or cord; an arrangement of intersecting railroad tracks designed to permit wheels to pass over the intersection without difficulty; a perforated holder for flower stems. *Slang* Hoarseness in the throat.

frol-ic (frol´ik) *n.* Merriness; a playful, carefree occasion. *v.* To romp about playfully; to have fun. **frolicker** *n.*

from (frum) *prep.* Starting at a particular time or place; used to indicate a specific point; used to indicate a specific source; used to indicate separation or removal; used to indicate differentiation, as knowing right from left.

frond (frond) *n.* A large leaf, as of a tropical fern, usually divided into smaller leaflets.

front (frunt) *n.* The forward surface of an object or body; the area or position located before or ahead; a position of leadership; a field of activity for disguising objectionable or illegal activities; an apparently respectable person, group, or business used as a cover for illegal or secret activities. *Meteor.* The line of separation between air masses of different temperatures. **frontal** *adj.* **frontally** *adv.*

front money *n.* Money paid in advance for a service or product that has been promised.

fron-tier (frun tēr´) *n.* A part of an international border or the area adjacent to it; an unexplored area of knowledge or thought. **frontiersman** *n.*

fron-tis-piece (frun´tis pēs´) *n.* An illustration that usually precedes the title page of a book or periodical.

front office *n.* The executive staff of an organization.

front-ward *adv.* Toward the front.

frost (frost) *n.* A feathery covering of minute ice crystals on a cold surface; the act or process of freezing. *v.* To cover with frost; to apply frosting to a cake. **frostily** *adv.* **frostiness** *n.* **frosty** *adj.*

Frost, Robert Lee *n.* (1874-1963). American poet.

frost-bite (frost´bīt´) *n.* The local destruc-

tion of bodily tissue due to exposure to freezing temperatures, often resulting in gangrene. **frostbite** *v.*

frost-ing (fro´sting) *n.* Icing; a mixture of egg whites, sugar, butter, etc.; a lusterless or frosted surface on glass or metal.

froth (froth) *n.* A mass of bubbles on or in a liquid, resulting from agitation or fermentation; a salivary foam, as of an animal, resulting from disease or exhaustion; anything unsubstantial or trivial. *v.* To expel froth. **frothily** *adv.* **frothiness** *n.* **frothy** *adj.*

frou-frou (frö´frö´) *n.* A rustling sound, as of silk; a frilly dress or decoration.

fro-ward (frö´wėrd) *adj.* Obstinate. **fro-wardness** *n.*

frown (froun) *v.* To contract the brow as in displeasure or concentration; to look on with distaste or disapproval. **frown** *n.* **frowningly** *adv.* **frowning** *v.*

frow-zy *or* **frow-sy (frou´zē)** *adj.* Appearing unkempt.

fro-zen (frö´zen) *adj.* Covered with, changed into, surrounded by, or made into ice; extremely cold, as a climate; immobilized or made rigid, as by fear; coldly reserved; unfriendly; kept at a fixed level, as wages; not readily available for withdrawal, sale, or liquidation, as from a bank.

fruc-tu-ous (fruk´chö us) *adj.* Fruitful; productive.

fru-gal (frö´gal) *adj.* Economical; thrifty. **frugality, frugalness** *n.* **frugally** *adv.*

fruit (fröt) *n. pl.* **fruit** *or* **fruits** The ripened, mature, seed-bearing part of a flowering plant, as a pod or berry; the edible, fleshy plant part of this kind, as an apple or plum; the fertile structure of a plant that does not bear seeds; the outcome or result. *v.* To produce or cause to produce fruit.

fruit-age *n.* The condition of bearing of fruit; the yield of fruit.

fruit cake *n.* A rich cake containing spices nuts, raisins, currants, other dried or candied fruits.

fruit fly *n.* Any of several small two-winged flies, whose larvae feed on fruit or rotting vegetable matter.

fru-i-tion (frŏ ish´an) *n.* Achievement or accomplishment of something worked for or desired; the state of bearing fruit.

fruit sugar *n.* Fructose.

frump-y (frump ē) *adj.* Unfashionable; dowdy. **frump, frumpiness** *n.*

frus-trate (frus´trāt) *v.* To keep from attaining a goal or fulfilling a desire; to thwart; to prevent the fruition of; to nullify. **frustration** *n.* **frustratingly** *adv.* **frustrating, frustrated** *v.*

fry (frī) *v.* To cook in hot fat or oil, especially over direct heat. *n.* A dish of any fried food; a social occasion at which foods are fried and eaten; a very young fish, especially a recently hatched one. **frying, fried** *v.*

fry-er (frī´ér) *n.* Something which is intended for the purpose of frying, such as a young chicken.

frying pan *n.* A type of metal pan that is used for the purpose of frying foods.

fub-sy *adj.* To be chubby and squat.

fuch-sia (fū´sha) *n.* A chiefly tropical plant widely grown for its drooping, four-petaled flowers of purple, red, or white.

fuch-sine (fek´sin) *n.* A type of dye that is made by the oxidation of a mixture of aniline and toluidines and it is a bright red.

fu-coid (fū´koid) *adj.* To be pertaining to or to be like rockweeds.

fu-cose *n.* A type of aldose sugar.

fu-co-xan-thin *n.* A type of brown pigment that occurs in the ova of brown algea.

fu-cus (fū´kus) *n.* A type of brown algea.

fud-dle (fud´l) *v.* To make someone or something confused.

fud-dy–dud-dy *n. pl.* **fuddy–duddies (fud´ē dud˝ē)** An old-fashioned person.

fudge (fuj) *n.* A soft, cooked candy containing sugar, butter, and a flavoring, as chocolate. *v.* To falsify; to adjust, make, or fit together in a clumsy way; to evade.

Fue-gian (fū ē´jē an) *n.* A person who is a member of the group of American Indians of Tierra del Fuego.

fuel (fū´el) *n.* A combustible matter con-sumed to generate energy, especially a material such as wood, coal, or oil burned to generat heat. *v.* To take in or supply with fuel; to stimulate, as an argument. **fueler** *n.*

fuel cell *n.* A kind of cell which will change the chemical energy of a fuel to an electrical energy.

fuel injection *n.* The forced spraying of fuel into the combustion chamber of an engine.

fuel oil *n.* An oil used for fuel, esp. one used as a substitute for coal.

fug (fug) *v.* To hang around or loll indoors in an atmosphere that is stuffy.

fu-ga-cious (fū gā´shus) *adj.* To be lasting a short time. **fugacity** *n.*

fu-gal (fū´gal) *adj.* To be pertaining to the style of a musical fugue.

fu-gi-tive (fū´ji tiv) *adj.* Fleeing or having fled, as from arrest, pursuit, etc. *n.* One who flees or tries to escape.

fu-gle *v.* To act in the manner a fugleman does.

fu-gle-man *n.* A person who heads a group.

fugue (fūg) *n., Mus.* A musical composition in which the theme is elaborately repeated by different voices or instruments; a psychological disturbance in which actions are not remembered after returning to a normal state.

fu-ji *n.* A type of spun silk fabric that was first made in Japan.

-ful *adj., suffix* Having the qualities of something; to be filled with or full of.

ful-crum (fel´krum) *n. pl.* **-crums** *or* **-cra** The point on which a lever turns.

ful-fill *or* **ful-fil (fel fil´)** *v.* To convert into actuality; to effect; to carry out; to satisfy.

ful-gent (ful´jent) *adj.* To be very or dazzling bright.

ful-gu-rant (fil´gur ant) *adj.* To be flashing like lightening flashes.

ful-gu-ra-tion *n.* The flashing as of lightning.

ful-gu-rite (ful´gū rīt) *n.* A type of tubular crust that is formed by the fusion of rock by lightening.

ful-gu-rous *adj.* To be giving off flashes

like that of lightening.

fu-lig-i-nous (fū lij´i nus) *adj.* To be murky or to have a color that is dark.

full (fel) *adj.* To have in something the maximum amount that the object is able to hold. **fullness** *n.*

full blood *n.* Pure extraction; an unmixed ancestry.

full–blood-ed *adj.* Of pure blood; thoroughbred; *fig.* vigorous; lusty.

full–bod-ied *adj.* Satisfying in flavor and strength.

full-fledged (fel´flejd´) *adj.* To have full plummage.

full-length *adj.* Of usual or standard length; unabridged.

full-size *adj.* To have the normal size of that of its kind.

full dress *n.* A style of dress that usually is found at a formal social gathering, very stylish.

full moon *n.* A phase of the moon where the whole side of the disk is able to be viewed.

full-scale *adj.* Equal in size to the original.

full tilt *adv.* At top potential.

full time *n.* The amount of time considered the normal amount for working; a 40-hour week.

ful-ly (fel´ē) *adv.* To be done in a manner that is full.

ful-mar (fel´mėr) *n.* A type of arctic seabird which is related to the petrels.

ful-mi-nate (ful´mi nāt) *v.* To condemn severely; to explode. **fulmination, fulminator** *n.* **fulminated, fulminating** *v.*

ful-some (fel´som) *adj.* Offensively insincere. **fulsomely** *adv.* **fulsomeness** *n.*

ful-vous (ful´vus) *adj.* Yellow; tawny.

fum-ble (fum´bl) *v.* To handle idly; to blunder; to mishandle a baseball or football. *n.* The act of fumbling; a fumbled ball. **fumbler** *n.* **fumbling, fumbled** *v.*

fume (fūm) *n.* An irritating smoke, gas, or vapor. To treat with or subject to fumes; to show or feel anger or distress.

fu-mi-gate (fū´mi gāt´) *v.* To subject to fumes in order to exterminate vermin or insects. **fumigation, fumigator** *n.*, **fumigated, fumigating** *v.*

fun *n.* That which is amusing, or mirthful; entertaining; recreation or play.

func-tion (fungk´shən) *n.* The characteristics or proper activity of a person or thing; specific occupation, duty, or role; an official ceremony; something depending upon or varying with another; in math, a quantity whose value is dependent on the value of another. *v.* To serve or perform a function as required or expected.

func-tion-al *adj.* Of or pertaining to functions; able to perform a regular function.

functional disease *n.*, *Pathol.* A disease with pathological changes in the function of an organ, but no structural alteration in the tissues involved.

fund (fund) *n.* A source of supply; a sum of money or its equivalent reserved for a specific purpose. *v.* To convert into long-term arrangements for paying something off; to furnish or accumulate a fund for.

fun-da-men-tal (fun˝da men´tal) *adj.* Basic or essential; of major significance; anything serving as the primary origin; most important. **fundamental** *n.* **fundamentally** *adv.*

fu-ner-al (fū´nėr al) *n.* The service performed in conjunction with the burial or cremation of a dead person.

funeral director *n.* A person who manages funerals.

funeral home *n.* The establishment where a dead person is prepared for burial or cremation and for viewing of the body.

fu-ne-re-al *adj.* Pertaining or relating to a funeral.

fun-gus (fung´gus) *n.* *pl.* **-gi** *or* **-guses** Any of numerous spore-bearing plants which have no chlorophyll that include yeasts, molds, mildews, and mushrooms. **fungous** *adj.* **fungal** *adj.*

fu-nic-u-lar (fū nik´ū lėr) *n.* A cable railway along which cable cars are drawn up a mountain, especially one with ascending and descending cars that counterbalance one another.

funk (fungk) *n.* Cowardly fright or panic; fear; a state of depression.

funk-y (fung´kē) *adj., Slang* Having an earthy quality that is characteristic of the blues. **funkiness** *n.*

fun-nel (fun´el) *n.* A cone-shaped utensil having a tube for channeling a substance into a container. *v.* To pass or cause to pass through a funnel.

fur *n.* The skin of certain animals, the hairy coating on such a skin; such skins that are used as a material for lining or trimming, or for entire garments.

fur-be-low (fer´be lō˝) *n.* A ruffle or frill on clothing; a piece of showy decoration or ornamentation.

fur-bish (fer´bish) *v.* To make bright, as by rubbing; to polish; to renovate.

fu-ri-ous (fer´ē us) *adj.* Extremely angry; marked by rage or activity. **furiously** *adv.*

furl (ferl) *v.* To roll up and secure to something, as a pole or mast; to curl or fold

fur-long (fer´long) *n.* A distance equal to approximately 201 meters or 230 yards.

fur-lough (fer´lō) *n.* Permission granted to be absent from duty, especially to members of the armed forces. **furlough** *v.*

fur-nace (fer´nis) *n.* A large enclosure designed to produce intense heat.

fur-nish (fer´nish) *v.* To outfit or equip, as with fittings or furniture. **furnisher** *n.*, **furnishing** *v.*

fur-ni-ture (fer´ni chėr) *n.* Movable articles, such as chairs and tables, used in a home, office, etc.

fu-ror (fūr´or) *n.* Violent anger; rage; great excitement; commotion; an uproar.

fur-row (fer´ō) *n.* A long, narrow trench in the ground, made by a plow or other tool; a deep wrinkle in the skin, especially of the forehead. **furrow** *v.*

fur-ther *adv.* At a more advanced point in time or space.

fur-ther-more *adv.* Moreover.

fur-ther-most *adj.* Most distant.

fur-tive (fer´tiv) *adj.* Done in secret; surreptitious; obtained underhandedly; stolen.

fu-ry (fūr´ē) *n. pl.* **-ies** Uncontrolled anger; turbulence; an angry or spiteful woman.

fuse (fūz) *n.* An electrical safety device containing a wire or strip of fusible metal that melts and interrupts the curcuit's flow when the current exceeds a particular amperage; a mechanical, electrical, or electronic device used to detonate explosives, such as bombs or grenades.

fu-see *or* **fu-zee (fū zē´)** *n.* A large-headed friction match capable of burning in the wind; a colored signal flare used as a railroad signal.

fu-se-lage (fū´se lij) *n.* The central section of an airplane, containing the wings and tail assembly.

fu-si-ble *adj.* Capable of being melted.

fu-si-lade *n.* A quickly repeated or simultaneous discharge of a number of firearms.

fu-sion (fū´zhan) *n.* The act or procedure of melting together by heat; a blend produced by fusion; a nuclear reaction in which nuclei of a light element combine to form more massive nuclei, with the release of huge amounts of energy.

fuss *n.* An excessive display of restless activity.

fus-tian (fus´chan) *n.* A sturdy, stout cotton cloth. *adj.* Pompous, pretentious language; bombastic.

fus-ti-gate *v.* To criticize.

fu-tile (fūt´il) *adj.* Ineffectual; being of no avail; without useful result; serving no useful purpose.

fu-ture (fū´chėr) *n.* The time yet to come; a prospective condition regarding advancement or success; the future tense or a verb form in the future tense.

fuzz (fuz) *n.* A mass of fine, loose particles, fibers, or hairs.

fuzz-y *adj.* Covered with fuzz; lacking in clarity.

fwd *abbr.* Forward.

FX *abbr.* Foreign exchange.

FYI *abbr.* For your information.

G, g (jē) The seventh letter of the English alphabet. *Mus.* The fifth tone in the scale of C major. *Slang* One thousand dollars; a grand. *Physiol.* A unit of force equal to that due to the earth's gravity.

g *abbr.* Gravity, gram.

gab (gab) *v., Slang* To talk or chat idly.

gab-ar-dine (gab´ėr dēn˝) *n.* A firm cotton, wool, or rayon material, having a diagonal raised weave, used for suits and coats.

gab-ble (gab´l) *v.* To speak rapidly or incoherently. **gabble** *n.*

gab-bro (gab´rō) *n.* A granular igneous rock. **gabbroci, gabbroitic** *adj.*

gab-fest *n.* Informal gathering or meeting where people engage in prolonged, general talk.

ga-ble (gā´bl) *n., Arch.* The portion of a building enclosed by the sloping ends.

gable roof *n.* A ridged roof that stops at both ends in a gable.

gable window *n., Arch.* A window under a gable.

Gabriel *n.* A special messenger of God mentioned in the Bible.

ga-boon (ga bōn´) *n.* An African tree with reddish-brown wood and is used mainly in furniture.

ga-by *n.* A foolish person; a dunce.

gad (gad) *v.* To wander about restlessly with little or no purpose. **gadder** *n.*

gad-a-bout (gad´a bout˝) *n. Slang* A person who goes about seeking excitement and fun.

gad-fly (gad´flī˝) *n.* A fly that bites or annoys cattle and horses; an irritating, critical, but often constructively provocative person; a person who is bothersome to others.

gadg-et (gaj´it) *n., Slang* A small device or tool used in performing miscellaneous jobs, especially in the kitchen.

ga-doid *adj.* Resembling or related to the cod family.

gad-o-lin-i-um (gad˝o lin´ē um) *n.* A metallic element, silvery-white in color, of the rare-earth series which is highly magnetic.

ga-droon (ga drōn´) *n.* The ornamental carving on a rounded molding.

gad-wall (gad´wal˝) *n.* A grayish brown duck.

Gaea *n.* In Greek mythology, the mother and wife of Uranus, the goddess of earth.

gaff (gaf) *n.* A sharp iron hook used for landing fish. *Naut.* A spar on the top edge of a fore-and-aft sail. *Slang* Abuse or harsh treatment. *v.* To land or hook with a gaff. To deceive.

gaffe (gaf) *n.* A social blunder; mistake; a faux pas.

gaf-fer (gaf´ėr) *n.* An old man.

gag (gag) *n.* Something as a wadded cloth, forced into or over the mouth to prevent someone from speaking or crying out; an obstacle to or any restraint of free speech, such as by censorship. *Slang* A practical joke or hoax. **to pull a gag** To perform a practical joke or trick on someone. *v.* To keep a person from speaking out by means of a gag; to choke on something. **gagger** *n.*

ga-ga (gä´gä) *adj., Slang* Crazy; silly.

gage (gāj) *n.* Something that is given as security for an action to be performed; a pledge; anything, as a glove, thrown down as a challenge to fight or a challenge for combat.

gag-gle (gag´l) *n.* A flock of geese; a group; a cluster.

gag rule *n.* A law or rule that prevents discussion or expression of an opinion.

gag-ster *n.* A person who plays practical jokes.

gahn-ite *n.* A dark-colored mineral containing zinc and aluminum.

gai-e-ty (gā´i tē) *n. pl.* **-ies** The state of being happy; cheerfulness; fun, festive activity.

gai-ly (gā´lē) *adj.* A gay or cheerful manner; showily or brightly.

gain (gān) *v.* To earn or acquire possession of something; to succeed in winning a victory; to develop an increase of; to put on weight; to secure as a profit; to improve progress; to draw nearer to.

gain-er (gā´nėr) *n.* A fancy dive used in diving competition; one who gains.

gain-ful (gān´ful) *adj.* Producing profits or advantage; lucrative. **gainfully** *adv.* **gainfulness** *n.*

gain-say (gān´sā´) *v.* To deny; to contradict; dispute. **gainsayer** *n.*

gait (gāt) *n.* A way or manner of moving on foot; one of the foot movements in which a horse steps or runs.

gai-ter (gā´tėr) *n.* A covering, as of leather or canvas, that covers the leg and extends from the knee to the instep; an old-fashioned shoe with a high top and elastic sides.

gal (gal) *n., Slang* A girl.

ga-la (gā´la) *n.* A festive celebration; party. **gala** *adj.*

ga-lac-tic (ga lak´tic) *adj.* Relating to the galaxy, or the Milky Way.

ga-lac-tose (ga lak´tōs) *n.* The sugar typically occurring in lactose.

ga-la-go *n.* A small nocturnal African primate with long ears, long tail, and long hind limbs enabling them to leap at great lengths.

ga-lah (ga lä´) *n.* A showy Australian cockatoo that is very destructive in wheat-growing areas.

gal-an-tine (gal´an tēn´) *n.* A cold dish that consists of fish or meat that has been poached, stuffed, and covered with aspic.

ga-lax *n.* An evergreen herb of the southeastern United States, whose leaves are widely used by florists.

gal-ax-y (gal´ak sē) *n. pl.* **-ies** *Astron.* Any of the very large systems of stars, nebulae, or other celestial bodies that constitute the universe; a brilliant, distinguished group or assembly. **Galaxy** The Milky Way.

gal-ba-num (gal´ba num) *n.* A greenish or brown aromatic, bitter gum resin used for medicinal purposes.

gale (gāl) *n., Meteor.* A very powerful wind stronger than a stiff breeze; an outburst, as of hilarity.

ga-le-na (ga lē´na) *n.* A metallic, dull gray mineral that is the principal ore of lead.

gal-i-lee *n.* A porch at the entrance of an English church.

Galiee, Sea of *n.* The freshwater lake that is bordered by Syria, Israel, and Jordan.

gal-i-ma-ti-as (gal´i mā´shē as) *n.* A confused mixture of words.

gal-i-ot, gal-li-ot *n.* A small galley or narrow sailing ship, moved by oars and sails.

gal-i-pot, gal-li-pot *n.* Turpentine removed from the stem of certain pine trees.

gall (gol) *n., Physiol.* The bitter fluid secreted by the liver; bile; bitterness of feeling; animosity; impudence; something that irritates. *v.* To injure the skin by friction; to chafe. **galling** *adj.*

gal-lant (gal´ant) *adj.* Dashing in appearance or dress; majestic; stately; chivalrously attentive to women; courteous; having a fine appearance; courage; heroic. **gallantly** *adv.*

gal-lant-ry (gal´an trē) *n. pl.* **-ries** Nobility and bravery; a gallant act.

gall-blad-der *or* **gall bladder** *n.* The small sac under the right lobe of the liver that stores bile.

gal-le-on (gal´ē on) *n.* A large, three-masted sailingship.

gal-ler-y (gal´e rē) *n. pl.* **-ries** A long, narrow passageway, as a corridor, with a roofed promenade, especially an open-sided one extending along an inner or outer wall of a building; a group of spectators, as at a golf tournament; a building where statues, paintings and other works of art are displayed; a room or building where articles are sold to the highest bidder; an underground passage in a mine. **galleried** *adj.* **gallery** *v.*

ga-lle-ta *n.* Forage grass grown in southwestern United States used as hay for cattle feeding.

gal-ley *n. pl.* **galleys (gal´ē)** A long medieval ship that was propelled by sails and oars; the long tray used by printers to hold set type; a printer's proof made from composed type, used to detect and correct errors.

galley—west *adv.* Into confusion or destruction.

galley proof *n.* The proof taken from type on a galley that permits corrections before the page is printed.

gal-ley slave *n.* A person who has been condemned to work at the oars on a galley; a person who is overworked; a drudge.

gall-fly *n.* An insect that causes yellow spots on plants by depositing eggs in the plant tissue.

gallic acid *n.* A slightly yellow crystalline acid found in plant galls and used as a developer in photography.

gal-li-gas-kins *n.* Very loose-fitting trousers of the 16th century.

gal-li-mau-fry (gal´i mo´frē) *n.* A hodgepodge; a jumbled mixture.

gal-li-nip-per *n.* A large mosquito.

gall-ing (go´ling) *adj.* Being very irritated; annoying; and vexing.

gal-li-nule *n.* A wading bird with dark iridescent plumage, having a frontal shield on the head and unlobed feet.

gal-li-um (gal´ē um) *n.* A silvery metallic element used in semiconductor technology and as a component of various low-melting alloys, symbolized by Ga.

gal-li-vant (gal´i vant˝) *v.* To roam about in search of amusement or pleasure; to flirt; to run about.

gall nut *n.* A gall resembling a nut that is often found on oak trees.

gal-lon (gal´on) *n.* A liquid measurement used in the United States, equal to 4 quarts; in Great Britain, a liquid measurement which equals 4 imperial quarts; a dry measurement that equals 1/8 bushel.

gal-loon (ga lön´) *n.* A trimming of lace, or embroidery with metallic threads.

gal-lop (gal´op) *n.* A horse's gait that is faster than a canter and characterized by regular leaps during which all four feet are off the ground at once. **gallop** *v.*

gal-low-glass *n.* A mercenary of an Irish chief.

gal-lows (gal´ōz) *n.* A framework of two or more upright beams and a crossbeam, used for execution by hanging.

gall-stone (gol´stōn´) *n., Pathol.* A small,

hard concretion of cholesterol crystals that sometimes form in the gall bladder or bile passages.

ga-loot (ga löt´) *n.* A strange or foolish person.

ga-lore (ga lōr´) *adj.* In great numbers; abundant; plentiful.

ga-losh (ga losh´) *n. pl.* **galoshes** Waterproof overshoes which are worn in bad weather.

ga-lump *v.* To bump or gallop along clumsily.

gal-van-ic (gal van´ik) *adj.* Produced by or pertaining to galvanism; stimulating or shocking.

gal-va-nism (gal´va niz´um) *n.* Electricity that is produced by chemical action. *Med.* A therapeutic application of continuous electric current from voltaic cells.

gal-va-nize (gal´va nīz˝) *v.* To stimulate or shock muscular action by an electric current; to protect iron or steel with rust resistant zinc. *Slang* To infuse with energy. **galvanization, galvanizer** *n.*

gal-va-nom-e-ter (gal˝va nom´i tėr) *n., Electr.* An apparatus for detecting the presence of an electric current and for determining its strength and direction. **galvanometric** *adj.*

gal-va-no-scope (gal´va no skōp˝) *n.* An instrument used to detect the direction and presence of an electric current by the deflecting of a magnetic needle.

gal-yak (gal´yak) *n.* A short-haired fur derived from the pelt of a stillborn lamb.

gam *n.* A school of whales.

gam-bit (gam´bit) *n.* In chess, an opening in which a piece is sacrificed for a favorable position; a maneuver that is carefully planned.

gam-ble (gam´bl) *v.* To take a chance on an uncertain outcome as a contest or a weekly lottery number. *n.* Any risky venture. **gambler** *n.*

gam-boge (gam bōj´) *n.* A gum resin that is orange to brown in color and is used as a yellow pigment.

gam-bol (gam´bol) *v.* To frolic, skip, or

leap about in play. *n*. Frolic; a playful leap or skip.

gambrel roof *n*., *Archit*. A ridged roof with the slope broken on each side, the lower slope steeper than the upper.

gam-bu-sia *n*. Any of various surface-feeding fishes which are stocked in fresh waters to eliminate mosquito larvae.

game (gām) *n*. A contest governed by specific rules; a way of entertaining oneself; amusement; a calculated way to do something; animals, fish, or birds that are hunted for sport or food. **gamer, gamest** *adj*. **gamely** *adv*. **gameness** *n*.

game bird *n*. A bird that may legally be hunted for sport of profit.

game-cock (gām'kok˝) *n*. The rooster bred and trained for cockfighting.

game fish *n*. A fish of a family that includes salmons, chars, and trouts.

game fowl *n*. A domestic fowl developed for the production of fighting cocks.

game-keep-er (gām'kē˝pėr) *n*. A person in charge of protecting and maintaining wildlife on a private preserve; a person who prevents illegal fishing or hunting.

gam-e-lan (gam'e lan˝) *n*. A string flute, and percussion orchestra of southeast Asia, that resembles the xylophone.

game-ly *adv*. In a courageous manner.

game plan *n*. A game where chance rather than skill determines the outcome.

games-man-ship (gāmz'man ship˝) *n*. The art or skill of winning games by somewhat dubious means but without breaking the rules.

game-some (gām'som) *adj*. Frolicsome; sportive; playful.

gam-e-tan-gi-um *n*. An organ or cell in which gametes are developed or produced.

gam-ete (gam'ēt) *n*., *Biol*. Either of two mature reproductive cells, an ovum or sperm, which produce a zygote when united.

gam-in (gam'in) *n*. A homeless child who wanders about the streets of a town or city.

gam-ma *n*. The third letter of the Greek alphabet; a scientific classification of third place.

gamma globulin *n*., *Biochem*. A globu-lin that is present in blood plasma and contains antibodies effective against certain infectious diseases.

gam-ma ray *n*., *Phys*. Electromagnetic radiation that has energy greater than several hundred thousand electron volts.

gam-mer (gam'ėr) *n*. An elderly woman.

gam-mon (gam'on) *n*. A cured ham; in the game of backgammon, a double victory in which a player removes all his pieces before the other player removes any.

gam-ut (gam'ut) *n*. The whole range series or extent of anything.

gam-y (gā'mē) *adj*. Having the strong flavor of game, especially when slightly tainted; scandalous. **gaminess** *n*.

gan-der (gan'dėr) *n*. A male goose. *Slang* A quick glance; a look or peek.

Gandhi, Mohandas Karamchand "Mahatma" *n*. Hindu leader of India, who was assassinated in 1948.

gandy dancer (gan'dē dan'sėr) *n*. A seasonal laborer or one who works in a railroad section gang.

ga-nef, go-nef *n*., *Slang*. Petty thief; rascal; an unscrupulous person.

gang (gang) *n*. A group of persons who are organized and work together or socialize regularly; a group of adolescent hoodlums or criminals. **gang up on** To attack as a group.

gang hook *n*. Two or three fishhooks with shanks joined together.

gang-land (gang'land˝) *n*. The underworld; organized criminal elements of society.

gan-gling (gang'gling) *adj*. Awkwardly tall and thin; lanky and loosely build.

gan-gli-on (gang'glē an) *n*. *pl*. -glia *or* ons *Physiol*. A collection of nerve cells located outside the spinal cord or brain.

gang-plank (gang'plangk˝) *n*. A temporary board or ramp used to board or leave a ship.

gang-plow *n*. A plow that is so designed to turn two, three or more rows at a time.

gan-grene (gang'grēn) *n*., *Pathol*. The

death and decay of tissue in the body caused by a failure in the circulation of the blood supply. **gangrene** *v.* **gangrenous** *adj.*

gang-ster (gang´stèr) *n.* A member of a crimminal gang; a racketeer; a mobster.

gang-way (gang´wā) *n.* A passageway through, into or out of an obstructed area. *Naut.* A passage on a ship's deck offering entrance to passengers or freight; gang-plank.

gan-net (gan´it) *n.* A large sea bird with white plumage and black wing tips, related to the pelican and heron.

gan-try (gan´trē) *n. pl.* **-ies** A bridge-like framework support, especially a movable vertical structure with platforms, that is used in assembling or servicing rockets before they are launched.

gaol (jāl) *n., Brit.* Jail. **gaol** *v.*

gap (gap) *n.* An opening or wide crack, as in a wall; a cleft; a deep notch or ravine in a mountain ridge, offering passage.

gape (gāp) *v.* To open the mouth wide, as in yawning; to stare in amazement with the mouth wide open; to become widely separated or open. **gape, gaper** *n*

gar (gär) *n.* A fish having a spearlike snout and elongated body covered with bony plates; a garfish.

ga-rage (ga razh´) *n.* A building or structure in which motor vehicles are stored, repaired, or serviced. **garage** *v.*

garb (gärb) *n.* Clothing; a particular way of dressing.

gar-bage (gär bij) *n.* Food wastes, consisting of unwanted or unusable pieces of meat, vegetables, and other food products; any unwanted or worthless material; trash.

gar-ble (gär´bl) *v.* To mix up or confuse; to change or distort the meaning of with the intent to mislead or misrepresent. *n.* The act or process of garbling. **garbler** *n.*

gar-den (gär´den) *n.* A place for growing flowers, vegetables, or fruit; a piece of ground commonly used as a public resort. *v.* To work in or make into a garden. *adj.* Produced or referring to or in a garden. **gardener, gardening** *n.*

garden heliotrope *n.* A large perennial herb with tiny, fragrant flowers.

gar-de-nia (gär dē´nya) *n.* A tropical shrub with glossy evergreen leaves and fragrant white flowers.

gar-den-ing *n.* The cultivating of a garden; the work or hobby of a gardener.

Garfield, James Abram *n.* (1831-1881). The 20th president of the United States, assassinated in 1881, after serving from March through September of 1881.

gar-gan-tu-an (gär gan´chö an) *adj.* Of enormous size; immense.

gar-gle (gär´gl) *v.* To force air from the lungs through a liquid held in the back of the mouth and throat. *n.* A liquid preparation used to wash the mouth and throat. **gargle** *n.*

gar-goyle (gär´goil) *n.* A waterspout made or carved to represent a grotesque animal or human figure, projecting from a gutter to throw rain away from the side of a building.

gar-ish (gâr´ish) *adj.* Too showy and bright; gaudy. **garishly** *adv.*

gar-land (gär´land) *n.* A wreath, chain, or rope of flowers or leaves. *v.* To decorate with or form into a garland. *Naut.* A ring of rope attached to a spar to aid in hoisting or to prevent chafing.

gar-lic (gär´lik) *n.* A plant related to the onion with a compound bulb which contains a strong odor and flavor, used as a seasoning.

garlic salt *n.* A condiment made of salt and ground dried garlic.

gar-ment (gär´ment) *n.* An article of clothing.

gar-ner (gär´nèr) *v.* To gather and store; to accumulate; to collect; to acquire.

gar-net (gär´nit) *n.* A dark-red silicate mineral used as a gemstone and as an abrasive.

garnet paper *n.* An abrasive paper coated with crushed garne.

gar-ni-er-ite *n.* A hydrous silicate consisting of nickel and magnesium: an important ore of nickel.

gar-nish (gär´nish) v. To add something to, as to decorate or embellish; to add decorative or flavorful touches to food or drink. **garnish** n.

gar-nish-ee (gär´ni shē´) v., Law To attach a debt or property with notice that no return or disposal is to be made until a court judgment is issued; to take a debtor's wages by legal authority.

gar-nish-ment (gär´nish ment) n. The act of garnishing; the legal proceeding that turns property belonging to a debtor over to his creditor.

gar-ni-ture (gär´ni chėr) n. Anything that is used to garnish or decorate.

gar-ret (gar´it) n. A room in an attic.

gar-ri-son (gar´i son) n. The military force that is permanently placed in a fort or town; a military post.

gar-ron (gar´on) n. A small workhorse.

gar-rote or **gar-rotte (ga rōt´)** n. The former Spanish method of execution by strangulation with an iron collar tightened by a screw-like device; the instrument used; throttling or strangulation. **garrote** v.

gar-ru-lous (gar´a lus) adj. Given to continual talkativeness; chatty. very talkative. **garrulity, garrulousness** n.

gar-ter (gär´tėr) n. A band or strap that is worn to hold a stocking in place; a band that holds up a sleeve.

garter snake n. A nonvenomous North American snake which is small, harmless and has brightly colored stripes.

garth (gärth) n. A small yard.

gas n. pl. **gases (gas)** A form of matter capable of expanding to fill a container and taking on the shape of the container; a combustible mixture used as fuel; gasoline; a gas used to produce an irritating, poisonous, or asphyxiating atmosphere. **gas** v. **gaseous, gassy** adj.

gas chamber n. An enclosure in which a condemned prisoner is put to death by the use of poisonous gas.

gas-con (gas´kon) n. A boastful person.

gas-con-ade n. A boasting; bravado; bragging.

gas engine n. An internal-combustion engine powered by a gas and air mixture.

gas-e-ous (gas´ē us) adj. Pertaining to or of the nature of gas.

gash (gash) n. A deep cut. v. To make a gash in.

gas-ket (gas´kit) n., Mech. A rubber seal, or ring used between machine parts or around pipe joints to prevent leakage.

gas-light (gas´līt´) n. A light made by burning illuminating gas; a lighting fixture.

gas-log n. An imitation log, that resembles firewood, used in a fireplace.

gas mask n. A protective respirator which covers the face and contains a chemical air filter to protect against poisonous gases.

gas-o-hol n. A fuel blended from unleaded gasoline and ethanol.

gas-o-line or **gas-o-lene (gas´o lēn´)** n. A colorless, highly flammable mixture of liquid hydrocarbons made from crude petroleum and used as a fuel and a solvent.

gas-om-e-ter n. A laboratory instrument for measuring or holding gases.

gasp (gasp) v. To inhale suddenly and sharply, as from fear or surprise; to make labored or violent attempts to breathe. **gasp** n.

gas–plant n. A perennial herbaceous plant with flowers that give off a flammable vapor in hot weather.

gas-ser n. An oil well that yields natural gas.

gas station n. A business where motor vehicles are serviced and gasoline, oil, etc., are sold.

gas-tral (ga stral´) adj. Relating to the stomach or digestive tract.

gas-terc-to-my n. The surgical removal of the stomach or a part of.

gas-tric (gas´trik) adj. Of or pertaining to the stomach.

gastric juice n., Biochem. The digestive fluid secreted by the stomach glands, containing several enzymes.

gastric ulcer n., Pathol. An ulcer formed on the stomach lining, often caused by excessive secretion of gastric juices.

gas-tri-tis (ga strī′tis) *n., Pathol.* Inflammation of the stomach lining. **gastritic** *adj.*

gas-tro-en-ter-ol-o-gy *n.* The medical study relating to the stomach and intestines. **gastroenterologist** *n.*

gas-tro-in-tes-ti-nal *adj.* Relating to or affecting the stomach and intestines.

gas-tron-o-my (ga stron′o mē) *n.* The art of good eating. **gastronome** *n.* **gastronomic** *adj.* **gastronomical** *adj.*

gas-tro-pod (gas′tro pod′) *n.* One of the large class of aquatic and terrestrial mollusks, including snails, slugs, limpets, having a single shell and a broad, muscular organ of locomotion. **gastropodan** *adj. & n.* **gastropodous** *adj.*

gas-tro-scope *n.* An instrument for viewing the interior of the stomach.

gas-trot-o-my *n.* The surgical operation of cutting into the stomach.

gas-tro-vas-cu-lar *adj.* Functioning in both circulation and digestion.

gas turbine *n.* A turbine engine activated by expansion of hot gases under pressure.

gas-works (gas′werks″) *n. pl.* **gasworks** An establishment where gas is manufactured.

gat (gat) *n., Slang* A pistol; short for Gatling gun.

gate (gāt) *n.* A movable opening in a wall or fence, commonly swinging on hinges, that closes or opens; a valve-like device for controlling the passage of gas or water through a conduit or dam; the total paid admission receipts or number in attendance at a public performance.

gate–crash-er (gāt′krash′ėr) *n.* One who gains admittance without an invitation or without paying.

gate-fold *n.* A foldout insert in a book larger in size than the other pages and is therefore folded.

gate-house *n.* A house near the front gate of an estate or prison entrance, used as quarters by the gatekeeper or guard.

gate-leg ta-ble (gāt′leg′ tā′bl) *n.* A table with legs that swing out to support drop leaves, the legs folding against the frame when the leaves are let down.

gate-way (gāt′wā″) *n.* The opening in a fence, etc. for a gate.

gath-er (gath′ėr) *v.* To bring or come together into one place or group; to harvest or pick; to increase or gain; to accumulate slowly; to fold or pleat a cloth by pulling it along a thread. **gathering** *n.*

gath-er-ing *n.* The act of assembling; that which is gathered.

gauche (gōsh) *adj.* Socially awkward; clumsy; boorish. **gauchely** *adv.*

gau-cho *n.* A cowboy of the South American.

gaud *n.* An ornament or trinket.

gaud-y (go′dē) *adj.* Too highly decorated to be in good taste. **gaudiness** *n.*

gauge *or* **gage (gāg)** *n.* A standard measurement, dimension, or capacity; an instrument used for measuring, testing, or registering; the distance between rails of a railroad; the diameter of the bore of a shotgun barrel. *v.* To determine the capacity, contents or volume of; to estimate; to evaluate. **gauger** *n.*

gaug-er *n.* A customs official who measures and inspects dutiable bulk goods.

gaunt (gont) *adj.* Thin and bony; haggard; gloomy or desolate in appearance.

gaunt-let *or* **gant-let (gont′lit)** *n.* A challenge to fight; a glove to protect the hand; a former military punishment which forced an offender to run between two lines of men armed with clubs with which to strike him; criticism from all sides.

gaur *n.* A very large, wild ox found in southeastern Asia and Malaysia.

gauze (goz) *n.* A loosely-woven, transparent material used for surgical bandages; any thin, open-mesh material; a mist. **gauzy** *adj.* **gauziness** *n.*

ga-vage *n.* Forced feeding, of nutrients into the stomach, by means of a flexible stomach tube and a force pump.

gave *v.* Past tense of give.

gav-el (gav´el) *n.* A mallet used to call for order or attention. **gavel** *v.*

gav-e-lock *n.* A crowbar.

ga-vi-al (gā´vē al) *n.* A large crocodile found in India, with long, slender jaws.

ga-votte (ga vot´) *n.* A French dance resembling a quick-moving minuet.

gawk (gok) *v.* To gape; to stare stupidly.

gawk-ish *adj.* Awkward; stupid.

gawk-y (go´kē) *adj.* Clumsy or awkward. **gawkiness** *n.*

gay (gā) *adj.* Merry; happy and carefree; brightly ornamental or colorful; homosexual. *n.* A homosexual. **gayness** *n.*

ga-yal *n.* A domesticated ox.

gaze (gāz) *v.* To look steadily or intently at something in admiration or wonder; to stare.

ga-ze-bo (ga zēbō) *n.* A freestanding structure open on all sides.

ga-zelle (ga zel´) *n.* A small, gracefully formed antelope of northern Arabia and Africa, having curved horns and large eyes.

ga-zette (ga zet´) *n.* A newspaper; an official publication. *v.* To publish or announce in a gazette.

gaz-et-teer (gaz´i tēr´) *n.* A dictionary consisting of geographical facts.

gaz-pa-cho (gaz po´chō) *n.* A cold soup made from vegetables, spices, oils, etc.

gds *abbr.* Goods.

ge-an-ti-cline *n.* An great upward fold encompassing of the earth's surface.

gear (gēr) *n., Mech.* A toothed wheel which interacts with another toothed part to transmit motion; an assembly of parts that work together for a special purpose; equipment. *v.* To regulate, match, or suit something. **gearing** *n.*

gear-box, gear box *n.* An enclosure for the protection of gears in a motor.

gear-ing *n.* The parts of a machine that transmits or changes motion.

gear-shift (gēr´shift˝) *n., Mech.* A mechanism used for engaging or disengaging the gears in a power transmission system.

gearwheel *or* **gear wheel (gēr´hwēl˝)** *Mech.* A cogwheel.

geck-o (gek´ō) *n. pl.* **geckos** *or* **geckoes** Any of various small lizards of warm regions having toes with adhesive pads enabling them to climb up or down vertical surfaces.

gee *interj.* A word command given to horses, or other work animals, directing them to turn right.

geese *n.* Plural of goose.

gee-zer (gēzėr) *n., Slang* An old odd or eccentric man.

ge-gen-schein *n.* A faint, round patch of light sometimes seen in the sky at night.

Ge-hen-na (gi hen´a) *n.* In the New Testament, hell; a place of torment.

ge-fil-te fish (gefil´te fish) *n.* Chopped fish mixed with crumbs, seasoning, and eggs, then cooked in a broth and served chilled in oval-shaped cakes or balls.

Geiger counter (gī´gėr koun´tėr) *n., Phys.* An instrument used to measure, detect, and record cosmic rays and nuclear radiation.

gei-sha (gā´sha) *n. pl.* **geisha** *or* **geishas** A Japanese girl who furnishes entertainment and companionship for men.

gel (jel) *n., Chem.* A colloid that is in a more solid than liquid form. *v.* To change into or take on the form of a gel.

gel-a-tin *or* **gel-a-tine (jel´a tin)** *n.* An almost tasteless, odorless, dried protein, soluble in water and derived from boiled animal tissues, used in making foods, drugs, and photographic film; a jelly made from gelatin. **gelatinous** *adj.*

ge-lat-i-nize *v.* To change into a jelly form.

geld (geld) *v.* To castrate or spay, especially a horse.

geld-ing (gel´ding) *n.* A gelded animal.

gel-id (jel´id) *adj.* Very cold; frigid. **gelidity** *n.*

gel-ig-nite *n.* Dynamite with an absorbent base of potassium or sodium nitrate.

gem (jem) *n.* A cut and polished precious or semiprecious stone; one that is highly treasured. *v.* To set or decorate with or as with gems.

gem-i-nate (jem´i nāt) *v.* To become paired

or arrange in pairs.

Gem-i-ni (jem´ī nī˝) *n.* The third sign of the zodiac; a person born between May 21 and June 21.

gem-mip-a-rous *adj.* Reproducing by buds.

gem-mule (jem´ūl) *n.* A small bud.

gem-ol-o-gy *or* **gem-mol-o-gy (je mol´o jē)** *n.* The study of gems. **gemological** *adj.*

gems-bok *n.* A large antelope, of southern Africa, strikingly marked and having long straight horns and a long tail.

Gem State *n.* Nickname of the state of Idaho.

gem-stone *n.* A precious stone that which can be refined by cutting and polishing and used in jewelry.

gen *abbr.* Gender; general; generally.

ge-ne-a-log-i-cal *adj.* Pertaining to genealogy.

gen-darme (zhän´därm) *n. pl.* **gendarmes** An armed policeman in France.

gen-der (jen´dėr) *n., Gram.* Any of two or more categories, as feminine, masculine, and neuter, into which words are divided and which determine agreement with or selection of modifiers or grammatical forms; the quality of being of the male or female sex.

gene (jēn) *n., Biol.* A functional hereditary unit which occupies a fixed location on a chromosome and controls or acts in the transmission of hereditary characteristics.

ge-ne-al-o-gy (jē´nē ol´o jē) *n. pl.* **-ies** A record, table, or account showing the descent of a family, group, or person from an ancestor; the study of ancestry. **genealogical** *adj.* **genealogically** *adv.* **genealogist** *n.*

gene mutation *n.* Alteration in an organism due to a chemical rearrangement within the molecules of a gene.

gen-er-a-ble *adj.* Capable of being generated or produced.

gen-er-al (jen´ėr al) *adj.* Pertaining to, including, or affecting the whole or every member of a group or class; common to or typical of most; not being limited to a special class; miscellaneous; not detailed or precise. *n., Milit.* An officer in the United States Army, Air Force, or Marine Corps ranking above a colonel. **generally** *adv.*

general admission *n.* A fee paid for an unreserved seating area.

general assembly *n.* A legislative body. **General Assembly** The supreme deliberative body of the United Nations.

general delivery *n.* A post office department in charge of mail that is held until called for by the addressee.

gen-er-a-list *n.* A person who is skilled and knowledgeable in several different fields.

gen-er-al-i-ty (jen´e ral´i tē) *n. pl.* **generalities** The state or quality of being general; an inadequate, inexact or vague statement or idea.

gen-er-al-i-za-tion (jen´ėr a lizā´shan) *n.* Something arrived at by generalizing, such as a broad, overall statement or conclusion.

gen-er-al-ize (jen´ėr a līz˝) *v.* To draw a general conclusion from particular facts, experiences, or observations.

general partner *n.* A partner with who has an unlimited liability for his company's debts.

general practitioner *n.* A doctor who treats a variety of medical problems rather than specializing in one.

general–purpose *adj.* Useful in two or more basic purposes; useful in several ways.

gen-er-al-ship (jen´ėr al ship˝) *n.* The office or rank of a general; leadership or management of any type.

general staff *n., Milit.* A group of officers who assist the commander in planning and supervising military operations.

general store *n.* A retail store selling a large variety of merchandise, but not subdivided into departments.

gen-er-ate (jen´e rāt˝) *v.* To cause to be; to produce; to bring into existence, especially by a chemical or physical process. **generative** *adj.*

gen-er-a-tion (jen´e rā´shan) *n.* A group of individuals born at about the same time; the average time interval between the birth of parents and that of their offspring. **generational** *adj.*

generative cell *n.* A male or female sexual reproductive cell.

gen-er-a-tor (jen´e rā´tèr) *n., Mech.* A machine that changes mechanical energy into electrical energy.

gen-er-a-trix *n.* A point, line, or surface whose motion generates a line, surface, figure, or solid.

ge-ner-ic (je ner´ik) *adj.* Relating to or characteristic of an entire class or group; pertaining to a class of or relating to a class of merchandise that does not have a trademark. **generically** *adv.*

gen-er-ous (jen´ēr us) *adj.* Sharing freely; abundant; overflowing. **generosity** *n.* **generously** *adv.*

gen-e-sis (jen´i sis) *n. pl.* **geneses** The act or state of originating. **Genesis** The first book of the Old Testament.

ge-net-ic (je net´ik) *adj.* Of or pertaining to the origin or development of something; of or relating to genetics. **genetically** *adv.*

genetic code *n., Biochem.* The biochemical basis of heredity that specifies the amino acid sequence in the synthesis of proteins and on which heredity is based.

ge-net-ics *n.* The science that deals with the hereditary and evolutionary differences and similarities of related organisms, as produced by the interaction of genes.

ge-ne-va (je nē´va) *n.* An alcoholic liquor flavored with juniper berries.

Ge-ne-va Con-ven-tion *n.* The international agreement signed at Geneva in 1864 which governs the war-time treatment of prisoners of war and of the wounded, sick, and the dead.

gen-ial (je nē´al) *adj.* Cheerful, kind, pleasant and good-humored in disposition or manner. **geniality** *n.* **genially** *adv.*

gen-ic (jen´ik) *adj.* Pertaining to a gene or genes.

ge-nic-u-late *adj.* Bent at an angle like the knee.

ge-nie (jē´nē) *n.* A supernatural creature, capable of taking on human form, who does

one's bidding.

genii *n.* In ancient mythology, a guardian spirit appointed to guide a person through life.

gen-i-tal (jen´i tal) *adj.* Of or pertaining to the reproductive organs or the process of reproduction.

genitals (jen´i talz) *n. pl.* The external sexual organs. **genitalia** *n.*

gen-i-tive (jen´i tiv) *adj., Gram.* Indicating origin, source, or possession. *n.* The genitive case. **genitival** *adj.*

gen-i-to-u-ri-nar-y (jen´i tō yer´iner´ē) *adj., Anat.* Of or pertaining to the genital and urinary organs or their functions.

gen-i-tor *n.* A male parent.

gen-ius (jēn´yus) *n. pl.* **genises** Exceptional intellectual ability or creative power; a strong, natural talent; a person who exerts powerful influence over another.

gen-o-cide (jen´o sīd´) *n.* The systematic extermination or destruction of a political, racial, or cultural group. **genocidal** *adj.*

gen-re *n.* A category of a specific artistic or literary accomplishment characterized by a particular form, technique, or subject matter.

gens (jenz) *n. pl.* **gentes** In ancient Rome, a clan that included families of the same name that have descended through the male line.

gent (jent) *n., Slang* A gentleman.

gen-teel (jen tēl´) *adj.* Refined or well-bred; elegant; polite; stylish or fashionable. **genteelly** *adv.* **genteelness** *n.*

gen-tian (jen´shan) *n.* An annual or perennial plant with showy blue, red, yellow, or white flowers.

Gen-tile (jen´tīl) *n.* A person, especially a Christian, who is not a Jew; of or relating to non-Mormons.

gen-til-i-ty (jen til´i tē) *n.* The quality of being genteel; the members of the upper class; well-born or well-bred persons collectively.

gen-tle (jen´tl) *adj.* Not harsh, severe, rough, or loud; easily handled or managed; docile; not sudden or steep; from a good family of high social standing. *Meteor.* A soft, moderate breeze. *v.* To tame. **gently** *adv.* **gentleness** *n.*

gen-tle-folk *or* **gen-tle-folks (jen´tl fōk˝)** *n. pl.* Nice people; persons from good family backgrounds.

gen-tle-man (jen´tl man) *n.* A man of noble birth and social position; a courteous or polite man; used as a form of address.

gen-tle-wom-an (jen´tl wum´an) *n.* A woman of noble birth and social position; a woman attendant upon a lady of rank; a well-bred or polite woman.

gen-try (jen´trē) *n.* People of good family or high social standing; the aristocracy; in England, the social class that is considered the upper ranks of the middle class.

ge-nu *n. pl.* **gennua** *Anat.* The knee.

gen-u-flect (jen´ū flekt˝) *v.* To bend down on one knee, as in worship.

gen-u-ine (jen´ū in) *adj.* Real; authentic; not counterfeit or spurious; not hypocritical; sincere. **genuinely** *adv.* **genuineness** *n.*

ge-nus (jē´nus) *n. pl.* **nera** *Biol.* A group or category of plants and animals usually including several species.

geo- *combining form* Ground; earth; soil.

ge-o-cen-tric (jē´ō sen´trik) *adj.* Of or relating to the earth's center; formulated on the assumption that the earth is the center of the universe. **geocentrically** *adv.* **geocentrical** *adj.*

ge-o-chem-is-try (jē´ō kem´i strē) *n.* A branch of chemistry that deals with the chemical composition of the earth's crust. **geochemical** *adj.* **geochemist** *n.*

ge-o-chro-nol-o-gy *n.* The earth's chronology determined by the study of geological data.

ge-ode (jē´ōd) *n., Geol.* A hollow rock having a cavity lined with crystals. **geodic** *adj.*

geodesic dome *n.* A vaulted or domed structure of lightweight straight elements that form interlocking polygons.

geodesic line (jē ō des´ik) *n.* In mathematics, the shortest line that connects two points on a given surface.

ge-od-e-sy (jē od´i sē) *n.* The geologic science dealing with the determination of the shape, area, and curvature of the earth. **geodesist** *n.* **geodetic** *adj.*

geo-duck *n.* An edible clam of the Pacific Coast.

ge-o-dy-nam-ics *n. pl.* The science that deals with the natural forces and processes, of the earth's interior and crust.

ge-og-no-sy *n.* That branch of geology that deals with the constituent parts of the earth, its description of land, air and water, its crust, and interior.

ge-og-ra-phy (jē og´ra fē) *n. pl.* **-phies** The science that deals with the earth's natural climate, resources, and population. **geographer** *n.* **geographic, geographical** *adj.* **geographically** *adv.*

ge-oid *n.* The surface around or within the earth which coincides with the mean sea level over the ocean and its extension under the continents.

ge-ol-o-gy (jē ol´o jē) *n. pl.* **geologies** The science that deals with the history, origin, and structure of the earth. **geologic, geological** *adj.* **geologically** *adv.*

ge-o-mag-net-ic *adj.* Relating to the earth's magnetism. **geomagnetism** *n.*

ge-om-e-ter *n.* A geometrid moth or its larva; a specialist in geometry.

ge-o-met-ric (jē´ō me´trik) *adj.* According to or pertaining to the rules and principles of geometry; increasing in a geometric progression.

ge-om-e-tri-cian *n.* A person skilled in geometry.

geometric progression *n.* A sequence of numbers, as 4, 8, 16, 32 where each term is the product of a constant factor and the term that precedes it.

ge-om-e-trid *n.* A small, delicate, slender-bodied moth having broad wings, whose larvae are commonly called inchworms.

ge-om-e-try (jē om´i trē) *n. pl.* **ies** The branch of mathematics that deals with the measurement, properties, and relationships of lines, angles, points, surfaces and solids.

ge-o-mor-phic *adj.* Relating to the form

or surface features of the earth.

ge-o-mor-phol-o-gy *n.* The science that deals with the origin, development, and characterisitics of the surface features of the earth.

ge-oph-a-gy *n.* The practice of eating earthy substances such as clay.

ge-o-phys-ics (jē'ō fiz'iks) *n. pl.* The study of the earth as the product of complex physico-chemical forces that act upon it internally from outer space, with reference to exploration of the less accessible regions.

ge-o-phyte *n.* A perennial plant, the surviving buds of which lie below the surface of the soil.

ge-o-pol-i-tics (jē'ō pol'i tiks) *n. pl.* The study of the influence of economic and geographical factors on the politics and policies of a nation or region. **geopolitical** *adj.*

geor-gette *n.* A fine transparent variety of silk crepe woven from hard-twisted yarns to give a dull pebby surface.

Georgia *n.* A state located in the southeastern part of the United States, statehood January 2, 1788, state capital Atlanta.

ge-o-strat-e-gy *n.* A group of factors, geographical, political, and strategic, are characteristic of a specific area.

ge-o-stroph-ic *adj.* Relating to the deflective force caused by the earth's rotation.

ge-o-tec-ton-ic *adj.* Relating to the structure form and arrangement of the earth's crust.

ge-o-ther-mal *or* **ge-o-ther-mic (jē'ō ther'mal)** *adj.* Relating to the internal heat of the earth.

ge-ot-ro-pism *n.* The tendency to turn gravitationally toward the earth.

ge-ra-ni-ol *n.* An unsaturated alcohol, chiefly used in soaps and perfumes.

ge-ra-ni-um (ji rā'nē um) *n.* A plant having rounded leaves and clusters of pink, red, or white flowers; a plant of the genus Pelargonium, with divided leaves and purplish or pink flowers.

ge-rar-di-a *n.* An herb belonging to the figwort family, having showy purple, pink, or yellow flowers with distended bases.

ger-a-tol-o-gy *n.* The study that addresses the decline of life, of animals threatened with extinction.

ger-bil (jer'bil) *n.* An animal of the rodent family found in the desert regions of Africa and Asia  Minor, having long hindlegs and a long tail; a popular pet.

ger-i-at-rics (jer'ē a'triks) *n. pl.* The medical study that deals with the structural changes, diseases, physiology, and hygiene of old age. **geriatric** *adj.* **geriatrician** *n.*

germ (jerm) *n.* A small cell or organic structure from which a new organism may develop; a microorganism which causes disease. *Biol.* A reproductive cell.

Ger-man (jer'man) *n.* The language of Germany; an inhabitant or native of Germany.

ger-mane (jer mān) *adj.* Relevant to what is being considered or discussed.

Ger-man-ic (jer man'ik) *n.* Relating to the language or customs of the Dutch, German, English, Afrikaans, Flemish, or Scandinavians. **Germanic** *adj.*

ger-ma-ni-um (jer mā'nē um) *n.* A grayish-white element widely used in electronics and optics, symbolized by Ge.

Ger-man meas-les *n., Pathol.* A contagious viral disease accompanied by sore throat, fever, and a skin rash; a disease capable of causing defects in infants born to mothers infected during the first stages of pregnanacy.

German Shepherd *n.* A large breed of dog, which is often trained to help the police and the blind.

germ cell *n.* An egg or sperm cell.

ger-mi-cide (jer'mi sīd") *n.* An agent used to destroy microorganisms or disease germs. **germicidal** *adj.*

ger-mi-nal (jer'mi nal) *adj.* Of or relating to a germ or germ cell; of or in the earliest stage of development.

ger-mi-nant *adj.* To gradually grow and develope.

ger-mi-nate (jer'mi nāt") *v.* To begin to

grow, develop, or sprout. **germination** *n.*

germ plasm *n., Biol.* The part of the protoplasm of a germ cell containing the chromosomes and genes.

ger-on-tol-gy (jer'*on* tol'*o* jē) *n.* The study of the processes and phenomena of aging. **gerontological** *adj.* **gerontologic** *adj.* **gerontologist** *n.*

ger-ry-man-der (jer'i man˝dėr) *v.* To divide a voting area so as to advance unfairly the interests of a political party; to adjust or adapt to one's advantage.

ger-und (jer'und) *n., Gram.* A verb form that is used as a noun.

ges-so (jes'ō) *n.* Plaster of paris prepared with glue used in painting, etc.

gest (jest) *n.* A notable deed or feat.

ge-stalt (g*e* shält') *n.* A pattern as a unified whole, with properties which cannot be derived by summation of its individual parts.

ge-sta-po (g*e* stä'pō) *n.* The secret police in Germany under the Nazi regime, known for its brutality.

ges-tate *v.* To conceive and gradually mature in the mind; to carry in the womb during pregnancy.

ges-ta-tion (je stā'sh*a*n) *n.* The carrying of a developing offspring in the uterus; pregnancy. **gestate** *v.* **gestational** *adj.*

ges-tic *adj.* Pertaining to motions or gestures of the body.

ges-tic-u-late (je stik'ū lāt') *v.* To make expressive or emphatic gestures, as in speaking.

ges-ture (jes'chėr) *n.* A bodily motion, especially with the hands in speaking, to emphasize some idea or emotion. *v.* To make gestures. **gesturer** *n.*

ge-sund-heit (g*e* zen'hīt) *Interj.* A German phrase used to wish good health to a person who has just sneezed.

get (get) *v.* To come into possession of, as by receiving, winning, earning, or buying. **to get ahead** To attain success. **to get back at** To revenge oneself on. **to get by** To manage; to survive. **to get one's goat** To make somebody angry.

get-a-way (get'*a* wā˝) *n.* The act of or instance of escaping by a criminal; a start, as of a race.

get-ta-ble, get-a-ble *adj.* Accessibly procured; obtainable.

get–to-geth-er (get'*to* geth˝ėr) *n.* A small, informal family or social gathering.

get-up (get'up˝) *n.* An outfit; a costume.

ge-um *n.* A perennial herb of the rose family with white, purple, or yellow flowers.

gew-gaw (gū'go) *n.* A little ornamental article of small value.

gey-ser (gī'zėr) *n.* A natural hot spring that intermittently ejects hot water and steam.

ghast-ly (gast'lē) *adj.* Horrible; terrifying; very unpleasant or bad; ghost-like in appearance; deathly pale.

ghat (gät) *n.* A broad flight of steps that leads down to the edge of a river; a mountain pass, range, or chain.

gher-kin (ger'kin) *n.* A very small, prickly cucumber pickled as a relish.

ghet-to (get'ō) *n.* A run-down section of a city in which a minority group lives because of poverty or social pressure.

ghost (gōst) *n.* The spirit of a dead person which is believed to appear to or haunt living persons; a spirit; a ghostwriter; a false, faint secondary television image. **ghostly** *adj.*

ghost-ly *adj.* Pertaining or relating to a ghost; suggestive of ghosts.

ghost town *n.* A town that once flourished but is now deserted.

ghost-writer *n.* A person hired to write for another person and to give credit for the writing to that other person.

ghoul (gōl) *n.* A person who robs graves; in Moslem legend, an evil spirit which plunders graves and feeds on corpses. **ghoulish** *adj.* **ghoulishly** *adv.* **ghoulishness** *n.*

GI (jē'ī') *n. pl.* **GIs** *or* **GI's** An enlisted person in the United States armed forces. *adj.* In conformity with military regulations or customs. *v.* To clean or scrub in preparation for or as if for a military inspection.

general issue.

gi-ant (jī´ant) *n.* A legendary man-like being of supernatural size and strength; one of great power, importance, or size; largest. **giantess** *n.*

giant powder *n.* A form of dynamite made of nitroglycerin and kieselguhr.

gib *n.* A thin plate of metal or other material to hold parts together or in place.

gib-ber (jib´ér) *v.* To talk or chatter incoherently or unintelligibly.

gib-ber-ish (jib´ér ish) *n.* Meaningless speech.

gib-bet (jib´it) *n.* A gallows. *v.* To execute by hanging on a gibbet.

gib-bon (gib´on) *n.* A slender, long-armed Asian ape.

gib-bous (gib´us) *adj.* The moon or a planet which is seen with more than half but not all of the apparent disk illuminated. **gibbously** *adv.* **gibbousness** *n.*

gibe (jīb) *v.* To ridicule or make taunting remarks. **gibe** *n.* **giber** *n.*

gib-let (jib´lit) *n.* or **giblets** The heart, liver, and gizzard of a fowl.

gid *n.* A disease of sheep caused by infestation of the brain caused by the larval of a tapeworm.

gid-dy (gid´ē) *adj.* Affected by a reeling or whirling sensation; dizzy; frivolous and silly; flighty. **giddily** *adv.* **giddiness** *n.*

gift (gift) *n.* Something that is given from one person to another; a natural aptitude; a talent.

gift-ed *adj.* The state of having a special ability.

gig (gig) *n.* A light, two-wheeled carriage drawn by one horse. *Naut.* A speedy, light; rowboat; a spear with forks or prongs used for fishing. *Slang* A job, especially an engagement to play music. *Milit., Slang* A demerit; a punishment to military personnel.

gi-gan-tic (jī gan´tik) *adj.* Of tremendous or extraordinary size; large; huge. **gigantically** *adv.*

gig-gle (gig´l) *v.* To laugh in high-pitched, repeated, short sounds. **giggle** *n.* **giggler**

n. **giggly** *adj.*

gig-o-lo (jig´o lō´) *n.* A man who is supported by a woman not his wife; a man who is paid to be an escort or dancing partner.

gigue *n.* A lively dance step.

Gila monster (hē´la mon´ster) *n.* A large, venomous lizard of the southwestern United States desert having an orange and black body.

gild (gild) *v.* To coat with a thin layer of gold; to brighten or adorn. **gilded** *adj.* **gilding, gilder** *n.*

gild-er *n.* **gild-ing** *n.* A thin coating of gold leaf; a superficially attractive appearance. *v.* To add unnecessary ornamentation.

gill (gil) *n., Zool.* The organ, as of fishes and various other aquatic invertebrates, used for taking oxygen from water. *n.* A liquid measure that equals 1/4 pint.

gilt (gilt) *adj.* Covered with or of the color of gold. *n.* A thin layer of gold or a gold-colored substance which is applied to a surface.

gilt-edge *or* **gilt-edged (gilt´ejd´)** *adj.* Of the highest value or the best quality.

gim-bal (jim´balz) *n.* A three ringed device that keeps an object supported on it level, as the compass of a ship.

gim-crack (jim´krak´) *n.* A cheap and useless object of little or no value.

gim-let (gim´lit) *n.* A small, sharp tool with a bar handle and a pointed, spiral tip which is used for boring holes.

gim-mal *n.* A series of interlocked rings.

gim-mick (gim´ik) *n.* A tricky feature that is obscured or misrepresented; a tricky device, especially when used dishonestly or secretly; a gadget. **gimmickry** *n.* **gimmicky** *adj.*

gimp (gimp) *n., Slang* A person who walks with a limp; a cripple. **gimp** *v.* **gimpy** *adj.*

gin (jin) *n.* An aromatic, clear, alcoholic liquor distilled from grain and flavored with juniper berries; a machine used to separate seeds from cotton fibers. *v.* To remove the seeds from cotton with a gin.

gin-ger (jin´jér) *n.* A tropical Asian plant

that has a pungent aromatic root, used in medicine and cooking.

ginger ale *n.* An effervescent soft drink flavored with ginger.

ginger beer *n.* A sweet nonalcoholic effervescing drink flavored with ginger.

gin-ger-bread (jin´jer bred) *n.* A dark, ginger and molasses flavored cake or cookie.

gin-ger-ly (jin´jer lē) *adv.* Doing something very cautiously; carefullly. **gingerliness** *n.* **gingerly** *adj.*

gin-ger-snap (jin´jer snap´) *n.* A brittle molasses and ginger cookie.

ging-ham (ging´am) *n.* A cotton fabric woven in solid colors and checks.

gin-gi-li (jin´ji lē) *n.* The sesame plant or its oil.

gin-gi-val *adj.* Referring to the gums.

gin-gi-vi-tis (jin˝ji vī´tis) *n., Pathol.* Inflammation of the gums.

gink-go (gingk´gō) *n. pl.* **ginkgoes** *or* **gingkoes** A large Chinese shade tree cultivated in the United States, with edible fruits and nuts.

gin rum-my *n.* A variety of the card game rummy.

gin-seng (jin´seng) *n.* An herb native to China and North America with an aromatic root believed to have medicinal properties.

Gip-sy (jip´sē) *n. & adj.* Variation of gypsy.

gi-raffe (ji raf´) *n. pl.*  **giraffes** *or* **giraffe** The tallest of all mammals, having an extremely long neck and very long legs, found in Africa.

gir-an-dole *n.* Radiating and showy fireworks; an ornamented branched candelstick.

gir-a-sol *n.* A variety of opal showing a reddish color when turned toward the light.

gird (gerd) *v.* To surround, encircle, or attach with or as if with a belt.

gird-er (ger´der) *n.* A strong, horizontal beam, as of steel or wood, which is the main support in a building.

gir-dle (ger´dl) *n.* A cord or belt worn a-

round the waist; a supporting undergarment worn by women to give support and to shape. **girdle** *v.*

girl (gerl) *n.* A female child or infant; a young, unmarried woman; any woman of any age; one's sweetheart. **girlish** *adj.* **girlishly** *adv.* **girlishness** *n.*

girl Friday *n.* A woman employee responsible for a variety of tasks.

girl friend *n.* A female friend; a regular or frequent female companion of a boy or man.

Girl Scout *n.* A member of the Girl Scouts of the United States, an organization for girls between 7 and 17 years of age.

girth (gerth) *n.* The circumference or distance around something; a strap that encircles an animal's body to secure something on its back, as a saddle.

gis-mo *n., Slang* A part or device whose name is unknown or forgotten; a gadget.

gist (jist) *n.* The central or main substance, as of an argument or question.

git-tern *n.* A medieval guitar strung with wire.

give (giv) *v.* To make a present of; to bestow; to accord or yield to another; to put into the possession of another; to convey to another; to donate or contribute; to apply; to devote; to yield as to pressure; to collapse; to furnish or provide; to deliver in exchange for pay. **giveaway** To hand over the bride to the bridegroom at a wedding ceremony. **give out** To collapse; to be exhausted. **give up** To surrender; to submit oneself. **give** *n.* **giver** *n.*

give–and–take *n.* To make a mutual exchange, as of conversation or opinions.

give-a-way (giv´awā˝) *n.* Something that is given free as a premium; something that betrays, generally unintentionally

giv-en (giv´n) *adj.* Bestowed; presented; specified or assumed.

given name *n.* The name bestowed or given at birth or baptism.

give up *v.* To surrender; to cease to do; hand over; to abandon all hope; quit.

giz-zard (giz´erd) *n.* The second stomach

in birds, where partly digested food is finely ground.

gla-brous (glā´brus) *adj. Biol.* Having no hair or down; having a smooth surface. **glabrousness** *n.*

gla-cial (glā´shal) *adj.* Of or pertaining to, caused by, or marked by glaciers; extremely cold. **glacially** *adv.*

glacial epoch *Geol.* A portion of geological time when ice sheets covered much of the earth's surface.

gla-ci-ate *v.* To convert into or cover with a glacier; to produce glacial effects.

gla-cier (glā´shėr) *n.* A large mass of compacted snow that moves slowly until it either breaks off to form icebergs or melts when it reaches warmer climates.

gla-ci-ol-o-gy *n.* Any branch of science dealing with snow or ice accumulation , geographical distribution, movement, or the effects of glaciers.

glad (glad) *adj.* Displaying, experiencing, or affording joy and pleasure; a state of being happy; being willing to help; grateful. *n.* Short for gladiolus.

glad-den (glad´n) *v.* To make glad.

glade (glād) *n.* A clearing in a forest or woods.

glad-hand *n.* A warm welcome to people you meet.

glad-i-a-tor (glad´ē ā˝tėr) *n.* An ancient Roman slave, captive, or paid freeman who entertained the public by fighting to the death; one who engages in an intense struggle or controversy. **gladiatorial** *adj.*

glad-i-o-lus (glad˝ē ō´lus) *n.* *pl.* **gladili** *or* **gladiluses** A plant with fleshy bulbs, sword-shaped leaves, and spikes of colorful flowers.

glad-some (glad´som) *adj.* Giving cheer; showing joy. **gladsomely** *adv.* **gladsomeness** *n.*

glam-or-ize *or* **glam-our-ize (glam´o rīz˝)** *v.* To make glamorous; to portray or treat in a romantic way.

glamour girl *n.* A woman considered to lead a glamorous life.

glam-our *or* **glam-or (glam´ėr)** *n.* Alluring fascination or charm. **glamorous** *adj.* **glamourous** *adj.*

glance (glans) *v.* To take a brief or quick look at something; to obliquely strike a surface at an angle and be deflected; to give light, brief touch; to brush against. **glancing** *adj.*, **glanced** *v.*

gland (gland) *n.. Anat.* Any of various body organs which excrete or secrete substances. **glandular** *adj.*

glan-du-lar *adj.* Relating to or involving glands.

glare (glâr) *v.* To stare fiercely or angrily; to shine intensely; to dazzle. *n.* An uncomfortably harsh or bright light.

glar-ing (glâr´ing) *adj.* Shining with an extremely bright light; painfully obvious. **glaringly** *adv.* **glaringness** *n.*

glass (glas) *n.* A hard, amorphous, brittle, usually transparent material which hardens from the molten state, preceded by rapid cooling to prevent crystallization; any substance made of or resembling glass; a mirror, tumbler, window pane, lens, or other material made of glass. **glasses** A pair of eyeglasses used as an aid to vision; glassware. **glass** *adj.* **glassy** *adj.*

glass blowing *n.* The art or process of shaping objects from molten glass by gently blowing air into them through a glass tube. **glassblower** *n.*

glass-ine *n.* A thin, dense, transparent paper highly resistent to air and grease.

glass-mak-er (glas´mā˝kėr) *n.* A person who makes glass or glassware.

glass-ware *n.* Articles made of glass.

glass-wool *n.* Glass fibers in a mass being used for thermal insulation and air filters.

glass-work *n.* The manufacture of glass and glassware; the fitting of glass; glazing; articles of glass.

glass-wort (glas´würt˝) *n.* A succulent, leafless plant of the goosefoot family, living in salt water marshes as well as alkaline regions.

glau-co-ma (glo kō´ma) *n., Pathol.* A disease of the eye characterized by abnormally high pressure within the eyeball and partial or complete loss of vision.

glau-cous (glo´kus) *adj.* Yellowish green.

glaze (glāz) *n.* A thin, smooth coating as on ceramics. *v.* To become covered with a thin glassy coating of ice; to coat or cover with a glaze; to fit with glass, as to glaze a window. **glazer** *n.* **glazing, glazed** *v.*

gla-zier (glā´zhėr) *n.* A person who sets glass **glaziery** *n.*

glaz-ing (glā´zing) *n.* The action or process of furnishing or fitting with glass.

gleam (glēm) *n.* A momentary ray or beam of light. *v.* To shine or emit light softly; to appear briefly. **gleamy** *adj.*

glean (glēn) *v.* To collect or gather facts by patient effort; to collect part by part; to pick bits of a crop left by a reaper. **gleanings** *pl. n.* **gleaner** *n.*

glean-ings *n. pl.* Things acquired a little at a time, or in slow stages.

glede *n.* A bird of prey.

glee (glē) *n.* Joy; merriment; an unaccompanied song for male voices. **gleeful** *adj.* **gleefully** *adv.*

glee club *n.* A singing group that is organized to sing short pieces of choral music.

gleet (glēt) *n.* An abnormal, transparent mucuous discharge of the urethra, caused by gonorrhea.

glen (glen) *n.* A small, secluded valley.

glen-gar-ry (glen gar´ē) *n.* A woolen cap worn by the Scottish people.

glen plaid *n.* A twill pattern of checks.

gli-a-din *n.* Any simple protein found in gluten, from wheat and rye.

glib (glib) *adj.* Spoken easily and fluently; superficial. **glibly** *adv.* **glibness** *n.*

glide (glīd) *v.* To pass or move smoothly with little or no effort; to fly without motor power. **glidingly** *adv.* **gliding** *v.*

glid-er (glī´dėr) *n.* One that glides; a swing gliding in a metal frame. *Aeron.* An aircraft without an engine, constructed to soar on air currents.

glim-mer (glim´ėr) *n.* A faint suggestion; an indication; a dim unsteady light. *v.* To give off a faint or dim light.

glimpse (glimps) *n.* A momentary look.

glint *v.* To be reflected; to give off a flash; or gleam.

glis-sade (gli säd´) *n.* A gliding ballet step; a controlled slide in either a sitting or standing position, used to descend a steep, snowy, or icy incline. **glissade** *v.*

glis-san-do (gli sän´dō) *n. pl.* **-di** A rapid passing from one tone to another by a continuous change of pitch.

glis-ten (glis´en) *v.* To shine softly as reflected by light; to shine or glow with a luster. **glisten** *n.* **glistened** *v.*

glitch *n.* A minor mishap or malfunction. *Elect.* A false signal caused by an unwanted surge of power.

glit-ter (glit´ėr) *n.* A brilliant sparkle; small bits of light-reflecting material used for decoration. *v.* To sparkle with brilliance. **glittery** *adj.* **glittering, glittered** *v.*

gloam-ing (glō´ming) *n.* Twilight; the dusk of early evening.

gloat (glōt) *v.* To express, feel, or observe with great malicious pleasure or self-satisfaction. **gloater** *n.* **gloating** *v.*

glob (glob) *n.* A drop of something; a rounded, large mass of something.

glob-al (glō´bal) *adj.* Spherical; involving the whole world. **globalize** *v.*

globe (glōb) *n.* A spherical object; anything that is perfectly rounded; the earth; anything like a sphere, such as a fishbowl; a spherical representation of the earth, usually including geographical and political boundaries.

globe-fish *n.* A fish with the capabilities to inflate themselves into a globular form.

globe–trotter *n.* One who travels all over the world.

glob-ule *n.* A very small particle of matter in the form of a ball.

glob-u-lin (glob´ū lin) *n., Biochem.* Any of a class of simple proteins found widely in blood, milk, tissue, muscle and plant seeds.

glo-chid-i-ate (glō kid´ē it) *adj.* Barbed at the tip; bearing barbs.

glom-er-ate (glom´ėr it) *adj.* Congregated; gathered into a round mass.

glom-er-ule *n.* A compact cluster, as of a single flower cluster that contains several flowers.

gloom (glŏm) *n.* Partial or total darkness; depression of the mind or spirits. **gloomily** *adv.* **gloominess** *n.* **gloomy** *adj.*

gloom-y *adj.* Partially or totally dark; low in spirits; lacking illumination.

glop (glob) *n, Slang* A messy mixture of food; something that is considered worthless.

glo-ri-fy (glŏr′*i* fi″) *v.* To worship and give glory to; to give high praise.

glo-ri-ole *n.* A halo.

glo-ri-ous (glŏr′ē us) *adj.* Magnificent; resplendent; delightful; illustrious; full of glory. **gloriously** *adv.*

glory (glŏr′ē) *n. pl.* **glories** Distinguished praise or honor; exalted reputation; adoration and praise offered in worship; a wonderful asset; the height of one's triumph, achievement, or prosperity. *v.* To rejoice with jubilation.

gloss (glos) *n.* The sheen or luster of a polished surface; a deceptively or superficially attractive appearance; a note that explains or translates a difficult or hard to understand expression. *v.* To cover over by falsehood in an attempt to excuse or ignore.

glos-sa-ry (glos′*a* rē) *n. pl.* **glossaries** A list of words and their meanings.

gloss-y (glos′ē) *adj.* Having a bright sheen; lustrous; superficially attractive. *n.* A photo print on smooth, shiny paper. **glossily** *adv.* **glossiness** *n.*

glost *n.* Ceramic glaze used on clay pottery.

glot-tis (glot′is) *n. pl.* **glottises** *or* **glottides** *Anat.* The opening or cleft between the vocal cords at the upper part of the larynx. **glottal** *adj.*

glove (gluv) *n.* A covering for the hand with a separate section for each finger; an oversized protective covering for the hand, as that used in baseball, boxing, or hockey. **gloved** *adj.*

glow (glō) *v.* To give off heat and light, especially without a flame; to have a bright,

warm, ruddy color. *n.* A warm feeling of emotion. **glowing** *adj.*

glow-er (glou′ėr) *v.* To look sullenly or angrily at; to glare. **glower** *n.*

glow-ing *adj.* Brilliantly luminous.

glow lamp *n.* Gas-discharged electric lamp in which electrons ionize a gas, emitting a glow.

glow-worm (glō′werm″) *n.* A European beetle; the luminous larva or grub-like female of an insect which displays phosphorescent light; the firefly.

glox-in-i-a (glok sin′ē *a*) *n.* A tropical South American plant with large, bell-shaped flowers.

glu-ca-gon *n.* A protein that increases the content of sugar in the blood by increasing the rate of breakdown of glycogen in the liver.

glu-cose (glō′kōs) *n., Chem.* A substance less sweet than cane sugar, found as dextrose in plants and animals and obtained by hydrolysis; a yellowish to colorless syrupy mixture of dextrose, maltose, and dextrins with a small amount of water, used especially in confectionery and baking.

glue (glō) *n.* Any of various adhesives in the form of a gelatin, made from animal substances, as bones or skins, and used to stick and hold items together. **glue** *v.* **gluey** *adj.*

glum (glum) *adj.* Moody and silent. **glumly** *adv.* **glumness** *n.*

glut (glut) *v.* To feed or supply beyond capacity; to provide with a supply that exceeds demand. *n.* An overabundance.

glutamic acid *n.* An amino acid that occurs in plant and animal proteins, used in the form of a sodium salt substitute and flavor enhancer.

glu-ten (glōt′en) *n.* A mixture of plant proteins that is used as an adhesive and as a substitute for flour. **glutenous** *adj.*

glu-te-us *n.* The large muscles of the buttock.

glut-ton (glut′n) *n.* Someone who eats immoderately; one who has a large capacity for work or punishment. **gluttonous** *adj.,* **gluttonously** *adv.*

glut-ton-ous *adj.* Marked by excessive eating; greedy.

glyc-er-ol (glis´e rōl˝) *n. Chem.* A sweet, oily, syrupy liquid derived from fats and oils and used as a solvent, sweetener, antifreeze, and lubricant.

gly-co-pro-tein *n.* A group of conjugated proteins in which the nonprotein group is a carbohydrate.

gly-co-side (glī´ko sīd˝) *n., Chem.* Any of a group of carbohydrates which, when decomposed, produce glucose or other sugar.

glyph *n.* An ornamental cavity or channel.

gly-phog-ra-phy (gli fog´ra fē) *n.* Electrotype process where a plate having a raised surface appropriate for printing is made from an engraved plate.

glyp-tic *n.* The art of carving or engraving on precious gems or related stones.

glyp-to-dont *n.* An extinct mallam that resembled an armadillo.

G–man (jē´man˝) *n. pl.* **G–men.** An agent of the Federal Bureau of Investigations.

gnarl (närl) *n.* A hard, protruding knot on a tree. **gnarled** *adj.*

gnash (nash) *v.* To grind or strike the teeth together, as in a rage or pain.

gnat (nat) *n.* A small, winged insect, specially one that bites or stings.

gnath-ic *adj.* Pertaining or relating to the jaw or jaws.

gnaw (no) *v.* To bite or eat away with persistence; to consume or wear away. **gnawer** *n.* **gnawing, gnawed** *v.*

gneiss (nīs) *n.* A banded, coarse-grained rock with minerals arranged in layers.

gnome (nōm) *n.* In folklore, a dwarf-like creature who lives underground and guards precious metals and treasures.

gno-mon (nō´mon) *n.* An object that by the position of its shadow is an indicator of the hour of the day.

GNP *abbr.* Gross National Product.

gnu (nō) *n. pl.* **gnus** *or* **gnu** South African antelope with an ox-like head, curved horns, a long tail, and a mane.

go (gō) *v.* To proceed or pass along; to leave; to move away from; to follow a certain course of action; to function; to function correctly; to be in operation; to be awarded or given; to have recourse; to resort to; to pass, as of time; to be abolished or given up *v.* ; to pass to someone, as by a will. *n.* An attempt; a try. **go back on** To abandon **go for** To try; to try to obtain. **go places** To be on the road to success. **go under** To suffer destruction or defeat. **going** *v.*

goad (gōd) *v.* To drive cattle to move; to incite or arouse.

go–a–head (gō´a hed˝) *n.* Permission; a signal to move ahead or proceed.

goal (gōl) *n.* A purpose; the terminal point of a race or journey; in some games, the area, space, or object into which participants must direct play in order to score.

goal-ie *n.* A goalkeeper.

goal-keep-er (gōl´kē˝pėr) *n.* The player responsible for defending the goal in hockey, soccer, and other games, preventing the ball or puck from passing over the goal for a score; a goal tender.

goal-post *n.* Two vertical poles with a crossbar which constitutes the goal line in some sports.

goat (gōt) *n.* A horned, cud-chewing mammal related to the sheep; a lecherous man. *Slang* One who is a scapegoat. **goatish** *adj.* **goatishly** *adv.* **goatishness** *n.*

goat-ee (gō tē´) *n.* A short, pointed beard on a man's chin.

goat-skin (gōt´skin˝) *n.* The skin of a goat, often used for leather.

go–be-tween (gō´bi twēn˝) *n.* A person who acts as an agent between two parties.

go–get-ter (gō´get´ėr) *n.* An enterprising, aggressive person.

gob (gob) *n.* A piece or lump of something. *Slang* A sailor.

gob-ble (gob´l) *v.* To eat and swallow food greedily; to take greedily; to grab.

gob-ble-dy-gook (gob´l dē gek) *n., Informal* Wordy and often unintelligible language.

gob-bler (gob´lẽr) *n.* A male turkey.

gob-let (gob´lit) *n.* A drinking glass, typically with a base and stem.

gob-lin (gob´lin) *n.* In folklore, an ugly, grotesque creature said to be mischievous and evil.

go-bo (gō´bō) *n.* A dark strip to shield a television camera from light.

go-by *n.* A small freshwater fish, often having the pelvic fins attached to form a ventral sucking cup enabling it to cling to rocks.

go-cart *n.* A small, gasoline-powered car, used for recreation or racing.

god (god) *n.* Someone considered to be extremely important or valuable; an image, symbol, or statue of such a being.

God (god) *n.* The Supreme Being; the ruler of life and the universe.

god-child (god´chīld´) *n.* A child for whom an adult serves as sponsor at baptism, circumcision, and other rites.

god-dess (god´is) *n.* A female of exceptional charm, beauty, or grace.

go-dev-il *n.* A small, gasoline propelled car used on railroad tracks to transport workers and supplies.

god-father (god´fä thẽr) *n.* A man who sponsors a child at his or her baptism or other such ceremony.

god-for-sak-en (god´fẽr sā˝kɛn) *adj.* In a remote desolate place.

god-head (god´hed´) *n.* Godhood; divinity. **Godhead** The essential and divine nature of God.

god-hood (god´hed) *n.* The state or quality of being a god; divinity.

god-less (god´lis) *adj.* Not recognizing a god. **godlessness** *n.*

god-ly (god´lē) *adj.* Filled with love for God.

god-mother (god´muth ẽr) *n.* A woman who sponsors a child at his or her baptism or other such ceremony.

god-par-ent (god´pâr´ɛnt) *n.* A godfather or godmother.

god-send (god´send´) *n.* Something received unexpectedly that is needed or wanted.

god-son *n.* A male godchild.

God-speed (god´spēd´) *n.* Best wishes for someone's venture or journey.

god-wit *n.* A long-billed wading bird related to snipes.

gof-fer *n.* An ornamental ruffled piece of lace as used on women's clothing.

go–get-ter (gō˝get´ẽr) *n.* An enterprising, aggressive person.

gog-gle (gog´l) *n. pl.* **goggles** Spectacles or eyeglasses to protect the eyes against dust, wind,  sparks, and other debris. *v.* To gaze or stare with bulging eyes.

go-ing (gō´ing) *n.* The act of moving, leaving, or departing; the condition of roads or ground that affects walking, riding, and other movement; a condition influencing activity or progress. **goings on** Actions or behavior, used to express disapproval.

goi-ter (goi´tẽr) *n., Pathol.* Any abnormal enlargement of the thyroid gland, visible as a swelling in the front of the neck. **goi-trous** *adj.*

gold (gōld) *n.* A soft, yellow, metallic element that is highly ductile and resistant to oxidation; used especially in coins and jewelry; a precious metal; a bright, vivid yellow; money; the element symbolized by Au.

gold-beat-er *n.* A person whose job it is to beat gold into thin leaves, as used in gilding.

gold-brick (gōld´brik) *n., Slang* A person who avoids work. **goldbricker** *n.*

gold digger *n., Slang* A woman who seeks money and gifts from men.

gold-en (gōl´dɛn) *adj.* Made of or containing gold; bright yellow in color; rich; lustrous; marked by prosperity.

golden age *n.* Any period marked by peace, happiness, prosperity, or excellence; the best of times.

golden anniversary *n.* The 50th anniversary.

Golden Gate *n.* A large bridge in San Francisco, California that connects the Pacific Ocean and San Francisco Bay.

gold-en-rod (gōl´den rod˝) *n.* A North American plant with small yellow flowers; the state flower of Alabama, Kentucky, and Nebraska.

golden rule *n.* The principle of treating others as one wants to be treated.

Golden State *n.* Nickname of the state of California.

gold–fill-ed (gōld´fild) *adj.* Made of a hard base metal over which a thick covering of gold is laid.

gold-finch (gōld´finch˝) *n.* A small bird, the male of which has yellow plumage with black forehead, tail, and wings.

gold-fish (gōld´fish˝) *n.* A reddish or brass-colored freshwater fish, cultivated as an aquarium fish.

gold foil *n.* Thin, pliable sheets of gold used primarily in grounding designs in enamel.

gold leaf *n.* Gold that has been hammered into extremely thin sheets, used primarily for gilding.

gold mine *n.* A mine which produces gold ore; any source of great riches or profit.

gold-smith *n.* A person who makes, or deals in gold items.

gold standard *n.* The monetary system based on gold of a specified weight and fineness as the unit of value and exchange.

golf (golf) *n.* A game played outdoors with a hard ball and various clubs, on a grassy course with 9 or 18 holes. **golf** *v.* **golfer** *n.*

Gol-go-tha (gol´go tha) *n.* A place near Jerusalem where Jesus was crucified; also known as Calvary.

Go-li-ath *n.* In the Bible, a giant Philistine killed by David with a stone from a sling shot.

gon-ad (gō´nad) *n., Anat.* The male or female sex gland where the reproductive cells develop; an ovary or testis. **gonadal, gonadial, gonadic** *adj.*

gon-do-la (gon´do la) *n.* A long, narrow, flat-bottomed boat propelled by a single oar and used on the canals of Venice.

gone (gon) *adj.* Past; bygone; dead; beyond hope; marked by faintness or weakness. **far gone** Exhausted; wearied; almost dead.

gon-er (go´nėr) *n., Slang* One that is ruined, close to death, or beyond all hope of saving.

gon-fa-lon (gon´fa lon) *n.* A banner hung from a cross piece and cut so as to end in streamers.

gong (gong) *n.* A heavy metal disk which produces a deep resonant tone when struck.

go-ni-om-e-ter *n.* An instrument used for measuring angles.

gon-o-coc-cus (gon´o kok´us) *n. pl.* **gon-ococci** The bacterium which causes gon-orrhea. **gonococcal, gonococcic** *adj.*

gon-or-rhe-a (go˝´o rē´a) *n., Pathol.* A contagious venereal infection transmitted chiefly by sexual intercourse.

goo (gō) *n.* Any sticky substance.

goo-ber (gö´bėr) *n., Regional* A peanut.

good (ged) *adj.* Having desirable or favorable qualities or characteristics; morally excellent; virtuous; well-behaved; tractable; proper; excellent in degree or quality; unspoiled; fresh; healthy; striking or attractive. **goods** Merchandise or wares; personal belongings; cloth; fabric. **for good** Forever; permanently. better, best.

Good Book *n.* The Bible.

good–by *or* **good–bye** (ged˝bī´) *interj.* Used to express farewell. *n.* A farewell; a parting word; an expression of farewell. *adj.* Final.

good fellow *n.* A good natured person.

good–for–nothing (ged´fėr nuth´ing) *n.* A person of little worth or usefulness.

Good Friday *n.* The Friday before Easter, a day observed by Christians as a commemoration of the crucifixion of Jesus.

good–heart-ed (ged´här´tid) *adj.* Having a kind and generous disposition. **good–heartedness** *n.*

good–hu-mored *adj.* Having a cheerful temper or mood; amiable. **good–humoredly** *adv.* **good–humoredness** *n.*

good–looking (ged´lek´ing) *adj.* Handsome; having a pleasing appearance.

good–na-tured (ged´nā´cherd) *adj.* Having an easy going and pleasant disposition; happy. **good–naturedly** *adv.* **good–na-turedness** *n.*

good-ness (ged´nis) *n.* The state or quality of being good.

good-will *n.* A desire for the well-being of others; the pleasant feeling or relationship between a business and its customers.

good-y (ged´ē) *n. pl.* **goodies** Something that is good to eat; a prissy person.

goof (gŏf) *n., Slang* A stupid or dull-witted person; a mistake. *v.* To blunder; to make a mistake.

goof–off *n.* A person who shuns responsibility or work. *v.* To be doing something else when there is work to be done.

goof-y (gō´fē) *adj.* Ridiculous; silly. **goofily** *adv.* **goofiness** *n.*

gook (gek) *n., Slang* A slimy, sludgy, or dirty substance.

goon (gōn) *n., Slang* A thug or hoodlum hired to intimidate or injure someone; a person hired to break strikes; a stupid person.

goose (gŏs) *n. pl.* **geese** A large water bird related to swans and ducks; a female goose. *Informal* A silly person.

goose-berry (gŏs´ber´ē) *n. pl.* **goose-berries** Greenish berry of a spiny shrub used for pies, jams, and other foods.

goose bumps *n. pl.* A prickling sensation of the skin caused by fear or cold, also known as goose pimples and goose skin.

goose egg *n.* A score of zero in a contest or game.

goose-neck (gŏs´nek˝) *n.* Any various devices curved like a goose's neck.

go-pher (gō´fer) *n.* A burrowing North American rodent with large cheek pouches.

gore (gōr) *v.* To stab or pierce. *n.* Blood that has been shed; a triangular or tapering piece of cloth as in a sail or skirt.

gorge (gorj) *n.* A deep, narrow ravine; deep or violent disgust. *v.* To eat or devour something greedily. **gorger** *n.*

gor-geous (gor´jus) *adj.* Beautiful; dazzling; extremely beautiful; magnificent. **gorgeously** *adv.* **gorgeousness** *n.*

Gor-gon-zo-la (gor˝gon zō´la) *n.* A pungent, strongly flavored Italian cheese.

go-ril-la (go ril´a) *n.* A large African jungle ape, having a massive, stocky body, long arms, and tusk-like canine teeth.

gorse (gors) *n.* A spiny plant bearing fragrant yellow flowers.

go-ry (gōr´ē) *adj.* Covered or stained with blood; resembling gore.

gosh *interj.* An expression of surprise.

gos-hawk (gos´hok˝) *n.* A large, short-winged hawk formerly used in falconry.

gos-ling (goz´ling) *n.* A young goose.

gos-pel *or* **Gos-pel** (gos´pel) *n.* The teachings of Christ and the apostles; any information which is accepted as unquestionably true; any of the first four books of the New Testament.

gospel music *n.* American religious music based on simple folk melodies blended with rhythmic and melodic elements of spirituals and jazz.

gos-port *n.* A flexible tube used as one-way communications between two people in an airplane cockpit.

gos-sa-mer (gos´a mer) *n.* The fine film or strands of a spider's web floating in the air; anything sheer, delicate, light, or flimsy.

gos-san *n.* Decomposed rock or vein material of a reddish or rusty color, often forming a large part of the outcrop of an iron-bearing vein.

gos-sip (gos´ip) *n.* Idle, often malicious talk; a person who spreads sensational or intimate facts. *v.* To spread or engage in gossip. **gossiper** *n.* **gossipy** *adj.*

got *v.* Past tense of get.

Goth (goth) *n.* A member of a Germanic people that invaded the Roman Empire early in the Christian era; a barbarian.

Goth-am *n.* A nickname for New York City.

Goth-ic (goth´k) *adj.* Of or pertaining to the Goths or to their lanugage; of or relating to an architectural style popular from about 1200 to 1500, which was characterized by pointed arches and ribbed vaulting.

gouache (gwäsh) *n.* A method of painting with opaque watercolors.

Gou-da cheese (gou´da chēz) *n.* A mild, yellow Dutch cheese made from milk.

gouge (gouj) *n.* A chisel with a scoop-shaped blade used for woodcarving; a groove or hole made with or as if with a gouge *v.* To make a hole or groove with a gouge; to cheat, as to charge exorbitant prices. **gouger** *n.*

gou-lash (gō´läsh) *n.* A stew made from beef or veal and vegetables seasoned chiefly with paprika.

gourd (gōrd) *n.* A vine fruit related to the pumpkin, squash, and cucumber and bearing inedible fruit with a hard rind; the dried, hollowed-out shell can be used as a drinking utensil.

gour-mand (ger´mand) *n.* A person who takes excessive pleasure in eating.

gour-met (ger´mā) *n.* Someone who appreciates and understands fine food and drink.

gout (gout) *n., Pathol.* A disease caused by a defect in metabolism and characterized by painful inflammation of the joints.

gov *abbr.* Government

gov-ern (guv´ern) *v.* To guide, rule, or control by right or authority; to control or guide the action of something; to restrain. **governable** *adj.* **governance** *n.*

gov-ern-ess (guv´er nis) *n.* A woman employed in a private household to train and instruct children.

gov-ern-ment (guv´ern ment) *n.* The authoritative administration of public policy and affairs of a nation, state or city; the system or policy by which a political unit is governed; any governed territory, dis-

trict, or area. **governmental** *adj.,* **governmentally** *adv.*

gov-er-nor (guv´er nėr) *n.* Someone who governs, as the elected chief executive of any state in the United States; an official appointed to exercise political authority over a territory. *Mech.* A device which will automatically control the speed of a machine. **governorship** *n.*

govt *abbr.* Government.

gow-an *n.* A yellow or white field flower.

gown (goun) *n.* A woman's dress, especially for a formal affair; any long, loose-fitting garment; a robe worn by certain officials, scholars, and clergymen.

GP *abbr.* General practitioner.

GPO *abbr.* General Post Office.

gr *abbr.* Grade; gross, grain.

grab (grab) *v.* To snatch or take suddenly; to take possession of by force or by dishonest means. *Slang* To capture the attention of someone or something. **grab** *n.* **grabber** *n.* **grabby** *adj.*

grab bag *n.* A bag or container full of miscellaneous unidentified articles from which one may draw an object at random.

grab-ble *v.* To search with the hand; grope.

gra-ben (grä´ben) *n., Geol.* An elongated depression in the earth, caused by the downward faulting of a portion of the earth's crust.

grab rope *n.* A rope or ropes along the side of a ship, for another boatman to hold on to if necesasry, when coming alongside.

grace (grās) *n.* Seemingly effortless beauty, ease, and charm of movement, proportion, or form; a charming quality or characteristic; an extension of time that is granted after a set date, as for paying a debt. **graceful** *adj.* **gracefully** *adv.*

grace-less *adj.* Lacking of grace or a pleasing quality.

grace period *n.* A time, after the actual due date of a payment when one may make payment without penalties.

gra-cious (grä´shus) *adj.* Marked by having or showing kindness and courtesy; full of compassion; merciful. **graciously** *adv.*

graciousness *n.*

grack-le (grak´l) *n.* Any of various New World blackbirds having long tails and iridescent blackish plumage.

grad *n., Slang* A graduate.

gra-date (grā´gāt) *v.* To shade into the next color or stage.

gra-da-tion (grā dā´shan) *n.* A gradual and orderly arrangement or progression according to quality, size, rank, or other value; the act of grading. **gradational** *adj.*

grade (grād) *n.* A step or degree in a process or series; a group or category; a level of progress in school, usually constituting a year's work; a letter or number indicating a level of achievement in school work; the degree to which something slopes, as a road, track, or other surface. *Milit.* Rank or rating. **grade** *v.*

grade crossing *n.* A crossing of highways, railroad tracks or walks on the same level.

grad-er (grā´dèr) *n.* A machine used to level earth.

grade school *n.* Elementary school, usually from kindergarten to grade 6 or grade 8.

gra-di-ent (grā´dē ent) *n.* A slope or degree of inclination. *Phys.* A rate of change in variable factors, as temperature or pressure.

gra-din (grā´din) *n.* One in a series of steps.

grad-u-al (graj´e al) *adj.* Moving or changing slowly by degrees; not steep or abrupt. **gradually** *adv.* **gradualness** *n.*

grad-u-ate (graj´ō āt˝) *v.* To receive or be granted an academic diploma or degree upon completion of a course of study; to divide into categories, grades or steps. *n.* A person who holds an academic degree; a container or beaker marked in units or degrees, used for measuring liquids.

graduate student A student who has received a college degree and is working toward an advanced or higher degree.

grad-u-a-tion (gra˝ō ā´shan) *n.* The state of graduating; a commencement ceremony; issuing of diplomas or degrees.

gra-dus *n.* A dictionary to assist in writing Greek or Latin verses.

graf-fi-to (gra fē´tō) *n. pl.* **graffiti** An inscription or drawing made on a public wall, subway train, rock, or any other surface.

graft (graft) *v.* To insert a shoot from a plant into another living plant so that the two will grow together as a single plant. *Surg.* To transplant a piece of tissue or an organ. *n.* Living tissue or skin used to replace damaged or destroyed tissue or skin; the act of acquiring or getting personal profit or advantage by dishonest or unfair means through one's public position.

gra-ham (grā´am) *n.* Whole wheat flour.

graham cracker *n.* A semisweet cracker made of whole wheat flour.

grail (grāl) *n.* The legendary cup used by Christ at the Last Supper; also called the Holy Grail.

grain (grān) *n.* A small, hard seed or kernel of cereal, wheat, or oats; the seeds or fruits of such plants as a group; a very small amount; a small, hard particle, as a grain of sand; the side of a piece of leather from which the hair has been removed; the characteristic markings or pattern of this side; texture; basic nature. **against the grain** Contrary to one's inclinations or temperament. **grainer** *n.* **grainless** *adj.*

grain alcohol *n.* Ethanol.

grain elevator *n.* A building used to store grain.

grain rust *n.* A rust which damages the stems of wheat, barley and other grains.

grain sorghum *n.* Any of several kinds of sorghum, cultivated, for grain or fodder.

grain-y (grā´nē) *adj.* Having a granular texture; resembling the grain of wood. **graininess** *n.*

gral-la-to-ri-al *adj.* Related or pertaining to large wading birds.

gram (gram) *n.* A metric unit of mass and weight equal to 1/1000 kilogram and nearly equal to one cubic centimeter of water at its maximum density.

gra-ma *n.* Any of several pasture grasses of the western United States.

gra-mer-cy *interj.* Used to express thanks;

an exclamation of astonishment or sudden feeling of surprise.

gram-i-ci-din *n.* Germicide used against bacteria in local infections.

gra-min-e-ous *adj.* Like or relating to grass.

gram-i-niv-o-rous *adj.* Surviving on grains or similar food.

gram-mar (gram´ėr) *n.* The study and description of the classes of words, their relations to each other, and their arrangement into sentences; the inflectional and syntactic rules of a language. **grammarian** *n.* **grammatical** *adj.* **grammatically** *adv.*

grammar school *n.* An elementary school. *Brit.* A secondary or preparatory school.

gram-mat-i-cal *adj.* Relating to the rules of grammar.

gram mol-e-cule (gram˝mo lek´ū lė) *n.* *Chem.* The quantity of a compound, expressed in grams, that is equal to the molecular weight of that compound.

gram-pus *n.* A large, marine mammal relating to the whale family.

gran-a-ry (grā´na rē) *n. pl.* **granaries** A building for storing threshed grain; an area or region where grain grows in abundance.

grand (grand) *adj.* To be large in size, extent, or scope; magnificent; of high rank or great importance; lofty; admirable; main or principal; highly satisfactory; excellent. *Slang* A thousand dollars. **grandly** *adv.* **grandness** *n.*

Grand Canyon State *n.* Nickname for the state of Arizona.

grand-child (gran´chīld˝) *n.* The child of one's son or daughter.

grand-dad *n.* The father of one's mother or father.

grand-daugh-ter (gran´do˝tėr) *n.* The daughter of one's son or daughter.

gran-deur (gran´jer) *n.* The quality or condition of being grand; splendor; magnificence.

grand-fa-ther (gran´fä˝thėr) *n.* The father of one's father or mother; an ancestor. **grandfatherly** *adv.*

grandfather clock *n.* A pendulum clock enclosed in a tall narrow cabinet.

gran-di-flo-ra *n.* A rose bush producing both single blooms and clusters of blooms on the same plant due to crossbreeding tea roses and floribunda.

gran-dil-o-quent (gran dil´o kwent) *adj.* Speaking in or characterized by a pompous or bombastic style.

gran-di-ose (gran´dē ōs˝) *adj.* Impressive and grand; pretentiously pompous; bombastic. **grandiosely** *adv.* **grandiosity** *n.*

grand jury *n.* A jury that listens to accusations against people who have committed a crime and passes judgment as to whether they are guilty or innocent.

grand mal (gran´mal´) *n., Pathol.* A form of epilepsy characterized by severe convulsions and loss of consciousness.

grand-moth-er (gran´muth˝ėr) *n.* The mother of one's father or mother; a female ancestor.

grand opera *n.* A form of opera having a serious and complex plot with the complete text set to music.

grand-par-ent (gran´pâr˝ent) *n.* A parent of one's mother or father.

grand piano *n.* A piano with the strings arranged horizontally in a curved, wooden case.

grand prix (grän prē´) *n.* An international long-distance car race through the streets.

grand slam *n.* In bridge, the taking of all the tricks; in baseball, a home run hit with runners on first, second, and third bases.

grand-son (gran´sun˝) *n.* A son of one's son or daughter.

grand-stand (gran´stand˝) *n.* A raised stand of seats, usually roofed, for spectators at a racetrack or sports event.

grange *n.* The farm buildings around a farmhouse; storage of grain.

grang-er-ize *v.* To illustrate a book using illustrations or prints taken from other sources.

gran-ite (gran´it) *n.* A hard, coarse-grained igneous rock composed chiefly of quartz, mica, and orthoclase, which is used for building material and in sculpture.

gran-ite-ware (gran´it wâr˝) *n.* Ironware

utensils coated with hard enamel.

gra-niv-o-rous *adj.* Feeding on seeds or grain.

gran-ny *or* **gran-nie (gran´ē)** *n.* A grandmother; an old woman; a fussy person.

gra-no-la *n.* Rolled oats mixed with dried fruit and seeds and eaten as a snack.

grano-lith (gran´o lith) *n.* An artificial stone made of crushed granite and cement.

gran-o-phyre *n.* Igneous rocks in which the ground mass is chiefly a mixture of quartz and feldspar crystals. **granophyric** *adj.*

grant (grant) *v.* To allow; to consent to; to admit something as being the truth; in law, to transfer property by a deed. *n.* That which is granted. **grantee, grantor** *n.*

grant-in-aid *n. pl.* **grants-in-aid** Financial support or subsidy for public use paid by a central government to local government for a public program or other public project.

gran-u-lar (gran´ū lėr) *adj.* The state of being composed or seeming to be composed or containing grains or granules. **granularity** *n.*

Grant, Ulysses S. *n.* The 18th president of the United States, from 1869-1877.

gran-u-lar (gran´ū lėr) *adj.* The state of being composed or seeming to be composed or containing grains or granules. **granularity** *n.*

gran-u-late (gran´ū lāt´) *v.* To make or form into granules or crystals; to become or cause to become rough and grainy.

gran-u-la-tion *n.* Tissue made up of minute projections of flesh that form in the process of healing.

gran-ule (gran´ūl) *n.* A very small grain or particle forming a larger unit.

gran-u-lo-cyte *n.* A white blood cell whose with the cytoplasm containing granules.

gran-u-lo-ma (gran´ūlō´ma) *n.* A nodule growth of inflamed tissue associated with the process of infection.

grape (grāp) *n.* Any of numerous woody vines bearing clusters of smooth-skinned, juicy, edible berries, having a dark purplish blue, red, or green color, eaten raw or dried and used in making wine.

grape-fruit (grāp´frŏt´) *n.* A tropical, large, round citrus fruit with a pale yellow rind and tart, juicy pulp; the tree bearing this fruit.

grape hy-a-cinth *n.* Several small bulbous spring flowering herbs of the lily family.

grape-shot (grāp´shot´) *n.* A shot consisting of a cluster of small iron balls, formerly used to charge a cannon.

grape sugar *n.* Dextrose.

grape-vine (grāp´vīn´) *n.* A climbing vine that produces grapes; a secret or informal means of transmitting information or rumor from person to person.

graph (graf) *n.* A diagram representing the relationship between sets of things.

graph-eme *n.* The smallest written unit of an alphabet, a single letter as used to represent one phoneme as the *(d)* in *drop*.

graph-ic *or* **graph-i-cal (graf´ik)** *adj.* Describing in full detail; of or pertaining to drawings or blueprints, as in architecture.

graph-ite (graf´īt) *n.* A soft black form of carbon having a metallic luster and slippery texture, used in lead pencils, lubricants, paints, and coatings. **graphitic** *adj.*

graph-i-tize *v.* To change into graphite, as part of the carbon in steel.

graph-ol-o-gy (gra fol´o jē) *n.* The study of handwriting for the purpose of analyzing a person's character or personality. **graphologist** *n.*

graph paper *n.* Paper ruled with lines for drawing graphs.

grap-nel (grap´nel) *n.* A small anchor with several flukes at the end.

grap-ple (grap´l) *n.* An instrument with iron claws used to fasten an enemy ship alongside for boarding. *v.* To struggle or contend with; to fasten, seize or drag as with a grapple. **grappler** *n.*

grasp (grasp) *v.* To seize and grip firmly; to comprehend; to understand. *n.* The power to seize and hold. **graspable** *adj.* **grasper** *n.*

grasp-ing (gras´ping) *adj.* Urgently desiring material possessions; greedy. **grasp-ingly** *adv.* **graspingness** *n.*

grass (gras) *n.* Any of numerous plants having narrow leaves and jointed stems; the ground on which grass is growing. *Slang* Marijuana. **grassiness** *n.* **grassy** *adj.*

grass court *n.* A tennis court made with a grass surface.

grass-hop-per (gras´hop˝ėr) *n.* Any of several jumping insects with long powerful hind legs. *Slang* Any small, lightweight airplane used for dusting crops and military observation.

grass-land (gras´land˝) *n.* Land in which grasses are the main vegetation, as a prairie.

grass-roots *n. pl.* A society of common people, thought of as having practical and highly independent views or interests. **grass-roots** *adj.*

grass widow *n.* A woman who is separated or divorced from her husband.

grass-y *adj.* Abounding or covered with grass.

grate (grāt) *v.* To reduce, shred or pulverize by rubbing against a rough or sharp surface; to make or cause to make a harsh sound. *n.* A rasping noise. **grater** n., **grating** *adj.* **gratingly** *adv.*

grate (grāt) *n.* A framework or bars placed over a window or other opening; an iron frame to hold burning fuel in a fireplace or furnace.

grate-ful *adj.* The state of being thankful or appreciative for benefits or kindness; expressing gratitude. **gratefully** adv.

grat-i-cule (grat´i kūl˝) *n.* The network of lines of latitude and longitude from which maps are drawn.

grat-i-fi-ca-tion *n.* The state of being gratified; that which affords pleasure, or enjoyment.

grat-i-fy (grat´i fī˝) *v.* To give pleasure or satisfaction to; to fulfill the desires of; to indulge. **gratification** *n.*

gra-tin (grat´in) *n.* A brown crust formed

on food cooked with a topping of crumbs or grated cheese.

grat-ing (grā´ting) *n.* A grate.

grat-is (grat´is) *adv. & adj.* Without requiring payment; free.

grat-i-tude (grat´i tŏd˝) *n.* The state of appreciation and gratefulness; thankfulness.

gra-tu-i-tous (gra tŏ´i tus) *adj.* Given or obtained without payment; unjustified; unwarranted. **gratuitously** *adv.* **gratuitousness** *n.*

gra-tu-i-ty (gra tŏ´i tē) *n. pl.* **gratuities** A gift, as money, given in return for a service rendered; a tip.

grau-pel *n.* Granules of soft hail or sleet.

gra-va-men (gra vā´men) *n. pl.* **grava-mens** *or* **gravamina** In law, the part of an accusation or charge weighing most heavily against the accused.

grave (grāv) *n.* A burial place for a dead body, usually an excavation in the earth. *adj.* Very serious or important in nature; filled with danger; critical. *v.* To sculpt or carve; to engrave. *Mus.* Solemn and slow. **gravely** *adv.* **graver** *n.*

grav-el (grav´el) *n.* Loose rock fragments often with sand. *Pathol.* The deposit of sand-like crystals that form in the kidneys; also known as kidney stones.

grave-stone (grāv´stōn˝) *n.* A stone that marks a grave; a tombstone.

grave-yard (grāv´yärd˝) *n.* An area set aside as a burial place; a cemetery.

graveyard shift *n.,* Slang A work shift that usually begins at midnight.

gra-vim-e-ter (gra vim´i tėr) *n.* An implement for determining specific gravity. **gravimetry** *n.*

grav-i-tate (grav´i tāt˝) *v.* To be drawn as if by an irresistible force; to sink or settle to a lower level.

grav-i-ta-tion (grav´i tā´shan) *n., Physics* The force or attraction any two bodies exert towards each other. **gravitational, gravitative** *adj.* **gravitationally** *adv.*

grav-i-ty (grav´i tē) *n. pl.* **gravities** The gravitational force manifested by the tendency of material bodies to fall toward the center of the earth; gravitation in general; weight; importance; seriousness.

gra-vy (grā´vē) *n. pl.* **gravies** The juices exuded by cooking meat; a sauce made by seasoning and thickening these juices. *Slang* Money or profit which is easily acquired.

gray *or* **grey (grā)** *adj.* A neutral color between black and white; gloomy; dismal; having gray hair; characteristic of old age. **grayish** *adj.* **grayness** *n.*

gray-beard (grā´bērd´) *n., Slang* An old man.

gray-lag *n.* A wild gray goose.

gray-ling (grā´ling) *n. pl.* **grayling** *or* **graylings** Any of several freshwater food and game fish with a small mouth and a large dorsal fin.

gray matter *n.* The grayish-brown nerve tissue of the spinal cord and brain, consisting mainly of nerve cells and fibers; brains.

graze (grāz) *v.* To feed upon growing grasses or herbage; to put livestock to feed on grass or pasturage; to brush against lightly in passing; to abrade or scrape slightly.

gra-zier (grā´zhėr) *n.* One who grazes cattle.

grease (grēs) *n.* Melted or soft animal fat; any thick fatty or oily substance, as a lubricant. *v.* To lubricate or coat with grease. **greasiness** *n.* **greasy** *adj.*

grease monkey *n.* An auto or airplane mechanic.

grease paint *n.* Makeup used for theatre performances.

grease-wood *n.* A shrub, of the goosefoot family common in alkaline regions of the western United States.

greasy (grē´sē) *adj.* Soiled with grease; oily in appearance.

greasy spoon *n.* A small cheap restaurant.

great (grāt) *adj.* Very large in size or volume; prolonged in duration or extent; more than ordinary; considerable; remarkable; impressive; eminent; renowned; very good or first-rate; a generation removed from a relative. **greatly** *adv.* **greatness** *n.*

great ape *n.* Any of the four modern anthropoid apes.

great–aunt (grāt´ant´) *n.* An aunt of either of one's parents.

Great Bear *n.* The constellation Ursa Major.

Great Britain *n.* The island which is located off the west coast of Europe, made up of England, Scotland and Wales; the United Kingdom.

great–grand-child *n.* A child of a grandchild.

great–grand-daugh-ter *n.* A daughter of a grandchild.

great–grand-fa-ther *n.* The father of a grandparent.

great–grand-mo-ther *n.* The mother of a grandparent.

great–grand-par-ent *n.* The father or mother of a grandparent.

great–grand-son *n.* The son of a grandchild.

great-heart-ed (grāt´här´tid) *adj.* Noble or generous in spirit; magnanimous. **greatheartedly** adv.

Great Lakes *n.* The group of five freshwater lakes of central North America located on either side of the boundary between the United States and Canada and including Lake Superior, Lake Michigan, Lake Huron, Lake Erie, and Lake Ontario.

great–neph-ew (grāt´nef´ū) *n.* A grandnephew.

great–niece (grāt´nēs´) *n.* A grandniece.

Great Pyr-e-nees *n.* A breed of large, heavy-coated, white dogs.

Great Salt Lake *n.* A lake composed of salt water located in the State of Utah.

great seal *n.* The chief seal of a government.

great–un-cle (grāt´ung´kl) *n.* An uncle of either of one's parents; granduncle.

greave *n.* An armor for the leg worn below the knee.

grebe (grēb) *n.* Any of various swimming and diving birds having partially webbed feet, very short tails, and a pointed bill.

greed (grēd) *n.* Selfish desire to acquire more than one needs or deserves.

greed-y (grē´dē) *adj.* Excessively eager to acquire or gain something; having an excessive appetite for drink and food; gluttonous. **greedily** *adv.* **greediness** *n.*

Greek (grēk) *n.* An inhabitant or native of Greece; the modern or ancient language of Greece. *adj.* Pertaining to or of the Greek Church; of or pertaing to the culture of Greece.

green (grēn) *adj.* Of the color between yellow and blue in the spectrum; not fully matured or developed; lacking in skill or experience. *n.* A grassy plot or lawn, especially an area of closely mowed grass at the end of a golf fairway. **greenish** *adj.,* **greenness** *n.*

green alga *n.* An alga of the family in which the chlorophyll not disguised by other pigments predominate.

green—eyed (grēn´īd˝) *adj.* Jealous.

green-back (grēn´bak˝) *n.* A United States; legal-tender currency note.

green bean *n.* A string bean; a vegetable commonly grown in private gardens.

green belt *n.* A group of parkways, lawns, farmlands, or wooded land that surrounds a planned community.

green-bri-er *n.* A climbing plant of the lily family, grown in the eastern United States.

green-er-y (grē´ne rē) *n. pl.* **-ies** Green foliage or plants.

green-gage *n.* A type of plum having a greenish or yellow-green skin.

green-gro-cer (grēen´grō˝sėr) *n.* A person who sells fresh vegetables and fruits.

green-horn (grēn´horn˝) *n.* An inexperienced person; a beginner; a person who is easily fooled.

green-house (grēn´hous˝) *n.* An enclosed structure equipped with heat and moisture designed for the cultivation of plants.

green-ing *n.* A type of green-skinned apple.

green light *n.* The traffic light which signs permission to proceed.

green manure *n.* A field of green plants, as the clover that is plowed under, while still growing and green, to decompose and enrich the soil.

green monkey *n.* A long-tailed monkey of West Africa that has greenish colored hair.

green onion *n.* Also called scallion; a flavorful young onion that is pulled from the ground while the bulb is still small, may be eaten alone or in salads.

green pepper *n.* The unripened fruit of various pepper plants.

green-room (grēn´rŏm˝) *n.* The room or lounge in a theatre used by performers when they are off stage.

greens fee *n.* The fee paid for playing golf on a golf course.

green thumb *n.* A special skill for making plants thrive.

green turtle *n.* A large edible green-shelled sea turtle.

greet (grēt) *v.* To address someone in a friendly way; to welcome; to meet or receive in a specified manner. **greeter** *n.*

greet-ing (grē´ting) *n.* A word of salutation on meeting.

gre-gar-i-ous (gri gâr´ē us) *adj.* Habitually associating with others as in groups, flocks, or herds; enjoying the company of others; sociable. **gregariously** *adv.* **gregariousness** *n.*

greige *n.* Woven fabric in an unbleached undyed state.

grei-sen *n.* A crystalline rock composed chiefly of quartz and mica.

grem-lin (grem´lin) *n.* A mischievous elf said to cause mechanical trouble in airplanes.

Gre-na-da *n.* An island in the West Indies.

gre-nade (gri nād´) *n.* A small explosive device detonated by a fuse and thrown by hand or projected from a rifle.

gren-a-dier (gren˝a dēr´) *n.* A member of a special European corps which was formerly armed with grenades.

gren-a-dine (gren˝a dēn´) *n.* A syrup made from pomegranates or red currants and used as a flavoring in mixed drinks.

grew *v.* Past tense of grow.

grey (grā) *n. & adj.* Variation of gray.

grey-hound (grā´hound´) *n.* One of a breed

of slender, swift-running dogs with long legs.

grib-ble (grib′l) *n.* A small marine crustacean which destroys submerged timber.

grid (grid) *n.* An arrangement of regularly spaced bars; the system of intersecting parallel lines that divide maps, charts, and aerial photographs, used as a reference for locating points.

grid-dle (grid′l) *n.* A flat pan used for cooking.

grid-dle cake (grid′l kāk″) *n.* A pancake.

grid-i-ron (grid′ī″ėrn) *n.* A metal framework used for broiling meat, fish, and other foods; a football field.

grief (grēf) *n.* Deep sadness or mental distress caused by a loss, remorse, or bereavement.

griev-ance (grē′vans) *n.* A real or imagined wrong which is regarded as cause for complaint or resentment; a complaint of unfair treatment.

grievance commitee *n.* A group formed by a labor union or employees jointly to discuss and try to eliminate problems.

grieve (grēv) *v.* To cause or feel grief or sorrow.

griev-ous (grē′vus) *adj.* Causing grief, sorrow, anguish, or pain; causing physical suffering. **grievously** *adv.*

grif-fin *or* **grif-fon (grif′on)** *n.* In Greek mythology, a fabulous beast with a lion's body, an eagle's head, and wings.

grift *v., Slang.* To obtain money by dishonest schemes, swindling, or cheating.

grig (grig) *n.* A lively young person.

grill (gril) *n.* A cooking utensil made from parallel metal bars; a gridiron; food cooked on a grill; a restaurant where grilled foods are a specialty. *v.* To broil on a grill.

gril-lage (gril′ij) *n.* A framework of lumber or steel for support in marshy soil.

grille *or* **grill (gril)** *n.* A grating with open metal work used as a decorative screen or room divider.

grilse *n.* A young, mature salmon returning from the sea to spawn for the first time.

grim (grim) *adj.* Stern or forbidding in appearance or character; unyielding; relentless; grisly; gloomy; dismal. **grimly** *adv.* **grimness** *n.*

grim-ace (grim′as) *n.* A facial expression of pain, disgust, or disapproval.

grime (grīm) *n.* Dirt, especially soot clinging to or coating a surface. **griminess** *n.* **grimy** *adj.*

grin (grin) *v.* To smile broadly. **grin** *n.*

grind (grīnd) *v.* To reduce to fine particles; to sharpen, polish, or shape by friction; to press or rub together; to work or study hard. *n.* A person who works hard or who studies very hard.

grind-er (grīn′dėr) *n.* One that grinds.

grinders *n. pl., Slang* The teeth.

grind-stone (grīnd′stōn″) *n.* A flat, circular stone which revolves on an axle and is used for polishing, sharpening, or grinding.

grip (grip) *n.* A firm hold; a grasp; the ability to seize or maintain a hold; the mental or intellectual grasp; a suitcase. *v.* To grasp and keep a firm hold on; to capture the imagination or attention. **gripper** *n.* **grippingly** *adv.*

gripe (grīp) *v.* To cause sharp pain or cramps in the bowels; to anger; to annoy; to com-plain.

grippe (grip) *n.* Influenza. **grippy** *adj.*

gri-saille *n.* A method of decorating in single colors especially in various shades of gray, making objects appear as three-dimensional.

gris-ly (griz′lē) *adj.* Ghastly; gruesome.

grist (grist) *n.* Grain that is to be ground; a batch of such grain.

gris-tle (gris′l) *n.* Cartilage of meat.

grist-mill *n.* A mill for grinding grain.

grit (grit) *n.* Small, rough granules, as of sand or stone; having great courage and fortitude. *v.* To clamp the teeth together. **gritty** *adj.*

grits (grits) *n. pl.* Coarsely ground hominy; coarse meal; eaten primarily in the southern states of the United States.

griz-zle (griz′l) *v.* To become or cause to become gray.

grizzly bear *n.* A large, grayish bear of western North America. **grizzlies** *n. pl., Slang* Grizzly bears.

groan (grōn) *v.* To utter a deep, prolonged sound of or as of disapproval or pain. **groan** *n.* **groaningly** *adv.*

groat (grōt) *n.* A former British coin worth four-pence; any grain without its hull; a tiny sum.

gro-cer (grō´sėr) *n.* A storekeeper who deals in foodstuffs and various household supplies.

gro-cer-ies *n. pl.* The merchandise sold in a grocery.

gro-cer-y (grō´se rē) *n. pl.* **groceries** A store in which foodstuffs and household staples are sold.

grog (grog) *n.* Any alcoholic liquor, especially rum, mixed with water.

grog-gy (grog´ē) *adj.* To be dazed, weak, or not fully conscious, such as from a blow or exhaustion; drunk. **groggily** *adv.* **grogginess** *n.*

gro-gram (grog´ram) *n.* A loosely woven fabric of silk and mohair or silk and wool.

grog-shop *n.* A low-class barroom.

groin (groin) *n., Anat.* The crease or fold where the thigh meets the abdomen. *Archit.* The curved edge of a building formed by two intersecting vaults.

grom-met (grom´it) *n.* A reinforcing eyelet through which a rope, cord, or fastening may be passed. *Naut.* A ring of rope or metal used to secure the edge of a sail.

grom-well *n.* Any plant of the borage family having hairy herbs and smooth, stony nuts.

groom (grōm) *n.* A male person hired to tend horses; a stableman; a bridegroom. *v.* To make neat in appearance; to prepare for a particular position, as for a political office.

grooms-man (grōmz´man) *n. pl.* **grooms-men** The best man at a wedding; any one of a bridegroom's attendants.

groove (grōv) *n.* A long, narrow channel or indentation; a fixed, settled habit or routine;

a rut. **groove** *v.*

groovy (grō´vē) *adj. Slang* A state or condition of being wonderful; delightful.

grope (grōp) *v.* The act of feeling about with or as with the hands, as in the dark; to look for uncertainly or blindly. **grope** *n.* **gropingly** *adv.*

gros-beak (grōs´bēk´) *n.* Any of several colorful birds related to the finch, with a stout, short beak.

gros-grain (grō´grān´) *n.* A heavy, horizontally corded silk or rayon fabric, woven as a ribbon.

gross (grōs) *adj.* Exclusive of deductions; of or relating to the total amount received; excessively large or fat; lacking refinement or delicacy; coarse; vulgar. *n.* The entire amount without deduction; an amount that equals 12 dozen or 144 items. **grossly** *adv.* **grossness** *n.*

gross national product *n.* The total market value of all goods and services produced by a nation in a year.

gross profit *n.* The total business receipts less cost of goods sold, before operating expenses and taxes are deducted.

gros-su-lar-ite *n.* A garnet of red, brown, yellow, green, or white.

gro-tesque (grō tesk´) *adj.* Distorted, incongruous or ludicrous in appearance or style; bizarre; outlandish. **grotesque, grotesqueness** *n.* **grotesquely** *adv.*

gro-tes-quer-y *n.* A grotesque representation; a group of absurdly represented characters.

grot-to (grot´ō) *n. pl.* **grottoes** *or* **grottos** A cave or cave-like structure.

grouch (grouch) *n.* An habitually irritable or complaining person. **grouch** *v.* **grouchily** *adv.* **grouchiness** *n.* **grouchy** *adj.*

ground (ground) *n.* The surface of the earth; soil, sand, and other natural material at or near the earth's surface; the connecting of an electric current to the earth through a conductor.

ground (ground) *v.* Past tense of grind.

ground ball *n.* A batted ball that bounds or rolls along the ground.

ground cherry *n.* A plant with round pulpy berries enclosed in a ribbed papery husk.

ground connection *n.* A grounding connection with the earth

ground cover *n.* A plant that forms a dense, extensive ground cover, prevents soil erosion.

ground crew *n.* The mechanics who maintain and service an airplane.

ground glass *n.* Glass that has been treated so that it is not fully transparent.

ground hog *n.* A woodchuck.

Groundhog Day *n.* February 2, on which if the groundhog sees his shadow, he goes underground again, because there will be six more weeks of winter.

ground ivy *n.* A trailing mint with rounded leaves, purple flowers.

ground-less (ground´lis) *adj.* Without foundation or basis.

ground plan *n.* A floor plan of a building; any first or basic plan.

ground rent *n.* Rent paid by a lessee for the use of land.

ground rule *n.* A basic rule; the rule in sports that modifies play on a particular field, course, or court.

grounds *n.* The land that surrounds a building; the basis for an argument, action or belief; the sediment at the bottom of a liquid, such as coffee or tea. *v.* To prevent an aircraft or pilot from flying. *Naut.* To run a boat aground.

ground sheet *n.* A waterproof cover to protect an area of ground, such as a baseball or football field.

ground swell *n.* Deep rolling of the sea, caused by a distant storm or gale.

ground wave *n.* A radio wave along the surface of the earth.

ground zero *n.* The point on the ground vertically beneath or above the point of detonation of an atomic bomb.

group (grŏp) *n.* A collection or assemblage of people, objects, or things having something in common.

grou-per (grŏ´pėr) *n.* A large fish related to the sea bass.

group-ie *n., Slang* A female follower of a rock group, especially when it is on tour.

group therapy *n.* Psychotherapy which involves sessions guided by a therapist and attended by several patients who discuss their problems.

grouse (grous) *n. pl.* **grouse** Any of a family of game birds characterized by mottled, brownish plumage and rounded bodies. *v.* To complain; to grumble.

grout (grout) *n.* A material used to fill cracks in masonry or spaces between tiles. **grout** *v.* **grouter** *n.*

grove (grōv) *n.* A small group of trees, lacking undergrowth.

grov-el (gruv´l) *v.* To lie or crawl face downward, as in fear; to act with abject humility. **groveler** *n.* **grovelingly** *adv.*

grow (grō) *v.* To increase in size, develop, and reach maturity; to expand; to increase; to come into existence. **to grow on** To become increasingly acceptable, necessary, or pleasing to. **grower** *n.*

growl (groul) *v.* To utter a deep, guttural, threatening sound, as that made by a hostile or agitated animal. **growl** *n.*

grown (grōn) *adj.* Fully matured; cultivated in a specified way.

grown-up (grōn´up´) *n.* A mature adult. **grownup** *adj.*

growth (grōth) *n.* The act or process of growing; a gradual increase in size or amount. *Pathol.* An abnormal formation of bodily tissue, as a tumor.

growth factor *n.* A substance that enhances the growth of an organism.

growth stock *n.* The common stock of a company with potential increase in business and profits.

grub (grub) *v.* To dig up by the roots; to lead a dreary existence; to drudge. *n.* The thick, worm-like larva of certain insects, as of the June beetle. *Slang* Food; to scrounge.

grub-by (grub´ē) *adj.* Sloppy, unkempt. **grubbily** *adv.* **grubbiness** *n.*

grub-stake (grub´stāk´) *n.* Funds and supplies furnished a miner until he can fend for himself.

grudge (gruj) *n.* A feeling of ill will, rancor, or deep resentment. *v.* To be displeased, resentful, or envious of the possessions or good fortune of another person. **grudger** *n.* **grudgingly** *adv.*

gru-el (grŏ´el) *n.* A thin liquid made by boiling meal in water or milk.

gru-el-ing *or* **gru-el-ling (grŏ´e ling)** *adj.* Very tired; exhausting. **gruelingly** *adv.*

grue-some (grŏ´som) *adj.* The state of causing horror or fright. **gruesomely** *adv.* **gruesomeness** *n.*

gruff (gruf) *adj.* Brusque and rough in manner; harsh in sound; hoarse. **gruffly** *adv.* **gruffness** *n.*

grum-ble (grum´bl) *v.* To complain in low, throaty sounds; to growl. **grumble** *n.* **grumbler** *n.* **grumbly** *adj.*

grump-y (grum´pē) *adj.* Irritable and moody; ill tempered. **grumpily** *adv.*

grun-gy *adj., Slang* Dirty, rundown, or inferior in condition or appearance.

grunt (grunt) *n.* The deep, guttural sound of a hog. **grunt** *v.*

grun-tle *v.* To put in a good mood.

G-string (jē´string´) *n.* A very narrow loincloth with a waistband, worn by stripteasers.

G-suit (jē´sŏt´) *n.* A flight garment designed to counteract the effects of high acceleration on a person by exerting pressure on the body parts.

GU *abbr.* Guam.

gua-ca-mo-le *n.* Mashed avocado seasoned with condiments.

gua-co *n.* A tropical climbing plant, of America, the leaves, or the substance from them, used as an antidote for snakebites.

gua-na-co (gwä nä´kō) *n.* A South American mammal with a fawn-colored coat, related to the camel but without a hump.

gua-neth-i-dine *n.* A drug used in treating severe high blood pressure.

gua-no (gwä´nō) *n.* The sea birds excrement used as a fertilizer.

guar *abbr.* Guaranteed.

guar-an-tee (gar´an tē´) *n.* The promise or assurance of the durability or quality of a product; something held or given as a pledge or security. *v.* To assume responsibility for the default or debt of; to certify; to vouch for.

guar-an-tor (gar´an tor´) *n.* One who gives a guarantee or guaranty.

guar-an-ty (gar´an tē´) *n. pl.* **guaranties** A pledge or promise to be responsible for the debt, duty, or contract of another person in case of default; something that guarantees.

guard (gärd) *v.* To watch over or shield from danger or harm; to keep watch as to prevent escape, violence, or indiscretion. *n.* A defensive position, as in boxing or fencing; in football, one of two linemen on either side of the center; in basketball, one of the two players stationed near the middle of the court; a device or piece of equipment that protects against damage, loss, or harm. **guarding, guarded** *v.*

guard hair *n.* The coarse, long outer hair forming a protective coating over the soft underfur of certain animals.

guard-house (gärd´hous´) *n.* A military jail; a building used by soldiers on guard duty.

guard-i-an (gär´dē an) *n.* One who is legally assigned responsibility for the care of the person and property of an infant, minor or person unable to do for himself because of physical or mental disability. **guardianship** *n.*

guard-rail *n.* The protective rail, as on a highway or any area that proposes a threat or danger.

guards-man (gärdz´man) *n.* A member of the United States National Guard.

guar gum *n.* A gum from ground guar seeds used as a thickening agent and as a sizing material.

gua-va (gwä´va) *n.* A tree or shrub of the myrtle family bearing small, pear-shaped, edible, yellow-skinned fruit.

gub-ba *v., Slang* To tickle the neck area, especially of young children and babies. *n.* The area that is tickled.

gu-ber-na-to-ri-al (gŏˮbêr nɑtōrˊē ɑl) *adj.* Of or pertaining to a governor.

gudgeon (gujˊon) *n.* A small European freshwater fish related to the carp.

gue-non (gᴇ nonˊ) *n.* A long-tailed arboreal African monkey.

guern-sey (gernˊzē) *n. pl.* **guernseys** A breed of brown and white dairy cattle.

guer-ril-la (gᴇ rilˊla) *n.* A member of an irregular military force that is capable of great speed and mobility, often operating behind enemy lines.

guess (ges) *v.* To make a judgment or form an opinion on uncertain or incomplete knowledge; to suppose; to believe.

guess-ti-mate (gesˊti mātˮ) *n., Slang* An estimate made without all the facts.

guest (gest) *n.* One who is the recipient of hospitality from another; a customer who pays for lodging.

guff (guf) *n., Slang* Nonsense or empty talk.

guf-faw (gu foˊ) *n.* A loud burst of laughter. **guffaw** *v.*

guid-ance (gīdˊɑns) *n.* The act, process, or result of guiding.

guide *n.* One who leads or directs another, as in a course of action; a person employed to conduct others on trips through museums and sightseeing tours. **guidable** *adj.* **guider** *n.*

guide-book (gīdˊbekˮ) *n.* A handbook containing directions and other information for tourists and visitors.

guided missile *n., Mil.* An unmanned mis-sile that can be controlled by radio signals while in flight.

guide-line *n.* Any suggestion, statement, or outline of policy or procedure; a rope or cord to guide a person over a difficult point.

guide-post *n.* A post to which a sign is attached for giving direction.

gui-don (gīˊdon) *n.* A small flag carried by a military unit as a unit marker.

guild (gild) *n.* An association of persons of the same trade or occupation.

guile *n.* Craft; duplicity; deceit.

guil-le-mot *n.* Birds of the auk family, that are native to the northern Atlantic coasts.

guil-loche *n.* Architectural ornament composed of two or more strands interlacing or combining other patterns.

guil-lo-tine (gilˊō tēnˮ) *n.* An instrument of capital punishment in France, used for beheading condemned prisoners.

guilt (gilt) *n.* The condition or fact of having committed a crime or wrongdoing; the feeling of responsibility for having done something wrong.

guilt-less *adj.* A state or condition of being without guilt; innocent.

guilt-y (gilˊtē) *adj.* Deserving of blame for an offense that has been committed; convicted of some offense; pertaining to, involving or showing guilt. **guiltily** *adv.,* **guiltiness** *n.*

guin-ea (ginˊē) *n.* Formerly, a British gold coin worth one pound and five pence.

guinea fowl (ginˊē foul) *n.* A widely domesticated bird of African origin with dark gray plumage speckled with white.

guinea hen *n.* The female guinea fowl.

guinea pig (ginˊē pig) *n.* A small, domesticated rodent usually with a short white tail, widely used for biological experimentation.

guinea worm *n.* A slender parasitic which can causes illness in man and animals.

gui-pure *n.* Heavy laces in which the pattern is connected by bars instead of worked on a net.

guise *n.* External appearance in dress; garb; an assumed appearance.

gui-tar (gi torˊ) *n.* A musical instrument with six strings, played by plucking or strumming.

gu-lar *adj.* Pertaining or relating to, or situated on the throat.

gulch (gulch) *n.* A deep cleft or ravine.

gulf (gulf) *n.* A large area of ocean or sea partially enclosed by land; a wide, impassable separation, as in social position or education.

gulf-weed *n.* A coarse branching olive-brown seaweed, found in tropical American waters.

gull (gul) *n.* A long-winged, web-footed

sea bird, usually white and gray with a hooked upper mandible.

gull (gul) *n.* A gullible person; one who is easily tricked.

gul-let (gul´it) *n., Pathol.* The passage from the mouth to the stomach; esophagus; the throat; the pharynx.

gul-li-ble (gul´i bl) *adj.* Easily cheated or fooled. **gullibility** *n.,* **gullibly** *adv.*

gul-ly (gul´ē) *n. pl.* **gullies** A ditch or channel cut in the earth by running water.

gulp (gulp) *v.* To swallow rapidly or in large amounts; to gasp or choke, as in nervousness; in computer science, small group of bytes that may be either data or instructions. **gulping, gulped** *v.*

gum (gum) *n.* A sticky, viscous substance exuded from various trees and plants, soluble in water and hardening on exposure to air; chewing gum; the firm connective fleshy tissue that surrounds the base of the teeth. *v., Slang* To bungle. **gummy** *adj.*

gum arabic *n.* The water-soluble gum of various species of acacia, which hardens in the air: used in the manufacturing of cine, inks, adhesives, confectionery and in medicine.

gum-bo (gum´bō) *n.* A thick soup or stew containing okra and other vegetable, chicken, meat or seafood.

gum-boil *n.* A small boil or abscess on the gum.

gum-drop (gum´drop˝) *n.* A small, round, firm piece of jelly-like, sugar-coated candy usually, colored and coated with sugar.

gum-mo-sis *n.* An abnormal gummy, discharge condition of plants.

gum-my (gum´ē) *adj.* Covered with or containing gum; sticky. **gumminess** *n.*

gump-tion (gump´shan) *n., Slang* Boldness; initiative; enterprise; personal initiative; practical common sense.

gum resin *n.* Various natural mixtures of gum and resin, obtained from certain plants.

gum-shoe (gum´shō˝) *n.* A shoe made of rubber. *Slang* A detective. **gumshoe** *v.*

gun (gun) *n.* A weapon made of metal from which a projectile is thrown by the force

of an explosion; a portable firearm. *v.* To shoot; to open up the throttle of an engine in order to accelerate. **gun for** To try to ruin, catch, or acquire.

gun-boat *n.* A small, armed ship of a shallow light draft.

gun-fight (gun´fit˝) *n.* A duel with pistols.

gunk *n.* Obnoxious sticky material; greasy, or messy material.

gun-man (gun´man) *n. pl.* **gunmen** One who is armed with a gun, especially an armed criminal.

gun moll *n., Slang.* A girlfriend or female companion of a gangster.

gun-ner-y (gun´e rē) *n.* The science and art of constructing and operating guns; the use of guns in general.

gun-ny (gun´ē rē) *n. pl.* **gunnies** A type of coarse, heavy fabric made of jute or hemp and used for making sacks.

gun-pow-der (gun´pou´dėr) *n.* An explosive powder used in blasting, fireworks, and guns.

gun-shot (gun´shot˝) *n.* A shot fired from a gun.

gun–shy (gun´shī˝) *adj.* Afraid of loud noises, as gunfire; wary.

gun-smith (gun´smith˝) *n.* A person who makes or repairs guns.

gun-wale *or* **gun-nel (gun´l)** *n.* The upper edge of a ship's side.

gup-py (gup´ē) *n. pl.* **guppies** A small, tropical freshwater fish, popular in home aquariums.

gur-gle (ger´gl) *v.* To flow in a broken, uneven current, making low, bubbling sounds. **gurgle** *n.* **gurglingly** *adv.*

gur-nard *n.* A marine fish with a spiny head and three pairs of free pectoral rays.

gush (gush) *v.* To flow or rush forth in volume and with sudden force; to be overly sentimental or enthusiastic. **gushy** *adj.*

gush-er *n.* An oil well with a plentiful natural flow of oil; a person who gushes.

gus-set (gus´it) *n.* A piece of armor that covers the joints in a suit of armor giving additional strength.

gust (gust) *n.* A sudden, violent rush of

wind or air; a sudden outburst, as of emotion. **gustily** *adv.* **gustiness** *n.* **gusty** *adj.*

gus-ta-to-ry (gus´ta tō˝rē) *adj.* Of or pertaining to the sense of taste or the act of tasting.

gust-o (gus´tō) *n.* Hearty enjoyment or enthusiasm.

gut (gut) *n.* The alimentary canal or part of it. *v.* To disembowel. **guts** Bowels; entrails; the prepared intestines of certain animals, used as strings for musical instruments and surgical sutures; fortitude; courage.

gut-less (gut´lis) *adj., Slang* Lacking courage. Appealing or expressing strongly to physical passions.

guts-y *n., Slang* Courageous.

gut-ta–per-cha *n.* A tough plastic from the latex of Malaysian trees, resembles rubber but has more resin and is used for electrical insulation and in dentistry.

gut-tate *adj.* Spotted, discolored by drops or droplike spots.

gut-ter *n.* A channel or ditch at the side of a street for carrying off surface water; a trough attached below or along the eaves of a house carrying off rain water from the roof.

gut-ter-snipe (gut´ėr snīp˝) *n.* A person of the lowest class or morals; a street urchin.

gut-tur-al (gut´ėr al) *adj.* Pertaining to the throat; having a harsh, muffled, or grating quality. **guttural** *n.* **gutturally** *adv.*

guy (gī) *n., Slang* A man; a fellow.

guz-zle (guz´l) *v.* To drink greedily, continually or to excess. **guzzler** *n.*,

gym (jim) *n., Informal* A gymnasium. An assortment of outdoor play equipment such as a seesaw, rings and a swing.

gym-na-si-um (jim nā´zē um) *n. pl.* **gymnasiums** *or* **gymnasia** A room or building equipped for indoor sports.

gym-nas-tic (jim nas´tik) *adj.* Of or pertaining to athletic exercises.

gym-nas-tics (jim nas´tiks) *n. pl.* A sport or physical exercises, especially those performed with a special apparatus in a gym;

athletic. **gymnast** *n.* **gymnastically** *adv.*

gym-no-spore *n.* A spore that does not have a protective covering.

gy-nan-dro-morph *n.* An abnormal individual exhibiting physical features characteristic of both sexes.

gy-nan-dry *n.* Hermaphroditism; the condition in an animal or plant where both male and female reproductive organs exist.

gy-ne-coid (jin´ekoid˝) *adj.* Having female characteristics; being typical of a woman.

gy-ne-col-o-gy (gī˝ne kol´o jē) *n.* The branch of medicine dealing with the female reproductive organs, female diseases, and female organs. **gynecological, gynecologic** *adj.* **gynecologist** *n.*

gyp (jip) *v., Informal* To swindle, cheat, or defraud. *n.* A fraud. **gypper** *n.*

gyp-sum (jip´sum) *n.* A mineral, hydrous calcium sulfate, used to make plaster of Paris, gypsum plaster, and plasterboard.

gypsy moth *n.* A moth whose larvae are destructive to foliage.

gy-rate (jī´rāt) *v.* To rotate or revolve around a fixed point or axis; to move or turn in a spiral motion. *adj.* Coiled or winding about. **gyrator** *n.* **gyratory** *adj.*

gyr-fal-con (jer´fol˝kon) *n.* A falcon with color phases ranging from black to white.

gy-ro-com-pass (jī´rō kum´pas) *n.* A compass that has a motor-driven gyroscope so mounted that its axis of rotation maintains a constant position with reference to the true or geographic north.

gyro pilot *n., Aeron.* An automatic pilot.

gy-ro-plane *n.* An airplane balanced and supported by the aerodynamic forces, such as a helicopter, having windmill-like wings that rotate horizontally.

gy-ro-scope (jī´ro skōp˝) *n.* A spinning wheel or disk whose spin axis maintains its angular orientation when not subjected to external torques. **gyroscopic** *adj.*

gy-ro-sta-bi-liz-er (jī˝ro stā´bi lī˝zėr) *n.* A gyroscopic instrument designed to reduce the rolling motion of ships.

gyve (jīv) *n.* A shackle for the legs. *v.* To chain; to shackle.

H, h (āch) The eighth letter of the English alphabet.

ha (hă) *interj.* An exclamation denoting joy, wonder, sudden emotion or surprise.

ha-ba-ne-ra (hä˝ba när´a) *n.* Cuban dance.

ha-be-as cor-pus (hä´bē as kor´pus) *n.* In law, a writ commanding a person to appear before a judge or court for the purpose of releasing that person from unlawful detention or restraint.

hab-er-dash-er (hab´ĕr dash˝ĕr) *n.* A person who deals in men's clothing and men's furnishings.

hab-er-dash-er-y *n. pl.* **haberdasheries** The goods sold by a haberdasher.

ha-ber-geon (hab´er jen) *n.* A medieval jacket.

hab-ile *adj.* Having skill; able.

ha-bil-i-ment (ha bil´i ment) *n. pl.* **habiliments** Clothing characteristic of an office, rank, or occasion.

ha-bil-i-tate (ha bil´i tāt˝) *v.* To furnish, as a mine, with money or equipment.

hab-it (hab´it) *n.* Involuntary pattern of behavior acquired by frequent repetition; manner of conducting oneself; an addiction. *Biol.* The characteristic form of a plant or animal. Clothing that indicated membership or rank in a religious order, or activity.

hab-it–form-ing (hab´it for˝ming) *adj.* Producing physiological addiction.

hab-it-a-ble (hab´i ta bel) *adj.* Suitable for habitation. **habitability, habitableness** *n.* **habitably** *adv.*

ha-bi-tant (hab´i tant) *n.* An inhabitant or settler; resident of a place.

hab-i-tat (hab´i tat˝) *n.* The region in which an animal or plant lives or grows; the place of residence of a person or group.

hab-i-ta-tion (hab˝i tā´shan) *n.* A place of residence; a house or other dwelling where man or animals dwell.

ha-bit-u-al (ha bich´ŏ al) *adj.* Practicing by or acting according to habit; resorted to on a regular basis; regular. **habitually** *adv.* **habitualness** *n.*

ha-bit-u-ate (ha bich´ŏ āt˝) *v.* To make; to familiar.

ha-chure (ha sher´) *n.* Shading used to denote surfaces in relief on a map.

ha-ci-en-da (hä˝sē en´da) *n.* A large estate or ranch in Spanish-speaking countries; the main building of a hacienda; a stock-raising ranch.

hack (hak) *v.* To cut with repeated irregular blows; to manage successfully. *n.* A tool used for hacking; a rough, dry cough; *Informal* A taxi driver.

hack-a-more (hak´a mōr˝) *n.* A bridle with a loop placed over the nose with a slip noose passed over the lower jaw used in place of a bit.

hack-ber-ry (hak˝ber´ē) *n.* Trees and shrubs of the elm family with small edible berries.

hack-le (hak´l) *n.* One of the long, slender, often narrow glossy feathers on the neck of a rooster; the hair on the back of the neck, especially of a dog, that rises in anger or fear.

hack-ney (hak´nē) *n.* A horse of medium size for ordinary driving or riding; a carriage or coach available for hire. *v.* To make common or frequent use of.

hackney coach *n.* A carriage drawn by two horses with seating for six persons.

hack-neyed *adj.* Trite; commonplace.

hack-saw (hak´so˝) *n.* A finetoothed saw in a narrow frame for cutting metal.

had *v.* Past participle and past tense of have.

had-dock (had´ok) *n.* A food fish that is usually smaller than the related cod and is found on both sides of the Atlantic.

Ha-des (hā´dēz) *n.* The underground abode of the dead in Greek mythology; hell.

had-n't (had´nt) *contraction* Had not.

hae-ma-tox-y-lon (hē˝ma tok´si lon˝) *n.* A small, tropical American tree with thorns.

haf-ni-um (haf´nē um) *n.* A metallic element that resembles zirconium chemical found in zirconium ores.

haft (haft) *n.* A handle of a weapon or tool.

haf-ta-rah (häf tor´ a) *n.* A biblical passage from the Book of Prophets which is read or chanted during a Jewish synagogue service, after reading the Parashah on the Sabbath and other holy days; also read at a Bar Mitzvah.

hag (hag) *n.* A malicious, ugly old woman; a witch. **haggish** *adj.*

hag-don (hag´ don) *n.* A group of seabirds having long, narrow wings.

hag-fish (hag´fish˝) *n.* A fish that resembles the eel but has a round mouth and horny teeth, surrounded by eight tentacles; which eats other fish.

Hag-ga-dah (h*a* **gä´d***a***)** *n.* Ancient Jewish lore forming especially the nonlegal part of the Talmud; the Jewish ritual for the Sedar.

hag-gard (hag´ėrd) A worn-out, exhausted, and gaunt look, as from hunger or fatigue; appearing wasted by suffering or want. **haggardly** *adv.* **haggardness** *n.*

hag-gle (hag´l) *v.* To argue or bargain on price or terms. *n.* The process or act of haggling someone. **haggler** *n.* **haggling, haggled** *v.*

hag-i-og-ra-phy *n. pl.* **-phies** Biography of the lives of saints or revered persons; an idolizing biography. **hagiographer** *n.* **hagiographic, hagiographical** *adj.*

ha–ha (hä˝hä´) *n. interj.* The sound of laughter, used to express amusement or joy.

haik (hīk) *n.* An oblong piece of usually white clothing used to cover the head and body, used as an outer garment in northern Africa.

hai-ku (hī´kŏ) *n.* An unrhymed Japanese verse form, having three short unrhymed lines; a poem using this style.

hail (hāl) *n.* Precipitation of small, hard lumps of ice and snow; a hailstone; an exclamation, greeting, acclamation *v.* To pour down as hail; to call loudly in greeting or welcome; to shout with enthusiasm; to signal in order to draw the attention of.

hail-stone (hāl´stōn˝) *n.* A single hard pellet of frozen snow and ice.

hair (hâr) *n.* One of the pigmented filaments that grow from the skin of most mammals; a covering of such structures, as on the

human head and on the skin; a slender margin. **hairy** *adj.*

hair-breadth (hâr´bredth˝) *n.* A very minute or small distance.

hair-brush (hâr´brush˝) *n.* A brush for grooming the hair.

hair-cloth (hâr´kloth˝) *n.* A very stiff and wiry fabric woven with either horse or camel hair and used for upholstery or to stiffen garments.

hair-do (hâr´dŏ˝) *n. pl.* **hairdos** Any arranged hair style for a woman's hair.

hair-dress-er (hâr´dres˝ėr) *n.* A person who styles or cuts hair.

hair follicle *n.* The tubular sheath that surrounds the lower part of the hair shaft providing the growing basal part of the hair with nourishment.

hair-less *adj.* Being bald; lacking hair. **hairlessness** *n.*

hair-pin (hâr´pin˝) *n.* A metal or plastic pin used to hold hair in place.

hair–rais-ing (hâr´rā´zing) *adj.* Causing fear or horror. **hairraiser** *n.*

hair-split-ing *n.* The process of making insignificant or petty distinctions. **hairsplitter** *n.*

hair-spring (hâr´spring´) *n.* A fine, coiled spring that regulates and controls the movement of the balance wheel in a clock or watch.

hair-streak (hâr´strēk˝) *n.* A small butterfly, with thin striped markings on the underside of their wings.

hair trigger *n.* A gun trigger set to react to the slightest pressure. **hair trigger** *adj.* Reacting immediately to the slightest provocation.

hake (hāk) *n.* An edible marine food fish related to the cod.

ha-kim (hă kēm) *n.* A Muslim physician, ruler or governor.

ha-la-tion *n.* A light that spreads beyond its proper boundaries in a developed photographic image.

hal-berd (hal´bėrd) *n.* A medieval weapon used in the 15th and 16th centuries, having both an ax-like blade and a steel spike on the end of a long pole.

hal-cy-on (hal′sē *on***)** *n.* A bird said to have the power of calming waves and winds during *adj* Calm and tranquil; peaceful; prosperous.

hale (hāl) *adj.* Healthy and robust, free from disease; free from defect. *v.* To compel to go. **haleness** *n.*

half (haf) *n. pl.* **halves** One of two equal parts into which a thing is divisible; art of a thing approximately equal to the remainder; one of a pair. Being one of two equal parts; being partial or incomplete. **half** *adj.*

half-and-half (haf′*an* **haf′)** *n.* A mixture of whole milk and cream.

half-back (haf′bak″) *n., Football.* One of two backs, positioned behind the line and usually on either side of the fullback.

half–baked (haf′bākt′) *adj.* Insufficiently cooked; imperfectly baked, as food; lacking in mature judgment or intelligence.

half binding *n.* A style of binding books in which the back and corners are leather and the sides are paper or cloth.

half–bred (hof′bred″) *adj.* A person born with one purebred parent; one born of different races, applies to the offspring of a white person and an American Indian.

half-breed (haf′brēd″) *n.* The off-spring of an American Indian and a white man; offspring of parents having different races.

half-brother *n.* A brother who is related through only one parent.

half–caste (haf′kast″) *n.* A person having one European and one Asian parent. **half–caste** *adj.*

half cock *n.* The position of the hammer of a firearm when about halfway retracted and held by the mechanism so that it cannot be operated.

half–dollar *n.* A coin representing one half of a dollar; 50 cents.

half gainer *n.* A dive performed in a diving competition.

half heart-ed (haf′här′tid) *adj.* Lacking in spirit or interest.

half-hitch *n.* A knot that is tied so it can be easily unfastened.

halfhour (haf′our′) *n.* Thirty minutes; time representing half of an hour.

half-length (haf′lengkth″) *n.* Something that represents only half the complete distance, height, or length.

half-life (haf′līf′) *n., Phys.* The length of time required for half the amount of a substance in a living system to be eliminated by a natural process.

half-light (haf′līt″) *n.* A partial obscured light.

half-mast (haf′mast′) *n.* A point or position halfway down or less below the top of a ship mast, or flag pole; the position of a flag in respect for the dead. *v.* To hang a flag at halfmast.

half note *n., Mus.* A note with the time value equivalent to one half of a whole note.

half pint *n.* A measurement equaling half of a pint; a nickname for a small person.

half-sister *n.* A sister that is related through one parent only.

half-slip (haf′slip″) *n.* A slip with an elasticized waistband and without a bodice; a petticoat.

half-sole (haf′sōl″) *v.* To repair shoes by replacing the sole that is worn out.

half step *n., Mus.* A semitone.

half time *n.* An intermission in the sport of football, basketball, etc.

half title *n.* The title of a book, often appearing alone on a right-hand page which immediately precedes the title page.

half-tone (haf′tōn″) *n., Photog.* A tone intermediate between the lightest and darkest shades of gray of a photograph; *photoengraving* A process in where an image is photographed through a screen and then etched to produce the image by a system of minute dots between fine intersecting black lines. **half tone** *n. Mus.* A semitone.

half–track (haf′trak′) *n.* A vehicle propelled by continuous rear treads and front wheels.

half-truth (haf′trōth″) *n.* A statement which is only partially true.

half volley *n*. A stroke, where as a ball in handball or tennis, is hit the instant it bounces from the playing area.

half-way (haf´wā´) *adv*. Half over the way; mid way between two points.

half–wit (haf´wit´) *n*. A mentally disturbed person; a feeble-minded person. **half–witted** *adj*.

halfway house *n*. A house for formerly institutionalized individuals which is designed to help them adjust to private life.

hal-i-but (hal´i but) *n*. Any of the edible flat fishes of the North Atlantic or Pacific waters.

hal-ide (hal´īd) *n., Chem.* A binary compound formed by the direct union of a halogen having a more electropositive element or radical.

hal-ite (hal´īt) *n*. Large crystal or masses of salt; saltrock.

hal-i-to-sis (hal´i tō´sis) *n*. A condition of having bad breath.

hal-le-lu-jah (hal´e lō´ya) *interj*. Used to express joy, praise, or jubilation.

hall-mark (hol´märk´) *n*. An official mark placed on gold and silver products to attest to their purity; an indication of quality or superiority; a distinctive characteristic.

Hall of Fame *n*. A building which houses memorials to famous individuals.

hal-low (hal´ō) *v*. To sanctify; to make holy; to honor.

Hal-low-een (hal´o wēn´) *n*. October 31, the eve of All Saint's Day, celebrated particularly by children.

hal-lu-ci-nate (ha-lō´si-nāt´) *v*. To affect with imaginary perceptions; to have a hallucination.

hal-lu-ci-na-tion (ha lō˝si nā´han) *n*. An illusion of seeing something that is non-existent; something one thinks is seen during a hallucination; a delusion. **hallucinate** *v*. **halucinational, hallucinative, hallucinatory** *adj*.

hal-lu-ci-no-gen (ha lō´si no jen˝) *n*. A drug or other agent which causes hallucination. **hallucinogenic** *adj*.

hal-lu-ci-no-sis (ha-lō˝si-nō´sis) *n., Psychi.* A mental disorder marked by hallucinations.

hal-lux (hal´uks) *n*. The innermost of the digit of the hind foot of air-breathing vertebrates.

hall-way (hol´wā˝) *n*. A corridor; an entrance hall.

ha-lo (hā´lō) *n*. A ring of colored light surrounding the head; an aura of glory.

hal-o-gen (hal´o jen) *n*. Any of the group of non-mentallic elements including flourine, chlorine, bromine, iodine,and astatine. **halogenous** *adj*.

hal-o-gen-ate (hal´o-je-nāt˝) *v., Chem.* To combine or treat with a halogen. **Halogenation** *n*.

hal-o-ge-ton *n*. An annual herb of the goosefoot family found in western America.

hal-oid (hal´oid) *adj*. A substance that resembles common table salt in composition; formed by the mixture of a halogen and a metal.

hal-o-mor-phic (hal´o-mor´fik) *a*. Influenced by the presence of an alkali or a neutral salt, or both.

halo-phile (hal´o fīl˝) *n*. An organism that grows in a salty environment.

hal-o-phyte (hal´o-fit˝) *n*. A plant that grows in a salty soil.

halt (holt) *v*. To bring to a stop.

hal-ter (hol´tėr) *n*. A rope or strap for leading or tying an animal; a noose for hanging a person; a woman's upper garment tied behind the neck and across the back.

hal-vah *n*. A flaky confection of sesame seeds in a base of syrup or honey.

halve (hav) *v*. To divide into two equal parts; to lessen by half. *Informal* Share equally.

hal-yard (hal´yėrd) *n*. A rope for hoisting or lowering a sail, flag, or yard.

ham (ham) *n*. The meat of a hog's thigh; the back of the knee or thigh. **ham** *v*.

ham-burg-er (ham´ber˝gėr) *n*. A patty of ground beef on a bun.

hame (hām) *n*. The curved projections attached to the collar of a draft horse to fasten the traces to.

ham-let (ham´lit) *n.* A small rural village or town.

ham-mer (ham´ėr) *n.* A hand tool with a heavy head used to drive or strike forcefully, especially nails; the part of a gun which strikes the primer or firing pin; any of the padded wooden levers which strike the strings of a piano. *v.* To strike or pound forcibly and repeatedly. **hammerer** *n.*

ham-mered (ham´ėrd) *adj.* Having indentions or marks on the surface on something produced by a hammer.

ham-mer-head (ham´ėr hed˝) *n.* A large, predatory shark of warm seas, whose eyes are set in long, fleshy projections at the sides of the head.

hammer-lock *n.* A hold in wrestling in which the opponent's arm is twisted upward behind his back.

ham-mer-toe *n.* A toe that is bent downward and malformed.

ham-mock (ham´ok) *n.* A hanging bed or couch of fabric or heavy netting, suspended from supports at each end.

ham-per (ham´pėr) *v.* To interfere with movement or progress of. *n.* A large, usually covered, receptacle used to store dirty laundry.

ham-ster (ham´stėr) *n.* Any of various rodents with large cheek pouches and a short tail.

ham-string (ham´string˝) *n.* Either of two tendons located at the back of the human knee; the large tendon at the back of the hock of four-footed animals. *v.* To cripple by cutting the hamstring; to frustrate.

ham-u-lus (ham´ūlus) *n.* A small hook or a hook process.

hand (hand) *n.* The part of the arm below the wrist, consisting of the palm, four fingers and a thumb; a unit of measure, four inches, used especially to state the height of a horse; a pointer on a dial, as of a clock, meter, or gauge; the cards dealt to or held by a player in one round of a game; a manual laborer, worker, or employee. *v.* To give, offer, or transmit with the hand; direct with the hands.

hand-bag (hand´bag˝) *n.* A woman's purse held in the hand or with a shoulder strap.

hand–me–down (hand´mē doun˝) *n.* Something, such as an article of clothing, used by a person after being outgrown or discarded by another. **hand-me-down** *adj.*

hand–to–mouth (hand´to mouth´) *adj.* Providing or having barely enough to exist.

hand-ball (hand´bol˝) *n.* A court game in which the players bat a small rubber ball against the wall with their hands.

hand-barrow *n.* A flat rectangular frame with handles at both ends for carrying loads.

hand-bill (hand´bil˝) *n.* A hand-distributed advertisement.

hand-book (hand´bek˝) *n.* A small guide or reference book giving information or instructions.

hand-breadth (hand´bredth˝) *n.* Various units of linear measure varying from 2½ to 4 inches.

hand-car (hand´kär˝) *n.* A small open four-wheeled railroad car propelled by a small motor or by hand.

hand-clasp (hand´klasp˝) *n.* Handshake; The clasping of hands by two persons to express a congratulation, or greeting.

hand-craft (hand´kraft˝) *v.* To make or create an item by hand. **handcrafted** *adj.*

hand-craft-man *n.* A person skilled in handicrafts.

hand-cuff (hand´kuf˝) *v.* To put handcuffs on; to make ineffective. **handcuffs** *pl. n.* A pair of circular metal shackles chained together that can be fastened around the wrists.

hand down *v.* To pass on in succession, from one relative to another; to deliver a courts decision.

hand-ful (hand´fel˝) *n.* As much as the hand will hold.

hand grenade *n.* An explosive that is

thrown by hand and explodes on impact or by the releasing of a fuse.

hand-gun (hand´gun˝) *n.* A gun that can be held and fired with one hand.

hand-i-cap (han´dē kap˝) *n.* A race or contest in which advantages or penalties are given to individual contestants to equalize the odds; any disadvantage that makes achievement unusually difficult; physical disablility; an obstacle. *v.* To give a handicap to.

hand-i-cap-per *n.* A person who predicts the winners in a race.

hand-i-craft *or* **hand-craft (han´dē kraft˝)** *n.* Skill and expertise in working with the hands; an occupation requiring manual dexterity; skilled work produced by the hands.

hand-i-ly (han´di-lē) *adv.* In a handy or convenient manner.

hand-i-work (han´dē-würk˝) *n.* Work exhibiting the hand skills of its maker.

hand-ker-chief (hang´kėr chif) *n.* A small piece of cloth used for wiping the face or nose; a kerchief or scarf.

han-dle (han´dl) *v.* To touch, pick up, or hold with the hands; to represent; to trade or deal in. **handler** *n.* **handleless, handleable** *adj.*

han-dle-bars (han´dl bär˝) *n.* A bent bar with a handle at each end used to steer a bicycle or similar vehicle.

han-dling (hand´ling) *n.* A touching; a manner of treatment.

hand-made *adj.* Made by hand or by a hand process.

hand-maid *or* **hand-maid-en** *n.* A female maid or personal servant.

hand-off (hand´of˝) *n., Football* The handing of the ball by one player, usually from the quarterback to a nearby teammate.

hand-out (hand´out˝) *n.* Free food, clothing, or cash given to the needy; a folder distributed free of charge; a flyer; a press release for publicity.

hand-pick (hand´pik´) *v.* To select with care.

hand-rail (hand´rāl˝) *n.* A narrow rail used for support.

hand-saw (hand´so˝) *n.* A saw operated with one hand.

hand-sel (hand´sel) *n.* A gift given as a token of good luck.

hand-set (hand´set´) *n.* A telephone receiver and transmitter combined in a single unit.

hand-shake (hand´shāk˝) *n.* The act of clasping hands by two people, as in greeting, agreement, or parting.

hand-some (han´som) *adj.* Very good-looking or attractive; very generous, as with money. **handsomely** *adv.* **handsomeness** *n.*

hand-spring (hand´spring˝) *n.* An acrobatic feat in which the body flips entirely backward or forward, while the feet pass quickly in an arc over the head.

hand-stand (hand´stand˝) *n.* The feat of supporting the body on the hands with the feet balanced in the air.

hand–to–mouth (hand´to mouth´) *adj.* Providing or having barely enough to exist.

hand truck *n.* A hand operated truck for moving heavy objects.

hand-weav-ing (hand´wē˝ving) *n.* The craft of weaving a fabric on a handloom.

hand-work (hand´werk˝´) *n.* Work done by hand.

hand-wo-ven (hand´wō´ven) *adj.* Produced by hand.

hand-writ-ing (hand´rī˝ting) *n.* Writing performed with the hand, especially cursive; the type of writing of a person. **handwriting on the wall.** An omen of one's unpleasant fate.

hand-y (han´dē) *adj.* Easy to use or reach; helpful or useful. **handily** *adv.*

handy-man (han´dē man˝) *n.* A person who does odd jobs.

hang (hang) *v.* To be attached to from above and unsupported from below; to fasten or be suspended so as to swing freely; to be put to death by hanging by the neck; to fasten or attach something as a picture to a wall. **hangout** *Slang* To spend one's time in a particular place. **up**

To end a telephone conversation by replacing the receiver on its cradle.

hang–up *n., Slang* A psychological or emotional problem; an obstacle.

han-gar (hang´ér) *n.* A building for housing aircraft.

han-ger (hang´ér) *n.* A device from which something may be hung or on which something hangs.

hang glider *n.* A device shaped like a kite from which a person hangs suspended in a harness while gliding through the air. **hang gliding** *n.* **hang glide** *v.*

hang-man (hang´man) *n. pl* **-men** One hired to execute people by hanging.

hang-nail (hang´nāl˝) *n.* The small piece of skin that hangs loose from the side or root of a fingernail.

hang-out (hang´out˝) *n.* A place one visits frequently.

hang-over (hang´ō˝vér) *n.* Something remaining from what has passed; the effects of excessive alcohol intake.

hang together *v.* To hold together; to be closely united.

hank (hangk) *n.* A loop, coil, or piece of hair, thread, or yarn.

han-ker (hang´kér) *v.* To have a yearning or craving for something. **hankerer, hankering** *n.*

han-som (han´som) *n.* A two-wheeled covered carriage with the driver's seat elevated behind the cab.

Ha-nuk-kah *or* **Ha-nu-kah (hä´nu ka)** *n.* An eight-day Jewish holiday remembering the rededication of the Temple in Jerusalem.

hao-le (hou´lē) *n.* A person who is not of the Hawaiian race, especially a Caucasian.

hap (hap) *n.* Chance or fortune.

hap-haz-ard (hap´haz˝érd) *adj.* Occurring by accident; happening by chance or at random; hit-or-miss. **haphazardly** *adv.* **haphazardness** *n.*

hap-less *adj.* Unfortunate; unlucky. **haplessly** *adv.* **haplessness** *n.*

hap-log-ra-phy (hap-log´ra-fē) *n.* The unintentional omission of a letter or letters in writing.

hap-ly (hap´lē) *adv.* By luck or chance; by accident; perhaps.

hap-pen (hap´n) *v.* To occur or come to pass; to take place; to discover by chance; to turn up or appear by chance.

hap-pen-ing (hap´e ning) *n.* A spontaneous event or performance; an important event.

happen-stance (hap´en stans˝) *n.* An event occurring by chance.

hap-pi-ness (hap´ē-nis) *n.* The quality of being content; pleasure.

hap-py (hap´ē) *adj.* Enjoying contentment and well-being; glad, joyous, satisfied or pleased. **happily** *adv.* **happiness** *n.*

happy–go–lucky (hap´ē gō luk´ē) *adj.* Carefree and unconcerned.

hap-ten (hap´ten) *n.* A substance which reacts with an antibody only when they are together in a synthetic environment.

ha-ra–ki-ri (här´a kēr´ē) *n.* A Japanese suicide ritual committed by ripping open the abdomen with a knife.

ha-rangue (ha rang´) *n.* A long, extravagant, speech; a lecture. **harangue** *v.* **haranguer** *n.*

ha-rass (har´as) *v.* To disturb or annoy constantly; to torment persistently. **harassment** *n.* **harasser** *n.*

har-bin-ger (här´bin´jér) *n.* A person that initiates or pioneers a major change; something that foreshadows what is to come.

har-bor (här´bér) *n.* A place of refuge or shelter; a bay or cove; an anchorage for ships. *v.* To provide shelter; to entertain, as a feeling or thought. **harborage, harborer** *n.*

harbor master *n.* The officer in charge of a harbor, one who enforces its regulations.

hard (härd) *adj.* Difficult to perform, endure, or comprehend; solid in texture or substance; resistant to cutting or penetration; containing salts which make lathering with soap difficult; high in alcoholic content. **hardness** *n.*

hard–and–fast (härd´an-fast´) *adj.* Firm and secure; strictly obligatory, not to be set aside or violated.

hard–bit-ten (härd´bit´en) *adj.* Hardened by conflict.

hard-board (härd´bōrd´) *n.* A composition board made by compressing wood chips

hard–boiled (härd´boild´) *adj.* Boiled or cooked in the shell to a hard or solid state.

hard candy *n.* A confection made of sugar and corn syrup.

hard cider *n.* Apple juice that has become fermented.

hard copy *n.* In computer science, the printed information or data from a com-puter.

hard–core *or* **hard-core (härd´kōr´)** *adj.* Extremely graphic in presentation; obstinately resistant to change.

hard disk *n.* In computer science, magnetic storage consisting of a rigid disk of aluminum coated with a magnetic recording substance; contained within a removable cartridge or mounted in the hard disk of a microcomputer.

hard-en (här´den) *v.* To make or become hard or harder; to make or become physically or mentally tough; to make or become callous or unsympathetic.

hard goods *n.* Merchandise made to last a relatively long time; durable.

hard hat (härd´hat´) *n.* A protective head covering made of rigid material, worn by construction workers.

hard-head-ed (härd´hed´) *adj.* Having a stubborn character; obstinate. **hardheadedly** *adv.* **hardheadedness** *n.*

hard-heart-ed (härd´här´tid) *adj.* Heartless; unfeeling. **hardheartedly** *adv.* **hardheartedness** *n.*

har-di-hood (här´dē hed) *n.* Resolute courage; audacious boldness; vitality; vigor.

har-di-ment (här´dē ment) *n.* A bold deed.

har-di-ness (här´dē-nis) *n.* The quality of being hardy; robustness.

hard labor *n.* Hard work required of criminals as additional punishment to their imprisonment.

hard-line (härd´līn´) *adj.* Holding fast to a rigid principle; favoring forceful action.

hard-ly (härd´lē) *adj. Slang* Very little; almost certainly not. *adv.* Forcefully; painfully; barely.

hard–of–hear-ing (härd´ov-hēr´ing) *adj.* Having an impaired but functional sense of hearing.

Harding, Warren Gamaliel *n.* (1865-1923) The 29th President of the United States, from 1921-1923, died in office.

har-ding-grass *n.* A perennial grass of Australia and Africa used as a forage grass.

hard palate *n.* The bony forward part of the palate that forms the roof of the mouth.

hard-pan (härd´pan´) *n.* A layer of very hard clay-like matter or subsoil which roots cannot penetrate.

hard put *adj.* In a difficult situation; not quite able.

hard rock *n.* Rock music featuring amplified sound and modulations, and feedback.

hard rubber *n.* Rubber processed with a vulcanizing agent as sulfur which unites its molecules into a comparably inflexible product.

hard sauce *n.* A mixture of butter and powdered sugar with cream and flavoring.

hard sell *n., Slang* A sales method involving aggressive, high-pressure selling and closing techniques.

hard-ship (härd´ship) *n.* A painful, difficult condition causing suffering.

hard-tack (härd´tak´) *n.* A hard, crackerlike biscuit made with flour and water.

hard-top (härd´top´) *n.* A car with a permanent top designed to resemble a convertible.

hard-ware (härd´wâr´) *n.* Manufactured machine parts, such as tools and utensils; the mechanical components of a computer installation.

hard-wood (härd´wed´) *n.* The wood of an angiospermous tree as opposed to that of a coniferous tree; a tree that yields hardwood.

har-dy (här´dē) *adj.* Bold and robust; able to survive very unfavorable conditions, as extreme cold; daring. **hardiness** *n.* **hardily** *adv.*

hare (hâr) *n.* Various mammals related to the rabbits but having longer ears and legs.
hare-bell (hâr-'bel") *n.* A small blue-flowered herb with leaves on the stem.
hare-brained (hâr 'brānd") *adj.* Foolish or silly.
hare-lip (hâr'lip") *n.* A congenital deformity in which the upper lip is split.
har-em (hâr'em) *n.* The women living in a Muslim residence; the living quarters of a harem.
har-i-cot (har'i-kō") *n.* A kind of thick mixture of meat and vegetables; the kidney bean or its pod or seed.
hark (härk) *v.* To listen closely.
har-le-quin (här'le kwin) *n.* A jester; a clown. *adj.* Patterned with vividly colored diamond shapes.
har-lot (här'lot) *n.* A prostitute.
harm (härm) *n.* Emotional or physical damage or injury. *v.* To cause harm to. **harmful** *adj.* **harmfully** *adv.* **harmfulness** *n.*
har-mat-tan (här"ma-tan') *n.* A seasonal dust-laden wind, on the west coast of Africa.
harm-less (härm'lis) *adj.* Without harm; lacking ability injure or harm.
har-mon-ic (här mon'ik) *adj.* Relating to musical harmony; in harmony; concordant. **harmonically** *adv.*
har-mon-i-ca (här mon'i ka) *n.* A small, rectangular musical instrument having a series of tuned metal reeds that vibrate with the player's breath.
har-mon-i-con (här-mon'i-kon) *n.* A harmonica or mouth organ.
har-mo-ni-ous (här mō'nē us) *adj.* Pleasing to the ear; characterized by agreement and accord; having components agreeably combined. **harmoniously** *adv.* **harmonious** *n.*
har-mo-nize (här'mo-nīz") *v.* To be in harmony. *Mus.* To perform in harmony. To bring into agreement.

har-mo-ny (här'mo nē) *n. pl.* **harmonies** Complete agreement, as of feeling or opinion; an agreeable combination of component parts; pleasing sounds; a combination of musical tones into chords. **harmonize** *v.* **harmonizer** *n.*
har-ness (här'nis) *n.* The working gear, other than a yoke, of a horse or other draft animal. **harnesser** *n.*
harness racing *n.* A racing sport in which horses are harnessed to a 2-wheeled sulky with a driver.
harp (härp) *n.* A musical instrument having a triangular upright frame with strings plucked with the fingers. *v.* To play a harp. **harp on** To write or talk about excessively. **harpist** *n.*
har-poon (här pōn') *n.* A barbed spear used in hunting whales and large fish. **harpoon** *v.*
harp-si-chord (härp'si kord') *n.* A piano-like instrument whose strings are plucked by using quills or leather points. **harpsichordist** *n.*
har-py (här'pē) *n. pl.* **harpies** A vicious woman; a predatory person.
har-ri-dan (har'i dan) *n.* A mean, hateful old woman.
har-ri-er (har'ē ėr) *n.* A slender, narrow-winged hawk that preys on small animals; a hunting dog; a cross-country runner.
Harrison, Benjamin *n.* (1833-1901). The 23rd president of the United States from 1889-1893.
Harrison, William Henry *n.* (1733-1841) The 9th president of the United States from March 4th-April 4th 1841; died in office.
har-row (har'ō) *n.* A cultivating tool with sharp teeth and spikes for breaking up and smoothing soil. *v.* To cultivate the soil with a harrow which is drawn across plowed soil to smooth the soil.
har-ry (har'ē) *v.* To harass.
harsh (härsh) *adj.* Disagreeable; extremely severe. **harshly** *adv.* **harshness** *n.*
hart (härt) *n.* A fully grown male deer after it has passed its fifth year.

harte-beest (här'tebēst") *n.* A large African antelope.

Hartford *n.* The capital of the state of Connecticut.

har-um–scar-um (här'*u*m skar'*u*m) *adj.* Reckless; irresponsible.

har-vest (här'vist) *n.* The process or act of gathering a crop; the season or time for gathering crops. *v.* To reap; to obtain as if by gathering. **harvester** *n.*

harvest home *n.* The gathering of the harvest feast.

harvest moon *n.* The full moon closest to the time of the September equinox.

harvest-time *n.* The time during which the annual crops are harvested.

has–been (haz'bin") *n.* One who has passed the period of his greatest effectiveness, achievement, or popularity.

ha-sen-pfef-fer (häsen fef'ėr) *n.* A highly seasoned stew made from rabbit meat.

hash (hash) *n.* A fried or baked mixture of chopped meat and potatoes. *v.* To chop up into small pieces. *Slang* To make a mess of; to discuss at great length.

hash-ish (hash'ēsh) *n.* The leaves and flowering tops of the hemp plant, which are chewed, drunk, or smoked for their intoxicating and narcotic effect.

hasp (hasp) *n.* A clasp or hinged fastener that passes over a staple and is secured by a pin, bolt, or padlock.

has-sle (has'l) *n., Slang* A type of quarrel or argument. **hassle** *v.*

has-sock (has'ok) *n.* A firm upholstered cushion used as a footstool.

haste (hāst) *n.* Speed; swiftness of motion or action; excessive eagerness to act. **make haste** To hurry.

has-ten (hā'sen) *v.* To act or move with haste or speed.

hast-y (hā'stē) *adj.* Rapid; swift; made or done with excessive speed. **hastily** *adv.* **hastiness** *n.*

hat (hat) *n.* A covering for the head with a crown and brim.

hat-band *n.* A strip of leather, cloth, etc. around the crown of a hat.

hat-box (hat'boks") *n.* A container or box used for storing or carrying hats.

hatch (hach) *n.* A small opening or door, as in a ship's deck. *v.* To bring forth, as young from an egg; to devise; to produce; to contrive secretly. **hatchery** *n.*

hatch-back *n.* An automobile with a sloped roof in the back that opens upward.

hatch-er-y (hach'e-rē) *n. pl.* **hatcheries.** A place for hatching eggs such as fish or poultry eggs.

hatch-et (hach'it) *n.* A small ax with a short handle.

hatchet face *n.* A thin face with sharp, prominent features.

hatchet man *n.* A person hired for murder, someone hired to perform unscrupulous tasks.

hatch-way (hach'wā") *n.* An opening covered by a hatch in a ship's deck.

hate (hāt) *v.* To feel hostility or animosity toward; to dislike intensely. **hatefully** *adv.* **hatefulness, hater** *n.*

ha-tred (hātrid) *n.* A deep-seated dislike or animosity.

hat-ter (hat'ėr) *n.* A person who makes, sells, or repairs hats.

hau-berk (ho'berk) *n.* A tunic of chain worn as defensive armor.

haugh-ty (ho'tē) *adj.* Arrogantly proud; disdainful. **haughtily** *adv.*

haul (hol) *v.* To pull or draw with force; to move or transport, as in a truck or cart. *n.* The distance over which someone travels or something is transported; an amount collected at one time.

haul-age (ho'lij) *n.* The process or act of hauling; a charge for hauling.

haunch (honch) *n.* The hip; the buttock and upper thigh of a human or animal; the loin and leg of a four-footed animal.

haunt (hont) *v.* To appear to or visit as a ghost or spirit; to visit frequently; to linger in the mind. **haunting** *adj.*

hau-sen (ho'zn) A large white fish, an outstanding source for caviar.

haus-tel-lum (ho-stel'*u*m) *n.* The sucking organ of insects, adapted to suck juices of plants or to suck blood.

haut-bois *or* **haut-boy (hō´boi, ō´boi)** *n.* An oboe. A double reed, wind instrument made of wood.

haute couture *n.* Designers who create exclusive fashions for women.

hau-teur (hō ter´) *n.* A disdainful arrogance.

Ha-van-a *n.* The capital of Cuba; a cigar made from Cuban tobacco.

have (hav) *v.* To hold or own, as a possession or as property. **have to** Need to; must. **have had it** Suffered or endured all that one can tolerate.

have-lock (hav´lok) *n.* A cap with a flap that covers the neck, protecting the neck from sun.

ha-ven (hā´ven) *n.* A place that offers a safe refuge; a harbor or port; an inlet which provides a place for ships to anchor.

hav-er-sack (hav´ėr sak˝) *n.* A bag for carrying supplies on a hike or march.

hav-oc (hav´ok) *n.* Mass confusion; widespread destruction; devastation.

haw (ho) *n.* A hesitating sound made by a speaker who is groping for words. *v.* To hesitate in speaking; to falter in speaking.

Ha-wai-i *or* **Ha-wai-ian Is-lands** A state and island group of the United States, located in the central Pacific, statehood August 21, 1959, state capital Honolulu.

Hawaiian guitar *n.* A guitar, with a fretted neck and six to eight strings, held horizontally and played by plucking the strings with pick and moving a sliding bar across the strings for pitch.

haw-finch *n.* A Eurasian finch with a large bill and a short thick neck.

hawk (hok) *n.* Any of several predatory birds, with a short, hooked bill and strong claws for seizing small prey; one who advocates a war-like foreign policy; one having an aggressive attitude. **hawkish** *adj.* **hawkishly** *adv.* **hawkishness** *n.*

hawks-bill (hoks´bil˝) *n.* A sea turtle with a hawk-like bill, whose shell provides a valuable commerical tortoise shell.

haw-ser (ho´zėr) *n.* A heavy cable or rope for towing or securing a ship.

haw-thorn (ho´thorn˝) *n.* A thorny shrub or tree bearing white or pink flowers and red fruit.

hay (hā) *n.* Alfalfa or grass that has been cut and dried for animal food.

hay-cock (hākok˝) *n.* A rounded pile of hay that is stacked and kept outdoors; a haystack.

Hayes, Rutherford Birchard *n.* (1822-1893) The 19th president of the United States from 1877-1881.

hay fever *n.* An acute allergy to certain airborne pollens, marked by severe irritation of the upper respiratory tract and the eyes.

hay-fork (hā´fork˝) *n.* A hand held or mechanical tool used to move hay.

hay-loft (hā´loft˝) *n.* A upper loft in a barn or stable used to store hay.

hay-mow (hā´mou˝) *n.* A large mound of hay stored in a loft.

hay-rack (hā´rak˝) *n.* A rack for holding hay from which livestock is fed; a rack of framework mounted on a wagon, for use in carrying hay or straw.

hay ride *n.* A pleasure ride on a wagon or truck party filled with straw or hay.

hay-seed (hā´sēd˝) *n.* The seeds from hay; a person from the country.

hay-stack (hā´stak˝) *n.* A pile of hay stored outdoors.

hay-wire (hā´wīėr˝) *adj., Slang* Broken; emotionally out of control; crazy.

haz-ard (haz´ėrd) *n.* A risk; chance; an accident; anger or source of danger. *v.* To take a chance on; to venture. **hazardous** *adj.*

haze (hāz) *n.* A fog-like suspension of dust, smoke, and vapor in the air; a confused or vague state of mind. *v.* To harass with disagreeable tasks.

ha-zel (hā´zel) *n.* A small tree or shrub bearing edible brown nuts with smooth shells; a light brown or yellowish brown.

hazel *adj.*

ha-zel-nut (hā′zel nut″) *n.* The edible nut of the hazel.

haz-y (hā′zē) *adj.* Lacking clarity; vague. **hazily** *adv.* **haziness** *n.*

hdqrs. *abbr.* Headquarters.

H–bomb (āch′bom″) *n.* Hydrogen bomb.

he (hē) *n.* A male person or animal.

he'd (hēd) *conj.* He had; he would.

he'll (hēl) He will.

he's (hēz) He has; he is.

he–man (hē′man′) *n.*, *Slang* A man marked by strength; a muscular man.

head (hed) *n.* The upper part of a human or animal body, containing the brain, the principal nerve centers, the eyes, ears, nose and mouth. **headed** *adj.*

head-ache (hed′āk″) *n.* A pain or ache in the head. *Slang* A bothersome problem. **headachy** *adj.*

head-band (hed′band″) *n.* A band of cloth worn around the head.

head-board (hed′bōrd″) *n.* A frame or panel that stands at the head of a bed.

head-cheese (hed′chēz″) *n.* A jellied loaf, preparation of parts of the head and feet of hogs; luncheon meat.

head cold *n.* A common cold or viral infection that centers primarily in the nasal passages.

head-dress (hed′dres″) *n.* An elaborate, ornamental head covering.

head-first (hed′ferst′) *adv.* With the head in a forward position; headlong.

head-gear (hed′gēr″) *n.* A protective covering worn on the head.

head-hunt-ing *n.* A tribal custom of decapitating slain enemies and preserving the heads as trophies.

head-ing (hed′ing) *n.* A title or caption that acts as a front, beginning, or upper part of anything; the direction or course of a ship or aircraft.

head-land (hed′land) *n.* A high ridge or cliff projecting into the water.

head-light (hed′līt″) *n.* A light with special lens mounted on the front of an automobile; a miners light worn on the head.

head-line (hed′lī′n″) *n.* A title, caption, or summarizing words of a newspaper story or article printed in large type. *v.* To provide with a headline; to serve as the star performer. **headliner** *n.*

head-lock (hed′lok) *n.* A wrestling hold in which the head of a wrestler is locked under the arm of his opponent.

head-long (hed′long″) *adv.* Headfirst; not having deliberation. **headlonging** *adj.*

head louse *n.* A common head louse, that lives chiefly on the scalp of man and attaches its eggs to the hair.

head-man (hed′man) *n.* A supervisor.

head-mas-ter (hed′mas′tèr) *n.* A school principal of a private school.

head-mis-tress (hed′mis′tris) *n.* A female school principal of a private school.

head-note (hed′nōt″) *n.* A prefixed note of explanation, such a statement preceding the report of a legal case.

head-phone (hed′fōn″) *n.* A phone held over the ear by a band worn on the head.

head-piece (hed′pēs″) *n.* A helmet, cap or other covering for the head; a headset.

head-quar-ters (hed′kwor″tèrz) *n. pl.* The official location from which a leader directs a military unit.

head-rest (hed′rest″) *n.* A pad at the top of the back of an automobile seat to support the head.

head-room (hed′rōm″) *n.* The vertical clear space that permits passage through a doorway or archway.

head-set (hed′set″) *n.* A pair of headphones.

head-stall (hed′stol″) *n.* The part of a bridle that goes over a horse's head.

head-stand *n.* The act of balancing the body's weight on the top of the head, with the aid of the arms.

head start *n.* An early or advance start; an advantage.

head-stone (hed′stōn″) *n.* A memorial stone marker at the head of a grave, indicating a name, date of birth and date of death.

head-strong (hed′strong″) *adj.* Not easily

restrained; obstinate.

heads up *n.* A warning given to look out for danger overhead.

head-wait-er (hed'wā''tėr) *n.* The waiter in charge of a restaurant or dining room staff.

head-wat-er (hed'wo'tėr) *n.* The source of a river or stream.

head-way (hed'wā'') *n.* Motion in a forward direction; progress toward a goal; clearance beneath an arch or ceiling.

head wind (hed'wind'') *n.* A wind blowing in the direction opposite the course of a ship or aircraft.

head-y (hed'ē) *adj.* Tending to intoxicate; affecting the senses; headstrong. **headily** *adv.* **headiness** *n.*

heal (hēl) *v.* To restore to good health; to mend. **healable** *adj.* **healer** *n.*

health (helth) *n.* The overall sound condition or function of a living organism at a particular time; freedom from disease or defect. **healthful** *adj,* **healthfully** *adv.* **healthfulness** *n.*

health-y (hel'thē) *adj.* In a state of or having good health; characteristic of a sound condition. **healthily** *adv.* **healthiness** *n.*

heap (hēp) *n.* A haphazard assortment of things; a large number or quantity. *v.* To throw or pile into a heap.

hear (hēr) *v.* To perceive by the ear; to listen with careful attention; to be informed of; to listen to officially or formally, as in a court of law. **hearer** *n.*

hear-ing (hēr'ing) *n.* One of the five senses; the range by which sound can be heard; an opportunity to be heard; in law, a preliminary examination of an accused person.

hearing aid *n.* An electronic device used to amplify the hearing of partially deaf persons.

heark-en (här'ken) *v.* To listen carefully.

hear-say (hēr'sā'') *n.* Information heard from another; common talk; rumor.

hearse (hers) *n.* A vehicle for conveying a dead body to the place of burial.

heart (härt) *n.* The hollow, primary muscular organ of vertebrates which circulates blood throughout the body; the emotional center, such as in love, hate, consideration, or compassion; the most essential part of something.

heart-ache (härt'āk'') *n.* Emotional grief; sorrow.

heart attack *n.* An acute malfunction or interrupted heart function.

heart-beat (härt'bēt'') *n.* A pulsation of the heart, consisting of one contraction and one relaxation.

heart block *n.* An impairment of the ventricular beats of the heart.

heart-break (härt'brāk'') *n.* Great sorrow; deep grief. **heartbreaking** *adj.,* **heartbreakingly** *adv.*

heart-brok-en (härt'brōken) *a.* Deeply grieved; overcome by sadness.

heart-burn (härt'bern'') *n.* A sensation of burning in the stomach and esophagus, usually caused by excess acid in the stomach.

heart disease *n.* An abnormality of the heart and or circulation.

heart-en (här'ten) *v.* To give courage to.

heart-felt (härt'felt'') *adj.* Deeply felt; sincere.

hearth (härth) *n.* The floor of a fireplace, furnace; the stone that forms the front of a fireplace.

heart-land (härt'land'') *n.* A strategically important central region, one regarded as vital to a nation's economy or defense.

heart-less (härt'lis) *adj.* Having no sympathy; lacking compassion. **heartlessness** *n.* **heartlessly** *adv.*

heart murmur *n.* An abnormal heart beat or sound.

heart-rend-ing (härt'ren''ding) *adj.* Causing great distress, suffering emotional anguish.

hearts-ease (härts'ēz) *n.* Emotional comfort; peace of mind; tranquillity.

heart-sick (härt'sik'') *adj.* Profoundly dejected. **heartsickness** *n.*

heart-strings (härt'stringz'') *n.* The deepest feelings and emotions.

heart-throb (härt'throb'') *n.* One pulsation

of the heart; tender emotion; a loved one.

heart–to–heart (härt´to härt´) *adj.* Sincere; frank.

heart–warm-ing *adj.* A feeling of warm sympathy.

heart-wood (härt´wŏd) *n.* The older, no longer active central wood of a tree.

heart-y (här´tē) *adj.* Marked by exuberant warmth; full of vigor; nourishing; substantial. **heartily** *adv.* **heartiness** *n.*

heat (hēt) *n.* A quality of being hot or warm; a degree of warmth; depth of feeling; a period of sexual ardor in female animals. *Slang* Pressure or stress. *v.* To make or become warm or hot. **heater** *n.*

heat engine *n.* A device that produces mechanical energy from heat, as an internal combustion engine.

heat exhaustion *n.* A reaction to intense heat, a mild form of heat stroke.

heath (hēth) *n.* An open tract of uncultivated wasteland covered with low-growing shrubs and plants.

hea-then (hē´then) *n.* A person or nation that does not recognize the God of Christianity, Judaism, or Islam; in the Old Testament, a Gentile; non-Jew. **heathen, heathenish** *adj.* **heathenism** *n.*

heath-er (heth´ér) *n.* A shrub that grows in dense masses and has small evergreen leaves and small pinkish flowers. **heather, heathery** *adj.*

heat lightning *n.* Flashes of electric light without thunder, seen near the horizon.

heat pump *n.* A heating plant for heating and cooling a building by transferring heat to a reservoir outside the building.

heat stroke (hēt´strōk˝) *n.* A state of collapse or exhaustion, accompanied by fever and marked by clammy skin, caused by excessive heat.

heat wave *n.* An extended period of unusually hot weather.

heave (hēv) *v.* To raise or lift, especially forcibly; to hurl or throw. *Naut.* To push, pull, or haul, as by a rope. *Slang* To vomit. *n.* The act of throwing.

heav-en-ly (hev´en-lē) *adj.* Relating to

heaven; celestial; delightful; holy.

heaves (hēvz) *n.* A disease of horses affecting the lungs and marked by coughing and difficult breathing.

heav-en (hev´en) *n.* The sky; the region above and around the earth; the abode of God, the angels, and the blessed souls of the dead; a state or place of blissful happiness. **heavenliness** *n.* **heavenly** *adj.* **heavenward** *adv. & adj.*

heav-i-ly (hev´i-lē) *adv.* In a heavy manner; with large weight, or burden; with great force.

heav-y (hev´ē) *adj.* Of great weight; very thick or dense; forceful; powerful; rough and violent, as stormy weather; of great significance; grave; painful, as bad news; oppressive. **heavily** *adv.* **heaviness** *n.*

heavy–du-ty (hev´ē dō´tē) *adj.* Designed for hard use.

heav-y–foot-ed (hev´ē-füt´id) *adj.* Awkward or slow in movement.

heavy–hand-ed (hev´ē han´did) *adj.* Clumsy; not tactful; oppressive. **heavy-handedly** *adv.* **heavy-handedness** *n.*

heavy–heart-ed (hev´ē här´tid) *adj.* Melancholy; depressed; sad. **heavy-heartedly** *adv.* **heavy–heartedness** *n.*

heavy–set (hev´ē set´) *adj.* Having a stocky build.

heavy water *n.* Water that contains more than the usual hydrogen in its heavier isotopic form, deuterium, used for scientific experiments.

heavy–weight (hev´ē wāt˝) *n.* A person of above average weight; a competitor in the heaviest class; a boxer weighing more that 175 pounds.

heb-e-tate (heb´i-tāt˝) *v.* To dull; to become dull or blunt.

heb-do-mad (heb´do mad˝) *n.* The period of seven days.

he-be-phre-nia (hē˝be frē´nē a) *n.* A schizophrenic reaction causing silliness, hallucinations and regression.

He-bra-ic *or* **He-bra-i-cal** *adj.* Of or relating to the Hebrews of their language or culture. **Hebraist** *n.*

He-brew (hēbrŏ) *n.* A member of a Semitic people claiming descent from Abraham, Isaac, and Jacob; the modern form of the language of the Hebrews. **Hebrew** *adj.*

heck (hek) *Slang.* An expression of disappointment; esp. as *oh heck.*

heck-le (hek´l) *v.* To badger or annoy, as with questions, comments, or gibes.

hec-tic (hek´tik) *adj.* Intensely active, rushed, or excited; marked by a persistent and fluctuating fever caused by a disease, such as tuberculosis; feverish; flushed.

hec-to-graph (hek´to graf´) *n.* A machine for making copies of a drawing on a gelatin surface.

hec-tor (hek´tèr) *n.* A bully; domineering person. *v.* To intimidate, to bully.

hed-dle (hed´l) *n.* A set of parallel cords or wires that guide warp threads in a loom.

hedge (hej) *n.* A boundary or fence formed of shrubs or low-growing trees; a means to guard against financial loss; a deliberately ambiguous statement. **hedge** *v.* **hedger** *n.*

hedge-hog (hej´hog´) *n.* A small nocturnal mammal with dense, erectile spines on the back, which are presented when the animal rolls itself into a ball in self-defense; a porcupine.

hedge-hop (hej´hop´) *v.* To fly an aircraft close to the ground, as in spraying crops. **hedgehopper** *n.*

hedge-row (hej´rō´) *n.* A dense row of bushes, shrubs, or trees forming a hedge.

hedge-spar-row *n.* A sparrow-like, European bird.

he-don-ics, *n. pl.* Branch of ethics relating to pleasure.

he-don-ism (hēd´o niz´um) *n.* The doctrine devoted to the pursuit of pleasure; the philosophy that pleasure is the principal good in life. **hedonist** *n.* **hedonistic** *adj.*

heed (hēd) *v.* To pay attention; to take notice of something. *n.* Attention. **heedful** *adj.* **heedfully** *adv.* **heedfulness** *n.*

heed-less (hēd´lis) *adj.* Without heed; inconsiderate; careless.

heel (hēl) *n.* The rounded back part of the human foot under and behind the ankle; the part of a shoe supporting or covering the heel; a lower or bottom part; the crusty ends of a loaf of bread. *v.* To follow along at one's heels.

heel-piece (hēl´pēs´) *n.* A small piece of material designed for the heel of a shoe.

heel-tap (hēl´tap´) *n.* The small amount of alcoholic that remains in a glass or bottle after drinking; a small piece of metal or leather designed for the heel of a shoe.

heft (heft) *n., Slang* Weight; bulk. *v.* To gauge or estimate the weight of by lifting; to lift up.

heft-y (hef´tē) *adj.* Bulky; heavy; sizable.

he-gem-o-ny (hi jem´o nē) *n.* Dominance or leadership, as of one country over another.

he-gi-ra (hi jī´ra) *n.* A journey or departure to flee an undesirable situation.

heif-er (hef´ér) *n.* A young cow, particularly one that has not produced a calf.

height (hīt) *n.* The quality of being high; the highest or most advanced point; the distance from the base of something; the apex; the distance above a specified level; altitude; the distance from head to foot.

height-en (hīt´en) *v.* To increase or become high in quantity or degree; to raise or lift.

Heimlich maneuver *n.* An emergency maneuver used to dislodge food from a choking person's throat; the closed fist is placed below the rib cage and pressed inward to force air from the lungs upward.

hei-nous (hā´nus) *adj.* Extremely wicked; hateful or shockingly wicked. **heinously** *adv.* **heinousness** *n.*

heir (âr) *n.* A person who inherits another's property or title.

heir apparent *n.* An heir who is legally assured of his right to inherit if he survives his ancestor.

heir-ess *n.* A female heir, especially to a large fortune.

heir-loom (âr´lŏm´) *n.* A family possession handed down from generation to generation; an article of personal property acquired by legal inheritance.

heist (hīst) *v., Slang* To take from; to steal. *n.* A robbery.

he-li-an-thus (hē-lē-an´thus) *n.* Herbaceous plants some of which are sunflowers.

hel-i-cal (hel´i kal) *adj.* Of or pertaining to the shape of a helix. **helically** *adv.*

hel-i-con (hel´i kon˝) *n.* A large, circular tuba that encircles the player's shoulder.

hel-i-cop-ter (hel´i kop˝tėr) *n.* An aircraft propelled by rotors which can take off verti-  cally rather than needing an approach or a rolling start.

he-li-o-cen-tric (hē˝lē-ō-sen´trik) *adj.* Referred to, measured or as seen from the sun's center.

he-lio-graph (hē´lē o graf˝) *n.* An apparatus for telegraphing using the sun's rays reflected from a mirror.

he-li-o-trope (hē´lē-ō-trōp˝) *n.* A garden plant having small, fragrant, purple flowers.

he-li-ot-ro-pism (hē˝lē-o´tro-piz˝um) *n.* The tendency of plants and other organisms to be influenced in growth by the direction of sun.

hel-i-port (hel´i pōrt˝) *n.* A designated area where helicopters land and take off.

he-li-um (hē´lē um) *n.* An extremely light, non-flammable, odorless, gaseous element, symbolized by He.

he-lix (hē´liks) *n.* Something that is spiral in form; a spiral line, as of wire winding around a tube; a coil.

hell *or* **Hell (hel)** *n.* The abode of the dead soals condemned to eternal punishment; a place of evil, torment, or destruction; great distress; anguish; a cause of trouble or misery. **hellish** *adj.* **hellishly** *adv.*

hell-bent (hel´bent˝) *adj., Slang.* Stubbornly determined; going ahead regardless of consequences.

hel-le-bore (hel´e bōr˝) *n.* A North American plant bearing white or greenish flowers and yielding a toxic alkaloid used in medicine.

Hel-le-nism (hel´e niz˝um) *n.* Ancient Greek civilization, character or culture; adoption of Greek thought, style, or cultural customs. **Hellenist** *n.*

hell hole *n.* A place of extreme wretchedness or horror.

hel-lion (hel´yon) *n.* A mischievous person.

hel-lo (he lō´) *n.* An expression of greeting.

helm (helm) *n.* A wheel or steering apparatus for a ship; a position or any place of control or command.

hel-met (hel´mit) *n.* A protective covering for the head made of metal, leather, or plastic.

hel-minth (hel´minth) *n.* An intestinal worm, as the tapeworm.

helms-man (helmz´man) *n.* One who guides a ship.

hel-ot *n.* A serf; a slave. **helotry** *n.*

help (help) *v.* To assist or aid. *n.* Assistance; relief; one that assists; one hired to help. **helper** *n.* **helpful** *adj.*

help-ing (hel´ping) *n.* A single serving of food.

help-less (help´lis) *adj.* Without help; powerless; lacking strength.

help-mate (help´māt˝) *n.* A helper, partner or companion.

Hel-sin-ki *n.* The capital of Finland.

hel-ter–skel-ter (hel´tėr skel´tėr) *adv.* In a confused or hurried manner; in an aimless way. *adj.* Rushed and confused. *n.* Great confusion; a tumult.

helve (helv) *n.* A handle on a tool such as an axe or hatchet.

hem (hem) *n.* A finished edge of fabric folded under and stitched. *interj.* A sound made as in clearing the throat, used especially to attract attention or to fill a pause in speech. *v.* To fold under and stitch down the edge of; to confine and surround.

he-mal (hē´mal) *a.* Pertaining to the blood or blood vessels; noting, pertaining to, or situated on that side of the spinal column containing the heart and great blood vessels.

hem-an-gi-o-ma *n.* A benign tumor that occurs as a reddish elevated area on the skin.

hem-a-tin-ic (hem″a tin′ik) *n.* A medicine, that tends to stimulate blood cell formation or increases the hemoglobin in the blood.

he-ma-tol-o-gy (hem″a tol′o jē) *n.* The branch of biological science that deals with blood and blood-generating organs. **hematologist** *n.*

he-ma-to-ma *n.* A tumor containing blood.

hem-i-cel-lu-lose (hem″i sel′ū lōs″) *n.* A natural carbohydrate less complex than cellulose, found mainly in the woody tissue of plants.

hem-i-cy-cle (hem′i sī″kl) *n.* A curved or half circle; a semicircular structure or building.

hemi-ple-gia *n.* The paralysis of one half of the body or part of it resulting from injury to the motor center of the brain.

he-mip-ter-an (hi mip′tėr an) *n.* A large insect that has a mouth adapted to piercing and sucking, among which are the true bugs, plant lice, cicadas, and other related insects, often having two sets of wings, and a life cycle that includes a partial metamorphosis.

hem-i-sphere (hem′i sfēr″) *n.* A half sphere that is divided by a plane passing through its center; either symmetrical half of an approximately spherical shape; the northern or southern half of the earth divided by the equator or the eastern or western half divided by a meridian. **hemispherical** *adj.*

hem-i-stitch (hem′i stik″) *n.* The decorative border stitch used in sewing.

hem-line (hem′līn″) *n.* The line formed at the lower edge of a garment as a skirt, or dress.

hem-lock (hem′lok″) *n.* An evergreen tree of North America and eastern Asia, having flat needles and small cones; the wood of a hemlock; any of several poisonous herbaceous plants, having compound leaves and small whitish flowers; a poison obtained from the hemlock plant.

he-mo-cy-to-me-ter (hē″mō sī tom′i tėr) *n.* The instrument used in counting blood corpuscles.

he-mo-dy-nam-ics *n.* The branch of phys-

iology that deals with the circulation of the blood.

he-mo-glo-bin (hē′mo glō″bin) *n.* The iron-containing protein respiratory pigment occuring in red corpuscles of vertebrates.

he-mo-ly-sin *n.* A substance which causes the dissolution of red blood cells.

he-mo-phil-i-a (hē″mo fil′ē a) *n., Pathol.* An inherited blood disease characterized by severe, protracted, sometimes spontaneous bleeding. **hemophiliac** *n.*

hem-or-rhage (hem′ėr ij) *n.* Bleeding, especially excessive bleeding. **hemorrhage** *v.*

hem-or-rhoid (hem′o roid″) *n., Pathol.* A painful mass of dilated veins in swollen anal tissue.

hemorrhoids *n. pl.* A condition in which hemorrhoids occur.

he-mo-stat (hē′mo stat″) *n.* An agent that stops bleeding; a clamp-like instrument for preventing or reducing bleeding.

hemp (hemp) *n.* An Asian herb; the female plant from which hashish and marijuana are produced; the tough fiber of the male plant from which coarse fabrics and rope are made. **hempen** *adj.*

hen (hen) *n.* A mature female bird, especially an adult female domestic fowl.

hence (hens) *adv.* From this place or time; from this source.

hence-forth / hence-for-ward (hens ′fōrth′) *adv.* From this time on.

hench-man (hench′man) *n.* A loyal and faithful follower; one who supports a political figure chiefly for personal gain.

hen-dec-a-gon (hen dek′a gon″) *n.* A plane figure with eleven sides and the same number of.

hen-e-quen (hen′ekin) *n.* A strong fiber obtained from the leaves of a tropical American plant, used for binder twine and course fabrics.

hen-na (hen′a) *n.* An Asian and North African ornamental tree bearing fragrant white or reddish flowers; a brownish-red dye derived from henna leaves and used as a cosmetic dye; a strong reddish brown.

heno-the-ism (hen'othē iz˝um) *n.* The worship of one god although not denying the existence of other gods.

hen-peck (hen'pek˝) *v.* To domineer over one's husband by persistent nagging.

Henry, Patrick *n.* (1736-1799). An American Revolutionary leader.

hep (hep) *adj., Slang* Knowledgeable about the styles, or tends.

hep-a-rin (hep'a rin) *n., Biochem* A substance found especially in liver tissue having the power to slow or prevent blood clotting.

he-pat-ic (hi pat'ik) *adj.* Of or like the liver.

he-pat-i-ca (hi pat'i ka) *n.* A small perennial herb having three-lobed leaves and white or lavender flowers.

hep-a-ti-tis (he˝a tī'tis) *n., Pathol.* Inflammation of the liver causing jaundice.

hep-a-tize (hep'a tīz˝) *v. ,Pathol.* To convert the spongy lung tissue, into liver-like tissue, caused by congestion.

hep-tad (hep'tad) n. A group of seven.

hep-ta-gon (hep'tagon˝) *n.* A polygon of seven angles and sides.

hep-tam-er-ous (hep tam'ėr us) *adj.* Containing seven parts.

her-ald (her'ald) *n.* A person who announces important news; one that comes before as a sign of what is to follow.

he-ral-dic (he ral'dik) *adj.* An official whose duty is to grant royal proclamations. *v.* To announce.

her-ald-ry (her'al drē) *n. pl.* **heraldries** The art or science of tracing genealogies and devising and granting coats of arms.

herb (erb) *n.* A soft-stemmed plant without woody tissue that usually withers and dies each year; an often pleasant-smelling plant. **herbal** *adj. & n.*

her-ba-ceous (her bā'shus) *adj.* Like, or consisting of herbs; green and leaf-like.

herb-age (hur'bij) *n.* Herbs collectively; herbaceous vegetation; the succulent parts, of herbaceous plants,as leaves and stems.

her-bal (hur'bal, ur'bal) *n.* A book on plants or herbs with reference to their medical properties.

herb-al-ist (her'ba list) *n.* One who gathers, grows, and deals in herbs.

her-bar-i-um (her bâr'ē um) *n. pl.* **herbariums** *or* **herbaria** A collection of dried plant specimens that are scientifically arranged for study; a place housing an herbarium.

her-bi-cide (er'bi sīd˝) *n.* A chemical agent used to kill weeds. **herbicidal** *adj.*

her-bi-vore (her'bi vō˝) *n.* A type of herbivorous animal.

her-biv-o-rous (her biv'ėr us) *adj.* Feeding chiefly on plant life or vegetables. **herbivorously** *adv.*

her-cu-le-an (hėr˝kū lē'an) *adj.* Of unusual size, force, or difficulty; having great strength.

Her-cu-les *n.* A mythical Greek hero famous for his great strength.

herd (hėrd) *n.* A number of cattle or other animals of the same kind, kept or staying together as a group; a large crowd of people. *v.* To bring together in a herd. **herder, herdsman** *n.*

here (hēr) *adv.* In or at this place; in a present life or state.

here-af-ter (hēr af'tėr) *adv.* From now on; at some future time. *n.* Existence after death.

here-by (hēr bī') *adv.* By means or by virtue of this.

he-red-i-tar-y (he red'i ter˝ē) *adj.* Passing or transmitted from an ancestor to a legal heir; having an inherited title or possession; transmitted or transmissible by genetic inheritance. **hereditarily** *adv.*

her-e-dit-a-ment (her˝i dit'a ment) *n.* Any heritable property.

he-red-i-ty (he red'i tē) *n.* The genetic transmission of physical traits from parents to offspring.

here-in (hēr in') *adv.* In or into this place.

here-of (hēr uv') *adv.* Relating to or in regard to this.

her-e-sy (her'i sē) *n. pl.* **heresies** A belief in conflict with orthodox religious beliefs; any belief contrary to set doctrine.

her-e-tic (her´i tik) *n.* A person holding opinions different from orthodox beliefs, especially religious beliefs. **heretical** *adj.*

here-to (hēr tō´) *adv.* To this matter, proposition, or thing.

here-to-fore (hēr´to fōr´) *adv.* Up to the present time; previously.

here-un-to (hēr˝un tō´) *adv.* Hereto; to this.

here-up-on (hēr˝u pon´) *adv.* Immediately following or resulting from this.

here-with (hēr with´) *adv.* Together or along with this; hereby.

her-i-ta-ble (her´i ta bl) *adj.* Something capable of being inherited.

her-i-tage (her´i tij) *n.* Property that is inherited; something handed down from past generations; a legacy.

herm (hèrm) *n.* Monument or statue, in the form of a square stone pillar, consisting of a head or bust.

her-maph-ro-dite (hèr maf´ro dīt´) *n.* A person having both male and female reproductive organs. **hermaphroditic** *adj.*

her-me-neu-tics (hur˝me nö´tiks) *n.* The study or art interpretation, especially when applied to Bible scriptures.

her-met-ic *or* **her-met-i-cal (her met´ik)** *adj.* Tightly sealed against air and liquids; made impervious to outside influences. **hermetically** *adv.*

her-mit (hèr´mit) *n.* A person who lives in seclusion, often for religious reasons.

her-mit-age (hèr´mi tij) *n.* The dwelling place or retreat of a hermit; a secluded hideaway.

hermit crab *n.* A chiefly marine decapod crustacean having soft abdomens and which occupy the empty shells of gastropods.

her-ni-a (hèr´nē a) *n.* The protrusion of a bodily organ, as the intestine, through an abnormally weakened wall that usually surrounds it; a rupture. **hernial** *adj.*

he-ro (hēr´ō) *n. pl.* **heroes** A figure in mythology and legend renowned for exceptional courage and fortitude. **heroic** *adj.* **heroically** *adv.*

he-ro-ic (hi rō´ik) *adj.* Relating or pertaining to heroes, impressive in power, size or extent; a great intensity; extreme.

heroic couplet *n.* A verse consisting of two rhyming lines of iambic pentameter.

her-o-in (her´ō in) *n.* A highly addictive narcotic derivative of morphine.

her-o-ine (her´ō in) *n.* A woman of heroic character; the principal female character in a story or play.

her-o-ism (her´ō iz˝um) *n.* Heroic behavior.

her-on (her´on) *n.* A bird having a long slender bill, long legs, and a long neck.

her-pes (hèr´pēz) *n., Pathol.* A viral infection, characterized by small blisters on the skin or mucous membranes. **herpetic** *adj.*

her-pe-tol-o-gy (hèr˝pi tol´o jē) *n.* The scientific study and treatment of reptiles and amphibians. **herpetologic, herpetological** *adj.* **herpetologically** *adv.* **herpetologist** *n.*

Herr *n. pl.* **Herren** A courtesy title of address to the name or a professional title of a German, equivelant to Mister.

her-ring (her´ing) *n.* A valuable food fish of the North Atlantic, the young of which are prepared as sardines, the adults are pickled, salted, or smoked.

her-ring-bone (her´ing bōn˝) *n.* A pattern utilizing rows of short slanted parallel lines with connected rows slanting in the opposite direction.

herring gull *n.* The most common large gull in North America, living on both the seashore and inland waters.

hertz *n.* A unit of frequency equalling one cycle per second.

hes-i-tant (hez´i tant) *adj.* Given to hesitating; lacking decisiveness.

hes-i-tate (hez´i tāt´) *v.* To pause or to be slow before acting, speaking, or deciding; to be uncertain. **hesitatingly** *adv.*

hes-i-ta-tion (hez˝i tā´shan) *n.* The act of hesitating; a state of doubt or pausing.

hes-sian (hesh´an) *n.* A German mercenary soldier.

het-er-o-chro-mat-ic (het˝èr o krō mat´ ik) *adj.* Of or relating to or containing different colors; made up of different frequencies or wavelengths.

het-er-o-cy-clic (het″ėr o sī′klik) *adj.* Relating to or characterized by an organic compound having a ring containing one or more atoms other than carbon.

het-er-o-dox (het′ėr o doks″) *adj.* Not in accord with established beliefs or religious doctrine; holding unorthodox opinions or beliefs. **heterodoxy** *n.*

het-er-oe-cious (het″e rē′shus) *adj.* Of a par-asite, passing through the different stages in the life cycle on often different hosts, as a certain fungi.

het-er-on-o-my (het″e ron′o mē) *n.* Subjection to something else.

het-er-o-nym (het′ėr o nim″) *n.* A word having the same spelling as another but a different meaning and pronunciation.

het-er-o-plas-ty (het′ėr o plas″tē) *n.* An operation in where lesions are repaired with grafted tissue taken from another organism or person.

het-er-o-sex-u-al (het″ėr o sek′shŏ al) *adj.* Of or having sexual desire to the opposite sex; involving different sexes. **heterosexual, heterosexuality** *n.*

het-er-o-sis (het″e rō′sis) *n.* An increased vigor or capacity for growth, often as the result of cross-breeding of plants or animals.

het-er-o-troph-ic (het″ėr o trof′ik) *adj., Biol.* Using organic matter as a source of food.

het-er-o-zy-gote (het″ėr o zī′gōt) *n.* A hybrid plant or animal that does not breed true because it contains a one pair of genes with different characteristics.

heu-ris-tic (hū ris′tik) *adj.* Involving a teaching method that utilizes self-educating or a method of trial and error to improve performance.

hew (hū) *v.* To make or shape with or as if with an axe; to adhere strictly; to conform.

hex (heks) *n.* One held to bring bad luck; a jinx. *v.* To put under an evil spell; to bewitch.

hex-a-gon (hek′sa gon″) *n.* A polygon having six sides and six angles. **hexagonal** *adj.* **hexagonally** *adv.*

hex-a-gram (hek′sa gram″) *n.* A six-pointed starlike figure formed by completing externally an equilateral triangle and on the opposite sides of the center.

hex-am-e-ter (hek sam′i tėr) *n.* A line of verse containing six metrical feet.

hex-a-pod (hek′sa pod″) *n.* Arthropods having six feet, comprising the true insects.

hey (hā) *interj.* An exclamation, used to express surprise or joy and used to call attention to.

hey-day (hā′dā″) *n.* A time of great power, prosperity or popularity; a peak.

HI *abbr.* Hawaii.

hi-a-tus (hī ātus) *n.* A slight gap, break, or lapse in time from which something is missing; a break. A break between shooting of television shows; a break in continuity.

hi-ba-chi *n. pl.* **hibachis** (hē bä′chē) A deep, portable charcoal grill used for cooking food.

hi-ber-nac-u-lum (hī″bėr nak′ū lum) *n.* A shelter occupied during the winter by a dormant animal.

hi-ber-nal (hī bur′nal) *adj.* Of, relating to belonging to the winter season; wintry.

hi-ber-nate (hī′bėr nāt″) *v.* To pass the winter in an inactive, dormant, sleep-like state. **hibernation, hibernator** *n.*

hi-bis-cus (hī bis′kus) *n.* A chiefly tropical shrub or tree, bearing large colorful flowers.

hic-cup *or* **hic-cough** (hik′up) *n.* An involuntary contraction of the diaphragm that occurs on inhalation and spasmodically closes the glottis, producing a short, sharp sound. **hiccup** *v.*

hick (hik) *n., Slang* A clumsy, unsophisticated country person. *adj.* Typical of hicks.

hick-o-ry (hik′o rē) *n. pl.* **hickories** A North American tree with a smooth or shaggy bark, hard edible nuts, and heavy, tough wood.

hi-dal-go (hi dal′go) *n, pl.* **hidalgoes** A

Spanish nobleman of lesser nobility.

hid-den (hid*e***n)** *adj.* Out of sight; away from the public eye.

hide (hīd) *v.* To put, or keep out of sight; to keep secret; to obscure from sight; to seek shelter. *n.* The skin of an animal.

hide-away (hīd*′a* **wā″)** *n.* A place to escape or retreat; a hideout.

hide-bound (hīd′bound″) *adj.* Obstinately narrow-minded or inflexible.

hid-e-ous (hid′ē us) *adj.* Physically repulsive; extremely ugly. **hideously** *adv.* **hideousness** *n.*

hide-out (hīd′out″) *n.* A place used for concealment, as a refuge from the authorities.

hi-dro-sis (hi drō′sis) *n.* Perspiration, esp. The excretion of sweat due to drugs, or a disease characterized by sweating.

hi-er-ar-chy (hī′*e* **rär″kē)** *n. pl.* **hierarchies** An authoritative body or group of things or persons arranged in successive order; a ranked series of persons or things. **hierachical, hierachic** *adj.*

hi-er-o-glyph-ic (hī′ĕr *o* **glif′ik)** *n.* A pictorial symbol representing an idea, object, or sound. **hieroglyphically** *adv.*

hi-er-o-phant (hī′ĕr *o* **fant″)** *n.* A priest in ancient Greece; one who interprets the rites of religion.

hi–fi (hī′fī″) *n.* High fidelity; electronic equipment, such as a phonograph, radio, or recording equipment capable of reproducing high fidelity sound.

hig-gle (hig′l) *v.* To bargain; to argue or haggle often over petty details.

high (hī) *adj.* Extending upward; located at a distance above the ground; more than normal in degree or amount.

high and dry *adv.* In a helpless position; away from the current or tide.

high-ball (hī′bol″) *n.* A mixed drink often served in a tall glass.

high-born (hī′born″) *adj.* Of noble birth or ancestry.

high-boy (hī′boi″) *n.* A tall chest of drawers often in two selections with the lower one mounted on four legs.

high-bred (hī′bred″) *adj.* Highborn; descending from superior breeding stock.

high-brow (hī′brou″) *n., Slang* One who claims to have superior knowledge or culture. **highbrow, highbrowed** *ad.j*

high chair (hī′chär″) *n.* A child's chair also used as a feeding table.

higher education *n.* An education beyond the secondary level; college education.

high-er–up (hī′ĕr up′) *n., Slang* A person having superior rank or status.

high-fa-lu-tin (hī″fa lōt′in) *adj.* Pretentious or extravagant in manner or speech.

high fashion *n.* The newest in fashion, style, or design.

high fidelity *n., Elect.* The reproduction of sound with minimal distortion, as on records or tapes.

high–flown (hī′flōn′) *adj.* Pretentious in language or style.

high frequency *n.* A radio frequency in the band from three to thirty megacycles.

high-grade (hī′grād) *n.* Having superior quality.

high–hand-ed (hī′han′did) *adj.* Overbearing and arbitrary. **highhandedly** *adv.* **highhandedness** *n.*

high–hat (hī′hat′) *adj., Slang* Supercilious; patronizing; snobbish; fashionable.

high jump *n.* A jump for height in athletics.

high-land (hī′land) *n.* Land elevated as a plateau. **highlands** *pl.* A hilly or mountainous region.

high–level (hī′lev′el) *a.* Having a high rank, status, or importance.

high–light (hī′līt′) *n.* A significant event or detail of special importance. *v.* To give emphasis to; to provide with highlights.

high–mind-ed (hī′mīn′did) *adj.* Possessing noble principles or behavior. **high–mindedness** *n.*

high-ness (hī′nis) *n.* The state of being high. **Highness** A title use for royalty.

high noon *n.* The middle of the day; 12:00 noon.

high–octane (hī′ok′tān) *adj.* Having a high octane number, indicating good antiknock properties and good performance.

high-pow-ered *n.* Having great energy.

high–pressure (hī´presh´er) *adj., Informal* Using insistent persuasive methods or tactics. *v.* To try to persuade by using high–pressure techniques.

high–rise *n.* An extremely tall building.

high roller *n.* A person who spends freely and gambles for high stakes.

high-road (hī´rōd´) *n.* A main road; a direct or guaranteed method or course.

high school *n.* A secondary school of grades nine through twelve or grades ten through twelve. high schooler *n.*

high seas *n. pl.* The open waters of an ocean or sea that are beyond the territorial jurisdiction of any one nation.

high–sound-ing (hī´soun´ding) *adj.* Pretentious or imposing in implication or sound.

high–spir-it-ed (hī´spir´i tid) *adj.* Unbroken in spirit; proud.

high–stick-ing *n.* In hockey, an offense in which a player holds the stick above the shoulders of other players or himself.

high–strung (hī´strung´) *adj.* Very nervous and excitable.

high tech *n.* An interior design that incorporates industrial materials or motifs; high technology.

high technology *n.* The technology that involves highly advanced or specialized systems or devices.

high–test (hī´test´) *adj.* Relating to gasoline with a high octane number.

high tide The highest level reached by the incoming tide each day.

high-water *adj.* A high state of water in a river.

high-way (hī´wā´) *adj.* A main or principal road or thoroughfare of some length which connects towns and cities and is open to the public.

high-way-man (hī´wā´man) *n.* Formerly, a robber who waylaid travelers on highways.

highway robbery *n.* An excessive profit derived from a business transaction.

high-jack (hī´jak´) *v., Slang* To seize illegally or steal while in transit; to coerce or compel someone; to commandeer a vehicle, especially an airplane in flight highjacker *n.*

hike (hīk) *v.* To walk for a lengthy amount of time usually through rugged terrain or woods; to pull up clothing with a sudden motion. hike *n.* hiker

hi-lar-i-ous (hi lâr´ē us) *adj.* Boisterously happy or cheerful. hilariously *adv.* hilarity *n.*

hill (hil) *n.* A rounded, elevation of the earth's surface, smaller than a mountain; a pile or heap; a small pile or mound, as of soil. *v.* To surround or cover with hills, as potatoes. hilliness *n.* hilly *adj.*

hill-ock (hil´ok) *n.* A small or low hill or mound. hillocky *adj.*

hill-side *n.* The side or slope of a hill.

hill-top *n.* The summit or top of a hill.

hilt (hilt) *n.* The handle of a dagger or sword. to the hilt Fully; completely; thoroughly.

him (him) *pron.* The objective case of the pronoun he.

Hi-ma-la-yas *n.* A mountain range in Asia.

hi-mat-i-on (hi mat´ē on´) *n.* A rectangular cloth draped over the left shoulder and body and worn as a garment in Greece.

him-self (him self´) *pron.* The identical male one; a form of the third person.

hind (hīnd) *adj.* Located at or toward the rear part; posterior.

hind-brain (hīnd´brān´) *n.* The posterior of the three primary divisions of the vertebrate brain including the pons, cerebellum, and medulla oblongata.

hin-der (hin´der) *v.* To interfere with the progress or action of. hinderer *n.*

Hin-di (hin´dē) *n.* The principal language of northern India. Hindi *adj.*

hind-most (hīnd´mōst´) *adj.* Farthest to the rear or back.

hind-quar-ter (hīnd´kwor´ter) *n.* The back or hind part of a side of meat. hindquarters *pl.* The rump.

hin-drance (hin´drans) *n.* The act of hindering or state of being hindered.

hind-sight (hīnd´sīt´) *n.* Comprehension

or understanding of an event after it has happened.

Hin-du (hin´dŏ) *n.* A native of India; a person whose religion is Hinduism.

Hin-du-ism (hin´dŏ iz˝um) *n.* The religion, philosophy, and cultural beliefs of the Hindus of India.

hinge (hinj) *n.* A jointed device which allows a part, as a door or gate, to swing or turn on another frame. *v.* To attach by or to equip with a hinge or hinges.

hin-ny (hin´ē) *n.* The hybrid or offspring of between a stallion and female donkey.

hint (hint) *n.* An indirect indication or suggestion. *v.* To make something known by a hint.

hin-ter-land (hin´tĕr land˝) *n.* A region remote from cities; an inland area immediately adjacent to a coastal area.

hip (hip) *n.* The part of the human body that projects outward below the waist and thigh; the hip joint.

hip (hip) *n.* The bright, red seed case of a rose. *adj., Slang* Said to be aware of or informed about current goings on.

hip-bone (hip´bōn´) *n.* The large, flat bone which forms a lateral half of the pelvis.

hip joint *n.* The joint between the hipbone and the thighbone.

hip-pie *or* **hip-py (hip´ē)** *pl.* **hippies** A young person who adopts unconventional dress and behavior along with the use of drugs to express withdrawal from middle class life and indifference to its values.

hip-po-drome (hip´o drōm˝) *n.* An oval stadium for chariot races in ancient Greece.

hip-po-pot-a-mus (hip˝o pot´a mus) *n.* A large, aquatic mammal, native to Africa, having short  legs, a massive, thick-skinned hairless body, and a broad wide-mouthed muzzle.

hip roof *n.* A roof with both sides and ends that slope.

hir-cine (hur´sīn) *adj.* A goat or a resemblance of a goat.

hire (hīer) *v.* To obtain the service of an-

other for pay. **hirer** *n.*

hir-sute (her´sŏt) *adj.* Covered with hair.

his (hiz) *adj.* The possessive case of the pronoun he.

His-pan-ic (hi span´ik) *adj.* Of or relating to the language, people, or culture of Spain or Latin America.

his-pid (his´pid) *adj.* Rough, shaggy, or covered with stiff bristles.

hiss (his) *n.* A sound resembling a prolonged, sibilant sound, as that of sss. *v.* To emit such a sound as an expression of disapproval. **hisser** *n.*

hist (hist) *interj.* A sibilant exclamation used to attract attention or command silence.

his-ta-mine (his´ta mēn˝) *n., Biochem.* A white, crystalline compound that is found in plant and animal tissue, responsible for reducing blood pressure and having a dilating effect which plays a major role in reducing the symptons of allergies. **histaminic** *adj.*

his-to-gen-e-sis (his˝to jen´i sis) *n.* The origin, development, and formation of tissues.

his-tol-o-gy (hi stol´o jē) *n. pl.* **histologies** The study of the minute structures of animal and plant tissues as seen through a microscope. **histological** *adj.*

his-tol-y-sis (hi stol´i sis) *n.* The dissolution and breaking down of bodily tissues.

his-tone (his´tōn) *n.* Any of a class of protein substances, as a globin, having a high proportion of basic amino acids.

his-to-ri-an (hi stōr´ē an) *n.* A person who specializes in the writing or study of history.

his-tor-ic (hi stor´ik) *adj.* Significant or famous in history; historical.

his-tor-i-cal (hi stor´i kal) *adj.* Relating to or taking place in history; serving as a source of knowledge of the past; historic. **historically** *adv.* **historicalness** *adj.*

his-to-ry (his´to rē) *n. pl.* **histories** Past events, especially those involving human affairs; an account or record of past events that is written in chronological order, especially those concerning a particular nation, people, activity, or knowledge; the study of the past and its significance.

his-tri-on-ics (his″trē on′iks) *n. pl.* Theatrical arts; feigned emotional display.

hit (hit) *v.* To give a blow to; to strike with force; to come forcibly in contact with; to collide with; to inflict a blow on; to move or set in motion by striking; in baseball, to make a successful hit while at bat.

hitch (hich) *v.* To fasten or tie temporarily, with a hook or knot. *Slang* To unite in marriage; to obtain a ride by hitch hiking. *n.* A delay or difficulty. *Milit.* A period of time in the armed forces.

hitch-hike (hich′hīk″) *v.* To travel by signaling and obtaining rides from passing drivers. **hitchhiker** *n.*

hith-er (hith′ėr) *adv.* To this place. *adj.* Situated toward this side.

hith-er-to (hith′ėr tŏ″) *adv.* Up to now.

hive (hīv) *n.* A natural or man-made structure serving as a habitation for honeybees; a beehive.

hives (hīvz) *n. pl.* Any of various allergic conditions marked by itching welts.

ho (hō) *interj.* An exclamation expressing surprise; used to attract attention; exultation.

hoar (hōr) *adj.* Having white or gray hair; grayish or white, as with frost.

hoard (hōrd) *n.* The accumulation of something stored away for safekeeping or future use. *v.* To amass and hide or store valuables, money, or supplies. **hoarder** *n.*

hoard-ing (hōr′ ding) *n.* A temporary enclosure, as a board fence put around a building under construction or repairs.

hoar-frost (hōr′frost″) *n.* The deposit of ice crystals that form on a cold surface exposed to moist air.

hoarse (hōrs) *adj.* Having a husky, gruff, or croaking voice. **hoarsely** *adv.*

hoars-en *v.* To become or make hoarse.

hoar-y *adj.* Ancient; aged; gray or white with age.

ho-at-zin (hō at′sin) *n.* A crested, olive-colored bird of South America, smaller than a pheasant and noted for the claws which grow out of its wings.

hoax (hōks) *n.* A trick or deception. *v.* To deceive by a hoax. **hoaxer** *n.*

hob (hob) *n.* The projection at the side or interior of a fireplace used to keep things warm; an elf or hobgoblin.

hob-ble (hob′l) *v.* To limp or walk with a limp; to progress irregularly or clumsily; to fetter a horse or other animal. *n.* A hobbling gait or walk.

hob-ble-de-hoy (hob′l dē hoi″) *n.* An awkward, adolescent boy.

hob-by (hob′e) *n. pl., hobbies* An activity or interest undertaken for pleasure during one's leisure time.

hobby-horse (hob′ē hors) *n.* A child's rocking horse; a long stick surmounted by a horse's head.

hob-gob-lin (hob′gob″lin) *n.* An imaginary cause of terror or dread.

hob-nail (hob′nāl″) *n.* A short, broad-headed nail used to stud the soles of heavy shoes against wear or slipping.

hob-nob (hob′nob″) *n.* To associate in a friendly manner; to be on familiar terms.

ho-bo (hō′bō) *n. pl.* **hoboes** *or* **hobos** A vagrant who travels aimlessly about; a tramp.

hock (hok) *n.* The joint of the hind leg of a horse, ox, or other animal which corresponds to the ankle in man.

hock-ey (hok′ē) *n.* A game played on ice between two teams of skaters whose object is to drive a puck into the opponent's goal using curved wooden sticks; a similar kind of hockey played on a field with a small ball instead of a puck.

ho-cus–po-cus (hō′kus pō′kus) *n.* Any deception or trickery, as misleading gestures; nonsense words or phrases used in conjuring or sleight of hand.

hod (hod) *n.* A V-shaped trough held over the shoulder to carry loads, as bricks or mortar.

hod carrier *n.* A laborer employed to carry supplies to bricklayers, plasterers, etc. on the job.

hodge-podge (hoj'poj") *n.* A jumbled mixture or collection.

Hodgkin's disease *n., Pathol.* A disease characterized by progressive enlargement of the lymph nodes, lymphoid tissue, and spleen, generally fatal.

hoe (hō) *n.* A tool with a long handle and flat blade used for weeding, cultivating, and loosening the soil. **hoer** *n.*

hoe-cake (hō'kāk") *n.* A thin, flat cake made of cornmeal.

hoe-down (hō'dou") *n., Slang* A lively country square dance; party.

hog (hog) *n.* A pig, especially one weighing more than 120 pounds and raised for the market; a greedy, selfish, or dirty person. *v.* To take something selfishly; to take more than one's share. **hoggish** *adj.* **hoggishly** *adv.* **hoggishness** *n.*

ho-gan (hō'gon) *n.* A building made of legs and mud and used as a dwelling by the Indians.

hog-back (hag'bak") *n.* A sharply crested ridge of land with steeply sloping sides.

hog cholera *n.* A highly contagious, sometimes fatal virus disease affecting swine.

hognose snake *n.* Any of several nonvenomous American snake with flat heads and prominent snouts.

hogs-head (hogz'hed") *n.* A large barrel or cask that holds from 63 to 140 gallons.

hog–tie (hog'tī") *v.* To tie together the four feet of an animal or the hands and feet of a person.

hog-wash (hog'wosh") *n.* Kitchen scraps fed to hogs; any nonsense; false or ridiculous talk or writing.

hoi pol-loi (hoi' po loi') *n.* The common people; the masses.

hoist (hoist) *v.* To haul or raise up. *n.* A machine used for raising large objects.

ho-kum (hō'kum) *n.* Material introduced into a speech or a device used to evoke laughter or a desired audience response.

hold (hōld) *v.* To take and keep as in one's hand; to grasp; to possess; to put or keep in a particular place, position, or relationship; to suppress; to keep under control.

n. A cargo storage area inside a ship or aircraft. **hold back** withhold; retain. **hold down,** to suppress. **hold in** to restrain or repress. **hold off** to keep from touching; to delay. **hold on** to continue, to endure, to cling to. **hold together** to remain united.

hold-er (hōl' dėr) *n.* A person that holds, as one who has the ownership, or use of something;

hold-ing (hōl'ding) *n.* Property, as land, money, or stocks.

holding company *n.* A company which owns controlling stock or interest in securities of other companies.

holding pattern *n.* A usually circular course that is flown by an aircraft awaiting clearance to land at an airport.

hold-out (hōld'out") *n.* One who refuses to participate; as in a group; *v.* To stretch forth, as the hand; to stand firm; to refuse to give in; to last.

hold-ov-er *n.* Something that remains from an earlier time.

hold-up (hōld'up") *n.* A robbery at gun point; a delay.

hole (hōl) *n.* A cavity or opening in a solid mass or body. **hole** *v.*

hol-i-day (hol'i dā") *n.* A day set aside by law to commemorate a special person or event; a day set aside for religious observance; a day free from work; any day of rest.

ho-li-ness (hō'lē nis) *n.* The state of being holy.

ho-lism (hō'liz um) *n.* The theory that living nature has an identity other than the total or sum of its parts.

hol-land (hol'and) *n.* An unbleached, linen or cotton fabric used in the manufacture of window shades, clothing and bookbindings.

hol-lan-daise sauce (hol'an dāz' sos)") *n.* A creamy sauce made from butter, egg yolks, and lemon juice or vinegar.

hol-ler (hol'ėr) *v.* To shout loudly; to yell. **holler** *n.*

hol-low (hol'ō) *adj.* Having a cavity or

space within; concaved or sunken; lacking significance or substance; not genuine; empty; meaningless. **hollowly** *adv.*

hol-ly (hol´ē) *n. pl.* **hollies** A tree or shrub that bears glossy spiny leaves and bright-red berries.

hol-ly-hock (hol´ē hok˝) *n.* A tall, cultivated plant of the mallow family, widely cultivated for its tall spikes of large, variously colored flowers.

Hol-ly-wood *n.* A district of Los Angeles CA., the capital of the American motion-picture industry.

hol-mi-um (hōl´mē um) *n.* A metallic element of the rare-earth group, symbolized by Ho.

hol-o-caust (hol´o kost˝) *n.* A wide-spread or total destruction, especially by fire.

hol-o-graph (hol´o graf˝) *n.* A handwritten document, as a letter or will, signed by the person who wrote it. **holographic, holographical** *adj.*

ho-lo-gram (hō´lo gram) *n.* A three-dimensional picture made on a photographic plate without the use of a camera and viewed with coherent light from behind.

hol-o-type (hol´o tīp˝) *n.* A single specimen selected for descriptive and taxonomical purposes as a represent for the entire species.

Hol-stein (hōl´stīn) *n.* One of a breed of black-and-white dairy cattle.

hol-ster (hōl´stėr) *n.* A leather case designed to hold a pistol or gun. **holstered** *adj.*

ho-ly (hō´lē) *adj.* Regarded with or characterized by divine power; sacred.

Holy Communion *n.* The Eucharist.

Holy Ghost *n.* The third person of the Trinity.

Holy Spirit *n.* The Holy Ghost.

ho-ly-stone (hō´lē stōn˝) *n.* A soft sandstone used by seamen to scrub the decks of ships.

hom-age (hom´ij) *n.* Great respect or honor, especially when expressed publicly.

hom-burg (hom´berg) *n.* A man's felt hat having a stiff brim and high crown creased lengthwise.

home (hōm) *n.* The place where one resides;

a place of origin; one's birthplace or residence during the formative years; a place one holds dear because of personal feelings or relationships; a place of security and comfort.

home-bod-y (hōm´bod˝ē) *n. pl.* **homebodies** One who prefers to stay at home or whose main interest centers around the home.

home-bred (hōm´bred´) *adj.* Originating or producing at home.

home-com-ing (hōm´kum˝ing) *n.* A return to one's home; a yearly celebration during which alumni return to visit their old schools.

home economics *n.* The principles of home management.

home-like (hōm´līk˝) *adj.* Having the charac-teristics of a home; warm, cozy, familiar.

home-ly (hōm´lē) *adj.* Having a simple, familiar, everyday character; having plain or ugly features; unattractive.

ho-me-op-a-thy (hō˝mē op´a thē) *n.* A system of treating a disease with minute doses of medicines that produce the symptoms of the disease being treated. **homeopath** *n.* **homeopathic** *adj.*

ho-me-o-sta-sis (hō˝mē o stā´sis) *n., Biol.* A state of equilibrium that occurs between different but related functions or elements.

home plate *n.* In baseball, the rubber slab or plate at which a batter stands when batting and which must be touched by a base runner in order to score.

ho-mer (hō´mėr) *n.* An ancient Hebrew unit of capacity equal to about 10-½ - 11-½ bushels dry measure; *v.* To hit a home run in a baseball or softball game.

home run *n.* In baseball, a hit that allows the batter to circle all the bases and to score.

home-sick (hōm´sik˝) *adj.* Longing or yearning for home and family.

home-spun (hōm´spun˝) *adj.* Something made, woven, or spun at home; anything that is simple and plain.

home-stead (hōm´sted) *n.* A house and

its land. *v.* To occupy land granted under the Homestead Act. **homesteader** *n.*

home-stretch (hōm′strech′) *n.* The straight portion of a racecourse between the last turn and the finish line; the last or final stage of anything.

home-ward (hōm′wėrd) *adj.* Being in the direction of one's home or native country.

home-work (hōm′werk′) *n.* Work done at home, especially school assignments.

home-y *or* **hom-y (hō′mē)** *adj.* Suggesting the coziness, intimacy, and comforts of home. **home-yness** *or* **hominess** *n.*

hom-i-cid-al (hom′̃i sīd′al) *adj.* Relating or pertaining to homicide.

hom-i-cide (hom′i sīd′) *n.* The killing of one person by another; a person killed by another.

hom-i-let-ic (hom′̃i let′ik) *n.* Pertaining to the nature of a sermon.

hom-i-ly (hom′i lē) *n. pl.* **homilies** A sermon, particularly one based on a Biblical text.

homing device *n.* Any device used to guide a missile to its home.

homing pigeon *n.* A pigeon trained to find its way home from great distances.

hom-i-ny (hom′i nē) *n.* Kernels of hulled and dried corn, often ground into a coarse white meal and boiled.

hominy grits *n.* Hominy in uniform particles served as a side dish in the South.

ho-mo-cer-cal (hō′̃mo sur′kal) *adj.* Having the upper and lower lobes of the tail fin in approximately equal size, and the vertebral column ending near the base.

ho-mo-ge-ne-ous (hō′̃mo jē′nē us) *adj.* Of a similar nature or kind. **homogeneity, homogeneousness** *n.* **homogeneously** *adv.*

ho-mog-e-nize (ho moj′e nīz′) *v.* To process milk by breaking up fat globules and dispersing them uniformly. **homogenization, homogenizer** *n.*

ho-mog-o-nous (ho mog′o nus) *adj.* Pertaining to a type of flower with equally long stamens and pistils.

ho-mo-graft (hō′mo graft′) *n.* A tissue taken from an individual and grafted to

another of the same species.

hom-o-graph (ho′mo graf′) *n.* A word that is identical to another in spelling, but different from it in origin and meaning.

ho-moi-ther-mal (hō moi′̃o thur′mal) *adj.* Having a relatively constant body temperature independent of the surroundings.

ho-mol-o-gate (ho mol′o gāt′) *v.* To approve; to ratify.

ho-mol-o-gous (ho mol′o gus) *adj.* Related or similar in structure, nature, position, or value.

ho-mo-mor-phic (hō′̃mo mar′fik, hom′̃o mar′ fik) *adj.* Having the same external form.

hom-o-nym (hom′o nim) *n.* A word that has the same sound and often the same spelling as another but a different meaning and origin.

hom-o-phone (hom′o fōn′) *n.* One of two or more words that have the same sound but different spelling, origin, and meaning.

Ho-mo sa-pi-ens (hō′mō sā′pēenz) *n.* The scientific name for the human race.

ho-mo-sex-u-al (hō′̃mo sek′shō al) *adj.* Having sexual attraction or desire for persons of the same sex. **homosexual, homosexuality** *n.*

hon-cho *n. pl.* **honchos** The main person in charge; the boss; the manager.

hone (hōn) *n.* A fine-grained stone used to sharpen cutting tools, such as knives or razors. *v.* To perfect something; to sharpen.

hon-est (on′ist) *adj.* Not cheating, or stealing; free from fraud. **honestly** *adv.* **honesty** *n.*

hon-es-ty (on′i stē) *n.* The quality of being honest; free from deceit or fraud; straightforwardness.

hon-ey (hun′ē) *n. pl.* **honeys** A sweet, sticky substance made by bees from the nectar gathered from flowers; sweetness. *Slang* Dear; darling.

hon-ey-bee (hun′ē bē′) *n.* Any of various bees living in colonies and producing honey.

hon-ey-comb (hun′ē kōm′) *n.* A structure

consisting of a series of hexagonal cells made by bees for the storage of honey, pollen, or their eggs.

hon-ey-dew (hun´ē dŏ˝) *n.* A sweet fluid deposited on plant leaves by certain insects.

hon-ey-dew mel-on *n.* A smooth-skinned, white melon with a sweet, greenish pulp.

hon-ey-moon (hun´ē mŏn˝) *n.* A trip taken by a newly-married couple. **honeymoon** *v.* **honey-mooner** *n.*

hon-ey-suck-le (hun´ē suk˝el) *n.* A shrub or vine bearing a tubular, highly fragrant flower.

honk (hongk) *n.* The harsh, loud sound made by a goose; the sound made by an automobile horn. **honk** *v.* **honker** *n.*

hon-ky–tonk (hong´ē tongk˝) *n., Slang* A cheap bar or nightclub.

Hon-o-lu-lu *n.* The capital of the state of Hawaii, located on the island of Oahu.

hon-or (on´ėr) *n.* High regard or respect; personal integrity; reputation; privilege; used as a title for mayors and judges. *v.* To accept something as valid. **honorer** *n.*

hon-or-a-ble (on´ėr a bl) *adj.* Worthy of honor.

hon-or-a-ble mention *n.* A distinction conferred on someone for exceptional merit but not deserving of top honors.

hon-o-rar-i-um (on˝o râr´ē um) *n.* A payment or reward given in recognition for a service performed on which custom propriety discourages a fixed fee.

hon-or-ar-y (on´o rer˝ē) *adj.* Relating to an office or title bestowed as an honor, without the customary powers, duties, or salaries.

honor guard *n.* A guard assigned to accompany a distinguished person or accompany a casket at a military funeral.

hon-or-if-ic (on˝o rif˝ik) *adj.* Granting honor; speaking about or addressing a social superior position.

honor system *n.* A system of management, whereby one is trusted to obey the regulations without supervision.

Hon-shu *n.* The largest island of Japan.

hood (hed) *n.* A covering for the head and neck, often attached to a garment; the movable metal hinged cover of an automobile engine.

-hood *suff.* The quality or state of; sharing a given quality or state.

hood-ed (hud´id) *adj.* Having a hood; having a crest that resembles a hood-shape.

hood-lum (hŏd´lum) *n.* A young, tough, wild, or destructive fellow.

hoo-doo (hŏ´dŏ) *n., Slang* One who is thought to bring bad luck.

hood-wink (hed´wingk˝) *v.* To deceive; to blindfold.

hoo-ey (hŏ´ē) *n. & interj., Slang* Nonsense.

hoof (hef) *n. pl.* **hooves** The horny covering of the foot in various mammals, as horses, cattle, and oxen. *Slang* To dance; to walk. **on the hoof** Alive; not butchered. **hoofed** *adj.*

hook (hek) *n.* A curved or bent piece of metal used to catch, drag, suspend, or fasten something; in golf, a stroke that sends the ball curving to the left; in boxing, to strike with a short, swinging blow; in hockey, to check illegally with the hockey stick. *Slang v.* To cause to become dependent or addicted. *Naut., Slang* An anchor. **by hook or by crook** In one way or another. **hook, line, and sinker** Unreservedly; entirely. **to hook up with** To marry; to form an association.

hook-ah (huk´a) *n.* An Oriental tobacco water pipe, constructed with a long pliable tube and water vase so that the smoke is cooked as it passes through the water.

hook-er (hek´ėr) *n., Slang* A prostitute.

hook-worm (hek´werm´) *n.* A parasitic intestinal worm with hooked mouth parts.

hook-y (hek´ē) *n., Slang* Truant. **to play hooky** To be out of school without permission.

hoo-li-gan (hŏ´li gan) *n.* A street hoodlum.

hoop (hŏp) *n.* A circular band of metal or wood used to hold staves of a cask or barrel together; in basketball, the basket.

hoop-la (hŏp´lä) *n., Slang* Noise and

excitement.

hoop skirt *n.* A bellshaped skirt stiffened with a framework of light, flexible hoops.

hoose-gow (hŏs´gou) *n., Slang* A jail.

Hoo-sier (hŏ´zhėr) *n., Slang* A native or resident of Indiana.

Hoosier State *n.* Nickname for the state of Indiana.

hoot (hŏt) *n.* The loud sound or cry of an owl. **hooter** *n.* **hoot** *v.*

hoot (hŏt) *n. Slang* A very insignificant amount. **not give a hoot** Not caring.

hoot-en-an-ny (hŏt´e nan˝ē) *n. pl.* **hootenannies** An informal gathering of folk singers for a public performance.

Hoo-ver, Herbert Clark *n.* (1874-1964). The 31st president of the United States, from 1929-1933.

hop (hop) *n.* A perennial herb with lobed leaves and green flowers that resemble pine cones; the dried flowers of the plant, yielding an oil used in brewing beer. *Slang* A dance; a quick trip on a plane. *v.* To move by making short leaps on one foot; to move with light springing motions.

hope (hōp) *v.* To want or wish for something with a feeling of confident expectation. **to hope against hope** To continue hoping for something even when it may be in vain. **hopeful** *adj. & n.* **hopefully** *adv.*

hope chest *n.* A chest in which a young unmarried woman collects articles as domestic furnishing in anticipation of marriage.

hope-ful (hōp´fu̇l) *adj.* Manifesting or full of hope. *n.* A young person who shows signs of succeeding. **hopefully** *adv.* **hopefulness** *n.*

hope-less (hōp´lis) *adj.* Totally without hope; despairing; having no grounds for hope. **hopelessly** *adv.* **hopelessness** *n.*

hopped–up *adj., Slang* Stimulated by narcotics; drugged.

hop-per (hop´ėr) *n.* One that hops; a jumping insect; a receptacle in which coal, sand, grain, or other materials are held ready for discharge through the bottom.

hop-scotch (hop´skoch˝) *n.* A child's game in which the player throws an object, as

a stone, into areas drawn on the ground and then hops on one foot over the lines of a diagram so as to recover the object.

horde (hōrd) *adj.* A large crowd.

hore-hound (hōr´hound) *n.* A whitish, bitter, aromatic plant, whose leaves yield a bitter extract used as a flavoring in candy.

ho-ri-zon (ho rī´zon) *n.* The line along which the earth and sky seem to meet; the bounds or limit of one's knowledge, experience or interest.

hor-i-zon-tal (ho˝i zon´tal) *adj.* Parallel to the horizon. **horizontal** *n.*

hor-mone (hor´mōn) *n., Physiol.* An internal secretion carried by the bloodstream to other parts of the body where it has a specific effect.

horn (horn) *n.* A hard, bone-like, permanent projection on the heads of certain hoofed animals, as  cattle, sheep, or deer; the two antlers of a deer which are shed annually. *Mus.* Any of the various brass instruments, formerly made from animal horns. **horn in** To join in a conversation or other activities without being invited. **horn** *adj.* **horny** *adj.*

horn-beam (harn´bēm˝) *n.* A tree of the birch family having smooth gray bark and hard white wood.

horn-blende (harn´blend) *n.* A dark green or black mineral which is a common form of aluminous amphibole.

horned (harnd) *adj.* Having horns.

horned pout *n.* Any of several fish having barbels on their heads common of the eastern United States, especially bullhead; catfish.

horned toad *n.* A lizard with a flat body, a short tail, and horn-like projections on the head.

hor-net (hor´nit) *n.* Any of various wasps which are capable inflicting a severe sting.

horn in *v. Slang,* To interrupt or participate without invitation.

horn-pipe (harn´pīp˝) n. A single-reed wind musical instrument similar to a clarinet.

horn-pout n. A freshwater catfish with a large head and barbels for navigation.

horn-stone (horn´stōn˝) n. A quartz mineral much like flint but more brittle.

horn-swog-gle (horn´swog˝l) v. To deceive.

horn-wort n. A rootless aquatic herb that has flowers with a single carpel.

hor-o-loge (har´olōj) n. A mechanism for keeping time; an older timepiece, as the sundial.

ho-rol-o-gy (ho rol´ojē) n. The scientific of measurng time.

hor-o-scope (hor´o skōp˝) n. A chart or diagram of the relative positions of the planets and signs of the zodiac at a certain time, as that of a person's birth; used to predict the future.

hor-ren-dous (ha ren´dus) adj. Dreadful; terrible.

hor-ri-ble (hor´i bl) adj. Shocking; inducing or producing horror. *Informal* Excessive; inordinate. **horribly** adv.

hor-rid (hor´id) adj. Horrible. **horridly** adv.

hor-ri-fy (hor´i fī˝) v. To cause a feeling of horror; to dismay or shock.

hor-rip-i-la-tion (ha rip˝i lā´shan) n. The standing on end of the hair as a result of fear in dogs and cats.

hor-ror (hor´ėr) n. The painful, strong emotion caused by extreme dread, fear, or repug-nance. *Informal* Something that is disagree-able or ugly.

hors d'oeuvre (or derv´) n. An appetizer served with cocktails before dinner.

horse (hors) n. A large, strong, hoofed quadruped mammal with a long mane and tail, used for riding and for pulling heavy objects; a device that generally has four legs, used for holding or supporting something; in gymnastics, a wooden block of wood four legs, used for vaulting and other exercises.

horse-car (hars´kär˝) n. A streetcar that was formerly drawn by horses. A car equipped for transporting horses.

horse chest-nut n. Any of several Eurasian trees with digitate leaves, clusters of flowers, and chestnut-like fruit.

horse-fly (hors´flī˝) n. A large fly, the female of which sucks the blood of various mammals, such as horses and cattle.

horse-hair (hors´hâr˝) n. The hair from a horse's tail or mane; a fabric made from such hair; haircloth.

horse-hide (hors´hīd˝) n. The hide of a horse; leather made from a horse's hide. *Informal* A baseball.

horse-laugh (hors´laf˝) n. A loud, scornful laugh.

horse-man (hors´man) n. A person who rides horseback; one who breeds or raises horses. **horsemanship** n.

horse-play (hors´plā˝) n. Rough, boisterous fun or play.

horse-pow-er (hors´pow˝ėr) n., *Mech.* A unit of power that is equal to 746 watts and nearly equivalent to the gravitational unit that equals 550 foot-pounds per second.

horse-rad-ish (hors´rad˝ish) n. A tall, coarse, white-flowered herb from the mustard family; the pungent root of this plant is used as a condiment.

horse sense n., *Slang* Common sense.

horse-shoe (hors´shō˝) n. A protective U-shaped shoe for a horse, consisting of a narrow plate of iron shaped to fit the rim of a horse's hoof. **horseshoes** A game in which the object is to encircle a stake with tossed horseshoes.

horse shoe crab n. Any closely related marine arthropod with a rounded body and a stiff pointed tail.

horse show n. An exhibition of horse skills such as riding, jumping, etc.

horse-whip (hors´hwip˝) n. A whip used to control horses. v. To whip or flog.

horst (horst) n. A block of the earth's crust

separated by faults from an adjacent block.

hort *abbr.* Horticultural; horticulture.

hor-ti-cul-ture (hor´ti kul˝chėr) *n.* The art or science of raising and tending fruits, vegetables, flowers, or ornamental plants. **horticultural** *adj.* **horticulturally** *adv.* **horticulturist** *n.*

hortus siccus *n.* A collection of plant specimens carefully dried and preserved.

ho-san-na (hō zan´a) *interj.* Used to praise or glorify God.

hose (hōz) *n.* A sock; a stocking; a flexible tube for carrying fluids or gases under pressure. *v.* To wash; to water; to squirt with a hose.

ho-sel (hō´zel) *n.* The socket in the head of a golf club that encloses the shaft.

ho-sier-y (hō´zhe rē) *n.* Stockings and socks.

hosp *abbr.* Hospital.

hos-pice (hos´pis) *n.* A lodging for travelers or the needy maintained by a religious order.

hos-pi-ta-ble (hos´pi ta bl) *adj.* Treating guests with warmth and generosity; receptive. **hospitably** *adv.*

hos-pi-tal (hos´pi tal) *n.* An institution where the injured or sick receive medical, surgical, and emergency care.

hos-pi-tal-i-ty (hos˝pi tal´i tē) *n.* Hospitable treatment, disposition, or reception.

hos-pi-tal-ize (hos´pi ta līz˝) *v.* To place or admit in a hospital as a patient for care or treatment. **hospitalization** *n.*

hospital ship *n.* A ship equipped as a hospital to assist the wounded, sick, or shipwrecked in time of war.

host (hōst) *n.* One who receives or entertains guests; one who provides a room or building for an event or function. *Biol.* A living organism, as a plant or an animal, on or in which a parasite lives. **host** *v.*

hos-tage (hos´tij) *n.* A person held as security that promises will be kept or terms met by a third party.

hos-tel (hos´tel) *n.* A low-priced, supervised lodging for young travelers.

hos-tel-ry *n.* An inn or hotel.

host-ess (hō´stis) *n.* A woman who entertains socially; a woman who greets patrons at a restaurant and escorts them to their tables.

hos-tile (hos´til) *adj.* Of or relating to an enemy; antagonistic. **hostilely** *adv.*

hos-til-i-ty (ho stil´i tē) *n. pl.* **-ies** A very deep-seated opposition or hatred; war.

hot (hot) *adj.* Having heat that exceeds normal body temperature; sexually excited or receptive; electrically charged, as a hot wire. *Slang* Recently and or illegally obtained.

hot air *n., Slang* Idle talk.

hot-bed (hot´bed˝) *n.* A glass-covered bed of soil heated by fermenting manure and used for raising seedlings; an environment that is conductive to rapid growth or development.

hot-blood-ed (hot´blud´id) *adj.* Excitable; inpulsive; irritable; adventuous.

hot cake *n.* A pancake.

hot dog *n.* A cooked frankfurter, served in a long roll. *Slang* A person who enjoys showing off.

hot-el (hō tel´) *n.* A business that provides lodging, meals, entertainment, and other services for the public.

hot flash *n.* A sudden sensation of heat that is caused by the dilation of skin capillaries and usually associated with menopausal endocrine imbalance.

hot-foot (hot´fet˝) *v.* To hasten.

hot-head (hot´hed˝) *n.* An impetuous person.

hot-headed (hot´hed´id) *adj.* To have a fiery temper. **hotheadedly** *adv.* **hotheadedness** *n.*

hot-house (hot´hous˝) *n.* A heated greenhouse used to raise plants.

hot line *n.* A direct telephone line that is in constant operation and ready to facilitate immediate communication.

hot plate *n.* A portable electric appliance for heating or cooking food.

hot potato *n.* An issue or problem that involves unpleasant or dangerous consequences for anyone dealing with it.

hot rod *n.* An automobile modified or rebuilt for greater power and speed. **rod-**

der *n.*

hot seat *n., Slang* An electric chair; a position of embarrassment or uneasiness.

hot spring *n.* A natural spring with water temperature above 98 degrees.

hound (hound) *n.* Any of several kinds of long-eared dogs with deep voices which follow their prey by scent; a person unusually devoted to something; a fan. *v.* To pursue or drive without letting up; to nag continuously.

hour (our) *n.* A measure of time equal to 60 minutes; one 24th of a day; the time of day or night. **hours** *pl.* A specific or certain period of time.

hour-glass (our´glas˝) *n.* A two-chambered glass instrument for measuring time with sand, water, or mercury trickling down from the top chamber to the bottom in order to measure the passage of an hour in time.

hour-ly (our´lē) *adj.* Something that happens or is done every hour. **hourly** *adv.*

house (hous) *n.* A building that serves as living quarters for one or more families; home; the shelter or refuge for a wild animal; a business firm; a legislative body of the U.S. government. *v.* To provide work space.

house-boat (hous´bōt˝) *n.* A boat equipped to serve as a dwelling or for cruising.

house-break *n.* To teach acceptable manners.

house-clean (hous´klēn˝) *v.* To get rid of unwanted items or people; maintain cleanliness and order in living quarters.

house-coat (hous´kōt˝) *n.* A woman's informal garment to be worn around the house.

house-hold (hous´hōld˝) *n.* Those living under the same roof and comprising a family.

house-keeper (hous´kē˝pėr) *n.* A woman employed to take care of the running of the house.

house-maid's knee *n.* The swelling of the knee due to an enlargement of the bursa in the front of the patella due to overuse of the knee usually.

house mother (hous´muth´ėr) *n.* A woman acting as a chaperone and sometimes a housekeeper in a residence for young people.

house of correction *n.* An institution where persons who have committed a minor offense are housed until they are removed and released back into society.

house–raising (hous´rā˝zing) *n.* A gathering of friends and neighbors for the purpose of building of a house.

house-warming (hous´wor˝ming) *n.* A party to celebrate a family moving into a new house.

house-wife (hous´wīf˝) *n.* A homemaker; a wife.

house-work (hous´wurk˝) *n.* The work involved in housekeeping, as cooking, cleaning, and managing a house.

housing development *n.* A group of usually individual dwellings or apartment houses typically of similar design.

housing project *n.* A publicly supported housing development planned for low-income families.

hov-el (hev´el) *n.* A small dirty house.

hov-er (hev´ėr) *n.* To remain suspended over something.

how (hou) *adv.* In what manner or way; to what effect; in what condition or state; for what reason; with what meaning.

how-dy *interj.* A word used to express a greeting.

how-ev-er (hou ev´ėr) *adv.* In whatever manner or way. *conj.* Nevertheless.

how-it-zer (hou´it sėr) *n.* A short cannon that fires projectiles at a high trajectory.

howl (houl) *v.* To utter a loud, sustained, plaintive sound, as the wolf.

howl-er (hou´lėr) *n.* One that howls; a ridiculous or stupid blunder.

how-so-ev-er (hou˝sō ev´ėr) *adv.* To whatever degree or extent.

hp *abbr.* Horsepower.

hr *abbr.* Hour.

HS *abbr.* High School.

ht *abbr.* Height.

hua-ra-che (wa rä´chē) *n.* A sandal with a low heel and an upper made of interwoven leather thongs.

hub (hub) *n.* The center of a wheel; the center of activity.

hub-bub (hub´ub) *n.* Confusion; a tumult; uproar.

hub-cap *n.* The removable metal cap that covers the end of an axle, such as one used on the wheel of a motor vehicle.

hu-bris (hū´bris, hŏ´bris) *n.* Arrogance cause by inordinate pride.

huck-le-ber-ry (huk´l ber˝ē) *n.* A type of bush, related to the blueberry and bearing glossy, blackish, usually acidic berries.

HUD *abbr.* Department of Housing and Urban Development.

hud-dle (hud´le) *n.* A crowd together; in football, a brief meeting of teammates to prepare for the next play. *v.* To nestle or crowd together; to confer.

hue (hū) *n.* A gradation of color running from red through yellow, green, and blue to violet; a particular color; a shade. **hued** *adj.*

huff (huf) *n.* A fit of resentment or of ill temper. *v.* To exhale or breathe heavily, as from extreme exertion. **huffily** *adv.* **huffiness** *n.* **huffy** *adj.*

hug (hug) *v.* To embrace; to hold fast; to keep, cling, or stay close to. **huggable** *adj.* **hugger** *n.*

huge (hūj) *adj.* Of great quantity, size, or extent. **hugely** *adv.* **hugeness** *n.*

hu-la (hŏ´la) *n.* A Hawaiian dance characterized by beautiful rhythmic movement of the hips and gestures with the hands.

hulk (hulk) *n.* A heavy, bulky ship; the body of an old ship no longer fit for service.

hulk-ing *adj.* Unwieldy or awkward.

hull (hul) *n.* The outer cover of a fruit or seed; the framework of a boat; the external covering of a rocket, spaceship, or guided missile.

hul-la-ba-loo (hul´a ba lŏ˝) *n.* A confused noise; a great uproar.

hum (hum) *v.* To make a continuous low-pitched sound; to be busily active; to sing with the lips closed. **hummer** *n.*

hu-man (hū´man) *adj.* Of, relating to, or typical of man; having or manifesting human form or attributes. **humanly** *adv.* **humanness** *n.*

hu-mane (hū mān´) *adj.* To be marked by compassion, sympathy, or consideration for other people or animals.

hu-man-sim (hū´ma niz˝um) *n.* Any method or mode of thought in which human interests are predominate.

hu-man-i-tar-i-an (hū man˝i târ´ē an) *n.* A person who is concerned for human welfare, especially through philanthropy. **humanitarian** *adj.*

hu-man-i-tar-i-an-ism (hū man˝i târ´ē a niz˝um) *n.* The principle which believes that mankind's chief obligation is to work for the welfare of human beings.

hu-man-i-ty (hū man´i tē) *n.* *pl.* **-ies** The quality or state of being human; humankind.

hu-man-ize (hū´ma nīz˝) *v.* To render human or humane; to represent as human. To become passionate, to become human.

hu-man-oid (hū´ma noid˝) *adj.* Of human form or characteristics.

hum-ble (hum´bl) *adj.* Marked by meekness or modesty; unpretentious; lowly. *v.* To make humble. **humbleness** *n.* **humbler** *n.* **humbly** *adv.*

hum-bug (hum´bug˝) *n.* A misleading trick, hoax, fraud, or pretense; a person who seeks to deceive others; something foolish.

hum-din-ger (hum´ding´ėr) *n.* *Slang* Someone or something that is marked as superior.

hum-drum (hum´drum˝) *n., Slang* Boring; dull.

hu-mec-tant (hū mek´tant) *n.* A substance, as glycerol, that promotes moisture retention.

hu-mer-us (hū´mėr us) *n.* *pl.* **meri** The long bone of the upper arm or forelimb extending from the shoulder to the elbow.

hu-mid (hū´mid) *adj.* Containing or characterized by a large amount of moisture;

damp.

hu-mid-i-fy (hū mid′i fī˝) *v.* To make humid or more moist. **humidifier** *n.*

hu-mid-i-stat (hū mid′i stat˝) *n.* An instrument that controls or maintains the degree of humidity.

hu-mid-i-ty (hū mid′i tē) *n.* A moderate amount of wetness in the air; dampness.

hu-mi-dor (hū′mi dor˝) *n.* A container used to keep cigars in which the air is kept properly humidified by a special device.

hu-mil-i-ate (hū mil′ē āt˝) *v.* To reduce one's dignity or pride to a lower position. **humiliation** *n.*

hum-ming-bird (hum′ing berd˝) *n.* A very small bird with narrow wings, long primaries, a slender bill, and a very extensile tongue.

hum-mock (hum′ok) *n.* A rounded knoll or hill of snow or dirt. **hummocky** *adj.*

hu-mor (hū′mėr) *n.* Something that is or has the ability to be comical or amusing. *Physiol.* Fluid contained in the body such as blood or lymph. **humorist** *n.* **humorousness** *n.* **humorous** *adj.*

hu-mor-ist (hū′mėr ist) *n.* A person who has a sense of humor; one who uses humor to amuse others.

hump (hump) *n.* The rounded lump or protuberance, as on the back of a camel. **over the hump** To be past the difficult or most critical state.

hu-mus (hū′mus) *n.* A complex material resulting from partial decomposition of plant or animal matter forming the organic portion of soil.

hunch (hunch) *n.* A strong, intuitive feeling about a future event or result. *v.* To bend into a crooked position or posture.

hunch-back (hunch′bak˝) *n.* A back deformed by a convex curvature of the spine, a person with this disorder.

hun-dred (hun′drid) *n. pl.* **-dreds** *or* **-dred** The cardinal number equal to 10 X 10. **hundredth** *n. adj. & adv.*

hun-ger (hung′gėr) *n.* A strong need or

desire for food; a craving for food. **hunger** *v.* **hungrily** *adv.* **hungry** *adj.*

hunk-y-dory (hung′kē dōr′ē) *adj., Slang* All right; quite satisfactory; comfortable.

hunt (hunt) *v.* To search or look for food; to pursue with the intent of capture; to look in an attempt to find. **hunter** *n.* **huntress** *n.*

hunt-er (hun′tėr) *n.* A person who hunts game; a dog or horse used in hunting; one who searches for something; as, a fortune.

hunt-ing (hun′ting) *n.* The act of one who or that which hunts; the pursuing of game; the chase.

hur-dle (hėr′dl) *n.* A portable barrier used to jump over in a race; an obstacle one must overcome. *v.* To leap over.

hur-dy-gur-dy (hėr′dē ger′dē) *n.* A musical instrument where the sound is produced by turnng a crank.

hurl (hėrl) *v.* To throw something with great force; in baseball, to pitch. **hurl** *n.* **hurler** *n.*

hur-rah (hu rä′) *interj.* Used to express approval, pleasure, or exultation. **hurrah** *n. & v.*

hur-ri-cane (her′i kān˝) *n.* A tropical cyclone with winds exceeding 74 miles per hour, usually accompanied by rain, thunder, and lightning.

hurricane lamp *n.* A lamp or candlestick with a glass chimney to protect the flame against wind.

hur-ry (her′ē) *v.* To move or cause to move with haste. *n.* The act of hurrying. **hurriedly** *adv.* **hurriedness** *n.*

hurt (hėrt) *v.* To experience or inflict with physical pain; to cause physical or emotional harm to; to damage. **hurtful** *adj.*

hur-tle (hėr′tl) *v.* To move rapidly as with a rushing sound to collide, with or against something.

hus-band (huz′band) *n.* A man who is married.

hus-band-ry (huz′ban drē) *n.* Agricultural cultivation, production of plants and animals, especilly through scientific control and management.

hush (hush) v. To make or become quiet; to calm; to keep secret; to suppress. n. A silence.

hush–pup-py (hush´pup˝ē) n. pl -ies A mixture of cornmeal that is shaped into small balls and deep fried.

husk (husk) n. The dry or membranous outer cover of certain vegetables, fruits, and seeds, often considered worthless.

husk-ing (hus´king) n. The act of removing husks from corn.

husk-y (hus´kē) adj. Having a dry cough or grating sound; burly or robust. **huskily** adv. **huskiness** n.

husk-y (hus´kē) n. pl. -ies A heavy-coated working dog of the arctic region.

hus-sy (hus´ē) n. pl -ies A saucy or mischievous girl; a woman with doubtful moral; a disreputable woman.

hus-tings n. pl. A platform used for making political speeches from.

hus-tle (hus´el) v. To urge or move hurriedly along; to work busily and quickly. Slang To make energetic efforts to solicit business or make money. **hustle, hustler** n.

hut (hut) n. A small and simply constructed dwelling or shack a cabin.

hutch (huch) n. A enclosed area for confining small animals.

huz-zah, huz-za (hu zä´) interj. An expression of appreciation or approval.

hy-a-cinth (hī´a sinth) n. A bulbous plant that has a cluster of variously colored, highly fragrant, bell-shaped flowers.

hy-a-lite (hī´a līt˝) n. A colorlesss opal, sometimes whitish and sometimes transparent-like glass.

hy-a-lu-ron-i-dase (hī˝a lu ron´i dās˝) n. An enzyme that breaks down the molecular structure of hyaluronic acid.

hy-brid (hī´brid) n. An offspring of two dissimilar plants or of two animals of different races, breeds, varieties, or species; something made up of mixed origin or makeup. **hybrid** adj.

hybrid computer A system which consists of a combination of analog and digital computer systems.

hy-brid-ize (hī´bri dīz˝) v. To cross, interbreed; to cause to form in a hybrid manner.

hy-da-tid (hī´da tid) n. A fluid-filled cyst that forms in the bodies of men and certain animals by the tapeworm larva.

hy-dran-gea (hī drän´ ja) n. A shrub cultivated for its showy clustered pink, white, or sometimes blue flowers.

hy-drant (hī´drant) n. A pipe with a valve and spout which supplies water from a main source.

hy-drate (hī´drāt) n. A chemical compound formed by the union of water with another substance in definite proportions. **hydrate** v. **hydration** n.

hy-drau-lic (hī dro´lik) adj. Operated, moved, or effected by the means of water; hardening or setting under water. **hydraulically** adv.

hy-drau-lics (hī dro´liks) n. pl. The scientific study that deals with practical applications of liquids in motion and the laws that govern its action.

hy-dric (hī´drik) adj. Characterized by or pertaining to, containing, or requiring moisture.

hy-dro-elec-tric (hī˝drō i lek´trik) n. Relating to the production of electricity by the use of waterpower.

hy-dro-foil (hī´dro foil˝) n. A motorboat built with metal plates and fins attached by struts for lifting the hull clear of the water as speed is attained.

hy-dro-gen (hī´dro jen) n. A colorless, normally odorless, highly flammable gas that is the simplest and lightest of the elements, symbolized by H.

hy-dro-gen-ate (hī´dro je nāt˝) v. To combine, or treat with hydrogen.

hydrogen bomb n. A bomb that is extremely destructive, with an explosive power obtained from the rapid release of atomic energy.

hydrogen peroxide n. A colorless, unstable, liquid compound that is used as an antiseptic solution and as a bleach.

hy-dro-pho-bi-a (hī˝dro fō´bē a) A fear

of water; rabies. **hydrophobic** *adj.*

hy-dro-plane (hī'dro plān″) *v.* To skim over water with only the hull more or less touching the surface. **hydroplane** *n.*

hy-dro-me-te-or (hī″drō mē'tē ėr) *n.* Any of the various products formed by condensation of atmospheric water vapors, as rain, hail, or fog.

hy-dro-phil-ic (hī″dro fil' ik) *a.* Having a strong attraction for water; having the ability of dissolving in water.

hy-dro-phone (hī'dro fōn″) *n.* A device for locating causes and transmitting sound under water.

hy-dro-pon-ics (hī″dro pon'iks) *n.* The method of growing plants in chemical solutions instead of soil.

hy-dro-scope (hī'dro skōp″) *n.* A mirror device which enables a person to see at a considerable distance below the surface of the water.

hy-dro–ski (hī'drō skē″) *n.* A hydrofoil, affixed to the fuselage of a seaplane in order to accelerate speed during takeoffs.

hy-dro-sphere (hī'dro sfēr″) *n.* The aqueous vapor on the surface of the globe, oceans, lakes, and all other waters.

hy-dro-stat (hī'dro stat″) *n.* The electrical device that detects the presence of water, as from leakage.

hy-dro-tax-is (hī″dro tak'sis) *n.* The reflex movement by an organism in the direction of water.

hy-dro-ther-a-py (hī″dro ther' a pē) *n.* The scientific use of water in the treatment of disease.

hy-dro-ther-mal (hī″dro ther'mal) *adj.* Referring or relating to heated water, esp. the action of heated water that dissolves or redistributes minerals.

hy-dro-tho-rax (hī″dro thōr'aks) *n.* The presence of excess serous fluid in the pleural cavities; especially The effusion that results from failing circulation of the heart or lungs.

hy-gro-scope (hī'gro skōp″) *n.* An instrument which shows the changes in humidity in the atmosphere.

hy-e-na (hī ē'na) *n.* Any of several strong carnivorous mammals of Africa and Asia, with coarse hair and very powerful jaws.

hy-e-tal (hī'i tal) *adj.* Relating to rain and its distribution with reference to different regions.

hy-giene (hī'jēn) *n.* The science of the establishment and maintenance of good health and the prevention of disease. **hygienic** *adj.* **hygienically** *adv.*

hy-gro-graph (hī'gro graf″) *n.* An instrument used to record automatically the variations of moisture content of the atmosphere.

hy-gro-ther-mo-graph (hī″gro ther'mo graf″) *n., Meteor.* The instrument used to register both relative humidity and the temperature on one chart.

hy-la (hī'la) *n.* The tree frog.

hy-men (hī'men) *n.* The thin membrane that partly closes the external vaginal orifice.

hymn (him) *n.* A song of praise giving thanks to God; a song of joy. **hymn** *v.*

hym-nal (him'nal) *n.* A book that contains hymns compiled for worshipping.

hym-nol-o-gy (him nol'o jē) *n.* The study, classification, and history of old hymns; the composition of hymns.

hy-oid (hī'oid) *adj.* Referring or relating to the U-shaped movable bone between the root of the tongue and larynx.

hype *v., Slang* To put on; to stimulate; to promote or publicize extravagantly.

hy-per *pref.* Excessive in anything that is performed or done physically.

hy-per-ac-tive (hī″pėr ak'tiv) *adj.* Excessively or abnormally active.

hyperbaric chamber *n., Med.* The airtight chamber that forces oxygen under pressure to a patient's heart and lungs.

hy-per-cho-les-te-remia *n.* A disease in which there is excessive cholesterol in the blood.

hy-per-chro-mica-ne-mi-a(hī˝pėrkro´mik *a* nē´mē *a*) *n.* An anemia which has an increase in the hemoglobin and a reduction in the number of red blood cells.

hy-per-crit-i-cal (hī˝pėr krit´i k*a***l)** *adj.* Being excessively critical.

hy-per-ga-my *n.* The act of marrying into an equal or higher social group.

hy-per-gly-ce-mia *n.* An excessive amount of sugar in the blood.

hy-per-gol-ic (hī´pėr ga´lik) *adj.* Referring to a rocket propellant that ignites upon contact of components without external aid.

hy-per-li-pe-mia *n.* The presence of excessive fat in the blood.

hy-perm-ne-sia *n.* The ability of having complete memory or recall of the past.

hy-per-os-to-sis *n.* An excessive thickening of bone tissue.

hy-per-pha-gia *n.* An abnormal desire for the consumption of food associated with injury to the hypothalamus.

hy-per-pnea *n.* Abnormally rapid breathing. **hyperpneic** *adj.*

hy-per-ten-sion (hī˝pėr ten´sh*a***n)** *n.* The condition of abnormally high blood pressure especially in the arteries.

hy-per-ven-ti-la-tion *n.* An excessive rate of respiration leading to loss of carbon dioxide from the blood.

hy-per-vi-ta-min-osis *n.* An abnormal condition resulting from the excessive use of one or more vitamins.

hy-phen (hī´f*en***)** *n.* A punctuation mark (-) used to show connection between two or more words. **hyphen** *v.*

hy-phen-ate (hī´f*e* **nāt´)** *v.* To separate or join with a hyphen. **hyphenation** *n.*

hyp-no-sis (hip nō´sis) *n. pl.* **hypnoses** A state that resembles sleep but is brought on or induced by another person whose suggestions are accepted by the subject.

hyp-not-ic (hip not´ik) *adj.* Inducing sleep. *n.* An agent, such as a drug, which induces sleep. **hypnotically** *adv.*

hyp-no-tism (hip´n*o* **tiz˝***u***m)** *n.* The study or act of inducing hypnosis. **hypnotist** *n.*

hyp-no-tize (hip´n*o* **tīz´)** *v.* To induce hyp-

nosis; to be dazzled by; to be overcome by suggestion.

hy-po (hī´pō) *n. pl.* **hypos** *Slang* A hypodermic needle or syringe.

hy-po-chon-dri-a (hī˝p*o* **kon´drē** *a*) *n.* A mental depression accompanied by imaginary physical ailments. **hypochondriac** *n. & adj.* **hypochondriacal** *adj.*

hy-po-der-mic sy-ringe (hī´p*o* **dėr ´mik)** *n.* A syringe and hypodermic needle used for injecting a substance into one's body.

hy-po-gly-ce-mia *n.* An unusual decrease of sugar in the blood.

hy-po-ten-sion (hī˝p*o* **ten´sh***a***n)** *n.* A condition marked by unusually low blood pressure.

hy-pot-e-nuse (hī pot´*e* **nŏs˝)** *n.* That side of a right triangle which is opposite the right angle.

hy-po-the-sis (hī poth´i sis) *n.* An assumption made in order to draw out and test the logical consequences.

hy-po-thy-roid-ism *n.* A condition which lowers the metabolic rate of the thyroid gland causing loss of vigor.

hy-po-xi-a (hī pok´sē *a*) *n.* A condition which causes a deficiency of oxygen reaching the tissue of the body.

hyp-sog-ra-phy (hip sog´rafē) *n.* The branch of geography which deals with the measurement of the varying elevations of the earth's surface.

hy-rax (hī´raks) *n.* A small ungulate mammal with a thickset body, short legs and ears, and a rudimentary tail.

hys-sop (his´*o***p)** *n.* An aromatic herb from the mint family.

hys-ter-ec-to-my (his˝te rek´to mē) *n. pl.* **-ies** Surgery on a female which partially or completely removes the uterus.

hys-ter-ia (hi stēr´ē *a*) *n.* A psychological condition characterized by emotional excess and or unreasonable fear.

hys-ter-ic *n.* A person suffering from hysteria. *n. pl.* A fit of uncontrollable laughter or crying; hysteria.

hys-ter-i-cal *adj.* Emotionally out of control. **hysterically** *adv.*

I, i (ī) The ninth letter of the English alphabet; the Roman numeral for one.

I (ī) *pron.* The person speaking or writing. *n.* The self; the ego.

I *or* **i** *abbr.* Island; isle.

IA *abbr.* Iowa.

i-amb *or* **i-am-bus** (ī´am) *n.* A metrical foot consisting of a short or unstressed syllable followed by an accented syllable. **iambic** *adj. & n.*

i-at-ric (ī at´rik) *adj.* Pertaining to medicine or a physician.

i-at-ro-gen-ic (ī a˝tro jen´ik) *adj.* Induced inadvertently by a physician or his treatment. **iatrogenically** *adv.*

ib *or* **ibid** *abbr.* Ibidem, in the same place.

I band *n.* A band of the striated muscle fiber.

I-beam (ī´bēm˝) *n.* A steel girder or crossbeam with an I-shaped cross section.

i-bex (ī´beks) *n.* An Old World mountain goat with long curved horns.

i-bi-dem (ib´i dem) *adv.* Used in footnotes to inicate a part of literary work that was just mentioned.

i-bis (ī´bis) *n.* A long-billed wading bird related to the heron and stork.

IBM *abbr.* Intercontinental ballistic missile.

Ibo *n.* A person of the Negro people who live around the area of the lower Niger.

ICA *abbr.* International Cooperation Administration.

ice (īs) *n.* Solidly frozen water; a dessert of crushed ice which is flavored and sweetened. *Informal* Extreme coldness of manner. **ice** *v.* To change into ice; to cool or chill; to cover with icing. **icily** *adv.* **iciness** *n.* **icy** *adj.*

ice age *n., Geol.* A time of widespread glaciation.

ice ax *n.* A pick and ax that has a spiked handle that is used for mountain climbing.

ice bag *n.* A small, flexible, waterproof bag designed to hold ice, used on parts of the body.

ice-berg (īs´berg) *n.* A thick mass of floating ice separated from a glacier.

ice-blink (īs´blingk˝) *n.* A luminous appearance under a cloud or near the horizon, caused by the reflection of light on distant formations of ice.

ice-boat (īs´bōt˝) *n.* A boat on runners that breaks a path through ice; an icebreaker.

ice-boating *n.* A sport of sailing in iceboats **iceboater** *n.*

ice-bound (īs´bound˝) *adj.* Obstructed or covered by ice so as to be inaccessible or immovable.

ice-box (īs´boks˝) *n.* A structure designed for holding ice in which food and other perishables are stored.

ice-break-er (īs´brā˝kėr) *n.* A sturdy vessel for breaking a path through icebound waters; a pier or dock apron for deflecting floating ice from the base of a pier or bridge.

ice cap (īs´kap˝) *n.* An extensive perennial covering of ice and snow that covers a large area of land.

ice–cold (īs´kōd´) *adj.* To be very cold; freezing.

ice cream *n.* A smooth mixture of milk, cream, flavoring, sweeteners, and other ingredients, beaten and frozen.

ice–cream chair *n.* An armless chair small in size having a circular seat.

ice–cream cone *n.* A crisp and edible cone for the purpose of holding ice cream.

ice-fall *n.* A waterfall which is frozen.

ice field *n.* Pieces of glaciers that have joined and frozen together causing a sheet of ice so large that one cannot see it end.

ice floe *n.* A mass of sea that floats free upon the water.

ice fog *n.* A type of fog that is composed of many ice particles.

ice hockey *n.* A version of hockey which is played on ice.

ice-house (īs´hous˝) *n.* A building where ice is stored.

Icel *abbr.* Icelandic.

Ice-land (īs´land) *n.* An island country in the North Atlantic Ocean near the Arctic Circle **Icelander** *n.* **Icelandic** *adj.*

Iceland moss *n.* A kind of lichen of the

Arctic areas which can be used for food.

Iceland poppy *n.* A type of perennial poppy having small pastel flowers.

ice-man (īs´man˝) *n.* A man who is able to travel upon the ice with ease; one who delivers and sells ice.

ice milk *n.* A food similar to ice cream but made with skim milk.

ice needle *n.* A slender ice particle which floats in the air in cold weather.

ice pack *n.* A large mass of floating, compacted ice; a folded bag filled with ice and applied to sore parts of the body.

ice pick *n.* A pointed tool used for breaking ice into small pieces.

ice plant *n.* An herb of the Old World that is related to the carpetweed.

ice point *n.* A temperature of zero degrees centigrade.

ice sheet *n.* A glacier.

ice show *n.* An entertaining show involving ice skaters.

ice skate (īs´skāt˝) *n.* A shoe or boot with a runner fixed to it for skating on ice. **ice–skate** *v.* **iceskater** *n.*

ice storm *n.* A type of storm with frozen rain.

ice water *n.* Water cooled by ice.

ich-neu-mon (ik nŏ´mon) *n.* An animal that feeds on snakes and rodents; a mongoose.

ich-nite (ik´nīt) *n.* A footprint.

ich-nog-ra-phy (ik nog´ra fē) *n.* The ground plan; the study or art of drawing ground plans.

ich-nol-ogy (ik nol´o jē) *n.* The study of fossil footprints of animals.

ich-thy-oid (ik´thē oid˝) *adj.* Resembling fishlike characteristics.

ich-thy-oi-dal (ik˝thē oi´dal) *n.* A fishlike organism.

ich-thy-ol-o-gy (ik˝thē ol´o jē) *n.* The zoological study of fishes. **ichthyologic, ichthyological** *adj.* **ichthologist** *n.*

ich-thy-or-nis (ik˝thē ar´nis) *n.* An extinct bird with teeth and vertebrae like those of fish.

ich-thy-o-sis (ik˝thē ō´sis) *n.* A hereditary skin disorder represented by thick, scaly skin.

i-ci-cle (ī´si kl) *n.* A hanging spike of ice formed by dripping water that freezes.

i-ci-ly (ī´si lē) *adv.* In an icy manner; coldly, having no warmth.

i-ci-ness (i´sē nis) *n.* The state of being very cold or icy.

ic-ing (ī´sing)*n.* A sweet preparation for frosting cakes and cookies.

i-con *or* **i-kon** (ī´kon) *n.* A sacred Christian pictorial representation of Jesus Christ, the Virgin Mary, or other sacred figures.

i-con-o-clasm (ī kon´o klaz˝um) *n.* The attitude or practice of an iconoclast. **iconoclastic** *adj.*

i-con-o-clast (ī kon´o klast˝) *n.* One who opposes the use of sacred images; one who attacks traditional or cherished beliefs. **iconoclasm** *n.* **iconoclastic** *adj.*

i-co-nog-ra-phy (ī˝ko nog´ra fē) *n.* A pictorial material illustrating a subject; a published work dealing with iconography.

i-co-nol-a-ter (ī˝ko nol´a tèr) *n.* A person who worships images or icons.

i-con-o-scope (ī kon´o skōp˝) *n.* A camera tube containing an electron gun and a mosaic screen which produces a charge proportional to the light intensity of the image on the screen.

ic-ter-us (ik´tèr us) *n.* A yellow appearance of certain plants after being exposed to cold and excess moisture; jaundice.

ic-tus (ik´tus) *n., Pathol.* A stroke, seizure, or fit.

i-cy (ī´sē) *adj.* Covered or consisting of ice; extremely cold; freezing; characterized by coldness.

id (id) *n., Psychol.* The unconscious part of the psyche associated with instinctual needs and drives.

I'd *contr.* I had; I should, I would.

ID *abbr.* Idaho.

ID *abbr.* Identification.

I-da-ho *n.* A state located in the northwest part of the United States; statehood July 3, 1890; state capital Boise.

i-de-a (ī dē´a) *n.* Something existing in the mind; conception or thought; an opinion; a plan of action.

i-de-al (ī dē´al) *n.* A concept or imagined state of perfection; highly desirable; perfect; an ultimate objective; an honorable principle or motive. **ideal** *adj.* Conforming to absolute excellence. **ideally** *adv.*

i-de-al-ism (ī dē´a liz˝um) *n.* The practice or tendency of seeing things in ideal form; pursuit of an ideal; a philosophical system believing that reality consists of ideas or perceptions. **idealist** *n.* **idealistic** *adj.*

i-de-al-ist (ī dē´a list) *n.* A person who practices or advocates idealism in writing.

i-de-al-is-tic (ī dē˝a lis´tik) *adj.* To be pertaining to idealism or idealists.

i-de-al-i-ty (ī˝dē al´i tē) *n.* The state of being ideal.

i-de-al-ize (ī dē´a līz) *v.* To regard or represent as ideal. **idealization** *n.*

i-de-al-ly (ī dē´a lē) *adv.* In respect to an ideal; theoretically.

ideal point *n.* The point added to a space to eliminate special cases.

i-de-ate (ī´dē āt˝) *v.* To make an idea of something.

i-de-a-tion (ī˝dē ā´shan) *n.* The act of forming ideas.

i-de-a-tion-al *adj.*To be pertaining to ideation; referring to ideas of objects not immediately present to the senses.

i-dem (ī´dem) *pron. & adj.* The same; used to indicate a previously mentioned reference.

i-dem-po-tent (ī´dem pō˝tent) *adj.* To be pertaining to a mathematical quantity that is not zero.

i-den-tic (ī den´tik) *adj.* Identical; constituting an expression in which governments follow precisely the same course.

i-den-ti-cal (ī den´ti kal) *adj.* Being the same; exactly equal or much alike; designating a twin or twins developed from the same ovum. **identically** *adv.*

i-den-ti-fi-a-ble (ī den´ti fī˝a bl) *adj.* Having the capability of being identified or recognized. **identifiably** *adv.*

i-den-ti-fi-ca-tion (ī den˝ti fi kā´shan) *n.* The act of identifying; the state of being identified; a means of identity.

i-den-ti-fi-er (ī den´ti fī˝er) *n.* A person who identifies someone or something.

i-den-ti-fy (ī den´ti fī˝) *v.* To recognize the identity of; to establish as the same or similar; to equate; to associate oneself with an individual or group.

i-den-ti-ty (ī den´ti tē) *n. pl.* **identities** The condition or state of being a specific person or thing and recognizable as such; the condition or fact of being the same as something else; individuality.

identity crisis *n.* A type of psychosocial confusion that arises when one is unable to attain psychological identification due to demands that conflict and other pressures.

identity element *n.* The element which leaves an element of a set to which it belongs unchanged when it is combined with that element such as, 1x 3=3, where 1 is the identity element.

id-e-o-gram *or* **id-e-o-graph** (id´ē o gram˝) *n.* A pictorial symbol used in a writing system to represent an idea or thing, as Chinese characters; a graphic symbol, as $ or %.

id-e-og-ra-phy (id˝ē og´ra fē) *n.* A representation of some ideas by the use of graphic symbols.

i-de-o-log-i-cal (ī˝dē o loj´i kal) *adj.* Concerned with ideas.

i-de-ol-o-gist (ī˝dē ol´o gist) *n.* A supporter of a particular ideology.

id-e-o-logue (ī dē´ o log) *n.* A person who adheres to a particular ideology.

i-de-ol-o-gy (ī˝dē ol´o jē) *n. pl.* **ideologies** A body of ideas that influence a person, group, culture, or political party. **ideological** *adj.*

i-de-o-mo-tor (ī˝dē o mō´ter) *adj.* Pertaining to involuntary and nonreflexive muscular movement which is the result of complete engrossment by an idea.

ides (īdz) *n.* In the ancient Roman calendar, the fifteenth day of March, May, July, and October or the thirteenth day of the other months.

-idin *n., suffix* A chemical compound that

is related in structure to another compound.

id-i-o *comb. form* Personal; distinct; separate.

id-i-o-blast (id´ē o blast″) *n.* A type of plant cell which differs from neighboring cells in a great manner. **idioblastic** *adj.*

id-i-o-cy (id´ē o sē) *n. pl.* **idiocies** A condition of an idiot; senseless folly.

id-i-o-graph-ic (id´ē o graf´ik) *adj.* Pertaining to the concrete or unique.

id-i-o-lect (id´ē o″lekt) *n.* The speech pattern of an individual at a period of time in his life. **idiolectal** *adj.*

id-i-om (id´ē om) *n.* A form of expression having a meaning that is not readily understood from the meaning of its component words; the dialect of people or a region; a kind of language or vocabulary. **idiomatic** *adj.* **idiomatically** *adv.*

id-i-o-mat-ic (id´ē o mat´ik) *adj.* Pertaining to an idiom; being peculiar to a group.

id-i-o-mor-phic (id´ē o mar´fik) *adj.* To have the right or proper shape.

id-i-o-path-ic (id´ē a path´ik) *adj.* To be peculiar to an individual.

id-i-o-syn-cra-sy (id´ē o sing´kra sē) *n. pl.* **idiosyncrasies** A peculiarity, as of behavior. **idiosyncratic** *adj.*

id-i-ot (id´ē ot) *n.* A mentally deficient person; an extremely foolish or stupid person.

id-i-ot-ic (id´ē ot´ik) *adj.* Showing of complete lack of thought or common sense by someone. **idiotically** *adv.* **idioticalness** *n.*

id-i-ot sa-vant (id´ē ot sa vänt´) *n.* A person who is mentally defective but exhibits exceptional skill in a specific area.

i-dle (īd´l) *adj.* Doing nothing; inactive; moving lazily; slowly; running at a slow speed or out of gear; unemployed or inactive. **idleness** *n.* **idler** *n.* **idly** *adv.*

idler pulley *n.* A type of guiding pulley that is used for a chain or a belt.

idler wheel *n.* A kind of wheel or roller which is used to transfer motion to something.

id-lesse (id´les) *n.* The state of being idle.

i-do-crase (ī´do krās″) *n.* A type of mineral which is a complex silicate of calcium, iron, magnesium, and aluminum.

i-dol (īd´ol) *n.* A symbol or representation of a god or deity that is worshiped; a person or thing adored.

i-dol-a-ter (ī dol´a tėr) *n.* One who worships idols; blind adoration; devotion.

i-dol-a-trous (ī dol´a trus) *adj.* Pertaining to idolatry; having a character of idolatry.

i-dol-a-try (ī dol´a trē) *n.* An immoderate attachment to something.

i-dol-ize (īd´o līz´) *v.* To admire with excessive admiration or devotion; to worship as an idol. **idolization** *n.* **idolizer** *n.*

IDP *abbr.* Integrated data processing.

i-dyll *or* **i-dyl** (īd´il) *n.* A poem or prose piece about country life; a scene, event, or condition of rural simplicity; a romantic interlude. **idyllic** *adj.* **idyllically** *adv.*

i-dyll-ist (īd´i list) *n.* A person who composes idylls.

IE *abbr.* Industrial engineer.

-ie *suff.* Little; dear.

IEA *abbr.* International Education Association.

IEEE *abbr.* Institute of Electrical and Electronic Engineers.

if (if) *conj.* On the condition that; allowing that; supposing or granting that.

if-fy (if´ē) *adj., Slang* Marked by unknown qualities or conditions.

IFO *abbr.* Identified flying object.

I formation *n.* A kind of offensive football formation where the players form a line directly behind the quarterback.

ig-loo (ig´lö) *n.* A dome-shaped Eskimo dwelling often made of blocks of snow.

ig-ne-ous (ig´nē us) *adj., Geol.* Relating to fire; formed by solidification from a molten magma.

ig-nes-cent (ig nes´ent) *adj.* To be capable of giving off sparks.

ignis fatuus (ig´nis fach´ö us) *n.* A type of light which will appear over marshy ground in the night; it is often attributable to the combustion of gas from organic matter that is decomposed.

ig-nite (ig nīt´) *v.* To start or set a fire; to render luminous by heat.

ig-ni-tion (ig nish´an) *n.* An act or action of igniting; a process or means for igniting the fuel mixture in an engine.

ig-ni-tron (ig´nī´trăn) *n.* A type of mercury-containing rectifier tube.

ig-no-ble (ig nō´bl) *adj.* Dishonorable in character or purpose; not of noble rank. **ignobly** *adv.* **ignobleness** *n.*

ig-no-min-i-ous (ig´no min´ē us) *adj.* Marked by or characterized by shame or disgrace; dishonorable. **ignominiousness** *n.* **ignominiously** *adv.*

ig-no-min-y (ig´no min´ē) *n.* A disgraceful conduct or action; dishonor; shame.

ig-no-ra-mus (ig´no rā´mus) *n.* A totally ignorant person.

ig-no-rance (ig´nėr ans) *n.* The state of being ignorant.

ig-no-rant (ig´nėr ant) *adj.* Lacking education or knowledge; not aware; lacking comprehension.

ig-no-ra-tio e-len-chi (ig´ne rät´ē ō i len˝kē) *n.* An act to disprove something that is not an issue.

ig-nore (ig nōr´) *v.* To pay no attention to; to reject. **ignorable** *adj.*

I-go-rot (ē˝ge rot´) *n.* Person who is a member of the group of people of Luzon, Phillipines.

i-gua-na (i gwä´na) *n.* A large, dark-colored tropical American lizard.

i-guan-o-don (i gwä´no don˝) *n.* A member of the genus of the gigantic herbivorous dinosaurs which are from the early Cretaceous period of England.

IGY *abbr.* International Geophysical Year.

IHP *abbr.* Indicated horsepower.

ike-ba-na (ik´ā bän˝e) *n.* A Japanese art of aranging flowers that emphasizes balance and form.

IL *abbr.* Illinois.

i-lang–i-lang (ē´läng ē´läng) *n.* A type of tree from the custard-apple family which has very fragrant greenish-yellow flowers.

-ile *adj. suffix* Capable of.

il-e-i-tis (il´ē ī´tis) *n.* Inflammation of the ileum.

il-e-um (il´ē um) *n. pl.* **ilea** The lower part of the small intestine between the jejunum and the large intestine.

il-e-us (il´ē us) *n.* A functional obstruction of the bowel.

i-lex (ī´lex) *n.* A type of European evergreen oak which is located in the southern region.

il-i-ac (il´ē ak) *n.* Pertaining to the ilium.

Il-i-ad (il´ē ad) *n.* An epic in the Homeric tradition; a series of disastrous events.

il-i-um (il´ē um) *n.* The largest bone of the pelvis.

ilk (ilk) *n.* Sort; kind.

ill (il) *adj.* Not healthy; sick; destructive in effect; harmful; hostile; unfriendly; not favorable; not up to standards. **ill** *adv.* In an ill manner; with difficulty; scarcely. **ill** *n.* Evil; injury or harm; something causing suffering.

Ill *abbr.* Illinois.

I'll *contr.* I will; I shall.

ill–ad-vised (il´ad vīzd´) *adj.* Done without careful thought or sufficient advice.

il-la-tion (i lā´shan) *n.* Action of inferring.

il-la-tive (i lā´tiv) *adj.* A phrase which introduces an inference. **illatively** *adv.*

il-laud-a-ble (il lad´dabl) *adj.* To be deserving no praise. **illaudably** *adv.*

ill–being *n.* The state of being deficient in one's health or prosperity.

ill–boding *adj.* To be boding evil.

ill–bred *adj.* Ill-mannered; impolite; rude; raised improper.

il-le-gal (i lē´gal) *adj.* Contrary to law or official rules; unlawful. **illegality** *n.* **illegally** *adv.*

il-le-gal-ize (i lē´gal īz) *v.* To declare illegal. **illegalization** *n.*

il-leg-i-ble (i lej´i bl) *adj.* Not readable; not legible; unable to read. **illegibly** *adv.* **illegibility** *n.*

il-le-git-i-mate (il˝i jit´i mit) *adj.* Against the law; unlawful; born out of wedlock. **illegitimacy** *n.* **illegitimately** *adv.*

ill–fat-ed (il´fā´tid) *adj.* Destined for misfortune; doomed; unlucky.

ill–fa-vored (il´fā´vėrd) *adj.* Unattractive;

objectionable; offensive; unpleasant.

ill–got-ten (il ´got´en) *adj.* Obtained in an illegal, dishonest, or improper way.

ill–hu-mored (il´hū´mėrd) *adj.* Irritable; cross.

il-lib-er-al (i lib´ėr al) *adj.* To be lacking or missing culture or refinement; narrow-minded; stingy. **illiberality** *n.*

il-lib-er-al-ism (i lib´ėr al izm) *n.* A lack of liberalism.

il-lic-it (i lis´it) *adj.* Not permitted by law; unlawful. **illicitly** *adv.*

il-lim-it-a-ble (i lim´i ta bl) *adj.* To be incapable of being bounded or limited in any way. **illimitably** *adv.* **illimitability** *n.*

Il-lin-ois *n.* A state located in the central part of the northern United States; statehood December 3, 1818; state capital Springfield. **Illinoisan** *adj. & n.*

il-liq-uid (il´lik´wed) *adj.* Not being readily convertible into cash. **illiquidity** *n.*

il-lite (il´īt´) *n.* A clay mineral that has essentially the crystal structure of muscovite. **illitic** *adj.*

il-lit-er-ate (i lit´ėr it) *adj.* Unable to read and write; uneducated; having or showing a lack of knowledge of fundamentals on a particular subject. **illiteracy** *n.* **illiterate** *n.* **illiterately** *adv.*

ill–mannered *adj.* Lacking or showing a lack of good manners; rude.

ill–natured *adj.* Disagreeable or unpleasant disposition. **illnaturedly** *adv.*

ill-ness (il´nis) *n.* Sickness; a state of being in poor health; the unhealthy condition of one's body or mind.

il-log-ic (i loj´ik) *n.* The state or quality of being illogical.

il-log-i-cal (i loj´i kal) *adj.* Contrary to the principles of logic; not logical. **illogicality** *n.* **illogically** *adv.*

ill–sorted (il´sōrt´ed) *adj.* To be not matched well.

ill tempered *adj.* Having or showing a cross temper or disposition.

ill–treat *v.* To treat someone or something improperly or cruelly. **ill–treatment** *n.*

il-lu-mi-nate (il ü˝me nāt) *v.* To give light;

to make clear; to provide with understanding; to decorate with pictures or designs; spiritually or intellectually enlightened. **illuminator** *n.*

il-lu-mi-na-tion (il ü´me nā˝shan) *n.* The action of illuminating to lighting or state of being illuminated.

il-lu-mi-na-tive (il ü˝me nāt iv) *adj.* Pertaining to or producing illumination.

il-lu-mi-nism (il ü˝me niz´em) *n.* A claim to a personal enlightenment which is not accessible to mankind in general.

ill–us-age (il yü˝sij) *n.* A harsh, abusive, or unkind treatment toward someone or something.

ill–use (il üz´) *v.* To treat cruelly or unjustly.

il-lu-sion (i lö´zhan) *n.* A misleading perception of reality; an overly optimistic idea or belief; misconception; the action of deceiving; a misleading image presented to ones vision. **illusive, illusory, illusional** *adj.*

il-lu-sion-ary (il ü˝zhe ner´ē) *adj.* To be factual; matter-of-fact.

il-lu-sion-ism (il ü˝zhe niz´em) *n.* The action of using artistic techniques that create an illusion of reality.

il-lus-trate (il´a strāt´) *v.* To explain or clarify, especially by the use of examples; to clarify by serving as an example; to provide a publication with explanatory features. **illustrator** *n.*

il-lus-tra-tion (il´es trā˝shen) *n.* The act of illustrating; an example or comparison used to illustrate.

il-lus-tra-tive (il´es tre tiv) *adj.* Serving to illustrate. **illustratively** *adv.*

il-lus-tri-ous (i lus´trē us) *adj.* Greatly celebrated; renowned. **illustriousness** *n.*

il-lu-vi-al (il ü˝vē el) *adj.* To be pertaining to or marked by illuviation.

il-lu-vi-ate (il ü˝vē āt´) *v.* To go through illuviation. *n.* The material drawn from one soil type and deposited in another.

il-lu-vi-a-tion (il ü´vē ā˝shen) *n.* A gathering of dissolved soil materials in an area as the result of eluviation from another.

il-lu-vi-um (il ū'vē em) *n*. The material that is leached from one soil horizon to another soil horizon.

ill will *n*. Unfriendly or hostile feelings; malice.

ill—wisher *n*. A person who wishes ill or harm to another.

il-men-ite (il'me nīt˝) *n*. A type of massive black mineral which is made of iron, oxygen, and titanium.

I'm (īm) *contr*. I am.

im-age (im'ij) *n*. A representation of the form and features of someone or something; an optically formed representation of an object made by a mirror or lens; a mental picture of something imaginary. **image** *v*. To make a likeness of; to reflect; to depict vividly.

im-ag-ery (im'ij rē) *n. pl.* **imageries** Mental pictures; existing only in the imagination; figurative language.

im-ag-in-a-ble (i maj'i na bl) *adj*. Capable of being imagined. **imaginably** *adv*.

im-ag-i-nar-y (i maj'i ner'ē) *adj*. Existing only in the imagination.

imaginary number *n*. A complex number where its imaginary part is not zero, as in $2 + 6i$.

imaginary part *n*. The portion of a complex number which has an imaginary unit as a factor, such as the 3i in $7 + 3i$.

imaginary unit *n*. A positive square root of negative one, -1.

im-ag-i-na-tion (i maj'i nā˝shan) *n*. The power of forming mental images of unreal or absent objects; such power used creatively; resourcefulness. **imaginative** *adj*. **imaginatively** *adv*.

im-ag-ine (im aj'in) *v*. To form a mental picture or idea of; to suppose; to guess.

im-ag-ism (im˝ij iz'em) *n*. The movement in poetry in the 20th century where expression of ideas and emotions are through precise images. **imagistically** *adj*.

i-ma-go (i mā'gō) *n. pl.* **imagoes** *or* **imagines** An insect in its sexually mature adult stage; the idealized image of self or another person.

i-mam (i măm') *n*. A prayer leader of Islam; rulers that claim descent from Muhammad.

i-mam-ate (i măm'āt) *n*. The country which is ruled over by an imam; the office of an imam.

i-ma-ret (i mär'et) *n*. A hospice of Turkey.

im-bal-ance (im bal'ans) *n*. A lack of functional balance; defective coordination.

im-be-cile (im'bi sil) *n*. A mentally deficient person. **imbecile** *adj*. **imbecilic** *adj*.

im-be-cil-i-ty (im'bi sil˝et ē) *n*. The state of being an imbecile.

im-bibe (im bīb') *v*. To drink; to take in. **imbiber** *n*.

im-bi-bi-tion (im'be bish˝en) *n*. The act of imbibing. **imbibitional** *adj*.

im-bri-cate (im'bri kāt) *adj*. With edges overlapping in a regular arrangement, as roof tiles or fish scales. **imbricately** *adv*.

im-bri-ca-tion (im'bri kā˝shen) *adj*. A pattern which shows overlapping or a regular arrangement.

im-bro-glio (im brōl'yō) *n. pl.* **imbroglios** A complicated situation or disagreement; a confused heap; a tangle.

im-brue (im brü') *v*. To drench something.

im-brute (im brüt') *v*. To degrade someone to the level of that of a brute.

im-bue (im bū') *v*. To saturate or penetrate, as with a stain or dye.

imdtly *abbr*. Immediately.

IMF *abbr*. International Monetary Fund.

im-id-az-ole (im'e daz˝ōl) *n*. A type of white crystalline which is an antimetabolite that is related to histidine.

im-ide (im'īd) *n*. A type of compound which contains the NH group and is derived from ammonia. **imidic** *adj*.

im-i-do (im'e dō˝) *adj*. To be pertaining to the group NH which is united to a radical which is not an acid radical.

im-ine (im ēn') *n*. A kind of compound that has an NH group and is derived from ammonia with the replacement of two hydrogen atoms by a hydrocarbon.

im-in-o (im e'no) *adj*. To be pertaining to the NH group which is united to a radical which is not an acid radical.

im-ip-ra-mine (im ip´re mēn´) *n.* A kind of antidepressant drug.

imit *abbr.* Imitation.

im-i-ta-ble (im´et a bl) *adj.* Capable or worthy of imitation.

im-i-tate (im´e tāt) *v.* To copy the actions or appearance of another; to adopt the style of; to duplicate; to appear like.

im-i-ta-tion (im´e tā´shan) *n.* An act of imitating; something copied from an original.

im-i-ta-tive (im´e tāt´iv) *adj.* To be marked by imitation. **imitatively** *adv.*

im-mac-u-la-cy (im ak´ū le sē) *n.* The state of something being immaculate.

im-mac-u-late (im ak´ū lit) *adj.* Free from sin, stain, or fault; impeccably clean. **immaculately** *adv.*

im-mane (im ān´) *adj.* To be large or monstrous in character.

im-ma-nence (im´a nens) *n.* The quality of being immanent.

im-ma-nent (im´a nent) *adj.* Existing within; restricted to the mind; subjective. **immanency** *n.* **immanently** *adv.*

im-ma-nent-ism (im´a nent iz´em) *n.* A theory according to which God or other spirit is immanent in the world. **immanentist** *n.*

im-ma-te-ri-al (im´a tēr´ē al) *adj.* Lacking material body or form; of no importance or relevance. **immaterially** *adv.* **immaterialness** *n.*

im-ma-te-ri-al-ism (im´a tēr´ē a liz´em) *n.* The theory which believes that external bodies are in essence mental.

im-ma-te-ri-al-i-ty (im´a tēr´ē al´et ē) *n.* The state of being immaterial.

im-ma-te-ri-al-ize (im´a tēr´ē a lī´) *v.* To cause or to make something immaterial.

im-ma-ture (im´a ter´) *adj.* Not fully grown; undeveloped; suggesting a lack of maturity. **immaturely** *adv.* **immaturity** *n.*

im-meas-ur-a-ble (i mezh´ėr a bl) *adj.* Not capable of being measured.

im-me-di-a-cy (i mē´dē a sē) *n. pl.* **immediacies** The quality of being immediate; directness; something of urgent importance.

im-me-di-ate (i mē´dē it) *adj.* Acting or happening without an intervening object, agent, or cause; directly perceived; occurring at once; close in time, location, or relation. **immediately** *adv.*

immediate constituent *n.* A meaningful constituent that directly forms a bigger linguistic construction, as a phrase or sentence.

im-me-di-ate-ly (i mē´dē it lē) *adv.* In direct relationship or connection.

im-me-mo-ri-al (im´e mōr´ē al) *adj.* Beyond the limits of memory, tradition, or records. **immemorially** *adv.*

im-mense (i mens´) *adj.* Exceptionally large. **immensely** *adv.* **immenseness** *n.*

im-men-si-ty (i men´sit ē) *n.* The state of something being immense, or very large in size.

im-merge (im erj´) *v.* To plunge or immerse someone or oneself into something such as water.

im-merse (i mėrs´) *v.* To put into a liquid; to baptize by submerging in water; to engross; to absorb.

im-mersed (i mersd´) *adj.* To be growing completely underwater such as a plant.

im-mers-i-ble (i mėr´se bl) *adj.* Having the capability of being totally under water without damaging any working parts.

im-mer-sion (i mėr´zhen) *n.* The act or state of being totally immersed.

im-me-thod-i-cal (im´e thäd´i kel) *adj.* Not being methodical.

im-mi-grant (im´i grant) *n.* One who leaves his country to settle in another.

im-mi-grate (im´i grāt´) *v.* To leave one country and settle in another.

im-mi-nent (im´i nent) *adj.* About to happen. **imminence** *n.* **imminently** *adv.*

im-min-gle (im in´gl) *v.* To intermingle or to blend into something such as a group; to intermix.

im-mis-ci-ble (im is´i bl) *adj* To be incapable of attaining homogeneity or mixing.

im-mit-i-ga-ble (im mit´i ga bl) *adj.* Not capable of being mitigated. **immitigableness** *n.* **immitigably** *adv.*

im-mix (im iks′) *v.* To mix something intimately.

im-mo-bile (i mō′bil) *adj.* Not moving or incapable of motion .**immobility** *n.*

im-mo-bi-lize (i mō′bi līz′) *v.* To render motionless; no movement. **immobilization** *n.* **immobilizer** *n.*

im-mod-er-a-cy (im mǎd′er a sē) *adj.* The lack of moderation.

im-mod-er-ate (i mod′ėr it) *adj.* Exceeding normal bounds. **immoderately** *adv.*

im-mod-est (i mod′ist) *adj.* Lacking modesty; indecent; boastful. **immodestly** *adv.* **immodesty** *n.*

im-mo-late (im′o lāt′) *v.* To kill, as a sacrifice; to destroy completely. **immolator** *n.*

im-mor-al (im or′al) *adj.* Not moral. **immorally** *adv.*

im-mor-al-ist (im or′al list) *n.* One who practices immorality.

im-mo-ral-i-ty (im′o ral′i tē) *n. pl.* **immoralities** Lack of morality; an immoral act or practice.

im-mor-tal (i mort′l) *adj.* Exempt from death; lasting forever, as in fame. **immortal** *n.* A person of lasting fame. **immortality** *n.* **immortally** *adv.*

im-mor-tal-ize (i mort′l īz) *adj.* To make something immortal. **immortalation** *n.* **immortilizer** *n.*

im-mo-tile (im ōt′l) *adj.* To be lacking motility.

im-mov-a-ble (i mō′va bl) *adj.* Not capable of moving or being moved. **immovably** *adv.*

immun *abbr.* Immunization.

im-mune (i mūn′) *adj.* Not affected or responsive; resistant, as to a disease. **immunity** *n.*

im-mu-ni-ty (im ū′nit ē) *n.* The state at which something is immune.

im-mu-nize (im′ū nīz′) *v.* To make immune. **immunization** *n.*

im-mu-no-as-say (im′ū nō as″ā) *n.* An identification of a substance by the way it acts as an antigen. **immunoassayable** *adj.*

im-mu-no-chem-is-try (im′ū nō kem″e str) *n.* The part of chemistry that deals with the chemical aspect of immunology. **immunochemical** *adj.* **immunochemist** *n.*

im-mu-no-dif-fu-sion (im′ū nō dif fūzhen) *n.* Immunodiffusion separation of antigens by the way they pass through a semipermeable membrane.

im-mu-no-gen-e-sis (im′ū nō jen″e sis) *n.* The production of immunity. **immunogenicity** *n.* **immunogenic** *adj.* **immunogenically** *adv.*

im-mu-no-gen-et-ics (im′ū nō je net″iks) *n.* A branch of immunology concerned with heredity, disease, and the immune system and its components. **immunogenetic** *adj.* **immunogenetically** *adv.*

im-mu-no-glob-u-lin (im′ū nō glăb′ū lin) *n.* A type of protein which is made up of heavy and light chains and is used as an antibody by the body.

immunol *abbr.* Immunology.

im-mu-nol-o-gy (im′ū nol′o jē) *n.* The study of immunity to diseases. **immunologic** *adj.* **immunological** *adj.* **immunologically** *adv.*

im-mu-no-pa-thol-o-gy (im′ū nō pa thǎl″e jē) *n.* The branch of medicine dealing with immunologic abnormalities. **immunopathologist** *n.* **immunopathological** *adj.*

im-mu-no-re-ac-tive (im′ū nō rē ak′tiv) *adj.* To be reacting to an antigen. **immunoreactivity** *n.*

im-mu-no-sup-pres-sion (im′ū nō se presh′en) *n.* The suppression of the body's natural immune responses. **immunosuppressant** *n. & adj.*

im-mu-no-sup-pres-sive (i mū′nō se pre′ siv) *adj.* Acting to suppress a natural immune response to an antigen.

im-mu-no-ther-a-py (im′ū nō ther′e pē) *n.* The treatment of disease by the means of antigenic preparations or with antigens.

im-mure (i mūr′) *v.* To confine by or as if by walls; to build into a wall.

im-mu-ta-ble (i mū′ta bl) *adj.* Unchanging or unchangeable. **immutability** *n.* **immutably** *adv.*

imp (imp) *n.* A mischievous child.

im-pact (im′pakt) *n.* A collision; the impetus or force produced by a collision; an initial, usually strong effect. **impact** *v.* To pack firmly together; to strike or affect forcefully.

im-pac-ted (im pak´tid) *adj.* Wedged together at the broken ends, as an impacted bone; wedged inside the gum in such a way that normal eruption is prevented, as an impacted tooth.

im-pac-tion (im pak´shen) *n.* Something wedged in a part of the body.

im-pact-or (im pak´ter) *n.* The one which impacts; a kind of tool or instrument which is used for the purpose of collecting samples of suspended particles.

im-pair (im pâr´) *v.* To diminish in strength, value, quantity, or quality. **impairment** *n.* **impairer** *n.*

im-pa-la (im pal´a) *n.* A large African antelope, the male of which has slender curved horns.

im-pale (im pāl´) *v.* To pierce with a sharp stake or point; to kill by piercing in this fashion. **impalement** *n.*

im-pal-pa-ble (im pal´pa bl) *adj.* Not perceptible to touch; not easily distinguished. **impalpability** *n.* **impalpably** *adv.*

im-pan-el (im pan´el) *v.* To enroll on a panel; to select a jury.

im-par-a-dise (im par´e dīs) *v.* To enrapture.

im-par-i-ty (im par´itē) *n.* Disparity; inequality.

im-part (im pärt´) *v.* To grant; to bestow; to make known; to communicate. **impartment** *n.* **impartation** *n.*

im-par-tial (im pär´shal) *adj.* Not partial; unbiased; not favoring one over another. **impartiality** *n.* **impartially** *adv.*

im-part-i-ble (im pär´ti bl) *v.* Being not subject to partition. **impartibly** *adv.*

im-pass-a-ble (im pas´a bl) *adj.* Impossible to travel over or across. **impassableness** *n.* **impassably** *adv.*

im-passe (im´pas) *n.* A road or passage having no exit; a difficult situation with no apparent way out; a deadlock.

im-pas-si-ble (im pas´i bl) *adj.* To be in-accessible to an injury; not to be moved by passion or sympathy.

im-pas-sion (im pash´an) *v.* To arouse the passions of someone by another person.

im-pas-sioned (im pash´and) *adj.* Filled with passion.

im-pas-sive (im pas´iv) *adj.* Unemotional; showing no emotion; expressionless. **impassively** *adv.*

im-paste (im pāst´) *v.* To make or form something into a crust or a paste

im-pas-to (im pas´tō) *n.* A kind of raised decoration on ceramic ware.

im-pa-tience (im pā´shens) *n.* The quality of being impatient.

im-pa-ti-ens (im´pā´shē enz˝) *n.* A type of watery-juiced annual herb that has irregular seccate flowers.

im-pa-tient (im pā´shent) *adj.* Unwilling to wait or tolerate delay; expressing or caused by irritation at having to wait; restlessly eager; intolerant. **impatience** *n.* **impatiently** *adv.*

im-pawn (im pän´) *v.* To put or place something in pawn.

im-peach (im pēch´) *v.* To charge with misconduct in public office before a proper court of justice; to make an accusation against. **impeachment** *n.*

im-pearl (im-perl) *v.* To form something into pearls.

im-pec-ca-ble (im pek´abl) *adj.* Having no flaws; perfect; not capable of sin. **impeccably** *adv.* **impeccability** *n.*

im-pe-cu-ni-ous (im´pe kū´nē us) *adj.* Having no money. **impecuniousness** *n.* **impecuniously** *adv.*

im-ped-ance (im pēd´ans) *n.* A measure of the total opposition to the flow of an electric current, especially in an alternating current circuit.

im-pede (im pēd´) *v.* To obstruct or slow down the progress of.

im-ped-i-ment (im ped´i ment) *n.* One that stands in the way; something that impedes, especially an organic speech defect.

im-ped-i-men-ta (im ped´i men´ta) *n.* Things that impede or encumber, such as baggage.

im-pel (im pel´) *v.* To spur to action; to provoke; to drive forward; to propel.

im-pel-ler (im pel´ėr) *n.* One who impels something.

im-pend (im pend´) *v.* To hover threateningly; to be about to happen.

im-pend-ent (im pend´ent) *adj.* To be near at hand.

im-pen-e-tra-bil-i-ty (im pen˝i tra bil´i tē) *n.* The inability of two parts of anything to occupy the same space at exactly the same time.

im-pen-e-tra-ble (im pen´i tra bl´) *adj.* Not capable of being penetrated; not capable of being seen through or understood; unfathomable. **impenetrably** *adv.*

im-pen-i-tence (im pen´i tens) *n.* The quality of being impenitent.

im-pen-i-tent (im pen´i tent) *adj.* Not sorry; unrepentant. **impenitently** *adv.*

im-per-a-tive (im per´a tiv) *adj.* Expressing a command or request; empowered to command or control; compulsory. **imperative** *n.* **imperatively** *adv.*

im-pe-ra-tor (im˝pe rā´tėr) *adj.* The commander in chief of the ancient Romans. **imperatorial** *adj.*

im-per-cep-ti-ble (im´per sep´ta bl) *adj.* Not perceptible by the mind or senses; extremely small or slight. **imperceptibly** *adv.* **imperceptibility** *n.*

im-per-cep-tive (im˝pėr sep´tiv) *adj.* Not being perceptive. **imperceptiveness** *n.*

im-per-cip-i-ence (im˝pėr sip´ē ens) *n.* The state of being imperceptive.

im-per-cip-i-ent (im˝pėr sip´ē ent) *adj.* Being not percipient.

imperf *abbr.* Imperfect; imperforate.

im-per-fect (im per´fikt) *adj.* Not perfect; of or being a verb tense which shows an uncompleted or continuous action or condition. **imperfect** *n.* The imperfect tense. **imperfectly** *adv.*

imperfect fungus *n.* A type of fungus of which only the conidial stage is known.

im-per-fec-tion (im´per fek´shan) *n.* The quality or condition of being imperfect; a

defect.

im-per-fec-tive (im per´fik˝tiv) *adj.* To be expressing action as being incomplete.

im-per-fo-rate (im per´fėr it)) *adj.* To have no opening; lacking a normal opening.

im-pe-ri-al (im pėr´ē al) *adj.* Of or relating to an empire or emperor; designating a nation or government having dependent colonies; majestic; regal. **imperial** *n.* A pointed beard on the lower lip or chin. **imperially** *adv.*

im-pe-ri-al-ism (im pėr´ē a liz´um) *n.* The national policy or practice of acquiring foreign territories or establishing dominance over other nations. **imperialist** *n.* **imperialistic** *adj.* **imperialistically** *adv.*

imperial moth *n.* A large New World moth with yellow wings and brownish or purplish markings.

im-per-il (im per´il) *v.* To put in peril; endanger.

im-pe-ri-ous (im pėr´ē us) *adj.* Commanding; domineering; urgent. **imperiousness** *n.* **imperiously** *adv.*

im-per-ish-a-ble (im per´i sha bl) *adj.* Not perishable; permanently enduring. **imperishably** *adv.* **imperishableness** *n.* **imperishability** *n.*

im-pe-ri-um (im pėr´ē um) *n.* An absolute dominion; the right to employ the force of the state.

im-per-ma-nence (im´perm e nents) *n.* The state of being impermanent.

im-per-ma-nen-cy (im´perm e nen sē) *n.* The state of something being impermanent.

im-per-ma-nent (im per´ma nent) *adj.* Not permanent; not enduring; temporary; transient. **impermanently** *adv.*

im-per-me-a-ble (im per´mē a bl) *adj.* Not permeable; impassable. **impermeability** *n.* **impermeableness** *n.*

im-per-mis-si-ble (im´pėr mis´a bl) *adj.* Not permissible; not allowed. **impermissibility** *n.* **impermissibly** *adv.*

im-per-son-al (im per´so nal) *adj.* Having no personal reference or connection; showing no emotion or personality. **imperson-ally** *adv.* **impersonality** *n.*

im-per-son-al-ize (im pŭr´so na līz″) *v.* To make something impersonal. **imperson-alization** *n.*

im-per-son-ate (im per´so nāt´) *v.* To as-sume the character or manner of. **imper-sonation** *n.* **impersonator** *n.*

im-per-ti-nence (im pŭr´ti nens) *n.* The in-stance of impertinence; rudeness in actions or speech.

im-per-ti-nent (im per´ti nent) *adj.* Overly bold or disrespectful; not pertinent; irrel-evant; rude. **impertinently** *adv.*

im-per-turb-a-ble (im´pėr ter´ba bl) *adj.* Not easily perturbed or agitated. **imper-turbability** *n.* **imperturbably** *adv.*

im-per-vi-ous (im per´vē us) *adj.* Incapable of being emotionally affected or influenced by argument. **imperviously** *adv.* **imper-viousness** *n.*

im-pe-tig-i-nous (im´pi tij´i nus) *adj.* To be pertaining to or related to impetigo.

im-pe-ti-go (im´pi tī´gō) *n.* A contagious skin disease marked by pustules.

im-pe-trate (im´pi trāt″) *v.* To obtain some-thing by a request. **impetration** *n.*

im-pet-u-os-i-ty (im pech″ū os´i tē) *n.* An action which is impetuous.

im-pet-u-ous (im pech´ū us) *adj.* Marked by sudden action or emotion; impulsive. **impetuousness** *n.* **impetuously** *adv.*

im-pe-tus (im´pi tus) *n.* A driving force; an incitement; a stimulus; momentum.

im-pi (im´pē) *n. pl.* **impies, impis** A brigade or large body of soldiers.

im-pi-e-ty (im pī´i tē) *n. pl.* **impieties** The quality of being impious; irreverence.

im-pinge (im pinj´) *v.* To strike or collide; to impact; to encroach. **impingement** *n.*

im-pi-ous (im´pē us) *adj.* Not pious; irrev-erent; disrespectful. **impiously** *adv.*

imp-ish (im´pish) *adj.* Mischievous. **imp-ishly** *adv.* **impishness** *n.*

im-pla-ca-ble (im plak´a bl) *adj.* Not cap-able of being placated or appeased. **im-placability** *n.* **implacably** *adv.*

im-plant (im plant´) *v.* To set in firmly; to

fix in the mind; to insert surgically. **im-plant** *n.* **implantation** *n.*

im-plau-si-ble (im plo´zi bl) *adj.* Difficult to believe; unlikely. **implausibility** *n.* **im-plausibly** *adv.*

im-plead (im plēd´) *v.* To prosecute by law.

im-ple-ment (im´ple ment) *n.* A utensil or tool. **implement** *v.* To put into effect; to carry out; to furnish with implements. **implementation** *n.*

im-pli-cate (im´pli kāt´) *v.* To involve, especially in illegal activity; to imply.

im-pli-ca-tion (im´pli kā´shan) *n.* The act of implicating or state of being implicated; the act of implying; an indirect expression; something implied. **implicatively** *adv.*

im-plic-it (im plis´it) *adj.* Contained in the nature of someone or something but not readily apparent; understood but not di-rectly expressed; complete; absolute.

im-plode (im plōd´) *v.* To collapse or burst violently inward. **implosion** *n.*

im-plore (im plōr´) *v.* To appeal urgently to. **implorer** *n.* **imploringly** *adv.*

im-plo-sion (im plō´shan) *n.* The action of bringing to a center. **implosive** *adj.*

im-ply (im plī´) *v.* To involve by logical necessity; to express indirectly; to suggest.

im-po-lite (im´po līt´) *adj.* Rude; uncivil. **impoliteness** *n.* **impolitely** *adv.*

im-pol-i-tic (im pol´i tik) *adj.* Not expe-dient; tactless. **impolitically** *adv.*

im-pon-der-a-ble (im pon´dèr a bl) *adj.* Incapable of being weighed or evaluated precisely. **imponderable** *n.* **imponder-ableness** *n.*

im-pone (im pōn´) *v.* To wager; bet.

im-port (im pōrt´) *v.* To bring in goods from a foreign country for trade or sale; to mean; to signify; to be significant. **im-port** *n.* Something imported; meaning; significance; importance. **importer** *n.* **im-portable** *adj.*

im-por-tance (im pir´tans) *n.* The quality of being important; significance.

im-por-tant (im pir´tant) *adj.* Likely to determine or influence events; significant; having fame or authority; prominent. **im-**

portantly *adv*.

im-por-ta-tion (im´pōr tā´shɑn) *n*. The act or business of importing goods; something which is imported by a country.

imported cabbageworm *n*. A type of small white butterfly which is a pest of cruciferous plants such as cabbage.

imported fire ant *n*. A type of small South American ant which is destructive in the southeastern United States.

im-por-tu-nate (im par´chɑ nit) *adj*. Urgent or persistent in pressing demands or requests; pertinacious. **importunately** *adv*.

im-por-tune (im˝ par tŏn´) *v*. To press with repeated requests; to harass or beset with solicitations; to beg or beg for urgently or persistently. **importuner** *n*.

im-por-tu-ni-ty (im˝par tŏ´ni tē) *n*. State of being importunate; persistence..

im-pose (im pōz´) *v*. To enact or apply as compulsory; to obtrude or force oneself or to be a burden on another; to take unfair advantage; to palm off. **imposer** *n*

im-pos-ing (im pō´zing) *adj*. Awesome; impressive. **imposingly** *adv*.

im-pos-i-tion (im˝pɒ zish´ɑn) *n*. The act of imposing upon someone or something; an excessive or uncalled for burden.

im-pos-si-ble (im pos´i bl) *adj*. Not capable of existing or happening; unlikely to take place or be done; unacceptable; difficult to tolerate or deal with. **impossibility** *n*. **impossibly** *adv*.

im-post (im´pōst) *n*. A tax or duty.

im-pos-tor *or* **im-pos-ter** (im pos´tėr) *n*. One who assumes a false identity or title for the purpose of deception.

im-pos-tume (im pos´chüm˝) *n*. A type of abscess.

im-pos-ture (im pos´chėr) *n*. Deception by the assumption of a false identity.

im-po-tent (im´pɒ tent) *adj*. Without strength or vigor; having no power; ineffectual; incapable of sexual intercourse. **impotence** *n*. **impotency** *n*.

im-pound (im pound´) *v*. To confine in or as if in a pound; to seize and keep in legal custody; to hold water, as in a reservoir.

im-pound-ment (im pound´ment) *n*. A type of a body of water which is formed by impounding.

im-pov-er-ish (im pov´ėr ish) *v*. To make poor; to deprive or be deprived of natural richness or fertility. **impoverishment** *n*.

im-pov-er-ish-ed (im pov´ėr isht) *v*. To be poor.

im-prac-ti-ca-ble (im prak´ti kɑ bl) *adj*. Incapable of being done or put into practice. **impracticableness** *n*. **impracticability** *n*. **impracticably** *adv*.

im-prac-ti-cal (im prak´ti kɑl) *adj*. Unwise to put into effect; unable to deal with practical or financial matters efficiently. **impracticality** *n*.

im-pre-cate (im´pre kāt˝) *v*. To utter curses or to invoke evil on someone or something.

im-pre-ca-tion (im´pre kā˝shɑn) *n*. The act of imprecating; a prayer that a curse will fall on someone. **imprecatory** *adj*.

im-pre-cise (im´pri sīs´) *adj*. Not precise.

im-preg-na-ble (im preg´nɑ bl) *adj*. To be beyond question or criticism.

im-preg-nate (im preg´nāt) *v*. To make pregnant; to fertilize, as an ovum; to fill throughout; to saturate. **impregnation** *n*. **impregnator** *n*.

im-pre-sa (im prā´sɑ) *n*. A device used in the 16th and 17th centuries with a motto; an emblem.

im-pre-sa-ri-o (im´pri sär´ē ō˝) *n*. *pl*. **impresarios** A theatrical manager or producer, especially the director of an opera company.

im-pre-scrip-ti-ble (im pri skrip´ti bl) *adj*. Not subject to prescription; referring to rights, not legally to be withdrawn or revoked.

im-press (im pres´) *v*. To apply or produce with pressure; to stamp or mark with or as if with pressure; to fix firmly in the mind; to affect strongly and usually favorably. **impress** *n*. The act of impressing; a mark made by impressing; a stamp or seal for impressing. **impressible** *adj*.

im-pres-sion (im presh´ɑn) *n*. A mark or

design made on a surface by pressure; an effect or feeling retained in the mind as a result of experience; an indistinct notion or recollection; a satiric or humorous imitation; the copies of a publication printed at one time.

im-pres-sion-a-ble (im presh´a na bl) *adj.* Easily influenced or impressed. **impressionably** *adv.*

im-pres-sion-ism (im presh´a niz˝um) *n.* A style of late nineteenth century painting in which the immediate appearance of scenes is depicted with unmixed primary colors applied in small strokes to simulate reflected light.

im-pres-sion-ist (im presh´an ist) *n.* A person who adheres to the theories of impressionism.

im-pres-sion-is-tic (im presh˝a nis´tik) *adj.* Pertaining to impressionism.

im-pres-sive (im pres´iv) *adj.* Making a strong impression; striking. **impressively** *adv.* **impressiveness** *n.*

im-press-ment (im pres´ment) *n.* The act of seizing men or property for public use.

im-pres-sure (im presh´er) *n.* A type of mark which is made by the application of pressure.

im-prest (im´prest) *n.* An advance of money.

im-pri-ma-tur (im´pri mä´ter) *n.* Official permission to print or publish; authorization.

im-pri-mis (im pri´mis) *adv.* In the first place.

im-print (im print´) *v.* To make or impress a mark or design on a surface; to make or stamp a mark on; to fix firmly in the mind. **imprint** *n.* A mark or design made by imprinting; a lasting influence or effect; a publisher's name, often with the date and place of publication, printed at the bottom of a title page.

im-print-ing (im prin´ting) *n.* A type of behavior pattern which is established early in the life of a member of a social species.

im-pris-on (im priz´on) *v.* To put in prison. **imprisonment** *n.*

im-prob-a-ble (im prob´a bl) *adj.* Not likely to occur or be true. **improbability** *n.* **improbably** *adv.*

im-pro-bi-ty (im prō´bi tē) *n.* Lack of principle; dishonest.

im-promp-tu (im promp´tö) *adj.* Devised or performed without prior planning or preparation. **impromptu** *n.* Something said or done without prior thought. **impromptu** *adv.* Off-handedly; extemporaneously.

im-prop-er (im prop´er) *adj.* Unsuitable; indecorous; incorrect. **improperly** *adv.*

improper fraction *n.* A fraction having a numerator larger than or the same as the denominator.

improper integral *n.* A type of definite integral.

im-pro-pri-ate (im prō´prē āt´) *v.* To place valuables, such as the profits of church property, in the hands of a layman. **impropriate** *adj.*

im-pro-pri-e-ty (im´pro prī´i tē) *n. pl.* **improprieties** The quality or state of being improper; an improper act or remark.

im-prove (im prōv´) *v.* To make or become better; to increase something's productivity or value. **improvable** *adj.*

im-prove-ment (im prōv´ment) *n.* The act or process of improving or the condition of being improved; a change that improves.

im-prov-i-dent (im prov´i dent) *adj.* Not providing for the future. **improvidence** *n.* **improvidently** *adv.*

im-prov-i-sa-tion (im prov˝i zā´shan) *n.* Something impromptu as music.

im-pro-vise (im´pro vīz´) *v.* To make up, compose, or perform without preparation; to make from available materials. **improviser** *n.* **improvisator** *n.* **improvisatory** *adj.* **improvisatorial** *adj.* **improvisatorially** *adv.*

im-pru-dent (im prōd´ent) *adj.* Not prudent; unwise. **imprudence** *n.*

im-pu-dent (im´pū dent) *adj.* Marked by rude boldness or disrespect. **impudence** *n.* **impudently** *adv.*

im-pu-dic-i-ty (im˝pū dis´i tē) *n.* Shamelessness; immodesty.

im-pugn (im pūn´) *v.* To attack as false; to cast doubt on. **impugner** *n.*

im-puis-sance (im pū´i sans) *n.* A weakness; impotence.

im-puis-sant (im pū´i sant) *adj.* Being weak.

im-pulse (im´puls) *n.* A driving force or the motion produced by it; a sudden spontaneous urge; a motivating force; a general tendency. *Physiol.* A transfer of energy from one neuron to another.

impulse buying *n.* The buying of items and merchandise on an impulse.

im-pul-sion (im pul´shan) *n.* The act of driving on or the resulting effect; impetus; a constraining action on the mind or conduct.

im-pul-sive (im pul´siv) *adj.* Acting on impulse rather than thought; resulting from impulse; uncalculated. **impulsively** *adv.* **impulsiveness** *n.*

im-pu-ni-ty (im pū´ni tē) *n.* Exemption from punishment.

im-pure (im pūr´) *adj.* Not pure; unclean; unchaste or obscene; mixed with another substance; adulterated; deriving from more than one source or style. **impurely** *adv.* **impurity** *n.*

im-pu-ta-tion (im˝pū ta´shan) *n.* An act of imputing.

im-pute (im pūt´) *v.* To attribute something, such as a mistake, to another; to charge.

IN *abbr.* Indiana.

in (in) *prep.* A function word that expresses inclusion or presence within a time, place, or circumstances. **in** *abbr.* Inch. **in** *adv.* Into a place, state, position, or a relationship; on the inside of a building.

in-a-bil-i-ty (in˝a bil´i tē) *n.* A lack of sufficient power or capacity.

in ab-sen-tia (in´ ab sen˝chē a) *adv.* In the absence of.

in-ac-ces-si-ble (in˝ak ses´i bl) *adj.* Not to be reached, or approached. **inaccessibility** *n.* **inaccessibly** *adv.*

in-ac-cu-ra-cy (in ak´yèr a sē) *n.* The state of being inaccurate. **inaccurately** *adv.*

in-ac-cu-rate (in ak´yèr it) *adj.* Not correct; not according to the truth.

in-ac-tion (in ak´shan) *n.* The lack of activity or action.

in-ac-ti-vate (in ak´ti vāt˝) *n.* To make someone or something inactive.

in-ac-tive (in ak´tiv) *adj.* Not active or inclined to be active; out of current use or service. **inactively** *adv.* **inactivity** *n.* **inactiveness** *n.*

in-ad-e-qua-cy (in ad´e kwi sē) *n. pl.* **inadequacies** The instance of being inadequate.

in-ad-e-quate (in ad´e kwit) *adj.* Not adequate. **inadequately** *adv.*

in-ad-mis-si-ble (in˝ad mis´i bl) *adj.* Not admissible; not proper to be allowed, or received.

in-ad-ver-tence (in´ad vèr´tens) *n.* The action of something being inadvertent; an oversight or careless mistake.

in-ad-ver-tent (in´ad vèr´tent) *adj.* Unintentional; accidental; inattentive. **inadvertently** *adv.*

in-ad-vis-a-ble (in˝ad vī´za bl) *adj.* Not advisable; unwise. **inadvisability** *n.*

in-al-ien-a-ble (in āl´ya na bl) *adj.* Not capable of being given up or transferred. **inalienably** *adv.* **inalienability** *n.*

in-al-ter-a-ble (in al´tèr a bl) *adj.* Being not alterable. **inalterability** *n.*

in-am-o-ra-ta (in am˝o rä´ta) *n.* The person with whom a person is in love.

in–and–in *adj. & adv.* Being in repeated generations of the same related stock families.

in-ane (i nān´) *adj.* Without sense or substance. **inanely** *adv.* **inanity** *n.*

in-an-i-mate (in an´i mit) *adj.* Not having the qualities of life; not animated. **inanimately** *adv.* **inanimateness** *n.*

in-a-ni-tion (in´a nish´an) *n.* Exhaustion, especially from malnourishment.

in-an-i-ty (i nan´i tē) *n. pl.* **inanities** The quality of being inane; the lack of substance, sense or ideas; senselessness; emptiness.

in-ap-par-ent (in´e par˝ent) *adj.* Being not apparent. **inapparently** *adv.*

in-ap-peas-a-ble (in˝ a pē´za bl) *adj.* Not

appeaseable.

in-ap-pe-tence (in ap´i t*e***ns)** *n.* The loss of the appetite.

in-ap-pli-ca-ble (in ap´li k*a* **bl)** *adj.* Not applicable; irrelevant; not suitable.

in-ap-po-site (in ap´*o* **zit)** *adj.* Not apposite.

in-ap-pre-cia-ble (in´*a* **prē´shē** *a* **bl)** *adj.* Too slight to be significant; negligible. **inappreciably** *adv.*

in-ap-pre-ci-a-tive (in´*a* **prē´shē** *a***˝tiv)** *adj.* Being not appreciative; lacking gratitude. **inappreciatively** *adv.*

in-ap-proach-a-ble (in´*a* **prō´ch***a* **bl)** *adj.* Being not approachable.

in-ap-pro-pri-ate (in´*a* **prō´prē it)** *adj.* Being not appropriate.

in-apt (in apt´) *adj.* Being not suitable or not apt. **inaptness** *n.* **inaptly** *adv.*

in-ap-ti-tude (in ap´ti tŏd) *n.* The lack of aptitude

in-arch (in-ärch´) *v.* To graft by combining a shoot to a stock without separating it from the parent tree.

in-ar-gu-a-ble (in-är´gū *e* **bl)** *v.* Being not arguable. **inarguably** *adv.*

in-ar-tic-u-late (in´är tik´ū lit) *adj.* Not uttering or forming intelligible words or syllables; unable to speak; speechless; unable to speak clearly or effectively; unexpressed. **inarticulately** *adv.* **inarticulateness** *n.*

in-ar-ti-fi-cial (in är´t*i* **fish´***a***l)** *adj.* Not artificial; natural.

in-ar-tis-tic (in´är tis´tik) *adj.* Not artistic; lacking artistic appreciation; uninformed on the principles of art.

in-as-much as (in´*a***z much´ az´)** *conj.* Because of the fact that; since.

in-at-ten-tion (in´*a* **ten´ sh***a***n)** *n.* The failure to pay attention.

in-at-ten-tive (in´*a* **ten´tiv)** *adj.* Not attentive; neglectful; heedless.

in-au-di-ble (in a´d*i* **bl)** *adj.* Not audible; incapable of being heard.

in-au-gu-ral (in a´gūr a*l***)** *adj.* Of or for an inauguration.

in-au-gu-rate (in i´gū rāt´) *v.* To put into office with a formal ceremony; to begin officially. **inauguration** *n.*

in-aus-pi-cious (in´*a* **spish´us)** *adj.* Not auspicious; unlucky; unfavorable.

in—be-tween (in´bē twēn´) *adj.* Intermediate. **in—between** *n.* An intermediate or intermediary.

in between *adv. & prep.* Between.

in-board (in´bōrd) *adj.* Within a ship's hull; close to or near the fuselage of an aircraft.

in-born (in´bōrn´) *adj.* Possessed at birth; natural; hereditary.

in-bound (in´bound´) *adj.* Incoming.

in-bounds (in´bounds´) *adj.* Pertaining to putting the ball into play by throwing or passing it onto a court such as with the game of basketball.

in-breathe (in´brēth´) *v.* To breathe something such as a small particle in the air into the lungs; to inhale..

in-bred (in´bred´) *adj.* To be rooted into someone's nature possibly by heredity.

in-breed (in´brēd´) *v.* To produce by repeatedly breeding closely related individuals.

in-breeding (in´brē´ding) *n.* The act of interbreeding individuals which are closely related in order to preserve desirable characteristics of the stock or thing being bred; as animals in the food chain.

in-built (in´bilt) *adj.* To be built into something.

inc *or* **Inc** *abbr.* Income; increase; incorporated.

In-ca (ing´ka) *n.* One of the dominant groups of South Americans Indians who maintained an empire in Peru until the Spanish conquest.

in-cal-cu-la-ble (in kal´ky*a* **l***a* **bl)** *adj.* Not calculable; indeterminate; unpredictable; very large. **incalculably** *adv.*

in-can-desce (in´k*a***n des´)** *v.* To become incandescent.

in-can-des-cence (in´k*a***n des´ens)** *n.* The quality of being incandescent.

in-can-des-cent (in´k*a***n des´ent)** *adj.* Giving off visible light when heated; shining brightly; ardently emotional or intense.

incandescent lamp *n.* A lamp in which a filament is heated to incandescence by an electric current.

in-can-ta-tion (in´kan tā´shan) *n.* A recitation of magic charms or spells; a magic formula for chanting or reciting.

in-ca-pa-ble (in kā´pa bl) *n.* Lacking the ability for doing or performing.

in-ca-pac-i-tate (in´ka pas´i tāt´) *v.* To render incapable; to disable; in law, to disqualify. **incapacitation** *n.*

in-ca-pac-i-ty (in´ka pas´i tē) *n. pl.* **in-capacities** Inadequate ability or strength; a defect; in law, a disqualification.

in-car-cer-ate (in kär´se rāt´) *v.* To confine; enclose.

in-car-na-dine (in kär´na dīn´) *v.* To redden, as the flesh.

incarnadine *adj.* Flesh-colored; pink; blood-red.

in-car-nate (in kär´nāt) *v.* To give actual form to; to embody in flesh. **incarnate** *adj.*

in-car-na-tion (in´kär nā´shan) *n.* The act of incarnating or state of being incarnated; the embodiment of God in the human form of Jesus; one regarded as personifying a given abstract quality or idea.

in-cen-di-ary (in sen´dē er´ē) *adj.* Causing or capable of causing fires; of or relating to arson; tending to inflame; inflammatory. **incendiary** *n.*

in-cense (in´sens) *v.* To make angry. **incense** *n.* A substance, as a gum or wood, burned to produce a pleasant smell; the smoke or odor produced.

in-cen-tive (in sen´tiv) *n.* Something inciting one to action or effort; a stimulus.

in-cep-tion (in sept´) *n.* A beginning; an origin. **inceptive** *adj.*

in-cer-ti-tude (in ser´ti tŏd´) *n.* Uncertainty; lack of confidence; instability.

in-ces-sant (in ses´ant) *adj.* Occurring without interruption; continuous; ongoing. **incessantly** *adv.*

in-cest (in´sest) *n.* Sexual intercourse between persons so closely related that they are forbidden by law to marry. **incestuous** *adj.* **incestuously** *adv.*

inch (inch) *n.* A unit of measurement equal to 1/12th of a foot. *v.* To move slowly.

in-cho-ate (in kō´it) *adj.* In an early stage; incipient; incomplete. **inchoately** *adv.* **inchoateness** *n.*

in-cho-a-tive (in kō´a tiv) *adj.* Denoting the beginning of an action or circumstance.

in-ci-dence (in´si dens) *n.* The extent or rate of occurrence.

in-ci-dent (in´si dent) *n.* An event; an event that disrupts normal procedure or causes a crisis.

in-ci-den-tal (in´si den´tal) *adj.* Occurring or likely to occur at the same time or as a result; minor; subordinate. **incidental** *n.* A minor attendant occurrence or condition. **incidentally** *adv.*

in-cin-er-ate (in sin´e rāt´) *v.* To burn up. **incineration** *n.*

in-cin-er-a-tor *n.* One that incinerates; a furnace for burning waste.

in-cip-i-ent (in sip´ē ent) *adj.* Just beginning to appear or occur. **incipience** *n.* **incipiently** *adv.*

in-cise (in sīz´) *v.* To make or cut into with a sharp tool; to carve into a surface; to engrave.

in-cised (in sīzd´) *adj.* Cut; made by cutting; to decorate with incised figures; having deep, uneven cuts.

in-ci-sion (in sizh´an) *n.* The act of incising; a cut or notch, especially a surgical cut.

in-ci-sive (in sī´siv) *adj.* Having or suggesting sharp intellect; penetrating; cogent and effective; telling. **incisively** *adv.* **incisiveness** *n.*

in-ci-sor (in sī´zėr) *n.* A cutting tooth at the front of the mouth.

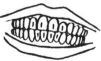

in-cite (in sīt´) *v.* To provoke to action. **incitement** *n.* **inciter** *n.*

in-ci-vil-i-ty (in´si vil´i tē) *n*. The state or quality of being uncivil.

in-clem-ent (in klem´ent) *adj*. Stormy or rainy; unmerciful. **inclemency** *n*.

in-clin-a-ble (in klī´na bl) *adj*. Having an inclination; favorably disposed.

in-cli-na-tion (in´kli nā´shan) *n*. An attitude; a disposition; a tendency to act or think in a certain way; a preference; a bow or tilt; a slope.

in-cline (in klīn´) *v*. To deviate or cause to deviate from the horizontal or vertical; to slant; to dispose or be disposed; to bow or nod. **incline** *n*. An inclined surface.

in-clined (in klīnd´) *adj*. Having a direction or inclination; favorably disposed toward something.

inclined plane *n*. Any plane surface making an obliquely angled toward the horizon.

in-cli-nom-e-ter (in´kli nom´i tėr) *n*. An appartus for indicating the direction of the earth's magnetic field in reference to the plane of the horizon.

in-clude (in klōd´) *v*. To have as a part or member; to contain; to put into a group or total. **included** *adj*.

in-clu-sion (in klō´zhan) *n*. The act or state of including; that which is included.

in-clu-sive (in klō´siv) *adj*. Embracing; comprehensive; including a great deal; covering the specified costs or limits. **inclusively** *adv*.

in-co-er-ci-ble (in´kō ür´si bl) *adj*. Not coercible; incapable of being confined or controlled.

in-cog-ni-to (in kog´ni tō´) *adj*. Having a hidden or assumed identity; unknown. *adv*. With the real identity concealed. *n*. A person who is in the state of disguise.

in-cog-ni-zance (in kog´ni zans) *n*. Failure to recognize, know or apprehend.

in-cog-ni-zant (in kog´ni zant) *adj*. Lacking awareness.

in-co-her-ence (in´kō hēr´ens) *n*. The quality of being incoherent; something incoherent.

in-co-her-ent (in´kō hēr´ent) *adj*. Lacking order, connection, or harmony; unable to think or speak clearly or consecutively. **in-**coherently *adv*.

in-com-bus-ti-ble (in´kom bus´ti bl) *adj*. Incapable of burning. **incombustible** *n*.

in-come (in´kum) *n*. Money or its equivalent received in return for work or as profit from investments.

income account *n*. Financial statement of profit and loss for a particular period.

income tax *n*. A tax on income earned by an individual or business.

in-com-ing (in´kum´ing) *adj*. Coming in or soon to come in.

in-com-men-su-ra-ble (in´ko men´shėr a bl) *adj*. Lacking a basis of comparison; utterly disproportionate.

in-com-men-su-rate (in´ko men´shėr it) *adj*. Not commensurate; disproportionate; inadequate. **incommensurately** *adv*.

in-com-mode (in´ko mōd´) *v*. To inconvenience; to disturb.

in-com-mu-ni-ca-ble (in´ko mū´ni ka bl) *adj*. Not communicable; incapable of being communicated; ineffable.

in-com-mu-ni-ca-do (in´ko mū´ni kä´dō) *adj. & adv*. Without being able to communicate with others; restrained from communication, as a prisoner in solitary confinement.

in-com-mu-ni-ca-tive (in´ko mū´ni ka ˈtiv) *adj*. Not communicative; not disposed to talk.

in-com-mut-a-ble (in´ko mū´ta bl) *adj*. Not commutable; unchangeable; incapable of being exchanged.

in-com-pa-ra-ble (in kom´pėr a bl) *adj*. Incapable of being compared; without rival. **incomparably** *adv*.

in-com-pat-i-ble (in´kom pat´a bl) *adj*. Not suited for combination or association; inconsistent. **incompatibility** *n*. **incompatibly** *adv*.

in-com-pe-tent (in kom´pi tent) *adj*. Not competent. **incompetence** *n*. **incompetency** *n*. **incompetent** *n*.

in-com-plete (in´kom plēt´) *adj*. Not complete; unfinished. **incompletely** *adv*. **incompleteness** *n*.

in-com-ple-tion (in´kom plē´shan) *n*. Lack

of completion.

in-com-pre-hen-si-ble (in˝kom pri hen´si bl) *adj.* Unable to be understood; unintelligible.

in-com-pre-hen-sion (in˝kom pri hen´shən) *n.* Lack of understanding.

in-com-put-a-ble (in˝kom pū´ta bl) *adj.* Incapable of being computed.

in-con-ceiv-a-ble (in˝kon sē´va bl) *adj.* Not imaginable; unthinkable; impossible to understand.

in-con-clu-sive (in˝kon klŏ´siv) *adj.* Having no definite result; indefinite.

in-con-den-sa-ble (in˝kon den´sa bl) *adj.* Incapable of being condensed.

in-con-dite (in kon´dit) *adj.* Being put together badly; crude.

in-con-gru-i-ty (in˝kong grŏ´i tē) *n. pl.* **incongruities** The quality or state of being incongruous; that which seems out of place.

in-con-gru-ous (in kong´grŏ us) *adj.* Not corresponding; disagreeing; made up of diverse or discordant elements; unsuited to the surroundings or setting; inappropriate. **incongruously** *adv.*

in-con-sec-u-tive (in˝kon sek´ū tiv) *adj.* Not successive.

in-con-se-quent (in kon´se kwent˝) *adj.* Not illogical; irrelevant; disconnected. **inconsequently** *adv.*

in-con-se-quen-tial (in´kon se kwen´shal) *adj.* Without importance; petty. **inconsequentially** *adv.*

in-con-sid-er-a-ble (in´kon sid´ėr a bl) *adj.* Not worthy of ones consideration; unimportant; trivial. **inconsiderably** *adv.*

in-con-sid-er-ate (in´kon sid´ėr it) *adj.* Not considerate for the feelings of others; thoughtless. **inconsiderately** *adv.* **inconsiderateness** *n.*

in-con-sis-tent (in´kon sis´tent) *adj.* Lacking firmness, harmony, or compatibility; incoherent in thought or actions; not consistent.

in-con-sol-a-ble (in˝kon sō´la bl) *adj.* Not capable of being consoled; sad. **inconsolably** *adv.*

in-con-so-nant (in kon´so nant) *adj.* Not

constant; likely to change.

in-con-spic-u-ous (in´kon spik´ū us) *adj.* Not readily seen or noticed. **inconspicuously** *adv.* **inconspicuousness** *n.*

in-con-stant (in kon´stant) *adj.* Likely to change; unpredictable; faithless; fickle. **inconstancy** *n.* **inconstantly** *adv.*

in-con-sum-a-ble (in´kon sŏ´ma bl) *adj.* Unfit to be consumed; incapable of being consumed.

in-con-test-a-ble (in˝kon tes´ta bl) *adj.* Not to be disputed; indisputable.

in-con-ti-nent (in kon´ti nent) *adj.* Not restrained; uncontrolled; unable to contain or restrain something specified; incapable of controlling the excretory functions. **incontinence** *n.* **incontinently** *adv.*

in-con-trol-la-ble (in˝kon trō´la bl) *adj.* Uncontrollable; unmanageable.

in-con-tro-vert-i-ble (in´kon tro vėr´ta bl) *adj.* Unquestionable; indisputable. **incontrovertibly** *adv.*

in-con-ven-ience (in´kon vēn´yens) *n.* The quality or state of being inconvenient; something inconvenient. **inconvenience** *v.* To cause inconvenience to; to bother.

in-con-ven-ient (in´kon vēn´yent) *adj.* Not convenient or handy; giving trouble. **inconveniently** *adv.*

in-con-vert-i-ble (in˝kon vür´ta bl) *adj.* Incapable of being or exchanged; currency that cannot be exchanged for foreign currency.

in-con-vin-ci-ble (in˝kon vin´si bl) *adj.* Incapable of being convinced.

in-cor-po-rate (in kor´po rāt˝) *v.* To combine into a unified whole; to unite; to form or cause to form a legal corporation; to give a physical form to; to embody. **incorporation** *n.* **incorporator** *n.*

in-cor-po-rat-ed (in kor´po rā´tid) *adj.* Constituted as a legal corporation; united as one.

in-cor-po-re-al (in˝kor pōr´ē al) *adj.* Without material form or substance. **incorporeally** *adv.*

in-cor-rect (in˝ko rekt´) *adj.* Not correct; inaccurate; not true; wrong; improper.

in-cor-ri-gi-ble (in kor´i ji bl) *adj.* Incapable of being corrected. **incorrigible** *n.* **incorrigibility** *n.* **incorrigibly** *adv.*

in-cor-rupt (in˜ko rupt´) *adj.* Incapable of corruption, or dissolution; free from error.

in-cor-rupt-i-ble (in´ko rup´ti bl) *adj.* Not capable of being corrupted morally; not subject to decay. **incorruptibility** *n.* **incorruptibly** *adv.*

in-cras-sate (in-kras´āt) *v.* To make thicker by evaporation or by adding another substance.

in-crease (in krēs´) *v.* To make or become greater or larger; to have offspring; to reproduce. **increase** *n.* The act of increasing; the amount or rate of increasing. **increasingly** *adv.*

in-cred-i-ble (in kred´i bl) *adj.* Too unlikely to be believed; unbelievable; extraordinary; astonishing. **incredibility** *n.* **incredibly** *adv.* **incredibleness** *n.*

in-cred-u-lous (in krej´u lus) *adj.* Skeptical; disbelieving; expressive of disbelief. **incredulity** *n.* **incredulously** *adv.*

in-cre-ment (in´kre ment) *n.* An increase; something gained or added, especially one of a series of regular additions. **incremental** *adj.*

in-cre-tion (in krē´shan) *n.* The substance secreted internally by an endocrine gland.

in-crim-i-nate (in krim´i nāt´) *v.* To involve in or charge with a wrongful act, as a crime. **incrimination** *n.* **incriminatory** *adj.*

in-crust (in krust´) *v.* To cover with a crust; to form a crust on the surface of something.

in-cu-bate (in´kū bāt´) *v.* To warm and hatch eggs, either by bodily heat or artificial means; to maintain a bacterial culture in favorable conditions for growth. **incubation** *n.*

in-cu-ba-tor (in´kū bā˜tėr) *n.* A cabinet in which a desired temperature can be maintained, used for bacterial culture; an enclosure for maintaining a premature infant in a controlled environment; a temperature-controlled enclosure for hatching eggs.

in-cu-bus (in´kū bus) *n. pl.* **incubuses** *or* **incubi** An evil spirit believed to seize or harm sleeping persons; a nightmare; a nightmarish burden.

in-cul-cate (in kul´kāt) *v.* To impress on the mind by frequent repetition or instruction. **inculcation** *n.* **inculcator** *n.*

in-cul-pa-ble (in kul´pa bl) *adj.* Not culpable; free from guilt or blame.

in-cul-pate (in kul´pāt) *v.* To incriminate.

in-cum-bent (in kum´bent) *adj.* Lying or resting on something else; imposed as an obligation; obligatory; currently in office. **incumbent** *n.* A person who is currently in an elective office. **incumbency** *n.* **incumbently** *adv.*

in-cu-nab-u-lum (in´kū nab´ū lum) *n. pl.* **incunabula** A book printed before 1501; earliest beginning of anything.

in-cur (in ker´) *v.* To become liable or subject to, especially because of one's own actions. **incurrence** *n.*

in-cur-a-ble (in kür´a bl) *adj.* Unable to be cured of a disease.

in-cu-ri-ous (in kür´ē us) *adj.* Lacking interest; detached.

in-cur-rent (in kür´ent) *n.* A current that flows inward.

in-cur-sion (in kür´zhan) *n.* A sudden hostile intrusion into another's territory.

in-cur-vate (in´ kür vāt´) *v.* To cause something to curve inward. **incurvate** *adj.*

in-curve (in kürv´) *v.* To curve or bend inward.

in-cus (ing´kus) *n. pl.* **incudes** An anvil-shaped bone in the middle ear of mammals.

in-cuse (in kūz´) *v.* To form or impress by striking or stamping.

Ind *abbr.* Indiana.

ind-amine (in´da mēn˜) *n.* Basic organic compounds which form blue and green salts, used to manufacture dyes.

in-debt-ed (in det´id) *adj.* Obligated to another, as for money or a favor; beholden. **indebtedness** *n.*

in-de-cent (in dē´sent) *adj.* Morally offensive or contrary to good taste. **indecency** *n.* **indecently** *adv.*

in-de-cid-u-ous (in˜di sij´ŏ us) *adj.* Not

deciduous.

in-de-ci-pher-a-ble (in´di sī´fėr a bl) *adj.* Not capable of being deciphered or interpreted.

in-de-ci-sion (in´di sizh´an) *n.* Inability to make up one's mind; irresolution.

in-de-ci-sive (in´di sī´siv) *adj.* Without a clear-cut result; marked by indecision. **indecisively** *adv.* **indecisiveness** *n.*

in-de-clin-able (in´di klī´na bl) *adj.* Not declinable.

in-dec-o-rous (in dek´ėr us) *adj.* Lacking good taste or propriety. **indecorously** *adv.* **indecorousness** *n.*

in-deed (in dēd´) *adv.* Most certainly; without doubt; in reality; in fact. **indeed** *interj.* Used to express surprise, irony, or disbelief.

in-de-fat-i-ga-ble (in´di fat´i ga bl) *adj.* Tireless. **indefatigably** *adv.*

in-de-fen-si-ble (in´di fen´si bl) *adj.* Incapable of being justified; not able to protect against a physical fight.

in-de-fin-a-ble (in´di fī´na bl) *adj.* Not capable of being defined. **indefinableness** *n.* **indefinably** *adv.*

in-def-i-nite (in def´i nit) *adj.* Not decided or specified; vague; unclear; lacking fixed limits. **indefinitely** *adv.* **indefiniteness** *n.*

in-del-i-ble (in del´i bl) *adj.* Not able to be erased or washed away; permanent. **indelibly** *adv.*

in-del-i-cate (in del´i kit) *adj.* Lacking sensitivity; tactless or crude. **indelicacy** *n.* **indelicately** *adv.*

in-dem-ni-fy (in dem´ni fī´) *v.* To secure against hurt, loss, or damage; to make compensation for hurt, loss, or damage. **indemnification** *n.* **indemnifier** *n.*

in-dem-ni-ty (in dem´ni tē) *n. pl.* **indemnities** Security against hurt, loss, or damage; a legal exemption from liability for damages; compensation for hurt, loss, or damage.

in-de-mon-stra-ble (in´di mon´stra bl) *adj.* Incapable of being demonstrated.

in-dent (in dent´) *v.* To set in from the margin, as the first line of a paragraph; to notch the edge of; to serrate; to make a dent or depression in; to impress; to stamp. **indent** *n.* An indentation.

in-den-ta-tion (in´den tā´shan) *n.* The act of indenting or the state of being indented; an angular cut in an edge; a recess in a surface.

in-den-ture (in den´chėr) *n.* A legal deed or contract; a contract obligating one party to work for another for a specified period of time. **indenture** *v.* To bind into the service of another.

in-de-pend-ence (in´di pen´dens) *n.* The quality or state of being independent.

Independence Day *n.* July 4, a legal holiday in the United States, commemorating the adoption of the Declaration of Independence in 1776.

in-de-pend-ent (in´di pen´dent) *adj.* Politically self-governing; free from the control of others; not committed to a political party or faction; not relying on others, especially for financial support; providing or having enough income to enable one to live without working. **independent** *n.* One who is independent, especially a candidate or voter not committed to a political party. **independently** *adv.*

in—depth *adj.* Thorough; detailed.

in-de-scrib-a-ble (in´di skrī´ba bl) *adj.* Surpassing description; incapable of being described. **indescribably** *adv.*

in-de-struc-ti-ble (in´di struk´ti bl) *adj.* Unable to be destroyed.

in-de-ter-mi-na-ble (in´di tėr´mi na bl) *adj.* Unable to determine, as certain, or fixed; not able to be decided.

in-de-ter-mi-nate (in´di tėr´mi nit) *adj.* Not determined; not able to be determined; unclear or vague. **indeterminacy** *n.* **indeterminately** *adv.*

in-de-ter-min-ism (in´di tėr´mi niz˝um) *n.* The theory maintaining that not every event has a cause.

in-dex (in´deks) *n. pl.* **indexes** *or* **indices** A list for aiding reference, especially an alphabetized listing in a printed work which gives the pages on which various names, places, and subjects are mentioned; something serving to guide or point out, especially a printed character calling attention to a paragraph or section; something that measures or indicates; a pointer, as in an instrument; in mathematics, a small number just above and to the left of a radical sign indicating what root is to be extracted; any number or symbol indicating an operation to be performed on an expression; a number or scale indicating change in magnitude, as of prices, relative to the magnitude at some specified point usually taken as one hundred (100). **index** *v.* To provide with or enter in an index; to indicate; to adjust through.

in-dex-a-tion (in´deks ā˝sha**n)** *n.* The linkage of economic factors, as wages or prices, to a cost-of-living index so they rise and fall within the rate of inflation.

index finger *n.* The finger next to the thumb.

index fossil *n.* The fossil having a narrow time span, used to establish the age of surrounding geological formations.

index number *n.* A number which indicates change in a factor, as the cost of living, from one year or reference point chosen arbitrarily to another specifed time.

index of refraction *n.* The quotient of the speed of light in a vacuum divided by the speed of light in a medium under consideration.

In-di-a (in´dē *a***)** *n.* A country in southern Asia.

in-di-an (in´dē *a***n)** *n.* A native or inhabitant of India; a member of various aboriginal peoples of the Americas.

In-di-an-a (in´dē *a***n** *a***)** *n.* A state located in the central part of the northern United States; statehood December 11, 1816; state capital Indianapolis. **Indianian** *n. & adj.*

Indian corn *n.* A tall American cereal grass bearing seeds on elongated ears.

Indian Ocean *n.* An ocean that extends from southern Asia to Antarctica and from eastern Africa to southeastern Australia.

Indian summer *n.* A period of mild weather in late autumn.

in-di-cate (in´di kāt´) *v.* To point out; to show; to serve as a sign or symptom; to signify; to suggest the advisability of; to call for. **indication** *n.* **indicator** *n.*

in-dic-a-tive (in dik´a tiv) *adj.* Serving to indicate; of or being a verb mood used to express actions and conditions that are objective facts. **indicative** *n.* The indicative mood; a verb in the indicative mood.

in-di-ca-tor (in´di kā˝tèr) *n.* A pressure gauge; a dial that registers pressure, speed, etc.

in-dict (in dīt´) *v.* To accuse of an offense; to charge; to make a formal accusation against by the findings of a grand jury. **indictable** *adj.* **indicter** *n.* **indictor** *n.* **indictment** *n.*

in-dif-fer-ence (in dif´èr *e***ns)** *n.* The quality of being different.

in-dif-fer-ent (in dif´èr ent) *adj.* Having no marked feeling or preference; impartial; neither good nor bad. **indifferently** *adv.*

in-di-gence (in´di jens) *n.* The condition of real hardship; poverty.

in-di-gene (in´di jēn˝) *n.* A native; a person originating from a particular area or country.

in-dig-e-nous (in dij´e nus) *adj.* Living or occurring naturally in an area; native.

in-di-gent (in´di jent) *adj.* Impoverished; needy.

in-di-gest-i-ble (in˝di jes´ti bl) *adj.* Not easily digestible.

in-di-ges-tion (in´di jes´cha**n)** *n.* Difficulty or discomfort in digesting food.

in-dig-nant (in dig´na**nt)** *adj.* Marked by or filled with indignation; displeasure. **indignantly** *adv.*

in-dig-na-tion (in´dig nā´sha**n)** *n.* Anger aroused by injustice, unworthiness, or unfairness.

in-dig-ni-ty (in dig´ni tē) *n. pl.* **indignities** Humiliating treatment; something that offends one's pride.

in-di-go (in´di gō´) *n. pl.* **indigos** *or* **indigoes** A blue dye obtained from a plant or produced synthetically; a dark blue.

indigo bunting *n.* A small North American bird, the male of which has deep blue plumage.

indigo snake *n.* A nonvenomous bluish-black snake found in the southern United States and northern Mexico.

in-di-rect (in´di rekt´) *adj.* Not taking a direct course; not straight to the point. **indirection** *n.* **indirectly** *adv.*

indirect lighting *n.* A type lighting where the light emitted is diffused and reflected, to minimize glare.

indirect object *n.* A word that usually follows a verb and represents the secondary goal of the recipient.

in-dis-cov-er-a-ble (in˝di skuv´ẽr a bl) *adj.* Undiscoverable.

in-dis-creet (in˝di skrēt´) *adj.* Lacking sound judgment; imprudent; not discreet. **indiscreetly** *adv.*

in-dis-crete(in˝di skrēt´)*adj.* Not consisting of distinct parts.

in-dis-cre-tion (in˝di skresh´an) *n.* The condition of being indiscreet; want of discretion; lack of discretion.

in-dis-crim-i-nate (in˝di skrim´i nit) *adj.* Not discriminate; haphazard.

in-dis-pen-sa-ble (in´di spen´sa bl) *adj* Necessary; essential. **indispensability** *n.* **indispensable** *n.* **indispensably** *adv.*

in-dis-pose (in˝di spōz´) *v.* To make or render unfit; to disqualify.

in-dis-posed *adj.* Mildly ill.

in-dis-put-a-ble (in˝di spū´ta bl) *adj.* Not disputable; incontrovertible.

in-dis-sol-u-ble (in˝di sol´ū bl) *adj.* Not capable of being dissolved; not capable of being broken.

in-dis-tinct (in˝di stingkt´) *adj.* Not distinct; not sharply outlined; blurred; not clear; confused.

in-dis-tinc-tive (in˝di stingk´ tiv) *adj.* Without distinctive characteristics.

in-dis-tin-guish-a-ble (in˝di sting´gwi sha bl) *adj.* Unable to determine in shape or structure; not clearly recognizable; lacking identity.

in-dite (in dīt´) *v.* To write; to compose; to put down in writing. **inditer** *n.*

in-di-um (in´dē um) *n.* A soft, silver-white, metallic element used for mirrors and transistor compounds, symbolized by In.

in-di-vid-u-al (in´di vij´ŏ al) *adj.* Of, for, or relating to a single human being. **individually** *adv.*

in-di-vid-u-al-ism (in˝di vij´ŏ a liz˝um) *n.* A theory advocating independent action of the individual; the habit of an individual or independent action.

in-di-vid-u-al-ist (in˝di vij´ŏ a list) *n.* A person markedly independent in his thoughts and actions.

in-di-vid-u-al-i-ty (in˝di vij´ŏ al´i tē) *n.* *pl.* **individualities** The condition of having a separate existence.

in-di-vis-i-ble (in´di viz´i bl) *adj.* Not able to be divided.

In-do-chi-na (in´dō chī na) *n.* The southeastern peninsula of Asia.

in-doc-ile (in dos´il) *adj.* Not docile; being difficult to control or train.

in-doc-tri-nate (in dok´tri nāt´) *v.* To instruct in a doctrine or belief; to train to accept a system of thought uncritically. **indoctrination** *n.*

In-do—Eu-ro-pe-an (in´dō ūr˝o pē´an) *n.* A family of languages comprising most of the languages of Europe and parts of southern Asia. **Indo—European** *adj.*

in-dole (in´dōl) *n.* A crystalline compound, of yellow or white that's produced in the intestines as a decomposition of protein.

in-do-lent (in´do lent) *adj.* Disinclined to exert oneself; lazy. **indolence** *n.*

in-dom-i-ta-ble (in dom´i ta bl) *adj.* Incapable of being subdued or defeated. **indomitably** *adv.*

In-do-ne-sia (in˝do nē´zē a) *n.* A country of southeastern Asis.

in-door (in´dōr˝) *adj.* Occurring inside a building or house rather than outdoors.

in-draft (in´draft˝) *n.* A drawing inward; an inward current.

in-drawn (in´drawn˝) *adj.* To be drawn in, as a breath.

in-du-bi-ta-ble (in dŏ´bi ta bl) *adj.* Certain; unquestionable.

in-duce (in dōs´) *v.* To move by persuasion or influence; to cause to occur; to infer by inductive reasoning. **inducer** *n.*

in-duce-ment (in dōs´ment) *n.* The act of inducing; something that induces.

in-duct (in dukt´) *v.* To place formally in office; to admit as a new member; to summon into military service. **inductee** *n.*

in-duc-tance (in duk´tans) *n.* A circuit element, usually a conducting coil, in which electromagnetic induction generates electromotive force.

in-duc-tile (in duk´til) *adj.* Not pliable; unyielding.

in-duc-tion (in duk´shan) *n.* The act of inducting or of being inducted; reasoning in which conclusions are drawn from particular instances or facts; the generation of electromotive force in a closed circuit by a magnetic field that changes with time; the production of an electric charge in an uncharged body by bringing a charged body close to it.

induction coil *n.* An electrical apparatus that interruptions in the direct current running through a primary coil which produces an induced current of high voltage, a secondary coil of a larger number of turns in which high voltage is induced.

in-duc-tive (in duk´tiv) *adj.* Inducing; leading on; introductory.

in-dulge (in dulj´) *v.* To give in to the desires of, especially to excess; to yield to; to allow oneself a special pleasure. **indulger** *n.*

in-dul-gence (in dul´jens) *n.* The practice of indulging; an indulgent act.

in-du-line (in´dū lēn) *n.* One of a large series of synthetic aniline dyes that yields a blue to purple color similar to true indigo.

in-dult (in dult´) *n.* A special dispensation granted in the Holy Roman Church.

in-du-pli-cate (in dō´pli kit) *adj.* Having the edges rolled inward, as a flower bud petal.

in-du-rate (in´dū rāt´) *v.* To make stubborn; to make hardy; to become hard. **indurative** *adj.* **induration** *n.*

in-du-si-um (in dō´zē um) *n.* The covering or outgrowth of a fern.

in-dus-tri-al (in dus´trē al) *adj.* Of, relating to, or used in industry involved in industrial products. **industrially** *adv.*

industrial arts *n.* A class or course of study, taught in schools, that trains technical skills in the use of tools and machinery.

in-dus-tri-al-ism (in dus´trē a liz˝um) *n.* An economic system where industrial interests predominate, as opposed to the interests of foreign or agriculture trade.

industrial school *n.* A school that specializes in the teaching of one or more branches of industry.

industrial union *n.* A labor union that admits membership regardless of occupation, skill, or craft.

in-dus-tri-ous (in dus´trē us) *adj.* Working steadily and hard; diligent. **industriously** *adv.* **industriousness** *n.*

in-dus-try (in´du strē) *n. pl.* **industries** The commercial production and sale of goods and services; a branch of manufacture and trade; industrial management as distinguished from labor; diligence.

in-dwell (in dwel´) *v.* To exist within; to occupy.

in-e-bri-ant (in ē´brē ant) *n.* Anything that intoxicates.

in-e-bri-ate (in ē´brē at´) *v.* To make drunk; to intoxicate. **inebriate** *n.* **inebriated** *adj.* **inebriation** *n.*

in-ed-i-ble (in ed´i bl) *adj.* Not edible; not useful as food.

in-ed-it-ed (in ed´i tid) *adj.* Not edited; unabridged.

in-ef-fa-ble (in ef´a bl) *adj.* Beyond expression; indescribable. **ineffably** *adv.*

in-ef-fec-tive (in˝i fek´tiv) *adj.* Not producing an intended or desired results; inefficient.

in-ef-fec-tu-al (in˝i fek´chō al) *adj.* Not producing the intended effect; unwilling to produce a required result.

in-ef-fi-ca-cious (in˝ef i kā´ shus) *adj.* Not having the power, or means to produce an intended effect.

in-ef-fi-ca-cy (in ef′*i* k*a* sē) *n*. Lack of the means or force to achieve the desired results.

in-ef-fi-cient (in′i fish′*e*nt) *adj*. Wasteful of time, energy, or materials. **inefficiency** *n*. **inefficiently** *adv*.

in-el-e-gant (in el′*e* g*a*nt) *adj*. Not elegant; lacking in grace or refinement.

in-el-i-gi-ble (in el′*i* ji bl) *adj*. Not eligible; not qualified or worthy of being chosen.

in-el-o-quent (in el′*o* kw*e*nt) *adj*. Not eloquent.

in-e-luc-ta-ble (in′i luk′t*a* bl) *adj*. Not capable of being avoided or overcome. **ineluctably** *adv*.

in-ept (in ept′) *adj*. Awkward or incompetent; not suitable. **ineptitude** *n*. **ineptness** *n*. **ineptly** *adv*.

in-e-qual-i-ty (in′i kwol′i tē) *n. pl.* **inequalities** The condition or quality of being unequal; the lack of evenness.

in-eq-ui-ta-ble (in ek′wi t*a* bl) *adj*. Not equitable; unfair.

in-eq-ui-ty *n. pl.* **inequities** Injustice; unfairness.

in-e-qui-valve (in ē′kw*i* valv″) *adj*. Having valves unequal in size and form, as in reference to a bivalve mollusk.

in-e-rad-i-ca-ble (in″i rad′*i* k*a* bl) *adj*. Not eradicable; incapable of being eradicated.

in-er-rant (in er′ *a*nt) adj. Free from any error.

in-ert (in ert′) *adj*. Not able to move or act; slow to move or act; sluggish; displaying no chemical activity. **inertly** *adv*.

in-er-tia (in er′sha) *n*. The tendency of a body to remain at rest or to stay in motion unless acted upon by an external force; resistance to motion or change. **inertial** *adj*. **inertially** *adv*.

inertial guidance *n*. An automatic system of navigation by means of automatically controlling devices that resond to inertial forces as aircraft, missiles, and space vehicles.

in-es-cap-a-ble (in″*e* skā′p*a* bl) *adj*. That which is unavoidable.

in-es-sen-tial (in″i sen′sh*a*l) *adj*. Not necessary or essential.

in-es-ti-ma-ble (in es′t*i* ma bl) *adj*. Unable of being estimated or computed; too great to be fully appreciated.

in-ev-i-ta-ble (in ev′i t*a* bl) *adj*. Not able to be avoided or prevented. **inevitability** *n*. **inevitably** *adv*.

in-ex-cus-a-ble (in″ik skū′z*a* bl) *adj*. Unpardonable; indefensible.

in-ex-haust-i-ble (in″ig zas′ti bl) *adj*. Not exhaustible; unfailing; tireless.

in-ex-ist-ence (in″ig zis′t*e*ns) *n*. Nonexistence.

in-ex-is-tent *adj*. Not existent.

in-ex-o-ra-ble (in ek′sėr *a* bl) *adj*. Not capable of being moved by entreaty; unyielding. **inexorably** *adv*.

in-ex-pe-di-ent (in″ik spē′dē *e*nt) *adj*. Not expedient; inappropriate.

in-ex-pen-sive (in″ik spen′siv) *adj*. Not expensive; cheep.

in-ex-pe-ri-ence (in″ik spėr′ē *e*ns) *n*. The lack of experience; without knowledge.

in-ex-pert (in eks′pėrt) *adj*. Unskilled.

in-ex-pi-a-ble (in eks′pē *a* bl) *adj*. Incapable of being atoned; unpardonable.

in-ex-pli-ca-ble (in eks′pl*i* k*a* bl) *adj*. Not capable of being explained; unable to be interpreted. **inexplicably** *adv*.

in-ex-pli-cit (in″ik splis′it) *adj*. Not explicit; not clearly stated.

in-ex-pres-sive (in″ik spres′iv) *adj*. Not expressive; wanting in meaning.

in-ex-pug-na-ble (in″ik spug′n*a* bl) *adj*. Cannot be overcome or taken by force; impregnable.

in-ex-tin-guish-a-ble (in ik sting′gwish*a* bl) *adj*. Not to be extinguished.

in ex-tre-mis (in ex trēm′is) *adv*. At the point of death.

in-ex-tri-ca-ble (in eks′tri k*a* bl) *adj*. Not capable of being untied or untangled; too complex to resolve. **inextricably** *adv*.

in-fal-li-ble (in fal′*i* bl) *adj*. Not capable of making mistakes; not capable of failing; never wrong. **infallibility** *n*. **infallibly** *adv*.

in-fa-mous (in′f*a* mus) *adj*. Having a very

bad reputation; shocking or disgraceful. **infamously** *adv.*

in-fa-my (in´fa mē) *n. pl.* **infamies** Evil notoriety or reputation; the state of being infamous; a disgraceful, publicly known act.

in-fan-cy (in´fan sē) *n. pl.* **infancies** The condition or time of being an infant; an early stage of existence; in law, minority.

in-fant (in´fant) *n.* A child in the first period of life; a very young child; in law, a minor.

in-fan-ti-cide (in fan´ti sīd´) *n.* The killing of an infant.

in-fan-tile (in´fan tīl´) *adj.* Of or relating to infants or infancy; immature; childish. **infantile paralysis** *n.* Poliomyelitis.

in-fan-ti-lism (in´fan ti liz˝um) *n.* Abnormal recurrence of childish characteristics; a lack of mature emotional development.

in-fan-try (in´fan trē) *n. pl.* **infantries** The branch of an army made up of soldiers who are trained to fight on foot.

in-farct (in färkt´) *n.* An area of dead tissue caused by an insufficient supply of blood. **infarcted** *adj.* **infarction** *n.*

in-fat-u-ate (in fach´ū āt´) *v.* To arouse an extravagant or foolish love in. **infatuated** *adj.* **infatuation** *n.*

in-fea-si-ble (in fē´zi bl) *adj.* Not feasible; impracticable.

in-fect (in fekt´) *v.* To contaminate with disease-producing organisms; to transmit a disease to; to affect as if by contagion. **infecter** *n.*

in-fec-tion (in fek´shan) *n.* Invasion of a bodily part by disease-producing organisms; the condition resulting from such an invasion; an infectious disease.

in-fec-tious (in fek´shus) *adj.* Causing infection; communicable by infection, as diseases; contagious; catching.

infectious hepatitis *n.* An acute liver inflammation caused by a virus and is transmitted in food and water that has been contaminated with fecal matter.

infectious mononucleosis *n.* An acute, contagious, viral disease characterized by fever and sore throat and the swelling of the lymph nodes.

in-fe-cund (in fē´kund) *adj.* Barren; not fruitful.

in-fe-lic-i-tous *adj.* Not happy; unfortunate; not apt, as in expression.

in-fe-lic-i-ty (in˝fe lis´i tē) *n. pl.* **infelicities** The state of being unhappy.

in-fer (in fer´) *v.* To conclude by reasoning; to deduce; to have as a logical consequence; to lead to as a result or conclusion. **inferable** *adj.*

in-fer-ence (in´fer ens) *n.* A conclusion based on facts and premises.

in-fe-ri-or (in fēr´ē er) *adj.* Located under or below; low or lower in order, rank, or quality. **inferior** *n.* **inferiority** *n.*

inferiority complex *n.* A condition of acute sense of personal inferiority resulting in timidity; withdrawal from social contact.

in-fer-nal (in fer´nal) *adj.* Of, like, or relating to hell; damnable; abominable. **infernally** *adv.*

in-fer-no (in fer´nō) *n.* A place or condition suggestive of hell.

in-fer-tile (in fer´til) *adj.* Not fertile or fruitful; barren. **infertility** *n.*

in-fest (in fest´) *v.* To spread in or over so as to be harmful or offensive.

in-fi-del (in´fi del) *n.* One who has no religion; an unbeliever in a religion, especially Christianity.

in-fi-del-i-ty (in˝fi del´i tē) *n. pl.* **infidelities** The lack of faith or belief; unfaithfulness to a moral obligation; adultery.

in-field (in´fēld˝) *n.* In baseball, the part of a playing field within the base lines.

in-fight-ing (in´fī˝ting) *n.* A prolonged struggle within an organization for leadership or power. **infighter** *n.*

in-fil-trate (in fil´trāt) *v.* To pass or cause to pass into something through pores or small openings; to pass through or enter gradually or stealthily. **infiltration** *n.*

in-fi-nite (in´fi nit) *adj.* Without boundaries; limitless; immeasurably great or large; in mathematics, greater in value than any specified number, however large; having measure that is infinite.

in-fin-i-tes-i-mal (in′fin i tes′i mal) adj. Immeasurably small. infinitesimally adv.

in-fin-i-tive (in fin′i tiv) n. A verb form which expresses the first person singular that performs the functions of a noun, usually preceded by to.

in-fin-i-ty (in fin′i tē) n. pl. infinities The quality or state of being infinite; unbounded space, time, or amount; an indefinitely large number.

in-firm (in ferm′) adj. Physically weak, especially from age; feeble; not sound or valid.

in-fir-ma-ry (in fer′ma rē) n. pl. infirmaries An institution for the care of the sick or disabled.

in-fir-mi-ty (in fur′mi tē) n. The state of being infirm; condition of feebleness.

in-fix (in fiks′) v. To fasten or fix; to instill; to insert; to fix, as thoughts or principles.

in-flame (in flām′) v. To set on fire; to arouse to strong or excessive feeling; to intensify; to produce, affect or be affected by inflammation.

in-flam-ma-ble (in flam′a bl) adj. Tending to catch fire easily; easily excited.

in-flam-ma-tion (in′fla mā′shan) n. Localized redness, swelling, heat, and pain in response to an injury or infection.

in-flam-ma-to-ry (in flam′a tōr″ē) adj. Tending to excite or anger, to inflame, anger. Med. Causing inflammation, usually accompanied by heat.

in-flate (in flāt′) v. To fill and expand with a gas; to increase unsoundly; to puff up; to raise prices abnormally. inflatable adj.

in-fla-tion (in flā′shan) n. The act or process of inflating; a period during which there is an increase in the monetary supply, causing a continuous rise in the price of goods.

in-flect (in flekt′) v. To turn; to veer; to vary the tone or pitch of the voice, especially in speaking; to change the form of a word to indicate number, tense, or person. inflective adj. inflection n.

in-flex-i-ble (in flek′si bl) adj. Not flexible; rigid; not subject to change; unalterable.

inflexibility n. inflexibly adv.

in-flict (in flikt′) v. To cause to be suffered; to impose. inflicter n. inflictor n. infliction n.

in-flo-res-cence (in′flō res′ens) n. A characteristic arrangement of flowers on a stalk. inflorescent adj.

in-flu-ence (in′flō ens) n. The power to produce effects, especially indirectly or through an intermediary; the condition of being affected; one exercising indirect power to sway or affect. influence v. To exert influence over; to modify. influential adj.

in-flu-ent (in′flō ent) adj. Flowing in. n. Something that flows in, as a tributary stream into a larger body of water.

in-flu-en-za (in′flō en′za) n. An acute, infectious viral disease marked by respiratory inflammation, fever, muscular pain, and often intestinal discomfort; the flu.

in-flux (in′fluks′) n. A stream of people or things coming in.

in-form (in form′) v. To communicate to give knowledge to; to make aware.

in-for-mal (in for′mal) adj. Not in usual form; unofficial; casual or relaxed.

in-for-mant (in for′mant) n. One who discloses or furnishes information which should remain secret.

in-for-ma-tion (in″fer mā′shan) n. The news communicated by word or in writing; data or facts; knowledge gained from reading of instruction, or gathered in another way.

information theory n. The statistical study or theory that deals with the processes and efficiency of transmitted messages, as in a computer or telecommunications.

in-for-ma-tive (in for′ma tiv) adj. Providing information; instructive.

in-frac-tion (in frak′shan) n. A violation of a rule.

in-fran-gi-ble (in fran′ji bl) adj. Not capable of being broken into parts; unbreakable.

in-fra-red (in´fra red´) *adj.* Of, being, or using electromagnetic radiation with wave lengths longer than those of visible light and shorter than those of microwaves.

in-fra-son-ic (in´fra son´ik) *adj.* Producing or using waves or vibrations with frequencies below those of audible sound.

in-fra-struc-ture (in´fra struk´chėr) *n.* An underlying base or foundation; the basic facilities needed for the functioning of a system.

in-fre-quent (in frē´kwent) *adj.* Seldom; not occurring frequently; rare; occasional. **infrequently** *adv.*

in-fringe (in frinj´) *v.* To break a law; to violate; to encroach; to trespass. **infringement** *n.*

in-fun-dib-u-li-form (in´fun dib´ū li form) *adj.* Having the form of a funnel; *Bot.* having a funnel-shaped flower.

in-fun-dib-u-lum (in´fun dib´ū lum) *n.* The funnel-shaped portion of the third ventricle in the brain that leads to the pituitary gland; the calyx of a kidney; the funnel-shaped abdominal opening of the fallopian tube.

in-fu-ri-ate (in fūr´ē āt´) *v.* To make very angry or furious; to enrage. **infuriatingly** *adv.* **infuriation** *n.*

in-fus-cate (in fus´kāt) *adj.* Darkened with a grayish or brownish-gray color, as the wing of an insect.

in-fuse (in fūz´) *v.* To introduce, instill or inculcate, as principles; to obtain a liquid extract by soaking a substance in water. **infusion** *n.*

-ing *suffix* Used in forming the present participle of verbs and adjectives resembling participles; activity or action; the result or a product of an action.

in-gath-er (in´gath ėr) *v.* To collect; bring in; to assemble or collect.

in-gem-i-nate (in jem´i nāt´) *v.* To repeat.

in-gen-ious (in jēn´yus) *adj.* Showing great ingenuity; to have inventive ability; clever. **ingeniously** *adv.* **ingeniousness** *n.*

in-ge-nu-i-ty (in´je nŏ´i tē) *n. pl.* **ingenuities** Cleverness; inventive skill.

in-gen-u-ous (in jen´ū us) *adj.* Frank and straightforward; lacking sophistication.

in-gest (in jest´) *v.* To take or put food into the body by swallowing. **ingestion** *n.* **ingestive** *adj.*

in-gle-nook (ing´gel nŭk´) *n.* A recessed area or corner near or beside a fireplace.

in-glo-ri-ous (in glōr´ē us) *adj.* Not showing courage or honor; dishonorable. **ingloriously** *adv.*

in-got (ing´got) *n.* A mass of cast metal shaped in a bar or block.

ingot iron *n.* Iron that has a high degree of purity, used in making special steels; a steel of high ductility and one that is rust resistant.

in-grain (in´grān´´) *v.* To impress firmly on the mind or nature. *n.* Fiber or yarn that is dyed before being spun or woven.

in-grained (in´grānd´´) *adj.* To be worked into the inmost texture; deep-seated.

in-grate (in´grāt) *n.* A person who is ungrateful.

in-gra-ti-ate (in grā´shē āt´) *v.* To gain favor or confidence of others by deliberate effort or manipulation. **ingratiatingly** *adv.* **ingratiation** *n.* **ingratiatory** *adj.*

in-grat-i-tude (in grat´i tŏd´) *n.* Lack of gratitude.

in-gra-ves-cent (in´´ gra ves´ant) *adj.* Increasing in severity. **ingravescence** *n.*

in-gre-di-ent (in grē´dē ent) *n.* An element that enters into the composition of a mixture; a part of anything.

in-gress (in´gres) *n.* A going in or entering of a building; an entrance. **ingression** *n.* **ingressive** *adj.*

in-grown (in´grōn´) *adj.* Growing into the flesh; growing abnormally within or into. **ingrowing** *adj.*

in-gui-nal (ing´gwi nal) *adj., Anat.* Of, pertaining to, or located in the groin.

in-gur-gi-tate (in gur´ji tāt´´) *v.* To swallow greedily or in great quantity.

in-hab-it (in hab´it) *v.* To reside in; to occupy as a home; where people live or work. **inhabitability** *n.* **inhabiter** *n.* **inhabitation** *n.* **inhabitable** *adj.*

in-hab-i-tant (in hab´i tant) *n.* A person who occupies a residence a permanently, as distinguished from someone who visits.

in-hal-ant (in hā´lant) *n.* Something that is inhaled. *adj.* Inhaling; used for inhaling.

in-ha-la-tion (in´ha lā´shan) *n.* The act of inhaling.

in-ha-la-tor (in´ha lā´tėr) *n.* A device that enables a person to inhale air, anesthetics, medicated vapors, or other matter.

in-hale (in´hāl´) *v.* To breathe or draw into the lungs, as air or tobacco smoke; the opposite of exhale.

in-hal-er (in´hāl´ėr) *n.* One that inhales; a respirator.

in-here (in her´) *v.* To be an essential or permanent feature; to belong.

in-her-ent (in hēr´ent) *adj.* Forming an essential element or quality of something. **inherently** *adv.*

in-her-it (in her´it) *v.* To receive something, as property, money, or other valuables, by legal succession or will. *n., Biol.* To receive traits or qualities from one's ancestors or parents. **inheritable** *adj.* **inheritor** *n.*

in-her-i-tance (in her´i tans) *n.* The act of inheriting; that which is inherited or to be inherited by legal transmission to an heir.

inheritance tax *n.* A tax imposed on an inherited estate.

in-he-sion (in hē´zhan) *n.* The fact of becoming a permanent part of something.

in-hib-it (in hib´it) *v.* To restrain or hold back; to prevent full expression. **inhibitable** *adj.* **inhibitor** *n.* **inhibiter** *n.* **inhibitive** *adj.* **inhibitory** *adj.*

in-hi-bi-tion (in´i bish´an) *n.* The act of restraining, especially a self-imposed restriction on one's behavior; a mental or psychological restraint.

in-hos-pi-ta-ble (in hos´pi ta bl) *adj.* Not showing hospitality; not friendly or receptive; uninviting. **inhospitableness** *n.* **inhospitably** *adv.* **inhospitality** *n.*

in—house (in hows´) *adj.* Of, relating to, or carried on within an organization.

in-human (in hū´man) *adj.* Lacking pity, emotional warmth, or kindness; monstrous; not being of the ordinary human type. **inhumanly** *adv.*

in-hu-mane (in´hū mān´) *adj.* Lacking compassion or pity; cruel. **inhumanely** *adv.*

in-hu-man-i-ty (in´hū man´i tē) *n. pl.* **inhumanities** The lack of compassion or pity; an inhumane or cruel act.

in-im-i-cal (i nim´i kal) *adj.* Harmful opposition; hostile; malign. **inimically** *adv.*

in-im-i-ta-ble (i nim´i ta bl) *adj.* Incapable of being matched; unique. **inimitably** *adv.*

in-iq-ui-ty (i nik´wi tē) *n. pl.* **iniquities** The grievous violation of justice; wickedness; sinfulness. **iniquitous** *adj.*

in-i-tial (i nish´al) *adj.* Of or pertaining to the beginning. **initial** *n.* The first letter of a name or word. **initial** *v.* To mark or sign with initials. **initially** *adv.*

in-i-ti-ate (i nish´ē āt´) *v.* To begin or start; to admit someone to membership in an organization, fraternity, or group; to instruct in fundamentals. **initiate** *adj.* Initiated. **initiator** *n.* **initiatory** *adj.*

in-i-ti-a-tive (i nish´ē a tiv) *n.* The ability to originate or follow through with a plan of action; the action of taking the first or leading step. *Govt.* The power or right to propose legislative measures.

in-ject (in jekt´) *v.* To force a drug or fluid into the body through a blood vessel or the skin with a hypodermic syringe; to throw in or introduce a comment abruptly. **injection** *n.*

in-ju-di-cious (in˝jŏ dish´us) *adj.* To act without discretion or sound judgment; unwise.

in-junc-tion (in jungk´shan) *n.* An authoritative command or order; in law, a court order requiring a person to refrain from some specified action. **injunctive** *adj.*

in-jure (in´jėr) *v.* To cause physical harm, damage, or pain.

in-ju-ri-ous (in jer´ē us) *adj.* Causing injury, damage or hurt; slanderous; abusive. **injuriously** *adv.* **injuriousness** *n.*

in-ju-ry (in´je rē) *n. pl.* **injuries** Damage or harm inflicted or suffered.

in-jus-tice (in jus´tis) *n.* The violation of another person's rights; an unjust act; a wrong.

ink (ingk) *n.* Any of variously colored liquids or pastes, used for writing, drawing, and printing; a dark fluid secreted by cephalopods such as squid for protecctive purposes. **inker** *n.* **inkiness** *n.*

ink-horn (ingk´horn˝) *n.* A small container to hold ink.

in-kle (ing´kl) *n.* A colored linen tape; also the linen thread it is made from.

ink-ling (ingk´ling) *n.* A slight suggestion or hint; a vague idea or notion.

ink-stand (ingk´stand˝) *n.* A stand or device for holding writing tools and ink.

ink-well (ingk´wel˝) *n.* A small container or reservoir for holding ink.

ink-y (ingk´ē) *adj.* Resembling ink in color; dark; black; containing or pertaining to ink.

in-laid (in´lād´) *adj.* Ornamented with wood, ivory, or other materials embedded flush with the surface.

in-land (in´land) *adj.* Pertaining to or located in the interior of a country. **inlander** *n.*

in–law (in´law) *n.* A relative by marriage.

in-lay (in´lā´) *v.* To set or embed something, as gold or ivory, into the surface of a decorative design.

in-let (in´let) *n.* A bay or stream that leads into land; a passage between nearby islands.

in-li-er (in´lī˝ėr) *n.* A rock formation completely surrounded by strata of a younger age.

in-mate (in´māt´) *n.* A person who dwells in a building with another; one confined in a prison, asylum, or hospital.

in memoriam (in me mōr´ē am) *prep. & adv.* In memory of; used in epitaphs.

in-most (in´mōst˝) *adj.* Farthest or deepest within; farthest from the surface or outside.

inn (in) *n.* A place of lodging where a traveler may obtain meals and lodging.

in-nards (in´ėrdz) *n., Slang* The internal organs or parts of the body, the inner parts of a machine.

in-nate (i nāt´) *adj.* Inborn and not acquired;

having as an essential part; inherent. **innately** *adv.*

in-ner (in´ėr) *adj.* Situated or occurring farther inside; relating to or of the mind or spirit.

inner ear *n.* The part of the ear which includes the semicircular canals, vestibule, and cochlea.

in-ner-most (in´ėr mōst´) *adj.* Most intimate; farthest within.

in-ner-sole (in´ėr sōl˝) *n.* The insole of a shoe.

inner space *n.* The space near the earth's surface; the ocean depths.

inner tube *n.* A flexible, inflatable rubber tube placed inside a pneumatic tire or used as a flotation device.

in-ner-vate (i nur´vāt) *v.* To supply with nerves. *n.* The communicating of nervous energy by means of nerves; the stimulation of some part or organ through its nerves.

in-nerve (i nurv´) *v.* To give nervous power or energy; invigorate.

in-ning (in´ing) *n.* In baseball, one of nine divisions of a regulation baseball game, in which each team has a turn at bat. **innings** *n. pl.* In the game of cricket, the time or period during which one side bats.

inn-keep-er (in´kē˝pėr) *n.* The proprietor or manager of an inn.

in-no-cent (in´o sent) *adj.* Free from sin, evil, or moral wrong; pure; legally free from blame or guilt; not maliciously intended; lacking in experience or knowledge; naive. **innocence** *n.* **innocent** *n.* **innocently** *adv.*

in-noc-u-ous (i nok´ū us) *adj.* Having no harmful qualities or ill effect; harmless.

in-nom-i-nate (i nom´i nit) *adj.* Anonymous; unnamed; untitled.

innominate bone *n., Anat.* One of the two large, irregular bones which form the sides of the pelvis.

in-no-vate (in´o vāt´) *v.* To introduce or begin something new. **innovative** *adj.* **innovator** *n.*

in-nu-en-do (in´ū en´dō) *n. pl.* **innuendos** *or* **innuendoes** An indirect or oblique comment, suggestion or hint.

in-nu-mer-a-ble (i nŏ´mėr *a* bl) *adj.* Too numerous; too much to be counted; countless.

in-ob-serv-ance (in˝*ob* zur´v*a*ns) *n.* Failure to heed or observe; inatttention; an intentional disregard.

in-oc-u-late (i nok´ū lāt´) *v.* To introduce a mild form of a disease or virus to a person or animal in order to produce immunity. **inoculation** *n.*

in-oc-u-lum (i nok´ū l*u*m) *n.* Material used for inoculation injections, usually made up of a bacteria or virus.

in-of-fen-sive (in˝*o* fen´siv) *adj.* Giving no harm, injury, or provocation.

in-op-er-a-ble (in op´ėr *a* bl) *adj.* Unworkable; incapable of being treated or improved by surgery.

in-op-er-a-tive (in op´ėr *a* tiv) *adj.* Not working; not functioning.

in-op-por-tune (in op´ėr tŏn´) *adj.* Inappropriate; untimely; unsuitable. **inopportunely** *adv.* **inopportuneness** *n.*

in-or-di-nate (in ir´d*i* nit) *adj.* Exceeding proper or normal limits; not regulated; unrestrained. **inordinately** *adv.*

in-or-gan-ic (in˝ir gan´ik) *adj.* Not having or involving living organisms, their remains, or products.

in-os-cu-late (in os´kū lāt˝) *v.* To unite or or join by connecting open ends, as nerve fibers and arteries.

in-o-si-tol (in nō´si tōl˝) *n.* A B complex vitamin essential to growth, found in animal and plant tissues.

in-pa-tient (in´pā´sh*e*nt) *n.* A patient admitted to a hospital for medical treatment.

in-per-so-nam (in pėr sō´nam) *adv.* Referring to a legal action against a person and not against specific things.

in-pour (in pōr´) *v.* To cause something as a liquid to flow into a container.

in-put (in´pŭt´) *n.* The amount of energy delivered to a machine; in computer science, information that is put into a data processing system. *n.* ,*Elect.* The voltage, current, or power that is delivered to a circuit.

in-quest (in´kwest) *n.* A legal investigation into the cause of death.

in-qui-line (in´kwi līn˝) *n.* An animal living with and sharing a habitation with another animal of another species.

in-quire (in kwīėr´) *v.* To ask a question; to make an investigation. **inquirer** *n.* **inquiringly** *adv.*

in-quir-y (in kwīėr´ē) *n. pl.* **inquiries** The act of seeking or inquiring; a request or question for information; a very close examination; an investigation or examination of facts or evidence.

in-qui-si-tion (in kwi´zish *a*n) *n.* A former Roman Catholic tribunal established to seek out and punish heretics; an interrogation that violates human rights; an investigation.

in-quis-i-tive (in kwiz´i tiv) *adj.* Curious; probing; questioning. **inquisitively** *adv.* **inquisitiveness** *n.*

in-quis-i-tor (in kwiz´i tėr) *n.* A person who inquires, makes inquisitions, or examines in an official or nonofficial way.

in-sa-lu-bri-ous (in˝s*a* lö´brē us) *adj.* Being unfavorable to ones health; unhealthy.

in-sane (in sān´) *adj.* Afflicted with a serious mental disorder impairing a person's ability to function; the characteristic of a person who is not sane. **insanely** *adv.*

in-san-i-tar-y (in san´i ter´ē) *adj.* Not sanitary; not hygienic; dangerous to one's health.

in-san-i-ty (in san´i tē) *n. pl.* **insanities** A deranged condition of being insane; a mental disorder; something completely unreasonable.

in-sa-tia-ble (in sā´sh*a* bl) *adj.* Incapable of being satisfied. **insatiability, insatiableness** *n.* **insatiably** *adv.*

in-scribe (in skrīb´) *v.* To write, mark, or engrave on a surface; to enter a name in a register or on a formal list; to write a short note on a card. To enclose one figure in another so that the latter encloses the former. **inscriber** *n.*

in-scrip-tion (in skrip´sh*a*n) *n.* A word

or something that is inscribed on a hard surface; the act of inscribing.

in-scru-ta-ble (in skrŏ´ta bl) *adj.* Difficult to interpret or understand; incomprehensible. **inscrutability** *n.* **inscrutableness** *n.* **inscrutably** *adv.*

in-seam (in´sēm˝) *n.* The inside seam, on a piece of clothing, as the leg of a pair of pants or slacks.

in-sect (in sekt´) *n.* *Zool.* Any of a numerous cosmopolitan class of small to minute winged invertebrate arthropods with three pairs of legs, a segmented body, and usually two pairs of wings.

in-sec-ti-cide (in sek´ti sīd˝) *n.* A substance for killing insects.

in-sec-ti-fuge (in sek´ti fūj˝) *n.* A substance used to repel insects.

in-sec-tiv-o-rous (in˝sek tiv´ér us) *adj.* Feeding on insects. **insectivore** *n.*

in-se-cure (in´si kūr´) *adj.* Troubled by anxiety and apprehension; threatened; not securely guarded; unsafe; liable to break, fail, or collapse. **insecurely** *adv.* **insecurity** *n.*

in-sem-i-nate (in sem´i nāt´) *v.* To introduce semen into the uterus of; to make pregnant; to sow or implant seed. **insemination** *n.* **inseminator** *n.*

in-sen-sate (in sen´sāt) *adj.* Showing a lack of humane feeling; unconscious.

in-sen-si-ble (in sen´si bl) *adj.* Deprived of consciousness; unconscious; incapable of perceiving or feeling; unmindful; unaware. **insensibility** *n.* **insensibly** *adv.*

in-sen-si-tive (in sen´si tiv) *adj.* Not responsive; lacking physical sensation or feeling.

in-sen-ti-ent (in sen´shē ent) *adj.* Without sensation or consciousness; lacking feelings. **insentience** *n.*

in-sep-a-ra-ble (in sep´ér a bl) *adj.* Incapable of being separated or parted. **inseparability** *n.* **inseparably** *adv.*

in-sert (in sert´) *v.* To put in place; to set. **insert** *n.* In printing, something inserted or to be inserted. **insertion** *n.*

in-ses-so-ri-al (in˝se sōr´ē al) *adj.* Habitu-

ally perching of a bird; suited for perching.

in-set (in set´) *v.* To set in; to implant; to insert. **inset** *n.*

in-shore (in´shōr´) *adj.* Near or moving toward the shore. **inshore** *adv.*

in-side (in´sīd´) *n.* The part, surface, or space that lies within. **insides** *n. pl.* The internal parts or organs. **inside** *adj.*

in-sid-er (in´sī´dér) *n.* One having special knowledge or access to confidential information.

in-sid-i-ous (in sid´ē us) *adj.* Cunning or deceitful; treacherous; seductive; attractive but harmful. **insidiously** *adv.* **insidiousness** *n.*

in-sight (in´sīt´) *n.* Perception into the true or hidden nature of things. **insightful** *adj.* **insightfully** *adv.*

in-sig-ni-a (in sig´nē a) *n. pl.* **insignia** *or* **insignias** A badge or emblem used to mark membership, honor, or office.

in-sig-nif-i-cant (in˝sig nif´i kant) *adj.* Lacking meaning importance, influence, or character; unimportant.

in-sin-cere (in´sin sēr´) *adj.* Not sincere; hypocritical. **insincerely** *adv.*

in-sin-u-ate (in sin´ū āt´) *v.* To suggest something by giving a hint; to introduce by using ingenious and sly means. **insinuating** *adv.*

in-sin-u-a-tion (in sin˝ū ā´shan) *n.* An indirect, derogatory suggestion; to suggest indirectly.

in-sip-id (in sip´id) *adj.* Lacking of flavor; tasteless; flat; dull; lacking interest. **insipidly** *adv.* **insipidness** *n.*

in-sist (in sist´) *v.* To demand or assert in a firm way; to dwell on something repeatedly, as to emphasize. **insistence** *n.* **insistent** *adj.* **insistently** *adv.*

in-so-bri-e-ty (in˝so brī´e tē) *n.* The lack of moderation; drunkenness.

in-so-far (in´so fär´) *adv.* To such an extent.

in-so-late (in´sō lāt˝) *v.* To dry in the sun's rays; to expose to the sun.

in-sole (in´sōl) *n.* The fixed inside sole of

a shoe or boot; a removable strip of material put inside a shoe for protection or comfort.

in-so-lent (in´so lent) *adj.* To be insultingly contemptuous in one's speech; overbearing. *n.* A rude disrespectful person. **insolently** *adv.*

in-sol-u-ble (in sol´ū bl) *adj.* Incapable of being dissolved; not soluble; not capable of being solved. **insolubility** *n.* **insolubleness** *n.* **insolubly** *adv.*

in-sol-vent (in sol´vent) *adj.* In law, unable to meet debts; bankrupt.

in-som-ni-a (in som´nē a) *n.* The chronic inability to sleep. **insomniac** *n.*

in-sou-ci-ant (in sŏ´sē ant) *adj.* Lighthearted and cheerful; unconcerned; not bothered. **insouciance** *n.*

in-spect (in spekt´) *v.* To examine or look at very carefully for flaws; to examine or review officially. **inspection** *n.*

in-spec-tor (in spek´tėr) *n.* One who reviews or examines something critically.

in-spi-ra-tion (in´spi rā´shan) *n.* The stimulation within the mind of some idea, feeling, or impulse which leads to creative action; a divine or holy presence which inspires; the act of inhaling air. **inspirational** *adj.* **inspirationally** *adv.*

in-spire (in spīėr´) *v.* To exert or guide by a divine influence; to arouse and create high emotion; to exalt; to inhale; breathe in. **inspirer** *n.* **inspiringly** *adv.*

inst *abbr.* Instant; institute; institution.

in-sta-bil-i-ty (in´sta bil´i tē) *n. pl.* **instabilities** Lacking stability.

in-stall (in stal´) *v.* To put into position for service; to place into an office or position; to settle. **installation** *n.* **installer** *n.*

in-stall-ment (in stal´ment) *n.* One of several payments due in specified amounts at specified intervals.

in-stance (in´stans) *n.* An illustrative case or example; a step in proceedings. **instance** *v.* To illustrate.

in-stant (in´stant) *n.* A very short time; a moment; a certain or specific point in time. **instant** *adj.* Instantaneously; immediate;

urgent.

in-stan-ta-ne-ous (in´stan tā´nē us) *adj.* Happening with no delay; instantly; completed in a moment. **instantaneously** *adv.*

in-stant-ly (in´stant lē) *adv.* Immediately; at once.

in-state (in stāt´) *v.* To set, establish, or install in place or in a particular position or office.

in-stead (in sted´) *adv.* In lieu of that just mentioned.

in-step (in´step´) *n., Anat.* The arched upper part of the human foot.

in-sti-gate (in´sti gāt´) *v.* To urge forward; to stir up; to foment; to provoke. **instigation** *n.* **instigator** *n.*

in-still (in stil´) *v.* To introduce by gradual instruction or effort; to pour in slowly by drops. **instillation** *n.* **instiller** *n.*

in-stinct (in´stingkt) *n.* The complex and normal tendency or response of a given species to act in ways essential to its existence, development, and survival. **instinctive** *adj.* **instinctual** *adj.* **instinctively** *adv.*

in-sti-tute (in´sti tōt´) *v.* To establish or set up; to find; to initiate; to set in operation; to start. **institute** *n.* An organization set up to promote or further a cause; an institution for educating.

in-sti-tu-tion (in´sti tō´shan) *n.* The principle custom that forms part of a society or civilization; an organization which performs a particular job or function, such as research, charity, or education; a place of confinement such as a prison or mental hospital. **institutionalize** *v.* **institutional** *adj.* **institutionally** *adv.*

in-sti-tu-tion-al-ism (in˝sti tō´sha na liz˝ um) *n.* Strong attachment or emphasis to established institutions, as of religion; the public system of institutional, or organized care of dependent persons.

in-struct (in strukt´) *v.* To impart skill or knowledge; to teach; to give orders or direction. **instructive** *adj.*

in-struc-tion (in struk´sh*a***n)** *n.* The act of teaching or instructing; important knowledge; a lesson; an order or direction.

in-struc-tor (in struk´tèr) *n.* One who instructs; a teacher; a low-rank college teacher, not having tenure. **instructorship** *n.* **instructress** *n.*

in-stru-ment (in´str*u* **m***e***nt)** *n.* A mechanical tool or implement; a device used to produce music; a person who is controlled by another; a dupe; in law, a formal legal document, deed, or contract.

in-stru-men-tal (in´str*u* **men´t***a***l)** *adj.* Acting or serving as a means; pertaining to, composed for, or performed on a musical instrument. **instrumentally** *adv.*

in-stru-men-tal-ist (in´str*u* **men´t***a* **list)** *n.* A person who plays or performs with a musical instrument.

in-stru-men-tal-i-ty (in´str*u* **men tal´i tē)** *n. pl.* **instrumentalities** Anything that serves to accomplish a purpose; means or agency.

in-stru-men-ta-tion (in´str*u* **men tā´sh***a***n)** *n.* The use of instruments or work performed with instruments. *n., Mus.* The arrangement of music for instruments.

in-sub-or-di-nate (in´s*u* **bor´d***i* **nit)** *adj.* Not obedient; not obeying orders. **insubordinately** *adv.* **insubordination** *n.*

in-sub-stan-tial (in´s*u***b stan´sh***a***l)** *adj.* Lacking substance or material nature; slight; imaginary; unreal; lacking firmness.

in-suf-fer-a-ble (in suf´èr *a* **bl)** *adj.* Not to be suffered; unendurable; intolerable. **insufferableness** *n.*

in-suf-fi-cient (in´s*u* **fish´***e***nt)** *adj.* Inadequate; not enough. **insufficiently** *adv.* **insufficiency** *n.*

in-suf-flate (in suf´lāt) *v.* To blow in; to breathe into or upon.

in-su-lar (in´s*u* **lèr)** *adj.* Of or related to an island; typical or suggestive of life on an island; narrow-minded; limited in customs, opinions, and ideas. **insularity** *n.*

in-su-late (in´s*u* **lāt´)** *v.* To isolate; to wrap or surround with nonconducting material in order to prevent the passage of heat, electricity, or sound into or out of; to protect with wrapping or insulation. **insulation** *n.* **insulator** *n.*

in-su-lin (in´s*u* **lin)** *n., Biochem.* The hormone released by the pancreas, essential in regulating the metabolism of sugar; a preparation of this hormone removed from the pancreas of a pig or an ox, used in the treatment of diabetes.

in-sult (in´sult) *v.* To speak or to treat with insolence or contempt; to abuse verbally. **insult** *n.* An act or remark that offends someone. **insulter** *n.* **insulting** *adj.* **insultingly** *adv.*

in-su-per-a-ble (in sō´pèr *a* **bl)** *adj.* Insurmountable; not able to be overcome. **insuperability** *n.* **insuperably** *adv.*

in-sup-press-i-ble (in´s*u* **pres´i bl)** *adj.* Incapable of being concealed or suppressed.

in-sur-a-ble (in shur´*a* **bl)** *adj.* Able to insure against the risk of harm or loss. **insurability** *n.*

in-sur-ance (in shur´*a***ns)** *n.* Protection against risk, loss, or ruin; the coverage an insurer guarantees to pay in the event of death, loss, or medical bills; a contract guaranteeing such protection on future specified losses in return for annual payments; any safeguard against risk or harm.

in-sure (in´shur´) *v.* To guarantee against loss of life, property, or other types of losses; to make certain; to ensure; to buy or issue insurance.

in-sured (in´shurd´) *n.* A person protected by an insurance policy.

in-sur-er (in shur´èr) *n.* The person or company which insures someone against loss or damage.

in-sur-mount-a-ble (in´sèr moun´t*a* **bl)** *adj.* Incapable of being overcome. **insurmountably** *adv.*

in-sur-rec-tion (in´s*u* **rek´sh***a***n)** *n.* An open revolt against an established government. **insurrectionary** *adj. & n.* **insurrectional** *adj.* **insurrectionist** *n.*

in-sus-cep-ti-ble (in´s*u* **sep´t***a* **bl)** *adj.* Immune; incapable of being infected. **insus-ceptibility** *n*.

in-tact (in takt´) *adj*. Remaining whole and not damaged in any way. **intactness** *n*.

in-take (in´tāk´) *n*. The act of taking in or absorbing; the amount or quantity taken in or absorbed.

in-tan-gi-ble (in tan´ji bl) *adj*. Incapable of being touched; vague or indefinite to the mind. **intangibility** *n*. **intangibleness** *n*. **intangibly** *adv*.

in-te-ger (in´ti jėr) *n*. Any of the numbers 1, 2, 3, etc., including all the positive whole numbers and all the negative numbers and zero; a whole entity.

in-te-gra-ble (in´te gra bl) *adj*. Capable of being integrated.

in-te-gral (in´te gral) *adj*. Being an essential and indispensable part of a whole; made up, from, or formed of parts that constitute a unity.

integral calculus *n*. A branch of mathematical concerned with integrals and integration, their use in the solution of differential equations and problems that involve lengths, volumes, and areas.

in-te-grant (in´te grant) *adj*. To make part of a whole; integral. *n*. A component portion or part.

in-te-grate (in´te grāt´) *v*. To make into a whole by joining parts together; to unify; to be open to people of all races or ethnic groups. **integration** *n*. **integrative** *adj*.

in-teg-ri-ty (in teg´ri tē) *n*. Uprightness of character; honesty; the condition, quality, or state of being complete or undivided.

in-teg-u-ment (in teg´ū ment) *n*. Something that covers or encloses, especially of an animal or plant body; a skin, membrane, rind, shell or husk.

in-tel-lect (in´te lekt´) *n*. The power of the mind to understand and to accept knowledge; the state of having a strong or brilliant mind; a person of notable intellect.

in-tel-lec-tu-al (in´te lek´chŏ al) *adj*. Pertaining to, possessing, or showing intellect; inclined to rational or creative thought. **intellectual** *n*. A person who pursues and

enjoys matters of the intellect and of refined taste. **intellectuality** *n*. **intellectually** *adv*.

in-tel-lec-tu-al-ize (in´te lek´chŏ a līz´) *v*. To examine objectively so as not to become emotionally involved. **intellectualization** *n*. **intellectualizer** *n*.

in-tel-li-gence (in tel´i jens) *n*. The capacity to perceive and comprehend meaning; information; news; the gathering of secret information, as by military or police authorities; information so collected.

in-tel-li-gent (in tel´i jent) *adj*. Having or showing intelligence. **intelligently** *adv*.

in-tel-li-gent-si-a (in tel´i jent´sē a) *n*. A group of intellectuals who form the social, artistic, political elite of a society.

in-tel-li-gi-ble (in tel´i ji bl) *adj*. Having the capabilities of being understood; understanding.

in-tem-per-ance (in tem´pėr ans) *n*. The lack of moderation, as in satisfying of the appetite or of one's passion for something; excess in anything.

in-tem-per-ate (in tem´pėr it) *adj*. To be not temperate. **intemperateness** *n*.

in-tend (in tend´) *v*. To have a plan or purpose in mind; to design for a particular use. **intender** *n*.

in-tend-ance (in ten´dans) *n*. The administrative department of some company or group.

in-tend-ant (in ten´dant) *n*. A type of administrative official such as a governor who is under the Spanish, French, or Portuguese monarchies.

in-tend-ed (in ten´did) *adj*. To be planned for the future. **intended** *n*., *Slang* One who is engaged to be married. **intendedness** *n*. **intendedly** *adv*.

in-tend-ing (in tend´ing) *adj*. Aspiring.

in-ten-er-ate (in ten˝e rāt´) *v*. To cause or to make something tender or softer than it was to begin with. **inteneration** *n*.

in-tense (in tens´) *adj*. Extreme in strength, effect, or degree; expressing strong emotion, concentration, or strain; profound. **intensely** *adv*. **intenseness** *n*.

in-ten-si-fi-er (in ten´si fī˝ér) *v.* The person who will intensify something.

in-ten-si-fy (in ten´si fī´) *v.* To become or make more intense or acute. **intensification** *n.*

in-ten-sion (in ten´shan) *n.* A connotation. **intentional** *adj.* **intentionally** *adv.*

in-ten-si-ty (in ten´si tē) *n. pl.* **intensities** The quality of being intense or acute; a great effect, concentration, or force.

in-ten-sive (in ten´siv) *adj.* Forceful and concentrated; marked by a full and complete application of all resources. **intensively** *adv.* **intensiveness** *n.*

intensive care *n.* The hospital care provided for a gravely ill patient in specially designed rooms with monitoring devices and life-support systems.

in-tent (in tent´) *n.* A purpose, goal, aim, or design. **intently** *adv.* **intentness** *n.*

in-ten-tion (in ten´shan) *n.* A plan of action; purpose, either immediate or ultimate.

in-ten-tion-al (in ten´shan al) *adj.* Deliberately intended or done. **intentionality** *n.* **intentionally** *adv.*

in-ter (in ter´) *v.* To place in a grave; bury. **interment** *n.*

in-ter- (in ter´) *prefix.* Mutually; with each other; together; among or between.

in-ter-act (in´tér akt´) *v.* To act on each other or with each other. **interactive** *adj.*

in-ter-ac-tant (in´tér ak´tant) *n.* A person or thing that will interact with something else.

in-ter-ac-tion (in´tér ak´shan) *n.* A reciprocal action or act. **interactional** *adv.*

in-ter al-ia (in´tér āl´ē a) *adv.* To be among other things.

inter alios (in´tér āl´ē ōs) *adv.* To be among other persons or people.

in-ter-a-tom-ic (in´tér a tom˝ik) *adj.* To be acting between atoms.

in-ter-brain (in´tér brān´) *n.* The diencephalon of the brain.

in-ter-breed (in´tér brēd´) *v.* To breed together by crossing one variety of plant or animal with another.

in-ter-ca-lar-y (in´tér ka ler˝ē) *adj.* To be inserted into a calendar.

in-ter-ca-late (in´tér ka lāt´) *v.* To place or to insert between existing elements.

in-ter-cede (in´tér sēd) *v.* To argue or plead on another's behalf. **interceder** *n.*

in-ter-cel-lu-lar (in´tér sel˝ u lér) *adj.* To be between cells.

in-ter-cept (in´tér sept´) *v.* To interrupt the path or course of; to seize or stop. **intercept** *n.*

in-ter-cep-tion (in´tér sep´shan) *n.* The state of being intercepted.

in-ter-cep-tor *or* **in-ter-cept-er** *n.* One who or that which intercepts; a fighter plane designed for the pursuit and interception of enemy aircraft.

in-ter-ces-sion (in´tér sesh´an) *n.* An entreaty or prayer on behalf of others. **intercessor** *n.* **intercessional** *adj.* **intercessory** *adj.*

in-ter-change (in´tér chānj´) *v.* To put each in the place of another; to give and receive in return. **interchange** *n.* The intersection of a highway which allows traffic to enter or turn off without obstructing other traffic. **interchangeably** *adv.* **interchanger** *n.*

in-ter-change-a-ble (in´tér chānj´a bl) *adj.* To be capable of being interchanged with something; an alternate; exchange. **interchangeableness** *n.*

in-ter-clav-i-cle (in˝tér klav´i kl) *n.* The bone which is located between the clavicles and in front of the sternum of reptiles. **interclavicular** *adj.*

in-ter-col-le-gi-ate (in´tér ko lē´jit) *adj.* Involving or pertaining to two or more colleges.

in-ter-co-lum-ni-a-tion (in´tér ko lum˝nē ā´shan) *n.* A space between the columns of a series.

in-ter-com (in´tér kom´) *n., Informal* A two-way communication system, as used in different areas of a home or business.

in-ter-com-mu-ni-cate (in´tér ko mū´ni kāt´) *v.* To communicate with each other. **intercommunication** *n.* **intercommunicative** *adj.*

intercommunication system *n.* A type of communication system that has a loudspeaker and microphone at both ends allowing for two-way talking.

in-ter-con-nect (in˝tėr ko nekt´) *v.* To connect two or more things with one another. **interconnection** *n.*

in-ter-con-ti-nen-tal (in´tėr kon´ti nen´tal) *adj.* Pertaining to or involving two or more continents.

in-ter-con-ver-sion (in´tėr kon ver´shan) *n.* A type of mutual conversion. **interconvertible** *adj.* **interconvertibility** *n.*

in-ter-cool-er (in´tėr kŏ˝lėr) *n.* A type of device that is for cooling a fluid between successive heat-generating processes.

in-ter-cos-tal (in´tėr kos´tal) *adj.* To be located or situated between the ribs. **intercostal** *n.* **intercostally** *adv.*

in-ter-course (in´tėr kōrs˝) *n.* Mutual exchange between persons or groups; communication; sexual intercourse.

in-ter-crop (in˝tėr krop´) *v.* To raise or grow a crop in between other crops.

in-ter-cross (in˝tėr kros´) *n.* A product of cross-breeding.

in-ter-cul-tur-al (in˝tėr kul´chėr al) *adj.* To be pertaining or related to two or more cultures. **interculturally** *adv.*

in-ter-cur-rent (in˝tėr kür´ent) *adj.* To be happening in the midst of a process.

in-ter-cut (in´tėr kut˝) *v.* To insert something such as a contrasting camera shot.

in-ter-de-nom-in-a-tion-al (in˝tėr di nom ˝i nā´sha nal) *adj.* To be occurring between denominations that are different. **interdenominationalism** *n.*

in-ter-den-tal (in˝tėr den´tal) *adj.* To be intended for use between the teeth.

in-ter-de-part-men-tal (in˝tėr dē˝pärt men´tal) *adj.* To be involving or to be between departments. **interdepartmentally** *adv.*

in-ter-de-pend (in˝tėr dē˝pend) *v.* To rely or to depend on another person.

in-ter-de-pend-ence (in˝tėr di pen´dens) *n.* A mutual dependence on someone or thing. **interdependency** *n.*

in-ter-de-pend-ent (in˝tėr di pen´dent) *adj.* To be mutually dependent.

in-ter-dict (in˝tėr dikt´) *v.* To forbid or prohibit by official decree. **interdiction** *n.* **interdictor** *n.* **interdictory** *adj.*

in-ter-dif-fuse (in˝tėr dif yüz´) *v.* To mix freely together to obtain a mixture which is homogeneous. **interdiffusion** *n.*

in-ter-dig-i-tate (in˝tėr dij´i tāt˝) *v.* To interlock, such as the fingers on one's hands are when folded together.

in-ter-dis-ci-pli-nar-y (in˝tėr dis´i pli nėr ˝ē) *adj.* To be involving or containing two or more artistic, academic, or scientific disciplines.

in-ter-est (in´tėr ist) *n.* Curiosity or concern about something; that which is to one's benefit; legal or financial right, claim, or share, as in a business; a charge for a loan of money, usually a percent of the amount borrowed.

in-ter-est-ed (in´tėr i stid) *adj.* Having or displaying curiosity; having a right to share in something. **interestedly** *adv.*

interest group *n.* The group of people who have a common identifying interest.

in-ter-est-ing (in´tėr i sting) *adj.* Stimulating interest, attention, or curiosity. **interesting** *adv.* **interestingness** *n.*

in-ter-face (in´tėr fās´) *n.* A surface forming a common boundary between adjacent areas; in computer science, the software or hardware connecting one device or system to another. **interfacial** *adj.*

in-ter-faith (in´tėr fāth´) *adj.* Involving or including persons of different religions faiths.

in-ter-fas-cic-u-lar (in´tėr fe´sik´ye ler) *adj.* To be located between fascicles.

in-ter-fere (in´tėr fēr´) *v.* To come between; to get in the way; to be an obstacle or obstruction. **interferer** *n.*

in-ter-fer-ence (in˝tėr fēr´ens) *n.* The process of interfering in something.

in-ter-fer-o-gram (in˝tėr fēr´o gram) *n.* A type of photographic record that is made by a device for recording optical interference phenomena.

in-ter-fer-om-e-ter (in˝tėr fe rom´i tėr) n. An instrument that utilizes the interference of light waves for precise measuring of distances and comparing wavelengths. interferometry n.

in-ter-fer-tile (in˝tėr fūr´til) adj. To be capable of interbreeding.

in-ter-file (in˝tėr fīl´) v. To place in or fit into an existing file.

in-ter-flu-ent (in˝tėr flō´ent) adj. The flowing or intermingling into each other.

in-ter-fuse (in˝tėr fūz´) v. To make or to cause something to pass into another. interfusion n.

in-ter-ga-lac-tic (in˝tėr ga lak´tik) adj. To be occurring between galaxies.

in-ter-gen-er-a-tion-al (in˝tėr jen´e rā´shen l) adj. To be ocurring between two or more generations.

in-ter-ge-ner-ic (in˝tėr je ner´ik) adj. To be existing between genera.

in-ter-gla-cial (in˝tėr glā´shal) adj. To be occurring between glacial epochs.

in-ter-gov-ern-men-tal (in˝tėr gov´ėrn ment l) adj. To be happening between two or more governments.

in-ter-gra-da-tion (in˝tėr grā dā´shan) n. A condition of a person or one who intergrades.

in-ter-grade (in˝tėr grād´) v. To come together or to merge gradually one with another, as different species do in the evolutionary process.

in-ter-group (in˝tėr grūp´) adj. To be occurring between two or more social groups.

in-ter-growth (in˝tėr grōth´) n. The growing together of two things.

in-ter-hem-i-spher-ic (in˝tėr hem´es fir´ik) adj. To be happening or existing between hemispheres.

in-ter-im (in˝tėr im) n. A time between events or periods. interim adj. Temporary.

in-ter-i-on-ic (in˝tėr ī on ik) adj. To be acting between two or more ions.

in-te-ri-or (in tēr´ē ėr) adj. Of, or contained in the inside; inner; away from the coast or border; inland; private; not exposed to view. interiority n.

interior decorator n. A person who will provide designs or supply furnishings for a home, office, or other internal area..

interior design n. The practice of planning and supervising the design for a home or other interior area in order to make it look better through the use of architectural interiors and the furnishings.

in-te-ri-or-ize (in tēr´ē ėr īz) v. To make something interior, such as a part of one's inner being. interiorization n.

interj abbr. Interjection.

in-ter-ject (in´tėr jekt´) v. To go between other parts or elements; to add something between other things. interjector n. interjectory adj.

in-ter-jec-tion (in´tėr jek´shan) n. A word used as an exclamation to express emotion, as Oh! Heavens! Super!

in-ter-jec-tion-al (in´tėr jek´shan l) adj. To be pertaining to or to be constituting an interjection. interjectionally adv.

in-ter-lace (in´tėr lās´) v. To join by weaving together; to intertwine; to blend.

in-ter-lam-i-nate (in´tėr lam´e nāt) v. To place or to insert between laminae. interlamination n.

in-ter-lay-er (in´tėr lā´ėr) n. The layer that is placed in between other layers. interlayering n.

in-ter-leaf (in´tėr lēf˝) n. pl. interleaves A blank sheet of paper that is bound or inserted between two other pages of a book.

in-ter-leave (in´tėr lēv˝) v. To place in alternating layers.

in-ter-li-brar-y (in´tėr lī˝brer˝ē) adj. To be taking place between two or more libraries.

in-ter-line (in˝tėr līn´) v. To mark or insert between the lines; to write between lines already written or printed.

in-ter-lin-e-ar (in´tėr lin´ē ėr) adj. Situated or inserted between lines of a text.

in-ter-lin-ing (in˝tėr līn´ing) n. A type of lining that is usually sewn between the outside fabric and the ordinary lining of a coat.

in-ter-link (in˝tėr lĭngk´) v. To put togther or to link things together. **interlink** n.

in-ter-lo-cal (in˝tėr lō´ kel´) adj. To be between localities.

in-ter-lock (in˝tėr lok´) v. To join closely.

in-ter-lo-cu-tion (in˝tėr lo kū shan) n. The interchange of speech with others; conversation; a dialogue or colloquy.

in-ter-loc-u-tor (in˝tėr lok´ū tėr) n. One who takes part in a conversation.

in-ter-loc-u-to-ry (in˝tėr lok´ū tōr´ē) adj. Having the nature of a dialogue; in law, pronounced while a suit is pending and temporarily in effect.

in-ter-lope (in˝tėr lōp´) v. To intrude or interfere in the rights of others.

in-ter-lude (in˝tėr lŏd´) n. A period of time that occurs in and divides some longer process; light entertainment between the acts of a show, play, or other more serious entertainment.

in-ter-lu-nar (in˝tėr lŏ´nėr) adj. To be pertaining to the interval that is between the new and old moon, where the moon is invisible.

in-ter-mar-riage (in˝tėr mar´ij) n. A marriage that takes place between the members of different groups.

in-ter-mar-ry (in˝tėr mar´ē) v. To marry someone who is not a member of one's own religion, class, race, or ethnic group.

in-ter-med-dle (in˝tėr med´l) v. To interfere with things. **intermeddler** n.

in-ter-me-di-a-cy (in˝tėr mē´dē e sē) n. The action of intermediating.

in-ter-me-di-ar-y (in˝tėr mē´dē er´ē) n. pl. **intermediaries** A mediator. **intermediary** adj. Coming between; intermediate.

in-ter-me-di-ate (in˝tėr mē´dē it) adj. Situated or occurring in the middle or between. **intermediately** adv. **intermediateness** n.

in-ter-me-di-a-tion (in˝tėr mē˝dē ā´shan) n. The action or the act of coming between two persons or two things.

in-ter-me-din (in˝tėr mē´din) n. A type of hormone that is secreted from the pituitary body and will induce the expansion of vertebrate chromatophores.

in-ter-ment (in˝tėr˝ment) n. The act or ceremony of interring.

in-ter-me-tal-lic (in˝tėr me tal´ik) adj. To be made of two or more metals.

in-ter-mez-zo (in˝tėr met´sō) n. The musical composition coming between the main sections or divisions of and extended musical work.

in-ter-min-a-ble (in tür´mi na bl) adj. To seem to have no end. **interminableness** n.

in-ter-min-gle (in˝tėr ming´gl) v. To blend or become mixed together.

in-ter-mis-sion (in˝tėr mish´an) n. A temporary interval of time between events or activities; the pause in the middle of a performance.

in-ter-mit (in˝tėr mit´) v. To cause something to cease for a certain amount of time.

in-ter-mit-tent (in˝tėr mit´ent) adj. Ceasing from time to time; coming at intervals.

intermittent current n. A type of electric current that will flow and stop at intervals but will not reverse.

in-ter-mix (in˝tėr miks´) v. To mix two or more things together.

in-ter-mo-lec-u-lar (in˝tėr mo lek´ū lėr) adj. To be acting between two or more molecules. **intermolecularly** adv.

in-tern (in tern´) n. A medical school graduate undergoing supervised practical training in a hospital. **intern** v. To confine as in wartime. **internship** n.

in-ter-nal (in ter´nal) adj. Of or pertaining to the inside; pertaining to the domestic affairs of a country; intended to be consumed by the body from the inside.

internal–combustion engine n. An engine in which fuel is burned inside the engine.

in-ter-nal-ize (in ter´na līz) adj. To incorporate within oneself. **internalization** n.

internal medicine n. The branch of medicine that studies and treats the nonsurgical diseases.

internal respiration n. The exchange of the gases, which are taken into the body through the lungs, between the cells and the blood in the body.

in-ter-na-tion-al (in˝tėr nash´*a* n*a*l) *adj.* Pertaining to or involving two or more nations. **internationally** *adv.*

in-ter-na-tion-al-ism (in˝tėr nash´*a* n*a* liz´ um) *n.* The policy of cooperation among nations where politics and economics are concerned. **internationalist** *n.*

in-ter-na-tion-al-ize (in˝tėr nash´*a* n*a* līz˝) *v.* To put or to place under control of an international organization.

international law *n.* Laws that affect the rights of different nations and their relations.

in-ter-ne-cine (in˝tėr nē´sēn) *adj.* Mutually destructive to both sides; involving struggle within a group.

in-tern-ee (in˝ter nē´) *n.* A person who is confined or interned.

in-ter-nist (in´tūr nist) *n.* A physician who is a specialist in internal medicine.

in-tern-ment (in tėrn´m*e*nt) *n.* The state of something being interned.

in-ter-node (in´tėr nōd˝) *n.* The interval that is between two nodes. **internodal** *adj.*

in-ter-nu-cle-ar (in´tėr nü˝klē´*e*r) *adj* To be happening or occurring between biological nuclei.

in-ter-nun-cial (in´tėr nun´sh*a*l) *adj.* To link motor and sensory neurons.

in-ter-nun-ci-o (in˝tėr nun´shē ō˝) *adj.* The messenger who is between two parties.

in-ter-pel-late (in˝tėr pel´āt) *v.* To question; to call upon formally; to ask for an explanation of an official action.

in-ter-pen-e-trate (in˝tėr pen´i trāt˝) *v.* To penetrate mutually; to penetrate between throughout, or within; to penetrate each other.

in-ter-per-son-al (in˝tėr pers´n*e*l) *adj.* To be relating to or pertaining to relations between people.

in-ter-plan-e-tar-y (in˝tėr plan´i ter´ē) *adj.* To be happening or operating between the planets.

in-ter-plant (in˝tėr plant´) *v.* To plant or place a crop between other crops.

in-ter-play (in´tėr plā´) *n.* Action, movement, or influence between or among peo-ple.

in-ter-plead (in˝ tėr plēd´) *v.* To litigate with each other in order to determine which is the rightful claimant against a third party.

in-ter-po-late (in ter´p*o* lāt´) *v.* To insert between other things or elements; to change something by introducing additions or insertions. **interpolation** *n.* **interpolative** *adj.*

in-ter-pose (in´tėr pōz´) *v.* To put between parts; to put in or inject a comment into a conversation or speech; to intervene. **interposer** *n.* **interposition** *n.*

in-ter-pret (in ter´prit) *v.* To convey the meaning of something by explaining or restating; to present the meaning of something, as in a picture; to take words spoken or written in one language and put them into another language. **interpretable** *adj.* **interpretation, interpreter** *n.*

in-ter-pre-ta-tive (in ter´pre tā´tiv) *adj* Of or based on interpreting; to provide an interpretation. **interpretatively** *adv.*

in-ter-pret-er (in ter´prit er) *v.* A person who will translates languages orally for others.

in-ter-pu-pil-lar-y (in´ter´pyü˝pi ler´ē) *adj.* To be located or extending between the pupils of one's eyes.

in-ter-ra-cial (in´tėr rā´sh*a*l) *adj.* Between, among, or affecting different races.

in-ter-reg-num (in´tėr reg´num) *n. pl.* **nums** An interval between two successive reigns; a break in continuity.

in-ter-re-late (in´tėr ri lāt´) *v.* To have or bring into a mutual relationship. **interrelation, interrelationship** *n.*

in-ter-re-lat-ed (in´tėr ri lāt´d) *adj.* To have a mutual relation with someone or something. **interrelatedly** *adv.*

in-ter-re-li-gious (in´tėr ri lij˝es) *adj.* To be existing between different religions.

in-ter-ro-gate (in ter´*o* gāt´) *v.* To question formally. **interrogation** *n.*

in-ter-rog-a-tive (ın´te rog´*a* tiv) *adj.* Asking or having the form of a question. *n.* A word used to ask a question. **interrog-**

atively *adv.*

in-ter-ro-ga-tor (in ter´o gā˝tėr) *n.* A person who will ask questions or interrogate.

in-ter-ro-gee (in ter´o gē´) *n.* A person who is interrogated.

in-ter-rupt (in´te rupt´) *v.* To break the continuity of something; to intervene abruptly while someone else is speaking or performing. **interrupter** *n.* **interruption** *n.* **interruptive** *adj.*

in-ter-scho-las-tic (in´tėr sko las´tik) *adj.* Conducted between or among schools.

in-ter se (in´ter sā´) *adj. or adv.* To be between or among friends.

in-ter-sect (in´tėr sekt´) *v.* To divide by cutting through or across; to form an intersection; to cross.

in-ter-sec-tion (in´tėr sek´shan) *n.* A place of crossing; a place where streets or roads cross; in mathematics, the point common to two or more geometric elements.

in-ter-ser-vice (in´ter ser ves) *adj.* To be relating to two or more of the armed forces.

in-ter-ses-sion (in´ter sesh en) *n.* The period that is between two academic sessions that can be used for brief, concentrated courses.

in-ter-space (in´tėr spās˝) *n.* A space between things; an intervening space or interval. *v.* To fill a space

in-ter-sperse (in´tėr spers´) *v.* To scatter among other things. **interspersion** *n.*

in-ter-sta-di-al (in´tėr stād˝ē el) *n.* The subdivision that is within a glacial stage and marking a temporary retreat of the ice.

in-ter-state (in´tėr stāt´) *adj.* Between, involving, or among two or more states.

in-ter-stel-lar (in´tėr stel´ėr) *adj.* Among or between the stars.

in-ter-stice (in tür´stis) *n.* The small space between things.

in-ter-sti-tial (in´tėr stish´ al) *adj.* To be situated within a tissue or an organ.

in-ter-sub-jec-tive ((in´tėr sub jek´tiv) *adj.* To be happening or occurring separate conscious minds. **intersubjectively** *adv.*

in-ter-till (in´tėr til´) *v.* To cultivate the ground between the rows of a crop. **intertillage** *n.*

in-ter-trop-i-cal (in´tėr trop´i kal) *adj.* To be located between the tropics.

in-ter-twine (in˝tėr twīn´) *v.* To unite by twisting together. **intertwinement** *n.*

in-ter-twist (in˝tėr twist´) *v.* To intertwine things together. **intertwist** *n.*

in-ter-ur-ban (in´tėr er´ban) *adj.* Between or among connecting urban areas.

in-ter-val (in´tėr val) *n.* The time coming between two points or objects; a period of time between events or moments. *Mus.* The difference in pitch between two tones.

in-ter-val-om-e-ter (in˝tėr va lom´i tėr) *n.* A type of device that operates a control such as one for the shutter of a camera.

in-ter-vene (in´tėr vēn) *v.* To interfere or take a decisive role so as to modify or settle something; to interfere with force in a conflict. **intervention** *n.*

in-ter-ven-or (in´tėr vēn ėr) *n.* A person who will intervene.

in-ter-ven-tion-ism (in˝tėr ven´shan izm) *n.* The practice of intervening in something. **interventionist** *n.*

in-ter-ver-te-bral (in´tėr vert˝e bral) *adj.* To be situated between the vertebrae, such as a disk.

intervertebral disk *n.* An elastic disk that is located between the vertebrae.

in-ter-view (in´tėr vū´) *n.* A conversation conducted by a reporter to elicit information from someone; a conversation led by an employer who is trying to decide whether to hire someone. **interview** *v.* **interviewer** *n.*

in-ter-view-ee (in´tėr vū´ē) *n.* The person who is being interviewed.

in-ter vi-vos (in˝tėr vē´vōs) *adj. & adv.* To be between living people; from one living person to another.

in-ter-vo-cal-ic (in˝tėr vō kal´ik) *n.* To be preceded and followed immediately by a vowel.

in-ter-war (in˝tėr war´) *n.* To be taking place between the wars.

in-ter-weave (in´tėr wēv´) *v.* To weave together; to intertwine.

in-ter-zon-al (in´tėr zōn´l) *adj.* To be carried on between two or more zones.

in-tes-ta-cy (in tes´ta sē) *n.* The state of being intestate.

in-tes-tate (in tes´tāt) *adj.* Having made no valid will; not disposed of by a will.

in-tes-ti-nal (in tes´ti nal) *adj.* To be pertaining to the intestines. **intestinally** *adv.*

intestinal fortitude *n.* Stamina of a person; courage.

in-tes-tine *or* **intestines (in tes´tin)** *n., Anat.* The section of the alimentary canal from the stomach to the anus.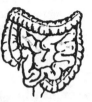

in-tim-a (in´ti ma) *n.* The covering of an organ which is the innermost and is made up of an endothelial layer and is backed by connective tissue. **intimal** *adj.*

in-ti-mate (in´ti mit) *adj.* Characterized by close friendship or association. **intimate** *n.* **intimately** *adv.* **intimacy** *n.* **intimateness** *n.*

in-tim-i-date (in tim´i dāt´) *v.* To make timid or fearful; to frighten; to discourage or suppress by threats or by violence. **intimidation** *n.* **intimidator** *n.*

in-tim-i-da-tor-y (in tim´i de´tōr ˝ē) *adj.* Tending to intimidate others.

in-tine (in tēn´) *n.* The layer that is innermost of a spore and is a cellular wall.

intitule (in tit´ūl) *v.* To give or furnish with a title.

intnl *abbr.* International.

in-to (in´tŏ) *prep.* To the inside of; to a form or condition of; to a time in the midst of.

in-tol-er-a-ble (in tol´ėr a bl) *adj.* Not tolerable; unbearable. **intolerability** *n.* **intolerableness** *n.* **intolerably** *adv.*

in-tol-er-ant (in tol´ėr ant) *adj.* Not able to endure; not tolerant of the rights or beliefs of others; bigoted. **intolerance** *n.* **intolerantly** *adv.*

in-to-nate (in´tŏ nāt˝) *v.* To utter something.

in-to-na-tion (in´tŏ nā˝shan) *n.* The manner of speaking, especially the meaning and melody given to speech by changing levels of pitch. **intonational** *adj.*

in-tone (in tōn´) *v.* To utter or recite in a monotone; to chant. **intoner** *n.*

in-tort (in tort´) *v.* To curl; to twist inward.

in-tor-tion (in tor´shan) *n.* A winding or twisting, usually inward, around an axis, as of a plant stem around a pole.

in to-to (in tō´tō) *adv.* Totally.

in-tox-i-cate (in tok´si kāt´) *v.* To make drunk; to elate or excite. **intoxicant** *n.* **intoxication** *n.*

in-tox-i-cat-ed (in tok´si kāt´d) *adj.* To be affected by alcohol.

in-tra- *prefix* Within.

in-tra-ar-te-ri-al (in´tra är tir˝ē al) *adj.* To be located or situated within an artery.

in-tra-car-di-ac (in´tra kär˝dē ak) *adj.* To be occurring within a being's heart.

in-tra-cel-lu-lar (in´tra sel˝ū lėr) *adj.* To be occurring within a cell or cells.

in-tra-cra-ni-al (in´tra krā nē al) *adj.* To be occurring within the skull.

in-trac-ta-ble (in trak´ta bl) *adj.* Hard to manage; difficult to cure or treat. **intractableness, intractability** *n.*

in-tra-cu-ta-ne-ous (in˝tra kū tā´nē us) *adj.* To be occurring between the layers of a being's skin. **intracutaneously** *adv.*

in-tra-der-mal (in˝tra dür˝mal) *adj.* To be done within the layers of a being's skin.

intradermal test *n.* A type of test which is used to evaluate the immunity to an antigen by injecting it under a layer of the skin and then watching for a reaction.

in-tra-dos (in´tra dos´) *n. pl.* **intrados** *or* **intradoses** The interior curve of an arch or vault.

in-tra-ga-lac-tic (in´tra ga lak˝tik) *adj.* To be occurring within a single galaxy.

in-tra-mo-lec-u-lar (in´tra mo lek˝ū lėr) *adj.* To be occurring or acting within a molecule.

in-tra-mu-ral (in´tra mūr´al) *adj.* Taking place within a school, college, or institution; competition limited to a school community.

in-tra-mus-cu-lar (in´tra mus´kū lėr) *adj.* Within a muscle.

in-trans *abbr.* Intransitive.

in-tran-si-gence (in tran′si jens) *n.* The state of something being intransigent.

in-tran-si-gent (in tran′si jent) *adj.* Refusing to moderate a position; uncompromising or unbending. **intransigency** *n.* **intransigent** *n.*

in-tran-si-tive (in tran′si tiv) *adj.* To be not transitive. **intransitiveness** *n.*

in-trant (in trant′) *n.* A person who is entering or going into a learning institution.

in-tra-oc-u-lar (in′tra ok′ū lėr) *adj.* To be located within the eyeball.

in-tra-per-i-to-ne-al (in′tra per″e ton ē′al) *adj.* To be going into the peritoneal cavity of the body.

in-tra-per-son-al (in′tra per″son al) *adj.* To be taking place among the members of a population.

in-tra-pop-u-la-tion (in′tra păp′ū lā′ shan) *adj.* To be taking place between the members of a population.

in-tra-psy-chic (in″tra sī′kik) *adj.* Arising or occurring within the psyche, mind, or personality.

in-tra-spe-cif-ic (in″tra spi sif′ik) *adj.* Occurring among or within a species or involving the members of the same species.

in-tra-state (in′tra stāt′) *adj.* Within a state.

in-tra-u-ter-ine (in′tra ū′tėr in) *adj.* Within the uterus.

intrauterine device *n.* A metal or plastic loop, ring, or spiral inserted into the uterus as a means of contraception; IUD.

in-tra-vas-cu-lar (in′tra vas″kū ler) *adj.* To be occurring within a vessel such as a blood vessel.

in-tra-ve-nous (in′tra vē′nus) *adj.* To be occurring within a vein. **intravenously** *adv.*

in-tra-vi-tam (in′tra vī′tam) *adj.* Happening during one's life; used on a living subject.

in-tra-zon-al (in′tra zōn″al) *adj.* To be pertaining to a soil group which is found to be marked with relatively well-developed characteristics which are, in turn, determined by local factors instead of climate or vegetation.

in-trep-id (in trep′id) *adj.* Courageous; unshaken by fear; bold. **intrepidly** *adv.* **intrepidness** *n.*

in-tri-ca-cy (in′tri ka sē) *n.* The state of something being intricate.

in-tri-cate (in′tri kit) *adj.* Having many perplexingly entangled parts or elements; complex; difficult to solve or understand. **intricately** *adv.*

in-tri-gant (in′tri gant) *n.* Someone or something that will intrigue.

in-trigue (in trēg′) *v.* To arouse the curiosity or interest; to fascinate; to plot; to conspire; to engage in intrigues. **intrigue** *n.* A secret or illicit love affair; a secret plot or plan. **intriguer** *n.*

in-tri-gu-ing (in tri′ging) *adj.* To be engaging the interest of something or of someone to a marked degree.

in-trin-sic (in trin′sik) *adj.* Belonging to the true or fundamental nature of a thing; inherent. **intrinsically** *adv.*

intrinsic factor *n.* A type of substance which is made by the gastrointestinal mucosa and is used for the purpose of the absorption of vitamin B12.

intro- *prefix* Into; in.

introd *abbr.* Introduction.

in-tro-duce (in′tro dōs′) *v.* To present a person face to face to another; to make acquainted; to bring into use or practice for the first time; to bring to the attention of. **introducer** *n.* **introductory** *adj.*

in-tro-duc-tion (in′tro duk′shan) *n.* A passage of a book that will introduce the story or the content of the book; something which introduces.

in-tro-duc-to-ry (in″tro duk′to rē) *adj.* Serving as an introduction, or being the first step that starts something; preliminary.

in-tro-gres-sion (in′tro gresh″en) *n.* The introduction of a gene from one gene complex to another gene complex.

in-tro-it (in′trō it) *n.* A hymn or psalm sung at the beginning of a Roman Catholic Mass; a piece of music played at the beginning of a religious service.

in-tro-ject (in´tro jekt´) *n.* To unconsciously incorporate ideas into someone's personality.

in-tro-mis-sion (in´tro mish´in) *n.* The process of intromitting.

in-tro-mit (in´tro mit) *v.* To put something in; insert.

in-trorse (in trors´) *adj.* To be facing inward.

in-tro-spect (in˝tro spekt´) *v.* To examine reflectively; to look into one's own feelings or thoughts. **introspection** *n.*

in-tro-ver-sion (in´tro vûr´zhan) *n.* The state of being introverted.

in-tro-vert (in´tro vert´) *n., Psychol.* A person who directs his interest to himself and not to friends or social activities. **introversive** *adj.* **introverted** *adj.*

in-trude (in tröd´) *v.* To thrust or push oneself in; to come in without being asked or wanted.

in-tru-sion (in trö´zhan) *n.* The act of intruding.

in-tru-sive (in trö´siv) *adj.* To be intruding where a person is not wanted or welcome. **intrusiveness** *n.* **intrusively** *adv.*

intsv *abbr.* Intensive.

in-tu-ba-tion (in´tü bā˝shan) *n.* The act of placing a tube in a hollow organ or oriface. **intubate** *v.*

in-tu-it (in tö´it) *v.* To understand through intuition. **intuitable** *adj.*

in-tu-i-tion (in´to ish´an) *n.* The direct knowledge or awareness of something without conscious attention or reasoning; knowledge that is acquired in this way. **intuitive** *adj.* **intuitively** *adv.*

in-tu-i-tion-ism (in´to ish´a niz˝um) *n.* A type of doctrine that states that objects of one's perception are intuitively known to be real.

in-tu-mesce (in˝tü mes´) *v.* To enlarge.

in-tu-mes-cence (in˝tü mes´ns) *n.* The swelling or the bubbling that can be caused by heat. **intumescent** *adj.*

in-tus-sus-cept (in˝tus su sept´) *v.* To undergo an intussusception.

in-tus-sus-cep-tion (in˝tus su sep´shan) *n.*

The pulling or drawing in of something, such as with the intestines in one's body. **intussusceptive** *adj.*

in-u-lin (in´ū lin) *n.* A type of white polysaccharide which can be found in the sap of the roots of composite plants.

in-unc-tion (in´ungk´shan) *n.* The act of placing ointment on a body part.

in-un-date (in´un dāt´) *v.* To overwhelm with abundance or excess, as with work. **inundation** *n.* **inundatory** *adj.*

in-ure (in ūr´) *v.* To become used to accepting something which is undesirable. **inurement** *n.*

in-u-tile (in ū´til) *adj.* To be unusable or useless.

in va-cu-o (in vak´ū ō˝) *adv.* To be done in a vacuum.

in-vade (in vād´) *v.* To enter by force with the intent to conquer or pillage; to penetrate and overrun harmfully; to violate; to encroach upon. **invader** *n.*

in vag-i-nate (in vaj´i nāt´) *v.* To sheathe something; to undergo an invagination.

in-va-lid (in´va lid) *n.* A chronically sick, bedridden, or disabled person. **invalid** *adj. & v.*

in-val-id (in val´id) *adj.* Not valid; unsound; having no force; without legal force or void, as a contract. **invalidity** *n.* **invalidly** *adv.*

in-val-i-date (in val´i dāt´) *v.* To nullify; to make invalid. **invalidation** *n.* **invalidator** *n.*

in-va-lid-ism (in´va´li diz˝um) *n.* A type of condition, which is chronic, of being an invalid.

in-val-u-a-ble (in val´ū a bl) *adj.* Priceless; of great value; to be of great help or use. **invaluably** *adv.* **invaluableness** *n.*

in-var-i-a-ble (in vâr´ē a bl) *adj.* Constant and not changing. **invariably** *adv.*

in-var-i-ance (in vâr´ē ans) *n.* The state of being invariable; constancy. **invariant** *adj.*

in-va-sion (in vā´zhan) *n.* The act of invading; an entrance made with the intent of overrunning or occupying.

in-va-sive (in vā´siv) *adj*. To be characterized by or to be similar to military aggression; intruding..

in-vec-tive (in vek´tiv) *adj*. To be characterized by abuse or insult. **invectively** *adv*.

in-veigh (in vā´) *v*. To angrily protest something. **inveigher** *n*.

in-vei-gle (in vā´gl) *v*. To win over by flattery. **inveiglement** *n*. **inveigler** *n*.

in-vent (in vent´) *v*. To devise or create by original effort or design. **inventor** *n*.

in-ven-tion (in ven´shan) *n*. The act or process of inventing; a new process, method, or device conceived from study and testing.

in-ven-tive (in ven´tiv) *adj*. Skillful at invention or contrivance; ingenious. **inventively** *adv*. **inventiveness** *n*.

in-ven-to-ry (in´ven tōr´ē) *n*. *pl*. **inventories** A list of items with descriptions and quantities of each; the process of making such a list. **inventory** *v*.

in-ver-ness (in˝vėr nes´) *n*. A type of loose belted coat with a cape.

in-verse (in vers´) *adj*. Reversed in order or sequence; inverted. **inverse** *n*. Something opposite. **inversely** *adv*.

in-ver-sion (in ver´zhan) *n*. The act of inverting or the state of being inverted; that which is inverted.

in-ver-sive (in ver´siv) *adj*. To be marked or characterized by inversion.

in-vert (in vert´) *v*. To turn upside down; to reverse the position, condition, or order of something. **inverter** *n*. **invertible** *adj*.

in-vert-ase (in ver´tās) *n*. A type of enzyme which is capable of inverting sucrose.

in-ver-te-brate (in vûr´te brit) *adj*. Lacking a backbone or spinal column.

inverted comma *n*. A type of comma that is inverted to be upside down and is placed at the top of a line.

in-vert-er (in vert´ėr) *n*. Someone or something that will invert.

in-vert-i-ble (in vert´i bl) *adj*. To be capable of being inverted.

invert sugar *n*. A type of dextrose that can be obtained from starch.

in-vest (in vest´) *v*. To use money for the purchase of stocks or property in order to obtain profit or interest; to place in office formally; to install; to make an investment. **investor** *n*.

in-ves-ti-gate (in ves´ti gāt´) *v*. To search or inquire into; to examine carefully. **investigative** *adj*. **investigation** *n*. **investigator** *n*.

in-ves-ti-ture (in ves´ti chėr) *n*. The ceremony or act of investing or installing someone in a high office.

in-vest-ment (in vest´ment) *n*. The act of investing money or capital to gain interest or income; property acquired and kept for future benefit.

in-vet-er-a-cy (in vet´ėr a sē) *n*. The state of being persistent.

in-vet-er-ate (in vet´ėr it) *adj*. To be confirmed in a habit. **inveterate** *adv*.

in-vi-a-ble (in vī´abl) *adj*. To be unable to survive. **inviability** *n*.

in-vid-i-ous (in vid´ē us) *adj*. To be causing animosity or discontent.

in-vig-o-rate (in vig´o rāt´) *v*. To give strength or vitality to. **invigoratingly** *adv*. **invigoration** *n*.

in-vin-ci-ble (in vin´si bl) *adj*. Incapable of being defeated. **invincibility** *n*. **invincibly** *adv*.

in-vi-o-la-ble (in vī´o la bl) *adj*. Secure from profanation; safe from assault. **inviolability** *n*. **inviolably** *adv*.

in-vi-o-late (in vī´o lit) *adj*. Not violated. **inviolately** *adv*. **inviolateness** *n*.

in-vis-cid (in vis´id) *adj*. To have zero viscosity.

in-vis-i-ble (in viz´i bl) *adj*. Not capable of being seen; not visible; not open to view; hidden. **invisibility** *n*. **invisibly** *adv*.

in-vi-ta-tion (in´vi tā´shan) *n*. The act of inviting; the means or words that request someone's presence or participation.

in-vi-ta-to-ry (in vī´ta tōr´ē) *adj*. Intending to invite; containing an invitation; to convey an invitation.

in-vite (in vīt´) *v*. To request the presence or participation of; to make a formal or polite request for; to provoke; to entice;

to issue an invitation.

in-vi-tee (in vi tē´) *n.* The person who is being invited to something or somewhere.

in-vit-ing (in vīt ing) *adj.* Tempting; attractive. **invitingly** *adv.*

in vi-tro (in vē´trō) *adv.* To be done outside the body, such as fertilization.

in vi-vo (in vē´vō) *adv.* To be in the living body of an animal or in a plant.

in-vo-cate (in´vo kāt´) *v.* To invoke someone or something into doing something.

in-vo-ca-tion (in´vo kā´shan) *n.* An appeal to a deity or other agent for inspiration, witness, or help; a prayer used at the opening of a ceremony or service.

in-voice (in´vois) *n.* An itemized list of merchandise shipped or services rendered, including prices, shipping instructions, and other costs; a bill. **invoice** *v.*

in-voke (in vōk´) *v.* To call upon for aid, support, or inspiration; to conjure. **invoker** *n.*

in-vol-u-cel (in vol´ū sel´) *n.* A small involucre often at the base of an individual flower or a small cluster of flowers.

in-vo-lu-cre (in´vo lŏ˝kėr) *n.* One or more whorls of bracts that are situated below and close to a flower cluster or fruit.

in-vo-lu-crum (in˝vo lü´krum) *n.* A type of surrounding sheath.

in-vol-un-tar-y (in vol´un ter´ē) *adj.* Not done by choice or willingly. **involuntary** *n., Physiol.* Muscles which function without an individual's control. **involuntariness** *n.*

in-vo-lute (in´vo lŏt˝) *v.* To return to the former condition; to be cleared up.

in-vo-lu-tion (in´vo lŏ´shan) *n.* The process where something returns itself to its former condition or state. **involutional** *adv.*

in-volve (in volv´) *v.* To include as a part; to make a participant of; to absorb; to engross. **involvement** *n.*

in-volved (in volvd´) *n.* To be complex in an extreme manner; not easily understood.

in-vul-ner-a-ble (in vul´nėr a bl) *adj.* To be immune to attack; impregnable; not able to be physically injured or wounded. **invulnerability** *n.* **invulnerably** *adv.*

in-wall (in wal´) *v.* To enclose within a wall. *n.* An interior wall.

in-ward (in´wėrd) *adj.* Situated toward the inside, center, or interior; of or existing in the mind or thoughts. **inwardness** *n.*

in-weave (in wēv´) *v.* To interlace something.

in-wrought (in rot´) *adj.* To have the decoration worked in, such as with embroidery.

IOC *abbr.* International Olympic Committee.

i-o-date (i´o dāt´) *v.* To treat something with iodine. **iodation** *n.*

i-od-ic (i´od´ik) *adj.* To be pertaining to or containing iodine.

iodic acid *n.* An oxidizing solid that is formed by the oxidation of iodine.

i-o-dide (i´o dīd´) *n.* A type of iodine compound that has a more electropositive element.

i-o-din-ate (i´o din āt´) *v.* To cause a compound to combine with iodine.

i-o-dine (ī´o dīn´) *n.* A grayish-black, corrosive, poisonous element, symbolized by I; a solution made up of iodine, alcohol, and sodium iodide or potassium iodide which is used as an antiseptic.

i-o-dize (i´o dīz´) *v.* To treat something with iodine or to treat with an iodide.

i-o-do-form (i ō´do form˝) *n.* A type of yellow compound that has a penetrating, persistent odor and is used as an antiseptic dressing.

i-o-do-phor (i ō´do for˝) *n.* A type of complex iodine and organic compound that will release iodine gradually and is used as a disinfectant.

i-o-dous (i ō´dus) *adj.* Pertaining to or containing iodine.

i-o-lite (ī´o līt˝) *n.* A mineral of a violet-blue color.

i-o moth (ī´o moth˝) *n.* A type of yellow American moth that has a large ocellated spot on both of its hind legs.

i-on (ī´on) *n., Physics* An atom or group of atoms which carries a positive or negative electric charge as a result of having lost or gained one or more electrons.

-ion *n. suffix* A process; a condition.

i-on-ize(ī´on īz˝) *v.* To convert completely or partially into ions. **ionizer** *n.* **ionization** *n.* **ionizable** *adj.*

i-on-o-sphere (ī on´o sfèr˝) *n.* An ionized region of the atmosphere; the earth's atomsphere beginning at an altitude of about 30 miles and a latitude of 300 miles above the earth's surface and extends upward approximately 200 miles.

i-o-ta (ī ō´ta) *n.* The ninth letter in the Greek alphabet.

IOU *abbr.* I owe you.

I-o-wa (ī ō´wa) *n.* A state which is located in the north central part of the United States.

ipecac (ip´e kak˝) *n.* A type of South American creeping plant that has flowers which droop and is found in tropical areas; the extract from its roots that is used as an emetic and expectorant.

i-pro-ni-a-zid (ī´pro nī˝a zid) *n.* A type of derivative of isoniazid that was formerly used to treat tuberculosis.

ip-se dix-it (ip´sē dik´set) *n* A type of assertion that is made but not proven.

ip-si-lat-er-al (ip´si lat˝èr al) *adj.* To be appearing on the same side of the body.

ip-so fac-to (ip´sō fak´tō) *adv.* By that very fact or act.

IQ *abbr.* Intelligence quotient.

Ir *abbr.* Irish.

i-ras-ci-ble (i ras´i bl) *adj.* Easily provoked to anger; quick-tempered. **irascibly** *adv.* **irascibility** *n.* **irascibleness** *n.*

i-rate (ī´rāt) *adj.* Raging; angry. **irately** *adv.* **irateness** *n.*

IRBM *abbr.* Intermediate range ballistic missile.

ire (īèr) *n.* Anger; wrath.

Ire *abbr.* Ireland.

i-ren-ic (ī ren´ik) *adj.* To be operating toward peace.

ir-i-da-ceous (ir˝i dā´shus) *adj.* To be pertaining to the iris family of flowers.

ir-i-des-cent (ir´i des´ent) *adj.* Displaying the colors of the rainbow in shifting hues and patterns. **iridescence** *n.*

i-rid-ic (i rid´ik) *adj.* To be pertaining to iridium or to the iris of the eye.

i-rid-i-um (i rid´ē um) *n.* A type of silver-white brittle and very hard metallic element of the platinum group.

ir-i-dos-mine (ir˝i doz´min) *n.* A compound of iridium and osmium alloy, that often contains some platinum and rhodium.

i-ris (ī´ris) *n. pl.* **irises** *or* **irides** The pigmented part of the eye which regulates the size of the pupil by contracting and expanding around it.  *Bot.* A plant with narrow sword-shaped leaves and handsome flowers, as the gladiolus and crocus.

iris diaphragm *n.* Adjustable diaphragm made of thin opaque plates that is turned by a ring, so as to change the diameter of a central opening such as the aperture of a lens.

I-rish (ī´rish) *n.* Pertaining to Ireland and its people or their language.

Irish coffee *n.* A type of hot, sweetened coffee that contains Irish whiskey and whipped cream.

Irish confetti *n.* A brick, rock, or fragment of either that is used as a missile.

Irish Gaelic *n.* The Celtic language that has been used in Ireland since the end of the medieval period.

I-rish-ism (ī´rish iz´im) *n.* A phrase or a word that is characteristic of the Irish.

Irish mail *n.* A child's toy with three or four wheels that is activated by a hand lever.

Irishman *n.* A male person who is native to or an inhabitant of Ireland.

Irish moss *n.* Red algar that has been dried and is used for thickening or emulsifying.

I-rish-ry (ī´rish rē) *adj.* To be Irish in character or in quality.

Irish setter *n.* A type of bird dog that has a chestnut or reddish coat.

Irish stew *n.* A type of stew that contains

meat (lamb, beef, or mutton) onions, and potatoes.

Irish terrier *n.* A type of medium-sized terrier dog that was developed in Ireland and has a reddish wiry coat.

Irish whiskey *n.* A type of whiskey, mainly of barley, that is made in Ireland.

Irish wolfhound *n.* A very large hound that resembles the Scottish deerhound but is much stronger and larger.

Irish woman *n.* A female person who was born in Ireland or is of Irish descnt.

irk (erk) *v.* To annoy or to weary someone or something.

irk-some (erk´sum) *adj.* Tending to annoy someone or something; aggravating.

i-ron (ī´ërn) *n.* A type of heavy, malleable, ductile and magnetic element that is silver-white and will rust easily in moist air. **iron** *v.* To smooth with an iron.

Iron Age *n.* The most recent of three early stages of human progress, following the Stone Age and the Bronze Age.

i-ron-bound (ī´ërn bound´) *adj.* Bound with iron; unyielding.

i-ron-clad (ī´ërn klad´) *adj.* Covered with protective iron plates; strict; unbreakable.

iron curtain *n.* An impenetrable political and ideological barrier between the Soviet bloc and the rest of the world.

i-ron-er (ī´ër nėr) *n.* A person who irons things, such as clothing.

i-ron-fis-ted (ī´ërn fis˝tid) *adj.* To be ruthless and mean.

iron gray *n.* A type of color which is neutral and slightly greenish dark gray.

iron hand *n.* The rigorous control of someone or of somthing. **ironhandedness** *n.* **ironhanded** *adj.*

ironhearted *adj.* To be hardhearted and cruel.

iron horse *n.* The engine of a train.

i-ron-ic (ī ron´ik) *adj.* Marked by or characterized by irony. **ironical** *adj.*

i-ron-ing (ī´ërn ing) *n.* The process or action of pressing or smoothing with a heated iron; clothes that have been ironed or are to be ironed.

i-ro-nist (ī´ro nist) *n.* A person who uses irony in developing of a literary work.

iron lung *n.* A tank which encloses the entire body with the exception of the head and regulates the respiration of a patient by alternately increasing and decreasing air pressure.

i-ron-ma-ster (ī´ërn mä˝stėr) *n.* The manufacturer of iron.

iron out *v.* To make harmonious or tolerable by modification of extremes.

i-ron-smith (ī´ërn smith˝) *n.* A person who works with iron, as a blacksmith.

i-ron-stone (ī´ërn stōn´) *n.* A heavy, white, glazed pottery.

i-ron-ware (ī´ërn wâr˝) *n.* Utensils, tools, and other articles made of iron; hardware.

i-ron-work (ī´ërn wurk) *n.* Any object that has been made from iron.

i-ro-ny (ī´ro nē) *n. pl.* **ironies** A literary device for conveying meaning by saying the direct opposite of what is really meant.

ir-ra-di-ance (i rā´dē ans) *n.* A ray of light or anything of such luster or splendor.

ir-ra-di-ate (i rā´dē āt´) *v.* To subject to ultraviolet light, radiation, or similar rays. **irradiation** *n.* **irradiator** *n.*

ir-ra-tion-al (i rash´a nal) *adj.* Unable to reason; contrary to reason; absurd; in mathematics, a number which is not expressible as an integer or a quotient of integers. **irrationality** *n.* **irrationally** *adv.*

ir-rec-on-cil-a-ble (i rek´on sī´la bl) *adj.* Not willing or able to be reconciled. **irreconcilability** *n.* **irreconcilably** *adv.*

ir-re-cov-er-a-ble (ir˝i kuv´ėr a bl) *adj.* Incapable of being regained or recovered; not capable of being remedied or restored.

ir-re-cu-sa-ble (ir˝i kū´za bl) *adj.* Not to be objected to.

ir-re-deem-a-ble (ir´i dē´ma bl) *adj.* Not capable of being recovered, bought back, or paid off; not convertible into coin.

ir-re-den-ta (ir˝i den´ta) *n.* Any region whose people are connected ethnically or historically to one country or area, but who are forced to accept the political jurisdiction of another state.

ir-re-duc-i-ble (ir´i dŏ´si bl) *adj.* Incapable of being reduced or simplified; not reducible.

ir-ref-ra-ga-ble (i ref´ra ga bl) *adj.* Incapable of being disproved; undeniable. **irrefragably** *n.*

ir-re-fran-gi-ble (ir˝i fran´ji bl) *adj.* Not to be violated; not to be broken.

ir-ref-ut-able (i ref´ū ta bl) *adj.* Cannot be disproved as truth. **irrefutability** *n.* **irrefutably** *adv.*

ir-reg-u-lar (i reg´ū lėr) *adj.* Not according to the general rule or practice; not straight, uniform, or orderly; uneven. **irregular** *n.* One who is irregular. **irregularity** *n.* **irregularly** *adv.*

ir-rel-a-tive (i rel´a tiv) *adj.* Not relative; without relationship; not related.

ir-rel-e-vant (i rel´e vant) *adj.* Not pertinent or related to the subject matter. **irrelevantly** *adv.* **irrelevance** *n.* **irrelevancy** *n.*

ir-re-lig-ious *adj.* Lacking in religion; opposed to religion. **irreligiously** *adv.* **irreligiousness** *n.* **irreligion** *n.*

ir-re-me-di-a-ble (ir˝i mē´dē a bl) *adj.* Incapable of being cured or remedied incurable.

ir-re-mis-si-ble (ir˝i mis´a bl) *adj.* Unpardonable, as for sin. **irremissibility** *n.*

ir-re-mov-a-ble (ir˝i mŏ´va bl) *adj.* Not removable. **irremovably** *adv.*

ir-rep-a-ra-ble (i rep´ėr a bl) *adj.* Unable to be set right or repaired. **irreparability** *n.* **irreparably** *adv.*

ir-re-peal-a-ble (ir˝i pē´la bl) *adj.* Impossible to revoke or repeal.

ir-re-place-a-ble (ir˝i plā´sa bl) *adj.* Unable to be replaced.

ir-re-press-i-ble (ir˝i pres´i bl) *adj.* Impossible to hold back or restrain. **irrepressibility** *n.* **irrepressibly** *adv.*

ir-re-proach-a-ble (ir˝i prō´cha bl) *adj.* Blameless; not meriting reproach. **irreproachableness** *n.* **irreproachably** *adv.*

ir-re-sist-i-ble (ir˝i zis´ti bl) *adj.* Completely fascinating; impossible to resist. **irresistibility** *n.* **irresistibly** *adv.*

ir-res-o-lu-ble (i re´zol´ū bl) *adj.* Admitting or having no explanation or solution.

ir-res-o-lute (i rez´o lŏt´) *adj.* Lacking resolution; indecisive; lacking firmness of purpose; hesitant. **irresolutely** *adv.* **irresoluteness** *n.*

ir-re-spec-tive (ir´i spek´tiv) *adj.* Regardless of; not related to certain conditions. **irrespective of** *prep.* Without regard to anything.

ir-re-spon-si-bil-i-ty (ir˝i spon´si bil´i tē) *n.* The quality of being irresponsible.

ir-re-spon-si-ble (ir˝i spon´si bl) *adj.* Lacking in responsibility; not accountable. **irresponsibly** *adv.*

ir-re-spon-sive (ir˝i spon´siv) *adj.* Unable to react or respond.

ir-re-triev-a-ble (ir´i trē´va bl) *adj.* Unable to be retrieved or recovered.

ir-rev-er-ence (i rev´ėr ens) *n.* A lack of reverence; a disrespectful action.

ir-rev-er-ent (i rev´ ėr ent) *adj.* Lacking the proper respect. **irreverently** *adv.*

ir-re-vers-i-ble (ir˝i ver´si bl) *adj.* Impossible to reverse. **irreversibility** *n.* **irreversibly** *adv.*

ir-rev-o-ca-ble (i rev´o ka bl) *adj.* Unable or incapable of being turned in the other direction; incapable of being repealed, annulled or undone. **irrevocability** *n.* **irrevocably** *adv.*

ir-ri-gate (ir´i gāt´) *v.* To water the land or crops artificially, as by means of ditches or sprinklers; to refresh with water. *Med.* To wash out with a medicated fluid or water. **irrigation** *n.* **irrigator** *n.* **irrigational** *adj.*

ir-ri-ta-ble (ir´i ta bl) *adj.* Easily annoyed; ill-tempered. *Pathol.* To respond abnormally to stimuli. **irritability** *n.* **irritableness** *n.* **irritably** *adv.*

ir-ri-tate (ir´i tāt´) *v.* To annoy or bother; to provoke; to be sore, chafed, or inflamed. **irritant** *adj. & n.* **irritator** *n.* **irritation** *n.* **irritatingly** *adv.*

ir-ri-ta-tive (ir´i tā˝tiv) *adj.* Serving to excite or irritate; produced or accompanied by an irritant or irritation.

ir-rupt (i rupt´) *v.* To burst or rush in; to invade. **irruption** *n.* **irruptive** *adj.* **irruptively** *adv.*

IRS *abbr.* Internal Revenue Service.

is (iz) *v.* Third person, singular, present tense of the verb to be.

Is *abbr.* Island; islands.

i-sa-gog-ic (ī´sa goj´ik) *adj.* To introduce one to the Bible. *pl.* **isagogics** *n.* The introductory study to the critical interpretation of the sacred writings of the Bible.

is-al-lo-bar (ī sal´o bär˝) *n.* A line on a chart which connects the locations of equal change of atmospheric pressure.

is-ba (iz bä´) *n.* The Russian log hut.

ISBN *abbr.* International Standard Book Number.

ISC *abbr.* International Space Congress; Interstate commerce.

is-che-mi-a (i skē´mē a) *n.* The tissue anemia that is localized due to an obstruction of the inflow of arterial blood.

is-chi-um (is´kēm um) *n. pl.* **ischia** The posterior bone of the pelvis at the hip joint of the body.

is-en-tro-pic (īs´en trō˝pik) *adj.* To be related to constant entropy.

-ish *suffix* Of or belonging to a nationality or ethnic group; characteristic of; the approximate age of; the approximate time of; somewhat.

Is-is (īs´is) *n.* The nature goddess of the Egyptians.

is-land (ī´land) *n.* A piece of land smaller than a continent, completely surrounded by water.

is-land-er (ī´lan dėr) *n.* A person who makes his home on an island.

island universe *n.* Any galaxy other than the Milky Way.

isle (īl) *n.* A small island.

is-let (ī´lit) *n.* A small island.

-ism *suffix* Practice; process; a manner of behavior characteristic of person or thing; a system of principles.

is-n´t (lz´ont) *contr.* Is not.

iso-ag-glu-ti nin (ī´sō a glŏt´i nin) *n.* A

clotting agent from one individual organism, effective in the cells of other individuals of the same species.

iso-bar (ī´so bär˝) *n.* An imaginary line or a line drawn on a map connecting places on the surface of the earth where the barometric pressure is the same for a given time.

iso-bath (ī´so bath˝) *n.* An imaginary line, or a line drawn on a map, connecting points that have the same depth below sea level.

iso-cli-nal (ī´so klīn´al) *adj.* To be having an equality of inclination.

iso-cy-clic (ī´sō sī˝klik) *adj.* Being or having a ring composed of atoms of only one element.

iso-di-a-met-ric (ī´so dī˝a me´trik) *adj.* Having equal axes or diameters; having a similar diameter throughout.

iso-e-lec-tron-ic (ī´sō i lek tron´ik) *adj.* To have the same number of electrons.

iso-gen-ic (ī´sō jen˝ik) *adj.* To be characterized by having identical genes.

iso-ge-o-therm (ī´so jē´o thurm˝) *n.* The imaginary line under the earth's surface which passes through points with the same mean temperature.

iso-gloss (ī´so glos˝) *n.* A boundary line that divides areas which differ in a particular linguistic feature. **isoglossal** *n.*

iso-gon-ic (ī´so gon˝ik) *adj.* To be growing so that sizes of parts remain equivalent.

iso-gram (ī´so gram˝) *n.* A line on a map or chart showing all points having constant value in relation to any climatic variable.

iso-late (ī´so lāt´) *v.* To set apart from the others; to put by itself; to place or be placed in quarantine. **isolation** *n.*

iso-la-tion-ism (ī´so lā´sha niz´um) *n.* A national policy of avoiding political or economic alliances or relations with other countries. **isolationist** *n.*

iso-mer (ī´so mėr) *n.* A compound having the same kinds and numbers of atoms as another compound but differing in chemical or physical properties due to the linkage or arrangement of the atoms.

isomeric *adj.*

isosceles triangle *n.*
A triangle which has
two equal sides.

iso-therm (ī′so
therm′) *n.* A line on
a map linking points
that have the same temperature.
isothermal *adj.*

iso-tope (ī′so tōp′) *n.* Any of two or more
species of atoms of a chemical element
which contain in their nuclei the same
number of protons but different numbers
of neutrons. **isotopic** *adj.*

iso-trop-ic (ī′so trop′ik) *adj.* Having the
same value in all directions. **isotropy** *n.*

Is-rae-li (iz rā′lē) *adj.* Of or pertaining to
the country of Israel or its inhabitants.
Israel *n.*

Is-ra-el-ite (iz rē e līt′) *n.* A Hebrew.

is-sue (ish′ö) *n.* The act of giving out; something that is given out or published; a matter
of importance to solve. *Med.* A discharge
as of pus or blood. **issue** *v.* To come forth;
to flow out; to emerge; to distribute or give
out, as supplies. **issuable** *adj.* **issuer** *n.*

it (it) *pron.* Used as a substitute for a specific
noun or name when referring to places,
things, or animals of unspecified sex; used
to refer to the general state of something.

I-tal-ian (i tal′yan) *adj.* Italian in character.
Italian *n.* A person living in Italy.

i-tal-ic (i tal′ik) *adj.* A style of printing type
in which the letters slant to the right. **italics**
n. pl. Italic typeface.

i-tal-i-cize (i tal′i sīz′) *v.* To print in italics.

I-tal-y (i′tal ē) *n.* A country in southern
Europe, bordered by the Mediterranean Sea.

itch (ich) *n.* A skin irritation which causes
a desire to scratch; a contagious skin disease accompanied by a desire to scratch;
a restless desire or craving. **itch** *v.* **itch-**
iness *n.* **itchy** *adj.*

-ite *suffix* A native or inhabitant of; an adherent of; a sympathizer or follower; a
descndant of; a rock or mineral.

i-tem (ī′tem) *n.* A separately-noted unit or
article included in a category or series; a

short article, as in a magazine or newspaper.

i-tem-ize (ī′te mīz″) *v.* To specify by item;
to list. **itemizer** *n.* **itemization** *n.*

it-er-ate (it′e rāt′) *v.* To state or do again;
to repeat. **iteration** *n.*

i-tin-er-ant (ī tin′ėr ant) *adj.* Traveling
from place to place; wandering around.
itinerant *n.*

i-tin-er-ar-y (ī tin′e rer″ē) *n. pl.* **itiner-**
aries A scheduled route of a trip.

it′ll (it′il) *contr.* It will; it shall.

it′s (its) *contr.* It is; it has.

its (its) *adj.* The possessive case of the
pronoun it.

-ity *n. suffix* Quality or state.

IUD *abbr.* Intrauterine device.

IV *abbr.* Intravenous.

i-vied (ī′vēd) To be overgrown with ivy.

i-vo-ry (ī′vo rē) *n.* A hard, smooth, yellowish-white material which forms the
tusks of elephants, walruses, and other
animals; any substance similar to ivory;
a yellow to creamy-white color. **ivories**
The teeth; the keys on a piano. **ivory** *adj.*

ivory–billed woodpecker *n.* A type of
large and almost extinct woodpecker living
in the southeastern United States.

ivory black *n.* A type of black pigment that
can be made by calcining ivory.

ivory nut *n.* A nutlike seed of South America's palm which can be used for carving;
used as a substitute for ivory to make
buttons, chessmen, or other such items.

ivory palm *n.* A low-growing tropical
American palm that produces the ivory
nut.

ivory tower *n.* A condition or attitude of
withdrawal from the world and reality;
seclusion.

ivory towered *adj.* To be divorced from
practical matters.

i-vy (ī′vē) *n. pl.* **ivies** A climbing plant
having glossy evergreen leaves.

-ization *suffix* The process, action, or result
of doing a specified thing.

-ize *suffix* To cause to become or resemble.

iz-zard (iz′ėrd) *n.* The letter Z.

J, j (jā) The tenth letter of the English alphabet.

JA *abbr.* Joint account; judge advocate.

jab (jab) *v.* To poke or thrust sharply with short blows; a rapid punch.

jab-ber (jab´ėr) *v.* To speak quickly or without making sense.

Jab-ber-wock-y (jab´ėr wok˝ē) *n.* A poem characterized by meaningless speech and nonsense syllables; an imitation of this in speech or in writing; gibberish.

jab-i-ru (jab´i rŏ˝) *n.* A wading bird of the stork family, usually white in color.

jab-ot (zha bō´) *n.* A ruffle or decoration on the front of a blouse, dress, or shirt; a lace decoration that was formerly worn by men.

ja-bot-i-ca-ba (ja bŏt˝i kāb´a) *n.* A tropical tree that yields an edible fruit that resembles the grape grown in warm climates such as Florida and California.

ja-cal (ha käl´) *n.* A small hut found in the southwestern United States and Mexico, with walls made of rows and rows of thin vertical poles filled in with mud.

jac-a-mar (jak´a mär˝) *n.* A tropical, brilliantly colored, insectivorous bird of tropical America.

ja-ca-na (zhä˝sa nä´) *n.* A small aquatic bird having long, straight claws that are adapted for walking on floating objects such as aquatic plants.

jac-a-ran-da (jak˝a ran´da) *n.* A tall tropical tree; or the fragrant wood of such a tree.

jack (jak) *n.* The playing card that ranks just below a queen and bears a representation of a knave; any of various tools or devices used for raising heavy objects; the male of certain animals; a man or boy; fellow; a small flag on a ship that indicates nationality *Electr.* A socket into which a plug is inserted to make an electric circuit.

jack-al (jak´al) *n.* An African or Asian doglike, carnivorous mammal; a person who works as a slave for another..

jack-a-napes (jak´a nāps) *n.* An impudent person, an impudent child.

jack-ass (jak´as˝) *n.* A male donkey or ass;

a stupid person or one who acts in a stupid fashion.

jack-boot (jak´bŏt˝) *n.* A heavy military boot which reaches above the knee.

jack-daw (jak´do˝) *n.* A glossy, black, crow-like bird.

jack-et (jak´it) *n.* A short coat worn by men and women; an outer protective cover for a book; the skin of a cooked potato. **jacketed, jacketless, jacketlike** *adj.*

Jack Frost *n.* A name given to frost or winter weather.

jack-hammer (jak´ham˝ėr) *n.* A tool operated by air pressure, used to break pavement and to drill rock.

jack–in–the–box (jak´in the boks˝) *n.* A toy consisting of a small box from which a puppet springs up when the lid is unfastened.

jack–in–the–pul-pit (jak´in the pel´pit) *n.* A common herb which grows from a turnip-shaped bulb.

Jack Ketch *n.* An executioner.

jack-knife (jak´nīf´) *n.* A large knife carried in a pocket; a dive executed by doubling the body forward with the knees unbent and the hands touching the ankles and then straightening before entering the water. **jackknife** *v.* To bend in the manner of a jackknife.

jack-leg (jak´leg˝) *adj.* Deficient in skill or training; having questionable practices; below professional quality or standards.

jack-light (jak´līt˝) *n.* A light used for hunting or fishing at night. **jacklight** *v.* To fish or hunt with a light.

jack mack-er-el *n.* A fish used for food, found along the California coast.

jack–of–all–trades (jak˝ov ol´trädz´) *n.* A person who is able to do many types of work.

jack–o–lan-tern (jak´o lan˝tėrn) *n.* A lantern made from a hollowed out pumpkin which has been carved to resemble a face.

jack pine *n.* A North American pine tree growing in barren or rocky areas.

jack-pot (jak´pot˝) *n.* Any post, prize, or pool in which the amount won is cumulative.

jack rabbit *n.* A large American hare with long back legs and long ears.

jacks *n.* A game played with a set of six-pronged metal pieces and a small ball.

jack-screw (jak′ skrŏ″) *n.* A jack used for lifting a heavy object a short distance.

Jackson, Andrew *n.* (1767-1845) The seventh president of the United States from 1829-1837.

jack stay (jak′ stā″) *n.* A yard or a gaff rod or rope used for bending a sail to.

jack tow-el *n.* A long towel with the ends sewn together that hangs on a roller.

Ja-cob (jā′kob) *n.* A Hebrew patriarch.

Jacob's ladder (jā′kobz lad′ėr) *n.* The ladder Jacob saw in his dreams, which extended from earth to heaven. *Naut.* A ladder with wooden or metal rungs and nonrigid sides. *Bot.* A plant with blue flowers with ladder-like leaflets.

jac-o-net (jak′ o net″) *n.* A cotton fabric. from India that is soft and light.

jac-ti-ta-tion (jak″ti tā′shan) *n.* An untrue statement which is insulting to another.

jac-u-late (jak′ū lāt″) *v.* To throw outwards; to hurl.

jade (jād) *n.* A hard, translucent, green gemstone; an old, worn-out, unmanageable horse; a mean old woman; hussy. **jade** *adj.* Worn-out; exhausted. **jade** *v.*

jad-ed (jā′did) *adj.* Tired; worn-out; bored.

jade green *n.* The color of jade, a light green tinted with blue.

Jade-ite (jā′ dīt) *n.* A highly valued kind of jade consisting of a silicate of sodium and aluminum; it ranges from pale green to emerald green in color.

jae-ger (yā′ gėr, jā′ gėr) *n.* Any of several sea birds that get food by forcing weaker birds to relinquish their prey.

jag (jag) *n.* A very sharp projection or point. *Slang* A binge or spree.

jag-ged *adj.* Having jags or sharp notches; serrated. **jaggedly** *adv.* **jaggedness** *n.*

jag-ger-y (jag′e rē) *n.* A brown sugar made from palm tree sap.

jag-uar (jag′wär) *n.* A large feline mammal of tropical America with a tawny coat and black spots.

ja-gua-run-di (jä′gwa run′dē) *n. pl.* **jaguarundis** A type of wildcat that is short-legged and slender.

jai alai (hī′lī″) *n.* A game similar to handball in which players catch and throw a ball with long, curved, wicker baskets strapped to their arms.

jail (jāl) *n.* A place of confinement for incarceration.

jail-bird (jāl′bėrd″) *n.* A prisoner or ex-prisoner.

jail-break (jāl′brāk″) *n.* A prison escape involving the use of force.

jail delivery *n.* The freeing of prisoners by force.

jail-er (jā′lėr) *n.* The officer in charge of a jail and its prisoners.

Jain-ism (jī′niz um) *n.* An ancient religion of India.

ja-lop-y (ja lop′ē) *n. pl.* **jalopies** *Slang* An old, run-down automobile.

ja-lou-sie (jal′o sē″) *n.* A window, blind, or door having adjustable horizontal slats.

jam (jam) *v.* To force or wedge into a tight position; to apply the brakes of a car suddenly; to be locked in a position; to block; to crush. *Mus.* To be a participant in a jazz session. *Slang* To be in a difficult situation or to be crowded together, as of people, cars; a difficult situation. **jam** *n.* A preserve of whole fruit boiled with sugar.

Jamaica ginger *n.* An extract of ginger used for flavoring made from ginger that is grown in Jamaica.

Ja-mai-can (ja mā′kan) *adj.* Relating to the island of Jamaica in the West Indies, or to its people.

Jamaica rum *n.* A dark brown rum made from Jamaican molasses.

jamb (jam) *n.* The vertical sidepiece of a door.

jam-ba-lay-a (jum″ba lī′a) *n.* A dish of rice that is cooked with vegetable, and various kinds of fish, meat, but usually shrimp or ham.

jam-beau (jam´bō) *n.* A medieval piece of armor worn to protect the lower leg.

jam-bo-ree (jam˝bo rē´) *n.* A large, festive gathering.

jam session *n.* An informal gathering of a group of jazz musicians, usually for their own enjoyment.

Jan. *abbr.* January.

Jane Doe *n.* A woman's name that is used in hypotheses, especially in a legal proceeding when a woman's name is unknown or unimportant.

jan-gle (jang´gl) *v.* To make a harsh, unmusical sound; to dispute something in an angry way; to cause to become angry, tense or mad. **jangle** *n.* A discordant sound; a dispute or quarrel. **jangle, jangler** *n.*

jan-i-tor (jan´i tėr) *n.* A person who cleans and cares for a building, office, school, apartment, etc. **janitorial** *adj.*

Jan-u-ar-y (jan´ū er˝ē) *n.* The first month of the year, having thirty-one days.

ja-pan (ja pan´) *n.* A black varnish used for coating metal, wood and other objects. **japan** *v.* To varnish an object with japan.

Ja-pan clo-ver *n.* A clover bush grown in the southern states of the United States and used as a forage crop.

Jap-a-nese (jap˝a nēz´) *adj.* Pertaining to Japan, its people, or their language.

Jap-a-nese an-drom-e-da (jap˝a nēz´ an drom´i da) *n.* An evergreen shrub found in Asia, bearing clusters of white flowers.

Jap-a-nese bee-tle *n.* A green and brown beetle which is very damaging to plants.

Japanese millet *n.* A coarse grass that is grown for its forage and its seeds used in bird feed.

Jap-a-nese per-sim-mon *n.* An edible fruit grown in the United States; the fruit itself, either red or orange in color.

Japanese quince *n.* A yellow-green fruit used to make preserves; the red-flowered shrub similar to a rose bush that bears the quince fruit.

Jap-a-nize (jap´a nīz) *n.* To conform to Japanese ideas or usages.

Japan wax *n.* A derivative from berries of Chinese and Japanese sumacs, used in the manufacturing of furniture and floor polishes.

jape (jāp) *v.* To joke; to make fun of or mock by words or actions. **jape, japer, japery** *n.*

Jap-o-nism (jap´oniz˝um) *n.* To adapt to Japanese styles or methods; any mannerism or trait that is characteristic of the Japanese.

jar (jär) *n.* A deep, cylindrical vessel with a wide mouth; a harsh sound. **jar** *v.* To strike against or bump into; to affect one's feelings unpleasantly.

jar-di-niere (jär´di nēr´) *n.* A decorative pot or stand for flowers or plants; a garnish for meat made from cooked and diced vegetables.

jar-gon (jär´gon) *n.* The technical or specialized vocabulary used among members of a particular profession. a type of speech containing pretentious or unfamiliar words; unintelligible writing or speech; gibberish. **jargonistic** *adj.*

jar-gon-ize (jär´g´o nīz´) *v.* To write or communicate jargon; a means of expressing onself with jargon.

jas-mine *or* **jes-sa-mine (jaz´min)** *n.* A shrub with fragrant yellow or white flowers.

jas-per (jas´pėr) *n.* An opaque red, brown, or yellow variety of quartz, having a high polish and often used for jewelry and vases.

ja-to (jā´tō) *n.* A takeoff of an airplane which is assisted by an auxilliary rocket engine.

jaun-dice (jon´dis) *n., Pathol.* A diseased condition of the liver due to the presence of bile pigments in the blood and characterized by yellowish staining of the eyes, skin, and body fluids.

jaun-diced (jon´dist) *adj.* To be affected with jaundice.

jaunt (jont) *n.* A short journey for pleasure. *v.* To make a short journey, trip, or excursion.

jaunting car *n.* A light weight, open air cart that has two seats, set back to back or facing each other, with an area in front for the driver.

jaun-ty (jon'tē) *adj.* Having a buoyantly carefree and self-confident air or manner about oneself. **jauntily** *adv.* **jauntiness** *n.*

Ja-va (jä'va) *n.* An Indonesian island. *Slang* Coffee; *Computer* Language used to program over the internet.

Jav-a-nese (jav˝a nēz') *n.* An inhabitant of Java or the language spoken there.

jave-lin (jav'lin) *n.* A light spear thrown as a weapon; a long spear with a wooden shaft, used in competitions of distance throwing.

jave-lin throw *v.* To wound or strike with a javelin.

jaw (jo) *n., Anat.* Either of the two bony structures forming the framework of the mouth and the teeth.

jaw-bone (jo'bōn˝) *n.* One of the bones of the jaw, especially the lower jaw or mandible.

jaw-break-er (jo'brā˝kėr) *n.* A very hard piece of candy. *Slang* A word which is hard to pronounce.

Jaws of Life *n.* A trademark for a metal device having pincer-like arms used to provide access to persons trapped inside a crushed vehicle.

jay (jā) *n.* Any of various corvine birds of brilliant coloring, as the blue jay.

Jay-cee (jā'sē') *n.* A young man belonging to an organization connected with a city's chamber of commerce.

jay-hawk-er (jā'ho˝kėr) *n.* The nickname for a person who is native to Kansas.

jay-walk (jā'wauk˝) *v., Slang* To cross a street carelessly, violating traffic regulations and or signals. **jaywalker** *n.*

jazz (jaz) *n.* A kind of music which has a strong rhythmic structure with frequent syncopation and often involving ensemble and solo improvisation. *Slang* Lying and exaggerated talk; idle and foolish talk; liveliness. **jazz up** To make more interesting; to enliven. **jazzer** *n.* **jazzy** *adj.*

jazz band *n.* A musical band that plays jazz, and typically uses the saxophone, clarinet, piano, trombone, and drums.

jazz-y (jaz'ē) *adj. Slang.* Lively; relating to or reminiscent of jazz music.

jct *abbr.* Junction.

jeal-ous (jel'us) *adj.* Suspicious or fearful of being replaced by a rival; resentful or bitter in rivalry; demanding exclusive love. **jealously** *adv.* **jealousness** *n.*

jeal-ous-y (jel'o sē) *n.* Envy; resentment against a rival or someone who possesses any coveted advantage.

jean (jēn) *n.* A strong, twilled cotton cloth. **jeans** *n. pl.* Pants made of denim.

jeep (jēp) *n.* A trademark for a small, military, and civilian vehicle with four-wheel drive.

jeer (jēr) *v.* To speak or shout derisively. **jeer, jeerer** *n.* **jeeringly** *adv.*

Jefferson City *n.* The capital of the state of Missouri.

Je-ho-vah (ji hō'va) *n.* God, in the Christian translations of the Old Testament.

je-june (ji jōn') *adj.* Lacking in substance or nourishment; immature.

je-ju-num (ji jō'num) *n., Anat.* The part of the small intestine which extends from the duodenum to the ileum.

jel-li-fy (jel'i fī) *v.* To prepare or turn into jelly.

jel-ly (jel'ē) *n. pl.* **jellies** Any food preparation made with pectin or gelatin and having a somewhat elastic consistency; a food made of boiled and sweetened fruit juice and used as a filler or spread. **jelly** *v.* To make into jelly; to become or take the form of jelly; to become gelatin-ous; to assume or cause to assume definite form.

jel-ly-bean (jel'ē bēn˝) *n.* A small candy having a hard, colored coating over a gelatinous center.

jel-ly-fish (jel'ē fish˝) *n. pl.* **jellyfishes** Any of a number of free-swimming marine animals of jellylike substance, often having bell or umbrella-shaped bodies with trailing tentacles; a person lacking determination; a spineless weakling.

jelly roll *n.* A rectangular layer of sponge cake, spread with jelly and then rolled up.

jen-net (jen´it) *n.* Name for a female donkey or a small Spanish horse.

jeop-ard-ize *v.* To put in jeopardy; to expose to loss or danger.

jeop-ard-y (jep´ėr dē) *n.* Exposure to loss or danger.

je-quir-i-ty (je kwir´i tē) *n.* The beans or seeds of the Indian licorice plant, black and scarlet in color, which contain abrin, a potent poison released when the seeds are broken open; the plant itself.

jer-bo-a (jėr bō´a) *n.* Any of a type of small, nocturnal rodent of Asia and Africa with long hind legs.

jer-e-mi-ad (jer˝e mī´ad) *n.* A lament or prolonged complaint.

Jer-e-mi-ah *n.* A Hebrew prophet of the seventh century B.C.

jerk (jerk) *v.* To give a sharp twist or pull to. **jerk** *n.* A sudden movement, as a tug or twist. *Physiol.* An involuntary contraction of a muscle resulting from a reflex action. *Slang* An annoying or foolish person. **jerky, jerkily** *adv.* **jerkiness** *n.*

jer-kin (jer´kin) *n.* A close-fitting jacket, usually sleeveless.

jerk-wa-ter (jerk´wo˝tėr) *adj.* Of little importance.

jer-o-boam (jer˝o bō´am) *n.* An extra-large wine bottle.

jer-ry-build (jer´ē bild˝) *v.* To build flimsily and cheaply. **jerrybuilt** *adj.*

jer-sey (jer´zē) *n. pl.* **jerseys** A soft ribbed fabric of wool, cotton, or other material; a knitted sweater, jacket, or shirt; fawn-colored, small dairy cattle which yield milk rich in butter fat.

Je-ru-sal-lem *n.* Capital of Israel.

jess (jes) *n.* A leather strap tied around each of the legs of a hawk, to which the falconer's leash is attached.

jest (jest) *n.* An action or remark intended

to provoke laughter; a joke; a playful mood. **jester** *n.*

Jes-u-it (jezh´ŏ it) *n.* A member of the Society of Jesus, a religious order founded in 1534.

Jesus (jē´zus) *n.* The founder of Christianity, son of Mary and regarded in the Christian faith as Christ the son of God, the Messiah; also referred to as Jesus Christ or Jesus of Nazareth.

jet (jet) *n.* A sudden spurt or gush of liquid or gas emitted through a narrow opening; a jet airplane; a hard, black mineral which takes a high polish and is used in jewelry; a deep glossy black.

jet engine *n.* An aircraft engine, which achieves its fast forward propulsion by discharging its oxidized fuel as hot air and gases through a rear exhaust system.

jet lag *n.* Mental and physical fatigue resulting from rapid travel through several time zones.

jet-lin-er (jet´lī˝nėr) *n.* A commercial jet plane carrying passengers and cargo.

jet–pro-pelled (jet´pro peld´) *adj.* Being moved by the power of a jet engine, usually referring to an airplane.

jet set *n.* An international social group of wealthy individuals who travel from one fashionable place to another for pleasure. **jet setter** *n.*

jet stream *n.* A high-velocity wind near the troposphere, generally moving from west to east often at speeds exceeding 250 mph.; a high-speed stream of gas or other fluid expelled from a jet engine or rocket.

jet-ti-son (jet´i son) *v.* To throw cargo overboard; to discard a useless or hampering item.

jet-ty (jet´ē) *n. pl.* **jetties** A wall, made by piling rocks or other material, which extends into a body of water to protect a harbor or influence the current; a pier.

Jew (jŏ) *n.* A descendant of the ancient Hebrew people; a person believing in Judaism.

jew-el (jŏ´el) *n.* A precious stone used for personal adornment; a person or thing of very rare excellence or value. **jewel** *v.* To furnish with jewels. **jewelry** *n.*

jew-el-er (jŏ´e lẽr) *n.* A person who makes or deals in jewelry.

jew-fish (jŏ´fish˝) *n.* A large fish of the sea bass family, found in the tropical waters of the Atlantic Ocean.

Jew-ish (jo´ish) *adj.* Of, relating to, or resembling the Jews, their customs, or their religion. **Jewishness** *n.*

Jew's harp (jŏz´härp˝) *n.* A small musical instrument held between the teeth when played, consisting of a U-shaped frame with a flexible metal piece attached which is plucked with the finger to produce twanging sounds.

Jez-e-bel (jez´e bel˝) *n.* The wife of Ahab, queen of Israel in the 9th century B.C., notorious for her evil actions.

jib (jib) *n., Naut.* A triangular sail set on a stay extending from the outer end of a jib boom. **jib** *v.* To swing or shift from one side of a vessel to the other.

jibe (jīb) *v.* To sail a course so that a vessel shifts from one side to the other; to be in agreement or in harmony.

jif-fy (jif´ē) *pl.* **jiffies** A very short time.

jig (jig) *n.* Any of a variety of fast, lively dances; the music for such a dance. *Mech.* A device used to hold and guide a tool.

jig-ger (jig´ẽr) *n.* A small measure holding 1-1/2 oz. used for measuring liquor. *Naut.* A small sail in the stern of a sailing craft. *Slang* A small item which does not have a particular name.

jig-ger-mast (jig´ẽr mast) *n.* A small mast in the stern of a small watercraft; the aftermost mast of a four-masted ship.

jig-gle (jig´l) *v.* To move or jerk lightly up and down. **jiggle** *n.* A jerky, unsteady movement.

jig saw *n.* A saw having a slim blade set vertically, used for cutting curved or irregular lines.

jig-saw puz-zle *n.* A puzzle consisting of many irregularly shaped pieces which fit together and form a picture.

jilt (jilt) *v.* To discard a lover. **jilt** *n.* A woman who discards a lover.

jim–dan-dy (jim´dan´dē) *adj.* Excellent; terrific; or admirable.

jim-jams (jim´jamz˝) *n., Slang.* Feelings of nervousness; delirium tremors.

jim-my (jim´ē) *n. pl.* **jimmies** A short crowbar, used by a burglar. **jimmy** *v.* To force open or break into with a jimmy.

jim-son weed (jim´son wēd) *n.* A tall, coarse, foul-smelling, poisonous annual weed with large, trumpet-shaped purplish or white flowers.

jin-gle (jing´gl) *v.* To make a light clinking or ringing sound. **jingle** *n.* A short, catchy song or poem, as one used for advertising.

jin-go (jing´gō) *n.* Self-proclaimed patriot who advocates a tough, warlike foreign policy. **jingoish** *adj.*

jin-go-ism *n.* Extreme nationalism which is marked by a belligerent foreign policy. **jingoist** *n.* **jingoistic** *adj.*

jink (jingk) *v.* To move with agility; to make a quick, evasive turn.

jinn (jin) *n. pl.* **jinni** *or* **jinn** In Moslem legend, a spirit with supernatural powers.

jin-rik-i-sha (jin rik´sha) *n.* A two-wheeled vehicle used in the Orient, which is pulled by one or more men.

jinx (jingks) *n., Slang* A person or thing thought to cause bad luck; a period of bad luck.

jit-ney (jit´nē) *n.* A vehicle carrying passengers for a small fee.

jit-ter (jit´ẽr) *v., Slang* To be intensely nervous. **jittery** *adj.*

jit-ter-bug (jit´ẽr bug˝) *n., Slang* A lively dance or one who performs this dance. **jitterbug** *v.*

jit-ters *n.* Nervousness.

jive (jīv) *n., Slang* Jazz or swing music and musicians.

job (job) *n.* Anything that is done; work that is done for a set fee; the project worked on; a position of employment. **jobless** *adj.* **joblessness** *n.*

job-ber (job´ėr) *n.* One who buys goods in bulk from the manufacturer and sells them to retailers; a person who works by the job; a pieceworker.

job-ber-y (job´e rē) *n.* Graft; dishonest use of a public office for private gain.

job-hold-er (job´hōl´dėr) *n.* Someone who is working at a steady job.

job–hop-ping (job´hop˝ing) *n.* The act of changing jobs at short intervals; often for better pay. **job–hopper** *n.*

job lot *n.* A mixed set of goods sold in a single deal, often at a reduced price.

job-name *n.* In Computer Science, a code that is assigned to a specific job instruction in a computer program, for the operator's use.

Job's–tears (jōbz´tērz´) *n.* A grass found in the tropics that has small oval fruits or seeds that have a resemblance to tears.

job work *n.* Work done by the job.

jock (jok) *n., Slang* A male athlete in college; a person who participates in athletics.

jock-ey (jok´ē) *n.* A person who rides a horse as a professional in a race; one who works with a specific object or device.

jock-ey club *n.* A group of officials and horse owners who are involved in racing which is formed to promote horse racing and detemine the rules for it.

jo-cose (jō kōs´) *adj.* To be joking and jesting; causing laughter; merry; playful.

joc-u-lar (jok´ū lėr) *adj.* Marked by joking; playful. **jocularity** *n.* **jocularly** *adv.*

joc-und (jok´and) *adj.* Cheerful; merry; suggestive of high spirits and lively mirthfulness. **jocundity** *n.* **jocundly** *adv.*

jodh-pur (jod´pėr) *n.* Riding breeches that are wide at the hips, narrow at the knees and fit tightly to the ankles.

joe–pye weed (jō˝pī´ wēd) *n.* A tall wild flower with clusters of pink to purple flowers that blooms in the summer.

jog (jog) *n.* A slight movement or a slight shake; the slow steady trot of a horse, especially when exercising or participating in a sport; a projecting or retreating part in a surface or line. **jog** *v.* To shift direction

abruptly; to exercise by running at a slow but steady pace. **jogger** *n.*

jog-gle (jog´l) *v.* To move or shake slightly. **joggle** *n.*

jog trot *n.* An easy, slow-paced trot, alternated with periods of fast walking, used for physical fitness; a slow gait of a horse.

john (jon) *n., Slang* Toilet; A prostitute's client.

John *n.* One of the twelve Apostles.

John Doe *n., Law* A person in a legal proceeding whose true name is unknown.

John Han-cock (jon han´kok) *n.* One of the signers of the Declaration of Independence. *Slang* A signature.

john-ny-cake (jon´ē kāk´) *n.* A thin bread made with cornmeal.

john-ny–come–late-ly *n. Slang* A late or recent arrival.

Johnson, Lyndon Baines *n.* (1908-1973) The 36th president of the United States from 1963-1969.

John the Baptist *n.* The baptizer of Jesus Christ.

join (join) *v.* To bring or put together so as to form a unit; to become a member of an organization; to participate.

join-er (joi´nėr) *n.* A person whose occupation is to build articles by joining pieces of wood; a cabinet maker; a carpenter.

joint (joint) *n.* The place where two or more things or parts are joined; a point where bones are connected. *Slang* A disreputable or shabby place of entertainment. **joint** *adj.* Marked by cooperation, as a joint effort.

joint res-o-lu-tion *n.* A resolution that is approved by the two houses of a legislature, which becomes law when signed by the chief executive.

joint-ress (join´tris) *n.* A woman who has received an estate after her husband's death.

joint return *n.* A tax report disclosing the income of a husband and a wife.

joint tenancy *n.* Equal ownership of property by two or more persons, with the property passing to the survivors in case of the death of a joint owner.

join-ture (join´chėr) *n., Law* A settlement of property arranged by a husband which is to be used for the support of his wife after his death.

joint-worm (joint´ wurm˝) *n.* The larva of a group of injurious insects that feeds in or near the joints of stalks of grain.

joist (joist) *n.* Any of a number of small parallel beams set from wall to wall to support a floor.

joke (jōk) *n.* Something said or done to cause laughter, such as a brief story with a punch line; something not taken seriously. **joke** *v.* To tell or play jokes. **jokingly** *adv.*

jok-er (jō´kėr) *n.* A person who jokes; a playing card, used in certain card games as a wild card; an unsuspected or unapparent fact which nullifies a seeming advantage.

jol-li-fi-ca-tion *n.* Merrymaking; festivity.

jol-ly (jol´ē) *adj.* Full of good humor; merry. **jollity** *n.* **jolly** *v.*

jolt (jōlt) *v.* To knock or shake about. **jolt** *n.* A sudden bump or jar, as from a blow.

Jon-ah (jō´na) *n.* An 8th or 9th century B.C. Hebrew prophet who was swallowed by a whale and then cast on the shore alive three days later; a person who brings bad luck.

jon-quil (jong´kwil) *n.* A widely grown species of narcissus related to the daffodil, having fragrant white or yellow flowers and long narrow leaves.

jo-rum (jōr´um) *n.* A large drinking vessel.

Jo-seph *n.* The husband of Mary, the mother of Jesus.

Joseph of Arimathea *n.* A very wealthy disciple of Christ who provided the tomb for his burial.

josh (josh) *v., Slang* To make good-humored fun of someone; to tease; to joke.

Jos-hu-a *n.* The successor of Moses.

joss (jos) *n.* A Chinese idol or image.

joss stick *n.* A stick of incense burnt by the Chinese.

jos-tle (jos´l) *v.* To make one's way through a crowd by pushing, elbowing, or shoving. **jostler** *n.*

jot (jot) *v.* To make a brief note of something. **jot** *n.* A tiny bit.

jounce (jouns) *v.* To bounce; to bump; to shake. **jounce** *n.* **jouncy** *adj.*

jour *abbr.* Journal; journalist.

jour-nal (jer´nal) *n.* A diary or personal daily record of observations and experiences; in bookkeeping, a book in which daily financial transactions are recorded. *Mech.* The part of an axle which rotates in or against a bearing.

jour-nal-ese (jer´na lēz´) *n.* The vocabulary and style of writing supposedly characteristic of most newspapers.

jour-nal-ism (jer´na liz˝um) *n.* The occupation, collection, writing, editing, and publishing of newspapers and other periodicals. **journalist** *n.* **journalistic** *adj.* **journalistically** *adv.*

jour-ney (jer´nē) *n.* A trip from one place to another over a long distance; the distance that is traveled. **journey** *v.* to make a trip; to travel a long distance.

jour-ney-man (jer´nē man) *n. pl.* **journeymen** A worker who has served an apprenticeship in a skilled trade.

joust (joust) *n.* A formal combat between two knights on horseback as a part of a medieval tournament.

Jove (jōv) *Interj.* A mild expression of surprise or emphasis.

jo-vi-al (jō´vē al) *adj.* Good-natured; good-humored; jolly. **joviality** *n.*

jowl (joul) *n.* The fleshy part of the lower jaw; the cheek. **jowly** *adj.*

joy (joi) *n.* A strong feeling of great happiness; delight; a state or source of contentment or satisfaction; anything which makes one delighted or happy. **joyful, joyless** *adj.* **joyfully** *adv.* **joyfulness** *n.* **joylessly** *adv.* **joylessness** *n.*

joy-ous (joi´us) *adj.* Joyful; causing or feeling joy. **joyously** *adv.* **joyousness** *n.*

joy ride *Slang* A ride taken for pleasure only.

joy stick *Slang* The control stick of an airplane or video game.

JP *abbr.* Justice of the Peace.

JR *abbr.* Junior.

jub-bah (jub´ba) *n.* An outer garment worn in Muslin countries by both men and women, which is long and has sleeves.

ju-bi-lant (jö´bi lant) *adj.* Exultantly joyful or triumphant; expressing joy. **jubilance** *n.* **jubilantly** *adv.*

ju-bi-la-tion (jö˝bi lā´shan) *n.* Rejoicing; exultation.

ju-bi-lee (jö´bi lē˝) *n.* A special anniversary of an event; any time of rejoicing.

Ju-dah *n.* In the Old Testament, a son of Jacob and Leah; the ancient kingdom in southern Palestine.

Ju-da-ic *or* **Judaical (jö dā´ik)** *adj.* Of or pertaining to Jews. **Judaically** *adv.*

Ju-da-ism (jö´dē iz˝um) *n.* The religious practices or beliefs of the Jews; a religion based on the belief in one God.

Ju-das (jö´das) *n.* One of the twelve Apostles; the betrayer of Jesus; one who betrays another under the guise of friendship.

Ju-de-a *n.* The southern part of ancient Palestine. **Judean** *adj. & n.*

judge (juj) *v., Law* A public officer who passes judgment in a court. **judge** *v.* To decide authoritatively after deliberation.

judge ad-vo-cate *n.* The staff officer appointed to prosecute during a court martial trial; a legal advisor.

judg-ment (juj´ment) *n.* The ability to make a wise decision or to form an opinion; the act of judging. *Law* The sentence or determination of a court. **judgmental** *adj.*

ju-di-ca-ble (jö´di ka bl) *adj.* Able to be judged or tried.

ju-di-ca-to-ry (jö´di ka tōr˝ē) *adj.* Pertaining to the administration of justice. **judicatory** *n.* A court of justice; a person or persons having judicial authority; processes used to administer justice.

ju-di-ca-ture (jö´di kā˝chèr) *n.* The function or action of administration of justice; law, courts, or judges as a whole.

ju-di-cial (jö dish´al) *adj.* Pertaining to the administering of justice, to courts of law, or to judges; enforced or decreed by a court of law. **judicially** *adv.*

ju-di-ci-ar-y (jö dish´ē er˝ē) *adj.* Of or pertaining to judges, courts, or judgments. **judiciary** *n.* The department of the government which administers the law; a system of courts of law.

ju-di-cious (jö dish´us) *adj.* Having, showing, or exercising good sound judgment. **judiciously** *adv.* **judiciousness** *n.*

Judith *n.* A Jewish heroine who rescued her countrymen by slaying the Assyrian general, Holofernes.

ju-do (jö´dō) *n.* A system or form of self-defense, developed from jujitsu in Japan in 1882, which emphasizes principles of balance and leverage.

ju-do-gi (jö dō´ gē) *n.* A loosely fitted white cotton costume, worn by judo wrestlers.

jug (jug) *n.* A small pitcher or similar vessel for holding liquids. *Slang* A jail.

ju-gal (jö´gal) *adj.* Relating to the bony arch of the cheek.

jug-ger-naut (jug´èr not˝) *n.* Any destructive force or object.

jug-gle (jug´l) *v.* To keep several objects continuously moving from the hand into the air; to practice fraud or deception.

ju-glan-da-ceous (jö˝glan dā´shus) *adj.* Belonging to the tree family that includes walnuts and hickories.

jug-u-lar (jug´ū lèr) *adj., Anat.* Of or pertaining to the throat or the jugular vein.

jugular vein *n., Anat.* One of the large veins on either side of the neck.

ju-gu-late (jö´gū lāt) *v.* To use extreme measures in order to suppress disease; to slit the throat.

ju-gum (jö´ gum) *n.* In some insects, an area at the base of the forewings which locks the forewings and hindwings together during flight.

juice (jös) *n.* The liquid part of a vegetable, fruit, or animal. *Slang* Electric current. **juice** *v.*

juic-er (jŏ'sėr) *n.* A device for extracting juice from fruit.

juic-y (jŏ'sē) *adj.* Full of; abounding with juice; full of interest; richly rewarding, especially financially. **juiciness** *n.*

ju-jit-su (jŏ jit'sŏ) *n.* A Japanese system of using holds, throws, and stunning blows to subdue an opponent.

juke-box (jŏk'boks˝) *n.* A large, automatic, coin-operated record player equipped with push buttons for the selection of records.

juke joint *n., Slang* A place of entertainment offering food, drinks, and dancing to juke-box music.

ju-lep (jū'lip) *n.* A mint julep.

ju-li-enne (jŏ˝lē en´) *adj.* Cut into thin strips. **julienne** *n.* A clear meat soup containing vegetables chopped or cut into thin strips.

Ju-ly (jū lī´) *n.* The seventh month of the year, having 31 days.

jum-ble (jum'bl) *v.* To mix in a confused mass; to throw together without order; to confuse or mix something up in the mind. **jumble** *n.*

jum-bo (jum'bō) *n.* A very large person, animal, or thing. **jumbo** *adj.* Extremely large.

jump (jump) *v.* To spring from the ground, floor, or other surface into the air by using a muscular effort of the legs and feet; to move in astonishment; to leap over; to increase greatly, as prices. *Informal* To attack by surprise. *Computer Science* To move from one set of instructions in a program to another set further behind or ahead.

jump-er (jum'pėr) *n.* One who or that which jumps; a sleeveless dress, usually worn over a blouse. *Electr.* A short wire used to by-pass or join parts of a circuit.

jump-ing bean *n.* The seed of certain shrubs from Mexico which jumps about due to the movements of the larva inside.

jumping jack *n.* A toy puppet whose joined limbs are moved by strings; an exercise performed by jumping to a position with legs spread wide and hands touching over-head and then back to a standing position

with arms down at the sides.

jump seat *n.* An extra seat, often folding, found in a limosine or a taxicab.

jump shot *n.* In basketball, a shot made at the highest point of a jump.

jump–start *v.* To start an automobile by connecting a jumper cable from its battery to one of another automobile and turning the engine over. **jump–start** *n.*

jump suit *n.* Originally, a uniform for parachutists; now, any one-piece garment.

jump-y *adj.* Nervous; jittery.

jun-co (jung'kō) *n.* Any of various small birds of North America, having mainly gray plumage.

junc-tion (jungk'shɑn) *n.* The place where lines or routes meet, as roads or railways; the process of joining or the act of joining.

junc-ture (jungk'chėr) *n.* The point where two things join; a crisis; an emergency; a point in time.

June (jūn) *n.* The sixth month of the year, having 30 days.

Ju-neau *n.* The capital of the state of A-laska.

June beetle *or* **June bug** *n.* A large, bright-ly colored beetle which flies in June and has larvae that live in the soil and often destroy crops.

jun-gle (jung'gl) *n.* A densely covered land with tropical vegetation, usually inhabited by wild animals. **jungle** *adj.*

jungle fever *n.* A disease that is commonly found in tropical regions; a severe, recur-ring fever.

jun-ior (jŏn'yėr) *adj.* Younger in years or rank, used to distinguish the son from the father of the same first name; the younger of two. **junior** *n.* The third year of high school or college.

junior college *n.* A college offering a two-year course which is equivalent to the first two years of a four year college.

junior high school *n.* A school which in-cludes the 7th, 8th, and 9th grades.

ju-ni-per (jŏ'nɪ pėr) *n.* An evergreen shrub or tree of Europe and America with dark blue berries, prickly foliage, and fragrant wood.

junk (jungk) *n.* Discarded material, as glass, scrap iron, paper, or rags; a flat-bottomed Chinese ship with battened sails; rubbish; worthless matter. *Slang* Heroin, narcotics or dope.

jun-ket (jung´kit) *n.* A party, banquet, or trip; a trip taken by a public official with all expenses paid for by public funds; a custard-like dessert of flavored milk set with rennet. **junket** *v.* **junketeer** *n.*

junk food *n.* Food containing very little nutritional value in proportion to the number of calories.

junk-ie (jung´kē) *n., Slang* A drug addict that uses heroin.

Ju-no (jŏ´nō) *n.* In Roman mythology, the queen of heaven.

Ju-no-esque (jŏ˝nō esk´) *adj.* Stately and beautiful.

jun-ta (hen´ta) *n.* A body of men or persons, as military officers, in power following a coup d'etat.

Ju-pi-ter (jŏ´pi tèr) *n., Astron.* The fifth planet from the sun; the largest planet in the solar system.

ju-ral (jur´al) *adj.* Pertaining to law; legal; pertaining to rights and obligations.

ju-rat (jur´at) *n., Law* The description on an affidavit that states when, where, before whom, and by whom the affidavit was made.

ju-ra-to-ry (jur´a tōr˝ē) *adj.* Referring to an oath.

ju-rid-i-cal (je rid´i kal) *adj.* Of or pertaining to the law and to the administration of justice.

ju-ris-con-sult (jur˝is kon sult´) *n.* An expert who gives opinions in cases of law.

ju-ris-dic-tion (jer˝is dik´shan) *n.* The lawful right or power to interpret and apply the law; the territory within which power is exercised. **jurisdictional** *adj.*

ju-ris-pru-dence (jur˝is prŏd´ens) *n.* The record of court decisions that are the basis for the formal principles upon which laws are based; the science of law.

ju-ror (jer´ér) *n.* A person who serves on a jury.

ju-ry (jer´ē) *n. pl.* **juries** A group of legally qualified persons summoned to serve on a judicial tribunal to give a verdict according to evidence presented.

just (just) *adj.* Fair and impartial in acting or judging; morally right; merited; deserved; based on sound reason. **just** *adv.* To the exact point; precisely; exactly right. **justly** *adv.* **justness** *n.*

jus-tice (jus´tis) *n.* The principle of moral or ideal rightness; conformity to the law; the abstract principle by which right and wrong are defined; a judge.

justice of the peace *n.* A local magistrate having limited jurisdiction with authority to try minor cases, administer oaths, and perform marriages.

jus-ti-ci-a-ble (ju stish´ē a bl) *adj.* Expected to be settled by court action or within the legal system.

jus-ti-fi-a-ble (jus´ti fī˝a bl) *adj.* Able to be defended or proven to be right.

justified margin *n.* A typing or type-setting margin with all the characters at the ends of the lines vertically aligned.

jus-ti-fy (jus´ti fī´) *v.* To be just, right, or valid; to declare guiltless; to adjust or space lines to the proper length. **justifiably** *adv.* **justification** *n.*

jut (jut) *v.* To extend beyond the main portion; to project.

jute (jŏt) *n.* A tall, annual Asian herb of the linden family, yielding a strong, coarse fiber used to make sacking and rope.

ju-ve-nile (jŏ´ve nĭl) *adj.* Young; youthful; not yet an adult. **juvenile** *n.* A young person; an actor who plays youthful roles; a child's book.

juvenile court *n.* A court which deals only with cases involving dependent, neglected, and delinquent children.

juvenile delinquent *n.* A person who is guilty of violations of the law, but is too young to be punished as an adult criminal; a young person whose behavior is out of control.

juvenile officer *n.* A police officer who

specializes in investigating, prosecuting, and looking after juvenile delinquents.

ju-ve-nil-i-a (jŏ˝ve nil´ē a) n. Works of art, such as writings or paintings, produced while young; any writings or artistic works intended to appeal to the young.

ju-ve-nil-i-ty (jŏ˝ve nil´i tē) n. Youthful looks or actions; a childish act; behaving in an immature manner.

jux-ta-pose (juk˝sta pōz´) v. To put side by side; to place together. **juxtaposed** adj. **juxtaposition** n.

K

K, k (kā) The eleventh letter of the English alphabet.

K abbr., Computer science A unit of storage capacity equal to 1024 bytes.

Kaa-ba (kä´ba) n. Building in the Great Mosque at Mecca that contains the sacred stone said to have been turned black in color, by the tears of the repentant pilgrims or by the sins of people who have rubbed or touched it.

ka-bob (ka bob´) n. Cubed meat and mushrooms, onions, and tomatoes placed on a skewer usually marinated, and broiled over an open fire.

ka-bu-ki (kä bō´kē) n. A traditional Japanese drama in which dances and songs are performed in a stylized fashion.

Kad-dish (kä´dēsh) n. A Jewish prayer recited by mourners after the death of a relative and during other daily prayers in the synagogue.

kaf-fee klatsch (kä´fā kläch˝) n. An informal get-to-gether to drink coffee and talk.

kaf-ir (kaf´ėr) n. A grain sorghum that is cultivated in dry areas having a tough leafy stalk and is used for fodder.

kai-nite (kī´nīt) n. A mineral that is used as a fertilizer and a source of magnesium and potassium.

ka-ka (kä´ka) n. A New Zealand parrot, having an olive-brown color.

ka-ka-po (kä˝kä pō´) n. A large parrot.

kale (kāl) n. A green cabbage having crinkled leaves which do not form a tight head.

ka-lei-do-scope (ka lī´do skōp˝) n. A tubular instrument rotated to make successive symmetrical designs by using mirrors reflecting the changing patterns made by pieces of loose, colored glass at the end of a tube; a series of continuously changing colors; changing events or phases. **kaleidoscopic** adj. **kaleidoscopical** adj. **kaleidoscopically** adv.

kaleyard school (kāl´yärd˝sköl) n. A school of writers from the 19th century who wrote about Scottish life in a very sentimental manner, using heavy dialect.

kal-mi-a (kal´mē a) n. An evergreen shrub of North America, having pink, white, or purple flowers.

kame (kām) n. A short ridge of gravel and sand that remains after glacial ice melts.

kam-ik (kăm´ik) n. Boot made of sealskin, knee-high in length and worn in the eastern arctic regions.

ka-mi-ka-ze (kä˝mi kä´zē) n. A Japanese pilot in World War II trained to make a suicidal crash; an aircraft loaded with explosives used in a suicide attack.

kam-pong (käm´pong) n. A group of dwellings or a local village in countries that speak Malay.

kan-ga-roo (kang˝ga rö´) n. pl. kangaroos or **kangaroo** Any of various herbivorous marsupials of Australia with short forelegs, large hind limbs capable of jumping, and a large tail.

kangaroo court n. A self-appointed, illegal court, usually marked by incompetence or dishonesty where the laws are deliberately totally disregarded or misinterpreted.

Kan-sas n. A state in the central United States; statehood January 29, 1861; state capital Topeka.

ka-o-lin or **ka-o-line (kā´o lin) n.** A fine clay which remains white after firing, used in ceramics and in manufacturing high quality porcelain.

ka-pok (kā´pok) *n.* A silky fiber manufactured from the fruit of the silk-cotton tree and used for stuffing cushions and life preservers, pillows, and sleeping bags and also used for insulation.

ka-put (kä pet´) *adj., Slang* Destroyed or out of order; something with no possibility of success.

kar-a-kul (kar´a kul) *n.* Any of a breed of fat-tailed sheep of central Asia, having a narrow body and coarse, wiry, brown fur.

kar-at (kar´at) *n.* A unit of measure for the fineness of gold; a measure of weight for precious gems.

ka-ra-te (ka rä´tē) *n.* A Japanese art of self-defense, in which a person uses his elbows, feet, and knees in quick, damaging blows to his opponent.

kar-ma (kär´ma) *n.* The overall effect of one's behavior, held in Hinduism and Buddhism to determine one's destiny in a future existence. **karmic** *adj.*

ka-ross (ka ros´) *n.* Animal skins sewn together into the shape of a square and worn by natives; a throw rug made from animal skins.

kar-y-o-lymph (kar´ē o limf´) *n., Biol.* The transparent substance surrounding the nucleus of a cell.

kar-y-o-type (kar´ē o tīp´) *n.* The characteristics of the nucleus of a cell, including its size, form, and chromosome number.

Kash-mir goat (kash´mēr gōt) *n.* A goat from India that is raised for its fine delicate wool, from which cashmere items are made.

ka-ty-did (kā´tē did) *n.* Any of various green insects related to grasshoppers and crickets having specialized organs on the wings of the male that make a shrill sound when rubbed together.

katz-en-jam-mer (kat´sen jam´ėr) *n.* A feeling of uneasiness, worry, or nervousness that follows intoxication.

kau-ri (kou´rē) *n.* A New Zealand tree which is the source of valuable resin used in varnish and timber used in construction.

ka-va (kä-va) *n.* A pepper shrub from Poly-

nesia; a beverage made from this shrub that can be intoxicating.

kay-ak (kī´ak) *n.* A watertight Eskimo boat, having a circular hole in the top for the occupant, and made from a light wooden frame with a sealskin cover.

kay-o (kā´ō´) *v.* To knock out an opponent, in boxing. **kayo** *n.* A knockout.

ka-zoo (ka zō´) *n.* A toy musical instrument with a paper membrane which vibrates simultaneously when a player hums into the tube.

ke-a (kā´a) *n.* A New Zealand parrot.

kedge (kej) *n.* A small anchor. **kedge** *v.* To pull a ship by the rope of an anchor.

keel (kēl) *n.* The central main stem on a ship or aircraft, which runs lengthwise along the center line from bow to stern, on which a frame is built upwards. **keel** *v.* To capsize. **keel over** To fall over suddenly; to turn upside down. **keelless** *adj.*.

keel-age (kē´lij) *n.* A fee for mooring a ship in port.

keel-boat (kēl´bōt´) *n.* A boat used on rivers; a shallow boat used for freight.

keel-haul (kēl´hol´) *v.* To drag a person under the keel of a ship as a form of punishment.

keel-son (kēl´son) *n., Naut.* A structural member fastened above and parallel to the keel to give additional strength.

keen (kēn) *adj.* Having a sharp edge or point; acutely painful or harsh; intellectually acute; strong; intense. *Slang* Great. **keen** *n.* Wailing lament, especially for the dead. **keen** *v.* **keenly** *adv.* **keenness, keener** *n.*

keep (kēp) *v.* To have and hold; to not let go; to maintain, as business records; to know a secret and not divulge it; to protect and defend.

keep back *v.* To withhold things; to prevent one from coming forward.

keep-er (kē´pėr) *n.* One who keeps, guards, or maintains something; a person who respects or observes a requirement; a device for holding something in place, as a latch, or clasp.

keep-ing (kē´ping) *n.* Charge or possession;

conformity or harmony; maintenance or support; be consistent with.

keep off *v.* To fend or avert off. **keep off** *v.* To stay back or remain at a distance.

keep-sake (kēp′sāk˝) *n.* A memento or souvenir; a token or remembrance of friendship.

keep up *v.* To persist in, sustain, or continue. To remain equal or even to; to stay informed; to continue without interruption.

kef (kāf) *n.* A tranquil and dreamy state; a narcotic.

keg (keg) *n.* A small barrel usually having the capacity of five to ten gallons; the unit of measure for nails which equals 100 pounds.

keg-ler (keg′lėr) *n.* A bowler.

Keller, Helen *n.* 1880-1968 American author and lecturer who was deaf, mute, and blind.

ke-loid (kē′loid) *n.* A scar formed from fibrous growth in the connective skin tissue.

kelp (kelp) *n.* Any of a large brown seaweed.

kel-pie (kel′pē) *n.* A sheep dog originally bred in Australia.

kemp *n.* A coarse hairlike fiber used in the making of carpet.

ken-nel (ken′el) *n.* A shelter for or a place where dogs or cats are bred, boarded, or trained. **kennel** *v.*

Ken-ny meth-od (ken′ē meth′od) *n., Med.* A treatment for poliomyelitis that involves both exercise and hot applications.

ke-no (kē′nō) *n.* A game of chance resembling bingo; a lottery game.

kent-ledge (kent′lij) *n.* Ship ballast for a ship made of pig iron.

Ken-tuck-y *n.* A state located in the east central United States; statehood June 1, 1792; state capital Frankfort. **Kentuckian** *adj.*

Ken-tuck-y cof-fee tree *n.* A tree that has thick, wood pods whose seeds were at one time used as a coffee bean substitute.

kep-i (kā′pē) *n.* A French military cap having a flat, round top and a visor.

ker-a-tin (ker′a tin) *n.* A fibrous protein which forms the basic substance of nails, hair, horns, and hooves. **keratinous** *adj.*

ker-a-to-plas-ty (ker′a tō plas˝tē) *n., Med.* An operation that replaces damaged corneal tissue with healthy corneal tissue. **kerato-**

plastic *adj.*

ker-a-to-sis (ker˝a tō′sis) *n.* An area of skin overgrown with horny tissue.

ker-chief (kėr′chif) *n.* A piece of cloth worn around the neck or on the head; scarf; a handkerchief.

kerf (kėrf) *n.* A slit or notch made by a saw or other cutting tool; the place where a branch is cut across.

ker-mes (kėr′mēz) *n.* A red dye consisting of the dried bodies of female scaled insects found in the Meditarranian area.

ker-mis (ker′mis) *n.* An annual fair of the Netherlands.

ker-nel (ker′nel) *n.* A grain or seed, as of corn, enclosed in a hard husk; the inner substance of a nut; the central, most important part. **kernally** *adj.*

ker-o-sene *or* **ker-o-sine (ker′o sēn˝)** *n.* An oil distilled from petroleum or coal and used for illumination.

ker-ri-a (ker′ē a) *n.* A shrub of Japan, having ridged, green stems and double or single flowers that are yellow in color.

ker-sey (ker′zē) *n.* A coarse cloth made from wool and cotton used mainly for rugged garments and outer wear.

ker-sey-mere (ker′zi mēr) *n.* A twill weave cloth made from fine wool; also sassimere.

ke-ryg-ma (ki rig′ma) *n.* The apostolic preaching of the life and teachings of Jesus Christ.

kes-trel (kes′trel) *n.* A small falcon that hovers in the air with its head in the direction of the wind, having a gray and brown plumage, common in Europe inhabitating coasts, moors, and farms.

ketch (kech) *n.* A small sailing vessel with two masts, one large mainmast toward the bow of the ship, and a smaller mizzenmast in the direction of the stern but before the rudder.

ketch-up (kech′up) *n.* A thick, smooth sauce made from tomatoes.

ke-tene (kē′tēn) *n.* A gas which is colorless and poisonous, having a penetrating odor.

ke-to (kē′tō) *adj.* Having or pertaining to a ketone.

ke-tol (kē´tol) *n.* Organic compound having both a ketone and alcohol group.

ke-tone (kē´tōn) *n.* An organic compound; used as a solvent; acetone. **ketonic** *adj.* **ketosis** *n.*

ket-tle (ket´l) *n.* A pot or vessel, usually made of metal, used for stewing or boiling liquids.

ket-tle-drum (ket´l drum´) *n.* A musical instrument with a parchment head which can be tuned by adjusting the tension.

ket-tle of fish *n.* A mess; an awkward situation; matter of consideration.

key (kē) *n.* An object used to open a lock; button or level pushed on a keyboard of a typewriter, piano, etc; the crucial or main element; an island. **key** *v.* **keyed** *adj.*

Key, Francis Scott *n.* 1779-1843 American poet and lawyer.

key-board (kē´bōrd´) *n.* A bank of keys, as on a piano, typewriter, or computer terminal. **keyboard** *v.* To set by means of a keyed typesetting machine; to generate letters by means of a word processor. **keyboarder** *n.*

key club *n.* A private club that offers entertainment and serves liquor; a nightclub.

key-hole (kē´hōl´) *n.* Lock; area or hole in a lock where a key is inserted.

key-note (kē´nōt´) *n., Mus.* The first and harmonically fundamental tone of a scale; main principle or theme.

keynote address *n.* An opening speech that outlines issues for discussion.

key-punch *n.* A machine operated from a keyboard that uses punched holes in tapes or cards for data processing systems. **keypunch** *v.* **keypuncher** *n.*

key ring *n.* A metal ring upon which keys are kept.

key-stone (kē´stōn´) *n.* The wedge-shaped stone at the center of an arch that locks its parts together; an essential part; the part upon which the other parts depend.

key-stroke *n.* A stroke of a key, as of a typewriter or computer keyboard.

key-way (kē´wā´) *n.* A slot cut in a wheel hub or shaft for the reception of a key.

key word *n.* A word having special significance in relation to other phrases, words, or concepts.

kg *abbr.* Kilogram.

khad-dar (kä´dėr) *n.* Cloth made from cotton.

khak-i (kak´ē) *n.* A yellowish brown or olive-drab color; a sturdy cloth which is khaki in color. **khakis** *n. pl.* A uniform of khaki cloth. **khaki** *adj.*

khan (kän) *n.* An Asiatic title of respect; a medieval Turkish, Mongolian or Tartar ruler. **khanate** *n.*

khe-dive (ke dēv´) *n.* A ruler of Egypt from 1867 to 1914, governing as a viceroy of the sultan of Turkey.

ki *abbr.* Kiloliter.

kib-ble (kib´l) *n.* A bucket used in the shaft of a mine for hoisting ore.

kib-butz (ki buts´) *n.* In Israel, a settlement or farm operated as a collective system.

kibe (kīb) *n.* An ulcerated chilblain, usually on the heel.

kib-itz (kib´its) *v., Slang* To look on and offer meddlesome advice to others. **kibitzer** *n.*

ki-bosh (kī´ bosh) *n., Slang* Something that acts as a check or stop.

kick (kik) *v.* To strike something with a force by the foot. **kick in** To put in money. **kick out** To expel with force. **kicker** *n.*

kick-back (kik´bak´) *n.* A secret payment to a person who can influence a source of income; repercussion; a strong reaction.

kick-off (kik´of) *n.* The play that begins a game of soccer or football.

kick-shaw (kik´sha´) *n.* Something of little substance or value; a trinket

kick-stand *n.* The swiveling bar for holding a two-wheeled vehicle upright.

kick turn *n.* In skiing, a half-turn done in place, accomplished by placing one ski at an angle to the other, and then placing the other ski in a position parallel to the first.

kid (kid) *n.* A young goat; leather made from the skin of a young goat. *Slang* A child; youngster. **kid** *v.* To mock or tease playfully; to deceive for fun; to fool. **kiddish** *adj.*

kid-nap (kid´nap) *v.* To seize and hold a person unlawfully, often for ransom.

kidnapper *n.* kidnapping *n.*

kid-ney (kid'nē) *n. pl.*  kidneys Either of two organs situated in the abdominal cavity of vertebrates whose function is to keep proper water balance in the body and to excrete wastes in the form of urine.

kidney bean *n.* A bean grown for its edible seeds.

kid-skin (kid'skin") *n.* A soft, pliable leather made from the skin of a young goat.

kidvid *n., Slang* Television programming for children.

kiel-ba-sa *n.* A smoked Polish sausage.

kier (kēr) *n.* A large-capacity tub or boiler used for bleaching and dyeing jobs.

kil-der-kin (kil'dėr kin) *n.* A measure of capacity of half a barrel; a vessel that holds this amount.

kill (kil) *v.* To put to death; to nullify; to cancel; to slaughter for food; to deprive of life; to neutralize or destroy the active qualities.

kill-deer (kil'dēr") *n. pl.* killdeer *or* killdeers A bird characterized by a plaintive, penetrating cry.

kill-er (kil'ėr) *n.* Anything that kills; a person or an animal given to killing. *Slang* Something or someone making a strong impression.

killer whale *n.* A black and white carnivorous whale, found in the colder waters of the seas.

kil-lick (kil'ik) *n.* An anchor for a boat usually consisting of a stone secured by wood.

kil-li-fish (kil'ē fish") *n.* A fish found in the waters of North America belonging to the family Cyprinodontidea.

kill-ing (kil'ing) *n.* The act of a person who kills; a slaying. killingly *adv.*

kill-joy (kil'joi") *n.* One who spoils the enjoyment of others.

kiln (kil) *n.* An oven or furnace for hardening or drying a substance, especially one for firing ceramics and pottery.

ki-lo (kil'ō) *n.* A kilogram.

kil-o-bit *n.* In computer science, one thousand binary digits.

kil-o-cal-o-rie (kil'o kal"o rē) *n.* One thousand gram calories.

ki-lo-cy-cle (kil'o sī"kl) *n.* A unit equal to one thousand cycles; one thousand cycles per second.

kil-o-gram (kil'o gram") *n.* A measurement of weight in the metric system equal to slightly more than one third of a pound.

kil-o-li-ter (kil'o lē"tėr) *n.* Metric measurement equal to one thousand litres.

kil-o-me-ter (kil'o mē"tėr) *n.* Metric measurement equal to one thousand meters.

kil-o-ton (kil'o tun") *n.* One thousand tons; an explosive power equal to that of one thousand tons of TNT.

kil-o-volt (kil'o vōlt") *n.* One thousand volts.

kil-o-watt (kil'o wot") *n.* A unit of power equal to one thousand watts.

kil-o-watt–hour (kil'o wot"our') *n.* A unit of electric power consumption of one thousand watts throughout one hour.

kilt (kilt) *n.* A knee-length wool skirt with deep pleats, usually of tartan, worn especially by men in the Scottish Highlands.

kil-ter (kil'tėr) *n.* Good condition; proper or working order.

ki-mo-no (ko mō'no) *n.* A loose Japanese robe with a wide sash; a loose robe.

kin (kin) *n.* One's relatives by blood; relatives collectively.

ki-nase (kī'nās) *n.* A catalyst that assists in changing a zymogen into an enzyme.

kind (kīnd) *n.* A characteristic; a particular variety of sort.

kind (kīnd) *adj.* Of a friendly or good-natured disposition; coming from a good-natured readiness to please others. kindness *n.*

kin-der-gar-ten (kin'dėr gär"ten) *n.* A school or class for young children from the ages of four to six to further their social, mental and physical development.

kin-der-gart-ner (kin'dėr gärt"nėr) *n.* A child who attends kindergarten.

kind-heart-ed (kīnd'här'tid) *adj.* Having much generosity and kindness.

kin-dle (kin'dl) *v.* To ignite; to catch fire; to stir up; to arouse; to excite, as the feelings.

kind-less (kīnd´lis) *adj.* Mean, cruel, unkind, unfriendly. **kindlessly** *adv.*

kin-dling (kind´ling) *n.* Easily ignited material, such as sticks, wood chips, or paper, used to start a fire.

kind-ly (kīnd´lē) *adv.* A kind nature, disposition, or character; benevolent. **kindliness** *n.*

kind-ness (kīnd´nis) *n.* An act of good will; state or quality of being kind; a kind act.

kin-dred (kin´drid) *n.* A person's relatives by blood. **kindred** *adj.* Having a like nature; similar. **kindredness** *n.*

kin-e-mat-ics (kin˝e mat´iks) *n.* The branch of dynamics that deals with motion, considered apart from force and mass. **kinematic** *adj.* **kinematical** *adj.*

kin-e-scope (kin´i skōp˝) *n.* A cathode-ray tube in a television set which translates received electrical impulses into a visible picture on a screen; a film of a television broadcast.

ki-ne-sics (ki nē´siks) *n.* To study the relationship between communication and nonverbal body language. **kinesic** *adj.* **kinesically** *adv.*

ki-ne-si-ol-o-gy (ki nē˝sē ol´o jē) *n.* Science that investigates organic and anatomy process in reference to human motion.

kin-es-the-sia (kin˝is thē´zha) *n.* The sense of muscular movement or effort. **kinesthesis** *n.* **kinesthetic** *adj.*

ki-net-ic (ki net´ik) *adj.* Of, pertaining to, or produced by motion.

ki-net-ic art *n.* The type of modern abstract art that attempts to present or indicate a sense of motion.

kinetic theory *n., Physics* The theory of matter that hypothesizes that the minute par-ticles of matter are constantly in very rapid random motion.

ki-ne-to-scope (ki nē´toskōp˝) *n.* The early form of the motion picture, where a series of pictures pass beneath a small opening for viewing at a high rate of speed.

kin-folk (kin´fōk˝) *n.* Relatives; family.

king (king) *n.* One who rules over a country; a male ruler; a playing card with a picture of a king; the main piece in the game of chess; a crowned checker in the game of checkers.

king-bird (king´berd˝) *n.* A North American bird belonging to the genus Tyrannus.

king-bolt (king´bōlt˝) *n.* A vertical, central bolt connecting a vehicle to the front axle.

king crab *n.* A large crab-like crustacean common in the coastal waters of Japan, Alaska, and Siberia.

king-craft (king´kraft˝) *n.* The art of ruling as a king; the profession and techniques used by a king.

king-dom (king´dom) *n.* The area or the country which is ruled by a king or queen. **kingdomless** *adj.*

king-fish (king´fish˝) *n.* A large fish used for food.

king-fish-er (king´fish˝ėr) *n.* A bright colored bird having a long stout bill and short tail that feeds on fish and insects.

King James Bible *n.* An English translation of the Bible from Hebrew and Greek, published in 1611, which was authorized by King James I of England.

king-let (king´lit) *n.* A very small bird; an unimportant king.

king-ly (king´lē) *adj.* Pertaining to or belonging to a king or kings; monarchical; splendid; befitting a king.

king-mak-er (king´mā˝kėr) *n.* A person or group that has enough power to influence the selection of a candidate for a position of political authority.

king-pin (king´pin˝) *n.* The foremost pin of a set arranged in order for bowling; the most important or essential person.

king post *n.* A post located between the tie beam and the apex of a roof truss.

king-ship (king´ship) *n.* A monarchy; the state, or dignity of a king.

king-size (king´sīz˝) *adj.* Very large; wider or longer, or both, than the standard size.

king snake *n.* Large snake found in the southern United States which is nonpoisonous.

king-wood (king´woud˝) *n.* Wood of Brazil with violet-colored stripes.

kink (kingk) *n.* A tight twist or knot-like curl; a sharp, painful muscle cramp; a mental quirk. **kink** *v.* To form or cause to form a kink.

kink-a-jou (king´k*a* jōˉ´) *n.* A tropical American mammal having large eyes, brown fur, and a long, prehensile tail.

kink-y *adj.* Tightly curled; sexually uninhibited. **kinkily** *adv.,* **kinkiness** *n.*

kin-ship(kin´ship) *n.* Family relationship; common blood bond.

kins-man (kinz´m*a*n) *n.* A blood relative, especially a male relative.

kins-wo-man (kinz´wum¨*a*n) *n.* A female blood relation.

ki-osk (kē osk´) *n.* A small building used as a refreshment booth or newsstand.

kip (kip) *n.* The untanned skin of a calf, a lamb and or an adult of any small breed; a bundle of such hides.

kip-per (kip´ẻr) *n.* A salted and smoked herring or salmon. **kipper** *v.* To cure by salting, smoking, or drying.

kirk (kerk) *n.* The Presbyterian Church of Scotland as opposed to the Episcopal Church of Scotland.

Kir-man (kir män´) *n.* An elaborate Persian rug having elaborate floral designs and soft colors.

kirsch (kērsh) *n.* A brandy made from the fermented juice of black cherries.

kir-tle (ker´tl) *n.* A woman's long skirt or petticoat; a man's tunic or coat.

kis-met (kiz´mit) *n.* Fate; appointed lot.

kiss (kis) *v.* To touch two lips together in greeting; between two people. **kissable** *adj.*

kit (kit) *n.* A collection of tools, supplies, or items for a special purpose.

kitch-en (kich´en) *n.* A room in a house or building used to prepare and cook food.

kitch-en cab-i-net *n.* A cupboard, often with drawers, made of wood or metal, used for storage of cooking utensils or imperishable foodstuffs.

kitch-en-ette (kich¨*e* net´) *n.* A small area that functions as a kitchen.

kitch-en-ware (kich´*en* wâr¨) *n.* Dishes, pots, pans, and other utensils that are used in a kitchen.

kite (kīt) *n.* A light-weight framework of wood and paper designed to fly in a steady breeze at the end of a string; any of various predatory birds of the hawk family having long, usually forked tails.

kith (kith) *n.* Acquaintances or family.

kitsch (kich) *n.* Anything that is pretentious and in poor taste.

kit-ten (kit´en) *n.* A young cat. **kittenish** *adj.* **kittenishly** adv.

kit-ty (kit´ē) *n.* A small collection of objects or money; a young cat or kitten.

kit-ty–cor-nered (kit´ē kor¨nẻr) *adj.* Diagonally; catty–cornered.

ki-va (kē´v*a*) *n.* A Pueblo Indian chamber, used in ceremonies, often underground.

Ki-wa-ni-an *n.* A member of a major national and international service club organized to promote higher business standards and to provide service to the community.

ki-wi (kē´wē) *n.* A flightless bird of New Zealand having vestigial wings and a long, slender bill; a vine, native to Asia, which yields a fuzzy-skinned, edible fruit; the fruit of this vine; a student who has not piloted a plane solo.

klatch *or* **klatsch** (klach) *n.* A social gathering devoted primarily to small talk and gossip.

klep-to-ma-ni-a (klep¨t*o* mā´nē *a*) *n.* Obsessive desire to steal or impulse to steal, especially without economic motive. **kleptomaniac** *n.*

kloof (klöf) *n.* A ravine; gorge; deep mountain cleft.

kludge *n.* A computer system that is made up of poorly matched components.

klutz *n., Slang* A stupid or clumsy person. **klutziness** *n.* **klutzy** *adj.*

km *abbr.* Kilometer.

knack (nak) *n.* A natural talent; aptitude; dexterity.

knack-wurst *or* **knock-wurst** *n.* A thick, short, heavily-seasoned sausage.

knap-sack (nap´sak¨) *n.* A supply or equipment bag, as of canvas or nylon, worn strapped across the shoulders.

knave (nāv) *n.* Tricky or dishonest person;

a rascal. **knavish** *adj.* **knavishly** *adv.* **knav-ishness** *n.*

knead (nēd) *v.* To work dough into a uniform mass; to shape by or as if by kneading. **kneader, kneadability** *n.* **kneadable** *adj.*

knee (nē) *n.* The joint in the human body which connects the calf with the thigh.

knee action *n.* The front-wheel suspension of an automobile that permits independent vertical movement of each front wheel.

knee-cap (nē´kap˝) *n.* Patella; bone covering the joint of the knee.

knee–deep (nē´dēp´) *adj.* So deep that it reaches one's knees.

knee–high (nē´hī´) *adj.* Reaching or rising upward toward the knee.

knee jerk *n.* An involuntary forward movement of the knee when the patellar tendon is lightly tapped.

kneel (nēl) *v.* To go down upon one's knees.

knell (nel) *v.* To sound a bell, especially when rung for a funeral; to toll. **knell** *n.* An act of knelling; a signal of disaster.

knick-ers (nik´ėrz) *n. pl.* Short, loose-fitting pants gathered at the knee.

knick-knack (nik´nak˝) *n.* A trinket; trifling article.

knife (nīf) *n.* An instrument used to cut an item. **knife** *v.*

knife edge *n.* A very sharp edge; the edge of a knife.

knife switch *n.* A metallic switch used to close an electric circuit.

knight (nīt) *n.* A medieval soldier serving a monarch; a chess piece in the shape of a horse's head.

knight bachelor *n.* A knight of the lowest and most ancient order of the English knights.

knight-hood (nīt´hed) *n.* The vocation and character of a knight.

knight-ly (nīt´lē) *adj.* Dealing with a knight; behaving according to the code of a knight.

knish *n.* Baked or fried dough stuffed with meat, cheese, or potatoes.

knit (nit) *v.* To form by intertwining thread or yarn by interlocking

loops of a single yarn by means of needles; to fasten securely; to draw together; to furrow the brow. **knitter, knitting** *n.*

knitting needle *n.* A long, slender, pointed rod for knitting.

knit-wear (nit´wâr˝) *n.* Clothing made from a fabric that was produced by knitting.

knob (nob) *n.* A rounded protuberance; a lump; a rounded mountain; a rounded handle. **knobbed, knobby** *adj.*

knock (nok) *v.* To hit or strike with a hard blow; to criticize; to collide; to make a noise, as that of a defective engine. **knock out** To render unconscious. **knock** *n.*

knock-down (nok´doun˝) *adj.* Designed to be easily assembled for storage or shipment. **knockdown** *n.*

knock down *v.* To strike to the ground with or as with a sharp blow.

knock–down–drag–out *adj.* Extremely violent or bitter.

knock-er (nok´ėr) *n.* One who or that which knocks; a metal ring for knocking on a door.

knock–knee (nok´nē˝) *n.* A condition in which one or both knees turn inward and knock or rub together while walking. **knock–kneed** *adj.*

knoll (nōl) *n.* A small, round hill; a mound.

knot (not) *n.* An intertwining of string or rope; a fastening made by tying together lengths of material, as string; a unifying bond, especially of marriage; a hard node on a tree from which a branch grows. *Naut.* A unit of speed, also called a nautical mile, which equals approximately 1.15 statute miles per hour. **knot** *v.* **knottiness** *n.*

knot-hole (not´hōl˝) *n.* A hole in lumber left by the falling out of a knot.

knot-ted (not´id) *adj.* Snarled; tied with or into knots; full of knots.

knout (nout) *n.* A whip or scourge for flogging criminals. **knout** *v.*

know (nō) *v.* To perceive directly as fact or truth; to believe to be true; to be certain of; to be familiar with or have experience of. **knowable** *adj.* **knower** *n.*

know–how (nō´hou˝) *n.* Knowing how to do something.

know-ing (nō´ing) *adj.* To be astute; to know secret knowledge. **knowingly** *adv.*

knowl-edge (nol´ij) *n.* Acquaintnce with facts and areas of study; having ability to know facts, information.

knowl-edge-a-ble (nol´i ja bl) *n.* The state of being intelligent.

know–nothing (nō´nuth¨ing) *n.* An extremely stupid person.

knuck-le (nuk´l) *n.* On the finger; the joint of the finger. **knuckly** *adj.*

knuck-le-ball *n.* A pitch used in baseball that is a slow pitch.

knuck-le-bone (nuk´l bōn¨) *n.* The bone of the finger which forms the knuckle.

knuck-le-head (nuk´l hed¨) *n.* A person who is not very smart; dumb.

knuck-le joint *n.* A finger joint; a machine joint formed like a knuckle.

knur (ner) *n.* A lump or knot of a tree.

knurl (nūrl) *n.* A ridge. **knurled, knurly** *adj.*

ko-a-la (kō ä´la) *n.* An Australian marsupial which has large hairy ears, and gray fur, and feeds on eucalyptus leaves.

Ko-di-ak bear (kō´dē ak¨ bâr) *n.* A large bear found in Alaska.

kohl (kōl) *n.* Dark powder used as cosmetics to darken under the eyes.

kohl-ra-bi (kōl rä´bē) *n. pl.* **kohlrabies** A variety of cabbage having a thick stem and eaten as a vegetable.

koi-ne (koi nā´) *n.* Any regional language or dialect which becomes the standard language of a larger region.

ko-la (kō´la) *n.* The tree which produces the kola nut.

ko-la nut *n.* The brownish nut used as a tonic or stimulant.

ko-lin-sky (ko lin´skē) *n.* A mink found in Asia.

kook (kōk) *n. Slang* A crazy or eccentric person. **kookiness** *n.* **kooky** *adj.*

Ko-ran (kō rän´) *n.* The sacred book of Islam, accepted as containing the revelations made to Mohammed by Allah through the angel Gabriel.

ko-sher (kō´shėr) *adj.* Serving food prepared according to Jewish dietary laws. *Slang* Appropriate; proper.

kow-tow (kou´tou´) *v.* To show servile deference.

kph *abbr.* Kilometers per hour.

kraal (krȧl) *n.* A village of southern African natives; an enclosure for animals in southern Africa.

K ration *n.* Emergency food pack used during W.W. II.

Krem-lin (krem´lin) *n.* The citadel of Moscow which houses the major Russian (formerly Soviet) government offices; the Russian or Soviet government.

krieg-spiel (krēg´ spēl´) *n.* A war game consisting of blocks representing troops, guns, and other military equipment which are moved around on model battlefields designed to teach military science.

krill (kril) *n.* A small crustacean living in open ocean waters and an important food source for whales.

kryp-ton (krip´ton) *n.* A white, inert gaseous chemical used mainly in fluorescent lamps, symbolized by Kr.

ku-chen (kō´chen) *n.* Any coffee cake made with a sweetened yeast-dough.

ku-dos (kō´dōs) *n.* Acclaim or prestige resulting from notable achievement or high position; glory; recognition; renown.

kum-quat (kum´kwot) *n.* A small, round orange fruit having a sour pulp and edible rind; the tree bearing this fruit..

kung fu *n.* A Japanese art of self-defense similar to karate.

kw *abbr.* Kilowatt.

kwash-i-or-kor *n.* Severe malnutrition, especially in children, caused by protein deficiency.

kwh *abbr.* Kilowatt-hour.

ky-mo-graph (kī´mo graf¨) *n.* A device for graphically recording variations in motion or pressure; a blood pressure graph.

ky-pho-sis (kī fō´sis) *n.* Abnormal curving of the spine; hunchback.

L, l (el) *n.* The twelfth letter of the English alphabet; the Roman numeral for fifty.

lab (lab) *n.* Laboratory.

la-bel (lā´bel) *n.* Something that identifies or describes. **label** *v.* To attach a label to.

la-bi-al (lā´bē el) *adj.* Pertaining to or of the labia or lips.

la-bi-um (lā´bē um) *n. pl.* **labia** Any of the four folds of the vulva.

la-bor (lā´bėr) *n.* Physical or manual work done for hire. *Med.* The physical pain and effort involved in childbirth. *v.* To work; to progress with great effort. **laborer** *n.*

lab-o-ra-to-ry (lab´ro tōr´ē) *n. pl.* **laboratories** A place equipped for conducting scientific experiments, research, or testing; a place where drugs and chemicals are produced.

labor camp *n.* A penal community where forced labor is required.

la-bored (lā bėrd) *adj.* Performed with labor.

la-bo-ri-ous (le´bōr ē es) *adj.* Characterized by hard work, devoted to labor.

la-bor-ite (lā be rīt) *n.* A political party member devoted to the interests of labor.

labor union *n.* An organization made up of wage earners designed to advance the general working conditions and the economic interests of its members.

lab-ra-dor-ite (lab´ra da rīt´) *n.* A kind of plagioclase feldspar mineral, distinguished by its iridescent colors.

la-bret (lā btet) *n.* A decoration or ornament worn through a hole in the lip.

la-bur-num (la bur´nam) *n.* A small ornamental tree; from the legume family, grown for its yellow flowers.

lab-y-rinth (lab´e rinth) *n.* A system of winding, intricate passages; a maze. **labyrinthian** *adj.*

lab-y-rin-thine (lab´e rin then) *adj.* Resembling or related to a labyrinth.

lac (lak) *n.* The resinous secretion left on certain trees by the lac insect and used in making paints and varnishes.

lac-co-lith (lak´e lith) *n.* A body of igneous rock between beds of overlying strata that causes the formation of domes.

lace (lās) *n.* A delicate open-work fabric of silk, cotton, or linen made by hand or on a machine; a cord or string used to fasten two edges together. **lace** *v.* To fasten or tie together; to interlace or intertwine.

lac-er-ate (las´e rāt´) *v.* To open with a jagged tear; to wound the flesh by tearing. **laceration** *n.*

lac-er-a-tion (las e´rā shan) *n.* The act of tearing; a jagged tear caused by lacerating.

lac-er-til-i-an (las˝e til´ian) *n.* Belonging to the family of lizards.

lace-wing (lās´wing˝) *n.* Any insects with bright eyes and lacelike wings, whose larvae prey on plant lice.

lach-es (lach´iz) *n.* Inexcusable delay in completing a duty or claiming a legal right.

lach-ry-mal *or* **lac-ri-mal (lak´ri mal)** Relating to or producing tears; relating to the glands that produce tears.

lach-ry-ma-to-ry (lak´ri ma tōr˝ē) *n.* A small vase found in ancient tombs that is said to have held tears from mourners.

lach-ry-mose (lak´ri mō) *adj.* Tearful; crying; trying to provoke tears.

lac-ing (lā´sing) *n.* The act of connecting or fastening; a cord used to draw tight; a trim or braid; a sprinkling of liquor in food or drink.

lack (lak) *n.* The deficiency or complete absence of something. *v.* To have little of something or to be completely without.

lack-a-dai-si-cal (lak˝a dā´zi kal) *adj.* Lacking life, interest, or spirit; melancholy. **lackadaisically** *adv.*

lack-a-day (lak´a dā´) *interj.* Exclamation used to express sorrow or regret.

lack-ey (lak´ē) *n.* A male servant of very low status.

lack-lus-ter (lak´lus´tėr) *adj.* Lacking sheen; dull.

la-con-ic (la kon´ik) *adj.* Short; concise, brief and to the point; expressing a great deal in a few words.

lac-quer (lak´ėr) *n.* A transparent varnish which is dissolved in a volatile solution and dries to give surfaces a glossy finish. **lacquer** *v.* **lacrimator**

la-crosse (la kros´) *n.* A game of American Indian origin played with a ball and long-handled rackets, by two teams of ten men each, trying to advance the ball into the opponents' goal.

lac-tase (lak´tās) *n.* An enzyme in intestinal juices in young mammals and in yeasts that catalyzes the production of galactose and glucose from lactose.

lac-tate (lak´tāt) *v.* To secrete or to milk. **lactation** *n.*

lac-te-al (lak´tēl) *adj.* Of, resembling, or like milk. *n., Anat.* Any of the lymphatic vessels carrying chyle from the small intestine to the blood.

lac-tes-cent (lak tes´ent) *adj.* Being or becoming milky; producing milk.

lactic acid *n.* A limpid, syrupy acid that is present in sour milk, molasses, some fruits, and wines.

lac-tif-er-ous (lak´tif e res) *adj.* Producing milk or a milky liquid substances.

lac-tone (lak´tōn) *n.* Any of a class of cyclic esters derived from hydroxy acids.

lac-tose (lak´tōs) *n.* A white, odorless, crystalline sugar that is found in milk.

la-cu-na (la kū´na) *n. pl.* **-nas, -nae** A space from which something is missing; a gap.

la-cu-nar (la kū´nėr) *n.* A ceiling with recessed panels.

la-cus-trine (lakus´trin) *adj.* Pertaining to a lake; living or formed in lakes, as various plants and animals.

lad (lad) *n.* A boy or young man.

lad-der (lad´ėr) *n.* An implement used for climbing up or down in order to reach another place or area.

lad-der-back (lad er bak) *adj.* Referring to the back of a chair with horizontal pieces connecting two vertical posts.

lade *v.* To load down, as with cargo or a burden; to dip or lift out.

lad-en (lād´en) *adj.* Heavily burdened; oppressed; weighed down; loaded.

la–di–da (lä´dē dä´) *adj.* An expression of ridicule aimed at pretentious or elegant manners.

lad-ing (lā´ding) *n.* Cargo; freight.

la-dle (lād´l) *n.* A cup-shaped vessel with a deep bowl and a long handle, used for dipping or conveying liquids. **ladle** *v.*

la-dy (lā´dē) *n. pl.* **ladies** A woman showing refinement, cultivation, and often high social position; the woman at the head of a household; an address or term of reference for any woman.

la-dy-bug *or* **la-dy-bird** *n.* Any of a family of brightly colored beetles, black with red spots which feed mainly on aphids and other insects.

lady–in–waiting (lā´dē in wā´ting) *n. pl.* **ladies–in–waiting** A lady appointed to wait on a queen or princess.

la-dy-like (lā´dē līk´) *adj.* Having the characteristics of a lady; delicate; gentle.

la-dy-love (lād ē lev) *n.* A mistress or sweetheart; a lady who is loved.

lady's slipper *n.* A species of orchids grown in North America, whose flowers resemble a slipper.

la-dy's–smock (lā´dēz smok´) *n.* A flower plant, with white or purple flowers; also called a cuckooflower.

lag (lag) *v.* To stray or fall behind; to move slowly; to weaken gradually. **lag** *n.* The process or act of retardation or falling behind; the amount or period of lagging.

lag-an (lag en) *n.* Something sunk at sea, but attached to a buoy in order to recover it.

la-ger (lä´ gėr) *n.* A light beer originated in Germany, which is brewed by slow fermentation and matured or aged under refrigeration.

lag-gard (lag erd) *adj.* Slow; backward; lagging. *n.* A person who lags behind everyone else; a loiterer.

lag-ging (lag´ing) *n.* A material used for

thermal insulation; a plank used to prevent cave-ins of earth walls; a support during construction

la-gniappe (lan yap´) *n.* A small gift which is given to a purchaser by a storekeeper; anything given as an extra bonus.

la-goon (*la*** gün)** *n.* A body of shallow water separated from the ocean by a coral reef or sandbars. **lagoonal** *adj.*

la-i-cism (lā *e* siz *e*m) *n.* A governmental system which is free from ecclesiastical influence or jurisdiction.

la-i-cize (lā *e* sīz) *v.* To take away the jurisdiction of the clergy. **laicization** *n.*

laid *v.* Past tense of lay.

laid back *adj., Slang* Casual or relaxed in character.

lain *v.* Past tense of lie.

lair (le*er*) *n.* The den or bed of a wild animal. **lair** *v.* To lie in a lair; to place in a lair.

lais-sez–faire (le sā´fa*er*) *n.* A policy stating that a government should exercise very little control in trade and industrial affairs; non-interference.

la-i-ty (lā´i tē) *n.* Laymen, the people of a religious group or faith as distinguished from clergy.

lake (lāk) *n.* A large inland body of either salt or freshwater.

lak-er (lā´k*e*r) *n.* One connected or associated with lakes; a fish living in or taken from a lake.

lake trout *n.* Any of various species of trout found in freshwater lakes.

lam (lam) *v., Slang* To beat; to thrash; to run or flee quickly. **lam** *n., Slang* A trip to escape; the escape.

Lamaze method *n.* A method of childbirth in which the mother is prepared psychologically and physically to give birth without the use of drugs.

lamb (lam) *n.* A young sheep; the meat of a lamb used as food; a gentle person.

lam-baste *or***lambast (lam bāst´)** *v., Slang* To thrash or beat.

lam-bent (lam´b*e*nt) *adj.* Lightly and playfully brilliant; flickering gently, softly radiant. **lambency** *n.* **lambently** *adv.*

lamb-skin (lam´skin) *n.* The skin of a lamb that is dressed with the fleece or wool attached, the leather made from this lamb's skin.

lame (lām) *adj.* Disabled or crippled, especially in the legs or feet so as to impair free movement; weak; ineffective; unsatisfactory. **lamely** *adv.* **lameness** *n.*

la-me (la mā´) *n.* A brocaded fabric woven with gold or silver thread, sometimes mixed with other fiber.

lame duck *n., Slang* An office holder who has been defeated in an election but continues in office until the inauguration of his or her successor.

la-mel-la (*la*** mel´a)** *n. pl.* **lamellae** A thin flat plate or scale; one composing the thin plates of the gills of certain mollusks.

la-mel-li-branch (lamel´i brangk˝) *n.* A species of mollusks, that include the oyster, mussel and clam.

la-ment (*la*** ment´)** *v.* To express sorrow; to mourn. *n.* An expression of regret or sorrow. **lamentable** *adj.* **lamentably** *adv.*

lam-en-ta-tion (lam˝en tā´sh*a*n) *n.* A wailing or expression of sorrow.

lam-i-na (lam´i n*a*) *n. pl.* **laminae** *or* **laminas** A thin scale or layer. *Bot.* The blade or flat part of a leaf.

laminar flow *n.* A smooth streamline flow of a glutinous material, in different layers of which move parallel at slightly varying rates.

lam-i-nate (lam´i nāt´) *v.* To form or press into thin sheets; to form layers by the action of pressure and heat. **lamination** *n.* **laminated** *adj.* **laminator** *n.*

lam-mer-gei-er (lam´*e*r gī´*e*r) *n.* The largest European bird of prey in the vulture family.

lamp (lamp) *n.* A device for generating heat or light.

lamp-black (lamp´blak˝) *n.* A black soot of very fine texture of pure carbon.

lamp-light-er (lamp´lī˝t*e*r) *n.* A person who lights street lamps; a torch or device for lighting lamps.

lam-poon (lam pün´) *n.* A satirical, but

often humorous, attack in verse or prose, especially one that ridicules a group, person, or institution. **lampoon** v.

lamp-post (lamp´pōst˝) n. A post used to support a lamp that lights a path or street.

lam-prey (lam´prē) n. pl. **lampreys** An eel-like fish having a circular, suctorial mouth with rasping teeth and no jaw.

lam-ster (lam´stèr) n., Slang A person who is fleeing from the law.

la-nate (lā´nāt) adj. Covered with a substance or growth that resembles wool.

lance (lans) n. A spear-like implement used as a weapon by mounted knights or soldiers.

lance corporal n., Mil. In the U.S. Marine Corps, an enlisted man who ranks above a private first class and below a corporal.

lance-let (lans´lit) n. A small fish-like marine animal, having a transparent body that is pointed at both ends, and usually found beneath sand in shallow waters.

lan-ce-o-late (lan´sē o lāt˝) adj. Shaped like a lance head; widening above the base and tapering to the apex.

lanc-er (lan´sèr) n. One such as a soldier who is armed with a lance.

lan-cet (lan´sit, län´sit) n. A small surgical instrument having a sharp pointed generally two-edged blade, used to open veins, abscesses or tumors.

lancet arch n. An arch having a sharply pointed apex.

lan-cet-ed (lan´si tid) adj. Characterized by lancet arches or lancet windows.

lancet window n. A narrow window characterized by a pointed apex.

lance-wood (lans´wud˝) n. Elastic wood that is used for fishing rods and archery bows.

lan-ci-nate (lan´si nāt˝) v. Pierce or stab; to tear. **lancination** n.

land (land) n. The solid, exposed surface of the earth as distinguished from the waters. **land** v. To arrive at a destination; to catch a fish; to get a new job. **landed** adj.

lan-dau (lan´do) n. A four-wheeled vehicle with a closed carriage and a back seat with a collapsible top.

land-er (lan der) n. A space vehicle for landing on a celestial body.

land-fill (land fil) n. A system of trash and garbage disposal in which the waste is burned in low-lying land so as to build up the ground surface; a section built up by landfill.

land grant n. A grant of land made by a government, especially for railroads, roads, or agricultural colleges.

land-hold-er (land´hōl˝dèr) n. An owner, holder, or proprietor of land.

land-ing (lan´ding) n. The act of coming, going, or placing ashore from any kind of vessel or craft; the act of descending and settling on the ground in an airplane.

landing craft n. A type of flat-bottomed naval vessel used for putting troops, equipment and necessary material ashore.

landing field n. A cleared area used for the takeoff and landing of aircraft.

landing gear n. The area under an aircraft that includes the wheels and their supporting frame.

landing strip n. The area on an airstrip where the planes actually touch the surface in takeoffs and landings; a secondary runway.

land-la-dy (land´lā˝ dē) n. A woman who rents and/or owns buildings or other property; a female landlord.

land-locked (land´lokt´) adj. Almost or completely surrounded by land.

land-lord (land´lord´) n. A person who owns property and rents or leases to another.

land-lub-ber (land´lub˝èr) n. An inexperienced person on a ship.

land-mark (land´märk´) n. A fixed object that serves as a boundary marker.

land mass n. A large body of land.

land measure n. A unit of measurement that is used in giving the area of land, such as an acre.

land office n. An office in which sales of public lands are recorded and open for public inspection.

land owner n. A person who owns land.

land reform n. A government program or

measures to redistribute farming and agricultural lands more equitably.

land-scape (land'skāp') *n.* A view or vista of natural scenery as seen from a single point. *v.* To change or improve the features of a section of ground by contouring the land and planting shrubs, trees, or flowers.

land-slide (land'slīd) *n.* The shifting or sliding of a large portion of soil from a higher level to a lower level.

lands-man (landz'man) *n.* An inexperienced seaman; a person who lives on the land.

land-ward (land'wėrd) *adj.* Facing, lying, or in the direction of land.

lane (lān) *n.* A small or narrow path between walls, fences, or hedges.

lang-syne (lang˝zīn') *n.* The time long ago; times past.

lan-guage (lang'gwij) *n.* The words, sounds, pronunciation and method of combining words used and understood by people.

lan-guet (lang'gwet) *n.* Something that resembles a tongue in shape, form or function.

lan-guid (lang'gwid) *adj.* Lacking in energy; drooping; weak. **languidly** *adv.* **languidness** *n.*

lan-guish (lang'gwish) *v.* To become weak; to be or live in a state of depression. **languisher** *n.* **languishment** *n.*

lan-guor (lang'gėr) *n.* Feebleness; physical exhaustion; listlessness; oppressive stillness. **languorous** *adj.* **languorously** *adv.*

la-ni-ar-y (lā'nē er˝ē) *n. pl.* **laniaries** A canine tooth, of a carnivorous animal.

la-nif-er-ous (la nif'ėr us) *adj.* Woolly.

lank (langk) *adj.* Slender; lean. **lankily** *adv.* **lankness** *n.*

lank-y (lang'kē) *adj.* Awkwardly tall and thin.

lan-o-lin (lan'o lin) *n.* Wool grease obtained from sheep's wool and refined for use in ointments and cosmetics.

lan-tern (lan'tėrn) *n.* A portable light having transparent or translucent sides.

lantern jaw *n.* A thin, long and projecting lower jaw.

lanthanide series *n.* The series of rare elements of increasing atomic numbers that start with lanthanum and ending with lutetium.

lan-tha-num (lan'tha num) *n.* The white soft metallic element of the rare-earth series, that has a valence of three, and is allied to aluminum.

la-nu-gi-nose or la-nu-gi-nous (la nō'ji nōs˝) *adj.* Downy; to be covered with down or fine soft hair.

la-nu-go (la nō'gō) *n., Biol.* A wooly or dense downy growth, as on the surface of a leaf or the hair that covers a newborn of some mammals.

lan-yard (lan'yėrd) *n.* A piece of rope or line used to secure objects on ships.

lap (lap) *n.* The surface of the upper thighs of the legs when a person is seated. **lap** *v.* To twist or wrap around; to enfold; to fold over; to lay a part above; to overlap.

lap-a-rot-o-my (lap˝arot'o mē) *n.* The cutting of the abdominal wall.

lap board (lap'bōrd˝) *n.* A thin board used on the lap as a writing surface or table.

lap dog *n.* A small dog that is easily held in the lap.

la-pel (la pel') *n.* The front part of a garment, especially that of a coat, that is turned back, usually a continuation of the collar.

lap-i-dar-y (lap'i der˝ē) *n. pl.* **lapidaries** A craftsman who polishes, cuts, and engraves precious stones and or gems.

lap-i-date (lap'i dāt˝) *v.* To pelt someone or something with stones; to stone to death.

la-pil-lus (la pil'us) *n.* A glassy volcanic fragment ejected during an eruption.

lap-in (lap'in) *n.* Rabbit fur that is sheared and dyed.

lapis lazuli *n.* A semiprecious stone that is azure blue in color, used in making jewelry

lap-pet (lap'it) *n.* A flap or fold on a headdress or on a garment.

lap robe *n.* A robe or blanket, used to cover the lap and legs as protection from the cold.

lapse (laps) *n.* A temporary deviation or fall to a less desirable estate. **lapse** *v.*

lap strake (lap´strāk˝) *adj.* A boat, constructed with each plank overlapping the one below it.

lar-ce-ny (lär´se nē) *n.* The unlawful taking of another person's property.

lard (lärd) *n.* The soft, white, solid or semisolid fat obtained after rendering the fatty tissue of the hog.

lar-der (lär´dėr) *n.* A place, such as a pantry or room, where food is stored.

large (lärj) *adj.* Greater than usual or average in amount or size. **at large** To be free and not confined.

large–heart-ed (lärj´här´tid) *adj.* Sympathetic; generous. **large–heartedness** *n.*

large intestine *n.* The portion of the intestine that extends from the end of the small intestine to the anus.

large–scale (lärj´skāl´) *adj.* Larger than others of the same kind; extensive; of or relating to a scale drawing to show detail.

lar-gess *or* **lar-gesse (lär jes´)** *n.* Liberal or excessive giving to an inferior; generosity.

lar-go (lär´gō) *adv.*, *Mus.* In a very slow, broad, and solemn manner. **largo** *n.*

lar-i-at (lar´ē at) *n.* A long, light rope with a running noose at one end to catch livestock.

lark (lärk) *n.* A bird having a melodious ability to sing; a merry or carefree adventure.

lark spur (lärk´spur˝) *n.* A annual, herbaceous plant from the crowfoot family that is cultivated for its blue, pink, or white flowers.

lar-ri-kin (lar´i kin) *n. Slang.* A rough and rowdy person. *adj.* Disorderly; rough.

lar-rup (lar´up) *v.* To flog or whip. **larrup** *n.* A blow; whipping.

lar-va (lär´va) *n. pl.* **larvae** The immature, wingless, often worm-like form of a newly hatched insect; the early form of an animal that differs greatly from the adult, such as

the tadpole. **larval** *adj.*

lar-vi-cide (lär´vi sīd˝) *n.* A chemical agent used to kill larvae.

la-ryn-ge-al (la rin´jē al) *adj.* Of or pertaining to the larynx. *n.* The sound made in the larynx.

lar-yn-gi-tis (lar´in jī´tis) *n.* Inflammation of the larynx.

lar-yn-gol-o-gy (lar˝ing gol´o jē) *n.* The study or branch of medicine that deals with the larynz and its diseases.

la-ryn-go-scope (la ring´go skōp˝) *n.* A reflecting instrument, used to examine the larynx. **laryngoscopically** *adv.*

lar-yn-got-o-my (lar˝ing got´o mē) *n.* The surgical removal of the larynx.

lar-ynx (lar´ingks) *n. pl.* **larynxes** The upper portion of the trachea which contains the vocal cords. **larynges** *adj.* **laryngeal** *adj.*

la-sa-gna *or* **la-sa-gne (le zän ye)** *n.* The traditional Italian dish of wide flat noodles baked with a sauce of tomatoes, meat, and cheese.

la-ser (lā´zėr) *n.* A device which utilizes the natural oscillations of molecules or atoms between energy levels for generating coherent electromagnetic radiation in the visible, ultraviolet, or infrared parts of the spectrum.

lash (lash) *v.* To strike or move violently or suddenly; to attack verbally; to whip. *n.* Eyelash. **lasher** *n.*

lass (las) *n.* A young girl or woman.

las-si-tude (las´i tüd´) *n.* A condition of weariness; fatigue.

las-so (las´ō) *n. pl.* **-sos, -soes** A long rope or long leather thong with a running noose used to catch horses and cattle. **lasso** *v.*

last (last) *adj.* Following all the rest; of the final stages, as of life; worst; lowest in rank. **last** *adv.* After all others in sequence or chronology. **last** *v.* To continue. **last** *n.* A form in the shape of a foot used to hold a shoe while it is repaired or to shape a shoe as it is being made.

last-ing (las´ting) *adj.* Enduring; or existing

a long time; durable; permanent.

last-ly (last´lē) *adv.* In the last place; finally; last word.

lat *abbr.* Latitude.

latch (lach) *n.* A device used to secure a gate or door, consisting of a bar that usually fits into a notch. **onto** To grab onto.

latch-et (lach´it) *n.* A narrow leather strap or thong used to fasten a shoe or sandal.

latch-key (lach´kē´) *n.* A key for opening an outside door.

latchkey child *n* A child who carries a key to the front door, because he or she returns home from school to an empty house.

latch-string (lach´string˝) *n.* A string that may be left on the outside of a door permitting raising of the latch and opening of the door from the outside.

late (lāt) *adj.* Coming, staying, happening after the proper or usual time; having recently died. **lateness** *n.* **lately** *adv.*

la-tent (lāt´ent) *adj.* Not apparent or visible although present and capable of becoming; not manifested.

latent heat *n.* Heat that is given off in a process as vaporization that changes the state of a body other than changing its temperature.

latent period *n.* The period of a disease between infection and the first symptoms.

la-ter (lā´tėr) *adv.* After the present; late in a greater degree.

lat-er-al (lat´ėr al) *adj.* Relating to or of the side. *n.* In football, an underhand pass thrown sideways or away from the line of scrimmage. **laterally** *adv.*

lateral pass *n.* A pass in the direction behind the passer or parallel to the goal line.

lat-er-ite (lat´e rīt˝) *n.* A porous residual product of rock decay, reddish in color having heavy concentrations of iron and aluminum hydroxides.

la-tex (lā´teks) *n.* The milky, white fluid that is produced by certain plants, such as the rubber tree; a water emulsion of synthetic rubber or plastic globules used in paints and adhesives.

lath (lath) *n.* A thin, narrow strip of wood

nailed to joists, rafters, or studding and used as a supporting structure for plaster.

lathe (lāth) *n.* A machine for holding material while it is spun and shaped by a tool.

lath-er (lath´ėr) *n.* A foam formed by detergent or soap and water. **latherer** *n.*

lath-y (lath´ē) *adj.* Thin.

lat-i-cif-er-ous (lat˝i sif´ėr us) *adj.* Containing latex, as in a plant cell.

Latin (lat´in) *n.* A member of the Latin people; language of the Roman Empire.

lat-i-tude (lat´i tūd´) *n.* The angular distance of the earth's surface north or south of the equator, measured in degrees along a meridian; freedom to act and to choose.

lat-i-tu-di-nar-i-an (lat˝i tŏd˝i när´ē an) *adj.* Permitting free and liberal thought and conduct, in religious beliefs.

la-trine (la trēn´) *n.* Something used as a toilet, as a hole or pit in the ground, in a military barracks or camp.

lat-ten (lat´en) *n.* A brass-like alloy formed in thin sheets.

lat-ter (lat´ėr) *adj.* Being the second of two persons or two things.

lat-tice (lat´is) *n.* A structure made of strips of wood, metal, or other materials, interlaced or crossed, framing regularly spaced openings. **lattice** *v.*

lat-tice-work (lat´is wurk˝) *n.* Any lattice work made of crossed strips of wood or metal in the pattern of a lattice.

laud (lod) *v.* To praise; to extol. **laudable** *adj.* **laudably** *adv.*

laud-a-ble (la´da bl) *adj.* Worthy of praise; commendable.

laud-a-to-ry (la´da tōr˝ē) *adj.* Containing relating to or expressing praise. **laudative, laudatorily,** *adv.*

laugh (laf) *v.* To express or show joy, merriment, or amusement; to display ridicule or to show a degree of contempt; to become amused; to produce the sound of laughter; to express by laughing; to compel with laughter. **laugh** *n.* The sound expressing amusement, joy, or ridicule. **laugher** *n.* **laughingly** *adv.*

laugh-ter (laf´tėr) *n.* The expression, sound, or act produced by laughing.

launch (lonch) *v.* To push or move a vessel into the water for the first time; to set a rocket or missile into flight; to put into operation.

laun-der (lon´dėr) *v.* To wash clothes or other materials in soap and water; to wash and iron. **launderer** *n.* **laundress** *n.*

laun-dro-mat (lōn´dro mat´) *n.* A place to wash and dry clothes in coin operated automatic machines.

laun-dry (lon´drē) *n. pl.* **laundries** An establishment where laundering is done professionally; clothes or other articles to be or that have been laundered.

laun-dry-man (lan´drē man´) *n. pl.* **laundrymen** A male employee who works at a laundry.

lau-re-ate (lor´ē it) *n.* A person honored for his accomplishment. **laureate** *v.*

lau-rel (lar´el) *n.* A small lauraceous evergreen tree having alternate leaves and small flowers.

la-va (lä´va) *n.* Molten rock which erupts or flows from an active volcano; the rock formed after lava has cooled and hardened.

lav-age (la väzh´) *n.* The washing out; the process of cleansing an organ by injection.

lava–lava (lä˝va lä´va) *n.* A printed rectangular cotton cloth worn as a kilt.

la-va-tion (la vā´shan) *n.* A cleansing.

lav-a-to-ry (lav´a tōr´ē) *n. pl.* **-ies** A room with permanently installed washing and toilet facilities.

lave (lāv) *v.* To bathe; of a river or the sea, to flow along or against.

lav-en-der (lav´en dėr) *n.* An aromatic plant having spikes of pale violet flowers; light purple in color. **lavender** *adj.*

la-ver (lā´ vėr) *n.* Any of several edible seaweeds or sea lettuce.

lav-ish (lav´ish) *adj.* Generous and extravagant in giving or spending. **lavisher** *n.* **lavishly** *adv.* **lavishness** *n.*

law (lo) *n.* A rule of conduct or action, recognized by custom or decreed by formal enactment, considered binding on the members of a nation, community, or group; a system or body of such rules.

law–a-bid-ing (lo´a bī´ding) *adj.* Abiding by the laws.

law-break-er (la´brä˝ kėr) *n.* A person who violates the law. **lawbreaking** *adj. or n.*

law-ful (la´ful) *adj.* To be in harmony with the law; allowed by law; agreeable to law; legitimate, rightful. **lawfully** *adv.* **lawfulness** *n.*

law-giv-er (la´giv˝ėr) *n.* A person who gives a code of laws; a legislator. **law-giving** *n.*

law-less (la´lis) *adj.* Not founded or regulated by or based on laws; disorderly. **lawlessness** *n.*

law-mak-er (la´mä˝ kėr) *n.* A legislator who makes laws. **lawmaking** *adj.*

law merchant *n.* The legal rules, that were formly applied to cases that regulated commerce.

lawn (lon) *n.* A stretch of ground near a house, park, or building covered with grass that is mowed regularly.

lawn mower *n.* A machine for cutting grass on lawns, operated by hand or by motor.

law-ren-ci-um (lo ren´sē um) *n.* A short-lived radioactive element, symbolized by LR.

law-suit (lo´süt´) *n.* A case or proceeding brought before a court of law for settlement.

law-yer (lo´yėr) *n.* A person trained in the legal profession who acts for and advises clients or pleads in court.

lax (laks) *adj.* Lacking disciplinary control; lacking rigidity or firmness. **laxity** *n.* **laxness** *n.* **laxly** *adv.*

lax-a-tion (lak sā´shan) *n.* The state of being relaxed; a loosening.

lax-a-tive (lak´sa tiv) *n.* A medicine taken to stimulate evacuation of the bowels. **laxative** *adj.*

lax-i-ty (lak´si-tē) *n.* The state or quality or being lax or loose; looseness.

lay (lā) *v.* To cause to lie; to place on a surface; past tense of lie.

lay-er (lā´er) *n.* A single thickness, coating, or covering that lies over or under another. **layered** *adj.* **layer** *v.*

lay-er-age (lā´ėr ij) *n.* The art or practice of reproducing plants by layering.

lay-ette (lā et´) *n.* The clothing, bedding, and equipment for a newborn child.

lay-man (lā´man) *n.* A person not belonging to a particular profession or specialty; one who is not a member of the clergy.

lay-off (lā´of´) *n.* A temporary dismissal of employees.

lay-out (lā´out´) *n.* A planned arrangement of something, such as a street, room, park, or building.

lay-o-ver (lā´ō˝ vėr) *n.* A delay; a stopover during a trip.

lay–up (lā ´up˝) *n.* A one-handed jump shot in basketball, aimed so the ball bounces off the backboard and in the basket.

lay up *v.* Confined by injury or illness.

laz-ar (laz´ėr) *n.* A person afflicted with a repulsive disease; a leper.

laz-a-ret-to (laz˝a ret´ō) n. pl. **lazarettos** A hospital for patients afflicted with contagious diseases; a ship, building or hospital used for quarantine purposes.

laze (lāz) *v.* To pass time lazily; to lounge or relax. **laze** *n.*

laz-u-lite (laz´a līt˝) *n.* An azure blue crystalline that ia a phosphate of aluminum, magnesium and iron.

la-zy (lā´zē) *adj.* Unwilling to work; moving slowly; sluggish. **lazily** *adv.* **laziness** *n.*

la-zy-bones (lā´zē bōnz´) *n., Slang* A lazy person.

lazy Susan *n.* A large revolving circular tray used to serve food or condiments.

lazy tongs *n.* Extendable tongs having a series of jointed and pivoted bars used to grasp objects at a distance.

lb *abbr.* Pound.

lea (lē) *n. ,Poetic* A grassy field or meadow.

leach (lēch) *v.* To cause a liquid to pass through a filter; to remove or wash out by filtering. **leachable** *adj.*

lead (lēd) *v.* To go ahead so as to show the way; to control the affairs or action of. **lead**

n. A soft, malleable, heavy, dull gray metallic element symbolized by Pb, used in solder, paints, and bullets; a graphite stick used as the writing material in pencils; in printing, the thin strip of type metal used to provide space between printed lines. **leadenness** *n.*

lead colic (led kol´ik) *n.* Severe stomach pain caused by lead poisoning.

lead-en (led´en) *adj.* Made of lead; heavy; dull gray in color.

lead glass (led glas) *n.* A refractive glass containing lead oxide and used to make lenses.

lead-ing (lē´ding) *adj.* Guiding; coming first; principal; foremost.

leading lady *n.* An actress performing the major feminine role in a production.

leading man *n.* An actor performing the major male role in a production.

leading question *n.* A question that suggests or guides an answer.

lead-off (lēd´of´) *n.* A beginning move or action; a person who is first to begin.

lead poisoning (led poi´zo ning) *n.* Poisoning of a person's system by the absorption of lead or any of its salts.

lead time (lēd tīm) *n.* The amount of time required from the beginning of a process to the end results.

leaf (lēf) *n. pl.* **leaves** A flat out-growth from a plant structure or tree, usually green in color and functioning  as the principal area of photosynthesis; a single page in a book. *v.* To turn the pages of a book. **leafless** *adj.* **leafy** *adj.*

leaf bud *n.* A bud which develops into a leafy shoot that consists of leaves and a stem, as distinguished from a flower bud.

leaf fat *n.* The animal fat that lines the abdominal cavity and encloses the kidneys of hogs.

leaf-hop-per (lēf´hop˝ėr) *n* Small, leaping, homopterous insects that suck the juices of plants.

leaf lard *n.* Lard made from the internal fat of the hog.

leaf-let (lēf´lit) *n.* A part or a segment of a compound leaf; a small printed handbill or circular, often folded.

leaf miner *n.* An type of insect characterized by species of flies, moths,and beetles that in the larval stage burrows in between the lower and upper surfaces of a leaf, and eats the tissue.

leaf mold *n.* A mixture of dead and decaying vegetable matter that helps to contribute to the fertility of the soil; a mold that affects foliage.

leaf-stalk (lēf´stak˝) *n.* The slender stem that supports the blade of a leaf.

leaf-y (lē´fē) *adj.* Furnished with or abounding or covered in leaves.

league (lēg) *n.* An association of persons, organizations, or states for common action or interest; an association of athletic competition; an underwater measurement of distance that equals 3 miles or approximately 4.8 km.

leak (lēk) *n.* An opening, as a flaw or small crack, permitting an escape or entrance of light or fluid. **leaky, leakage** *n.*

leak-age (lē´kij) *n.* The act or process of leaking; the amount or something that leaks.

leak-y (lē´kē) *adj.* Allowing fluid, water, or air to leak in or out.

lean (lēn) *v.* To rest or incline the weight of the body for support; to rest or incline anything against a large object or wall; to rely or depend on; to have a tendency or preference for; to tend towards a suggestion or action. **lean** *adj.* having little or no fat; thin. **leanly** *adv.* **leanness** *n.*

lean-ing (lē´ning) *n.* An inclination; a predispositon.

lean–to (lēn´tū´) *n.* A structure of branches, sloping to the ground from a raised support, usually an outside wall.

leap (lēp) *v.* To rise or project oneself by a sudden thrust from the ground with a spring of the legs; to spring, to jump. **leap** *n.* **leaper** *n.*

leap-frog (lēp´frog´) *n.* A game in which two players leap over each other by placing one's hands on the back of another who is bending over and leaping over him in a straddling position.

leap year *n.* A year containing 366 days, occurring every 4th year, with the extra day added to make 29 days in February

learn (lern) *n.* The process of acquiring knowledge, understanding, or mastery of a study or experience. **learner** *n.* **learnable** *adj.* **learn** *v.*

learn-ed (lur´nid) *adj.* Characterized by or associated with learning; acquired or obtained by study.

learn-ing (lur´ning) *n.* Knowledge or skill acquired by study; the act of a person that learns; the process of obtaining knowledge.

lease (lēs) *n.* A contract for the temporary use or occupation of property or premises in exchange for payment of rent. **lease** *v.*

leash (lēsh) *n.* A strong cord or rope for restraining a dog or other animal.

least-wise (lēst wīz) *adv., Slang* At least; at any rate.

leath-er (leth´er) *n.* An animal skin or hide with the hair removed, prepared for use by tanning.

leath-er-back (leth´er bak˝) *n.* A largest existing marine turtle having a flexible, leathery shell.

leath-er-neck (leth´er nek´) *n., Slang* A United States Marine.

leave (lēv) *v.* To go or depart from; to permit to remain behind or in a specified place or condition; to forsake; to abandon; to bequeath, as in a will. **leave** *n.* Official permission for absence from duty.

leav-en (lev´en) *n.* An agent of fermentation, as yeast, used to cause batters and doughs to rise; any pervasive influence that produces a significant change.

leav-ing (lē´ving) *n.* Residue; something that is left. **leavings** Refuse or remains.

lech-er-y (lech erē) *n.* Unrestrained indulgence in sexual activity. **lecher** *n.* **lecherous** *adj.* **lecherously** *adv.*

lec-i-thin (les´i thin) *n.* Any of a group of

phosphorus containing compounds found in plant and animal tissues, commercially derived from egg yolks, corn, and soybeans, and used in the production of foods, cosmetics, pharmaceuticals, and plastics.

lec-tern (lek´tern) *n.* A stand or tall desk, usually with a slanted top, on which a speaker or instructor may place books or papers.

lec-tion (lek´shan) *n.* A varient reading of a text or passage in a manuscript.

lec-ture (lek´cher) *n.* A speech on a specific subject, delivered to an audience for information or instruction. *v.* To give a speech or lecture; to criticize or reprimand.

led *v.* Past tense of lead.

ledge (lej) *n.* A narrow, shelf-like projection forming a shelf, as on a wall or the side of a rocky formation.

ledg-er (lej´er) *n.* A book in which sums of money received and paid out are recorded.

lee (lē) *n.* The side of a ship sheltered from the wind.

leech (lēch) *n.* Any of various carnivorous or bloodsucking worms; a person who clings or preys on others.

leek (lēk) *n.* A culinary herb of the lily family, related to the onion, with a slender, edible bulb.

leer (lēr) *n.* A sly look or sideways glance expressing desire or malicious intent.

lee tide *n.* A tide running in the same direction in which the wind is blowing.

lee-ward (lē´werd) *adj., Naut.* Pertaining to the side of a ship which is sheltered from the wind; opposite to windward. **leeward** *n.* A shelt-ered side.

lee-way (lē´wā´) *n., Naut.* The lateral drift of a plane or ship away from the correct course.

left (left) *adj.* Pertaining to or being on the side of the body that faces north when the subject is facing east.

left–hand (left´hand´) *adj.* Situated on or to the left; left-handed.

left-o-ver (left´ō´ver) *n.* Something remaining or left over; unconsumed food from a meal.

left wing, *n.* A political party, faction or group with leftist principles.

leg (leg) *n.* A limb or appendage serving as a means of support and movement in animals and man; a part or division of a journey or trip.

leg-a-cy (leg´a sē) *n. pl.* **-ies** Personal property, money, and other valuables that are bequeathed by will; anything that is handed down from an ancestor, predecessor, or earlier era.

le-gal (lē´gal) *adj.* Of, pertaining to, or concerned with the law or lawyers; something based on or authorized by law. **legality** *n.* **legalization** *n.* **legalize** *v.*

legal holiday *n.* A holiday established by legal authority, on which official business is resticted.

le-gal-ism (lē´ga liz´um) *n.* A strict conformity to the law, especially when stressing the letter and forms of the law rather than the spirit of justice. **legalist** *n.* **legalistic** *adj.*

le-gal-i-ty (lē gal´ i tē) *n. pl.* **legalities** The quality of being legal; the observance of law.

le-gal-ize (lē´ga līz˝) *v.* To make legal; to give legal authority or sanction.

legal reserve *n.* The minimum sum of money that banks or life insurance companies are legally required to put aside for security purposes.

legal tender *n.* Money that is legally valid as payment of a bill or debt and which must be accepted by the creditor.

le-ga-tion (li gā´shan) *n.* The official diplomatic mission in a foreign country, headed by a minister; the official residence or business premises of a diplomatic minister of lower rank than an ambassador.

le-ga-to (le gä´tō) *adv., Music* Smooth and flowing with successive notes connected. **legato** *n.*

leg-end (lej´end) *n.* An unverifiable story handed down from the past; a body of such stories, as those connected with a culture or people.

leg-en-dar-y (lej´en der´ē) *adj.* Presented

as, based on, or of the nature of a legend. **legendary** *adv.*

leg-er-de-main (lej˝ẽr de mān´) *n.* Sleight of hand; a deceptive performance, a display of skill.

leg-gy (leg´ē) *adj.* Having long attractive legs.

leg-horn (leg´horn´) *n.* A hat made from finely plaited wheat straw.

leg-i-ble (lej´i bl) *adj.* Capable of being read or deciphered. **legibility** *n.* **legibly** *adv.*

le-gion (lē´jon) *n.* In ancient Rome, an army unit that comprised between 4,200 and 6,000 men; any of various honorary or military organizations, usually national in character.

leg-is-late (lej´is lāt´) *v.* To pass or make laws.

leg-is-la-tion (lej˝is lā´shan) *n.* The act or procedures of passing laws; lawmaking; an officially enacted law.

leg-is-la-tive (lej´is lā´tiv) *adj.* Of or pertaining to legislation or a legislature; having the power to legislate.

leg-is-la-tor (lej´is lā˝tẽr) *n.* A lawmaker; a member of a legislative body.

leg-is-la-ture (lej´is lā´chẽr) *n.* A body of persons officially constituted and empowered to make and change laws.

le-gist (lē´jist) *n.* A person who specializes in law.

le-git-i-mate (li jit´imit) *adj.* Accordant with the laws and established rules or principles; to conform to accepted standards; born of parents legally married; of the regular type; genuine; in accordance with established laws or reasoning.

le-git-i-mist (li jit´i mist) *n.* A person who supports legitimate authority *adj.* Relating to, or upholding legitimate authority.

leg-man (leg´man˝) *n.* An assistant who gathers needed information, or run errands, and performs tasks.

leg-ume (leg´ūm, li gūm´) *n.* A simple, one-cell, dried, dehiscent, fruit which splits along two seams that are attached to a ventral suture.

le-gu-min (li gū´min) *n.* A protein resem-

bling casein, obtained from the seeds of leguminous plants.

leg-work *n., Slang* A chore, task, or gathering of information accomplished by going about on foot.

le-hu-a (lā hŏ´ă) *n.* A tropical, hardwood, tree of the myrtle family, that has bright red flowers that bloom in large clusters.

lei (lā´ē) *n. pl.* **leis** A wreath of flowers worn around the neck; the customary greeting of welcome in the state of Hawaii.

leis-ter (lē´stẽr) *n.* A barbed spear used to catch fish.

lei-sure (lē´zhẽr) *n.* The time of freedom from work or duty.

lei-sure-ly (lē´zhẽr lē) *adv.* Acting, without haste.

lem-nis-cus (lem nis´kus) *n.* A long band of nerve fibers of the brain.

lem-on (lem´on) *n.* An oval citrus fruit grown on a tree, having juicy, acid pulp and a yellow rind that yields an essential oil used as a flavoring and as a perfuming agent. *Slang* Something, as an automobile, that proves to be defective or unsatisfactory.

lem-on-ade (lem´o nād´) *n.* A drink made from water, lemon juice, and sugar.

lemon verbena *n.* A subtropical shrub of the garden variety.

lend (lend) *v.* To allow the temporary use or possession of something with the understanding that it is to be returned; to offer oneself as to a specific purpose.

length (lengkth) *n.* The linear extent of something from end to end, usually the longest dimension of a thing as distinguished from its thickness and width; the measurement of something to estimate distance. **lengthy** *adj.*

length-en (lengk´then) *v.* To make longer or to become longer.

length-wise (lengkth´wīz´) *adv. & adj.* Of or in the direction or dimension of length; longitudinally.

length-y (lengk´thē) *adj.* Long, extended or moderately long; protracted.

le-ni-ent (lē´nē *ent*) *adj.* Gentle, forgiving, and mild; merciful; undemanding; tolerant. **leniency** *n.* **lenience** *n.*

len-i-tive (len´i tiv) *adj.* Having the ability to softening or moderate, as with medicines. **lenitive** *n.*

lens (lenz) *n.* In optics, the curved piece of glass or any other transparent substance that is used to refract light rays so that they converge or diverge to form an image; the transparent structure in the eye, situated behind the iris, which serves to focus an image on the retina.

lent (lent) *v.* Past tense of lend.

Lent (lent) *n.* The period of forty days, excluding Sundays, of fasting and penitence observed by many Christians from Ash Wednesday until Easter. **Lenten** *adj.*

len-tan-do (len tän´dō) *adj.* In a slackening manner; gettting slower.

len-ti-cel (len´ti sel) *n.* A pore in shape, in the bark of woody stems through which the gases are exchanged between the stem tissue and the atmosphere.

len-ti-go (len tī´gō) *n.* A freckle or a freckly condition.

len-til (len´til) *n.* A leguminous plant, having broad pods that contain edible seeds and leafy stalks used as fodder.

leop-ard (lep´ėrd) *n.* A large member of the cat family of Africa and Asia, having a tawny coat with dark brown or black spots grouped in rounded clusters, also called a panther. **leopardess** *n.*

le-o-tard (lē´o tärd´) *n.* A close-fitting garment worn by dancers and acrobats.

lep-er (lep´ėr) *n.* One who suffers from leprosy.

lep-i-dop-ter-an (lep˜i dop´tėr *an*) *n.* Any insects comprising the butterfly, moth, or skipper.

lep-i-dote (lep´i dōt˝) *adj.* Covered with scurf or scurfy spots or scales.

lep-re-chaun (lep´re kon´) *n.* A mischief-making elf of Irish folklore, supposed to own hidden treasure.

lep-ro-sy (lep´ro sē) *n.*, *Pathol.* A chronic communicable disease characterized by nodular skin lesions and the progressive destruction of tissue. **leprous** *adj.*

lep-ton (lep´ton) *n.* A small coin; small in mass, as an electron.

les-bi-an (lez´bē *an*) *n.* A homosexual woman. **lesbian** *adj.*

lese majesty *n.* An offense against a ruler or supreme power of state.

le-sion (lē´zhan) *n.* An injury; a wound; any well-defined bodily area where the tissue has changed in a way that is characteristic of a disease.

less (les) *adj.* Smaller; of smaller or lower importance or degree. **less** *prep.* With the subtraction of; minus.

-less *suffix* Without; lacking.

les-see (le sē´) *n.* One who leases a property.

less-en (les´en) *v.* To decrease or make smaller or less; to become smaller; to diminish.

les-son (les´on) *n.* An instance from which something is to be or has been learned; an assignment to be learned or studied as by a student.

les-sor (les´or) *n.* One who grants a lease to another.

let (let) *v.* To give permission; to allow. **let** *n.* An invalid stroke in a game such as tennis, that must be repeated because of some interruption or hindrance of playing conditions. **let's** (lets) *contr.* Let us.

let-down (let´doun´) *n.* A decrease or slackening, as in energy or effort. *Slang* A disappointment.

le-thal (lē´thal) *adj.* Pertaining to or being able to cause death. **lethally** *adv.*

lethal gene *n.* A gene that may affect, prevent development, or cause death of an organism at any stage of its life.

le-thar-gic (le thär´jik) *adj.* Affected with or characterized by lethargy; sluggish; inclined to sleep; dull.

leth-ar-gy (leth´ėr jē) *n.*, *Pathol.* A state

of excessive drowsiness or abnormally deep sleep; laziness. **lethargic** *adj.*

let-ter (let´ér) *n.* A standard character or sign used in writing or printing to represent an alphabetical unit or speech sound; a written or printed means of communication sent to another person.

let-tered (let´érd) *adj.* Learned or educated; characterized by learning; to be versed in literature.

letter of credit *n.* A bank certification that entitles the person named to draw a specified amount of money from that bank or an affiliate.

let-ter-head (let´ér hed´) *n.* Stationery printed with a name and address, usually of a company or business establishment.

letter–perfect (let´ér per´fikt) *adj.* Absolutely correct; perfect.

let-tuce (let´is) *n.* A plant having crisp, edible leaves that are used especially in salads.

let-up (let´up´) *n.* A pause or lessening of intensity.

leu-co-ma-ine (lōkō´ma ēn´) *n.* A poisonous nitrogen compound that is present in animal tissue as a by-product of metabolism.

leu-ke-mi-a (lü kē´mē a) *n., Pathol.* A generally fatal disease of the blood in which white blood cells multiply in uncontrolled numbers. **leukemic** *adj.*

le-vant-er (li van´tér) *n.* A forceful wind that blows in an easterly direction.

le-vee (lev´ē) *n.* An embankment along the shore of a body of water, especially a river, built to prevent overflowing.

lev-el (lev´el) *n.* A relative position, rank, or height on a scale; a standard position from which other heights and depths are measured. *adj.* Balanced in height; even. *v.* To make or become flat or level. **leveler** *n.* **levelness** *n.* **levelly** *adv.*

level–headed (lev´el hed´id) *adj.* Showing good judgment and common sense. **level–headedness** *n.*

leveling rod *n.* A graduated rod used to measure the vertical distance from a point on the ground and the sight line of a surveyor's level.

le-ver (lev´ér) *n.* A handle that projects and is used to operate or adjust a mechanism.

lev-er-age (lev´e-rij) *n.* The use of a lever; the mechanical advantage gained by using a lever; power to act effectively.

lev-i-gate (lev´i gāt´) *v.* To make a smooth paste; to rub or grind to a fine smooth powder.

lev-i-tate (lev´i tāt´) *v.* To rise and float in the air in apparent defiance of gravity. **levitation** *n.*

lev-i-ty (lev´i tē) *n. pl.* **-ies** Lack of seriousness; frivolity; lightness.

le-vo-ro-ta-tion (lē´vō rō tā´shan) *n.* Rotation toward the left; a counterclockwise rotation or direction.

lev-y (lev´ē) *v.* To impose and collect by authority or force, as a fine or tax; to draft for military service; to prepare for, begin, or wage war. **levy** *n.*

lewd (lüd) *adj.* Preoccupied with sex; lustful. **lewdly** *adv.* **lewdness** *n.*

lex-i-cal (lek´si kal) *adj.* Pertaining or relating to words or vocabulary of a language, as distinguished from its construction and grammar.

lex-i-cog-ra-phy (lek´si kog´ra fē) *n.* The practice or profession of compiling dictionaries. **lexicographer, lexicographic** *adj.* **lexicographical** *adj.*

lex-i-con (lek´si kon´) *n.* A dictionary; a vocabulary or list of words that relate to a certain subject, occupation, or activity. **lexical** *adj.*

li (lē) *n.* A Chinese linear unit of measure equivalent to about ⅓ mile or 0.5 kilometer.

li-a-bil-i-ty (lī´a bil´i tē) *n. pl.* **-ies** The condition or state of being liable; that which is owed to another.

li-a-ble (lī´a bl) *adj.* Legally or rightly responsible.

li-ai-son (lē´ā zon´) *n.* A communication, as between different parts of an armed force or departments of a government; a close connection or relationship; an illicit love affair.

li-ar (lī´ér) *n.* A person who tells falsehoods.

lib (lib) *n., Slang* Liberation.

li-bel (lī´bel) *n., Law* A written statement in published form that damages a person's character or reputation. **libel** *v.* **libelous** *adj.*

li-bel-ant (lī´be lant) *n.* A person who institutes a libel suit.

li-bel-ee (lī´be lē´) *n.* The defendant in a libel lawsuit that has been brought to court.

lib-er-al (lib´er al) *adj.* Characterized by generosity or lavishness in giving; abundant; ample; inclining toward opinions or policies that favor progress or reform, such as religion or politics. **liberalism** *n.* **liberality** *n.* **liberalize** *v.* **liberally** *adv.*

liberal arts *n. pl.* Academic courses that include literature, philosophy, history, languages, etc., which provide general cultural information.

lib-er-al-i-ty (lib´e ral´i tē) *n.* The quality or state of being liberal.

lib-er-ate (lib´e rāt´) *v.* To set free, as from bondage, oppression, or foreign control. **liberation** *n.*

lib-er-tar-i-an (lib´er târ´ē an) *n.* A person who upholds the doctrine of the free will; one who advocates unrestricted liberty.

li-ber-ti-cide (li bur´ri sīd´) *n.* The destruction of liberty; a destroyer of liberty.

lib-er-tine (lib´er tēn´) *n.* A person lacking moral or sexual restraint; one who leads a unscrupulous life.

lib-er-ty (lib´er tē) *n. pl.* **-ies** The state of being free from oppression, tyranny, confinement, or slavery; freedom; in Navy terms, the permission to be absent from one's ship or duty for less that 48 hours.

li-bi-do (li bē´dō) *n.* One's sexual desire or impulse; the psychic energy drive that is behind all human activities. **libidinal** *adj.* **libidinous** *adj.*

li-brar-i-an (lī brer ē en) *n.* A person in charge of a library; one who specializes in library work.

li-brar-y (lī´brer´ē) *n. pl.* **libraries** A collection of books, pamphlets, magazines, and reference books kept for reading, reference, or borrowing; a commercial estab-

lishment, usually in connection with a city or school, which lends or rents books.

lice *n.* Plural of louse.

li-cense (lī´sens) *n.* An official document that gives permission to engage in a specified activity or to perform a specified act. **license** *v.* **licensee** *n.* **licenser** *n.*

li-cen-ti-ate (lī sen´shē it) *n.* A person licensed to practice a specified profession.

li-cen-tious (lī sen´shus) *adj.* Lacking in moral restraint; immoral. **licentiously** *adv.* **licentiousness** *n.*

li-chen (lī´ken) *n.* Any of various flowerless plants consisting of fungi, commonly growing in flat patches on trees and rocks. **lichened** *adj.* **lichenous** *adj.*

lic-it (lis´it) *adj.* Lawful. **licitly** *adv.* **licitness** *n.*

lick (lik) *v.* To pass the tongue over or along the surface of. *Slang* To beat; to thrash.

lickety-split (lik´i tē split´) *adv.* Full speed; rapidly.

lick-ing (lik´ing) *n.* A setback; a beating or thrashing; a defeat.

lick-spit-tle (lik´spit´l) *n.* A person who seeds favor through flatterer.

lic-o-rice (lik´o ris) *n.* A perennial herb of Europe, the dried root of which is used to flavor medicines and candy.

lid (lid) *n.* A hinged or removable cover for a container; an eyelid. **lidded** *adj.*

li-dar (lī där) *n.* A radar system that emits pulsed laser light instead of microwaves.

lie (lī) *v.* To be in or take a horizontal recumbent position; to recline. *n.* A false or untrue statement.

lie detector *n.* A machine which detects and records tracings of physical changes, as blood pressure, pulse rate, and tension that accompanies lying or falsity of.

lie down *v.* To neglect or fail to perform one's duties deliberately.

liege (lēj) *n.* A feudal lord or sovereign. *adj.* Loyal; faithful.

lien (lēn) *n.* The legal right to claim, hold, or sell the property of another to satisfy a debt or obligation. **li-en-ter-y (lī´en ter´ē)** *n.* A condition or type of diarrhea, where the food is discharged undigested.

lieu (lū) *n.* Place; instead of; in place of.

lieu-ten-ant (lū ten′ant) *n.* A commissioned officer in the United States Army, Air Force, or Marine Corps who ranks below a captain.

life (līf) *n. pl.* **lives** The form of existence that distinguishes living organisms from dead organisms or inanimate matter in the ability to carry on metabolism, respond to stimuli, reproduce, and grow.

life-blood (līf′blud″) *n.* That which is vital or essential to life and existence.

life-boat (līf′bōt″) *n.* A strong boat constructed and equipped for saving lives.

life buoy *n.* A buoyant life preserving device, in various forms, that allows a person to keep afloat until rescued.

life cycle *n.* The series of activities or processes that an organism undergoes during its lifetime.

life expectancy *n.* The average number of years that a person is likely to live.

life-guard (līf′gärd′) *n.* An expert swimmer employed to protect people in and around water.

life-less (līf′lis) *adj.* To be deprived of life; dead; lacking qualities of life or spirit; inactive. **lifelessly** *adv.* **lifelessness** *n.*

life-like (līf′līk″) *adj.* Resembling, representing or simulating life.

life-long (līf′lang″) *adj.* Lasting or continuing throughout life.

life-net *n.* A strong net used to catch persons jumping from a burning building.

life of Riley *n., Slang* An enjoyable, carefree way of living.

life preserver *n.* A buoyant device, one in the shape of a ring or jacket, used to keep a person afloat in water.

lifer (lī′fèr) *n., Slang* A person sentenced to life in prison.

life-raft *n.* A raft made of wood or an inflatable material used by people who have been forced into the water.

life-sav-er (līf′sā″vèr) *n.* A person trained to save others from drowning.

life–size (līf′sīz′) *adj.* Of the natural size of the original.

life–support system *n.* A system giving a person all or some of the items, such as oxygen, water, food, and control of temperature, necessary for a person's life and health while in a spacecraft or while exploring the surface of the moon; a system used to sustain life in a critical health situation.

life-time (līf′tīm′) *n.* The period between one's birth and death.

life-work (līf′werk′) *n.* The main work of a person's lifetime.

life zone *n.* A biogeographic zone.

lift (lift) *v.* To raise from a lower to a higher position; to elevate; to take from; to steal.

lift *n.* The act or process of lifting; force or power available for lifting; an elevation of spirits; a device or machine designed to pick up, raise, or carry something; an elevator. **lifter** *n.*

lift–off (lift′of′) *n.* The vertical take off or the instant of takeoff of an aircraft or spacecraft.

lig-a-ment (lig′a ment) *n.* A tough band of tissue joining bones or holding a body organ in place. **ligamentous** *adj.*

li-gate (lī′gāt) *v.* To tie with a ligature.

lig-a-ture (lig′a chèr) *n.* Something, as a musical cord, that is used to bind; a thread used in surgery; something that unites or connects; a printing character that combines two or more letters.

light (līt) *n.* Electromagnetic radiation that can be seen by the naked eye; brightness; a source of light; spiritual illumination; enlightenment; a source of fire, such as a match. *adj.* Having light; bright; of less force, quantity, intensity, weight, than normal; having less calories or alcoholic content; dizzy; giddy. **light** *v.* **lightness** *n.*

light–year *or* **light year** (līt′yēr′) *n.* A measure equal to the distance light travels in one year, approximately 5.878 trillion miles.

light-en (līt′en) *v.* To make lighter or less dark; to grow brighter; to lessen as in weight.

light-er (līˊtèr) *n.* A device used to light a pipe, cigar or cigarette; a barge used to load and unload a cargo ship.

light fast *adj.* Resistant to sunlight.

light–foot-ed (lītˊfutˊed) *adj.* Nimble; light and springy step.

light–hand-ed (lītˊhanˊdid) *adj.* Having a delicate or light touch.

light–heart-ed (lītˊhärˊ tid) *adj.* Free from anxiety or care; hopefull and optimistic.

light-ning (lītˊning) *n.* The flash of light produced by a high-tension natural electric discharge into the atmosphere. *adj.* Moving with or as if with the suddenness of light-ning.

lightning bug *n.* A firefly.

lightning rod *n.* A grounded metal rod positioned high on a building to protect it from lightning.

light opera *n.* An operetta.

lights (līts) *n.* The lungs, especially of a slaughtered animal.

light-ship (lītˊshipˊ) *n.* A ship, having a powerful light or horn, that is anchored in dangerous waters to warn other vessels.

light show *n.* A display of colored lights in kaleidoscopic patterns, often accompanied by film, slides, or music.

light-weight (lītˊwātˊ) *n.* A person who weighs very little; a boxer or wrestler weighing between 127 and 135 pounds. **lightweight** *adj.*

lig-ne-ous (ligˊnē us) *adj.* Of or resembling wood; woody.

lig-ni-fy (ligˊni fīˊ) *v.* To make or become woody or wood-like.

lig-nin (ligˊnin) *n.* An organic substance associated with cellulose that forms the woody cell walls of plants.

lg-nite (ligˊnīt) *n.* A brownish-black soft coal, especially one in which the texture of the original wood is distinct.

lig-no-cel-lu-lose (ligˊnō selˊū lōsˊ) *n.* An association of lignin and cellulose that contains the essential part of woody cell walls and the fibrous tissue in plants.

lig-ro-in (ligˊrō in) *n.* A volatile, flammable fraction of petroleum used as a solvent.

like (līk) *adj.* Of the same form, appearance, kind, character, or amount. *n.* A counter-part one that is like a another; the match or equal.

like–mind-ed (līkˊmīnˊdid) *adj.* Of the same way of thinking.

lik-en (līˊken) *v.* To describe as being like; to compare.

like-ness (līkˊnis) *n.* Resemblance; a copy.

like-wise (līkˊwīzˊ) *adv.* In a similar way.

lik-ing (līˊking) *n.* A favorable regard to something.

li-lac (līˊlak) *n.* A shrub widely grown for its large, fragrant purplish or white flower cluster; a pale purple. **lilac** *adj.*

lilt (lilt) *n.* A light song; a rhythmical way of speaking.

lil-y (lilˊē) *n.* *pl.* **lilies** Any of various plants bearing trumpet-shaped flowers; a plant similar or related to the lily, as the water lily.

lil-y–liv-ered (lilˊē livˊèrd) *adj.* Timid; cowardly.

lily pad *n.* The large floating leaf of the water lily, sometimes accompanied with a flower.

lily–white (lilˊē hwītˊ, lilˊwītˊ) *adj.* To be white and as pure as lily.

lima bean (līˊma bēn) *n.* Any of several varieties of tropical American plants hav-ing flat pods with light green edible seeds.

limb (lim) *n.* A large bough of a tree; an animal's appendage used for movement or grasping; an arm or leg.

lim-bate (limˊbāt) *adj.* Bordered, in color as a leaf or flower with one color sur-rounded by an edging of another.

lim-ber (limˊbèr) *adj.* Bending easily; pli-able; moving easily; agile. **limber** *v.* To make or become limber. **limberly** *adv.*

lim-bo *or* **Lim-bo** (limˊbō) *n.* The abode of souls kept from entering Heaven; a place or condition of oblivion or neglect.

lime (līm) *n.* A tropical citrus tree with

evergreen leaves, fragrant white flowers, and edible green fruit; calcium oxide.

lime-light (līm´līt) *n.* A focus of public attention; the center of attention.

lim-er-ick (lim´ėr ik) *n.* A humorous verse of five lines.

lime-stone (līm´stōn´) *n.* A form of sedimentary rock composed mainly of calcium carbonate which is used in building and in making lime and cement.

lime-sul-fur (līm´sul˝fėr) *n.* Product composed of sulfur, lime, and water that have been boiled together; used as an insecticide.

lime-wa-ter (līm´wa˝tėr) *n.* An alkaline water solution of calcium hydroxide, in medicine used as an antacid.

lim-it (lim´it) *n.* A boundary; a maximum or a minimum number or amount; a restriction on frequency or amount. *v.* To restrict; to establish bounds or boundaries. **limitation** *n.*

lim-i-ta-tion (lim˝i tā´shan) *n.* The instance or act of limiting; that which limits; a certain period of time that limits.

lim-i-ted (lim´i-tid) *adj.* Confined within the limits; restricted.

limn (lim) *v.* To describe; to depict by drawing. **limner** *n.*

li-mo-nite (lī´mo nīt´) *n.* A natural iron oxide used as an ore of iron.

lim-ou-sine (lim´o zēn´) *n.* A luxurious large vehicle; a small bus used to carry passengers to airports and hotels.

limp (limp) *v.* To walk lamely. *adj.* Lacking or having lost rigidity; not firm or strong. **limply** *adv.* **limpness** *n.*

lim-pet (lim´pit) *n.* Any of numerous marine gastropod mollusks having a conical shell and adhering to tidal rocks.

lim-pid (lim´pid) *adj.* Transparently clear. **limpidity** *n.* **limpidly** *adv.*

lin-age (lī´nij) *n.* The number of printed or written lines on a page.

linch-pin (linch´pin´) *n.* A locking pin inserted through a shaft to keep a wheel from slipping off.

Lincoln *n.* The capital of the state of Nebraska.

lin-den (lin´den) *n.* Any of various shade trees having heart-shaped leaves.

line (līn) *n.* A mark made with a pencil, pen, or other writing tool, on a surface; the spoken words of a play; a short written note. *Math.* The shortest distance between two points. **line–up** A line of persons formed for the purpose of inspection or identification; the members of a team who take part in a game; a group of television programs that are aired sequentially.

lin-e-age (lin´ē ij) *n.* A direct line of descent from an ancestor.

lin-e-a-ment (lin´ē a ment) *n.* A contour, shape, or feature of the body and especially of the face.

lin-e-ar (lin´ē ėr) *adj.* Of, pertaining to, or resembling a line; long and narrow.

linear acceletator *n., Phys.* A device for accelerating charged particles in a straight line by successive impulses from a series of electric fields.

linear measure *n.* A measure of length, or the system that measures length, as in contrast with area or volume.

linear perspective *n.* A technique in painting and drawing in which parallel lines converge to give the illusion of distance and depth.

lin-e-a-tion (lin˝ē ā´shan) *n.* Marking with or tracing by lines; an arrangement of lines.

line-back-er (līn´bak´ėr) *n.* In football, one of the defensive players positioned directly behind the line of scrimmage.

line-breed-ing (līn´brē˝ding) *n., Biol.* The interbreeding of individuals to develop and maintain desirable characteistics of individuals in the same ancestral line.

line cut *n.* The photo engraving of lines and solid areas.

line drawing *n.* A drawing composed of a solid line without color.

line drive *n.* In baseball, a ball hit with force whose path approximates a straight line parallel or nearly parallel to the ground.

line engraving *n.* An engraving cut directly in the plate with incised lines of varying thickness and density.

line gauge *n.* A printers ruler that shows printing point sizes, marked off in agates and picas.

line-man (līn´man) *n.* A person who works on telephone or electric power lines; a player on the forward line of a team, especially football.

lin-en (lin´en) *n.* Thread, yarn, or fabric made of flax; household articles, such as sheets and pillow cases, made of linen or a similar fabric. **linen** *adj.*

line of force *n., Phys.* A theoretical line in a field of force, an electric or magnetic field which corresponds to the force and direction of that field.

line of scrimmage *n.* In football, an imaginary line that extends across the field from the position of the football on any given play.

line of sight *n.* The imaginary line that extends from the viewer's eye to the distant point to which he is looking.

lin-er (lī´nėr) *n.* A ship belonging to a ship line or an aircraft belonging to an airline; one that lines or serves as a lining.

line score *n.* In baseball, a statistical record of each inning of a game.

lines-man (līnz´man) *n.* An official in a court game, as tennis or volleyball, who calls shots which fall out–of–bounds; an official in football who marks the downs.

line squall *n.* A thunderstorm, or a series of storms that build on a cold front, that is characterized by a drop in temperature and a change in the wind direction.

line storm *n.* A raging, violent rain storm that occurrs about the same time as the equinox.

ling (ling) *n.* Any of various marine food fishes related to the cod.

ling-cod (ling´kod´) *n.* A large greenish in color, food fish of the North Pacific, similar to the common greenlings family.

lin-ger (ling´gėr) *v.* To be slow in parting or reluctant to leave; to be slow to act; to procrastinate. **lingerer** *n.* **lingeringly** *adv.*

lin-ge-rie (län´zhe rā´) *n.* Women's undergarments.

lingo (ling´gō) *n. pl. goes* Language that is unfamiliar; a specialized vocabulary.

lin-gual (ling´gwal) *adj.* Relating or pertaining to the tongue; relating to the surface of the tooth laying next to the tongue.

lin-guist (ling´gwist) *n.* One who is fluent in more than one language; a person specializing in linguistics.

linguistic atlas *n.* A series of maps where speech variations are recorded.

linguistic form *n.* An understandable unit of speech, as a sentence also called the speech form.

linguistic geography *n.* A regional language and dialectic distribution among regions and peoples.

lin-guis-tics (ling gwis´tiks) *n.* The study of the origin, structure, and history of language.

lin-i-ment (lin´i ment) *n.* A liquid or semi-liquid medicine applied to the skin.

li-nin (lī´nin) *n., Biol.* The substance that forms the net-like formation which connects the chromatin granules in a cell nucleus.

lin-ing (lī´ning) *n.* A material which is used to cover an inside surface.

link (lingk) *n.* One of the rings forming a chain; something in the form of a link; a tie or bond; a cuff link. *v.* To connect by or as if by a link or links.

link-age (ling´kij) *n.* The act or process of linking; a system of connecting structures.

linking verb *n., Gram.* A verb which links a subject to the predicate of a sentence: as *become, be, feel, seem.*

links (lingks) *n. pl.* A golf course.

link-work (lingk´wurk´) *n.* Work that is composed of links, as a chain.

lin-net (lin´it) *n.* A small Old World finch.

li-no-le-um (li nō´lē um) *n.* A floor covering consisting of a surface of hardened linseed oil and a filler, as wood or powdered cork, on a canvas or burlap backing.

lin-seed (lin´sēd´) *n.* The seed of flax, used in paints and varnishes.

linsey–woolsey (lin´zē wel´zē) *n.* A coarse, sturdy fabric of wool and linen or cotton.

lin-stock (lin´stok˝) *n.* A staff with a fork tip and formally used to hold a lighted match.

lin-tel (lin´tel) *n.* A horizontal beam across the top of a door which supports the weight of the structure above it.

lint-er (lin´tèr) *n.* A machine used to remove fibers that remain on cotton seeds after the first ginning.

li-on (lī´on) *n.* A large carnivorous mammal of the cat family, found in Africa and India, having a short, tawny coat and a long, heavy mane in the male; a person of great importance or prestige. **lioness** *n.*

li-on–heart-ed (lī´on här´tid) *adj.* Very courageous.

li-on-ize (lī´o nīz´) *v.* To treat someone as a celebrity.

lion's share *n.* The largest portion or share.

li-pase (lī´pās, lip´ās) *n., Biochem.* An enzyme, that occurrs in the liver and pancreas that accelerates the breaking down of fats into fatty acids and glycerin.

li-pid (lī´pid) *n., Biochem.* Substances of an organic material, including sterols, fats, and waxes, that are insoluble in water but are able to be metabolized.

lip-oid (lip´oid) *adj., Biochem.* Resembling fat.

lip–read (lip´rēd˝) *v.* To understand a person's speech, by watching his lips form words.

liq-ue-fac-tion (lik˝we fak´shan) *n.* The act of making liquid or becoming liquid.

liq-ue-fy (lik´ we fī˝) *v.* To convert or reduce to a liquid state.

li-queur (li ker´) *n.* A sweet alcoholic beverage flavored with fruit, spices or nuts; a cordial.

liq-ui-date (lik´wi dāt´) *v.* To settle a debt by payment or other settlement; to close a business by settling accounts and dividing

up assets; to get rid of, especially to kill. **liquidation** *n.* **liquidator** *n.*

liq-ui-da-tor (lik we dāt er) *n.* A person who liquidates usually appointed by law to liquidate assets.

liquid measure *n.* The units of capacity used in measuring liquids.

liq-uor (lik´ér) *n.* A distilled alcoholic beverage; a liquid substance, as a watery solution of a drug.

lisle (līl) *n.* A fine, tightly twisted cotton thread.

lisp (lisp) *n.* A speech defect or mannerism marked by lisping. **lisp** *v.* To mispronounce the s and z sounds, usually as th.

lis-some (lis´om) *adj.* Nimble. **lissomely** *adv.* **lissomeness** *n.*

list (list) *n.* A series of numbers or words; a tilt to one side. **list** *v.*

list-ed (lis´tid) *adj.* Set down or to make a list, as a telephone number.

lis-ten (lis n) *v.* To monitor or tune in to conversation or a broadcast.

list-ing (lis´ting) *n.* The act or process of making or putting in a list; the entry on a list; a directory.

list-less (list´lis) *adj.* Lacking energy or enthusiasm. **listlessly** *adv.*

list price *n.* The basic price of an item.

lit (lit) *abbr.* Literary; literature.

lit-a-ny (lit´e nē) *n. pl.* **litanies** A prayer in which phrases, recited by a leader are alternated with answers from the congregation.

li-tchi *or* **li-chee (lē´chē)** *n.* A Chinese tree, bearing edible fruit; the fruit of the tree.

lit-er-a-c y (lit´ér a sē) *n.* The state or quality of being literate, having the skills of reading and writing.

lit-er-al (lit´ér al) *adj.* Conforming to the exact meaning of a word; concerned primarily with facts; without embellishment or exaggeration. **literally** *adv.*

lit-er-al-ism (lit´ér a liz´um) *n.* Adherence to the explicit sense of a given test; literal portrayal; realism. **literalist** *n.*

lit-er-ar-y (lit´e rer´ē) *adj.* Pertaining to literature; appropriate to or used in literature; of or relating to the knowledge of literature. **literarily** *adv.*

lit-er-ate (lit´ėr it) *adj.* Having the ability to read and write; showing skill in using words. **literacy** *n.* **literate** *n.*

lit-er-a-ti (lit´e rä´tē) *n.* *pl.* The educated class.

lit-er-a-ture (lit´ėr *a* chėr) *n.* Printed material, as leaflets for a political campaign; written words of lasting excellence.

li-tharge (lith´ärj) *n.* The yellowish-red oxide of lead, that is used for glazing earthenware.

lithe (līth) *adj.* Bending easily; supple. **lithely** *adv.* **litheness** *n.*

li-thi-a-sis (li thī´*a* sis) *n.*, *Pathol.* The formation of stony solid concretions in any part of the body, as in the gallbladder.

lith-ic (lith´ik) *adj.* Pertaining or relating to or consisting of stone; *Pathol.* Pertaining to stones in the body, as in the bladder.

lith-i-um (lith´ē *u*m) *n.* A metallic element, the lightest metal know.

li-thog-ra-phy (li thog´ra fē) *n.* A printing process in which a flat surface is treated so that the ink adheres only to the portions that are to be printed. **lithograph** *n.* & *v.* **lithographer** *n.* **lithographic** *adj.* **lithographical** *adj.*

li-thol-o-gy (li thol´o jē) *n.* The microscopic study and classification of rocks.

lith-o-marge (lith´o märj˝) *n.* A compact clay.

lith-o-sphere (lith´o sfēr˝) *n.* The crust or outer surface of the solid earth, thought to be approximately 50 miles thick.

lit-i-gate (lit´*i* gāt´) *v.* To conduct a legal contest by judicial process. **litigant** *n.* **litigation** *n.* **litigator** *n.*

lit-mus (lit´m*u*s) *n.* A blue powder obtained from lichens which turns red in acid solutions and blue in alkaline solutions, used as an acid-base indicator.

litmus paper *n.* Unsized paper that is treated with litmus and used as an indicator.

lit-ter (lit´ėr) *n.* A covered and curtained couch, mounted on shafts and used to convey a single passenger; a stretcher used

to carry a sick or injured person; material used as bedding for animals; the offspring at one birth of a multiparous animal; an accumulation of waste material. **litter** *v.* **litterer** *n.*

lit-ter-bug (lit´ėr bug´) *n.* One who litters a public area.

lit-tle (lit´l) *adj.* Small in size or extent; not large; short in time; small in amount or quantity.

Little Dipper *n.* Ursa Minor.

lit-to-ral (lit´ėr al) *adj.* Relating to or existing on a shore. *n.* A shore.

lit-ur-gy (lit´ėr jē) *n.* *pl.* -ies A prescribed rite or body of rites for public worship. **liturgical** *adj.* **liturgically** *adv.*

liv-a-ble (liv´abl) *adj.* Endurable; suitable for living in.

live (liv) *v.* To have life; to be alive; capable of performing vital functions; to remain effective; not to perish; to pass through or spend life in a particular manner.

live (līv) *adj.* Being in life, living, or alive; of or pertaining to life or living beings.

live-li-hood (līv´lē hed´) *n.* A means of support or subsistence.

live-long (liv´lang˝) *adj.* Enduring; lasting a long time.

live-ly (līv´lē) *adj.* Vigorous. **liveliness** *n.*

liv-er (liv´ėr) *n.* The large, very vascular, glandular organ of vertebrates which secretes bile.

liv-er-wurst (liv´ėr werst´) *n.* A kind of sausage made primarily of liver.

liv-er-y (liv´e rē) *n.* *pl.* -ies A uniform worn by servants; the care and boarding of horses for pay; a concern offering horses and vehicles for rent. **liveried** *adj.*

liv-er-y-man (liv´e rē man) *n.* A keeper or employee of a livery stable.

live-stock (līv´stok´) *n.* Farm animals raised for human use.

live wire *n.*, *Slang* An energetic person.

liv-id (liv´id) *adj.* Discolored from a bruise; very angry.

liv-ing (liv´ing) *n.* The act or condition of being alive; one who or that which lives; manner or course of life.

living room *n.* A room in a home for family use and social activity; a sitting room.

living wage *n.* A wage sufficient for an earner to suppport himself and dependents at an acceptable standard of living.

liz-ard (liz´ẻrd) *n.* One of various reptiles, usually with an elongated scaly body, four legs, and a tapering tail.

lizard fish *n.* A bottom-dwelling fish, having a lizard-like head and dwelling in warm waters of the seas.

lla-ma (lä´ma) *n.* A South American ruminant, related to the camel family and raised for its soft wool.

loach (lōch) *n.* A small, freshwater fish that's related to the carp family.

load (lōd) *n.* A mass or weight that is lifted or supported; anything, as cargo, put in a ship, aircraft, or vehicle for conveyance; something that is a heavy responsibility; a burden. **loader** *n.* **loading** *n.* **load** *v.*

load-ed (lō´did) *adj.* Intended to trick or trap. *Slang* Drunk; rich.

loaf (lōf) *n. pl.* **loaves** A food, especially bread, that is shaped into a mass. To spend time in idleness. **loafer** *v.*

loam (lōm) *n.* Soil that consists chiefly of sand, clay, and decayed plant matter.

loan (lōn) *n.* Money lent with interest to be repaid; something borrowed for temporary use. *v.* To lend.

loan shark *n.* One who lends money to individuals at exorbitant rates of interest. **loan sharking** *n.*

loath (lōth) *adj.* Averse.

loathe (lōth) *v.* To dislike intensely.

loath-ing (lō´thing) *n.* Intense dislike; abhorrence.

loath-some (lōth´som) *adj.* Arousing disgust. **loathsomely** *adv.* **loathsomeness** *n.*

lob (lob) *v.* To hit or throw in a high arc; to move in an arc. **lob** *n.*

lob-by (lob´ē) *n. pl.* **lobbies** A foyer, as in a hotel or theatre; a group of private persons trying to influence legislators. **lobbyist** *n.* **lobby** *v.*

lobe (lōb) *n.* A curved or rounded projection or division, as the fleshy lower part of the ear. **lobar** *adj.* **lobed** *adj.*

lob-lol-ly (lob´lol´ē) *n. pl.* **loblollies** A mudhole; mire.

lo-bo (lō´bō) *n.* The gray wolf, as referred to by those who reside in the western United States.

lo-bot-o-my (lō bot´o mē) *n. pl.* **lobotomies** Surgical severance of nerve fibers by incision into the brain. **lobotomize** *v.*

lob-ster (lob´stẻr) *n.* Any of several large, edible marine crustaceans with five pairs of legs, the first pair being large and claw-like.

lobster pot *n.* An oblong trap with a funnel-shaped net used for catching lobsters.

lob-ule (lob´ūl) *n.* A small lobe; a subdivision of a lobe. **lobular** *adj.*

lo-cal (lō´kẻl) *adj.* Pertaining to, being in, or serving a particular area or place. **locally** *adv.*

lo-cale (lō kal´) *n.* A locality where a particular event takes place; the setting or scene, as of a novel.

local government *n.* The administration of a specific local area of a town or district by its inhabitants.

lo-cal-ism (lō´ka liz˝um) *n.* A local idiom of speaking or acting; a local custom; affection for a particular place.

lo-cal-i-ty (lō kal´i tē) *n. pl* **localities** A particular place, a specific neighborhood or district.

lo-cal-ize (lō´ka līz˝) *v.* To assign or keep to a particular place; to check, control, or restrict to a specific area. **localization** *n.*

lo-cate (lō´kāt) *v.* To determine the place, position, or boundaries of; to look for and find; to establish or become established; to settle. **locator** *n.*

lo-ca-tion (lō kā´shan) *n.* The process or act of locating; a place where something is or can be located; a site outside a motion picture or television studio where a movie is shot.

loch (lok) *n.* A lake.

lock (lok) *n.* A device used, as on a door, to secure or fasten; a part of a waterway closed off with gates to allow the raising or lowering of boats by changing the level of the water; a strand or curl of hair. **lock** *v.*

lock-er (lok´ẽr) *n.* A compartment, drawer, closet or the like, for storing personal items, may be locked.

lock-et (lok´it) *n.* A small, ornamental case for a keepsake, often a picture, worn as a pendant on a necklace.

lock-jaw (lok´jo´) *n.* Tetanus; a form of tetanus in which a spasm of the jaw muscles locks the jaws closed.

lock-smith (lok´smith´) *n.* A person who makes or repairs locks.

lock stitch *n.* A sewing machine stitch that loops together two threads one on the top and one on the bottom of the material.

lock-up (lok´up´) *n.* A place of temporary confinement or detention of persons under arrest.

lo-co (lō´kō) *adj., Slang* Insane.

lo-co-mo-tion (lō˝ko mō´shan) *n.* The act or power of moving from place to place.

lo-co-mo-tive (lō´ko mō´tiv) *n.* A self-propelled vehicle that is generally electric or diesel-powered and is used for moving railroad cars.

locomotor ataxia *n., Pathol.* A disease that is marked by intense pain and affects the spinal cord; causes difficulty in coordination and eventually paralysis, caused by syphilis.

lo-co-weed (lō´kō wēd´) *n.* Any of several plants found throughout the western and central United States which are poisonous to livestock.

loc-u-late (lok´ūlāt´) *adj., Biol.* Composed or divided into cells or loculi.

lo-cus (lō´kus) *n. pl.* **lo-ci** *or* **lo-ca** A place; locality; the center of activity.

lo-cust (lō´kust) *n.* Any of numerous grasshoppers which often travel in swarms and damage vegetation; any of various hardwooded leguminous trees, such as carob, black locust, or honey locust.

lo-cu-tion (lōkū´shan) *n.* A particular form of a phrase; a style of verbal expression.

lode-star (lōd´stär) *n.* The North Star, used as a reference point or a guiding star.

lode-stone (lōd´stōn˝) *n.* The mineral, magnetite, which possesses magnetic polarity and strongly attracts.

lodge (loj) *n.* A house, such as a cabin, used as a temporary or seasonal dwelling or shelter; an inn; the den of an animal, such as a beaver; a local chapter of a fraternal organization; the meeting hall of such a chapter. **lodge** *v.*

lodg-er (lăj er) *n.* One who rents a room in another's house.

lodg-ing (loj´ing) *n.* A temporary place to dwell; abode; accommodation in a house; sleeping accommodations

lodg-ment (loj´ment) *n.* An act of lodging; a place for lodging; an accumulation or deposit.

lod-i-cule (lod´i kūl) *n., Bot.* One of the delicate membranous scales at the base of a grass.

loft (loft) *n.* One of the upper, generally unpartitioned floors of an industrial or commercial building, such as a warehouse; an attic; a gallery in a church or hall.

loft-y (laf´tē, lof´tē) *adj.* Extremely high; elevated in condition, position, or character.

log (lag, log) *n.* A bulky piece of timber either from a branch or a tree trunk. The record of a ship or aircraft travel.

lo-gan-ber-ry (lō´gan ber´ē) *n.* A prickly plant cultivated for its edible, acidic, red fruit.

log-book (lag´buk˝) *n.* A book which contains the trip record of a truck, ship, or aircraft.

loge (lōzh) *n.* A small compartment, especially a box in a theatre; a small partitioned area, as a separate forward section of a theatre mezzanine or balcony.

log-ger-head (lo´gėr hed´) *n.* Any of various large marine turtles, especially the carnivorous turtle found in the warm waters of the western Atlantic. **at logger-**

heads In a state of contention; at odds.

log-gi-a (loj´a) *n.* A roofed but open arcade along the front of a building; an open balcony in a theatre.

log-ic (loj´ik) *n.* The science dealing with the principles of reasoning, especially of the method and validity of deductive reasoning; something that forces a decision apart from or in opposition to reason.

log-i-cal (loj´i kal) *adj.* Relating to; or in accordance with logic; something marked by consistency of reasoning. **logically** *adv.*

lo-gi-on (lō´gē on˝) *n. pl.* **logions** *or* **logia** Traditional saying attributed to Jesus.

lo-gis-tics (lō jis´tiks) *n.* The methods of procuring, maintaining, and replacing material and personnel, as in a military operation. **logistic** *adj.*

log-jam (lag´jam˝) *n.* A jumble or group of logs wedged together in a river; deadlock.

lo-gom-a-chy (lō gom´a kē) *n. pl.* **logomachies** A dispute over or about words; a verbal disagreement

lo-go-type (lo´go tīp´) *n.* Identifying symbol for a company or publication.

log-roll (lag´rōl˝) *v.* To promote successfully passage of a bill; rolling of logs in water.

lo-gy (lō´gē) *adj.* Something marked by sluggishness. **loginess** *n.*

loin (loin) *n.* The area of the body located between the ribs and pelvis; a cut of meat from an animal.

loin-cloth (loin´kloth´) *n.* A cloth worn about the loins.

loins (loinz) *n.* The thighs and groin; the reproductive organs.

loi-ter (loi´tėr) *v.* To stay for no apparent reason; to dawdle or delay. **loiterer** *n.*

loll (lol) *v.* To move or act in a lax, lazy or indolent manner; to hang loosely or laxly. **loller** *n.*

lol-li-pop *or* **lol-ly-pop (lol´ē pop´)** *n.* A piece of flavored hard candy on a stick.

lol-ly-gag (lol ē gag) *v., Slang* To fool around.

lo-ment (lō´ment) *n., Bot.* A dry indehiscent one-cell fruit, produced from a single ovary, which separates at maturity into numerous segments.

lone (lōn) *adj.* Single; isolated; sole; unfrequented.

lone-ly (lōn´lē) *adj.* Being without companions; dejected from being alone. **loneliness** *n.*

lon-er (lō ner) *n.* A person who avoids the company of others.

lone-some (lōn´som) *adj.* Dejected because of the lack of companionship. **lonesomely** *adv.* **lonesomeness** *n.*

long (lang, long) *adj.* Having a greater length than usual; considerable extent; not short; unusually great; prolonged past the usual time. *n.* A long length of time; a long sounding syllable.

long *abbr.* Longitude.

long-boat (lang´bōt˝) *n.* The largest boat carried by a sailing ship.

long-bow (long´bō´) *n.* A wooden bow that is approximately five to six feet in length.

long distance *n.* The service handling by telephone communications; calls between a location and out of state or out of country. **long distance** *adv.* Connecting distant places; over a long distance.

long division *n., Math.* Arithmetical division, where several steps are involved in finding the answer, in which all steps are indicated in writing.

lon-gev-i-ty (lon jev´i tē) *n.* Long duration; length or duration of life; long continuance; length of service.

long-hair (long´hâr´) *n.* A lover of the arts, especially classical music; a person with long hair.

long-hand (long´hand´) *n.* Cursive handwriting.

long-horn (long´horn´) *n.* One of the long-horned cattle of Spanish derivation, formerly common in the southwestern United States; a firm-textured cheddar cheese ranging from white to orange in color and from mild to sharp in flavor.

long house *n.* A communal dwelling house of North American Indians.

long-ing (lang´ing) *n.* A strong and earnest desire; a yearning.

lon-gi-tude (lon´ji tūd´) *n.* The angular distance that is east and west of the prime meridian at Greenwich, England.

lon-gi-tu-di-nal (lon´ji tūd´i nal) *adj.* Of or relating to the length; relating to longitude. **longitudinally** *adv.*

long–lived (lang´līvd´, long´līvd´) *adj.* Having a long life; lasting for a long time.

long–range (lang´rānj, long´rānj´) *adj.* Relating to long distance; extended distances; taking into account a long period of time.

long-shore-man (long´shōr´man) *n.* A dockhand who loads and unloads cargo.

long shot *n.* An adventure offering little hope of success but promising great gains if achieved.

long-sight-ed (lang´sī´tid) *adj.* Farsighted; the ability to see at a distance; having foresight. **longsightedness** *n.*

long-some (lang´som) *adj.* Tiresome due to the of length; tediously lone.

long–suf-fer-ing (lang´suf´fèr ing) *adj.* Sustaining injuries for a long time; patient. **long–suffering** *n.* Lengthy adversity.

long–term (lang´turm˝) *adj.* Happening over a long period of time.

lon-gueur (lang gur´) *n.* A tedious section passage in a book.

long–wind-ed(lang´win´did)*adj.* Tediously long in length; capable of exertion or talking for a long period without being out of breath.

look (lek) *v.* To examine with the eyes; to see; to glance, gaze, or stare at. **look** *n.* The act of looking; the physical appearance of something or someone.

look-er (luk´ėr) *n.* One who looks. *Slang* A person with an attractive appearance.

look-out (lek´out´) *n.* A person positioned to keep watch or look for something or someone.

loom (lüm) *v.* To come into view as a image; to seem to be threatening. *n.* A machine used for interweaving thread or yarn to produce cloth.

loon (lōn) *n.* An idle or worthless man; a crazy person; a fish-eating diving bird of the northern hemisphere.

loo-ny *or* **loo-ney (lü´nē)** *n.* Crazy; foolish.

loop (lüp) *n.* A circular length of line folded over and joined at the ends; a loop-shaped pattern, figure, or path. **loop** *v.* To form into a loop; to join, fasten, or encircle with a loop.

loop-hole (lüp´hōl´) *n.* A means of escape; a legal way to circumvent the intent of a law.

loose (lüs) *adj.* Not tightly fastened; not confined or fitting; free.

loose end *n.* Something left unattached or hanging loose; unfinished business.

loose–jointed (lōs´join´tid) *adj.* Having loose joints of unusually free movement.

loos-en (lōs´en) *v.* To make looser, or less firm, compact, or tight; to relax.

loot (lüt) *n.* Goods, usually of significant value, taken in time of war; goods that have been stolen. **loot** *v.* To plunder; to steal. **looter** *n.*

lop (lop) *v.* To remove branches from; to trim; to cut off with a single blow.

lope (lōp) *v.* To run with a steady gait. **lope** *n.* **lopper** *n.*

lop–eared (lop´ērd˝) *adj.* Having ears that droop or hang down.

lop-sid-ed (lop´sī´did) *adj.* Larger or heavier on one side than on the other; tilting to one side. **lopsidedly** *adv.*

lo-qua-cious (lō kwā´shus) *adj.* Talkative; given to excessive or continual talking; **loquaciously** *adv.* **loquacity** *n.*

lo-quat (lō´kwot, lō´kwat) *n.* A small Asian evergreen tree.

lo-ran (lōr´an) *n.* A system by which a navigator determines the position of his airplane or ship based in part on the measurement of arrival times and signals sent out by ground stations.

Lord (lord) *n.* God. A man having dominion and power over other people; the owner of a feudal estate.

lore (lōr) *n.* Traditional fact; knowledge that has been gained through education or experience.

lor-gnon (lor nyon´) *n.* A pair of eyeglasses

or opera glasses.

lorn (larn) *adj.* Forsaken; abandoned; desolate.

lose (loz) *v.* To mislay; to fail to keep; misplace. **loser** *n.*

loss (los) *n.* The suffering or damage used by losing; someone or something that is lost. **losses** *pl.* Killed, wounded, or captured soldiers; casualties.

loss ratio *n.* The ratio between insurance premiums and insurance losses in a given period of time.

lost (lost) *adj.* Unable to find one's way.

lot (lot) *n.* Fate; fortune; a parcel of land having boundaries; a plot.

lo-ta (lō ta) *n.* A small spherical water vessel of copper or brass used in India.

lo-tic (lō'tic) *adj.* Living in or related to actively moving water.

lo-tion (lō'shan) *n.* A liquid medicine for external use on the hands and body.

lot-ter-y (lot'e rē) *n. pl.* **-ies** A contest in which winners are selected by a random drawing.

lot-to (lot'ō) *n.* A game of chance that resembles bingo.

lo-tus (lō'tus) *n.* An aquatic plant having fragrant pink flowers and large leaves; any of several plants similar or related to the lotus.

lo-tus–eater (lō'tus ē'tėr) *n.* One of a people represented in the Odyssey of Homer as eating the lotus fruit and living in the dreamy indolence it produced.

loud (loud) *adj.* Marked by intense sound and high volume. **loudly** *adv.* **loudness** *n.*

loud-en (loud'en) *v.* To make or become loud; an increase in sound.

loud-mouthed (loud'mouthd") *adj.* Loud and offensive talk that irritates others.

loud-speak-er (loud'spē"kėr) *n.* A device that amplifies sound as music or a speaker's voice.

lounge (lounj) *v.* To move or act in a lazy, relaxed manner. *n.* A room, as in a hotel or theatre, where people may wait; a couch. **lounger** *n.*

loupe (lōp) *n.* A small magnifying glass, that attaches to eyeglasses, or is held close to the eye for viewing an object up close.

louse (lous) *n. pl.* **lice** A small, wingless sucking and biting insect that lives on various animals as well as human beings. *Slang* A contemptible person.

louse up *v., Slang.* To botch or mess up.

lous-y (lou'zē) *adj.* Lice- infested. *Slang* Mean; poor; inferior; abundantly supplied. **lousily** *adv.*

lout (lout) *n.* An awkward, stupid person. **loutish** *adj.*

lou-ver *or* **lou-vre (lü'vėr)** *n.* An opening in a wall fitted with movable, slanted slats which let air in, but keep precipitation out; one of the slats used in a louver. **louvered** *adj.*

love (luv) *n.* Intense affection for another arising out of kinship or personal ties; a strong feeling of attraction resulting from sexual desire; enthusiasm or fondness; a score of zero in tennis. **love** *v.* **lovable** *adj.* **loving** *adj.*

love-bird (luv'berd') *n.* Any of various Old World parrots which show great affection for their mates.

love-less (luv'lis) *adj.* Having no love; devoid of or unaccompanied by love; not loved. **lovelessly** *adv.* **lovelessness** *n.*

love-lorn (luv'larn") *adj.* Forsaken by one's lover; deprived of lover.

love-ly (luv'lē) *adj.* Beautiful. **loveliness** *n.* **lovely** *n.*

lov-er (luv'ėr) *n.* A person who loves another; a sexual partner.

love seat *n.* A small sofa, or upholstered chair for two people.

love–sick (luv'sik) *adj.* Languishing with love; expressing a lover's yearning. **love–sickness** *n.*

loving cup *n.* A large, ornamental cup with two or more handles, often given as an award or trophy.

low (lō) *adj.* Not high; being below or under

normal height, rank, or level; depressed or lacking in health or vigor; soft in pitch; small in number; cheap in price. **low** *v.* To moo, as a cow.

low beam *n.* A low-intensity headlight.

low-boy (lō´boi) *n.* A low chest of drawers or side table approximately three feet high, usually with drawers.

low-bred (lō´bred´) *adj.* Of an inferior class; characteristic of vulgar or rude.

low-brow (lō´brou´) *n.* An uncultured person. **lowbrow** *adj.*

low-down (lō´doun´) *n.* The whole truth; all the facts. **lowdown** *adj.* Despicable; mean; depressed.

low-er (lō´ėr) *adj.* Relatively low in position; in a position considered inferior to others in value or rank; located beneath or under something. **lower** *v.* To make lower in position; to reduce the value of.

low-er–case (lō´ėr kās´) *adj.* Having as its typical form a, b, c, or u, v, w rather than A, B, C, or U,V, W.

lower class *n.* The group in society that ranks below the middle class in social and economic status.

lowest common denominator *n.* The least common multiple of the denominators of a set of fractions.

lowest common multiple *n.* Least common multiple.

low frequency *n.* A radio-wave frequency between 30 and 300 kilohertz.

low-key (lō´kē´) *adj.* Restrained.

low-land (lō´land) *n.* Land that is lower than the adjacent neighboring country; level or low country.

low–lev-el (lō´lev´el) *adj.* Being of minor importance; done, placed or occurring at a low level.

low-ly (lō´lē) *adj.* Low in position or rank. **lowliness** *n.*

low–pres-sure (lō´presh´ėr) *adj.* Having or operation under a low degree of steam or water pressure.

low profile *n.* A deliberately inconspicuous lifestyle or posture.

low–rise *adj.* Having only one or two levels

and no elevator.

low–ten-sion (lō´ten´shan) *adj.* Having a low voltage; built to be used at low voltage.

low tide *n.* The lowest level of the tide; the time of day when this occurs.

lox (loks) *n.* Smoked salmon; liquid oxygen.

loy-al (loi´al) *adj.* Faithful in allegiance to one's country and government; faithful to a person, cause, ideal, or custom. **loyalty** *n.*

loy-al-ist (loi´ al ist) *n.* One who is or remains loyal to a political cause, party, government, or sovereign.

loz-enge (loz´inj) *n.* Small medicated candy, normally having the shape of a lozenge.

LSD (el´es´dē´) *n.* Lysergic acid diethylamide, a hallucinogenic drug that induces psychotic symptoms, producing changes in thought, perception, mood, and behavior.

lu-au (lü ou´) *n.* A traditional Hawaiian feast.

lub-ber (lub´ėr) *n.* An awkward, clumsy or stupid person; an inexperienced sailor.

lu-bri-cant (lü´bri kant) *n.* A material, as grease or oil, applied to moving parts to reduce friction.

lu-carne (lō kärn´) *n.* A window set vertically in a steeple.

lu-cid (lü´sid) *adj.* Easily understood; mentally clear; rational; shining. **lucidity** *n.* **lucidness** *n.* **lucidly** *adv.*

luck (luk) *n.* Good fortune; the force or power which controls odds and which brings good fortune or bad fortune. **lucky** *adj.* **luckily** *adv.* **luckiness** *n.*

lu-cra-tive (lü´kra tiv) *adj.* Producing profits or great wealth. **lucratively** *adv.*

lu-cre (lü´kėr) *n.* Money; profit.

lu-cu-brate (lü´kū brāt´) *v.* To study or work laboriously.

lu-di-crous (lü´di krus) *adj.* Amusing or laughable through obvious absurdity; ridiculous. **ludicrously** *adv.* **ludicrousness** *n.*

luff (luf) *v.* To turn a sailing vessel toward the wind.

lug (lug) *n.* An ear-like handle or projection used as a hold; a tab. **lug** *v.* To carry with difficulty.

luge (lüzh) *n.* A small sled similar to a toboggan which is ridden in a supine position and used in competitions like the Olympics..

lug-gage (lug´ij) *n.* Something that is lugged, especially suitcases or a traveler's baggage.

lu-gu-bri-ous (le gü´brē us) *adj.* Mournful; dejected; especially exaggeratedly or affectedly so. **lugubriously** *adv.* **lugubriousness** *n.*

luke-warm (lük´worm´) *adj.* Mildly warm; tepid; unenthusiastic; soothing. **lukewarmly** *adv.*

lull (lul) *v.* To cause to rest or sleep; to cause to have a false sense of security. **lull** *n.* A temporary period of quiet or rest.

lul-la-by (lul´a bī´) *n. pl.* **lullabies** A song to lull a child to sleep.

lum-ba-go (lum bā´gō) *n.* Painful rheumatic pain of the muscles and tendons of the lumbar region.

lum-bar (lum´bėr) *adj.* Part of the back and sides between the lowest ribs and the pelvis.

lum-ber (lum´bėr) *n.* Timber, sawed or split into boards. *v.* To walk clumsily.

lum-ber-ing (lum´bėr ing) *v.* To move in a clumsy or awkward way.

lum-ber-jack (lum´bėr jak´) *n.* One who cuts and prepares timber for the sawmill.

lum-ber-yard (lum´bėr yärd´) *n.* A business place where lumber and other building materials are sold.

lu-mi-nar-y (lü´mi ner´ē) *n. pl.* **-ies** A celestial body, as the sun; a notable person.

lu-mi-nes-cence (lü´mi nes´ens) *n.* An emission of light without heat, as in fluorescence.

lu-mi-nous (lü´mi nus) *adj.* Emitting or reflecting light; bathed in steady light; illuminated; easily understood; clear. **luminously** *adv.*

luminous paint *n.* A paint that glows in the dark.

lum-mox (lum´uks) *n.* A clumsy oaf.

lump (lump) *n.* A projection; a protuberance; a swelling, as from a bruise or infection.

lump *v.* To group things together.

lum-pen (lum´pen) *adj.* Relating to groups of people who have been uprooted from their normal routine or economic status.

lump-ish (lum´pish) *adj.* Stupid or dull. **lumpishly** *adv.* **lumpiness** *n.*

lump-y (lum´pē) *adj.* Covered or full of lumps.

lu-na-cy (lü´na sē) *n. pl.* **lunacies** Insanity.

lu-nar (lü´nėr) *adj.* Of, relating to, caused by the moon.

lunar eclipse *n.* An eclipse where the moon passes partially or wholly through the umbra of the earth's shadow.

lu-nate (lö´nāt) *adj.* Having the form or shape like the half-moon; crescent-shaped.

lu-na-tic (lü´na tik) *n.* A crazy person.

lunatic fringe *n.* Members of a political or extremist expressing extreme or eccentric views.

lunch (lunch) *n.* A meal served between breakfast and supper.

lunch-eon (lun´chon) *n.* A lunch.

lunch-room (lunch´röm´) *n.* Room in a school, business or establishments where individual may eat lunch.

lung (lung) *n.* One of the two spongy organs that constitute the basic respiratory organ of air breathing vertebrates.

lunge (lunj) *n.* A sudden forward movement. **lunge** *v.*

lu-pine (lö´pīn) *adj.* To be wolf-like; wolfish.

lu-pu-lin (lö´pū lin) *n.* A yellow powder that is obtained from hops and used as a sedative.

lu-pus (lü´pus) *n.* A bacterial disease of the skin.

lurch (lürch) *v.* To heave something to one side.

lure (ler) *n.* A decoy; something appealing; an artificial bait to catch fish. **lure** *v.* To attract or entice with the prospect of reward or pleasure.

lu-rid (lūr´id) *adj.* Sensational; shining with a fiery glare; fierce passion. **luridly** *adv.* **luridness** *n.*

lurk (lerk) *v.* To lie in concealment, as in an ambush.

lus-cious (lush´us) *adj.* Very pleasant to smell or taste; appealing to the senses. **lusciously** *adv.* **lusciousness** *n.*

lush (lush) *adj.* Producing luxuriant growth or vegetation. *Slang* An alcoholic. **lushly** *adv.* **lushness** *n.*

lust (lust) *n.* Intense sexual desire; an intense longing; a craving. **lustful** *adj.*

luster (lus´ter) *n.* A glow of reflected light; sheen; brilliance or radiance; brightness. **lustrous** *adj.* **lusterless** *adj.*

lus-ter-ing (lus´ter ing) *n.* The process that gives a luster to cloth.

lus-ter-ware (lus´ter wâr˝) *n.* A glossy and often iridescent piece of pottery.

lust-ful (lust´ful) *adj.* Having a strong desire for sexual satisfaction.

lust-ral (lus´tral) *adj.* Pertaining to a rite of purification.

lus-trate (lus´trāt) *v.* To purify by a ceremony.

lus-trous (lus´trus) *adj.* Characterized by sheen; bright; luminous. **lustrously** *adv.* **lustrousness** *n.*

lust-y (lus´tē) *adj.* Vigorous; healthy; robust; lively. **lustily** *adv.* **lustiness** *n.*

lusus naturae (lō´sus na tūr´ē) *n.* An abnormally formed animal, person, or plant; a freak of nature.

lu-tan-ist (lōt´a nist) *n.* A person who plays the lute.

lute (lūt) *n.* A medieval musical stringed instrument with a fretted fingerboard, a pear-shaped body, and usually a bent neck.

lute-string (lōt´string) *n.* A glossy silk fabric formerly used for women's ribbons and dresses.

lu-te-ti-um *or* **lu-te-ci-um (lū tē´shē um)** *n.* A silvery rare-earth metallic element symbolized by Lu.

lux-ate (luk´sāt) *v.* To dislocate a limb, as a shoulder, arm, or hip. **luxation** *n.*

lux-u-ri-ant (lug zher´ē ant) *adj.* Growing or producing abundantly; lush; plentiful. **luxuriance** *n.* **luxuriantly** *adv.*

lux-u-ri-ate (lug zher´ē āt) *v.* To enjoy luxury or abundance; to grow abundantly; pleasure.

lux-u-ry (luk´sha rē) *n. pl.* **-ies** Something desirable but costly or hard to get; something which adds to one's comfort or pleasure but is not absolutely necessary; sumptuous surroundings or living.

ly-can-thro-py (lī kan´thro pē) *n.* An insanity where the patient supposes himself to be a wolf; the delusional transformation of a human into the form of a wolf.

ly-ce-um (lī sē´um) *n.* A hall where public programs are presented; an organization which sponsors such programs as lectures and concerts.

lye (lī) *n.* A powerful caustic solution yielded by leaching wood ashes; potassium hydroxide; sodium hydroxide.

ly-ing–in (lī´ing in´) *n.* Confinement in childbirth.

lymph node *n.* A roundish body of lymphoid tissue; lymph gland.

lym-pho-ma (lim˝fo´ma) *n. pl.* **lymphomas** *Pathol.* A tumor located in the lymphoid tissue.

lynch (linch) *v.* To execute without authority or the due process of law.

lynx (lingks) *n.* A wildcat. **lynx-eyed** *adj.* Having acute eyesight.

lyre (līer) *n.* A harp-like stringed instrument of Ancient Greece.

lyr-ic (lir´ik) *adj.* Concerned with thoughts and feelings; romantic; appropriate for singing. *n.* A lyric poem. **lyrics** The words of a song. **lyrical** *adj.* **lyrically** *adv.*

lysergic acid diethylamide *n.* An organic compund which induces psychotic symptoms similar to those of schizophrenia; LSD.

ly-sis (lī´sis) *n., Med.* The gradual decline of a disease.

M, m (em) The thirteenth letter of the English alphabet; the Roman numeral for 1,000.

m *abbr.* Mile.

ma (mä) *n., Slang* Mother.

MA *abbr.* Massachusetts. *abbr.* Master of Arts.

ma'am (mam) *n.* Madam.

mac *n.* An address for a man whose name is unknown.

ma-ca-bre (ma **kab´re)** *adj.* Suggesting death and decay.

mac-ad-am (ma **kad´**a**m)** *n.* Pavement for roads consisting of layers of compacted, broken stone, usually cemented with asphalt and tar. **macadamize** *v.*

mac-a-ro-ni (mak´a **rō´nē)** *n.* Dried pasta made into short tubes and prepared as food.

mac-a-roon (mak´a **rŏn´)** *n.* A small cookie made of sugar, egg whites, coconut, and ground almonds.

ma-caw (ma **ko´)** *n.* Any of various tropical American parrots with long tails, brilliant plumage, and harsh voices.

mac-e-doine (mas˝i dwän´) *n.* A jellied salad; mixture of diced vegetables or fruits.

mace (mās) *n.* An aromatic spice made by grinding the cover of the nutmeg.

mac-er-ate (mas´e rāt´) *v.* To make a solid substance soft by soaking in liquid; to cause to grow thin. **macerater** *or* **macerator** *n.* **maceration** *n.*

ma-chet-e (ma **shet´ē)** *n.* A large, heavy knife with a broad blade, used as a weapon.

mach-i-nate (mak´i **nāt´)** *v.* To plot. **machination** *n.* **machinator** *n.*

ma-chine (ma **shēn´)** *n.* A device or system built to use energy to do work; a political organization. *v.* To produce precision tools.

machine language *n.* In Computer Science, the system of numbers or instructions for coding input data.

ma-chin-er-y (ma **shē´n**e **rē)** *n. pl.* **-ies** A collection of machines as a whole; the mechanism or operating parts of a machine.

machine shop *n.* A work area where materials, especially metals, are cut and designed by machine tools.

machine tool *n.* A machine that is power-driven and used for shaping or cutting metals, wood.

ma-chin-ist (ma **shē´nist)** *n.* One skilled in the operation or repair of machines.

ma-chis-mo *n.* An exaggerated sense of masculinity **macho** *Slang* Exhibiting machismo.

mach-me-ter *n.* An indicator that measures airspeed relative to the speed of sound, and then indicates the speed that an airplane using such as indicator, can exceed without sustaining damage due to compressibility effects.

ma-cho *adj., Slang* Exhibiting machismo.

mack-er-el (mak´ẽr e**l)** *n.* A fish with dark, wavy bars on the back and a silvery belly, found in the Atlantic Ocean.

mack-er-el sky *n.* The sky dotted with small, white in color, fleecy clouds.

Mack-i-naw *n.* A short coat of blanket-like material and thickness.

mack-in-tosh *or* **macintosh (mak´in tosh´)** *n.* A lightweight waterproof overgarment or cloak; a rain coat.

mack-le (mak´l) *n.* To become blurred.

ma-cle *n.* The double crystal of a diamond.

mac-ra-me (mak´ra **mā´)** *n.* The craft or hobby of tying knots into a pattern.

mac-ro-bi-ot-ic *adj.* Relating to or being on an extremely restricted diet to promote longevity, consisting mainly of whole grain, vegetables and fish.

mac-ro-cosm *n.* A large scale model of something that is smaller. **-ic** *adj.* **macrocosmically** *adv.*

mac-ro-cyte *n.* A red blood cell that is larger than normal. **macrocytic** *adj.*, **macrocytosis** *n.*

mac-ro-graph *n.* A drawing or photograph that is at least life-size or larger.

ma-crog-ra-phy *v.* To investigate something by the use of the naked eye.

ma-cron *n.* A short mark (-) placed over a vowel to indicate the pronunciation as a long sound.

ma-cron (mā´kron) *n.* A mark (-) placed over a vowel to indicate a long sound.

mac-ro-scop-ic *or* **macroscopical (mak´-**

ro skop´ik) *adj.* Large enough to be seen by the naked eye. **macroscopical, macroscopically** *adv.*

mac-u-la (mak´ū la) n. A discolored spot on the skin. **macular** *adj.*

mad (mad) *adj.* Angry; afflicted with a mental disorder; insane.

mad-am (mad´am) *n. pl.* A title used to addressa married woman; used without a name as a courtesy title when addressing a woman.

mad-cap *adj.* Impulsive, rash or reckless; hare brained.

mad-den *v.* To craze; to enrage; to make mad. *v.* To become mad.

mad-ding *adj.* Behaving senselessly; acting mad; inducing madness.

made (mād) *v.* Past tense of make. *adj.* Constructed not natural; invented or constructed.

mad-e-moi-selle *n. pl.* **mademoiselles** *or* **mesdemoiselles** An unmarried French girl or woman.

made–to–order *adj.* Custom-made.

made–up (mād´up´) *adj.* Fabricated; invented; having only makeup on.

mad-house (mad´hous´) *n. Slang* A place of confusion and disorder.

Madison, James *n.* (1751-1836). The 4th United States president of the United States from 1809-1817.

mad-man *n.* A lunatic.

mad-ness *n.* The state of being mad; extreme excitement.

Ma-don-na *n.* Virgin Mary.

mad-ri-gal (mad´ri gal) *n., Music* An unaccompanied song, usually for four to six voices, developed during the early Renaissance.

mael-strom (māl´strom) *n.* Any irresistible or dangerous force.

maes-tro (mī´strō) *n. pl.* **-tros** *or* **-tri** A person mastering any art, but especially a famous conductor of music.

Ma-fi-a (mä´fē a) *n.* A secret criminal organization in Sicily; an international criminal organization believed to exist in many countries, including the United States.

mag-a-zine (mag´a zēn´) *n.* A publication with a paper cover containing articles, stories, illustrations and advertising; the part of a gun which holds ammunition ready for feeding into the chamber.

mag-da-len *n.* A prostitute that has been reformed; a house used for the purpose of reforming prostitutes.

ma-gen-ta (ma jen´ta) *n.* A purplish red color.

mag-got (mag´ot) *n.* The legless larva of any of various insects, as the housefly, often found in decaying matter.

Ma-gi (mā´jī) *n. pl.* **Magus** The three wise men of the East who traveled to Bethlehem to pay homage to the baby Jesus.

mag-ic (maj´ik) *n.* The art which seemingly controls foresight of natural events and forces by means of supernatural agencies. **magic** *adj.* **magical** *adj.* **magically** *adv.*

magician *n.* A person who is skilled in magic and performs magic.

mag-is-te-ri-al *adj.* Pertaining to the office or a magistrate; arrogant; pompous; authoritative.

mag-is-trate (maj´i strāt´) *n.* A civil officer with the power to enforce the law.

mag-ma (mag´ma) *n. pl.* **-mata** *or* **-mas** *Geol.* The molten rock beneath the earth's surface from which igneous rocks are formed.

Magna Carta (mag´na kär´ta) *n.* The Great Charter of English liberties which the barons forced King John to sign on June 19, 1215; any document constituting a guarantee of rights and privileges.

mag-nan-i-mous (mag nan´i mus) *adj.* Generous in forgiving insults or injuries. **magnanimity** *n.* **magnanimousness** *n.* **magnanimously** *adv.*

mag-nate (mag´nāt) *n.* A person notable or powerful, especially in business.

mag-ne-sia (mag nē´zha) *n., Chem.* A light, white powder used in medicine as an antacid and laxative.

mag-ne-si-um (mag nē´zē um) *n.* A light, silvery metallic element which burns with a very hot, bright flame and is used in lightweight alloys, symbolized by Mg.

mag-net (mag´nit) *n.* A body having the property of attracting iron and other magnetic material. **magne- tism** *n.*

mag-net-ic (mag net´ik) *adj.* Pertaining to mag- netism or a magnet; capable of being attracted by a magnet; having the power or ability to attract. **magnetically** *adv.*

magnetic field *n.* The area in the neighbor- hood of a magnet or of an electric current, marked by the existence of a detectable magnetic force in every part of the region.

mag-net-ite (mag´ni tīt´) *n.* A black iron oxide in mineral form, which is an impor- tant iron ore.

mag-net-ize (mag´ni tīz´) *v.* To have mag- netic properties; to attract by personal charm or influence. **magnetizable** *adj.* **magnetization** *n.* **magnetizer** *n.*

mag-ne-to (mag nē´tō) *n.* A small alternator which works by means of magnets that are permanently attached, inducing an electric current for the spark in some engines.

mag-ne-tom-e-ter (mag´ni tom´i tėr) *n.* An instrument used for measuring the direction and intensity of magnetic forces.

mag-ne-to-sphere (mag nē´to sfēr´) *n.* *Physics.* A region of the upper atmosphere extending from about 500 to several thousand km above the surface, forming a band of ionized particles trapped by the earth's magnetic field.

mag-ni-fi-ca-tion *n.* The act of magnifying; magnified reproduction.

mag-nif-i-cent (mag nif´i sent) *adj.* Having an extraordinarily imposing appearance; beautiful; outstanding; exceptionally pleas- ing.

mag-ni-fy (mag´ni fī´) *v.* To increase in size; to cause to seem more important or greater; to glorify or praise someone or something. **magnification** *n.* **magnifier** *n.*

mag-nil-o-quent (mag nil´o kwent) *adj.* Speaking or spoken in a lofty and extrav-

agant manner. **magniloquence** *n.* **mag- niloquently** *adv.*

mag-ni-tude (mag´ni tŏd´) *n.* Greatness or importance in size or extent. *Astron.* The relative brightness of a star expressed on a numerical scale, ranging from one for the brightest to six for those just visible.

mag-no-lia (mag nōl´ya) *n.* An ornamental flowering tree or shrub with large, fragrant flowers of white, pink, purple, or yellow.

Magnolia State *n.* Nickname of the state of Mississippi.

mag-num (mag´num) *n.* A wine bottle holding about two quarts or approximately 2/5 gallon.

mag-num o-pus *n.* A great work of art; literary or artistic masterpiece; the greatest single work of an artist, writer, or other creative person.

mag-pie (mag´pī´) *n.* Any of a variety of large, noisy bird found the world over having long tapering tails and black and white plumage.

ma-ha-ra-ja *or* **ma-ha-ra-jah (mä´ harä´ ja)** *n.* A king or prince who rules an In- dian state.

ma-ha-ra-ni *or* **ma-ha-ra-nee (mä´harä´ nē)** *n.* The wife of a maharajah.

ma-hat-ma (ma hät´ma) *n.* In some Asian religions, a person venerated for great knowledge; a title of respect.

ma-hog-a-ny (ma hog´a nē) *n. pl.* **-ies** Any of various tropical trees having hard, reddish-brown wood, much used for cab- inet work and furniture.

maid (mād) *n.* A young unmarried woman or girl; a female servant. **maiden** *n.*

maid-en-hair (mād´en hâr´) *n.* A delicate fern with dark stems and light-green, feathery fronds.

maiden head *n.* Virginity.

maiden name *n.* A woman's family name before marriage.

maid of honor *n.* An unmarried woman who is the main attendant of a bride at a wedding.

maid-ser-vant *n.* Female servant.

mail (māl) *n.* Letter, printed matter, or parcel handled by the postal system. *v.* To send something through the mail; to put in a mailbox for delivery.

mail-a-ble *adj.* Having the capabilities of being mailed. **mailability** *n.*

mail-bag *n.* A bag in which mail is carried and transported.

mail-box *n.* A box used to deposit mail waiting for delivery and collection; a box at a private residence that receives mail.

mail-er *n.* A box or other container used to send mail in.

mail-lot *n.* The close fitting clothing worn by dancers, gymnasts, and acrobats.

mail-man *n.* A person who carries and delivers mail; also postman.

mail order *n.* Goods which are ordered and sent by mail.

maim (mām) *v.* To disable or to deprive of the use of a body part; to impair.

main (mān) *adj.* Being the most important part of something. *n.* A large pipe used to carry water, oil, or gas. **mainly** *adv.*

Maine *n.* A state located in the northeastern corner of the United States; statehood March 15, 1820; state capital Augusta.

main-land (mān'land') *n.* The land part of a country as distinguished from an island.

main-line *v., Slang* To inject a drug directly into a vein.

main-stream (mān'strēm') *n.* A main direction or line of thought. **mainstream** *v.*

main-tain (mān tān') *v.* To carry on or to keep in existence; to preserve in a desirable condition. **maintenance** *n.*

maize (māz) *n.* Corn.

maj-es-ty (maj'i stē) *n. pl.* -ies Stateliness; exalted dignity. **majestic** *adj.*

ma-jor (mā'jėr) *adj.* Greater in importance, quantity, number, or rank; serious. *n.* An officer in the United States Army, Air Force or Marines who ranks above a captain and below a lieutenant colonel; a subject or field of academic study. *Music* A major musical scale, interval, key, or mode.

ma-jor-do-mo *n.* A butler who manages a large household.

ma-jor-ette (mā'jo ret') *n.* A young woman or girl who marches and twirls a baton with a band.

major general *n.* Military officer just below a lieutenant general, but above a brigadier general.

ma-jor-i-ty (ma jor'i tē) *n. pl.* -ies The greater number of something; more than half; the age at which a person is considered to be an adult, usually 21 years old; a number of voters in agreement; a political party group with the most votes.

majority rule *n.* A majority vote that consists of at least one vote over half of the total.

ma-jor med-i-cal (mā'jėr med'i cal) *n.* An insurance policy which pays for most of the medical charges incurred during an illness.

make (māk) *v.* To cause something to happen; to create; to provide, as time; to manufacture a line of goods. *n.* A brand name, as a make of a car. **with** To carry off. **hay** To take advantage of a given opportunity in the early stages. **bones** To perform unhesitating. **make away** *v.* **make** *n.* **maker** *n.*

make-be-lieve (māk'bi lēv') *n.* A pretending to believe. *v.* To pretend. **make-believe** *adj.*

make do *v.* To carry on or manage with minimal materials.

make-ready *n.* The procedure used to make a form ready for printing by the use of overlays and underlays in order to produce a distinct impression.

make-shift *n.* A temporary substitute. **makeshifty, makeshiftness** *n.*

make-up (māk'up') *n.* The manner in which something is formed together or assembled; constructions; the qualities of physical or mental constitution; cosmetics. *v.* To invent a story.

make-weight *n.* Anything added to something to cover a deficiency.

mak-ing *n.* The act of one who or something that forms, or produces; the process of being constructed.

mal-a-chite (mal´a kīt´) *n.* A green basic copper carbonate, used as a common ore of copper and for decorating stoneware.

mal-ad-min-is-ter *v.* To conduct dishonestly. **maladministration** *n.*

mal-a-droit (mal´a droit´) *adj.* Lacking skill; awkward; clumsy. **maladroitly** *adv.* **maladroitness** *n.*

mal-a-dy (mal´a dē) *n. pl.* **-ies** A chronic disease or sickness.

mal-aise (ma lāz´) *n.* The vague discomfort sometimes indicating the beginning of an illness.

mal-a-prop-ism (mal´a prop iz´um) *n.* A foolish misuse of a word. **malaprop, malapropian** *adj.*

mal-ap-ro-pos (mal´ap ro pō´) *adj.* Not appropriate. **malapropos** *adv.*

ma-lar-i-a (ma lâr´ē a) *n., Pathol.* The infectious disease introduced into the blood by the bite of the infected female anopheles mosquito and characterized by cycles of fever, chills, and profuse sweating.

ma-lar-key (ma lär´kē) *n., Slang* Foolish or insincere talk; nonsense.

mal-con-tent (mal´kon tent´) *adj.* Unhappy with existing conditions or affairs. **malcontent** *n.*

mal de mer *n.* Seasickness.

male (māl) *adj.* Of or belonging to the sex that has organs to produce spermatozoa. *Bot.* A plant with stamens but no pistil. *n.* A male person or animal. **maleness** *n.*

male alto *n.* The unusually high adult male voice.

mal-e-dic-tion (mal´i dik´shan) *n.* A curse; execration. **maledictory** *adj.*

mal-e-fac-tor (mal´e fak´ter) *n.* A person who commits a crime or an unlawful act; a criminal. **malefaction** *n.*

ma-lef-i-cent *n.* Harmful; doing evil or wrong. **maleficence** *n.*

ma-lev-o-lent (ma lev´o lent) *adj.* Full of spite or ill will for another; malicious. **malevolently** *adv.* **malevolence** *n.*

mal-for-ma-tion (mal´for mā´shan) *n.* Defective structure or form. **malformed** *adj.*

mal-func-tion (mal fungk´shan) *n.* Failure to function correctly. **malfunction** *v.*

mal-ice (mal´is) *n.* The direct intention or desire to harm others. *Law* The willfully formed design to injure another without just reason or cause.

ma-lign (ma līn´) *v.* To speak slander or evil of. **maligner** *n.*

ma-lig-nant (ma lig´nant) *adj., Pathol.* Of or relating to tumors and abnormal or rapid growth, and tending to metastasize; opposed to benign; causing death or great harm. **malignancy** *n.* **malignity** *n.* **malignantly** *adv.*

ma-lin-ger (ma ling´gėr) *v.* To pretend injury or sickness so as to avoid responsibility or work. **malingerer** *n.*

mall (mol) *n.* A walk or other shaded public promenade; a street with shops, restaurants, and businesses which is closed to vehicles.

mal-lard (mal´ėrd) *n. pl.* **mallard** *or* **-ards.** A wild duck having brownish plumage, the male of which has a green head and neck.

mal-le-a-ble (mal´ē a bl) *adj.* Able to be bent, shaped, or hammered without breaking; capable of being molded, altered, or influenced. **malleability** *n.* **malleableness** *n.* **malleably** *adv.*

mal-let (mal´it) *n.* A hammer with a head made of wood or rubber and a short handle; a tool for striking an object without marring it.

mal-le-us (mal´ē us) *n., Anat.* The club-shaped bone of the middle ear or the largest of three small bones; also called the hammer.

mal-nour-ished (mal´ner´isht) *adj.* Undernourished.

mal-nu-tri-tion (mal´nō trish´an) *n.* Insufficient nutrition.

mal-o-dor *n.* An offensive stench; odor.

mal-oc-clu-sion (mal´o klō´zhan) *n.* Improper alignment of the teeth.

mal-o-dor-ous (mal ō´dėr us) *adj.* Having

a disagreeable or foul odor. **malodorously** *adv.* **malodorousness** *n.*

mal-po-si-tion *n., Pathol.* Wrong position as of a fetus in the uterus or a body organ.

mal-prac-tice (mal prak´tis) *n.* Improper treatment of a patient by his doctor during surgery or treatment which results in damage or injury; failure to perform a professional duty in a proper, careful, or correct fashion, resulting in injury, loss, or other problems.

malt (molt) *n.* Grain, usually barley, used chiefly in brewing and distilling; an alcoholic beverage.

mal-tose (mol´tōs) *n.* A white, crystalline sugar found in malt.

mal-treat (mal trēt´) *v.* To treat badly, unkindly, or roughly. **maltreatment** *n.*

mal-ver-sa-tion *n.* Improper behavior in a position of trust.

ma-ma (mam´a) *n.* Mother.

mam-ba (măm´bä) *n.* A venomous snake found in the tropics and in southern Africa.

mam-bo (măm´bō) *n.* A dance resembling the rumba of Latin America.

mam-mal (mam´al) *n.* Any member of a class whose females secrete milk for nourishing their young, including man. **mammalian** *n.*

mam-ma-ry gland (mam´a rē) *n.* The milk-producing organ of the female mammal, consisting of small cavity clusters with ducts ending in a nipple.

mam-mog-ra-phy *n.* An x-ray examination of the breast for early detection of cancer.

mam-moth (mam´oth) *n.* An extinct, early form of elephant whose tusks curved upwards and whose body was covered with long hair; any thing of great or huge size.

man (man) *n. pl.* **men** An adult or fully-grown male; the human race; Husband; an expression of pleasure or surprise.

man-a-cle (man´a kl) *n.* A device for restraining the hands; handcuffs. **manacle** *v.*

man-age (man´ij) *v.* To direct or control the affairs or use of; to organize. **manageability** *n.* **manageable** *adj.* **manageably** *adv.*

man-age-ment *n.* The act of directing, or managing for a purpose; administration.

man-ag-er (man´i jer) *n.* One in charge of managing an enterprise or business. **managerial** *adj.* **managership** *n.*

man-a-tee (man´a tē´) *n.* An aquatic mammal of the coastal waters of Florida, West Indies, and the Gulf of Mexico.

man-date (man´dāt) *n.* An authoritative order or command. *Law* A judicial order issued by a higher court to a lower one. **mandate** *v.*

man-da-to-ry (man´da tōr´ē) *adj.* Required by, having the nature of, or relating to a mandate; obligatory.

man-di-ble (man´di bl) *n.* The lower jaw bone. *Biol.* Either part of the beak of a bird. **mandibular** *adj.*

man-do-lin (man´do lin) *n.* A musical instrument having a pear-shaped body and a fretted neck.

man-drake (man´drāk) *n.* A plant having purplish flowers and a branched root sometimes resembling the human form.

man-drel *or* **mandril (man´drel)** *n.* A spindle or shaft on which material is held for working on a lathe.

man-drill (man´dril) *n.* A large, fierce West African baboon.

mane (mān) *n.* The long hair growing on the neck of some animals, as the lion, and horse.

man–eater (man´ē´tėr) *n.* An animal which feeds on human flesh, such as a shark or a tiger.

ma-nege (ma nezh´) *n.* The art of training and riding horses; the performance of a horse so trained.

ma-neu-ver (ma nö´vėr) *n., Milit.* A planned strategic movement or shift, as of warships, or troops; any planned, skillful, or calculated move. **maneuver** *v.* **maneuverability** *n.* **maneuverable** *adj.*

man Friday *n.* A person devoted to another as a servant, aide, or employee.

man-ful (man´fŭl) *adj.* Having a manly spirit. **manfully** *adv.* **manfulness** *n.*

man-ga-nese (mang´gả nēs´) *n.* A hard, brittle, gray-white metallic element which forms an important component of steel alloys, symbolized by Mn.

mange (mānj) *n.* A contagious skin disease of dogs and other domestic animals caused by parasitic mites and marked by itching and hair loss. **mangy** *adj.*

man-ger (mān´jẻr) *n.* A trough or box which holds livestock feed.

man-gle (mang´gl) *v.* To disfigure or mutilate by bruising, battering, or crushing; to spoil. **mangler** *n.*

man-go (mang´gō) *n.* *pl.* **-goes** *or* **-gos** A tropical evergreen tree that produces a fruit having a slightly acid taste.

man-grove (mang´grōv) *n.* A tropical evergreen tree or shrub having aerial roots which form dense thickets along tidal shores.

man-han-dle (man´han´dl) *v.* To handle very roughly.

man-hole (man´hōl´) *n.* A circular covered, opening usually in a street, through which one may enter a sewer, drain, or conduit.

man-hood (man´hed) *n.* The state of being an adult male.

man–hour (man´our´) *n.* The amount of work that one person can complete in one hour.

man-hunt *n.* An extensive organized hunt for a person, especially one who has committed a crime. **manhunter** *n.*

ma-ni-a (mā´nē ả) *n.* An extraordinary enthusiasm or craving for something; intense excitement and physical overactivity, often a symptom of manic depressive psychosis.

-mania *suffix.* Unreasonable or intense desire or infatuation with.

ma-ni-ac (mā´nē ak´) *n.* A violently insane person. **maniac** *adj.* **maniacal** *adj.*

man-ic–de-pres-sive (man´ik di pres´iv) *adj.* Of a mental disorder characterized by alternating periods of manic excitation and depression. **manic–depressive** *n.*

man-i-cot-ti *n.* Pasta shaped like a tube, filled with meat or ricotta cheese and served with hot tomato sauce.

man-i-cure (man´i kūr) *n.* The cosmetic care of the hands and finger nails. **manicure** *v.* **manicurist** *n.*

man-i-fest (man´i fest´) *adj.* Clearly apparent; obvious. *v.* To display, reveal or show. *n.* A list of cargo or passengers. **manifestly** *adv.*

man-i-fes-ta-tion (man´i fe stā´shản) *n.* The act or state of being manifest; making clear to the understanding; display; that which reveals; a person who participates in public demonstrations.

manifest content *n.* The images that take place within a dream.

man-i-fes-to (man´i fes´tō) *n.* *pl.* **-toes** *or* **-tos** A public or format explanation of principles or intentions, usually of a political nature

man-i-fold (man´i fōld´) *adj.* Having many and varied parts, forms, or types; having an assortment of features. *Mech.* A pipe with several or many openings, as for the escaping of exhaust gas. **manifoldly** *adv.* **manifoldness** *n.*

man-i-kin *or* **mannikin (man´i kin)** *n.* A little man; a dwarf; a mannequin.

Ma-nil-a (mả nil´ả) *n.* The capital of the Philippines.

Manila hemp *n.* The fiber of the banana plant, used for making paper, rope, and cord.

Manila paper *n.* Strong, light brown paper, originally made from Manila hemp but now made of various fibers.

ma-nip-u-late (mả nip´ū lāt´) *v.* To handle or manage shrewdly and deviously for one's own profit. **manipulation** *n.* **manipulator** *n.* **manipulative** *adj.*

man-kind (man´kīnd´) *n.* The human race; men collectively, as opposed to women.

man-like *adj.* Resembling a man.

man-ly (man´lē) *adj.* Pertaining to or having qualities which are traditionally attributed to a man. **manly** *adv.*

man–made (man´mād) *adj.* Made by human beings and not developed by nature.

man-na (man´a) *n.* The food which was miraculously given to the Israelites in the wilderness on their flight from Egypt; anything of value that one receives unexpectedly.

manned (mand) *adj.* Operated by a human being.

man-ne-quin (man´e kin) *n.* A life-sized model of a human figure, used to fit or display clothes; a woman who models clothes.

man-ner (man´er) *n.* The way in which something happens or is done; an action or style of speech; one's social conduct and etiquette. **mannered** *adj.*

man-ner-ism (man´e riz´um) *n.* A person's distinctive behavioral trait or traits. **mannerist** *n.* **manneristic** *adj.*

man-ner-ly (man´er lē) *adj.* Well-behaved; polite. **mannerliness** *n.*

man-nish (man´ish) *adj.* Resembling a man; masculine. **mannishly** *adv.*

man–of–war (man´ov wor´) *n. pl.* **men–of–war** A warship.

ma-nom-e-ter (ma nom´i tèr) *n.* An instrument used to measure pressure, as of gases or liquids. **manometric** *adj.*

man-or (man´er) *n.* A landed estate; the house or hall of an estate. **manorial** *adj.*

man pow-er (man´pou´èr) *n.* The force of human physical power; the number of men whose strength and skill are readily available to a nation, army, project, or other venture.

man-que *adj.* Lacking fulfillment; frustrated.

man-sard (man´särd) *n., Archit.* A curved roof with the lower slope almost vertical and the upper almost horizontal.

manse (mans) *n.* The house of a clergyman.

man-sion (man´shan) *n.* A very large, impressive house.

man–size *or* **man–sized (man´sīzd´)** *Slang* Quite large.

man-slaugh-ter (man´slo´tèr) *n., Law* The unlawful killing without malice of a person by another.

man-slay-er *n.* One who murders or kills a

human being.

man-ta (man´ta) *n.* A rough-textured cotton fabric; any of several very large fishes having large, very flat bodies with winglike fins.

man-teau (man´tō) *n. pl.* **-teaus** *or* **-teaux** A robe or cloak.

man-tel *also* **mantle (man´tl)** A shelf over a fireplace; the ornamental brick or stone around a fireplace.

man-til-la (man til´a) *n.* A light scarf worn over the head and shoulders by women in Latin America and Spain.

man-tis (man´tis) *n. pl.* **mantises** *or* **mantes** A tropical insect with a long body, large eyes, and swiveling head, which stands with its forelegs folded as if in prayer.

man-tle (man´tl) *n.* A loose-fitting coat which is usually sleeveless; something that covers or conceals; a device consisting of a sheath of threads, used in gas lamps to give off brilliant illumination when heated by a flame. **mantle** *v.*

man-u-al (man´ū al) *adj.* Used or operated by the hands. *n.* A small reference book which gives instructions on how to operate or work something. **manually** *adv.*

man-u-fac-ture (man´ū fak´chèr) *v.* To make a product; to invent or produce something. **manufacturer** *n.*

ma-nure (ma ner´) *n.* The fertilizer used to fertilize land, obtained from animal dung. **manure** *v.*

man-u-script (man´ū skript´) *n.* A typed or written material copy of an article, book, or document, which is being prepared for publication.

man-wise *adv.* According to the nature of men.

many (men´ē) *adj.* A mounting to a large or indefinite number or amount.

man-y-sid-ed *adj.* Having many aspects or sides, talents or capabilities.

map (map) *n.* A plane surface representation of a region. *v.* To plan anything in detail. **mapmaker** *n.* **mapper** *n.*

maple (mā´pl) *n.* A tall tree having lobed

leaves and a fruit of two joined samaras; the wood of this tree, amber-yellow incolor when finished and used for furniture and flooring.

maple sugar *n.* Sugar made from the sap of the maple tree.

maple syrup *n.* The refined sap of the sugar maple.

mar *v.* To scratch or deface; to blemish; to ruin; to spoil.

Mar *abbr.* March.

mar-a-bou (mar´a bŏ´) *n.* A stork of Africa, whose soft down is used for trimming women's garments.

ma-ra-ca (ma rä´ka) *n.* A percussion instrument made from gourds containing dried beans or pebbles.

mar-a-schi-no (mar´a skē´nō) *n.* A cherry preserved in a cordial distilled from the fermented juice of the small wild cherry and flavored with cracked cherry pits.

mar-a-thon (mar´a thon´) *n.* A foot race of 26 miles, usually run on the streets of a city; any contest of endurance.

mar-ble (mär´bl) *n.* A limestone which is partly crystallized and irregular in color. *v.* To contain sections of fat, as in meat. **marbles** A game played with balls of glass. A person's common sense or sanity.

march (märch) *v.* To walk with measured, regular steps in asolemn or dignified manner. *Mus.* A musical composition.

March (märch) *n.* The third month of the year, containing 31days.

Mar-di Gras (mär´dē grä´) *n.* The Tuesday before Ash Wed nesday, often celebrated with parades and costumed merrymaking.

mare (mâr) *n.* The female of the horse and other equine animals.

ma-re (mär´a) *n. pl., Astron.* Any of the dark areas on the surface of the moon.

mare clausum *n.* The body of water that is controlled by one nation.

ma-re li-be-rum *n.* A body of water that is available to all nations for travel and navi-gation.

mare's nest *n.* An accomplishment found to be worthless.

mar-ga-rine (mär´jer in) *n.* A butter substitute made from vegetable oils and milk.

mar-gin (mär´jin) *n.* The edge or border around the body of written or printed text; the difference between the selling price and cost of an item.

mar-gi-na-li-a *n. pl.* The notes in the margin of a book.

ma-ri-a-chi *n.* A Mexican band; the music performed by a musician playing in a mariachi.

Marie Antoinette *n.* (1755-1793). The queen of Louis XVI of France from 1774-1793.

mar-i-gold (mar´i gōld´) *n.* Any of a variety of plants having golden-yellow flowers.

mar-i-jua-na *or* **marihuana (mar´i wä´na)** *n.* Hemp; the dried flower tops and leaves of this plant, capable of producing dis-orienting or hallucinogenic effects when smoked in cigarettes or in gested.

ma-ri-na (ma rē´na) *n.* A docking area for boats, furnishing moorings and supplies for small boats.

mar-i-nade (mar´i nād´) *n.* A brine made from vinegar or wine and oil with various herbs and spices for soaking meat, fowl, or fish before cooking.

mar-i-nate (mar´i nāt´) *v.* To soak meat in a marinade.

ma-rine (ma rēn´) *adj.* Of, pertaining to, existing in, or formed by the sea. *n.* A soldier trained for service on land and at sea. **Marine** A member of the Marine Corps.

ma-rine glue *n.* A water-insoluble glue used to coat areas on a ship's deck.

mar-i-ner *n.* A person whose job is to assist or navigate ships and seaman through an area.

mar-i-o-nette (mar´ē o net´) *n.* A small jointed animal or human figure of wood which is manipulated from above by attached strings or wires.

mar-i-tal (mar´i tal) *adj.* Pertaining to marriage. **maritally** *adv.*

mar-i-time (mar´i tīm´) *adj.* Located or situated on or near the sea; pertaining to the sea and its navigation and commerce.

mark (märk) *n.* A visible impression, trace, dent, or stain; an identifying seal, inscription, or label.

Mark *n.* The evangelist who wrote the second Gospel narratives in the New Testament; the second Gospel of the New Testament; Saint Mark.

mar-ket (mär´kit) *n.* The trade and commerce in a certain service or commodity; a public place for purchasing and selling merchandise; the possible consumers of a particular product. *v.* To sell. **marketability** *n.* **marketable** *adj.*

mar-ket-place (mär´kit plās´) *n.* A place, such as a public square, where ideas, opinions, and works are traded and tested.

marks-man (märks´man) *n.* A person skilled in firing a gun and hitting the mark. **markswoman** *n.*

mark-up *n.* The amount of increase in price from the cost to the selling price. *v.* To raise the price.

mar-lin (mär´lin) *n.* A large marine game fish of the Atlantic; the striped marlin found in the Pacific.

mar-line-spike (mär´lin spīk´) *n., Naut.* A pointed tool used in splicing ropes.

mar-ma-lade (mär´ma lād´) *n.* A preserve made from the pulp and rind of fruits.

ma-roon (ma rōn´) *v.* To put ashore and abandon on a desolate shore. *n.* A dull purplish red.

mar-que-try (mär´ki trē) *n.* Inlaid work of wood or ivory used for decorating furniture.

mar-quis (mär´kwis) *n.* The title of a nobleman ranking below a duke.

mar-qui-sette (mär´ki zet´) *n.* A fabric of cotton, silk, nylon, or a combination of these, used in curtains, clothing, and mosquito nets.

mar-riage (mar´ij) *n.* The state of being married; wedlock; the act of marrying or the ceremony entered into by a man and woman so as to live together as husband and wife. **marriageability** *n.* **marriageable** *adj.*

mar-row (mar´ō) *n.* The soft, vascular tissue which fills bone cavities; the main part or essence of anything.

mar-row-bone *n.* A bone that is rich in marrow.

mar-ry (mar´ē) *v.* To take or join as husband or wife; to unite closely.

Mars (märz) *n.* The 4th planet from the sun.

marsh (märsh) *n.* An area of low, wet land; a swamp. **marshy** *adj.*

mar-shal (mär´shal) *n.* A military officer of high rank in foreign countries; the person in the United States in charge of a police or fire department. *v.* To bring troops together to prepare for a battle.

marsh-mal-low (märsh´mel´ō) *n.* A soft, white confection made of sugar, corn syrup, starch, and gelatin and coated with powdered sugar.

mar-su-pi-al (mär sō´pē al) *n.* An animal, such as a kangaroo, koala, or opossum, which has no placenta, but which in the female has an abdominal pouch with teats to feed and carry the off spring.

mart (märt) *n.* A trading market; a center.

mar-ten (mär´ten) *n.*

A weasel-like mammal of eastern North America with arboreal habits; the valuable brown fur of the marten.

mar-tial (mär´shal) *adj.* Of, pertaining to, or concerned with war or the military life.

martial arts *n. pl.* Oriental arts of self-defense, such as karate or judo, which are practiced as sports.

martial law *n.* Temporary rule by military forces over the citizens in an area where civil law and order no longer exist.

mar-tin (mär´tin) *n.* A bird of the swallow family with a tail that is less forked than that of the common swallow.

mar-ti-ni (mär tē´nē) *n. pl.* **-nis** A cocktail

of gin and dry vermouth, served with an olive or lemon peel.

mar-tyr (mär′tẻr) *n.* A person who would rather die than renounce his religious principles; one making great sacrifices to advance a cause, belief, or principle. **martyr** *v.* **martyrdom** *n.*

mar-vel (mär′vel) *n.* Anything causing surprise, wonder, or astonishment.

mar-vel-ous *or* **marvellous (mär′ve lus)** Informal Excellent; very good,admirable. **marvelously** *adv.* **marvelousness** *n.*

Marx-ism (märk′siz um) *n.* The body of socialist doctrines developed by Karl Marx. **Marxist** *n.*

Mary (mâr′ē) *n.* The mother of Jesus.

Mary-land *n.* A state located on the eastern coast of the United States; statehood April 28, 1788; state capital Annapolis.

mar-zi-pan (mär′zi pan′) *n.* A confection of grated almonds, sugar, and egg whites.

masc *abbr.* Masculine.

mas-car-a (ma skar′a) *n.* A cosmetic preparation used for coloring or darkening the eyelashes.

mas-cot (mas′kot) *n.* A person, animal, or object thought to bring good luck.

mas-cu-line (mas′kū lin) *adj.* Of or pertaining to the male sex; male; the masculine gender. **culinity** *n.*

ma-ser (mä′zẻr) *n., Physics* One of several devices which are similar to the laser but which operate with microwaves rather than light.

mash (mash) *n.* A soft, pulpy mass or mixture used to distill alcohol or spirits. *v.* To crush into a soft, pulpy mass. **masher** *n.*

mask (mask) *n.* A covering used to conceal the face in order to disguise or protect. *v.* To hide or conceal.

mas-o-chism (mas′o kiz um) *n.* A condition in which sexual gratification is marked by pleasure in being subjected to physical pain or abuse. **masochist** *n.* **masochistic** *adj.*

ma-son (mä′son) *n.* A person working with brick or stone.

ma-son-ic (ma son′ik) *adj.* Pertaining to or like Freemasonry or Freemasons.

masque (mask) *n.* An elaborately staged dramatic performance, popular during the 16th and 17th centuries in England; a masquerade.

mas-quer-ade (mas′ke rād′) *n.* A costume party in which the guests are masked and dressed in fancy costumes. *v.* To disguise oneself. **masquerader** *n.*

mass (mas) *n.* A body of matter that does not have definite shape but is relatively large in size; physical volume; the measure of a body's resistance to acceleration.

Mass *or* **mass (mas)** *n.* A celebration in the Roman Catholic and some Protestant churches; the service including this celebration.

Mass *or* **Ma** *abbr.* Massachusetts.

Mass-a-chu-setts *n.* A state located in the northeastern part of the United States; statehood February 6, 1788; state capital Boston.

mas-sa-cre (mas′a kẻr) *n.* The indiscriminate and savage killing of human beings in large numbers. **massacre** *v.*

mas-sage (ma säzh′) *n.* The manual or mechanical manipulation of the skin to improve circulation and to relax muscles. **massage** *v.*

mas-seur (ma ser′) *n.* A man who gives massages.

mas-seuse (ma sös′) *n.* A woman who gives massages.

mas-sive (mas′iv) *adj.* Of great intensity, degree, and size. **massively** *adv.* **massiveness** *n.*

mast (mast) *n.* The upright pole or spar which supports the sails and running rigging of a sail boat.

mas-tec-to-my (ma stek′to mē) *n. pl.* -ies The surgical removal of breast.

mas-ter (mas′tẻr) *n.* A person with control or authority over others; one who is exceptionally gifted or skilled in an art, science, or craft; the title given for respect or in address. *v.* To learn a skill, craft, or job; to overcome defeat. **mastership** *n.*

master key *n.* A key which will open many different locks whose keys are not the same.

mas-ter-ly *adj.* Characteristic of a master. **masterliness** *n.*

mas-ter-mind (mas´tėr mīnd´) *n.* A person who plans and directs at the highest levels of policy and strategy. *v.* To plan or direct an undertaking.

master of ceremonies *n.* A person who hosts a formal event or program.

mas-ter-piece (mas´tėr pēs´) *n.* Something having notable excellence; an unusually brilliant achievement which is considered the greatest achievement of its creator.

master plan *n.* A plan providing complete instructions.

mast-head (mast´hed´) *n.* The top of a mast; the listing in a periodical giving the names of the editors, staff, and owners.

mas-ti-cate (mas´ti kāt´) *v.* To chew. **mastication** *n.*

mas-to-don (mas´to don´) *n.* A large, extinct mammal which resembles an elephant.

mas-toid (mas´toid) *n., Anat.* The nipple shaped portion at the rear of the temporal bone behind the ear.

mas-tur-ba-tion (mas´tėr bā´shan) *n.* The act of stimulating the sexual organs by hand or other means without sexual intercourse. **masturbate** *v.* **masturbator** *n.*

mat (mat) *n.* A flat piece of material made of fiber, rubber, rushes, or other material and used to cover floors; the border around a picture, which serves as a contrast between the picture and the frame.

mat-a-dor (mat´a dor´) *n.* A bullfighter who kills the bull after completing various maneuvers with a cape.

match (mach) *n.* Anything that is similar or identical to another; a short, thin piece of wood or cardboard with a specially treated tip which ignites as a result of friction. *v.* To equal; to oppose successfully. **matchable** *adj.* **matcher** *n.*

match-maker (mach´mā´kėr) *n.* A person who arranges a marriage.

mate (māt) *n.* A spouse; something matched, joined, or paired with another; in chess, a move which puts the opponent's king in-

jeopardy. *Naval* A petty officer. **mate** *v.*

ma-te-ri-al (ma tēr´ē al) *n.* The substance from which anything is or may be composed or constructed of; anything that is used in creating, working up, or developing something.

ma-te-ri-al-ism (ma tēr´ē aliz´um) *n.* The doctrine that physical matter is the only reality and that everything, including thought, feeling, will, and mind, is explainable in terms of matter; a preference for material objects as opposed to spiritual or intellectual pursuits. **materialist, materialistic** *n.* **materialistically** *adj.*

ma-te-ri-al-ize (ma tēr´ē alīz´) *v.* To give material or actual form to something; to assume material or visible appearance; to take form or shape. **materialization** *n.* **materializer** *n.*

ma-te-ri-el (ma tēr´ē el´) *n.* The equipment and supplies of a military force, including guns and ammunition.

ma-ter-nal (ma ter´nal) *adj.* Relating to a mother or motherhood; inherited from one's mother.

ma-ter-ni-ty (ma ter´ni tē) *n.* The state of being a mother; the qualities of a mother; the department in a hospital for the prenatal and postnatal care of babies and their mothers.

math (math) *n.* Mathematics.

math-e-mat-ics (math´e mat´iks) *n.* The study of form, arrangement, quantity, and magnitude of numbers and operational symbols. **mathematical** *adj.* **mathematically** *adv.* **mathematician** *n.*

mat-i-nee (mat´i nā´) *n.* An afternoon performance of a play, concert, movie, etc.

ma-tri-arch (mā´trē ärk´) *n.* A woman ruler of a family, tribe, or clan. **matriarchal** *adj.* **matriarchy** *n.*

mat-ri-cide (ma´tri sīd´) *n.* The killing of one's own mother; one who kills his mother. **matricidal** *adj.*

ma-tric-u-late (ma trik´ū lāt´) *v.* To enroll, or to be admitted into a college or university. **matriculation** *n.*

mat-ri-mo-ny (ma´tri mō´nē) *n.* The condition of being married; the act, sacrament, or ceremony of marriage. **matrimonial** *adj.* **matrimonially** *adv.*

ma-trix (mā´triks) *n. pl.* **-rixes** *or* **-rices** Something within which something else develops, originates, or takes shape; a mold or die.

ma-tron (mā´tron) *n.* A married woman or widow of dignity and social position; the woman supervisor in a prison. **matronly** *adv.* **matronliness** *n.*

mat-ter (mat´ér) *n.* Something that makes up the substance of anything; that which is material and physical, occupies space, and is perceived by the senses; something that is sent by mail; something that is written or printed.

mat-tock (mat´ok) *n.* A tool having a blade on one side and a pick on the other or one with a blade on each side.

mat-tress (ma´tris) *n.* A large cloth case filled with soft material and used on or as a bed.

mat-u-rate (mach´e rāt´) *v.* To ripen or mature. **maturation** *n.*

ma-ture (ma ter´) *adj.* Completely developed; at full growth; something, as a bond at a bank, that is due and payable. **mature** *v.* **maturely** *adv.* **maturity** *n.*

mat-zo (mät´sa) *n. pl.* **-zos** *or* **-zot** A large, flatpiece of unleavened bread eaten during Passover.

maud-lin (mod´lin) *adj.* Overly sentimental; tearfully and overwhelmingly emotional.

maul (mol) *n.* A heavy hammer or mallet used to drive wedges, piles, and other materials. *v.* To handle roughly; to abuse.

maun-der (mon´dér) *v.* To wander or talk in an incoherent manner.

mau-so-le-um (mo´so lē´um) *n. pl.* **-leums** *or* **-lea** A large and stately tomb.

mauve (mōv) *n.* A purplish rose shade; a moderately reddish to gray purple.

mav-er-ick (mav´ér ik) *n.* An unbranded or orphaned calf or colt. *Slang* A person who is unorthodox in his ideas or attitudes.

maw (mo) *n.* The jaws, mouth, or gullet of a hungry or ferocious animal; the stomach.

mawk-ish (mo´kish) *adj.* Disgustingly sentimental; sickening or insipid. **mawkishly** *adv.* **mawkishness** *n.*

max *abbr.* Maximum.

max-i *n.* A floor-length garment, such as a skirt or coat.

max-il-la (mak sil´a) *n. pl.* **-lae** *or* **-las** The upper jaw or jawbone. **maxillary** *adj.*

max-im (mak´sim) *n.* A brief statement of truth, general principle, or rule of conduct.

max-i-mize (mak´si mīz´) *v.* To increase as greatly as possible; to intensify to the maximum.

max-i-mum (mak´si mum) *n. pl.* **-mums** *or* **-ma** The greatest possible number, measure, degree, or quantity. **maximum** *adj.*

may (mā) *v.* To be permitted or allowed; used to express a wish, purpose, desire, contingency, or result.

May (mā) *n.* The fifth month of the year, having 31 days.

may-be (mā´bē) *adv.* Perhaps; possibly.

May Day (mā´dā´) *n.* The first day of May, traditionally celebrated as a spring festival and in some countries as a holiday honoring the labor force.

may-flow-er (mā´flou´ér) *n.* A wide variety of plants which blossom in May.

Mayflower (mā´flou´ér) *n.* The ship on which the Pilgrims came to America in 1620.

may-hem (mā´hem) *n., Law* The offense of injuring a person's body; any situation brought on by violence, confusion, noise, or disorder.

may-o *n., Slang* Mayonnaise.

may-on-naise (mā´o nāz´) *n.* A dressing for salads, made by beating raw egg yolk, oil, lemon juice, or vinegar and seasonings.

may-or (mā´ér) *n.* The chief magistrate of a town, borough, municipality, or city. **mayoral** *adj.* **mayoralty** *n.* **mayorship** *n.*

may-pole (mā´pōl´) *n.* A decorated pole hung with streamers around which May Day dancing takes place.

maze (māz) *n.* A complicated, intricate network of passages or pathways; a labyrinth; a state of uncertainty, bewilderment, or perplexity. **maze** *v.*

MBA *abbr.* Master of Business Administration.

MC *abbr.* Master of ceremonies.

McKinley, William *N.* (1843-1901) The 25th president of the United States, from 1897- 1901, assassinated while in office.

MD *abbr.* Maryland *or* Md. *abbr.* Doctor of Medicine.

mdse *abbr.* Merchandise.

me (mē) The objective case of the pronoun I.

ME *abbr.* Maine.

mead (mēd) *n.* An alcoholic beverage made from fermented honey and water with yeast and spices added.

mead-ow (med´ō) *n.* A tract of grassland used for grazing or growing hay.

mead-ow-lark (med´ō lärk´) *n.* A songbird of North America.

mea-ger *or* **mea-gre (mē´gėr)** *adj.* Thin; lean; deficient in quantity, richness, vigor, or fertility. **meagerly** *adv.* **meagerness** *n.*

meal (mēl) *n.* The edible seeds of coarsely ground grain; any powdery material; the food served or eaten at one sitting at certain times during the day; the time or occasion of taking such food. **mealy** *adj.*

meal-ticket *n., Slang* One who is a source of financial support for another; a ticket or card bought for a specified price and redeemable at a restaurant for food.

meal-y–mouthed (mē´lē mouthd´) *adj.* Unable to speak plainly and frankly; evasive.

mean (mēn) *v.* To have in mind as a purpose or intent; to be of a specified importance or significance. *adj.* Poor or inferior in appearance or quality. *n.* The medium point. **means** The method or instrument by which some end is or may be accomplished; the available resources.

me-an-der (mē an´dėr) *v.* To wander about without a certain course or a fixed direction. **meander** *n.*

mean-ing (mē´ning) *n.* That which is meant or intended; the aim, end, or purpose; the significance; an interpretation. **meaningful** *adj.* **meaningfulness** *adj.*

mean-time (mēn´tīm´) *n.* The time or period between or during the intervening time.

mean-while (mēn´hwīl´) *adv.* At the same time.

mea-sles (mē´zelz) *n.* A contagious viral disease usually occurring in children, characterized by the eruption of redspots.

mea-sly (mē´zlē) *adj., Slang* Very small; meager.

meas-ure (mezh´ėr) *n.* The range, dimension, extent, or capacity of anything. *Mus.* The group of beats marked off by regularly recurring primary accents; the notes and rests between two successive bars on a musical staff. *v.* To determine the range, dimension, extent, volume, or capacity of anything. **measurable** *adj.* **measurably** *adv.* **measurer** *n.*

meas-ure-ment (mezh´ėr ment) *n.* The process or act of measuring.

meat (mēt) *n.* The flesh of an animal which is used as food; the core or essential part of something. **meatiness** *n.* **meaty** *adj.*

mech *abbr.* Mechanical; mechanics.

me-chan-ic (me kan´ik) *n.* A person skilled in the making, operation, or repair of machines or tools.

me-chan-i-cal (me kan´i kal) *adj.* Involving or having to do with the construction, operation, or design of tools or machines; produced or operated by a machine. **mechanically** *adv.*

mechanical drawing *n.* A drawing done with the aid of squares, compasses, or other instruments.

me-chan-ics (me kan´iks) *n. pl.* The scientific study and analysis of the action of forces and motion on material bodies.

mech-a-nism (mek´a niz´um) *n.* The arrangement or parts of a machine; the technique or process by which something works.

mech-a-nize (mek´a nīz´) *v.* To make

mechanical; to equip with tanks, trucks, mechanical and other equipment, as in the military. **mechanization** *n.*

med *abbr.* Medical.

med-al (med´al) *n.* A small piece of metal with a commemorative image or inscription which is presented as an award.

med-al-ist (med´a list) *n.* A person who designs, col-lects, or makes medals; one who has been awarded or received a medal.

me-dal-lion (me dal´yan) *n.* A large circular or oval medal which is used as a decorative element.

med-dle (med´l) *v.* To interfere or participate in another person's business or affairs. **meddler** *n.* **meddlesome** *adj.*

med-i-a (mē´dē a) *n. pl.* The instruments of news communication, as radio, television, and newspapers.

me-di-al (mē´dē al) *adj.* Pertaining to or situated in the middle; ordinary.

me-di-an (mē´dē an) *n.* Something that is halfway between two different parts. *adj.* Relating to or constituting the median of a set of numbers.

median strip *n.* The strip which divides highway traffic lanes which are going in opposite directions.

me-di-ate (mē´dē āt´) *v.* To help settle or reconcile opposing sides in a dispute. **mediation** *n.* **mediator** *n.*

med-ic (med´ik) *n., Slang* A physician or intern; a medical student; in the armed forces, a corpsman or enlisted person trained to give first aid.

Med-i-caid *or* **medicaid (med´i kād´)** *n.* A governmental medical care or health insurance program providing medical aid for people who are unable to pay their own medical expenses.

med-i-cal (med´i kal) *adj.* Relating to the study or practice of medicine. **medically** *adv.*

medical examiner *n.* A physician who is

authorized by a governmental body to ascertain causes of death.

Med-i-care *or* **medicare (med´i kâr´)** *n.* The program under the Social Security Administration which provides medical care for elderly people.

med-i-cate (med´i kāt´) *v.* To treat an injury or illness with medicine. **medication** *n.*

med-i-cine (med´i sin) *n.* Any agent or substance used in the treatment of disease or in the relief of pain; the science of diagnosing and treating disease; the profession of medicine.

medicine ball *n.* A large, heavy ball used for physical exercise.

medicine man *n.* In primitive cultures, a person believed to have supernatural powers for healing.

me-di-e-val *or* **mediaeval (mē´dēē´val)** *adj.* Like or characteristic of the Middle Ages. **medievalism, medievalist** *n.* **medievally** *adv.*

me-di-o-cre (mē´dē ō´kėr) *adj.* Common; fair; undistinguished.

med-i-tate (med´i tāt´) *v.* To be in continuous, contemplative thought; to think about doing something. **meditative** *adj.* **meditation** *n.*

Med-i-ter-ra-ne-an *n.* A sea bounded by Africa, Asia, and Europe, which connects with the Atlantic Ocean through the Straits of Gibraltar. *adj.* Of or relating to the people or countries bounded by the Mediterranean.

me-di-um (mē´dē um) *n. pl.* **-dia** *or* **-ums** Something which occupies a middle position between two extremes; the means of communicating information or ideas through publishing, radio, or television.

med-ley (med´lē) *n.* A mixture or confused mass of elements; a jumble. *Music* A musical composition made up of parts of different songs.

me-dul-la (mi dul´a) *n., Anat.* The center of certain vertebrate structures, such as bone marrow.

medulla oblongata (mi dul´a ob´longgä´

ta) n. The mass of nerve tissue found at the base of the brain, controlling bodily functions such as breathing and circulation.

meek (mēk) *adj.* Showing patience and a gentle disposition; lacking spirit or backbone; submissive. **meekly** *adv.* **meekness** *n.*

meet (mēt) *v.* To come upon; to encounter; to come into conjunction or contact with someone or something; to cope or deal with; to handle; to fulfill an obligation or need.

meet-ing (mē´ting) *n.* An assembly or gathering of persons; a coming together.

meg-a-bucks *n., Slang* One million dollars; a lot of money.

meg-a-hertz *n. pl.* **-hertz** *Physics.* One million cycles per second, used as a radio-frequency unit.

meg-a-lo-ma-ni-a (meg´a lō mā´nēa) *n.* A mental disorder marked by fantasies of power, wealth, or omnipotence. **megalomaniac** *n.* **megalomaniacal** *adj.*

meg-a-lop-o-lis (meg´a lop´o lis) *n.* A very large urban complex.

meg-a-phone (meg´a fōn´) *n.* A funnel-shaped device which is used to amplify or direct the voice.

meg-a-ton (meg´a tun´) *n.* One million tons; the unit equal to the explosive power of one million tons of TNT.

meg-a-watt (meg´a wot´) *n.* A unit of electrical power equal to one million watts.

mei-o-sis (mī ō´sis) *n., Biol.* The process by which undeveloped sex cells, sperm and ovum, mature by reduction division so that they contain only half of the full number of chromosomes. **meiotic** *adj.*

mel-an-cho-li-a (mel´an kō´lē a) *n., Psychi.* A mental disorder of great depression of spirits and excessive brooding without apparent cause. **melancholiac** *n.*

mel-an-chol-ic (mel´an kol´ik) *adj.* Depressed; sad.

mel-an-chol-y (mel´an kol´ē) *adj.* Excessively gloomy or sad.

me-lange (mā länzh´) *n.* A medley or mixture.

mel-a-nin (mel´a nin) *n., Biochem.* The brownish-black pigment which is contained in animal tissues, as the hair and skin.

mel-a-nism (mel´a niz´um) *n.* An abnormally dark pigmentation of the skin.

mel-a-no-ma (mel´a nō´ma) *n. pl.* **-mas** *or*-**mata** A dark-colored tumor or malignant mole.

Mel-ba toast (mel´ba tōst´) *n.* Very thinly sliced bread which is toasted until brown and crisp.

meld (meld) *v.* In pinochle and other card games, to declare or announce a combination of cards for inclusion in one's total score. *n.* The card or combination of cards declared for a score.

me-lee (mā´lā) *n.* The confused and tumultuous mingling of a crowd.

mel-io-rate (mel´ya rāt´) *v* To cause to improve or to make better. **meliorative** *& n.* **melioration** *n.*

mel-lif-er-ous (me lif´ėr us) *adj.* Producing or bearing honey.

mel-lo *adj.* Sweet and soft; rich and full-flavored; rich and soft in quality, as in sounds or colors.

me-lo-di-ous (me lō´dē us) *adj.* Characterized by a melody; tuneful; pleasant to hear. **melodiously** *adv.*

mel-o-dra-ma (mel´o drä´ma) *n.* A very dramatic presentation which is marked by suspense and romantic sentiment; sensational and highly emotional language or behavior. **melodramatic** *adj.* **melodramatically** *adv.*

mel-o-dy (mel´o dē) *n. pl.* **-ies** An agreeable succession of pleasing sounds. **melodic** *adj.* **melodically** *adv.*

mel-on (mel´on) *n.* The large fruit of any of various plants of the gourd family, as the watermelon.

melt (melt) *v.* To change from a solid to a liquid as a result of pressure or heat.

melt-down *n.* The melting of a nuclear-reactor core.

melting pot *n.* A place where immigrants of different cultures or races are assimilated.

mem-ber (mem´bẻr) *n.* A person who belongs to a society, party, club, or other organization. *Biol.* An organ or part of an animal or person's body, especially a limb.

mem-ber-ship (mem´bẻr ship´) *n.* The state or fact of being a member.

mem-brane (mem´brān) *n.* A thin, pliable, sheet-like layer of tissue which covers body surfaces and separates or connects body-parts. **membranous** *adj.*

me-men-to (me men´tō) *n. pl.* -tos *or* -toes A keepsake.

mem-o (mem´ō) *n.* A memorandum.

mem-oir (mem´wär) *n.* Personal records or reminiscences; an autobiography.

mem-o-ra-ble (mem´ẻr a bl) *adj.* Worth remembering or noting. **memorably** *adv.*

mem-o-ran-dum (mem´o ran´dum) *n. pl.* -dums *or* -da A brief, informal note written as a reminder.

me-mo-ri-al (me mōr´ē al) *n.* Something that serves to keep in remembrance, as a person or event. *adj.* Perpetuating remembrance. **memorialize** *v.*

Memorial Day *n.* The holiday that recognizes members of the armed forces killed in wars, celebrated on the last Monday in May.

mem-o-rize (mem´o rīz´) *v.* To commit something to memory. **memorization** *n.* **memorizer** *n.*

mem-ory (mem´o rē) *n. pl.* -ries The mental function or capacity of recalling or recognizing something that has been previously learned or experienced.

men *n. pl.* The plural of man.

men-ace (men´is) *n.* Something or someone who threatens; an annoying person. **menace** *v.* **menacingly** *adv.*

me-nar-che *n.* The beginning or the first occurrence of menstruation.

mend (mend) *v.* To fix; to repair; to correct.

men-da-cious (men dā´shus) *adj.* Prone to lying; deceitful; untrue; false. **mendaciously** *adv.* **mendacity** *n.*

men-de-le-vi-um (men´de lē´vē um) *n.* A short-lived radioactive element of the actinide series, symbolized by Md.

me-ni-al (mē´nē al) *adj.* Relating to a household servant or household chores requiring little responsibility or skill. **menially** *adv.*

men-in-gi-tis (men´in jī´tis) *n., Pathol.* An inflammation of the membranes which enclose the brain and spinal cord.

me-ninx (mē´ningks) *n. pl.* **meninges** The membrane which encloses the spinal cord and brain. **meningeal** *adj.*

men-o-pause (men´o poz´) *n., Physiol.* The time of final menstruation, occurring normally between the ages of 45 and 50. **menopausal** *adj.*

men-ses (men´sēz) *n. pl.* The blood and dead cell debris which are discharged from the uterus through the vagina by women who are not pregnant; menstruation, occurring at monthly intervals between puberty and menopause.

men-stru-ate (men´strŏ āt´) *v.* To discharge the menses, approximately every 28 days. **menstrual** *adj.*

men-stru-a-tion (men´strŏ ā´shan) *n. Physiol.* The process, act, or periodical flow of bloody fluid from the uterus, also called period.

-ment *suffix* The result or product of achievement; action; process.

men-tal (men´tal) *adj.* Relating to or of the mind. **mentally** *adv.*

mental deficiency *n.* Subnormal intellectual development, marked by deficiencies ranging from impaired learning ability to social incompetence.

men-tal-i-ty (men tal´i tē) *n. pl.* -ies Mental faculties or powers; mental activity; habit of mind.

mental retardation *n.* A mental deficiency.

men-thol (men´thŏl) *n., Chem.* The white, waxy crystalline alcohol which is obtained from and has the odor of peppermint oil. **mentholated** *adj.*

men-tion (men´shan) *v.* To refer to incidentally, in passing, or briefly. **mention-**

able, mentioner *adj.*

men-tor (men´tėr) *n.* A wise and trusted person.

men-u (men´ū) *n.* A list of food or dishes available at a restaurant; in computer science, a list of options displayed on the screen from which the operator may choose.

me-ow (mē ou´) *n.* The cry of a cat.

me-phi-tis (me fī´tis) *n.* A sickening or foul smell; a stench emitted from the earth.

mer-can-tile (mer´kan tēl´) *adj.* Of or relating to merchants, trading, or commerce.

mer-ce-nar-y (mer´se ner´ē) *n.* A person who is concerned only with making money and obtaining material gain; a person paid to serve as a soldier in a foreign country. **mercenary** *adj.*

mer-cer-ize (mer´se rīz´) *v.* To treat cotton yarn or thread with sodium hydroxide so as to give strength and receptiveness to dyes.

mer-chan-dise (mer´chan dīz´) *n.* Commodities or goods that are bought and sold. *v.* To buy and sell.

mer-chant (mer´chant) *n.* A person who operates a retail business for profit.

mer-chant-man (mer´chant man) *n.* A ship used for commercial shipments.

mer-cu-ry (mŭr´kū rē) *n.* A silvery, metallic, liquid element used in thermometers and barometers, symbolized by Hg.

mer-cy (mer´sē) *n. pl.* **-ies** Compassionate and kind treatment. **merciful** *adj.* **merciless** *adj.* **mercifully** *adv.* **mercilessly** *adv.*

mere (mēr) *adj.* Absolute; no more than what is stated. **merest** *adj.* **merely** *adv.*

merge (merj) *v.* To unite or bring together as one; in computer science, to combine two or more files into one, retaining the internal order of both.

merger (mer´jėr) *n.* The act of combining two or more corporations into one.

me-ringue (me rang´) *n.* A mixture of stiffly beaten egg whites and sugar, used as a topping for cakes and pies or baked into crisp shells.

me-ri-no (me rē´nō) *n. pl.* **-nos** A Spanish breed of hardy, white, fine-wooled sheep;

a soft, lightweight fabric originally made of merino wool. **merino** *adj.*

mer-it (mer´it) *n.* A characteristic act or trait which is worthy of praise. *v.* To earn; to be worthy of.

mer-i-toc-ra-cy *n. pl.* **-ies** A system which bases advancement on ability or achievement.

mer-i-to-ri-ous (mer´i tōr´ē us) *adj.* Deserving honor, praise or reward. **meritoriously** *adv.*

mer-maid (mer´mād´) *n.* An imaginary sea creature having the upper body of a woman and the tail of a fish. **merman** *n.*

mer-ry (mer´ē) *adj.* Delightful; gay; entertaining; festive; happy; joyous. **merrily** *adv.* **merriness** *n.*

mer-ry–go–round (mer´ē gō round´) *n.* A circular, revolving platform often with benches and animal figures, usually found in circuses and amusement parks.

me-sa (mā´sa) *n.* A flat-topped hill or small plateau with steep sides.

mesh (mesh) *n.* Open spaces in a thread, wire or cord net; something that entraps or snares; the fitting or coming together of gear teeth for transmitting power. **mesh** *v.*

mes-mer-ize (mez´me rīz´) *v.* To hypnotize or put into a trance.

Mes-o-po-ta-mi-a *n.* The area between the Euphrates and Tigris rivers.

mes-quite (me skēt´) *n.* A thorny, deep-rooted shrub or small tree which grows in the southwestern United States and in Mexico.

mess (mes) *n. pl.* **messes** A disorderly or confused heap; a jumble; a dish or portion of soft or liquid food; a meal eaten by a group of persons, usually in the military.

mes-sage (mes´ij) *n.* Any information, command, or news transmitted from one person to another.

mes-sen-ger (mes´en jėr) *n.* A person who carries a message or does an errand for another person or company.

Mes-si-ah (mi sī´a) *n.* The anticipated or expected king of the Jews; Jesus Christ.

mess-y *adj.* Untidy; upset; dirty; lacking neatness. **messily** *adv.* **messiness** *n.*

met *v.* Past tense of meet.

me-tab-o-lism (me tab´o liz´um) *n.* The chemical and physical changes in living cells which involve the maintenance of life. **metabolic** *adj.*

meta-car-pus (met´a kăr´pus) *n.* The part of the forefoot or hand which connects the bones of the toes or fingers to the ankle or wrist.

met-a-gal-ax-y (met´a gal´ak sē) *n.* The universe; the entire system of galaxies.

metal (met´al) *n.* One of a category of opaque, fusible, ductile, and typically lustrous elements. **metallic** *adj.* **metallically** *adv.*

met-al-lur-gy (met´a ler´jē) *n.* The technology and science which studies methods of extracting metals from their ores and of preparing them for use. **metallurgical** *adj.* **metallurgist** *n.*

met-a-mor-pho-sis (met´a mor´fo sis) *n.* The transformation and change in the structure and habits of an animal during normal growth, as the metamorphosis of a tadpole into a frog. **metamorphism** *n.* **metamorphose** *v.*

met-a-phor (met´a for´) *n.* A figure of speech in which the context demands that a word or phrase not be taken literally, as the sun is smiling; a comparison which doesn't use like or as.

me-tas-ta-sis (me tas´ta sis) *n.* A spread of cancer cells from the original tumor to one or more additional sites within the body. **metastasize** *v.* **metastatic** *adj.*

met-a-tar-sus (met´a tăr´sus) *n. pl.* **-si** The part of the human foot which forms the instep and contains five bones between the ankle and the toes; the hind foot of four-legged animals. **metatarsal** *adj.*

me-te-or (mē´tē ėr) *n.* A moving particle in the solar system which appears as a trail or streak in the sky as it comes into contact with the atmosphere of the earth.

me-te-or-ic (mē´tē or´ik) *adj.* Of or relating to a meteor or meteors; resembling a meteor in speed, brilliance, or brevity.

me-te-or-ite (mē´tē o rīt´) *n.* A stony or metallic mass of a meteor which reaches the earth after partially burning in the atmosphere.

me-te-or-ol-o-gy (mē´tē o rol´ojē) *n.* The science concerned with the study of weather, weather conditions and weather forecasting. **meteorological** *adj.* **meteorologic** *adj.* **meteorologically** *adv.* **meteorologist** *n.*

me-ter (mē´tėr) *n.* The arrangement of words, syllables, or stanzas in verse or poetry; a measure equaling 39.37 inches.

meth-a-done (meth´a dōn´) *n.* A man-made narcotic used in the treatment of heroin addiction.

meth-ane (meth´ān) *n.* A colorless, odorless flammable gas used as a fuel; a product of the decomposition of organic matter.

meth-a-nol (meth´a nōl´) *n.* A colorless, odorless flammable alcohol that is used as an antifreeze, as a fuel, and as a raw material in chemical synthesis.

me-thinks (mi thingks´) *v.* It seems to me.

meth-od (meth´od) *n.* A manner, a process, or the regular way of doing something; the orderly arrangement, development, or classification. **methodical** *adj.* **methodic** *adj.* **methodically** *adv.*

Meth-od-ist (meth´o dist) *n.* A member of a Protestant denomination which was developed from a religious club formed by John and Charles Wesley in 1729. **Methodism** *n.* **Methodist** *adj.*

Methuselah (me thŏ´ze la) *n.* A Biblical ancestor of Noah who is said to have lived to the age of 969.

meth-yl (meth´il) *n.* An alkyl radical derived from methane which occurs in several organic compounds.

me-tic-u-lous (me tik´ū lus) *adj.* Very precise; careful; concerned with small details. **meticulously** *adv.* **meticulousness** *n.*

me-tis (mā tēs´) *n.* A person of mixed blood, usually of French and Indian ancestry.

met-ric (me´trik) *adj.* Of or relating to the metric system. **metrical** *adj.* **metrication** *n.*

metric system *n.* A decimal system of weights and measures based on the meter as a unit of length and the kilogram as a unit of mass, originated in France around 1790.

met-ri-fy (me´tri fi´) *v.* To adopt or convert to the metric system. **metrification** *n.*

met-ro (me´trō) *n.* A subway system for transportation.

met-ro-nome (me´tro nōm´) *n.* An instrument designed to mark time by means of a series of clicks at exact intervals. **metronomic** *adj.*

me-trop-o-lis (me trop´o lis) *n.* A large or capital city of a state, region, or country. **metropolitan** *adj.*

mew (mū) *n.* A hideaway; a secret place.

Mexico *n.* A large country located in south western North America.

mez-za-nine (mez´a nēn´) *n.* A low story between two main stories of a building; the lowest balcony in a theatre.

mfg *abbr.* Manufacturing.

mfr *abbr.* Manufacturer.

MI *abbr.* Michigan.

mi *abbr.* Mile; miles.

MIA *abbr.* Missing in action.

mice *pl. n.* The plural of mouse.

Michelangelo *n.* Italian Renaissance painter and sculptor.

Mich-i-gan *n.* A state located in the mid-western part of the United States; statehood January 26, 1837; state capital Lansing.

mi-crobe (mī´krōb) *n.* A germ, plant, or animal so small that is can be seen only with the aid of a microscope.

mi-cro-bi-ol-o-gy (mī´krō bī ol´ojē) *n.* The scientific study of microorganisms. **microbiological** *adj.* **microbiologist** *n.*

mi-cro-ceph-a-ly *n.* A condition of abnormal smallness of the head, usually associated with mental defects.

mi-cro-cir-cuit *n.* An electronic circuit composed of very small components.

mi-cro-com-put-er *n.* A computer which uses a microprocessor.

mi-cro-film (mī´kro film´) *n.* A film used to photograph printed matter at a greatly reduced size.

micro-or-gan-ism (mī´krō or´ganiz´um) *n.* An organism too small to see without the aid of a microscope.

mi-cro-phone (mī´kro fōn´) *n.* An instrument which converts acoustical waves into electrical signals and feeds them into a recorder, amplifier or broadcasting transmitter. **microphonic** *adj.*

mi-cro-proc-es-sor *n.* In Computer Science, a semiconductor processing unit which is contained on an integrated circuit chip.

mi-cro-scope (mī´kro skōp´) *n.* An optical instrument consisting of a lens or combination of lenses, used to produce magnified images of very small objects.

mi-cro-scop-ic (mī´kro skop´ik) *adj.* Too small to be seen by the eye alone. **microscopical** *adv.*

mi-cro-sur-ger-y *n.* Surgery performed by means of a microscope and laser beam. **microsurgical** *adj.*

mi-cro-wave (mī´krō wāv´) *n.* A very short electromagnetic wave.

microwave oven *n.* An oven which uses microwaves to heat and cook food.

mid (mid) *adj.* In the middle or center; central.

mid-air *n.* A point in the air just above the ground surface.

mid-day (mid´dā´) *n.* Noon; the middle of the day.

mid-den *n.* A refuse heap or dunghill.

mid-dle (mid´l) *adj.* Being equally distant from extremes or limits; the central. *n.* Anything which occupies a middle position; the waist.

middle age *n.* A period of life from about 40 to 60 years.

Middle Ages *n. pl.* The period of European history from about 500 to 1500.

Middle America *n.* The midwestern states of the United States; the class of American citizens with conservative values and attitudes, considered to have an average income and education. **Middle American** *adj.*

middle class (mid´l klas´) *n.* The social class of people between a high income and low income status.

middle ear *n.* A small membrane-lined cavity between the tympanic membrane and the inner ear through which sound waves are carried.

middle-man (mid´l man´) *n.* A person who serves as an agent between the producer of a product and the consumer.

middle school *n.* A school which usually includes grades 6, 7, and 8.

mid-dle-weight (mid´l wāt´) *n.* A boxer weighing between 148 and 160 pounds.

midg-et (mij´it) *n.* A very small person.

mid-i *n., Slang* A dress, skirt, or coat which extends to the calf.

mid-night (mid´nīt´) *n.* 12 o'clock p.m.; the middle of the night.

mid-point (mid´point´) *n.* A point at or near the middle.

mid-riff (mid´rif) *n.* The mid-section of the human torso; the diaphragm.

mid-ship-man (mid´ship´man) *n.* A person in training for a naval commission; a student at the United States Naval Academy.

midst (midst) *n.* The central or middle part or position; a person positioned among others in a group.

mid-sum-mer (mid´sum´ér) *n.* The middle of summer.

mid-term (mid´term´) *n.* The middle of an academic term.

mid-way (mid´wā´) *n.* The section of a carnival or fair where shows and rides are located.

mid-week (mid´wēk´) *n.* The middle of a calendar week.

mid-wife (mid´wīf´) *n.* A woman who gives assistance in the birth of a baby. **mid-wifery** *n.*

mid-win-ter (mid´win´tér) *n.* The middle of the winter months.

mid-year (mid´yēr´) *n.* The middle of a calendar year; academic examinations which are given in the middle of the academic year.

miff (mif) *n.* Ill humor; displeasure. **miff** *v.*

might (mīt) *n.* Force, power, or physical strength. *v.* To indicate a present condition contrary to fact; to ask permission politely.

might-y (mī´tē) *adj.* Showing or having great power.

mi-graine (mī´grān) *n.* A condition of severe, recurring headaches often accompanied by nausea.

mi-grant (mī´grant) *n.* A person who moves from one place to another to find work in the fields.

mi-grate (mī´grāt) *v.* To move from one place to another or from one climate to another. **migration** *n.* **migrational** *adj.* **migratory** *adj.*

mike (mīk) *n., Slang* Microphone.

mil (mil) *n.* A unit of measure equal to 1/1000 of an inch, used in measuring wire.

mild (mild) *adj.* Gentle in manner, behavior, or disposition; not severe or extreme. **mildly** *adv.* **mildness** *n.*

mil-dew (mil´dō´) *n.* A fungal growth which is usually white in color. **mildew** *v.* **mildewy** *adj.*

mile (mīl) *n.* A unit of measurement equaling 5,280 feet.

mile-age (mī´lij) *n.* The distance traveled or measured in miles; an allowance given for traveling expenses at a set rate per mile; the average distance of miles a vehicle will travel on a gallon of gas.

mile-post (mīl´pōst´) *n.* A number posted along the side of a highway indicating the distance to a given place, also called a mile marker.

mile-stone (mīl´stōn´) *n.* A stone marker

serving as a millpost; an important point in development or progress.

mil-i-tant (mil´i tant) *adj.* Engaged in warfare or combat; aggressive. **militancy** *n.* **militant** *n.*

mil-i-ta-rize (mil´i ta rīz´) *v.* To train or equip for war.

mil-i-tar-y (mil´i ter´ē) *adj.* Of or related to arms, war, or soldiers. *n.* A nation's armed forces. **militarily** *adv.*

mi-li-tia (mi lish´a) *n.* A military service or armed forces called upon in case of an emergency.

milk (milk) *n.* A whitish fluid produced by the mammary glands of all mature female mammals as a source of food for their young. *v.* To draw milk from the breast or udder. *Slang* To take advantage of every possibility in a given situation. **milkiness** *n.* **milky** *adj.*

milk glass *n.* An opaque glassware used especially for ornamental and novelty objects.

milk of magnesia *n.* A milk-white liquid suspension of magnesium hydroxide, used as an antacid and laxative.

milk shake *n.* A refreshing drink made from milk flavoring and ice cream, which is thoroughly blended or shaken.

milk-sop (milk´sop´) *n.* A man who lacks manly qualities.

milk-weed (milk´wēd´) *n.* Any of various plants which secrete latex and have pointed pods that open to release seeds and downy flowers.

Milky Way (mil´kē) *n.* The broad, luminous galaxy in which the solar system is located.

mill (mil) *n.* A building housing machinery for grinding grain into meal or flour; any of various machines which grind, crush, or press; a unit of money which equals 1/1000 of a United States dollar. *v.* To grind. **miller** A person who operates, works, or owns a grain mill; a moth whose wings are covered with a powdery substance.

mil-li-ner (mil´i nėr) *n.* Someone who designs, sells, or makes women's hats.

mil-lion (mil´yon) *n.* A very large number

equal to 1,000 x 1,000. **millionth** *adj.* **million** *adj.*

mil-lion-aire (mil´ya när´) *n.* A person whose wealth is estimated at $1,000,000 or more.

mime (mīm) *v.* To act a part or performance without using words. *n.* An actor who portrays a part, emotion, or situation using only gestures and body language. **mimer** *n.*

mim-e-o-graph (mim´ē o graf´) *n.* A duplicating machine that makes duplicates of typed or drawn information from a stencil through which ink is pressed.

mim-ic (mim´ik) *v.* To imitate another person's behavior or speech.

mince (mins) *v.* To cut or chop something into small pieces.

mince-meat (mins´mēt´) *n.* A pie filling made from spiced raisins, apples, and meat that have been cut into small pieces.

mind (mīnd) *n.* The element of a human being which controls perception, thought, feeling, memory, and imagination. *v.* To obey; to take care of; to bring; to remember; to object to.

mind-less *adj.* Destitute of consciousness or mind.

mine (mīn) *n.* A pit or underground excavation from which metals or coal can be uncovered and removed. The one that belongs to me. **mine** *v.* **miner** *n.*

mine *pron.* The one that belongs to me.

mine-lay-er *n.* A navy ship used to lay underwater mines.

min-er-al (min´ėr al) *n.* A solid inorganic substance, such as silver, diamond, or quartz, which is taken from the earth. **mineral** *adj.* **mineralize** *v.*

min-e-stro-ne (min´i strō´nē) *n.* A very thick vegetable soup that may contain pasta and beans.

mine-sweep-er *n.* A warship used to neutralize or remove mines by dragging the bottom.

min-gle (ming´gl) *v.* To mix or come together. **mingler** *n.*

min-i-a-ture (min´ē a chėr) *n.* A copy or

model of something that has been greatly reduced in size.

min-i-com-put-er *n.* In computer science, a computer designed on a very small scale.

mini-disk *n.* Computer Science The 5 1/4 inch floppy disk which is used for storing information.

min-i-mize *v.* To reduce something to a minimum.

min-i-mum (min´*i* m*u*m) *n. pl.* **-ums** or **-uma** The least, smallest, or lowest a-mount, degree, number, or position.

mini-skirt *n.* A woman's skirt that has a hemline several inches above the knee.

min-is-ter (min´i stėr) *n.* The pastor of a Protestant church; a high officer of state who is in charge of a governmental division.

mink (mingk) *n. pl.*
mink or **minks** A semiaquatic animal of the weasel family whose thick, lustrous fur is used for making fur coats.

Min-nes-o-ta *n.* A state located in the central part of the United States; statehood May 11, 1858; state capital St. Paul.

min-now (min´ō) *n.* A small, freshwater fish used as bait.

mi-nor (mī´nėr) *adj.* Not of legal age; lesser in degree, size or importance.

mi-nor-i-ty (mi nor´i tē) *n. pl.* **-ies** The smaller in number of two groups making a whole; a part of the population that differs, as in race, sex, or religion.

min-ster (min´stėr) *n.* A large cathedral or church.

min-strel (min´strel) *n.* A medieval traveling musician or poet.

mint (mint) *n.* A place where coins are made by a government; any of a variety of aromatic plants used for flavoring; candy flavored by such a plant. **minty** *adj.*

min-u-end (min´ū end´) *n.* A number of quantity from which another is to be subtracted.

min-u-et (min´ū et´) *n.* A slow, stately dance.

mi-nus (mī´n*u*s) *prep.* Reduced, by

subtraction. *n.* The minus sign (-); a negative number.

mi-nus-cule (min´*u* skūl´) *n.* Rather dim, or small in size.

min-ute (min´it) *n.* The unit of time which equals 60 seconds.

mi-nute (mī nŏt´) *adj.* Extremely small in size.

mir-a-cle (mir´*a* kl) *n.* A supernatural event or happening regarded as an act of God.

mi-rage (mi räzh´) *n.* An optical illusion in which nonexistent bodies of water with reflections of objects are seen.

mire (mīėr) *n.* Soil or heavy mud.

mir-ror (mir´ėr) *n.* A surface of glass which reflectslight, forming the image of an object.

mirth (merth) *n.* Merriment or joyousness expressed by laughter.

mis- *prefix* Wrong, bad, or ill.

mis-ad-ven-ture (mis´*a*d ven´chėr) *n.* An unlucky mishap; a misfortune.

mis-an-thrope (mis´*a*nthrōp´) *n.* Someone who hates mankind.

mis-ap-pre-hend (mis´ap ri hend´) *v.* To understand something incorrectly; to misunderstand. **misapprehension** *n.*

mis-ap-pro-pri-ate (mis´*a* prō´prēāt´) *v.* To embezzle money; to use wrongly for one's own benefit.

misc *abbr.* Miscellaneous.

mis-car-riage (mis kar´ij) *n.* The premature birth of a fetus from the uterus.

mis-ce-ge-na-tion (mis´i j*e* nā´sh*a*n) *n.* The marriage between two people of different races.

mis-cel-la-ne-ous (mis´*e* lā´nē us) *adj.* Consisting of a mixed variety of parts, elements, or characteristics.

mis-chance (mis chans´) *n.* Bad luck or mishap.

mis-chief (mis´chif) *n.* Behavior which causes harm, damage, or annoyance.

mis-chie-vous (mis´ch*i* vus) *adj.* Tending to behave in a play fullyannoying way. **mischievously** *adv.*

mis-ci-ble (mis´i bl) *adj., Chem.* Capable of being mixed. **miscibility** *n.*

mis-con-ceive (mis´kon sēv´) v. To misunderstand the meaning. **misconceiver** n. **misconception** n.

mis-con-duct (mis kon´dukt) n. Improper conduct or behavior; bad management.

mis-count (mis kount´) v. To count incorrectly; to miscalculate.

mis-cre-ant (mis´krē ant) n. A person who is involved in criminal or evil acts; a heretic. **miscreant** adj.

mis-cue (mis kū´) n. An error; a mistake.

mis-deed (mis dēd´) n. A wrong or improper act; an evil deed.

mis-de-mean-or (mis´di mē´nėr) n., Law A crime-less serious than a felony.

mis-er (mī´zėr) n. A person who hoards money; a person who lives a meager life in order to hoard his money.

mis-er-a-ble (miz´ėr a bl) adj. Very uncomfortable or unhappy; causing misery. **miserableness** n. **miserably** adv.

mis-er-y (miz´e rē) n. A state of great unhappiness, distress, or pain.

mis-feed n. In computer science, the failure of paper or other media to pass through a printer or other device properly.

mis-fire (mis fīėr´) v. To fail to explode, ignite, or fire. **misfire** n.

mis-fit (mis fit´) n. A person who is not adjusted to his environment; anything which does not fit correctly.

mis-for-tune (mis for´chan) n. Bad luck or fortune.

mis-giv-ing (mis giv´ing) n. A feeling of doubt.

mis-guide (mis gīd´) v. To guide incorrectly; to misdirect. **misguidance** n. **misguidedly** adv.

mis-han-dle (mis han´dl) v. To handle clumsily; to manage inefficiently.

mis-hap (mis´hap) n. An unfortunate accident; bad luck.

mish-mash (mish´mash´) n. A jumble or hodgepodge.

mis-in-ter-pret (mis´in ter´prit) v. To understand or explain incorrectly. **misinterpretation** n.

mis-judge (mis juj´) v. To make a mistake in judgment **misjudgment** n.

mis-lay (mis lā´) v. To lose; to put something in a place and not remember where.

mis-lead (mis lēd´) v. To lead in a wrong direction; to deliberately deceive. **misleader** n. **misleading** adj.

mis-no-mer (mis nō´mėr) n. A wrong or inappropriate name.

mis-pro-nounce (mis´pro nouns´) v. To pronounce a word incorrectly.

mi-sog-a-my (mi sog a mē) n. Hatred of marriage.

mi-sog-y-ny (mi soj´i nē) n. Hatred of women.

mis-place (mis plās´) v. To mislay; to put in a wrong place.

mis-read (mis rēd´) v. To read or interpret incorrectly.

mis-rep-re-sent (mis´rep ri zent´) v. To represent wrongly, misleadingly, or falsely. **misrepresentation** n.

mis-rule (mis rōl´) n. Misruling; the condition of being misruled; disorder.

Miss (mis) n. The proper title for an unmarried woman or girl. v. To fail to hit, reach, or make contact with something; to omit; to feel the absence or loss of.

mis-sal (mis´al) n. A book containing prayers and services, used in the Roman Catholic Church throughout the year.

mis-shape (mis shāp´) v. To deform; to shape badly; to distort. **misshapen** adj.

mis-sile (mis´il) n. An object that is thrown or shot at a target. **missilery** n.

mis-sion (mish´an) n. An instance or the act of sending; an assignment or task to be carried out.

mis-sion-ar-y (mish´a ner´ē) n. pl. -ies A person sent to do religious or charitable work, usually in a foreign country.

Miss-i-ssip-pi n. A state located in the south central part of the United States; statehood December 10, 1817; state capital Jackson.

Miss-ou-ri n. A state located in the central part of the United States; statehood August 10, 1821; state capital Jefferson

City.

mis-spell (mis spel´) v. To spell a word incorrectly. **misspelling** n.

mis-take (mi stāk´) n. A wrong statement, action, or decision. **mistaken** adj. **mistakable** adj. **mistakably** adv. **mistake** v.

Mis-ter (mis´tėr) n. A courtesy title used before a man's name, abbreviated as Mr.

mis-tle-toe (mis´l tō´) n. A parasitic plant with thick leaves, small yellowish flowers and white berries.

mis-treat (mis trēt´) v. To treat badly or wrongly. **mistreatment** n.

mis-tress (mis´tris) n. A woman having authority, ownership, or a position of control; a woman having a sexual relationship with a man who is not her husband.

mis-tri-al (mis trī´al) n. A trial that is invalid because of an error during the procedure.

mis-trust (mis trust´) v. To have doubt; to lack trust in something or someone. **mistrust** n. **mistrustful** adj. **mistrustfully** adv.

mis-un-der-stand (mis´un dėr stand´) v. To interpret incorrectly; to fail to understand.

mite (mīt) n. A very small insect; a small amount of money.

mi-ter (mī´tėr) n. A joint made by cutting two pieces at an angle and then fitting them together.

mit-i-gate (mit´i gāt´) v. To make or become less severe or painful.

mi-to-sis (mī tō´sis) n. pl. **mitoses** A process of cell division in which chromatin divides into chromosomes.

mitt (mit) n. A women's glove that covers only the wrist and hand, leaving the fingers exposed; in baseball, a glove for a catcher or first baseman made in the style of a mitten.

mix (miks) v. To blend or combine into one; to come or bring together. **mixable** adj.

mixed number n. A number representing the sum of an integer and a fraction, such as 5 1/2.

mix-ture (miks´chėr) n. The state of being mixed; the process or act of mixing; a combination of two or more substances.

mix-up (miks´up´) n. An instance or state of confusion.

MN abbr. Minnesota.

MO abbr. Missouri.

mo abbr. Money order; mail order.

moan (mōn) n. A very low, dull sound indicative of pain or grief. v. To make a moan.

moat (mōt) n. A deep and wide trench surrounding a castle, usually filled with water.

mob (mob) n. A large, unruly crowd. v. To overcrowd.

mo-bi-lize (mō´bi līz´) v. To put into motion; to make ready. **mobilization** n.

moc-ca-sin (mok´a sin) n. A heelless shoe or slipper made of a soft leather.

mo-cha (mō´ka) n. An Arabian coffee of superior quality; a flavoring with coffee, often used with chocolate.

mock (mok) v. To treat with contempt or scorn; to imitate a mannerism or sound closely; to mimic. adv. In an insincere manner. n. An imitation; a copy. **mockingly** adv.

mock-er-y (mok´e rē) n. pl. **-ies** Insulting or contemptuous action or speech; a subject of laughter or sport; a false or counterfeit appearance; something that's ridiculous.

mock–he-ro-ic (mok´hi rō´ik) n. A satirical imitation of the heroic manner or style.

mock-ing-bird (mok´ing berd´) n. A common bird that is remarkable for its exact imitations of the notes of other birds.

mock-up or **mock–up (mok´up´)** n. A model of a structure used for study, testing, or demonstration.

mod n. A modern and unusual style of dress. adj. Modern.

mode (mōd) *n.* A way or method of doing something; a particular manner or form; the value or score that occurs most frequently in a set of data; the current fashion or style, as in dress.

mod-el (mod´el) *n.* A small representation of an object; a pattern that something will be based on; a design or type; one serving as an example; one who poses for an artist or photographer. **model** *v.* **modeler** *n.*

mod-er-ate (mod´ėr it) *adj.* Not excessive; tending toward the mean or average extent or quality; opposed to extreme political views. **moderate** *v.* **moderation** *n.*

mod-er-a-tor (mod´e rā´tėr) *n.* A person who moderates; a person who presides over a discussion or meeting but takes no sides.

mod-ern (mod´ėrn) *adj.* Typical of the recent past or the present; advanced or up-to-date. **modern** *n.* **modernity** *n.* **modernly** *adv.*

mod-ern-ism (mod´ėr niz´um) *n.* A thought, action, or belief characteristic of modern times. **modernistic** *adj.*

mod-ern-ize (mod´ėr nīz´) *v.* To make or become modern. **modernization** *n.*

mod-est (mod´ist) *adj.* Placing a moderate estimate on one's abilities or worth; retiring or reserved; limited in size or a-mount. **modesty** *n.*

mod-i-cum (mod´i kum) *n.* A small amount.

mod-i-fy (mod´i fī´) *v.* To alter; to make different in character or form; to change to less extreme; to moderate. **modified** *adj.* **modifiable** *adj.* **modification** *n.* **modifier** *n.*

mod-ish (mō´dish) *adj.* Fashionable. **modishly** *adv.* **modishness** *n.*

mo-diste (mō dēst´) *n.* A person dealing in fashionable clothing for women.

mod-u-late (moj´u lāt´) *v.* To soften; to temper; to vary the intensity of. *Music* To change from one key to another; to vary the tone or intensity of. **modulation** *n.* **modulator** *n.* **modulative** *adj.* **modulatory** *adj.*

mod-ule (moj´öl) *n.* One of a series of standardized components which work

together in a system. *Electr.* A self-contained subassembly of electronic components, as a computer stage; the self-contained area of a spacecraft for performing a particular task. **modular** *adj.*

mod-us op-er-an-di (mō´dus op´eran´dī) *n.* A method of operating or proceeding.

mod-us vi-ven-di (mō´dus vi ven´dī) *n.* A compromise which avoids difficulties.

mo-gul (mō´gul) *n.* A very great or important person; a small hill or bump of ice and snow on a ski slope.

mo-hair (mō´hâr´) *n.* The fabric or yarn made from the silky hair of the Angora goat.

Mo-ham-med *n.* The Arab founder of Islam.

Mo-ham-med-an (mō ham´i dan) *adj.* Moslem. **Mohammedan** *n.* **Mohammedanism** *n.*

Mohs scale (mōz´ skāl´) *n.* A scale that classifies the hardness of minerals ranging from one for the softest, which is talc, to fifteen for the hardest, which is diamond.

moi-e-ty (moi´e tē) *n. pl.* **-ies** A half; any portion; part or share.

moil (moil) *v.* To work hard; to drudge. **moil** *n.*

moi-re (mwä rā´) *n.* Fabric, especially silk or rayon having a wavy pattern.

moist (moist) *adj.* Slightly wet; damp; saturated with moisture or liquid. **moistly** *adv.* **moistness** *n.*

mois-ten (moi´sen) *v.* To make or become moist or slightly wet. **moistener** *n.*

mois-ture (mois´chėr) *n.* Liquid diffused or condensed in a relatively small quantity; dampness. **moisturize** *v.* **moisturizer** *n.*

Mo-ja-ve *or* **Mo-ha-ve** *n.* A desert region located in southern California.

mol (mōl) *abbr.* Molecular; molecule.

mo-lar (mō´lėr) *n.* A grinding tooth which has a broad surface for grinding food, located in the back of the mouth. **molar** *adj.*

mo-las-ses (mo las´iz) *n.* A thick, dark syrup produced when sugar is refined.

mold (mōld) *n.* A superficial, often woolly growth produced on damp or decaying organic matter or on living organisms; a fungus that produces such a growth; crumbling, soft, pliable earth suited to plant growth; distinctive nature or character; the frame on or around which an object is constructed; a cavity in which an object is shaped; general shape; form. **mold moldable** *adj.*

mold-board (mōld´bōrd´) *n.* The curved blade of a plow.

mold-er (mōl´dėr) *v.* To crumble or decay gradually and turn to dust.

mole (mōl) *n.* A pigmented spot or mark on the human skin; a small, insectivorous mammal that lives mostly underground  and has an arrow snout, small eyes, and silky fur; a large wall of stone or masonry used as a breakwater or pier.

mo-lec-u-lar (mō lek´ū lėr) *adj.* Of, relating to, or caused by molecules.

molecular biology *n.* The branch of biology dealing with the structure and development of biological systems which are studied in terms of their molecular constituents. **molecular biologist** *n.*

mol-e-cule (mol´e kūl´) *n.* The simplest structural unit into which a substance can be divided and still retain its identity.

mole-hill (mōl´hil´) *n.* A small ridge of earth thrown up by a mole.

mole-skin (mōl´skin´) *n.* The dark gray pelt of the mole; a heavy, durable cotton fabric with a short, thick velvety nap on one side.

mo-lest (mo lest´) *v.* To bother, annoy, or persecute; to accost sexually. **molestation** *n.* **molester** *n.*

mol-li-fy (mol´i fi´) *v.* To make less angry; to soften; to make less intense or severe. **mollification** *n.*

mol-lusk *or* **mol-lusc** (mol´usk) *n.* Any of various largely marine invertebrates, including the edible shellfish.

mol-ly-cod-dle (mol´ē kod´l) *v.* To spoil by pampering; to coddle.

Mol-o-tov cocktail (mol´o tof´kok´tāl´) *n.* A homemade, flammable bomb consisting

of a combustible liquid in a breakable bottle fitted with a rag that is ignited before the bomb is thrown.

molt (mōlt) *v.* To cast off or shed an external covering, as horns, feathers, or skin, which is periodically replaced by new growth. **molt** *n.*

mol-ten (mōl´ten) *adj.* Transformed to liquid form by heat.

mo-lyb-de-num (mo lib´de num) *n.* A hard, gray metallic element used to harden steel alloys, symbolized by Mo.

mo-men-tar-i-ly (mō´men târ´ile) *adv.* For just a moment; soon; from moment to moment.

mo-men-tar-y (mō´menter´ē) *adj.* Lasting just a moment; occurring presently or at every moment.

mo-men-tous (mō men´tus) *adj.* Of great importance or consequence; significant. **momentously** *adv.* **momentousness** *n.*

mo-men-tum (mō men´tum) *n.* *pl.* **-ta** *or* **-tums** A property of a moving body which determines the length of time required to bring it to rest when under the action of a constant force.

Mon *abbr.* Monday.

mon-arch (mon´ark) *n.* A person who reigns over a kingdom or empire; a large orange and black butterfly. **monarchic** *adj.* **monarchical** *adj.*

mon-ar-chism (mon´ėr kiz´um) *n.* The principles or system of a monarchic government. **monarchist** *n.* **monarchistic** *adj.*

mon-ar-chy (mon´ėr kē) *n.* *pl.* **-chies** Government by a monarch; sovereign control; a government or nation ruled by a monarch.

mon-as-ter-y (mon´a ster´ē) *n.* *pl.* **-ies** A house for persons under religious vows. **monasterial** *adj.*

mo-nas-tic (mo nas´tik) *adj.* Of, relating to, or typical of monasteries, monks, or life in monasteries.

mo-nas-ti-cism (mo nas´ti siz´um) *n.* The monastic lifestyle or system.

mon-au-ral (mon är´al) *adj.* Of or relating

to a system of transmitting or recording sound by techniques in which one or more sources are channeled into one carrier.

Mon-day (mun´dē) *n.* The second day of the week.

Monet, Claude *n.* (1840-1926) French Impressionist painter.

mon-e-tar-y (mon´i ter´ē) *adj.* Of or relating to money or how it is circulated. **monetarily** *adv.*

mon-ey (mun´ē) *n.* Anything which has or is assigned value and is used as a medium of exchange.

mon-ey-lend-er *n.* Someone whose business is lending money to others with interest.

mon-ger (mung´gėr) *n.* One who attempts to stir up or spread something that is undesirable; one who deals.

Mon-gol (mong´gol) *n.* A native or inhabitant of Mongolia; a member of one of the chiefly pastoral Mongoloid peoples of Mongolia.

Mon-go-li-a *n.* A region of Asia that extends from Siberia to northern China; a country in Asia.

Mon-go-li-an (mong gō´lē an) *n.* A native or inhabitant of Mongolia; a member of the Mongoloid ethnic division. **Mongolian** *adj.*

Mon-gol-ism (mong´go liz´um) *n.* Down's syndrome.

Mon-gol-oid (mong´go loid´) *adj.* Of, constituting, or characteristic of a people native to Asia, including peoples of northern and eastern Asia, Malaysians, Eskimos, and American Indians. **Mongoloid** Of, affected with, or pertaining to Down's syndrome. **Mongoloid** *n.*

mon-goose (mong´gōs´) *n. pl.* **-ses** A chiefly African or Asian mammal which has the ability to kill venomous snakes.

mon-grel (mung´grel) *n.* An animal or plant, especially a dog, produced by interbreeding.

mo-ni-tion (mō nish´an) *n.* A caution or warning, as for an impending danger.

mon-i-tor (mon´i tėr) *n.* A student assigned to assist a teacher; a receiver used to view the picture being picked up by a television

camera; the image being generated by a computer. **monitorial** *adj.*

mon-i-to-ry (mon´i tōr´ē) *adj.* Giving a caution or conveying a warning.

monk (mungk) *n.* A man who is a member of a religious order and lives in a monastery. **monkish** *adj.* **monkishly** *adv.*

monkey (mung´kē) *n. pl.* **-keys** A member of the older primates, excluding man, having a long tail; a smaller species as distinguished from the larger apes. *v.* To play or fool around; to tamper with.

monkey wrench *n.* A tool which has one adjustable jaw. *Slang* Something that hinders or stops a normally flowing system or procedure.

monk's cloth *n.* A sturdy cotton cloth having a coarse basket weave.

monks-hood (mungks´hed´) *n.* A normally poisonous plant of the genus Aconitum, having variously colored hooded flowers.

mon-o *n.* Mononucleosis.

mon-o-chro-mat-ic (mon´o krō mat´ik) *adj.* Of, consisting of, or having one color. **monochromatically** *adv.*

mon-o-cle (mon´o kl) *n.* An eyeglass for one eye.

mon-o-cot-y-le-don (mon´o kot´ilēd´on) *n.* Any of various plants having a single embryonic seed leaf appearing at germination. **monocotyledonous** *adj.*

mo-noc-u-lar (mo nok´ū lėr) *adj.* Of, relating to, or having one eye.

mo-nog-a-my (mo nog´a mē) *n.* Marriage or sexual relationship with only one person at a time. **monogamist** *n.* **monog-amous** *adj.*

mon-o-gram (mon´o gram´) *n.* A design consisting of one or more initials. **monogram** *v.*

mon-o-graph (mon´o graf´) *n.* A scholarly pamphlet or book on a particular and usually limited subject. **monographic** *adj.*

mon-o-lin-gual (mon´*o* ling´gw*a*l) *adj.* Knowing only one language.

mon-o-lith (mon´*o* lith) *n.* A single block of stone, as one used in architecture or sculpture. **monolithic** *adj.*

mon-o-logue *or* **mon-o-log** (mon´*o* log´) *n.* A speech by one person which precedes conversation; a series of jokes and stories delivered by a comedian. **monologist** *n.*

mon-o-ma-ni-a (mon´*o* mā´nē *a*) *n.* A pathological obsession or mental disorder in which a person is totally obsessed with a single idea. **monomaniac** *n.* **monomaniacal** *adj.*

mo-no-mi-al (mō nō´mē *a*l) *n.* An algebraic expression consisting of only one term. **monomial** *adj.*

mon-o-nu-cle-ar (mon´*o* nŏ´klē ėr) *adj.* Having only one nucleus.

mon-o-nu-cle-o-sis (mon´*o* nŏ´klēō´sis) *n.* An infectious disease marked by an abnormal increase of too many cells having one nucleus.

mon-o-nu-cle-o-tide *n.* A nucleotide containing one molecule each of a phosphoric acid, a pentose, and either a purine or pyrimidine base.

mon-o-phon-ic (mon´*o* fon´ik) *adj.* Having only one part; a solo voice with accompaniment, as a piano.

mon-o-plane (mon´*o* plān´) *n.* An aircraft with one wing or one set of wings.

mo-nop-o-ly (m*o* nop´*o* lē) *n.* *pl.* **-ies** Exclusive ownership or control, as of a service or commodity, by a single group, person, or company; a group, person, or company having a monopoly; exclusive possession; a service or commodity controlled by a single group. **monopolist** *n.* **monopolization** *n.* **monopolistic** *adj.* **monopolize** *v.*

mon-o-rail (mon´*o* rāl´) *n.* A single rail serving as a track on which a wheeled vehicle can travel; a vehicle that travels on such a rail.

mon-o-so-di-um glu-ta-mate (mon´*o* sō´dē*u*m glŏ´t*a* māt´) *n.* Sodium glutamate used as a seasoning, abbreviated as

MSG.

mon-o-syl-la-ble (mon´*o* sil´*a* bl) *n.* A word of one syllable. **monosyllabic** *adj.* **monosyllabically** *adv.*

mon-o-the-ism (mon´*o* thē iz´*u*m) *n.* The belief that there is just one God. **monotheist** *n.* **monotheistic** *adj.*

mon-o-tone (mon´*o* tōn´) *n.* The utterance of sounds, syllables, or words in a single unvarying tone.

mo-not-o-nous (m*o* not´*o* nus) *adj.* Spoken in a monotone; lacking in variety. **monotonously** *adv.* **monotony** *n.*

mon-ox-ide (mon ok´sīd) *n.* An oxide that contains one oxygen atom per molecule.

Monroe, James *n.* (1758-1831). The 5th president of the United States.

Mon-si-gnor (mon sē´ner) *n. pl.* **-ors** *or* **-ori** A title given to Roman Catholic priests who have received papal honors.

mon-soon (mon sŏn´) *n.* A periodic wind, especially in the Indian Ocean and southern Asia; the season of the monsoon in India and parts of Asia.

mon-ster (mon´stėr) *n.* An animal or plant having an abnormal form or structure; an animal, plant, or object having a frightening or deformed shape; one unusually large for its kind. **monstrosity** *n.* **monstrousness** *n.* **monstrous** *adj.* **monstrously** *adv.*

mon-tage (mon täzh´) *n.* A composite picture made by combining several separate pictures or parts of several pictures; a rapid succession of images in a motion picture, designed to illustrate an association of ideas.

Mon-tan-a *n.* A state located in the northwestern United States; statehood November 8, 1889; state capital Helena.

Mont-gom-er-y *n.* The capital of the state of Alabama.

month (munth) *n.* One of the twelve divisions of a calendar year.

month-ly (munth´lē) *adj.* Occurring, done, or payable each month. *n.* A publication issued once a month. **monthly** *adv.*

Mont-pe-lier *n.* The capital of the state of

Vermont.

mon-u-ment (mon´ū ment) *n.* An object, such as a statue, built as a memorial to a person or an event; a burial vault; an area set aside for public use by a government because of its aesthetic, historical, or ecological significance.

mon-u-men-tal (mon´ū men´tal) *adj.* Serving as or similar to a monument; massive; extremely important. **monumentally** *adv.*

mooch (mōch) *v., Slang* To acquire by begging; to steal. **moocher** *n.*

mood (mōd) *n.* A conscious yet temporary state of mind or emotion; the prevailing spirit; a verb form or set of verb forms inflected to show the understanding of the person speaking regarding the condition expressed.

mood-y (mō´dē) *adj.* Subject to moods, especially depression; gloomy. **moodily** *adv.* **moodiness** *n.*

moon (mōn) *n.* The earth's only natural satellite; a natural satellite which revolves around a planet. *v.* To dream.

moon-beam (mōn´bēm´) *n.* A ray of moonlight.

moon-light (mōn´līt´) *n.* The light of the moon. *v.* To hold a second job in addition to a regular one. **moonlighter** *n.*

moon-lit (mōn´lit´) *adj.* Lit by the moon.

moon-rise (mōn´rīz´) *n.* The rising of the moon above the horizon; the time of the moon's rising.

moon-scape (mōn´skāp´) *n.* The surface of the moon as seen or as depicted.

moon-set (mōn´set´) *n.* The descent of the moon below the horizon; the time of the moon's setting.

moon-shine (mōn´shīn´) *n.* Moonlight; empty talk; nonsense; intoxicating liquor, especially illegally distilled corn whiskey.

moon-shin-er (mōn´shī´nėr) *n., Informal* A maker or seller of illicit whiskey; usually distributed in the night.

moon shot *n.* The launching of a spacecraft to the moon or its vicinity.

moon-stone (mōn´stōn´) *n.* A transparent or translucent feldspar of pearly or opaline luster used as a gem.

moon-struck (mōn´struk´) *adj.* Mentally unbalanced; lunatic; romantically sentimental.

moon-ward *adv.* Toward the moon.

moor (mer) *v.* To make fast with cables, lines, or anchors. *n.* An expanse of open, rolling, infertile land. **moorage** *n.*

Moor (mer) *n.* Ancient North African people of mixed Berber and Arab descent who invaded and conquered Spain in the eighth century. **Moorish** *adj.*

moor-ing *n.* A place where a ship or aircraft can be secured; a stabilizing device.

moose (mōs) *n. pl.* **moose** A very large North American deer having a large broad muzzle.

moot (mōt) *v.* To bring up as for debate or discussion; to argue. *adj.* Open to debate; having no legal significance.

mope (mōp) *v.* To be uncaring or dejected; to move in a leisurely manner. **moper** *n.*

mo-ped *n.* A motorbike that can be pedaled.

mop-pet (mop´it) *n.* A child; a darling baby.

mop-up *n.* The process of completing a task.

mo-raine (mo rān´) *n.* An accumulation of earth and stones carried and finally deposited by a glacier.

mor-al (mor´al) *adj.* Of or pertaining to conduct or character from the point of right and wrong; teaching a conception of right behavior. *n.* The lesson to be learned from a story, event, or teaching. **morals** Standards of right and wrong.

mo-rale (mo ral´) *n.* An individual's state of mind with respect to the tasks he or she is expected to perform; esprit decorps.

mor-al-ist (mor´a list) *n.* Someone concerned with moral principles and questions; someone who practices morality. **moralism** *n.* **moralistic** *adj.*

moralistically *adv.*

mo-ral-i-ty (mo ral´i tē) *n. pl.* **-ies** The quality of being morally right; moral behavior.

mor-al-ize (mor´a līz´) *v.* To think, discuss, or judge in a moral sense. **moralization** *n.* **moralizer** *n.*

mo-rass (mo ras´) *n.* A marsh or bog; low-lying wet, soft ground; something which hinders or overwhelms.

mor-a-to-ri-um *n. pl.* **-iums** *or* **-ia** A temporary pause in activity; an authorization given legally to a debtor to suspend payments for a period of time.

mo-ray (mōr´ā) *n.* Any of various marine eels found usually in tropical waters.

mor-bid (mor´bid) *adj.* Of, pertaining to, or affected by disease; suggesting an unhealthy mental state of being; gruesome. **morbidity** *n.* **morbidness** *n.* **morbidly** *adv.*

mor-da-cious (mor dā´shus) *adj.* Violent in action; prone to biting. **mordacity** *n.*

mor-dant (mor´dant) *adj.* Biting and caustic in thought, manner, or style. **mordancy** *n.* **mordantly** *adv.*

more (mōr) *adj.* Greater number, size, or degree; additional. *n.* An additional or greater number, degree, or amount. *adv.* To a greater extent or degree; in addition. *pron.* Additional things or persons.

mo-rel (mo rel´) *n.* An edible mushroom having a sponge-like cap or hood.

more-o-ver (mōr ō´vėr) *adv.* Furthermore; besides.

mo-res (mōr´āz) *n. pl.* The moral customs and traditional customs of a social group.

morgue (morg) *n.* A place in which dead bodies are kept until claimed or identified; the reference file at a newspaper or magazine office.

mor-i-bund (mor´i bund´) *adj.* Approaching extinction; at the point of death. **moribundity** *n.*

Mor-mon (mor´mon) *n.* A member of the Church of Jesus Christ of Latterday Saints. **Mormonism** *n.*

morn (morn) *n.* Morning.

morn-ing (mor´ning) *n.* The early part of the day; the time from midnight to noon.

morn-ing–glo-ry (mor ning glōr´ē) *n.* A usually twining, climbing plant with funnel-shaped flowers which are open in the morning, but closed later in the day.

morning star *n.* A planet seen in the eastern part of the sky just before or at sunrise.

Mo-roc-co *n.* A country located in northwestern Africa.

mo-roc-co (mo rok´ō) *n.* A soft, textured leather made of goatskin.

mo-ron (mōr´on) *n.* An adult exhibiting an intelligence equal to that of a seven to twelve year old child; a very stupid person. **moronic** *adj.* **moronically** *adv.*

mo-rose (mo rōs´) *adj.* Having a sullen disposition; marked by gloom. **morosely** *adv.* **moroseness** *n.*

mor-pheme (mor´fēm) *n.* A meaningful unit which cannot be divided into smaller meaningful parts. **morphemic** *adj.* **morphemically** *adv.*

mor-phi-a (mor´fē a) *n.* Morphine.

mor-phine (mor´fēn) *n.* A highly addictive narcotic derived from opium which can be used as either a sedative or to dull pain.

mor-phol-o-gy (mor fol´o jē) *n.* The study of the form and structure of living organisms, considered separate from function; the study and description of word formation in a language. **morphological** *adj.* **morphologically** *adj.* **morphologist** *n.*

mor-ris (mor´is) *n.* An old English folk dance.

mor-row (mor´ō) *n.* The next day.

Morse code (mors kōd) *n.* Either of two codes, developed by S. F. B. Morse, consisting of dots and dashes, long and short sounds, or long and short flashes of light.

mor-sel (mor´sel) *n.* A small piece or quantity of food; a tasty dish.

mor-tal (mor´tal) *adj.* Having caused or about to cause death; fatal; subject to death; very tedious or prolonged; unrelentingly hostile; of, relating to, or connected with death. *n.* A human being. **mortally** *adv.*

mor-tal-i-ty (mor tal′i tē) *n. pl.* **-ies** The state or condition of being mortal; the death rate; deaths.

mor-tar (mor′tėr) *n.* A strong vessel in which materials can be crushed or ground with a pestle; a muzzle-loading cannon for firing shells at short ranges and at high angles; a mixed building material, as cement with sand and water, which hardens and is used with masonry or plaster.

mor-tar-board (mor′tėr bōrd′) *n.* A square-board with a handle, for holding mortar; an academic cap topped by a stiff, flat square.

mort-gage (mor′gij) *n.* A temporary conveyance of property to a creditor as security for the repayment of a debt; a contract or deed defining the terms of a mortgage. *v.* To pledge or transfer by means of a mortgage. **mortgagee** *n.* **mortgagor** *n.*

mor-ti-cian (mor tish′an) *n.* An undertaker.

mor-ti-fy (mor′ti fī′) *v.* To destroy the strength or functioning of; to subdue or deaden through pain or self-denial; to subject to severe humiliation; to become gangrenous. **mortification** *n.*

mor-tise (mor′tis) *n.* A usually hollowed out rectangular hole in a piece of wood which receives a tenon of another piece to form a joint.

mor-tu-ar-y (mor′chŏ er′ē) *n. pl.* **-ies** A place in which dead bodies are temporarily held until burial or cremation.

mo-sa-ic (mō zā′ik) *n.* A decorative inlaid design of small pieces, as of colored glass or tile, in cement. **mosaic** *adj.*

Mos-es *n.* Hebrew prophet and law-giver; in the Old Testament, the person who lead the Israelites out of Egypt to the Promised Land; the person whom God presented the Ten Commandments to.

mo-sey (mō′zē) *v., Slang* To move slowly; to shuffle along.

Mos-lem (moz′lem) *n.* A believer of Islam. **Moslem** *adj.*

mosque (mosk) *n.* A Moslem house of worship.

mos-qui-to (mo skē′tō) *n. pl.* **-toes** *or* **-tos** Any of various winged insects of which the females suck the blood of animals or humans.

mosquito net *n.* A fine net or screen to keep out mosquitoes.

moss (mos) *n.* Delicate, small green plants which of ten form a dense, mat-like growth. **mossiness** *n.* **mossy** *adj.*

moss-back (mos′bak′) *n.* An old-fashioned person.

moss rose *n.* An old-fashioned garden rose which has a glandular, mossy calyx and flower stalk.

most (mōst) *adj.* The majority of. *n.* The greatest amount. *pron.* The largest part or number. *adv.* In or to the highest degree.

most-ly (mōst′lē) *adv.* For the most part; principally.

mot (mō) *n.* A short, witty saying.

mote (mōt) *n.* A particle, as of dust; a speck of dust.

mo-tel (mō tel′) *n.* A temporary, roadside dwelling for motorists with rooms opening directly onto a parking area.

mo-tet (mō tet′) *n.* A polyphonic vocal composition, based on a religious text and usually sung without accompaniment.

moth (moth) *n.* A usually nocturnal insect having antennae that are often feathered, duller in color and with wings smaller than the butterflies.

moth-ball (moth′bol′) *n.* A ball, usually of camphor, used to repel moths from clothing during storage. **mothballs** A condition of protective storage.

moth–eat-en (moth′ēt′en) *adj.* Partially eaten by moths; in a state of disrepair.

moth-er (muth′ėr) *n.* A female parent; one who holds a maternal relationship toward another; an old or elderly woman; a woman in a position of authority. *adj.* Of, relating to, or being a mother. *v.* To give birth to; to care for or protect like a mother. **motherhood** *n.* **motherliness** *n.*

mother–in–law (muth′ėr in lo′) *n* The mother of one's spouse.

mother-land (muth′ėr land′) *n.* The

country or land of one's birth.

moth-er-of-pearl (muth´ẽr *ov* **perl´)** *n.* The pearly iridescent internal layer of a mollusk shell.

mo-tif (mō tēf´) *n.* An underlying main element or theme that recurs in a musical, artistic, or literary work.

mo-tile (mōt´il) *adj.* Exhibiting or capable of movement.

mo-tion (mō´shan) *n.* The act or process of changing position; a purposeful movement of the body or a bodily part; a formal proposal or suggestion that action be taken. **motion** *v.* **motionless** *adj.*

motion picture *n.* A sequence of filmed pictures that gives the illusion of continuous movement, when projected on a screen.

motion sickness *n.* Dizziness; nausea brought on by motion as traveling by land or water.

mo-ti-vate (mō´ti vāt´) *v.* Causing to act.

mo-tive (mō´tiv) *n.* Something, as a need or desire, which causes a person to act; a musical motif. *adj.* Causing or having the power to cause motion.

mot-ley (mot´lē) *adj.* Composed of a variety of components.

mo-tor (mō´tẽr) *n.* Any of various devices which develop energy or impart motion. *adj.* Imparting or producing motion; driven by or equipped with a motor; of, relating to or designed for motor vehicles; of, relating to, or involving muscular movement. *v.* To travel or transport by motor vehicle. **motorist** *n.*

motor-bike (mō´tẽr bīk´) *n.* A small motorcycle.

mo-tor-boat (mō´tẽr bōt´) *n.* A boat propelled by an internal-combustion engine or an electric motor.

mo-tor-cade (mō´tẽr kād´) *n.* A procession of motor vehicles.

mo-tor-car (mō´tẽr kär´) *n.* An automobile.

mo-tor-cy-cle (mō´tẽr sī´kl) *n.* A two-wheeled automotive vehicle. **motorcycle** *v.* **motorcyclist** *n.*

motor home *n.* A motor vehicle built on a truck frame and equipped to provide a self-contained home during travel.

mo-tor-ize (mō´to rīz´) *v.* To equip with a motor; to supply with motor-propelled vehicles. **motorization** *n.*

mo-tor-man (mō´tẽr *man*) *n.* An operator of a locomotive engine, streetcar, or subway train.

motor scooter *n.* A small two-wheeled vehicle similar to a scooter but having a low-powered gasoline engine.

motor vehicle *n.* A motor-powered vehicle which travels freely without the need for rails.

mot-tle (mot´l) *v.* To mark or be marked with spots or streaks of different colors or shades; to blotch. *n.* A blotch.

mot-to (mot´ō) *n. pl.* **-toes** *or* **-tos** A sentence, phrase,or word expressing purpose, character, or conduct; an appropriate phrase inscribed on something.

moue (mō) *n.* A grimace, as of disapproval or disdain.

mound (mound) *n.* A small hill of earth, sand, gravel or debris; the slightly elevated ground in the middle of a baseball diamond on which the pitcher stands.

mount (mount) *v.* To rise or ascend; to get up on; climb upon; to increase in amount or extent; to organize and equip; to launch and carry out. *n.* A horse or other animal used for riding; a support to which something is fixed.

moun-tain (moun´tin) *n.* A land mass that rises above its surroundings and is higher than a hill.

mountain ash *n.* Any of various deciduous trees bearing clusters of small white flowers and orange-red berries.

moun-tain-eer (moun´ta nẽr´) *n.* An inhabitant of a mountainous region; one who climbs mountains for sport. **mountaineer** *v.*

mountain goat *n.* A long-haired Rocky Mountain goat.

mountain laurel *n.* A low-growing evergreen shrub with poisonous leaves and clusters of pink or white flowers.

mountain lion *n.* A large wildcat; puma.

moun-tain-ous (moun´ta nus) *adj.* Of or relating to a region with many mountains.

moun-tain-side (moun´tan sīd´) *n.* The side of a mountain.

moun-tain-top (moun´tan top´) *n.* The top of amountain.

moun-te-bank(moun´tebangk´)*n.* A quack doctor; a false and boastful pretender; a charlatan.

Mountie Mounty *n.* A member of the Canadian Mounted Police.

mount-ing (moun´ting) *n.* A supporting frame or structure of an article.

mourn (mōrn) *v.* To express grief; to feel grief or sorrow; to follow the religious customs and rituals surrounding the death of a loved one.

mouse (mous) *n. pl.* **mice** A small rodent that frequents human habitations; a timid person.

mousse (mōs) *n.* A light frozen dessert.

mouth (mouth) *n. pl.* **mouths** The bodily opening through which food is taken in.

mouth-off *v.* To speak disrespectfully.

mouth–to–mouth (mouth´tō mouth´) *adj.* Pertaining to a method of artificial resuscitation.

move (mōv) *v.* To set in motion; to change one's place or location; to make a recommendation in a formal manner. **movable** *adj.* **moveable** *adj.* **moveably** *adv.*

move-ment (mōv´ment) *n.* The act of moving; a part of a musical composition; an excretion of the bowels.

mov-er *n.* One that moves; a person employed to help in moving the contents of a home or business.

mov-ie (mō´vē) *n.* A motion picture; motion picture industry.

mow (mō) *v.* To cut down, as with a machine. *n.* The part of the barn where hay or grain is stored. **mower** *n.*

Mozart, Wolfgang Amadeus *n.* (1756-1791). Austrian composer.

moz-za-rel-la *n.* A soft white cheese with a mild flavor.

MP *abbr.* Military Police.

mpg *abbr.* Miles per gallon.

mph *abbr.* Miles per hour.

Mr *abbr.* Mister.

Mrs *abbr.* Mistress.

Ms *abbr.* A form of address used for a woman when her marital status is irrelevant or unknown.

MS *abbr.* Mississippi.

MST *abbr.* Mountain Standard Time.

much (much) *adj.* In great amount, quantity, degree, or extent. *adv.* To a great extent. *n.* Something impressive.

mu-ci-lage (mū´si lij) *n.* A sticky substance that is similar to plant gums.

muck (muk) *n.* Moist farmyard manure; moist, sticky soil or filth. *v.* To dirty with or as with muck. **mucky** *adj.*

muck-rake (muk´rāk´) *v.* To search out and publicly expose real or apparent misconduct on the part of well-known persons. **muckraker** *n.*

mu-co-sa (mū kō´sa) *n.* A mucous membrane.

mu-cous (mū´kus) *adj.* Of, pertaining to, or secreting mucus.

mucous membrane *n.* A membrane secreting mucus which lines bodily channels that come into contact with air.

mu-cus (mū´kus) *n.* The viscous liquid secreted by glands by the mucous membrane.

mud (mud) *n.* A mixture of water and earth. *Slang* A slanderous remark. **muddy** & *v.* **muddily** *adv.* **muddiness** *n.*

mud-dle (mud´l) *v.* To make muddy; to mix up or confuse; to make a mess of; to think or act in a confused way. **muddler** *n.*

mud-guard (mud´gärd´) *n.* A piece of material applied to a wheel well to prevent mud from splashing onto a vehicle.

mud-sling-er *n.* One who makes malicious statements or charges against a political opponent. **mudslinging** *n.*

muff (muf) *n.* An arm, tubular covering for the hands; a bungling performance. *v.* To handle awkwardly; to act or do something stupidly or clumsily.

muf·fin (muf´in) *n.* A soft, cup-shaped bread that is cooked in a muffin pan and often served hot.

muf·fle (muf´l) *v.* To wrap up so as to conceal or protect; to deaden the sound of; to suppress.

muf·fler (muf´lėr) *n.* A scarf worn around the neck; a device which deadens noise, especially one forming part of the exhaust system of an automotive vehicle.

mug (mug) *n.* A large drinking cup; a person's face; a photograph of someone's face. *v.* To make funny faces; to assault viciously, usually with the intent to rob. **mugger** *n.*

mug·gy (mug´ē) *adj.* Warm, humid and sultry. **muggily** *adv.* **mugginess** *n.*

mug·wump (mug´wump´) *n.* A defector from the Republican Party in 1884; anyone who acts independently, especially in politics.

Mu·ham·mad·an (me ham´i dan) *n.* A Moslem. **Muhammadan** *adj.* **Muhammadanism** *n.*

muk·luk (muk´luk) *n.* A boot made from the skin of seals or reindeer, worn by Eskimos; a slipper that resembles a mukluk.

mu·lat·to (mu lat´ō) *n. pl.* **-tos** *or* **-toes** A person with one white parent and one black parent; a person of mixed black and white ancestry.

mul·ber·ry (mul´ber´ē) *n.* Any of several trees having an edible, berry-like fruit.

mulch (mulch) *n.* A loose protective covering, as of sawdust or compost, or wood chips spread on the ground to prevent moisture evaporation, to protect roots from freezing, and to retard the growth of weeds. **mulch** *v.*

mulct (mulkt) *n.* A financial penalty or fine. *v.* To punish by fining; to obtain by fraud or theft.

mule (mul) *n.* A hybrid animal that is the offspring of a female horse and a male ass. *Slang* A stubborn person. **mulish** *adj.* **mulishly** *adv.* **mulishness** *n.*

mule deer *n.* A long-eared deer of western North America, heavier built and larger than the white-tail deer.

mule–foot *adj.* Having a solid foot; not cleft.

mule-skinner *n.* A muleteer.

mu·le·teer (mū´le tēr´) *n.* A person who drives mules.

mu·ley (mū´lē) *adj.* Naturally without horns.

mull (mul) *v.* To mix or grind thoroughly; to ponder; to think about.

mul·lah (mul´a) *n.* A Muslim leader and clergyman.

mul·lein (mul´en) *n.* A plant having yellow flowers and downy leaves.

mul·let (mul´it) *n.* An edible marine and freshwater fish.

mul·li·gan stew (mul´i gan) *n.* A stew made of various vegetables and meats.

multi- *prefix* Much, many, multiple; more than two.

mul·ti·dis·ci·plin·ary *adj.* Using or related to a combination of several disciplines for a common cause.

mul·ti·far·i·ous (mul´ti fâr´ē us) *adj.* Having much diversity. **multifariously** *adv.*

mul·ti·form (mul´ti form´) *adj.* Having many appearances or forms. **multiformity** *n.*

mul·ti·lane *adj.* Having several lanes.

mul·ti·lat·er·al (mul´ti lat´ėr al) *adj.* Having many sides; involving or participated in by more than two parties or nations. **multilaterally** *adv.*

mul·ti·lin·gual (mul´ti ling´gwal) *adj.* Expressed in several languages. **multilingualism** *n.*

mul·ti·mil·lion·aire (mul´tē mil´yanâr´) *n.* A person whose fortune is worth many millions of dollars.

mul·ti·na·tion·al *adj.* Involving or relating to several countries.

mul·tip·a·rous *adj.* Producing more than one at a birth.

mul·ti·ple (mul´ti pl) *adj.* Relating to or consisting of more than one individual, part, or element. *Math.* A number into which another number can be divided with no remainders.

multiple–choice (mul´ti pl chois´) *adj.* Offering several answers from which the correct one is to be chosen.

multiple sclerosis *n.* A degenerative condition marked by patches of hardened tissue in the spinal cord or the brain.

multi-plex (mul´ti pleks) *n.* A communications system in which two or more messages can be transmitted simultaneously on the same circuit. **multiplex** *v.*

mul-ti-pli-ca-tion(mul´ti plikā´shan)*n.* The mathematical operation by which a number indicates how many times another number is to be added to itself.

mul-ti-plic-i-ty (mul´ti plis´i tē) *n. pl.* **-ies** A large number or variety.

mul-ti-pli-er (mul´ti plī´ér) *n.* A number that is or is to be multiplied by another number.

mul-ti-ply (mul´ti plī´) *v.* To increase in amount or number; to combine by multiplication.

mul-ti-sense *adj.* Having several meanings.

mul-ti-stage (mul´ti stāj´) *adj.* Consisting of propulsion units which operate in turn.

mul-ti-tude (mul´ti tŏd´) *n.* A very large amount or number. **multitudinous** *adj.*

mul-ti-vi-ta-min *n.* A pill containing several vitamins that are essential to health.

mum (mum) *adj.* Silent, not speaking.

mum-ble (mum´bl) *v.* To speak or utter in a low, confused manner. **mumble** *n.* **mumbler** *n.*

mum-ble-ty–peg (mum´bl tē peg´) *n.* A game in which players try to throw a knife from various positions so that the blade will stick into the ground.

mum-bo jum-bo (mum´bō jum´bō) *n.* A complicated or obscure ritual; a confusing and complicated language or activity.

mum-mer (mum´ér) *n.* A performer who acts in a pantomime.

mum-mery (mum´e rē) *n. pl.* **-ies** A hypocritical or ridiculous ceremony.

mum-mi-fy (mum´i fī´) *v.* To dry and

embalm as a mummy; to cause to shrivel and dry up. **mummification** *n.*

mum-my (mum´ē) *n. pl.* **-ies** A body embalmed or treated for burial in the manner of the ancient Egyptians. **mummify** *v.*

mumps (mumps) *n. pl.* An acute, contagious viral disease marked by fever and swelling of the salivary glands.

mun *abbr.* Municipal; municipality.

munch (munch) *v.* To chew noisily. **muncher** *v.*

mun-dane (mun dān´) *adj.* Pertaining to or relating to the world; characterized by the ordinary and practical. **mundanely** *adv.*

Mu-nich *n.* A city located in southwest Germany.

mu-nic-i-pal (mū nis´i pal) *adj.* Relating to or typical of a municipality; having self-government in local affairs. **municipally** *adv.* **municipality** *n.*

mu-nif-i-cent (mū nif´i sent) *adj.* Very liberal in giving; lavish. **munificence** *n.* **munificently** *adv.*

mu-ni-tions *n. pl.* Guns and ammunition. **munition** *v.*

mu-ral (mer´al) *n.* A painting created on a wall. **muralist** *n.*

mur-der (mer´dér) *n.* The crime of unlawfully killing a person. *Slang* Something very dangerous, difficult, or uncomfortable. *v.* To kill a person unlawfully and with premeditated malice. **murderer** *n.*

mur-der-ous (mer´dér us) *adj.* Intending or having the purpose or capability of murder. **murderously** *adv.*

murk (merk) *n.* Darkness; gloom. **murkily** *adv.* **murkiness** *n.* **murky** *adj.*

mur-mur (mer´mér) *n.* A low, indistinct, and often continuous sound; a gentle or soft utterance. **murmur** *v.*

mur-mur-ous *adj.* Characterized by murmurs. **murmurously** *adv.*

Murphy bed (mer´fē bed) *n.* A bed which folds into a closet.

mur-rain (mer´in) *n.* A plague affecting plants or domestic animals.

mur-rey (mer´ē) *n.* Mulberry colored;

purplish-black.

mus *abbr.* Museum; musical; musician.

muscae volitantes A condition of spots before the eyes due to cells and cell fragments in the vitreous humor and lens.

mus-cle (mus′l) *n.* Bodily tissue which consists of long cells that contract when stimulated. **muscle** *v.*

mus-cle–bound (mus′l bound′) *adj.* Having muscles which are overdeveloped and lack the capacity to flex fully, usually caused by too much exercise.

mus-cu-lar (mus′kū lėr) *adj.* Relating to or consisting of muscle; brawny; having well-developed muscles. **muscularity** *n.*

muscular dystrophy *n.* A noncontagious hereditary disease characterized by gradual but irreversible muscular deterioration.

mus-cu-la-ture (mus′kū la chėr) *n.* The muscles of an animal's body.

muse (mūz) *n.* A state of deep thought.

Muse (mūz) *n.* One of the nine Greek goddesses in mythology, who are the inspiration for creativity, as music and art.

mu-sette (mū zet′) *n.* A small bagpipe having a soft, sweet tone or sound; a small bag with a shoulder strap.

mush (mush) *n.* A thick porridge of corn meal boiled in water or milk; soft matter. **mushiness** *n.* **mushy** *adj.*

mush-room(mush′rŏm) *n.* A fungus having an umbrella-shaped cap on a stalk. *v.* To grow or multiply quickly.

mu-sic (mu′zik) *n.* Organized tones in sequences and combinations which make up a continuous composition. **musical** *adj.*

music box *n.* A box enclosing an apparatus which produces music when activated.

mu-si-cian (mū zish′an) *n.* A composer or performer of music. **musicianly** *adj.* **musicianship** *n.*

mu-si-col-o-gy (mū′zi kol′o jē) *n.* The scientific and historical study of music. **musicological** *adj.* **musicologist** *n.*

musk (musk) *n.* A substance with a strong,

powerful odor which is secreted by the male musk deer. **muskiness** *n.* **musky** *adj.*

mus-keg (mus′keg) *n.* A bog formed by moss, leaves, and decayed matter resembling peat.

mus-ket (mus′kit) *n.* A heavy, large-caliber shoulder gun with a long barrel.

musk-mel-on (musk′mel′on) *n.* A sweet melon having a rough rind and juicy, edible flesh.

musk-rat (musk′rat′) *n.* A rodent of North America with brown fur.

Mus-lim (muz′lim) *n.* A follower of Islam. **Muslim** *adj.*

mus-lin (muz′lin) *n.* A plain-woven, sheer, or coarse fabric.

muss (mus) *v.* To make messy or untidy. *Slang* A confused conflict. **mussily** *adv.*

mus-sel (mus′el) *n.* A freshwater bivalve mollusk.

must (must) *v.* To be forced to; to have to; to be obligated to do something; to be necessary to do something. *n.* A requirement; absolute; something indispensable.

mus-tache *also* **mous-tache** *n.* The hair growing on the human upper lip, especially on the male upper lip.

mus-tang (mus′tang) *n.* A wild horse of the western plains.

mus-tard (mus′tėrd) *n.* A condiment or medicinal preparation made from the seeds of the mustard plant.

mustard gas *n.* An irritating liquid chemical used as a war gas.

mus-ter (mus′tėr) *v.* To come or bring together; to convene; to bring or call forth. *n.* The act of examining or inspecting critically.

mustn't *contr.* Must not.

mus-ty (mus′tē) *adj.* Moldy or stale in odor or taste. **mustily** *adv.* **mustiness** *n.*

mu-ta-ble (mū′ta bl) *adj.* Prone to or capable of change. **mutability** *n.* **mutableness** *n.*

mu-tant (mūt′ant) *n.* An individual or organism which differs from the parental strain as a result of mutation. **mutant** *adj.*

mu-tate (mū´tāt) *v.* To undergo or cause to undergo mutation. **mutative** *adj.*

mute (mūt) *adj.* Unable to speak. *n.* A person who cannot speak. **mutely** *adv.* **muteness** *n.*

mu-ti-late (mūt´i lāt´) *v.* To deprive of an essential part, as a limb of the body; to maim or cripple; to make imperfect. **mutilation** *n.* **mutilator** *n.*

mu-ti-ny (mūt´i nē) *n. pl.* **-ies** Open revolt against lawful authority. **mutineer** *n.* **mutinous** *adj.* **mutiny** *v.*

mutt (mut) *n., Slang* A mongrel; a dog of mixed breed.

mut-ter (mut´ėr) *v.* To speak or utter in a low voice; to grumble; to complain. **mutter** *n.*

mut-ton (mut´on) *n.* The flesh of a fully grown sheep, used for food. **muttony** *adj.*

mut-ton-chops *n. pl.* The whiskers on the side of the face which are narrow at the temple and broad and round by the lower jaw.

mu-tu-al (mū´chŏ al) *adj.* Having the same relationship; received and directed in equal amounts. **mutuality** *n.*

mutual fund *n.* An investment company which invests its shareholders' money in diversified ways.

muu-muu *n.* A dress which hangs loosely, originally given to the native women of Hawaii by missionaries.

muz-zle (muz´l) *n.* The projecting mouth of certain animals; the open end or mouth of an implement such as the barrel of a gun. **muzzler** *n.*

my (mī) *adj.* Relating to or of myself or one. *interj.* Used to express surprise, dismay, or pleasure.

my-ce-li-um (mī sē´lē um) *n. pl.* **-lia** A mass of interwoven filaments which form the main growing structure of a fungus. **mycelial** *adj.*

my-col-o-gy (mī kol´o je) *n.* A branch of botany; the scientific study of fungi. **mycological** *adj.* **mycologist** *n.*

my-e-li-tis *n.* An inflammation of the spinal cord or bone marrow.

my-elo-ma *n.* A tumor of the bone marrow.

myo-car-dio-graph (mī´o kär´dē ograf´) *n.* A recording tool which traces the action of the heart muscles.

myo-car-di-um *n.* The muscular layer of the heart, located in the middle of the heart wall. **myocardial** *adj.*

my-o-pia (mī ō´pē a) *n.* A visual defect in which visual images come to a focus in front of the retina of the eye rather than on the retina, causing fuzzy images. **myopic** *adj.* **myopically** *adv.*

myr-tle (mer´tl) *n.* An evergreen shrub.

my-self (mī self´) *pron.* The one identical with me; used reflexively; my normal, healthy state or condition.

mys-te-ri-ous (mi stēr´ē us) *adj.* Relating to or being a mystery; impossible or difficult to comprehend. **mysteriously** *adv.* **mysteriousness** *n.*

mys-ter-y (mis´te rē) *n. pl.* **-ies** Something not understood; a problem or puzzle; an enigma; a Christian sacrament.

mys-tic (mis´tik) *adj.* Relating to mystics, mysticism, or mysteries. *n.* A person practicing or believing in mysticism. **mystical** *adj.* **mystically** *adv.*

mys-ti-cism (mis´ti siz´um) *n.* The spiritual discipline of communion with God.

mys-ti-fy (mis´ti fī) *v.* To perplex, to bewilder. **mystification** *n.* **mystifyingly** *adv.*

myth (mith) *n.* A traditional story dealing with supernatural ancestors; a person or thing having only an unverifiable or imaginary existence. **mythical** *adj.* **mythic** *adj.* **mythically** *adv.*

my-thol-o-gy (mi thol´o jē) *n. pl.* **-ies** A body of myths dealing with gods and heroes. **mythological** *adj.* **mythologist** *n.*

my word *interj.* An expression of astonishment or surprise.

myx-e-de-ma *n.* A disease that is caused by the decreased activity of the thyroid gland and marked by the loss of mental and physical vigor; dry skin and hair. **myxedematous** *adj.*

N, n (en) The fourteenth letter of the English alphabet.

nab (nab) *v., Slang* To seize; to arrest; to catch suddenly.

na-celle (na sel') *n.* The housing of an airplane that usually contains the engine.

na-cho *n.* A tortilla, often small and triangular in shape, topped with cheese or chili sauce and baked.

na-dir (nā'dėr) *n.* The lowest point.

nag (nag) *v.* To bother by scolding or constant complaining. **nag** *n.* A worthless horse. **nagger** *n. & adj.* **nagging** *adj.*

na-ga-na (na gä'na) *n.* A disease of horses caused by flies.

nai-ad (nā'ad) *n., Mythol.* A nymph presiding over and living in springs, brooks, and fountains.

nail (nāl) *n.* A thin pointed piece of metal for hammering into wood and other materials to hold pieces together. **nailer** *n.*

nail-head (nāl'hed") *n.* The enlarged end of a nail, the area that is hit when driving into a surface. **nailheaded** *adj.*

nail-set *n.* A steel punch used to drive a nail below the surface of wood.

na-ive (nä ēv') *adj.* Simple and trusting; not sophisticated. **naively** *adv.* **naiveness** *n.*

na-ked (nā'kid) *adj.* Without clothes on the body; nude; exposed; uncovered. **nakedly** *adv.* **nakedly, nakedness** *n.*

nam-by–pam-by (nam'bē pam'bē) *adj.* Weak; indecisive; lacking in substance or character.

name (nām) *n.* A title or word by which something or someone is known. *v.* To give a name. **namable** *n.* **namable** *adj.*

name-drop (nām'drop") *v.* To refer to a prominent person in a familar and close associated way in order to impress others.

name-less (nām'lis) *adj.* Having no name; anonymous.

name-sake (nām'sāk') *n.* A person named after someone with the same name.

nap (nap) *n.* A short rest or sleep, often during the day. *v.* The surface of a piece of leather or fabric.

na-palm (nā'päm) *n.* A mixture of aluminum soaps used in jelling gasoline for use in bombs or by flame throwers.

nape (nāp) *n.* The back of the neck.

na-per-y (nāp'e rē) *n.* Linens in general that are used for domestic purposes.

naph-tha (naf'tha) *n.* A volatile, colorless, liquid, that is used especially as a solvent or fuel.

na-pi-form (nāpi form") *adj.* Having the globular shape of a turnip.

nap-kin (nap'kin) *n.* A cloth or soft paper, used at the dinner table for wiping the lips and fingers.

na-po-le-on (na pō'lē an) *n.* A pastry of several flaky layers filled with custard cream.

nap-py (nap'ē) *n. pl.* **nappies.** A small rimless, shallow serving.

na-prap-a-thy (na prap'a thē) *n.* A system of treatment of a disease, that is based on the theory that an illness is caused by disordered connective tissues, and that using massage, manipulation, and dietary measures, healing is achieved.

nar-cis-sus (när sis'us) *n.* A widely grown type of bulbous plant which includes the jonquil, narcissus, and daffodil.

nar-co-ma-ni-a (när'o mä'nē a) *n.* The abnormal craving for a narcotic.

nar-co-sis (när kō'sis) *n.* A deep drug-induced state of stupor or unconsciousness.

nar-cot-ic (när kot'ik) *n.* A drug which dulls the senses, relieves pain, and induces a deep sleep; if abused, it can become habit-forming and cause convulsions or comas.

nard (närd) *n.* An aromatic medicial, ointment that is obtained from the rhizomes of an East Asian plant.

nar-is (när'is) *n. pl.* **nares.** The Nasal passage or opening; the nostril.

nar-rate (när'rāt) *v.* To tell a story or give a description in detail. **arration** *n.* **narrator** *v.*

nar-ra-tion (na rā'shan) *n.* The act of narrating; a narrative; a story accompanying a visual presentation.

nar-ra-tive (när'ativ) *n.* Something that

is narrated; the technique or practice of narration.

nar-row (nar´ō) *adj.* Slender or small in width; of less than standard width. **narrowly** *adj.* **narrowness** *n.*

narrow–mind-ed (nar´ō mīn´did) *adj.* Lacking sympathy or tolerance.

nar-whal (när´wəl) *n.* An aquatic mammal of the Arctic regions, closely related to the white whale, having a long, twisted, protruding tusk in the male.

nar-y (nâr´ē) *adj.* Never a; not a; not; not one.

na-sal (nā´zəl) *adj.* Of or pertaining to the nose; producing a nasal speech sound.

na-sal-ize (nā´zə līz´) *v.* To produce or speak in a nasal manner.

nas-tic (nas´tik) *adj., Bot.* Relating to the movement of a plant part, as a result of changing cellular pressure on the surface.

na-stur-tium (nə ster´shim) *n.* A five-petaled garden plant usually having red, yellow, or orange flowers.

nas-ty (nas´tē) *adj.* Dirty, filthy, or indecent; unpleasant. **nastily** *adv.*

na-tal (nāt´əl) *adj.* Pertaining to or associated with birth.

na-tant (nāt´ənt) *adj.* Swimming or floating; in or on water.

na-ta-tion (nā tā´shən) *n.* The act or part of swimming. **natator** *n.* A swimmer.

na-ta-to-ri-al (nā˝ tə tōr´ē əl) *adj.* Pertaining to, adapted for, or characterized by swimming.

na-ta-to-ri-um (nā˝ tə tōr´ē um) *n. pl.* **natatoriums** An indoor swimming pool.

na-tes (nā´tēz) *n. pl.* The buttocks.

na-tion (nā´shən) *n.* A group of people made up of one or more nationalities under one government. **national** *adj.* **nationally** *adv.*

na-tion-al (nash´ə nəl) *adj.* Pertaining or relating to a nation or people; maintained by a nation as an independent political unit; devoted totally to one's own nation, welfare, and interests; to be patriotic.

national bank *n.* A bank associated with other financial institutions; a bank chartered by the federal government.

national income *n., Econ.* The combination of earnings from a nation's current production to include interest, rental property income and business profits after taxes.

na-tion-al-ism (nash´ə nə liz´um) *n.* Devotion to or concern for one's nation; a movement or desire for national independence.

na-tion-al-i-ty (nash´ə nal´i tē) *n.* The fact or condition of belonging to a nation.

na-tion-al-ize (nash´ə nə līz´) *v.* To place a nation's resources and industries under the control of the state.

national park *n.* A special area of land noted for its scenic beauty or historical interest, that is maintained by the national government for public recreational purposes.

na-tion-wide (nā´shən wīd˝) *adj.* Extending throughout a nation.

na-tive (nā´tiv) *n.* A person born in a country or place. *adj.* Belonging to one by nature or birth.

na-tiv-ism (nā´ti viz˝um) *n.* The policy of protecting and favoring native inhabitants from immigrants.

na-tiv-i-ty (nə tiv´i tē) *n.* Birth, circumstances, or conditions; the birth of Christ.

nat-ro-lite (na´trə līt˝) *n.* A hydrolous silicate of sodium and aluminum, that occurs occasionally in white, needle-shaped crystals.

na-tron (nā´tron) *n.* Native carbonate of soda found in solution found in some mineral springs and lakes, used in previous times as an embalming agent.

nat-ty (nat´ē) *adj.* Tidy; neatly dressed; of a neat appearance.

nat-u-ral (nach´ėr əl) *adj.* Produced or existing by nature; not artificial. *Mus.* A note that is not sharp or flat. **naturalness, naturally** *adv.*

natural childbirth *n.* Childbirth with little stress or pain; childbirth requiring training for the mother and father and medical supervision, but without the use of drugs, anesthesia, or surgery.

natural gas *n.* A combustible gas coming from the earth's surface, formed naturally in the earth.

natural history *n.* The study or description of normal nature objects; in its widest sense, from an amateur or popular point of view approach.

nat-u-ral-ize (nach´ẻr *a* **līz´)** *v.* To confer the privileges and rights of full citizenship. **naturalization** *n.*

natural law *n.* A rule or body of law founded on the natural ethics of man, religion, or nature, that is considered to be morally binding upon the human society in the absence of positive law.

natural resource *n.* The industrial materials and the capacities that are supplied by nature such as minerals, oil, forests, and water.

natural science *n.* Any science, that deals with matter such as, biology, geology, or chemistry.

natural selection *n.* The theory that a natural process results in the survival of individuals best adjusted to conditions under and in the environment in which they live.

na-ture (nā´chẻr) *n.* The universe and its phenomena; kind, sort, or type; one's own character or temperament. **natured** *adj.*

naught (not) *n.* Nothing; the number 0; zero.

naugh-ty (no´tē) *adj.* Unruly; not proper; ill-behaved. **naughtily** *adv.*

nau-se-a (no´zē *a***)** *n.* An upset stomach with a feeling that one needs to vomit. **nauseous** *adj.* **nauseate** *v.* **nauseatingly** *adv.*

nau-se-ate (na´ze āt˝) *v.* To feel nausea or be sick to ones stomach; to be inclined to vomit.

nau-seous (na´shus) *adj.* Disgusting, nausreating; to cause a feeling of nausea. **nauseously** *adj.* **nauseousness** *n.*

nau-ti-cal (no´ti k*a***l)** *adj.* Pertaining to ships or seamanship. **nautically** *adv.*

na-val (nā´v*a***l)** *adj.* Of or relating to ships; maritime.

na-vel (nā´v*e***l)** *n.* A small mark or scar on the abdomen where the umbilical cord was attached.

na-vic-u-lar (n*a* **vik´ū lẻr)** *adj.* Having the shape of a boat. *n.* The bone of the ankle or wrist.

nav-i-ga-ble (nav´i g*a* **bl)** *adj.* Sufficiently deep and wide enough to allow ships to pass.

nav-i-gate (nav´i gāt´) *v.* To plan the course of a ship or aircraft; to steer a course. **navigator** *n.* **navigation, navigational** *adj.*

nav-i-ga-tion (nav´i gā´shan) *n.* The act or science of navigating ships; the science of determining the location, speed, destination, and direction of airplanes and other crafts and moving them from place to place.

nav-i-ga-tor (nav´i gā˝tẻr) *n.* A person who is trained in the methods of navigation or one who navigates.

na-vy (nā´vē) *n.* One of a nation's organizations for defense; a nation's fleet of ships; a very dark blue.

NBA *abbr.* National Basketball Association; National Boxing Association.

NC *abbr.* North Carolina.

ND *abbr.* North Dakota.

NE *n.* Nebraska.

Ne-an-der-thal (nē an´dẻr thol´) *adj.* Suggesting a caveman in behavior or appearance; primitive or crude. **Neanderthal** *n.*

neap tide (nēp) *n.* A tide in the minimum range which occurs during the first and third quarter of the moon or twice a month.

near (nēr) *adv.* At, to, or within a short time or distance. *adj.* Closely or intimately related. **nearness** *n.*

near-by (nēr´bī´) *adj. & adv.* Close by; near at hand; adjacent.

near point (nēr´point˝) *n.* The point nearest the eye at which point the eye can accurately focus.

near-sight-ed (nēr´sī´tid) *adj.* Able to see clearly at short distances only.

neat (nēt) *adj.* Tidy and clean; free from

disorder and dirt. *Slang* Great, fine, or wonderful. **neatly** *adv.* **neatness** *n.*

neat's–foot oil *n.* A pale yellow light oil made from the bones of cattle and used as a lubricant or softener for leather.

neb-bish (neb′ish) *n.* A timid, ineffectual person.

Neb-ras-ka *n.* A state located in the central part of the United States; statehood March 1, 1867; state capital Lincoln.

neb-u-lize (neb′ū liz″) *v.* Reduce to fine spray .

neb-u-lous (neb′ū lus) *adj.* Confused or vague; hazy, cloudy, or misty.

nec-es-sar-y (nes′i ser′ē) *adj.* Unavoidable; required; essential; needed.

ne-ces-si-tate (ne ses′i tāt′) *v.* To make necessary; to oblige; to require; to force or be forced.

ne-ces-si-ty (ne ses′i tē) *n. pl.* -ies The condition of being necessary; the condition making a particular course of action necessary; a requirement; something inevitable.

neck (nek) *n.* The part of the body which connects the head and trunk; a narrow part or projection, as of land, a stringed instrument, or bottle. *v.* To caress and kiss.

neck-line (nek′līn′) *n.* The open part of a women's garment which outlines the neck.

neck-tie (nek′tī′) *n.* A narrow strip of material worn around the neck and tied so that the two ends hang down in the front of a shirt.

ne-crol-o-gy (ne krol′o jē) *n. pl.* **ne-crol-o-gies** A death notice or list of the most recent dead.

nec-tar (nek′tėr) *n.* A good-tasting beverage; a sweet fluid in various flowers, gathered by bees to help make honey.

nec-tar-ine (nek″ta rēn′) *n.* A variety of the common peach, whose fruit at maturity is smooth like a plum.

nee (nā) *n.* Born; the surname a woman was born with.

need (nēd) *n.* The lack of something desirable, useful, or necessary; misfortune or poverty; a necessity.

nee-dle (nēd′l) *n.* A slender, pointed steel implement which contains an eye through which thread is passed. *v.* To tease.

needle-point (nēd′l point′) *n.* Decorative stitching done on canvas in even stitches across counted threads.

need-n't (nēd′ant) Need not.

ne-far-i-ous (ni fâr′ē us) *adj.* Extremely wicked;despicable.

ne-gate (ni gāt′) *v.* To nullify; to deny; to rule out. **negation** *n.*

neg-a-tive (neg′a tiv) *adj.* Expressing denial or disapproval; not positive. *n.* In photography, a negative photo. **negatively** *adj.* **negativeness** *n.*

neg-a-tiv-ism (neg′a ti viz″um) *n.* A philosophy attitude characterized by skepticism; a tendency to refuse to do something or to do the opposite or at least a variation of what was asked.

neg-a-tron (neg′a tron″) *n.* An electron.

neglect (ni glekt′) *v.* To ignore; to pay no attention to; to fail to perform.

neg-li-gee (neg′li zhā′) *n.* A woman's loose fitting dressing gown.

neg-li-gence (neg′li jens) *n.* The act or condition of being negligent, an act of being habitually neglectful.

neg-li-gent (neg′li jent) *adj.* To neglect what needs to be done; neglectful.

neg-li-gi-ble (neg′li ji ble) *adj.* So unimportant or small that it may be safely disregarded, warranting little or no attention.

ne-go-ti-a-ble (ni gō′shē a bl) *adj.* Capable of being negotiated.

ne-go-ti-ate (ni gō′shē āt′) *v.* To confer with another person to reach an agreement; to accomplish successfully.

ne-gus (nēgus) *n.* A beverage made of wine, hot water, sugar, lemon and nutmeg or other spices.

neigh (nā) *v.* To make the cry of a horse.

neigh-bor (nā′bėr) *n.* One who lives near another; fellowman. **neighboring** *adj.*

neigh-bor-hood (nā′bėr hed′) *n.* A section or small region that possesses a specific quality; the people living in such a region.

nei-ther (nē´thėr) *adj.* Not one or the other. *pron.* Not the one or the other. *conj.* Not either; also not.

nek-ton (nek´ton) *n.* Free-swimming aquatic animals in the middle depths of the sea, that are independent of wave patterns and currents.

nem-a-to-cyst (nem´a to sist) *n.* A minute stinging apparatus of coelenterate animals, that is used in kill its prey.

neo *prefix* Recent; new.

ne-o-clas-sic (nē´ō klas´ik) *adj.* Pertaining to a renewal of a classic style, as literature.

neo-dym-i-um (nē´ō dim´ē um) *n.* A metallic element of the rare-earth group, symbolized by Nd.

ne-ol-o-gism (nē ol´o jiz˝um) *n.* A new word or phrase; that is often disapproved of because of its newness.

ne-o-my-cin (nē˝ō mī´sin) *n.* An antibiotic, developed from microorganisms, and used in a variety of local skin infections.

ne-on (nē´on) *n.* An inert gaseous element used in lighting fixtures, symbolized by Ne.

ne-o-nate (nē´o nāt´) *n.* A newborn child less than a month old.

ne-o-na-tol-o-gy *n.* The medical study of the first 60 days of a baby's life.

neo-phyte (nē´o fīt´) *n.* A novice; a beginner.

ne-o-plasm (nē´o plaz´um) *n.* A tumor tissue serving no physiologic function.

ne-ot-e-ny (nē ot´e nē) *n.* The achievement of sexual maturity during the larval stage.

neph-e-line (nef´e li nit˝) *n.* A heavy, dark-colored rock of volcanic origin.

neph-ew (nef´ū) *n.* The son of one's sister, brother, sister-in-law, or brother-in-law.

ne-phrid-i-um (ne frid´ē um) *n.* *pl.* **ne-phridia** A primitive excretory organ or structure in annelids, mollusks, and other invertebrates, like the kidney and functioning in some cases in reproduction.

neph-rite (nef´rīt) *n.* A white to dark green variety of actinolite, a form of jade.

ne-phrit-ic *adj.* Relating to the kidneys; afflicted with an inflammation of the kidneys.

nep-o-tism (nep´o tiz´um) *n.* The act of showing favoritism to relatives or friends in the work force. **nepotist** *n.*

Nep-tune (nep´tōn) *n.* The planet eighth in order from the sun.

nep-tu-ni-um (nep tō´nē um) *n.* A radioactive metallic element, symbolized by Np.

ne-rit-ic (ne rit´ik) *adj.* Of or pertaining to the region of shallow water immediately adjoining the seacoast.

neroli oil *n.* The fragrant essential oil made from orange tree flowers and used in the manufacture of perfume and as a flavoring.

nerve (nerv) *n.* The bundles of fibers which convey sensation and originate motion through the body. *Slang* Impudent.

nerve cell *n.* Any of the cells constituting the cellular element of nerve tissue; neuron.

nerve gas *n.* A gas which interferes with the central nervous system resulting in extreme weakness.

nerve impulse *n.* Transmission of a wave of sensation that activates or inhibits a nerve cell.

nerv-ous (ner´vus) *adj.* Affecting the nerves or the nervous system; agitated; worried. **nervously** *adv.* **nervousness** *n.*

nervous breakdown *n.* Nervous exhaustion; emotional or mental weakness, that results from extended mental strain.

nervous system *n.*, *Physiol.* The body system that coordinates, regulates, and controls the various internal functions and responses to stimuli.

ner-vure (nür´vūr) *n.* The vein of a leaf.

nes-cience (nesh´ens) *n.* The lack of knowledge; ignorance

nest (nest) *n.* A place, shelter, or home built by a bird to hold its eggs and young.

nest egg *n.* A supply of money accumulated or saved for future use.

nest-er (nes´tėr) *n.*, *Slang* Formely, a homesteader who established a farm, usually by squatting, on open land.

nes-tle (nes´l) *v.* To settle snugly; to lie close to. **nestler** *n.*

nest-ling (nest´ling) *n.* A young bird still living in the nest.

net (net) *n.* A meshed fabric made of cords, ropes, threads, or other material knotted or woven together; the profit, weight, or price which remains after all additions, subtractions, or adjustments have been made.

neth-er (neth´ėr) *adj.* Situated below or beneath.

net-tle (net´l) *n.* A plant having toothed leaves covered with stinging hairs. *v.* To provoke; to sting.

net-work (net´werk´) *n.* A system of interlacing tracks, channels, or lines; an interconnected system; a group of broadcasting stations.

neu-ral (ner´al) *adj.* Relating to a nerve or the nervous system.

neu-ral-gia (ne ral´ja) *n.* Pain that occurs along the course of a nerve.

neu-ri-lem-ma (nur˝i lem´a) *n.* The delicate plasma membrane sheath of a nerve fiber.

neu-ri-tis (ne rī´tis) *n.* An inflammation of a nerve which causes pain, the loss of reflexes, and muscular decline. **neurotic** *adj.*

neu-ro-cir-cu-la-to´-ry (nur˝ō sur´kū la tōr˝ē) *adj.* Pertaining to the circulatory and nervous systems of the human body.

neu-ro-fi-bril (nür˝o fī´bril) *n., Anat.* The minute fibrils in the nerve cells.

neu-ro-gen-ic (nür˝o jen´ik) *adj., Med.* Beginning in a nerve or the nerve tissue.

neu-rog-li-a (nü rog´lē a) *n.* The delicate connective tissue that binds together and supports the necessary parts of the nervous tissue.

neu-rol-o-gy (ne rol´o jē) *n.* The medical and scientific study of the nervous system and its disorders. **neurological** *adj.* **neurologist** *n.*

neu-ro-ma (nü rō´ma) *n. pl.* **neuromas** *Pathol.* A tumor or mass that is growing from or comprised of nerve tissue.

neu-ron *or* **neu-rone (ner´ on)** *n., Anat.* A granular cell nerve which is the main functional unit of the nervous system.

neu-rop-ter-an (nü rop´tėr an) *n.* Insects having two pairs of net-like membranous wings.

neu-ro-sis (ne rō´sis) *n.* Any one of various functional disorders of the mind or emotions having no physical cause. **neurotic** *adj.* **neurotically** *adv.*

neu-ro-tox-ic (nür˝ō tok´sik) *adj.* Poisonous to nerves or to nerve tissue such as the brain.

neu-ter (nō´tėr) *adj.* Neither feminine nor masculine. *n.* A castrated animal.

neu-tral (nō´tral) *adj.* Not supporting either side of a debate, quarrel, or party; a color which does not contain a decided hue. *Chem.* Neither alkaline nor acid. **neutrality** *n.* **neutrally** *adv.*

neu-tral-ize (nō´tra līz´) *v.* To make or declare neutral.

neu-tri-no (nō trē´nō) *n., Phys.* The uncharged elementary particle having a mass nearing zero.

neu-tron (nō´tron) *n.* An uncharged particle in the nucleus of an atom present in all atomic nuclei except the hydrogen nucleus.

Ne-va-da *n.* A state located in the western part of the United States; statehood October 31, 1864; state capital Carson City.

nev-er (nev´ėr) *adv.* Not ever; absolutely not.

nev-er-more (nev´ėr mōr´) *adv.* Never again.

nev-er–nev-er (nev˝ėr nev˝ėr) *adj.* Imaginary.

nev-er-the-less (nev´ėr the les´) *adv.* Nonetheless; however.

ne-vus (nē´vus) *n. pl.* **nevi** A congenital pigmented mark, or blemish; a birthmark.

new (nō) *adj.* Not used before; unaccustomed; unfamiliar. **newness** *n.*

New Deal *n.* The legislative and social programs of President F. D. Roosevelt designed for relief, economic recovery, and social security during the 1930's.

New Hampshire *n.* A state located in the northeastern part of the United States;

statehood June 21, 1788; state capital Concord.

New Jersey *n.* A state located on the eastern coast of the United States; statehood December 18, 1787; state capital Trenton.

new-ly (nŏ´lē) *adv.* Lately; freshly; recently; anew; afresh.

New Mexico *n.* A state located in the southwestern part of the United States; statehood January 6, 1912; state capital Santa Fe.

news (nŏz) *n. pl.* Current happenings; matter considered newsworthy.

news agency *n.* An organization that gathers news items for periodicals, newspapers, and news reporters.

news-boy (nŏz´boi˝) *n.* A boy who sells or delivers newspapers.

news-break (nŏz´brāk˝) *n.* Any newsworthy occurrence, incident, or event.

news-cast (nŏz´kast´) *n.* A television or radio newsbroadcast.

news conference *n.* A meeting for reporters called by a government official, celebrity or other noteable person to release information and to answer reporter's questions.

news-man (nŏz´man˝) *n. pl.* **newsmen** A person who collects and reports the news; one who sells magazines and newspapers.

news-mon-ger (nŏz´mung˝gėr) *n.* One who actively repeats the news; gossip.

news-pa-per (nŏz´pā´pėr) *n.* A weekly or daily publication which contains recent news and information.

news-print (nŏz´print´) *n.* An inexpensive machine-finished paper made from wood pulp and used chiefly for newspapers and some paperback books.

newt *n.* A small, colorful, semiaquatic salamander found in North America, Europe, and Asia.

New Testament *n.* The second part of the Christian Bible containing the Gospels, Acts, Epistles, and the Book of Revelation.

New World *n.* North and South America.

New Year *n.* The new year about to start. The first few days of the new year.

New Year's Day *n.* January 1st, the first day of the year.

New York *n.* A state located on the eastern coast of the United States; statehood July 26, 1788; state capital Albany.

next (nekst) *adj.* Immediately following or proceeding; nearest in space or position.

next friend *n., Law* A court appointed person, other than a legal guardian who acts in the benefit of an infant or other person lacking the full ability to act for himself.

nex-us (nek´sus) *n. pl.* **nexus** A connected group; connection; connector; a linked series.

NH *abbr.* New Hampshire.

nib-ble (nib´l) *v.* To bite a little at a time; to take small bites. **nibble, nibbler** *n.*

nic-co-lite (nik´o līt˝) *n.* A pale copper-red mineral with a metallic luster that consists mainly of nickel arsenide.

nice (nīs) *adj.* Pleasing; enjoyable; polite and courteous; refined. **nicely** *adv.* **niceness** *n.*

ni-ce-ty (nī´si tē) *n. pl.* **niceties** A delicate point; a fine distinstion. The characteristic of being nice; precision.

niche (nich) *n.* A recess or alcove in a wall, usually used for displays.

nick (nik) *n.* A small chip or cut on a surface; the final critical moment.

nick-el (nik´el) *n.* A hard, silver, metallic element used in alloys and symbolized by Ni; a United States coin worth five cents.

nick-el-o-de-on (nik´e lō´dē an) *n.* A movie theatre which charged five cents for admission; a coin-operated juke box.

nick-name (nik´nām´) *n.* The familiar form of a propername, expressed in a shortened form. **nickname** *v.*

nic-o-tine *or* **nicotin (nik´o tēn´)** *n.* A poisonous alkaloid found in tobacco and used in insecticides and medicine.

nic-ti-tate (nik´ti tāt˝) *v.* To wink.

ni-dic-o-lous (nī dik´o lus) *adj.* Sharing the nest of another; raised for a time in a nest.

ni-dif-u-gous (nī dif´ū gus) *adj.* Indicating a bird that leaves a nest soon after it is hatched.

ni-dus (nīdus) *n.* A nest or breading place; a place where insects deposit their eggs.

niece (nēs) *n.* A daughter of one's sister or brother or one's sister-in-law or brother-in-law.

ni-el-lo (nē el'ō) *n.* The art of decorating silver plates with incised designs filled with a black metallic composition.

nig-gle (nig'l) *v.* To triffle; to find fault in a petty way; to work ineffectively.

nigh (nī) *adv.* Near in relationship, time, or space.

night (nīt) *n.* The time between dusk and dawn or the hours of darkness.

night blindness *n.* A condition of the eyes where the visual capacity is reduced in faint or dim light.

nightcap (nīt'kap') *n.* An alcoholic drink usually taken before retiring for the night.

night club *n.* A place of intertainment that serves liquor and food from night until the early morning.

night-in-gale (nīt'in gāl') *n.* A songbird with brownish plumage, noted for the sweet, nocturnal song of the male.

night-mare (nīt'mâr) *n.* A frightening and horrible dream.

night owl *n.* A person who stays up late at night.

night-time (nīt'tīm") *n.* The time between evening and morning, or dusk to dawn.

night-walker (nīt'wä"ker) *n.* A person who walks around at night.

ni-gres-cent (nī gres'ent) *adj.* Blackish; a shade of black. **nigrescence** *n.*

nig-ri-tude (nig'ri tŏd") *n.* Complete darkness.

ni-gro-sine (nī'gro sēn") *n.* A blue-black dye that is used commercially as a dyeing agent.

ni-hil-ism (nī'i liz"um) *n.* An extreme form of skepticism where traditional values and beliefs are unfounded; the total disbelief in religion or moral obligations and principles.

nil (nil) *v.* Nothing.

nill (nil) *v.* To be unwilling.

nim-ble (nim'bl) *adj.* Marked by a quick, light movement;quick-witted. **nimbleness** *n.* **nimbly** *adv.*

nim-bo-stra-tus (nim"bō strātus) *n. pl.* **nimbostratus** *Meteor.* A low, dark gray cloud often producing rain.

nin-com-poop (nin'kom pŏp') *n.* A silly or stupid person.

nine (nīn) *n.* The cardinal number that is equal to 8+1. **nine** *adj. & pron.*

nine-teen (nīn'tēn') *n.* The cardinal number which follows 18.

nine-ty (nīn'tē) *n. pl.* **nineties** The cardinal number which follows 89.

nin-ny (nin'ē) *n. pl.* **ninnies** A fool; a simpleton.

ni-non (nē non') *n.* A smooth sheer fabric, as chiffon, used for curtains, and women's clothing.

ni-o-bi-um (nī ō'bē um) *n.* A gray, metallic element used in alloys, symbolized by Nb.

nip (nip) *v.* To pinch, bite, or grab something. *n.* A pinch, bite, or grab; a sharp, stinging feeling caused by cold temperatures. **nipper** *n.*

ni-pa (nē'pa) *n.* A fruit-bearing palm; a shelter made from the leaves of the nipa palm.

nip-ping (nip'ing) *adj.* Pertaining to something that is sharp or biting, as cold or wind.

nip-ple (nip'l) *n.* The small projection of a mammary gland through which milk passes; an artificial teat usually made from a type of rubber which a bottle-fed baby nurses.

nip-py (nip'ē) *adj.* Inclined to be biting cold, as chilly weather.

Ni-sei (nē'sā') *n.* A native American of Japanese ancestry.

ni-sus (nīsus) *n. pl.* **nisus** Endeavor; effort; striving; an impulse.

nit (nit) *n.* The egg of a louse or other similar parasitic insects.

nit-id (nit'id) *adj.* Bright; shining; lustrous.

nit–pick (nit'pik") *v., Slang* To be overly critical with unimportant details.

ni-trate (nī′trāt) *n., Chem.* A salt or ester of nitric acid; potassium or sodium nitrate, used as a fertilizer.

ni-tro-gen (nī′tro jen) *n.* A nonmetallic gaseous element which is essential to life, symbolized by N.

nitrogen balance *n.* Equivalent of the intake and loss of nitrogen in an organism or in soil.

ni-tro-glyc-er-in (nī′tro glis′ěr in) *n.* A highly flammable, explosive liquid, used to make dynamite and in medicine, to dilate blood vessels.

nit-wit (nit′wit′) *n.* A stupid person.

ni-val (nīval) *adj.* Pertaining to snow.

nix (niks) *n.* A water spirit usually small and either good or bad.

Nixon, Richard M. *n.* Born in 1913, the 37th president of the United States from 1969-1974 resigned August 9, 1974 due to Watergate scandal.

NM *abbr.* New Mexico.

no (nō) *adv.* Used to express rejection, disagreement, or denial; not so; not at all.

no-bel-i-um (nō bē′lē um) *n.* A radioactive element, symbolized by No.

Nobel prize (nō bel′ prīz) *n.* An award given to people with achievements in literature, economics, medicine, and other fields, established by the last will and testament of Alfred Nobel.

no-bil-i-ty (nō bil′i tē) *n.* The state or quality of being noble; the rank or status of a noble.

no-ble (nō′bl) *adj.* Morally good; superior in character or nature. *n.* A person of rank or noble birth. **nobleman, noblemen, nobleness** *n.* **nobly** *adv.*

no-blesse (nō bles′) *n.* Nobility; person of noble rank collectively.

noblesse oblige *n.* The obligation of people of wealth and social position to behave with honor and generosity.

no-bod-y (nō′bod′ē) *pron.* Not anybody; no person.

no-cent (nō sent) *adj.* Harmful; hurtful, or injuries.

noc-tur-nal (nok ter′nal) *adj.* Pertaining to or occurring during the night; active at night and quiet during the daylight hours. **nocturnally** *adv.*

noc-u-ous (nok′ū us) *adj.* Harmful; injuries.

nod (nod) *n.* A quick downward motion of the head as one falls off to sleep; a downward motion of the head indicating acceptance or approval. *v.* To move the head down and then up again.

nod-dy (nod′ē) *n. pl.* **noddies** A simpleton; a fool; a stupid person.

node (nōd) *n.* A swollen or thickened enlargement.

nod-ule (noj′ōl) *n.* A little knot or lump.

no-dus (nō′dus) *n.* A difficult situation.

no-el (nō el′) *n.* A Christmas carol.

no-et-ic (nō et′ik) *adj.* Pertaining to the mind or intellect.

nog (nog) *n.* A wooden peg or block; a strong ale.

nog-gin (nog′in) *n.* A small mug or cup; a small quantity of a beverage.

nog-ging (nog′ing) *n.* Brick masonry used to fill the spaces of a wooden frame.

no-hitter (nō′hit′ěr) *n., Baseball* A game with no hits.

no-how (nō′hou″) *adv.* In no way or manner; not at all.

noil (noil) *n.* A short fiber of wool, cotton, or silk often separated during combing and often separately spun into yarn.

noise (noiz) *n.* A sound which is disagreeable or loud; in computer science, unwanted data in an electronic signal.

noise-less (noiz′lis) *adj.* Making no noise; silent; quiet.

noi-some (noi′som) *adj.* Offensive to the sense of smell; noxious; harmful.

nois-y (noi′zē) *adj.* Making an excessive amount noise; abounding in or attended with noise.

no-mad (nō′mad) *n.* A member of a group of people who wander from place to place. **nomadic** *adj.* **nomadism** *n.*

nom de guerre (nom″ de gâr′) *n.* An assumed name that one pursues in a profession.

no-men-cla-tor (nōmen klā″těr) *n.* An inventor of names.

no-men-cla-ture (nŏ′mɛn klā′chėr) *n*. The set of names used to describe the elements of art, science, and other fields.

nom-i-nal (nom′i nal) *adj*. Of or relating to something that is in name or form only. **nominally** *adv*.

nom-i-nate (nom′i nāt′) *v*. To select a candidate for an elective office; to appoint or designate to a position. **nomination, nominator** *n*.

nom-i-nee (nom′i nē′) *n*. A person nominated for a position or office.

no-mism (nŏ′miz um) *n*. Conduct based on moral or religious beliefs.

no-mol-o-gy (nō mol′ojē) *n*. The science of the formulation of law; the science that deals directly with the laws of reason.

non- *prefix* Not.

non-a-bra-sive (non″a brā′siv) *adj*. Not causing wear by friction.

non-ab-sorb-ent (non″ab sor′bent) *adj*. Unable to absorb liquids.

non-ac-cept-ance (non″ak sep′tans) *n*. Failure to accept.

non-ad-he-sive (non″ad hē′siv) *adj*. Not having the quality to adhere.

non-ad-min-is-tra-tive (non″ad min′i strā″tiv) *adj*. Not pertaining to the executive staff of an organization.

non-a-ge-nar-i-an (non″a je nâr′ēan) *adj*. A person between the ages of 90 and 100 years.

non-a-gon (non′a gon″) *n*. A geometric figure with nine sides and nine angles.

non-al-co-hol-ic (non″al ko ho′lik) *adj*. Not containing alcohol.

non-ap-pear-ance (non″a pēr′ans) *n*. The failure to appear.

non-be-liev-er (non″bi lē′vėr) *n*. One who does not believe; a person who does not believe in God.

non-cha-lant (non′sha länt′) *adj*. Giving an effect of casual unconcern. **nonchalance** *n*. **nonchalantly** *adv*.

non-col-le-gi-ate (non″ko lē′jit) *adj*. Not belonging to a college.

non-com (non′kom″) *n*. A noncommis-

sioned officer.

non-com-bat-ant (non kom′ba tant) *n*. A member of the armed forces whose duties or direct responsibility does not involve actual fighting.

non-com-bus-ti-ble (non″kom bus′ti bl) *adj*. Not easily ignitable.

non-com-mu-ni-ca-ble (non″ka mū′i ka bl) *adj*. Not transmissible through personal contact, as a disease.

non com-pos men-tis (non kom′pos men′tis) *adj*. Mentally unbalanced; not of sound mind.

non-con-duc-tor (non″kon duk′tėr) *n*. A substance which conducts with difficulty or in a very small degree, such as electricity, heat, or sound.

non-con-form-ist (non′kon for′mist) *n*. One who does not feel compelled to follow or accept traditions. **nonconformity** *n*.

non-con-tagious (non″kon tā′jus) *adj*., *Med*. Of a disease, not transmissable by contact.

non-co-op-er-a-tion (non″kō op″e rā shan) *n*. Failure to cooperate with an individual, party, or organization.

non-cor-ro-sive (non″ko rō′sive) *adj*. Unable to corrode, as certain acids.

non-de-duct-i-ble (non″di duk′ti bl) *adj*. Unable to subtract.

non-de-liv-er-y (non″di liv′e rē) *n*. Unable to deliver due to a contract or expectation.

non-de-script (non″di skript′) *n*. A person or something not easily classed or described.

non-de-struct-ive (non″di stuk′tiv) *adj*. Not causing destruction, or ruin.

non-dis-tinc-tive (non″di stingk′tiv) *adj*. Not distinctive.

none (nun) *adj*. Not any; not one.

non-ef-fec-tive (non″i fek′tiv) *adj*. Without the necessary power to cause or produce effect.

non-en-ti-ty (non en′ti tē) *n. pl*. **nonentities.** Nonexistence; something that does not exist.

non-es-sen-tial (non″i sen′shal) *adj*. Not essential; not absolutely necessary. *n*. An unnecessary person or thing.

none-the-less (non˝the les´) *adv.* Never the less.

non-ex-empt (nun˝ig zempt´) *adj.* Not exempt from liability.

non-ex-por-ta-tion (non˝eks pōr tā´shan) *n.* Failure to export.

non-sec-tar-i-an (non´sek târ´ē an) *adj.* Not associated with or restricted to one religion, faction, or sect.

non-sense (non´sens) *n.* Something that seems senseless or foolish; something which is very unimportant.

non seq-ui-tur (non sek´wi tėr) *n.* An inference that does not follow as the logical result of what has preceded it.

non-sex-ist *adj.* Not discriminating on the basis of gender.

noo-dle (nōd´l) *n.* A flat strip of dried dough made with eggs and flour. *Slang* The head.

nook (nek) *n.* A corner, recess, or secluded place.

noon (nōn) *n.* The middle of the day; 12: 00 o'clock.

noose (nōs) *n.* A loop of rope secured by a slipknot, allowing it to decrease in size as the rope is pulled.

nor (nor) *conj.* Not either; or not.

norm (norm) *n.* A rule, model, or pattern typical for a particular group.

nor-mal (nor´mal) *adj.* Ordinary, average, usual; having average intelligence; standard. **normalcy, normality** *n.* **normally** *adv.*

north (north) *n.* The direction to a person's left while facing east.

North Carolina *n.* A state located in the southeastern part of the United States; statehood November 21, 1789; state capital Raleigh.

North Dakota *n.* A state located in the north central part of the United States; statehood November 2, 1889; state capital Bismarck.

nose (nōz) *n.* The facial feature containing the nostrils; the sense of smell. *v.* To discover by smell.

nose-bleed (nōz´blēd˝) *n.* Bleeding from the nose.

nose cone *n., Aeron.* A cone-shaped, heat-resistant front portion or section of a missile or rocket.

nose-dive *n.* A sudden plunge as made by an aircraft.

nose-piece (nōz´pēs˝) *n.* A piece, on a helmet that covers the nose; the part on eyeglasses that rests or the nose.

no-sol-o-gy (nō sol´o jē) *n. pl.* **nosologies** A systematic list of diseases; the branch of medical science that deals with the grouping of diseases.

nos-tal-gia (no stal´ja) *n.* A yearning to return to the past. **nostalgic** *adj.*

nos-tril (nos´tril) *n.* The external openings of the nose.

nos-trum (nos´trum) *n.* A secret remedy for a medical condition.

nos-y *or* **nos-ey (nō´zē)** *adj.* Snoopy; inquisitive; prying.

not (not) *adv.* In no manner; used to express refusal or denial.

no-ta-ble (nō´ta bl) *adj.* Remarkable, distinguished. *n.* A person or thing which is notable. *v.* To acknowledge and certify as a notary public. **notably** *adv.*

notary public *n.* A person who is legally authorized as a public officer to witness and certify documents.

no-ta-tion (nō tā´shan) *n.* A process or system of figures or symbols used in specialized fields to represent quantities, num-bers, or values. **notational** *adj.*

notch (noch) *n.* A v-shaped indentation or cut. **notch** *v.*

note (nōt) *n.* A record or message in short form. *Mus.* A tone or written character. **note** *v.*

note-book (nōt´bük˝) *n.* A blank book for writting notes or memoranda.

not-ed (nō´tid) *adj.* Famous; well-known.

note-wor-thy (nōt´wür˝thē) *adj.* Significant; worthy of observation or attention. **noteworthily** *adv.* **noteworthiness** *n.*

noth-ing (nuth´ing) *n.* Not anything; no part or portion. *adv.* In no way; not at all.

no-tice (nō´tis) *n.* An announcement; a noti-

fication. *v.* To give notice; to become a-
ware of. **noticeable** *adj.* **noticeably** *adv.*
no-ti-fi-ca-tion (nō″ti fi kā′shan) *n.* The act
of notifying; a notice in words of writing;
anything which gives information.
no-ti-fy (nō′ti fī′) *v.* To give notice of; to
announce. **notifier, notification** *n.*
no-tion (nō′shan) *n.* An opinion; a general
concept; an idea. *pl.* Small useful articles,
as thread or buttons. **notions** *n.*
no-tion-al (nō′sha nal) *adj.* Referring to
or expressing ideas, concepts.
no-to-ri-ous (nō tōr′ē us) *adj.* Having a
widely known and usually bad reputation.
not-with-stand-ing (not′with stan′ding)
In spite of. *adv.* Nevertheless; anyway. *conj.*
Although.
nou-gat (nō′gat) *n.* A confection made of
sugar , honey, or corn syrup, contains nuts
and fruit pieces.
noun (noun) *n.* A word which names a person, place, or thing.
nour-ish (ner′ish) *v.* To furnish with the
nutriment and other substances needed for
growth and life; to support. **nourishing** *adj.*
nourishment *n.*
nour-ish-ment (nür′ish ment) *n.* Food, the
act of nourishing.
nou-veau riche (nō′vō rēsh′) *n.* A person
who has recently become rich.
no-va (nō′va) *n. pl.* -vae *or* -vas A star
which flares up and fades away after a few
years or months.
nov-el (nov′el) *n.* An inventive narrative
dealing with human experiences; a book.
novelist *n.*
nov-el-ty (nov′el tē) *n. pl.* -ies Something
unusual or new.
No-vem-ber (nō vem′bėr) *n.* The 11th
month of the calendar year, having 30 days.
nov-ice (nov′is) *n.* A person who is new and
unfamiliar with an activity or business.
now (nou) *adv.* At the present time; immediately.
now-a-days (nou′a dāz″) *adv.* At the present
time.
no-way (nō′wā″) *adv.* Not at all.
no-where (nō′hwâr′) *adv.* Not in or at any

place.
nox-ious (nok′shus) *adj.* Harmful; obnoxious; corrupt.
noz-zle (noz′l) *n.* A projecting spout or vent
of something.
nu-ance (nō′äns) *n.* A gradation or variation by which a color passes from the
lightest possible shade to its darkest shade.
nub (nub) *n.* A knob; a small piece or lump.
nub-bin (nub′in) *n.* A small piece.
nu-bile (nō′bil) *adj.* Suitable or ready for
marriage; of the right age for marriage.
nu-bi-lous (nō′bi lus) *adj.* Cloudy; foggy;
vague.
nu-cha (nō′ka) *n. pl.* **nuchae** The nape of
the neck.
nu-cle-ar (nō′klē ėr) *adj.* Pertaining to and
resembling a nucleus; relating to atomic
energy.
nuclear force *n.* The powerful and explosive interaction between the nucleons
which holds the atomic nuclei together.
nu-cle-ase (nō′klē ās″) *n.* An enzyme which
breaks down nucleic acids.
nu-cle-ate (nō′klē it) *v.* To form into a nucleus; to gather round or form a nucleus.
adj. Having a nucleus.
nucleation particles *n. pl.* Microscopic salt
grains and other articles in the atmosphere
that form the nucleus around which rain-
drops develope.
nu-cle-on (nō′klē on″) *n., Phys.* An elementary particle of the atomic nucleus,
a proton or neutron.
nu-cle-on-ics *n. pl.* The science dealing
with the practical application of nuclear
physics.
nu-cle-us (nō′klē us) *n.* The main element
around which all other elements group;
the central core of an atom.
nude (nōd) *adj.* Unclothed; naked. **nudity,
nudist** *n.*
nu-di-cau-lous (nō″di ko′lus) *adj., Bot.*
having leafless stems.
nud-ism (nō′diz um) *n.* The practice of
going naked as a means of healthful living.
nudist *n.*
nu-ga-to-ry (nō′ga tōr″ē) *adj.* Trifling;

worthless; inoperative.

nudge (nuj) *v.* To poke or push gently.

nug-get (nug´it) *n.* A lump, as of precious metal.

nui-sance (nŏ´sans) *n.* A source of annoyance or inconvenience.

null (nul) *adj.* Invalid; having no value or consequence. **nullification** *n.*

nul-li-fy (nul´i fī´) *v.* To counteract.

numb (num) *adj.* Lacking physical sensation; paralyzed or stunned. **numb** *v.* **numbness** *n.*

num-ber (num´bėr) *n.* A word or symbol which is used in counting or which indicates how many or which one in a series.

number-less *adj.* Too many to be counted.

nu-men (nŏ´min) *n. pl.* **numina** A divine spiritual force or influence, one thought to dwell within an object.

nu-meral (nŏ´mėr al) *n.* A symbol, figure, letter, word, or a group of these which represents a number.

nu-mer-a-tion (nŏ˝me rā´shan) *n.* The act of numbering or calculating.

nu-mer-a-tor (nŏ´me rā´tėr) *n.* The term in mathematics indicating how many parts are to be taken; the number in a fraction which appears above the line.

nu-mer-ous (nŏ´mėr us) *adj.* Consisting or made up of many units, things, or individuals.

num-mu-lar (num´ū lėr) *adj.* Characterized by circular lesions.

nun (nun) *n.* A woman who has joined a religious group and has taken vows to give up worldly goods and never to marry.

nup-tial (nup´shal) *adj.* Of or pertaining to a wedding. **nuptials** *n. pl.* A wedding.

nurse (ners) *n.* A person who is specially trained to care for disabled or sick persons. *v.* To feed a baby from a mother's breast;to provide care to a sick or disabled person.

nurse-maid (nŭrs´mād˝) *n.* A maid servant employed to take care of children.

nurs-er-y (ners´se rē) *n. pl.* **-ies** A room reserved for the special use of infants or small children; a business or place where trees, shrubs, and flowers are raised and sold.

nursery bottle *n.* A bottle with a nipple, used for feeding infants.

nurs-er-y-man (nŭr´se rē man) *n. pl.* **nurserymen** A person who owns or is employed at a nursery.

nursery rhyme *n.* A story for children written in rhyme.

nursery school *n.* A school for children under the age of five.

nur-ture (ner´chėr) *n.* The upbringing, care, or training of a child. **nurture** *v.* **nurturer** *n.*

nut (nut) *n.* A hard-shelled fruit or seed which contains an inner, often edible kernal. *Slang* A person who does crazy or silly things.

nu-ta-tion (nŏ tā´shan) *n.* The involuntary nodding of the head.

nut-crack-er (nut´krak´ėr) *n.* A hinged tool for cracking nuts.

nut-let (nut´lit) *n.* A small nut or nut-like fruit or seed.

nut-meg (nut´meg) *n.* The hard seed of a tropical evergreen tree, which is grated and used as a spice.

nut-pick (nut´pik˝) *n.* A small sharp, pointed instrument, used to pick the soft kernal from nuts.

nu-tri-ent (nŏ´trē ent) *n.* A substance which nourishes. **nutrient** *adj.*

nu-tri-tion (nŏ trish´an) *n.* The process by which a living being takes in food and uses it to live and grow. **nutritive, nutritional** *adj.* **nutritionally** *adv.* **nutritionist** *n.*

nu-tri-tious (nŏ trish´us) *adj.* Containing or serving as nourishment.

nuts (nuts) *adj., Slang* Foolish, crazy.

nut-ty (nut´ē) *adj.* Producing nuts; tasting like nuts. *Slang* silly; eccentric; crazy. **nuttiness** *n.*

nuz-zle (nuz´l) *v.* To gently rub against something with the nose; to cuddle.

NV *abbr.* Nevada.

NY *abbr.* New York.

NYC *abbr.* New York City.

nyc-ta-lo-pi-a (nik˝ta lō´pē a) *n.* A condition of the eyes where the sight is good during day or bright light but abnormally poor at night or in dim light; night blindness.

ny-lon (nī´lon) *n.* A strong, elastic material; yarn or fabric made from nylon. *pl.* **nylons** Stockings made of nylon.

nymph (nimf) *n.* Nature goddesses who lived in woods, rivers, and trees; various immature insects, especially the larva which undergoes incomplete metamorphosis.

O

O o (ō) The 15th letter of the English alphabet.

O (ō) *n.* A word used before a name when talking to that person; an interjection.

oaf (ōf) *n.* A stupid or clumsy person. **oafish** *adj.* **oafishly** *adv.*

oak (ōk) *n.* A large tree of durable wood bearing acorns. **oaken** *adj.*

oar (ōr) *n.* A long pole, flat at one end, used in rowing a boat.

oasis (ō ā´sis) *n. pl.* **oases** A fertile section in the desert which contains water; anything that can provide refuge.

oat (ōt) *n.* A cultivated cereal grass whose grain or seed is used as food for humans as well as animals.

oath (ōth) *n.* A solemn promise in the name of God or on a Bible that a person will speak only the truth.

oat-meal (ōt´mēl´) *n.* A cooked cereal food made from rolled oats.

ob-du-rate (ob´de rit) *adj.* Stubborn; hardhearted; not giving in. **obduracy** *n.*

o-be-di-ent (ō bē´dē ent) *adj.* Obeying or willing to do what one is told.

ob-e-lisk (ob´e lisk) *n.* A tall, four-sided stone pillar which slopes from a pointed top.

o-bese (ō bēs´) *adj.* Very fat. **obesity** *n.*

o-bey (ō bā´) *v.* To carry out instructions; to be guided or controlled; to follow directions. **obeyer** *n.*

o-bit-u-ar-y (ō bich´ō er´ē) *n. pl.* **-ies** A published announcement that a person has died, often containing a short biography of the person's life.

ob-ject (ob jekt´) *v.* To voice disapproval; to protest. *n.* Something that is visible or can be touched. A word in a sentence which explains who or what is acted upon.

ob-jec-tion (ob jek´shan) *n.* A feeling of opposition or disagreement, etc.; the reason for a disagreement.

ob-jec-tive (ob jek´tiv) *adj.* Pertaining to or dealing with material objects rather than mental concepts. *n.* Something that one works toward, a goal; a purpose. **objectivity** *n.*

ob-la-tion (o blā´shan) *n.* A religious offering or the act of sacrifice; that which is offered.

ob-li-ga-tion (ob´li gā´shan) *n.* A promise or feeling of duty; something one must do because one's conscience or the law demands it; a debt which must be repaid.

o-blige (o blīj´) *v.* To constrain; to put in one's debt by a service or favor; to do a favor. **obliger** *n.* **obligingly** *adv.*

o-blique (o blēk´) *adj.* Inclined; not level or straight up and down; slanting; indirect. **obliqueness** *n.* **obliquity** *n.*

o-blit-er-ate (o blit´e rāt´) *v.* To blot out or eliminate completely; to wipe out. **obliteration** *n.* **obliterator** *n*

o-bliv-i-on (o bliv´ē an) *n.* The condition of being utterly forgotten; the act of forgetting.

ob-liv-i-ous (o bliv´ē us) *adj.* Not aware or conscious of what is happening; unmindful. **obliviously** *adv.*

ob-long (ob´long´) *adj.* Rectangular; longer in one direction than the other; normally, the horizontal dimension; the greater in length. **oblong** *n.*

ob-nox-ious (ob nok´shus) *adj.* Very unpleasant; repugnant. **obnoxiousness** *n.*

o-boe (ō´bō) *n.* A double reed, tube-shaped woodwind instrument. **oboist** *n.*

ob-scene (ob sēn´) *adj.* Indecent;

disgusting. **obscenity** *n.*

ob-scure (*ob* skūr´) *adj.* Remote; not clear; faint. *v.* To make dim; to conceal by covering. **obscurely** *adv.* **obscurity** *n.*

ob-ser-va-tion (*ob´*zer vā´sh*a*n) *n.* The act of observing something; that which is observed; a judgment or opinion. **observational** *adj.* **observationally** *adv.*

ob-ser-va-to-ry (*ob* zer´vatōr´ē) *n. pl.* -ies A building or station furnished with instruments for studying the natural phenomenon; a high tower affording a panoramic view.

ob-serve (*ob* zerv´) *v.* To pay attention; to watch. **observable** *adj.* **observant** *adj.* **observably** *adv.* **observer** *n.*

ob-sess (*ob* ses´) *v.* To preoccupy the mind with an idea or emotion; to be abnormally preoccupied. **obsession** *n.*

ob-so-lete (*ob´so* lēt´) *adj.* No longer in use; out-of-date; no longer current. **obsolescence** *n.* **obsolescent** *adj.*

ob-sta-cle (*ob´sta* kl) *n.* An obstruction; anything which opposes or stands in the way of.

ob-ste-tri-cian (*ob´*sti trish *a*n) *n.* A physician who specializes in the care of a woman during pregnancy and childbirth.

ob-stet-rics (*ob* ste´triks) *n.* The branch of medicine which deals with pregnancy and childbirth.

ob-sti-nate (*ob´sti* nit) *adj.* Stubbornly set to an opinion or course of action; difficult to control or manage; hardheaded. **obstinacy** *n.* **obstinately** *adv.*

ob-strep-er-ous (*ob* strep´ẽr us) *adj.* Noisy, unruly, or boisterous in resistance to advice or control. **obstreperously** *adv.* **obstreperousness** *n.*

ob-struct (*ob* strukt´) *v.* To block, hinder or impede. **obstructor** *n.* **obstruction** *n.*

ob-tain (*ob* tān´) *v.* To acquire or gain possession of. **obtainable** *adj.* **obtainer** *n.*

ob-trude (*ob* trŏd´) *v.* To thrust forward without request or warrant; to call attention to oneself.

ob-tuse (*ob* tŏs´) *adj.* Lacking acuteness of feeling; insensitive; not distinct or clear to

the senses, as pain or sound. *Bot.* Rounded or blunt at the end, as a petal or leaf.

ob-vi-ate (*ob´*vē āt´) *v.* To counter or prevent by effective measures; to provide for.

ob-vi-ous (*ob´*vē us) *adj.* Easily seen, discovered, or understood.

oc-ca-sion (*o* kā´zh*a*n) *n.* The time an event occurs; the event itself; a celebration. *v.* To bring about; to cause.

oc-ca-sion-al (*o* kā´zh*a* n*a*l) *adj.* Appearing or occurring irregularly or now and then; intended, made, or suitable for a certain occasion; incidental.

oc-ci-den-tal (ok´si den´t*a*l) *adj.* Western.

oc-cip-i-tal bone (ok sip´i t*a*l) *n., Anat.* The bone which forms the back of the skull.

oc-cult (*o* kult´) *adj.* Concealed. *n.* The action or influence of supernatural agencies or secret knowledge of them.

oc-cu-pan-cy (ok´kū p*a*n sē) *n.* The state or act of being occupied; the act of holding in possession; the time or term during which something is occupied.

oc-cu-pa-tion (ok´ū pā´sh*a*n) *n.* A job, profession, or vocation; a foreign military force which controls an area.

occupational therapy *n., Med.* The treatment of mental, nervous, or physical disabilities by means of work designed to promote recovery or readjustment.

oc-cu-py (ok´ū pī´) *v.* To take and retain possession of; to live in. **occupier** *n.*

oc-cur (*o* ker´) *v.* To suggest; to have something come to mind; to happen.

o-cean (ō´sh*a*n) *n.* An immense body of salt water which covers 3/4 of the earth's surface; one of the oceans. **oceanic** *adj.*

o-ce-an-og-ra-phy (ō´shē *a* nog´rafē) *n.* The science of oceanic phenomena dealing with underwater research.

o'clock (*o* klok´) *adv.* Of, or according to the clock.

Oct *abbr.* October.

oc-ta-gon (ok´t*a* gon´) *n.* A polygon with eight angles and eight sides. **octagonal** **octagonally** *adv.*

oc-tave (ok′tiv) *n.*, *Music* A tone on the eighth degree above or below another tone.

Oc-to-ber (ok tō′bėr) *n.* The 10th month of the calendar year, having 31 days.

oc-to-ge-nar-i-an (ok′to je nâr′ēan) *n.* A person between the ages of 80 and 90.

oc-to-pus (ok′to pus) *n.* *pl.* **-es** *or* **-pi** A cephalopod with a sac-like body and eight tentacles containing double rows of suckers.

oc-u-lar (ok′ū lėr) *adj.* Of or relating to the eye; perceived or done by the eye.

OD *n.* *Slang* An overdose of a drug; one who has taken an overdose. *v.* To overdose; to die from an overdose.

odd (od) *adj.* Unusual; strange; singular; left over; not even. **oddly** *adv.* **oddness** *n.*

odds (odz) *n.* An equalizing advantage given to a weaker opponent; a ratio between the probability against and the probability for something happening or being true.

odds and ends *n.* Miscellaneous things; remnants; scraps.

ode (ōd) *n.* A lyric poem usually honoring a person or event.

o-dom-e-ter (ō dom′i tėr) *n.* A device in a vehicle used to measure distance traveled. **odometry** *n.*

o-dor (ō′dėr) *n.* A smell; a sensation which occurs when the sense of smell is stimulated.

od-ys-sey (od′i sē) *n.* A long voyage marked by many changes of fortune; a spiritual quest.

oedipus complex (ed′i pus kom′pleks) *n.* An unconscious sexual feeling a child develops towards the parent of the opposite sex.

of (uv) *prep.* Proceeding; composed of; relating to.

off (of) *adv.* From a position or place; no longer connected or on. *adj.* Canceled. *prep.* Away from. *interj.* Go away.

of-fend (o fend′) *v.* To make angry; to arouse resentment; to break a law **offender** *n.*

of-fense (o fens′) *n.* A violation of a duty, rule, or propriety; the act of causing displeasure; the act of assaulting or attacking; in football and other sports, the team having possession of the ball.

of-fen-sive (o fen′siv) *adj.* Disagreeable or unpleasant; causing resentment; insulting.

of-fer (o′fėr) *v.* To present for acceptance or rejection; to present as an act of worship; to make available; to present in order to satisfy a requirement.

of-fer-ing (o′fėr ing) *n.* The act of one who offers; a contribution, as money, given to the support of a church.

off-hand (of′hand′) *adv. or adj.* Without preparation or premeditation.

of-fice (o′fis) *n.* A place where business or professional duties are conducted; an important job, duty, or position.

of-fi-cer (o′fi sėr) *n.* A person who holds a title, position of authority, or office; a policeman.

of-fi-cial (o fish′al) *adj.* Something derived from proper authority. *n.* One who holds a position or office; a person who referees a game such as football, basketball, or soccer. **officialism** *n.* **officially** *adv.*

of-fi-ci-ate (o fish′ē at′) *v.* To carry out the duties and functions of a position or office.

of-fi-cious (o fish′us) *adj.* Offering one's services or advice in an unduly forward manner. **officiously officiousness** *n.*

off-spring (of′spring′) *n.* *pl.* **-springs** The descendants of a person, plant, or animal.

of-ten (o′fen) *adv.* Frequently; many times.

oh (ō) Used to express surprise, fear, or pain.

OH *abbr.* Ohio.

O-hi-o *n.* A state in the midwestern section of the United States; statehood March 1, 1803; state capital Columbus.

ohm (ōm) *n.* A unit of electrical resistance equal to the resistance of a conductor in which one volt produces a current of one ampere.

oil (oil) *n.* Any of various substances,

usually thick, which can be burned or easily melted; a lubricant. *v.* To lubricate.

oilcloth (oil´kloth´) *n.* A cloth treated with oil which therefore becomes waterproof.

oil field *n.* An area rich in petroleum; an area which has been made ready for oil production.

oil slick *n.* A layer of oil floating on water.

oint-ment (oint´ment) *n.* An oily substance used on the skin as an aid to healing or to soften the skin.

OK *abbr.* Oklahoma.

Ok-la-ho-ma *n.* A state in the south central part of the United States; statehood November 16, 1907; state capital Oklahoma City.

o-kra (ō´kra) *n.* A tall tropical and semi-tropical plant with green pods that can be either fried or cooked in soups.

ok-tane (ok´tān) *n.* Any of several hydrocarbon compounds which occur in petroleum.

old (ōld) *adj.* Having lived or existed for a long time; of a certain age. *n.* Former times.

old-en (ōl´den) *adj.* Of or relating to times long past; ancient.

old–fash-ioned (ōld´fash´ond) *adj.* Pertaining to or characteristic of former times or old customs; not modern or up-to-date.

Old Glory *n.* The flag of the United States of America.

Old Testament *n.* The first of two parts of the Christian Bible, containing the history of the Hebrews, the laws of Moses, the writings of the prophets, the Holy Scriptures of Judaism, and other material.

Old World (ōld´werld´) *n.* The eastern hemisphere, including Asia, Europe, and Africa.

ol-fac-tory (ol fak´to rē) *adj.* Pertaining to the sense of smell.

oli-gar-chy (ol´i gär´kē) *n. pl.* -ies A government controlled by a small group for corrupt and selfish purposes; the group exercising such control.

ol-ive (ol´iv) *n.* A small oval fruit from an evergreen tree with leathery leaves and yellow flowers, valuable as a source of oil.

Olympic Games (ō lim´pik) *n. pl.* International athletic competition held every four years, based on an ancient Greek festival.

om-buds-man (om´bŏdz man´) *n.* -men A government official appointed to report and receive grievances against the government.

om-e-let *or* **om-e-lette** (om´e lit) *n.* A dish made from eggs and other items, such as bacon, cheese, and ham, and cooked until set.

o-men (ō´men) *n.* A phenomenon which is thought of as a sign of something to come, whether good or bad.

om-i-nous (om´i nus) *adj.* Foreshadowed by an omen or by a presentiment of evil; threatening.

o-mis-sion (ō mish´an) *n.* The state or act of being omitted; anything neglected or left out.

o-mit (ō mit´) *v.* To neglect; to leave out; to overlook.

om-ni-bus (om´ni bus´) *n.* A public vehicle designed to carry a large number of people; a bus. *adj.* Covering a complete collection of objects or cases.

om-nip-o-tent (om nip´o tent) *adj.* Having unlimited or infinite power or authority.

om-nis-cient (om nish´ent) *adj.* Knowing all things; having universal or complete knowledge.

om-niv-or-ous (om niv´er us) *adj.* Feeding on both vegetable and animal substances; absorbing everything. **omnivorously** *adv.*

on (on) *prep.* Positioned upon; indicating proximity; indicating direction toward; with respect to. *adv.* In a position of covering; forward.

once (wuns) *adv.* A single time; at any one time. *conj.* As soon as.

once-over (wuns´ō´ver) *n., Slang* A swift but comprehensive glance.

on-col-o-gy (ong kol´o jē) *n.* The study of tumors. **oncological, oncologic** *adj.* **oncologist** *n.*

one (wun) *adj.* Single; undivided. *n.* A single person; a unit; the first cardinal number (1). **oneself** *pron.* One's own self.

one–sid-ed (wun´sī´did) *adj.* Partial to one side; unjust. **one–sidedness** *n.*

on-ion (un´yon) *n.* An edible bulb plant having a pungent taste and odor.

on–line (on´līn´) *adj., Computer Science* Controlled directly by a computer.

on-ly (ōn´lē) *adj.* Sole; for one purpose alone. *adv.* Without anyone or anything else. *conj.* Except; but.

on-shore (on´shōr´) *adj.* Moving or coming near or onto the shore. **onshore** *adv.*

on-slaught (on´slot´) *n.* A fierce attack.

on-to (on´tö) *prep.* To a position or place; aware of.

o-nus (ō nus) *n.* A burden; a responsibility or duty which is difficult or unpleasant; the blame.

on-ward (on´wèrd) *adv.* Moving forward in time or space. **onwards** *adj.*

on-yx (on´iks) *n.* A gemstone; a chalcedony in layers of different colors.

oo-dles (öd´lz) *n. pl., Slang* A great or large quantity.

ooze (öz) *n.* A soft deposit of slimy mud on the bottom of a body of water; muddy or marshy ground; a bog. *v.* To flow or leak slowly; to disappear little by little.

o-pal (ō´pal) *n.* A translucent mineral composed of silicon, often marked with an iridescent play of colors. **opaline** *adj.*

o-paque (ō pāk´) *adj.* Not transparent; dull; obscure. **opacity** *n.* **opaqueness** *n.*

OPEC *abbr.* Organization of Petroleum Exporting Countries.

o-pen (ō´pen) *adj.* Having no barrier; not covered, sealed, locked, or fastened. *n.* A contest for both amateurs and professionals. *v.* To begin or start. **openness** *n.* **openly** *adv.*

open–and–shut (ō´pen an shut´) *adj.* Easily settled; simple to decide.

op-era (ō´pèr a) *n.* A drama having music as a dominant factor, an orchestral accompaniment, acting, and scenery.

op-er-ate (op´e rāt´) *v.* To function, act, or work effectively; to perform an operation, as surgery. **operative** *adj.*

op-er-a-tion (op´e rā´shan) *n.* The process of operating; the system or method of operating; a series of acts to effect a certain purpose; a process; a procedure performed on the human body with surgical instruments to restore health; various mathematical or logical processes.

op-er-a-tor (op´e rā´tèr) *n.* A person who operates a machine; the owner or person in charge of a business. *Slang* A shrewd person.

oph-thal-mol-o-gy (of´thal mol´o jē) *n.* A branch of medical science dealing with diseases of the eye, its structure, and functions.

o-pin-ion (o pin´yan) *n.* A judgment held with confidence; a conclusion held without positive knowledge.

o-pi-um (ō´pē um) *n.* A bitter, highly addictive drug; a narcotic.

o-pos-sum (o pos´um) *n. pl.* **-sum** *or* **-sums** An octurnal animal which hangs by its tail and carries its young in a pouch.

op-po-nent (o pō´nent) *n.* An adversary; one who opposes another.

op-por-tune (op´èr tön´) *adj.* Occurring at the right or appropriate time. **opportunist** *n.* **opportunely** *adv.*

op-por-tu-ni-ty (op´èr tö´ni tē) *n. pl.* **-ies** A favorable position; a chance for advancement.

op-pose (o pōz´) *v.* To be in direct contention with; to resist; to be against. **opposable** *adj.* **opposition** *n.*

op-po-site (op´o zot) *adj.* Situated or placed on opposing sides. **oppositeness** *n.*

op-press (o pres´) *v.* To worry or trouble the mind; to weigh down; to burden as if to enslave. **oppression** *n.* **oppressor** *n.*

op-tic (op´tik) *adj.* Pertaining or referring to sight or the eye.

op-ti-cal (op´ti kal) *adj.* Pertaining to sight; constructed or designed to assist vision. **optically** *adv.*

op-ti-cian (op tish´an) *n.* A person who makes eyeglasses and other optical articles.

op-ti-mism (op´ti miz´um) *n.* A doctrine which emphasizes that everything is for the best.

op-ti-mum (op´ti mum) *n. pl.* **-ma** The degree or condition producing the most favorable result. *adj.* Conducive to the best result.

op-tion (op´shan) *n.* The act of choosing or the power of choice; a choice.

op-tion-al *adj.* Left to one's decision; elective; not required.

op-tom-e-try (op tom´i trē) *n.* The occupation or profession of examining the eyes and prescribing corrective lenses.

op-u-lence (op´ū lens) *n.* Wealth in abundance; affluence.

or (or) *conj.* A word used to connect the second of two choices or possibilities, indicating uncertainty. *suffix* Indicating a person or thing which does something.

OR *abbr.* Oregon.

or-a-cle (or´a kl) *n.* A seat of worship where ancient Romans and Greeks consulted the gods for answers; a person of unquestioned wisdom. **oracular** *adj.*

o-ral (ōr´al) *adj.* Spoken or uttered through the mouth; taken or administered through the mouth. **orally** *adv.*

oral contraceptive *n.* A pill containing hormones, taken monthly to prevent pregnancy.

or-ange (or´inj) *n.* A citrus fruit which is round and orange in color. *adj.* Yellowish red.

o-rang-u-tan (ō rang´e tan´) *n. pl.* **-tans** A large, anthropoid ape, having brownish-red hair and very long arms.

o-rate (ō rāt´) *v.* To speak in an elevated manner.

orb (orb) *n.* A globe or sphere.

or-bit (or´bit) *n.* The path of a celestial body or a man-made object. *v.* To revolve or move in an orbit; to circle. **orbital** *adj.*

or-chard (or´chėrd) *n.* Land that is devoted to the growing of fruit trees.

or-ches-tra (or´ki stra) *n.* A group of musicians performing together on various instruments. **orchestral** *adj.*

orchestra pit *n.* In theatres, the space reserved for musicians.

or-chid (or´kid) *n.* A plant found the world over having three petals in various colors.

or-dain (or dān´) *v.* To appoint as a minister, priest, or rabbi by a special ceremony; to decree.

or-deal (or dēl´) *n.* A painful or severe test of character or endurance.

or-der (or´dėr) *n.* A condition where there is a logical arrangement or disposition of things; sequence or succession; method; an instruction for a person to follow; a request for certain objects. *v.* To command; to demand.

orderly (or´dėr lē) *adj.* Neat, tidy.

or-di-nance (or´di nans) *n.* A command, rule, or order; a law issued by a municipal body.

or-di-nar-y (or´di ner´ē) *adj.* Normal; having no exceptional quality; common; average; plain.

ore (ōr) *n.* A natural underground substance, as a mineral or rock, from which valuable matter is extracted.

o-reg-a-no (o reg´a nō´) *n.* A bushy perennial herb of the mint family, used as a seasoning for food.

Or-e-gon (or´e gon) *n.* A state in the northwestern part of the United States; statehood February 14, 1859; state capital Salem.

or-gan (or´gan) *n.* A musical instrument of pipes, reeds, and keyboards which produces sound by means of compressed air; a part of an animal, human, or plant that performs a definite function, as the heart, a kidney, or a stamen.

or-gan-dy *or* **or-gan-die (or´gan dē)** *n.* A translucent, stiff fabric of cotton or silk.

or-gan-ic (or gan´ik) *adj.* Effecting or pertaining to the organs of an animal or plant. **organically** *adv.*

or-gan-i-za-tion (or´ga ni zā´shan) *n.* The state of being organized or the act of organizing; a group of people united for a particular purpose. **organizational** *adj.*

or-gan-ize (or´ga nīz´) v. To assemble or arrange with an orderly manner; to arrange by planning. **organization** n.

or-gasm (or´gaz um) n., Physiol. Intensive emotional excitement; the culmination of a sexual act.

o-ri-ent (ōr´ē ent´) v. To determine the bearings or right direction with respect to another source.

Orient (ōr´ē ent) n. The countries located east of Europe. **Oriental** adj.

or-i-fice (or´i fis) n. An opening through which something may pass; a mouth.

or-i-gin (er´i jin) n. The cause or beginning of something; the source; a beginning place.

o-rig-i-nal (o rij´i nal) adj. Belonging to the first or beginning. n. A new idea produced by one's own imagination; the first of a kind. **originality** n. **originally** adv.

or-i-ole (ōr´ē ōl´) n. A songbird having brightly colored yellow and black plumage in the males.

or-na-ment (or´na ment) n. A decoration. v. To adorn or beautify. **ornamental** adj. **ornamentally** adv. **ornamentation** n.

or-nate (or nāt´) adj. Excessively ornamental; elaborate; showy, as a style of writing.

or-phan (or´fan) n. A child whose parents are deceased. **orphan** v. **orphanage** n.

or-ris (or´is) n. Any of several species having a fragrant root and used in medicine, perfumes, and cosmetics.

or-tho-don-tics (or´tho don´tiks) n. The branch of dentistry dealing with the correction and prevention of irregularities of the teeth.

or-tho-dox (or´tho doks´) adj. Following established traditions and beliefs, especially in religion.

Orthodox Judaism n. The branch of Jewish faith which accepts the Mosaic Laws as interpreted in the Talmud.

or-tho-pe-dics or **or-tho-pae-dics (or´thōpē´diks)** n. pl. A branch of surgery that deals with correcting skeletal deformities.

os-cil-late (os´i lāt) v. To swing back and forth with regular motion, as a pendulum.

oscillation n. **oscillator** n.

os-mi-um (oz´mē um) n. A hard, but brittle metallic element symbolized as OS.

os-mo-sis (oz mō´sis) n. The tendency of fluids separated by a semipermeable membrane to pass through it and become mixed and equal in strength. **osmotic** adj.

os-ten-ta-tion (os´ten tā´shan) n. The act of displaying pretentiously in order to excite.

osteo n., comb. form Bone; pertaining to the bones.

os-te-op-a-thy (os´tē op´a thē) n. A medical practice based on the theory that diseases are due chiefly to abnormalities of the body, which can be restored by manipulation of the parts by therapeutic measures.

os-teo-po-ro-sis n. A disorder causing gradual deterioration of bone tissue, usually occurring in older women.

os-tra-cize (os´tra sīz´) v. To exile or exclude from a group; to shut out.

oth-er (uth´ėr) adj. Additional; alternate; different from what is implied or specified. pron. A different person or thing.

oth-er-wise (uth´ėr wīz´) adv. Under different conditions of circumstances.

ot-ter (ot´ėr) n. pl. -ter or -ters Web-footed aquatic mammals, related to the weasel.

ouch (ouch) n., interj. An exclamation to express sudden pain.

ought (ot) v. Used to show or express a moral duty or obligation; to be advisable or correct.

ounce (ouns) n. A unit of weight which equals 1/16 of a pound.

our (our) adj. Of or relating to us ourselves. pron. The possessive case of the pronoun we.

oust (oust) v. To eject; to remove with force.

out (out) adv. Away from the center or inside. adj. Away. n. A means of escape. prep. Through; forward from.

out-age (ou´tij) n. A loss of electricity.

out-break (out´brāk´) n. A sudden outburst; an occurrence.

out-cast (out´kast´) *n.* A person who is excluded; a homeless person.

out-come (out´kum´) *n.* A consequence or result.

out-dated *adj.* Old-fashioned and obsolete.

out-do (out´dŏ´) *v.* To excel in achievement.

out-fit (out´fit) *n.* The equipment or tools required for a specialized purpose; the clothes a person is dressed in. *v.* To supply.

out-land-ish (out lan´dish) *adj.* Extremely ridiculous, unusual, or strange.

out-law (out´lo´) *n.* A person who habitually defies or breaks the law; a criminal. *v.* To ban; prohibit; to deprive of legal protection.

out-let (out´let) *n.* An exit.

out-line (out´līn´) *n.* A rough draft showing the main features of something. **outline** *v.*

out-look (out´lek´) *n.* A person's point of view; an area offering a view of something.

out-num-ber (out´num´bėr) *v.* To go over or exceed in number.

out-pa-tient (out´pā´shent) *n.* A patient who visits a clinic or hospital for treatment but does not spend the night.

out-post (out´pōst´) *n.* Troops stationed at a distance away from the main group as a guard against attack; a frontier or outlying settlement.

out-put (out´pet´) *n.* Production or yield during a given time.

out-rage (out´rāj) *n.* An extremely violent act of violence or cruelty; the violent emotion such an act engenders. **outrageous** *adj.* **outrage** *v.*

out-right (out´rīt´) *adj.* Free from reservations or complications; complete; entire.

out-side (out´sīd´) *n.* The area beyond the boundary lines or surface; extreme. *adv.* Outdoors.

out-spo-ken (out´spō´ken) *adj.* Spoken without reserve; candid. **outspokenly** *adv.*

out-stand-ing (out´stan´ding) *adj.* Excellent; prominent; unsettled, as a bill owed; projecting.

out-ward (out´wėrd) *adj.* Pertaining to the outside or exterior; superficial. **outwards** *adv.*

out-wit (out´wit´) *v.* To trick, baffle, or outsmart with ingenuity.

o-val (ō´val) *adj.* Having the shape of an egg; an ellipse.

o-va-ry (ō´va rē) *n. pl.* **-ies** One of the pair of female reproductive glands.

o-va-tion (ō vā´shan) *n.* An enthusiastic display of approval for a person or a performance; applause.

ov-en (uv´en) *n.* An enclosed chamber used for baking, drying, or heating.

o-ver (ō´vėr) *prep.* Above; across; upon. *adv.* Covering completely; thoroughly; again; repetition. *adj.* Higher; upper. *prefix* Excessive, as overcrowded.

over-act (ō´vėr akt´) *v.* To act in an exaggerated way.

over-all (ō´vėr ol´) *adj.* Including or covering everything; from one side or end to another; generally. *n.* Pants with a bib and shoulder straps.

over-arm (ō´vėr ärm´) *adj.* Thrown or executed with the arms raised above the shoulders.

over-bear (ō´vėr bâr´) *v.* To crush or bear down by superior force or weight. **overbearing** *adj.*

over-board (ō´vėr bōrd´) *adv.* Over the side of a boat or ship into the water.

over-cast (ō´vėr kast´) *adj.* Gloomy; obscured. *Meteor.* Clouds covering more than 9/10 of the sky.

over-coat (ō´vėr kōt´) *n.* A coat worn over a suit for extra warmth.

over-come (ō´vėr kum´) *v.* To prevail; to conquer or defeat. **overcomer** *n.*

over-con-fi-dence (ō´vėr kon´fi dens) *n.* Extreme or excessive confidence.

over-do (ō´vėr dŏ´) *v.* To do anything excessively; to overcook.

over-dose (ō´vėr dōs´) *n.* To take an excessive dose of medication, especially narcotics.

over-draw (ō´vėr dro´) *v.* To withdraw money over the limits of one's credit.

over-drive (ō´vėr drīv´) *n.* A gearing device in a vehicle that turns a drive shaft at a greater speed than that of the engine, therefore decreasing power output.

over-due (ō´vėr dō´) *adj.* Past the time of return or payment.

over-flow (ō´vėr flō´) *v.* To flow beyond the limits of capacity; to overfill.

over-hand (ō´vėr hand´) *v.* To execute something with the hand above the level of the elbow or shoulder. **overhanded** *adv.*

over-haul (ō´vėr hol´) *v.* To make all needed repairs.

over-head (ō´vėr hed´) *n.* The operating expenses of a company, including utilities, rent, and upkeep. *adj.* Situated above the level of one's head.

over-look (ō´vėr lek´) *v.* To disregard or fail to notice something purposely; to ignore.

over-night (ō´vėr nīt´) *adj.* Lasting the whole night; from dusk to dawn.

over-pass (ō´vėr pas´) *n.* A raised section of highway which crosses other lines of traffic. *v.* To cross, pass over, or go through something; to overlook.

over-ride (ō´vėr rīd´) *v.* To disregard; to take precedence over; to declare null and void.

over-rule (ō´vėr rŏl´) *v.* To put aside by virtue of higher authority.

over-run (ō´vėr run´) *v.* To spread out; to extend or run beyond.

over-seas (ō´vėr sēz´) *adv.* Abroad, across the seas. **overseas** *adj.*

over-see (ō´vėr sē´) *v.* To supervise; to direct. **overseer** *n.*

over-sexed (ō´vėr sekst´) *adj.* Having an overactive interest in sex.

over-shoe (o´vėr shŏ´) *n.* A galosh worn over a shoe for protection from snow or water.

over-sight (ō´vėr sīt´) *n.* A mistake made inadvertently.

over-size *or* **oversized** (ō´vėr sīz´) *adj.* Larger than the average size of something.

over-step (ō´vėr step´) *v.* To go beyond a limit or restriction.

overt (ō vert´) *adj.* Open to view.

over–the–counter (ō´vėr the koun´tėr) *adj.* Not traded on an organized security exchange; of or relating to drugs or medicine which can be purchased without a prescription.

over-throw (ō´vėr thrō´) *v.* To remove from power by force; to bring about destruction.

over-time (ō´vėr tīm´) *n.* The time worked beyond or before the specified hours.

over-whelm (ō´vėr hwelm´) *v.* To overcome completely; to make helpless.

o-void (ō´void) *adj.* Having the shape of an egg.

ovu-late (ō´vū lāt´) *n.* To discharge or produce eggs from an ovary.

o-vum (ō´vum) *n. pl.* **ova** The female reproductive cell.

owe (ō) *v.* To be in debt for a certain amount; to have a moral obligation.

owl (oul) *n.* A predatory nocturnal bird, having large eyes, a short, hooked bill, and long powerful claws. **owlish** *adj.*

own (ōn) *adj.* Belonging to oneself. *v.* To possess; to confess; to admit. *v.* To have as property. **owner** *n.*

ox (oks) *n. pl.* **oxen** A bovine animal used domestically in much the same way as a horse; an adult castrated bull.

ox-ford (oks´fėrd) *n.* A shoe which is laced and tied over the instep.

ox-ide (ok´sīd) *n.* A compound of oxygen and another elements.

ox-y-gen (ok´si jen) *n.* A colorless, odorless, tasteless gaseous element essential to life, symbolized by O.

oxygen mask *n.* A device worn over the mouth and nose through which a person can receive oxygen as an aid to breathing.

oys-ter (oi´stėr) *n.* An edible marine mollusk having an irregularly shaped shell.

oyster bed *n.* A breading area or place for oysters.

o-zone (ō´zōn) *n.* A pale-blue gas formed of oxygen with an odor like chlorine, formed by an electrical discharge in the air. *Slang* Fresh air.

P, p (pē) The 16th letter of the English alphabet.

PA *n. abbr.* Pennsylvania; power of attorney; per annum.

PABA *n. abbr.* The para-aminobenzoic acid.

pab-u-lom (pan´ū l*u***m)** *n.* Type of food such as an absorable solution.

Pac *n. abbr.* Pacific.

pa-ca (pä´k*a***)** n. A large brown with white spots, rodent from Central and South America.

pace (pās) *n.* A person's step in walking or the length of a person's step; stride; the gait of a horse in which the legs on the same side are moved at the same time. **pacer** *n.*

pace car *n.* The automobile that leads a field of competitors around the track, in order to warm up the engines then falls out and does not continue in the race.

pace lap *n.* The warm-up lap before the start of a car race.

pace-mak-er (pās´mā´kėr) *n.* The person who sets the pace for another in a race; a surgically implanted electronic instrument used to stabilize or stimulate the heartbeat.

pacer (pā´sėr) *n.* One that sets a particular speed or pace.

pa-chi-si (p*a* **chē´zē)** *n.* Another name for the game Parcheesi; ancient board game played with dice.

pach-y-derm (pak´i dürm˝) *n.* A group of animals including the elephant, the rhinoceros, and hippo; animals having thick skins. **pachydermal** *adj.*

pach-y-san-dra (pak˝i san´dr*a***)** *n.* A type of evergreen trailing herbs of the box family and grown for the purpose of ground cover in shaded areas.

Pa-cif-ic (p*a* **sif´ik)** *n.* The largest ocean on the earth, extending from North & South America westward to Asia and Australia.

pa-cif-i-ca-tion (pas˝i fi kā´sh*a***n)** *n.* The state of something being pacified or calmed.

pac-i-fi-er (pas´i fī˝ėr) *n.* A person or something that will pacify another; nipple-shaped device for babies to suck on.

pac-i-fism (pas´i fiz˝*u***m)** *n.* The policy dealing with the establishment of universal peace between all nations; opposition to violence or war as a means of settling problems or disputes. **pacifist** *n.*

pac-i-fy (pas´i fī) *v.* To quiet or soothe anger or distress; to calm.

pack (pak) *n.* A bundle; a group or number of things tied or wrapped up; a full set of associated or like things, such as a pack of cards; a group of wolves or wild dogs that hunt together. *v.* To put things together in a trunk, box, or suitcase; to put away for storage. **packing** To force to leave with haste and without ceremony.

package (pak´ij) *n.* Something tied up, wrapped or bound together.

package deal *n.* An agreement or offer that involves a number of related items, the items offered.

package store *n.* A retail establishment that sells alcoholic beverages only in sealed containers.

pack animal *n.* An animal used to carry heavy packs.

pack-board (pak bōrd) *n.* A metal frame that is usually covered with canvas, used to carry goods and equipment over one's shoulder.

packed (pakt) *adj.* To be filled to capacity.

pack-er (pak´ėr) *n.* A person who packs; one who works in an establishment that packs meat; a machine that automatically packs.

pack-et (pak´it) *n.* A type of parcel or package that is small in size and can be used to carry or hold small items.

pack-ing (pak´ing) *n.* The action of a person who packs.

packing house *n.* A place where food, such as meats, are made and packed in order to be sent to the market for sale.

pack-man (pak´m*a***n)** *n.* A person who carries a pack and tries to sell his wares; a peddler.

pack rat *n.* A type of rodent located in North America that has a habit of hiding or hoarding the items that it finds; one who collects useless items.

pack-sack (pak´sak˝) *n.* A flexible baglike

case of material or leather designed with straps for carrying items on one's back.

pack-sad-dle (pak´sad˝l) *n.* A saddle that is used on pack animals for carrying objects.

pack-thread (pak´thred˝) *n.* The twine or rope that is used for the purpose of binding packages together to make them easier for carrying. **packthreaded** *adj.*

pact (pakt) *n.* An agreement between nations, groups, or people.

pad (pad) *n.* Anything stuffed with soft material and used to protect against blows; a cushion; a drawing or writing tablet of paper gummed together at one edge; the cushion-like part of the foot on some animals, as the dog. *Slang* A person's home. *v.* To stuff, line,or protect with soft material; to extend or lengthen something by inserting unnecessary matter; to travel by foot in a soft and nearly inaudible way.

pad-ding (pad ing) *n.* The material, as cotton, or synthetic fibers, which is used for the purpose of protecting something.

pad-dle(pad´l)*n.* A broad-bladed implement usually made from wood, used to steer and propel a small boat; a tool used for mixing, turning, or stirring; a small wooden, rounded racket used in table tennis. **paddle** *v.* **paddler** *n.*

pad-dle-fish (pad´l fish˝) *n.* A type of fish that is located in the Mississippi River and has a snout which is shaped like a paddle.

paddle wheel *n.* A wheel with boards for propelling vessels.

pad-dock (pad´ok) *n.* The area that is located near the racetrack and is used for the purpose of mounting and tending to the horses that will or have already run in a race.

pad-dy (pad´ē) *n.* Land usually in China, which is flooded with water and used for the purpose of growing rice.

paddy wagon *n., Slang* A police vehicle for transporting suspects.

pad-lock (pad´lok) *n.* A detachable lock, having a pivoted u-shaped hasp which can be inserted through a ring and then locked. **padlock** *v.*

pa-dre (pä´drā) *n.* A title used in Spain and Italy for a priest.

pa-dro-ne (pa drō´nē) *n.* The person who is master of a vessel; the owner or operator of a business; an innkeeper.

pad-u-a-soy (paj´ŏ a soi˝) *n.* A corded, rich silk fabric.

pae-an (pē´an) *n.* A song of praise or joy.

pae-do-gen-e-sis (pē˝do jen´i sis) n. The reproduction by immature animals.

pae-on (pē´on) *n.* A type of metrical foot that is made up of four syllables, one long and three short.

pa-gan (pā´gan) *n.* A person who does not acknowledge God in any religion; a heathen. **pagan** *adj.* **paganism** *n.*

pa-gan-ism (pā´ga niz˝um) *n.* The belief in and the worship of a false god; heathenism.

pa-gan-ize (pā´ga nīz˝) *v.* To make someone a pagan or to become a pagan. **paganizer** *n.*

page (pāj) *n.* A person hired to deliver messages or run errands; one side of the leaf of a book or letter. *v.* To call or summon a person.

pag-eant (paj´ent) *n.* An elaborate exhibition or spectacular parade for public celebration; anything having a showy appearance.

pag-eant-ry (paj´en trē) *n.* A type of exhibition that is showy; a spectacle.

pag-i-nate (paj´i nāt˝) *v.* To number or to place numbers on a page showing the order in which they should be placed in order to read.

pa-go-da (pa gō´da) *n.* A sacred Buddhist tower, built as a memorial or shrine.

paid *v.* Past tense of pay.

pail (pāl) *n.* A cylindrical container usually having a handle; a bucket.

pail-ful (pāl´fūl˝) *adj.* The total amount that a pail is able to hold.

pail-lasse (pal yas´) *n.* A type of mattress that is filled with wood shavings and can be used under another mattress for support.

pail-lon (pä yän´) *n.* A type of metallic foil

which is used for the purpose of enamel work.

pain (pān) *n.* The unpleasant feeling resulting from injury or disease; any distress or suffering of the mind; sorrow. *v.* To cause or experience pain. **painful** *adj.*

pain-ful (pān'fʉl) adj. To be distressing or having or causing pain to something or to someone. **painfulness** *n.* **painfully** *adv.*

pain-kill-er (pān kil'ėr) *n.* Medication that relieves pain. **painkilling** *adj.*

pains-tak-ing (pānz'tā˝king) *adj.* To be given to taking pains; done with carefulness and diligence. **painstakingly** *adv.*

paint (pānt) *n.* A mixture of colors or pigments which are spread on a surface as protection or as a decorative coating; makeup for the face, as rouge. *v.* To apply paint to a surface; the practice of using paint to express oneself on canvas. **painter** *n.* **painting** *n.*

paint-brush (pānt'brush˝) *n.* A type of brush that is used for painting surfaces.

painted bunting *n.* A type of bird that is found in North America and is brightly colored.

paint-er (pān'tėr) *n.* The person who paints for a living or for self enjoyment.

painter's colic *n.* The lead poisoning which is markd by acute pain in the stomach area and a pulse which is slowed.

paint-ing (pān'ting) *n.* The piece of art that is made by a painter and can be hung on one's wall for decoration.

pair (pâr) *n. pl.* **pairs** *or* **pair** Two things which are similar and used together; something made of two parts which are used together; two persons or animals which live or work together.

pair–oar (pâr'ōr˝) *n.* A type of boat where the rowers sit in front of one another and pull one oar in order to move the boat. **pair-oared** *adj.*

pais-ley (pāz'lē) *adj.* To have colors that are bright and patterned into a design which is typical of paisley.

pa-ja-mas (pa jäm'az) *n. pl.* A loose fitting garment for sleeping, consisting of a jacket and pants.

pal (pal) *n.* A good friend.

pal-ace (pal'is) *n.* The royal residence of a sovereign, as of a king; a mansion. **palatial** *adj.*

pal-a-din (pal'a din) *n.* One who is an eminent hero.

pa-laes-tra (pa les'tra) *n.* A type of school of ancient Greece that was used to teach athletics.

pal-at-a-ble (pal'a ta bl) *adj.* Pleasant to the taste; agreeable to one's feelings or mind.

pal-a-tal (pal'a tal) *adj.* To be pertaining or to be related to the palate.

pal-ate (pal'it) *n.* The muscular tissue at the roof of a person's mouth, opposite the tongue; sense of taste.

pa-la-tial (pa lā'shal) *adj.* Pertaining to a palace. **palatialness** *n.*

pal-a-tine (pal'a tīn˝) *adj.* To be related to the palate of one's mouth. *n.* A lord invested with royal privileges within his territory.

pa-lav-er (pa lav'ėr) *n.* A type of discussion; superfluous talk.

pale (pāl) *n.* The pointed stake of a fence; a picket; an area that is enclosed within bounds. *adj.* Having a whitish or lighter than normal complexion; pallid; weak. **palely** *adv.*

pa-le-eth-nol-o-gy (pā˝lē eth nol'o jē) *n.* A part or branch of ethnology which deals with the earliest human races known.

pale-face (pāl'fās˝) *n.* A person who has white skin; term first used by the American Indians.

pa-le-o-bot-a-ny (pā˝lē ō bot'a nē) *n.* A study of plants which are discovered in their fossilized state or condition.

pa-le-og-ra-phy (pā˝lē og'ra fē) *n.* The study of ancient writings. **paleographically** *adv.* **paleographer** *n.*

pa-le-o-lith (pā'lē o lith) *n.* A stone implement that is from the Paleolithic period.

pa-le-on-tol-o-gy (pā˝lē on tol'o jē) *n.* The study and the science which deals with ancient life and how they lived.

pa-le-o-zo-ol-o-gy (pā˝lē ō zō ol´o jē) *n.* The science or the study of the fossil animals.

pal-ette (pal´it) *n.* A thin oval board with a hole for the thumb, on which an artist lays and mixes colors.

palette knife *n.* A knife which has a rounded blade.

pal-frey (pol´frē) *n.* A type of small horse that is used by a lady.

pal-imp-sest (pal´imp sest˝) *n.* A piece of writing paper from which something has been erased and another writing has been written over, leaving the first faintly visible.

pal-in-drome (pal´in drōm´) *n.* A word, number, or sentence which reads the same backward or forward, such as toot or 1991.

pal-ing(pā´ling) *n.* A type of fence which is made from pales or pickets.

pal-in-gen-e-sis (pal´in jen´i sis) *n.* The regeneration or the rebirth of someone or something. **palingenetically** *adv. adj.*

pal-i-node (pal´i nōd˝) *n.* A poem that contains something from a previous piece; a recantation. **palinodist** *n.*

pal-i-sade (pal´i sād´) *n.* A fence made of stakes forprotection. **palisade** *v.*

pall (pol) *n.* A heavy cloth used to cover a bier or coffin; avery gloomy atmosphere.

pal-la-di-um (pa lā´dē um) *n.* A silvery-white metallic element symbolized by Pd.

pall-bear-er (pol´bâr´ér) *n.* A person who assists in carrying a coffin at a funeral.

pal-let (pal´it) *n.* A wooden platform on which material for freight shipments can be moved or stored.

pal-let-ize (pal´i tīz˝) *v.* To load items on pallets for transportation and storing.

pal-li-al (pal´ē al) *adj.* To be related to or pertaining to pallium.

pal-li-ate (pal´ē āt˝) *v.* To conceal something with an excuse.

pal-lid (pal´id) *adj.* Deficient in color; lacking sparkle.

pal-lor (pal´ér) *n.* Lacking color; paleness.

palm (pām) *n.* The inner area of the hand between the fingers and wrist; any of a large group of tropical evergreen trees, having an unbranched trunk with a top or crown of fan-like leaves. *v.* To hide something small in or about the hand.

pal-mar (pal´mėr) *adj.* To be located or situated in the palm of one's hand.

palm-er-worm (pä´mėr würm˝) *n.* A caterpillar that is very destructive to vegetation.

pal-met-to (pal met´ō) *n.* A type of palm tree that has fan-shaped leaves. *Palmetto* The nickname for the state of South Carolina.

palm-is-try (pä´mi strē) *n.* The practice of fortune telling by the configurations of the palms of the hands.

palmitic acid *n.* A type of fatty acid that is used for the making of soap.

pal-mi-tin (pal´mi tin) *n.* A type of colorless compound that is found in palm oil and can be used in the making of soap.

palm oil *n.* The vegetable fat that is obtained from the fruit of an oil palm and used for the making of soap.

palm-y (pä´mē) *adj.* To be prosperous.

pal-my-ra (pal mī´ra) *n.* A type of palm that is used for the making of stiff brushes.

pal-o-min-o (pal˝o mē´nō) *n.* A type of horse that has a coat which is golden in color and a mane that is flaxen.

pal-pa-ble (pal´pa bl) *adj.* To be capable of being touched or felt by someone or something; easily detected; obvious; plain. **palpably** *adv.* **palpability** *n.*

pal-pate (pal´pāt) *v.* To check something through the use of touch, such as a doctor would examine a patient.

pal-pe-bral (pal´pe bral) *adj.* To be located near the eyelid of someone or something.

pal-pus (pal´pus) *n.* A type of organ found on certain insects and is used for the purpose of sensing.

pal-sy (pol´zē) *n. pl.* **-ies** Paralysis; the loss of ability to control one's movements. **palsy** *v.*

pal-ter (pol´tė) *v.* To haggle over something, such as the price of a good.

pal-try (pol´trē) *adj.* To be worthless or

inferior. **paltriness** *n.*

pa-lu-dal (pa lŏd´al) *adj.* To be related to or referring to a marsh.

pal-u-drine (pal´ū drēn˝) *n.* A type of drug which is used for the purpose of treating malaria in people.

pam-pas (pam´paz) *n.* The grassy plains that can be found in South America.

pam-per (pam´pėr) *v.* To treat with extreme care.

pam-pe-ro (păm pâr´ō) *n.* The strong and cold wind that blows in the pampas of South America and coming from the Andes mountain chain.

pam-phlet (pam´flit) *n.* A brief publication which is not permanently bound.

pan (pan) *n.* A type of vessel that is usually made of metal and is used for the cooking of foods over heat.

pan-a-ce-a (pan´a sē´a) *n.* A remedy for all diseases, difficulties, or ills; a cure-all.

pa-nache (pa nash´) *n.* A type of showy plume that is worn on a cap.

pan-cake (pan´kāk´) *n.* A thin, flat cake made from batter and fried on a griddle, served with butter, powdered sugar, syrup, and other toppings.

pancake ice *n.* Type of ice pieces that float on the water and are too small to interfere with navigation of the ships.

pan-chro-mat-ic (pan˝krō mat´ik) *adj.* To be sensitive to the light of all of the colors.

pan-cra-ti-um (pan krā´shē a) *n.* A type of gymnastic context that was held in ancient Greece and contained a combination of wrestling and boxing.

pan-cre-as (pan´krē as) *n., Anat.* A large, irregularly shaped gland situated behind the stomach which releases digestive enzymes and produces insulin. **pancreatic** *adj.*

pan-cre-at-ec-to-my (pan´krēt omē) *n.* The surgical removal of any part or all of the pancreas.

pancreatic juice *n.* A type of alkaline fluid that contains digestive enzymes and is secreted by the pancreas into the duodenum of the small intestine.

pan-da (pan´da) *n.* A large bear-like animal of China and Tibet with black and white fur and rings around the eyes; a racoon-like animal of the southeastern Himalayas with a ringed tail and reddish fur.

pan-de-mo-ni-um (pan´de mō´nē um) *n.* A place marked with disorder and wild confusion; disorder; confusion.

pan-der *or* **panderer (pan´dėr)** *n.* A go-between in sexual affairs; a pimp; one who profits from the base desires or passions of others. *v.* To act as a panderer for someone.

pan-dit (pan´dėt) *n.* A man who is respected highly.

pan-dow-dy (pan dou´dē) *n.* A type of deep-dish pie that has been made with apples.

pan-e-gry-ic (pan˝i jir´ik) *n.* A type of writing about a person that praises them.

pan-el (pan´el) *n.* A flat, rectangular piece of material, often wood, which forms a part of a surface; a group of people selected to participate in a discussion group or to serve on a jury. **panelist** *n.* **panel** *v.*

pan-eling (pan´el ing) *n.* A type of wood that has been made into panels and is used to cover walls for decoration.

panel truck *n.* A type of truck that is used for small deliveries and is enclosed.

pan-e-tel-la (pan˝i tel´a) *n.* A type of cigar that has one end that is slender.

pang (pang) *n.* A sudden and sharp pain that does not last for very long.

pan-go-lin (pang gō´lin) *n.* A type of scaled mammal that has a pointed tail and eats ants, found in Africa.

pan-han-dle (pan´han˝dl) *n.* A projecting strip of land that is not a peninsula, such as the state of Texas.

pan-ic (pan´ik) *n.* A sudden unreasonable fear which overpowers. *v.* To cause or to experience panic. **panicky** *adj.*

panic grass *n.* A type of grass that is grown and cut for forage.

pan-ic–strick-en (pan´ik strik˝en) *adj.* To be overcome by great and intense fear.

panne (pan) *n.* A type of light-weight velvet.

pan-nier (pan´yėr) *n.* One of a pair of large baskets which are carried on either side of an animal or over a person's back.

pan-ni-kin (pan´*i* kin) *n.* A small cup or pan.

pan-o-cha (p*a* nō´cha) *n.* A type of sugar that has a course grade and can be found in Mexico.

pan-o-ply (pan´*o* plē) *n. pl.* -lies The complete equipment of a warrior, including his armor and weapons.

pan-o-ram-a (pan´*o* ram´*a*) *n.* An unlimited or complete view in all directions of what is visible.

pan-sy (pan´zē) *n.* A garden plant with flowers bearing blossoms in a variety of colors.

pant (pant) *v.* To breathe in rapid or short gasps; to yearn. *n.* A short breath.

pan-ta-lets (pan˝*ta* lets´) *n.* A type of underpants that are long and have a fringed bottom.

pan-tech-ni-con *n.* A type of storehouse that is used to store furniture.

pan-the-ism (pan´thē iz´*u*m) *n.* The belief that the laws and forces of nature are all manifestations of God. **pantheist** *n.* **pantheistic** *adj.*

pan-the-on (pan´thē on˝) *n.* A type of building or temple that was built in order to honor all the gods. **pantheonic** *adj.*

pan-ther (pan´thėr) *n.* A black leopard in its unspotted form. **pantheress** *n.*

pan-ther-ess (pan´thėr is) *n.* The female panther.

pan-to-mime (pan´*to* mīm´) *n.* Communication done solely by means of facial and body gestures. *v.* To express or act in pantomime.

pan-to-then-ic ac-id (pan´*to* then´ik as´id) *n.* A type of vitamin belonging to the B complex that promotes cell growth.

pan-try (pan´trē) *n.* A closet or room for the storage of food, dishes, and other kitchen items.

pants (pants) *n.* Trousers; underpants.

pan-zer (pan´zėr) *n.* A type of German tank.

pap (pap) *n.* A soft food for invalids or babies.

pa-pa-cy (pā´p*a* sē) *n.* The dignity or jurisdiction of a pope; a pope's term in office.

pa-pa-in (p*a* pā´ in) *n.* A type of enzyme that is found in the juice of the unripe fruit of the papaya tree.

pa-pa-ya (p*a* p*a*´ya) *n.* A type of tropical tree that will yield melon-like fruits.

pa-per (pā´pėr) *n.* A substance made of pulp from wood and rags, formed into sheets for printing, wrapping and writing.

pa-per-back (pā´pėr bak˝) *n.* A book with its cover made of paper.

paper birch *n.* A type of tree found in North America and having white bark that will peel into layers.

paper cutter *n.* A type of device which has been designed to cut many sheets of paper at one time.

pa-per-hang-er (pā´pėr hang˝ėr) *n.* A person employed to hang wallpaper.

paper mulberry *n.* A type of tree of China and of Japan used for making paper.

pa-per-weight (pā´pėr wāt˝) *n.* A heavy object that is placed upon papers to keep them from moving.

pa-pier–ma-che (pā´pėr m*a* shā) *n.* A material consisting of paper mixed with glue or paste which can be molded when wet and becomes hard when dry.

pap-il-lo-ma (pap´*i* lō´m*a*) *n.* A type of benign tumor that exists on mucous membranes or the skin.

pa-poose (p*a* pōs´) *n.* A North American Indian child or baby.

pa-pri-ka (p*a* prē´k*a*) *n.* A dark red seasoning powder made by grinding red peppers.

Pap test *n.* A test in which a smear of bodily secretion from the uterus is examined for the early detection of cancer.

pap-ule (pap´ūl) *n.* A type of elevation in the skin that does not contain pus, but is inflammatory. **papular** *adj.*

pa-py-rus (pa pī´rus) *n.* A reedlike plant used as paper in early Egypt, to write upon.

par-a-bi-o-sis (par˝a bī ō´sis) *n.* The joining or fusion of two separate organisms, such as Siamese twins.

par-a-ble (par´a bl) *n.* A short, fictitious story which illustrates a moral lesson.

par-a-chute (par´a shŏt´) *n.* A folding umbrella-shaped apparatus of light fabric used to make a safe landing after a free fall from an airplane. **parachutist** *n.*

pa-rade (pa rād´) *n.* An organized public procession; a march. **parade** *v.* **parader** *n.*

par-a-di-chlor-ben-zene (par˝a dī klōr˝ ben´zēn) *n.* A white compound used as an insecticide.

par-a-dise (par´a dīs´) *n.* A state or place of beauty, bliss or delight; heaven. **paradisiac** *adj.* **paradisiacal** *adj.*

par-a-dox (par´a doks´) *n.* A statement which seems opposed to common sense or contradicts itself, but is perhaps true. **paradical** *adj.* **paradoxically** *adv.*

par-aes-the-sia (par˝is thē´zha) *n.* An abnormal sensation, as the prickling of the skin.

par-af-fin (par´a fin) *n.* A white, waxy substance derived from petroleum and used to make lubricants, candles, and sealing materials. **paraffin** *v.*

par-a-gen-e-sis (par˝a jen´i sis) *n.* A type of formation of minerals where they are too close together and impact on one another's development. **paragenetic** *n.* **paragenetically** *adv.*

par-ago-ge (par˝a gō´jē) *n.* An addition of a letter or syllable to the end of a word that is incorrect.

par-a-gon (par´a gon´) *n.* A pattern or model of excellence or perfection.

par-a-graph (par´a graf´) *n.* A section of a composition dealing with a single idea, containing one or more sentences with the first line usually indented.

par-a-keet (par´a kēt´) *n.* A small parrot with a long, wedge-shaped tail.

par-al-de-hyde (pa ral´de hīd´) *n.* A type of colorless liquid that can be used in medicine as a hypnotic.

par-al-lel (par´a lel´) *adj.* Moving in the same direction but separated by a distance, as railroad tracks. *n.* A parallel curve, line, or surface; a comparison; one of the imaginary lines which circle the earth paralleling the equator and mark the latitude. **parallel** *v.* **parallelism** *n.*

parallel bars *n.* One pair of bars that are horizontal and supported by uprights.

par-al-lel-o-gram (par´a lel´o gram´) *n.* A four-sided figure having parallel opposite sides which are equal.

pa-ral-o-gism (pa ral´o jiz˝um) *n.* A type of argument that is fallacious.

pa-ral-y-sis (pa ral´i sis) *n. pl.* **-ses** Complete or partial loss of the ability to feel sensation or to move.

par-a-lyze (par´a līz´) *v.* To cause to be inoperative or powerless.

par-a-mat-ta (par˝a mat´a) *n.* A type of light twilled fabric that can be used for the making of dresses.

par-a-med-ic (par´a med´ik) *n.* A person trained to give emergency medical treatment until a doctor is available.

par-am-ne-sia (par˝am nē´zha) *n.* The illusion of remembering things that have not yet been experienced.

par-a-mount (par´a mount´) *adj.* Superior to all others in rank, importance, and power.

par-a-mour (par´a mür) *n.* An unlawful lover.

pa-rang (pä´räng) *n.* A type of knife that is large and heavy.

par-a-noi-a (par´a noi´a) *n.* Mental insanity marked by systematic delusions of persecution or grandeur.

par-a-noid (par´a noid˝) *adj.* To be marked by paranoia.

par-a-nor-mal (par″a nor′mal) *adj.* To be supernatural in character.

par-a-pet (par′a pit) *n.* A type of covering or wall that is used to protect the soldiers from the attacks of the enemy in front of them.

par-a-pher-na-lia (par′a fėr nāl′ya) *n.* Personal effects or belongings; the apparatus or articles used in some activities; equipment.

par-a-phrase (par′a frāz′) *v.* To put something written or spoken into different words while retaining the same meaning.

par-a-phras-tic (par″a fras′tik) *adj.* To be making or forming a paraphrase.

par-a-ple-gi-a (par″a plē′jē a) *n.* The paralysis of the lower trunk and of both legs.

par-a-site (par′a sīt′) *n., Biol.* An organism which lives, grows, feeds, and takes shelter in or on another organism; a person depending entirely on another without providing something in return.

par-a-sit-i-cide (par″a sit′i sīd″) *n.* A type of agent that is used to destroy parasites.

par-a-si-tize (par′a si tīz″) *v.* To live upon another object as a parasite.

par-a-sol (par′a sol′) *n.* A small umbrella used as protection from the sun.

par-a-thi-on (par″a thī′on) *n.* A type of insecticide that is very poisonous.

parathyroid gland *n.* The four glands that are located in or near the thyroid gland and are used for the control of calcium in the blood.

par-a-troops (par′a trö″ps) *n. pl.* Troops which are equipped and trained to parachute behind enemy lines.

par-a-ty-phoid (par″a tī′foid) *n.* A type of very infectious bacterial disease that has symptoms which are like those of typhoid fever.

par-boil (pär′boil′) *v.* To precook something in boiling water.

par-cel (pär′sel) *n.* A wrapped package; a bundle; a portion or plat of land.

parch (pärch) *v.* To become very dry from intense heat; to become dry from thirst or the lack of water.

parch-ment (pärch′ment) *n.* Goatskin or sheepskin prepared with a pumice stone and used as a material for writing or drawing.

par-don (pär′don) *v.* To forgive someone for an offense; in law, to allow a convicted person freedom from the penalties of an office or crime. **pardonable** *adj.* **pardonably** *adv.* **pardon** *n.*

pare (pâr) *v.* To cut away or remove the outer surface gradually. **parer** *n.*

par-e-go-ric (par′e gor′ik) *n.* A medication used to relieve stomach pains.

par-ent (pâr′ent) *n.* A mother or father; a forefather; an ancestor; a source. **parentage** *n.* **parenthood** *n.*

par-ent-age (pâr′en tij) *n.* The origin or birth of someone.

par-en-ter-al (pa ren′tėr al) *adj.* To be introduced into the body by means other than the digestive tract. **parentally** *adv.*

pa-ren-the-sis (pa ren′thi sis) *n. pl.* **-ses** One of a pair of curved lines ( ) used to enclose a qualifying or explanatory remark.

pa-re-sis (pa rē′sis) *n.* A type of paralysis that is incomplete and affecting only movement. **paretic** *adj.*

par-fleche (pär′flesh) *n.* The hide of an animal that has been dried upon a frame, such as the buffalo.

par-get (pär′jit) *v.* To cover something with plaster.

pa-ri-ah (pa rī′a) *n.* A person who is thought of as an outcast.

pa-ri-e-tal (pa rī′i tal) *adj.* Referring to the two bones of the skull which form the side and the top.

par-ing (pâr′ing) *n.* The action of cutting or of paring a piece of a vegetable off, such as with a potato.

par-ish (par′ish) *n.* In association with the Roman Catholic Church, the district under the charge of a priest; the members of a parish.

par-i-ty (par″i tē) *n.* The number which is used to state the fact of having borne children.

park (pärk) *n.* A tract of land used for recreation. *v.* To leave something temporarily in a parking garage or lot, as a car.

par-ka (pär'ka) *n.* A cloth jacket with an attached hood.

parking lot *n.* A cleared area that is used for the storage and parking of cars, such as at a mall.

Parkinson's disease *n., Pathol.* A progressive disease marked by partial facial paralysis, muscular tremor, weakness, and impaired muscular control.

park-way (pärk'wā') *n.* A type of thoroughfare that is lined with trees.

par-lia-ment (pär'li ment) *n.* The assembly which constitutes the law making body of various countries, as the United Kingdom.

par-lia-men-ta-ry *adj.* To be relating or pertaining to a parliament.

par-lor (pär'lér) *n.* A room for entertaining visitors or guests; a business offering a personal service, as beauty parlor, ice cream parlor, or funeral parlor.

parlor car *n.* A type of railroad car that requires an extra fare but containing individual cars.

parlor maid *n.* A person who is employed as a maid to take care of a parlor.

par-lous *adj.* To be dangerous; clever.

pa-ro-chi-al (pa rō'kē al) *adj.* Belonging to a local parish; having to do with a parish.

pa-ro-chi-al-ism (pa rō'kē a liz"um) *n.* A condition or state of being parochial.

parochal school *n.* A type of school which is maintined by the parish.

par-o-dy (par'o dē) *n. pl.* **-ies** A composition, song, or poem which mimics another in a ridiculous way.

pa-rol (pa rōl') *n.* An oral statement.

pa-role (pa rōl') *n.* The conditional release of a prisoner before his sentence expires. **parole** *adj.*

parotid gland *n.* A type of salivary gland that is located in front of each ear.

pa-rot-i-di-tis (pa rot"i dī'tis) *n.* The sweling and inflammation of the parotid glands.

par-ox-ysm (par'ok siz'um) *n.* A violent attack or outburst; a spasm.

par-quet (pär kā) *n.* A main floor of the theater which will extend back from the orchestra pit.

parquet circle *n.* Those seats which are located at the rear of the main floor in a theater.

parr (pär) *n.* A type of salmon when it is young and has not yet entered the salt waters.

par-ri-cide (par'i sīd') *n.* One who murders his mother or father; the crime of murdering parents. **parricidal** *adj.*

par-rot (par'ot) *n.* A brightly colored, semitropical bird with a strong, hooked bill. *v.* To imitate or repeat.

par-rot-fish (par'ot fish') *n.* A type of fish that is tropical and has bright colors.

par-ry (par'ē) *v.* To avoid something; to turn aside. **parry** *n.*

parse (pärs) *v.* To identify the parts of speech in a sentence and to indicate their relationship to each other.

par-si-mo-ny (pär'si mō'nē) *n.* Extreme reluctance to use one's resources or to spend money. **parsimonious** *adj.* **parsimoniously** *adv.*

pars-ley (pärs'lē) *n.* An herb with curly leaves which is used for seasoning and garnishing.

pars-nip (pär'snip) *n.* A plant from the carrot family cultivated for its long, edible root.

par-son (pär'son) *n.* A pastor or clergyman.

parsonage (pär'so nij) *n.* The home provided by a church for its parson.

part (pärt) *n.* A segment, portion, or division of a whole; a component for a machine; the role of a character, as in a play; the line which forms where the hair is parted by combing or brushing. *v.* To leave or go away from; to be separated into pieces; to give up control or possession.

par-take (pär tāk´) v. To have a share or part; to take; to take a part in something.

par-tial (pär´shal) adj. Incomplete; inclined to favor one side more than the other. **partiality** n. **partially** adv.

par-tic-i-pate (pär tis´i pāt´) v. To join in or share; to take part. **participant** n. **participation** n. **participator** n. **participatory** adj.

par-ti-cle (pär´ti kl) n. A very small piece of solid matter. *Gram.* A group of words, such as articles, prepositions, and conjunctions which convey very little meaning but help to connect, specify, or limit the meanings of other words.

par-tic-u-lar (pėr tik´ū lėr) adj. Having to do with a specific person, group, thing, or category; noteworthy; precise.

part-ing (pär´ting) n. A division; a separation; the place where a division or separation occurs. adj. Done, given, or said on departing.

par-ti-tion (pär tish´an) n. A separation or division. v. To divide.

part-ner (pärt´nėr) n. One who shares something with another.

part-ner-ship (pärt´nėr ship) n. Two or more persons who run a business together and share in the profits and losses.

par-tridge (pär´trij) n. pl. **partridges** A plump or stout-bodied game bird.

par-ty (pär´tē) n. pl. **-ies** A group of persons who gather for pleasure or entertainment; a group of persons associated together for a common purpose; a group which unites to promote or maintain a policy, a cause, or other purposes, as a political group; n. in law, a person or group of people involved in a legal proceeding.

pass (pas) v. To proceed; to move; to transfer; to go away or come to an end; to get through a course, trial or test; to approve; to vote for; to give as an opinion or judgment; to hit or throw a ball to another player. n. A ticket or note that allows a person to come and go freely. **pass** To happen. **away** To die or cease to live. **over** To leave out, to ignore.

pas-sage (pas´ij) n. The act of going, proceeding, or passing; the enactment by a legislature of a bill into law; a small portion or part of a whole book or speech; something, as a path or channel, through, over or along which something else may pass.

pas-sen-ger (pas´en jėr) n. One who travels in a vehicle, car, plane, boat, or other conveyance.

pas-sion (pash´an) n. A powerful feeling; lust; sexual desire; an outburst of strong feeling; violence or anger. **Passion** The suffering of Christ which followed the Last Supper to the time of his death. **passionless** adj. **passionate** adj.

pas-sive (pas´iv) adj. Not working, acting, or operating; inactive; acted upon, influenced, or affected by something external. *Gram.* Designating the form of a verb which indicates the subject is receiving the action. **passively** adv **passivity** n. **passiveness** n.

Pass-o-ver (pas´ō´vėr) n. The Jewish holiday which commemorates the Exodus from Egypt.

pass-port (pas´pōrt) n. An official permission issued to a person allowing him to travel out of this country and to return; a document of identification.

pass-word (pas´werd´) n. A secret word allowing a person to prove authorization to pass or enter.

past (past) adj. Having to do with or existing at a former time. n. Before the present time; a person's history or background. adv. To go by. prep. After; beyond in time; beyond the power, reach, or influence.

paste (pāst) n. A mixture usually made from water and flour, used to stick things together; dough used in making pastry; a brilliant glass used in imitating precious stones. **paste** v.

pas-tel (pa stel´) n. A crayon made of ground pigments; a drawing made with crayons of this kind. adj. Pale and light in color or shade.

pas-teur-i-za-tion (pas´che rī¯zėr) n. The process of killing disease-producing microorganisms by heating the liquid to a high temperature for a period of time.

pas-time (pas´tīm´) n. Spending spare time in a pleasant way; a diversion.

pas-tor (pas´tėr) n. A Christian clergyman in charge of a church or congregation.

pas-tor-al (pas´tėr al) adj. Referring to the duties of a pastor; pertaining to life in the country; rural or rustic. n. A poem dealing with country life.

past participle n. A participle used with reference to actions and conditions in the past.

pas-try (pā´strē) n. Food made with dough or having a crust made of dough, as pies, tarts, or other desserts.

pas-ture (pas´chėr) n. An area for grazing of domestic animals. **pastured** v. **pasturing** v. **pasturage** n. **pasturer** n.

pat (pat) v. To tap lightly with something flat. n. A soft, caressing stroke.

patch (pach) n. A piece of fabric used to repair a weakened or torn area in a garment; a piece of cloth with an insignia which represents an accomplishment. v. To repair or put together hastily. **patchy** adj. **patchable** adj. **patcher** n.

pat-ent (pat´ent) n. A governmental protection assuring an inventor the exclusive right of manufacturing, using, exploiting, and selling an invention. adj. Evident; obvious. **patentee, patency** n. **patently** adv.

pa-ter-nal (pa ter´nal) adj. Relating to or characteristic of a father; inherited from a father. **paternally** adv. **paternalism** n.

path (path) n. A track or course; a route; a course of action or life.

pa-thet-ic (pa thet´ik) adj. A rousing pity, tenderness, or sympathy. **pathetically** adv.

pa-thol-o-gy (pa thol´o jē) n. The science that deals with facts about diseases, their nature and causes. **pathologic** adj. **pathological** adj. **pathologist** n.

pa-thos (pā´thos) n. A quality in a person that evokes sadness or pity.

pa-tience (pā´shens) n. The quality, state, or fact of being patient; the ability to be patient.

pa-tient (pā´shent) adj. Demonstrating uncomplaining endurance under distress. n. A person under medical care.

pa-ti-o (pat´ē ō´) n. An area attached to a house, used for enjoyment and entertainment.

pa-tri-arch (pā´trē ärk´) n. The leader of a tribe or family who rules by paternal right; a very old and revered man. **patriarchal** adj. **patriarchy** n.

pa-tri-ot (pā´trē ot) n. A person who loves and defends his country. **patriotic** adj. **patriotically** adv. **patriotism** n.

pa-trol (pa trōl´) n. Walking around an area for the purpose of maintaining or observing security; a person or group carrying out this action. **patrol** v.

pa-tron (pā´tron) n. A person who fosters, protects, or supports some person, enterprise, or thing; a regular customer. **patroness** n.

pat-sy (pat´sē) n. pl. -ies Slang A person who is taken advantage of.

pat-tern (pat´ern) n. Anything designed or shaped to serve as a guide in making something else; a sample. v. To make according to a pattern.

pat-ty (pat´ē) n. pl. -ies A small, flat piece of chopped meat.

pau-per (po´pėr) n. A very poor person who depends on charity. **pauperism** n. **pauperize** v.

pause (poz) v. To linger, hesitate, or stop for a time. **pause** n.

pave (pāv) v. To surface with gravel, concrete, asphalt, or other material.

pave-ment (pāv´ment) n. A surface that has been paved.

pa-vil-ion (pa vil´yon) n. A large, roofed structure used for shelter.

paw (po) n. The foot of an animal. v. To

handle clumsily or rudely.

pawn (pon) *n*. Something given as security for a loan; a hostage; a chessman of little value. **pawn** *v*.

pawn-broker (pon´brō´kėr) *n*. A person who lends money on pledged personal property.

pay (pā) *v*. To give a person what is due for a debt, purchase, or work completed; to compensate; to suffer the consequences.

pay-ment (pā´m*e*nt) *n*. The act of paying.

pay-roll (pā´rōl) *n*. The amount of money to be paid to a list of employees.

pea (pē) *n*. A round edible seed contained in a pod and grown on a vine.

peace (pēs) *n*. A state of physical or mental tranquillity; calm; serenity; the absence of war; the state of harmony between people. **peaceable** *adj*. **peaceful** *adj*. **peaceably** *adv*. **peacefully** *adv*.

peach (pēch) *n*. A round, sweet, juicy fruit having a thin, downy skin, a pulpy yellow flesh, and a hard, rough single seed.

pea-cock (pē´kok´) *n*. A male bird with brilliant blue or green plumage and a long iridescent tail that fans out to approximately six feet.

peak (pēk) *n*. A projecting edge or point; the summit of a mountain; the top. *v*. To bring to the maximum.

peal (pēl) *n*. The ring of bells; the long, loud sound of thunder or laughter. *v*. To ring.

pea-nut (pē´nut´) *n*. A nut-like seed which ripens underground; the plant bearing this nut.

pear (pâr) *n*. A juicy, edible fruit which grows on a tree.

pearl (perl) *n*. A smooth, rounded deposit formed around a grain of sand in the shell of various mollusks, especially the oyster; anything which is precious, rare, or fine. **pearly** *adj*.

peas-ant (pez´*a*nt) *n*. A farmhand or rustic workman; an uneducated person of the lowest class. *Slang* Uneducated or uncouth.

peat (pēt) *n*. The black substance formed when plants begin to decay in wet ground, as bogs. **peaty** *adj*.

peat moss *n*. A moss which grows in very wet areas, used as plant food and mulch.

peb-ble (peb´l) *n*. A small, smooth stone. *v*. To treat, as to give a rough texture.

pe-can (pi kăn´) *n*. A large tree of the central and southern United States with an edible oval, thin-shelled nut.

peck (pek) *v*. To strike with the beak; to eat without any appetite, taking only small bites. *n*. A measure which equals 1/4 of a bushel.

pec-tin (pek´tin) *n*. A complex carbohydrate found in ripe fruits and used in making jelly. **pectic** *adj*.

pe-cu-liar (pi kūl´yėr) *adj*. Odd; strange. **peculiarity** *n*. **peculiarly** *adv*.

ped-al (ped´*a*l) *n*. A lever usually operated by the foot. **pedal** *v*.

ped-dle (ped´l) *v*. To travel around in an attempt to sell merchandise.

ped-es-tal (ped´i st*a*l) *n*. A support or base for a statue. **pedestal** To hold something in high respect.

pe-des-tri-an (p*e* des´trē *a*n) *n*. A person traveling by foot.

pe-di-at-rics (pē´dē a´triks) *n*. The branch of medicine dealing with the care of children and infants. **pediatric** *adj*. **pediatrician** *n*.

ped-i-cure (ped´i kūr´) *n*. The cosmetic care of the toenails and feet.

ped-i-gree (ped´i grē´) *n*. A line of ancestors, especially of an animal of pure breed.

ped-i-ment (ped´i ment) *n*. A broad, triangular architectural or decorative part above a door.

pe-dom-e-ter (p*e* dom´i tėr) *n*. An instrument which indicates the number of miles one has walked.

pe-dun-cle (pi dung´kl) *n*., *Biol*. A stalk-like support in some plants and animals.

peek (pēk) *v*. To look shyly or quickly from a place of hiding; to glance. **peek** *n*.

peel (pēl) *n*. The natural rind or skin of a fruit. *v*. To pull or strip the skin or bark off; to remove in thin layers. *Slang* To undress. **peeler** *n.*

peep (pēp) *v.* To utter a very small and weak sound, as of a young bird.

peer (pēr) *v.* To look searchingly; to come partially into one's view. *n.* An equal; a member of the British nobility, as a duke or earl.

pee-vish (pē´vish) *adj.* Irritable in mood; cross. **peevishly** *adv.* **peevishness** *n.*

peg (peg) *n.* A small pin, usually of wood or metal; a projecting pin on which something may be hung. *Slang* An artificial leg, often made of wood.

pei-gnoir (pān wär´) *n.* A woman's loose fitting dressing gown.

pe-koe (pē´kō) *n.* A superior black tea made from young or small leaves.

pel-i-can (pel´i kan) *n.* A large, web-footed bird with a large pouch under the lower bill for the temporary storage of fish.

pel-let (pel´it) *n.* A small round ball made from paper or wax; a small bullet or shot.

pelt (pelt) *n.* The skin of an animal with the fur.

pel-vis (pel´vis) *n. pl.* **-vises** *or* **-ves** The structure of the vertebrate skeleton which rests on the lower limbs, supporting the spinal column.

pen (pen) *n.* An instrument used for writing.

pe-nal (pēn´al) *adj.* Of or pertaining to punishment or penalties.

pen-al-ty (pen´al tē) *n. pl.* **-ties.** The legal punishment for an offense or crime; something which is forfeited when a person fails to meet a commitment; in sports, a punishment or handicap imposed for breaking a rule.

pen-ance (pen´ans) *n.* A voluntary act to show sorrow or repentance for sin.

pen-cil (pen´sil) *n.* A writing or drawing implement made from graphite. *v.* To make, write, or draw with a pencil.

pend-ing (pen´ding) *adj.* Not yet decided; imminent. *prep.* During; until.

pen-du-lous (pen´ja lus) *adj.* Hanging downward so as to swing; wavering.

pen-du-lum (pen´ja lum) *n.* A suspended

object free to swing back and forth.

pen-e-trate (pen´i trāt´) *v.* To force a way through or into; to pierce; to enter; to pass through something. **penetrable** *adj.* **penetrating** *adj.* **penetration** *n.*

pen-guin (pen´gwin) *n.* A web-footed, flightless, marine bird of the southern hemisphere.

pen-i-cil-lin (pen´i sil´in) *n.* A powerful antibiotic derived from mold and used to treat certain types of bacterial infections.

pen-in-su-la (pe nin´sa la) *n.* A piece of land projecting into water from a larger land mass. **peninsular** *adj.*

pe-nis (pē´nis) *n. pl.* **-nises** *or* **-nes** The male sex organ; the male organ through which urine leaves the body.

pen-i-tent (pen´i tent) *adj.* Having a feeling of guilt or remorse for one's sins or misdeeds; sorry. **penitence** *n.* **penitential** *adj.*

Penn-syl-va-nia *n.* A state located in the mid-eastern part of the United States; statehood; December 12, 1787; state capital Harrisburg.

pen-ny (pen´ē) *n. pl.* **-ies** A United States coin worth one cent ($.01).

pen-sion (pen´shan) *n.* The amount of money a person receives regularly after retirement. *v.* To pay a person his pension

pen-sive (pen´siv) *adj.* Involved in serious, quiet reflection; causing melancholy thought. **pensively** *adv.* **pensiveness** *n.*

pen-ta-gon (pen´ta gon´) *n.* Any object or building having five sides and five interior angles. **Pentagon** The five-sided office building in Arlington, Va. which houses the Defense Department.

Pen-te-cost (pen´te kost´) *n.* The seventh Sunday after Easter, celebrated by Christians as commemoration of the descent of the Holy Ghost on the Apostles. **Pentecos** *n.* **Pentecostal** *n.*

pent-house (pent´hous) *n.* An apartment built on the roof of a building.

pe-on (pē´on) n. A servant; a person engaged in menial work. peonage n.

pe-o-ny (pē´o nē) n. pl. -nies A plant with a large, fragrant red, white, or pink flower.

peo-ple (pē´pl) n. pl. people Human beings; a body of persons living in the same country, under the same government, and speaking the same language; one's relatives or family. people v.

pep-per (pep´ėr) n. A strong, aromatic condiment. v. To pelt or sprinkle.

pep-tic (pep´tik) adj. Pertaining to or aiding digestion.

per an-num (pėr an´um) adv. For, by, or in each year; annually.

per-cale (pėr kāl´) n. A closely woven cotton fabric.

per–cap-i-ta (pėr kap´i ta) adj. & adv. Of each individual.

per-ceive (pėr sēv´) v. To become aware of by the senses; to understand; to feel or observe. perceivable adj. perceivably adv.

per-cent-age (pėr sen´tij) n. The rate per hundred; a part or proportion in relation to a whole. Slang Profit; advantage.

per-cept (per´sept) n. A mental impression of something perceived; the immediate knowledge obtained from perceiving.

perch (perch) n. A place on which birds rest or light; any place for standing or sitting; a small, edible freshwater fish having tender white meat.

per-cip-i-ent (pėr sip´ent) adj. Having the power of perception. percipience n. percipiency n.

per-co-late (per´ko lāt´) v. To pass or cause to pass through a porous substance; to filter. percolation n. percolator n.

per-cus-sion (pėr kush´an) n. The sharp striking together of one body against another; the striking of a cap in a firearm. Music. An instrument which makes music when it is struck, as a drum or cymbal.

per-en-ni-al (pe ren´ē al) adj. Lasting from year to year; perpetual. n. A plant which lives through the winter and blooms again in the spring. perennially adv.

per-fect (per´fikt) adj. Having no defect or fault; flawless; accurate; absolute. v. To make perfect. perfectly adv.

per-form (pėr form´) v. To execute or carry out an action; to act or function in a certain way; to act; to give a performance or exhibition. performable adj. performer n. performance n.

per-fume (per´fūm) n. A fragrant substance which emits a pleasant scent; one distilled from flowers. perfume v.

per-haps (pėr haps´) adv. Possibly; maybe; not sure.

per-i-gee (per´i jē´) n. The point of an orbit when a satellite of the earth is closest to the earth; the lowest part of an orbit.

per-il (per´il) n. A source of danger; exposure to the chance of injury; danger. perilous adj. perilously adv.

pe-ri-od (pēr´ē od) n. An interval of time marked by certain conditions; an interval of time that is regarded as a phase in development; menstruation; the punctuation mark (.) which indicates the end of a sentence or an abbreviation.

pe-riph-er-y (pe rif´e rē) n. pl. -ies The outer part, boundary, or surface. peripheral adj.

per-ish (per´ish) v. To ruin or spoil; to suffer an untimely or violent death.

per-i-win-kle (per´i wing´kl) n. Any of several edible marine snails; a trailing evergreen plant with blue and sometimes white flowers.

per-jure (per´jėr) v. To give false testimony while under oath. perjury n.

per-ma-nent (per´ma nent) adj. Continuing in the same state; lasting indefinitely; enduring. n. A hair wave which gives long lasting curls or body to the hair. permanence n. permanency n. permanently adv.

per-me-ate (per´mē āt´) v. To spread through; to pervade; to pass through the pores. permeation n. permeable adj.

per-mis-sion (pėr mish´an) n. The act of permitting something; consent.

per-mit (pėr mit´) v. To consent to; to allow. n. An official document giving permission for a specific activity.

per-ni-cious (pĕr nish´us) *adj.* Very harmful; malicious. **perniciously** *adv.* **perniciousness** *n.*

per-ox-ide (pe rok´sīd) *n.*, *Chem.* Oxide containing the highest proportion of oxygen for a given series; a chemical used with other ingredients to bleach the hair.

per-pen-dic-u-lar (per´pen dik´ū lĕr) *adj.* Being at right angles to the plane of the horizon. *Math.* Meeting a plane or given line at right angles. **perpendicular** *n.* **perpendicularity** *n.* **perpendicularly** *adv.*

per-pe-trate (per´pi trāt´) *v.* To perform; to commit; to be guilty. **perpetration** *n.* **perpetrator** *n.*

per-pet-u-al (pĕr pech´ŏ al) *adj.* Lasting or continuing forever or an unlimited time. **perpetually** *adv.*

per-plex (pĕr pleks´) *v.* To confuse or be confused; to make complicated. **perplexing** *adj.* **perplexingly** *adv.* **perplexedly** *adv.* **perplexity** *n.*

per-se-cute (per´se kūt´) *v.* To harass or annoy persistently; to oppress because of one's religion, beliefs, or race. **persecution** *n.* **persecutor** *n.* **persecutive** *adj.*

per-se-vere (per´se vēr´) *v.* To persist in any purpose or idea; to strive in spite of difficulties or obstacles. **perseverance** *n.* **perseveringly** *adv.*

per-sim-mon (pĕr sim´on) *n.* A tree having reddish-orange, edible fruit.

per-sist (pĕr sist´) *v.* To continue firmly despite obstacles; to endure. **persistence** *n.* **persistency** *n.* **persistent** *adj.* **persistently** *adv.*

per-son (per´son) *n.* A human being; an individual; the personality of a human being. *Law* Any human being, corporation, or other entity having legal rights and duties.

per-son-al (per´so nal) *adj.* Belonging to a person or persons; of the body or person; relating to oneself; done by oneself.

per-son-i-fy (pĕr son´i fī´) *v.* To think of or represent as having human qualities or life; to be a symbol of. **personifier** *n.*

personification *n.*

per-son-nel (per´so nel´) *n.* The body of people working for a business or service.

per-spec-tive (pĕr spek´tiv) *n.* A painting or drawing technique in which objects seem to have depth and distance.

per-spi-ra-tion (per´spi rā shan) *n.* The salty fluid excreted from the body by the sweat glands.

per-spire (pĕr spīĕr´) *v.* To give off perspiration.

per-suade (pĕr swād´) *v.* To cause to convince or believe by means of reasoning or argument. **persuader** *n.* **persuasiveness** *n.* **persuasive** *adj.*

per-tain (pĕr tān´) *v.* To relate to; to refer to; to belong as a function, adjunct or quality; to be appropriate or fitting.

per-ti-na-cious (per´ti nā´shus) *adj.* Adhering firmly to an opinion, belief, or purpose; stubbornly persistent. **pertinaciously** *adv.* **pertinacity** *n.*

per-ti-nent (per´ti nent) *adj.* Relating to the matter being discussed; or the matter at hand.

per-turb (pĕr terb´) *v.* To disturb, make anxious, or make uneasy; to cause confusion. **perturbation** *n.*

per-vade (pĕr vād´) *v.* To spread through every part of something; to permeate. **pervasive** *adj.*

per-ver-sion (pĕr ver´zhan) *n.* The act of being led away from the accepted course; a deviant form of sexual behavior.

per-vert (pĕr vert´) *v.* To lead away from the proper cause; to use in an improper way. *n.* A person practicing or characterized by sexual perversion. **perverted** *adj.* **pervertible** *adj.*

pes-si-mism (pes´i miz´um) *n.* The tendency to take a gloomy view of affairs or situations and to anticipate the worst. **pessimist** *n.* **pessimistic** *adj.* **pessimistically** *adv.*

pest (pest) *n.* A person or thing which is a nuisance; an annoying person or thing;

a destructive insect, plant, or animal.

pes-ter (pes´tėr) *v.* To harass with persistent annoyance; to bother.

pes-ti-cide (pes´ti sīd´) *n.* A chemical substance used to destroy rodents, insects, and pests. **pesticidal** *adj.*

pes-ti-lence (pes´ti lens) *n.* A widespread and often fatal infectious disease, as bubonic plague or cholera.

pet (pet) *n.* An animal, bird, or fish one keeps for companionship; any favorite or treasured thing. *adj.* Treated or tamed as a pet. *v.* To stroke or caress gently. *Slang* To make love by fondling and caressing.

pet-al (pet´al) *n. Bot.* One of the leaf-like parts of a flower.

pe-tite (pe tēt´) *adj.* Small in size; little. **petiteness** *n.*

pet-it four (pet´ē fōr´) *n. pl.* **fours** A small decorated cake.

pe-ti-tion (pe tish´an) *n.* A solemn request or prayer; a formal written request addressed to a group or person in authority. **petitioner** *n.*

pet-ri-fy (pe´tri fī´) *v.* To convert into a stony mass; to make fixed or immobilize, as in the face of danger or surprise. **petrification** *n.* **petrifactive** *adj.*

pe-tro-le-um (petrō´lē um) *n.* An oily, thick liquid which developes naturally below the ground surface, used in products such as gasoline, fuel oil, and kerosene.

pet-ti-coat (pet´ē kōt´) *n.* A woman's skirt-like garment worn as an underskirt.

pet-ty (pet´ē) *adj.* To have little importance or value; insignificant; trivial; having a low position or rank; minor; small minded. **pettiness** *n.*

petty cash *n.* Cash held on hand for minor bills or expenditures.

pe-tu-nia (pe tõ´nē a) *n.* A widely grown tropical plant having a funnel shaped flower in various colors.

pew (pū) *n.* A row of bench-like seats for seating people in church.

pew-ter (pū´tėr) *n.* An alloy of tin with copper, silver-gray in color and used for tableware and kitchen utensils.

pfen-nig *n. pl.* **-nigs** *or* **-nige** A small coin of Germany, equal to one hundredth of a Deutschemark.

phal-lus (fal´us) *n. pl.* **-li** *or* **-luses** A representation of the penis, often as a symbol of generative power. **phallic** *adj.*

phan-tasm (fan´taz um) *n.* The creation of an imaginary image; a fantasy; a phantom. **phantasmal** *adj.* **phantasmic** *adj.*

phan-tom (fan´tom) *n.* Something which exists but has no physical reality; a ghost.

phar-ma-ceu-ti-cal (fär´ma sõ´ti kal) *adj.* Pertaining or relating to a pharmacy or pharmacists.

phar-ma-cy (fär´ma sē) *n. pl.* **-cies.** A place of business which specializes in preparing, identifying, and disbursing drugs; a drugstore.

phar-ynx (far´ingks) *n. pl.* **-ynges** *or* **-ynxes.** The part of the throat located between the palate and the esophagus, serving as a passage for air and food. **pharyngeal** *adj.*

phase (fāz) *n.* Any decisive stage in development or growth. *Astron.* One of the forms or appearances of a planet.

pheas-ant (fez´ant) *n.* A long-tailed game bird noted for the beautiful plumage of the male.

phe-nom-e-non (fi nom´e non´) *n. pl.* **-na** *or* **-nons** Something that can be observed or perceived; a rare occurrence. *Slang* An outstanding person with remarkable power, ability, or talent.

phi-lan-der (fi lan´dėr) *v.* To make love without feeling or serious intentions. **philanderer** *n.*

phi-lat-e-ly (fi lat´e lē) *n.* The collection and study of postage stamps and postmarked material. **philatelic** *adj.* **philatelist** *n.*

phil-har-mon-ic (fil´här mon´ik) *adj.* Pertaining to a symphony orchestra. **philharmonic** *n.*

phi-los-o-phy (fi los´o fē) *n. pl.* **-ies** The logical study of the nature and source of human knowledge or human values; the set of values, opinions, and ideas of a group or individual.

pho-bi-a (fō´bē a) *n*. A compulsive fear of a specified situation or object.

phone (fōn) *n.*, *Slang* A telephone. *v*. To call or communicate by telephone.

phon-ic (fon´ik) *adj*. Pertaining to sounds in speech; using the same symbol for each sound. **phonetically** *adv*. **phonetics** *n*.

pho-no-graph (fō no graf´) *n*. A machine which uses a needle to reproduce sound from a grooved disc or record.

pho-ny (fō´nē) *adj.*, *Informal* Counterfeit; fraudulent; not real or genuine.

phos-phate (fos´fāt) *n.*, *Chem.* A salt or phosphoric acid which contains mostly phosphorus and oxygen.

phos-pho-rus (fos´fèr us) *n*. A highly flammable, poisonous, nonmetallic element used in safety matches, symbolized by P.

pho-to (fō´tō) *n*. *Slang* A photograph.

pho-to-cop-y (fō´to kop´ē) *v*. To reproduce printed material using a photographic process. **photocopier** *n*. **photocopy** *n*.

pho-to-graph (fō´to graf´) *n*. A picture or image recorded by a camera and then reproduced on a photosensitive surface. **photography** *n*.

pho-to-stat (fō´to stat´) *n*. A trademark for a camera designed to reproduce documents and graphic material.

pho-to-syn-the-sis (fō´to sin´thi sis) *n.*, *Biochem.* The chemical process by which plants use light to change carbon dioxide and water into carbohydrates, releasing oxygen as a by-product. **photosynthesize** *v*. **photosynthetic** *adj*.

phrase (frāz) *n.*, *Gram.* A brief or concise expression which does not contain a predicate.

phre-nol-o-gy (fri nol´o jē) *n*. The study of or the theory that the conformation of the human skull indicates the degree of intelligence and character.

phys-i-cal (fiz´i kal) *adj*. Relating to the human body apart from the mind or emotions; pertaining to material rather than imaginary subjects. *n*. A medical exam to determine a person's physical condition.

physically *adv*.

phy-si-cian (fi zish´an) *n*. A person licensed to practice medicine.

phys-ics (fiz´iks) *n*. The scientific study which deals with energy, matter, motion, and related areas of science.

phys-i-ol-o-gy (fiz´ē ol´o jē) *n*. *pl*. -ies The scientific study of living animals, plants, and their activities and functions; the vital functions and processes of an organism. **physiological** *adj*. **physiologic** *adj*. **physiologist** *n*.

phys-i-o-ther-a-py (fiz´ē ō ther´ape) *n*. The treatment of disease or physical defects by the use of heat and massage.

pi-an-o (pē an´ō) *n*. A musical instrument with a manual keyboard and felt-covered hammers which produce musical tones when struck upon steel wires.

pi-az-za (pē az´a) *n*. A public square or an open area in an Italian town or city.

pi-ca (pī´ka) *n*. A printer's type size of 12 points, equal to about 1/6 inch; a typewriter type size with 10 characters to an inch.

pic-co-lo (pik´o lō´) *n*. A small flute with a brilliant sound pitched an octave above the flute.

pick (pik) *v*. To select or choose from a number or group; to remove the outer area of something with the fingers or a pointed instrument; to remove by tearing away little by little; to open a lock without using a key; to harass or tease someone or something; to pluck *v*. A musical instrument. *n*. A pointed metal tool sharpened at both ends, used to break up hard surfaces. *Music* A small flat piece of plastic or of bone, used to pluck or strum the strings of an instrument, as a guitar or banjo.

pick-et (pik´it) *n*. A pointed stake driven into the ground as support for a fence; a person positioned outside of a place of employment during a strike. *Mil.* A soldier posted to guard a camp.

pick-le (pik´l) *n*. A cucumber preserved in a solution of brine or vinegar. *Slang* A troublesome situation.

pick-pock-et (pik′ok′it) *n.* A person who steals from another's purse or pocket.

pic-nic (pik′nik) *n.* An outdoor social gathering where food is provided usually by the people attending. **picnicker** *n.*

pic-ture (pik′chėr) *n.* A visual represen-tation on a surface, which is printed, drawn or photographed; the mental image or im-pression of an event or situation.

piece (pēs) *n.* An element, unit, or part of a whole; a musical or literary work. *Slang* A firearm.

piece-meal (pēs′mēl′) *adv.* Gradually, bit by bit.

pier (pēr) *n.* A structure extending into the water, used to secure, protect, and provide access to vessels.

pierce (pērs) *v.* To penetrate or make a hole in something; to force into or through. **piercing** *adj.*

pi-e-ty (pī′i tē) *n. pl.* **-ties** Devoutness to-ward God.

pig (pig) *n.* A cloven-hoofed mammal with short legs, bristly hair, and a snout for rooting; the edible meat of a pig; pork. *Slang* A greedy or gross person.

pi-geon (pij′on) *n.* A bird with short legs, a sturdy body, and a small head.

pig-gy-back (pig′ē bak′) *adv.* Carried on the back and shoulders. **piggyback** *adj.*

pig-head-ed (pig′hed′id) *adj.* Stubborn. **pigheadedly** *adv.*

pig-ment (pig′ment) *n.* A material used as coloring matter, suitable for making paint. *Biol.* Any substance such as melanin and chlorophyll which imparts color to vege-table tissue or animals.

pig-skin (pig′skin′) *n.* Something made from the skin of a pig. *Slang* A football.

pike (pīk) *n.* A long pole with a sharp, point-ed steel head; a large edible freshwater fish with a long snout and a slender body. *Slang* A turnpike or a major highway.

pile (pīl) *n.* A quantity of anything thrown in a heap; a massive or very large building or a group of buildings.

pil-fer (pil′fėr) *v.* To steal in little quan-tities; to steal items of little value. **pilfer-age** *n.*

pil-grim (pil′grim) *n.* A person who travels to a sacred place; a wanderer. **Pilgrims** The English Puritans who founded the Plymouth colony in New England in the year 1620.

pill (pil) *n.* A small tablet containing med-icine which is taken by mouth; someone or something which is disagreeable but must be dealt with. **pill** An oral contra-ceptive drug taken by women.

pil-lar (pil′ėr) *n.* A freestanding column which serves as a support.

pil-low (pil′ō) *n.* A cloth case filled with feathers or other soft material, used to cushion the head during sleep.

pi-lot (pī′lot) *n.* A person who is licensed to operate an aircraft; someone who is trained and licensed to guide ships in and out of port. *v.* To act or serve as a pilot.

pi-men-to (pi men′tō) *n.* A sweet pepper used as a stuffing for olives or as a relish.

pimp (pimp) *n.* A person who arranges customers for prostitutes in exchange for a share of their money.

pim-ple (pim′pl) *n.* A small eruption of the skin, having an inflamed base. **pimpled** *adj.* **pimply** *adj.*

pin (pin) *n.* A small, stiff piece of wire with a blunt head and a sharp point, used to fasten something, usually temporarily; one of the rounded wooden clubs serving as the target in bowling.

pin-a-fore (pin′a fōr′) *n.* A sleeveless apron-like garment.

pin-cers (pin′chėrz) *n.* An implement hav-ing two handles and a pair of jaws working on a pivot, used to hold objects.

pinch (pinch) *v.* To squeeze between a finger and thumb causing pain or discom-fort; to be miserly. *n.* The small amount that can be held between the thumb and forefinger.

pine (pīn) *n., Bot.* Any of various conebearing evergreen trees; the wood of such a tree.

pine-ap-ple (pīn′ap′l) *n.* A tropical American plant with spiny, curved leaves bearing a large edible fruit. *Slang* A hand grenade.

pine-cone *n.* The cone of a pinetree.

pink (pingk) *n.* Any of various plants related to the carnation, having fragrant flowers; a light or pale hue of crimson; the highest or best possible degree.

pink-eye (pingk′ī′) *n., Pathol.* An acute, contagious conjunctivitis of the eye.

pin-na-cle (pin′a kl) *n.* The highest peak; a sharp point;a pointed summit.

pi-noch-le *or* **pi-noc-le (pē′ nuk l)** *n.* A card game for two, three, or four people, played with a double deck of 48 cards.

pint (pīnt) *n.* A liquid or dry measurement equal to half of a quart or two cups.

pin-to (pin′tō) *n. pl.* **-tos** *or* **-toes** A horse with spots; a spotted bean of the southwestern United States.

pin-wheel (pin′hwēl′) *n.* A toy with revolving paper or plastic fastened to a stick; a fireworks display featuring a revolving wheel of colored flames.

pin-worm (pin′werm′) *n.* A nematode parasite which infests the human intestines and rectum.

pi-o-neer (pī′o nēr′) *n.* One of the first settlers of a new region or country; the first developer or investigator in a new field of enterprise, research, or other endeavor.

pi-ous (pī′us) *adj.* Reverently religious; devout. **piously** *adv.* **piousness** *n.*

pipe (pīp) *n.* A hollow cylinder for conveying fluids; a small bowl with a hollow stem for smoking tobacco. *Music* A tubular flute.

pipe-line (pīp′līn′) *n.* A pipe used to transfer gas or oil over long distances; a means for conveying information.

pique (pēk) *n.* A feeling of resentment or irritation.

pi-rate (pī′rat) *n.* A robber of the high seas. *Slang* Someone who uses or reproduces someone else's work without authorization. **piracy** *n.* **piratical** *adj.*

pis-ta-chi-o (pi stash′ē ō′) *n.* A small tree of western Asia; the edible fruit from this tree.

pis-til (pis′til) *n.* The seed-producing female reproductive organ of a flower.

pis-tol (pis′tol) *n.* A small hand-held firearm.

pis-ton (pis′ton) *n.,* Mech. A solid cylinder fitted in a larger cylinder, moving back and forth under liquid pressure.

pit (pit) *n.* An artificial or manmade hole in the ground; a slight indentation in the skin, as a scar from the chicken pox; an area for refueling or repair at a car race; the stone in the middle of some fruit, as peaches. *the pits* Anything at its worst.

pitch (pich) *n.* A thick, sticky, dark substance which is the residue of the distillation of petroleum or coal tar; the degree of slope of an incline; the property of a musical tone which makes it high or low. *v.* To cover with pitch; to throw; to throw out; to slope.

pitch–black (pich′blak′) *adj.* Extremely dark.

pitch-er (pich′ėr) *n.* The person who throws the ball to the batter; a container for holding and pouring liquids.

pitch-fork (pich′fork′) *n.* A large fork with a wide prong span, used as a garden or farm tool.

pith (pith) *n., Bot.* The sponge-like soft tissue at the center of the branch or stem of many plants.

pit-i-ful (pit′i ful) *adj.* Evoking or meriting pity. **pitifully** *adv.*

pit-y (pit′ē) *n. pl.* **-ies** A feeling of compassion or sorrow for another's misfortune. **pity** *v.*

piv-ot (piv′ot) *n.* A thing or person upon which development, direction, or effect depends. *v.* To turn.

piz-za (pēt′sa) *n.* An Italian food consisting of a doughy crust covered with tomato sauce, cheese, and other toppings and then baked.

pkg *abbr.* Package.

place (plās) *n.* A region; an area; a building or location used for a special purpose; the position of something in a series or sequence. *v.* To put in a particular order or place.

place-ment (plās′ment) *n.* The act of being placed; a business or service which finds positions of employment for applicants.

pla-cen-ta (pla sen′ta) *n. pl.* **-tas** *or* **-tae** *Anat.* The vascular, membranous structure which supplies a fetus with nourishment before its birth.

plague (plāg) *n.* Anything that is troublesome. *Pathol.* A highly contagious and often fatal epidemic disease, as the bubonic plague.

plaid (plad) *n.* A rectangular wool cloth or garment, usually worn by men and women, having a crisscross or checkered design.

plain (plān) *adj.* Level; flat; clear; open, as in view; not rich or luxurious; not highly gifted or cultivated. **plainly** *adv.*

plain-tiff (plān′tif) *n.* A person who brings suit.

plan (plan) *n.* A scheme or method for achieving something; a drawing to show proportion and relationship to parts. *v.* To have in mind as an intention or purpose.

plane (plān) *n.* A tool for smoothing or leveling a wood surface. *Geom.* A surface as a straight line that joins any two points on it. *Slang* Airplane. **plane** *v.*

plan-et (plan′it) *n., Astron.* A celestial body which is illuminated by light from the star around which it revolves. **planetary** *adj.*

plan-e-tar-i-um (plan′i târ′ē um) *n. pl.***-iums** *or* **- ia** A device for exhibiting celestial bodies as they exist at any time and for any place on earth.

plank (plangk) *n.* A broad piece of wood; one of the issues or principles of a political platform.

plant (plant) *n.* A living organism belonging to the vegetable kingdom, having cellulose cell walls. *v.* To place a living organism in the ground for growing; to place so as to deceive or to spy.

plaque (plak) *n.* A flat piece, made from metal, porcelain, ivory, or other materials, engraved for mounting; the bacteria deposit which builds up on the teeth.

plas-ma (plaz′ma) *n.* The clear fluid part of blood, used for transfusions.

plas-ter-board (plas′tėrbōrd′) *n.* A building material of layered gypsum bonded to outer layers of paper.

plas-tic (plas′tik) *adj.* Pliable; capable of being molded. *n.* A synthetically made material which is molded and then hardened into objects. **plasticity** *n.*

plastic surgery *n.* Surgery dealing with the restoration or repair of deformed or destroyed parts of the body or skin.

plate (plāt) *n.* A flat flexible, thin piece of material, as metal; a shallow, flat vessel made from glass, crockery, plastic, or other material from which food is served or eaten; a piece of plastic, metal, or vulcanite fitted to the mouth to hold one or more artificial teeth. *n., Baseball* The place or object marking home base. *v.* To cover something, as jewelry, with a thin layer of gold, silver, or other metal.

pla-teau (pla tō′) *n.* An extensive level of elevated land; a period of stability.

plat-form (plat′form) *n.* Any elevated or raised surface used by speakers, or by other performers or for display purposes; a formal declaration of principles or policy of a political party.

plat-i-num (plat′i num) *n.* A silver-white, metallic element, corrosive-resistant, used in jewelry; symbolized by Pt.

pla-toon (pla tōn′) *n.* A military unit subdivision commanded by a lieutenant.

plat-ter (plat′ėr) *n.* A large, oblong, shallow dish for serving food.

plau-si-ble (plo′zi bl) *adj.* Seeming to be probable; appearing to be trustworthy or believable.

play (plā) *v.* To entertain, as in recreation; to take part in a game; to perform in a dramatic role; to perform with a musical instrument; in fishing, to allow a hooked fish to tire itself out; to pretend to do something. *n.* A dramatic presentaton.

playful (plā´ful) *adj.* Lightly humorous; full of high spirits.

playground (plā´ground´) *n.* The area set aside for children's recreation.

play–off *n.* A sports contest to break a tie; a series of games to decide the winner or championship.

pla-za (plä´za) *n.* An open-air market place or square; a shopping mall.

plea (plē) *n.* An urgent request; in law, an allegation made by either party in a law suit.

plea bargaining *v.* Making a pretrial agreement to plead guilty to a lesser charge if a more serious one will be dropped.

plead (plēd) *v.* To argue for or against something in court; to ask earnestly.

pleas-ant (plez´ant) *adj.* Giving or promoting the feeling of pleasure; very agreeable. **pleasantly** *adv.* **pleasantness** *n.*

please (plēz) *v.* To make happy; to give pleasure; to be the will or wish of; to prefer.

pleas-ur-a-ble (plezh´er a bl) *adj.* Pleasant; gratifying.

pleas-ure (plezh´er) *n.* A feeling of satisfaction or enjoyment; one's preference or wish.

pleat (plēt) *n.* A fold in a cloth made by doubling the cloth back and fastening it down.

plebe (plēb) *n.* A freshman or first year student at the United States Naval Academy.

pledge (plej) *n.* A solemn promise; a deposit of something as security for a loan; a promise to join a fraternity; a person who is pledged to join a fraternity. *v.* To promise or vow.

plen-ti-ful (plen´ti ful) *adj.* Having great abundance. **plentifully** *adv.*

plen-ty (plen´tē) *n.* An ample amount; prosperity or abundance.

pleu-ra (pler´a) *n. pl.* **pleurae** *Anat.* The membranous sac which covers the inside of the thorax membrane, which covers the lungs.

pli-a-ble (plī´a bl) *adj.* Flexible; easily

controlled or persuaded. **pliability** *n.* **pliableness** *n.* **pliably** *adv.*

pli-ers (plī´erz) *n.* A pincers-like tool used for holding, bending, or cutting.

plight (plīt) *n.* A distressing circumstance, situation, or condition.

plod (plod) *n.* To walk in a heavy, slow way.

plot (plot) *n.* A small piece of ground usually used for a special purpose; the main story line in a piece of fiction; a plan; an intrigue; a conspiracy. *v.* To represent something by using a map or chart; to scheme secretly. **plotter** *n.*

plow (plou) *n.* An implement for breaking up or turning over the soil. *v.* To dig out. *Slang* To hit with force.

pluck (pluk) *v.* To remove by pulling out or off; to pull and release the strings on a musical instrument. *Slang* To swindle. **plucker** *n.*

plug (plug) *n.* Anything used to stop or close a hole or drain. *Electr.* A two-pronged device attached to a cord and used in a jack or socket to make an electrical connection. *Slang* To advertise favorably; to give a recommendation or a piece of publicity for someone.

plum (plum) *n.* A small tree bearing an edible fruit with a smooth skin and a single hard seed; the fruit from such a tree.

plum-age (plö´mij) *n.* The feathers of a bird.

plumb (plum) *n.* A lead weight tied to the end of a string, used to test the exact perpendicular line of something.

plumb-er (plum´er) *n.* A person who repairs or installs plumbing in a home or business.

plumb-ing (plum´ing) *n.* The profession or trade of a plumber; the connecting of pipes and fixtures used to carry water and waste.

plume (plöm) *n.* A feather used as an ornament.

plun-der (plun´der) *v.* To deprive of goods or property in a violent way.

plunge (plunj) *v.* To thrust or cast something, as into water; to submerge; to descend sharply or steeply.

plunk (plungk) *v.* To put down or place suddenly; to pluck or strum a banjo. **plunker** *n.*

plu-ral (pler´al) *adj.* Consisting of or containing more than one. **plural** *n.*

plus (plus) *n.* The symbol (+) which indicates addition; increase; extra quantity.

plu-to-ni-um (plŏtō´nēum) *n.* A radioactive metallic element symbolized by Pu.

ply (plī) *v.* To mold, bend, or shape. *n.* A layer of thickness; the twisted strands of thread, yarn, or rope.

ply-wood (plī´wed´) *n.* A structural material consisting of thin layers of wood which have been glued and pressed together.

pneu-mo-nia (ne mōn´ya) *n.* An inflammation caused by bacteria, virus of the lungs, or irritation.

poach (pōch) *v.* To cook in a liquid just at the boiling point; to trespass on another's property with the intent of taking fish or wild game. **poacher** *n.*

pock-et (pok´it) *n.* A small pouch within a garment, having an open top and used for carrying items. *v.* To put in or deposit in a pocket.

pod (pod) *n., Bot.* A seed vessel, as of a bean or pea. *Aeron.* A separate and detachable compartment in a spacecraft.

po-di-a-try *n.* Professional care and treatment of the feet.

po-di-um (pō´dē um) *n. pl.* **-ia** *or* **-iums** A small raised platform for an orchestra conductor or a speaker.

po-em (pō´im) *n.* A composition in verse with language selected for its beauty and sound.

po-et (pō´it) *n.* A person who writes poetry.

po-et-ry (pō´i trē) *n.* The art of writing stories, poems, and thoughts into verse.

poin-set-ti-a (poin set´ē a) *n.* A tropical plant having large scarlet leaves, used in Christmas decorations.

point (point) *n.* The sharp or tapered end

of something; a mark of punctuation, as a period (.); a geometric object which does not have property or dimensions other than locaton; a degree, condition, or stage; a particular or definite spot in time. *v.* To aim; to indicate direction by using the finger.

poise (poiz) *v.* To bring into or hold one's balance. *n.* Equilibrium; self-confidence; the ability to stay calm in all social situations.

poi-son (poi´zon) *n.* A substance which kills, injures, or destroys. **poisoner** *n.* **poisonous** *adj.*

poke (pōk) *v.* To push or prod at something with a finger or other implement.

pok-er (pō´kėr) *n.* A card game, played by two or more people in which the players bet on the cards dealt to them.

po-lar (pō´lėr) *adj.* Having to do with the poles of a magnet or sphere; relating to the geographical poles of the earth.

po-lar-ize (pō´la rīz´) *v.* To cause something to vibrate in an exact pattern; to break up into opposite groups.

pole (pōl) *n.* Either of the two ends of the axis of a sphere, as the earth; the two points called the North and South Poles, where the axis of the earth's rotation meets the surface; a long, slender rod.

po-lice (po lēs´) *n.* A division or department organized to maintain order; the members of such a department. *v.* To patrol; to enforce the law and maintain order.

po-liceman (po lēs´man) *n.* A member of the police force. **policewoman** *n.*

pol-i-cy (pol´i sē) *n. pl.* **-ies** Any plan or principle which guides a persons or gourps decision making.

pol-i-o-my-e-li-tis (pō´lē ōmī´e lī´tis) *n.* Inflammation of the spinal cord causing paralysis; also polio.

pol-ish (pol´ish) *v.* To make lustrous and smooth by rubbing; to become refined or elegant.

po-lite (po līt´) *adj.*

Refined, mannerly, and courteous.

po-lit-i-cal (p*o* **lit´i k***a***l)** *adj.* Concerned with or pertaining to government; involved in politics.

pol-i-ti-cian (pol´i tish´*a***n)** *n.* A person active in governmental affairs or politics.

pol-i-tics (pol´i tiks) *n.* The activities and methods of a political party.

poll (pōl) *n.* The recording of votes in an election; a public survey taken on a given topic. **poll** *v.*

pol-len (pol´*e***n)** *n.* The yellow dust-like powder which contains the male reproductive cells of a flowering plant.

pol-lute (p*o* **löt´)** *v.* To contaminate; to make unclear or impure; to dirty. **pollution** *n.*

po-lo (pō´lō) *n.* A game played on horseback in which players try to drive a wooden ball through the opposing team's goal using long-handled mallets. **poloist** *n.*

po-lo-ni-um (p*o* **lō´nē** *u***m)** *n.* A radioactive metallic element symbolized by PO.

pol-ter-geist (pōl´tėr gīst´) *n.* A mischievous spirit which makes noise.

pol-y-es-ter (pol´ē es´tėr) *n.* A strong lightweight synthetic resin used in fibers.

pol-y-gon *n.* A closed figure bounded by straight lines.

pol-y-graph (pol´ē graf´) *n.* A machine designed to record different signals given off by the body, as respiration, blood pressure, or heartbeats; may be used to detect a person who may be lying.

pol-y-he-dron (pol´ē hē´dr*o***n)** *n. pl.* **-dra** or **-drons** *Geom.* A solid bounded by polygons.

pom-pa-dour (pom´p*a* **dōr´)** *n.* A hairstyle which is puffed over the forehead.

pomp-ous (pom´pus) *adj.* A showing or appearance of dignity or importance.

pond (pond) *n.* A body of still water, smaller in size than a lake.

pon-der (pon´dėr) *v.* To think about very carefully; to meditate.

pon-der-ous (pon´dėr us) *adj.*

Massive; having great weight.

pon-tiff (pon´tif) *n.* A pope.

po-ny (pō´nē) *n. pl.* **-ies** A small horse.

pool (pōl) *n.* A small body of water; the collective stake in gambling games.

poor (per) *adj.* Lacking possessions and money; not satisfactory; broke; needy; destitute.

pop (pop) *v.* To cause something to burst; to make a sharp, explosive sound. *Slang* Soda. **popper** *n.*

pop-corn (pop´korn´) *n.* A variety of corn which explodes when heated, forming white puffs.

pope (pōp) *n.* The head of the Roman Catholic Church.

pop-lar (pop´lėr) *n.* A rapid growing tree having a light, soft wood.

pop-u-lar (pop´ū lėr) *adj.* Approved of; widely liked; suited to the means of the people.

pop-u-la-tion (pop´ū lā´sh*a***n)** *n.* The total number of people in a given area, country, or city.

por-ce-lain (pōr´s*e* **lin)** *n.* A hard, translucent ceramic which has been fired and glazed.

porch (pōrch) *n.* A covered structure forming the entrance to a house.

por-cu-pine (por´kū pīn´) *n.* A clumsy rodent covered with long sharp quills.

pore (pōr) *v.* To ponder or meditate on something. *n.* A minute opening, as in the skin.

pork (pōrk) *n.* The edible flesh of swine. *Informal* Favors given by a government for political reasons and not public necessity.

por-no *n., Slang* Pornography.

por-nog-ra-phy (por nog´ra fē) *n.* Pictures, films, or writing which deliberately arouse sexual excitement.

por-poise (por´p*o***s)** *n.* An aquatic mammal with a blunt, rounded snout.

port (pōrt) *n.* A city or town with a harbor for loading and unloading cargo from ships; the left side of a ship; a dark red, sweet, fortified wine.

port-a-ble (pōr´ta bl) *adj.* Capable of being moved easily.

por-ter (pōr´tėr) *n.* A person hired to carry baggage.

port-fo-li-o (pōrt fō´lē ō´) *n.* A carrying case for holding papers, drawings, and other flat items.

port-hole (pōrt´hōl´) *n.* A small opening in the side of a ship providing light and ventilation.

por-tion (pōr´shan) *n.* A section or part of a whole; a share. *v.* To allot; to assign.

por-tray (pōr trā´) *v.* To represent by drawing, writing, or acting.

pose (pōz) *v.* To place or assume a position, as for a picture.

po-si-tion (po zish´an) *n.* The manner in which something is placed; an attitude; a viewpoint; a job; employment. *v.* To place in proper order.

pos-i-tive (poz´i tiv) *adj.* Containing, expressing, or characterized by affirmation; very confident; absolutely certain; not negative. **positively** *adv.* **positiveness** *n.*

pos-se (pos´ē) *n.* A deputized group or squad.

pos-ses-sion (po zesh´an) *n.* The fact or act of possessing property; the state of being possessed, as by an evil spirit.

pos-ses-sive (po zes´iv) *adj.* Having a strong desire to possess; not wanting to share. *n.* The noun or pronoun case which indicates ownership.

pos-si-ble (pos´i bl) *adj.* Capable of being true, happening, or being accomplished. **possibility** *n.* **possibly** *adv.*

post (pōst) *n.* An upright piece of wood or metal support; a position or employment. *v.* To put up information in a public place. *prefix.* After; in order; or time; behind.

post-age (pō´stij) *n.* The charge or fee for mailing something.

pos-te-ri-or (po stēr´ē ėr) *adj.* Located in the back. *n.* The buttocks.

post-mor-tem (pōst mor´tem) *adj.* The examination of a body after death; an autopsy.

post-pone (pōst pōn´) *v.* To put off; to defer to a later time. **postponable** *adj.* **postponement** *n.* **postponer** *n.*

post-script (pōst´skript´) *n.* A short message added at the end of a letter.

pos-ture (pos´chėr) *n.* The carriage or position of the body.

pot (pot) *n.* A rounded, deep container used for cooking and other domestic purposes. *Slang* A large sum of money which is shared by all members of a group; marijuana. **potful** *n.*

po-tas-si-um (po tas´ē um) *n.* A silvery-white, highly reactive metallic element symbolized by K.

po-ta-to (po tā´tō) *n. pl.* **-toes** A thick, edible, underground tuber plant native to America.

po-tent (pōt´ent) *adj.* Having great strength or physical powers; having a great influence on the mind or morals; sexually competent.

po-ten-tial (po ten´shal) *adj.* Possible, but not yet actual; having the capacity to be developed. *Electr.* The potential energy of an electric charge that depends on its position in an electric field.

pot-pour-ri (pō´pe rē´) *n.* A mixture of sweet-smelling dried flower petals and spices, kept in an airtight jar.

pot-ter-y (pot´e rē) *n. pl.* **-ies** Objects molded from clay and fired by intense heat.

pouch (pouch) *n.* A small bag or other container for holding or carrying money, tobacco, and other small articles. *Zool.* The sac-like structure in which some animals carry their young.

poul-try (pōl´trē) *n.* Domestic fowl as ducks and hens, which are raised for eggs or meat.

pound (pound) *n. pl.* **pound** A measure of weight equal to sixteen ounces; a public enclosure where stray animals are fed and housed. To strike repeatedly or with force; to throb or beat violently or rapidly. **pounds** *v.*

pov-er-ty (pov´ėr tē) *n.* The condition or

state of being poor and needing money.

POW (pē´ō´dub´lū´) *abbr.* Prisoner of war.

pow-der (pou´dèr) *n.* A dry substance which has been finely ground or pulverized; dust; an explosive, such as gunpowder. *v.* To dust or cover.

pow-er-ful (pou´èr ful) *adj.* Possessing energy or great force; having authority.

power of attorney *n.* A legal document in which one person gives another the authority to act for him.

prac-ti-cal (prak´ti kal) *adj.* Serving an actual use or purpose; inclined to act instead of thinking or talking about something; useful.

pract-ice (prak´tis) *n.* A custom or habit of doing something. *v.* To work at a profession; to apply; to put into effect; to exercise or rehearse.

prai-rie (prâr´ē) *n.* A wide area of level or rolling land with grass and weeds but no trees.

praise (prāz) *v.* To express approval; to glorify.

prank (prangk) *n.* A mischievous, playful action or trick. **prankster** *n.*

pra-seo-dym-i-um (prā´zē ō dim´ēum) *n.* A metallic element of the rare-earth group, symbolized by Pr.

prawn (pron) *n.* An edible shrimp-like crustacean found in both salt and fresh water.

pray (prā) *v.* To address prayers to God; to ask or request.

prayer (prâr) *n.* A devout request; the act of praying; a formal or set group of words used in praying.

praying mantis *n.* An insect which holds its front legs folded as, in prayer.

preach (prēch) *v.* To advocate; to proclaim; to deliver a sermon. **preacher** *n.* **preach-ment** *n.* **preachy** *adj.*

pre-am-ble (prē´am´bl) *n.* An introduction to something, as a law, which states the purpose and reasons for the matter which follows.

pre-cau-tion (pri ko´shan) *n.* A measure of caution or care taken in advance to guard against harm.

pre-cede (pri sēd´) *v.* To be or go before in time, position, or rank. **precedence** *n.*

prec-e-dent (pres´i dent) *n.* An instance which may serve as a rule or example in the future.

pre-cept (prē´sept) *n.* A rule, order, or commandment meant to guide one's conduct.

pre-cinct (prē´singkt) *n.* An electoral district of a county, township, city, or town; an enclosure with definite boundaries.

pre-cious (presh´us) *adj.* Having great worth or value; beloved; cherished.

pre-cip-i-ta-tion (pri sip´i tā´shan) *n.* Condensed water vapor which falls as snow, rain, sleet or hail. *Chem.* The act of causing crystals to separate and fall to the bottom of a liquid.

pre-cip-i-tous (pri sip´i tus) *adj.* Very steep; marked with very steep cliffs.

pre-cise (pri sīs´) *adj.* Exact; definite; strictly following rules; very strict.

pre-ci-sion (pri sizh´an) *n.* Exactness; the quality of being precise; accuracy.

pre-clude (pri klōd´) *v.* To shut out; to make impossible; to prevent.

pre-co-cious (pri kō´shus) *adj.* Showing and developing skills and abilities very early in life.

pre-con-ceive (prē´kon sēv´) *v.* To form a notion or conception before knowing all the facts. **preconception** *n.*

pre-da-cious (pri dā´shus) *adj.* Living by preying on other animals.

pred-a-tor (pred´a tèr) *n.* A person who lives or gains by stealing from another person; an animal that survives by killing and eating other animals.

pre-des-ti-na-tion (pri des´ti nā´shan) *n.* Destiny; fate; the act by which God has predestined all events.

pred-i-ca-ble (pred´i ka bl) *adj.* Capable of being predicated to foretell.

pred-i-cate (pred´i kāt´) *n., Gram.* The word or words which say something about the subject of a clause or sentence; the part of a sentence which contains the verb. *v.*

To establish.

pre-dict (pri dikt´) v. To tell beforehand; to foretell; to forcast. **predictability** n. **predictable** adj. **predictably** adv. **prediction** n.

pre-dom-i-nant (pri dom´i nant) adj. Superior in strength, authority, number, or other qualities.

pree-mie n., *Slang* A baby born before the expected due date.

pre-empt (prē empt´) v. To take or get hold of before someone else; to take the place of; to do something before someone else has a chance to do it. **preemption** n. **preemptive** adj.

pre-fab-ri-cate (prē fab´ri kāt´) v. To construct in sections beforehand. **prefabrication** n.

pref-ace (pref´is) n. The introduction at the beginning of a book or speech.

pre-fect (prē´fekt) n. A high administrative official. **prefecture** n.

pre-fer (pri fer´) v. To select as being the favorite; to promote; to present.

pref-er-ence (pref´ėr ens) n. A choice; a special liking for anything over another. **preferential** adj.

pre-fix (prē fiks´) v. To put at the beginning; to put before.

preg-nant (preg´nant) adj. Carrying an unborn fetus; significant. **pregnancy** n.

pre-his-tor-i-cal (prē´hi stor´ik) adj. Of or related to the period before recorded history.

pre-judge (prē juj´) v. To judge before one knows all the facts. **prejudgment** n.

prej-u-dice (prej´a dis) n. A biased opinion based on emotion rather than reason; bias against a group, race, or creed.

pre-lim-i-nar-y (pri lim´i ner´ē) adj. Leading up to the main action.

prel-ude (prel´ūd) n. An introductory action. *Music* The movement at the beginning of a piece of music.

pre-ma-ture (prē´ma ter´) adj. Occurring or born before the natural or proper time. **prematurely** adv.

pre-med-i-tate (pri med´i tāt´) v. To plan in advance or beforehand.

pre-mi-er (pri mēr´) adj. First in rank or importance. n. The chief executive of a government. **premiership** n.

pre-mi-um (prē´mē um) n. An object offered free as an inducement to buy; the fee or amount payable for insurance; an additional amount of money charged above the nominal value.

pre-na-tal (prē nāt´al) adj. Existing prior to birth.

pre-oc-cu-py (prē ok´ū pī´) v. To engage the mind or attention completely.

prep (prep) *Slang* Preparatory school; preparation.

prep-a-ra-tion (prep´a rā´shan) n. The process of preparing for something.

pre-par-a-to-ry (pri pâr´a tōr´ē) adj. Serving as preparation.

pre-pare (pri pâr´) v. To make ready or qualified; to equip. **preparedly** adv.

pre-pay (prē pā´) v. To pay for in advance.

pre-pon-der-ate (pri pon´de rāt´) v. To have superior importance, weight, force, influence, or other qualities. **preponderance** n. **preponderancy** n. **preponderantly** adv.

prep-o-si-tion (prep´o zish´an) n., *Gram.* A word placed in front of a noun or pronoun to show a connection with or to something or someone.

pre-pos-ter-ous (pri pos´tėr us) adj. Absurd; ridiculous; beyond all reason.

prep-pie (prep ē) n., *Slang* A student attending a prep school; a young adult who behaves and dresses very traditionally.

pre- *pref* Earlier or prior to something; in front.

pre-rog-a-tive (pri rog´a tiv) n. The unquestionable right belonging to a person.

pres-age (pres´ij) n. An omen or indication of something to come; a premonition. **presage** v.

pre-school (prē´skōl´) adj. Of or for children usually between the ages of two and five. **preschooler** n.

pre-scribe (pri skrīb´) v. To impose as a guide; to recommend.

pre-scrip-tion (pri skrip´shan) *n., Med.* A physician's written order for medicine.

pres-ence (prez´ens) *n.* The state of being present; the immediate area surrounding a person or thing; poise.

pres-ent (prez´ent) *adj.* Now going on; not past or future. *Gram.* Denoting a tense or verb form which expresses a current state or action. *v.* To bring into the acquaintance of another; to introduce; to make a gift of. *n.* A gift. *adv.* Currently.

pres-en-ta-tion (prez´en tā´shan) *n.* A formal introduction of one person to another; to present something as an exhibition, show, or product.

pre-serv-a-tive (pri zer´va tiv) *adj.* Keeping something from decay or injury. **preservation** *n.* **preservable** *adj.*

pre-serve (pri zerv´) *v.* To keep or save from destruction or injury; to prepare fruits or vegetables to prevent spoilage or decay. **preserves** Fruit which has been preserved with sugar.

pre-shrunk (prē shrungk´) *adj.* Material which has been washed during the manufacturing process to minimize shrinkage later.

pre-side (pri zīd´) *v.* To have a position of authority or control; to run or control a meeting.

pres-i-dent (prez´i dent) *n.* The chief executive officer of a government, corporation, or association. **presidency** *n.* **presidential** *adj.*

press (pres) *v.* To act upon or exert steady pressure or force; to squeeze out or extract by pressure; to smooth by heat and pressure; to iron clothes. *n.* A machine used to produce printed material.

pres-sure (presh´ér) *n.* The act of or the state of being pressed; a constraining moral force; any burden, force, painful feeling, or influence; the depressing effect of something hard to bear.

pres-tige (pre stēzh´) *n.* Importance based on past reputation and achievements.

pres-to (pres´tō) *adv., Music* Very fast and quick; at once.

pre-sume (pri zŏm´) *v.* To take for granted; to take upon oneself without permission; to proceed overconfidently. **presumable** *adj.* **presumably** *adv.* **presumer** *n.*

pre-sump-tion (pri zump´shan) *n.* Arrogant conductor speech; something that can be logically assumed true until disproved.

pre-tend (pri tend´) *v.* To make believe; to act in a false way. **pretender** *n.*

pre-tense (pri tens´) *n.* A deceptive and false action or appearance; a false purpose.

pre-ten-tions (pri ten´shan) *n.* Having or making claims to worth, excellence, etc.; showy.

pre-text (prē´tekst) *n.* A motive assumed in order to conceal the true purpose.

pret-ty (prit´ē) *adj.* Pleasant; attractive; characterized by gracefulness; pleasing to look at. **pretty** In a favorable position; good circumstances. **sitting** *adj.* **prettier** *adj.* **prettiest** *adj.*

pret-zel (pret´sel) *v.* A hard, cooked dough usually twisted in a knot and sprinkled with salt.

pre-vail (pri vāl´) *v.* To succeed; to win control over something; to predominate. **prevailer** *n.* **prevailingly** *adv.*

pre-vent (pri vent´) *v.* To keep something from happening; to keep from doing something.

pre-ven-tive *or* **preventative (pri ven´tiv)** *adj.* Protecting or serving toward off harm, disease, or other problems.

pre-view *or* **prevue (prē´vū´)** *n.* An advance showing or viewing to invited guests.

pre-vi-ous (prē´vē us) *adj.* Existing or occurring earlier. **previously** *adv.*

price (prīs) *n.* The set amount of money expected or given for the sale of something.

prick (prik) *n.* A small hole made by a sharp point. *v.* To pierce something lightly.

pride (prīd) *n.* A sense of personal dignity; a feeling of pleasure because of something achieved, done, or owned. **pride** *v.*

priest (prēst) *n.* A clergyman in the Catholic church who serves as mediator between God and His worshipers.

pri-ma-ry (prī´mer ē) *adj.* First in origin, time, series, or sequence; basic; fundamental.

prime (prīm) *adj.* First in importance, time, or rank. *n.* A period of full vigor, success, or beauty. *v.* To make ready by putting something on before the final coat, as to prime wood before painting.

prim-i-tive (prim´i tiv) *adj.* Of or pertaining to the beginning or earliest time; resembling the style or manners of an earlier time.

primp (primp) *v.* To dress or arrange with superfluous attention to detail.

prince (prins) *n.* The son of a king; a king.

prin-cess (prin´sis) *n.* The daughter of a king.

prin-ci-pal (prin´sĭ pal) *adj.* Chief; most important. *n.* The headmaster or chief official of a school; a sum of money invested or owed which is separate from the interest.

prin-ci-ple (prin´sĭ pl) *n.* The fundamental law or truth upon which others are based; a moral standard.

print (print) *n.* An impression or mark made with ink; the design or picture which is transferred from an engraved plate or other impression. *v.* To stamp designs; to publish something in print, as a book or magazine.

printer (print´tėr) *n.* A person whose occupation is printing.

print-out (print´out´) *n., Computer Science* The output of a computer, printed on paper.

pri-or (prī´ėr) *adj.* Previous in order or time.

pri-or-i-ty (prī or´i tē) *n.* Something which takes precedence; something which must be done or taken care of first.

prism (priz´um) *n.* A solid figure with triangular ends and rectangular sides, used to disperse light into a spectrum.

pris-on (priz´on) *n.* A place of confinement where people are kept while waiting for a trial or while serving time for breaking the law; jail. **prisoner** *n.*

pri-vate (prī´vit) *adj.* Secluded or removed from the public view; secret; intimate; owned or controlled by a group or person rather than by the public or government. *n.* An enlisted person holding the lowest rank in military service.

priv-i-lege (priv´i lij) *n.* A special right or benefit granted to a person.

priv-i-leged (priv´i lijd) *adj.* To have or enjoy a given privilege.

prize (prīz) *n.* An award or something given to the winner of a contest; something exceptional or outstanding.

pro (prō) *n.* An argument in favor of or supporting something. *Slang* A professional or an expert in a given field.

prob-a-bil-i-ty (prob´a bil´i tē) *n. pl.* **-ies** The state or quality of being probable; a mathematical statement or prediction of the odds of something happening or not happening.

prob-a-ble (prob´a bl) *adj.* Likely to become a reality, but not certain or proved.

pro-bate (prō´bāt) *n.* The act of legally proving that a will is genuine.

pro-ba-tion (prō bā´shan) *n.* A period used to test the qualifications and character of a new employee; the early release of law breakers who must be under supervision and must report as requested to a probation officer.

probe (prōb) *n.* An instrument used for investigating an unknown environment; a careful investigation or examination.

prob-lem (prob´lem) *n.* A perplexing situation or question; a question presented for consideration, solution, or discussion. **problem** *adj.* **problematic** *adj.*

pro-ce-dure (pro sē´jėr) *n.* A certain pattern or way of doing something; the normal methods or forms to be followed.

pro-ceed (pro sēd´) *v.* To carry on or continue an action or process. *Law* To begin or institute legal action.

pro-ceeds (prō´sēdz) *n. pl.* The profits received from a fund raising venture.

proc-ess (pros´es) *n.* The course, steps, or methods toward a desired result. *Law* Any judicial request or order; in Computer Science, the sequence of operations which gives a desired result. *v.* To compile, compute, or assemble; data.

pro-ces-sion (pro sesh´an) *n.* A group which moves along in a formal manner; a parade.

pro-ces-sion-al (pro sesh´a nal) *n.* A hymn sung during a procession; *adj.* The opening of a church service; of or relating to a procession.

pro-ces-sor (pros´es or) *n. Computer Science* The central unit of a computer which processes data.

pro-claim (prō klām´) *v.* To announce publicly.

proc-la-ma-tion (prok´la mā´shan) *n.* An official public declaration or announcement.

pro-cras-ti-nate (prō kras´ti nāt´) *v.* To put off, defer, or postpone to a later time. **procrastination** *n.* **procrastinator** *n.*

proc-tor (prok´tėr) *n.* A person in a university or college whose job it is to see that order is maintained during exams. **proctorial** *adj.*

pro-cure (prō kūr´) *v.* To acquire; to accomplish.

prod (prod) *v.* To arouse mentally; to poke with a pointed instrument. *n.* A pointed implement used to prod or poke.

prod-i-gal (prod´i gal) *adj.* Wasteful expenditure of money, strength, or time; extravagance. *n.* One who is a spendthrift or is wasteful.

pro-duce (pro dōs´) *v.* To bear or bring forth by a natural process; to manufacture; to make; to present or bring into view. **producer** *n.*

prod-uct (prod´ukt) *n.* Something produced, manufactured, or obtained *Math.* The answer obtained by multiplying.

pro-duc-tion (pro duk´shan) *n.* The process or act of producing; something produced, as a play.

pro-fane (pro fān´) *adj.* Manifesting disrespect toward sacred things; vulgar.

pro-fess (pro fes´) *v.* To admit or declare openly; to make an open vow.

pro-fes-sor (pro fes´ėr) *n.* A faculty member of the highest rank in a college or university; a highly skilled teacher.

pro-fess-sion-al (pro fesh´a nal) *adj.* Having to do with a job or profession; referring to or engaging in an occupation, usually a sport for money rather than for fun.

pro-fi-cient (pro fish´ent) *adj.* Highly skilled in a field of knowledge. **proficiency** *n.* **proficiently** *adv.*

pro-file (prō´fil) *n.* The outline of a person's face or figure as seen from the side; a short biographical sketch indicating the most striking characteristics.

prof-it (prof´it) *n.* The financial return after all expenses have been accounted for. *v.* To gain an advantage or a financial reward. **profitable** *adj.*

pro-found (pro found´) *adj.* Deeply held or felt; intellectually penetrating.

pro-fuse (pro fūs´) *adj.* Extravagant; giving forth lavishly; overflowing. **profusely** *adv.* **profuseness** *n.*

prog-e-ny (proj´e nē) *n. pl.* -ies One's offspring, children, or descendants.

prog-no-sis (prog nō´sis) *n. pl.* -noses A prediction of the outcome and course a disease may take.

pro-gram (prō´gram) *n.* Any prearranged plan or course; a show or performance, as one given at a scheduled time; in Computer Science, a sequence of commands which tell a computer how to perform a task or sequence of tasks. **program** *v.*

prog-ress (prog´res) *n.* Forward motion or advancement to a higher goal; an advance; steady improvement.

pro-hib-it (prō hib´it) *v.* To forbid legally; to prevent.

pro-ject (proj´ekt´) *n.* A plan or course of action; a proposal; a large job. *v.* To give an estimation on something.

pro-jec-tile (pro jek´til) *n.* Anything hurled forward through the air.

pro-jec-tion (pro jek´shan) *n.* The act or state of being projected; the state or part that sticks out.

pro-lif-er-ate (prō lif´e rāt´) *v.* To grow or produce with great speed, as cells in tissue formation.

pro-logue (prō´log) *n.* An introductory statement at the beginning of a poem, song, or play.

pro-long (pro long´) *v.* To extend or lengthen in time.

prom-e-nade (prom´e nād´) *n.* An unhurried walk for exercise or amusement; a public place for such a walk, as the deck of a ship.

prom-i-nent (prom´i nent) *adj.* Jutting out; widely known; held in high esteem.

pro-mis-cu-ous (pro mis´kū us) *adj.* Lacking selectivity or discrimination, especially in sexual relationships.

prom-ise (prom´is) *n.* An assurance given that one will or will not do something; a pledge. **promise** *v.*

Promised Land *n.* Heaven.

prom-i-see *n., Law* A person to whom a promise is given.

prom-is-ing (prom´i sing) *adj.* Giving hopeful and favorable promises of future success. **promisingly** *adv.*

prom-i-sor (prom˝i sor´) *n., Law* A person who promises.

promissory note *n.* A written document or agreement that contains a promise to pay a debt to a particular person by a specified date or on demand.

prom-on-to-ry (prom´on tōr˝ē) *n.* A projecting rock that extends into the sea.

pro-mote (pro mōt´) *v.* To raise to a higher rank or position; to work on behalf of. **promotion** *n.* **promotional** *adj.*

pro-mot-er (pro mō´tėr) *n.* A person who encourages; one who aids in promoting a financial understanding; a person who starts or sets up a business venture.

pro-mo-tion (pro mō´shan) *n.* Elevation in rank; state of being raised in status; advancement. **promotional** *adj.*

prompt (prompt) *adj.* Arriving on time; punctual; immediate. *v.* To suggest or inspire.

prompt-book (prompt´būk˝) *n.* A copy of a play to be used by the director or the prompter.

prompt-er (promp´tėr) *n.* One who prompts.

promp-ti-tude (promp´ti tŏd˝) *n.* Promptness.

prom-ul-gate (prom´ul gāt´) *v.* To proclaim; to make known to the public.

prone (prōn) *adj.* Lying flat; face down. **pronely** *adv.* **proneness** *n.*

prong (prong) *n.* A pointed, projecting part, as the end of a sharp instrument or the end of an antler.

pronghorn (prong´horn˝) *n.* An antelope having hollow horns that fall off seasonally.

pro-nom-i-nal (prō nom´inal) *adj.* Belonging to the nature of a pronoun. **proniminally** *adv.*

pro-noun (prō´noun´) *n., Gram.* A word which can be used in the place of a noun or noun phrase.

pro-nounce (pro nouns´) *v.* To deliver officially; to articulate the sounds. **pronounceable** *adj.* **pronunciation** *n.*

pro-nounced (pro nounst´) *adj.* Strongly defined; decided. **pronouncedly** *adv.*

pro-nounce-ment (pro nouns´ment) *n.* Act of pronouncing a word or letter; a decision.

pron-to (pron´tō) *adv.* Quickly; promptly.

pro-nun-ci-a-tion (pro nun˝sē ā´shan) *n.* The art of uttering. **pronunciational** *adj.*

proof (prŏf) *n.* The establishment of a fact by evidence; the act of showing that something is true; a trial impression from the negative of a photograph. *v.* To proofread; to mark and make corrections.

proof-read (prŏf rēd´) *v.* To read in order to detect and mark errors in a printer's proof.

proofreader's marks *n. pl.* The symbols that indicate changes that are to be made by the typesetter.

proof spirit *n.* Alcoholic liquor that contains a standard amount of alcohol.

prop (prop) *n.* A support to keep something upright. *v.* To sustain.

prop-a-gate (prop´a gāt´) *v.* To reproduce or multiply by natural causes; to pass on qualities or traits. **propagation** *n.*

pro-pel (pro pel´) *v.* To thrust or cause to move forward; to motivate.

prop-er (prop´ér) *adj.* Appropriate; especially adapted or suited; conforming to social convention; correct.

proper adjective *n.* An adjective whose form is obtained from that of a proper noun.

proper fraction *n.* A fraction with a larger denominator than numerator.

prop-er-ly (prop´ér lē) *adv.* In a suitable manner; fitly; correctly.

proper noun *n.* A noun denoting a specific person, place, or thing and is capitalized.

prop-er-ty (prop´ér tē) *n. pl.* **-ies** Any object of value owned or lawfully acquired, as real estate; a piece of land. **propertied, propertyless** *adj.*

property man *n.* A person employed by a theater to take care of the stage properties.

proph-e-cy (prof´i sē) *n. pl.* **-ies** A prediction made under divine influence.

proph-et (prof´it) *n.* One who delivers divine messages; one who foretells the future. **prophetess** *n.*

pro-pi-ti-ate (pro pish´ē āt´) *v.* To win the goodwill of; to stop from being angry. **propitiation** *n.*

pro-po-nent (pro pō´nent) *n.* One who supports or advocates a cause.

pro-por-tion (pro pōr´shan) *n.* The relation of one thing to another in size, degree, or amount. *v.* To adjust or arrange with balance and harmony. **proportional** *adj.* **proportionate** *adj.* **proportionally** *adv.*

pro-por-tion-a-ble *adj.* In proportion; a due comparative relation. **proportionably** *adv.*

pro-pose (pro pōz´) *v.* To present or put forward for consideration or action; to suggest someone for an office or position; to make an offer; to offer marriage. **proposal** *n.*

prop-o-si-tion (prop´o zish´an) *n.* A scheme or plan offered for consideration; a subject or idea to be proved or discussed. *v.* To make a sexual suggestion.

pro-pri-e-tor (pro prī´i tér) *n.* The person who owns property and has the exclusive title or legal right.

pro-pri-e-ty (pro prī´i tē) *n. pl.* **-ies** The quality or state of being proper in accordance with recognized principles or usage.

prop root *n., Bot.* The root of plants, as corn, that grows into the soil and provides the main support of the stalk.

pro-pul-sion (pro pul´shan) *n.* The act or process of propelling. **propulsive** *adj.*

pro-pul-sis *n.* The outward protuberance of an organ.

pro-rate (prō rāt´) *v.* To distribute or divide proportionately. **proration** *n.*

pro-scribe (prō skrīb´) *v.* To banish; to outlaw; to prohibit.

prose (prōz) *n.* Ordinary language, speech, or writing which is not poetry.

pros-e-cute (pros´e kūt´) *v.* To carry on. *Law* To bring suit against a person; to seek enforcement for legal process. **prosecution** *n.*

pros-pect (pros´pekt) *n.* Something that has the possibility of future success; a possible customer. *v.* To explore. **prospective** *adj.* **prospectively** *adv.*

pros-per (pros´pér) *v.* To be successful; to achieve success. **prosperous** *adj.*

pros-tate (pros´tāt) *n.* A small gland at the base of the male bladder.

pros-ti-tute (pros´ti tōt´) *n.* One who sells the body for the purpose of sexual intercourse.

pros-trate (pros´trāt) *adj.* Lying with the face down to the ground. *v.* To overcome; to adopt a submissive posture. **prostrative** *adj.* **prostrator** *n.*

prot-ac-tin-i-um (prō´tak tin´ē um) *n.* A radioactive metallic element symbolized by Pa.

pro-tect (pro tekt´) *v.* To guard or shield from attack or injury; to shield. **protective** *adj.* **protectively** *adv.*

pro-tein (prō´tēn) *n., Biochem.* Any of a very large group of highly complex nitrogenous compounds occurring in living matter and composed of amino acids which are essential for tissue repair and growth.

pro-test (pro test´) *v.* To make a strong

formal objection; to object to. *n.* The act of protesting. **protester** *n.*

pro-to-col (prō′to kol′) *n.* The code and rules of diplomatic and state etiquette.

pro-ton (prō′ton) *n., Physics* A unit of positive charge equal in magnitude to an electron.

pro-tract (prō trakt′) *v.* To extend in space; to protrude.

pro-trude (prō trōd′) *v.* To project; to thrust outward. **protrusion** *n.*

proud (proud) *adj.* Showing or having a feeling that one is better than the others; having a feeling of satisfaction; having proper self-respect or proper self-esteem.

prove (prōv) *v.* To show with valid evidence that something is true. **provable** *adj.* **provably** *adv.*

prov-erb (prov′erb) *n.* An old saying which illustrates a truth. **Proverbs** The book contained in the Bible which has many sayings supposed to have come from Solomon and others.

pro-vide (pro vīd′) *v.* To supply or furnish with what is needed.

prov-i-dence (prov′i dens) *n.* The supervision of God over his people.

pro-vi-sion (pro vizh′an) *n.* A supply of food or needed equipment.

pro-voke (pro vōk′) *v.* To cause to be angry; to annoy. **provocation** *n.*

prox-i-mate (prok′si mit) *adj.* Immediate; direct; close.

prox-y (prok′sē) *n. pl.* **-ies** The authority, usually written, to act for another.

prude (prōd) *n.* A person who is very modest, especially in matters related to sex. **prudery** *n.* **prudishness** *n.*

pru-dent (prōd′ent) *adj.* Cautious; discreet; managing very carefully.

prune (prōn) *n.* The dried fruit of a plum. *v.* To cut off that which is not wanted or not necessary.

psalm (säm) *n.* A sacred hymn, taken from the Book of Psalms in the Old Testament.

psalm-book (säm′bŭk′) *n.* A type of book which has the psalms in it.

psalm-ist (sä′mist) *n.* A person who writes psalms.

psal-tery (sol′tėr) *n.* A type of musical instrument that was used many years ago.

pseu-do (sŏ′dō) *adj.* To be counterfeit or fake.

pseu-do-nym (sŏ′do nim) *n.* A name that is a fake. **pseudonymous** *adj.*

psi (sī) *n.* The twenty-third letter that is found in the Greek alphabet.

psil-o-cy-bin (sil′o sī′bin) *n.* A type of an alkaloid of the fungus.

pso-ri-a-sis (so rī′a sis) *n., Pathol.* A non-contagious, chronic, inflammatory skin disease characterized by reddish patches and white scales.

psych (sī′kē) *v., Slang* To prepare oneself emotionally or mentally; to outwit or outguess.

psy-chas-the-ni-a (sī″kas thē′nē a) *n.* A type of emotional disorder that is caused by morbid fears. **psychasthenic** *adj.*

psych-e-del-ic (sī″ki del′ik) *adj.* To be causing extraordinary alterations in the consciousness of a person.

psy-chi-a-trist (si kī′a trist) *n.* A person who is a specialist in the field of psychiatry.

psy-chi-a-try (si kī′a trē) *n.* The branch of medicine which deals with the diagnosis and treatment of mental disorders.

psy-chic (sī′kik) *adj.* Cannot be explained by natural or physical laws. *n.* A person who communicates with the spirit world.

psy-cho-a-nal-y-sis (sī″kō a nal′i sis) *n.* The way of studying and analyzing one's subconscious thoughts.

psy-cho-an-a-lyst (sī″kō an′a list) *n.* The person who has been trained and is qualified to practice psychoanalysis on others.

psy-cho-bi-ol-o-gy (sī″kō bī ol′o jē) *n.* The science of the study of the relationships between the body and the mind.

psy-cho-gen-e-sis (sī″kō jen′i sis) *n.* The development of the mind.

psy-chol-o-gy (sī kol′o jē) *n. pl.* **-ies** The science of emotions, behavior, and the mind. **psychologist** *n.*

psy-cho-path (sī'ko path') *n.* A person suffering from a mental disorder characterized by aggressive antisocial behavior. **psychopathic** *adj.*

ptar-mi-gan (tär'mi gan) *n.* A type of species of grouse that has feathered feet and can be located in the cold regions.

PT boat (pē'tē'bōt) *n.* A type of small vessel of the navy.

pter-i-dol-o-gy (ter"i dol'o jē) *n.* The section or part of botany concerned with the study of ferns.

pter-o-dac-tyl (ter"o dak'til) *n.* A type of flying reptile that is now extinct and is believed to have lived thousands of years ago.

pter-o-saur (ter'o sor") *n.* A type of flying reptile that is now extinct.

pto-maine (tō'mān) *n.* A type of compound that can be very poisonous and produced by an animal.

pto-sis (tō'sis) *n.* The drooping of a body organ. **ptotic** *adj.*

pty-a-lin (tī'a lin) *n.* A type of enzyme that is found in saliva of man and used to digest starch into maltose and dextrin.

pty-a-lism (tī'a liz"um) *n.* The excessive production of saliva in one's mouth.

pub (pub) *n.* A type of tavern.

pu-ber-ty (pū'bėr tē) *n.* The stage of development in which sexual reproduction can first occur; the process of the body which culminates in sexual maturity. **pubertal** *adj.* **puberal** *adj.*

pu-ber-u-lent (pū ber'ū lent) *adj.* To be covered or to have down.

pu-bes-cence (pū bes'ens) *n.* The arrival of the stage of puberty in a person.

pubis (pū'bis) *n.* The part of the bone that forms the pelvis which is located in the front.

pub-lic (pū'bik) *adj.* Pertaining to or affecting the people or community; for everyone's use; widely or well known. **public-ness** *n.*

public–address system *n.* An amplifying system that amplifies sound through a series of loud speakers and microphones.

pub-li-can (pub'li kan) *n.* A person who collects taxes in a town or city; any collector of public revenues.

pub-li-ca-tion (pub'li kā'shan) *n.* The business of publishing; any pamphlet, book, or magazine.

public defender *n.* The attorney who defends someone without cost because they cannot afford to furnish an attorney for themselves.

public domain *n.* Public property; a published work whose copyrights have expired.

public enemy *n.* A person who is considered to be a threat or menace to the public; government regarded as an enemy.

public house *n.* A type of inn.

pub-li-cist (pub'li sist) *n.* A press or publicity agent; a person who is a specialist in public relations; a specialist on international law.

pub-lic-i-ty (pu blis'i tē) *n.* The state of being known to the public; common knowledge.

pub-li-cize (pub'li sīz") *v.* To give publicity to; advertise.

public law *n.* A type of statute that has been adapted for the public as a whole by the nation.

pub-lic-ly (pub'lik lē) *adv.* Public manner; without concealment.

public property *n.* The property which is owned by the public.

public sale *n.* A type of sale which is made after a public notice.

public servant *n.* A person who works for the government.

public speaking *n.* An art of speaking effectively to the public.

pub-lish (pub'lish) *v.* To print and distribute a book, magazine, or any printed matter to the public. **publishable** *adj.* **publisher** *n.*

pub-lish-er (pub'li shėr) *n.* A person who will publish the works of others as in books.

puc-coon (pa kön') *n.* A type of North American herb that has yellow flowers and can grow in the dry sandy soils.

puce (pūs) *adj.* To be a reddish brown.

puck (puk) *n.* A hard rubber disk used in playing ice hockey.

puck-er (puk´ėr) *v.* To gather or group something into small wrinkles.

puck-ish (puk´ish) *adj.* Elfish in character.

pud-dle (pud´l) *n.* A small pool of water.

pu-den-cy (pūd´en sē) *n.* The modesty of someone.

pudg-y (puj´ē) *adj.* To be fat and short.

pueb-lo (pweb´lō) *n.* A type of village of grouped houses that can be found in New Mexico, used by the Pueblo Indians of North America.

pu-er-ile (pū´ėr il) *adj.* To be childish in character and actions.

pu-er-per-al (pū ûr´pėr al) *adj.* To be related to childbirth.

puff (puf) *n.* A brief discharge of air or smoke. *v.* To breathe in short heavy breaths.

puff adder *n.* A type of large African viper that will puff up its body when it becomes agitated.

puff-ball (puf´bol˝) *n.* A type of fungus that is rounded and will discharge its spores in a mass of smoke.

puff-er (puf´ėr) *n.* A person or something that puffs.

puff-er-y (puf´e rē) *n.* A type of praise which is very exaggerated.

puf-fin (puf´in) *n.* A type of sea bird that has a red bill and can be found in the North Atlantic regions.

pug (pug) *n.* A type of dog which looks like a small bulldog.

pug-na-cious (pug nā´shus) *adj.* To be inclined to fight. **pugnaciousness** *n.*

pug-ree (pug´rē) *n.* A type of turban that is worn to keep the rays of the sun off one's head.

pu-is-sance (pū´i sans) *n.* Might; strength.

puke (pūk) *v.* To throw up or vomit food.

puk-ka (puk´a) *adj.* To be good.

pull (pel) *v.* To apply force; to cause motion toward or in the same direction of; to remove from a fixed place; to stretch.

pull-back (pül´bak˝) *n.* The action or the process of pulling something back.

pul-let (pül´it) *n.* A young chicken.

pull-o-ver (pül´ō˝vėr) *n.* A type of clothing that is put on the body by pulling it over the head.

pul-lu-late (pul´ya lāt˝) *v.* To send off or forth buds.

pul-mo-nar-y (pul´mo ner˝ē) *adj.* To be referring to the lungs.

pulmonary artery *n.* The artery which is going from the heart to the lungs and is carrying unoxygenated blood.

pulmonary vein *n.* A vein which comes from the lungs to the heart and is carrying the blood which has received oxygen in the lungs and is ready to be pumped through the rest of the body.

pulp (pulp) *n.* The soft juicy part of a fruit; a soft moist mass; inexpensive paper.

pul-pit (pel´pit) *n.* The elevated platform lectern used in a church from which a service is conducted.

pulp-wood (pulp´wüd˝) *n.* A type of soft wood which is found in the pine and spruce, and it is used for the purpose of making paper.

pul-sate (pul´sāt) *v.* To beat rhythmically. **pulsation** *n.* **pulsator** *n.*

pul-sa-tile (pul´sa til) *adj.* To be throbbing.

pul-sa-tion (pul sā´shan) *n.* The action or the process of beating.

pul-sa-tor (pul´sā tėr) *n.* Something which will pulsate, such as the heart.

pulse (puls) *n., Physiol.* The rhythmical beating of the arteries caused by the action of the heart. **pulse** *v.*

pul-sim-e-ter (pul sim´i tėr) *n.* A type of device that is used to measure the rate and the strength of one's pulse.

pul-ver-a-ble (pul´vėr a bl) *adj.* To be capable of being changed or reduced to dust.

pul-ver-ize (pul´ve rīz´) *v.* To be reduced to dust or powder by crushing.

pul-ver-u-lent (pul ver´ya lent) *adj.* To be made up of fine powder.

pul-vil-lus (pul vil´us) *n.* A type of cushion-like mass that is found on the feet of certain insects.

pu-ma (pū´ma) n. A type of large cat that is tawny in color and is located in North and South America.

pump (pump) n. A mechanical device for moving a gas or liquid. v. To raise with a pump; to obtain information through persistent questioning.

pum-per-nick-el (pum´pėr nik˝el) n. A type of coarse bread that is made from rye.

pump-kin (pump´kin) n. A large, edible yellow-orange fruit having a thick rind and many seeds.

pump-kin-seed (pump´kin sēd˝) n. A type of sunfish that can be found in fresh water of eastern North America.

pu-na (pō´nä) n. A type of plateau that is arid.

punch (punch) n. A tool used for perforating or piercing; a blow with the fist; a drink made of an alcoholic beverage and a fruit juice or other nonalcoholic beverage. v. To use a punch on something; to hit sharply with the hand or fist.

punch bowl n. A typeof bowl that is large in size and used to serve punch.

pun-cheon (pun´chon) n. A type of tool used to punch holes into something.

pun-chi-nel-lo (pun´chon) n. A person who is grotesque.

punching bag n. A type of leather bag that is stuffed and used to punch on for practice.

punc-tate (pungk´tāt) adj. To be ending with a point; marked with dots, that are variously scattered over a surface. **punctation** n.

punc-til-i-ous (pungk til´ē us) adj. To be formal in one's behavior.

punc-tu-al (pungk´chō al) adj. Prompt; arriving on time.

punc-tu-ate (pungk´chō āt´) v. To mark words or written material with punctuation; to give or show emphasis.

punc-ture (pungk´chėr) v. To prick or pierce with a pointed instrument. n. The act or effect of puncturing.

pun-gent (pun´jent) adj. Sharp or acrid in smell or taste.

pun-ish (pun´ish) v. To subject a person to confinement or impose a penalty for a crime.

punishment (pun´ish ment) n. A penalty which is imposed for breaking the law or a rule.

punk (pungk) n., Slang A young, inexperienced boy. adj. Of or relating to a bizarre style of clothing; relating to punk rock bands.

pun-kah (pung´ka) n. A type of fan that is hung from the ceiling and is operated by servants.

punk-ie (pung´kē) n. A type of midge that sucks blood and can be found along the beach of the northeastern United States.

pun-ster (pun´stė) n. A person who likes to make puns.

punt (punt) n. A narrow, long, flat-bottomed boat; in football, a kick of a football dropped from the hands. v. To kick a football.

pun-ty (pun´tē) n. A rod that is made of iron and is used for the making of glassworks.

pu-ny (pū´nē) adj. To be weak and underdeveloped; insignificant or petty.

pup (pup) n. A puppy, young dog, or the young of other animals.

pu-pa (pū´pa) n. The stage in the evelopment of an insect that is between the larva and the adult stage.

pupil (pū´pil) n. A person who attends school and receives instruction by a teacher.

pu-pil-age (pū´pi lij) n. The state of being a pupil.

pup-pet (pup´it) n. A small figure of an animal or person which is manipulated by hand or by strings. **puppeteer** n. **puppetry** n.

pup-py (pup´ē) n. The young of a dog.

pup tent n. A type of tent that sleeps only a few people.

pur-blind (pür´blīnd˝) adj. To be lacking in insight. **purblindness** n.

pur-chase (per´chas) v. To receive by paying money as an exchange.

pure (pūr) adj. Free from anything that damages, weakens, or contaminates; innocent; clean. **pureness** n.

pur-ga-tive (pūr´ga tiv) n. A type of medicine that is used to clean the bowels in preparation for surgery.

purge (perj) v. To make clean; to free from guilt or sin; to rid of anything undesirable, as unwanted persons. *Med.* To cause or induce emptying of the bowels. **purge** n.

pu-ri-fy (pūr´i fī´) v. To make clean or pure. **purification** n. **purifier** n.

pu-ri-ty (pūr´i tē) n. The quality of being pure; freedom from guilt or sin.

pur-ple (per´pl) n. A color between red and violet. **purplish** adj.

pur-port (per´pōrt) v. To give the appearance of intending; to imply, usually with the intent to deceive.

pur-pose (per´pos) n. A desired goal; an intention. **purposeful** adj. **purposeless** adj. **purposely** adv.

purr (per) n. The low, murmuring sound characteristic of a cat. **purr** v.

purse (pers) n. A small pouch or bag for money; a handbag; a pocketbook; the sum of money offered as a prize.

pur-sue (pėr sö´) v. To seek to achieve; to follow in an attempt to capture.

pur-suit (pėr söt´) n. The act of pursuing an occupation.

pur-vey (pėr vā´) v. To supply provisions as a service. **purveyance** n. **purveyor** n.

pus (pus) n. A yellowish secretion formed in infected tissue which contains bacteria.

push (pesh) v. To move forward by exerting force; to force oneself through a crowd; to sell illegally. *Slang* To sell illegal drugs.

push-cart (pūsh kärt´) n. A type of light cart that can be pushed by the hands.

push-pin (pūsh´pin˝) n. A type of pin with a large head used to hold papers up on a wall or corkboard.

pus-sy (pūs´ē) adj. To be containing or to be filled with pus.

pus-tu-late (pus´cha lāt˝) v. To cause blis-ters.

put (pet) v. To cause to be in a location; to bring into a specific relation or state; to bring forward for debate or consideration, as to put up for. **down** To humiliate.

pu-ta-tive (pū´ta tiv) adj. Commonly supposed.

pu-tre-fy (pū´tre fī´) v. To cause to decay; to decay. **putrefaction** n.

putt (put) n. In golf, a light stroke made on a putting green to get the ball into the hole.

puz-zle (puz´l) v. To bewilder; to confuse. n. A toy, board game, or word game which tests one's patience and skills.

pyg-my (pig´mē) n. pl. **-ies** A very small person or animal; a dwarf.

py-lon (pī´lon) n. A tower serving as a support for electrical power lines.

py-or-rhe-a (pī´o rē´a) n., *Pathol.* Inflammation of the gums and sockets of the teeth. **pyorrheal** adj.

py-ral-i-did n. A type of moth that has a slender body.

pyr-a-mid (pir´a mid) n. A solid structure with a square base and sides which meet at a point.

pyre (pī´er) n. A pile of combustible material for burning a dead body.

py-ro-ma-ni-a (pī´ro mā´nē a) n. A compulsion to set fires.

py-rom-e-ter (pī rom´ tėr) n. A type of device that can measure very high temperatures. **pyrometrically** adv. **pyrometrical** adj.

py-rope (pī´rōp) n. A type of deep-red garnet.

py-ro-pho-bi-a (pī˝ro fō´bē a) n. A fear of fire that is considered to be abnormal.

py-ro-phor-ic (pī˝ro for´ik) adj. To be highly flammable.

pyr-rhic (pir´ik) n. A metrical foot containing two short syllables.

Pyrrhic victory n. A victory acquired at too great a cost.

pyr-rhu-lox-i-a (pir″a lok′sē a) *n.* A type of gray grosbeak that has a rose-colored breast and crest.

py-thon (pī′thon) *n.* A large nonvenomous snake which crushes its prey.

py-u-ri-a (pi ūr′ē a) *n., Pathol.* The condition where there is pus in the urine.

pyx-ie (pik′sē) *n.* A type of evergreen plant located in the eastern United States.

pyx-is (pik′sis) *n.* A small box, used by the Romans to hold jewelry.

Q

Q, q (kū) The seventeenth letter of the English alphabet.

qat *n.* A small plant found in Africa, the fresh leaf is chewed for a stimulating effect.

qi-vi-ut *n.* Yarn spun from the fine, soft hair of the musk ox.

qt. *abbr.* Quart.

quack (kwak) *n.* The harsh, croaking cry of a duck; someone who pretends to be a doctor. **quack** *v.* **quackery** *n.*

quad-ran-gle (kwod′rang′gl) *n., Math* A plane figure with four sides and four angles.

quad-rant (kwod′rant) *n.* A quarter section of a circle, subtending or enclosing a central angle of 90 degrees.

qua-draph-o-ny *n.* The recording of sound using four transmission channels.

quad-rate (kwod′rit) *adj.* Being square or almost square.

qua-drat-ics (kwo drat′iks) *n.* A branch of algebra concerned with equations.

quad-ra-ture *n.* An arrangement of two celestial bodies with a separation of 90 degrees.

qua-dren-ni-um (kwo dren′ē um) *n.* A period consisting of four years.

quad-ri-cen-ten-ni-al *n.* An anniversary celebrating 400 years.

quad-ri-ceps (kwod′ri seps″) *n.* The muscle located in the front of the thigh.

qua-dri-ga *n.* A chart pulled by four horses.

qua-drille *n.* A square dance with five or six figures executed by four couples.

quad-ril-lion (kwo dril′yon) *n.* A thousand trillions; one followed by fifteen zeros.

quad-ri-par-tite *adj.* Consisting of four persons or parts.

quad-ri-ple-gic *n.* A person who is paralyzed in both arms and both legs.

qua-dru-ma-na *n.* A group of primates distinguished by hand-shaped feet.

quad-ru-ped (kwod′re ped′) *n.* Any animal having four feet.

quad-ru-ple (kwo drŏ′pl) *adj.* Consisting of four parts; multiplied by four.

qua-dru-plet (kwo drup′lit) *n.* One of four infants born at the same time.

qua-dru-pli-cate (kwo drŏ′pli kit) *n.* Consisting of four identical parts.

quag-ga (kwag′a) *n.* A wild ass of Africa related to the zebras.

quag-mire (kwag′mīěr′) *n.* An area of soft muddy land that gives way underfoot; a marsh.

qua-hog (kwo′hog) *n.* A clam found in the Atlantic Ocean.

quail (kwāl) *n. pl.* A small game bird, about the same size as the piegon.

quaint (kwānt) *adj.* Pleasing in an old-fashioned, unusual way.

quake (kwāk) *v.* To shake or tremble violently.

quak-er (kwā′kėr) *n.* The religious sect called the Society of Friends.

qual-i-fi-ca-tion An act of qualifying; the ability, skill, or quality which makes something suitable for a given position.

qual-i-fy (kwol′i fī′) *v.* To prove something able; restrict; limit; modify.

qual-i-ty (kwol′i tē) *n. pl.* **ties** A distinguishing character; a high degree of excellence.

qualm (kwăm) *n.* A sudden feeling of sickness; sensation of uneasiness or doubt.

quan-da-ry (kwon′da rē) *n.* A state of perplexity.

quan-ti-ty (kwon′ti tē) *n.* Number; amount; bulk; weight; a portion; as a large amount.

quan-tum (kwon′tum) *n. pl.* **quanta** An amount or quantity.

quar-an-tine (kwor′an tēn′) *n.* A period

of enforced isolation for a specified period of time used to prevent the spread of a contagious disease. **quarantine** *v.*

quar-rel (kwor´el) *n.* An unfriendly or angry disagreement; a cause for dispute. *v.* To find fault with.

quarrier (kwor´ē ėr) *n.* A person who works in a stone quarry.

quar-ry (kwor´ē) *n. pl.* **quarries** An animal hunted for food; an open pit or excavation from which limestone or other material is being extracted.

quart (kwort) *n.* A unit of measurement equaling four cups.

quartan (kwor´tan) n. Something happening every four days.

quar-ter (kwor´tėr) *n.* One of four equal parts into which anything may be divided; a place of lodging, as a barracks; a United States coin equal to 1/4 of a dollar.

quar-ter-back (kwor´tėr bak´) *n., Football* The offensive player who directs the plays for his team.

quarterdeck *n.* The part of a deck used for ceremonial and official use only.

quarter horse *n.* A horse capable of high speed and great endurance.

quarterly *adj.* Payable in three month intervals.

quar-ter-mas-ter (kwor´tėr mas´tėr) *n.* The officer in charge of supplies for army troops; a navy officer who steers a ship and handles signaling equipment.

quar-tet (kwor tet´) *n.* A musical composition for four voices or instruments; any group or set of four.

quartz (kworts) *n.* A hard, transparent crystallized mineral.

qua-sar (kwā´sär) *n.* One of the most distant and brightest bodies in the universe; a quasar producing intense visible radiation but not emitting radio signals.

quash (kwosh) *v.* To nullify or suppress by judicial action.

quay *n.* A landing place beside water for loading and unloading ships.

quea-sy (kwē´zē) *adj.* Nauseated; sick. **queasiness** *n.*

que-bra-cho *n.* A tree of the sumac family which has hard wood found in South America.

queen (kwēn) *n.* The wife of a king; a woman sovereign or monarch; in chess, the most powerful piece on the board, which can move any number of squares in any direction; the fertile female in a colony of social insects.

quell (kwel) *v.* To put down with force; to quiet; to pacify.

quench (kwench) *v.* To extinguish or put out; to cool metal by thrusting into water; to drink to satisfy a thirst.

quer-cit-ron *n.* A large oak tree rich in tannin used in dyeing and tanning.

quer-u-lous (kwer´a lus) *adj.* Complaining or fretting; expressing complaints.

que-ry (kwēr´ē) n. An injury; a question. *v.* To question.

quest (kwest) *n.* A search; pursuit; an expedition to find something.

ques-tion (kwes´chan) *n.* An expression of inquiry which requires an answer; a problem; an unresolved matter; the act of inquiring or asking. *v.* To ask; to inquire.

ques-tion-able *adj.* Being in doubt; not certain or sure.

question mark *n.* A mark of punctuation, (?), used in writing to indicate a question.

ques-tion-naire (kwes´cha nâr´) *n.* A written series of questions to gather statistical information often used for a survey.

queue (kū) *n. Computer Science* A sequence of stored programs or data on hold for processing. *v.* To form a line; to stand in line.

quib-ble (kwib´l) *v.* To raise trivial objection. **quibble** *n.* **quibbler** *n.*

quiche *n.* Unsweetened custard baked in a pastry shell, usually with vegetables or seafood.

quick (kwik) *adj.* Moving swiftly; occurring in a short time; responding, thinking, or understanding something rapidly and easily. **quickly** *adv.* **quickness** *n.*

quick-en *adj.* To become faster; to increase

in pace.

quick-sand (kwik´sand´) *n.* A bog of very fine, wet sand of considerable depth, that engulfs and sucks down objects, people, or animals.

quick–temp-ered (kwik´tem´pėrd) *adj.* Being easily angered or upset.

quick–wit-ted (kwik´wit´id) *adj.* Being quick to understand something.

quid (kwid) *n.* A small portion of tobacco; a cow's cud.

qui-es-cent (kwē es´ent) *adj.* Being in a state of quiet repose.

qui-et (kwī´it) *adj.* Silent; making very little sound; still; tranquil; calm. *v.* To become or make quiet. *n.* The state of being quiet.

quill (kwil) *n.* A strong bird feather; a spine from a porcupine; a writing instrument made from a long stiff feather.

quilt (kwilt) *n.* A bed coverlet made of two layers of cloth with a soft substance between and held in place by lines of stitching. *v.* To sew or stitch together.

quince *n.* A fruit that resembles a yellow apple used for making marmalade, jellys, etc.

quin-i-dine *n.* An alkaloid used in treating cardiac rhythm irregularities.

qui-nine (kwī´nīn) *n., Chem.* A very bitter, colorless, crystalline powder used in the treatment of malaria.

quin-quen-ni-al *adj.* Happening or being done every five years.

quin-sy (kwin´zē) *n., Pathol.* A severe inflammation of the tonsils, which is accompanied by fever.

quin-tes-sence (kwin tes´ens) *n.* The most essential and purest form of anything.

quin-tet (kwin tet´) *n.* A musical composition written for five people; any group of five.

quin-til-lion (kwin til´yon) *n.* A thousand quadrillions, one followed by eighteen zeros.

quin-tu-ple (kwin tö´pl) *adj.* Increased five times; multiplied by five; consisting of five parts. *v.* To make five times larger.

quip (kwip) *n.* A sarcastic remark.

quire (kwī´ėr) *n.* Twenty-five sheets of paper removed from a complete ream of paper; a set of all the sheets of paper necessary to form a book.

quirk (kwerk) *n.* A sudden, sharp bend or twist; a personal mannerism.

quis-ling (kwiz´ling) *n.* A person who is a traitor, working against his own country from within.

quit (kwit) *v.* To cease; to give up; to depart; to abandon; to resign or leave a job or position.

quite (kwīt) *adv.* To the fullest degree; really; actually; to a great extent.

quittance *n.* A documnt which releases someone from an obligation.

quiv-er (kwiv´ėr) *v.* To shake with a trembling motion. *n.* The arrows used in archery; the case in which arrows are kept.

quix-ot-ic (kwik sot´ik) *adj.* Extravagantly romantic; impractical.

quiz (kwiz) *v.* To question, as with an informal oral or written examination. **quiz** *n.* **quizzer** *n.*

quo-rum (kwōr´um) *n.* The number of members needed in order to validate a meeting.

quo-ta (kwō´ta) *n.* An allotment or proportional share; a proportion or share required from each person, state, or group in order to meet a certain number required.

quo-ta-tion (kwō tā´shan) *n.* The exact quoting of words as a passage; the stated current price.

quotation mark *n.* The marks of punctuation (" ") showing a direct quote.

quote (kwōt) *v.* To repeat exactly what someone else has previously stated; to state the price of an item.

quo-tid-i-an- (kwō tid´ē an) *adj.* Occurring or recurring daily.

quo-tient (kwō´shent) *n., Math* The amount or number which results when one number is divided by another.

R, r (är) The eighteenth letter of the English alphabet.

R *abbr.* Radius.

ra-ba-to (ra **bā′tō)** *n.* A wide lace-edged collar of the early 17th century.

rab-bet (rab′it) *n.* A recess or groove along the edge of a piece of wood cut to fit another piece to form a joint. *v.* To join the edges of in a rabbet joint.

rab-bi (rab′ī) *n.* An ordained leader of Jews; the leader and teacher of a Jewish congregation. **rabbinic** *adj.*

rab-bin-ate *n.* The dignity of a rabbi.

rab-bin-i-cal (ra **bin′i k**a**l)** *adj.* To be referring or pertaining to the rabbis. **rabbinically** *adv.*

rab-bit (rab′it) *n.* A burrowing mammal re-lated to but smaller than the hare.

rabbit ears *n.* Indoor television antenna, having two extensible rods, connected to a base forming a V shape.

rab-bit-eye *n.* A blueberry found in the southeastern part of the United States.

rabbit punch *n.* A hit that is aimed at the back of one's head.

rab-bit-ry *n.* The location where rabbits are kept.

rab-ble (rab′l) *n.* A disorderly crowd. **rabbling** *v.* **rabbled** *v.*

rab-ble-ment *n.* A rabble; a tumult.

rab-ble-rous-er (rab′l rou″ze**r)** *n.* A person who stirs masses of people to riot.

rab-id (rab′id) *adj.* Affected with rabies; mad; furious. **rabidly** *adv.*

ra-bies (rā′bēz) *n.* An acute, infectious viral disease of the central nervous system, often fatal, which is transmitted by the bite of an infected animal.

rac-coon (ra **kōn′)** *n. pl.* **-coons, -coon** A nocturnal mammal with a black, mask-like face and a black-and white ringed, bushy tail.

race (rās) *n.* A contest which is judged by speed; any contest, such as a race for an elective office. **raced, racer** *n.*

race (rās) *n.* The zoological division of the human population having common origin and physical traits, such as hair form and pigmentation; a group of people having such common characteristics or appearances; people united by a common nationality.

race course *n.* The track on which a race takes place.

race horse *n.* A type of horse which is bred strictly for the purpose of racing.

ra-ceme (rā sēm′) *n.* A type of plant bearing flowers along its stalk. **racemed** *adj.*

rac-er (rā′se**r)** *n.* A person who takes part in a race; one who runs in a race.

racetrack *n.* The course which is used for the purpose of racing horses.

raceway *n.* The channel for water to pass through; a racetrack.

ra-chis (rā′kis) *n.* A type of axial structure.

ra-cial (rā′sha**l)** *adj.* A characteristic of a race of people. **racially** *adv.*

rac-ism (rā′siz *u***m)** *n.* A thought or belief that one race is better than another race. **-ist** *n.* A thought or belief that one race is better than another race.

rack (rak) *n.* An open framework or stand for displaying or holding something; an instrument of torture used to stretch the body; a triangular frame used to arrange the balls on a pool table. *Mech.* A metal bar with teeth designed to move a cogged bar and produce a rotary or linear motion. *v.* To strain, as with great effort in thinking.

rack-et *or* **racquet** *n.* A light-weight bat-like object with netting stretched over an oval frame, used in striking a tennis ball or a shuttlecock.

rack-et-eer (rak′i tēr′) *n.* A person who engages in acts which are illegal.

rack-e-ty (rak′i tē) *adj.* To be noisy.

rack-rent *n.* A rent that is very high.

ra-clette *n.* A Swiss dish with cheese melted over a fire then scraped onto bread or potatoes.

rac-on-teur *n.* One who is skilled in the act of telling stories.

rac-y (rā′sē) *adj.* Having a spirited or strongly marked quality; slightly improper or immodest. **racily** , **raciness** *n.*

ra-dar (rā′där) *n.* A system which uses radio signals to detect the presence of an object or the speed the object is traveling.

ra-dar as-tron-o-my *n.* Astronomy that deals with investigations of the celestial bodies of the solar system by comparing characteristics of reflected radar wave with characteristics of ones transmitted from earth.

ra-dar-scope (rā′där skōp′) *n.* A screen or oscilloscope that serves as a visual indicator in a radar receiver.

rad-dled *adj.* To be in a state of confusion; broken down; worn; lacking composure.

ra-di-al (rā′dē al) *adj.* Pertaining to or resembling a ray or radius; developing from a center axis.

ra-di-ance (rā′dē ans) *n.* The quality of being shiny; the state of being radiant; relating or emitting to radiant heat.

ra-di-ant (rā′dē ant) *adj.* Emitting rays of heat or light; beaming with kindness or love; projecting a strong quality. **radiantly** *adv.*

ra-di-ant en-er-gy *n.* The energy traveling as a wave motion.

ra-di-ant heat *n.* Heat that is transmitted by radiation.

ra-di-a-tion (rā′dē ā′shan) *n.* An act of radiating; the process or action of radiating; the process of emitting radiant energy in the form of particles or waves. **radiationless, radiative** *adj.*

ra-di-a-tor (rā′dē ā′tėr) *n.* Something which radiates; a system of pipes for heating or cool in gexternal or internal substances.

rad-i-cal (rad′i kal) *adj.* Proceeding from a foundation or root; drastic; making extreme changes in views, conditions, or habits; carrying convictions or theories to their fullest application. **radically** *adv.*, **radicalness** *n.*

rad-i-cal-ism (rad′i ka liz″um) *n.* A following of views which are extreme in character.

rad-i-cand *n.* Term within the radical sign.

rad-i-cate *v.* To take root.

rad-i-cle (rad′i kl) *n.* The lower part of a plant embryo or seedling.

radii *pl. of* radius.

ra-di-o (rā′dē ō′) *n.* The technique of communicating by radio waves; the business of broadcasting programmed material to the public via radio waves. **radioing** *v.* **radioed** *v.*

ra-di-o-ac-tive (rā′dē ō ak′tiv) *adj.* Exhibiting radioactivity. **radioactively** *adv.*

ra-di-o-ac-tiv-i-ty *n., Physics* A spontaneous emission of electro-magnetic radiation, as from a nuclear reaction.

ra-di-o-broad-cast *n.* A broadcasting or transmission of messages by a radio.

ra-di-o-chem-is-try *n.* The part of chemistry that deals with radioactive bodies. **radiochemical** *adj.*

ra-di-o-fre-quen-cy (rā′dē ōfrē′kwen sē) *n.* A frequency which is above 15,000 cycles per second that is used in radio transmission.

ra-di-o-gram (rā′dē ō gram′) *n.* A type of radiograph.

ra-di-o-graph *n.* A picture which is made by rays from a radioactive substance. **radiographically** *adv.* **radiographic** *adj.*

ra-di-o-lar-o-an *n.* A member of the group of minute marine protozoans and having an amoeboid body.

ra-di-o-lo-ca-tion *n.* The finding of the location of something with the use of radar.

ra-di-ol-o-gy (rā′dē ol′o jē) *n.* A science which deals with rays for a radioactive substance and use for medical diagnosis. **radiologist, radiological** *adj.*

ra-di-o-lu-cen-cy *n.* The state of being permeable to radiation.

ra-di-o-man (rā′dē ō man″) *n.* A person who operates a radio.

ra-di-o-pho-to *n.* A picture transmitted via radio.

ra-di-o-sonde *n.* A miniature radio transmitter with instruments for broadcasting the humidity, pressure, and temperature.

rad-ish (rad′ish) *n.* The pungent, edible root of the radish plant.

ra-di-um (rā′dē um) *n* A radioactive metallic element symbolized by Ra.

ra-di-us (rā′dē us) *n. pl.* **-dii** *or* **-uses** A line from the center of a circle to its surface or circumference.

ra-dix *n.* The origin of something; as a root.

RADM *abbr.* Rear admiral.

ra-dome *n.* A plastic housing which protects the antenna assembly on an airplane.

ra-don (rā′don) *n.* A heavy, colorless, radioactive gaseous element symbolized by Rn.

rad-u-la (raj′e la) *n.* The chitinous band in a mollusk's mouth that is used to break up its food. **radular** *adj.*

raff (raf) *n.* The rabble of a group or town.

raf-fi-a (raf′ē a) *n.* A fiber from an African palm tree used for making baskets, hats, and other woven articles.

raf-fi-nose (raf′i nōs′) *n.* A slightly sweet sugar obtained commercially from cotton seed meal.

raff-ish (raf′ish) *adj.* Something that is marked by crudeness or flashy vulgarity. **raffishly, raffishness** *n.*

raf-fle (raf′l) *n.* A game of chance; a lottery in which one buys chances to win some thing.

raf-fle-sia *n.* A type of plant that has foul-smelling flowers and appears to be stemless.

raft (raft) *n.* A floating structure made from logs or planks and used for water transportation.

raft-er (raf′tèr) *n.* A timber of a roof which slopes; a person who maneuvers logs into position.

rafts-man *n.* A person who engages in rafting.

rag (rag) *n.* A cloth which is useless and sometimes used for cleaning purposes.

ra-ga (rä′ga) *n.* Ancient melodic patterns in Indian music.

rag-a-muf-fin (rag′a muf′in) *n.* A child who is unkempt.

rag bag *n.* A miscellaneous grouping or collection; a bag for holding scrap pieces of material.

rag doll *n.* A child's doll that is usually made from scrap material and has a hand painted face.

rage (rāj) *n.* Violent anger; intense feelings. **raging** *adj.* **ragingly** *adv.*

rag-ged (rag′id) *adj.* To be torn or ripped; unkempt. **raggedness** *n.* **raggedly** *adv.*

rag-ged rob-in *n.* A perennial herb having pink flowers with narrow-lobed petals.

rag-gle (rag′l) *n.* A small groove cut in masonry.

rag-i (rag′ē) *n.* An East Indian cereal grass used as a staple food in the Orient.

rag-lan (rag′lan) *n.* A loose fitting coat with extra wide sleeves.

raglan sleeve *n.* A sleeve with slanted seams from the underarm to the neck.

rag-man *n.* A person who collects objects which have been discarded by others.

ra-gout *n.* A highly seasoned meat and vegetable dish with a thick sauce.

rag picker *n.* A person who collects refuse for a living.

rag-time *n.* A type of music with a ragtime rhythm.

rag-weed *n.* A type of plant whose pollen can cause hay fever.

rag-wort (rag′wert′) *n.* A type of herb which has yellow-rayed flowers.

raid (rād) *n.* A sudden invasion or seizure.

rail (rāl) *n.* A horizontal bar of metal, wood, or other strong material supported at both ends or at intervals; the steel bars used to support a track on a railroad.

rail-bird *n.* A person who sits on or near a racetrack rail and watches a race or workout.

rail-head (rāl′hed′) *n.* A section on a railroad where traffic may begin or start.

rail-ing (rā′ling) *n.* A barrier of wood.

rail-ler-y *n.* A teasing that is good-humored.

rail-road *n.* A road having a line of rails providing a track for cars driven by a locomotive. **railroader** *n.*

rail-road-ing *n.* The operation of railroads.

railroad worm *n.* A fruit fly's larva.

rail-split-ter *n.* A person who chops logs into fence rails.

rai-ments (rā´ment) *n.* Garments.

rain (rān) *n.* The condensed water from atmospheric vapor, which falls to earth in the form of drops.

rain-bird *n.* A type of American cuckoo that has a series of rapid calls.

rain-bow (rān´bō´) *n.* An arc that contains bands of colors of the spectrum and is formed opposite the sun and reflects the sun's rays, usually visible after a light rain shower.

rainbow trout *n.* A large stout-bodied fish of western North America.

rain check *n.* A coupon or stub for merchandise which is out of stock; the assurance of entrance or availability at a later date.

rain-coat (rān´kōt´) *n.* A water-resistant or waterproof coat.

rain-fall (rān´fol´) *n.* The amount of measurable precipitation.

rain forest *n.* A tropical woodland that has an annual rainfall of at least 100 inches.

rain gauge *n.* An instrument used to measure rain fall.

rain-mak-ing *n.* The act or process of producing or attempting to produce rain by the use of artificial means.

rain-proof *adj.* To be impervious to rain.

rain spout *n.* A pipe which drains rain from the roof.

rain-wear *n.* Waterproof clothing.

rain-y (rā´nē) *adj.* To be wet from the rain. **raininess, rainily** *adv.*

raise (rāz) *v.* To cause to move upward; to build; to make greater in size, price, or amount; to increase the status; to grow; as plants; to rear as children; to stir one's emotions; to obtain or collect as funds or money.

raised (rāzd) *adj.* To be elevated.

rai-sin (rā´zin) *n.* A grape dried for eating.

ra-ja (rä´ja) *n.* An Indian prince or chief.

rake (rāk) *n.* A tool with a long handle at the end and a set of teeth at the other end used to gather leaves and other matter; a

slope or incline, as the rake of an auditorium. **rake** *v.* **raker** *n.*

rak-ish *adj.* Having a stylish appearance. **rakishness** *n.*

ral-len-tan-do (rä˝len tän´dō) adj. In music, a gradual de-crease in tempo.

ral-ly (ral´ē) *v.* To call together for a purpose. *n.* A rapid recovery, as from depression, exhaustion, or any setback; in a meeting whose purpose is to rouse or create support; an automobile run over public roads at average speeds between checkpoints over a route unfamiliar to the participants.

ral-ly-ing *n.* The sport of driving automobiles in rallies.

ram (ram) *n.* A male sheep; an implement used to drive or crush by impact; to cram or force into place.

RAM *abbr.* Random access memory.

ram-ble (ram´bl) *v.* To stroll or walk without a special destination in mind; to talk without sequence of ideas. **ramble** *n.* **ramblingly** *adv.*

ram-bler *n.* A climbing rose with small flowers in large clusters.

Ram-bouil-let (ram´bü lā˝) *n.* A large sheep raised in France.

ram-bunc-tious (ram bungk´shus) *adj.* Rough or boisterous; unruly. **rambunctiousness** *n.*

ram-bu-tan *n.* A bright red spiny fruit found on the soapberry plant.

ram-e-kin (ram´e kin) n. A dish made of cheese with bread crumbs or eggs baked in a mold; a baking dish.

ra-men-tum (ra men´tum) *n.* A type of scaly material that adheres to the leaves and the stems of certain ferns.

ra-met *n.* A member of a clone.

ra-mie (ram´ē) *n.* A perennial plant with strong fibers used in the manufacture of clothing.

ram-i-form (ram´i form˝) adj. To have the shape of a branch.

ram-i-fy (ram´i fī´) *v.* To send forth branches.

ra-mose (rā´mōs) *adj.* To have branching.

ramp (ramp) *n.* An incline which connects two different levels; movable staircase allows passengers to enter or leave an aircraft.

ram-page (ram pāj´) *n.* A course of destruction or violent behavior. *v.* To storm about in a rampage. **rampageous, rampageously** *adv.* **rampageousness** *n.*

ram-pan-cy (ram´pan sē) *n.* The state or quality of being rampant.

ram-pant (ram´pant) *adj.* Exceeding or growing without control; wild in actions; standing on the hind legs and elevating both forelegs. **rampantly** *adv.*

ram-part (ram´pärt) *n.* An embankment raised as a fortification or barrier.

ram-pike (ram´pīk˝) *n.* An erect dead tree.

ram-pi-on *n.* A tuberous root bellflower with leaves which can be used in salads.

ram-rod (ram´rod´) *n.* A metal rod used to drive or plunge the charge into a muzzle-loading gun or pistol; the rod used for cleaning the barrels of a rifle or other firearm.

ram-shack-le (ram´shak´l) *adj.* Likely to fall apart from poor construction or maintenance.

rams-horn (ramz´horn´) *n.* A snail used in an aquarium as a scavenger.

ram-til *n.* A tropical herb grown for its oil seeds.

ram-u-lose (ram´ya lōs´) *adj.* To have small branches.

ranch (ranch) *n.* A large establishment for raising cattle, sheep, or other livestock; a large farm that specializes in a certain crop or animals. **rancher** *n.*

ranch house *n.* A one story house with a low-pitched roof.

ran-cho (ran´chō) *n.* A small Mexican ranch.

ran-cid (ran´sid) *adj.* Having a rank taste or smell. **rancidness** *n.*

ran-cor (rang´kėr) *n.* Bitter ill will. **rancorous, rancorousness** *n.*

ran-dom (ran´dom) *adj.* Done or made in a way that has no specific pattern or purpose; to select from a group whose members all had an even chance of being chosen. **randomly** *adv.* **randomness** *n.*

ran-dom-iz-a-tion *n.* An arrangement to simulate a chance distribution.

R and R *abbr.* Rest and relaxation.

rang *v.* Past tense of ring.

range (rānj) *n.* An area over which anything moves; an area of activity; a tract of land over which animals such as cattle and horses graze; an extended line or row especially of mountains; an open area for shooting at a target; large cooking stove with burners and oven *v.* To arrange in a certain order; to extend or proceed in a particular direction.

range finder *n.* Instrument that is used in gunnery to determine the distance of a target.

rang-er (rān´jėr) *n.* A person who is hired to tend the public forests.

rang-y (rān´jē) *adj.* To be adapted for moving around. **ranginess** *n.*

ra-ni (rä´nē) *n.* A Hindu queen.

ra-nid *n.* A large family of frogs.

rank (rank) *n.* A degree of official position or status. *v.* To place in order, class, or rank. *adj.* A strong and disagreeable odor, smell, or taste. **rankly** *adv.* **rankness** *n.*

ran-kle (rang´kl) *v.* To cause anger or deep bitterness.

ran-sack (ran´sak) *v.* To search or plunder through every part of something.

ran-som (ran´som) *n.* The price demanded or paid for the release of a kidnapped person; the payment for the release of a person or property detained. **ransom** *v.*

rant (rant) *v.* To talk in a wild, excited loud way. **ranter** *n.*

ran-u-la (ran´ū la) *n.* A type of cyst that can occur under the tongue due to a blockage in a duct.

rap (rap) *v.* To talk with people with similar interest and problems.

ra-pa-cious *adj.* Living on prey seized alive; taking by force; plundering.

rape (rāp) *n.* The crime of forcible sexual intercourse; abusive treatment.

rape oil *n.* Type of oil that is from the

rapeseed and is used in making ribbert substitutes.

rap-id (rap´id) *adj.* Having great speed; completed quickly or in a short time. **rapidity** *n.* **rapidness** *n.*

rap-id–fire *adj.* Pertaining to firing shots in close succession to one another.

rap-id trans-it *n.* The train system that runs within a city and in the area around it.

ra-pi-er (rā´pē ėr) *n.* A long, slender, straight sword with two edges.

rap-ine (rap´in) *n.* The forcible taking of another's property.

rap-pa-ree *n.* An Irish soldier or bandit.

rap-pee (ra pē´) *n.* A snuff made from dark tobacco leaves.

rap-pel (ra pel´) *n.* A descent from a cliff using a rope under one thigh, across the back and over the opposite shoulder.

rap-pi-ni (rap skal on) *n.* An immature turnip plant used for its greens.

rap-port (ra pōr´) *n.* A harmonious relationship.

rap-proche-ment (rä prosh män´) *n.* The establishment of cordial relations.

rap-scal-ion (rap skal´yon) n. A rascal.

rapt (rapt) *adj.* Deeply absorbed or carried away with something and not noticing anything else. **raptness** *n.* **raptly** *adv.*

rap-tor (rap´tōr) *n.* A bird of prey.

rap-to-ri-al (rap tōr´ē al) adj. Having the ability to seize prey.

rap-ture (rap´chėr) *n.* An experience of being carried away by emotion. **rapturous** *adj.* **rapturously** *adv.*

rare (râr) *adj.* Scarce; infrequent; often held in high esteem or admiration because of infrequency. **rareness** *n.*

rare-bit (râr´bit) *n.* A dish made of cheese poured over toast or crackers.

rar-e-fy *v.* To make thin or less dense.

rare-ly *adv.* Seldom; not often.

rar-ing *adj.* Being full of eagerness and enthusiasm.

rar-i-ty *n.* The quality of something being rare.

ras-bo-ra (raz bōr´a) *n.* A breed of brightly colored fish often kept in tropical aquariums.

ras-cal (ras´kal) *n.* A person full of mischief; a person who is not honest.

ras-cal-i-ty *n.* Behavior which is mischievous.

rash (rash) *adj.* Acting without consideration or caution. *n.* A skin irritation or eruption caused by an allergic reaction.

rash-er *n.* A thin slice of bacon; a portion of several slices of bacon.

ra-so-ri-al (ra sōr´ē al) *adj.* Scratching the ground in search of food.

rasp *n.* A file with coarse raised and pointed projections. *v.* To scrape or rub with a coarse file; to utter something in a rough, grating voice. **rasper** *n.* **raspy** adj.

rasp-ber-ry (raz´ber´ē) *n.* A small edible fruit, red or black in color and having many small seeds. *Slang* Contemptuous sound made by expelling air with the tongue between the lips in order to make a vibration.

rasp-y (ras´pē) *adj.* Grating; irritable.

ras-ter *n.* An area onto which an image is reproduced in a kinescope.

rat (rat) *n.* A rodent similar to the mouse, but having a longer tail. *Slang* A despicable person who betrays his friends or associates. **ratlike** *adj.*

rat-a-fia (rat´a fē´a) *n.* A liqueur flavored with kernels of fruit and almonds.

rat-a-tat (rat´a tat´) *n.* A sharp tapping, or repeated knocking.

rat-bite fe-ver *n.* A kind of disease that can be transmitted through the bite of a rat and is characterized by muscle soreness and fever.

ratch-et (rach´it) *n.* A mechanism consisting of a pawl that allows a wheel or bar to move in one direction only.

ratchet wheel *n.* A wheel with teeth that is held in place with an engaging handle.

rate (rāt) *n.* The measure of something to a fixed unit; the degree of price or value; a fixed ratio or amount. *v.* To appraise.

ra-tel (rāt´el) *n.* An African nocturnal carnivorous mammal resembling a badger.

rate of ex-change *n.* The amount of one currency which equals the given amount of another.

rathe (rāth) *adj.* To be before the normal time.

rath-er (rath´ėr) *adv.* Preferably; with more reason or justice; more accurate or precise.

rath-skel-ler *n.* A basement restaurant patterned after the German city hall and in which beer is sold.

rat-i-cide (rat´i sīd´) *n.* A material that is used tokill rats.

rat-i-fy (rat´i fī´) *v.* To approve something in an official way. **ratification** *n.*

ra-ti-ne (rat´i nā´) *n.* A nubby ply yarn made by twisting a thick and a thin yarn under pressure.

rat-ing (rā´ting) *n.* A relative evaluation or estimate of something.

ra-tio (rā´shō) *n. pl.* **-tios** The relationship between two things in amount, size, degree, expressed as a proportion.

ra-ti-o-ci-na-tion (rash˝ē os˝i nā´shan) *n.* A reasoned train of thought.

ra-tion (rash´an) *n.* A fixed portion or share. *v.* To provide or allot in rations. **rationing** *n.* **rationed** *v.*

ra-tion-al (rash´a nal) *adj.* Having the faculty of reasoning; being of sound mind. **rationality** *n.* **rationally** *adv.*

ra-tion-ale *n.* An explanation of principles of opinion, belief, or phenomena.

ra-tio-nal-ize *v.* To provide plausible but not truthful reasons for conduct.

ra-toon (ra tōn´) *v.* To grow or sprout up from the root.

rat race *n.* A strenuous activity or rush.

rats-bane (rats´bān´) *n.* A material that is poisonous to rats.

rat snake *n.* A large, harmess rat-eating snake.

rat-tail *n.* A horse's tail which has very little hair.

rattail file *n.* A slender, round, tapered file.

rat-tan (ra tan´) *n.* An Asian palm whose strong stems are used to make wicker works.

rat-teen *n.* A woolen fabric which is coarse in texture.

rat-ter *n.* A person who likes to catch rats.

rat-tle (rat´l) *v.* To make a series of rapid, sharp noises in quick succession; to talk rapidly; chatter. *n.* A baby's toy made to rattle when shaken.

rat-tle-brain (rat´l brān˝) *n.* A thoughtless person. **rat-tlebrained** *adj.*

rat-tler (rat´lėr) *n. Slang* A venomous snake which has a series of horny, modified joints which make a rattling sound when moved; a rattlesnake; one that rattles.

rat-tle-snake *n.* An American venomous snake with a tail that makes a sharp rattling sound when shaken.

rattlesnake root *n.* A plant formerly believed to be effective against their venom.

rattlesnake weed *n.* A woody herb with purple-veined leaves grown in the western United States related to the carrot.

rat-tle-trap (rat´l trap´) *n.* Something that is rickety or rattly; an old car.

rat-trap (rat´trap˝) *n.* An instrument or device that is used to catch rats.

rat-ty (rat´ē) *adj.* Shabby; unkempt.

rau-cous (ro´kus) *adj.* Loud and rowdy; having a rough, hoarse sound; disorderly. **raucously raucousness** *n.*

raun-chy *adj.* Being dirty, slovenly.

rau-wol-fi-a *n.* A type of shrub which is used as a source of the drug reserpine.

rav-age (rav´ij) *v.* To bring on heavy destruction; devastate. **ravaged** *v.* **ravagement, ravager** *n.*

rave (rāv) *v.* To speak incoherently; to speak with enthusiasm. *n.* The act of raving.

rav-el (rav´el) *v.* To separate fibers or threads; to unravel.

rav-el-ment *n.* A confusion.

ra-ven (rā´ven) *n.* A large bird, with shiny black feathers. *adj.* Of or relating to the glossy sheen or color of the raven.

rav-en-ing *adj.* To be hunting in order to

devour something.

rav-en-ous (rav´e nus) adj. Being very hungry and eager for food.

rav-in (rav´n) n. Something seized as prey.

ra-vine (ra vēn) n. A deep gorge with steep sides in the earth's surface, usually created by flowing water.

rav-ing (rav´ ing) adj. An incoherent, wild, or extravagant outburst.

rav-i-o-li (rav´ē ō´lē) n. A small piece of dough filled with meat or cheese served in a tomato sauce.

rav-ish (rav´ish) v. To seize and carry off; to rape. **ravishment, ravisher** n.

rav-ish-ing adj. Unusually striking.

raw (ro) adj. Uncooked; in natural condition; not processed; inexperienced; damp, sharp, or chilly. **rawly** adv. **rawness** n.

raw-boned (ro´bōnd´) adj. Having a coarse, lean appearance.

raw-hide (ro´hīd´) n. The untanned hide of cattle.

raw material n. Material that is existing in its natural form.

ray (rā) n. A thin line of radiation or light; a small trace or amount; one of several lines coming from a point.

ray-less (rā´lis) adj. Having no rays; dark.

ray-on (rā´on) n. A synthetic cellulose yarn; any fabric made from such yarn.

raze (rāz) v. To destroy or demolish.

ra-zor (rā´zėr) n. A sharp cutting instrument used especially for shaving.

ra-zor-back (rā´zėr bak) n. A wild hog of the south-eastern United States.

ra-zor-bill n. A North American auk.

razor clam n. A type of bivalve mollusk having a shell that is long and narrow.

razz (raz) v. Slang To heckle; to tease.

raz-zle-daz-zle (raz´l daz´l) n. A state of complete confusion.

re- prefix Again, anew, or reverse action.

reach (rēch) v. To stretch out; to be able to grasp. n. The act of stretching out. **reach-able** adj. **reacher** n.

re-act (rē akt´) v. To act in response to. Chem. To undergo a chemical change; to experience a chemical reaction; to move in a reverse direction; to cause to react.

re-ac-tant (rē ak´tant) n. Substance which enters into and is altered by the course of a chemical reaction.

re-ac-tion (rē ak´shan) n. The mental or bodily response to an activity; the process or act of reacting; the action that is induced by vital resistance to another action; exhaustion caused by excessive exertion or stimulation; an emotional disorder forming a person's response to his life; the force that a body exerts when encountering force from another body in the opposite direction; a chemical change; the state resulting from an interaction of chemical entities. **reactional** adj. **reactionally** adv.

re-ac-tion-ar-y adj. Marked by, or relating to political reaction. **reactionarism** n.

reaction engine n. A jet engine or one similar that develops thrust by expelling a jet of fluid.

re-ac-ti-vate v. To activate something again. **reactively** adv. **reactiveness** n. **reactivity** n.

re-ac-tor (rē ak´tėr) n. A person, object, device, or substance which reacts to something.

read (rēd) v. To visually go over something, as a book, and to understand its meaning; to learn or be informed; to perceive something in a meaning which may or may not actually be there; to become acquainted with or look at the contents; to recognize the nature of by observing outward expression or signs.

read-able (rē´da bl) adj. Able to be read with ease. **readableness, readability** n. **readably** adv.

read-er (rē´dėr) n. A person who has been instructed to read to others.

read-er-ship n. The state or quality of being a reader; the office of a reader; a particular group of readers.

readi-ly (red´i lē) adj. Without hesitation; without a lot of difficulty.

read-ing n. An interpretation of something; the act of reading; a particular interpretation or version; the indication of a state of affairs.

reading desk *n.* A desk used to support a book and allow a person to read in a standing position.

read-out (rēd′out′) *n.* In computer science, the process of removing information from a computer and displaying it in an understandable form; the process of reading something; the radio transmission of pictures or information from a space vehicle either immediately upon acquisition or by tape recording playback.

read-y (red′ē) *adj.* Prepared for use or action; quick or prompt. **readiness** *n.*

ready-made *n.* Something made beforehand for sale to the public; something that is lacking individuality or originality.

ready room *n.* An area where pilots are briefed before flying.

ready-to-wear *n.* Clothing manufactured to sell to the general public.

Rea-gan, Ronald Wilson *n.* The 40th president of the United States from 1981-1988.

re-a-gent (rē ā′jent) *n.* Any substance which causes a chemical reaction.

re-ag-gre-gate *v.* To reform into a whole. **reaggregate, reaggregation** *n.*

re-al (rē′al) *adj.* Something which is existing, genuine, true, or authentic. *Law* Property which is regarded as permanent, fixed, or immovable; not illusory, artificial, or fraudulent. **realness** *n.*

real estate *n.* The property in land and buildings.

re-al-gar *n.* An orange-red mineral consisting of arsenic sulfide with a resinous luster.

re-alia (rē ā′lē a) *n.* Objects used to relate classroom teaching to the real life of people studied.

re-al-ism (rē′a liz′um) *n.* Concern or interest with actual facts and things as they really are. **realist** *n.* **realistic** *adj.*

re-al-i-ty (rē al′i tē) *n. pl.* The fact or state of being real or genuine; an actual situation or real event; something that is neither dependent nor derivative but exists necessarily.

re-al-ize (rē′a līz′) *v.* To understand correctly; to make real; to make or cause to seem real. **realizable** *adj.* **realizer, realization** *n.*

re-al-ly (rē′a lē) *adv.* Actually; truly; indeed; unquestionably. **realizable** *adj.* **realizer** *n.*

realm (relm) *n.* A scope or field of any power or influence.

re-al-po-li-tik *n.* Politics that are based on material and practical factors and not on ethical or theoretical objectives.

Re-al-tor (rē′al tėr) *n.* A real estate agent who belongs to the National Association of Realtors.

re-al-val-ued *adj.* Using only real numbers for values.

ream (rēm) *n.* A quantity of paper containing 500 sheets; *v.* To widen the opening of something.

ream-er (rē′mėr) *n.* A rotating tool with cutting edges used to enlarge or shape a hole; a fruit juice extractor that has a ridged and pointed center that rises from a shallow bowl.

reap (rēp) *v.* To harvest a crop with a sickle or other implement; to cut with a scythe, sickle, or other harvesting machine.

reap-er (rē′pėr) *n.* A machine used to reap grain.

reap-hook *n.* An implement that is held by the hand and has a hook-shaped blade used in reaping grain.

rear (rēr) *n.* The back. *adj.* Of or at the rear. *v.* To raise up on the hind legs; to raise as an animal or child; to erect by building something. **rearer** *n.*

rear admiral *n.* A commissioned officer in the Navy who ranks above a captain.

rear echelon *n.* A military unit or headquarters located at a considerable distance from the front line.

rear guard *n.* A military detachment detailed to protect the rear of a main body of men.

re-arm (rē ärm′) *v.* To supply with new or better weapons. **rearmament** *n.*

rear-most (rēr′mōst′) *adj.* Being farthest

in the rear.

rearview mirror *n.* A mirror on the side of an automobile which gives a view of the area behind the vehicle.

rea-son (rē′zon) *n.* A statement given to confirm or justify a belief, promise, or excuse; the ability to decide things, to obtain ideas, to think clearly, and to make logical and rational choices and decisions. *v.* To discuss something logically. **reasoning** *adj.* **reasoner** *n.*

rea-son-a-ble (rē′zo na bl) *adj.* Moderate; rational; not excessive or extreme. **reasonableness** *n.* **reasonably** *adv.*

rea-son-ing (rē′zo ning) *n.* Conclusions drawn through the use of reason.

re-as-sur-ance *n.* The act of reassuring; reinsurance.

re-as-sure (rē′a sher′) *v.* To restore confidence. **reassuringly** *adv.*

reave *v.* To carry away. **reaver** *n.*

re-bar-ba-tive *adj.* The act of being repellent. **rebarbatively** *adv.*

re-bate (rē′bāt) *n.* A deduction allowed on items sold; a discount; money which is returned to the purchaser from the original payment. *v.* To return part of the payment. **rebater** *n.*

reb-be *n.* A Jewish spiritual leader.

re-bec *n.* An ancient musical instrument with a pear-shaped body and slender neck.

re-bel (ri bel′) *v.* To refuse allegiance; to resist any authority; to react with violence; to take arms against a government.

re-bel-lion (ri bel′yon) *n.* An organized uprising to change or overthrow an existing authority.

re-bel-lious (ri bel′yus) *adj.* Engaged in rebellion; relating to a rebel or rebellion; characteristic of a rebellion. **rebelliously** *adv.* **rebelliousness** *n.*

rebel yell *n.* A high-pitched yell given by Confederate soldiers in the Civil War.

re-birth (rē berth′) *n.* A revival or renaissance; reincarnation; spiritual regeneration.

re-bound (ri bound′) *v.* To spring back; to recover from a setback or frustration; to gain possession of a rebound ball in bas-

ketball. *n.* Recoil.

re-bound-er *n.* A basketball player skilled at rebounding the ball.

re-bo-zo *n.* A long scarf worn by Mexican women.

re-broad-cast (rē brod′kast′) *v.* To repeat or broadcast again at a later time or date. **rebroadcast** *n.* **rebroadcaster** *n.*

re-buff (ri buf′) *v.* To refuse abruptly; to snub.

re-build (rē bild′) *v.* To restore or make extensive changes to a building; to reconstruct; remodel.

re-buke (ri būk′) *v.* To reprimand; to criticize sharply; to turn back. *n.* Strong disapproval. **rebuker** *n.*

re-bus (rē′bus) *n.* A riddle using words or syllables whose names resemble the intended words or syllables in sound.

re-but (ri but′) *v.* To try and prove someone wrong by argument or evidence; to contradict by formal argument.

re-but-tal *n.* An argument that rebuts.

re-but-ter (ri but′er) *n.* The reply of a defendant to the plaintiff's surrejoinder.

rec *abbr.* Recreation; receipt; record.

re-cal-ci-trant (ri kal′si trant) *adj.* Being difficult to handle or operate.

re-cal-cu-late (rē kal′kū lāt′) *v.* To calculate again to discover an error or formulate new conclusions. **recalculation** *n.*

re-ca-les-cence *n.* An increase in temperature occurring while cooling metal.

re-call (ri kol′) *v.* To order or summon to return to ask for something to be returned; so that defects can be fixed or repaired; to remember; to recollect. **recallability** *n.* **recallable** *adj.* **recaller** *n.*

re-cant (ri kant′) *v.* To formally admit that a previously held belief was wrong by making public confession; to withdraw; renounce. **recantation** *n.*

re-cap (rē′kap′) *v.* To restore an old tire; to review or summarize something. **recappable** *adj.*

re-cap-i-tal-i-za-tion *n.* A revision of the capital structure of a corporation.

re-ca-pit-u-la-tion *n.* A concise summary;

the third section of a sonata.

re-cap-ture *v.* To take possession of again.

re-cast (rē kast´) *v.* To cast new people in a play; to cast once again.

re-cede (ri sēd´) *v.* To move back; as flood-water; to withdraw from an agreement; to grow less or smaller.

re-ceipt (ri sēt´) *n.* The written acknowledgment of something received. *pl.,* **receipts** The amount of money received.

re-ceiv-ables (ri sē´va blz) n. The amount of money received.

re-ceive (ri sēv´) *v.* To take or get something; to greet customers or guests; to accept as true or correct; to assimilate through senses.

re-ceiv-er (ri sē´vėr) *n.* A person that receives something.

receiving blanket *n.* A small lightweight blanket to wrap an infant.

receiving line *n.* A group of people who individually welcome arriving guests.

re-cen-sion (ri sen´shan) *n.* A revision of a text.

re-cent (rē´sent) *adj.* Happening at a time just before the present; relating to a short time ago. **recently** *adv.* **recentness** *n.*

re-cep-ta-cle (ri sep´ta kl) *n.* Anything which holds something; an electrical outlet designed to receive a plug.

re-cep-tion (ri sep´shan) *n.* The act or manner of receiving something; a formal entertainment of guests, as a wedding reception.

re-cep-tion-ist (ri sep´sha nist) *n.* An employee who greets callers and answers the telephone for a business.

re-cep-tive (ri sep´tiv) *adj.* Able to receive; open and responsive to ideas. **receptively** *adv.* **receptiveness** *n.* **receptivity** *n.*

re-cep-tor (ri sep´tėr) *n.* A group of cells that receive stimuli.

re-cess (ri ses´) *n.* A break in the normal routine of something; a depression or niche in a smooth surface.

re-ces-sion (ri sesh´an) *n.* The act of receding; withdrawal; a period or time of reduced economic activity.

re-ces-sion-al (ri sesh´a nal) n. A musical piece at the conclusion of a service.

re-ces-sive *adj.* Having a tendency to go backward. **recessively**

re-charge *v.* To restore the active materials in a battery; to make a new attack. **recharger** *n.* **rechargeable** *adj.*

re-cheat *n.* A hunting call on a horn to assemble the hounds.

re-cid-i-vism *n.* A tendency to relapse into a previous mode of behavior.

rec-i-pe (res´i pē´) *n.* The directions and a list of ingredients for preparing food.

re-cip-i-ent (ri sip´ē ent) *n.* A person who receives.

re-cip-ro-cal (ri sip´ro kal) *adj.* To return the same way.

reciprocal pronoun *n.* A pronoun to denote mutual action between members in a plural subject.

re-cip-ro-cate (ri sip´ro kāt´) *v.* To give and return mutually, one gift or favor for another. **reciprocator** *n.*

re-cip-ro-ca-tion *n.* A mutual exchange; an alternating motion. **reciprocative** *adj.*

rec-i-proc-i-ty *n.* Mutual exchange of privileges; the state of being reciprocal.

re-cit-al (ri sīt´al) *n.* A performance given by an individual musician or dancer. **recitalist** *n.*

rec-i-ta-tion *n.* An instance of repeating aloud; a student's oral reply to questions.

re-cite (ri sīt´) *v.* To repeat something from memory; give an account of something in detail. **reciter** *n.*

reck-less (rek´lis) *adj.* State of being careless and rash when doing something. **recklessness** *n.* **recklessly** *adv.*

reck-on (rek´on) *v.* To calculate; to compute; to estimate; to consider; to assume. **with** Take into consideration.

reck-on-ing (rek´o ning) *n.* The act of calculation or counting.

re-claim (ri klām´) *v.* To redeem; to reform; to recall; to change to a more desirable condition or state. **reclaimable** *adj.*

rec-la-ma-tion (rek´la mā´shan) *n.* The state of being reclaimed.

re-cline (ri klīn´) *v.* To assume a prone position.

re-clos-able *adj.* Capable of being shut or closed again.

rec-luse (rek´lōs) *n.* A person who chooses to live in seclusion.

rec-og-ni-tion (rek´og nish´an) *n.* An acknowledgment which is formal; the action of recognizing something; special attention or notice.

re-cog-ni-zance (ri kog´ni zans) *n.* An amount of money which will be forfeited for a nonperformance of an obligation.

rec-og-nize (rek´og nīz´) *v.* To experience or identify something or someone as having been known previously; to be appreciative. **recognizable** *adj.* **recognizably** *adv.* **recognizer** *n.* **recognizability** *n.*

re-coil (ri koil´) *v.* To fall back or to rebound; to spring back under pressure. **recoilless** *adj.*

rec-ol-lect (rek´o lekt´) *v.* To remember or recall to the mind. **recollection** *n.* **recollected** *adj.*

rec-om-mend (rek˝o mrnd´) v. To suggest to another as desirable; advise. **recommendation** *n.* **recommendable** *adj.*

re-com-mit (rē˝ko mit´) *v.* To refer back to; to entrust or consign again. **recommitment, recommital** *n.*

rec-om-pense (rek´om pens´) *v.* To reward with something for a service.

re-com-pose (rē´kom pōz´) *v.* To restore the composure of. **recomposition** *n.*

rec-on-cile (rek´on sīl´) *v.* To restore a friendship after an estrangement. **reconcileably** *adv.* **reconcileable** *adj.* **reconciler** *n.* **reconcilement** *n.*

rec-on-dite (rek´on dīt´) *adj.* Being obscure. **reconditely** *adv.* **reconditeness** *n.*

re-con-di-tion (rē´kon dish´an) *v.* To return to a good condition.

re-con-firm (rē´kon ferm´) *v.* Confirm something again. **reconfirmation** *n.*

re-con-nais-sance (ri kon´i sans) *n.* An observation of territory such as that of the enemy.

re-con-noi-ter (rē´ko noi´tèr) *v.* To survey a region. **reconnoitering** *v.*

re-con-sid-er (rē´kon sid´èr) *v.* To think

about again with a view to changing a previous action or decision. **reconsideration** *n.*

re-con-sti-tute *v.* To restore to a former condition. **reconstitution** *n.*

re-con-struct *v.* To build something again. **reconstructible, reconstructive** *adj.* **reconstructor** *n.*

re-con-struc-tion (rē´kon struk´shan) *n.* Something which has been reconstructed or rebuilt.

re-con-ver-sion *n.* Returning back to the previous or original state.

re-con-vey *v.* To return back to a previous position or owner. **reconveyance** *n.*

re-cord (ri kord´) *v.* To write down for future use or permanent reference; to preserve sound on a tape or disk for replay; a phonograph record. *n.* Information which is recorded and kept permanently.

record changer *n.* A device that automatically positions and plays each of a stack of records.

re-cord-er (ri kor´dèr) *n.* A person who records things such as official transactions.

re-cord-ing (ri kor´ding) *n.* The act of making a transcription of sounds.

record player *n.* The machine which is used to play recordings.

re-count (rē kount´) *v.* To tell the facts; narrate or describe in detail; to count again. *n.* A second count to check the results of the first count. **recounter** *n.*

re-coup (ri köp´) *v.* To be reimbursed; to recover. **recoupable** *adj.*

re-course (rē´kōrs) *n.* A turning to or an appeal for help; a source of help.

re-cov-er (ri kuv´èr) *v.* To regain something which was lost; to be restored to good health. *Law* To obtain a judgment for damages. **recoverability** *n.* **recoverable** *adj.* **recoverer** *n.*

re-cov-er-y (ri kuv´e rē) *n.* The power to regain something.

rec-re-ant (rek´rē ant) *adj.* Cowardly; unfaithful.

re-cre-ate (rē´krē āt´) *v.* To create again,

to form in the imagination. **recreative** *adj.*
recreatable *adj.* **recreative** *adj.*

rec-re-a-tion (rek´rē ā´shan) *n.* Refreshment of body and mind; a pleasurable occupation or exercise. **recreational** *adj.*

rec-re-a-tion-ist *n.* A person seeking recreation out of doors.

re-cre-a-tion room *n.* A room used for relaxation and play; a public room in a hospital for social activities.

re-crim-i-nate *v.* The charging of another of the same account. **recriminatory, recriminative** *adj.* **recrimination** *n.*

re-cru-desce (rē´krŏ des´) *v.* To break out; become raw again. **recrudescence** *n.*

re-cruit (ri krŏt´) *v.* To enlist someone for military or naval purposes; to look for someone as for a service or employment. *n.* A newly enlisted person. **recruiter, recruitment** *n.*

rec-tal (rek´tal) *adj.* Referring to the rectum of the body. **rectally** *adv.*

rec-tan-gle (rek´tang´gl) *n.* A parallelogram with all right angles. **rectangular, rectangularity** *n.*

rec-ti-fi-er (rek´ti fī´ér) *n.* That which rectifies something. **rectifiable** *adj.*

rec-ti-fy (rek´ti fī´) *v.* To make correct. *Chem.* To purify by repeated distillations. *Electr.* To make an alternating current a direct current. **rectification** *n.*

rec-ti-lin-ear (rek´ti lin´ē ér) *adj.* Made up of or indicated by straight lines; bounded by straight lines. **rectilinearly** *adv.*

rec-ti-tude (rek´ti tŏd´) *n.* Rightness in principles and conduct; correctness.

rec-to (rek´tō) *n.* The right-hand page of a book.

rec-tor (rek´tér) *n.* A member of the clergy in charge of a parish; a priest in charge of a congregation, church, or parish; the principal or head of a school or of a college. **rectorate** *n.* **rectorial** *adj.* **rectorship** *n.*

rec-to-ry (rek´to rē) *n.* The rector's residence.

rec-trix *n.* The quill feathers of a bird's tail that are important in controlling flight.

rec-tum (rek´tum) *n., Anat.* The lower terminal portion of the large intestine connecting the colon and anus.

re-cum-bent (ri kum´bent) *adj.* Lying down or reclining. **recumbently** *adv.*

re-cu-per-ate (ri kŏ´pe rāt´) *v.* To regain strength or to regain one's health; to recover from a financial loss. **recuperation** *n.* **recuperative** *adj.*

re-cur (ri ker´) *v.* To happen, to return, or to appear again. **recurrence** *n.* **recurrent** *adj.*

re-cur-rent (ri kūr´ent) *adj.* Happening time after time. **recurrently** *adv.*

re-cu-san-cy *n.* The refusal to accept established authority.

re-cy-cle *v.* To return to an earlier usable condition. **recyclable** *adj.*

red (red) *n.* Having the color which resembles blood, as pigment or dye which colors red. *Slang* A communist; one who is in favor of the overthrow of an existing political or social order; a condition indicating a loss, as in the red.

re-dact (ri dakt´) *v.* To adapt for publication. **redactional** *adj.*

red-breast (red brest´) *n.* A bird with a reddish colored breast.

red-brick (red brik´) *n.* A commonly used brick in construction.

red-bud (red bud´) *n.* An American tree with a pale pinkish-rose flower.

red-cap *n.* A porter who carries luggage at railroad stations, airports, etc.

red carpet *n.* A greeting reserved for very important people.

red clover *n.* A clover with reddish purple flowers cultivated as forage and a cover crop.

red-coat *n.* A British soldier in America during the Revolutionary War.

red coral *n.* A hard stony skeleton of a delicate red or pink color used for jewelry and ornaments found in the Atlantic Ocean.

Red Cross *n.* An organization which helps

people in need, collects and preserves human blood for use in emergencies, and responds with help in time of disaster.

rede (rēd) *v.* To advise or counsel.

re-dec-o-rate (rē dek´o rāt´) *v.* To change in appearance; to refurbish. **redecorator** *n.* **redecoration** *n.*

re-deem (ri dēm´) *v.* To buy back; to pay off; to turn something in, as coupons or rain checks and receive something in exchange. **redeemable** *adj.* **redeemer** *n.*

re-de-fine (*v.* To examine with a view to change. **redefinition** *n.*

re-demp-tion (ri demp´shan) *n.* The act of redeeming; rescue; ransom; that which redeems; salvation. **redemptional** *adj.*

re-demp-tion-er (ri demp´shan ėr) *n.* An immigrant to America who obtained passage by becoming a servant.

re-demp-tive (ri demp´tiv) *adj.* Relating to redemption.

re-de-ploy (rē´di ploi´) *v.* To move men and equipment from one location to another.

re-de-scribe *v.* To give a more updated version of something.

re-de-sign (rē´di zīn´) *v.* To change or revise the appearance or function of something.

re-de-vel-op-ment *n.* The renovation of a rundown area.

red-hand-ed (red´han´did) *adj.* Caught in the act of committing a crime.

red-hot (red´hot´) *adj.* Extremely hot. *n.* A small red candy flavored with cinnamon.

red-in-gote (red´ing gōt´) *n.* A fitted double-breasted coat with wide flat cuffs and collar worn by men in the 18th century.

red ink *n.* A business loss.

red-in-te-grate (red in´te grāt´) *v.* To restore to a former sound state.

re-di-rect (rē´di rekt´) *v.* To change the course of. **redirection** *n.*

re-dis-trib-ute (rē´di strib´ūt) *v.* To spread to different areas. **redistributive** *adj.* **redistribution** *n.*

red light *n.* A traffic signal; a warning device.

re-double *v.* To make something twice in size or amount.

re-doubt (ri dout´) *n.* A small enclosed fortification.

re-doubt-a-ble *adj.* To be dreaded. **redoubtably** *adv.*

re-dound (ri dound´) *v.* To have an effect on something.

red pencil *v.* To correct; to censor.

re-dress (ri dres´) *v.* To put something right; to remedy. **redresser** *n.*

red ribbon *n.* The ribbon which designates second place winner in a contest.

red-root (red´rŏt´) *n.* An herb of the blood-wort family of the eastern United States.

red-snap-per *n.* A saltwater fish which is red in color and can be found in the Gulf of Mexico and near Florida.

red squirrel *n.* A squirrel reddish in color but smaller than the grey squirrel .

red-start (red´stärt´) *n.* An American warbler which is brightly colored.

red tape *n.* Routines which are rigid and may cause a delay in a process.

red tide *n.* The presence of large numbers of dinoflagellates in seawater which is fatal to many forms of marine life.

re-duce (ri dŏs´) *v.* To decrease; lessen in number, degree, or amount; to put into order; to lower in rank; to lose weight by dieting. **reducer** *n.* **reducible** *adj.*

re-duc-tion (ri duk´shan) *n.* The state of being reduced. **reductional** *adj.*

re-dun-dant (ri dun´dant) *adj.* Exceeding what is necessary; repetitive. **redundantly** *adv.* **redundancy** *n.*

re-du-pli-cate (ri dŏ´pli kāt´) *v.* To repeat something. **reduplication** *n.* **reduplicative** *adj.* **reduplicatively** *adv.*

red-wood *n.* A tree found in California which is very tall and wide.

re-ech-o *v.* To reverberate again.

reed (rēd) *n.* Tall grass with a slender stem, which grows in wet areas; a thin tongue of wood, metal, cane, or plastic; placed in the mouthpiece of an instrument to produce sounds by vibrating. **reediness, reedy** *adj.*

reed-buck *n.* An African antelope.

re-ed-u-cate *v.* To train again through education; rehabilitate. **reeducation** *n.* **re-educative** *adj.*

reed-y (rē′dē) *adj.* Having the tone quality of a reed instrument.

reef (rēf) *n.* A chain of rocks, coral, or sand at or near the surface of the water.

reef-er (rē′fėr) *n.* A double-breasted jacket which is close-fitting.

reef knot *n.* A square knot used on a sail.

reek (rēk) *v.* To emit vapor or smoke; to give off a strong offensive odor.

reel (rēl) *n.* A device which revolves on an axis and is used for winding up or letting out fishing line, rope, or other string-like material; a lively and fast dance; a bobbin for sewing thread.

re-e-lect (rē″i lekt) *v.* The act of electing someone again for an office.

reel-to-reel *adj.* Pertaining to magnetic tape which is threaded to a take-up reel, which moves from one reel to another.

re-em-pha-size (rē em′fa sīz′) *v.* To stress something or an idea again.

re-em-ploy (rē′em ploi′) *v.* To rehire someone who previously worked for you.

re-en-act (rē′en akt′) *v.* To perform again; to repeat the actions of a previous event.

re-en-list *v.* To enlist or join a group or an armed force again. **reenlistment** *n.*

re-en-ter (rē en′tėr) *v.* To enter a room or area again.

re-en-try (rē en′trē) *n.* The return of a space craft after a mission into outer space.

reeve (rēv) *n.* A medieval English manor officer responsible for overseeing feudal obligations.

re-ex-am-ine (rē′ig zam′in) *v.* Examine something or someone another time or again. **reexamination** *n.*

ref *n.* The person who controls sports games.

re-fer-to-ry (ri fek′to rē) *n.* The place in colleges where students dine.

re-fer (ri fer′) *v.* To direct for treatment, information, or help; to classify within a general category or cause.

ref-e-ree *n.* A person who supervises a game, making sure all the rules are followed.

ref-er-ence (ref′ėr ens) *n.* The act of refer-

ring someone to someplace or to something.

reference mark *n.* A mark, such as an asterisk, to direct the reader's attention to a footnote.

ref-er-en-dum (ref′e ren′dum) *n.* A public vote on an item for final approval or for rejection.

ref-er-ent (ref′ėr ent) *n.* What is referred to, such as a person; the thing that a word or sign stand for. **referent** *adj.*

re-fill (rē fil′) *v.* To fill something with an item again. **refillable** *adj.*

re-fine (ri fin′) *v.* To purify by removing unwanted substances or material; to improve. **refined** *adj.* **refinement** *n.*

re-fin-er-y (ri fi′ne rē) *n.* A place or location which is used for the purpose of refining, such as sugar.

re-fin-ish *v.* The act of putting a new surface onto something, such as wood.

re-fit (rē fit′) *v.* To repair something.

re-flect (rē flekt′) *v.* To throw back rays of light from a surface; to give an image, as from a mirror; to ponder or think carefully about something. **reflection, reflectiveness** *n.* **reflectively** *adv.*

re-flec-tom-e-ter (rē″flek tom′i tėr) *n.* A device for measuring radiant energy.

re-flec-tor *n.* Something which is able to reflect things, such as light.

re-flex (rē′fleks) *adj.* Turning, casting, or bending backward. *n.* An involuntary reaction of the nervous system to a stimulus.

re-flex-ive (ri flek′siv) *adj.* A relation that exists between an entity and itself. **reflexiveness** *n.* **reflexivity** *n.*

re-flex-ol-gy *n.* The science of behavior of simple and complex reflexes.

re-flo-res-cent *adj.* Blooming again.

re-flow *v.* To flow back again.

re-fo-cus (rē fō′kus) *v.* To change the direction of.

re-for-est (rē for′ist) *v.* The act of replanting a forest or wooded area with trees.

re-forge (rē fōrj′) *v.* To make over.

re-form (ri form′) *v.* To reconstruct, make

over, or change something for the better; improve; to abandon or give up evil ways. **reformer** *n*. **reformed** *adj*.

re-for-ma-to-ry *n*. A jail-like institution for young criminals.

Reform Judaism *n*. The branch of Judaism which has adopted a simpler and more liberal approach to religious rites and observances.

re-fract (ri frakt´) *v*. The deflecting of something, such as a ray of light. **refractive** *adj*.

re-frac-to-ry *adj*. Unmanageable; obstinate; difficult to melt; resistant to heat. *n*. Something which does not change significantly when exposed to high temperatures. **refactorily** *adv*. **refactoriness** *n*.

refractory period *n*. The period immediately following the response of a muscle before it recovers to make a second response.

re-frain (ri frān´) *v*. To hold back; to keep oneself from following a passing impulse. *n*. A recurring phrase at the end of each stanza of a poem or song.

re-fresh (ri fresh´) *v*. To freshen something again; to restore strength. **refreshing** *adj*. **refreshingly** *adv*. **refresher** *n*.

re-fresh-er *n*. A course taken to review what has been previously learned.

re-fresh-ment (ri fresh´ment) *n*. Something which will refresh someone, such as a cold drink or snack.

re-frig-er-ant (ri frij´ĕr ant) *n*. An agent which cools something.

re-frig-er-a-tor *n*. A box-like piece of equipment which chills food and other matter.

re-fu-el (rē fū´el) *v*. To put fuel into something again; take on additional fuel.

ref-uge *n*. Shelter or protection from harm; any place one may turn for relief or help.

ref-u-gee (ref´ū jē´) *n*. A person who flees to find safety. **refugeeism** *n*.

re-ful-gent (ri ful´jent) *adj*. State of being radiant or putting off a bright light.

re-fund (ri fund´) *v*. To return or pay back; to reimburse. **refundable** *adj*. **refund** *n*.

re-fur-bish *v*. To make clean; to renovate. **refurbisher, refurbishment** *n*.

re-fus-al (ri fū´zal) *n*. The denial of something which is demanded.

re-fuse (ri fūz´) *v*. To decline; to reject; to deny.

re-fute (ri fūt´) *v*. To overthrow or to disprove with the use of evidence. **refutable** *adj*. **refutably** *adv*. **refuter** *n*.

re-gain (ri gān´) *v*. To recover; to reach again.

re-gal (ri gāl´) *adj*. Of or appropriate for royalty. **regally** *adv*.

re-gale (ri gāl´) *v*. To entertain or delight; to give pleasure.

re-ga-li-a (ri gā´lē a) *n*. Something which represents royalty such as a scepter.

re-gard (ri gärd´) *v*. To look upon closely; to consider; to have great affection for. *n*. Careful attention or thought; esteem or affection. **regards** Greetings of good wishes.

re-gard-ful *adj*. State of being mindful. **regardfulness** *n*. **regardfully** *adv*.

re-gard-less *adj*. State of being careless or showing no regard towards something or someone. **regardlessness** *n*.

re-gat-ta (ri gat´a) *n*. A boat race.

re-gen-cy (rē´jen sē) *n. pl.* **-ies** The jurisdiction or office of a regent.

re-gen-er-ate *v*. To reform spiritually or morally; to make or create anew; to refresh or restore. **regenerateness** *n*.

re-gent (rē´jent) *n*. One who rules and acts as a ruler during the absence of a sovereign, or when the ruler is underage.

reg-i-cide *n*. A person who kills a king.

re-gime (re zhem´) *n*. An administration.

reg-i-men (rej´i men´) *n*. Government control; therapy; a systematic plan to improve the health.

reg-i-ment *n*. A military unit of ground troops which is composed of several battalions. **regimental** *adj*.

re-gion (rē´jan) *n*. An administrative, political, social, or geographical area.

re-gion-al (rēja nal) adj. Typical or pertaining to a geographic region; limited to a particular region.

re-gion-al-ize *v*. To divide into regions or

districts.

regional library *n.* A public library serving several counties within the same state.

reg-is-ter (rej´i stėr) *n.* Something which contains names or occurrences; a book of public records.

reg-is-tered (rej´i stėrd) *adj.* Recorded with the owner's name; recorded on the basis of pedigree of an animal.

registered mail *n.* Mail registered in the post office and guaranteed special care in delivery.

registered nurse *n.* A trained graduate nurse who is licensed by a state and who has passed qualifying examinations for registration.

reg-is-trar *n.* The person who keeps a register; an office of an educational institution who is in charge of registration, keeping academic records, and evaluating their credentials.

reg-is-tra-tion *n.* An act of recording things or names.

reg-is-try *n.* The nationality of a ship in a register; an official record book.

reg-let (reg´lit) *n.* A narrow strip of molding.

re-gress *v.* To return to a previous state or condition. **regressor** *adj.* **regressive** *n.*

re-gres-sion *n.* The progressive decline of a disease; a shift toward a lower state; gradual loss of memory and acquired skills. **regressive** *adj.* **regressiveness** *n.*

re-gret (ri gret´) *v.* To feel disappointed or distressed about; to be sorry for. *n.* A sense of loss or expression of grief; a feeling of sorrow. **regretably, regretfully** *adv.* **regretable, regretful** *adj.*

re-group (rē grōp´) *v.* To reorganize after a setback in an activity.

reg-u-lar *adj.* Usual; normal; customary; conforming to set principles, procedures, or discipline; well-ordered; not varying. **regularity** *n.* **regularly** *adv.*

reg-u-lar-ize (reg´ya lāt´) *v.* To conform to laws, rules, and customs.

reg-u-late (reg´ya lāt´) *v.* To adjust to a specification or requirement; to bring order or authority. **regulative** *adj.* **regulatory**

adj. **regulator** *n.*

reg-u-la-tion *n.* A rule that is set down in order to govern an area or people.

reg-u-lus (reg´a lus) *n.* A star in the constellation Leo.

re-gur-gi-tate (ri g *v.* To pour something forth. **regurgitation** *n.*

re-ha-bil-i-tate *v.* To restore to a former state by education and therapy. **rehabilitation** *n.* **rehabilitative** *adv.*

re-hash (rē hash´) *v.* To rework or go over old material; to discuss again.

re-hears-al *n.* The act of practicing for a performance; a practice session.

re-hu-man-ize *v.* To restore to a full life; restore human rights and dignity.

re-hy-drate (rē hī´drāt) *v.* To return fluid lost due to dehydration.

reichs-mark *n.* A German coin.

reign (rān) *n.* The period in time when the monarch rules over an area.

reign of terror *n.* A period in history marked by violence committed by those in power which produced widespread terror.

re-im-burse (rē´im bers´) *v.* To repay; to make restitution. **reimbursement** *n.*

rein (rān) *n.* One of a pair of narrow, leather straps attached to the bit of a bridle and used to control a horse.

re-in-car-na-tion *n.* The state of rebirth in new forms of life.

rein-deer *n.* A large deer found in northern regions, both sexes having antlers.

re-in-force (rē´in fōrs´) *v.* To support; to strengthen with additional people or equipment. **reinforcement** *n.*

re-in-state (rē´in stāt´) *v.* To restore something to its former position or condition. **reinstatement** *n.*

re-in-te-grate *v.* To reunite with something.

re-in-vent *v.* To remake something that has already been invented.

re-in-vest (rē´in vest´) *v.* To invest money in additional securities.

re-in-vig-o-rate *v.* To restore vigor.

re-is-sue (rē ish´ŏ) *v.* To make available again.

re-it-er-ate *v.* To say or do something over and over again. **reiteration** *n.*

re-ject (ri jekt´) *v.* To refuse; to discard as useless. **reject** *n.* **rejection** *n.*

re-jec-tion *n.* The process in which the body rejects an organ transplant or tissue.

re-joice *v.* To fill with joy; to be filled with joy. **rejoicer** *n.* **rejoicingly** *adv.*

re-joic-ing (ri jois´ing) *n.* An occasion or expression of joy.

re-join *v.* To respond or to answer someone.

re-join-der (ri join´dėr) *n.* The answer to a reply made by someone to another.

re-ju-ve-nate (ri jŏ´ve nāt´) *v.* To restore to youthful appearance or vigor. **rejuvenation** *n.*

re-ju-ve-nes-cence *n.* A renewal of youthfulness. **rejuvensecent** *adj.*

re-kin-dle (rē kin´dl) *v.* To inflame something again. **rekindler** *n.*

re-lapse (ri laps´) *v.* To fall back or revert to an earler condition. **relapser** *n.*

re-late (ri lāt´) *v.* To tell the events of; to narrate; to bring into natural association. **relater** *n.* **relatable** *adj.*

re-lat-ed *adj.* To be in the same family; connected to each other by blood or marriage.

re-la-tion (ri lā´shan) *n.* The relationship between people by marriage or blood lines.

re-la-tion-ship (ri lā´shan ship˝) *n.* A connection by blood or family; kinship; friendship; a natural association.

rel-a-tive (rel´a tiv) *adj.* Relevant; connected; considered in comparison or relationship to other. *n.* A member of one's family. **relatively** *adv.* **relativeness** *n.*

relative humidity *n.* The ratio of the amount of water vapor actually present in the air to the amount possible at the same temperature.

rel-a-tiv-i-ty (rel´a tiv´i tē) *n.* A condition or state of being relative.

re-lax (ri laks´) *v.* To make loose or lax; to relieve something from effort or strain; to become less formal or less reserved. **relaxation** *n.* **relaxedly** *adv.*

re-lax-a-tion (rē˝lak sā´shan) *n.* A period of recreational activity or pastime.

re-laxed *adj.* Being at rest or ease. **relaxedly** *adv.* **relaxedness** *n.*

re-lay (rē´lā) *n.* A race in which a fresh team replaces another. *v.* To pass from one group to another.

re-lease *v.* To set free from confinement; to unfasten; to free; to relinquish a claim on something. *n.* A release from an obligation. **releaser** *n.*

rel-e-gate (rel´e gāt´) *v.* To banish someone or something. **relegation** *n.*

re-lent (ri lent´) *v.* To soften in temper, attitude, or determination; to slacken. **relentless, relentlessness** *adj.*

rel-e-vant (rel´e vant) *adj.* Related to matters at hand. **relevantly** *adv.*

re-li-a-ble (ri lī´a bl) *adj.* Dependable; capable of being relied upon.

re-li-ance (ri lī´ans) *n.* Confidence and trust; something which is relied upon.

re-li-ant (ri lī´ant) *adj.* State of being confident or having reliance.

re-lic (rel´ik) *n.* Something which is very old; a keepsake; an object whose cultural environment has disappeared.

re-lic-tion *n.* The recession of water from land leaving it permanently uncovered.

re-lief (ri lēf´) *n.* Anything which decreases or lessens anxiety, pain, discomfort, or other unpleasant conditions or feelings.

relief map *n.* A map which outlines the contours of the land.

relief pitcher *n.* In baseball, a pitcher who relieves another pitcher due to ineffectiveness.

re-lieve *v.* To lessen or ease pain, anxiety, embarrassment, or other problems; to release or free from a duty by providing a replacement. **reliever** *n.* **relievable** *adj.*

re-lig-ion *n.* An organized system of beliefs, rites, and celebrations centered on a supernatural being; belief pursued with devotion.

re-li-gi-ose *adj.* Being excessively religious.

re-lin-quish (ri ling´kwish) *v.* To release something or someone; withdraw from; to give up. **relinquishment** *n.*

rel-i-quary (rel´i kwer´ē) *n.* A shrine in

which sacred relics are kept.

re-lish (rel´ish) v. Pleasure; a spicy condiment taken with food to lend it flavor.

re-live(rē liv´) v. To experience something again in the imagination or fantasy.

re-lo-cate v. To move to another area; establish in another place. **relocation** n.

re-luct (ri lukt´) v. To revolt; to feel opposition.

re-luc-tance n. An unwillingness; opposition by a magnetic substance to magnetic flux.

re-luc-tant (ri lik´tant) adj. Unwilling, not yielding. **reluctation** n.

re-lume (ri lōm´) v. To light again.

re-ly (ri lī´) v. To trust or depend; to have confidence in someone.

REM abbr. Rapid eye movement.

re-main (ri mān´) v. To continue without change; to stay after the departure of others.

re-main-der (ri mān dėr) n. Something left over. Math The difference which remains after division or subtraction.

re-mains (ri mān´z) n. What is left after all other parts have been taken away; corpse.

re-make v. To revise an old movie, etc.

re-mand (ri mand´) v. To order back; to send to another court or agency for further action; to return to custody pending trial.

re-man-u-fac-ture v. To make into a new product. **remanufacturer** n.

re-mark (ri märk´) n. A brief expression or comment; to take notice; to observe; to comment.

re-mark-a-ble adj. Extraordinary.

re-match (rē´mach) n. A second contest between the same contestants or teams.

rem-e-di-a-ble (ri mē´dē a bl) adj. Being able to be remedied.

re-me-di-al (ri mē´dē al) adj. Concerned with the correction of study habits.

rem-e-dy (rem´i dē) n. pl. -ies A therapy or medicine which relieves pain; something which corrects an error or fault. v. To cure or relieve a disease; to rectify.

re-mem-ber v. To bring back or recall to the mind; to retain in the mind carefully; to keep a person in one's thoughts; to recall a person to another as a means of greetings.

rememberability, rememberer n. **rememberable** adj.

re-mem-brance n. Something which is remembered by someone.

re-mex (rē´meks) n. A quill feather in the wing of a bird. **remigial** adj.

re-mil-i-ta-rize v. To equip again with military installations.

re-mind (ri mīnd´) v. To cause or help to remember. **reminder** n.

rem-i-nisce (rem´i nis´) v. To recall the past things which have happened.

rem-i-nis-cence n. The practice or process of recalling the past. **reminiscent** adj.

re-mint v. To make old coins into a new coins by melting down the old coins.

re-mise (ri mīz´) v. To release a claim to.

re-miss adj. Lax in performing one's duties; negligent. **remissness** n.

re-mis-sion n. A forgiveness; act of remitting; a temporary state of a disease when it doesn't progress; forgiveness.

re-mit (ri mit´) v. To send money as payment for goods; to forgive, as a crime or sin; to slacken, make less violent, or less intense. **remittance, remitter** n.

re-mit-tance (ri mit´ans) n. A sum of money sent to reduce a debt.

re-mit-tent adj. Marked by periods of abatement and increase of symptoms.

rem-nant (rem´nant) n. A small piece or a scrap of something; an unsold end of a material.

re-mod-el v. To reconstruct something making it like new; to alter the structure of a building or house.

re-mon-e-tize (rē mon´i tīz´) v. To restore to use as legal tender. **remonetization** n.

re-mon-strance n. Statement of reasons against an idea or something.

re-mon-strate v. Giving strong reasons against an act or an idea. **remonstrative** adj. **remonstration** n.

rem-o-ra (rem´ėr a) n. Any of several fishes that have anterior dorsal fin converted into a disk on the head thereby allowing them to cling to other fishes or ships.

re-morse (ri mors´) n. Deep moral regret

for past misdeeds. **remorseful** *adj.* **remorsefully** *adv.* **remorsefulness** *n.*

re-mote *adj.* Distant in time, space, or relation. **remotely** *adv.* **remoteness** *n.*

re-mount (rē mount´) *v.* To mount something again.

re-mov-a-ble (ri mŏ´va bl) adj. Being able to be removed. **removeableness** *n.*

re-mov-al *n.* The change of a site or place; the act of removing from a post.

re-move (ri mŏv´) *v.* To get rid of; to extract; to dismiss from office; to change one's business or residence. *n.* An act of moving. **removable** *adj.* **removal** *n.*

re-moved *adj.* State of being separate from others.

re-mu-da (ri mŏ´da) *n.* A herd of horses from which they chose the horses to be used for the day.

re-mu-ner-ate (ri mū´ne rāt´) *v.* Pay an equivalent for a service; to reward. **remunerator, remuneration** *n.*

ren-ais-sance *n.* A revival or rebirth; the humanistic revival of classical art, literature, and learning in Europe which occurred during the 14th through the 16th centuries.

re-nal *adj.* Of or relating to the kidneys.

re-nas-cence (ri nas´ens) *n.* A revival or a rebirth.

re-na-ture *v.* To restore to an original condition.

ren-con-tre (ren kon´tèr) *n.* A hostile contest between forces or individuals.

ren-coun-ter (ren koun´tèr) *v.* A casual meeting; a duel; a debate.

rend (rend) *v.* To remove from with violence; to split. **renderable** *adj.*

ren-der *v.* To give or make something available; to submit or give; to represent artistically; to liquify or melt fat by means of heat. **rendering** *n.* **renderable** *adj.*

ren-dez-vous *n.* A meeting place that has been prearranged; an appointment made between two or more people. *v.* To meet at a particular time and place.

ren-di-tion (ren dish´an) n. An interpretation or a translation.

ren-dzi-na *n.* A grayish brown intrazonal soil developed in grassy regions of high humidity; a rich limy soil.

ren-e-gade (ren´e gād´) n. A person who rejects one allegiance for another; an outlaw; a traitor. **renegade** *adj.*

re-nege (ri nig´) *v.* To fail to keep one's word. **reneger** *n.*

re-new (ri nŏ´) *v.* To make new or nearly new by restoring; to resume.

re-ni-tent (ri nīt´ent) *adj.* Resisting pressure; opposed.

ren-net (ren´it) *n.* An extract taken from a calf's stomach and used to curdle milk for making cheese.

ren-nin (ren´in) *n.* An enzyme that coagulates milk used in making cheese.

re-nom-i-nate (rē nom´i nāt´) *v.* To nominate for a succeeding term.

re-nounce (ri nouns´) *v.* To reject something. **renouncement** *n.*

ren-o-vate (ren´o vāt´) *v.* To return or to restore to a good condition; to make new. **renovation, renovator** *n.*

re-nown (ri noun´) *n.* The quality of being widely honored. **renowned** *adj.*

rent (rent) *n.* The payment made for the use of another's property. *v.* To obtain occupancy in exchange for payment. **rental** *n.* **rentable** *adj.*

rent control *n.* A government regulation of the amount charged for housing.

rent-er *n.* The leasee of a property.

rent strike *n.* The refusal of tenants to pay rent in protest of an increase in price.

re-nun-ci-a-tion (ri nun´sē ā´shan) *n.* Renouncing. **renunciative** *adj.*

re-o-pen (rē ō´pen) v. To resume again, as a discus-sion or session.

re-or-der (rē or´dèr) *n.* An order for more of the same kind as previously ordered.

re-or-gan-i-za-tion (rē´or ga nizā´shan) *n.* The process of reorganizing something.

rep (rep) *n.*, *Slang* Representative. *v.* To represent.

re-pack-age *v.* To wrap into a more efficient and attractive form.

re-pair (ri pâr´) *v.* To restore to good or usable condition; to renew; refresh. **re-**

pairable *adj.*

re-pair-man *n.* The person who makes repairs of things that are broken; a person who makes his living repairing things.

re-pand (ri pand´) *adj.* Having a slightly wavy margin.

rep-a-ra-ble *adj.* Being able to be corrected.

rep-a-ra-tion (rep˝a rā´shan) n. The act of repairing something.

re-par-a-tive (ri par´a tiv) *adj.* Able to make amends.

rep-ar-tee *n.* A quick, witty response or reply; an interchange of clever retorts.

re-pass (rē pas´) *v.* To pass through again.

re-past (ri past´) *n.* Something taken as food; food which comprises a meal.

re-pa-tri-ate (rē pātrē āt´) *v.* To go back to one's own country; to return to the country of one's origin. **repatriation** *n.*

re-pay (ri pā) *v.* To pay back money; to recompensate; to do something in return.

re-peal (ri pel´) *v.* To withdraw officially; to rescind; to revoke. **repealable** *adj.* **repeal** *n.* **repealer** *n.*

re-peat (ri pēt´) *v.* To utter something again; to do an action again.

re-peat-ed *adj.* Recurring again and again.

re-peat-er (ri pē´tèr) *n.* Something or person which repeats.

re-pel (ri pel´) *v.* To discourage; to force away; to create aversion.

re-pel-lent (ri pel´ent) adj. Able to repel; tending to drive away or ward off.

re-pent (ri pent´) *v.* To feel regret for something which has occurred; to change one's sinful way. **repentance** *n.* **repentant** *adj.* **repenter** *n.*

re-per-cus-sion (rē˝pèr kush´an) n. An unforeseen effect produced by an action.

rep-er-toire (rep´èr twär˝) *n.* The accomplishments or skills of a person.

rep-er-to-ry *n.* A collection of things.

rep-e-tend *n.* A repeated sound or refrain.

rep-e-ti-tion (rep´i tish´an) *n.* The act of doing something over and over again; the act of repeating.

re-pine *v.* To feel discontent; to complain.

re-place *v.* To return something to its previ-

ous place. **replaceable** *adj.* **replacement** *n.* **replacer** *n.*

re-plant *v.* To provide with new plants; to move plants to a new location.

re-play *v.* To play something again.

re-plen-ish (ri plen´ish) *v.* To add to something to replace what has gone or been used. **replenisher** *n.* **replenishment** *n.*

re-plete (ri plēt´) *adj.* Having plenty; abounding; full. **repleteness** *n.*

re-ple-tion (ri plē´shan) n. An act of eating too much food.

rep-li-ca (rep´li ka) *n.* A reproduction or copy of something. **replicate** *v.*

re-ply (ri plī´) *v.* To give an answer to either verbally or in writing. **reply** *n.*

re-port (ri pōrt´) *n.* A detailed account; usually in a formal way. *v.* To tell about; to make oneself available; to give details of. **reportable** *adj.* **reporter** *n.*

re-port-age (ri pōr tij) *n.* The process of reporting something.

report card *n.* The report of the student's progress in school submitted to the parents for review.

re-port-ed-ly (ri pōr´tid lē) *adv.* To be according to a report.

re-pos-al (ri pō´zal) *n.* An act or action of reposing.

re-pose (ri pōz´) *n.* The act of being at rest. *v.* To lie at rest. **reposeful** *adj.*

re-pos-it (ri poz´it) *v.* To put something back into place.

re-po-si-tion (rē´po zish´an) n. The state of something being repositioned.

re-pos-i-tor-y *n.* The location where things may be placed for preservation; a side altar in a Catholic church.

re-pos-sess (rē´po zes´) *v.* To restore ownership of something.

re-pow-er *v.* To return power anew to something or someone.

rep-re-hend (rep´ri hend´) *v.* To show or express disapproval of. **reprehension** *n.* **reprehensible** *adj.*

rep-re-hen-sive (rep˝ri hen ziv) *adj.* To be conveying reproof.

rep-re-sent *v.* To stand for something; to

serve as the official representative for.

re-pre-sent-a-tion *n.* The act of representing. **representational** *adj.*

rep-re-sent-a-tive *n.* A person or thing serving as an example or type. *adj.* Of or relating to government by representation; typical. **representatively** *adv.*

re-press (ri pres´) *v.* To restrain; hold back; to remove from the conscious mind. **repressive** *adj.* **repressibility** *n.* **repression** *n.* **re-pressiveness** *n.* **repressively** *adv.*

re-press-ed *adj.* To be marked by repression.

re-pres-sor *n.* Someone or something that will repress.

re-priev e (ri prēv´) *v.* To postpone punishment; to provide temporary relief; a temporary suspension of an execution. **reprieveable** *adj.* To postpone punishment; to provide temporary relief; a temporary suspension of an execution. **reprieve** *n.* **reprieving** *v.*

rep-ri-mand (rep´ri mand) *v.* To censure severely; rebuke. **repripand** *n.*

re-print (rē print´) *n.* An additional printing of a book exactly as the previous one. **reprint** *v.* **reprinter** *n.*

re-pri-sal *n.* Retaliation with intent to inflict injury in return for injury received; a sum of money paid in restitution.

re-prise (ri prīz´) *v.* To take back by force.

re-proach (ri prōch´) *v.* To blame; to rebuke. **reproachful** *adj.*

rep-ro-bate (rep´ro bāt´) *adj.* The state of being morally depraved. *v.* To condemn as unacceptable or evil.

re-pro-cess *v.* To treat in a special way in preparation for reuse.

re-pro-duce (rē´pro dŏs´) *v.* To produce an image or copy. *Biol.* To produce an offspring; to recreate or produce again. **reproducer** *n.* **reproducible** *adj.* **reproduction** *n.* **reproductive** *adj.*

re-pro-gram *v.* To rewrite an existing program for a computer.

re-proof (ri prŏf´) *n.* A censure.

re-prove (ri prŏv´) *v.* To tell or express a disapproval of something.

rep-tile *n.* A cold-blooded, egg-laying verte-brate, as a snake, lizard, or turtle. **reptilian** *n., adj.*

re-pub-lic (ri pub´lik) *n.* A political unit or state where representatives are elected to exercise the power.

re-pub-li-can (ri pub´li kan) *adj.* Having the character of a republic; one of two political parties of the United States.

re-pub-li-can-ism (ri pub´li ka niz˝um) *n.* The Republican principles.

Republican Party *n.* One of the two political parties in the United States.

re-pu-di-ate (ri pū´dē āt´) *v.* To cast away; to refuse to pay something.

re-pugn (ri pūn´) *v.* To offer resistance.

re-pug-nance (ri pug´nans) *n.* The state or condition of being opposed.

re-pug-nant (ri pug´nant) *adj.* Distasteful; repulsive; offensive.

re-pulse (ri puls´) *v.* To repel or drive back; to repel or reject rudely; to disgust or be disgusted. **repulsion** *n.*

re-pul-sive (ri pul´siv) *adj.* State of causing aversion. **repulsively** *adj.*

rep-u-ta-ble (rep´ū ta bl) *adj.* Considered to be honor-able; held in high esteem. **reputably** *adv.* **reputability** *n.*

rep-u-ta-tion *n.* The commonly held evaluation of a person's character.

rep-ute (ri pūt´) *v.* To account or to consider something. **reputedly** *adj.*

re-quest *v.* To ask for something.

re-qui-em (rek´wē em) *n.* The Roman Catholic mass for a deceased person.

re-quire (ri kwī´ėr) *v.* To demand or insist upon. **requirement** *n.*

req-ui-site (rek´wi zit) *adj.* Absolutely needed; necessary.

req-ui-si-tion (rek˝wi zish´an) *n.* A request; a demand by one government to another for release of prisoners.

re-quit-al *n.* The act of requiting something.

re-quite (ri kwīt´) *v.* To reward; to repay someone. **requiter** *n.*

rere-dos (rēr´dos) *n.* An ornamental screen or partition wall behind an altar.

re-run (rē run) *n.* A television show which is shown again.

re-sale (rē′sā) *n*. The act of selling something again. **resalable** *adj*.

re-scind (ri sind′) *v*. To repeal; to void. **rescinder** *n*. **rescindment** *n*.

res-cue (res′kū) *v*. To free from danger. *n*. An act of deliverance. **rescuer** *n*.

re-search *n*. A scientific or scholarly investigation. *v*. To carefully seek out.

re-sec-tion (ri sek′shan) *n*. The surgical removal of a action of an organ.

re-se-da (ri sē′da) *n*. An herb of the mignonette family with greyish-green leaves.

re-sem-ble (ri zem′bl) *v*. To have similarity to something. **resemblance** *n*.

re-send *v*. To send back.

re-sent (ri zent′) *v*. To feel angry about. **resentful** *adj*. **resentment** *n*.

res-er-va-tion (rez″ẽr vā′shan) *n*. The act of keeping something back.

re-serve (ri zerv′) *v*. To save for a special reason; to set apart; to retain; to put off. *n*. Something that is saved for a future point in time; the portion of a country's fighting force kept inactive until called upon.

re-serve-clause *n*. A clause in an athlete's contract which gives the club the exclusive rights of the athletes services until he is traded or released.

res-er-voir (rez′ẽr vwär′) *n*. A body of water stored for the future; large reserve; a supply.

re-shape (rē shāp′) *v*. To give new form to.

re-side (ri zīd′) *v*. To dwell permanently; to exist as a quality or attribute; live in or at. **residence** *n*.

res-i-den-cy (rez′i den sē) *n*. A period of training in a medical field.

res-i-due (rez′i dö′) *n*. Matter remaining after treatment or removal of a part; something which remains.

re-sign *v*. To give up; to submit to something as being unavoidable; to quit.

res-ig-na-tion *n*. A formal notification stating the resignation of one's job, etc.

re-sil-ience (ri zil′yens) *n*. The ability to recover from a shock without permanent aftereffects.

res-in *n*. A plant substance from certain plants and trees used in varnishes and lacquers. **resinous** *n*.

re-sist (ri zist′) *v*. To work against or actively oppose; to withstand. **resistible** *adj*.

re-sist-er *n*. A person who is opposed to the policies of the government.

re-sis-tor (ri zis′tẽr) *n*. An electrical device used in an electric circuit for protection or current control.

res-ju-di-ca-ta *n*. A matter decided on its merits by a court and not subject to litigation again between the same parties.

res-o-lute (rez′o löt′) *adj*. Coming from or characterized by determination. **resolutely resolution** *n*.

re-solve (ri zolv′) *v*. To make a firm decision on something; to find a solution. **resolvable** *adj*. **resolver, resolution** *n*.

res-o-nance *n*. The increase of sound by the vibration of other bodies.

res-o-na-tor (rez′o nā′tẽr) *n*. A device for increasing sounds of a musical instrument.

re-sort (ri zort′) *v*. To go frequently or customarily. *n*. A place, or recreation, for rest and for a vacation.

re-sound (ri zound′) *v*. To be filled with echoing sounds; to reverberate; to ring or sound loudly. **resounding** *adj*. **resoundingly** *adv*.

re-source (rē′sōrs) *n*. A source of aid or support which can be drawn upon if needed. **resources** *n*. One's available capital or assets. **resourceful** *adj*.

re-spect (ri spekt′) *v*. To show consideration or esteem for; to relate to. *n*. Courtesy or considerate treatment. **respectfully** *adv*. **respectful** *adj*. **respectability** *n*.

res-pi-ra-tion *n*. The process or act of inhaling and exhaling; the act of breathing; the process in which an animal or person takes in oxygen from the air and releases carbon dioxide. **respirator** *n*. **respirational, respiratory** *adj*.

re-spire (ri spīẽr′) *v*. To inhale and exhale air; take in oxygen.

res-pi-rom-e-ter *n*. An instrument for studying the extent and character of respiration.

res-pite (res´pit) *n.* A temporary postponement.

re-splen-dent (ri splen´dent) *adj.* Having a shining appearance. **resplendently** *adj.*

re-spond (ri spond´) *v.* To answer or reply; to act when prompted by something or someone.

re-sponse (ri spons´) *n.* A reply; the act of replying. **responsive** *adj.*

re-spon-si-ble *adj.* Trustworthy; in charge; having authority; being answerable for one's actions or the actions of others. **responsibility** *n.* **responsibly** *adv.*

re-spon-sum *n.* A formal opinion from a rabbinic authority to a submitted question or problem.

rest (rest) *n.* A cessation of all work, activity, or motion. *Mus.* An interval of silence equal in time to a note of same value. *v.* To stop work; to place or lay. **restful** *adj.* **rester** *n.* **restfully** *adv.*

res-tau-rant (res´tèr ant) *n.* A place which serves meals to the public.

res-tau-ran-teur (res˝tèr a tür´) *n.* The owner of a restaurant.

rest home *n.* An establishment for the aged or the convalescent.

res-ti-tu-tion (res´ti tö´shan) *n.* The act of restoring something to its rightful owner; compensation for injury, loss, or damage.

res-tive (res´tiv) *adj.* Nervous or impatient because of adelay; resisting control. **restively** *adv.* **restiveness** *n.*

re-store (ri stôr´) *v.* To bring back to a former condition or original state; to make restitution of. **restoration** *n.*

re-strain (ri strän´) *v.* To hold back or be held back; to control, limit, or restrict. **restrainer** *n.* **restraint** *n.*

restraining order *n.* A legal document issued to keep a situation unchanged.

re-strict (ri strikt´) *v.* To confine within limits. **restriction** *n.* **restrictive** *adj.* **restrictively** *adv.*

re-sult (ri zult´) *v.* To happen or exist in a particular way. *n.* The consequence of an action, course, or operation.

re-sume (rizöm´) *v.* To start again after an interruption. **resumption** *n.*

res-u-me (rez´e mä´) *n.* A summary of one's personal history, background, work, and education.

re-su-pi-nate (ri sö´pi nät´) *adj.* To bend backward to an inverted position.

res-ur-rec-tion *n.* The act of Christ rising from the dead.

re-sus-ci-ate (ri sus´i tät) *v.* To return to life; to revive; give mouth-to-mouth breathing technique to help a person to start breathing again. **resuscitation, resuscitator** *n.*

re-tail *n.* The sale of goods or commodities to the public. *v.* To sell to the consumer. **retail** *adj.* **retailer** *n.*

re-tain (ri tän´) *v.* To hold in one's possession; to remember; to employ someone, as for his services.

re-tain-er *n.* A person or thing that retains; a fee paid for one's services.

re-tal-i-ate (ri tal´ē ät´) *v.* To seek revenge against someone. **retaliation** *n.*

re-tard (ri tärd´) *v.* To delay or slow the progress of. **retardant** *n. & adj.*

re-tar-da-tion *n.* A condition in which mental development is slow or delayed; a condition of mental slowness.

re-ten-tion (ri ten´shan) *n.* The act or condition of being retained.

re-ten-tive *adj.* Having the capacity of retaining knowledge with ease.

ret-i-cent (ret´i sent) *adj.* Being uncommunicative in speech; reserved.

re-tic-u-late (ri tik´ya lit) *v.* To divide or construct as to form a network.

ret-i-na (ret´i na) *n. pl.* **-nas, nae** The light sensitive membrane lining the inner eyeball connected by the optic nerve to the brain. **retinal** *adj.*

re-tire (ri tïèr´) *v.* To depart for rest; to remove oneself from the daily routine of working. *Baseball* To put a batter out. **retirement, retiree** *n.*

re-tired (ri tïèd´) *adj.* No longer working at one's profession.

re-tir-ing *adj.* Being shy or withdrawn.

re-tort (ri tort´) *n.* A witty or cutting reply to another person.

re-touch (rē tuch´) *v.* To alter a negative to produce a more desirable picture.

re-trace (ri trās´) *v.* To go back over.

re-tract (ri trakt´) *v.* To draw back or to take back something that has been said. **re-tractable** *adj.* **retraction** *n.*

re-tral *adj.* Toward the back.

re-tread (rē tred´) *v.* To replace the tread of a worn tire. **retread** *n.*

re-treat *n.* The act of withdrawing from danger; a time of study, prayer, and meditation in a quiet, isolated location.

ret-ri-bu-tion (re´tri bū´shan) *n.* An act of getting revenge against another person. **retributively** *adv.* **retributive** *adj.*

re-trieve (ri trēv´) *v.* To regain; to find something and carry it back. **retrievable** *adj.* **retrieval** *n.*

ret-ro-ac-tive *adj.* Taking effect on a date prior to enactment; extending to a prior time. **retroactively** *adv.*

ret-ro-grade (re´tro grād´) *adj.* Moving backward; contrary to normal order.

ret-ro-gres-sion *n.* A reversal in development from a higher to a lower state.

ret-ro-pack *n.* A system of rockets on a spacecraft which produce thrust used to reduce speed.

ret-ro-re-flec-tor *n.* A device that reflects radiation.

ret-ro-rock-et *n.* A rocket on an airplane or spacecraft which produces thrust in the opposite direction to the motion of the craft for deceleration.

ret-ro-spect (re´tro spekt´) *n.* A review of things in the past. **retrospectively** *adv.* **retrospective** *adj.*

re-turn *v.* To come back to an earlier condition; to reciprocate. *n.* The act of sending, bringing, or coming back. **returns** *n.* A yield or profit from investments; a report on the results of an election. **returnable** *adj.* **return-ee, returner** *n.*

re-un-ion (rē ūn´yan) *n.* A reuniting; the coming together of a group which has been separated for a period of time.

re-us-able (rē ū´za bl) *adj.* Capable of using something over and over again.

re-val-u-ate (rē val´ū āt´) *v.* To increase the value of something.

re-val-ue (rē val´ū) *v.* To reappraise something as jewelry.

re-vamp (rē vamp´) *v.* Patch or reconstruct some thing again.

re-veal (ri vēl´) *v.* To disclose or make known; to expose or bring into view.

rev-eil-le (rev´e lē) *n.* The sounding of a bugle used to awaken soldiers in the morning.

rev-el (rev´el) *v.* To take great delight in. **reveler** *n.*

rev-e-la-tion (rev´e lā´shan) *n.* An act of or something revealed; a manifestation of divine truth. **Revelation** The last book in the New Testament.

re-venge (ri venj´) *v.* To impose injury in return for injury received. **revengeful** *adj.* **revenger** *n.*

rev-e-nue (rev´en ū´) *n.* Income returned by an investment.

revenue stamp *n.* A stamp which serves as evidence of payment of a tax.

re-verb *n.* An echo effect produced electronically in recorded music.

re-vere (ri vēr´) *v.* To honor and respect.

re-ver-sal (ri ver´sal) *n.* An act of overthrowing a legal proceeding or judgment.

re-verse (ri vers´) *adj.* Turned backward in position. *n.* The opposite of something; a change in fortune usually from better to worse; change or turn to the opposite direction; to transpose or exchange the positions of. *Law* To revoke a decision. **reverser** *n.*

re-vert (ri vert´) *v.* To return to a former practice or belief. **reversion** *n.*

re-view (ri vū´) *v.* To study or look over something again; to give a report on. *n.* A reexamination; a study which gives a critical estimate of something.

re-vile (ri vīl´) *v.* To use verbal abuse.

re-vise (ri vīz´) *v.* To look over something again with the intention of improving or correcting it. **reviser, revision** *n.*

re-vi-tal-ize (rē vīt´a līz´) v. To give new life or energy to. **revitalization** n.

re-viv-al (ri vī´val) n. The act or condition of reviving; the return of a film or play which was formerly presented; a meeting whose purpose is religious reawakening.

re-vive (ri vīv´) v. To restore, refresh, or recall; to return to consciousness or life. **revivable** adj. **reviver** n.

re-voke (ri vōk´) v. To nullify or make void by recalling. **revocation** n.

re-volt (ri vōlt´) n. To try to overthrow authority; to fill with disgust.

rev-o-lu-tion (rev´o lō´shan) n. The act or state of orbital motion around a point; the abrupt overthrow of a government; a sudden change in a system.

re-volve (ri volv´) v. To move around a central point; to spin; to rotate.

re-volv-ing charge ac-count (ri vol´ving) n. A charge account in which payment is made in monthly installments.

re-vue (ri vū´) n. A musical show consisting of songs, dances, skits, and other similar entertainment.

re-ward (ri word´) n. Something given for a special service. v. To give a reward.

R.F.D. abbr. Rural Free Delivery.

rhab-do-man-cy (rab´do man´sē) n. The discovery of things that are concealed in the ground by the use of a divining rod.

rham-na-ceous (ram nā´shus) adj. To be pertaining to or belonging to the buckthorn family of plants.

rhap-sod-ic (rap sod´ik) adj. To have the characteristics of a rhapsody.

rhap-so-dist (rap´so dist) n. A person who speaks in a rhapsodical way or manner.

rhap-so-dize (rap´so dīz´) v. To recite rhapsodies.

rhap-so-dy (rap´so dē) n. pl. -ies An excessive display of enthusiasm.

rhat-a-ny (rat´a nē) n. A type of South American shrub whose roots are used as an astringent.

rhea (rē´a) n. A large flightless South American bird that resembles the African ostrich but is smaller and has three toes.

rhe-ni-um (rē´nē um) n. A metallic element symbolized by Re.

rhe-ol-o-gy (rē ol´o jē) n. The study of the behavior of a liquid matter.

rhe-om-e-ter (rē om´i tėr) n. A type of device that is used for measuring the flow of liquids.

rhe-sus (rē´sus) n. A light-brown monkey that is used for laboratory tests.

rhe-tor (rē´tėr) n. One who is an orator.

rhet-o-ric (ret´ėr ik) n. Effective expression in writing or speech; language which is not sincere.

rhe-tor-i-cal (ri tor´i kal) adj. To be involving rhetoric. **rhetoricalness** n.

rhetorical question n. A kind of question that is used for an effect and no answer is expected.

rhet-o-ri-cian (ret´o rish´an) n. A person who writes elaborate prose.

rheum (rōm) n. A fluid that is discharged from the mucus glands of the body.

rheumatic fever n. A severe infectious disease that is characterized by the swelling of the heart lining and the heart valves.

rheu-ma-tism (rō´ma tiz´um) n. A kind of inflammation that affects the joints and muscles of the body and can be very painful.

Rh fac-tor n. A substance found in the red blood cells of 85% of all humans; the presence of this factor is referred to as RH positive; the absence as RH negative.

rhi-nal (rīn´al) adj. To be referring to the nose.

rhi-ni-tis (rī nī´tis) n. An inflammation that occurs in the nose or the membranes of the nose.

rhi-noc-er-os (rī nos´ėr os) n. A very large mammal with one or two upright horns on the snout.

rhi-noc-er-os bee-tle n. A beetle, large in size, that has a projecting horn on the top of its head.

rhi-zan-thous (rī zan´thus) adj. To be

bearing very short-stemmed flowers.

rhi-zo-bi-um (rī zō´bē *um***)** *n.* A type of bacteria that is important in maintaining the soil's fertility.

rhi-zo-ceph-a-lan (rī´zō sef´*a* **l***a***n)** *n.* A kind of crustacean that lives off a host and causes the host to lose its ability to reproduce.

rhi-zoid (rī´zoid) *n.* The hair-like structure that provides a root for ferns and mosses.

rhi-zome (rī´zōm) *n.* A subterranean plant stem thickened by deposits of reserve food material which produces shoots above and roots below.

rhi-zo-mor-phous (rī´zō mor´fus) *adj.* To be shaped like a root.

rhi-zo-pus (rī´zō p*u***s)** *n.* A type of mold fungus.

rho-da-mine (rō´d*a* **mēn´)** *n.* A red dye.

Rhode Island *n.* A state located in the northeastern part of the United States; statehood May 29, 1790; state capital Providence.

Rhode Island bent *n.* A kind of European grass that is used as a lawn grass.

Rhode Island Red *n.* An American breed of domestic fowl with rich brownish red plumage.

Rhode Island White *n.* A domestic chicken that has white feathers and is like the Rhode Island Red.

rho-di-um (rō´dē um) *n.* A metallic element symbolized by Rh.

rho-do-chro-site (rō´d*o* **krō´sīt)** *n.* A kind of mineral that is made of manganese carbonate and is pink in color.

rho-do-den-dron (rō´d*o* **den´dr***o***n)** *n.* A variety of cultivated shrubs and trees with showy flowers and evergreen leaves.

rho-do-lite (rōd´*o* **līt´)** *n.* A type of garnet that is rose-red in color.

rho-do-ra (rō dōr´*a***)** *n.* A shrub found in Canada and New England having delicate pink flowers produced before the leaves in spring.

rhom-boid (rom´boid) *n.* A parallelogram where the angles are oblique and adjacent sides are unequal. **rhombic** *adj.*

rhom-bus (rom´b*u***s)** *n.* A four sided figure whose sides are equal in length.

rhon-chus (rong´k*u***s)** *n.* A type of rale that occurs in the bronchial tubes of the airway.

rhu-barb (rō´bärb) *n.* A garden plant with large leaves and edible stalks used for pies.

rhyme (rīm) *n.* A word having a sound similar to another. **rhymer** *n.*

rhy-thm (rith´*u***m)** *n.* Music, speech, or movements which are characterized by equal or regularly alternating beats. **rhythmic, rhythmical** *adv.*

rhyth-mics (rith´miks) *n.* The science of rhythms.

RI *abbr.* Rhode Island.

ri-al-to (rē al´tō) *n.* The theatre district.

ri-ant (rī´*a***nt)** *adj.* To be smiling; happy.

rib (rib) *n.* One of a series of curved bones enclosed in the chest of man and animals. *Slang* To tease. **ribber** *n.*

rib-ald (rib´*a***ld)** *adj.* To be using indecent humor.

rib-band (rib´band´) *n.* A narrow strip used in ship building to hold frames in position during construction.

rib-bon (rib´*o***n)** *n.* A narrow band or strip of fabric, such as satin, used for trimming.

rib-bon fish (rib´*o***n fish´)** *n.* A kind of marine fish that has a long and flat body.

ri-bo-fla-vin (rī´bō flā´vin) *n.* A B complex vitamin that is found in milk, leafy vegetables, and liver.

rib-wort (rib´wûrt´) *n.* A type of weed having a flower head and three-ribbed leaves.

rice (rīs) *n.* A cereal grass grown extensively in warm climates.

rice-bird (rīs´bûrd´) *n.* A type of small bird that can be found in rice field in the southern United States.

rice pa-per *n.* A paper made from rice paper tree pith.

rice pa-per tree (rīs´pā´pėrtrē´) *n.* The tree that is grown in China to make ricepaper.

ric-er (rī´sėr) *n.* A kitchen utensil thru which soft foods are pressed in order to produce strings about the diameter of rice grain.

rich (rich) *adj.* Having great wealth; of great value; satisfying and pleasing in voice, color, tone, or other qualities; extremely productive; as soil or land.

rich-es (rich´iz) *n.* One's wealth.

rich-ly (rich´lē) *adv.* To be done in a rich manner or way.

Richter scale *n.* An instrument which measures a seismic disturbance such as an earthquake with 1.5 being the smallest and 8.5 being a very devastating earthquake.

ri-cin (rī´sin) *n.* A white powder that is poisonous and is used to cause the agglutination of the red corpuscles.

rick-ets (rik´its) *n.* A childhood disease which is caused by lack of inadequate sunlight or vitamin D resulting in severely deformed bones.

rick-ett-si-a (ri ket´sē a) *adj.* A microorganism that is passed from arthropods to humans.

rick-et-y (rik´i tē) *adj.* To be ready to fall apart or fall down. **ricketiness** *n.*

rick-rack (rik´rak´) *n.* A zigzag braid used in trimming.

rick-sha (rik´sho´) *n.* A small 2-wheeled vehicle that is pulled by one man and that originated in Japan.

ric-o-chet (rik´o shā´) *n.* A glancing blow off a flat surface.

ri-cot-ta *n.* A white whey cheese of Italy resembling cottage cheese.

ric-tus (rik´tus) *n.* An opening.

rid (rid) *v.* To make free from anything objectionable. **ridable** *adj.*

rid-dance (rid´ans) *n.* The getting rid of something or someone that is unwanted.

rid-dle (rid´l) *v.* To perforate with numerous holes. *n.* A puzzling problem or question which requires a clever solution. **riddled** *v.* **riddling** *v.*

ride (rīd) *v.* To travel in a vehicle or on an animal; to sit on and drive, as a motorcycle. **ride for a fall** To flirt with danger. **ride high** To experience great success. **ride roughshod over** To treat with abuse.

rid-er (rī´dėr) *n.* One who rides as a

passenger; a clause, usually having little relevance, which is added to a document.

ridge (rij) *n.* A long, narrow crest; a horizontal line formed where two sloping surfaces meet. **ridge** *v.*

ridge-pole (rij´pōl´) *n.* Timber located at the top of a roof which is horizontal.

rid-i-cule (rid´i kūl´) *n.* Actions or words intended to make a person or thing the object of mockery. **ridiculer** *n.*

ri-dic-u-lous (ri dik´ū lus) *adj.* To be causing derision or ridicule; to be laughable. **ridiculousness** *n.* **ridiculously** *adv.*

rid-ing (rī´ding) *n.* An action of a person who rides.

riding habit *n.* An outfit that is worn by women while they ride.

rid-ley (rid´lē) *n.* A marine turtle found in the Atlantic Ocean off the coast of the United States.

ri-dot-to *n.* A place of entertainment in masquerade popular in the 18th century England.

rife (rīf) *adj.* State of being abundant or abounding. **rifely** *adv.*

rif-fle (rif´l) *n.* Ripply water which is caused by a ridge.

rif-fler *n.* A small scraping tool.

riff-raff (rif´raf´) *n.* The rabble; low persons in society; a disreputable person.

ri-fle (rī´fl) *n.* A firearm having a grooved bore designed to be fired from the shoulder.

rifle bird *n.* Type of Australian bird that has a velvety-black plumage.

ri-fle-man (rī´fl man) *n.* A person skilled in the shooting of a rifle.

ri-fling (rī´fling) *n.* The act of putting or cutting spiral grooves in the barrel of a gun.

rift (rift) *n.* A fault; disagreement; a lack of harmony; a shallow place in a stream.

rig (rig) *v.* To outfit with necessary equipment. *n.* The arrangement of sails, masts, and other equipment on a ship; the apparatus used for drilling water or oil wells.

rig-a-doon (rig´a dōn´) *n.* A lively dance of the 17th and 18th century.

rig-a-to-ni (rig´a tō´nē) *n.* A curved macaroni with fluted edges.

rig-ger (rig´ẻr) *n.* A long pointed paintbrush; a ship with special rigs.

rig-ging (rig´ing) *n.* The lines used aboard a ship in working sails and supporting masts and spars; ropes, etc. used to support and manipulate scenery in the theatre.

right (rīt) *adj.* In accordance with or conform able to law, justice, or morality; proper and fitting; properly adjusted, disposed, or placed; orderly; sound in body or mind. *n.* The right side, hand, or direction; the direction opposite left. *adv.* Immediately; completely; according to justice, morality, or law.

right angle *n., Geom.* An angle of 90 degrees; an angle with two sides perpendicular to each other.

right a-way *adv.* Immediately, without hesitation.

right-eous (rī´chus) *adj.* Free from guilt; morally right; acting in accordance with moral or divine law. **righteousness** *n.*

right-ful (rīt´ful) *adj.* Having a legal claim.

right-hand-ed (rīt´hand´did) *adj.* Using the right hand more easily than the left; designed to be used with the right. **righthandedness righthandedly** *adv.* **right-handed** *adv.*

right-ly (rīt´lē) *adv.* To be done suitably.

right–of–way *n.* A tract of land used by a public utility company.

right tri-an-gle *n.* A type of triangle where one angle is 90 degrees.

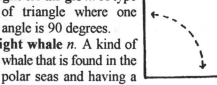

right whale *n.* A kind of whale that is found in the polar seas and having a large head.

right wing *n.* One who is a member of a conservative political party. **rightwinger** *n.* **rightwing** *adj.*

rig-id (rij´id) *adj.* Not bending; inflexible; severe; stern. **rigidity** *n.* **rigidness** *n.*

ri-gid-i-fy (ri jid´i fī´) *v.* To make something rigid. **rigidification** *n.*

rig-ma-role (rig´ma rōl´) *n.* A meanless or complex procedure.

rig-or (rig´ẻr) *n.* The condition of being rigid or stiff; stiffness of temper; harshness. **rigorous , rigorously** *adv.*

rig-or-ism (rig´o riz´um) *n.* A strictness in practice.

rig-or mor-tis (rig´ẻr mor´tis) *n.* The rigidity of muscles occurring after death.

rile (rīl) *v.* To make angry.

rill-et (ril´it) *n.* A small brook.

rim (rim) *n.* The outer edge or border of something; the outer part of a wheel joined to the hub on a car. **rimless** *adj.*

rime (rīm) *n.* An accumulation of granular ice on the windward sides of exposed objects formed from supercooled fog or clouds.

ri-mose (rī´mōs) *adj.* To be filled with fissures. **rimosity** *n.* **rimosely** *adv.*

rim-rock (rim´rok´) *n.* An overlying strata of rock on a plateau that outcrops to form a vertical face.

rind (rīnd) *n.* A tough outer layer which may be taken off or peeled off.

rin-der-pest (rin´dẻr pest´) *n.* A kind of contagious disease that affects the ruminant animals.

ring (ring) *n.* A circular mark, line, or object; a small circular band worn on a finger; a group of persons acting together; especially in an illegal way. *v.* To make a clear resonant sound, as a bell when struck. *n.* The sound made by a bell.

ring-bone (ring´bōn´) *n.* The callus growth that occurs on the pastern bones of a horse.

ring-dove (ring´duv´) *n.* A kind of very large European pigeon.

ring-er (ring´ẻr) *n.* A person who sounds bells by ringing; in the game of horseshoes, a shoe that encircles the peg.

ring finger *n.* The third finger on the left hand usually where the wedding band is worn.

ring-lead-er (ring´lē´dẻr) *n.* The person who is the leader of a group, usually one that will violate the law.

ring-let (ring´lit) *n.* A small curl of hair.

ring-mas-ter (ring´mas´tėr) *n.* The person in charge of performances in the circus.

ring–necked pheasant *n.* A chicken- like bird that has a whitering around its neck and is found in the northern regions of the United States.

ring-side (ring´sīd´) *n.* A section or area that is located right around the ring, such as in a boxing match.

ring-taw *n.* A game where marbles are placed in a circle with the object being for the shooter to knock the marbles out of the ring.

ring-toss (ring´tos´) *n.* A type of game where rings are tossed in an attempt to get them around a small upright pole some distance away.

ring-worm (ring´werm´) *n., Pathol.* A contagious skin disease caused by fungi and marked by discolored, ring-shaped, scaly patches on the skin.

rink (ringk) *n.* A smooth area covered with ice used for hockey or ice-skating; a smooth wooden surface for roller-skating.

rinse (rins) *v.* To wash lightly with water. *n.* The act of rinsing; a hair coloring or conditioning solution. **rinser, rinsed** *v.*

rins-ing (rin´sing) *n.* The action or act of a person who rinses.

ri-ot (ri´ot) *n.* A wild and turbulent public disturbance. *Slang* An irresistibly amusing person. **riotous** *adj.* **rioter** *n.*

rip (rip) *v.* To tear apart violently; to move violently or quickly. *n.* A torn place. **rip-off** To steal.

ri-par-i-an (ri pâr´ē an) *adj.* To be located on the bank by water, such as a lake.

rip cord *n.* A cord which, when pulled, releases a parachute from its pack.

rip cur-rent *n.* A strong surface current flowing outward from shorewhich results from the return flow of waves.

ripe (rīp) *adj.* Fully developed or aged; mature. **ripeness** *n.*

rip-en (rī´pen) *v.* To age; to develop to maturity.

ri-poste (ri pōst´) *n.* A quick return thrust used in fencing; a verbal outbreak.

rip-per (rip´ėr) *n.* A machine used to break up rock, ore, etc.

rip-ping (rip´ing) *adj.* To be pertaining to the tearing of something.

rip-ple (rip´l) *v.* To cause to form small waves on the surface of water; to waver gently. **rippler** *n.*

rip rap (rip´rap´) *n.* A foundation wall of stones thrown together in random fashion.

rip–roar-ing *adj.* To be noisy and loud.

rip saw (rip´so´) *n.* A coarse-toothed saw used to cut wood in the direction of the grain.

rip tide (rip´tīd´) *n.* Water made rough by the meeting of opposite tides and currents.

rise (rīz) *v.* To move from a lower position to a higher one; to extend upward; to meet a challenge or demand. *n.* The act of going up or rising; an elevation in condition or rank.

ris-er (rī´zėr) *n.* A person who rises; the upright part of a stairway.

ris-i-bil-i-ty (riz´i bil´i tē) *n.* The ability to laugh.

ris-i-ble (riz´i bl) *adj.* Being inclined to or causing laughter.

ris-ing (rī´zing) *adj.* To be growing in height; to be more active.

risk (risk) *n.* A chance of suffering or encountering harm or loss; danger; a person who is a hazard to an insurer.

risk-y (ris´kē) *adj.* To be hazardous or full of risk. **riskiness** *n.*

ri-sot-to (ri so´tō) *n.* Rice cooked in meat stock, seasoned with cheese.

rite (rīt) *n.* A formal religious ceremony; any formal custom or practice.

rit-u-al (rich´ō al) *n.* A prescribed method for performing a religious ceremony. *adj.* Pertaining to or practiced as a rite. **ritualism** *n.* **ritually** *adv.*

ritzy (rit´sē) *adj.* To be fashionable; having a high fashion.

ri-val (rī´val) *n.* One who strives to compete with another; one who equals or almost equals another.

ri-val-ry (rī´val rē) *n.* Competition.

rive (rīv) *v.* To tear or to rip. **river** *n.*

riv-er (riv´ėr) *n.* A relatively large natural

stream of water, usually fed by another body of water.

river bed (riv´ĕr bed´) *n.* The channel thru which the river flows.

riv-er-ine (riv´e rīn´) *adj.* To be caused or formed by a river.

riv-er-weed (riv´ĕr wēd´) *n.* A type of submerged freshwater plant.

ri-vet (riv´it) *n.* A metal bolt that is used to secure two or more objects.

riv-u-let (riv´ū lit) *n.* A small stream.

RN *abbr.* Registered Nurse.

RNA *abbr.* Ribonucleic acid.

roach (rōch) *n.* A European freshwater fish; cockroach. *Slang* The butt of a marijuana cigarette.

roach back *n.* A back that is curved.

road (rōd) *n.* A public highway used for vehicles, people, and animals; a path or course; a course toward the achievement of something.

road-a-bil-i-ty (rō´*da* bil´i tē)*n.* In reference to a car, its ability to ride over all types of roads.

road-bed (rōd´bed´)*n.* The surface of which a road is constructed.

road block (rōd´blok´) *n.* An obstruction in a road, which prevents passage.

road hog *n.* A type of driver that drives in the center of the road preventing others from passing.

road-house (rōd´hous´) *n.* An inn outside city limits which serves liquor, meals, etc. and often has gambling.

road met-al *n.* The material, such as stones, that is used for repairing a road.

road racing *n.* A race over public roads instead of a race track.

road-run-ner (rōd´run´ĕr) *n.* A large bird of the cuckoo family that is a speedy runner found in the southwestern part of the United States.

road show *n.* A theatrical show given by a traveling troupe on tour.

road-side (rōd´sīd´) *n.* The side or the edge of a road.

road-stead (rōd´sted´)*n.* The covered place for ships that may anchor off the shore.

road-ster (rōd´stĕr) *n.* The early kind of car that has a single seat for two people and a rumble seat in the rear.

road test *n.* The test for a car to know how it will handle on the road in normal conditions.

road-way (rōd´wā´) *n.* The land the road passes through.

roam (rōm) *v.* To travel aimlessly or without a purpose. **roamer** *n.*

roan (rōn) *n.* The color of a horse; a sheepskin tanned with sumac.

roar (rōr) *v.* To utter a deep prolonged sound of excitement;to laugh loudly; a boisterous outcry. **roar** *n.* **roarer** *n.*

roar-ing (rōr´ing) *n.* A loud sound or cry that is given off by something.

roast (rōst) *v.* To cook meat by using dry heat in an oven. *n.* A cut of meat.

roast-er (rō´stĕr) *n.* A person that roasts.

rob (rob) *v.* To take property unlawfully from another person. **robber** *n.*

rob-a-lo (rob´*a* lō´) *n.* A type of marine fish that is found in the West Indian waters.

ro-band *n.* A piece of woven yarn used to fasten the sail to a spar.

rob-ber (rob´ĕr) *n.* A person who steals from others.

rob-ber fly *n.* A large predatory fly.

rob-ber-y (rob´e rē) *n.* The act of larceny from a person by violence or threat.

robe (rōb) *n.* A long loose garment usually worn over nightclothes; a long flowing garment worn on ceremonial occasions.

rob-in (rob´in) *n.* A large North American bird with a black head and reddish breast.

Robinson Crusoe *n.* A shipwrecked sailor who lived many years on a desert island.

ro-ble (rō´blä) *n.* Type of white oak tree that is found mainly in California.

ro-bot (rō´b*o*t) *n.* A machine capable of performing human duties.

ro-bot bomb *n.* Type of missile with a bomb and is directed to its target with an automatic pilot.

ro-bot ize (rō´bo tīz´) *v.* To make something automatic. **robotization** *n.*

ro-bust (rō bust´) *adj.* Full of strength and health; rich; vigorous. **robustly** *adv.* **robustness** *n.*

ro-bus-tious (rō bus´chus) *adj.* To be sturdy or strong. **robustiousness** *n.*

roc-am-bole (rok´am bōl´) *n.* One type of garlic that is cultivated.

roch-et (roch´it) *n.* A white linen vestment with close-fitting sleeves worn by bishops and prelates.

rock (rok) *n.* A hard naturally formed material. *Slang* One who is dependable.

rock-a-way (rok´a wā´) *n.* A carriage having three or four wheels and a top that stands.

rock bass (rok´ bas´) *n.* The striped bass.

rock-bottom *n.* The lowest part.

rock–bound (rok´bound´) *adj.* To be surrounded by rocks.

rock brake *n.* A kind of fern that will grow in places which are rocky.

rock candy *n.* Candy made from boiling sugar and water and crystallized on string.

rock dove *n.* A type of pigeon that has a fan-shaped tail and is bluish-grey in color.

rock-er (rok´ėr) *n.* A curved piece, usually of wood, on which a cradle or chair rocks.

rocker arm *n.* A pivoted lever to push an engine valve down.

rock-et (rok´it) *n.* A device propelled with the thrust from a gaseous combustion. *v.* To move rapidly.

rock-e-teer (rok´i tēr´) *n.* One who operates rockets.

rocket plane *n.* An airplane propelled by rockets.

rock-et-ry (rok´i trē) *n.* The study of rockets.

rock-fish (rok´fish´) *n.* The striped bass.

rock garden *n.* Type of garden that is grown in or on rocks.

rocking horse *n.* Toy horse that is mounted on rockers and a child can rock back and forth on.

rock-ling (rok´ling) *n.* A little codfish.

rock-oon (rok´ön) *n.* A research rocket carried by a balloon to a high altitude and then fired.

rock–ribbed (rok´ribd´) *adj.* Being firm and unyielding.

rock-rose (rok´rōz´) *n.* Type of flowering shrub.

rock salt *n.* Salt that is artificially prepared in large crystals, sometimes used in the preparation of ice cream made at home.

rock tripe *n.* An edible lichen that can be found on the rocks in the arctic areas.

rock-weed (rok´wēd´) *n.* Type of seaweed that can be found on rocks during the low tide.

rock wool *n.* A mineral wool made by blowing steam through molten rock and used for heat and sound insulation.

rock-y (rok´ē) *adj.* Unsteady or unstable; full of rocks. **rockiness** *n.*

Rocky Mountain spotted fever *n.* A disease contracted from the bite of a wood tick characterized by fever, chills, and pains in muscles and joints.

rod (rod) *n.* A straight stick growing from a tree or bush; a pole with a line attached for fishing. **rodlike** *adj.*

rode *v.* Past tense of ride.

ro-dent (rōd´ent) *n.* A mammal, such as a rat, mouse, or beaver having large incisors used for gnawing.

ro-den-ti-cide (rō den´ti sīd´) *n.* A material that is used to destroy rodents.

ro-de-o (rō´dē ō´) *n.* A public show, contest, or demonstration of ranching skills, as riding and roping.

rod-man (rod´man) *n.* A surveyor's assistant.

rod-o-mon-tade (rō´do mon tād´) *n.* Boasting that is vain.

roe (rō) *n.* The eggs of a female fish.

roent-gen-o-gram (rent´ge no gram´) *n.* Type of photograph which is made with the use of x-rays. **roentgenographic** *adj.*

roent-gen-o-ther-a-py (rent´ge nō ther´ apē) *n.* Kind of medical treatment using x-rays.

rogue (rōg) *n.* A scoundrel or dishonest person; a mischievous or playful person. **roguishness** *n.* **roguishly** *adv.*

rogue elephant *n.* The elephant that has been excluded from the herd.

roil (roil) *v.* To make one angry.

role (rōl) *n.* The position or character that an actor or actress plays.

roll (rōl) *v.* To move in any direction by turning over and over; to sway or rock from side to side, as a ship; to make a deep prolonged sound as thunder. *n.* A list of names. *Slang* A large amount of money.

roll call *n.* The act of calling out the names on a list in order to determine who is present.

roll-er (rō´lėr) *n.* A cylinder for crushing, smoothing or rolling something; any of a number of various cylindrical devices.

rol-lick (rol´ik) *v.* To frolic about.

rolling mill *n.* A type of mill where metal is rolled into sheets.

rolling pin *n.* A long cylinder having two handles and is rolled over dough in order to flatten it out.

roll up *v.* To collect items together.

ro-maine (rō mān´) *n.* Type of lettuce that has narrow leaves.

ro-mance (rō mans´) *n.* A love affair, usually of the young, characterized by ideals of devotion and purity; a fictitious story filled with extravagant adventures. **romance, romancer** *n.*

Roman numeral *n.* The letter or letters of the Roman system of numbering still used in formal contexts, as I=1, V=5, X=10, L=50, C=100, D=500, M=1000.

ro-man-tic (rō man´tik) *adj.* Very amorous; referring to romance.

romp (romp) *v.* To run, play, or frolic in a carefree way.

romp-er (rom´pėr) *n.* A person who romps around.

ron-dure (ron´jėr) *n.* A form that is gracefully curved.

rood (rōd) *n.* A measurement of land which equals 1/4 acre.

roof (rōf) *n.* The top or covering of a house or other building keeping the elements of weather out. **rooflike** *adj.*

roof garden *n.* The garden that can be found on top of a building.

roof-ing (rō´fing) *n.* The supplies and material that are used to cover a roof.

rook (rek) *n.* A kind of European crow.

rook-er-y (rek´e rē) *n.* The location which is used by the rooks for nesting.

rook-ie (rek´ē) *n.* An untrained person; a novice or inexperienced person.

room (rōm) *n.* A section or area of a building set off by partitions or walls. *v.* To occupy or live in a room.

room-er (rō´mėr) *n.* Person who rents a room from someone and pays rent.

room-ful (rōm´fel) *n.* The amount that a room is able to hold.

rooming house *n.* A place or house where the rooms are rented out.

room-mate (rōm´māt´) *n.* A person who will share or live in the same room with another.

room-y (rō´mē) *adj.* To be spacious. **roomily** *adv.*

roost (rōst) *n.* A place or perch on which birds sleep or rest; a piece of meat which has been or is to be roasted.

roost-er (rō´stėr) *n.* The male chicken.

root (rōt) *n.* The part of a plant which grows in the ground. *Math* A number when multiplied by itself, will produce a given quantity. **root** *v.* To search or rummage for something; to turn up the earth with the snout, as a hog.

root-age (rō´tij) *n.* The action of taking root into.

root beer *n.* A non-alcholic beverage flavored with extracts of herbs and roots.

root borer *n.* Type of insect that will tunnel into the roots of plants.

root cellar *n.* A place that is used to store vegetables.

root crop *n.* A crop that is grown for its enlarged roots.

root-ed-ness *n.* The state of having roots.

root-hold *n.* The anchorage of a plant in the soil by the growing and spreading of its roots.

root-less (rŏt´lis) *adj.* Having no roots at all.

root-let (rŏt´lit) *n.* A small root.

root out *v.* To discover something.

root rot *n.* A plant disease which is recognized by the decaying of it's roots.

root-y (rō´tē) *adj.* To have a lot of roots.

rope (rōp) *n.* A heavy cord of twisted fiber. **know the ropes** To be familiar with all of the conditions at hand.

rope-walk (rōp´wok´) *n.* A long building, or a room where ropes are made.

rope yarn *n.* The strands of hemp that makes up a rope.

ro-que-laure *n.* A knee-length coat that was worn in the 18th and 19th centuries.

ror-qual (ror´kwal) *n.* Large whale.

ro-sa-ry (rō´za rē) *n. pl.* **-ies** A string of beads for counting prayers; a series of prayers.

rose (rōz) *n.* A shrub or climbing vine having sharp prickly stems and variously colored fragrant flowers.

ro-se-ate (rō´zē it) *adj.* To be of a deep pink color. **roseately** *adv.*

rose-bay (rōz´bā´) *n.* A flowering shrub.

rose-bud (rōz´bud´) *n.* The state of the rose just before it blooms.

rose–col-ored (rōz´kul´ėrd) *adj.* To be optimistic and bright.

rose fever *n.* The allergy that is associated to rose pollen.

rose-fish (rōz´fish´) *n.* Type of marine fish which is red in color and can be found in the North Atlantic.

ro-se-o-la (rō zē´o la) *n.* A rash that is rose colored and appearing on the skin.

rose slug *n.* A larva of the sawfly that will feed on the leaves of roses.

ro-sette (rō zet´) *n.* An ornament gathered to resemble a rose and made of silk or ribbon.

rose wa-ter *n.* A fragrant product made from rose petals, steeped in water, and used in cosmetics.

rose-wood (rōz´wed´) *n.* A tropical tree found in South America that yields a fine wood for building objects.

Rosh Hashanah (rōsh´ ha shä´na) *n.* The Jewish New Year.

ros-i-ly (rō´zi lē) *adv.* In a cheerful manner; with a rosy color.

ros-in-weed (roz´in wēd´) *n.* A sunflower-like plant that is found in North America.

ros-ter (ros´tėr) *n.* A list of names.

ros-y (rō´zē) *adj.* To be pink, like the color of roses. **rosiness** *n.*

rot (rot) *v.* To break down or decompose.

ro-ta-ry (rō´ta rē) *adj.* Turning or designed to turn; of or relating to axial rotation.

ro-tate (rō´tāt) *v.* To turn on an axis; to alternate something in sequence. **rotation** *n.* **rotator** *n.* **rotatory** *adj.*

ROTC *abbr.* Reserve Officers Training Corps.

rote (rōt) *n.* Repetition of sounds.

ro-te-none (rōt´e nōn´) *n.* Type of compound that is used as an insecticide.

ro-tis-ser-ie (rō tis´e rē) *n.* A rotation device with spits for roasting food.

ro-tor (rō´tėr) *n.* A rotating part of a mechanical device.

rot-ten (rot´en) *adj.* Decomposed; morally corrupt; very bad.

rot-ten-stone (rot´en stōn´) *n.* Type of soft stone that is used for polishing brass.

rot-ter (rot´ėr) *n.* A person who is really bad.

ro-tund (rō tund´) *adj.* Plump; rounded.

ro-tun-da (rō tun´da) *n.* A building that is round having a domed roof.

rouge (rōzh) *n.* A cosmetic coloring for the cheeks.

rough (ruf) *adj.* Having an uneven surface; violent or harsh. **rough** *n.* The part of a golf course with tall grass. **rough** *v.* To treat roughly. **roughly** *adv.* In a very rude manner; approximately. **roughness** *n.*

rough-age (ruf´ij) *n.* Material that is coarse in texture.

rough–and–ready (ruf´an red´ē) *adj.* Crude in method but effective in action.

rough bluegrass *n.* Type of grass having bluish-green stems.

rough-en (ruf´en) *v.* To cause something to become rough.

rou-leau (rŏ lō′) *n.* A trimming for hats that is rolled.

rou-lette (rŏ let′) *n.* A gambling game in which players bet on which slot a small ball will land in.

round (round) *adj.* Curved; circular; spherical. **round** *v.* To become round; to surround. **round** *adv.* Throughout; prescribed duties, places, or actions. **roundness** *n.*

round-a-bout (round′a bout′) *adj.* To be going round something.

rouse (rouz) *v.* To awaken or stir up.

rout (rout) *v.* To dig something up, such as a root.

route (rŏt) *n.* A course of travel. **route** *v.* To send in a certain direction.

rou-tine (rŏ tēn′) *n.* Activities done regularly. **routine** *adj.* Ordinary.

rove (rōv) *v.* To wander over a wide area. **rover** *n.* **roving** *adj.*

rove beetle *n.* A beetle that has slender body and is able to run quickly.

row (rō) *n.* A number of things positioned next to each other; a continuous line. **row** *v.* To propel a boat with oars.

row-an tree (rō′an trē) *n.* Type of smooth-barked tree that has clusters of red berries.

row-dy (rou′dē) *n.* A person who is disorderly. **rowdily** *adv.* **rowdiness** *n.*

roy-al (roi′al) *adj.* Relating to a king or queen.

royal blue *n.* A dark and deep shade of blue.

roy-al-ist (roi′a list) *n.* A person who supports the king.

royal palm *n.* Type of palm tree that is located in California and Florida.

roy-al-ty *n. pl.* **royalties** Monarchs and their families; a payment to someone for the use of his invention, copyright, or services.

R.S.V.P. *abbr.* Respondez s'il vous plait; please reply.

rub (rub) *v.* To move over a surface with friction and pressure; to cause to become worn or frayed.

rub-ber (rub′ĕr) *n.* A resinous elastic material obtained from the coagulated and processed sap of tropical plants or produced synthetically. **rubbery** *adj.*

rubber cement *n.* A type of adhesive that is liquid and made of rubber.

rub-ber-ize (rub′e rīz′) *v.* Coat or cover something with rubber.

rub-ber-neck (rub′ĕr nek′) *v.* To turn the head in order to see something.

rubber plant *n.* Type of plant that is found in East India and yields rubber.

rubber stamp *n.* A type of rubber plate which is coated with ink and used for the purpose of leaving prints on paper or other objects.

rub-bing (rub′ing) *n.* The action or act of a person or thing that rubs.

rub-bish (rub′ish) *n.* Worthless trash; nonsense.

rub-ble (rub′l) *n.* The pieces of broken material or stones.

rub-down (rub′doun′) *n.* A type of quick and brisk massage.

ru-be-fa-cient (rō′be fā′shent) *n.* A type of substance which will turn the area of skin it is applied to red. **rubefaction** *n.*

ru-bel-la (rō bel′a) *n.* The German measles.

ru-bel-lite (rō bel′īt) *n.* A red gem stone.

ru-be-o-la (rō bē′o la) *n.* The German measles. **rubeoloid** *adj.* **rubeolar** *adj.*

ru-bi-cund (rō′bi kund′) *adj.* State of being of a red color or hue.

ru-bid-i-um (rō bid′ē um) *n.* A silvery, highly reactive element symbolized by Rb.

ru-bi-ous (rō′bē us) *adj.* Being red in color.

ru-bric (rō′brik) *n.* A heading, title, or initial letter of a manuscript which appears in red. **rubrically** *adv.* **rubrical** *adj.*

ru-bri-cate (rō′bri kāt′) *v.* To color something red. **rubricator** *n.*

ru-by (rō′bē) *n. pl.* **-ies** A deep-red precious stone. **rubylike** *adj.*

ruby glass *n.* Type of red glass.

ruby spi-nal *n.* A gem stone, red in color.

ruche (rōsh) *n.* Piece of crimped fabric which is used to trim a woman's clothes.

ruck-sack (ruk′sak′) *n.* A knapsack that is carried by hikers.

ruck-us *n., Slang* A noisy uproar, or commotion.

rud-der (rud´ėr) *n., Naut.* A broad, flat, hinged device attached to the stern of a boat used for steering.

rud-dock (rud´ok) *n.* The robin that is found in Europe.

rud-dy (rud´ē) *adj.* Being red in color or hue.

ru-di-ment (rö´di ment) *n.* A first step, element, skill, or principle. *Biol.* An undeveloped organ. **rudimentariness** *n.*

rue (rö) *v.* To repent.

rue anemone *n.* A type of woodland flower of North America having pinkish flowers.

rue-ful (rö´ful) *adj.* To be causing sorrow or remorse. **ruefully** *adv.*

ru-fes-cent (rö fes´ent) *adj.* To be red in color or tint. **rufescence** *n.*

ruff (ruf) *n.* A stiff collar which has pleats in it.

ruffed grouse *n.* A bird, like the chicken, and living in North America having a fan-shaped tail and tufted feathers at the neck.

ruf-fi-an (ruf´ē an) *n.* A lawless, rowdy person. **ruffianly** *adj.* **ruffianism** *n.*

ruf-fle (ruf´l) *n.* A pleated strip or frill; a decorative band. *v.* To disturb or destroy the smoothness.

ru-fous (rö´fus) *adj.* To be red in color or tint.

rug (rug) *n.* A heavy textile fabric used to cover a floor.

ru-ga (rö´ga) *n.* A wrinkle or fold in something.

Rugby *n.* A game similar to football in which the ball is propelled toward the opponent's goal by carrying or kicking.

rug-ged (rug´id) *adj.* Strong; rough; having an uneven or rough surface. **ruggedness** *n.* **ruggedly** *adv.*

ru-gose (rö´gōs) *adj.* To be filled with folds and wrinkles. **rugous** *adj.* **rugosely** *adv.*

ru-in (rö´in) *n.* Total destruction. **ruin** *v.* To destroy. **ruination** *n.* **ruinous** *adj.*

rule (röl) *n.* Controlling power; an authoritative direction or statement which regulates the method of doing something; a standard procedure. **rule** *v.* To have control

over; to make a straight line using a ruler; to be in command.

rule out *v.* To omit something.

rul-er (rö´lėr) *n.* A straight edge used for measuring; a person who rules as a sovereign.

rul-ing (rö´ling) *n.* A type of decision which is handed down by a judge in a trial.

rum (rum) *n.* A type of liquor made from molasses and is distilled.

rum-ba (rum´ba) *n.* A type of dance which has a complex rhythm.

rum-ble (rum´bl) *v.* To make a heavy, continuous sound. *n.* A long, deep rolling sound.

rumble seat *n.* A seat that is uncovered and located in the back of a vehicle, such as an early roadster.

rum-bly (rum´blē) *adj.* To be characterized by a rumble.

ru-men (rö´min) *n.* The first stomach of ruminant animals, such as a cow or goat.

ru-mi-nant (rö´mi nant) *n.* A cud-chewing animal; as a cow, deer, sheep, or giraffe; an animal which chews something which was swallowed. **ruminantly** *adv.*

ru-mi-nate (rö´mi nāt´) *v.* To chew a cud; to ponder at length. **rumination** *n.* **ruminative** *adj.* **ruminator** *n.*

rum-mage (rum´ij) *v.* To look or search thoroughly by digging or turning things over; to ransack.

rummage sale *n.* A sale of second-hand objects, conducted to make money.

rum-my (rum´ē) *n.* A card game in which each player tries to get rid of his hand in sequences of three cards or more of the same suit.

ru-mor (rö´mėr) *n.* An uncertain truth which is circulated from one person to another; gossip. **rumor** *v.* To spread by rumor.

rump (rump) *n.* The fleshy hind quarter of an animal; the human buttocks.

rum-ple (rum´pl) *v.* To form into creases or folds; to wrinkle.

rum-pus (rum´pus) *n.* A loud noise or disturbance.

rumpus room *n.* A type of room which is used for parties.

run (run) *v.* To hurry busily from place to place; to move quickly in such a way that both feet leave the ground for a portion of each step; to make a rapid journey; to be a candidate seeking an office; to drain or discharge. *Law* To be effective, concurrent with. **run** *n.* A speed faster than a walk; a streak, as of luck; the continuous extent or length of something; an outdoor area used to exercise animals. In baseball, the method of scoring a point by running the bases and returning to home plate.

run-a-bout (run′*a* bout′) *n.* A type of boat which is open.

run-a-way (run′*a* wā′) *n.* A person who leaves home without telling anyone where they are going and does not plan on coming back.

rung (rung) *n.* A bar or board which forms a step of a ladder.

run-nel (run′*el*) *n.* A small stream.

run-ner (run′ėr) *n.* The person who runs in a race.

run-ner–up (run′ėr up′) *n.* A contestant who finishes second in a competition.

run-ning (run′ing) *adj.* State of moving fast or rapidly.

run-ny (run′ē) *adj.* To be tending to run.

run-off (run′of′) *n.* That which runs off of something.

run–of–the–mill (run′ov the mil′) *adj.* Ordinary; not special; average.

runt (runt) *n.* The smallest animal in a litter. **runty** *adj.* **runtiness** *n.*

run–through (run′thrō′) *n.* The rehearsal of a play.

run-way (run′wā′) *n.* A path over which something runs; a platform which extends from a stage into the middle of an auditorium; a strip of paved ground for the landing and takeoff of airplanes.

rup-ture (rup′chėr) *n.* A state of being broken; the act of bursting.

ru-ral (rer′al) *adj.* Pertaining to the country or country life. **ruralist** *n.*

ru-ral-ize (rer′*a* līz′) *v.* The act of moving to or living in the country or the rural area. **ruralization** *n.*

rural route *n.* A mail route which runs through the country.

rush (rush) *v.* To move quickly; to hurry; to be in a hurry. **rushy** *adj.*

rusk (rusk) *n.* A piece of toasted and sweet bread.

rus-set (rus′it) *n.* A reddish or yellowish brown color

rust (rust) *n.* Ferric oxide which forms a coating on iron material exposed to moisture and oxygen; deterioration through neglect. **rust** *v.* To form rust.

rus-tic (rus′tik) *adj.* Characteristic of country life. **rustic** *n.* A simple person.

rus-ti-cate (rus′ti kāt′) *v.* Living and staying in the country or rural area.

rus-tic-i-ty (ru stis′i tē) *n.* The quality of being rustic.

rus-tle (rus′l) *v.* To move making soft sounds, such as those made by leaves of a tree.

rus-tler (rus′lėr) *n.* A person who steals cattle.

rust-proof (rust′prōf′) *adj.* Being unable to rust.

rust-y (rus′tē) *adj.* To be covered by rust. **rustiness** *n.* **rustily** *adv.*

rut (rut) *n.* An indented track made by the wheels of vehicles.

ru-ta-ba-ga (rō′ta bā′ga) *n.* A vegetable of the mustard family which makes an underground white tuber.

ruth (rōth) *n.* Grief; sorrowful for another.

ru-the-ni-um (rō thē′nē um) *n.* A metallic element symbolized by Ru.

ruth-ful (rōth′ful) *adj.* To be mournful. **ruthfulness** *n.*

ruth-less (rōth′lis) *adj.* Merciless.

ru-ti-lant (rōt′i lant) *adj.* To have a glow that is reddish in color or tine.

rut-ty (rut′ē) *adj.* A state of having many ruts.

Rx *abbr.* A prescription for medicine.

rye (rī) *n.* A cultivated cereal grass used to make flour and whiskey.

rye whiskey *n.* Whiskey distilled from rye.

S, s (es) The nineteenth letter of the English alphabet.

SA *abbr.* Salvation Army.

Saa-nen *n.* A member of the Swiss breed that is a white hornless goat.

sab-a-dil-la (sab´*a* **dil´***a)* n. A type of Mexican plant of the lily family whose seeds can be used for insecticides.

sab-bat (sab´*a***t)** n. The midnight assembly of the diabolists.

Sab-ba-tar-i-an *n.* A person who observes the Sabbath on Saturday.

Sab-bath *n.* The seventh day of the week; sundown on Friday to sundown on Saturday; a day set aside as the day of worship for Jews and some Christians; Sunday, the first day of the week, a day set apart as the day of worship by most Christians.

sab-bat-i-cal (sa bat´ik) *adj.* To be relating to the sabbath.

Sa-bel-li-an *n.* The member of the early Italian peoples which includes the Sabines and Samnited.

sa-ber (sā´bėr) *n.* A lightweight sword.

saber saw *n.* A type of light and portable electric saw.

saber–toothed tiger *n.* A type of extinct cat which was characterized by the great development of the upper canines.

sa-bin *n.* The unit of acoustic absorption.

Sa-bine *n.* The member of the people of the Apennines of the ancient times.

sa-ble (sā´bl) *n.* A carnivorous mammal having soft, black or dark fur.

sa-ble-fish (sā´bl fish˝) *n.* A type of large spiny-finned fish which is grey or black and of the Pacific coast.

sa-bot (sab´ō) *n.* The kind of wooden shoe which is worn by the people in various European countries.

sab-o-tage (sab´*o* **täzh´)** n. An act of malicious destruction, intended to obstruct production of war material by the opposing side.

sab-o-teur *n.* A person who commits sabotage.

sac (sak) *n., Biol.* A membranous pouch in an animal or plant, containing a liquid.

SAC *abbr.* Strategic Air Command.

sa-ca-huis-te *n.* A kind of bear grass that has long linear leaves and is used for forage.

sac-cade *n.* A type of small rapid jerky movements of the eye.

sac-cate (sak´it) *adj.* To have the form of a pouch.

sac-cha-rate *n.* A type of a compound of sugar usually with a bivalent metal.

sac-char-i-fy *v.* To break some compound into a simple sugar.

sac-cha-rim-e-ter *n.* A kind of device which is used for the purpose of measuring the amount of sugar in a solution.

sac-cha-rin (sak´*a* **rin)** n. A white, crystalline powder used as a noncaloric sugar substitute.

sac-cha-rine (sak´ *a* **rin)** adj. Pertaining to or like sugar.

sac-cha-roi-dal *adj.* Being of fine granular texture.

sac-cha-rom-e-ter *n.* A type of hydrometer that has a special scale.

sac-cu-lar *adj.* To be resembling a sac.

sac-cu-late *adj.* To be formed of a series of saccular expansions.

sac-cule *n.* A chamber which is the smaller of the membranous labyrinth of the ear.

sac-er-do-tal (sas˝ė dōt´*a***l)** adj. Pertaining to the priesthood or to priests.

sa-chem (sā´chem) *n.* A kind of North American Indian chief.

sa-chet (sa shā´) *n.* A small bag of a sweet smelling powder used to scent clothes.

sack (sak) *n.* A strong bag for holding articles. *Slang* Dismissal from a position or job; sleeping bag or bed.

sack-cloth (sak´kloth˝) *n.* A type of garment which is made of sackcloth and is worn as a sign of mourning.

sack coat *n.* A type of man's jacket that has a straight and unfitted back.

sacking (sak´ing) *n.* The material that sacks are constructed from.

sack out *v.* To go or to get into bed.

sack race *n.* Type of race where the contestants jump inside a sack to the finish line.

sacque (sak) *n.* A type of infant jacket that is short and fastens at the neck.

sa-cral *adj.* Pertaining to the sacrum.

sac-ra-ment (sak´ra ment) *n., Eccl.* A formal Christian rite performed in a church, as a baptism. **Sacrament** The consecrated bread and wine of the Eucharist; the Lord's Supper.

sac-ra-ment-al *adj.* The use of the sacramental acts or rites.

sa-crar-i-um *n.* A kind of ancient Roman shrine which holds sacred articles.

sa-cred (sā´krid) *adj.* Dedicated to worship; holy. **sacredly** *adv.* **sacredness** *n.*

sacred mushroom *n.* A type of New World hallucinogenic fungi.

sac-ri-fice (sak´ri fīs´) *n.* The practice of offering something, as an animal's life, to a deity. **sacrifice** *v.* To give up something of value for something else. **sacrificial** *adj.*

sac-ri-lege *n.* A technical violation of what is sacred because consecrated to God. **sacrilegious** *adj.* **sacrilegiousness** *n.*

sac-ris-tan *n.* A type of person who is in charge of the sacristy equipment.

sa-cro-il-i-ac *adj.* Pertaining to the region of juncture of the sacrum and the ilium.

sa-crum *n.* The section or part of the vertebral column which is directly connected with the pelvis and in man is made up of five fused vertebrae.

sad (sad) *adj.* Marked by sorrow; unhappy; causing sorrow; deplorable. **sadly** *adv.* **sadness** *n.*

sadden *v.* To become or to make sad.

sad-dle (sad´l) *n.* A seat for a rider, as on the back of a horse or bicycle; a cut of meat which includes the backbone. *v.* To put a saddle on; to load down; to burden.

saddlebag *n.* A covered pouch which is put across the back of the horse.

saddle blanket *n.* A type of folded blanket which is placed under the saddle to prevent galling the horse.

saddlebow *n.* The pieces which form the front of the saddle.

saddlecloth *n.* A type of cloth which is placed under the saddle.

saddle horn *n.* The prolongation of the pommel of a saddle.

saddle horse *n.* A type of horse which is used for riding.

saddle leather *n.* A type of leather which is made from the hide of cattle that is vegetable-tanned and used for making saddles.

sad-dler (sad´lėr) *n.* A person who makes or sells saddles.

saddle roof *n.* A type of roof having one ridge and two gables.

sad-dler-y *n.* The things and items which are for sale in the shop of a saddler.

saddle seat *n.* A type of slightly concave chair as a Windsor chair.

saddle soap *n.* A type of mild soap used for the purpose of cleaning leather.

saddle sore *n.* An open sore which will develop on the back of a horse at the points of pressure from the saddle.

sad-i-ron (sad´ī ėrn) *n.* A type of flatiron which is pointed at both ends.

sa-dism (sad´iz um) *n., Psychol.* A condition in which sexual gratification comes from inflicting pain on others; cruelty. **sadist** *n.* **sadistic** *adj.* **sadistically** *adv.*

sad sack *n.* A kind of person who is inept.

sa-fa-ri (sa fär´ē) *n. pl.* **safaris** A trip or journey; a hunting expedition in Africa.

safe (sāf) *adj.* Secure from danger, harm, or evil; unharmed; not likely to cause harm. **safe** *n.* A strong metal container used to protect and store important documents or money. **safely** *adv.*

safe–conduct *n.* The protection which is given to a person that is passing through a military zone.

safe-crack-er *n.* A person who breaks into a safe for stealing the things inside.

safe–deposit box *n.* A box which can be found in a bank and used for the purpose of protecting the valuables of the one who uses it.

safe-guard *n.* A kind of precautionary measure.

safe-keeping *n.* The process of keeping safe.

safe-light *n.* A kind of darkroom lamp which has a filter to screen out the rays which can be harmful to film.

safe-ty (sāf'tē) *n.* A condition of being safe from injury or hurt.

safety belt *n.* A type of belt that is used to prevent a person from injury or falling.

safety glass *n.* A type of material that is transparent and is used for windows that are easily or likely to be broken.

safety pin *n.* A type of pin with a clasp that has a guard to cover its point.

safety valve *n.* A type of valve that is used to release pressure.

saf-flow-er *n.* A type of Old World herb that has large red and orange flowers.

saf-fron *n.* A type of purple-flowerd crocus which is used to flavor foods.

saf-ra-nine *n.* Any of the various mixtures of safranine salts which are used in dyeing.

saf-role *n.* A type of poisonous ether that is used for perfuming and flavoring.

sag *v.* To droop; to sink from pressure or weight; to lose strength;decline in amount.

sa-ga (sä'ga) *n.* A long heroic story.

sa-ga-cious (sa gä'shus) *adj.* Being of keen penetration and judgment.

sa-gac-i-ty *n.* The state of being sagacious.

sag-a-more (sag'a mōr") *n.* The subordinate chief of the Algonquian Indians who are of the north Atlantic coast.

sage (sāj) *n.* A person recognized for judgment and wisdom. **sage** *adj.*

sagebrush *n.* A type of North American undershrubs that have a bitter juice and odor.

sage cheese *n.* A type of cheese which is similar to a mild cheddar and is flavored with sage.

sag-ger (sag'ėr) *n.* A type of box which is made of fireclay.

sag-it-tal *adj.* Pertaining to the suture between the parietal bones of the skull.

Sag-it-ta-ri-us *n.* The ninth sign of the zodiac; a person born between November 22 - December 21.

sag-it-tate (saj'i tāt") *adj.* To be shaped like an arrowhead.

sa-go *n.* A type of powdered starch that is made from the pith of a sago palm.

sago palm *n.* A type of plant which yields sago.

sa-gua-ro *n.* A type of arborescent cactus which grows in the southwestern United States and Mexico.

said (sed) *v.* Past tense of say.

sail (sāl) *n.* A strong fabric used to catch the wind and cause a ship to move; a trip on a sailing vessel or boat. **sail** *v.* To travel on a sailing vessel.

sail-board *n.* A type of small flat sailboat made for two passengers.

sail-boat (sāl'bōt") *n.* A type of boat which is propelled with a sail.

sail-cloth (sāl'kloth") *n.* A type of canvas which is used for boat sails.

sail-er (sā'lėr) *n.* A boat which has specified sailing qualities.

sail-fish (sāl'fish") *n.* A type of pelagic fish that has a large dorsal fin.

sailing *n.* The skill of managing a ship.

sailor (sā'lėr) *n.* The person that sails a boat or a ship.

sail-plane (sāl'plān") *n.* A type of glider.

sain-foin (sān'foin) *n.* A type of herb that has pink flowers.

saint (sānt) *n.* A person of great purity who has been officially recognized as such by the Roman Catholic Church; a person who has died and is in heaven.

Saint Bernard *n.* A type of Swiss alpine bred of working dog.

saint-dom *n.* The state of being a saint.

saint-ed (sān'tid) *adj.* Pertaining or relating to a saint.

saint-ly (sānt'lē) *adj.* Resembling a saint.

Saint Patrick's Day *n.* A day which is observed by the Roman Catholic Church on March 17th in honor of St Patrick and is celebrated in Ireland.

Saint Valentine's Day *n.* A day on which St. Valentine is honored on February 14th.

sake (sāk) *n.* Motive or reason for doing something.

sa-ker *n.* A type of Old World falcon.

sal-a-ble (sā′la bl) *adj.* Fit to be sold.

sa-la-cious *adj.* To be appealing to sexual desire. **salaciousness** *n.*

sal-ad (sal′ad) *n.* A dish usually made of green vegetables, fruit, or meat tossed with dressing.

salad days *n.* The time of youthful indiscretion.

salad dressing *n.* A type of dressing used for the flavoring of a salad such as French, Ranch, Italian, etc.

salad oil *n.* A type of vegetable oil which is used for salad dressings.

sal-a-man-der (sal′a man′dėr) *n.* A lizard-like amphibian with porous, scaleless skin.

sa-la-mi (sa lä′mē) *n.* A spiced sausage made of beef and pork.

sa-lar-i-at *n.* A body of salaried persons.

sa-la-ry (sal′a rē) *n. pl.* **salaries** A set compensation paid on a regular basis for services rendered. **salaried** *adj.*

sale (sāl) *n.* An exchange of goods for a price; disposal of items at reduced prices. **salable** *adj.*

sa-lep *n.* The dried tubers of various Old World orchids.

sal-er-a-tus *n.* A kind of leavening agent.

sales *adj.* Pertaining to selling.

sales-clerk *n.* A person who sells in a store.

sales-man *n.* A person who sells in a store or a given area.

sales tax *n.* A tax which is placed on the sale of goods.

sal-i-cin (sal′i sin) *n.* A bitter white glucoside that is found in the bark of willows.

sa-lic-y-late *n.* The ester of salicylic acid.

sa-li-ence *n.* The state of being salient.

sa-li-ent (sā′lē ent) *adj.* Projecting beyond a line; conspicuous.

sa-li-tian *n.* Any of the group of amphibians which consists of frogs, toads, and tree toads.

sa-lim-e-ter *n.* Type of hydrometer for indicating a percentage of salt in a solution.

sa-li-nize *v.* To impregnate with salt.

sa-li-nom-e-ter *n.* A type of instrument used for the purpose of measuring salt in a so-lution.

sa-li-va (sa lī′va) *n.* Tasteless fluid secreted in the mouth which aids in digestion.

sal-i-var-y *adj.* Pertaining to saliva or the glands of the body that secrete saliva.

sal-i-vate *v.* To produce or make an abnormal flow of saliva.

Salk vaccine (salk′ vak sēn′) *n.* A vaccine used to immunize against polio.

sal-let *n.* A type of 15th century helmet.

sal-low (sal′ō) *n.* A type of Old World broad-leaved willow.

sal-ly *n. pl.* **sallies** A sudden rush to launch an assault on something or someone.

sally port *n.* A passage in a fortified place.

sal-ma-gun-di *n.* A kind of salad plate made with eggs, meats, and vegetables.

sal-mi *n.* A ragout of roasted game that is stewed in a rich sauce.

salm-on (sam′on) *n. pl.* **salmon** *or* **salmons** A large game fish with pinkish flesh.

salm-on-ber-ry *n.* A type of red-flowered raspberry found on the Pacific coast.

sal-mon-el-la *n.* A type of aerobic rod-shaped bacteria that causes food poisoning.

sal-mo-nel-lo-sis *n.* A disease that is caused by salmonellae.

sal-mo-nid *n.* A member of the family of elongated soft-finned fishes.

Salmon pink *n.* A yellowish pink which is lighter and redder than salmon.

sa-lon (sa lon′) *n.* A large drawing room; a business establishment pertaining to fashion.

sa-loon (sa lōn′) *n.* A place where alcoholic drinks are sold; a barroom.

sa-loop (sa lōp′) *n.* A hot drink which is made from sassafras and dried tubers of orchids.

sal-pa *n.* An oceanic tunicate which is found to be abundant in warm seas.

sal-pin-gian *adj.* Pertaining to or relating to a salpinx.

sal-pin-gi-tis *n.* The swelling or inflammation of a fallopian tube or a eustachian tube.

sal-si-fy *n.* A type of European biennial

herb that has an edible root.

sal soda *n.* A crystalline hydrated sodium carbonate.

salt (solt) *n.* A white crystalline solid, mainly sodium chloride, found in the earth and sea water, used as a preservative and a seasoning. **salt** *adj.* Containing salt. **salt** *v.* To season or preserve with salt. **salty** *adj.*

sal-ta-rel-lo (sal″ta rel′ō) *n.* A type of Italian dance with a lively hop at the beginning of the measures.

sal-ta-tion (sal tā′shan) *n.* The process of jumping or leaping.

sal-ta-to-ri-al *adj.* To be adapted for leaping.

sal-ta-to-ry *adj.* Pertaining to dancing.

salt away *v.* To put or lay away something safely such as money.

salt-box *n.* A type of dwelling with two stories that has a roof with a long rear slope.

salt-bush *n.* A type of shrubby plant that is able to thrive in alkaline soil.

salt-cel-lar (solt′sel″ẻr) *n.* A vessel used for holding salt at the table.

salt dome *n.* An anticline in sedimentary rock which has a mass of rock salt located within its core.

salt-ed *adj.* Being immune to a disease because one was infected earler and recovered.

salt-er *n.* A person who makes or sells salt.

sal-tern *n.* A location where salt is made.

salt gland *n.* The gland of a marine bird which is able to excrete a concentraed salt solution.

salt grass *n.* A type of grass which is native to a habitat which is alkaline.

sal-tine (sol tēn′) *n.* A crisp cracker which is sprinkled with salt.

salt-ing *n.* An area which is flooded by tides.

salt lake *n.* A lake that has become salty.

salt marsh *n.* An area of flat land which is subject to the overflow by salt water.

salt–marsh caterpillar *n.* A type of American moth whose larva has been found to be very destructive to crops.

salt out *v.* To separate from a solution by adding salt.

salt-pe-ter (solt′pē″tẻr) *n.* Potassium nitrate.

salt pork *n.* The fat pork that has ben cured

in brine or salt.

salt shaker *n.* A type of container which is used for the purpose of sprinkling salt onto foods through a perforated top.

salt–water *n.* Pertaining to salt water.

salt-works (solt′würks″) *n.* The plant or place where salt is made.

salt-wort *n.* A plant of the goosefoot family which is used in making soda ash.

salty *adj.* To be containing salt.

sa-lu-bri-ous (sa lō′brē us) *adj.* To be promoting well-being or health.

sa-lu-ki *n.* A type of old northern African and Asiatic breed of hunting dogs.

sal-u-tar-y (sal′ū ter″ē) *adj.* Wholesome; healthful; beneficial.

sal-u-ta-tion (sal′ū tā′shan) *n.* An expression; a greeting of good will, as used to open a letter.

sa-lu-ta-to-ri-an *n.* A student that usually has the second highest rank in the class.

sa-lu-ta-to-ry *adj.* Pertaining to a salutation.

sa-lute (sa lōt′) *v.* To show honor to a superior officer by raising the right hand to the forehead. **salute** *n.* An act of respect or greeting by saluting.

salv-a-ble *adj.* Capable of being salvaged.

sal-vage (sal′vij) *v.* The act of rescuing a ship, its cargo, or its crew; property which has been saved. **salvage** *v.* To save from destruction; to rescue.

sal-va-tion (sal vā′shan) *n.* The means which effect salvation; the deliverance from the effects of sin.

sal-va-tion-ism *n.* The religious teachings which emphasize the saving of the soul.

Sal-va-tion-ist *n.* An officer of the Salvation Army.

salve (sav) *n.* A medicated ointment used to soothe the pain of a burn or wound.

sal-ver (sal′vẻr) *n.* A type of tray which is used for serving food and drinks.

sal-ver-form *adj.* Being tubular with a spreading limb.

sal-vi-a *n.* Type of herbs of the mint family that have a two-lipped open calyx.

sal-vif-ic *adj.* To have the intent to save or

to redeem.

sal-vo (sal'vō) *n. pl.* **-vos** *or* **-voes** The discharge of a number of guns at the same time.

sal volatile *n.* A solution of ammonium carbonate in alcohol.

SAM *abbr.* Surface-to-Air-Missile.

sa-ma-ra *n.* A dry indehiscent, one-seeded winged fruit.

Sa-mar-i-tan (*sa* mar'i t*a*n) *n.* A person who is ready to help others in need.

sa-mar-i-um (*sa* mâr'ē *u*m) *n.* A metallic element symbolized by Sm.

sa-mar-skite *n.* A black orthorhombic mineral which is a complex oxide.

sam-ba *n.* A type of Brazilian dance.

sam-bar *n.* A kind of large Asiatic deer that has long, coarse hair on its neck.

sam-bo *n.* A type of international wrestling with judo techniques.

same (sām) *adj.* Identical; exactly alike; similar; not changing. *pron.* The very same one or thing. **sameness** *n.*

sa-mekh *n.* The 15th letter which is found in the Hebrew alphabet.

sam-i-sen *n.* A type of Japanese musical instrument having three strings.

sa-mite (sam'īt) *n.* A type of medieval silk fabric made with gold or silver which is interwoven.

Sam-nite *n.* A person who belongs to the ancient people of central Italy.

sam-o-var *n.* A type of Russian urn used to boil water for the making of tea.

samp *n.* A coarse homini.

sam-phire (sam'fī ėr") *n.* A common glasswort that is sometimes pickled.

sam-ple (sam'pl) *n.* A portion which represents the whole. *v.* To try a little.

sam-pler (sam'plėr) *n.* A person who collects or examines samples.

sample room *n.* The room where samples are displayed.

sampling *n.* A small section, art, or portion which is collected as a sample or analysis.

sam-shu *n.* A type of alcoholic liquor that is distilled in China from large millet or rice.

sam-u-rai *n.* The warrior aristocracy of Japan.

san-a-to-ri-um (san'*a* tōr'ē *u*m) *n. pl.* **-ums** An institution for treating chronic diseases.

sanc-ti-fy (sangk'ti fī') *v.* To make holy. **sanctification** *n.*

sanc-ti-mo-ni-ous *adj.* To be possessing sanctity. **sanctimoniousness** *n.*

sanc-ti-mo-ny *n.* A hypocritical holiness.

sanc-tion (sangk'sh*a*n) *n.* Permission from a person of authority; a penalty to ensure compliance. *v.* To officially approve an action.

sanc-tu-ar-y (sangk'chŏ er'ē) *n. pl.* **sanctuaries** A sacred, holy place, as the part of a church, where services are held; a safe place; a refuge.

sanc-tum *n.* A place which is sacred.

sand (sand) *n.* Fine grains of disintegrated rock found in deserts and on beaches. *v.* To smooth or polish with sandpaper; to sprinkle or toss sand. **sandy** *adj.*

san-dal (san'd*a*l) *n.* A shoe which is fastened to the foot by straps attached to the sole; a low shoe or slipper with an ankle strap.

san-dal-wood (san'd*a*l wed') *n.* A fragrant Asian tree used in wood carving and cabinet making.

san-dal-wood oil *n.* The oil which is obtained from the sandalwood.

san-dar-ac (san'd*a* rak") *n.* A resin that is aromatic and brittle obtained from the African sandarac tree.

sandarac tree *n.* A type of northern African tree of the pine family.

sand-bag (sand'bag') *n.* A sand-filled bag, used to hold backwater.

sand-bank (sand'bangk") *n.* A deposit of sand which can be large in size.

sand-bar *n.* A sand ridge which has been built by currents of the water.

sand-blast *n.* A stream of sand that is projected by steam used for cleaning.

sand—blind *adj.* To have very poor eyesight.

sand-box *n.* A receptacle that contains loose

sand.

sand-bur *n*. A type of weed that has burry fruit and occurs in waste places.

sand-cast (sand′kast) *v*. To make a casting by pouring the metal into a mold which is made of sand.

sand-casting *n*. A casting which is made from a mold in sand.

sand crack *n*. A crack or fissure in the hoof of a horse which may cause lameness.

sand dollar *n*. A flat circular sea urchin that lives in shallow water on the sandy bottom.

sand-er *n*. A person who sands.

sand-er-ling *n*. A type of small sandpiper that has gray-and-white plumage.

sand flea *n*. A type of flea that may be found on the sand.

sand fly *n*. A type of small biting fly that has two wings.

sand fly fever *n*. A disease of short duration that is characterized by a headache, fever, and malaise and is transmitted through the bite of the sand fly.

sand-glass *n*. A type of instrument for measuring the passing of time with the running of sand through it.

sand grouse *n*. Type of bird that is closely related to the pigeons and can be found in southern Europe, Africa, and Asia.

sandhill crane *n*. The crane that is bluish-grey tinged and can be found in central and eastern North America.

sand-hog (sand′hog′) *n*. A person who works in a caisson.

sand jack *n*. The device which is for lowering a heavy weight by allowing the sand that supports it to run out.

sand lance *n*. A slender type marine fish that swims in schools and remains buried in the sand at ebb tide.

sand lily *n*. A type of western North American herb of the lily family.

sand-ling *n*. A young or small flounder.

sand myrtle *n*. A low-branching evergreen shrub of the heath family.

sand-paper *n*. A type of paper that is covered on one side with sand used for the purpose of smoothing rough edges.

sand-pile *n*. A large pile of sand that children can play in.

sand-pip-er *n*. A small shorebird having a long soft-tipped bill.

sand rat *n*. A type of rodent that inhabits sandy areas.

sand-soap *n*. A type of soap that is gritty and can be used for all-purpose cleaning.

sand-stone *n*. A type of sedimentary rock.

sand-storm *n*. A storm in the desert that can drive clouds of sand in front of it.

sand trap *n*. A hazard on the golf course which is filled with sand.

sand-wich (sand′wich) *n*. Two or more slices of bread between which a filling, such as cheese or meat, is placed.

sand-worm *n*. A type of polychaete worm that lives in sand.

sand-wort *n*. A type of low tufted herb that will usually grow in a sandy region.

san-dy (san′dē) *adj*. Containing or consisting of sand.

sane (sān) *adj*. Having a healthy, sound mind; showing good judgment. **sanely** *adv*. **sanity** *n*.

san-ga-ree (sang″ga rē) *n*. An iced drink of wine, beer, ale, or liquor which has been garnished with nutmeg.

sang-froid (sän frwä′) *n*. A self-possession or imperturbability.

san-gui-nar-ia *n*. The roots and rhizome of the bloodroot which can be used as an emetic or as an expectorant.

san-guine (sang′gwin) *adj*. To be relating to the blood. **sanguinely** *adv*.

san-guin-e-ous *adj*. Pertaining to bloodshed; consisting of blood.

san-guin-o-lent *adj*. To be tinged by blood or to contain blood.

san-guin-o-pu-ru-lent *adj*. To be containing pus and blood in the discharge.

san-i-cle *n*. A type of plants that sometimes are held to have healing powers.

sa-ni-ous *adj*. To be slightly blood tinged.

san-it *abbr*. Sanitation; sanitary.

san-i-tar-i-an *n*. One who is a specialist in sanitary science and the public health.

san-i-tar-i-ly *adv*. Doing something in a

sanitary manner or way.

san-i-tar-y (san´i ter´ē) *adj.* Free from bacteria or filth which endanger health. **sanitary** *n.*

sanitary ware *n.* The ceramic plumbing fixtures such as sinks or toilet bowls.

san-i-tate *v.* To make something sanitary.

san-i-ta-tion (san˝i tā´shan) *n.* The process of making something sanitary.

san-i-tize (san´i tīz´) *v.* To make sanitary; to make clean or free of germs.

san-i-ty *n.* The state of being sane.

sank *v.* Past tense of sink.

san-nup (san´up) *n.* An American Indian male who is married.

sans-cu-lotte *n.* One who is of a lower class and lacking culture or refinement.

san-se-vie-ria *n.* A member of the group of tropical herbs of the lily family that yield a strong fiber.

Santa Claus *n.* The symbol of Christmas, represented as a jolly, fat, white-bearded old man dressed in a red suit.

sap (sap) *n.* The liquid which flows or circulates through plants and trees. *v.* To weaken or wear away gradually. *Slang* A gullible person; fool.

sa-pi-ent (sā´pē ent) *adj.* Wise.

sap-phire (saf´ī ėr) *n.* A clear, deep-blue gem, used in jewelry.

sar-casm (sär´kaz um) *n.* An insulting or mocking statement or remark. **sarcastic** *adj.* **sarcastically** *adv.*

sar-dine (sär dēn´) *n.* A small edible fish of the herring family, often canned in oil.

sar-don-ic (sär don´ik) *adj.* Scornful; mockingly cynical.

sa-ri (sär´ē) *n.* A garment consisting of a long piece of lightweight material wrapped around the body and over the shoulder of Hindu women.

sar-sa-pa-ril-la (sas´pa ril´a) *n.* The dried root of a tropical American plant, which is used as flavoring.

sash (sash) *n.* A band worn over the shoulder or around the waist.

sass (sas) *n., Slang* Rudeness; a disrespectful manner of speech. *v.* To talk with disrespect.

sas-sa-fras (sas´a fras´) *n.* The dried root of a North American tree, used as flavoring.

Sat *abbr.* Saturday.

Sa-tan (sāt´an) *n.* The devil.

sat-el-lite (sat´e līt´) *n.* A natural or manmade object which orbits a celestial body.

sat-in (sat´in) *n.* A smooth, shiny fabric made of silk, nylon, or rayon, having a glossy face and dull back.

sat-ire (sat´ī ėr) *n.* The use of mockery, sarcasm, or humor in a literary work to ridicule or attack human vice.

sat-is-fac-tion (sat´is fak´shan) *n.* Anything which brings about a happy feeling; the fulfillment of a need, appetite, or desire; a source of gratification.

sat-is-fy *v.* To fulfill; to give assurance to.

sat-u-rate (sach´a rāt´) *v.* To make completely wet; to soak or load to capacity. **saturable** *adj.* **saturation** *n.*

sat-yr (sā´tėr) *n., Myth.* A Greek woodland god having a human body and the legs, horns, and ears of a goat.

sauce (sos) *n.* A liquid or dressing served as an accompaniment to food.

sau-cer (so´sėr) *n.* A small shallow dish for holding a cup.

sau-er-kraut (sour´krout´) *n.* Shredded and salted cabbage cooked in its own juices until tender and sour.

sau-na (sou´nä) *n.* A steam bath in which one is subjected to heat produced by water poured over heated rocks.

sau-sage (so´sij) *n.* Chopped meat, usually pork, which is highly seasoned, stuffed into a casing and cooked.

sav-age (sav´ij) *adj.* Wild; not domesticated; uncivilized; brutal. *n.* A vicious or crude person. **savagery** *n.*

save (sāv) *v.* To rescue from danger, loss, or harm; to prevent loss or waste; to keep for another time in the future; to be delivered from sin. **saver** *n.*

sav-ior (sāv´yėr) *n.* One who saves. Christ Savior.

sa-voir–faire (sav´wär fâr´) *n.* Social skill;

the ability to say and do the right thing.

sa-vor (sā´vėr) *n.* The taste or smell of something. *v.* To have a particular smell; to truly enjoy. **savory** *adj.*

saw (so) *n.* A tool with a sharp metal blade edged with teeth-like points for cutting. *v.* Past tense of see; to cut with a saw.

sax-o-phone (sak´so fōn´) *n.* A brass wind instrument having finger keys and a reed mouthpiece. **saxo-phonist** *n.*

say (sā) *v.* To speak aloud; to express oneself in words; to indicate; to show. *n.* The chance to speak; the right to make a decision.

sb *abbr.* Substantive.

SB *abbr.* Simultaneous broadcast; south-bound.

SBA *abbr.* Small Business Administration.

SBN *abbr.* Standard Book Number.

SC *abbr.* South Carolina.

scab (skab) *n.* The stiff, crusty covering which forms over a healing wound. *Slang* A person who continues to work while others are on strike.

scab-bard (skab´ėrd) *n.* A type of sheath for a bayonet or a dagger.

scab-ble *v.* To dress something, such as stone, with a rough furrowed surface.

scab-by *adj.* To be diseased with scab.

sca-bies (skā´bēz) *n.* A contagious skin disease characterized by severe itching, caused by a mite under the skin.

sca-bi-o-sa *n.* A type of herb of the teasel family.

sca-brous (skab´rus) *adj.* To be rough to the touch. **scabrousness** *n.*

scad (skad) *n.* A type of caragid fish.

scaf-fold (skaf´old) *n.* A temporary support of metal or wood erected for workers who are building or working on a large structure.

scaf-fold-ing *n.* The system of scaffolds.

scal-a-ble *adj.* Able to be scaled.

sca-lar *adj.* To have an uninterrupted series of steps such as a staircase.

sca-lar-i-form *adj.* To be like or resembling

a ladder.

scal-a-wag (skal´a wag´) *n., Slang* A rascal.

scald (skold) *v.* To burn with steam or a hot liquid; to heat a liquid to a temperature just under boiling.

scald-ing *adj.* To be able to cause a sensation of scalding.

scale (skāl) *n.* A flat plate which covers certain animals, especially fish and reptiles; a device for weighing; a series of marks indicating the relationship between a map or model and the actual dimensions. *Music* A sequence of eight musical notes in accordance with a specified scheme of intervals. **scaly** *adj.*

scale armor *n.* A type of armor covered by small metallic scales.

scale–down *n.* A kind of reduction that is according to a fixed ratio.

scale leaf *n.* A type of scaly leaf that is small in size.

scale-like *adj.* To resemble a scale.

sca-lene (skā lēn´) *adj.* To have three sides that are not equal in their lengths.

scale-pan *n.* A kind of pan which is used for the purpose of weighing things.

scal-er (skā´lėr) *n.* Someone or something that scales an object.

scale–up *n.* The increase that is according to a ratio which is fixed.

scall (skol) *n.* A type of scabby disorder which can occur on the skin.

scal-lion *n.* A type of onion that will form a thick basal part but without a bulb.

scal-lop (skol´op) *n.* A marine shellfish with a fan-shaped, fluted bivalve shell; the fleshy edible muscle of the scallop. **scalloper** *n.*

scalp (skalp) *n.* The skin which covers the top of the human head where hair normally grows. *v.* To tear or remove the scalp from. *Slang* To buy or sell something at a greatly inflated price. **scalper** *n.*

scal-pel (skal´pel) *n.* A small, straight knife with a narrow, pointed blade, used in surgery.

scalp lock *n.* A tuft of the hair on the crown

of an otherwise shaved head.

scamp (skamp) *n*. A scheming or tricky person.

scamp-er *v*. To run playfully about.

scamp-i *n*. A type of large shrimp that is prepared with a garlic sauce.

scan (skan) *v*. To examine all parts closely; to look at quickly; to analyze the rhythm of a poem. *Electron*. To move a beam of radar in search of a target. **scanner** *n*.

scan-dal (skan´dal) *n*. Something which brings disgrace when exposed to the public; gossip.

scan-dal-ize (skan´da līz´) *v*. To offend someone in a moral sense.

scan-dal-mon-ger (skan´dal mung´gėr) *n*. One who circulates scandal.

scan-dal-ous *adj*. Being offensive to morality. **scandalously** *adv*.

scan-dent *adj*. To be characterized by a climbing means of growth.

Scan-di-an *n*. To be pertaining or related to the languages of Scandinavia.

Scan-di-na-vian *adj*. A person of Scandinavian descent.

scan-di-um (skan´dē um) *n*. A metallic element symbolized by Sc.

scant (skant) *adj*. Not plentiful or abundant; inadequate. **scantly** *adv*. **scantness** *n*.

scant-ling (skant´ling) *n*. The dimensions of material used in building, as wood and brick.

scant-y (skan´tē) *adj*. To be somewhat less than is normal. **scantiness** *n*.

scape (skāp) *n*. The shaft of a column.

scape-goat *n*. A person bearing a blame for others.

scape-goating *n*. The process of casting blame for failure on an innocent individual.

scape-grace (skāp´grās´) *n*. A rascal.

scaph-oid *adj*. To be shaped like a boat.

sca-pose *adj*. To be consisting of a scape.

scap-u-la (skap´ū la) *n. pl.* -lae One pair of large, flat, triangular bones which form the back of the shoulder.

scap-u-lar *adj*. To be pertaining to or related to the scapula or the shoulder.

scar (skär) *n*. A permanent mark which

remains on the skin after a sore or injury has healed. **scar** *v*.

scar-ab *n*. The scarabaeid beetle.

scar-a-bae-id *n*. A type of stout-bodied beetle.

scarce (skârs) *adj*. Not common or plentiful; rare. **scarceness** *n*.

scarce-ly *adv*. Being done by a slight margin.

scar-ci-ty *n*. The state of being scarce.

scare (skâr) *v*. To become scared or to frighten someone suddenly.

scare-crow *n*. A human figure usually placed in a garden for the purpose of scaring off animals and preventing them from eating what is being grown.

scar-ed *adj*. The state of fear one may be thrown into by another who frightens them.

scared-y–cat *n*. A person who is very fearful.

scare up *v*. To get together with considerable difficulty.

scarf (skärf) *n*. A wide piece of cloth worn around the head, neck, and shoulders for warmth.

scarf-skin (skärf´skin´) *n*. The skin which forms the cuticle of the nail.

scar-i-fi-ca-tion *n*. The marks which can be made by scarifying.

scar-i-fy (skar´i fī´) *v*. To make small cuts into the skin. **scarifier** *n*.

scar-i-ous (skâr´ē us) *adj*. To be membranous in texture.

scar-la-ti-na (skär´la tē´na) *n*. A mild form of scarlet fever.

scar-let (skär´lit) *n*. A bright or vivid red.

scarlet fever *n*. A communicable disease caused by streptococcus and characterized by a sore throat, vomiting, high fever, and a rash.

scarlet letter *n*. A scarlet A which is worn by a woman as a punitive mark representing the act of adultery.

scarlet runner *n*. A type of American high-climbing bean that is grown as an ornamental tool.

scarlet sage *n*. A type of garden salvia

found in Brazil with intense scarlet flowers.

scarlet tanager *n.* A type of American tanager bird.

scar tissue *n.* A connective tissue that forms a scar and is made mostly of fibroblasts.

scar-y (skâ´ē) *adj.* To be able to scare; to be easily scared.

SCAT *abbr.* School and College Ability Test.

scathe (skāth) *v.* To assail something with withering denunciation.

scath-ing (skā´thing) *adj.* To be bitterly severe. **scathingly** *adv.*

scat-ter (skat´ėr) *v.* To spread around; to distribute in different directions.

scat-ter-a-tion *n.* The process of scattering things.

scat-ter-brain *n.* A heedless person.

scat-ter-good (skat´ėr gŭd˝) *n.* A person who is very wasteful.

scat-ter-ing (skat´ėr ing) *n.* The process of something being scattered.

scatter pin *n.* A type of pin which is worn for decoration on one's clothes.

scatter rug *n.* A type of rug small enough so that several can be used in one room.

scaup (skop) *n.* A type of diving bird.

scav-enge *v.* To salvage something from being discarded; to take away from an area.

scav-en-ger (skav´in jėr) *n.* An animal, as a vulture, which feeds on decaying or dead animals or plant matter.

SCCA *abbr.* Sports Car Club of America.

sce-na *n.* A solo vocal that consists of a recitative.

sce-nar-i-o (si nâr´ē ō´) *n.* A synopsis of a dramatic plot.

sce-nar-ist (si nâr´ist) *n.* A person who creates and writes a scenario.

scend (send) *v.* To heave up under the influence of a natural force.

scene (sēn) *n.* A view; the time and place where an event occurs; a public display of temper; a part of a play.

scene dock *n.* An area or space which is near the stage in a theater and is used for the storage of the scenery.

scen-er-y *n.* Painted screens or other accessories that are used with a play.

scene-shift-er *n.* The person who moves the scenes around in a theater.

sce-nic (sē´nik) *adj.* Pertaining to the stage or setting in a play.

scent (sent) *n.* A smell; an odor. *v.* To smell; to give something a scent.

scent-ed *adj.* To have a smell or a scent.

scep-ter (sep´tėr) *n.* A rod or staff carried by a king as a sign of authority.

scep-tered *adj.* To be invested with a scepter.

sch *abbr.* School.

scha-den-freu-de *n.* The enjoyment that is obtained through the troubles of others.

sched-ule (skej´ōl) *n.* A list or written chart which shows the times at which events will happen, including a plan given for work and specified deadlines.

schee-lite (shā´līt) *n.* A type of mineral that consists of the tungstate of calcium and is a source of tungsten.

sche-ma (skē´ma) *n.* A presentation which is diagrammatic.

sche-mat-ic *adj.* To be pertaining to a schema. **schematically** *adv.*

sche-ma-tize *v.* To form a scheme. **schematization** *n.*

scheme (skēm) *n.* A plan of action; an orderly combination of related parts; a secret plot.

schem-ing *adj.* To be given to forming schemes.

schil-ler (shil´ėr) *n.* A type of bronzy iridescent luster.

schism (siz´um) *n.* A formal separation from a religious body.

schis-mat-ic (siz mat´ik) *n.* The person who creates schism.

schis-ma-tize *v.* To take part in schism.

schist *n.* A type of metamorphic rock that has a closely foliated structure.

schis-tose *adj.* To be pertaining to schist.

schiz-o-carp *n.* A type of dry compound fruit that will split at its maturity.

schiz-ont *n.* A type of multinucleate sporozoan that will reproduce by schizogony.

schle-miel *n.* A bungler who is unlucky.

schnapps *n.* A type of distilled liquors.

schnau-zer *n.* A type of dog that has a long head, small ears, and a wiry coat.

schnit-zel (shnit´sel) *n.* A type of garnished and seasoned veal cutlet.

schnor-rer *n.* A person who wheedles other people into supplying his wants.

schol-ar (skol´er) *n.* A student with a strong interest in learning. **scholarly** *adj.*

schol-ar-ly (skol´er lē) *adj.* To be suitable to learned persons.

schol-ar-ship *n.* A grant of money which is given to a students to enable them to go to school.

scho-las-tic (sko las´tik) *adj.* Pertaining to the schools. **scholastically** *adv.*

scho-li-ast *n.* The maker of scholia.

scho-li-um *n.* A comment which is marginal.

school (skōl) *n.* A place for teaching and learning; a group of persons devoted to similar principles.

school age *n.* The time of one' life when one is able to attend school and required to do so by the law.

school-bag *n.* A bag which is used for the purpose of toting one's school books.

school board *n.* The board of people who are in charge of the public schools.

school-book *n.* A textbook which is used for the schoolwork done in schools.

school bus *n.* A vehicle that is used to take children to and from school.

school-house *n.* The building that is used for teaching and school.

school-ing (skō´ling) *n.* The instruction that is given in school.

school-room (skōl´rōm˝) *n.* A classroom that is used for teaching.

school-time *n.* The time that is designated for the beginning of a session of school.

school-work (skōl´würk˝) *n.* The lessons which are done in school.

schoon-er (skō´ner) *n.* A sailing vessel with two or more masts.

Schwann cell *n.* A type of cell of the neurilemma of the fiber of the nerve.

sci *abbr.* Science; scientific.

sci-ae-nid *n.* A type of carnivorous marine percoid fish such as the croaker.

sci-at-ic (sī at´ik) *adj.* Relating to being located near the hip area of the body.

sciatic nerve *n.* The largest nerve of the body that runs down both legs.

sci-ence (sī´ens) *n.* The study and theoretical explanation of natural phenomena in an orderly way; knowledge acquired through experience. **scientific** *adj.* **scientifically** *adv.* **scientist** *n.*

sci-en-tism *n.* The attitudes that are typical of the natural scientist.

sci-fi *abbr.* Science fiction.

scil *abbr.* Scilicet.

scil-la *n.* A type of Old World herb of the lily family that has pink, blue, or white flowers.

scim-i-tar (sim´i ter) *n.* A type of saber that is made of a curved blade and is used by the Turks and the Arabs.

scin-til-late (sin´ti lāt˝) *v.* To give off or emit quick flashes. **scintillator** *n.*

scir-rhus *n.* A type of malignant tumor that has a preponderance of fibrous tissue.

scis-sion (sizh´an) *n.* The process of splitting or cutting.

scis-sors (siz´erz) *n. pl.* A cutting tool con-sisting of two blades joined and pivoted so that the edges are close to each other.

scis-sor-tail *n.* A type of flycatcher that lives in Mexico and the southern U.S. having a tail that is deeply forked.

scler-a *n.* A dense fibrous white outer coat that will enclose the eyeball exept the section which is covered by the cornea.

scler-ite (sklēr´īt) *n.* A type of hard chitinous plate or piece.

scle-ro-der-ma (sklēr˝o dur´ma) *n.* A kind of disease of the skin that causes thickening of the subcutaneous tissues.

scle-rom-e-ter *n.* A device which is used for the purpose of determining the hardness of something.

scle-ro-pro-tein *n.* A type of protein that can be found in the skeletal and the connective tissues of the body.

scle-ro-sis (skli rō´sis) *n. pl.* **-ses** A hardening of a part of the body, as an artery.

scle-rot-ic *adj.* Pertaining to the sclera.

scler-o-ti-za-tion *n.* The state of being sclerotized.

scler-o-tized *adj.* To be made hard by a substance other than chitin.

scoff *n.* The expression of derision or scorn. **scoffer** *n.*

scold (skōld) *v.* To accuse or reprimand harshly.

scold-ing (skōld ing) *n.* The action of a person who scolds another person.

sco-lex (skōleks) *n.* A head of the tapeworm in the stages of its life.

sco-li-o-sis (skō˝lē ō´sis) *n.* The lateral curvature of the spine. **scoliotic** *adj.*

sconce (skons) *n.* A wall bracket for holding candles.

scoop (skŏp) *n.* A small, shovel-like tool. *v.* To lift up or out. *Slang* An exclusive news report.

scoot (skōt) *v.* To go suddenly and quickly.

scoot-er *n.* Type of child's foot-operated riding toy that is a board mounted between two wheels and having a steering handle.

scop *n.* A poet of the Old English.

scope (skōp) *n.* The range or extent of one's actions; the space to function or operate in.

-scope *suff.* A device for seeing or discovering.

sco-pol-a-mine (sko pol´a mēn˝) *n.* A kind of poisonous alkaloid that can be found in the roots of some plants belonging to the nightshade family.

scop-u-la *n.* A tuft of bushy hairs.

scor-bu-tic *adj.* To be like or resembling scurvy. **scorbutically** *adv.*

scorch (skorch) *v.* To burn slightly, changing the color and taste of something; to parch with heat.

scorched *adj.* To be discolored by scorching.

scorch-er (skor´chėr) *n., Slang* A very hot day.

score (skōr) *n.* A numerical record of total points won in a game or other contest; the result of an examination; a grouping of twenty items; a written musical composition which indicates the part to be per-

formed by each person; a groove made with a pointed tool. *v.* To achieve or win; to arrange a musical score for.

score-board *n.* A board which is used to display the score of a game.

score-card *n.* A card which is used for the recording of the score in a game.

score-keep-er *n.* The person in the game who is in charge of keeping the score.

score-less *adj.* Having no points scored in a game.

sco-ria *n.* A refuse from the melting of metals. **scoriaceous** *adj.*

scorn (skorn) *n.* Contempt; disdain. *v.* To treat with scorn. **scornful** *adj.*

scorn-ful *adj.* Being full of scorn. **scornfulness** *n.*

scor-pae-nid *n.* A member of the group or family of marine spiny-finned fishes, having large mouths and sharp teeth.

Scor-pi-o *n.* The eighth sign of the zodiac; a person born between October 23 - November 21.

scor-pi-oid *adj.* To be curved or circular at the end like the tail of the scorpion.

scor-pi-on (skor´pē on) *n.* An arachnid having an upright tail tipped with a poisonous sting.

scor-pi-on fish *n.* A type of fish that has a venomous spine on the dorsal fin.

Scor-pi-us *n.* The southern constellation that is located partly in the Milky Way and next to Libra.

Scot *n.* A member of the Gaelic people of northern Ireland that settled on Scotland around the year 500 A.D.

Scot *abbr.* Scotland; Scottish.

scotch *v.* To stamp something out.

Scotch broth *n.* A type of soup that has been made from beef and vegetables and then thickened with barley.

Scotch-man (skots´man) *n.* A man who is of Scotch descent.

Scotch pine *n.* A type of pine that is found in Asia and northern Europe yielding very hard wood used for building purposes.

Scotch whisky *n.* A type of whisky that is distilled from malted barley.

sco-ter *n.* A type of sea duck of the northern coasts of Europe and North America.

scot–free *adj.* To be totally free from harm or penalty.

Scot-ic *adj.* Pertaining to the ancient Scots.

sco-to-ma *n.* A dark spot in the visual field.

Scot-ti-cism *n.* The characteristic feature of Scottish English.

Scottish Gaelic *n.* The Gaelic language of the country of Scotland.

Scottish terrier *n.* A type of old Scottish breed of the terrier having short legs, broad chest, wiry hair, and a large head.

scoun-drel *n.* A villain or a robber.

scour (skour) *v.* To clean by rubbing with an abrasive agent; to clean thoroughly.

scour-er (skour´ẻr) *n.* Someone or something that scours.

scout (skout) *v.* To observe activities in order to obtain information. *n.* A person whose job is to obtain information; a member of the Boy Scouts or Girl Scouts.

scout-ing (skou´ting) *n.* The action or activities of a person who scouts.

scow (skou) *n.* A large barge with a flat bottom and square ends used to transport freight, gravel, or other cargo.

scowl (skoul) *v.* To make an angry look; to frown. **scowl** *n.*

SCPO *abbr.* Senior chief petty officer.

scrab-ble (skrab´l) *v.* To scratch about frantically, as if searching for something. **scrabble** *n.* **scrabbler** *n.*

scrag *v.* To kill or to execute by hanging.

scrag-gly (skrag´lē) *adj.* Messy; irregular.

scram *v.* To leave or to go away at once.

scram-ble *v.* To move with panic.

scrap (skrap) *n.* A small section or piece. *v.* To throw away waste.

scrap-book (skrap´bŭk˝) *n.* A book that contains miscellaneous items.

scrape (skrāp) *v.* To rub a surface with a sharp object in order to clean. *Slang* An embarrassing situation.

scrap heap *n.* A large pile of metal which has been discarded.

scra-pie *n.* A kind of viral disease of sheep where they become itchy, excited, excessively thirsty, weak, and eventually a paralysis occurs.

scrap-pi-ness *n.* The state of being scrappy.

scratch (skrach) *v.* To mark or make a slight cut on; to mark with the fingernails. *n.* The mark made by scratching; a harsh, unpleasant sound.

scratch hit *n.* A batted ball that is not hit hard enough but is still credited to the batter as a base hit.

scratch line *n.* The starting line of a race.

scratch pad *n.* A pad of paper that is used to jot down notes.

scratch paper *n.* The paper that is used just to take notes upon.

scratch test *n.* A type of test for allergic susceptibility that involves placing an extract of an allergy-producing substance into a scratch on the skin.

scratch-y (skrach´ē) *adj.* To be marked with scratches. **scratchiness** *n.*

scrawl (skrol) *n.* To write or draw quickly and often illegibly. **scrawl** *n.*

scraw-ny (skro´nē) *adj.* Very thin; skinny. **scrawniness** *n.*

screak *v.* To make or produce a shrill noise.

scream (skrēm) *v.* To utter a long, sharp cry, as of fear or pain. *n.* A long piercing cry. *Slang* A very funny person.

scream-er *n.* A person who screams.

scream-ing-ly (scrē´ming lē) *adv.* To do something to an extreme degree.

scree (skrē) *n.* A gathering of stones lying on a slope.

screech (skrēch) *v.* To make a shrill, harsh noise.

screech owl *n.* A type of owl that has a tuft of feathers on its head.

screed *n.* A piece of writing that is informal.

screen (skrēn) *n.* A movable object used to keep something from view, to divide, or to decorate; a flat reflecting surface on which a picture is projected. *v.* To keep from view.

screen-ing (skrē´ning) *n.* A metal mesh that may be used to cover a window.

screen pass *n.* A type of forward pass in the game of football to a receiver at or behind the line of scrimmage.

screen test *n.* A type of short film sequence testing the abilities of a prospective movie actor.

screen writer *n.* A person who writes screenplays.

screw (skrŏ) *n.* A metal piece that resembles a nail, having a spiral thread which is used for fastening things together; a propeller on a ship. *v.* To join by twisting. **screw up** To make a mess of.

screw-ball *n.* A type of pitch in baseball where the ball spins and breaks in the opposite direction to a curve.

screw bean *n.* A type of leguminous shrub of the southwestern U.S.

screw-driver (skrŏ´drī˝vėr) *n.* A type of tool which is used for turning screws.

screw up *n.* To tighten.

screw-worm *n.* A type of fly whose larva is found to develop in the nostrils of mammals, including man.

screw-y *adj.* To be very unusual.

scrib-ble *v.* To write without thought.

scribe (skrīb) *n.* A person whose profession is to copy documents and manuscripts.

scrib-er *n.* A sharp tool for the purpose of making marks in material to be cut.

scrieve *v.* To move along smoothly.

scrim (skrim) *n.* A type of durable cotton fabric used for clothing and curtains.

scrim-mage (skrim´ij) *n.* In football, a practice game. **scrimmage** *v.*

scrimp (skrimp) *v.* To make something too small or short.

scrim-shaw (skrim´sho´) *n.* The art of carving designs on whale ivory or whalebone.

scrip *n.* A type of small wallet.

script *n.* The written text of a play.

scrip-tur-al *adj.* According to a sacred writing. **scripturally** *adv.*

scrip-ture (skrip´chėr) *n.* A sacred writing. **Scriptures** The Bible.

script-writ-er *n.* A person who writes screenplays and other scripts.

scriv-en-er *n.* A public copyist or writer.

scrod (skrod) *n.* A type of young fish such as the haddock or the cod.

scrof-u-la (skrof´ū la) *n.* A tuberculosis of the lymph glands.

scrof-u-lous *adj.* To be affected with scroful.

scroll (skrōl) *n.* A roll of parchment or similar material used in place of paper.

scroll saw *n.* A type of thin handsaw that is used for the purpose of cutting curves and designs.

scroll-work *n.* An ornamentation that is characterized by scrolls.

scrooge *n.* A type of person who is miserly.

scro-tum (skrō´tum) *n. pl.* **-ta** The external sac of skin which encloses the testes. **scrotal** *adj.*

scrounge *v.* To collect by foraging.

scrub (skrub) *v.* To clean something by rubbing. *Slang* To cancel.

scrub-ber *n.* One that is able to scrub.

scrub brush *n.* A type of rush which is used for the purpose of scrubbing.

scrub-land *n.* An area of land which has been covered with scrub.

scrub pine *n.* A type of tree which is not used for lumber due to its size.

scruff *n.* The region on the back of the neck.

scrump-tious (skrump´shus) *adj., Slang* Delightful.

scru-ple (skrŏ´pl) *n.* A principle which governs one's actions. **scrupulous** *adj.*

scru-pu-los-i-ty *n.* The state of being scrupulous.

scru-pu-lous (skrŏ´pū lus) *adj.* To have moral integrity. **scrupulously** *adv.*

scru-ta-ble (skrŏ´ta bl) *adj.* To be able to be deciphered.

scru-ta-ter *n.* An examiner.

scru-ti-neer *n.* The person who examines.

scru-ti-nize *v.* To look at or to examine something very carefully.

scru-ti-ny *n.* An inspection of something.

sct *abbr.* Scout.

sctd *abbr.* Scattered.

scu-ba (skŏ´ba) *n.* An apparatus used by divers for underwater breathing; from the initials for self-contained underwater breathing apparatus.

scuba diver *n.* A person who swims under the water with the use of scuba gear.

scud *v.* To move or to go quickly.

scuff (skuf) *v.* To drag or scrape the feet while walking. *n.* A rough spot.

scuf-fle (skuf′l) *v.* To struggle in a confused manner. **scuffle** *n.*

scuffle hoe *n.* A type of hoe which has both edges sharpened.

scull (skul) *n.* An oar mounted at the stern of a boat, which is moved back and forth to produce forward motion.

scul-ler-y (skul′e rē) *n.* A room used for storing and cleaning dishes.

scul-lion *n.* A type of kitchen helper.

scul-pin (skul′pin) *n.* A type of large-headed scaleless fish.

sculpt *v.* To carve; to make a sculpture.

sculp-tor (skulp′tėr) *n.* A person who creates statues from clay, marble, or other material.

sculp-ture (skulp′chėr) *n.* The art of processing a hard or soft material into another form, such as a statue.

scum (skum) *n.* A thin layer of waste matter floating on top of a liquid.

scum-ble *v.* To make something less brilliant by covering it with a thin coat of color.

scun-ner *v.* To be in a state of irritation.

scup-per-nong *n.* A type of white aromatic table wine that is made from scuppernongs.

scurf (skerf) *n.* Flaky dry skin; dandruff.

scur-ril-i-ty *n.* The state of being scurrilous.

scur-ri-lous *adj.* To be vulgar and evil.

scur-ry (sker′ē) *v.* To move quickly; to scamper.

scur-vy *n.* A type of disease that is caused by the lack of ascorbic acid and is characterized by bleeding gums and bleeding into the skin.

scut *n.* A type of tail which is short and erect.

scu-tage *n.* A kind of tax that is levied on a tenant of a knight's land in the place of service for the military.

scutch-er *n.* A type of machine used for the purpose of scutching cotton.

scute *n.* An external horny plate.

scu-tel-late (skū tel′it) *adj.* To be resembling scutellum.

scu-tel-lum (skū tel′um) *n.* A small shield-shaped plant structure.

scut-tle *n.* A small opening with a movable lid in the hull of a ship. *v.* To deliberately sink a boat or other floating object by cutting or making holes in the bottom or sides.

scut-tle-butt *n.* A type of cask on a shipboard that contains fresh water that is to be used during that day.

scu-tum *n.* A type of horny and bony plate.

scy-pho-zo-an (sī′fo zō′an) *n.* A type of coelenterates of the group of jellyfish and lacking a true polyp.

scythe (sīth) *n.* A tool with a long handle and curved, single-edged blade, used for cutting hay, grain and grass.

Scyth-i-an *n.* A member of the people that inhabited Scythia and were nomads.

SD *abbr.* South Dakota.

sea *n.* The body of salt water which covers most of the earth; a large body of salt water.

seacoast *n.* Land that borders the sea.

seal (sēl) *n.* A device having a raised emblem, displaying word or symbol, used to certify a signature or the authenticity of a document; a tight closure which secures; a large aquatic mammal with a sleek body and large flippers; the fur or pelt of a seal. **seal** *v.* To hunt seals. **sealer** *n.* **sealant** *n.*

sea level *n.* The level of the sea's surface, used as a standard reference point in measuring the height of land or the depth of the sea.

seam (sēm) *n.* The line formed at the joint of two pieces of material.

sear (sēr) *v.* To wither or dry up; to shrivel; to burn or scorch.

search (serch) *v.* To look over carefully; to find something; to probe. **search** *n.*

searcher *n.*

sea-son (sē´zon) *n.* One of the four parts of the year; spring, summer, fall or autumn, and winter; a time marked by particular activities or celebrations. *v.* To add flavorings or spices; to add interest or enjoyment. **seasonal** *adj.* **seasonally** *adj.*

seat (sēt) *n.* A place or spot, as a chair, stool, or bench, on which to sit; the part of the body used for sitting; the buttocks.

se-cede (si sēd´) *v.* To withdraw from an organization or group. **secession** *n.* **secessionist** *n.*

se-clude (si klōd´) *v.* To isolate; to keep apart.

sec-ond (sek´ond) *n.* A unit of time equal to 1/60 of a minute; a very short period of time; an object which does not meet first class standards. *Math* A unit of measure equal to 1/60 of a minute of angular measurement.

sec-on-dar-y (sek´on der´ē) *adj.* Not being first in importance; inferior; pertaining to a secondary school; high school.

se-cret (sē´krit) *n.* Knowledge kept from others; a mystery. **secretly** *adv.* **secret** *n.* **secrecy** *n.*

sec-re-tary (sek´ri ter´ē) *n. pl.* **-ies** A person hired to write and keep records for an executive or an organization; the head of a government department. **secretarial** *adj.*

se-crete (si krēt´) *v.* To produce and give off; to release or discharge.

sec-tion (sek´shan) *n.* A part or division of something; a separate part. *v.* To divide or separate into sections.

sec-tor (sek´tèr) *n.* An area or zone in which a military unit operates; the part of a circle bounded by two radii and the arc they cut. *v.* *Math* To divide.

sec-u-lar (sek´ya lèr) *adj.* Relating to something worldly; not sacred or religious.

se-cure (si kūr´) *adj.* Safe and free from doubt or fear; sturdy or strong; not likely to fail. *v.* To tie down, fasten, lock, or otherwise protect from risk or harm; to ensure. **securely** *adv.*

se-cu-ri-ty (si kūr´i tē) *n. pl.* **-ies** The state of being safe and free from danger or risk; protection; an object given to assure the fulfillment of an obligation; in computer science, the prevention of unauthorized use of a device or program.

se-dan (si dan´) *n.* A closed, hard-top automobile with a front and back seat.

se-date (si dāt´) *adj.* Serene and composed. *v.* To keep or be kept calm through the use of drugs. **sedative** *n.*

sed-i-ment (sed´i ment) *n.* Material which floats in or settles to the bottom of a liquid. **sedimentary** *adj.*

se-duce (si dōs´) *v.* To tempt and draw away from proper conduct; to entice someone to have sexual intercourse. **seducer** *n.* **seduction** *n.* **seductive** *adj.*

see (sē) *v.* To have the power of sight; to understand; to experience; to imagine; to predict. **see red** To be extremely angry.

seed (sēd) *n.* A fertilized plant ovule with an embryo, capable of producing an offspring. *v.* To plant seeds; to remove the seeds from.

seek (sēk) *v.* To search for; to try to reach; to attempt. **seeker** *n.*

seem (sēm) *v.* To appear to be; to have the look of. **seeming** *adj.* **seemingly** *adv.*

seep (sēp) *v.* To leak or pass through slowly. **seepage** *n.*

seer (sē´ér) *n.* A person who predicts the future.

see-saw (sē´so´) *n.* A board supported in the center which allows children to alternate being up and down.

seg-ment (seg´ment) *n.* Any of the parts into which a thing is divided. *v.* To divide. **segmental** *adj.* **segmentation** *n.*

seg-re-gate (seg´re gāt´) *v.* To separate or isolate from others.

seg-re-ga-tion (seg´re gā´shan) *n.* The act of separating people based on the color of their skin.

seine (sān) *n.* A fishing net with weights on one edge and floats on the other.

seize (sēz) *v.* To grasp or take possession forcibly.

sel-dom (sel´dom) *adv.* Not often.

se-lect (si lekt´) v. To choose from a large group; to make a choice. **selection, select** n. **selector** n. **selectness** n.

se-le-ni-um (si lē´nē um) n. An element symbolized by Se.

self (self) n. pl. **-selves** The complete and essential being of a person; personal interest, advantage or welfare.

self–de-fense (self´di fens´) n. The act of defending oneself or one's belongings.

sell (sel) v. To exchange a product or service for money; to offer for sale. **seller** n.

se-man-tics (si man´tiks) n. The study of word meanings and the relationships between symbols and signs.

sem-a-phore (sem´a fōr´) n. A system for signaling by using flags, lights or arms in various positions. **semaphore** v.

se-men (sē´men) n. The secretion of the male reproductive system, thick and whitish in color and containing sperm.

se-mes-ter (si mes´tėr) n. One of two periods of time in which a school year is divided.

sem-i-an-nu-al (sem´ē an´ū al) adj. Occurring twice a year.

sem-i-co-lon (sem´i kō´lon) n. A punctuation mark (;) having a degree of separation stronger than a comma but less than a period.

sem-i-nar (sem´i när´) n. A course of study for students engaged in advanced study of a particular subject.

sem-i-nar-y (sem´i ner´ē) n. pl. **-ies** A school that prepares ministers, rabbis, or priests for their religious careers. **seminarian** n.

sen-ate (sen´it) n. The upper house of a legislature, as the United States Senate.

send (send) v. To cause something to be conveyed from one place to another; to dispatch.

se-nile (sē´nīl) adj. Having a mental deterioration often associated with old age. **senility** n.

sen-ior (sēn´yėr) adj. Being the older of two; of higher office or rank; referring to the last year of high school or college. n. One who

is older or of higher rank.

sen-ior-i-ty (sēn yor´i tē) n. Priority over others based on the length of time of service.

sen-sa-tion (sen sā´shan) n. An awareness associated with a mental or bodily feeling; something that causes a condition of strong interest.

sense (sens) n. Sensation; feeling; the physical ability which allows a person to be aware of things around him; the five senses; taste, smell, touch, sight, and hearing; an ethical or moral attitude; the meaning of a word; v. To feel through the senses; to have a feeling about.

sen-si-bil-i-ty (sen´si bil´i tē) n. pl. **-ies** The ability to receive sensations.

sen-si-ble (sen´si bl) adj. Capable of being perceived through the senses; sensitive; having good judgment. **sensibly** adv.

sen-si-tive (sen´si tiv) adj. Capable of intense feelings; affected by the emotions or circumstances of others; tender-hearted; of or relating to secret affairs of state. **sensitively** adv. **sensitivity** n. **sensitiveness** n.

sen-sor (sen´sėr) n. A device which responds to a signal.

sen-su-al (sen´shŏ al) adj. Preoccupied with the gratification of the senses. **sensually** adv. **sensualist** n. **sensuality** n. **sensuous** adj.

sent v. Past tense of send.

sen-tence (sen´tens) n. A series of words arranged to express a single complete thought; a prison term for a convicted person, determined by a judge or jury. v. To impose or set the terms of punishment.

sen-ti-ment (sen´ti ment) n. Feelings of affection; an idea, opinion, thought, or attitude based on emotion rather than reason.

sen-ti-men-tal (sen´ti men´tal) adj. Emotional ; affected by sentiment.

sen-ti-nel (sen´ti nel) n. One who guards.

se-pal (sē´pal) n. One of the leaves which forms a calyx in a flower.

sep-a-rate (sep´a rāt´) v. To divide or keep

apart by placing a barrier between; to go in different directions; to set apart from others. *adj.* Single; individual.

sep·a·ra·tion (sep´a rā´shan) *n.* The process of separating or being separated; an interval which separates.

Sept *abbr.* September.

September *n.* The ninth month of the calendar year, having 30 days.

se·quel (sē´kwel) *n.* A new story which follows or comes after an earlier one and which uses the same characters.

se·quence (sē´kwens) *n.* A set arrangement; a number of connected events; the regular order; the order in which something is done. **sequential** *adj.* **sequentially** *adv.*

ser·e·nade (ser´e nād´) *n.* Music performed as a romantic expression of love.

se·rene (se rēn´) *adj.* Calm; peaceful. **se·renity** *n.*

serf (serf) *n.* A slave owned by a lord during the Middle Ages.

serge (serj) *n.* A twilled, durable woolen cloth.

ser·geant (sär´jent) *n.* A noncommissioned officer who ranks above a corporal but below a lieutenant.

se·ri·al (sēr´ē al) *adj.* Arranged in a series with one part presented at a time.

se·ries (sēr´ēz) *n.* A number of related items which follow one another.

se·ri·ous (sēr´ē us) *adj.* Sober; grave; not trivial; important. **seriously** *adv.* **seriousness** *n.*

ser·mon (ser´mon) *n.* A message or speech delivered by a clergyman during a religious service.

ser·pent (ser´pent) *n.* A snake.

ser·rate (ser´it) *adj.* Having sharp teeth; having a notched edge. **serration** *n.*

se·rum (sēr´um) *n.* *pl.* **-rums** *or* **-ra** The yellowish fluid part of the blood which remains after clotting; the fluid extracted from immunized animals and used for the prevention of disease.

ser·vant (ser´vant) *n.* One employed to care for someone or his property.

serve (serv) *v.* To take care of; to wait on;

to prepare and supply; to complete a term of duty; to act in a certain capacity; to start the play in some sports. *n.* The manner of serving or delivering a ball.

serv·ice (ser´vis) *n.* Help given to others; a religious gathering; the military; a set of dishes or utensils. *v.* To repair; to furnish a service to something or someone.

ses·a·me (ses´a mē) *n.* A tropical plant and its edible seeds.

ses·sion (sesh´an) *n.* A meeting or series of meetings; a meeting set for a specific purpose; the period during the day or year during which a meeting takes place.

set (set) *v.* To put or place; to cause to do; to regulate; to adjust; to arrange; to place in a frame or mounting; to go below the horizon; to establish or fix. *n.* A group of things which belong together; a piece of equipment made up of many pieces; a young plant. *adj.* Established; ready.

set·tee (set ē´) *n.* A small couch or bench with arms and a back.

set·ting (set´ing) *n.* The act of placing or putting something somewhere; the scenery for a show or other production; the place where a novel, play, or other fictional work takes place; a jewelry mounting.

set·tle (set´l) *v.* To arrange or put in order; to restore calm or tranquillity to; to come to an agreement on something; to resolve a problem or argument; to establish in a new home or business.

sev·en (sev´en) *n.* The cardinal number 7, after 6 and before 8. **seven** *adj. & pron.* **seventh** *adj., adv. & n.*

sev·en·teen (sev´en tēn´) *n.* The cardinal number 17, after 16 and before 18. **seventeen** *adj. & pron.* **seventeenth** *adj., adv. & n.*

sev·en·ty (sev´en tē) *n.* *pl.* **-ies** The cardinal number 70, after 69 and before 71. **seventy** *adj. & pron.* **seventieth** *adj., adv.*

sev·er (sev´ér) *v.* To cut off or separate. **severance** *n.*

sev·er·al (sev´ér al) *adj.* Being more than one or two, but not many; separate. **severally** *adv.*

se-vere (si vēr´) *adj.* Strict; stern; hard; not fancy; extremely painful; intense. **severely** *adv.* **severity** *n.*

sew (sō) *v.* To fasten or fix; to make stitches with thread and needle.

sew-age (sō´ij) *n.* The solid waste material carried away by a sewer.

sew-er (sō´ėr) *n.* A conduit or drain pipe used to carry away waste.

sex (seks) *n.* One of two divisions, male and female, into which most living things are grouped; sexual intercourse.

sex-tet (seks tet´) *n.* A group of six people or things; music written for six performers.

sgt *abbr.* Sergeant.

sh *abbr.* Share.

shab-by (shab´ē) *adj.* Worn-out; ragged. **shabbily** *adv.* **shabbiness** *n.*

shack (shak) *n.* A small, poorly built building.

shack-le (shak´l) *n.* A metal band locked around the ankle or wrist of a prisoner; anything that restrains or holds. *v.* To restrain with shackles.

shad (shad) *n. pl.* **shad** *or* **shads** An edible fish which swims upstream to spawn.

shad-ber-ry (shad´ber´ē) *n.* A fruit that is grown by the serviceberry.

shad-dock *n.* A type of pear-shaped citrus fruit that is related to the grapefruit.

shade (shād) *n.* A shadow that will gather with the coming of darkness; a comparative darkness due to the interception of the rays of the sun by an object.

shade–grown *n.* To be grown in the shade.

shad-ing *n.* A filling up with color within outlines to give the object a three-dimensional shape or look.

shad-ow (shad´ō) *n.* An area from which light is blocked; a shaded area. *v.* To cast or throw a shadow on. **shadowy** *adj.*

shadow dance *n.* A type of dance that is shown by throwing shadows of the actors upon a screen.

shad-y (shā´dē) *n.* Being sheltered or protected from the rays of the sun.

shaft (shaft) *n.* A long, narrow part of something; a beam or ray of light; a long, narrow underground passage; a tunnel; a narrow, vertical opening in a building for an elevator.

shaft-ing (shaf´ting) *n.* The materials that are used for shafting.

shag *n.* A long matted fiber orcovering.

shag-gy (shag´ē) *adj.* To be covered with long, matted, or coarse hair.

shak-a-ble *n.* Being capable of being shaken.

shake (shāk) *v.* To move or to cause a back-and-forth or up-and-down motion; to tremble; to clasp hands with another, as to welcome or say farewell; to upset or disturb. **shake** *n.* **shaky** *adj.*

shake-down (shāk´doun´) *n.* Type of search which is very thorough.

shak-er (shā´kėr) *n.* Someone or something that shakes.

sha-ko (shak´ō) *n.* A type of stiff military hat that has a plume and high crown.

shale *n.* A type of fissile rock which is made by the consolidation of mud or clay and has a finely stratified structure.

shale oil *n.* A type of dark oil which is obtained from oil shale by heating.

shall (shal) *v. pl.* Past tense of should; used with the pronouns I or we to express future tense; with other nouns or pronouns to indicate promise, determination or a command.

shal-loon *n.* The twilled fabric of wool which is used for linings of coats.

shal-lop *n.* A type of small boat that can be propelled with oars or sails.

shal-lot (sha lot´) *n.* A type of perennial herb that resembles an onion and is used for seasoning.

shal-low (shal´ō) *adj.* Not deep; lacking intellectual depth.

sham (sham) *n.* A person who is not genuine but pretends to be; a cover for pillows. *v.* To pretend to have or feel something.

sham-ble (sham´bl) *v.* To walk while dragging one's feet. **shambles** A scene or state of complete destruction.

sham-bling *adj.* To be characterized with

or by slow awkward movements.

shame (shām) *n.* A painful feeling of embarrassment or disgrace brought on by doing something wrong; dishonor; disgrace; a disappointment.

shame-faced (shām´fāst´) *adj.* To be showing shame. **shamefacedness** *n.*

shame-ful (shām´ful) *adj.* To be arousing the feeling of shame within someone.

shame-less (shām´lis) *adj.* To be showing a lack of shame. **shamelessness** *n.*

sham-poo (sham pō´) *n.* A soap used to cleanse the hair and scalp; a liquid preparation used to clean upholstery and rugs; the process of cleaning with shampoo. **shampoo** *v.*

sham-rock (sham´rok) *n.* A form of clover with three leaflets on a single stem; regarded as the national flower and emblem of Ireland.

shan-dy (shan´dē) *n.* A type of drink which is made of beer and lemonade.

shan-dy-gaff (shan´dē gaf´) *n.* A type of drink which is made of beer and ginger ale.

shang-hai (shang´hī) *v.* To put someone on board a ship with the help of a drug.

shank (shangk) *n.* The portion of the leg between the ankle and the knee; a cut of meat from the leg of an animal, such as a lamb.

shan-ty-man (shan´tē man) *n.* A person who resides in a shanty.

shan-ty-town (shan´tē toun´) *n.* A type of town where the buildings are shanties.

shap-a-ble *n.* To be capable of being shaped.

shape (shāp) *n.* The outline or configuration of something; the form of a human body; the condition of something; the finished form in which something may appear. *v.* To cause to take a particular form.

shape-less (shāp´lis) *adj.* To have no real or definite shape; without shape. **shape-lessness** *n.*

shape-ly (shāp´lē) *adj.* To have a pleasant or pleasing shape to the form.

shard (shärd) *n.* A fragment of a substance which is brittle.

share (shâr) *n.* A part or portion given to or by one person; one of equal parts, as the capital stock in a corporation. *v.* To divide or distribute portions. **sharer** *n.*

share-a-ble *adj.* To be capable of being shared. **shareability** *n.*

share-hold-er *n.* A person who holds a share in a piece of property.

shark (shärk) *n.* A large marine fish which eats other fish and is dangerous to man; a greedy, crafty person.

shark-skin *n.* The skin or hide of the shark that can be made into goods of leather.

sharp (shärp) *adj.* Having a thin edge or a fine point; capable of piercing or cutting; clever; quick-witted; intense; painful. *Slang* Nice looking. *n., Music* A note raised half a tone above a given tone. **sharpness** *n.* **sharply** *adv.*

sharp-en *v.* To make something sharp.

sharp-eyed *adj.* To have sight that is keen.

sharp–nosed *adj.* To be keen in smelling.

sharp–shinned hawk *n.* A type of hawk who eats birds and can be found in North America with a square-tipped tail.

sharp-tongued (shärp–tungd´) *adj.* To have bitter or harsh speech.

shat-ter (shat´ėr) *v.* To burst suddenly into pieces.

shave (shāv) *v.* To remove a thin layer; to cut body hair, as the beard, by using a razor; to come close to. *n.* The act of shaving.

shav-er (shā´vėr) *n.* The person who shaves; the tool used to shave.

shawl (shol) *n.* An oblong or square piece of fabric worn over the head or shoulders.

she (shē) *pron.* A female previously indicated by name.

shea butter *n.* A type of pale solid fat that is from the seeds of the shea tree and can be used in candles and soap.

shear (shēr) *v.* To trim, cut, or remove the fleece or hair with a sharp instrument; to clip. **shearer** *n.*

shear-water *n.* A type of oceanic birds that are related to the albatrosses.

sheat-fish *n.* A type of large catfish.

sheath (shēth) *n.* A cover or case for a blade, as a sword.

sheath-bill (shēth´bil˝) *n.* A white shore bird that has a horny sheath on the base of the upper mandible.

sheath knife *n.* A type of knife that has a fixed blade and is designed to be carried in a sheath.

shea tree *n.* A type of tree of Africa that produces fatty nuts which yield shea butter.

sheave *n.* A wheel that is grooved.

she-been (she bēn´) *n.* A type of drinking establishment that is operated illegally.

shed (shed) *v.* To pour out or cause to pour; to throw off without penetrating; to cast off or leave behind, especially by a natural process. *n.* A small building for shelter or storage.

shed-der *n.* Something that sheds something such as skin.

sheen (shēn) *n.* Luster.

sheep (shēp) *n., pl.* **sheep** A cud-chewing thick-fleeced mammal, widely domesticated for meat and wool; a meek or timid person.

sheep-ber-ry *n.* A type of viburnum of North America that is shrubby having white flowers.

sheep dog *n.* A type of dog that is raised for the purpose of herding or watching over sheep.

sheep-fold *n.* A shelter for sheep.

sheep-herd-er *n.* A person who is in charge of a herd of sheep.

sheep-ish *adj.* To be like a sheep in meekness. **sheepishness** *n.*

sheep-shear-er *n.* A person who removes the wool of sheep.

sheep-shear-ing *n.* The act of removing the wool off of sheep.

sheep-skin *n.* The leather that is prepared from the skin of the sheep.

sheep walk *n.* A range for the sheep.

sheer (shēr) *adj.* Very thin; almost transparent; complete; absolute; very steep, almost perpendicular.

sheet (shēt) *n.* A large piece of cloth for covering a bed; a single piece of paper; a continuous, thin piece of anything.

sheet anchor *n.* A type of anchor that was carried in the waist of a ship.

sheet glass *n.* A type of glass which is processed into sheets.

sheet metal *n.* A type of metal that is in the form of a sheet.

shelf (shelf) *n. pl.* **shelves** A flat piece of wood, metal, plastic, or other rigid material attached to a wall or within another structure, used to hold or store things; something which resembles a shelf, as a ledge of rocks.

shelf ice *n.* An ice sheet that starts on land and continues out to sea and out to where it rests on the floor of the ocean.

shell (shel) *n.* The hard outer covering of certain organisms; something light and hollow which resembles a shell; the framework of a building under construction; a case containing explosives which are fired from a gun. *v.* To remove the shell from. **sheller** *n.*

shel-lac (she lak´) *n.* A clear varnish used to give a smooth, shiny finish to furniture and floors. *Slang* To defeat. **shellac** *v.*

shell bean *n.* A type of bean that is grown for its seeds which are edible.

shelled *adj.* To have a shell.

shel-ter (shel´tėr) *n.* Something which gives protection or cover. *v.* To give protection.

shel-ter-belt *n.* The barrier of trees that protects crops from storms and winds.

shel-ter tent *n.* A type of tent that is made of two interchangeable pieces of waterproof cotton duck.

shelve (shelv) *v.* To put aside; to place on a shelf.

shelv-ing *n.* The degree of sloping of something.

shep-herd (shep´ėrd) *n.* A person who takes care of a flock of sheep; a person who takes care of others.

shep-herd-ess *n.* A girl who tends to sheep.

shepherd's pie *n.* A type of pie that is made

with meat and has a mashed potato crust.

sher-bet (sher´bit) *n.* A sweet frozen dessert made with fruit juices, milk or water, egg white, and gelatin.

sher-iff (sher´if) *n.* A high ranking law-enforcement officer.

sher-ry (sher´ē) *n.* A type of wine that is of Spanish origin and has a nutty taste.

SHF *abbr.* Super high frequency.

shield (shēld) *n.* A piece of protective metal or wood held in front of the body; anything which serves to conceal or protect; a badge or emblem. **shield** *v.* **shielder** *n.*

shield law *n.* The law that protects journalists from being forced to reveal confidential sources.

shiel-ing *n.* A type of hut which is used by shepherds in the mountains for shelter.

shift (shift) *n.* A group of people who work together; a woman's loose-fitting dress. *v.* To change direction or place; to change or move the gears in an automobile.

shift-less (shift´lis) *adj.* To be lacking in ambition. **shiftlessness** *n.*

shill *n.* A person or thing that acts as a decoy.

shim-mer (shim´ėr) *v.* To shine with a faint sparkle. **shimmery** *adj.*

shin (shin) *n.* The front part of the leg from the knee to the ankle. *v.* To climb a rope or pole by gripping and pulling with the hands and legs.

shin-bone *n.* The tibia in the lower leg.

shin-dig *n.* A party or social gathering.

shine (shīn) *v.* To give off light; to direct light; to make bright or glossy; to polish shoes. *n.* Brightness.

shin-er (shī´nėr) *n.* A black eye.

shin-gle (shing´gl) *n.* A thin piece of material, as asbestos, used to cover a roof or side of a house. *v.* To apply shingles to.

shin-gles (shing´glz) *n. pl., Pathol.* An acute, inflammatory viral infection, characterized by skin eruptions along a nerve path.

shin-ing *adj.* To be reflecting light.

shin-ner-y *n.* A growth of trees that is dense.

shin-splints *n.* The inflammation and injury to the muscles of the lower leg due to running on hard surfaces.

ship (ship) *n.* A large vessel for deep-water travel or transport. *v.* To send or transport.

ship-board *n.* A side of a ship.

ship-borne *adj.* To be designed to be carried or transported by a ship.

ship-build-er *n.* A peron who builds ships. **shipbuilding** *n.*

ship-mas-ter (ship´mas˝tėr) *n.* The commander of a ship that is not a warship.

ship-ment (ship´ment) *n.* The process of shipping goods from one port to another.

ship-worm *n.* A type of marine clam that will burrow into the wharf and wooden ships causing damage to them.

ship-wreck (ship´rek´) *n.* The loss of a ship; destruction; ruin. *v.* To wreck.

ship-wright *n.* The carpenter who is skilled in the repair and construction of ships.

ship-yard (ship´yärd´) *n.* A place where ships are built or repaired.

shire (shī´ėr) *n.* The administrative division such as a county.

shire town *n.* The town in which is located a court of jurisdiction.

shirt (shert) *n.* A garment worn on the upper part of the body.

shirt-ing (shür´ting) *n.* The fabric which can be used to make shirts.

shirt-maker *n.* A person who is capable of making shirts.

shirt-tail *n.* The section of the shirt which falls below the waist in the back.

shiv-er (shiv´ėr) *v.* To tremble or shake with excitement or chill. **shivery** *adj.*

shoal (shōl) *n.* Large group.

shoat *n.* A hog less than one year old.

shock (shok) *n.* A sudden blow or violent impact; an unexpected, sudden upset of mental or emotional balance; a serious weakening of the body caused by the loss of blood pressure or sudden injury. *v.* To strike with great surprise, disgust, or outrage; to give an electric shock.

shock absorber *n.* A device which is used for absorbing the energy of impulses to something.

shock-er (shok´ėr) *n.* Something that produces shock into something or someone.

shocking pink *n.* A shade of pink that is intense.

shock-proof *n.* To be incapable of being shocked.

shod *adj.* To be equipped with a shoe.

shoe (shōō) *n.* An outer cover for a foot; the part of a brake which presses against the drum or wheel to slow or stop the motion. *v.* To put on shoes.

shoe-bill *n.* A type of large wading bird that is located in the valley of the White Nile and is related to the herons and storks.

shoe-horn *n.* Type of curved piece of material that is used to put on a shoe.

shoe tree (shōō´trē˝) *n.* A device that is foot-shaped and placed into the shoe to help it maintain the shape of the shoe.

shone *v.* Past tense of shine.

shoo-fly (shōō´flī˝) *n.* A type of plant that is believed to repel flies.

shoot (shōōt) *v.* To kill or wound with a missile, as a bullet, fired from a weapon; to discharge or throw rapidly; to push forward or begin to grow by germinating. *Slang* To inject drugs directly into the veins.

shoot–em–up *n.* A type of show or movie where there is a large amount of bloodshed and shooting.

shooting gallery *n.* A range that is usually covered and having targets to shoot at for practice.

shooting star *n.* A meteor that appears in the sky as a temporary streak of light.

shoot–out *n.* A fight with handguns.

shop (shop) *n.* A small business or small retail store; a place where certain goods are produced. *v.* To visit a store in order to examine or buy things. **shopper** *n.*

shop-keep-er *n.* A person who runs a store.

shop-lift (shop´lift´) *v.* To take something from a store without paying for it.

shop-lift-er *n.* The person who takes things from a store without paying for them.

shopping center *n.* A group of stores that are gathered in one area for easier access.

shop-talk (shop´tok˝) *n.* The subject matter that is peculiar to an occupation.

shore (shōr) *n.* The land bordering a body of water.

shore dinner *n.* A meal or dinner that consists of mainly seafoods.

shore-front *n.* The land which is located along a shore.

shore-line *n.* A line or location where a body of water and the shore meet.

short (short) *adj.* Having little height or length; less than normal in distance, time, or other qualities; less than the needed amount. **shorts** Underpants or outerpants which end at the knee or above. **shortage** A lack in the amount needed. **short-change** To give less than the correct a-mount, as change for money. **short circuit** An electrical malfunction.

short-bread *n.* A type of cookie that is made from sugar, flour, and shortening.

short-cut *n.* A type of route that is more direct than the one that is usually taken.

short-en-ing (shor´te ning) *n.* A fat, such as butter, used to make pastry rich and light.

short-fall (short´ fol) *n.* The failure to accomplish a goal.

short-hand (short´hand˝) *n.* A type of writing where words and phrases are substituted by symbols and characters.

short-horn *n.* A breed of roan, red, or white beef cattle that originated in England.

short–horned grasshopper *n.* A type of grasshopper that has short antennae.

shortleaf pine *n.* A type of pine that has short leaves and can be found in the southern United States.

short-lived (short´līvd´) *adj.* Not lasting long; or living long.

short order (short´or´dėr) *n.* An order, usually for food, which can be quickly prepared and served.

short-sight-ed (short´sī´tid) *adj.* To be missing or lacking one's foresight.

shot (shot) *n.* The discharging of a gun, rocket, or other device; an attempt; a try; an injection; a photograph. *Slang* Useless; ruined.

shot hole *n.* The hole which is drilled for dynamite to be exploded in.

should (shed) *v.* Past tense of shall, used to express obligation, duty, or expectation.

shoul-der (shōl´dẽr) *n.* The part of the body located between the neck and upper arm; the side of the road. *v.* To use the shoulder to push or carry something; to take upon oneself.

shoul-der bag *n.* A type of bag that can be carried on the shoulder.

shoul-der patch *n.* A patch which is worn on the arm just below the shoulder.

should-n't (shed´ant) *contr.* Should not.

shout (shout) *v.* To yell. *n.* A loud cry.

shouting distance *n.* A distance that is short.

shove *v.* To push something or someone in a manner that may be rough.

shov-el (shuv´el) *n.* A tool with a long handle and a scoop, used for picking up material or for digging. *v.* To move, dig, or scoop up with a shovel; to push or move large amounts rapidly.

shov-el-er *n.* Someone or something that will shovel things such as dirt and debris.

shov-el-head *n.* A type of fish that has a head which looks like a shove.

shov-el-man *n.* A person who works with a shovel.

shov-el–nosed *n.* To have a flat nose that may resemble a shovel.

show (shō) *v.* To put within sight; to point out; to explain; to put on display. *n.* A display; a movie, play or similar entertainment.

show bill *n.* A type of poster which may be used for advertising purposes.

show-er (shou´ẽr) *n.* A short period of rain; a party with gifts given in honor of someone; a bath with water spraying down on the bather. *v.* To take a shower; to be extremely generous; to pour down in a shower. **showery** *adj.*

shrank *v.* Past tense of shrink.

shrap-nel (shrap´nel) *n. pl.* **shrapnel** A large shell containing metal fragments; fragments of metal that are exploded with great force.

shred (shred) *n.* A narrow strip or torn fragment; a small amount. *v.* To rip, tear, or cut into shreds.

shrew (shrō) *n.* A small mouse-like mammal, having a narrow, pointed snout.

shriek (shrēk) *n.* A loud, sharp scream or noise. **shriek** *v.*

shrill (shril) *adj.* A high-pitched, sharp sound.

shrimp (shrimp) *n. pl.* **shrimp** *or* **shrimps** A small, edible shellfish. A small person.

shrine (shrīn) *n.* A place for sacred relics; a place considered sacred because of an event or person associated with it.

shrink (shringk) *v.* To make or become less or smaller; to pull back from; to flinch. *Slang* A psychiatrist.

shroud (shroud) *n.* A cloth in which a body is wrapped for burial. *v.* To cover.

shrub (shrub) *n.* A woody plant which grows close to the ground and has several stems beginning at its base.

shrug (shrug) *v.* To raise the shoulders briefly to indicate doubt or indifference. **shrug** *n.*

shrunk *v.* Past tense of shrink.

shuck (shuk) *n.* The outer husk that covers an ear of corn. **shuck** *v.*

shud-der (shud´ẽr) *v.* To tremble uncontrollably, as from fear. **shudder** *n.*

shuf-fle (shuf´l) *v.* To drag or slide the feet; to mix together in a haphazard fashion; to rearrange or change the order of cards. **shuffle** *n.*

shun (shun) *v.* To avoid deliberately.

shut (shut) *v.* To move a door, drawer, or other object to close an opening; to block an entrance; to lock up; to cease or halt operations.

shut-tle (shut´l) *n.* A device used to move thread in weaving; a vehicle, as a train or plane, which travels back and forth from one location to another.

shy (shī) *adj.* Bashful; timid; easily frightened. *v.* To move suddenly from fear. **shy-ly** *adv.* **shyness** *n.*

si-al-a-gogue *n.* A kind of agent that will promote the flow of saliva.

si-al-ic *adj.* Pertaining to the light rock which is rich in alumina and silica.

Siamese twin *n.* One of a pair of twins that

are united at some part of the body with the other twin.

sib-ling (sib´ling) *n.* One of two or more children from the same parents.

sick (sik) *adj.* In poor health; ill; nauseated; morbid. **sickness** *n.*

sick bay *n.* A room on a ship that can be used as a hospital.

sick-en (sik´en) *v.* To become sick.

sick-en-er (sik´e nėr) *n.* Something that disgusts or sickens.

sick-ish *adj.* To be somewhat sick.

sick-le (sik´l) *n.* A tool with a curved blade attached to a handle, used for cutting grass or grain.

sick leave *n.* The absence from one's work that is permitted due to an illness.

sick-le cell *n.* An abnormal red blood cell which will take the shape of a crescent.

sickle feather *n.* A long curved tail feather of the cock.

sick-ly *adj.* To be somewhat unwell.

sick pay *n.* The wages which are paid to an employee while they are on sick leave.

sick-room *n.* A room where a person who is sick remains.

side (sīd) *n.* A surface between the front and back or top and bottom of an object; either surface of a flat object; the part to the left or right of a vertical axis; the right or left portion of the human body; the space beside someone or something; an opinion or point of view which is the opposite of another. *v.* To take a stand and support the opinion of a particular side. *adj.* Supplementary; peripheral.

side-arm *adj.* To be pertaining to a baseball pitching style where the arm is raised above the shoulder.

side-band *n.* A band of frequencies that are produced by modulation.

side bearing *n.* A space which is provided at the side of a typeset letter to prevent it from touching another letter.

side-burns *n.* The short side-whiskers that are worn by the man on the side of his face.

sideburned *adj.*

side-car *n.* A type of car that is attached to the side of a motorcycle for the use of a passenger.

side effect *n.* The secondary effect.

side-glance *n.* A look that is directed to the side.

side issue *n.* The issue that is apart from the main point.

side-light (sād´līt˝) *n.* The light that is produced for the side.

side-lin-er *n.* The person that remains on the sidelines during a sport or activity.

side-long *adj.* To be inclining on the side.

si-de-re-al (sī dēr´ē al) *adj.* To be pertaining to the stars.

sid-er-ite *n.* A type of ferrous carbonate that is an iron ore.

sid-er-it-ic *adj.* Pertaining to siderite.

side-sad-dle *n.* A type of saddle usually for women which allows the rider to place both legs on the same side of the horse.

side-split-ting *adj.* To be very funny.

side-step *v.* To step to the side.

side-stroke *n.* A type of swimming stroke where the swimmers are on their sides.

side-walk *n.* A type of paved walk that is used by pedestrians at the side of the street.

side-wall *n.* A wall which forms the side of something.

side-ward *adj.* To move toward the side.

side-wind-er *n.* A type of snake which moves by thrusting its body diagonaly forward.

SIDS *abbr. n.* Sudden infant death syndrome; an unexpected death of a seemingly healthy baby, occurring during sleep in the first four months of life.

siege (sēj) *n.* The action of surrounding a town or port in order to capture it; a prolonged sickness.

si-er-ra (sē er´a) *n.* A rugged chain of mountains or hills.

si-es-ta (sē es´ta) *n.* A rest or short nap.

sie-va bean *n.* A type of bean which is closely related to the lime bean.

sieve (siv) *n.* A meshed or perforated device

which allows small particles to pass through but which holds back larger particles; a device for separating liquids from solids.

sieve plate *n.* A wall which is perforated located at the end of one of the cells that make up a sieve tube.

sieve tube *n.* A type of tube that is made of thin-walled cells.

sift (sift) *v.* To separate coarse particles from small or fine ones by passing through a sieve. **through** To carefully examine. **sift** *n.* **sifter** *n.*

sig *abbr.* Signature; signal.

SIG *abbr.* Special interest group.

sigh (sī) *v.* To exhale a long, deep breath, usually when tired, sad, or relieved.

sight (sīt) *n.* The ability to see with the eyes; the range or distance one can see; a view; a device mounted on a firearm used to guide the eye or aim.

sighted *adj.* To have sight.

sight gag *n.* A comic episode where the effect is created by a camera shot rather than by the words.

sight-less *adj.* To be lacking or missing the sense of sight. **sightlessness** *n.*

sight-ly (sīt´lē) *adj.* To be pleasing to the sight. **sightliness** *n.*

sight-see (sīt´sē) *v.* To travel about and see sights that are of interest.

sig-il (sij´il) *n.* A word that is supposed to have occult power in magic.

sig-ma (sig´ma) *n.* The 18th letter in the Greek alphabet.

sig-moid *adj.* To be curved in two directions.

sign (sīn) *n.* A piece of paper, wood, metal, etc., with information written on it; a gesture that tells or means something. *v.* To write one's name on.

sig-nal (sig´nal) *n.* A sign which gives a warning; the image or sound sent by television or radio. *v.* To make or send a signal to.

sig-nal-ize (sig´na līz´) *v.* To make signals to someone. **signalization** *n.*

sig-nal-man *n.* A person who works with signals or signals others.

sig-nal-ment *n.* The description of some-

thing or someone by characteristic marks.

sig-na-ture (sig´na chėr) *n.* The name of a person, written by that person; a distinctive mark which indicates identity. *Music* A symbol indicating the time and key.

sign-board *n.* A type of board that is used for the purpose of being noticed.

sig-net *n.* A type of seal which is used to give personal authority to a document or papers instead of using a signature.

signet ring *n.* A type of ring that is engraved with a signet.

sig-ni-fi-a-ble *adj.* Being represented with a symbol or a sign of some sort.

sig-nif-i-cance (sig nif´i kans) *n.* The quality of being important; the meaning of something which is considered important.

sig-ni-fi-er *n.* Something that signifies.

sig-ni-fy (sig´ni fī´) *v.* To express or make known by a sign; to indicate. **signification** *n.* **significant** *adj.*

sign in *v.* To record the arrival of someone at a particular time by the signing of a list or the punching of the time clock.

sign language *n.* A means of communicating by using hand gestures; the language of deaf people.

sign manual *n.* The signature of a king which is on a royal grant and is placed at the top or beginning of the document.

sign off *v.* To tell or to announce the end of a program or of a broadcast.

sign on *n.* To tell or to announce the beginning of the the broadcast for the day.

si-gnor *n.* An Italian man of the gentility.

si-gno-ra *n.* An Italian woman who is married and is usually of the gentility.

si-gno-ri-na (sēn˝yo rē´na) *n.* Italian woman who is not yet married.

si-gno-ri-no (sēn˝yo rē´nō) *n.* Italian boy.

sign out *v.* To tell of one's departure by signing a list depicting when a person left.

sign-post *n.* A type of post that bears signs on it for the use of giving directions.

sike (sīk) *n.* A type of stream which is small in size.

si-lage (sīlij) *n.* The fodder which is converted into feed for livestock.

sild *n.* A herring at a young age in its development but older than a brisling.

si-lence (sī´lens) *n.* The state or quality of being silent; quiet. *v.* To make quiet. **silencer** *n.*

si-lenc-er (sī´len sėr) *n.* Someone or something which will cause silence.

si-lent (sī´lent) *adj.* Making no sound; not speaking; mute; unable to speak; an unpronounced letter, as the "g" in gnat.

si-lents *n.* A kind of motion picture in which there is not a spoken dialogue.

silent treatment *n.* The act of ignoring another person completely.

sil-hou-ette (sil´ŏ et´) *n.* The outline of something, as a human profile, filled in with a solid color, as black; the outline of an object. *v.* To make a silhouette.

sil-i-con (sil´*i* k*o*n) *n.* The second most common chemical element, found only in combination with another substance, symbolized as Si.

silicone rubber *n.* A type of rubber that is made from silicone elastomers and is flexible over a wide range of different temperatures.

silk (silk) *n.* A soft, thread-like fiber spun by silkworms; thread or fabric made from silk. **silken** *adj.* **silky** *adj.*

silk-a-line *n.* A type of cotton fabric that has a smooth finish like that of silk.

silk cotton *n.* A type of silky covering that can be found on the seeds of various silk-cotton trees.

silk–cotton tree *n.* A type of tropical tree that has large fruits with the seeds covered by silk cotton.

silk gland *n.* The gland that will produce the fluid which is excreted in filaments and then hardens into silk when it comes into contact with the air.

silk oak *n.* A type of timber tree of Australia that has mottled wood which is used for the purpose of making cabinets.

silk stocking *n.* A person who is dressed in a fashionable manner.

silk-worm *n.* A type of larva that spins a large amount of silk when it is making its cocoon.

sill (sil) *n.* The horizontal support that forms the bottom part of the frame of a window or door.

sil-ly (sil´ē) *adj.* Foolish; lacking good sense, seriousness, or substance.

si-lo (sī´lō) *n.* A tall, cylindrical structure for storing food for farm animals; an underground shelter or storage for guided missiles.

silt *n.* A deposit of soil and sediment that may have been caused by a river.

silt-stone *n.* A type of stone which is composed of silt.

sil-u-roid *n.* A member of the suborder of the fishes which contains the catfish.

sil-va *n.* The trees of a country or region.

sil-ver (sil´vėr) *n.* A soft, white metallic element used in tableware, jewelry, and coins, symbolized by Ag. *v.* To coat with silver. *adj.* Of the color silver.

silver age *n.* A period in history that is secondary to the gold age.

silver bell *n.* A type of tree located in the southeastern United States that is grown for its bell-shaped flowers.

sil-ver-ber-ry *n.* A type of shrub which is found in North America and is related to the buffalo berry.

silver fir *n.* A fir that has leaves that are silver that are silver colored on the underneath.

sil-ver-fish *n.* A small wingless insect which has been known to be injurious to clothing and paper.

silver fox *n.* A color phase of the red fox which is genetic and the coat is white with black tips.

silver hake *n.* A type of hake that is found off the northern New England coast and is used as an important food fish.

silver lining *n.* A hopeful prospect.

silver maple *n.* A type of maple of North America that has leaves which are silvery white beneath.

sil-vern *adj.* To be made of silver.

silver paper *n.* A metallic paper, such as tinfoil, that has a silver-like coating.

silver perch *n.* A type of fish which is silvery in color and resembles the perch.

sil-ver-sides *n.* A type of fish that has a silver stripe down both sides of its body.

sil-ver-smith *n.* A person who makes goods and articles out of silver.

sil-ver-y *adj.* To have a musical tone which is clear and soft.

sil-vics *n.* A study of the characteristics and ecology of forest trees.

sim-i-lar (sim´i lėr) *adj.* Almost the same, but not identical.

sim-i-lar-i-ty *n.* The state of two things or people being like or similar.

sim-i-le (sim´i lē) *n.* A structure of speech which is used for the purpose of comparing two things that are often unlike.

sim-mer (sim´ėr) *v.* To cook just below boiling; to be near the point of breaking, as with emotion.

simmer down *v.* To calm.

sim-nel *n.* A bread that is made of fine wheat flour.

si-mo-nize *v.* To polish something with wax.

si-moom *n.* A type of dry wind that is found to be from the deserts of Africa and Asia.

sim-ple (sim´pl) *adj.* Easy to do or understand; not complicated; ordinary; not showy; lacking intelligence or education. **simpleness** *n.* **simply** *adv.*

simple closed curve *n.* A type of curve that does not intersect itself.

simple fraction *n.* A type of fraction where the denominator and the numerator are of whole numbers.

simple motion *n.* A type of motion that is in a straight line.

sim-plic-i-ty (sim plis´i tē) *n.* The state of being easy to understand; naturalness; sincerity.

sim-pli-fy (sim´pli fī´) *v.* To make easy or simple. **simplification** *n.*

sim-u-late (sim´ū lāt´) *v.* To have the appearance, effect, or form of. **simulation** *n.*

simulator *n.*

sim-u-lat-ed rank *n.* The status of a civilian that is equal to a military rank.

si-mul-ta-ne-ous *adj.* Occurring at exactly the same time. **simultaneously** *adv.*

sin (sin) *n.* The breaking of a religious law or a law of God. *v.* To do something which is morally wrong. **sinless** *adj.* **sinner** *n.*

since (sins) *adv.* At a time before the present. *prep.* During the time later than; continuously from the time when something occurs.

sin-cere (sin sēr´) *adj.* Honest; not deceitful; genuine; true. **sincerely** *adv.* **sincerity** *n.*

sin-cer-i-ty *n.* The state of being sincere.

sin-cip-i-tal *adj.* To be pertaining to the sinciput.

sin-ci-put *n.* The upper half or section of the skull.

sine *n.* A function in trigonometry.

sine qua non *n.* Something which is indispensable.

sin-ful *n.* To be tainted with sin. **sinfulness** *n.* **sinfully** *adv.*

sing (sing) *v.* To use the voice to make musical tones; to make a humming or whistling sound. **singer** *n.*

singe (sinj) *v.* To slightly burn the surface of something; to remove feathers.

sin-gle (sing´gl) *adj.* Of or referring to only one, separate; individual; unmarried. *n.* A separate, individual person or item; a dollar bill; in baseball, a hit that allows the batter to progress to first base.

single–breasted *adj.* To have a center closing that has one row of buttons.

single cross *n.* The first generation hybrid that is between two selected lines.

sin-gle file *n.* A type of line where the people are one right behind each other.

single–handed *adj.* To be done by one person. **single-handedly** *adv.*

sin-gle–minded *adj.* To have one overriding purpose.

sin-gle-ness *n.* The state of being single.

sin-gle-stick *n.* Fencing with a wooden stick that is held in one hand.

single tax *n.* A type of tax that is levied on a single item.

sin-gu-lar (sing´gū lėr) *adj.* Separate; one; extraordinary; denoting a single unit, thing or person.

sin-gu-lar-i-ty (sing˝gū lar´i tē) *n.* A unit that is separate; a state of being singular.

sin-gu-lar-ize *v.* To make something singular.

sin-is-ter (sin´i stėr) *adj.* To be evil or causing evil. **sinisterness** *n.* **sinisterly** *adv.*

sink (singk) *v.* To submerge beneath a surface; to go down slowly; to become less forceful or weaker. *n.* A basin for holding water, attached to a wall and connected to a drain. **sinkable** *adj.*

sink-age (sing´kij) *n.* The degree of sinking.

sink-er *n.* A weight that is used for the purpose of sinking a fishing line into the water.

sink-hole *n.* A type of hollow depression where drainage is able to collect.

si-no-logue *n.* A person who is a specialist in sinology.

si-nol-o-gy *n.* A study of the Chinese and the culture, history, and language. **sinological** *adj.* **sinologist** *n.*

sin-u-ate (sin´ū it) *adj.* To have a margin that has indentations. **sinuately** *adv.*

sin-u-os-i-ty *n.* The state of being sinuous.

sin-u-ous (sin´ū us) *adj.* To be marked with strong lithe movements. **sinuousness** *n.*

si-nus (sī´nus) *n., Anat.* A body cavity; one of eight air spaces in the bones of the face which drain into the nasal cavity.

si-nus-i-tis *n.* The swelling and inflammation of the sinuses of the skull.

sip (sip) *v.* To drink in small amounts.

si-phon (sī´fon) *also* **syphon**. A tube through which liquid from one container can be drawn into another by forced air pressure. **siphon** *v.*

si-pho-no-phore *n.* A type of free-swimming hyfrozoans that are transparent and have specialized zooids.

sip-pet (sip´it) *n.* A small piece of toast used for garnishing.

sir (ser) *n.* A respectful term used when addressing a man.

sir-dar (sėr där´) *n.* The person who holds a responsible position in India.

si-ren (sī´ren) *n.* A whistle which makes a loud wailing noise, as a warning or signal; a seductive woman.

si-re-ni-an *n.* A type of aquatic herbivorous mammal including the manatee.

sir-loin (sūr´loin) *n.* The cut of meat that is from the hindquarter.

sis-ter (sis´tėr) *n.* A female having the same parents as another; a woman in membership with others, as in a church group or sorority.

sis-ter-hood *n.* The state of being a sister.

sis-ter-ly (sis´tėr lē) *adj.* The state of being a sister; acting like a sister.

sis-trum *n.* A type of percussion instrument that was used in Egypt in ancient times.

sit (sit) *v.* To rest the body with the weight on the buttocks; to cover eggs for hatching; to pose for a portrait.

si-tar *n.* A type of Indian lute that has a long neck and varying number of strings.

site (sīt) *n.* A location of planned buildings.

sit-ting (sit´ing) *n.* An act of one that sits.

sitting ducks *n.* A defenseless target.

sit-u-a-tion *n.* A way in which something or someone is placed, with its surroundings. **situationally** *adv.* **situational** *adj.*

six (siks) *n.* The cardinal number 6, after five and before seven.

six-fold (siks´fōld) *adj.* To have six members.

six-pack *n.* The container for six bottles so that they can be bought together.

six–penny nail *n.* A type of nail that is about two inches in length.

six-teen (siks´tēn´) *n.* The cardinal number 16, after fifteen and before seventeen.

six-ty (siks´tē) *n.* The cardinal number 60, after fifty-nine and before sixty-one.

siz-a-ble (sī´za bl) *adj.* Large in size or dimensions.

size (sīz) *n.* The measurement or dimensions of something; a sticky substance used to glaze walls, before applying wallpaper. *v.* To arrange according to size.

siz-ed *adj.* To have a size which is specified.

siz-zle (siz´l) *v.* To make a hissing sound, as of fat frying. **sizzle** *n.*

sizzler *n.* The one that will sizzle.

skald *n.* Type of ancient Scandinavian poet. **skaldic** *adj.*

skat *n.* A kind of three-handed game of cards where each player bids for the privilege to attempt any of the several contracts.

skate (skāt) *n.* A device with rollers which attaches to the shoe and allows one to glide over ice or roll over a wooden or cement surface; a shoe fitted with rollers. **ice skate** *v.* **roller skate** *v.*

skate-board *n.*

A narrow piece of wood with wheels attached.

skat-er *n.* A person who is able to skate.

skat-ing *n.* The action or the art of gliding on skates.

ska-tole *n.* A kind of foul smelling substance which is found in the intestines.

ske-dad-dle *v.* To leave or to run away from something or someone.

skeet *n.* The sport of trapshooting where the targets are made of clay and thrown in a way which resembles the manner in which birds fly.

skee-ter *n.* A type of iceboat that has one sail.

skeg *n.* A stern of the keel of a boat or ship which is near the sternpost.

skeigh *adj.* To be spirited.

skein (skān) *n.* A piece of thread which is wound onto a reel.

skel-e-tal *adj.* Pertaining to or relating to the skeleton.

skel-e-ton (skel´i ton) *n.* The framework of bones that protects and supports the soft tissues and organs.

skel-e-ton-ize *v.* To reduce something to skeleton form.

skeleton key *n.* A type of key that has been filed in order to be able to open many locks and can be used as a master key.

skep (skep) *n.* A type of hive that is doomed and has been made of twisted straw.

skep-sis *n.* A philosophic doubt as to the reality of something.

skep-tic (skep´tik) *n.* A person who doubts or questions. **skepticism** *n.* **skeptical** *adj.* **skeptically** *adv.*

sker-ry *n.* A island which is rocky.

sketch (skech) *n.* A rough drawing or outline; a brief literary composition.

sketch-book *n.* A kind of book which is used for the purpose of sketching things.

skew (skū) *v.* To turn or slant. *n.* A slant.

skew-bald *adj.* To be marked with spots of white or another color or colors.

skew curve *n.* A type of curve which is three-dimensional and does not lie in the same plane or single plane.

skew-er *n.* A piece of metal used as a pin for the purpose of fastening foods together in order to broil them on a grill

skew lines *n.* Type of lines which are straight and do not intersect and are not located within the same plane.

skew-ness *n.* The lack of symmetry or of straightness of an object such as a line or curve.

ski (skē) *n. pl.* **skis** One of a pair of long, narrow pieces of wood worn on the feet for gliding over snow or water. To travel on skis. **skier** *v.*

ski-a-gram *n.* The figure which is formed by shading the outline of a shadow that is created by the figure.

ski-ag-ra-phy *n.* The art of making skiagrams.

ski boot *n.* A rigid boot which is attached to the ski and is used to hold the ski on the foot.

skid (skid) *v.* To slide to the side of the road; to slide along without rotating.

skid-der *n.* A person who uses a skid or who skids.

skid-dy *adj.* Being likely to cause skidding.

skid road *n.* A type of road where logs are skidded along.

skill (skil) *n.* Ability gained through practice; expertise. **skilled** *adj.*

skiff (skif) *n.* A type of small and light sailing ship.

ski-ing (skē´ing) *n.* The sport of jumping

and moving on skis.

ski jump *n.* The jump which is made by someone who is wearing skis and usually jumps off of a large ramp.

ski lift *n.* A type of conveyor that is used to bring the skiers to the top of the hill that they will then ski down.

skill (skil) *n.* Ability gained through practice; expertise.

skilled (skild) *adj.* To have acquired a skill for something.

skil-let (skil´it) *n.* A type of pot that has feet and is used for the purpose of cooking foods on the hearth.

skill-ful (skil´ful) adj. To be displaying a skill. **skillfully** *adv.*

skil-ling (skil´ing) *n.* Type of old Scandinavian unit of value, such as a coin.

skill-less (skil´lis) *adj.* To have no skill for anything. **skilllessness** *n.*

skim (skim) *v.* To remove the top layer; to remove floating matter; to read over material quickly; to travel over lightly and quickly. **skimmer** *n.*

ski mask *n.* A type of face covering that is made of fabric and can be worn while one is skiing for protection from the elements.

skim milk *n.* A type of milk where the cream has been taken out.

skim-ming (skim´ing) *n.* The substance or that which is skimmed from a liquid.

skimp (skimp) *v.* To economize; to hold back. **skimpy** *adj.*

skin (skin) *n.* The tough, outside covering of man and some animals; the outside layer of a vegetable or fruit; the fur or pelt of an animal. **skin** *v.* **skinless** *adj.*

skin–deep *adj.* To be as deep as the skin; very thin.

skin diving *n.* A sport that involves swimming under the water without a breathing device.

skin-flint (skin´flint˝) *n.* A type of person who would extort or save money any way that is possible.

skin game *n.* A kind of game that involves a trick or swindling of the person.

skin graft *n.* A section of the skin that is removed from one area and placed in an area where the skin has been removed or damaged.

skin grafting *n.* The process of placing or or making a skin graft.

skin-head (skin´hed) *n.* A person whose hair is very short.

skink *v.* To serve something like a drink.

skink-er *n.* A person who serves liquor.

skin-ner (skin´ėr) *n.* A person who deals or sells skins.

skin-ny (slin´ē) *adj.* To be lacking a sufficient amount of flesh on the body, making one look thin.

skin-tight (skin´tīt) *adj.* To be closely fitted to one's body.

skip (skip) *v.* To move in light jumps or leaps; to go from one place to another, missing what is between. **skip** *n.*

skip-jack *n.* A type of fish that will jump above the surface of the water.

ski pole *n.* The type of pole that is used in the sport of skiing for the purpose of pushing the skier along the snow.

skirl (skürl) *n.* The high shrill sound which is produced by a bagpipe.

skir-mish *n.* A small and minor fight.

skirr *n.* To look or to search about in.

skirt (skert) *n.* A piece of clothing that extends down from the waist. *v.* To extend along the boundary; to avoid the issue.

skirt-ing (skür´ting) *n.* The fabric which is suitable for the making of skirts.

ski run *n.* The trail which is used for the sport of skiing.

skit (skit) *n.* A type of humorous story.

ski tow *n.* A conveyor that is used for the purpose of bringing the skiers back up to the top of the hill so that they can ski back down.

skit-tish (skit´ish) *adj.* To be frightened easily.

skiv-er (skī´vėr) *n.* A type of thin leather that is made from sheepskin.

ski-wear *n.* The clothing that is used while one is skiing to keep warm.

skulk *v.* To conceal something out of fear; to move in a furtive way or manner. **skulk**

n. A person who skulks around.

skull (skul) *n.* The bony part of the skeleton which protects the brain.

skull-cap (skul´kap˝) *n.* A type of cap that is close-fitting.

skull practice *n.* A type of meeting for a discussion or the exchanging of ideas.

skunk (skungk) *n.* A black mammal with white streaks down its back, which sprays an unpleasant smelling liquid when annoyed or frightened.

skunk cab-bage *n.* A type of herb that has a very foul odor and is found in the eastern part of North America.

sky (skī) *n. pl.* **skies** The upper atmosphere above the earth; the celestial regions.

sky blue *n.* A color which may range from light blue to pale blue.

sky-cap *n.* A person who has the job of handling the luggage at an airport.

sky-div-ing *n.* The sport of jumping out of an airplane while it is flying in the air.

sky-ey (skīē) *adj.* Pertaining to or resembling the sky.

sky-high (skī´hī) *adv. or adj.* To be located high in the air; to do in a manner which is exorbitant.

ski-lark *n.* A type of lark which is large in size and is especially noted for its song.

sky-light *n.* The light of the sky; a window in the roof to admit natural light.

sky-line *n.* The outline of a building or other very large object against the sky.

sky-phos (skī´fos) *n.* A type of drinking vessel that was used in ancient Greece and had two handles.

sky-scrap-er (skīskrā˝pėr) *n.* A type of building which is very tall and therefore seems to scrape the sky.

sky-ward *adj.* To be moving toward the sky.

sky-way (skī´wā˝) *n.* The route which is used by airplanes.

sky-write *v.* To write letters or words in the sky.

sky-writ-ing *n.* The writing which is formed in the sky with the use of smoke.

sl *abbr.* Slightly.

SL *abbr.* Sea level; south latitude.

slab (slab) *n.* A thick piece or slice.

slab-sid-ed *adj.* To have sides which are flat.

slack (slak) *adj.* Not taut or tense; sluggish; lacking in strength. *v.* To make slack. *n.* A part of something which hangs loose. **slacks** Long pants or trousers.

slack-baked *n.* To be underdone.

slack-en *v.* To slow something down.

slack-er *n.* One who shirks an obligation.

slain *v.* Past tense of slay.

sla-lom *n.* A type of skiing where the skier zig-zags down the hill between upright obstacles such as flags.

slam (slam) *v.* To shut with force; to strike with a loud impact. *n.* A loud noise produced by an impact.

slam–bang *adj.* Being very loud or violent.

slam-mer *n., Slang* Jail or prison.

slan-der (slan´dėr) *n.* A false statement that deliberately does harm to another's reputation. **slanderous** *adj.*

slang (slang) *n.* Informal language that contains made-up words or common words used in a different or uncommon way.

slant (slant) *v.* To lie in an oblique position; to slope; to report on something giving only one side or viewpoint. *n.* An incline or slope.

slap (slap) *n.* A sharp blow with an open hand. **slap** *v.*

slap-hap-py *adj.* To be recklessly foolish.

slap shot *n.* The shot which is taken in ice hockey that is made with a swinging stroke.

slap-stick *n.* A type of comedy that stresses or contains horseplay and silly expressions.

slash (slash) *v.* To cut with a fast sweeping stroke; to reduce or limit greatly. *n.* A long cut.

slash-ing *n.* The process of slashing something. **slashingly** *adv.*

slash pine *n.* A type of southern pine which

is a source of lumber and of turpentine.

slat *n*. A narrow piece of wood.

slate (slāt) *n*. A fine grained rock that splits into thin layers, often used as a writing surface or roofing material. **slate** *v*.

slate black *n*. A color that is purplish black.

slat-er *n*. A person who slates.

slath-er *v*. To spread something in a thick manner onto something else.

slat-ing *n*. The work that is done by a slater.

slat-tern-ly (slat´ėrn lē) *adj*. To be dirty because of neglect.

slat-y *adj*. To have the characteristic of slate.

slaugh-ter (slo´tėr) *v*. To kill livestock for food; to kill in great numbers. *Slang* To soundly defeat. **slaughterer** *n*.

slaugh-ter-house *n*. A place where one butchers or slaughters animals.

slaugh-ter-ous *adj*. Pertaining to slaughter.

Slav *n*. One who is able to speak a Slavic language for his native tongue.

slave (slāv) *n*. A person held against his will and made to work for another.

slave ant *n*. A type of ant that is enslaved by the slave-making ant of the colony.

slave driver *n*. A person who is the supervisor of slaves.

slave-hold-er *n*. A person who is the owner of the slaves.

Slav-ic *adj*. To be pertaining to the Slavs or the language that they speak.

Slav-i-cist *n*. A person who is a specialist in the Slavic language.

slav-ish (slā´vish) *adj*. Pertaining to the characteristics of a slave.

slay (slā) *v*. To kill or to destroy something in a violent manner.

sleave (slēv) *v*. To separate something such as silk fibers into filaments.

sleave silk *n*. A type of floss silk that is easily separated into filaments.

sled (sled) *n*. A vehicle with runners, used to travel on snow or ice.

sled dog *n*. A type of dog which has been trained to pull a sledge.

sledge *n*. A kind of vehicle that has low runners and is used for the purpose of transporting loads over the snow and is pulled by dogs.

sledge-ham-mer *n*. A type of hammer which is very heavy and must be wielded with both hands.

sleek (slēk) *adj*. Smooth and shiny; neat and trim. **sleekly** *adv*. **sleekness** *n*.

sleep (slēp) *n*. A natural state of rest for the mind and body. *v*. To rest in sleep.

sleeping bag *n*. The bag which is lined and is used for sleeping.

sleep-ing car *n*. A car of a train that has accommodations allowing a person to sleep.

sleeping pill *n*. A type of drug which is taken to help a person fall asleep.

sleep-less *adj*. Being not able to get to sleep. **sleeplessness** *n*.

sleep out *v*. To sleep away in a place that is not one's home.

sleep-walk-er *n*. A person who is able to walk while still asleep.

sleep-y (slē´pē) *adj*. Pertaining to sleep; needing sleep.

sleet (slēt) *n*. Rain that is partially frozen; a combination of snow and rain. **sleet** *v*. **sleety** *adj*.

sleeve (slēv) *n*. The part of a garment which covers the arm; a case for something.

sleeve-let *n*. A kind of covering which is worn on the forearm in order to protect the clothing from dirt and wear.

sleigh (slā) *n*. A vehicle mounted on runners, usually pulled over ice and snow by horses.

sleigh bell *n*. A type of bell that is attached to a sleigh.

slen-der (slen´dėr) *adj*. Slim; inadequate in amount. **slenderly** *adv*.

slept *v*. Past tense of sleep.

sleuth *n*. A detective.

slew *n*. A large amount of something.

slice (slīs) *n*. A thin cut; a portion or share; in sports, a ball in flight that curves off to the right of its target. *v*. To cut into slices. **slicer** *n*.

slice bar *n*. A type of steel bar that has a flat blade used for chipping.

slick (slik) *adj*. Smooth and slippery; quick;

smart; clever; attractive for the present time but without quality or depth. *n.* Water with a thin layer of oil floating on top.

slick-en-side *n.* A striated surface that is produced on a rock by moving along a fault.

slick-er (slik´ẽr) *n.* A raincoat made of yellow oilcloth.

slide (slīd) *v.* To move smoothly across a surface without losing contact. *n.* The act of sliding; a slanted smooth surface usually found on playgrounds; a transparent picture which can be projected on a screen; a small glass plate for examining specimens under a microscope.

slid-er *n.* Something that slides.

slide valve *n.* A kind of valve which opens and closes something such as a passageway.

slide-way *n.* The way which something slides.

slid-ing seat *n.* The rower's seat which will slide aft and fore.

slight (slīt) *adj.* Minor in degree; unimportant. *v.* To ignore. **slightly** *adv.*

slight-ing *adj.* To be characterized by disrespect. **slightingly** *adv.*

slim (slim) *adj.* Slender; meager; not much. **slimness** *n.*

slime (slīm) *n.* A wet, slippery substance. **slimy** *adj.*

slim-ming *adj.* To be giving the appearance or effect of slenderness.

slim-sy *adj.* Being frail.

sling (sling) *n.* A piece of material, as leather, or a strap which secures something; a piece of fabric worn around the neck used to support an injured hand or arm; a weapon made of a strap, used to throw a stone.

sling-shot *n.* A type of v-shaped device which has an elastic band and is used to propel objects such as rocks through the air.

slink-y (sling´ke) *adj.* To be sinuous and sleek in moving.

slip (slip) *v.* To move in a smooth, quiet way; to fall or lose one's balance. *Slang* To become less active, alert, or strong. *n.* The action of slipping; the place between two piers used for docking a boat; a woman's undergarment; a small piece of paper; a

portion of a plant used for grafting.

slip-case (slip´kās´) *n.* A type of container that has one end open in order to slide books into for protection.

slip-cov-er *n.* A type of cover that can be slipped on and off of something.

slip-knot *n.* A type of knot that will slip along the rope of which it is made.

slip-o-ver *n.* A type of garment that will slip on and off with ease.

slip-page *n.* The process of slipping.

slip-per-y (slip´e rē) *adj.* To cause something to slip. **slipperiness** *n.*

slip-sheet *v.* To put in or to insert a slip sheet between other sheets.

slip sheet *n.* A type of paper that is put between newly printed sheets.

slip-sole *n.* A type of thin insole.

slip stitch *n.* A type of stitch which is used for concealing folded edges in sewing.

slip up *v.* Make a blunder or mistake.

slit *v.* To cut a slit into something. *n.* A narrow opening or cut into something.

slith-er (slith´ẽr) *v.* To slide or slip in an indirect manner; to move like a snake. **slithery** *adj.*

slit trench *n.* A trench which is narrow and is used as shelter in a battle from shell fragments.

sliv-er (sliv´ẽr) *n.* A thin, narrow piece of something that has been broken off.

slob (slob) *n.* One who is slovenly.

slob-ber (slob´ẽr) *v.* To dribble from the mouth. **slobber** *n.*

sloe gin *n.* A type of sweet liquor that is made of grain spirits and is flavored with sloes.

slog *v.* To plod along slowly and heavily.

slo-gan (slō´gan) *n.* A phrase used to express the aims of a cause.

slo-gan-ize *v.* To use something as a slogan.

sloop (slōp) *n.* A type of boat with one mast which is rigged fore-and-aft.

slop (slop) *n.* A tasteless liquid food.

slop chest *n.* The store which is on a merchant ship and supplies the crew with goods such as tobacco.

slope (slōp) *v.* To slant upward or downward. *n.* An upward or downward incline, as a ski slope.

slop jar *n.* A type of pail that is large in size and is used for the purpose of receiving and holding the waste water from a washbowl.

slop-py *adj.* To be wet so that it spatters easily.

slosh (slosh) *v.* To splash in a liquid, as water. **sloshy** *adj.*

slot (slot) *n.* A narrow, thin groove or opening. *Slang* A place or scheduled time for an event.

slot-back *n.* The offensive halfback in the game of football that lines up behind and between the tackle and the offensive end.

sloth (sloth) *n.* Laziness; a slow mammal found in SouthAmerica.

sloth-ful *adj.* To be inclined to sloth. **slothfulness** *n.*

slouch (slouch) *n.* A drooping or sagging posture; a lazy person. *v.* To sit or walk with poor posture.

slouch hat *n.* A kind of hat that has a wide flexible brim.

slouch-y *adj.* To be lacking good posture. **slouchiness** *n.*

slough *n.* The skin which is cast off from a snake as he sheds it.

Slo-vak *n.* A person who is a member of the Slavic people of eastern Czecholslovakia.

slo-ven (sluv′en) n. A person who is habitually negligent of cleanliness.

slov-en-ly (sluv′en lē) adj. To be untidy as in one's personal appearance.

slow (slō) *adj.* Moving at a low rate of speed; requiring more time than usual; not lively; sluggish; not interesting. *adv.* At less speed; in a slow manner. *v.* To make slower. **slowly** *adv.* **slowness** *n.*

slow–foot-ed *adj.* To be moving at a slow pace. **slow-footedness** *n.*

slow-poke *n.* A person who is slow.

slow–witted *adj.* To be mentally slow.

sludge *n.* A mass which is slushy.

slue *v.* To cause something to skid.

slug (slug) *n.* A slow animal related to the snail; a bullet or a lump of metal. *v.* To strike forcefully with the fist or a heavy object.

slug-fest *n.* A type of fight which is marked by the exchange of blows that are heavy.

slug-gard (slug′ėrd) *n.* A person who is habitually lazy. **sluggardly** *adj.*

slug-ger *n.* A person who strikes with heavy blows such as a fighter.

slug-gish *adj.* To be slow to respond to a treatment or to a stimulation. **sluggishness** *n.* **sluggishly** *adv.*

sluice (slŏs) *n.* A man-made ditch used to move water; a sloping trough used for floating logs. *v.* To wash with flowing water.

sluice-way (slŏs′wā) *n.* A channel which is artifical and into which water is admitted from a sluice.

slum (slum) *n.* A crowded urban neighborhood marked by poverty. **slum** *v.*

slum-ber (slum′bėr) *v.* To sleep; to doze. *n.* Sleep. **slumberer** *n.*

slum-ber-ous (slum′bė us) *adj.* Being able to induce slumber.

slumber party *n.* A type of overnight gathering usually of girls at someone's house.

slum-my *adj.* To be pertaining to a slum.

slump (slump) *v.* To fall or sink suddenly. **slump** *n.*

slung *v.* Past tense of sling.

slur (sler) *v.* To slide over without careful consideration; to pronounce unclearly. *n.* An insult. *Music* Two or more notes connected with a curved line to indicate they are to be slurred.

slurp (slürp) *v.* To make or produce a sucking noise while one is drinking.

slur-ry (slür′ē) *n.* A type of watery mixture of matter which is insoluble.

slush (slush) *n.* Melting snow; snow which is partially melted. **slushy** *adj.*

slut (slut) *n.* A woman of bad character; a prostitute. **sluttish** *adj.*

SLV *abbr.* Satellite launch vehicle.

sly (slī) *adj.* Cunning; clever; sneaky; underhanded. **slyly** *adv.* **slyness** *n.*

sly-boots *n.* A person who is sly.

sm *abbr.* Small.

SMA *abbr.* Sergeant major of the army.

smack (smak) *v.* To slap; to press and open the lips with a sharp noise. *n.* The act or noise of slapping something. *adv.* Directly.

smack-er *n.* A person who smacks.

smack-ing (smak´ing) *adj.* To be lively.

Smaj *abbr.* Sergeant major.

small (smol) *adj.* Little in size, quantity, or extent; unimportant. *n.* The part that is less than the other. **smallness** *n.*

small ale *n.* A kind of weak ale that is brewed with little malt and is a cheap drink.

small arm *n.* A type of firearm which can be fired while it is held in the hands.

small change *n.* The coins of a low demonination.

small-clothes *n.* The close-fitting knee breeches which were worn in the 18th century.

small–fry *adj.* To be pertaining to a child.

small hours *n.* The hours which occur in the early morning.

small intestines *n.* The section of the intestines which is located between the colon and the stomach.

small-mouth bass *n.* Type of black bass which can be found in clear lakes and rivers.

small-pox (smol´poks´) *n.* An acute, contagious disease marked by high fever and sores on the skin.

small–scale *adj.* To be small in scope.

small-sword *n.* A type of light tapering sword that is used for thrusting in fencing.

small talk *n.* A casual conversation.

smalt-ite *n.* A type of white or grey mineral which is an arsenide of nickel and cobalt.

smal-to *n.* A type of colored glass that can be used for mosaic work.

smarm-y *adj.* To be marked by a smug.

smart (smärt) *adj.* Intelligent; clever. **smartly** *adv.* **smartness** *n.*

smart-en *v.* To make someone smarter.

smart-weed *n.* A polygonums that has a strong acid juice.

smash (smash) *v.* To break into small pieces; to move forward violently, as to shatter; to ruin. *n.* The act or sound of crashing. *adj.* Outstanding. **smasher** *n.*

smat-ter *v.* To speak with a superficial knowledge.

smaze *n.* The combination of smoke and haze that is similar to smog in its appearance only.

smear (smēr) *v.* To spread or cover with a sticky, oily, or moist substance. *Slang* To discredit one's reputation. **smear** *n.*

smear-y *adj.* To be marked with smears.

smell (smel) *v.* To notice an odor by means of the olfactory sense organs. *n.* An odor; the ability to perceive an odor; the scent of something.

smel-ly (smel´ē) *adj.* To have an odor.

smelt (smelt) *v.* To heat metals or their ores to a high temperature in order to obtain pure metallic constituents.

smelt-er *n.* Something or someone that smelts.

smew (smū) *n.* A bird of northern Europe and Asia; the male of this species has a white crest.

smid-gen (smij´en) *n.* A small amount.

smi-lax *n.* A type of twinning plant which has ovate bright green cladophylls.

smile (smīl) *n.* A grin; a facial expression in which the corners of the mouth turn upward, indicating pleasure. **smile** *v.*

smirch (smürch) *v.* To make something stained or dirty.

smirk (smerk) *v.* To smile in a conceited way. **smirk** *n.* **smirker** *n.*

smite (smīt) *v.* To hit with great force using the hand.

smith (smith) *n.* One who repairs or shapes metal.

smith-er-y *n.* The art of a smith.

smith-son-ite *n.* A type of zinc which is white.

smock (smok) *n.* A loose-fitting garment worn as a protection for one's clothes while working. *v.* To gather fabric into very small pleats or gathers.

smock frock *n.* An outer garment which is loose-fitting and is worn by workmen.

smog (smog) *n.* A mixture of smoke and fog. **smoggy** *adj.*

smoke (smōk) *n.* A cloud of vapor released

into the air when something is burning. *v.* To preserve or flavor meat by exposing it to smoke. **smokeless** *adj.* **smoky** *adj.* **smoker** *n.*

smoke-house *n.* A place or building where meat and fish are cured by using smoke.

smoke jumper *n.* A type of forest fighter who will parachute to the aea of a fire that may have become hard to reach by land.

smoke out *v.* To force or drive out with the use of smoke.

smoke-stack *n.* The chimney through which gases and smoke are able to be discharged.

smoke tree *n.* A type of shrubby tree belonging to the sumac family.

smok-ing jack-et *n.* A type of jacket which is worn by the man at home.

smolder (smōl′dėr) *v.* To burn slowly without a flame and with little smoke.

smolt *n.* A young sea trout or salmon.

smooth (smŏyth) *adj.* Not irregular; flat; without lumps, as in gravy; without obstructions or impediments. *adv.* Evenly. *v.* To make less difficult; to remove obstructions.

smooth-en *v.* To make something smooth.

smooth-y *n.* A type of person who has manners which are greatly polished.

smor-gas-bord (smor′gas bōrd′) *n.* A buffet meal with a variety of foods to choose from.

smother (smuth′ėr) *n.* Failure to receive enough oxygen to survive. *v.* To conceal; to be overly protective. **smothery** *adj.*

smudge (smuj) *v.* To soil by smearing with dirt. *n.* A dirty mark or smear; a fire made to fill the air with smoke in order to protect fruit trees from frost.

smug (smug) *adj.* Complacent with oneself; self-satisfied. **smugly** *adv.* **smugness** *n.*

smug-gle (smug′l) *v.* To import or export goods illegally without paying duty fees. **smuggler** *n.*

smug-ly *adv.* To be done in a smug manner.

smut *n.* A type of matter or substance which will soil something.

smut-ty *adj.* To be tainted or soiled by smut. **smittiness** *n.*

SMV *abbr.* Slow moving vehicle.

snack (snak) *n.* A small amount of food taken between meals. **snack** *v.*

snack bar *n.* An eating place for the public that serves snacks at a counter.

snaf-fle *n.* A jointed bit used with a bridle.

sna-fu *v.* To be someone in a confused state.

snag (snag) *n.* A stump or part of a tree that is partly hidden under the surface of water; a pull in a piece of fabric. *v.* To tear on a rough place. *Slang* To catch unexpectedly; to snatch.

snail (snāl) *n.* A type of gastropod mollusk that can live in a spiral shell.

snail-paced *adj.* To be moving at a slow pace.

snake (snāk) *n.* Any of a large variety of scaly reptiles, having a long tapering body. *Slang* An untrustworthy person.

snake-bite *n.* A bite of a snake on the skin.

snake charmer *n.* A person who exhibits his power to charm a snake.

snake-mouth *n.* A type of bog orchid that is located in eastern North America and Japan and has pink flowers.

snake-skin *n.* The leather that has been prepared from the skin of a snake.

snake-weed (snā′kēd′) *n.* A plant that is associated with snakes and used in the treatment of snake bites.

snak-y *adj.* To be entwined with snakes.

snap (snap) *v.* To break suddenly with a sharp, quick sound; to fly off under tension; to snatch something suddenly.

snap back *n.* A type of football snap; a sudden recovery.

snap bean *n.* A type of bean which is grown for its pods that are broken and cooked.

snap-drag-on *n.* A type of plant of the figwort family and having white, yellow, or crimson flowers.

snap-per (snap′ėr) *n.* A type of fish found in warm seas.

snapper–back *n.* In the game of football, a center.

snap-pish (snap′ish) *adj.* To be given to curt irritable speech. **snappishness** *n.*

snap-shot *n.* A type of photograph which

is made by an amateur with a small camera.

snare (snâr) *n.* Anything that entangles or entraps; a trap with a noose, used to catch small animals.

snare drum *n.* A type of drum that has snares stretched across the lower end.

snarl (snärl) *v.* To speak in an angry way; to cause confusion; to tangle or be tangled. *n.* A growl.

snatch (snach) *v.* To seize or grasp something suddenly. *n.* The act of taking something; a brief or small part.

snatch block *n.* A type of block which can be opened on one side in order to get the bight of a rope.

snaz-zy *adj.* To be flashily attractive.

sneak (snēk) *v.* To act or move in a quiet, sly way. *n.* A person who acts in a secret, underhanded way.

sneak-ing *adj.* To be characteristic of a sneak. **sneakingly** *adv.*

sneak pre-view *n.* An advance showing of a motion picture.

sneak thief *n.* A type of thief that will steal whatever he can without using violence.

sneak-y *adj.* To be marked by shiftiness.

sneer (snēr) *v.* To express scorn by the look on one's face.

sneeze (snēz) *v.* To expel air from the nose suddenly and without control. **sneeze** *n.*

sneeze-weed (snēz'wēd˝) *n.* A type of plant such as the North American yellow-flowered herb.

sneeze-wort *n.* A type of strong-scented herb found in Eurasia.

snee-zy *adj.* To be causing sneezing.

SNG *abbr.* Substitute natural gas.

snick *v.* To cut at something slightly.

snide (snīd) *adj.* To be unworthy of esteem; malicious.

sniff *v.* To inhale through the nose in short breaths with a noise; to show scorn. **sniff** *n.*

sniff-er *n.* Someone or something that sniffs.

sniff-ish *adj.* Expressing an attitude.

snif-ter *n.* A type of drink of liquor that has been distilled.

snig-gle *n.* To try to catch an eel by putting

the baited hook into the place where they hide.

snip (snip) *v.* To cut off in small pieces and with quick strokes. *n.* A small piece.

snipe (snīp) *n.* *pl.* **snipe** *or* **snipes** A bird with a long bill which lives in marshy places. *v.* To shoot at people from a hidden position. **sniper** *n.*

snip-pet (snip´it) *n.* A small part or thing.

snips *n.* A type of hand shears that can be used for the purpose of cutting metal.

sniv-el (sniv´l) *v.* To whine with snuffling.

snob (snob) *n.* A person who considers himself better than anyone else and who looks down on those he considers to be his inferiors.

snob-ber-y *n.* A snobbish conduct.

snob-bish (snob´ish) *adj.* Being like a snob.

snood (snŏd) *n.* A type of band that can be worn on a woman's hair.

snook (snŏk) *n.* A type of fish that is large and can be used as food or for sport.

snook-er *n.* A type of pool which is played with six colored balls and fifteen red balls.

snoop (snŏp) *v., Slang* To prowl or spy. *n.* One who snoops.

snoop-y *adj.* To be given to snooping.

snoot (snŏt) *n.* An expression of contempt.

snooze (snŏz) *n.* To sleep for a short amount of time.

snore (snōr) *v.* To breath with a harsh noise while sleeping. **snore** *n.* **snorer** *n.*

snor-kel (snor´kel) *n.* A tube that extends above the water, used for breathing while swimming face down.

snort (snort) *n.* To force air through the nostrils with a loud, harsh noise. *Slang* To inhale a narcotic through the nose.

snort-er *n.* Someone or something that snorts.

snout (snout) *n.* A nose of an animal such as a swine.

snout beetle *n.* A type of beetle that has a head which has projected into a snout.

snow (snō) *n.* Vapor that forms crystals in cold air and falls to the ground in white flakes. *Slang* To charm or overwhelm. **snow** *v.*

snow-ball *n.* A mass of snow which is usually round in shape and pressed together.

snow-bank *n.* A slope of snow.

snow-ber-ry (snŏn´ber˝ē) *n.* A type of white-beried shrub that has pink flowers.

snow-bird (snō´bŭrd˝) *n.* A type of small bird that can be seen in the winter.

snow–blind (snō´blīnd˝) *adj.* To be affected with snow blindness.

snow-bound (snō´bound˝) *adj.* To be blocked in by a large amount of snow.

snow-brush *n.* A type of white-flowered shrub that can be found in North America.

snow-cap (snō´kap˝) *n.* A cap of snow that appears on the tops of mountains.

snow-flake *n.* A small crystal of snow.

snow leopard *n.* A large cat having light-colored fur with black spots.

snow line *n.* The margin of a perennial snow-field.

snow-man (snō´man˝) *n.* A figure which is made out of snow and usually resembles a man or woman.

snow-mo-bile (snō´mo bēl˝) n. A type of vehicle that is used for the purpose of traveling on the snow. **snowmobiling** *n.*

snow plant *n.* A type of California herb that is able to grow at high altitudes and will usually appear just before the snow melts.

snow-plow *n.* A machine which is used for the purpose of removing the snow from an area where it is not desired, such as a street.

snow-shed *n.* A type of shelter which is used for protection against snow slides.

snow-shoe (snō´shŏ˝) *n.* A type of shoe which is used to travel on top of the snow.

snow-storm (snō´storm) *n.* A storm that is made up of snow.

snow tire *n.* A type of tire that is used by a car when there is snow on the street in order to get better traction.

snow-y (snō´ē) *adj.* To be covered with snow. **snowily** *adv.* **snowiness** *n.*

snub (snub) *v.* To treat with contempt or in an unfriendly way. **snub** *n.*

snub-ber (snub´ėr) *n.* Someone who snubs.

snub–nosed *adj.* To have a stubby nose.

snuff (snuf) *v.* To draw air in through the nostrils. **snuff** *n.*

snuff-box (snuf´boks˝) *n.* A type of small box that can be used for holding snuff.

snuff-er *n.* A type of device used for dropping and holding the snuff of a candle.

snuf-fle *v.* To breathe through a nose that is obstructed producing a sniffing sound.

snug (snug) *adj.* Warm, pleasant, comfortable and safe.

snug-gle (snug´l) *v.* To curl up to someone in an af-fectionate manner.

so (sō) *adv.* To a degree or extent as a result; likewise; also; indeed. *conj.* In order that; therefore.

soak (sōk) *v.* To pass through something with the use of pores. **soaker** *n.*

soak-age (sōk´āj) *n.* The amount of liquid that is gained through absorption.

soap (sōp) *n.* A cleansing agent made of an alkali and a fat, and used for washing. *v.* To rub with soap.

soap-ber-ry (sōp´ber´e) *n.* A type of tropical woody plant.

soap-box (sōp´boks˝) *n.* A platform that is used by an informal orator.

soap bubble *n.* A type of hollow globe which is formed by blowing a small film of soapsuds.

soap-less *adj.* Containing no soap.

soap plant *n.* A type of plant which has a part that can be used in the place of soap.

soap-y (sō´pē) *adj.* To be covered or smeared with soap.

soar (sōr) *v.* To glide or fly high without any noticeable movement; to rise higher than usual.

sob (sob) *v.* To weep with short, quick gasps.

so-ber (sō´bėr) *adj.* Not drunk or intoxi-cated; serious; solemn; quiet. **soberly** *adv.* **soberness** *n.*

soc-cer (sok´ėr) *n.* A game in which two teams of eleven people each try to kick a ball into the opposing team's goal.

so-cia-ble (sō´sha bl) *adj.* Capable of friendly social relations; enjoying the company of others. **sociably** *adv.*

so-cial (sō´shɑl) *adj.* Having to do with

people living in groups; enjoying friendly companionship with others. *n.* An informal party or gathering.

so-cial-ism (sō′shɑ liz′um) *n.* A system in which people as a whole, and not individuals, control and own all property.

so-ci-e-ty (so sī′i tē) *n. pl.* **-ies** People working together for a common purpose; companionship.

so-ci-ol-o-gy (sō′sē ol′o jē) *n.* The study of society and the development of human society. **sociologic** *adj.* **sociological** *adj.*

sock (sok) *n.* A short covering for the foot, ankle, and lower part of the leg; a hard blow. *Slang* To hit with force.

sock-et (sok′it) *n.* A hollow opening into which something is fitted.

Soc-ra-tes *n.* Greek philosopher.

so-da (sō′dɑ) *n.* Sodium carbonate; a flavored, carbonated drink.

sod-den (sod′en) *adj.* Completely saturated; very wet; lacking in expression.

so-di-um (sō′dē um) *n.* A metallic element symbolized by Na.

sod-om-y (sod′o mē) *n.* Anal sexual intercourse.

so-fa (sō′fɑ) *n.* An upholstered couch with arms and a back.

soft (soft) *adj.* Not stiff or hard; not glaring or harsh; mild or pleasant; gentle in sound.

soft-ball (soft′bol′) *n.* A game played on a smaller diamond than baseball, with a larger, softer ball.

soft-ware (soft′wâr′) *n.* In computer science, data, as routines, programs and languages, which is essential to the operation of computers.

sog-gy (sog′ē) *adj.* Saturated with a liquid or moisture.

sol-ace (sol′is) *n.* Comfort in a time of trouble, grief, or misfortune. **solace** *v.*

so-lar (sō′lėr) *adj.* Relating to or connected with the sun; utilizing the sun for power or light; measured by the earth's movement around the sun.

so-lar-i-um (sō lâr′ē um) *n. pl.* **-ia** *or* **-ums** A glassed-in room exposed to the sun's rays.

solar system *n.* The sun and the planets, asteroids, and comets that orbit it.

sol-der (sod′ėr) *n.* Any alloy, as lead or tin, which is melted and used to mend or join other pieces of metal. *v.* To join or mend with solder. **soldered** *adj.*

sol-dier (sōl′jėr) *n.* An enlisted person who serves in the military.

sole (sōl) *n.* The bottom of a foot or shoe; single, the only one; a flat fish very popular as seafood.

sol-emn (sol′em) *adj.* Very serious; characterized by dignity; sacred. **solemnity** *n.* **solemnness** *n.*

so-lic-it (so lis′it) *v.* To try to obtain; to ask earnestly; to beg or entice a person persistently. **solicitation** *n.*

sol-id (sol′id) *adj.* Having a definite firm shape and volume; having no crevices; not hollow; having height, weight and length; without interruption; reliable, sound and upstanding. *n.* A solid substance. **solidification** *n.* **solidness** *n.* **solidify** *v.*

sol-i-taire (sol′i târ′) *n.* A single gemstone set by itself; a card game played by one person.

sol-i-tude (sol′i tōd′) *n.* The act of being alone or secluded; isolation.

so-lo (sō′lō) *n.* A musical composition written for and performed by one single person or played by one instrument.

sol-stice (sol′stis) *n.* Either of the two times in a twelve month period at which the sun reaches an extreme north or south position.

sol-u-ble (sol′ū bl) *adj.* Capable of being dissolved; able to be solved or explained. **solubility** *n.* **solubly** *adv.*

solve (solv) *v.* To find the answer to. **solvable** *adj.*

som-ber (som′bėr) *adj.* Dark; gloomy; melancholy.

some (sum) *adj.* Being an indefinite number or quantity; unspecified. *pron.* An undetermined quantity. *adv.* An approximated degree. **somebody** A person unknown. **somehow** In a way. **someday** *adv.* At an unspecified future time.

som-er-sault (sum´ĕr solt´) *n.* The act or acrobatic stunt in which one rolls the body in a complete circle, with heels over head.

som-nam-bu-lism (som nam´by*a* liz´*u*m) *n.* The act of walking during sleep. **somnambulant** *adj.*

son (sun) *n.* A male offspring.

so-na-ta (s*o* nä´t*a*) *n.* An instrumental composition with movements contrasting in tempo and mood but related in key.

song (song) *n.* A piece of poetry put to music; the act or sound of singing.

son-ic (son´ik) *adj.* Pertaining to sound or the speed of sound.

son-net (son´it) *n.* A poem made up of fourteen lines.

soon (sŏn) *adv.* In a short time; in the near future; quickly.

soot (set) *n.* The black powder generated by incomplete combustion of a fuel, such as coal or wood.

soothe (sŏth) *v.* To make comfortable; to calm.

sop (sop) *v.* To soak up a liquid; to absorb. *n.* Anything softened by a liquid; something given as a conciliatory offering.

soph-o-more (sof´*o* mōr´) *n.* A second year college or high school student.

so-pran-o (s*o* pran´ō) *n.* The highest female singing voice.

sor-cery (sor´s*e* rē) *n.* The use of supernatural powers.

sor-did (sor´did) *adj.* Filthy, very dirty; morally corrupt.

sore (sōr) *adj.* Tender or painful to the touch, as an injured part of the body; severe or extreme. *n.* A place on the body which has been bruised, inflamed, or injured in some way. **sorely** *adv.*

sor-ghum (sor´g*u*m) *n.* A cane-like grass grown for its sweet juices and used as fodder for animals; the syrup prepared from the sweet juices.

so-ror-i-ty (s*o* ror´i tē) *n. pl.* **-ies** A social organization for women.

sor-rel (sor´*e*l) *n.* Any of several herbs with sour-tasting leaves, used in salads.

sor-row (sor´ō) *n.* Anguish; mental suffering; an expression of grief. **sorrowful** *adj.* **sorrowfully** *adv.*

sor-ry (sor´ē) *adj.* Feeling or showing sympathy or regret; worthless.

sort (sort) *n.* A collection of things having common attributes or similar qualities. *v.* to arrange according to class, kind, or size.

sor-tie (sor´tē) *n., Mil.* An attack on enemy forces; a combat mission flown by an aircraft.

SOS (es´ō´es´) *n.* A call for help; the international distress signal; a call made when a rescue is needed, especially by a ship or plane.

souf-fle (sŏ flā´) *n.* A fluffy dish made of egg yolks, whipped egg whites, and other ingredients, served as a main dish or sweetened as a dessert.

sought *v.* Past tense of seek.

soul (sōl) *n.* The spirit in man that is believed to be separate from the body and is the source of a person's emotional, spiritual, and moral nature. *Slang* A spirit or attitude derived from Blacks and their culture.

sound (sound) *n.* A sensation received by the ears from air, water, noise, and other sources. *v.* To make a sound; to make noise. *adj.* Free from flaw, injury, disease, or damage. **soundless** *adj.* **soundly** *adv.*

soup (sŏp) *n.* A liquid food made by boiling meat and/or vegetables, in water.

sour (sour) *adj.* Sharp to the taste; acid; unpleasant; disagreeable. *v.* To become sour or spoiled. **sourly** *adv.*

source (sōrs) *n.* Any point of origin or beginning; the beginning or place of origin of a stream or river.

south (south) *n.* The direction opposite of north. *adv.* To or towards the south. *adj.* From the south. **southerly** *adj.& adv.* **southern** *adj.* **southward** *adj.* **southerner** *n.*

South Carolina *n.* A state located in the southeastern part of the United States; statehood May 23, 1788; state capital

Columbia.

South Dakota *n.* A state located in the central northwestern part of the United States; statehood November 2, 1889; state capital Pierre.

south-paw (south′po′) *n.* A left-handed person. **southpaw** *adj.*

South Pole *n.* The southern most part of the earth.

south-west (south′west′) *n.* The direction between south and west. **southwestern** *adj.*

sou-ve-nir (sŏ′ve nēr′) *n.* An item kept as a remembrance of something or someplace.

sov-er-eign (sov′rin) *n.* A ruler with supreme power; a monarch. *adj.* Possessing supreme jurisdiction or authority.

So-vi-et *n.* The elected governmental council of the USSR. **soviet** *adj.* Having to do with the Soviet Union.

sow (sō) *v.* To scatter or throw seeds on the ground for growth. *n.* A female pig.

space (spās) *n.* The unlimited area in all directions in which events occur and have relative direction; an interval of time; the area beyond the earth's atmosphere.

spade (spād) *n.* A tool with a flat blade used for digging, heavier than a shovel.

spa-ghet-ti (spa get′ē) *n.* Long thin pasta.

span (span) *n.* The extent of space from the end of the thumb to the end of the little finger of a spread hand; the section between two limits or supports. *v.* To extend across.

span-iel (span′yel) *n.* A dog with large drooping ears and short legs.

spank (spangk) *v.* To strike or slap the buttocks with an open hand as a means of punishment.

spare (spâr) *v.* To refrain from injuring, harming or destroying; to refrain from using; to do without. *n.* An extra, as a spare tire.

spark (spärk) *n.* A glowing or incandescent particle, as one released from a piece of burning wood or one produced by means of friction. *v.* To give off sparks.

spar-kle (spär′kl) *v.* To emit or reflect light.

spar-row (spar′ō) *n.* A small bird with grayish or brown plumage.

sparse (spärs) *adj.* Scant; thinly distributed. **sparsely** *adv.* **sparsity** *n.*

spasm (spaz′um) *n.* An involuntary muscle contraction.

spat-ter (spat′er) *v.* To scatter or splash a liquid.

spat-u-la (spach′a la) *n.* A kitchen utensil with a flexible blade for mixing soft substances.

spawn (spon) *n.* The eggs of fish or other water animals, as oysters or frogs. *v.* To lay eggs.

speak (spēk) *v.* To utter words; to express a thought in words.

speak-er (spē′ker) *n.* A person who speaks, usually before an audience.

spear (spēr) *n.* A weapon with a long shaft and a sharply pointed head. *v.* To strike, pierce, or stab with a spear.

spear-mint (spēr′mint′) *n.* A mint plant yielding an aromatic oil used as a flavoring.

spe-cial-ist (spesh′a list) *n.* A person, such as a doctor, who devotes his practice to one particular field.

spe-cial-ize (spesh′a līz′) *v.* To focus one's efforts or interests in one field of activity or study.

spec-i-men (spes′ i men) *n.* A sample; a representative of a particular thing.

speck (spek) *n.* A small particle, mark, or spot. *v.* To cover or dot with specks.

spec-ta-cle (spek′ta kl) *n.* A public display of something strange and unusual. *pl.* Eyeglasses.

spec-trum (spek′trum) *n., Physics* The band of colors produced when light is passed through a prism or by other means, separating the light into different wave lengths.

spec-u-late (spek′ū lāt′) *v.* To reflect and think deeply; to take a chance on a business venture in hopes of making a large profit. **speculation** *n.*

speech (spēch) *n.* The ability, manner, or act of speaking; a talk before the public. **speechless** *adj.*

speed (spēd) *n.* Rate of action or movement; quickness; rapid motion. *Slang* A drug used strictly as a stimulant.

spell (spel) *v.* To say out loud or write in proper order the letters which make up a word; to relieve. *n.* The state of being controlled by magic; a short period of time; a time or period of illness; an attack.

spell-bind *v.* To fascinate or hold as if by magic.

spend (spend) *v.* To give out; to use up; to pay; to exhaust.

sperm (sperm) *n.* The male cell of reproduction; semen. **spermatic** *adj.*

sphere (sfēr) *n., Math* A round object with all points the same distance from a given point; globe, ball, or other rounded object. **spherical** *adj.* **spherically** *adv.*

sphinx (sfingks) *n. pl.* **sphinxes** *or* **sphinges** An ancient Egyptian figure having the head of a man, male sheep, or hawk and the body of a lion; a very mysterious person.

spice (spīs) *n.* A pungently aromatic plant used as flavoring in food, as nutmeg, cinnamon, pepper, or curry. **spice** *v.* **spicy** *adj.*

spi-der (spī'dėr) *n.* An eight-legged insect with a body divided into two parts spinning webs to use as a means of capturing and holding its prey.

spike (spīk) *n.* A large, thick nail; a pointed metal piece on the sole of a shoe to prevent slipping, as on a sports shoe. **spike** *v.*

spill (spil) *v.* To allow or cause something to flow or run out of something. *n., Slang* A fall from a horse; to make known.

spin (spin) *v.* To draw out fibers and twist into thread; to run something around and around; to resolve. *Slang* A short drive or ride in an auto. **spinner** *n.*

spin-ach (spin'ich) *n.* A widely cultivated plant with dark green leaves which are used in salads.

spin-dle (spin'dl) *n.* A rod with a slit in the top and a piece of wood at the other end, used to hold yarn or thread; a needle-like rod mounted on a base, used to hold papers.

spine (spīn) *n.* The spinal column; the backbone; the back of a bound book, inscribed with the title.

spin-ster (spin'stėr) *n.* An unmarried woman; an old maid.

spir-it (spir'it) *n.* The vital essence of man, considered divine in origin; the part of a human being characterized by personality and self-consciousness; the mind; the Holy Ghost; the creative power of God; a supernatural being, as a ghost or angel.

spir-i-tual (spir'i chŏ al) *adj.* Of, like, or pertaining to the nature of spirit; relating to religion; sacred. *n.* A religious song originating among the Blacks of the southern United States. **spirituality** *n.* **spiritualize** *v.*

spite (spīt) *n.* Hatred or malicious bitterness; a grudge; ill will. **spite** *v.* **spiteful** *adj.* **spitefully** *adv.*

spit-toon (spi tön') *n.* A cuspidor or receptacle for spit.

spitz (spits) *n.* A small dog with a tail which curls over its back.

splash (splash) *v.* To spatter a liquid; to wet or soil with liquid; to make a splash. **splash** *n.* **splashy** *adj.*

splash-down (splash'doun') *n.* The landing of a missile or spacecraft in the ocean.

spleen (splēn) *n., Anat.* A highly vascular, flattened organ which filters and stores blood, located below the diaphragm.

splen-did (splen'did) *adj.* Illustrious; magnificent.

splice (splīs) *v.* To join together by wearing, overlapping, and binding the ends.

splint (splint) *n.* A device used to hold a fractured or injured limb in the proper position for healing. **splint** *v.*

splotch (sploch) *n.* A discolored and irregularly shaped spot.

splutter (splut'ėr) *v.* To make a slight, short spitting sound. **splutter** *n.*

spoil (spoil) *v.* To destroy the value, quality, or usefulness; to overindulge as to harm the character. **spoils** *n.* **spoilage** *n.*

spoke (spōk) *n.* One of the rods that serve to connect and support the rim of a wheel.

v. Past tense of speak.

spokes-man (spōks′man) *n.* One who speaks on behalf of another.

sponge (spunj) *n.* Any of a number of marine creatures with a soft, porous skeleton which soaks up liquid. *v.* To clean with a sponge. **sponger, spongy** *adj.*

spon-sor (spon′sėr) *n.* A person who is responsible for a debt or duty of another; a business that finances a television or radio program that in turn advertises its product. **sponsor** *v.* **sponsorship** *n.*

spon-ta-ne-ous (spon tā′nē us) *adj.* Done from one's own impulse without apparent external cause. **spontaneity** *n.* **spontaneously** *adv.*

spoof (spōf) *n.* A deception; nonsense.

spook (spōk) *n., Slang* A ghost. *v.* To scare or frighten. **spooky** *adj.*

spool (spōl) *n.* A small cylinder for holding thread, tape or wire.

spoon (spōn) *n.* An eating or cooking utensil; a shiny metallic fishing lure. *Slang* To make love, as by kissing or caressing.

spo-rad-ic (spō rad′ik) *adj.* Occurring occasionally or at irregular intervals.

spore (spōr) *n., Bot.* The reproductive single-celled structure produced by nonflowering plants; any cell capable of developing into a new organism, seed, or germ.

sport (spōrt) *n.* An interesting diversion; a particular game or physical activity with set rules; a person who leads a fast life. *Slang* To amuse and have a good time. *adj.* Relating or pertaining to sports.

sport-ing (spōr′ting) *adj.* Of or relating to risk taking or gambling; displaying sportsmanship.

sports-man-ship (spōrts′man ship′) *n.* Fair play; the ability to win or lose graciously.

spot (spot) *n.* A small area that differs in size, portion, or color. *adj.* Delivered or made immediately. *Slang* A dangerous or difficult situation. **spot** *v.* **spotless** *adj.* **spotlessly** *adv.* **spotlessness** *n.*

spot-light (spot′līt′) *n.* A powerful light thrown directly at one area.

spouse (spous) *n.* One's husband or wife;

a marriage partner.

spout (spout) *v.* To pour out forcibly, as under pressure; to cause to shoot forth. *Slang* To orate pompously; to declaim.

sprain (sprān) *n.* A wrenching or twisting of a muscle or joint.

sprawl (sprol) *v.* To sit or lie in an ungraceful manner; to develop haphazardly. **sprawl** *n.* **sprawler** *n.*

spray (sprā) *n.* A liquid dispersed in a fine mist or droplets. *v.* To disperse or send forth in a spray. **sprayer** *n.*

spread (spred) *v.* To unfold or open fully; to apply or distribute over an area; to force apart; to extend or expand. **spread** *v.*

spree (sprē) *n.* An excessive indulgence in an activity; a binge.

spright-ly (sprīt′lē) *adj.* Vivacious, lively. **sprightliness** *n.*

sprin-kle (spring′kl) *v.* To scatter in small particles or drops; to rain in small drops. **sprinkle** *n.*

sprint (sprint) *n.* A short, fast race.

sprock-et (sprok′it) *n., Mech.* A tooth-like projection from the rim of a wheel.

spruce (sprōs) *n.* An evergreen tree with needle-like foliage, cones, and soft wood.

sprung *v.* Past tense of spring.

spry (sprī) *adj.* Quick; brisk; energetic.

spud (spud) *n., Slang* A potato.

spur (sper) *n.* A sharp, projecting device worn on a riders boot, used to nudge a horse. *v.* To urge on.

sput-nik (spet′nik) *n.* An unmanned Soviet earth satellite.

sput-ter (sput′ėr) *v.* To throw off small particles in short bursts; to speak in a confused or agitated manner.

spu-tum (spū′tum) *n. pl.* -ta Saliva or mucus that is expectorated.

spy (spī) *n. pl.* **spies** A secret agent who obtains information; one who watches other people secretly.

squab *n.* A type of fledging bird.

squab-ble (skwob′l) *v.* To engage in a petty argument. **squabble** *n.*

squad (skwod) *n.* A small group organized

to perform a specific job.

squad car *n.* A type of police car.

squad-ron (skwod'ron) *n.* A type of naval unit that has two or more divisions.

squa-lene *n.* A type of acyclic hydrocarbon that is widely distributed in nature.

squal-id (skwol'id) *adj.* To be marked by degradation from poverty or neglect.

squall (skwol) *v.* To cry out.

squa-lor *n.* The state of being squalid.

squa-ma-tion *n.* A state of something being scaly or having an arrangement of scales.

squa-mo-sal)skwa mō'sal) adj. Pertaining to the membrance bone of the skull.

squa-mous (skwā'mus) *n.* To be consisting of scales. **squamously** *adv.*

squamous cell *n.* A type of cell which is derived from squamous epithelium.

squan-der (skwon'dėr) *v.* To spend extra-vagantly or wastefully.

square (skwâr) *n.* A parallelogram with four equal sides; an implement having a T or L shape used to measure right angles. *Math.* To multiply a number by itself. *Slang* An unsophisticated person; a person who is not aware of the latest fads or trends.

square dance *n.* A type of dance that involves couples forming a hollow square. **square dancing** *n.*

square deal *n.* A fair trade.

square knot *n.* A kind of knot that is comprised of two reverse half-knots.

squar-er (skwâr'ėr) *n.* Someone who squares something.

square rig *n.* A type of sailing-ship rig where the main sails are extended on yards which are fastened to the masts on the center and horizontally.

square root *n.* A number which when multiplied by itself gives the given number.

square shooter *n.* A person who is honest.

square–toed (skwâr'tōd') *adj.* To have a toe that is shaped like a square.

squar-ish (skwār'ish) *adj.* To be slightly square in appearance.

squash (skwosh) *n.* An edible fruit of the gourd family; a sport

played in a walled court with a hard rubber ball and racket. *v.* To press or squeeze into a soft pulp.

squash bug *n.* A type of large black American bug that can be injurious to squash vines.

squat (skwot) *v.* To sit on the heels; to crouch; to settle on a piece of land in order to obtain legal title. **squatter** *n.*

squaw (skwo) *n.* An American Indian woman.

squaw-fish *n.* A type of cyprinid fish found in western North America.

squawk (skwok) *v.* To protest something in a loud manner.

squawk box *n.* A type of intercom speaker.

squaw-root (skwo'rŏt˝) *n.* A type of herb of North America which is a parasitic on hemlock and oak roots.

squeak (skwēk) *v.* To utter a sharp, penetrating sound. **squeak** *n.* **squeaky** *adj.*

squeak-er *n.* Someone or something that squeaks.

squeal (skwēl) *v.* To produce or to make a shrill cry. **squealer** *n.*

squea-mish (skwē'mish) *adj.* Easily shocked or nauseated. **squeamishly** *adv.*

squea-mish-ness *n.* State of being squeamish.

squee-gee (skwē'jē) *n.* A tool having a stout rubber blade across a wooden handle, used to wash windows. **squeegee** *v.*

squeeze (skwēz) *v.* To press together; to extract by using pressure. *n.* An instance of squeezing for pleasure; a hug.

squeeze bottle *n.* A kind of bottle which is flexible and will dispense its contents when one squeezes the bottle.

squeg *v.* To oscillate in a manner which is irregular.

squelch (skwelch) *n.* The process or act of suppressing. **squelchy** *adv.*

squib (skwib) *n.* A firecracker that does not explode.

squid (skwid) *n.* A type of 10-armed cephalopod that has a tapered body.

squig-gle *n.* The short wavy line or twist.

squil-la (skwil'a) n. A type of stomatopod

crustacean that will dig into the mud.

squinch *v.* To make something more compact.

squint (skwint) *v.* To view something through partly closed eyes; to close the eyes in this manner. **squint** *n.*

squint–eyed *adj.* To have eyes that squint.

squire (skwī´ėr) *n.* An old-fashioned title for a rural justice of the peace, lawyer, or judge; a man who escorts a woman; a young man who ranks just below a knight.

squire-ar-chy (skwīėr´ȧr kē) *n.* The gentry.

squirm (skerm) *n.* To twist the body in a wiggling motion. **squirm** *v.*

squir-rel (skwer´el) *n.*
A rodent with gray or brown fur, having a long bushy tail and dark eyes. **squirrel** *v.*

squir-rel cage *n.* A type of cage that is used for small animals and has a rotatable cylinder for exercising.

squir-rel-ly (squir rel y) *adj.* To be odd.

squirrel monkey *n.* A kind of monkey of South America that has a long tail that is not used for grasping.

squirt (skwert) *v.* To eject in a thin stream or jet; to wet with a squirt. *n.* The act of squirting.

squirting cucumber *n.* A type of plant of the Mediterranean that belongs to the gourd family and will burst to eject its seeds when it is ripe.

squish-y *adj.* To be soft and damp.

Sr. *abbr.* Senior.

SRB *abbr.* Solid rocket booster.

sta-bi-lize (stā´bi līz´) *v.* To make firm; to keep from changing. **stabilization** *n.* **stabilizer** *n.*

sta-ble (stā´bl) *n.* A building for lodging and feeding horses or other farm animals. *adj.* Standing firm and resisting change.

stac-ca-to (sta kä´tō) *adj., Music* Marked by sharp emphasis. **staccato** *n. & adv.*

stack (stak) *n.* A large pile of straw or hay; any systematic heap or pile; a chimney. *v.* To fix cards so as to cheat.

sta-di-um (stā´dē um) *n. pl.* **-dia** A large structure for holding athletic events or other large gatherings.

staff (staf) *n. pl.* **staffs** *or* **staves** A pole or rod used for a specific purpose; the people employed to assist in the day-to-day affairs of running a business, organization, or government. *Mil.* A group of people on an executive or advisory board. *Music* The horizontal lines on which notes are written. **staff** *v.*

stag (stag) *n.* The adult male of various animals; a man who attends a social gathering without a woman companion; a social event for men only. *adj.* For men only.

stag-ger (stag´ėr) *v.* To walk unsteadily; to totter. *adj.* Strongly affected by defeat, misfortune, or loss of strength.

stag-nant (stag´nant) *adj.* Not flowing; standing still; foul from not moving; inactive. **stagnate** *v.*

stair (stâr) *n.* A step or a series of steps.

staircase (stâr´kās´) *n.* A series or a flight of steps that connect one level to another.

stake (stāk) *n.* A bet placed on a game of chance; a sharpened piece of wood for driving into the ground. **stake** *v.*

stale (stāl) *adj.* Having lost freshness; deteriorated; lacking in interest; dull; inactive.

stale-mate (stāl´māt´) *n.* A position in chess when a player cannot move without placing his king in check.

stalk (stok) *n.* The main axis of a plant. *v.* To approach in a stealthy manner.

stall (stol) *n.* An enclosure in a barn, used as a place to feed and confine animals; a sudden loss of power in an engine; a booth used to display and sell. *v.* To try to put off doing something; to delay.

stal-lion (stal´yan) *n.* An uncastrated, fully grown male horse.

sta-men (stā´men) *n. pl.* **stamens** *Bot.* The pollen-producing organs of a flower.

stam-i-na (stam´i na) *n.* Physical or moral endurance.

stam-mer (stam´ėr) *v.* To make

involuntary halts or repetitions of a sound or syllable while speaking. **stammer** *n*.

stamp (stamp) *v*. To put the foot down with force; to imprint or impress with a die, mark, or design. *n*. The act of stamping; the impression or pattern made by a stamp; a postage stamp.

stam-pede (stam pēd′) *n*. A sudden rush of panic, as of a herd of horses or cattle. *v*. To cause a stampede.

stance (stans) *n*. The posture or position of a standing person or animal.

stand (stand) *v*. To be placed in or maintain an erect or upright position; to take an upright position; to remain unchanged; to maintain a conviction; to resist. *n*. The act of standing; a device on which something rests; a small booth for selling or displaying items.

stand-ard (stan′dėrd) *n*. A model which stands for or is accepted as a basis for comparison. **standard** *adj*.

stand-ing (stan′ding) *n*. A status, reputation, or achievement; a measure of esteem. *adj*. Unchanging; stationary; not moving.

sta-ple (stā′pl) *n*. A principle commodity grown in an area; a major element; a metal fastener designed to hold materials such as cloth or paper. **staple** *v*. **stapler** *n*.

star (stär) *n*., *Astron*. A self-luminous body that is a source of light; any of the celestial bodies that can be seen in the night sky; a symbol having five or six points and resembling a star.

star-board (stär′bėrd) *n*. The right side of a ship or boat. **starboard** *adj. & adv.*

starch (stärch) *n*. Nutrient carbohydrates that are found in foods such as rice and potatoes. *v*. To stiffen clothing by using starch. **starchiness** *n*. **starchy** *adj*.

stare (stâr) *v*. To look with an intent, direct gaze. **stare** *n*. **starer** *n*.

stark (stärk) *adj*. Bare; total; complete; forbidding in appearance. **starkly** *adv*.

star-ling (stär′ling) *n*. A common black or brown bird.

star-tle (stär′tl) *v*. To cause a sudden surprise; to shock. **startle** *n*.

starve (stärv) *v*. To suffer or die from not having food; to suffer from the need of food, love, or other necessities.

state (stāt) *n*. A situation, mode, or condition of something; a nation; the governing power or authority of; one of the subdivisions or areas of a federal government, as the United States. *v*. To make known verbally.

stat-ic (stat′ik) *adj*. Not moving. *n*. A random noise heard on a radio.

sta-tion (stā′shan) *n*. The place where someone or something is directed to stand; a scheduled stopping place; the place from which radio and television programs are broadcast.

sta-tion-ar-y (stā′sha ner′ē) *adj*. Not movable; unchanging.

sta-tion-er-y (stā′sha ner′ē) *n*. Writing paper and envelopes.

sta-tis-tic (sta tis′tik) *n*. An estimate using an average or mean on the basis of a sample taken; numerical data.

stat-ue (stach′ö) *n*. A form sculpted from wood, clay, metal, or stone.

stave (stāv) *n* A narrow piece of wood used in forming part of a container, as a barrel. **stave** *v*.

stay (stā) *v*. To remain; to pause; to maintain a position; to halt or stop; to postpone or delay an execution. *n*. A short visit.

stead (sted) *n*. The position, place, or job of another.

stead-fast (sted′fast′) *adj*. Not changing or moving; firm in purpose; true; loyal. **steadfastly** *adv*. **steadfastness** *n*.

stead-y (sted′ē) *adj*. Firmly placed, fixed or set; not changing; constant; uninterrupted.

steal (stēl) *v*. To take another person's property; to move in a sly way; to move secretly. *Baseball* To take a base without the ball being hit. *Slang* A real bargain.

steam (stēm) *n*. Water in the form of vapor; the visible mist into which vapor is condensed by cooling. **steam** *v*. **steamy** *adj*.

steel (stēl) *n*. A various mixture of iron, carbon, and other elements; a strong material that can be shaped when heated. **steely** *adj.*

stem (stem) *n.* The main stalk of a plant; the main part of a word to which prefixes and suffixes may be added. *v.* To stop or retard the progress or flow of something.

sten-cil (stenʹsĭl) *n.* A form cut into a sheet of material, as cardboard or plastic, so that when ink or paint is applied, the pattern will reproduce on paper or another material.

ste-nog-ra-phy (ste nogʹra fē) *n.* The skill of writing in shorthand. **stenographer** *n.* **stenographic** *adj.*

step (step) *n.* A single completed movement in walking, dancing, or running; the distance of such a step; the part of a ladder that one places the feet on in ascending or descending. *Music* A musical scale; a degree.

ste-re-o (sterʹē ō´) *n.* A record player with stereophonic sound. **stereo** *adj.*

ste-re-o-phon-ic (sterʹē o fonʹik) *adj.* Relating to or giving a three-dimensional effect of auditory perspective.

ster-e-o-type (sterʹē o tīp´) *n.* A conventional opinion or belief; a metal printing plate.

ster-ile (sterʹil) *adj.* Free from microorganisms; sanitary; unable to reproduce.

ster-ling (sterʹling) *n.* An alloy of 92.5% silver and another metal, as copper.

stern (stern) *adj.* Inflexible; harsh. *n.* The rear of a boat or ship. **sternly** *adv.*

ster-num (sterʹnum) *n. pl* **-nums** *or* **-na** A long, flat bone located in the chest wall, connecting the collarbones and the cartilage of the first seven pairs of ribs. **sternal** *adj.*

steth-o-scope (stethʹo skōp´) *n.* An instrument used to listen to the internal sounds of the body.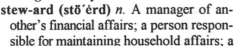

stew (stŏ) *v.* To cook slowly; to simmer; to boil. *n.* A dish of stewed meat and potatoes. *Slang* To worry.

stew-ard (stŏʹerd) *n.* A manager of another's financial affairs; a person responsible for maintaining household affairs; a

male attendant on an airplane or ship. **stewardess** *n.* **stewardship** *n.*

stick (stik) *n.* A slender piece of wood; a club, rod, or walking stick. *v.* To put a hole in something; to pierce; to cling; to become jammed.

stiff (stif) *adj.* Not flexible; not easily bent; awkward. *n., Slang* A dead body.

sti-fle (stīʹfl) *v.* To suffocate; to cut off; to suppress; to keep back.

stig-ma (stigʹma) *n. pl.* **-mata** *or* **-mas** A mark of disgrace. **stigmata** The part of a flower where pollen is deposited at pollination; wounds resembling the crucifixion scars of Jesus Christ.

still (stil) *adj.* Silent; calm; peaceful; until now or another time. *adv.* Nevertheless. **still** *v.* **stillness** *n.*

still-birth (stilʹberth´) *n.* The birth of a dead fetus.

stilt (stilt) *n.* One of a pair of long poles with foot supports, used for walking.

stim-u-lant (stimʹū lant) *n.* An agent which arouses or accelerates physiological activity.

stim-u-late (stimʹū lāt´) *v.* To excite to a heightened activity; to quicken. **stimulation** *n.*

stim-u-lus (stimʹū lus) *n.* Something that excites to action.

sting (sting) *v.* To prick with something sharp; to feel or cause to feel a smarting pain; to cause or feel sharp pain, either physical or mental. *n.* The act of stinging; the injury or pain caused by the stinger of a bee or wasp. **stinger** *n.*

stin-gy (stinʹjē) *adj.* Not giving freely; cheap.

stink (stingk) *v.* To give off a foul odor that is highly offensive.

stip-u-late (stipʹū lāt´) *v.* To settle something by agreement; to establish conditions of agreement. **stipulation** *n.*

stir (ster) *v.* To mix a substance by moving round and round; to agitate or provoke. **stirrer** *n.*

stir-rup (sterʹup) *n.* A loop extending from a horse's saddle, used to support the rider's foot.

stitch (stich) *n.* In scwing, a single loop formed by a needle and thread; the section of loop of thread, as in sewing. *v.* To join with a stitch.

stock (stok) *n.* A supply of goods kept on hand; animals living on a farm; a share in ownership, as in a company or corporation; the raw material or the base used to make something. *v.* To provide with stock. *adj.* Regular, common, or typical.

stock-ade (sto kād') *n.* A barrier placed around a fort for protection.

stock-ing (stok'ing) *n.* A knitted covering for the foot.

stock-y (stok'ē) *adj.* Short and plump; built sturdily.

stole (stōl) *n.* A long, narrow scarf that is usually worn around a woman's shoulders, as a mink stole. *v.* Past tense of steal.

stom-ach (stum'ak) *n., Anat.* The organ into which food passes from the esophagus; one of the primary organs of digestion. *v.* To tolerate or stand; to put up with.

stone (stōn) *n.* Rock; compacted earth or mineral matter; a gem or jewel; the seed or pit of certain fruits. *Med.* A hard rock that forms inside a body organ, as the kidney. **stoned** To be overcome by an excessive amount of alcohol or drugs.

stood *v.* Past tense of stand.

stool (stōl) *n.* A seat without a backrest and arms; a small version of this on which to rest the feet; a bowel movement.

stoop (stōp) *v.* To bend the body forward and downward from the waist. *n.* A porch attached to a house.

stop (stop) *v.* To cease; to halt; to refrain from moving, operating, or acting; to block or obstruct; to visit for a short time. *v.* A location where a bus, train, or other means of mass transportation may pick up or drop off passengers. **stoppage** *n.*

stor-age (stōr'ij) *n.* The act of storing or keeping; in Computer Science, the part of a computer in which all information is held; the memory.

store (stōr) *n.* A business offering mer-chandise for sale; a supply to be used in the future. *v.* To supply; to accumulate.

stork (stork) *n.* A large, wading bird.

storm (storm) *n.* An atmospheric condition marked by strong winds with rain, sleet, hail, or snow. *v.* To charge or attack with a powerful force. **stormy** *adj.*

sto-ry (stōr'ē) *n. pl.* **-ies** A narration of a fictional tale or account; a lie; a level in a building or house.

stout (stout) *adj.* Strong; sturdy; substantial; courageous. **stoutly** *adv.*

stove (stōv) *n.* An apparatus in which oil, electricity, gas, or other fuels are consumed to provide the heat for cooking.

stow (stō) *v.* To pack or put away.

strad-dle (strad'l) *v.* To sit or stand with the legs on either side of something; to favor both sides of an issue.

straight (strāt) *adj.* Being without bends, angles, or curves; upright; erect; honest; undiluted; unmodified; heterosexual. *n.* In poker, a numerical sequence of five cards not of the same suit. **straightly** *adv.* **straightness** *n.*

strain (strān) *v.* To stretch beyond a proper limit; to injure by putting forth too much effort; to pass through a sieve to separate small particles from larger ones.

strait (strāt) *n.* A narrow passageway which connects two bodies of water.

strand (strand) *n.* Land that borders a body of water; one of the threads that are twisted together to form a rope. *v.* To leave in a difficult situation.

strange (strānj) *adj.* Not previously known or experienced; odd; peculiar; inexperienced; alien. **strangely** *adv.* **strangeness** *n.*

stran-ger (strān'jėr) *n.* A person unknown; a newcomer; an alien.

stran-gle (strang'gl) *v.* To kill by choking. **strangler** *n.*

strap (strap) *n.* A long, narrow strip of leather or other material used to secure objects. **strap** *v.*

strat-e-gy (strat'i jē) *n. pl.* **-ies** The skillful planning and managing of an activity. **strategic** *adj.* **strategist** *n.*

stra-tum (strā´tum) *n. pl.* **-ta** *or* **-tums** A horizontal layer, as of the earth's crust.

straw (stro) *n.* A stalk of dried, threshed grain; a slender, plastic or paper straw used to suck up a liquid. *adj.* Yellowish brown.

straw-ber-ry (stro´ber´ē) *n.* A low plant with white flowers and red fruit; the fruit of this plant.

stray (strā) *v.* To roam or wander. *n.* A lost or wandering animal or person. *adj.* Lost. **strayer** *n.*

streak (strēk) *n.* A narrow line or stripe that is different from the surrounding area; a run of good or bad luck. *v.* To rush or move rapidly; to make a streak. **streaky** *adj.*

stream (strēm) *n.* A small body of flowing water; a steady or continuous succession or procession. *v.* To flow in or like a stream.

street (strēt) *n.* A public thoroughfare in a town or city with buildings on either or both sides.

strength (strengkth) *n.* The quality of being strong; power in general; degree of concentration or potency.

strength-en (strengk´then) *v.* To grow strong or stronger.

stren-u-ous (stren´ū us) *adj.* Necessitating or characterized by vigorous effort or exertion. **strenuously** *adv.*

stress (stres) *n.* Special significance; an emphasis given to a specific syllable, word, action, or plan; strain or pressure.

stretch (strech) *v.* To extend fully; to extend forcibly beyond proper limits; to prolong. *n.* The state or act of stretching. **stretchable** *adj.* **stretchy** *adj.*

strew (strō) *v.* To scatter about.

strick-en (strik´en) *adj.* Suffering, as from an emotion, illness, or trouble.

strict (strikt) *adj.* Holding to or observing rules exactly; imposing absolute standards. **strictly** *adv.* **strictness** *n.*

stride (strīd) *v.* To walk with a long, sweeping step. **stride** *n.*

strike *v.* To hit with the hand; to ignite, as with a match; to afflict suddenly with a disease; to discover; to conclude or make; to stop working as a protext against some-

thing or in favor of rules or demands presented to an employer. **strike** *n.*

string *n.* A strip of thin twine, wire, or catgut used on stringed musical instruments; a series of related acts, items, or events; in Computer Science, data arranged in an ascending or descending sequence according to a command within the data.

strin-gent (strin´jent) *adj.* Of or relating to strict requirements; marked by obstructions or scarcity. **stringency** *n.*

strip *v.* To take off the outer covering; to divest or pull rank; to remove one's clothes; to rob. **strip** *n.* **stripper** *n.*

stripe *n.* A streak, band, or strip of a different color or texture; a piece of material or cloth worn on the sleeve of a uniform to indicate rank, award, or service..

stroke (strōk) *n.* The movement of striking; a sudden action with a powerful effect; a single movement made by the hand or as if by a brush or pen. *Path.* A sudden interruption of the blood supply to the brain. *v.* To pass the hand over gently.

stroll (strōl) *v.* To walk in a slow, leisurely way. **stroll** *n.*

strong (strong) *adj.* Exerting or possessing physical power; durable; difficult to break. **strongly** *adv.*

stron-ti-um (stron´shē um) *n.* A metallic element symbolized by Sr.

struc-ture (struk´cher) *n.* A construction made up of a combination of related parts. **structure** *v.* **structural** *adj.*

strug-gle (strug´l) *v.* To put forth effort against opposition. **struggle** *n.* **struggler** *n.* **strugglingly** *adv.*

strych-nine (strik´nin) *n.* An extremely poisonous alkaloid derived from certain plants, used to kill rodents and as a neural stimulant.

stub (stub) *n.* A short, projecting part; the short end of something after the main part has been removed or used. **stub** *v.*

stub-born (stub´ern) *adj.* Inflexible; difficult to control, handle, or manage.

stuc-co (stuk´ō) *n. pl.* **-coes** *or* **-cos** Fine plaster used to coat exterior walls and to decorate interior walls.

stud (stud) *n.* An upright post, as in a building frame, to which sheets of wallboard or paneling are fastened; a small removable button used as an ornament; a male horse used for breeding. **stud** *v.*

stu-dent (stŏd´ent) *n.* A person who studies at a school or college.

stu-di-o (stŏ´dē ō´) *n.* The place of work for an artist, photographer, or other creative person; a place for filming movies.

stud-y (stud´ē) *n. pl.* **-ies** The process of applying the mind to acquire knowledge.

stum-ble (stum´bl) *v.* To trip and nearly fall over something; to come upon unexpectedly. **stumble** *n.*

stump (stump) *n.* The part of a tree which remains after the top is cut down. *v.* To puzzle or be puzzled; to walk heavily; to campaign.

stun (stun) *v.* To render senseless by or as if by a blow.

stu-pen-dous (stŏ pen´dus) *adj.* Astonishing or highly impressive. **stupendousness** *n.* **stupendously** *adv.*

stu-pid (stŏ´pid) *adj.* Slow in apprehension or understanding. **stupidity** *n.*

stur-dy (ster´dē) *adj.* Possessing robust strength and health. **sturdily** *adv.* **sturdiness** *n.*

stur-geon (ster´jen) *n.* A large freshwater fish highly valued as a source of caviar.

stut-ter (stut´er) *v.* To speak with involuntary repetitions of sound. **stutter** *n.*

sty (stī) *n. pl.* **sties** An inflammation of the edge of an eyelid.

style (stīl) *n.* A method, manner, or way of performing, speaking, or clothing; elegance, grace, or excellence in performance or appearance. **style** *v.* **stylish** *adj.*

suave (swäv) *adj.* Ingratiating; smoothly pleasant in manner.

sub- (sub) *prefix.* Beneath, under, or below.

sub (sub) *abbr.* Substitute.

sub-con-scious (sub kon´shus) *adj.* Below the level of consciousness.

sub-due (sub dō´) *v.* To bring under control by influence, training, persuasion or force.

sub-ject (sub´jikt) *n.* The word in a sentence that defines a person or thing; a person who is under the control of another's governing power. *v.* To subdue or gain control over. **subjection** *n.*

sub-jec-tive (sub jek´tiv) *adj.* Taking place within, relating to or proceeding from an individual's emotions or mind. **subjectively** *adv.* **subjectivity** *n.*

sub-ma-rine (sub´ma rēn´) *adj.* Operating or existing beneath the surface of the sea. *n.* A ship that travels underwater. **submariner** *n.*

sub-merge (sub merj´) *v.* To plunge under the surface of the water. **submergible** *adj.* **submergence** *n.*

sub-mit (sub mit´) *v.* To give in to or surrender to another's authority. **submission** *n.* **submittal** *n.* **submissive** *adj.*

sub-or-di-nate (su bor´di nit) *adj.* Being of lower class or rank; minor; inferior. **subordinate** *v.* **subordination** *n.* **subordinative** *adj.*

sub-poe-na (su pē´na) *n.* A legal document requiring a person to appear in court for testimony.

sub-se-quent (sub´se kwent) *adj.* Following in time, place, or order. **subsequently** *adv.* **subsequentness** *n.*

sub-side (sub sīd´) *v.* To move to a lower level or sink; to become less intense.

sub-sid-i-ar-y (sub sid´ē er´ē) *adj.* Providing assistance in a lesser capacity. **subsidiary** *n.*

sub-si-dy (sub´si dē) *n. pl.* **-dies.** Financial aid granted directly to a private commercial enterprise from the government.

sub-sist (sub sist´) *v.* To have continued existence.

sub-soil (sub´soil´) *n.* The layer of earth that comes after the surface soil.

sub-stance (sub´stans) *n.* Matter or material of which anything consists.

sub-sti-tute (sub´sti tōt´) *n.* Something or someone that takes the place of another. **substitute** *v.*

sub-ten-ant (sub ten´ant) *n.* A person who rents property from a tenant.

sub-ter-ra-ne-an (sub´te rā´nē an) *adj.* Located, situated, or operating underground.

sub-ti-tle (sub´tīt´l) *n.* An explanatory title, as in a document, book, etc.; a written translation that appears at the bottom of a foreign motion picture screen.

sub-tract (sub trakt´) *v.* To deduct or take away from.

sub-trop-i-cal (sub trop´i kal) *adj.* Pertaining to regions adjacent to the tropics.

sub-urb (sub´erb) *n.* A residential community near a large city. **suburban** *adj.*

sub-way *n.* An underground electrically-powered train, usually used as a means of transportation.

suc-ceed (suk sēd´) *v.* To accomplish what is attempted; to come next or to follow.

suc-cess (suk ses´) *n.* Achievement of something intended or desired; attaining wealth, fame, or prosperity.

suc-ces-sion (suk sesh´an) n. The act or process of following in order; sequence; series; the order, sequence, or act by which something changes hands.

suc-ces-sive (suk ses´iv) *adj.* Following in order or sequence. **successively** *adv.* **successiveness** *n.*

suc-cu-lent (suk´u lent) *adj.* Juicy; full of juice or sap. **succulence** *n.* **succulently** *adv.*

such (such) *adj.* Of this or that kind or thing; a great degree or extent in quality. *pron.* Of a particular degree or kind; a person or thing of such.

suck (suk) *v.* To pull liquid into the mouth by means of a vacuum created by the lips and tongue. **suck** *n.*

su-crose (sō´krōs) *n.* Sugar obtained from the sugar beet or sugar cane.

suc-tion (suk´shan) *n.* The process or act of sucking.

sud-den (sud´en) *adj.* Happening very quickly without warning or notice; sharp; abrupt; marked by haste. **suddenly** *adv.* **suddenness** *n.*

suds *n.* Bubbles or soapy water. *Slang* Beer.

suede (swād) *n.* Leather with a soft, napped finish.

su-et (sō´it) *n.* The hard fat around the kidney and loins of sheep.

suf-fer (suf´er) *v.* To feel pain or distress; to sustain injury, loss, or damage.

suf-fi-cient (su fish´ent) *adj.* As much as is needed or desired. **sufficiency** *n.* **sufficiently** *adv.*

suf-fix (suf´iks) *n.* A form affixed to the end of a word.

suf-fo-cate (suf´o kāt´) *v.* To kill by depriving something or someone of oxygen. **suffocation** *n.*

sugar (sheg´er) *n.* A sweet, water-solable, crystalline carbohydrate. *Slang* A nickname for someone.

sug-gest (sug jest´) *v.* To give an idea for action or consideration; to imply; hint or intimate.

sug-ges-tion (sug jes´chan) *n.* The act of suggesting; a slight insinuation; hint.

su-i-cide (sō´i sīd´) *n.* The act of taking one's own life. **suicidal** *adj.*

suit (sōt) *n.* A set of articles, as clothing, to be used or worn together; in cards, one of the four sets: spades, hearts, clubs, and diamonds, that make up a deck. *v.* To meet the requirements of; to satisfy.

sul-fur *also* **sul-phur (sul´fer)** *n.* A light, yellow, nonmetallic element occurring naturally in both combined and free form, used in making matches, gunpowder and medicines.

sulk (sulk) *v.* To be sullenly silent.

sul-len (sul´en) *adj.* Ill-humored, melancholy; gloomy; depressing.

sul-try (sul´trē) *adj.* Hot and humid; muggy.

sum (sum) *n.* The result obtained by adding; the whole amount, quantity, or number; summary.

sum-ma-ry (sum´a rē) *n. pl.* **-ries.** Giving the sum or substance. *adj.* A statement covering the main points. **summarily** *adv.*

sum-mer (sum´er) *n.* The warmest of the four seasons, following spring and coming before autumn. **summery** *adj.*

sum-mit (sum´it) *n.* The top and highest point, degree, or level.

sum-mons (sum´onz) *n. pl.* **-monses** An

order or command to perform a duty; a notice to appear at a certain place.

sun (sun) *n.* The star around which other planets of the solar system orbit; the energy, visible light, and heat, that is emitted by the sun; sunshine. **sunny** *adj.*

Sun-day *n.* The Christian holy day; the first day of the week.

sun-down (sun´doun´) *n.* The time of day the sun sets.

sunk-en (sung´ken) *adj.* Submerged or deeply depressed in.

su-per (sŏ´pẻr) *adj.* Exceeding a norm; in excessive intensity or degree; surpassing most others; superior in rank, status or position; excellent. *n., Slang* Superintendent of a building.

su-perb (se perb´) *adj.* Of first-rate quality. **superbly** *adv.*

su-per-fi-cial (sŏ´pẻr fish´al) *adj.* Pertaining to a surface; concerned only with what is not necessarily real.

su-pe-ri-or (su pẻr´ē ẻr) *adj.* Of higher rank, grade, or dignity. *n.* A person who surpasses another in rank or excellence. **superiority** *n.* **superiorly** *adv.*

su-per-la-tive (su per´la tiv) *adj.* Of the highest degree of excellence; pertaining to the degree of comparison of an adverb or adjective that shows extreme extent or level. **superlatively** adv.

su-per-nat-u-ral *adj.* An order of existence beyond the natural world; pertaining to a divine power. **supernaturally** *adv.*

su-per-sede (sŏ´pẻr sēd´) *v.* To take the place of; to set aside.

su-per-son-ic (sŏ´pẻr son´ik) *adj., Aero.* Characterized by a speed greater than that of sound.

su-per-sti-tion (sŏ´pẻr stish´an) *n.* A belief held, despite evidence that it is irrational; a belief, resulting from faith in magic or chance. **superstitious** *adj.*

su-per-vise (sŏ´pẻr vīz´) *v.* To have charge in directing the work of other people. **supervision** *n.* **supervisor** *n.*

sup-per (sup´ẻr) *n.* The last or evening meal of the day.

sup-ple-ment (sup´le ment) *n.* A part that compensates for what is lacking. **supplementary** *adj.* **supplemental** *adj.*

sup-ply (su plī´) *v., n. pl.* **-plies** To provide with what is needed; to make available. **supplier** *n.*

sup-port (su pōrt´) *v.* To bear or hold the weight of; to tolerate; to give assistance or approval. *n.* The act of supporting. **supportable** *adj.* **supportive** *adj.*

sup-pose (su pōz´) *v.* To think or assume as true; to consider probable. **supposed** *adj.* **supposedly** *adv.*

sup-pos-i-to-ry (su poz´i tōr´ē) *n. pl.* **-ries** A medication, in solid form, that melts when inserted into the body cavity, as the rectum.

su-preme (su prēm´) *adj.* Of the highest authority, rank, or power.

sur-charge (ser´chärj´) *n.* An extra fee added to the cost of something; to overcharge.

sure (sher) *adj.* Firm and sturdy; being impossible to doubt; inevitable; not liable to fail. **surer** *adj.* **surest** *adj.* **surely** *adv.*

sur-face (ser´fis) *n.* The exterior or outside boundary of something; outward appearance. *adj.* Situated on a surface.

surge (serj) *v.* To increase suddenly. *n.* A large swell of water.

sur-geon (ser´jon) *n.* A physician who practices surgery.

sur-ger-y (ser´je rē) *n. pl.* **-ies.** The branch of medicine in which physical deformity or disease is treated by an operative procedure.

sur-mise (sẻr mīz´) *v.* To guess; to conjecture.

sur-mount (sẻr mount´) *v.* To overcome; to be at the top.

sur-name (ser´nām´) *n.* A person's family's last name.

sur-pass (sẻr pas´) *v.* To go beyond the limits of; to be greater than.

sur-plus (ser´plus) *n.* An amount beyond what is needed.

sur-prise (sẻr prīz´) *v.* To come upon unexpectedly or suddenly; to cause to feel amazed or astonished. **surprise** *n.* **sur-priser** *n.* **surprisingly** *adv.*

sur-ren-der (su ren´dèr) *v.* To give up or yield possession or power. *n.* The act of surrendering.

sur-rey (ser´ē) *n. pl.* **-reys.** A four-wheeled, horse-driven carriage.

sur-ro-gate (ser´o gāt´) *n.* A person who puts himself in the place of another. **surrogate** *v.*

sur-round (su round´) *v.* To extend around all edges of something; to enclose or shut in.

sur-veil-lance (sèr vā´lans) *n.* Close observation kept over one, especially as a suspect.

sur-vey (sèr vā´) *v., n. pl.* **-veys.** To examine in detail; to determine area, boundaries, or position and elevation of a section of the earth's surface. **surveyor** *n.*

sur-vive (sèr vīv´) *v.* To continue to exist; to outlast; to outlive. **survival** *n.*

su-shi *n.* A Japanese dish of thin slices of fresh, raw fish.

sus-pect (su spekt´) *v.* To have doubt or distrust; to have a suspicion or inkling of someone or something. **suspect** *n.*

sus-pend (su spend´) *v.* To bar from a privilege for a certain time, as a means of punishment; to hang so as to allow free movement.

sus-pense (su spens´) *n.* The feeling of being insecure or undecided, resulting from uncertainty.

sus-pi-cion (su spish´an) *n.* The instance of suspecting something wrong without proof. **suspicious** *adj.* **suspiciously** *adv.*

sus-tain (su stān´) *v.* To hold up and keep from falling; to suffer or undergo an injury.

su-ture (sō´chèr) *n.* The stitching together or joining the edges of an incision or cut. **suture** *v.*

swab (swäb) *n.* A small stick with a wad of cotton on both ends, used to apply medication. *Slang* A sailor. **swab** *v.*

swad-dle (swäd´l) *v.* To wrap closely, using a long strip of flannel or linen.

swal-low (swäl´ō) *v.* To cause food to pass

from the mouth to the stomach; to retract or take back, as words spoken. *n.* The act of swallowing.

swap (swäp) *v.* To trade something for something in return. **swap** *n.*

swarm (sworm) *n.* A large number of insects, as bees; a large group of persons or things. **swarm, swarmer** *n.*

swat (swät) *v.* To hit something with a sharp blow.

swatch (swäch) *n.* A strip of cloth cut off a larger piece, used as a sample.

swath (swoth) *n.* The area or width of grass cut by a machine. **swathe** *v.*

sway (swā) *v.* To move or swing from right to left or side to side; to exert influence or control. *n.* Dominating power.

swear (swâr) *v.* To make an affirmation under oath. **swearer** *n.*

sweat (swet) *v.* To excrete a salty moisture from the pores of the skin. *Informal* To work hard; to cause to sweat. *Slang* Being impatient; having anxiety.

sweat-er (swet´èr) *n.* A knitted or crocheted garment with or without sleeves attached.

sweat gland *n., Anat.* One of the tubular glands that secrete sweat externally through pores.

sweep (swēp) *v.* To touch very lightly; to remove or clear away with a brush, broom, etc.; to move with an even action.

sweet (swēt) *adj.* Having a sugary, agreeable flavor; arousing pleasant emotions; a beloved or dear person.

swell (swel) *v.* To increase in size or bulk; to grow in volume. *n.* The process, effect, or act of swelling; a continuous wave that is long and billowing. *Informal* Fine; excellent; smart.

swel-ter (swel´tèr) *v.* To suffer from extreme heat.

swerve (swerv) *v.* To turn aside from the regular course.

swift (swift) *adj.* Moving with great speed; accomplished or occurring quickly. **swiftly** *adv.* **swiftness** *n.*

swim (swim) *v.* To move oneself through

water by moving parts of the body, as arms, head, and legs.

swin-dle (swin′dl) v. To cheat out of property or money; to practice fraud. **swindle** n. **swindler** n.

swine (swīn) n. pl. **swine** A hoofed mammal with a snout, related to pigs and hogs; a low, despicable person. **swinish** adj.

swing (swing) v. To move freely back and forth; to hang or to be suspended. n. The act of a swing; a seat that hangs from chains or ropes. Music Jazz played by a large band and developed by using simple harmonic patterns. **swinger** n.

swirl (swerl) v. To move with a whirling, rotating motion. **swirl, swirly** adj.

switch (swich) n. A small, thin, flexible stick, twig or rod. Electr. A device for opening or closing an electric circuit; to shift to another train track by using a switch; to exchange.

swiv-el (swiv′el) n. A coupling device, ring, or pivot that allows attached parts to rotate or move freely. **swivel** v.

sword (sōrd) n. A weapon with a long, pointed cutting blade.

Syb-a-rite n. One who is a native to the ancient city of Sybaris.

syc-a-more (sik′a mōr′) n. A North American tree that is used widely for shade.

syce n. One who is an attendant as in India.

sy-cee n. The silver money which was once used in China.

sy-co-ni-um n. A type of fleshy fruit where the ovaries are borne in an enlarged receptacle.

sy-co-phan-cy n. The behavior of a sycophant.

sy-co-phant n. A self-seeking flatterer.

sy-co-phan-tic adj. Pertaining to a sycophant. **sycophantically** adv.

sy-co-sis n. An inflammatory disorder of the hair follicles.

syl-la-bar-y n. A listing of syllables.

syl-lab-ic adj. Pertaining to or denoting syllables.

syl-la-bic-i-ty n. The state of being a syllable.

syl-la-ble (sil′a bl) n., Phonet. A word or part of one that consists of a single vocal impulse, usually consisting of one or more vowels or consonants.

syl-la-bub n. A type of desert that is made by curdling milk with an acid such as wine.

syl-la-bus n. An outline of a course of study.

syl-lo-gism (sil′o jiz′um) n. An argument with a major premise, a minor premise and a conclusion that is logically drawn from the premises. **syllogistic** adj.

syl-lo-gist n. A person who applies syllogistic reasoning.

sylph n. A slender woman who is very graceful. **sylphlike** adj.

sylph-id n. A diminutive sylph.

syl-van adj. To be living or located in the woods.

syl-va-nite n. A kind of mineral which will often occur in crystals.

syl-vat-ic adj. To be affecting wild animals.

syl-vite n. A mineral which is a natural potassium chloride and occurs in colorless cubes.

sym-bi-ont n. An organism that is living in symbiosis.

sym-bi-o-sis n. A living together in close union of two dissimilar organisms.

sym-bol (sim′bol) n. Something that stands for or represents something else. **symbolic** adj. **symbolical** adj. **symbolically** adv.

sym-bol-ism n. The practice of using symbols.

sym-bol-ist n. A person who is skilled in the interpretation of symbols.

sym-bol-iz-a-tion n. An instance of symbolizing.

sym-bol-ize v. To serve as a symbol of or for something.

sym-bol-o-gy n. The interpretation of a symbol or symbols.

sym-met-ri-cal adj. Involving symmetry. **symmetricalness** n.

sym-me-trize v. To make something symmetrical in form or size.

sym-me-try (sim′i trē) n. pl. **-tries**

Balance in form, size, and position of parts that are on two sides of an axis.

sym-pa-thet-ic (sim´pa thet´ik) *adj.* Having or showing kindness or sympathy for others. **sympathetically** *adv.* **sympathize** *v.*

sympathetic nervous system *n.* Part of the body's nervous system which when stimulated will decrease muscle tone and constriction of the blood vessels and will depress secretions.

sympathetic vibration *n.* The vibration which is produced in a body by another body.

sym-pa-thin *n.* The substance which is produced by the sympathetic nerve endings in the body.

sym-pa-thize *v.* To respond to someone or something with sympathy.

sym-pa-tho-lyt-ic *adj.* To be tending to oppose physiological results of the sympathetic nervous activity.

sym-pa-tho-mi-met-ic *adj.* To be able to simulate the sympathetic nervous system in effect and action.

sym-pa-thy (sim´pa thē) *n. pl.* **-thies** Mutual understanding or affection during a time of sadness or loss.

sym-pat-ric (sim pa´trik) *adj.* To be happening or occurring in the same area.

symphonic poem *n.* An extended composition for a symphony orchestra in a freer form than a symphony.

sym-pho-ni-ous (sim fō´nē us) *adj.* To be agreeing such as in sound.

sym-pho-nist *n.* One who composes or writes symphonies.

sym-pho-ny (sim´fo nē) *n. pl.* **-nies.** A large orchestra with wind, percussion and string sections. **symphonic** *adj.*

sym-phy-se-al *adj.* Pertaining to or related to a symphysis.

sym-po-di-al *adj.* To be involving the formation of a main axis from a secondary axis. **sympodially** *adv.*

sym-po-si-arch *n.* The person who will preside over a symposium.

sym-po-si-um *n.* A gathering or meeting where several specialists will give short

speeches on a topic or on subjects which are related.

symp-tom (simp´tom) *n.* A sign of change in a bodys functions or appearance.

symp-tom-at-ic *adj.* To be having the characteristics of a particular disease but arising from something else.

symp-tom-at-ol-ogy *n.* The part of medical science that deals with symptoms of a disease or diseases.

syn *abbr.* Synonymous; synonym.

syn-aes-the-sis *n.* The harmony of opposing impulses which are produced by a piece of art.

syn-a-gogue (sin´a gog´) *n.* A place for Jewish worship and prayer.

syn-a-loe-pha (sin˝a lē´fa) *n.* A reduction to one syllable of two vowels of syllables which are adjacent.

syn-apse (sin´aps) *n.* A point where a nervous impulse passes from one neuron to the next neuron.

syn-ar-thro-di-al *adj.* Pertaining to or related to a synarthrosis.

syn-ar-thro-sis (sin˝är thrō´sis) *n.* A joining of bones that is immovable and is united by fibrous connective tissues.

syn-car-pous *adj.* To have the carpels of gynoecium to unite in a compound ovary.

syn-chro-mesh *adj.* To be designed for effecting synchronized gear shifting.

syn-chro-nism (sing´kro niz˝um) *n.* The state of being synchronous.

syn-chro-ni-za-tion (sing˝kro ni zā´shan) *n.* A result of synchronizing.

syn-chro-nize (sing´kro nīz´) *v.* To operate or take place at the same time.

syn-chro-nous *adj.* To be existing at precisely the same time.

syn-chro-ny *n.* A synchronistic treatment or occurrence.

syn-cli-nal *adj.* To be inclined down from opposite directions so they meet.

syn-co-pate (sing´ko pāt˝) *v.* To produce by a synscope. **syncopator** *n.*

syn-co-pated (sing´kopā˝tid) *adj.* To be exhibiting syncopation.

syn-cret-ic *adj.* To be brought about by

suncretism.

syn-cret-ism *n.* A combination of different beliefs or practices.

syn-cy-ti-um *n.* The multinucleate mass made of protoplasm which is formed from the fusion or the joining of cells.

syn-det-ic *adj.* To be marked by a conjunctive. **syndetically** *adv.*

syn-dic *n.* A type of municipal magistrate in other countries.

syn-di-cate (sin´*di* kit) *n.* An organization set up to carry out business transactions; a company that sells materials for simultaneous publication at a number of different locations.

syn-drome (sin´drōm) *n.* A set of concurrent symptoms that indicate or characterize a disorder or disease.

syn-e-col-o-gy *n.* A section or branch of ecology which deals with the development, structure, and distribution of ecological communities. **synecologic** *adj.*

syn-eph-rine *n.* A type of crystalline sympathomimetic amine.

syn-ere-sis *n.* A separation of a liquid from a gel due to constraction.

syn-er-gic *adj.* To be working together. **synergically** *adv.*

syn-er-gid *n.* A small cell lying near the micrpyle of the embryo sac of the seed plant.

syn-er-gist *n.* One that will enhance the effects of an active agent.

syn-er-gis-tic *adj.* Pertaining or relating to synergism.

syn-er-gy *n.* An operation as of the muscles.

syn-ga-my *n.* A type of sexual reproduction through the uniting of the gametes.

syn-o-nym (sin´*o* nim) *n.* A word that means the same or nearly the same as another. **synonymous** *adj.* **synonymy** *n.*

syn-op-sis (si nop´sis) *n. pl.* **-ses** A shortened statement or narrative.

syn-os-to-sis *n.* The joining or the union of bones which are separate to form a single bone.

sy-no-vi-al (si nō´vē *a*) *adj.* Pertaining to or relating to synovia, a lubricating substance that resembles the white of a egg.

sy-no-vi-tis (sin´´*o*vī´tis) n. The inflammation or the swelling of a synovial membrane.

syn-tax (sin´taks) *n.* The way in which words are put together or arranged to form sentences and phrases. **syntactic** *adj.* **syntactical** *adj.*

syn-the-sis (sin´thi sis) *n., pl.* A production of a substance by the joining of chemical elements.

syn-the-size *v.* To produce or to make with synthesis.

syn-thet-ic *adj.* To be involving synthesis. **synthetically** *adv.*

syph-i-lis (sif´*i* lis) *n.* An infectious venereal disease transmittible by direct contact and usually progressing in severity.

syph-i-lol-o-gist *n.* One who specializes in the treatment and the diagnosis of syphilis.

syph-i-lol-o-gy *n.* The branch of medicine that deals with the disease syphilis.

sy-ringe (si rinj´) *n.* A medical instrument used to inject or draw fluids from the body. **syringe** *v.*

sy-rin-go-my-el-ia *n.* A progressively chronic disease of the spinal cord associated with muscle atrophy, spasticity, and sensory disturbances.

syr-up (sir´*u*p) *n.* A sticky, thick, sweet liquid, used as a topping for food.

sys-tal-tic (si stol´tik) *adj.* To be marked by regular dilatation and contraction.

sys-tem (sis´t*e*m) *n.* A method or way of doing something; the human body or related parts of the body that perform vital functions; an orderly arrangement. **systematic** *adj.* **systematically** *adv.*

sys-to-le (sis´t*o* lē´) *n., Physiol.* The regular rhythmic contraction of the heart that pumps blood through the aorta and pulmonary artery.

sy-zy-gy *n.* A configuration of three celestial bodies in one gravitational system such as the moon, the sun, and earth when an eclipse is taking place.

T, t (tē) The twentieth letter of the English alphabet.

tab (tab) *n.* A strip, flap, or small loop that projects from something. *Slang* A bill or total, as for a meal.

tab-ard (tabèrd) *n.* A type of sleeveless coat that is worn as a tunic by a knight over top the armor.

tab-by (tab´ē) *n.* A type of domestic cat that has a coat which is mottled and striped.

tab-er-na-cle (tab´ér nak´l) *n.* A portable shelter or structure used by the Jews during their journey out of Egypt; a place of worship.

ta-bes (tāb´bēz) *n.* The wasting that comes with or is accompanying a chronic disease.

tabes forsalis *n.* A type of syphilitic disorder that affects the nervous system and is marked with wasting, incorrdination, and pain.

ta-bla (tab´la) *n.* A type of drum which is usually used in pairs of different sizes in the Hindu music.

ta-ble (tā´bl) *n.* An article of furniture having a flat top, supported by legs; a collection of related signs, values, or items. **table** *v.* To put off or postpone the discussion of something until another time.

tab-leau (tab´lō) *n. pl.* **tableaux** *or* **tableaus** A vivid representation; a stage scene represented by motionless and silent people who stand in an appropriate arrangement.

ta-ble-cloth (tā´bl kloth´) *n.* A type of covering that is placed on the top of tables for protection or for decoration.

tab-le-ful (tā´bl fül) *n.* The amount that a table is able to accommodate.

ta-ble–hop *v.* To go from one table to another in order to talk with one's friends such as in a restaurant. **table–hopper** *n*

ta-ble-land *n.* An area of land which is flat and is elevated, such as a table.

table salt *n.* The salt that is suitable for use in cooking and at the table for food.

ta-ble-spoon (tā´bl spōn´) *n.* A unit of measure; a large spoon for serving food. **table-spoonful** *n. pl.*

table sugar *n.* A type of white sugar which

is granulated and used in foods.

tab-let (tab´lit) *n.* A pad used for writing; a thin, flat piece of stone or wood which is fit for or has an inscription.

table talk *n.* The conversation which is informal and takes place at the dinner table.

table tennis *n.* A type of game that is like lawn tennis and is played on a table top with a plastic ball and wooden paddles.

ta-ble-top (tā´bl top´) *n.* A top of a table.

ta-ble-ware (tā´bl wâr´) *n.* The utensils such as forks, knives, and plates that are used on the table to eat food with.

table wine *n.* A type of wine that is served with the food and does not have more that 14 percent alcohol.

tab-loid (tab´loid) *n.* A small newspaper with news reported by means of pictures and concise reporting.

ta-boo (ta bŏ´) *n.* A custom or rule against doing, using, or mentioning something. *adj.* Forbidden by social authority, convention, or custom.

ta-bor (tā´bèr) *n.* A type of small drum that has one head made of calf skin.

tab-o-ret (tab´rit) *n.* A type of cylindrical seat that is without a back or arms.

tab-u-lar (tab´ū lèr) *adj.* Pertaining to or arranged in a table or list. **tabularly** *adv.*

tabula rasa *n.* A person's mind in its hypothetical empty state before receiving an impression from the outside.

tab-u-late (tab´ū lāt´) *v.* To put something in a tabular form. **tabulation** *n.*

tab-u-la-tor (tab´ū lā˝tèr) *n.* Something or someone that tabulates.

ta-chom-e-ter (ta kom´i tèr) *n.* An instrument for measuring velocity and speed.

tach-y-car-dia (tak˝i kär´dē a) *n.* A rapid heart beat.

tach-y-lyte (tak´ilit˝) *n.* A type of black basalt, glossy in appearance.

ta-chym-e-ter (ta kim´i tè) *n.* A device that is used to determine bearings or distances quickly.

tac-it (tas´it) *adj.* Understood; expressed or implied nonverbally; implicit. **tacitly** *adv.* **tacitness** *n.*

tac-i-turn *adj.* To be temperamentally disinclined to speak or talk.

tack (tak) *n.* A small, short nail with a flat head; a sewing stitch used to hold something temporarily; the changing of a sailboat from one direction to another. *v.* To attach or fasten with tacks; to change the direction in which a sailboat is going. **tacker** *n.*

tack-board *n.* A type of board that can be made of cork and used for the purpose of tacking notices up.

tack claw *n.* A small tool used to remove tacks.

tack-i-fy *v.* To cause or to make something tacky. **tackifier** *n.*

tack-ily *adv.* To be done in a tacky manner.

tacki-ness *n.* The state of being tacky.

tack-le (ta´kl) *n.* Equipment used for fishing or other sports or occupations; an apparatus of ropes and pulley blocks for pulling and hoisting heavy loads; in football, a position on a football team; the lineman between the guard and end. **tackle** *v.* **tackler** *n.*

tack-y (tak´ē) *adj.* Slightly sticky; shabby; lacking style or good taste; flashy.

ta-co (tä´kō) *n. pl.* **-cos** A type of Mexican or Spanish food made of a tortilla folded over with a filling inside.

tac-o-nite *n.* A type of flint-like rock which can be considered a low-grade iron ore.

tact (takt) *n.* Having the ability to avoid what would disturb or offend someone. **tactful** *adj.* **tactfully** *adv.* **tactfulness** *n.*

tac-tic (tak´tik) *n.* A way or method of working toward a goal; the art of using strategy to gain military objectives or other goals. **tactical** *adj.* **tactician** *n.*

tac-tics (tak´tiks) *n. pl.* The art of disposing of forces in combat or war.

tac-til-i-ty *n.* The responsiveness of someone or something to stimulation of the sense of touch.

tact-less *adj.* To be marked by a lack of tact. **tactlessness** *n.* **tactless** *adj.* **tactlessly** *adv.*

tad (tad) *n.* A small boy; an insignificant degree or amount.

tad-pole (tad´pōl´) *n.*

The early stage in the growth of a frog or toad during which it breathes by external gills, has a long tail, and lives in the water; a polliwog.

tae-ni-a (tē´nē a) *n.* A type of Greek fillet of ancient times.

tae-nia-cide *n.* The agent which will kill or destroy tapeworms.

tae-ni-a-sis *n.* A type of disease that can be caused by tapeworms.

taf-fe-ta (taf´i ta) *n.* A stiff, smooth fabric of rayon, nylon, or silk.

taf-fe-tized *adj.* To have a finish that is crisp in nature.

taff-rail (taf´rāl´) *n.* The rail around the stern of a boat or ship.

taf-fy (taf´ē) *n.* A type of candy which is boiled and is made of brown sugar and is pulled until it becomes porous.

taf-i-a (taf´ē a) *n.* A type of rum of West India that is made from distilled sugar cane juice.

tag (tag) *n.* A piece of plastic, metal, paper, or other material that is attached to something in order to identify it; a children's game in which one child is "it" and tries to catch another child, who then becomes "it." **tagger** *n.*

tag-along *n.* The person that follows the lead of another person.

tag-board *n.* A type of cardboard that is used for the making of shipping tags.

tag end *n.* A random bit.

tag up *v.* To touch base in the game of baseball before one runs after a fly ball is caught.

Ta-hi-tian *n.* A person who is a native or living in Tahiti.

tah-sil-dar (ta sēl där´) *n.* One who is a revenue officer in the country of India.

Tai *n.* A group of people of southeast Asia.

tai-ga *n.* The moist subarctic forest which will begin where the tundra ends and contains firs and spruces.

tail (tāl) *n.* The posterior extremity, extending from the end or back of an animal. **tails** *n. pl.* The opposite side of a coin from heads; formal evening dress for men.

tail v. To follow or keep close watch on someone.

tail-back (tāl´bak˝) n. The position in football that is the farthest back on the offensive side from the line of scrimmage.

tail-coat n. A type of coat that has tails.

tail end n. The end of something or one.

tail fin n. The fin that is located on the tail of a fish.

tail-gate (tāl´gāt´) n. The hinged gate at the back of a truck or automobile for loading and unloading. v. To follow very closely in a car.

taille (tāl) n. A type of tax that was levied by a French king on his subjects or the land that they held in their possession.

tail light n. A red light that is at the rear of a car or other vehicle for the purpose of warning other cars behind it.

tai-lor (tā´lėr) n. One whose profession is making, mending, and altering clothing. **tailor** v. To adapt for a specific purpose.

tailor's chalk n. A type of chalk that is used by tailors in order to make a temporary mark on the cloth they are using.

tai-lor-bird (tā´lėr bürd˝) Type of warbler that will stitch leaves together in order to build their nests.

tai-lored (tā´lėrd) adj. Made by a tailor.

tail-or-ing (tā´lėr ing) n. The occupation of a tailor.

tail pipe n. A pipe that will discharge gases from the muffler.

tail-spin (tāl´spin˝) n. An emotional collapse.

tail-wa-ter n. The water which can be found below a dam.

taint (tānt) v. To spoil, contaminate, or pollute. n. A blemish or stain.

tai-pan n. One who is a foreigner and living in China wielding economic power.

take (tāk) v. To seize or capture; to get possession of; to receive, swallow, absorb, or accept willingly; to attack and surmount; to move, convey, or conduct to a different place; to require; to choose or pick. Slang To cheat; to subtract. **take** n. The process of acquiring; the total receipts for admission at an event.

take back v. To make or state a retraction of something such as a statement.

take down v. To lower the vanity of someone.

take in v. To receive as a lodger; to encompass something within the limits of something else.

take on v. To deal with something or someone.

talc (talk) n. A soft, fine-grained, smooth mineral used in making talcum powder.

talcum powder n. A type of powder that is made of talc and an antiseptic.

tale (tāl) n. A story or recital of relating events that may or may not be true; a malicious or false story; gossip.

tale-bear-er (tāl´bâr˝ėr) n. One who will spread gossip. **talebearing** adj. & n.

tal-ent (tal´ent) n. The aptitude, disposition, or characteristic ability of a person. **talented** adj. **talentless** adj.

talent scout n. A person who discovers and recruits people with talent for a specialized activity or field.

talent show n. A type of show which consists of a series of individual performances which are done by amateurs.

ta-ler n. A silver coin which was issued by German states in the 15th to the 19th centuries.

talk (tok) v. To communicate by words or speech; to engage in chatter or gossip. **talk** n. A speech or lecture, usually given to a group of people. Slang To boast; to brag. **talker, talkativeness** n. **talkative** adj. **talkatively** adv.

talk down v. To belittle someone by talking; to speak in a condescending manner.

talk over v. To consider something in a conversation between persons.

talky (to´kē) adj. To be containing or having too much talk in something.

tall (tol) adj. Of greater than average height; of a designated or specified height; imaginary, as a tall tale. **tallish** adj.

tal-lage (tal´ij) n. A fee that is paid a lord for his feudal tenant.

tall-boy (tol´boi˝) n. A type of chest of

drawers where the top section is smaller than the lower section.

tal-low (tal´ō) *n.* Hard fat rendered from sheep or cattle, used to make candles, lubricants, and soap. **tallow** *adj.*

tal-ly (tal´ē) *n. pl.* **tallies** A record or counting of money, amounts, or scores. *v.* To agree with; to reckon or figure a score; to count.

tal-ly-man (tal´ē man) *n.* The person who checks or has a record of counting.

tal-on (tal´on) *n.* A long, curved claw found on birds or animals, used to kill or capture prey. **taloned** *adj.*

ta-lus *n.* The slope which is formed by the gathering or accumulation of rock debris.

ta-ma-le (ta mä´lē) *n.* The meat that is seasoned with chili and then is rolled into a cornmeal dough and is steamed.

tam-a-rind *n.* A type of leguminous tree that has hard yellowish wood and red-striped yellow flowers; the tree's fruit.

tam-bour (tam´bür) *n.* A type of frame that can be used for the purpose of embroidering.

tam-bou-rine (tam´bo rēn´) *n.* A percussion instrument made of a small drum with jingling metal disks around the rim.

tame (tām) *adj.* Not wild or ferocious; domesticated or manageable. **tame** *v.* To make docile or calm. **tamely** *adv.* **tamer** *n.* **tameness** *n.*

tame-less (tām´lis) *adj.* Being unable to be tamed.

tam-per (tam´pėr) *v.* To change, meddle, or alter something; to use corrupt measures to scheme. **tamperproof** *adj.*

tan (tan) *v.* To cure a hide into leather by using chemicals. *Slang* To spank a child. **tan** *n.* A brownish skin tone caused by exposure to the sun.

tan-a-ger *n.* A type of American passerine bird which can be found in the woodlands.

tan-bark *n.* A type of bark that is rich in tannin and is used in the tanning process.

tan-dem (tan´dem) *n.* Any arrangement that involves two or more things, animals or persons arranged one behind the other.

tandem bicycle *n.* A type of bicycle that was built for two persons.

tang (tang) *n.* A sharp, distinct taste, smell, or quality; a slender shank that projects from a tool and connects to a handle.

tan-ge-lo *n.* The hybrid that is between a tangerine and a pomelo or grapefruit.

tan-gent (tan´jent) *n.* A line that touches a curved line but does not intersect or cross it; a sudden change from one course to another. **tangency** *n.* **tangential** *adj.*

tan-ger-ine (tan´je rēn) *n.* A small citrus fruit with an easily peeled orange skin, resembling an orange.

tan-gi-ble (tan´ji bl) *adj.* Capable of being appreciated or felt by the sense of touch; capable of being realized. **tangibleness, tangibility** *n.* **tangibly** *adv.*

tan-gle (tang´gl) *v.* To mix, twist, or unite in a confused manner making separation difficult. **tangle** *n.* **tanglement** *n.*

tangled *adj.* To be in a state of disorder.

tangly *adj.* To be full of tangles.

tan-go (tang´gō) *n.* A ballroom dance with long, gliding steps. **tango** *v.*

tangram *n.* A type of Chinese puzzle that is made by cutting a square of material into different shapes, such as five triangles, a rhomboid, and a square and they are able to be combined in different figures.

tank (tangk) *n.* A large container for holding or storing a gas or liquid. **tankful** *n.*

tankage *n.* The contents of a tank.

tank-ard (tang´kėrd) *n.* A large drinking mug, usually with a hinged top.

tanker *n.* A type of boat that is fitted with tanks for the carrying of liquid in bulk.

tank farm *n.* An area that has tanks and is used for the purpose of storing oil.

tan-nage (tan´ij) *n.* A process of tanning something.

tan-nery *n.* The place where tanning is done.

tan-ning (tan´ing) *n.* The browning of the skin with an exposure to the sun.

tan oak *n.* A type of evergreen oak that will yield tan bark.

tan-tal-ic (tan tal´ik) *adj.* To be pertaining to tanlaum.

tan-ta-lite (tan´ta līt˝) *n.* The mineral that is made of dark oxide of iron, tantalum, manganise, and columbium.

tan-ta-lize (tan´ ta līz´) *v.* To tease or tempt by holding or keeping something just out of one's reach. **tantalizingly** *adv.*

tan-ta-liz-ing (tan´ta līz˝) *adj.* To have a quality that stimulates an interest.

tan-ta-lum (tan´ta lūm) *n.* A metallic element symbolized by Ta.

tan-ta-mount (tan´ta mount˝) *adj.* To be equivalent in effect, significance, or value.

tan-ta-ra (tan´tèr a) *n.* A blare of the horn or trumpet.

tan-trum (tan´trum) *n.* A fit; an outburst or a rage of bad temper.

tan-yard *n.* The part of the tannery that is used to house the tanning vats.

tan-za-nite *n.* A type of mineral that is a blue variety of zoisite.

tap (tap) *v.* To strike repeatedly, usually while making a small noise; to strike or touch gently; to make secret contact with something; in medicine, to remove fluids from the body. **tapper** *n.*

tap dance *n.* A type of step dance that is tapped out by the means of shoes that have metal taps on them.

tape (tāp) *n.* A narrow strip of woven fabric; a string or ribbon stretched across the finish line of a race. **tape** *v.*

tape grass *n.* A type of submerged plant that has leaves which are long and ribbonlike.

tape measure *n.* A strip of cloth or other material that is marked off in units of measure and is used to measure things.

ta-per (tā´pèr) *n.* A very slender candle. *v.* To become gradually smaller or thinner at one end.

ta-per-er *n.* The person who bears or carries a taper in a religious procession.

tap-es-tried *adj.* To be decorated

with tapestry.

tap-es-try (tap´i strē) *n. pl.* **-ies** A thick fabric woven with designs and figures.

ta-pe-tum *n.* The layer of the nutritive cells that is found in the sporogenous tissue.

tape-worm (tāp´würm˝) *n.* A type of cestode worm that is parasitic and found in the intestine of animals or of man.

tap-i-o-ca (tap´ē ō´ka) *n.* A bead-like substance used for thickening and for puddings.

ta-pis *n.* The tapestry material that is used for table coverings and hangings.

tappet hen *n.* A hen that is crested.

tap-ping *n.* Process where something is tapped.

tap-root *n.* A root that will grow vertically downward and has other lateral roots.

taps (taps) *n. pl., Milit.* A bugle call that signals lights out, also sounded at memorial and funeral services.

tap-ster (tap´stèr) *n.* The person who is hired to dispense liquors in a barroom.

tar (tär) *n.* A black bituminous viscous liquid that is made or obtained by the destructive distillation of organic matter.

tar-an-tel-la (tar˝an tela) *n.* A type of folk dance of Italy.

ta-ran-tu-la (ta ran´cha la) *n.* A type of spider which is hairy and slow and not poisonous to man.

ta-rax-a-cum (ta rak´sa kum) *n.* A dried root of the dandelion which can be used as a tonic and diuretic.

tar-dy (tär´dē) *adj.* Late; not on time. **tardily, tardiness** *n.*

tare (târ) *n.* An element which is undesirable.

targe *n.* A type of light shield.

tar-get (tär´git) *n.* An object marked to shoot at; an aim or goal.

target date *n.* A date which has been set for the completion of something.

tar-iff (tar´if) *n.* Duty or tax on merchandise coming into or going out of a country.

tar-la-tan (tär´la tan) *n.* A type of cotton fabric that is heavily sized for stiffness.

tarn (tärn) *n.* A type of steep-banked mountain pool.

tar-nish (tär'nish) *v.* To become discolored or dull; to lose luster; to spoil. **tarnish, tarnishable** *adj.*

tar-nish (tär'nish) *v.* To become discolored or dull; to lose luster; to spoil. **tarnish** *n.* **tarnishable** *adj.*

tarnished plant bug *n.* A type of bug that is destructive to plants because it will suck the sap from the leaves, buds, and fruits.

ta-ro *n.* A type of plant of the arum family that is grown in the tropics for its root stocks which can be eaten.

tar-ok *n.* The card game that was popular in Europe and was played with a deck of 40, 52, or 56 cards.

tar-ot *n.* A set of 22 cards used for for-tune-telling, each card showing a virtue, an elemental force, or a vice.

tar paper *n.* A type of paper which is heavy and is impregnated with tar and used in building.

tar-pau-lin (tär pa'lin) *n.* A sheet of waterproof canvas used as a protective covering.

tar-ra-gon (tar'a gon") *n.* A type of European wood that is grown for its aromatic foliage.

tar-ry (tar'ē) *v.* To linger, delay, or hesitate.

tar-sal *adj.* To be pertaining to the tarsus.

tar-si-er *n.* A type of nocturnal mammal of East India which is related to the lemurs.

tar-sus (tär'sus) *n.* A bone of the foot or hand which makes up the ankle or the wrist.

tart (tärt) *adj.* Sharp; sour; cutting, biting in tone or meaning. **tartly, tartness** *n.*

tar-tan (tär'tan) *n.* A plaid fabric pattern of Scottish origin. **tartan** *adj.*

tar-tar (tär'tèr) *n.* The reddish, acidic, crust-like deposit which forms as grape juice turns to wine; a hard deposit which forms on the teeth, composed of secretions, food, and calcium salts. **tartaric** *adj.*

TAS *abbr.* Telephone answering service.

task (task) *n.* A bit of work, usually assigned by another; a job.

task-mas-ter *n.* A person who imposes labor upon another person.

task-mis-tress *n.* A woman who is a taskmaster.

tasse *n.* An overlapping plate in a suit of armor which will make a short skirt below the waist.

tas-sel (tas'el) *n.* An ornamental decoration made from a bunch of string or thread.

taste (tāst) *n.* The ability to sense or determine flavor in the mouth; a personal liking or disliking. *v.* To test or sense flavors in the mouth. **tasteless, tasteful** *n.*

taste bud *n.* An organ on the tongue that will mediate the sensation of taste.

taste-mak-er *n.* A person who will set a standard of what is fashionable.

tasty *adj.* To have a taste which is pleasing. **tastiness** *n.*

TAT *abbr.* Thematic apperception test.

ta-ta-mi *n.* The straw matting which is used as a covering for the floor in the Japanese home.

tat-ter (tat'ēr) *n.* A torn scrap of cloth. *v.* To become or make ragged.

tat-ter-de-ma-lion (tat"ēr di māl'yon) *n.* One who is dressed in clothing that is ragged.

tat-tered (tat'ērd) *adj.* To be torn into pieces or shreds.

tat-ter-sail (tat'ēr sāl") *n.* The pattern of colored lines which form squares.

tat-ting (tat'ing) *n.* A type of handmade lace.

tat-tle (tat'l) *v.* To reveal the secrets of another by gossiping. **tattler** *n.*

tattle-tale (tat'l tāl') *n.* One who betrays secrets concerning others; a person, usually a child, who informs on others.

tat-too (ta tö') *n.* A permanent design or mark made on the skin by pricking and inserting an indelible dye. **tattooer** *n.*

tat-ty *adj.* To be frayed.

taught (tot) *v.* Past tense of teach.

taunt (tont) *v.* To mock or insult someone.

taupe *n.* A color which is a brownish gray.

tau-rine (tor'ēn) *adj.* To be pertaining to a bull.

Tau-rus *n.* The second sign of the zodiac; a person born between April 20-May 20.

taut (tot) *adj.* Tight; emotionally strained. **tautly** *adv.* **tautness** *n.*

tau-tog *n.* A type of fish that is found along the Atlantic coast of the United States.

tau-tol-o-gy (ta´tol´*o* **jē)** *n. pl.* **-ies** Redundancy; a statement which is an unnecessary repetition of the same idea.

tau-to-mer-ic *adj.* To be pertaining to tautomerism.

tav-ern (tav´ĕrn) *n.* An inn; an establishment or business licensed to sell alcoholic drinks. **taverner** *n.*

tav-ern-er *n.* A person who runs a tavern.

taw *v.* To dress such as skins by a dry process.

taw-dry (to´drē) *adj.* To be gaudy in appearance. **tawdriness** *n.*

taw-pie *n.* A person who is foolish.

tax (taks) *n.* A payment imposed and collected from individuals or businesses by the government. *v.* To strain. **taxable** *adj.* **tax-ation** *n.* **taxer** *n.* **taxpayer** *n.*

tax--ex-empt (taks´igzempt) *adj.* Exempted from tax; bearing tax-free interest on federal or state income.

tax evasion *n.* The failure, which is deliberate, to pay taxes.

tax-i (tak´sē) *v.* To move along the ground or water surface on its own power before taking off.

tax-i-cab (tak´sē kab´) *n.* A vehicle for carrying passengers for money.

tax-i-der-my (tak´si dur´mē) *n.* The art or profession of preparing, stuffing, and mounting animal skins. **taxidermist** *n.*

tax-i-me-ter *n.* The device which is used in a taxicab to record the money that is owed by the passenger.

tax-i-stand *n.* The place where a taxi will park while the driver waits for a passenger.

tax-pay-er (taks´pā˝ĕr) *n.* A person who pays a tax.

tax-pay-ing *adj.* Pertaining to the paying of taxes by someone.

tax shelter *n.* A credit or allowance that reduces taxes on current earnings for an individual investor or corporation.

tax stamp *n.* The stamp which is placed on something to show that the tax for it has been paid.

Taylor, Zachary *n.* The 12th president of the United States from 1849-1850, died in office.

TBA *abbr.* To be announced.

tbs *abbr.* Tablespoon.

tchr *abbr.* Teacher.

TDY *abbr.* Temporary duty.

tea (tē) *n.* A small tree or bush which grows where the climate is very hot and damp; a drink made by steeping the dried leaves of this shrub in boiling water.

tea bag *n.* A filter paper bag that holds tea.

tea-board *n.* A type of tray which is used for the purpose of serving tea.

tea-bowl *n.* A type of teacup that does not have a handle.

teach (tēch) *v.* To communicate skill or knowledge; to give instruction or insight. **teaching, teachability** *adj.* **teachableness** *adj.* **teachable** *adj.*

teach-er (tē´chĕr) *n.* A person who teaches; one who instructs.

teacher's pet *n.* A student in the class who gets the special attention of the teacher.

teach-er-ship *n.* A position of teaching.

teaching aid *n.* The device which is used to help reinforce the classroom instructions.

tea-cup *n.* A type of cup that is used for hot beverages. **teacupful** *n.*

teak *n.* A type of tall tree of East India that can be used for shipbuilding.

teal blue *n.* A color which is a greenish blue.

team (tēm) *n.* Two or more players on one side in a game; a group of people trained or organized to work together; two or more animals harnessed to the same implement. *v.* To join or work together.

tea mak-er *n.* A type of covered spoon which is used for making tea in a cup.

team-mate *n.* A person who is on a team with others.

team-ster (tēm´stĕr) *n.* A person who drives a team of animals or a vehicle as an occupation.

tea party *n.* A gathering that takes place in the afternoon where tea is served.

tea-pot *n.* A container that tea is brewed in.

tea-poy *n.* A type of stand for a tea service.

tear (tēr) *n.* A fluid secreted by the eye to moisten and cleanse. *v.* To cry.

tear (târ) *v.* To become divided into pieces; to separate; to rip into parts or pieces; to move fast; to rush. *n.* A rip or torn place.

tear-down *n.* The process of taking something apart.

tear-ful *adj.* To be accompanied by tears. **tearfulness** *n.*

tear gas *n.* A type of gaseous substance that will blind the eyes with tears.

tear jerker *n.* A story that is pathetic. **tear-jerking** *n.*

tea-room *n.* A type of room in a restaurant that is designed for the female clientele.

tea rose *n.* A type of rose that descends from the Chinese rose.

tear-stain *n.* The streak that is left by a tear. **tearstained** *adj.*

tear up *v.* To remove or to damage something.

teary *adj.* To be stained with tears.

tease (tēz) *v.* To make fun of; to bother; to annoy; to tantalize. *n.* A person who teases. **teaser, teasingly** *adv.*

teasel *n.* A type of herb which is prickly and is used in the wool industry.

tea service *n.* The set of china which contains the items needed to serve tea, such as a tray, cups, and a teapot.

teat *n.* The protuberance that milk flows out of.

tea-time (tē´tīm˝) *n.* A time for serving the tea.

tec *abbr.* Technician.

tech *abbr.* Technical; technician.

tech-ne-tium (tek nē´shē um) *n.* A metallic element symbolized by Tc.

tech-ne-tron-ic *adj.* To be pertaining to a society that is shaped by the impact of technology.

tech-ni-cal (tek´ni kal) *adj.* Expert; derived or relating to technique; relating to industry or mechanics. **technically** *adv.*

tech-ni-cal-i-ty (tek˝ni kal´i tē) *n.* The state of something being technical.

tech-ni-cian *n.* A person who is a specialist in the technical details of a subject.

tech-nique (tek nēk´) *n.* A technical procedure or method of doing something.

tech-no-crat *n.* A person who is a member of a technocracy.

tech-no-crat-ic *adj.* To be pertaining to a technocracy.

technol *abbr.* Technology.

tech-nol-o-gist *n.* A person who is a specialist in technology.

tech-nol-o-gy (tek nol´o jē) *n. pl.* **-ies** The application of scientific knowledge to serve man in industry, commerce, medicine and other fields.

tec-ton-ic (tek ton´ik) *adj.* To be pertaining to the deformation of the crust of the earth. **tectonically** *adv.*

tec-ton-ics *n.* The art of construction and building of things, such as a building.

ted (ted) *v.* To turn and scatter something, such as grass for drying purposes.

ted-der (ted´ėr) *n.* Someone or something that teds.

teddy bear *n.* A type of bear that is stuffed and used as a child's toy.

te-di-ous (tē´de us) *adj.* Boring; taking a longtime. **tediously** *adv.*

tedium *n.* The state of being tedious.

tee (tē) *n.* A peg used to hold a golf ball on the first stroke toward a hole or goal post; a peg used to support a football during a field goal attempt. **teed off**

teem (tem) *v.* To abound; to be full of; to swarm or crowd.

teen-ag-er (tēn´ā˝jėr) *n.* A young adult who is in the teen years of life, such as 13 to 19 years old.

teens (tēnz) *n. pl.* The ages between 13 and 19; the years of one's life between 13 and 19.

tee-ter (tē´tėr) *v.* To move about in an unsteady manner.

teeth *n. pl.* The plural of tooth.

teethe (tēth) *v.* To grow one's teeth.

teeth-er *n.* An object which can be used by

babies while they are cutting teeth.

teff *n.* A type of grass which is grown for its grain in Africa.

tel-e-cast (tel´ē kast´) *n.* A television broadcast. **telecast** *v.*

tel-e-com-mu-ni-ca-tion *n.* The communication between two points which are a great distance away from each other.

tel-e-course *n.* A school course which can be taught over the television.

tel-e-film *n.* A movie or picture which has been made or produced for television.

tel-e-gram (tel´e gram) *n.* A message sent or received by telegraph. **telegram** *v.*

tel-e-graph (tel´e graf) *n.* A system for communicating; a transmission sent by wire or radio. *v.* To send messages by electricity over wire. **telegraphist, telegrapher** *n.* **telegraphic** *adj.*

telegraph plant *n.* A type of tick trefoil of East India whose leaflets move up and down.

te-le-ost *n.* The group of fishes that have a bony skeleton. **teleostean** *adj.*

te-lep-a-thy (telep´a thē) *n.* Communication by means of mental processes rather than ordinary means. **telepathic** *n.*

tel-e-phone (tel´e fōn´) *n.* A system or device for transmitting conversations by wire. **telephone** *v.* **telephoner** *n.*

telephone booth *n.* The booth where a telephone can be located and one makes a call while standing up.

telephone directory *n.* The book which lists numbers, names, and addresses of people who have a telephone.

telephone number *n.* The number which has been given to a person and one is able to call this person with this number.

tel-e-phon-ic (tel´´e fon´ik) *adj.* To be able to convey sound. **telephonically** *adv.*

tel-e-pho-to (tel´ē fō´tō) *adj.* Relating to a camera lens which produces a large image of a distant object. **telephotograph** *n.*

tel-e-pho-to (tel´e fō´´tō) *adj.* Relating to a camera lens which produces a large image of a distant object. **telephotograph** *n.*

tel-e-pho-to-graph-ic *adj.* To be pertaining

to the process of telephotography.

tel-e-play (tel´e plā´´) *n.* A type of play which has been written for the television.

tel-e-scope (tel´i skōp´) *n.* An instrument which contains a lens system which makes distant objects appear larger and nearer. **telescopic** *adj.*

tel-e-sis *n.* The progress which is directed and planned in an intelligent manner.

tel-e-thon (tel´e thon´) *n.* A long telecast used to raise money for a worthy cause.

tel-e-view *v.* To watch something by the means of a television receiver.

tel-e-vise (tel´e vīz´´) *v.* To broadcast some show with the use of a television.

tel-e-vi-sion (tel´e vizh´an) *n.* Reception and transmission of images on a screen with sound; the device that reproduces television sounds and images.

tel-e-vis-or *n.* The apparatus that will transmit or will receive for a television.

tel-ex *n.* Teletype communications by means of automatic exchanges.

te-lio-spore *n.* A type of chlamydospore that is thick-walled and in its final stage in the life cycle of the rust fungus.

tell (tel) *v.* To relate or describe; to command or order. **telling, tellable** *n.*

tell-er *n.* A person who will relate or tell.

tell-tale *n.* The device for recording something.

tel-lu-ri-an (te lür´ē an) *adj.* To be pertaining to the earth.

tel-lu-ri-um (te lur´ē um) *n.* An element symbolized by Te.

tel-lu-rom-e-ter *n.* The device that will measure a distance with the use of microwaves.

tel-lu-rous (tel´yer us) *adj.* To be pertaining to tellurium.

temp *abbr.* Temperature.

tem-per (tem´pèr) *n.* The state of one's feelings. *v.* To modify something, making it flexible or hard. **temperable** *adj.*

tem-per-a-ment (tem´pèr a ment) *n.* Personality; a characteristic way of thinking, reacting, or behaving.

tem-per-ance (tem´pèr ans) n. Moderation; restraint; moderation or abstinence from drinking alcoholic beverages.

tem-per-ate (tem´ėr it) *adj.* Avoiding extremes; moderate. **temperately** *adj.* **temperateness** *n.*

tem-per-a-ture (tem´pėr *a* **cher)** *n.* A measure of heat or cold in relation to the body or environment; an elevation in body temperature above the normal 98.6 degrees Fahrenheit.

tem-pest (tem´pist) *n.* A severe storm, usually with snow, hail, rain, or sleet.

tem-ple (tem´pl) *n.* A place of worship; the flat area on either side of the forehead.

tem-po (tem´po) *n.* *pl.* **-pos** *or* **-pi** *Mus.* The rate of speed at which a musical composition is to be played.

tem-po-rar-y (tem´po rer´ē) *adj.* Lasting for a limited amount of time; not permanent.

tempt (tempt) *n.* To encourage or draw into a foolish or wrong course of action; to lure. **temptation** *n.* **tempter** *n.*

ten (ten) *n.* The cardinal number equal to 9 + 1; the number before eleven.

te-na-cious (te nā´ shus) *adj.* Persistent; stubborn. **tenaciousness** *n.*

ten-ant (ten´ant) *n.* A person who pays rent to occupy another's property. **tenantless** *adj.* **tenantable** *adj.*

Ten Commandments *n.* The ten rules of moral behavior which were given to Moses by God.

tend (tend) *v.* To be inclined or disposed; to be directed; to look after.

ten-den-cy (ten´den sē) *n.* *pl.* **-ies** A disposition to act or behave in a particular way; a particular direction, mode, outcome, or direction.

ten-der (ten´dėr) *adj.* Fragile; soft; not hard or tough; painful or sore when touched. *n.* Something offered as a formal bid or offer; compassionate; a supply ship. *v.* To make an offer to buy or purchase; to present, as a resignation. **tenderly** *adj.* **tenderhearted** *adj.* **tenderness** *n.*

ten-der-loin (ten´dėr loin´) *n.* A cut of tender pork or beef.

ten-don *n.* A band of tough, fibrous tissues

that connect, a muscle and bone.

ten-dril (ten´dril) *n.* A thread-like part of a climbing plant which attaches itself to a support. **tendriled** *or* **tendrilled** *adj.*

ten-nis (ten´is) *n.* A sport played with a ball and racket by 2 or 4 people on a rectangular court.

ten-or (ten´ėr) *n.* An adult male singing voice, above a baritone.

tense (tens) *adj.* Taut or stretched tightly; nervous; under strain. **tense** *v.*

ten-sion (ten´shan) *n.* The condition of stretching or the state of being stretched. **tensional** *adj.* **tensionless** *adj.*

tent (tent) *n.* A portable shelter made by stretching material over a supporting framework.

ten-ta-cle (ten´ta kl) *n.* A long, unjointed, flexible body part that projects from certain invertebrates, as the octopus. **tentacular** *adj.* **tentacled** *adj.*

ten-ta-tive (ten´ta tiv) *adj.* Experimental; subject to change; not definite.

ten-ure (ten´yėr) *n.* The right, state, or period of holding something, as an office or property. **tenurial, tenured, tenurially** *adv.*

te-pee (tā´pē) *n.* A tent made of hides or bark used by the Indians of North America.

tep-id (tep´id) *adj.* Lukewarm. **tepidly** *adj.* **tepidness** *n.*

te-qui-la *n.* A type of Mexican liquor.

te-rai *n.* A type of wide-brimmed felt hat that is worn by the people in subtropical areas.

ter-a-to-log-i-cal *adj.* To be abnormal in structure of growth.

ter-a-to-ma *n.* A type of tumor that is made up of a heterogeneous mixture of the tissues. **teratomatous** *adj.*

ter-bi-um (tŭr'bē ŭm) *n*. A metallic element of the rare-earth group symbolized by Tb.

ter-cen-ten-a-ry (ter sen'te ner'ē) *n. pl.* **-ries.** The time span of 300 years; a 300th anniversary. **tercentenary** *adj*.

ter-cet *n*. A group of three lines of verse.

ter-e-binth (ter'e binth) *n*. A type of European tree that belongs to the sumac family and yeilds turpentine.

ter-e-bin-thine (ter˝e bin'thin) *adj*. To be pertaining to or resembling turpentine.

te-rete *adj*. To be almost cylindrical but to be tapering at both ends.

ter-gi-ver-as-tion *n*. The evasion of a clear-cut statement.

ter-gum (tür'gum) *n*. A plate of an rthropod that is a dorsal section.

ter-i-ya-ki *n*. A Japanese dish where the ingrediants are marinated in soy sauce then grilled.

term *n*. A phrase or word; a limited time or duration; a phrase having a precise meaning. *Math* The quantity of two numbers either added together or subtracted.

ter-mi-nal (ter'mi nal) *adj*. Of, forming, or located at the end; final. *n*. A station at the end of a bus line, railway, or airline; in Computer Science, the instrument through which data enters or leaves a computer.

ter-mi-nate (tür'mi nāt˝) *v*. To bring to a conclusion or end; to finish; to fire someone from a job. **termination** *n*.

ter-mite (tee'mīt) *n*. The winged or wing-lessinsect which lives in large colonies feeding on wood.

terr *abbr*. Territory.

ter-race (ter'as) *n*. An open balcony or porch; a level piece of land that is higher than the surrounding area; a row of houses built on a sloping or raised site.

ter-ra cot-ta *n*. A hard, baked clay used in ceramic pottery.

ter-rain (te rān') *n*. The surface of an area, as land.

ter-ra-pin (ter'a pin) *n*. An edible turtle of North America, living in both fresh and salt water.

ter-res-tri-al (te res'trē al) *adj*. Something earthly; not heavenly; growing or living on land.

ter-ri-ble (ter'i bl) *adj*. Causing fear or terror; intense; extreme; horrid; difficult. **terribly** *adv*. **terribleness** *n*.

ter-ri-er (ter'ē èr) *n*. A very active small dog, originally bred by hunters to dig for burrowing game, now kept as a family pet.

ter-rif-ic (te rif'ik) *adj*. Terrifying. *Informal* Excellent; causing amazement.

ter-ri-fy (ter'i fī') *v*. To fill with fear or terror; to frighten; to menace. **terrified** *adj*. **terrifying** *adj*.

ter-ri-to-ry (ter'i tōr'ē) *n. pl.* **-ies** An area, usually of great size, which is controlled by a particular government; a district or area assigned to one person or group. **territorial** *adj*. **territorially** *adv*.

ter-ror (ter'èr) *n*. Extreme fear; one who causes terror.

ter-ror-ism *n*. The state of being terrorized or the act of terrorizing; the use of intimidation to attain one's goals or to advance one's cause.

terse (ters) *adj*. Brief; using as few words as possible without loss of force or clearness. **tersely** *adv*. **terseness** *n*.

test (test) *n*. An examination or evaluation of something or someone; an examination to determine one's knowledge, skill, intelligence or other qualities. **tester** *n*.

tes-ta-ment (tes'ta ment) *n*. A legal document which states how one's personal property is to be distributed upon his death. **Testament** One of the two sections of the Bible; the Old Testament and the New Testament. **testamentary** *adj*.

tes-tate (tes'tāt) *adj*. Having left a valid will.

tes-ti-fy (tes'ti fī') *v*. To give evidence while under oath; to serve as proof. **testifier** *n*.

tes-ti-mo-ni-al (tes'ti mō'nē al) *n*. A formal statement; a gift, dinner, reception, or other sign of appreciation given to a person as a token of esteem.

tes-ti-mo-ny (tes'ti mō'nē) *n. pl.* **-ies** A

solemn affirmation made under oath; an outward expression of a religious experience.

tes-tis (tes'tis) *n. pl.* **testes** The sperm producing gland of the male.

test tube *n.* A thin glass tube closed at one end, used in biology and chemistry.

test–tube baby *n.* A baby conceived outside of the womb by fertilizing an egg removed from a woman and then returning the fertilized egg to the womb.

tet-a-nus (tet'a nus) *n., Pathol* An often fatal disease marked by muscular spasms, commonly known as lockjaw.

teth-er (teth'er) *n.* A rope or chain which fastens an animal to something but allows limited freedom to wander within its range.

text (tekst) *n.* The actual wording of an author's work distinguished his from notes; the main part or body of a book. **textual, textually** *adv.*

text-book (tekst'bek') *n.* A book used by students to prepare their lessons.

tex-tile (teks'til) *n.* A cloth made by weaving; yarn or fiber for making cloth.

tex-ture (teks'cher) *n.* The look, surface, or feel of something; the basic makeup. **textural** *adj.* **texturally** *adv.*

thal-li-um (thal'ē um) *n.* A metallic element resembling lead, symbolized by Tl.

than (than) *conj.* In comparison with or to something.

thank (thangk) *v.* To express one's gratitude; to credit.

thank-ful (thangk'ful) *adj.* Feeling or showing gratitude; grateful. **thankfully** *adv.* **thankfulness** *n.* **thankless** *adj.*

thanks (thangks) *n. pl.* An expression of one's gratitude.

Thanksgiving Day *n.* A United States holiday, set apart as a legal holiday for public thanksgiving, celebrated on the fourth Thursday of November.

that (that) *adj. pl.* **those** The person or thing present or being mentioned. Used to introduce a clause stating what is said.

thatch (thach) *n.* Grass, straw, or similar material used to make a roof. *v.* To overlay or cover with or as if with thatch.

thaw (tho) *v.* To change from a frozen state to a liquid or soft state; to grow warmer; to melt. **thaw** *n.*

the-a-tre (thē'a tėr) *n.* A building adapted to present dramas, motion pictures, plays, or other performances; a performance.

the-at-ri-cal (thē a'tri kal) *adj.* Extravagant; designed for show, display, or effect. **theatricals** *n.*

the *definite adj. or article* Used before nouns and noun phrases as a determiner, designating particular persons or things. *adv.* Used to modify words in the comparative degree; by so much; by that much.

theft (theft) *n.* The act or crime of stealing; larceny.

their (thâr) *adj. & pron.* The possessive case of they; belonging to two or more things or beings previously named.

the-ism (thē'iz um) *n.* The belief in the existence of God. **theist, theistic** *adj.*

them (them) *pron.* The objective case of they.

theme (thēm) *n.* The topic or subject of something. *Mus.* A short melody of a musical composition. **thematic** *adj.*

them-selves (them selvz') *pron.* Them or they; a form of the third person plural pronoun.

then (then) *adv.* At that time; soon or immediately. *adj.* Being or acting in or belonging to or at that time.

thence (thens) *adv.* From that place, event, fact, or origin.

the-oc-ra-cy (thē ok'ra sē) *n. pl.* **-ies** Government by God or by clergymen who think of themselves as representatives of God. **theocrat** *n.* **theocratic** *adj.*

the-ol-o-gy (thē ol'o' jē) *n. pl.* **-ies** The religious study of the nature of God, beliefs, practices, and ideas. **theologian** *n.*

the-o-rize (thē'o rīz') *v.* To analyze theories. **theoretician** *n.* **theorization** *n.* **theorizer** *n.* **the-orist** *n.*

the-o-ry (thē'o rē) *n. pl.* -ies A general principle or explanation which covers the known facts; an offered opinion which may possibly, but not positively, be true.

ther-a-peu-tics (ther'a pū'tiks) *n.* The medical treatment of disease.

ther-a-py (ther'a pē) *n. pl.* -ies The treatment of certain diseases; treatment intended to remedy an undesirable condition. therapist *n.*

there (thâr) *adv.* In, at, or about that place; toward, into, or to. thereabouts *adv.* thereafter *adv.* thereby *adv.* therefore *adv.* therefrom *adv.* therein *adv.*

ther-mal (ther'mal) *adj.* Having to do with or producing heat.

ther-mom-e-ter (thèr mom'i tèr) *n.* A glass tube containing mercury which rises and falls with temperature changes. thermometric *adj.*

ther-mo-plas-tic (ther'mo plas'tik) *adj.* Pliable and soft when heated or warm but hard when cooled. thermoplastic *n.*

ther-mo-stat (ther'mo stat') *n.* A device that automatically responds to temperature changes and activates equipment such as air conditioners and furnaces to adjust the temperature to correspond with the setting on the device. thermostatic *adj.*

the-sau-rus (thi so'us) *n. pl.* -ruses *or* -ri A book which contains synonyms.

these *pron.* The plural of this.

the-sis (thē'sis) *n. pl.* -ses A formal argument or idea; a paper written by a student that develops an idea or point of view.

they (thā) *pron.* The two or more beings just mentioned.

they'd (thād) *contr.* They had.

they'll (thāl) *contr.* They will.

they're (thār) *contr.* They are.

they've (thāv) *contr.* They have.

thick (thik) *adj.* Having a heavy or dense consistency; having a considerable extent or depth from one surface to its opposite.

Slang Excessive. thickly *adv.* thickness *n.* thicken *v.*

thief (thēf) *n. pl.* thieves A person who steals.

thieve (thēv) *v.* To take by theft.

thigh (thī) *n.* The part of the leg between the hip and the knee of man.

thim-ble (thim'bl) *n.* A small cap-like protection for the finger, worn while sewing. thimbleful *n.*

thin (thin) *adj.* Having very little depth or extent from one side or surface to the other; not fat; slender. *v.* To make or become thin. thinly *adv.* thinness *n.*

thing (thing) *n.* Something not recognized or named; an idea, conception, or utterance; a material or real object.

things *n.* One's belongings.

think (thingk) *v.* To exercise thought; to use the mind; to reason and work out in the mind; to visualize. thinkable *adj.* thinker *n.*

third (therd) *n.* Next to the second in time or place; the last in a series of three. *Mech.* The 3rd forward gear in an automo-bile, truck, tractor, or other vehicle.

thirst (therst) *n.* An uncomfortably dry feeling in the throat and mouth accompanied by an urgent desire for liquids. thirsty *adj.*

thir-teen (ther'tēn) *n.* The cardinal number equal to $12 + 1$.

this (this) *pron. pl.* these The person or thing that is near, present, or just mentioned; the one under discussion.

this-tle (this'l) *n.* A prickly plant usually producing a purplish or yellowish flower.

thith-er (thith'èr) *adv.* To that place; there; on the farthest side.

thong (thong) *n.* A narrow strip of leather used for binding.

tho-rax (thōr'aks) *n. pl.* -raxes *or* -races The section or part of the human body between the neck and abdomen, supported by the ribs and breastbone. thoracic *adj.*

tho-ri-um (thōr'ē um) *n.* A radioactive metallic element symbolized by Th.

thorn (thorn) *n.* A sharp, pointed, woody

projection on a plant stem. **thorniness** *n.* **thorny** *adj.*

thor-ough (ther'ō) *adj.* Complete; intensive; accurate; very careful; absolute. **thoroughness** *n.* **thoroughly** *adv.*

thor-ough-bred (ther'ō bred') *adj.* Being of a pure breed of stock.

thor-ough-fare (ther'ō fâr') *n.* A public highway, road or street.

those *adj. & pron.* The plural of that.

though (thō) *adv.* Nevertheless; in spite of.

thought (thot) *n.* The process, act, or power of thinking; a possibility; an idea. **thoughtful** *adj.* **thoughtless** *adj.*

thou-sand (thou'zand) *n.* The cardinal number equal to 10 X 100.

thrash (thrash) *v.* To beat or strike with a whip; to move violently about; to defeat. **thrasher** *n.*

thread (thred) *n.* A thin cord of cotton or other fiber; the ridge going around a bolt, nut or screw. *v.* To pass a thread through, as to thread a needle. **thready** *adj.*

thread-bare (thred'bâr') *adj.* Shabby.

threads *n. pl., Slang* Clothes.

threat (thret) *n.* An expression or warning of intent to do harm; anything holding a possible source of danger. **threaten** *v.* **threatener** *n.* **threateningly** *adv.*

three (thrē) *n.* The cardinal number equal to 2 + 1.

three-D *or* **3-D** (thrē'dē') *n.* A three-dimensional form.

thresh (thresh) *v.* To separate seed from a harvested plant mechanically; to strike severely.

thresh-old (thresh'ōld) *n.* A horizontal piece of wood or other material which forms a doorsill; a beginning point.

threw *v.* Past tense of throw.

thrice (thrīs) *adv.* Three times.

thrift (thrift) *n.* The careful use of money and other resources. **thriftily** *adv.* **thriftiness** *n.* **thrifty** *adj.*

thrill (thril) *n.* A feeling of sudden intense excitement, fear, or joy. **thrilling** *adj.* **thrillingly** *adv.*

thrive (thrīv) *v.* To prosper; to be healthy;

to do well in a position.

throat (thrōt) *n.* The front section or part of the neck containing passages for food and air.

throb (throb) *v.* To beat, move, or vibrate in a pulsating way; to pulsate. **throb** *n.*

throm-bo-sis (throm bō'sis) *n. pl.* **-ses** The development of a blood clot in a blood vessel or in the heart cavity.

throng (throng) *n.* A large group or crowd. *v.* To crowd around or into.

throt-tle (throt'l) *n.* The valve which controls the flow of fuel to an engine. *v.* To control the speed or fuel with a throttle.

through (thrö) *prep.* From the beginning to the end; in one side and out the opposite side. *Slang* Completed; finished.

through-out (thrö out') *prep., adv.* In every place; everywhere; at all times.

throw (thrō) *v.* To toss or fling through the air with a motion of the arm; to hurl with force. *Slang* To entertain, as to throw a party. **throw up** To vomit. **throw out** To discard something.

thru (thrö) *prep., adv., & adj.* Through.

thrush (thrush) *n.* A small songbird having a brownish upper body and spotted breast.

thrust (thrust) *v.* To push; to shove with sudden or vigorous force. *n.* A sudden stab or push.

thru-way *or* **throughway** (thrö'wā') *n.* A major highway; an expressway.

thud (thud) *n.* A heavy, dull thumping sound.

thug (thug) *n.* A tough or violent gangster. **thuggish** *adj.*

thumb (thum) *n.* The short first digit of the hand; the part of the glove that fits over the thumb. *v.* To browse through something quickly. *Slang* To hitchhike.

thump (thump) *n.* A blow with something blunt or heavy. **thump** *v.*

thun-der (thun'der) *n.* The loud explosive sound made as air is suddenly expanded by heat and then quickly contracted again.

thun-der-bolt (thun'der klap') *n.* A flash of lightning immediately followed by thunder.

thun-der-cloud (thun´dėr kloud´) *n*. A dark cloud carrying an electric charge and producing lightning and thunder.

thun-der-show-er (thun´dėr shou´ėr) *n*. A brief rainstorm with thunder and lightning.

thus (thus) *adv*. In this or that way; therefore.

thwack (thwak) *v*. To strike hard, using something flat.

thwart (thwort) *v*. To prevent from happening; to prevent from doing something. *n*. A seat positioned crosswise in a boat.

thy (thī) *adj*. Pertaining to oneself; your.

thyme (tīm) *n*. An aromatic mint herb whose leaves are used in cooking.

thy-roid (thī´roid) *adj., Anat*. Pertaining to the thyroid gland. *n*. The gland in the neck of man that produces hormones which regulate food use and body growth.

thy-rox-ine (thī rok´sēn) *n*. A hormone secreted by the thyroid gland.

ti-ar-a (tē ar´a) *n*. A bejeweled crown in the form of a half circle and worn by women at formal occasions.

tick (tik) *n*. One of a series of rhythmical tapping sounds made by a clock; a small bloodsucking parasite, many of which are carriers of disease.

tick-et (tik´it) *n*. A printed slip of paper or cardboard allowing its holder to enter a specified event or to enjoy a privilege; a list of candidates who represent a political party.

tick-le (tik´l) *v*. To stroke lightly so as to cause laughter; to amuse or delight. **tickle** *n*. **tickler** *n*.

tidal wave *n*. An enormous rise of destructive ocean water caused by a storm or earthquake.

tid-bit (tid´bit´) *n*. A choice bit of food, news, or gossip.

tide (tīd) *n*. The rise and fall of the surface level of the ocean which occurs twice a day due to the gravitational pull of the sun and moon on the earth.

tid-ings (tī´dingz) *n. pl*. News; information about events.

ti-dy (tī´dē) *adj*. Well arranged; neat; orderly. *v*. To make orderly and neat. **tidily** *adv*. **tidiness** *n*.

tie (tī) *v*. To secure or bind with a rope, line, cord or other similar material; to make secure or fasten with a rope; to make a bow or knot in; to match an opponent's score. *n*. A string, rope, cord or other material used to join parts or hold something in place; a necktie; a beam that gives structural support. **tie** A device, as timber, laid crosswise to support train tracks.

tier (tēr) *n*. A layer or row placed one above the other. **tiered** *adj*.

ti-ger (tī´gėr) *n*. A large carnivorous cat having tawny fur with black stripes.

tiger-eye (tī´gėr ī´) *n*. A yellow-brown gemstone.

tight (tīt) *adj*. Set closely together; bound or securely firm; not loose; taut; difficult. *adv*. Firmly. *Slang* Intoxicated.

tight-en (tīt´en) *v*. To become or make tighter. **tightener** *n*.

tight-rope (tīt´rōp´) *n*. A tightly stretched horizontal rope high above the ground for the use of acrobats.

tights (tīts) *n. pl*. A skintight stretchable garment, covering the lower half of the body.

TIL *abbr., Med*. Tumor-infiltrating lymphocytes.

tile (tīl) *n*. A thin, hard, flat piece of plastic, asphalt, baked clay, or stone used to cover walls, floors, and roofs. *v*. To cover with tile.

till (til) Until; unless or before. *v*. To cultivate; to plow. *n*. A small cash register or drawer for holding money.

till-er (til´ėr) *n*. A machine or person that tills land.

tilt (tilt) *v*. To tip, as by raising one end. *n*. The state of tilting or being tilted.

tim-ber (tim´bėr) *n*. Wood prepared for building; a finished piece of wood or plank.

timber line *n*. The height on a mountain beyond which trees cannot grow.

time (tīm) *n*. A continuous period measured by clocks, watches, and calendars; the period or moment in which something happens or takes place. *adj*. Of or pertaining to time; pertaining to paying in, installments. *Slang* A period of imprisonment.

time–shar-ing *n*. The joint ownership of property with each individual sharing the use of the property.

time tri-al *n*. A race or competition where each participant is timed individually over a set distance.

tim-id (tim´id) *adj*. Lacking selfconfidence; shy.

tin (tin) *n*. A white, soft, malleable metallic element, symbolized by Sn; a container made of tin. *adj*. Made of tin.

tinc-ture (tingk´chẻr) *n*. A tinge of color; an alcohol solution of some medicial substance. *v*. To tint.

tin-der (tin´dẻr) *n*. A readily combustible substance or material used for kindling.

tin-der-box (tin´dẻr boks´) *n*. A portable metal box for holding tinder; a building which is a fire hazard; a situation which is about to explode with violence.

tine (tīn) *n*. A narrow pointed spike or prong, as of a fork or antler.

tinge (tinj) *v*. To impart a faint trace of color; to tint. *n*. As light trace of added color.

tin-gle (ting´gl) *v*. To feel a stinging or prickling sensation. **tingle** *n*. **tingly** *adj*.

tink-er (ting´kẻr) *n*. A person who mends domestic household utensils; one who does repair work of any kind. *v*. To work as a tinker; to attempt to fix, mend, or repair something in a bumbling, unprofessional manner.

tin-kle (ting´kl) *v*. To produce a slight, sharp series of metallic ringing sounds. **tinkle** *n*.

tin-ny (tin´ē) *adj*. Pertaining to or composed of tin.

tin-sel (tin´sẻl) *n*. Thin strips of glittering material used for decorations. **tinsel** *adj*.

tint (tint) *n*. A slight amount or trace of color.

v. To color.

ti-ny (tī´nē) *adj*. Minute; very small.

tip (tip) *v*. To slant from the horizontal or vertical. *n*. Extra money given as an acknowledgment of a service; a gratuity; a helpful hint.

tip-ple (tip´l) *v*. To drink an alcoholic beverage to excess.

tip-sy (tip´sē) *adj*. Partially intoxicated. **tipsiness** *n*.

ti-rade (tī´rād) *n*. A long, violent speech or outpouring, as of censure.

tire (tīẻr) *v*. To become or make weary; to be fatigued; to become bored. *n*. The outer covering for a wheel, usually made of rubber, serving to absorb shock and to provide traction.

tire-less *adj*. Untiring. **tirelessly** *adv*.

tis-sue (tish´ŏ) *n*., *Biol*. Similar cells and their products developed by plants and animals; a soft, absorbent piece of paper, consisting of two layers.

tissue paper *n*. Thin, almost transparent paper used for wrapping or protecting delicate articles.

ti-ta-ni-um (tī tā´nē um) *n*. A metallic element symbolized by Ti.

tithe (tīth) *n*. A tenth of one's income given voluntarily for the support of a church. **tithe** *v*. **tither** *n*.

tit-il-late (tit´i lāt´) *v*. To excite or stimulate in a pleasurable way. **titillating** *adj*. **titillative** *adj*. **titillatingly** *adv*. **titillation** *n*.

ti-tle (tīt´l) *n*. An identifying name of a book, poem, play, or other creative work; a name or mark of distinction indicating a rank or an office; in law, the evidence giving legal right of possession or control of something; in sports, a championship. *v*. To give a title or name to.

to (tŏ) *prep*. Toward, opposite or near; in contact with; as far as; used as a function word indicating an action, movement, or condition suggestive of movement; indicating correspondence, dissimilarity, similarity, or proportion; indicating the one for which something is done or exists. *adv*. In the state, direction, or condition.

toad (tōd) *n.* A tailless amphibian, resembling the frog but without teeth in the upper jaw and having a rougher, drier skin.

toad-stool (tōd´stōl´) *n.* A poisonous mushroom or inedible fungus, shaped like an umbrella.

toast (tōst) *v.* To heat and brown over a fire or in a toaster. *n.* Sliced bread browned in a toaster. **toasty** *adj.*

toaster (tō´stėr) *n.* A device for toasting bread.

to-bac-co (to bak´ō) *n.* A tropical American plant widely cultivated for its leaves, which are prepared in various ways, as for chewing or smoking.

to-bog-gan (to bog´an) *n.* A long sled-like vehicle without runners, having long thin boards curved upwards at the forward end. **tobogganist** *n.* **toboggan** *v.*

to-day (to dā´) *adv.* On or during the present day. *n.* The present time, period, or day.

tod-dle (tod´l) *v.* To walk unsteadily with short steps.

toddler *n.* A small child learning to walk.

tod-dy (tod´ē) *n. pl.* **-ies** A drink made with hot water, sugar, spices, and liquor.

toe (tō) *n.* One of the extensions from the front part of a foot; the part of a stocking, boot or shoe that covers the toes. *v.* To kick, reach, or touch with the toe or toes.

tof-fee (to´fē) *n.* A chewy candy made of butter and brown sugar.

to-geth-er (te geth´ėr) *adv.* In or into one group, mass, or body; regarded jointly; in time with what is happening or going on. **togetherness** *n.*

toil (toil) *v.* To labor very hard and continuously. *n.* A difficult task. **toilsome** *adj.*

toi-let (toi´lit) *n.* A porcelain apparatus with a flushing device, used as a means of disposing body wastes.

toi-lette (toi let´) *n.* The act of washing, dressing, or grooming oneself.

toi let water *n.* A liquid with a scent stronger than cologne and weaker than perfume.

to-ken (tōk´en) *n.* A keepsake; a symbol of authority or identity; a piece of imprinted metal used in place of money. *adj.* Done

as a pledge or indication.

tol-er-ate (tol´e rāt´) *v.* To put up with; to recognize and respect the opinions and rights of others; to endure; to suffer. **toleration** *n.* **tolerance** *adj.* **tolerant** *adj.*

toll (tōl) *n.* A fixed charge for travel across a bridge or along a road. *v.* To sound a bell in repeated single, slow tones.

tom (tom) *n.* A male turkey or cat.

tom-a-hawk (tom´a hok´) *n.* An ax used as a weapon or tool by North American Indians.

to-ma-to (to mā´tō) *n. pl.* **-toes** A garden plant cultivated for its edible fruit; the fruit of such a plant.

tomb (tōm) *n.* A vault for burying the dead; a grave.

tom-boy (tom´boi´) *n.* A girl whose behavior is characteristic of a boy. **tomboyish** *adj.*

tomb-stone (tōm´stōn´) *n.* A stone used to mark a grave.

tom-cat (tom´kat´) *n.* A male cat.

to-mor-row (to mor´ō) *n.* The day after the present day. *adv.* On the day following today.

ton (tun) *n.* A measurement of weight equal to 2,000 pounds. *Slang* A large amount.

tone (tōn) *n.* A vocal or musical sound that has a distinct pitch, loudness, quality, and duration; the condition of the body and muscles when at rest. *v.* To change or soften the color.

tongs (tongz) *n. pl.* An implement with two long arms joined at one end, used for picking up or lifting.

tongue (tung) *n.* The muscular organ attached to the floor of the mouth, used in tasting, chewing, and speaking; anything shaped like a tongue, as the material under the laces or buckles of a shoe.

ton-ic (ton´ik) *n.* A medicine or other agent used to restore health; in music, the first note of a scale. *Slang* Flavored carbonated soda.

to-night (to nīt´) *n.* This night; the night of this day; the night that is coming. *adv.* On or during the present or coming night.

ton-sil (ton´sil) *n.* One of a pair of tissue similar to lymph nodes, found on either side of the throat.

ton-sil-lec-to-my (ton´si lek´to mē) *n.* The surgical removal of tonsils.

too (tō) *adv.* Also; as well; more than is needed.

tool (tōl) *n.* An implement used to perform a task; anything needed to do one's work. *v.* To make or shape with a tool.

tooth (tōth) *n. pl.* **teeth** One of the hard, white structures rooted in the jaw and used for chewing and biting; the small, notched, projecting part of any object, such as a gear, comb or saw. **toothless** *adj.*

top (top) *n.* The highest part or surface of anything; a covering or lid; the above-ground part of a rooted plant; the highest degree; a toy having a symmetric body with a tapered end upon which it spins.

to-paz (tō´paz) *n.* A gemstone, usually yellow in color.

top-coat (top´kōt´) *n.* An outer coat.

top-ic *n.* The subject discussed in an essay, thesis, speech or other discourse; the theme.

to-pog-ra-phy (to pog´ra fē) *n. pl.* **-ies** A detailed description of a region or place; a physical outline showing the features of a region or place.

top-ple (top´l) *v.* To fall; to overturn.

top-sy–tur-vy (top´sē ter´vē) *adv.* With the top side down; upside down. *adj.* In a confused state. *n.* Confusion.

To-rah (tōr´a) *n.* The body of law and wisdom contained in Jewish Scripture and oral tradition; a parchment scroll that contains the first five books of the Old Testament.

torch (torch) *n.* A stick of resinous wood which is burned to give light; any portable device which produces hot flame. *Slang* To set fire to.

tor-ment (tor´ment) *n.* Extreme mental anguish or physical pain; a source of trouble or pain. *v.* To cause terrible pain; to pester, harass, or annoy. **tormentingly** *adv.* **tormentor** *n.*

tor-na-do (tor nā´dō) *n. pl.* **-does** *or* **-dos** A whirling, violent windstorm accompanied by a funnel-shaped cloud that travels a narrow path over land; a whirlwind.

tor-pe-do (tor pē´dō) *n. pl.* **-oes** A large, self–propelled, underwater missile launched from a ship, containing an explosive charge.

tor-pid (tor´pid) *adj.* Having lost the power of motion or feeling; dormant. **torpidity** *n.* **torpidly** *adv.*

tor-rent (tor´ent) *n.* A swift, violent stream; a raging flood. **torrential** *adj.*

tor-rid (tor´id) *adj.* Parched and dried by the heat. **torridly** *adv.*

tor-sion (tor´shan) *n.* The act or result of twisting; the stress produced when one end is held fast and the other turned.

tor-so (tor´sō) *n. pl.* **-sos** *or* **-si** The trunk of the human body.

tort (tort) *n., Law* A wrongful act requiring compensation for damages.

tor-toise (tor´tos) *n.* A turtle that lives on the land; a person or thing regarded as slow.

tor-tu-ous (tor´chŏ us) *adj.* Marked by repeated bends, turns, or twists; devious. **tortuousness** *n.*

tor-ture (tor´chèr) *n.* The infliction of intense pain as punishment; something causing anguish or pain. *v.* To subject or cause intense suffering; to wrench or twist out of shape. **torturer** *n.* **torturously** *adv.*

toss (tos) *v.* To fling or throw about continuously; to throw up in the air. *n.* A throw.

tot (tot) *n.* A young child; a toddler.

to-tal (tōt´al) *n.* The whole amount or sum; the entire quantity. *adj.* Absolute; complete. **total** *v.* **totally** *adv.*

to-tal-i-tar-i-an *adj.* Characteristic of a government controlled completely by one party; exercising complete political control. **totalitarian** *n.*

tote (tōt) *v.* To carry something on one's arm or back. *n.* A load.

to-tem (tō´tem) *n.* An animal or plant

regarded as having a close relationship to some family clan or group; a representation or symbol.

tot-ter (tot´ẽr) *v.* To walk unsteadily; to shake or sway as if about to fall.

tou-can (tõ´kan) *n.*
A brightly colored tropical bird having a very large thin bill.

touch (tuch) *v.* To allow a part of the body, as the hands, to feel or come into contact with; to hit or tap lightly; to eat or drink; to join; to come next to; to have an effect on; to move emotionally. *n.* An instance or act of touching; the feeling, fact, or act of touching or being touched; a trace; a tiny amount; a method, manner, or style of striking the keys of an instrument with a keyboard. **touchable** *adj.*

tough (tuf) *adj.* Resilient and strong enough to withstand great strain without breaking or tearing; strong; hardy; very difficult; difficult to cut or chew. *n.* An unruly person; a thug. **toughly** *adv.* **toughness** *n.*

tou-pee (tõ pā) *n.* A small wig piece worn to cover a bald spot on one's head.

tour (ter) *n.* A trip with visits to points of interest; a journey; a period or length of service at a single place or job. **tourism** *n.* **tourist** *n.*

tour-na-ment (ter´na ment) *n.* A contest involving a number of competitors for a title or championship.

tour-ni-quet (ter´ni kit) *n.* A device used to temporarily stop the flow of blood through an artery.

tou-sle (tou´zl) *v.* To mess up; to disarrange.

tout (tout) *v.* To solicit customers. *Slang* In horse racing, a person who obtains information on racehorses and sells it to bettors. **touter** *n.*

tow (tõ) *v.* To drag or pull, as by a chain or rope. *n.* An act of being pulled; a rope or line for pulling or dragging; coarse broken flax, hemp, or jute fiber prepared for spinning.

to-ward *or* **towards (tõrd)** *prep.* In the direction of; just before; some what before; regard-ing; with respect to.

tow-el (tou´el) *n.* An absorbent piece of cloth used for drying or wiping. **towel** *v.*

tow-er (tou´ẽr) *n.* A very tall building or structure; a skyscraper; a place of security or defense. **towering** *adj.*

town (toun) *n.* A collection of houses and other buildings larger than a village and smaller than a city.

town-ship (toun´ship) *n.* A subdivision of a county having corporate powers of municipal government.

tox-e-mi-a (tok sē´mē a) *n., Pathol.* Blood poisoning; a condition in which the blood contains toxins.

tox-ic (tok´sik) *adj.* Relating to a toxin; destructive, deadly, or harmful.

tox-in (tok´sin) *n.* A poisonous substance produced by chemical changes in plant and animal tissue.

toy (toi) *n.* An object designed for the enjoyment of children; any object having little value or importance; a small trinket; a bauble; a dog of a very small breed. *v.* To amuse or entertain oneself.

trace (trās) *n.* A visible mark or sign of a thing, person, or event; something left by some past agent or event. *v.* To follow the course or track of; to copy by drawing over the lines visible through a sheet of transparent paper. **traceable** *adj.* **traceably** *adv.* **tracer** *n.*

track (trak) *n.* A mark, as a footprint, left by the passage of anything; a regular course; a set of rails on which a train runs; a circular or oval course for racing. *v.* To follow the trail of footprints of. **trackable** *adj.* **tracker** *n.*

tract (trakt) *n.* An extended area, as a stretch of land. *Anat.* An extensive region of the body, one comprising body organs and tissues that together perform a specialized function.

trac-tion (trak´shan) *n.* The act of drawing, as a load over a surface; the state of being drawn or pulled; rolling friction that prevents a wheel from skidding over the surface on which it runs.

trac-tor (trak'tėr) *n.* A diesel or gasoline-powered vehicle used in farming to pull another piece of machinery.

tractor trailer *n.* A large truck having a cab and no body, used to pull large trailers.

trade (trād) *n.* A business or occupation; skilled labor; a craft; an instance of selling or buying; a swap. **trade** *v.* **tradeable** *adj.* **trader** *n.*

trade-mark (trād'märk') *n.* A brand name which is legally the possession of one company and cannot be used by another. **trademark** *v.*

trade–off *n.* A compromise of possibilities when all cannot be attained at the same time; a surrender of one consideration in order to obtain another.

tra-di-tion (tra dish'an) *n.* The doctrines, knowledge, practices, and customs passed down from one generation to another. **traditional** *adj.* **traditionally** *adv.*

tra-duce (tra dŏs') *v.* To betray. **traducement** *n.* **traducer** *n.*

traf-fic (traf'ik) *n.* The passage or movement of vehicles; trade, buying and selling; the signals handled by a communications system. **trafficker** *n.*

trag-e-dy (traj'i dē) *n. pl.* **-ies** An extremely sad or fatal event or course of events; a story, play, or other literary work which arouses terror or pity by a series of misfortunes or sad events.

trail (trāl) *v.* To draw, drag, or stream along behind; to follow in the tracks of; to follow slowly behind or in the rear; to let hang so as to touch the ground. *n.* Something that hangs or follows along behind; a rough path through a wooded area.

trail-er (trā'lėr) *n.* One who trails; a large vehicle that transports objects and is pulled by another vehicle.

train (trān) *n.* The part of a long gown that trails behind the wearer; a long moving line of vehicles or persons; a group of railroad cars. *v.* To instruct so as to make skillful or capable of doing something; to aim; to

direct. **trainable** *adj.* **trainer** *n.* **training** *n.* **trainee** *n.*

trait (trāt) *n.* A quality or distinguishing feature, such as one's character.

trai-tor (trā'tėr) *n.* A person who betrays his country, a cause, or another's confidence.

tra-jec-to-ry (tra jek'to rē) *n. pl.* **-ies** The curved line or path of a moving object.

tram-mel (tram'el) *n.* A long, large net used to catch birds or fish; something that impedes movement. **trammeler** *n.*

tramp (tramp) *v.* To plod or walk with a heavy step. *n.* A homeless person or vagrant who travels about aimlessly.

tram-ple (tram'pl) *v.* To tread heavily; to stomp; to inflict injury, pain, or loss by heartless or brutal treatment. **trample** *n.* **trampler** *n.*

tram-po-line (tram'po lēn') *n.* A canvas device on which an athlete or acrobat may perform. **trampolinist** *n.*

trance (trans) *n.* A stupor, daze, mental state, or condition, such as produced by drugs or hypnosis.

tran-quil (trang'kwil) *adj.* Very calm, quiet, and free from disturbance. **tranquilly** *n.* **tranquillity** *n.* **tranquilize** *v.*

trans-act (tran sakt') *v.* To perform, carry out, conduct, or manage business in some way. **transaction** *n.* **transactor** *n.*

tran-scend (tran send') *v.* To pass beyond; to exceed; to surpass. **transcendent, transcendence** *n.*

tran-scribe (tran skrīb') *v.* To make copies of something; to adopt or arrange.

tran-script (tran'skript) *n.* A written copy.

trans-crip-tion (tran skrip'shan) *n.* The process or act of transcribing.

trans-fer (trans fer') *v.* To remove, shift, or carry from one position to another. **transferable** *adj.* **transference** *n.*

trans-fig-ure (trans fig'yėr) *v.* To change the outward appearance or form; to exalt; to glorify. **transfiguration** *n.*

trans-fix (trans fiks') *v.* To pierce; to hold motionless, as with terror, awe or amazement. **transfixion** *n.*

trans-form (trans form´) v. To change or alter completely in nature, form or function. **transformable** adj. **transformation** n. **transformer** n.

trans-fuse (trans fūz´) v. To transfer liquid by pouring from one place to another. *Med.* To pass blood from the blood vessels of one person into the vessels of another. **transfusion** n. **transfuser** n.

trans-gress (trans gres´) v. To go beyond the limit or boundaries; to sin against or violate. **transgression** n. **transgressor** n. **transgressive** adj.

tran-sient (tran´shent) adj. Not staying or lasting very long; moving from one location to another. **transient** n.

tran-sit (tran´sit) n. Passage or travel from one point to another; an instrument for surveying that measures horizontal and vertical angles.

trans-late (trans lāt´) v. To change from one language to another while retaining the original meaning; to explain. **translation** n. **translator** n.

trans-lu-cent (trans lö´sent) adj. Diffusing and admitting light but not allowing a clear view of the object.

trans-mis-sion (trans mish´an) n. The act or state of transmitting. *Mech.* The gears and associated parts of an engine which transmit power to the driving wheels of an automobile or other vehicle.

trans-mit (trans mit´) v. To dispatch or convey from one thing, person, or place to another. **transmissible** adj. **transmittable** adj. **transmitter** n.

trans-mute (trans mūt´) v. To change in nature, kind, or substance.

tran-som (tran´som) n. A small, hinged window over a doorway; the horizontal crossbar in a window.

trans-par-ent (trans pâr´en sē) adj. Admitting light so that images and objects can be clearly viewed; easy to understand; obvious. **transparency** n. **transparently** adv.

tran-spire (tran spīèr´) v. To give off waste products through plant or animal pores in the form of vapor; to happen; to take place.

transpiration n.

trans-plant (trans plant´) v. To remove a living plant from where it is growing and plant it in another place; to remove a body organ from one person and implant it in the body of another, as a kidney transplant; to remove skin from one area of the body and move it to another area of the body, as a skin graft. **transplant** n. **transplantable** adj.

trans-port (trans pōrt´) v. To carry or move from one place to another. n. A vessel or ship used to carry military supplies and troops; the process or act of transporting. **transportable** adj. **transportation** n.

trans-pose (trans pōz´) v. To reverse the place or order of. *Mus.* To perform or write music in a key different from the one it was originally written in.

trans-sex-u-al n. A person whose sex has been changed surgically.

trap (trap) n. A device for holding or catching animals; v. To catch in a trap; to place in an embarrassing position. *Slang* The mouth.

tra-peze (tra pēz´) n. A short horizontal bar suspended by two ropes, used for acrobatic exercise or stunts.

trau-ma (trou´ma) n. pl. **-mas** or **-mata** A severe wound caused by a sudden physical injury; an emotional shock causing lasting and substantial damage to a person's psychological development.

tra-vail (tra vāl´) n. Strenuous mental or physical exertion; labor in childbirth. v. To undergo the sudden sharp pain of childbirth.

trav-el (trav´el) v. To journey or move from one place to another. n. The process or act of traveling. **traveler** n.

tra-verse (trav´èrs) v. To pass over, across, or through. n. A path or route across; something that lies across something else. **traversable** adj. **traversal** n.

trawl (trol) n. A strong fishing net which is dragged through water.

tray (trā) n. A flat container having a low

rim, used for carrying, holding, or displaying something.

treach-er-ous (threch´ėr us) *adj.* Disloyal; deceptive; unreliable. **treacherously** *adv.* **treachery** *n.*

tread (tred) *v.* To walk along, on, or over; to trample. *n.* The act or manner of treading; the part of a wheel which comes into contact with the ground.

trea-son (trē´zon) *n.* Violation of one's allegiance to a sovereign or country, as giving or selling state secrets to another country or attempting to overthrow the government. **treasonable** *adj.* **treasonous** *adj.*

treas-ure (trezh´ėr) *n.* Hidden riches; something regarded as valuable. *v.* To save and accumulate for future use; to value.

treasurer (trezh´ėr ėr) *n.* A person having charge and responsibilities for funds.

treas-ur-y (trezh´a rē) *n. pl.* **-ies** A place where public or private funds are kept. **Treasury** The executive department of the United States Government in charge of collection, management, and expenditure of public revenue.

treat (trēt) *v.* To behave or act toward; to regard in a given manner; to provide entertainment or food for another at one's own expense or cost. *n.* A pleasant surprise; something enjoyable which was unexpected. **treatable** *adj.* **treater** *n.*

treat-ment (trēt´mėnt) *n.* The manner or act of treating; medical care.

treb-le (treb´l) *adj.* Multiplied by three; having three. *Mus.* Performing or having the highest range, part, or voice. *n.* A high-pitched sound or voice. **treble** *v.*

tree (trē) *n.* A tall woody plant, usually having a single trunk of considerable height; a diagram resembling a tree, as one used to show family descent. *Slang* To get the advantage of something. **tree** *v.* **treeless** *adj.*

tre-foil (trē´foil) *n.* Any of various plants having three leaflets with red, purple, yellow, or pink flowers.

trek (trek) *v.* To make a slow and arduous journey. **trek** *n.* **trekker** *n.*

trel-lis (trel´is) *n.* A lattice work frame used for supporting vines and other climbing plants.

trem-ble (trem´bl) *v.* To shake involuntarily, as with fear or from cold; to express or feel anxiety. **tremble** *n.* **trembler** *n.* **trembly** *adj.*

tre-men-dous (trimen´dus) *adj.* Extremely huge, large, or vast. *Slang* Wonderful.

trem-or (trem´ėr) *n.* A quick, shaking movement; any continued and involuntary trembling or quavering of the body.

trench (trench) *n.* A ditch; a long, narrow excavation in the ground. *v.* To cut deep furrows for protection. **trencher** *n.*

trend (trend) *n.* A general inclination, direction, or course; a fad. *v.* To have or take a specified direction. **trendsetter** *n.*

tres-pass (tres´pas) *v.* To infringe upon another's property; in law, to invade the rights, property, or privacy of another without consent or knowledge.

tri-al (trī´al) *n.* In law, the examination and hearing of a case before a court of law in order to determine the case; an attempt or effort; an experimental treatment or action to determine a result. *adj.* Pertaining to or of a trial; performed or used during an experiment or test.

tri-an-gle (trī´ang´gl) *n., Geom.* A plane figure bounded by three sides and having three angles. **triangular** *adj.* **triangularity** *n.*

tribe (trīb) *n.* A group of people composed of several villages, districts, or other groups which share a common language, culture, and name.

trib-u-la-tion (trib´ū lā´shan) *n.* Great distress or suffering caused by oppression.

trib-ute (trib´ūt) *n.* An action of respect or gratitude to someone; money or other goods given by one country to another showing obedience and insuring against invasion.

tri-ceps (trī´seps) *n., Anat.* The large muscle at the back of the upper arm.

trick (trik) *n*. An action meant to fool, as a scheme; a prank; a feat of magic. *v*. To deceive or cheat. **tricky** *adj*.

trick-er-y (trik´e rē) *n*. Deception.

trick-le (trik´l) *v*. To flow in droplets or a small stream. **trickle** *n*.

tri-cy-cle (trī´si kl) *n*. A small vehicle having three wheels, propelled by pedals.

tri-dent (trīd´ent) *n*. A long spear with three prongs, used as a weapon.

tried (trīd) *adj*. Tested and proven reliable or useful.

tri-en-ni-al (trī en´ē al) *adj*. Happening every third year; lasting for a time period of three years. **triennial** *n*. **triennially** *adv*.

tri-fle (trī´fl) *n*. Something of little value or importance; a dessert made with cake, jelly, wine, and custard. *v*. To use or treat without proper concern.

trig-ger (trig´er) *n*. A lever pulled to fire a gun; a device used to release or start an action. *v*. To start.

trill *n*. A tremulous utterance of successive tones. *v*. To utter with a fluttering sound.

tril-lion (tril´yon) *n*. The cardinal number equal to one thousand billion.

trim (trim) *v*. To clip or cut off small a-mounts in order to make neater; to decorate. *adj*. Neat. **trim** *n*.

tri-ni-tro-tol-u-ene (trī nī´trōtol´ū ēn´) *n*. A very powerful explosive, abbreviated as TNT.

trin-ket (tring´kit) *n*. A small piece of jewelry.

tri-o (trē´ō) *n*. A set or group of three.

trip (trip) *n*. Travel from one place to another; a journey; a loss of balance. *v*. To stumble. *Slang* A hallucinatory effect induced by drugs.

tripe (trīp) *n*. The stomach lining of oxen or similar animals, used as food. *Slang* Nonsense.

trip-le (trip´l) *adj*. Having three parts. *v*. To multiply by three; in baseball, a three-base hit.

trip-let (trip´lit) *n*. One of three born at the same time.

trip-li-cate (trip´li kāt´) *n*. A group of three identical things. **triplicate** *v*.

tri-pod (trī´pod) *n*. A three–legged stand or frame.

trite (trīt) *adj*. Used too often; common.

tri-umph (trī´umf) *v*. To be victorious. *n*. A victory. **triumphant** *adj*.

triv-i-al (triv´ē al) *adj*. Insignificant; of little value or importance; ordinary.

trol-ley (trol´ē) *n*. A streetcar powered by electricity from overhead lines; a small container or basket used to convey material, as in an underground tunnel or mine.

trom-bone (trom bōn´) *n*. A brass musical instrument, larger and lower in pitch than a trumpet.

troop (trōp) *n*. A group or assembly of people or animals; a group of Boy Scouts or Girl Scouts having an adult leader; a military unit. **trooper** *n*.

tro-phy (trō´fē) *n. pl.* **-ies** A prize or object, such as a plaque, awarded to someone for his success, victory, or achievement.

trop-ic (trop´ik) *n*. Either of two imaginary parallel lines which constitute the Torrid Zone. **Tropics** The very warm region of the earth's surface between the Tropic of Cancer and the Tropic of Capricorn. **tropical** *adj*.

tro-po-sphere (trop´o sfēr´) *n*. The lowest atmosphere between the earth's surface and the stratosphere.

trot (trot) *n*. The gait of a horse or other four-footed animal, between a walk and a run, in which the hind leg and opposite front leg move at about the same time.

troth (troth) *n*. Good faith; the act of pledging one's fidelity. **troth** *v*.

trou-ble (trub´l) *n*. Danger; affliction; need; distress; an effort; physical pain, disease or malfunction. *v*. To bother; to worry; to be bothered; to be worried. **troubler** *n*. **troublingly** *adv*.

trough (trof) *n*. A long, narrow, shallow container, especially one that holds food or water for animals.

troupe (trōp) *n.* A group, especially of the performing arts. **troupe** *v.*

trou-sers (trou´zėrz) *n. pl.* An outer garment that covers the body from the waist down.

trout (trout) *n.* A freshwater game or food fish.

trowel (trou´el) *n.* A flat-bladed garden tool with a pointed blade, used for digging. **trowel** *v.* **troweler** *n.*

tru-ant (trō´ant) *n.* A person who is absent from school without permission.

truce (trōs) *n.* An agreement to stop fighting; a cease fire.

truck (truk) *n.* An automotive vehicle used to carry heavy loads; any of various devices with wheels designed to move heavy loads; garden vegetables for sale. **trucker** *n.*

trudge (truj) *v.* To walk heavily; to plod.

true (trō) *adj.* In accordance with reality or fact; not false; real; loyal; faithful. *adv.* Truthfully. **truly** *adv.*

trump (trump) *n.* In cards, a suit of any cards which outrank all other cards for a selected period of time.

trum-pet (trum´pit) *n., Mus.* A brass instrument having a flared bell, valves, and a mouthpiece. *v.* To proclaim something loudly.

trunk (trungk) *n.* The main part of a tree; the human body, excluding the head, arms and legs; a sturdy box for packing clothing, as for travel or storage; the long snout of an elephant. **trunks** Men's clothing worn for swimming or athletics.

truss (trus) *v.* To fasten or tie securely. *Med.* A support or device worn to keep a hernia in place.

trust (trust) *n.* Confidence or faith in a person or thing; care or charge. *Law* The confidence or arrangement by which property is managed and held for the good or benefit of another person. *v.* To have confidence or faith in; to believe; to expect; to entrust; to depend on.

truth (trōth) *n. pl.* **truths** The facts corresponding with actual events or happen-

ings; sincerity or honesty. **truthful** *adj.* **truthfully** *adv.* **truthfulness** *n.*

try (trī) *v.* To make an attempt; to make an effort; to strain; to hear or conduct a trial; to place on trial. **trying** *adj.*

tsp *abbr.* Teaspoon.

tub (tub) *n.* A round, low, flat-bottomed, vessel with handles on the side, as one used for washing.

tu-ba (tō´ba) *n.* A large, brass wind instrument having a low range.

tube (tōb) *n.* A hollow cylinder, made of metal, rubber, glass or other material, used to pass or convey something through. **tube** *adj.* **tubal** *adj.*

tu-ber (tō´bėr) *n.* The underground stem of certain plants, as the potato, with buds from which new plants arise.

tu-ber-cu-lo-sis *n.* A contagious lung disease of humans and animals caused by micro-organisms; abbreviated as TB.

tuck (tuk) *n.* A flattened fold of material, usually stitched in place. *v.* To sew or make a tuck in material; to put in a safe place; to make secure.

tuft (tuft) *n.* A small cluster of feathers, threads, hair, or other material fastened or growing closely together.

tug (tug) *v.* To strain and pull vigorously. *n.* A hard pull; a strong force.

tu-i-tion (tō ish´an) *n.* Payment for instruction, as at a private school or college.

tu-lip (tō´lip) *n.* A bulb-bearing plant, having upright cup-like blossoms.

tum-ble (tum´bl) *v.* To fall or cause to fall; to perform acrobatic rolls, somersaults, and similar maneuvers; to mix up; to turn over and over. **tumbler** *n.* **tumble** *n.*

tum-ble-down (tum´bl doun´) *adj.* Ramshackle; in need of repair.

tu-mor (tō´mėr) *n., Pathol.* A swelling on or in any part of the body; an abnormal growth which may be malignant or benign.

tu-mult (tō´mult) *n.* The confusion and noise of a crowd; a riot; any violent commotion. **tumultuous** *adj.*

tu-na (tō´na) *n. pl.* **-na** *or* **-nas** Any of several large marine food fish.

tune (tŏn) *n.* A melody which is simple and easy to remember; agreement; harmony. *v.* To adjust. **tunable** *adj.* **tunably** *adv.*

tu-nic (tō´nik) *n.* A loose garment extending to the knees, worn by ancient Romans and Greeks.

tun-nel (tun´el) *n.* An underground or underwater passageway. **tunnel** *v.*

tur-ban (ter´ban) *n.* A Moslem headdress that consists of a long scarf wound around the head.

tur-bine (ter´bin) *n.* A motor having one or more rotary units mounted on a shaft, which are turned by the force of gas or a liquid.

tur-bu-lent (ter´bya lent) *adj.* Marked by a violent disturbance. **turbulence** *n.* **turbulently** *adv.*

tu-reen (te rēn´) *n.* A large dish, often having a cover, used to serve soup or stew.

turf (terf) *n.* A layer of earth with its dense growth of grass and matted roots. *Slang* Home territory or ground.

tur-key (ter´kē) *n.* A large game bird of North America, having a bare head and extensible tail; the meat of this bird. *Slang* A failure.

tur-moil (ter´moil) *n.* A state of confusion or commotion.

turn (tern) *v.* To move or cause to move around a center point; to revolve or rotate; to transform or change; to move so that the bottom side of something becomes the top and the top becomes the bottom.

turn-buck-le (tern´buk´l) *n.* A metal coupling, used to regulate the distance or tension between two metal rods or wires.

turn-down (tern´doun´) *n.*, *Slang* A rejection or refusal.

tur-nip (ter´nip) *n.* An edible root from the mustard family of plants.

turn-key (tern´kē´) *n.* The person in charge of the keys at a prison.

turn-off *n.* A road branching off from a main highway. *Slang* Something which causes one to lose interest.

turn on *v.*, *Slang* To cause a person to experience with intense stimulation, as by means of LSD or marijuana.

turn-over (tern´ō´vėr) *n.* The process or act of turning over; an upset; a change or reversal; the number of times merchandise is bought, sold, and restocked in a certain period of time; the number of people hired in a given period of time to replace those who have left; *n.* a piece of pastry made by putting a filling on one half of the dough and turning the other half over to enclose the filling.

tur-pen-tine (ter´pen tīn´) *n.* The thick sap of certain pine trees; a clear liquid manufactured from this sap, used to thin paint.

tur-quoise (ter´koiz) *n.* A blue-green gemstone; a light bluish-green color.

tur-ret (ter´it) *n.* A small ornamental tower on a building; a raised, usually rotating, section of a ship, tank, or plane where the gunner sits. **turreted** *adj.*

tur-tle (ter´tl) *n.* A scaly-skinned animal having a softbody covered with a hard shell into which the head, legs, and tail can be retracted.

tur-tle-neck (ter´tl nek´) *n.* A high collar that fits closely around the neck.

tusk (tusk) *n.* A long, curved tooth, as of an elephant or walrus.

tus-sle (tus´l) *n.* A hard fight or struggle with a problem or person. **tussle** *v.*

tu-tor (tō´tėr) *n.* A person who teaches another person privately. *v.* To teach, coach, or instruct privately.

tut-ti–frut-ti (tō´tē frō´tē) *n.* An ice cream flavor that contains different types of candied fruits.

tu-tu (tō´tō) *n.* A very short ballet skirt.

tux-e-do (tuk sē´dō) *n.* A semiformal dress suit worn by men.

twang (twang) *n.* A sharp, ringing sound like that of a violin or other stringed instrument. *v.* To cause or make a twang.

tweak (twēk) *v.* To pinch and twist sharply. **tweak** *n.*

tweed (twēd) *n.* A coarse woolen fabric, woven in two or more colors. **tweeds**

Clothing made of tweed.

tweez-ers (twē´zẻrz) *n. pl.* A small, pincer-like implement used to grasp or pluck small objects.

twelve (twelv) *n.* The cardinal number equal to 11 + 1.

twen-ty (twen´tē) *n.* The cardinal number equal to 19 + 1 or 2 X 10.

twice (twīs) *adv.* Double; two times.

twid-dle (twid´l) *v.* To turn or twirl in an aimless way.

twig (twig) *n.* A small branch which grows from a larger branch on a tree.

twi-light (twī´līt´) *n.* The soft light of the sky between sunset and complete darkness.

twill (twil) *n.* A weave that produces the parallel rib on the surface of a fabric.

twin (twin) *n.* One of two persons born at the same time to the same mother; one of two similar persons or things. *adj.* Having two similar or identical parts.

twine (twīn) *v.* To weave or twist together. *n.* A strong cord or thread made by twisting many threads together.

twinge (twinj) *n.* A sudden, sharp pain; a brief emotional or mental pang.

twin-kle (twing´kl) *v.* To gleam or shine with quick flashes; to sparkle.

twirl (twerl) *v.* To rotate or cause to turn around and around. **twirl** *n.*

twist (twist) *v.* To wind two or more pieces of thread, twine, or other materials together to make a single strand; to curve; to bend; to distort or change the meaning of; to injure and wrench. *n.* The act of twisting.

twit (twit) *v.* To tease about a mistake. *n.* A taunting reproach.

twitch (twich) *v.* To move or cause to move with a jerky movement. *n.* A sudden tug.

twit-ter (twit´ẻr) *v.* To utter a series of chirping sounds; to chatter nervously. **twittery** *adj.*

two (tŏ) *n.* The cardinal number of 1 + 1; the second in a sequence.

two-bit (tŏ´bit´) *adj.* Insignificant. **bits** Twenty-five cents. **faced** Double-dealing. **twofold.** Being double as much or as many.

two–time (tŏ´tīm´) *v., Slang* To be unfaith-

fulto. **two-timer** *n.*

ty-coon (tī kŏn´) *n., Slang* A business person of wealth and power.

tyke (tīk) *n.* A small child.

type (tīp) *n.* A class or group of persons or things; letters, numbers, and other symbols typewritten on paper or another surface; in printing, the piece of plastic, metal, or wood having the character or characters that are printed; a model or example of. *v.* To identify according to some sort of classification; to typewrite.

typecast To use repeatedly in the same kind of role.

type-face (tīp´fās´) *n.* A style or design of printing type.

type-set-ter (tīp´set´ẻr) *n.* A person who arranges or sets type. **typesetting** *n.*

ty-phoid (tī´foid) *n., Pathol.* An acute, infectious disease caused by germs in drink or food, resulting in high fever and intestinal hemorrhaging. **typhoid** *adj.*

ty-phoon (tī fŏn´) *n.* A tropical hurricane, especially one in the western part of the Pacific Ocean.

typ-i-cal (tip´i kȧl) *adj.* Exhibiting the characteristics of a certain class or group. **typically** *adv.*

typ-i-fy (tip´i fī´) *v.* To be characteristic or typical of; to show all the traits or qualities of. **typified** *adj.* **typifying** *adj.*

typ-ist (tī´pist) *n.* The operator of a typewriter.

ty-po (tī´pō) *n., Slang* An error in typewriting or in setting type; any printed error which was not the fault of the author.

tyr-an-nize *v.* To rule or control completely.

ty-ran-no-sau-rus (ti ran´o sor˝) *n.* A large, flesh-eating dinosaur which walked on its hind legs.

tyr-an-ny (tir´a nē) *n.* Harsh, absolute, and unfair rule by a government, king or other ruler.

ty-rant (tī´rant) *n.* An absolute, unjust, or cruel ruler; one who exercises power or control unfairly.

ty-ro *also* **ti-ro (tīrō)** *n.* A novice or a beginner.

U, u (ū) The twenty-first letter of the English alphabet.

UAW *abbr.* United Automobile Workers.

U-ban-gi *n.* A woman of Africa that has lips which are distended with wooden disks.

ubiq-ui-none *n.* The quinone which is able to function as an electron transfer agent in the Kreb's cycle.

ubiq-ui-tous (ū bik′wi tus) *adj.* To be everywhere at the same point in time.

ubiq-ui-ty (ū bik′wi tē) *n.* A presence in many places or locations at the same time.

U–boat (ū′bōt″) *n.* A type of submarine which is used by the Germans.

UDC *abbr.* Universal decimal classification.

ud-der (ud′er) *n.* The milk-producing organ pouch of some female animals, having two or more teats.

UFO (ū′ef′ō′) *n.* Unidentified flying object.

UFT *abbr.* United Federation of Teachers.

UG *abbr.* Underground.

Uga-rit-ic (ö″ga rit′ik) *adj.* Pertaining to the ancient city of Ugarit.

ugh (ŏch) Used to express disgust or horror.

ug-li-fy (ug′li fī) v. To make something or someone ugly.

ug-ly (ug′lē) *adj.* Offensive; unpleasant to look at.

ugly duckling *n.* Someone or something which at first appears unpromising but in the end is found to have great potential.

UGPA *abbr.* Undergraduate gradepoint average.

ug-some *adj.* To be loathsome.

ugt *abbr.* Urgent.

uh *interj.* To express hesitation.

uh–huh *interj.* Used for the purpose of showing or indicating agreement.

uhf *abbr.* Ultra high frequency.

uh-lan (ö′län) *n.* Part of a body of the Prussian light cavalry that was originally modeled on Tartar lancers.

uin-ta-ite *n.* A type of black asphalt which can be found especially in Utah.

ukase *n.* The proclamation by a russian government that has the force of law.

uki-yo-e *n.* A kind of Japanese art movement which flourished during the 17th to the 19th century.

u-ku-le-le (ū′ka lā′lē) *n.* A small, four-stringed musical instrument, orginally from Hawaii.

ula-ma n. Body of mullahs.

-u-lar *adj., suffix* To be relating to.

ul-cer (ul′sėr) *n.* A festering, inflamed sore on a mucous membrane or on the skin that results in the destruction of the tissue. **ul-cerous** *adj.*

ul-cero-gen-ic *adj.* To be tending to develop into an ulcer.

-ule *n., suffix* Small or little one.

-u-lent *adj., suffix* That abounds in.

ulex-ite *n.* A kind of mineral that occurs in loose fibers that is able to transmit light lengthwise with very little diminished intensity.

ul-lage (ul′ij) *n.* That amount a container lacks from being full.

ul-na (ul′na) *n., Anat.* One of the two bones of the forearm.

-u-lose *n., suffix* Ketose sugar.

ulot-ri-chous (ū lo′ti kus) *adj.* To have crisp or woolly hair.

-u-lous *adj., suffix* Being slightly.

ul-ster (ul′stėr) *n.* A type of long loose overcoat that is of Irish origin and is made of heavy material.

ult *abbr.* Ultimo; ultimate.

ul-te-ri-or (ul tēr′ē ėr) *adj.* To be located or situated on the further side of something or someone.

ultima *n.* A last syllable of a word.

ul-ti-ma ra-tio *n.* A final argument or the last resort to a problem or discussion.

ul-ti-mate (ul′ti mit) *adj.* Final; ending; most extreme; maximum; most.

ul-ti-ma-tum (ul′ti mā′tum) *n. pl* **-tums, -ta** A final demand, proposal, or choice, as in negotiating.

ul-ti-mo (ul′ti mō″) *adj.* To be happening or occurring in the month which precedes the present.

ul-ti-mo-gen-i-ture (ul″ti mō jen′i chėr) *n.* The system of inheritance where the youngest boy succeeds to the estate.

ultra *adj.* To be going beyond others.

ul-tra- (ul'tra) *prefix* Beyond the scope, range, or limit of something.

ul-tra-ba-sic *adj.* To be extremely basic. **ultrabasic** *n.*

ul-tra-cen-trif-u-gal *adj.* Pertaining to being obtained by the means or methods of ultracentrifuge.

ul-tra-cen-tri-fuge (ul″tra sen′tri fūj″) *n.* A kind of high speed centrifuge that is able to sediment colloidal and other small particles.

ul-tra-con-ser-va-tive (ul″tra kon sür′va tiv) *adj.* To be extremely cautious.

ul-tra-fash-ion-able *adj.* Being up-to-date with fashions and customs.

ul-tra-fiche *n.* A type of microfiche whose microimages are of printed matter which has been reduced 90 times or more.

ul-tra-fil-tra-tion *n.* The act of filtrating small particles through a membrane and holding back the larger particles.

ul-tra-high *adj.* To be exceedingly high.

ul-tra-ism (ul′tra iz″um) *n.* An example of radicalism. **ultraist** *n. or adj.*

ul-tra-lib-er-al *adj.* To be very liberal. **ultraliberal** *n.*

ul-tra-ma-rine (ul″tra ma rēn′) *adj.* To be situated beyond the sea or the ocean.

ul-tra-mi-cro *adj.* To be referring or dealing with something which is smaller than micro.

ul-tra-mi-cro-scope (ul″tra mī′kro skōp″) *n.* A type of instrument used for the purpose of viewing objects which are too small to be viewed through a regular microscope.

ul-tra-mi-cro-scop-ic *adj.* Being too small in size to be viewed with a regular microscope. **ultramocroscopically** *adv.*

ul-tra-mi-cro-tome *n.* A type of microtome that is made or designed to cut very thin sections off of something for the purpose of examining it. **ultramicrotomy** *n.*

ul-tra-mil-i-tant *adj.* To be very militant. **ultramilitant** *n.*

ul-tra-min-ia-ture *adj.* Extremely small; below miniature; tiny. **ultraminiaturization** *n.*

ul-tra-mod-ern (ul′tra mod′ẻrn) *adj.* Extremely advanced or modern in style or ideas.

ul-tra-mon-tane (ul″tra mon tān′) *adj.* Pertaining to the people beyond the mountains such as the Alps. **ultramontanism** *n.*

ul-tra-na-tion-al-ism *n.* An excessive devotion to national interests.

ul-tra-pure *adj.* To be of the utmost purity. **ultrapurely** *adv.*

ul-tra-se-cret *adj.* To be highly secret.

ul-tra-short *adj.* To be short in duration.

ul-tra-son-ic (ul″tra son′ik) *adj.* Relating to sound frequencies inaudible to humans. **ultrasonically** *adv.*

ul-tra-son-ics *n.* The science of the ultrasonic happenings and phenomena.

ul-tra-so-phis-ti-cat-ed *adj.* To be very sophisticated.

ult-ra-sound *n.* The vibrations of the same physical nature as sound.

ul-tra-struc-ture (ul′tra struk″chẻr) *n.* The invisible physio-chemical make up of protoplasm. **ultrastructurally** *adv.*

ul-tra-vi-o-let (ul′tra vī′o lit) *adj.* Producing radiation having wave lengths just shorter than those of visible light and longer than those of x-rays.

ultraviolet light *n.* The ultraviolet radiation.

ultra vires *adv.* Beyond the scope of legal authority.

ul-u-lant *adj.* To have a howling sound or noise. **ululation** *n.*

ul-u-late *v.* To howl like a wolf of dog; to wail very loud.

um-bel (um′bel) *n.* The racemose inflorescence which is found in the carrot family where the axis is very contracted so the pedicels appear to come from the same point.

um-bel-late *adj.* To be consisting of umbels.

um-bel-li-fer *n.* A member or plant of the carrot family.

um-bel-lif-er-ous (um″be lif′ẻr us) *adj.* Pertaining to the carrot family.

um-ber *n.* A moderate brown color.

um-bil-i-cal *adj.* Pertaining to the navel.

umbilical cord *n.* The structure by which a fetus is attached to its mother, serving to supply food and dispose of waste.

um-bil-i-cate *adj.* To be depressed such as the navel in appearance.

um-bil-i-cus (um bil′*i* k*u*s) *n.* A little depression occurring in the abdominal wall where the umbilical cord was attached to the embryo.

um-bles (um′b*e*lz) *n.* Entrails of an animal such as a deer which used to be used as food.

um-bo (um′bō) *n.* The elevation of the tympanic membrane of the ear.

um-bra *n.* The conical shadow that excludes all light from the given source.

um-brage (um′brij) *n.* A reason for doubt.

um-bra-geous *adj.* To be filled with shadows. **umbrageousness** *n.*

um-brel-la (um brel′*a*) *n.* A collapsible frame covered with plastic or cloth, held above the head as protection from sun or rain.

umbrella bird *n.* A type of tropical bird that is related to the fly catchers.

umbrella leaf *n.* A kind of North American herb belonging to the barberry family.

umbrella plant *n.* A type of African sedge which has whorls of slender leaves.

umbrella tree *n.* A type of American magnolia that has clusters of leaves.

Um-bri-an *n.* A person who is a member of ancient Italy and occupying Umbria.

Um-bun-du *n.* The Congo language of Angola.

umi-ak (ŏ′mē ak″) *n.* An open flat bottom Eskimo boat propelled with broad paddles.

ump *v., Slang* To act or to behave as an umpire such as in the game of baseball.

um-pir-age *n.* An act of umpiring.

um-pire (um′pī ėr) *n.* In sports, the person who rules on plays in a game. *v.* To act as an umpire.

ump-teen (ump′tēn′) *adj., Slang* An indefinitely large number.

UN *abbr.* United Nations.

un- *prefix* The reverse or opposite of an act; removal or release from.

un-a-bat-ed *adj.* To be not abated. **unabatedly** *adv.*

un-able (un ā′bl) *adj.* Not having the mental capabilities.

un-abridged *adj.* To be the most complete of a group or of a class.

un-ac-cept-able (un″ak sep′t*a* bl) *adj.* To be not welcome. **unacceptably** *adv.*

un-ac-com-mo-dat-ed (un″*a* kom′*o* dā″ tid) *adj.* To be not accommodated.

un-ac-com-pa-nied *adj.* Alone; without a companion. *Mus.* Solo.

un-ac-count-a-ble (un′*a* koun′t*a* bl) *adj.* Without an explanation; mysterious; not responsible. **unaccountably** *adv.*

un-ac-count-ed *adj.* Not being accounted for.

un-ac-cus-tomed (un′*a* kus′tomd) *adj.* Not used to or in the habit of; not ordinary.

una corda *adv.* With the soft pedal pressed downward, such as with a piano.

un-adorned (un″*a* dornd′) *n.* Being without decorations.

un-adorn-ment *n.* The state of being unadorned.

un-adul-ter-at-ed *adj.* To be pure. **unadulteratedly** *adv.*

un-ad-vised (un″ad vīzd′) *adj.* To do something or an action without consideration.

un-af-fect-ed (un″*a* fek′tid) *adj.* Not being affected in any way by something or someone.

un-af-fec-tion-ate *adj.* Without or lacking affection.

un-al-loyed (un″*a* loid′) *adj.* To be not alloyed; pure.

un-al-ter-able (un ol′tėr *a* bl) *adj.* Incapable of being changed. **unalterableness** *n.*

un-am-biv-a-lent *adj.* Being not ambivalent. **unambivalently** *adv.*

unan *abbr.* Unanimous.

un-an-chor *v.* To remove or to loosen for an anchor, as a boat.

un-anes-the-tized *adj.* Not having been subject to the anesthetic.

u-na-nim-i-ty *n.* The state of being unanimous.

u-nan-i-mous (ū nan´*i* mus) *adj.* Agreed to completely; based on the agreement of all. **unanimously** *adv.*

un-an-tic-i-pat-ed *adj.* To be not anticipated. **unanticipatedly** *adv.*

un-apol-o-get-ic *adj.* To be put forward without an apology.

un-ap-peas-able *adj.* Not to be appeased.

un-ap-proach-able (un´*a* prō´cha bl) *adj.* To be physically inaccessible.

un-apt (un apt´) *adj.* Not likely.

un-armed (un ermd´) *adj.* Lacking means for protection.

un-ar-tic-u-lat-ed *adj.* To be not carefully reasoned before something is done.

una-ry *adj.* To consist of a single item.

un-a-shamed (un´*a* shāmd´) *adj.* To be without guilt. **unashamedly** *adv.*

un-as-sail-a-ble (un´*a* sā´la bl) *adj.* Being not liable to attack. **unassailableness** *n.*

un-as-ser-tive (un´*a* sür´tiv) *adj.* Not being assertive.

un-as-sist-ed (un´*a* sis´tid) *adj.* To be made without being assisted by another.

un-as-sum-ing (un´*a* sö´ming) *adj.* Modest and not showy. **unassumingness** *n.*

un-at-tach-ed (un´*a* tacht´) *adj.* Not engaged, going steady, or married.

un-at-trac-tive *adj.* Not attactive or pretty; dull.

un-a-vail-ing (un´*a* vā´ling) *adj.* To be not availing.

un-a-void-a-ble (un´*a* void´*a* bl) *adj.* Inevitable; unstoppable. **avoidably** *adv.*

un-a-ware (un´*a* wâr´) *adj.* Not realizing. **unawareness** *n.* **unawarely** *adv.*

un-backed *adj.* To be lacking aid or support from another.

un-bal-ance (un bal´*a*ns) *v.* To put someone or something out of balance.

un-bal-anced (un bal´*a*nst) *adj.* Not in balance.

un-bal-last-ed *adj.* Not steadied with ballast.

un-ban-dage *adj.* To take off or to remove

a bandage from a wound.

un-bar-bered *adj.* To have unkempt long hair.

un-barred *adj.* Not being fixed or secured with a bar.

un-be *v.* To cease to have being.

un-bear-a-ble (un bâr´*a* bl) *adj.* Not possible to endure; intolerable.

un-beat-able (un bēt´*a* bl) *adj.* To be possessing unsurpassable qualities.

unbeaten *adj.* Being not pounded.

un-be-coming (un´bi kum´ing) *adj.* Unattractive; not pleasing; not proper, polite or suitable for the situation or occasion. **unbecomingness** *n.*

un-be-known *or* **un-be-knownst (un´bin-ōnst´)** *adj.* Not known; without one's knowledge.

un-be-lief *n.* The skepticism in the matters such as one's religious faith.

un-be-liev-able (un´bi lēv´*a* bl) *adj.* Incredible; hard to accept; not to be believed. **unbelievably** *adv.*

un-be-liev-er (un´bi lē´vėr) *n.* A person who does not believe certain things as being true.

un-belt-ed *adj.* To not be belted or furnished with a belt.

un-bend (un bend´) *v.* To make something straight. **unbendable** *adj.*

un-bend-ing (un ben´ding) *adj.* To not bend.

un-bi-ased *adj.* To be not biased.

un-bib-li-cal *adj.* To be unsanctioned by the Bible.

un-bid-den (un bid´*e*n) *adj.* To be not bidden.

un-bind (un bīnd´) *v.* To take or remove a band from something or from someone.

un-blessed (un blest) *adj.* To be not blessed.

un-blind-ed *adj.* Existing free from illusion.

un-blink-ing *adj.* Not showing any emotions such as crying.

un-block *v.* To free something from being blocked by something else.

un-bod-i-ed (un bod´ēd) *adj.* To have no body.

un-bolt (un bōlt´) v. To unfasten with the withdrawal of a bolt such as with a lock on a door.

un-born (un born) adj. To be existing without birth.

un-bo-som (un būz´om) v. To disclose or tell the thoughts of oneself to another.

un-bound (un bound´) adj. Being free or not fastened to anything or by anything.

un-box v. To remove something from a box.

un-brace (un brās´) v. To detach as if removing a brace or a band from something or someone.

un-braid v. To take apart grouped strands of hair or cloth.

un-branched (un brancht´) adj. To have no or be without branches.

un-bred (un bred´) adj. Being not taught.

un-bri-dle v. To free from or to unfasten a bridle.

un-bro-ken (un brō´ken) adj. Being not violated or broken; being in one piece.

un-buck-le (un buk´l) v. To loosen or remove the buckle of something such as a belt.

un-budg-ing adj. Unable to be moved or changed.

un-build (un bild) v. To take down such as a house.

un-bun-dle v. To price or place something separately.

un-bur-den (un būr´den) v. To relieve from a burden; to free from fears or problems.

un-but-tered adj. Being without butter.

un-but-ton (un but´on) v. To open the hatches; to loosen the buttons of a jacket or of a coat in order to remove the object from the body.

un-but-toned adj. Not provided with buttons.

un-cage v. To set something or someone free from a cage or the object that holds them.

un-cal-cu-lat-ed adj. Not thought about or out before it occurs.

un-called for (un kåld´får´) adj. Not necessary or needed; not requested.

un-can-did adj. Not honest.

un-can-ny (un kan´ē) adj. Strange, odd, or mysterious; exceptional. **uncannily** adv.

uncanniness n.

un-cap (un kap´) v. To remove covering or lid of something.

un-caused adj. Having no cause or reason.

un-ceas-ing adj. To never cease or end. **unceasingly** adv.

un-cel-e-brat-ed adj. Not being famous or well-known.

un-cer-e-mo-ni-ous (un´ser e mō´nē us) adj. To be informal; not ceremonious.

un-cer-tain (un ser´tan) adj. Doubtful; not sure; not known; hard to predict.

un-cer-tain-ty (un sūr´tan tē) n. The state of being uncertain or unsure.

un-change-able (un chān´ja bl) adj. To be not changing. **unchangeableness** n.

un-changed adj. Having nothing new or different.

un-char-ac-ter-is-tic adj. Being not typical.

un-charged (un chärjd´) adj. Not being charged with something.

un-char-i-ta-ble (un char´i ta bl) adj. To be lacking in charity. **uncharitableness** n.

un-chart-ed (un chär´tid) adj. Not plotted such as on a map.

un-chas-ti-ty n. The state of being unchaste.

un-chiv-al-rous adj. Not being chivalrous. **unchivalrously** adv.

un-choke v. To unblock an obstruction such as a piece of food in the throat.

un-church (un chürch´) v. To expel someone from a church. **unchurched** adj.

un-ci-al (un´shē al) n. A style of writing used in Greek and Latin manuscripts.

un-ci-form (un´si form˝) adj. To be hook shaped.

un-ci-nar-ia n. A type of parasitic worm in the shape of a hook; hookworm.

un-ci-nate (un´si nit) adj. To be bent at the end or the tip.

un-cir-cum-cised (un sūr´kum sīzd˝) adj. Being spiritually impure.

un-civ-il (un siv´il) adj. Being not civil.

un-civ-i-lized (un siv´i līzd´) adj. Without culture or refinement; without an established cultural and social way of living.

un-clamp *v.* To remove the clamp off of something.

un-clar-i-ty *n.* A lack of clarity.

un-clasp (un klasp´) *v.* To remove the clasp of or open the clasp of something.

un-clas-si-cal *adj.* Not being classical.

un-clas-si-fied *adj.* To not be subject to a security classification.

un-cle (ung´kl) *n.* The brother of one's mother or father; the husband of an aunt.

un-clean (un klēn´) *adj.* Immoral; dirty; not decent.

un-clench (un klench´) *v.* To open something from a clenched position.

un-climb-a-ble *adj.* Unable to be climbed. **unclimbableness** *n.*

un-cloak (un klōk´) *v.* To remove a cover from.

un-closed *adj.* Not being settled.

un-clothe (un klōth´) *v.* To uncover or undress.

un-cloud-ed *adj.* Not being covered by clouds. **uncloudedly** *adv.*

un-clut-ter (un klut´ėr) *v.* To take clutter from an area; to make neat.

un-cock *v.* To take away the hammer from such as a gun.

un-cof-fin *v.* To take out of a coffin.

un-coil (un koil´) *v.* To release from a coiled state; to unwind.

un-coined (un koind´) *adj.* Not being minted.

un-com-fort-a-ble (un kumf´ta bl) *adj.* Disturbed; not at ease physically or mentally; causing discomfort. **uncomfortably** *adv.*

un-com-mer-cial *adj.* Not related to commerce.

un-com-mit-ted (un˝ko mit´id) *adj.* Not being committed to something or to someone.

un-com-mon (un kom´on) *adj.* Rare; odd; unusual; extraordinary. **uncommonly** *adv.*

un-com-mu-ni-ca-ble *adj.* Being unable to communicate something.

un-com-mun-i-ca-tive (un˝komū´nikā˝tiv) *adj.* Not able to give information about something.

un-com-pas-sion-ate *adj.* Being unfeeling; not compassionate.

un-com-pet-i-tive *adj.* Being unable to compete in a competition or sport.

un-com-plain-ing *adj.* Not complaining. **un-complainingly** *adv.*

un-com-pli-cat-ed *adj.* To be not complex or complicated; simple.

un-com-pli-men-ta-ry(un˝komplimen´ta rē) *adj.* Not being complimentary.

un-com-pre-hend-ing(un˝komplimen´ta rē) *adj.* To be lacking in understanding of something.

un-com-pro-mis-ing (un kom´pro mī´zing) *adj.* Firm; unwilling to give in or to compromise.

un-con-cern (un´kon sern´) *n.* Lack of interest; disinterest; indifference.

un-con-cern-ed *adj.* The state of not having any interest in something or someone. **un-concernedness** *n.*, **unconcernedly** *adv.*

un-con-di-tion-al (un´kon dish´a nal) *adj.* Without conditions or limits. **unconditionally** *adv.*

un-con-di-tioned *adj.* Not subject to conditioning.

un-con-form-a-ble (un˝kon for´ma bl) *adj.* Not conforming to anything such as ideals.

un-con-for-mi-ty *n.* The lack of conformity.

un-con-ge-nial *adj.* Not being compatible to something or to someone.

un-con-ge-nial-i-ty *n.* The state of being uncongenial.

un-con-quer-a-ble (un kong´kė a bl) *adj.* Being unable to be conquered by someone.

un-con-scio-na-ble(un kon´sha na bl) *adj.* To be not guided by the conscience. **un-conscionability, unconscionableness** *n.*

un-con-scious (un kon´shus) *adj.* Not mentally aware; done without thought; not on purpose.

un-con-sid-ered (un˝kon sid´ėrd) *adj.* To be not worth considering.

un-con-sol-i-dat-ed *adj.* To be arranged loosely.

un-con-sti-tu-tion-al (un˝kon sti tō´sha nal) *adj.* Contrary to the constitution or the basic laws of a state or country.

un-con-straint *adj.* To be free from constraint.

un-con-trol-la-ble (un˝k*o***n trō´l***a* **bl)** *adj.* To exist free from the control of another.

un-con-ven-tion-al (un˝k*o***n ven´sh***a* **n***a***l)** *adj.* Not in accordance with convention.

un-con-vinc-ing *adj.* To not be convincing. **unconvincingly** *adv.*

un-cool *adj.* To be lacking or without assurance.

un-cork (un kork´) *v.* To release from a container that has been sealed with a cork.

un-cor-set-ed *adj.* To not be wearing a corset.

un-cou-ple (un kup´l) *v.* To release or disconnect from railroad cars.

un-couth (un kŏth´) *adj.* Acting or speaking crudely, unrefined; clumsy or awkward. **uncouthness** *n.*

un-cov-er (un kuv´ėr) *v.* To remove the cover from something; to disclose.

un-cre-at-ed (un˝krē ā´tid) *adj.* To not exist because of creation.

un-crit-i-cal (un krit´i k*a***l)** *adj.* To be lacking in discrimination.

un-cross *v.* To remove or to change something from a crossed position.

un-crown *v.* To remove the crown from someone such as a king.

un-crum-ple *v.* To return something to its original smooth condition.

un-crush-a-ble *adj.* Not being able to be crushed by something or by someone.

unc-tion *n.* An ointment which is used for the purpose of anointing an injury.

unc-tu-ous (ungk´chŏ us) *adj.* To be smooth in texture; have organic matter and be easily workable.

un-curl (un kürl´) *v.* To straighten something from a curled position.

un-cut (un kut´) *adj.* Not being cut into.

un-cyn-i-cal *adj.* Not being cynical.

un-daunt-a-ble *adj.* To be incapable of being daunted.

un-daunt-ed (un don´tid) *adj.* Being courageously resolute. **undauntedly** *adv.*

un-de-bat-a-ble *adj.* Being not subject to debate. **undebatably** *adv.*

un-de-cid-ed (un´di sī´did) *adj.* Unsettled; having made no firm decision; open to change. **undecidedly** *adv.*

undecylenic acid *n.* Type of acid that is found in perspiration.

un-de-fend-ed *adj.* Being not defended or protected.

un-dem-o-crat-ic *adj.* To not be agreeing with the ideals of the democratic party.

un-de-mon-stra-tive (un˝demon´stra tiv) *adj.* Being restrained in the expression of one's feelings or emotions. **undemonstrativeness** *n.*

un-de-ni-able (un´di nī´a bl) *adj.* Not open to doubt or denial; not possible to contradict. **undeniably** *adv.*

un-der (un´dėr) *prep.* Below, in place or position; in a place lower than another; less in degree, number, or other quality; inferior in rank, quality, or character; during the reign or period; in accordance with. **under** *adv.* Into; in a position underneath or below something; less than the required amount; insufficient.

under (un´dėr) *prefix* Location beneath or below; lower in importance or rank, degree or amount.

un-der-a-chiev-er (un˝dėr *a* chē´vėr) *n.* A kind of student that fails to achieve his or her scholastic potential.

un-der-act (un˝dėr akt´) *v.* To perform something in a feeble manner.

un-der-ac-tiv-i-ty *n.* A low level of activity which is thought of as not being normal.

un-der-age (un˝dėr āj´) *adj.* Being less than legal age.

un-der-arm (un´dėr ärm) *n.* The armpit.

un-der-bel-ly (un´dėr bel˝ē) *n.* The parts or sections of the body which are low.

un-der-bid (un˝dėr bid´) *v.* To bid for something at a level which is too low.

un-der-bod-y (un´dėr bod˝ē) *n.* The parts or sections of the body which are low.

un-der-bred (un˝dėr bred´) *adj.* Being of an inferior breed.

un-der-brim *n.* The area on the underside of a hat's brim.

un-der-brush (un´dėr brush´) *n.* Small bushes, vines, and plants that grow under tall trees.

un-der-bud-get-ed *adj.* To be provided with a budget which is inadequate.

un-der-car-riage (un´dėr kar˝ij) *n.* The landing gear of an airplane.

un-der-charge (un˝dėr chärj´) *v.* To charge too little for something that one buys.

un-der-class (un˝dėr klas´) *n.* The class which is lower such as in high school.

un-der-class-man (un˝dėr klas´man) *n.* A person who is a member of the freshman class in high school.

un-der-clothes (un´dėr klōz´) *n.* Clothes worn next to the skin; underwear.

un-der-coat (un´dėr kōt) *n.* A jacket which can be worn under another jacket.

un-der-coating *n.* A kind of waterproof coating which is applied to the underside of cars for the prevention of rusting and other types of wear.

un-der-cover (un˝dėr kuv´ėr) *adj.* To be executed in a secret manner; engaged in spying for one's country, etc.

un-der-croft (un´dėr kroft˝) *n.* A type of room which is subterranean.

un-der-cur-rent (un´dėr kür˝ent) *n.* The current that is located below the surface currents in the water.

un-der-cut *v.* To sell something at a price which is lower than the competitor's price to get the business of the one being offered the price.

un-der-de-vel-oped (un´dėr di vel´apt) *adj.* Not fully mature or grown; lacking modern communications and industry.

un-der-de-vel-op-ment *n.* The state of being underdeveloped.

un-der-do (un˝dėr dō) *v.* To do something less thoroughly than one is able to do it.

un-der-done (un´dėr dun´) *adj.* To be not completely cooked.

un-der-dress *n.* A piece of clothing which is made to be worn under the dress of a woman when the dress is sheer.

un-der-ed-u-cat-ed *adj.* Being educated poorly.

un-der-em-ployed *adj.* To have less than adequate employment.

un-der-es-ti-mate (un˝dėr es´ti māt˝) *v.* To place or to put a value or price on something which is too low. **underestimation** *n.*

un-der-feed (un˝dėr fēd´) *v.* To feed someone or something too little food.

un-der-foot (un´dėr fot´) *adj.* Underneath or below the feet; being so close to one's feet as to be in the way.

un-der-fur (un´dėr für˝) *n.* A thick and soft fur that is lying under the long and coarse hair of a mammal.

un-der-gar-ment (un´dėr gär˝ment) *n.* A kind of garment that is made to be worn under another piece of garment, such as underwear.

un-der-gird (un˝dėr gürd´) *v.* To make the foundation of something.

un-der-glaze (un´dėr glāz˝) *adj.* Suitable for applying before glaze is applied to something.

un-der-go (un´dėr gō´) *v.* To have the experience of; to be subjected to.

un-der-grad-u-ate (un´dėr graj´ō it) *n.* A college or university student studying for a bachelor's degree.

un-der-ground (un´dėr ground´) *adj.* A channel or space which is subterranean. *n.* A group which functions outside of the law.

un-der-ground-er *n.* The member of the underground.

un-der-growth *n.* A type of growth which is found growing on the floor of the forest.

un-der-hand (un´dėr hand´) *adj.* Done deceitfully and secretly; sly; sneaky. **underhandedly** *adv.*

un-der-hung *adj.* To have an underhung jaw; protruding or projecting beyond the upper jaw.

un-der-insured *adj.* Being not sufficiently insured.

un-der-laid (un˝dėr lād´) *adj.* To be placed beneath something.

un-der-lay (un˝dėr lā) *v.* To cover the bottom of something.

un-der-let (un˝dėr let) *v.* To be below the real value.

un-der-lie (un´dėr lī´) *v.* To be at the basis of something.

un-der-line (un´dėr līn´) *v.* To draw a line directly under something. **underline** *n.*

un-der-ling (un´dėr ling) *n.* The person who is under the orders of another person.

un-der-lip (un´dėr lip˝) *n.* The lower lip of a person's mouth.

un-der-ly-ing (un´dėr lī˝ing) *adj.* To be lying below something.

un-der-manned *adj.* Being inadequately staffed.

un-der-mine (un´dėr mīn´) *v.* To weaken; to make less strong.

un-der-most (un´dėr mōst˝) *adj.* The lowest in position.

un-der-neath (un´dėr nēth´) *adv.* Beneath or below; on the under side; lower. **underneath** *prep.* Under; below.

un-der-nour-ished *n.* To be supplied with less than the minimum amount of the needed food. **undernourishment** *n.*

un-der-nu-tri-tion *n.* The lacking or deficient bodily nutrition which is due to inadequate food intake.

un-der-paid *adj.* To receive less than enough or adequate pay.

un-der-pants (un´dėr pants˝) *n.* The pants that are worn under another garment.

un-der-part *n.* An auxiliary part or section.

un-der-pass (un´dėr pas´) *n.* A road or walk that goes under another.

un-der-pin (un´dėr pin´) *v.* To strengthen the foundation of something.

un-der-pin-ning (un´dėr pin˝ing) *n.* The material which is used for the support of a structure.

un-der-play (un´dėr plā´) *v.* To act with restraint.

un-der-plot *n.* A kind of dramatic plot in a play that is subordinate to the main action or plot.

un-der-powered *adj.* To be driven by an engine that is not sufficiently powered.

un-der-priv-i-leged (un´dėr priv´i lijd) *adj.* Deprived of economic and social advantages.

un-der-pro-duc-tion *n.* A type of production which is unable to satisfy the demand.

un-der-pro-duc-tive *adj.* Being unable to produce something adequately.

un-der-proof *adj.* To be containing less alcohol than the proof spirit.

un-der-rate (un´dėr rāt´) *v.* To rate or value below the true worth.

un-der-re-port *v.* To report something as being less than it actually is.

un-der-ripe (un´dėr rīp´) *adj.* To be insufficiently ripe.

un-der-run *v.* To pass something along under in order to look at it or examine it.

un-der-sat-u-rat-ed *adj.* To be less than normally saturated or wet with a liquid.

un-der-score (un´dėr skōr´) *v.* To emphasize. **underscore** *n.*

un-der-sea (un´dėr sē˝) *adj.* Being carried under the sea or under the surface of the sea.

un-der-sec-re-tar-i-at *n.* The staff which is under the secretary.

un-der-sell (un´dėr sel´) *v.* To sell for less than a competitor.

un-der-shirt *n.* A shirt that is worn under another.

un-der-side (un´dėr sīd´) *n.* The side or part on the bottom.

un-der-stand (un´dėr stand´) *v.* To comprehend; to realize; to know the feelings and thoughts of.

un-der-stand-a-ble (un´dėr stan´da bl) *adj.* Able to sympathize or comprehend. **understandably** *adv.*

un-der-state (un´dėr stāt´) *v.* To make too little of the actual situation. **understatement** *n.*

un-der-stood (un´dėr sted´) *adj.* Agreed upon by all.

un-der-stud-y (un´dėr stud´ē) *v.* To learn, another person's part or role in order to be able to replace him if necessary. **understudy** *n.*

un-der-take (un´dėr tāk´) *v.* To set about to do a task; to pledge oneself to a certain job; to attempt. **undertaking** *n.*

un-der-tak-er (un´dėr tā´kėr) *n.* A person who prepares the dead for burial.

un-der-tone (un´dẻr tōn´) *n.* A low, quiet voice; a pale or subdued color visible through other colors.

un-der-tow (un´dẻr tō´) *n.* The underwater current which runs in the opposite direction of the surface current.

un-der-wa-ter (un´dẻr wå´tẻr) *adj.* Occurring, happening or used beneath the surface of the water. **underwater** *adv.*

un-der-write (un´dẻr rīt´) *v.* To sign or write at the end of something; to finance; to assume a risk by means of insurance. To assume responsibility for; to undertake to pay a written pledge of money. **underwriter** *n.*

un-de-sir-a-ble (un´di zī´ẻr *a* bl) *adj.* Offensive; not wanted. **undesirably** *adv.*

un-do (un dö´) *v.* To cancel; to reverse; to loosen or unfasten; to open a package.

un-done *adj.* Not finished; unfastened; ruined.

un-du-late (un´ja lāt´) *v.* To move from side to side with a flowing motion; to have a wavy shape. **undulation** *n.*

un-dy-ing (un dī´ing) *adj.* Without end.

un-earth (un erth´) *v.* To dig up from the earth; to find or discover.

unearthly (un erth´lē) *adj.* Strange; not from this world.

un-eas-y (un ē´zē) *adj.* Feeling or causing distress or discomfort; embarrassed; awkward; uncertain. **uneasily** *adv.*

un-em-ployed (un´em ploid´) *adj.* Without a job; without work. **unemployment** *n.*

un-en-thu-si-as-tic *adj.* Not being excited about something.

un-e-qual (un ē´kwal) *adj.* Not even; not fair; not of the same size or time; lacking sufficient ability.

un-equiv-o-cal *adj.* Being clear; having no doubt.

UNESCO *abbr.* United Nations Educational, Scientific, and Cultural Organization.

un-es-sen-tial *adj.* Not being important.

un-e-ven (un ē´ven) *adj.* Not equal; varying inconsistency or form; not balanced.

un-e-vent-ful (un´i vent´ful) *adj.* Lacking

insignificance; calm.

un-expect-ed (un´ik spek´tid) *adj.* Surprising; happening without warning. **unexpectedly** *adv.*

un-fail-ing (un fā´ling) *adj.* Constant, unchanging.

un-fair (un fâr´) *adj.* Not honest; marked by a lack of justice. **unfairly** *adv.* **unfairness** *n.*

un-faith-ful (un fāth´ful) *adj.* Breaking a promise or agreement; without loyalty; guilty of adultery.

un-fa-mil-iar (un´fa mil´yẻr) *adj.* Not knowing; strange; foreign.

un-fath-om-able *adj.* Being unable to comprehend.

un-fa-vor-able (un fā´vẻr *a* bl) *adj.* Undesired; harmful.

un-feel-ing (un fē´ling) *adj.* Without sympathy; hardhearted; without sensation. **unfeelingly** *adv.*

un-fin-ished *adj.* At loose ends; not completed.

un-fit (un fit´) *adj.* Not suitable; not qualified; in poor body or mental health.

un-fold (un fōld´) *v.* To open up the folds of and lay flat; to reveal gradually. **unfoldment** *n.*

un-fore-seen (un´fōr sēn´) *adj.* Not anticipated or expected.

un-for-get-ta-ble (un´fẻr get´*a* bl) *adj.* Impossible or hard to forget; memorable. **unforgettably** *adv.*

un-for-tu-nate (un for´cha nit) *adj.* Causing or having bad luck, damage, or harm. *n.* A person who has no luck.

un-found-ed (un foun´did) *adj.* Not founded or based on fact; groundless; lacking a factual basis.

un-friend-ly (un frend´lē) *adj.* Showing a lack of kindness; not friendly; not favorable.

un-frock *v.* To remove from a position of honor; to relieve from the duties of an office, post, etc.

un-furl (un ferl´) *v.* To unroll or unfold; to open up or out.

un-fur-nished (un fer´nisht) *adj.* Without

furniture.

un-god-ly (un god'lē) *adj.* Wicked; evil; lacking reverence for God.

un-grate-ful (un grāt'ful) *adj.* Not thankful; showing no appreciation.

un-guent (ung'gwent) *n.* A healing or soothing salve; ointment.

un-gu-late *n.* A group of hoofed mammals, many having horns.

un-happy (un hap'ē) *adj.* Sad; without laughter or joy; not satisfied or pleased. **unhappily** *adv.* **unhappiness** *n.*

un-healthy *adj.* Sickly; not enjoying good health.

un-heard (un herd') *adj.* Not heard; not listened to.

un-heard–of (un herd'uv') *adj.* Not known or done before; without precedent.

un-ho-ly *adj.* Wicked.

un-hook (un hek') *v.* To release or undo from a hook.

un-hur-ried *adj.* At a leisurely pace. **un-hurriedly** *adv.*

UNICEF *abbr.* United Nations Children's Fund.

u-ni-corn (ū'ni kårn') *n.* A mythical animal resembling a horse, with a horn in the center of its forehead.

u-ni-cy-cle (ū'ni sī'kl) *n.* A one wheeled vehicle with pedals.

unidentified flying object *n.* A flying object that cannot be explained or identified, abbreviated as UFO.

uni-fac-to-ri-al *adj.* Controlled by a single gene.

u-ni-form (ū'ni form') *n.* Identical clothing worn by the members of a group to distinguish them from the general population. **uniformly** *adv.*

u-ni-fy (ū'ni fī') *v.* To come together as one; to unite.

uni-lat-er-al *adj.* Affecting only one side of a subject.

uni-lin-ear *adj.* Developing in a series of stages from primitive to advanced.

un-in-hab-it-ed *adj.* Not lived in; empty.

un-in-ter-est-ed (un in'tėr i stid) *adj.* Having no interest or concern in; not interested.

un-ion (ūn'yon) *n.* The act of joining together of two or more groups or things; a group of countries or states joined under one government; a marriage; an organized body of employees who work together to upgrade their working conditions and wages. **Union** The United States, especially the federal government during the Civil War.

union card *n.* A card which certifies membership in good standing in a union.

u-nip-ar-ous (ū nip'ėr us) *adj.* Having produced one egg or offspring at a time.

u-nique (ū nēk') *adj.* Unlike any other; sole.

u-ni-sex *adj.* Adaptable and appropriate for both sexes.

u-ni-son (ū'ni son) *n.* In music, the exact sameness of pitch, as of a tone; harmonious agreement.

u-nit (ū'nit) *n.* Any one of several parts regarded as a whole; an exact quantity that is used as a standard of measurement; a special section or part of a machine.

u-ni-tar-i-an (ū'ni târ'ē an) *n.* A member of a denomination that believes the deity exists in one person.

u-nite (ū nīt') *v.* To join or come together for a common purpose.

United Nations *n.* An international organization formed in 1945; comprised of nearly all the countries of the world whose purpose is to promote security, economic development, and peace.

unit rule *n.* A ruling which allows a delegation to a Democratic national convention to cast its entire vote as a unit by majority vote.

u-ni-ty (ū'ni tē) *n. pl.* **unities** The fact or state of being one; accord; agreement; harmony.

u-ni-valve (ū'ni valv') *n.* A mollusk having a one-piece shell, such as a snail.

u-ni-ver-sal (ū'n*i* ver'sal) *adj.* Having to do with the world or the universe in its entirety.

u-ni-verse (ū'n*i* vers') *n.* The world, stars, planets, space, and all that is contained.

u-ni-ver-si-ty (ū'n*i* ver'si tē) *n. pl.* **universities** An educational institution offering undergraduate and graduate degrees in a variety of academic areas.

un-just (un just') *adj.* Not fair; lacking justice or fairness. **unjustly** *adv.*

un-kempt (un kempt') *adj.* Poorly groomed; messy; untidy.

un-kind (un kīnd') *adj.* Harsh; lacking in sympathy, concern, or understanding. **unkindly** *adj.* **unkindness** *n.*

un-known (un nōn') *adj.* Strange; unidentified; not known; not familiar or famous. **unknown** *n.*

un-lead-ed (un led'id) *adj.* Containing no lead.

un-like (un līk') *adj., prep* Dissimilar; not alike; not equal in strength or quantity.

un-lim-it-ed (un lim'i tid) *adj.* Having no boundaries or limitations.

un-load (un lōd') *v.* To take or remove the load; to unburden; to dispose or get rid of by selling in volume.

un-lock (un lok') *v.* To open, release, or unfasten a lock; open with a key.

un-loose (un lōs') *v.* To loosen or undo; to release.

un-luck-y (un luk'ē) *adj.* Unfortunate; having bad luck; disappointing or unsuitable. **unluckily** *adv.*

un-manned (un mand') *adj.* Designed to operate or be operated without a crew of people.

un-mask *v.* To reveal the truth of one's identity; to expose.

un-men-tion-a-ble (un men'sha na bl) *adj.* Improper or unsuitable.

un-mis-tak-a-ble (un'mi stā'ka bl) *adj.* Very clear and evident; understood; obvious. **unmistakably** *adv.*

un-mor-al (un mor'al) *adj.* Having no moral knowledge.

un-nat-u-ral (un nach'ėr al) *adj.* Abnormal or unusual; strange; artificial.

un-nec-es-sar-y (un nes'i ser'ē) *adj.* Not needed; not appropriate.

un-nerve (un nerv') *v.* To frighten; to upset.

un-num-bered (un num'bėrd) *adj.* Countless; not identified by number.

un-oc-cu-pied (un ok'ya pīd') *adj.* Empty; not occupied.

un-pack (un pak') *v.* To remove articles out of trunks, suitcases, boxes, or other storage places.

un-pleas-ant (un plez'ant) *adj.* Not agreeable; not pleasant. **unpleasantly** *adv.* **unpleasantness** *n.*

un-pop-u-lar (un pop'ya lėr) *adj.* Not approved or liked. **unpopularity** *n.*

un-pre-dict-a-ble (un'pri dik'ta bl) *adj.* Not capable or being foretold; not reliable. **unpredictably** *adj.*

un- *prefix* The reverse or opposite of an act; removal or release from.

un-pre-pared (un'pri pârd') *adj.* Not equipped or ready.

un-pro-fes-sion-al (un'pro fesh'a nal) *adj.* Contrary to the standards of a profession; having no professional status.

un-prof-it-a-ble (un prof'i ta bl) *adj.* Showing or giving no profit; serving no purpose.

un-qual-i-fied (un kwol'i fīd') *adj.* Lacking the proper qualifications; unreserved.

un-ques-tion-able *adj.* Being indisputable.

un-rav-el (un rav'el) *v.* To separate threads; to solve; to clarify; to come apart.

un-re-al (un rē'al) *adj.* Having no substance or reality.

un-rea-son-a-ble (un rē'zo na bl) *adj.* Not according to reason; exceeding all reasonable limits.

un-re-lent-ing *adj.* Not weakening in vigor or determination.

un-re-li-a-ble (un'ri lī'a bl) *adj.* Unable to betrusted; not dependable.

un-re-served (un'ri zervd') *adj.* Done or given without reserve; unlimited.

un-re-strained (un'ri strānd') *adj.* Not

held back, forced, or affected.

un-ripe *adj.* Immature, not ready to harvest. **unripeness** *n.*

un-ruf-fled *adj.* Serene and calm in the face of setbacks.

un-ru-ly (un rŏ´lē) *adj.* Disorderly; difficult to subdue or control.

un-sat-is-fac-to-ry (un´sat is fak´to rē) *adj.* Unacceptable; not pleasing.

un-sa-vor-y *adj.* Disagreeable; morally offensive.

un-screw (un skrŏ´) *v.* To loosen or unfasten by removing screws from.

un-scru-pu-lous (un skrŏ´pya lus) *adj.* Without morals, guiding principles, or rules. **unscrupulously** *adv.* **unscrupulousness** *n.*

un-seat (un sēt´) *v.* To cause to lose one's seat; to force out of office.

un-seg-re-gat-ed *adj.* Being free from racial segregation.

un-sel-fish (un sel´fish) *adj.* Willing to share; thinking of another's well-being before one's own. **unselfishly** *adv.* **unselfishness** *n.*

un-set-tle (un set´l) *v.* To cause to be upset or excited; to disturb. **unsettled** *adj.*

un-sheathe (un shēth´) *v.* To draw a sword from a sheath or other case.

un-sight-ly (un sīt´lē) *adj.* Not pleasant to look at; ugly.

un-skilled (un skild´) *adj.* Having no skills or training in a given kind of work.

un-skill-ful (un skil´ful) *adj.* Lacking in proficiency. **unskillfully** *adv.* **unskillfulness** *n.*

un-sound (un sound´) *adj.* Having defects; not solidly made; unhealthy in body or mind. **unsoundly** *adv.* **unsoundness** *n.*

un-speak-a-ble (un spē´ka bl) *adj.* Of or relating to something which cannot be expressed or described. **unspeakably** *adv.*

un-sta-ble (un stā´bl) *adj.* Not steady or firmly fixed; having the tendency to fluctuate or change.

un-stead-y (un sted´ē) *adj.* Not secure; unstable; variable. **unsteadily** *adv.* **unsteadiness** *n.*

un-sub-stan-tial (un´sub stan´shal) *adj.* Lacking strength, weight, or solidity; unreal.

un-suit-a-ble (un sŏ´ta bl) *adj.* Unfitting; not suitable; not appropriate for a specific circumstance. **unsuitably** *adv.* **unsuitableness** *n.*

unswerving *adj.* Being loyal and steady.

un-tan-gle (un tang´gl) *v.* To free from snarls or entanglements.

un-thank-ful (un thangk´ful) *adj.* Ungrateful.

un-think-a-ble (un thing´ka bl) *adj.* Unimaginable.

un-ti-dy (un tī´dē) *adj.* Messy; showing a lack of tidiness. **untidily** *adv.*

un-tie (un tī´) *v.* To unfasten or loosen; to free from a restraint or bond.

un-til (un til´) *prep.* Up to the time of. *conj.* To the time when; to the degree or place.

un-time-ly (un tīm´lē) *adj.* Premature; before the expected time.

un-told (un tōld´) *adj.* Not revealed; not told; inexpressible; cannot be described or revealed.

un-touch-a-ble (un tuch´a bl) *adj.* Cannot be touched; incapable of being obtained or reached.

un-true (un trŏ´) *adj.* Not true; contrary to the truth; not faithful; disloyal.

un-truth (un trŏth´) *n.* Something which is not true; the state of being false. **untruthful** *adj.* **untruthfully** *adv.* **untruthfulness** *n.*

un-used (un ūzd´) *adj.* Not put to use; never having been used.

un-u-su-al (un ū´zhō al) *adj.* Not usual; uncommon. **unusually** *adv.* **unusualness** *n.*

un-ut-ter-a-ble (un ut´er a bl) *adj.* Incapable of being described or expressed; unpronounceable. **unutterably** *adv.*

un-veil (un vāl´) *v.* To remove a veil from; to uncover; to reveal.

un-war-y (un wâr´ē) *adj.* Not cautious or careful; careless.

un-wa-ver-ing (un wā´ver ing) *adj.* Steady; not moving; steadfast.

un-whole-some (un hōl´s*o*m) *adj.* Unhealthy; morally corrupt or harmful.

un-will-ing (un wil´ing) *adj.* Reluctant; not willing. **unwillingly** *adv.*

un-wind (un wīnd´) *v.* To undo or reverse the winding of; to untangle.

un-wise (un wīz´) *adj.* Lacking good judgment or common sense. **unwisely** *adv.*

un-wor-thy (un wer´thē) *adj.* Not deserving; not becoming or befitting; lacking merit or worth; shameful.

up (up) *adv.* From a lower position to a higher one; on, in, or to a higher level, position, or place; to a greater degree or amount; in or into a specific action or an excited state, as they stirred up trouble; to be even with in time, degree, or space, as up to date; under consideration, as up for discussion; in a safe, protected place, as vegetables are put up in jars; totally, completely, as the building was burned up; in baseball, at bat or, as up to bat. **up front** To be honest.

up-beat (up´bēt´) *n., Mus.* The relatively unaccented beat preceding the down beat. **upbeat** *adj.* Optimistic; happy.

up-bring-ing (up´bring´ing) *n.* The process of teaching and rearing a child.

up-com-ing (up´kum´ing) *adj.* About to take place or appear.

up-date (up dāt´) *v.* To revise or bring up-to-date; to modernize. **update** *n.*

up-draft (up´draft´) *n.* An upward current of air.

up-grade (up´grād´) *v.* To increase the grade, rank, or standard of. *n.* An upward slope.

up-hill (up´hil´) *adv.* Up an incline. *adj.* Hard to accomplish; going up a hill or incline.

up-hold *v.* To support.

up-hol-ster (up hōl´stèr) *v.* To cover furniture with fabric covering, cushions, and padding. **upholsterer** *n.* **upholstery** *n.*

up-keep (up´kēp´) *n.* The cost and work needed to keep something in good condition.

up-land (up´land) *n.* A piece of land which is elevated or higher than the land around it.

up-lift (up lift´) *v.* To raise or lift up; to improve the social, economic, and moral level of a group or of a society.

up-on (*u* pon´) *adv., prep.* On.

up-per (up´ér) *adj.* Higher in status, position or location. **upper** *n.* The part of a shoe to which the sole is attached. *Slang* A drug used as a stimulant. **case** The large or capital case of letters.

up-per–class (up´ér klas´) *adj.* Economically or socially superior.

up-per-class-man (up´ér klas´m*a*n) *n.* A junior or senior at a high school or college.

up-right (up´rīt´) *adj.* Having a vertical direction or position; honest. **upright** *n.* Something standing vertically, such as a beam in a building.

up-ris-ing (up´rī´zing) *n.* A revolt; a rebellion; an insurrection.

up-roar (up´rōr´) *n.* A confused, loud noise; a commotion.

up-root (up rōt´) *v.* To detach completely by pulling up the roots. **uprooter** *n.*

up-set (up set´) *v.* To capsize; to turn over; to throw into confusion or disorder; to overcome; to beat unexpectedly. **upset** *adj.* Capsized; overturned; distressed; troubled.

up-stage (up´stāj´) *adj. & adv.* Toward or at the backpart of a stage. *Slang* To steal the show or scene from.

up-stairs (up´stârz´) *adv.* Up one or more flights of stairs. **upstairs** *adj.* Situated on the upper floor.

up-stand-ing (up stan´ding) *adj.* Straightforward; honest; upright.

up-start (up´stärt´) *n.* One who has risen quickly to power or wealth, especially one who is conceited.

up-stream (up´strēm´) *adv.* Toward the origin of a stream; against the current.

up-tight *adv.* Nervous, tense, or anxious.

up–to–date (up´*to* dāt´) *adj.* Most current or recent; appropriate to the present time.

up-town (up´toun´) *adv.* Toward or in the upper part of town. *n.* The upper part of town or city. **uptown** *adv.*

up-ward *or* **up-wards** *adv.* From a lower position to or toward a higher one **upward** *adj.* Directed toward a higher position.

u-ra-ni-um (ū rā′nē *u*m) *n.* A hard, heavy, shiny metallic element that is radioactive, used especially in research and in nuclear weapons and fuels, symbolized by U.

ura-nog-ra-phy *n.* The science concerned with the description of the heavens and the celestial bodies.

ura-nom-e-try (ūr″*a* nom′i trē) *n.* A chart of celestial bodies.

U-ra-nus *n.* The seventh planet of the solar system in distance from the sun.

ur-ban (er′b*a*n) *adj.* Pertaining to a city or having characteristics of a city; living or being in a city. **urbanite** *n.*

ur-ban-ol-o-gy *n.* The study dealing with the problems of a city such as education, politics, planning, etc.

urge (erj) *v.* To encourage, push, or drive; to recommend persistently and strongly. *n.* An influence, impulse, or force.

ur-gent (er′jent) *adj.* Requiring immediate attention. **urgency** *n.* **urgently** *adv.*

urine (ūr′in) *n.* In man and other mammals, the yellowish fluid waste produced by the kidneys.

us (us) *pron. pl.* The objective case of we; used as an indirect object, direct object, or object of a preposition.

us-a-ble *or* **useable** (ū′z*a* bl) *adj.* Fit or capable of being used. **usably** *adv.*

us-age (ū′sij) *n.* The way or act of using something; the way words are used.

use (ūz) *v.* To put into action; to employ for a special purpose; to employ on a regular basis; to exploit for one's own advantage. *n.* The state or fact of being used; the act or way of using something; the reason or purpose for which something is used; the function of something; the occupation or utilization of property. **used** *adj.* **useful** *adj.* **useless** *adj.*

ush-er (ush′ėr) *n.* A person who directs people to the correct seats in a theatre. *v.* To show or escort someone to a place; to go before as a representative or sign of something that comes later.

u-su-al (ū′zhŏ *a*l) *adj.* Ordinary or common; regular; customary. **usually** *adv.* **usualness** *n.*

u-surp (ū serp′) *v.* To take over by force without authority. **usurpation** *n.*

usu-ry *n.* An exorbitant rate of interest charged to a borrower.

u-ten-sil (ū ten′s*i*l) *n.* A tool, implement, or container, especially one for the kitchen.

u-ter-ine (ū′tėr in) *adj.* Referring to birth by the same mother but by a different father.

u-ter-us (ū′tėr *u*s) *n.* An organ of female mammals within which young develop and grow before birth. **uterine** *adj.*

u-til-i-ty (ū til′i tē) *n. pl.* **-ies** The state or quality of being useful; a company which offers a public service, as water, heat, or electricity.

u-til-ize (ūt′*i* līz′) *v.* To make or put to use.

ut-most (ut′mōst′) *adj.* Of the greatest amount or degree; most distant. **utmost** *n.*

u-to-pi-a (ū tō′pē *a*) *n.* A condition or place of perfection or complete harmony and peace.

ut-ter (ut′ėr) *v.* To say or express verbally; to speak. *adv.* Absolute; complete. **utterly** *adv.* **utterance** *n.* **uttermost** *adj.*

ut-ter-most *n.* To do or perform to our highest ability.

u-vu-la (ū′vy*a* la) *n.* The fleshy projection which hangs above the back of the tongue. **uvular** *adj.*

ux-or-i-cide (uk sōr′i sīd″) *adj.* Murder of a wife by her husband.

V

V, v (vē) The twenty-second letter of the English alphabet; the Roman numeral for the number 5.

va-cant (vā′k*a*nt) *adj.* Empty; not occupied; without expression or thought.

va-cate (vā′kāt) *v.* To leave; to cease to occupy.

va-ca-tion (vā kā´shan) *n.* A period of time away from work for pleasure, relaxation, or rest. *v.* To take a vacation.

vac-ci-nate (vak´si nāt´) *v.* To inject with a vaccine so as to produce immunity to an infectious disease, as measles or smallpox.

vac-ci-na-tion (vak´si nā´shan) *n.* The inoculation with a vaccine.

vac-cine (vak sēn´) *n.* A solution of weakened or killed microorganisms, as bacteria or viruses, injected into the body to produce immunity to a disease.

vac-u-um (vak´ū um) *n. pl.* **vacuums** *or* **vacuua** A space which is absolutely empty; a void; a vacuum cleaner. **vacuum** *v.* To clean with a vacuum cleaner.

vag-a-bond (vag´a bond´) *n.* A homeless person who wanders from place to place; a tramp; a wanderer. **vagabond** *adj.*

va-gar-y (va gâr´ē) *n. pl.* **-ies** An eccentric or capricious action or idea.

va-gi-na (va jī´na) *n. pl.* **vaginas, vaginae** *Anat.* The canal or passage extending from the uterus to the external opening of the female reproductive system.

vaginitis (vaj´i nī´tis) *n.* An inflammation of the vagina.

va-grant (vā´grant) *n.* A person who wanders from place to place. *adj.* Roaming from one area to another without a job. **va-grancy** *n.*

vague (vāg) *adj.* Not clearly expressed; not sharp or definite. **vaguely** *adv.*

vain (vān) *adj.* Conceited; lacking worth or substance; having too much pride in oneself.

val-ance (val´ans) *n.* A decorative drapery across the top of a window.

vale (vāl) *n.* A valley.

val-e-dic-to-ri-an (val´i dik tōr´ē an) *n.* The student ranking highest in a graduating class, who delivers a speech at the commencement.

val-en-tine (val´en tīn´) *n.* A card or gift sent to one's sweetheart on Valentine's Day, February 14th.

val-et (val´it) *n.* A man who takes care of another man's clothes and other personal needs; a hotel employee who attends to personal services for guests.

val-iant (val´yant) *adj.* Brave; exhibiting valor. **valiance, valor** *n.*

val-id (val´id) *adj.* Founded on facts or truth. *Law* Binding; having legal force. **validity, validate** *n.*

val-ley (val´ē) *n. pl.* **-leys** Low land between ranges of hills or mountains.

val-or (val´er) *n.* Bravery. **valorous** *adj.* **valorously** *adv.*

val-u-a-ble (val´ū a bl) *adj.* Of great value or importance; having a high monetary value; having a worthy quality or value. **valuableness** *n.*

val-ue (val´ū) *n.* The quality or worth of something that makes it valuable; material worth; a principle regarded as worthwhile or desirable. *Math* A calculated numerical quantity. *v.* To estimate the value or worth of; to regard very highly; to rate according to importance, worth, or usefulness.

valve (valv) *n.* The movable mechanism which opens and closes to control the flow of a substance through a pipe or other passageway. *Anat.* A membranous structure in a vein or artery that prevents or slows the backward movement of fluid. **valveless** *adj.*

va-moose (va mŏs´) *v., Slang* To leave in a hurry.

vam-pire (vam´pīer) *n.* In folklore, a dead person believed to rise from the grave at night to suck the blood of sleeping persons; a person who preys on others.

vampire bat *n.* A tropical bat that feeds on the blood of living mammals.

van (van) *n.* A large closed wagon or truck.

va-na-di-um (va nā´dē um) *n.* A metallic element symbolized by V.

van-dal-ism (van´da liz´um) *n.* The malicious defacement or destruction of private or public property.

vane (vān) *n.* A metal device that turns in the direction the wind is blowing; a thin rigid blade of an electric fan, propeller, or windmill.

va-nil-la (*va* **nil´***a***)** *n.* A flavoring extract used in cooking and baking; prepared from the vanilla bean.

van-ish (van´ish) *v.* To disappear suddenly; to drop out of sight; to go out of existence.

van-i-ty (van´i tē) *n.* *pl.,* *-ies* Conceit; extreme pride in one's ability, possessions, or appearance.

van-tage (van´tij) *n.* A superior position; an advantage.

va-por (vā´pėr) *n.* Moisture or smoke suspended in air, as mist or fog. **vaporish, vaporous** *adj.* **vaporize** *v.*

var-i-able (vâr´ē *a* **bl)** *adj.* Changeable; tending to vary; inconstant. *n.* A quantity or thing which can vary. **variableness** *n.* **variably** *adv.*

var-i-ance (vâr´ē *a***ns)** *n.* The state or act of varying; difference; conflict.

var-i-a-tion (vâr´ē ā´sh*a***n)** *n.* The result or process of varying; the degree or extent of varying. *Mus.* A different form or version of a given theme, with modifications in rhythm, key, or melody.

var-i-e-gat-ed (vâr´ē *e* **gāt´tid)** *adj.* Having marks of different colors.

va-ri-e-ty (v*a* **rī´i tē)** *n.* The state or character of being varied or various; a number of different kinds; an assortment.

var-i-ous (vâr´ē us) *adj.* Of different kinds. **variousness** *n.*

var-mint (vär´m*i***nt)** *n., Slang* A troublesome animal; an obnoxious person.

var-nish (vär´nish) *n.* A solution paint used to coat or cover a surface with a hard, transparent, shiny film. *v.* To put varnish on.

var-si-ty (vär´si tē) *n.* *pl.* *-ies* The best team representing a college, university, or school.

var-y (vâr´ē) *v.* To change; to make or become different; to be different; to make of different kinds.

vas-cu-lar (vas´ky*a* **lėr)** *adj., Biol.* Having to do with vessels circulating fluids, as blood.

va-sec-to-my (va sek´to mē) *n.* *pl.* *-ies* Method of male sterilization involving the surgical excision of a part of the tube which conveys semen.

vast (vast) *adj.* Very large or great in size. **vastly** *adv.* **vastness** *n.*

vault (volt) *n.* An arched structure that forms a ceiling or roof; a room for storage and safekeeping, as in a bank, usually made of steel; a burial chamber. *v.* To supply or construct with a vault; to jump or leap with the aid of a pole.

vb *abbr.* Verb; verbal.

VCR *abbr.* Videocassette recorder.

veg-e-ta-ble (vej´t*a* **bl)** *n.* A plant, as the tomato, greenbeans, lettuce, raised for the edible part. *adj.* Resembling a vegetable in activity; passive; dull.

veg-e-tar-i-an (vej´i târ´ē *a***n)** *n.* A person whose diet is limited to vegetables. *adj.* Consuming only plant products. **vegetarianism** *n.*

veg-e-ta-tion (vej´i tā´sh*a***n)** *n.* Plants or plant life which grow from the soil.

ve-hi-cle (vē´i kl) *n.* A motorized device for transporting goods, equipment, or passengers; any means by which something is transferred, expressed, or applied.

veil (vāl) *n.* A piece of transparent cloth worn on the head or face for concealment or protection; anything that conceals from view. *v.* To cover or conceal, as with a veil.

vein (vān) *n., Anat.* A vessel which transports blood back to the heart after passing through the body; one of the branching support tubes of an insect's wing; a long wavy, irregularly colored streak, as in marble, or wood. **vein** *v.*

ve-lour (v*e* **ler´)** *n.* A soft velvet-like woven cloth having a short, thick nap.

vel-vet (vel´vit) *n.* A fabric made of rayon, cotton, or silk, having a smooth, dense pile. **velvety** *adj.*

vend-er (ven´dẻr) *n.* A person who sells, as a peddler.

ven-det-ta (ven det´a) *n.* A fight or feud between blood-related persons, involving revenge killings.

ven-er-a-ble (ven´ẻr a bl) *adj.* Meriting or worthy of respect by reason of dignity, position, or age.

venereal disease *n.* A contagious disease, as syphilis, or gonorrhea, which is typically acquired through sexual intercourse.

ve-ne-tian blind *n.* A window blind having thin, horizontal slats which can be adjusted to desired angles so as to vary the amount of light admitted.

ven-i-son (ven´i son) *n.* The edible flesh of a deer.

ven-om (ven´om) *n.* A poisonous substance secreted by some animals, as scorpions or snakes, usually transmitted to their prey or an enemy through a bite or sting. **venomous** *adj.*

ve-nous (vē´nus) *adj.* Of or relating to veins. *Physiol.* Returning blood to the heart after passing through the capillaries, supplying oxygen for the tissues, and becoming charged with carbon dioxide. **venously** adv.

vent (vent) *n.* A means of escape or passage from a restricted area; an opening which allows the escape of vapor, heat, gas, or liquid. *v.* To discharge by way of a vent.

ven-ti-late (ven´ti lāt´) *v.* To expose to a flow of fresh air for refreshing, curing, or purifying purposes; to cause fresh air to circulate through an area; to expose to public discussion or examination. **ventilation ventilator** *n.*

ven-ture (ven´chẻr) *n.* A course of action involving risk, chance, or danger, especially a business investment. *v.* To take a risk.

ven-ue (ven´ŏ) *n.* The place where a crime or other cause of legal action occurs; the locale of a gathering or public event.

verb (verb) *n.* The part of speech which expresses action, existence, or occurrence.

ver-bal (ver´bal) *adj.* Expressed in speech; expressed orally; not written; relating to or derived from a verb. *n.* An adjective, noun, or other word which is based on a verb and retains some characteristics of a verb. **verbally** *adv.* **verbalize** *v.*

ver-ba-tim (vẻr bā´tim) *adv.* Word for word.

ver-be-na (vẻr bē´na) *n.* An American garden plant having variously colored flower clusters.

verge (verj) *n.* The extreme edge or rim; margin; the point beyond which something begins. *v.* To border on.

ver-min (ver´min) *n. pl.* **vermins** A destructive, annoying animal which is harmful to one's health.

Ver-mont *n.* A state located in the northeastern part of the United Sates; statehood March 4, 1791; state capital Montpelier.

ver-sa-tile (ver´sa til) *adj.* Having the capabilitiesof doing many different things; having many functions or uses.

verse (vers) *n.* Writing that has a rhyme; poetry; a subdivision of a chapter of the Bible. *v.* To make verse; to tell or celebrate in verse; to familiarize by close association or study.

ver-sion (ver´zhan) *n.* An account or description told from a particular point of view; a translation from another language, especially a translation of the Bible; a form or particular point of view; a condition in which an organ, such as the uterus, is turned; manual turning *n.* Of a fetus in the uterus to aid delivery. **versional** *adj.*

ver-so (ver´sō) *n. pl.* **-sos** The left-hand page.

ver-sus (ver´sus) *prep.* Against; in contrast to; as an alternative of.

ver-te-bra (ver´te bra) *n. pl.* **-brae, -bras** One of the bony or cartilaginous segments making up the spinal column.

ver-tex (ver´teks) *n. pl.* **-es, -tices** The highest or top most point; the pointed top of a triangle, opposite the base; the point at which two lines meet to form an angle.

ver-ti-cal (ver´ti kal) *adj.* In a straight up-and-down direction; being perpendicular to the plane of the horizon or to a primary axis; upright. **vertically** *adv.*

ver-y (ver´ē) *adv.* To a high or great degree; truly; absolutely; exactly; actually; in actual fact.

ves-per (ves´pėr) *n.* An evening prayer service; a bell to call people to such a service.

ves-sel (ves´el) *n.* A hollow or concave utensil, as a bottle, kettle, container, or jar; a hollow craft designed for navigation on water, one larger than a rowboat. *Anat* . A tube or duct for circulating a bodily fluid.

vest (vest) *n.* A sleeveless garment open or fastening in front, worn over a shirt.

ves-tige (ves´tij) *n.* A trace or visible sign of something that no longer exists. **vestigial** *adj.* **vestigially** *adj.*

ves-try (ves´trē) *n. pl.* **vestries** A room in a church used for meetings and classes.

vet (vet) *n., Slang* A veterinarian; a veteran.

vet-er-an (vet´ėr *an*) *n.* A person with a long record or experience in a certain field; one who has served in the military.

Veterans Day *n.* A day set aside to commemorate the end of World War I in 1918, celebrated on November 11th of each year; national holiday.

vet-er-i-nar-i-an (vet´ėr *i* nâr´ēan) *n.* One who is trained and authorized to give medical treatment to animals.

vet-er-i-nar-y (vet´ėr *i* ner´ē) *adj.* Pertaining to or being the science and art of prevention and treatment of animals.

ve-to (vē´tō) *n. pl.* **vetoes** The power of a government executive, as the President or a governor, to reject a bill passed by the legislature. *v.* To reject a bill passed by the legislature.

vex (veks) *v.* To bother; or annoy; to torment.

vexed *adj.* Annoyed by something.

vi-a (vī´*a*) *prep.* By way of; by means of.

vi-a-duct (vī´*a* dukt´) *n.* A bridge, resting on a series of arches, carrying a road or railroad.

vi-al (vī´*al*) *n.* A small, closed container used especially for liquids.

vi-brate (vī´brāt) *v.* To move or make move back and forth or up and down. **vibration** *n.*

vi-car-i-ous (vī kâr´ē us) *adj.* Undergoing or serving in the place of someone or something else; experienced through sympathetic or imaginative participation in the experience of another.

vice (vīs) *n.* An immoral habit or practice; evil conduct. *prefix* One who takes the place of another.

vice-ge-rent *n.* A substitute for someone having his or her powers to make decisions on their behalf.

vi-ce ver-sa (vī´se ver´sa) *adv.* With the order or meaning of something reversed.

vi-chy-ssoise (vish´ē swäz´) *n.* A soup made from potatoes, chicken stock, and cream, flavored with leeks or onions and usually served cold.

vi-cin-i-ty (vi sin´i tē) *n. pl.* **-ies** The surrounding area or district; the state of being near in relationship or space.

vi-cious (vish´us) *adj.* Dangerously aggressive; having the quality of immorality. **viciously** *adv.* **viciousness** *n.*

vic-tim (vik´tim) *n.* A person who is harmed or killed by another; a living creature which is slain and offered as sacrifice; one harmed by circumstance or condition. **victimize** *v.*

vic-tor (vik´tėr) *n.* A person who conquers; the winner.

vic-to-ri-ous (vik tōr´ē us) *adj.* Being the winner in a contest. **victoriously** *adv.*

vic-to-ry (vik´to rē) *n. pl.* **-ies** A defeat of those on the opposite side.

vid-e-o (vid´ē ō´) *adj.* Being, related to, or used in the reception or transmission of television.

video disc *n.* A disc containing recorded images and sounds which may be played on a television set.

video game *n.* A computerized game displaying on a display screen, controlled by a player or players.

video terminal *n., Computer Science* A computer device having a cathode-ray tube for displaying data on a screen.

vie (vī) v. To strive for superiority.

view (vū) n. The act of examining or seeing; a judgment or opinion; the range or extent of one's sight; something that is kept in sight. v. To watch or look at attentively; to consider.

vig-il (vij´il) n. A watch with prayers kept on the night before a religious feast; a period of surveillance.

vig-or (vig´ėr) n. Energy or physical strength; intensity of effect or action. **vigorous** adj.

Vi-king (vī´king) n. One of the pirate Scandinavian people who plundered the coasts of Europe from the eighth to the tenth century.

vile (vīl) adj. Morally disgusting, miserable, and unpleasant. **vilely** adv. **vileness** n.

vil-la (vil´a) n. A luxurious home in the country; a country estate.

vil-lage (vil´ij) n. An incorporated settlement, usually smaller than a town.

vil-lain (vil´an) n. An evil or wicked person; a criminal; an uncouth person. **villainous** adj. **villainy** n.

vin-ai-grette (vin´a gret´) n. A small ornamental bottle with a perforated top, used for holding an aromatic preparation such as smelling salts.

vin-di-cate (vin´di kāt´) v. To clear of suspicion; to set free; to provide a defense or justification for. **vindication** n.

vin-dic-tive (vin dik´tiv) adj. Showing or possessing a desire for revenge; spiteful.

vine (vīn) n. A plant whose stem needs support as it climbs or clings to a surface.

vin-e-gar (vin´e gėr) n. A tart, sour liquid derived from cider or wine and used in flavoring and preserving food.

vin-tage (vin´tij) n. The grapes or wine produced from a particular district in one season.

vi-nyl (vī´nil) n. A variety of shiny plastics, similar to leather, often used for clothing and for covering furniture.

vi-o-la (vē ō´la) n. A stringed instrument, slightly larger and deeper in tone than a violin.

vi-o-late (vī´o lāt´) v. To break the law or a rule; to disrupt or disturb a person's privacy. **violation** n.

vi-o-lence (vī´o lens) n. Physical force or activity used to cause harm, damage, or abuse.

vi-o-let (vī´o lit) n. A small, low-growing plant with blue, purple, or white flowers; a purplish-blue color.

vi-o-lin (vī´o lin´) n. A small stringed instrument, played with a bow.

VIP (vē´ī´pē´) abbr. Very important person.

vi-per (vī´pėr) n. A poisonous snake; an evil or treacherous person.

vir-gin (ver´jin) n. A person who has never had sexual intercourse. adj. In an unchanged or natural state.

Vir-gin-ia n. A state located in the eastern part of the United States; statehood June 25, 1788; state capital Richmond.

Virgo n. The sixed sign of the zodiac; a person born between August 23rd and September 22nd.

vir-ile (vir´il) adj. Having the qualities and nature of a man; capable of sexual performance in the male. **virility** n.

vir-tu (vėr tö´) n. The love or knowledge of fine objects of art.

vir-tue (ver´chö) n. Morality, goodness or uprightness; a special type of goodness. **virtuous** adj. **virtuously** adv.

vi-rus (vī´rus) n. Any of a variety of microscopic organisms which cause diseases.

vi-sa (vē´za) n. An official authorization giving permission on a passport to enter a specific country.

vis-cid (vis´id) adj. Sticky; having an adhesive quality.

vise or **vice** (vīs) n. A tool in carpentry and metal work having two jaws to hold things in position.

vis-i-bil-i-ty (viz´i bil´i tē) n. pl. -ies The degree or state of being visible; the distance that one is able to see clearly.

vis-i-ble (viz´i bl) *adj.* Apparent; exposed to view.

vi-sion (vizh´an) *n.* The power of sight; the ability to see; an image created in the imagination; a supernatural appearance.

vis-it (viz´it) *v.* To journey to or come to see a person or place. *n.* A professional or social call. *Slang* To chat. **visitor, visitation** *n.*

vi-sor (vī´zėr) *n.* A brim on the front of a hat which protects the eyes from glare, the sun, wind, and rain.

vi-su-al (vizh´ŏ al) *adj.* Visible; relating to seeing or sight.

vi-tal (vīt´al) *adj.* Essential to life; very important. **vitally** *adv.*

vital signs *n. pl., Med.* The pulse rate, body temperature, blood pressure, and respiratory rate of a person.

vi-ta-min (vī´ta min) *n.* Any of various substances which are found in foods and are essential to good health.

vit-re-ous (vi´trē us) *adj.* Related to or similar to glass.

vit-ri-fy (vi´tri fī´) *v.* To convert into glass or a substance similar to glass, by heat and fusion.

vi-va-cious (vi vā´shus) *adj.* Filled with vitality or animation; lively.

viv-id (viv´id) *adj.* Bright; brilliant; intense; having clear, lively, bright colors; realistic. **vividly** *adv.*

viv-i-fy (viv´i fī´) *v.* To give life to. **vivifiction** *n.*

vo-cab-u-lar-y (vō kab´ya ler´ē) *n.* A list or group of words and phrases, usually in alphabetical order; all the words that a person uses or understands.

vo-cal (vō´kal) *adj.* Of or related to the voice; uttered by the voice; to speak freely and loudly. *n.* A vocal sound. **vocally** *adv.*

vocal cords *n. pl.* The lower of two folds or bands in the throat which produce sound when made tighter or loosened when air is breathed out while speaking or singing.

vo-ca-tion (vō kā´shan) *n.* A career, occupation, or profession.

vo-cif-er-ate (vō sif´e rāt´) *v.* To utter or cry out loudly; to shout. **vociferation** *n.* **vociferous** *adj.* **vociferously** *adv.*

vod-ka (vod´ka) *n.* A colorless liquor of neutral spirits distilled from fermented rye or wheat mash.

vogue (vōg) *n.* The leading style or fashion; popularity. **vogue** *adj.*

voice (vois) *n.* The sounds produced by speaking; the ability or power to produce musical tones. *v.* To express; to utter; to give voice.

void (void) *adj.* Containing nothing; empty; not inhabited; useless; vain; without legal force or effect; null. *n.* Empty space; the quality or state of being lonely. *v.* To make void; to discharge; to emit.

voile (voil) *n.* A fine, soft, sheer fabric used for making light clothing and curtains.

vol-ley (vol´ē) *n. pl.* **-leys** A simultaneous discharge of a number of missile weapons; the shooting or eruption of similar things at one time; in the game of tennis, a shot in which the ball is hit before touching the ground.

volt-age (vōl´tij) *n.* The amount of electrical power, given in terms of the number of volts.

vol-ume (vol´ūm) *n.* The capacity or amount of space or room; a book; a quantity; the loudness of a sound.

vol-un-tar-y (vol´an ter´ē) *adj.* Done cooperatively or willingly; from one's own choice.

vol-un-teer (vol´un tēr´) *n.* One who offers himself for a service of his own free will. *adj.* Consisting of volunteers. *v.* To offer voluntarily.

vo-lup-tuous (vo lup´chŏ us) *adj.* Full of pleasure; delighting the senses; sensuous; luxury. **voluptuousness** *n.*

vom-it (vom´it) *v.* To eject contents of the stomach through the mouth. *n.* The food or matter ejected from the stomach by vomiting.

voo-doo (vō´dŏ) *n.* A religious cult derived from African ancestor worship; a cure or spell resulting from magical powers. **voodooism** *n.*

vo-ra-cious (vō rā´shus) *adj.* Having a large appetite; insatiable. **voraciously** *adv.*

vote (vōt) *n.* The expression of one's choice by voice, by raising one's hand, or by secret ballot. *v.* To express one's views. **voteless** *adj.* **voter** *n.*

vo-tive (vō´tiv) *adj.* Performed in fulfillment of a vow or in devotion.

vouch (vouch) *v.* To verify or support as true; to guarantee. **voucher (vou´chèr)** *n.*

vow (vou) *n.* A solemn pledge or promise, especially one made to God; a marriage vow. *v.* To make a vow.

vow-el (vou´el) *n.* A sound of speech made by voicing the flow of breath within the mouth; a letter representing a vowel, as a, e, i, o, u, and sometimes y.

voy-age (voi´ij) *n.* A long trip or journey.

vul-gar (vul´gèr) *adj.* Showing poor manners; crude; improper; immoral or indecent. **vulgarity** *n.*

vul-ner-a-ble (vul´nèr a bl) *adj.* Open to physical injury or attack. **vulnerability** *n.* **vulnerably** *adv.*

vul-ture (vul´chèr) *n.* A large bird of the hawk family, living on dead animals; a greedy person; one who feeds on the mistakes or bad luck of others.

W

W, w (dub´l ū´) The twenty-third letter of the English alphabet.

WA *abbr.* Washington.

WAC *abbr.* Women's Army Corps.

wacky *adj.* Amusingly or absurdly irrational. **wackiness** *n.*

wad (wod) *n.* A small crumpled mass or bundle; a soft plug used to hold shot or gunpowder charge in place. *Slang* A large roll of money. **wad** *v.*

wad-able *adj.* Capable of being wadded.

wad-ding *n.* Wads or materials for making wads; a sheet of loose fibers that is used for stuffing or padding.

wad-dle (wod´l) *v.* To walk with short steps and swing from side to side. **waddle** *n.* **waddler** *n.*

wade (wād) *v.* To walk through a substance as mud or water which hampers one's steps.

wader *n.* A person that wades; a name for high top waterproof boots.

wading bird *n.* A long-legged bird such as the sandpiper or snipe.

wading pool *n.* A portable shallow pool that is filled with water and used by children.

wae-sucks *interj.* A Scottish phrase used to express pity.

wa-fer (wā´fèr) *n.* A small, thin, crisp cracker, cookie, or candy.

waf-fle (wof´l) *n.* Pancake batter cooked in a waffle iron.

waft (waft) *v.* To drift or move gently, as by the motion of water or air. **waft** *n.*

waft-age *n.* The state or act of being wafted.

waf-ture *n.* A wavelike motion.

wag (wag) *v.* To move quickly from side to side or up and down. *n.* A playful, witty person. **waggish** *adj.*

wage (wāj) *n.* A payment of money for labor or services. *v.* To conduct.

wage earner *n.* A person who works for a salary or wages.

wage level *n.* The approximate position of wages at any given time.

wa-ger (wā´jèr) *v.* To make a bet; to gamble. **wager** *n.*

wag-on (wag´on) *n.* A four-wheeled vehicle used to transport goods; a station wagon; a child's four-wheeled cart with a long handle.

wag-on-er *n.* A person who drives a wagon.

wagon master *n.* The person in charge of one or more wagons while transporting freight or other items.

wag-tail *n.* An Old World bird having a slender body and long tail.

wa-hi-ne *n.* A Polynesian girl or woman.

waif (wāf) *n.* An abandoned, homeless, or lost child; a piece of property found without the owner; a stray animal.

wail (wāl) *n.* A loud, mournful cry or weep. *n.* To make such a sound.

waist (wāst) *n.* The narrow part of the body between the thorax and hips; the middle part or section of something which is narrower than the rest. **waisted** *adj.*

waist-band *n.* The band on clothing that encircles the waist.

wait (wāt) *v.* To stay in one place in expectation of; to await; to put off until a later time or date; to be ready or prepared. *n.* A time of waiting.

wait-er (wā´tẻr) *n.* A man who serves food at a restaurant.

wait-ress (wā´tris) *n.* A woman who serves food at a restaurant.

waive (wāv) *v.* To forfeit of one's own free will; to postpone or dispense with.

waiv-er *n.* The act of intentionally abandoning a privilege or right.

wake (wāk) *v.* To come to consciousness, as from sleep. *n.* A vigil for a dead body; the surface turbulence caused by a vessel moving through water.

walk (wok) *v.* To move on foot over a surface; to pass over, go on, or go through by walking; in baseball, to advance to first base after four balls have been pitched. **walker** *n.*

walk-ie-talk-ie *n.* A battery-operated radio transmitting and receiving set.

walk--in *n.* A walk-in freezer or refrigerator; a person who walks in without an appointment.

walking delegate *n.* Labor union personnel who have been appointed to visit with their members and their companies to enforce the union agreements and rules.

walking stick *n.* A stick usually made of wood, used to aid a person in walking.

walk--on *n.* A small non-speaking part in a play.

walk-out (wok´out´) *n.* A labor strike against a company.

walk-way *n.* A passage that is used for walking.

wall (wol) *n.* A vertical structure to separate or enclose an area. *v.* To provide or close up, as with a wall.

wal-la-by (wol´a bē) *n.* A small or medium sized kangaroo.

wal-lah *n.* A person who performs a specific service or duty.

wal-let (wol´it) *n.* A flat folding case for carrying paper money.

wall-flow-er *n.* A person who shys away from a group; one who is unpopular and stays away from other people.

wal-lop (wol´op) *n.* A powerful blow; an impact. *v.* To move with disorganized haste. **walloper** *n.*

wall-pa-per (wol´pā´pẻr) *n.* Decorative paper for walls, usually having a colorful pattern.

Wall Street *n.* The street in New York City where the New York Stock Exchange is located.

wal-nut (wol´nut) *n.* An edible nut with a hard, light- brown shell; the tree on which this nut grows.

wal-rus (wol´rus) *n.* A large marine mammal of the northern seas having flippers, ivory tusks, and a tough hide.

waltz (wolts) *n.* A ballroom dance in 3/4 time; music for a waltz. *v.* To dance a waltz; to advance successfully and easily.

wam-pum (wom´pum) *n.* Polished shells, once used as currency by North American Indians. *Slang* Money.

wand (wond) *n.* A slender rod used by a magician.

wan-der (won´dẻr) *v.* To travel about aimlessly; to roam; to stray. **wanderer** *n.*

wane (wān) *v.* To decrease in size or extent; to decrease gradually. *n.* A gradual deterioration.

wan-gle (wang´gl) *v.* To resort to devious methods in order to obtain something wanted. **wangler** *n.*

want (wont) *v.* To wish for or desire; to need; to lack; to fail to possess a required amount; to hunt in order to apprehend. *n.* The state of lacking a required or usual amount. **wanting** *adj.*

war (wor) *n.* An armed conflict among

states or nations; a state of discord; the science of military procedures.

ward (word) *n.* A section in a hospital for certain patients requiring similar treatment; a person under protection or surveillance. *v.* To keep watch over someone or some thing.

ware (wâr) *n.* Manufactured items of the same general kind; items or goods for sale.

ware-house (wâr'hous') *n.* A large building used to store merchandise. **warehouse** *v.*

warm (worm) *adj.* Moderate heat; neither hot or cold; comfortably established; marked by a strong feeling; having pleasant feelings.

warn (worn) *v.* To give notice or inform beforehand; to call to one's attention; to alert.

warp (worp) *v.* To become bent out of shape; to deviate from a proper course. *n.* The condition of being twisted or bent; threads running down the length of a fabric.

war-rant (wor'ant) *n.* A written authorization giving the holder legal power to search, seize, or arrest. *v.* To provide a reason; to give proof. **warrantable** *adj.* **warrantor** *n.*

war-ri-or (wor'ē ėr) *n.* One who fights in a war or battle.

war-y (wâr'ē) *adj.* Marked by caution; alert to danger.

wash (wosh) *v.* To cleanse by the use of water; to remove dirt; to move or deposit as if by the force of water. *n.* A process or instance of washing; a group of soiled clothes or linens.

wash–and–wear *adj.* Requiring little or no ironing after washing.

wash-board (wosh'bōrd') *n.* A corrugated board on which clothes are rubbed in the process of washing; an uneven surface as a washboard.

washed–out (wosht'out') *adj., Slang* Tired.

wash-er (wosh'ėr) *n.* A small disk usually made of rubber or metal having a hole in the center, used with nuts and bolts; a washing machine.

wash-ing (wosh'ing) *n.* Clothes and other

articles that are washed or to be washed; cleaning.

Wash-ing-ton *n.* A state located in the northwestern part of the United States, statehood November 11, 1889. State capital Olympia.

Washington, George *n.* (1732-1799) The first president of the United States from 1789-1797.

was-n't (wuz'ant) Was not.

wasp (wasp) *n.* Any of various insects, having a slim body with a constricted abdomen, the female capable of inflicting a painful sting.

waste (wāst) *v.* To be thrown away; to be available but not used completely. *n.* A barren region; the instance of wasting; useless material produced as a by-product. *Slang* To destroy or murder. **wasteful** *adj.* **waster** *n.*

watch (woch) *v.* To view carefully; to guard; to keep informed. *n.* The act of staying awake to guard or protect; a small timepiece worn on the wrist, designed to keep the correct time of day.

watch-dog (woch'dog') *n.* A dog trained to guard someone or his property.

watch-ful (woch'ful) *adj.* Carefully observant or attentive. **watchfully** *adv.*

watch-man (woch'man) *n.* A person hired to keep watch; a guard.

wa-ter (wo'tėr) *n.* The clear liquid making up oceans, lakes, and streams; the body fluids as tears or urine. *v.* To pour or spray water on something or someone; to give water to drink; to weaken or dilute with water.

water moccasin *n.* A venomous snake from the lowlands and swampy areas of the southern United States.

water polo *n.* A water game between two teams, the object of which is to get a ball into the opponent's goal.

water power *n.* The power of energy produced by swift-moving water.

wa-ter-proof (wo'tėr prōf') *adj.* Capable of preventing water from penetrating. *v.* To make or treat in order to make waterproof. *n.* A material or fabric which is waterproof.

wa-ter–re-pel-lant (wo´tėr ri pel´ent) *adj.* A material or product treated to resist water, but not completely waterproof.

wa-ter-shed *n.* The raised area between two regions that divides two sections drained by different river sources.

wa-ter--ski (wo´tėr skē´) *v.* To travel over water on a pair of short, broad skis while being pulled by a motorboat.

wa-ter-spout (wo´tėr spout´) *n.* A tube or pipe through which water is discharged; a funnel-shaped column of spray and mist whirling over an ocean or lake.

water table *n.* The upper limit of the portion of the ground completely saturated with water.

wa-ter-tight (wo´tėr tīt´) *adj.* Closed or sealed so tightly that no water can enter, leaving no chance for evasion.

wa-ter-way (wo´tėr wā´) *n.* A navigable body of water; a channel for water.

wa-ter-y (wo´te rē) *adj.* Containing water; diluted; lacking effectiveness.

watt (wot) *n.* A unit of electrical power represented by current of one ampere, produced by the electromotive force of one volt.

wave (wāv) *v.* To move back and forth or up and down; to motion with the hand. *n.* A swell or moving ridge of water; a curve or curl, as in the hair.

wa-ver (wā´vėr) *v.* To sway unsteadily; to move back and forth; to weaken in force. **waver** *n.* **waveringly** *adv.*

wax (waks) *n.* A natural yellowish substance made by bees, solid when cold and easily melted or softened when heated. **waxy** *adj.*

way (wā) *n.* A manner of doing something; a tendency or characteristic; a habit or customary manner of acting or living; a direction; freedom to do as one chooses.

way-far-er (wā´fâr´ėr) *n.* A person who travels on foot.

way-lay (wā´lā´) *v.* To attack by ambush.

way-ward (wā´wėrd) *adj.* Unruly; unpredictable.

we (wē) *pron. pl.* Used to refer to the person speaking and one or more other people.

weak (wēk) *adj.* Having little energy or strength; easily broken; having inadequate skills; not reasonable or convincing. **weakness** *n.* **weakly** *adv.*

wealth (welth) *n.* An abundance of valuable possessions or property; all goods and resources having monetary value.

wealth-y (wel´thē) *adj.* Having much wealth or money; abundant; rich.

wean (wēn) *v.* To accustom an infant or small child to food other than a mother's milk or bottle.

weap-on (wep´on) *n.* A device used in fighting a war; advice which can be used to harm another person.

wear (wâr) *v.* To have on or put something on the body; to display. *n.* The act of wearing out or using up; the act of wearing, as clothing. **wearable** *adj.*

wea-ri-some (wēr´ē som) *adj.* Tedious, boring or tiresome.

wea-ry (wēr´ē) *adj.* Exhausted; tired; feeling fatigued. *v.* To make or become tired; to become fatigued. **wearily** *adv.*

wea-sel (wē´zel) *n.* A mammal with a long tail and short legs; a sly, sneaky person.

weath-er (weth´ėr) *n.* The condition of the air or atmosphere in terms of humidity, temperature, and similar features. *v.* To become worn by the actions of weather; to survive.

weath-er-man (weth´ėr man´) *n.* A man who reports or forecasts the weather.

weather vane *n.* A device that turns, indicating the direction of the wind.

weave (wēv) *v.* To make a basket, cloth, or other item by interlacing threads or other strands of material. **weaver** *n.*

web (web) *n.* A cobweb; a piece of interlacing material which forms a woven structure; something constructed as an entanglement; a thin membrane that joins the toes of certain water birds.

wed (wed) *v.* To take as a spouse; to marry.

Wed *abbr.* Wednesday.

we'd (wēd) *contr.* We had; we should.

wed-ding (wed´ing) *n.* A marriage ceremony; an act of joining together in close association.

wedge (wej) *n.* A tapered, triangular piece of wood or metal used to split logs, to add leverage, and to hold something open or ajar. *v.* To force or make something fit tightly.

wed-lock (wed´lok) *n.* Marriage; the state of being married.

Wed-nes-day *n.* The fourth day of the week.

weed (wēd) *n.* An unwanted plant which interferes with the growth of grass, vegetables, or flowers.

week (wēk) *n.* A period of seven days, beginning with Sunday and ending with Saturday; the time or days normally spent at school or work.

week-day (wēk´dā´) *n.* Any day of the week except Saturday or Sunday.

week-end (wēk´end´) *n.* The end of the week from the period of Friday evening through Sunday evening.

week-ly (wēk´lē) *adv.* Every week; once a week. *adj.* Taking place or done every week of or relating to a week.

weep (wēp) *v.* To shed tears; to express sorrow, joy, or emotion; by shedding tears; to cry. **weeper** *n.*

wee-vil (wē´vil) *n.* A small beetle having a downward-curving snout, which damages plants.

weigh (wā) *v.* To determine the heaviness of an object by using a scale; to consider carefully in one's mind; to be of a particular weight; to oppress or burden.

weight (wāt) *n.* The amount that something weighs; heaviness; a heavy object used to hold or pull something down; an overpowering force; the quality of a garment for a particular season. *v.* To make heavy.

weight-less (wāt´lis) *adj.* Lacking the pull of gravity; having little weight.

weight-y (wā´tē) *adj.* Burdensome; important.

weird (wērd) *adj.* Having an extraordinary or strange character. **weirdly** *adv.*

weird-o *n.*, *Slang* A person who is very strange.

wel-come (wel´kom) *v.* To extend warm hospitality; to accept gladly. *adj.* Received warmly. *n.* A greeting upon one's arrival.

weld (weld) *v.* To unite metallic parts by applying heat and sometimes pressure, allowing the metals to bond together. *n.* A joint formed by welding.

wel-fare (wel´fâr´) *n.* The state of doing well; governmental aid to help the disabled or disadvantaged.

well (wel) *n.* A hole in the ground which contains a supply of water; a shaft in the ground through which gas and oil are obtained. *adj.* Being in good health; in an agreeable state.

we'll (wēl) *contr.* We will; we shall.

well–be-ing (wel´bē´ing) *n.* The state of being healthy, happy, or prosperous.

well–done (wel´dun´) *adj.* Completely cooked; done properly.

well–groomed (wel´grömd´) *adj.* Clean, neat, and properly cared for.

well–known (wel´nōn´) *adj.* Widely known.

well–man-nered *adj.* Polite; having good manners.

well–mean-ing (wel´mē´ning) *adj.* Having good intentions.

well–to–do (wel´to dö´) *adj.* Having more than enough wealth.

welsh (welsh) *v.*, *Slang* To cheat by avoiding a payment to someone; to neglect an obligation. **welsher** *n.*

welt (welt) *n.* A strip between the sole and upper part of a shoe; a light swelling on the body, usually caused by a blow to the area. *v.* To hit severly.

wel-ter-weight (wel´tėr wāt´) *n.* A boxer weighing between 136 and 147 pounds.

went *v.* Past tense of go.

wept *v.* Past tense of weep.

were (wer) *v.* Second person singular past

plural of be.

we're (wēr) *contr.* We are

were-n't (wernt) *contr.* Were not.

west (west) *n.* The direction of the setting sun; the direction to the left of a person standing north. *adj.* At, of, or from the west. *adv.* To or toward the west. **western** *adj.*

West Virginia *n.* A state located in the eastern part of the United States; statehood June 20, 1863; state capital Charleston.

whack (hwak) *v.* To strike with a hard blow, to slap. *n.* An attempt.

whale (hwāl) *n.* A very large mammal resembling a fish which lives in salt water. *Slang* An outstanding or impressive example.

wharf (hworf) *n.* A pier or platform built at the edge of water so ships can load and unload.

what (hwut) *pron.* Which one; which things; which type or kind. *adv.* In which way. *adj.* Which particular one.

what-ev-er (hwut ev´ėr) *pron.* Everything or anything. *adj.* No matter what. *Slang* Which thing or things.

what's *contr.* What is.

wheat (hwēt) *n.* A grain ground into flour, used to make breads and similar foods.

wheel (hwēl) *n.* A circular disk which turns on an axle; an apparatus having the same principles of a wheel; something which resembles the motion or shape of a wheel. *v.* To move on or as if by wheels; to turn around a central axis; to rotate, pivot, or turn around.

wheel-bar-row (hwēl´bar´ō) *n.* A vehicle having one wheel, used to transport small loads.

wheel-chair (hwēl´châr´) *n.* A mobile chair for disabled persons.

wheel-er (hwē´lėr) *n.* Anything that has wheels.

wheeze (hwēz) *v.* To breathe with a hoarse whistling sound. *n.* A high whistling sound.

whelk (hwelk) *v.* Any of various large water

snails, sometimes edible.

when (hwen) *adv.* At what time; at which time. *pron.* What or which time. *conj.* While; at the time that; although.

whence (hwens) *adv.* From what source or place; from which.

when-ev-er (hwen ev´ėr) *adv.* At any time; when. *conj.* At whatever time.

where (hwâr) *adv.* At or in what direction or place; in what direction or place.

where-a-bouts (hwâr´a bouts´) *adv.* Near, at, or in a particular location. *n.* The approximate location.

where-as (hwâr az´) *conj.* It being true or the fact; on the contrary.

where-by (hwâr bī´) *conj.* Through or by which.

wher-ev-er *adv.* In any situation or place.

whet (hwet) *v.* To make sharp; to stimulate.

wheth-er (hweth´ėr) *conj.* Indicating a choice; alternative possibilities; either.

whet-stone (hwet´stōn´) *n.* A stone used to sharpen scissors, knives, and other implements.

whew (hwū) *n., interj.* Used to express relief; or tiredness.

whey (hwā) *n.* The clear, water-like part of milk that separates from the curd.

which (hwich) *pron.* What one or ones; the one previously; whatever one or ones; whichever. *adj.* What one; any one of.

which-ev-er (hwich ev´ėr) Any; no matter which or what.

whiff (hwif) *n.* A slight puff; a light current of air; a slight breath or odor.

while (hwīl) *n.* A length or period of time. *conj.* During the time that; even though; at the same time; although.

whim (hwim) *n.* A sudden desire or impulse.

whim-per (hwim´pėr) *v.* To make a weak, soft crying sound. **whimper** *n.*

whim-si-cal (hwim´zi kal) *adj.* Impulsive; erratic; light and spontaneous. **whimsically** *adv.*

whine (hwīn) *v.* To make a squealing, plaintive sound; to complain in an irritating, childish fashion.

whin-ny (hwin´ē) v. To neigh in a soft gentle way.

whip (hwip) v. To spank repeatedly with a rod or stick; to punish by whipping; to move in a motion similar to whipping or beating. n. A flexible stick or rod used to herd or beat animals; a dessert made by whipping ingredients; the utensil used to do so. *Slang* To overcome. **whipper** n.

whip-lash (hwip´lash´) n. An injury to the spine or neck caused by a sudden jerking motion of the head.

whip-poor-will (hwip´ėr wil´) n. A brownish nocturnal bird of North America.

whir (hwer) v. To move with a low purring sound.

whirl (hwerl) v. To rotate or move in circles; to twirl; to move, drive, or go very fast. n. A rapid whirling motion.

whirl-pool (hwerl´pōl´) n. A circular current of water.

whirl-wind (hwerl´wind´) n. A violently whirling mass of air; a tornado.

whirl-y-bird (hwer´lē berd´) n., *Slang* A helicopter.

whisk (hwisk) v. To move with a sweeping motion; to move quickly or lightly. n. A sweeping movement; a utensil used in cooking; to stir.

whisk-er (hwis´kėr) n. The hair that grows on a man's face; the long hair near the mouth of dogs, cats, and other animals. **whiskers** A man's beard.

whis-key (hwis´kē) n. An alcoholic beverage distilled from rye, barley, or corn.

whis-per (hwis´pėr) v. To speak in a very low tone; to tell in secret. n. A low rustling sound; the act of whispering.

whis-tle (hwis´l) v. To make a clear shrill sound by blowing air through the teeth, through puckered lips, or through a special instrument. n. A device used to make a whistling sound. **whistler** n.

white (hwīt) n. The color opposite of black; the part of something that is white or light in color, as an egg or the eyeball; a member of the Caucasian group of people. *adj.* Having a light color; pale; pure; blameless, without sin.

white-cap (hwīt´kap n. A wave having a top of white foam.

white--col-lar (hwīt´kol´ėr) *adj.* Relating to an employee whose job does not require manual labor.

White House n. The official residence of the President of the United States, located in Washington, D.C.

white-wash (hwīt´wosh´) n. A mixture made of lime and other ingredients and used for whitening fences and exterior walls. v. To cover up a problem; to pronounce someone as being innocent without really investigating.

whith-er (hwith´ėr) *adv.* To what state, place, or circumstance; wherever.

whither (with´ėr) v. To dry up or wilt from a lack of moisture; to lose freshness or vigor.

whit-tle (hwit´l) v. To cut or carve off small shavings from wood with a knife; to remove or reduce gradually. **whittler** n.

whiz (hwiz) v. To make a whirring or buzzing sound, a projectile passing at a high rate of speed through the air. *Slang* A person having notable expertise, as with a computer.

who (hŏ) *pron.* Which or what certain individual, person, or group; referring to a person pre-viously mentioned.

who'd *contr.* Who would; who had.

who-ev-er (hŏ ev´ėr) *pron.* Whatever person; all or any persons.

whole (hōl) *adj.* Complete; having nothing missing; not divided or in pieces; a complete system or unity; everything considered. *Math* Not a fraction. **wholeness** n.

whole-heart-ed (hōl´här´tid) *adj.* Sincere; totally committed; holding nothing back.

whole-sale (hōl´sāl´) n. The sale of goods in large amounts to a retailer. *adj.* Relating to or having to do with such a sale. v. To sell wholesale. **wholesaler** n.

whole-some (hōl´som) *adj.* Contributing

to good mental or physical health. **wholesomely** *adv.* **wholesomenes** *n.*

whole wheat (hōl´hwēt´) *adj.* Made from the wheat kernel with nothing removed.

who'll *contr.* Who shall; who will.

whol-ly (hō´lē) *adv.* Totally; exclusively.

whom (hŏm) *pron.* The form of who used as the direct object of a verb or the object of a preposition.

whom-ev-er (hŏm ev´ėr) *pron.* The form of whoever used as the object of a preposition or the direct object of a verb.

whooping cough (hō´ping kăf) *n.* An infectious disease of the throat and breathing passages in which the patient has spasms of coughing often followed by gasps for breath.

whooping crane *n.* A large bird of North America, nearly extinct, having long legs and a high, shrill cry.

whoosh (hwŏsh) *v.* To make a rushing or gushing sound, as a rush of air.

whop-per (hwop´ėr) *n.* Something of extra ordinary size. *Slang* A lie.

whore (hōr) *n.* A prostitute.

who's *contr.* Who is; who has.

whose (hŏz) *pron.* Belonging to or having to do with one's belongings. *adj.* Relating to *which* or *whom*.

why (hwī) *adj.* For what reason or purpose. *conj.* The cause, purpose, or reason for which. *interj.* Expressing surprise or disagreement.

WI *abbr.* Wisconsin.

wick (wik) *n.* The soft strand of fibers which extends from a candle or lamp and draws up the fuel for burning.

wick-er (wik´ėr) *n.* A thin, pliable twig used to make furniture and baskets.

wick-et (wik´it) *n.* A wire hoop in the game of croquet; a small door, window, or opening used as a box office.

wide (wīd) *adj.* Broad; covering a large area; completely extended or open. *adv.* Over a large area; full extent.

wide-spread (wīd´spred´) *adj.* Fully spread out; over a broad area.

wid-ow (wid´ō) *n.* A woman whose husband is no longer living.

wid-ow-er (wid´ō ėr) *n.* A man whose wife is no longer living.

width (width) *n.* The distance or extent of something from side to side.

wield (wēld) *v.* To use or handle something skillfully; to employ power effectively.

wie-ner (wē´nėr) *n.* A frankfurter; a hot dog.

wife (wīf) *n.* A married female.

wig (wig) *n.* Artificial or human hair woven together to cover baldness or a bald spot on the head.

wig-gle (wig´l) *v.* To squirm; to move with rapid side-to-side motions. **wiggler** *n.*

wig-wam (wig´wom) *n.* An Indian dwelling place.

wild (wīld) *adj.* Living in a natural, untamed state; not occupied by man; not civilized; strange and unusual. *adv.* Out of control. *n.* A wilderness region not cultivated or settled by man.

wild-cat (wīld´kat´) *n.* A medium-sized wild, feline animal; one with a quick temper. *v.* To drill for oil or gas in an area where such products are not usually found. *adj.* Not approved or legal.

wil-der-ness (wīl´dėr nis) *n.* An unsettled area; a region left in its uncultivated or natural state.

wild-life (wīld´līf´) *n.* Animals and plants living in their natural environments.

will (wil) *n.* The mental ability to decide or choose for oneself; strong desire or determination; a legal document stating how one's property is to be distributed after death. *v.* To bring about by an act of a will; to decide as by decree; to give or bequeath something in a will.

wil-low (wil´ō) *n.* A large tree, usually having narrow leaves and slender flexible twigs.

Wilson, Woodrow *n.* (1856-1924) The 28th president of the United States from 1913-1921.

wilt (wilt) *v.* To cause or to become limp; to lose force; to deprive of courage or energy.

win (win) *v.* To defeat others; to gain victory in a contest; to receive. *n.* Victory; the act of winning. **winner** *n.*

winch (winch) *n.* An apparatus with one or more drums on which a cable or rope is wound, used to lift heavy loads.

wind (wīnd) *n.* A natural movement of air. *v.* To become short of breath. **windy** *adj.*

wind (wind) *v.* To wrap around and around something; to turn, to crank. *n.* A turning or twisting.

wind-bag (wind′bag′) *n., Slang* A person who talks excessively without saying anything of importance.

wind-fall (wind′fol′) *n.* A sudden or unexpected stroke of good luck.

wind instrument (wind′in′stru ment) *n.* A musical instrument which produces sound when a person forces his breath into it.

wind-mill (wind′mil′) *n.* A machine operated or powered by the wind.

win-dow (win′dō) *n.* An opening built into a wall for light and air; a pane of glass.

win-dow–shop (win′dō shop′) *v.* To look at merchandise in store windows without going inside to buy. **window–shopper** *n.*

wind-pipe (wind′pīp′) *n.* The passage in the neck used for breathing; the trachea.

wine (wīn) *n.* A drink containing 10-15% alcohol by volume, made by fermenting grapes.

wing (wing) *n.* One of the movable appendages that allow a bird or insect to fly; one of the airfoils on either side of an aircraft, allowing it to glide or travel through the air. *v.* To move as if on wings; to fly.

wing-spread (wing′spred′) *n.* The extreme measurement from the tips or outer edges of the wings of an aircraft, bird, or other insect.

wink (wingk) *v.* To shut one eye as a signal or message; to blink rapidly. *n.* The act of winking; a short period of rest; a nap.

win-ning (win′ing) *adj.* Defeating others; captivating. *n.* Victory.

win-some (win′som) *adj.* Very pleasant; charming.

win-ter (win′tėr) *n.* The coldest season, coming between autumn and spring. *adj.* Relating to or typically of winter.

win-ter-green (win′tėr grēn′) *n.* A small plant having aromatic evergreen leaves which yield an oil, used as flavoring or medicine.

wipe (wīp) *v.* To clean by rubbing; to take off by rubbing. *n.* The act or instance of wiping.

wire (wīėr) *n.* A small metal rod used to conduct electricity; thin strands of metal twisted together to form a cable; the telephone or telegraph system; the finish line of a race. *v.* To equip with wiring. *Slang* To convey a message by telegram or telegraph; something completed at the last possible time.

Wis-con-sin *n.* A state located in the north central part of the United States; statehood May 29, 1848; state capital Madison.

wis-dom (wiz′dom) *n.* The ability to understand what is right, true, or enduring; good judgment; knowledge.

wise (wīz) *adj.* Having superior intelligence; having great learning; having a capacity for sound judgment marked by deep understanding. **wisely** *adv.*

wise-crack (wīz′krak′) *n. Slang* A witty remark or joke usually showing a lack of respect.

wish (wish) *v.* To desire or long for something; to command or request. *n.* A longing or desire.

wish-bone (wish′bōn′) *n.* The bone of a bird, which, according to the superstition, when broken brings good luck to the person who has the longer end.

wish-ful (wish′ful) *adj.* Having or expressing a wish; hopeful. **wishfully** *adv.*

wish-y–wash-y (wish′ē wosh′ē) *adj. , Slang* Not purposeful; indecisive.

wisp (wisp) *n.* A tuft or small bundle of hay, straw, or hair; a thin piece. **wispy** *adj.*

wit (wit) *n.* The ability to use words in a clever way; a sense of humor.

witch (wich) *n.* A person believed to have magical powers; a mean, ugly, old woman.

with (with) In the company of; near or

alongside; having, wearing or bearing; in the judgment or opinion of; containing; in the possession or care of; supporting; a-mong; occurring at the same time. *v.* To take away or back; to retreat.

with-draw (with dro´) *v.* To take away; to take back; to remove; to retreat.

with-draw-al (with dro´al) *n.* The process of withdrawing; a retreat; the act of re-moving money from an account; the process of discontinuing or no longer using a drug which is addictive.

with-hold (with hōld´) *n.* To hold back or keep.

withholding tax *n.* The tax on income held back by an employer in payment of one's income tax.

with-in (with in´) *adv.* Inside the inner part; inside the limits; inside the limits of time, distance, or degree. *n.* An inside area.

with-out (with out´) *adv.* On the outside; not in possession of. *prep.* Something or someone lacking.

with-stand (with stand´) *v.* To endure.

wit-ness (wit´nis) *n.* A person who has seen, experienced, or heard something; something serving as proof or evidence. *v.* To see or hear something; to give proof or evidence of; to give testimony.

wit-ty (wit´ē) *adj.* Amusing or cleverly humorous.

wiz-ard (wiz´ėrd) *n.* A very clever person; a person thought to have magical powers. *Slang* One with amazing skill.

wob-ble (wob´l) *v.* To move unsteadily from side to side, as a rocking motion.

woe (wō) *n.* Great sorrow or grief; misfor-tune.

wok *n.* A convex metal cooker for stir-frying food.

woke *v.* Past tense of wake.

wolf (welf) *n.* A carnivorous animal found in northern areas; a fierce person. *v.* To eat quickly and with greed. **wolfish** *adj.* **wolf-ishly** *adv.*

woman (wem´an) *n.* The mature adult human female; a person who has feminine qualities.

womanhood (wem´an hed´) *n.* The state of being a woman.

womb (wōm) *n.* The uterus; the place where development occurs.

won (wun) *v.* Past tense of win.

won-der (wun´dėr) *n.* A feeling of amaze-ment or admiration. *v.* To feel admiration; to feel uncertainty. **wonderful** *adj.*

won-der-ment (wun´dėr ment) *n.* A feeling or state of amazement.

won-drous (wun´drus) *adj.* Wonderful; marvelous.

won't (wōnt) *contr.* Will not.

won-ton *n.* A noodle dumpling filled with minced pork and served in soup.

wood (wed) *n.* The hard substance which makes up the main part of trees. *adj.* Made of wood. **woods** A growth of trees smaller than a forest.

wood-chuck (wed´chuk´) *n.*A rodent having short legs and a heavyset body, which lives in a burrow.

wood-en (wed´en) *adj.* Made of wood; resembl-ing wood; stiff; lifeless; lacking flexibility. **wood-enly** *adv.*

wood-peck-er (wed´pek´ėr) *n.* A bird which uses its bill for drilling holes in trees looking for insects to eat.

wood-wind (wed´wind´) *n.* Musical instruments which produce sounds when air is blown through the mouthpiece, as the clarinet, flute, and oboe.

wool (wel) *n.* The soft, thick hair of sheep and other such mammals; a fabric made from such hair.

word (werd) *n.* A meaningful sound which stands for an idea; a comment; a brief talk; an order or command. *v.* To express orally. **wording** *n.*

word processing *n.* A system which pro-duces typewritten documents with auto-mated type and editing equipment.

work (werk) *n.* The action or labor required to accomplish something; employment; a job; a project or assignment; something requiring physical or mental effort. *v*. To engage in mental or physical exertion; to labor to have a job; to arrange.

work-book (werk´bek´) *n*. A book containing exercises and problems designed to be written in; usually advancing in difficulty from kindergarten through grade 6; ranging in subjects as math, reading, spelling, science.

work-er (wer´ker) *n*. A person who works for wages; an employee; a bee or other insect which performs special work in the colony in which it lives.

work-ing (wer´king) *adj*. Adequate to permit work to be done; assumed to permit further work.

work-man-ship (werk´man ship´) *n*. The skill or art of a craftsman; the quality given to something in the process of making it.

work-out (werk´out´) *n*. A period of strenuous exercise.

world (werld) *n*. The planet Earth; the universe; the human race; a field of human interest or effort.

worldly (werld´le) *adj*. Interested in pleasure rather than religious or spiritual matters.

worm (werm) *n*. A small, thin animal having a long, flexible, rounded or flattened body. *Slang* A crude person.

worn (worn) *adj*. Made weak or thin from use; exhausted.

wor-ry (wer´e) *v*. To be concerned or troubled; to tug at repeatedly; to annoy; to irritate. *n*. Distress or mental anxiety.

wor-ship (wer´ship) *n*. Reverence for a sacred object; high esteem or devotion for a person. *v*. To revere; attend a religious service. **worshiper** *n*.

worst (werst) *adj*. Bad; most inferior; most disagreeable. *adv*. In the worst degree.

worth (werth) *n*. The quality or value of something; personal merit; the quantity that can be purchased for a certain amount of money.

wor-thy (wer´the) *adj*. Valuable or useful; deserving admiration or honor.

would-n't (wed´nt) *contr*. Would not.

wound (wond) *n*. A laceration of the skin. *v*. To injure by tearing, cutting, or piercing the skin.

wow (wou) *interj*. An expression of amazement, surprise, or excitement.

wran-gle (rang´gl) *v*. To quarrel noisily. **wrangler** *n*.

wrap (rap) *v*. To fold in order to protect something; to encase or enclose. *n*. A coat, shawl, or other outer protection. *Slang* To finish doing something, to finish producing or making something.

wrath (rath) *n*. Violent anger or fury.

wreak (rek) *v*. To inflict punishment upon another person.

wreath (reth) *n*. A decorative ring-like form of intertwined flowers, bows, and other articles.

wreck (rek) *v*. To ruin or damage by accident or deliberately; to spoil. *n*. Destruction; the remains of something wrecked or ruined; someone in poor condition.

wren (ren) *n*. A small brown songbird having a slender beak, short tail, and rounded wings.

wrench (rench) *n*. A tool used to grip, turn, or twist an object as a bolt or nut. *v*. To turn or twist violently; to give emotional pain.

wrest (rest) *v*. To twist or pull away in a violent way. *n*. A forcible twist.

wres-tle (res´l) *v*. To struggle with an opponent in order to pin him down. *n*. The instance of wrestling. **wrestler** *n*.

wretch (rech) *n*. An extremely unhappy person; a miserable person. **wretched** *adj*.

wrig-gle (rig´l) *v*. To squirm; to move by turning and twisting.

wring (ring) *v*. To squeeze and twist by hand or machine; to press together.

wrin-kle (ring´kl) *n*. A small crease on the skin or on fabric. *v*. To have or make wrinkles.

wrist (rist) *n*., *Anat*. The joint of the body between the hand and forearm; the part of a sleeve which encircles the wrist.

wrist-watch *n*. A timepiece worn on the wrist.

writ (rit) *n.*, *Law* A written court document directed to a public official or individual ordering a specific action.

write (rīt) *v.* To form symbols or letters; to form words on a surface; to communicate by writing; to earn a living by writing books.

write down *v.* To record in writing; to put visually on paper or another surface.

writer's cramp *n.* A muscle contraction, causing pain in the fingers or hands.

writhe (rīth) *v.* To twist, as in pain; to suffer greatly with pain.

writ-ing (rī'ting) *n.* A book or other written work; handwriting; the process of forming letters into words; the occupation of a writer.

wrong (rong) *adj.* Incorrect; against moral standards; not suitable; immoral; unsuitable; in appropriate. *n.* An act which is wicked or immoral. *v.* To do wrong; to injure or hurt. **wrongly** *adv.*

wrote *v.* Past tense of write.

wrought (rot) *adj.* Fashioned; formed; beatened or hammered into shape.

wrung *v.* Past tense of wring.

WV *abbr.* West Virginia.

WY *abbr.* Wyoming.

Wy-o-ming *n.* A state located in the western part of the United States; statehood July 10, 1890; state capital Cheyenne.

X

X, x (eks) The twenty-fourth letter of the English alphabet.

Xan-a-du (zan' a du) *n.* A place having idyllic beauty.

xan-thate (zan'thāt) *n.* Ester or slat of a xanthic acid.

xan-thic (zan'thik) *adj.* The color yellow or all colors that tend toward the color yellow when relating to flowers.

xan-thin (zan'thin) *n.* A carotinoid pigment that is soluble in alcohol.

xan-thine (zan'thēn) *n.* A crystalline nitrogen compound, closely related to uric acid, found in blood, urine, and certain plant and animal tissues.

xan-tho-chroid (zan'tho kroid") *adj.* Pertaining to the light-complexioned Caucasoid race.

xan-tho-ma (zan thō'ma) *n.* A skin condition of the eyelids marked by small, yellow, raised nodules or plates.

X chro-mo-some (eks'krō'mosōm) *n.* The sex female chromosome, associated with female characteristics; occurs paired in the female and single in the male chromosome pair.

xe-bec (zē'bek) *n.* A small vessel with three masts having both lateen and square sails.

xe-nic *adj.* Relating to, or employing a culture medium that contains one or more unidentified organisms.

xe-non (zē'non) *n.* The colorless, odorless gaseous element found in small quantities in the air, symbolized by Xe.

xe-no-phile *n.* One attracted to foreign people, styles, manners, etc.

xen-o-phobe (zen'o fōb') *n.* A person who dislikes, fears, and mistrusts foreigners or anything stranger. **xenophobia** *n.*

xe-rarch (zērärk) *adj.* Originating or developing in a dry place.

xe-ric (zēr'ik) *adj.* Relating to or requiring only a small amount of moisture. **xerically** *adv.*

xe-roph-i-lous (zi rof'i lus) *adj.* Tolerant or characteristic of xeric environments. **xerophily** *n.*

xe-roph-thal-mi-a (zēr'of thal'mē a) *n.* An itching soreness of the eyes that is caused by an insufficient amount of vitamin A.

xe-ro-phyte (zēr'o fīt") *n.* A plant that can live in a surrounding of extreme heat and drought. **xerophytic** *adj.* **xerophytically** *adv.* **xerophytism** *n.*

XL *abbr.* Extra large.

X-mas (eks'mas) *abbr.*, *n.* Christmas.

X–Ra-di-a-tion *n.* Treatment with X-rays.

X ray (eks'rā') *n.* Energy that is radiated with a short wavelength and high penetrating power; a black and white negative image or picture of the interior of the body.

x–sec-tion *n.* Cross section of something. **x–sectional** *adj.*

xy-lo-phone (zī´lo fōn´) *n.* A musical instrument consisting of mounted wooden bars which produce a ringing musical sound when struck with two small wooden hammers. **xylophonist** *n.*

xy-lose (zī´lōs) *n., Chem.* A crystalline aldose sugar.

xy-lot-o-mous (zī lot´o mus) *adj.* Capable of cutting or boring wood. **xylotomic** *adj.*

Y

Y, y (wī) The twenty-fifth letter of the English alphabet.

yacht (yot) *n.* A small sailing vessel powered by wind or motor, used for pleasure cruises. **yacht** *v.*

yacht-ing (yot´ing) *n.* The sport of sailing in a yacht.

yachts-man (yots´man) *n.* A person who sails a yacht. **yachtsmanship** *n.*

yak (yak) *n.* A long haired ox of Tibet and the mountains of central Asia.

yam (yam) *n.* An edible root; a variety of the sweet potato.

Yan-kee (yang´kē) *n.* A native of the northern United States. **Yankee** *adj.*

yap (yap) *v.* To bark in a high pitched, sharp way. *Slang* To talk in a relentless, loud, or stupid manner.

yard (yärd) *n.* A unit of measure that equals 36 inches or 3 feet; the ground around or near a house or building.

yard goods *n.* Fabric that is sold by the yard.

yard-man (yärd´man) *n.* A person employed as a worker in a railroad yard.

yard-mas-ter (yärd´mas˝tèr) *n.* A person in charge of a railroad yard.

yard-stick (yärd´stik´) *n.* A graduated measuring stick that equals 1 yard or 36 inches.

yarn (yarn) *n.* Twisted fibers, as of wool, used in knitting or weaving. *Slang* An involved tale or story.

yawn (yon) *v.* To inhale a deep breath with the mouth open wide. **yawner** *n.*

yawn-ing (yo´ning) *adj.* Expressing tiredness by a yawn.

Y-Chro-mo-some (wī´krō´mosōm) *n.* The sex chromosome associated with male characteristics.

ye (yē) *pron.* You, used especially in religious contexts, as hymns.

yea (yā) *adv.* Yes; indeed; truly.

yeah *adv., Slang* Yes.

year (yēr) *n.* A period of time starting on January 1st and continuing through December 31st, consisting of 365 days or 366 days in a leap year, which occurs every four years.

year-book (yēr´būk˝) *n.* A book printed each year giving facts about the year; a book printed each year for a high school, college, etc.

year-ling (yēr´ling) *n.* An animal that is one year old.

year-ly (yēr´lē) *adj.* Pertaining to something that happens, appears, or comes once a year, every year.

yearn (yern) *v.* To feel a strong craving.

year–round *adj.* Lasting or continuing for an entire year.

yeast (yēst) *n.* Fungi or plant cells used to make baked goods rise or fruit juices ferment.

yell (yel) *v.* To cry out loudly. *n.* A loud cry; a cheer to show support for an athletic team.

yel-low (yel´ō) *n.* The bright color of a lemon; the yolk of an egg. *v.* To make or become yellow. *adj.* Of the color yellow. *Slang* Cowardly.

yellow fever *n.* An acute infectious disease of the tropics, spread by the bite of a mosquito.

yellow jacket *n.* A small wasp that has

bright yellow markings and usually makes its nest below ground level.

yelp *n.* A quick, sharp, shrill cry, as from pain.

yen (yen) *n.* An intense craving or longing.

yeo-man (yō´man) *n.* The owner of a small farm; a petty officer who acts as a clerk.

yeo-man-ly *n.* The rank of a yoeman; befitting a yeoman.

Yeoman's service *n.* Useful, good, or substantial service.

yes (yes) *adv.* To express agreement or consent.

yes-ter-day (yes´tĕr dē) *n.* The day before today; a former or recent time. *adv.* On the day before the present day.

yes-ter-year *n.* Time just recently past; last year.

yet (yet) *adv.* Up to now; at this time; even now; more so. *conj.* Nevertheless; but.

yet-i *n.* The abominable snowman.

yew (ū) *n.* An evergreen tree having poisonous flat, dark-green needles and poisonous red berries.

Yid-dish (yid´ish) *n.* A language spoken by Jews combining German and Hebrew; spoken by Jews. **Yiddish** *adj.*

yield (yēld) *v.* To bear or bring forward; to give up the possession of something; to give way to. *n.* An amount that is produced; the act of prducing.

yield-ing (yēl´ding) *adj.* Ready to yield, comply, or submit; unresisting. **yieldingly** *adv.*

YMCA (wī´em´sē´ā´) *n., abbr.* Young Men's Christian Association.

yo-del (yōd´el) *v.* To sing in a way so that the voice changes from normal to a high shrill sound and then back again.

yo-ga (yō´ga) *n.* A system of exercises which helps the mind and the body in order to achieve tranquillity and spiritual insight.

yo-gurt (yō´gĕrt) *n.* A thick custard-like food made from curdled milk and often mixed with fruit.

yoke (yōk) *n.* A wooden bar used to join together two oxen or other animals working together; the section of a garment fit-

ting closely around the shoulders. *v.* To join with a yoke.

yo-kel (yōkel) *n.* A very unsophisticated country person; a bumpkin.

yolk (yōk) *n.* The yellow nutritive part of an egg.

Yom Kip-pur (yom kip´ĕr) *n.* The Jewish holiday observed with fasting and prayer for the forgiveness of sins.

you (ū) *pron.* The person or persons addressed.

you all (ū ol´) *pron., Slang* **y'all** A southern variation used for two or more people in direct address.

you'd (ūd) *contr.* You had; you would.

you'll (ūl) *contr.* You will; you shall.

young (yung) *adj.* Of or relating to the early stage of life; not old. *n.* The offspring of an animal. **youngster** *n.*

your (yer) *adj.* Belonging to you or yourself or the person spoken to.

you're (ūr) *contr.* You are.

your-self (yer self´) *pron.* A form of you for emphasis when the object of a verb and the subject is the same.

youth (ūth) *n.* The appearance or state of being young; the time of life when one is not considered an adult; a young person.

youth-ful (ūth´ful) *adj.* Being of a young age or early stage in life. **youthfully** *adv.*

you've (ūv) *contr.* You have.

yowl (youl) *v.* To make a loud, long cry or howl. **yowl** *n.*

yo-yo (yō´yō) *n.* A grooved spool toy with a string wrapped around the spool so it can be spun or moved up and down.

yt-ter-bi-um (i ter´bē um) *n.* A metallic element of the rare-earth group symbolized by Yb.

yt-tri-um (i´trē um) *n.* A metallic element symbolized by Y.

yuc-ca (yuk´a) *n.* A tropical plant having large, white flowers and long, pointed leaves.

yule (ūl) *n.* Christmas.

yule-tide (ūl´tīd´) *n.* The Christmas season.

YWCA *abbr., n.* Young Women's Christian Association.

YWHA *abbr.*, *n.* Young Women's Hebrew Association.

Z

Z, z (zē) The twenty-sixth letter of the English alphabet.

za-ny (zā′nē) *n. pl.* **-nies** A clown; a person who acts silly or foolish. *adj.* Typical of being clownish. **zaniness** *n.* **zannily** *adv.*

zap *v.*, *Slang* To destroy; to do away with.

zeal (zēl) *n.* Great interest or eagerness.

zeal-ot (zel′ot) *n.* A fanatical person; a fanatic.

zeal-ous (zel′us) *adj.* Full of interest; eager; passionate. **zealously** *adv.*

ze-bra (zē′bra) *n.* An African mammal of the horse family having black or brown stripes on a white body.

zeph-yr (zef′ėr) *n.* A gentle breeze.

ze-ro (zēr′ō) *n. pl.* **-ros, -roes** The number or symbol "0"; nothing; the point from which degrees or measurements on a scale begin; the lowest point. *v.* To aim, point at, or close in on. *adj.* Pertaining to zero; nonexisting.

zest (zest) *n.* Enthusiasm; a keen quality. **zestful** *adj.* **zestfully** *adj.* **zesty** *adj.*

zig-zag (zig′zag′) *n.* A pattern with sharp turns in alternating directions. *adv.* To move in a zigzag course or path.

zilch *n.*, *Slang* Nothing; zero.

zil-lion (zil′yon) *n.*, *Slang* An extremely large number.

zinc (zingk) *n.* A bluish-white crystalline metallic element, used as a protective coating for steel and iron, symbolized by Zn.

Zi-on (zī′on) *n.* The Jewish homeland, symbolic of Judaism; the Jewish people.

zip (zip) *n.* To act or move with vigor or speed. *v.* To move with energy, speed, or facility; to open or close with a zipper. *Slang* Energy; zero; nothing.

zip code *n.* The system to speed the delivery of mail by assigning a five digit number, plus four to each postal delivery location in the United States.

zip-per (zip′ėr) *n.* A fastener consisting of two rows of plastic or metal teeth that are interlocked by means of sliding a tab.

zir-co-ni-um (zėr kō′nē um) *n.* A metallic element symbolized by Zr.

zit *n.*, *Slang* A pimple.

zo-di-ac (zō′dē ak′) *n.* The celestial sphere; the unseen path followed through the heavens by the moon, sun, and most planets; this area divided into twelve parts or twelve astrological signs, each bearing the name of a constellation.

zom-bie (zom′bē) *n.* A person who resembles the walking dead, as a supernatural power; a person who has a strange appearance or behavior.

zone (zōn) *n.* An area or region set apart from its surroundings by some characteristic.

zonk *v.*, *Slang* To stun; to render senseless with alcohol or drugs.

zoo (zō) *n.*, *pl.* **zoos** A public display or collection of living animals.

zo-ol-o-gy (zō ol′o jē) *n.* The science that deals with animals, animal life, and the animal kingdom. **zoologist** *n.*

zoom (zōm) *v.* To move with a continuous, loud, buzzing sound; to move upward sharply; to move toward a subject with great speed.

zuc-chi-ni (zō kē′nē) *n. pl.* **-ni** A summer squash that is long and narrow and has a dark-green, smooth rind.

zwie-back (zwī′bak′) *n.* A sweetened bread which is baked, sliced, and toasted to make it crisp.

zy-mol-o-gy (zī mol′o jē) *n.* The branch of science dealing with ferments and fermentation. **zymologic** *n.*

zy-mo-scope (zī′mo skōp) *n.* An instrument that measures yeast's fermenting power.

zy-mot-ic (zī mot′ik) *adj.* Relating or pertaining to fermentation.

zy-mur-gy (zī′mer jē) *n.* The chemistry that deals with the fermentation processes.

THESAURUS

DEFINITION OF THESAURUS

SYNONYMS:

Words having the same meaning.

Example:

Always *(SYN.)* eternally, everlasting, forever.

ANTONYMS:

Words having the opposite meaning.

Example:

Always *(ANT.)* never, occasionally, sometimes.

a *(SYN.)* any, one.

abandon *(SYN.)* relinquish, resign, surrender, leave, give up, cease, forsake, waive, desert, quit, vacate, abjure, entirely, abdicate, leave undone, discard, evacuate, wicked, deserted, desolate, forsaken, rejected, cast off, profligate, loose, unrestrained, marooned.

(ANT.) support, keep, fulfill, uphold, depend, stay, maintain, embrace, cherish, favor, adopt, join, engage, unite, retain.

abandoned *(SYN.)* depraved, deserted.

(ANT.) befriended, cherished, chaste, moral, respectable, virtuous, righteous.

abase *(SYN.)* make humble, reduce, bring down, degrade, demote, mock, scorn, belittle, shame, despise, humiliate.

(ANT.) exalt, cherish, elevate, uplift, respect, dignify.

abash *(SYN.)* disconcert, bewilder, confuse, discompose, nonplus.

(ANT.) comfort, relax, hearten, nerve.

abashed *(SYN.)* confused, ashamed, embarrassed, humiliated.

abate *(SYN.)* lessen, curtail, reduce, decrease, restrain, decline, stop, moderate, subside, slow, diminish, slacken.

(ANT.) grow, prolong, increase, extend, quicken, enhance, accelerate.

abbey *(SYN.)* nunnery, convent, cloisters, monastery.

abbot *(SYN.)* friar, monk.

abbreviate *(SYN.)* shorten, lessen, abridge, condense, curtail, reduce, cut, compress, trim, restrict, clip.

(ANT.) lengthen, increase, expand, extend, prolong, enlarge, augment.

abbreviation *(SYN.)* abridgment, reduction, condensation.

(ANT.) expansion, amplification, lengthening, dilation.

abdicate *(SYN.)* relinquish, renounce, vacate, waive, desert, abolish, quit, abandon, resign.

(ANT.) maintain, defend, stay, retain, uphold.

abdomen *(SYN.)* paunch, belly, stomach.

abduct *(SYN.)* take, kidnap.

aberrant *(SYN.)* capricious, devious, irregular, unnatural, abnormal, unusual.

(ANT.) methodical, regular, usual, fixed, ordinary.

aberration *(SYN.)* oddity, abnormality, irregularity, deviation, quirk, abortion, eccentricity.

(ANT.) norm, conformity, standard, normality.

abet *(SYN.)* support, connive, encourage, conspire, help, incite, aid, assist.

(ANT.) deter, check, hinder, frustrate, oppose, discourage, resist.

abettor *(SYN.)* accomplice, ally, confederate, associate, accessory.

(ANT.) opponent, rival, enemy.

abeyance *(SYN.)* inaction, cessation, pause, inactivity, rest, recess, dormancy, remission.

(ANT.) ceaselessness, continuation.

abhor *(SYN.)* dislike, hate, loathe, execrate, avoid, scorn, detest, despise.

abhorrent *(SYN.)* loathsome, horrible, detestable, nauseating, hateful, despicable, disgusting, foul, offensive, terrible, revolting.

abide *(SYN.)* obey, accept, tolerate, endure, dwell, stay, reside.

ability *(SYN.)* aptness, capability, skill, dexterity, faculty, power, talent, aptitude, efficiency, aptitude, capacity, effectiveness,

(ANT.) incapacity, incompetency, ineptitude, inability, disability.

abject *(SYN.)* sordid, infamous, wretched, mean, base, contempt.

abjure *(SYN.)* relinquish, renounce, vacate, waive, desert, quit, leave, forsake, forewear, abdicate, resign, surrender.

(ANT.) cling to, maintain, uphold, stay.

able *(SYN.)* qualified, competent, fit, capable, skilled, having power, efficient, clever, talented, adequate, skillful.

(ANT.) inadequate, trained, efficient, incapable, weak, incompetent, unable.

abnegation *(SYN.)* rejection, renunciation, abandonment, refusal, relinquishment, abjuration.

abnormal *(SYN.)* uncommon, unnatural, odd, irregular, eccentric, insane, unusual, weird, strange.

(ANT.) standard, natural, usual, normal, average.

aboard *(SYN.)* on board.

abode *(SYN.)* dwelling, habitat, hearth, home, residence, address, quarters, lodging place, domicile.

abolish *(SYN.)* end, eradicate, annul, cancel, revoke, destroy, invalidate, overthrow, obliterate, abrogate, erase, eliminate.

(ANT.) promote, restore, continue, establish, sustain.

abominable *(SYN.)* foul, dreadful, hateful, revolting, vile, odious, loathsome, detestable, bad, horrible, terrible, awful, nasty, obnoxious, disgusting, unpleasant.

(ANT.) delightful, pleasant, agreeable, commendable, admirable, noble, fine.

abominate *(SYN.)* despise, detest, hate, dislike, abhor, loathe.

(ANT.) love, like, cherish, approve, admire.

abomination *(SYN.)* detestation, hatred, disgust, loathing, revulsion, antipathy, horror.

abort *(SYN.)* flop, fizzle, miscarry, abandon, cancel.

abortion *(SYN.)* fiasco, disaster, failure, defeat.

abortive *(SYN.)* unproductive, vain, unsuccessful, failed, futile.

(ANT.) rewarding, effective, profitable, successful.

abound *(SYN.)* swarm, plentiful, filled, overflow, teem.

(ANT.) scarce, lack.

about *(SYN.)* relating to, involving, concerning, near, around, upon, almost, approximately, of, close to, nearby, ready to, nearly.

about-face *(SYN.)* reversal, backing out, shift, switch.

above *(SYN.)* higher than, overhead, on, upon, over, superior to.

(ANT.) under, beneath, below.

aboveboard *(SYN.)* open, frank, honest, overt, plain, straightforward, guileless, trustworthy.

(ANT.) underhand, ambiguous, sneaky, wily.

abracadabra *(SYN.)* voodoo, magic, charm, spell.

abrasion *(SYN.)* rubbing, roughness, scratching, scraping, friction, chap, chafe, scrape.

abrasive *(SYN.)* hurtful, sharp, galling, annoying, grating, cutting, irritating, caustic.

(ANT.) pleasant, soothing, comforting, agreeable.

abreast *(SYN.)* beside, side by side, alongside.

abridge *(SYN.)* condense, cut, abbreviate, contract, shorten, reduce, summarize, curtail.

(ANT.) increase, lengthen, expand, extend.

abridgment *(SYN.)* digest, condensation, summary, abbreviation.

(ANT.) lengthening, expansion, enlargement.

abroad *(SYN.)* away, overseas, broadly, widely.

(ANT.) at home, privately, secretly.

abrogate *(SYN.)* rescind, withdraw, revoke, annul, cancel, repeal.

abrupt *(SYN.)* sudden, unexpected, blunt, curt, craggy, precipitous, sharp, hasty, unannounced, harsh, precipitate, brusque, rude, rough, short, steep.

(ANT.) foreseen, smooth, warm, courteous, gradual, smooth, expected, anticipated.

abscess *(SYN.)* pustule, sore, wound, inflammation.

absence *(SYN.)* nonexistence, deficiency, need, shortcoming.

(ANT.) attendance, completeness, existence, presence.

absent *(SYN.)* away, truant, abroad, departed, inattentive, lacking, not present, out, off.

(ANT.) attending, attentive watchful, present.

absentminded *(SYN.)* inattentive, daydreaming, preoccupied, absorbed, distrait, forgetful.

(ANT.) observant, attentive, alert.

absolute *(SYN.)* unconditional, entire, actual, complete, thorough, total, perfect, essential, supreme, ultimate, unrestricted, positive, unqualified, whole.

(ANT.) partial, conditional, dependent accountable, restricted, qualified, limited, fragmentary, imperfect, incomplete.

absolutely *(SYN.)* positively, really, doubtlessly.

(ANT.) doubtfully, uncertainly.

absolution *(SYN.)* pardon, forgiveness, acquittal, mercy, dispensation, amnesty, remission.

absolutism *(SYN.)* autarchy, dictatorship,

absolve *(SYN.)* exonerate, discharge, acquit, pardon, forgive, clear, excuse.
(ANT.) blame, convict, charge, accuse.

absorb *(SYN.)* consume, swallow up, engulf, assimilate, imbibe, engage, engross, take in, integrate, incorporate, occupy.
(ANT.) discharge, dispense, emit, exude, leak, eliminate, bore, tire, weary, drain.

absorbent *(SYN.)* permeable, spongy, pervious, porous.
(ANT.) moisture proof, waterproof, impervious.

absorbing *(SYN.)* engaging, exciting, engrossing, entertaining, thrilling, intriguing, pleasing, fascinating.
(ANT.) dull, boring, tedious, tiresome.

abstain *(SYN.)* forbear, forego, decline, resist, hold back, withhold, refrain.
(ANT.) pursue.

abstemious *(SYN.)* abstinent, sparing, cautious, temperate, ascetic, self-disciplined, continent, sober.
(ANT.) uncontrolled, indulgent, abandoned, excessive.

abstinence *(SYN.)* fasting, self-denial, continence, forbearance, sobriety, refrain, abstention.
(ANT.) gluttony, greed, excess, self-indulgence, pursue.

abstract *(SYN.)* part, appropriate, steal, remove, draw from, separate, purloin, unconcrete, abridge, summarize.
(ANT.) return, concrete, unite, add, replace, specific, clear, particular, restore.

abstracted *(SYN.)* parted, removed, stolen, abridged, taken away.
(ANT.) replaced, returned, alert, united, added.

abstraction *(SYN.)* idea, image, generalization, thought, opinion, impression, notion.
(ANT.) matter, object, thing, substance.

abstruse *(SYN.)* arcane, obscure, complicated, abstract, refined, mandarin, esoteric, metaphysical.
(ANT.) uncomplicated, direct, obvious, simple.

absurd *(SYN.)* ridiculous, silly, unreasonable, foolish, irrational, nonsensical, impossible, inconsistent, preposterous, self-contradictory, unbelievable.
(ANT.) rational, sensible, sound, meaningful, consistent, reasonable.

absurdity *(SYN.)* foolishness, nonsense, farce, drivel, joke, paradox, senselessness, folly.

abundance *(SYN.)* ampleness, profusion, large amount, copiousness, plenty.
(ANT.) insufficiency, want, absence, dearth, scarcity.

abundant *(SYN.)* ample, overflowing, plentiful, rich, teeming, large amount, profuse, abounding.
(ANT.) insufficient, scant, not enough, scarce, deficient, rare, uncommon, absent.

abuse *(SYN.)* maltreatment, misuse, reproach, defamation, dishonor, mistreat, damage, ill-use, reviling, aspersion, desecration, invective, insult, outrage, profanation, perversion, upbraiding, disparagement, misemploy, misapply, hurt, harm, injure, scold, berate.
(ANT.) plaudit, respect, appreciate, commendation. protect, praise, cherish.

abusive *(SYN.)* harmful, insulting, libelous, hurtful, slanderous, nasty, defamatory, injurious, scathing, derogatory.
(ANT.) supportive, helpful, laudatory, complimentary.

abut *(SYN.)* touch, border, meet, join, verge on, connect with.

abutment *(SYN.)* pier, buttress, bulwark, brace, support.

abysmal *(SYN.)* immeasurable, boundless, endless, stupendous, profound, unbelievable, infinite, overwhelming, consummate.

abyss *(SYN.)* depth, chasm, void, infinitude, limbo, unknowable.

academic *(SYN.)* learned, scholarly, theoretical, erudite, bookish, formal, pedantic.
(ANT.) ignorant, practical, simple, uneducated.

academy *(SYN.)* college, school.

accede *(SYN.)* grant, agree, comply, consent, yield, endorse, accept, admit.
(ANT.) dissent, disagree, differ, oppose.

accelerate *(SYN.)* quicken, dispatch, facilitate, hurry, rush, speed up, forward, hasten, push, expedite.

(ANT.) hinder, retard, slow, delay, quicken.

accent *(SYN.)* tone, emphasis, inflection, stress, consent.

accept *(SYN.)* take, approve, receive, allow, consent to, believe, adopt, admit.

(ANT.) ignore, reject, refuse.

acceptable *(SYN.)* passable, satisfactory, fair, adequate, standard, par, tolerable, unobjectionable.

(ANT.) poor, substandard, inadmissible.

access *(SYN.)* entrance, approach, course, gateway, door, avenue.

accessible *(SYN.)* nearby, attainable, achievable, affable, democratic, accommodating.

(ANT.) remote, unobtainable, unachievable, standoffish, forbidding, unfriendly.

accessory *(SYN.)* extra, addition, assistant, supplement, contributory, accomplice.

accident *(SYN.)* casualty, disaster, misfortune, mishap, chance, calamity, contingency, fortuity, misadventure, mischance, injury, event, catastrophe.

(ANT.) purpose, intention, calculation.

accidental *(SYN.)* unintended, chance, casual, fortuitous, contingent, unplanned, unexpected, unforeseen.

(ANT.) calculated, planned, willed, intended, intentional, on purpose, deliberate.

acclaim *(SYN.)* eminence, fame, glory, honor, reputation, credit, applaud, distinction, approve, notoriety.

(ANT.) infamy, obscurity, disapprove, reject, disrepute.

acclimated *(SYN.)* adapted, habituated, acclimatized, accommodated, seasoned, inured, used to, weathered, reconciled.

accolade *(SYN.)* praise, honor, acclaim, recognition, applause, kudos, bouquet, crown, testimonial, acclamation, salute.

accommodate *(SYN.)* help, assist, aid, provide for, serve, oblige, hold, house.

(ANT.) inconvenience.

accommodating *(SYN.)* obliging, helpful, willing, kind, cooperative, gracious, cordial, sympathetic, unselfish.

(ANT.) unfriendly, selfish, hostile, uncooperative.

accommodation *(SYN.)* change, alteration, adaptation, convenience, adjustment, acclimatization, aid, help, boon, kindness, service, courtesy.

(ANT.) inflexibility, rigidity, disservice, stubbornness, disadvantage.

accommodations *(SYN.)* housing, lodgings, room, place, quarters, board.

accompany *(SYN.)* chaperon, consort with, escort, go with, associate with, attend, join.

(ANT.) abandon, quit, leave, desert, avoid, forsake.

accomplice *(SYN.)* accessory, ally, associate, partner in crime, assistant, sidekick, confederate.

(ANT.) opponent, rival, enemy, adversary.

accomplish *(SYN.)* attain, consummate, achieve, do, execute, carry out, fulfill, complete, effect, perform, finish.

(ANT.) fail, frustrate, spoil, neglect, defeat.

accomplished *(SYN.)* proficient, skilled, finished, well-trained, gifted, masterly, polished, able.

(ANT.) unskilled, amateurish, crude.

accomplishment *(SYN.)* deed, feat, statute, operation, performance, action, achievement, transaction.

(ANT.) cessation, inhibition, intention, deliberation.

accord *(SYN.)* concur, agree, award, harmony, conformity, agreement, give, tale, sum, statement, record, grant.

(ANT.) difference, quarrel, disagreement.

accordingly *(SYN.)* consequently, therefore, hence, so, thus.

accost *(SYN.)* approach, greet, speak to, address.

(ANT.) avoid, shun.

account *(SYN.)* description, chronicle, history, narration, reckoning, rate, computation, detail, narrative, relation, recital, consider, believe, deem, record, explanation, report, tale, story, anecdote, reason, statement, tale, ledger.

(ANT.) confusion, misrepresentation, distortion.

accountable *(SYN.)* chargeable, answerable, beholden, responsible, obliged, liable.

account for *(SYN.)* justify, explain, substantiate, illuminate, clarify, elucidate.

accredited *(SYN.)* qualified, licensed, deputized, certified, commissioned, vouched for, empowered.

(ANT.) illicit, unofficial, unauthorized.

accrue *(SYN.)* amass, collect, heap, increase, accumulate, gather, hoard.

(ANT.) disperse, dissipate, waste, diminish.

accrued *(SYN.)* accumulated, totaled, increased, added, enlarged, amassed, expanded.

accumulate *(SYN.)* gather, collect, heap, increase, accrue, assemble, compile, hoard, amass.

(ANT.) spend, give away, diminish, dissipate.

accumulation *(SYN.)* heap, collection, pile, store, hoard, stack, aggregation.

accurate *(SYN.)* perfect, just, truthful, unerring, meticulous, correct, all right.

(ANT.) incorrect, mistaken, false, wrong.

accursed *(SYN.)* ill-fated, cursed, doomed, ruined.

(ANT.) fortunate, hopeful.

accusation *(SYN.)* charge, incrimination, indictment, arraignment.

(ANT.) pardon, exoneration, absolve.

accuse *(SYN.)* incriminate, indict, censure, tattle, denounce, charge, arraign, impeach, blame.

(ANT.) release, vindicate, exonerate, acquit, absolve, clear.

accustom *(SYN.)* addict, familiarize, condition.

accustomed *(SYN.)* familiar with, used to, comfortable with.

(ANT.) strange, unusual, rare, unfamiliar.

ace *(SYN.)* champion, star, king, queen, winner, head.

acerbity *(SYN.)* bitterness, harshness, unkindness, sourness, acidity, unfriendliness, acrimony, coldness, sharpness.

(ANT.) sweetness, gentleness, kindness, tenderness.

ache *(SYN.)* hurt, pain, throb.

achieve *(SYN.)* do, execute, gain, obtain, acquire, accomplish, perform, complete, accomplish, finish, fulfill, reach, attain, secure,

procure.

(ANT.) fail, lose, fall short.

achievement *(SYN.)* feat, accomplishment, attainment, exploit, realization, performance, completion, deed.

(ANT.) botch, dud, mess, omission, defeat, failure.

acid *(SYN.)* tart, sour, bitter, mordant, biting, vinegary.

(ANT.) pleasant, friendly, bland, mild, sweet.

acknowledge *(SYN.)* allow, admit, agree to, concede, recognize, answer, grant, accept, receive.

(ANT.) reject, refuse, disavow, refute, deny.

acme *(SYN.)* summit, top, zenith, peak, crown.

(ANT.) bottom.

acquaint *(SYN.)* inform, teach, enlighten, notify, tell.

acquaintance *(SYN.)* fellowship, friendship, cognizance, knowledge, intimacy, familiarity, companionship, associate, colleague, companion.

(ANT.) inexperience, unfamiliarity, ignorance.

acquiesce *(SYN.)* submit, agree, concur, assent, comply, consent, succumb.

(ANT.) refuse, disagree, rebel, argue.

acquire *(SYN.)* attain, earn, get, procure, assimilate, obtain, secure, gain, appropriate.

(ANT.) miss, surrender, lose, forego, forfeit.

acquirement *(SYN.)* training, skill, learning, achievement, attainment, education, information.

acquisition *(SYN.)* procurement, gift, purchase, proceeds, possession, grant.

acquisitive *(SYN.)* greedy, avid, hoarding, covetous.

acquit *(SYN.)* forgive, exonerate, absolve, cleanse, pardon, excuse, discharge, found not guilty.

(ANT.) doom, saddle, sentence, condemn.

acrid *(SYN.)* bitter, sharp, nasty, stinging, harsh.

(ANT.) pleasant, sweet.

acrimonious *(SYN.)* sharp, sarcastic, acerb, waspish, cutting, stinging, testy.

(ANT.) soft, kind, sweet, pleasant, soothing.

acrobat *(SYN.)* athlete, gymnast.

act *(SYN.)* deed, doing, feat, execution, accomplishment, performance, action, operation, transaction, law, decree, statute, edict, achievement, exploit, statute, judgment, routine, pretense.

(ANT.) inactivity, deliberation, intention, cessation.

acting *(SYN.)* officiating, substituting, surrogate, temporary, delegated.

action *(SYN.)* deed, achievement, feat, activity, exploit, movement, motion, play, behavior, battle, performance, exercise.

(ANT.) idleness, inertia, repose, inactivity, rest.

activate *(SYN.)* mobilize, energize, start, propel, nudge, push.

(ANT.) paralyze, immobilize, stop, deaden.

active *(SYN.)* working, operative, alert, agile, nimble, supple, sprightly, busy, brisk, lively, quick, industrious, energetic, vigorous, industrious, occupied, vivacious, dynamic, engaged.

(ANT.) passive, inactive, idle, dormant, lazy, lethargic.

activism *(SYN.)* engagement, confrontation, agitation, commitment, aggression, fervor, zeal.

(ANT.) detachment, lethargy, disengagement, fence-sitting.

activist *(SYN.)* militant, doer, enthusiast.

activity *(SYN.)* action, liveliness, motion, vigor, agility, exercise, energy, quickness, enterprise, movement, briskness.

(ANT.) idleness, inactivity, dullness, sloth.

actor *(SYN.)* performer, trouper, entertainer.

actual *(SYN.)* true, genuine, certain, factual, authentic, concrete, real.

(ANT.) unreal, fake, bogus, nonexistent, false.

actuality *(SYN.)* reality, truth, deed, occurrence, fact, certainty.

(ANT.) theory, fiction, falsehood, supposition.

acute *(SYN.)* piercing, severe, sudden, keen, sharp, perceptive, discerning, shrewd, astute, smart, intelligent.

(ANT.) bland, mild, dull, obtuse, insensitive.

adamant *(SYN.)* unyielding, firm, obstinate.

(ANT.) yielding.

adapt *(SYN.)* adjust, conform, accommodate, change, fit, alter, vary, modify.

(ANT.) misapply, disturb.

add *(SYN.)* attach, increase, total, append, sum, affix, augment, adjoin, unite, supplement.

(ANT.) remove, reduce, deduct, subtract, detach, withdraw.

address *(SYN.)* greet, hail, accost, speak to, location, residence, home, abode, dwelling, speech, lecture, greeting, oration, presentation.

(ANT.) avoid, pass by.

adept *(SYN.)* expert, skillful, proficient.

(ANT.) unskillful.

adequate *(SYN.)* capable, commensurate, fitting, satisfactory, sufficient, enough, ample, suitable, plenty, fit.

(ANT.) lacking, scant, insufficient, inadequate.

adhere *(SYN.)* stick fast, grasp, hold, keep, retain, cling, stick to, keep, cleave.

(ANT.) surrender, abandon, release, separate, loosen.

adherent *(SYN.)* follower, supporter.

(ANT.) renegade, dropout, defector.

adjacent *(SYN.)* next to, near, bordering, adjoining, touching, neighboring.

(ANT.) separate, distant, apart.

adjoin *(SYN.)* connect, be close to, affix, attach.

(ANT.) detach, remove,

adjoining *(SYN.)* near to, next, next to, close to, touching, bordering.

(ANT.) distant, remote, separate.

adjourn *(SYN.)* postpone, defer, delay, suspend, discontinue, put off.

(ANT.) begin, convene, assemble.

adjust *(SYN.)* repair, fix, change, set, regulate, settle, arrange, adapt, accommodate, modify, very, alter, fit.

administer *(SYN.)* supervise, oversee, direct, manage, rule, govern, control, conduct, provide, give, execute, preside, apply, contribute, help.

administration *(SYN.)* conduct, direction,

management, supervision.

admirable *(SYN.)* worthy, fine, deserving, commendable, excellent.

admiration *(SYN.)* pleasure, wonder, esteem, approval.

(ANT.) disdain, disrespect, contempt.

admire *(SYN.)* approve, venerate, appreciate, respect, revere, esteem, like.

(ANT.) abhor, dislike, despise, loathe, detest, hate.

admissible *(SYN.)* fair, justifiable, tolerable, allowable, permissible.

(ANT.) unsuitable, unfair, inadmissible.

admission *(SYN.)* access, admittance, entrance, pass, ticket.

admit *(SYN.)* allow, assent, permit, acknowledge, welcome, concede, agree, confess, accept, grant.

(ANT.) deny, reject, dismiss, shun, obstruct.

admittance *(SYN.)* access, entry, entrance.

admonish *(SYN.)* caution, advise against, warn, rebuke, reprove, censure.

(ANT.) glorify, praise.

admonition *(SYN.)* advice, warning, caution, remainder, tip.

ado *(SYN.)* trouble, other, fuss, bustle, activity, excitement, commotion, action, hubbub, upset, confusion, turmoil.

(ANT.) tranquillity, quietude.

adolescent *(SYN.)* young, youthful, immature, teenage.

(ANT.) grown, mature, adult.

adoration *(SYN.)* veneration, reverence, glorification, worship homage.

adore *(SYN.)* revere, venerate, idolize, respect, love, cherish, esteem, honor.

(ANT.) loathe, hate, despise.

adorn *(SYN.)* trim, bedeck, decorate, ornament, beautify, embellish, glamorize, enhance, garnish, embellish.

(ANT.) mar, spoil, deform, deface, strip, bare.

adrift *(SYN.)* floating, afloat, drifting, aimless, purposeless, unsettled.

(ANT.) purposeful, stable, secure, well-organized.

adroit *(SYN.)* adept, apt, dexterous, skillful, clever, ingenious, expert.

(ANT.) awkward, clumsy, graceless, unskill-

ful, oafish.

adult *(SYN.)* full-grown, mature.

(ANT.) infantile, immature.

advance *(SYN.)* further, promote, bring forward, propound, proceed, aggrandize, elevate, improve, adduce, allege, propose, progress, move, advancement, improvement, upgrade.

(ANT.) retard, retreat, oppose, hinder, revert, withdraw, flee, retardation.

advantage *(SYN.)* edge, profit, superiority, benefit, mastery, leverage, favor, vantage, gain.

(ANT.) handicap, impediment, obstruction, disadvantage, detriment, hindrance, loss.

adventure *(SYN.)* undertaking, occurrence, enterprise, happening, event, project, occurrence, incident, exploit.

adventurous *(SYN.)* daring, enterprising, rash, bold, chivalrous.

(ANT.) cautious, timid, hesitating.

adversary *(SYN.)* foe, enemy, contestant, opponent, antagonist.

(ANT.) ally, friend.

adverse *(SYN.)* hostile, counteractive, unfavorable, opposed, disastrous, contrary, antagonistic, opposite, unlucky, unfriendly, unfortunate.

(ANT.) favorable, propitious, fortunate, friendly, beneficial.

adversity *(SYN.)* misfortune, trouble, calamity, distress, hardship, disaster.

(ANT.) benefit, happiness.

advertise *(SYN.)* promote, publicize, make known, announce, promulgate.

advertisement *(SYN.)* commercial, billboard, want ad, handbill, flyer, poster, brochure, blurb.

advice *(SYN.)* counsel, instruction, suggestion, warning, information, caution, exhortation, admonition, recommendation, plan, tip, guidance, opinion.

advisable *(SYN.)* wise, sensible, prudent, suitable, fit, proper, fitting.

(ANT.) ill-considered, imprudent, inadvisable.

advise *(SYN.)* recommend, suggest, counsel, caution, warn, admonish.

adviser *(SYN.)* coach, guide, mentor, counselor.

advocate *(SYN.)* defend, recommend, support, urge.

(ANT.) opponent, adversary, oppose.

aesthetic *(SYN.)* literary, artistic, sensitive, tasteful, well-composed.

(ANT.) tasteless.

affable *(SYN.)* pleasant, courteous, sociable, friendly, amiable, gracious, approachable, communicative.

(ANT.) unfriendly, unsociable.

affair *(SYN.)* event, occasion, happening, party, occurrence, matter, festivity, business, concern.

affect *(SYN.)* alter, modify, concern, regard, move, touch, feign, pretend, influence, sway, transform, change, impress.

affected *(SYN.)* pretended, fake, sham, false.

affection *(SYN.)* fondness, kindness, emotion, love, feeling, tenderness, attachment, disposition, endearment, liking, friendly, friendliness, warmth.

(ANT.) aversion, indifference, repulsion, hatred, repugnance, dislike, antipathy.

affectionate *(SYN.)* warm, loving, tender, fond, attached.

(ANT.) distant, unfeeling, cold.

affirm *(SYN.)* aver, declare, swear, maintain, endorse, certify, state, assert, ratify, pronounce, say, confirm, establish.

(ANT.) deny, dispute, oppose, contradict, demur, disclaim.

afflict *(SYN.)* trouble, disturb, bother, agitate, perturb.

(ANT.) soothe.

affliction *(SYN.)* distress, grief, misfortune, trouble.

(ANT.) relief, benefit, easement.

affluent *(SYN.)* wealthy, prosperous, rich, abundant, ample, plentiful, well-off, bountiful, well-to-do.

(ANT.) poor.

afford *(SYN.)* supply, yield, furnish.

affront *(SYN.)* offense, slur, slight, provocation, insult.

afraid *(SYN.)* fainthearted, frightened, scared, timid, fearful, apprehensive, cowardly, terrified.

(ANT.) assured, composed, courageous, bold, confident.

after *(SYN.)* following, subsequently, behind, despite, next.

(ANT.) before.

again *(SYN.)* anew, repeatedly, afresh.

against *(SYN.)* versus, hostile to, opposed to, in disagreement.

(ANT.) pro, with, for, in favor of.

age *(SYN.)* antiquity, date, period, generation, time, senility, grow old, senescence, mature, dotage, ripen, mature, era, epoch.

(ANT.) youth, childhood.

aged *(SYN.)* ancient, elderly, old.

(ANT.) youthful, young.

agency *(SYN.)* office, operation.

agent *(SYN.)* performer, worker, actor, operator.

aggravate *(SYN.)* intensify, magnify, annoy, irritate, increase, heighten, nettle, make worse, irk, vex, provoke, embitter, worsen.

(ANT.) soften, soothe, appease, pacify, mitigate, ease, relieve.

aggregate *(SYN.)* collection, entirety, sum, accumulate, total, amount to, compile, conglomeration.

(ANT.) part, unit, ingredient, element.

aggression *(SYN.)* assault, attack, invasion, offense.

(ANT.) defense.

aggressive *(SYN.)* offensive, belligerent, hostile, attacking, militant, pugnacious.

(ANT.) timid, withdrawn, passive, peaceful, shy.

aghast *(SYN.)* surprised, astonished, astounded, awed, thunderstruck, flabbergasted, bewildered.

agile *(SYN.)* nimble, graceful, lively, active, alert, fast, quick, athletic, spry.

(ANT.) inept, awkward, clumsy.

agility *(ANT.)* quickness, vigor, liveliness, energy, activity, motion.

(ANT.) dullness, inertia, idleness, inactivity.

agitate *(SYN.)* disturb, excite, perturb, rouse, shake, arouse, disconcert, instigate, inflame, provoke, jar, incite, stir up, toss.

(ANT.) calm, placate, quiet, ease, soothe.

agitated *(SYN.)* jumpy, jittery, nervous, restless, restive, upset, disturbed, ruffled.

agony *(SYN.)* anguish, misery, pain, suffering, torture, ache, distress, throe, woe, torment, grief.

(ANT.) relief, ease, comfort.

agree *(SYN.)* comply, coincide, conform, occur, assent, accede, tally, settle, harmonize, unite, yield, consent.

(ANT.) differ, disagree, protest, contradict, argue, refuse.

agreeable *(SYN.)* amiable, charming, gratifying, pleasant, suitable, pleasurable, welcome, pleasing, acceptable, friendly, cooperative.

(ANT.) obnoxious, offensive, unpleasant, disagreeable, quarrelsome, contentious, touchy.

agreement *(SYN.)* harmony, understanding, unison, contract, pact, stipulation, alliance, deal, bargain, treaty, contract, arrangement, settlement, accord, concord.

(ANT.) variance, dissension, discord, disagreement, difference, misunderstanding.

agriculture *(SYN.)* farming, gardening, tillage, husbandry, cultivation, agronomy.

ahead *(SYN.)* before, leading, forward, winning, in advance.

(ANT.) behind.

aid *(SYN.)* remedy, assist, helper, service, support, assistant, relief, help.

(ANT.) obstruct, hinder, obstacle, impede, hindrance.

ail *(SYN.)* bother, trouble, perturb, disturb, suffer, feel sick.

ailing *(SYN.)* sick, ill.

(ANT.) hearty, hale, well.

ailment *(SYN.)* illness, disease, affliction, sickness.

aim *(SYN.)* direction, point, goal, object, target, direct, try, intend, intention, end, objective.

aimless *(SYN.)* directionless, adrift, purposeless.

air *(SYN.)* atmosphere, display, reveal, expose, publicize.

(ANT.) conceal, hide.

airy *(SYN.)* breezy, light, gay, lighthearted, graceful, fanciful.

aisle *(SYN.)* corridor, passageway, lane, alley, opening, artery.

ajar *(SYN.)* gaping, open.

akin *(SYN.)* alike, related, connected, similar, affiliated, allied.

alarm *(SYN.)* dismay, fright, signal, warning, terror, apprehension, affright, consternation, fear, siren, arouse, startle, bell.

(ANT.) tranquillity, composure, security, quiet, calm, soothe, comfort.

alarming *(SYN.)* appalling, daunting, shocking.

(ANT.) comforting, calming, soothing.

alcoholic *(SYN.)* sot, drunkard, tippler, inebriate.

alert *(SYN.)* attentive, keen, clear-witted, ready, vigilant, watchful, observant.

(ANT.) logy, sluggish, dulled, listless.

alias *(SYN.)* anonym, assumed name.

alibi *(SYN.)* story, excuse.

alien *(SYN.)* adverse, foreigner, strange, remote, stranger, different, extraneous.

(ANT.) germane, kindred, relevant, akin, familiar, accustomed.

alight *(SYN.)* debark, deplane, detrain, disembark.

(ANT.) embark, board.

alive *(SYN.)* existing, breathing, living, live, lively, vivacious, animated.

(ANT.) inactive, dead, moribund.

allay *(SYN.)* soothe, check, lessen, calm, lighten, relieve, soften, moderate, quite.

(ANT.) excite, intensify, worsen, arouse.

allege *(SYN.)* affirm, cite, claim, declare, maintain, state, assert.

(ANT.) deny, disprove, refute, contradict, gainsay.

allegiance *(SYN.)* faithfulness, duty, devotion, loyalty, fidelity, obligation.

(ANT.) treachery, disloyalty.

allegory *(SYN.)* fable, fiction, myth, saga, parable, legend.

(ANT.) history, fact.

alleviate *(SYN.)* diminish, soothe, solace, abate, assuage, allay, soften, mitigate, extenuate, relieve, lot up, ease, slacken, relax, weaken.

(ANT.) increase, aggravate, augment, irritate.

alley *(SYN.)* footway, byway, path, passageway, aisle, corridor, opening, lane.

alliance *(SYN.)* combination, partnership, union, treaty, coalition, association, confederacy, marriage, pact, agreement, relation, interrelation, understanding, relationship.

(ANT.) separation, divorce, schism.

allot *(SYN.)* divide, mete, assign, give, measure, distribute, allocate, share, grant, dispense, deal, apportion.

(ANT.) withhold, retain, keep, confiscate, refuse.

allow *(SYN.)* authorize, grant, acknowledge, admit, let, permit, sanction, consent, concede, mete, allocate.

(ANT.) protest, resist, refuse, forbid, object, prohibit.

allowance *(SYN.)* grant, fee, portion, ration, allotment.

allude *(SYN.)* intimate, refer, insinuate, hint, advert, suggest, imply, mention.

(ANT.) demonstrate, specify, state, declare.

allure *(SYN.)* attract, fascinate, tempt, charm, infatuate, captivate.

ally *(SYN.)* accomplice, associate, confederate, abettor, assistant, friend, partner.

(ANT.) rival, enemy, opponent, foe, adversary.

almighty *(SYN.)* omnipotent, powerful.

almost *(SYN.)* somewhat, nearly.

(ANT.) completely, absolutely.

alms *(SYN.)* dole, charity, donation, contribution.

aloft *(SYN.)* overhead.

alone *(SYN.)* desolate, unaided, only, isolated, lone, secluded, lonely, deserted, solitary, single, apart, solo, separate.

(ANT.) surrounded, attended, accompanied, together.

aloof *(SYN.)* uninterested, uninvolved, apart, away, remote, unsociable, standoffish, separate, disdainful, distant.

(ANT.) warm, outgoing, friendly, cordial.

also *(SYN.)* in addition, likewise, too, besides, furthermore, moreover, further.

alter *(SYN.)* adjust, vary, deviate, modify, reserved, change.

(ANT.) maintain, preserve, keep.

alteration *(SYN.)* difference, adjustment, change, modification.

(ANT.) maintenance, preservation.

altercation *(SYN.)* controversy, dispute, argument, quarrel.

alternate *(SYN.)* rotate, switch, spell, interchange.

(ANT.) fix.

alternative *(SYN.)* substitute, selection, option, choice, replacement, possibility.

although *(SYN.)* though, even if, even though, despite, notwithstanding.

altitude *(SYN.)* elevation, height.

(ANT.) depth.

altogether *(SYN.)* totally, wholly, quite, entirely, thoroughly, completely.

(ANT.) partly.

altruism *(SYN.)* kindness, tenderness, generosity, charity, benevolence, liberality.

(ANT.) selfishness, unkindness, cruelty, inhumanity.

always *(SYN.)* evermore, forever, perpetually, ever, unceasingly, continually, constantly, eternally, everlastingly.

(ANT.) never, rarely, sometimes, occasionally.

amalgamate *(SYN.)* fuse, unify, unite, commingle, merge, blend, combine, consolidate.

(ANT.) decompose, disintegrate, separate.

amass *(SYN.)* collect, accumulate, heap up, gather, increase, compile, assemble, store up.

(ANT.) disperse, dissipate, spend.

amateur *(SYN.)* beginner, dilettante, learner, dabbler, neophyte, apprentice, novice, nonprofessional, tyro.

(ANT.) expert, master, adept, professional, authority.

amaze *(SYN.)* surprise, flabbergast, stun, dumbfound, astound, bewilder, aghast, thunderstruck, astonish.

(ANT.) bore, disinterest, tire.

ambiguous *(SYN.)* uncertain, vague, obscure, dubious, equivocal, unclear, deceptive.

(ANT.) plain, clear, explicit, obvious, unequivocal, unmistakable, certain.

ambition *(SYN.)* eagerness, goal, incentive, aspiration, yearning, longing, desire.

(ANT.) indifference, satisfaction, indolence, resignation.

ambitious *(SYN.)* aspiring, intent upon.
(ANT.) indifferent.

amble *(SYN.)* saunter, stroll.

ambush *(SYN.)* trap, hiding place.

amend *(SYN.)* change, mend, better, correct, improve.
(ANT.) worsen.

amends *(SYN.)* compensation, restitution, payment, reparation, remedy, redress.

amiable *(SYN.)* friendly, good-natured, gracious, pleasing, agreeable, outgoing, kindhearted, kind, pleasant.
(ANT.) surly, hateful, churlish, disagreeable, ill-natured, ill-tempered, cross, captious, touchy.

amid *(SYN.)* among, amidst, surrounded by.

amiss *(SYN.)* wrongly, improperly, astray, awry.
(ANT.) properly, rightly, right, correctly, correct.

ammunition *(SYN.)* shot, powder, shells, bullets.

among *(SYN.)* between, mingled, mixed amidst, amid, betwixt, surrounded by.
(ANT.) separate, apart.

amorous *(SYN.)* amatory, affectionate, loving.

amount *(SYN.)* sum, total, quantity, number, price, value, measure.

ample *(SYN.)* broad, large, profuse, spacious, copious, liberal, plentiful, full, bountiful, abundant, great, extensive, generous, wide, enough, sufficient, roomy.
(ANT.) limited, insufficient, meager, small, lacking, cramped, confined, inadequate.

amplification *(SYN.)* magnification, growth, waxing, accrual, enhancement, enlargement, heightening, increase.
(ANT.) decrease, diminishing, reduction, contraction.

amplify *(SYN.)* broaden, develop, expand, enlarge, extend.
(ANT.) confine, restrict, abridge, narrow.

amuse *(SYN.)* divert, please, delight, entertain, charm.
(ANT.) tire, bore.

amusement *(SYN.)* diversion, pastime, entertainment, pleasure, enjoyment, recreation.
(ANT.) tedium, boredom.

amusing *(SYN.)* pleasant, funny, pleasing, entertaining, comical.
(ANT.) tiring, tedious, boring.

analogous *(SYN.)* comparable, corresponding, like, similar, correspondent, alike, correlative, parallel, allied, akin.
(ANT.) different, opposed, incongruous, divergent.

analysis *(SYN.)* separation, investigation, examination.

analyze *(SYN.)* explain, investigate, examine, separate.

ancestral *(SYN.)* hereditary, inherited.

ancestry *(SYN.)* family, line, descent, lineage.
(ANT.) posterity.

anchor *(SYN.)* fix, attach, secure, fasten.
(ANT.) detach, free, loosen.

ancient *(SYN.)* aged, old-fashioned, archaic, elderly, antique, old, primitive.
(ANT.) new, recent, current, fresh.

anecdote *(SYN.)* account, narrative, story, tale.

anesthetic *(SYN.)* opiate, narcotic, sedative, painkiller, analgesic.

angel *(SYN.)* cherub, archangel, seraph.
(ANT.) demon, devil.

angelic *(SYN.)* pure, lovely, heavenly, good, virtuous, innocent, godly, saintly.
(ANT.) devilish.

anger *(SYN.)* exasperation, fury, ire, passion, rage, resentment, temper, indignation, animosity, irritation, wrath, displeasure, infuriate, arouse, nettle, annoyance, exasperate.
(ANT.) forbearance, patience, peace, self-control.

angry *(SYN.)* provoked, wrathful, furious, enraged, incensed, maddened, indignant, irate, mad, inflamed.
(ANT.) happy, pleased, calm, satisfied, content, tranquil.

anguish *(SYN.)* suffering, torment, torture, distress, pain, heartache, grief, agony, misery.
(ANT.) solace, relief, joy, comfort, peace,

ecstasy, pleasure.

animal *(SYN.)* beast, creature.

animate *(SYN.)* vitalize, invigorate, stimulate, enliven, alive, vital, vigorous.
(ANT.) dead, inanimate.

animated *(SYN.)* gay, lively, spry, vivacious, active, vigorous, chipper, snappy.
(ANT.) inactive.

animosity *(SYN.)* grudge, hatred, rancor, spite, bitterness, enmity, opposition, dislike, hostility, antipathy.
(ANT.) good will, love, friendliness, kindliness.

annex *(SYN.)* join, attach, add, addition, wing, append.

annihilate *(SYN.)* destroy, demolish, end, wreck, abolish.

announce *(SYN.)* proclaim, give out, make known, notify, publish, report, herald, promulgate, advertise, broadcast, state, tell, declare, publicize.
(ANT.) conceal, withhold, suppress, bury, stifle.

announcement *(SYN.)* notification, report, declaration, bulletin, advertisement, broadcast, promulgation, notice, message.
(ANT.) silence, hush, muteness, speechlessness.

annoy *(SYN.)* bother, irk, pester, tease, trouble, vex, disturb, inconvenience, molest, irritate, harry, harass.
(ANT.) console, gratify, soothe, accommodate, please, calm, comfort.

annually *(SYN.)* once a year.

anoint *(SYN.)* grease, oil.

answer *(SYN.)* reply, rejoinder, response, retort, rebuttal, respond.
(ANT.) summoning, argument, questioning, inquiry, query, ask, inquire.

antagonism *(SYN.)* opposition, conflict, enmity, hostility, animosity.
(ANT.) geniality, cordiality, friendliness.

antagonist *(SYN.)* adversary, rival, enemy, foe, opponent.
(ANT.) ally, friend.

antagonize *(SYN.)* against, provoke, counter, oppose, embitter.
(ANT.) soothe.

anthology *(SYN.)* garland, treasury, collection.

anticipate *(SYN.)* await, foresee, forecast, hope for, expect.

anticipated *(SYN.)* expected, foresight, hoped, preconceived.
(ANT.) dreaded, reared, worried, doubted.

antics *(SYN.)* horseplay, fun, merrymaking, pranks, capers, tricks, clowning.

antipathy *(SYN.)* hatred.

antiquated *(SYN.)* old, out-of-date, outdated, old-fashion.

antique *(SYN.)* rarity, curio, old, ancient, old-fashioned, archaic, out-of-date.
(ANT.) new, recent, fresh.

anxiety *(SYN.)* care, disquiet, fear, concern, solicitude, trouble, worry, apprehension, uneasiness, distress, foreboding.
(ANT.) nonchalance, assurance, confidence, contentment, peacefulness, placidity, tranquillity.

anxious *(SYN.)* troubled, uneasy, perturbed, apprehensive, worried, concerned, desirous, bothered, agitated, eager, fearful.
(ANT.) tranquil, calm, peaceful.

anyway *(SYN.)* nevertheless, anyhow.

apartment *(SYN.)* suite, flat, dormitory.

apathy *(SYN.)* unconcern, indifference, lethargy.
(ANT.) interest, feeling.

aperture *(SYN.)* gap, pore, opening, cavity, chasm, abyss, hole, void.
(ANT.) connection, bridge, link.

apex *(SYN.)* acme, tip, summit, crown, top.

apologize *(SYN.)* ask forgiveness.

apology *(SYN.)* defense, excuse, confession, justification, alibi, explanation, plea.
(ANT.) denial, complaint, dissimulation, accusation.

apostate *(SYN.)* nonconformist, unbeliever, dissenter, heretic, schismatic.
(ANT.) saint, conformist, believer.

appall *(SYN.)* shock, stun, dismay, frighten, terrify, horrify.
(ANT.) edify, please.

appalling *(SYN.)* fearful, frightful, ghastly, horrid, repulsive, terrible, dire, awful.
(ANT.) fascinating, beautiful, enchanting,

enjoyable.

apparatus *(SYN.)* rig, equipment, furnishings, gear, tackle.

apparel *(SYN.)* clothes, attire, garb, clothing, garments, dress, robes.

apparent *(SYN.)* obvious, plain, self-evident, clear, manifest, transparent, unmistakable, palpable, unambiguous, ostensible, illusory, visible, seeming, evident, understandable.

(ANT.) uncertain, indistinct, dubious, hidden, *mysterious.*

apparition *(SYN.)* illusion, ghost, phantom, vision, fantasy, dream.

appeal *(SYN.)* plea, petition, request, entreaty, plead, beseech, beg, entreat, attract, solicitate.

(ANT.) repulse, repel.

appear *(SYN.)* look, arrive, emanate, emerge, arise, seem, turn up.

(ANT.) vanish, withdraw, exist, disappear, evaporate.

appearance *(SYN.)* advent, arrival, aspect, demeanor, fashion, guise, apparition, manner, mien, look, presence.

(ANT.) disappearance, reality, departure, vanishing.

appease *(SYN.)* calm, compose, lull, quiet, relieve, assuage, pacify, satisfy, restraint, lesson, soothe, check, ease, alleviate, still, allay, tranquilize.

(ANT.) excite, arouse, incense, irritate, inflame.

append *(SYN.)* supplement, attach, add.

appendage *(SYN.)* addition, tail, supplement.

appetite *(SYN.)* zest, craving, desire, liking, longing, stomach, inclination, hunger, thirst, relish, passion.

(ANT.) satiety, disgust, distaste, repugnance.

appetizer *(SYN.)* hors d'oeuvre.

applaud *(SYN.)* cheer, clap, hail, approve, praise, acclaim.

(ANT.) disapprove, denounce, reject, criticize, condemn.

appliance *(SYN.)* machine, tool, instrument, device, utensil, implement.

applicable *(SYN.)* fitting, suitable, proper, fit, usable, appropriate, suited.

(ANT.) inappropriate, inapplicable.

apply *(SYN.)* affix, allot, appropriate, use, employ, petition, request, devote, avail, pertain, attach, ask, administer, assign, relate, utilize.

(ANT.) give away, demand, detach, neglect, ignore.

appoint *(SYN.)* name, choose, nominate, designate, elect, establish, assign, place.

(ANT.) discharge, fire, dismiss.

appointment *(SYN.)* rendezvous, meeting, designation, position, engagement, assignment.

(ANT.) discharge, dismissal.

appraise *(SYN.)* value, evaluate, place a value on.

appreciate *(SYN.)* enjoy, regard, value, prize, cherish, admire, go up, improve, rise, respect, think highly of, esteem, appraise.

(ANT.) belittle, misunderstand, apprehend, degrade, scorn, depreciate, undervalue.

apprehend *(SYN.)* seize, capture, arrest, understand, dread, fear, grasp, perceive.

(ANT.) release, lose.

apprehension *(SYN.)* fear, misgiving, dread, uneasiness, worry, fearfulness, anticipation, capture, seizure.

(ANT.) confidence, composure, self-assuredness.

apprehensive *(SYN.)* worried, afraid, uneasy, bothered, anxious, concerned, perturbed, troubled, fearful.

(ANT.) relaxed.

apprentice *(SYN.)* amateur, recruit, novice, learner, beginner.

(ANT.) experienced, professional, master.

approach *(SYN.)* greet, inlet, come near, advance, access, passageway.

(ANT.) avoid, pass by, retreat.

appropriate *(SYN.)* apt, particular, proper, fitting, suitable, applicable, loot, pillage, purloin, rob, steal, embezzle, assign, becoming, apportion, authorize.

(ANT.) improper, contrary, inappropriate, buy, repay, restore, return, unfit, inapt.

approval *(SYN.)* commendation, consent, praise, approbation, sanction, assent, endorsement, support.

(ANT.) reproach, censure, reprimand,

disapprove.

approve *(SYN.)* like, praise, authorize, confirm, endorse, appreciate, think well of, ratify, commend, sanction.
(ANT.) criticize, nullify, disparage, frown on, disapprove, deny.

approximate *(SYN.)* near, approach, roughly, close.
(ANT.) correct.

apt *(SYN.)* suitable, proper, appropriate, fit, suited, disposed, liable, inclined, prone, clever, bright, alert, intelligent, receptive.
(ANT.) ill-becoming, unsuitable, unlikely, slow, retarded, dense.

aptness *(SYN.)* capability, dexterity, power, qualification, skill, ability, aptitude.
(ANT.) incompetency, unreadiness, incapacity.

aptitude *(SYN.)* knack, talent, gift, ability.

aqueduct *(SYN.)* gully, pipe, canal, waterway, channel.

arbitrary *(SYN.)* unrestricted, absolute, despotic, willful, unreasonable, unconditional, authoritative.
(ANT.) contingent, qualified, fair, reasonable, dependent, accountable.

arbitrate *(SYN.)* referee, settle, mediate, umpire, negotiate.

architecture *(SYN.)* structure, building, construction.

ardent *(SYN.)* fervent, fiery, glowing, intense, keen, impassioned, fervid, hot, passionate, earnest, eager, zealous, enthusiastic.
(ANT.) indifferent, nonchalant, apathetic.

ardor *(SYN.)* enthusiasm, rapture, spirit, zeal, fervent, eager, glowing, eagerness.
(ANT.) unconcern, apathy, disinterest, indifference.

arduous *(SYN.)* laborious, hard, difficult, burdensome, strenuous, strained.
(ANT.) easy.

area *(SYN.)* space, extent, region, zone, section, expanse, district, neighborhood, size.

argue *(SYN.)* plead, reason, wrangle, indicate, prove, show, dispute, denote, imply, object, bicker, discuss, debate, disagree.
(ANT.) reject, spurn, ignore, overlook, agree, concur.

argument *(SYN.)* debate, dispute, discussion,

controversy.
(ANT.) harmony, accord, agreement.

arid *(SYN.)* waterless, dry, flat, dull, unimaginative, stuffy.
(ANT.) fertile, wet, colorful.

arise *(SYN.)* enter, institute, originate, start, open, commence, emerge, appear.
(ANT.) terminate, end, finish, complete, close.

aristocrat *(SYN.)* noble, gentleman, peer, lord, nobleman.
(ANT.) peasant, commoner.

arm *(SYN.)* weapon, defend, equip, empower, fortify.

armistice *(SYN.)* truce, pact, deal, understanding, peace, treaty, contract, alliance, agreement.

army *(SYN.)* troops, legion, military, forces, militia.

aroma *(SYN.)* smell, odor, fragrance, perfume, scent.

arouse *(SYN.)* stir, animate, move, pique, provoke, kindle, disturb, excite, foment, stimulate, awaken.
(ANT.) settle, soothe, calm.

arraign *(SYN.)* charge, censure, incriminate, indict, accuse.
(ANT.) acquit, release, vindicate, exonerate, absolve.

arraignment *(SYN.)* imputation, charge, accusation, incrimination.
(ANT.) pardon, exoneration, exculpation.

arrange *(SYN.)* classify, assort, organize, place, plan, prepare, devise, adjust, dispose, regulate, order, group, settle, adapt, catalog, systematize, prepare.
(ANT.) jumble, scatter, disorder, confuse, disturb, disarrange.

arrangement *(SYN.)* display, grouping, order, array.

array *(SYN.)* dress, adorn, attire, clothe, arrange, order, distribute, arrangement, display, exhibit.
(ANT.) disorder, disorganization, disarray.

arrest *(SYN.)* detain, hinder, restrain, seize, withhold, stop, check, obstruct, apprehend, interrupt, catch, capture.
(ANT.) free, release, discharge, liberate.

arrival *(SYN.)* advent, coming.

(ANT.) leaving, departure.

arrive *(SYN.)* come, emerge, reach, visit, land, appear.

(ANT.) exit, leave, depart, go.

arrogance *(SYN.)* pride, insolence.

(ANT.) humbleness, modesty, humility.

arrogant *(SYN.)* insolent, prideful, scornful, haughty, cavalier, proud.

(ANT.) modest, humble.

art *(SYN.)* cunning, tact, artifice, skill, aptitude, adroitness, painting, drawing, design, craft, dexterity, composition, ingenuity.

(ANT.) clumsiness, innocence, unskillfulness, honesty.

artery *(SYN.)* aqueduct, pipe, channel.

artful *(SYN.)* clever, sly, skillful, knowing, deceitful, tricky, crafty, cunning.

(ANT.) artless.

article *(SYN.)* story, composition, treatise, essay, thing, report, object.

artifice *(SYN.)* trick, clever, scheme, device.

artificial *(SYN.)* bogus, fake, affected, feigned, phony, sham, unreal, synthetic, assumed, counterfeit, unnatural, manmade, manufactured, false, pretended.

(ANT.) genuine, natural true, real, authentic.

artisan *(SYN.)* worker, craftsman, mechanic.

artist *(SYN.)* actor, actress, painter, sculptor, singer, designer.

artless *(SYN.)* innocent, open, frank, simple, honest, candid, natural, unskilled, ignorant, truthful, sincere.

(ANT.) artful.

ascend *(SYN.)* rise, scale, tower, mount, go up, climb.

(ANT.) fall, sink, descend, go down.

ascertain *(SYN.)* solve, learn, answer.

ascribe *(SYN.)* attribute, assign.

ashamed *(SYN.)* shamefaced, humiliated, abashed, mortified, embarrassed.

(ANT.) proud.

ask *(SYN.)* invite, request, inquire, query, question, beg, solicit, demand, entreat, claim, interrogate, charge, expect.

(ANT.) order, reply, insist, answer.

askance *(SYN.)* sideways.

askew *(SYN.)* disorderly, crooked, awry, twisted.

(ANT.) straight.

asleep *(SYN.)* inactive, sleeping, dormant.

(ANT.) alert, awake.

aspect *(SYN.)* appearance, look, view, outlook, attitude, viewpoint, phase, part, feature, side.

aspersion *(SYN.)* dishonor, insult, misuse, outrage, reproach, defamation, abuse, disparagement.

(ANT.) plaudit, respect, commendation, approval.

asphyxiate *(SYN.)* suffocate, stifle, smother, choke, strangle, throttle.

aspiration *(SYN.)* craving, desire, hope, longing, objective, passion, ambition.

aspire *(SYN.)* seek, aim, wish for, strive, desire, yearn for.

ass *(SYN.)* mule, donkey, burro, silly, dunce, stubborn, stupid, fool.

assail *(SYN.)* assault, attack.

assassinate *(SYN.)* purge, kill, murder.

assault *(SYN.)* invade, strike, attack, assail, charge, bombard, onslaught.

(ANT.) protect, defend.

assemble *(SYN.)* collect, gather, meet, congregate, connect, manufacture.

(ANT.) disperse, disassemble, scatter.

assembly *(SYN.)* legislature, congress, council, parliament.

assent *(SYN.)* consent to, concede, agree, approval, accept, comply, permission.

(ANT.) deny, dissent, refusal, denial, refuse.

assert *(SYN.)* declare, maintain, state, claim, express, defend, press, support, aver, uphold, consent, accept, comply, affirm, allege, emphasize.

(ANT.) deny, refute, contradict, decline.

assertion *(SYN.)* statement, affirmation, declaration.

(ANT.) contradiction, denial.

assess *(SYN.)* calculate, compute, estimate, levy, reckon, tax, appraise.

asset *(SYN.)* property, wealth, capitol, resources, goods.

assign *(SYN.)* apportion, ascribe, attribute, cast, allot, choose, appropriate, name, elect, appoint, distribute, designate, specify.

(ANT.) release, relieve, unburden, discharge.

assignment *(SYN.)* task, job, responsibility, duty.

assimilate *(SYN.)* digest, absorb, blot up.

assist *(SYN.)* help, promote, serve, support, sustain, abet, aid, back.
(ANT.) prevent, impede, hinder, hamper.

assistance *(SYN.)* backing, help, patronage, relief, succor, support.
(ANT.) hostility, resistance, antagonism, counteraction.

assistant *(SYN.)* accomplice, ally, associate, confederate, abettor.
(ANT.) rival, enemy, adversary.

associate *(SYN.)* affiliate, ally, join, connect, unite, combine, link, mingle, partner, mix.
(ANT.) separate, disconnect, divide, disrupt, estrange.

association *(SYN.)* organization, club, union, society, fraternity, sorority, companionship, fellowship.

assorted *(SYN.)* varied, miscellaneous, classified, different, several, grouped, various.
(ANT.) alike, same.

assortment *(SYN.)* collection, variety, mixture, conglomeration.

assuage *(SYN.)* calm, quiet, lessen, relieve, ease, allay, moderate, alleviate, restrain.

assume *(SYN.)* arrogate, affect, suspect, believe, appropriate, take, pretend, usurp, simulate, understand, postulate, presume, suppose.
(ANT.) doff, demonstrate, prove, grant, concede.

assumption *(SYN.)* presumption, guess, theory, supposition, conjecture, postulate.

assurance *(SYN.)* confidence, conviction, self-reliance, surety, firmness, courage, promise, pledge, certainty, assertion, security, word, assuredness.
(ANT.) humility, shyness, suspicion, modesty.

assure *(SYN.)* promise, convince, warrant, guarantee, pledge.
(ANT.) equivocate, deny.

astonish *(SYN.)* astound, amaze, surprise, shock.
(ANT.) tire, bore.

astound *(SYN.)* shock, amaze, astonish, stun, surprise, floor.

asunder *(SYN.)* divided, separate, apart.
(ANT.) together.

asylum *(SYN.)* shelter, refuge, home, madhouse, institution.

athletic *(SYN.)* strong, active, ablebodied, gymnastic, muscular, well-built.

atone *(SYN.)* repay, make up.

atrocious *(SYN.)* horrible, savage, brutal, ruthless, dreadful, awful, horrifying, horrid, unspeakable, ghastly.
(ANT.) good, kind.

attach *(SYN.)* connect, adjoin, annex, join, append, stick, unite, adjoin, affix.
(ANT.) unfasten, untie, detach, separate, disengage.

attachment *(SYN.)* friendship, liking, regard, adherence, affection, devotion.
(ANT.) estrangement, opposition, alienation, aversion.

attack *(SYN.)* raid, assault, besiege, abuse, censure, offense, seige, onslaught, denunciation, aggression, bombardment, push, criticism, invade.
(ANT.) surrender, defense, opposition, aid, defend, protect, repel.

attain *(SYN.)* achieve, acquire, accomplish, gain, get, reach, win, complete, finish, secure, procure, arrive, fulfill, obtain, effect.
(ANT.) relinquish, discard, abandon, desert.

attainment *(SYN.)* exploit, feat, accomplishment, realization, performance.
(ANT.) omission, defeat, failure, neglect.

attempt *(SYN.)* essay, experiment, trial, try, undertaking, endeavor, effort.
(ANT.) laziness, neglect, inaction.

attend *(SYN.)* accompany, escort, watch, be serve, care for, follow, lackey, present, frequent, protect, guard.
(ANT.) desert, abandon, avoid.

attendant *(SYN.)* waiter, servant, valet.

attention *(SYN.)* consideration, heed, circumspection, notice, watchfulness, observance, application, reflection, study, care, alertness, mindfulness.
(ANT.) negligence, indifference, omission, oversight, disregard.

attentive *(SYN.)* careful, awake, alive, con-

siderate, heedful, mindful, wary, assiduous, diligent, aware, alert.
(ANT.) indifferent, unaware, oblivious, apathetic.
attest *(SYN.)* testify, swear, vouch, certify.
attire *(SYN.)* apparel, dress, clothe.
attitude *(SYN.)* standpoint, viewpoint, stand, pose, aspect, position, disposition, opinion.
attorney *(SYN.)* lawyer.
attract*(SYN.)*enchant,interest,pull,fascinate, draw, tempt, infatuate, entice, lure, charm, captivate, allure.
(ANT.) deter, repel, repulse, alienate.
attractive *(SYN.)* enchanting, winning, engaging, pleasant, pleasing, seductive, magnetic, charming, inviting, alluring.
(ANT.) unattractive, obnoxious, repellent, repulsive, forbidding.
attribute *(SYN.)* give, apply, place, trait, characteristic, feature, nature, credit, assign, ascribe.
audacious *(SYN.)* daring, bold, arrogant, foolhardy, cavalier, haughty, insolent.
(ANT.) humble, shy.
audacity *(SYN.)* effrontery, fearlessness, temerity, boldness.
(ANT.) humility, meekness, circumspection, fearfulness.
audible *(SYN.)* distinct, bearable, plain, clear.
(ANT.) inaudible.
augment *(SYN.)* enlarge, increase, raise, expand, broaden, extend.
auspicious *(SYN.)* lucky, timely, favorable, promising, fortunate.
(ANT.) untimely, unfortunate.
austere *(SYN.)* stern, severe, harsh, strict.
(ANT.) lenient, soft.
authentic *(SYN.)* real, true, genuine, pure, accurate, reliable, legitimate, factual, actual, correct, verifiable, authoritative.
(ANT.) false, spurious, artificial, counterfeit, erroneous.
authenticate *(SYN.)* validate, warrant, guarantee, verify, certify.
author *(SYN.)* father, inventor, originator, writer, composer.
authoritative *(SYN.)* certain, secure, commanding, sure, tried, safe, influential, de-

pendable.
(ANT.) uncertain, unreliable, dubious, fallible, questionable.
authority *(SYN.)* dominion, justification, power,permission,importance,supremacy.
(ANT.) incapacity, denial, prohibition, weakness, impotence.
authorize *(SYN.)* permit, sanction, legalize, approve, empower.
(ANT.) forbid, prohibit.
autocrat *(SYN.)* monarch, ruler, tyrant, dictator.
autograph *(SYN.)* endorse, sign, approve.
automatic *(SYN.)* self-acting, mechanical, spontaneous, uncontrolled, involuntary, self-working.
(ANT.) hand-operated, intentional, deliberate, manual.
automobile *(SYN.)* auto, car.
auxiliary *(SYN.)* assisting, helping, aiding.
avail *(SYN.)* help, profit, use, value, benefit, serve, advantage.
available *(SYN.)* obtainable, convenient, ready, handy, accessible, prepared.
(ANT.) unavailable, out of reach, inaccessible, unobtainable.
avarice *(SYN.)* lust, greed.
average *(SYN.)* moderate, ordinary, usual, passable, fair, intermediate, medium, median, mediocre, mean, middling.
(ANT.) outstanding, exceptional, extraordinary, unusual.
averse *(SYN.)* unwilling, opposed, forced, against, involuntary.
(ANT.) willing.
aversion *(SYN.)* disgust, dislike, distaste, hatred, loathing, abhorrence, antipathy.
(ANT.) devotion, enthusiasm, affection, love.
avert *(SYN.)* avoid, prevent, prohibit.
(ANT.) invite.
avid *(SYN.)* greedy, eager.
avocation *(SYN.)* sideline, hobby.
avoid *(SYN.)* elude, forestall, evade, escape, dodge, avert, forbear, eschew, free, shun.
(ANT.) oppose, meet, confront, encounter, seek.
award *(SYN.)* reward, prize, medal, gift,

trophy.

aware *(SYN.)* mindful, perceptive, apprised, realizing, conscious, observant, knowing, cognizant.

(ANT.) unaware, insensible, ignorant, oblivious.

away *(SYN.)* absent, departed, distracted, gone, not at home.

(ANT.) present, attentive, at home, attending.

awe *(SYN.)* surprise, respect, dread, astonishment, alarm.

awful *(SYN.)* frightful, horrible, dire, terrible, unpleasant, imposing, solemn, appalling, cruel, wicked, brutal, savage, dreadful.

(ANT.) humble, lowly, pleasant, nice, commonplace.

awkward *(SYN.)* inept, unpolished, clumsy, gauche, rough, ungraceful, ungainly, cumbersome.

(ANT.) adroit, graceful, polished, skillful.

awry *(SYN.)* askew, wrong, twisted, crooked, disorderly.

(ANT.) straight, right.

axiom *(SYN.)* fundamental, maxim, principle, theorem, adage, apothegm, byword, aphorism.

B

babble *(SYN.)* twaddle, nonsense, gibberish, prattle, balderdash, rubbish, chatter, baby talk, poppycock, jabber, maunder, piffle.

baby *(SYN.)* newborn, infant, neonate, babe, teeny, small, wee, little, undersized, midget, papoose, protect, cosset, pamper.

babyish *(SYN.)* infantile, childish, baby, whiny, unreasonable, immature, puerile, foolish, dependent.

(ANT.) mature, adult, sensible, reasonable, grown-up.

back *(SYN.)* help, assist, endorse, support, second, ratify, approve, posterior, rear, finance.

(ANT.) anterior, front, face, undercut, veto, undermine, progress, flow, close, accessible, near.

backbiting *(SYN.)* gossip, slander, abuse, malice, cattiness, aspersion, derogation, badmouthing.

(ANT.) compliments, praise, loyalty, friendliness, approval.

backbone *(SYN.)* vertebrae, spine, pillar, prop, skeleton, support, staff, mainstay, basis, mettle, courage, firmness, determination.

(ANT.) timidity, weakness, cowardice, spinelessness.

backbreaking *(SYN.)* exhausting, fatiguing, tough, tiring, demanding, wearying, wearing, difficult.

(ANT.) light, relaxing, undemanding, slight.

back down *(SYN.)* accede, concede, surrender, acquiesce, yield.

(ANT.) persevere, insist.

backer *(SYN.)* underwriter, benefactor, investor, patron, sponsor.

backfire *(SYN.)* flop, boomerang, fail, founder, disappoint.

(ANT.) succeed.

background *(SYN.)* training, knowledge, experience.

backing *(SYN.)* help, support, funds, money, assistance, grant, advocacy, subsidy, endorsement.

(ANT.) criticism, detraction, faultfinding.

backlog *(SYN.)* inventory, reserve, hoard, amassment, accumulation.

backslide *(SYN.)* relapse, revert, return, weaken, regress, renege.

backward *(SYN.)* dull, sluggish, stupid, loath, unwilling, regressive, rearward, slow, retarded.

(ANT.) progressive, precocious, civilized, advanced, forward.

bad *(SYN.)* unfavorable, wrong, evil, immoral, sinful, faulty, improper, unwholesome, wicked, corrupt, tainted, harmful, injurious, defective, poor, imperfect, inferior, substandard, contaminated, inappropriate, unsuited, rotten, unsuitable, sorry, upset, sick, suffering, unpleasant, disagreeable, spoiled, depraved.

(ANT.) good, honorable, reputable, moral, excellent.

badger *(SYN.)* tease, question, annoy, pester, bother, taunt, bait, provoke, torment, harass, hector.

baffle *(SYN.)* confound bewilder, perplex, puzzle, mystify, confuse.
(ANT.) inform, enlighten.

bag *(SYN.)* catch, snare, poke, sack.

bait *(SYN.)* enticement, captivate, ensnare, tease, torment, pester, worry, entrap, question, entice, lure, trap, harass, tempt, badger.

balance *(SYN.)* poise, stability, composure, remains, residue, equilibrium, compare, equalize.
(ANT.) unsteadiness, instability.

bald *(SYN.)* bare, hairless, nude, open, uncovered, simple.
(ANT.) covered, hairy.

baleful *(SYN.)* evil, immoral, sinful, destructive, detrimental, noxious, wicked, bad, villainous, injurious.
(ANT.) good, moral, reputable, excellent, harmless.

balk *(SYN.)* unwilling, obstinate, stubborn, hesitate, check, stop.
(ANT.) willing.

ball *(SYN.)* cotillion, dance, globe, sphere, spheroid.

ballad *(SYN.)* poem, song, ditty.

ballot *(SYN.)* choice, vote, poll.

balmy *(SYN.)* soft, gentle, soothing, fragrant, mild.
(ANT.) tempestuous, stormy.

ban *(SYN.)* prohibit, outlaw, disallow, block, bar, exclude, obstruct, prohibition, taboo, forbid.
(ANT.) allow, permit.

banal *(SYN.)* hackneyed, corny, vapid, trite, overused, stale.
(ANT.) striking, original, fresh, stimulating, novel.

band *(SYN.)* company, association, crew, body, group, society, belt.

bandit *(SYN.)* thief, robber, highwayman, outlaw, marauder.

bang *(SYN.)* hit, strike, slam.

banish *(SYN.)* drive away, eject, exile, oust, deport, dismiss, expel.
(ANT.) receive, accept, shelter, admit, harbor, embrace, welcome.

bank *(SYN.)* barrier, slope, storage, treasury, row, series, string, shore, embankment.

banner *(SYN.)* colors, standard, pennant, flag.

banquet *(SYN.)* feast, celebration, festival, dinner, regalement, affair, entertainment.

banter *(SYN.)* joke, tease, jest.

bar *(SYN.)* counter, impediment, saloon, exclude, obstacle, barricade, obstruct, hindrance, forbid, block, barrier, obstruction.
(ANT.) allow, permit, aid, encouragement.

barbarian *(SYN.)* brute, savage, boor, ruffian, rude, uncivilized, primitive, uncultured, coarse, cruel, barbaric, crude, barbarous.

barber *(SYN.)* coiffeur, hairdresser.

bare *(SYN.)* naked, nude, uncovered, undressed, unclothed, unfurnished, plain, barren, empty, disclose, reveal, expose, scarce.
(ANT.) dressed, garbed, conceal, covered, hide, disguise, clothed.

barefaced *(SYN.)* impudent, bold, insolent, brazen, shameless, audacious, rude, unabashed.

barely *(SYN.)* hardly, scarcely, just.

bargain *(SYN.)* agreement, arrangement, deal, contract, arrange, sale, agree.

baroque *(SYN.)* ornamented, elaborate, embellished, ornate, decorated.

barren *(SYN.)* unproductive, bare, unfruitful, infertile, blank, sterile.
(ANT.) productive, fruitful, fertile.

barricade *(SYN.)* fence, obstruction, fortification, barrier.
(ANT.) free, open, release.

barrier *(SYN.)* fence, wall, bar, railing, obstacle, hindrance, fortification, obstruction, restraint, impediment, limit, barricade.
(ANT.) assistance, encouragement.

barter *(SYN.)* exchange, deal, trade.

base *(SYN.)* bottom, rest, foundation, establish, found, immoral, evil, bad, wicked, depraved, selfish, worthless, cheap, debased, poor, support, stand, low, abject, menial, lowly.
(ANT.) exalted, righteous, lofty, esteemed, noble, honored, refined, valuable.

bashful *(SYN.)* timorous, abashed, shy, coy,

timid, diffident, modest, sheepish, embarrassed, shame-faced, humble, recoiling, uneasy.
(ANT.) fearless, adventurous, gregarious, aggressive, daring.
basic *(SYN.)* underlying, chief, essential, main, fundamental.
(ANT.) subsidiary, subordinate.
basis *(SYN.)* presumption, support, base, principle, underpinning, bottom, presupposition, foundation, postulate, ground, assumption, premise, essential.
(ANT.) implication, trimming, derivative, superstructure.
basket *(SYN.)* hamper, creel, bassinet.
bastion *(SYN.)* mainstay, support, staff, tower, stronghold.
bat *(SYN.)* strike, hit, clout, stick, club, knock, crack.
batch *(SYN.)* group, set, collection, crowd, lot, cluster, bunch, mass.
bath *(SYN.)* washing, shower, tub, wash, dip, soaping.
bathe *(SYN.)* launder, drench, swim, cover, medicate, immerse, wet, dip, soak, rinse, saturate.
bathing suit *(SYN.)* maillot, swimsuit, trunks.
bathos *(SYN.)* mawkishness, soppiness, slush, sentimentality.
bathroom *(SYN.)* powder room, toilet, bath, lavatory.
baton *(SYN.)* mace, rod, staff, billy, crook, stick, fasces.
battalion *(SYN.)* mass, army, swarm, mob, drove, horde, gang, legion, regiment.
batten *(SYN.)* thrive, flourish, fatten, wax, expand, bloom, boom.
(ANT.) decrease, weaken, fail.
batter *(SYN.)* pound, beat, hit, pommel, wallop, mixture, strike.
battery *(SYN.)* series, troop, force, rally, muster, set.
battle *(SYN.)* strife, fray, combat, struggle, contest, skirmish, conflict, fight, war, flight, warfare, action, campaign, strive against.
(ANT.) truce, concord, agreement, settlement, harmony, accept, concur, peace.
battlement *(SYN.)* parapet, crenellation,

rampart, fort, bastion, stronghold, escarpment.
bauble *(SYN.)* plaything, toy, trinket.
bawd *(SYN.)* procuress, prostitute.
bawdy *(SYN.)* vulgar, smutty, filthy, dirty, obscene, pornographic.
bawl *(SYN.)* sob, shout, wail, cry loudly, bellow, weep, cry.
bawl out *(SYN.)* scold, upbraid, censure, reprove, reprimand.
bay *(SYN.)* inlet, bayou, harbor, lagoon, cove, sound, gulf.
bazaar *(SYN.)* fair, market, marketplace.
beach *(SYN.)* sands, seashore, seaside, strand, coast, shore.
beacon *(SYN.)* light, signal, watchtower, guide, flare, warning, alarm.
bead *(SYN.)* globule, drop, pill, blob.
beak *(SYN.)* nose, bill, proboscis.
beam *(SYN.)* gleam, ray, girder, cross-member, pencil, shine, glisten, smile, glitter, gleam.
beaming *(SYN.)* joyful, bright, happy, radiant, grinning.
(ANT.) sullen, gloomy, threatening, scowling.
bear *(SYN.)* carry, support, take, uphold, suffer, convey, allow, stand, yield, endure, tolerate, produce, sustain, brook, transport, undergo, spawn, permit, suffer, abide, tolerate.
(ANT.) evade, shun, avoid, refuse, dodge.
bearable *(SYN.)* sufferable, supportable, manageable, tolerable.
(ANT.) terrible, painful, unbearable, awful, intolerable.
bearing *(SYN.)* course, direction, position, posture, behavior, manner, carriage, relation, reference, connection, application, deportment, air, way, conduct.
bearings *(SYN.)* orientation, whereabouts, location, direction, position, reading, course.
bear on *(SYN.)* affect, relate to.
bear out *(SYN.)* confirm, substantiate, justify, verify, prove.
bear up *(SYN.)* carry on, endure.
bear with *(SYN.)* tolerate, forbear.
beast *(SYN.)* monster, savage, brute, crea-

ture, animal.

beastly *(SYN.)* detestable, mean, low, hateful, loathsome, nasty, unpleasant, despicable, obnoxious, brutal, brutish, offensive.
(ANT.) considerate, sympathetic, refined, humane, fine, pleasant, great.

beat *(SYN.)* pulse, buffet, pound, defeat, palpitate, hit, thump, belabor, knock, overthrow, thrash, pummel, rout, smite, throb, punch, subdue, pulsate, dash, strike, overpower, vanquish, conquer, batter, conquer.
(ANT.) stroke, fail, defend, surrender, shield.

beaten *(SYN.)* disheartened, dejected, licked, discouraged, hopeless, downcast, enervated, down, depressed.
(ANT.) eager, hopeful, cheerful.

beatific *(SYN.)* uplifted, blissful, blessed, elated, happy, wonderful, joyful, divine.
(ANT.) awful, hellish, ill-fated, accursed.

beating *(SYN.)* caning, whipping, drubbing, flogging, lashing, scourging, walloping.

beau *(SYN.)* lover, suitor, swain, admirer.

beautiful *(SYN.)* pretty, fair, beauteous, lovely, charming, fine, comely, handsome, elegant, attractive.
(ANT.) repulsive, hideous, unsightly, foul, homely, plainness, unattractive, ugly, ugliness.

beauty *(SYN.)* handsomeness, fairness, charm, pulchritude, attractiveness, loveliness, comeliness, grace, allegiance.
(ANT.) ugliness, disfigurement, homeliness, plainness, deformity, eyesore.

becalm *(SYN.)* calm, quiet, smooth, still, hush, repose, settle.

because *(SYN.)* inasmuch as, as, since, for.

because of *(SYN.)* as a result of, as a consequence of.

beckon *(SYN.)* call, signal, summon, motion, gesture, wave.

becloud *(SYN.)* obfuscate, confuse, befog, confound, obscure, muddle, screen.
(ANT.) illuminate, clarify, solve.

become *(SYN.)* change, grow, suit, be appropriate, befit.

becoming *(SYN.)* suitable, meet, befitting, appropriate, fitting, seemly, enhancing, attractive, pleasing, flattering, tasteful, smart,

adorning, ornamental.
(ANT.) unsuitable, inappropriate, incongruent, ugly, unattractive, improper.

bed *(SYN.)* layer, cot, vein, berth, stratum, couch, accumulation, bunk, deposit, cradle.

bedazzle *(SYN.)* glare, blind, dumbfound, flabbergast, stun, bewilder, furbish, festoon.

bedeck *(SYN.)* deck, adorn, beautify, smarten, festoon, garnish.

bedevil *(SYN.)* worry, fret, irk, torment, harass, pester, nettle, tease, vex, plague.
(ANT.) soothe, calm, delight, please.

bedlam *(SYN.)* tumult, uproar, madhouse, commotion, confusion, racket, rumpus, pandemonium.
(ANT.) calm, peace.

bedraggled *(SYN.)* shabby, muddy, sodden, messy, sloppy.
(ANT.) dry, neat, clean, well-groomed.

bedrock *(SYN.)* basis, foundation, roots, basics, essentials, fundamentals, bottom, bed, substratum, core.
(ANT.) top, dome, apex, nonessentials.

bedroom *(SYN.)* chamber, bedchamber.

beef *(SYN.)* brawn, strength, heft, gripe, sinew, fitness, huskiness, might.

beef up *(SYN.)* reinforce, vitalize, nerve, buttress, strengthen.
(ANT.) sap, weaken, enervate, drain.

beefy *(SYN.)* solid, strong, muscular, heavy, stocky.

befall *(SYN.)* occur, come about, happen.

before *(SYN.)* prior, earlier, in advance, formerly.
(ANT.) behind, following, afterward, latterly, after.

befriend *(SYN.)* welcome, encourage, aid, stand by.
(ANT.) dislike, shun, desert, avoid.

befuddle *(SYN.)* stupefy, addle, confuse, rattle, disorient.

beg *(SYN.)* solicit, ask, implore, supplicate, entreat, adjure, petition, beseech, pray, crave, request, importune, entreat, implore.
(ANT.) grant, cede, give, bestow, favor.

beget *(SYN.)* sire, engender, produce, create, propagate, originate, breed, generate, procreate, father.

(ANT.) murder, destroy, kill, abort, prevent, extinguish.

beggar *(SYN.)* scrub, tatterdemalion, pauper, wretch, ragamuffin, vagabond, starveling.

begin *(SYN.)* open, enter, arise, initiate, commence, start, inaugurate, originate, institute, create.

(ANT.) terminate, complete, finish, close, end, stop.

beginner *(SYN.)* nonprofessional, amateur, apprentice.

(ANT.) veteran, professional.

beginning *(SYN.)* outset, inception, origin, source, commencement, start, opening, emergence, initiation, inauguration.

(ANT.) termination, completion, end, close, consummation, closing, ending, finish.

begrime *(SYN.)* soil, dirty, smear, muddy, splotch, tarnish.

(ANT.) wash, clean, freshen, launder.

begrudge *(SYN.)* resent, envy, stint, withhold, grudge.

begrudging *(SYN.)* hesitant, reluctant, resentful, unwilling, forced, loath.

(ANT.) willing, eager, quick, spontaneous.

beguiling *(SYN.)* enchanting, interesting, delightful, intriguing, engaging, bewitching, attractive, enthralling, captivating.

(ANT.) boring, dull, unattractive, tedious.

behalf *(SYN.)* benefit, welfare, support, aid, part, interest.

behave *(SYN.)* deport, comport, manage, act, demean, bear, interact, carry, operate, conduct.

(ANT.) rebel, misbehave.

behavior *(SYN.)* manners, carriage, disposition, action, deed, bearing, deportment, conduct, demeanor.

(ANT.) rebelliousness, misbehavior.

behead *(SYN.)* decapitate, guillotine, decollate.

behest *(SYN.)* order, command, decree, mandate, bidding.

behind *(SYN.)* after, backward, at the back, in back of.

(ANT.) frontward, ahead, before.

behold *(SYN.)* look, see, view, notice, observe, perceive, sight.

(ANT.) overlook, ignore.

being *(SYN.)* life, existing, existence, living, actuality, organism, individual.

(ANT.) death, nonexistence, expiration.

belabor *(SYN.)* repeat, reiterate, pound, explain, expatiate, din.

belated *(SYN.)* late, delayed, overdue, tardy.

(ANT.) well-timed, early.

belch *(SYN.)* emit, erupt, gush, disgorge, bubble, eructation, burp.

beleaguered *(SYN.)* bothered, beset, annoyed, harassed, badgered, vexed, plagued, victimized.

belie *(SYN.)* distort, misrepresent, twist, disappoint.

belief *(SYN.)* trust, feeling, certitude, opinion, conviction, persuasion, credence, confidence, reliance, faith, view, creed, assurance.

(ANT.) heresy, denial, incredulity, distrust, skepticism, doubt.

believe *(SYN.)* hold, apprehend, fancy, support, accept, conceive, suppose, imagine, trust, credit.

(ANT.) doubt, reject, distrust, disbelieve, question.

believer *(SYN.)* adherent, follower, devotee, convert, zealot.

(ANT.) doubter, critic, scoffer, skeptic.

belittle *(SYN.)* underrate, depreciate, minimize, decry, disparage, diminish, demean, slight, discredit, aggressive, militant, humiliate.

(ANT.) esteem, admire, flatter, overrate, commend.

bell *(SYN.)* pealing, ringing, signal, tolling, buzzer, chime.

belligerent *(SYN.)* aggressive, warlike, hostile, offensive, combative, militant.

(ANT.) easygoing, compromising, peaceful.

bellow *(SYN.)* thunder, roar, scream, shout, yell, howl.

bellwether *(SYN.)* leader, pilot, guide, ringleader, boss, shepherd.

belly *(SYN.)* stomach, abdomen, paunch.

belonging *(SYN.)* community, loyalty, relationship, kinship, acceptance, rapport.

belongings *(SYN.)* property, effects, possessions.

beloved *(SYN.)* adored, sweet, loved, cherished, prized, esteemed, valued, darling.

below *(SYN.)* under, less, beneath, underneath, lower.

(ANT.) aloft, overhead, above, over.

belt *(SYN.)* girdle, sash, strap, cummerbund, band, waistband, whack, hit, wallop, punch.

bemoan *(SYN.)* mourn, lament, grieve, sorrow, regret, deplore.

bend *(SYN.)* turn, curve, incline, submit, bow, lean, crook, twist, yield, stoop, crouch, agree, suppress, oppress, mold, kneel, deflect, subdue, influence.

(ANT.) resist, straighten, break, stiffen.

beneath *(SYN.)* under, below.

(ANT.) above, over.

benediction *(SYN.)* thanks, blessing, prayer.

beneficial *(SYN.)* salutary, good, wholesome, advantageous, useful, helpful, serviceable, profitable.

(ANT.) harmful, destructive, injurious, deleterious, detrimental.

benefit *(SYN.)* support, help, gain, avail, profit, account, favor, aid, good, advantage, serve, interest, behalf, service.

(ANT.) handicap, calamity, trouble, disadvantage, distress.

benevolence *(SYN.)* magnanimity, charity, tenderness, altruism, humanity, philanthropy, generosity, liberality, beneficence, good will, kindness.

(ANT.) malevolence, unkindness, cruelty, selfishness, inhumanity.

benevolent *(SYN.)* kindhearted, tender, merciful, generous, altruistic, obliging, kind, good, well-wishing, philanthropy, liberal, unselfish, kindly, disposed, openhearted, humane, benign, friendly.

(ANT.) malevolent, greedy, wicked, harsh.

bent *(SYN.)* curved, crooked, resolved, determined, set, inclined, firm, decided.

(ANT.) straight.

berate *(SYN.)* scold.

beseech *(SYN.)* appeal, entreat, plead, ask, beg, implore.

beset *(SYN.)* surround, attack.

besides *(SYN.)* moreover, further, except for, in addition, also, as well, furthermore.

besiege *(SYN.)* assault, attack, siege, bombard, raid, charge.

bespeak *(SYN.)* engage, reserve, indicate, show, signify, express.

best *(SYN.)* choice, prime, select.

(ANT.) worst.

bestial *(SYN.)* brutal, beastly, savage, cruel.

bestow *(SYN.)* confer, place, put, award, give, present.

(ANT.) withdraw, withhold.

bet *(SYN.)* gamble, give, stake, wager, pledge, ante.

betray *(SYN.)* reveal, deliver, expose, mislead, trick, deceive, exhibit, show.

(ANT.) shelter, protect, safeguard.

betrothal *(SYN.)* marriage, engagement, contract.

better *(SYN.)* superior, preferable, improve.

(ANT.) worsen.

between *(SYN.)* among, betwixt.

beware *(SYN.)* take care, watch out, look sharp, be careful.

bewilder *(SYN.)* perplex, confuse, mystify, baffle, puzzle, overwhelm.

(ANT.) clarify, enlighten.

bewitch *(SYN.)* captivate, charm, delight, enchant.

beyond *(SYN.)* past, farther, exceeding.

bias *(SYN.)* slant, inclination, proneness, turn, bent, penchant, tendency, disposition, propensity, partiality, predisposition, leaning, proclivity, prejudice, bend, influence, slanting, predilection.

(ANT.) fairness, justice, even-handedness, equity, impartiality.

bible *(SYN.)* guide, handbook, gospel, manual, sourcebook, guidebook.

bibulous *(SYN.)* guzzling, intemperate, wine-bibbing, sottish, alcoholic.

(ANT.) sober, moderate.

bicker *(SYN.)* dispute, argue, wrangle, quarrel.

(ANT.) go along with, agree.

bid *(SYN.)* order, command, direct, wish, greet, say, offer, instruct, invite, purpose, tender, proposal.

bidding *(SYN.)* behest, request, decree, call, charge, beck, summons, solicitation, invitation, instruction, mandate.

bide *(SYN.)* stay, tarry, delay, wait, remain.

big *(SYN.)* large, huge, bulky, immense, co-lossal, majestic, august, monstrous, hulking, gigantic, massive, great, enormous, tremen-dous, outgoing, important, considerable, generous, grand.

(ANT.) small, little, tiny, immature, petite.

big-hearted *(SYN.)* good-natured, liberal, generous, unselfish, open-handed, un-stinting, charitable, magnanimous.

(ANT.) cold, selfish, mean, uncharitable.

bigoted *(SYN.)* intolerant, partial, prejudiced, biased, unfair, chauvinist.

bigotry *(SYN.)* bias, blindness, intolerance, unfairness, prejudice, ignorance, mind-lessness, passion, sectarianism.

(ANT.) acceptance, open-mindedness.

big-shot *(SYN.)* somebody, brass hat, big gun.

(ANT.) underling, nobody, nebbish, cipher.

bijou *(SYN.)* gem, bauble, jewel, ornament.

bile *(SYN.)* spleen, rancor, anger, bitterness, peevishness, ill-humor, nastiness, resentment, discontent, irascibility.

(ANT.) cheerfulness, affability, pleasantness.

bilge *(SYN.)* hogwash, drivel, gibberish, rub-bish, bosh, foolishness, twaddle.

bilious *(SYN.)* petulant, crabby, ill-natured, cross, peevish, crotchety, cranky.

(ANT.) happy, agreeable, pleasant, good-natured.

bilk *(SYN.)* defraud, trick, cheat, hoodwink, deceive, fleece, rook, bamboozle.

bill *(SYN.)* charge, invoice, account, statement.

billet *(SYN.)* housing, quarters, berth, shelter, barrack, installation.

billingsgate *(SYN.)* swearing, scurrility, cursing, abuse, vulgarity, gutter, profanity.

billow *(SYN.)* surge, swell, rise, rush, peaking, magnification, amplification, augmentation, increase, intensification.

(ANT.) lowering, decrease.

bin *(SYN.)* cubbyhole. box, container, chest, cubicle, crib, receptacle, can.

bind *(SYN.)* connect, restrain, band, fasten, oblige, obligate, engage, wrap, connect, weld, attach, tie, require, restrict.

(ANT.) unlace, loose, unfasten, untie, free.

binding *(SYN.)* compulsory, obligatory, mandatory, compelling, unalterable, im-perative, indissoluble, unconditional, un-changeable, hard-and-fast.

(ANT.) adjustable, flexible, elastic, change-able.

binge *(SYN.)* fling, spree, carousal, toot.

birth *(SYN.)* origin, beginning, infancy, inception.

(ANT.) finish, decline, death, disappear-ance, end.

biscuit *(SYN.)* bun, roll, cake, muffin, bread, rusk.

bit *(SYN.)* fraction, portion, scrap, fragment, particle, drop, speck, harness, small amount, restraint, morsel, sum.

bite *(SYN.)* gnaw, chew, nip, sting, pierce, mouthful, snack, morsel.

biting *(SYN.)* cutting, sharp, acid, sneering, sarcastic.

(ANT.) soothing, kind, gentle, agreeable.

bitter *(SYN.)* distasteful, sour, acrid, pun-gent, piercing, vicious, severe, biting, dis-tressful, stinging, distressing, ruthless, hat-ed, hostile, grievous, harsh, painful, tart.

(ANT.) sweet, mellow, pleasant, delicious.

bizarre *(SYN.)* peculiar, strange, odd, un-common, queer, unusual.

(ANT.) usual, everyday, ordinary, incon-spicuous.

black *(SYN.)* sooty, dark, ebony, inky, soiled, filthy, dirty, stained, somber, depressing, sad, dismal, gloomy.

(ANT.) white, clean, pristine, glowing, pure, cheerful, light-skinned, sunny, bright.

blackball *(SYN.)* turn down, ban, blacklist, exclude, snub, reject, debar.

(ANT.) accept, include, invite, ask, bid.

blacken *(SYN.)* tar, ink, black, darken, be-soot, smudge, begrime, discredit, defile, dull, dim, tarnish, ebonize, denounce, sully, libel, blemish, defame.

(ANT.) exalt, honor, whiten, brighten, shine, bleach.

blackmail *(SYN.)* bribe, payment, bribery, extortion, shakedown, coercion.

blackout *(SYN.)* faint, coma, uncon-sciousness, oblivion, amnesia, stupor.

bladder *(SYN.)* saccule, sac, vesicle, pouch, pod, cell, blister, container, cyst.

blade *(SYN.)* cutter, lancet, knife, sword.

blah *(SYN.)* lifeless, flat, jejune, lukewarm, stale, insipid, tasteless, pedestrian, tedious, dreary, uninteresting.

(ANT.) spirited, fascinating, vibrant, vigorous.

blame *(SYN.)* upbraid, criticize, fault, guilt, accuse, rebuke, charge, implicate, impeach, tattle, condemn, indict, responsibility, censure, denounce, reproach.

(ANT.) exonerate, credit, honor, absolve.

blameless *(SYN.)* moral, innocent, worthy, faultless.

(ANT.) blameworthy, culpable, guilty.

blanch *(SYN.)* whiten, bleach, decolorize, peroxide, fade, wash out, dim, dull.

bland *(SYN.)* soft, smooth, gentle, agreeable, vapid, insipid, mild, polite.

(ANT.) harsh, outspoken, disagreeable.

blandish *(SYN.)* praise, compliment, overpraise, cajole, puff, adulate, salve, fawn, court, toady, butter up, please, jolly.

(ANT.) insult, deride, criticize, belittle.

blandisher *(SYN.)* adulator, booster, sycophant, eulogist, apple polisher, flunkey.

(ANT.) knocker, faultfinder, belittler.

blandishment *(SYN.)* applause, cajolery, honey, adulation, plaudits, acclaim, fawning, compliments.

(ANT.) carping, belittling, criticism, deprecation.

blank *(SYN.)* unmarked, expressionless, uninterested, form, area, void, vacant, empty.

(ANT.) marked, filled, alert, animated.

blanket *(SYN.)* quilt, coverlet, cover, comforter, robe, padding, carpet, wrapper, mantle, envelope, housing, coat, comprehensive, universal, across-the-board, panoramic, omnibus.

(ANT.) limited, detailed, restricted, precise.

blare *(SYN.)* roar, blast, resound, jar, scream, swell, clang, peal, trumpet, toot, hoot.

blasphemous *(SYN.)* profane, irreverent, impious, godless, ungodly, sacrilegious, irreligious.

(ANT.) reverent, reverential, religious, pious.

blasphemy *(SYN.)* profanation, impiousness, cursing, irreverence, sacrilege, abuse, ecration, swearing, contempt.

(ANT.) respect, piety, reverence, devotion.

blast *(SYN.)* burst, explosion, discharge.

blasted *(SYN.)* blighted, withered, ravaged, decomposed, spoiled, destroyed.

blastoff *(SYN.)* launching, expulsion, launch, shot, projection.

blatant *(SYN.)* shameless, notorious, brazen, flagrant, glaring, bold, obvious.

(ANT.) deft, subtle, insidious, devious.

blaze *(SYN.)* inferno, shine, flare, marking, fire, outburst, holocaust, notch, flame.

(ANT.) die, dwindle.

bleach *(SYN.)* pale, whiten, blanch, whitener.

(ANT.) darken, blacken.

bleak *(SYN.)* dreary, barren, cheerless, depressing, gloomy, windswept, bare, cold, dismal, desolate, raw, chilly.

(ANT.) lush, hopeful, promising, cheerful.

bleary *(SYN.)* hazy, groggy, blurry, fuzzy, misty, clouded, overcast, dim, blear.

(ANT.) clear, vivid, precise, clear-cut.

bleed *(syn.)* pity, lose blood, grieve, sorrow.

blemish *(SYN.)* injury, speck, flaw, scar, disgrace, imperfection, stain, fault, blot.

(ANT.) purity, embellishment, adornment, perfection.

blend *(SYN.)* beat, intermingle, combine, fuse, unify, consolidate, unite, amalgamate, conjoin, mix, coalesce, intermix, join, merge, compound, combination, stir, mixture, commingle, mingle.

(ANT.) separate, decompose, analyze, disintegrate.

bless *(SYN.)* thank, celebrate, extol, glorify, adore, delight, praise, gladden, exalt.

(ANT.) denounce, blaspheme, slander, curse.

blessed *(SYN.)* sacred, holy, consecrated, dedicated, hallowed, sacrosanct, beatified, joyful, delighted, joyous, sainted, canonized, blissful.

(ANT.) miserable, sad, dispirited, cheerless.

blessing *(SYN.)* benison, sanction, favor, grace, benediction, invocation, approbation, approval, compliment, bounty, windfall, gift, benefit, advantage, kindness, felicitation, invocation.

(ANT.) disapproval, execration, curse, denunciation, malediction, rebuke, displeasure, condemnation, adversity, misfortune, mishap, calamity.

blight *(SYN.)* decay, disease, spoil, sickness, wither, ruin, damage, harm, decaying, epidemic, affliction, destroy.

blind *(SYN.)* sightless, unmindful, rash, visionless, ignorant, unsighted, unconscious, discerning, heedless, oblivious, purblind, unknowing, screen, unaware, thoughtless, shade, unthinking, cover, curtain, without thought, headlong.

(ANT.) discerning, sensible, calculated, perceiving, perceptive, aware.

blink *(SYN.)* bat, glance, flicker, wink, twinkle.

bliss *(SYN.)* ecstasy, rapture, glee, elation, joy, blessedness, gladness, happiness, delight, felicity, blissfulness.

(ANT.) woe, sadness, sorrow, grief, unhappiness, torment, wretchedness, misery.

blissful *(SYN.)* happy, elated, rapturous, esctatic, paradisiacal, joyous, enraptured.

blister *(SYN.)* bleb, swelling, welt, sore, blob, bubble, inflammation, boil, canker.

blithe *(SYN.)* breezy, merry, airy, lighthearted, light, gay, fanciful, graceful.

(ANT.) morose, grouchy, low-spirited, gloomy.

blitz *(SYN.)* strike, onslaught, thrust, raid, lunge, drive, incursion, assault, sally.

blizzard *(SYN.)* storm, snowstorm, snowfall, gale, tempest, blast, blow, swirl.

bloat *(SYN.)* distend, puff up, inflate, swell.
(ANT.) deflate.

blob *(SYN.)* bubble, blister, pellet, globule.

block *(SYN.)* clog, hinder, bar, impede, close, obstruct, barricade, blockade, obstruction, hindrance, obstacle, impediment, retard, check, stop.

(ANT.) forward, promote, aid, clear, advance, advantage, assist, further, open.

blockade *(SYN.)* barrier, fortification, obstruction, barricade.

blockhead *(SYN.)* dunce, dolt, fool, sap, idiot, simpleton, chump, booby, bonehead, woodenhead.

blood *(SYN.)* murder, gore, slaughter, bloodshed, ancestry, lineage, heritage.

bloodcurdling *(SYN.)* terrifying, alarming, chilling, stunning, scary.

bloodless *(SYN.)* dead, torpid, dull, drab, cold, colorless, passionless, lackluster.

(ANT.) passionate, vital, ebullient, animated, vivacious.

bloodshed *(SYN.)* murder, killing, slaying, blood bath, massacre, carnage.

bloodthirsty *(SYN.)* murderous, cruel.

bloody *(SYN.)* cruel, pitiless, bloodthirsty, inhuman, ruthless, ferocious, murderous.

(ANT.) kind, gentle.

bloom *(SYN.)* thrive, glow, flourish, blossom, flower.

(ANT.) wane, decay, dwindle, shrivel, wither.

blooming *(SYN.)* flush, green, vigorous, thriving, vital, abloom, healthy, fresh, booming.

(ANT.) flagging, declining, whithering.

blooper *(SYN.)* muff, fluff, error, bungle, botch, blunder, fumble, howler, indiscretion.

blossom *(SYN.)* bloom, flower, flourish.
(ANT.) shrink, wither, dwindle, fade.

blot *(SYN.)* stain, inkblot, spot, inkstain, blemish, dishonor, disgrace, spatter, obliterate, soil, dry.

blot out *(SYN.)* wipe out, destroy, obliterate, abolish, annihilate, cancel, expunge, strike out, shade, darken, shadow, overshadow, obfuscate, cloud, eclipse.

blow *(SYN.)* hit, thump, slap, cuff, box, shock, move, drive, spread, breeze, puff, whistle, inflate, enlarge.

blowout *(SYN.)* blast, explosion, burst.

blue *(SYN.)* sapphire, azure, gloomy, sad, unhappy, depressed, dejected, melancholy.

(ANT.) cheerful, optimistic, happy.

blueprint *(SYN.)* design, plan, scheme, chart, draft, prospectus, outline, proposal, conception, project, layout.

blues *(SYN.)* dumps, melancholy, depression, doldrums, moodiness, dejection, despondency, gloominess, moroseness.

bluff *(SYN.)* steep, perpendicular, vertical, abrupt, precipitous, rough, open, frank, hearty, blunt, fool, mislead, pretend, deceive, fraud, lie, fake, deceit.

blunder *(SYN.)* error, flounder, mistake, stumble.

blunt *(SYN.)* solid, abrupt, rough, dull, pointless, plain, bluff, edgeless, unceremonious, obtuse, rude, outspoken, unsharpened, rounded, worn, crude, direct, impolite, short, curt, gruff.

(ANT.) tactful, polite, subtle, polished, suave, sharp, keen, pointed, diplomatic.

blur *(SYN.)* sully, dim, obscure, stain, dull, confuse, cloud, smear, stain, smudge.

(ANT.) clear, clarify.

blush *(SYN.)* redden.

board *(SYN.)* embark, committee, wood, mount, cabinet, food, get on, lumber.

boast *(SYN.)* vaunt, flaunt, brag, glory, crow, exaggerate, bragging.

(ANT.) humble, apologize, minimize, deprecate.

body *(SYN.)* remains, bulk, mass, carcass, form, company, corpus, society, firmness, group, torso, substance, collection, cadaver, trunk, group, throng, company, crowd, band.

(ANT.) spirit, intellect, soul.

bogus *(SYN.)* counterfeit, false, pretend, fake, phony.

(ANT.) genuine.

boil *(SYN.)* seethe, bubble, pimple, fume, cook, swelling, rage, foam, simmer, smolder, stew.

boisterous *(SYN.)* rough, violent, rowdy, noisy, tumultuous.

(ANT.) serene.

bold *(SYN.)* daring, forward, pushy, striking, brave, dauntless, rude, prominent, adventurous, fearless, insolent, conspicuous, defiant, arrogant, cavalier, brazen, unafraid, intrepid, courageous, valiant, heroic, gallant, disrespectful, impudent, shameless.

(ANT.) modest, bashful, cowardly, timid, retiring, flinching, fearful, timorous, polite, courteous, deferential.

bolt *(SYN.)* break away, fastener, flee, take flight, lock.

bombard *(SYN.)* shell, open fire, bomb, rake, assail, attack.

bond *(SYN.)* fastener, rope, tie, cord, connection, attachment, link, promise.

(ANT.) sever, separate, untie, disconnect.

bondage *(SYN.)* slavery, thralldom, captivity, imprisonment, servitude, confinement, vassalage, enslavement.

(ANT.) liberation, emancipation, free, independence, freedom.

bonds *(SYN.)* chains, cuffs, fetters, shackles, irons, bracelets.

bone up *(SYN.)* learn, master, study, relearn.

bonus *(SYN.)* more, extra, premium, gift, reward, bounty.

bony *(SYN.)* lean, lank, thin, lanky, rawboned, fleshless, skinny, gangling, weight.

(ANT.) plump, fleshy, stout.

book *(SYN.)* manual, textbook, work, booklet, monograph, brochure, tract, volume, pamphlet, treatise, publication, hardcover, paperback, novel, workbook, text.

bookish *(SYN.)* formal, scholarly, theoretical, academic, learned, scholastic, erudite.

(ANT.) simple, ignorant.

boom *(SYN.)* advance, grow, flourish, progress, gain, increase, roar, beam, rumble, reverberate, thunder, prosper, swell, thrive, pole, rush.

(ANT.) decline, fail, recession.

booming *(SYN.)* flourishing, blooming, thriving, vigorous, prospering, exuberant.

(ANT.) waning, dying, failing, declining,

boon *(SYN.)* gift, jolly, blessing, pleasant, godsend, windfall.

boondocks *(SYN.)* sticks, backwoods.

boor *(SYN.)* lout, clown, oaf, yokel, rustic, vulgarian, ruffian.

boorish *(SYN.)* coarse, churlish, uncivil, ill-mannered, ill-bred, uncivilized, crude, uncouth.

(ANT.) polite, genteel cultivated, well-mannered.

boost *(SYN.)* push, lift, help, hoist, shove.

(ANT.) depress, lower, belittle, submerge, disparage, decrease, decline, reduction, downturn.

booster *(SYN.)* supporter, fan, rooter, plugger, follower.

boot *(SYN.)* shoe, kick.

booth *(SYN.)* enclosure, cubicle, stand, compartment, box.

bootless *(SYN.)* purposeless, ineffective, profitless, useless.

(ANT.) favorable, successful, useful.

bootlicker *(SYN.)* flunky, fawner, toady, sycophant.

booty *(SYN.)* prize, plunder, loot.

booze *(SYN.)* spirits, drink, liquor, alcohol.

border *(SYN.)* fringe, rim, verge, boundary, edge, termination, brink, limit, brim, outskirts, frontier, margin.

(ANT.) interior, center, mainland, core, middle.

borderline *(SYN.)* unclassifiable, indeterminate, halfway, obscure, inexact, indefinite, unclear.

(ANT.) precise, absolute, definite.

border on *(SYN.)* approximate, approach, resemble, echo, parallel, connect.

bore *(SYN.)* tire, weary, hole, perforate, pierce, drill.

(ANT.) arouse, captivate, excite, interest.

boredom *(SYN.)* ennui, doldrums, weariness, dullness, tedium.

(ANT.) stimulation, motive, activity, stimulus, excitement.

boring *(SYN.)* monotonous, dull, dead, flat, tedious, wearisome, trite, prosaic, humdrum.

born *(SYN.)* hatched, produced.

borrow *(SYN.)* copy, adopt, simulate, mirror, assume, usurp, plagiarize, take.

(ANT.) allow, advance, invent, originate, credit, lend.

bosom *(SYN.)* chest, breast, feelings, thoughts, mind, interior, marrow, heart.

boss *(SYN.)* director, employer, oversee, direct, foreman, supervisor, manager.

(ANT.) worker, employee, underling.

bossy *(SYN.)* overbearing, arrogant, domineering, lordly, tyrannical, highhanded, arbitrary, oppress.

(ANT.) flexible, easy-going, cooperative.

botch *(SYN.)* blunder, bungle, fumble, goof, muff, mishandle, mismanage.

(ANT.) perform, realize.

bother *(SYN.)* haunt, molest, trouble, annoy, upset, fleeting, transient, harass, inconven-

ience, momentary, disturb, passing, pester, tease, irritate, worry, vex.

(ANT.) prolonged, extended, long, protracted, lengthy, comfort, solace.

bothersome *(SYN.)* irritating, vexatious, worrisome, annoying, distressing, troublesome, disturbing.

bottle *(SYN.)* container, flask, vessel, decanter, vial, ewer, jar.

bottleneck *(SYN.)* obstacle, obstruction, barrier, block, blockage, detour.

bottom *(SYN.)* basis, fundament, base, groundwork, foot, depths, lowest part, underside, foundation, seat, buttocks, rear, behind.

(ANT.) top, peak, apex, summit, topside.

bough *(SYN.)* branch, arm, limb.

bounce *(SYN.)* recoil, ricochet, rebound.

bound *(SYN.)* spring, vault, hop, leap, start, surrounded, jump, limit, jerk, boundary, bounce, skip, tied, shackled, trussed, fettered, certain, sure, destined, compelled, required.

(ANT.) unfettered, free.

boundary *(SYN.)* bound, limit, border, margin, outline, circumference, perimeter, division, frontier, edge.

boundless *(SYN.)* limitless, endless, inexhaustible, unlimited, eternal, infinite.

(ANT.) restricted, narrow, limited.

bounteous *(SYN.)* plentiful, generous, liberal, abundant.

(ANT.) scarce.

bountiful *(SYN.)* bounteous, fertile, plentiful, generous, abundant.

(ANT.) sparing, infertile, scarce.

bounty *(SYN.)* generosity, gift, award, bonus, reward, prize, premium.

bourgeois *(SYN.)* common, ordinary, commonplace, middle-class, conventional.

(ANT.) upper-class, unconventional, loose, aristocratic.

bout *(SYN.)* round, contest, conflict, test, struggle, match, spell, fight.

bow *(SYN.)* bend, yield, kneel, submit, stoop.

bowels *(SYN.)* entrails, intestines, innards, guts, stomach.

bowl *(SYN.)* container, dish, pot, pottery,

crock, jug, vase.

bowl over *(SYN.)* fell, floor, overturn, astound, nonplus, stagger, jar.

bow out *(SYN.)* give up, withdraw, retire, resign, abandon.

box *(SYN.)* hit, fight, crate, case, container.

boxer *(SYN.)* prizefighter, fighter.

boy *(SYN.)* male, youngster, lad, kid, fellow, buddy, youth.

(ANT.) girl, man.

boycott *(SYN.)* picket, strike, ban, revolt, blackball.

boy friend *(SYN.)* date, young man, sweetheart, courtier, beau.

brace *(SYN.)* strengthen, tie, prop, support, tighten, stay, strut, bind, truss, crutch.

bracelet *(SYN.)* armband, bangle, circlet.

bracing *(SYN.)* stimulating, refreshing, restorative, fortifying, invigorating.

bracket *(SYN.)* join, couple, enclose, relate, brace, support.

brag *(SYN.)* boast, flaunt, vaunt, bluster, swagger.

(ANT.) demean, debase, denigrate, degrade, depreciate, deprecate.

braid *(SYN.)* weave, twine, wreath, plait.

brain *(SYN.)* sense, intelligence, intellect, common sense, understanding, reason.

(ANT.) stupid, stupidity.

brake *(SYN.)* decelerate, stop, curb.

(ANT.) accelerate.

branch *(SYN.)* shoot, limb, bough, tributary, offshoot, part, division, expand, department, divide, spread, subdivision.

brand *(SYN.)* make, trademark, label, kind, burn, trade name, mark, stamp, blaze.

brave *(SYN.)* bold, daring, gallant, valorous, adventurous, heroic, magnanimous, chivalrous, audacious, valiant, courageous, fearless, intrepid, unafraid.

(ANT.) weak, cringing, timid, cowardly, fearful, craven.

brawl *(SYN.)* racket, quarrel, fracas, riot, fight, melee, fray, disturbance, dispute, disagreement.

brawn *(SYN.)* strength, muscle.

(ANT.) weakness.

brazen *(SYN.)* immodest, forward, shameless, bold, brassy, impudent, insolent, rude.

(ANT.) retiring, self-effacing, modest, shy.

breach *(SYN.)* rupture, fracture, rift, break, crack, gap, opening, breaking, quarrel, violation.

(ANT.) observation.

break *(SYN.)* demolish, pound, rack, smash, burst, rupture, disobey, violate, crack, infringe, crush, squeeze, transgress, fracture, shatter, wreck, crash, atomize, disintegrate, collapse, splinter, crack, gap, breach, opening, rupture.

(ANT.) restore, heal, join, renovate, mend, repair.

breed *(SYN.)* engender, bear, propagate, father, beget, rear, conceive, train, generate, raise, procreate, nurture, create, mother, produce, originate, generate, raise, train, nurture.

(ANT.) murder, abort, kill.

breeze *(SYN.)* air, wind, zephyr, breath.

(ANT.) calm.

breezy *(SYN.)* jolly, spry, active, brisk, energetic, lively, carefree, spirited.

brevity *(SYN.)* briefness, conciseness.

(ANT.) length.

brew *(SYN.)* plot, plan, cook, ferment, prepare, scheme.

bribe *(SYN.)* buy off.

bridle *(SYN.)* control, hold, restrain, check, harness, curb, restraint, halter.

(ANT.) release, free, loose.

brief *(SYN.)* curt, short, fleeting, passing, compendious, terse, laconic, succinct, momentary, transient, temporary, concise, compact, condensed.

(ANT.) long, extended, prolonged, lengthy, protracted, comprehensive, extensive, exhaustive.

brigand *(SYN.)* bandit, robber, thief.

bright *(SYN.)* luminous, gleaming, clever, witty, brilliant, lucid, vivid, clear, smart, intelligent, lustrous, clever, shining, shiny, sparkling, shimmering, radiant, cheerful, lively, gay, happy, lighthearted, keen, promising, favorable, encouraging.

(ANT.) sullen, dull, murky, dark, gloomy, dim, lusterless, boring, colorless, stupid,

backward, slow.

brilliant *(SYN.)* bright, clear, smart, intelligent, sparkling, shining, alert, vivid, splendid, radiant, glittering, talented, ingenious, gifted.
(ANT.) mediocre, dull, lusterless.

brim *(SYN.)* border, margin, lip, rim, edge.
(ANT.) middle, center.

bring *(SYN.)* fetch, take, carry, raise, introduce, propose.
(ANT.) remove, withdraw.

brink *(SYN.)* limit, verge, rim, margin, edge.

brisk *(SYN.)* fresh, breezy, cool, lively, spry, refreshing, spirited, jolly, energetic, quick, active, animated, nimble, agile, sharp, keen, stimulating, invigorating.
(ANT.) musty, faded, stagnant, decayed, hackneyed, slow, lethargic, sluggish, still, dull, oppressive.

briskness *(SYN.)* energy, exercise, motion, rapidity, agility, action, quickness, activity, vigor, liveliness, movement.
(ANT.) inertia, idleness, sloth, dullness, inactivity.

bristle *(SYN.)* flare up, anger, rage, seethe, get mad.

brittle *(SYN.)* crumbling, frail, breakable, delicate, splintery, crisp, fragile, weak.
(ANT.) tough, enduring, unbreakable, thick, strong, sturdy, flexible, elastic, supple.

broach *(SYN.)* set afoot, introduce, inaugurate, start, mention, launch, advance.

broad *(SYN.)* large, wide, tolerant, expanded, vast, liberal, sweeping, roomy, expansive, extended, general, extensive, full.
(ANT.) restricted, confined, narrow, constricted, slim, tight, limited, negligible.

broadcast *(SYN.)* distribute, announce, publish, scatter, circulate, spread, send, transmit, relay.

broaden *(SYN.)* spread, widen, amplify, enlarge, extend, increase, add to, expand, stretch, deepen, magnify.
(ANT.) tighted, narrow, constrict, straiten.

broad-minded *(SYN.)* unprejudiced, tolerant, liberal, unbigoted.
(ANT.) prejudiced, petty, narrow-minded.

brochure *(SYN.)* booklet, pamphlet, leaflet, mailing, circular, tract, flier.

broil *(SYN.)* cook, burn, heat, roast, bake, scorch, fire, grill, singe, sear, toast.

broken *(SYN.)* flattened, rent, shattered, wrecked, destroyed, reduced, smashed, crushed, fractured, ruptured, interrupted, burst, separated.
(ANT.) whole, integral, united, repaired.

brokenhearted *(SYN.)* disconsolate, forlorn, heartbroken, sad, grieving.

bromide *(SYN.)* banality, platitude, stereotype, commonplace, slogan.

brooch *(SYN.)* clasp, pin, breastpin, broach.

brood *(SYN.)* study, consider, ponder, reflect, contemplate, meditate, young, litter, offspring, think, muse, deliberate.

brook *(SYN.)* rivulet, run, branch, stream, creek.

brother *(SYN.)* comrade, man, kinsman, sibling.
(ANT.) sister.

brotherhood *(SYN.)* kinship, kindness, fraternity, fellowship, clan, society, brotherliness, bond, association, relationship, solidarity.
(ANT.) strife, discord, acrimony, opposition.

brotherly *(SYN.)* affectionate, fraternal, cordial, sympathetic, benevolent, philanthropic, kindred, communal, altruistic.

brow *(SYN.)* forehead, eyebrow.

browbeat *(SYN.)* bully, domineer, bulldoze, intimidate, henpeck, oppress, grind.

brown study *(SYN.)* contemplation, reflection, reverie, musing, thoughtfulness, deliberation, rumination, self-communion.

browse *(SYN.)* look, skim, scan, graze, read, feed.

bruise *(SYN.)* hurt, injure, wound, damage, abrasion, injury, contusion, harm.

brunt *(SYN.)* force, impact, shock, strain, oppression, severity.

brush *(SYN.)* rub, wipe, clean, bushes, remove, shrubs, broom, whisk, paintbrush, hairbrush, underbrush, thicket.

brush-off *(SYN.)* dismissal, snub, slight, rebuff, turndown.

brusque *(SYN.)* sudden, curt, hasty, blunt, rough, steep, precipitate, rugged, craggy, gruff, surly, abrupt, short, bluff.

(ANT.) smooth, anticipated, courteous, expected, gradual, personable.

brutal *(SYN.)* brute, cruel, inhuman, rude, barbarous, gross, sensual, ferocious, brutish, coarse, bestial, carnal, remorseless, ruthless, savage, mean, pitiless, barbaric.

(ANT.) kind, courteous, humane, civilized, gentle, kindhearted, mild.

brute *(SYN.)* monster, barbarian, beast, animal, wild, savage.

bubble *(SYN.)* boil, foam, seethe, froth.

buccaneer *(SYN.)* sea robber, privateer, pirate.

buck *(SYN.)* spring, jump, vault, leap.

bucket *(SYN.)* pot, pail, canister, can.

buckle *(SYN.)* hook, fastening, fastener, bend, wrinkle, clip, clasp, distort, catch, strap, fasten, collapse, yield, warp.

bud *(SYN.)* develop, sprout.

buddy *(SYN.)* companion, comrade, friend, partner, pal.

budge *(SYN.)* stir, move.

budget *(SYN.)* schedule, ration.

buff *(SYN.)* shine, polish, burnish, rub, wax.

buffet *(SYN.)* bat, strike, clout, blow, knock, beat, crack, hit, slap, cabinet, counter, server.

buffoon *(SYN.)* jester, fool, clown, jokester, zany, comedian, chump, boor, dolt.

bug *(SYN.)* fault, hitch, defect, catch, snag, failing, rub, flaw, snarl, weakness, annoy, pester, hector, vex, nag, nettle.

bugbear *(SYN.)* bogy, specter, demon, devil, fiend.

build *(SYN.)* found, rear, establish, constructed, raise, set up, erect, assemble.

(ANT.) raze, destroy, overthrow, demolish, undermine.

building *(SYN.)* residence, structure, house, edifice.

buildup *(SYN.)* gain, enlargement, increase, praise, commendation, promotion, jump, expansion, uptrend, testimonial, plug, puff, blurb, endorsement, compliment.

(ANT.) reduction, decrease, decline.

bulge *(SYN.)* lump, protuberance, bump, swelling, protrusion, extend, protrude.

(ANT.) hollow, shrink, contract, depression.

bulk *(SYN.)* lump, magnitude, volume, mass, most, majority.

bulky *(SYN.)* great, big, huge, large, enormous, massive, immense, monstrous, clumsy, cumbersome, unwieldy.

(ANT.) tiny, little, small, petite, handy, delicate.

bull *(SYN.)* push, force, press, drive, thrust, bump.

bulldoze *(SYN.)* cow, bully, coerce, thrust, push.

bulletin *(SYN.)* news, flash, message, statement, newsletter.

bullheaded *(SYN.)* dogged, stiff-necked, stubborn, mulish, rigid.

(ANT.) flexible, submissive, compliant.

bully *(SYN.)* pester, tease, intimidate, harass, domineer.

bulwark *(SYN.)* wall, bastion, abutment, bank, dam, rampart, shoulder, parapet, backing, maintainer, embankment, safeguard, reinforcement, sustainer.

bum *(SYN.)* idler, loafer, drifter, hobo, wretch, beggar, vagrant.

bumbling *(SYN.)* bungling, inept, blundering, clumsy, incompetent, awkward, maladroit, ungainly.

(ANT.) facile, handy, dexterous, proficient.

bump *(SYN.)* shake, push, hit, shove, prod, collide, knock, bang.

bumpkin *(SYN.)* hick, yokel, rustic.

bumptious *(SYN.)* arrogant, self-assertive, conceited, forward, overbearing, swaggering, pushy.

(ANT.) sheepish, self-effacing, shrinking, unobtrusive, diffident.

bumpy *(SYN.)* uneven, jolting, rough, jarring, rocky, coarse.

(ANT.) flat, smooth, flush, polished, level.

bunch *(SYN.)* batch, bundle, cluster, company, collection.

bundle *(SYN.)* package, mass, collection, batch, parcel, packet, box.

bungalow *(SYN.)* ranch house, cabana, cabin, cottage, lodge.

bungle *(SYN.)* tumble, botch, foul up, boggle, mess up, blunder.

bunk *(SYN.)* berth, rubbish, nonsense, couch, bed, cot.

buoyant *(SYN.)* light, jolly, spirited, effervescent, blithe, sprightly, lively, resilient, vivacious, afloat, floating, cheery.
(ANT.) hopeless, dejected, sullen, depressed, despondent, sinking, low, pessimistic, downcast, glum.

burden *(SYN.)* oppress, afflict, trouble, encumber, tax, weight, load, worry, contents, trial, lade.
(ANT.) lighten, alleviate, ease, mitigate, console, disburden.

burdensome *(SYN.)* arduous, cumbersome, bothersome, oppressive, irksome, trying, hard, difficult.

bureau *(SYN.)* office, division, department, unit, commission, board, chest, dresser.

bureaucrat *(SYN.)* clerk, official, functionary, servant, politician.

burglar *(SYN.)* thief, robber.

burial *(SYN.)* interment, funeral.

burly *(SYN.)* husky, beefy, heavy-set, brawny, strapping.
(ANT.) skinny, scrawny.

burn *(SYN.)* scorch, blaze, scald, sear, char, incinerate, fire, flare, combust, flame, consume.
(ANT.) quench, extinguish.

burnish *(SYN.)* polish, shine, buff, wax, rub.

burrow *(SYN.)* tunnel, search, seek, dig, excavate, hunt, den, hole.

burst *(SYN.)* exploded, broken, erupt.

bury *(SYN.)* hide, inhume, conceal, immure, cover, entomb, secrete.
(ANT.) reveal, display, open, raise, disinter.

business *(SYN.)* employment, profession, trade, work, art, engagement, vocation, occupation, company, concern, firm, partnership, corporation.
(ANT.) hobby, avocation, pastime.

bustle *(SYN.)* noise, flurry, action, trouble, fuss, stir, excitement.
(ANT.) calmness, composure, serenity, peacefulness.

bustling *(SYN.)* humming, busy, stirring, vibrant, bubbling, alive, active, moving, jumping, astir.

busy *(SYN.)* careful, industrious, active, patient, assiduous, diligent, perseverant, hardworking, occupied, engaged, employed.
(ANT.) unconcerned, indifferent, apathetic, lethargic, careless, inactive, unemployed, lazy, indolent.

busybody *(SYN.)* gossip, tattletale, pry, meddler, snoop.

but *(SYN.)* nevertheless, yet, however, though, although, still.

butcher *(SYN.)* kill, murder, slaughter, assassinate, slay, massacre, execute.
(ANT.) save, protect, vivify, animate, resuscitate.

butt *(SYN.)* bump, ram, bunt, shove, jam, drive, punch, blow, push, thrust, propulsion.

buttocks *(SYN.)* hind end, rump, posterior, backside, behind, bottom, rear, butt.

button *(SYN.)* clasp, close, fasten, hook.

buttress *(SYN.)* support, brace, stay, frame, prop, reinforcement, bulwark, backing, encourage, sustain, reassure, boost, bolster.

buxom *(SYN.)* well-developed, chesty, ample, fleshy, full-figured.

buy *(SYN.)* procure, get, purchase, acquire, obtain.
(ANT.) vend, sell.

buzz *(SYN.)* whir, hum, thrum, drone, burr.

by *(SYN.)* near, through, beside, with, from, at, close to.

bygone *(SYN.)* bypast, former, earlier, past, older, erstwhile, onetime, forgotten.
(ANT.) immediate, present, current, modern.

bypass *(SYN.)* deviate from, go around, detour around.

by-product *(SYN.)* offshoot, spin-off, effect, extra, outgrowth.

bystander *(SYN.)* passerby, onlooker, watcher, viewer, observer.

byway *(SYN.)* passage, detour, path.

byword *(SYN.)* adage, proverb, commonplace, axiom, shibboleth, apothegm, motto, slogan.

C

cab *(SYN.)* coach, taxi, car, hack, taxicab, carriage.

cabin *(SYN.)* cottage, shack, shanty, hut, dwelling, house.

cabinet *(SYN.)* ministry, council, committee, case, cupboard.

cable *(SYN.)* wire, cord, rope, telegraph.

cache *(SYN.)* bury, hide, cover, store.

cad *(SYN.)* knave, rascal, scoundrel, rogue.

cafe *(SYN.)* coffeehouse.

cafeteria *(SYN.)* cafe, diner, restaurant.

cagey *(SYN.)* cunning, wary, clever, tricky, cautious, shrewd, evasive.
(ANT.) innocent, straight-foward, guileless, naive.

calamity *(SYN.)* ruin, disaster, casualty, distress, hardship, trouble, misfortune, bad luck.
(ANT.) blessing, fortune, welfare.

calculate *(SYN.)* count, compute, figure, estimate, consider, tally, determine, measure, subtract, add, divide, multiply, judge.
(ANT.) guess, miscalculate, assume, conjecture.

calculating *(SYN.)* crafty, shrewd, scheming, cunning.
(ANT.) simple, guileless, direct, ingenuous.

calculation *(SYN.)* figuring, reckoning, computation, estimation.
(ANT.) guess, assumption.

calendar *(SYN.)* timetable, schedule, diary.

call *(SYN.)* designate, name, yell, cry, ask, shout, speak, cry out, call out, exclaim, command, term, label, phone, ring up, collect, waken, awaken, ring, wake, arouse, rouse, outcry, need.

callous *(SYN.)* insensitive, impenitent, obdurate, unfeeling, indurate, hard, insensible, heartless.
(ANT.) soft, compassionate, tender.

calm *(SYN.)* appease, lull, quiet, soothe, composed, tranquilize, dispassionate, still, imperturbable, peaceful, pacify, alloy, assuage, unruffled, mild, tranquil.
(ANT.) tempestuous, disturbed, emotional, turmoil, incite, inflame, excite, upset, disturb, arouse.

campaign *(SYN.)* movement, cause, crusade.

can *(SYN.)* tin, container.

canal *(SYN.)* gully, duct, waterway.

cancel *(SYN.)* eliminate, obliterate, erase, delete, nullify, repeal, revoke, cross out, expunge, void, recall, set aside, abolish, rescind.
(ANT.) perpetuate, confirm, ratify, enforce, enact.

candid *(SYN.)* free, blunt, frank, plain, open, sincere, honest.
(ANT.) sly, contrived, scheming.

candidate *(SYN.)* applicant, aspirant, nominee.

canine *(SYN.)* pooch, dog, puppy.

canny *(SYN.)* artful, skillful, shrewd, clever, cautious, cunning.

canopy *(SYN.)* awning, screen, shelter, cover.

cant *(SYN.)* dissimulation, patois, jargon, shoptalk, deceit, argot.
(ANT.) honesty, frankness, truth.

cantankerous *(SYN.)* crabby, grouchy, irritable, surly, ill-natured, grumpy, irascible.

canyon *(SYN.)* gulch, gully, arroyo, ravine, gorge.

cap *(SYN.)* top, cover, crown, lid.

capability *(SYN.)* aptness, ability, capacity, aptitude, dexterity, power, efficiency, qualification.
(ANT.) incapacity, disability, incompetency.

capable *(SYN.)* clever, qualified, able, efficient, competent, skilled, fit, skillful, accomplished, fitted.
(ANT.) unfitted, incapable, incompetent, inept, inadequate.

capacity *(SYN.)* capability, power, ability, talent, content, skill, volume, size.
(ANT.) inability, stupidity, incapacity, impotence.

cape *(SYN.)* pelisse, cloak, mantle, neck, point, headland, peninsula.

caper *(SYN.)* romp, frisk, cavort, frolic, gambol.

capital *(SYN.)* leading, chief, important, property, wealth, money, city, cash, assets, principal, resources, primary, first, funds.
(ANT.) unimportant, trivial, secondary.

capricious *(SYN.)* undependable, erratic, inconstant, fickle, changeable, irregular, inconsistent.

captain *(SYN.)* commander, authority, supervisor, leader, commander, officer.

caption *(SYN.)* heading, title, headline.

captivate *(SYN.)* fascinate, charm, delight.

captive *(SYN.)* convict, prisoner, hostage.

captivity *(SYN.)* detention, imprisonment, custody, confinement, bondage, slavery. *(ANT.)* liberty, freedom.

capture *(SYN.)* catch, grip, apprehend, clutch, arrest, snare, seize, nab, seizure, catching, grasp, take prisoner, recovery. *(ANT.) set free, lose, liberate, throw, free, release.*

car *(SYN.)* auto, automobile, motorcar, vehicle.

carcass *(SYN.)* remains, frame, corpse, form, bulk, mass, corpus, association, body, cadaver. *(ANT.) mind, spirit, intellect, soul.*

cardinal *(SYN.)* chief, primary, important, prime, major, essential. *(ANT.) subordinate, secondary, auxiliary.*

care *(SYN.)* concern, anxiety, worry, caution, solicitude, charge, ward, attention, regard, supervision, consider, consideration, keeping, protection, attend, watch, supervise, guardianship. *(ANT.) neglect, disregard, indifference, unconcern, negligence.*

career *(SYN.)* occupation, profession, job, calling, vocation, trade.

carefree *(SYN.)* lighthearted, happy, unconcerned, breezy, jolly.

careful *(SYN.)* prudent, thoughtful, attentive, cautious, painstaking, scrupulous, heedful, circumspect, vigilant, guarded, discreet, watchful, wary, concerned, meticulous. *(ANT.) nice, careful, heedless, messy, careless, accurate, incautious, sloppy, meticulous.*

careless *(SYN.)* imprudent, heedless, unconcerned, inattentive, lax, indiscreet, desultory, reckless. *(ANT.) careful, nice, cautious, painstaking, prudent, accurate.*

caress *(SYN.)* hug, fondle, embrace, pet, pat, stroke, kiss, cuddle. *(ANT.) vex, buffet, annoy, tease.*

cargo *(SYN.)* freight, load, freightload, shipment.

carnage *(SYN.)* massacre, liquidation, slaughter, genocide, butchery, extermination.

carnal *(SYN.)* base, corporeal, animal, lustful, worldly, sensual, bodily, gross, fleshy, voluptuous. *(ANT.) intellectual, spiritual, exalted, temperate.*

carnival *(SYN.)* fete, fair, jamboree, festival.

carol *(SYN.)* hymn, song, ballad.

carp *(SYN.)* pick, praise, complain.

carpet *(SYN.)* mat, rug.

carping *(SYN.)* discerning, exact, captions, accurate, important. *(ANT.) superficial, cursory, approving, encouraging, unimportant, insignificant.*

carriage *(SYN.)* bearing, conduct, action, deed, behavior, disposition, deportment.

carry *(SYN.)* convey, transport, support, bring, sustain, bear, hold, move, transfer, take. *(ANT.) drop, abandon.*

carry off *(SYN.)* seize, abduct, capture, kidnap. *(ANT.) set free, let go. liberate.*

carry on *(SYN.)* go on, continue, proceed, misbehave. *(ANT.) stop.*

carry out *(SYN.)* succeed, complete, fulfill, accomplish, effect.

carve *(SYN.)* hew, shape, cut, whittle, chisel, sculpt.

case *(SYN.)* state, covering, receptacle, condition, instance, example, happening, illustration, sample, suit, action, claim, lawsuit, crate, container, carton, box.

cash *(SYN.)* currency, money.

casket *(SYN.)* coffin, box, crate.

cast *(SYN.)* fling, toss, throw, pitch, form, company, shape, sort, mold, hurl, sling, shed, direct, impart, turn, actors, players, type, variety.

caste *(SYN.)* class, grade, order, category, status, elegance, set, rank, station, social standing, denomination, excellence, genre.

castle *(SYN.)* mansion, palace, chateau.

casual *(SYN.)* chance, unexpected, informal, accidental, incidental, offhand, unplanned, relaxed, fortuitous, spontaneous. *(ANT.) planned, expected, calculated, formal, deliberate, dressy, premeditated,* *pretentious.*

casualty *(SYN.)* calamity, fortuity, mishap, loss, injured, dead, wounded, accident, victim.
(ANT.) design, purpose, intention, calculation.

catalog *(SYN.)* classify, group, list, inventory, directory, index.

catastrophe *(SYN.)* mishap, calamity, disaster, adversity, accident.
(ANT.) fortune, boon, triumph, blessing, advantage, welfare.

catch *(SYN.)* hook, snare, entrap, ensnare, capture, grip, apprehend, grasp, take, grab, nab, arrest, contract, snare, seize, apprehension, bolt, pin, clasp, trap.
(ANT.) lose, free, liberate, throw, release.

catching *(SYN.)* contagious, pestilential, communicable, infectious, virulent.
(ANT.) noncommunicable, healthful.

category *(SYN.)* class, caste, kind, order, genre, rank, classification, sort, type, set, excellence.

cater *(SYN.)* coddle, oblige, serve, humor, baby, mollycoddle, pamper, spoil, indulge, provide.

cause *(SYN.)* effect, incite, create, induce, inducement, occasion, incentive, prompt, principle, determinant, reason, origin, motive.

caustic *(SYN.)* bitter, disagreeable, distasteful, acrid, sour, spiteful, pungent, tart, painful, cruel, insulting, peevish, mean, ruthless.
(ANT.) mellow, sweet, delicious, pleasant.

caution *(SYN.)* heed, vigilance, care, prudence, counsel, warning, wariness, advice, warn, injunction.
(ANT.) carelessness, heedlessness, incaution, abandon, recklessness.

cautious *(SYN.)* heedful, scrupulous, attentive, prudent, thoughtful, discreet, guarded, circumspect, vigilant, wary, careful.
(ANT.) improvident, headstrong, foolish, forgetful, indifferent.

cavalcade *(SYN.)* column, procession, parade.

cavalier *(SYN.)* contemptuous, insolent, haughty, arrogant.

cave *(SYN.)* grotto, hole, shelter, lair, den, cavern.

cave in *(SYN.)* fall in, collapse.

cavity *(SYN.)* pit, hole, crater.

cavort *(SYN.)* caper, leap, frolic, hop, prance.

cease *(SYN.)* desist, stop, abandon, discontinue, relinquish, end, terminate, leave, surrender, resign.
(ANT.) occupy, continue, persist, begin, endure, stay.

cede *(SYN.)* surrender, relinquish, yield.

celebrate *(SYN.)* honor, glorify, commemorate, keep, solemnize, extol, observe, commend, praise.
(ANT.) decry, overlook, profane, disregard, disgrace.

celebrated *(SYN.)* eminent, glorious, distinguished, noted, illustrious, famed, well-known, popular, renowned, famous.
(ANT.) obscure, hidden, anonymous, infamous, unknown.

celebrity *(SYN.)* somebody, personage, heroine, hero, dignitary.

celestial *(SYN.)* godlike, holy, supernatural, divine, paradisiacal, transcendent, superhuman.
(ANT.) diabolical, profane, mundane, wicked.

cement *(SYN.)* solidify, weld, fasten, secure.

cemetery *(SYN.)* graveyard.

censure *(SYN.)* denounce, reproach, upbraid, blame, disapproval, reprehend, condemn, criticism, disapprove, reprove.
(ANT.) commend, approval, forgive, approve, praise, applaud, condone.

center *(SYN.)* heart, core, midpoint, middle, nucleus, inside.
(ANT.) rim, boundary, edge, border, periphery, outskirts.

central *(SYN.)* chief, necessary, main, halfway, dominant, mid, middle, inner, focal, leading, fundamental, principal.
(ANT.) side, secondary, incidental, auxiliary.

ceremonious *(SYN.)* correct, exact, precise, stiff, outward, external.
(ANT.) material, unconventional, easy, heartfelt.

ceremony *(SYN.)* observance, rite, parade, pomp, ritual, protocol.
(ANT.) informality, casualness.

certain *(SYN.)* definite, assured, fixed, inevitable, sure, undeniable, positive, confident, particular, insecure, unquestionable.
(ANT.) probable, uncertain, doubtful, questionable.

certainly *(SYN.)* absolutely, surely, definitely.
(ANT.) dubiously, doubtfully, questionably.

certainty *(SYN.)* confidence, courage, security, assuredness, firmness, assertion, statement.
(ANT.) humility, bashfulness, modest, shyness.

certificate *(SYN.)* affidavit, document.

certify *(SYN.)* validate, affirm, verify, confirm, authenticate.

certitude *(SYN.)* confidence, belief, conviction, feeling, faith, trust.
(ANT.) doubt, incredulity, denial, heresy.

cessation *(SYN.)* ending, finish, stoppage, termination, conclusion, end.

chafe *(SYN.)* heat, rub, warm, annoy, disturb.

chagrin *(SYN.)* irritation, mortification, embarrassment, annoyance, vexation, worry, bother, shame, annoy, irk, humiliation, irritate, vex, frustrate, humiliate, embarrass, mortify, exasperate.

chain *(SYN.)* fasten, bind, shackle, restrain.

chairman *(SYN.)* speaker.

challenge *(SYN.)* question, dare, call, summon, threat, invite, threaten, demand.

chamber *(SYN.)* cell, salon, room.

champion *(SYN.)* victor, winner, choice, best, conqueror, hero, support, select.

chance *(SYN.)* befall, accident, betide, disaster, opportunity, calamity, occur, possibility, prospect, happen, luck, fate.
(ANT.) design, purpose, inevitability, calculation, certainty, intention.

change *(SYN.)* modification, alternation, alteration, mutation, variety, exchange, shift, alter, transfigure, veer, vary, variation, substitution, substitute.
(ANT.) uniformity, monotony, settle, remain, endure, retain, preserve, steadfastness, endurance, immutability, stability.

changeable *(SYN.)* fitful, fickle, inconstant, unstable, shifting.
(ANT.) stable, uniform, constant, unchanging.

channel *(SYN.)* strait, corridor, waterway, artery, duct, canal, way, trough, groove, passageway.

chant *(SYN.)* singing, incantation, hymn, sing, carol, psalm, song.

chaos *(SYN.)* confusion, jumble, turmoil, anarchy, disorder, muddle.
(ANT.) organization, order, tranquillity, tidiness, system.

chaotic *(SYN.)* confused, disorganized, disordered, messy.
(ANT.) neat, ordered, systematic, organized.

chap *(SYN.)* break, fellow, person, crack, split, man, rough, individual, boy.

chaperon *(SYN.)* associate with, escort, convoy, accompany, consort with.
(ANT.) avoid, desert, leave, abandon, quit.

chapter *(SYN.)* part, section, division.

char *(SYN.)* scorch, singe, burn.

character *(SYN.)* description, class, kind, repute, mark, individuality, disposition, traits, personality, reputation, symbol, features, quality, eccentric, nature.

characteristic *(SYN.)* exclusive, distinctive, special, mark, feature, property, typical, unique, attribute, distinguishing, trait, quality.

charge *(SYN.)* arraignment, indictment, accusation, sell for, attack, assail, assault, indict, blame, allegation, custody, imputation.
(ANT.) pardon, flee, exculpation, excuse, absolve, exoneration.

charitable *(SYN.)* benevolent, generous, liberal, altruistic, kind, obliging, considerate, unselfish.
(ANT.) petty, mean, harsh, wicked, greedy, stingy, malevolent.

charity *(SYN.)* benevolence, kindness, magnanimity, altruism.
(ANT.) malevolence, cruelty, selfishness.

charm *(SYN.)* allure, spell, enchantment, attractiveness, magic, witchery, amulet, talisman, lure, enchant, bewitch, fascinate.

charmer *(SYN.)* siren, temptress, enchantress, vamp, seducer, enchanter.

charming *(SYN.)* attractive, enchanting, fascinating, alluring, appealing, winsome, agreeable.

chart 801 choice

(ANT.) revolting, repugnant, repulsive.

chart *(SYN.)* design, plan, cabal, plot, sketch, stratagem, map, diagram, conspiracy, graph.

charter *(SYN.)* lease, hire, rent, alliance.

chase *(SYN.)* hunt, run after, pursue, trail, follow, persist.
(ANT.) escape, flee, abandon, elude, evade.

chasm *(SYN.)* ravine, abyss, canyon, gorge.

chaste *(SYN.)* clear, immaculate, innocent, sincere, bare, clean, modest, pure, decent, virtuous, virginal, sheer, absolute, spotless.
(ANT.) polluted, tainted, foul, impure, sinful, worldly, sullied, defiled.

chasten *(SYN.)* chastise, restrain, punish, discipline.

chastise *(SYN.)* punish, castigate, correct.
(ANT.) release, acquit, free, exonerate.

chat *(SYN.)* argue, jabber, blab, plead, consult, converse, lecture, discuss, talk, conversation, tattle.

chatter *(SYN.)* dialogue, lecture, speech, conference, talk, discourse.
(ANT.) silence, correspondence, writing.

cheap *(SYN.)* poor, common, inexpensive, shabby, low-priced, beggary, low-cost, shoddy, mean, inferior.
(ANT.) honorable, dear, noble, expensive, costly, well-made, elegant, dignified.

cheat *(SYN.)* deceive, fool, bilk, outwit, victimize, dupe, gull, hoodwink, circumvent, swindler, cheater, trickster, fraud, defraud, charlatan, crook, chiseler, con artist, hoax, swindle.

check *(SYN.)* dissect, interrogate, analyze, contemplate, inquire, question, scrutinize, arrest, stop, halt, block, curb, control, investigate, review, examine, test, counterfoil, stub, barrier, watch.
(ANT.) overlook, disregard, advance, foster, continue, promote, omit, neglect.

checkup *(SYN.)* medical examination, physical.

cheek *(SYN.)* nerve, effrontery, impudence, gall, impertinence.

cheer *(SYN.)* console, gladden, comfort, encourage, applause, encouragement, joy, glee, gaiety, mirth, soothe, sympathize, approval, solace.

(ANT.) depress, sadden, discourage, derision, dishearten, discouragement, antagonize.

cheerful *(SYN.)* glad, jolly, joyful, gay, happy, cherry, merry, joyous, lighthearted.
(ANT.) mournful, sad, glum, depressed, gloomy, sullen.

cherish *(SYN.)* prize, treasure, appreciate, nurse, value, comfort, hold dear, foster, nurture, sustain.
(ANT.) disregard, neglect, deprecate, scorn, reject, undervalue, abandon.

chest *(SYN.)* bosom, breast, coffer, box, case, trunk, casket, dresser, commode, cabinet, chifforobe.

chew *(SYN.)* gnaw, munch, bite, nibble.

chic *(SYN.)* fashionable, modish, smart, stylish, trendy.

chide *(SYN.)* admonish, rebuke, scold, reprimand, criticize, reprove.
(ANT.) extol, praise, commend.

chief *(SYN.)* chieftain, head, commander, captain, leader, principal, master, boss, leading, ruler.
(ANT.) servant, subordinate, secondary, follower, incidental, accidental, auxiliary, attendant.

chiefly *(SYN.)* mainly, especially, mostly.

childish *(SYN.)* immature, childlike, infantile, babyish.
(ANT.) mature, adult, seasoned, grownup.

chill *(SYN.)* coolness, cold, cool, coldness, brisk, frosty.
(ANT.) hot, warm, heat, heated, warmth.

chilly *(SYN.)* cold, frigid, freezing, arctic, cool, icy, passionless, wintry, unfeeling.
(ANT.) fiery, heated, passionate, ardent.

chirp *(SYN.)* peep, cheep, twitter, tweet, chirrup.

chivalrous *(SYN.)* noble, brave, polite, valorous, gallant, gentlemanly, courteous.
(ANT.) crude, rude, impolite, uncivil.

chivalry *(SYN.)* courtesy, nobility, gallantry, knighthood.

choice *(SYN.)* delicate, elegant, fine, dainty, exquisite, pure, refined, subtle, splendid, handsome, option, selection, beautiful, minute, pretty, pick, select, uncommon, rare, precious, valuable, thin, small.

(ANT.) coarse, rough, thick, blunt, large.

choke *(SYN.)* throttle, gag, strange.

choose *(SYN.)* elect, determine, pick, select, cull, opt.

(ANT.) reject, refuse.

chop *(SYN.)* hew, cut, fell, mince.

chore *(SYN.)* routine, task, job, duty, work.

chronic *(SYN.)* persistent, constant, lingering, continuing, perennial, unending, sustained, permanent.

(ANT.) fleeting, acute, temporary.

chronicle *(SYN.)* detail, history, narrative, account, description, narration, recital.

(ANT.) misrepresentation, confusion, distortion.

chuckle *(SYN.)* titter, laugh, giggle.

chum *(SYN.)* friend, pal, buddy, companion.

cinema *(SYN.)* effigy, film, etching, appearance, drawing, engraving, illustration, likeness, image, panorama, painting, picture, photograph.

circle *(SYN.)* disk, ring, set, group. class, club, surround, encircle, enclose, round.

circuit *(SYN.)* circle, course, journey, orbit, revolution, tour.

circuitous *(SYN.)* distorted, devious, indirect, roundabout swerving, crooked, tortuous.

(ANT.) straightforward, straight, direct, honest.

circular *(SYN.)* chubby, complete, curved, bulbous, cylindrical, round, ringlike, globular, entire, rotund.

(ANT.) straight.

circumference *(SYN.)* border, perimeter, periphery, edge.

circumspection *(SYN.)* care, worry, solicitude, anxiety, concern, caution, attention, vigilance.

(ANT.) neglect, negligence, indifference.

circumstance *(SYN.)* fact, event, incident, condition, happening, position, occurrence, situation.

circumstances *(SYN.)* facts, conditions, factors, situation, background, grounds, means, capital, assets, rank, class.

cite *(SYN.)* affirm, assign, allege, advance, quote, mention, declare, claim, maintain.

(ANT.) refute, gainsay, deny, contradict.

citizen *(SYN.)* native, inhabitant, national, denizen, subject, dweller, resident.

city *(SYN.)* metropolis, municipality, town.

civil *(SYN.)* courteous, cultivated, accomplished, public, municipal, respectful, genteel, polite, considerate, gracious, urban.

(ANT.) uncouth, uncivil, impertinent, impolite, boorish.

civilization *(SYN.)* cultivation, culture, education, breeding, enlightenment, society, refinement.

(ANT.) ignorance, vulgarity.

civilize *(SYN.)* refine, tame, polish, cultivate, instruct, teach.

claim *(SYN.)* aver, declare, allege, assert, affirm, express, state, demand, maintain, defend, uphold.

(ANT.) refute, deny, contradict.

clamor *(SYN.)* cry, din, babel, noise, racket, outcry, row, sound tumult, shouting, shout, uproar.

(ANT.) hush, serenity, silence, tranquillity, stillness, quiet.

clan *(SYN.)* fellowship, kindness, solidarity, family, association, fraternity.

(ANT.) discord, strife, opposition, acrimony.

clandestine *(SYN.)* covert, hidden, latent, private, concealed, secret, unknown.

(ANT.) exposed, known, conspicuous, obvious.

clarify *(SYN.)* educate, explain, expound, decipher, illustrate, clear, resolve, define, interpret, unfold.

(ANT.) darken, obscure, baffle, confuse.

clash *(SYN.)* clank, crash, clang, conflict, disagreement, opposition, collision, struggle, mismatch, contrast, disagree, collide, interfere.

(ANT.) accord, agreement, harmony, blend, harmonize, match, agree.

clasp *(SYN.)* grip, hold, grasp, adhere, clutch, keep, have, maintain, possess, occupy, retain, support, confine, embrace, fastening, check, detain, curb, receive.

(ANT.) relinquish, vacate, surrender, abandon.

class *(SYN.)* category, denomination, caste, kind, genre, grade, rank, order, elegance, classification, division, sort, family, species, set, excellence.

classic *(SYN.)* masterpiece.

classification *(SYN.)* order, category, class, arrangement, ordering, grouping, organization.

classify *(SYN.)* arrange, class, order, sort, grade, group, index.

clause *(SYN.)* condition, paragraph, limitation, article.

claw *(SYN.)* hook, talon, nail, scratch.

clean *(SYN.)* mop, tidy, neat, dustless, clear, unsoiled, immaculate, unstained, untainted, pure, dust, vacuum, scour, decontaminate, wipe, sterilize, cleanse, scrub, purify, wash, sweep. *(ANT.)* stain, soil, pollute, soiled, impure, dirty.

cleanse *(SYN.)* mop, purify, wash, sweep. *(ANT.)* stain, soil, dirty, pollute.

clear *(SYN.)* fair, sunny, cloudless, transparent, apparent, limpid, distinct, intelligible, evident, unmistakable, understandable, unclouded, uncloudy, light, bright, certain, manifest, lucid, plain, obvious, unobstructed. *(ANT.)* obscure, unclear, muddled, confused, dark, cloudy, blocked, obstructed, questionable, dubious, blockaded, foul, overcast.

clearly *(SYN.)* plainly, obviously, evidently, definitely, surely, certainly. *(ANT.)* questionably, dubiously.

clemency *(SYN.)* forgiveness, charity, compassion, grace, mercy, leniency, pity, mildness. *(ANT.)* punishment, vengeance, retribution.

clerical *(SYN.)* ministerial, pastoral, priestly, celestial, holy, sacred, secretarial.

clerk *(SYN.)* typist, office worker, office girl, saleslady, salesperson, salesclerk.

clever *(SYN.)* apt, dexterous, quick, adroit, quick-witted, talented, bright, skillful, witty, ingenious, smart, intelligent, shrewd, gifted, expert, sharp. *(ANT.)* unskilled, slow, stupid, backward, maladroit, bungling, dull, clumsy.

cleverness *(SYN.)* intellect, intelligence, comprehension, mind, perspicacity, sagacity, fun.

(ANT.) sobriety, stupidity, solemnity, commonplace, platitude.

client *(SYN.)* patron, customer.

cliff *(SYN.)* scar, bluff, crag, precipice, escarpment.

climate *(SYN.)* aura, atmosphere, air, ambience.

climax *(SYN.)* apex, culmination, peak, summit, consummation, height, acme, zenith. *(ANT.)* depth, base, anticlimax, floor.

climb *(SYN.)* mount, scale, ascend. *(ANT.)* descend.

clip *(SYN.)* snip, crop, cut, mow, clasp.

cloak *(SYN.)* conceal, cover, disguise, clothe, cape, guard, envelop, hide, mask, protect, shield. *(ANT.)* divulge, expose, reveal, bare, unveil.

clod *(SYN.)* wad, hunk, gobbet, lump, chunk, clot, gob, dunce, dolt, oaf, fool.

clog *(SYN.)* crowd, congest, cram, overfill, stuff.

cloister *(SYN.)* monastery, priory, hermitage, abbey, convent.

close *(SYN.)* adjacent, adjoining, immediate, unventilated, stuffy, abutting, neighboring, dear, oppressive, mean, impending, nearby, near, devoted. *(ANT.)* afar, faraway, removed, distant.

close *(SYN.)* seal, shut, clog, stop, obstruct, cease, conclude, complete, end, terminate, occlude, finish. *(ANT.)* unlock, begin, open, unbar, inaugurate, commence, start.

closet *(SYN.)* cabinet, locker, wardrobe, cupboard.

cloth *(SYN.)* fabric, goods, material, textile.

clothe *(SYN.)* garb, dress, apparel. *(ANT.)* strip, undress.

clothes *(SYN.)* array, attire, apparel, clothing, dress, garb, garments, raiment, drap-ery, vestments. *(ANT.)* nudity, nakedness.

clothing *(SYN.)* attire, clothes, apparel, array, dress, drapery, garments, garb, vestments. *(ANT.)* nudity, nakedness.

cloud *(SYN.)* fog, mist, haze, mass, collection, obscure, dim, shadow.

cloudy *(SYN.)* dim, dark, indistinct, murky,

mysterious,indefinite,vague,sunless,cloud-ed, obscure, overcast, shadowy.
(ANT.) sunny, clear, distinct, limpid, lucid, clarified,cloudless, clearheaded, brilliant, bright.

club *(SYN.)* society, association, set, circle, organization, bat, cudgel, stick, blackjack.

clue *(SYN.)* sign, trace, hint, suggestion.

clumsy *(SYN.)* bungling, inept, rough, un-polished, bumbling, awkward, ungraceful, gauche, ungainly, unskillful, untoward.
(ANT.) polished, skillful, neat, graceful, dexterous, adroit.

cluster *(SYN.)* batch, clutch, group, bunch, gather, pack, assemble, crowd.

clutch *(SYN.)* grip, grab, seize, hold.

coalition *(SYN.)* combination, association, alliance,confederacy,entente,league,treaty.
(ANT.) schism, separation, divorce.

coarse *(SYN.)* unpolished, vulgar, refined, rough, smooth, impure, rude, crude, gruff, gross, cultivated, delicate, cultured.
(ANT.) delicate, smooth, refined, polished, genteel, cultivated, suave, fine, cultured.

coast *(SYN.)* seaboard, seashore, beach, shore, drift, glide, ride.

coax *(SYN.)* urge, persuade, wheedle, cajole.
(ANT.) force, bully, coerce.

coddle *(SYN.)* pamper, baby, spoil, indulge.

code *(SYN.)* crypt, cryptogram, cipher.

coerce *(SYN.)* constrain, compel, enforce, force, drive, oblige, impel.
(ANT.) prevent, persuade, convince, induce.

coercion *(SYN.)* emphasis, intensity, energy, dint, potency, power, vigor, strength, compulsion, force, constraint, violence.
(ANT.) impotence, frailty, feebleness, weakness, persuasion.

cognizance *(SYN.)* apprehension, erudition, acquaintance, information, learning, knowl-edge, lore, science, scholarship, under-standing.
(ANT.) illiteracy, misunderstanding, ignorance.

cognizant *(SYN.)* conscious, aware, apprised informed, mindful, observant, perceptive.
(ANT.) unaware, ignorant, oblivious, insensible.

coherent *(SYN.)* logical, intelligible, sensible, rational, commonsensical, reasonable.

coiffeur *(SYN.)* hairdresser.

coiffure *(SYN.)* haircut, hairdo.

coincide *(SYN.)* acquiesce, agree, accede, assent,consent,comply,correspond,concur, match, tally, harmonize, conform.
(ANT.) differ, disagree, protest, contradict.

coincidence *(SYN.)* accident, chance.
(ANT.)plot,plan,prearrangement,scheme.

coincident *(SYN.)* identical, equal, equiv-alent, distinguishable, same.
(ANT.) distinct, contrary, disparate, op-posed.

coincidental *(SYN.)* unpredicted, unexpected, chance, unforeseen, accidental, fortuitous.

cold *(SYN.)* cool, freezing, chilly, frigid, icy, frozen, wintry, arctic, unfriendly, indif-ferent, phlegmatic, stoical, passionless, chill, unemotional, heartless, unfeeling.
(ANT.) hot, torrid, fiery, burning, ardent, friendly, temperate, warm, passionate.

collapse *(SYN.)* descend, decrease, diminish, fail, downfall, failure, decline, fall, drop, sink, subside, topple.
(ANT.) soar, steady, limb, mount, arise.

colleague *(SYN.)* companion, attendant, comrade, associate, crony, mate, friend, partner.
(ANT.) enemy, stranger, adversary.

collect *(SYN.)* assemble, amass, concentrate, pile, accumulate, congregate, obtain, heap, gather, solicit, secure, procure, raise, get, mass, hoard, consolidate.
(ANT.) divide, dole, assort, dispel, dis-tribute, disperse.

collected *(SYN.)* cool, calm, composed, peaceful, imperturbable, placid, sedate, quiet.
(ANT.) excited, violent, aroused, agitated.

collection *(SYN.)* amount, conglomeration, sum, entirety, aggregation, hoard, accumu-lation, pile, store, aggregate, total, whole.
(ANT.) part, unit, particular, element, in-gredient.

collide *(SYN.)* hit, smash, crash, strike.

collision *(SYN.)* conflict, combat, duel, battle, encounter, crash, smash, fight, contention, struggle, discord.

(ANT.) concord, amity, harmony, consonance.

collusion *(SYN.)* combination, cabal, intrigue, conspiracy, plot, treason, treachery.

color *(SYN.)* hue, paint, pigment, complexion, dye, shade, tone, tincture, stain, tint, tinge.

(ANT.) paleness, transparency, achromatism.

colorful *(SYN.)* impressive, vivid, striking, full-color, multicolored, offbeat, weird, unusual.

(ANT.) flat, dull, uninteresting.

colossal *(SYN.)* enormous, elephantine, gargantuan, huge, immense, gigantic, prodigious.

(ANT.) little, minute, small, miniature, diminutive, microscopic, tiny.

combat *(SYN.)* conflict, duel, battle, collision, encounter, fight, contest, oppose, war, contention, struggle, discord.

(ANT.) consonance, harmony, concord, yield, surrender, succumb, amity.

combination *(SYN.)* association, confederacy, alliance, entente, league, compounding, mixture, blend, composite, federation, mixing, compound, blending, union.

(ANT.) separation, division, schism, divorce.

combine *(SYN.)* adjoin, associate, accompany, conjoin, connect, link, mix, blend, couple, unite, join.

(ANT.) detach, disjoin, divide, separate, disconnect.

come *(SYN.)* near, approach, reach, arrive, advance.

(ANT.) depart, leave, go.

comedian *(SYN.)* comic, wit, humorist, gagman, wag.

comely *(SYN.)* charming, elegant, beauteous, beautiful, fine, lovely, pretty, handsome lovely.

(ANT.) hideous, repulsive, foul, unsightly.

come-on *(SYN.)* lure, inducement, enticement, temptation.

comfort *(SYN.)* contentment, ease, enjoyment, relieve, consolation, relief, cheer, console, calm, satisfaction, soothe, encourage, succor, luxury, solace.

(ANT.) depress, torture, discomfort, upset, misery, disturb, agitate, affliction, discompose, uncertainty, suffering.

comfortable *(SYN.)* pleasing, agreeable, convenient, cozy, welcome, acceptable, relaxed, restful, gratifying, easy, contented, rested, satisfying, pleasurable.

(ANT.) miserable, distressing, tense, strained, troubling, edgy, uncomfortable.

comical *(SYN.)* droll, funny, humorous, amusing, ludicrous, witty, ridiculous, odd, queer.

(ANT.) sober, solemn, sad, serious, melancholy.

command *(SYN.)* class, method, plan regularity, rank, arrangement, series, sequence, point, aim, conduct, manage, guide, bid, system, succession, bidding, direct, order, demand, direction, rule, dictate, decree.

(ANT.) consent, obey, misdirect, distract, deceive, misguide, license, confusion.

commandeer *(SYN.)* take, possession, seize, confiscate, appropriate.

commanding *(SYN.)* imposing, masterful, assertive, authoritative, positive.

commence *(SYN.)* open, start.

(ANT.) stop, end, terminate, finish.

commend *(SYN.)* laud, praise, applaud, recommend.

(ANT.) censure, blame, criticize.

commendable *(SYN.)* deserving, praiseworthy.

(ANT.) bad, deplorable, lamentable.

commendation *(SYN.)* approval, applause, praise, recommendation, honor, medal.

(ANT.) criticism, condemnation, censure.

commensurate *(SYN.)* keep, celebrate, observe, honor, commend, extol, glorify, laud, praise, honor.

(ANT.) decry, disgrace, disregard, overlook, profane, dishonor.

comment *(SYN.)* assertion, declaration, annotation, explanation, review, commentary, report, remark, observation, utterance, criticism, statement.

commerce *(SYN.)* business, engagement, employment, art, trade, marketing, enterprise, occupation.

(ANT.) hobby, pastime, avocation.

commission *(SYN.)* board, committee, command, permit, order, permission, delegate, authorize, deputize, entrust.

commit *(SYN.)* perpetrate, perform, obligate, do, commend, consign, relegate, bind, delegate, empower, pledge, entrust, authorize, trust.

(ANT.) neglect, mistrust, release, free, miscarry, fail, loose.

commitment *(SYN.)* duty, promise, responsibility, pledge.

committee *(SYN.)* commission, bureau, board, delegate, council.

commodious *(SYN.)* appropriate, accessible, adapted, favorable, handy, fitting, timely.

(ANT.) inconvenient, troublesome, awkward.

commodity *(SYN.)* article, merchandise, wares, goods.

common *(SYN.)* ordinary, popular, familiar, mean, low, general, vulgar, communal, mutual, shared, natural, frequent, prevalent, joint, conventional, plain, usual, universal.

(ANT.) odd, exceptional, scarce, noble, extraordinary, different, separate, outstanding, rare, unusual, distinctive, refined.

commonplace *(SYN.)* common, usual, frequent, ordinary, everyday.

(ANT.) distinctive, unusual, original.

commonsense *(SYN.)* perceptible, alive, apprehensible, aware, awake, cognizant, conscious, comprehending, perceptible.

(ANT.) unaware, impalpable, imperceptible.

commotion *(SYN.)* confusion, chaos, disarray, ferment, disorder, stir, tumult, agitation.

(ANT.) tranquillity, peace, certainty, order.

communicable *(SYN.)* infectious, virulent, catching, transferable, contagious.

(ANT.) hygienic, noncommunicable, healthful.

communicate *(SYN.)* convey, impart, inform, confer, disclose, reveal, relate, tell, advertise, publish, transmit, publicize, divulge.

(ANT.) withhold, hide, conceal.

communication *(SYN.)* disclosure, transmission, declaration, announcement, notification, publication, message, report, news, information.

communicative *(SYN.)* unreserved, open, frank, free, straightforward, unrestrained.

(ANT.) close-mouthed, secretive.

communion *(SYN.)* fellowship, participation, association, sacrament, union.

(ANT.) nonparticipation, alienation.

community *(SYN.)* public, society, city, town, village, township.

compact *(SYN.)* contracted, firm, narrow, snug, close, constricted, packed, vanity, treaty, agreement, tense, taught, tight, parsimonious, compressed, stingy.

(ANT.) slack, open, loose, relaxed, unconfined, unfretted, sprawling, lax.

companion *(SYN.)* attendant, comrade, consort, friend, colleague, partner, crony, mate, associate.

(ANT.) stranger, enemy, adversary.

companionship *(SYN.)* familiarity, cognizance, acquaintance, fellowship, knowledge, intimacy.

(ANT.) unfamiliarity, inexperience, ignorance.

company *(SYN.)* crew, group, band, party, throng, house, assemblage, troop, fellowship, association, business, concern, partnership, corporation, companionship, firm.

(ANT.) seclusion, individual, solitude, dispersion.

comparable *(SYN.)* allied, analogous, alike, akin, like, correspondent, correlative, parallel.

(ANT.) opposed, incongruous, dissimilar, unalike, different, divergent.

compare *(SYN.)* discriminate, match, differentiate, contrast, oppose.

comparison *(SYN.)* likening, contrasting, judgment.

compartment *(SYN.)* division, section.

compassion *(SYN.)* mercy, sympathy, pity, commiseration, condolence.

(ANT.) ruthlessness, hardness, brutality, inhumanity, cruelty.

compassionate *(SYN.)* sympathizing, benign, forbearing, good, tender, affable, humane, indulgent, kind, sympathetic, kindly.

(ANT.) inhuman, merciless, unkind, cold-hearted, unsympathetic, cruel.

compatible *(SYN.)* consistent, agreeing, conforming, accordant, congruous, harmonious, cooperative, agreeable, constant, consonant, correspondent.

(ANT.) discrepant, paradoxical, disagreeable, contradictory.

compel *(SYN.)* drive, enforce, coerce, constrain, force, oblige, impel.

(ANT.) induce, coax, prevent, wheedle, persuade, cajole, convince.

compensate *(SYN.)* remunerate, repay, reimburse, recompense.

compensation *(SYN.)* fee, earnings, pay, payment, recompense, allowance, remuneration, remittance, settlement, stipend, re- payment, salary, wages.

(ANT.) present, gratuity, gift.

compete *(SYN.)* rival, contest, oppose, vie.

(ANT.) reconcile, accord.

competence *(SYN.)* skill, ability, capability.

competent *(SYN.)* efficient, clever, capable, able, apt, proficient, skillful, fitted, qualified.

(ANT.) inept, incapable, unfitted, awkward, incompetent, inadequate.

competition *(SYN.)* contest, match, rivalry, tournament.

competitor *(SYN.)* rival, contestant, opponent.

(ANT.) ally, friend, colleague.

complain *(SYN.)* lament, murmur, protest, grouch, grumble, regret, moan, remonstrate, whine, repine.

(ANT.) rejoice, praise, applaud, approve.

complaint *(SYN.)* protest, objection, grievance.

complement *(SYN.)* supplement, complete.

(ANT.) clash, conflict.

complete *(SYN.)* consummate, entire, ended, full, thorough, finished, full, whole, concluded, over, done, terminate, unbroken, total, undivided.

(ANT.) unfinished, imperfect, incomplete, start, partial, begin, commence, lacking.

completion *(SYN.)* achievement, attainment, end, conclusion, close, finish, windup, accomplishment, realization.

(ANT.) omission, neglect, failure, defeat.

complex *(SYN.)* sophisticated, compound, intricate, involved, perplexing, elaborate, complicated.

(ANT.) basic, simple, rudimentary, uncompounded, uncomplicated, plain.

complexion *(SYN.)* paint, pigment hue, color, dye, stain, tincture, tinge, tint, shade.

(ANT.) paleness, transparency, achromatism.

compliant *(SYN.)* meek, modest, lowly, plain, submissive, simple, unostentatious, unassuming, unpretentious.

(ANT.) proud, vain, arrogant, haughty, boastful.

complicated *(SYN.)* intricate, involved, complex, compound, perplexing.

(ANT.) simple, plain, uncompounded.

compliment *(SYN.)* eulogy, flattery, praise, admiration, honor, adulation, flatter, commendation, tribute.

(ANT.) taunt, affront, aspersion, insult, disparage, criticism.

complimentary *(SYN.)* gratis, free.

comply *(SYN.)* assent, consent, accede, acquiesce, coincide, conform, concur, tally.

(ANT.) differ, dissent, protest, disagree.

component *(SYN.)* division, fragment, allotment, moiety, apportionment, scrap, portion, section, share, segment, ingredient, organ.

(ANT.) whole, entirety.

comport *(SYN.)* carry, conduct, behave, act, deport, interact, operate, manage.

compose *(SYN.)* forge, fashion, mold, make, construct, create, produce, shape, form, constitute, arrange, organize, make up, write, invent, devise, frame.

(ANT.) misshape, dismantle, disfigure, destroy.

composed *(SYN.)* calm, cool, imperturbable, placid, quiet, unmoved, sedate, peaceful, collected, tranquil.

(ANT.) aroused, violent, nervous, agitated, perturbed, excited.

composer *(SYN.)* author, inventor, creator, maker, originator.

composition *(SYN.)* paper, theme, work, essay, compound, mixture, mix.

composure *(SYN.)* calmness, poise, control, self-control, self-possession.

(ANT.) anger, rage, turbulence, agitation.

compound *(SYN.)* blend, confound, jumble, consort, aggregate, complicated, com-

bination, combined, mixture, complex, join.
(ANT.) segregate, separate, divide, simple, sort.
comprehend *(SYN.)* apprehend, discern, learn, perceive, see, grasp, understand.
(ANT.) mistake, misunderstand, ignore.
comprehension *(SYN.)* insight, perception, understanding, awareness, discernment.
(ANT.) misconception, insensibility.
comprehensive *(SYN.)* wide, inclusive, complete, broad, full.
(ANT.) fragmentary, partial, limited, incomplete.
compress *(SYN.)* press, compact, squeeze, pack, crowd.
(ANT.) spread, stretch, expand.
comprise *(SYN.)* contain, hold, embrace.
(ANT.) emit, encourage, yield, discharge.
compulsion *(SYN.)* might, energy, potency, strength, vigor.
(ANT.) persuasion, impotence, frailty.
compulsory *(SYN.)* required, obligatory, necessary, unavoidable.
(ANT.) elective, optional, free, unrestricted.
computation *(SYN.)* reckoning, record.
(ANT.) misrepresentation.
compute *(SYN.)* count, calculate, determine, figure, reckon.
(ANT.) conjecture, guess, miscalculate.
comrade *(SYN.)* attendant, companion, colleague, associate, friend.
(ANT.) stranger, enemy, adversary.
con *(SYN.)* cheat, bamboozle, trick, swindle.
conceal *(SYN.)* disguise, cover, hide, mask, screen, secrete, veil, withhold.
(ANT.) reveal, show, disclose, expose.
concede *(SYN.)* permit, suffer, tolerate, grant, give, admit, acknowledge, allow, yield.
(ANT.) forbid, contradict, protest, refuse, deny, negate, resist.
conceit *(SYN.)* pride, vanity, complacency, conception, idea, egotism, self-esteem, caprice, fancy, whim.
(ANT.) humility, meekness, humbleness, modesty.
conceited *(SYN.)* proud, arrogant, vain, smug, egotistical.
(ANT.) humble, modest, self-effacing.

conceive *(SYN.)* design, create, imagine, understand, devise, concoct, perceive, frame, grasp, invent.
(ANT.) imitate, reproduce, copy.
concentrate *(SYN.)* localize, focus, condense, ponder, meditate, center, scrutinize.
(ANT.) scatter, diffuse, dissipate, disperse.
concentrated *(SYN.)* compressed, thick, dense.
(ANT.) sparse, quick, dispersed.
concept *(SYN.)* fancy, conception, image, notion, idea, sentiment, thought.
(ANT.) thing, matter, substance, entity.
conception *(SYN.)* consideration, deliberation, fancy, idea, notion, regard, thought, view.
concern *(SYN.)* matter, anxiety, affair, disturb, care, business, solicitude, interest, affect, involve, touch, trouble, interest, worry.
(ANT.) unconcern, negligence, disinterest, tire, bore, calm, soothe, indifference.
concerning *(SYN.)* regarding, about, respecting.
concerted *(SYN.)* united, joint, combined.
(ANT.) individual, unorganized, separate.
concession *(SYN.)* admission, yielding, granting.
(ANT.) insistence, demand.
concise *(SYN.)* pity, neat, brief, compact, succinct, terse.
(ANT.) wordy, lengthy, verbose, prolix.
conclude *(SYN.)* decide, achieve, close, complete, end, finish, terminate, arrange, determine, settle, perfect, perform.
(ANT.) start, begin, commence.
concluding *(SYN.)* extreme, final, last, terminal, utmost.
(ANT.) first, foremost, opening, initial.
conclusion *(SYN.)* end, finale, termination, deduction, close, settlement, decision, finish, resolution, determination, completion, issue, judgment.
(ANT.) commencement, inception, opening, start, beginning.
conclusive *(SYN.)* decisive, eventual, final, terminal, ultimate.
(ANT.) original, first, inaugural.

concord *(SYN.)* agreement, unison, understanding, accordance, stipulation.
(ANT.) disagreement, discord, dissension.
concrete *(SYN.)* solid, firm, precise, definite, specific.
(ANT.) undetermined, vague, general.
concur *(SYN.)* agree, assent, consent, accede.
(ANT.) dissent, protest, differ.
condemn *(SYN.)* denounce, reproach, blame, upbraid, convict, rebuke, doom, judge, censure, reprehend, punish, reprobate, sentence.
(ANT.) condone, forgive, absolve, praise, applaud, extol, approve, pardon, laud, excuse, commend.
condense *(SYN.)* shorten, reduce, abridge, abbreviate, concentrate, digest, compress, diminish.
(ANT.) enlarge, increase, swell, expand.
condition *(SYN.)* circumstance, state, situation, case, plight, requirement, position, necessity, stipulation, predicament, provision, term.
conditional *(SYN.)* dependent, relying.
(ANT.) casual, original, absolute.
condolence *(SYN.)* commiseration, concord, harmony, pity, sympathy, warmth.
(ANT.) harshness, indifference, unconcern.
conduct *(SYN.)* control, deportment, supervise, manage, behavior, deed, actions, act, behave, manners.
confederate *(SYN.)* ally, abettor, assistant.
(ANT.) enemy, rival, opponent, adversary.
confederation *(SYN.)* combination, league, union, marriage, treaty.
(ANT.) separation, divorce.
confer *(SYN.)* gossip, grant, speak, tattle, blab, chat, deliberate, consult, award, give, bestow, talk, mutter.
(ANT.) retrieve, withdraw.
confess *(SYN.)* avow, acknowledge, admit, concede, grant, divulge, reveal.
(ANT.) disown, renounce, deny, conceal.
confession *(SYN.)* defense, justification, excuse, apology.
(ANT.) dissimulation, denial, complaint.
confidence *(SYN.)* firmness, self-reliance, assurance, faith, trust, pledge, declaration, self-confidence, reliance, self-assurance,

courage, statement.
(ANT.) distrust, shyness, mistrust, bashfulness, diffidence, doubt, modesty, suspicion.
confident *(SYN.)* certain, sure, dauntless, self-assured.
(ANT.) uncertain, timid, shy.
confine *(SYN.)* enclose, restrict, hinder, fence, limit, bound.
(ANT.) release, expose, free, expand, open.
confirm acknowledge, establish, settle, substantiate, approve, fix, verify, assure, validate, ratify, corroborate, strengthen.
(ANT.) disclaim, deny, disavow.
confirmation *(SYN.)* demonstration, experiment, test, trail, verification.
(ANT.) fallacy, invalidity.
confirmed *(SYN.)* regular, established, habitual, chronic.
(ANT.) occasional, infrequent.
conflict *(SYN.)* duel, combat, fight, collision, discord, encounter, interference, inconsistency, contention, struggle, opposition, clash, oppose, battle, controversy, contend, engagement, contest, variance.
(ANT.) consonance, harmony, amity.
confiscate *(SYN.)* capture, catch, gain, purloin, steal, take, clutch, grip, seize, get, obtain, bear.
conflagration *(SYN.)* flame, glow, heat, warmth, fervor, passion, vigor.
(ANT.) apathy, cold, quiescence.
conform *(SYN.)* adapt, comply, yield, submit, obey, adjust, agree, fit, suit.
(ANT.) misapply, misfit, rebel, vary, disagree, disturb.
conformity *(SYN.)* congruence, accord, agreement, correspondence.
confound *(SYN.)* confuse, baffle, perplex, puzzle, bewilder.
confront *(SYN.)* confront, defy, hinder, resist, thwart, withstand, bar.
(ANT.) submit, agree, support, succumb.
confuse *(SYN.)* confound, perplex, mystify, dumbfound, baffle, puzzle, jumble, mislead, mix up, mistake, bewilder.
(ANT.) explain, instruct, edify, illumine, enlighten, illuminate, solve.

confused *(SYN.)* deranged, indistinct, disordered, muddled, bewildered, disconcerted, disorganized, perplexed.
(ANT.) organized, plain, clear, obvious.

confusion *(SYN.)* commotion, disarray, agitation, disorder, chaos, ferment, stir, perplexity, tumult, bewilderment, disarrangement, uncertainty, muss, mess, turmoil.
(ANT.) order, tranquillity, enlightenment, comprehension, understanding, tidiness, organization, peace.

congregate *(SYN.)* gather, foregather, meet, convene.
(ANT.) scatter, dispel, disperse, dissipate.

congress *(SYN.)* parliament, legislature, assembly.

congruous *(SYN.)* agreeing, conforming, constant, correspondent.
(ANT.) incongruous, inconsistent, discrepant.

conjecture *(SYN.)* law, supposition, theory.
(ANT.) proof, fact, certainty.

conjunction *(SYN.)* combination, junction, connection, link.
(ANT.) separation, disconnection, separation, diversion.

connect *(SYN.)* adjoin, link, combine, relate, join, attach, unite, associate, attribute, affix.
(ANT.) detach, separate, disjoin, untie, dissociation, disconnect, disassociation, unfasten.

connection *(SYN.)* conjunction, alliance, link, affinity, bond, tie, association, relationship, union.
(ANT.) isolation, dissociation, separation, disassociation, disunion.

conquer *(SYN.)* master, beat, humble, defeat, overcome, rout, win, succeed, achieve, gain, overpower, quell, subdue, crush, vanquish.
(ANT.) cede, yield, retreat, surrender.

conquest *(SYN.)* triumph, victory, achievement.
(ANT.) surrender, failure, defeat.

conscientious *(SYN.)* upright, straight, honest, incorruptible, scrupulous.
(ANT.) careless, irresponsible, slovenly.

conscious *(SYN.)* cognizant, informed, perceptive, aware, intentional, sensible, awake, purposeful, deliberate.

(ANT.) unaware, insensible, asleep, comatose, ignorant.

consecrate *(SYN.)* exalt, extol, hallow, honor.
(ANT.) mock, degrade, debase, abuse.

consecrated *(SYN.)* holy, divine, devout, spiritual.
(ANT.) evil, worldly, secular.

consent *(SYN.)* permission, leave, agree, let, assent, agreement, license, permit.
(ANT.) refusal, opposition, denial, dissent, prohibition.

consequence *(SYN.)* outcome, issue, result, effect, significance, importance.
(ANT.) impetus, cause.

consequential *(SYN.)* significant, important, weighty.
(ANT.) trivial, unimportant, minor, insignificant.

consequently *(SYN.)* hence, thence, therefore.

conservative *(SYN.)* conventional, reactionary, cautious, moderate, careful.
(ANT.) radical, liberal, rash, foolhardy, reckless.

conserve *(SYN.)* save, retain, reserve, guard, keep, support, sustain.
(ANT.) dismiss, neglect, waste, reject, discard.

consider *(SYN.)* heed, ponder, contemplate, examine, study, weigh, reflect, think about, regard, deliberate, respect.
(ANT.) ignore, overlook, disdain, disregard, neglect.

considerable *(SYN.)* much, noteworthy, worthwhile, significant, important.

considerate *(SYN.)* careful, considerate, heedful, prudent, kind, thoughtful, polite, introspective, reflective.
(ANT.) thoughtless, heedless, inconsiderate, selfish, rash.

consideration *(SYN.)* kindness, care, heed, politeness, empathy, notice, watchfulness, kindliness, thoughtfulness, courtesy, concern, sympathy, thought, attention, reflection, fee, pay, study.
(ANT.) omission, oversight, negligence.

consistent *(SYN.)* conforming, accordant,

compatible, agreeing, faithful, constant, harmonious, expected, regular, congruous, correspondent.
(ANT.) paradoxical, discrepant, contrary, antagonistic, opposed, eccentric, inconsistent, incongruous.

consolation *(SYN.)* enjoyment, sympathy, relief, ease, contentment, comfort, solace.
(ANT.) discomfort, suffering, discouragement, torture, burden, misery.

console *(SYN.)* solace, comfort, sympathize with, assuage, soothe.
(ANT.) worry, annoy, upset, disturb, distress.

consolidate *(SYN.)* blend, combine, conjoin, fuse, mix, merge, unite.
(ANT.) decompose, separate, analyze, disintegrate.

consort *(SYN.)* companion, comrade, friend.
(ANT.) stranger, enemy, adversary.

conspicuous *(SYN.)* distinguished, clear, manifest, salient, noticeable, striking, obvious, prominent, visible.
(ANT.) hidden, obscure, neutral, common, inconspicuous.

conspiracy *(SYN.)* machination, combination, treason, intrigue, cabal, treachery, plot, collusion.

conspire *(SYN.)* plan, intrigue, plot, scheme.

constancy *(SYN.)* devotion, faithfulness, accuracy, precision, exactness.
(ANT.) faithlessness, treachery, perfidy.

constant *(SYN.)* continual, invariable, abiding, permanent, faithful, invariant, true, ceaseless, enduring, unchanging, steadfast, unchangeable, loyal, stable, immutable, staunch, steady, fixed.
(ANT.) fickle, irregular, wavering, off-and-on, infrequent, occasional, mutable.

constantly *(SYN.)* eternally, ever, evermore, forever, unceasingly.
(ANT.) rarely, sometimes, never, occasionally.

consternation *(SYN.)* apprehension, dismay, alarm, fear, fright, dread, horror, terror.
(ANT.) bravery, courage, boldness, assurance.

constitute *(SYN.)* compose, found, form, establish, organize, create, appoint, delegate,

authorize, commission.

constitution *(SYN.)* law, code, physique, health, vitality.

constrain *(SYN.)* necessity, indigence, need, want, poverty.
(ANT.) luxury, freedom, uncertainty.

construct *(SYN.)* build, form, erect, make, fabricate, raise, frame.
(ANT.) raze, demolish, destroy.

construction *(SYN.)* raising, building, fabricating.

constructive *(SYN.)* useful, helpful, valuable.
(ANT.) ruinous, destructive.

construe *(SYN.)* explain, interpret, solve, render, translate.
(ANT.) distort, confuse, misconstrue.

consult *(SYN.)* discuss, chatter, discourse, gossip, confer, report, rumor, deliberate, speech, talk.
(ANT.) writing, correspondence, silence.

consume *(SYN.)* engulf, absorb, use up, use, expend, exhaust, devour, devastate, destroy, engross.
(ANT.) emit, expel, exude, discharge.

consumer *(SYN.)* user, buyer, purchaser.

consummate *(SYN.)* close, conclude, do, finish, perfect, terminate.

consummation *(SYN.)* climax, apex, culmination, peak.
(ANT.) depth, base, floor.

contact *(SYN.)* meeting, touching.

contagious *(SYN.)* infectious, virulent, communicable, catching.
(ANT.) noncommunicable, healthful, hygienic.

contain *(SYN.)* embody, hold, embrace, include, accommodate, repress, restrain.
(ANT.) emit, encourage, yield, discharge.

contaminate *(SYN.)* corrupt, sully, taint, defile, soil, pollute, dirty, infect, poison.
(ANT.) purify.

contemplate *(SYN.)* imagine, recollect, consider, study, reflect upon, observe, deliberate, muse, ponder, plan, intend, view, regard, think about, reflect, think, mean.
(ANT.) forget, guess, conjecture.

contemplative *(SYN.)* simultaneous, meditative, thoughtful, contemporaneous, studious.

(ANT.) inattentive, indifferent, thoughtless.

contemporary *(SYN.)* modern, present, simultaneous, fashionable, coexisting, contemporaneous, up-to-date.

(ANT.) old, antecedent, past, ancient, succeeding, bygone.

contempt *(SYN.)* detestation, malice, contumely, disdain, derision, scorn.

(ANT.) respect, reverence, admiration, esteem, awe.

contemptible *(SYN.)* base, mean, vile, vulgar, nasty, low, detestable, selfish, miserable, offensive.

(ANT.) generous, honorable, noble, exalted, admirable.

contemptuous *(SYN.)* disdainful, sneering, scornful, insolent.

(ANT.) modest, humble.

contend *(SYN.)* dispute, combat, contest, assert, claim, argue, maintain.

content *(SYN.)* pleased, happy, contented, satisfied.

(ANT.) restless, dissatisfied, discontented.

contented *(SYN.)* delighted, fortunate, gay, happy, joyous, lucky, merry.

(ANT.) gloomy, blue, depressed.

contention *(SYN.)* combat, duel, struggle, discord, battle, variance.

(ANT.) concord, harmony, amity, consonance.

contentment *(SYN.)* delight, happiness, pleasure, satisfaction.

(ANT.) misery, sorrow, grief, sadness, despair.

contest *(SYN.)* dispute, debate, competition, tournament, oppose, discuss, quarrel, squabble.

(ANT.) allow, concede, agree, assent.

continence *(SYN.)* forbearance, temperance.

(ANT.) self-indulgence, excess, intoxication.

contingency *(SYN.)* likelihood, possibility, occasion, circumstance.

contingent *(SYN.)* depending, subject.

(ANT.) independent, original, casual.

continual *(SYN.)* constant, unceasing, everlasting, unremitting, endless, continuous, uninterrupted, regular, connected, consecutive, ceaseless.

(ANT.) periodic, rare, irregular, occasional, interrupted.

continue *(SYN.)* proceed, extend, endure, persist, resume, renew, recommence, last, remain, prolong, pursue.

(ANT.) check, cease, discontinue, stop, suspend.

continuous *(SYN.)* continuing, uninterrupted, ceaseless, unceasing, incessant, constant.

(ANT.) intermittent, irregular, sporadic.

contract *(SYN.)* condense, diminish, reduce, bargain, restrict, agreement, compact, pact, shrink, get, treaty, shorten.

(ANT.) lengthen, extend, swell, expand, elongate.

contraction *(SYN.)* reduction, shortening.

(ANT.) enlargement, expansion, extension.

contradict *(SYN.)* gainsay, counter, oppose, confute, dispute.

(ANT.) verify, confirm, agree, support.

contradictory *(SYN.)* inconsistent, conflicting, incompatible, paradoxical, unsteady.

(ANT.) congruous, consistent, correspondent.

contrary *(SYN.)* disagreeable, perverse, hostile, stubborn, opposite, opposing, opposed, disagreeing, disastrous, conflicting, headstrong, unlucky.

(ANT.) lucky, agreeable, propitious, favorable, like, obliging, similar, complementary, tractable, fortunate.

contrast *(SYN.)* differentiate, compare, distinction, disagreement, distinguish, differ, discriminate, difference, oppose.

(ANT.) agreement, similarity, likeness.

contribute *(SYN.)* grant, give, donate, bestow, provide, offer.

(ANT.) deny, withhold.

contribution *(SYN.)* grant, gift, offering, donation.

contrition *(SYN.)* grief, regret, self-reproach.

(ANT.) self-satisfaction, complacency.

contrive *(SYN.)* devise, intend, plan, make, invent, plot, hatch, form, project, arrange, manage, maneuver, scheme, sketch.

control *(SYN.)* govern, regulate, rule, command, dominate, direct, manage, check, repress, curb, management, mastery, direction, restraint, superintend, restrain. *(ANT.) ignore, forsake, follow, submit, abandon.*

controversy *(SYN.)* disagreement, dispute, debate. *(ANT.) agreement, harmony, accord, concord, decision.*

convenience *(SYN.)* accessibility, aid, benefit, help, service, availability. *(ANT.) inconvenience.*

convenient *(SYN.)* adapted, appropriate, fitting, favorable, handy, suitable, accessible, nearby, ready, available, advantageous, timely. *(ANT.) inconvenient, troublesome, awkward.*

convention *(SYN.)* meeting, conference, assembly, practice, custom, rule.

conventional *(SYN.)* common, regular, usual, everyday, habitual, routine, accustomed. *(ANT.) exotic, unusual, bizarre, extraordinary.*

conversant *(SYN.)* aware, intimate, familiar, versed, close, friendly, sociable. *(ANT.) affected, distant, cold, reserved.*

conversation *(SYN.)* colloquy, dialogue, chat, parley, discussion, talk.

converse *(SYN.)* jabber, talk, argue, comment, harangue, plead, rant, spout, discuss, chat, speak, reason.

conversion *(SYN.)* alteration, change, mutation, modification, metamorphosis.

convert *(SYN.)* change, alter, turn, transform, shift, modify, exchange, win over, vary, veer. *(ANT.) establish, stabilize, settle, retain.*

convey *(SYN.)* carry, bear, communicate, transport, transmit, support, sustain. *(ANT.) drop, abandon.*

conveyance *(SYN.)* van, car, train, truck, plane.

convict *(SYN.)* felon, offender, criminal.

conviction *(SYN.)* opinion, position, view, faith, belief, confidence, feeling, reliance, trust. *(ANT.) doubt, heresy, incredulity, denial.*

convince *(SYN.)* persuade, assure, exhort, induce, influence. *(ANT.) deter, compel, restrain, dissuade.*

convivial *(SYN.)* jolly, social, jovial, gregarious. *(ANT.) solemn, stern, unsociable.*

convoy *(SYN.)* with, attend, chaperone. *(ANT.) avoid, desert, quit, leave.*

cool *(SYN.)* frosty, chilly, icy, cold, wintry, quiet, composed, collected, distant, unfriendly, moderate. *(ANT.) hot, warm, heated, overwrought, excited, hysterical, friendly, outgoing.*

cooperate *(SYN.)* unite, combine, help, contribute, support.

coordinate *(SYN.)* attune, harmonize, adapt, match, balance.

copious *(SYN.)* ample, abundant, bountiful, overflowing, plentiful, profuse, rich. *(ANT.) scant, scarce, insufficient, meager, deficient.*

copy *(SYN.)* facsimile, exemplar, imitation, duplicate, reproduction, likeness, print, carbon, transcript. *(ANT.) prototype, original.*

cordial *(SYN.)* polite, friendly, affable, genial, earnest, gracious, warm, ardent, warmhearted, hearty, sincere. *(ANT.) unfriendly, cool, aloof, hostile, ill-tempered, reserved.*

core *(SYN.)* midpoint, heart, kernel, center, middle. *(ANT.) outskirts, border, surface, outside, boundary, rim.*

corporation *(SYN.)* business, organization, crew, group, troop, society, company, conglomerate, firm. *(ANT.) individual, dispersion, seclusion.*

corpse *(SYN.)* cadaver, carcass, remains, body, form. *(ANT.) spirit, soul, mind, intellect.*

corpulent *(SYN.)* obese, portly, chubby, stout. *(ANT.) slim, thin, slender, lean, gaunt.*

correct *(SYN.)* true, set right, faultless, impeccable, proper, accurate, precise, mend, right, rebuke, punish, amend, rectify, better, emend, caution, discipline, exact, strict. *(ANT.) condone, aggravate, false, inaccurate, wrong, untrue, faulty.*

correction *(SYN.)* order, improvement, reg-

ulation, instruction, amendment, remedy, rectification, repair, training, punishment.
(ANT.) confusion, turbulence, chaos.

correlative *(SYN.)* allied, correspondent, like, similar, parallel.
(ANT.) different, opposed, divergent.

correspond*(SYN.)* compare, coincide, match, agree, suit, fit, write.
(ANT.) differ, diverge, vary.

correspondent *(SYN.)* allied, alike, comparable, like, parallel, similar.
(ANT.) different, opposed, divergent, dissimilar.

corridor *(SYN.)* hallway, hall, foyer, passage, lobby, passageway.

corrode *(SYN.)* erode.

corrupt *(SYN.)* crooked, untrustworthy, treacherous, debased, unscrupulous, wicked, evil, low, contaminated, perverted, bribe, depraved, corrupted, demoralize, degrade, venal, putrid, tainted, dishonest, impure.
(ANT.) upright, honest, pure, sanctify, edify, purify, sanctified, scrupulous.

corrupted*(SYN.)* crooked, dishonest, impure, spoiled, unsound.

cost *(SYN.)* price, value, damage, charge, loss, sacrifice, penalty.

costly *(SYN.)* dear, expensive.
(ANT.) cheap, inexpensive.

costume *(SYN.)* dress, clothes, apparel, clothing, garb.

couch *(SYN.)* davenport, sofa, loveseat.

council *(SYN.)* caution, instruction, committee, cabinet, board, suggestion.

counsel *(SYN.)* guidance, attorney, lawyer, counselor, hint, imply, opinion, advice, offer, advise.
(ANT.) declare, dictate, insist.

count *(SYN.)* consider, number, enumerate, total, figure, compute, tally, estimate.
(ANT.) conjecture, guess, miscalculate.

countenance *(SYN.)* visage, face, aspect, support, appearance, approval, encouragement, favor.
(ANT.) forbid, prohibit.

counteract *(SYN.)* thwart, neutralize, offset, counterbalance, defeat.

counterfeit *(SYN.)* false, fraudulent, pretended,

pretend, sham, imitate, forgery, artificial, bogus, fake, spurious, imitation, unreal.
(ANT.) authentic, natural, real, genuine, true.

country *(SYN.)* state, nation, forest, farmland.
(ANT.) city.

couple *(SYN.)* team, pair, accompany, associate, attach, combine, connect, brace, join, link, unite.
(ANT.) detach, separate, disjoin, disconnect.

courage *(SYN.)* fearlessness, boldness, chivalry, fortitude, mettle, spirit, daring, bravery, prowess, intrepidity, valor, resolution.
(ANT.) fear, timidity, cowardice.

courageous *(SYN.)* bold, dauntless, brave, daring, intrepid, valorous, plucky, fearless, heroic, valiant.
(ANT.) fearful, weak, timid, cowardly.

course *(SYN.)* passage, advance, path, road, progress, way, direction, bearing, route, street, track, trail, way.

courteous *(SYN.)* civil, respectful, polite, genteel, well-mannered, gracious, refined.
(ANT.) discourteous, rude, uncivil, impolite, boorish.

courtesy *(SYN.)* graciousness, politeness, respect.
(ANT.) discourtesy, rudeness.

covenant *(SYN.)* agreement, concord, harmony, unison, compact, stipulation.
(ANT.) variance, discord, dissension, difference.

cover *(SYN.)* clothe, conceal, disguise, curtain, guard, envelop, mask, cloak, shield, hide, screen, protect, embrace, top, lid, covering, stopper, protection, refuge, spread, overlay, include, veil.
(ANT.) bare, expose, reveal.

covert *(SYN.)* potential, undeveloped, concealed, dormant.
(ANT.) explicit, visible, manifest.

covetous *(SYN.)* grasping, greedy, acquisitive, avaricious.
(ANT.) generous.

coward *(SYN.)* dastard, milquetoast, cad.
(ANT.) hero.

cowardice *(SYN.)* dread, dismay, fright, dismay, panic, terror, timidity.
(ANT.) fearlessness, courage, bravery.
cowardly *(SYN.)* fearful, timorous, afraid, faint-hearted, yellow, pusillanimous, spineless.
cower *(SYN.)* wince, flinch, cringe, quail, tremble.
coy *(SYN.)* embarrassed, sheepish, shy, timid.
(ANT.) fearless, outgoing, bold, adventurous, daring.
crack *(SYN.)* snap, break, split.
craft *(SYN.)* talent, skill, expertness, ability, cunning, guile, deceit, trade, profession, occupation.
crafty *(SYN.)* covert, clever, cunning, skillful, foxy, tricky, sly, underhand, shrewd.
(ANT.) frank, sincere, gullible, open, guileless, ingenuous.
craggy *(SYN.)* rough, rugged, irregular, uneven.
(ANT.) level, sleek, smooth, fine, polished.
crank *(SYN.)* cross, irritable, bad-tempered, testy.
(ANT.) cheerful, happy.
crash *(SYN.)* smash, shatter, dash.
crave *(SYN.)* want, desire, hunger.
(ANT.) relinquish, renounce.
craving *(SYN.)* relish, appetite, desire, liking, longing, passion.
(ANT.) renunciation, distaste, disgust.
crazy *(SYN.)* delirious, deranged, idiotic, mad, insane, imbecilic, demented, foolish, maniacal.
(ANT.) sane, sensible, sound, rational, reasonable.
creak *(SYN.)* squeak.
create *(SYN.)* fashion, form, generate, engender, formulate, make, originate, produce, cause, ordain, invent, beget, design, construct, constitute.
(ANT.) disband, abolish, terminate, destroy, demolish.
creative *(SYN.)* imaginative, ingenious, original, resourceful, clever, inventive, innovative.
(ANT.) unromantic, dull, literal.
credence *(SYN.)* confidence, faith, feeling, opinion, trust.
(ANT.) doubt, incredulity, denial.
credit *(SYN.)* believe, accept, belief, trust, faith, merit, honor, apprehend, fancy, hold, support.
(ANT.) doubt, question, distrust.
creditable *(SYN.)* worthy.
(ANT.) dishonorable, shameful.
credulous *(SYN.)* trusting, naive, believing, gullible, unsuspicious.
(ANT.) suspicious.
creed *(SYN.)* belief, precept, credo, faith, teaching.
(ANT.) practice, deed, conduct, performance.
creek *(SYN.)* brook, spring, stream.
crime *(SYN.)* offense, insult, aggression, wrongdoing, wrong.
(ANT.) right, innocence, morality.
criminal *(SYN.)* unlawful, crook, gangster, outlaw, illegal, convict, delinquent, offender, malefactor, felonious, felon, transgressor.
cripple *(SYN.)* hurt, maim, injure.
crisis *(SYN.)* conjuncture, emergency, pass, pinch, acme, climax, contingency, juncture, exigency.
(ANT.) calm, normality, stability, equilibrium.
crisp *(SYN.)* crumbling, delicate, frail, brittle.
(ANT.) calm, normality, stability.
criterion *(SYN.)* measure, law, rule, principle, gauge, proof.
(ANT.) fancy guess, chance, supposition.
critic *(SYN.)* reviewer, judge, commentator, censor, defamer.
critical *(SYN.)* exact, fastidious, caviling, faultfinding, accurate, condemning, reproachful, risky, dangerous, momentous, carping, acute, hazardous, hypercritical.
(ANT.) shallow, uncritical, approving, trivial, unimportant.
criticize *(SYN.)* examine, analyze, inspect, blame, censure, appraise, evaluate, scrutinize, reprehend.
(ANT.) neglect, overlook, approve.
critique *(SYN.)* criticism, inspection, review.
crony *(SYN.)* colleague, companion, chum, buddy, comrade, friend.

(ANT.) stranger, enemy, adversary.

crooked *(SYN.)* twisted, corrupt, hooked, curved, criminal, dishonest, bent, impaired.
(ANT.) improved, raised, straight, honest, upright, enhanced.

crop *(SYN.)* fruit, produce, harvest, cut, mow, reaping, result, yield.

cross *(SYN.)* mix, mingle, traverse, interbreed, annoyed, irritable, cranky, testy, angry, mean.
(ANT.) cheerful.

crouch *(SYN.)* duck, stoop.

crow *(SYN.)* boast, brag.

crowd *(SYN.)* masses, flock, host, squeeze, mob, multitude, populace, press, throng, swarm.

crown *(SYN.)* coronet, apex, crest, circlet, pinnacle, tiara, skull, head, top, zenith.
(ANT.) base, bottom, foundation, foot.

crude *(SYN.)* rude, graceless, unpolished, green, harsh, rough, coarse, ill-prepared, unfinished, raw, boorish, unrefined, uncouth.
(ANT.) finished, refined, polished, cultured, genteel, cultivated.

cruel *(SYN.)* ferocious, mean, heartless, unmerciful, malignant, savage, brutal, pitiless, inhuman, ruthless, merciless, barbarous.
(ANT.) humane, forbearing, kind, compassionate, gentle.

cruelty *(SYN.)* harshness, meanness, savagery, brutality.
(ANT.) compassion, kindness.

crumb *(SYN.)* jot, grain, mite, particle, shred.
(ANT.) mass, bulk, quantity.

crunch *(SYN.)* champ, gnaw, nibble.

crush *(SYN.)* smash, break, crash.

cry *(SYN.)* yowl, yell, roar, shout, scream, wail, weep, bawl, sob.

cryptic *(SYN.)* puzzling, mysterious, enigmatic, hidden, secret, vague, obscure, occult, unclear.

cull *(SYN.)* elect, choose, select.
(ANT.) reject, refuse.

culprit *(SYN.)* delinquent, felon, offender.

cultivate *(SYN.)* plant, seed, farm, till, refine, educate, teach.

cultivation *(SYN.)* farming, horticulture, tillage, agriculture.

culture *(SYN.)* humanism, upbringing, cultivation, breeding, education, learning, civilization, enlightenment, refinement.
(ANT.) illiteracy, vulgarity, ignorance.

cultured *(SYN.)* sophisticated, worldly.
(ANT.) crude, simple, uncouth, ingenuous.

cumbersome *(SYN.)* bulky, clumsy, awkward, unmanageable.
(ANT.) handy.

cunning *(SYN.)* clever, wily, crafty, foxy, skillful, tricky, ingenious, foxiness, ability, skill, wiliness, devious, shrewdness, cleverness.
(ANT.) honest, naive, openness, straightforward, simple, direct.

curb *(SYN.)* check, restraint, hinder, hold, limit, control, stop.
(ANT.) aid, loosen, incite, encourage.

cure *(SYN.)* help, treatment, heal, medicine, relief, remedy.

curiosity *(SYN.)* marvel, rarity, phenomenon, admiration, amazement, bewilderment, wonder.
(ANT.) apathy, indifference, expectation.

curious *(SYN.)* interrogative, interested, peculiar, queer, nosy, peeping, prying, inquisitive, unusual.
(ANT.) unconcerned, incurious, ordinary, indifferent, uninterested.

current *(SYN.)* up-to-date, contemporary, present, new, tide, stream.
(ANT.) antiquated, old, bygone, ancient, past.

curse *(SYN.)* ban, oath, denounce, swear, condemn.
(ANT.) boon, blessing, advantage.

cursory *(SYN.)* frivolous, shallow, slight.
(ANT.) complete, deep, profound, thorough.

curt *(SYN.)* hasty, short, abrupt, brusque, brief, blunt, rude, harsh.
(ANT.) friendly, smooth, gradual, polite, courteous.

curtail *(SYN.)* condense, contract, reduce, limit, abbreviate.
(ANT.) lengthen, extend.

curtain *(SYN.)* blind, drapery, drape, shade.

curve *(SYN.)* crook, deflect, bend, incline, turn, twist.
(ANT.) resist, stiffen, straighten.

cushion *(SYN.)* pillow, pad, check, absorb.

custodian *(SYN.)* guard, keeper, guardian, watchman.

custody *(SYN.)* guardianship, care.

(ANT.) neglect, disregard, indifference.

custom *(SYN.)* fashion, rule, routine, practice, usage.

customary *(SYN.)* common, usual, regular, everyday, general.

(ANT.) exceptional, irregular, rare, unusual, abnormal.

customer *(SYN.)* client, buyer.

cut *(SYN.)* slash, gash, prick, slit, sever, cleave, mow, incision, chop, lop, slice.

cut back *(SYN.)* decrease, reduce.

cut in *(SYN.)* butt in, interfere.

cut off *(SYN.)* cease, terminate.

cylindrical *(SYN.)* circular, curved, plump, rotund, spherical, round.

D

dab *(SYN.)* coat, pat, smear.

dabble *(SYN.)* splatter, toy, splash, fiddle, putter.

dabbler *(SYN.)* amateur, dilettante, tinkerer, trifler.

(ANT.) master, expert, scholar, specialist, authority.

daft *(SYN.)* crazy, foolish, insane.

dagger *(SYN.)* knife, dirk, blade.

daily *(SYN.)* every day, diurnal, regularly.

dainty *(SYN.)* slender, pleasing, delicate, frail, pleasant, pretty, petite, graceful, fine, elegant.

(ANT.) uncouth, vulgar, coarse, tough.

dally *(SYN.)* dawdle, linger, lag, delay, loiter.

(ANT.) rush, hurry, dash, get going, bustle.

dam *(SYN.)* dike, levee, barrier, slow, stop, check, obstruct, block.

(ANT.) free, release, loose, unleash.

damage *(SYN.)* spoil, deface, impair, mar, hurt, injury, impairment, destruction, injure, harm.

(ANT.) repair, benefit, mend, rebuild, improve, ameliorate.

dame *(SYN.)* woman, lady.

damn *(SYN.)* denounce, descry, curse, reprove, blame.

(ANT.) bless, honor, glorify, praise, accept, applaud, consecrate.

damnable *(SYN.)* blameworthy, evil, detestable, execrable, outrageous, bad, sinful, horrible.

(ANT.) good, commendable, worthy, praiseworthy.

damp *(SYN.)* humid, dank, moisture, wetness, humidity.

(ANT.) arid, dry.

dampen *(SYN.)* wet, depressed, moisten, dull, suppress, sprinkle, discouraged, retard, slow, inhibit, deaden, muffle.

(ANT.) dehumidify, increase, encourage.

dance *(SYN.)* bounce, flit, skip, sway, prance, bob, glide, caper, cavort, frisk.

dandle *(SYN.)* jounce, joggle, bounce, jiggle, nestle, cuddle, caress.

dandy *(SYN.)* coxcomb, fop, swell, great, fine, wonderful, excellent.

(ANT.) rotten, terrible, awful, miserable, slob.

danger *(SYN.)* jeopardy, risk, threat, hazard, uncertainty, peril.

(ANT.) safety, immunity, security, defense.

dangerous *(SYN.)* risky, insecure, threatening, critical, perilous, unsafe, uncertain, hazardous.

(ANT.) trustworthy, secure, protected, safe.

dangle *(SYN.)* droop, swing, flap, hang, sag.

dank *(SYN.)* moist, muggy, wet.

(ANT.) dry.

dapper *(SYN.)* spruce, trim, natty, well-tailored, dashing, neat.

(ANT.) untidy, sloppy, shabby, messy, unkempt.

dappled *(SYN.)* spotted, flecked, brindled, variegated, piebald, pied.

(ANT.) uniform, solid, unvaried.

dare *(SYN.)* brave, call, question, defy, risk, challenge.

daredevil *(SYN.)* lunatic, thrill-seeker, madcap, adventurer.

daring *(SYN.)* foolhardy, chivalrous, rash, fearless, courageous, intrepid, valiant, courage, bravery, brave, precipitate, bold.

(ANT.) timid, cowardice, timidity, cautious.

dark *(SYN.)* somber, obscure, gloomy, black, unilluminated, dim, evil, hidden, secret, swarthy, murky, opaque, dismal, mournful, sable, sullen, shadowy, sinister, dusky, mystic, shadowy, unlit, sunless, shaded, wicked, occult.

(ANT.) lucid, light, happy, cheerful, illuminated, pleasant.

darling *(SYN.)* dear, adored, sweetheart, favorite, cherished.

(ANT.) uncherished, unlovable, disagreeable, rejected, forlorn.

darn *(SYN.)* repair, mend.

dart *(SYN.)* scurry, arrow, barb, hurry, dash, throw, missile, run, hasten, scamper, toss, rush, cast.

dash *(SYN.)* pound, thump, beat, smite, buffet, thrash, smash, break, scurry, run, dart, rush, scamper, hint, pinch, hit, strike.

(ANT.) stroke, hearten, encourage, defend.

dashing *(SYN.)* swashbuckling, dapper, flamboyant, handsome.

(ANT.) dull, colorless, shabby, lifeless.

dastardly *(SYN.)* craven, cowardly, mean, rotten, villainous, dishonorable.

(ANT.) heroic, brave, high-minded, courageous.

data *(SYN.)* information, statistics, proof, facts, evidence.

date *(SYN.)* interview, appointment, commitment, engagement, meeting, rendezvous, regale, entertain.

dated *(SYN.)* out-of-date, old-fashioned, outmoded.

(ANT.) latest, now, current, fashionable, hot.

daub *(SYN.)* coat, grease, soil, scribble, cover, stain, smear, scrawl.

daunt *(SYN.)* discourage, dishearten, intimidate, frighten, deter.

(ANT.) enspirit, encourage.

dauntless *(SYN.)* fearless, brave, bold, courageous, intrepid, valiant.

(ANT.) fearful, timid, cowardly.

dawn *(SYN.)* sunrise, start, outset, day-break, origin, commencement.

(ANT.) dusk, sunset, nightfall, end, con- *clusion, finish.*

daydream *(SYN.)* woolgather, muse.

daze *(SYN.)* perplex, stun, puzzle, bewilder, upset, confuse, ruffle, confusion, stupor, bewilderment.

dazzle *(SYN.)* surprise, stun, astonish, impress, bewilder, stupefy.

dead *(SYN.)* departed, lifeless, deceased, insensible, inanimate, dull, defunct, gone, unconscious, inoperative, inactive, inert, motionless, spiritless.

(ANT.) animate, functioning, active, living, alive, stirring.

deaden *(SYN.)* anesthetize, numb, paralyze.

deadlock *(SYN.)* standstill, impasse, stalemate.

deadly *(SYN.)* lethal, mortal, fatal, deathly, baleful.

deaf *(SYN.)* stone-deaf, unhearing, unheeding, unaware, unheedful, stubborn, oblivious, inattentive.

(ANT.) aware, conscious.

deafening *(SYN.)* vociferous, noisy, stentorian, resounding, loud.

(ANT.) soft, inaudible, subdued.

deal *(SYN.)* act, treat, attend, cope, barter, trade, bargain, apportion, give, distribute, deliver.

dear *(SYN.)* valued, esteemed, expensive, beloved, costly, darling, high-priced, loved, precious.

(ANT.) hateful, reasonable, inexpensive, cheap, unwanted.

dearth *(SYN.)* shortage, lack, scarcity.

death *(SYN.)* decease, extinction, demise, passing.

(ANT.) life.

debase *(SYN.)* lower, degrade, alloy, adulterate, defile, humiliate, depress, abase, pervert, corrupt.

(ANT.) restore, improve, vitalize, enhance.

debate *(SYN.)* wrangle, discuss, plead, argue, discussion, contend, argument, controversy, dispute.

(ANT.) agreement, reject, accord, ignore, spurn.

debonair *(SYN.)* urbane, sophisticated, refined, dapper, well-bred.

debris *(SYN.)* rubbish, litter, junk, wreckage, refuse, detritus, ruins, trash, residue.

debt *(SYN.)* amount due, liability, obligation.

decay *(SYN.)* decrease, spoil, ebb, decline, waste, disintegrate, wane, dwindle, molder, deteriorate, perish, wither, rot, collapse, putrefy, die, decompose.
(ANT.) progress, rise, increase, grow, flourish.

deceased *(SYN.)* lifeless, departed, dead, insensible, defunct.
(ANT.) living, alive.

deceit *(SYN.)* duplicity, cheat, fraud, chicanery, trick, cunning, deception, guile, beguilement, deceitfulness, dishonesty, wiliness.
(ANT.) truthfulness, openness, forthrightness, honesty, candor.

deceitful *(SYN.)* false, fraudulent, insincere, dishonest, deceptive.
(ANT.) sincere, honest.

deceive *(SYN.)* cheat, defraud, hoodwink, mislead, swindle.

decency *(SYN.)* decorum, dignity, property, respectability.

decent *(SYN.)* befitting, fit, suitable, becoming, respectable, adequate, seemly, fitting, comely, appropriate, proper, tolerable, decorous.
(ANT.) vulgar, gross, improper, unsuitable, indecorous, reprehensible, indecent, coarse.

deception *(SYN.)* trick, cheat, sham, deceit, trickery, craftiness, treachery, beguilement, cunning.
(ANT.) openness, frankness, candor, probity, truthfulness, honesty.

deceptive *(SYN.)* specious, fallacious, deceitful, false, delusive, unreliable, illusive, tricky, dishonest, deceiving, misleading, delusory.
(ANT.) honest, real, genuine, true, truthful, authentic.

decide *(SYN.)* resolve, determine, terminate, conclude, close, settle, adjudicate, choose, end.
(ANT.) waver, hesitate, vacillate, doubt, suspend.

decipher *(SYN.)* render, unravel, construe, solve, decode, translate, elucidate, determine.

(ANT.) misconstrue, distort, misinterpret, confuse.

decision *(SYN.)* resolution, determination, settlement.

decisive *(SYN.)* determined, firm, decided, unhesitating, resolute.

declaration *(SYN.)* pronouncement, notice, affirmation, statement, announcement, assertion.

declare *(SYN.)* assert, promulate, affirm, tell, broadcast, express, proclaim, aver, say, pronounce, profess, announce.
(ANT.) deny, withhold, conceal, suppress.

decline *(SYN.)* descend, decay, dwindle, refuse, incline, wane, sink, depreciate, deny, diminish, weaken.
(ANT.) accept, ascend, ameliorate, increase.

decompose *(SYN.)* rot, disintegrate, molder, decay, crumble.

decorate *(SYN.)* trim, paint, deck, enrich, color, beautify, enhance, furbish, furnish, adorn, ornament.
(ANT.) uncover, mar, deface, defame, debase.

decoration *(SYN.)* ornamentation, embellishment, adornment, furnishing, award, citation, medal.

decoy *(SYN.)* lure, bait.

decrease *(SYN.)* lessen, wane, deduct, diminish, curtail, deduct, remove, lessening, decline.
(ANT.) expansion, increase, enlarge, expand, grow.

decree *(SYN.)* order, edict, statute, declaration, announce, act.

decrepit *(SYN.)* feeble, puny, weakened, infirm, enfeebled, languid, rickety, weak, run-down, tumble-down, dilapidated, faint.
(ANT.) strong, forceful, vigorous, energetic, lusty.

decry *(SYN.)* lower, belittle, derogate, minimize, undervalue.
(ANT.) praise, commend, magnify, aggrandize.

dedicate *(SYN.)* sanctify, consecrate, hallow, devote, assign.

dedicated *(SYN.)* disposed, true, affectionate, fond, wedded.

(ANT.) indisposed, detached, untrammeled, disinclined.

deduct *(SYN.)* lessen, shorten, abate, remove, eliminate, curtail, subtract.

(ANT.) grow, enlarge, add, increase, amplify, expand.

deed *(SYN.)* feat, transaction, action, performance, act, operation, achievement, document, certificate, title, accomplishment.

(ANT.) intention, cessation, inactivity, deliberation.

deem *(SYN.)* hold, determine, believe, regard, reckon, judge, consider, account, expound, view.

deep *(SYN.)* bottomless, low, unplumbed, acute, obscure, involved, absorbed.

(ANT.) shallow.

deface *(SYN.)* spoil, impair, damage, mar, hurt, scratch, mutilate, disfigure, injure, harm.

(ANT.) mend, benefit, repair, enhance.

defamation *(SYN.)* invective. reproach, upbraiding, abuse, insult, outrage, reviling, desecration.

(ANT.) respect, approval, laudation, commendation.

default *(SYN.)* loss, omission, lack, failure, want, dereliction.

(ANT.) victory, achievement, sufficiency, success.

defeat *(SYN.)* quell, vanquish, beat, overcome, overthrow, subdue, frustrate, spoil, conquest.

(ANT.) submit, retreat, cede, yield, surrender, capitulate, lose.

defect *(SYN.)* shortcoming, fault, omission, blemish, imperfection, forsake, leave, weakness, failure.

(ANT.) perfection, flawlessness, support, join, completeness.

defective *(SYN.)* faulty, imperfect, inoperative, flawed, inoperable.

(ANT.) flawless, perfect, faultless.

defend *(SYN.)* screen, espouse, justify, protect, vindicate, fortify, assert, guard, safeguard, shield.

(ANT.) oppose, assault, submit, attack, deny.

defense *(SYN.)* resistance, protection, bulwark, fort, barricade, trench, rampart, fortress.

defer *(SYN.)* postpone, delay.

(ANT.) speed, hurry, expedite.

deference *(SYN.)* fame, worship, adoration, reverence, admiration, respect, fame, dignity, homage.

(ANT.) dishonor, derision, reproach, contempt.

defiant *(SYN.)* rebellious, antagonistic, obstinate.

(ANT.) yielding, submissive.

deficient *(SYN.)* lacking, short, incomplete, defective, scanty, insufficient, inadequate.

(ANT.) enough, ample, sufficient, adequate.

defile *(SYN.)* pollute, march, corrupt, dirty, file, debase, contaminate.

(ANT.) purify.

define *(SYN.)* describe, fix, establish, label, designate, set, name, explain.

definite *(SYN.)* fixed, prescribed, certain, specific, exact, determined, distinct, explicit, correct.

(ANT.) indefinite, confused, undetermined, equivocal.

definitely *(SYN.)* certainly, assuredly, absolutely, positively, surely.

definition *(SYN.)* sense, interpretation, meaning, explanation.

deft *(SYN.)* handy, adroit, clever, adept, dexterous, skillful, skilled.

(ANT.) inept, clumsy, maladroit, awkward.

defunct *(SYN.)* lifeless, dead, departed, expired, extinct, spiritless, inanimate.

(ANT.) living, alive, stirring.

defy *(SYN.)* hinder, oppose, withstand, attack, resist, confront, challenge, flout, dare, thwart.

(ANT.) yield, allow, relent, surrender, submit, accede.

degenerate *(SYN.)* dwindle, decline, weaken, deteriorate, decrease.

(ANT.) ascend, ameliorate, increase, appreciate.

degrade *(SYN.)* crush, reduce, subdue, abash, humble, lower, shame, demote, downgrade, abase, mortify.

(ANT.) praise, elevate, honor.

degree *(SYN.)* grade, amount, step, measure, rank, honor, extent.

deign *(SYN.)* condescend, stoop.

dejected *(SYN.)* depressed, downcast, sad, disheartened, blue, discouraged.
(ANT.) cheerful, happy, optimistic.

delectable *(SYN.)* tasty, delicious, savory, delightful, sweet, luscious.
(ANT.) unsavory, distasteful, unpalatable, acrid.

delegate *(SYN.)* emissary, envoy, ambassador, representative, commission, deputize, authorize.

delete *(SYN.)* erase, cancel, remove.
(ANT.) add.

deleterious *(SYN.)* evil, unwholesome, base, sinful, bad, wicked, immoral, destructive, injurious, hurtful, damaging, detrimental, unsound.
(ANT.) moral, excellent, reputable, healthful, healthy, helpful, constructive, good.

deliberate *(SYN.)* studied, willful, intended, contemplated, premeditated, planned, methodical, designed.
(ANT.) fortuitous, hasty, accidental.

delicate *(SYN.)* frail, critical, slender, dainty, pleasing, fastidious, exquisite, precarious, demanding, sensitive, savory, fragile, weak.
(ANT.) tough, strong, coarse, clumsy, hearty, hale, vulgar, rude.

delicious *(SYN.)* tasty, luscious, delectable, sweet, savory.
(ANT.) unsavory, distasteful, unpalatable, unpleasant, acrid.

delight *(SYN.)* joy, bliss, gladness, pleasure, ecstasy, happiness, rapture.
(ANT.) revolt, sorrow, annoyance, displeasure, disgust, displease, revulsion, misery.

delightful *(SYN.)* pleasing, pleasant, charming, refreshing, pleasurable.
(ANT.) nasty, disagreeable, unpleasant.

delirious *(SYN.)* raving, mad, giddy, frantic, hysterical, violent.

deliver *(SYN.)* impart, publish, rescue, commit, communicate, free, address, offer, save, give, liberate,
(ANT.) restrict, confine, capture, enslave, withhold, imprison.

deluge *(SYN.)* overflow, flood.

delusion *(SYN.)* mirage, fantasy, phantasm, vision, dream, illusion, phantom, hallucination.
(ANT.) substance, actuality.

delve *(SYN.)* dig, look, search, scoop, explore, hunt.

demand *(SYN.)* claim, inquire, ask, need, require, obligation, requirement, ask for, necessitate.
(ANT.) tender, give, present, waive, relinquish, offer.

demean *(SYN.)* comport, bear, operate, carry, act, manage, deport.

demeanor *(SYN.)* manner, way, conduct, actions, behavior.

demented *(SYN.)* insane, crazy, mad, mental, psychotic, lunatic.

demolish *(SYN.)* ruin, devastate, ravage, annihilate, wreck, destroy, raze, exterminate, obliterate.
(ANT.) erect, make, save, construct, preserve, build, establish.

demolition *(SYN.)* wrecking, destruction.
(ANT.) erection, construction.

demon *(SYN.)* fiend, monster, devil, ogre, spirit.

demonstrate *(SYN.)* evince, show, prove, display, illustrate, describe, explain, manifest, exhibit.
(ANT.) hide, conceal.

demonstration *(SYN.)* exhibit, show, presentation, exhibition, display, rally.

demur *(SYN.)* waver, falter, delay, stutter, doubt, vacillate, hesitate, scruple.
(ANT.) proceed, decide, resolve, continue.

demure *(SYN.)* meek, shy, modest, diffident, retiring, bashful, coy.

den *(SYN.)* cave, lair, cavern.

denial *(SYN.)* disallowance, proscription, refusal, prohibition.

denounce *(SYN.)* condemn, blame, reprove, reprehend, censure, reproach, upbraid, reprobate.
(ANT.) condone, approve, forgive, commend, praise.

dense *(SYN.)* crowded, slow, close, obtuse, compact, dull, stupid, compressed, thick, concentrated, packed, solid.
(ANT.) sparse, quick, dispersed, clever, dissipated, empty, smart, bright.

dent *(SYN.)* notch, impress, pit, nick.

deny *(SYN.)* refuse, withhold, dispute, disavow, forbid, refute, contradict, abjure, confute, gainsay.

(ANT.) confirm, affirm, admit, confess, permit, allow, concede, assert.

depart *(SYN.)* quit, forsake, withdraw, renounce, desert, relinquish, die, perish, decease.

(ANT.) tarry, remain, come, abide, stay, arrive.

departure *(SYN.)* valediction, farewell.

depend *(SYN.)* trust, rely, confide.

dependable *(SYN.)* secure, trustworthy, certain, safe, trusty, reliable, tried.

(ANT.) unreliable, fallible, dubious, uncertain.

dependent *(SYN.)* relying, contingent, subordinate, conditional.

(ANT.) original, casual, absolute, independent.

depict *(SYN.)* explain, recount, describe, portray, characterize, relate, narrate.

deplore *(SYN.)* repine, lament, bemoan, wail, bewail, weep, grieve, regret.

deport *(SYN.)* exile, eject, oust, banish, expel, dismiss, ostracize, dispel, exclude.

(ANT.) receive, admit, shelter, accept, harbor.

deportment *(SYN.)* deed, behavior, manner, action, carriage, disposition, bearing, demeanor.

deposit *(SYN.)* place, put, bank, save, store, sediment, dregs, addition, entry.

(ANT.) withdraw, withdrawal.

depreciate *(SYN.)* dwindle, decrease, decay, belittle, disparage, weaken, minimize, descend, deteriorate.

(ANT.) ascend, ameliorate, praise, increase, applaud, appreciate.

depress *(SYN.)* deject, dishearten, sadden, dampen, devaluate, devalue, lessen, lower, cheapen, reduce, dispirit, discourage, sink.

(ANT.) exalt, cheer, exhilarate.

depression *(SYN.)* hopelessness, despondency, pessimism, dip, cavity, pothole, hole, despair, gloom, melancholy, sadness, sorrow, recession, decline, desperation, discouragement.

(ANT.) eminence, elation, optimism, hap-

piness, confidence, elevation, hope.

deprive *(SYN.)* bereave, deny, strip.

(ANT.) provision, supply, provide.

derelict *(SYN.)* decrepit, shabby, dilapidated, neglected, forsaken, deserted, remiss, abandoned, lax.

dereliction *(SYN.)* want, lack, failure, miscarriage, loss, default, deficiency, omission, fiasco.

(ANT.) sufficiency, success, achievement, victory.

derision *(SYN.)* irony, satire, banter, raillery, sneering, gibe, ridicule.

derivation *(SYN.)* source, birth, inception, start, beginning, spring, commencement, foundation, origin.

(ANT.) issue, end, outcome, harvest, product.

derive *(SYN.)* obtain, acquire, get, receive.

descend *(SYN.)* wane, lower, move, slope, incline, decline, slant, sink.

(ANT.) increase, appreciate, ameliorate, ascend.

descendant *(SYN.)* child, issue, progeny, offspring.

describe *(SYN.)* portray, picture, recount, depict, relate, characterize, represent, narrate.

description *(SYN.)* history, record, recital, account, computation, chronicle, reckoning, narration, detail, narrative.

(ANT.) misrepresentation, confusion, caricature.

desecration *(SYN.)* profanation, insult, defamation, reviling, abuse, maltreatment, aspersion, perversion, dishonor.

(ANT.) respect, commendation, approval, laudation.

desert *(SYN.)* forsake, wilderness, resign, abjure, abandon, wasteland, waste, leave, surrender, abdicate, quit, barren, uninhabited.

(ANT.) uphold, defend, stay, maintain, accompany, join, support.

deserter *(SYN.)* runaway, renegade, fugitive, defector.

deserts *(SYN.)* right, compensation, due, reward, requital, condign.

deserve *(SYN.)* earn, warrant, merit.

design *(SYN.)* drawing, purpose, outline, devise, intend, draw, contrive, draft, cunning, plan, artfulness, delineation, scheming, sketch, intent, invent, objective, mean, contrivance, plotting, intention, create.

(ANT.) candor, accident, result, chance.

designate *(SYN.)* manifest, indicate, show, specify, denote, reveal, name, appoint, select, assign, disclose, signify, imply, nominate, intimate.

(ANT.) divert, mislead, conceal, falsify, distract.

desirable *(SYN.)* coveted, wanted.

desire *(SYN.)* longing, craving, yearning, appetite, lust, long for, crave, covet, want, request, ask, need, wish, aspiration, urge.

(ANT.) hate, aversion, loathing, abomination, detest, loathe, abhor, distaste.

desist *(SYN.)* cork, stop, cease, hinder, terminate, abstain, halt, interrupt, seal, arrest, plug, bar.

(ANT.) promote, begin, speed, proceed, start.

desolate *(SYN.)* forlorn, waste, bare, lonely, abandoned, wild, deserted, uninhabited, empty, sad, miserable, wretched, unhappy, bleak, forsaken.

(ANT.) crowded, teeming, populous, happy, cheerful, fertile, attended.

despair *(SYN.)* discouragement, pessimism, depression, hopelessness, despondency, gloom, desperation.

(ANT.) elation, optimism, hope, joy, confidence.

desperado *(SYN.)* criminal, crook, thug, gangster, hoodlum.

desperate *(SYN.)* reckless, determined, despairing, wild, daring, hopeless, despondent, audacious.

(ANT.) optimistic, composed, hopeful, collected, calm, assured.

despicable *(SYN.)* vulgar, offensive, base, vile, contemptible, selfish, low, mean, worthless, nasty.

(ANT.) noble, exalted, admirable, generous, worthy, dignified.

despise *(SYN.)* hate, scorn, detest, loathe, disdain, abhor, condemn, dislike, abominate.

(ANT.) honor, love, approve, like, admire.

despite *(SYN.)* notwithstanding.

despoil *(SYN.)* plunder, rob, loot.

despondent *(SYN.)* sad, dismal, depressed, somber, ejected, melancholy, doleful, sorrowful.

(ANT.) joyous, cheerful, merry, happy.

despot *(SYN.)* tyrant, ruler, oppressor, dictator.

despotic *(SYN.)* authoritative, unconditional, absolute, tyrannous, entire, unrestricted.

(ANT.) dependent, conditional, qualified, accountable.

destiny *(SYN.)* fate, portion, outcome, consequence, result, fortune, doom, lot.

destitute *(SYN.)* poor, penurious, needy, impecunious, poverty-stricken, impoverished, indigent.

(ANT.) opulent, wealthy, affluent, rich.

destroy *(SYN.)* raze, devastate, ruin, end, demolish, wreck, extinguish, annihilate, exterminate, obliterate, waste, slay, kill, eradicate.

(ANT.) make, construct, start, create, save, establish.

destroyed *(SYN.)* rent, smashed, interrupted, flattened, wrecked, broken, ruptured, crushed.

(ANT.) whole, repaired, integral, united.

destruction *(SYN.)* ruin, devastation, extinction, demolition.

(ANT.) beginning, creation.

destructive *(SYN.)* deadly, baneful, noxious, deleterious, injurious, pernicious, fatal, detrimental.

(ANT.) salutary, beneficial, creative.

detach *(SYN.)* deduct, remove, subtract, curtail, divide, shorten, decrease, disengage, reduce, separate, diminish.

(ANT.) hitch, grow, enlarge, increase, connect, amplify, attack, expand.

detail *(SYN.)* elaborate, commission, part, itemize, portion, division, fragment, assign, circumstance, segment.

detain *(SYN.)* impede, delay, hold back, retard, arrest, restrain, stay.

(ANT.) quicken, hasten, expedite, forward, precipitate.

detect *(SYN.)* discover, reveal, find, ascertain, determine, learn, originate, devise.
(ANT.) hide, screen, lose, cover, mask.
determinant *(SYN.)* reason, incentive, source, agent, principle, inducement.
(ANT.) result, effect, consequence, end.
determine *(SYN.)* decide, settle, end, conclude, ascertain, induce, fix, verify, resolve, establish, necessitate.
detest *(SYN.)* loathe, hate, despise.
(ANT.) savor, appreciate, like, love.
detriment *(SYN.)* injury, harm, disadvantage, damage.
(ANT.) benefit.
detrimental *(SYN.)* hurtful, mischievous, damaging, harmful.
(ANT.) salutary, advantageous, profitable, beneficial.
develop *(SYN.)* evolve, unfold, enlarge, amplify, expand, create, grow, advance, reveal, unfold, mature, elaborate.
(ANT.) wither, contract, degenerate, stunt, deteriorate, compress.
development *(SYN.)* growth, expansion, progress, unraveling, elaboration, evolution, maturing, unfolding.
(ANT.) compression, abbreviation, curtailment.
deviate *(SYN.)* deflect, stray, divert, diverge, wander, sidetrack, digress.
(ANT.) preserve, follow, remain, continue, persist.
device *(SYN.)* tool, utensil, means, channel, machine, agent, vehicle, gadget, apparatus, tools, instrument, contrivance.
(ANT.) preventive, impediment, hindrance, obstruction.
devilish *(SYN.)* diabolical, fiendish, diabolic, satanic, demonic.
devious *(SYN.)* tortuous, winding, distorted, circuitous, tricky, crooked, roundabout, cunning, erratic, indirect.
(ANT.) straight, direct, straightforward, honest.
devise *(SYN.)* create, concoct, invent, originate.
devote *(SYN.)* assign, dedicate, give, apply.
(ANT.) withhold, relinquish, ignore, with-

draw.
devoted *(SYN.)* attached, dedicated, prone, wedded, addicted, ardent, earnest, loyal, disposed, inclined, fond, affectionate, faithful.
(ANT.) untrammeled, disinclined, detached, indisposed.
devotion *(SYN.)* piety, zeal, ardor, loyalty, dedication, religiousness, consecration, affection, love, devoutness, fidelity, attachment.
(ANT.) unfaithfulness, aversion, alienation, indifference.
devour *(SYN.)* consume, gulp, gorge, waste, eat, ruin, swallow, destroy.
devout *(SYN.)* sacred, religious, spiritual, holy, theological, pietistic, pious, sanctimonious, reverent.
(ANT.) profane, skeptical, atheistic, secular, impious.
dexterity *(SYN.)* talent, capability, qualification, aptness, skill, ability.
(ANT.) unreadiness, incapacity, disability, incompetence.
dexterous *(SYN.)* clever, adroit, handy, deft, facile, skillful, skilled, proficient.
(ANT.) awkward, clumsy.
dialect *(SYN.)* slang, jargon, cant, speech, idiom, tongue, diction, vernacular.
(ANT.) nonsense, drivel, babble, gibberish.
dialogue *(SYN.)* interview, chat, discussion, conference, exchange, talk, conversation.
diary *(SYN.)* memo, account, journal, words.
dicker *(SYN.)* haggle, bargain, negotiate.
dictate *(SYN.)* deliver, speak, record, command, order, direct.
dictator *(SYN.)* oppressor, tyrant, despot, persecutor, overlord, autocrat.
die *(SYN.)* fade, wane, cease, depart, wither, decay, decline, sink, expire, perish, decease, go, diminish, fail, languish, decrease.
(ANT.) live, begin, grow, survive, flourish.
difference *(SYN.)* inequality, variety, disparity, discord, distinction, dissension, dissimilarity, disagreement, contrast, separation.
(ANT.) harmony, similarity, identity, agreement, likeness, compatibility, kinship,

resemblance.

different *(SYN.)* unlike, various, distinct, miscellaneous, divergent, sundry, contrary, differing, diverse, variant, incongruous, divers, unlike, changed, dissimilar, opposite.
(ANT.) similar, congruous, same, alike, identical.

differentiate *(SYN.)* separate, discriminate, distinguish, perceive, detect, recognize, discern.
(ANT.) confuse, omit, mingle, confound, overlook.

difficult *(SYN.)* involved, demanding, arduous, trying, complicated, hard, laborious, perplexing, hard, intricate.
(ANT.) simple, easy, facile, effortless.

difficulty *(SYN.)* trouble, hardship, fix, predicament, trouble.
(ANT.) ease.

diffuse *(SYN.)* spread, sparse, scattered, scanty, dispersed, thin, rare.
(ANT.) concentrated.

dig *(SYN.)* burrow, excavate, appreciate, understand.

digest *(SYN.)* consume, eat, reflect on, study, shorten, consider, summarize, abridge, abstract, abridgment, synopsis.

dignified *(SYN.)* serious, solemn, noble, stately, elegant.

dignify *(SYN.)* honor, elevate.
(ANT.) shame, degrade, humiliate.

dignity *(SYN.)* stateliness, distinction, bearing.

digress *(SYN.)* divert, wander, bend, stray, deflect, sidetrack, crook.
(ANT.) preserve, continue, remain, follow, persist.

dilate *(SYN.)* increase, widen, amplify, enlarge, augment, expand.
(ANT.) shrink, contract, restrict, abridge.

dilemma *(SYN.)* fix, strait, condition, scrape, difficulty, plight.
(ANT.) ease, calmness, satisfaction, comfort.

diligent *(SYN.)* patient, busy, hard-working, active, perseverant, assiduous, industrious, careful.
(ANT.) unconcerned, indifferent, apathetic, lethargic, careless.

dim *(SYN.)* pale, shadowy, faint, faded, unclear, vague, darken, dull, indistinct.
(ANT.) brighten, brilliant, bright, illuminate, glaring.

dimension *(SYN.)* size, importance, measure, extent.

diminish *(SYN.)* suppress, lower, decrease, shrink, wane, abate, reduce, lessen, assuage.
(ANT.) enlarge, revive, amplify, increase.

diminutive *(SYN.)* small, wee, tiny, little, minute.
(ANT.) large, big, great, gigantic, huge.

din *(SYN.)* tumult, clamor, sound, babble, outcry, row, noise, racket.
(ANT.) quiet, stillness, hush.

dine *(SYN.)* lunch, eat, sup, feed.

dingy *(SYN.)* dull, dark, dismal, dirty, drab, murky, gray.
(ANT.) cheerful, bright.

dip *(SYN.)* immerse, plunge, submerge, wet, swim.

diplomacy *(SYN.)* knack, dexterity, skill, address, poise, tact, finesse.
(ANT.) vulgarity, blunder, awkwardness, incompetence.

diplomatic *(SYN.)* politic, adroit, tactful, discreet, judicious, gracious, polite, discriminating.
(ANT.) rude, churlish, gruff, boorish, impolite, coarse.

dire *(SYN.)* horrible, terrible, appalling, fearful, harrowing, grievous, ghastly, awful, horrid, terrifying, dreadful, frightful, horrifying, monstrous, horrendous, repulsive.
(ANT.) lovely, enchanting, fascinating, beautiful, enjoyable.

direct *(SYN.)* rule, manage, bid, order, level, command, conduct, regulate, point, indicate, show, aim, control, sight, guide, instruct, train, govern.
(ANT.) swerving, untruthful, misguide, distract, indirect, crooked, deceive.

direction *(SYN.)* way, order, course, instruction, tendency, management, route, trend, guidance, administration, supervision, inclination.

directly *(SYN.)* immediately, straight.

dirt *(SYN.)* pollution, soil, filthiness, filth.
(ANT.) cleanliness, cleanness.

dirty *(SYN.)* muddy, base, pitiful, filthy, shabby, foul, soiled, nasty, mean, grimy, low, obscene, untidy, indecent, unclean, messy, squalid, contemptible, sloppy.
(ANT.) pure, neat, wholesome, clean, presentable.

disability *(SYN.)* inability, weakness, handicap, incapacity, injury, unfitness, incompetence, impotence.
(ANT.) power, ability, strength, capability.

disable *(SYN.)* weaken, incapacitate, cripple.
(ANT.) strengthen.

disabled *(SYN.)* deformed, limping, weak, crippled, maimed, defective, unsatisfactory, halt, unconvincing, feeble.
(ANT.) vigorous, athletic, sound, agile, robust.

disadvantage *(SYN.)* drawback, hindrance, handicap, inconvenience, obstacle.
(ANT.) advantage, benefit, convenience.

disagree *(SYN.)* quarrel, dispute, differ, conflict.
(ANT.) agree.

disagreement *(SYN.)* nonconformity, variance, difference, objection, challenge, remonstrance, dissent.
(ANT.) assent, acceptance, compliance, agreement.

disappear *(SYN.)* end, fade out, vanish.
(ANT.) emerge, appear.

disappoint *(SYN.)* fail, displease, mislead, dissatisfy.
(ANT.) please, satisfy, gratify.

disappointment *(SYN.)* dissatisfaction, defeat, discouragement, failure.
(ANT.) pleasure, satisfaction, gratification.

disapprove *(SYN.)* object to, disfavor, oppose.
(ANT.) approve.

disarm *(SYN.)* paralyze, demilitarize.

disaster *(SYN.)* casualty, mishap, misfortune, catastrophe, accident, adversity, ruin, calamity.
(ANT.) fortune, advantage, welfare.

disavow *(SYN.)* reject, revoke, disclaim, retract, disown.
(ANT.) recognize, acknowledge.

disband *(SYN.)* scatter, split, dismiss, separate.

disbelief *(SYN.)* doubt, incredulity, skepticism.
(ANT.) certainty, credulity.

discard *(SYN.)* scrap, reject.

discern *(SYN.)* distinguish, see, descry, separate, differentiate, perceive, discriminate, detect, observe, recognize.
(ANT.) omit, confuse, overlook, mingle, confound.

discernment *(SYN.)* perception, sharpness, intelligence, perspicacity, acuity, keenness.
(ANT.) dullness, stupidity.

discharge *(SYN.)* remove, relieve, dismiss, banish, unburden, shoot, fire, explosion, eject, detonation, liberation, release, unload, discard, send.
(ANT.) retain, employ, enlist, hire, accept, recall, detain.

disciple *(SYN.)* learner, follower, student, adherent, supporter, scholar, pupil, votary, devotee.
(ANT.) guide, leader.

discipline *(SYN.)* training, order, instruction, drill, restraint, regulation, practice, correction, control, self-control, train, teach, exercise.
(ANT.) carelessness, sloppiness, confusion, negligence, messiness, chaos, turbulence.

disclaim *(SYN.)* retract, reject, deny, renounce, disavow, revoke.
(ANT.) recognize, acknowledge.

disclose *(SYN.)* show, divulge, betray, uncover, discover, reveal, expose.
(ANT.) hide, cloak, mask, cover, obscure, conceal.

discomfit *(SYN.)* malaise, concern, confuse, baffle, perplex, disconcert.

discomfort *(SYN.)* malaise, concern, anxiety, uneasiness.

disconcerted *(SYN.)* disturbed, agitated, upset.

disconnect *(SYN.)* divide, separate, unhook, disengage.
(ANT.) connect, bind, attach, unify, engage.

disconsolate *(SYN.)* depressed, downcast, sorrowful, dejected, dismal, sad, unhappy, wretched, somber, cheerless, morose, miserable, mournful.

(ANT.) delightful, merry, glad, cheerful, happy.

discontent *(SYN.)* displeased, disgruntled, unhappy, dissatisfied, vexed.

discontinue *(SYN.)* postpone, delay, adjourn, stay, stop, defer, suspend, end, cease, interrupt.

(ANT.) prolong, persist, continue, start, begin, proceed, maintain.

discord *(SYN.)* disagreement, conflict.

(ANT.) concord, accord, agreement.

discourage *(SYN.)* hamper, obstruct, restrain, block, dishearten, retard, check, dispirit, thwart, depress, hinder, stop.

(ANT.) expedite, inspire, encourage, promote, inspirit, assist, further.

discourteous *(SYN.)* gruff, rude, vulgar, blunt, impolite, saucy, uncivil, boorish, rough.

(ANT.) stately, courtly, civil, dignified, genteel.

discover *(SYN.)* find out, invent, expose, ascertain, devise, reveal, learn, determine, detect.

(ANT.) hide, screen, cover, conceal, lose.

discredit *(SYN.)* disbelieve, dishonor, doubt, disgrace, shame.

discreet *(SYN.)* politic, discriminating, judicious, adroit, prudent, cautious, wise, tactful, careful, diplomatic.

(ANT.) incautious, rude, coarse, boorish, tactless, imprudent, indiscreet, careless, gruff.

discrepant *(SYN.)* incompatible, wavering, contrary, irreconcilable, unsteady, illogical, contradictory.

(ANT.) correspondent, compatible, consistent.

discriminating *(SYN.)* exact, particular, critical, accurate, discerning.

(ANT.) unimportant, shallow, insignificant, superficial.

discrimination *(SYN.)* perspicacity, discernment, racism, wisdom, bias, sagacity, prejudice, intelligence, understanding.

(ANT.) thoughtlessness, senselessness, arbitrariness.

discuss *(SYN.)* gossip, plead, discourse, blab, lecture, talk, chat, spout, mutter, deliberate, consider, reason, comment.

discussion *(SYN.)* speech, chatter, lecture, conference, talk, dialogue, conversation, rumor.

(ANT.) silence, correspondence, writing.

disdain *(SYN.)* derision, hatred, contempt, scorn, contumely, reject, haughtiness, detestation.

(ANT.) respect, esteem, reverence, admire, prize, honor, admiration, awe, regard.

disdainful *(SYN.)* haughty, scornful, arrogant, contemptuous.

(ANT.) awed, admiring, regardful.

disease *(SYN.)* malady, disorder, ailment, illness, affliction, infirmity, complaint, sickness.

(ANT.) soundness, health, vigor.

disentangle *(SYN.)* unwind, untie, clear, unravel, unknot, unsnarl, untangle.

disfigured *(SYN.)* deformed, marred, defaced, scarred.

disgrace *(SYN.)* odium, chagrin, shame, mortification, embarrassment, humiliate, scandal, dishonor.

(ANT.) renown, glory, respect, praise, dignity, honor.

disgraceful *(SYN.)* ignominious, shameful, discreditable, disreputable, scandalous, dishonorable.

(ANT.) renowned, esteemed, respectable, honorable.

disguise *(SYN.)* excuse, simulation, pretension, hide, camouflage, make-up, cover-up, mask, conceal, screen, affectation, pretext.

(ANT.) show, reality, actuality, display, reveal, sincerity, fact.

disgust *(SYN.)* offend, repulse, nauseate, revolt, sicken.

(ANT.) admiration, liking.

disgusting *(SYN.)* repulsive, nauseating, revolting, nauseous, repugnant

dish *(SYN.)* serve, container, give, receptacle.

dishearten *(SYN.)* depress, sadden, discourage.

disheveled *(SYN.)* misused, sloppy, rumpled, untidy.

dishonest *(SYN.)* crooked, impure, unsound, false, contaminated, venal, corrupt, putrid, thievish, vitiated, tainted.

(ANT.) upright, honest, straightforward.

dishonor *(SYN.)* disrepute, scandal, indignity, chagrin, mortification, shame, obloquy, defamation, humiliation, disgrace.

(ANT.) renown, glory, praise, honor, dignity.

disinclined *(SYN.)* unwilling, reluctant, loath.

disingenuous *(SYN.)* tricky, deceitful, scheming, dishonest, underhanded, cunning, artful, crafty, insidious.

disintegrate *(SYN.)* decompose, dwindle, spoil, decay, wane, ebb, decline, rot.

(ANT.) increase, flourish, rise, grow.

disinterested *(SYN.)* unbiased, open-minded, neutral, impartial, unprejudiced.

dislike *(SYN.)* aversion, dread, reluctance, abhorrence, disinclination, hatred, repugnance.

(ANT.) devotion, affection, enthusiasm, attachment.

disloyal *(SYN.)* false, treasonable, apostate, unfaithful, recreant, treacherous, untrue, perfidious, traitorous, faithless.

(ANT.) true, devoted, constant, loyal.

dismal *(SYN.)* dark, lonesome, somber, bleak, dull, sad, doleful, sorrowful, cheerless, depressing, dreary, funeral, gloomy, melancholy.

(ANT.) lively, gay, happy, lighthearted, charming, cheerful.

dismantle *(SYN.)* take apart, wreck, disassemble.

dismay *(SYN.)* disturb, bother, dishearten, horror, alarm, bewilder, frighten, scare, discourage, confuse.

(ANT.) encourage, hearten.

dismiss *(SYN.)* remove, discharge, discard, release, liberate, exile, banish, eject, oust.

(ANT.) retain, detain, engage, hire, accept, recall.

disobedient *(SYN.)* refractory, forward, unruly, insubordinate, defiant, rebellious, undutiful.

(ANT.) submissive, compliant, obedient.

disobey *(SYN.)* invade, break, violate, infringe, defile.

disorder *(SYN.)* tumult, chaos, jumble, confusion, muddle, turmoil, anarchy.

(ANT.) organization, neatness, system, order.

disorganization *(SYN.)* jumble, confusion, muddle, anarchy.

(ANT.) system, order.

disorganized *(SYN.)* muddled, confused, indistinct, bewildered, mixed.

(ANT.) organized, lucid, clear, plain.

disown *(SYN.)* deny, renounce, reject, repudiate, forsake, disinherit.

disparaging *(SYN.)* belittling, deprecatory, discrediting, deprecating.

disparage *(SYN.)* undervalue, depreciate, lower, belittle, derogate, minimize, decry, discredit.

(ANT.) exalting, praise, aggrandize, magnify, commend.

disparagement *(SYN.)* lowering, decrying, undervaluing, belittling, minimizing.

(ANT.) praise, exalting, aggrandizement, magnification.

dispassionate *(SYN.)* calm, cool, composed, controlled, unemotional, imperturbable.

dispatch *(SYN.)* throw, impel, transmit, emit, cast, finish, report, message, send, speed, achieve, conclude, communication, promptness, discharge.

(ANT.) reluctance, get, retain, bring, slowness, hold.

dispel *(SYN.)* disseminate, scatter, disperse, separate, diffuse.

(ANT.) collect, accumulate, gather.

dispense *(SYN.)* deal, give, allot, assign, apportion, mete, distribute, grant, allocate, measure.

(ANT.) refuse, withhold, confiscate, retain, keep.

disperse *(SYN.)* dissipate, scatter, disseminate, diffuse, separate, dispel.

(ANT.) collect, amass, gather, assemble, accumulate.

dispirited *(SYN.)* unhappy, dejected, disheartened, sad, depressed, melancholy.

(ANT.) cheerful, happy, optimistic.

displace *(SYN.)* remove, transport, lodge, shift, move.

(ANT.) retain, leave, stay, remain.

display *(SYN.)* parade, exhibit, show, expose, reveal, demonstrate, showing, uncover, flaunt.

(ANT.) hide, cover, conceal.

displeasure *(SYN.)* dislike, disapproval, dissatisfaction, distaste, discontentment.

disposal *(SYN.)* elimination, adjustment, removal, release, arrangement, administration, settlement.

dispose *(SYN.)* settle, adjust, arrange.

disposition *(SYN.)* behavior, character, deed, deportment, action, manner, bearing, temperament, nature, demeanor, personality, carriage.

dispossess *(SYN.)* eject, expel, evict, oust, dislodge.

disprove *(SYN.)* refute, deny, invalidate, controvert.

dispute *(SYN.)* squabble, debate, argument, controversy, contention, disagreement, bicker, contest, argue, contend, quarrel, contradict, discuss, deny, oppose, altercate.
(ANT.) harmony, concord, agreement, allow, concur, agree, concede, decision.

disregard *(SYN.)* slight, omit, ignore, inattention, oversight, skip, neglect, overlook.
(ANT.) regard, include.

disrepair *(SYN.)* ruin, decay, dilapidation, destruction.

disreputable *(SYN.)* dishonored, notorious, dishonorable, disgraced.

disrespectful *(SYN.)* fresh, impertinent, rude, impolite, impudent.
(ANT.) polite, respectful, courteous.

dissect *(SYN.)* examine, cut, analyze.

disseminate *(SYN.)* publish, circulate, spread, publish, broadcast.

dissent *(SYN.)* objection, challenge, disagreement, protest, remonstrance, difference, nonconformity, variance, noncompliance.
(ANT.) assent, acceptance, compliance, agreement.

dissertation *(SYN.)* thesis, treatise, disquisition.

dissimilar *(SYN.)* diverse, unlike, various, distinct, contrary, sundry, different, miscellaneous.
(ANT.) same, alike, similar, congruous.

dissimulation *(SYN.)* pretense, deceit, sanctimony, hypocrisy, cant.
(ANT.) honesty, candor, openness, frankness, truth.

dissipate *(SYN.)* misuse, squander, dwindle, consume, waste, lavish, diminish.
(ANT.) save, conserve, preserve, accumulate, economize.

dissolve *(SYN.)* liquefy, end, cease, melt, fade, disappear.

distant *(SYN.)* stiff, cold, removed, far, afar, unfriendly, remote, faraway, separated, aloof, reserved.
(ANT.) nigh, friendly, close, cordial, near.

distasteful *(SYN.)* disagreeable, unpleasant, objectionable.

distend *(SYN.)* swell, widen, magnify, expand, enlarge.

distinct *(SYN.)* plain, evident, lucid, visible, apparent, different, separate, individual, obvious, manifest, clear.
(ANT.) vague, indistinct, uncertain, obscure, ambiguous.

distinction *(SYN.)* importance, peculiarity, trait, honor, fame, characteristic, repute, quality, renown, prominence, attribute, property.
(ANT.) nature, substance, essence, being.

distinctive *(SYN.)* odd, exceptional, rare, individual, eccentric, special, strange.
(ANT.) ordinary, general, common, normal.

distinguish *(SYN.)* recognize, differentiate, divide, classify, descry, discern, separate, perceive, detect.
(ANT.) mingle, conjoin, blend, found, omit, confuse, overlook.

distinguished *(SYN.)* eminent, illustrious, renowned, celebrated, elevated, noted, important, famous, prominent.
(ANT.) ordinary, common, unknown, undistinguished, obscure, unimportant.

distort *(SYN.)* contort, falsify, twist, misrepresent.

distract *(SYN.)* occupy, bewilder, disturb, divert, confuse.
(ANT.) focus, concentrate.

distracted *(SYN.)* abstracted, preoccupied, absent.
(ANT.) attentive, attending, watchful, present.

distraction *(SYN.)* entertainment, confusion, amusement, diversion.

distress *(SYN.)* torment, misery, trouble, worry, pain, agony, torture, anguish, anxiety, disaster, wretchedness, peril, danger, suffering.
(ANT.) joy, solace, comfort, relief.

distribute *(SYN.)* deal, sort, allot, mete, classify, share, issue, dole, apportion, allocate, dispense, group.

district *(SYN.)* domain, place, territory, country, region, division, neighborhood, section, area, land.

distrust *(SYN.)* scruple, unbelief, suspect, mistrust, hesitation, suspense, uncertainty, doubt, suspicion, ambiguity.
(ANT.) faith, conviction, trust, belief, determination.

disturb *(SYN.)* perturb, vex, confuse, worry, agitate, derange, unsettle, perplex, rouse, bother, trouble, annoy, interrupt, discompose.
(ANT.) quiet, order, calm, settle, pacify, soothe.

disturbance *(SYN.)* disorder, commotion, confusion, riot, fight, brawl.
(ANT.) calm, tranquillity, serenity.

disturbed *(SYN.)* neurotic, psychopathic, psychoneurotic, psychotic.
(ANT.) normal.

diverge *(SYN.)* fork, separate.
(ANT.) converge, join, merge.

diverse *(SYN.)* unlike, various, different, several.

diversify *(SYN.)* change, modify, alter.

diversion *(SYN.)* entertainment, sport, distraction, amusement, recreation.

divert *(SYN.)* detract, amuse, confuse, distract, deflect, entertain, tickle.
(ANT.) tire, bore, weary.

divide *(SYN.)* share, split, detach, cleave, apportion, sunder, part, distribute, allocate, disunite, estrange, separate, allot, sever.
(ANT.) merge, unite, convene, join, gather, combine.

divine *(SYN.)* holy, supernatural, godlike, transcendent, celestial, heavenly.
(ANT.) mundane, wicked, blasphemous, profane, diabolical.

division *(SYN.)* partition, separation, sharing, section, segment, part, portion.

(ANT.) union, agreement.

divorce *(SYN.)* disjoin, disconnect, separate, divide.

divulge *(SYN.)* discover, release, expose, show, betray, reveal, admit, disclose, uncover.
(ANT.) hide, conceal, cloak, cover.

dizzy *(SYN.)* staggering, unsteady, giddy, light-headed, confused.
(ANT.) rational, clear-headed, unconfused.

do *(SYN.)* effect, conduct, perform, work, suffice, accomplish, finish, transact, serve, discharge, execute, complete, carry on, make, settle, conclude, fulfill, consummate, produce, terminate, observe, practice.

docile *(SYN.)* pliant, tame, complaint, teachable, obedient, submissive, yielding.
(ANT.) unruly, obstinate, ungovernable, mulish.

dock *(SYN.)* moor, clip, anchor, tie.

doctor *(SYN.)* heal, treat, medic, remedy, cure.

doctrine *(SYN.)* tenet, precept, belief, dogma, teaching, principle, creed.
(ANT.) deed, practice, conduct, perform.

doctrinaire *(SYN.)* formal, dogmatic, overbearing, authoritarian, formal, arrogant, magisterial.
(ANT.) skeptical, indecisive, fluctuating.

document *(SYN.)* report, minute, memorial, vestige, account, note, trace.

dodge *(SYN.)* equivocate, recoil, elude, evade, avoid, duck.

dogma *(SYN.)* tenet, doctrine, belief, teaching, creed.
(ANT.) deed, practice, conduct, performance.

dogmatic *(SYN.)* formal, domineering, authoritarian, doctrinaire, opinionated, dictatorial, positive, arrogant, authoritative, overbearing, doctrinal, magisterial.
(ANT.) skeptical, indecisive, fluctuating.

doing *(SYN.)* feat, performance, act, deed, action, accomplishment, transaction.
(ANT.) intention, inactivity, cessation, inhibition.

dole *(SYN.)* deal, spread, allot, relief, divide, apportion, alms, welfare, distribute, dispense.

doleful *(SYN.)* dark, depressed, sad, dismal, dejected, bleak, dull, blue, sorrowful, unhappy, morose, lonesome, mournful, somber.
(ANT.) gay, lively, cheerful, joyous.

dolt *(SYN.)* blockhead, dunce.

domain *(SYN.)* place, division, region, territory, empire, country, charge, kingdom, realm, quarter, dominion, bailiwick, jurisdiction, land.

domestic *(SYN.)* family, tame, native, servant, homemade, household, internal.
(ANT.) alien, foreign, outside.

domesticate *(SYN.)* train, tame, housebreak, teach.

domicile *(SYN.)* dwelling, residence, home, abode.

dominate *(SYN.)* control, manage, rule, influence, command, govern, tyrannize, direct, regulate.
(ANT.) follow, ignore, abandon, submit, forsake.

domination *(SYN.)* mastery, sway, ascendancy, transcendence.

don *(SYN.)* wear, slip on.

donation *(SYN.)* gift, bequest, present, benefaction, grant, contribution, offering, largess, boon.
(ANT.) earnings, purchase, deprivation, loss.

done *(SYN.)* complete, concluded, finished, over, terminated.

doom *(SYN.)* fortune, issue, result, destruction, destiny, consequence, fate, outcome, destine, ruin, death, lot.

doomed *(SYN.)* fated, predestined, destined, foreordained.

dormant *(SYN.)* unemployed, inert, lazy, unoccupied, idle, indolent.
(ANT.) working, employed, occupied, active, industrious.

dose *(SYN.)* quantity, amount, portion.

dote *(SYN.)* indulge, treasure, coddle, pamper, spoil.
(ANT.) ignore.

double *(SYN.)* copy, fold, duplicate.

doubt *(SYN.)* distrust, incredulity, suspicion, hesitation, uncertainty, question, scruple, ambiguity, skepticism, suspect, mistrust, unbelief, suspense.
(ANT.) conviction, belief, determination, trust, certainty.

doubtful *(SYN.)* uncertain, unsettled, dubious, questionable, unsure, undetermined.

doubtless *(SYN.)* certainly, undoubtedly, assuredly, positively, unquestionably.

dour *(SYN.)* gloomy, sulky, crabbed, morose, fretful.
(ANT.) joyous, pleasant, amiable, merry.

douse *(SYN.)* immerse, quench, dip, dunk, extinguish.

dowdy *(SYN.)* messy, unkempt, untidy, sloppy, shabby, frowzy.

downcast *(SYN.)* sad, disheartened, unhappy, down-hearted, dejected, dispirited, discourage, depressed, glum.

downfall *(SYN.)* destruction, comedown.

downgrade *(SYN.)* reduce, lower, diminish, decrease, depreciate.
(ANT.) improve, upgrade, appreciate.

downhearted *(SYN.)* glum, discouraged, depressed, gloomy, downcast, sad, dejected.
(ANT.) enthusiastic, cheerful, happy.

downpour *(SYN.)* cloudburst, deluge, flood.

downright *(SYN.)* totally, positively, completely, definitely.

dowry *(SYN.)* endowment, gift, settlement, talent, ability.

drab *(SYN.)* flat, dull, lifeless, unattractive.

draft *(SYN.)* air, induction, wind, enrollment, drawing, outline.

drag *(SYN.)* heave, pull, tug, crawl, draw, tarry, tow, haul, delay.

drain *(SYN.)* empty, deprive, dry, filter, spend, tap, exhaust, waste, sap, use.
(ANT.) fulfill, fill.

drama *(SYN.)* show, play, production, piece.

dramatist *(SYN.)* playwright.

drape *(SYN.)* flow, cover, hang.

drastic *(SYN.)* severe, rough, extreme, violent, tough, intense.

draw *(SYN.)* tug, obtain, trace, lure, drag, attract, persuade, induce, haul, write, remove, extend, stretch, take out, allure, pull, prolong, extract, tow, draft, delineate, unsheathe, lure, depict, entice, sketch.

(ANT.) shorten, contract, propel, alienate, drive.

drawback *(SYN.)* snag, hitch, disadvantage, deficiency, difficulty, check, obstacle, hindrance, impediment.

(ANT.) gain, benefit, windfall, advantage.

drawing *(SYN.)* likeness, print, view, engraving, portrait, sketch, illustration, picture, scene.

drawn *(SYN.)* tired, haggard, taut, strained, harrowed, weary, tense, sapped, spent.

(ANT.) rested, relaxed, energetic, fresh.

draw out *(SYN.)* protract, extend, persist, prolong, lengthen, sustain, continue.

(ANT.) reduce, curtail, shorten, abridge.

draw up *(SYN.)* draft, write out, prepare, compose, indite, formulate, wait, stay.

dread *(SYN.)* awe, horror, fear, terror, alarm, reverence, apprehension.

(ANT.) courage, boldness, assurance, confidence.

dreadful *(SYN.)* dire, inspiring, ghastly, appalling, horrid, impressive, terrible, awful, frightful, horrible, bad, hideous, awesome, outrageous, repulsive.

(ANT.) fascinating, beautiful, enjoyable, enchanting, lovely.

dream *(SYN.)* fantasy, wish, hope, vision, daydream, reverie, imagine, fantasize, fancy, invent, muse.

dream up *(SYN.)* cook up, create, concost, contrive, originate, imagine, devise.

dreary *(SYN.)* dull, sad, bleak, lonesome, gloomy, chilling, somber, depressing, dismal, cheerless, dark.

(ANT.) lively, hopeful, gay, cheerful, bright, joyous.

dregs *(SYN.)* riffraff, scum, outcasts, dross, leftovers, flotsam.

drench *(SYN.)* wet, bathe, flood, soak, saturate.

dress *(SYN.)* garb, frock, gown, clothing, costume, apparel, attire, wardrobe, garments, vesture, clothes, wear, don, robe, raiment.

(ANT.) undress, strip, divest, disrobe.

dresser *(SYN.)* dude, fop, dandy.

dressing *(SYN.)* bandage, seasoning, medicine, sauce.

dressy *(SYN.)* flashy, swank, showy, dapper.

(ANT.) dowdy, drab, frumpy, shabby, tacky.

dribble *(SYN.)* fall, drip, leak, slaver, slobber.

drift *(SYN.)* roam, tendency, meander, sail, float, direction, intention, stray.

drifter *(SYN.)* hobo, tramp, vagabond.

drill *(SYN.)* employment, lesson, task, use, activity, operation, training.

(ANT.) relaxation, indolence, rest, idleness, repose.

drink *(SYN.)* gulp, swallow, imbibe, beverage, refreshment, potion.

drip *(SYN.)* dribble, drop, trickle.

drive *(SYN.)* impel, coerce, oblige, force, push, direct, constrain, journey, urge, enforce, trip, handle, ride, propel, control, run, compel.

drivel *(SYN.)* slaver, drool, spit, spittle, dribble, slobber, saliva, nonsense, twaddle, rubbish, babble, gibberish.

driver *(SYN.)* motorist, operator, teamster, trucker, motorman, pilot, coachman.

droll *(SYN.)* laughable, funny, amusing, witty, comical.

(ANT.) sober, sad, solemn, melancholy.

drone *(SYN.)* buzz, hum, loafer, idler, nonworker.

drool *(SYN.)* drivel, slaver, dribble, spit, gibber, jabber, twaddle, trickle, salivate.

droop *(SYN.)* dangle, weaken, hang, sink, fail, settle, sag, weary, languish, despond.

(ANT.) stand, tower, extend, rise, straighten.

drop *(SYN.)* droop, dribble, topple, collapse, downward, drip, trickle, tumble, gob, droplet, reduction, slump, slip, fall, dismiss, decline.

(ANT.) ascend, mount, steady, arise, soar.

drop out *(SYN.)* back out, withdraw, stop, forsake, abandon, leave, quit.

droppings *(SYN.)* faces, dung, waste, manure, excrement, ordure, guano.

dross *(SYN.)* dregs, impurity, leftovers, residue, debris, leavings, remains.

drove *(SYN.)* flock, herd.

drown *(SYN.)* sink, inundate, submerge, immerse.

drowse *(SYN.)* nap, doze, catnap, snooze,

sleep, slumber, rest, drop off, repose.

drowsy *(SYN.)* dozing, torpid, soothing, dreamy, sleepy, comatose, sluggish, lulling, calming, restful, lethargic.

(ANT.) alert, awake, sharp, keen, acute.

drub *(SYN.)* wallop, thrash, beat, thump, cane, flog, rout, outclass, overcome, pummel, defeat, outplay.

drubbing *(SYN.)* walloping, flogging, beating, pounding, pommeling, thrashing, rout, licking, clobbering.

drudge *(SYN.)* work, labor, hack, slave, toil, grub, grind, toiler, flunky, menial, servant.

drudgery *(SYN.)* toil, travail, effort, task, work, endeavor, labor.

(ANT.) recreation, indolence, leisure.

drug *(SYN.)* remedy, medicine, stupefy, anesthetize, numb, benumb.

drugged *(SYN.)* numb, doped, numbed, stupefied, dazed, groggy, benumbed.

druggist *(SYN.)* apothecary, chemist, pharmacologist.

drunk *(SYN.)* tight, intoxicated, soused, drunken, inebriated, alcoholic, besotted, sot, toper, boozer, wino, rummy, dipsomaniac, lush, tipsy.

drunkard *(SYN.)* sot, drunk, alcoholic, lush.

dry *(SYN.)* thirsty, dehydrated, vapid, plain, arid, uninteresting, drained, parched, barren, waterless, dull, tedious, boring, desiccated, tiresome.

(ANT.) fresh, wet, soaked, fascinating, attractive, lively, moist, interesting.

dub *(SYN.)* nickname, name, christen, call, style, term, confer, bestow, denominate, characterize, tag, label.

dubious *(SYN.)* unsure, uncertain, undecided, hesitant, spurious, unreliable, puzzling, untrustworthy, questionable, ambiguous.

(ANT.) decided, fixed, irrefutable, definite, genuine, unquestionable, sound, authentic, trustworthy.

duck *(SYN.)* douse, dip, submerse, submerge, immerse, plunge, wet, souse, drench, engulf, avoid, shun, lower, bob, hedge, shy, evade, swerve, quail.

(ANT.) raise, confront, face, elevate, cope with, undertake, assume, face up to.

duct *(SYN.)* pipe, tube, passage, vein, canal, funnel, gutter, main, trough, artery.

due *(SYN.)* payable, unpaid, owing, owed, imminent, expected.

duel *(SYN.)* competition, contest, engagement, rivalry, combat, strife, encounter, battle, conflict, dispute, strive.

dues *(SYN.)* assessment, fees, cost, levy, admission, fare, toll, demand, contribution.

duffer *(SYN.)* bungler, slouch, blunderer, novice, incompetent, fumbler, lummox.

(ANT.) master, expert, pro.

dull *(SYN.)* commonplace, slow, sad, dreary, boring, stupid, uninteresting, blunt, tedious, dulled, dumb, tiring, monotonous, obtuse, tiresome, dense, unimaginative, unfeeling, dead, lifeless, dismal.

(ANT.) clear, animated, interesting, lively.

dullard *(SYN.)* dolt, dunce, moron, clod, blockhead, numskull.

dumb *(SYN.)* dull, witless, ignorant, mute, speechless, brainless, dense, stupid, senseless.

(ANT.) discerning, bright, alert, clever, intelligent.

dumbfound *(SYN.)* stagger, stun, nonplus, stupefy, overwhelm, amaze, confuse, bewilder, surprise, astonish.

dumfounded *(SYN.)* shocked, astonished, flabbergasted, astounded, stunned.

dump *(SYN.)* heap, fling down, drop, empty, unload, clear out, dispose of, tipple, discharge, overturn, dismiss, abandon.

(ANT.) store, fill, load, hoard, pack.

dunce *(SYN.)* deadhead, nitwit, booby, idiot, ignoramus, numskull, noddy, fool.

dungeon *(SYN.)* jail, prison, keep, cell.

dunk *(SYN.)* plunge, douse, submerge, dip.

(ANT.) uplift, elevate, recover.

dupe *(SYN.)* sucker, victim, gull, pushover, fool, cheat, deceive, defraud.

duplicate *(SYN.)* replica, replicate, facsimile, copy, reproduce, clone, double, twin, transcript.

(ANT.) prototype.

duplicity *(SYN.)* dissimulation, deception, hypocrisy, deceitfulness, insincerity, cant, guile.

(ANT.) openness, artlessness, candor, straightforwardness, genuineness.

durability *(SYN.)* might, strength, force, sturdiness, intensity, potency, vigor.
(ANT.) weakness, frailty, feebleness.

durable *(SYN.)* constant, firm, fixed, unchangeable, enduring, abiding, lasting.
(ANT.) unstable, temporary, perishable, transitory.

duration *(SYN.)* time, term, period, while, stage, era, epoch, interim.

duress *(SYN.)* force, demand, compulsion, emergency, pressure.

dusky *(SYN.)* sable, black, dark, darkish, swarthy, tawny, gloomy, overcast, misty, opaque, shadowy.
(ANT.) light, fair, white, pale, shining, clear, bright.

dusty *(SYN.)* sooty, unclean, dirty, musty, grubby, unswept, crumbly, friable, chalky, messy, grimy.
(ANT.) polished, immaculate, clean, shiny.

dutiful *(SYN.)* docile, faithful, obedient.
(ANT.) disobedient, willful, unruly, headstrong.

duty *(SYN.)* bond, responsibility, accountability, faithfulness, function, obligation, conscience, assignment, part, engagement.
(ANT.) freedom, choice.

dwarf *(SYN.)* midget, runt, reduce, minimize, tiny.
(ANT.) mammoth, colossus, monster, giant.

dwell *(SYN.)* inhabit, roost, settle, abide, live, reside.

dwelling *(SYN.)* seat, quarters, abode, home, hearth, residence, house, domicile.

dwell on *(SYN.)* insist, linger over, harp on, emphasize.
(ANT.) skip, neglect, skim over, disregard.

dwindle *(SYN.)* wane, decrease, diminish, fade, subside, ebb, shrivel, lessen.
(ANT.) enlarge, wax, increase, grow, gain.

dying *(SYN.)* failing, expiring, waning, passing, final, declining, receding, dwindling, vanishing, disappearing,
(ANT.) thriving, growing, booming, flourishing.

dynamic *(SYN.)* active, forceful, kinetic, energetic, motive, mighty, vigorous.
(ANT.) sleepy, stable, inert, fixed, dead, still, uninspiring, ineffectual, listless.

E

eager *(SYN.)* avid, hot, anxious, fervent, enthusiastic, impatient, ardent, impassioned, yearning.
(ANT.) unconcerned, apathetic, impassioned, dull, uninterested, indifferent.

early *(SYN.)* betimes, opportune, first, advanced, soon, shortly.
(ANT.) retarded, late, tardy, belated, overdue.

earmark *(SYN.)* peculiarity, characteristic, brand, sign, stamp.

earn *(SYN.)* attain, win, get, achieve, obtain, gain, deserve, collect, net, acquire, merit.
(ANT.) waste, consume, forfeit.

earnest *(SYN.)* sincere, decided, determined, serious, eager.
(ANT.) indifferent, frivolous, insincere.

earnings *(SYN.)* wages, pay, salary, income.

earth *(SYN.)* globe, dirt, land, world, turf, soil, sod, ground.

earthly *(SYN.)* mundane, everyday, worldly.
(ANT.) heavenly.

earthy *(SYN.)* earthlike, coarse, earthen, crude, unrefined, vulgar.
(ANT.) elegant, polished, refined.

ease *(SYN.)* lighten, alleviate, pacify, soothe, allay, comfort, contentedness, assuage, reduce, rest, facilitate, relaxation, calm, mitigate, contentment, relax.
(ANT.) worry, disturb, confound, aggravate, difficulty, trouble, intensify, distress.

easily *(SYN.)* readily, effortlessly, smoothly, naturally.
(ANT.) hardly, arduously, painfully, laboriously.

easiness *(SYN.)* repose, comfort, satisfaction, contentment, liberty, leisure, facility, simplicity.
(ANT.) unrest, torment, arduousness, difficulty, discomfort.

easy *(SYN.)* light, simple, facile, gentle, effortless, unhurried, comfortable, cozy,

relaxed, plain, uncomplicated, restful.
(ANT.) hard, demanding, awkward, strict, difficult, formal.
eat *(SYN.)* consume, swallow, dine, corrode, chew, lunch, devour.
eavesdrop *(SYN.)* spy, listen, snoop, overhear.
eavesdropper *(SYN.)* monitor, listener, snoop, spy.
ebb *(SYN.)* diminish, recede, decline, decrease, retreat, lessen.
(ANT.) wax, grow, thrive, increase, swell.
ebullient *(SYN.)* vivacious, buoyant, exuberant.
(ANT.) lethargic, sad, gloomy, depressed.
eccentric *(SYN.)* odd, irregular, unusual, abnormal, peculiar.
(ANT.) ordinary, conventional, normal.
eccentricity *(SYN.)* kink, idiosyncrasy, whim, freak, caprice, foible, quirk, oddness, aberration.
(ANT.) normality, conventionality, ordinariness.
ecclesiastical *(SYN.)* religious, churchly, clerical.
echelon *(SYN.)* rank, level, grade, place, status.
echo *(SYN.)* response, imitation, suggestion, trace, reaction, imitate, repeat.
eclectic *(SYN.)* selective, diverse, broad, liberal, comprehensive.
(ANT.) limited, narrow, rigid, confined.
eclipse *(SYN.)* conceal, screen, hide, cover, obscure, overcast.
economical *(SYN.)* saving, thrifty, careful, frugal, provident, sparing.
(ANT.) wasteful, extravagant, lavish, improvident, prodigal.
economize *(SYN.)* pinch, scrimp, save.
economy *(SYN.)* saving, thrift.
ecstasy *(SYN.)* frenzy, gladness, delight, madness, joy, glee, exaltation, pleasure, trance, rapture.
(ANT.) misery, melancholy, sadness.
ecstatic *(SYN.)* overjoyed, thrilled, delighted, happy, elated.
edge *(SYN.)* margin, brim, verge, brink, border, keenness, extremity, rim, boundary, trim.
(ANT.) dullness, center, bluntness.

edgy *(SYN.)* tense, touchy, nervous, irritable.
edict *(SYN.)* declaration, order, ruling, decree, pronouncement, command, law, proclamation.
edifice *(SYN.)* construction, building, establishment.
edit *(SYN.)* check, revise, correct, amend.
educate *(SYN.)* instruct, teach, school, train.
education *(SYN.)* training, development, knowledge, learning, cultivation, schooling, instruction, study.
eerie *(SYN.)* weird, fearful, ghastly, spooky, strange.
efface *(SYN.)* obliterate, erase.
effect *(SYN.)* produce, consequence, evoke, cause, make, complete, outcome, result, determine.
effective *(SYN.)* efficient, practical, productive.
(ANT.) useless, wasteful, ineffective.
efficiency *(SYN.)* efficacy, capability, effectiveness, competency.
(ANT.) wastefulness, inability.
efficient *(SYN.)* efficacious, skillful, capable, adept, competent, useful, effectual, effective, apt, proficient.
(ANT.) inefficient, unskilled, ineffectual, incompetent.
effort *(SYN.)* labor, endeavor, pains, essay, trial, exertion, struggle, strain, try, attempt.
effortless *(SYN.)* simple, easy.
egg *(SYN.)* stir, ovum, incite, urge, arouse, embryo, provoke.
egoism *(SYN.)* self-interest, conceit, pride, selfishness, egotism.
(ANT.) modesty, generosity, selflessness.
eject *(SYN.)* expel, remove, oust, eliminate.
(ANT.) include.
elaborate *(SYN.)* detail, develop, decorated, decorative, ornate.
(ANT.) simplify, simple, unadorned.
elapse *(SYN.)* expire.
elastic *(SYN.)* yielding, flexible, adaptable, pliable.
elated *(SYN.)* delighted, rejoicing, overjoyed, jubilant.
(ANT.) sad, unhappy.
elder *(SYN.)* senior.

(ANT.) younger.

elderly (SYN.) aged, old.

(ANT.) young, youthful.

elect (SYN.) pick, appoint, choose.

electrify (SYN.) shock, charge, stir, upset, generate, agitate.

elegant (SYN.) tasteful, refined, cultivated, choice, polished, fine.

(ANT.) crude, coarse, unpolished, tasteless.

elementary (SYN.) simple, primary, basic, fundamental.

(ANT.) involved, complex, sophisticated, complicated.

elevate (SYN.) raise, lift.

(ANT.) lower, drop.

elf (SYN.) devil, fairy, imp.

elicit (SYN.) summon.

eligible (SYN.) fit, suitable, qualified.

eliminate (SYN.) expel, eject, remove, dislodge, extirpate, erase.

(ANT.) admit, involve.

elite (SYN.) nobility, upperclass, aristocracy, gentry.

(ANT.) mob, proletariat.

elongate (SYN.) extend, prolong, lengthen.

elope (SYN.) escape, flee.

eloquent (SYN.) expressive, fluent, articulate, glib, meaningful.

(ANT.) inarticulate.

else (SYN.) different, another, other.

elude (SYN.) escape, miss, avoid, dodge.

(ANT.) add, include.

emaciated (SYN.) wasted, thin, starved, withered, shriveled, gaunt, shrunken, drawn.

emancipate (SYN.) liberate, free, deliver, save.

(ANT.) restrain.

embankment (SYN.) shore, dam, bank, fortification, buttress.

embargo (SYN.) prohibition, restriction, restraint.

embark (SYN.) board, depart.

embarrass (SYN.) discomfit, rattle, distress, hamper, fluster, entangle, abash, mortify, hinder, perplex, confuse, shame, trouble.

(ANT.) relieve, encourage, help.

embassy (SYN.) ministry, legation, consulate.

embed (SYN.) root, inset, enclose, plant.

embellish (SYN.) adorn, decorate, ornament.

embezzle (SYN.) pilfer, misuse, rob, misappropriate, steal, take.

embitter (SYN.) provoke, arouse, anger, inflame.

emblem (SYN.) token, mark, symbol, badge.

embody (SYN.) comprise, cover, embrace, include.

embrace (SYN.) espouse, accept, receive, comprehend, contain, welcome, comprise, clasp, include, adopt, hug.

(ANT.) spurn, reject, bar, exclude, repudiate.

embroider (SYN.) decorate, adorn, stitch, trim, overstate, embellish, ornament, exaggerate, magnify.

emerge (SYN.) surface, show, appear.

emergency (SYN.) strait, pass, crisis, urgency, predicament.

eminent (SYN.) renowned, glorious, distinguished, noted, celebrated, elevated, glorious, important, conspicuous, prominent.

(ANT.) ordinary, commonplace, unknown, undistinguished, common.

emissary (SYN.) envoy, minister, delegate, agent, spy.

emit (SYN.) expel, breathe, shoot, hurl, ooze, vent, belch, discharge.

emotion (SYN.) passion, turmoil, perturbation, affection, sentiment, feeling, trepidation, agitation.

(ANT.) dispassion, indifference, tranquillity, calm, restraint.

emotional (SYN.) ardent, passionate, stirring, zealous, impetuous, overwrought, enthusiastic.

(ANT.) tranquil, calm, placid.

emphasis (SYN.) accent, stress, insistence.

emphatic (SYN.) positive, definite, forceful, energetic, strong.

(ANT.) lax, quiet, unforceful.

employ (SYN.) avail, use, devote, apply, utilize, engage, sign, hire, retain, service, contract.

(ANT.) reject, discard.

employee (SYN.) laborer, worker, servant.

(ANT.) boss, employer.

employer *(SYN.)* owner, boss, proprietor, manager, superintendent, supervisor.
(ANT.) employee, worker.

employment *(SYN.)* occupation, work, business, position, job, engagement.
(ANT.) leisure, idleness, slothfulness.

empower *(SYN.)* enable, sanction, permit, warrant.

empty *(SYN.)* void, devoid, unfilled, barren, senseless, unoccupied, unfurnished, vacant, blank, evacuate, unload, hollow.
(ANT.) supplied, full, occupied.

emulate *(SYN.)* follow, imitate, copy.

enable *(SYN.)* authorize, empower, sanction, qualify.

enact *(SYN.)* legislate, portray, pass, stage, represent.

enchant *(SYN.)* charm, titillate, fascinate, bewitch, delight, thrill, captivate.
(ANT.) tire, bore.

encircle *(SYN.)* comprise, include, bound, encompass.

enclose *(SYN.)* envelop, confine, bound, surround, encompass, encircle.
(ANT.) open, exclude, distend, expose, develop.

encompass *(SYN.)* include, surround, encircle.

encore *(SYN.)* repetition, repeat, again.

encounter *(SYN.)* battle, meet, oppose, run into, face, collide.

encourage *(SYN.)* incite, favor, cheer, impel, countenance, inspirit, exhilarate, animate, hearten, embolden, support.
(ANT.) deter, dispirit, deject, dissuade.

encroach *(SYN.)* interfere, trespass, intrude, infringe.

encumber *(SYN.)* hamper, load, burden.

end *(SYN.)* completion, object, close, aim, result, conclusion, finish, extremity, intent, halt, stop, limit, purpose, cessation, expiration, termination.
(ANT.) opening, start, introduction, beginning, launch, inception.

endanger *(SYN.)* imperil, hazard, risk.
(ANT.) secure.

endear *(SYN.)* allure, charm.

endeavor *(SYN.)* strive, struggle, exertion, attempt, try, labor.

endless *(SYN.)* constant, nonstop, continuous, incessant, everlasting.

endorse *(SYN.)* approve, accept, sign, confirm, pass.

endow *(SYN.)* provide, furnish, bestow, give, contribute.
(ANT.) divest.

endure *(SYN.)* experience, undergo, sustain, last, bear, continue, remain, undergo, persist, brook, tolerate, suffer.
(ANT.) wane, die, perish, succumb, fail.

enemy *(SYN.)* foe, antagonist, rival, opponent, competitor, adversary, opposition.
(ANT.) colleague, ally, friend, accomplice.

energy *(SYN.)* strength, vim, force, power, stamina, vigor, might.
(ANT.) feebleness, lethargy.

enervate *(SYN.)* enfeeble, weaken, debilitate, exhaust, devitalize.
(ANT.) invigorate.

enfold *(SYN.)* clasp, surround, wrap, embrace, hug.

enforce *(SYN.)* make, drive, compel, execute, force.

engage *(SYN.)* absorb, occupy, employ, hold, involve, hire, agree, engross, retain, promise, commit, entangle.
(ANT.) fire, disengage, discharge, dismiss.

engaged *(SYN.)* affianced, betrothed, busy, occupied.

engaging *(SYN.)* fascinating, appealing, enticing, interesting, tempting, lovely, beguiling, charming, enchanting, engrossing, delightful, exquisite.
(ANT.) ordinary, boring.

engender *(SYN.)* develop, breed, cause, generate, produce.

engineer *(SYN.)* direct, conduct, guide, lead, manage.

engrave *(SYN.)* print, cut, impress, inscribe, carve, sketch.

engross *(SYN.)* engage, enthrall, occupy, fascinate, absorb.

engulf *(SYN.)* flood, swallow.

enhance *(SYN.)* better, uplift, improve.

enigma *(SYN.)* mystery, stumper, riddle.

enigmatic *(SYN.)* perplexing, confusing, puzzling, baffling, mystifying.

enjoy *(SYN.)* savor, like, relish.

enjoyment *(SYN.)* pleasure, delight, gratification.

(ANT.) abhorrence, displeasure.

enlarge *(SYN.)* widen, distend, amplify, broaden, extend, increase, augment, expand, dilate.

(ANT.) diminish, shrink, contract, decrease, wane, restrict.

enlighten *(SYN.)* inform, illuminate, clarify, teach, instruct.

(ANT.) confuse.

enlist *(SYN.)* enroll, prompt, join, induce, enter, register, persuade.

(ANT.) quit, leave, abandon.

enliven *(SYN.)* inspire, brighten, stimulate.

enmity *(SYN.)* antagonism, hatred, animosity, malignity, ill-will, antipathy, hostility, unfriendliness.

(ANT.) love, like, friendliness.

enormity *(SYN.)* heinousness, wickedness, barbarity, atrociousness.

enormous *(SYN.)* vast, huge, colossal, immense, gargantuan, elephantine, gigantic, stupendous, large.

(ANT.) small, slight, tiny, minute, infinitesimal, diminutive, little.

enough *(SYN.)* ample, adequate, sufficient, plenty.

(ANT.) inadequate, insufficient.

enrage *(SYN.)* anger, provoke, madden, inflame.

(ANT.) appease, soothe, calm.

enrich *(SYN.)* better, improve.

enroll *(SYN.)* record, list, recruit, register, enlist, write, induct.

(ANT.) quit, leave, abandon.

enshrine *(SYN.)* bury, entomb.

ensign *(SYN.)* banner, colors, flag, officer.

enslave *(SYN.)* keep, hold, capture.

ensue *(SYN.)* arise, succeed, follow, result.

ensure *(SYN.)* guarantee, assure, protect, defend, cover.

entangle *(SYN.)* confuse, snare, involve, ravel, snarl, tangle, trap.

enter *(SYN.)* join, go inside.

enterprise *(SYN.)* fete, deed, venture, project, adventure, undertaking, ambition, business, exploit.

enterprising *(SYN.)* energetic, resourceful.

(ANT.) lazy, indolent, sluggish, unresourceful.

entertain *(SYN.)* cheer, gladden, hold, consider, please, contemplate, divert, amuse, harbor, fascinate, interest.

(ANT.) repulse, tire, bore, disgust, annoy.

enthrall *(SYN.)* captivate, fascinate, enchant, charm, thrill.

enthusiasm *(SYN.)* fervor, fanaticism, zeal, ardor, intensity, devotion, excitement, eagerness, fervency, earnestness.

(ANT.) indifference, ennui, apathy, unconcern, detachment.

enthusiastic *(SYN.)* earnest, zealous, eager.

(ANT.) aloof, indifferent, unconcerned.

entice *(SYN.)* lure, attract, seduce.

entire *(SYN.)* complete, intact, whole, undivided.

(ANT.) divided, separated, incomplete, partial.

entirely *(SYN.)* altogether, thoroughly, wholly, solely.

entitle *(SYN.)* call, label, name, empower, allow, authorize, license, title.

entourage *(SYN.)* train, company, retinue, escort.

entrance *(SYN.)* inlet, portal, doorway, fascinate, entry, intrigue, door, thrill.

(ANT.) exit.

entreat *(SYN.)* implore, beg, plead.

entreaty *(SYN.)* plea, appeal.

entrust *(SYN.)* commit, charge, assign, delegate, consign, commission.

enumerate *(SYN.)* count, tally, list, number.

enunciate *(SYN.)* announce, express, speak, state.

envelop *(SYN.)* embrace, cover, conceal, surround, wrap.

environment *(SYN.)* neighborhood, habitat, surroundings, setting.

envision *(SYN.)* picture, imagine, visualize.

envoy *(SYN.)* delegate, emissary, representative, agent, messenger.

envy *(SYN.)* covetousness, jealousy, spitefulness, covet.

(ANT.) indifference, generosity.

epicure *(SYN.)* gourmand, gourmet, connoisseur, aesthete.

epidemic *(SYN.)* prevalent, scourge, plague, catching, widespread, pestilence, infectious.

episode *(SYN.)* happening, affair, occurrence, event, experience.

epoch *(SYN.)* age.

equal *(SYN.)* even, uniform, like, alike, equitable, same, identical, commensurate, equivalent, regular, parallel.

(ANT.) different, unequal, irregular, uneven.

equilibrium *(SYN.)* stability, steadiness, balance, firmness.

equip *(SYN.)* fit, rig, provide, outfit, prepare, furnish.

equipment *(SYN.)* utensils, material, apparatus.

equitable *(SYN.)* square, rightful, fair, due, just, fit.

(ANT.) partial, biased, unjust, uneven.

equity *(SYN.)* impartiality, fairness, justness, justice, evenhandedness.

equivalent *(SYN.)* match, rival, equal, like, replacement.

equivocal *(SYN.)* oblique, ambiguous, vague, indeterminate, uncertain, obscure.

(ANT.) clear, precise, explicit, certain, clearcut, definite.

equivocate *(SYN.)* temporize, evade, hedge, quibble, fudge, waffle, straddle.

era *(SYN.)* epoch, cycle, age, time, period.

eradicate *(SYN.)* remove, demolish, eliminate.

erase *(SYN.)* obliterate, remove, cancel.

(ANT.) add, include.

erect *(SYN.)* upright, build, straight, raise, construct, vertical.

(ANT.) flat, horizontal, raze, flatten, demolish.

erection *(SYN.)* building, construction, raising, fabrication.

erode *(SYN.)* rust, consume, disintegrate.

erotic *(SYN.)* carnal, fleshy, amatory, prurient, lewd, wanton, passionate, lecherous.

err *(SYN.)* slip, misjudge.

errand *(SYN.)* chore, duty, task, exercise.

errant *(SYN.)* roving, rambling, wandering, vagrant.

erratic *(SYN.)* irregular, abnormal, uneven, occasional, sporadic, changeable, unsteady, odd, eccentric, strange, extraordinary, unconventional, bizarre, peculiar, uncertain, unusual, unstable.

(ANT.) regular, steady, normal, ordinary.

erroneous *(SYN.)* wrong, mistaken, incorrect, inaccurate, false, untrue.

(ANT.) true, right, correct, accurate.

error *(SYN.)* inaccuracy, fault, slip, oversight, fallacy, mistake, blunder.

erudite *(SYN.)* sage, wise, learned, deep, profound.

erupt *(SYN.)* vomit.

escapade *(SYN.)* caper, antic, stunt, trick, prank.

escape *(SYN.)* shun, avoid, flee, decamp, elude, flight, avert, departure, abscond, fly, evade.

(ANT.) meet, confront, invite, catch.

escort *(SYN.)* conduct, lead, attend, accompany, protection, guard, guide, convoy, usher, squire.

especially *(SYN.)* unusually, principally, mainly, particularly, primarily.

essay *(SYN.)* test, thesis, undertake, paper, try.

essence *(SYN.)* substance, character, nature, principle, odor, basis, smell, perfume.

essential *(SYN.)* vital, intrinsic, basic, requisite, indispensable, critical, requirement, necessity, necessary, important.

(ANT.) dispensable, unimportant, inessential.

establish *(SYN.)* prove, fix, found, settle, institute, raise, verify, conform, form, sanction, begin, organize.

(ANT.) upset, discontinue, scatter, disperse, refute, abolish, unsettle.

esteem *(SYN.)* revere, deem, appreciate, honor, value, think, admire, respect, hold, prize, reverence, regard.

(ANT.) scorn, disdain, depreciate, disregard, contempt, abhor.

estimate *(SYN.)* calculate, gauge, judge, rate, evaluate, compute, value, figure.

estimation *(SYN.)* judgment, viewpoint, opinion.

etch *(SYN.)* stamp, engrave, impress.

eternal *(SYN.)* undying, immortal, ceaseless, infinite, everlasting, deathless, perpetual, endless, timeless.
(ANT.) mortal, transient, finite, brief, temporary, passing.

etiquette *(SYN.)* decorum, formality.

evacuate *(SYN.)* withdraw, depart, leave, vacate.

evade *(SYN.)* miss, avoid, bypass.
(ANT.) confront, meet, face.

evaluate *(SYN.)* value, appraise, assay.

evaporate *(SYN.)* disappear, vanish.
(ANT.) condense, appear.

even *(SYN.)* smooth, level, still, square, same, flat, balanced, equal, parallel, identical.
(ANT.) irregular, bumpy, unbalanced, unequal, divergent.

evening *(SYN.)* twilight, dusk, sunset.
(ANT.) sunrise, dawn.

event *(SYN.)* issue, end, result, circumstance, occurrence, incident, consequence, happening, episode.

even-tempered *(SYN.)* composed, calm, cool.
(ANT.) hotheaded.

eventual *(SYN.)* consequent, ultimate.
(ANT.) present, current.

eventually *(SYN.)* ultimately.

ever *(SYN.)* continuously, always, constantly.
(ANT.) never.

everlasting *(SYN.)* permanent, ceaseless, endless, continual.

evermore *(SYN.)* always.

everyday *(SYN.)* common, usual, ordinary, customary.
(ANT.) rare.

evict *(SYN.)* oust, put out, expel.

evidence *(SYN.)* grounds, clue, facts, testimony, data, sign, proof.

evident *(SYN.)* apparent, clear, obvious, indubitable, plain, conspicuous, patent, manifest.
(ANT.) hidden, unclear, uncertain, obscure, concealed.

evil *(SYN.)* immoral, harmful, badness, sinful, woe, bad, wicked.
(ANT.) goodness, moral, useful, upright, virtuous, advantageous.

evoke *(SYN.)* summon, prompt.

evolve *(SYN.)* grow, advance, develop, result, emerge, unfold.

exact *(SYN.)* correct, faultless, errorless, detailed, accurate.
(ANT.) inaccurate, inexact, faulty.

exaggerate *(SYN.)* stretch, expand, amplify, embroider, heighten, overstate, caricature, magnify.
(ANT.) understate, minimize, diminish, depreciate.

exalt *(SYN.)* erect, consecrate, raise, elevate, extol, dignify.
(ANT.) humble, degrade, humiliate.

examination *(SYN.)* investigation, inspection, test, scrutiny.

examine *(SYN.)* assess, contemplate, question, review, audit, notice, inquire, analyze, check, investigate, dissect, inspect, survey.
(ANT.) omit, disregard, overlook.

example *(SYN.)* pattern, archetype, specimen, illustration, model, instance, prototype, sample.
(ANT.) rule, concept, principle.

exasperate *(SYN.)* aggravate, anger, madden, irritate.

excavate *(SYN.)* dig, burrow.

exceed *(SYN.)* excel, beat, surpass.

exceedingly *(SYN.)* extremely, very, especially, surprisingly.

excel *(SYN.)* better, beat, surpass.

excellence *(SYN.)* distinction, superiority.
(ANT.) poorness, inferiority, badness.

excellent *(SYN.)* wonderful, fine, marvelous, superior.
(ANT.) poor, terrible, bad, inferior.

except *(SYN.)* omitting, barring, reject, excluding, save, exclude.

exception *(SYN.)* affront, offense, exclusion, deviation, omission.

exceptional *(SYN.)* different, irregular, strange, unusual.

excerpt *(SYN.)* abstract, extract.

excess *(SYN.)* surplus, intemperance, extravagance, immoderation, abundant, profuse.
(ANT.) want, sparse, lack, dearth.

exchange *(SYN.)* barter, interchange, substitute, trade, change.

excite *(SYN.)* arouse, incite, agitate, stimulate, awaken.

(ANT.) lull, quiet, bore, pacify.

exclaim *(SYN.)* vociferate, cry, call out, cry out, ejaculate, shout.

exclamation *(SYN.)* shout, outcry, clamor.

exclude *(SYN.)* omit, restrain, hinder, bar, except, prevent.

(ANT.) welcome, involve, embrace, admit, accept, include.

exclusion *(SYN.)* exception, bar, rejection.

(ANT.) inclusion.

exclusive*(SYN.)*restricted,limited,restrictive, choice, selective, fashionable.

(ANT.) common, general, ordinary, unrestricted, unfashionable.

excursion *(SYN.)* voyage, tour, trip.

excuse *(SYN.)* exculpate, forgive, remit, acquit, free, pardon, condone, explanation, overlook, exempt, reason, justify, absolve.

(ANT.) revenge, punish, convict.

execute*(SYN.)*complete,accomplish,achieve, kill, perform.

exemplify *(SYN.)* show, illustrate.

exempt *(SYN.)* excuse, free, except, release.

exercise *(SYN.)* drill, task, use, activity, lesson, training, exertion, application, gymnastics, operation, practice.

(ANT.) rest, indolence, repose.

exertion *(SYN.)* attempt, effort, strain, endeavor.

exhale *(SYN.)* blow, breathe out.

exhaust *(SYN.)* drain, tire, empty, wear out, use, finish, fatigue.

(ANT.) renew, refresh, replace.

exhaustive *(SYN.)*comprehensive,thorough, extensive, complete.

(ANT.) incomplete.

exhibit *(SYN.)* demonstrate, display, reveal, present, show, flaunt.

(ANT.) hide conceal, disguise.

exhilarate *(SYN.)* gladden, refresh, cheer, excite, stimulate.

exhort *(SYN.)* advise, coax, press, urge, prompt.

exile *(SYN.)* expulsion, proscription, deportation,ostracism,expatriation,deport,extradition.

(ANT.) retrieval, welcome, recall, admittance,

reinstatement.

exist *(SYN.)* stand, live, occur, be.

exit *(SYN.)* leave, depart.

exodus *(SYN.)* leaving, exit, parting, departure.

exonerate *(SYN.)* acquit, clear.

exorbitant *(SYN.)* unreasonable, outrageous, overpriced, preposterous, excessive.

(ANT.) normal, reasonable.

exotic *(SYN.)* strange, vivid, foreign, gay.

(ANT.) dull, native.

expand *(SYN.)* unfold, enlarge, broaden, inflate, swell, grow.

(ANT.) contract, shrivel, shrink.

expect *(SYN.)* await, think, hope, anticipate.

expedient *(SYN.)* helpful, desirable, rush, hasten, useful.

(ANT.) delay.

expedition *(SYN.)* trek, speed, trip, haste, voyage, journey, hurry.

expel *(SYN.)* exile, dislodge, discharge, excommunicate, oust, eject, dismiss, banish, disown.

(ANT.) favor, recall, invite, admit.

expend *(SYN.)* consume, waste, spend, exhaust.

(ANT.) ration, reserve, conserve.

expense *(SYN.)*charge,cost,payment,price.

experience *(SYN.)* occurrence, episode, sensation, happening, existence, background, feeling, living, encountering, knowledge.

experienced *(SYN.)* expert, qualified, accomplished, skilled.

(ANT.) untutored, inexperienced, naive.

experiment *(SYN.)* trial, test, prove, research, examine, try.

expert *(SYN.)* adept, handy, skillful, clever, specialist, authority, skilled, knowledgeable, ingenious.

(ANT.)untrained,unskilled,inexperienced.

expire *(SYN.)* terminate, die, cease, perish, pass, end, disappear.

(ANT.) commence, continue.

explain *(SYN.)* illustrate, decipher, expound, clarify, resolve, define, unravel, unfold, justify, interpret.

(ANT.) darken, baffle, obscure.

explanation *(SYN.)* definition, description, interpretation, account, reason, justification.

explicit *(SYN.)* lucid, definitive, specific, express, clear, manifest.

(ANT.) vague, implicit, ambiguous.

exploit *(SYN.)* feat, deed, accomplishment, adventure.

explore *(SYN.)* research, hunt, probe, search, investigate, look.

explosion *(SYN.)* bang, boom, blowup, blast, detonation, outbreak, convulsion, furor, tantrum.

explosive *(SYN.)* fiery, rabid, eruptive, volcanic, inflammatory.

(ANT.) stable, inert, peaceful, calm.

exponent *(SYN.)* explicator, spokesman, supporter, expounder, interpreter.

expose *(SYN.)* uncover, display, bare, open, unmask, reveal.

(ANT.) hide, conceal, mask, covered.

exposition *(SYN.)* fair, bazaar, show, expo, exhibition.

expound *(SYN.)* clarify, present, explain, lecture, demonstrate.

express *(SYN.)* voice, tell, send, say, ship, declare, precise, specific, swift, describe.

expressive *(SYN.)* suggestive, meaningful, telling, significant.

(ANT.) unthinking, meaningless, nondescript.

expressly *(SYN.)* precisely, exactly, definitely, clearly.

(ANT.) tentatively, vaguely, ambiguously.

expulsion *(SYN.)* ejection, discharge, removal, elimination.

expunge *(SYN.)* blot out, erase, cancel, obliterate, delete, efface.

expurgate *(SYN.)* cleanse, purge, censor, edit, emasculate, abridge.

exquisite *(SYN.)* delicate, delightful, attractive, beautiful, elegant, fine, superb.

(ANT.) vulgar, dull, ugly, unattractive.

extant *(SYN.)* subsisting, remaining, surviving, present, existing.

(ANT.) lost, defunct, extinct, vanished.

extemporaneous *(SYN.)* casual, impromptu, offhand.

extemporize *(SYN.)* improvise, devise.

extend *(SYN.)* lengthen, stretch, increase, offer, give, grant, magnify, expand.

(ANT.) abbreviate, shorten, curtail.

extension *(SYN.)* expansion, increase, stretching, enlargement.

extensive *(SYN.)* vast, wide, spacious, broad.

(ANT.) narrow, cramped, confined, restricted.

extent *(SYN.)* length, degree, range, amount, measure, size, compass, reach, magnitude.

extenuating *(SYN.)* exculpating, excusable, qualifying, justifying.

exterior *(SYN.)* surface, face, outside, covering, outer, external.

(ANT.) inside, lining, interior, inner, internal.

exterminate *(SYN.)* slay, kill, destroy.

external *(SYN.)* outer, exterior, outside.

(ANT.) inner, internal, inside, interior.

externals *(SYN.)* images, effects, look, appearance, veneer, aspect.

extinct *(SYN.)* lost, dead, gone, vanished.

(ANT.) present, flourishing, alive, extant.

extinction *(SYN.)* eclipse, annihilation, obliteration, death.

extinguish *(SYN.)* suppress, smother, quench.

extol *(SYN.)* laud, eulogize, exalt, praise.

(ANT.) denounce, belittle, discredit, disparage.

extra *(SYN.)* surplus, spare, additional.

extract *(SYN.)* remove, withdraw, essence.

(ANT.) penetrate, introduce.

extraordinary *(SYN.)* unusual, wonderful, marvelous, peculiar, remarkable, exceptional.

(ANT.) commonplace, ordinary, usual.

extravagant *(SYN.)* excessive, exaggerated, lavish, wasteful, extreme.

(ANT.) prudent, frugal, thrifty, economical, provident.

extreme *(SYN.)* excessive, overdone, outermost, limit, greatest, utmost, furthest, extravagant.

(ANT.) reasonable, moderate.

extricate *(SYN.)* rescue, free, clear, release.

exuberant *(SYN.)* buoyant, ebullient, vivacious.

(ANT.) sad, depressed.

exult *(SYN.)* rejoice, delight.

fable *(SYN.)* legend, parable, myth, fib, fiction, tale, story.

fabled *(SYN.)* legendary, famous, famed, historic.

fabric *(SYN.)* goods, textile, material, cloth, yard goods.

fabricate *(SYN.)* assemble, make, construct, produce, create.

(ANT.) raze, destroy, demolish.

fabrication *(SYN.)* deceit, lie, falsehood, untruth, forgery, deception.

(ANT.) verity, reality, actuality, truth, fact.

fabulous *(SYN.)* amazing, marvelous, unbelievable, fantastic, astounding, astonishing, striking.

(ANT.) ordinary, commonplace, credible, proven, factual.

facade *(SYN.)* deception, mask, front, show, pose, veneer, guise.

face *(SYN.)* cover, mug, front, assurance, countenance, audacity, visage, expression, look, features, facade, meet, surface.

(ANT.) rear, shun, avoid, evade, back, timidity.

facet *(SYN.)* perspective, view, side, phase.

facetious *(SYN.)* jocular, humorous, funny, clever, droll, witty, playful, jesting.

(ANT.) sober, serious, grave, weighty.

face to face *(SYN.)* opposing, nose to nose, confronting.

facile *(SYN.)* simple, easy, quick, clever, uncomplicated, fluent.

(ANT.) complex, difficult, complicated, hard, ponderous, arduous.

facilitate *(SYN.)* help, speed, ease, promote, accelerate, expedite.

facilities *(SYN.)* aid, means, resources, conveniences.

facility *(SYN.)* ability, skill, ease, skillfulness, material.

(ANT.) effort, difficulty, labor.

facsimile *(SYN.)* reproduction, likeness, replica.

fact *(SYN.)* reality, deed, certainty, incident, circumstance, event, occurrence, truth, actuality.

(ANT.) falsehood, fiction, delusion.

faction *(SYN.)* clique, party, sect.

factitious *(SYN.)* false, sham, artificial, spurious, unnatural, affected.

(ANT.) natural, real, genuine, artless.

factor *(SYN.)* part, certain, element, basis, cause.

factory *(SYN.)* installation, plant, mill, works.

factual *(SYN.)* true, correct, accurate. sure, genuine, authentic.

(ANT.) incorrect, erroneous, fabricated, invented.

faculty *(SYN.)* power, capacity, talent, staff, gift, qualification, ability, skill.

fad *(SYN.)* fashion, vogue, rage.

faddish *(SYN.)* ephemeral, modish, temporary, passing, fleeting.

(ANT.) lasting, permanent, enduring, classic.

fade *(SYN.)* pale, bleach, weaken, dim, decline, sink, discolor.

fagged *(SYN.)* exhausted, tired, weary, pooped, worn.

fail *(SYN.)* neglect, weaken, flunk, miss, decline, disappoint, fade.

(ANT.) succeed, achieve, accomplish.

failing *(SYN.)* fault, foible, imperfection, frailty, defect, peccadillo, shortcoming.

(ANT.) steadiness, strength, integrity, firmness.

failure *(SYN.)* miscarriage, omission, decline, deficiency, fiasco, lack, dereliction, failing, unsuccessfulness, loss, default, want.

(ANT.) conquest, accomplishment, success, triumph, victory, hit, luck, achievement.

faint *(SYN.)* timid, faded, languid, halfhearted, dim, pale, wearied, feeble, indistinct, weak.

(ANT.) strong, sharp, forceful, glaring, clear, distinct, conspicuous, brave.

faint-hearted *(SYN.)* shy, cowardly, timid, bashful.

(ANT.) fearless, brave, stouthearted, courageous.

fair *(SYN.)* pale, average, light, just, sunny, mediocre, bright, clear, lovely, blond, honest, equitable, impartial, reasonable.

(ANT.) *ugly, fraudulent, foul, outstanding, dishonorable, unfair.*

fair-minded *(SYN.)* reasonable, fair, just, honest, unprejudiced, impartial, even-handed.

(ANT.) *bigoted, narrow-minded, unjust, closeminded, partisan.*

fairness *(SYN.)* equity, justice, honesty.

(ANT.) *favoritism, partiality, bias, one-sidedness.*

fairy *(SYN.)* leprechaun, gnome, elf, pixie, sprite.

faith *(SYN.)* dependence, trust, reliance, creed, loyalty, doctrine, confidence, dogma, tenet, persuasion, credence, fidelity, religion.

(ANT.) *mistrust, disbelief, doubt, infidelity.*

faithful *(SYN.)* staunch, true, devoted, trusty, loyal, constant, credible, steadfast, strict, trustworthy, accurate.

(ANT.) *untrustworthy, faithless, inaccurate, wrong, false, disloyal, treacherous.*

fake *(SYN.)* falsify, distort, pretend, feign, fraud, counterfeit, cheat, artificial, phony, imitation.

(ANT.) *honest, pure, real, genuine, authentic.*

falderal *(SYN.)* foolery, jargon, nonsense, gibberish, blather, balderdash.

fall *(SYN.)* drop, decline, diminish, droop, topple, decrease, sink, hang, descend, subside, plunge.

(ANT.) *soar, climb, steady, rise, ascend.*

fallacious *(SYN.)* untrue, false, wrong, erroneous, deceptive, illusory, delusive.

(ANT.) *accurate, true, exact, real, factual.*

fallacy *(SYN.)* mistake, error, illusion, misconception, deception.

fall back *(SYN.)* retreat, recede, withdraw, concede.

(ANT.) *progress, advance, gain, prosper, proceed.*

fallow *(SYN.)* idle, unprepared, unproductive. inactive.

(ANT.) *prepared, productive, cultivated.*

false *(SYN.)* incorrect, wrong, deceitful, fake, imitation, counterfeit.

(ANT.) *genuine, loyal, true, honest.*

falsehood *(SYN.)* untruth, lie, fib, story.

(ANT.) *truth.*

falsify *(SYN.)* misquote, distort, mislead, adulterate.

falter *(SYN.)* stumble, tremble, hesitate, flounder.

fame *(SYN.)* distinction, glory, mane, eminence, credit, reputation, renown, acclaim, notoriety.

(ANT.) *infamy, obscurity, anonymity, disrepute.*

famed *(SYN.)* known, renowned, famous.

(ANT.) *obscure, unknown, anonymous.*

familiar *(SYN.)* informal, intimate, close, acquainted, amicable, knowing, cognizant, versed, unreserved, friendly, sociable, affable, aware, known.

(ANT.) *unfamiliar, distant, affected, reserved.*

familiarity *(SYN.)* sociability, acquaintance, awareness, intimacy, understanding, knowledge.

(ANT.) *distance, ignorance, reserve, presumption, constraint, haughtiness.*

family *(SYN.)* kin, tribe, folks, group, relatives.

famine *(SYN.)* want, deficiency, starvation, need.

(ANT.) *excess, plenty.*

famous *(SYN.)* distinguished, noted, glorious, illustrious, famed, celebrated, well-known, eminent, renowned, prominent.

(ANT.) *obscure, hidden, unknown.*

fan *(SYN.)* arouse, spread, admirer, enthusiast, devotee, stir.

fanatic *(SYN.)* bigot, enthusiast, zealot.

fancy *(SYN.)* love, dream, ornate, imagine, suppose, imagination, fantasy, ornamented, elaborate.

(ANT.) *plain, undecorated, simple, unadorned.*

fantastic *(SYN.)* strange, unusual, odd, wild, unimaginable, incredible, unbelievable, bizarre.

(ANT.) *mundane, ordinary, staid, humdrum.*

fantasy *(SYN.)* illusion, dream, whim, hallucination, delusion, caprice, mirage, daydream, fancy.

(ANT.) bore.

far *(SYN.)* removed, much, distant, remote, estranged, alienated.

(ANT.) close, near.

fare *(SYN.)* prosper, eat, passenger, thrive, toll, progress, succeed.

farewell *(SYN.)* good-by, valediction, departure, leaving.

(ANT.) welcome, greeting.

farm *(SYN.)* grow, harvest, cultivate, ranch, hire, charter, plantation.

fascinate *(SYN.)* charm, enchant, bewitch, attract, enthrall.

fashion *(SYN.)* create, shape, style, mode, make, custom, form, method, way, vogue.

fashionable *(SYN.)* chic, smart, stylish, mod-ish, elegant, voguish.

(ANT.) dowdy, unfashionable.

fast *(SYN.)* fleet, firm, quick, swift, inflexible, stable, secure, expeditious, rapid, steady, constant, speedy.

(ANT.) insecure, sluggish, unstable, loose, slow, unsteady.

fasten *(SYN.)* secure, bind, tie, join, fix, connect, attach, unite.

(ANT.) open, loose, free, loosen, release, separate.

fastidious *(SYN.)* choosy, selective, discriminating, picky, meticulous.

fat *(SYN.)* stout, plump, chubby, pudgy, obese, oily, fleshy, greasy, fatty, portly, corpulent, paunchy, wide, thick, rotund.

(ANT.) slim, gaunt, emaciated, thin, slender.

fatal *(SYN.)* killing, lethal, doomed, disastrous, deadly, fateful, mortal.

(ANT.) nonfatal.

fate *(SYN.)* end, fortune, doom, issue, destiny, necessity, portion, result, lot, chance, luck, outcome, consequence, kismet.

father *(SYN.)* cause, sire, breed, originate, founder.

fatherly *(SYN.)* protective, paternal, kind, paternalistic.

fathom *(SYN.)* penetrate, understand, interpret, comprehend.

fatigue *(SYN.)* weariness, lassitude, exhaus-

tion, enervation, languor, tiredness.

(ANT.) vivacity, rejuvenation, energy, vigor.

fault *(SYN.)* defect, flaw, mistake, imperfection, shortcoming, error, weakness, responsibility, omission, blemish, blame, failure.

(ANT.) perfection, completeness.

faulty *(SYN.)* imperfect, broken, defective, damaged, impaired.

(ANT.) flawless, perfect, whole.

favor *(SYN.)* rather, resemble, liking, service, prefer, approval, like, support, patronize, benefit.

(ANT.) deplore, disapprove.

favorite *(SYN.)* prized, pet, choice, darling, treasured, preferred.

favoritism *(SYN.)* prejudice, bias, partiality.

(ANT.) fairness, impartiality.

fear *(SYN.)* horror, terror, fright, trepidation, alarm, consternation, dismay, cowardice, panic, anxiety, dread, scare, apprehension.

(ANT.) fearlessness, boldness, courage, assurance.

fearless *(SYN.)* bold, brave, courageous, gallant, dauntless, confident.

(ANT.) timid, fearful, cowardly.

feast *(SYN.)* dinner, banquet, barbecue.

feat *(SYN.)* performance, act, operation, accomplishment, achievement, doing, transaction, deed.

(ANT.) intention, deliberation, cessation.

feature *(SYN.)* trait, quality, characteristic, highlight, attribute.

fee *(SYN.)* payment, pay, remuneration, charge, recompense.

feeble *(SYN.)* faint, puny, exhausted, impair, delicate, weak, enervated, frail, powerless, forceless, sickly, decrepit, ailing.

(ANT.) strong, forceful, powerful, vigorous, stout.

feed *(SYN.)* satisfy, nourish, food, fodder, forage.

feel *(SYN.)* sense, experience, perceive.

feeling *(SYN.)* opinion, sensibility, tenderness, affection, impression, belief, sen-

sation, sympathy, thought, passion, sentiment, attitude, emotion.
(ANT.) fact, imperturbability, anesthesia, insensibility.

fellowship *(SYN.)* clan, society, brotherhood, fraternity, camaraderie, companionship, comradeship, association.
(ANT.) dislike, discord, distrust, enmity, strife, acrimony.

felonious *(SYN.)* murderous, criminal, larcenous.

feminine *(SYN.)* womanly, girlish, lady-like, female, maidenly, womanish.
(ANT.) masculine, male, virile.

ferocious *(SYN.)* savage, fierce, wild, bloodthirsty, brutal.
(ANT.) playful, gentle, harmless, calm.

fertile *(SYN.)* rich, fruitful, teeming, plenteous, bountiful, prolific, luxuriant, productive, fecund.
(ANT.) unproductive, barren, sterile.

festival *(SYN.)* feast, banquet, celebration.

festive *(SYN.)* joyful, gay, joyous, merry, gala, jovial, jubilant.
(ANT.) sad, gloomy, mournful, morose.

fetching *(SYN.)* charming, attractive, pleasing, captivating, winsome.

feud *(SYN.)* dispute, quarrel, strife, argument, conflict, controversy.
(ANT.) amity, understanding, harmony, peace.

fiber *(SYN.)* line, strand, thread, string.

fickle *(SYN.)* unstable, capricious, restless, changeable, inconstant, variable.
(ANT.) stable, constant, trustworthy, steady, reliable, dependable.

fiction *(SYN.)* fabrication, romance, falsehood, tale, allegory, narrative, fable, novel, story, invention.
(ANT.) verity, reality, fact, truth.

fictitious *(SYN.)* invented, make-believe, imaginary, fabricated, unreal, counterfeit, feigned.
(ANT.) real, true, genuine, actual, proven.

fidelity *(SYN.)* fealty, devotion, precision, allegiance, exactness, constancy, accuracy, faithfulness, loyalty.
(ANT.) treachery, disloyalty.

fidget *(SYN.)* squirm, twitch, wriggle.

fiendish *(SYN.)* devilish, demonic, diabolical, savage, satanic.

fierce *(SYN.)* furious, wild, savage, violent, ferocious, vehement.
(ANT.) calm, meek, mild, gentle, placid.

fight *(SYN.)* contend, scuffle, struggle, battle, wrangle, combat, brawl, quarrel, dispute, war, skirmish, conflict.

figure *(SYN.)* design, pattern, mold, shape, form, frame, reckon, calculate, compute, determine.

fill *(SYN.)* glut, furnish, store, stuff, occupy, gorge, pervade, content, stock, fill up, supply, replenish, satisfy.
(ANT.) void, drain, exhaust, deplete, empty.

filter *(SYN.)* screen, strainer, sieve.

filth *(SYN.)* pollution, dirt, sewage, foulness.
(ANT.) cleanliness, innocence, purity.

filthy *(SYN.)* foul, polluted, dirty, stained, unwashed, squalid.
(ANT.) pure, clean, unspoiled.

final *(SYN.)* ultimate, decisive, concluding, ending, terminal, last, conclusive, eventual, latest.
(ANT.) inaugural, rudimentary, beginning, initial, incipient, first, original.

finally *(SYN.)* at last, eventually, ultimately.

find *(SYN.)* observe, detect, discover, locate.

fine *(SYN.)* thin, pure, choice, small, elegant, dainty, splendid, handsome, delicate, nice, powdered, beautiful, minute, exquisite, subtle, pretty, refined.
(ANT.) thick, coarse, rough, blunt, large.

finicky *(SYN.)* fussy, meticulous, finical, fastidious, prim.

finish *(SYN.)* consummate, close, get done, terminate, accomplish, conclude, execute, perform, complete, end, achieve, fulfill, do, perfect.
(ANT.) open, begin, start, beginning.

fire *(SYN.)* vigor, glow, combustion, passion, burning, conflagration, ardor, flame, blaze, intensity, fervor.
(ANT.) apathy, cold.

firm *(SYN.)* solid, rigid, inflexible, stiff,

unchanging, steadfast, dense, hard, unshakable, compact, business, company, corporation, partnership.
(ANT.) weak, limp, soft, drooping.
first *(SYN.)* chief, primary, initial, pristine, beginning, foremost, primeval, earliest, prime, primitive, original.
(ANT.) subordinate, last, least, hindmost, latest.
fishy *(SYN.)* suspicious, questionable, doubtful.
(ANT.) believable, credible.
fit *(SYN.)* adjust, suit, suitable, accommodate, conform, robust, harmonize, belong, seizure, spasm, attack, suited, appropriate, healthy, agree, adapt.
(ANT.) misfit, disturb, improper.
fitful *(SYN.)* variable, restless, fickle, capricious, unstable, changeable.
(ANT.) trustworthy, stable, constant, steady.
fitting *(SYN.)* apt, due, suitable, proper.
(ANT.) improper, unsuitable, inappropriate.
fix *(SYN.)* mend, regulate, affix, set, tie, repair, attach, settle, link, bind, determine, establish, define, place, rectify, stick, limit, adjust, fasten.
(ANT.) damage, change, mistreat, displace, alter, disturb, mutilate.
fixation *(SYN.)* fetish, obsession, infatuation, compulsion.
flair *(SYN.)* style, dash, flamboyance, drama, gift, knack, aptitude.
flamboyant *(SYN.)* showy, flashy, ostentatious, gaudy, ostentatious.
flame *(SYN.)* blaze, fire.
flash *(SYN.)* flare, flame, wink, twinkling, instant, gleam.
flashy *(SYN.)* tawdry, tasteless, pretentious, garish, flamboyant.
flat *(SYN.)* vapid, stale, even, smooth, tasteless, horizontal, dull, level, insipid, uninteresting, boring.
(ANT.) tasty, racy, hilly, savory, stimulating, interesting, broken, sloping.
flattery *(SYN.)* compliment, praise, applause, blarney, acclaim.
flaunt *(SYN.)* exhibit, show off, display, parade.

(ANT.) conceal, hide, disguise.
flavor *(SYN.)* tang, taste, savor, essence, quality, character, season, spice.
flaw *(SYN.)* spot, imperfection, blemish, fault, deformity, blotch.
flee *(SYN.)* fly, abscond, hasten, escape, run away, decamp, evade.
(ANT.) remain, appear, stay, arrive.
fleece *(SYN.)* filch, rob, purloin, swindle, defraud, pilfer, cheat.
fleet *(SYN.)* rapid, swift, quick, fast.
(ANT.) unhurried, sluggish, slow.
fleeting *(SYN.)* brief, swift, passing, temporary.
(ANT.) stable, fixed, lasting, permanent.
fleshy *(SYN.)* overweight, chubby, stocky, plump, obese, stout.
(ANT.) spare, underweight, skinny.
flexible *(SYN.)* lithe, resilient, pliable, tractable, complaint, elastic, yielding, adaptable, easy, agreeable, supple, pliant, ductile.
(ANT.) hard, unbending, firm, brittle, inflexible, rigid, fixed.
flighty *(SYN.)* giddy, light-headed, frivolous, irresponsible.
(ANT.) solid, responsible, steady.
flimsy *(SYN.)* wobbly, weak, frail, fragile, unsteady, delicate, thin.
(ANT.) durable, stable, firm, strong.
fling *(SYN.)* pitch, throw, toss, fun, celebration, party.
flippant *(SYN.)* disrespectful, sassy, insolent, brazen, rude, impertinent.
(ANT.) courteous, polite, mannerly.
flit *(SYN.)* flutter, scurry, hasten, dart, skim.
flock *(SYN.)* gathering, group, flight, swarm, herd, school.
flog *(SYN.)* thrash, lash, switch, strike, paddle.
flood *(SYN.)* overflow, deluge, inundate, cascade.
florid *(SYN.)* gaudy, fancy, ornate, embellished.
(ANT.) spare, simple, plain, unadorned.
flourish *(SYN.)* succeed, grow, prosper, wave, thrive, bloom.
(ANT.) wither, wane, die, decline.

flout *(SYN.)* disdain, scorn, spurn, ignore, taunt, ridicule, mock.

flow *(SYN.)* proceed, abound, spout, come, stream, run, originate, emanate, result, pour, squirt, issue, gush, spurt.

fluctuate *(SYN.)* vary, oscillate, change, waver, hesitate, vacillate.

(ANT.) persist, stick, adhere, resolve.

fluent *(SYN.)* graceful, glib, flowing.

fluid *(SYN.)* liquid, running, liquefied.

flush *(SYN.)* abundant, flat, even, level.

fluster *(SYN.)* rattle, flurry, agitate, upset, perturb, quiver, vibrate.

fly *(SYN.)* flee, mount, shoot, decamp, hover, soar, flit, flutter, sail, escape, rush, spring, glide, abscond, dart, float.

(ANT.) sink, descend, plummet.

foam *(SYN.)* suds, froth, lather.

foe *(SYN.)* opponent, enemy, antagonist, adversary.

(ANT.) associate, ally, friend, comrade.

fog *(SYN.)* haze, mist, cloud, daze, confusion, stupor, vapor, smog.

foible *(SYN.)* frailty, weakness, failing, shortcoming, kink.

foist *(SYN.)* misrepresent, insinuate, falsify.

fold *(SYN.)* lap, double, overlap, clasp, pleat, tuck.

follow *(SYN.)* trail, observe, succeed, ensue, obey, chase, comply, accompany, copy, result, imitate, heed, adopt.

(ANT.) elude, cause, precede, avoid, flee.

follower *(SYN.)* supporter, devotee, henchman, adherent, partisan, votary, attendant, disciple, successor.

(ANT.) master, head, chief, dissenter.

following *(SYN.)* public, disciples, supporters, clientele, customers.

folly *(SYN.)* imprudence, silliness, foolishness, indiscretion, absurdity, imprudence, imbecility, stupidity, extravagance.

(ANT.) reasonableness, judgment, sense, prudence, wisdom.

fond *(SYN.)* affectionate, loving, attached, tender, devoted.

(ANT.) hostile, cool, distant, unfriendly.

fondness *(SYN.)* partiality, liking, affection.

(ANT.) hostility, unfriendliness.

food *(SYN.)* viands, edibles, feed, repast, nutriment, sustenance, diet, bread, provisions, meal, rations, victuals, fare.

(ANT.) want, hunger, drink, starvation.

fool *(SYN.)* oak, dunce, jester, idiot, simpleton, buffoon, harlequin, dolt, blockhead, numskull, clown, dope, trick, deceive, nincompoop.

(ANT.) scholar, genius, sage.

foolish *(SYN.)* senseless, irrational, crazy, silly, brainless, idiotic, simple, nonsensical, stupid, preposterous, asinine.

(ANT.) sane, sound, sensible, rational, judicious, wise, reasonable, prudent.

footing *(SYN.)* base, basis, foundation.

footloose *(SYN.)* uncommitted, free, detached, independent.

(ANT.) engaged, rooted, involved.

forbearance *(SYN.)* moderation, abstinence, abstention, continence.

(ANT.) greed, excess, intoxication.

forbid *(SYN.)* disallow, prevent, ban, prohibit, taboo, outlaw.

(ANT.) approve, let, allow, permit.

forbidding *(SYN.)* evil, hostile, unfriendly, sinister, scary, repulsive.

(ANT.) pleasant, beneficent, friendly.

force *(SYN.)* energy, might, violence, vigor, intensity, dint, power, constraint, coercion, vigor, compel, compulsion, oblige, make, coerce, strength.

(ANT.) weakness, frailty, persuasion, feebleness, impotence, ineffectiveness.

forceful *(SYN.)* dynamic, vigorous, energetic, potent, drastic, intense.

(ANT.) lackadaisical, insipid, weak.

foreboding *(SYN.)* misgiving, suspicion, apprehension, presage, intuition.

forecast *(SYN.)* prophesy, predict, predetermine.

foregoing *(SYN.)* above, former, preceding, previous, prior.

(ANT.) later, coming, below, follow.

foreign *(SYN.)* alien, strange, exotic, different, unfamiliar.

(ANT.) commonplace, ordinary, familiar.

foreigner *(SYN.)* outsider, alien, newcomer, stranger.

(ANT.) native.

foreman *(SYN.)* super, boss, overseer, supervisor.

forerunner *(SYN.)* harbinger, proclaimer, informant.

foresee *(SYN.)* forecast, expect, anticipate, surmise, envisage.

forest *(SYN.)* grove, woodland, wood, copse, woods.

forestall *(SYN.)* hinder, thwart, prevent, obstruct, repel.

foretell *(SYN.)* soothsay, divine, predict.

forever *(SYN.)* evermore, always, everlasting, hereafter, endlessly.

(ANT.) fleeting, temporarily.

forfeit *(SYN.)* yield, resign, lose, sacrifice.

forgive *(SYN.)* exonerate, clear, excuse, pardon.

(ANT.) impeach, accuse, blame, censure.

forgo *(SYN.)* relinquish, release, surrender, waive, abandon.

(ANT.) keep, retain, safeguard.

forlorn *(SYN.)* pitiable, desolate, dejected, woeful, wretched.

(ANT.) optimistic, cherished, cheerful.

form *(SYN.)* frame, compose, fashion, arrange, construct, make up, devise, create, invent, mold, shape, forge, organize, produce, constitute, make.

(ANT.) wreck, dismantle, destroy, misshape.

formal *(SYN.)* exact, stiff, correct, outward, conformist, conventional, affected, regular, proper, ceremonious, decorous, methodical, precise, solemn, external, perfunctory.

(ANT.) heartfelt, unconstrained, easy, unconventional.

former *(SYN.)* earlier, onetime, previous, erstwhile, prior.

formidable *(SYN.)* alarming, frightful, imposing, terrible, terrifying, dire, fearful, forbidding.

(ANT.) unimpressive, ordinary.

forsake *(SYN.)* abandon, desert, forgo, quit, discard, neglect.

forte *(SYN.)* gift, capability, talent, specialty, aptitude, bulwark.

forth *(SYN.)* out, onward, forward.

forthright *(SYN.)* honest, direct, candid, outspoken, blunt sincere, plain, explicit.

forthwith *(SYN.)* instantly, promptly, immediately.

(ANT.) afterward, later, ultimately, slowly.

fortify *(SYN.)* bolster strengthen, buttress, barricade, defend.

fortuitous *(SYN.)* successful, benign, lucky, advantageous, propitious, happy, favored.

(ANT.) unlucky, condemned, persecuted.

fortunate *(SYN.)* happy, auspicious, fortuitous, successful, favored, advantageous, benign, charmed, lucky, felicitous, blessed, propitious, blissful.

(ANT.) ill-fated, cheerless, unlucky, unfortunate, cursed, condemned.

fortune *(SYN.)* chance, fate, lot, luck, riches, wealth, destiny.

fortuneteller *(SYN.)* soothsayer, clairvoyant, oracle, medium.

forward *(SYN.)* leading, front, promote, elevate, advance, first, ahead, onward, further, foremost.

(ANT.) withhold, retard, hinder, retreat, oppose.

foul *(SYN.)* base, soiled, dirty, mean, unclean, polluted, impure, vile, evil, muddy, wicked, rainy, stormy, despicable, filthy.

(ANT.) pure, neat, wholesome, clean.

found *(SYN.)* organize, establish.

foundation *(SYN.)* support, root, base, underpinning, groundwork, establishment, substructure.

(ANT.) top, cover, building.

foxy *(SYN.)* cunning, sly, artful, crafty, wily, sharp, shrewd, slick.

fraction *(SYN.)* fragment, part, section, morsel, share, piece.

fracture *(SYN.)* crack, break, rupture.

fragile *(SYN.)* delicate, frail, weak, breakable, infirm, brittle, feeble.

(ANT.) tough, hardy, sturdy, strong, stout, durable.

fragment *(SYN.)* scrap, piece, bit, remnant, part, splinter, segment.

fragrance *(SYN.)* odor, smell, scent, perfume, aroma.

fragrant *(SYN.)* aromatic, scented, perfumed.

frail *(SYN.)* feeble, weak, delicate, breakable, fragile.

(ANT.) sturdy, strong, powerful.

frame *(SYN.)* support, framework, skeleton, molding, border, mount.

frank *(SYN.)* honest, candid, open, unreserved, direct, sincere.

(ANT.) tricky, dishonest.

frantic *(SYN.)* frenzied, crazed, raving, panicky.

(ANT.) composed, stoic.

fraud *(SYN.)* deception, guile, swindle, deceit, artifice, imposture, trick, cheat, imposition.

(ANT.) sincerity, fairness, integrity.

fraudulent *(SYN.)* tricky, fake, dishonest, deceitful

fray *(SYN.)* strife, fight, battle, struggle, tussle, combat, brawl.

(ANT.) truce, agreement, peace, concord.

freak *(SYN.)* curiosity, abnormality, monster, oddity.

free *(SYN.)* munificent, clear, autonomous, immune, open, freed, bountiful, liberated, unfastened, immune, emancipated, unconfined, unobstructed, easy, artless, loose, familiar, bounteous, unrestricted, liberal, independent.

(ANT.) stingy, clogged, illiberal, confined, parsimonious.

freedom *(SYN.)* independence, privilege, familiarity, unrestraint, liberty, exemption, liberation.

(ANT.) servitude, constraint, bondage, slavery, necessity.

freight *(SYN.)* chipping, cargo, load, shipment.

frenzy *(SYN.)* craze, agitation, excitement.

frequent *(SYN.)* usual, habitual, common, often, customary.

(ANT.) unique, rare, solitary, uncommon, infrequent, scanty.

fresh *(SYN.)* recent, new, additional, modern, further, refreshing, natural, brisk, novel, late, current, sweet, pure, cool.

(ANT.) stagnant, decayed, musty, faded.

fret *(SYN.)* torment, worry, grieve, anguish.

fretful *(SYN.)* testy, irritable, touchy, peevish, short-tempered.

(ANT.) calm.

friend *(SYN.)* crony, supporter, ally, companion, intimate, associate, advocate, comrade, mate, patron, acquaintance, chum.

(ANT.) stranger, adversary.

friendly *(SYN.)* sociable, kindly, affable, genial, companionable, social, neighborly, amicable.

(ANT.) hostile, antagonistic, reserved.

friendship *(SYN.)* knowledge, familiarity, fraternity, acquaintance, intimacy, fellowship, comradeship, cognizance.

(ANT.) unfamiliarity, ignorance.

fright *(SYN.)* alarm, fear, panic, terror.

frighten *(SYN.)* scare, horrify, daunt, affright, appall, terrify, alarm, terrorize, astound, dismay, startle, panic.

(ANT.) soothe, embolden, compose, reassure.

frigid *(SYN.)* cold, wintry, icy, glacial, arctic, freezing.

fringe *(SYN.)* hem, edge, border, trimming, edging.

frisky *(SYN.)* animated, lively, peppy, vivacious.

frolic *(SYN.)* play, cavort, romp, frisk, gambol.

front *(SYN.)* facade, face, start, border, head.

(ANT.) rear, back.

frontier *(SYN.)* border, boundary.

frugal *(SYN.)* parsimonious, saving, stingy, provident, temperate, economical.

(ANT.) extravagant, wasteful, self-indulgent, intemperate.

fruitful *(SYN.)* fertile, rich, bountiful, teeming, fecund, productive, luxuriant, prolific.

(ANT.) lean, unproductive, barren, sterile.

fruitless *(SYN.)* barren, futile, vain, sterile, unproductive.

(ANT.) fertile, productive.

frustrate *(SYN.)* hinder, defeat, thwart, circumvent, outwit, foil, baffle, disappoint, discourage.

(ANT.) promote, fulfill, accomplish, further.

fugitive *(SYN.)* refugee, deserter, runaway.

fulfill *(SYN.)* do, effect, complete, accomplish, realize.

full *(SYN.)* baggy, crammed, entire, satiated, flowing, perfect, gorged, soaked, complete, filled, packed, extensive, plentiful, voluminous.

(ANT.) lacking, devoid, partial, empty, depleted.

full-fledged *(SYN.)* schooled, expert, professional, adept, qualified, senior, trained, able.

(ANT.) inexperienced, green, untried, untrained.

full-grown *(SYN.)* ripe, adult, mature, developed, complete.

(ANT.) green, young, unripe, adolescent.

fullness *(SYN.)* glut, repletion, enough, satiety, satiation, sufficiency, all, totality, satisfaction, sum, aggregate, everything.

(ANT.) need, want, hunger, lack, insufficiency, privation, emptiness, incompleteness.

fulsome *(SYN.)* disgusting, repulsive, nauseating, revolting.

fume *(SYN.)* gas, steam, smoke, rage, rave, vapor.

fun *(SYN.)* merriment, pleasure, enjoyment, gaiety, sport, amusement.

function *(SYN.)* operation, activity, affair, ceremony, gathering, party.

fundamental *(SYN.)* basic, essential, primary, elementary.

furious *(SYN.)* angry, enraged.

(ANT.) serene, calm.

furnish *(SYN.)* yield, give, endow, fit, produce, equip, afford, decorate, appoint.

(ANT.) divest, denude, strip.

furor *(SYN.)* commotion, tumult, turmoil.

furthermore *(SYN.)* moreover, also, further.

furtive *(SYN.)* surreptitious, secret, hidden, clandestine.

(ANT.) honest, open.

fury *(SYN.)* wrath, anger, frenzy, rage, violence, fierceness.

(ANT.) calmness, serenity.

fuss *(SYN.)* commotion, bother, pester, annoy, irritate.

futile *(SYN.)* pointless, idle, vain, useless, worthless, minor.

(ANT.) weighty, important, worthwhile, serious, valuable.

future *(SYN.)* approaching, imminent, coming, impending.

(ANT.) former, past.

fuzzy *(SYN.)* indistinct, blurred.

(ANT.) lucid, clear.

G

gab *(SYN.)* jabber, babble, chatter, prattle, gossip.

gabble *(SYN.)* chatter, babble, jabber, blab, prate, gaggle, prattle.

gabby *(SYN.)* chatty, talkative, wordy, verbose.

gad *(SYN.)* wander, roam, rove, ramble, meander, cruise.

gadabout *(SYN.)* gypsy, wanderer, rambler.

gadget *(SYN.)* contrivance, device, doodad, jigger, thing, contraption.

gaffe *(SYN.)* blunder, boner, mistake, gaucherie, error, howler.

gag *(SYN.)* witticism, crack jest, joke.

gaiety *(SYN.)* joyousness, cheerfulness, lightheartedness.

(ANT.) melancholy, sadness, depression.

gain *(SYN.)* acquire, avail, account, good, interest, attain, favor, achieve, get, secure, advantage, earn, profit, procure, service, obtain, improvement, increase, behalf, net, reach, win, benefit.

(ANT.) trouble, lose, calamity, forfeit, handicap, lose, distress.

gainful *(SYN.)* lucrative, rewarding, profitable, beneficial, payable, productive.

(ANT.) unproductive, unprofitable, unrewarding.

gainsay *(SYN.)* refute, contradict, controvert, deny, refuse, inpugn, contravene, disavow, differ.

(ANT.) maintain, aver, affirm, asseverate.

gait *(SYN.)* stride, walk, tread, step.

gala *(SYN.)* ball, party, carnival, fete, festival.

gale *(SYN.)* burst, surge, outburst.

gall *(SYN.)* nerve, audacity, impudence,

annoy, vex, anger.

gallant *(SYN.)* bold, brave, courageous, valorous, valiant, noble, polite, fearless, heroic.

gallantry *(SYN.)* valor, daring, courage, prowess, heroism, manliness, dauntlessness, graciousness, attentiveness, coquetry.

(ANT.) timidity, cowardice, cravenness, cloddishness.

gallery *(SYN.)* passageway, hall, aisle, hallway, passage, corridor.

galling *(SYN.)* vexing, irritating, annoying, distressful, irksome.

galore *(SYN.)* abounding, plentiful, profuse, rich, overflowing.

gamble *(SYN.)* game, wager, bet, hazard, risk, venture, chance.

gambol *(SYN.)* romp, dance, cavort, frolic.

game *(SYN.)* fun, contest, merriment, pastime, match, play, amusement, recreation, entertainment, competition, sport.

(ANT.) labor, hardship, work, business.

gamut *(SYN.)* extent, scope, sweep, horizon, range.

gang *(SYN.)* group, troop, band, company, horde, crew.

gangling *(SYN.)* rangy, lean, skinny, tall, lanky.

gangster *(SYN.)* crook, hoodlum, gunman, criminal.

gap *(SYN.)* cavity, chasm, pore, gulf, aperture, abyss, interval, space, hole, void, pore, break.

gape *(SYN.)* ogle, stare, gawk.

garb *(SYN.)* clothing, dress, vesture, array, attire, clothes, drapery, apparel, garments, costume.

(ANT.) nudity, nakedness.

garbage *(SYN.)* refuse, waste, trash, rubbish.

garbled *(SYN.)* twisted, confused, distorted.

gargantuan *(SYN.)* colossal, monumental, giant, large, enormous.

garments *(SYN.)* drapery, dress, garb, apparel, array, attire, clothes, raiment, clothing.

(ANT.) nakedness, nudity.

garnish *(SYN.)* decorate, embellish, trim, adorn, enrich, beautify.

(ANT.) expose, strip, debase, uncover,

defame.

garrulous *(SYN.)* chatty, glib, verbose, talkative, communicative.

(ANT.) silent, uncommunicative, laconic, reticent, taciturn.

gash *(SYN.)* lacerate, slash, pierce, cut, hew, slice.

gasp *(SYN.)* pant, puff, wheeze.

gather *(ANT.)* assemble, collect, garner, harvest, reap, deduce, judge, amass, congregate, muster, cull, glean, accumulate, convene.

(ANT.) scatter, disperse, distribute, disband, separate.

gathering *(SYN.)* meeting, crowd, throng, company, assembly.

gaudy *(SYN.)* showy, flashy, loud, bold, ostentatious.

gaunt *(ANT.)* lank, diaphanous, flimsy, gauzy, narrow, rare, scanty, meager, gossamer, emaciated, scrawny, tenuous, thin, fine, lean, skinny, spare, slim, slight, slender, diluted.

(ANT.) wide, fat, thick, broad, bulky.

gay *(SYN.)* merry, lighthearted, joyful, cheerful, sprightly, jolly, happy, joyous, gleeful, jovial, colorful, bright, glad.

(ANT.) glum, mournful, sad, depressed, sorrowful, sullen.

gaze *(SYN.)* look, stare, view, watch, examine, observe, glance, behold, discern, seem, see, survey, witness, inspect, goggle, appear.

(ANT.) hide, overlook, avert, miss.

geld *(SYN.)* neuter, alter, castrate.

gem *(SYN.)* jewel, semiprecious stone.

general *(SYN.)* ordinary, universal, usual, common, customary, regular, vague, miscellaneous.

(ANT.) definite, particular, exceptional, singular, rare, particular, precise, exact, specific.

generally *(SYN.)* ordinarily, usually, customarily, normally, mainly.

(ANT.) seldom, infrequently, rare.

generate *(SYN.)* produce, bestow, impart, concede, permit, acquiesce, cede, relent, succumb, surrender, pay, supply, grant, relent, bear, afford, submit, waive, allow, breed, accord, accede, abdicate, resign, relinquish.

(ANT.) assert, refuse, struggle, resist, dissent, oppose, deny, strive.

generation *(SYN.)* age, date, era, period, seniority, senescence, senility, time, epoch.

(ANT.) infancy, youth, childhood.

generosity *(SYN.)* magnanimity, benevolence, humanity, kindness, philanthropy, altruism, liberality.

(ANT.) selfishness, malevolence, cruelty, inhumanity, unkindness.

generous *(SYN.)* giving, liberal, unselfish, magnanimous, bountiful, munificent, charitable, big, noble.

(ANT.) greedy, stingy, selfish, covetous, mean, miserly.

genesis *(SYN.)* birth, root, creation, source, origin, beginning.

genius *(SYN.)* intellect, adept, intellectual, sagacity, proficient, creativity, ability, inspiration, faculty, originality, brain, gift.

(ANT.) dullard, stupidity, dolt, moron, ineptitude, obtuseness.

genre *(SYN.)* chaste, order, set, elegance, class, excellence, kind, caste, denomination, grade.

genteel *(SYN.)* cultured, polished, polite, refined, elegant.

(ANT.) discourteous, churlish, common.

gentle *(SYN.)* peaceful, placid, tame, serene, relaxed, docile, benign, soothing, calm, soft, mild, friendly, kindly, cultivated.

(ANT.) nasty, harsh, rough, fierce, mean, violent, savage.

genuine *(SYN.)* real, true, unaffected, authentic, sincere, bona fide, unadulterated, legitimate, actual, veritable, definite, proven.

(ANT.) false, sham, artificial, fake, counterfeit, bogus, pretended, insincere, sham.

genus *(SYN.)* kind, race, species, sort, type, variety, character.

germ *(SYN.)* pest, virus, contamination, disease, pollution, taint, infection, contagion, ailment.

germinate *(SYN.)* vegetate, pullulate, sprout, develop, grow.

gesture *(SYN.)* omen, signal, symbol, emblem, indication, note, sign, token, symptom, movement.

get *(SYN.)* obtain, receive, attain, gain, achieve, acquire, procure, earn, fetch, carry, remove, prepare, take, ready, urge, induce.

(ANT.) lose, surrender, forfeit, leave, renounce.

ghastly *(SYN.)* frightful, horrible, horrifying, frightening, grisly, hideous, dreadful.

ghost *(SYN.)* phantom, spook, apparition, specter, trace, hint, vestige, spirit.

ghoulish *(SYN.)* weird, eerie, horrifying, gruesome, sinister, scary.

giant *(SYN.)* monster, colossus, mammoth, superman, gigantic.

(ANT.) small, tiny, dwarf, runt, midget, infinitesimal.

gibe *(SYN.)* sneer, jeer, mock, scoff, boo, hoot, hiss.

(ANT.) approve.

giddy *(SYN.)* reeling, dizzy, flighty, silly, scatterbrained.

(ANT.) serious.

gift *(SYN.)* endowment, favor, gratuity, bequest, talent, charity, present, largess, donation, grant, aptitude, boon, offering, faculty, genius, benefaction.

(ANT.) purchase, loss, ineptitude, deprivation, earnings, incapacity.

gigantic *(SYN.)* huge, colossal, immense, large, vast, elephantine, gargantuan, prodigious, mammoth, monumental, enormous.

(ANT.) small, tiny, minute, diminutive, little.

giggle *(SYN.)* chuckle, jeer, laugh, roar, snicker, titter, cackle, guffaw, mock.

gild *(SYN.)* cover, coat, paint, embellish, sweeten, retouch, camouflage.

gingerly *(SYN.)* gentle, cautiously, carefully, gently.

(ANT.) roughly.

gird *(SYN.)* wrap, tie, bind, belt, encircle, surround, prepare.

(ANT.) untie.

girl *(SYN.)* female, lass, miss, maiden, damsel.

girth *(SYN.)* measure, size, width, dimensions, expanse, proportions.

gist *(SYN.)* explanation, purpose, significance, acceptation, implication, interpretation, meaning.
(ANT.) redundancy.

give *(SYN.)* bestow, contribute, grant, impart, provide, donate, confer, deliver, present, furnish, yield, develop, offer, produce, hand over, award, allot, deal out, bend, sacrifice, supply.
(ANT.) withdraw, take, retain, keep, seize.

given *(SYN.)* handed over, presented, supposed, stated, disposed, assumed, inclined.

glacier *(SYN.)* frigid, icy, iceberg.

glad *(SYN.)* happy, cheerful, gratified, delighted, joyous, merry, pleased, exulting, charmed, thrilled, satisfied, tickled, gay, bright.
(ANT.) sad, depressed, dejected, melancholy, unhappy, morose, somber, despondent.

gladness *(SYN.)* bliss, contentment, happiness, pleasure, well-being, beatitude, delight, satisfaction, blessedness.
(ANT.) sadness, sorrow, despair, misery, grief.

glade *(SYN.)* clearing.

gladiator *(SYN.)* battler, fighter, competitor, combatant, contender, contestant.

glamorous *(SYN.)* fascinating; spellbinding, alluring, charming, bewitching, entrancing, captivating, enchanting, attractive, appealing, enticing, enthralling.

glamour *(SYN.)* charm, allure, attraction, magnetism, fascination.

glance *(SYN.)* eye, gaze, survey, view, examine, inspect, discern, look, see, witness, peek, regard, skim, reflect, glimpse, behold, observe.
(ANT.) hide, miss, avert, overlook.

glare *(SYN.)* flash, dazzle, stare, glower, glow, shine, glaze, burn, brilliance, flare, blind, scowl.

glaring *(SYN.)* flagrant, obvious, blatant, prominent, dazzling.

glass *(SYN.)* cup, tumbler, goblet, pane, crystal.

glassy *(SYN.)* blank, empty, emotionless, vacant, fixed, expressionless.

glaze *(SYN.)* buff, luster, cover, wax, gloss, coat, polish, shellac.

gleam *(SYN.)* flash, glimmer, glisten, shimmer, sparkle, twinkle, glare, beam, glow, radiate, glimmering, shine, burn, reflection, blaze.

glean *(SYN.)* reap, gather, select, harvest, pick, separate, cull.

glee *(SYN.)* mirth, joy, gladness, enchantment, delight, bliss, elation, merriment.
(ANT.) depression, misery, dejection.

glen *(SYN.)* ravine, valley.

glib *(SYN.)* smooth, suave, flat, plain, polished, sleek, urbane.
(ANT.) rough, rugged, blunt, harsh, bluff.

glide *(SYN.)* sweep, sail, fly, flow, slip, coast, cruise, move easily, skim, slide.

glimmer *(SYN.)* blink, shimmer, flicker, indication, hint, clue, suggestion.

glimpse *(SYN.)* notice, glance, peek, see, impression, look, flash.

glint *(SYN.)* flash, gleam, peek, glance, glimpse, sparkle, glitter.

glisten *(SYN.)* shimmer, shine, glimmer, twinkle, glitter, glister, sparkle.

glitch *(SYN.)* mishap, snag, hitch, malfunction.

glitter *(SYN.)* glisten, glimmer, sparkle, shine, twinkle.

gloat *(SYN.)* triumph, exult, glory, rejoice, revel.

global *(SYN.)* universal, international, worldwise.

globe *(SYN.)* orb, ball, world, earth, map, universe, sphere.

gloom *(SYN.)* bleakness, despondency, misery, sadness, woe, darkness, dejection, obscurity, blackness, shadow, shade, dimness, shadows, melancholy.
(ANT.) joy, mirth, exultation, cheerfulness, light, happiness, brightness, frivolity.

gloomy *(SYN.)* despondent, dismal, glum, somber, sorrowful, sad, dejected, disconsolate, dim, dark, morose, dispirited, moody, grave, pensive.

(ANT.) happy, merry, cheerful, high-spirited, bright, sunny, joyous.

glorify *(SYN.)* enthrone, exalt, honor, revere, adore, dignify, enshrine, consecrate, praise, worship, venerate.

(ANT.) mock, dishonor, debase, abuse, degrade.

glorious *(SYN.)* exalted, high, noble, splendid, supreme, elevated, lofty, raised, majestic, famous, noted, stately, distinguished, celebrated, renowned, famed, magnificent, grand, proud, impressive, elegant, sublime.

(ANT.) ridiculous, low, base, ignoble, terrible, ordinary.

glory *(SYN.)* esteem, praise, respect, reverence, admiration, honor, dignity, worship, eminence, homage, deference.

(ANT.) dishonor, disgrace, contempt, reproach, derision.

gloss *(SYN.)* luster, shine, glow, sheen.

glossary *(SYN.)* dictionary, thesaurus, wordbook, lexicon.

glossy *(SYN.)* smooth, glistening, shiny, sleek, polished.

(ANT.) matte, dull.

glow *(SYN.)* beam, glisten, radiate, shimmer, sparkle, glare, blaze, scintillate, shine, light, gleam, burn, flare, flame, radiate, dazzle, blush, redden, heat, warmth.

glower *(SYN.)* scowl, stare, frown, glare.

(ANT.) beam, grin, smile.

glowing *(SYN.)* fiery, intense, passionate, zealous, enthusiastic, ardent, eager, fervent, impassioned, complimentary, vehement.

(ANT.) cool, indifferent, apathetic, nonchalant.

glue *(SYN.)* bind, fasten, cement, paste.

glum *(SYN.)* morose, sulky, fretful, crabbed, sullen, dismal, dour, moody.

(ANT.) joyous, merry, amiable, gay, pleasant.

glut *(SYN.)* gorge, sate, content, furnish, fill, pervade, satiate, stuff, replenish, fill up, satisfy, stock.

(ANT.) empty, exhaust, deplete, void, drain.

glutton *(SYN.)* pig, hog, greedy eater.

gluttony *(SYN.)* ravenousness, piggishness, devouring, hoggishness, insatiability, swinishness, voraciousness.

(ANT.) satisfaction, fullness.

gnarled *(SYN.)* twisted, knotted, rugged, nodular.

gnash *(SYN.)* gnaw, crunch, grind.

gnaw *(SYN.)* chew, eat, gnash, grind, erode.

go *(SYN.)* proceed, depart, flee, move, vanish, exit, walk, quit, fade, progress, travel, become, fit, agree, leave, suit, harmonize, pass, travel, function, operate.

(ANT.) stay, arrive, enter, stand, come.

goad *(SYN.)* incite, prod, drive, urge, push, shove, jab, provoke, stimulate.

goal *(SYN.)* craving, destination, desire, longing, objective, finish, end, passion, aim, object, aspiration.

gobble *(SYN.)* devour, eat fast, gorge, gulp, stuff.

goblet *(SYN.)* cup, glass.

goblin *(SYN.)* troll, elf, dwarf, spirit.

godlike *(SYN.)* holy, supernatural, heavenly, celestial, divine, transcendent.

(ANT.) profane, wicked, blasphemous, diabolical, mundane.

godly *(SYN.)* pious, religious, holy, pure, divine, spiritual, righteous, saintly.

golden *(SYN.)* shining, metallic, bright, fine, superior, nice, excellent, valuable.

(ANT.) dull, inferior.

gong *(SYN.)* chimes, bells.

good *(SYN.)* honest, sound, valid, cheerful, honorable, worthy, conscientious, moral, genuine, humane, kind, fair, useful, skillful, adequate, friendly, genial, proficient, pleasant, exemplary, admirable, virtuous, reliable, precious, benevolent, excellent, pure, agreeable, gracious, safe.

(ANT.) bad, imperfect, vicious, undesirable, unfriendly, unkind, evil.

good-by *(SYN.)* so long, farewell.

good-bye *(SYN.)* farewell.

good-hearted *(SYN.)* good, kind, thoughtful, kind-hearted, considerate.

(ANT.) evil-hearted.

good-humored *(SYN.)* pleasant, good-natured, cheerful, sunny, amiable.

(ANT.) petulant, cranky.

goodness *(SYN.)* good, honesty, integrity, virtue, righteousness.
(ANT.) sin, evil, dishonesty, corruption, badness.

goods *(SYN.)* property, belongings, holdings, possessions, merchandise, wares.

good will *(SYN.)* agreeability, harmony, willingness, readiness.

gore *(SYN.)* impale, penetrate, puncture, gouge.

gorge *(SYN.)* ravine, devour, stuff, gobble, valley, defile, pass, cram, fill.

gorgeous *(SYN.)* grand, ravishing, glorious, stunning, brilliant, divine, splendid, dazzling, beautiful, magnificent.
(ANT.) homely, ugly, squalid.

gory *(SYN.)* bloody.

gossamer *(SYN.)* dainty, fine, filmy, delicate, sheer, transparent.

gossip *(SYN.)* prate, rumor, prattle, hearsay, meddler, tattler, chatter, talk, chat, blabbermouth.

gouge *(SYN.)* scoop, dig, carve, burrow, excavate, chisel, notch.

gourmet *(SYN.)* gourmand, gastronome, connoisseur.

govern *(SYN.)* manage, oversee, reign, preside over, supervise, direct, command, sway, administer, control, regulate, determine, influence, guide, lead, head, rule.
(ANT.) assent, submit, acquiesce, obey, yield.

government *(SYN.)* control, direction, rule, command, authority.

governor *(SYN.)* controller, administrator, director, leader, manager.

gown *(SYN.)* garment, robe, frock, dress, costume, attire.

grab *(SYN.)* snatch, grip, clutch, seize, grasp, capture, pluck.

grace *(SYN.)* charm, beauty, loveliness, dignify, fairness, honor, distinguish, sympathy, attractiveness, elegance, clemency, excuse, pardon, thanks, blessing, prayer, pulchritude.
(ANT.) eyesore, homeliness, deformity, ugliness, disfigurement.

graceful *(SYN.)* elegant, fluid, natural, supple, beautiful, comely, flowing, lithe.
(ANT.) clumsy, awkward, gawky, ungainly, deformed.

gracious *(SYN.)* warm-hearted, pleasing, friendly, engaging, agreeable, kind, amiable, kindly, nice, good, courteous, polite, generous, good-natured.
(ANT.) surly, hateful, churlish, rude, disagreeable, impolite, thoughtless, discourteous, ill- natured.

grade *(SYN.)* kind, rank, elegance, denomination, sort, arrange, category, classify, rate, group, place, mark, incline, slope, excellence, caste, order.

gradual *(SYN.)* deliberate, sluggish, dawdling, laggard, slow, leisurely, moderate, easy, delaying.
(ANT.) quick, swift, fast, speedy, rapid.

graduate *(SYN.)* pass, finish, advance.

graft *(SYN.)* fraud, theft, cheating, bribery, dishonesty, transplant, corruption.

grain *(SYN.)* speck, particle, plant, bit, seed, temper, fiber, character, texture, markings, nature, tendency.

grand *(SYN.)* great, elaborate, splendid, royal, stately, noble, considerable, outstanding, distinguished, impressive, prominent, majestic, fine, dignified, large, main, principal.
(ANT.) unassuming, modest, insignificant, unimportant, humble.

grandeur *(SYN.)* resplendence, majesty, distinction, glory.

grandiose *(SYN.)* grand, lofty, magnificent, stately, noble, pompous, dignified, imposing, sublime, majestic.
(ANT.) lowly, ordinary, common, undignified, humble.

grandstand *(SYN.)* bleachers, gallery.

granite *(SYN.)* stone, rock.

grant *(SYN.)* confer, allocate, deal, divide, mete, appropriation, assign, benefaction, distribute, allowance, donate, award, mete out, deal out, consent, bestow, give, measure.
(ANT.) refuse, withhold, confiscate, keep, retain.

granular *(SYN.)* grainy, sandy, crumbly,

rough, gritty.

graph *(SYN.)* design, plan, stratagem, draw up, chart, sketch, cabal, machination, outline, plot, scheme, diagram.

graphic *(SYN.)* vivid, lifelike, significant, meaningful, pictorial, descriptive, representative.

grapple *(SYN.)* grip, seize, clutch, clasp, grasp, fight, struggle.

grasp *(SYN.)* clutch, grip, seize, apprehend, capture, snare, hold, clasp, comprehend, reach, grab, understand, grapple, possession, control, domination, command, perceive, trap.

(ANT.) release, lose, throw, liberate.

grasping *(SYN.)* possessive, greedy, selfish, acquisitive, mercenary.

(ANT.) liberal, unselfish, generous.

grate *(SYN.)* file, pulverize, grind, scrape, scratch, scrape, annoy, irritate.

grateful *(SYN.)* beholden, obliged, appreciative, thankful, indebted.

(ANT.) ungrateful, unappreciative, grudging, thankless.

gratify *(SYN.)* charm, gladden, please, satisfy.

(ANT.) frustrate.

gratifying *(SYN.)* contentment, solace, relief, comfort, ease, succor, consolation, enjoyment.

(ANT.) suffering, torment, affliction, discomfort, torture, misery.

grating *(SYN.)* harsh, rugged, severe, stringent, coarse, gruff, jarring, rigorous, strict.

(ANT.) smooth, melodious, mild, gentle, soft.

gratis *(SYN.)* complimentary, free.

gratitude *(SYN.)* gratefulness, thankfulness, appreciation.

(ANT.) ungratefulness.

gratuity *(SYN.)* tip, bonus, gift, donation.

grave *(SYN.)* sober, grim, earnest, serious, important, momentous, sedate, solemn, somber, imposing, vital, essential, staid, consequential, thoughtful.

(ANT.) light, flighty, trivial, insignificant, unimportant, trifling, merry, gay, cheery, frivolous.

gravel *(SYN.)* stones, pebbles, grain.

gravitate *(SYN.)* incline, tend, lean, approach, toward.

gravity *(SYN.)* concern, importance, pull, seriousness, movement.

(ANT.) triviality.

graze *(SYN.)* scrape, feed, rub, brush, contact, skim.

grease *(SYN.)* fat, oil, lubrication.

greasy *(SYN.)* messy, buttery, waxy, fatty.

great *(SYN.)* large, numerous, eminent, illustrious, big, gigantic, enormous, immense, vast, weighty, fine, important, countless, prominent, vital, huge, momentous, serious, famed, dignified, excellent, critical, renowned, majestic, elevated, noble, grand.

(ANT.) minute, common, menial, ordinary, diminutive, small, paltry, unknown.

greed *(SYN.)* piggishness, lust, desire, greediness, avarice, covetousness.

(ANT.) unselfishness, selflessness, generosity.

greedy *(SYN.)* selfish, devouring, ravenous, avaricious, covetous, rapacious, gluttonous, insatiable, voracious.

(ANT.) full, generous, munificent, giving, satisfied.

green *(SYN.)* inexperienced, modern, novel, recent, further, naive, fresh, natural, raw, unsophisticated, undeveloped, immature, unripe, additional, brisk, artless.

(ANT.) hackneyed, musty, decayed, faded, stagnant.

greenhorn *(SYN.)* tenderfoot, beginner, apprentice, amateur, novice.

greenhouse *(SYN.)* hothouse.

greet *(SYN.)* hail, accost, meet, address, talk to, speak to, welcome, approach.

(ANT.) pass by, avoid.

gregarious *(SYN.)* outgoing, civil, affable, communicative, hospitable, sociable.

(ANT.) inhospitable, antisocial, disagreeable, hermitic.

grief *(SYN.)* misery, sadness, tribulation, affliction, heartache, woe, trial, anguish, mourning, distress, lamentation.

(ANT.) happiness, solace, consolation, comfort, joy.

grief-stricken *(SYN.)* heartsick, ravaged, devastated, wretched, forlorn, desolate, wretched.

(ANT.) joyous, blissful, content.

grievance *(SYN.)* injury, wrong, injustice, detriment, complaint, damage, prejudice, evil, objection, protest, accusation, harm.

(ANT.) improvement, benefit, repair.

grieve *(SYN.)* lament, brood over, mourn, weep, wail, sorrow, distress, bemoan, hurt, deplore.

(ANT.) revel, carouse, celebrate, rejoice, gladden, soothe.

grieved *(SYN.)* contrite, remorseful, beggarly, mean, pitiful, shabby, vile, sorrowful, pained, hurt, sorry, contemptible, worthless.

(ANT.) splendid, delighted, cheerful, impenitent, unrepentant.

grievous *(SYN.)* gross, awful, outrageous, shameful, lamentable, regrettable.

(ANT.) agreeable, comforting, pleasurable.

grill *(SYN.)* cook, broil, question, interrogate, barbecue, grating, gridiron, cross-examine.

grim *(SYN.)* severe, harsh, strict, merciless, fierce, horrible, inflexible, adamant, ghastly, frightful, unyielding, rigid, stern.

(ANT.) pleasant, lenient, relaxed, amiable, congenial, smiling.

grimace *(SYN.)* expression, sneer, scowl, mope.

grimy *(SYN.)* unclean, grubby, soiled.

grin *(SYN.)* beam, smile, smirk.

grind *(SYN.)* mill, mash, powder, crush, crumble, pulverize, smooth, grate, sharpen, even.

grip *(SYN.)* catch, clutch, apprehend, trap, arrest, grasp, hold, bag, suitcase, lay hold of, clench, command, control, possession, domination, comprehension, seize.

(ANT.) release, liberate, lose, throw.

gripe *(SYN.)* protest, lament, complaint, grumbling.

grit *(SYN.)* rub, grind, grate, sand, gravel, pluck, courage, stamina.

groan *(SYN.)* sob, wail, howl, moan, whimper, wail, complain.

groggy *(SYN.)* dazed, dopy, stupefied, stunned, drugged, unsteady.

(ANT.) alert.

groom *(SYN.)* tend, tidy, preen, curry, spouse, consort.

groove *(SYN.)* furrow, channel, track, routine, slot, scratch.

groovy *(SYN.)* marvelous, delightful, wonderful.

grope *(SYN.)* fumble, feel around.

gross *(SYN.)* glaring, coarse, indelicate, obscene, bulky, great, total, whole, brutal, grievous, aggregate, earthy, rude, vulgar, entire, enormous, crass, rough, large.

(ANT.) appealing, delicate, refined, proper, polite, cultivated, slight, trivial, decent.

grotesque *(SYN.)* strange, weird, odd, incredible, fantastic, monstrous, absurd, freakish, bizarre, peculiar, deformed, disfigured.

grotto *(SYN.)* tunnel, cave, hole, cavern.

grouch *(SYN.)* protest, remonstrate, whine, complain, grumble, murmur, mope, mutter, repine.

(ANT.) praise, applaud, rejoice, approve.

grouchy *(SYN.)* cantankerous, grumpy, surly.

(ANT.) cheerful, contented, agreeable, pleasant.

ground *(SYN.)* foundation, presumption, surface, principle, set, underpinning, premise, base, bottom, fix, basis, soil, land, earth, root, support, establish, dirt, presupposition.

(ANT.) implication, superstructure, derivative.

groundless *(SYN.)* baseless, unfounded, unwarranted, needless.

grounds *(SYN.)* garden, lawns, dregs, foundation, leftovers, reason, sediment, cause, premise, motive.

groundwork *(SYN.)* support, bottom, base, underpinning, premise, presupposition, principle, basis.

(ANT.) trimming, implication, derivative, superstructure.

group *(SYN.)* crowd, clock, party, troupe, swarm, bunch, brook, assembly, herd,

band, mob, brood, class, throng, cluster, flock, lot, collection, pack, horde, gathering.
(ANT.) disassemble.

grouse *(SYN.)* mutter, grumble, gripe, scold, growl, complain.

grovel *(SYN.)* creep, crawl, cower, cringe, slouch, stoop, scramble.

groveling *(SYN.)* dishonorable, lowly, sordid, vile, mean, abject, despicable, ignoble, menial, servile, vulgar, ignominious.
(ANT.) lofty, noble, esteemed, exalted, righteous.

grow *(SYN.)* extend, swell, advance, develop, enlarge, germinate, mature, expand, flower, raise, become, cultivate, increase.
(ANT.) wane, shrink, atrophy, decay, diminish, contract.

growl *(SYN.)* complain, snarl, grumble, gnarl, clamor, bellow.

grown-up *(SYN.)* adult, of age, mature, big, senior.
(ANT.) little, childish, budding, junior, juvenile.

growth *(SYN.)* expansion, development, maturing, progress, elaboration, evolution.
(ANT.) degeneration, deterioration, curtailment, compression.

grub *(SYN.)* gouge, dig, scoop out, burrow, tunnel, excavate, plod.

grubby *(SYN.)* unkempt, grimy, slovenly, dirty.
(ANT.) tidy, spruce, neat, clean, well-groomed.

grudge *(SYN.)* malevolence, malice, resentment, bitterness, spite, animosity, enmity, rancor, ill will.
(ANT.) kindness, love, benevolence, affection, good will, toleration.

grudgingly *(SYN.)* reluctantly, unwillingly, involuntarily.

grueling *(SYN.)* taxing, exhausting, excruciating, trying, grinding.
(ANT.) easy, light, simple.

gruesome *(SYN.)* hideous, frightful, horrible, loathsome, horrifying, grisly.
(ANT.) agreeable, soothing, delightful, charming.

gruff *(SYN.)* scratchy, crude, incomplete,

unpolished, stormy, brusque, rude, rough, uncivil, churlish, violent, harsh, imperfect, craggy, irregular, deep, husky, approximate, tempestuous, blunt.
(ANT.) civil, courteous, polished, calm, even, sleek, smooth, finished, gentle, placid, pleasant, tranquil.

grumble *(SYN.)* protest, mutter, complain.

grumpy *(SYN.)* cranky, grouchy, surly, crabbed, fractious, pettish.
(ANT.) winsome, amiable, pleasant, cheery.

guarantee *(SYN.)* bond, pledge, token, warrant, earnest, surety, bail, commitment, promise, secure, swear, assure, sponsor, certify, warranty, insure, endorse.

guarantor *(SYN.)* voucher, sponsor, warrantor, signatory, underwriter, surety.

guaranty *(SYN.)* warranty, token, deposit, earnest, pledge, collateral, stake.

guard *(SYN.)* protect, shield, veil, cloak, conceal, disguise, envelop, preserve, hide, defend, cover, sentry, protector, shroud, curtain.
(ANT.) unveil, expose, ignore, bare, reveal, disregard, divulge.

guardian *(SYN.)* curator, keeper, protector, custodian, patron.

guess *(SYN.)* estimate, suppose, think, assume, reason, believe, reckon, speculate, notion, surmise, hypothesis, imagine.
(ANT.) know.

guest *(SYN.)* caller, client, customer, visitor, company.
(ANT.) host.

guide *(SYN.)* manage, supervise, conduct, direct, lead, steer, escort, pilot, show, squire, usher, control, influence, regulate.
(ANT.) follower, follow.

guild *(SYN.)* association, union, society.

guile *(SYN.)* deceitfulness, fraud, wiliness, trick, deceit, chicanery, cunning, deception, craftiness, sham, sneakiness, cheat.
(ANT.) sincerity, openness, honesty, truthfulness, candor, frankness.

guileless *(SYN.)* open, innocent, naive, sincere, simple, candid.
(ANT.) treacherous, plotting.

guise *(SYN.)* aspect, pretense, mien, look,

air, advent, apparition, appearance, dress, garb, coat, cover.

gulch *(SYN.)* gorge, valley, gully, ravine, canyon.

gulf *(SYN.)* ravine, cut, break, crack, chasm, canyon, abyss, cleft, separation, bay, sound, inlet.

gullible *(SYN.)* trustful, naive, innocent, unsuspecting, deceivable, unsuspicious, believing.

(ANT.) skeptical, sophisticated.

gully *(SYN.)* ditch, gorge, ravine, valley, gulch, gulf.

gulp *(SYN.)* devour, swallow, gasp, repress, choke.

gun *(SYN.)* fire, shoot, weapon, pistol, firearm, revolver.

gush *(SYN.)* pour, spurt, stream, rush out, spout, flood, flush.

gust *(SYN.)* blast, wind, outbreak, outburst, eruption.

gymnasium *(SYN.)* playground, arena, court, athletic field.

gymnastics *(SYN.)* drill, exercise, acrobatics, calisthenics.

gyp *(SYN.)* swindle, cheat, defraud.

gypsy *(SYN.)* nomad.

H

habit *(SYN.)* usage, routine, compulsion, use, wont, custom, disposition, practice, addiction.

habitation *(SYN.)* abode, domicile, lodgings, dwelling, home.

habitual *(SYN.)* general, usual, common, frequent, persistent, customary, routine, often.

(ANT.) solitary, unique, exceptional, occasional, unusual, scanty, rare.

habituated *(SYN.)* used, accustomed, adapted, acclimated, comfortable, familiarized, addicted.

hack *(SYN.)* cleave, chop, slash, hew, slice, pick, sever.

hag *(SYN.)* beldam, crone, vixen, granny, ogress, harridan, virage.

haggard *(SYN.)* drawn, debilitated, spent, gaunt, worn.

(ANT.) bright, fresh, clear-eyed, animated.

haggle *(SYN.)* dicker, bargain.

hail *(SYN.)* welcome, approach, accost, speak to, address, greet.

(ANT.) pass by, avoid.

hair-raising *(SYN.)* horrifying, exciting, alarming, thrilling, startling, frightful, scary.

hairy *(SYN.)* bearded, shaggy, hirsute, bewhiskered.

hale *(SYN.)* robust, well, wholesome, hearty, healthy, sound, strong, salubrious.

(ANT.) noxious, frail, diseased, delicate, infirm, injurious.

half-baked *(SYN.)* crude, premature, makeshift, illogical, shallow.

half-hearted *(SYN.)* uncaring, indifferent, unenthusiastic, cool.

(ANT.) eager, enthusiastic, earnest.

half-wit *(SYN.)* dope, simpleton, nitwit, dunce, idiot, fool.

hall *(SYN.)* corridor, lobby, passage, hallway, vestibule, foyer.

hallow *(SYN.)* glorify, exalt, dignify, aggrandize, consecrate, elevate, ennoble, raise, erect.

(ANT.) dishonor, humiliate, debase, degrade.

hallowed *(SYN.)* holy, sacred, beatified, blessed, divine.

hallucination *(SYN.)* fantasy, mirage, dream, vision, phantasm, appearance, aberration, illusion.

halt *(SYN.)* impede, obstruct, terminate, stop, hinder, desist, check, arrest, abstain, discontinue, hold, end, interrupt, bar.

(ANT.) start, begin, proceed, speed, beginning, promote.

halting *(SYN.)* imperfect, awkward, stuttering, faltering, hobbling, doubtful, limping, wavering.

(ANT.) decisive, confident, smooth, graceful, facile.

hammer *(SYN.)* beat, bang, whack, pound, batter, drive, tap, cudgel.

hamper *(SYN.)* prevent, impede, thwart, restrain, hinder, obstruct.

(ANT.) *help, assist, expedite, encourage, facilitate.*

hamstrung *(SYN.)* disabled, helpless, paralyzed.

hand *(SYN.)* assistant, helper, support, aid, laborer.

handicap *(SYN.)* retribution, penalty, disadvantage, forfeiture, hindrance, chastisement.

(ANT.) *reward, pardon, compensation, remuneration.*

handle *(SYN.)* hold, touch, finger, clutch, grip, manipulate, feel, grasp, control, oversee, direct, treat, steer, supervise, regulate.

hand out *(SYN.)* disburse, distribute, deal, mete, circulate.

hand over *(SYN.)* release, surrender, deliver, yield, present.

handsome *(SYN.)* lovely, pretty, fair, comely, beautiful, charming, elegant, good-looking, generous.

(ANT.) *repulsive, ugly, unattractive, stingy, small, mean, petty, meager, homely, foul, hideous.*

handy *(SYN.)* suitable, adapted, favorable, fitting, near, ready, close, nearby, clever, helpful, useful, timely, accessible.

(ANT.) *inopportune, troublesome, awkward, inconvenient.*

hang *(SYN.)* drape, hover, dangle, suspend, kill, sag, execute, lynch.

hanker *(SYN.)* wish, yearn, long, desire, pine, thirst, covet.

haphazard *(SYN.)* aimless, random, purposeless, casual, indiscriminate, accidental.

(ANT.) *determined, planned, designed, deliberate.*

hapless *(SYN.)* unfortunate, ill-fated, jinxed, luckless, wretched.

happen *(SYN.)* occur, take place, bechance, betide, transpire, come to pass, chance, befall.

happening *(SYN.)* episode, event, scene, incident, affair, experience.

happiness *(SYN.)* pleasure, gladness, delight, beatitude, bliss, contentment, satisfaction, joy, joyousness, blessedness, joyfulness, felicity, elation, well-being.

(ANT.) *sadness, sorrow, despair, misery, grief.*

happy *(SYN.)* gay, joyous, cheerful, fortunate, glad, merry, contented, satisfied, lucky, blessed, pleased, opportune, delighted.

(ANT.) *gloomy, morose, sad, sorrowful, miserable, depressed, blue.*

harangue *(SYN.)* oration, diatribe, lecture, tirade, exhortation.

harass *(SYN.)* badger, irritate, molest, pester, taunt, torment, provoke, tantalize, worry, aggravate, annoy, nag, plague, vex.

(ANT.) *please, soothe, comfort, delight, gratify.*

harbinger *(SYN.)* sign, messenger, proclaim, forerunner, herald.

harbor *(SYN.)* haven, port, anchorage, cherish, entertain, protect, shelter.

hard *(SYN.)* difficult, burdensome, arduous, rigid, puzzling, cruel, strict, unfeeling, severe, stern, impenetrable, compact, tough, solid, onerous, rigorous, firm, intricate, harsh, perplexing.

(ANT.) *fluid, brittle, effortless, gentle, tender, easy, simple, plastic, soft, lenient, flabby, elastic.*

hard-boiled *(SYN.)* unsympathetic, tough, harsh, unsentimental.

harden *(SYN.)* petrify, solidify.

(ANT.) *loose, soften.*

hardly *(SYN.)* barely, scarcely.

hardship *(SYN.)* ordeal, test, effort, affliction, misfortune, trouble, experiment, proof, essay, misery, examination, difficulty.

(ANT.) *consolation, alleviation.*

hardy *(SYN.)* sturdy, strong, tough.

(ANT.) *frail, feeble, weak, fragile.*

harm *(SYN.)* hurt, mischief, misfortune, mishap, damage, wickedness, cripple, injury, evil, detriment, ill, infliction, wrong.

(ANT.) *favor, kindness, benefit.*

harmful *(SYN.)* damaging, injurious, mischievous, detrimental, deleterious.

(ANT.) *helpful, salutary, profitable, advantageous, beneficial.*

harmless *(SYN.)* protected, secure, snag, dependable, certain, painless, innocent, trustworthy.
(ANT.) perilous, hazardous, insecure, dangerous, unsafe.

harmonious *(SYN.)* tuneful, melodious, congenial, amicable.
(ANT.) dissonant, discordant, disagreeable.

harmony *(SYN.)* unison, bargain, contract, stipulation, pact, agreement, accordance, concord, accord, understanding, unity.
(ANT.) discord, dissension, difference, variance, disagreement.

harness *(SYN.)* control, yoke.

harry *(SYN.)* vex, pester, harass, bother, plague.

harsh *(SYN.)* jarring, gruff, rugged, severe, stringent, blunt, grating, unpleasant, tough, stern, strict, unkind, rigorous, cruel, coarse.
(ANT.) smooth, soft, gentle, melodious, soothing, easy, mild.

harvest *(SYN.)* reap, gather, produce, yield, crop, gain, acquire, fruit, result, reaping, product, proceeds, glean, garner.
(ANT.) plant, squander, lose, sow.

haste *(SYN.)* speed, hurry, rush, rapidity, flurry, scramble.
(ANT.) sloth, sluggishness.

hasten *(SYN.)* hurry, sprint, quicken, rush, precipitate, accelerate, scurry, run, scamper, dispatch, press, urge, dash, expedite, speed.
(ANT.) retard, tarry, detain, linger, dawdle, delay, hinder.

hasty *(SYN.)* quick, swift, irascible, lively, nimble, brisk, active, speedy, impatient, sharp, fast, rapid.
(ANT.) slow, dull, sluggish.

hat *(SYN.)* helmet, bonnet.

hatch *(SYN.)* breed, incubate, brood.

hate *(SYN.)* loathe, detest, despise, disfavor, hatred, abhorrence, abominate, abhor, dislike.
(ANT.) love, cherish, approve, admire, like.

hateful *(SYN.)* loathsome, detestable, offensive.
(ANT.) likable, loving, admirable.

hatred *(SYN.)* detestation, dislike, malevolence, enmity, rancor, ill will, loathing,

hate, hostility, abhorrence, aversion, animosity.
(ANT.) friendship, love, affection, attraction.

haughty *(SYN.)* proud, stately, vainglorious, arrogant, disdainful, overbearing, supercilious, vain.
(ANT.) meek, ashamed, lowly, humble.

haul *(SYN.)* draw, pull, drag, tow.

have *(SYN.)* own, possess, seize, hold, control, occupy, acquire, undergo, maintain, experience, receive, gain, affect, include, contain, get, take, obtain.
(ANT.) surrender, abandon, renounce, lose.

havoc *(SYN.)* devastation, ruin, destruction.

hazard *(SYN.)* peril, chance, dare, risk, offer, conjecture, jeopardy, danger.
(ANT.) safety, defense, protection, immunity.

hazardous *(SYN.)* perilous, precarious, threatening, unsafe, dangerous, critical, menacing, risky.
(ANT.) protected, secure, safe.

hazy *(SYN.)* uncertain, unclear, ambiguous, obscure, undetermined, vague, unsettled, indefinite.
(ANT.) specific, clear, lucid, precise, explicit.

head *(SYN.)* leader, summit, top, culmination, director, chief, master, commander, supervisor, start, source, crest, beginning, crisis.
(ANT.) foot, base, bottom, follower, subordinate, underling.

headstrong *(SYN.)* obstinate, stubborn, willful.
(ANT.) easygoing, amenable.

headway *(SYN.)* movement, progress.

heady *(SYN.)* thrilling, intoxicating, exciting, electrifying.

heal *(SYN.)* restore, cure.

healthy *(SYN.)* wholesome, hale, robust, sound, well, vigorous, strong, hearty, healthful, hygienic, salubrious, salutary.
(ANT.) noxious, diseased, unhealthy, delicate, frail, infirm, injurious.

heap *(SYN.)* collection, mound, increase,

store, stack, pile, gather, accumulate, a-mass, accrue, accumulation, collect.
(ANT.) dissipate, scatter, waste, diminish, disperse.

hear *(SYN.)* heed, listen, detect, harken, perceive, regard.

heart *(SYN.)* middle, center, sympathy, nucleus, midpoint, sentiment, core, feeling, midst.
(ANT.) outskirts, periphery, border, rim, boundary.

heartache *(SYN.)* anguish, mourning, sadness, sorrow, affliction, distress, grief, lamentation, tribulation.
(ANT.) happiness, joy, solace, comfort, consolation.

heartbroken *(SYN.)* distressed, forlorn, mean, paltry, worthless, contemptible, wretched, disconsolate, downhearted, comfortless, low.
(ANT.) noble, fortunate, contented, significant.

hearten *(SYN.)* encourage, favor, impel, urge, promote, sanction, animate, cheer, exhilarate, cheer.
(ANT.) deter, dissuade, deject, discourage, dispirit.

heartless *(SYN.)* mean, cruel, ruthless, hardhearted, pitiless.
(ANT.) sympathetic, kind.

heart-rending *(SYN.)* heart-breaking, depressing, agonizing.

hearty *(SYN.)* warm, earnest, ardent, cordial, sincere, gracious, sociable.
(ANT.) taciturn, aloof, cool, reserved.

heat *(SYN.)* hotness, warmth, temperature, passion, ardor, zeal, inflame, cook, excitement, warm.
(ANT.) cool, chill, coolness, freeze, coldness, chilliness, iciness, cold.

heated *(SYN.)* vehement, fiery, intense, passionate.

heave *(SYN.)* boost, hoist, raise.

heaven *(SYN.)* empyrean, paradise.

heavenly *(SYN.)* superhuman, god-like, blissful, saintly, holy, divine, celestial, angelic, blessed.
*(ANT.) wicked, mundane, profane, blas-*phemous, diabolical.

heavy *(SYN.)* weighty, massive, gloomy, serious, ponderous, cumbersome, trying, burdensome, harsh, grave, intense, dull, grievous, concentrated, severe, oppressive, sluggish.
(ANT.) brisk, light, animated.

heckle *(SYN.)* torment, harass, tease, hector, harry.

heed *(SYN.)* care, alertness, circumspection, mindfulness, consider, watchfulness, reflection, study, attention, notice, regard, obey, ponder, respect, meditate, mind, observe, deliberate, examine, contemplate, weigh, esteem.
(ANT.) negligence, oversight, overlook, neglect, ignore, disregard, indifference, omission.

heedless *(SYN.)* sightless, headlong, rash, unmindful, deaf, unseeing, oblivious, ignorant, inattentive, disregardful, blind.
(ANT.) perceiving, sensible, aware, calculated, discerning.

height *(SYN.)* zenith, peak, summit, tallness, mountain, acme, apex, elevation, altitude, prominence, maximum, pinnacle, culmination.
(ANT.) base, depth, anticlimax.

heighten *(SYN.)* increase, magnify, annoy, chafe, intensify, amplify, aggravate, provoke, irritate, concentrate, nettle.
(ANT.) soothe, mitigate, palliate, soften, appease.

heinous *(SYN.)* abominable, grievous, atrocious.

hello *(SYN.)* greeting, good evening, good afternoon, good morning.
(ANT.) farewell, good-bye, so long.

help *(SYN.)* assist, support, promote, relieve, abet, succor, back, uphold, further, remedy, encourage, aid, facilitate, mitigate.
(ANT.) afflict, thwart, resist, hinder, impede.

helper *(SYN.)* aide, assistant, supporter.

helpful *(SYN.)* beneficial, serviceable, wholesome, useful, profitable, advantageous, good, salutary.
(ANT.) harmful, injurious, useless, worth-

less, destructive, deleterious, detrimental.

helpfulness *(SYN.)* assistance, cooperation, usefulness, serviceability, kindness, neighborliness, willingness, collaboration, supportiveness, readiness.

(ANT.) antagonism, hostility, opposition.

helpless *(SYN.)* weak, feeble, dependent, disabled, inept, incapable, incompetent.

(ANT.) resourceful, competent, enterprising.

helplessness *(SYN.)* impotence, feebleness, weakness, incapacity, ineptitude, shiftless, awkwardness.

(ANT.) power, strength, might, potency.

helter-skelter *(SYN.)* haphazardly, chaotically, irregularly.

hem *(SYN.)* bottom, border, edge, rim, margin, pale, verge, flounce, boundary, fringe, brim, hedge, frame.

hem in *(SYN.)* enclose, shut in, confine, restrict, limit.

hence *(SYN.)* consequently, thence, therefore, so, accordingly.

herald *(SYN.)* harbinger, crier, envoy, forerunner, precursor, augury, forecast.

herculean *(SYN.)* demanding, heroic, titanic, mighty, prodigious, laborious, arduous, overwhelming, backbreaking.

herd *(SYN.)* group, pack, drove, crowd, flock, gather.

heretic *(SYN.)* nonconformist, sectarian, un-believer, sectary, schismatic, apostate, dis-senter.

heritage *(SYN.)* birthright, legacy, patrimony, inheritance.

hermit *(SYN.)* recluse, anchorite, eremite.

hero *(SYN.)* paladin, champion, idol.

heroic *(SYN.)* bold, courageous, fearless, gallant, valiant, valorous, brave, chivalrous, adventurous, dauntless, intrepid, magnanimous.

(ANT.) fearful, weak, cringing, timid, cowardly.

heroism *(SYN.)* valor, bravery, gallant, dauntless, bold, courageous, fearless.

hesitant *(SYN.)* reluctant, unwilling, disinclined, loath, slow, averse.

(ANT.) willing, inclined, eager, ready,

disposed.

hesitate *(SYN.)* falter, waver, pause, doubt, demur, delay, vacillate, wait, stammer, stutter, scruple.

(ANT.) proceed, resolve, continue, decide, persevere.

hesitation *(SYN.)* distrust, scruple, suspense, uncertainty, unbelief, ambiguity, doubt, incredulity, skepticism.

(ANT.) determination, belief, certainty, faith, conviction.

hidden *(SYN.)* undeveloped, unseen, dormant, concealed, quiescent, latent, inactive.

(ANT.) visible, explicit, conspicuous, evident.

hide *(SYN.)* disguise, mask, suppress, withhold, veil, cloak, conceal, screen, camouflage, shroud, pelt, skin, leather, cover.

(ANT.) reveal, show, expose, disclose, uncover, divulge.

hideous *(SYN.)* frightful, ugly, shocking, frightening, horrible, terrible, horrifying, terrifying, grisly, gross.

(ANT.) lovely, beautiful, beauteous.

high *(SYN.)* tall, eminent, exalted, elevated, high-pitched, sharp, lofty, proud, shrill, raised, strident, prominent, grave, important, powerful, expensive, dear, high-priced, costly, serious, extreme, towering.

(ANT.) low, mean, tiny, stunted, short, base, lowly, deep, insignificant, unimportant, inexpensive, reasonable, trivial, petty, small.

highly *(SYN.)* extremely, very, extraordinarily, exceedingly.

high-minded *(SYN.)* lofty, noble, honorable.

(ANT.) dishonorable, base.

high-priced *(SYN.)* dear, expensive, costly.

(ANT.) economical, cheap.

high-strung *(SYN.)* nervous, tense, intense.

(ANT.) calm.

highway *(SYN.)* parkway, speedway, turnpike, superhighway, freeway.

hilarious *(SYN.)* funny, side-splitting, hysterical.

(ANT.) depressing, sad.

hinder *(SYN.)* hamper, impede, block, retard, stop, resist, thwart, obstruct, check, prevent, interrupt, delay, slow, restrain.
(ANT.) promote, further, assist, expedite, advance, facilitate.

hindrance *(SYN.)* interruption, delay, interference, obstruction, obstacle, barrier.

hinge *(SYN.)* rely, depend, pivot.

hint *(SYN.)* reminder, allusion, suggestion, clue, tip, taste, whisper, implication, intimate, suspicion, mention, insinuation.
(ANT.) declaration, affirmation, statement.

hire *(SYN.)* employ, occupy, devote, apply, enlist, lease, rent, charter, rental, busy, engage, utilize, retain, let.
(ANT.) reject, banish, discard, fire, dismiss, discharge.

history *(SYN.)* narration, relation, computation, record, account, chronicle, detail, description, narrative, annal, tale, recital.
(ANT.) confusion, misrepresentation, distortion, caricature.

hit *(SYN.)* knock, pound, strike, hurt, pummel, beat, come upon, find, discover, blow, smite.

hitch *(SYN.)* tether, fasten, harness, interruption, hindrance, interference.

hoard *(SYN.)* amass, increase, accumulate, gather, save, secret, store, cache, store, accrue, heap.
(ANT.) dissipate, scatter, waste, diminish, squander, spend, disperse.

hoarse *(SYN.)* deep, rough, husky, raucous, grating, harsh.
(ANT.) clear.

hoax *(SYN.)* ploy, ruse, wile, device, cheat, deception, antic, imposture, stratagem, stunt, guile, fraud.
(ANT.) openness, sincerity, candor, exposure, honesty.

hobbling *(SYN.)* deformed, crippled, halt, lame, unconvincing, unsatisfactory, defective, feeble, disabled maimed, weak.
(ANT.) robust, vigorous, agile, sound.

hobby *(SYN.)* diversion, pastime, avocation.
(ANT.) vocation, profession.

hobo *(SYN.)* derelict, vagrant, vagabond, tramp.

hoist *(SYN.)* heave, lift, elevate, raise, crane, elevator, derrick.

hold *(SYN.)* grasp, occupy, possess, curb, contain, stow, carry, adhere, have, clutch, keep, maintain, clasp, grip, retain, detain, accommodate, restrain, observe, conduct, check, support.
(ANT.) vacate, relinquish, surrender, abandon.

holdup *(SYN.)* heist, robbery, stickup, delay, interruption, slowdown.

hole *(SYN.)* cavity, void, pore, opening, abyss, chasm, gulf, aperture, tear, pit, burrow, lair, den, gap.

hollow *(SYN.)* unfilled, vacant, vain, meaningless, flimsy, false, hole, cavity, depression, hypocritical, depressed, empty, insincere.
(ANT.) sound, solid, genuine, sincere, full.

holocaust *(SYN.)* fire, burning, extermination, butchery, disaster, massacre.

holy *(SYN.)* devout, divine, blessed, consecrated, sacred, spiritual, pious, sainted, religious, saintly, hallowed.
(ANT.) worldly, sacrilegious, unconsecrated, evil, profane, secular.

homage *(SYN.)* reverence, honor, respect.

home *(SYN.)* dwelling, abode, residence, seat, quarters, hearth, domicile, family, house, habitat.

homely *(SYN.)* uncommonly, disagreeable, ill-natured, ugly, vicious, plain, hideous, unattractive, deformed, surly, repellent, spiteful.
(ANT.) fair, handsome, pretty, attractive, comely, beautiful.

homesick *(SYN.)* lonely, nostalgic.

honest *(SYN.)* sincere, trustworthy, truthful, fair, ingenuous, candid, conscientious, moral, upright, open, frank, forthright, honorable, straightfoward.
(ANT.) fraudulent, tricky, deceitful, dishonest, lying.

honesty *(SYN.)* frankness, openness, fairness, sincerity, trustworthiness, justice, candor, honor, integrity, responsibility, uprightness.
(ANT.) deceit, dishonesty, trickery, fraud,

cheating.

honor *(SYN.)* esteem, praise, worship, admiration, homage, glory, respect, admire, heed, dignity, revere, value, deference, venerate, reverence, consider, distinction, character, principle, uprightness, honesty, adoration.

(ANT.) scorn, dishonor, despise, neglect, abuse, shame, reproach, disdain, contempt, derision, disgrace.

honorable *(SYN.)* fair, noble, creditable, proper, reputable, honest, admirable, true, trusty, eminent, respectable, esteemed, just, famed, illustrious, noble, virtuous, upright.

(ANT.) infamous, disgraceful, shameful, dishonorable, ignominious.

honorary*(SYN.)* gratuitous, complimentary.

hoodlum *(SYN.)* crook, gangster, criminal, hooligan, mobster.

hop *(SYN.)* jump, leap.

hope *(SYN.)* expectation, faith, optimism, anticipation, expectancy, confidence, desire, trust.

(ANT.) pessimism, despair, despondency.

hopeful *(SYN.)* optimistic, confident.

(ANT.) despairing, hopeless.

hopeless *(SYN.)* desperate, despairing, forlorn, fatal, incurable, disastrous.

(ANT.) promising, hopeful.

hopelessness*(SYN.)* gloom, discouragement, depression, pessimism, despondency.

(ANT.) hope, optimism, confidence, elation.

horde *(SYN.)* host, masses, press, rabble, swarm, throng, bevy, crush, mob, multitude, crowd, populace.

horizontal *(SYN.)* even, level, plane, flat, straight, sideways.

(ANT.) upright, vertical.

horrendous *(SYN.)* awful, horrifying, terrible, dreadful, horrid, ghastly.

(ANT.) splendid, wonderful.

horrible *(SYN.)* awful, dire, ghastly, horrid, terrible, repulsive, frightful, appalling, horrifying, dreadful, ghastly, fearful.

(ANT.) enjoyable, enchanting, beautiful, lovely, fascinating.

horrid *(SYN.)* repulsive, terrible, appalling, dire, awful, frightful, fearful, shocking,

horrible, horrifying, horrid, ghastly, revolting, hideous.

(ANT.) fascinating, enchanting, enjoyable, lovely, beautiful.

horror *(SYN.)* dread, awe, hatred, loathing, foreboding, alarm, apprehension, aversion, terror.

(ANT.) courage, boldness, assurance, confidence.

horseplay *(SYN.)* tomfoolery, clowning, shenanigans.

hospital *(SYN.)* infirmary, clinic, sanatorium, rest home, sanitarium.

hospitality *(SYN.)* warmth, liberality, generosity, graciousness, welcome.

hostile *(SYN.)* unfriendly, opposed, antagonistic, inimical, adverse, warlike.

(ANT.) friendly, favorable, amicable, cordial.

hostility *(SYN.)* grudge, hatred, rancor, spite, bitterness, enmity, malevolence.

(ANT.) love, friendliness, good will.

hot *(SYN.)* scorching, fervent, hot-blooded, passionate, peppery, ardent, burning, fiery, impetuous, scalding, heated, sizzling, blazing, frying, roasting, warm, intense, torrid, pungent.

(ANT.) indifferent, apathetic, impassive, passionless, bland, frigid, cold, freezing, cool, phlegmatic.

hot air *(SYN.)* bombast, blather, jabber, gabble.

hotbed *(SYN.)* sink, nest, well, den, nursery, cradle, source, incubator, seedbed.

hot-blooded *(SYN.)* passionate, ardent, excitable, wild, fervent, fiery, impetuous, rash, brash, intense, impulsive.

(ANT.) stolid, impassive, cold, staid.

hotel *(SYN.)* hostel, motel, inn, hostelry.

hotheaded *(SYN.)* rash, touchy, reckless, unruly.

(ANT.) levelheaded, coolheaded, calm.

hound*(SYN.)* harry, pursue, pester, harass.

hourly *(SYN.)* frequently, steadily, constantly, unfailingly, periodically, perpetually, ceaselessly, continually, incessantly.

(ANT.) occasionally, seldom.

house *(SYN.)* building, residence, abode, dwelling.

housebreaker *(SYN.)* robber, thief, prowler, cracksman, burglar.

household *(SYN.)* manage, family, home.

householder *(SYN.)* homeowner, occupant.

housing *(SYN.)* lodgings, shelter, dwelling, lodgment, case, casing, quarters, domicile, enclosure, console, bracket.

hovel *(SYN.)* cabin, hut, sty, shack, hole, shed.

hover *(SYN.)* hang, drift, poise, stand by, linger, impend, waver, hand around.

however *(SYN.)* notwithstanding, still, nevertheless, but, yet.

howl *(SYN.)* bellow, yowl, wail, yell, cry.

hub *(SYN.)* pivot, center, core, heart, axis, basis, focus, nucleus.

hubbub *(SYN.)* uproar, tumult, commotion, clamor, bustle, turmoil, racket, confusion. *(ANT.)* peacefulness, stillness, silence, quiet, quiescence.

huckster *(SYN.)* peddler, adman, hawker, salesman, pitchman.

hue *(SYN.)* pigment, tint, shade, dye, complexion, paint, stain, color, tone, tincture. *(ANT.)* transparency, achromatism, paleness.

huffy *(SYN.)* sensitive, vulnerable, testy, offended, thin-skinned, touchy, irascible, cross, offended. *(ANT.)* tough, placid, stolid, impassive.

hug *(SYN.)* embrace, coddle, caress, kiss, pet, press, clasp, fondle, cuddle. *(ANT.)* tease, vex, spurn, buffet, annoy.

huge *(SYN.)* great, immense, vast, ample, big, capacious, extensive, gigantic, enormous, tremendous, large, wide, colossal. *(ANT.)* short, small, mean, little, tiny.

hulking *(SYN.)* massive, awkward, bulky, ponderous, unwieldy, overgrown, lumpish, oafish.

hullabaloo *(SYN.)* clamor, uproar, din, racket, tumult, hubbub, commotion, noise. *(ANT.)* calm, peace, silence.

hum *(SYN.)* whir, buzz, whizz, purr, croon, murmur, intone.

human *(SYN.)* manlike, hominid, mortal, fleshly, individual, person, tellurian.

humane *(SYN.)* lenient, tender, tolerant, compassionate, clement, forgiving, kind, forbearing, thoughtful, gentle, merciful. *(ANT.)* remorseless, cruel, heartless, pitiless, unfeeling, brutal.

humanist *(SYN.)* scholar, sage, classicist, savant.

humanitarian *(SYN.)* benefactor, philanthropist.

humanitarianism *(SYN.)* good will, beneficence, philanthropy, welfarism, humanism.

humanity *(SYN.)* generosity, magnanimity, tenderness, altruism, beneficence, kindness, charity. *(ANT.)* selfishness, unkindness, cruelty, inhumanity.

humble *(SYN.)* modest, crush, mortify, simple, shame, subdue, meek, abase, break, plain, submissive, compliant, unpretentious, unassuming, abash, lowly, polite, courteous, unpretending. *(ANT.)* praise, arrogant, exalt, illustrious, boastful, honor, elevate.

humbly *(SYN.)* deferentially, meekly, respectfully, unassumingly, diffidently, modestly, subserviently, submissively. *(ANT.)* insolently, proudly, grandly, arrogantly.

humbug *(SYN.)* drivel, gammon, bosh, nonsense, rubbish, inanity.

humdrum *(SYN.)* commonplace, prosy, mundane, insipid, tedious, routine, dull, boring. *(ANT.)* interesting, stimulating, arresting, striking, exciting.

humid *(SYN.)* moist, damp, misty, muggy, wet, watery, vaporous. *(ANT.)* parched, dry, desiccated.

humiliate *(SYN.)* corrupt, defile, depress, pervert, abase, degrade, disgrace, adulterate, humble, shame, lower, deprave, depress. *(ANT.)* restore, raise, enhance, improve, vitalize.

humiliation *(SYN.)* chagrin, dishonor, ignominy, scandal, abasement, mortification, odium, disgrace, shame.

(ANT.) honor, praise, glory, dignity, renown.

humor *(SYN.)* jocularity, wit, temperament, sarcasm, irony, amusement, facetiousness, joke, disposition, fun, clowning, satire.

(ANT.) sorrow, gravity, seriousness.

humorous *(SYN.)* funny, ludicrous, witty, curious, queer, amusing, comical, farcical, laughable, droll.

(ANT.) sober, unfunny, melancholy, serious, sad, solemn.

hunger *(SYN.)* desire, longing, inclination, stomach, zest, craving.

(ANT.) satiety, repugnance, disgust, distaste, renunciation.

hungry *(SYN.)* famished, thirsting, craving, avid, starved, ravenous.

(ANT.) gorged, satisfied, full, sated.

hunt *(SYN.)* pursuit, investigation, examination, inquiry, pursue, track, chase, search, quest, seek, probe, scour, exploration.

(ANT.) cession, resignation, abandonment.

hurl *(SYN.)* throw, cast, propel, fling, toss, pitch, thrust.

(ANT.) pull, draw, haul, hold.

hurried *(SYN.)* rushed, hasty, swift, headlong, impulsive, superficial.

(ANT.) deliberate, slow, dilatory, thorough, prolonged.

hurry *(SYN.)* quicken, speed, ado, rush, accelerate, run, hasten, race, urge, bustle, expedite.

(ANT.) retard, tarry, hinder, linger, dawdle, delay, hinder.

hurt *(SYN.)* damage, harm, grievance, detriment, pain, injustice, injure, abuse, distress, disfigured, mar, afflict, spoil, affront, insult, wound, dishonor, wrong.

(ANT.) improvement, repair, compliment, help, praise, benefit.

hurtful *(SYN.)* harmful, damaging, maleficent, injurious, baleful.

(ANT.) remedial, beneficial, good, salutary.

hurtle *(SYN.)* charge, collide, rush, crash, lunge, bump.

hush *(SYN.)* quiet, silence, still.

husk *(SYN.)* shell, hull, pod, skin, covering, crust, bark.

husky *(SYN.)* strong, brawny, strapping, muscular.

(ANT.) feeble, weak.

hustle *(SYN.)* hasten, run, race, hurry, speed.

hutch *(SYN.)* box, chest, locker, trunk, coffer, bin.

hybrid *(SYN.)* mule, mixture, crossbreed, cross, mongrel, mutt, composite.

hygiene *(SYN.)* cleanliness, sanitation, health, hygienics.

hygienic *(SYN.)* robust, strong, well, wholesome, healthy, sound.

(ANT.) frail, noxious, infirm, delicate, diseased, injurious.

hyperbole *(SYN.)* puffery, exaggeration, embellishment, overstatement, ballyhoo, amplification, magnification.

hypercritical *(SYN.)* faultfinding, captious, censorious, finicky, exacting, carping, querulous, nagging, finical, hairsplitting.

(ANT.) lax, easygoing, indulgent, lenient, tolerant.

hypnotic *(SYN.)* soothing, opiate, sedative, soporific, entrancing, arresting, charming, engaging.

hypnotize *(SYN.)* entrance, dazzle, mesmerize, fascinate, spellbind.

hypocrisy *(SYN.)* pretense, deceit, dissembling, fakery, feigning, pharisaism, cant, dissimulation.

(ANT.) openness, candor, truth, directness, honesty, frankness.

hypocrite *(SYN.)* cheat, deceiver, fake, pretender, fraud, charlatan.

hypocritical *(SYN.)* dissembling, two-faced, insincere, dishonest, duplicitous, deceitful, phony.

(ANT.) true, genuine, honest.

hypothesis *(SYN.)* law, theory, supposition, conjecture.

(ANT.) proof, fact, certainty.

hypothetical *(SYN.)* conjectural, speculative, theoretical.

(ANT.) actual.

I

idea *(SYN.)* conception, image, opinion,

sentiment, concept, notion, thought, impression.

(ANT.) thing, matter, entity, object, substance.

ideal *(SYN.)* imaginary, supreme, unreal, visionary, perfect, faultless, fancied, exemplary, utopian.

(ANT.) imperfect, actual, material, real, faulty.

idealistic *(SYN.)* extravagant, dreamy, fantastic, fanciful, ideal, maudlin, imaginative, mawkish, sentimental, poetic, picturesque.

(ANT.) practical, literal, factual, prosaic.

identify *(ANT.)* recollect, apprehend, perceive, remember, confess, acknowledge, name, describe, classify.

(ANT.) ignore, forget, overlook, renounce, disown, repudiate.

identity *(SYN.)* uniqueness, personality, character, individuality.

ideology *(SYN.)* credo, principles, belief.

idiom *(SYN.)* language, speech, vernacular, lingo, dialect, jargon, slang, tongue.

(ANT.) babble, gibberish, drivel, nonsense.

idiot *(SYN.)* buffoon, harlequin, dolt, jester, dunce, blockhead, imbecile, simpleton, oaf, moron.

(ANT.) philosopher, genius, scholar, sage.

idiotic *(SYN.)* asinine, absurd, brainless, irrational, crazy, nonsensical, senseless, preposterous, silly, ridiculous, simple, stupid, foolish, inane, moronic, half-witted, simpleminded, dimwitted.

(ANT.) prudent, wise, sagacious, judicious, sane, intelligent, bright, brilliant, smart.

idle *(SYN.)* unemployed, dormant, lazy, inactive, unoccupied, indolent, slothful, inert, unused.

(ANT.) occupied, working, employed, busy, active, industrious, engaged.

idol *(SYN.)* unoccupied, unused, inactive, unemployed.

idolize *(SYN.)* revere, worship, adore.

(ANT.) despise.

ignoble *(SYN.)* dishonorable, ignominious, lowly, menial vile, sordid, vulgar, abject, base, despicable, groveling, mean, vile.

(ANT.) righteous, lofty, honored, esteemed, noble, exalted.

ignominious *(SYN.)* contemptible, abject, despicable, groveling, dishonorable, ignoble, lowly, low, menial, mean, sordid, vulgar, vile.

(ANT.) lofty, noble, esteemed, righteous, exalted.

ignorant *(SYN.)* uneducated, untaught, uncultured, illiterate, uninformed, unlearned, unlettered, untrained, unaware.

(ANT.) cultured, literate, educated, erudite, informed, cultivated, schooled, learned, lettered.

ignore *(SYN.)* omit, slight, disregard, overlook, neglect, skip.

(ANT.) notice, regard, include.

ill *(SYN.)* diseased, ailing, indisposed, morbid, infirm, unwell, unhealthy, sick, unsound.

(ANT.) robust, strong, healthy, well, sound, fit.

ill-use *(SYN.)* defame, revile, vilify, misemploy, disparage, abuse, asperse, misapply, misuse.

(ANT.) protect, cherish, respect, honor, praise.

ill-advised *(SYN.)* injudicious, ill-considered, imprudent.

illegal *(SYN.)* prohibited, unlawful, criminal, illicit, outlawed.

(ANT.) permitted, lawful, honest, legal, legitimate.

illiberal *(SYN.)* fanatical, bigoted, narrowminded, intolerant, dogmatic, prejudiced.

(ANT.) progressive, liberal radical.

illicit *(SYN.)* illegitimate, criminal, outlawed, unlawful, prohibited, illegal, unauthorized.

(ANT.) legal, honest, permitted, lawful, licit.

ill-natured *(SYN.)* crabby, cranky, grouchy, cross, irascible.

illness *(SYN.)* complaint, infirmity, ailment, disorder, sickness.

(ANT.) healthiness, health, soundness, vigor.

illogical *(SYN.)* absurd, irrational, preposterous.

ill-tempered *(SYN.)* crabby, cranky, cross, grouchy.

illuminate *(SYN.)* enlighten, clarify, irradiate, illustrate, light, lighten, explain, interpret, elucidate, brighten, illumine.

(ANT.) obscure, confuse, darken, obfuscate, shadow, complicate.

illusion *(SYN.)* hallucination, vision, phantom, delusion, fantasy.

(ANT.) actuality, reality.

illusive *(SYN.)* fallacious, delusive, false, specious, misleading, deceptive, deceitful, delusory.

(ANT.) real, truthful, authentic, genuine, honest.

illustrate *(SYN.)* decorate, illuminate, adorn, show, picture, embellish, demonstrate.

illustration *(SYN.)* likeness, painting, picture, print, scene, sketch, view, engraving, drawing, panorama, photograph, cinema, etching, effigy, film, appearance, resemblance, image, portrait.

illustrator *(SYN.)* painter, artist.

illustrious *(SYN.)* prominent, eminent, renowned, famed, great, vital, elevated, majestic, noble, excellent, dignified, big, gigantic, enormous, immense, huge, vast, large, countless, numerous, celebrated, critical, momentous.

(ANT.) menial, common, minute, diminutive, small, obscure, ordinary, little.

image *(SYN.)* reflection, likeness, idea, representation, notion, picture, conception.

imaginary *(SYN.)* fanciful, fantastic, unreal, whimsical.

(ANT.) actual, real.

imagination *(SYN.)* creation, invention, fancy, notion, conception, fantasy, idea.

imaginative *(SYN.)* inventive, poetical, fanciful, clever, creative, mystical, visionary.

(ANT.) prosaic, dull, unromantic, literal.

imagine *(SYN.)* assume, surmise, suppose, conceive, dream, pretend, conjecture, fancy, opine, think, envision, guess, picture.

imbecile *(SYN.)* idiot, simpleton, blockhead, dolt, dunce, jester, buffoon, harlequin, oaf, fool.

(ANT.) scholar, sage, genius, philosopher.

imbibe *(SYN.)* absorb, consume, assimilate, engulf, engage, occupy, engross.

(ANT.) dispense, exude, discharge, emit.

imitate *(SYN.)* duplicate, mimic, follow, reproduce, mock, ape, counterfeit, copy, impersonate.

(ANT.) invent, distort, alter, diverge.

imitation *(SYN.)* replica, reproduction copy, duplicate, facsimile, transcript, exemplar.

(ANT.) prototype, original.

immaculate *(SYN.)* clean, spotless, unblemished.

(ANT.) dirty.

immature *(SYN.)* young, boyish, childish, youthful, childlike, puerile, girlish, juvenile, callow.

(ANT.) old, senile, aged, elderly, mature.

immeasurable *(SYN.)* unlimited, endless, eternal, immense, interminable, unbounded, boundless, illimitable, infinite.

(ANT.) limited, confined, bounded, finite, circumscribed.

immediate *(SYN.)* present, instant, instantaneous, near, close, next, prompt, direct.

(ANT.) distant, future.

immediately *(SYN.)* now, presently, forthwith, instantly, promptly.

(ANT.) sometime, hereafter, later, shortly, distantly.

immense *(SYN.)* enormous, large, gigantic, huge, colossal, elephantine, great, gargantuan, vast.

(ANT.) small, diminutive, little, minuscule, minute, petit, tiny.

immensity *(SYN.)* hugeness, enormousness, vastness.

immerse *(SYN.)* plunge, dip, dunk, sink, submerge, engage, absorb, engross, douse.

(ANT.) uplift, elevate, recover.

immigration *(SYN.)* settlement, colonization.

(ANT.) exodus, emigration.

imminent *(SYN.)* nigh, impending, overhanging, approaching, menacing, threatening.

(ANT.) retreating, afar, distant, improbable, remote.

immoderation *(SYN.)* profusion, surplus, extravagance, excess, intemperance, super-abundance.
(ANT.) lack, want, deficiency, dearth, paucity.

immoral *(SYN.)* sinful, wicked, corrupt, bad, indecent, profligate, unprincipled, anti-social, dissolute.
(ANT.) pure, high-minded, chaste, virtuous, noble.

immortal *(SYN.)* infinite, eternal, timeless, undying, perpetual, endless, deathless, ever-lasting.
(ANT.) mortal, transient, finite, ephemeral, temporal.

immune *(SYN.)* easy, open, autonomous, un-obstructed, free, emancipated, clear, inde-pendent, unrestricted, exempt, liberated, familiar, loose, unconfined, frank.
(ANT.) confined, impeded, restricted, sub-ject.

immutable *(SYN.)* constant, faithful, invari-ant, persistent, unchanging, unalterable, continual, ceaseless, enduring, fixed, per-manent, perpetual, unwavering.
(ANT.) mutable, vacillating, wavering, fickle.

impact *(SYN.)* striking, contact, collision.

impair *(SYN.)* harm, injure, spoil, deface, destroy, hurt, damage.
(ANT.) repair, mend, ameliorate, enhance, benefit.

impart *(SYN.)* convey, disclose, inform, tell, reveal, transmit, notify, confer, communi-cate, relate.
(ANT.) hide, withhold, conceal.

impartial *(SYN.)* unbiased, just, honest, reasonable, equitable.
(ANT.) fraudulent, dishonorable, partial.

impartiality *(SYN.)* indifference, unconcern, impartiality, neutrality, disinterestedness, apathy, insensibility.
(ANT.) passion, ardor, fervor, affection.

impasse *(SYN.)* standstill, deadlock, stale-mate.

impede *(SYN.)* hamper, hinder, retard, thwart, check, encumber, interrupt, bar, clog, delay, obstruct, block, restrain, stop.

(ANT.) assist, promote, help, advance, further.

impel *(SYN.)* oblige, enforce, drive, coerce, force, constrain.
(ANT.) induce, prevent, convince, per-suade.

impending *(SYN.)* imminent, nigh, threat-ening, overhanging, approaching, menac-ing.
(ANT.) remote, improbable, afar, distant, retreating.

impenetrable *(SYN)* rigid, tough, harsh, strict, unfeeling, rigorous, intricate, ardu-ous, penetrable, cruel, difficult, severe, stern, firm.
(ANT.) soft, simple, gentle, tender, fluid, lenient, easy, effortless.

imperative *(SYN.)* critical, instant, im-portant, necessary, serious, urgent, cogent, compelling, crucial, pressing, impelling, importunate.
(ANT.) trivial, insignificant, unimportant, petty.

imperceptible *(SYN.)* invisible, indiscerni-ble, indistinguishable.
(ANT.) seen, evident, visible, perceptible.

imperfection *(SYN.)* flaw, shortcoming, vice, defect, blemish, failure, mistake, fault, error.
(ANT.) correctness, perfection, complete-ness.

imperil *(SYN.)* jeopardize, risk, endanger, hazard, risk.
(ANT.) guard, insure.

impersonal *(SYN.)* objective, detached, disinterested.
(ANT.) personal.

impersonate *(SYN.)* mock, simulate, imi-tate, ape, counterfeit, mimic, copy, dupli-cate.
(ANT.) alter, diverge, distort.

impertinence *(SYN)* impudence, presump-tion, sauciness, effrontery, audacity, rude-ness, assurance, boldness, insolence.
(ANT.) truckling, politeness, diffidence, subserviency.

impertinent *(SYN.)* rude, offensive, inso-lent, disrespectful, arrogant, brazen, impudent, insulting, contemptuous, abusive. *(ANT.) polite, respectful, considerate, courteous.*

impetuous *(SYN.)* rash, heedless, quick, hasty, careless, passionate. *(ANT.) cautious, reasoning, careful, thoughtful, calculating.*

implicate *(SYN.)* reproach, accuse, blame, involve, upbraid, condemn, incriminate, censure. *(ANT.) exonerate, absolve, acquit.*

implore *(SYN.)* beg, pray, request, solicit, crave, entreat, beseech, ask, importune, supplicate, adjure, appeal, petition. *(ANT.) give, bestow, favor, grant.*

imply *(SYN.)* mean, involve, suggest, connote, hint, mention, indicate, insinuate, signify. *(ANT.) assert, declare, express.*

impolite *(SYN.)* rude, unpolished, impudent, boorish, blunt, discourteous, rough, saucy, surly, savage, insolent, gruff, uncivil, coarse, ignorant, crude, illiterate, raw, primitive, vulgar, untaught. *(ANT.) genteel, courteous, courtly, dignified, stately, noble, civil.*

import *(SYN.)* influence, significance, stress, emphasis, importance, value, weight. *(ANT.) triviality, insignificance.*

important *(SYN.)* critical, grave, influential, momentous, well-known, pressing, relevant, prominent, primary, essential, weighty, material, considerable, famous, principle, famed, sequential, notable, significant. *(ANT.) unimportant, trifling, petty, trivial, insignificant, secondary, anonymous, irrelevant.*

impose *(SYN.)* levy, require, demand.

imposing *(SYN.)* lofty, noble, majestic, magnificent, august, dignified, grandiose, high, grand, impressive, pompous, stately. *(ANT.) ordinary, undignified, humble, common, lowly.*

imposition *(SYN.)* load, onus, burden.

impossible *(SYN.)* preposterous.

impregnable *(SYN.)* safe, invulnerable, secure, unassailable. *(ANT.) vulnerable.*

impress *(SYN.)* awe, emboss, affect, mark, imprint, influence.

impression *(SYN.)* influence, indentation, feeling, opinion, mark, effect, depression, guess, thought, belief, dent, sensibility. *(ANT.) fact, insensibility.*

impressive *(SYN.)* arresting, moving, remarkable, splendid, thrilling, striking, majestic, grandiose, imposing, commanding, affecting, exciting, stirring. *(ANT.) regular, unimpressive, commonplace.*

impromptu *(SYN.)* casual, unprepared, offhand, extemporaneous.

improper *(SYN.)* unfit, unsuitable, inappropriate, naughty, indecent, unbecoming. *(ANT.) fitting, proper, appropriate.*

improve *(SYN.)* better, reform, refine, ameliorate, amend, help, upgrade, rectify. *(ANT.) debase, vitiate, impair, corrupt, damage.*

improvement *(SYN.)* growth, advance, progress, development, advancement, progression. *(ANT.) relapse, regression, decline, retrogression, delay.*

imprudent *(SYN.)* indiscreet, thoughtless, desultory, lax, neglectful, remiss, careless, inattentive, heedless, inconsiderate, reckless, ill-advised, irresponsible, unconcerned. *(ANT.) careful, meticulous, accurate.*

impudence *(SYN.)* boldness, insolence, rudeness, sauciness, assurance, effrontery, impertinence, presumption, audacity. *(ANT.) politeness, truckling, subserviency, diffidence.*

impudent *(SYN.)* forward, rude, abrupt, prominent, striking, bold, fresh, impertinent, insolent, pushy, insulting, brazen. *(ANT.) bashful, flinching, polite, courteous, cowardly, retiring, timid.*

impulse *(SYN.)* hunch, whim, fancy, urge, caprice, surge, pulse.

impulsive *(SYN.)* passionate, rash, spontaneous, heedless, careless, hasty, quick, impetuous. *(ANT.) reasoning, calculating, careful,* *prudent, cautious.*

impure *(SYN.)* dishonest, spoiled, tainted, contaminated, debased, corrupt, profligate, unsound, putrid, corrupted, crooked, depraved, vitiated, venal.

imputation *(SYN.)* diary, incrimination, arraignment, indictment.

(ANT.) exoneration, pardon, exculpation.

inability *(SYN.)* incompetence, incapacity, handicap, disability, impotence, weakness.

(ANT.) power, strength, ability, capability.

inaccurate *(SYN.)* false, incorrect, mistaken, untrue, askew, wrong, awry, erroneous, fallacious, imprecise, faulty, amiss.

(ANT.) right, accurate, true, correct.

inactive *(SYN.)* lazy, unemployed, indolent, motionless, still, inert, dormant, idle, unoccupied.

(ANT.) employed, working, active, industrious, occupied.

inadequate *(SYN.)* insufficient, lacking, short, incomplete, defective, scanty.

(ANT.) satisfactory, enough, adequate, ample, sufficient.

inadvertent *(SYN.)* careless, negligent, unthinking, thoughtless.

inane *(SYN.)* trite, insipid, banal, absurd, silly, commonplace, vapid, foolish, stupid, hackneyed.

(ANT.) stimulating, novel, fresh, original, striking.

inanimate *(SYN.)* deceased, spiritless, lifeless, gone, dull, mineral, departed, dead, insensible, vegetable, unconscious.

(ANT.) living, stirring, alive, animate.

inattentive *(SYN.)* absent-minded, distracted, abstracted, preoccupied.

(ANT.) watchful, attending, attentive.

inaugurate *(SYN.)* commence, begin, open, originate, start, arise, launch, enter, initiate.

(ANT.) end, terminate, close, complete, finish.

incense *(SYN.)* anger, enrage, infuriate.

incentive *(SYN.)* impulse, stimulus, inducement, encouragement.

(ANT.) discouragement.

inception *(SYN.)* origin, start, source, open-ing, beginning, outset, commencement.

(ANT.) end, termination, close, completion, consummation.

incessant *(SYN.)* perennial, uninterrupted, continual, ceaseless, continuous, unremitting, eternal, constant, unceasing, unending, perpetual, everlasting.

(ANT.) rare, occasional, periodic, interrupted.

incident *(SYN.)* happening, situation, occurrence, circumstance, condition, event, fact.

incidental *(SYN.)* casual, contingent, trivial, undesigned, chance, fortuitous, accidental, secondary, unimportant, unintended.

(ANT.) intended, fundamental, planned, calculated, willed, decreed.

incidentally *(SYN.)* by the way.

incinerate *(SYN.)* sear, char, blaze, scald, singe, consume, scorch, burn.

(ANT.) quench, put out, extinguish.

incisive *(SYN.)* neat, succinct, terse, brief, compact, condensed, neat, summary, concise.

(ANT.) wordy, prolix, verbose, lengthy.

incite *(SYN.)* goad, provoke, urge, arouse, encourage, cause, stimulate, induce, instigate, foment.

(ANT.) quiet, bore, pacify, soothe.

inclination *(SYN.)* bent, preference, desire, slope, affection, bent, bias, disposition, bending, penchant, incline, attachment, predisposition, predication, tendency, prejudice, slant, lean, leaning.

(ANT.) nonchalance, apathy, distaste, aversion, reluctance, disinclination, uprightness, repugnance.

incline *(SYN.)* slope, nod, lean.

(ANT.) straighten.

include *(SYN.)* contain, hold, accommodate, embody, encompass, involve, comprise, embrace.

(ANT.) omit, exclude, discharge.

income *(SYN.)* earnings, salary, wages, pay, revenue, return, receipts.

incomparable *(SYN.)* peerless, matchless, unequaled.

incompetency *(SYN.)* inability, weakness, handicap, impotence, disability, incapacity.
(ANT.) strength, ability, power, capability.
incomprehensible *(SYN.)* unintelligible, indecipherable.
inconceivable *(SYN.)* unbelievable, unimaginable, impossible.
(ANT.) possible, believable.
incongruous *(SYN.)* inconsistent, contrary, incompatible, irreconcilable, contradictory, unsteady, incongruous, wavering, paradoxical, vacillating, discrepant, illogical.
(ANT.) consistent, compatible, correspondent.
inconsiderate *(SYN.)* unthinking, careless, unthoughtful, unmindful.
(ANT.) logical, consistent.
inconsistency *(SYN)* discord, variance, contention, conflict, controversy, interference.
(ANT.) harmony, concord, amity, consonance.
inconsistent *(SYN.)* fickle, wavering, variable, changeable, contrary, unstable, illogical, contradictory, irreconcilable, discrepant, paradoxical, incompatible, self-contradictory, incongruous, unsteady, fitful, shifting.
(ANT.) unchanging, steady, logical, stable, uniform, constant.
inconspicuous *(SYN.)* retiring, unnoticed, unostentatious.
(ANT.) obvious, conspicuous.
inconstant *(SYN.)* fickle, shifting, changeable, fitful, vacillating, unstable, wavering.
(ANT.) stable, constant, steady, uniform, unchanging.
inconvenient *(SYN.)* awkward, inappropriate, untimely, troublesome.
(ANT.) handy, convenient.
incorrect *(SYN.)* mistaken, wrong, erroneous, inaccurate.
(ANT.) proper, accurate, suitable.
increase *(SYN.)* amplify, enlarge, grow, magnify, multiply, augment, enhance, expand, intensify, swell, raise, greaten, prolong, broaden, lengthen, expansion, accrue, extend, heighten.
(ANT.) diminish, reduce, atrophy, shrink,

shrinkage, decrease, lessening, lessen, contract.
incredible *(SYN.)* improbable, unbelievable.
(ANT.) plausible, credible, believable.
incriminate *(SYN.)* charge, accuse, indict, arraign, censure.
(ANT.) release, exonerate, acquit, absolve, vindicate.
incrimination *(SYN.)* imputation, indictment, accusation, charge, arraignment.
(ANT.) exoneration, pardon, exculpation.
indebted *(SYN.)* obliged, grateful, beholden, thankful, appreciative.
(ANT.) unappreciative, thankless.
indecent *(SYN.)* impure, obscene, pornographic, coarse, dirty, filthy, smutty, gross, disgusting.
(ANT.) modest, refined, decent, pure.
indeed *(SYN.)* truthfully, really, honestly, surely.
indefinite *(SYN.)* unsure, uncertain, vague, confused, unsettled, confusing.
(ANT.) decided, definite, equivocal.
independence *(SYN.)* liberation, privilege, freedom, immunity, familiarity, liberty, exemption, license.
(ANT.) necessity, constraint, compulsion, reliance, dependence, bondage, servitude.
independent *(SYN.)* free, unrestrained, voluntary, autonomous, self-reliant, uncontrolled, unrestricted.
(ANT.) enslaved, contingent, dependent, restricted.
indestructible *(SYN.)* enduring, lasting, permanent, unchangeable, abiding, constant, fixed, stable, changeless.
(ANT.) unstable, temporary, transitory, ephemeral.
indicate *(SYN.)* imply, denote, specify, intimate, designate, symbolize, show, manifest, disclose, mean, reveal.
(ANT.) mislead, falsify, distract, conceal, falsify.
indication *(SYN.)* proof, emblem, omen, sign, symbol, token, mark, portent, gesture, signal.

indict *(SYN.)* charge, accuse, incriminate, censure, arraign.
(ANT.) acquit, vindicate, absolve, exonerate.

indictment *(SYN.)* incrimination, arraignment, imputation, charge.
(ANT.) pardon, exoneration, exculpation.

indifference *(SYN.)* unconcern, apathy, impartiality, disinterestedness, insensibility, neutrality.
(ANT.) ardor, passion, affection, fervor.

indifferent *(SYN.)* uncaring, insensitive, cool, unconcerned.
(ANT.) caring, concerned, earnest.

indigence *(SYN.)* necessity, destitution, poverty, want, need, privation, penury.
(ANT.) wealth, abundance, plenty, riches, affluence.

indigenous *(SYN.)* inborn, native, inherent, domestic, aboriginal, plenty, endemic, innate, natural.

indigent *(SYN.)* wishing, covetous, demanding, lacking, requiring, wanting, claiming, craving.

indignant *(SYN.)* irritated, irate, angry, aroused, exasperated.
(ANT.) calm, serene, content.

indignation *(SYN.)* ire, petulance, passion, choler, anger, wrath, temper, irritation, exasperation, animosity, resentment, rage.
(ANT.) self-control, peace, forbearance, patience.

indignity *(SYN.)* insolence, insult, abuse, affront, offense.
(ANT.) homage, apology, salutation.

indirect *(SYN.)* winding, crooked, devious, roundabout, cunning, tricky, tortuous, circuitous, distorted, erratic, swerving.
(ANT.) straightforward, direct, straight, honest.

indiscretion *(SYN.)* imprudence, folly, absurdity, extravagance.
(ANT.) prudence, sense, wisdom, reasonableness, judgment.

indispensable *(SYN.)* necessary, fundamental, basic, essential, important, intrinsic, vital.
(ANT.) optional, expendable, peripheral,

extrinsic.

indistinct *(SYN.)* cloudy, dark, mysterious, vague, blurry, ambiguous, cryptic, dim, obscure, enigmatic, abstruse, hazy, blurred, unintelligible.
(ANT.) clear, lucid, bright, distinct.

indistinguishable *(SYN.)* identical, like, coincident, equal, same, equivalent.
(ANT.) dissimilar, opposed, contrary, disparate, distinct.

individual *(SYN.)* singular, unique, specific, distinctive, single, particular, undivided, human, apart, marked, person, different, special, separate.
(ANT.) universal, common, general, ordinary.

individuality *(SYN.)* symbol, description, mark, kind, character, repute, class, standing, sort, nature, disposition, reputation, sign.

indolent *(SYN.)* slothful, lazy, idle, inactive, slow, sluggish, torpid, supine, inert.
(ANT.) diligent, active, assiduous, vigorous, zestful, alert.

indomitable *(SYN.)* insurmountable, unconquerable, invulnerable, impregnable, unassailable.
(ANT.) weak, puny, powerless, vulnerable.

induce *(SYN.)* evoke, cause, influence, persuade, effect, make, originate, prompt, incite, create.

inducement *(SYN.)* incentive, motive, purpose, stimulus, reason, impulse, cause, principle, spur, incitement.
(ANT.) result, attempt, action, effort, deed.

induct *(SYN.)* instate, establish, install.
(ANT.) eject, oust.

indulge *(SYN.)* humor, satisfy, gratify.

indulgent *(SYN.)* obliging, pampering, tolerant, easy.

indurate *(SYN.)* impenitent, unfeeling, hard, insensible, tough, obdurate, callous.
(ANT.) sensative, soft, compassionate, tender.

industrious *(SYN.)* hard-working, perseverant, busy, active, diligent, assiduous, careful, patient.
(ANT.) unconcerned, indifferent, lethar-

gic, careless, apathetic, lazy, indolent, shiftless.

inebriated *(SYN.)* drunk, tight, drunken, intoxicated, tipsy.

(ANT.) sober, clearheaded, temperate.

ineffective *(SYN.)* pliant, tender, vague, wavering, defenseless, weak, inadequate, poor, irresolute, frail, decrepit, delicate, vacillating, assailable, exposed, vulnerable.

(ANT.) sturdy, robust, strong, potent, powerful.

inept *(SYN.)* clumsy, awkward, improper, inappropriate.

(ANT.) adroit, dexterous, adept, appropriate, proper, apt, fitting.

inequity *(SYN.)* wrong, injustice, unfairness, grievance, injury.

(ANT.) righteousness, lawfulness, equity, justice.

inert *(SYN.)* lazy, dormant, slothful, inactive, idle, indolent, motionless, unmoving, fixed, static.

(ANT.) working, active, industrious, occupied.

inertia *(SYN.)* indolence, torpidity, idleness, slothfulness, indolence, sluggishness, supineness.

(ANT.) assiduousness, activity, alertness, diligence.

inevitable *(SYN.)* definite, fixed, positive, sure, undeniable, indubitable, certain, assured, unquestionable, secure.

(ANT.) uncertain, probable, doubtful, questionable.

inexpensive *(SYN.)* low-priced, cheap, inferior, mean, beggarly, common, poor, shabby, modest, economical.

(ANT.) expensive, costly, dear.

inexperienced *(SYN.)* naive, untrained, uninformed, green.

(ANT.) experienced, skilled, sophisticated, trained, seasoned.

inexplicable *(SYN.)* hidden, mysterious, obscure, secret, dark, cryptic, enigmatical, incomprehensible, occult, recondite, inscrutable, dim.

(ANT.) plain, simple, clear, obvious, explained.

infamous *(SYN.)* shocking, shameful, scandalous.

infantile *(SYN.)* babyish, naive, immature, childish.

(ANT.) mature, grownup, adult.

infect *(SYN.)* pollute, poison, contaminate, defile, sully, taint.

(ANT.) purify, disinfect.

infection *(SYN.)* virus, poison, ailment, disease, pollution, pest, germ, taint, contamination, contagion.

infectious *(SYN.)* contagious, virulent, catching, communicable, pestilential, transferable.

(ANT.) noncommunicable, hygienic, healthful.

infer *(SYN.)* understand, deduce, extract.

inference *(SYN.)* consequence, result, conclusion, corollary, judgment, deduction.

(ANT.) preconception, foreknowledge, assumption, presupposition.

inferior *(SYN.)* secondary, lower, poorer, minor, subordinate, mediocre.

(ANT.) greater, superior, better, higher.

infinite *(SYN.)* immeasurable, interminable, unlimited, unbounded, eternal, boundless, illimitable, immense, endless, vast, innumerable, limitless.

(ANT.) confined, limited, bounded, circumscribed, finite.

infinitesimal *(SYN.)* minute, microscopic, tiny, submicroscopic.

(ANT.) gigantic, huge, enormous.

infirm *(SYN.)* feeble, impaired, decrepit, forceless, languid, puny, powerless, enervated, weak, exhausted.

(ANT.) stout, vigorous, forceful, lusty, strong.

infirmity *(SYN.)* disease, illness, malady, ailment, sickness, disorder, complaint.

(ANT.) soundness, health, vigor, healthiness.

inflame *(SYN.)* fire, incite, excite, arouse.

(ANT.) soothe, calm.

inflammation *(SYN.)* infection, soreness, irritation.

inflammatory *(SYN.)* instigating, inciting, provocative.

inflate *(SYN.)* expand, swell, distend.
(ANT.) collapse, deflate.

inflexible *(SYN.)* firm, stubborn, headstrong, immovable, unyielding, uncompromising, dogged, contumacious, determined, obstinate, rigid, unbending, unyielding, steadfast.
(ANT.) submissive, compliant, docile, amenable, yielding, flexible, giving, elastic.

inflict *(SYN.)* deliver, deal, give, impose, apply.

influence *(SYN.)* weight, control, effect, sway.

influenced *(SYN.)* sway, affect, bias, control, actuate, impel, stir, incite.

influential *(SYN.)* important, weighty, prominent, significant, critical, decisive, mo-mentous, grave, relevant, material, pressing, consequential.
(ANT.) petty, irrelevant, mean, trivial, insignificant.

inform *(SYN.)* apprise, instruct, tell, notify, advise, acquaint, enlighten, impart, warn, teach, advise, relate.
(ANT.) delude, mislead, distract, conceal.

informal *(SYN.)* simple, easy, natural, unofficial, familiar.
(ANT.) formal, distant, reserved, proper.

informality *(SYN.)* friendship, frankness, liberty, acquaintance, sociability, intimacy, unreserved.
(ANT.) presumption, constraint, reserve, distance, haughtiness.

information *(SYN.)* knowledge, data, intelligence, facts.

informative *(SYN.)* educational, enlightening, instructive.

informer *(SYN.)* tattler, traitor, betrayer.

infrequent *(SYN.)* unusual, rare, occasional, strange.
(ANT.) commonplace, abundant, usual, ordinary, customary, frequent, numerous.

ingenious *(SYN.)* clever, skillful, talented, adroit, dexterous, quick-witted, bright, smart, witty, sharp, apt, resourceful, imaginative, inventive, creative.
(ANT.) dull, slow, awkward, bungling, unskilled, stupid.

ingenuity *(SYN.)* cunning, inventiveness, resourcefulness, aptitude, faculty, cleverness, ingenuousness.
(ANT.) ineptitude, clumsiness, dullness, stupidity.

ingenuous *(SYN.)* open, sincere, honest, candid, straightforward, free, plain, frank, truthful, naive, innocent, unsophisticated, simple.
(ANT.) scheming, sly, contrived, wily.

ingredient *(SYN.)* component, element, constituent.

inhabit *(SYN.)* fill, possess, absorb, dwell, occupy, live.
(ANT.) relinquish, abandon, release.

inherent *(SYN.)* innate, native, congenital, inherent, intrinsic, inborn, inbred, natural, real.
(ANT.) extraneous, acquired, external, extrinsic.

inhibit *(SYN.)* curb, constrain, hold back, restrain, bridle, hinder, repress, suppress, stop, limit.
(ANT.) loosen, aid, incite, encourage.

inhuman *(SYN.)* merciless, cruel, brutal, ferocious, savage, ruthless, malignant, barbarous, barbaric, bestial.
(ANT.) kind, benevolent, forbearing, gentle, compassionate, merciful, humane, humane.

inimical *(SYN.)* hostile, warlike, adverse, antagonistic, opposed, unfriendly.
(ANT.) favorable, amicable, cordial.

iniquitous *(SYN.)* baleful, immoral, pernicious, sinful, wicked, base, bad, evil, noxious, unsound, villainous.
(ANT.) moral, good, excellent, honorable, reputable.

iniquity *(SYN.)* injustice, wrong, grievance, unfairness, injury.
(ANT.) lawful, equity, righteousness, justice.

initial *(SYN.)* original, first, prime, beginning, earliest, pristine, chief, primeval, primary, foremost, basic, elementary.
(ANT.) latest, subordinate, last, least, hindmost, final, terminal.

initiate *(SYN.)* institute, enter, arise, inaugurate, commence, originate, start, open, begin.

(ANT.) terminate, complete, end, finish, close, stop.

initiative *(SYN.)* enthusiasm, energy, vigor, enterprise.

injure *(SYN.)* harm, wound, abuse, dishonor, damage, hurt, impair, spoil, disfigure, affront, insult, mar.

(ANT.) praise, ameliorate, help, preserve, compliment, benefit.

injurious *(SYN.)* detrimental, mischievous, damaging, hurtful, deleterious, harmful, destructive.

(ANT.) profitable, helpful, advantageous, salutary, beneficial, useful.

injury *(SYN.)* harm, detriment, damage, injustice, wrong, prejudice, grievance, mischief.

(ANT.) repair, benefit, improvement.

injustice *(SYN.)* unfairness, grievance, iniquity, wrong, injury.

(ANT.) righteousness, justice, equity, lawfulness.

inmate *(SYN.)* patient, prisoner.

inn *(SYN.)* motel, lodge, hotel.

innate *(SYN.)* native, inherent, congenital, innate, real, inborn, natural, intrinsic, inbred.

(ANT.) extraneous, acquired, external, extrinsic.

innocent *(SYN.)* pure, sinless, blameless, innocuous, lawful, naive, faultless, virtuous, not guilty.

(ANT.) guilty, corrupt, sinful, culpable, sophisticated, wise, worldly.

innocuous *(SYN.)* naive, pure, innocent, blameless, virtuous, lawful, faultless, innocuous, sinless.

(ANT.) sinful, corrupt, unrighteous, culpable, guilty.

inquire *(SYN.)* ask, solicit, invite, demand, claim, entreat, interrogate, query, beg, request, question, investigate, examine.

(ANT.) dictate, insist, reply, command, order.

inquiring *(SYN.)* prying, searching, curious, inquisitive, peering, snoopy, peeping, med-

dling, interrogative.

(ANT.) unconcerned, indifferent, uninterested, incurious.

inquiry *(SYN.)* investigation, quest, research, examination, interrogation, exploration, query, question, scrutiny, study.

(ANT.) inattention, inactivity, disregard, negligence.

inquisitive *(SYN.)* meddling, peeping, nosy, interrogative, peering, searching, prying, snoopy, inquiring, curious.

(ANT.) unconcerned, indifferent, incurious, uninterested.

insane *(SYN.)* deranged, mad, foolish, idiotic, demented, crazy, delirious, maniacal, lunatic.

(ANT.) sane, rational, reasonable, sound, sensible, coherent.

insanity *(SYN.)* delirium, aberration, dementia, psychosis, lunacy, madness, frenzy, mania, craziness, derangement.

(ANT.) stability, rationality, sanity.

insecure *(SYN.)* uneasy, nervous, uncertain, shaky.

(ANT.) secure.

insensitive *(SYN.)* unfeeling, impenitent, callous, hard, indurate, obdurate, tough.

(ANT.) soft, compassionate, tender, sensitive.

insight *(SYN.)* intuition, acumen, penetration, discernment, perspicuity.

(ANT.) obtuseness.

insignificant *(SYN.)* trivial, paltry, petty, small, frivolous, unimportant, insignificant, trifling.

(ANT.) momentous, serious, important, weighty.

insincere *(SYN.)* false, dishonest, deceitful.

(ANT.) honest, sincere.

insinuate *(SYN.)* imply, mean, suggest, connote, signify, involve.

(ANT.) express, state, assert.

insipid *(SYN.)* tasteless, dull, stale, flat, vapid.

(ANT.) racy, tasty, savory, exciting.

insist *(SYN.)* command, demand, require.

insolence *(SYN.)* boldness, presumption, sauciness, effrontery, audacity, assurance, impertinence, rudeness.

(ANT.) politeness, truckling, diffidence, subserviency.

insolent *(SYN.)* arrogant, impertinent, insulting, rude, brazen, contemptuous, abusive, offensive, disrespectful.

(ANT.) respectful, courteous, polite, considerate.

inspect *(SYN.)* observe, discern, eye, behold, glance, scan, stare, survey, view, regard, see, watch, witness, examine, investigate.

(ANT.) overlook, miss, avert, hide.

inspection *(SYN.)* examination, retrospect, survey, revision, reconsideration, critique, criticism, review.

inspiration *(SYN.)* creativity, aptitude, gift, genius, originality, ability, faculty, sagacity, talent, proficient, master, adept, intellectual, thought, impulse, idea, notion, hunch.

(ANT.) dullard, moron, shallowness, ineptitude, stupidity, obtuseness, dolt.

install *(SYN.)* establish.

instance *(SYN.)* occasion, illustration, occurrence, example, case.

instant *(SYN.)* flash, moment.

instantaneous *(SYN.)* hasty, sudden unexpected, rapid, abrupt, immediate.

(ANT.) slowly, anticipated, gradual.

instantly *(SYN.)* now, presently, directly, forthwith, immediately, straight-away, at once, instantaneously.

(ANT.) sometime, distantly, hereafter, later, shortly.

instinct *(SYN.)* intuition, feeling.

instinctive *(SYN.)* offhand, voluntary, willing, spontaneous, automatic, impulsive, extemporaneous.

(ANT.) rehearsed, planned, compulsory, prepared, forced.

institute *(SYN.)* ordain, establish, raise, form, organize, sanction, fix, found, launch, begin, initiate.

(ANT.) overthrow, upset, demolish, abolish, unsettle.

instruct *(SYN.)* teach, tutor, educate, inform, school, instill, train, inculcate, drill.

(ANT.) misinform, misguide.

instruction *(SYN.)* advise, warning, information, exhortation, notification, admonition, caution, recommendation, counsel, suggestion, teaching, training, education, command, order.

instrument *(SYN.)* channel, device, utensil, tool, agent, apparatus, means, vehicle, medium, agent, implement.

(ANT.) obstruction, hindrance, preventive, impediment.

insubordinate *(SYN.)* rebellious, unruly, defiant, disorderly, disobedient, undutiful, refractory, intractable, mutinous.

(ANT.) obedient, compliant, submissive, dutiful.

insufficient *(SYN.)* limited, lacking, deficient, short, inadequate.

(ANT.) ample, protracted, abundant, big, extended.

insulation *(SYN.)* quarantine, segregation, seclusion, withdrawal, isolation, loneliness, alienation, solitude.

(ANT.) union, communion, association, fellowship, connection.

insult *(SYN.)* insolence, offense, abuse, dishonor, affront, insult, indignity, offend, humiliate, outrage.

(ANT.) compliment, homage, apology, salutation, flatter, praise.

integrated *(SYN.)* mingled, mixed, combined, interspersed, desegregated, nonsectarian, interracial.

(ANT.) separated, divided, segregated.

integrity *(SYN.)* honesty, openness, trustworthiness, fairness, candor, justice, rectitude, sincerity, uprightness, soundness, wholeness, honor, principle, virtue.

(ANT.) fraud, deceit, cheating, trickery, dishonesty.

intellect *(SYN.)* understanding, judgment.

intellectual *(SYN.)* intelligent.

intelligence *(SYN.)* reason, sense, intellect, understanding, mind, ability, skill, aptitude.

(ANT.) feeling, passion, emotion.

intelligent *(SYN.)* clever, smart, knowledgeable, well-informed, alert, discerning, astute, quick, enlightened, smart, bright, wise.

(ANT.) insipid, obtuse, dull, stupid, slow, foolish, unintelligent, dumb.

intend *(SYN.)* plan, prepare, scheme, contrive, outline, design, sketch, plot, project, delineate.

intense *(SYN.)* brilliant, animated, graphic, lucid, bright, expressive, vivid, deep, profound, concentrated, serious, earnest.

(ANT.) dull, vague, dusky, dim, dreary.

intensify *(SYN.)* accrue, augment, amplify, enlarge, enhance, extend, expand, heighten, grow, magnify, raise, multiply.

(ANT.) reduce, decrease, contract, diminish.

intent *(SYN.)* purpose, design, objective, intention, aim.

(ANT.) accidental, result, chance.

intensity *(SYN.)* force, potency, power, toughness, activity, durability, fortitude, vigor, stamina.

(ANT.) weakness, feebleness, infirmity, frailty.

intention *(SYN.)* intent, purpose, objective, plan, expectation, aim, object.

(ANT.) chance, accident.

intentional *(SYN.)* deliberate, intended, studied, willful, contemplated, premeditated, designed, voluntary, purposeful, planned.

(ANT.) fortuitous, accidental, chance.

intentionally *(SYN.)* purposefully, deliberately, maliciously.

(ANT.) accidentally.

interest *(SYN.)* attention, concern, care, advantage, benefit, profit, ownership, credit, attract, engage, amuse, entertain.

(ANT.) apathy, weary, disinterest.

interested *(SYN.)* affected, concerned.

(ANT.) unconcerned, indifferent, uninterested.

interesting *(SYN.)* engaging, inviting, fascinating, attractive.

(ANT.) boring, tedious, uninteresting, wearisome.

interfere *(SYN.)* meddle, monkey, interpose, interrupt, tamper, butt in, intervene.

interference *(SYN.)* prying, intrusion, meddling, obstacle, obstruction.

interior *(SYN.)* internal, inmost, inner, inward, inside, center.

(ANT.) outer, adjacent, exterior, external, outside.

interject *(SYN.)* intrude, introduce, insert, inject, interpose.

(ANT.) overlook, avoid, disregard.

interminable *(SYN)* immense, endless, immeasurable, unlimited, vast, unbounded, boundless, eternal, infinite.

(ANT.) limited, bounded, circumscribed, confined.

internal *(SYN.)* inner, interior, inside, intimate, private.

(ANT.) outer, external, surface.

interpose *(SYN.)* arbitrate, inject, intervene, meddle, insert, interject, introduce, intercede, intrude, interfere.

(ANT.) overlook, avoid, disregard.

interpret *(SYN.)* explain, solve, translate, construe, elucidate, decode, explicate, render, unravel, define, understand.

(ANT.) misinterpret, falsify, confuse, distort, misconstrue.

interrogate *(SYN.)* quiz, analyze, inquire, audit, question, contemplate, assess, dissect, notice, scan, review, view, check, survey, scrutinize, examine.

(ANT.) overlook, omit, neglect, disregard.

interrupt *(SYN.)* suspend, delay, postpone, defer, adjourn, stay, discontinue, intrude, interfere.

(ANT.) prolong, persist, continue, maintain, proceed.

interval *(SYN.)* pause, gap.

intervene *(SYN.)* insert, intercede, meddle, inject, introduce, interpose, mediate, interfere, interrupt, intrude.

(ANT.) overlook, avoid, disregard.

intimacy *(SYN.)* fellowship, friendship, acquaintance, frankness, familiarity, unreserved, liberty.

(ANT.) presumption, distance, haughtiness, constraint, reserve.

intimate *(SYN.)* chummy, confidential, friendly, loving, affectionate, close, familiar, near, personal, private, secret.

(ANT.) conventional, formal, ceremonious, distant.

intimation *(SYN.)* reminder, implication, allusion, hint, insinuation.
(ANT.) declaration, statement, affirmation.

intolerant *(SYN.)* fanatical, narrow-minded, prejudiced, bigoted, illiberal, dogmatic, biased.
(ANT.) tolerant, radical, liberal, progressive, broad-minded, fair.

intoxicated *(SYN.)* inebriated, tipsy, drunk, tight, drunken, high.
(ANT.) sober, temperate, clearheaded.

intrepid *(SYN.)* brave, fearless, insolent, abrupt, rude, pushy, adventurous, daring, courageous, prominent, striking, forward, imprudent.
(ANT.) timid, bashful, flinching, cowardly, retiring.

intricate *(SYN.)* compound, perplexing, complex, involved, complicated.
(ANT.) simple, plain, uncompounded.

intrigue *(SYN.)* design, plot, cabal, machination, stratagem, scheme, attract, charm, interest, captivate.

intrinsic *(SYN.)* natural, inherent, inbred, congenital, inborn, native.
(ANT.) extraneous, acquired, external, extrinsic.

introduce *(SYN.)* acquaint, present, submit, offer, propose.

introduction *(SYN.)* preamble, prelude, beginning, prologue, start, preface.
(ANT.) finale, conclusion, end, epilogue, completion.

intrude *(SYN.)* invade, attack, encroach, trespass, penetrate, infringe, interrupt.
(ANT.) vacate, evacuate, abandon, relinquish.

intruder *(SYN.)* trespasser, thief, prowler, robber.

intuition *(SYN.)* insight, acumen, perspicuity, penetration, discernment, instinct, clairvoyance.

invade *(SYN.)* intrude, violate, infringe, attack, penetrate, encroach, trespass.
(ANT.) vacate, abandon, evacuate, relinquish.

invalidate *(SYN.)* annul, cancel, abolish, revoke, abrogate.

(ANT.) promote, restore, sustain, establish, continue.

invaluable *(SYN.)* priceless, precious, valuable.
(ANT.) worthless.

invasion *(SYN.)* assault, onslaught, aggression, attack, intrusion.
(ANT.) surrender, opposition, resistance, defense.

invective *(SYN.)* insult, abuse, disparagement, upbraiding, reproach, defamation, aspersion.
(ANT.) laudation, plaudit, commendation.

invent *(SYN.)* devise, fabricate, design, concoct, frame, conceive, contrive, create, originate.
(ANT.) reproduce, copy, imitate.

inventive *(SYN.)* fanciful, imaginative, visionary, clever, creative.
(ANT.) unromantic, literal, dull, prosaic.

inventiveness *(SYN)* cunning, cleverness, ingenuousness, aptitude.
(ANT.) ineptitude, clumsiness, dullness, stupidity.

invert *(SYN.)* upset, turn about, transpose, countermand, revoke, reverse, overturn, repeal.
(ANT.) stabilize, endorse.

investigate *(SYN.)* look, probe, ransack, scrutinize, ferret, examine, seek, explore, search, scour, inspect, study.

investigation *(SYN.)* exploration, interrogation, quest, question, scrutiny, inquiry, query, examination, study, research.
(ANT.) inattention, disregard, inactivity, negligence.

invigorating *(SYN.)* bracing, fortifying, vitalizing, stimulating.

invincible *(SYN.)* insurmountable, unconquerable, impregnable, indomitable, unassailable.
(ANT.) powerless, weak, vulnerable.

invisible *(SYN.)* indistinguishable, unseen, imperceptible.
(ANT.) evident, visible, seen, perceptible.

invite *(SYN.)* bid, ask, encourage, request, urge.

inviting *(SYN.)* appealing, tempting, luring,

alluring, attractive.

(ANT.) unattractive, uninviting.

involuntary *(SYN.)* reflex, uncontrolled, automatic, unintentional.

(ANT.) voluntary, willful.

involve *(SYN.)* include, embrace, entangle, envelop, incriminate, embroil, implicate, contain, complicate, confuse.

(ANT.) separate, disconnect, extricate, disengage.

invulnerable *(SYN.)* indomitable, unassailable, invincible, unconquerable, impregnable.

(ANT.) powerless, vulnerable.

irate *(SYN.)* incensed, enraged, angry.

ire *(SYN.)* indignation, irritation, wrath, anger, animosity, fury, passion, temper, exasperation.

(ANT.) peace, patience, conciliation, self-control, forbearance.

irk *(SYN.)* irritate, bother, disturb, pester, trouble, vex, tease, chafe, annoy, inconvenience, provoke.

(ANT.) console, soothe, accommodate, gratify.

irrational *(SYN.)* inconsistent, preposterous, self-contradictory, unreasonable, absurd, foolish, nonsensical, ridiculous.

(ANT.) sensible, sound, rational consistent, reasonable.

irregular *(SYN.)* eccentric, unusual, aberrant, devious, abnormal, unnatural, capricious, variable, unequal, disorderly, unsettled, random, disorganized.

(ANT.) regular, methodical, fixed, usual, ordinary, even.

irrelevant *(SYN.)* foreign, unconnected, remote, alien, strange.

(ANT.) germane, relevant, akin, kindred.

irresolute *(SYN.)* frail, pliant, vacillating, ineffective, wavering, weak, yielding, fragile, pliable.

(ANT.) robust, potent, sturdy, strong, powerful.

irresponsible *(SYN.)* unreliable.

irritable *(SYN.)* hasty, hot, peevish, testy, irascible, fiery, snappish, choleric, excitable, touchy.

(ANT.) composed, agreeable, tranquil, calm.

irritate *(SYN.)* irk, molest, bother, annoy, tease, disturb, inconvenience, vex, trouble, pester.

(ANT.) console, gratify, accommodate, soothe, pacify, calm.

irritable *(SYN.)* peevish, testy, sensitive, touchy.

(ANT.) happy, cheerful.

irritation *(SYN.)* chagrin, mortification, vexation, annoyance, exasperation, pique.

(ANT.) pleasure, comfort, gratification, appeasement.

isolate *(SYN.)* detach, segregate, separate, disconnect.

(ANT.) happy, cheerful.

isolated *(SYN.)* lone, single, alone, desolate, secluded, solitary, deserted, sole.

(ANT.) surrounded, accompanied.

isolation *(SYN.)* quarantine, seclusion, separation, solitude, alienation, loneliness, withdrawal, segregation, detachment.

(ANT.) fellowship, union, association, communion, connection.

issue *(SYN.)* flow, proceed, result, come, emanate, originate, abound, copy, number, edition, problem, question, concern, publish, distribute, circulate, release.

itemize *(SYN.)* register, detail, record.

J

jab *(SYN.)* thrust, poke, nudge, prod, shove, jolt, boost, tap, slap, rap, thwack, push.

jabber *(SYN.)* mumble, gossip, prattle, chatter, gab, palaver.

jacent *(SYN.)* level, flatness, plane, proneness, recline.

jacinth *(SYN.)* decoration, ornament, embellishment.

jack *(SYN.)* fellow, guy, boy, toiler, guy, man, worker.

jacket *(SYN.)* wrapper, envelope, coat, sheath, cover, casing, folder, enclosure.

jack-of-all-trades *(SYN.)* man friday, expert, proficient, amateur, adept, handyman, dab.

jade *(SYN.)* hussy, wanton, trollop, harlot, common, whore, ignoble, wench, hag, shrew.

jaded *(SYN.)* exhausted, bored, tired, fatigued, satiated, weary, hardened.

jag *(SYN.)* notch, snag, protuberance, barb, dent, cut, nick, serration, indentation, point.

jagged *(SYN.)* crooked, bent, ragged, pointy, notched, aquiline, furcated, aduncous, serrated.

(ANT.) smooth.

jail *(SYN.)* stockade, prison, reformatory, penitentiary, keep, dungeon, brig, confine, lock up, detain, imprison, hold captive, coop, cage, incarcerate.

jailbird *(SYN.)* convict, parolee, con, inmate, prisoner.

jailer *(SYN.)* guard, keeper, turnkey, warden.

jam *(SYN.)* force, pack, ram, crowd, push, wedge, squeeze, stuff, load, cram, press, crush, marmalade, jelly, conserve, preserve.

jamboree *(SYN.)* celebration, fete, spree, festival, festivity, carousal.

jangle *(SYN.)* rattle, vibrate, clank, clatter, dissonance, discord, quarrel, din, discord, dispute.

janitor *(SYN.)* custodian, door-keeper, caretaker, superintendent, gatekeeper.

jape *(SYN.)* lampoon, banter, joke, jest, tease, ridicule.

jar *(SYN.)* rattle, shake, bounce, jolt.

jargon *(SYN.)* speech, idiom, dialect, vernacular, diction, argot, phraseology, language, parlance, slang.

(ANT.) gibberish, babble, nonsense, drivel.

jaundiced *(SYN.)* biased, prejudiced.

(ANT.) fair.

jaunt *(SYN.)* journey, trip, tour, excursion, outing, voyage, expedition.

jaunty *(SYN.)* lively, vivacious, bouyant, winsome, frisky, showy, dapper, breezy, airy.

jazzy *(SYN.)* garish, vivacious, loud, splashy, exaggerated, flashy.

jealous *(SYN.)* covetous, desirous of, envious.

jealousy *(SYN.)* suspicion, envy, resentfulness, greed, covetousness.

(ANT.) tolerance, indifference, geniality, liberality.

jeer *(SYN.)* taunt, mock, scoff, deride, make fun of, gibe, sneer.

(ANT.) flatter, praise, compliment, laud.

jell *(SYN.)* finalize, congeal, set, solidify, take form.

jeopardize *(SYN.)* risk, dare, expose, imperil, chance, venture, hazard, endanger.

(ANT.) know, guard, determine.

jerk *(SYN.)* quiver, twitch, shake, spasm, jolt, yank, fool.

jerkwater *(SYN.)* remote, hick, backwoods, unimportant, one-horse.

jest *(SYN.)* mock, joke, tease, fun, witticism, quip.

jester *(SYN.)* fool, buffoon, harlequin, clown.

(ANT.) sage, genius, scholar, philosopher.

jet *(SYN.)* squirt, spurt, gush, inky, coal-black, nozzle.

jettison *(SYN.)* heave, discharge, throw, eject, cast off, dismiss.

jetty *(SYN.)* pier, breakwater, bulwark, buttress.

jewel *(SYN.)* ornament, gemstone, gem, bauble, stone.

jib *(SYN.)* shrink, shy, dodge, retreat, balk.

jig *(SYN.)* caper, prance, jiggle, leap, skip.

jiggle *(SYN.)* shimmy, agitate, jerk, twitch, wiggle.

jilt *(SYN.)* abandon, get rid of, reject, desert, forsake, leave.

jingle *(SYN.)* chime, ring, tinkle.

jinx *(SYN.)* hex, whammy, nemesis, curse, evil eye.

jittery *(SYN.)* jumpy, nervous, quivering, shaky, skittery.

job *(SYN.)* toil, business, occupation, post, chore, stint, career, duty, employment, profession, trade, work, situation, labor, assignment, position, undertaking, calling, task.

jobless *(SYN.)* idle, unoccupied, inactive, unemployed.

jocularity *(SYN.)* humor, wit, joke, face-

tiousness, waggery.
(ANT.) sorrow, gravity.
jocund *(SYN.)* mirthful, elated, pleasant, cheerful, merry, gay, jovial, frolicsome.
jog *(SYN.)* gait, trot, sprint, run, lope.
join *(SYN.)* conjoin, attach, accompany, associate, assemble, fit, couple, combine, fasten, unite, clasp, put together, go with, adjoin, link, connect.
(ANT.) separate, disconnect, split, sunder, part, divide, detach.
joint *(SYN.)* link, union, connection, junction, coupling, common, combined, mutual, connected.
(ANT.) divided, separate.
joke *(SYN.)* game, jest, caper, prank, anecdote, quip, tease, antic, banter, laugh.
joker *(SYN.)* wisecracker, humorist, wit, comedian, trickster, comic, jester, punster.
jolly *(SYN.)* merry, joyful, gay, happy, sprightly, pleasant, jovial, gleeful, spirited, cheerful, glad.
(ANT.) mournful, depressed, sullen, glum.
jolt *(SYN.)* sway, waver, startle, rock, jar, totter, jerk, quake, bump, shake.
josh *(SYN.)* poke fun at, kid, tease, ridicule.
jostle *(SYN.)* shove, push, bump, thrust.
jot *(SYN.)* note, write, record.
jounce *(SYN.)* bounce, jolt, bump, jostle, jar, shake.
journal *(SYN.)* account, diary, log, chronicle, magazine, newspaper, record.
journey *(SYN.)* tour, passage, cruise, voyage, pilgrimage, jaunt, trip, outing, expedition, excursion, travel.
joust *(SYN.)* tournament, contest, skirmish, competition, fight.
jovial *(SYN.)* good-natured, kindly, merry, good-humored, good-hearted, joyful, jolly, gleeful.
(ANT.) solemn, sad, serious, grim.
joy *(SYN.)* pleasure, glee, bliss, elation, mirth, felicity, rapture, delight, transport, exultation, gladness, happiness, festivity, satisfaction, merriment, ecstasy.
(ANT.) grief, depression, unhappiness, sorrow, misery, gloom, sadness, affliction.
joyful *(SYN.)* gay, lucky, opportune, cheer-

ful, happy, blissful, jovial, merry, gleeful, delighted, glad, contented, fortunate.
(ANT.) gloomy, sad, blue, solemn, serious, grim, morose, glum, depressed.
joyous *(SYN.)* jolly, gay, blithe, merry, gleeful, cheerful, jovial.
(ANT.) sad, gloomy, sorrowful, melancholy.
jubilant *(SYN.)* exulting, rejoicing, overjoyed, triumphant, gay, elated, delighted.
(ANT.) dejected.
jubilee *(SYN.)* gala, holiday, celebration, festival, fete.
judge *(SYN.)* umpire, think, estimate, decide, arbitrator, condemn, decree, critic, appreciate, adjudicator, determine, arbiter, magistrate, arbitrate, justice, consider, mediate, referee, evaluate.
judgment *(SYN.)* wisdom, perspicacity, discernment, decision, common sense, estimation, verdict, understanding, intelligence, discretion, opinion, sense.
(ANT.) thoughtlessness, senselessness, arbitrariness.
judicial *(SYN.)* legal, judicatory, forensic.
judicious *(SYN.)* sensible, wise, thoughtful.
(ANT.) ignorant.
jug *(SYN.)* bottle, jar, flask, flagon, pitcher.
juice *(SYN.)* broth, liquid, sap, distillation, serum, fluid.
jumble *(SYN.)* disarrangement, tumult, agitation, ferment, turmoil, commotion, confuse, mix, muddle, scramble, disorder.
(ANT.) peace, arrange, compose, certainty, tranquillity.
jumbo *(SYN.)* huge, big, immense, enormous, giant, colossal, monstrous, mammoth, gigantic, tremendous.
(ANT.) mini, midget, dwarf, small, little, tiny.
jump *(SYN.)* leap, skip, bound, jerk, vault, hop, spring.
jumpy *(SYN.)* touchy, excitable, nervous, sensitive.
(ANT.) tranquil, calm, unruffled.
junction *(SYN.)* coupling, joining, union, crossroads, intersection, weld, connection, linking, meeting, seam, joint.

(ANT.) separation.

jungle (SYN.) woods, thicket, undergrowth, forest, bush.

junior (SYN.) secondary, inferior, minor, lower, younger.

junk (SYN.) rubbish, scraps, trash, waste, dump, discard, castoffs, debris.

jurisdiction (SYN.) power, commission, warrant, authority, authorization, magistracy, sovereignty.

just (SYN.) fair, trustworthy, precise, exact, candid, upright, honest, impartial, lawful, rightful, proper, legal, truthful, merely, only, conscientious.

(ANT.) tricky, dishonest, unjust, corrupt, lying, deceitful.

justice (SYN.) justness, rectitude, equity, law, impartiality, right.

(ANT.) unfairness, inequity, wrong, partiality.

justifiable (SYN.) allowable, tolerable, admissible, warranted.

(ANT.) unsuitable, inadmissible.

justify (SYN.) uphold, excuse, acquit, exonerate, absolve, clear, vindicate.

(ANT.) convict.

jut (SYN.) project, protrude, stick out.

(ANT.) indent, recess.

juvenile (SYN.) puerile, youthful, childish, babyish, youngster, young, child.

(ANT.) old, aged, adult, mature.

K

kaiser (SYN.) czar, caesar, caliph, mogul, padishah, tycoon, khan, landamman, cazique.

kavass (SYN.) badel, macebearer, constable.

keck (SYN.) vomit, belch, retch.

keen (SYN.) clever, cunning, acute, penetrating, exact, severe, shrewd, wily, astute, sharp, bright, intelligent, smart, sharp-witted, witty, cutting, fine, quick, energetic, lively.

(ANT.) stupid, shallow, dull, blunted, slow, bland, gentle, obtuse, blunt.

keep (SYN.) maintain, retain, observe, protect, confine, sustain, continue, preserve, save, guard, restrain, reserve, obey, support, honor, execute, celebrate, conserve, have, tend, detain, remain, hold on.

(ANT.) abandon, disobey, dismiss, discard, ignore, neglect, lose, relinquish.

keeper (SYN.) warden, jailer, ranger, guard, turnkey, watchman, escort, custodian.

keeping (SYN.) congeniality, uniformity, consentaneousness, conformance, congruity, union.

keepsake (SYN.) reminder, memorial, relic, souvenir, memento, remembrance.

keg (SYN.) container, drum, tub, barrel, receptacle, reservatory, cask, tank.

kelpie (SYN.) sprite, nixie, naiad, pixy.

kelson (SYN.) bottom, sole, toe, foot, root, keel.

kempt (SYN.) neat, trim, tidy, spruce, cleaned.

ken (SYN.) field, view, vision, range, scope.

kennel (SYN.) swarm, flock, covy, drove, herd, pound, doghouse.

kerchief (SYN.) neckcloth, hankerchief, scarf, headpiece, babushka.

kern (SYN.) peasant, carle, serf, tike, tyke, countryman.

kernel (SYN.) corn, seed, grain, marrow, pith, backbone, soul, heart, core, nucleus.

ketch (SYN.) lugger, cutter, clipper, ship, barge, sloop.

kettle (SYN.) pan, caldron, vat, pot, teapot, vessel, receptacle, receiver, tureen.

key (SYN.) opener, explanation, tone, lead, cause, source, note, answer, clue.

keynote (SYN.) core, model, theme, pattern, standard.

khan (SYN.) master, czar, kaiser, padishah, caesar.

kick (SYN.) punt, remonstrate, boot, excitement, pleasure, abandon, stop, hit.

kickback (SYN.) repercussion, backfire, rebound.

kickoff (SYN.) beginning, opening, start, commencement, outset.

kid (SYN.) joke, tease, fool, jest, tot, child.

kidnap (SYN.) abduct, snatch, shanghai.

kill (SYN.) execute, put to death, slay, butcher, assassinate, murder, cancel, destroy, slaughter, finish, end, annihilate, massacre.

(ANT.) save, protect, animate, resuscitate, vivify.

killer *(SYN.)* assassin, murderer.

killing *(SYN.)* massacre, genocide, slaughter, carnage, butchery, bloodshed.

kin *(SYN.)* relatives, family, folks, relations.

kind *(SYN.)* humane, affable, compassionate, benevolent, merciful, tender, sympathetic, breed, indulgent, forbearing, kindly, race, good, thoughtful, character, benign, family, sort, species, variety, class, type, gentle.

(ANT.) unkind, cruel, merciless, severe, mean, inhuman.

kindle *(SYN.)* fire, ignite, light, arouse, excite, set afire, stir up, trigger, move, provoke, inflame.

(ANT.) pacify, extinguish, calm.

kindred *(SYN.)* family, relations, relatives, consanguinity, kinsfolk, affinity.

(ANT.) strangers, disconnection.

kinetic *(SYN.)* vigorous, active, dynamic, energetic, mobile, forceful.

king *(SYN.)* sovereign, ruler, chief, monarch, potentate.

kingdom *(SYN.)* realm, empire, monarchy, domain.

kingly *(SYN.)* kinglike, imperial, regal, royal, majestic.

kink *(SYN.)* twist, curl, quirk, complication.

kinship *(SYN.)* lineage, blood, family, stock, relationship.

kismet *(SYN.)* fate, end, fortune, destiny.

kiss *(SYN.)* pet, caress, fondle, cuddle, osculate, embrace.

(ANT.) vex, spurn, annoy, tease, buffet.

kit *(SYN.)* outfit, collection, furnishings, equipment, rig, gear, set.

knack *(SYN.)* cleverness, readiness, deftness, ability, ingenuity, skill, talent, aptitude, talent, know-how, art, adroitness, skillfulness.

(ANT.) inability, clumsiness, awkwardness, ineptitude.

knave *(SYN.)* rogue, rascal, villain, scoundrel.

knead *(SYN.)* combine, massage, blend.

knife *(SYN.)* sword, blade.

knightly *(SYN.)* valiant, courageous, gallant, chivalrous, noble.

knit *(SYN.)* unite, join, mend, fasten, connect, combine.

knob *(SYN.)* doorknob, handle, protuberance.

knock *(SYN.)* thump, tap, rap, strike, hit, jab, punch, beat, pound, bang, hammer.

knockout *(SYN.)* stunning, overpowering, stupefying, overwhelming.

knoll *(SYN.)* hill, elevation, hump, mound, butte.

knot *(SYN.)* cluster, gathering, collection, group, crowd, twist, snarl, tangle, connection, junction, link, loop, tie.

know *(SYN.)* perceive, comprehend, apprehend, recognize, understand, discern, discriminate, ascertain, identify, be aware, distinguish.

(ANT.) doubt, suspect, dispute, ignore.

know-how *(SYN.)* skill, ability, proficiency.

knowing *(SYN.)* smart, wise, clever, sagacious, shrewd.

knowledge *(SYN.)* information, wisdom, erudition, learning, apprehension, scholarship, cognizance, acquirements, understanding, intelligence, education, experience.

(ANT.) ignorance, stupidity, illiteracy.

knowledgeable *(SYN.)* understanding, informed, aware.

(ANT.) lacking, unaware.

knurl *(SYN.)* gnarl, knot, projection, burl, node, lump, bulge, bump.

kooky *(SYN.)* odd, wild, unpredictable, weird.

(ANT.) conservative, predictable.

kosher *(SYN.)* permitted, okay, fit, proper, acceptable.

kowtow *(SYN.)* stoop, bend, kneel, genuflect, bow, flatter.

kudos *(SYN.)* acclaim, praise, approbation, approval, applause, cheer, credit, honor.

L

label *(SYN.)* mark, tag, title, name, marker,

stamp, sticker, ticket, docket, identity.

labor *(SYN.)* toil, travail, effort, task, childbirth, work, parturition, striving, workers, effort, industry, workingmen, strive, exertion, employment, drudgery, endeavor.
(ANT.) recreation, indolence, idleness, leisure.

laboratory *(SYN.)* lab, workroom, workshop.

laborer *(SYN.)* wage earner, helper, worker, blue-collar worker.

laborious *(SYN.)* tiring, difficult, hard, burdensome, industrious.
(ANT.) easy, relaxing, restful.

labyrinth *(SYN.)* complex, maze, tangle.

lace *(SYN.)* openwork, fancywork, embroidery, edging.

lacerate *(SYN.)* mangle, tear roughly.

laceration *(SYN.)* cut, wound, puncture, gash, lesion, injury.

lack *(SYN.)* want, need, shortage, dearth, scarcity, require.
(ANT.) quantity, plentifulness.

lackey *(SYN.)* yesman, stooge, flatterer, flunky.

lacking *(SYN.)* insufficient, short, deficient, incomplete, defective.
(ANT.) satisfactory, enough, ample, sufficient, adequate.

lackluster *(SYN.)* dull, pallid, flat, lifeless, drab, dim.

laconic *(SYN.)* short, terse, compact, brief, curt, succinct, concise.

lacquer *(SYN.)* polish, varnish, gild.

lad *(SYN.)* youth, boy, fellow, stripling.

laden *(SYN.)* burdened, loaded, weighted.

ladle *(SYN.)* scoop, dipper.

lady *(SYN.)* matron, woman, dame, gentlewoman.

ladylike *(SYN.)* feminine, womanly, maidenly, womanish, female.
(ANT.) masculine, male, virile, mannish, manly.

lag *(SYN.)* dawdle, loiter, linger, poke, straggle, delay, tarry.

laggard *(SYN.)* dallier, idler, lingerer, slowpoke, dawdler.

lair *(SYN.)* retreat, burrow, den, nest, mew, hole.

lame *(SYN.)* feeble, maimed, disabled, crippled, deformed, hobbling, unconvincing, weak, poor, inadequate, defective, limping.
(ANT.) vigorous, convincing, plausible, athletic, robust, agile, sound.

lament *(SYN.)* deplore, wail, bemoan, bewail, regret, grieve, mourning, lamentation, moaning, wailing, weep, mourn, sorrow.
(ANT.) celebrate, rejoice.

lamentable *(SYN.)* unfortunate, deplorable.

lampoon *(SYN.)* skit, tirade, burlesque, parody, satire.

lance *(SYN.)* cut, pierce, perforate, stab, puncture, impale, knife.

land *(SYN.)* earth, continent, ground, soil, domain, estate, field.

landmark *(SYN.)* keystone, monument, point, cornerstone.

landscape *(SYN.)* scenery, panorama, countryside, scene.

landslide *(SYN.)* rockfall, glissade, avalanche.

lane *(SYN.)* alley, way, road, path, aisle, pass, avenue, passage.

language *(SYN.)* dialect, tongue, speech, lingo, jargon, cant, diction, idiom, patter, phraseology, vernacular, words, lingo, talk.
(ANT.) gibberish, nonsense, babble, drivel.

languid *(SYN.)* feeble, drooping, irresolute, debilitated, dull, lethargic, weak, faint, listless.
(ANT.) forceful, strong, vigorous.

languish *(SYN.)* decline, sink, droop, wither, waste, fail, wilt.
(ANT.) revive, rejuvenate, refresh, renew.

languor *(SYN.)* weariness, depression, torpor, inertia, apathy.

lanky *(SYN.)* skinny, gaunt, lean, scrawny, slender, thin.
(ANT.) chunky, stocky, obese, fat.

lantern *(SYN.)* torch, light, lamp, flashlight.

lap *(SYN.)* drink, lick, fold over.

lapse *(SYN.)* decline, sink, go down, slump.

larceny *(SYN.)* pillage, robbery, stealing, theft, burglary, plunder.

lard *(SYN.)* grease, fat.

large *(SYN.)* great, vast, colossal, ample, extensive, capacious, sizable, broad, massive, grand, immense, big, enormous, huge.
(ANT.) tiny, little, short, small.

largely *(SYN.)* chiefly, mainly, principally, mostly.

lariat *(SYN.)* lasso, rope.

lark *(SYN.)* fling, frolic, play, fun, spree, joke, revel.

lascivious *(SYN.)* lecherous, raunchy, lustful, wanton, lewd.

lash *(SYN.)* thong, whip, rod, cane, blow, strike, hit, beat, knout.

lass *(SYN.)* maiden, girl, damsel.
(ANT.) woman.

lasso *(SYN.)* lariat, rope, noose, snare.

last *(SYN.)* terminal, final, ultimate, remain, endure, concluding, latest, utmost, end, conclusive, hindmost, continue.
(ANT.) first, initial, beginning, opening, starting, foremost.

latch *(SYN.)* clasp, hook, fastener, lock, closing, seal, catch.

late *(SYN.)* overdue, tardy, behind, advanced, delayed, new, slow.
(ANT.) timely, early.

lately *(SYN.)* recently, yesterday.

latent *(SYN.)* potential, undeveloped, unseen, dormant, secret, concealed, inactive, hidden, obscured, covered.
(ANT.) visible, evident, conspicuous, explicit, manifest.

lather *(SYN.)* suds, foam, froth.

lateral *(SYN.)* sideways, glancing, tangential, marginal, skirting.

latitude *(SYN.)* range, scope, freedom, extent.

latter *(SYN.)* more recent, later.
(ANT.) former.

lattice *(SYN.)* grating, screen, frame, trellis, openwork, framework, grid.

laud *(SYN.)* commend, praise, extol, glorify, compliment.
(ANT.) criticize, belittle.

laudable *(SYN.)* creditable, praiseworthy, commendable, admirable.

laudation *(SYN.)* applause, compliment, flattery, praise, commendation, acclaim, glorification.
(ANT.) criticizing, condemnation, reproach, disparagement, censure.

laugh *(SYN.)* chuckle, giggle, snicker, cackle, titter, grin, smile, roar, guffaw, jeer, mock.

laughable *(SYN.)* funny, amusing, comical, humorous, ridiculous.

launch *(SYN.)* drive, fire, propel, start, begin, originate, set afloat, initiate.
(ANT.) finish, stop, terminate.

launder *(SYN.)* bathe, wash, scrub, scour.

laurels *(SYN.)* glory, distinction, recognition, award, commendation, reward, honor.

lavatory *(SYN.)* toilet, washroom, bathroom, latrine.

lavish *(SYN.)* squander, waste, dissipate, scatter, abundant, free, plentiful, liberal, extravagant, ample, wear out, prodigal.
(ANT.) economize, save, conserve, accumulate, stingy, preserve.

law *(SYN.)* decree, formula, statute, act, rule, ruling, standard, principle, ordinance, proclamation, regulation, order, edict.

lawful *(SYN.)* legal, permissible, allowable, legitimate, authorized, constitutional, rightful.
(ANT.) prohibited, criminal, illicit, illegal, illegitimate.

lawless *(SYN.)* uncivilized, uncontrolled, wild, savage, untamed.
(ANT.) obedient, law-abiding, tame.

lawlessness *(SYN.)* chaos, anarchy.

lawn *(SYN.)* grass, meadow, turf.

lawyer *(SYN.)* counsel, attorney, counselor.

lax *(SYN.)* slack, loose, careless, vague, lenient, lazy.
(ANT.) firm, rigid.

lay *(SYN.)* mundane, worldly, temporal, place, dispose, bet, wager, hazard, risk, stake, site, earthly, profane, laic, arrange, location, put, set, ballad, deposit, position.
(ANT.) spiritual, unworldly, remove, misplace, disturb, mislay, disarrange,

ecclesiastical, religious.

lay off *(SYN.)* discharge, bounce, fire, dismiss.

layout *(SYN.)* plan, arrangement, design.

lazy *(SYN.)* slothful, supine, idle, inactive, sluggish, inert, indolent.

(ANT.) alert, ambitious, forceful, diligent, active, assiduous.

lea *(SYN.)* pasture, meadow.

leach *(SYN.)* remove, extract, seep, dilute, wash out.

lead *(SYN.)* regulate, conduct, guide, escort, direct, supervise, command, steer, control.

(ANT.) follow.

leader *(SYN.)* master, ruler, captain, chief, commander, principal, director, head, chieftain.

(ANT.) follower, servant, disciple, subordinate, attendant.

leading *(SYN.)* dominant, foremost, principal, first, main, primary.

league *(SYN.)* entente, partnership, association, confederacy, coalition, society, alliance, federation.

(ANT.) separation, schism.

leak *(SYN.)* dribble, flow, drip, opening, perforation.

lean *(SYN.)* rely, tilt, slim, slender, slope, incline, tend, trust, bend, tendency, slant, depend, spare, scant, lanky, thin, meager, inclination, narrow, sag.

(ANT.) rise, heavy, fat, erect, straighten, portly, raise.

leaning *(SYN.)* trend, proclivity, bias, tendency, bent, predisposition, proneness.

(ANT.) disinclination, aversion.

leap *(SYN.)* vault, skip, caper, dive, hurdle, jump, bound, start, hop, plunge, spring.

learn *(SYN.)* gain, find out, memorize, acquire, determine.

learned *(SYN.)* erudite, knowing, enlightened, deep, wise, discerning, scholarly, intelligent, educated, sagacious.

(ANT.) simple, uneducated, ignorant, illiterate, foolish.

learning *(SYN.)* science, education, lore, apprehension, wisdom, knowledge, scholarship.

(ANT.) misunderstanding, ignorance, stupidity.

lease *(SYN.)* charter, let, rent, engage.

leash *(SYN.)* chain, strap, shackle, collar.

least *(SYN.)* minutest, smallest, tiniest, trivial, minimum, fewest, slightest.

(ANT.) most.

leave *(SYN.)* give up, retire, desert, abandon, withdraw, relinquish, will, depart, quit, liberty, renounce, go, bequeath, consent, allowance, permission, freedom, forsake.

(ANT.) come, stay, arrive, tarry, remain, abide.

lecherous *(SYN.)* lustful, sensual, carnal, lascivious.

lecture *(SYN.)* talk, discussion, lesson, instruct, speech, conference, sermon, report, recitation, address, oration, discourse.

(ANT.) writing, meditation, correspondence.

ledge *(SYN.)* eaves, ridge, shelf, rim, edge.

lee *(SYN.)* shelter, asylum, sanctuary, haven.

leech *(SYN.)* barnacle, bloodsucker, parasite.

leer *(SYN.)* eye, grimace, ogle, wink, squint.

leeway *(SYN.)* reserve, allowance, elbowroom, slack, clearance.

leftovers *(SYN.)* scraps, remains, residue, remainder.

legacy *(SYN.)* bequest, inheritance, heirloom.

legal *(SYN.)* legitimate, rightful, honest, allowable, allowed, permissible, lawful, permitted, authorized.

(ANT.) illicit, illegal, prohibited, illegitimate.

legalize *(SYN.)* authorize, ordain, approve, sanction.

legate *(SYN.)* envoy, agent, representative, emissary.

legend *(SYN.)* saga, fable, allegory, myth, parable, tale, story, folklore, fiction, chronicle.

(ANT.) history, facts.

legendary *(SYN.)* fictitious, traditional, mythical, imaginary, fanciful.

legible *(SYN.)* plain, readable, clear, distinct. *(ANT.)* *illegible.*

legion *(SYN.)* outfit, unit, troop, regiment, company, battalion, force, army, team, division.

legislation *(SYN.)* resolution, ruling, law-making, regulation, enactment, statute, decree.

legislator *(SYN.)* statesman, congressman, senator, politician, lawmaker.

legitimate *(SYN.)* true, real, bona fide, lawful, proper, right, valid, correct, unadulterated, authentic, rightful, legal, sincere. *(ANT.)* *sham, counterfeit, artificial, false.*

leisure *(SYN.)* respite, intermission, ease, relaxation, rest, calm, tranquillity, recreation, peace, pause. *(ANT.)* *motion, commotion, tumult, agitation, disturbance.*

leisurely *(SYN.)* sluggish, laggard, unhurried, relaxed, casual, dawdling, slow, deliberate. *(ANT.)* *hurried, swift, pressed, rushed, forced, fast, speedy, quick.*

lend *(SYN.)* entrust, advance, confer.

length *(SYN.)* reach, measure, extent, distance, span, longness, stretch.

lengthen *(SYN.)* stretch, prolong, draw, reach, increase, grow, protract, extend. *(ANT.)* *shrink, contract, shorten.*

leniency *(SYN.)* grace, pity, compassion, mildness, charity, mercy, clemency. *(ANT.)* *vengeance, punishment, cruelty.*

lenient *(SYN.)* tender, humane, clement, tolerant, compassionate, merciful, relaxed, forgiving, gentle, mild, lax, kind. *(ANT.)* *unfeeling, pitiless, brutal, remorseless.*

leprechaun *(SYN.)* gnome, imp, goblin, fairy, elf, sprite, banshee.

lesion *(SYN.)* wound, blemish, sore, trauma, injury.

less *(SYN.)* fewer, smaller, reduced, negative, stinted. *(ANT.)* *more.*

lessen *(SYN.)* shorten, reduce, deduct, subtract, curtail, diminish, shrink, dwindle, decline, instruction, teaching, remove, decrease. *(ANT.)* *swell, grow, enlarge, increase, expand, multiply, amplify.*

lesson *(SYN.)* exercise, session, class, assignment, section, recitation.

let *(SYN.)* admit, hire out, contract, allow, permit, consent, leave, grant, rent. *(ANT.)* *deny.*

letdown *(SYN.)* disillusionment, disappointment.

lethal *(SYN.)* mortal, dangerous, deadly, fatal, devastating.

lethargic *(SYN.)* sluggish, logy, slow, listless, phlegmatic, lazy. *(ANT.)* *vivacious, energetic.*

lethargy *(SYN.)* numbness, stupor, daze, insensibility, torpor. *(ANT.)* *wakefulness, liveliness, activity, readiness.*

letter *(SYN.)* note, mark, message, character, symbol, sign, memorandum.

letup *(SYN.)* slowdown, slackening, lessening, abatement, reduction.

levee *(SYN.)* dike, breakwater, dam, embankment.

level *(SYN.)* smooth, even, plane, equivalent, uniform, horizontal, equal, flatten, equalize, raze, demolish, flat. *(ANT.)* *uneven, sloping, hilly, broken.*

level-headed *(SYN.)* reasonable, sensible, calm, collected, cool.

leverage *(SYN.)* clout, power, influence, weight, rank.

levity *(SYN.)* humor, triviality, giddiness, hilarity, fun, frivolity.

levy *(SYN.)* tax, duty, tribute, rate, assessment, exaction, charge, custom. *(ANT.)* *wages, remuneration, gift.*

lewd *(SYN.)* indecent, smutty, course, gross, disgusting, impure. *(ANT.)* *pure, decent, refined.*

liability *(SYN.)* indebtedness, answerability, obligation, vulnerability.

liable *(SYN.)* answerable, responsible, likely, exposed to, subject, amenable, probable, accountable. *(ANT.)* *immune, exempt, independent.*

liaison *(SYN.)* union, coupling, link, connection, alliance.

liar *(SYN.)* fibber, falsifier, storyteller, fabricator, prevaricator.

libel *(SYN.)* slander, calumny, vilification, aspersion, defamation.
(ANT.) defense, praise, applause, flattery.

liberal *(SYN.)* large, generous, unselfish, open-handed, broad, tolerant, kind, unprejudiced, open-minded, lavish, plentiful, ample, abundant, extravagant, extensive.
(ANT.) restricted, conservative, stingy, confined.

liberality *(SYN.)* kindness, philanthropy, beneficence, humanity, altruism, benevolence, generosity, charity.
(ANT.) selfishness, cruelty, malevolence.

liberate *(SYN.)* emancipate, loose, release, let go, deliver, free, discharge.
(ANT.) subjugate, oppress, jail, confine, restrict, imprison.

liberated *(SYN.)* loose, frank, emancipated, careless, liberal, freed, autonomous, exempt, familiar.
(ANT.) subject, clogged, restricted, impeded.

liberty *(SYN.)* permission, independence, autonomy, license, privilege, emancipation, self-government, freedom.
(ANT.) constraint, imprisonment, bondage, captivity.

license *(SYN.)* liberty, freedom, liberation, permission, exemption, authorization, warrant, allow, consent, permit, sanction, approval, unrestraint.
(ANT.) servitude, constraint, bondage, necessity.

lick *(SYN.)* taste, lap, lave.

lid *(SYN.)* top, cover, cap, plug, cork, stopper.

lie *(SYN.)* untruth, fib, illusion, delusion, falsehood, fiction, equivocation, prevarication, repose, location, perjury, misinform, site, recline, similitude.
(ANT.) variance, truth, difference.

life *(SYN.)* sparkle, being, spirit, vivacity, animation, buoyancy, vitality, existence, biography, energy, liveliness, vigor.
(ANT.) demise, lethargy, death, languor.

lift *(SYN.)* hoist, pick up, elevate, raise, heft.

light *(SYN.)* brightness, illumination, beam, gleam, lamp, knowledge, brilliance, fixture, bulb, candle, fire, ignite, burn, dawn, incandescence, flame, airy, unsubstantial, dainty, luminosity, shine, radiance, giddy, enlightenment, weightless, understanding.
(ANT.) darken, gloom, shadow, extinguish, darkness.

lighten *(SYN.)* diminish, unburden, reduce, brighten.

light-headed *(SYN.)* giddy, silly, dizzy, frivolous.
(ANT.) sober, clear-headed, rational.

lighthearted *(SYN.)* carefree, merry, gay, cheerful, happy, glad.
(ANT.) somber, sad, serious, melancholy.

like *(SYN.)* fancy, esteem, adore, love, admire, care for, prefer, cherish.
(ANT.) disapprove, loathe, hate, dislike.

likely *(SYN.)* liable, reasonable, probable, possible.

likeness *(SYN.)* similarity, resemblance, representation, image, portrait.
(ANT.) difference.

likewise *(SYN.)* besides, as well, also, too, similarly.

liking *(SYN.)* fondness, affection, partiality.
(ANT.) antipathy, dislike.

limb *(SYN.)* arm, leg, member, appendage, part, bough.

limber *(SYN.)* bending, flexible, elastic, pliable.
(ANT.) inflexible, stiff.

limbo *(SYN.)* exile, banishment, purgatory.

limelight *(SYN.)* spotlight, notice, notoriety, fame, prominence.

limerick *(SYN.)* jingle, rhyme.

limit *(SYN.)* terminus, bound, extent, confine, border, restriction, boundary, restraint, edge, frontier, check, end, limitation.
(ANT.) endlessness, vastness, boundlessness.

limn *(SYN.)* depict, portray, sketch, paint, illustrate.

limp *(SYN.)* soft, flabby, drooping, walk,

limber, supple, flexible, hobble, stagger.
(ANT.) stiff.

limpid *(SYN.)* clear, open, transparent, unobstructed.
(ANT.) cloudy.

line *(SYN.)* row, file, series, array, sequence, wire, seam, wrinkle, crease, boundary, arrangement, kind, type, division.

lineage *(SYN.)* race, family, tribe, nation, strain, folk, people, ancestry, clan.

linger *(SYN.)* wait, rest, bide, delay, dwadle, stay, loiter, remain, dilly-dally, tarry.
(ANT.) leave, expedite.

lingo *(SYN.)* vernacular, dialect, language, jargon, speech.

link *(SYN.)* unite, connector, loop, couple, attach, connective, connection, coupling, juncture, bond.
(ANT.) separate, disconnect, split.

lip *(SYN.)* edge, brim, rim.

liquid *(SYN.)* watery, fluent, fluid, flowing.
(ANT.) solid, congealed.

liquidate *(SYN.)* pay off, settle, defray.

liquor *(SYN.)* spirits, alcohol, drink, booze.

lissom *(SYN.)* nimble, quick, lively, flexible, agile.

list *(SYN.)* roll, register, slate, enumeration, series.

listen *(SYN.)* overhear, attend to, heed, hear, list, hearken.
(ANT.) ignore, scorn, disregard, reject.

listless *(SYN.)* uninterested, tired, lethargic, unconcerned, apathetic.
(ANT.) active.

literal *(SYN.)* exact, verbatim, precise, strict, faithful.

literally *(SYN.)* actually, exactly, really.

literate *(SYN.)* informed, educated, learned, intelligent, versed, knowledgeable.
(ANT.) unread, illiterate, ignorant, unlettered.

literature *(SYN.)* books, writings, publications.

lithe *(SYN.)* supple, flexible, bending, limber, pliable.
(ANT.) stiff.

litigious *(SYN.)* quarrelsome, disputatious, argumentative.

litter *(SYN.)* rubbish, trash, scatter, clutter, strew, debris, rubble, disorder.

little *(SYN.)* tiny, petty, miniature, diminutive, puny, wee, significant, small, short, brief, bit, trivial.
(ANT.) huge, large, big, long, immense.

liturgy *(SYN.)* ritual, sacrament, worship, service.

live *(SYN.)* dwell, reside, abide, survive, exist, alive, occupy, stay, active, surviving.
(ANT.) die.

livelihood *(SYN.)* keep, sustenance, support, subsistence, job, trade, profession, vocation.

lively *(SYN.)* blithe, vivaciousness, clear, vivid, active, frolicsome, brisk, fresh, animated, energetic, live, spry, vigorous, quick, nimble, bright, exciting, supple.
(ANT.) stale, dull, listless, slow, vapid.

livestock *(SYN.)* animals, cattle.

livid *(SYN.)* grayish, furious, pale, enraged.

living *(SYN.)* support, livelihood, existent, alive.

load *(SYN.)* oppress, trouble, burden, weight, freight, afflict, encumber, pack, shipment, cargo, lade, tax.
(ANT.) lighten, console, unload, mitigate, empty, ease.

loafer *(SYN.)* loiterer, bum, idler, sponger, deadbeat.

loan *(SYN.)* credit, advance, lend.

loath *(SYN.)* reluctant, unwilling, opposed.

loathe *(SYN.)* dislike, despise, hate, abhor, detest, abominate.
(ANT.) love, approve, like, admire.

loathsome *(SYN.)* foul, vile, detestable, revolting, abominable, atrocious, offensive, odious.
(ANT.) pleasant, commendable, alluring, agreeable, delightful.

lob *(SYN.)* toss, hurl, pitch, throw, heave.

lobby *(SYN.)* foyer, entry, entrance, vestibule, passageway, entryway.

local *(SYN.)* limited, regional, restricted, particular.

locality *(SYN.)* nearness, neighborhood, district, vicinity.
(ANT.) remoteness.

locate *(SYN.)* discover, find, unearth, site, situate, place.

located *(SYN.)* found, residing, positioned, situated, placed.

location *(SYN.)* spot, locale, station, locality, situation, place, area, site, vicinity, position, zone, region.

lock *(SYN.)* curl, hook, bolt, braid, ringlet, plait, close, latch, tuft, fastening, bar, hasp, fasten, tress.
(ANT.) open.

locker *(SYN.)* wardrobe, closet, cabinet, chest.

locket *(SYN.)* case, lavaliere, pendant.

locomotion*(SYN.)* movement, travel, transit, motion.

locution *(SYN.)* discourse, cadence, manner, accent.

lodge *(SYN.)* cabin, cottage, hut, club, chalet, society, room, reside, dwell, live, occupy, inhabit, abide, board, fix, settle.

lodger *(SYN.)* guest, tenant, boarder, occupant.

lofty *(SYN.)* high, stately, grandiose, towering, elevated, exalted, sublime, majestic, scornful, proud, grand, tall, pompous.
(ANT.) undignified, lowly, common, ordinary.

log *(SYN.)* lumber, wood, board, register, record, album, account, journal, timber.

logical *(SYN.)* strong, effective, telling, convincing, reasonable, sensible, rational, sane, sound, cogent.
(ANT.) crazy, illogical, irrational, unreasonable, weak.

logy *(SYN.)* tired, inactive, lethargic, sleepy, weary.

loiter *(SYN.)* idle, linger, wait, stay, tarry, dilly-dally, dawdle.

loll *(SYN.)* hang, droop, recline, repose, relax.

lone *(SYN.)* lonely, sole, unaided, single, deserted, isolated, secluded, apart, alone, solitary.
(ANT.) surrounded, accompanied.

loner *(SYN.)* recluse, maverick, outsider, hermit.

loneliness *(SYN.)* solitude, isolation, seclusion, alienation.

lonely *(SYN.)* unaided, isolated, single, solitary, lonesome, unaccompanied, deserted, alone, desolate.
(ANT.) surrounded, attended.

lonesome *(SYN.)* secluded, remote, unpopulated, barren, empty, desolate.

long *(SYN.)* lengthy, prolonged, wordy, elongated, extended, lingering, lasting, protracted, extensive, length, prolix, prolonged.
(ANT.) terse, concise, abridged, short.

long-standing *(SYN.)* persistent, established.

long-winded *(SYN.)* boring, dull, wordy.
(ANT.) curt, terse.

look *(SYN.)* gaze, witness, seem, eye, behold, see, watch, scan, view, appear, stare, discern, glance, examine, examination, peep, expression, appearance, regard, study, contemplation, survey.
(ANT.) overlook, hide, avert, miss.

loom *(SYN.)* emerge, appear, show up.

loop *(SYN.)* ringlet, noose, spiral, fastener.

loose *(SYN.)* untied, unbound, lax, vague, unrestrained, dissolute, limp, undone, baggy, disengaged, indefinite, slack, careless, heedless, unfastened, free, wanton.
(ANT.) restrained, steady, fastened, secure, tied, firm, fast, definite, bound, inhibited.

loosen *(SYN.)* untie, undo, loose, unchain.
(ANT.) tie, tighten, secure.

loot *(SYN.)* booty, plunder, take, steal, rob, sack, rifle, pillage, ravage, devastate.

lope *(SYN.)* run, race, bound, gallop.

lopsided *(SYN.)* unequal, twisted, uneven, askew, distorted.

loquacious *(SYN.)* garrulous, wordy, profuse, chatty, verbose.

lord *(SYN.)* peer, ruler, proprietor, boss, nobleman, master, owner, governor.

lore *(SYN.)* learning, knowledge, wisdom, stories, legends beliefs, teachings.

lose *(SYN.)* misplace, flop, fail, sacrifice, forfeit, mislay, vanish, surrender.
(ANT.) succeed, locate, place, win, discover, find.

loss *(SYN.)* injury, damage, want, hurt, need, bereavement, trouble, death, failure, deficiency.

lost *(SYN.)* dazed, wasted, astray, forfeited, preoccupied, used, adrift, bewildered, missing, distracted, consumed, misspent, absorbed, confused, mislaid, gone, destroyed.
(ANT.) found, anchored.

lot *(SYN.)* result, destiny, bunch, many, amount, fate, cluster, group, sum, portion, outcome, number, doom, issue.

lotion *(SYN.)* cosmetic, salve, balm, cream.

lottery *(SYN.)* wager, chance, drawing, raffle.

loud *(SYN.)* vociferous, noisy, resounding, stentorian, clamorous, sonorous, thunderous, shrill, blaring, roaring, deafening.
(ANT.) soft, inaudible, murmuring, subdued, quiet, dulcet.

lounge *(SYN.)* idle, loaf, laze, sofa, couch, davenport, relax, rest, lobby, salon, divan.

louse *(SYN.)* scoundrel, knave, cad, rat.

lousy *(SYN.)* revolting, grimy, rotten, dirty, disgusting.

lovable *(SYN.)* charming, attractive, delightful, amiable, sweet, cuddly, likable.

love *(SYN.)* attachment, endearment, affection, adoration, liking, devotion, warmth, adore, tenderness, friendliness, worship, like, cherish, fondness.
(ANT.) loathing, detest, indifference, dislike, hate, hatred.

loveliness *(SYN.)* grace, pulchritude, elegance, charm, attractiveness, comeliness, fairness, beauty.
(ANT.) ugliness, eyesore, disfigurement, deformity.

lovely *(SYN.)* handsome, fair, charming, pretty, attractive, delightful, comely, beautiful, beauteous, exquisite.
(ANT.) ugly, unsightly, homely, foul, hideous, repulsive.

lover *(SYN.)* fiance, suitor, courter, sweetheart, beau.

loving *(SYN.)* close, intimate, confidential, affectionate, friendly.
(ANT.) formal, conventional, ceremonious, distant.

low *(SYN.)* mean, vile, despicable, vulgar, abject, groveling, contemptible, lesser, menial.
(ANT.) righteous, lofty, esteemed, noble.

lower *(SYN.)* subordinate, minor, secondary, quiet, soften, disgrace, degrade, decrease, reduce, diminish, lessen, inferior.
(ANT.) greater, superior, increase, better.

low-key *(SYN.)* subdued, muted, calm, controlled, restrained, understated, gentle.

lowly *(SYN.)* lowborn, humble, base, low, mean, common, average, simple, modest.
(ANT.) royal, noble.

loyal *(SYN.)* earnest, ardent, addicted, inclined, faithful, devoted, affectionate, prone, fond, patriotic, dependable, true.
(ANT.) indisposed, detached, disloyal, traitorous, untrammeled.

loyalty *(SYN.)* devotion, steadfastness, constancy, faithfulness, fidelity, patriotism, allegiance.
(ANT.) treachery, falseness, disloyalty.

lubricate *(SYN.)* oil, grease, anoint.

lucent *(SYN.)* radiant, beaming, vivid, illuminated, lustrous.

lucid *(SYN.)* plain, visible, clear, intelligible, unmistakable, transparent, limpid, translucent, open, shining, light, explicit, understandable, distinct.
(ANT.) unclear, vague, obscure.

luck *(SYN.)* chance, fortunate, fortune, lot, fate, fluke, destiny, karma, providence.
(ANT.) misfortune.

lucky *(SYN.)* favored, favorable, auspicious, fortunate, successful, felicitous, benign.
(ANT.) unlucky, condemned, unfortunate, persecuted.

lucrative *(SYN.)* well-paying, profitable, high-paying, productive, beneficial.

ludicrous *(SYN.)* absurd, ridiculous, preposterous.

lug *(SYN.)* pull, haul, drag, tug.

luggage *(SYN.)* bags, valises, baggage, suitcases, trunks.

lugubrious *(SYN.)* mournful, sad, gloomy, somber, melancholy.

lukewarm *(SYN.)* unenthusiastic, tepid,

spiritless, detached, apathetic, mild.

lull *(SYN.)* quiet, calm, soothe, rest, hush, stillness, pause, break, intermission, recess, respite, silence.

lumber *(SYN.)* logs, timber, wood.

luminous *(SYN.)* beaming, lustrous, shining, glowing, gleaming, bright, light, alight, clear.

(ANT.) murky, dull, dark.

lummox *(SYN.)* yokel, oaf, bumpkin, clown, klutz.

lump *(SYN.)* swelling, protuberance, mass, chunk, hunk, bump.

lunacy *(SYN.)* derangement, madness, aberration, psychosis.

(ANT.) stability, rationality.

lunge *(SYN.)* charge, stab, attack, thrust, push.

lurch *(SYN.)* topple, sway, toss, roll, rock, tip, pitch.

lure *(SYN.)* draw, tug, drag, entice, attraction, haul, attract, temptation, persuade, pull, allure.

(ANT.) drive, alienate, propel.

lurid *(SYN.)* sensational, terrible, melodramatic, startling.

lurk *(SYN.)* sneak, hide, prowl, slink, creep.

luscious *(SYN.)* savory, delightful, juicy, sweet, pleasing, delectable, palatable, delicious, tasty.

(ANT.) unsavory, nauseous, acrid.

lush *(SYN.)* tender, succulent, ripe.

lust *(SYN.)* longing, desire, passion, craving, aspiration, urge.

(ANT.) hate, loathing, distaste.

luster *(SYN.)* radiance, brightness, glister, honor, fame, effulgence, gloss, sheen, shine, gleam, glow, glitter, brilliance, splendor.

(ANT.) dullness, obscurity, darkness.

lustful *(SYN.)* amorous, sexy, desirous, passionate, wanton, lubricious, want, concupiscent.

lusty *(SYN.)* healthy, strong, mighty, powerful, sturdy, strapping, hale, hardy, rugged, hefty.

(ANT.) weak, sick, unhealthy, frail.

luxuriant *(SYN.)* abundant, flourishing, dense, lush, rich.

luxurious *(SYN.)* rich, lavish, deluxe, splendid, magnificent.

(ANT.) simple, crude, sparse.

luxury *(SYN.)* frills, comfort, extravagance, wealth, elegance, splendor, prosperity, swankiness, plush, well-being, grandeur, prodigality, finery, ease.

(ANT.) poverty, without, poor, shabby.

lyric *(SYN.)* musical, text, words, libretto, singing, tune.

lyrical *(SYN.)* poetic, musical.

M

macabre *(SYN.)* ghastly, grim, horrible, gruesome.

maceration *(SYN.)* dilution, washing.

machination *(SYN.)* hoax, swindle, card-sharping, cunning, plot, cabal, conspriracy.

machinator *(SYN.)* stragetist, schemer, schemist.

machine *(SYN.)* motor, mechanism, device, contrivance.

machinist *(SYN.)* engineer.

macilent *(SYN.)* gaunt, lean, lank, meager, emaciated.

mactation *(SYN.)* immolation, self-immolation, infanticide.

macula *(SYN.)* mole, patch, freckle, spot.

maculate *(SYN.)* bespot, stipple.

maculation *(SYN.)* irisation, striae, iridescence, spottiness.

mad *(SYN.)* incensed, crazy, insane, angry, furious, delirious, provoked, enraged, demented, maniacal, exasperated, wrathful, crazy, deranged, infuriated.

(ANT.) sane, calm, healthy, rational, lucid, cheerful, happy, composed, reasonable.

madam *(SYN.)* dame, woman, lady, matron, mistress.

madden *(SYN.)* anger, annoy, infuriate, enrage, provoke, convulse, asperate, outrage.

(ANT.) please, mollify, calm.

madder *(SYN.)* ruddle.

madness *(SYN.)* derangement, delirium, aberration, mania, insanity, craziness, psychosis.

(ANT.) *stability, rationality.*

maelstrom *(SYN.)* surge, rapids, eddy, white water, riptide.

magazine *(SYN.)* journal, periodical, arsenal, armory.

magic *(SYN.)* sorcery, wizardry, charm, legerdemain, enchantment, black art, necromancy, conjuring, bewitchery, spell.

magical *(SYN.)* mystical, marvelous, magic, miraculous, bewitching, spell-binding.

magician *(SYN.)* conjuror, sorcerer, wizard, artist, trickster.

magistrate *(SYN.)* judge, adjudicator.

magnanimous *(SYN.)* giving, bountiful, beneficent, unselfish, chivalrous, generous. *(ANT.)* *stingy, greedy, selfish.*

magnate *(SYN.)* leader, bigwig, tycoon, chief, giant.

magnet *(SYN.)* enticer, enticement, lure, temptation.

magnetic *(SYN.)* pulling, attractive, alluring, drawing, enthralling, seductive.

magnetism *(SYN.)* allure, irresistibility, attraction, appeal.

magnificence *(SYN.)* luxury, grandeur, splendor, majesty, dynamic.

magnificent *(SYN.)* rich, lavish, luxurious, splendid, wonderful, extraordinary, impressive. *(ANT.)* *simple, plain.*

magnify *(SYN.)* heighten, exaggerate, amplify, expand, stretch, increase, enhance, intensify. *(ANT.)* *compress, understate, depreciate, belittle.*

magnitude *(SYN.)* mass, bigness, size, area, volume, dimensions, greatness, extent, measure, importance, consequence, significance.

maid *(SYN.)* chambermaid, servant, maidservant.

maiden *(SYN.)* original, foremost, first, damsel, lass, miss. *(ANT.)* *accessory, secondary.*

mail *(SYN.)* dispatch, send, letters, post, correspondence.

maim *(SYN.)* disable, cripple, hurt, wound, injure, mangle, mutilate, incapacitate.

main *(SYN.)* essential, chief, highest, principal, first, leading, cardinal, supreme, foremost. *(ANT.)* *supplemental, subordinate, auxiliary.*

mainstay *(SYN.)* buttress, pillar, refuge, reinforcement, support.

maintain *(SYN.)* claim, support, uphold, defend, vindicate, sustain, continue, allege, contend, preserve, affirm, keep, justify. *(ANT.)* *neglect, oppose, discontinue, resist, deny.*

maintenance *(SYN.)* subsistence, livelihood, living, support, preservation, upkeep.

majestic *(SYN.)* magnificent, stately, noble, august, grand, imposing, sublime, lofty, high, grandiose, dignified, royal, kingly. *(ANT.)* *humble, lowly, undignified, common, ordinary.*

majesty *(SYN.)* grandeur, dignity, nobility, splendor, distinction.

major *(SYN.)* important, superior, larger, greater, uppermost. *(ANT.)* *inconsequential, minor.*

make *(SYN.)* execute, cause, produce, establish, assemble, create, shape, compel, fashion, construct, build, fabricate, manufacture, form, accomplish. *(ANT.)* *unmake, break, undo, demolish.*

make-believe *(SYN.)* pretend, imagined, simulated, false, fake.

maker *(SYN.)* inventor, creator, producer, builder, manufacturer.

makeshift *(SYN.)* proxy, deputy, understudy, expedient, agent, lieutenant, alternate, substitute. *(ANT.)* *sovereign, head, principal.*

make-up *(SYN.)* composition, formation, structure, cosmetics.

malady *(SYN.)* disease, illness, sickness, ailment, infirmity, disorder, affliction. *(ANT.)* *vigor, healthiness, health.*

malaise *(SYN.)* anxiety, apprehension, dissatisfaction, uneasiness, nervousness, disquiet, discontent.

male *(SYN.)* masculine, virile. *(ANT.)* *female, womanly, feminine.*

malcontent *(SYN.)* displeased, ill- humored, querulous, discontented, quarrelsome.

malefactor *(SYN.)* perpetrator, gangster, hoodlum, wrongdoer, troublemaker, criminal, scoundrel, evildoer, law-breaker.

malevolence *(SYN.)* spite, malice, enmity, rancor, animosity.
(ANT.) love, affection, toleration, kindness.

malfunction *(SYN.)* flaw, breakdown, snag, glitch, failure.

malice *(SYN.)* spite, grudge, enmity, ill will, malignity, animosity, rancor, resentment, viciousness, grudge, bitterness.
(ANT.) love, affection, toleration, benevolence, charity.

malicious *(SYN.)* hostile, malignant, virulent, bitter, rancorous, malevolent, spiteful.
(ANT.) kind, benevolent, affectionate.

malign *(SYN.)* misuse, defame, revile, abuse, traduce, asperse.
(ANT.) praise, protect, honor.

malignant *(SYN.)* harmful, deadly, killing, lethal, mortal, destructive.
(ANT.) benign, harmless.

malingerer *(SYN.)* quitter, idler, gold-brick.

malleable *(SYN.)* meek, tender, soft, lenient, flexible, mild, compassionate, supple.
(ANT.) tough, rigid, unyielding, hard.

malodorous *(SYN.)* reeking, fetid, noxious, vile, rancid, offensive,

malpractice *(SYN.)* wrongdoing, misdeed, abuse, malfeasance, error, mismanagement, dereliction, fault, sin, misconduct.

maltreat *(SYN.)* mistreat, ill-treatment, abuse.

maltreatment *(SYN.)* disparagement, perversion, aspersion, invective, defamation, profanation.
(ANT.) respect, approval, laudation, commendation.

mammoth *(SYN.)* enormous, immense, huge, colossal, gigantic, gargantuan, ponderous.
(ANT.) minuscule, tiny, small.

man *(SYN.)* person, human being, society, folk, soul, individual, mortal, fellow, male, gentleman.
(ANT.) woman.

manacle *(SYN.)* chain, shackle, cuff, handcuff, bond.

manage *(SYN.)* curb, govern, direct, bridle, command, regulate, repress, check, restrain, dominate, guide, lead, supervise, superintend, control, rule.
(ANT.) forsake, submit, abandon, mismanage, bungle.

manageable *(SYN.)* willing, obedient, docile, controllable, tractable, submissive, governable, wieldy, untroublesome.
(ANT.) recalcitrant, unmanageable, wild.

management *(SYN.)* regulation, administration, supervision, direction, control.

manager *(SYN.)* overseer, superintendent, supervisor, director, boss, executive.

mandate *(SYN.)* order, injunction, command, referendum, dictate, writ, directive, commission.

mandatory *(SYN.)* compulsory, required, obligatory, imperative.
(ANT.) optional.

maneuver *(SYN.)* execution, effort, proceeding, enterprise, working, action, operation, agency.
(ANT.) rest, inaction, cessation.

mangle *(SYN.)* tear apart, cut, maim, wound, mutilate, injure.

mangy *(SYN.)* shoddy, frazzled, seedy, threadbare, shabby.

manhandle *(SYN.)* maltreat, maul, abuse, ill-treat.

manhood *(SYN.)* maturity, manliness.
(ANT.) youth.

mania *(SYN.)* insanity, enthusiasm, craze, desire, madness.

manic *(SYN.)* excited, hyped up, agitated.

manifest *(SYN.)* open, evident, lucid, clear, distinct, unobstructed, cloudless, apparent, intelligible, apparent.
(ANT.) vague, overcast, unclear, cloudy, hidden, concealed.

manifesto *(SYN.)* pronouncement, edict, proclamation, statement.

manifold *(SYN.)* various, many, multiple, numerous, abundant.
(ANT.) few.

manipulate *(SYN.)* manage, feel, work, operate, handle, touch.

manly *(SYN.)* strong, brave, masculine, courageous, stalwart.

man-made *(SYN.)* artificial.

(ANT.) natural.

manner *(SYN.)* air, demeanor, custom, style, method, deportment, mode, habit, practice, way, behavior, fashion.

mannerism *(SYN.)* eccentricity, quirk, habit, peculiarity, idiosyncrasy, trait.

mannerly *(SYN.)* well-bred, gentlemanly, courteous, suave, polite, genteel.

manor *(SYN.)* land, mansion, estate, domain, villa, castle, property, palace.

manslaughter *(SYN.)* murder, killing, assassination, homicide, elimination.

mantle *(SYN.)* serape, garment, overgarment, cover, cloak, wrap.

manual *(SYN.)* directory, guidebook, handbook, physical, laborious, menial.

manufacture *(SYN.)* construct, make, assemble, fabricate, produce, fashion, build.

manure *(SYN.)* fertilizer, droppings, waste, compost.

manuscript *(SYN.)* copy, writing, work, paper, composition, document.

many *(SYN.)* numerous, various, divers, multitudinous, sundry, multifarious, several, manifold, abundant, plentiful.

(ANT.) infrequent, meager, few, scanty.

map *(SYN.)* sketch, plan, chart, graph, itinerary.

mar *(SYN.)* spoil, hurt, damage, impair, harm, deface, injure.

(ANT.) repair, benefit, mend.

marathon *(SYN.)* relay, race, contest.

maraud *(SYN.)* invade, plunder, loot, ransack, ravage, raid.

march *(SYN.)* promenade, parade, pace, hike, walk, tramp.

margin *(SYN.)* boundary, border, rim, edge.

marginal *(SYN.)* unnecessary, nonessential, borderline, noncritical.

(ANT.) essential.

marine *(SYN.)* naval, oceanic, nautical, ocean, maritime.

mariner *(SYN.)* seafarer, gob, seaman, sailor.

marionette *(SYN.)* doll, puppet.

maritime *(SYN.)* shore, coastal, nautical.

mark *(SYN.)* stain, badge, stigma, vestige, sign, feature, label, characteristic, trace, brand, trait, scar, indication, impression, effect, imprint, stamp, brand.

marked *(SYN.)* plain, apparent, noticeable, evident, decided, noted, special, noteworthy.

market *(SYN.)* supermarket, store, bazaar, mart, stall, marketplace, plaza, emporium.

maroon *(SYN.)* desert, leave behind, forsake, abandon, jettison.

marriage *(SYN.)* wedding, matrimony, nuptials, espousal, union, alliance, association.

(ANT.) divorce, celibacy, separation.

marrow *(SYN.)* center, core, gist, essential, soul.

marry *(SYN.)* wed, espouse, betroth.

marsh *(SYN.)* bog, swamp, mire, everglade, estuary.

marshal *(SYN.)* adjutant, officer, order, arrange, rank.

mart *(SYN.)* shop, market, store.

martial *(SYN.)* warlike, combative, militant, belligerent.

(ANT.) peaceful.

martyr *(SYN.)* victim, sufferer, tortured, torment, plague, harass, persecute.

marvel *(SYN.)* phenomenon, wonder, miracle, astonishment, sensation.

marvelous *(SYN.)* rare, wonderful, unusual, exceptional, miraculous, wondrous, amazing, astonishing, astounding.

(ANT.) usual, common, ordinary. commonplace.

mascot *(SYN.)* pet, amulet, charm.

masculine *(SYN.)* robust, manly, virile, strong, bold, male, lusty, vigorous, hardy, mannish.

(ANT.) weak, emasculated, feminine, female, effeminate, womanish, unmasculine.

mash *(SYN.)* mix, pulverize, crush, grind, crumble, granulate.

mask *(SYN.)* veil, disguise, cloak, secrete, withhold, hide, cover, protection, protector, camouflage, conceal, screen.

(ANT.) uncover, reveal, disclose, show, expose.

masquerade *(SYN.)* pretend, disguise, pose, impersonate, costume party.

mass *(SYN.)* society, torso, body, remains, association, carcass, bulk, company, pile, heap, quantity, aggregation.

(ANT.) spirit, mind, intellect.

massacre *(SYN.)* butcher, murder, carnage, slaughter, execute, slay, genocide, killing, butchery, extermination.

(ANT.) save, protect, vivify, animate.

massage *(SYN.)* knead, rub, stroke.

masses *(SYN)* populace, crowd, multitude, people.

massive *(SYN.)* grave, cumbersome, heavy, sluggish, ponderous, serious, burdensome, huge, immense, tremendous, gigantic.

(ANT.) light, animated, small, tiny, little.

mast *(SYN.)* pole, post.

master *(SYN.)* owner, employer, leader, ruler, chief, head, lord, teacher, manager, holder, commander, overseer, expert, maestro, genius, captain, director, boss.

(ANT.) slave, servant.

masterful *(SYN.)* commanding, bossy, domineering, dictatorial, cunning, wise, accomplished, skillful, sharp.

masterly *(SYN.)* adroit, superb, skillful, expert.

(ANT.) awkward, clumsy.

mastermind *(SYN.)* prodigy, sage, guru, mentor.

masterpiece *(SYN.)* prizewinner, classic, perfection, model.

mastery *(SYN.)* sway, sovereignty, domination, transcendence, ascendancy, influence, jurisdiction, prestige.

masticate *(SYN.)* chew.

mat *(SYN.)* cover, rug, pallet, bedding, pad.

match *(SYN.)* equivalent, equal, contest, balance, resemble, peer, mate.

matchless *(SYN.)* peerless, incomparable, unequaled, unrivaled, excellent.

(ANT.) ordinary, unimpressive.

mate *(SYN.)* friend, colleague, associate, partner, companion, comrade.

(ANT.) stranger, adversary.

material *(SYN.)* sensible, momentous, germane, bodily, palpable, important, physical, essential, corporeal, tangible, substance, matter, fabric.

(ANT.) metaphysical, spiritual, insignificant, mental, immaterial, irrelevant, intangible.

materialize *(SYN.)* take shape, finalize, embody, incarnate, emerge, appear.

maternal *(SYN.)* motherly.

(ANT.) fatherly.

mathematics *(SYN.)* measurements, computations, numbers, add, calculation, figures.

matrimony *(SYN.)* marriage, wedding, espousal, union.

(ANT.) virginity, divorce.

matrix *(SYN.)* template, stamp, negative, stencil, mold, form, die, cutout.

matron *(SYN.)* lady.

matted *(SYN.)* tangled, clustered, rumpled, shaggy, knotted, gnarled, tousled.

matter *(SYN.)* cause, thing, substance, occasion, material, moment, topic, stuff, concern, theme, subject, consequence, affair, business, interest.

(ANT.) spirit, immateriality.

mature *(SYN.)* ready, matured, complete, ripe, consummate, mellow, aged, seasoned, full-grown.

(ANT.) raw, crude, undeveloped, young, immature, innocent.

maudlin *(SYN.)* emotional, mushy, sentimental, mawkish.

maul *(SYN.)* pummel, mistreat, manhandle, beat, batter, bruise, abuse.

mausoleum *(SYN.)* shrine, tomb, vault.

maverick *(SYN.)* nonconformist, oddball, outsider, dissenter, loner.

mawkish *(SYN.)* sentimental, emotional, nostalgic.

maxim *(SYN.)* rule, code, law, proverb, principle, saying, adage, motto.

maximum *(SYN.)* highest, largest, head, greatest, supremacy, climax.

(ANT.) minimum.

may *(SYN.)* can, be able.

maybe *(SYN.)* feasibly, perchance, perhaps,

possibly.

(ANT.) definitely.

mayhem *(SYN.)* brutality, viciousness, ruthlessness.

maze *(SYN.)* complex, labyrinth, network, muddle, confusion, snarl, tangle.

meadow *(SYN.)* field, pasture, lea, range, grassland.

meager *(SYN.)* sparse, scanty, mean, frugal, deficient, slight, paltry, inadequate.

(ANT.) ample, plentiful, abundant, bountiful.

meal *(SYN.)* refreshment, dinner, lunch, repast, breakfast.

mean *(SYN.)* sordid, base, intend, plan, propose, expect, indicate, denote, say, signify, suggest, express, average, nasty, middle, contemptible, offensive, vulgar, unkind, cruel, despicable, vile, low.

(ANT.) dignified, noble, exalted, thoughtful, gentle, openhanded, kind, generous, admirable.

meander *(SYN.)* wind, stray, wander, twist

meaning *(SYN.)* gist, connotation, intent, purport, drift, acceptation, implication, sense, import, interpretation, denotation, signification, explanation, significance.

meaningful *(SYN.)* profound, deep, expressive, important, crucial.

meaningless *(SYN.)* nonsensical, senseless, unreasonable, preposterous.

means *(SYN.)* utensil, channel, agent, money, riches, vehicle, apparatus, device, wealth, support, medium, instrument.

(ANT.) preventive, impediment, hindrance.

measly *(SYN.)* scanty, puny, skimpy, meager, petty.

measure *(SYN.)* law, bulk, rule, criterion, size, volume, weight, standard, dimension, breadth, depth, test, touchstone, trial, length, extent, gauge.

(ANT.) guess, chance, supposition.

measureless *(SYN.)* immeasurable, immense, boundless, limitless, infinite, vast.

(ANT.) figurable, ascertainable, measurable.

meat *(SYN.)* lean, flesh, food.

mecca *(SYN.)* target, shrine, goal, sanctuary, destination.

mechanic *(SYN.)* repairman, machinist.

mechanism *(SYN.)* device, contrivance, tool, machine, machinery.

medal *(SYN.)* decoration, award, badge, medallion, reward, ribbon, prize, honor.

meddle *(SYN.)* tamper, interpose, pry, snoop, intrude, interrupt, interfere, monkey. '

meddlesome *(SYN.)* forward, bothersome, intrusive, obtrusive.

media *(SYN.)* tools, instruments, implements.

mediate *(SYN.)* settle, intercede, umpire, intervene, negotiate, arbitrate, referee.

medicinal *(SYN.)* helping, healing, remedial, therapeutic, corrective.

medicine *(SYN.)* drug, medication, remedy, cure, prescription.

mediocre *(SYN.)* medium, mean, average, moderate, fair, ordinary.

(ANT.) outstanding, exceptional.

meditate *(SYN.)* remember, muse, think, judge, mean, conceive, plan, contemplate, deem, suppose, purpose, consider, picture, reflect, believe, reckon.

medium *(SYN.)* modicum, average, middling, median.

(ANT.) extreme.

medley *(SYN.)* hodgepodge, mixture, assortment, conglomeration, mishmash, miscellany.

meek *(SYN.)* subdued, dull, tedious, flat, docile, domesticated, tame, insipid, domestic.

(ANT.) spirited, exciting, savage, wild.

meet *(SYN.)* fulfill, suffer, find, collide, gratify, engage, connect, converge, encounter, unite, join, satisfy, settle, greet, answer, undergo, meeting, contest, match, assemble, discharge, gather, con-vene, congregate, confront, intersect.

(ANT.) scatter, disperse, separate, cleave.

melancholy *(SYN.)* disconsolate, dejected, despondent, glum, somber, pensive, moody, dispirited, depressed, gloomy, dismal, doleful, depression, sad, downcast, gloom, sadness, grave, downhearted, sorrowful.

(ANT.) happy, cheerful, merry.

meld *(SYN.)* unite, mix, combine, fuse, merge, blend, commingle, amalgamate.

melee *(SYN.)* battle royal, fight, brawl, free-for-all, fracas.

mellow *(SYN.)* mature, ripe, aged, cured, sweet, smooth, melodious, develop, soften.

(ANT.) unripened, immature.

melodious *(SYN.)* lilting, musical, lyric, dulcet, mellifluous, tuneful.

melodramatic *(SYN.)* dramatic, ceremonious, affected, stagy, histrionic, overwrought, sensational, stagy.

(ANT.) unemotional, subdued, modest.

melody *(SYN.)* strain, concord, music, air, song, tune, harmony.

melt *(SYN.)* dissolve, liquefy, blend, fade out, vanish, dwindle, disappear, thaw.

(ANT.) freeze, harden, solidify.

member *(SYN.)* share, part, allotment, moiety, element, concern, interest, lines, faction, role.

(ANT.) whole.

membrane *(SYN.)* layer, sheath, tissue, covering.

memento *(SYN.)* keepsake, token, reminder, trophy, sign, souvenir, remembrance.

memoirs *(SYN.)* diary, reflections, experiences, autobiography, journal, confessions.

memorable *(SYN.)* important, historic, significant, unforgettable, noteworthy, momentous, crucial.

(ANT.) passing, forgettable, transitory, commonplace.

memorandum *(SYN.)* letter, mark, token, note, indication, remark.

memorial *(SYN.)* monument, souvenir, ritual, memento, remembrance, eulogizing honoring, commemoration, reminiscent, testimonial.

memorize *(SYN.)* study, remember.

memory *(SYN.)* renown, remembrance, reminiscence, fame, retrospection, recollection.

(ANT.) oblivion.

menace *(SYN.)* warning, threat, intimidation, warn, threaten, imperil, forebode.

menagerie *(SYN.)* collection, zoo, kennel.

mend *(SYN.)* restore, better, refit, sew, remedy, patch, correct, repair, rectify, ameliorate, improve, reform, recover, fix.

(ANT.) hurt, deface, rend, destroy.

mendacious *(SYN.)* dishonest, false, lying, deceitful, deceptive, tricky.

(ANT.) honest, truthful, sincere, creditable.

mendicant *(SYN.)* ragamuffin, vagabond, beggar.

menial *(SYN.)* unskilled, lowly, degrading, tedious, humble.

mental *(SYN.)* reasoning, intellectual, rational, thinking, conscious, mad, thoughtful, psychotic.

(ANT.) physical.

mentality *(SYN.)* intellect, reason, understanding, liking, disposition, judgment, brain, inclination, faculties, outlook.

(ANT.) materiality, corporeality.

mention *(SYN.)* introduce, refer to, reference, allude, enumerate, speak of.

mentor *(SYN.)* advisor, tutor, sponsor, guru, teacher, counselor, master, coach.

mercenary *(SYN.)* sordid, corrupt, venal, covetous, grasping, avaricious, greedy.

(ANT.) liberal, generous.

merchandise *(SYN.)* stock, wares, goods, sell, commodities, promote, staples, products.

merchant *(SYN.)* retailer, dealer, trader, storekeeper, salesman, businessman.

merciful *(SYN.)* humane, kind-hearted, tender, clement, sympathetic, forgiving, tolerant, forbearing, lenient, compassionate, tenderhearted, kind.

(ANT.) remorseless, cruel, unjust, mean, harsh, unforgiving, vengeful, brutal, unfeeling, pitiless.

merciless *(SYN.)* carnal, ferocious, brute, barbarous, gross, ruthless, cruel, remorseless, bestial, savage, rough, pitiless, inhuman.

(ANT.) humane, courteous, merciful, open-hearted, kind, civilized.

mercurial *(SYN.)* fickle, unstable, volatile, changeable, inconstant, capricious, flighty.

mercy *(SYN.)* grace, consideration,

ness, clemency, mildness, forgiveness, pity, charity, sympathy, leniency, compassion. *(ANT.) punishment, retribution, ruthlessness, cruelty, vengeance.*

mere *(SYN.)* only, simple, scant, bare. *(ANT.) substantial, considerable.*

merely *(SYN.)* only, barely, simply, hardly.

meretricious *(SYN.)* gaudy, sham, bogus, tawdry, flashy, garish.

merge *(SYN.)* unify, fuse, combine, unite, amalgamate, blend, commingle. *(ANT.) separate, decompose, analyze.*

merger *(SYN.)* cartel, union, conglomerate, trust, incorporation, combine, pool.

meridian *(SYN.)* climax, summit, pinnacle, zenith, peak, acme, apex, culmination.

merit *(SYN.)* worthiness, earn, goodness, effectiveness, power, value, virtue, goodness, quality, deserve, excellence, worth. *(ANT.) sin, fault, lose, consume.*

merited *(SYN.)* proper, deserved, suitable, adequate, earned. *(ANT.) unmerited, improper.*

meritorious*(SYN.)* laudable, excellent, commendable, good, deserving.

merry *(SYN.)* hilarious, lively, festive, joyous, sprightly, mirthful, blithe, gay, cheery, joyful, jolly, happy, gleeful, jovial, cheerful. *(ANT.) sorrowful, doleful, morose, gloomy, sad, melancholy.*

mesh *(SYN.)* grid, screen, net, complex.

mesmerize *(SYN.)* enthrall, transfix, spellbind, bewitch, charm, fascinate, hypnotize.

mess *(SYN.)* dirtiness, untidiness, disorder, confusion, muddle, trouble, jumble, difficulty, predicament, confuse, dirty.

message *(SYN.)* letter, annotation, memo, symbol, indication, sign, note, communication, memorandum, observation, token.

messenger *(SYN.)* bearer, agent, runner, courier, liaison, delegate, page.

messy *(SYN.)* disorderly, dirty, confusing, confused, disordered, sloppy, untidy, slovenly. *(ANT.) orderly, neat, tidy.*

metallic *(SYN.)* grating, harsh, clanging, brassy, brazen.

metamorphosis *(SYN.)* transfiguration, change, alteration, rebirth, mutation.

mete *(SYN.)* deal, assign, apportion, divide, give, allocate, allot, measure. *(ANT.) withhold, keep, retain.*

meteoric *(SYN.)* flashing, blazing, swift, brilliant, spectacular, remarkable.

meter *(SYN.)* record, measure, gauge.

method *(SYN.)* order, manner, plan, way, mode, technique, fashion, approach, design, procedure. *(ANT.) disorder.*

methodical *(SYN.)* exact, definite, ceremonious, stiff, accurate, distinct, unequivocal. *(ANT.) easy, loose, informal, rough.*

meticulous *(SYN.)* precise, careful, exacting, fastidious, fussy, perfectionist.

metropolitan *(SYN.)* civic, city, municipal.

mettle *(SYN.)* intrepidity, resolution, boldness, prowess, bravery, fearlessness. *(ANT.) fear, timidity, cowardice.*

microscopic *(SYN.)* tiny, precise, fine, detailed, minute, infinitesimal, minimal. *(ANT.) general, huge, enormous.*

middle *(SYN.)* midpoint, nucleus, center, midst, median, central, intermediate, core. *(ANT.) end, rim, outskirts, beginning, border, periphery.*

middleman *(SYN.)* dealer, agent, distributor, broker, representative, intermediary, liaison.

midget *(SYN.)* gnome, shrimp, pygmy, runt, dwarf. *(ANT.) giant.*

midst *(SYN.)* center, heart, middle, thick.

midway *(SYN.)* halfway, midmost, inside, central, middle.

mien *(SYN.)* way, semblance, manner, behavior, demeanor, expression, deportment, style.

miff *(SYN.)* provoke, rile, chagrin, irk, irritate, affront, offend, annoy, exasperate.

might *(SYN.)* force, power, vigor, potency, ability, strength. *(ANT.) frailty, vulnerability, weakness.*

mighty *(SYN.)* firm, fortified, powerful, athletic, potent, muscular, robust, strong, cogent.

(ANT.) feeble, weak, brittle, insipid, frail, delicate.

migrant *(SYN.)* traveling, roaming, straying, roving, rambling, transient, meandering.
(ANT.) stationary.

migrate *(SYN.)* resettle, move, emigrate, immigrate, relocate, journey.
(ANT.) stay, remain, settle.

migratory *(SYN.)* itinerant, roving, mobile, vagabond, unsettled, nomadic, wandering.

mild *(SYN.)* soothing, moderate, gentle, tender, bland, pleasant, kind, meek, calm, amiable, compassionate, temperate, peaceful, soft.
(ANT.) severe, turbulent, stormy, excitable, violent, harsh, bitter.

milieu *(SYN.)* environment, background, locale, setting, scene, circumstances.

militant *(SYN.)* warlike, belligerent, hostile, fighting, pugnacious, aggressive, combative.
(ANT.) peaceful.

military *(SYN.)* troops, army, service, soldiers.

milksop *(SYN.)* weakling, sissy, coward.

mill *(SYN.)* foundry, shop, plant, factory, manufactory.

millstone *(SYN.)* load, impediment, burden, encumbrance, hindrance.

mimic *(SYN.)* simulate, duplicate, copy, imitate, mock, counterfeit, simulate.
(ANT.) invent, distort, alter.

mince *(SYN.)* shatter, fragment, chop, smash.

mind *(SYN.)* intelligence, psyche, disposition, intention, understanding, intellect, spirit, brain, inclination, mentality, soul, wit, liking, sense, watch, faculties, judgment, reason.
(ANT.) matter, corporeality.

mindful *(SYN.)* alert, aware, watchful, cognizant, watchful, sensible, heedful.

mine *(SYN.)* shaft, lode, pit, excavation, drill, dig, quarry, source.

mingle *(SYN.)* unite, coalesce, fuse, merge, combine, amalgamate, unify, conjoin, mix, blend, commingle.
(ANT.) separate, analyze, sort, disintegrate.

miniature *(SYN.)* small, little, tiny, midget, minute, minuscule, wee, petite, diminutive.
(ANT.) outsize.

minimize *(SYN.)* shorten, deduct, belittle, decrease, reduce, curtail, lessen, diminish, subtract.
(ANT.) enlarge, increase, amplify.

minimum *(SYN.)* lowest, least, smallest, slightest.
(ANT.) maximum.

minister *(SYN.)* pastor, clergyman, vicar, parson, curate, preacher, prelate, chaplain, cleric, deacon, reverend.

minor *(SYN.)* poorer, lesser, petty, youth, inferior, secondary, smaller, unimportant, lower.
(ANT.) higher, superior, major, greater.

minority *(SYN.)* youth, childhood, immaturity.

minstrel *(SYN.)* bard, musician.

mint *(SYN.)* stamp, coin, strike, punch.

minus *(SYN.)* lacking, missing, less, absent, without.

minute *(SYN.)* tiny, particular, fine, precise, jiffy, instant, moment, wee, exact, detailed, microscopic.
(ANT.) large, general, huge, enormous.

miraculous *(SYN.)* spiritual, supernatural, strange, wonderful, marvelous, incredible, preternatural.
(ANT.) commonplace, natural, common, plain, everyday, human.

mirage *(SYN.)* vision, illusion, fantasy, dream, phantom.
(ANT.) reality, actuality.

mire *(SYN.)* marsh, slush, slime, mud.

mirror *(SYN.)* glass, reflector, reflect.

mirth *(SYN.)* joy, glee, jollity, joyousness, gaiety, joyfulness, laughter, merriment.
(ANT.) sadness, gloom, seriousness.

misadventure *(SYN.)* accident, adversity, reverse, calamity, catastrophe, hardship, mischance, setback.

misappropriate *(SYN.)* embezzle, steal, purloin, plunder, cheat, filch, defraud.

misbehave *(SYN.)* trespass, act badly.
(ANT.) behave.

miscalculate *(SYN.)* miscount, blunder,

confuse, err, mistake, misconstrue.

miscarriage *(SYN.)* omission, want, decay, fiasco, default, deficiency, loss, abortion, prematurity.

(ANT.) success, sufficiency, achievement.

miscarry *(SYN.)* flounder, fall short, falter, fail.

(ANT.) succeed.

miscellaneous *(SYN.)* mixed, diverse, motley, indiscriminate, assorted, sundry, heterogeneous, varied.

(ANT.) classified, selected, homogeneous, alike, ordered.

miscellany *(SYN.)* medley, gallimaufry, jumble, potpourri, mixture, collection.

mischief *(SYN.)* injury, harm, damage, evil, ill, prankishness, rascality, roguishness, playfulness, wrong, detriment, hurt.

(ANT.) kindness, boon, benefit.

mischievous *(SYN.)* roguish, prankish, naughty, playful.

(ANT.) well-behaved, good.

misconduct *(SYN.)* transgression, delinquency, wrongdoing, negligence.

miscreant *(SYN.)* rascal, wretch, rogue, sinner, criminal, villain, scoundrel.

miscue *(SYN.)* blunder, fluff, mistake, error, lapse.

misdemeanor *(SYN.)* infringement, transgression, violation, offense, wrong.

miser *(SYN.)* cheapskate, tightwad, skinflint.

(ANT.) philanthropist.

miserable *(SYN.)* abject, forlorn, comfortless, worthless, pitiable, low, distressed, heartbroken, disconsolate, despicable, wretched, uncomfortable, unhappy, poor, unlucky, paltry, contemptible, mean.

(ANT.) fortunate, happy, contented, joyful, content, wealthy, honorable, lucky, noble, significant.

miserly *(SYN.)* stingy, greedy, acquisitive, tight, tightfisted, cheap, mean, parsimonious, avaricious.

(ANT.) bountiful, generous, spendthrift, munificent, extravagant, openhanded, altruistic.

misery *(SYN.)* suffering, pain, woe, evil, agony, torment, trouble, distress, anguish, grief, unhappiness, tribulation, calamity, sorrow.

(ANT.) fun, pleasure, delight, joy.

misfit *(SYN.)* crank, loner, deviate, fifth wheel, individualist.

misfortune *(SYN.)* adversity, distress, mishap, calamity, accident, catastrophe, hardship, ruin, disaster, affliction.

(ANT.) success, blessing, prosperity.

misgiving *(SYN.)* suspicion, doubt, mistrust, hesitation, uncertainty.

misguided *(SYN.)* misdirected, misled, misinformed, wrong, unwise, foolish, erroneous, unwarranted, ill-advised.

mishap *(SYN.)* misfortune, casualty, accident, disaster, adversity, reverse.

(ANT.) intention, calculation, purpose.

mishmash *(SYN.)* medley, muddle, gallimaufry, hodgepodge, hash.

misjudge *(SYN.)* err, mistake, miscalculate.

mislay *(SYN.)* misplace, lose.

(ANT.) discover, find.

mislead *(SYN.)* misdirect, deceive, misinform, deceive, delude.

misleading *(SYN.)* fallacious, delusive, deceitful, false, deceptive, illusive.

(ANT.) real, genuine, truthful, honest.

mismatched *(SYN.)* unfit, unsuitable, incompatible, unsuited.

misplace *(SYN.)* lose, mislay, miss.

(ANT.) find.

misrepresent *(SYN.)* misstate, distort, falsify, twist, belie, garble, disguise.

miss *(SYN.)* lose, want, crave, yearn for, fumble, drop, error, slip, default, omit, lack, need, desire, fail.

(ANT.) suffice, have, achieve, succeed.

misshapen *(SYN.)* disfigured, deformed, grotesque, malformed, ungainly, gnarled, contorted.

missile *(SYN.)* grenade, shot, projectile.

missing *(SYN.)* wanting, lacking, absent, lost, gone, vanished.

mission *(SYN.)* business, task, job, stint, work, errand, assignment, delegation.

missionary *(SYN.)* publicist, evangelist, propagandist.

mist *(SYN.)* cloud, fog, haze, steam, haze.

mistake *(SYN.)* slip, misjudge, fault, blunder, misunderstand, confuse, inaccuracy, misinterpret, error.
(ANT.) truth, accuracy.

mistaken *(SYN.)* false, amiss, incorrect, awry, wrong, misinformed, confused, inaccurate, askew.
(ANT.) true, correct, suitable, right.

mister *(SYN.)* young man, gentleman, esquire, fellow, buddy.

mistreat *(SYN.)* wrong, pervert, oppress, harm, maltreat, abuse.

mistrust *(SYN.)* suspect, doubt, distrust, dispute, question, skepticism, apprehension.
(ANT.) trust.

misunderstand *(SYN.)* misjudge, misinterpret, jumble, confuse, mistake.
(ANT.) perceive, comprehend.

misunderstanding *(SYN)* clash, disagreement, dispute, conflict, misinterpretation.

misuse *(SYN.)* defame, malign, abuse, misapply, traduce, asperse, revile, vilify.
(ANT.) protect, honor, respect, cherish.

mite *(SYN.)* particle, mote, smidgen, trifle, iota, corpuscle.

mitigate *(SYN.)* soften, soothe, abate, assuage, relieve, allay, diminish.
(ANT.) irritate, agitate, increase.

mix *(SYN.)* mingle, blend, consort, fuse, alloy, combine, jumble, fraternize, associate, concoct, commingle, amalgamate, join, confound, compound.
(ANT.) divide, sort, segregate, dissociate, separate.

mixture *(SYN.)* diversity, variety, strain, sort, change, kind, confusion, heterogeneity, jumble, mess, mix, assortment, breed, hodgepodge, subspecies.
(ANT.) likeness, sameness, homogeneity, monotony.

moan *(SYN.)* wail, groan, cry, lament.

moat *(SYN.)* fortification, ditch, trench, entrenchment.

mob *(SYN.)* crowd, host, populace, swarm, riot, bevy, horde, rabble, throng, multitude.

mobile *(SYN.)* free, movable, portable.
(ANT.) stationary, immobile, fixed.

mock *(SYN.)* taunt, jeer, deride, scoff, scorn, fleer, ridicule, tease, fake, imitation, sham, gibe, sneer, fraudulent, flout.
(ANT.) praise, applaud, real, genuine, honor, authentic, compliment.

mockery *(SYN.)* gibe, ridicule, satire, derision, sham, banter, irony, sneering, scorn, travesty, jeering.
(ANT.) admiration, praise.

mode *(SYN.)* method, fashion, procedure, design, manner, technique, way, style, practice, plan.
(ANT.) disorder, confusion.

model *(SYN.)* copy, prototype, type, example, ideal, imitation, version, facsimile, design, style, archetype, pattern, standard, mold.
(ANT.) reproduction, imitation.

moderate *(SYN.)* lower, decrease, average, fair, reasonable, abate, medium, conservative, referee, umpire, suppress, judge, lessen, assuage.
(ANT.) intensify, enlarge, amplify.

moderation *(SYN.)* sobriety, forbearance, self-control, restraint, continence, temperance.
(ANT.) greed, excess, intoxication.

moderator *(SYN.)* referee, leader, arbitrator, chairman, chairperson, master of cermonies, emcee.

modern *(SYN.)* modish, current, recent, novel, fresh, contemporary, new.
(ANT.) old, antiquated, past, bygone, ancient.

modernize *(SYN.)* refurnish, refurbish, improve, rebuild, renew, renovate.

modest *(SYN.)* unassuming, virtuous, bashful, meek, shy, humble, decent, demure, unpretentious, prudish, moderate, reserved.
(ANT.) forward, bold, ostentatious, conceited, immodest, arrogant.

modesty *(SYN.)* decency, humility, propriety, simplicity, shyness.
(ANT.) conceit, vanity, pride.

modicum *(SYN.)* particle, fragment, grain, trifle, smidgen, bit.

modification *(SYN.)* alternation, substitution, variety, change, alteration.

(ANT.) uniformity, monotony.

modify *(SYN.)* shift, vary, alter, change, convert, adjust, temper, moderate, curb, exchange, transform, veer.
(ANT.) settle, establish, retain, stabilize.

modish *(SYN.)* current, fashionable, chick, stylish, voguish.

modulate *(SYN.)* temper, align, balance, correct, regulate, adjust, modify.

module *(SYN.)* unit, measure, norm, dimension, component, gauge.

modus operandi *(SYN.)* method, technique, system, means, process, workings, procedure.

mogul *(SYN.)* bigwig, personage, figure, tycoon, magnate, potentate.

moiety *(SYN.)* part, scrap, share, allotment, piece, division, portion.

moist *(SYN.)* damp, humid, dank, muggy, clammy.

moisten *(SYN.)* wet, dampen, sponge.
(ANT.) dry.

moisture *(SYN.)* wetness, mist, dampness, condensation, evaporation, vapor, humidity.
(ANT.) aridity, dryness.

mold *(SYN.)* make, fashion, organize, produce, forge, constitute, create, combine, construct, form, pattern, format.
(ANT.) wreck, dismantle, destroy, misshape.

moldy *(SYN.)* dusty, crumbling, dank, old, deteriorating.

molest *(SYN.)* irk, disturb, trouble, annoy, pester, bother, vex, inconvenience.
(ANT.) console, accommodate.

mollify *(SYN.)* soothe, compose, quiet, humor, appease, tranquilize, pacify.

molt *(SYN.)* slough off, shed, cast off.

molten *(SYN.)* fusible, melted, smelted, redhot.

moment *(SYN.)* flash, jiffy, instant, twinkling, gravity, importance, consequence, seriousness.

momentary *(SYN.)* concise, pithy, brief, curt, terse, laconic, compendious.
(ANT.) long, extended, prolonged.

momentous *(SYN.)* critical, serious, essential, grave, material, weighty, consequen-

tial, decisive, important.
(ANT.) unimportant, trifling, mean, trivial, tribial, insignificant.

momentum *(SYN.)* impetus, push, thrust, force, impulse, drive, vigor, propulsion, energy.

monarch *(SYN.)* ruler, king, queen, empress, emperor, sovereign.

monastic *(SYN.)* withdrawn, dedicated, austere, unworldly, celibate, abstinent, ascetic.

monastery *(SYN.)* convent, priory, abbey, hermitage, cloister.

money *(SYN.)* cash, bills, coin, notes, currency, funds, specie, capital.

monger *(SYN.)* seller, hawker, huckster, trader, merchant, shopkeeper, retailer, vendor.

mongrel *(SYN.)* mixed-breed, hybrid, mutt.

monitor *(SYN.)* director, supervisor, advisor, observe, watch, control.

monkey *(SYN.)* tamper, interfere, interrupt, interpose.

monogram *(SYN.)* mark, stamp, signature

monograph *(SYN.)* publication, report, thesis, biography, treatise, paper, dissertation.

monologue *(SYN.)* discourse, lecture, sermon, talk, speech, address, soliloquy, oration.

monomania *(SYN.)* obsessiveness, passion, single-mindedness, extremism.

monopoly *(SYN.)* corner, control, possession.

monotonous *(SYN.)* dull, slow, tiresome, boring, humdrum, dilatory, tiring, irksome, tedious, burdensome, wearisome.
(ANT.) interesting, riveting, quick, fascinating, exciting, amusing.

monsoon *(SYN.)* storm, rains.

monster *(SYN.)* brute, beast, villain, demon, fiend, wretch.

monstrous *(SYN.)* tremendous, huge, gigantic, immense, enormous, revolting, repulsive, shocking, horrible, hideous, terrible.
(ANT.) diminutive, tiny, miniature, small.

monument *(SYN.)* remembrance, landmark,

memento, commemoration, headstone, souvenir, statue, shrine.

monumental *(SYN.)* enormous, huge, colossal, immense, gigantic, important, significant.

mood *(SYN.)* joke, irony, waggery, temper, disposition, temperament, sarcasm.

(ANT.) sorrow, gravity.

moody *(SYN.)* morose, fretful, crabbed, changeable, sulky, dour, short-tempered, testy, temperamental, irritable, peevish, glum.

(ANT.) good-natured, even-tempered, merry, gay, pleasant, joyous.

moor *(SYN.)* tether, fasten, tie, dock, anchor, bind.

moorings *(SYN.)* marina, slip, harbor, basin, landing, dock, wharf, pier, anchorage.

moot *(SYN.)* unsettled, questionable, problematical, controversial, contestable.

mop *(SYN.)* wash, wipe, swab, scrub.

mope *(SYN.)* gloom, pout, whine, grumble, grieve, sulk, fret.

(ANT.) rejoice.

moral *(SYN.)* just, right, chaste, good, virtuous, pure, decent, honest, upright, ethical, righteous, honorable, scrupulous.

(ANT.) libertine, immoral, unethical, licentious, amoral, sinful.

morale *(SYN.)* confidence, spirit, assurance.

morality *(SYN.)* virtue, strength, worth, chastity, probity, force, merit.

(ANT.) fault, sin, corruption, vice.

morals *(SYN.)* conduct, scruples, guidelines, behavior, life style, standards.

morass *(SYN.)* fen, march, swamp, mire.

morbid *(SYN.)* sickly, unwholesome, awful, unhealthy, ghastly, horrible, shocking, decaying.

(ANT.) pleasant, healthy.

more *(SYN.)* further, greater, farther, extra, another.

(ANT.) less.

moreover *(SYN.)* further, in addition, also, furthermore, besides.

mores *(SYN.)* standards, rituals, rules, customs, conventions, traditions.

moron *(SYN.)* subnormal, dunce, blockhead, imbecile, retardate, simpleton.

morose *(SYN.)* gloomy, moody, fretful, crabbed, sulky, glum, dour, surly, downcast, sad, unhappy.

(ANT.) merry, gay, amiable, joyous, pleasant.

morsel *(SYN.)* portion, fragment, bite, bit, scrap. amount, piece, taste, tidbit.

(ANT.) whole, all, sum.

mortal *(SYN.)* fatal, destructive, human, perishable, deadly, temporary, momentary, final.

(ANT.) superficial, divine, immortal.

mortgage *(SYN.)* stake, post, promise, pledge.

mortician *(SYN.)* funeral director, embalmer.

mortified *(SYN.)* embarrassed, humiliated, abashed, ashamed.

mortify *(SYN.)* humiliate, crush, subdue, abase, degrade, shame.

(ANT.) praise, exalt, elevate.

mortuary *(SYN.)* morgue, crematory, funeral parlor.

most *(SYN.)* extreme, highest, supreme, greatest, majority.

(ANT.) least.

mostly *(SYN.)* chiefly, generally, largely, mainly, principally, especially, primarily.

mother *(SYN.)* bring about, produce, breed, mom, mama, watch, foster, mind, nurse, originate, nurture.

(ANT.) father.

motif *(SYN.)* keynote, topic, subject, theme.

motion *(SYN.)* change, activity, movement, proposition, action, signal, gesture, move, proposal.

(ANT.) stability, immobility, equilibrium, stillness.

motionless *(SYN.)* still, undisturbed, rigid, fixed, stationary, unresponsive, immobilized.

motivate *(SYN.)* move, prompt, stimulate, induce, activate, propel, arouse.

motive *(SYN.)* inducement, purpose, cause, incentive, reason, incitement, idea, ground, principle, stimulus, impulse, spur.

(ANT.) deed, result, attempt, effort.

motley *(SYN.)* heterogeneous, mixed, assorted, sundry, diverse, miscellaneous.
(ANT.) ordered, classified.

motor *(SYN.)* engine, generator, machine.

mottled *(SYN.)* streaked, flecked, dappled, spotted, speckled.

motto *(SYN.)* proverb, saying, adage, byword, saw, slogan, catchword, aphorism.

mound *(SYN.)* hillock, hill, heap, pile, stack, knoll, accumulation, dune.

mount *(SYN.)* scale, climb, increase, rise, prepare, ready, steed, horse, tower.
(ANT.) sink, descend.

mountain *(SYN.)* alp, mount, pike, peak, ridge, height, range.

mountebank *(SYN.)* faker, rascal, swindler, cheat, fraud.

mounting *(SYN.)* backing, pedestal, easel, support, framework, background.

mourn *(SYN.)* suffer, grieve, bemoan, sorrow, lament, weep, bewail.
(ANT.) revel, celebrate, carouse.

mournful *(SYN.)* sorrowful, sad, melancholy, gloomy, woeful, rueful, disconsolate.
(ANT.) joyful, cheerful, happy.

mourning *(SYN.)* misery, trial, distress, affliction, tribulation, sorrow, woe.
(ANT.) happiness, solace, comfort, joy.

mousy *(SYN.)* quiet, reserved, dull, colorless, withdrawn, shy, bashful.

move *(SYN.)* impel, agitate, persuade, induce, push, instigate, advance, stir, progress, propel, shift, drive, retreat, proceed, stir, transfer, budge, actuate.
(ANT.) halt, stop, deter, rest.

movement *(SYN.)* activity, effort, gesture, move, proposition, crusade, action, change, motion.
(ANT.) stillness, immobility, equilibrium.

moving *(SYN.)* poignant, stirring, touching.

mow *(SYN.)* prune, cut, shave, crop, clip.

much *(SYN.)* abundance, quantity, mass, ample, plenty, sufficient, substantial.

mucilage *(SYN.)* adhesive, glue, paste.

muck *(SYN.)* filth, mire, dirt, rot, sludge, sewage.

muddle *(SYN.)* disorder, chaos, mess.

muddled *(SYN.)* disconcerted, confused, mixed, bewildered, perplexed.
(ANT.) plain, lucid, organized.

muff *(SYN.)* blunder, bungle, spoil, mess, fumble.

muffle *(SYN.)* soften, deaden, mute, quiet, drape, shroud, veil, cover.
(ANT.) louden, amplify.

mug *(SYN.)* cup, stein, goblet, tankard.

muggy *(SYN.)* damp, warm, humid, stuffy, sticky, dank.

mulct *(SYN.)* amerce, punish, penalize.

mulish *(SYN.)* obstinate, stubborn, headstrong, rigid, tenacious, willful.

multifarious *(SYN.)* various, many, numerous, diversified, several.
(ANT.) scanty, infrequent, scarce, few.

multiply *(SYN.)* double, treble, increase, triple, propagate, spread.
(ANT.) lessen, decrease.

multitude *(SYN.)* crowd, throng, mass, swarm, host, mob, army, legion.
(ANT.) scarcity, handful.

mum *(SYN.)* mute, silent, quiet, still, closemouthed, secretive.

mumble *(SYN.)* stammer, whisper, hesitate, mutter.
(ANT.) shout, yell.

mundane *(SYN.)* temporal, earthly, profane, worldly, lay, secular.
(ANT.) unworldly, religious, extraordinary, rare.

municipal *(SYN.)* urban, metropolitan.

munificent *(SYN.)* bountiful, full, generous, forthcoming, satisfied.
(ANT.) voracious, insatiable, grasping, ravenous, devouring.

murder *(SYN.)* homicide, kill, slay, slaughter, butcher, killing, massacre, assassinate, execute.
(ANT.) save, protect, vivify, animate.

murderer *(SYN.)* slayer, killer, assassin.

murky *(SYN.)* gloomy, dark, obscure, unclear, impenetrable.
(ANT.) cheerful, light.

murmur *(SYN.)* mumble, whine, grumble, whimper, lament, mutter, complaint, remonstrate.
(ANT.) praise, applaud, rejoice.

muscle *(SYN.)* brawn, strength, power, fitness, vigor, stamina, robustness, authority, force, muscularity, might.
(ANT.) flab, weakness, frail, helpness, soft.

muse *(SYN.)* ponder, brood, think, meditate, ruminate, reflect.

museum *(SYN.)* exhibit hall, treasure house, gallery, repository.

mushroom *(SYN.)* multiply, proliferate, flourish, spread, grow, pullulate.

music *(SYN.)* symphony, harmony, consonance.

musical *(SYN.)* tuneful, melodious, dulcet, lyrical, harmonious.

muss *(SYN.)* mess, disarray, rumple, litter, clutter, disarrange.
(ANT.) fix, arrange.

must *(SYN.)* ought to, should, duty, obligation, ultimatum.

muster *(SYN.)* cull, pick, collect, harvest, accumulate, garner, reap, deduce.
(ANT.) separate, disband, scatter.

musty *(SYN.)* mildewed, rancid, airless, dank, stale, decayed, rotten, funky.

mute *(SYN.)* quiet, noiseless, dumb, taciturn, hushed, peaceful, speechless, uncommunicative.
(ANT.) raucous, clamorous, noisy, talkative, audible.

mutilate *(SYN.)* tear, cut, clip, amputate, lacerate, dismember, deform, castrate.

mutinous *(SYN.)* revolutionary, rebellious, unruly, insurgent, turbulent, riotous.
(ANT.) dutiful, obedient, complaint.

mutiny *(SYN.)* revolt, overthrow, rebellion, rebel, coup, uprising, insurrection.

mutter *(SYN.)* complain, mumble, whisper, grumble.

mutual *(SYN.)* correlative, interchangeable, shared, alternate, joint, common, reciprocal.
(ANT.) unshared, unrequited, separate, dissociated, exclusive, uncommon.

muzzle *(SYN.)* restrain, silence, bridle, bind, curb, suppress, gag, stifle, censor.
(ANT.) loose, free, set loose, liberate, untie.

myopia *(SYN.)* incomprehension, folly, shortsightedness, obtuseness, insensibility.

myriad *(SYN.)* considerable, many.

mysterious *(SYN.)* hidden, mystical, secret, cryptic, incomprehensible, occult, dim, dark, inexplicable, enigmatical, inscrutable, obscure, recondite, puzzling.
(ANT.) simple, obvious, clear, plain.

mystery *(SYN.)* riddle, difficulty, enigma, puzzle, strangeness.
(ANT.) solution, key, answer, resolution.

mystical *(SYN.)* secret, cryptic, hidden, dim, obscure, dark, cabalistic, transcendental, inexplicable.
(ANT.) simple, explained, plain, clear.

mystify *(SYN.)* puzzle, confound, bewilder, floor, bamboozle.

myth *(SYN.)* fable, parable, allegory, fiction, tradition, lie, saga.
(ANT.) history.

mythical *(SYN.)* fictitous, unreal, imaginary, story, fiction, untrue, nonexistent, false.
(ANT.) actual, true, real.

N

nag *(SYN.)* badger, harry, provoke, tease, bother, annoy, molest, taunt, vex, torment, worry, pester, irritate, pick on, scold, plague.
(ANT.) please, comfort, soothe.

nail *(SYN.)* hold, fasten, secure, fix, catch, snare, hook, capture.
(ANT.) release.

naive *(SYN.)* frank, unsophisticated, natural, artless, ingenuous, simple, candid, open, innocent.
(ANT.) worldly, cunning, crafty.

naked *(SYN.)* uncovered, unfurnished, nude, bare, open, unclad, stripped, exposed, plain, mere, simple, barren, unprotected, bald, defenseless, unclothed, undressed.
(ANT.) covered, protected, dressed, clothed, concealed, suppressed.

name *(SYN.)* title, reputation, appellation, style, fame, repute, renown, denomination, call, appoint, character, designation, surname, distinction, christen, denominate,

lable, mention, specify, epithet, entitle.
(ANT.) anonymity, hint, misname.
nap *(SYN.)* nod, doze, sleep, snooze, catnap, siesta, slumber, drowse, forty winks.
narcissistic *(SYN.)* egotistical, egocentric, self-centered.
narcotics *(SYN.)* opiates, drugs, sedatives, tranquilizers, barbiturates.
narrate *(SYN.)* recite, relate, declaim, detail, rehearse, deliver, review, tell, describe, recount.
narrative *(SYN.)* history, relation, account, record, chronicle, detail, recital, description, story, tale.
(ANT.) distortion, caricature, misrepresentation.
narrow *(SYN.)* narrow-minded, illiberal, bigoted, fanatical, prejudiced, close, restricted, slender, cramped, confined, meager, thin.
(ANT.) progressive, liberal, wide,
nascent *(SYN.)* prime, introductory, emerging, elementary.
nasty *(SYN.)* offensive, malicious, selfish, mean, disagreeable, unpleasant, foul, dirty, filthy, loathsome, disgusting, polluted, obscene, indecent, sickening, nauseating, obnoxious, odious.
(ANT.) generous, dignified, noble, admirable, pleasant.
nation *(SYN.)* state, community, realm, nationality, commonwealth, kingdom, country, republic, land, society, tribe.
native *(SYN.)* domestic, inborn, inherent, natural, aboriginal, endemic, innate, inbred, indigenous, hereditary, original, local.
(ANT.) alien, stranger, foreigner, outsider, foreign.
natty *(SYN.)* chic, well-dressed, sharp, dapper.
natural *(SYN.)* innate, genuine, real, unaffected, characteristic, native, normal, regular, inherent, original, simple, inbred, inborn, hereditary, typical, authentic, legitimate, pure, customary.
(ANT.) irregular, false, unnatural, formal, abnormal.
nature *(SYN.)* kind, disposition, reputation,

character, repute, world, quality, universe, essence, variety, features, traits.
naught *(SYN.)* nought, zero, nothing.
naughty *(SYN.)* unmanageable, insubordinate, disobedient, mischievous, unruly, bad, misbehaving, disorderly, wrong, evil, rude, improper, indecent.
(ANT.) obedient, good, well- behaved.
nausea *(SYN.)* sickness, vomiting, upset, queasiness, seasickness.
nauseated *(SYN.)* unwell, sick, queasy, squeamish.
nautical *(SYN.)* naval, oceanic, marine, ocean.
near *(SYN.)* close, nigh, dear, adjacent, familiar, at hand, neighboring, approaching, impending, proximate, imminent, bordering.
(ANT.) removed, distant, far, remote.
nearly *(SYN.)* practically, close to, approximately, almost.
neat *(SYN.)* trim, orderly, precise, clear, spruce, nice, tidy, clean, well-kept, clever, skillful, adept, apt, tidy, dapper, smart, proficient, expert, handy, well-done, shipshape, elegant.
(ANT.) unkempt, sloppy, dirty, slovenly, messy, sloppy, disorganized.
nebulous *(SYN.)* fuzzy, indistinct, indefinite, clouded, hazy.
(ANT.) definite, distinct, clear.
necessary *(SYN.)* needed, expedient, unavoidable, required, essential, indispensable, urgent, imperative, inevitable, compelling, compulsory, obligatory, needed, exigent.
(ANT.) optional, nonessential, contingent, casual, accidental, unnecessary, dispensable, unneeded.
necessity *(SYN.)* requirement, fate, destiny, constraint, requisite, poverty, exigency, compulsion, want, essential, prerequisite.
(ANT.) option, luxury, freedom, choice, uncertainty.
necromancy *(SYN.)* witchcraft, charm, sorcery, conjuring, wizardry.
need *(SYN.)* crave, want, demand, claim, desire, covet, wish, lack, necessity,

requirement, poverty, require, penniless-ness.

needed *(SYN.)* necessary, indispensable, essential, requisite.
(ANT.) optional, contingent.

needle *(SYN.)* goad, badger, tease, nag, prod, provoke.

needless *(SYN.)* nonessential, unnecessary, superfluous, useless, purposeless.

needy *(SYN.)* poor, indigent, impoverished penniless, destitute.
(ANT.) affluent, well-off, wealthy.

nefarious *(SYN.)* detestable, vicious, wicked, atrocious, horrible, vile.

negate *(SYN.)* revoke, void, cancel, nullify.

neglect *(SYN.)* omission, default, heedless-ness, carelessness, thoughtlessness, disre-gard, negligence, oversight, omission, ig-nore, slight, failure, overlook, omit, skip, pass over, be inattentive, miss.
(ANT.) diligence, do, protect, watchfulness, care, attention, careful, attend, regard, concern.

negligent *(SYN.)* imprudent, thoughtless, lax, careless, inattentive, indifferent, remiss, neglectful.
(ANT.) careful, nice, accurate, meticulous.

negligible *(SYN.)* trifling, insignificant, trivial, inconsiderable.
(ANT.) major, vital, important.

negotiate *(SYN.)* intervene, talk over, medi-ate, transact, umpire, referee, arbitrate, arrange, settle, bargain.

neighborhood *(SYN.)* environs, nearness, locality, district, vicinity, area, section, lo-cality.
(ANT.) remoteness.

neighboring *(SYN.)* bordering, near, ad-jacent, next to, surrounding, adjoining.

neighborly *(SYN.)* friendly, sociable, ami-able, affable, companionable, congenial, kind, cordial, amicable.
(ANT.) distant, reserved, cool, unfriendly, hostile.

neophyte *(SYN.)* greenhorn, rookie, ama-teur, beginner, apprentice, tyro, student.

nepotism *(SYN.)* bias, prejudice, partiality, partronage, favoritism.

nerve *(SYN.)* bravery, spirit, courage, bold-ness, rudeness, strength, stamina, bravado, daring, impudence, mettle, impertinence.
(ANT.) frailty, cowardice, weakness.

nervous *(SYN.)* agitated, restless, excited, shy, timid, upset, disturbed, shaken, rattle, high-strung, flustered, tense, jittery, strain-ed, edgy, perturbed, fearful.
(ANT.) placid, courageous, confident, calm, tranquil, composed, bold.

nest *(SYN.)* den, refuge, hideaway.

nestle *(SYN.)* cuddle, snuggle.

net *(SYN.)* snare, trap, mesh, earn, gain, web, get, acquire, secure, obtain.

nettle *(SYN.)* irritate, vex, provoke, annoy, disturb, irk, needle, pester.

neurotic *(SYN.)* disturbed, psychoneurotic.

neutral *(SYN.)* nonpartisan, uninvolved, detached, impartial, cool, unprejudiced, indifferent, inactive.
(ANT.) involved, biased, partisan.

neutralize *(SYN.)* offset, counteract, nulli-fy, negate.

nevertheless *(SYN.)* notwithstanding, how-ever, although, anyway, but, regardless.

new *(SYN.)* modern, original, newfangled, late, recent, novel, young, firsthand, fresh, unique, unusual.
(ANT.) antiquated, old, ancient, obsolete, outmoded.

newborn *(SYN.)* baby, infant, cub.

news *(SYN.)* report, intelligence, informa-tion, copy, message, advice, tidings, knowl-edge, word, story, data.

next *(SYN.)* nearest, following, closest, suc-cessive, succeeding, subsequent.

nibble *(SYN.)* munch, chew, bit.

nice *(SYN.)* pleasing, pleasant, agreeable, thoughtful, satisfactory, friendly, enjoy-able, gratifying, desirable, fine, good, cordial.
(ANT.) nasty, unpleasant, disagreeable, unkind, inexact, careless, thoughtless.

niche *(SYN.)* corner, nook, alcove, cranny, recess.

nick *(SYN.)* cut, notch, indentation, dash, score, mark.

nickname *(SYN.)* byname, sobriquet.

nigh *(SYN.)* close, imminent, near, adjacent, approaching, bordering, neighboring, impending.
(ANT.) removed, distant.

nightmare *(SYN.)* calamity, horror, torment, bad dream.

nil *(SYN.)* zero, none, nought, nothing.

nimble *(SYN.)* brisk, quick, active, supple, alert, lively, spry, light, fast, speedy, swift, agile.
(ANT.) slow, heavy, sluggish, clumsy.

nincompoop *(SYN.)* nitwit, fool, moron, blockhead, ninny, idiot, simpleton.

nip *(SYN.)* bite, pinch, chill, cold, squeeze, crispness, sip, small.

nippy *(SYN.)* chilly, sharp, bitter, cold, penetrating.

nit-picker *(SYN.)* fussbudget, precise, purist, perfectionist.

nitty-gritty *(SYN.)* essentials, substance, essence.

noble *(SYN.)* illustrious, exalted, dignified, stately, eminent, lofty, grand, elevated, honorable, honest, virtuous, great, distinguished, majestic, important, prominent, magnificent, grandiose, aristocratic, upright, well-born.
(ANT.) vile, low, base, mean, dishonest, common, ignoble.

nocturnal *(SYN.)* nightly.

nod *(SYN.)* bob, bow, bend, tip, signal.

node *(SYN.)* protuberance, growth, nodule, cyst, lump, wen.

noise *(SYN.)* cry, sound, din, babel, racket, uproar, clamor, outcry, tumult, sounds, hubbub, bedlam, commotion.
(ANT.) quiet, stillness, hush, silence, peace.

noisome *(SYN.)* repulsive, disgusting, revolting, obnoxious, malodorous, rotten.

noisy *(SYN.)* resounding, loud, clamorous, vociferous, stentorian, tumultuous.
(ANT.) soft, dulcet, subdued, quiet, silent, peaceful.

nomad *(SYN.)* gypsy, rover, traveler, roamer, migrant, vagrant, wanderer.

nominate *(SYN.)* propose, choose, select.

nomination *(SYN.)* appointment, naming, choice, selection, designation.

nominee *(SYN.)* sapirant, contestant, candidate, competitor.

nonbeliever *(SYN.)* skeptic, infidel, atheist, heathen.

nonchalant *(SYN.)* unconcerned, indifferent, cool, casual, easygoing.

noncommittal *(SYN.)* neutral, tepid, undecided, cautious, uncommunicative.

nonconformist *(SYN.)* protester, rebel, radical, dissenter, renegade, dissident, eccentric.

nondescript *(SYN.)* unclassifiable, indescribable, indefinite.

nonentity *(SYN.)* nothing, menial, nullity.

nonessential *(SYN.)* needless, unnecessary.

nonpareil *(SYN.)* unsurpassed, exceptional, paramount, unrivaled.

nonplus *(SYN.)* confuse, perplex, dumfound, mystify, puzzle, baffle, bewilder.
(ANT.) illumine, clarify, solve, explain.

nonsense *(SYN.)* balderdash, rubbish, foolishness, folly, ridiculousness, stupidity, absurdity, poppycock, trash.

nonsensical *(SYN.)* silly, preposterous, absurd, unreasonable, foolish, irrational, stupid, senseless.
(ANT.) sound, consistent, reasonable.

nonstop *(SYN.)* constant, continuous, unceasing, endless.

nook *(SYN.)* niche, corner, recess, cranny, alcove.

noose *(SYN.)* snare, rope, lasso, loop.

normal *(SYN.)* ordinary, uniform, natural, unvaried, customary, regular, healthy, sound, whole, usual, typical, characteristic, standard.
(ANT.) rare, erratic, unusual, abnormal.

normally *(SYN.)* regularly, frequently, usually, customarily.

nosy *(SYN.)* inquisitive, meddling, peering, searching, prying, snooping.
(ANT.) unconcerned, incurious, uninterested.

notable *(SYN.)* noted, unusual, uncommon, noteworthy, remarkable, conspicuous, distinguished, distinctive, celebrity, starts, important, striking, special, memorable, extraordinary, rare, exceptional.

(ANT.) commonplace, ordinary, usual.

notch *(SYN.)* cut, nick, indentation, gash.

note *(SYN.)* sign, annotation, letter, indication, observation, mark, symbol, comment, remark, token, message, memorandum, record, memo, write, list, notice.

noted *(SYN.)* renowned, glorious, celebrated, famous, illustrious, well-known, distinguished, famed.

(ANT.) unknown, hidden, infamous.

noteworthy *(SYN.)* consequential, exceptional, prominent.

notice *(SYN.)* heed, perceive, hold, mark, behold, descry, recognize, observe, attend to, remark, note, regard, see, sign, announcement, poster, note, advertisement, observation, warning.

(ANT.) overlook, disregard, skip.

notify *(SYN.)* apprise, acquaint, instruct, tell, advise, warn, teach, inform, report, remind, announce, reveal.

(ANT.) mislead, delude, conceal.

notion *(SYN.)* image, conception, sentiment, abstraction, thought, idea, view, opinion.

(ANT.) thing, matter, substance, entity.

notorious *(SYN.)* celebrated, renowned, famous, well-known, popular, infamous.

nourish *(SYN.)* strengthen, nurse, feed, nurture, sustain, support.

nourishment *(SYN.)* nutriment, food, sustenance, support.

(ANT.) starvation, deprivation.

novel *(SYN.)* fiction, narrative, allegory, tale, fable, story, romance, invention, different, unusual, original, new, unique, fresh.

(ANT.) verity, history, truth, fact.

novice *(SYN.)* beginner, amateur, newcomer, green-horn, learner, apprentice, freshman.

(ANT.) expert, professional, adept, master.

now *(SYN.)* today, at once, right away, immediately, present.

(ANT.) later.

noxious *(SYN.)* poisonous, harmful, damaging, toxic, detrimental.

(ANT.) harmless.

nucleus *(SYN.)* core, middle, heart, focus, hub, kernel.

nude *(SYN.)* naked, unclad, plain, open,

mere, bare, exposed, unprotected, stripped, uncovered.

(ANT.) dressed, concealed, protected, clothed, covered.

nudge *(SYN.)* prod, push, jab, shove, poke, prompt.

nugget *(SYN.)* clump, mass, lump, wad, chunk, hunk.

nuisance *(SYN.)* annoyance, bother, irritation, pest.

nullify *(SYN.)* abolish, cross out, delete, invalidate, obliterate, cancel, annul, revoke, rescind.

(ANT.) perpetuate, confirm, enforce.

numb *(SYN.)* unfeeling, dull, insensitive, deadened, anesthetized, stupefied.

number *(SYN.)* quantity, sum, amount, volume, aggregate, total, collection, sum, numeral, count, measure, portion, bulk, figure, multitude, digit.

(ANT.) zero, nothing, nothingness.

numeral *(SYN.)* figure, symbol, digit.

nuptials *(SYN.)* marriage, wedding, espousal, wedlock, matrimony.

(ANT.) virginity, divorce, celibacy.

nurse *(SYN.)* tend, care for, nourish, nurture, feed, foster, train, mind, attend.

nurture *(SYN.)* hold dear, foster, sustain, appreciate, prize, bring up, rear, value, treasure, cherish.

(ANT.) dislike, disregard, abandon.

nutriment *(SYN.)* food, diet, repast, meal, fare, edibles.

(ANT.) hunger, want, starvation.

nutrition *(SYN.)* nourishment, sustenance, food, nutriment.

O

oaf *(SYN.)* boor, clod, clown, lummox, fool, lout, dunce, bogtrotter.

oasis *(SYN.)* shelter, haven, retreat, refuge.

oath *(SYN.)* promise, pledge, vow, profanity, curse, agreement, commitment, swearword.

obdurate *(SYN.)* insensible, callous, hard, tough, unfeeling, insensitive, impenitent, indurate.

(ANT.) soft, compassionate, tender.

obedience *(SYN.)* docility, submission, subservience, compliance.

(ANT.) rebelliousness, disobedience.

obedient *(SYN.)* dutiful, yielding, tractable, compliant, submissive.

(ANT.) rebellious, intractable, insubordinate, obstinate.

obese *(SYN.)* portly, fat, pudgy, chubby, plump, rotund, stout, thickset, corpulent, stocky.

(ANT.) slim, gaunt, lean, thin, slender.

obey *(SYN.)* submit, yield, mind, comply, listen to, serve, conform.

(ANT.) resist, disobey.

obfuscate *(SYN.)* bewilder, complicate, fluster, confuse.

object *(SYN.)* thing, aim, intention, design, end, objective, particular, mark, purpose, goal, target.

(ANT.) assent, agree, concur, approve, acquiesce.

objection *(SYN.)* disagreement, protest, rejection, dissent, challenge, noncompliance, difference, nonconformity, recusancy, disapproval, criticism, variance.

(ANT.) acceptance, compliance, agreement, assent.

objectionable *(SYN.)* improper, offensive, unbecoming, deplorable.

objective *(SYN.)* aspiration, goal, passion, desire, aim, hope, purpose, drift, design, ambition, end, object, intention, intent, longing.

(ANT.) biased, subjective.

objectivity *(SYN.)* disinterest, neutrality, impartiality.

obligate *(SYN.)* oblige, require, pledge, bind, force, compel.

obligation *(SYN.)* duty, bond, engagement, compulsion, account, contract, ability, debt.

(ANT.) freedom, choice, exemption.

oblige *(SYN.)* constrain, force, impel, enforce, coerce, drive, gratify.

(ANT.) persuade, convince, allure, free, induce, disoblige, prevent.

obliging *(SYN.)* considerate, helpful, thoughtful, accommodating.

(ANT.) discourteous.

obliterate *(SYN.)* terminate, destroy, eradicate, raze, extinguish, exterminate, annihilate, devastate, wipe out, ravage, erase.

(ANT.) make, save, construct, establish, preserve.

oblivious *(SYN.)* sightless, unmindful, headlong, rash, blind, senseless, ignorant, forgetful, undiscerning, preoccupied.

(ANT.) sensible, aware, calculated, perceiving, discerning.

oblong *SYN.)* rectangular, elliptical, elongated.

obloquy *(SYN.)* defamation, rebuke, censure.

obnoxious *(SYN.)* hateful, offensive, nasty, disagreeable, repulsive, loathsome, vile, disgusting, detestable, wretched, terrible.

obscene *(SYN.)* indecent, filthy, impure, dirty, gross, lewd, pornographic, coarse, disgusting, bawdy, offensive, smutty.

(ANT.) modest, pure, decent, refined.

obscure *(SYN.)* cloudy, enigmatic, mysterious, abstruse, cryptic, dim, dusky, ambiguous, dark, indistinct, unintelligible, unclear, shadowy, fuzzy, blurred.

(ANT.) clear, famous, distinguished, noted, illumined, lucid, bright, distinct.

obsequious *(SYN.)* fawning, flattering, ingratiating.

observance *(SYN.)* protocol, ritual, ceremony, rite, parade, pomp, solemnity, formality.

(ANT.) omission.

observant *(SYN.)* aware, alert, careful, mindful, watchful, heedful, considerate, attentive, conscious, anxious, circumspect, cautious.

(ANT.) unaware, indifferent, oblivious.

observation *(SYN.)* attention, watching, comment, opinion, remark, notice, examination.

observe *(SYN.)* note, behold, discover, notice, perceive, eye, detect, inspect, keep, commemorate, mention, utter, watch, examine, mark, view, express, see.

(ANT.) neglect, overlook, disregard, ignore.

observer *(SYN.)* examiner, overseer, lookout, spectator, bystander, witness, watcher.

obsession *(SYN.)* preoccupation, mania, compulsion, passion, fetish, infatuation.

obsolete *(SYN.)* old, out-of-date, ancient, archaic, extinct, old-fashioned, discontinued, obsolescent, venerable, dated.
(ANT.) modern, stylish, current, recent, fashionable, extant.

obstacle *(SYN.)* block, hindrance, barrier, impediment, snag, check, deterrent, stoppage, hitch, bar, difficulty, obstruction.
(ANT.) help, aid, assistance, encouragement.

obstinate *(SYN.)* firm, head-strong, immovable, stubborn, determined, dogged, intractable, uncompromising, inflexible, willful, bullheaded, contumacious, obdurate, unbending, unyielding.
(ANT.) yielding, docile, amenable, submissive, pliable, flexible, compliant.

obstruct *(SYN.)* clog, barricade, impede, block, delay, hinder, stop, close, bar.
(ANT.) promote, clear, aid, help, open, further.

obstruction *(SYN.)* block, obstacle, barrier, blockage, interference.

obtain *(SYN.)* get, acquire, secure, win, procure, attain, earn, gain.
(ANT.) surrender, forfeit, lose, forego, miss.

obtrusive *(SYN.)* blatant, garish, conspicuous.

obtuse *(SYN.)* blunt, dull, slow-witted, unsharpened, stupid, dense, slow.
(ANT.) clear, interesting, lively, bright, animated, sharp.

obviate *(SYN.)* prevent, obstruct, forestall, preclude, intercept, avert, evade.

obvious *(SYN.)* plain, clear, evident, palpable, patent, self-evident, apparent, distinct, understandable, unmistakable.
(ANT.) concealed, hidden, abstruse, obscure.

obviously *(SYN.)* plainly, clearly, surely, evidently, certainly.

occasion *(SYN.)* occurrence, time, happening, excuse, opportunity.

occasional *(SYN.)* random, irregular, sporadic, infrequent, periodically, spasmodic.
(ANT.) chronic, regular, constant.

occasionally *(SYN.)* seldom, now and then, infrequently, sometimes, irregularly.
(ANT.) regularly, often.

occlude *(SYN.)* clog, obstruct, choke, throttle.

occupant *(SYN.)* tenant, lodger, boarder, dweller, resident, inhabitant.

occupation *(SYN.)* employment, business, enterprise, job, trade, vocation, work, profession, matter, interest, concern, affair, activity, commerce, engagement.
(ANT.) hobby, pastime, avocation.

occupy *(SYN.)* dwell, have, inhabit, absorb, hold, possess, fill, keep.
(ANT.) relinquish, abandon, release.

occur *(SYN.)* take place, bechance, come about, befall, chance, transpire, betide, happen.

occurrence *(SYN.)* episode, event, issue, end, result, consequence, happening, circumstance.

ocean *(SYN.)* deep, sea, main, briny.

odd *(SYN.)* strange, bizarre, eccentric, unusual, single, uneven, unique, queer, quaint, peculiar, curious, unmatched, remaining.
(ANT.) matched, common, typical, normal, even, usual, regular.

odious *(SYN.)* obscene, depraved, vulgar, despicable, mean, wicked, sordid, foul, base, loathsome, depraved, vicious, displeasing, hateful, revolting, offensive, repulsive, horrible, obnoxious, vile.
(ANT.) decent, upright, laudable, attractive, honorable.

odor *(SYN.)* fume, aroma, fragrance, redolence, smell, stink, scent, essence, stench.

odorous *(SYN.)* scented, aromatic, fragrant.

odyssey *(SYN.)* crusade, quest, journey, voyage.

offbeat *(SYN.)* uncommon, eccentric, strange, unconventional, peculiar.

off-color *(SYN.)* rude, improper, earthy, suggestive, salty.

offend *(SYN.)* annoy, anger, vex, irritate, displease, provoke, hurt, grieve, pain, disgust, wound, horrify, stricken, insult, outrage.

(ANT.) flatter, please, delight.

offender *(SYN.)* criminal, culprit, lawbreaker, miscreant.

offense *(SYN.)* indignity, injustice, transgression, affront, outrage, misdeed, sin, insult, atrocity, aggression, crime.

(ANT.) morality, gentleness, innocence, right.

offensive *(SYN.)* attacking, aggressive, unpleasant, revolting, disagreeable, nauseous, disgusting.

(ANT.) pleasing, defending, defensive, pleasant, attractive, agreeable.

offer *(SYN.)* suggestion, overture, proposal, present, suggest, propose, try, submit, tender.

(ANT.) withdrawal, denial, rejection.

offhand *(SYN.)* informal, unprepared, impromptu, spontaneous.

(ANT.) considered, planned, calculated.

office *(SYN.)* position, job, situation, studio, berth, incumbency, capacity, headquarters, duty, task, function, work, post.

officiate *(SYN.)* regulate, administer, superintend, emcee.

offset *(SYN.)* compensate, counterbalance, cushion, counteract, neutralize, soften, balance.

offshoot *(SYN.)* outgrowth, addition, supplement, appendage, accessory, branch.

offspring *(SYN.)* issue, children, progeny, descendants.

often *(SYN.)* frequently, repeatedly, commonly, generally, recurrently.

(ANT.) seldom, infrequently, rarely, occasionally, sporadically.

ogle *(SYN.)* gaze, stare, eye, leer.

ogre *(SYN.)* monster, devil, demon.

ointment *(SYN.)* lotion, pomade, balm, emollient.

old *(SYN.)* antique, senile, ancient, archaic, old-fashioned, superannuated, obsolete, venerable, antiquated, elderly, abandoned, aged.

(ANT.) new, youthful, recent, modern, young.

old-fashioned *(SYN.)* outmoded, old, dated, ancient, nostalgic.

(ANT.) modern, fashionable, current, new.

olio *(SYN.)* potpourri, variety, mixture, jumble, conglomeration.

omen *(SYN.)* sign, gesture, indication, proof, portent, symbol, token, emblem, signal.

ominous *(SYN.)* unfavorable, threatening, sinister, menacing.

omission *(SYN.)* failure, neglect, oversight, default.

(ANT.) inclusion, notice, attention, insertion.

omit *(SYN.)* exclude, delete, cancel, eliminate, ignore, neglect, skip, leave out, drop, miss, overlook.

(ANT.) insert, notice, enter, include, introduce.

omnipotent *(SYN.)* all-powerful, almighty, divine.

oncoming *(SYN.)* imminent, approaching, arriving, nearing.

onerous *(SYN.)* intricate, arduous, hard, perplexing, difficult, burdensome, puzzling.

(ANT.) simple, easy, facile, effortless.

one-sided *(SYN.)* unfair, partial, biased, prejudiced.

(ANT.) impartial, neutral.

ongoing *(SYN.)* advancing, developing, continuing, progressive.

onlooker *(SYN.)* witness, spectator, observer, bystander.

only *(SYN.)* lone, sole, solitary, single, merely, but, just.

onset *(SYN.)* commencement, beginning, opening, start, assault, attack, charge, offense, onslaught.

(ANT.) end.

onslaught *(SYN.)* invasion, aggression, attack, assault, offense, drive, criticism, onset, charge.

(ANT.) vindication, defense, surrender, opposition, resistance.

onus *(SYN.)* load, weight, burden, duty.

onward *(SYN.)* ahead, forward, frontward.

(ANT.) backward.

ooze *(SYN.)* seep, leak, drip, flow, filter.

opacity *(SYN.)* obscurity, thickness, imperviousness.

opaque *(SYN.)* murky, dull, cloudy, filmy, unilluminated, dim, obtuse, indistinct, shadowy, dark.

(ANT.) light, clear, bright.

open *(SYN.)* uncovered, overt, agape, unlocked, passable, accessible, unrestricted, candid, plain, clear, exposed, unclosed, unobstructed, free, disengaged, frank, unoccupied, honest, ajar.

open *(SYN.)* unbar, unfold, exhibit, spread, unseal, expand, unfasten.

(ANT.) close, shut, conceal, hide.

open-handed *(SYN.)* kind, generous, charitable, lavish, extravagant, bountiful.

(ANT.) mean, stingy.

openhearted *(SYN.)* frank, honest, candid, sincere, ingenuous.

(ANT.) insincere, devious.

opening *(SYN.)* cavity, hole, void, abyss, aperture, chasm, pore, gap.

openly *(SYN.)* sincerely, frankly, freely.

(ANT.) secretly.

open-minded *(SYN.)* tolerant, fair, just, liberal, impartial, reasonable, unprejudiced.

(ANT.) prejudiced, bigoted.

operate *(SYN.)* comport, avail, behave, interact, apply, manage, utilize, demean, run, manipulate, employ, act, exploit, exert, exercise, practice, conduct.

(ANT.) neglect, waste.

operation *(SYN.)* effort, enterprise, mentality, maneuver, action, instrumentality, performance, working, proceeding, agency.

(ANT.) inaction, cessation, rest, inactivity.

operative *(SYN.)* busy, active, industrious, working, effective.

(ANT.) inactive, dormant.

opiate *(SYN.)* hypnotic, tranquilizer, narcotic.

opinion *(SYN.)* decision, feeling, notion, view, idea, conviction, belief, judgment, sentiment, persuasion, impression.

(ANT.) knowledge, fact, misgiving, skepticism.

opinionated *(SYN.)* domineering, over-

bearing, arrogant, dogmatic, positive, magisterial, obstinate.

(ANT.) questioning, fluctuating, skeptical, open-minded, indecisive.

opponent *(SYN.)* competitor, foe, adversary, contestant, enemy, rival, contender, combatant.

(ANT.) comrade, team, ally, confederate.

opportune *(SYN.)* fitting, suitable, appropriate, proper, favorable.

opportunity *(SYN.)* possibility, chance, occasion, time, contingency, opening.

(ANT.) obstacle, disadvantage, hindrance.

oppose *(SYN.)* defy, resist, withstand, combat, bar, counteract, confront, thwart, struggle, fight, contradict, hinder, obstruct.

(ANT.) submit, support, agree, cooperate, succumb.

opposed *(SYN.)* opposite, contrary, hostile, adverse, counteractive, unlucky, antagonistic, unfavorable, disastrous.

(ANT.) lucky, benign, propitious, fortunate, favorable.

opposite *(SYN.)* reverse, contrary, different, unlike, opposed.

(ANT.) like, same, similar.

opposition *(SYN.)* combat, struggle, discord, collision, conflict, battle, fight, encounter, controversy, inconsistency, variance.

(ANT.) harmony, amity, concord, consonance.

oppress *(SYN.)* harass, torment, vex, afflict, annoy, harry, pester, hound, worry, persecute.

(ANT.) encourage, support, comfort, assist, aid.

oppression *(SYN.)* cruelty, tyranny, persecution, injustice, despotism, brutality, abuse.

(ANT.) liberty, freedom.

oppressive *(SYN.)* difficult, stifling, burdensome, severe, domineering, harsh, unjust, overbearing, overwhelming.

oppressor *(SYN.)* bully, scourge, slave-driver.

opprobrium *(SYN.)* disgrace, contempt, reproach, shame, discredit.

opt *(SYN.)* choose, prefer, pick, select.

optical *(SYN.)* seeing, visual.

optimism *(SYN.)* faith, expectation, optimism, anticipation, trust, expectancy, confidence, hope.

(ANT.) despair, pessimism, despondency.

optimistic *(SYN.)* happy, cheerful, bright, glad, pleasant, radiant, lighthearted.

(ANT.) pessimistic.

option *(SYN.)* preference, choice, selection, alternative, election, self-determination.

optional *(SYN.)* selective, elective, voluntary.

(ANT.) required.

opulence *(SYN.)* luxury, abundance, fortune, riches, wealth, plenty, affluence.

(ANT.) need, indigence, want, poverty.

opulent *(SYN.)* wealthy, rich, prosperous, well-off, affluent, well-heeled.

oracle *(SYN.)* authority, forecaster, wizard, seer, mastermind, clairvoyant.

oral *(SYN.)* voiced, sounded, vocalized, said, uttered, verbal, vocal, spoken.

(ANT.) recorded, written, documentary.

orate *(SYN.)* preach, lecture, sermonize.

oration *(SYN.)* address, lecture, speech, sermon, discourse, recital, declamation.

orb *(SYN.)* globe, sphere, ball, moon.

orbit *(SYN.)* path, lap, course, circuit, revolution, revolve, circle.

orchestra *(SYN.)* ensemble, band.

orchestrate *(SYN.)* coordinate, direct, synchronize, organize.

ordain *(SYN.)* constitute, create, order, decree, decide, dictate, command, rule, bid, sanction, appoint.

(ANT.) terminate, disband.

ordeal *(SYN.)* hardship, suffering, test, affliction, trouble, fortune, proof, examination, trial, experiment, tribulation, misery.

(ANT.) consolation, alleviation.

order *(SYN.)* plan, series, decree, instruction, command, system, method, aim, arrangement, class, injuction, mandate, instruct, requirement, dictate, bidding.

(ANT.) consent, license, confusion, disarray, irregularity, permission.

order *(SYN.)* guide, command, rule, direct,

govern, manage, regulate, bid, conduct.

(ANT.) misguide, deceive, misdirect, distract.

orderly *(SYN.)* regulated, neat, well-organized, disciplined, methodical, shipshape.

(ANT.) sloppy, messy, haphazard, disorganized.

ordinarily *(SYN.)* commonly, usually, generally, mostly, customarily, normally.

ordinary *(SYN.)* common, habitual, normal, typical, usual, conventional, familiar, accustomed, customary, average, standard, everyday, inferior, mediocre, regular, vulgar, plain.

(ANT.) uncommon, marvelous, extraordinary, remarkable, strange.

ordance *(SYN.)* munitions, artillery.

organ *(SYN.)* instrument, journal, voice.

organic *(SYN.)* living, biological, animate.

organism *(SYN.)* creature, plant, microorganism.

organization *(SYN.)* order, rule, system, arrangement, method, plan, regularity, scheme, mode, process.

(ANT.) irregularity, chaos, disarrangement, chance, disorder, confusion.

organize *(SYN.)* assort, arrange, plan, regulate, systematize, devise, categorize, classify, prepare.

(ANT.) jumble, disorder, disturb, confuse, scatter.

organized *(SYN.)* planned, neat, orderly, arranged.

orient *(SYN.)* align, fit, accustom, adjust.

orifice SYN.) vent, slot, opening, hole.

origin *(SYN.)* birth, foundation, source, start, commencement, inception, beginning, derivation, infancy, parentage, spring, cradle.

(ANT.) product, issue, outcome, end.

original *(SYN.)* primary, fresh, new, initial, pristine, creative, first, primordial, inventive, primeval, novel, introductory.

(ANT.) banal, trite, subsequent, derivative, later, modern, terminal.

originality *(SYN.)* unconventionality, genius, novelty, creativity, imagination.

originate *(SYN.)* fashion, invent, cause,

create, make, initiate, inaugurate, organize, institute, produce, engender, arise, commence, found, establish, form, begin, generate, formulate.
(ANT.) demolish, terminate, annihilate, disband, destroy.

originator *(SYN.)* creator, inventor, discoverer.
(ANT.) follower, imitator.

ornament *(SYN.)* decoration, ornamentation, adornment, embellishment, trimming, garnish.

ornamental *(SYN.)* ornate, decorative.

ornate *SYN.)* florid, overdone, elaborate, showy, flowery, pretentious.

ornery *(SYN.)* disobedient, firm, unruly, stiff, rebellious, stubborn, headstrong, willful, contrary, rigid, mean, difficult, malicious, cross, disagreeable.
(ANT.) pleasant.

orthodox *(SYN.)* customary, usual, conventional, correct, proper, accepted.
(ANT.) different, unorthodox.

oscillate *(SYN.)* vary, change, hesitate, waver, undulate, fluctuate, vacillate.
(ANT.) persist, resolve, adhere, stick, decide.

ostentation *(SYN.)* parade, show, boasting, pageantry, vaunting, pomp, display, flourish.
(ANT.) reserve, humility, unobtrusiveness, modesty.

ostentatious *(SYN.)* flashy, showy, overdone, fancy, pretentious, garish.

ostracize *(SYN.)* hinder, omit, bar, exclude, blackball, expel, prohibit, shout out, prevent, except.
(ANT.) welcome, accept, include, admit.

other *(SYN.)* distinct, different, extra, further, new, additional, supplementary.

ought *(SYN.)* must, should, be obliged.

oust *(SYN.)* eject, banish, exclude, expatriate, ostracize, dismiss, exile, expel.
(ANT.) shelter, accept, receive, admit, harbor.

ouster *(SYN.)* expulsion, banishment, ejection, overthrow.

outbreak *(SYN.)* riot, revolt, uprising, dis-

turbance, torrent, eruption, outburst.

outburst *(SYN.)* outbreak, eruption, torrent, ejection, discharge.

outcast *(SYN.)* friendless, homeless, deserted, abandoned, forsaken, disowned, derelict, forlorn, rejected.

outclass *(SYN.)* outshine, surpass.

outcome *(SYN.)* fate, destiny, necessity, doom, portion, consequence, result, end, fortune, effect, issue, aftermath.

outcry *(SYN.)* scream, protest, clamor, noise, uproar.

outdated *(SYN.)* old-fashioned, unfashionable, old, outmoded.
(ANT.) stylish.

outdo *(SYN.)* outshine, defeat, excel, beat, surpass.

outer *(SYN.)* remote, exterior, external.

outfit *(SYN.)* garb, kit, gear, furnish, equip, rig, clothing, provisions.

outgoing *(SYN.)* leaving, departing, friendly, congenial, amicable.
(ANT.) unfriendly, incoming.

outgrowth *(SYN.)* effect, outcome, upshot, fruit, result, consequence, product, by-product, development.

outing *(SYN.)* journey, trip, excursion, jaunt, expedition, junket.

outlandish *(SYN.)* peculiar, odd, weird, curious, strange, queer, exotic, bazaar.
(ANT.) ordinary, common.

outlast *(SYN.)* survive, endure, outlive.

outlaw *(SYN.)* exile, bandit, outcast, badman, convict, criminal, fugitive, desperado.

outlay *(SYN.)* expense, costs, spending, disbursement, expenditure, charge.

outlet *(SYN.)* spout, opening, passage.

outline *(SYN.)* form, sketch, brief, draft, figure, profile, contour, chart, diagram, skeleton, delineation, plan, silhouette.

outlook *(SYN.)* viewpoint, view, prospect, opportunity, position, attitude, future.

outlying *(SYN.)* external, remote, outer, out-of-the-way, surburban, rural.

outmoded *(SYN.)* unfashionable, old-fashioned.
(ANT.) up-to-date, modern.

outnumber *(SYN.)* exceed.

output *(SYN.)* yield, crop, harvest, proceeds, productivity, production.

outrage *(SYN.)* aggression, transgression, vice, affront, offense, insult, indignity, atrocity, misdeed, trespass, wrong.
(ANT.) morality, right, gentleness, innocence.

outrageous *(SYN.)* shameful, shocking, disgraceful, insulting, nonsensical, absurd, foolish, crazy, excessive, ridiculous, bizarre, preposterous, offensive.
(ANT.) prudent, reasonable, sensible.

outright *(SYN.)* entirely, altogether, completely, quite, fully, thoroughly.

outset *(SYN.)* inception, origin, start, commencement, opening, source.
(ANT.) end, completion, termination, consummation, close.

outside *(SYN.)* covering, exterior, surface, facade, externals, appearance.
(ANT.) intimate, insider.

outsider *(SYN.)* immigrant, stranger, foreigner, alien, newcomer, bystander.
(ANT.) countryman, friend, acquaintance, neighbor, associate.

outsmart *(SYN.)* outmaneuver, outwit.

outspoken *(SYN.)* rude, impolite, unceremonious, brusque, unrestrained, vocal, open, straight-foward, blunt, unreserved, frank, forthright, rough.
(ANT.) suave, tactful, shy, polished, polite, subtle.

outstanding *(SYN.)* well-known, important, prominent, leading, eminent, distinguished, significant, conspicuous.
(ANT.) insignificant, unimportant.

outward *(SYN.)* apparent, outside, exterior, visible.

outweigh *(SYN.)* predominate, supersede, counteract, dwarf.

outwit *(SYN.)* baffle, trick, outsmart, bewilder, outdo, outmaneuver, confuse.

oval *(SYN.)* egg-shaped, elliptical, ovular.

ovation *(SYN.)* fanfare, homage, applause, tribute, cheers, acclamation.

overall *(SYN.)* comprehensive, complete, general, extensive, wide-spread, entire.

overbearing *(SYN.)* domineering, masterful, autocratic, dictatorial, arrogant, imperious, haughty.
(ANT.) humble.

overcast *(SYN.)* dim, shadowy, cloudy, murky, dark, mysterious, gloomy, somber, dismal, hazy.
(ANT.) sunny, bright, distinct, limpid, clear.

overcome *(SYN.)* quell, beat, crush, surmount, rout, humble, conquer, subjugate, defeat, subdue, upset.
(ANT.) retreat, surrender, capitulate, cede, lose.

overconfident *(SYN.)* egotistical, presumptuous, arrogant, conceited.

overdo *(SYN.)* stretch, exaggerate, enlarge, magnify, exhaust, overexert, strain.

overdue *(SYN.)* tardy, advanced, slow, delayed, new.
(ANT.) timely, early, beforehand.

overflow *(SYN.)* run over, flood, spill, cascade, inundate.

overflowing *(SYN.)* ample, plentiful, teeming, abundant, copious.
(ANT.) insufficient, scant, deficient, scarce.

overhang *(SYN.)* protrude, extend, projection.

overhaul *(SYN.)* recondition, rebuild, service, repair, revamp.

overhead *(SYN.)* high, above, aloft, expenses, costs.

overjoyed *(SYN.)* enchanted, delighted, ecstatic, enraptured, elated, blissful.
(ANT.) depressed.

overlap *(SYN.)* overhang, extend, superimpose.

overload *(SYN.)* burden, weight, oppress, afflict, weigh, encumber.
(ANT.) ease, lighten, console, alleviate, mitigate.

overlook *(SYN.)* miss, disregard, exclude, cancel, omit, skip, ignore, drop, delete, neglect, exclude, watch, eliminate.
(ANT.) notice, enter, include, introduce, insert.

overly *(SYN.)* exceedingly, needlessly, unreasonably.

overpass *(SYN.)* span, bridge, viaduct.

overpower *(SYN.)* overcome, conquer, defeat, surmount, vanquish, overwhelm.
(ANT.) surrender.

overrated *(SYN.)* exaggerated, misrepresented.

overrule *(SYN.)* disallow, nullify, cancel, override, repeal, revoke.

overrun *(SYN.)* spread, exceed, beset, infest, flood, abound.

oversee *(SYN.)* direct, run, operate, administer, superintend, boss, manage, supervise.

overseer *(SYN.)* leader, ruler, master, teacher, chief, commander, lord, employer, manager.
(ANT.) slave, servant.

overshadow *(SYN.)* dominate, control, outclass, surpass, domineer.

oversight *(SYN.)* omission, charge, superintendence, surveillance, inattention, error, inadvertence, neglect, mistake, inspection, control, negligence, management.
(ANT.) scrutiny, care, attention, observation.

overstep *(SYN.)* surpass, exceed, trespass, transcend, impinge, violate, intrude.

overt *(SYN.)* honest, candid, frank, plain, open, apparent.

overtake *(SYN.)* outdistance, reach, catch, pass.

overthrow *(SYN.)* defeat, demolish, upset, overcome, destroy, ruin, rout, vanquish, subvert, reverse, supplant, overturn, overpower.
(ANT.) revive, restore, construct, regenerate, reinstate.

overture *(SYN.)* offer, bid, proposal, prelude, introduction, presentation, recommendation.
(ANT.) finale.

overturn *(SYN.)* demolish, overcome, vanquish, upset, supplant.
(ANT.) uphold, construct, build, preserve, conserve.

overweight *(SYN.)* pudgy, stout, heavy, obese, fat.

overwhelm *(SYN.)* crush, surmount, vanquish, conquer, astonish, surprise, bewilder, astound, startle, overcome.

overwrought *(SYN.)* distraught, hysterical.

owe *(SYN.)* be liable, be indebted.

own *(SYN.)* monopolize, possess, maintain, have.

owner *(SYN.)* landholder, partner, proprietor, possessor.

P

pace *(SYN.)* rate, gait, step.

pacific *(SYN.)* peaceful, calm, serene, undisturbed, composed, imperturbable, placid, still, tranquil, unruffled, peaceable, quiet.
(ANT.) turbulent, wild, excited, frantic.

pacify *(SYN.)* appease, lull, relieve, quell, soothe, allay, assuage, calm, satisfy, placate, alleviate.
(ANT.) incense, inflame, arouse, excite.

pack *(SYN.)* prepare, stow, crowd, stuff, bundle, parcel, load, crowd, gang, mob.

package *(SYN.)* parcel, packet, load, bundle, box, bottle, crate.

packed *(SYN.)* filled, complete, plentiful, crammed, fall, replete, gorged, satiated, copious, entire.
(ANT.) lacking, depleted, devoid, vacant, insufficient, partial, empty.

pageant *(SYN.)* show, display, spectacle.

pain *(SYN.)* twinge, ache, pang, agony, distress, grief, anguish, paroxysm, suffering, misery.
(ANT.) happiness, pleasure, comfort, relief, ease, delight, joy.

painful *(SYN.)* hurting, galling, poignant, bitter, grievous, agonizing, aching.
(ANT.) sweet, pleasant, soothing.

painting *(SYN.)* image, picture, portrayal, scene, view, sketch, illustration, panorama.

pair *(SYN.)* team, couple, mate, match.

palatial *(SYN.)* majestic, magnificent, sumptuous, luxurious.

pale *(SYN.)* colorless, white, pallid, dim, faint, whiten, blanch.
(ANT.) flushed, ruddy, bright, dark.

pamphlet *(SYN.)* leaflet, brochure.

pang *(SYN.)* throb, pain, hurt.

panic *(SYN.)* fear, terror, fright, alarm, apprehension, trembling, horror, dread.
(ANT.) tranquillity, composure, calmness, serenity, calm, soothe.

pant *(SYN.)* wheeze, puff, gasp.

pantry *(SYN.* cupboard, storeroom.

paper *(SYN.)* journal, newspaper, document, article, essay.

parable *(SYN.)* fable, saga, legend, myth, allegory, chronicle, fiction.
(ANT.) history, fact.

parade *(SYN.)* procession, cavalcade, succession, train, file, cortege, retinue, sequence, march, review, pageant, strut.

paradise *(SYN.)* utopia, heaven.

paradoxical *(SYN.)* unsteady, contradictory, discrepant, incompatible, inconsistent, vacillating, wavering, illogical.
(ANT.) correspondent, compatible, congruous, consistent.

parallel *(SYN.)* allied, analogous, comparable, corresponding, akin, similar, correlative, alike, like, resembling, equal, counterpart, likeness, correspondence, resemble, equal, match.
(ANT.) opposed, different, incongruous.

paralyze *(SYN.)* numb, deaden.

paraphernalia *(SYN.)* effect, gear, belonging, equipment.

parcel *(SYN.)* packet, package, bundle.

parched *(SYN.)* dry, arid, thirsty, drained, dehydrated, desiccated.
(ANT.) moist, damp.

pardon *(SYN.)* absolution, forgiveness, remission, acquittal, amnesty, excuse, exoneration, forgive, acquit.
(ANT.) sentence, penalty, conviction, punishment, condemn.

pardon *(SYN.)* condone, overlook, remit, absolve, acquit, forgive, excuse.
(ANT.) punish, chastise, accuse, condemn, convict.

pare *(SYN.)* skin, peel, reduce, trim, shave, crop.

parley *(SYN.)* interview, talk, conference, chat, dialogue, colloquy.

paroxysm *(SYN.)* twinge, pang, ache, pain.
(ANT.) ease, relief, comfort.

parsimonious *(SYN.)* avaricious, miserly, penurious, stingy, acquisitive, greedy.
(ANT.) munificent, extravagant, bountiful, altruistic, generous.

part *(SYN.)* piece, section, allotment, portion, segment, element, member, concern, side, interest, lines, role, apportionment, division, share, fragment, ingredient, organ, party, moiety, fraction, participation, divide.
(ANT.) whole, entirety.

part *(SYN.)* separate, sever, divide, sunder.
(ANT.) join, combine, unite, convene.

partake *(SYN.)* dispense, parcel, allot, assign, distribute, partition, appropriate, divide, share.
(ANT.) condense, aggregate, combine.

partial *(SYN.)* unfinished, undone, incomplete, prejudiced, unfair.
(ANT.) comprehensive, complete, entire.

partiality *(SYN.)* preconception, bias, predisposition, bigotry.
(ANT.) reason, fairness, impartiality.

participant *(SYN.)* associate, colleague, partner, shareholder.

participate *(SYN.)* join, share, partake.

participation *(SYN.)* communion, sacrament, union, intercourse, association, fellowship.
(ANT.) nonparticipation, alienation.

particle *(SYN.)* mite, crumb, scrap, atom, corpuscle, grain, iota, smidgen, grain, speck, bit, spot.
(ANT.) quantity, bulk, mass.

particular *(SYN.)* peculiar, unusual, detailed, specific, fastidious, individual, distinctive, singular, circumstantial, exact, careful, squeamish, special.
(ANT.) general, rough, universal, comprehensive, undiscriminating.

partisan *(SYN.)* follower, successor, adherent, attendant, henchman, devotee, disciple.
(ANT.) leader, chief, master, head.

partition *(SYN.)* distribution, division, separation, screen, barrier, separator, divider, wall.
(ANT.) unification, joining.

partly *(SYN.)* comparatively, partially, somewhat.

partner *(SYN.)* colleague, comrade, friend, crony, consort, associate, companion, mate, participant.

(ANT.) stranger, enemy, adversary.

party *(SYN.)* company, gathering, crowd, group.

pass *(SYN.)* proceed, continue, move, go, disregard, ignore, exceed, gap, permit, permission, toss, admission, throw.

(ANT.) note, consider, notice.

pass by *(SYN.)* dodge, avert, elude, free, ward, shun, eschew avoid, forbear.

(ANT.) meet, confront, oppose, encounter.

passable *(SYN.)* fair, average, mediocre, acceptable, adequate, satisfactory.

(ANT.) worst, excellent, first-rate, exceptional, extraordinary, superior.

passage *(SYN.)* section, passageway, corridor, section, voyage, tour, crossing.

passenger *(SYN.)* traveler, tourist, rider, voyager, commuter.

passion *(SYN.)* feeling, affection, turmoil, sentiment, perturbation, agitation, emotion, trepidation, zeal, rapture, excitement, desire, love, liking, fondness, enthusiasm.

(ANT.) tranquillity, indifference, calm, restraint, dispassion, apathy, coolness.

passionate *(SYN.)* fiery, ardent, burning, glowing, irascible, fervid, excitable hot, impetuous, emotional, impulsive, excited, zealous, enthusiastic, earnest, sincere.

(ANT.) quiet, calm, cool, apathetic, deliberate.

passive *(SYN.)* relaxed, idle, stoical, enduring, inert, inactive, patient, submissive.

(ANT.) dynamic, active, aggressive.

password *(SYN.)* watchword.

past *(SYN.)* done, finished, gone, over, former.

(ANT.) future, present, ahead.

pastime *(SYN.)* match, amusement, diversion, fun, play, sport, contest, merriment, recreation, entertainment, hobby.

(ANT.) quiescence, labor, apathy, business.

patch *(SYN.)* restore, fix, repair, ameliorate, correct, rectify, remedy, sew, mend, better.

(ANT.) rend, deface, destroy, hurt, injure.

patent *(SYN.)* conspicuous, apparent, obvious, clear, evident, unmistakable, open, overt, manifest, indubitable, protection, control, copyright, permit.

(ANT.) hidden, concealed, obscure, covert.

path *(SYN.)* avenue, street, trail, walk, course, road, route, thoroughfare, channel, way, track, lane, footpath, pathway, walkway.

pathetic *(SYN.)* piteous, sad, affecting, moving, poignant, pitiable, touching, pitiful, touching.

(ANT.) funny, comical, ludicrous.

patience *(SYN.)* perseverance, composure, endurance, fortitude, long-suffering, forbearance, calmness, passiveness, serenity, courage, persistence.

(ANT.) restlessness, nervousness, impatience, unquite, impetuosity.

patient *(SYN.)* indulgent, stoical, forbearing, composed, assiduous, passive, uncomplaining, persistent, untiring, persevering, submissive, resigned, serene, calm, quiet, unexcited, unruffled.

(ANT.) turbulent, high-strung, chafing, clamorous, hysterical.

patrol *(SYN.)* inspect, watch, guard.

patron *(SYN.)* purchaser, buyer, client, customer.

patronize *(SYN.)* support.

pattern *(SYN.)* guide, example, original, model, design, figure, decoration.

paunchy *(SYN.)* fat, pudgy, stout, plump, portly, rotund, corpulent, obese, stocky.

(ANT.) slim, slender, gaunt, lean, thin.

pause *(SYN.)* falter, hesitate, waver, demur, doubt, scruple, delay, vacillate, hesitation, rest, interruption, break, delay, intermission, recess.

(ANT.) proceed, continue, decide, resolve, persevere, continuity, perpetuate.

pawn *(SYN.)* tool, puppet, stooge.

pay *(SYN.)* earnings, salary, allowance, stipend, wages, payment, compensation, recompense.

(ANT.) gratuity, present, gift.

payable *(SYN.)* unpaid, due, owed, owing.

peace *(SYN.)* hush, repose, serenity, tranquillity, silence, stillness, calmness, quiescence, calm, quietude, rest, quiet, peacefulness, pact.
(ANT.) noise, tumult, agitation, disturbance, excitement.

peaceable *(SYN.)* mild, calm, friendly, peaceful, amiable, gentle, pacific.
(ANT.) aggressive, hostile, warlike.

peaceful *(SYN.)* pacific, calm, undisturbed, quiet, serene, mild, placid, gentle, tranquil, peaceable.
(ANT.) noisy, violent, agitated, turbulent, disturbed, disrupted, riotous.

peak *(SYN.)* climax, culmination, summit, zenith, height, acme, consummation, apex, top, point, crest.
(ANT.) depth, floor, base, anticlimax, base, bottom.

peculiar *(SYN.)* odd, eccentric, extraordinary, unusual, individual, particular, striking, rare, exceptional, distinctive, strange, unfamiliar, uncommon, queer, curious, outlandish.
(ANT.) ordinary, common, normal, general, regular, unspecial.

peculiarity *(SYN.)* characteristic, feature, mark, trait, quality, attribute, property, distinctiveness.

pedantic *(SYN.)* formal, scholastic, erudite, academic, learned, bookish, theoretical, scholarly.
(ANT.) simple, commonsense, ignorant, practical, unlearned.

peddle *(SYN.)* sell, vend, hawk.

pedestrian *(SYN.)* stroller, walker.

pedigree *(SYN.)* descent, line, parentage, lineage, ancestry, family.

peek *(SYN.)* glimpse, look, peer, peep.

peel *(SYN.)* rind, skin, peeling.

peep *(SYN.)* squeak, cheep, chirp.

peer *(SYN.)* match, rival, equal, parallel, peep, glimpse, examine, peek, scrutinize.

peeve *(SYN.)* nettle, irk, irritate, annoy, vex.

peevish *(SYN.)* ill-natured, irritable, waspish, touchy, petulant, snappish, fractious, ill-tempered, fretful.
(ANT.) pleasant, affable, good-tempered,

genial, good-natured.

pen *(SYN.)* coop, enclosure, cage.

penalize *(SYN.)* dock, punish.

penalty *(SYN.)* fine, retribution, handicap, punishment, chastisement, disadvantage, forfeiture, forfeit.
(ANT.) remuneration, compensation, reward, pardon.

penchant *(SYN.)* disposition, propensity, tendency, partiality, inclination, bent, tendency, slant, bias.
(ANT.) justice, fairness, equity, impartiality.

penetrate *(SYN.)* bore, hole, pierce, enter.

penetrating *(SYN.)* profound, recondite, abstruse, deep, solemn, piercing, puncturing, boring, sharp, acute.
(ANT.) superficial, trivial, shallow, slight.

peninsula *(SYN.)* spit, headland, neck, point.

penitent *(SYN.)* remorseful, sorrowful, regretful, contrite, sorry, repentant.
(ANT.) remorseless, objurgate.

penniless *(SYN.)* poor, destitute, impecunious, needy, poverty-stricken, needy.
(ANT.) rich, wealthy, affluent, opulent, prosperous, well-off.

pensive *(SYN.)* dreamy, reflect, meditative, thoughtful, introspective, reflective, contemplative.
(ANT.) thoughtless, heedless, inconsiderate, precipitous, rash.

penurious *(SYN.)* avaricious, greedy, parsimonious, miserly, stingy, acquisitive, tight.
(ANT.) munificent, extravagant, bountiful, generous, altruistic.

penury *(SYN.)* poverty, want, destitution, necessity, indigence, need, privation.
(ANT.) riches, affluence, abundance, plenty, wealth.

people *(SYN.)* humans, person.

perceive *(SYN.)* note, conceive, see, comprehend, understand, discern, recognize, apprehend, notice, observe, distinguish, understand, grasp.
(ANT.) overlook, ignore, miss.

perceptible *(SYN.)* sensible, appreciable,

apprehensible.

(ANT.) imperceptible, absurd, impalpable.

perception *(SYN.)* understanding, apprehension, conception, insight, comprehension, discernment.

(ANT.) misconception, ignorance, misapprehension, insensibility.

perceptive *(SYN.)* informed, observant, apprised, cognizant, aware, conscious, sensible, mindful, discerning, sharp, acute, observant.

(ANT.) unaware, ignorant, oblivious, insensible.

perfect *(SYN.)* ideal, whole, faultless, immaculate, complete, superlative, absolute, unqualified, utter, sinless, holy, finished, blameless, entire, excellent, pure, flawless, ideal.

(ANT.) incomplete, defective, imperfect, deficient, blemished, lacking, faulty, flawed.

perfectionist *(SYN.)* purist, pedant.

perform *(SYN.)* impersonate, pretend, act, play, do, accomplish, achieve, complete.

performance *(SYN.)* parade, entertainment, demonstration, movie, show, production, ostentation, spectacle, presentation, offering.

performer *(SYN.)* entertainer, actress, actor.

perfume *(SYN.)* cologne, scent, essence.

perfunctory *(SYN.)* decorous, exact, formal, external, correct, affected, methodical, precise, stiff, outward, proper, solemn.

(ANT.) unconventional, easy, unconstrained, natural, heartfelt.

perhaps *(SYN.)* conceivable, possible, maybe.

(ANT.) absolutely, definitely.

peril *(SYN.)* jeopardy, risk, danger, hazard.

(ANT.) safety, immunity, protection, defense, security.

perilous *(SYN.)* menacing, risky, hazardous, critical, dangerous, precarious, unsafe, insecure, threatening.

(ANT.) safe, firm, protected, secure.

period *(SYN.)* era, age, interval, span, tempo, time, epoch, duration, spell, date.

periodical *(SYN.)* uniform, customary,

orderly, systematic, regular, steady.

(ANT.) exceptional, unusual, abnormal, rare, erratic.

perish *(SYN.)* die, sink cease, decline, decay, depart, wane, wither, languish, expire, cease, pass away.

(ANT.) grow, survive, flourish, begin, live.

perishable *(SYN.)* decomposable, decayable.

permanent *(SYN.)* constant, durable, enduring, abiding, fixed, changeless, unchangeable, lasting, indestructible, stable, continuing, long-lived, persistent, persisting, everlasting, unchanging, unaltered.

(ANT.) unstable, transient, ephemeral, temporary, transitory, passing, inconstant, fluctuating.

permeate *(SYN.)* penetrate, pervade, run through, diffuse, fill, saturate, infiltrate.

permissible *(SYN.)* allowable, fair, tolerable, admissible, justifiable, probable, warranted.

(ANT.) unsuitable, inadmissible, irrelevant.

permission *(SYN.)* authorization, liberty, permit, authority, consent, leave, license, freedom.

(ANT.) refusal, prohibition, denial, opposition.

permissive *(SYN.)* easy, tolerant, open-minded, unrestrictive.

(ANT.) restrictive.

permit *(SYN.)* let, tolerate, authorize, sanction, allow, grant, give.

(ANT.) refuse, resist, forbid, protest, object, prohibit, disallow.

perpendicular *(SYN.)* standing, upright, vertical.

(ANT.) horizontal.

perpetrate *(SYN.)* commit, perform, do.

(ANT.) neglect, fail, miscarry.

perpetual *(SYN.)* everlasting, immortal, ceaseless, endless, timeless, undying, infinite, eternal, unceasing, continuing, continual, continuous, permanent, constant.

(ANT.) transient, mortal, finite, temporal ephemeral, inconstant, intermittent, fluc-

tuating.

perpetually *(SYN.)* continually, ever, incessantly, eternally, forever, always, constantly.

(ANT.) rarely, sometimes, never, occasionally, fitfully.

perplex*(SYN.)* confuse, dumbfound, mystify, puzzle, bewilder, confound, nonplus.

(ANT.) solve, explain, illumine, instruct, clarify.

perplexed *(SYN.)* confused, disorganized, mixed, bewildered, deranged, disordered, muddled, disconcerted.

(ANT.) plain, obvious, clear, lucid, organized.

perplexing *(SYN.)* intricate, complex, involved, compound, complicated.

(ANT.) uncompounded, plain, simple.

persecute *(SYN.)* harass, hound, torment, worry, vex, torture, harry, afflict, annoy, oppress, pester, ill-treat, victimize, maltreat.

(ANT.) support, comfort, assist, encourage, aid.

persevere *(SYN.)* remain, abide, endure, last, persist, continue.

(ANT.) vacillate, desist, discontinue, cease, waver, lapse.

perseverance*(SYN.)* persistency, constancy, pertinacity, steadfastness, tenacity, industry.

(ANT.) sloth, cessation, laziness, idleness, rest.

persist *(SYN.)* endure, remain, abide, persevere, continue, last.

(ANT.) vacillate, waver, desist, cease, discontinue, stop.

persistence *(SYN.)* persistency, constancy, perseverance, steadfastness, tenacity.

(ANT.) cessation, rest, sloth, idleness.

persistent *(SYN.)* lasting, steady, obstinate, stubborn, fixed, enduring, immovable, constant, indefatigable.

(ANT.) wavering, unsure, hesitant, vacillating.

person *(SYN.)* human, individual, somebody, someone.

personal *(SYN.)* secret, private.

(ANT.) general, public.

personality *(SYN.)* make-up, nature, dis-

position, character.

perspicacity *(SYN.)* intelligence, understanding, discernment, judgment, wisdom, sagacity.

(ANT.) thoughtlessness, stupidity, arbitrariness, senselessness.

persuade *(SYN.)* entice, coax, exhort, prevail upon, urge, allure, induce, influence, win over, convince.

(ANT.) restrain, deter, compel, dissuade, coerce, discourage.

persuasion*(SYN.)* decision, feeling, notion, view, sentiment, conviction, belief, opinion.

(ANT.) knowledge, skepticism, fact, misgiving.

persuasive *(SYN.)* winning, alluring, compelling, convincing, stimulating, influential.

(ANT.) dubious, unconvincing.

pertain *(SYN.)* refer, relate, apply.

pertinacious *(SYN.)* firm, obstinate, contumacious, head-strong, dogged, inflexible, obdurate, uncompromising, determined, immovable, unyielding.

(ANT.) yielding, docile, amenable, submissive, compliant.

pertinent *(SYN.)* apt, material, relevant, relating, applicable, to the point, germane, apropos, apposite, appropriate.

(ANT.) unrelated, foreign, alien, extraneous.

perturbed *(SYN.)* agitated, disturbed, upset, flustered.

pervade *(SYN.)* penetrate, saturate, fill, diffuse, infiltrate, run through, permeate.

perverse *(SYN.)* obstinate, ungovernable, sinful, contrary, fractious, peevish, forward, disobedient, wicked, intractable, petulant.

(ANT.) docile, agreeable, tractable, obliging.

perversion *(SYN.)* maltreatment, outrage, desecration, abuse, profanation, misuse, reviling.

(ANT.) respect.

pervert *(SYN.)* deprave, humiliate, impair, debase, corrupt, degrade, abase, defile.

(ANT.) improve, raise, enhance.

perverted *(SYN.)* wicked, perverse, sinful.

pest *(SYN.)* annoyance, nuisance, bother, irritant, irritation.

pester *(SYN.)* disturb, annoy, irritate, tease, bother, chafe, inconvenience, molest, trouble, vex, harass, torment, worry.
(ANT.) console, soothe, accommodate, gratify.

pet *(SYN.)* darling, favorite, caress.

petition *(SYN.)* invocation, prayer, request, appeal, entreaty, supplication, suit, plea, application, solicitation, entreaty.

petty *(SYN.)* paltry, trivial, frivolous, small, unimportant, trifling, insignificant.
(ANT.) important, serious, weighty, momentous, grand, vital, significant, generous.

petulant *(SYN.)* irritable, ill-natured, fretful, snappish, peevish, ill-tempered, waspish, touchy.
(ANT.) pleasant, affable, good-tempered, genial, good-natured.

phantom *(SYN.)* apparition, ghost, specter.

phase *(SYN.)* period, stage, view, condition.

phenomenon *(SYN.)* occurrence, fact, happening, incident.

philanthropy *(SYN.)* kindness, benevolence, charity, generosity, tenderness, liberality, humanity, magnanimity, altruism.
(ANT.) unkindness, inhumanity, cruelty, malevolence, selfishness.

phlegmatic *(SYN.)* unfeeling, passionless, listless, cold, lethargic, sluggish, slow, lazy.
(ANT.) passionate, ardent, energetic.

phony *(SYN.)* counterfeit, artificial, ersatz, fake, synthetic, unreal, spurious, feigned, assumed, bogus, sham, false, forged.
(ANT.) real, genuine, natural, true.

phrase *(SYN.)* expression, term, word, name.

physical *(SYN.)* material, bodily, carnal, corporeal, natural, somatic, corporal.
(ANT.) spiritual, mental.

pick *(SYN.)* cull, opt, select, elect, choose.
(ANT.) reject, refuse.

picture *(SYN.)* etching, image, painting, portrait, print, representation, sketch, appearance, cinema, effigy, engraving, scene, view, illustration, panorama, resemblance, likeness, drawing, photograph.

piece *(SYN.)* portion, bit, fraction, morsel, scrap, fragment, amount, part, quantity, unit, section.
(ANT.) sum, whole, entirety, all, total.

piecemeal *(SYN.)* gradually, partially.
(ANT.) whole, complete, entire.

pierce *(SYN.)* puncture, perforate.

pigheaded *(SYN.)* inflexible, stubborn, obstinate.

pigment *(SYN.)* shade, tint, color, dye, hue, complexion, tincture, stain, tinge.
(ANT.) transparency, paleness.

pile *(SYN.)* accumulation, heap, collection, amass.

pilgrim *(SYN.)* wanderer, traveler.

pilgrimage *(SYN.)* trip, journey, tour, expedition.

pillar *(SYN.)* support, prop, column, shaft.

pillow *(SYN.)* bolster, cushion, pad.

pilot *(SYN.)* helmsman, aviator, steersman.

pin *(SYN.)* clip, fastening, peg, fastener.

pinch *(SYN.)* squeeze, nip.

pinnacle *(SYN.)* crown, zenith, head, summit, chief, apex, crest, top.
(ANT.) bottom, foundation, base, foot.

pioneer *(SYN.)* guide, pilgrim, pathfinder, explorer.

pious *(SYN.)* devout, religious, spiritual, consecrated, divine, hallowed, holy, saintly, sacred, reverent.
(ANT.) worldly, sacrilegious, evil, secular, profane, irreligious, impious.

pirate *(SYN.)* plunderer, buccaneer, privateer.

pistol *(SYN.)* gun, revolver, weapon, handgun.

pit *(SYN.)* well, cavity, hole, excavation.

pitch *(SYN.)* throw, cast, toss, propel, hurl, fling, thrust, establish.
(ANT.) retain, draw, hold, pull, haul.

pitcher *(SYN.)* jug.

piteous *(SYN.)* poignant, touching, affecting, moving, pitiable, sad, pathetic.
(ANT.) funny, ludicrous, comical.

pitfall *(SYN.)* lure, snare, wile, ambush,

bait, intrigue, trick, trap, artifice, net, snare.

pitiable *(SYN.)* poignant, touching, moving, affecting, sad.

(ANT.) ludicrous, funny, comical.

pitiful *(SYN.)* distressing, pathetic, pitiable.

pitiless *(SYN.)* unmerciful, mean, unpitying, merciless, cruel.

(ANT.) gentle, kind.

pity *(SYN.)* sympathy, commiseration, condolence, compassion, charity, mercy.

(ANT.) ruthlessness, hardness, cruelty, inhumanity, brutality, vindictiveness.

pivotal *(SYN.)* crucial, critical, essential, central.

(ANT.) peripheral, unimportant.

place *(SYN.)* lay, arrange, dispose, put, deposit, space, region, location, plot, area, spot.

(ANT.) mislay, remove, disarrange, disturb, misplace.

placid *(SYN.)* pacific, serene, tranquil, calm, imperturbable, composed, peaceful, quiet, still, undisturbed, unruffled.

(ANT.) wild, frantic, turbulent, stormy, excited.

plagiarize *(SYN.)* recite, adduce, cite, quote, paraphrase, repeat, extract.

(ANT.) retort, contradict, misquote, refute.

plague *(SYN.)* hound, pester, worry, harass, annoy, persecute, torment, vex, afflict, badger, torture, epidemic, trouble.

(ANT.) encourage, aid, comfort, assist, support.

plain *(SYN.)* candid, simple, flat, smooth, clear, evident, sincere, unpretentious, level, distinct, absolute, visible, open, frank, palpable, undecorated, ordinary, unembellished, unadorned.

(ANT.) embellished, abstruse, abrupt, rough, broken, insincere, adorned, fancy, elaborate, beautiful, ornamented.

plan *(SYN.)* design, purpose, sketch, devise, invent, contrive, intend, draw, create, scheme, plot, method, procedure.

plane *(SYN.)* level, airplane.

plastic *(SYN.)* pliable, moldable, supple, flexible, synthetic.

platform *(SYN.)* stage, pulpit.

plausible *(SYN.)* likely, practical, credible, feasible, possible, probable.

(ANT.) impracticable, impossible, visionary.

play *(SYN.)* entertainment, amusement, pastime, sport, game, fun, diversion, recreation, show, performance, drama, theatrical.

(ANT.) work, labor, boredom, toil.

playful *(SYN.)* sportive, frolicsome, frisky.

plaything *(SYN.)* game, trinket, toy, gadget.

playwright *(SYN.)* scriptwriter, dramatist.

plea *(SYN.)* invocation, request, appeal, entreaty, supplication, petition, suit.

plead *(SYN.)* beseech, defend, rejoin, supplicate, discuss, beg, appeal, ask, implore, argue, entreat.

(ANT.) deprecate, deny, refuse.

pleasant *(SYN.)* agreeable, welcome, suitable, charming, pleasing, amiable, gratifying, acceptable, pleasurable, enjoyable, nice, satisfying, satisfactory, acceptable, affable, mild, friendly.

(ANT.) offensive, disagreeable, obnoxious, unpleasant, horrid, sour, difficult, nasty.

please *(SYN.)* satisfy, suffice, fulfill, content, appease, gratify, satiate, compensate, remunerate.

(ANT.) dissatisfy, annoy, tantalize, frustrate, displease, vex.

pleasing *(SYN.)* luscious, melodious, sugary, delightful, agreeable, honeyed, mellifluous, enjoyable, welcome, pleasant, charming.

(ANT.) repulsive, sour, acrid, bitter, offensive, irritating, annoying.

pleasure *(SYN.)* felicity, delight, amusement, enjoyment gratification, happiness, joy, satisfaction, gladness, well-being.

(ANT.) suffering, pain, vexation, trouble, affliction, discomfort, torment.

pledge *(SYN.)* promise, statement, assertion, declaration, assurance, agreement, oath, commitment, agree, vow, swear.

pledge *(SYN.)* bind, obligate, commit.

(ANT.) renounce, release, neglect, mistrust.

plentiful *(SYN.)* ample, profuse, replete, bountiful, abundant, plenteous, luxurious, fullness, fruitful, copious.

(ANT.) rare, scanty, deficient, scarce, insufficient.

plenty *(SYN.)* fruitfulness, bounty, fullness, abundance.

(ANT.) want, scarcity, need.

pliable *(SYN.)* elastic, supple, flexible, compliant, pliant, resilient, ductile.

(ANT.) rigid, unbending, hard, brittle, stiff.

plight *(SYN.)* dilemma, situation, difficulty, condition, predicament, fix, scrape, state.

(ANT.) satisfaction, ease, comfort, calmness.

plot *(SYN.)* design, plan, scheme, cabal, conspiracy, diagram, sketch, graph, chart, machination, intrigue.

plotting *(SYN.)* cunning, scheming, objective, artfulness, contrivance, purpose, intent, design.

(ANT.) accident, chance, result, candor, sincerity.

ploy *(SYN.)* ruse, guile, antic, deception, hoax, subterfuge, wile, cheat, artifice, fraud, trick.

(ANT.) honesty, sincerity, openness, exposure, candor.

pluck *(SYN.)* yank, snatch, jerk, pull.

plug *(SYN.)* cork, stopper.

plump *(SYN.)* obese, portly, stout, thickset, rotund, chubby, fat, paunchy, stocky, corpulent, pudgy, fleshy.

(ANT.) slim, thin, gaunt, lean, slender, skinny.

plunder *(SYN.)* ravage, strip, sack, rob, pillage, raid, loot.

plunge *(SYN.)* immerse, dip, submerge.

pocketbook *(SYN.)* purse, handbag.

poem *(SYN.)* lyric, verse, poetry.

poetry *(SYN.)* rhyme, verse.

pogrom *(SYN.)* massacre, carnage, slaughter, butchery.

poignant *(SYN.)* pitiable, touching, affecting, impressive, sad, tender, moving, heart-rending.

point *(SYN.)* direct, level, train, aim, locality, position, spot, location.

(ANT.) distract, misguide, deceive, misdirect.

pointed *(SYN.)* keen, sharp, penetrating, shrewd, witty, quick, acute, cutting, piercing, astute, severe.

(ANT.) shallow, stupid, bland, blunt, gentle.

pointless *(SYN.)* vain, purposeless.

poise *(SYN.)* composure, self-possession, equanimity, equilibrium, carriage, calmness, balance, self-control, assurance, control, dignity.

(ANT.) rage, turbulence, agitation, anger, excitement.

poison *(SYN.)* corrupt, sully, taint, infect, befoul, defile, contaminate, venom, toxin, virus.

(ANT.) purify, disinfect.

poke *(SYN.)* punch, stab, thrust, jab.

policy *(SYN.)* procedure, system, rule, approach, tactic.

polish *(SYN.)* brighten, shine, finish, brightness, gloss.

(ANT.) tarnish, dull.

polished *(SYN.)* glib, diplomatic, urbane, refined, sleek, suave, slick.

(ANT.) rough, blunt, bluff, harsh, rugged.

polite *(SYN.)* civil, refined, well-mannered, accomplished, courteous, genteel, urbane, well-bred, cultivated, considerate, thoughtful, mannerly, respectful.

(ANT.) uncouth, impertinent, rude, boorish, uncivil, discourteous.

pollute *(SYN.)* contaminate, poison, taint, sully, infect, befoul, defile, dirty.

(ANT.) purify, disinfect, clean, clarify.

pomp *(SYN.)* flourish, pageantry, vaunting, show, boasting, ostentation, parade, display.

(ANT.) reserve, humility, modesty.

pompous *(SYN.)* high, magnificent, stately, august, dignified, grandiose, noble, majestic, lofty, imposing, arrogant, vain, pretentious.

(ANT.) lowly, undignified, humble, common, ordinary.

ponder *(SYN.)* examined, study, contemplate, investigate, meditate, muse, scrutinize, cogitate, reflect, weigh, deliberate, consider.

ponderous *(SYN.)* burdensome, trying, gloomy, serious, sluggish, massive, heavy, cumbersome, grievous, grave, dull, weighty.
(ANT.) light, animated, brisk.

poor *(SYN.)* penniless, bad, deficient, destitute, inferior, shabby, wrong, scanty, pecunious, indigent, needy, poverty-stricken, unfavorable, impoverished, penniless.
(ANT.) wealthy, prosperous, rich, fortunate, good, excellent.

poppycock *(SYN.)* rubbish, babble, twaddle, nonsense.

popular *(SYN.)* favorite, general, common, familiar, prevalent, liked, prevailing, well-liked, approved, accepted, celebrated, admired, ordinary.
(ANT.) unpopular, esoteric, restricted, exclusive.

populous *(SYN.)* dense, thronged, crowded.

porch *(SYN.)* patio, veranda.

pornographic *(SYN.)* impure, indecent, obscene, coarse, dirty, filthy, lewd, smutty, offensive, disgusting.
(ANT.) refined, modest, pure, decent.

port *(SYN.)* harbor, refuge, anchorage.

portable *(SYN.)* transportable, movable.

portal *(SYN.)* entry, doorway, opening, inlet, entrance.
(ANT.) exit, departure.

portend *(SYN.)* foreshadow, presage, foretoken.

portentous *(SYN.)* significant, critical, momentous.
(ANT.) trivial.

portion *(SYN.)* share, bit, parcel, part, piece, section, fragment, division, quota, segment, allotment.
(ANT.) whole, bulk.

portly *(SYN.)* majestic, grand, impressive, dignified, stout, fat, heavy, obese.
(ANT.) slender, thin, slim.

portrait *(SYN.)* painting, representation, picture, likeness.

portray *(SYN.)* depict, picture, represent, sketch, describe, delineate, paint.
(ANT.) misrepresent, caricature, suggest.

pose *(SYN.)* model.

position *(SYN.)* caste, site, locality, situation, condition, standing, incumbency, office, bearing, posture, berth, place, job, pose, rank, attitude, location, place, spot, station, situation, occupation.

positive *(SYN.)* sure, definite, fixed, inevitable, undeniable, indubitable, assured, certain, unquestionable, unmistakable.
(ANT.) uncertain, doubtful, questionable, probably, unsure, dubious, confused, negative, adverse.

positively *(SYN.)* unquestionably, surely, certainly, absolutely.

possess *(SYN.)* own, obtain, control, have, seize, hold, occupy, affect.
(ANT.) surrender, abandon, lose, renounce.

possessed *(SYN.)* entranced, obsessed, consumer, haunted, enchanted.

possession *(SYN.)* custody, ownership, occupancy.

possessions *(SYN.)* commodities, effects, goods, property, stock, merchandise, wares, wealth, belongings.

possible *(SYN.)* likely, practical, probable, feasible, plausible, credible, practicable.
(ANT.) visionary, impossible, improbable.

possibility *(SYN.)* opportunity, chance, contingency, occasion.
(ANT.) obstacle, disadvantage, hindrance.

possible *(SYN.)* feasible, practical, practicable, doable.

possibly *(SYN.)* perchance, perhaps, maybe.

post *(SYN.)* position, job, berth, incumbency, situation, shaft, pole, fort, base, station.

postpone *(SYN.)* delay, stay, suspend, discontinue, defer, adjourn, interrupt, put off.
(ANT.) persist, prolong, maintain, continue, proceed.

postulate *(SYN.)* principle, adage, saying, proverb, truism, byword, aphorism, axiom, fundamental, maxim.

potency *(SYN.)* effectiveness, capability, skillfulness, efficiency, competency, ability.

(ANT.) wastefulness, inability, ineptitude.

potent *(SYN.)* mighty, influential, convincing, effective.

(ANT.) feeble, weak, powerless, impotent.

potential *(SYN.)* likely, possible, dormant, hidden, latent.

pouch *(SYN.)* container, bag, sack.

pound *(SYN.)* buffet, beat, punch, strike, thrash, defeat, subdue, pulse, smite, belabor, knock, thump, overpower, palpitate, rout, vanquish.

(ANT.) fail, surrender, stroke, defend, shield.

pour *(SYN.)* flow.

pout *(SYN.)* brood, sulk, mope.

poverty *(SYN.)* necessity, need, want, destitution, privation, indigence, distress.

(ANT.) plenty, abundance, wealth, riches, affluence, richness, comfort.

power *(SYN.)* potency, might, authority, control, predominance, capability, faculty, validity, force, vigor, command, influence, talent, ability, dominion, competency.

(ANT.) incapacity, fatigue, weakness, disablement, impotence, ineptitude.

powerful *(SYN.)* firm, strong, concentrated, enduring, forcible, robust, sturdy, tough, athletic, forceful, hale, impregnable, hardy, mighty, potent.

(ANT.) feeble, insipid, brittle, delicate, fragile, weak, ineffectual, powerless.

practical *(SYN.)* sensible, wise, prudent, reasonable, sagacious, sober, sound, workable, attainable.

(ANT.) stupid, unaware, impalpable, imperceptible, absurd, impractical.

practically *(SYN.)* almost, nearly.

practice *(SYN.)* exercise, habit, custom, manner, wont, usage, drill, tradition, performance, action, repetition.

(ANT.) inexperience, theory, disuse, idleness, speculation.

practiced *(SYN.)* able, expert, skilled, adept.

(ANT.) inept.

prairie *(SYN.)* plain, grassland.

praise *(SYN.)* applaud, compliment, extol,

laud, glorify, commend, acclaim, eulogize, flatter, admire, celebrate, commendation, approval.

(ANT.) criticize, censure, reprove, condemn, disparage, disapprove, criticism, negation.

pray *(SYN.)* supplicate, importune, beseech, beg.

prayer *(SYN.)* plea, suit, appeal, invocation, supplication, petition, entreaty, request.

preach *(SYN.)* teach, urge, moralize, lecture.

preamble *(SYN.)* overture, prologue, beginning, introduction, prelude, start, foreword, preface.

(ANT.) end, finale, completion, conclusion, epilogue.

precarious *(SYN.)* dangerous, perilous, threatening, menacing, critical, risky, unsafe, hazardous.

(ANT.) secure, firm, protected, safe.

precaution *(SYN.)* foresight, forethought, care.

precedence *(SYN.)* preference, priority.

precedent *(SYN.)* model, example.

precept *(SYN.)* doctrine, tenet, belief, creed, teaching, dogma.

(ANT.) practice, conduct, performance, deed.

precious *(SYN.)* dear, useful, valuable, costly, esteemed, profitable, expensive, priceless, dear.

(ANT.) poor, worthless, cheap, mean, trashy.

precipice *(SYN.)* bluff, cliff.

precipitate *(SYN.)* speedy, swift, hasty, sudden.

precipitous *(SYN.)* unannounced, sudden, harsh, rough, unexpected, sharp, abrupt, hasty, craggy, steep, precipitate.

(ANT.) expected, smooth, anticipated, gradual.

precise *(SYN.)* strict, exact, formal, rigid, definite, unequivocal, prim, ceremonious, distinct, accurate, correct.

(ANT.) loose, easy, vague, informal, careless, erroneous.

precisely *(SYN.)* specifically, exactly.

precision *(SYN.)* correction, accuracy, exactness.

preclude *(SYN.)* hinder, prevent, obstruct, forestall, obviate, thwart, impede.
(ANT.) permit, aid, expedite, encourage, promote.

preclusion *(SYN.)* omission, exception, exclusion.
(ANT.) standard, rule, inclusion.

predicament *(SYN.)* dilemma, plight, situation, condition, fix, difficulty, strait, scrape.
(ANT.) satisfaction, comfort, east, calmness.

predict *(SYN.)* forecast, foretell.

prediction *(SYN.)* forecast, prophecy.

predilection *(SYN.)* attachment, inclination, affection, bent, desire, penchant, disposition, preference.
ANT.) repugnance, aversion, apathy, distaste, nonchalance.

predominant *(SYN.)* highest, paramount, cardinal, foremost, main, first, leading, supreme, principal, essential, prevalent, dominant, prevailing.
(ANT.) subsidiary, auxiliary, supplemental, minor, subordinate.

predominate *(SYN.)* prevail, outweigh, rule.

preface *(SYN.)* foreword, introduction, preliminary, prelude, prologue, preamble.

prefer *(SYN.)* select, favor, elect, fancy.

preference *(SYN.)* election, choice, selection, alternative, option.

prejudice *(SYN.)* bias, favoritism, unfairness, partiality.

prejudiced *(SYN.)* fanatical, narrow-minded, dogmatic, bigoted, illiberal, intolerant.
(ANT.) radical, liberal, tolerant, progressive.

preliminary *(SYN.)* introductory, preparatory, prelude, preface.

premature *(SYN.)* early, untimely, unexpected.
(ANT.) timely.

premeditated *(SYN.)* intended, voluntary, contemplated, designed, intentional, willful, deliberate, studied.
(ANT.) fortuitous, accidental.

premeditation *(SYN.)* intention, deliberation, forethought, forecast.
(ANT.) hazard, accident, impromptu, extemporization.

premise *(SYN.)* basis, presupposition, assumption, postulate, principle, presumption.
(ANT.) superstructure, derivative, trimming, implication.

preoccupied *(SYN.)* abstracted, distracted, absorbed, meditative, inattentive, absent, absent-minded.
(ANT.) attentive, alert, conscious, present, attending, watchful.

prepare *(SYN.)* contrive, furnish, ready, predispose, condition, fit, arrange, plan, qualify, make ready, get ready.

preposterous *(SYN.)* foolish, nonsensical, silly, contradictory, unreasonable, absurd, inconsistent, irrational, self-contradictory.
(ANT.) sensible, rational, consistent, sound, reasonable.

prerequisite *(SYN.)* essential, requirement, necessity, condition, demand.

prerogative *(SYN.)* grant, right, license, authority, privilege.
(ANT.) violation, encroachment, wrong, injustice.

prescribe *(SYN.)* order, direct, designate.

presence *(SYN.)* nearness, attendance, closeness, vicinity, appearance, bearing, personality.

present *(SYN.)* donation, gift, today, now, existing, current, largess, donate, acquaint, introduce, being, give, gratuity, boon, grant.
(ANT.) reject, spurn, accept, retain, receive.

presentable *(SYN.)* polite, well-bred, respectable, well-mannered.

presently *(SYN.)* shortly, soon, directly, immediately.

preserve *(SYN.)* protect, save, conserve, maintain, secure, rescue, uphold, spare, keep, can, safeguard, defend, rescue.
(ANT.) impair, abolish, destroy, abandon, squander, injure.

preside *(SYN.)* officiate, direct, administrate.

press*SYN.)* impel, shove, urge, hasten, push, compress, squeeze, hug, crowd, propel, force, drive, embrace, smooth, iron, insist on, pressure, promote, urgency, jostle.
(ANT.) oppose, pull, falter, drag, retreat, ignore.

pressing *(SYN.)* impelling, insistent, necessary, urgent, compelling, imperative, instant, serious, important, cogent, exigent, importunate.
(ANT.) unimportant, trifling, insignificant, petty, trivial.

pressure *(SYN.)* force, influence, stress, press, compulsion, urgency, constraint, compression.
(ANT.) relaxation, leniency, ease, recreation.

prestige *(SYN.)* importance, reputation, weight, influence, renown, fame, distinction.

presume *(SYN.)* guess, speculate, surmise, imagine, conjecture, apprehend, believe, think, assume, suppose, deduce.
(ANT.) prove, ascertain, demonstrate, know, conclude.

presumption *(SYN.)* boldness, impertinence, insolence, rudeness, assurance, effrontery, impudence, assumption, audacity, supposition, sauciness.
(ANT.) politeness, truckling, diffidence.

presumptuous *(SYN.)* bold, impertinent, fresh, imprudent, rude, forward, arrogant.

presupposition *(SYN.)* basis, principle, premise, assumption, postulate.
(ANT.) superstructure, derivative, implication.

pretend *(SYN.)* feign, stimulate, act, profess, make believe, imagine, fake, sham, affect.
(ANT.) expose, reveal, display, exhibit.

pretense *(SYN.)* mask, pretext, show, affection, disguise, garb, semblance, simulation, fabrication, lie, excuse, falsification, deceit, subterfuge.
(ANT.) sincerity, actuality, truth, fact, reality.

pretentious *(SYN.)* gaudy, ostentatious.
(ANT.) simple, humble.

pretty *(SYN.)* charming, handsome, lovely, beauteous, fair, comely, attractive, beautiful, elegant.
(ANT.) repulsive, foul, unsightly, homely, plain, hideous.

prevail *(SYN.)* win, succeed, predominate, triumph.
(ANT.) yield, lose.

prevailing *(SYN.)* common, current, general, habitual, steady, regular, universal.

prevalent *(SYN.)* ordinary, usual, common, general, familiar, popular, prevailing, wide-spread, universal, frequent.
(ANT.) odd, scarce, exceptional, extraordinary.

prevent *(SYN.)* impede, preclude, forestall, stop, block, check, halt, interrupt, deter, slow, obviate, hinder, obstruct, thwart.
(ANT.) expedite, help, allow, abet, aid, permit, encourage, promote.

previous *(SYN.)* former, anterior, preceding, prior, antecedent, earlier, aforesaid, foregoing.
(ANT.) subsequent, following, consequent, succeeding, later.

prey *(SYN.)* raid, seize, victimize.

price *(SYN.)* worth, cost, expense, charge, value.

pride *(SYN.)* self-respect, vanity, glory, superciliousness, haughtiness, conceit, arrogance, self-importance, pretension, egotism, satisfaction, fulfillment, enjoyment, self-esteem.
(ANT.) modesty, shame, humbleness, lowliness, meekness, humility.

prim *(SYN.)* formal, puritanical, priggish, prudish.

primarily *(SYN.)* mainly, chiefly, firstly, essentially, originally.
(ANT.) secondarily.

primary *(SYN.)* first, principal, primeval, pristine, beginning, original, initial, fundamental, elementary, chief, foremost, earliest, main, prime.
(ANT.) subordinate, last, secondary, least, hindmost, latest.

prime *(SYN.)* first, primary, chief, excellent, best, superior, ready.

primeval *(SYN.)* fresh, primary, novel, inventive, creative, primordial, original, first, new, initial.

(ANT.) trite, modern, subsequent, banal, later, terminal, derivative.

primitive *(SYN.)* antiquated, early, primeval, prehistoric, uncivilized, uncultured, simple, pristine, old, aboriginal, unsophisticated, rude, rough, primary.

(ANT.) sophisticated, modish, civilized, cultured, cultivated, late.

primordial *(SYN.)* pristine, inventive, novel, creative, original, first, initial, new, primary.

(ANT.) trite, terminal, banal, modern, derivative, subsequent, later.

principal *(SYN.)* first, leading, main, supreme, predominant, chief, foremost, highest, prime, primary, leader, headmaster, paramount, essential, cardinal.

(ANT.) supplemental, secondary, auxiliary, subsidiary, accessory, minor, subordinate.

principle *(SYN.)* law, method, axiom, rule, propriety, regulation, maxim, formula, order, statute.

(ANT.) exception, hazard, chance, deviation.

print *(SYN.)* issue, reprint, publish, letter, sign, fingerprint, mark, picture, lithograph, engraving, etching.

prior *(SYN.)* previous, aforesaid, antecedent, sooner, earlier, preceding, former, foregoing.

(ANT.) succeeding, following, later, consequent, subsequent.

prison *(SYN.)* brig, jail, stockade, penitentiary.

pristine *(SYN.)* primordial, creative, first, original, fresh, inventive, novel, primary, initial.

(ANT.) trite, terminal, derivative, modern, banal, subsequent, plagiarized, later.

private *(SYN.)* concealed, hidden, secret, clandestine, unknown, personal, surreptitious, covert, individual, particular, special, latent.

(ANT.) exposed, known, closed, general, public, conspicuous, disclosed, obvious.

privation *(SYN.)* necessity, penury, destitution, need, poverty, want.

(ANT.) wealth, affluence, abundance, plenty, riches.

privilege *(SYN.)* liberty, right, advantage, immunity, freedom, license, favor, sanction.

(ANT.) restriction, inhibition, prohibition, disallowance.

prize *(SYN.)* compensation, bonus, award, premium, remuneration, rate, reward, bounty, esteem, value, recompense, requital.

(ANT.) charge, punishment, wages, earnings, assessment.

probable *(SYN.)* presumable, likely.

probe *(SYN.)* stretch, reach, investigate, examine, examination, scrutiny, scrutinize, inquire, explore, inquiry, investigation, extend.

(ANT.) miss, short.

problem *(SYN.)* dilemma, question, predicament, riddle, difficulty, puzzle.

procedure *(SYN.)* process, way, fashion, form, mode, conduct, practice, manner, habit, system, operation, management, plan.

proceed *(SYN.)* progress, continue, issue, result, spring, thrive, improve, advance, emanate, rise.

(ANT.) retard, withhold, withdraw, hinder, retreat, oppose.

proceeding *(SYN.)* occurrence, business, affair, deal, negotiation, transaction, deed.

proceedings *(SYN.)* account, record, document.

proceeds *(SYN.)* result, produce, income, reward, intake, fruit, profit, store, yield, product, return, harvest, crop.

process *(SYN.)* method, course, system, procedure, operation, prepare, treat.

procession *(SYN.)* cortege, parade, sequence, train, cavalcade, file, retinue, succession.

proclaim *(SYN.)* declare, assert, make known, promulgate, state, broadcast, aver, express, announce, advertise, tell, publish, profess.

proclamation *(SYN.)* statement, declaration, announcement, promulgation, notice, manifesto.

procrastinate *(SYN.)* waver, vacillate, defer, hesitate, delay, postpone.

procreate *(SYN.)* generate, produce, beget, engender, originate, propagate, sire, create, father.
(ANT.) murder, destroy, abort, kill, extinguish.

procure *(SYN.)* secure, gain, win, attain, obtain, get, acquire, earn.
(ANT.) lose.

prod *(SYN.)* goad, nudge, jab, push.

prodigious *(SYN.)* astonishing, enormous, immense, monstrous, huge, remarkable, marvelous, amazing, astounding, monumental.
(ANT.) insignificant, commonplace, small.

produce *(SYN.)* harvest, reaping, bear, result, originate, bring about, store, supply, make, create, crop, proceeds, bring forth, occasion, breed, generate, cause, exhibit, show, demonstrate, fabricate, hatch, display, manufacture, exhibit, give, yield.
(ANT.) conceal, reduce, destroy, consume, waste, hide.

product *(SYN.)* outcome, result, output, produce, goods, commodity, stock, merchandise.

productive *(SYN.)* fertile, luxuriant, rich, bountiful, fruitful, creative, fecund, teeming, plenteous, prolific.
(ANT.) wasteful, unproductive, barren, impotent, useless, sterile.

profanation *(SYN.)* dishonor, insult, outrage, aspersion, defamation, invective, misuse, abuse, reviling, maltreatment, desecration, perversion.
(ANT.) plaudit, commendation, laudation, respect, approval.

profane *(SYN.)* deflower, violate, desecrate, pollute, dishonor, ravish, debauch.

profess *(SYN.)* declare, assert, make known, state, protest, announce, aver, express, broadcast, avow, tell.
(ANT.) suppress, conceal, repress, withhold.

profession *(SYN.)* calling, occupation, vocation, employment.

(ANT.) hobby, avocation, pastime.

proffer *(SYN.)* extend, tender, volunteer, propose, advance.
(ANT.) reject, spurn, accept, receive, retain.

proficient *(SYN.)* competent, adept, clever, able, cunning, practiced, skilled, versed, ingenious, accomplished, skillful, expert.
(ANT.) untrained, inexpert, bungling, awkward, clumsy.

profit *(SYN.)* gain, service, advantage, return, earnings, emolument, improvement, benefit, better, improve, use, avail.
(ANT.) waste, loss, detriment, debit, lose, damage, ruin.

profitable *(SYN.)* beneficial, advantageous, helpful, wholesome, useful, gainful, favorable, serviceable, salutary, productive, good.
(ANT.) harmful, destructive, injurious, deleterious, detrimental.

profligate *(SYN.)* corrupt, debased, tainted, unsound, vitiated, venal, contaminated, crooked, depraved, impure.

profound *(SYN.)* deep, serious, knowing, wise, intelligent, knowledgeable, recondite, solemn, abstruse, penetrating.
(ANT.) trivial, slight, shallow, superficial.

profuse *(SYN.)* lavish, excessive, extravagant, improvident, luxuriant, prodigal, wasteful, exuberant, immoderate, plentiful.
(ANT.) meager, poor, economical, sparse, skimpy.

profusion *(SYN.)* immoderation, superabundance, surplus, extravagance, intemperance, superfluity.
(ANT.) lack, paucity, death, want, deficiency.

program *(SYN.)* record, schedule, plan, agenda, calendar.

progress *(SYN.)* advancement, improvement, development, betterment, advance, movement, improve, progression.
(ANT.) delay, regression, relapse, retrogression, decline.

progression *(SYN.)* gradation, string, train, chain, arrangement, following, arrangement, order.

prohibit *(SYN.)* hinder, forbid, disallow, obstruct, prevent, stop, ban, interdict, debar.
(ANT.) help, tolerate, allow, sanction, encourage, permit.
prohibition *(SYN.)* prevention, ban, embargo, restriction.
(ANT.) allowance, permission.
prohibitive *(SYN.)* forbidding, restrictive.
project *(SYN.)* design, proposal, scheme, contrivance, outline, homework, activity, purpose, bulge, protrude, throw, cast, device, plan.
(ANT.) production, accomplishment, performance.
prolific *(SYN.)* fertile, rich, fruitful, teeming, fecund, bountiful, luxuriant, productive, plenteous.
(ANT.) unproductive, barren, sterile, impotent.
prolong *(SYN.)* extend, increase, protract, draw, stretch, lengthen.
(ANT.) shorten.
prominent *(SYN.)* distinguished, illustrious, outstanding, renowned, influential, famous, well-known, noted, notable, important, conspicuous, eminent, leading, celebrated.
(ANT.) vulgar, ordinary, common.
promise *(SYN.)* assurance, guarantee, pledge, undertaking, agreement, bestowal, word, contract, oath, vow.
promote *(SYN.)* advance, foster, encourage, assist, support, further, aid, help, elevate, raise, facilitate, forward.
(ANT.) obstruct, demote, hinder, impede.
prompt *(SYN.)* punctual, timely, exact, arouse, evoke, occasion, induce, urge, ineffect, cite, suggest, hint, cause, mention, propose, make, precise, originate.
(ANT.) laggardly, slow, tardy, dilatory.
promptly *(SYN.)* immediately, instantly, straightway, forthwith, directly, instantaneously, presently.
(ANT.) later, sometime, hereafter, distantly, shortly.
promulgate *(SYN.)* declare, known, protest, affirm, broadcast, profess, assert, proclaim, state, aver, tell.
(ANT.) repress, conceal, withhold.

prone *(SYN.)* apt, inclined, disposed, likely, predisposed.
pronounce *(SYN.)* proclaim, utter, announce, articulate, enunciate.
pronounced *(SYN.)* clear, definite.
(ANT.) minor, unnoticeable.
proof *(SYN.)* evidence, verification, confirmation, experiment, demonstration, testimony, trial, protected, impenetrable, corroboration, test.
(ANT.) fallacy, invalidity, failure.
propagate *(SYN.)* create, procreate, sire, beget, breed, father, originate, produce.
(ANT.) extinguish, kill, abort, destroy.
propel *(SYN.)* drive, push, transfer, actuate, induce, shift, persuade, move.
(ANT.) stay, deter, halt, rest, stop.
propensity *(SYN.)* leaning, proneness, trend, drift, aim, inclination, bias, proclivity, tendency, predisposition.
(ANT.) disinclination, aversion.
proper *(SYN.)* correct, suitable, decent, peculiar, legitimate, right, conventional, decent, just, well-mannered, seemly, fit, appropriate, fitting, respectable, special.
property *(SYN.)* real estate, effects, possessions, quality, characteristic, merchandise, stock, possession, land, wealth, belongings, attribute, trait.
(ANT.) poverty, destitution, want, deprivation.
prophecy *(SYN.)* augury, prediction.
prophesy *(SYN.)* foretell, predict, augur.
prophet *(SYN.)* fortuneteller, oracle, seer, soothsayer, clairvoyant.
propitious *(SYN.)* lucky, opportune, advantageous, favorable, fortunate, promising, happy.
proportion *(SYN.)* steadiness, poise, composure, relation, balance, equilibrium, comparison, section, part, arrange, adjust, symmetry.
(ANT.) unsteadiness, imbalance, fall.
proposal *(SYN.)* plan, proposition, tender, scheme, program, offer, suggestion, overture.
(ANT.) rejection, acceptance, denial.
propose *(SYN.)* offer, proffer, recommend,

plan, mean, expect, move, design, propound, present, tender.
(ANT.) fulfill, perform, effect.
proposition *(SYN.)* proposal, motion.
propound *(SYN.)* bring forward, offer, advance, allege, propose, assign.
(ANT.) retreat, hinder, withhold, retard.
proprietor *(SYN.)* master, owner.
(ANT.) slave, servant.
prosaic *(SYN.)* commonplace, common, everyday, ordinary, routine.
(ANT.) exciting, different, extraordinary.
proscribe *(SYN.)* forbid, ban, prohibit.
(ANT.) permit, allow.
prospect *(SYN.)* anticipation, expectation, candidate, buyer, explore, search.
prospective *(SYN.)* planned, proposed.
prosper *(SYN.)* succeed, win, achieve, gain, rise, prevail, flourish, thrive.
(ANT.) miscarry, wane, miss, fail.
prosperous *(SYN.)* rich, wealthy, affluent, well-to-do, sumptuous, well-off, flourishing, thriving, opulent, luxurious.
(ANT.) impoverished, indigent, beggarly, needy, destitute, poor.
prostrate *(SYN.)* prone, supine, overcome, recumbent, crushed.
protect *(SYN.)* defend, preserve, save, keep, conserve, safeguard, maintain, guard, shield, secure.
(ANT.) impair, abandon, destroy, abolish, injure.
protection *(SYN.)* safeguard, shelter, security, bulwark, fence, guard, safety, assurance, defense, refuge, shield.
protest *(SYN.)* dissent, noncompliance, disagree, objection, disagreement, challenge, difference, complaint, nonconformity, variance, opposition, remonstrate, reject, disapprove, complain, object, rejection.
(ANT.) acquiesce, assent, compliance, concur, comply, acceptance, approval.
prototype *(SYN.)* model, archetype, specimen, instance, illustration, example, pattern, sample.
(ANT.) rule, concept, precept, principle.
protract *(SYN.)* extend, strain, distend, expand, spread, stretch, elongate, distort,

lengthen.
(ANT.) tighten, contract, loosen, shrink.
protuberance *(SYN.)* prominence, projection, bulge, protrusion, swelling.
proud *(SYN.)* overbearing, vain, arrogant, haughty, stately, vain, glorious, disdainful, prideful, conceited, egotistical, self-important, supercilious.
(ANT.) humble, meek, ashamed, lowly.
prove *(SYN.)* manifest, verify, confirm, demonstrate, establish, show, affirm, examine, corroborate, try, test.
(ANT.) contradict, refute, disprove.
proverb *(SYN.)* maxim, byword, saying, adage, saw, motto, apothegm.
proverbial *(SYN.)* common, well-known.
provide *(SYN.)* supply, endow, afford, produce, yield, give, fit, equip, furnish, bestow, fit out.
(ANT.) strip, denude, divest, despoil.
provident *(SYN.)* saving, thrifty, economical, frugal, sparing.
(ANT.) wasteful, lavish, extravagant.
provision *(SYN.)* supply, fund, condition, arrangement, accumulation, reserve, store, hoard.
provisions *(SYN.)* stock, supplies, store.
provoke *(SYN.)* excite, stimulate, agitate, arouse, incite, stir up, vex, bother, disquiet, excite, irritate, annoy, anger.
(ANT.) quell, allay, pacify, calm, quiet.
prowess *(SYN.)* fortitude, mettle, boldness, fearlessness, courage, chivalry, bravery, resolution.
(ANT.) pusillanimity, fear, cowardice, timidity.
prowl *(SYN.)* sneak, slink, lurk.
proximate *(SYN.)* nigh, imminent, adjacent, neighboring, bordering, close, impending, approaching.
(ANT.) removed, distant, far.
proximity *(SYN.)* vicinity, nearness.
proxy *(SYN.)* representative, equivalent, makeshift, alternate, deputy, substitute, expedient, lieutenant.
(ANT.) sovereign, head, principal, master.
prudence *(SYN.)* watchfulness, care, heed, vigilance, wariness, carefulness, tact, judg-

ment, wisdom, common, foresight, caution.
(ANT.) rashness, recklessness, abandon, foolishness, carelessness.

prudent *(SYN.)* reasonable, sensible, sound, discreet, practical, judicious, sagacious, sensible, provident, sage, intelligent, sober, careful, wise.
(ANT.) stupid, unaware, absurd.

pry *(SYN.)* peer, peep, meddle, peek.

prying *(SYN.)* inquisitive, meddling, curious, inquiring, nosy, peering, searching, interrogative, snoopy.
(ANT.) unconcerned, incurious, indifferent, uninterested.

psyche *(SYN.)* judgment, reason, understanding, brain, intellect, mentality, soul, mind, faculties, spirit.
(ANT.) materiality, body, matter, corporality.

psychosis *(SYN.)* derangement, insanity, madness, delirium, dementia, frenzy, lunacy, mania, aberration.
(ANT.) stability, rationality, sanity.

public *(SYN.)* common, civil, governmental, federal, unrestricted, people, society, open.

publish *(SYN.)* distribute, issue, declare, announce, reveal, proclaim, publicize, bring out.

pulchritude *(SYN.)* elegance, grace, loveliness, attractiveness, comeliness, fairness, charm, beauty.
(ANT.) ugliness, eyesore, deformity, homeliness, disfigurement.

pull *(SYN.)* attract, induce, prolong, draw, tow, drag, remove, take out, persuade, allure, entice, extract.
(ANT.) shorten, alienate, drive, propel.

pulsate *(SYN.)* beat, throb, palpitate.

pummel *(SYN.)* punish, correct, castigate, discipline, chastise, strike.
(ANT.) release, acquit, free, exonerate.

pump *(SYN.)* interrogate, question, ask, inquire, quiz, examine, query.
(ANT.) state, answer, respond, reply.

punctual *(SYN.)* timely, prompt, exact, ready, nice, precise.
(ANT.) laggardly, tardy, dilatory, late.

punish *(SYN.)* correct, pummel, chasten,

reprove, strike, castigate, chastise.
(ANT.) release, exonerate, reward, pardon, acquit, free.

punishment *(SYN.)* correction, discipline.
(ANT.) turbulence, chaos, confusion.

puny *(SYN.)* feeble, impaired, exhausted, infirm, unimportant, frail, decrepit, trivial, enervated, powerless, forceless, delicate.
(ANT.) strong, forceful, lusty, vigorous.

pupil *(SYN.)* learner, student, undergraduate.

purchase *(SYN.)* get, procure, buy, shopping, acquire, obtain.
(ANT.) sell, dispose of, vend.

pure *(SYN.)* chaste, absolute, clean, immaculate, untainted, spotless, guiltless, modest, virgin, bare, unmixed, simple, undiluted, uncontaminated, innocent, chaste, undefiled, genuine, clear.
(ANT.) corrupt, mixed, defiled, foul, tainted, adulterated, polluted, tarnished.

purely *(SYN.)* entirely, completely.

purify *(SYN.)* cleanse, wash, clean, mop, sweep.
(ANT.) soil, dirty, stain, pollute.

puritanical *(SYN.)* prim, stiff.
(ANT.) permissive.

purloin *(SYN.)* loot, plagiarize, steal, pilfer, burglarize, plunder, pillage, snitch, embezzle, swipe.
(ANT.) repay, return, refund, buy.

purport *(SYN.)* import, meaning, explanation, acceptation, drift, sense, significance, intent, gist.

purpose *(SYN.)* intention, end, goal, aim, objective, application, use, drift, object, intent, design.
(ANT.) hazard, accident, fate.

pursue *(SYN.)* persist, track follow, hunt, chase, trail.
(ANT.) evade, abandon, flee, elude.

pursuit *(SYN.)* hunt, chase.

push *(SYN.)* jostle, shove, urge, press, thrust, force, drive, crowd, hasten, shove, propel, promote.
(ANT.) ignore, halt, drag, oppose.

pushy *(SYN.)* impudent, abrupt, prominent, insolent, forward, brazen, conspicuous, bold, striking.

(ANT.) retiring, timid, cowardly, bashful.

put *(SYN.)* set, place, state, express, assign, attach, establish.

putrefy *(SYN.)* disintegrate, decay, rot, waste, spoil, decompose.

(ANT.) grow, increase, luxuriate.

putrid *(SYN.)* decayed, rotten, moldy, decomposed.

puzzle *(SYN.)* mystery, mystify, confound, perplex, riddle, conundrum, confusion, question, bewilder, confuse, enigma, problem.

(ANT.) key, solution, solve, explain, answer, resolution, clue.

Q

quack *(SYN.)* faker, fake, fraud, gaggle, clack, gabble, bluffer, cackle, dissembler, charlatan, impostor.

quackery *(SYN.)* charlatanism, deceit, make-believe, fakery, duplicity, dissimulation, pretense, fraudulence, sham, counterfeiting, show.

(ANT.) integrity, probity, veracity, sincerity, honesty.

quaff *(SYN.)* swig, swill, swallow, lap up, sip, drink, ingurgitate, guzzle, imbibe.

quagmire *(SYN.)* swamp, bog, fen, ooze, morass, slough, marsh, plight, predicament, dilemma, impasse, fix, entanglement, quicksand, hole, quandary.

quail *(SYN.)* recoil, cower, flinch, blench, wince, falter, shrink, shake, hesitate, faint.

(ANT.) brave, resist, defy, withstand.

quaint *(SYN.)* odd, uncommon, old-fashioned, antique, antiquated, queer, unusual, curious, eccentric, peculiar, picturesque, singular, whimsical, droll, charming, fanciful, droll, strange.

(ANT.) usual, normal, common, novel, ordinary, modern, current, commonplace, familiar.

quake *(SYN.)* shake, tremble, shudder, quiver, pulsate, stagger, shiver, temblor, vibrate, throb, earthquake.

qualification *(SYN.)* efficiency, adaptation, restriction, aptness, skill, ability, faculty, talent, power, aptitude, competence, suitability, capability, fitness, condition, dexterity.

(ANT.) unreadiness, incapacity, disability.

qualified *(SYN.)* clever, skillful, efficient, suitable, able, capable, fit, fitted, suited, bounded, limited, contingent, eligible, delimited, adept, modified, competent.

(ANT.) deficient, inept, impotent, categorical, unlimited, unfit, incapable, unsuitable, inadequate.

qualify *(SYN.)* fit, suit, befit, ready, prepare, empower, lessen, moderate, soften, capacitate, condition, adapt, label, designate, name, call, equip, train, restrict, restrict, limit, change.

(ANT.) unfit, incapacitate, disable, disqualify, enlarge, reinforce, aggravate.

quality *(SYN.)* trait, feature, attribute, value, peculiarity, grade, caliber, character, distinction, rank, condition, status, characteristic, kind, nature, constitution, mark, type, property.

(ANT.) nature, inferiority, mediocrity, triviality, indifference, inferior, shoddy, secondrate, being, substance, essence.

qualm *(SYN.)* doubt, uneasiness, anxiety, suspicion, skepticism, question, pang, compunction, twinge, regret, uncertainty, demur, fear, remorse, misgiving.

(ANT.) security, comfort, confidence, easiness, invulnerability, firmness.

quandary *(SYN.)* predicament, perplexity, confusion, uncertainty, puzzle, plight, bewilderment, fix, difficulty, entanglement, impasse, dilemma, crisis.

(ANT.) ease, relief, certainty, assurance.

quantity *(SYN.)* sum, measure, volume, content, aggregate, bulk, mass, portion, amount, number, multitude, extent.

(ANT.) zero, nothing.

quarantine *(SYN.)* segregate, separate, confine, isolate, seclude.

quarrel *(SYN.)* contention, argument, affray, dispute, altercation, squabble, feud, difference, disagree, bicker, differ, spar, fight, bickering, argue, disagreement, spat.

(ANT.) *peace, friendliness, reconciliation, amity, agreement, sympathy, accord, concur, agree, unity, harmony.*

quarrelsome *(SYN.)* testy, contentious, edgy, peevish, irritable, snappish, argumentative, disputatious, cranky, belligerent, combative.

(ANT.) *genial, friendly, peaceful, easygoing, peaceable, tempered.*

quarry *(SYN.)* prey, quest, game, victim, goal, aim, prize, objective.

quarter *(SYN.)* place, source, fount, well, origin, mainspring, ruth, mercy, pity, compassion, clemency, benevolence, forbearance.

(ANT.) *ruthlessness, brutality, cruelty, barbarity, harshness, ferocity.*

quarters *(SYN.)* residence, rooms, lodgings, dwelling, flat, billets, chambers, accommodations.

quash *(SYN.)* void, annul, overthrow, nullify, suppress, cancel, quench, quell, repress, invalidate.

(ANT.) *reinforce, sustain, authorize, sanction, validate, incite.*

quasi *(SYN.)* wouldbe, partial, synthetic, nominal, imitation, bogus, sham, counterfeit, mock.

(ANT.) *certified, real, legitimate.*

quaver *(SYN.)* tremble, shake, hesitate, trill, oscillate, waver, vibrate, shiver, quiver, falter, quake.

quay *(SYN.)* dock, wharf, pier, jetty, bank.

queasy *(SYN.)* sick, squeamish, nauseated, uneasy, restless, nauseous, uncomfortable.

(ANT.) *untroubled, comfortable, easy, relaxed.*

queen *(SYN.)* empress, diva, doyenne, goddess, star.

queer *(SYN.)* odd, quaint, curious, unusual, droll, strange, peculiar, extraordinary, singular, uncommon, eccentric, weird, funny, nutty, screwy, wacky, deviant, whimsical.

(ANT.) *familiar, usual, normal, common, commonplace, plain, patent, conventional, ordinary.*

queerness *(SYN.)* oddity, oddness, freakishness, strangeness, singularity, outlandishness, weirdness.

(ANT.) *normality, familiarity, commonness, standardization.*

quell *(SYN.)* subdue, calm, pacify, quiet, cool, hush, appease, lull, mollify, reduce, crush, smother, suppress, stifle, extinguish, overpower, repress.

(ANT.) *encourage, foment, arouse, foster, incite.*

quench *(SYN.)* extinguish, stop, suppress, sate, allay, abate, stifle, slacken, put out, slake, satisfy, appease, refresh.

(ANT.) *set, light, begin, start, kindle.*

querulous *(SYN.)* faultfinding, fretful, carping, critical, complaining, censorious, captious, petulant.

(ANT.) *pleased, easygoing, contented, carefree.*

query *(SYN.)* inquire, interrogate, demand, investigate, probe, examine, question, inquiry, ask.

(ANT.) *answer.*

quest *(SYN.)* investigation, interrogation, research, examination, search, question, exploration, seek, pursue, journey, hunt, pursuit, explore, query.

(ANT.) *negligence, inactivity, disregard.*

question *(SYN.)* interrogate, quiz, doubt, ask, pump, challenge, inquiry, uncertainty, interview, suspect, inquire, dispute, demand, examine, query.

(ANT.) *accept, solution, reply, assurance, rejoinder, state, answer, result, response, attest, avow, confidence, respond.*

questionable *(SYN.)* uncertain, doubtful, dubious, implausible, debatable, hypothetical, unlikely.

(ANT.) *obvious, assured, indubitable, proper, unimpeachable, seemly, conventional, sure, certain.*

queue *(SYN.)* file, row, line, series, chain, tier, sequence, string.

quibble *(SYN.)* cavil, shift, evasion, dodge, equivocation, sophism, prevaricate, quiddity, palter, objection, evade.

quick *(SYN.)* rapid, touchy, shrewd, active, hasty, testy, nimble, irascible, discerning, fast, swift, precipitate, excitable, speedy, sharp, impatient, acute, abrupt, curt, brisk, clever, keen, lively.

(ANT.) inattentive, dull, gradual, patient, slow, unaware, unhurried, backward, deliberate, sluggish.

quicken *(SYN.)* expedite, forward, rush, hurry, accelerate, push, hasten, dispatch, facilitate, speed.

(ANT.) slow, impede, hinder, hamper, delay, kill, deaden, retard, block.

quickly *(SYN.)* soon, rapidly, fast, at once, promptly, presently, swiftly, hastily, fleety, headlong, immediately, now.

(ANT.) deliberately, slowly, later, gradually.

quickness *(SYN.)* energy, vigor, intensity, action, movement, briskness, exercise, motion, rapidity, agility, enterprise.

(ANT.) sloth, idleness, inertia, dullness.

quick-witted *(SYN.)* astute, shrewd, alert, keen, penetrating, quick, knowing, intelligent, clever.

(ANT.) slow, dull, unintelligent, gradual, plodding.

quiescent *(SYN.)* latent, resting, silent, tranquil, undeveloped, still, quiet, dormant, secret, inactive.

(ANT.) visible, aroused, evident, active, patent, astir, manifest.

quiet *(SYN.)* meek, passive, hushed, peaceful, calm, patient, quiescent, motionless, tranquil, gentle, undisturbed, mild, peace, silent, quiescence, hush, modest, quietude, rest, tranquillity, calmness, repose, silence, placid, serenity, soundless.

(ANT.) disturbed, agitation, excitement, loud, disturbance, restless, noisy, boisterous, anxious, perturbed, noise, agitated.

quietness *(SYN.)* tranquillity, repose, calm, silence, quietude, calmness, stillness, quietism, muteness, noiselessness, placidity, seclusion.

(ANT.) flurry, disturbance, fuss, turbulence, agitation, uproar, tumult.

quintessence *(SYN.)* heart, soul, extract, essence, distillation, core.

(ANT.) contingency, adjunct, excrescence, nonessential.

quip *(SYN.)* jest, sally, wisecrack, witticism, joke, jibe, pleasantry, sarcasm, retort.

quirk *(SYN.)* mannerism, idiosyncrasy, foible, peculiarity, oddity, quiddity, vagary, habit, trait, eccentricity.

quirky *(SYN.)* odd, weird, whimsical, peculiar, pixilated, erratic, kinky.

(ANT.) normal, conventional, steady.

quisling *(SYN.)* collaborationist, traitor, subversive, betrayer.

(ANT.) partisan, loyalist.

quit *(SYN.)* leave, stop, desist, depart, abandon, resign, withdraw, refrain, retreat, cease, vacate, end, relinquish, discontinue, halt, lay off, surrender, conclude, go.

(ANT.) perservere, remain, stay, endure, persist, abide, continue.

quite *(SYN.)* somewhat, rather, completely, truly, absolutely, really, entirely.

(ANT.) hardly, merely, barely, somewhat.

quitter *(SYN.)* shirker, dropout, defeatist, piker, loser, malingerer, deserter, stop, desist.

quiver *(SYN.)* quake, shake, shudder, tremble, vibrate, shiver.

quixotic *(SYN.)* unrealistic, romantic, visionary, impractical, idealistic, chimerical, lofty, fantastic, fey.

(ANT.) pragmatic, realistic, prosaic, practical.

quiz *(SYN.)* challenge, interrogate, inquire, pump, doubt, question, ask, dispute, test, query, examine, questioning, investigate.

(ANT.) reply, say, inform, respond, accept, answer, state.

quizzical *(SYN.)* teasing, coy, mocking, derisive, insolent, arch, bantering, puzzled, questioning, baffled.

(ANT.) respectful, obsequious, uninterested, normal, everyday, usual, serious, attentive.

quota *(SYN.)* share, portion, apportionment, ratio, proportion, allotment.

quotation *(SYN.)* quote, selection, excerpt, repetition, cutting, reference.

quote *(SYN.)* refer to, recite, paraphrase, adduce, repeat, illustrate, cite, echo, plagiarize, excerpt, extract.

(ANT.) retort, contradict, refute.

rabble *(SYN.)* throng, mob, horde, crowd.

rabid *(SYN.)* frantic, frenzied, violent, raging, raving, zealous.

(ANT.) normal, sound, sober, moderate.

race *(SYN.)* meet, run, clan, stock, lineage, strain, match, course, stream, hasten, compete, folk, competition, dash, contest, contend, hurry, speed, tribe.

(ANT.) linger, dawdle, dwell.

rack *(SYN.)* frame, frame-work, bracket, scaffold, skeleton.

racket *(SYN.)* sound, cry, babel, noise, uproar, hubbub, clamor, fuss, disturbance, din, tumult, fracas, clatter.

(ANT.) stillness, hush, silence, quiet, tranquillity, peace.

racy *(SYN.)* interesting, vigorous, spirited, animated, entertaining.

radiance *(SYN.)* luster, brilliancy, brightness, splendor, effulgence, glowing.

(ANT.) gloom, darkness, obscurity.

radiant *(SYN.)* showy, superb, brilliant, illustrious, dazzling, grand, shining, bright, effulgent.

(ANT.) dark, unimpressive, dull, dim, lusterless, ordinary.

radiate *(SYN.)* spread, emit, diffuse, shed, irradiate, shine, gleam.

radical *(SYN.)* ultra, innate, essential, organic, complete, revolutionary, insurgent, natural, total, extreme, basic, original.

(ANT.) extraneous, moderate, conservative, superficial, established.

radius *(SYN.)* orbit, reach, extent, scope, sphere, range, sweep.

raft *(SYN.)* pontoon, platform, float.

rag *(SYN.)* dishcloth, dishrag, cloth.

ragamuffin *(SYN.)* tatterdemalion, wretch, beggar, vagabond.

rage *(SYN.)* passion, ire, exasperation, fashion, fad, vogue, craze, anger, temper, fury, irritation, mania, rave, rant, storm, fume.

(ANT.) peace, forbearance, conciliation, patience.

raging *(SYN.)* raving, severe, passionate, boisterous, violent, fierce, wild, passionate, acute.

(ANT.) feeble, soft, calm, quiet.

ragged *(SYN.)* tattered, torn, worn, shredded, threadbare, shabby.

raid *(SYN.)* assault, attack, invasion, arrest, invade, seizure.

rail *(SYN.)* railing, fence, bar.

railing *(SYN.)* balustrade, banister, barrier, fence.

rain *(SYN.)* shower, drizzle, rainstorm, sprinkle, deluge.

raise *(SYN.)* grow, muster, elevate, heave, cultivate, awake, rouse, excite, enlarge, increase, rise, breed, hoist, bring up, rear, gather, exalt.

(ANT.) destroy, decrease, lessen, cut, depreciate, lower, abase, debase, drop, demolish, level.

rakish *(SYN.)* dapper, dashing, smart, debonair, natty, swanky, showy.

rally *(SYN.)* muster, convoke, summon, convene, convention, assemblage.

ramble *(SYN.)* err, amble, saunter, wander, roam, walk, meander deviate, stroll, digress, stray.

(ANT.) stop, linger, stay, halt, settle.

rambling *(SYN.)* incoherent, erratic.

(ANT.) straightfoward, coherent.

rambunctious *(SYN.)* stubborn, defiant, unruly, aggressive, contrary.

ramification *(SYN.)* aftermath, extension, branch, offshoot, result, consequence.

rampage *(SYN.)* tumult, outbreak, uproar, rage, frenzy, ebullition, storm.

rampant *(SYN.)* excessive, flagrant, boisterous, menacing.

(ANT.) bland, calm, mild.

ramshackle *(SYN.)* rickety, decrepit, flimsy, dilapidated, shaky.

rancid *(SYN.)* spoiled, rank, tainted, sour, musty, putrid, rotten, purtrescent.

(ANT.) pure, fresh, wholesome, fragrant.

rancor *(SYN.)* spite, grudge, malice, animosity, malevolence, hostility.

(ANT.) kindness, toleration, affection.

random *(SYN.)* haphazard, chance, unscheduled, unplanned, casual.

(ANT.) intentional, specific, particular.

range *(SYN.)* expanse, extent, limit, area, grassland, pasture, plain, change, wander, roam, travel, rove.

rank *(SYN.)* estate, blood, range, grade, standing, hue, eminence, level, class, order, classify, dense, wild, rotten, degree, standing, arrange, sort, row.

(ANT.) shame, disrepute, stigma, humiliation.

ransack *(SYN.)* pillage, loot, rummage, plunder, despoil, ravish, search.

ransom *(SYN.)* release, deliverance, compensation, redeem.

rant *(SYN.)* declaim, rave, harangue.

rap *(SYN.)* thump, knock, blow, whack.

rapacious *(SYN.)* greedy, wolfish, avaricious, ravenous, grasping, predatory.

rapid *(SYN.)* speedy, quick, swift, fast.

(ANT.) deliberate, halting, sluggish, slow.

rapidity *(SYN.)* motion, enterprise, action, vigor, liveliness, activity, quickness, exercise, energy.

(ANT.) sloth, dullness, inertia, idleness.

rapine *(SYN.)* destruction, pillage, robbery, marauding, spoiling.

rapport *(SYN.)* harmony, fellowship, agreement, mutuality, accord, empathy.

rapture *(SYN.)* joy, gladness, ecstasy, bliss, transport, exultation, delight, happiness, enchantment, ravishment.

(ANT.) woe, misery, wretch, depression.

rare *(SYN.)* unique, strange, precious, uncommon, infrequent, choice, singular, occasional, unusual, fine, matchless, undone, incomparable, scarce.

(ANT.) worthless, common, commonplace, usual, everyday, customary.

rarely *(SYN.)* scarcely, hardly infrequently, occasionally, sparingly, barely.

(ANT.) usually, continually, often.

rascal *(SYN.)* scoundrel, villain, trickster, rogue, scamp, swindler, imp, prankster.

rash *(SYN.)* quick, careless, passionate, thoughtless, hotheaded, reckless, foolhardy, eruption, dermatitis, heedless.

(ANT.) thoughtful, considered, prudent, reasoning, calculating, careful.

raspy *(SYN.)* gruff, harsh, dissonant, grinding, hoarse, grating, strident.

rate *(SYN.)* try, adjudicate, consider, decide, condemn, decree, estimate, speed, pace, measure, judge, arbitrate, velocity, ratio, evaluate.

ratify *(SYN.)* validate, certify, confirm, establish, support, endorse, uphold.

rating *SYN.)* assessment, position, assignment, status, classification.

ration *(SYN.)* portion, allowance, distribute, measure, allotment, share, percentage.

rational *(SYN.)* sound, wise, sane, intelligent, sensible, judicious, sober.

(ANT.) irrational, absurd, insane.

rationality *(SYN.)* cause, aim, intelligence, reason, basis, mind, understanding, ground, argument, sense.

raucous *(SYN.)* raspy, harsh, grating, hoarse, discordant, rowdy.

(ANT.) dulcet, pleasant, sweet.

ravage *(SYN.)* ruin, despoil, strip, waste, destroy, pillage, plunder, sack, havoc.

(ANT.) conserve, save, accumulate.

rave *(SYN.)* rage, storm, laud, praise.

ravenous *(SYN.)* hungry, voracious, craving, starved, gluttonous, famished.

(ANT.) replete, gorged, satiated, full.

ravine *(SYN.)* chasm, gorge, crevasse, canyon, abyss.

ravish *(SYN.)* violate, debauch.

ravishing *(SYN.)* enchanting, captivating, bewitching, fascinating, alluring.

(ANT.) loathsome, disgusting, repulsive.

raw *(SYN.)* harsh, rough, coarse, unrefined, undone, uncooked, crude, unprocessed, unpolished, natural.

(ANT.) finished, refined, processed.

ray *(SYN.)* beam.

raze *(SYN.)* ravage, wreck, destroy, flatten, annihilate, obliterate, demolish.

(ANT.) make, erect, construct, preserve, establish, save.

reach *(SYN.)* overtake, arrive at, extent, distance, scope, range, extend, attain, stretch.

(ANT.) fail, miss.

react *(SYN.)* result, reply, respond.

(ANT.) overlook, disregard.

reaction *(SYN.)* result, response, reception,

repercussion.

readable *(SYN.)* understandable, distinct, legible, plain, clear, comprehensible.
(ANT.) obliterated, illegible, defaced.

readily *(SYN.)* quickly, promptly, easily.

ready *(SYN.)* mature, ripe, complete, seasonable, done, arrange, prompt, prepared, completed, quick, mellow.
(ANT.) undeveloped, immature, green.

real *(SYN.)* true, actual, positive, authentic, genuine, veritable.
(ANT.) counterfeit, unreal, fictitious, false, sham, supposed.

realization *(SYN.)* completion, achievement, performance, accomplishment, comprehension, insight.
(ANT.) failure.

realize *(SYN.)* discern, learn, comprehend, appreciate, perfect, actualize, understand, apprehend, know, see.
(ANT.) misunderstand, misapprehend.

really *(SYN.)* truly, actually, honestly, undoubtedly, positively, genuinely.
ANT.) questionably, possibly, doubtfully.

realm *(SYN.)* land, domain, farm, kingdom, sphere, department, estate, world.

reap *(SYN.)* gather, harvest, gain, glean, produce, cut, pick, acquire, garner.
(ANT.) plant, seed, sow, lose, squander.

reaping *(SYN.)* proceeds, result, crop, yield, fruit, produce.

rear *(SYN.)* posterior, raise, lift, train, nurture, rump, back, elevate, construct, build, foster.

reason *(SYN.)* intelligence, objective, understanding, mind, aim, argument, cause, judgment, common sense, sanity, gather, assume, sake, motive.

reasonable *(SYN.)* prudent, rational, logical, sage, sound, moderate, intelligent, sensible, discreet.
(ANT.) unaware, imperceptible, insane, absurd, stupid, illogical, irrational.

rebel *(SYN.)* revolutionary, traitor, mutineer, mutiny, revolt, disobey.

rebellion *(SYN.)* revolt, uprising, coup, overthrow, insurrection, revolution.
(ANT.) submission, obedience, repression,

peace.

rebellious *(SYN.)* unruly, forward, defiant, undutiful, disobedient.
(ANT.) obedient, compliant, submissive.

rebirth *(SYN.)* renascence, renaissance, revival.

rebuff *(SYN.)* snub, oppose, resist, reject, refuse, slight, opposition.
(ANT.) welcome, encourage, support.

rebuild *(SYN.)* restore, renew, refresh, reconstruct, renovate.

rebuke *(SYN.)* chide, scold, reproach, censure, upbraid, scolding, condemn.
(ANT.) praise, exonerate, absolve.

rebuttal *(SYN.)* contradiction, defense, answer.
(ANT.) argument, validation, corroboration.

recall *(SYN.)* recollect, remembrance, withdraw, retract, remember, recollection, reminisce, mind, memory, remind.
(ANT.) forget, overlook, ignore.

recede *(SYN.)* withdraw, ebb, retire, retreat.

receive *(SYN.)* entertain, acquire, admit, accept, shelter, greet, obtain, welcome.
(ANT.) reject, offer, give, bestow, discharge, impart.

recent *(SYN.)* novel, original, late, new, newfangled, fresh, modern, current.
(ANT.) old, antiquated, ancient.

reception *(SYN.)* gathering, party.

recess *(SYN.)* hollow, opening, nook, cranny, dent, respite, rest, break, pause.
(ANT.) gather, convene.

recession *(SYN.)* slump, depression.

recipe *(SYN.)* instructions, formula, prescriptions, procedure, method.

recital *(SYN.)* history, account, relation, chronicle, narrative, detail, narration.
(ANT.) distortion, confusion, misrepresentation.

recite *(SYN.)* describe, narrate, declaim, rehearse, tell, mention, repeat, detail, recapitulate, report, list, relate, deliver.

reckless *(SYN.)* thoughtless, inconsiderate, careless, imprudent, rash, indiscreet, unconcerned.
(ANT.) careful, nice, accurate.

reclaim *(SYN.)* reform, rescue, reinstate, regenerate, recycle.

recline *(SYN.)* stretch, sprawl, repose, rest, lounge, loll, incline.

recluse *(SYN.)* hermit, eremite, loner, anchorite.

recognize *(SYN.)* remember, avow, own, know, admit, apprehend, recollect, recall, concede, acknowledge, confess.
(ANT.) disown, ignore, renounce.

recollect *(SYN.)* recall, remember, memory, reflect, call to mind, reminisce.
(ANT.) forget.

recollection *(SYN.)* remembrance, retrospection, impression, recall.
(ANT.) forgetfulness, oblivion.

recommend *(SYN.)* hind, refer, advise, commend, suggest, counsel, allude, praise, approve, intimate, advocate.
(ANT.) disapprove, declare, insist.

recommendation *(SYN.)* instruction, justice, trustworthiness, counsel, admonition, caution, integrity, uprightness.
(ANT.) fraud, deceit, trickery, cheating.

reconcile *(SYN.)* meditate, unite, adapt, adjust, settle, reunite, appease.

recondition *(SYN.)* rebuild, overhaul, restore, service.

reconsider *(SYN.)* ponder, reevaluate, mull over, reflect, reassess.

record *(SYN.)* enter, write, register, chronicle, history, account, document.

recount *(SYN.)* report, convey, narrate, tell, detail, recite, describe, repeat.

recoup *(SYN.)* regain, recover, repay, retrieve.

recover *(SYN.)* regain, redeem, recapture, retrieve, salvage, better, improve, mend, heal.
(ANT.) debilitate, succumb, worsen.

recreation *(SYN.)* entertainment, amusement, enjoyment, diversion, fun.

recrimination *(SYN.)* vindication, reproach, dissension, accusation, countercharge.

recruit *(SYN.)* trainee, beginner, volunteer, draftee, select, enlist, novice.

recuperate *(SYN.)* regain, retrieve, cure, recapture, redeem, rally, convalesce, revive, recover, repossess, restore.
(ANT.) sicken, weaken, lose, regress, forfeit.

redeem *(SYN.)* claim, recover, repossess, regain, reclaim, cash in, retrieve.

reduce *(SYN.)* lessen, decrease, lower, downgrade, degrade, suppress, abate, diminish.
(ANT.) enlarge, swell, raise, elevate, revive, increase, amplify.

reduction *(SYN.)* shortening, abridgment, abbreviation.
(ANT.) amplification, extension, enlargement.

reek *(SYN.)* odor, stench, stink, smell.

refer *(SYN.)* recommend, direct, commend, regard, concern, relate, suggest, mention.

referee *(SYN.)* judge, arbitrator, umpire, arbiter, moderator, mediator, intermediary.

reference *(SYN.)* allusion, direction, mention, concern, respect, referral.

refine *(SYN.)* purify, clarify, improve, clean.
(ANT.) pollute, debase, muddy, downgrade.

refined *(SYN.)* purified, cultured, cultivated, courteous, courtly.
(ANT.) rude, coarse, crude, vulgar.

refinement *(SYN.)* culture, enlightenment, education, civilization.
(ANT.) vulgarity, ignorance, boorishness.

reflect *(SYN.)* muse, mirror, deliberate, cogitate, think, reproduce, ponder, consider, reason, meditate, contemplate.

reflection *(SYN.)* warning, conception, intelligence, appearance, likeness, image, cogitation, notification.

reform *(SYN.)* right, improve, correction, change, amend, improvement, better, betterment, correct, rectify.
(ANT.) spoil, damage, aggravate, vitiate.

refresh *(SYN.)* exhilarate, renew, invigorate.
(ANT.) exhaust, tire.

refreshing *(SYN.)* bracing, cool, brisk, fresh.

refreshment *(SYN.)* food, snack, drink, nourishment, exhilaraton, stimulation.

refuge *(SYN.)* safety, retreat, shelter, asylum, sanctuary, harbor.
(ANT.) peril, exposure, jeopardy, danger.
refuse *(SYN.)* spurn, rebuff, decline, reject, trash, rubbish, withhold, disallow, waste, garbage, deny, demur.
(ANT.) allow, accept, welcome, grant.
refute *(SYN.)* rebut, disprove, confute, falsify, controvert, contradict.
(ANT.) prove, confirm, accept, establish.
regain *(SYN.)* redeem, retrieve, recover, repossess, recapture.
(ANT.) lose.
regalement *(SYN.)* feast, dinner, celebration, entertainment.
regard *(SYN.)* estimate, value, honor, affection, notice, care, consideration, consider, relation, respect, attend, thought, reference, care, attention, esteem, concern, liking.
(ANT.) neglect, disgust, antipathy.
regards *(SYN.)* salutations, greetings, good wishes, respects, remembrances.
regenerate *(SYN.)* improve, reconstruct, remedy, reestablish, rebuild.
regime *(SYN.)* direction, government, administration, management, dynasty, command, leadership.
regimented *(SYN.)* ordered, directed controlled, orderly, rigid, disciplined.
(ANT.) loose, free, unstructured.
region *(SYN.)* belt, place, spot, territory, climate, area, zone, locality, station, locale.
register *(SYN.)* catalog, record, book, list, roll, enter, roster, chronicle.
regressive *(SYN.)* revisionary, retrograde.
(ANT.) progressive, civilized, advanced.
regret *(SYN.)* sorrow, qualm, lament, grief, compunction, bemoan, concern, scruple, misgiving, remorse, contrition.
(ANT.) obduracy, complacency.
regular *(SYN.)* steady, orderly, natural, normal, customary, usual, habitual, even, uniform, systematic, unvaried, methodical, symmetrical.
(ANT.) odd, exceptional, unusual, irregular, abnormal, rare.
regulate *(SYN.)* control, manage, govern, direct, legislate, set, adjust, systematize.

regulation *(SYN.)* method, rule, axiom, guide, control, standard, canon, precept, restraint, requirement.
(ANT.) chaos, deviation, hazard, turbulence, confusion.
rehabilitate *(SYN.)* renew, restore, rebuild, reestablish, repair, reconstruct.
rehearse *(SYN.)* repeat, practice, train, learn, coach, prepare, perfect, direct.
reign *(SYN.)* dominion, power, rule, sovereignty, govern, domination.
reimburse *(SYN.)* recompense, remunerate, compensate, remit.
rein *(SYN.)* restriction, bridle, check, deterrent, curb, restraint, barrier, control.
reinforce *(SYN.)* brace, strengthen, fortify, intensify, support.
reiterate *(SYN.)* reproduce, recapitulate, duplicate, repeat, rephrase.
reject *(SYN.)* spurn, rebuff, decline, renounce, expel, discard, withhold, deny, refuse.
(ANT.) endorse, grant, welcome, accept.
rejection *(SYN.)* dissent, nonconformity, variance, challenge, remonstrance, difference, noncompliance.
(ANT.) assent, acceptance, compliance.
rejoice *(SYN.)* celebrate, delight, enjoy, revel, exhilarate, elate.
rejuvenate *(SYN.)* refresh, rekindle, overhaul, revitalize, animate, invigorate.
(ANT.) deplete, weaken, exhaust, eneverate.
relapse *(SYN.)* worsen, deteriorate, regress, weaken, fade, worsen, sink, fail.
(ANT.) strengthen, progress, advance, get well, rehabilitate.
relate *(SYN.)* refer, beat, report, describe, tell, correlate, narrate, recount, compare, connect.
relation *(SYN.)* entente, compact, coalition, alliance, connection, relationship, association, partnership, similarity, kinsman, treaty, marriage.
(ANT.) separation, divorce.
relationship *(SYN.)* link, tie, alliance, connection, union, bond, affinity, conjunction.
(ANT.) separation, disunion.

relative *(SYN.)* dependent, proportional, about, pertinent, regarding.

relax *(SYN.)* slacken, loosen, repose, rest, recline, unwind.

(ANT.) increase, tighten, intensify.

relaxation *(SYN.)* comfort, ease, rest, enjoyment, lull, recess, breather, loafing.

relaxed *(SYN.)* welcome, pleasing, casual, acceptable, informal, restful, agreeable.

(ANT.) formal, planned, wretched, distressing, troubling.

release *(SYN.)* liberate, emancipate, relinquish, proclaim, publish, liberation, announce, deliver, free, discharge.

(ANT.) restrict, imprison, subjugate.

relegate *(SYN.)* entrust, authorize, remand, refer, assign.

relent *(SYN.)* cede, yield, surrender, give, relax, abdicate, relinquish, waive.

(ANT.) strive, assert, struggle.

relentless *(SYN.)* eternal, stubborn, tenacious, dogged, ceaseless, incessant, ceaseless, persistent, determined.

relevant *(SYN.)* related, material, apt, applicable, fit, relating, germane.

(ANT.) foreign, alien, unrelated.

reliable *(SYN.)* trusty, tried, certain, secure, trustworthy, dependable.

(ANT.) unreliable, eccentric, questionable, erratic, dubious.

reliance *(SYN.)* faith, confidence, trust.

(ANT.) mistrust, doubt, skepticism.

relic *(SYN.)* remains, fossil, throwback, heirloom, souvenir, keepsake, heirloom.

relief *(SYN.)* help, aid, comfort, ease, backing, patronage, alms, support.

(ANT.) hostility, defiance, antagonism, resistance.

relieve *(SYN.)* diminish, soothe, calm, abate, pacify, ease, lessen, replace, spell, lighten, comfort, alleviate.

(ANT.) disturb, irritate, agitate, trouble, aggravate, worry.

religion *(SYN.)* tenet, belief, dogma, faith, creed, persuasion.

religious *(SYN.)* godly, reverent, faithful, devout, zeal, pious, divine, holy, devoted, sacred, theological.

(ANT.) profane, irreligious, skeptical, impious, lax, atheistic.

religiousness *(SYN.)* love, zeal, affection, devoutness, fidelity, ardor.

(ANT.) indifference, apathy, unfaithfulness.

relinquish *(SYN.)* capitulate, submit, yield, abandon, cede, sacrifice, disclaim.

(ANT.) overcome, conquer, rout, resist.

relish *(SYN.)* enjoyment, satisfaction, delight, gusto, appreciation, condiment, like, enjoy, enthusiasm.

(ANT.) distaste, antipathy, disfavor, dislike.

reluctance *(SYN.)* disgust, hatred, repulsion, abhorrence, distaste, repugnance, aversion.

(ANT.) enthusiasm, affection, devotion.

reluctant *(SYN.)* slow, averse, hesitant, unwilling, loath, disinclined, balky.

(ANT.) ready, eager, willing, disposed.

rely *(SYN.)* confide, trust, lean, depend.

(ANT.) mistrust, disbelieve, question, distrust.

remain *(SYN.)* survive, rest, stay, abide, halt, endure, dwell, tarry, continue, linger.

(ANT.) finish, leave, terminate, dissipate.

remainder *(SYN.)* leftover, residue, rest, surplus, balance, excess.

remains *(SYN.)* residue, balance, rest, remnants, relics, discards, waste, junk.

remark *(SYN.)* comment, state, utterance, mention, note, observe, observation, annotation, declaration, statement.

remarkable *(SYN.)* exciting, impressive, overpowering, unusual, affecting, thrilling, splendid, special, noteworthy, extraordinary, touching, august.

(ANT.) ordinary, unimpressive, commonplace, average, regular.

remedy *(SYN.)* redress, help, cure, relief, medicine, restorative, rectify, alleviate, medication, correct, reparation.

remember *(SYN.)* recollect, reminisce, recall, memorize, mind, retain, remind.

(ANT.) forget, overlook, disregard.

remembrance *(SYN.)* monument, memory, recollection, memento, recall, keepsake, souvenir, retrospection.

remiss *(SYN.)* delinquent, lax, careless, negligent, oblivious, forgetful, absentminded, sloppy, irresponsible.

remit *(SYN.)* send, pay, forward, forgive, pardon, overlook, excuse, reimburse.

remittance *(SYN.)* payment.

remnant *(SYN.)* remains, remainder, rest, residue, trace, relic.

remodel *(SYN.)* remake, reshape, rebuild, redecorate, renovate, modify, change, alter, convert, refurbish, update.

remonstrate *(SYN.)* grouch, protest, complain, grumble, murmur, repine, dispute.
(ANT.) rejoice, applaud, praise.

remorse *(SYN.)* sorrow, qualm, contrition, regret, compunction, repentance.
(ANT.) obduracy, complacency.

remorseless *(SYN.)* savage, unrelenting, crude, barbaric, merciless, cruel, fiendish, brutal, callous.
(ANT.) kind, refined, polite, civilized.

remote *(SYN.)* inconsiderable, removed, slight, far, unlikely, distant, inaccessible, unreachable, isolated, sequestered.
(ANT.) visible, nearby, current, near, close.

remove *(SYN.)* transport, eject, move, vacate, withdraw, dislodge, transfer, doff, displace, eliminate, murder, kill, oust, extract.
(ANT.) insert, retain, leave, stay, keep.

removed *(SYN.)* aloof, distant, cool, remote.

remuneration *(SYN.)* wages, payment, pay, salary, compensation, reimbursement, reward.

render *(SYN.)* become, make, perform, do, offer, present, give, submit.

rendition *(SYN.)* interpretation, version, depiction, expression, characterization.

renegade *(SYN.)* defector, insurgent, dissenter, rebel, maverick, mutineer, betrayer.

renege *(SYN.)* let down, doublecross, deceive.

renew *(SYN.)* restore, renovate, overhaul, revise, modernize, reshape, redo.

renounce *(SYN.)* resign, disown, revoke, abandon, quit, retract, forgo, leave, forsake, abdicate, reject, relinquish, deny.

(ANT.) assert, uphold, recognize, maintain.

renovate *(SYN.)* restore, rehabilitate, rebuild, refresh, renew, overhaul, redesign.

renown *(SYN.)* honor, reputation, eminence, acclaim, glory, repute, luster, fame, notability.
(ANT.) obscurity, anonymity, disgrace.

renowned *(SYN.)* noted, famous, distinguished, well-known, glorious, celebrated.
(ANT.) unknown, infamous, hidden, obscure.

rent *(SYN.)* payment, rental, let, lease, hire.

repair *(SYN.)* rebuilding, mend, renew, tinker, correct, patch, restore, adjust, reconstruction, remedy, amend, rehabilitation, retrieve.
(ANT.) harm, break.

repartee *(SYN.)* badinage, banter.

repast *(SYN.)* feast, banquet, meal, refreshment, snack.

repeal *(SYN.)* end, cancel, nullify, annul, quash, abolish, cancellation, rescind, abolition, abrogate.

repeat *(SYN.)* reiterate, restate, redo, rehearse, quote, remake, relate, iterate, reproduce.

repeated *(SYN.)* continuous, frequent, recurrent, continual.

repel *(SYN.)* check, repulse, rebuff, reject, decline, discourage.
(ANT.) lure, attract.

repellent *(SYN.)* sickening, offensive, disgusting, nauseating, repugnant, obnoxious.

repent *(SYN.)* deplore, regret, rue, lament.

repentance *(SYN.)* penitence, remorse, sorrow, compunction, qualm, grief.
(ANT.) obduracy, complacency.

repentant *(SYN.)* regretful, sorrowful, contrite, sorry, penitent.
(ANT.) remorseless, obdurate.

repetitious *(SYN.)* repeated, monotonous, boring, tiresome, humdrum.

repine *(SYN.)* protest, lament, complain, whine, regret, grouch, murmur, grumble.
(ANT.) rejoice, applaud, praise.

replace *(SYN.)* alternate, return, reinstate.

replacement *(SYN.)* understudy, proxy,

second, alternate, substitute, replica, surrogate.

replenish *(SYN.)* store, pervade, fill, stock, occupy, supply.

(ANT.) empty, void, deplete, exhaust, drain.

replica *(SYN.)* reproduction, copy, exemplar, imitation, duplicate, facsimile.

(ANT.) prototype.

reply *(SYN.)* retort, rejoinder, answer, retaliate, respond, confirmation.

(ANT.) summoning, inquiry.

report *(SYN.)* declare, herald, publish, announce, summary, publish, advertise.

(ANT.) suppress, conceal, withhold, bury.

reporter *(SYN.)* journalist.

repose *(SYN.)* hush, quiet, tranquillity, rest, peace, slumber, calm, stillness, sleep, calmness, dormancy.

(ANT.) tumult, excitement, agitation.

reprehensible *(SYN.)* criminal, immoral, damnable, culpable, wrong, wicked.

represent *(SYN.)* picture, draw, delineate, portray, depict, denote, symbolize.

(ANT.) misrepresent, caricature.

representation *(SYN.)* effigy, film, likeness, portrait, print, scene, appearance, drawing, scene, view, cinema.

representative *(SYN.)* delegate, agent, substitute, surrogate.

repress *(SYN.)* limit, stop, check, bridle, curb, restrain, constrain, suppress.

(ANT.) loosen, aid, incite, liberate, encourage.

reprimand *(SYN.)* rate, scold, vituperate, berate, lecture, blame, admonish, upbraid.

(ANT.) praise, approve.

reproach *(SYN.)* defamation, dishonor, insult, profanation, abuse, disparagement, misuse, reviling.

(ANT.) respect, laudation, approval, plaudit.

reproduction *(SYN.)* replica, copy, exemplar, transcript, duplicate, photocopy.

reproof *(SYN.)* rebuke, punishment, blame, censure, disapproval, scorn, disdain, admonition.

repugnance *(SYN.)* disgust, hatred, reluctance, abhorrence, aversion, loathing, antipathy, distaste, repulsion.

(ANT.) devotion, affection, enthusiasm, attachment.

repulsive *(SYN.)* repellent, ugly, homely, deformed, horrid, offensive, plain, uncomely.

(ANT.) fair, pretty, attractive, handsome.

reputable *(SYN.)* honest, upstanding, trustworthy, straightforward, upright, reliable.

(ANT.) notorious, corrupt, disreputable.

reputation *(SYN.)* class, nature, standing, name, fame, kind, renown, prominence, character, distinction, disposition, repute.

repute *(SYN.)* class, nature, standing, kind, character, reputation, disposition, sort.

request *(SYN.)* sue, implore, petition, desire, appeal, question, entreaty, beseech, ask, pray, supplicate.

(ANT.) require.

require *(SYN.)* exact, need, order, command, order, lack, claim, demand, want.

requirement *(SYN.)* demand, need, necessity, condition, provision, prerequisite.

requisite *(SYN.)* vital, necessary, basic, fundamental, indispensable, essential, needed.

(ANT.) casual, nonessential, peripheral, accidental.

rescind *(SYN.)* annul, quash, revoke, abolish, invalidate, abrogate, withdraw.

rescue *(SYN.)* liberate, ransom, release, deliver, deliverance, liberation.

research *(SYN.)* exploration, quest, scrutiny, exploration, interrogation, query, examination, study, investigation.

(ANT.) inattention, disregard, negligence.

resemblance *(SYN.)* parity, similitude, analogy, likeness, correspondence.

(ANT.) distinction, difference.

resemble *(SYN.)* duplicate, mirror, look like.

resentfulness *(SYN.)* envy, jealousy, covetousness, suspicion.

(ANT.) liberality, geniality, tolerance, difference.

resentment *(SYN.)* displeasure, bitterness, indignation, rancor, outrage, hostility.

(ANT.) complacency, understanding, good

will.

reservation *(SYN.)* skepticism, restriction, objection, limitation, doubt.

reserve *(SYN.)* fund, hold, keep, store, accumulation, save, stock, maintain, supply.
(ANT.) waste, squander.

reserved *(SYN.)* cautious, fearful, timorous, wary, aloof, chary, sheepish, restrained, proper, unfriendly, bashful, diffident.
(ANT.) forward, bold, wild, immodest, brazen, abandoned, friendly.

reside *(SYN.)* inhabit, dwell, abide, live, lie.

residence *(SYN.)* home, dwelling, stay, seat, abode, quarters, domicile, living quarters.

residue *(SYN.)* balance, remainder, rest, ashes, remnants, dregs, leftovers, ends.

resign *(SYN.)* vacate, withdraw, leave, surrender, quit.

resignation *(SYN.)* perseverance, endurance, fortitude, composure, forbearance.
(ANT.) unquiet, nervousness, impatience.

resigned *(SYN.)* forbearing, stoical, assiduous, passive, accepting, composed, uncomplaining.
(ANT.) turbulent, chafing.

resilience *(SYN.)* rubbery, springy, buoyant, elasticity.
(ANT.) unresponsive, fixed, rigid, stolid.

resist *(SYN.)* defy, attack, withstand, hinder, confront, oppose.
(ANT.) relent, allow, yield, accede.

resolute *(SYN.)* firm, resolved, set, determined, decided.
(ANT.) irresolute, wavering, vacillating.

resolution *(SYN.)* resolve, courage, determination, persistence, statement, verdict, recommendation, decision, steadfastness, dedication, perseverance.
(ANT.) indecision, inconstancy.

resolve *(SYN.)* determination, resolution, courage, settle, decide, persistence, determine, confirm, decision, steadfastness.
(ANT.) integrate, indecision, inconstancy.

resort *(SYN.)* motel, lodge, hotel, solve.

resound *(SYN.)* echoe, ring, reverberate.

resource *(SYN.)* store, source, supply, reserve.

resourceful *(SYN.)* inventive, ingenious, creative, clever, imaginative, skillful.

respect *(SYN.)* honor, approval, revere, heed, value, admire, esteem, point, detail, admiration, reverence, regard, feature, particular, venerate, consider.
(ANT.) disrespect, neglect, abuse, scorn, disregard, despise.

respectable *(SYN.)* becoming, respected, proper, seemly, tolerable, decent, acceptable, fair, adequate, passable, suitable, honorable, valuable.
(ANT.) unsavory, vulgar, gross, disreputable, reprehensible.

respectful *(SYN.)* courteous, polite, well-behaved, well-bred, compliant, submssive.
(ANT.) disobedient, impertinent, rude, flippant.

respite *(SYN.)* deferment, adjournment, suspension.

respond *(SYN.)* rejoin, answer, reply, acknowledge, retort.
(ANT.) overlook, disregard.

response *(SYN.)* reply, acknowledgment, answer, retort, rejoinder.
(ANT.) summoning, inquiry.

responsibility *(SYN.)* duty, obligation, accountability, trust-worthiness, trust, liability, commitment.

responsible *(SYN.)* answerable, chargeable, trustworthy, liable, accountable, able, capable, upstanding, reliable, solid, indebted, creditable.
(ANT.) careless, free, negligent.

rest *(SYN.)* ease, intermission, calm, quiet, balance, surplus, repose, lounge, inactivity, motionlessness, immobility, standstill, relax, remainder, excess, surplus, relaxation, slumber, peace, tranquillity, leisure.
(ANT.) tumult, commotion, motion, agitation.

restful *(SYN.)* peaceful, quiet, tranquil, calm.
(ANT.) tumultuous, upsetting, agitated, disturbed.

restitution *(SYN.)* recompense, satisfaction, refund, amends, retrieval.

restive *(SYN.)* balky, disobedient, fractious, impatient, unruly, fidgety, uneasy.

restless *(SYN.)* sleepless, unquiet, transient, active, agitated, disturbed, jumpy, nervous, uneasy, disquieted, irresolute.

(ANT.) quiet, tranquil, calm, peaceable.

restore *(SYN.)* repair, recover, rebuild, re-establish, renovate, return, renew, mend, reinstall, revive, rehabilitate, replace.

restrain *(SYN.)* limit, curb, constraint, stop, bridle, control, reserve, constrain, repress, check, suppress, hinder.

(ANT.) incite, aid, loosen.

restraint *(SYN.)* order, self-control, reserve, control, regulation, limitation, confinement.

(ANT.) freedom, liberty, confusion.

restrict *(SYN.)* fetter, restrain, confine, limit, engage, attach, connect, link, tie, bind.

(ANT.) broaden, enlarge, untie, loose, free.

restriction *(SYN.)* curb, handicap, check, boundary, ban, limitation, control, deterrent.

result *(SYN.)* effect, issue, outcome, resolve, end, consequence, happen, determination, conclusion, reward, aftermath.

(ANT.) cause, beginning, origin.

resume *(SYN.)* restart, continue, recommence, reassume.

resurgence *(SYN.)* rebirth, comeback, recovery, revival, resuscitation, rejuvenation, renewal.

resuscitate *(SYN.)* restore, revive, resurrect.

retain *(SYN.)* keep, hold, recall, remember, employ, hire, engage.

retainer *(SYN.)* aide, assistant, lackey, attendant, servant.

retaliate *(SYN.)* repay, revenge, return, avenge.

(ANT.) condone, forgive, overlook, excuse, forget.

retard *(SYN.)* detain, slacken, defer, impede, hold back, delay, postpone.

(ANT.) accelerate, speed, hasten, rush.

retention *(SYN.)* reservation, acquisition, holding, tenacity, possession.

reticent *(SYN.)* reserved, subdued, quiet, shy, withdrawn, restrained, bashful, silent.

(ANT.) outspoken, forward, opinionated.

retire *(SYN.)* resign, quit, abdicate, depart, vacate.

retiring *(SYN.)* timid, bashful, withdrawn, modest, reticent, quiet, reserved.

(ANT.) gregarious, assertive, bold.

retort *(SYN.)* reply, answer, response, respond, rejoin, rejoinder, retaliate.

(ANT.) summoning, inquiry.

retreat *(SYN.)* leave, depart, retire, withdraw, retirement, withdrawal, departure, shelter, refuge.

(ANT.) advanced.

retrench *(SYN.)* reduce, scrape, curtail.

retribution *(SYN.)* justice, vengeance, reprisal, punishment, comeuppance, vindictiveness, revenge, retaliation.

retrieve *(SYN.)* regain, recover, recapture, repossess, reclaim, salvage, recoup.

retrograde *(SYN.)* regressive, backward, declining, deteriorating, worsening.

(ANT.) onward, progression, advanced.

return *(SYN.)* restoration, replace, revert, recur, restore, retreat.

(ANT.) keep, take, retain.

reveal *(SYN.)* discover, publish, communicate, impart, uncover, tell, betray, divulge, disclose.

(ANT.) conceal, cover, obscure, cloak, hide.

revel *(SYN.)* rejoice, wallow, bask, enjoy, delight, savor, gloat, luxuriate, relish.

revelation *(SYN.)* hallucination, dream, phantoms, apparition, ghost, mirage, specter, daydream, suprise, shocker.

(ANT.) verity, reality.

revelry *(SYN.)* merriment, merry-making, carousal, feasting, gala, festival.

revenge *(SYN.)* vindictiveness, reprisal, requital, vengeance, repayment, repay, retribution, reparation.

(ANT.) reconcile, forgive, pity.

revenue *(SYN.)* take, proceeds, income, profit, return.

revere *(SYN.)* admire, honor, worship, respect, venerate, adore.

(ANT.) ignore, despise.

reverence *(SYN.)* glory, worship, homage, admiration, dignity, renown, respect, esteem, veneration, adoration, honor.

(ANT.) dishonor, derision, reproach.

reverent *(SYN.)* honoring, respectful, ador-

ing, pious, devout, humble.
(ANT.) impious, disrespectful.
reverse *(SYN.)* overthrow, unmake rescind, opposite, invert, contrary, rear, back, misfortune, defeat, catastrophe, upset, countermand, revoke.
(ANT.) vouch, stabilize, endorse, affirm.
revert *(SYN.)* revive, relapse, backslide, rebound, retreat, recur, go back.
(ANT.) keep, take, appropriate.
review *(SYN.)* reconsideration, examination, commentary, retrospection, restudy, journal, synopsis, study, reexamine, critique, inspection.
revile *(SYN.)* defame, malign, vilify, abuse, traduce, asperse, scandalize, smear.
(ANT.) honor, respect, cherish, protect.
revise *(SYN.)* change, alter, improve, correct, amend, update, rewrite, polish.
revision *(SYN.)* inspection, survey, retrospection, commentary, critique.
revival *(SYN.)* renaissance, exhumation, resurgence, renewal, revitalization.
revive *(SYN.)* refresh, lessen, decrease, renew, reduce, lower, abate, reanimate, diminish, reawaken, rejuvenate, suppress.
(ANT.) increase, amplify, intensify.
revoke *(SYN.)* nullify, cancel, abolish, quash, rescind, abrogate.
revolt *(SYN.)* mutiny, rebel, disgust, revolution, uprising, rebellion, upheaval, take over, insurgence, abolish.
revolting *(SYN.)* hateful, odious, abominable, foul, vile, detestable, loathsome, repugnant, obnoxious, sickening.
(ANT.) delightful, agreeable, pleasant.
revolution *(SYN.)* rebellion, mutiny, turn, coup, revolt, overthrow, cycle, spin, uprising.
revolutionary *(SYN.)* insurgent, extremist, radical, subversive, mutinous.
revolve *(SYN.)* spin, wheel, rotate, circle, circle, turn, whirl, gyrate.
(ANT.) travel, proceed, wander.
revolver *(SYN.)* gun, pistol.
revulsion *(SYN.)* reversal, rebound, backlash, withdrawal, recoil.
reward *(SYN.)* bounty, premium, meed,

award, compensation, prize, recompense, bonus, remuneration, accolade, wages.
(ANT.) charge, wages, punishment.
rewarding *(SYN.)* pleasing, productive, fruitful, profitable, favorable, satisfying, gratifying, fulfilling.
rhetoric *(SYN.)* style, verbosity, expressiveness, eloquence, fluency, flamboyance.
rhyme *(SYN.)* poem, verse, poetry, ballad, ditty, rhapsody, sonnet.
ribald *(SYN.)* suggestive, off-color, indecent, spicy, rude, vulgar.
rich *(SYN.)* ample, costly, wealthy, fruitful, prolific, abundant, well-off, affluent, plentiful, fertile, bountiful, luxuriant.
(ANT.) poor, unfruitful, beggarly, barren, impoverished, scarce, scanty, unproductive, destitute.
rickety *(SYN.)* unsound, unsteady, flimsy, unstable, shaky, decrepit, wobbly.
(ANT.) steady, solid, sturdy.
ricochet *(SYN.)* recoil, backfire, rebound, bounce, deviate, boomerang.
rid *(SYN.)* free, clear, shed, delivered, eliminate, disperse, unload, purge.
riddle *(SYN.)* puzzle, mystery, conundrum, problem, question, enigma.
(ANT.) key, solution, answer, resolution.
ride *(SYN.)* tour, journey, motor, manage, drive, control, guide.
ridge *(SYN.)* hillock, backbone, spine, crest, mound, hump.
ridicule *(SYN.)* gibe, banter, mock, jeering, deride, tease, taunt, satire, mockery, derision.
(ANT.) praise, respect.
ridiculous *(SYN.)* silly, nonsensical, absurd, accurate, inconsistent, farcical, proper, laughable, apt, preposterous, foolish.
(ANT.) sound, reasonable, consistent.
rife *(SYN.)* widespread, abundant, innumerable, rampant, teeming.
rifle *(SYN.)* plunder, pillage, rummage, ransack, rob, steal.
rift *(SYN.)* crevice, fault, opening, crack, flaw, fissure, split, breach, opening.
right *(SYN.)* correct, appropriate, suitable, ethical, fit, real, legitimate, justice, factual,

just, directly, virtue, true, definite, straight, honorably, seemly.

(ANT.) immoral, unfair, wrong, bad, improper.

righteous *(SYN.)* ethical, chaste, honorable, good, virtuous, good, noble.

(ANT.) sinful, libertine, amoral, licentious.

rigid *(SYN.)* strict, unyielding, stiff, stern, austere, rigorous, inflexible, stringent, unbendable, severe, harsh, unbending.

(ANT.) supple, flexible, mild, compassionate, pliable, limp, relaxed.

rigorous *(SYN.)* unfeeling, rough, strict, blunt, cruel, hard, severe, grating, coarse, jarring, stern, stringent.

(ANT.) soft, mild, tender, gentle, smooth.

rile *(SYN.)* irritate, nettle, hector, exasperate, provoke, gripe.

rim *(SYN.)* verge, frontier, border, outskirts, edge, brink, lip, limit, termination, boundary, fringe, brim, margin.

(ANT.) core, mainland, center.

rind *(SYN.)* layer, cover, skin, hide, peel, crust, bark.

ring *(SYN.)* fillet, band, loop, circlet, circle, surround, encircle, peal, sound, resound, jingle, tinkle.

ringleader *(SYN.)* provoker, troublemaker, leader, instigator, chief, inciter, agitator.

rinse *(SYN.)* launder, cleanse, wash, soak, immerse, laundering, flush, rinsing, bathe, clean.

riot *(SYN.)* disturbance, disorder, outburst, commotion, insurgence, uproar, panic, boisterousness, lark, hoot, wow, sensation, caper, roister, frolic, eruption, confusion, tumult, revolt.

riotous *(SYN.)* boisterous, wild, rambunctious, roisterous, tumultuous, turbulent, noisy, loud, rowdy, rollicking.

rip *(SYN.)* tear, rend, wound, rive, cleave, cut, slit, slash, lacerate, shred, scramble, dart, dash, split, disunite.

(ANT.) unite, join, repair.

ripe *(SYN.)* ready, finished, mature, complete, full-grown, develop, mellow, seasonable, full-fledged, primed, disposed, keen, avid, consummate.

(ANT.) raw, crude, undeveloped, premature, unprepared, unripe, immature.

ripen *(SYN.)* grow, season, age, mature, mellow, develop, progress, maturate.

rip into *(SYN.)* assail, lash out at, attack, charge.

rip-off *(SYN.)* fraud, dishonesty, gyp, racket, swindle, exploitation, heist, theft, extortion, thievery, larceny, shakedown.

riposte *(SYN.)* rejoinder, comeback, quip, retort, response, reply, wise-crack.

ripple *(SYN.)* wave, ruffle, wavelet, gurgle, undulate, corrugation, rumple, crumple, spurtle, dribble, bubble.

rise *(SYN.)* thrive, awaken, ascend, climb, mount, tower, arise, wake, scale, flourish, prosper, advance, proceed, soar.

(ANT.) fall, drop, plunge, fade, slump, decline, sinking, depression, waning, comedown, setback, retrogression, descend.

risk *(SYN.)* hazard, peril, danger, endanger, chance, jeopardy, threat, vulnerability, contingency, precariousness, shakiness.

(ANT.) protection, safety, immunity, defense.

risky *(SYN.)* menacing, chancy, threatening, critical, perilous, insecure, unsafe, dicey, unsound, dangerous.

(ANT.) guarded, safe, certain, firm, secure.

rite *(SYN.)* pomp, solemnity, ceremony, observance, ceremonial, formality.

ritual *(SYN.)* pomp, solemnity, ceremony, parade, rite, ritualism, routine, custom, tradition.

rival *(SYN.)* enemy, opponent, contestant, compete, foe, adversary, oppose, competitor, contest, antagonist.

(ANT.) colleague, confederate, allay, collaborator, helpmate, teammate.

rivalry *(SYN.)* contest, struggle, duel, race, vying, opposition, contention, competition.

(ANT.) alliance, collaboration, partnership, cooperation, teamwork, coalition.

river *(SYN.)* brook, stream, headstream, watercourse, tributary, creek.

rivet *(SYN.)* weld, bolt, fasten, attach, secure, bind, join, staple, nail, couple.

road *(SYN.)* street, way, highway, pike, drive, highway, expressway.

roam *(SYN.)* err, saunter, deviate, rove, range, wander, digress, ramble, stroll. *(ANT.)* stop, linger, stay, halt, settle.

roar *(SYN.)* cry, bellow, yell, shout, yowl, howl, bawl, hoot, bang, boom, blast, blare, scream, whoop, holler, yelp.

roast *(SYN.)* deride, ridicule, kid, ride, mock, tease, twit, parody, burlesque.

rob *(SYN.)* fleece, steal, despoil, pilfer, pillage, sack, loot, plunder, burglarize, ransack, hold up, rip off, thieve.

robbery *(SYN.)* larceny, plundering, thievery, stealing, theft, pillage, swiping, caper, snatching, burglary, plunder.

robe *(SYN.)* housecoat, bathrobe, dressing gown, caftan, muumuu, smock, cape.

robot *(SYN.)* computer, android, automaton, pawn, workhorse, drudge, laborer.

robust *(SYN.)* well, hearty, hale, sound, healthy, strong, able-bodied, stalwart. *(ANT.)* fragile, feeble, debilitated, reserved, refined, puny, frail, delicate, infirm.

rock *(SYN.)* pebble, boulder, stone, gravel, granite, roll, sway, swagger, limestone.

rocky *(SYN.)* unstable, faint, rocklike, stony, pebbly, gravelly, trembly, rough, bumpy, formidable, quavering, challenging, unsteady, dizzy. *(ANT.)* effortless, easy, slight, simple, sound, rugged, stout, hardy, strong, robust.

rod *(SYN.)* bar, pole, wand, stick, pike, staff, billy, baton.

rogue *(SYN.)* criminal, rascal, outlaw, scoundrel, scamp, good-for-nothing, villain.

roguish *(SYN.)* prankish, playful, mischievous, elfish, waggish, devilish, tricky. *(ANT.)* grave, humorless, solemn, staid, lawabiding.

roil *(SYN.)* churn, muddy, rile, mire, disturb.

roister *(SYN.)* bluster, swagger, swashbuckle, vaunt, bluff, flourish, rollick.

role *(SYN.)* task, part, function, portrayal, face, character.

roll *(SYN.)* revolve, rotate, whirl, swing, rock, waver, reel, lumber, swagger, stagger, progress, proceed, turn, spin.

rollicking *(SYN.)* spirited, animated, frolicsome, exuberant, lighthearted, carefree.

roll up *(SYN.)* amass, collect, accumulate, gather.

romance *(SYN.)* affair, enchantment, novel, tale, adventure, enterprise, daring, story.

romantic *(SYN.)* poetic, mental, dreamy, fanciful, imaginative, extravagant, impractical, exaggerated, wild, idealistic, mawkish, ideal, maudlin. *(ANT.)* homely, familiar, unromantic, pessimistic, unemotional, cynical, prosaic, factual.

romp *(SYN.)* caper, gambol, frolic, play, conquer, triumph, horseplay, frisk. *(ANT.)* defeat, rout.

room *(SYN.)* enclosure, cell, chamber, space, stay, lodge, cubicle, reside.

roomy *(SYN.)* broad, large, wide, sizable, generous, capacious, ample, spacious, extensive, commodious, vast. *(ANT.)* tight, limited, crowded, confined, narrow.

roost *(SYN.)* coop, henhouse, perch, hutch, residence, abode, hearth, lodgings.

root *(SYN.)* reason, bottom, base, groundwork, cause, support, underpinning, beginning, mainspring, source, basis. *(ANT.)* cover, top, building.

rooted *(SYN.)* fixed, fast, firm, steadfast, immovable, stationary.

root for *(SYN.)* back, support, boost, sponsor, promote, bolster, encourage, hail, cheer.

root out *(SYN.)* dispose of, uproot, cut out, pluck out.

rope *(SYN.)* string, wire, cord, cable, line, strand, rigging, ropework, cordage.

ropy *(SYN.)* wiry, stringy, viscous, threadlike, viscoid.

roster *(SYN.)* list, census, muster, enrollment, listing, register.

rosy *(SYN.)* reddish, pink, healthy, fresh, cheerful, bright, happy, glowing, promising, favorable. *(ANT.)* pale, pallid, gray, wan, disheartening, ashen, unfavorable, gloomy.

rot *(SYN.)* putrefy, waste, decay, mold, decompose, dwindle, spoil, decline, decomposition, wane, rotting, ebb.

(ANT.) increase, rise, grow, luxuriate.

rotary *(SYN.)* axial, rotating, turning, gyral, revolving, rolling, whirling, rotational.

rotate *(SYN.)* spin, twirl, wheel, circle, twist, orbit, invert, swivel, gyrate, wind, alternate, recur.

(ANT.) stop, arrest, stand.

rotation *(SYN.)* turning, rolling, succession, gyration, revolution, return, rhythm, swirling, spinning.

rote *(SYN.)* repetition, system, convention, routine, mechanization, habitude, habit, custom, perfunctoriness.

rotten *(SYN.)* decayed, decomposed, spoiled, putrid, contaminated, tainted.

(ANT.) unspoiled, pure, sweet, fresh.

rough *(SYN.)* jagged, scratchy, crude, incomplete, severe, craggy, stormy, rugged, unpolished, approximate, uneven, irregular, bumpy, coarse, rude.

(ANT.) calm, polished, civil, mild, refined, placid, gentle, smooth, sleek, sophisticated, suave.

roughly *(SYN.)* nearly, about, approximately.

round *(SYN.)* rotund, chubby, curved, bulbous, entire, complete, spherical, circular, bowed.

(ANT.) slender, trim, slim, thin, lean.

roundness *(SYN.)* sphericalness, globualrity, rotundity, globularness, sphericity.

rouse *(SYN.)* waken, awaken, stimulate, excite, summon, arise, stir.

(ANT.) rest, calm, sleep, restrain, sedate.

rousing *(SYN.)* exciting, galvanic, stimulating, electric, moving, exhilarating, stirring, inciting.

(ANT.) flat, uninteresting, drab, monotonous, boring, tiresome, slow, dull.

rout *(SYN.)* defeat, beat, quell, vanquish, conquer, humble, subdue, scatter.

(ANT.) cede, retreat, surrender.

route *(SYN.)* street, course, trail, way, avenue, passage, thoroughfare, track, road, path.

routine *(SYN.)* way, habit, use, custom, practice, fashion, method, system, channel, circuit.

(ANT.) unusual, rate, uncommon.

rover *(SYN.)* traveler, adventurer, wanderer, voyager.

row *(SYN.)* file, order, series, rank, progression, sequence, arrangement.

rowdy *(SYN.)* disorderly, unruly, brawling, roughneck, scrapper.

royal *(SYN.)* lordly, regal, noble, courtly, ruling, stately, dignified, supreme, majestic, sovereign.

(ANT.) servile, common, low, humble, vulgar.

rub *(SYN.)* shine, polish, scour, scrape.

rubbish *(SYN.)* debris, garbage, trash, waste, junk, clutter.

ruddy *(SYN.)* rosy, reddish, healthy, robust, blushing, sanguine.

rude *(SYN.)* gruff, impudent, blunt, impolite, boorish, insolent, saucy, rough, crude, coarse, impertinent.

(ANT.) courtly, civil, stately, genteel, calm, dignified, polished, courteous, cultivated, polite.

rudimentary *(SYN.)* essential, primary, fundamental, original.

rue *(SYN.)* lament, repine, sorrow, deplore, regret, bemoan.

ruffian *(SYN.)* crook, hoodlum, thug.

ruffle *(SYN.)* rumple, disarrange, disorder, disturb, trimming, frill.

rug *(SYN.)* carpet.

rugged *(SYN.)* jagged, craggy, scratchy, irregular, uneven, harsh, severe, tough.

(ANT.) smooth, level, even.

ruin *(SYN.)* wreck, exterminate, devastate, annihilate, raze, demolish, spoil, wreck, destroy, destruction, devastation, disintegration, decay.

(ANT.) save, establish, preserve.

ruination *(SYN.)* obliteration, annihilation, havoc, catastrophe.

rule *(SYN.)* law, guide, order, regulation, sovereignty, control.

ruler *(SYN.)* commander, chief, leader, governor, yardstick.

ruling *(SYN.)* judgment, decision.

ruminate *(SYN.)* brood, reflect, meditate, ponder, consider, speculate, mull, think about.

rummage *(SYN.)* root, scour, ransack.

rumor *(SYN.)* innuendo, hearsay, gossip.

rumple *(SYN.)* tousle, furrow, crease, wrinkle, dishevel.

run *(SYN.)* race, hurry, speed, hasten, sprint, dart, scamper, dash.

runaway *(SYN.)* refugee, deserter, fugitive.

run-down *(SYN.)* ramshackle, dilapidated, weakened, unhealthy, summary, outline, draft.

rupture *(SYN.)* fracture, fissure, cleft, severance.

rural *(SYN.)* country, farm, rustic, backwoods.
(ANT.) citified, urban.

rush *(SYN.)* dash, speed, hurry, hasten, run, scoot, hustle, scurry, acceleration, demand, movement.
(ANT.) tarry, linger, stop, stay, halt.

rut *(SYN.)* road, trench, walkway, ditch, passageway, trail, path.

ruthless *(SYN.)* cruel, heartless, savage, brutal, barbaric.

S

sabotage *(SYN.)* subversion, treason, treachery, damage.

sack *(SYN.)* pouch, bag.

sacrament *(SYN.)* communion, fellowship, intercourse, participation, union.
(ANT.) nonparticipation, alienation.

sacred *(SYN.)* consecrated, blessed, devout, divine, holy, hallowed, pious, religious, spiritual.
(ANT.) profane, evil, sacrilegious, worldly, secular, blasphemous.

sad *(SYN.)* dejected, cheerless, despondent, depressed, disconsolate, doleful, glum, saddening.
(ANT.) cheerful, glad, merry.

safe *(SYN.)* dependable, certain, harmless, secure, trustworthy.
(ANT.) hazardous, dangerous, unsafe, *insecure, perilous.*

safeguard *(SYN.)* fence, bulwark, protection, shelter, refuge, shield, guard, defense, security.

sag *(SYN.)* incline, bend, lean, slant, tend, depend, rely, trust.
(ANT.) rise, raise, erect, straighten.

sagacity *(SYN.)* erudition, discretion, foresight, insight, information, judgment, intelligence, knowledge, learning, reason.
(ANT.) foolishness, imprudence, stupidity, nonsense.

sage *(SYN.)* intellectual, disciple, learner, savant, scholar, pupil, student, wise, judicious, sagacious, rational, logical, expert.
(ANT.) dunce, fool, dolt, idiot.

saintly *(SYN.)* virtuous, moral, holy, devout, righteous, good.

sake *(SYN.)* motive, reason, purpose, benefit, advantage.

salary *(SYN.)* compensation, allowance, earnings, pay, fee, payment, recompense, wages.
(ANT.) gratuity, present, gift.

salient *(SYN.)* distinguished, clear, manifest, noticeable, prominent.
(ANT.) hidden, obscure.

salubrious *(SYN.)* healthy, hale, sound, robust, strong, well, hygienic, salutary.
(ANT.) diseased, delicate, frail, infirm, noxious.

saloon *(SYN.)* pub, bar.

salutary *(SYN.)* beneficial, advantageous, profitable, useful.
(ANT.) destructive, deleterious, detrimental, harmful.

salute *(SYN.)* receive, greet.

salvage *(SYN.)* retrieve, rescue, recover.

salvation *(SYN.)* release, rescue, deliverance.

same *(SYN.)* equal, coincident, equivalent, like, indistinguishable.
(ANT.) disparate, contrary, dissimilar, opposed, distinct.

sample *(SYN.)* example, case, illustration, model, instance, pattern, prototype, specimen, token.

sanction *(SYN.)* approval, approbation, authorization, authority, let, permit.

(ANT.) reproach, reprimand, stricture, censure, forbid, refuse, resist.

sanctuary *(SYN.)* harbor, haven, asylum, refuge, retreat, shelter.

(ANT.) danger, hazard, exposure, jeopardy, peril.

sane *(SYN.)* balanced, rational, normal, reasonable.

(ANT.) crazy, insane, irrational.

sanguinary *(SYN.)* bloody, sanguineous, gory.

sanguine *(SYN.)* confident, optimistic.

sanitary *(SYN.)* purified, clean, hygienic, disinfected.

(ANT.) soiled, fouled, unclean, dirty.

sap *(SYN.)* undermine, exhausted, drain, weaken.

sarcastic *(SYN.)* biting, acrimonious, cutting, caustic, derisive, sardonic, satirical, ironic, sneering.

(ANT.) agreeable, affable, pleasant.

sardonic *(SYN.)* bitter, caustic, acrimonious, harsh.

(ANT.) mellow, pleasant, sweet.

satanic *(SYN.)* demonic, fiendish, diabolic, diabolical.

sate *(SYN.)* fill, occupy, furnish, stuff, pervade, stock, replenish, store, supply, content, satiate.

(ANT.) empty, drain, deplete, void.

satiate *(SYN.)* compensate, appease, content, please, gratify.

(ANT.) displease, dissatisfy, annoy, frustrate, tantalize.

satire *(SYN.)* cleverness, fun, banter, humor, irony, raillery.

(ANT.) platitude, sobriety, commonplace, solemnity, stupidity.

satirical *(SYN.)* biting, caustic, acrimonious, cutting, ironic, derisive, sarcastic, sneering.

(ANT.) agreeable, affable, pleasant.

satisfaction *(SYN.)* blessedness, beatitude, bliss, delight, contentment, felicity, pleasure.

(ANT.) grief, misery, sadness, despair.

satisfactory *(SYN.)* ample, capable, adequate, commensurate, enough, sufficient, fitting.

(ANT.) scant, lacking, deficient, unsatisfactory, poor.

satisfy *(SYN.)* compensate, appease, content, gratify, fulfill.

(ANT.) displease, dissatisfy, annoy, frustrate, tantalize.

saturate *(SYN.)* fill, diffuse, infiltrate, penetrate, permeate.

saucy *(SYN.)* insolent, bold, impudent, impertinent.

(ANT.) shy, demure.

savage *(SYN.)* brutal, cruel, barbarous, ferocious, inhuman, merciless, malignant, ruthless, wild, uncivilized, uncultivated, rough.

(ANT.) compassionate, forbearing, benevolent, gentle, humane, kind, merciful, tame, cultivated.

save *(SYN.)* defend, conserve, keep, maintain, guard, preserve, protect, safeguard, rescue, secure, uphold, spare, free, liberate.

(ANT.) abolish, destroy, abandon, impair, injure.

savory *(SYN.)* delectable, delightful, delicious, palatable, luscious.

(ANT.) distasteful, nauseous, acrid, unpalatable, unsavory.

say *(SYN.)* converse, articulate, declare, express, discourse, harangue, talk, speak, tell, utter.

(ANT.) hush, refrain, be silent.

saying *(SYN.)* aphorism, adage, byword, maxim, proverb, motto.

scalding *(SYN.)* hot, scorching, burning, torrid, warm, fervent, ardent, fiery, impetuous, pungent.

(ANT.) cool, cold, freezing, passionless, frigid, bland.

scale *(SYN.)* balance, proportion, ration, range, climb, mount.

scamp *(SYN.)* troublemaker, rascal.

scan *(SYN.)* examine, study.

scandal *(SYN.)* chagrin, humiliation, abashment, dishonor, disgrace, disrepute, odium.

(ANT.) glory, honor, dignity, praise.

scandalize *(SYN.)* asperse, defame, abuse, disparage, revile, vilify.

(ANT.) honor, respect, cherish.

scandalous *(SYN.)* disgraceful, discreditable, dishonorable, ignominious, disreputable.

(ANT.) honorable, renowned, esteemed.

scant *(SYN.)* succinct, summary, concise, terse, inadequate, deficient, insufficient, limited.

(ANT.) ample, big, extended, abundant, protracted.

scanty *(SYN.)* inadequate, scarce, sparse, insufficient, meager.

(ANT.) abundant, plentiful.

scarce *(SYN.)* occasional, choice, infrequent, exceptional, incomparable, precious, singular, rare, uncommon, unique, sparse.

(ANT.) frequent, ordinary, usual, abundant, numerous, worthless.

scarcely *(SYN.)* barely, hardly.

scarcity *(SYN.)* want, insufficiency, lack, need, dearth.

(ANT.) abundance.

scare *(SYN.)* alarm, papal, affright, astound, dismay, daunt, frighten, intimidate, horrify.

(ANT.) compose, reassure, soothe.

scared *(SYN.)* apprehensive, afraid, frightened, fearful.

(ANT.) bold, assured, courageous, composed, sanguine.

scarf *(SYN.)* kerchief.

scatter *(SYN.)* dispel, disperse, diffuse, disseminate, separate, dissipate, spread.

(ANT.) assemble, accumulate, amass, gather, collect.

scene *(SYN.)* exhibition, view, display.

scent *(SYN.)* fragrance, fume, aroma, incense, perfume, odor, redolence, stench, stink, smell.

schedule *(SYN.)* program, timetable.

scheme *(SYN.)* conspiracy, cabal, design, machination, intrigue, plot, plan, chart, stratage, diagram, graph, sketch, program, delineate, devise.

scheming *(SYN.)* create, design, intend, mean, draw, sketch.

scholar *(SYN.)* intellectual, pupil, learner, disciple, sage, student, teacher, professor.

(ANT.) dunce, idiot, fool, ignoramus.

scholarly *(SYN.)* bookish, erudite, formal, academic, learned, pedantic, theoretical, scholastic.

(ANT.) practical, simple, ignorant.

scholarship *(SYN.)* cognizance, erudition, apprehension, information, learning, science, wisdom.

(ANT.) illiteracy, stupidity, ignorance, misunderstanding.

science *(SYN.)* enlightenment, discipline, knowledge, scholarship.

(ANT.) superstition, ignorance.

scoff *(SYN.)* ridicule, belittle, mock.

scold *(SYN.)* berate, blame, lecture, rate, rebuke, censure, admonish, reprehend, reprimand.

(ANT.) commend, praise, approve.

scope *(SYN.)* area, compass, expanse, amount, extent, magnitude, degree, measure, reach.

scorch *(SYN.)* burn, char, consume, blaze, incinerate, sear, singe.

(ANT.) put out, quench, extinguish.

score *(SYN.)* reckoning, tally, record, mark, rating.

scorn *(SYN.)* contumely, derision, contempt, detestation, hatred, disdain, despise, hate, spurn.

(ANT.) esteem, respect, awe.

scornful *(SYN.)* disdainful, contemptuous.

scoundrel *(SYN.)* rogue, villain, cad.

scour *(SYN.)* wash, clean, scrub.

scourge *(SYN.)* affliction, lash, whip.

scowl *(SYN.)* glower, frown, glare.

scramble *(SYN.)* combine, mix, blend, hasten, clamber, climb.

scrap *(SYN.)* fragment, rag, apportionment, part, portion, piece, section, share, segment, crumb.

(ANT.) whole, entirety.

scrape *(SYN.)* difficulty, dilemma, condition, fix, predicament, plight, situation, strait, scour.

(ANT.) comfort, ease, calmness.

scratch *(SYN.)* scrape, scar.

scrawny *(SYN.)* gaunt, skinny, spindly.

(ANT.) husky, burly.

scream (SYN.) screech, shriek, yell.

screech (SYN.) yell, cry, scream.

screen (SYN.) partition, cover, separation, protection.

scrimp (SYN.) skimp, save, economize, conserve.

script (SYN.) penmanship, hand, handwriting, text, lines.

scrounge (SYN.) sponge, borrow.

scrub (SYN.) cleanse, mop, purify, clean, sweep, wash, scour.

(ANT.) pollute, dirty, stain, sully.

scrupulous (SYN.) conscientious, candid, honest, honorable, fair, just, sincere, truthful, critical.

(ANT.) dishonest, fraudulent, lying, deceitful, tricky, careless.

scrutinize (SYN.) criticize, appraise, evaluate, examine, inspect.

(ANT.) neglect, overlook, approve.

scurrilous (SYN.) insulting, outrageous.

scurry (SYN.) scamper, scramble, hasten, hustle, hurry.

scuttle (SYN.) swamp, ditch, sink.

seal (SYN.) emblem, stamp, symbol, crest, signet.

search (SYN.) exploration, examination, investigation, inquiry, pursuit, quest, explore, scrutinize, investigate, hunt, probe, rummage, ransack, seek, scour.

(ANT.) resignation, abandonment.

searching (SYN.) inquiring, inquisitive, interrogative, nosy, curious, peering, prying.

(ANT.) indifferent, unconcerned, incurious, uninterested.

season (SYN.) mature, perfect, ripen, develop, age.

seasoned (SYN.) veteran, skilled.

secede (SYN.) quit, withdraw, resign.

secluded (SYN.) deserted, desolate, isolated, alone, lonely, lone, unaided, only, sole, solitary, single, separate, isolated, sheltered.

(ANT.) attended, surrounded, accompanied.

seclusion (SYN.) insulation, isolation, loneliness, alienation, quarantine, segregation, separation, retirement.

(ANT.) fellowship, union, connection, as-

sociation, communion.

secondary (SYN.) minor, poorer, inferior, lower, subordinate.

(ANT.) greater, higher, superior.

secret (SYN.) concealed, hidden, latent, covert, private, surreptitious, unknown.

(ANT.) disclosed, exposed, known, conspicuous, open, public.

secrete (SYN.) clothe, conceal, cover, cloak, curtain, envelop, disguise, hide, mask, guard, protect.

(ANT.) divulge, reveal, expose, unveil.

sect (SYN.) segment, denomination, faction, group.

section (SYN.) district, country, domain, dominion, division, land, place, province, territory.

secular (SYN.) lay earthly, laic, mundane, temporal, profane, worldly, temporal.

(ANT.) religious, spiritual, unworldly, ecclesiastical.

secure (SYN.) certain, definite, fixed, assured, indubitable, positive, inevitable, undeniable, sure.

(ANT.) probable, questionable, doubtful, loose, endangered, free.

security (SYN.) bond, earnest, pawn, bail, guaranty, pledge.

sedate (SYN.) controlled, serene, calm, composed, unruffled.

sediment (SYN.) residue, lees, dregs, grounds.

see (SYN.) contemplate, descry, behold, discern, espy, distinguish, glimpse, inspect, look at, observe, perceive, scan, watch, view, witness, regard, examine, study.

seek (SYN.) explore, hunt, examine, look, investigate, probe, ransack, search, scour, rummage.

seem (SYN.) look, appeal.

(ANT.) exist, be, disappear, withdraw, vanish.

segment (SYN.) apportionment, division, fragment, moiety, allotment, part, portion, piece, scrap, share, section, element, faction.

(ANT.) whole, entirety.

segregate *(SYN.)* exclude, separate. *(ANT.)* include, combine.

seize *(SYN.)* check, detain, hinder, apprehend, arrest, obstruct, stop, restrain, grab, grasp, clutch. *(ANT.)* free, liberate, release, activate, discharge, loosen.

seldom *(SYN.)* infrequently, rarely.

select *(SYN.)* cull, opt, pick, choose, elect, prefer. *(ANT.)* reject, refuse.

selection *(SYN.)* election, choice, alternative, option, preference.

self-denial *(SYN.)* abstinence, continence, abstention, forbearance, fasting, sobriety, temperance. *(ANT.)* gluttony, excess, greed, intoxication, self-indulgence.

self-important *(SYN.)* egotistical, proud, conceited, egocentric.

self-indulgence *(SYN.)* egotism, narrowness, self-seeking, stinginess, ungenerousness. *(ANT.)* charity, magnanimity, altruism, liberality.

selfish *(SYN.)* illiberal, narrow, self-centered, stingy, ungenerous, greedy, mean, miserly. *(ANT.)* charitable.

sell *(SYN.)* market, retail, merchandise, vend, trade, barter.

send *(SYN.)* discharge, emit, dispatch, cast, propel, impel, throw, transmit, forward, ship, mail. *(ANT.)* get, hold, retain, receive, bring.

senescence *(SYN.)* dotage, senility, age, seniority. *(ANT.)* infancy, youth, childhood.

senile *(SYN.)* antiquated, antique, aged, ancient, archaic, obsolete, old, elderly, venerable. *(ANT.)* new, youthful, young, modern.

senior *(SYN.)* superior, older, elder. *(ANT.)* minor, junior.

sensation *(SYN.)* feeling, image, impression, apprehension, sense, sensibility, perception. *(ANT.)* insensibility, torpor, stupor, apathy.

sensational *(SYN.)* exciting, marvelous, superb, thrilling, startling.

sense *(SYN.)* drift, connotation, acceptation, explanation, gist, implication, intent, import, interpretation, purport, meaning, purpose, signification, significance.

sense *(SYN.)* perception, sensation, feeling, awareness, insight, consciousness, appreciate.

sensibility *(SYN.)* sensation, emotion, feeling, passion, tenderness. *(ANT.)* coldness, imperturbability, anesthesia, insensibility, fact.

sensible *(SYN.)* apprehensible, perceptible, appreciable, alive, aware, awake, cognizant, comprehending, perceiving, conscious, sentient, intelligent, discreet, practical, judicious, prudent, reasonable, sober, wise. *(ANT.)* impalpable, imperceptible, absurd, stupid, unaware, foolish.

sensitive *(SYN.)* perceptive, prone, impressionable, responsive, susceptible, sentient, tender, sore, delicate, tender, tense, touchy. *(ANT.)* dull, hard, callous, insensitive.

sensual *(SYN.)* lascivious, earthy, lecherous, carnal, sensory, voluptuous, wanton, erotic, sexual. *(ANT.)* chaste, ascetic, abstemious, virtuous, continent.

sentence *(SYN.)* convict, condemn. *(ANT.)* pardon, absolve acquit.

sentiment *(SYN.)* affection, emotion, sensation, feeling, passion, tenderness, impression, opinion. *(ANT.)* coldness, imperturbability, anesthesia, insensibility, fact.

sentimental *(SYN.)* extravagant, fanciful, fantastic, dreamy, fictitious, idealistic, ideal, maudlin, imaginative, mawkish, poetic. *(ANT.)* literal, practical, prosaic.

separate *(SYN.)* part, sever, sunder, divide, allot, dispense, share, distribute, disconnect, split, isolate, segregate, different. *(ANT.)* convene, join, combine.

separation *(SYN.)* insulation, isolation, loneliness, alienation, quarantine, seclusion, retirement. *(ANT.)* communion, fellowship, union, association, connection.

sequence *(SYN.)* chain, graduation, order,

progression, arrangement, following, series, succession.

serene *(SYN.)* composed, imperturbable, calm, dispassionate, pacific, placid, peaceful, quiet. tranquil, still, undisturbed.

(ANT.) frantic, turbulent, wild, excited, stormy, agitated, turbulent.

serenity *(SYN.)* calmness, hush, calm, quiet, peace, quiescence, quietude, rest, repose, stillness, silence, tranquillity.

(ANT.) tumult, excitement, noise, agitation, disturbance.

series *(ANT.)* following, chain, arrangement, graduation, progression, order, sequence, train.

serious *(SYN.)* important, momentous, great, earnest, grave, sedate, sober, staid, alarming, solemn, critical, dangerous, risky, solemn.

(ANT.) trivial, informal, relaxed, small.

servant *(SYN.)* attendant, butler, domestic, valet, manservant.

serve *(SYN.)* assist, attend, help, succor, advance, benefit, answer, promote, content, satisfy, suffice, supply, distribute, wait on, aid.

(ANT.) command, direct, dictate, rule.

service *(SYN.)* advantage, account, avail, benefit, behalf, good, gain.

(ANT.) distress, calamity, trouble, handicap.

serviceable *(SYN.)* beneficial, good, helpful, advantageous, profitable, salutary, wholesome.

(ANT.) destructive, deleterious, detrimental, injurious, harmful.

servile *(SYN.)* base, contemptible, despicable, abject, groveling, dishonorable, ignoble, lowly, low, menial, mean, sordid, vulgar, vile.

(ANT.) honored, exalted, lofty, esteemed, righteous, noble.

servitude *(SYN.)* confinement, captivity, bondage, slavery.

(ANT.) liberation, freedom.

set *(SYN.)* deposit, dispose, lay, arrange, place, put, position, pose, station, appoint, fix, assign, settle.

(ANT.) mislay, misplace, disturb, remove, disarrange.

settle *(SYN.)* close, conclude, adjudicate, decide, end, resolve, agree upon, establish, satisfy, pay, lodge, locate, reside, determine.

(ANT.) suspend, hesitate, doubt, vacillate, waver.

settlement *(SYN.)* completion, close, end, finale, issue, conclusion, termination, deduction, decision, inference.

(ANT.) commencement, prelude, start, inception, beginning.

sever *(SYN.)* part, divide, sunder, split, cut, separate.

(ANT.) convene, connect, gather, join, unite, combine.

several *(SYN.)* some, few, a handful.

severe *(SYN.)* arduous, distressing, acute, exacting, hard, harsh, intense, relentless, rigorous, sharp, stern, rigid, stringent, strict, cruel, firm, unyielding, unmitigated, difficult, unpleasant, dangerous, violent.

(ANT.) genial, indulgent, lenient, yielding, merciful, considerate.

sew *(SYN.)* mend, patch, fix, stitch, refit, restore, repair.

(ANT.) destroy, hurt, deface, injure.

shabby *(SYN.)* indigent, impecunious, needy, penniless, worn, ragged, destitute, poor, threadbare, deficient, inferior, scanty.

(ANT.) rich, wealthy, ample, affluent, opulent, right, sufficient, good.

shack *(SYN.)* hovel, hut, shanty, shed.

shackle *(SYN.)* chain, fetter, handcuff.

shade *(SYN.)* complexion, dye, hue, paint, color, stain, pigment, darkness, shadow, tincture, dusk, gloom, darken, conceal, screen, tint.

(ANT.) transparency, paleness.

shadowy *(SYN.)* dark, dim, gloomy, murky, black, obscure, dusky, unilluminated, dismal, evil, gloomy, sinister, indistinct, hidden, vague, wicked, indefinite, mystic, secret, occult.

(ANT.) bright, clear, light, pleasant, lucid.

shady *(SYN.)* shifty, shaded, questionable,

devious.

shaggy *(SYN.)* hairy, unkempt, uncombed, woolly.

shake *(SYN.)* flutter, jar, jolt, quake, agitate, quiver, shiver, shudder, rock, totter, tremble, vibrate, waver.

shaky *(SYN.)* questionable, uncertain, iffy, faltering, unsteady.

(ANT.) sure, definite, positive, certain.

shallow *(SYN.)* exterior, cursory, flimsy, frivolous, slight, imperfect, superficial.

(ANT.) complete, deep, abstruse, profound, thorough.

sham *(SYN.)* affect, act, feign, assume, pretend, simulate, profess.

(ANT.) exhibit, display, reveal, expose.

shame *(SYN.)* chagrin, humiliation, abashment, disgrace, mortification, dishonor, ignominy, embarrassment, disrepute, odium mortify, humiliate, abash, humble, opprobrium, scandal.

(ANT.) pride, glory, praise, honor.

shameful *(SYN.)* disgraceful, dishonorable, disreputable, discreditable, humiliating, ignominious, scandalous.

(ANT.) honorable, renowned, respectable, esteemed.

shameless *(SYN.)* unembarrassed, unashamed, brazen, bold, impudent.

(ANT.) demure, modest.

shape *(SYN.)* create, construct, forge, fashion, form, make, produce, mold, constitute, compose, arrange, combine, organize, frame, outline, figure, invent, appearance, pattern, cast, model, devise.

(ANT.) disfigure, misshape, dismantle, wreck.

shapeless *(SYN.)* rough, amorphous, vague.

shapely *(SYN.)* attractive, well-formed, curvy, alluring.

(ANT.) shapeless.

share *(SYN.)* parcel, bit, part, division, portion, ration, piece, fragment, allotment, partake, apportion, participate, divide, section.

(ANT.) whole.

shared *(SYN.)* joint, common, reciprocal, correlative, mutual.

(ANT.) unrequited, dissociated.

sharp *(SYN.)* biting, pointed, cunning, acute, keen, barbed rough, fine, cutting, shrill, pungent, witty, acrid, blunt, steep, shrewd.

(ANT.) gentle, bland, shallow, smooth, blunt.

sharpen *(SYN.)* whet, hone, strop.

shatter *(SYN.)* crack, rend, break, pound, smash, burst, demolish, shiver, infringe.

(ANT.) renovate, join, repair, mend.

shattered *(SYN.)* fractured, destroyed, reduced, separated, broken, smashed, flattened, rent, wrecked.

(ANT.) united, integral, whole.

shawl *(SYN.)* stole, scarf.

sheepish *(SYN.)* coy, embarrassed, shy, humble, abashed, timid, modest, timorous.

(ANT.) daring, outgoing, adventurous, gregarious.

sheer *(SYN.)* thin, transparent, clear, simple, utter, absolute, abrupt, steep.

sheet *(SYN.)* leaf, layer, coating, film.

shelter *(SYN.)* retreat, safety, cover, asylum, protection, sanctuary, harbor, guard, haven, security.

(ANT.) unveil, expose, bare, reveal.

shield *(SYN.)* envelop, cover, clothe, curtain, protest, protection, cloak, guard, conceal, defense, shelter, hide, screen, veil, shroud.

(ANT.) unveil, divulge, reveal, bare.

shift *(SYN.)* move, modify, transfer, substitute, vary, change, alter, spell, turn, transfigure.

(ANT.) settle, establish, stabilize.

shifting *(SYN.)* wavering, inconstant, changeable, fitful, variable, fickle.

(ANT.) uniform, stable, unchanging.

shiftless *(SYN.)* idle, lazy, slothful.

(ANT.) energetic.

shifty *(SYN.)* shrewd, crafty, tricky.

shilly-shally *(SYN.)* fluctuate, waver, hesitate, vacillate.

shimmer *(SYN.)* glimmer, shine, gleam.

(ANT.) dull.

shine *(SYN.)* flicker, glisten, glow, blaze, glare, flash, beam, shimmer, glimmer, radiate, brush, polish, twinkle, buff, luster, gloss, scintillate, radiance, gleam.

shining *(SYN.)* dazzling, illustrious, showy, superb, brilliant, effulgent, magnificent, splendid, bright.

(ANT.) ordinary, dull, unimpressive.

shiny *(SYN.)* bright, glossy, polished, glistening.

(ANT.) lusterless, dull.

shipshape *(SYN.)* clean, neat.

(ANT.) sloppy, messy.

shiver *(SYN.)* quiver, quake, quaver, tremble, shudder, shake, break, shatter.

shock *(SYN.)* disconcert, astonish, surprise, astound, amaze, clash, disturbance, bewilder, outrage, horrify, revolt, agitation, stagger, blow, impact, collision, surprise, startle, upset, stun.

(ANT.) prepare, caution, admonish.

shocking *(SYN.)* hideous, frightful, severe, appalling, horrible, awful, terrible, dire, fearful.

(ANT.) safe, happy, secure, joyous.

shore *(SYN.)* seaside, beach, coast.

(ANT.) inland.

short *(SYN.)* abrupt, squat, concise, brief, low, curtailed, dumpy, terse, inadequate, succinct, dwarfed, small, abbreviated, lacking, abridge, undersized, slight, little.

(ANT.) extended, ample, protracted.

shortage *(SYN.)* deficiency, deficit, shortfall.

(ANT.) surplus, enough.

shortcoming *(SYN.)* error, vice, blemish, failure, flaw, omission, failing.

(ANT.) perfection, completeness.

shorten *(SYN.)* curtail, limit, cut, abbreviate, reduce, abridge, lessen, restrict.

(ANT.) lengthen, elongate.

shortening *(SYN.)* reduction, abridgment, abbreviation.

(ANT.) enlargement, amplification.

short-handed *(SYN.)* understaffed.

shortly *(SYN.)* soon, directly, presently.

shortsighted *(SYN.)* myopic, nearsighted, unimaginative, unthinking, thoughtless.

shout *(SYN.)* cry, yell, roar, vociferate, bellow.

(ANT.) whisper, intimate.

shove *(SYN.)* propel, drive, urge, crowd, jostle, force, push, promote.

(ANT.) retreat, falter, oppose, drag, halt.

shovel *(SYN.)* spade.

show *(SYN.)* flourish, parade, point, reveal, explain, array, movie, production, display, exhibit, note, spectacle, demonstrate, entertainment, tell, usher, guide, prove, indicate, present, lead.

showy *(SYN.)* ceremonious, stagy, affected, theatrical, artificial.

(ANT.) unaffected, modest, unemotional, subdued.

shred *(SYN.)* particle, speck, iota, mite, bit, smidgen, tear, slit, cleave, rip, disunite, rend, mince, tatter, lacerate.

(ANT.) bulk, unite, quantity, mend, aggregate, repair.

shrewd *(SYN.)* cunning, covert, artful, stealthy, foxy, astute, ingenious, guileful, crafty, sly, surreptitious, wily, tricky, clever, intelligent, clandestine.

(ANT.) frank, sincere, candid, open.

shriek *(SYN.)* screech, scream, howl, yell.

shrill *(SYN.)* keen, penetrating, sharp, acute, piercing, severe.

(ANT.) gentle, bland, shallow.

shrink *(SYN.)* diminish, shrivel, dwindle.

shrivel *(SYN.)* wizen, waste, droop, decline, sink, dry, languish, wither.

(ANT.) renew, refresh, revive, rejuvenate.

shun *(SYN.)* escape, avert, forestall, avoid, forbear, evade, ward, elude, dodge.

(ANT.) encounter, confront, meet.

shut *(SYN.)* seal, finish, stop, close, terminate, conclude, clog, end, obstruct.

(ANT.) begin, open, start, unbar, inaugurate, unlock, commence.

shy *(SYN.)* reserved, fearful, bashful, retiring, cautious, demure, timid, shrinking, wary, chary.

(ANT.) brazen, bold, immodest, self-confident, audacious.

sick *(SYN.)* ill, morbid, ailing, unhealthy, diseased, infirm.

(ANT.) sound, well, robust, strong.

sickness *(SYN.)* illness, ailment, disease, complaint, disorder.

(ANT.) soundness, healthiness, vigor.

side *(SYN.)* surface, face, foe, opponent, rival, indirect, secondary, unimportant.

siege *(SYN.)* blockade.

sieve *(SYN.)* screen, strainer, colander.

sight *(SYN.)* eyesight, vision, scene, view, display, spectacle, eyesore.

sightless *(SYN.)* unmindful, oblivious, blind, unseeing, heedless, ignorant.

(ANT.) sensible, discerning, aware, perceiving.

sign *(SYN.)* omen, mark, emblem, token, suggestion, indication, clue, hint, approve, authorize, signal, gesture, symbol, portent.

signal *(SYN.)* beacon, sign, alarm.

significance *(SYN.)* connotation, drift, acceptation, explanation, implication, gist, importance, interpretation, intent, weight, meaning, purpose, signification.

significant *(SYN.)* grave, important, critical, material, indicative, meaningful, crucial, momentous, telling, vital, weighty.

(ANT.) irrelevant, insignificant, meaningless, unimportant, negligible.

signify *(SYN.)* designate, imply, denote, intimate, reveal, indicate, mean, communicate, show, specify.

(ANT.) distract, divert, mislead, conceal, hide.

silence *(SYN.)* motionless, peaceful, placid, hushed, stillness, quiescent, still, soundlessness, quiet, tranquil, noiselessness, hush, muteness, undisturbed.

(ANT.) strident, loud, racket, disturbed, clamor, agitated, perturbed.

silent *(SYN.)* dumb, hushed, mute, calm, noiseless, quiet, peaceful, still, soundless, speechless, tranquil, uncommunicative, taciturn.

(ANT.) communicative, loud, noisy, raucous, talkative, clamorous.

silhouette *(SYN.)* contour, delineation, brief, draft, form, figure, outline, profile, plan, sketch.

silly *(SYN.)* asinine, brainless, crazy, absurd, foolish, irrational, witless, nonsensical, ridiculous, stupid.

(ANT.) sane, wise, judicious, prudent.

similar *(SYN.)* alike, akin, allied, comparable, analogous, correlative, corresponding, correspondent, parallel, resembling, like.

(ANT.) dissimilar, divergent, opposed, different, incongruous.

similarity *(SYN.)* likeness, parity, analogy, correspondence, resemblance.

(ANT.) distinction, variance, difference.

simple *(SYN.)* effortless, elementary, pure, easy, facile, mere, single, uncompounded, homely, humble, unmixed, plain, artless, naive, frank, natural, unsophisticated, open, asinine, foolish, credulous, silly.

(ANT.) artful, complex, intricate, adorned, wise.

simpleton *(SYN.)* idiot, fool, ignoramus.

simulate *(SYN.)* copy, counterfeit, duplicate, imitate, impersonate, mock, mimic.

(ANT.) distort, diverge, alter, invent.

sin *(SYN.)* evil, crime, iniquity, transgress, guilt, offense, ungodliness, trespass, vice, wickedness, wrong.

(ANT.) purity, goodness, purity, virtue, righteousness.

sincere *(SYN.)* earnest, frank, heartfelt, genuine, candid, honest, true, straightforward, faithful, truthful, up-right, trustworthy.

(ANT.) hypocritical, insincere, affected, dishonest, untruthful.

sincerity *(SYN.)* fairness, frankness, honesty, justice, candor, integrity, openness, responsibility, rectitude.

(ANT.) deceit, dishonesty, cheating.

sinful *(SYN.)* bad, corrupt, dissolute, antisocial, immoral, licentious, profligate, evil, indecent, vicious.

(ANT.) pure, noble, virtuous.

sing *(SYN.)* chant, croon, hum, carol, lilt, warble.

singe *(SYN.)* burn, char, consume, blaze, incinerate, scorch, sear, scald.

(ANT.) put out, quench, extinguish.

single *(SYN.)* individual, marked, particular, distinctive, separate, special, specific, lone, one, solitary, sole, unwed, unmarried, singular, unique.

(ANT.) ordinary, universal, general.

singular *(SYN.)* exceptional, eccentric, odd, peculiar, rate, extraordinary, strange, unusual, striking, characteristic, remarkable, rare, individual, distinctive, uncommon, special.

(ANT.) general, normal, ordinary.

sink *(SYN.)* diminish, droop, subside, hang, decline, fall, extend, drop, descend.

(ANT.) mount, climb, soar, steady, arise.

sinless *(SYN.)* faultless, holy, immaculate, perfect, blameless, holy, consummate, ideal, excellent, superlative, supreme.

(ANT.) defective, faulty, blemished, imperfect.

sip *(SYN.)* drink, taste, swallow.

sire *(SYN.)* breed, create, father, engender, beget, generate, procreate, originate, produce, propagate.

(ANT.) destroy, ill, extinguish, murder, abort.

site *(SYN.)* place, position, location, station, locality.

situation *(SYN.)* circumstance, plight, state, site, location, locale, predicament, position, condition.

size *(SYN.)* bigness, bulk, dimensions, area, expanse, amplitude, measurement, extent, largeness, magnitude, mass, volume.

skeptic *(SYN.)* doubter, infidel, agnostic, deist, questioner, unbeliever.

(ANT.) believer, worshiper, adorer.

skepticism *(SYN.)* hesitation, questioning, wavering, distrust, mistrust, suspicion.

(ANT.) confidence, reliance, trust.

sketch *(SYN.)* draft, figure, form, outline, contour, delineation, drawing, picture, represent, silhouette, draw, profile.

sketchy *(SYN.)* indefinite, vague, incomplete, indistinct.

(ANT.) definite, detailed, complete.

skill *(SYN.)* cunning, deftness, dexterity, ability, adroitness, cleverness, talent, readiness, skillfulness.

(ANT.) ineptitude, inability.

skillful *(SYN.)* adept, clever, able, accomplished, competent, expert, ingenious, cunning, proficient, practiced, versed, skilled.

(ANT.) untrained, inept, clumsy, bungling,

awkward.

skimpy *(SYN.)* cheap, scanty, meager.

(ANT.) abundant, generous.

skin *(SYN.)* outside, covering, peel, rind, shell, pare.

skinny *(SYN.)* gaunt, thin, raw-boned.

(ANT.) fat, hefty, heavy.

skip *(SYN.)* drop, eliminate, ignore, exclude, cancel, delete, disregard, omit, overlook neglect, miss.

(ANT.) notice, introduce, include, insert.

skirmish *(SYN.)* brawl, battle, conflict, combat, dispute, encounter, contend, quarrel, squabble, scuffle, wrangle, struggle.

slack *(SYN.)* lax, limp, indefinite, free, disengaged, unbound, untied, unfastened, vague, dissolute, heedless, careless, unrestrained, limp, lazy, loose, inactive, sluggish, wanton.

(ANT.) restrained, tied, right, stiff, taunt, rigid, fast, inhibited.

slander *(SYN.)* libel, calumny, backbiting, aspersion, scandal, vilification.

(ANT.) praise, flattery, commendation, defense.

slang *(SYN.)* jargon, dialect.

slant *(SYN.)* disposition, inclination, bias, bent, partiality, slope, tilt, pitch, penchant, prejudice, proneness, proclivity, turn, incline, lean, tendency.

(ANT.) justice, fairness, impartiality, equity.

slash *(SYN.)* gash, cut, slit, lower, reduce.

slaughter *(SYN.)* butcher, kill, massacre, slay, butchering, killing.

slave *(SYN.)* bondservant, serf.

slavery *(SYN.)* captivity, imprisonment, serfdom, confinement, bondage, thralldom, servitude.

(ANT.) freedom, liberation.

slay *(SYN.)* assassinate, kill, murder.

sleek *(SYN.)* smooth, polished, slick.

(ANT.) blunt, harsh, rough, rugged.

sleep *(SYN.)* drowse, nap, nod, catnap, repose, doze, rest, slumber, snooze.

sleepy *(SYN.)* tired, drowsy, nodding.

slender *(SYN.)* lank, lean, meager, emaciated, gaunt, scanty, rare, skinny, scrawny,

slight, spare, trim, slim, tenuous, thin.
(ANT.) fat, broad, overweight, thick, wide, bulky.

slide *(SYN.)* glide, slip, skim, skid.

slight *(SYN.)* lank, lean, meager, emaciated, gaunt, fine, narrow, scanty, scrawny, skinny, sparse, small, rare, slender, spare, insignificant, tenuous, unimportant, slim, thin.
(ANT.) regard, notice, enormous, large, major, huge, include.

slim *(SYN.)* thin, slender, lank, slight, weak, insignificant, unimportant.

slip *(SYN.)* error, fault, inaccuracy, shift, err, slide, mistake, glide, blunder.
(ANT.) precision, truth, accuracy.

slipshod *(SYN.)* sloppy, careless.
(ANT.) careful.

slit *(SYN.)* slash, cut, tear, slot.

slogan *(SYN.)* catchword, motto.

slope *(SYN.)* incline, leaning, inclination, bending, slant.

sloth *(SYN.)* indolence, idleness, inactivity, inertia, supineness, sluggishness, torpidity.
(ANT.) alertness, assiduousness, diligence, activity.

slothful *(SYN.)* indolent, idle, inactive, lazy, inert, supine, sluggish, torpid.
(ANT.) alert, diligent, active, assiduous.

slovenly *(SYN.)* sloppy, bed-raggled, unkempt, messy.
(ANT.) meticulous, neat.

slow *(SYN.)* deliberate, dull, delaying, dawdling, gradual, leisurely, tired, sluggish, unhurried, late, delayed.
(ANT.) rapid, quick, swift, speedy, fast.

sluggish *(SYN.)* dull, deliberate, dawdling, delaying, laggard, gradual, leisurely, tired, slow, lethargic.
(ANT.) quick, rapid, fast, speedy, swift, energetic, vivacious.

slumber *(SYN.)* drowse, catnap, nod, doze, repose, sleep, rest, snooze.

slump *(SYN.)* drop, decline, descent.

sly *(SYN.)* covert, artful, astute, crafty, clandestine, foxy, furtive, cunning, insidious, guileful, stealthy, subtle, shrewd, tricky, surreptitious, wily, secretive.
(ANT.) sincere, ingenuous, open, candid.

small *(SYN.)* little, minute, petty, diminutive, puny, wee, tiny, trivial, slight, miniature.
(ANT.) immense, enormous, large, huge.

smart *(SYN.)* dexterous, quick, skillful, adroit, apt, clever, bright, witty, ingenious, sharp, intelligent.
(ANT.) foolish, stupid, unskilled, awkward, clumsy, bungling, slow, dumb.

smash *(SYN.)* burst, crush, demolish, destroy, break, crack, fracture, pound, fringe, rack, rupture, shatter, rend.
(ANT.) mend, renovate, restore, repair.

smear *(SYN.)* wipe, rub, spread.

smell *(SYN.)* fragrance, fume, odor, perfume, incense, aroma, fetidness, stench, stink, scent, sniff, detect, bouquet.

smidgen *(SYN.)* crumb, mite, small, bit, particle, shred, speck, scrap.
(ANT.) bulk, mass, quantity, aggregate.

smile grin.
(ANT.) frown.

smite *(SYN.)* knock, hit, dash, beat, belabor, buffet, pound, punch, pummel, thrash, thump, defeat, overthrow, overpower, subdue, vanquish, rout.
(ANT.) surrender, fail, defend, shield, stroke.

smooth *(SYN.)* polished, sleek, slick, glib, diplomatic, flat, level, plain, suave, urbane, even, unwrinkled.
(ANT.) rugged, harsh, rough, blunt, bluff, uneven.

smother *(SYN.)* suffocate, asphyxiate, stifle.

smutty *(SYN.)* disgusting, filthy, impure, coarse, dirty, lewd, offensive, obscene, pornographic.
(ANT.) modest, refined, decent, pure.

snag *(SYN.)* difficulty, bar, barrier, check, hindrance, obstruction.
(ANT.) assistance, help, encouragement.

snappish *(SYN.)* ill-natured, ill-tempered, fractious, irritable, fretful, peevish, testy, touchy, petulant.
(ANT.) good-tempered, pleasant, good-natured, affable, genial.

snappy *(SYN.)* quick, stylish, chic.

snare *(SYN.)* capture, catch, arrest, clutch, grasp, grip, apprehend, seize, trap, net.
(ANT.) throw, release, lose, liberate.

snarl *(SYN.)* growl.

snatch *(SYN.)* grasp, seize, grab.

sneak *(SYN.)* steal, skulk, slink.

sneer *(SYN.)* fleer, flout, jeer, mock, gibe, deride, taunt, scoff, scorn.
(ANT.) laud, flatter, praise, compliment.

sneering *(SYN.)* derision, gibe, banter, jeering, mockery, raillery, sarcasm, ridicule, satire.

sniveling *(SYN.)* whimpering, sniffling, weepy, whining, blubbering.

snobbish *(SYN.)* uppity, conceited, snooty, snobby, snotty.

snoopy *(SYN.)* inquisitive, interrogative, curious, inquiring, meddling, peeping, prying, peering.
(ANT.) uninterested, incurious, unconcerned, indifferent.

snub *(SYN.)* rebuke, insult, slight.

snug *(SYN.)* constricted, close, contracted, compact, firm, narrow, taut, tense, stretched, tight, cozy, comfortable, sheltered.
(ANT.) loose, lax, slack, relaxed, open.

soak *(SYN.)* saturate, drench, steep, wet.

soar *(SYN.)* flutter, fly, flit, float, glide, sail, hover, mount.
(ANT.) plummet, sink, fall, descend.

sob *(SYN.)* weep, cry, lament.

sober *(SYN.)* sedate, serious, staid, earnest, grave, solemn, moderate.
(ANT.) ordinary, joyful, informal, boisterous, drunk, fuddled, inebriated.

sobriety *(SYN.)* forbearance, abstinence, abstention, self-denial, moderation, temperance.
(ANT.) self-indulgence, excess, intoxication.

social *(SYN.)* friendly, civil, gregarious, affable, communicative, hospitable, sociable, group, common, genial, polite.
(ANT.) inhospitable, hermitic, antisocial, disagreeable.

society *(SYN.)* nation, community, civilization, organization, club, association, fraternity, circle, association, company, companionship.

soft *(SYN.)* gentle, lenient, flexible, compassionate, malleable, meek, mellow, subdued, mild, tender, supple, yielding, pliable, elastic, pliant.
(ANT.) unyielding, rough, hard, tough, rigid.

soften *(SYN.)* assuage, diminish, abate, allay, alleviate, mitigate, relieve, soothe, solace.
(ANT.) irritate, increase, aggravate, agitate.

soil *(SYN.)* defile, discolor, spot, befoul, blemish, blight, stain, earth, dirt, loam, dirty.
(ANT.) purify, honor, cleanse, bleach, decorate.

solace *(SYN.)* contentment, ease, enjoyment, comfort, consolation, relief, succor.
(ANT.) torture, torment, misery, affliction, discomfort.

sole *(SYN.)* isolated, desolate, deserted, secluded, unaided, lone, alone, only, single, solitary.
(ANT.) surrounded, accompanied, attended.

solemn *(SYN.)* ceremonious, imposing, formal, impressive, reverential, ritualistic, grave, sedate, earnest, sober, staid, serious, dignified.
(ANT.) ordinary, joyful, informal, boisterous, cheerful, gay, happy.

solicit *(SYN.)* beg, beseech, request, seek, pray.

solicitous *(SYN.)* anxious, concerned.

solicitude *(SYN.)* concern, worry, anxiety, care, attention, regard, vigilance, caution, wariness.
(ANT.) indifference, disregard, neglect, negligence.

solid *(SYN.)* hard, dense, compact, firm.
(ANT.) loose.

solitary *(SYN.)* isolated, alone, lonely, deserted, unaided, secluded, only, single, lone, sole.
(ANT.) surrounded, attended, accompanied.

solitude *(SYN.)* loneliness, privacy, refuge, retirement, seclusion, retreat, alienation, asylum, concealment.

(ANT.) publicity, exposure, notoriety.

solution *(SYN.)* explanation, answer.

solve *(SYN.)* explain, answer, unravel.

somatic *(SYN.)* corporeal, corporal, natural, material, bodily, physical.

(ANT.) spiritual, mental.

somber *(SYN.)* dismal, dark, bleak, doleful, cheerless, natural, physical, serious, sober, gloomy, grave.

(ANT.) lively, joyous, cheerful, happy.

sometimes *(SYN.)* occasionally.

(ANT.) invariably, always.

soon *(SYN.)* shortly, early.

(ANT.) tardy, late, overdue, belated.

soothe *(SYN.)* encourage, console, solace, comfort, cheer, gladden, sympathize, calm, pacify.

(ANT.) dishearten, depress, antagonize, aggravate, disquiet, upset, unnerve.

soothing *(SYN.)* gentle, benign, docile, calm, mild, placid, peaceful, serene, relaxed, tractable, tame.

(ANT.) violent, savage, fierce, harsh.

sophisticated *(SYN.)* cultured, worldly, blase, cultivated, urbane, cosmopolitan, suave, intricate, complex, advanced.

(ANT.) uncouth, ingenuous, simple, naive, crude.

sorcery *(SYN.)* enchantment, charm, black, magic, voodoo, witchcraft, wizardry.

sordid *(SYN.)* vicious, odious, revolting, obscene, foul, loathsome, base, depraved, debased, vile, vulgar, abject, wicked, ignoble, despicable, mean, low, worthless, wretched, dirty, unclean.

(ANT.) upright, decent, honorable.

sore *(SYN.)* tender, sensitive, aching, hurting, painful.

sorrow *(SYN.)* grief, distress, heartache, anguish, misery, sadness, mourning, tribulation, gloom, depression.

(ANT.) consolation, solace, joy, happiness, comfort.

sorrowful *(SYN.)* dismal, doleful, dejected, despondent, depressed, disconsolate, gloomy, melancholy, glum, moody, somber, sad, grave, aggrieved.

(ANT.) merry, happy, cheerful, joyous.

sorry *(SYN.)* hurt, pained, sorrowful, afflicted, grieved, contrite, repentant, paltry, poor, wretched, remorseful, mean, shabby, contemptible, vile, regretful, apologetic.

(ANT.) delighted, impenitent, cheerful, unrepentant, splendid.

sort *(SYN.)* class, stamp, category, description, nature, kind, type, variety.

(ANT.) peculiarity, deviation.

sound *(SYN.)* effective, logical, telling, binding, powerful, weighty, legal, strong, conclusive, valid.

(ANT.) weak, null, counterfeit.

sour *(SYN.)* glum, sullen, bitter, peevish, acid, rancid, tart, acrimonious, sharp, bad-tempered, cranky.

(ANT.) *wholesome, kindly, genial, benevolent, sweet.*

source *(SYN.)* birth, foundation, agent, determinant, reason, origin, cause, start, incentive, motive, spring, principle, beginning.

(ANT.) product, harvest, outcome, issue, consequence, end.

souvenir *(SYN.)* memento, monument, commemoration, remembrance.

sovereign *(SYN.)* monarch, king, emperor, queen, empress.

sovereignty *(SYN.)* command, influence, authority, predominance, control.

(ANT.) debility, incapacity, disablement, ineptitude, impotence.

space *(SYN.)* room, area, location.

spacious *(SYN.)* capacious, large, vast, ample, extensive, wide, roomy.

(ANT.) limited, confined, narrow, small, cramped.

span *(SYN.)* spread, extent.

spare *(SYN.)* preserve, safeguard, uphold, conserve, protect, defend, rescue, reserve, additional, unoccupied.

(ANT.) impair, abolish, injure, abandon.

sparing *(SYN.)* economical, thrifty, frugal.

(ANT.) lavish.

sparkle *(SYN.)* gleam, glitter, twinkle, beam, glisten, radiate, shine, blaze.

spat *(SYN.)* quarrel, dispute, affray, wrangle, altercation.
(ANT.) peace, friendliness, agreement, reconciliation.

spawn *(SYN.)* yield, bear.

speak *(SYN.)* declare, express, say, articulate, harangue, converse, talk, utter.
(ANT.) refrain, hush, quiet.

special *(SYN.)* individual, uncommon, distinctive, peculiar, exceptional, unusual, extraordinary, different.
(ANT.) general, wide-spread, broad, prevailing, average, ordinary.

specialist *(SYN.)* authority, expert.

species *(SYN.)* variety, type, kind, class, sort.

specific *(SYN.)* limited, characteristic, definite, peculiar, explicit, categorical, particular, distinct, precise.
(ANT.) generic, general, nonspecific.

specify *(SYN.)* name, call, mention, appoint, denominate, designate, define.
(ANT.) miscall, hint.

specimen *(SYN.)* prototype, example, sample, model, pattern, type.

speck *(SYN.)* scrap, jot, bit, mite, smidgen, crumb, iota, particle, spot.
(ANT.) quantity, bulk, aggregate.

spectacle *(SYN.)* demonstration, ostentation, movie, array, exhibition, show, display, performance, parade, splurge.

spectator *(SYN.)* viewer, observer.

speculate *(SYN.)* assume, deduce, surmise, apprehend, imagine, consider, view, think, guess, suppose, conjecture.
(ANT.) prove, demonstrate, conclude.

speech *(SYN.)* gossip, discourse, talk, chatter, lecture, conference, discussion, address, dialogue, articulation, accent.
(ANT.) silence, correspondence, writing, meditation.

speed *(SYN.)* forward, push, accelerate, hasten, rapidity, dispatch, swiftness.
(ANT.) impede, slow, block, retard.

spellbound *(SYN.)* fascinated, entranced, hypnotized, mesmerized, rapt.

spend *(SYN.)* pay, disburse, consume.
(ANT.) hoard, save.

spendthrift *(SYN.)* squanderer, profligate.

sphere *(SYN.)* globe, orb, ball, environment, area, domain.

spherical *(SYN.)* round, curved, globular.

spicy *(SYN.)* indecent, off-color, suggestive, indelicate.

spin *(SYN.)* revolve, turn, rotate, whirl, twirl, tell, narrate, relate.

spine *(SYN.)* vertebrae, backbone.

spineless *(SYN.)* weak, limp, cowardly.
(ANT.) brave, strong, courageous.

spirit *(SYN.)* courage, phantom, verve, fortitude, apparition, mood, soul, ghost.
(ANT.) listlessness, substance, languor.

spirited *(SYN.)* excited, animated, lively, active, vigorous, energetic.
(ANT.) indolent, lazy, sleepy.

spiritless *(SYN.)* gone, lifeless, departed, dead, insensible, deceased, unconscious.
(ANT.) stirring, alive, living.

spiritual *(SYN.)* sacred, unearthly, holy, divine, immaterial, supernatural.
(ANT.) material, physical, corporeal.

spite *(SYN.)* grudge, rancor, malice, animosity, malevolence, malignity.
(ANT.) kindness, toleration, affection.

spiteful *(SYN.)* vicious, disagreeable, surly, ill-natured.
(ANT.) pretty, beautiful, attractive, fair.

splendid *(SYN.)* glorious, illustrious, radiant, brilliant, showy, superb, bright.
(ANT.) ordinary, mediocre, dull.

splendor *(SYN.)* effulgence, radiance, brightness, luster, magnificence, display.
(ANT.) darkness, obscurity, dullness.

splinter *(SYN.)* fragment, piece, sliver, chip, shiver.

split *(SYN.)* rend, shred, cleave, disunite, sever, break, divide, opening, lacerate.
(ANT.) repair, unite, join, sew.

spoil *(SYN.)* rot, disintegrate, waste, decay, ruin, damage, mold, destroy.
(ANT.) luxuriate, grow, flourish.

spoken *(SYN.)* verbal, pronounced, articulated, vocal, uttered, oral.
(ANT.) written, documentary.

spokesman *(SYN.)* agent, representative.

spontaneous *(SYN.)* impulsive, voluntary,

automatic, instinctive, willing, extemporaneous, natural, unconscious.

(ANT.) planned, rehearsed, forced, studied, prepared.

sport *(SYN.)* match, play, amusement, fun, pastime, entertainment, athletics.

sporting *(SYN.)* considerate, fair, sportsmanlike.

spot *(SYN.)* blemish, mark, stain, flaw, blot, location, place, site, splatter.

spotty *(SYN.)* erratic, uneven, irregular, inconsistent.

(ANT.) regular, even.

spout *(SYN.)* spurt, squirt, tube, nozzle.

spray *(SYN.)* splash, spatter, sprinkle.

spread *(SYN.)* unfold, distribute, open, disperse, unroll, unfurl, scatter, jelly.

(ANT.) shut, close, hide, conceal.

sprightly *(SYN.)* blithe, hopeful, vivacious, buoyant, lively, light, nimble.

(ANT.) hopeless, depressed, sullen, dejected, despondent.

spring *(SYN.)* commencement, foundation, start, beginning, inception, jump, cradle, begin, birth, bound, originate.

(ANT.) issue, product, end.

sprinkle *(SYN.)* strew, spread, scatter, rain.

spruce *(SYN.)* orderly, neat, trim, clear, nice.

(ANT.) unkempt, sloppy, dirty.

spry *(SYN.)* brisk, quick, agile, nimble, energetic, supple, alert, active, lively.

(ANT.) heavy, sluggish, inert, clumsy.

spur *(SYN.)* inducement, purpose, cause, motive, impulse, reason, incitement.

(ANT.) effort, action, result, attempt.

squabble *(SYN.)* bicker, debate, altercate, contend, discuss, argue, quarrel.

(ANT.) concede, agree, assent.

squalid *(SYN.)* base, indecent, grimy, dirty, pitiful, filthy, muddy, nasty.

(ANT.) wholesome, clean, pure.

squander *(SYN.)* scatter, lavish, consume, dissipate, misuse.

(ANT.) preserve, conserve, save, accumulate.

squeamish *(SYN.)* particular, careful.

stab *(SYN.)* stick, gore, pierce, knife, spear, bayonet.

stability *(SYN.)* steadiness, balance, proportion, composure, symmetry.

(ANT.) imbalance, fall, unsteadiness.

stable *(SYN.)* firm, enduring, constant, fixed, unwavering, steadfast, steady.

(ANT.) irresolute, variable, changeable.

stack *(SYN.)* mass, pile, mound, heap, accumulate.

staff *(SYN.)* pole, stick, club, personnel, crew, employees.

stage *(SYN.)* frame, platform, boards, theater, scaffold, period, phase, step, direct, produce, present.

stagger *(SYN.)* totter, sway, reel, vary, falter, alternate.

staid *(SYN.)* solemn, sedate, earnest, sober, grave.

(ANT.) joyful, informal, ordinary.

stain *(SYN.)* blight, dye, tint, befoul, spot, defile, mark, dishonor, disgrace, smirch, blot, blemish, discolor, color, tinge.

(ANT.) honor, bleach, decorate, purify.

stair *(SYN.)* staircase, stairway, steps.

stake *(SYN.)* rod, pole, picket, post, pale, bet, wager, concern, interest.

stale *(SYN.)* tasteless, spoiled, old, inedible, dry, uninteresting, trite, flat, dull, vapid, insipid.

(ANT.) new, fresh, tasty.

stalk *(SYN.)* dog, follow, track, shadow, hunt.

stall *(SYN.)* hesitate, stop, delay, postpone.

stammer *(SYN.)* falter, stutter.

stamp *(SYN.)* crush, trample, imprint, mark, brand, block, seal, die.

stand *(SYN.)* tolerate, suffer, stay, stand up, endure, bear, abide, halt, arise, rise, remain, sustain, rest.

(ANT.) run, yield, advance.

standard *(SYN.)* law, proof, pennant, emblem, measure, example, gauge, model, banner, symbol, test.

(ANT.) guess, chance, irregular, unusual, supposition.

standing *(SYN.)* rank, position, station.

standpoint *(SYN.)* position, viewpoint, attitude.

staple *(SYN.)* main, principal, chief, essential, necessary.

stare *(SYN.)* gaze.

stark *(SYN.)* utter, absolute, sheer, complete, rough, severe, harsh, grim.

start *(SYN.)* opening, source, commence, onset, surprise, shock, beginning, origin, begin, initiate, jerk, jump, advantage, lead, commencement, outset.

(ANT.) end, completion, termination, close.

startle *(SYN.)* astonish, disconcert, aback, alarm, shock, agitate, surprise, astound, amaze, stun.

(ANT.) caution, prepare, admonish, forewarn.

starved *(SYN.)* longing, voracious, hungry, craving, avid, famished.

(ANT.) satisfied, sated, gorged, full.

state *(SYN.)* circumstance, predicament, case, situation, condition, affirm, declare, express, nation, country, status, recite, tell, recount.

(ANT.) imply, conceal, retract.

stately *(SYN.)* lordly, elegant, regal, sovereign, impressive, magnificent, courtly, grand, imposing, majestic, noble, supreme, dignified.

(ANT.) low, common, mean, servile, humble, vulgar.

statement *(SYN.)* announcement, mention, allegation, declaration, thesis, assertion, report.

station *(SYN.)* post, depot, terminal, position, place.

statuesque *(SYN.)* imposing, stately, regal, majestic, dignified.

status *(SYN.)* place, caste, standing, condition, state, rank, position.

statute *(SYN.)* law, ruling, decree, rule.

(ANT.) intention, deliberation.

staunch *(SYN.)* faithful, true, constant, reliable, loyal, devoted.

(ANT.) treacherous, untrustworthy.

stay *(SYN.)* delay, continue, hinder, check, hold, hindrance, support, brace, line, rope, linger, sojourn, abide, halt, stand, rest, remain, tarry, arrest, wait.

(ANT.) hasten, progress, go, depart,

advance, leave.

stead *(SYN.)* place.

steadfast *(SYN.)* solid, inflexible, constant, stable, unyielding, secure.

(ANT.) unstable, insecure, unsteady.

steadfastness *(SYN.)* persistence, industry, tenacity, constancy, persistency.

(ANT.) laziness, sloth, cessation.

steady *(SYN.)* regular, even, unremitting, stable, steadfast, firm, reliable, solid.

steal *(SYN.)* loot, rob, swipe, burglarize, pilfer, shoplift, embezzle, snitch.

(ANT.) restore, buy, return, refund.

stealthy *(SYN.)* sly, secret, furtive.

(ANT.) direct, open, obvious.

steep *(SYN.)* sharp, hilly, sheer, abrupt, perpendicular, precipitous.

(ANT.) gradual, level, flat.

steer *(SYN.)* manage, guide, conduct, lead, supervise, escort, navigate, drive, control, direct.

stem *(SYN.)* stalk, trunk, arise, check, stop, orginate, hinder.

stench *(SYN.)* odor, fetor, fetidness, stink, aroma, smell, fume, scent.

step *(SYN.)* stride, pace, stage, move, action, measure, come, go, walk.

stern *(SYN.)* harsh, rigid, exacting, rigorous, sharp, severe, strict, hard, unyielding, unmitigated, stringent.

(ANT.) indulgent, forgiving, yielding, lenient, considerate.

stew *(SYN.)* ragout, goulash, boil, simmer.

stick *(SYN.)* stalk, twig, rod, staff, pole, pierce, spear, stab, puncture, gore, cling, adhere, hold, catch, abide, remain, persist.

stickler *(SYN.)* nitpicker, perfectionist, disciplinarian.

sticky *(SYN.)* tricky, delicate, awkward.

stiff *(SYN.)* severe, unbendable, unyielding, harsh, inflexible, unbending, rigid, firm, hard, solid, rigorous.

(ANT.) supple, yielding, compassionate, mild, lenient, resilient.

stifle *(SYN.)* choke, strangle, suffocate.

stigma *(SYN.)* trace, scar, blot, stain, mark, vestige.

still *(SYN.)* peaceful, undisturbed, but,

mild, hushed, calm, patient, modest, nevertheless, motionless, meek, quiescent, stationary, besides, however, quiet, tranquil, serene, placid.
(ANT.) agitated, perturbed, loud.

stimulate *(SYN.)* irritate, excite, arouse, disquiet, rouse, activate, urge, invigorate, animate, provoke.
(ANT.) quell, calm, quiet, allay.

stimulus *(SYN.)* motive, goad, arousal, provocation, encouragement.
(ANT.) discouragement, depressant.

stingy *(SYN.)* greedy, penurious, avaricious, mean, cheap, selfish, miserly, tight, tightfisted.
(ANT.) munificent, generous, giving, extravagant, open-handed, bountiful.

stipend *(SYN.)* payment, earnings, salary, allowance, pay, compensation, wages.
(ANT.) gratuity, gift.

stipulate *(SYN.)* require, demand.

stir *(SYN.)* instigate, impel, push, agitate, induce, mix, rouse, move, propel.
(ANT.) halt, stop, deter.

stock *(SYN.)* hoard, store, strain, accumulation, supply, carry, keep, provision, fund, breed, sort.
(ANT.) sameness, likeness, homogeneity, uniformity.

stoical *(SYN.)* passive, forbearing, uncomplaining, composed, patient.
(ANT.) turbulent, chafing, hysterical.

stolid *(SYN.)* obtuse, unsharpened, dull, blunt, edgeless.
(ANT.) suave, tactful, polished, subtle.

stone *(SYN.)* pebble, gravel, rock.

stony *(SYN.)* insensitive, unsentimental, cold.

stoop *(SYN.)* bow, bend, lean, crouch.

stop *(SYN.)* terminate, check, abstain, hinder, arrest, close, bar, cork, halt, end, conclude, obstruct, finish, quit, pause, discontinue, stay, impede, cease.
(ANT.) start, proceed, speed, begin.

store *(SYN.)* amass, hoard, collect, market, shop, reserve, supply, deposit, bank, save, accrue, increase, stock.
(ANT.) dissipate, waste, disperse.

storm *(SYN.)* gale, tempest, tornado, thunderstorm, hurricane, rage, rant, assault, besiege.

stormy *(SYN.)* rough, inclement, windy, blustery, roaring, tempestuous.
(ANT.) quiet, calm, tranquil, peaceful.

story *(SYN.)* yarn, novel, history, tale, falsehood, account, fable, anecdote, narrative, fabrication, lie, level, floor, fiction, report.

stout *(SYN.)* plump, obese, chubby, fat, paunchy, overweight, portly, heavy, sturdy, strong, pudgy, thickset.
(ANT.) thin, slender, flimsy, gaunt, slim.

straight *(SYN.)* erect, honorable, square, just, direct, undeviating, unbent, right, upright, honest, uncurving, directly, moral, correct, orderly, vertical.
(ANT.) dishonest, bent, circuitous, twisted, crooked.

straightforward *(SYN.)* forthright, direct, open, candid, aboveboard.
(ANT.) devious.

strain *(SYN.)* stock, kind, variety, stretch, breed, tighten, harm, injure, screen, filter, sprain, sort.

strainer *(SYN.)* colander, sieve, filter.

strait *(SYN.)* fix, situation, passage, dilemma, channel, trouble, predicament, difficulty, distress, crisis.
(ANT.) ease, calmness, satisfaction, comfort.

strange *(SYN.)* bizarre, peculiar, odd, abnormal, irregular, unusual, curious, uncommon, singular, extraordinary, foreign, eccentric, unfamiliar, queer.
(ANT.) regular, common, familiar, conventional.

stranger *(SYN.)* foreigner, outsider, newcomer, alien, outlander, immigrant.
(ANT.) friend, associate, acquaintance.

strap *(SYN.)* strip, belt, thong, band.

stratagem *(SYN.)* design, ruse, cabal, plot, machination, subterfuge, trick, wile, conspiracy.

strategy *(SYN.)* technique, management, tactics, approach.

stray *(SYN.)* ramble, rove, deviate, lost,

strayed, wander, digress, roam, stroll.
(ANT.) linger, stop, halt, settle.
stream *(SYN.)* issue, proceed, brook, flow, come, abound, spout, run.
street *(SYN.)* way, road, boulevard, avenue.
strength *(SYN.)* power, might, toughness, durability, lustiness, soundness, vigor, potency.
(ANT.) weakness, frailty, feebleness.
strengthen *(SYN.)* verify, assure, confirm, fix, sanction, ratify, substantiate.
strenuous *(SYN.)* forceful, energetic, active, vigorous, determined.
stress *(SYN.)* urgency, press, emphasize, accentuate, accent, weight, strain, importance, compulsion, pressure.
(ANT.) relaxation, lenience, ease.
stretch *(SYN.)* strain, expand, elongate, extend, lengthen, spread, distend, protract, distort.
(ANT.) tighten, loosen, slacken, contract.
strict *(SYN.)* rough, stiff, stringent, harsh, unbending, severe, rigorous.
(ANT.) easygoing, lenient, mild.
strife *(SYN.)* disagreement, conflict, discord, quarrel, difference, unrest.
(ANT.) tranquillity, peace, concord.
strike *(SYN.)* pound, hit, smite, beat, assault, attack, affect, impress, overwhelm, sitdown, walkout, slowdown.
striking *(SYN.)* arresting, imposing, splendid, august, impressive, thrilling, stirring, awesome, aweinspiring.
(ANT.) ordinary, unimpressive, commonplace, regular.
stringent *(SYN.)* harsh, rugged, grating, severe, gruff.
strip *(SYN.)* disrobe, undress, remove, uncover, peel, ribbon, band, piece.
stripped *(SYN.)* open, simple, bare, nude, uncovered, exposed, bald, plain, naked, barren, defenseless.
(ANT.) protected, dressed, concealed.
strive *(SYN.)* aim, struggle, attempt, undertake, design, endeavor, try.
(ANT.) omit, abandon, neglect, decline.
stroke *(SYN.)* rap, blow, tap, knock, feat, achievement, accomplishment, caress.

stroll *(SYN.)* amble, walk, ramble.
strong *(SYN.)* potent, hale, athletic, mighty, sturdy, impregnable, resistant.
(ANT.) feeble, insipid, brittle, weak, bland, fragile.
structure *(SYN.)* construction, arrangement.
struggle *(SYN.)* fray, strive, fight, contest, battle, skirmish, oppose, clash.
(ANT.) peace, agreement, truce.
stubborn *(SYN.)* obstinate, firm, determined, inflexible, obdurate, uncompromising, contumacious, rigid, unbending, in-tractable.
(ANT.) docile, yielding, amenable, submissive.
student *(SYN.)* pupil, observer, disciple, scholar, learner.
studio *(SYN.)* workroom, workshop.
study *(SYN.)* weigh, muse, master, contemplate, reflect, examination, examine.
stuff *(SYN.)* thing, subject, material, theme, matter, substance, fill, ram, cram, pack, textile, cloth, topic.
(ANT.) spirit, immateriality.
stumble *(SYN.)* sink, collapse, tumble, drop, topple, lurch, trip, fall.
(ANT.) steady, climb, soar, arise.
stun *(SYN.)* shock, knock out, dumbfound, take, amaze, alarm.
(ANT.) forewarn, caution, prepare.
stunning *(SYN.)* brilliant, dazzling, exquisite, ravishing.
(ANT.) drab, ugly.
stunt *(SYN.)* check, restrict, hinder.
stupid *(SYN.)* dull, obtuse, half-witted, brainless, foolish, dumb, witless, idiotic.
(ANT.) smart, intelligent, clever, quick, bright, alert, discerning.
stupor *(SYN.)* lethargy, torpor, daze, languor, drowsiness, numbness.
(ANT.) wakefulness, liveliness, activity.
sturdy *(SYN.)* hale, strong, rugged, stout, mighty, enduring, hardy, well-built.
(ANT.) fragile, brittle, delicate.
style *(SYN.)* sort, type, kind, chic, smartness, elegance.
subdue *(SYN.)* crush, overcome, rout, beat,

reduce, lower, defeat, vanquish.
(ANT.) retreat, cede, surrender.
subject *(SYN.)* subordinate, theme, case, topic, dependent, citizen, matter.
sublime *(SYN.)* lofty, raised, elevated, supreme, exalted, splendid, grand.
(ANT.) ordinary, vase, low, ridiculous.
submerge *(SYN.)* submerse, dunk, sink, dip, immerse, engage, douse.
(ANT.) surface, rise, uplift, elevate.
submissive *(SYN.)* deferential, yielding, dutiful, compliant.
(ANT.) rebellious, intractable, insubordinate.
submit *(SYN.)* quit, resign, waive, yield, tender, offer, abdicate, cede, surrender.
(ANT.) fight, oppose, resist, struggle, deny, refuse.
subordinate *(SYN.)* demean, reduce, inferior, assistant, citizen, liegeman.
(ANT.) superior.
subsequent *(SYN.)* later, following.
(ANT.) preceding, previous.
subside *(SYN.)* decrease, lower, sink, droop, hang, collapse.
(ANT.) mount, steady, arise, climb.
subsidy *(SYN.)* support, aid, grant.
substance *(SYN.)* stuff, essence, importance, material, matter.
(ANT.) spirit, immaterial.
substantial *(SYN.)* large, considerable, sizable, actual, real, tangible, influential.
(ANT.) unimportant, trivial.
substantiate *(SYN.)* strengthen, corroborate, confirm.
substitute *(SYN.)* proxy, expedient, deputy, makeshift, replacement, alternate, representative, surrogate, exchange, equivalent.
(ANT.) sovereign, master, head.
substitution *(SYN.)* change, mutation, vicissitude, alteration, modification.
(ANT.) uniformity, monotony.
subterfuge *(SYN.)* pretext, excuse, cloak, simulation, disguise, garb, pretension.
(ANT.) reality, truth, actuality, sincerity.
subtle *(SYN.)* suggestive, indirect.
(ANT.) overt, obvious.
subtract *(SYN.)* decrease, reduce, curtail,

deduct, diminish, remove.
(ANT.) expand, increase, add, enlarge, grow.
succeed *(SYN.)* thrive, follow, replace, achieve, win, flourish.
(ANT.) flop, miscarry, anticipate, fail, precede.
success *(SYN.)* advance, prosperity, luck.
(ANT.) failure.
successful *(SYN.)* fortunate, favorable, lucky, triumphant.
succession *(SYN.)* chain, course, series, order, string, arrangement, progression, train, following.
successive *(SYN.)* serial, sequential.
succinct *(SYN.)* pithy, curt, brief, short, compendious, terse.
(ANT.) prolonged, extended, long, protracted.
succor *(SYN.)* ease, solace, comfort, enjoyment, consolation.
(ANT.) suffering, discomfort, torture, affliction, torment.
sudden *(SYN.)* rapid, swift, immediate, abrupt, unexpected, unforeseen, hasty.
(ANT.) slowly, anticipated.
suffer *(SYN.)* stand, experience, endure, bear, feel, allow, let, permit, sustain.
(ANT.) exclude, banish, overcome.
suffering *(SYN.)* distress, ache, anguish, pain, woe, misery, torment.
(ANT.) ease, relief, comfort.
sufficient *(SYN.)* fitting, enough, adequate, commensurate.
(ANT.) scant, deficient.
suffix *(SYN.)* ending.
(ANT.) prefix.
suggest *(SYN.)* propose, offer, refer, advise, hint, insinuate, recommend, allude.
(ANT.) dictate, declare, insist.
suggestion *(SYN.)* exhortation, recommendation, intelligence, caution, admonition, advice.
suit *(SYN.)* conform, accommodate, fit.
(ANT.) misapply, disturb.
suitable *(SYN.)* welcome, agreeable, acceptable, gratifying.
(ANT.) offensive, disagreeable.

sullen *(SYN.)* fretful, morose, crabbed, dismal, silent, sulky, bitter, sad, somber, glum, gloomy.
(ANT.) pleasant, joyous, merry.

sultry *(SYN.)* close, hot, stifling.

sum *(SYN.)* amount, total, aggregate, whole, increase, add.
(ANT.) fraction, reduce, deduct.

summary *(SYN.)* digest, outline, abstract, synopsis, concise, brief.

summit *(SYN.)* peak, top, head, crest, zenith, crown, pinnacle.
(ANT.) bottom, foundation, base.

summon *(SYN.)* invoke, call, invite.
(ANT.) dismiss.

sundry *(SYN.)* miscellaneous, several, different, various, divers.
(ANT.) similar, identical, alike, same, congruous.

superannuated *(SYN.)* old, archaic, aged, senile, ancient, venerable, elderly.
(ANT.) youthful, modern, young.

superb *(SYN.)* splendid, wonderful, extraordinary, marvelous.

supercilious *(SYN.)* contemptuous, snobbish, overbearing, vainglorious, arrogant, haughty, stately.
(ANT.) meek, ashamed, lowly.

superficial *(SYN.)* flimsy, shallow, cursory, slight, exterior.
(ANT.) thorough, deep, abstruse, profound.

superintend *(SYN.)* rule, control, govern, command, manage.
(ANT.) ignore, follow, submit, abandon.

superintendent *(SYN.)* manager, supervisor, overseer, director, administrator.

superior *(SYN.)* greater, finer, better, employer, boss.
(ANT.) inferior.

superlative *(SYN.)* pure, consummate, sinless, blameless, holy, perfect, faultless, ideal, unqualified, immaculate.
(ANT.) lacking, defective, imperfect, deficient, blemished.

supervise *(SYN.)* rule, oversee, govern, command, direct, superintend, manage, control.
(ANT.) submit, forsake, abandon.

supervision *(SYN.)* oversight, inspection, charge, management.

supervisor *(SYN.)* manager, boss, foreman, director.

supplant *(SYN.)* overturn.
(ANT.) uphold, conserve.

supple *(SYN.)* lithe, pliant, flexible, limber, elastic, pliable.
(ANT.) stiff, brittle, unbending.

supplement *(SYN.)* add, extension, complement, addition, extend.

supplicate *(SYN.)* beg, petition, solicit, adjure, beseech, entreat.
(ANT.) cede, give, bestow, grant.

supplication *(SYN.)* invocation, plea, appeal, request, entreaty.

supply *(SYN.)* provide, inventory, hoard, reserve, store, accumulation, stock, furnish, endow, give.

support *(SYN.)* groundwork, aid, favor, base, prop, assistance, comfort, basis, succor, living, subsistence, encouragement, backing, livelihood, help, maintain.
(ANT.) discourage, abandon, oppose, opposition, attack.

supporter *(SYN.)* follower, devotee, adherent, henchman, attendant, disciple, votary.
(ANT.) master, head, chief.

suppose *(SYN.)* believe, presume, deduce, apprehend, think, assume, imagine, speculate, guess.
(ANT.) prove, demonstrate, ascertain.

supposition *(SYN.)* theory, conjecture.
(ANT.) proof, fact.

suppress *(SYN.)* diminish, reduce, overpower, abate, lessen, decrease, subdue, lower.
(ANT.) revive, amplify, intensify, enlarge.

supremacy *(SYN.)* domination, predominance, ascendancy.

supreme *(SYN.)* greatest, best, highest, main, principal, cardinal, first, chief, foremost, paramount.
(ANT.) supplemental, minor, subsidiary, auxiliary.

sure *(SYN.)* confident, fixed, inevitable, certain, positive, trustworthy, reliable, unquestionable, convinced, steady, assured, unfailing, stable, firm, safe, solid, destined, fated.

(ANT.) probable, uncertain, doubtful.

surface *(SYN.)* outside, exterior, cover, covering.

surge *(SYN.)* heave, swell, grow.

(ANT.) wane, ebb, diminish.

surly *(SYN.)* disagreeable, hostile, unfriendly, ugly, antagonistic.

surmise *(SYN.)* judge, think, believe, assume, suppose, presume, guess, thought, suspect.

surname *(SYN.)* denomination, epithet, title, name, appellation.

surpass *(SYN.)* pass, exceed, excel, outstrip, outdo.

surplus *(SYN.)* extravagance, intemperance, superabundance, excess, immoderation, remainder, extra, profusion, superfluity.

(ANT.) want, lack, dearth, paucity.

surprise *(SYN.)* miracle, prodigy, wonder, awe, phenomenon, marvel, bewilderment, wonderment.

(ANT.) expectation, triviality, indifference, familiarity.

surrender *(SYN.)* relinquish, resign, yield, abandon, sacrifice.

(ANT.) overcome, rout, conquer.

surreptitious *(SYN.)* sneaky, sneaking, underhead, sly, furtive.

(ANT.) openhanded, open, straight-forward.

surround *(SYN.)* confine, encompass, circle, encircle, girdle, fence, circumscribe, limit, envelop.

(ANT.) open, distend, expose, enlarge.

surveillance *(SYN.)* inspection, oversight, supervision, management, control.

survey *(SYN.)* scan, inspect, view, examine, inspection, examination.

survive *(SYN.)* live, remain, continue, persist.

(ANT.) die, fail, succumb.

suspect *(SYN.)* waver, disbelieve, presume, suppose, mistrust, distrust, question, suspected, assume, defendant, questionable.

(ANT.) decide, believe, trust.

suspend *(SYN.)* delay, hang, withhold, interrupt, postpone, dangle, adjourn, poise,

defer.

(ANT.) persist, proceed, maintain.

suspicious *(SYN.)* suspecting, distrustful, doubtful, doubting, questioning, suspect, skeptical.

suspicion *(SYN.)* unbelief, distrust, suspense, uncertainty, doubt.

(ANT.) determination, conviction, faith, belief.

sustain *(SYN.)* bear, carry, undergo, foster, keep, prop, help, advocate, back, encourage, maintain, assist, suffer, approve.

(ANT.) discourage, betray, oppose, destroy.

sustenance *(SYN.)* fare, food, diet, rations, nutriment, edibles, victuals, repast, feed.

(ANT.) hunger, want, drink.

swallow *(SYN.)* gorge, gulp, eat, mouthful.

swallow up *(SYN.)* consume, absorb, engulf, assimilate.

(ANT.) exude, dispense, expel, discharge.

swamp *(SYN.)* fen, bog, marsh, quagmire, morass, flood, overcome, deluge.

swarm *(SYN.)* throng, horde, crowd.

swarthy *(SYN.)* sable, dark.

(ANT.) bright, light.

sway *(SYN.)* control, affect, stir, actuate, impel, impress, bend, wave, swing, persuade, influence.

swear *(SYN.)* declare, state, affirm, vouchsafe, curse, maintain.

(ANT.) demur, oppose, deny, contradict.

sweat *(SYN.)* perspiration, perspire.

sweeping *(SYN.)* extensive, wide, general, broad, tolerant, comprehensive, vast.

(ANT.) restricted, confined.

sweet *(SYN.)* engaging, luscious, pure, clean, fresh, melodious, winning, unsalted, pleasant.

(ANT.) bitter, harsh, nasty, irascible, discordant, irritable, acrid.

swell *(SYN.)* increase, grow, expand, enlarge.

(ANT.) diminish, shrink.

swift *(SYN.)* quick, fast, fleet, speedy, rapid, expeditious.

swindle *(SYN.)* bilk, defraud, con, deceive, cheat, guile, imposture, deception, artifice,

deceit, trick.
(ANT.) sincerity, honesty, fairness.
swing *(SYN.)* rock, sway, wave.
switch *(SYN.)* shift, change, turn.
swoon *(SYN.)* faint.
symbol *(SYN.)* sign, character.
sympathetic *(SYN.)* considerate, compassionate, gentle, benevolent, good, tender, affable.
(ANT.) unkind, merciless, unsympathetic, indifferent, intolerant, cruel.
sympathize *(SYN.)* gladden, sheer, solace, comfort, encourage.
(ANT.) depress, antagonize.
sympathy *(SYN.)* compassion, agreement, tenderness, commiseration, pity.
(ANT.) indifference, unconcern, antipathy, malevolence.
symptom *(SYN.)* indication, sign.
synopsis *(SYN.)* outline, digest.
synthetic *(SYN.)* counterfeit, artificial, phony, unreal, bogus, sham.
(ANT.) natural, true, genuine.
system *(SYN.)* organization, procedure, regularity, arrangement.
(ANT.) confusion, chance, disorder.
systematic *(SYN.)* orderly, organized, grouped, classified, measured, constant, methodical.
(ANT.) irregular, random, disorganized, erratic.

T

table *(SYN.)* catalog, list, schedule, postpone, chart, index, shelve, delay, put off.
tablet *(SYN.)* pad, notebook, capsule, pill, sketchpad, pill, paper,
taboo *(SYN.)* banned, prohibited, forbidden, restriction, limitation.
(ANT.) accepted, allowed, sanctioned.
tacit *(SYN.)* understood, assumed, implied, unspoken, acknowledged, inferred, expected.
(ANT.) said, spoken.
taciturn *(SYN.)* quiet, reserved, silent.
(ANT.) talkative.
tack *(SYN.)* add, join, attach, clasp, fasten.

tackle *(SYN.)* rigging, gear, apparatus, equipment, grab, seize, catch, down, try, undertake.
(ANT.) evade, avoid.
tacky *(SYN.)* gummy, sticky, gooey.
tact *(SYN.)* dexterity, poise, diplomacy, judgment, savoirfaire, skill, finesse, sense, prudence.
(ANT.) incompetence, vulgarity, blunder, rudeness, awkwardness, insensitivity, grossness.
tactful *(SYN.)* discreet, considerate, judicious, adroit, sensitive, diplomatic, skillful, discriminating, politic.
(ANT.) coarse, gruff, tactless, boorish, unfeeling, churlish, rude.
tactical *(SYN.)* foxy, cunning, proficient, adroit, clever, expert.
(ANT.) blundering, gauche, clumsy, inept.
tactics *(SYN.)* plan, strategy, approach, maneuver, course.
tag *(SYN.)* sticker, label, mark, identification, marker, name.
tail *(SYN.)* rear, back, follow, end, shadow, pursue, trail, heel.
tailor *(SYN.)* modiste, couturier, modify, redo, shape, fashion.
taint *(SYN.)* spot, stain, tarnish, soil, mark, discolor.
(ANT.) cleanse, disinfect, clean.
tainted *(SYN.)* crooked, impure, vitiated, profligate, debased, spoiled, corrupted, depraved, dishonest, contaminated, putrid.
take *(SYN.)* accept, grasp, catch, confiscate, clutch, adopt, assume, receive, attract, claim, necessitate, steal, ensnare, capture, demand, select, appropriate, obtain, captivate, hold, seize, win, escort, note, record, rob, shoplift, get, remove, gain, choose.
taking *(SYN.)* charming, captivating, winning, attractive.
takeover *(SYN.)* revolution, merger, usurpation, confiscation.
tale *(SYN.)* falsehood, history, yarn, chronicle, account, fable, fiction, narration, story, narrative.
talent *(SYN.)* capability, knack, skill,

endowment, gift, cleverness, aptitude, ability, genius.

(ANT.) ineptitude, incompetence, stupidity.

talented *(SYN.)* skillful, smart, adroit, dexterous, clever, apt, witty, ingenious.

(ANT.) dull, clumsy, awkward, unskilled, stupid, slow.

talk *(SYN.)* conversation, gossip, report, speech, communicate, discuss, confer, chatter, conference, preach, dialogue, reason, jabber, discourse, lecture, communication, consul, plead, argue, converse, rant, chat, mutter, speak, rangue, rumor, deliberate, discussion.

(ANT.) silence, correspondence, meditation, writing.

talkative *(SYN.)* glib, communicative, chattering, loquacious, voluble, garrulous.

(ANT.) uncommunicative, laconic, reticent, silent.

tall *(SYN.)* elevated, high, towering, big, lofty, imposing, gigantic.

(ANT.) tiny, low, short, small, stunted.

tally *(SYN.)* score, count, compute, reckon, calculate, estimate, list, figure, correspond, agree, match.

tame *(SYN.)* domesticated, dull, insipid, docile, broken, uninteresting, gentle, subdued, insipid, flat, unexciting, boring, empty, break, domesticate, mild, tedious.

(ANT.) spirited, savage, wild, exciting, animated, undomesticated.

tamper *(SYN.)* mix in, interrupt, interfere, meddle, interpose.

tang *(SYN.)* zest, sharpness, tartness, taste.

tangible *(SYN.)* material, sensible, palpable, corporeal, bodily.

(ANT.) metaphysical, mental, spiritual.

tangle *(SYN.)* confuse, knot, snarl, twist, ensnare, embroil, implicate.

tangy *(SYN.)* pungent, peppery, seasoned, sharp, tart.

tantalize *(SYN.)* tease, tempt, entice, titillate, stimulate, frustrate.

tantrum *(SYN.)* outburst, fit, fury, flare-up, conniption, rampage.

tap *(SYN.)* pat, rap, hit, strike, blow, faucet, spout, spigot.

tape *(SYN.)* ribbon, strip, fasten, bandage, bind, record, tie.

taper *(SYN.)* narrow, candle, decrease, lessen.

tardy *(SYN.)* slow, delayed, overdue, late, belated.

(ANT.) prompt, timely, punctual, early.

target *(SYN.)* aim, goal, object, objective.

tariff *(SYN.)* duty, tax, levy, rate.

tarnish *(SYN.)* discolor, blight, defile, sully, spot, befoul, disgrace, stain.

(ANT.) honor, purify, cleanse, bleach, decorate, gleam, sparkle.

tarry *(SYN.)* dawdle, loiter, linger, remain, delay, procrastinate.

tart *(SYN.)* sour, acrid, pungent, acid, sharp, distasteful, bitter.

(ANT.) mellow, sweet, delicious, pleasant.

task *(SYN.)* work, job, undertaking, labor, chore, duty, stint.

taste *(SYN.)* tang, inclination, liking, sensibility, flavor, savor, try, sip, sample, zest, experience, undergo, appreciation, relish, discernment, judgment.

(ANT.) indelicacy, disinclination, antipathy, insipidity.

tasteful *(SYN.)* elegant, choice, refined, suitable, artistic.

(ANT.) offensive, unbecoming.

tasteless *(SYN.)* flavorless, insipid, unpalatable, rude, unrefined, uncultivated, boorish, uninteresting.

tasty *(SYN.)* delectable, delicious, luscious, palatable, tempting.

tattered *(SYN.)* ragged, torn, shoddy, shabby, frazzled, frayed.

tattle *(SYN.)* inform, divulge, disclose, blab, reveal.

taunt *(SYN.)* tease, deride, flout, scoff, sneer, mock, annoy, pester, bother, ridicule, jeer.

(ANT.) praise, compliment, laud, flatter.

taunting *(SYN.)* ironic, caustic, cutting, sardonic, derisive, biting, acrimonious, sarcastic, satirical.

(ANT.) pleasant, agreeable, affable, amiable.

taut *(SYN.)* tight, constricted, firm, stretched, snug, tense, extended.

(ANT.) slack, loose, relaxed, open, lax.

tavern *(SYN.)* pub, bar, cocktail lounge.

tawdry *(SYN.)* pretentious, showy, vulgar, tasteless, sordid, garish.

tax *(SYN.)* duty, assessment, excise, levy, toll, burden, strain, tribute, tariff, assess, encumber, overload, custom, exaction, rate.

(ANT.) reward, gift, remuneration, wages.

taxi *(SYN.)* cab, taxicab.

teach *(SYN.)* inform, school, educate, train, inculcate, instruct.

(ANT.) misinform, misguide.

teacher *(SYN.)* tutor, instructor, professor, lecturer.

team *(SYN.)* company, band, party, crew, gang, group.

teamwork *(SYN.)* cooperation.

tear *(SYN.)* rend, shred, sunder, cleave, rip, lacerate, teardrop, disunite, rend, divide, drop, wound, split, slit, sever.

(ANT.) mend, join, unite, sew.

tearful *(SYN.)* sad, weeping, crying, sobbing, weepy, lachrymose.

tease *(SYN.)* badger, harry, bother, irritate, nag, pester, taunt, vex, annoy, disturb, harass, worry, tantalize, plague, aggravate, provoke.

(ANT.) please, delight, soothe, comfort, gratify.

technical *(SYN.)* industrial, technological, specialized, mechanical.

technique *(SYN.)* system, method, routine, approach, procedure.

tedious *(SYN.)* boring, dilatory, humdrum, sluggish, monotonous, dull, irksome, dreary, tiring, burdensome, tiresome, wearisome.

(ANT.) interesting, entertaining, engaging, exciting, amusing, quick.

teem *(SYN.)* abound, swarm.

teeming *(SYN.)* overflowing, bountiful, abundant, ample, profuse, plenteous, rich, copious.

(ANT.) scant, scarce, deficient, insufficient.

teeter *(SYN.)* sway, hesitate, hem and haw, waver.

telecast *(SYN.)* broadcast.

televise *(SYN.)* telecast.

tell *(SYN.)* report, mention, state, betray, announce, recount, relate, narrate, rehearse, mention, utter, confess, disclose, direct, request, acquaint, instruct, notify, inform, determine, reveal, divulge.

telling *(SYN.)* persuasive, convincing, forceful, effective.

telltale *(SYN.)* revealing, informative, suggestive, meaningful.

temerity *(SYN.)* rashness, foolhardiness, audacity, boldness, recklessness, precipitancy.

(ANT.) prudence, wariness, caution, hesitation, timidity.

temper *(SYN.)* fury, choler, exasperation, anger, passion, petulance, disposition, nature, rage, soothe, soften, wrath, indignation, irritation, pacify, animosity, mood, resentment.

(ANT.) peace, self-control, forbearance, conciliation.

temperament *(SYN.)* humor, mood, temper, nature, disposition.

temperamental *(SYN.)* testy, moody, touchy, sensitive, irritable.

(ANT.) calm, unruffled, serene.

temperance *(SYN.)* abstinence, sobriety, forbearance, abstention.

(ANT.) intoxication, excess, self-indulgence, gluttony, wantonness.

temperate *(SYN.)* controlled, moderate, cool, calm, restrained.

(ANT.) excessive, extreme, prodigal.

tempest *(SYN.)* draft, squall, wind, blast, gust, storm, hurricane, commotion, tumult, zephyr.

(ANT.) calm, tranquillity, peace.

tempo *(SYN.)* measure, beat, cadence, rhythm.

temporal *(SYN.)* mundane, earthly, lay, profane, worldly, laic.

(ANT.) spiritual, ecclesiastical, unworldly, religious, heavenly.

temporary *(SYN.)* brief, momentary, short-lived, fleeting, ephemeral, passing, short.

(ANT.) lasting, permanent, immortal, everlasting, abiding.

tempt *(SYN.)* entice, allure, lure, attract,

seduce, invite, magnetize.

tenacious *(SYN.)* persistent, determined, unchanging, unyielding.

tenable *(SYN.)* correct, practical, rational, reasonable, sensible.

tenacity *(SYN.)* perseverance, steadfastness, industry, constancy, persistence, pertinacity.

(ANT.) laziness, rest, idleness, sloth.

tenant *(SYN.)* renter, lessee, lodger, leaseholder, dweller, resident.

tend *(SYN.)* escort, follow, care for, lackey, watch, protect, take care of, attend, guard, serve.

tendency *(SYN.)* drift, inclination, proneness, leaning, bias, aim, leaning, disposition, predisposition, propensity, trend, impulse.

(ANT.) disinclination, aversion, deviation.

tender *(SYN.)* sympathetic, sore, sensitive, painful, gentle, meek, delicate, fragile, proffer, bland, mild, loving, offer, affectionate, soothing, propose, soft.

(ANT.) rough, severe, fierce, chewy, tough, cruel, unfeeling, harsh.

tenderfoot *(SYN.)* novice, apprentice, beginner, amateur.

tenderhearted *(SYN.)* kind, sympathetic, merciful, softhearted, understanding, sentimental, affectionate, gentle, sensitive.

tenet *(SYN.)* dogma, belief, precept, doctrine, creed, opinion.

(ANT.) deed, conduct, practice, performance.

tense *(SYN.)* strained, stretched, excited, tight, nervous.

(ANT.) loose, placid, lax, relaxed.

tension *(SYN.)* stress, strain, pressure, anxiety, apprehension, distress.

tentative *(SYN.)* hypothetical, indefinite, probationary, conditional.

tenure *(SYN.)* administration, time, regime, term.

tepid *(SYN.)* temperate, mild, lukewarm.

(ANT.) boiling, scalding, passionate, hot.

term *(SYN.)* period, limit, time, boundary, duration, name, phrase, interval, session, semester, expression, word.

terminal *(SYN.)* eventual, final, concluding, decisive, ending, fatal, latest, last, ultimate, conclusive.

(ANT.) original, first, rudimentary, incipient, inaugural.

terminate *(SYN.)* close, end, finish, abolish, complete, cease, stop, conclude, expire, culminate.

(ANT.) establish, begin, initiate, start, commence.

terminology *(SYN.)* vocabulary, nomenclature, terms, phraseology.

terms *(SYN.)* stipulations, agreement, conditions, provisions.

terrible *(SYN.)* frightful, dire, awful, gruesome, horrible shocking, horrifying, terrifying, horrid, hideous, appalling, shocking.

(ANT.) secure, happy, joyous, pleasing, safe.

terrific *(SYN.)* superb, wonderful, glorious, great, magnificent, divine, colossal, sensational, marvelous.

terrify *(SYN.)* dismay, intimidate, startle, terrorize, appall, frighten, petrify, astound, alarm, affright, horrify, scare.

(ANT.) soothe, allay, reassure, compose, embolden.

territory *(SYN.)* dominion, province, quarter, section, country, division, region, domain, area, place, district.

terror *(SYN.)* fear, alarm, dismay, horror, dread, consternation, fright, panic.

(ANT.) calm, security, assurance, peace.

terse *(SYN.)* concise, incisive, succinct, summary, condensed, compact, neat, pithy, summary.

(ANT.) verbose, wordy, lengthy, prolix.

test *(SYN.)* exam, examination, trial, quiz, analyze, verify, validate.

testify *(SYN.)* depose, warrant, witness, state, attest, swear.

testimony *(SYN.)* evidence, attestation, declaration, proof, witness, confirmation.

(ANT.) refutation, argument, disproof, contradiction.

testy *(SYN.)* ill-natured, irritable, snappish, waspish, fractious, fretful, touchy, peevish, petulant.

(ANT.) pleasant, affable, good- tempered, genial, good-natured.

tether *(SYN.)* tie, hamper, restraint, bridle.

text *(SYN.)* textbook, book, manual.

textile *(SYN.)* material, cloth, goods, fabric.

texture *(SYN.)* construction, structure, composition, grain, finish.

thankful *(SYN.)* obliged, grateful, appreciative.

(ANT.) ungrateful, resenting.

thaw *(SYN.)* liquefy, melt, dissolve.

(ANT.) solidify, freeze.

theater *(SYN.)* arena, playhouse, battlefield, stadium, hall.

theatrical *(SYN.)* ceremonious, melodramatic, stagy, artificial, affected, dramatic, showy, dramatic.

(ANT.) unemotional, subdued, modest, unaffected.

theft *(SYN.)* larceny, robbery, stealing, plunder, burglary, pillage, thievery, depredation.

theme *(SYN.)* motive, topic, argument, subject, thesis, text, point, paper, essay, composition.

theoretical *(SYN.)* bookish, learned, scholarly, pedantic, academic, formal, erudite.

(ANT.) practical, ignorant, commonsense, simple.

theory *(SYN.)* doctrine, guess, presupposition, postulate, assumption, speculation.

(ANT.) practice, verity, fact, proof.

therefore *(SYN.)* consequently, thence so, accordingly, hence, then.

thick *(SYN.)* compressed, heavy, compact, viscous, close, concentrated, crowded, dense.

(ANT.) watery, slim, thin, sparse, dispersed, dissipated.

thief *(SYN.)* burglar, robber, criminal.

thin *(SYN.)* diluted, flimsy, lean, narrow, slender, spare, emaciated, lank, diaphanous, gauzy, meager, slender, tenuous, slim, rare, sparse, scanty, gossamer, scanty, slight.

(ANT.) fat, wide, broad, thick, bulky.

think *(SYN.)* picture, contemplate, ponder, esteem, intend, mean, imagine, deliberate, contemplate, recall, speculate, recollect,

deem, apprehend, consider, devise, plan, judge, purpose, reflect, suppose, assume, meditate, muse.

(ANT.) forget, conjecture, guess.

thirst *(SYN.)* appetite, desire, craving, longing.

thirsty *(SYN.)* craving, arid, dry, dehydrated, parched, desirous.

(ANT.) satisfied.

thorn *(SYN.)* spine, barb, prickle, nettle, bramble.

thorough *(SYN.)* entire, complete, perfect, total, finished, unbroken, careful, thoroughgoing, consummate, undivided.

(ANT.) unfinished, careless, slapdash, imperfect, haphazard, lacking.

thoroughfare *(SYN.)* avenue, street, parkway, highway, boulevard.

(ANT.) byway.

though *(SYN.)* in any case, notwithstanding, however, nevertheless.

thought *(SYN.)* consideration, pensive, attentive, heedful, prudent, dreamy, reflective, introspective, meditation, notion, view, deliberation, sentiment, fancy, idea, impression, reasoning, contemplation, judgment, regard.

(ANT.) thoughtlessness.

thoughtful *(SYN.)* considerate, attentive, dreamy, pensive, provident, introspective, meditative, cautious, heedful, kind, courteous, friendly, pensive.

(ANT.) thoughtless, heedless, inconsiderate, rash, precipitous, selfish.

thoughtless *(SYN.)* inattentive, unconcerned, negligent, lax, desultory, inconsiderate, careless, imprudent, inaccurate, neglectful, indiscreet, remiss.

(ANT.) meticulous, accurate, nice, careful.

thrash *(SYN.)* whip, beat, defeat, flog, punish, flog, strap, thresh.

thread *(SYN.)* yarn, strand, filament, fiber, string, cord.

threadbare *(SYN.)* shabby, tacky, worn, ragged, frayed.

threat *(SYN.)* menace, warning, danger, hazard, jeopardy, omen.

threaten *(SYN.)* caution, warning, forewarn, menace, intimidate, loom.

threatening *(SYN.)* imminent, nigh, approaching, impending, overhanging, sinister, foreboding.

(ANT.) improbable, retreating, afar, distant, remote.

threshold *(SYN.)* edge, verge, start, beginning, doorsill, commencement.

thrift *(SYN.)* prudence, conservation, saving, economy.

thrifty *(SYN.)* saving, economical, sparing, frugal, provident, stingy, saving, parsimonious.

(ANT.) wasteful, spendthrift, intemperate, self-indulgent, extravagant.

thrill *(SYN.)* arouse, rouse, excite, stimulation, excitement, tingle.

(ANT.) bore.

thrive *(SYN.)* succeed, flourish, grow, prosper.

(ANT.) expire, fade, shrivel, die, fail, languish.

throb *(SYN.)* pound, pulsate, palpitate, beat, pulse.

throe *(SYN.)* pang, twinge, distress, suffering, pain, ache, grief, agony.

(ANT.) pleasure, relief, ease, solace, comfort.

throng *(SYN.)* masses, press, crowd, bevy, populace, swarm, rabble, horde, host, mass, teem, mob, multitude.

throttle *(SYN.)* smother, choke, strangle.

through *(SYN.)* completed, done, finished, over.

throughout *(SYN.)* all over, everywhere, during.

throw *(SYN.)* propel, cast, pitch, toss, hurl, send, thrust, fling.

(ANT.) retain, pull, draw, haul, hold

thrust *(SYN.)* jostle, push, promote, crowd, force, drive, hasten, push, press, shove, urge.

(ANT.) ignore, falter, retreat, drag, oppose, halt.

thug *(SYN.)* mobster, hoodlum, mugger, gangster, assassin, gunman.

thump *(SYN.)* blow, strike, knock, jab, poke, pound, beat, clout, bat, rap, bang.

thunderstruck *(SYN.)* amazed, astounded, astonished, awed, flabbergasted, surprised, dumb-founded, bewildered, spellbound.

thus *(SYN.)* hence, therefore, accordingly, so, consequently.

thwart *(SYN.)* defeat, frustrate, prevent, foil, stop, baffle, circumvent, hinder, obstruct, disappoint, balk, outwit.

(ANT.) promote, accomplish, fulfill, help, further.

ticket *(SYN.)* stamp, label, tag, seal, token, pass, summons, certificate, ballot, sticker, slate, citation.

tickle *(SYN.)* delight, entertain, thrill, amuse, titillate, excite.

ticklish *(SYN.)* fragile, delicate, tough, difficult.

tidings *(SYN.)* message, report, information, word, intelligence, news.

tidy *(SYN.)* trim, clear, neat, precise, spruce, orderly, shipshape.

(ANT.) disheveled, unkempt, sloppy, dirty, slovenly.

tie *(SYN.)* bond, join, relationship, bind, restrict, fetter, connect, conjunction, association, alliance, union, fasten, engage, attach, restrain, oblige, link, affinity.

(ANT.) separation, disunion, unfasten, open, loose, untie, free, isolation.

tier *(SYN.)* line, row, level, deck, layer.

tiff *(SYN.)* bicker, squabble, argue, row, clash, dispute, altercation.

tight *(SYN.)* firm, taut, penny-pinching, constricted, snug, taut, parsimonious, secure, fast, strong, sealed, fastened, watertight, locked, close, compact, stingy.

(ANT.) slack, lax, open, relaxed, loose.

till *(SYN.)* plow, work, moneybox, depository, cultivate, vault.

tilt *(SYN.)* slant, slope, incline, tip, lean.

timber *(SYN.)* lumber, wood, logs.

time *(SYN.)* epoch, span, term, age, duration, interim, period, tempo, interval, space, spell, season.

timeless *(SYN.)* unending, lasting, perpetual, endless, immemorial.

(ANT.) temporary, mortal, temporal.

timely *(SYN.)* prompt, exact, punctual,

ready, precise.

(ANT.) slow, dilatory, tardy, late.

timepiece *(SYN.)* clock, watch.

timetable *(SYN.)* list, schedule.

timid *(SYN.)* coy, humble, sheepish, abashed, embarrassed, modest, bashful, diffident, shamefaced, retiring, fearful, faint-hearted, shy, timorous.

(ANT.) gregarious, bold, daring, adventurous, fearless, outgoing.

tinge *(SYN.)* color, tint, dye, stain, flavor, imbue, season, impregnate.

tingle *(SYN.)* shiver, chime, prickle.

tinker *(SYN.)* potter, putter, fiddle with, dawdle, dally, dabble.

tinkle *(SYN.)* sound, peal, ring, jingle, chime, toll.

tint *(SYN.)* color, tinge, dye, stain, hue, tone, shade.

tiny *(SYN.)* minute, little, petty, wee, slight, diminutive, miniature, small, insignificant, trivial, puny.

(ANT.) huge, large, immense, big, enormous.

tip *(SYN.)* point, end, top, peak, upset, tilt, reward, gift, gratuity, clue, hint, suggestion, inkling.

tirade *(SYN.)* outburst, harangue, scolding.

tire *(SYN.)* jade, tucker, bore, weary, exhaust, weaken, wear out, fatigue.

(ANT.) restore, revive, exhilarate, amuse, invigorate, refresh.

tired *(SYN.)* weary, exhausted, fatigued, run-down, sleepy, faint, spent, wearied, worn, jaded.

(ANT.) rested, fresh, hearty, invigorated, energetic, tireless, eager.

tireless *(SYN.)* active, enthusiastic, energetic, strenuous.

(ANT.) exhausted, wearied, fatigued.

tiresome *(SYN.)* dull, boring, monotonous, tedious.

(ANT.) interesting.

titan *SYN.)* colossus, powerhouse, mammoth.

title *(SYN.)* epithet, privilege, name, appellation, claim, denomination, due, heading, ownership, right, deed, designation.

toast *(SYN.)* salutation, pledge, celebration.

toddle *(SYN.)* stumble, wobble, shuffle.

toil *(SYN.)* labor, drudgery, work, travail, performance, business, achievement, employment, occupation, slave, sweat, effort.

(ANT.) recreation, ease, vacation, relax, loll, play, leisure, repose.

token *(SYN.)* mark, sign, sample, indication, evidence, symbol.

tolerant *(SYN.)* extensive, vast, considerate, broad, patient, large, sweeping, liberal, wide.

(ANT.) intolerant, bigoted, biased, restricted, narrow, confined.

tolerate *(SYN.)* endure, allow, bear, authorize, permit, brook, stand, abide.

(ANT.) forbid, protest, prohibit, discriminating, unreasonable.

toll *(SYN.)* impost, burden, rate, assessment, duty, custom, excise, tribute, levy, burden, strain.

(ANT.) reward, wages, gift, remuneration.

tomb *(SYN.)* vault, monument, catacomb, grave, mausoleum.

tone *(SYN.)* noise, sound, mood, manner, expression, cadence.

tongs *(SYN.)* tweezers, hook, grapnel, forceps.

tongue *(SYN.)* diction, lingo, cant, jargon, vernacular, dialect, idiom, speech, phraseology.

(ANT.) nonsense, drivel, babble, gibberish.

too *(SYN.)* furthermore, moreover, similarly, also, in addition, besides, likewise.

tool *(SYN.)* devise, medium, apparatus, agent, implement, utensil, agent, vehicle, instrument.

(ANT.) preventive, hindrance, impediment, obstruction.

top *(SYN.)* crown, pinnacle, peak, tip, cover, cap, zenith, apex, crest, chief, head, summit.

(ANT.) bottom, foundation, base, foot.

topic *(SYN.)* subject, thesis, issue, argument, matter, theme, point.

topple *(SYN.)* collapse, sink, fall, tumble.

torment *(SYN.)* pain, woe, pester, ache, distress, misery, harass, throe, annoy, vex, torture, anguish, suffering, misery.

(ANT.) relief, comfort, ease, gratify, delight.

torpid *(SYN.)* sluggish, idle, lazy, inert, inactive, supine, slothful, indolent, motionless, lethargic.

(ANT.) alert, assiduous, diligent, active.

torpor *(SYN.)* lethargy, daze, numbness, stupor, drowsiness, insensibility, languor.

(ANT.) wakefulness, liveliness, activity, alertness, readiness.

torrent *(SYN.)* flood, downpour, deluge.

torrid *(SYN.)* scorching, ardent, impetuous, passionate, scalding, warm, fiery, hot-blooded, sultry, tropical, intense, sweltering, burning, hot.

(ANT.) passionless, impassive, cold, frigid, apathetic, freezing, phlegmatic, indifferent, temperate.

torso *(SYN.)* form, frame, body.

(ANT.) soul, mind, spirit, intellect.

torture *(SYN.)* anguish, badger, plague, distress, ache, torment, pester, pain, hound, agony, woe, worry, vex, persecute, suffering, throe, afflict, misery.

(ANT.) aid, relief, comfort, ease, support, encourage, mitigation.

toss *(SYN.)* throw, cast, hurl, pitch, tumble, thrust, pitch, fling, propel.

(ANT.) retain, pull, draw, haul, hold.

total *(SYN.)* entire, complete, concluded, full, finished, thorough, whole, entirely, collection, aggregate, conglomeration, unbroken, perfect, undivided, consummate.

(ANT.) part, element, imperfect, unfinished, ingredient, particular, lacking.

tote *(SYN.)* move, transfer, convey, drag, carry.

totter *(SYN.)* falter, stagger, reel, sway, waver, stumble, wobble.

touch *(SYN.)* finger, feel, handle, move, affect, concern, mention, hint, trace, suggestion, knack, skill, ability, talent.

touch-and-go *(SYN.)* dangerous, risky, perilous, hazardous.

touching *(SYN.)* pitiable, affecting, moving, sad, adjunct, bordering, tangent, poignant, tender, effective, impressive, adjacent.

(ANT.) removed, enlivening, animated,

exhilarating.

touchy *(SYN.)* snappish, irritable, fiery, choleric, testy, hot, irascible, nervous, excitable, petulant, sensitive, jumpy, peevish.

(ANT.) composed, agreeable, tranquil, calm, serene, stolid, cool.

tough *(SYN.)* sturdy, difficult, trying, vicious, incorrigible, troublesome, hard, stout, leathery, strong, laborious, inedible, sinewy, cohesive, firm, callous, obdurate, vicious.

(ANT.) vulnerable, submissive, easy, brittle, facile, weak, fragile, compliant, tender, frail.

toughness *(SYN.)* stamina, sturdiness, fortitude, durability, intensity, force, might, stoutness, power, sturdiness, vigor.

(ANT.) weakness, feebleness, infirmity, frailty.

tour *(SYN.)* rove, travel, go, visit, excursion, ramble, journey, roam.

(ANT.) stop, stay.

tourist *(SYN.)* traveler, sightseer, vagabond, voyager.

tournament *(SYN.)* tourney, match, contest, competition.

tout *(SYN.)* vend, importune, peddle, solicit, sell, hawk.

tow *(SYN.)* tug, take out, unsheathe, haul, draw, remove, extract, pull, drag.

(ANT.) propel, drive.

towering *(SYN.)* elevated, exalted, high, lofty, tall, proud, eminent.

(ANT.) base, mean, stunted, small, tiny, low.

town *(SYN.)* hamlet, village, community, municipality.

toxic *(SYN.)* deadly, poisonous, fatal, lethal, harmful.

(ANT.) beneficial.

toy *(SYN.)* play, romp, frolic, gamble, stake, caper, plaything, wager, revel.

trace *(SYN.)* stigma, feature, indication, trait, mark, stain, scar, sign, trial, trace, suggestion, characteristic, vestige, symptoms.

track *(SYN.)* persist, pursue, follow, sign,

mark, spoor, trace, path, route, road, carry, hunt, chase.

(ANT.) escape, evade, abandon, flee, elude.

tract *(SYN.)* area, region, territory, district, expanse, domain.

tractable *(SYN.)* yielding, deferential, submissive, dutiful, compliant, obedient.

(ANT.) rebellious, intractable, insubordinate, obstinate.

trade *(SYN.)* business, traffic, commerce, dealing, craft, occupation, profession, livelihood, swap, barter, exchange.

trademark *(SYN.)* logo, brand name, identification, emblem, insignia, monogram.

tradition *(SYN.)* custom, legend, folklore, belief, rite, practice.

traduce *(SYN.)* defame, malign, vilify, revile, abuse, asperse, scandalize, disparage.

(ANT.) protect, honor, cherish, praise, respect, support, extol.

tragedy *(SYN.)* unhappiness, misfortune, misery, adversity, catastrophe.

tragic *(SYN.)* miserable, unfortunate, depressing, melancholy, mournful.

(ANT.) happy, cheerful, comic.

trail *(SYN.)* persist, pursue, chase, follow, drag, draw, hunt, track.

(ANT.) evade, flee, abandon, elude, escape.

train *(SYN.)* direct, prepare, aim, point, level, teach, drill, tutor, bid, instruct, order, command.

(ANT.) distract, deceive, misguide, misdirect.

traipse *(SYN.)* roam, wander, saunter, meander.

trait *(SYN.)* characteristic, feature, attribute, peculiarity, mark, quality, property.

traitor *(SYN.)* turncoat, betrayer, spy, double-dealer, conspirator.

traitorous *(SYN.)* disloyal, faithless, apostate, false, recreant, perfidious, treasonable, treacherous.

(ANT.) devoted, true, loyal, constant.

tramp *(SYN.)* bum, beggar, rover, hobo, march, stamp, stomp, vagabond, wanderer, vagrant.

(ANT.) laborer, worker, gentleman.

trample *(SYN.)* crush, stomp, squash.

tranquil *(SYN.)* composed, calm, dispassionate, imperturbable, peaceful, pacific, placid, quiet, still, serene, undisturbed, unruffled.

(ANT.) frantic, stormy, excited, disturbed, upset, turbulent, wild.

tranquillity *(SYN.)* calmness, calm, hush, peace, quiet, quiescence, quietude, repose, serenity, rest, stillness, silence, placid.

(ANT.) disturbance, agitation, excitement, tumult, noise.

transact *(SYN.)* conduct, manage, execute, treat, perform.

transaction *(SYN.)* business, deal, affair, deed, settlement, occurrence, negotiation, proceeding.

transcend *(SYN.)* overstep, overshadow, exceed.

transcribe *(SYN.)* write, copy, rewrite, record.

transfer *(SYN.)* dispatch, send, transmit, remove, transport, transplant, consign, move, shift, reasign, assign, relegate.

transform *(SYN.)* change, convert, alter, modify, transfigure, shift, vary, veer.

(ANT.) establish, continue, settle, preserve, stabilize.

transgression *(SYN.)* atrocity, indignity, offense, insult, outrage, aggression, injustice, crime, misdeed, trespass, sin, wrong, vice.

(ANT.) innocence, morality, gentleness, right.

transient *(SYN.)* ephemeral, evanescent, brief, fleeting, momentary, temporary.

(ANT.) immortal, abiding, permanent, lasting, timeless, established.

transition *(SYN.)* change, variation, modification.

translate *(SYN.)* decipher, construe, decode, elucidate, explicate, explain, interpret, solve, render, unravel.

(ANT.) distort, falsify, misinterpret, confuse, misconstrue.

transmit *(SYN.)* confer, convey, communicate, divulge, disclose, impart, send, inform, relate, notify, reveal, dispatch, tell.

(ANT.) withhold, hide, conceal.

transparent *(SYN.)* crystalline, clear, limpid, lucid, translucent, thin, evident, manifest, plain, explicit, obvious, open.
(ANT.) opaque, muddy, turbid, thick, questionable, ambiguous.

transpire *(SYN.)* befall, bechance, betide, happen, chance, occur.

transport *(SYN.)* carry, bear, convey, remove, move, shift, enrapture, transfer, lift, entrance, ravish, stimulate.

transpose *(SYN.)* change, switch, reverse.

trap *(SYN.)* artifice, bait, ambush, intrigue, net, lure, pitfall, ensnare, deadfall, snare, ruse, entrap, bag, trick, stratagem, wile.

trash *(SYN.)* refuse, garbage, rubbish, waste.

trashy *(SYN.)* insignificant, worthless, slight.

trauma *(SYN.)* ordeal, upheaval, jolt, shock, disturbance.

travail *(SYN.)* suffering, torment, anxiety, distress, anguish, misery, ordeal.

travel *(SYN.)* journey, go, touring, ramble, rove, voyage, cruise, tour, roam.
(ANT.) stop, stay, remain, hibernate.

travesty *(SYN.)* farce, joke, misrepresentation, counterfeit, mimicry.

treachery *(SYN.)* collusion, cabal, combination, intrigue, conspiracy, disloyalty, betrayal, treason, plot.
(ANT.) allegiance, steadfastness, loyalty.

treason *(SYN.)* cabal, combination, betrayal, sedition, collusion, intrigue, conspiracy, machination, disloyalty, treachery, plot.

treasure *(SYN.)* cherish, hold dear, abundance, guard, prize, appreciate, value, riches, wealth, foster, sustain, nurture.
(ANT.) disregard, neglect, dislike, abandon, reject.

treat *(SYN.)* employ, avail, manipulate, exploit, operate, utilize, exert, act, exercise, practice, handle, manage, deal, entertain, indulge, host, negotiate, tend, attend, heal, use.
(ANT.) neglect, overlook, ignore, waste.

treaty *(SYN.)* compact, agreement, pact, bargain, covenant, alliance, marriage.
(ANT.) schism, separation, divorce.

trek *(SYN.)* tramp, hike, plod, trudge.

tremble *(SYN.)* flutter, jolt, jar, agitate, quake, quiver, quaver, rock, shake shudder, shiver, sway, vibrate, waver.

trembling *(SYN.)* apprehension, alarm, dread, fright, fear, horror, terror, panic.
(ANT.) composure, calmness, tranquillity, serenity.

tremendous *(SYN.)* enormous, huge, colossal, gigantic, great, large.

tremor *(SYN.)* flutter, vibration, palpitation.

trench *(SYN.)* gully, gorge, ditch, gulch, moat, dugout, trough.

trenchant *(SYN.)* clear, emphatic, forceful, impressive, meaningful.

trend *(SYN.)* inclination, tendency, drift, course, tendency, direction.

trendy *(SYN.)* modish, faddish, stylish, voguish, popular, current.

trepidation *(SYN.)* apprehension, alarm, dread, fright, fear, horror, panic, terror.
(ANT.) boldness, bravery, fearlessness, courage, assurance.

trespass *(SYN.)* atrocity, indignity, affront, insult, outrage, offense, aggression, crime, misdeed, injustice, vice, wrong, sin.
(ANT.) evacuate, vacate, relinquish, abandon.

trespasser *(SYN.)* invader, intruder, encroacher.

trial *(SYN.)* experiment, ordeal, proof, test, examination, attempt, effort, endeavor, essay, affliction, misery, hardship, suffering, difficulty, misfortune, tribulation, trouble.
(ANT.) consolation, alleviation.

tribe *(SYN.)* group, race, clan, bunch.

tribulation *(SYN.)* anguish, distress, agony, grief, misery, sorrow, torment, suffering, woe, disaster, calamity, evil, trouble, misfortune.
(ANT.) elation, delight, joy, fun, pleasure.

tribunal *(SYN.)* arbitrators, judges, decisionmakers, judiciary.

trick *(SYN.)* artifice, antic, deception, device, cheat, fraud, hoax, guile, imposture, ruse, ploy, stratagem, trickery, deceit, jest, joke, prank, defraud, subterfuge, wile, stunt.

(ANT.) *exposure, candor, openness, honesty, sincerity.*

trickle *(SYN.)* drip, drop, dribble, leak, seep.

tricky *(SYN.)* artifice, antic, covert, cunning, foxy, crafty, furtive, guileful, insidious, sly, shrews, stealthy, surreptitious, subtle, underhand.

(ANT.) *frank, candid, ingenuous, sincere, open.*

trifling *(SYN.)* insignificant, frivolous, paltry, petty, trivial, small, unimportant.

(ANT.) *momentous, serious, important, weighty.*

trigger *(SYN.)* generate, provoke, prompt, motivate, activate.

trim *(SYN.)* nice, clear, orderly, precise, tidy, spruce, adorn, bedeck, clip, shave, prune, cut, shear, compact, neat, decorate, embellish, garnish.

(ANT.) *deface, deform, spoil, mar, important, serious, momentous, weighty.*

trimmings *(SYN.)* accessories, adornments, decorations, garnish, ornaments.

trinket *(SYN.)* bead, token, memento, bauble, charm, knickknack.

trio *(SYN.)* threesome, triad, triple.

trip *(SYN.)* expedition, cruise, stumble, err, journey, jaunt, passage, blunder, bungle, slip, excursion, tour, pilgrimage, voyage, travel.

trite *(SYN.)* common, banal, hackneyed, ordinary, stereotyped, stale.

(ANT.) *modern, fresh, momentous, stimulating, novel, new.*

triumph *(SYN.)* conquest, achievement, success, prevail, win, jubilation, victory.

(ANT.) *succumb, failure, defeat.*

triumphant *(SYN.)* celebrating, exultant, joyful, exhilarated, smug.

trivial *(SYN.)* insignificant, frivolous, paltry, petty, trifling, small, unimportant.

(ANT.) *momentous, important weighty, serious.*

troops *(SYN.)* militia, troopers, recruits, soldiers, enlisted men.

trophy *(SYN.)* award, memento, honor, testimonial, prize.

tropical *(SYN.)* sultry, sweltering, humid, torrid.

trouble *(SYN.)* anxiety, affliction, calamity, distress, hardship, grief, pain, misery, sorrow, woe, bother, annoyance, care, embarrassment, irritation, torment, pains, worry, disorder, problem, disturbance, care, effort, exertion, toil, inconvenience, misfortune, labor.

(ANT.) *console, accommodate, gratify, soothe, joy, peace.*

troublemaker *(SYN.)* rebel, scamp, agitator, demon, devil, ruffian.

troublesome *(SYN.)* bothersome, annoying, distressing, irksome, disturbing, trying, arduous, vexatious, difficult, burdensome, laborious, tedious.

(ANT.) *amusing, accommodating, gratifying, easy, pleasant.*

trounce *(SYN.)* lash, flog, switch, whack, punish, whip, stomp.

truant *(SYN.)* delinquent, absentee, vagrant, malingerer.

truce *(SYN.)* armistice, ceasefire, interval, break, intermission, respite.

trudge *(SYN.)* march, trek, lumber, hike.

true *(SYN.)* actual, authentic, accurate, correct, exact, genuine, real, veracious, veritable, constant, honest, faithful, loyal, reliable, valid, legitimate, steadfast, sincere, trustworthy.

(ANT.) *erroneous, counterfeit, false, spurious, fictitious, faithless, inconstant, fickle.*

truly *(SYN.)* indeed, actually, precisely, literally, really, factually.

truncate *(SYN.)* prune, clip, pare, shorten.

truss *(SYN.)* girder, brace, framework, shoring.

trust *(SYN.)* credence, confidence, dependence, reliance, faith, trust, depend on, rely on, reckon on, believe, hope, credit, commit, entrust, confide.

(ANT.) *incredulity, doubt, skepticism, mistrust.*

trusted *(SYN.)* trustworthy, reliable, true, loyal, staunch, devoted.

trustworthy *(SYN.)* dependable, certain, reliable, secure, safe.

(ANT.) fallible, dubious, questionable, un-reliable, uncertain.

truth *(SYN.)* actuality, authenticity, accuracy, correctness, exactness, honesty, fact, rightness, truthfulness, veracity, verity.
(ANT.) falsity, falsehood, fiction, lie, untruth.

truthful *(SYN.)* frank, candid, honest, sincere, open, veracious, accurate, correct, exact, reliable.
(ANT.) misleading, sly, deceitful.

try *(SYN.)* endeavor, attempt, strive, struggle, undertake, afflict, test, prove, torment, trouble, essay, examine, analyze, investigate, effort, aim, design, aspire, intend.
(ANT.) decline, ignore, abandon, omit, neglect, comfort, console.

trying *(SYN.)* bothersome, annoying, distressing, irksome, disturbing, troublesome, arduous, vexatious, difficult, tedious.
(ANT.) amusing, easy, accommodating, pleasant, gratifying.

tryout *(SYN.)* audition, trial, chance, test.

tryst *(SYN.)* rendezvous, meeting, appointment.

tub *(SYN.)* basin, vessel, sink, bowl.

tube *(SYN.)* hose, pipe, reed.

tubular *(SYN.)* hollow, cylindrical.

tuck *(SYN.)* crease, fold, gather, bend.

tuft *(SYN.)* bunch, group, cluster.

tug *(SYN.)* pull, wrench, tow, haul, draw, yank, jerk.

tuition *(SYN.)* instruction, schooling, teaching, education.

tumble *(SYN.)* toss, trip, fall, sprawl, wallow, lurch, flounder, plunge, topple, stumble.

tumult *(SYN.)* chaos, agitation, commotion, confusion, disarray, disarrangement, disorder, noise, hubbub, ferment, stir, to do, ado, disturbance, uproar, turmoil.
(ANT.) peacefulness, order, peace, certainty, tranquillity.

tune *(SYN.)* song, concord, harmony, air, melody, strain.
(ANT.) aversion, discord, antipathy.

tunnel *(SYN.)* passage, grotto, cave.

turbid *(SYN.)* dark, cloudy, thick, muddy, murky.

turbulent *(SYN.)* gusty, blustery, inclement, rough, roaring, stormy, tempestuous, disorderly, violent, tumultuous, unruly, windy.
(ANT.) clear, calm, quiet, peaceful, tranquil.

turf *(SYN.)* lawn, grassland, sod, grass.

turmoil *(SYN.)* chaos, agitation, commotion, confusion, disarray, disarrangement, disorder, jumble, uproar, ferment, pandemonium.
(ANT.) order, peace, certainty, quiet, tranquillity.

turn *(SYN.)* circulate, circle, invert, rotate, revolve, spin, twist, twirl, whirl, wheel, avert, reverse, become, sour, spoil, ferment, deviate, deflect, divert, swerve, change, alter, transmute.
(ANT.) fix, stand, arrest, stop, continue, endure, proceed, perpetuate.

turncoat *(SYN.)* renegade, defector, deserter, betrayer, traitor.
(ANT.) loyalist.

turret *(SYN.)* watchtower, belfry, steeple, tower, cupola, lookout.

tussle *(SYN.)* wrestle, struggle, contend, battle, fight, scuffle.

tutor *(SYN.)* instruct, prime, school, teach, train, prepare, drill.

tweak *(SYN.)* squeeze, pinch, nip.

twig *(SYN.)* sprig, branch, shoot, stem.

twilight *(SYN.)* sunset, sundown, nightfall, eventide, dusk.

twin *(SYN.)* lookalike, imitation, copy, double, replica.

twine *(SYN.)* string, cordage, rope, cord.

twinge *(SYN.)* smart, pang, pain.

twinkle *(SYN.)* shine, gleam, glisten, sparkle, glitter, shimmer, scintillate.

twirl *(SYN.)* rotate, spin, wind, turn, pivot, wheel, swivel, whirl.

twist *(SYN.)* bow, bend, crook, intertwine, curve, incline, deflect, lean, braid, distort, contort, warp, interweave, stoop, turn.
(ANT.) resist, break, straighten, stiffen.

twitch *(SYN.)* fidget, shudder, jerk.

two-faced *(SYN.)* deceitful, insincere, hypocritical, false, untrustworthy.

(ANT.) straightforward, honest.

tycoon *(SYN.)* millionaire, industrialist, businessman.

tyke *(SYN.)* rascal, urchin, brat, ragamuffin, imp.

type *(SYN.)* mark, emblem, sign, category, symbol, character, class, description, nature, kind, variety, example, sample, sort, stamp, model, exemplar, pattern.

(ANT.) deviation, monstrosity, eccentricity, peculiarity.

typhoon *(SYN.)* hurricane, cyclone, storm, tornado, whirlwind, twister.

typical *(SYN.)* common, accustomed, conventional, familiar, customary, habitual ordinary, characteristic, normal, plain, representative, regular, usual.

(ANT.) marvelous, extraordinary, remarkable, odd, atypical, uncommon, strange.

typify *(SYN.)* symbolize, illustrate, signify, represent, incarnate.

tyrannize *(SYN.)* oppress, victimize, threaten, brutalize, coerce.

tyrannous *(SYN.)* arbitrary, absolute, authoritative, despotic.

(ANT.) conditional, accountable, contingent, qualified, dependent.

tyrant *(SYN.)* dictator, autocrat, despot, oppressor, slave driver, disciplinarian, persecutor.

tyro *(SYN.)* amateur, beginner, novice, freshman, rookie, student, apprentice.

(ANT.) professional, veteran.

U

ugly *(SYN.)* hideous, homely, plain, deformed, repellent, uncomely, repulsive, ill-natured, unsightly, nasty, unpleasant, wicked, disagreeable, spiteful, surly, vicious.

(ANT.) beautiful, fair, pretty, attractive, handsome, comely, good, harmless, pleasant.

ultimate *(SYN.)* extreme, latest, final, concluding, decisive, hindmost, last, terminal, utmost, greatest, maximum.

(ANT.) foremost, opening, first, beginning,

initial.

umbrage *(SYN.)* anger, displeasure, resentment, better.

(ANT.) happy, harmony.

umbrella *(SYN.)* cover, shade, parasol, shield.

unable *(SYN.)* ineffective, ineffectual, inept.

(ANT.) effective.

umpire *(SYN.)* judge, referee, arbitrator.

unadulterated *(SYN.)* genuine, clear, clean, immaculate, spotless, pure, absolute, untainted, sheer, bare.

(ANT.) foul, sullied, corrupt, tainted, polluted, tarnished, defiled.

unalterable *(SYN.)* fixed, unchangeable, steadfast, inflexible.

unanimity *(SYN.)* accord, unity, agreement.

unannounced *(SYN.)* hasty, precipitate, abrupt, unexpected.

(ANT.) courteous, expected, anticipated.

unassuming *(SYN.)* humble, lowly, compliant, modest, plain, meek, simple, unostentatious, retiring, submissive, unpretentious.

(ANT.) haughty, showy, pompous, proud, vain, presumptuous, arrogant, boastful.

unattached *(SYN.)* apart, separate, unmarried, single, free, independent.

(ANT.) committed, involved, entangled.

unavoidable *(SYN.)* inescapable, certain, inevitable, unpreventable.

unawares *(SYN.)* abruptly, suddenly, unexpectedly, off guard.

unbalanced *(SYN.)* crazy, mad, insane, deranged.

unbearable *(SYN.)* insufferable, intolerable, unacceptable, oppressive.

(ANT.) tolerable, acceptable, bearable.

unbeliever *(SYN.)* dissenter, apostate, heretic, schismatic, nonconformist, sectary, sectarian.

unbending *(SYN.)* firm, inflexible, decided, determined, obstinate.

(ANT.) flexible.

unbiased *(SYN.)* honest, equitable, fair, impartial, reasonable, unprejudiced, just.

(ANT.) partial, fraudulent, dishonorable.

unbroken *(SYN.)* complete, uninterrupted,

continuous, whole.

unburden *(SYN.)* clear, disentangle, divest, free.

uncanny *(SYN.)* amazing, remarkable, extraordinary, strange.

uncertain *(SYN.)* dim, hazy, indefinite, obscure, indistinct, unclear, undetermined, unsettled, ambiguous, unsure, doubtful, questionable, dubious, vague.
(ANT.) explicit, lucid, specific, certain, unmistakable, precise, clear.

uncertainty *(SYN.)* distrust, doubt, hesitation, incredulity, scruple, ambiguity, skepticism, uncertainty, suspense, suspicion, unbelief.
(ANT.) faith, belief, certainty, conviction, determination.

uncivil *(SYN.)* impolite, rude, discourteous.
(ANT.) polite.

uncivilized *(SYN.)* barbaric, barbarous, barbarian, brutal, crude, inhuman, cruel, merciless, rude, remorseless, uncultured, savage, unrelenting.
(ANT.) humane, kind, polite, civilized, refined.

unclad *(SYN.)* exposed, nude, naked, bare, stripped, defenseless, uncovered, open, unprotected.
(ANT.) concealed, protected, clothed, covered, dressed.

uncommon *(SYN.)* unusual, rare, odd, scarce, strange, peculiar, queer, exceptional, remarkable.
(ANT.) ordinary, usual.

uncompromising *(SYN.)* determined, dogged, firm, immovable, contumacious, headstrong, inflexible, obdurate, intractable, obstinate, pertinacious, stubborn, unyielding.
(ANT.) docile, compliant, amenable, yielding, submissive, pliable.

unconcern *(SYN.)* disinterestedness, impartiality, indifference, apathy, insensibility, neutrality.
(ANT.) affection, fervor, passion, ardor.

unconditional *(SYN.)* unqualified, unrestricted, arbitrary, absolute, pure, complete, actual, authoritative, perfect, entire, ulti-

mate, tyrannous.
(ANT.) conditional, contingent, accountable, dependent, qualified.

unconscious *(SYN.)* lethargic, numb, comatose.

uncouth *(SYN.)* green, harsh, crude, coarse, ill-prepared, rough, raw, unfinished, unrefined, vulgar, rude, impolite, discourteous, unpolished, ill-mannered, crass.
(ANT.) well-prepared, cultivated, refined, civilized, finished.

uncover *(SYN.)* disclose, discover, betray, divulge, expose, reveal, impart, show.
(ANT.) conceal, hide, cover, obscure, cloak.

undependable *(SYN.)* changeable, unstable, uncertain, shifty, irresponsible.
(ANT.) stable, dependable, trustworthy.

under *(SYN.)* beneath, underneath, following, below, lower, downward.
(ANT.) over, above, up, higher.

undercover *(SYN.)* hidden, secret.

undergo *(SYN.)* endure, feel, stand, bear, indulge, suffer, sustain, experience, let, allow, permit, feel, tolerate.
(ANT.) overcome, discard, exclude, banish.

underhand *(SYN.)* sly, secret, sneaky, secretive, stealthy, crafty.
(ANT.) honest, open, direct, frank.

undermine *(SYN.)* demoralize, thwart, erode, weaken, subvert, sabotage.

underscore *(SYN.)* emphasize, stress.

understand *(SYN.)* apprehend, comprehend, appreciate, conceive, discern, know, grasp, hear, learn, realize, see, perceive.
(ANT.) misunderstand, mistake, misapprehend, ignore.

understanding *(SYN.)* agreement, coincidence, concord, accordance, concurrence, harmony, unison, compact, contract, arrangement, bargain, covenant, stipulation.
(ANT.) variance, difference, discord, dissension, disagreement.

understudy *(SYN.)* deputy, agent, proxy, representative, agent, alternate, lieutenant, substitute.
(ANT.) head, principal, sovereign, master.

undertake *(SYN.)* venture, attempt.

undertaking *(SYN.)* effort, endeavor, attempt, experiment, trial, essay.

(ANT.) laziness, neglect, inaction.

undersigned *(SYN.)* casual, chance, contingent, accidental, fortuitous, incidental, unintended.

(ANT.) decreed, planned, willed, calculated.

undesirable *(SYN.)* obnoxious, distasteful, objectionable, repugnant.

(ANT.) appealing, inviting, attractive.

undivided *(SYN.)* complete, intact, entire, integral, total, perfect, unimpaired, whole.

(ANT.) partial, incomplete.

undoing *(SYN.)* ruin, downfall, destruction, failure, disgrace.

undying *(SYN.)* endless, deathless, eternal, everlasting, ceaseless, immortal, infinite, perpetual, timeless.

(ANT.) transient, mortal, temporal, ephemeral, finite, impermanent.

unearthly *(SYN.)* metaphysical, ghostly, miraculous, marvelous, preternatural, superhuman, spiritual, foreign, strange, weird, supernatural.

(ANT.) physical, plain, human, natural, common, mundane.

uneducated *(SYN.)* uncultured, ignorant, illiterate, uninformed, unlearned, untaught, unlettered.

(ANT.) erudite, cultured, educated, literate, formed.

unemployed *(SYN.)* inert, inactive, idle, jobless, unoccupied.

(ANT.) working, occupied, active, industrious, employed.

uneven *(SYN.)* remaining, single, odd, unmatched, rugged, gnarled, irregular.

(ANT.) matched, even, flat, smooth.

unexceptional *(SYN.)* commonplace, trivial, customary.

unexpected *(SYN.)* immediate, hasty, surprising, instantaneous, unforeseen, abrupt, rapid, startling, sudden.

(ANT.) slowly, expected, gradual, predicted, anticipated, planned.

unfaithful *(SYN.)* treacherous, disloyal, deceitful, capricious.

(ANT.) true, loyal, steadfast, faithful.

unfasten *(SYN.)* open, expand, spread, exhibit, unbar, unlock, unfold, unseal.

(ANT.) shut, hide, conceal, close.

unfavorable *(SYN.)* antagonistic, contrary, adverse, opposed, opposite, disastrous, counteractive, unlucky.

(ANT.) benign, fortunate, lucky, propitious.

unfeeling *(SYN.)* hard, rigorous, cruel, stern, callous, numb, hard, strict, unsympathetic, severe.

(ANT.) tender, gentle, lenient. humane.

unfold *(SYN.)* develop, create, elaborate, amplify, evolve, mature, expand.

(ANT.) wither, restrict, contract, stunt, compress.

unfurnished *(SYN.)* naked, mere, bare, exposed, stripped, plain, open, simple.

(ANT.) concealed, protected, covered.

ungainly *(SYN.)* clumsy, awkward, bungling, clownish, gawky.

(ANT.) dexterous, graceful, elegant.

unhappy *(SYN.)* sad, miserable, distressed, depressed, wretched.

(ANT.) joyful, happy, joyous, cheerful.

unhealthy *(SYN.)* infirm, sick, diseased, sickly.

(ANT.) vigorous, well, healthy, hale.

uniform *(SYN.)* methodical, natural, customary, orderly, normal, consistent, ordinary, regular, unvarying, unchanging, systematic, steady, unvaried.

(ANT.) rare, unusual, erratic, abnormal, exceptional, changeable.

unimportant *(SYN.)* petty, trivial, paltry, trifling, insignificant, indifferent, minor, petty.

uninformed *(SYN.)* illiterate, uncultured, uneducated, ignorant, unlearned, untaught, unlettered.

(ANT.) informed, literate, erudite, cultured, educated.

uninhibited *(SYN.)* loose, open, liberated, free.

(ANT.) constrained, tense, suppressed.

unintelligible *(SYN.)* ambiguous, cryptic, dark, cloudy, abstruse, dusky, mysterious, indistinct, obscure, vague.

(ANT.) lucid, distinct, bright, clear.

uninteresting *(SYN.)* burdensome, dilatory, dreary, dull, boring, slow humdrum, monotonous, sluggish, tedious, tardy, wearisome, tiresome.

(ANT.) entertaining, exciting, quick, amusing.

union *(SYN.)* fusion, incorporation, combination, joining, concurrence, solidarity, agreement, unification, concord, harmony, alliance, unanimity, coalition, confederacy, amalgamation, league, concert, marriage.

(ANT.) schism, disagreement, separation, discord.

unique *(SYN.)* exceptional, matchless, distinctive, choice, peculiar, singular, rare, sole, single, incomparable, uncommon, solitary, unequaled.

(ANT.) typical, ordinary, commonplace, frequent, common.

unison *(SYN.)* harmony, concurrence, understanding, accordance, concord, agreeable, coincidence.

(ANT.) disagreement, difference, discord, variance.

unite *(SYN.)* attach, blend, amalgamate, combine, conjoin, associate, connect, embody, consolidate, join, link, fuse, unify, merge.

(ANT.) sever, divide, separate, sever, disrupt, disconnect.

universal *(SYN.)* frequent, general, popular, common, familiar, prevailing, prevalent, usual.

(ANT.) scarce, odd, regional, local, extraordinary, exceptional.

unkempt *(SYN.)* sloppy, rumpled, untidy, messy, bedraggled.

(ANT.) presentable, well-groomed, tidy, neat.

unkind *(SYN.)* unfeeling, unsympathetic, unpleasant, cruel, harsh.

(ANT.) considerate, sympathetic, amiable, kind.

unlawful *(SYN.)* illegitimate, illicit, illegal, outlawed, criminal, prohibited.

(ANT.) permitted, law, honest, legal, legitimate, authorized.

unlike *(SYN.)* dissimilar, different, distinct, contrary, diverse, divergent, opposite, incongruous, variant, miscellaneous, divers.

(ANT.) conditional, accountable, contingent, qualified, dependent.

unlucky *(SYN.)* cursed, inauspicious, unfortunate.

(ANT.) prosperous, fortunate, blessed.

unmerciful *(SYN.)* cruel, merciless, heartless, brutal.

unmistakable *(SYN.)* clear, patent, plain, visible, obvious.

unnecessary *(SYN.)* pointless, needless, superfluous, purposeless.

unoccupied *(SYN.)* empty, vacant, uninhabited.

unparalleled *(SYN.)* peerless, unequaled, rare, unique, unmatched.

unpleasant *(SYN.)* offensive, disagreeable, repulsive, obnoxious, unpleasing.

unqualified *(SYN.)* inept, unfit, incapable, incompetent, unquestioned, absolute, utter.

unreasonable *(SYN.)* foolish, absurd, irrational, inconsistent, nonsensical, ridiculous, silly.

(ANT.) reasonable, sensible, sound, consistent, rational.

unruffled *(SYN.)* calm, smooth, serene, unperturbed.

unruly *(SYN.)* unmanageable, disorganized, disorderly, disobedient.

(ANT.) orderly.

unsafe *(SYN.)* hazardous, insecure, critical, dangerous, perilous, menacing, risky, precarious, threatening.

(ANT.) protected, secure, firm, safe.

unselfish *(SYN.)* bountiful, generous, liberal, giving, beneficent, magnanimous, openhanded, munificent.

(ANT.) miserly, stingy, greedy, selfish, covetous.

unsightly *(SYN.)* ugly, unattractive, hideous.

unsophisticated *(SYN.)* frank, candid, artless, ingenuous, naive, open, simple, natural.

(ANT.) sophisticated, worldly, cunning, crafty.

unsound *(SYN.)* feeble, flimsy, weak, fragile, sick, unhealthy, diseased, invalid, faulty, false.

unstable *(SYN.)* fickle, fitful, inconstant, capricious, restless, variable.

(ANT.) steady, stable, trustworthy, constant.

unswerving *(SYN.)* fast, firm, inflexible, constant, secure, stable, solid, steady, steadfast, unyielding.

(ANT.) sluggish, insecure, unsteady, unstable, loose, slow.

untainted *(SYN.)* genuine, pure, spotless, clean, clear, unadulterated, guiltless, innocent, chaste, modest, undefiled, sincere, virgin.

(ANT.) polluted, tainted, sullied, tarnished, defiled, corrupt, foul.

untamed *(SYN.)* fierce, savage, uncivilized, barbarous, outlandish, rude, undomesticated, frenzied, mad, turbulent, impetuous, wanton, boisterous, wayward, stormy, extravagant, wild, tempestuous, foolish, rash, giddy, reckless.

(ANT.) quiet, gentle, calm, civilized, placid.

untidy *(SYN.)* messy, sloppy, disorderly, slovenly.

untoward *(SYN.)* disobedient, contrary, peevish, fractious, forward, petulant, obstinate, intractable, stubborn, ungovernable.

(ANT.) docile, tractable, obliging, agreeable.

unusual *(SYN.)* capricious, abnormal, devious, eccentric, aberrant, irregular, variable, remarkable, extraordinary, odd, peculiar, uncommon, strange, exceptional, unnatural.

(ANT.) methodical, regular, usual, fixed, ordinary.

unyielding *(SYN.)* fast, firm, inflexible, constant, solid, secure, stable, steadfast, unswerving, steady.

(ANT.) sluggish, slow, insecure, loose, unsteady, unstable.

upbraid *(SYN.)* blame, censure, berate, admonish, rate, lecture, rebuke, reprimand, scold, vituperate.

(ANT.) praise, commend, approve.

uphold *(SYN.)* justify, espouse, assert, defend, maintain, vindicate.

(ANT.) oppose, submit, assault, deny, attack.

upright *(SYN.)* undeviating, right, unswerving, direct, erect, unbent, straight, fair, vertical.

(ANT.) bent, dishonest, crooked, circuitous, winding.

uprising *(SYN.)* revolution, mutiny, revolt, rebellion.

uproar *(SYN.)* noise, disorder, commotion, tumult, disturbance.

upset *(SYN.)* disturb, harass, bother, annoy, haunt, molest, inconvenience, perplex, pester, tease, plague, trouble, worry, overturned, toppled, upend, capsize, fluster, agitate.

(ANT.) soothe, relieve, please, gratify.

upshot *(SYN.)* conclusion, result, outcome.

urbane *(SYN.)* civil, considerate, cultivated, courteous, genteel, polite, accomplished, refined.

(ANT.) rude, uncouth, boorish, uncivil.

urge *(SYN.)* craving, desire, longing, lust, appetite, aspiration, yearning, incite, coax, entice, force, drive, prod, press, plead, persuade, recommend, advise.

(ANT.) loathing, hate, distaste, aversion, coerce, deter, restrain, compel, dissuade, discourage.

urgency *(SYN.)* emergency, exigency, pass, pinch, strait, crisis.

urgent *(SYN.)* critical, crucial, exigent, imperative, impelling, insistent, necessary, instant, serious, pressing, cogent, important, importunate, immediate.

(ANT.) trivial, unimportant, petty, insignificant.

usage *(SYN.)* use, treatment, custom, practice, tradition.

use *(SYN.)* custom, practice, habit, training, usage, manner, apply, avail employ, operate, utilize, exert, exhaust, handle, manage, accustom, inure, train, exploit, manipulate, spend, expend, consume, exercise, work.

(ANT.) disuse, neglect, waste, ignore, overlook, idleness.

useful *(SYN.)* beneficial, helpful, good, serviceable, wholesome, advantageous.
(ANT.) harmful, injurious, deleterious, destructive, detrimental.

usefulness *(SYN.)* price, merit, utility, value, excellence, virtue, worthiness.
(ANT.) useless, cheapness, valuelessness, uselessness.

useless *(SYN.)* bootless, empty, idle, pointless, vain, valueless, worthless, abortive, fruitless, unavailing, ineffectual, vapid.
(ANT.) profitable, potent, effective.

usher *(SYN.)* guide, lead.

usual *(SYN.)* customary, common, familiar, general, normal, habitual, accustomed, everyday, ordinary, regular.
(ANT.) irregular, exceptional, rare, extraordinary, abnormal.

utensil *(SYN.)* instrument, tool, vehicle, apparatus, device, implement.
(ANT.) preventive, hindrance, obstruction.

utilize *(SYN.)* use, apply, devote, busy, employ, occupy, avail.
(ANT.) reject, banish, discharge, discard.

utopian *(SYN.)* perfect, ideal, faultless, exemplary, supreme, visionary, unreal.
(ANT.) real, material, imperfect, actual, faulty.

utter *(SYN.)* full, perfect, whole, finished, entire, speak, say, complete, superlative, supreme, total, absolute, pronounce, unqualified, downright, express, voice, declare.
(ANT.) imperfect, deficient, lacking, faulty, incomplete.

utterance *(SYN.)* expression, speech, articulation, communication, remark.

V

vacancy *(SYN.)* void, emptiness, vacuum, hollowness, blankness, vacuity, depletion, nothingness.
(ANT.) plenitude, fullness, profusion, completeness.

vacant *(SYN.)* barren, empty, blank, bare, unoccupied, void.
(ANT.) filled, packed, employed, full, replete, busy, engaged.

vacate *(SYN.)* abjure, relinquish, abdicate, renounce, abandon, resign, surrender, desert, waive.
(ANT.) stay, uphold, maintain.

vacation rest, holiday, break.
(ANT.) labor, work, routine.

vacillate *(SYN.)* hesitate, oscillate, undulate, change, fluctuate, vary.
(ANT.) persist, stick, decide.

vacillating *(SYN.)* contrary, illogical, contradictory, contrary, inconsistent, incongruous, incompatible, paradoxical, irreconcilable, unsteady, wavering.
(ANT.) correspondent, congruous, consistent, compatible.

vacuity *(SYN.)* space, emptiness, vacuum, void, blank, nothingness, ignorance, unawareness, senselessness, mindlessness, chatter, nonsense, froth, absurdity.
(ANT.) matter, fullness, content, substance, knowledge, intelligence.

vacuous *(SYN.)* dull, blank, uncomprehending, foolish, thoughtless, distracted, absentminded.
(ANT.) responsive, alert, attentive, bright, intelligent, aware.

vacuum *(SYN.)* void, gap, emptiness, hole, chasm, nothingness.

vagabond *(SYN.)* pauper, ragamuffin, scrub, beggar, mendicant, hobo, starveling, tramp.
(ANT.) responsible, established, rooted, installed, reliable.

vagary *(SYN.)* notion, whim, fantasy, fancy, daydream, caprice, conceit, quirk, whimsy, impulse.

vagrant *(SYN.)* hobo, rover, tramp, beggar, wanderer, vagabond.
(ANT.) settled, worker, laborer, rooted, ambitious, gentleman.

vague *(SYN.)* indefinite, hazy, dim, indistinct, ambiguous, obscure, undetermined, unclear, unsure.
(ANT.) certain, spelled out, specific, lucid, clear, definite, distinct, explicit, precise, unequivocal.

vain *(SYN.)* fruitless, empty, bootless, futile, idle, abortive, ineffectual, una-

vailing, vapid, pointless, valueless, useless, trivial, unfruitful, unsuccessful, conceited.
(ANT.) meek, modest, potent, rewarding, self-effacing, diffident, profitable, effective, humble.

vainglory (SYN.) conceit, pride, self-esteem, arrogance, superciliousness, haughtiness, vanity.
(ANT.) shame, modesty, meekness, humility, lowliness.

valet (SYN.) groom, dresser, attendant, man-servant.

valiant (SYN.) bold, brave, courageous, adventurous, audacious, chivalrous, daring, fearless, dauntless, heroic, brave, gallant, magnanimous, intrepid, unafraid.
(ANT.) weak, cowardly, timid.

valid (SYN.) cogent, conclusive, effective, convincing, binding, efficacious, logical, powerful, legal, sound, weighty, well-founded, real, genuine, actual, true, trustworthy, authentic, strong, telling, logical, satisfactory.
(ANT.) weak, unconvincing, void, unproved, spurious, counterfeit.

validate (SYN.) corroborate, substantiate, support, confirm, prove, uphold, sustain, authenticate.
(ANT.) contradict, cancel.

valise (SYN.) satchel, bag, baggage.

valley (SYN.) dale, dell, lowland, basin, gully, vale, ravine.
(ANT.) hill, upland, headland.

valor (SYN.) courage, heroism, bravery, boldness, intrepidity.

valuable (SYN.) profitable, useful, costly, precious, dear, expensive, worthy, important, esteemed.
(ANT.) poor, cheap, worthless.

value (SYN.) price, merit, usefulness, value, virtue, utility, appreciate, prize, hold dear, treasure, excellence, benefit, cost, rate, evaluate, appraise, esteem, importance, worthiness.
(ANT.) uselessness, cheapness.

vanish (SYN.) evaporate, disappear.
(ANT.) appear.

vanity (SYN.) complacency, egotism, pride, self-esteem, conceit, caprice, fancy, idea, conception, notion, haughtiness, self- respect, whim, smugness, vainglory, arrogance, imagination.
(ANT.) humility, diffidence.

vanquish (SYN.) defeat, crush, humble, surmount, master, beat, conquer, overcome, rout, quell.
(ANT.) surrender, cede, lose, retreat, capitulate.

vapid (SYN.) hackneyed, inane, insipid, trite, banal, commonplace.
(ANT.) striking, novel, fresh, original, stimulating.

vapor (SYN.) steam, fog, mist, smog, haze, steam.

variable (SYN.) fickle, fitful, inconstant, unstable, shifting, changeable, unsteady, vacillating.
(ANT.) unchanging, uniform, stable, steady, constant.

variant (SYN.) dissimilar, different, distinct, contrary, diverse, divergent, opposite, unlike, incongruous, divers, various.
(ANT.) similar, same, congruous, identical, alike.

variation (SYN.) change, alternation, alteration, substitution, variety, substitute, exchange.
(ANT.) uniformity, stability, monotony.

variety (SYN.) dissimilarity, diversity, heterogeneity, assortment, change, difference, medley, mixture, miscellany, variousness, form, type, class, breed, sort, kind, strain, stock.
(ANT.) likeness, monotony, uniformity, sameness, homogeneity.

various (SYN.) miscellaneous, sundry, divers, several, contrary, distinct, dissimilar, divergent, unlike, opposite, different.
(ANT.) identical, similar, same, alike, congruous.

vary (SYN.) exchange, substitute, alter, change, modify, shift, convert, transform, transfigure, diversify.
(ANT.) settle, stabilize, continue, establish, preserve.

vassalage *(SYN.)* confinement, captivity, imprisonment, slavery, thralldom.
(ANT.) liberation, freedom.

vast *(SYN.)* big, capacious, extensive, huge, great, ample, immense, wide, unlimited, enormous, measureless, large.
(ANT.) tiny, small, short, little.

vault *(SYN.)* caper, jerk, jump, leap, bound, crypt, sepulcher, hop, spring, safe, start, tomb, grave, catacomb, skip.

vaunt *(SYN.)* crow, flaunt, glory, boast.
(ANT.) minimize, humble, deprecate, apologize.

vaunting *(SYN.)* flourish, display, ostentation, parade, show, pomp.
(ANT.) modesty, reserve, humility.

vehement *(SYN.)* excitable, fervent, ardent, burning, fiery, glowing, impetuous, hot, irascible, passionate.
(ANT.) calm, quiet, cool, apathetic, deliberate.

veil *(SYN.)* clothe, conceal, cover, cloak, web, hide, curtain, disguise, gauze, film, envelop, screen, mask, shield.
(ANT.) reveal, unveil, bare, divulge.

velocity *(SYN.)* quickness, rapidity, speed, swiftness.

venal *(SYN.)* greedy, mercenary, sordid, corrupt.
(ANT.) liberal, honorable, generous.

venerable *(SYN.)* antiquated, aged, antique, ancient, elderly, old, superannuated, old-fashion.
(ANT.) young, new, youthful, modern.

venerate *(SYN.)* approve, esteem, admire, appreciate, wonder, respect.
(ANT.) dislike, despise.

vengeance *(SYN.)* requital, reprisal, reparation, retribution, revenge.
(ANT.) forgiveness, remission, pardon, mercy.

venom *(SYN.)* toxin, poison, bitterness, spite, hate.

vent *(SYN.)* eject, emit, expel, shoot, spurt, emanate, hurl, shed, belch, discharge, breathe.

venture *(ANT.)* speculate, attempt, test, dare, hazard, gamble, chance, risk.

(ANT.) insure, secure, protect.

verbal *(SYN.)* oral, spoken, literal, unwritten, vocal.
(ANT.) printed, written, recorded.

verbose *(SYN.)* communicative, glib, chattering, chatty, garrulous, loquacious, talkative.
(ANT.) uncommunicative, silent.

verbosity *(SYN.)* long-windedness, verboseness, redundancy, wordiness.
(ANT.) terseness, laconic, conciseness.

verdict *(SYN.)* judgment, finding, opinion, decision.

verge *(SYN.)* lip, rim, edge, margin, brink, brim.

verification *(SYN.)* confirmation, demonstration, evidence, proof, test, experiment, testimony, trial.
(ANT.) terseness, laconic, conciseness.

verify *(SYN.)* confirm, substantiate, acknowledge, determine, assure, establish, approve, fix, settle, ratify, strengthen, corroborate, affirm, sanction.

veritable *(SYN.)* authentic, correct, genuine, real, true, accurate, actual.
(ANT.) false, fictitious, spurious, erroneous, counterfeit.

versed *(SYN.)* conversant, familiar, intimate, knowing, acquainted, aware.
(ANT.) inclined, level, prone, oblique.

version *(SYN.)* interpretation, rendition.

vertical *(SYN.)* erect, perpendicular, upright.
(ANT.) horizontal.

very *(SYN.)* exceedingly, extremely, greatly, considerably.

vessel *(SYN.)* craft, boat, ship.

vestige *(SYN.)* stain, scar, mark, brand, stigma, characteristic, trace, feature, trait, symptoms, hint, token, suggestion, indication.

veto *(SYN.)* refusal, denial, refuse, deny, negate, forbid, prohibit.
(ANT.) approve, approval.

vex *(SYN.)* embitter, exasperate, aggravate, annoy, chafe, bother, provoke, pester, plague, nettle, anger.
(ANT.) soften soothe, palliate, mitigate.

vexation *(SYN.)* chagrin, irritation, annoyance, mortification, irritation, pique.
(ANT.) comfort, pleasure, appeasement, gratification.

vibrate *(SYN.)* flutter, jar, quake, jolt, quaver, agitate, transgression, wickedness, ungodliness, tremble, wrong.

vice *(SYN.)* iniquity, crime, offense, evil, guilt, sin, ungodliness, wickedness, depravity, corruption, wrong.
(ANT.) righteousness, virtue, goodness, innocence, purity.

vicinity *(SYN.)* district, area, locality, neighborhood, environs, proximity, nearness, adjacency.
(ANT.) remoteness, distance.

vicious *(SYN.)* bad, evil, wicked, sinful, corrupt, cruel, savage, dangerous.

victimize *(SYN.)* cheat, dupe, swindle, deceive, take advantage of.

victor *(SYN.)* champion, winner.
(ANT.) loser.

victory *(SYN.)* conquest, jubilation, triumph, success, achievement, ovation.
(ANT.) defeat, failure.

view *(SYN.)* discern, gaze, glance, behold, eye, discern, stare, watch, examine, witness, prospect, vision, vista, sight, look, panorama, opinion, judgment, belief, impression, perspective, range, regard, thought, observation, survey, scene, conception, outlook, inspect, observe.
(ANT.) miss, overlook, avert, hide, be neutral, thoughtless.

viewpoint *(SYN.)* attitude, standpoint, aspect, pose, disposition, position, stand, posture.

vigilant *(SYN.)* anxious, attentive, careful, alert, circumspect, cautious, observant, wary, watchful, wakeful.
(ANT.) inattentive, neglectful, careless.

vigor *(SYN.)* spirit, verve, energy, zeal, fortitude, vitality, strength, liveliness.
(ANT.) listlessness.

vigorous *(SYN.)* brisk, energetic, active, blithe, animated, frolicsome, strong, spirited, lively, forceful, sprightly, vivacious, powerful, supple.

(ANT.) vapid, dull, listless, insipid.

vile *(SYN.)* foul, loathsome, base, depraved, debased, sordid, vulgar, wicked, abject, ignoble, mean, worthless, sinful, bad, low, wretched, evil, offensive, objectionable, disgusting.
(ANT.) honorable, upright, decent, laudable, attractive.

vilify *(SYN.)* asperse, defame, disparage, abuse, malign, revile, scandalize.
(ANT.) protect, honor, praise, cherish.

village *(SYN.)* hamlet, town.
(ANT.) metropolis, city.

villain *(SYN.)* rascal, rogue, cad, brute, scoundrel, devil, scamp.

villainous *(SYN.)* deleterious, evil, bad, base, iniquitous, unsound, sinful, unwholesome.
(ANT.) honorable, reputable, moral, good, excellent.

vindicate clear, assert, defend, absolve, excuse, acquit, support.
(ANT.) accuse, convict, abandon.

violate *(SYN.)* disobey, invade, defile, break, infringe, desecrate, pollute, dishonor, debauch, profane, deflower, ravish.
(ANT.) obey, protect, respect, honor.

violence *(SYN.)* constraint, force, compulsion, coercion.
(ANT.) weakness, persuasion, feebleness, impotence, frailty.

violent *(SYN.)* strong, forceful, powerful, forcible, angry, fierce, savage, passionate, furious.
(ANT.) gentle.

virgin *(SYN.)* immaculate, genuine, spotless, clean, clear, unadulterated, chaste, untainted, innocent, guiltless, pure, untouched, modest, maiden, sincere, unused, undefiled, pure.
(ANT.) foul, tainted, defiled, sullied, polluted, corrupt.

virile *(SYN.)* hardy, male, mannish, lusty, bold, masculine, strong.
(ANT.) feminine, unmanly, weak, effeminate, emasculated.

virtue *(SYN.)* integrity, probity, purity,

chastity, goodness, rectitude, effectiveness, force, honor, power, efficacy, quality, strength, merit, righteousness, advantage. *(ANT.) fault, vice, corruption.*

virtuous *(SYN.)* good, ethical, chaste, honorable, moral, just, pure, righteous, upright. *(ANT.) licentious, unethical, amoral, sinful, libertine, immoral.*

virulent *(SYN.)* hostile, malevolent, malignant, bitter, spiteful, wicked. *(ANT.) affectionate, benevolent.*

vision *(SYN.)* dream, hallucination, mirage, eyesight, sight, fantasy, illusion, specter, revelation, phantom, spook, ghost, imagination, foresight, apparition. *(ANT.) verity, reality.*

visionary *(SYN.)* faultless, ideal, perfect, unreal, supreme. *(ANT.) real, actual, faulty.*

visit *(SYN.)* attend, see, call on, appointment.

visitor *(SYN.)* caller, guest.

vista *(SYN.)* view, scene, aspect.

vital *(SYN.)* cardinal, living, paramount, alive, essential, critical, basic, indispensable, urgent. *(ANT.) lifeless, unimportant, inanimate, nonessential.*

vitality *(SYN.)* buoyancy, being, life, liveliness, existence, spirit. *(ANT.) death, dullness, demise.*

vitiate *(SYN.)* allay, abase, corrupt, adulterate, debase, defile, depress, deprave, degrade, impair, humiliate, pervert, improve, restore, vitalize, restore.

vivacious *(SYN.)* lively, spirited.

vivid *(SYN.)* brilliant, striking, clear, bright, intense, lively. *(ANT.) dim, vague, dull, dreary.*

vocal *(SYN.)* said, uttered, oral, spoken, definite, outspoken.

vocation *(SYN.)* commerce, employment, business, art, job, profession, trade, occupation, career, calling, work, trading. *(ANT.) pastime, hobby, avocation.*

void *(SYN.)* barren, emptiness, space, annul, cancel, empty, bare, unoccupied, meaningless, invalid, useless, invalidate, vacant, vacuous.

(ANT.) employed, replete, engaged.

volatile *(SYN.)* effervescent, resilient, buoyant, animated, cheerful, hopeful, lively, spirited. *(ANT.) depressed, sullen, hopeless, dejected, despondent.*

volition *(SYN.)* desire, intention, pleasure, preference, choice, decision, resolution, testament, wish. *(ANT.) disinterest, compulsion, indifference.*

voluble *(SYN.)* glib, communicative, verbose, loquacious, chatty. *(ANT.) silent, uncommunicative, laconic, taciturn.*

volume *(SYN.)* capacity, skill, power, talent, faculty, magnitude, mass, book, dimensions, quantity. *(ANT.) stupidity, inability, impotence, incapacity.*

voluntary *(SYN.)* extemporaneous, free, automatic, spontaneous. *(ANT.) forced, planned, required, rehearsed, compulsory, prepared.*

volunteer *(SYN.)* extend, offer, advance, propose, tender, sacrifice. *(ANT.) receive, spurn, reject, accept, retain.*

voodoo *(SYN.)* art, conjuring, legerdemain, magic, wizardry.

vow *(SYN.)* oath, pledge, promise.

voyage *(SYN.)* journey, excursion.

vulgar *(SYN.)* ordinary, popular, common, general, crude, coarse, low, rude, obscene, unrefined. *(ANT.) polite, refined, select, aristocratic.*

vulnerable *(SYN.)* unguarded, defenseless, unprotected.

W

wacky *(SYN.)* strange, crazy, peculiar.

wad *(SYN.)* hunk, clump, chunk.

wafer *(SYN.)* cracker, lozenge.

waft *(SYN.)* convey, glide, sail, float.

wage *(SYN.)* payment, salary, earnings, compensation, income, conduct, pursue, make.

wager *(SYN.)* stake, bet, play, gamble, speculate, risk, chance.

wages *(SYN.)* payment, compensation, fee, allowance, pay, salary, earnings, rate, recompense.

wagon *(SYN.)* carriage, buggy, cart, surrey, stagecoach.

waif *(SYN.)* guttersnipe, ragamuffin, tramp, vagrant, urchin.

wail *(SYN.)* mourn, moan, cry, bewail, lament, bemoan, sorrow, weep, sob.

wait *(SYN.)* linger, tarry, attend, bide, watch, delay, await, abide, stay, serve, pause, remain, postponement, rest, expect.
(ANT.) hasten, act, leave, commence, start, expedite.

waive *(SYN.)* renounce, abandon, surrender, relinquish, forgo, yield, drop.
(ANT.) uphold, maintain.

wake *(SYN.)* awaken, rouse, waken, arouse, stimulate, activate.
(ANT.) doze, sleep.

waken *(SYN.)* wake, arouse, rouse, awaken, stimulate, activate.
(ANT.) doze, sleep.

walk *(SYN.)* step, stroll, march, amble, saunter, hike, lane, path, passage, traverse.

wall *(SYN.)* barricade, divider, partition, panel, stockade, screen, fence, obstruction.

wallow *(SYN.)* plunge, roll, flounder, grovel.

wan *(SYN.)* colorless, haggard, gaunt, pale, pallid, pasty.

wander *(SYN.)* rove, stroll, deviate, ramble, digress, roam, traipse, range, err, meander, saunter.
(ANT.) linger, stop, conform, settle.

wane *(SYN.)* abate, weaken, fade, ebb, decrease, wither, subside, decline, dwindle.
(ANT.) expand, increase.

want *(SYN.)* penury, destitution, crave, desire, requirement, poverty, wish, require, need.
(ANT.) wealth, plenty, satisfy, abundance. comfortable.

wanton *(SYN.)* lecherous, immoral, loose, lewd, salacious, lustful, wayward, impulsive.

war *(SYN.)* battle, hostilities, combat, fight, strife, contention.

warble *(SYN.)* sing, trill, chirp.

ward *(SYN.)* annex, wing, section, precinct, zone.

warden *(SYN.)* custodian, guard, guardian, keeper, turnkey, jailer, curator, gamekeeper.

ward off *(SYN.)* repel, thwart, deflect, foil, deter, forestall, repulse.

wardrobe *(SYN.)* chiffonier, bureau, closet, armoire.

warehouse *(SYN.)* arsenal, storehouse, depository, stockroom, storeroom, depot.

wares *(SYN.)* merchandise, staples, inventory, commodities, goods, products, stock.

wariness *(SYN.)* heed, care, watchfulness, caution, vigilance.
(ANT.) carelessness, abandon.

warlike *(SYN.)* hostile, unfriendly, combative, belligerent, antagonistic, pugnacious, bellicose, opposed, aggressive.
(ANT.) cordial, peaceful, amicable.

warm *(SYN.)* sincere, cordial, hearty, earnest, sympathetic, ardent, heated, gracious, temperate, enthusiastic, lukewarm, tepid, eager, sociable.
(ANT.) cool, aloof, taciturn, brisk, indifferent.

warmhearted *(SYN.)* loving, kind, kindhearted, friendly, generous, compassionate.

warmth *(SYN.)* friendliness, cordiality, geniality, understanding, compassion.
(ANT.) chilly, coolness.

warn *(SYN.)* apprise, notify, admonish, caution, advise, inform.

warning *(SYN.)* advice, information, caution, portent, admonition, indication, notice, sign, notification.

warp *(SYN.)* turn, bend, twist, distort, deprave.

warrant *(SYN.)* pledge, assurance, warranty, guarantee, authorize, approve, mandate, sanction.

warrior *(SYN.)* combatant, fighter, soldier, mercenary, guerrilla.

wary *(SYN.)* careful, awake, watchful, heedful, attentive, alive, mindful, cautious, thoughtful.
(ANT.) unaware, indifferent, careless, apathetic.

wash *(SYN.)* launder, cleanse, rub, touch, reach, border, wet, clean, scrub, bathe.
(ANT.) soil, dirty, stain.

washed-out *(SYN.)* bleached, dull, faded, pale, discolored, pallid.

waspish *(SYN.)* irritable, petulant, fractious, ill-tempered, testy, snappish, touchy.
(ANT.) pleasant, genial.

waste *(SYN.)* forlorn, bleak, wild, solitary, dissipate, abandoned, spend, deserted, bare, consume, dwindle, decay, misspend, decrease, wither, wear, effluent, useless, unused, garbage, rubbish, refuse, trash, squander, uninhabited.
(ANT.) cultivated, attended.

wasteful *(SYN.)* wanton, costly, lavish, extravagant.

watch *(SYN.)* inspect, descry, behold, distinguish, guard, attend, observe, contemplate, espy, perceive, look at, protect, chronometer, timepiece, patrol, vigil, duty, shift, regard, note, view, scan, sentinel, watchman, sentry, discern.

watchdog *(SYN.)* lookout, guard, sentinel, sentry.

watchful *(SYN.)* alert, careful, attentive, vigilant, wary, cautious.

waterfall *(SYN.)* cascade, cataract.

watertight *(SYN.)* impregnable, firm, solid.

wave *(SYN.)* ripple, whitecap, undulation, breaker, surf, swell, sea, surge, tide, flow, stream.

waver *(SYN.)* question, suspect, flicker, deliberate, doubt, distrust, hesitate, falter, stagger.
(ANT.) confide, trust, believe, decide.

wavering *(SYN.)* fickle, shifting, variable, changeable, vacillating, fitful.
(ANT.) unchanging, constant, uniform.

wavy *(SYN.)* rippling, serpentine, curly.

wax *(SYN.)* raise, heighten, expand, accrue, enhance, extend, multiply, enlarge, augment, amplify.

(ANT.) contract, reduce, atrophy, diminish.

way *(SYN.)* habit, road, course, avenue, route, mode, system, channel, track, fashion, method, walk, approach, manner, technique, means, procedure, trail, proceed, progress, path, style.

waylay *(SYN.)* surprise, accost, ambush, attack, pounce, intercept.

wayward *(SYN.)* stubborn, headstrong, contrary, obstinate, naughty, disobedient, rebellious, refractory.

weak *(SYN.)* frail, debilitated, delicate, poor, wavering, infirm, bending, lame, defenseless, vulnerable, fragile, pliant, feeble, watery, diluted, undecided, assailable, irresolute, unsteady, yielding, tender.
(ANT.) strong, potent, sturdy, powerful.

weaken *(SYN.)* exhaust, sap, disable, devitalize.

weakling *(SYN.)* sissy, nambypamby, milksop, milquetoast.

weakness *(SYN.)* incompetence, inability, impotence, handicap, fondness, liking, affection, disability, incapacity, feebleness.
(ANT.) strength, ability, dislike, power.

wealth *(SYN.)* fortune, money, riches, possessions, means, abundance, opulence, affluence, property, quantity, profession, luxury.
(ANT.) want, need.

wealthy *(SYN.)* rich, exorbitant, prosperous, affluent, successful.
(ANT.) poverty-stricken, poor, indigent, impoverished, beggarly, destitute, needy.

wear *(SYN.)* erode, fray, grind, apparel, clothes, garb, attire.

wearied *(SYN.)* weak, languid, faint, irresolute, feeble, timid.
(ANT.) brave, vigorous.

weary *(SYN.)* faint, spent, worn, tired, fatigued, exhausted, tiresome, bored, wearied, tedious, jaded.
(ANT.) rested, hearty, fresh.

weasel *(SYN.)* cheat, traitor, betrayer.

weave *(SYN.)* lace, interlace, plait, intertwine, braid, knit.

web *(SYN.)* netting, network, net, cobweb, trap, entanglement.

wed *(SYN.)* espouse, marry.

wedlock *(SYN.)* marriage, union, espousal, wedding, matrimony.

wedge *(SYN.)* chock, jam, lodge.

wee *(SYN.)* small, tiny, miniature, petite, microscopic, minute.

weep *(SYN.)* mourn, sob, bemoan, cry, lament, whimper, wail.

weigh *(SYN.)* heed, deliberate, consider, study, ponder, contemplate, reflect, evaluate.
(ANT.) neglect, ignore.

weight *(SYN.)* importance, emphasis, load, burden, import, stress, influence, heaviness, pressure, value, gravity, significance.
(ANT.) triviality, levity, insignificance, lightness, buoyancy.

weird *(SYN.)* odd, eerie, strange, unnatural, peculiar, spooky.

welcome *(SYN.)* take, entertain, greet, accept, receive, reception, gain, greeting, shelter.
(ANT.) reject, bestow, impart, discharge.

weld *(SYN.)* solder, connect, fuse, bond.

welfare *(SYN.)* good, well-being, prosperity.

well *(SYN.)* hearty, happy, sound, hale, beneficial, good, convenient, expedient, healthy, favorably, fully, thoroughly, surely, adequately, satisfactorily, competently, certainly, completely, trim, undoubtedly, fit, profitable.
(ANT.) infirm, depressed, weak.

well-being *(SYN.)* delight, happiness, satisfaction, contentment, gladness.
(ANT.) sorrow, grief, sadness, despair.

well-bred *(SYN.)* cultured, polite, genteel, courtly, refined, cultivated.
(ANT.) crude, vulgar, boorish, rude.

well-known *(SYN.)* famous, illustrious, celebrated, noted, eminent, renowned.
(ANT.) unknown, ignominious, obscure, hidden.

wet *(SYN.)* moist, dank, soaked, damp, drenched, dampen, moisten.
(ANT.) arid, dry, parched.

wharf *(SYN.)* pier, dock.

wheedle *(SYN.)* coax, cajole, persuade.

whim *(SYN.)* fancy, notion, humor, quirk, caprice, whimsy, inclination, vagary.

whimsical *(SYN.)* quaint, strange, curious, odd, unusual, droll, queer, eccentric, peculiar.
(ANT.) normal, common, usual, familiar.

whine *(SYN.)* whimper, cry, moan, complain.

whip *(SYN.)* scourge, thrash, beat, lash.

whirl *(SYN.)* rotate, twirl, spin, revolve, reel.

whole *(SYN.)* total, sound, all, intact, complete, well, hale, integral, unimpaired, healed, entire, uncut, undivided, unbroken, undamaged, intact, perfect.
(ANT.) partial, defective, imperfect, deficient.

wholesome *(SYN.)* robust, well, hale, sound, salubrious, good, hygienic, salutary, nourishing, healthful, strong, nutritious, hearty.
(ANT.) frail, noxious, infirm, delicate, injurious, diseased.

wicked *(SYN.)* deleterious, iniquitous, immoral, bad, evil, base, ungodly, unsound, sinful, bitter, blasphemous, malicious, evil-minded, profane, baleful, hostile, rancorous, unwholesome.
(ANT.) moral, good, reputable, honorable.

wide *(SYN.)* large, broad, sweeping, extensive, vast, expanded.
(ANT.) restricted, narrow.

width *(SYN.)* wideness, extensiveness, breadth.

wield *(SYN.)* handle, brandish, employ, flourish.

wild *(SYN.)* outlandish, uncivilized, untamed, irregular, wanton, foolish, mad, barbarous, rough, waste, desert, uncultivated, boisterous, unruly, savage, primitive, giddy, unrestrained, silly, wayward, uncontrolled, impetuous, crazy, ferocious, undomesticated, desolate.
(ANT.) quiet, gentle, placid, tame, restrained, civilized.

willful *(SYN.)* intentional, designed, contemplated, studied, premeditated.
(ANT.) fortuitous.

will *(SYN.)* intention, desire, volition, decision, resolution, wish, resoluteness, choice, determination, pleasure.

(ANT.) disinterest, coercion, indifference.

willing *(SYN.)* agreeing, energetic, enthusiastic, consenting, agreeable, eager.

wilt *(SYN.)* sag, droop, weaken.

wily *(SYN.)* cunning, foxy, sly, crafty.

win *(SYN.)* gain, succeed, prevail, achieve, thrive, obtain, get, acquire, earn, flourish.

(ANT.) lose, miss, forfeit, fail.

wind *(SYN.)* gale, breeze, storm, gust, blast, air, breath, flurry, puff, blow, hurricane, typhoon, cyclone, tornado, suggestion, hint, clue, zephyr, squall, coil, crank, screw, meander, wander, twist, weave, draft.

winsome *(SYN.)* winning, charming, agreeable.

wisdom *(SYN.)* insight, judgment, learning, sense, discretion, reason, prudence, erudition, foresight, intelligence, sageness, knowl-edge, information, sagacity.

(ANT.) nonsense, foolishness, stupidity, ignorance.

wise *(SYN.)* informed, sagacious, learned, penetrating, enlightened, advisable, prudent, profound, deep, erudite, scholarly, knowing, sound, intelligent, expedient, discerning.

(ANT.) simple, shallow, foolish.

wish *(SYN.)* crave, hanker, long, hunger, yearning, lust, craving, yearn, want, appetite, covet, longing, desire, urge.

(ANT.) hate, aversion, loathing, distaste.

wit *(SYN.)* sense, humor, pleasantry, satire, intelligence, comprehension, understanding, banter, mind, wisdom, intellect, wittiness, fun, drollery, humorist, wag, comedian, raillery, irony, witticism.

(ANT.) solemnity, commonplace, sobriety.

witch *(SYN.)* magician, sorcerer, enchanter, sorceress, enchantress, warlock.

witchcraft *(SYN.)* enchantment, magic, wizardry, conjuring, voodoo.

withdraw *(SYN.)* renounce, leave, abandon, recall, retreat, go, secede, desert, quit, retire, depart, retract, remove, forsake.

(ANT.) enter, tarry, abide, place, stay.

wither *(SYN.)* wilt, languish, dry, shrivel, decline, fade, decay, sear, waste, wizen, weaken, droop, sink, fail, shrink.

(ANT.) renew, refresh, revive.

withhold *(SYN.)* forbear, abstain, repress, check, refrain.

(ANT.) persist, continue.

withstand *(SYN.)* defy, contradict, bar, thwart, oppose, hinder, combat, resist, counteract.

(ANT.) succumb, cooperate, support.

witness *(SYN.)* perceive, proof, spectator, confirmation, see, attestation, watch, observe, eyewitness, declaration, notice, testimony.

(ANT.) refutation, contradiction, argument.

witty *(SYN.)* funny, talented, apt, bright, adroit, sharp, clever.

(ANT.) foolish, slow, dull, clumsy, awkward.

wizard *(SYN.)* magician, conjuror, sorcerer.

wizardry *(SYN.)* voodoo, legerdemain, conjuring, witchcraft, charm.

woe *(SYN.)* sorrow, disaster, trouble, evil, agony, suffering, anguish, sadness, grief, distress, misery, torment, misfortune.

(ANT.) pleasure, delight, fun.

womanly *(SYN.)* girlish, womanish, female, ladylike.

(ANT.) mannish, virile, male, masculine.

wonder *(SYN.)* awe, curiosity, miracle, admiration, surprise, wonderment, marvel, conjecture, amazement, question, astonishment.

(ANT.) expectation, familiarity, indifference, apathy, triviality.

wonderful *(SYN.)* extraordinary, marvelous, astonishing, amazing, remarkable, astounding.

wont *(SYN.)* practice, use, custom, training, habit, usage, manner.

(ANT.) inexperience, disuse.

word *(SYN.)* phrase, term, utterance, expression, articulate.

wordy *(SYN.)* talkative, verbose, garrulous.

work *(SYN.)* opus, employment, achievement, performance, toil, business, exertion, occupation, labor, job, product, ac-

complishment, travail, effort.
(ANT.) recreation, leisure, vacation, ease.
working *(SYN.)* busy, active, industrious.
(ANT.) lazy, dormant, passive, inactive.
world *(SYN.)* globe, earth, universe.
worldly *(SYN.)* bodily, fleshy, animal, carnal, corporeal, gross, voluptuous, base.
(ANT.) refined, temperate, exalted, spiritual.
worn *(SYN.)* tired, jaded, exhausted, wearied, faint, weary.
(ANT.) invigorated, fresh, rested.
worry *(SYN.)* concern, trouble, disquiet, anxiety, fear, pain, harry, gall, grieve, persecute, annoy, disturb, fidget, chafe, agonize, bother, haze, pester, uneasiness, fret.
(ANT.) console, comfort, contentment, satisfaction, peace.
worship *(SYN.)* honor, revere, adore, idolize, reverence, glorify, respect, deify, venerate.
(ANT.) curse, scorn, blaspheme, despise.
worth *(SYN.)* value, price, deserving, excellence, usefulness, utility, worthiness, merit.
(ANT.) uselessness, valuelessness, cheapness.
worthless *(SYN.)* empty, idle, abortive, ineffectual, bootless, pointless, vain, unavailing.
(ANT.) meek, effective, modest, potent.
wound *(SYN.)* mar, harm, damage, hurt, dishonor, injure, injury, spoil, wrong, disfigure.
(ANT.) compliment, benefit, preserve, help.
wrangle *(SYN.)* spat, bickering, affray, argument, dispute, quarrel, altercation, contention, squabble, disagreement.
(ANT.) peace, friendliness, reconciliation, harmony.
wrap *(SYN.)* cover, protect, shield, cloak, mask, clothe, curtain, guard, conceal.
(ANT.) reveal, bare, unveil, expose.
wrath *(SYN.)* fury, anger, irritation, rage, animosity, passion, temper, petulance, choler, resentment.
(ANT.) patience, conciliation, peace.
wreck *(SYN.)* ravage, devastation, extinguish, destroy, annihilate, damage, raze, de-molish, destruction, ruin, devastate.

(ANT.) make, construct, preserve, establish.
wrench *(SYN.)* tug, jerk, twist.
wrestle *(SYN.)* fight, tussle, grapple.
wretch *(SYN.)* cad, knave, scoundrel, rogue.
wretched *(SYN.)* forlorn, miserable, comfortless, despicable, paltry, low, worthless, disconsolate, sorry, mean, heart-broken.
(ANT.) noble, contented, happy, significant.
wring *(SYN.)* twist, extract.
writer *(SYN.)* creator, maker, author, father, composer.
writhe *(SYN.)* twist, squirm.
wrong *(SYN.)* awry, incorrect, improper, amiss, naughty, inappropriate, criminal, faulty, erroneous, bad, evil, imprecise, inaccurate, askew, sin, incorrectness, false, unsuitable, impropriety, wickedness, immoral.
(ANT.) proper, true, correct, suitable, perfect, appropriate, accurate.
wry *(SYN.)* amusing, witty, dry, droll, quizzical, sarcastic, displaced, awry.

Y

yacht *(SYN.)* sailboat, boat, cruiser.
yank *(SYN.)* pull, wrest, draw, haul, tug, jerk, wrench, heave, extract, pluck, grab.
yap *(SYN.)* howl, bark.
yard *(SYN.)* pen, confine, court, enclosure, compound, garden, backyard, patio, grounds.
yardstick *(SYN.)* measure, criterion, gauge, example, guideline, rule.
yarn *(SYN.)* wool, tale, narrative, thread, story, fiber, anecdote, spiel.
yaw *(SYN.)* tack, change course, pitch, toss, roll.
yawn *(SYN.)* open, gape.
yearly *(SYN.)* annually.
yearn *(SYN.)* pine, long for, want, desire, crave, hope, wish.
yearning *(SYN.)* hungering, craving, desire, longing, appetite, lust, urge, aspiration, wish.

(ANT.) *distaste, loathing, abomination, hate.*

yell *(SYN.)* call, scream, shout, whoop, howl, roar, holler, wail, bawl, bellow, screech, yelp.

yellow *(SYN.)* fearful, cowardly, chicken, weak, unreliable, scared.
(ANT.) *daring, bold, brave, courageous, manly.*

yelp *(SYN.)* screech, squeal, howl, bark.

yen *(SYN.)* longing, craving, fancy, appetite, desire, lust, hunger, longing, concupiscence, want,

yet *(SYN.)* moreover, also, additionally, although, but, further, besides.

yield *(SYN.)* produce, afford, breed, grant, accord, cede, relent, succumb, bestow, allow, permit, give way, submit, bear, surrender, supply, fruits, give up, abdicate, return, impart, harvest, permit, accede, acquiesce, crop, capitulate, pay, concede, defer, generate, resign, waive, cede, relinquish.
(ANT.) *assert, deny, refuse, resist, overpower, struggle, master, oppose, forbid, prevent, overcome, strive.*

yielding *(SYN.)* dutiful, submissive, compliant, obedient, tractable, succumb, accede, relent.
(ANT.) *rebellious, intractable, insubordinate.*

yoke *(SYN.)* tether, leash, bridle, harness, bond, collar, burden, weight.

yokel *(SYN.)* hick, peasant, hayseed, innocent, ignoramus, oaf.
(ANT.) *sophisticate, refined, cultured, worldly.*

young *(SYN.)* immature, undeveloped, youthful, underdeveloped, juvenile, junior, underage, growing, adolescent, untested, vigorous, dynamic, spirited, inexperienced, minor.
(ANT.) *old, mature, elderly, adult, experienced, aged, developed.*

youngster *(SYN.)* kid, lad, stripling, minor, youth, child, fledgling, kid.
(ANT.) *adult, elder.*

youthful *(SYN.)* childish, immature, young, boyish, childlike, girlish, puerile.
(ANT.) *old, elderly, senile, aged, mature.*

yowl *(SYN.)* yell, shriek, cry, wail, whoop, howl, scream.

yummy *(SYN.)* good, great, delicious, appetizing, pleasing, joyable, tasty, savory,
(ANT.) unappetizing, tastless, unsavory.

Z

zany (SYN.) clownish, comical, foolish, silly, scatterbrained.

zap *(SYN.)* drive, vim, pep, determination.

zeal *(SYN.)* fervor, eagerness, passion, feverency, vehemence, devotion, intensity, excitement, earnestness, inspiration, warmth, ardor, fanaticism, enthusiasm.
(ANT.) *unconcern, ennui, apathy, indifference.*

zealot *(SYN.)* champion, crank, fanatic, bigot.

zealous *(SYN.)* enthusiastic, fiery, keen, eager, fervid, ardent, intense, vehement, fervent, glowing, hot, impassioned, passionate.
(ANT.) *cool, nonchalant, apathetic.*

zenith *(SYN.)* culmination, apex, height, acme, consummation, top, summit, pinnacle, climax, peak.
(ANT.) *floor, nadir, depth, base, anticlimax.*

zero *(SYN.)* nonexistent, nil, nothing, none.

zest *(SYN.)* enjoyment, savor, eagerness, relish, satisfaction, gusto, spice, tang, pleasure, thrill, delight, exhilaration.

zestful *(SYN.)* delightful, thrilling, exciting, stimulating, enjoyable, gusto, zeal, passion, spirit.

zip *(SYN.)* vigor, vim, energy, vitality, spirited, animation, provocative.

zone *(SYN.)* region, climate, tract, belt, sector, section, district, area, circuit, commune band, locality, precinct, territory, location, neighborhood, site, ward, terrain.

zoo *(SYN.)* menagerie.

zoom (SYN.) zip, fly, speed, whiz, roar, race.

COMPUTER

TERMS

AND

REFERENCE

SECTION

abend – abnormal ending; the termination of processing due to program or system fault.

abort – to terminate a process before completion.

access – to call up a program or data.

access code – the user name or security code required to use a computer, program or certain files.

access time – the interval between a request for data from storage by the computer and the moment when it is available to the user.

accounting check – a routine, such as cross totals, to assure that data has been entered accurately.

acoustic coupler – a device for connecting the computer to a telephone hand set.

active document – in a system that allows viewing of multiple items on the screen, the document currently selected and avail-able to the user.

active file – a computer file visible to the user and ready to be manipulated.

active window – the screen area where the active file is viewed.

adapter– a device or routine for making disparate hardware or software elements compatible.

adaptive system – a computer program that learns by keeping a record of corrections to its activity, such as errors in optical character recognition.

ADC – Analog to Digital Converter; a device that converts analog signals to digital data.

add–on – a supplement to enhance performance of an existing program or device.

ADP – Automatic Data Processing; the manipulation of data with the use of a computer.

algebraic expression – a formula that follows the conventions for mathematical syn-tax.

algorithm – precise instructions for performing a specific task.

alias – a name assigned to a file or a block of data to address it for processing.

alignment – the placement of type, as flush right, centered, etc.; the positioning of a frame containing graphics or type.

allocation – the assignment of computer resources for a specific purpose, such as setting aside an area of memory for the operation of a TSR.

alphameric – same as alphanumeric.

alphanumeric– short for alphabetic num-eric; of a string that is able to contain both letters and numbers.

Alternate key (Alt) – an alternate shift key used in conjunction with other keys to execute commands.

ALU– Arithmetic and Logic Unit; the part of the CPU that performs arithmetic and logic functions.

ambiguous–imprecise; of a program command or formula that is stated in such a way that it may yield an undesirable result.

analog – descriptive of data represented as a continuous variable, such as sound.

analog to digital converter – a device that converts analog data to digital data.

analyst – one skilled in identifying the source of problems and correcting them.

anchor, anchor point – the starting point for selection of a block of computer copy as for editing, printing, etc.; the linking of copy or graphics to related material in a computer file.

annotation – an explanatory note in a program or document; a feature in some word processing programs that allows commentary within a document without changing the original document.

ANSI – American National Standards Institute; an organization concerned with standardization of computer elements.

anti–virus – a program or routine designed to detect unauthorized alteration of a computer program.

application – a computer program designed for a particular use, such as a word pro-cessor or spreadsheet; a particular use to which a program is applied, as for compiling financial transactions or inventory records.

application generator – a program feature that assists the user in creating custom designed applications.

architecture – the design of a computer that defines such things as type of processor, speed, bus size, etc.

argument – a variable in a formula, as in $2+4$, wherein $+$ is the operator, and both 2 and 4 are arguments.

arithmetic expression – a formula that uses a mathematical operator and returns a numeric value.

arithmetic relation – an expression that uses a mathematical operator to show the relationship between two values, such as $=$ (equal to), $\neq$ (not equal to), $>$ (greater than), etc.

arrangement – the way that items are located or displayed in a set or array.

array – an ordered group of like elements; a *one dimensional array* may be a list of numbers representing total expense for each department in a company; to show expense by type, a *two dimensional array* is necessary, with a column for each department and rows for each type of expense; a *three dimensional array* may be prepared with layers to represent similar data for other periods.

artificial intelligence – descriptive of the ability of a computer to simulate human intelligence, as by recording corrections to its output and adjusting for future transactions.

artificial language – a programming language with a distinct set of rules and vocabulary.

ascending sort – an alphabetical or numerical arrangement from lowest to highest.

ASCII– American Standard Code for Information Exchange; a standard code for representing characters in the computer.

ASK – a computer programmed query that requires input from the user, often for inputting information to a database.

assembler – a program that translates a programming language into instructions that are understood directly by the computer.

assignment statement – a command that assigns the value of an expression to a variable name, as $A=A+1$, in which the value of A increase by one for each iteration of the command.

attribute – a characteristic, as of a file that is read–only, archived or hidden.

augment– to expand the capabilities of a computer, as by increasing processing speed or memory size.

audio system – a computer capable of responding to voice commands.

automatic backup – a program that creates a backup copy of files; a program that backs up data in the computer at a predetermined time.

automatic link – a connection between embedded objects that provides for the update of all instances of the object when a change is made in one place.

automatic load – a program in computer memory that is brought on line by a predetermined signal, as of a timer, often used to create backup files during the night.

available resources – all of the processing capacity, memory, storage and peripherals available in a computer system; that which remains ready for use after discounting those occupied by primary processing, such as the RAM space remaining after a program is loaded.

axis, *pl.* **axes** – a straight reference line on a graph, horizontal, vertical or on a plane that is perpendicular to both the horizontal and vertical lines.

B

background noise – extraneous matter in a

scanned image or in electronic transmission.

background processing – computer operations taking place out of view, such as printing from a buffer, while the user is manipulating data in the foreground.

back up – to make a copy of data for safe keeping.

backup copy – a copy of data files and programs held as protection against corruption of the originals.

backup system – computer hardware available to take over processing in the event of a failure in the primary system; the procedure for recording and manipulating data in the event of a primary system failure.

backward compatibility – an upgraded program's ability to use files created by an earlier version.

bar chart – a diagram that shows quantities as columns of varying length according to their relative magnitude.

baseline – an imaginary line on which a row of type is arranged.

BASIC – Beginner's All-purpose Symbolic Instruction Code; a programming language.

batch – a group of files or commands that are processed as a unit.

batch command – a single command that causes the execution of a number of commands contained in a batch file.

batch file – a program file containing a series of commands that are processed in order.

baud – a measure of transmission speed.

BBS – Bulletin Board Service; a message center that may be accessed by computer users via telephone lines.

binary code – the representation of characters by the use of binary numbers.

binary digit – 0 or 1, the digits in a binary system.

binary logic – a type of reasoning in computer formulae that returns one of two possible variables, as true or false, yes or no.

binary system – a number system in base 2.

BIOS – Basic Input/Output System; that part of the operating system controlling communication.

bit – short for binary digit, the basic unit in the binary system.

bit mapping – creation of an image of tiny dots (pixels), each of which is assigned a series of bits to record its precise location.

blank – the absence of data; not a space or zero.

block an assembly of data, files, etc. manipulated as a unit.

block command – an instruction that acts on

all elements in a block of text or files.

bomb– a situation wherein the computer locks up and must be restarted.

bookmark– a user–inserted reference marker in a data file that allows instant return from another location.

Boolean algebra – a system of calculation based on Boolean logic.

Boolean logic – a logic system based on a return of one of two variables, as true or false, yes or no.

boot – to initialize a computer.

bootleg software – a program obtained outside of normal channels, such as proprietary software transferred illegally to a second user.

bootstrap – a disc or device that loads the operating system into a computer enabling it to function.

branch– a command to jump to another section of a program; an *unconditional branch* directs a move to a specific location; a *conditional branch* first calls for a test, then directs a move when certain conditions are met.

brightness – descriptive of the reflective quality of the medium holding copy to be scanned.

Break (key) – a command key that temporarily suspends processing.

buffer – an area for temporary data storage, often used to compensate for differences in transmission speed between devices.

bug– a defect in a computer system or program.

bundled – descriptive of computer hardware and software sold together as a package.

burn–in– a method of testing for weak components in a computer.

bus – the collection of lines along which data travels.

business application – a program designed for business use, such as for payroll or inventory control.

byte – a basic data unit manipulated by the computer, usually eight bits.

C

cable – the transmission link between devices in a computer system.

cache – a buffer for holding frequently called data.

CAD/CAM– Computer Aided Design/ Computer Aided Manufacturing; a program that assists in planning and production.

CADD– Computer Aided Design and Drafting; a graphics program that assists in the creation of engineering drawings.

CAL – Computer Augmented Learning; the reinforcement of learning with the use of the computer.

cancel – a command to abandon a change or stop a procedure.

capacity – the size of a storage device; the ability of a computer to handle a particular task.

carpel tunnel syndome – an injury or strain to the wrist caused by performing a repetitive task, such as computer data entry.

carriage – the device on a printer that holds the paper.

Cartesian coordinates – numbers that locate a point in space on a two or three dimensional array.

case – a property of text, as capitals or bold face, so called for the shallow case in which type is stored.

case conversion – a program feature that changes the property of type, as from capitals to lower case, bold, italics, etc.

case sensitive – descriptive of a command or search instruction that must follow exactly the type format, as capital or lower case, in order to obtain the correct results.

catenate – to link in series.

CD – Compact Disk; a digital disk from which data is read by laser.

CD ROM – Compact Disk Read–Only Memory; a CD containing data that cannot be altered.

cell – the area that holds a unit of information, as for a spreadsheet cell.

CGA – Color Graphics Adaptor; an early standard for the display on a color monitor screen.

character – any of the set of letters, numbers and punctuation marks available on the computer keyboard.

character code – a set of binary digits that represents a specific symbol.

character pitch – the number of characters per inch of a type font.

character recognition – identification of text or special symbols by any of several computer input devices.

character string – a set of characters processed as a unit.

chart – to set up a graph that shows the relationships among a group of associated values; the graphic representation of those values; to diagram the steps in a procedure.

chip – a semiconductor in which an integrated circuit is formed.

circuit – a complete path for the flow of electrical current.

click – to press and release a mouse button to place the cursor or make a selection.

clip art – generic artwork that can be used to embellish a document.

clone – a computer using the same operating system as IBM® microcomputers.

closed loop – a condition in which output modifies input, so that a final value is never reached, such as a spreadsheet formula in cell *B* that calls for the value of *A+B* that cannot be attained, as *B* changes each time the command is executed.

code – a combination of symbols recognized by the computer as instructions.

cold boot – restarting a computer that is completely shut down.

column– the vertical arrangement of data in a two or three dimensional array.

command – a key word directing performance of a function; an instruction to the computer.

command character – a character that expresses a control function.

command driven – descriptive of an interactive computer program that acts on each user command as it is issued.

command line – the position at which instructions are entered by the user to direct computer processing.

communication buffer – a device that provides temporary storage of data, sent or received, to allow for differences in the speed of various devices.

communication link – hardware or software that allows the transfer of data between devices.

communication protocol –standards for the transfer of data between devices.

communication software – a program that enables contact between modems.

compare– a command that contrasts files, documents, etc. for ordering or verification.

compatibility – descriptive of the ability of hardware and software to function in harmony.

compiler – a program that translates programming language into machine language.

component – any of the main elements in a computer system.

COM port – communications port; any of the connections to a computer that allow the transfer of data.

compression– the technique of compacting data for more efficient storage or transmission.

compression utility – a program that compresses files for storage to save space and restores them as required for normal use.

computer art – artwork created with the aid of a computer.

computer game – a program designed for amusement or instruction.

computer graphics – charts, graphs, diagrams or pictures produced with the aid of the computer.

computer language – characters and symbols that are understood directly by the computer.

computer system – all of the hardware and software that make up a particular computer.

concatenate – to link two or more character strings.

conditional branch – a computer instruction that is executed only if certain specific conditions are met.

configuration – the way a computer and peripherals are programmed and connected to function together.

connect time – the time a user is on line with a BBS or other telephone line.

constant – a symbol or name that represents a fixed value.

context sensitive help – the ability of some programs to pop up a help screen with information about the feature highlighted.

contrast – the relative difference between image and non–image areas in copy to be scanned.

control character – a non-printing ASCII character that issues a command to the computer.

Control key (Ctrl) – a shift key used in conjunction with other keys to execute commands.

conversational language – programming language commands that are similar to the spoken language.

conversion – the changing of a data file format to make it acceptable for a different use or a different program.

converter – software for formatting data to use in a different program; a hardware connector that permits linking of devices that would otherwise be incompatible.

coordinate system – the use of symbols to locate an element or point in a two or three dimensional array.

coprocessor – an auxiliary chip that augments the functions of the CPU.

copy – to make a duplicate, as of a file; to duplicate copy for insertion elsewhere in a document.

corona wire – the wire in an electrostatic printer that attracts toner to the surface of the paper.

cpi – characters per inch; descriptive of a type font.

cps – characters per second, a measure of the speed of a printer.

CPU – Central Processing Unit; the integrated circuits that control the operation of a microcomputer.

crash– computer or program failure; a disk failure caused by the read/write head striking the disk.

CR– Carriage Return; a reference to typewriters with moveable carriage and fixed printing head, the comparable move on a computer screen-in effect, a cursor return.

crop– in desktop publishing, trimming off any unwanted parts of a picture, drawing or other graphic image.

CRT– Cathode Ray Tube; a type of picture tube used as a computer monitor screen.

cursor – the line or block that marks the insertion point for text or graphics in a word processing or similar program.

cursor arrows – arrows on the keyboard that serve to move the insertion point up, down, right or left.

cursor control key – any key that moves the insertion point without altering copy, as arrow keys, Tab, End, Home, Page Up and Page Down.

cut and paste – the act of removing copy from one location and inserting it at another.

D

daisy wheel – a type of impact printer in which raised characters are mounted on a rotating wheel.

data – *sing*. datum; information processed by the computer.

data bank – a stockpile of information available to the computer.

database – a collection of specific related information.

database file – a file comprised of records of information in distinct, related fields.

data block – a selection of data based on a specific search criterion.

data conversion – an altering of selected data for transfer to a different program or format, as from a database file to a spreadsheet file.

data entry – the recording or updating of information to a computer file.

data field – any of the areas in a database dedicated to a particular item of information, as a date or name.

data format – the type of data acceptable in a particular field, as date, number, alphameric, etc.

data link – a connection between computer systems that allows information sharing; a validation formula in a spreadsheet or database that limits entry of data into a cell or field based on a previous entry; a link between documents containing similar information that automatically updates all documents when one is changed.

data management – the process of recording and manipulating data in the conduct of a business.

data parsing – breaking a data string down to its basic elements for conversion to another file format, as from database fields to spreadsheet cells.

data processing – manipulation of information, as by sorting or creating a report.

data record – the set of fields that comprise a unique entry in a database file.

data set – a block of related database records.

data structure – the way in which database records are organized.

data transmission – the transfer of information through a computer system or between computer systems.

data validation – a means for verifying that data in a field is of the correct type or magnitude, such as by checking for a date format

date number – the numeric value for a specific date, as by the number of the day, month and year or the number of days from a base date.

DCA – Document Content Architecture; a word processing file format.

dead file – a data file that is no longer active.

debug – to find and correct errors in a computer program or the operation of a piece of equipment.

decimal number – a value represented in base 10.

dedicated – set aside for a specific purpose, as an area in computer memory or a transmission line.

default – failure to issue specific instructions for the operation of a device or program.

default configuration – instructions or formatting for a device or program in the absence of instructions by the user.

define – to set a value for a symbol or variable.

delete – to erase or cancel, as a block of text or a file.

delimiter – a symbol such as a comma or quotation marks, used to separate items of information in a data string.

descending sort – an alphabetical or numerical arrangement from highest to lowest.

desktop – a set of computer accessory programs that emulate items found on a desk, as a calendar, calculator or note pad.

desktop computer – a personal or micro computer, designed to fit on a desk.

desktop publishing – creation of type and graphics on a desktop computer.

destination – the file, computer or peripheral to which data is being transmitted.

destructive read – a computer read–out that simultaneously erases the source file.

device– any component or peripheral that is a part of a computer system.

device driver – a program that interprets instructions for the operation of a peripheral, such as a printer

diagnostic – descriptive of a system to detect and isolate errors or malfunction in programs or equipment.

diagnostic message – an error message that describes the source of the error.

dialog box – a panel that appears on screen as a part of a program to furnish instructions, information or to request user input.

digit – a symbol representing an integer in a numbering system, as 0-9 in decimal notation or 0-F in hexadecimal.

digital – represented by a distinct value.

digital camera – a camera that records images in digital format for downloading and viewing on a computer screen.

digital data – information recorded according to a system of numbers, as binary for the computer.

digital recording – sound recorded as discrete values.

DIP switch – Dual In–line Package switch; an integrated circuit that can be programmed with the use of a series of toggle switches.

directory – in the hierarchical file structure, a division that holds related program or data files and sub-directories.

disk – a computer storage device.

disk crash – destruction of a disk and the data it holds as a result of the read/write head coming in contact with the surface of the disk; any disk failure, sometimes recoverable.

disk drive – the device that holds, spins and reads from or writes to the disk.

diskette – a floppy or removable disk.

disk formatting – a series of reference points recorded on a disk that allow orderly storage and retrieval of data.

disk fragmentation – a condition that occurs after many reads and writes to a disk in that data for a single file is scattered throughout the disk rather than being stored in contiguous sectors.

disk sector – a section of a disk track.

disk tracks – concentric circles of a disk where data is stored.

display console – a screen where the user views data and monitors the operation of the computer.

dithered image – a pattern of black or colored dots of varying size that create the image of a full range of gray or color tones on a computer monitor screen.

document – a page of data; a printed copy of the information held in computer memory.

documentation – information or instructions relating to a program, procedure, etc.

document reader – a device that is able to recognize an image on paper and convert it to digital data.

document retrieval – a system for identifying and retrieving data stored in the computer.

DOS – Disk Operating System; a program that controls all of the basic operations of the computer.

dot matrix – printing in which characters are formed by numerous dots arranged according to the pattern established for the character.

double click – pressing and releasing a button of a mouse twice in succession, used to activate a selection in some programs.

double density disk – a diskette on which data is packed in order to double its capacity.

double–sided disk – a diskette on which data is stored on both sides.

download – the transfer of data to another computer or peripheral device.

downward compatible – descriptive of the ability of a program to run with data or formatting created by an earlier version.

dpi – dots per inch; a measure of the quality of image from a scanner or printer; the more dots per inch, the finer the image appears to the eye.

drag – to press and hold a mouse button down while moving the cursor, thereby moving the image under the cursor.

DRAM – Dynamic Random Access Memory; memory that must be constantly refreshed to be retained and that is erased when the power is off.

drive – the device that moves a disk or tape past the read/write head in order to access or store data.

drive designation – the letter assigned to a drive in order to identify it for sourcing.

driver – a program or routine that translates and conveys messages between a computer and a peripheral.

drop down menu – a program feature that presents a list of options on screen when a menu title is selected.

dump – to transfer the entire contents of a file to a printer, monitor or storage device.

E

EBCDIC – Extended Binary Coded Decimal Interchange Code; a standard code for numeric representation of alphanumeric characters.

echo – in a DOS program, command or information lines that are displayed on the monitor screen.

edit – to make changes, as additions or deletions, to a file or document.

edit commands – commands in a program that facilitate the process of editing, such as *move, copy, paste*, etc.

edit key – any of the special keyboard keys, such as *insert* or *delete*, used to edit text.

edlin – a line by line text editor available in DOS.

EDP – Electronic Data Processing; any manipulation of data by electronic means.

EGA – Enhanced Graphics Adapter; a standard for the display on a color monitor screen.

EIS, executive information system – a computer software package that permits storage and retrieval of a variety of material, such as appointments, customer contacts, or financial data.

electronic bulletin board – a computer message center.

electronic mail – messages exchanged with the use of a computer through an internal network or the services of an outside vendor.

electronic spreadsheet – a computer version of a worksheet with data organized in rows and columns.

electrostatic printer – a device that creates images through the adherence of a toner to charged portions of a receiver.

embed – to fix an element from one docu-ment or file into another.

embedded commands – program instructions that establish and maintain the appearance, position and special characteristics of a text or graphics element.

embedded object – a drawing, chart, sound recording, etc. that is fixed in a text based document.

embedded pointer – the link between an embedded object and its source file, as the link between a chart and its spreadsheet source data.

emulation software – a program that directs a peripheral to imitate another, usually to improve performance, as the emulation of laser quality by a dot matrix printer.

enabled – allowed to operate, as by computer command.

encryption – jumbling or coding of sensitive data for security purposes.

END – a program code indicating the final command.

End key – a cursor movement key that sends the cursor to the end of a line of text and, used in conjunction with other keys, to the bottom right of the screen, the bottom of the page or the end of the file.

end of page indicator – a command embedded in a document to indicate the end of a printed page; the sensor on a printer that signals the end of a sheet of paper.

enter – to add information, as text to a document, records to a database, etc.

Enter key – a function key used to signal the end of a block of copy or enable a selected command; also expressed as CR or carriage return or Return.

envelope feeder – a device that attaches to the printer to allow the automatic feeding of envelopes for addressing.

environment – referring to the type of operating system, the peripherals and programs that make up a computer system.

equation – an expression of equality, as in a spreadsheet formula.

equipment compatibility – the quality of computers and peripherals to share data without translation.

erase – to delete, as a block of copy or a file, from storage.

errorlevel – in a program or batch file, a value that is tested to signal a branch.

error message – a message from an operating system or program displayed on the monitor or printer indicating that an error in processing has occurred, often citing the source of the error.

escape – to discontinue processing, or to return to a previous menu or operating level.

escape character – ASCII control character 027 signaled by the Escape key and used in certain program sequences to signal the start of a printer or monitor control code.

Escape key (Esc) – a function key that triggers the escape command.

escape sequence – a character string prefaced by the escape code (ASCII 027) so that computer will recognize it as a command.

execute – to carry out an instruction or set of instructions.

execution – performance of an operation.

exit – a program branch that returns control to the next higher level; to leave a subroutine and return to the main application program or to leave an application and return to the operating system.

expansion card – a board that is installed in the computer to provide additional memory or functions.

expansion slots – positions in the computer reserved for the installation of expansion or control boards.

expression– a symbol or symbols that describe a mathematical operation.

F

face– all of the styles of a type of a particular design; see also, *font*.

fan fold paper – a continuous stream of computer paper with equally spaced feed holes along the borders, perforated between pages and folded accordion–style so as to lie flat.

fax – facsimile; a copy of a document sent to a remote terminal by a fax machine or computer modem over telephone lines; to send such a copy.

fax card – a controller board in a computer that enables the transmission of a facsimile.

feed holes – holes along the sides of continuous feed computer paper, engaged by a sprocket wheel for feeding into the printer.

fetch – to retrieve data or a file from storage.

field – the part of a data base record that contains a specific item of information; the basic unit of a data base record.

field mark – a code that signals the begin-ning or end of a database field.

field name – the identification of a specific field in a database record.

file – a set of related information, as spreadsheets, database, etc., identified by name and manipulated as a unit.

file attributes – special nature of a file for identification or protection such as read- only, archived or hidden.

file conversion – the transfer of a file's formatting codes to allow access by another program.

file maintenance – correcting and updating files and directories to reflect the most recent data available and purging the system of outdated files.

file management – the organization and tracking of files by the operating system and the user.

file manager – a software utility designed to simplify the task of locating and organizing files.

file name – the designation that identifies a data file.

file name extension – a tag of up to three characters following a file name that aids in identification by the operating system, a program or the user.

file protection – a file attribute that identifies a data file as read-only; a device on a floppy disk that can be set to make the files on the disk read–only.

file server – a computer that stores a library of program and data files for a number of users in a network.

filter – that which refines output by sifting input according to user- or program-designated criterion; user input that restricts output to a certain class or group of information; machine controls that eliminate extraneous signals.

financial planning software – a program that assists the user in budgeting, saving, investment decisions, etc.

fixed disk – a computer disk that is permanently mounted in its drive.

floppy disk – a removable memory storage device; also, *diskette*.

floppy disk controller – the hardware and software that manages the operation of a disk drive.

flow chart – a graphic representation of the progression through a series of operations, as of a computer program or the paperwork in an office.

font – traditionally descriptive of one type face and style in one size; with the introduction of scalable fonts, one font often refers to a type face in a single style in a wide range of sizes.

font cartridge – a device that attaches to a printer to make additional fonts available to it.

forecasting – the process of attempting to predict future conditions based on a study of past conditions.

foreground – that taking place in the view of, and usually under the control of, the user; processing that has priority over all others.

form – a document designed for the orderly entry of data; the configuration or arrangement of data in a report.

format – to initialize a disk to accept data; the system by which data is held in a particular file, such as spreadsheet or database; the layout, or arrangement, of information in a document.

form feed – a command to the printer to advance the paper the length of one form or one page.

formula – a string of symbols that calculate to a value, as in a spreadsheet cell that calls for the total of the values in other specified cells, or that calculates to a logical *true* or *false* as in a conditional branch command.

fragmentation– broken into parts; a condition wherein files on a disk are recorded to scattered rather than contiguous seg-ments.

frame – a window on a monitor screen that provides a view of information displayed by a program.

friction feed – a type of printer feed, usually used for single sheets.

full screen access – descriptive of a program feature that allows editing of data anywhere on the monitor screen.

function code – any symbol or set of symbols that generates an instruction to the computer.

Function keys (F*n*) – where *n* equals a number, one of a set of ten or twelve keys that alone or in conjunction with Ctrl, Alt or Shift execute commands in certain programs.

G

GET– a program instruction to fetch data, a file or command from a non-contiguous source.

gigabyte – one thousand million (one billion) bytes

GIGO – Garbage In Garbage Out, the axiom that the quality of information from computer proc-essing is directly related to the quality of data entered into the computer.

global– descriptive of formatting or instructions that affect all of the elements in a file or all of the files created by a program.

global search – descriptive of a search through every directory, sub–directory or file on a disk; a command to find all occurrences of a string in a file, in a group of files or anywhere on the disk.

GOTO– a program instruction to branch off to a new set of commands.

grammar checker – a program that inspects a file or document for grammatical errors, advises the user of the error and suggests alternatives.

graph– a chart that displays the relative magni-tude of associated elements as bars, columns, or sections of a pie.

graphic display – the depiction of graphic ele-ments on a computer monitor screen.

graphics capability – a computer monitor with a graphic interface that permits the depiction of picture elements on screen; a printer that has the ability to print picture elements.

gray scale – a graduated series of dot patterns to depict various shades of gray on the monitor.

grid – a pattern of columns and rows for recording data as for a spreadsheet or for posi-

tioning elements as for optical character recognition.

H

hacker – one who has acquired skill in the use of computers for personal pleasure.

halt – the untimely termination of computer processing.

hand held computer – a computer small enough to be held in the hand, often used to keep track of appointments and addresses.

handshaking – the protocol for identification and communication between two pieces of equipment.

hang–up – a temporary halt in processing.

hard copy – information to be input through the keyboard or scanner; a printout of informa-tion.

hard disk – a disk that is mounted with its own drive, usually installed in the computer case.

hard error – an equipment malfunction or mistake in processing caused by hardware.

hardware – the computer itself and any of the peripheral devices that are a part of the system.

head – the read/write head in a disk drive; the device on an impact or ink jet printer that transfers characters to paper.

head crash – a circumstance in which the read/write head contacts the surface of the disk.

header – a headline on a document or report.

Help – a feature in most programs that offers guidance to the user; see also, *context sensitive help*.

help screen – on screen guidance for the user, often interactive, allowing a selection of sub-jects about which the program offers informa-tion.

hexadecimal – a numbering system in base sixteen used in computer notation.

hierarchical – referring to a system arranged in order of rank; in the computer, a system of directories and files wherein the *root directory* is of the highest order.

high level language – a programming language that is somewhat similar to spoken language.

highlighted – an element on the screen that is set apart from others by underlining, reverse video or contrasting color; of a block of copy or graphic element that has been selected for some purpose.

Home (key) – a cursor movement key that sends the cursor to the beginning of a line of text and, used in conjunction with other keys, to the top left of the screen, the top of the page or the beginning of a file.

hopper – the tray that holds single sheets of paper for feeding into a printer.

hot key – a key combination that executes a macro or command that would otherwise require several key strokes.

hot line – a telephone number provided by an equipment or software manufacturer or dealer through which a user may access technical help.

housekeeping – the process of deleting old files, arranging files in their proper directories and maintaining an orderly file structure for efficient operation.

I

icon– a graphic image on a monitor screen that represents a directory, file, utility, etc. and that can be selected with a mouse click.

IF (statement) – a select word in a conditional branch specifying that IF a condition exists, the first set of instructions is to be followed, otherwise, follow a different set of instructions.

illegal character – a symbol that is unacceptable in a specific situation, as those symbols not available in a particular type font or a letter placed in a database number field.

illegal instruction – a reserved word or command in a formula that is not available in that particular program.

image enhancement – altering or improving a graphic image such as art or a photograph by use of a computer program.

imaging – to create or modify a graphic representation with the use of a computer.

impact printer – a printer that creates an image by striking the paper.

inclusive – incorporating as part of the whole, such as the part of a formula in which terms or values joined by the reserved word *AND*, often enclosed by parenthesis, must both be considered in evaluating the formula.

information – any data that can be stored, retrieved and manipulated by a computer.

information management – the systems and techniques involved in effectively compiling and manipulating useful data.

information processing – the manipulation of compiled data and the compilation of reports from the data.

information retrieval – descriptive of the techniques for accessing data from storage in the form or pattern that the user desires.

initialize – to format a disk to accept data; to boot up a computer by loading the system files it needs to become functional.

ink jet printer – a printer that forms images from tiny jets of ink spayed on paper.

input – information conveyed to a computer or peripheral from the keyboard, a disk or other memory device, or an external source, such as a telephone line.

input buffer – the area of computer memory that accepts and stores input for transfer to its destination.

input device – any equipment linked to the computer that enters source data, such as a keyboard, an optical scanner or a modem.

input/output (I/O) – a reference to the conventions for transmitting data between a computer and its peripherals or an external device.

inquiry routine – the technique for seeking specific records from a database.

installation – the process of setting up and configuring a computer system or program; the computer system so installed.

instruction – a direction to the computer to set a parameter or execute an operation.

instruction code – the language understood by a particular computer or program.

instruction format – the syntax required by a particular program for issuing a command.

integrated circuit – an electronic device that contains a number of circuit elements working together.

integrated software – descriptive of applications that are able to share data; a program package that offers a combination of features, such as a word processor, spreadsheet, and database capability.

integrated system – a combination of computers and peripherals that are compatible.

interactive program – an application that responds to each user command as it is entered, then waits for the next command.

interface – hardware or software that forms a link between devices and allows them to communicate with each other.

interleaving – a routine that directs the computer to switch between applications, thus appearing to run both at the same time, such as printing in the background while accepting new data entered in the foreground.

internal storage – data storage that is built into, and directly accessible by, the computer.

interrupt – a control signal that directs the computer to halt processing on one level and move to another.

interrupt priority – the order of precedence in which signals are processed, for example, input from the keyboard usually has priority over background printing.

inventory control program – a system for creating an accounting of goods in inventory by adjusting for additions and withdrawals, often in conjunction with accounts receivable and accounts payable so that the quantity and value of inventory is adjusted with each transaction.

I/O – Input/Output.

I/O buffer – a portion of memory dedicated to the temporary storage of data received or to be sent by the computer—the buffer compensates for differences in communication speeds between devices and prevents the interruption of other operations.

I/O bus – a group of lines that carries signals between devices.

I/O port – the physical connector between the computer and its peripherals.

iterate – to say or do again, as a search command that is repeated numerous times with different values.

J

job – a task or series of tasks to be accomplished by the computer.

job cost system – a cost accounting procedure that isolates the costs associated with the manufacture of a specific quantity of a product.

job entry system – a procedure whereby data relative to a manufacturing process, such as materials requisitioned and labor expended, are recorded for later evaluation; the procedure for setting up the com-puter to perform a task or series of tasks.

job processing – the execution of a particular task or series of tasks by the computer.

justify – to space text so that it is lined up at both side margins; also called *full justify*.

K

kerning – descriptive of proportional spacing between typeset characters.

keyboard – a panel of buttons containing the alphabet, numbers and various symbols used as the primary device for entering data into a computer.

keyboard lockout – a program feature that prevents further entry from the keyboard while the computer is processing; a security device to prevent access to the computer by an unauthorized user.

keypad – a small, special purpose keyboard with a limited number of buttons.

key word – a word or words in a formula that indicate the operation to be performed.

kilobyte (KB) – one thousand bytes.

L

label – a name that identifies a computer disk, file, program routine, etc.

LAN – Local Area Network; a group of computers that are linked to share common programs, data, output devices, etc.

language – a precise system of vocabulary and syntax for writing programs; *absolute* or *machine* language refers to instructions that can be understood directly by the computer; an *artificial* or *high level* language more closely emulates spoken English to make programming easier.

laptop computer – a portable computer complete with monitor and keyboard as a unit, smaller in size than a desktop, larger than a notebook computer.

laser – light amplification by stimulated emission of radiation; a device that emits intense light of a precise wavelength.

laser disk – a storage disk that is read using laser technology.

laser printer – an electrostatic printer that uses laser technology to create images on paper.

layer – the third dimension in a three dimensional array.

LCD – Liquid Crystal Display; a monitor screen that uses liquid crystals to create an image.

leader – in typesetting, a series of symbols joining two character strings, often periods, dashes or a line; a symbol represented by a set of three periods (...) usually representing an incomplete expression.

letter quality – descriptive of the quality of characters printed on a typewriter, a measure of the relative quality of the image from a computer printer.

level – descriptive of the separation or division of otherwise similar elements, as the level of a directory in the hierarchical structure; denoting relative position in value, performance, etc.

library – a collection, as of programs, databases, etc.

light sensitive – descriptive of a material that reacts to the stimulus of light.

limiting – descriptive of a device that, because of its slower speed or capacity, restricts processing.

line feed – a command to the printer to advance the paper one line.

link – the connection between two computers or a computer and peripherals; the connection between an embedded object and its source that permits updating in one instance to update all instances of the object.

linked documents – records or files that are connected so that data from one will be automatically entered in another, such as billing records that are automatically added to the accounts receivable file.

load – to call up a program or data to the computer's main memory from a storage device.

lockout– denial of access to the computer by a security system; in a program, temporary denial of access to commands during processing.

log – a record of times and dates the computer is accessed by each user.

logic– correct reasoning; the use of symbols in a formula to test the relationship between elements.

logic circuit – computer circuitry that controls logic functions.

logic formula – a group of symbols that calculates to a logical *true* or *false*, as for a conditional branch.

logic operator – a symbol used in logic formulas.

log in or **log on** – to type the password that allows access to the computer.

lookup table – a set of variables arranged in a two dimensional array.

loop– a set of program instructions that are executed until a specific condition is met.

loop ender – a value expressed in a loop instruction to signal a branch and prevent unnecessary iterations of the loop.

loop feedback – the output value that modi-fies input for the next iteration of a loop instruction.

loosely coupled – descriptive of computers that are connected, but that operate independent of one another.

M

machine dependent – a program that can only function on a particular computer or type of computer.

machine error – a program error caused by an equipment malfunction.

machine readable – characters or symbols that can be read directly into a computer.

macro – a set of computer instructions that are executed by a single command or a hot key combination.

macro library – a collection of macros available to the user.

magnetic disk – a computer storage medium, a hard disk or floppy disk.

mail merge – a program feature that combines

a mailing list with the body of a letter.

main memory – the internal memory of a computer from which programs are run.

manual link – a data link between documents or files that is updated only at the command of the user.

manufacturer's software – a system program or driver that is supplied by the OEM for a specific piece of equipment.

margin – the limits of a body of copy on a page; the unprinted area around a block of copy.

mask – a pattern of bits used in search and comparison operations.

master – a template or formatted document to which variable data is entered; a primary or main file, such as a database, to which data is entered only after verification.

math coprocessor – a chip that works in conjunction with the CPU to perform high speed arithmetic calculations.

mathematical operator – a symbol that governs an arithmetic computation.

matrix – a pattern for comparison of elements in optical character recognition; a two dimensional array.

megabyte (MB) – one million bytes.

megahertz (MHz) – one million cycles per second.

memory – that part of a computer where data is stored.

memory card – a computer add-on to provide additional memory storage.

memory resident – descriptive of a program or utility that is loaded in RAM.

menu – a list of user options.

menu–driven – descriptive of a program that offers menus for the user to select options.

merge – to combine, as a file or database.

merged sort – to combine and arrange in a particular order, as alphabetically, sets of database files.

microcomputer – a small computer driven by a single integrated circuit.

microprocessor – a chip that is the central processing unit for a microcomputer.

MIDI – Musical Instrument Digital Interface; the protocol for interaction between a digitized musical instrument and a computer.

minicomputer – a computer smaller than a mainframe and larger than a microcomputer, designed to support multiple users.

MIS – Management Information System; an organization's facilities for gathering, storing, and managing data for use in decision making.

mnemonics–memory aids; commands designed so as to make remembering their function easier, as *Q* for *quit*, or *P* for *print*.

modem– modulator/demodulator; a device for translating digital signals to telephone signals and back, used to communicate between computers via telephone lines.

modular– descriptive of a computer program made up of a series of routines that perform special tasks.

module – a device that is part of a larger unit, designed for a specific function.

modulo (MOD) – a program command that gives the remainder of a division.

monitor– a display screen that permits viewing of the user's interaction with a computer.

monochrome– a monitor that displays data in one color or shades of one color.

motherboard – the primary circuit board in a computer.

mouse– a hand held device that is moved on a flat surface to position the cursor on a monitor screen, often with programmable buttons so as to issue commands to the computer.

move– a command that copies text or a graphic element to a new location and deletes the original.

multimedia– descriptive of the ability to embed a combination of sight and sound elements in a computer program, such as a section of video tape or sound in a text document.

multiplexer– a system that manages signals between two or more devices simultaneously.

multitasking– the ability of a CPU to execute two or more programs or routines at the same time, either by independent processing or by *interleaving*.

multi–user system– a computer system designed to mange input and output from several terminals at the same time.

N

name – a designation that identifies a data set, a file, a database field, a spreadsheet range, etc.

near letter quality (NLQ) – a designation of the ability of a printer to emulate typewriter quality printing.

network– a number of computers and peripherals interconnected so as to share information and resources.

network server – a computer that stores and manages programs and data for other computers in the network.

non breaking space – a feature in some word processing programs that keeps two words from being separated at the end of a line.

nondestructive read – access of a computer file while maintaining a copy of the file in storage.

non printing character – a command or formatting character in computer code.

NOT – an exclusive operator used in programming, as for a spreadsheet formula.

notation – the combination of symbols, mnemonics, etc. used to designate computer commands.

notebook computer– a portable computer with monitor screen and keyboard contained in a single unit, smaller in physical size than a laptop, but often as powerful as a desktop.

number crunching – manipulation of numeric data, as for financial reports from a spreadsheet.

O

object linking and embedding (OLE) – connecting text or graphics data between documents and applications-linking implies that a change of data in one position changes all occurrences of the same data.

OCR – Optical Character Recognition; a program capability that reads graphic text from a hard copy or computer file to translate it into characters that can be manipulated by the user.

octal – a numbering system in base eight.

OEM – Original Equipment Manufacturer; the manufacturer, as contrasted to the distributor, of hardware.

office automation – use of the computer to accomplish the tasks associated with running a business.

off line – descriptive of equipment that is not directly connected to or controlled by the computer; equipment that is turned off.

on line – a reference to equipment that is turned on and connected to a controller.

op code – operation code; a symbol or set of characters that directs the computer to execute a command.

open – a file that has been copied from memory storage to RAM and is available to the user.

operator – a symbol that represents a mathematical or logical function, as +, =, >, etc.

options – choices available to the user.

OR – a selective operator used in programming, as for a spreadsheet formula.

order – to arrange in sequence.

output – any information transferred from one device to another in the computer system; processed information delivered to the user, as by a printout.

output device – a peripheral unit that delivers

information to the user, as a printer or plotter.

overhead– volatile memory that is used by various operating and utility functions, and is therefore not available for programs.

overload – a condition that can cause a crash, brought on by an attempt to transfer more data than memory can hold or transferring data faster than the CPU can process it.

overwrite – to save information to storage already occupied, thus obliterating the old data.

P

pack– to compress data for more efficient use of disk storage space.

packaged software – a program adaptable to a variety of uses that is available on the open market.

page – a unit of memory used by the computer to manipulate data in storage; a single sheet of output from the printer.

pagination– the numbering of printed pages in a document or file.

paper feeder – the device that controls the flow of paper through the printer.

parallel – descriptive of operations that occur simultaneously.

parallel interface – a multichannel interface that allows the transfer of a full computer word at one time.

parallel port – a connection on the computer for communicating with a peripheral device, such as a printer.

parameter – a limit or characteristic, as of a program or operating system.

parse – to break down into parts, as in separating the elements of a data string from a database into columns for a spreadsheet.

partition – a divider, as on a disk for file management or for processing a database sort.

password– a series of characters or symbols by which a user gains access to a computer, application or file.

path– the course followed by the computer in seeking programs and files.

pattern recognition – the technique used by a program to identify elements through comparison with a standard matrix as in optical character recognition.

PC– personal computer; a microcomputer originally designed for individual use at home or in business.

PDA, personal digital assistant – A communications device featuring an electronic note pad that records written notes, retrieves electronic mail, and transfers information to a fax, personal computer, or another PDA via cellular phone.

peripheral – a device that is connected to a computer and controlled by it.

peripheral program – a utility; a program that adds to the capabilities of a computer or another program, such as a memory manager or grammar checker.

permanent memory – a storage medium, such as a computer disk, that retains its memory when power is off.

PIM, Personal Information Manager – a compute program for recording personal data, such as notes or appointments.

pin feed – a device that feeds a continuous form through a printer by engaging a series of holes along the edges of the form; same as *tractor feed* or *sprocket feed*.

pirated software – programs obtained outside of normal or legal channels.

pitch – the number of characters per inch of a type font.

pixel – picture element; a basic component of a computer picture.

platen – the roller that paper rests against while images are being formed by an impact printer.

plotter – a computer peripheral that produces charts or graphs as output.

point of sale system – a computer network that accepts input from remote terminals located at a retailer's cash register and uses the data to perform a variety of tasks such as creating sales reports, updating inventory records, etc.

point and click – to select an object by moving the mouse cursor to it, then pressing and releasing the mouse button.

poll – an I/O function that scans transmission lines to check their status and ascertain when data is to be sent or received.

port – any of the connections to a computer that allow the transfer of data.

power supply – a device that converts AC power to low level DC power for the computer.

power surge – a sudden increase in electrical energy that can damage a computer's system and files.

power up – to turn on a piece of equipment.

precedence – the order in which arithmetic operations in a formula are processed by the computer.

preprocessing – configuring data before it is entered into a program, such as converting spreadsheet rows to comma separated values for entering into a database.

print control character – any of the symbols

that control the operation or output of the printer, as for line spacing, double width characters, etc.

printed circuit – a circuit created by applying a conductor to an insulated board.

printer fonts – type fonts built into a printer or a printer cartridge.

Print Screen (key) – the function key that commands the computer to copy the data on the monitor screen to the printer.

processing – the manipulation of data by the computer.

production control program – a system for scheduling and allocating materials and processes associated with a manufacturing operation.

program – a set of directions that instruct the computer in the performance of a task.

program compatibility – descriptive of the ability of programs to work together or to share data.

programmable – descriptive of a device whose function can be altered by the user.

programmable function key – a function key to which a command or series of commands may be assigned.

programmable mouse – a mouse whose buttons may be assigned a command or series of commands, usually in conjunction with key combinations.

programmer – an individual who creates or alters routines for a computer.

programming language – a precise system of vocabulary and syntax for writing instructions for the computer; a high level language.

program package – all of the files and manuals needed to run a program; descriptive of the qualities of a program; a set of applications, as for accounting functions, that make up a program.

prompt – a cursor; a highlight on the monitor screen that indicates where the next character will be entered; a program query or instruction.

proportional spacing – descriptive of the display of type so that the white space between characters is approximately the same regardless of the width of the char-acter itself.

proprietary software – packaged software that is sold with the provision that the seller retains ownership and the buyer purchases only the license to use the software subject to the provisions of a licensing agreement.

protected field – a block of text, formula, etc. that cannot be altered.

protected files – read–only files; computer memory that may be read, but that cannot be altered.

protocol – the rules governing the transfer of data between a computer and peripherals or another computer.

public domain software – programs that are not copyrighted and may be used or altered by anyone.

Q

qualifier – a symbol or set of symbols in a formula that limits or clearly defines an element.

query – a request for data, as a record or set of records from a database.

query language – formal notation for requesting specific data, as from a database.

queue – a list for processing, such as for a printer

QWERTY keyboard – a keyboard with letters arranged the same as those on a typewriter.

R

ragged right – descriptive of type that is lined up with the left margin, but not the right.

RAM – Random Access Memory; memory that may be accessed independent of the previous call.

range – all of the values that a variable may assume; in a spreadsheet or database, user–defined limits of data affected by a command.

read–only – descriptive of a computer file that may be accessed, but not altered.

read/write head – the device in a disk drive that reads from and writes to the storage disk.

record – the group of fields that make up a unique entry in a database.

recording head – the part of a disk drive that writes data to the disk.

reformat – to change the style of text; to convert a file for use by a different application.

refresh – to revive or renew volatile memory so as to maintain or alter it, such as to redraw the image on the monitor screen.

relational database – a database that has a field in common with another so that information may be drawn from both and combined.

relational operator – a mathematical symbol that represents the relationship between two values.

remote – descriptive of a computer or peripheral that is not in the immediate area of the host computer.

remote access – the ability of a computer to connect and interact with a computer or peripheral that is not in the immediate area.

remote entry system – a data entry terminal

that is located at a distance from the host computer.

repeat key – a program feature that directs a function key or key combination to repeat the last entry from the keyboard, such as a line of typing or a formatting command.

report – a document on disk or hard copy that summarizes the output from data processing.

reserved word or **symbol** – a word or symbol in a programming language that has a special meaning.

reset– to command a return to an original state; to restart the computer.

resolution– the relative quality of the image on a monitor screen or produced by a print-er.

resources – the sum of all the capabilities of a computer system determined by its hardware and software configuration.

restore – to return to a previous state, as a program feature that deletes the effect of the last entry from the keyboard, such as typing or for-matting.

Return (key) – Same as *Enter key*.

reverse video – the display, on a monitor screen, of dark characters on a light background.

right justified – type aligned along the right margin of a document.

ROM– Read–Only Memory; memory, as on a compact disk, that can be accessed, but cannot be altered.

root directory – the primary directory in a hier-archical file structure containing the command and system configuration files.

routine– a set of computer instructions that per-forms a particular task.

row – the horizontal arrangement of data in a two or three dimensional array.

run time – the period required for a computer to perform a particular task, such as a mail merge.

S

scalable font – descriptive of a type font that can be reproduced in a wide range of sizes.

scanner – an optical device for reading hard copy and translating it to digital data.

screen – the device that displays information from the computer and monitors its activity..

screen blanker– a program that prevents burning an image into a monitor screen by blacking it out after a specified period of inactivity.

screen refresh – constant renewal of the monitor screen to provide an image that does not flicker.

screen saver – a *screen blanker* that displays a random, moving pattern on the screen.

scrolling – movement of the image on a monitor screen to view elements outside its borders.

search – a feature in some programs that locates a word or phrase in text files, records in a data base file, or a particular file.

search object – the element, as a name or symbol, that is the basis for a search command.

select – to choose from the alternatives offered.

sequential – ordered; descriptive of data, files, etc. arranged or accessed in a particular order.

sequential search – an orderly progression through data, files, etc. until the object of the search is found.

serial interface – a single line connector that transmits data sequentially, one bit a time.

serial port – a connection on the computer for communicating with a peripheral device.

server – a computer that stores and manages programs and data for other computers or terminal in a network.

shared resources – descriptive of devices or peripherals that serve two or more computers or terminals.

shift – to change position or function; shift keys (Shift, Ctrl, Alt) in combination with other keys are often used to execute commands.

shortcut key – a combination of a character or function key with a shift key, used to exe-cute a command.

shovelware – computer programs or data distinguished by volume rather than quality.

simultaneous processing – the processing, by a computer, of two or more tasks at the same time.

slot – a position in a computer frame designed to hold a controller board.

soft carriage return – in some word proces-s-ing programs, a forced end to a line of text within a paragraph.

soft hyphen – a hyphen that appears between syllables only when the word is broken at the end of a line.

software– any program, such as an applic-ation, system file, device driver, etc. that furnishes instructions to the computer.

software documentation – instructions for the loading and operation of software.

software utilities – programs that assist in the operation of the computer as by improving performance, managing files, etc.

sort – to place data or files in a predetermined order, as alphabetical, by number, by date, by size, etc.

sort field – in a database file, the field on which the sort is based.

sound driver – the program that controls the

recording, manipulation and reproduction of sound in a multimedia computer.

source data – data that has been entered into the computer for manipulation.

space – an interval that is not occupied by a character, a zero, or a blank.

special character – any character that is not a letter or a number, such as a punctuation mark or mathematical symbol.

speech recognition – a computer that accepts and acts on speech commands.

speech synthesis – the emulation of human speech by a computer.

speed key – a combination of a character or function key with a shift key, used to execute a command.

spell checker – a feature in some word processors that checks and corrects spellinging in a document.

spike – a momentary sharp increase in electrical current that may damage the computer or its memory; a program feature that permits a number of independent elements to be removed from a document to be inserted elsewhere as a unit.

split screen – a program feature that per-mits viewing different program elements at the same time.

spooler – a hardware or software device for storing computer output to be sent to the printer at a later time.

spreadsheet – a document with data, arranged in rows and columns, that can be adjusted for the entry of additional data and manipulated for reporting.

sprocket feed – a printer device that feeds a continuous form through the printer by engaging a series of holes along the edges of the form; same as *pin feed* or *tractor feed*.

stack – an area of memory in RAM reserved for temporary storage of data.

standard interface – connection between a computer and peripherals that complies with an industry standard.

statistical analysis – the evaluation of a body of numerical data relating to a particular subject.

step – any one of a series of related actions.

storage – the area in a computer, as a hard disk, or an external device, as a diskette or tape, where copies of program and data files are kept for future use.

storage capacity – the volume of data, expressed in bytes, that can be contained in a storage device.

string – a series of characters or symbols processed as a unit.

subscript – in typesetting, a character that is positioned below the baseline of the body of text, as H_2SO_4

suffix – an addendum to a computer file name, separated from the name by a period, that aids in identifying the file contents, as *.SYS* for a system file, *.TXT* for a text file, etc.

summarize – to abbreviate by discarding unnecessary detail; to condense data by totaling like elements.

superscript – in typesetting, a character that is positioned above the baseline of the body of text, as x^2.

Super VGA – a technology that creates a monitor display of higher resolution than VGA.

support services – ongoing help available to the user from hardware or software manufacturers or vendors, usually via a toll free hot line or bulletin board.

surge – an increase in electrical current that may damage the computer or its memory

surge suppresser – a device that protects the computer and peripherals from power surges.

symbol – any of the characters available from the computer keyboard; a program defined element, as a mark or word, that represents a command or instruction.

symbolic logic – the use of symbols in a formula to test the relationship between elements.

symbolic name – a label that identifies a program, a file, a data field, a range of data, etc.

syntax – the rules governing the precise way that statements must be constructed in a programming language.

system – an orderly arrangement of related elements, as all of the hardware devices that make up a *computer system* or all of the hardware, software and procedures that make up an *accounting system*.

system backup – a reserved copy of all of the program and data files in a computer; a second set of hardware that can replace the primary hardware in the event of equipment failure.

system disk – a disk that contains the basic files the computer needs to operate.

system prompt – the symbols or characters on a monitor screen that indicate the command line where instructions to the operating system are to be typed.

system resources – all of the elements unique to a particular computer system, as peripheral devices, type of CPU, memory, etc.

system software – the programs that control the operation of the computer and its peripherals.

T

tab – tabulator; a user–defined position on a text line to which the cursor can be advanced with a single key stroke; to move by activating the *tab key*.

tab key – a cursor control key that moves the insertion point according to program instructions, such as to a fixed position on a line of text, to the adjacent cell in a spreadsheet or to the next item on a menu.

table – an orderly arrangement of related data in rows and columns; a two dimensional array.

tape backup – a reserve copy of computer programs and data on magnetic tape.

target – objective, as a file or device to which data is to be transmitted, or a directory to which a file is to be copied or saved.

task – a job assigned to the computer.

temporary storage – the computer's main memory; the area that holds program and data files that are active.

terminal – a device connected to a main computer or file server usually comprised of an input device, as a keyboard, and a monitor screen.

test – to subject to diagnostics or sample problems to ascertain that a hardware device or program is working properly.

test data – data whose output is known for a particular formula or routine.

test run – to operate with test data to confirm the validity of a formula or routine.

text – the body of a document; any set of character and symbols that conveys a message.

text editor – a basic program for altering text without formatting.

three dimensional array – an ordered group of like elements, aligned in rows, columns and layers.

three dimensional graphics – the simulation, on a computer monitor screen, of a three dimensional object.

toggle – a switch that may be in either of two states; to select one of two options.

touch terminal – a device that allows selection or entry of data by touching areas of the monitor screen.

trackball – a hand held device, similar to a mouse, but with a fixed base holding a sphere that is manipulated to move the cursor.

tractor feed – a device that feeds a continuous form through a printer by engaging a series of holes along the edges of the form; same as *pin feed* or *sprocket feed*.

transaction – a completed action.

transaction file – a record of recent transactions, used to update a master file, such as a recording of daily sales used to update the sales account, receivables, cash account, inventory, etc.

transaction terminal – a device that permits remote input of data directly to the computer, such as on a shop floor or at a cash register.

transfer – to move data or files from one location, storage device or computer to another.

transient – temporary, as a file that is created by a program while it is processing, then deleted when processing is completed.

translate – to change signals to a different format, as from analog to digital; to adapt data files to a format that can be read by a different program.

transmission – the transfer of signals between parts of a computer system.

transmission speed – the rate at which data can be sent and received.

transparent – descriptive of computer processing that is taking place in the background, not under the direct supervision of, or apparent to, the user.

tree – a graphic representation of a directory structure showing the directories that branch from the root directory, then their subdirectories, etc.

troubleshoot – to attempt to locate the source of a hardware or software problem and correct it.

truncate – to shorten by eliminating less significant parts, as by rounding off a decimal number or eliminating leading zeros in a number.

TSR – terminate and stay resident; a program feature, such as a pop-up note pad, that remains in RAM when not in use, available to be called up in the active window as needed.

tutorial – an adjunct to a program that teaches the user how to use the program.

two dimensional array – an ordered group of like elements, formed in rows and columns.

type ahead buffer – an area of memory that stores key strokes entered faster than they can be processed.

U

uniform spacing – descriptive of a type font in which every character occupies exactly the same space regardless of the width of the character itself.

uninterruptible power supply – a sophisticated backup power supply that automatically furnishes power to a computer system when the primary power source is interrupted, permitting continued operation or an orderly shutdown.

up and running – descriptive of computers and peripherals that are on line and functioning properly.

update – to add or alter data to reflect the most recent information available.

up time – the period that a computer is on line and functioning properly.

upward compatibility – descriptive of features built into a computer to permit upgrading.

user friendly – descriptive of a computer system or program that is intuitive, making it easier to use.

user hot line – a telephone number provided by an equipment or software manufacturer or dealer through which a user may access

technical help.

utilities – computer programs that improve performance or productivity of the computer or the user.

V

vaporware - non-existing software, promised by a developer and discussed in the media as though it existed.

variable – a symbol or code that represents a value that changes during processing.

variable name – a label that represents an element that can assume a changing value, such as a range of cells in a spreadsheet.

VGA – video graphics array; a standard for high resolution display on a color monitor screen.

video card – a board in the computer that controls the display on the monitor.

virtual memory – an extension of the computer's main memory in disk storage.

virus – unauthorized instructions in the computer that disrupt its normal operation.

vocabulary – the collection of reserved words that are acceptable for use in a particular programming language.

volatile – descriptive of computer memory that is erased when power is turned off.

volume label – the name given to a hard or floppy disk to identify it.

W

warm boot – a restart of the computer system after it has been running.

wild card – a symbol within a command that represents an unknown.

window – a viewing area on the monitor screen.

word processor – a text editor, often with enhancements that allow special formatting.

word wrap – a word processor program feature that enables text to overflow to the next line without a carriage return or around a graphic element.

write protect – a feature that prevents the overwriting of a file or specified data in the file.